W9-BZY-680

THE
PULPIT COMMENTARY

THE
PULPIT COMMENTARY

Edited by

H. D. M. Spence

and

Joseph S. Exell

Volume 4
RUTH
I & II SAMUEL

Wm. B. Eerdmans Publishing Company, *Grand Rapids, Michigan*

THE PULPIT COMMENTARY

Edited by
H. D. M. Spence *and* Joseph S. Exell

This large-type edition republished
from new plates by

WM. B. EERDMANS PUBLISHING COMPANY
Grand Rapids, Michigan

ISBN 0-8028-8061

Reprinted, November 1981

PHOTOLITHOPRINTED BY EERDMANS PRINTING COMPANY
GRAND RAPIDS, MICHIGAN, UNITED STATES OF AMERICA

RUTH

EXPOSITION AND HOMILETICS BY

JAMES MORISON

HOMILIES BY VARIOUS AUTHORS

W. M. STATIIAM   J. R. THOMSON

THE BOOK OF RUTH

INTRODUCTION.

§ 1. THE STORY.

SOME time during that period of chequered Hebrew history when the Judges ruled, a famine prevailed over the whole land. There was "cleanness of teeth" everywhere. Even the most fertile districts, such as that of which Bethlehem (the house of bread) is the centre, suffered severely. Among the sufferers were a respectable family, consisting of Elimelech, a proprietor in the locality, his wife Naomi, and their two sons, Machlon and Chilion. This family, being hard pressed by the *Hungersnoth*, resolved to emigrate for a season to the adjoining country of Moab, where apparently there was exemption from the widespread agricultural calamity. Accordingly, setting out from the place of their nativity, they reached the place of their destination, and were, it would appear, hospitably welcomed by the inhabitants (ch. i. 1, 2).

Unhappily, however, Elimelech, subject it would seem to some constitutional weakness, was prematurely cut off (ver. 3).

After his decease his two sons married Moabitish wives, called respectively Orpah and Ruth, and all seemed to go well for a season. There was, however, no family, no mirth of little ones, in either home. And in the course of some ten years from their entrance into the land of Moab, both Machlon and Chilion, in consequence apparently of delicacy inherited from their father, sickened and died (vers. 4, 5).

The three widows were left behind, desolate and destitute. The mother-in-law, Naomi, did not see how she could live in comfort, or maintain herself in respectability, in a foreign land. Still less could she see how it would be possible for her to stand between her daughters-in-law and want. Hence she resolved to return to Bethlehem. Her sorrowing daughters-in-law made up their minds to accompany her (vers. 6, 7).

Naomi, however, felt that it would be too great a burden of responsibility for her to undertake to make her daughters-in-law comfortable in Bethlehem. Hence, after allowing them to give her a convoy for some distance, she insisted that they should return to their mothers' homes, warmly expressing her prayer and her hope that they might soon have sweet and restful homes of their own (vers. 8—13).

The thought of leaving their esteemed and beloved mother-in-law was like a barbed arrow in the heart of both Orpah and Ruth. But at length, after much pleading and remonstrance, Orpah yielded, and returned to her mother (ver. 14). Ruth, however, would not give one moment's entertainment to the proposal. How could she allow the beloved old lady to pursue in solitude her weary way homeward? How could she brook the thought of leaving her to live in solitude after the old home should be reached? Her mind was made up firmly and inflexibly to accompany her much-loved mother-in-law as her companion and attendant. All the nobler feelings of her soul rose, as she thought of her duty, into a heroic mood, while a spirit of deep poetical pathos seized her utterances, as, in unconscious rhythm, she said—

> " Insist not on me forsaking thee,
> To return from following thee :
> For whither thou goest, I will go ;
> And wheresoever thou lodgest, I will lodge :
> Thy people is my people,
> And thy God my God :
> Wheresoever thou diest, I will die,
> And there will I be buried.
> So may Yahveh do to me,
> And still more,
> If ought but death part thee and me " (vers. 15—17).

Naomi could insist no more ; and the two widows consequently, with their hearts knit together for ever, wended their weary way toward Bethlehem, which at length they reached. On entering the city gate, travel-worn, and sore, and creeping along the streets in quest of some humble lodging, Naomi was recognised, and soon there was quite a commotion among the matrons and others who had known her of old. The news of her arrival, in the company of an interesting and pensive-looking young woman, flew from house to house, till wondering groups of excited females gathered in the streets, and exclaimed to one another, Is THAT NAOMI? The name *Naomi*, which brought up to the mind the idea of the *sweetness of Jah*, suggested for the moment a painful contrast to the sorely-disheartened widow. And hence, in her anguish, she begged the people not to call her *Naomi*, as of old, but *Mara*, inasmuch as the Lord had been dealing very *bitterly* with her (vers. 18—21).

It was fortunately just at the commencement of the barley-harvest that Naomi and Ruth arrived in Bethlehem (ver. 22). Hunger was imminent. Perhaps it had already seized on the two widows, gnawingly. Hence, without delay, Ruth begged permission from her mother-in-law to go out in quest of gleaning. It was humiliating employment, but honest. The permission asked was granted.   And so Ruth went out of the house, passed out of the city gate, and, casting her eyes over the wide expanse of golden fields, right and left, ripe for the sickle, and already alive with reapers and binders and gleaners, she was inwardly guided to a field that belonged to Boaz, a substantial yeoman, and, as it happened, near of kin to the late Elimelech.   Ruth knew nothing of his near relationship, but courteously requested from the overseer permission to glean (ch. ii. 1—7).   The overseer, perceiving that there was about this petitioner a certain air of superiority that he had never before witnessed in gleaners, got from her some particulars of her history, and made her heartily welcome to take her place on the field (ver. 7).   So she went to work " with a will."

By and by, as the dayspring advanced in the sky, the proprietor himself, Boaz, came out of the city to see how his reapers were getting on with their pleasant work.   As he reached them and passed along, he courteously saluted them all—*Yahveh be with you!*   The grave, kindly courtesy was heartily reciprocated by the workers—*May Yahveh bless thee!* (ver. 4).

His eye speedily caught sight of the elegant and diligent gleaner, and so he directed his steps to the overseer, and asked, *Whose is this young woman?* (ver. 5).   The overseer informed him, and praised her modesty and industry.   Boaz, passing back again along the row of workers, enjoined on the young men to be respectful to the stranger.   Then he went direct toward her, and, addressing her as a father might speak to his daughter, he made her most heartily welcome to continue in his fields as long as the harvest continued (ver. 8).   He informed her that he had given strict injunctions to the young men to refrain from all improper freedoms ; and he graciously added that she was to avail herself at will of the water which was drawn for the workers, and carried into the field (vers. 4.—9).

Ruth was filled with wonder and gratitude for such unexpected favours, and bowed herself in obeisance to the ground (ver. 10).

Boaz was stricken with admiration, and informed her that he had got, with much satisfaction, full particulars of her devoted attention to her mother-in-law. He prayed that she might receive abundant recompense from Yahveh the God of Israel, under the shadow of whose outstretched wings she had come to trust (vers. 11, 12).

As Boaz was about to turn away to attend to his affairs, Ruth ventured, with beautiful respectfulness, to solicit a continuance for the future of that graciousness which he had already showed to her, and which had brought comfort to her heart (ver. 13).

Then they separated.   But, at the time of the mid-day siesta and refreshment, Boaz returned to her, and conducted her to the booth, under whose cooling shade all the workers were wont to assemble at mid-day.   He requested her to be seated beside the reapers, and to partake of the bread and vinegar which had been provided.   He likewise prepared for her a bunch of delicious " parched corn," of which she gratefully partook, reserving, after she was satisfied, a portion for her mother-in-law to give her a glad surprise (ver. 14).

After the siesta was completed, and Ruth had returned to her labour, Boaz told the reapers to let her glean " even among the sheaves." And not only so, he wished them now and again to pull stalks out of the bundles, with express design, and leave them lying about, that she might gather them. They were, moreover, to be most particular not to affront her by any unkind insinuation (vers. 15, 16).

The work went on merrily till near sunset, when Ruth, collecting together her gatherings, and threshing them, found that she had about an ephah of barley (ver. 17). She took up the welcome load, and made for her humble home, where she had a long story to tell, and many a long story to hear, regarding Boaz (vers. 18—22).

All the harvest through, Ruth continued to glean in the fields of Boaz (ver. 23). But after the reaping and gleaning were ended, and there were no more out-of-door engagements, and no more interviews day after day with Boaz, such a change came over her tender and desolate spirit that the keen eye of her mother-in-law saw that some other step required to be taken. She had had, apparently, interviews with Boaz, and clearly perceived that a mutual attachment had sprung up ; but for some reason or other a seal was on his lips. To remove that seal Naomi contrived a plan, which would have been in the highest degree improper had there not been, on the one hand, a peculiar Oriental custom in vogue, and, on the other, absolute reason for absolute confidence in the incorruptible purity of both Boaz and Ruth. The plan was for Ruth to take the position allowed her by the Levirate law. That would at once put Boaz on his honour in reference to the deceased Machlon and the living widow (ch. iii. 1—4). Ruth yielded to her mother-in-law's wishes, and the plan was carried into effect (vers. 5—7). Ruth placed herself by night at the feet of her kinsman while he slept, and, when discovered, was not only heartily welcomed, but warmly commended, and thanked. He was indeed advanced in years, and he could not, for that reason, have ventured to offer himself for her acceptance. But since his age was not to her an obstacle, and she wished to show every possible respect to the deceased, it would be his joy to mingle his lot with hers (vers. 8—11).

There was, however, one obstacle in the way. There was an individual who was nearer of kin than himself to the deceased. According to the Levirate law, that individual had a prior claim on all the prerogatives attaching to priority of kinship ; and with these prerogatives were bound up the duties of the nearest of kin. He consequently must, first of all, receive full consideration ; and if he insisted on performing the kinsman's part, why then the matter would pass out of the sphere of personal preference, and the result would be accepted as the outcome of the Will that is higher than man's. But if that nearest kinsman should have no desire to act the kinsman's part, then with joy would Boaz step into his place, and show respect to the deceased (vers. 12, 13).

The watches of the night passed rapidly on, no doubt amid many mutual consultations and explanations. And just as the first thinning of the darkness into dusk gave augury of the coming morning, Ruth rose to return home. She bore a present with her, which would carry its own tangible meaning to Naomi. By and by home would be reached, and Naomi saluted her daughter in law by saying, with a peculiar interrogative significance, *Who art thou?* After the whole story was told, "Sit still, my daughter," said Naomi, "until thou know how the matter will end, for the man will not rest until this very day he have brought the affair to its consummation" (vers. 14—18).

It was as Naomi conjectured. Early in the morning Boaz took his place at the gate of the city, and made arrangements for transacting important business in the presence of elders and other witnesses. The near kinsman was passing by. Boaz requested him to be seated, as he had some business to discharge in which they both were interested. The kinsman complied with the respectful request, and ere long a full court of casual witnesses assembled. In the presence and hearing of these elders and others Boaz informed his friend that Naomi, who had lately returned from Moab, had determined, in consequence of reduced circumstances, to sell the property that had belonged to her deceased husband Elimelech (ch. iv. 1—3). He added, "Buy it before the inhabitants of the city, and the elders of the people, if thou art willing to act the kinsman's part." The kinsman intimated that he was willing (ver. 4). Boaz then added that the property would require to be purchased from the hand, not of Naomi only, but of Ruth likewise, the prospective heiress, *who, moreover, was to go with it as a fixed appurtenant*, "in order that the name of her deceased husband might be raised up on his inheritance" (ver. 5).

The anonymous kinsman, however, was not willing to acquire the estate on the terms offered (ver. 6). Hence, perceiving that Boaz was quite willing, he resigned his right in his favour, and pulling off his shoe, handed it to his friend (vers. 7, 8). All the people were witnesses that the nearest kinsman had voluntarily surrendered his peculiar prerogative.

The story thenceforward hastens to its conclusion. Boaz, in presence of the people, acquired the estate, and along with it Ruth, its living and priceless appurtenant (vers. 9, 10). "We are witnesses," shouted the assembled conclave, and then they lifted up their voices and prayed that showers of blessings might descend on the bridal pair (vers. 11, 12). Ruth thus became the wife of Boaz, and bore him a son, whom the matrons who clustered around insisted on calling *Obed*. Naomi took the child to her bosom, and nursed it with tenderness and care which no other care and tenderness could surpass. He was (1) the lineal descendant of Judah, the head of the royal tribe, and (2) the lineal ancestor of David (vers. 13—22).

Taking a broad survey of the contents of the little Book, we may say that it consists of a series of pen-and-ink pictures, or idylls in prose, representing, firstly, the remarkable attachment of a young Moabitish woman, herself a widow, to Naomi, her desolate Hebrew mother-in-law; and, secondly, the remarkable reward with which, in God's providence, her self-sacrifice was crowned.

§ 2. AIM OF THE WRITER.

Edward Topsell, one of the Puritan commentators on the Book, gave, as the leading title of his exposition, 'THE REWARD OF RELIGION,' in that way indicating what he supposed to have been the aim of the writer.

The title is not entirely satisfactory, for certainly it is not the *religion* or *religiousness* of Ruth that is the principal feature of character portrayed in the Book. There is not, it is true, the least shadow of reason for casting the least shadow of suspicion on the genuine piety of the heroine of the story. There is no room for taking exception to her theology. There is still less, if that be possible, for raising objections to her sweet and simple religiousness. Though probably no skilful theologian, she had come to Bethlehem-Judah, to put her trust " under the wings of the God of Israel " (ch. ii. 12). She believed that He " is," and that He is " the rewarder of them that diligently seek Him " (Heb. xi. 6).

Still it is not Ruth's religiousness that is the outstanding feature of the character that is delineated in the Book. It is not her love to the great Divine Object, the God of Israel, that is portrayed. It is her love to a good and worthy human object, Naomi, her mother-in-law. Topsell was right in assigning to *religion* or *religiousness* a higher pedestal than can be accorded to any other devotedness; but he misled himself when, in his eagerness to do homage to that which is highest, he assumed that it was the highest ideal of human character that is bodied forth in the succession of literary photographs which are found in the Book of Ruth.

Many have supposed that the true *raison d'être* of the Book is a matter of genealogy. The ground on which this opinion is maintained is the fact that there is a little bit of genealogy in the five verses with which the Book is wound up. This bit of genealogy connects Pharez the son of Judah with David the son of Jesse. The line passed through Boaz, the husband of Ruth. It is an important historical relationship, more especially to us Christians; for as Christ was " the Son of David," he was the Son of Boaz too, and consequently the Son of Ruth the Moabitess—a Gentile link. The fact is all the more significant and suggestive as, in ascending the genealogical ladder upward to Abraham, the father of the Messianic people, we discover that there were other Gentile links which connected the favoured descendants of the patriarch with the outlying " families of the earth," and which likewise show, in consequence of the moral peculiarity attaching to them, how wondrous was the boon conferred upon men, when the Lord of glory humbled himself to become the "kinsman" and the "friend" of those whose name is "sinners."

But in the genealogy that is appended to the Book of Ruth, the succession is carried no further down than to King David. The genealogy is thus, so far as the discoverable aim of the genealogist is concerned, rather Davidic than Messianic. The interest in it that was manifestly felt by the writer, and that may have been extensively felt by his cotemporaries, was an interest that gathered round "great David" himself, rather than "great David's greater Son."

Yet it seems preposterous to assume that the whole graphic story of Ruth was composed simply in consequence of this genealogical interest. The assumption looks like an inversion of the natural, and the substitution in its place of the unnatural.

Why not rather suppose that the writer wrote just because he was charmed with the facts of Ruth's character, and because he rejoiced over the reward with which, in the providence of God, the heroine's devotedness was so signally crowned? Why not accept the narrative of the Book as being simply what it appears to be? Why not suppose that the writer may have simply sought to reproduce, in the literature of words, the delineation of character and reward that had already been so charmingly executed in the literature of facts? Why hesitate to assume that he may have undertaken his task in the spirit of literary spontaneity, feeling a wide sympathy in his heart, seeing a meaning in everything, and resting assured that there must be a very peculiar meaning and lesson in all those things that are the outcome of noble effort, noble endurance, and noble love.

The writer must, we conceive, have been, though perhaps unconsciously, and in a comparatively limited sphere of activity, *a true litterateur*. He loved literature for its own sake, and had a true appreciation of its mission and responsibilities. Hence, though a Hebrew, he did not turn aside his eyes and his heart from beholding and admiring facts full of interest, and instruction, because they occurred in connection with an alien race. Nor did he make apologies for finding excellences in Gentiles, and recording them with vivid zest and delight. There is a noteworthy absence of Hebrew bigotry in the spirit of the Book.

The title which is given to his commentary on the book by Richard Bernard, another of the Puritan expositors, brings out admirably what appears to have been the aim of the Hebrew writer—'RUTH'S RECOMPENSE.'

§ 3. THE BOOK'S LITERARY CHARACTER.

The Book of Ruth is not a history; nor is it a biography. It is only a little biographical episode in a history. It is *a story;* but, without doubt, *a true story.*

True? How is that evinced? What is there even to suggest the story's objective truthfulness or authenticity?

Much. The Book comes before us as a narrative of facts; and, although making no parade of its veracity, it has, in its own inimitable simplicity and crystalline transparency, all the appearance of being an honest representation of objective realities.

The material of the story, moreover, is of such a nature that its unreality, if it had not been honest, would at once have been detected and exposed. The stuff out of which the story is woven consisted, so to speak, of very sensitive filaments. It had to do with the genealogy of the royal family. The principal personages in the story were the ancestors of King David.

That there was a Moabitish link in the chain of his genealogy must have been well known to the king himself, and to all his household, and to a large proportion of the people of Israel in general. It must likewise have been well known that this Moabitish link did not lie far back in the line. The existence of such a link was too great a peculiarity to be treated with indifference. We cannot doubt that the whole history of the case would be a frequent topic of narration, conversation, and comment at once within and around the royal court. The probability, therefore, is, that the writer would be careful to do no violence to the facts of the case. Any alloy of fiction or romance on such a subject would have been at once resented, alike by the royal family and by the great body of the people, the devoted admirers of the king.

It is, hence, one should suppose, in a mood of literary waywardness that Bertholdt contends that the Book is *not* a narrative of facts, but merely a "historical fiction"—a family picture painted on a canvas of romance.* The writer, he alleges, has himself betrayed the fact of his work's fictitiousness. "He forgot himself for once," he says.† For although, according to one part of his story, he represents Naomi, with her husband and sons, as reduced to such extremity of poverty that they required to abandon their mortgaged property and take refuge in Moab; yet, in utter forgetfulness of this representation, he introduces Naomi, at a later stage of the story, as saying to the matrons in Bethlehem that "she went out *full*, and came back empty." A mere romance writer, Bertholdt alleges, might easily run into such a contradiction, and care nothing about it; but a narrator of actual facts would speedily have detected the blunder, and have got it rectified. The blunder! It is demonstrably Bertholdt's own. He has, in fact, committed a double blunder. (1) He has misunderstood what is said of the condition of the family before their departure, and (2) he has likewise misapprehended what Naomi said after her return. The family is not represented as reduced to absolute destitution before their emigration; there was abundance of scope for much further descent. And, on the other hand, there is not an

---

* Section 551 of the 'Einleitung' is entitled "Das Buch enthält reine Dichtung."
† "Der Verfasser hat sich einmal vergessen."

atom of evidence to establish the objector's conjecture, that, when Naomi after her return referred to her 'fulness' before her departure, she had simply her financial condition in view.

§ 4. DATE OF COMPOSITION.

There is not the least likelihood that the little Book could have been written just immediately after the occurrence of the events narrated. For, in the first place, the writer, in the very opening sentence of the Book, comes down beyond the age of the Judges. He speaks of what came to pass "in the days when the Judges judged." It is implied that these days were, by his time, at some considerable distance in the past. Then, in the second place, he speaks in ch. iv. of a custom that "in former time" obtained in Israel in reference to important transactions, involving the transfer of property, or the surrender of property-rights, which custom was observed by Boaz and his kinsman. At the time when the writer lived the custom had become obsolete, so that a considerable period must have elapsed between the date of the events narrated and the date of the narrative of them in the Book of Ruth. Then, in the third place, the genealogy at the close of the Book is carried down to David, and thus far beyond the time "when the Judges judged."

It might be said indeed that the genealogical appendix may have been added by a later hand. True; *it may.* And if it should ever be proved that it has been, then all the logical effects involved in the proof will be willingly conceded. Until, however, the desiderated proof be forthcoming, we may be excused for accepting the Book in its integrity.

No opinion, on the whole, wears a greater aspect of verisimilitude than that which assigns the composition of the Book to the reign of King David. That epoch was among the Hebrews a literary age. The king himself was a man of letters. He would draw literary men around his throne. He was a man, besides, of deep human sympathies; and thus he would no doubt be intensely interested in the Moabitish incident. He would be master of all its details. They had come down to him only through a very limited succession of remembrancers. "Boaz begat Obed; Obed begat Jesse; and Jesse begat David." No wonder that even the conversations and the salient sayings of Naomi, Ruth, and Boaz should have been sharply imprinted on the brief succession of memories.

King David, moreover, was free from many narrownesses of spirit that belittle multitudes of other minds. He recognised the gracious relationship of the God of Israel to all the families of the earth. He believed that there was a tide of goodness and tender mercy flowing from the inexhaustible depths of the Divine heart to all nations and peoples, even to the uttermost parts of the earth. Hence he would not be ashamed of the Moabitish link in his genealogy. He would be proud of it, and all the more, it is likely, because at a peculiarly critical period of his own history he had been on terms of amity, intimacy, and confidence with the cotemporary king of Moab. At the time when he had to flee for his life from the presence of Saul, and take refuge in the cave of Adullam, it is said, in 1 Sam. xxii. 3, 4, that he went to Mizpeh of Moab, "and said unto the king of Moab, Let my father and my mother, I pray thee, come forth, and be with you, till I know what God will do for me. And he brought them before the king of Moab: and they dwelt with him all the while that David was in the hold." It would not be doing violence to verisimilitude were we to suppose that, in David's communication with the king of Moab, he made mention of the Moabitish link in his genealogy, and of the incidents connected with it. If Ruth, an ancestor of his own, had been hospitably received in Judah, would it be asking too much if the grandson of that ancestor might, with his wife, be hospitably received for a season in Moab?

No other time, it would appear, can be fixed upon as furnishing a more likely date for the composition and publication of the Book.

Not an earlier time; for the custom of pulling off a shoe and giving it to the contracting party was observed in the days of Boaz, but had gone into desuetude at the date of the Book's publication. It could scarcely have died out much sooner than in two or three generations.

Not a later time; for the minute incidents recorded, and the minute conversations and observations reported — all of them apparently unfictitious — would, if unpublished, have faded from the memories of the personages principally concerned. Then the genealogy, at the close of the fourth chapter, *is carried down to King David, and stops there.* Why should it stop there, and by stopping at that particular stage suggest and indicate a particular date? Had the writer some political object in view that required a false date to be given to his publication? There is no trace of such a *motif.* Had he some distinctively theocratic object in view that could be best subserved in his judgment by indicating a false date? There is no evidence of such a *motif.* Had he then some literary object in view that might be furthered by a fabrication, in the colophon, of the date of composition? There is not the slightest evidence of the presence in his mind of such a *motif.*

Ewald, indeed, and Bertheau, following other critics of earlier date, and having themselves many followers of later date, conjecture that the Book is not nearly so old. They would ascribe it to the exilic epoch. Bertholdt asks if it should not be ascribed to the post-exilic epoch.* This, their conjecture of postponement to a date far removed from the time of King David, is based for the most part on considerations that have to do generically with a large proportion of the Old Testament writings. It is hence a question which, falling to be discussed on its own wide arena, is, to a large extent, ruled out of this specific Introduction.

---

* "Ob es vielleicht gar in die Zeiten nach dem Exil gehört." § 553.

The specific reasons that are adduced in favour of the application of the postponing theory to the particular Book of Ruth are not to us of much or very weighty significance. One is that there are some coincidences of expression discoverable in Ruth, on the one hand, and in the Books of 1 and 2 Samuel and 1 and 2 Kings on the other. These coincidences, it is contended, are evidences that the writer of the Book of Ruth must have been acquainted with the Books of Samuel and Kings. For instance, it is said in Ruth i. 17, "May Yahveh do so to me, and more also, if," &c.; and the same formula is found in 1 Sam. iii. 17; 1 Kings ii. 23; xx. 10; 2 Kings vi. 31. Again, it is said in Ruth i. 19, "the whole city got into commotion;" and the same expression occurs in 1 Kings i. 45, where it is rendered in King James's version, "the city rang again." Then in Ruth iv. 4 we read, "I will uncover thine ear" (so as to give thee information); and in 1 Sam. xxii. 8, and elsewhere, it is written, "There is none that uncovereth mine ear" (to inform me). Ewald thinks that "we distinctly hear an echo from the Book of Job, not merely in the general style, but even in some single words and phrases" ('Geschichte,' vol. i. p. 155). He instances Job xxvii. 2, where the simple name "(the) Almighty" is used instead of the complex name "God Almighty" (see Gen. xvii. 1, &c.). Ewald thinks that this shorter form of the name "was evidently rendered possible" in Ruth i. 20 "only through the grand example of the Book of Job." He would infer, therefore, on the one hand, that the writer of the Book of Ruth was familiar with the Book of Job, and he assumes, on the other, that the Book of Job belongs to a late period of literary activity. With the assumption we have here nothing to do. But his inference in reference to the age of the Book of Ruth, and the concurrent inference that is deduced by the advocates in general of exilic or post-exilic origination, from those coincidences of expression of which we have made mention, are surely extremely precarious, or rather absolutely baseless. The simple name "(the) Almighty" occurs not only again and again in Job, but likewise in Gen. xlix. 25, and also in Num. xxiv. 4, 16. If the writer of the story of Ruth must needs be held as borrowing, why might he not have borrowed from Genesis and Numbers in place of Job. And is not the whole argument reversible? Why not infer from coincidences of expression that the writers of the Books of Samuel and Kings borrowed from the Book of Ruth? And, besides, what is to hinder us from supposing that all of the expressions specified lived and moved and had their being for generations as part and parcel of the common idioms of the country, so that various writers of various ages might at pleasure make use of them as constituent elements of the unappropriated language of the people? Peculiar expressions, like peculiar single words, have their lifetime in a people's language. They are born, they grow, they culminate, they wane, grow old, drop off, and are buried. Why might not all the expressions referred to by the critics of the Book of Ruth be "living" at all the successive epochs doing which the writers themselves were living, from whose writings the coincident words and phrases have been culled ?

Ewald thought that he detected evidence of late exilic composition not merely in the echoes of earlier books, but likewise in the "antiquarian lore" that is characteristic of the writer. He refers in particular to the statement that is made in the fourth chapter, in reference to the antique custom of taking off a shoe, and presenting it to the contracting party, when rights of property were surrendered (see ver. 7). He thought, moreover, that such a custom, unearthed by successful antiquarian research, "could only have ceased with the national existence" ('Geschichte,' *ut sup.*). The argument is thus twofold. 1. One branch of it consists in the evidence of successful antiquarian research. 2. Another resolves itself into the peculiarity of the custom itself. It was of such a nature, and manifestly so tenacious of life, that it could not have come to an end so long as the national existence continued.

But surely both of these branches of argumentation are insufficient to carry much weight, or even any weight at all. One might know that a peculiar custom once prevailed, and yet be undistinguished for extensive and accurate "antiquarian lore." The word-of-mouth tradition that sufficed to convey to the writer of the Book of Ruth the actions, and conversations, and remarks of Naomi, Ruth, and Boaz respectively, would likewise suffice to be the vehicle of information regarding the old-fashioned symbolism that was observed when certain legal rights were readjusted. And is it not a matter of well-known fact that legal symbolisms, connected with the transfer of rights of property, *have changed* in various nations whose national existence remains intact? In some nations, for instance, the delivery of land symbolically by the delivery of earth and stones of the land, or other representative elements, though not so very long ago a binding formality, has now ceased to be imperative, or even customary. If there is to be evidence of the exilic or post-exilic composition of the Book of Ruth, it must be found elsewhere.

Some have supposed that this evidence is found in several Chaldaisms of expression. In ch. i. 13, 20 ; ii. 8, 9, 21 ; iii. 3, 4 ; iv. 7, there are certainly some peculiar forms of words. Sanctius supposed that they might be Moabitisms. Dereser conjectured that they might be Bethlehemitish provincialisms. They remind one undoubtedly of forms that are common in Chaldee. But it is at the same time to be borne in mind that there were no hard and fast lines separating, in the olden times, between the various members of the Semitic group of languages. They overlapped one another in various details ; and as originally the fathers of the affiliated nations literally lived in one home, so, even after long periods of distinctive linguistic evolution, there were floating about, in waving lines of mutual intercourse, expressions that were in some cases survivals of original unity, and in others the direct result of subsequent familiar contact. One thing is evident, that the Hebrew which is found in the Books

of the Bible, even the oldest of them, is comparatively modern. It is the survival of a much older Hebrew. The manifold verbal abbreviations are evidence
(see Raabe's ' Zurückführung des Hebräischen Textes des Buches Ruth auf die
ursprünglichen Wortformen '). And nothing is more evident than that the
expressions in ch. ii. 8, 9, 21 ; iii. 3, 4, called Chaldaisms, and not improperly
so called, are in reality Hebrew archaisms.

We see then no reason whatever for postponing the date of the Book of Ruth
to exilic or post-exilic times. All the weightiest evidence seems to be in the
scale that assigns the composition of the Book to the literary age of King David.
And yet, even with these strong convictions, we would bear in mind that the real
interest of the story is independent of any chronological theory. The Book is a
literary gem in ancient Hebrew literature ; and it speaks, by what Ewald calls
" the pre-eminent beauty of its pictures and descriptions," not to the hearts of
Hebrews only, but to universal man.

§ 5. THE AUTHOR.

The authorship is utterly unknown, and guesses need not be multiplied.
Many attribute it to Samuel. Abarbanel ascribes it to the writer of Joshua.
Others have imagined that Hezekiah, and others still that Ezra, is the author.
Heumann thinks that King David himself was the penman. He conceives that
any other writer would, in the genealogical table at the close, have given its
royal honour to his name. It is too slender and too precarious a basis on which
to establish his guess. It is in vain to guess, although we deem it probable
that the incidents of the story would be preserved with interest in the family
of David, and often narrated within the precincts of his home.

§ 6. THE BOOK'S PLACE IN THE OLD TESTAMENT CANON.

Editors of the Old Testament Canon have freely availed themselves of their
right to hold their own opinions, and to act upon them. The Hebrew editors
have relegated the little Book of Ruth to the ' Hagiographa,' the group of
' Sacred Miscellanies,' which comprehends, among other works, the Psalms,
the Proverbs, Job, the Song of Songs, Lamentations, and Ecclesiastes. In the
Hebrew Bibles in current use Ruth stands between the Song of Songs and
Lamentations, as if with sorrow on the left hand, and joy on the right. In other
editions it stands at the head of the entire group. In the Septuagint, on the
other hand, followed by the Vulgate, the Book is found at the close of the Book
of Judges, as if it were a little biographical additament to that larger historical work. Origen expressly says that the Hebrews—he must mean the
Hellenistic Hebrews—count Judges and Ruth as forming one book.[*] Luther
followed in the wake of the Vulgate, and so did Bishop Miles Coverdale and the

---

[*] See Eusebius's ' Ecclesiastical History,' vi. 25.

authors of King James's English version. Hence the Book's position in our English Bibles. We may doubtless assume that Josephus attached the Book to Judges as one parcel, as did Origen's Jews, for we could not otherwise make out his enumeration when, in his 'Cont. Apion.,' i. 8, he says that the Hebrew sacred writings consisted of twenty-two books.

§ 7. STYLE OF COMPOSITION.

There is no artistic elaboration in the style. There is not a vestige of aim at fine writing. No whip is laid on the imagination to impart gleam or lustre to what is said. Yet there are in the Book graces of diction that are the native and apparently unconscious outcome of ardent and devoted attachment on the one hand, and of kindly feeling and admiration on the other. The composition is simple, clear, transparent, and with quite a noticeable amount of that additive or aggregative and agglutinative method of joining thing to thing, that is a feature of Hebrew composition in general. There are eighty-five verses in the Book, and yet there are only eight of them that do not commence with the conjunction *and*. Throughout the little Book this earliest of conjunctions occurs about 250 times in all.

§ 8. LITERATURE.

Passing over those expositions of the Book of Ruth which form part and parcel of serial commentaries on the whole, or on certain great sections, of the Bible, it will suffice, for our purpose, to take note almost exclusively of such exegetical, homiletical, and critical works as are monographs, constituting a specialist literature on Ruth.

The annotations of Victorinus Strigel, 1571, and Feuardentius, 1582, are only of antiquarian interest. So, too, are the homilies of Rudolph Gualter, John Wolph, and Ludowick Lavater, who all flourished in the second half of the sixteenth century. All three were famous in their day for Latin sermons, and were, to a remarkable degree, prolific in that kind of literature. Lavater's book on Ruth, for example, contained "homilias XXVIII.," and it had, as companion volumes, one on Joshua containing LXXIII. homilies, one on Judges containing CVII., one on Ezra containing XXXVIII., one on Nehemiah containing LVIII., one on Esther containing XLVII., and one on Job—enough to try a little his readers' "patience"—containing CXLI. He was fortunate in finding, for his sermons on Ruth, an English translator of the name of E. Pagett, who published his version in the year 1586.

To these homilies may be added Alexander Manerba's volume, published in Venice, and entitled, 'Peregrinatio Ruth Moabitidis per Commentarium et Sermones descripta,' 1604; as also Didacus de Celada's 'Commentarii litterales et morales in Rutham,' with a twofold appendix, 'de Boozi convivio mystico, id est, Eucharistico, et de Maria virgine, in Ruth figurata,' 1614. Schleupner's little 'Explicatio,' 1632, need not be overlooked.

To English students the works of Edward Topsell, Richard Bernard, and Dr. Thomas Fuller, all of the seventeenth century, will afford more interest. The first and second are conspicuous for conscientious and earnest elaboration, the third for a delightful might, mastery, and sparkle of thought. Topsell's volume is entitled, 'The Reward of Religion, delivered in sundrie Lectures upon the Booke of Ruth, wherein the godly may see their daily both inward and outward trialls, with the presence of God to assist them, and his mercies to recompense them,' 1613. The author, in his 'Epistle Dedicatorie,' speaks humbly of his "slender studies, which are but as smoak, being compared with the burning coales of others' knowledge." There are certainly but few scintillations in the work. Richard Bernard's work, a quarto, is entitled, 'Ruth's Recompense; or, a Commentarie upon the Book of Ruth, wherein is showed her happy calling out of her owne country and people, into the fellowship and society of the Lord's inheritance, her virtuous life and holy carriage amongst them, and then her reward in God's mercy. Delivered in several Sermons, the brief sum whereof is now published for the benefit of the Church of God, 1628. Elaborately earnest, and earnestly elaborate, like Topsell's volume, but with more mental grasp in it; albeit, like Topsell's, of scarcely any *exegetical* value. Bernard, unlike Topsell, could emit flashes, and he did emit many of them. But there is often something lurid in them, as when he takes occasion to strike out against "the roaring boys and damned crew"—"the tobacconists, the drunkards, the riotous," who "congee and compliment, or hunt and hawk, and then curse and swear as the furies of hell" (ch. ii. 17). Dr. Thomas Fuller's 'Comment on Ruth,' 1650, unfortunately breaks off at the end of the second chapter. It bears evidence of having been hastily thrown off, but nevertheless it is aglow with wit and bright felicities of illustration and practical application. The commentaries of both Bernard and Fuller were republished in 1865 by James Nichol of Edinburgh.

A different style of book altogether is John Drusius's 'Historia Ruth, ex Ebræo Latine conversa, et commentario explicata. Ejusdem Historiæ Tralatio Græca ad exemplar Complutense, et notæ in eandem,' 1632. The dedication to Archbishop Whitgift is dated Lambeth, 1584. This thin quarto is a gem in its way, so far as the sphere of grammar is concerned. Drusius said of himself, "I am no theologian, and I am not sure whether I am capable of sustaining the character of a grammarian; but," adds he, "I am a Christian."

An invaluable book to the student is John Benedict Carpzov's 'Collegium Rabbinico-biblicum in libellum Ruth,' 1703, published in Leipzig. It contains, on verse after verse—(1) the Chaldee Targum of Jonathan, in the original, and translated into Latin; (2) the notes of the lesser and larger Masora, with translations and explanatory annotations; (3) the expositions of the great Hebrew commentators Rashi and Ibn Esra, as also of Ibn Melech and others, all in the original, and translated into Latin; and then (4) Carpzov's own elaborate exposition, in which he discusses the views of preceding expositors and critics. The author belonged to a literary family. He himself was John Benedict Carpzov the Second. The latter part of the work was compiled from the author's classroom notes by John Benedict Carpzov the Third, father of John Benedict Carpzov the Fourth, the famous Helmstädt professor of poetry and Greek, who wrote 'Theological and Critical Strictures on the Epistle to the Romans,' and 'Sacred Exercitations on the Epistle to the Hebrews, out of Philo of Alexandria.' The great scholar, Gottlob Carpzov—greater than all the Benedicts—was cousin to John Benedict the Third.

Perhaps the best of all helps for such as have just begun to study Hebrew is Werner's 'Liber Ruth illustratus, duplici quidem interpretatione, quarum altera verba sacra in fonte exhibita de verbo ad verbum exprimit, altera secundum idiotismos linguæ sanctæ,' &c., 1740. The book is full of sound, old-fashioned scholarship.

To the same eighteenth century belongs C. A. Heumann's 'Spicilegium ad Historiam Ruth,' 1722—1725. It was published in three successive parts of his 'Pœcile,' vol. i. pp. 177—187, 353—376; vol. ii. pp. 153—170. Heumann was a Free Lance, and of great capacity; but he was too hasty, too self-assertatory and self-assured, too fond of differing, and too little aware that there is a moral element in literary taste.

Toward the beginning of the same eighteenth century, in 1711, Outhof's 'Exposition of the Book of Ruth,' in Dutch, was published. It was much prized by his own countrymen for its profusion of erudition. Toward the end of the century, in 1781, John Macgowan's 'Discourses on Ruth, and other important subjects, wherein the wonders of Providence, the riches of grace, the privileges of believers, and the contrition of sinners are judiciously and faithfully exemplified and improved,' was published. The author, says Mr. Spurgeon, " is well known for originality and force." "The discourses," he adds, "are good reading."

Coming down to the nineteenth century, there is quite a considerable group of practical and homiletical works, such as Lawson's 'Lectures on the whole Book of Ruth,' 1805; Hughes' 'Ruth and her Kindred,' 1839 ; Macartney's 'Observations on Ruth,' 1842 ; Dr. Stephen Tyng's 'Rich Kinsman, or the History of Ruth,' 1856 ; Aubrey Price's 'Six Lectures on the Book of Ruth,' 1869 ; B. Philpot's 'Ruth—Six Lectures,' 1872; Bishop Oxenden's 'Story of Ruth,' 1873; and W. Braden's 'Beautiful Gleaner,' 1874. The oldest of these, viz., Dr. George Lawson's Lectures, is as fresh as the latest. The excellent author had the pen of a ready writer, and, guiding that pen, a large endowment of sanctified common sense. Two other recent works fall to be added to the same group, only the publishing firms from which they are issued desire them, for other than literary reasons and purposes, to be *dateless*. They are, firstly, Samuel Cox's Book of Ruth, a Popular Exposition,' and Dr. Andrew Thomson's 'Home Life in Ancient Palestine, or Studies in the Book of Ruth,' both of them fresh and charming little volumes.

A very different and much more scholarly group of works consists of such as the following :—Dereser's 'Büchlein Ruth, ein Gemälde häuslicher Tugenden. Aus dem Hebräischen übersetzt, erklart, und fur Pfarrer auf dem Lande bearbeitet,' 1806 ; Riegler's 'Das Buch Ruth. Aus dem Hebräischen ins Deutsche übersetzt, mit einer vollständigen Einleitung, philologischen und exegetischen Erläuterungen,' 1812 ; Mezger's 'Liber Ruth ex Hebræo in Lat. versus perpetuaque interpretatione illustratus,' 1856. To these may be added ' Ruth ein Familien-gemälde,' in Augusti's 'Memorabilien des Orients,' pp. 65—96, 1802 ; and Umbreit's 'Ueber Geist und Zweck des Buchs Ruth,' in the 'Studien und Kritiken' of 1834. In this group of works Riegler's volume, in particular, is conspicuous for its taste. The author had a good ear for detecting and appreciating the rhythmic element in the style of the ancient story, and in this respect he anticipated the judgment of Ewald, who takes special note of the rhythmic elevation of the composition in ch. i. 20, 21 for example ('Geschichte,' vol. i. p. 154, Eng. trans.).

To this group of expositions we may add, as deserving of special notice for the interpretation of Ruth, Bertheau's Commentary in the 'Kurzgefasstes exegetisches Handbuch zum Alten Testament,' and the Commentary of Cassel, as contained in Lange's 'Bibelwerk.' The former appeared in 1845 ; the latter in 1865. An excellent English translation of the latter, with valuable notes, by P. H. Steenstra, appeared in New York in 1872, as part and parcel of the English reproduction of Lange's 'Bibelwerk.'

A very important appendix to the more critical expositions of the Book of Ruth consists of—(1) Charles H. H. Wright's 'Book of Ruth in Hebrew, with a critically-revised Text, various readings, &c., including a grammatical and critical Commentary ; to which is appended the Chaldee Targum, with various readings, grammatical notes, and a Chaldee Glossary,' 1864. (2) Raabe's 'Das Buch Ruth und das Hohe Lied im urtext nach neuester Kenntniss der Sprache behandelt, übersetzt, mit Anmerkungen und einem Glossar versehen,' 1879. The former of these two works will be of the utmost value to young students of Hebrew, as an assistant and guide. The latter is of high philological significance, resting as it does on the most recent lines of linguistic science.

ARRANGEMENT OF THE BOOK IN SECTIONS.

For the purposes of this Commentary the following arrangement into sections has been adopted :—

Section 1 (ch. i. 1—5). A certain Hebrew family, driven by stress of famine, emigrated from Bethlehem to Moab, where still greater trials befell them.

Section 2 (ch. i. 6—14).   The widowed mother of the family, Naomi, resolved to return to Bethlehem.

Section 3 (ch. i. 15—22).   Ruth, her Moabitish daughter-in-law, attaches herself indissolubly to Naomi ; and the two widows, sadly reduced in circumstances, journey on foot to Bethlehem, which they reach at the commencement of the barley-harvest.

Section 4 (ch. ii i—9).   Ruth obtains permission from her mother-in-law to go out in quest of gleaning, and lighted on the fields of Boaz, a kinsman of her late husband.   Boaz met her in the rear of his reapers, and took an instant interest in her.

Section 5 (ch. ii. 10—17).   Ruth, profoundly affected by the kindness of Boaz, received from him still greater attention and kindness, and gathered during the day about an ephah of barley.

Section 6 (ch. ii. 18—23).   In the evening she returned with her precious load to her mother-in-law, who informed her of the kinship of Boaz, and poured out her heart in thanksgivings to God.

Section 7 (ch. iii. 1—18).   At the close of the harvest, Naomi, having watched the growth of an attachment between Boaz and Ruth, adopted the principle of the Levirate law to effect their complete union in heart and hand, and thus to secure a " rest " for her devoted daughter-in-law.   The scheme was in all respects successful, and most agreeable to Boaz.

Section 8 (ch. iv. 1—12).   As there were, however, some technical obstacles in the way of the union, Boaz took steps to have these honourably surmounted in the presence of the elders of the city, and he succeeded.

Section 9 (ch. iv. 13—22).   The bridal of Boaz and Ruth was consummated, and Obéd was born, the lineal descendant of Judah, and the grandfather of King David.

THE BOOK OF RUTH

EXPOSITION.

CHAPTER I. 1—5.

Ver. 1.—Now it came to pass. Or, more literally, "And it came to pass." The "And" is somewhat remarkable, standing at the commencement of the Book. But as it is also found at the commencement of Exodus, Leviticus, Numbers, Joshua, Judges, 1 and 2 Samuel, 1 and 2 Kings, 2 Chronicles, Ezekiel, Esther, and Ezra, its use, though inartistic, must be amenable to some literary law. The Books specified, even including Ezekiel, are historical. They are parcels of history, each narrating events that had their genesis in more or less significant antecedent occurrences. This historical genesis, so very different from an "absolute commencement" of things, is indicated, though probably in unreflective spontaneity, by the copulative "And." **In the days when the judges ruled.** Or, more literally, "when the judges judged." In primitive times there was no function that was more important for society than that of judiciously settling disputes between man and man. Every such settlement, besides conferring a benefit on society, and in particular on the individuals at variance, would increase the moral influence and social elevation of the judge. By and by his moral and social superiority would, in favourable circumstances, grow into authority, specifically judicial on the one hand, and generically political, or semi-political, on the other. When military prowess and skill in strategy were added, a ruler, champion, or leader would be the result. Many such leaders rose up among the Hebrews ere yet society was compactly organised. They were variously endowed; but most of them were only very partially equipped for the judicious administration of the affairs of the commonwealth. All, however, were called *judges;* and the discharge of their high duties was denominated *judging*, even when it was entirely inconspicuous as regards judicial ability or judicious determinations. The Hebrew word for *judge* is שֹׁפֵט *shofet;* and it is an interesting evidence of the very close kinship of Hebrew and Phœnician, that in Carthage the chief magistrate, as we learn from Livy and other Roman writers, was called *sufes* (originally, as we see from the inflection, *sufet*). **That there was a famine.** An admirable though free rendering. In the original the structure of the whole statement is exceedingly primitive and "agglutinative"—*And (it) was in the days of the judging of the judges, and (there) was a famine.* **In the land.** Namely, of Israel. The non-specification of the particular country referred to is evidence that the writer was living in it, as one at home. Josephus says that it was under the judgeship of Eli, the high priest, that the famine spoken of occurred ('Antiquities,' v. 9, 1). But here the historian speaks "without book," and without any particular plausibility. Several expositors, such as Bishop Patrick, have antedated, by a very long way, the calculation of Josephus. They would assign the famine to the period when the Midianites and Amalekites came up, "as grasshoppers for multitude, to destroy the land," so that Israel was greatly impoverished (see Judges vi.). But it is in vain to multiply guesses. The date of the famine is not given, and it is futile to make inquisition for it. **And a certain man.** The interpolation of the individualising word "certain" is quite uncalled for, and now quite archaic. The simplicity of the original is sufficient, "And a man." **Of Bethlehem-judah.** Or, as it might be still more literally represented, "of Bethlehem, Judah." There is no such single name as Bethlehem-judah.

There is only the apposition, for discrimination's sake, of one geographical name to another, just as we may say, in English, *Boston, Lincolnshire,* or *Alexandria, Dumbartonshire.* The localisation of the main name is thus effectually indicated. There is another Alexandria in Egypt; there is another Boston in the United States of America; and there was in Palestine another Bethlehem, namely, in the canton of Zebulun (see Josh. xix. 15). Bethlehem, Judah, lies about six miles to the south of Jerusalem. "Its appearance," says Dr. Porter, "is striking. It is situated on a narrow ridge, which projects eastward from the central mountain range, and breaks down in abrupt terraced slopes to deep valleys on the north, east, and south. The terraces, admirably kept, and covered with rows of olives, intermixed with the fig and the vine, sweep in graceful curves round the ridge, regular as stairs" ('Syria and Palestine,' p. 199). The valleys below are exceptionally fertile, and have been so from time immemorial. Hence indeed the name *Beth-lehem,* or *Bread-house.* Its modern name is *Beit-lahm,* or *Flesh-house.* **Went to sojourn in the land of Moab.** We have no word in English that exactly corresponds to the verb גּוּר rendered *sojourn.* The cognate noun is uniformly translated, in King James's version, *stranger,* and means *foreigner.* The verb means *to dwell as a foreigner,* but its root-idea is yet undetermined. The Latin *peregrinari* admirably corresponds. The man of Bethlehem, Judah, went forth from his own country to "peregrinate" (Greek, παροικῆσαι) "in the land of Moab;" literally, "in the fields of Moab," that is, "in the pastoral parts of the territory of Moab." It was not a very great way off, this land of his "peregrination." Its blue mountains, rising up luridly beyond the silver thread of the Jordan and the gleaming expanse of the Dead Sea, are distinctly visible from the Mount of Olives and the heights about Bethlehem. **He, and his wife, and his two sons.** The resumptive *he* is employed for the purpose of linking on to him, in his "peregrination," the other members of the little household. He emigrated "along with his wife and two sons." He had fought hard to keep the wolf of hunger from his door, but was like to be beaten. One after another the props of his hope that better days would soon dawn had been swept from under him, and he saw no alternative but to leave for a season the land of his fathers.

Ver. 2.—**And the name of the man was Elimelech.** That is, "God is King," not, as the older critics were accustomed to interpret it, "My God is King." The intermediate *i* is not the possessive pronoun,

but the vowel of union. The name would be originally significant of strong religious sentiments, perhaps mingled with strong political principles. The imposition of it on a son would be something like a manifesto of the father's creed. **And the name of his wife Naomi.** Or rather "No-o-mi." The precise import of the word is not absolutely ascertained; but it is probable that it is somewhat abbreviated in its termination, and means "God is sweet," or, very literally, "Jah is sweetness." It had been originally imposed as a name by some grateful and happy mother, who, by gracious providences, or by other gracious revelations, had been led to think that "sweet are the ways, sweet are the dealings, and sweet is the character of God." The word does not mean *beautiful,* as some suppose; nor *gracious,* as others suppose; nor *my delight,* as others still suppose. It was not intended to describe the character of the person who was to bear the name. It was intended to signalise, in the spirit of a manifesto, a much-prized feature in the Divine character—that feature, namely, that is displayed when "he deals sweetly with men." Gesenius is doubtless right when he makes *sweetness* the fundamental idea of the whole group of affiliated words (see his 'Thesaurus,' *in voc.*). The cognate Hebrew adjective is rendered *sweet* in 2 Sam. xxiii. 1 and Prov. xxiii 8 (comp. Prov. xvi. 24 and the margin of 2 Sam. i. 23). In the light of this interpretation, and of it alone, can the full significance of what Naomi said on her return to Bethlehem be apprehended: "Call me not *Naomi,* call me *Mara:* for *the Almighty hath dealt very bitterly* with me" (ver. 20). **And the name of his two sons.** In our idiom we should say, "and the names of his two sons." The two sons, however, were for the moment regarded as a unity among the other units of the household. **Mahlon,** or rather "Machlon," **and Chilion.** We need not dip deeply into the etymological import of these names, or attach to them, as applied to Elimelech's children, any peculiar significance. The names, unlike those of the parents, are devoid of theological tinge, and, in these modern times at all events, their import is liable to endless debate. One would at the first blush of consideration suppose that the one meant *sickliness,* and the other *consumptiveness,* or *consumption*—rather uninteresting and melancholy ideas. But they are peculiarly confounding when we consider that the individuals, so named in our story, had apparently inherited a delicate constitution, which developed in both of them into premature *sickliness* and *decay.* The names have the aspect of being prophetic. And yet, even though we should assume that Elimelech, in virtue of some element of bodily delicacy, was afflicted with feelings of morbid despondency, it is hard to come to the conclusion that he would deliberately stereotype his most hypochondriacal anticipations in the names of his children. The probability is, that the names, as names, would originally have some other import. Dr. Cassel supposes that they meant, respectively, *joy* and *ornament*, but he trusts to impossible etymologies. Raabe, taking his cue from Sanscrit roots, interprets the one thus— "He who brings gifts with him;" and the other thus—"He who conceals his wife in his house." Werner, taking his cue from Chaldee cognates, interprets the former of the two names as meaning *ready to forgive*, and the latter as holding forth the idea of *hopeful*. All of them unlikely derivations. And yet something quite distinct from the ideas of *sickliness* and *consumption*, but lying so far on parallel lines of thought, may be conceived. The primary import of מָחַל, the root of *Machlon*, is apparently *to be tender*. Thence the word came by one line of thought to mean *to be physically tender*, that is, *to be sick;* and by another that runs out in Chaldee it came to mean *to be morally tender, to be mild* or *forgiving*. Machlon may mean *mildness* or *tender-heartedness*. Again, the primary idea of כָּלָה, the root of Chilion, is *to complete*. But, besides the completion that is realised in *consuming, consumption*, or *ending*, there is moral *completeness*, the *completeness* or *finish* that is realised in *perfection* (see Ps. cxix. 96: "I have seen an end of all *perfection*"). This idea of *beautiful completeness*, or *perfection*, is more likely to be the meaning of the name than the idea of *consumptiveness*, or *consumption*. **Ephrathites of Bethlehem Judah.** It is not simply the two sons who are so designated. It is the whole group. They were Ephrathites, that is, Bethlehemites, for the old name of Bethlehem was Ephrath, or Ephratha. As, however, the word Ephrathite also meant Ephraimite (see Judges xii. 5 ; 1 Sam. i. 1 ; and 1 Kings xi. 26), it gave precision to the designation, although at the expense of a little redundancy, to say "Ephrathites of Bethlehem Judah." **And they came into the country of Moab.** The Hebrew emigrants reached the *fields* or *pastoral territory* of Moab. **And continued there.** The phrase in the original is of primitive simplicity—"and were there." It has been asked by theological critics whether Elimelech was justifiable in removing to an "idolatrous country" to avoid the inconveniences of a famine in the land of his nativity. It is enough to say in reply that there is no hint in the text itself

that the step taken was blamable or blamed. "No man ought," says Lawson, "to be condemned, whether dead or alive, without proofs of guilt ; and no certain proofs of guilt appear in the present case." "The beam of Elimelech's judgment," says Dr. Thomas Fuller, "is *justly* weighed down to go from Bethlehem, Judah, into the land of Moab."

Vers. 3—5. — "In these words," says Fuller, "we have two marriages ushered and followed by funerals."

Ver. 3.—**And Elimelech Naomi's husband died.** Apparently soon after the settlement of the family. No details, however, are given, as, on the one hand, no blame is attached to the conduct of Elimelech, and as, on the other, the line of biographical interest runs in another direction. **And she was left, and her two sons.** Not only was the mother her husband's *relict;* they were all *left behind*. He had gone somewhither in advance, and they "remained." So the word is frequently rendered.

Ver. 4.—**And they took to themselves wives of the women of Moab.** It was their own act. Josephus, reproducing the narrative from memory, represents the event as occurring in the father's lifetime, and as brought about by his arrangement. He says of Elimelech, "Coming into the territory of Moab, he sojourns there, and, things prospering according to his mind, he gives in marriage to his sons (ἄγεται τοῖς υἱοῖς) Moabitish wives." Theological critics have here again raised the question, Was it sinful in these emigrant Hebrews to take in marriage daughters of the land? The Chaldee Targumist did not hesitate in his decision. He begins his paraphrase of the verse thus : "And they transgressed the edict of the word of the Lord, and took to themselves alien wives of the daughters of Moab." Dr. Thomas Fuller represents Naomi as passionately remonstrating with her sons. He says of himself, "My mouth denieth to be the orator of an unjust action." "Nothing can be brought," he adds, "for the defence of these matches. Something may be said for the excuse of them, but that fetched not from piety, but from policy." It is noteworthy, however, that in the text itself, and throughout the entire Book, there is nothing of the nature of condemnation, not the least hint of blame. There was a law, indeed, which laid an interdict upon marriages with Canaanites (see Deut. vii. 3). But these Canaanites occupied a peculiar relation to the Hebrews. They were within the line of that Canaan which had become the land of Israel. Israelites and Canaanites were thus living within the same borders as rival claimants of the same territory. It was no wonder that the Canaanites' claim was not to be recognised by the Hebrews. The Moabites, however, living within the lines or "coasts" of their own distinct territory, stood in quite a different relation. And while, for purity's sake, great restrictions were to be laid upon all overtures for naturalisation (Deut. xxiii. 3—6), yet the law could never be intended to apply to the families of Hebrews who were settlers in Moab, or to Moabitish females living in their own land, and rather awarding than seeking the prerogatives of natives. **The name of the one was Orpah, and the name of the other Ruth.** No doubt native Moabitish names. Much ingenuity has been expended on that of the more interesting person. Some have unwarrantably assumed that *Ruth* is a contraction of the Hebrew word רְעוּת meaning a *female companion* or *friend*. Still more unwarrantable, though more captivating to the æsthetic imagination, is the signification which is given to the word by Werner and Eadie, namely, *beauty*. It is founded on an impossible derivation from the Hebrew רָאָה. Still more æsthetically captivating is the conjecture of Cassel, that the name is the ancient Semitic form of the Indo-European word *rodon* or *rose*. "At all events," says he, "the thought of Ruth as *the Rose of Moab* is in itself too attractive not to be proposed as a conjecture." It is certainly most attractive and most admirable as a *jeu d'esprit*, but too imaginative to be vindicated on grounds of comparative philology. **And they dwelt there.** Or, "settled themselves there;" literally, "sat there." We still call a gentleman's mansion his *seat*. **About ten years,**

which, however, are treated by the writer as a mere blank in his story. He hastens on.

Ver. 5.—**And, to make a long story short, Machlon and Chilion died also both of them.** "Like green apples," says Fuller, "cudgelled off the tree." But why "cudgelled"? There is no evidence in the text of Divine displeasure, and the Christian expositor, when going beyond the text in quest of principles, should not forget the tower of Siloam, and the victims of Pilate's bloodthirstiness (see Luke xiii. 1—5). **And the woman was left of her two children and of her husband.** That is, "of her two children as well as of her husband." She became as it were their *relict* too. She remained behind after they had gone on before. If all sentiment were to be taken out of the expression, it might then be simply said, in very commonplace prose, *she survived them.* Poor woman! "Of the two sexes," says Fuller, "the woman is the weaker; of women, old women are most feeble; of old women, widows most woeful; of widows, those that are poor, their plight most pitiful; of poor widows, those who want children, their case most doleful; of widows that want children, those that once had them, and after lost them, their estate most desolate; of widows that have had children, those that are strangers in a foreign country, their condition most comfortless. Yet all these met together in Naomi, as in the centre of sorrow, to make the measure of her misery pressed down, shaken together, running over. I conclude, therefore, many men have had affliction—none like Job; many women have had tribulation—none like Naomi."

HOMILETICS.

Vers. 1—5.—*The emigrants and their trials.* We are introduced to the Hebrew family into which the Moabitess Ruth was married.

I. The BEAUTIFUL SIGNIFICANCE OF THE NAMES of both the Hebrew parents.

II. THE WOLF OF HUNGER HAD COME PROWLING TO THE HEBREWS' DOOR. In those conditions of society in which there is little commerce to unite people to people, or when a city is in a state of siege, the consequences of famine are inexpressibly sad and harrowing. Examples:—The recurring famines in India; the famine in Jerusalem when besieged by the Romans, and as narrated by Josephus; the famine in Leyden, when that city was, in 1573, besieged by the Spaniards, and when one of the patriotic magistrates—a noble soul—said to the hungry and mutinous people, "Friends, here is my body. Divide it among you to satisfy your hunger; but banish all thoughts of surrendering to the cruel and perfidious Spaniard." As commerce, however, grows under the fostering care of those Christian influences that aim at realising the brotherhood of all earth's nations, local famines become more and more amenable to control and neutralisation.

III. THE HEBREW FAMILY WAS CONSTRAINED TO EMIGRATE. Many tender ties get ruptured when emigration takes place. But the heart is pulled onward by new hopes. Consider the importance of emigration from old and over-crowded countries to the numerous rich fields lying fallow abroad. These fields are just awaiting the presence of the cultivator to pour forth into the lap of industry overflowing riches of food for the teeming millions of mother countries, and corresponding riches of raw material for the skilled and skilful hands of manufacturers.

IV. THE EMIGRANTS SEEM TO HAVE GOT A CORDIAL WELCOME IN MOAB. It was creditable to the Moabites. Kindness and sympathy should always be shown to strangers, and to all who are far removed from the sweet influences of home.

V. MORTALITY SOON SADLY RAVAGED THE HEBREW HOME. All are mortal. All must die. But in Christ—"the Resurrection and the Life"—we may get the victory even over death. He has "brought life and immortality to light." He who believeth in Him "shall never see death" (John viii. 51; xi. 26). He "hath," and "shall have," everlasting life.

HOMILIES BY VARIOUS AUTHORS.

On the Book of Ruth.—That the Book of Ruth is included in the canon of Scripture need excite no surprise.

I. IT IS A CHAPTER FROM THE HISTORY OF THE HUMAN HEART. Contrast it with the Book of Judges, to which it is a supplement, and which records feats of arms, deeds of heroism, treachery, violence, and murder. Here we are led aside from the highway of Hebrew history into a secluded by-path, a green lane of private life. Here are simple stories of heart and home. In human life, home, with its affections and relationships, plays an important part. In this Book we have a glimpse into the domestic life of Israel, with its anxieties, sorrows, and sweetness. Women and children, honest work and homely talk; deaths, births, and marriages; loves, memories, and prayers, are all here. The Bible is the book of man as God has made him.

II. IT IS A RECORD OF HUMAN VIRTUE, AND THE PROVIDENTIAL CARE AND REWARD ASSURED TO VIRTUE. Human kindness, filial piety, affectionate constancy, uncomplaining toil, true chastity, sweet patience, strong faith, noble generosity, simple piety—are all here, and they are all observed by God, and are shown to be pleasing to him, who rewards them in due time.

III. IT IS A PROOF OF THE SUPERIORITY OF HUMANITY TO NATIONALITY. The Hebrews are often blamed for intense exclusiveness and bigotry, yet no ancient literature is so liberal and catholic as the inspired books of the Old Testament. This narrative shows no trace of national narrowness; it proves that "God is no respecter of persons; but in every nation he that feareth him, and worketh righteousness, is accepted with him." A pure and gentle Moabitess is welcomed into a Hebrew home.

IV. IT SUPPLIES A LINK IN THE CHAIN OF THE GENEALOGY OF DAVID, AND OF THAT SON OF DAVID WHO WAS DAVID'S LORD. Ruth was one of three foreign women whose names are preserved in the table of our Lord's descent from Abraham.—T.

Vers. 1, 2.—*A family of Bethlehem.* This Book is precious as a record of domestic life. The peaceful, prosperous, happy home of the Ephrathite is rather suggested than described.

I. The TIME and STATE of society. "The days when the judges ruled." The preceding Book enables us to picture what times of unsettlement, and occasionally of anarchy, these were. The customs of the time were primitive, and the habits of the people were simple. The elders sat at the gates of the little city. Business was transacted with primitive simplicity. The tranquil course of agricultural life diversified by a feast at sheep-shearing, or a mirthful harvest-home.

II. The SCENE. "Bethlehem-judah." The fields of Bethlehem, in the territory of Judah, are among the classic, the sacred spots of earth. 1. In Old Testament history. The home of Boaz; the scene of Ruth's gleaning, and of her marriage. In these pastures was trained, in the household of Jesse, and among his stalwart sons, the youthful David, who became the hero and the darling, the minstrel and the king, of Israel. 2. In New Testament history. Between the pastures of Bethlehem and the stars of heaven was sung the angels' song of good-will and peace. Here was born the Son of David, who was the Son of God. The visit of the shepherds and the wise men. Herod's massacre of the babes, &c.

III. The PURSUITS of rural life. In Bethlehem-Ephratah Elimelech had his inheritance. Here, for a time, he, like his fathers, tilled the fields and fed the flocks he owned in peace. Even in times of trouble and disorder some secluded spots are quiet; the bleating of the sheep is familiar, and the shouts of war are unheard. In most men's breasts the scenes and pursuits of rural life are cherished; perhaps it is hereditary. "God made the country." A simple and natural piety is fed by fellowship with nature, the work of God's own hands.

IV. The PEACEFUL JOYS of home. In the sweet society of his wife Naomi ("the pleasant"), his young sons Mahlon and Chilion, growing by his side in stature and intelligence, the freeholder of Bethlehem passed the jocund days. How can we think and speak quite worthily of the *family* and the *home?* Here is the Divine nursery of the soul, the Divine school of life! Let us have no terms with the fanatics who would reconstruct society upon another basis than domestic life. The great lesson—gratitude to Providence for peace, congenial occupation, and a happy home.—T.

Vers. 1, 2.—*Famine and impoverishment.* The former scene one bright and joyous. An honest Hebrew, of the tribe of Judah, living upon the land of his inheritance, with the wife of his heart and the children of his youth. Thus were formed the bonds which prosperity could not dissolve and adversity could not snap. Here were learned the hereditary and traditional lessons of faith, patience, forbearance, piety, and hope. A contrast follows.

I. FAMINE. Probably from some incursion of the hostile forces of Midian into the vale of Bethlehem; or, if not so, from a succession of bad harvests, or a failure of pasture, scarcity and famine invaded the abodes of plenty and of peace.

II. IMPOVERISHMENT. Upon Elimelech the pressure of the times was peculiarly severe, compelling him to break up his home, quit the modest but cherished inheritance of his fathers, and seek subsistence elsewhere.

Lessons :—1. Change of circumstances is a common incident in human life. Every person has either experienced some such change, or has witnessed such reverse in the condition of kindred or acquaintance. A fall from comfort, or even affluence, to poverty frequently happens among occupiers, and even owners, of land, and still more frequently in manufacturing and commercial communities. 2. Religion teaches sympathy with those in reduced circumstances. When a neighbour is deprived not only of the usual conveniences of life, but of the means of educating his children and of providing for his old age, we should not offer reproach, or even cold, hard advice, but, if possible, substantial help, and always considerate sympathy. 3. Religion has consolation for those in adversity. A message from heaven bids them "be of good cheer!" Let diligence and frugality contend with circumstances! Be patient and uncomplaining, and avoid that sign of a petty and broken spirit, the dwelling fondly upon bygone prosperity! The sun of prosperity may yet break through the clouds. Even if it be not so appointed, there may still remain those blessings which are dearer than fortune's gifts—wife, child, a good conscience, health, fortitude, hope! If calamity has come upon you through your own fault, repent, and learn "the sweet uses of adversity." If through the fault of others, refrain your heart from malice and revenge, and your lips from cursing. Think rather of what Heaven has left than of what Heaven has taken. "Lay up for yourselves treasures in heaven." Remember that, if Christians, " all things are yours! "—T.

Vers. 1, 2.—*Emigration.* Picture the removal of this family from the home they loved. Taking with them, it may be, the remnant of their cattle, they bade adieu to the familiar scenes where they had known content and plenty, where they had formed their friendships and alliances. The best prospect for them lay towards the east, and eastwards accordingly they travelled. Whether they struck southwards by the foot of the Salt Sea, or crossed the Jordan at the ford, they must soon have reached the verdant highlands of Moab. Here it was they were to seek a settlement and make a home.

I. These CHANGES of abode are IN ACCORDANCE WITH PROVIDENTIAL APPOINTMENT. Migrations have at all times been common among pastoral, nomadic people. The tillers of the soil and the dwellers in cities have been more stationary. Emigration a great fact in the social life of Britain in our time. Owing to the increase of population, to geographical discovery, to the application of steam to ocean voyages, emigration common among our artisan and agricultural classes. Some become colonists through the pressure of the times; others from love of adventure, and desire for a freer life. All of us have friends who have emigrated. Thus God replenishes his earth.

II. THESE CHANGES AFFECT DIFFERENTLY DIFFERENT PERSONS. Naomi would feel the severance most keenly, and would look forward with least interest and hope to new surroundings and acquaintances. Her sons would not realise the bitterness of change; the novelty of the circumstances would naturally excite and charm them. Picture the emigrants, the friends they leave behind, the scenes awaiting them, &c.

III. THESE CHANGES SHOULD BE WATCHED BY CHRISTIANS WITH WISE AND PRAYERFUL INTEREST. Remember that the undecided are yonder free from many restraints. By prayer and correspondence seek to retain them under the power of the truth. Guide emigration into hopeful channels; induce colonists to provide for themselves the word of God, the means of education, the ministry of the gospel.—T.

Ver. 3.—*Widowhood.* In the country of Moab Elimelech and his family found a home. A period of repose seems to have been granted them. They learned to reconcile themselves to new scenes and associations. But life is full of vicissitude. "Boast not thyself of to-morrow." O, to live as those whose treasure and whose heart are above! "Elimelech, Naomi's husband, died; and she was left." A brief, pathetic record!

I. The widow's SORROW. The observation of all, the experience of some hearers, may fill up the outline. In every social circle, in every religious assembly, are women who have been called upon to part with those upon whom they had leaned for support and guidance, to whom they gave their hearts in youth, to whom they had borne sons and daughters.

II. The widow's LOT. It is often one of hardship and trouble. As in the case before us, it may be aggravated by—1. Poverty. 2. Distance from home and friends. 3. The charge and care of children, who, though a blessing, are a burden and responsibility.

III. The widow's CONSOLATION. 1. The promise of God: "Thy Maker is thy husband." 2. Opportunity of Christian service. How different the widow's condition in Christian communities from that of such among the heathen! The honour and the work of "widows indeed."

Lessons:—1. Submission and patience under bereavement. 2. Sympathy with the afflicted and desolate.—T.

Ver. 4.—*Marriage.* The notes of time found in this narrative are meagre. It is not easy to decide to what the "ten years" here mentioned refer. After the death of Elimelech, the two sons were spared to be the occupation and the solace of the widow's life. Naomi saw them grow up to manhood. Then the young men "took them wives of the women of Moab."

I. MARRIAGE IS LAWFUL BETWEEN PERSONS OF DIFFERENT NATIONS. There was nothing in the law of Moses to prevent these young men from acting as they did, although the children of Israel were not allowed to intermarry with the Canaanites. Later in Jewish history Nehemiah interpreted the law as forbidding marriage with the children of Moab. But he seems to have acted with unjust severity. These Moabitish women were virtuous, kind, devoted; conformed to the religion of their husbands, and one of them found a solid satisfaction in the worship of Jehovah. The conduct of the young men seems to have been natural and blameless.

II. MARRIAGE SHOULD ONLY BE-ENTERED UPON AFTER SERIOUS AND PRAYERFUL DELIBERATION, AND WITH A CONVICTION OF ITS ACCEPTABLENESS TO GOD. Sensible and Christian people should discountenance the practice of treating marriage with levity. Consideration should be given to time, to circumstances, and, above all, to character. Confidence and esteem must be, with affection, the basis of wedded happiness; and these cannot exist in their completeness where there is dissimilarity of conviction and aim—where one party is living to the world, and the other would live unto the Lord. Error here involves misery, and perhaps disaster and ruin.

Lessons:—1. Let elders inculcate just views of the marriage relationship upon the young. 2. Let the young avoid committing themselves to a contract of marriage until a fair experience of life has been acquired. 3. Let Christians marry " only in the Lord."—T.

Ver. 5.—*Double desolation.* In the happiness of her children Naomi would revive the happy years of her own early married life. But the bright sky was soon clouded over by the shadow of death. Perhaps inheriting their father's constitution, her sons died in early manhood. She became a childless widow. Three widows were in one house, each bearing in her silent heart her own burden of grief.

I. Some are called upon to endure repeated bereavements. Households there are which have been visited again and again by the angel of death. Youthful lives are snapt asunder; youthful hearts are left desolate. Some are called upon to endure prolonged age, whilst children and friends, the joy of their hearts, are taken from them. Here and there is one who can exclaim, " All thy waves and thy billows are gone over me."

II. For such God has promises of grace and purposes of mercy. 1. The assurances of the Divine remembrance and kindness. " The mountains shall depart," &c. 2. The sympathy of the Divine High Priest. The miracle of the raising of the widow's son at Nain is an illustration. 3. Grace of submission shall be imparted. " The Lord gave, and the Lord hath taken away; blessed be the name of the Lord." 4. Intentions of Divine wisdom shall be accomplished. Thus shall the heart be weaned from earth; thus shall Christian character be matured; thus shall saints be prepared for glory. How can the vicissitudes of life be borne by those who are strangers to Christian principles, to Christian consolations, to Christian hopes? May ours be the happy lot of the Christian, from whom (as from all the children of men) the future is hidden; but who knows himself to be the object of a Father's love and a Saviour's care, and to whose heart comes day by day a voice from heaven, saying, " I will never leave thee! I will never forsake thee!"—T.

Ver. 1.—" In the days when the judges ruled." This is the age in which the story happened which constitutes Ruth's history, beautiful as an epic, and touching as a pathetic drama of home life. The judges. Whether the earlier or later we know not. Whether in the days of Deborah or the days of Gideon. Probably, however, the latter, as history tells then of a famine through the invasion of the Midianites. The judges. Religion means law, order, mutual respect, and, with all diversity of circumstance, equality in the eyes of the law. A nation that perverts justice has undermined the foundations of the commonwealth.

I. All judges are representatives and interpreters of the law. They are not creators of it; they are not allowed to govern others according to their own will, but they are to be fair and wise interpreters of the national jurisprudence. Law is a beautiful thing if it is founded on the Divine sanctions; it means protection for the weak, safety for the industrious.

II. The best administration cannot meet the want caused by wars. Famine came! The Midianites came up and " destroyed the increase of the earth." " And Israel was greatly impoverished because of the Midianites." Here are the old border wars. Nature was as beautiful as ever, and the flowers of Palestine as fragrant, and the corn as golden; but the enamelled cup of the flower was soon filled with the blood of slaughter, and the beautiful sheaves were pillaged to supply the overrunning enemies of Israel. Such is the heart of man. In every age out of that come forth wars; and although modern legislation is enabled to fill the empty granary from other shores, yet in the main it still remains true, war means, in the end, not only bloodshed and agony, but want.

III. All earthly rulership is the symbol of a higher government. As the

fatherly relationship is symbolical of the Divine Fatherhood, and the monarchical of the Divine King, so the earthly judge is to be the emblem of a Divine Ruler, whose reign is righteousness, and who hath appointed a day in which he will judge the world. There are schools of thought that question human responsibility, that teach a doctrine of irresistible law, the predicate of which is, that sin is not so much criminal or vicious, as the result of innate tendencies which come under the dominion of resistless inclinations. But it is to be noticed that these teachers would not excuse the thief who has robbed *them*, or the murderer who has slain *their* child. To be consistent, however, they ought ; for they object to punishment in the plan of the Divine government. Human instinct, however, and Divine revelation are at one in this ; alike they ask, "Wherefore should a man complain, a man for the punishment of his sin ? " In all ages and amongst all races where society is secure, and progress real, and innocence safe, they are " those where the judges rule."—W. M. S.

Ver. 1.—" There was a famine in the land." Providence led Elimelech, his wife Naomi, and his two sons Mahlon and Chilion, into the land of Moab, on the other side of Jordan. Whilst there was scarcity of bread in Israel, there was plenteous supply in Moab. So they left their fatherland and home in Bethlehem. We carry "home" with us when we go with wife and children. It is the exile's solitary lot that is so sad. It is when God setteth the solitary in families, and the child is away from home in a foreign land, amongst strange faces, that the heart grows sick. We ought always to remember in prayer the exile and the stranger. Sometimes, amongst the very poor, a man has to go and seek substance far away from wife and child ; but in this case sorrow was mitigated by mutual sympathy and help.

I. THERE ARE WORSE FAMINES THAN THIS. It was famine of another sort that led Moses from Egypt, when he feared not the wrath of the king, that he might enjoy the bread of God ; and it was religious hunger that led the Pilgrim Fathers first to Amsterdam, and then to New England, that they might find liberty to worship God. In the day of famine we read Elimelech could not be satisfied. No. And it is a mark of spiritual nobility never to be contented where God is dishonoured and worship demoralised. The word "Bethlehem" signifies the house of bread ; but there was barrenness in the once wealthy place of harvest. And the name of Church cannot suffice when the place is no longer the house of God, which the word Church means.

II. IN THIS FAMINE ELIMILECH'S NAME WAS A GUARANTEE OF GUIDANCE AND SUPPLY. It means, " My God is King." Beautiful that. He reigns, and will cause all things to work together for good. Mark the words, My God ; for as Paul says, " My God shall supply all your need." King ! Yes, " the earth is the Lord's, and the fulness thereof," and he will not let his children want bread. They go without escort, but the Lord goes before them. There are no camels or caravanserai behind them, but the Lord God of Israel is their rereward. So is Divine promise translated into family history.

III. THE TROUBLE THAT SEEMS LEAST LIKELY OFTEN COMES. Bread wanting in Bethlehem, "the house of bread." Yes ! But have not we often seen this ? The sorrows of life are often such surprises. They do not take the expected form of the imagination, but they assume shapes which we never dreamed of. The king not only loses his crown, but becomes an exile and a stranger in a strange land. The rich man in health loses all in a night. A sudden flicker, and the lamp of health which always burned so brightly goes out in an hour.

IV. BETHLEHEM WAS A QUIET, RESTFUL ABODE. Nestling in its quiet beauty, ten miles or so from time-beloved Jerusalem, who would have thought that the golden ring of corn-fields which surrounded it would ever have been taken off its hand ? Very early in history it was productive. Here Jacob fed his sheep in the olden times. Famine in a city impoverished and beleaguered we can understand ; but famine in Bethlehem ! So it is. The rural quietness does not always give us repose. There too the angel with the veiled face comes—the angel of grief and want and death. Happy those who have a Father in heaven who is also their Father and their King. —W. M. S.

Vers. 4, 5.—*A foreign land.* "And they dwelled there about ten years." Memorable years! Marriages and births had given place to separation and bereavement. Elimelech the father died; so also did the two sons Mahlon and Chilion. Thus we have the sad picture of three widows.

I. WE CAN FLY FROM FAMINE, BUT NOT FROM DEATH. We need not enter upon the argument of some expositors, as to whether Elimelech did right to leave Bethlehem; whether by famine is not meant insufficiency of plenty rather than actual want. We must be content with the fact that he thought it prudent and wise to go. And now with fulness of bread came the saddest experience of all. How often it happens that when circumstances improve, those we hoped to enjoy them with are taken away. We climb the hill together, and then with new and fair prospect comes the desolation of death amid the beauties and blessings of earth and sky. These are darker clouds than covered them in Bethlehem. We never know how dear are the living till they are gone; then we see it was their presence that gave life and peace to so many scenes, that gave inspiration to labour and sweetness to success.

II. TROUBLES OFTEN COME WAVE UPON WAVE. Ten years! and lo, three out of the four pilgrims are at rest. No more fatigue, no more distress for them. True; but those that are left! What of them? It is often easier to go than to remain. It is all summed up in the consciousness, I have but to live, and to live without them. Nor is this a morbid feeling. It is a most sacred emotion. True, time will alleviate; but there will always be graves in the heart, and men and women who have lost their beloved ones can never be the same again. Character will be softened, purified, elevated. Heaven will be nearer and dearer to the heart. Ten years! How fleetly they fly, and yet what a long volume of experience may be bound up in them.

III. EVERY HOME IS BUT AS A TENT LIFE. They dwelled there. Got used to the new people, the new skies, the new ways. After a time, to a family removed to another shore, there are always some tendrils gathering round the place, and in time they feel in leaving *that* a sense of loss. Strange as it all seemed at first, in time touches of experience make it homelike to them. Still the old first home, the dear village of childhood and youth, nestles in the heart. How many in life's evening like to go back and live near the abode of the morning. We dwell! So it seems; and we look at the picture of the world's life-pilgrimage as though, like some panorama, it was all *outside* us. But we pass onward too, and ere long grey hairs are here and there upon us, though we know it not. At times we look back. Ten years! And their experience is within us, as well as behind us.—W. M. S.

EXPOSITION.

CHAPTER I. 6—14.

Ver. 6.—**Then**—the conjunction in Hebrew is the common generic copulative *and*— **she arose.** She had been *sitting*, as it were, where her husband had settled, and she now rose up to depart (see ver. 4). **She, and her daughters-in-law.** The word for "her daughters-in-law"—כַּלֹּתֶיהָ—is literally "her brides," that is, the brides of her sons. **That she might return**—an admirable rendering into English idiom. The phrase in the original is simply " and she returned," that is, " and she began to return." **From the country of Moab: for she had heard in the country of Moab how that the Lord had visited his people in giving them bread.** Or, more literally, " for she heard in the country of Moab that Jehovah"—or, rather, "Yahveh," or, as Epiphanius gives it, 'Ιαβέ —"had visited his people to give them bread." There is no warrant, however, and no need, to add, with the Chaldee Targumist, that the news was conveyed *by the mouth of an angel.* And the representation is not that Yahveh, in giving bread to his people, had thereby visited them; it is that he had visited them "to give them bread." The word פָּקַד, rendered *visited*, is quite peculiar, with no analogue in English, German, Greek, or Latin. Yahveh had *directed his attention* to his people, and had, so to speak, *made inquisition into their state*, and had hence taken steps to give them bread (see Exod. iii. 16; iv. 31). They had already got it, or, as the Septuagint translates, they had got *loaves* (ἄρτους). The Vulgate translates it *meats* (escas). It is assumed in the tidings that the seasons and their products, and all beneficent influences in nature, belong to Yahveh. It is likewise assumed that the Hebrews were his people, albeit not in such a sense as to secure for them more " bread " and "milk and honey" than other peoples

enjoyed. Their chief prerogatives were spiritual and moral. *They were his Messianic people.* That is the key to unlock the secret of the whole Old Testament Scriptures.

Ver. 7.—**And so she went forth out of the place where she was.** There is no attempt on the part of the writer to localise the spot. **And her two daughters-in-law with her.** They had kept, it seems, on terms of affectionate sympathy with their mother-in-law. The jealousies that so often disturb the peace of households had no place within the bounds of Naomi's jurisdiction. The home of which she was the matronly centre had been kept in its own beautiful orbit by the law of mutual respect, deference, affection, and esteem—the law that insures happiness to both the loving and the loved. "If there were more Naomis," says Lawson, "there might be more Orpahs and Ruths." **And they went on the way to return to the land of Judah.** Having left her Moabitish abode, and got into the frequented track which led in the direction of her native land, she journeyed onward for a stage or two, accompanied by her daughters-in-law. Such is the picture. It must be subsumed in it that her daughters-in-law had made up their minds to go with her to the land of her nativity. The subject had been often talked over and discussed. Naomi would from time to time start objections to their kind intention. They, on their part, would try to remove her difficulties, and would insist on accompanying her. So the three widows journeyed onward together, *walking.* Adversity had pressed hard on their attenuated resources, and they would not be encumbered with burdensome baggage.

Ver. 8.—**And Naomi said to her two daughters-in-law, Go, return each to her mother's house.** She reverted, with deeper earnestness, to their theme of discussion. She acknowledged that most kindly had they acted toward her. Her heart was filled with gratitude. It was likewise agitated with grief at the prospect of bidding them a final farewell. Nevertheless, she felt that it would be unreasonable and unkind to invite them to be, to any further degree, sharers of her adversity. Hence, thanking them for their loving convoy, she would remind them that every step further on would only increase the length of their return-journey; and she said, Go, return each to her mother's home. There, in the females' apartment, and in the bosom of their mothers, they would surely find a welcome and a refuge. She judges of their mothers by herself, and she refers rather to them than to their fathers, partly, perhaps, because she bears in mind her own motherhood, but principally, no doubt, because, in those Oriental countries, it lay very particularly within the province of mothers to make arrangements in reference to their daughters. **May Yahveh deal kindly with you, as ye have dealt with the deceased, and with me.** It is beautiful gratitude, and at the same time a touching monument to the faithfulness and gentleness that had characterised and adorned the young widows. Her simple Hebrew theology, moreover, comes finely out. She assumes that her own Yahveh reigned in Moab as in Judah, and that all blessing descended from him. There is a little peculiarity in the Hebrew pronouns in this clause. They are masculine instead of feminine. The influence of the stronger sex overrides grammatically, for the moment, the influence of the weaker.

Ver. 9.—**May Yahveh grant to you that ye may find rest, each in the house of her husband.** Naomi again, when the current of her tenderest feelings was running full and strong, lifts up her longing heart toward her own Yahveh. He was the God not of the Hebrews only, but of the Gentiles likewise, and ruled and overruled in Moab. The prayer is, in its form, full of syntactical peculiarity: "May Yahveh give to you," and, as the result of his giving, "may you find rest, each [in] the house of her husband." The expression, "the house of her husband," is used locatively. It is an answer to the suppressed question, "Where are they to find rest?" And hence, in our English idiom, we must insert the preposition, "*in* the house of her husband." As to the substance of the prayer, it has, as truly as its grammatical syntax, its own tinge of Orientalism. Young females in Moab had but little scope for a life of usefulness and happiness, unless shielded round and round within the home of a pure and devoted husband. Naomi was well aware of this, and hence, in her motherly solicitude for her virtuous daughters-in-law, she gave them to understand that it would be the opposite of a grief to her if they should seek, in the one way open to them in that comparatively undeveloped state of society, to brighten the homes of the lonely. In such homes, it circumstances were propitious, they would find deliverance from unrest and anxiety. They would find *rest.* It would be a position in which they could *abide,* and in which their tenderest feelings and most honourable desires would find satisfaction and *repose.* The peculiar force of the Hebrew מְנוּחָה is finely displayed by the texture of the associated expressions in Isa. xxxii. 17, 18: "And the work of righteousness shall be *peace;* and the effect of righteousness *quietness* and *assurance for ever;* and my people shall dwell in *a peaceable habitation,* and in *sure dwellings,* and in *quiet resting-places*"

(מִנֻּחֹת). **And she kissed them,** locking them lingeringly and lovingly in a farewell embrace. "Kissed them." The preposition *to*, according to the customary Hebrew idiom, stands before the pronoun. In kissing, Naomi imparted herself passionately *to* her beloved daughters-in-law, and clung *to* them. There would be full-hearted reciprocation, and each to each would cling "in their embracement, as they grew together" (Shakespeare, *Henry VIII.*). **And they lifted up their voice and wept.** The idea is not that all three wept aloud. The pronoun "they" refers to the daughters-in-law, as is evident both from the preceding and from the succeeding context. The fine idiomatic version of the Vulgate brings out successfully and unambiguously the true state of the case—*quæ elevata voce flere cœperunt*. The *lifting up of the voice* in weeping must be thought of according to the measure of Oriental, as distinguished from Occidental, custom. In the East there is less self-restraint in this matter than in the West.

Ver. 10.—**And they said unto her, Surely we will return with thee unto thy people.** So King James's version. The expression in the original is broken at the commencement: "And they said to her, For with thee we shall return to thy people." It is as if they had said, "Do not insist on our return to our mothers' homes, *for with thee we shall return to thy people.*" Note the expression, "we shall return," instead of "we shall go with thee in thy return to thy people." For the moment they identify themselves with their mother-in-law, as if they had come with her from Judah.

Ver. 11.—**And Naomi said, Turn back, my daughters. To what purpose should you go with me? Have I yet sons in my womb, that might be husbands to you?** According to the old Levirate law—a survival of rude and barbarous times—Orpah and Ruth, having had husbands who died without issue, would have been entitled to claim marriage with their husbands' brothers, if such surviving brothers there had been (see Deut. xxv. 5—9; Matt. xxii. 24—28). And if the surviving brothers were too young to be married, the widows, if they chose, might wait on till they reached maturity (see Gen. xxxviii.). It is in the light of these customs that we are to read Naomi's remonstrances. The phraseology in the second interrogation is very primitive, and primitively 'agglutinative.' "Are there yet to be sons in my womb, and they shall be to you for husbands?" (see on ver. 1).

Ver. 12.—**Turn back, my daughters, go; for I am too old to have a husband. But even if I could say, I have hope; yea, even if I had a husband this very night; yea, even if I had already given birth to sons;**

(ver. 13) **would ye therefore wait till they grew up? would ye therefore shut yourselves up so as not to have husbands? nay, my daughters; for my lot is exceedingly bitter, more than even yours, for the hand of Yahveh has gone out against me.** Most pathetic pleading, and not easily reproduced on lines of literal rendering. "Go, for I am too old to have a husband." A euphemistic rendering; but the original is euphemistic too, though under another phraseological phase. "But even if I could say, I have hope." The poverty of the Hebrew verb, in respect of provision to express "moods," is conspicuous: "that," *i. e.* "suppose that I said, I have hope." Mark the climactic representation. *Firstly,* Naomi makes, for argument's sake, the supposition that she might yet have sons; then, *secondly,* she carries her supposition much higher, namely, that she might that very night have a husband; and then, *thirdly,* she carries the supposition a great deal higher still, namely, that even already her sons were brought forth: "Would you therefore wait?" Note the *therefore.* Ibn Ezra, the Septuagint, the Vulgate, and King James's version assume that לָהֵן means *for them.* The feminine pronoun, however, as applied to Naomi's sons, is, on that supposition, all but inexplicable. It is much better to assume, with the majority of modern critics, that it is equivalent to לָכֵן, whether we call it a Chaldaism or not. Certainly it was current in Chaldee (see Dan. ii. 6, 9). But it may have floated in circles of Semitic society that were never included within Chaldæa proper. Indeed, there were no precise limits bounding off the Chaldee language from the kindred dialects, just as there are no such limits in English or in German, or in any member of a linguistic group. Idioms often overlap. In the two interrogative clauses, "Would ye for that purpose wait till they grew up? Would ye for that purpose seclude yourselves, so as not to have husbands?" there is a parallelism; only, in the second clause, the representation rises. "For my lot is exceedingly bitter, more than even yours;" literally, "for it is bitter to me exceedingly, beyond you." The verb is used impersonally. Naomi means that her case was even more lamentable than theirs, so that she could not encourage them to hang their dependence on her help, or to hope for a retrieval of their circumstances in becoming partakers of her fortunes. The translation of King James's version, "for your sakes," though decidedly supported by the Septuagint, is unnatural. Pagnin and Drusius both give the correct rendering, "more than you." So do Michaelis and Wright. But Bertheau and Gesenius agree with King James's version. The Syriac Peshito, strange to say, gives both translations, "I feel very bitterly for you, and to me it is more bitter than to you."

Ver. 14.—**And they,** the daughters-in-law, **lifted up their voice** in unison and unity, as if instead of two voices there had been but one. Hence the propriety of the singular number, as in ver. 9. **And wept again.** The "again" doubles back on the statement in ver. 9. With uplifted voice, in shrill Oriental wail, and amid streams of tears, they bemoaned their hapless lot. Then, after the paroxysm of grief had somewhat spent itself, Orpah yielded to her mother-in-law's dissuasives, and at length imprinted on her, reluctantly and passionately, a farewell kiss. Then, not waiting to ascertain the ultimate decision of Ruth, or rather, perhaps, having now a fixed presentiment what it would be, she moved regretfully and tearfully away. She was afraid, perhaps, that if she, as well as Ruth, should insist on accompanying her mother-in-law, the two might be unreason-ably burdensome to the aged widow. Perhaps, too, she was not without fear that her own burden in a foreign land, amid strangers, might be too heavy to be borne. There is not, however, the slightest need for suppos-ing that she was, in any respect, deficient in attachment to her mother-in-law. **But,** it is added, **Ruth clave to her mother-in-law,** all reasonings, remonstrances, dissuasives on Naomi's part notwithstanding. Ruth would not be parted from her. "Clave." It is the same word that is used in the primitive law of marriage. "Therefore shall a man leave his father and his mother, and shall *cleave* to his wife, and they shall be one flesh" (Gen. ii. 24). It occurs again in Ps. lxiii. 8: "My soul *followeth hard* after thee;" and in Ps. cxix. 31: "I have *stuck* to thy testimonies." Joshua said, "*Cleave* unto the Lord thy God" (Josh. xxiii. 8); and many have had sweet, while others have had bitter, experience of the truth that "there is a friend that *sticketh closer* than a brother" (Prov. xviii. 24).

HOMILETICS.

Vers. 6—14.—*Longing for the old home.* Brings to view (1) Naomi's resolution to return to the land of Judah, and then it records (2) a touching scene that occurred at her departure.

I. NAOMI'S RESOLUTION. No wonder that she formed it; for—1. The ties that bound her to the land of Moab had been snapped by the hand of death. In the death of her *husband* there was the disruption of the *house-band.* In the deaths of her two sons who had become *husbands,* the only other *bands* or *bonds* that could keep together for Naomi a home in Moab were burst. Matthew Henry says, "The land of Moab was now become a melancholy place to her. It is with little pleasure that she can breathe in that air in which her husband and sons had expired; or go on that ground in which they lay buried out of her sight, but not out of her thoughts." 2. Her heart had got sick for the home of her youth, that home which was now to her imagination and recollection "home, sweet home." "Heaven," she remembered, "lay around her" in her childhood. And such feelings as then thrilled within her are the stuff out of which, as years roll on, patriotism is woven. 3. She was reduced to absolute poverty. Diseases and death are costly, especially in a strange land, among strangers. And pitiable is the condition of those who, in a strange land and among strangers, are unable to "pay their way." 4. She would shrink, moreover, from the possibility of being burdensome to her daughters-in-law, who might, in consequence of their own widowhood, have difficulty in lending efficient assistance. However much she was pulled down in her circumstances, in her spirit her fine womanly independence stood erect. 5. She had learned that brighter days had dawned on the land of her early love. "The Lord had visited his people to give them bread." And "bread," as Dr. Thomas Fuller remarks, "is a dish in every course. Without it can be no feast; with it can be no famine." The Lord gave it. "The miracle of the loaves was a sudden putting forth of God's bountiful hand from behind the veil of his ordinary providence; the miracle of the harvest is the working of the same bountiful hand, only unseen, giving power to the living grains to drink the dew and imbibe the sunshine, and appropriate the nourishment of the soil during the long bright days of summer. I understand the one miracle in the light of the other" (Macmillan's Bible Teachings in Nature,' p. 92).

II. SCENE AT NAOMI'S DEPARTURE. 1. Her daughters-in-law, who had "dealt kindly" with their husbands, had likewise dealt kindly with her. What was to become of them ?   2. They convoyed Naomi for some distance, and then, as they all halted, she reminded them that every step in advance took them further from their mothers' homes, and she insisted on their returning.   Not for her own sake, however, but for theirs.   In their own land their prospects would be brighter than in Judæa.   Their mothers were still living, and would no doubt be motherly.   Their other relatives would be at hand.   They themselves might each be the means of brightening some solitary home.   She prayed that they might have " rest."   This word, so sweet to the weary and the distracted, reveals one element that is essential to the comfort of a home, whether that home be a cottage or a castle.   3. Naomi's words overwhelm the hearts of her daughters-in-law.   They passionately express their desire to accompany her to her old home.   But she persists firmly, though tenderly and meltingly, in her dissuasives.   It is a scene of weeping—a valley of Baca.   At length Orpah yields, and tears herself away.   But Ruth would not yield.   She "clave to her mother-in-law."   The character of both the young widows is beautiful, but that of Ruth is heroic.   This world is a constantly chequered scene of arrivals and departures.   Looming in the near or more remote future, there is one departure which must be made " in solemn loneliness."   Whither ?   With what convoy ?

HOMILIES BY VARIOUS AUTHORS.

Ver. 8.—*Kindness.*   Tidings reached Naomi that peace and plenty had returned to Judah, and she resolved to return to Bethlehem.   She acknowledged the Lord's goodness, who " had visited his people in giving them bread."   Doubtless she sought the Lord's guidance with reference to her return.   It must have needed courage on her part to form and carry out this resolution.   Her affectionate daughters-in-law accompanied her part of the way.   Then came the hour of separation.   As Naomi bade the young widows return, she uttered words of testimony to their kindness, words of prayer that Heaven might deal kindly with them.   Coming from her lips, this witness was precious.   They had dealt kindly with the dead—their husbands, her sons.   They had dealt kindly with her, in her bereavements and loneliness ; they had sympathised with her, and now were willing to accompany her to the land of her birth and early days.   I. The FOUNDATION of kindness.   We must seek this below what is called "good nature ;" and, taught by Christianity, must find it in the brotherhood of man, the fatherhood of God.   The sacrifice of Christ is the power and the model of true Christian kindness.   II. The SPHERE of kindness.   The family, as in the passage before us, comes first.   "Kind" is related, as a word, to "kin."   "Charity begins at home."   But, as has been remarked, it does not end there.   Kindness should be shown to our fellow-creatures, as Christians, as neighbours, as fellow-countrymen, as members of the human race.   III. The DIFFICULTIES in the way of kindness.   It is not always easy for persons of one nation to agree with those of another ; foreigners are often foes.   It is not always easy for mothers-in-law to agree with daughters-in-law.   Yet these difficulties may be overcome, as in this narrative.   IV. The RECOMPENSE of kindness.   Naomi's prayer was answered, and the Lord dealt kindly with those who had shown kindness.   True kindness will breathe many a prayer.   And the Lord's loving-kindness, condescending, unmerited, and free, is his people's most precious possession ; it is " better than life ! "—T.

Vers. 10—14.—*Separation.*   These three women were bound together by the memory of common happiness, by the memory of common sorrows.   The proposal that they should part, however reasonable and just, could not but reopen the flood-gates of their grief.   Orpah found her consolation in her home in Moab, and Ruth found hers in Naomi's life-long society and affection.   But as the three stand before us on the borders of the land, as Naomi begs her daughters-in-law to return, the sorrow and the sanctity of human separations are suggested to our minds.
I. SEPARATIONS BETWEEN LOVING FRIENDS ARE OFTEN EXPEDIENT AND NECESSARY.

II. SEPARATIONS ARE SOMETIMES THE OCCASION OF ALMOST THE BITTEREST SORROWS OF HUMAN LIFE.

III. SEPARATIONS MAY, BY GOD'S GRACE, BE MADE A DISCIPLINE OF THE SOUL'S HEALTH AND WELFARE.

IV. SEPARATIONS MAY BE OVERRULED, BY GOD'S PROVIDENCE, FOR THE REAL GOOD, PROSPERITY, AND HAPPINESS OF THOSE WHO ARE PUT APART.

V. SEPARATIONS REMIND US OF HIM WHO HAS SAID, "I WILL NEVER LEAVE THEE; I WILL NEVER FORSAKE THEE!"—T.

Vers. 6, 7.—*Home returning.* "Then she arose with her daughters-in-law, that she might return. . . . And they went on their way to return." Home again! The first step is everything! "She arose." It was all well with the prodigal when he *did* that. Not simply when he said, I will arise; but when he arose and went to his father. Directly the eye and the heart and the step agree, then the whole is settled. We read nothing of the preliminaries of departure. Who does not know the power of the loadstone when it first begins to act? When the breeze swells the sail from the foreign port, the sailor sees *not* the intervening waters, but the home cottage under the familiar cliffs. There are many beautiful home-returnings in the Bible, but the best of all is the son seeking the father's house.

I. HEARTS ARE UNITED BY COMMON EXPERIENCES. These daughters-in-law were not of her land, nor of her religion; they were not Hebrews; but they were widows! A common sorrow is a welding power, uniting hearts more closely than before. It is said that a babe in a house is a new clasp of affection between husband and wife. True; but an empty cradle has done more than a living child. During the time of these ten years these two wives remained still heathen. We do not know what family they sprang from, or if they were sisters. We do know that Naomi exercised no control or domination over their religious principles. She respects their personal liberty and responsibility; she even urges Ruth not to let natural affection for her override her religious convictions, but to go back to "her gods," as Orpah did. "Behold, thy sister-in-law is gone back unto her people, and unto her gods: return thou after thy sister-in-law." What a sorrow it must have been to her that her sons had married heathen women. We can respect that sorrow. And we can see that Naomi did not *slight* her own religion when she said these words, but used them as a test of the sincerity of Ruth. A common sorrow had brought them all very close together. "For," as Bailey says in Festus, "the world is one, and hath one great heart."

II. RETURN JOURNEYS HAVE A TOUCHING ELOQUENCE IN THEIR SCENES. There were the places Naomi had traversed with her husband and her boys; places of rest under the shadow of the rocks, and of refreshment at the wells. Much must there have been, to recall conversations touched with anxiety concerning their future in the land of Moab. So would many places speak to us to-day. There, care gazed at us wistfully, and we remember all the thoughts it suggested. There she heard the tinkling of the bells of the camels, as the little trading cavalcade passed by her. What reminiscences! And they would all remind her of the good hand which had led her on, and never forgotten or forsaken her.

III. RETURN JOURNEYS REMIND US OF LITTLE EPISODES OF LIFE THAT ARE OVER FOR EVER. We cannot in the ordinary course of an unbroken and unshifting home realise the flight of time so well as when we have marked changes, which by their very abruptness divide life into chapters, which, like volumes, have their commencement and close. A new nest has to be built, and new trees have to be sought to build it in. Thus with ordinary observation we may notice how those who have had to seek new homes find the pilgrim-nature of life more marked in their thought than those who are born and brought up and settled through the long years in one home. There is a dreamy sense of continuance unbroken in some lives! "That she might return!" But she would not, could not take all of herself with her. She would leave, as we all do, a memory of character, an influence of good or evil over those who had been associated with her in the foreign land.—W. M. S.

Ver. 8.—*Benedictions.* The Hebrews were fond of benedictions. "The Lord bless thee and keep thee." "And Jacob blessed Joseph, and said, The God which fed me all

my life long unto this day, the angel which redeemed me from all evil, bless the lads."
"The Lord bless thee out of Zion."   These Scriptures of olden time touch us so
tenderly, because they recognise the living hand, the loving heart of God.   It is this
which will make them never grow old.   It is this which makes their inspiration
living, and keeps their fountains of consolation open still.   We are always meeting
and parting, journeying forth and returning home.   Our families are broken up, our
churches have gates of entrance and departure, and the picture of life is always one
of a tent-life.   We are pilgrims and strangers, as all our fathers were.   The key-
note of all that I have to say to you from this text is in that word "kindly."   The
argument is this.   We can understand kindness in the sphere of the human, and
rise from that to a prayer for the Divine kindness.   No society in any age can be
cemented together by force alone.   Feudalism, for instance, in olden times, was not
all terror.   The baron could command his dependents in time of war, as he fed and
housed and clothed them in times of peace; but, as the old chroniclers tell us, there
was often a rare hospitality, a hearty cheerfulness, a chivalrous affection in the somewhat stern relationship ; nor will any political economy of government ever be able
to preserve nations in allegiance to each other,. or at peace amongst themselves,
without the cultivation of Christian brotherhood.

I. THE LORD KNOWS BEST WHAT KINDNESS IS.   The Lord deal kindly with you.   Has
he been kind ? that is the question for us all.   At times we should have been tempted
to answer, No !   The vine is blighted, the fig tree withered, the locusts have spoiled
the green of spring, the little lambs have died.   Kindly ?   Yes, we shall answer one
time when we stand in our lot at the end of days.   For kindness is not indulgence.   I am thankful that this once common word has dropped out of our prayers—
Indulgent Father.   No word in the English language describes a feebler state of
being than the word indulgence ; it refers always to the weaker side of our nature ;
that which is pleasant to us, that which eases us of pain and of discipline and
effort.   Prayer like this goes to the heart ; more especially from the Naomis of the
universe who have had so hard a time of it, to whom life has been so full of bereavement and battle.   But if you study life, you will see it is the indulged who complain ;
it is those nursed in the lap of luxury who whine and whimper if the sun does not
shine, if the pomegranate, and the fig, and the grape do not supplement the bread.
Indulgence breeds supercilious mannerism and contempt for common things in them ;
and all seems so very strange if men, and women, and things are not ready for their
comfort.   God's kindness to us may take forms which surprise us.   At the heart of
his severest judgments there is mercy, in the bitter spring there is healing water, in
the desolated altar there is the downfall of idolatry.   Abba, Father, we cry, and he
seems not to hear us.   The wild winds seem to waft away into empty space our
cries for help and pity, but he who sitteth in the heavens hears and answers according to the wisdom of his own will.   The kindest things God has ever done for us
have been, perhaps, the strangest and severest.   So it was with Daniel, and Jacob,
and Joseph, and Abraham our father.   All God's ways are done in truth, and truth
is always kindness, for the music of the universe is set in that key.   The throne of
the Almighty himself has its firm pillars planted on that.   Away we go to business
and duty.   Farewell to son and daughter.   Go thy way, pilgrim of life, with knap-
sack and staff; henceforth our paths are separate, and for you there will come battles
when we cannot fight beside you, burdens we cannot help you to bear.   To another
hearth you will come at evening, when the day's work is done, and the anodynes of
sympathy are needed for the worker's heart.   "Go thy way.   The Lord deal kindly
with thee."

II. THE LORD ALONE WILL BE WITH US ALL THROUGH OUR FUTURE PILGRIMAGE.
Apart from Divine power, which we have not to bless with, there is Divine presence
which we all need.   Christ will be with us to the end.   Never will come a battle, a
temptation, a solitude, a sorrow, a needful sacrifice, but the Lord will be at hand.
The sceptre will never be laid in front of an empty throne.   The Lord reigns.   It
is touching to see the struggles of modern thought in the minds of men who have
drifted away from the incarnation and resurrection of our Lord.   "The ocean en-
croaches more and more each year "—to use a figure of one who has marked the
" ebb " of thought—" and he watches his fields eaten up from year to year."   Yes,

says the same writer, who is depicting the drift:—"The meadow-land, whereon he played in the innocent delights of childhood, has now become a marshy waste of sand. The garden where he gathered flowers, an offering of love and devotion to his parents, is now sown with sea-salt. The church where he offered up his childish prayers, and wondered at the high mysteries of which his teachers spoke, stands tottering upon the edge of a crumbling cliff that the next storm may bring down in ruin." And this is rightly called "an experience of spiritual misery." Pathetic, indeed, is this. The picture is most touching and saddening! Who can feel it more than those who suffer the eclipse of faith? We, who worship here, trust in the living God, who as we believe revealed himself to our fathers by the prophets, and who in these last days has spoken to us by his Son, whom he hath made heir of all things, anhath given us this testimony, in that he hath raised him from the dead.—W. M. S.

Ver. 8.—"As you have dealt with the dead and me." This beautiful analogy, which has its root idea in love and home, is very suggestive.

I. THE LORD KNOWS BEST WHAT OTHERS HAVE BEEN TO US. "As you have dealt with the dead and me." You have been good and true to them, Naomi says, with a voice that trembles with remembrances of the old days gone for ever. It is a touching little sentence. The dead. So silent now. Never to come back for us to touch imperfectness into riper good; never to charm away with pleasant thoughts the dull hours; never to fill with deeper meanings of love the half-empty words; never to make more Divine the common service of life; never to put the best interpretation upon conduct; never to lift the leaden crown of care from the anxious brow; never to help to transfigure the mean and lowly with heavenly hopes and aspirations. Gone! What a world of vacancy, and silence, and subtle mystery! Is it strange we should wish well to those who were kind to the dead? And Naomi links her own being with them still. "The dead and me." And with true hearts they never can be disassociated. Anniversaries of remembrance make our separations no more distant. They soften them. They give place for comforting remembrances; but the dead are near as ever. "The dead and me!" Who shall separate? None. Christ died, yea, rather is risen again, and he will raise us up together to the heavenly places. What a blessing so to live, so to fill our place as sons and daughters, so to sweeten, sublime, and sanctify life that others may make our conduct a plea with that God who has known our heart and life, and say, "The Lord deal kindly with you, as you have dealt with the dead and me."

II. THE LORD HAS GIVEN US GUARANTEES OF HIS KINDNESS. We are not left to meditate on rain and fruitful seasons only. Not the green of spring, nor the south wind of summer, nor the gold of autumn alone proclaim his goodness. So long as the story of the cross has Divine meaning for us, so long as we believe it, not alone as the spirit of a good man's life, but as the revelation of God manifest in the flesh, so long can we exclaim, "Herein is love, not that we loved God, but that he loved us." Nor can we exclude conscience from our argument; that, too, is a guarantee that the Almighty cares for us, that he will not let us sin and suffer without the very voice Divine awakening, alarming, and arresting us. None but a good Being would have put conscience there, and made it universal, and filled it with such sweet benedictions for the soul. We are surrounded by evidences of the Eternal pity. God who spared not his own Son, will with him also freely give us all things—for man is still his child, and he has a desire to the work of his hands. When we pray, therefore, "The Lord deal kindly with thee," we only ask him to be like himself, we only put him in remembrance of his promise to hear when we call upon him. Some would think God kind, indeed, if he were less severe on sin; to them all law is baneful, and the sorest evils are only evidences of an imperfect brain, or an untrained mind, or an ungovernable power of impulse. How, then, should the law of God be other than dislikable—nay, detestable to them; but he who prepared the light, prepared also the throne of his judgment, and he will by no means clear the guilty—for the love of God would be but a weak sentiment if it were not harmonised with a law which means order, truth, righteousness, and justice in all domains of his eternal empire. We only predicate that love is the root of law, as it is also the essence of mercy, and how God's kindness even on the cross shows that justice and mercy blend with each other.

III. THE LORD LOOKS FOR OUR LOVE TO HIM IN OUR LOVE TO EACH OTHER. If we love him we shall feed his lambs, forgive our enemies, and fulfil the whole law of love. How many there have been who, professing even an extreme sanctity, have robbed their partners, deluded their followers, and sometimes darkened for ever a brightly opening life. It is saddening to think what religion has suffered from those whose countenances advertise asperity and contempt, selfishness and pride, whilst they carry their Bibles under their arms, and seem shocked at the exuberance of a healthy joy. Deal kindly? Not they. Their silken words are often the soft sheaths of dagger purposes, and their sham friendship is often only the occasion of stealing mental photographs of you to distribute among their friends. Deal kindly? Why they sleep as well when they have wounded as when they have healed, and they do not understand what the plan of salvation has to do with a conscientious rectitude, a tender consideration, and a warm and loving heart. Deal kindly. Let the Church arise and shine, and put on her beautiful garments. Let the venerable Apostle John take his place once more in the midst of the Churches, and say, "Beloved, let us love one another, for love is of God; and every one that loveth is born of God, for God is love." "If we love one another, God dwelleth in us, and his love is perfected in us." "My little children, let us not love in word, neither in tongue, but in deed and truth." "He that loveth his brother abideth in the light, and there is none occasion of stumbling in him." How true we feel all this to be, and yet how hard in such a world as this. God *is* light, God is love, but unless we walk in the light with him we know nothing of it at all. It is still more popular to discuss a mystery than to seek after a Divine ideal. It is still true that many appraise their goodness by their greater enlightenment on some disputable points of religion, and they greatly hope their friend and brother will come to *see* like themselves. Alas! alas! all the while we may perchance be so untrue to Christ, we may be experiencing no sensitive grief that we are unlike the chief Shepherd of the sheep, so worldly, so captious, so dull in all Divine sensibilities. Naomi's prayer, therefore, may teach us much to-day about God—our Saviour; much, too, about ourselves. This, at all events, is true. If the harvests of love come late, they are very real and very precious. Years alone can reveal character. We know what *others* are in times of test and trial, as Naomi did in a strange land. She was a mother-in-law, and that is a hard part to fulfil, often the subject of satire, too often, indeed, an experience which awakens slender sympathy; she yet gained the crown of trust, and honour, and love. And now, how can she speak better for others than by speaking to God for them? The God who has never left her, the God who has been the husband of the widow, the God who sent her human solace in the trying hours of her bereavement in the far away land. "The Lord deal kindly with you." When once in the hush of death a girl stood at the threshold of the door, trembling, as childhood does, in the presence of death, the mother, bending over the quiet sleeper, beckoned her in. She regained confidence then, and taking up the cold hand kissed it, and said of her dead brother, "Mother, that hand never struck me." How beautiful! Can we say the same, that we never wounded the dead? Can we say it of the Christ himself, that we never crucified the Son of God afresh? And now we look up to the great Father of our spirits, and the God of our salvation, and pray him to bless all we love, to make them his own now and evermore. His kindness is truer, deeper, wiser than our own. "The Lord bless them and keep them." "The Lord deal kindly with them."—W. M. S.

EXPOSITION.

CHAPTER I. 15—22.

Ver. 15.—**And she said, Behold, thy sister-in-law is gone back to her people, and to her gods: return thou after thy sister-in-law.** The expression that stands in King James's version thus, "and to her

gods," is rendered by Dr. Cassel "and to her God." The same interpretation, it is noteworthy, is given in the Targum of Jonathan, who renders the expression, "and to her Fear" (וּלְוַת דְּחַלְתָּהּ). Such a translation assumes that the Moabites were not only theists, but monotheists. And yet in the mythology, or primitive theology, of Moab, we read both of Baal-Peor and of Chemosh. As to the former, see Num. xxv. 3, 5 ; Deut. iv. 3 ; Ps. cvi. 28 ; Hosea ix. 10. As to the latter, see Judges xi. 24 ; 1 Kings xi. 7, 33 ; Jer. xlviii. 7, 13. In Numbers, moreover, xxi. 29, and in Jeremiah xlviii. 46, the Moabites are called *the people of Chemosh*, and frequently is their national god called Chemosh in the inscription of King Mesha on *the Moabitish Stone*, so recently discovered and deciphered. It is supposed, not without reason, that the two names belonged to one deity, Chemosh being the old native name. Nevertheless, the translation "to her god" is an interpretation, not a literal rendering, and, on the other hand, the translation "to her gods" would, on the hypothesis of the monotheism of the Moabites, be unidiomatic. The original expression, "to her Elohim," does not tell anything, and was not intended by Naomi to tell anything, or to hint anything, of a numerical character concerning the object or objects of the Moabitish worship. *It was an expression equally appropriate whether there was, or was not, a plurality of objects worshipped.* It might be liberally rendered, *and to her own forms of religious worship.* The word *elohim* was a survival of ancient polytheistic theology and worship, when a plurality of powers were held in awe. "For," says Fuller, "the heathen, supposing that the whole world, with all the creatures therein, was too great a diocese to be daily visited by one and the same deity, they therefore assigned sundry gods to several creatures." The time arrived, however, when the great idea flashed into the Hebrew mind, *The Powers are One!* and hence the plural noun, with its subtended conception of unity, became construed with verbs and adjectives in the singular number. It was so construed when applied to the one living God ; but it readily retained its original applicability to a plurality of deities, and hence, in such a passage as the one before us, where there is neither adjective nor verb to indicate the number, the word is quite incapable of exact rendering into English. Orpah had returned to her people and her Elohim. **Return thou after thy sister-in-law.** Are we then to suppose that Naomi desired Ruth to return to her Moabitish faith ? Is it with a slight degree of criticism that she referred to Orpah's palinode ? Would she desire that Ruth should, in this matter, follow in her sister-in-law's wake ? We touch on tender topics. Not unlikely she had all along suspected or seen that Orpah would not have insuperable religious scruples. And not unlikely, too, she would herself be free from narrow religious bigotry, at least to the extent of dimly admitting that the true worship of the heart could reach the true God, even when offensive names, and forms, and symbolisms were present in the outer courts of the creed. Nevertheless, when she said to Ruth, "Return thou after thy sister-in-law," she no doubt was rather putting her daughter-in-law to a final test, and leading her to thorough self-sifting, than encouraging her to go back to her ancestral forms of worship. "God," says Fuller, "wrestled with Jacob with desire to be conquered ; so Naomi no doubt opposed Ruth, hoping and wishing that she herself might be foiled."

Ver. 16.—**And Ruth said, Insist not on me forsaking thee : for whither thou goest, I will go.** Ruth's mind was made up. Her heart would not be wrenched away from her mother-in-law. The length of the journey, its dangers, and the inevitable fatigue accompanying it, moved not, by so much as a jot, her resolution. Had not her mother-in-law the same distance to travel, the same fatigue to endure, the same perils to encounter ? Might not the aged traveller, moreover, derive some assistance and cheer from the company of a young, ready-handed, and willing-hearted companion ? She was resolved. Nothing on earth would separate them. **Wheresoever thou lodgest, I will lodge.** A better version than Luther's, "Where thou stayest, I will stay" (*wo du bleibest, da bleibe ich auch*). The reference is not to the ultimate destination, but to the nightly halts. לין is the verb employed ; and it is rendered "to tarry all night" in Gen. xxiv. 54 ; xxviii. 11 ; xxxi. 54 ; Judges xix. 6, &c. It is the Latin *pernoctare* and the German *übernachten*, the former being the rendering of the Vulgate, and the latter the translation in the *Berlenburger Bibel*. **Thy people (is) my people, and thy God my God.** There being no verb in the original, it is well to supply the simplest copula. Ruth claims, as it were, Naomi's people and Naomi's God as her own already.

Ver. 17.—**Where thou diest, will I die, and there will I be buried.** She wished to be naturalised for life in Naomi's fatherland. Nor did she wish her remains to be conveyed back for burial to the land of her nativity. **So may Yahveh do to me, and still more, but death only shall part me and thee.** She appeals to the God of the Israelites, the one universal God. She puts herself on oath, and invokes his severest penal displeasure if she should suffer anything less uncontrollable than death to part her from her mother-in-law. "So may Yahveh do to me." It was thus that the Hebrews made their most awful appeals to Yahveh. They signified their willingness to suffer some dire calamity if they should either do the evil deed repudiated or fail to do the good deed promised. *So* stands in misty indefiniteness; not, as Fuller supposes, by way of "leaving it to the discretion of God Almighty to choose that arrow out of his quiver which he shall think it most fit to shoot," but as a kind of euphemism, or cloudy veil, two-thirds concealing, and one-third revealing, whatever horrid infliction could by dramatic sign be represented or hinted. *And still more*—a thoroughly Semitic idiom, *and so may he add* (*to do*)! There was first of all a full imprecation, and then an additional 'bittock,' to lend intensity to the asseveration. "But death only shall sever between me and thee!" Ruth's language is broken. Two formulas of imprecation are flung together. One, if complete, would have been to this effect: "So may Yahveh do to me, and so may he add to do, 'if' (אִם) aught but death sever between me and thee!" The other, if complete, would have run thus: "I swear by Yahveh 'that' (כִּ֜י) death, death only, shall part thee and me!" In the original the word *death* has the article, *death emphatically*. It is as if she had said *death, the great divider*. The full idea is in substance *death alone*. This divider alone, says Ruth, "shall sever between me and thee;" literally, "between me and between thee," a Hebrew idiom, repeating for emphasis' sake the two-sided relationship, but taking the repetition in reverse order, *between me* (*and thee*) and *between thee* (*and me*).

Ver. 18.—**And she perceived.** In our idiom we should have introduced the proper name, "And Naomi perceived." **That she was determined to go with her.** She saw that Ruth was fixed in her resolution. **And she left off speaking to her.** She "gave in." Ruth, as Fuller has it, was "a fixed star."

Ver. 19. — **And they two went**—they trudged along, the two of them—**until they came to Bethlehem.** In the expression "the two of them" the masculine pronoun (הֶם for הֵן) occurs, as in verses 8 and 9. It mirrors in language the actual facts of relationship in life. The masculine is sometimes assumptively representative of both itself and the feminine. And sometimes, even apart from the representative element, it is the overlapping and overbearing gender. **And it came to pass, as they entered Bethlehem, that the whole city got into commotion concerning them, and they said, Is this Naomi?** Naomi, though greatly altered in appearance, besides being travel-worn and weary, was recognised. But who was that pensive and beautiful companion by her side? Where was Elimelech? Where was Machlon and Chilion? Why are they not with their mother? Such would be some of the

questions started, and keenly talked about and discussed. Then on both the wayfarers the finger-marks of poverty, involuntary signals of distress, would be unconcealable. Interest, sympathy, gossip would be alive throughout the little town, especially among the female portion of the population, and loud would be their exclamations of surprise. The verb *they said* is feminine in Hebrew, וַתֹּאמַרְנָה, a nicety which cannot be reproduced in English without obtruding too prominently the sex referred to, as in Michaelis's version—"and all the women said." So the Vulgate. The verb which we have rendered *got into commotion* is found in 1 Sam. iv. 5—"the earth *rang again;*" and in 1 Kings i. 45—"the city *rang again.*"

Ver. 20.—**And she said to them, Call me not Naomi, call me Mara: for the Almighty hath dealt very bitterly with me.** Salutations were respectfully addressed to her as she walked along in quest of some humble abode. And when thus spoken to by the sympathetic townspeople, she was called, of course, by her old *sweet* name. But as it fell in its own rich music on her ears, its original import flashed vividly upon her mind. Her heart "filled" at the contrast which her circumstances represented, and she said, "Address me not as Naomi, call not to me (לִי) Naomi: address me as Mara,"—that is, *bitter*,—"for the Almighty has caused bitterness to me exceedingly" (see on ver. 2). *The Almighty*, or שַׁדַּי, an ancient polytheistic name that had at length—like אֱלֹהִים and אֲדֹנָי — been reclaimed in all its fulness for the one living and true God. It had become a thorough proper name, and hence it is used without the article. In the Septuagint it is sometimes rendered, as here, ὁ ἱκανός, *the Sufficient*; in Job, where it frequently occurs, ὁ παντοκράτωρ, *the Omnipotent*. But it is one of those peculiar nouns that never can be fully reproduced in any Aryan language. Naomi's theology, as indicated in the expression, "the Almighty hath caused bitterness to me exceedingly," need not be to its minutest jot endorsed. God was not the only agent with whom she had had to do. Much of the bitterness of her lot may have been attributable to her husband or to herself, and perhaps to forefathers and foremothers. It is not fair to ascribe all the embittering element of things to God. Much rather might the sweetness, which had so often relieved the bitterness, be traced to the hand of him who is "the Lord God, merciful and gracious, abundant in goodness."

Ver. 21.—**I went forth full, and Yahveh has caused me to return in emptiness. Why should you call me Naomi, and Yahveh has** testified against me, and the Almighty has brought evil upon me? She went forth "full," with husband and sons, not to speak of goods. She was under the necessity of returning *in emptiness*, or *with empty hands*. The Hebrew word רֵיקָם does not exactly mean *empty*, as it is rendered in the Septuagint, the Vulgate, and King James's version. It is not an adjective, but an adverb, *emptily*. This lamentable change of circumstances she attributed to the action of Yahveh. He had, she believed, been testifying against her by means of the trials through which she had passed. She was right in a certain conditional acceptation of her language ; but only *on condition of that condition*. And, let us condition her declarations as we may, she was probably in danger of making the same mistake concerning herself and her trials which was made by Job's comforters in reference to the calamities by which he was overwhelmed. In so far as *penal evil* is concerned, it may be traced directly or circuitously to the will and government of God. "Shall there be evil—*that is*, penal evil—in a city, and the Lord hath not done it?" (Amos iii. 6). *But there are many sufferings that are not penal.* The evil that is penal is only one segment of physical evil ; and then there is besides, metaphysical evil, or the evil that consists in the inevitable imperfection of finite being. It is noteworthy that the

participle of the Hiphilic verb הֵרַע employed by Naomi is always translated in King James's version *evil doer*, or *wicked doer*, or *evil*, or *wicked*. Naomi, in using such a term, and applying it to Yahveh, was walking on a theological precipice, where it is not needful that we should accompany her. Instead of the literal expression, '*and*' Yahveh, we may, with our English wealth of conjunctions freely say, '*when*' Yahveh. There is a charm in the original simplicity. There is likewise a charm in the more complex structure of the free translation.

Ver. 22.—**So Naomi returned.** The narrator pauses to recapitulate his narrative of the return, and hence the recapitulatory *so* is, in English, very much to be preferred to the merely additive *and* of the original. **And Ruth the Moabitess, her daughter-in-law, with her, who returned out of the land of Moab.** The cumulative and apparently redundant expression, "who returned out of the land of Moab," is remarkable at once for its simplicity and for its inexactitude. Ruth, strictly speaking, had not returned, but she took part in Naomi's return. **And they arrived in Bethlehem at the commencement of barley-harvest.** Barley ripened before wheat, and began to be reaped sometimes as early as March, but generally in April, or Abib. By the time that the barley-harvest was finished the wheat crop would be ready for the sickle.

HOMILETICS.

Vers. 15—22.—*Devoted attachment.* I. Ruth was fixed in her desire and determination to CAST IN HER LOT WITH HER DESOLATE AND DESTITUTE MOTHER-IN-LAW. The absolute unselfishness of this determination is noteworthy, for—1. Be it noted that Naomi was not one of those who are always murmuring and complaining because they do not receive sufficient consideration. 2. Still less did she claim as a right, or urge as a duty, that her daughter-in-law should become her companion in travel, and wait upon her as an attendant. 3. On the contrary, she was careful to put Ruth in an attitude of entire freedom, so that, if she had a secret wish to go back to her Moabitish friends, she could have gratified her desire without laying herself open to the imputation of coldness or ingratitude. 4. Ruth was tested nevertheless, as all of us in our respective relations have either already been or will be. Eve, for instance, was emphatically tested. So was Adam. Abraham too. Joseph also. Very particularly the second Adam, our Lord Jesus Christ, when he was led up by the Spirit into the wilderness. Judas was tested when the demon of cupidity entered into his heart. So was Peter when he stood warming himself at the fire in the court of the high priest's palace. All who are *tried* are tested. And all men without exception have to endure *trial* and *trials*. It was as regards the strength of her attachment to her mother-in-law that Ruth was tested. Not only did Naomi hold out no hopes of home-comfort in Judah, she expressly said, dissuasively, when Orpah had gone back, "Behold, thy sister-in-law has gone back to her people, and to her Elohim : return thou after thy sister-in-law" (ver. 15). 5. Ruth stood the test. Not so did Eve. Not so Adam. But Abraham stood it. So Joseph. Emphatically did Jesus stand it, so that he knows how to succour those who are tempted. Judas did not stand the test. Nor at first did Peter, though afterwards he repented, and, when reconverted, was able to strengthen his brethren. Ruth, for love to Naomi, was able to say in her heart, " Farewell, Melchom! Farewell, Chemosh! Farewell, Moab! Welcome, Israel! Welcome, Canaan! Welcome, Bethlehem!" (Fuller). 6. She witnessed a good and most noble confession of love and devotedness (see vers. 16, 17). She said, " Insist not on me forsaking thee ; for whither thou goest, I will go ; wheresoever thou lodgest, I will lodge ; thy people is my people, and thy God my God : where thou diest, will I die, and there will I be buried. So may Yahveh do to me, and still more, if aught but death part thee and me." "Nothing," says Matthew Henry, " could be said more fine, more brave." " Truly," says Dr. Kitto, " the simple eloquence of the mouth that speaks out of the abundance of the heart never found more beautiful and touching expression than in these words of this young widow " (' Daily Bible-Illustrations '). "Her vow," says S. Cox, "has stamped itself on the very heart of the world ; and that not because of the beauty of its form simply, though even in our English version it sounds like a sweet and noble music, but because it expresses in a worthy form, and once for all, the utter devotion of a genuine and self-conquering love. It is the spirit which informs and breathes through these melodious words that make them so precious to us, and that also renders it impossible to utter any fitting comment on them " (' Book of Ruth,' pp. 72, 73). Be it borne in mind that something of the same enthusiasm of love, that dwelt in the heart of Ruth, should be found in *the centre of every home*. Wheresoever a heart is swayed and dominated by the might and mastery of a great affection, the entire character becomes clothed with mingled dignity and beauty.

II. THE ENTRY OF THE TWO WIDOWS INTO BETHLEHEM. There was no more talk, no more thought, of turning back. The hearts of the two widows were locked together for ever. Hence they travelled on from stage to stage, until, worn and wearied, they entered Bethlehem. 1. Note the effect on the citizens, especially the female portion of them (see ver. 19). Naomi, passing along through the streets, was recognised. The news flew from individual to individual, from house to house, from lane to lane. There was a running to and fro of excited mothers and maidens. All were eager to see the returned emigrant, and her pensive Moabitish companion. Her old acquaint-ances, in particular, when they had seen and identified her, broke up into groups, and talked, and said, Is that Naomi ? That, Naomi! Is this Naomi ? This, Naomi! " So unlike is the rose when it is withered to what it was when it was blooming." 2. Note the effect on Naomi herself. As she looked on old scenes, and witnessed the excitement and commotion of old neighbours and acquaintances, her heart felt over-whelmed within her, and she said to the sympathising friends who clustered around her, "Call me not Naomi, call me Mara : for the Almighty hath dealt very bitterly with me " (see vers. 20, 21). But it surely will be permitted to us not only to mingle our tears with those of the afflicted widow, but likewise to pause reverently ere we unreservedly accept or endorse her attribution of all her trials and woes to the hand and heart of the Lord. It should nevertheless be borne in mind that even those trials that come most directly from men's own acts or choices come to pass by the per-mission of the Almighty, and are so overruled by him that they will be made to work for good to them who love him (Rom. viii. 28).

HOMILIES BY VARIOUS AUTHORS.

Vers. 16—18.—*Constancy.* For simple pathos and unstudied eloquence, this lan-guage is unsurpassed. " One touch of nature makes the whole world kin." Here is the fervent outpouring of a true heart. Love and resolution are at their height. Thousands of human souls have expressed their mutual attachment in these words. They are not words of extravagance or of passion, but of feeling, of principle, of a fixed and changeless mind. Constancy must be admired, even by the inconstant.

I. THERE WERE INFLUENCES OPPOSED TO RUTH'S CONSTANCY. 1. Early associations and friendships would have tied her to Moab. 2. The entreaty of Naomi that she would return set her perfectly free to do so, if she had been disposed. 3. The example of her sister-in-law, Orpah, could not but have some weight. Orpah had been, like Ruth, kind alike to the living and the dead, yet she wept, kissed her mother-in-law, and returned. 4. The religion of her childhood could scarcely have been without attractions for her.   Could she leave the temples, the deities, the observances of her earliest days behind ?

II. THERE WERE MANIFESTATIONS OF PIOUS CONSTANCY IN RUTH'S RESOLVES.   **1.** She would go with Naomi, though by an unknown route.   **2.** She would dwell with Naomi, though in an unknown home.   **3.** She would die with Naomi, though to be buried in an unknown grave.

III. THERE WAS A RELIGIOUS FOUNDATION FOR RUTH'S CONSTANCY.   **1.** Apparent from the resolution—" Thy people shall be my people, and thy God my God."   **2.** Apparent from the adjuration she employed—" The Lord do so," &c.

IV. THE TRIUMPH AND RECOMPENSE OF RUTH'S CONSTANCY.   **1.** Her fidelity and devotion were reciprocated by Naomi.   **2.** In the providence of God Ruth was rewarded by an honourable position and a happy life.—T.

Vers. 19—21.—*Heart wounds reopened.*   Return after long absence to scenes of youth always affecting ; he who returns is changed ; they who receive him are changed too.   Observe the reception which Naomi met from her former neighbours at Bethlehem.   Their question, " Is this Naomi ? " evinces—1. Surprise.   She is living !   We see her again !   Yet how is she changed !   2. Interest.   How varied has been her experience whilst absent !   And she loves Bethlehem so that she returns to it in her sorrow !   3. Compassion.   " All the city was moved about them."   How could those who remembered her fail to be affected by the calamities she had passed through ?   Consider the sentiments expressed by Naomi upon her return.

I. HER GRIEF WAS NATURAL AND BLAMELESS.   " I went out full," *i. e.* in health, in youth, with some earthly property ; above all, with husband and sons.   " The Lord hath brought me home again empty," *i. e.* aged, broken down in health and spirits, poor, without kindred or supporters.   " Call me not Naomi," *i. e.* pleasant ; " call me Mara," *i. e.* bitter.   Her lot was sad.   Religion does not question the fact of human trouble and sorrow.   And she was not wrong in feeling, in the circumstances, the peculiar pressure of grief and distress.   We remember that " Jesus wept."

II. HER RECOGNITION OF GOD'S PROVIDENCE WAS RIGHT ; WAS A SIGN OF PIETY.   She attributes all to the Almighty, to the Lord.   Observe that in two verses this acknowledgment is made four times.   In a world over which God rules we should acknowledge his presence and reign in all human experience.   If trouble comes to us by means of natural laws, those laws are ordered by his wisdom.   If by human agency, that agency is the result of the constitution with which he has endowed man.   If as the result of our own action, he connects actions with their consequences.   Therefore, let us reverently recognise his hand in all that happens to us !

III. HER INTERPRETATION OF GOD'S PROVIDENCE WAS MISTAKEN.   " The Lord," said Naomi, " hath testified against me."   Men frequently imagine that if God could prevent afflictions, and yet permits them, he cannot regard the afflicted in a favourable and friendly light.   But this is not so.   " Whom he loveth he chasteneth."   The Book of Job warns us against misunderstanding the meaning of calamity.   Christ has also warned us against supposing that Divine anger is the explanation of human griefs and sufferings.   " All things work together for good unto those who love God."   How often is it true, as the poet Cowper knew and sang—

> " Behind a frowning providence
> God hides a smiling face ! "   T.

Vers. 16, 17.—" Entreat me not to leave thee."   A mother and a daughter-in-law are to go together.   The daughter wishes it, and petitions with most eloquent ardour that it shall be so.   A mother-in-law is sometimes—alas, too often—the subject of criticism and satire.   It is a difficult position to fill, and many bitterly unkind and untrue caricatures have been made upon the relationship.   In this case Naomi had made herself beloved by both Orpah and Ruth, and it was only through Naomi's words, " Turn again," that Orpah went back ; for they had both said, " Surely we will return with thee unto thy people."   Ruth, however, remained firm, and her fidelity has made these words quickening to many undecided souls.

I. ENTREATY MAY PROVE TOO EARNEST.   " Entreat me not."   It is the language of a heart that feels what limits there are to the power of resistance within us. Test may turn in unwise hands into overpowering temptation. Naomi knew where to stop, and Ruth remains to us a picture of heroic devotion. Orpah failed in courage, but was not destitute of affection, for her farewell is accompanied with a kiss of love. In her character we see impulse without strength. But "Ruth clave unto her." And it was no light sacrifice to leave fatherland and home. We can hardly call the test at first a religious one, for it is evident that Ruth's love for her mother-in-law was the immediate occasion of her cleaving to her, and leaving the Moabitish gods. In time, doubtless, her nominal faith turned into a living heritage.

II. LOVE CREATES THE FINEST ELOQUENCE. There is no utterance in the Old Testament more pathetic and melodious than these words. They are idyllic in their eloquence. There is nothing stilted or artificial in them, and they have in them a rhythm of melody which is more beautiful than a mere rhyme of words. Courage and sacrifice, love and devotion, breathe all through them. They condense too all that is prophetic of coming experience—the lodging and the loneliness, the weary pilgrimage and the grave in a foreign land. The mind cannot frame sentences like these without the glow of a sincere and sacrificial heart. We feel as we read them what grandeur there is in human nature when love evokes all its depth of power. It is not a skilful touch that can do this, but a soul alive to the calls of love and duty.

III. NO TRUE LIFE WAS EVER LIVED IN VAIN. It was what Naomi had been to her, what she was in herself, that made this sacrifice possible. Love creates love. The charm of friendship may be merely intellectual, and then, after the feast of reason, all is over. But Naomi's character was rooted in religion. She did not carry the mere roll of the prophets in her hand; she carried the spirit of the Holy Book in her heart. Ruth had never been in synagogue or temple; she had listened to no Rabbi, and never sat at the feet of the doctors; but as "the earliest piety is mother's love," so the character of a true mother is a stem around which the tendrils of the young heart climb to the mother's God. None of us liveth to himself. And so from the flower of piety, the seed drops into other hearts, and brings forth fruit after many days.—W. M. S.

Ver. 18.—*Moral steadfastness.* "When she saw that she was steadfastly minded." "Then she left speaking." The test had done a true work, and we see the heroine who could stand fast. Yes; "having done all, to stand," is something in the great emergencies and temptations of life. There are times when to stand in the rush of the stream, as the river breaks into spray around us, is as much for the hour as we can do, and God knows and honours that.

I. THE STEADFAST MIND GIVES THE STEADFAST STEP. A double-minded man is unstable in all his ways. Veering here and there like the wind, there is no dependence on the direction he may take. The man or the woman is made by something within them invisible to the world. When Christ was led as a lamb to the slaughter, the great conflict had been fought out in Gethsemane, and then the steps were calm and steadfast. What an hour is that in which, in common parlance, "the mind is made up," the resolution taken. This is firmness, as opposed to obstinacy, which acts without reasons, and often in the teeth of them. The misery caused in this world by obstinate people is to be seen sometimes in the home, where sulkiness of temper makes the lives of others miserable. Firmness is the result of the thoughtful decision of an enlightened mind and a consecrated heart.

II. THE STEADFAST MIND MAKES THE BEST COMPANION. Ruth was ready for the companion journey back to Bethlehem. And in all our life journeys nothing is so precious as a steadfast heart. There are times of misinterpretation in all lives—times of disheartenment, times of shadow and darkness. In such hours a steadfast companion is God's richest gift to us. What consolation it is to know that even humanly every support will not give way, that there will always be one eye to brighten, one hand to help, one heart to love, one mind to appreciate. The fickle and irresolute may have a transient beauty and a winning manner, but these are poor endowments without a steadfast mind.

III. THE STEADFAST MIND IS FREED FROM THE INFINITUDE OF LESSER WORRIES.

It is made up. It is not open to every solicitation. It is negative to doubt and distrust. This is the *right* way, and nought can move it. The feeble and irresolute have a restless life. They are constantly balancing expediences and advantages. Christ our Divine Lord set his face steadfastly to go to Jerusalem. The hardest journey of all to the shame and spitting, the awful darkness and the cruel cross. If we are firm and decided in our purposes we shall not be wasting either time or strength upon the solicitations of the popular or profitable. A voice within will say, "This is the way, walk ye in it."—W. M. S.

Ver. 19.—"So they two went till they came to Bethlehem." "They two!" Sometimes it is husband and wife. Sometimes it is two sisters commencing life together in the great city where they have to earn their bread. Sometimes it is two lovers who have large affection and little means, and who have to wait and work and hope on. Sometimes it is widow and child. "They two!" What unrecorded histories of heroism there are written in God's book all unknown to us.

I. HERE IS THE COMMENCEMENT AND CLOSE OF A PILGRIMAGE. They went. They came. So is it of the life history itself. All is enfolded in these brief words. What a multitude of figures in Scripture suggest the brevity of life. A tale that is told. A post. A weaver's shuttle. The morning flower. So indeed it is. What a multitude of incidents would be included even in this brief journey of Naomi's ; but these are the two clasps of the volume of life. They went. They came. "Every beginning holds in it the end, as the acorn does the oak."

II. HERE IS THE SIGHT OF A CITY. Bethlehem. Cities with them were not like cities with us. Even Bethlehem was called a city. But the old dwelling-places, after ten years, have a mute eloquence about them. Other feet come to the well. Little children who gathered flowers on the wild hills are now bearing pitchers to the well. But after a weary journey how refreshing to the Easterns was the glimpse of the white houses on the hills. We look for a city. A city which hath foundations. A city where our beloved are ; for God is not the God of the dead, but of the living. We do not think of it in health and strength and excitement of human interest, but one day we shall look with quiet longing for the city gates. The evening of life will come upon us, and we shall pray, "Let me go, for the day breaketh."

III. HERE IS A PILGRIMAGE ENDED. Better is the end of a thing than the beginning, said the wise man. And so it is. "I have finished my course." How much is included in that. When the battered ship comes into harbour we take more interest in her than the spick and span new vessel with trim decks, and untorn sails, and scarless masts. When the battle is over we think more of the shot-pierced flag than of the new banner borne out by the troops with martial music. We like to see the pilgrim start. But some pilgrims turn back. We like to *hear* Ruth's resolve. How much better is it to *see* the resolve written in letters of living history. We can call no man hero, no woman heroine, till the march is over and the victory won.—W. M. S.

Ver. 19.—Never seemed there a sadder contrast. Naomi left Bethlehem in the full bloom of womanhood, with a husband and two sons. Elimelech, her husband, died, we read, "and she was left and her two sons." They took them wives, and, as mothers do, she lived in the hopes and honours of their new homes ; but, after dwelling in Moab about ten years, we read Mahlon and Chilion died also, both of them, and the woman was left of her two sons and her husband. A strange land is not *so* strange when we carry home with us ; but it *is* strange when all that made home *home*, is gone. We need not wonder, therefore, that not alone for the bread of harvest, but for the bread of love, she and her daughters-in-law "went on the way to *return* to the land of Judah." But, with a fine instinct, Naomi felt that what would be home again for her would be an alien land to them ; and the tender narrative tells us how she suggested they should remain, and find rest, each of them, in the place of their people. We well know the sequel to the words of Naomi, "Turn again my daughters ; " for Ruth has become with us all a beautiful picture of true-hearted womanhood, and a very household name. But it is with the question, "Is this Naomi ?" that we now have to deal. She went out full. Not wealthy, perhaps, —though love is always wealthy, for it alone gives that which worlds want wealth to buy. She is coming home "empty," as many have done since Naomi did, in all the generations. Bent, and sad, and grey, her worn dress tells of her poverty, her garb bespeaks the widow. All in a few years; all crowded into these few opening verses. The pathway of the past is an avenue now, along which she looks to the opening days, when the light flooded her steps, and she walked in the warm glow of companionship and love. Is this Naomi? And have not *we* had this to say again and again concerning those whose early days we knew? There we heard the merry shout of children, and there we saw manhood in its strength and prime. Naomi it cannot be : *that* the face we knew as a bride and as a mother! Never! Yet so it is. They went out full and came home empty. Yet not empty, if, like Naomi, they keep their fellowship with God.

I. Naomi is a returning pilgrim. Home has been but a tent life, and the curtains have been rent by sorrow and death. She tells us the old, old story. *Here* have we no continuing city. Beautiful was the land to which she returned, and in that dear land of promise there never was a fairer time than barley-harvest. Many and many a harvest-time had come and gone since Naomi went forth, and many a reaper's song was silent evermore. As she passed the vines and the oleanders fringing the broad fields, bronzed and bright-eyed faces were directed towards her; and here, in the distance, was Bethlehem, its little white houses dotting the green slopes, its well by the wayside. Bethlehem—home! Oh! that strange longing to live through the closing years in the country places where we were born! It is a common instinct. The Chinese have it, and will be buried nowhere else. It is a beautiful instinct too — to look with the reverent eyes of age on the tombstones we used to spell out in the village, to hear the old rush of the river, the old murmur of the sea. Strange thoughts fill this woman's mind, as the old picture is there with a new peopling of forms and faces. Yet not *all* new. The workers turn to the passing figure, and a gleam of recognition, doubtful at first, lights up their eyes. And then the word passes from one to the other, Is this Naomi? It is the same world in which we live to-day. There is also something to remind us that we are pilgrims and strangers, that unresting time will not wait one hour for us. The unseen angels hurry us on through love and grief and death. Happy for us if we say *plainly* that we seek a country, for the only escape from the *ennui* of life is the satisfaction of the immortal thirst within us by the gospel revelation of eternal life through Jesus Christ our Lord.

II. Naomi is a godly pilgrim. Travel-worn and weary, with sandaled feet, she is coming to a city sanctified by the faith of her fathers. She had lived in a heathen country so devoutly, that Ruth could say, " Thy God shall be my God "—a beautiful testimony to Naomi's fidelity, to her victory over idolatrous usages, to her own personal influence over others. Thy God! How serious the eye, how sober the mien, of this woman as she comes into the city. She has had a battle of life to fight, and she has fought it well. How brave and noble and faithful a woman she is! Is this Naomi? If there is not so much of what the world calls beauty in her face, there is character there, experience there. The young Christian starting on his pilgrimage is cheerful enough. His armour is bright and new, his enthusiasm is fresh and keen. He goes forth full of enterprise and hope. Do not be surprised if in the after years you ask, Is this Naomi? How careful, how anxious, how dependent on God alone! What bright visions once filled his soul, how ready he was to criticise Christian character, how determined and unflinching he looked! Well, it *was* a noble promise, and where would the world be without the enthusiasm of youth? Be not surprised now if he looks worn and weary. He has had battles to fight that the world knows not of. He has made strange discoveries in the continent of his own heart; he has been well-nigh overcome, and casting himself entirely on his Lord, he says, " By the grace of God I am what I am." Look at that weary heart. Is that Luther? Look at that faithless spirit. Is that Peter? Look at that worn soldier. Is that Paul? But the Lord is with them! Empty, indeed, in a human sense was Naomi. Call me not Naomi, she said; it has lost its meaning. Life is no longer pleasant. Call me Mara, for life is bitter. True-hearted soul! She knew that it was bitter, indeed, though it was God's will ; " for the Almighty hath dealt very bitterly with me." Very bitterly! And are we to cover over that? Can we sing—

"Thy will is sweetest to me when
 It triumphs at my cost"?

We may *sing* it; but it is hard to *live* it.   It is glorious to believe in God at such times at all, and to bow with the pain all through our hearts, and to say, "*My* God."—W. M. S.

Ver. 22; ii. 1—3.—Naomi's history may now be carried on in the light of these texts.

I. NAOMI IS AN ANCESTRAL PILGRIM.   Ancestor of whom?   Turn to Matt. i. 5, and you will find in the genealogy of our Lord the name of Ruth.   The earlier part of that Divine life, how fresh and beautiful it is—the advent, the angels, the shepherds' songs!   The mother, the first visit to the temple, the doctors!   And beautiful ministry too.   Power wedded to mercy, miracles of healing, mighty deeds of love, sermons amid the mountains and the cities.   True!   But stand here a moment.   It is an *early* evening of life, I admit; but it *is* evening.   Do you see in the blue distance One coming from the judgment hall?   Do you hear the wild cry of the mob, "Away with him!   Away with him!   Crucify him!   Crucify him!"?   Do you mark the crush of the crowd round one fallen form, who fainted beneath the burden of that cross which he bore for us all?   Follow him on to the slopes, while Simon, the Cyrenian, helps to bear his cross.   The soldiers mock him.   The crowd insult him.   They spat upon him, they smote him with their hands, they buffeted him.   And now his hands and feet are nailed; his pale face is bowed.   Come nearer and gaze.   Behold the man!   As the reapers asked, "Is this Naomi?" so we ask, "Is this Jesus?"   Is this he whose sweet face lay in the manger?   Is this he whose bright inquisitive face was in the temple?   Is this he who passed the angels at heaven's high gate, and *came* to earth, saying, "Lo!   I come to do thy will, O God."   Yes!   Bowed, bruised, broken for us.   The same Saviour, who now endures the cross, despising the shame.   Well may we wonder and adore!   He saved others, himself he cannot—will not—save!   More beautiful now than in the stainless infancy of the Holy Child.   More beautiful now than when by the shores of Galilee's lake, he spake words which mirrored heaven more purely and clearly than those waters the gold and crimson of the sky.   It is the bowed, broken, forsaken, suffering, dying Lord that moves the world's heart.   He knew it all   In that hour, when his soul was made an offering for sin, he, being lifted up, had power to draw all hearts unto him.   Is this Naomi?   Well might angels ask, Is this the eternal Son of the Father?   Is this he of whom the Almighty said, "He is my fellow."   Is this he to whom command was given, Let all the angels of God worship him?   Yes!   It is he.   It is finished.   "Lift up your heads, O ye gates, and be ye lift up, ye everlasting doors, and the King of glory shall come in."

II. NAOMI IS A PROVIDED-FOR PILGRIM.   Back to Bethlehem; but how to live?   how to find the roof-tree that should shelter again?   She knew the Eternal's name, "Jehovah-Jireh," the Lord will provide.   A kinsman of her husband's, a mighty man of wealth, lived there: of the family of Elimelech; his name was Boaz.   We must not mind criticism when we talk of chance, or happening.   The Bible does.   It is simply one way of stating what seems to us accidental; although in reality we know that the least secrets are in the good hand of him "to whom is nothing trivial."   Ruth wants to glean!   And Naomi says, Go, my daughter; "and her *hap*—her chance—was to light on the part of a field belonging unto Boaz."   We know that the same old love story, which is new in every generation begins again; so Boaz took Ruth, and she was his wife.   So that a new home begins, and a smile plays through the tears of the lonely widow.   Naomi has some human light again in her landscape; she will see the children's children, and take them by the hand into the coming barley-harvests; she will have some appropriate hopes and joys and interests still.   Life to her will not be desolate, because she has still a God above her and a world around her to call forth interest and hope.   Her sorrow was not greater than she could bear, and the summer over, even autumn had its tender beauties before life's winter came.   So it ever is.   Trust in the Lord, and you shall never want any good thing.   Believe still in your Saviour, and provided for you will be with all weapons of fence, all means of consolation, all prosperity that shall not harm your soul. So *true*, then, is the Bible to the real facts of human life. It is not a book of gaiety, for life is real and earnest, and its associations are mortal and mutable. It consecrates home joy, and yet reminds us that every garden has its grave, every dear union its separation. But, on the other hand, there are no utterances of unbearable grief, or unmitigated woe. It says ever to us, Jehovah-Jireh, the Lord will provide. And the facts of experience in every age endorse its truth. As the snows hide flowers even in the Alps, so beneath all our separations and sorrows there are still plants of the Lord, peace, and hope, and joy, and rest in him. Blessed, indeed, shall we be if we can rest in the Lord, and wait patiently for him. We, too, shall all change. Time and sorrow will write their experiences on our brow. There will be hours in which we feel like Naomi, empty, oh! *so* empty. The cup of affection poured out on the ground, the forest without its songsters, the garden without its flowers, the home without its familiar faces. We shall see these pictures every day, and wonder, more and more, how any hearts can do without a Brother and a Saviour in Jesus Christ. But if character be enriched and trained, all is well; for this very end have we had Divine discipline, and the Lord will perfect that which concerneth us for the highest ends of eternal life in him. The baptism with which our Lord was baptised changed his face, altered his mien, enlarged even his Divine experience. He was made "perfect through suffering," and became the Author of eternal salvation to all who trust in him. Coming back even to Bethlehem is only for a season. As Naomi returns, nature alone remains the same; the blue roller-bird would flash for a moment across her path, the music of the turtle-dove remind her of the melody of nature in her childhood;—the peasant garb would tell her of the old unchanged ways; and the line of hills against the sky would remind her that the earth abideth for ever. But for her there was a still more abiding country, where Elimelech, like Abraham, lived, and where Mahlon and Chilion waited for the familiar face that had made their boyhood blessed. And so we wait. The redemption we celebrate here is a passover, a memorial of deliverance and a prophecy of home. Home where sorrow and sighing, night and death, will flee away; where, no longer pilgrims, we shall no more go out, and where the worn face and the weary heart shall be transfigured into the immortal life.—W. M. S.

Ver. 21. "I went out full, and the Lord hath brought me home again empty." It seemed, indeed, a *via dolorosa*, this path homeward. How expressive the words.

I. LOVE MAKES LIFE FULL. Why, I thought they went out poor? Yes. Seeking bread? Yes. Yet Naomi's description is true and beautiful. We are "full" when we have that which makes home, home indeed, and we are poor if, having all wealth of means, we have not love. Well, indeed, has it been said that "the golden moments in the stream of life rush past us, and we see nothing but sand; the angels come to visit us, and we only know them when they are gone." We never know how empty life is till the loved are lost to us.

II. THE LORD IS THE DISPOSER OF ALL EVENTS. "The Lord hath brought me home." We talk of Providence when all goes well with us, when the harvests are ripened, and the fruits hang on the wall. But we must not limit Providence to the pleasant. The Lord "takes away" as well as gives. It is said that, in the order of reading at the family altar, when the late John Angell James was about to conduct worship after a severe bereavement, the Psalm to be read was the hundred and third. The good man stopped, tears rolled down his face; and then, gathering up his strength, he said, "Why not? It is the Father!" and he read on, "Bless the Lord, O my soul!"

III. THE FULLEST HOME MAY SOON BE EMPTIED. Yes! We too should feel it so. A husband and two sons gone! What converse there had been! what interest in each other's pursuits! what affectionate concern for each other's weal and happiness! and what a wealth of love for Naomi, the centre of all! We feel at such seasons that death would be blessed relief for us. The thought comes across us, "I have got to live;" to live on from day to day, attending to the minutiæ of duty, and coming here and there so often on the little relics of the dead. Home again! That has music in it for the school-children, who come back to the bright home ; but to the widow, oh, how different ! Home again, but how empty ! Yet we may learn, even from Naomi. that rest and refreshment come to hearts that trust in God their Saviour; and we may learn too what mistakes we make. Naomi said, "Why call ye me Naomi, seeing that the Lord hath testified against me ? " Natural enough ; but life was still to have a pleasant side for her.—W. M. S.

EXPOSITION.

CHAPTER II. 1—9.

It is by way of introduction to the remaining narrative that the writer says—
Ver. 1.—**And Naomi had, on her husband's side, a friend.** The C'tib reading מְיֻדָּע (absolute מְיֻדָּע) is much to be preferred to the K'ri מוֹדַע. But מְיֻדָּע is ambiguous in import. It primarily means *known*, *well-known*, *acquainted*, *an acquaintance* (see Job xix. 14 ; Ps. lv. 13 ; lxxxviii. 8, 18). But as intimate acquaintances, especially in a primitive and comparatively unwelded state of society, are generally found within the circle of kinsfolk, the word may be used, and is here used, in reference to a *kinsman*. The Vulgate translates it *consanguineus*. The translation is interpretatively correct ; but the original term is less definite, and hence, in virtue of the ambiguity, there is not absolute redundancy in the appended clause, *of the family* or *clan of Elimelech*. This friend of Naomi on her husband's side is said, in King James's version, to be **a mighty man of wealth.** But the expression so rendered has, in the very numerous passages in which it occurs, a conventional import that stretches out in a different and nobler direction. It is the expression that is so frequently translated "a mighty man of valour" (see Josh. i. 14 ; vi. 2 ; viii. 3 ; x. 7 ; Judges vi. 12 ; xi. 1, &c.). In only one other passage is it rendered as it is by King James's translators in the passage before us, viz., in 2 Kings xv. 20. There it is correctly so translated, interpretatively. Here there seems to be a leaning in the same direction, and yet it is not strongly pronounced. Cassel, however, takes the other cue, and translates "a valiant hero." "Probably," says he, "he had distinguished himself in the conflicts of Israel with their enemies." The expression originally means "strong in strength" (δυνατὸς ἰσχύϊ, Sept.), but is ambiguous in consequence of the many-sided import of the latter word חַיִל, which means originally, either *strength*, and then *valour ;* or, *clannish following* (see Raabe), and then *military host*, or *force*, or *forces ;* also, *faculty* or *ability*, and then, as so often "answering all things," *riches* or *wealth*. The idea of the writer seems to be that the friend of the widow's husband was *a strong and substantial yeoman.* He was **of the family** or **clan of Elimelech.** The word *family* is conventionally too narrow, and the word *clan* too broad, to represent the import of מִשְׁפָּחָה as here used. The idea intended lies somewhere between. **And his name was Boaz.** The root of this name is not found, apparently, in Hebrew, as was supposed by the older philologists, and hence its essential idea is as yet undetermined. Raabe finds its original form in the Sanscrit *bhuvanti*, which yields the idea of *prosperousness*.
Ver. 2.—**And Ruth the Moabitess said to Naomi, Let me go, I pray thee, to the cornfields, that I may glean among the ears after whosoever shall show me favour.** In modern style one would not, in referring, at this stage of the narrative, to Ruth, deem it in the least degree necessary or advantageous to repeat the designation "the Moabitess." The repetition is antique, and calls to mind the redundant particularisation of legal phraseology — "the aforesaid Ruth, the Moabitess." She was willing and wishful to avail herself of an Israelitish privilege accorded to the poor, the privilege of gleaning after the reapers in the harvest-fields (see Levit. xix. 9 ; xxiii. 22 ; Deut. xxiv. 19). Such gleaning was a humiliation to those who had been accustomed to give rather than to get. But Ruth saw, in the pinched features of her mother-in-law, that there was now a serious difficulty in keeping the wolf outside the door. And hence, although there would be temptation in the step, as well as humiliation, she resolved to avail herself of the harvest season to gather as large a store as possible of those nutritious cereals which form the staff of life, and which they would grind for themselves in their little handmill or quern. She said, with beautiful courtesy, "Let me go, I pray thee ;" or, "I wish to go, if you will please to allow me." Such is the force of the peculiar Hebrew idiom. "There is no place," says Lawson, "where our tongues ought to be better governed than in our own houses." **To the cornfields.** Very literally, "to the field." It is the language of townspeople, when referring to the land round about the town that was kept under tillage. It was not customary to separate cornfield from

cornfield by means of walls and hedges. A
simple furrow, with perhaps a stone here
and there, or a small collection of stones,
sufficed, as in Switzerland at the present
day, to distinguish the patches or portions
that belonged to different proprietors. Hence
the singular word *field*, as comprehending
the sum-total of the adjoining unenclosed
ground that had been laid down in grain.
"Though the gardens and vineyards," says
Horatio B. Hackett, "are usually surrounded
by a stone wall or hedge of prickly pear, the
grain-fields, on the contrary, though they
belong to different proprietors, are not separated by any enclosure from each other.
The boundary between them is indicated by
heaps of small stones, or sometimes by single
upright stones, placed at intervals of a rod
or more from each other. This is the ancient
landmark of which we read in the Old
Testament" ('Illustrations of Scripture,' p.
110). The word *field* in Hebrew, שָׂדֶה, denotes radically, not so much *plain*, as
ploughed land (see Raabe's 'Glossar'). In
English there is a slightly varied though
corresponding idiom lying at the base of the
Teutonic term in use. A *field* (German *Feld*)
is a *clearance*, a place where the trees of the
original forest have been *felled*. The expression, **that I may glean 'among' the
ears,** proceeds on the assumption that Ruth
did not expect that she would "make a
clean sweep" of all the straggled ears. There
might likely be other gleaners besides herself, and even though there should not, she
could not expect to gather all. **After whosoever shall show me favour.** A peculiarly
antique kind of structure in the original:
"after whom I shall find favour in his eyes."
Ruth speaks as if she thought only of one
reaper, and he the proprietor. She, as it
were, instinctively conceives of the labourers
as "hands." **And she said to her, Go, my
daughter.** Naomi yielded; no doubt at first
reluctantly, yet no doubt also in a spirit of
grateful admiration of her daughter-in-law,
who, when she could not lift up her circumstances to her mind, brought down her mind
to her circumstances.

Ver. 3.—Ruth, having obtained the consent of her mother-in-law, **went, and came,
and gleaned in the field after the reapers.**
That is, she "went forth," viz., from the
city, "and came to the cornfields, and
gleaned." "There are some," says Lawson,
"whose virtue and industry lie only in their
tongues. They say, and do not. But Ruth
was no less diligent in business than wise
in resolution." The later Jews had a set of
fantastic bye-laws concerning gleaning, detailed by Maimonides. One of them was,
that if only one or two stalks fell from the
sickle or hand of the reaper, these should be
left lying for the gleaners; but if *three stalks*

fell, then the whole of them belonged to the
proprietor (see Carpzov's 'Collegium Rabbinico-Biblicum,' p. 242). Happily for Ruth,
her steps were so ordered that the field which
she entered as a gleaner belonged to Elimelech's kinsman, Boaz. **And it so happened,**
runs the story, **that it was the portion of
the fields that belonged to Boaz, who was
of the kindred of Elimelech.**

Ver. 4.—On the very day that the Moabitess entered on her gleaning, Boaz, in accordance with his wont, as a good and wise
master, visited his harvest-field. **And, behold, Boaz came from Bethlehem.** The
law of kindness was on his lips; and while
benevolence was beaming from his countenance, piety was ruling within his heart.
He **said to the reapers, Yahveh be with
you! And they said to him, Yahveh bless
thee!** Courtesy met courtesy. It is a
charming scene, and we may reasonably assume that there was reality in the salutations. Such civilities of intercourse between
proprietors and their labourers are still, says
Dr. W. M. Thomson, common in the East.
"*The Lord be with you!* is merely the
Allah m'akum! of ordinary parlance; and
so too the response, *The Lord bless thee!*"
('The Land and the Book,' p. 648). Modern
Moslems are particular in the matter of
salutations. "Abuhurairah reports that he
heard Mohammed say, *You will not enter
into paradise until you have faith, and you
will not complete your faith until you love
one another, and that is shown by making
salaam to friends and strangers*" (Kitto's
'Bible Illustrations,' *in loc.*).

Ver. 5.—**And Boaz said to the young
man who was set over the reapers, Whose
is that young woman?** His eye had been
instantaneously arrested by the handsome
stranger. Perhaps, as Jarchi remarks, he
took note of the modest and graceful carriage
of her person while she picked up indus-
triously the straggled stalks. It is too
Rabbinic, however, and artificial, finical,
bizarre, to suppose with the same Jewish
annotator that Boaz would notice with
admiration that, while she picked up zealously all available couples of stalks, she left
the triplets in the field unappropriated!
The question which he put to the overseer
is not *who* but *whose is that young woman?*
She had not the gait or air of an ordinary
pauper, and hence he wondered if she could
belong to any of the families in Bethlehem.

Ver. 6.—**And the young man who was
set over the reapers replied and said, She
is a Moabitish young woman who returned
with Naomi from the land of Moab.** The
young man had already received, no doubt
from her own lips, particulars regarding the
attractive stranger. Instead of the free
definitive rendering of Luther and King

James's English version, "*the* Moabitish damsel," it is better, with Michaelis, Wright, Raabe, to adhere to the original indefiniteness, "*a* Moabitish maiden." Note the Zeugmatic use of the word *returned* as applied here, as well as in ch. i. 22, not only to Naomi, but also to Ruth. It is thus used on the same Zeugmatic principle as the word *die* in Gen. xlvii. 19 : "Wherefore shall we *die* before thine eyes, both *we* and *our land?*"

Ver. 7.—The steward continues his account of Ruth. She had respectfully solicited leave to glean. **She said, Let me glean, I pray thee, and gather in bundles after the reapers.** The expression, "and gather in bundles," is in Hebrew וְאָסַפְתִּי בָעֳמָרִים, and is rendered in King James's version, as also by Coverdale, Tremellius, Castellio, Luther, Michaelis, "and gather among" or "beside the sheaves." But such a request on the part of Ruth would seem to be too bold, the more especially as we find Boaz afterwards giving instructions to the young men to allow her, without molestation, to glean "even between the sheaves" (ver. 15). Hence Pagnin's free version is to be preferred, "and gather bundles" (*et congregabo manipulos*). Carpzov pleads for the same interpretation, and translates thus: "Let me, I pray thee, glean, and collect the gleanings into bundles" (*colligam obsecro spicas, collectasque accumulem in manipulos*). Montanus too adopts it, and Raabe likewise (*und sammele zu Haufen*). The steward praises Ruth's industry. **And she came, and has remained ever since the morning until just now.** She had worked diligently, with scarcely any intermission, from early morning. Drusius says that the following expression, rendered in King James's version **that she tarried a little in the house**, occasioned him critical torture (*locus hic et diu et acriter me torsit*). Coverdale also had been inextricably perplexed. He renders it, "And within a litel whyle she wolde have bene gone home agayne." The word *house* troubled these and many other interpreters, as if the reference were to Naomi's dwelling-house in the town. The reference, however, is evidently to a temporary hut, shed, tent, or booth erected in the harvest-field for the siesta of the workers, and the accommodation of the master, when he was visiting by day, or exercising supervision by night. We would translate the clause thus—"Her resting at the hut (has been) little." Her siesta in the shade of the hut was but brief. She felt as if she could not afford a long repose.

Ver. 8.—**And Boaz said to Ruth.** We are to suppose that Boaz, having communicated with his overseer, and having given some instructions to his reapers, and likewise to the young women who bound the reaped corn into sheaves, moved onward to the place where Ruth, keeping modestly far in the rear, was gleaning. He entered into conversation with her, and, among other things, said to her, **Hearest thou not, my daughter?** A grave antique way of drawing special attention to what is about to follow. "My daughter" is a fatherly expression, appropriate on the part of an elderly person when addressing a young woman. **Do not go to glean in the other field.** Pointing, no doubt, as he spoke, to a 'parcel' of adjoining fields, belonging to a neighbour proprietor. Boaz's interest and sympathy went out strong, all at once, toward the daughter-in-law of his deceased relative. His heart was smitten with admiration for the modest and fascinating widow. He said further to her, as he walked on along with her in the direction of the reapers, **and also do not pass on hence.** The expression is not a redundant repetition of the preceding utterance. It was intended, apparently, to direct Ruth to a particular line of gleaning-ground, probably right behind the sheaf-binders, which it would be advantageous for her to occupy. He would point it out with his hand. **And so keep close by my young women.** Their proximity would give the stranger a feeling of security, and her nearness to them in their work would be manifestly for her benefit.

Ver. 9.—Boaz continues his talk, led on by an interest that was, probably, surprising to himself. **Let thine eyes be on the field which they are reaping.** He feels increasingly anxious concerning the fascinating stranger, and gives her excellent counsel. "Let not thine eyes be wiled away, wanderingly, from the work on which thou art so praiseworthily engaged." **And go thou behind 'them.'** The reference is not to the same parties, who are indeterminately spoken of in the preceding clause—"which 'they' are reaping." A determinate feminine pronoun makes it evident that the reference is to the maidens, who were working in the rear of the reapers (אַחֲרֵיהֶן *post eas*). **Have not I charged the young men not to touch thee?** A fine euphemistic injunction ; that was best obeyed, however, when most literally construed. **And when thou thirstest, go to the jars, and drink of whatever the young men may draw.** Most likely it would be from the well that was "by the gate" of the city that the young men would draw—that very well of which her illustrious descendant, King David, spake, when he "longed, and said, O that one would give me drink of the water of the well in Bethlehem, which is by the gate" (see 2 Sam. xxiii. 14, 15 ; 1 Chron. xi. 17, 18). When the water was drawn by the young men, then the maidens would carry the filled jars upon their heads to the resting-place. Gleaners could not be expected to get the freedom of the water which was thus so laboriously drawn, and then fatiguingly carried from a distance. But Boaz made Ruth free, and thus conferred on her a distinguishing privilege, that must have been at once most acceptable and most valuable. The Vulgate renders the last clause too freely—" of which the young men ' drink.' " The familiar well referred to "appears," says Dean Stanley, "close by the gate" of the town ('Sinai and Palestine,' p. 163). Yet not very close. "It is," says Dr. John Wilson, "less than half a mile distant from the present village, and is in a rude enclosure, and consists of a large cistern with several small apertures" ('Lands of the Bible,' vol. i. p. 399). Dr. Wilson has no doubt of its identity, though Dr. Robinson hesitated to come to the same conclusion ('Researches,' vol. ii. p. 158).

HOMILETICS.

Vers. 1—9.—*The harvest-field.* RUTH WAS EAGER TO WORK (see ver. 2). 1. Work is honourable ; it is wholesome ; inspiriting too ; the best antidote to *ennui.* If not immoderate, nothing is so efficacious in giving full development to man's *physique;* nothing is so potent to put reins upon passions, and a curb on the tendency to morbid imaginations. All great men and women have been diligent workers. Jesus worked. He who is his Father and ours "worketh hitherto." 2. Ruth did not hesitate to stoop to very lowly work. She was willing and wishful to glean in the harvest-fields (see ver. 2). She humbled herself, and was free from the pride which goes before a fall. She "descended ascendingly." It was in the school of adversity that she had been taught. All honest work is honourable. Dignity is lent to the humblest labours when they are undertaken in a spirit of magnanimity. 3. Ruth expressed her wish to her mother-in-law, and solicited her approval. "Let me go, I pray thee, to the cornfields, that I may glean among the ears after whosoever shall show me favour" (ver. 2). The request was put in a beautifully deferential way. Nowhere is courtesy so precious as in the home. It is comely when displayed by juniors to seniors. It is charming when displayed by seniors to juniors. 4. Naomi yielded to Ruth's request, and said, "Go, my daughter." But we may be sure that it would cost her a pang to give her consent. The tears would start as she turned aside and said, "Is it come to this ? " of it. 5. "A Divinity" was "shaping Ruth's ends," and leading her by a way she knew not. She was unconsciously led, as if by a guardian angel sent forth to minister, until she lighted on a field belonging to Boaz, a near kinsman of her own. "And she went forth, and came to the cornfields, and gleaned, and it so happened that it was the portion of the fields that belonged to Boaz, who was of the kindred of Elimelech" (ver. 3). While the Divinity was thus "shaping her ends" for her, she was herself, to the utmost of her little ability, busy in "rough-hewing them." God's agency does not supersede man's, nor does man's supersede God's. Each of us should be able to say, "My Father worketh hitherto, *and so do I.*"

BOAZ ENTERS ON THE SCENE. 1. He had some preparation for the part he was about to act in the nearness of his relationship to Elimelech. In the absence of infinite comprehensiveness, it is right, as well as natural, for friends to take a special interest in friends. 2. Though not a "husband," he was a "husbandman." He had a *house,* and was a *house-band.* He was likewise conspicuous for good *husbandry.* He was in some respects a model *husbandman.* Note his habit of personal inspection and superintendence (see ver. 4, and ch. iii. 3). Note his courtesy to his workers as he passed along: "Yahveh be with you ! " (ver. 4). Note the hearty response which his courtesy elicited from his men: "Yahveh bless *thee !* " Note his habit of making inquiries of his overseer in reference to the state of his affairs (ver. 5). 3. In position he was a substantial yeoman (ver. 1). Stout in person, we may suppose. Stout in principle. Substantial in those resources that make *wealth* contribute to *weal.* 4. The reason of his loneliness at home is not hinted at. Perhaps some great sorrow lay buried in his breast ; perhaps some bright, sylph-like form lay buried in the grave. 5. He was now, as regards years, an elder in Bethlehem. Most likely all hopes of a brightened home had been for long lying dormant in his spirit. As to his age, it may be inferred from the fatherly way in which he addressed Ruth: "Hearest thou, *my daughter ?* " (ver. 8).

Boaz and Ruth. 1. Scarcely had Boaz entered his field, when his eye was arrested by the vision of an elegant and beautiful gleaner, altogether unlike all the rest whom he saw in his field, or had ever seen before. He said to his steward, " Whose young woman is this ? " 2. His question was answered, and other information of a highly satisfactory description was communicated. The young woman was a Moabite, who had accompanied home Naomi, her unfortunate mother-in-law (ver. 6). She had, with unwonted respectfulness, solicited liberty to glean. " She said, Let me glean, I pray thee, and gather in bundles, after the reapers " (ver. 7). She had been peculiarly diligent since early morning. " She came, and has remained ever since the morning, till just now " (ver. 7). Nor had she availed herself much of the siesta-booth. " Her resting at the hut has been little " (ver. 7). She seemed to grudge every moment that was not devoted to work. 3. Having obtained this information, Boaz wended his way to Ruth, speaking to the young men as he passed. When he came up to her, he was at once thrilled with admiration. He expressed to her his desire that she should continue on his fields all through the harvest season. " Hearest thou not, my daughter ? Go not to glean on other fields." He showed her, moreover, where she could glean to the best advantage. " Pass not on hence ; keep close by my young women." He informed her that, in passing along, he had enjoined the young men not to annoy her. " Have I not charged the young men not to touch thee ? " He added that she was to be sure to make full use of the water that was drawn by the young men, and carried to the field by the maidens. " When thou art thirsty, go to the jars, and drink of what the young men have drawn " (ver. 9). In all this we see the beginning of the reward which was, in the providence of God, conferred on noble, self-surrendering, self-sacrificing Ruth. The heart of Boaz was moving toward her. The blessing of the Most High was descending on her. So, in one form or another, will it descend on all who, in their different spheres, carry with them, according to the measure of their capacity, the spirit that, in beautiful activity, stirred and heaved within the heart of the Moabitish gleaner.

HOMILIES BY VARIOUS AUTHORS.

Ch. i. 22 ; ii. 3.—*The gleaner.* Bethlehem, " the house of bread," was famous for the pastures of its hills, and for the rich cornfields in its fertile valleys. The barley-harvest usually happened in April, and it was then that Naomi and Ruth returned to the village of Judah with which their names are associated. The Mosaic law sanctioned the practice of gleaning, commanded that the produce of the fields and vineyards should not be wholly removed, but that a portion should be left " for the stranger, the fatherless, and the widow." Ruth had, therefore, a right to glean.

I. Ruth's gleaning indicates THE POVERTY OF HER CONDITION. None but the necessitous would undertake such an occupation. Naomi and she must indeed have returned empty. In our land, and in our days, happily for the poor, there is always more remunerative work to be had by the industrious poor than this, which accordingly has, with the growing prosperity of the country, almost dropped out of use.

II. Ruth's ABSENCE OF PRIDE is very apparent. The family into which she had married had owned some of the adjoining land ; but in changed circumstances she was not too proud to mingle with the gleaners, and in lowly guise to gather ears of corn.

III. We cannot but admire Ruth's VIRTUOUS INDUSTRY. Boaz afterwards said, in praise of her conduct, " Thou followedst not young men." She chose a blameless, though laborious, life. An example to all to avoid dependence, and to cultivate the habit of self-reliance and diligence.

IV. Remark Ruth's FILIAL LOVE. She worked not only for herself, but for her mother-in-law, and found a pleasure in supporting her.

V. SUCCESS attends Ruth's honest toil. She gathered barley with her hands ; special favour was shown to her ; a friend was raised up to assist her ; prosperity crowned her efforts. " Thy bread shall be given thee, and thy water shall be sure."—T.

Ver. 3.—*Her hap.* Words could hardly be more suggestive than these. They may be applied to circumstances in the life of every one of us. There have been turning-points in our history ; we took one path rather than another, and with results (as we now see) how momentous to ourselves! So was it with Ruth of Moab, the gleaner.

I. MANY OF OUR ACTIONS ARE PERFORMED WITHOUT ANY THOUGHT OR INTENTION REGARDING THEIR RESULTS. In ordinary affairs how often do we decide and act without any special sense of the wisdom of one course rather than another! And there are positions in which our choice seems quite immaterial. It seemed of little consequence in which field this young foreigner, this friendless widow, went to glean a few ears of barley. So is it often with us. Shall we go to such a place? shall we pay such a visit? shall we form such an acquaintance? shall we read such a book? shall we venture on such a remark? shall we write such a note?

II. UNFORESEEN AND IMPORTANT ISSUES MAY DEPEND UPON CASUAL ACTIONS. Though it seemed of little consequence in which field Ruth gleaned, "*her hap* was to light on a part of the field belonging unto Boaz," and from this fact sprang results of the greatest importance. "Her hap" determined her marriage, her wealth, her happiness and that of her mother-in-law, her union with Israel, her motherhood, her position as an ancestress of David and of Christ. In such seemingly insignificant causes originate the most momentous issues. Thus oftentimes it comes to pass that family relationships are formed, a professional career is determined; nay, religious decision may be brought about, life-work for Christ may be appointed, eternal destiny is affected.

Lessons:—1. Regard nothing as insignificant. 2. Look out for, and follow, the leadings of Divine providence. 3. "In all thy ways acknowledge him, and he shall direct thy paths!"—T.

Ver. 4.—*Salutations.* It is a pleasant picture of old-world life among the ancient Hebrews, this of the "mighty man of wealth" coming down from his house to his cornfields to watch the work of the reapers, the progress of the harvest. Boaz seems to have lived on friendly terms with those in his employment, and to have taken an interest in them and in their toils. A lesson for all masters and employers of labour. And how picturesque the scene when the proprietor meets his labourers, and they exchange the customary greeting of the East, sanctified by Hebrew piety! Salutations are—

I. SANCTIONED BY SCRIPTURAL USAGE. *E. g.* When the mower filleth his hand, and he that bindeth sheaves his bosom, "they which go by say, The blessing of the Lord be upon you: we bless you in the name of the Lord!" (Ps. cxxix.). *E. g.* Angels are represented as greeting those they are commissioned to visit. Gideon was saluted thus: "The Lord is with thee;" and Mary thus: "Hail, highly favoured one! the Lord is with thee." *E. g.* Christ himself was wont to greet his disciples, saying, "Peace be with you!" *E. g.* The apostles closed their letters with greetings and benedictions. "The Lord of peace himself give you peace always by all means: the Lord be with you all!"

II. FOUNDED UPON DIVINELY-IMPLANTED PRINCIPLES OF HUMAN NATURE. They presume our social existence and nature. They imply sympathy. They express friendly and benevolent feelings.

III. CONDUCIVE TO THE EASY AND PLEASANT INTERCOURSE OF HUMAN SOCIETY. We all feel the influence of courteous address, polite expressions, and the minor benevolences of life. Christians should not be offended or contemptuous when well-meaning persons accost them with hand-shaking and minute inquiries after health, &c.; if well meant, courtesies should be kindly accepted.

IV. In the case of pious persons, EXPRESSIVE OF PRAYERFUL WISHES FOR GOOD. How many of our common salutations have their origin in piety and prayer! So, in the text, The Lord be with you! The Lord bless thee! So with such phrases as, Adieu! Good-bye! Good morning! God bless you! Farewell! They all convey a desire, a prayer. Let our salutations be sincere. and let our language and our conduct prove that they are so.—T.

Vers. 5—14.—*Filial piety and fidelity recognised and recompensed.* As "the whole city was moved" at Naomi's return, it is not surprising that the foreman over the reapers was able to answer the inquiry of Boaz—"Whose damsel is this?"

Though Boaz had not seen her before, he knew her story, and was evidently pleased to meet her. His judgments were just, his feelings were appropriate, his language was considerate, his conduct was generous. The character of Boaz commands our respect; and his treatment of Ruth, from beginning to end, was not only blameless, it was admirable. As we follow the simple and interesting narrative, we observe—

I. FILIAL PIETY AWAKENING INTEREST. The beauty of the Moabitess, though in complexion or figure she was "not like unto one of the handmaidens" of Boaz, her modest demeanour and graceful movements, all excited remark and admiration; but, probably, had he not known of her coming back with Naomi, and of all she had done unto her mother-in-law, he would not have addressed her. His interest expressed itself in kindly language and treatment, such as were very suitable in the circumstances. In ver. 11 Boaz acknowledges, in appreciative language, her disinterested devotion.

II. FILIAL PIETY PROMPTS AN OBSERVER'S FERVENT PRAYER. In ver. 12 Boaz is recorded to have said, "The Lord recompense thy work, and a full reward be given thee of the Lord God of Israel, under whose wings thou art come to trust." Who can contemplate a life of self-sacrifice, of affectionate devotion and service, without asking God to reward it with a recompense not in man's power to bestow? No prayers are purer and more effectual than those presented for a devoted, dutiful, affectionately ministering daughter!

III. FILIAL PIETY SECURES A GENEROUS AND PRACTICAL RECOMPENSE. Boaz was so gratified by what he heard of Ruth's conduct, and what he observed in her bearing and language, that he became the agent of Providence in rewarding her excellence. He bade her abide in his fields; he charged the young men to treat her with respect; he bade her take with welcome of the water, the wine, the bread, and the parched corn provided for the reapers. She found favour in his sight, and he comforted her by his friendly words.

Lesson:—Divine providence does not overlook human virtue. Not that man has merit before God; but the fruits of the spirit are pleasing to the Giver of the Spirit And God will raise up ministers of recompense for the comfort of his faithful children!—T.

Ver. 4.—"The Lord be with you. And they answered him, The Lord bless thee." Nothing is more beautiful in national history than good feeling between masters and men. Religion alone can inspire this feeling. It fails before mere expediency, and can only be secured by mutual dependence on God and on each other.

I. THE LIVING PRESENCE. The Lord with us means courage and consolation—courage to face difficulty, and consolation in all times of depression and disheartenment. Christ has given us his own gracious promise, "Lo, I am with you alway, even unto the end of the world."

II. THE HARVEST TOIL. "Said unto the reapers." It is hard work everywhere in the glaring heat to put in the sickle, and to gather up the sheaves. We may learn from the spectacle the blessed lesson of our duty in relation to others. Let us try to cheer and inspire. Some are full of cold indifference, and others of critical complaint. We little know what a word of cheer does for others. Blame makes the hands hang down, and quenches that music of the heart which makes work pleasant and successful. Encouragement is like fresh strength to weary hearts.

III. THE KIND RESPONSE. The benediction of Boaz awakens a corresponding benediction from the reapers. The harp answers to the hand that sweeps it. Men are to us very much what we are to them. "The Lord bless thee." We need never despair of this reward. Love begets love. Confidence begets confidence. Blessing awakens blessing. This is what we long and pray for—cessation of war between capital and labour, and mutual benediction.—W. M. S.

Ver. 7.—"I pray thee let me glean." In rural life no sight is pleasanter than the hour when the gleaners come in and "gather after the reapers among the sheaves." It bespeaks "something to spare." It is like the "commons" or the grass by the roadside for the poor man's cattle. We all like the spectacle of plenty; we all like the consciousness that the overflowings of the cup of plenty are to be tasted by others.

I. THERE IS WORK FOR THE HUMBLEST TO DO. We may not be permitted to take a leading part even in God's great harvest-field, but we can all do something. We can glean words of comfort to carry to the bedsides of the sick and the homes of the poor. We can glean in the fields of Scripture lessons for the little ones, and promises for the broken-hearted. Thank God there is a place in the world for gleaners as well as reapers.

II. THERE IS WORK TO BE SOUGHT OUT. It is asked for. "I pray thee." How many complain that no one finds a service for them. They are waiters and idlers because no one gives them a commission, or secures them a suitable field. They wait to be sought out, instead of saying, "Here am I, send me." They wait to be besought, instead of beseeching for work. What a glorious day for the Church of Christ everywhere when men seek for the honour of service.

III. ALL WORK DEMANDS PERSEVERANCE. How constant Ruth is! "She came, and hath continued from the morning until now." How much spasmodic energy there is; how many ploughs are left mid-furrow; how many begin and do not finish. It is not genius that wins the goal, but plodding earnestness. Ye did run well, glean well; what doth hinder you?—W. M. S.

EXPOSITION.

CHAPTER II. 10—17.

Ver. 10.—RUTH did not seize the opportunity for bewailing the hardship of the lot to which she had been reduced, and which now constrained her to undertake a species of work which at one time she little anticipated. With beautiful humility and modesty, and in the profoundest gratitude, she accepted wonderingly the kindness of Boaz. **And she fell on her face.** A rather remarkable expression, physiologically viewed. Her face was part of herself. How then could she fall on it? It was part of that which fell, and yet she is said to fall *upon* (עַל) it, as if it had been underneath the self-hood that fell. It was what was undermost as she bowed herself, so that the pressure of the sum-total of the body fell on it as she gracefully stooped. **And prostrated herself to the ground.** Thus completing, and doubtless in no sprawling or clumsy way, her respectful obeisance. Her face would be made, with æsthetic delicacy of movement, to touch the ground. **Wherefore have I found favour in thine eyes?** She was surprised, amazed, bewildered. **So that thou takest notice of me, and I a stranger!** Boaz had done far more than merely *take notice* of her. But, with equal gratitude and felicity, she specifies not the culminating acts of kindness, but the very first step that her benefactor had taken. He began by *taking notice* of her. There is an interesting *paranomasia* in the two words הַכִּירֵנִי and נָכְרִיָּה. A foreigner, though *unknown*, and just indeed because *unknown*, is naturally *noted* and *noticed*.

Ver. 11.—Boaz's interest and admiration grew. **And Boaz answered and said to her, It has been fully showed to me, all that thou hast done toward thy mother-in-law since the death of thy husband: and that thou hast left thy father and thy mother, and the land of thy nativity, and hast come to a people whom heretofore thou knewest not.** When Boaz says, "It has been fully showed to me," he probably refers to the information which he had received from his overseer. The expression rendered "fully showed" is a fine specimen of a very antique idiom, *showed-showed* (הֻגֵּד הֻגַּד). "Toward thy mother-in-law." The preposition which we render "toward" is literally "with," which, indeed, when laid side by side with the Hebrew preposition, looks as if it were organically identical. (אֵת = *eth*. Compare the old Hebrew *etha* with the Sanscrit *itáh*. See Raabe's 'Glossar'). The expression which we render "heretofore" is literally "yesterday and the day before," a very primitive way of representing *time past*. It must have been like balm to the anxious heart of Ruth to hear from the lips of such a man as Boaz so hearty a "well-done." "Ruth," says the venerable Lawson, "showed no disposition to praise herself. She did not claim a right to glean from what she had done for Naomi, but wondered that such kindness should be showed by Boaz to her who was a stranger, and she hears the voice of praise from the mouth of one whose commendations were a very great honour. No saying was oftener in the mouth of Jesus than this, *He that exalteth himself shall be abased, and he that humbleth himself shall be exalted.*"

Ver. 12.—**May Yahveh requite thy work, and may thy recompense be complete from**

Yahveh God of Israel, to trust under whose wings thou art come. Already there were streaks of light shooting athwart Boaz's horizon. His very phraseology is getting tipped with unwonted beauty. He sees Ruth cowering trustfully under the outstretched wings of Him who is "good to all, and whose tender mercies are over all his works" in all lands (see Ps. xci. 1—4). The metaphor, says Fuller, "is borrowed from a hen, which, with her clucking, summons together her straggling chickens, and then outstretcheth the fan of her wings to cover them." "Who would not," says Topsell, "forsake the shadow of all the trees in the world to be covered under 'such' wings?"

Ver. 13.—**May I continue to find favour, sir, in thine eyes, for indeed thou hast comforted me, and cheered the heart of thine handmaid, and yet I have not the position of one of thy maidens.** To be one of his maidens was, in her estimation, to be in a most desirable condition. She could not aspire to that. But as he had spoken so graciously to her heart, and soothed its sorrows, she trusted he would still befriend her. אֶמְצָא should not be rendered, with the Vulgate, "I have found" (*inveni*); nor, with Tremellius and Junius, "I find" (*invenio*); but, with Piscator, optatively, "may I find" (*inveniam*), that is, "may I still find, may I continue to find." So Luther, Coverdale, and Michaelis. The courtesy-expression, rendered in King James's version "my lord" (אֲדֹנִי = *Mein-Herr* or *Monsieur*), is used, as Carpzov remarks, in "humility and civility."

Ver. 14.—**And Boaz, at meal-time, said to her, Come along hither.** Luther, Coverdale, and King's James's English translators took the expression "at meal-time" as part of the report of Boaz's words: "And Boaz said, *At meal-time come along hither.*" But it is evidently to be taken, in accordance with the Masoretic punctuation, as the historical statement of the narrator: "At meal-time, Boaz said, *Come along hither.*" At meal-time Boaz rejoined Ruth, and said to her, "Come along hither." Then they would walk along in company, till they reached the siesta-hut. **And eat of the bread,** that is going, **and dip thy morsel in the vinegar,** or the *sour wine* that was quite a favourite beverage with out-door workers. It had a peculiarly cooling and refreshing effect. It corresponded to the *posca* used by the Roman soldiery, and would, according to circumstances and individual taste, be taken either "neat" or diluted with water. **And she sat by the side of the reapers.** Probably along with the other young women, although the reference to them is accidentally overlapped by the specification of the male workers. **And he prepared for her a bunch of parched corn.** יִצְבָּט is only conjecturally rendered "reached" in King James's version, and by many other translators. The rendering is given under the leadership of the Chaldee Paraphrast, who explains the word by אוֹשִׁיט, which is a pure Chaldee word for "reached." But light is thrown on the old Hebrew word by both Arabic and Sanscrit cognates, as well as by the Septuagint version (ἐβούνισε). It meant *to bind into a bunch* or *bunches* (see Fürst and Raabe). The word is illustrated by modern Oriental usage. Dr. W. M. Thomson says, "Harvest is the time for parched corn. It is made thus:—A quantity of the best ears, not too ripe, are plucked with the stalks attached. These are tied into small parcels; a blazing fire is kindled with dry grass and thorn bushes, and the corn-heads are held in it until the chaff is mostly burnt off. The grain is thus sufficiently roasted to be eaten, and it is a favourite article all over the country" ('The Land and the Book,' p. 648). Mr. Legh, in like manner, states, in MacMichael's 'Journey, 1819, that, travelling in harvest-time in the country east of the Dead Sea, they one day rested near some cornfields, "where one of the Arabs, having plucked some green ears of corn, parched them for us by putting them into the fire, and then, when roasted, rubbing out the grain in his hands" (Kitto's 'Pictorial Bible,' *in loc.*). Sometimes, however, the parched corn is otherwise prepared. Dr. Robinson says, "In one field, as we approached Kubeibeh, nearly 200 reapers and gleaners were at work; the latter being nearly as numerous as the former. A few were taking their refreshment, and offered us some of their 'parched corn.' In the season of harvest the grains of wheat, not yet fully dry and hard, are roasted in a pan or on an iron plate, and constitute a very palatable article of food. This is eaten with bread, or instead of it. Indeed, the use of it is so common at this time among the labouring classes, that this parched wheat is sold in the markets; and it was among our list of articles to be purchased at Hebron for our journey to Wady Mûsa. The Arabs, it was said, prefer it to rice; but this we did not find to be the case. The whole scene of the reapers and gleaners, and their 'parched corn,' gave us a lively representation of the story of Ruth and the ancient harvest-time in the fields of Boaz" ('Biblical Researches,' vol. ii. p. 394, ed. 1841). Boaz had given Ruth a kind of Benjamin's portion of parched corn. She could not use it all. **And she ate, and was satisfied, and left over.** Carefully reserving, however, and "basketing up" the liberal surplus.

Ver. 15.—**And she rose to glean : and Boaz charged his young men, saying, Even between the sheaves let her glean, and do not affront her.** Boaz would probably thus speak in the hearing of Ruth herself, so that, without any fear of reproach, she might feel free to take full advantage of the privilege accorded her. Boaz wished her to gather a large gleaning, no doubt rightly conjecturing that there must have been for some time past but little superfluity in the larder of Naomi. The space "between the sheaves," as distinguished from the spaces outside their line, would probably be the part whither the maidens conveyed their collected armfuls, and where they bound them into sheaves. It would thus be the place where there would be the greatest number of 'waifs.' It would also be the place in which unprincipled gleaners might have the best opportunity for stealing from the sheaves. Boaz felt unbounded confidence in Ruth, and said to the reapers, "Affront her not," namely, by saying or insinuating anything to the effect that she was either pilfering, on the one hand, or making herself too forward, on the other. The Vulgate version completely merges out of sight the poetic beauty and tenderness of the injunction by rendering it thus : "Do not hinder her."

Ver. 16.—**And even of set purpose draw out for her from the bundles, and leave them, and let her glean them, and do not find fault with her.** His kindness grows as he sees her, or speaks concerning her. He gives additional injunctions in her favour, both to the young men and to the maidens, though the line of distinction between the two sexes dips at times entirely out of sight. When the sheaf-makers had gathered an armful of stalks, and there seemed to be so clean a sweep that none were left behind, then they were of set purpose (*de industria*) to draw out some from the bunches or bundles, and leave them lying. The act of deliberate, as opposed to unintentional, drawing, is expressed by the emphatic repetition of the verb שֹׁל־תָּשֹׁלּוּ. The verb thus repeated was a puzzle to the older expositors, inclusive of all the Hebrew commentators. But comparative philology has clearly determined its radical import, and thus illuminated its use in the passage before us. It does not here mean "spoil," though that is its usual signification. Nor can it mean "let fall," as in King James's version. It means *draw out*. **Do not find fault with her.** The word is almost always rendered *rebuke* in our English version ; but the force of the preposition may be represented thus : "do not chide 'with' her." "It was," says Dr. Andrew Thomson, "a thoughtful and delicate form of kindness to Ruth, thus

to increase her gleanings, and yet to make them all appear the fruit of her own industry." "There are persons to be met with in social life who, while possessing the more solid qualities of moral excellence, are singularly deficient in the more graceful. They have honesty, but they have no sensibility ; they have truth, but they are strangely wanting in tenderness. They are distinguished by *whatsoever things are just and pure*, but not by those which are *lovely and of good report*. You have the marble column, but you have not the polish or the delicate tracery on its surface ; you have the rugged oak, but you miss the jasmine or the honeysuckle creeping gracefully around it from its roots. But the conduct of Boaz, as we stand and hear him giving these directions to his reapers, proves the compatibility of those two forms of excellence, and how the strong and the amiable may meet and harmonise in the same character. Indeed, they *do* always meet in the highest forms of moral greatness" ('Studies on the Book of Ruth,' pp. 119, 120).

Ver. 17.—**And she gleaned in the field until the evening, and beat out what she had gleaned, and it was about an ephah of barley.** Gathering together her various sheaves, lots, or bundles (see ver. 7), she threshed them with some suitable rod or simple 'flail' (*flagellum*), which she had either brought with her in the morning, as part of her equipment as a gleaner, or had obtained at the hut; or perhaps, like many others, she would make use of a convenient stone. Speaking of the village of Hûj, near Gaza, Robinson says, "We found the lazy inhabitants still engaged in treading out the barley harvest, which their neighbours had completed long before. *Several women were beating out with a stick handfuls of the grain which they seemed to have gleaned.* One female was grinding with a handmill, turning the mill with one hand, and occasionally dropping in the grain with the other" ('Researches,' vol. ii. p. 385). "In the evening," says Dr. W. M. Thomson, "you might see some poor woman or maiden, that had been permitted to glean on her own account, sitting by the roadside, and beating out with a stick or a stone what she had gathered, as Ruth did. I have often watched this process in various parts of the country" ('The Land and the Book,' p. 647). The diligent gleaner on Boaz's field found, after threshing, that she had nearly an ephah of barley. It would be a considerable load for a female to carry—about a bushel. Josephus mentions incidentally, in his 'Antiquities' (xv. 9, 2), that the Hebrew *cor* or *homer* was equivalent to ten Attic μέδιμνοι. But as the ephah was exactly the tenth part of a cor or homer, it follows that the Hebrew ephah was equivalent to the Attic μέδιμνος. Moreover, just as the ephah was the tenth part of a homer, so the omer was the tenth part of an ephah (Exod. xvi. 36) ; and thus, if an omer of barley would be somewhat equivalent for nutritive purposes to an omer of manna, it would be a sufficient daily allowance for a man (see Exod. xvi. 16). Hence Ruth would take home with her what would suffice for several days' sustenance to Naomi and herself.

HOMILETICS.

Vers. 10—17.—*The harvest-field again.* Let us return to the Oriental harvest-field. Harvest-fields in general are lively scenes. Emphatically so in the East, where bright weather may be calculated on with almost absolute certainty. Pleasantry and work go hand in hand. Dr. W. M. Thomson, speaking of Philistia, says, "When the fog dispersed, the whole plain appeared to be dotted over with harvesting parties ; men reaping, women and children gleaning and gathering the grain into bundles, or taking care of the flocks, which followed closely upon the footsteps of the gleaners. All seemed to be in good humour, enjoying the cool air of the morning. There was singing, alone and in chorus, incessant talking, home-made jokes, and laughing loud and long" ('The Land and the Book,' p. 543). The harvest scene as represented on the shield of Achilles may be recalled (see the eighteenth book of the 'Iliad'). 1. We find Boaz and Ruth still standing where we left them (vers. 9, 10). Surely some great attraction is detaining the busy husbandman, a 'man of affairs.' 2. A group of Graces are tripping round about Ruth. There is, firstly, *gratitude*, always lovely and welcome. If in any soul it be meagre, stinted, stunted, the soil of that soul is shallow. There is, secondly, *respectfulness*. "She fell on her face, and did obeisance to the ground" (ver. 10). Respectfulness is the homage that is due to a noble nature, and to him who is the Creator of it. We are to "honour the king." True ; but we are likewise to "honour all men" (1 Pet. ii. 17), for there is something kingly after all in the nature of all. Then there is, thirdly, *wonder*. "Why have I found favour in thine eyes, so that thou takest notice of me, and I a stranger ?" (ver. 10). Some accept attentions and kindnesses as things of course. Some almost exact them, as if they were dues. Not so the nobler souls. They wonder when distinction is conferred on them. Moses wondered : "Who am I, that I should go unto Pharaoh, and that I should bring forth the children of Israel out of Egypt ?" (Exod. iii. 11). David wondered : "Who am I, O Lord God ? and what is my house, that thou hast brought me hitherto ?" (2 Sam. vii. 18). Paul wondered : "Unto me, who am less than the least of all saints, is this grace given, that I should preach among the Gentiles the unsearchable riches of Christ" (Eph. iii. 8). 3. Boaz explained to the wondering stranger why it gratified him to show her attention. "It hath been fully showed unto me, all that thou hast done toward thy mother-in-law since the death of thy husband : and that thou hast left thy father and thy mother, and the land of thy nativity, and hast come to a people whom heretofore thou knewest not" (ver. 11). His spirit seems to kindle as he proceeds, so that his words become tipped with brightness and beauty. He "winds the robes of ideality around the bareness" of mere facts (J. Ingelow). He says, "The Lord requite thy work, and may thy recompense be complete from the Lord God of Israel, to trust under whose wings thou art come" (ver. 12). Words "fitly spoken!" "Words spoken in due season!" "How good they are!" A word, in particular, of well-deserved appreciation and commendation is peculiarly "good." It goes to the heart, and is often mighty to animate to victorious courage and hope. Nobler in its aims than "fame," it is yet, like "fame," a "spur, that the clear spirit doth raise, to scorn delights and live laborious days" (Milton). 4. Note the fine expression, "to trust under whose wings thou art come." Compare what the Psalmist says : "He that dwelleth in the secret place of the Most High shall abide under the shadow of the Almighty." "He shall cover thee with his feathers, *and under his wings shalt thou trust*" (Ps. xci. 1, 4). Compare what Jesus said : "O Jerusalem, Jerusalem, how often would I have gathered thy children together, even as a hen gathereth her chickens under her wings, and ye would not" (Matt. xxiii. 37). Compare what the Christian poet says:

" All my trust on thee is stayed ;
  All my help from thee I bring ;
  Cover my defenceless head
  With the shadow of thy wing."

5. Just as Boaz was turning to complete the supervision of his harvest-field, Ruth, with delicate acknowledgments for the past, prefers a humble request for the future. " May I continue, sir, to find favour in thine eyes; for indeed thou hast comforted me, and cheered the heart of thine handmaid, and yet I have not the position of one of thy maidens " (ver. 13). Thus from one to the other, under the impulse of some subtle spontaneity, was the shuttle of respectful feeling shot and re-shot. 6. The scene is now shifting. The two separate. Boaz proceeds to attend to the various details of his husbandry. Ruth returns to the monotony of her gleaning. Both exhibit a worthy example of painstaking industry. 7. Time advances. The work proceeds. The sun hastens towards its zenith. The hour for siesta is at hand. Boaz turns once more in the direction of Ruth. He rejoins her, and invites her to accompany him to the place of temporary shelter, refreshment, and rest. " At meal-time Boaz said to her, Come along hither, and eat of the bread, and dip thy morsel in the vinegar " (ver. 14). All the workers—but of course not the gleaners—assemble around the master. Ruth is seated among the rest, and is carefully attended to. " She sat beside the reapers : and Boaz prepared for her a bunch of parched corn, and she ate, and was satisfied, and left over " (ver. 14). Then there is more work. Boaz gives still more liberal instructions to the young men. " Even between the sheaves let her glean, and do not affront her " (ver. 15). " And even of set purpose draw out for her from the bundles, and leave them, and let her glean them, and do not find fault with her " (ver. 16). At length, at the close of the day, Ruth gathered her bundles together, and threshed them, and found that she had about an ephah of barley—as much as a woman could be expected to carry. Thus is the dawn of Ruth's prosperity growing brighter and brighter, and giving promise of a day that shall be as " the bridal of the earth and sky." The Lord is " recompensing her work." The shadows are fleeing.

" As morning in the east,
  Stands winged to mount in day,
  So for a swift surprise of joy
  Our God prepares his way " (Gibbons).

So assuredly will there be a corresponding dayspring from on high to all who, in the midst of thickening trials, maintain their integrity, and engage in " works of faith " and " labours of love." There may be, there will be, differences in the degree of prosperity and reward, even as star differeth from star in magnitude and lustre. It is not to be expected that all shall have such reversions on earth as were granted to Job and to Ruth. Nevertheless, none will be forgotten. Every several blade of grass will have its own drop of dew. Love on the part of man will be crowned with love on the part of God. And when love rises to Jesus, the ideal Son of man, then it is capped with more love ; for, says he, " my Father will love him, and we will come unto him, and make our abode with him " (John xiv. 23). All three will " sup together " (Rev. iii. 20). " Sorrow and sighing will flee away."

HOMILIES BY VARIOUS AUTHORS.

Vers. 15—17.—*Liberality to the poor.* The customs recorded in these chapters remain — many of them — to the present day. As to *gleaning,* Robinson says, " The way led us through open fields, where the people were in the midst of the wheat-harvest. The beautiful tracts of grain were full of reapers of the Henâdy Arabs, and also of gleaners almost as numerous. These were mostly women ; and this department seemed almost as important as the reaping itself, since the latter is done in so slovenly a manner, that not only much falls to the ground, but also many stalks remain uncut. In one field nearly 200 reapers and gleaners were at work, the latter being nearly as numerous as the former." As to *threshing,* Robinson mentions that "several women were beating out with a stick handfuls of the grain which they seemed to have gleaned." As to the *parching of corn*, the same writer says, "The grains of wheat, not yet fully dry and hard, are roasted in a pan or on an iron plate, and eaten along with bread, or instead of it." Boaz showed his practical sympathy with the widows of the narrative by giving parched corn to Ruth to eat, and by securing that her gleaning should be even more successful and abundant than was usual with the maidens.

I. Liberality to the poor should ACCORD WITH THE CIRCUMSTANCES OF THE GIVER.

II. It should TAKE A FORM ADAPTED TO THE WANTS OF THE RECIPIENT.

III. It should BE UNGRUDGING AND GRACEFUL IN ITS BESTOWAL.

IV. It should BE INSPIRED BY THE MEMORY OF THE UNDESERVED BOUNTY OF THE GREAT GIVER, GOD.

V. It should NOT COUNT UPON, though it may have occasion to rejoice in, THE GRATITUDE OF THE BENEFICIARY.—T.

Ver. 10.—"I am a stranger!" What a touching word. In some cities there is the strangers' burying-ground. There they sleep as they lived, separated from their brethren.

I. THE HEBREWS WERE KIND TO STRANGERS. Their Divine revelation gave them injunctions concerning the stranger within their gates. They were to be considerate and kind to the cattle; how much more to those made in the image of God like themselves! The young learnt this lesson; from earliest years they were taught the law while "sitting in the house." Boaz knew all this, and he "lived" it.

II. STRANGERS HAVE SENSITIVE HEARTS. Their experiences make them quick to feel insult or blessing. Never can they quite escape the consciousness, "I am a stranger." In other lands, under other skies, the stranger carries far-away visions of the heart within, which make the spirit pensive. Consequently, care and love are intensely appreciated by them. Religion is the life of love and the death of selfishness wherever it lives and reigns in the heart.

III. STRANGERS IN TIME MAKE A FATHERLAND OF THE NEW HOME. So did Ruth. New ties sprang up; for love looks forward. Children take the place of ancestors, and we live in *them*. How often we are tempted to forget our own lot. "Remember that ye were strangers," therefore deal kindly with them. Think how precious to you was the fellowship of hearts that stole away your sadness as a stranger at school, or in the new city of life and duty. What a consolation it is that we are never strangers in our Father's sight, and that everywhere we may find "home" in God.—W. M. S.

Vers. 12, 13.—"The Lord recompense thy work, and a full reward be given thee." Here we see that the character of God is gloriously revealed. It is understood by Boaz that God is a God of "rewards," and we need not fear that a mistaken notion of rewards and punishments will prevail amongst students of the Bible. God's highest blessings are given to the soul; but it remains true that even in the earthly life the outworking of duty is blessing.

I. HERE IS THE HISTORIC NAME. "The Lord God of Israel." What memories cluster around that significant sentence! We see in it a "miniature" of all Hebrew deliverance and mercy.

II. HERE IS THE COMPREHENSIVE BLESSING. "A full reward." *That* must refer to the inner self—to the consciousness of heroic fidelity and filial love. Many rewards are precious, but no reward is full that does not "bless us indeed."

III. HERE IS THE HOMELY ANALOGY. "Under whose wings," &c. All nature is taken into the illustrative record of the inspired word. The wing! How strong without. How easily outspread. How "downy" within. So soft! so warm! The rain cannot reach through the outward covering. Notice how roof-like are the arrangements of the feathers, and notice also how *complete* is the canopy.

IV. HERE IS THE PERSONAL TRUST. "Thou art come to trust." We must not forget not alone what God reveals himself as, to us, but what responsibility rests on us, to "rest in the Lord."—W. M. S.

EXPOSITION.

CHAPTER II. 18—23.

Ver. 18.—**And she lifted it up, and went into the city: and her mother-in-law beheld what she had gleaned. She likewise brought forth, and gave to her, what she had left over after she was satisfied.** It would be with gratitude and pride that Ruth would let her heavy burden slip off into the hands of Naomi. It would be with gratitude and wonder that Naomi would *behold* the precious load. Other gentle emotions would stir within the mother-in-law's hungry heart when her beloved daughter-in-law produced and presented the remains of her delightfully refreshing repast at the tent. The expression, "after she was satisfied," is literally, "from her satiety."

Ver. 19.—**And her mother-in-law said to her, Where hast thou gleaned to-day? and where hast thou worked? May he who took notice of thee be blessed!** The grateful eagerness of the mother-in-law to get full information overflows in a delightful redundancy. "Where hast thou gleaned to-day? and where hast thou worked?" She saw at a glance, from the magnitude of the load, from the bright and beaming countenance of her daughter-in-law, and from the delicious parched corn which the master had given with his own hands, that the day had been crowned with peculiar blessings. The lines had fallen in pleasant places. Hence her womanly and motherly interest to get full particulars. Ruth, on her part, would feel as if a kind of inspiration had seized upon her tongue. **And she showed to her mother-in-law with whom she had worked; and she said, The name of the man with whom I worked to-day is Boaz.** A thrill would shoot through Naomi's heart as that once familiar name fell upon her ears.

Ver. 20.—**And Naomi said to her daughter-in-law, Blessed 'of' Yahveh be he who—.** The expression is literally, "Blessed 'to' Yahveh be he who," that is, "Blessed in relation to Yahveh be he who," or "Blessed be he! I carry the desire and prayer up to Yahveh," which just amounts, in meaning, to this: "Blessed 'by' Yahveh be he who." See other instances of the same construction in Gen. xiv. 19, and Ps. cxv. 15. **Who has not let go his kindness to the living and to the dead.** Some take these words to be descriptive of Yahveh. Others take them to be descriptive of Boaz. If they be regarded in the former point of view, then the foregoing clause must be rendered, not, "Blessed by Yahveh be he who," but, "Blessed be he by Yahveh who." Dr. Cassel assumes, but without any formal

reasoning or apparent reason, that the reference of the relative is to Yahveh, and hence he makes out an ingenious argument in defence of the doctrine, *that those who are dead to us are yet alive to God*—the doctrine of immortality. It is strained. Yet Raabe thinks that the reference is to Yahveh, inasmuch as Naomi had as yet no evidence of Boaz's kindness to the deceased. The reason thus given for carrying the reference up to God is certainly unsatisfactory; for, looking at the subject from the human point of view, it is obvious that Boaz's peculiar kindness to the living *was* his kindness to the deceased; whereas, if we look at the case from the Divine point of view, it is difficult, if not impossible, to account for the discrimination between the living and the dead. The first feeling that sprang up in the heart of Naomi at the mention of the name of Boaz was one of adoration. The next was a generous desire in reference to Boaz himself. She prayed that he might be graciously recompensed by Yahveh for the kindness he had shown that day, both toward the living —Ruth and herself—and toward the deceased—Elimelech and his sons. A man of less noble nature might have been ready, in reference to relatives in reduced circumstances, to ignore the present, and to bury in oblivion the past. After giving scope to her feelings of adoration and benediction, Naomi, with the prompt and practical directness of a true woman, said to her daughter-in-law, **The man is near to us,** adding immediately, and with a rapid glance at bright contingencies that were in the region of the possible, **He is one of our peculiar kinsmen** (our *Goëlim*). She meant that he was one of those peculiarly near kinsmen who had a right of redemption over whatever lands may have formerly belonged to her, and the first right of purchase over whatever lands might yet remain in the possession of herself or of her daughter-in-law. Naomi and Ruth, though greatly reduced in circumstances, and painfully pent up in present straits, were far from being paupers. They were proprietors (see ch. iv. 3, 5). But their property was not, for the time being, available for income or sustenance. It had either been farmed out on usufruct or allowed to lie waste. In the absence of the *yod* in מְגֹאֲלֵנוּ we have an instance of *scriptio defectiva*, as distinguished from *scriptio plena*. Such defective manuscription might be expected to occur occasionally in transcription from dictation, when, as here, the presence or the absence of the letter made no difference in the pronunciation of the reader. Michaelis, however ('Mosaisches Recht,' § 137), and Gesenius ('Thesaurus,' *in voc.*), instead of regarding the absence of the *yod* as an instance of *scriptio defectiva*, have conjectured that מִנְאָל is a noun, or name, meaning *the second in order of the Goëlim*. But, notwithstanding the ingenuity of the conjecture, there is not a shadow of evidence to evince that the Hebrews themselves ever knew of such a word. Nor does the supposition or subsumption of such a word in the least facilitate the construction on the one hand, or illumine the narrative on the other.

Ver. 21.—**And Ruth the Moabitess said.** It seems *to us* rather remarkable that Ruth should be here again particularised formally as "the Moabitess." There is apparently no discoverable reason for the re-repetition. It is simply antique particularity, not amenable to any literary law "the said Moabitess." There is a peculiar abruptness in the initial words of what follows:—**Yea also he said to me.** Carpzov and Wright understand them thus: "'Yea' blessed be he, 'for' he said to me." But the word *blessed*, as used by Naomi, is too far removed to make it natural for the *yea* of Ruth's remark to fall back upon it. Her mind and heart were full. She was profoundly affected by the kindness that had been shown to her. Hence she piles up her representation. "*Also,*"—so *may I well speak,*—"*for he said to me.*" **Keep close by my young men, until they have finished all my harvest.** The "young men" are not here discriminated from the "young women" (see ver. 8). The idea, consequently, is not that Ruth was to keep close to them in distinction from the young women. It was understood that she should work behind the young women, who followed in the rear of the young men. But it was the express desire of Boaz that, instead of exposing herself among strangers, on any adjoining harvest-fields, she should maintain her position behind his reapers as long as there remained any golden crops to reap.

Ver. 22.—**And Naomi said to Ruth her daughter-in-law, It is good, my daughter, that thou shouldest go with his young women, and that thou be not set upon in another field.** Here again we have the archaic repetition, "Ruth her daughter-in-law." Naomi was grateful for Boaz's invitation. Compliance with it would be "good," both immediately and prospectively. In particular, it would save Ruth from running the risk of being rudely handled by utter, and perhaps rough and unprincipled, strangers. "It is good," says Naomi, "that 'they' do not set upon thee in another field." She says "they," but allows the parties she had

in view to remain, dimly visible, in the shade. No doubt, however, she refers to the reapers, binders, gleaners, and other workers who might have to be encountered "in another field." "Meaning," says homely Richard Bernard, "some lewd and lustful men whom Naomi would not so much as make mention of." The verb פָּגַע־בְּ is often rendered in our English version *fall upon.* It originally means *to light upon,* whether for good or for evil.

Ver. 23.—**And she kept close by Boaz's young women to glean.** Wright translates thus: "And she kept gleaning along with the maidens of Boaz." But the maidens of Boaz are not represented as gleaning. The historical statement of the verse is to be explained from the hortatory statement of ver. 8: "Keep close to my young women." **Till the end of the barley-harvest and the wheat-harvest.** Ruth's gleaning labours extended to the close of the wheat-harvest, during which time, no doubt, there would be frequent opportunities for a growing intimacy between the beautiful gleaner and the worthy proprietor. Often too, we may rest assured, would Boaz be a visitor in the humble home of Naomi. "The harvest upon the mountains," says Dr. Robinson, "ripens of course later than in the plains of the Jordan and the sea-coast. The barley-harvest precedes the wheat-harvest by a week or fortnight. On the 4th and 5th of June the people of Hebron were just beginning to gather their wheat; on the 11th and 12th the threshing-floors on the Mount of Olives were in full operation. We had already seen the harvest in the same stage of progress on the plains of Gaza on the 19th of May; while at Jericho, on the 12th of May, the threshing-floors had nearly completed their work" ('Biblical Researches,' vol. ii. p. 99). "The Syrian harvest," says Dr. W. M. Thomson, "extends through several months. On the plain of Philistia it commences in April and ends in June; and this not only gives ample time, but it has this great advantage, that the villagers from the mountains can assist the farmers on the plain, since their own crops are not yet ripe. I was struck with this fact while at Mesmia. Several Christians from Bethlehem, who had thus come to reap, spent the evening at my tent, and one of them explained to me the advantages from thus labouring on the plain. He not only received wages for his own and his wife's labour, but his children were permitted to follow after them and glean on their own account, as Boaz allowed Ruth to do in their native village" ('The Land and the Book,' p. 544). When it is said, in the last clause of the verse, **and she dwelt with her mother-in-law,** the reference is not to be restricted to the time that succeeded the period of harvesting. The Vulgate indeed connects the clause with the following verse, and renders it, "After she returned to her mother-in-law," pointing the verb thus וַתֵּשֶׁב instead of וַתֵּשֶׁב. The same translation is given to the verb by Luther and Coverdale. But there is no evidence whatever that Ruth slept anywhere else than under her mother-in-law's roof. The clause was written, apparently, for the very purpose of bringing out clearly before the mind of the reader her stainless innocence, and sweet simplicity, and never-tiring devotion to her noble mother-in-law.

HOMILETICS.

Vers. 18—23.—*Home from the harvest-field.* Evening begins to draw her curtains around the little city of Bethlehem. Let us *look on this picture, and on that.* 1. "On this picture." See Naomi. She is wistfully and longingly looking out for her daughter-in-law's return. So many a matron looks, evening after evening, for the safe return of her husband, her son, her daughter. 2. "And on that." See Ruth toiling slowly along under her "ephah." Her strength is taxed; yet she is thankful for the precious burden. She is picturing to herself the reception she would receive under the lowly roof of her mother-in-law, and ruminating pleasantly on the cheer which both herself and her burden would bring to the anxious heart of the dear old lady. She is happy, though fatigued. Happy are all other bread-winners who, amid the monotony and weariness of daily toil, are cheered with the prospect of ministering to the comfort of wife, mother, grandmother or grandfather, sick sister perhaps, or little children. 3. At length the long-looked-for gleaner arrives. What a glad welcome she receives!—a model welcome, hearty and animating, such as should always be accorded to the good and faithful bread-winner. See with what pride and gratitude she lets slip off her burden into the hands of Naomi. We read, "And her mother-in-law *beheld* what she had gleaned" (ver. 18). What a *looking*, what a *gazing* there would be. *All that, my daughter? What a wonderful gleaner you must be! How could you gather all that? How good to us has Yahveh been! Here is good food for days to come.* In this matter of gratitude millions should be as conspicuous as Naomi. "Goodness and mercy" have accompanied them all the days of their life. "A table has been spread for them" every day of every year. In looking back over life, for ten, twenty, forty, sixty years, they cannot remember one single day when they had no food to eat. Even in heathen lands "God has not left himself without witness, in that *he does good*, and gives rain from heaven, and fruitful seasons, filling men's hearts with food and gladness" (Acts xiv. 17). Every year is "crowned by him with his goodness" (Ps. lxv. 11). 4. When Naomi's spirit had become somewhat calmed, and she was about, as we may suppose, to prepare a portion of the gleanings for their simple evening repast, Ruth produced what she had "left over" of her delicious "parched corn." "She brought forth, and gave to her, what she had left over after she was satisfied" (ver. 18). Naomi's astonishment, gratitude, delight would mount up rapidly. She could restrain herself no longer. "Where hast thou gleaned to-day? and where hast thou worked? May he who took notice of thee be blessed!" "She doth here," says Dr. Thomas Fuller, "dart out and ejaculate a prayer, *and that at rovers*, aiming at no particular mark. '*Blessed be he who took notice of thee.*' Yet, no doubt, was it not in vain; but God made it light on the head of bountiful Boaz, who deserved it." It seems to be in the nature of all great gratitude to ascend to God in praise or prayer. For indeed "every good and perfect gift cometh down from him" (James i. 17). 5. Ruth did not keep her mother-in-law in suspense. "She showed her with whom she had worked; and she said, The name of the man with whom I worked to-day is Boaz" (ver. 19). It augurs well for both daughters and mothers when there are unreserved intercommunications between them. But mothers would require to be confidential if they would have their daughters to be confiding. There will be danger of tragedies in the home if daughters are reticent in reference to the affairs that are of chief concern at once to their own hearts and to the hearts of their parents. The tragedies will be more tragic still if husbands and sons have haunts of which mention cannot be made in the bosom of domestic confidence. "Boaz!" The name would thrill through Naomi. It instantaneously recalled tender memories of the past ; and side by side with these recollections there flitted in before her view visions of the future. But her first utterance was a benison, no longer shot "at rovers." She gratefully lifted aloft her heart, and said, " Blessed of the Lord be he, who has not let go his kindness to the living and to the dead " (ver. 20). He had, it seems, been kind to her and hers long ago. The recollection came fresh to her mind. And now there was abundant and gratifying evidence that he was not " weary of well-doing." He had still the old kind heart, perhaps kinder than ever. With " Boaz " as the theme of conversation, there would not be in all Bethlehem a brighter or happier home that evening than the humble cot of Naomi. The genea- logical relationship and former kindnesses of their worthy friend would be fully elucidated (ver. 20), and Ruth would be sure to dwell at length on the invitation she had received to continue in his fields all the harvest through (ver. 21). The evening would glide rapidly on. While they talked, and while, in the intervals of talk, they " mused," the fire within the breast would burn. As it burned, the flame would flicker, now to this side, now to that, but still ever upward toward God. Boaz had said to Ruth—and her heart responded heartily as he said it—that it was under the wings of the God of Israel that she had come to cower and be covered. She had come, he said, to "trust " in Yahveh. She was resolved that she would. Even Naomi would encourage her, and would herself be disposed to revert to the sweet significance of her own name—*Jah is sweet, and deals sweetly*. The hard thoughts which she had been tempted in the time of her anguish to entertain would be sensibly beginning to thaw and melt. And if one could have read the hearts of both, as at length they laid themselves down to rest, perhaps the thoughts of each might have been found to be running in the strain of the words of a great descendant, as he said and sang, "Thou hast put gladness in my heart, more than in the time that their corn and their wine increased. I will both lay me down in peace, and sleep: for thou, Lord, only makest me dwell in safety " (Ps. iv. 6—8). "Tired nature's sweet restorer " would not need to be sedulously wooed, on the part of the gleaner at least ; and if Naomi's slumber was not so easily obtained, or so uninterruptedly retained, yet she would "commune with her own heart on her bed, and be still." May we not assume that, when both awoke in the early morning, they were "still with God " ?

HOMILIES BY VARIOUS AUTHORS.

Ver. 20.—*Kindred and kindness.* When Naomi and Ruth returned to Bethlehem they could scarcely have found friends there, but they found kinsmen. They do not seem, in their circumstances, to have sought assistance from relatives, or even to have brought themselves under the notice of such. Still, Naomi had not lost sight of Elimelech's family connections ; and when the name of Boaz was mentioned, she recognised it as the name of one of her husband's nearest kindred.

I. KINDRED IS A DIVINE INSTITUTION. Men have many artificial associations ; bonds of sympathy, and of locality, and of common occupation bind them together. But kindred is the Divine, the natural tie.

II. KINDRED IS AT THE FOUNDATION OF SOCIAL AND POLITICAL LIFE. The patriarchal economy was the earliest. The family is the first social unit, out of which springs the tribe, the clan, the nation.

III. KINDRED INVOLVES AN OBLIGATION TO CONSIDERATION AND REGARD. We cannot always cherish feelings of congeniality or of respect with reference to all who are our kindred according to the flesh. But relatives should not lose sight of one another—should not, if it can be avoided, be estranged from one another.

IV. KINDRED MAY, IN CERTAIN CASES, INVOLVE THE DUTY OF PRACTICAL HELP. Christian wisdom must here be called in to the counsels of Christian kindness.

V. KINDRED IS SUGGESTIVE AND EMBLEMATIC OF DIVINE RELATIONS. Apart from human relationship, how could we conceive of God as our Father ? of Christ Jesus as our elder Brother ? of Christians as our brethren and sisters in a spiritual family ?—T.

Ver. 23.—*Harvest-time.* This Book of Ruth is emphatically the book of the hus- bandman. It pictures the barley-harvest and the wheat-harvest of ancient days.

The primitive manners and usages are interesting, and deserve attentive study. But harvest—as here so vividly brought before us—is full of lessons of a spiritual kind. *E. g.*—

I. HARVEST WITNESSES TO THE ATTRIBUTES OF THE DIVINE CREATOR. To his power and wisdom. To his goodness. To his faithfulness to his promise: "Seed-time and harvest shall not cease."

II. HARVEST IS A SUMMONS TO MAN'S GRATITUDE AND CONFIDENCE.

III. HARVEST IS SUGGESTIVE OF GREAT SPIRITUAL TRUTHS. There is a moral harvest in the history of the human character and of human society. Seed and soil are presumed. Development and growth are evidenced. The law operates: "Whatsoever a man soweth, that shall he also reap." The fruit is matured and gathered in. The Husbandman—God himself—is interested in the result. To us the result is infinitely important.—T.

Ver. 20.—"Who hath not left off his kindness to the living and the dead." The prayers of the poor for their helpers are very precious. Naomi remembers the former kindnesses that Boaz had shown to the husband of her youth and to her two boys.

I. HERE IS CONTINUITY OF CHARACTER. Some leave off kindness because they meet with experiences of ingratitude and callousness. The once warm deep within them is frozen up by these wintry experiences. But as God continues his mercy through all generations, so those who are followers of God as dear children walk in love; that is, it becomes the spirit and habit of their lives. Boaz had not left off his kindness. Ruth now drinks at the same fountain of considerate care that had refreshed Elimelech.

II. HERE IS THE GOOD WORD OF A MOTHER. It is well when the mother *respects* the man who may become allied in marriage to one who is akin to her. Naomi says to her daughter, "Blessed be he of the Lord." Let those who have become sceptical concerning Christianity ask themselves this: Whether should I like to give my child in marriage to a Christian or an infidel? This practical query would suggest many thoughts tending to renewed faith, and would stifle for ever many superficial doubts.—T.

EXPOSITION.

CHAPTER III.

Ver. 1.—**And Naomi, her mother-in-law, said to her, My daughter, shall not I seek out for thee a rest, that it may be well with thee?** When Ruth had nothing more to do on the harvest-fields, where Boaz appeared daily, and was unremittingly gracious to her, she may have fallen into a pensive mood. Naomi was quick to note the varying '*nuances*' of feeling, and said "My daughter, shall I not seek out for thee a rest?" The expression *rest*, or *resting-place*, though in itself of generic import, was, when used in such circumstances as environed Ruth, quite specific in application, and would be at once understood. It was *a home* to which Naomi pointed, a home for her daughter's heart. In such a home, if warm and pure, there would be repose for the affections. "That it may be well with thee," or, "which shall (or may) be good for thee." Either translation is warrantable and excellent. The latter is the most simple, and is given by Carpzov and Rosenmüller; but the former is in accordance with a frequent idiomatic use of the expression, in which there is a change from *the relative in result* to *the relative in*

aim, so that אֲשֶׁר יִיטַב is equivalent to לְמַעַן יִיטַב (see Deut. iv. 40; vi. 3, 18; x. 11, 25, 28). Naomi did not distinguish between *rests* that would be 'good,' and other *rests* which would not be 'good.' Nor did she moralise on the idea of a *rest*, and affirm that it would be 'good' for her widowed daughter-in-law. She assumed that every true *rest* was 'good,' and, on the basis of that assumption, she sought out one for her devoted Ruth. Hence the superiority of the rendering that expresses *aim* to that which expresses the mere prediction of *result*.

Ver. 2.—**And now is not Boaz, with whose young women thou wast, our relative?** Naomi opens her case. She had been studying Boaz all through the harvest season. She had been studying Ruth too. She saw unmistakable evidence of mutual responsiveness and attachment. And now she had a matured scheme in her head. Hence she brings up Boaz's name at once, and says, "Is he not our relative?" מוֹדַעַת, an abstract term used concretely, meaning literally "acquaintance," but here "relative," or "kinsman" (see ch. ii. 1). **Lo, he is**

winnowing barley on the threshing-floor to-night. Literally, "Lo, he is winnowing the threshing-floor of barley." The Hebrews could idiomatically speak of "the threshing-floor of barley," meaning "the threshing-floor-ful of barley." The barley lay heaped up in Boaz's threshing-floor, and he was engaged in winnowing it. He threw up against the wind the mingled mass that was on his floor, after the stalks had been carefully trodden or beaten. "Not far," says Dr. Horatio Hackett, "from the site of ancient Corinth, I passed a heap of grain, which some labourers were employed in winnowing. They used for throwing up the mingled wheat and chaff a three-pronged wooden fork, having a handle three or four feet long" ('Illustrations,' p. 106). "The winnowing," says Dr. Kitto, "was performed by throwing up the grain with a fork against the wind, by which the chaff and broken straw were dispersed, and the grain fell to the ground. The grain was afterwards passed through a sieve to separate the morsels of earth and other impurities, and it then underwent a final purification by being tossed up with wooden scoops, or short-handed shovels, such as we see sculptured on the monuments of Egypt" ('Illustrations,' *in loc.*, p. 40). In some of the Egyptian sculptures the winnowers are represented as having scoops in both hands. הַלַּיְלָה, *to-night* (Scotticé, "*the* nicht"). The agriculturist in Palestine and the surrounding districts would often carry on his winnowing operations after sunset, taking advantage of the evening breeze that then blows. The Chaldee Targumist makes express reference to this breeze, explaining the word *to-night* as meaning *in the wind which blows by night.*

Ver. 3. — **So then wash thyself, and anoint thyself, and dress thyself.** This latter phrase is in the original, "and put thy garments on thee." The verb וְשַׂמְתְּ, with its final yod, was the archaic form of the second person feminine, though still much cut down and contracted from its oldest form. See Raabe's 'Zurückführing,' and note the conduct of the verb, in its relation to the pronominal suffixes, when these are affixed. **And go down to the threshing-floor.** The town of Bethlehem lay on the summit of "the narrow ridge of a long gray hill" (Stanley's 'Sinai and Palestine,' p. 163), while the corn-fields, that gave the fortified place its name of *Bread-town*, stretched out expandingly in the valleys below. Dr. Robinson says, "We ascended gradually toward Bethlehem around the broad head of a valley running N.E. to join that under Mâr Elyâs. The town lies on the E. and

N.E. slope of a long ridge; another deep valley, Wady Ta'âmirah, being on the south side, which passes down north of the Frank Mountain toward the Dead Sea, receiving the valley under Mâr Elyâs not far below. Toward the west the hill is higher than the village, and then sinks down very gradually toward Wady Ahmed" ('Biblical Researches,' vol. ii. p. 158). **Let not your presence be known to the man before he has finished eating and drinking.** It would have been imprudent and impolitic to have discovered her presence while his servants and himself were busied in operations which required to be actively prosecuted while the breeze was favourable, and the light of the moon serviceable. Ruth was to wait till the servants, having finished their work and their repast, had retired to their respective homes. The master, as Naomi knew, would remain gratefully and joyfully on the spot, to keep watch in the midst of his cereal treasures, and under the still magnificence of the broad canopy of heaven. Speaking of Hebron, Dr. Robinson says, "Here we needed no guard around our tent. The owners of the crops came every night and slept upon their threshing-floors to guard them, and this we had found to be universal in all the region of Gaza. We were in the midst of scenes precisely like those of the Book of Ruth, when Boaz winnowed barley in his threshing-floor, and laid himself down at night to guard the heap of corn" ('Biblical Researches,' vol. ii. p. 446). Boaz's heart, when all was quiet around him, would be full of calm and comfort. He would pace about his well-heaped threshing-floor contentedly, contemplatively; and, as he paced, and thought, and adored, the figure of the beautiful and industrious gleaner might persist in coming in within the field of meditation. It might linger there, and be gladly allowed to linger.

Ver. 4. — **And let it be, when he lies down, that thou take note of the place where he lies; and go, and uncover the parts about his feet, and lay thee down; and he shall declare to thee what thou shalt do.** The denominative word מַרְגְּלֹתָיו—freely rendered in King James's version "his feet"—we have rendered "the parts about his feet." It is the exact opposite of מְרַאֲשֹׁתָיו, which never means "his head," but is always translated correctly either "his pillows" or "his bolster." It denotes "the supports on which the head was laid in lying;" and מַרְגְּלוֹת, having reference to members of the body which do not need such supports as the head, simply means "the places occupied by the feet." Naomi ventured on a bold expedient to bring speedy 'rest' to her daughter-in-law. But we assume that, with unmistaking feminine intuition, she saw, on the one hand, that Boaz was already deeply attached to Ruth, and, on the other, that Ruth reciprocated his attachment with pure intensity. Most probably we should also assume that she detected in Boaz a peculiar diffidence that caused him to shrink from making decisive advances in the way of declaring his affection. He had, however, unconsciously revealed himself, and made it clear to Naomi that he wished to divulge in words the depth of his honourable feelings. But again and again, as we may suppose, his sensitiveness overcame his resolutions. Hence Naomi's scheme to bring him to the point of declaration. It would have been reprehensible in the extreme had she not been absolutely certain of his wishes, on the one hand, and of his perfect honour and uncontaminable purity on the other. And even with that qualification, the scheme would have been imprudent and improper, and utterly unfeminine, had it not been the case that, in virtue of an ancient and much-prized Hebrew law, Ruth was entitled to call upon her nearest of kin to fulfil the various duties of a responsible kinsman. Still, notwithstanding the existence of this law, we may rest assured that the sensitive gleaner would never have summoned up courage to ask Boaz to discharge to her the duties of kinship, unless she had been sure that the thrills that vibrated within her own heart were responsive to subtle touches, on his part, of spirit with spirit.

Ver. 5.—**And she said, All that thou sayest I will do.** There is no need for adopting into the text the K'ri "to me," after the expression "All that thou sayest." It is a mere "tittle," indeed, whether we omit or insert the pronoun; yet it was not found in the manuscripts that lay before the Septuagint and Vulgate translators.

Vers. 6, 7.—**And she went down to the threshing-floor, and did according to all that her mother-in-law had enjoined. And Boaz ate and drank, and his heart was comfortable; and he went to lie down at the end of the heap; and she came softly, and uncovered the parts about his feet, and laid herself down.** The translation in King James's version, "and his heart was *merry*," is perhaps stronger than there is any occasion for. The word rendered "was *merry*,"—viz., יִיטַב.—is literally "was *good*." The Septuagint word is ἠγαϑύνϑη. After the labours of the evening, Boaz had a relish for his simple repast. It was *good* to him. Hence he ate and drank to his heart's content, enjoying with grateful spirit the bounties of a gracious Providence. By and by he retired to rest, amid visions perchance of a brightened home, which just helped to reflect on his conscious-

ness a stronger resolution than he had ever formed before to make known his affection. At length he slept. The Syriac translator adds interpretatively, "in a sweet sleep on the floor." Ruth then stepped cautiously forth to play her delicate part. She stole softly to the sheltered spot where he lay. She gently uncovered the margin of the cloak, which lay over the place where his feet were laid. She laid herself down noiselessly. The Arabic translator adds, "and slept beside him"—a most unhappy interpretation. Nothing but sin would be so far away as sleep from the eyes, and mind, and heart of the anxious suitor.

Ver. 8.—**And it came to pass at midnight that the man started in a fright; and he bent himself over, and lo, a woman was lying at his feet.** He had awaked, and, feeling something soft and warm at his feet, he was startled and affrighted. What could it be? In a moment or two he recovered his self-possession, and bending himself up and over, or "*crooking* himself," to see and to feel, lo, a woman was lying at his feet. The Chaldee Targumist tumbles into a ludicrous bathos of taste when endeavouring to emphasise the startle and shiver which Boaz experienced. He says, "He trembled, *and his flesh became soft as a turnip* from the agitation." How could the most peddling and paltering of Rabbis succeed in betraying himself into such a laughable puerility and absurdity? The explanation, though of course it is not the least atom of justification, lies in the fact that the Chaldee word for "turnip" is לֶפֶת, while the verb that denotes "he bent himself" is the niphal of לָפַת. The use of the expression "the man," in this and several of the adjoining verses, is apt to grate a little upon English ears. Let us explain and vindicate the term as we may, the grating is still felt. No matter though we know that "the rank is but the guinea stamp," the grating is felt inevitably. It is a result of that peculiar growth in living language that splits generic terms into such as are specific or semi-specific. We have *gentleman* as well as *man*, and embarrassment is not infrequently the result of our linguistic wealth. In the verse before us, and in some of those that go before, we should be disposed, in our English idiom, to employ the proper name: "And it came to pass at midnight that 'Boaz' started in a fright."

Ver. 9.—**And he said, Who art thou? And she said, I am Ruth, thy handmaid; and thou hast spread thy wings over thy handmaid, for thou art kinsman.** The Syriac translator spoils the question of Boaz by metamorphosing it from "Who art thou?" into "What is thy message?" Tremulous would be the voice of Ruth as she replied,

"I am Ruth, thy handmaid." What she said in continuance has been very generally, and by Driver, among others ('Hebrew Tenses,' p. 135), misapprehended. Not by Raabe, however. It has been regarded as a petition presented to Boaz—"Spread thy wings (or, *thy wing*) over thy handmaid, for thou art kinsman." The literal translation, however, and far the more delicate idea, as also far the more effective representation, is, "And thou hast spread thy wings over thy handmaid, for thou art kinsman." Ruth explains her position under Boaz's coverlet as if it were his own deliberate act. Such is her felicitous way of putting the case. It is as if she had said, "The position in which thy handmaid actually is exhibits the true relation in which thou standest to thy handmaid. She is under thy wings. Thou hast benignantly spread them over her, for thou art kinsman." The Masorites have correctly regarded כנפך as a *scriptio defectiva* for the dual of the noun, and hence have punctuated it כְּנָפֶךָ, "thy wings." The majority of interpreters, however, have assumed that the word is singular, and have hence translated it as if it had been punctuated כְּנָפֶךָ. The dual reading is to be preferred. Boaz himself had represented Ruth as having come trustfully under the wings of Yahveh (see ch. ii. 12). She accepted the representation. It was beautifully true. But, as she was well aware that God often works through human agency, she now recognised the Divine hand in the kindness of Boaz. "*Thou hast spread thy wings* over thine handmaid." She was under his wings because she had come under the wings of Yahveh. She felt like a little timid chicken; but she had found a refuge. It is the wings of tender, gentle, sheltering care that are referred to. There is only indirect allusion to the typical coverlet under which she lay. **For thou art kinsman** (see ch. ii. 20). The native modesty of Ruth led her to account for her position by a reference to the law of kinship. She had rights, and she stood upon them. She conceived that Boaz had correlative duties to discharge; but we may be sure that she would never have made the least reference to her rights, or to the correlative duties which she regarded as devolving on Boaz, had she not known that his heart was already hers.

Ver. 10.—**And he said, Blessed be thou of Yahveh, my daughter; thou hast made thy latter kindness better than the former, in not going after any young man, whether poor or rich.** This verse is full of satisfactory evidence that Naomi was perfectly right in conjecturing that Boaz, deep in love, was restrained only by diffidence from formally declaring himself. It shows us too that the chief ground of his diffidence was his age.

He had been an acquaintance, and the equal in years, of Ruth's father-in-law, Elimelech, and the impression had got hold on him that the handsome young widow might feel repugnance to his suit. Hence, instead of being in the least degree offended by the steps she had taken, he was relieved, and felt full of gratification on the one hand, and of gratitude on the other. **Blessed be thou by Yahveh.** Literally, "to Yahveh," *i. e.* "in relation to Yahveh" (see ch. ii. 20). **My daughter.** His relative elderliness was in his mind. **Thou hast made thy latter kindness better than the former.** Michaelis has seized the true meaning of these words: "The kindness which thou art showing to thy husband, now that he is gone, is still greater than what thou didst show to him while he lived." Her employment of the word "kinsman," or *goël*, was evidence to Boaz that she was thinking of the respect which she owed to her husband's memory. Her concern in discharging that duty of 'piety' struck the heart of Boaz; and all the more as, in his opinion, she might easily have found open doors, had she wished for them, in quarters where there was no connection of kinship with her deceased husband. "She did not go after any young man, whether poor or rich." She preferred, above all such, her first husband's elderly "kinsman." In the original the construction is peculiar—"in not going after the young men, whether a poor one or a rich one." He does not simply mean that she was free from vagrant courses and desires. Her character lay, to his eye, on a far higher level. His meaning is that she deliberately refrained from "thinking of any young man." The plural "young men" is to be accounted for on the principle that when an alternate is assumed or postulated, there is, in actual contemplation, a plurality of individuals.

Ver. 11.—**And now, my daughter, fear not: all that thou sayest I shall do to thee, for it is on all hands known in the gate of my people that thou art a truly capable woman.** The word חַיִל in the expression אֵשֶׁת חַיִל is of many-sided import, and has no synonym in English, German, Latin, or Greek. But every side of its import brings into view one or other or more of such affiliated ideas as *strength, force, forces, capability*—whether mental and moral only, or also financial; *competency, substantiality, ability, bravery*. All who had taken notice of Ruth perceived that she was mentally and morally, as well as physically, a *substantial* and *capable* woman. She was possessed of *force*, both of mind and character. She was, in the New England sense of the expression, *a woman* of "faculty." She was *full of resources*, and thus adequate to the position which, as Boaz's wife, she would be required to fill. There was no levity about her, "no nonsense." She was earnest, industrious, virtuous, strenuous, brave. There was much of *the heroine* in her character, and thus the expression connects itself with the masculine application of the distinctive and many-sided word, "a mighty man *of valour.*" The expression אֵשֶׁת חַיִל occurs in Prov. xii. 4, where, in King James's version, it is, as here and in Prov. xxxi. 10, translated "a virtuous woman"—"a virtuous woman is a crown to her husband." But it is not so much to *moral virtue* that there is a reference as to that general capacity which consists in "large discourse, looking before and after" ('Hamlet,' iv. 4). Compare the masculine expression אַנְשֵׁי־חַיִל in Exod. xviii. 21, 25, rendered, in King James's version, "able men," and meaning *capable* or *substantial men*, who, however, as we learn from the additional characteristics that are specified, were to be likewise conspicuous for high moral worth. In Prov. xxxi. 10 there is the same reference to *general capacity*, as is evidenced by the graphic representation that follows—a representation that by no means exhausts itself in the idea of *moral virtue*. Ibn Esra takes the whole soul out of the expression when he interprets it, both here and in Proverbs, as meaning "a woman possessed of riches." When Boaz says, "All that thou sayest I will do to thee," he means, "All that thou hast só winsomely and yet so modestly referred to in what thou didst say, I am prepared to do to thee." There was only one obstacle in the way, and that of a somewhat technical description. If that should be honourably surmounted, nothing would be more agreeable to Boaz's heart than to get nearer to Ruth. "For," said he, "it is on all hands known in the gate of my people that," &c. Literally the phrase is, "for all the gate of my people know," a strangely inverted but picturesque mode of expression. It was not "the gate of the people," but "the people of the gate," that knew.

Ver. 12.—**And now it is the case of a truth that while I am a kinsman, there is yet a kinsman nearer than I.** Or the rendering might with greater brevity be given thus: **And now of a truth I am a kinsman; and yet there is a kinsman nearer than I.** The survivals of a very ancient style of elaborately-detailed composition are here preserved. The archaism, however, was not quite appreciated by the Mazorites, who, in accordance with the spirit of the age in which they flourished, took but little note of the philological development, historical and prehistorical, of the language they were handling. Hence they suppressed the אִם in

K'ri, though faithfully preserving it in C'tib. The particles, standing up and semi-isolated, palæolithic-wise, might be accounted for in some such way as is shown in the following paraphrase: "*And now* (I declare) '*that*' *of a truth* (it is the case) '*that if*' (I declare the whole truth) *I* (am) *a kinsman, and also there is a kinsman nearer than I.*" Boaz was of that strictly honourable cast of mind that he could not for a moment entertain any project that might amount to a disregard of the rights of others, even although these rights should fly violently in the teeth of his own personal desires.

Ver. 13.—**Abide here to-night; and it shall come to pass in the morning, if he will act to thee the part of a kinsman, well; he shall act the kinsman's part: and if it please him not to act to thee the kinsman's part, then sure as Yahveh is alive, I will act to thee the kinsman's part. Lie still till the morning.** Love is quickwitted. Boaz's plan of operations would formulate itself on the spur of the moment; but the remainder of the night would doubtless be spent in maturing the details of procedure. The aim would be to secure, as far as honour would permit, the much-wished-for prize. There would be, moreover, we need not doubt, much conversation between them, and mutual consultation, and arrangement. A large letter, a *majuscula*, occurs in the first word of the verse—לִינִי—which the smaller Masora ascribes to the Oriental or Babylonian textualists. It had, no doubt, been at first either a merely accidental, or a finically capricious, enlargement; but, being found, mysteries had to be excogitated to account for it;—all mere rubbish. "To-night" is a perfect translation of הַלַּיְלָה, for the *to* is simply the common definite article in one of its peculiar forms, perhaps peculiarly crushed and defaced (see note on ch. iii. 2).

Ver. 14.—**And she lay at the place of his feet until morning: and she arose ere yet a man could distinguish his neighbour.** In the original it is "the places of his feet" (see ver. 4). Time would rapidly fly past. Sleep there would be none to either the one or the other. In mutual modesty they guarded each other's honour. Thoughts and feelings, narratives and projects, would be freely interchanged. Their mutual understanding would become complete. At length there began to be the first faint tinge of paleness streaking into the dark. Ruth arose, and prepared to depart. It is added, **For he had said,**—or, more literally, "And he had said,"—**Let it not be known that 'the' woman came to the threshing-floor.** This has been to critics a puzzling clause. The conjunction in the foreground, a mere copulative, has occasioned difficulty. It is thoroughly Hebraistic. But of course it does not here introduce to notice something merely added to what goes before, of the nature of a parting injunction or request addressed to Ruth. The articulated phrase "*the* woman," as distinguished from "*a* woman," the expression in King James's version, renders such an interpretation impossible. The Targumist explains thus: "and he said *to his young men*." But the whole tenor of the preceding narrative proceeds on the assumption that there were no servants on the premises or at hand. Other Rabbis, and after them Luther and Coverdale, interpret thus: "and he said *in his heart*," or, "and he thought." Unnatural. The difficulty is to be credited, or debited, to simplicity of composition, and the habit of just adding thing to thing aggregatively, instead of interweaving them into a complex unity. In the course of their many interchanges of thought and feeling, Boaz had expressed a desire, both for Ruth's sake and for his own, that it should not be known that she had come by night to the threshing-floor. The narrator, instead of introducing this expression of desire in the way in which it would directly fall from the lips of Boaz, "Let it not be known that *thou didst* come," gives it in the indirect form of speech, the *oratio obliqua*, as his own statement of the case. It is as if he had introduced a parenthesis or added a note in the margin. The ἄπαξ λεγόμενον טְרוֹם—instead of טֶרֶם— was most probably not a later form, as Bertheau supposes, but an older Hebrew form that had died out of use long before the days of the Masorites.

Ver. 15.—**And he said, Allow me the wrapper which is upon thee, and hold on by it; and she held on by it; and he measured six measures of barley; and he put it on her, and went to the city.** The expression "Allow me," literally, "Give (me)," was a current phrase of courtesy. The verb employed—יָהַב—was common Semitic property, ere yet the mother-tongue was subdivided into Hebrew, Syriac, Chaldee, Arabic. **The wrapper which is upon thee.** The word for *wrapper* occurs nowhere else except in Isa. iii. 22, where it is translated, in King James's version, "wimple." Here it is rendered "vail," and, in the margin, "sheet or apron,"—all of them unhappy translations. So is the rendering of the Targumist, סוּדְרָא, i. e. *sudarium*, or "napkin." N. G. Schröder discusses the word at great length in his masterly 'Commentarius Philologico-Criticus de Vestitu Mulierum Hebræarum,' pp. 247—277. He would render it *pallium* or *palla*. In consequence of national peculiarities in articles of dress, especially in

ancient times, it is best to avoid a specific, and to employ a generic translation. When Boaz said, "Give me the wrapper," he did not ask that it should be handed to him. He had already put his hand upon it, and was engaged in hollowing out a scoop or cavity. Hence he said, on the one hand, "Allow me," and, on the other, "Hold on by it." **And he measured six measures of barley.** The particular measure referred to is unspecified. It is not only mere dream on the part of the Targumist, but it is dream involving almost sheer impossibility, that the measures were *seahs*, i. e. two ephahs. The Targumist had to bolster up his dream by adding another, viz., that Ruth got miraculously strength to carry the load. Load, indeed, there undoubtedly was; and no doubt it would be as great as she could conveniently carry. And likewise, in accordance with the primitive simplicity of manners, the magnitude of the burden would be demonstration to Naomi of Boaz's satisfaction with the "*measures*" which, in full motherliness of spirit, she had planned. **And he went to the city.** The Vulgate and Syriac versions, as also Castellio, Coverdale, and various other translators, but not Luther, have assumed that we should read וַתָּבֹא, "and she went," instead of וַיָּבֹא, "and he went." So too Wright. But there seems to be no good reason for making the change. If there had been no division into verses, then the departure of both Boaz and Ruth on their respective routes, or in their respective order of sequence, would have been recorded close together: "and 'he' went to the city, and 'she' went to her mother-in-law"—each, let us bear in mind, with the heart elate.

Ver. 16.—**And she went to her mother-in-law. And she said, Who art thou, my daughter? And she narrated to her all that the man had done to her.** The question, "Who art thou, my daughter?" is not put by Naomi, as Drusius supposes, because it was still so dusk that she could not properly distinguish Ruth. The address, "My daughter," shows that she had no difficulty in determining who the visitor was. But there is *something arch* intended. "Art thou Boaz's betrothed?" Michaelis translates, "What art thou?" Unwarrantably as regards the letter, but correctly as regards the spirit of the interrogatory.

Ver. 17.—**And she said, These six measures of barley he gave to me; for he said, Thou must not go empty to thy mother-in-law.** The C'tib omission of "to me" after "for he said" is most likely to be the original reading. A fastidious Rabbi would rather originate this insertion than the omission.

Ver. 18.—**And she said, Sit still, my daughter, till that thou know how the affair**

will fall out, for the man will not rest unless he complete the affair to-day. In saying, "Sit still, my daughter," it is as if Naomi had said, "There is no occasion for restless anxiety. Let your heart be at ease till that thou know how the affair will fall out." In the Hebrew the noun is without the article. But in English it must be supplied, unless a plural be employed—"how 'things' will fall out." דָּבָר, *thing*, i. e. *think.* Compare the corresponding relation between the German *sache* and *sagen*.

HOMILETICS.

Ch. iii.—*Naomi's maternal solicitude.* This is one of those paragraphs of Scripture which require delicate handling, but which, for that very reason, are full of suggestiveness that comes home to the bosom. Under strange, old-fashioned forms of things there was often much real virtue and true nobility of character. 1. It may be regarded as certain that while the harvest lasted Boaz and Ruth would be coming daily into contact with each other. 2. It may likewise be assumed as certain that their minds would from day to day grow into one another, in interest and esteem. As intimacy increased, it would reveal, on either side, points of character that were fitted to evoke admiration and sincere respect. 3. It is reasonable to suppose that Naomi's humble home in Bethlehem would be again and again visited by Boaz. There would be various attractions. Naomi herself, as an old and now a far-travelled friend, would be able to tell much that would be interesting to the kinsman of Elimelech. 4. The Palestinian harvest season would that year, as well as on other years, be a lively time. The harvest-home, in particular, would be a joy and a rural triumph. It may well be so in all countries. The golden grain is more precious by far than grains of gold. It is emphatically the "staff" on which terrestrial life has to lean. One of the chief uses of gold is to buy from the agriculturist, directly or circuitously, for the use of those who live in towns and cities, the superfluity of cereals raised in the harvest-fields. Harvesting operations are thus always interesting and stirring. Ruth would feel an interest; and, in consequence of the hearty sympathy and favour of Boaz, her whole nature would be stirred. 5. But it is far from being improbable that when the gleaning season was ended, so that Ruth had to exchange out-of-door for indoor activities, she may have acquired, to the eye of her solicitous mother-in-law, an unusually pensive appearance. 6. Naomi would no doubt make Ruth a constant study. Every mother, every father, should make every individual child in the family circle an individual study. It is not every child, it is not every young man, or young woman, whose whole heart can be read off at a sitting. Many a mind is many-volumed. Naomi did her best day by day to understand her devoted and deeply affectionate daughter-in-law, and seems to have felt increasingly solicitous as she noticed her unwonted thoughtfulness and reticence. 7. Then we must bear in mind that in such a state of society as then prevailed in Bethlehem and Judah, there must have been extremely little scope for female energy and industry in business directions. Happily in our time there is, so far as Great Britain is concerned, considerable interest taken by philanthropic minds in the subject of female education, literary and technical. There are, moreover, even already many spheres in which females, not otherwise provided for, can find, in affairs congenial to their tastes and idiosyncrasies, remuneration and employment. In many government offices, and in other spheres of activity, females now occupy important positions. Not only do they excel in works of taste: whatever requires careful attention, combined with delicate manipulation, can be intrusted to their hands. There is still, it is true, much to be done to promote the employment and independence of single females; but a beginning has been made, and a point or two beyond that beginning have been reached. In the time and sphere of Naomi, however, there were no open doors of this kind. And hence, when she was looking out for the settlement of her daughter-in-law, she naturally thought only of a 'rest' for her in a home of her own. In reference to such a 'rest,' it is the duty of all mothers and mothers-in-law to be solicitous, though never obtrusive, in behalf of their children. Advice may be tendered, caution may be suggested; but there must be true sympathy on the one hand, and true delicacy of feeling on the other.

To turn now more particularly to Boaz—1. It is reasonable to suppose that Naomi had noticed that he looked on Ruth with longing eyes. 2. It is also reasonable to suppose that, from some cause or other, Boaz felt himself under an unconquerable spell of reticence. The cause seems to be revealed in his use again and again of the fatherly expression, *My daughter*, as applied to Ruth. He was evidently well advanced in years. This seems to have been the soil on which his insuperable diffidence grew. How to get this diffidence plucked up by the roots was the problem which the solicitous Naomi set herself to solve. 3. There was only one way, as it appeared to her, in which Boaz's mind could be set free from the spell which put a seal on his lips. That was to bring Ruth into such relationship to him that he would learn her true sentiments on the one hand, and feel put upon his honour on the other. Naomi, to effect this consummation, took advantage of a time-honoured custom, which had come down from very remote and primitive times, and was still in full force among the Hebrews. She thought of *the Levirate law*. This was a law that gave a widow, if an heiress, the right to claim, from the nearest of kin to her deceased husband, conjugal assistance in the management of her estate. The nearest of kin, if thus appealed to for the purpose indicated, had a right to refuse the widow's claim, provided he was willing to submit to certain indignities and unpleasant formalities, such as being stripped of one of his shoes, and then twitted and hooted as *Barefoot* (Deut. xxv. 5—10). But if it should happen to be the case that his feelings were the reverse of repugnance, then the act of compliance would be at once the highest meed of respect which could be paid to the memory of the deceased, and the greatest gratification that could be enjoyed by the living. In the case of Ruth and Boaz, two just conclusions had been arrived at by Naomi. One had reference to Ruth, and was to the effect that, while it would be impossible for her to initiate action that might be regarded as terminating on herself, it would yet be both possible for and becoming in her to undertake the initiation of action that had for its aim what was due to the name and honour of her deceased husband. The other had reference to Boaz, and was to the effect that his diffidence, otherwise unconquerable, would be conquered if he were put upon his honour, and saw his way clear to discharge a duty to a deceased kinsman. 4. We must, in addition, suppose that Naomi, in making arrangement for the midnight interview, had unfaltering confidence in the incorruptible innocence of Ruth, and in the incontaminable purity of Boaz. 5. We are likewise entitled to assume that the method of claiming a kinsman's interposition, which she laid down for her daughter-in-law's guidance, was no gratuitous invention of her own. It is natural to regard it as having been the normal and accredited formula of procedure that was in use in " society," for the initiation of such measures as were requisite in the application of the Levirate law. 6. It is on this assumption alone that we can account for the fact that no apology was made by Ruth, and that no surprise was expressed by Boaz. Instead of surprise, there was only devout admiration of Ruth's entire demeanour in relation to her deceased husband. He said, " Blessed be thou of the Lord, my daughter ; thou hast made thy latter kindness better than the former, in not going after any young man, whether poor or rich." It is her kindness to the deceased, not her kindness to himself, of which he speaks. The kindness she was showing after her husband's decease was, in Boaz's estimation, still greater than the kindness she had showed him, or had been able to show him, during his life. A woman, so attractive and so capable as she, might have readily found among the young men many open doors to rest, and ease, and affluence. But she did not for one moment wish to avail herself of any of these openings. She wished to do honour to the name and memory of her lamented Machlon, more especially in her capacity as the prospective heiress of his property. 7. We may be sure, however, that Naomi would never have availed herself of the customs that had got fixed by " use and wont " in relation to the Levirate law, unless she had been certain that it would be in accordance with the deepest desires of both her friends that they should get together in life.

In the light of these remarks we may now re-read the entire chapter, interposing, as we go along the successive verses, whatever expository or practical remark may seem to be called for.

Ver. 1.—There is something radically wrong in every home which is not a " rest " to its inmates ; and life without a home is emphatically a life of unrest.

Vers. 2—4.—Naomi's solicitude for her devoted daughter-in-law is beautiful and motherly. But the form into which it ran and took shape can never recur in the midst of the culture and customs of European society. Even the method of winnowing the golden grain of the harvest-field, as referred to in ver. 2, is antique and obsolete. So, too, is the method which Boaz adopted to watch over his cereal treasures. He constituted himself his own watchman and police-man.

Ver. 5.—Ruth's confidence in Naomi's kindness and wisdom is noteworthy. It was no upstart prepossession and blindfold feeling. Naomi had earned it by a long-continued course of prudence and sympathy. Boaz too had earned a correspond-ing confidence, and hence she did not hesitate to intrust herself to his honour. She felt that she was safe.

Vers. 6, 7.—The expression "his heart was merry" just means that he felt physic-ally comfortable, and ready for quiet and sound repose.

Ver. 8.—When it is said that "the man was afraid, *and turned himself*," the meaning of the latter clause, as it stands in King James's version, would require some modification. The idea is not that Boaz *turned from one side to another*. It is that, having started in a fright, in consequence of the presence, to his indis-tinct consciousness, of something unusual about his feet, he raised himself up and bent forward to feel what it was.

Ver. 9.—His touch had satisfied him that it was a woman who was at his feet. Who was she? Ruth at once declared herself, no doubt in accents of sweet modesty. The statement with which she follows up the declaration of herself is variously inter-preted. In King James's version there are two departures from literality. 1. The word *skirt* is not a literal rendering of the Hebrew term. *Wings* is the proper trans-lation. 2. The entreaty *Spread therefore* is also a departure from literality. The verb is not in the *imperative*, but in the *affirmative—And thou hast spread*. It is Ruth's own interpretation of the position of affairs. She had come to Judæa to take shelter *under the wings of Jehovah;* and Boaz had, on his part, in harmony with the heavenly kindness of Jehovah, spread over her his wings of terrestrial kindness. She thus does not speak at all of Boaz's *skirt*, or *skirts*. There was beautiful delicacy in her representation. She did not need to enter into particular details. Her posi-tion, viewed in the light of custom, explained the whole case.

Vers. 10, 11.—"And now, my daughter, fear not"—give not thyself any anxious concern in reference to the result. "All the people in the gate of my city know that thou art *a virtuous woman*." Yes, she *was* virtuous; and yet she was much more. She was endowed with all the *capabilities* which fitted her for the position she was willing to occupy (see the *Exposition*).

Ver. 12.—Note the highly honourable character of Boaz. There was one nearer in kinship to Ruth than himself. This person, therefore, must receive the first offer. Had the case come before Boaz as simply one of personal affection, he would in all probability have made no reference to the nearer kinsman. But as it had come before him in its relation to the deceased, and connected itself with Ruth because of her relation to the deceased, he felt that he must act in strictest honour. There were rights of property at stake, as well as affections of the heart, and Boaz could be no party to deprive any one of such rights. Still we need not doubt that his heart thrilled at the thought that the rights involved would not prove an insurmountable barrier between himself and Ruth.

Ver. 13.—Boaz's mind still runs on the lines of a kinsman's duty. There was hence something that might be thrust in between the desires of his heart and the object toward whom they trembled.

Ver. 14.—Boaz was desirous to guard the fair name and fame of Ruth, as well as to keep untarnished his own unsullied reputation.

Ver. 15.—He wished that Naomi might have some tangible evidence of his satis-faction.

Ver. 16.—The question *Who art thou?* sprang from Naomi's hope that the entire scheme would issue in success.

Ver. 17.—The present was, in one point of view, inconsiderable; but, in another point of view, it was a most suitable gift from one who desired indeed to show sym pathy, gratitude, and kindness, but who did not wish, at that stage of the affair, to raise unconditioned expectation which might never be realised.

Ver. 18.—Naomi, as it were, said to Ruth and to her own heart, *Peace, peace. All will be well. All is well. The hand of the Almighty is dealing " sweetly," not " bitterly,"* with all the parties concerned.

HOMILIES BY VARIOUS AUTHORS.

Ver. 1.—*Marriage, a woman's rest.* If Ruth was unselfish, so also was Naomi. The mother-in-law acted towards the young Moabitess as if she had been her own daughter. In seeking a husband for her daughter-in-law Naomi followed the customs of her country and her age. (Our English custom is intermediate between the French custom, according to which the husband is provided by the negotiations of the parents, and the American custom, which leaves daughters to select for themselves.) The case before us was not an ordinary one. For whilst marriage was almost universally looked forward to by Hebrew youths and maidens, there were very special reasons why Naomi should seek a husband for Ruth. As is implied in the text, Naomi desired that her daughter-in-law might find in marriage with Boaz—

I. A HOME, which should be a rest from her wanderings.

II. A PROVISION, which should deliver her from the misery and the temptations of poverty.

III. HAPPINESS, which should compensate her for the sorrows of her widowhood.

IV. PIOUS COMPANIONSHIP, which should be a relief from long friendlessness.

Lessons:—1. Parents should take thought for their children, and not leave them to choose companions and friends and life-associates by chance. Nothing could be more disastrous than such neglect and thoughtlessness. 2. Marriage should be thought of with deliberation and prayer, both by the young, and by their parents or natural guardians. 3. Those who have found rest and prosperity in marriage should not omit the duty of gratitude and praise for the care and direction of Divine providence.—T.

Ver. 2.—*Diligence in business.* Boaz is an example of a thorough man of business. He was wont himself to see to it that the land was well tilled and well reaped. He was personally acquainted with the labourers. He even noticed the gleaners. He watched the reaping. He superintended the winnowing. He slept on the winnowing-floor, to protect his corn from the designs of robbers.

I. A RELIGIOUS MAN IS BOUND TO ATTEND TO THE CALLING HE EXERCISES. Whether a landowner, a farmer, a merchant, a tradesman, or a professional man, he ought to give his attention to his occupation, and not to neglect his own business to be a meddler in that of others. His business is thus more likely to prosper, and his example to younger men will be influential and beneficial.

II. AN EMPLOYER OF LABOUR IS BOUND TO STUDY THE WELFARE OF HIS SERVANTS. The present state of society is very different from that in the time of Boaz. Society is less patriarchal, and more democratic. But there is still room, both in the household and in commercial and agricultural and manufacturing life, for the exercise of wise and kindly supervision over those who are employed to labour.

III. DILIGENCE IN BUSINESS PROCURES A MAN MANY ADVANTAGES. It is foolish to despise wealth, though it is easy to over-estimate it. From the narrative it is clear that the wealth of Boaz enabled him to secure a charming and virtuous wife, gave him great consideration amongst his neighbours and fellow-townsmen. If a man neglects the opportunity of acquiring property in order to pursue learning, or to do good, he deserves respect; but if from sloth and heedlessness, he is despised. Wealth is good if it be used for good purposes — for the education of children, for the encouragement of learning and virtue, for the well-being of the people at large.—T

Vers. 5, 6.—*Filial obedience.* Ruth was not Naomi's daughter, yet she acted, and with good reason and great propriety, as though she had been such. What holds good, therefore, of the relationship described in this book holds good, *à fortiori*, of the relation between parents and children. In modern society the bonds of parental discipline are, especially among the working class, lamentably relaxed. Christian people should, in the interests alike of patriotism and religion, do all they can to strengthen these bonds. The text affords us a beautiful example of filial obedience.

I. MOTIVES to filial obedience. Gratitude should lead the child to obey the parent, to whom he owes so very much. The constraint should be the sweet constraint of love. Reason should lead to the reflection—The parent has experience of human life, in which I am necessarily lacking; is not a parent's judgment far more likely to be sound than is a child's, or even a youth's? Divine legislation commands children to obey their parents. *E. g.* the fifth commandment, under the old covenant; apostolical admonitions, under the new. The example of the Holy Child, Jesus!

II. The ADVANTAGES of filial obedience. Usually, obvious temporal advantages ensue upon such a course. This is proverbial and unquestionable. The satisfaction of a good conscience is a compensation not to be despised for any sacrifice of personal feeling in this matter. The approval of God is most emphatically pronounced upon those who honour and obey their parents. And this is usually followed by the confidence and admiration of fellow-men.

Lessons:—1. Expostulate with the disobedient. 2. Encourage the obedient.—T.

Ver. 7.—*The joy of harvest.* There is brightness and pleasantness in the view this passage gives us of a harvest-time in the vale of Bethlehem. Poets and painters have interpreted the heart of humanity in the pictures and the songs in which they have represented " the joy of harvest." Boaz, the mighty man of wealth, was not only rich and prosperous—he was happy, and free from the moroseness which sometimes accompanies riches; he was generous, and free from the miserliness and penuriousness which often grows with prosperity; he was considerate, and observed and recognised individual cases of need.

I. IT IS RIGHT TO PARTAKE OF THE BOUNTIES OF GOD'S PROVIDENCE. Gluttony and drunkenness meet with no encouragement from this, or from any other portion of Scripture. But no countenance is given to asceticism God "daily loadeth us with benefits;" he giveth not only seed to the sower, but "bread to the eater." We should eat, drink, and give thanks to him who "openeth his hand and satisfieth the wants of every living thing." Sincerity and thoughtfulness should accompany the daily blessing and breaking of bread. Christ "came eating and drinking."

II. IT IS RIGHT TO BE HAPPY AND MIRTHFUL WHEN GOD HAS DEALT BOUNTIFULLY WITH US. There is mirth of a kind attending the carousals and the debaucheries of sinners. This mirth is hollow, and will soon be succeeded by regrets. But when God's children sit at their Father's table and partake of his bounty, what more natural and just than that they should rejoice and sing aloud of his goodness? These gifts and "all things" are theirs!

III. IT IS RIGHT TO REST WHEN DUTY HAS BEEN FULFILLED AND TASKS ACHIEVED. Some zealous Christians seem to think all repose is sinful, as manifesting indifference to the magnitude of the work to be done. But God has made the body so that it needs rest, the mind so that it needs relaxation. The quality of the work will not suffer, but will gain, by timely and moderate repose.—T.

Ver. 10.—*Benediction.* A blessing comes appropriately from a senior; a father blesses his son, a venerable patriarch his youthful colleague. Boaz was an elderly man, and it seems appropriate that, addressing Ruth, the young widow of his kinsman, he should use language of benediction: "Blessed be thou of the Lord, my daughter!"

I. BENEDICTION PROCEEDS FROM A BENEVOLENT DISPOSITION. It is the opposite of cursing. Sometimes language of benediction is used when there is no spiritual reality behind it. In such cases it is a mockery, a counterfeit of benevolence and piety.

II. BENEDICTION IMPLIES PIETY. Belief in God, and in God's willingness to bless. There is a looking up to God on behalf of him who is to be blessed. Without this the language of blessing is meaningless.

III. BENEDICTION IS THE ACKNOWLEDGMENT THAT FROM GOD ALL GOOD MUST COME, COMBINED WITH THE DESIRE AND PRAYER THAT HE WILL BE GRACIOUS. It is the hallow-ing of our best affections ; it is the making real and personal of our most solemn religious beliefs.

IV. BENEDICTION, IF HARMONIOUS WITH GOD'S WILL, SECURES GOD'S FAVOUR. It is a wish, but a wish realised ; a prayer, but a prayer heard and answered in heaven. —T.

Ver. 11.—*A virtuous woman.* The circumstances of the narrative read strangely to us. But one nation and one age cannot fairly apply its standards to another. Nothing is more certain than that the conduct of Naomi, of Ruth, and of Boaz was perfectly correct, and probably Ruth's proceeding was wise and justifiable. Upon her character no breath of suspicion rested ; she was, in the language of the text, " a virtuous woman."

I. RUTH'S VIRTUE WAS MANIFESTED BY HER CIRCUMSPECT CONDUCT WITH REFERENCE TO YOUNG MEN. "Thou followedst not young men, whether rich or poor."

II. HER VIRTUE WAS APPARENT IN HER OBEDIENCE TO HER MOTHER-IN-LAW. Instead of taking counsel of her own comparative inexperience, she listened to the advice of the sage and prudent Naomi.

III. HER VIRTUE WAS ACKNOWLEDGED BY ALL HER ACQUAINTANCE. "All the city of my people doth know." If there had been anything in the conduct of the poor, friendless young foreigner inconsistent with virtue, it would not have been hid. She escaped calumny.

IV. HER VIRTUE LED TO AN HONOURABLE MARRIAGE AND POSITION IN ISRAEL. "A virtuous woman is a crown to her husband." We can believe that Ruth verified the beautiful description given in Prov. xxxi.—T.

Vers. 12, 13.—*Respect for others' rights.* The situation in which Boaz found himself was very singular. All that he had heard and all that he had observed of this young Moabitess had impressed him favourably. His language and his conduct show that Ruth had made an impression upon his heart. And it was honourable to him that it was so. Her youth, her beauty, her misfortunes, her industry, her cheerfulness, her filial devotedness, her virtue, her piety, all commended her to the judgment and the affections of the upright and conscientious Boaz. And now, with the most perfect modesty, and in the presentation of an undoubted claim upon him, Ruth offered herself to him as his lawful, rightful wife. What hindered him from immediately complying with her request, and taking her to his heart and his home ? There was one impediment. Another had, if he chose to exercise it, a prior claim. Another had the first right to redeem the field of Elimelech, and to espouse the heiress, and raise up seed to the departed. And until this person — the nameless one—had exercised his option, Boaz did not feel at liberty to act upon the suggestion of his heart.

I. PERSONAL FEELINGS ALWAYS INCREASE THE URGENCY OF THE CLAIMS OF SELFISHNESS. "By nature and by practice" men seek their own interest. But experience shows us that strong emotion increases the danger of our yielding to such impulses.

II. WHERE PERSONAL FEELINGS ARE CONCERNED THERE IS NEED OF WATCHFULNESS AND PRAYER. It is so easy to wrong others for the sake of our own gratification, that it is well to question the arguments and pleas by which our interests are commended. Boaz must have been tempted, in the circumstances, to say nothing about the nearer kinsman, but quietly to accept the proposal of Ruth.

III. TRUE PRINCIPLE, AIDED BY THE POWER OF RELIGION, WILL ENABLE A MAN TO DO THE RIGHT, EVEN THOUGH HIS OWN INTERESTS AND HIS OWN FEELINGS ARE OPPOSED TO SUCH A COURSE. Boaz gained the victory over himself, and consented to abide the issue of an appeal to the nearer kinsman, although he risked thereby the loss of Ruth. Many of the highest illustrations of the nobility possible to man turn upon some such situation, and the course which honour and virtue prescribe is the course in which true and lasting happiness will be found.—T.

Vers. 15—17.—*Generosity.* Boaz was " a mighty man of wealth," and Naomi and Ruth were poor, widowed, friendless, and comparatively strangers. All through the narrative Boaz appears as thoughtful, liberal, unselfish, honourable, munificent. He is an example to those whom Providence has endowed with wealth.

I. WEALTH IS GIVEN TO THE RICH not for their own sake only, but FOR THE SAKE OF OTHERS. Men are not the owners, but the stewards, of their possessions. How imperfectly this truth is recognised! The only way in which we can give to Christ is by giving to his people.

II. GENEROSITY SHOULD BE PROPORTIONATE TO THE MEANS OF THE GIVER. Both his means absolutely and his means relatively, *i. e.* considering the claims upon him by virtue of his family, his position, &c.

III. GENEROSITY SHOULD BE PROPORTIONATE TO THE NEEDS OF THE RECIPIENT. Those should have the preference who are old, crippled, and helpless; the widow and the orphan.

IV. GENEROSITY SHOULD BE UNOSTENTATIOUS AND SYMPATHETIC in its spirit. "Let not thy left hand know what thy right hand doeth." Hardness of manner may spoil beneficence. "Rich gifts wax poor when givers prove unkind."—T.

Ver. 18.—*Sit still!* Naomi showed in her whole conduct not only tender feeling and sympathy, and sincere piety, but much shrewdness, foresight, tact, and knowledge of human nature. When there was anything for Ruth to do she was forward in urging her to action. But she knew that there is always a time to wait, as well as a time to work; and she reminded Ruth that now events must be left to others—indeed, must be left to God!

I. The OCCASION for sitting still. According to some, the belief that God works is inconsistent with the obligation to work ourselves. The whole idea of the religious life, as apprehended by some mistaken minds, is to do nothing, and to leave God to do everything. And some, who do not go so far as this, still are blind to the privilege of being "workers together with God." When we have done our part, then is the time to sit still. The workman has first to labour, then to rest. The day of toil comes first, and the night of repose follows. When we can do no more, then is the time to sit still. Ask yourself whether you have or have not this reason for refraining from effort. We sometimes come to the end of our ability; we have done our part, and for us nothing now remains to do.

II. MOTIVES which should induce thus to sit still. We have to consider that in certain cases to do otherwise would be utterly useless. In these cases it is a waste of power to make further effort, and a waste of feeling to allow anxiety to distress the heart. Thus any other course would be injurious, would destroy or disturb our peace of mind. And there are occasions when to be quiet is to trust in the providential rule and care of God. So it was with Ruth at this conjuncture. The example of Christ should not be overlooked. There came a time when he was silent before his foes.

III. The BLESSING which follows sitting still. 1. Peace of heart. "Rest in the Lord." 2. Strength. "Your strength is to sit still." "In quietness and confidence shall be your strength." 3. If God will, prosperity. "He shall give thee thy heart's desire." 4. In any case the glory of God, who desires that his people should do his will, and leave results to him.—T.

Ver. 1.—*Thoughtful love.* "Shall not I seek rest for thee?" How natural. We cannot ever be with those we love. Marriage is God's own ideal, and it is the happiest estate if his fear dwells in our hearts.

I. THERE IS NO EARTHLY REST LIKE THE REST OF HOME. Judges, warriors, statesmen enjoy the honours of life, and are conscious of pleasure in promotion and distinction, but their biographies tell us how they turn to home as the highest joy of all. Yes! Nothing can compensate for the loss of a happy home, and we should seek in every way to make it a refreshment and a delight by doing our best to promote its peace and purity.

II. THE EARTHLY HOME IS A PARABLE OF HEAVEN. Our Saviour touches our hearts at once when he says, "My Father's house," and when he speaks the exquisite parable of the prodigal son. No analogies of city or temple are so powerful in their influence over us as the analogy of home.—W. M. S.

Ver. 2.—*The work of winnowing.* "Behold, he winnoweth barley to-night." A world-old process this, the winnowing of the chaff from the wheat. Customs change, and commercial life increases and creates ever new demands; but the agricultural life is still the basis of all. You may make new threshing-machines, but you must still have *bread*. It may be winnowed by steam or hand, but it must be *winnowed*. A pleasant Eastern sight: work done in the cool of the evening—"to-night."

I. WORK IS EVER ASSOCIATED BY GOD WITH HIS BLESSINGS TO MAN. We must plant and dig and reap. God sends the sunshine, the sweet air, and the shower. If a man will not work, neither shall he eat. A paradise of idlers would soon be a Gehenna indeed. No curse can come to a nation so sad as this: "Abundance of idleness was in her sons and her daughters."

II. WORK IS NEVER UNDIGNIFIED OR TO BE DISDAINED. A gentleman is gentle in his work—not because he does no work. It is a false pride that dislikes handiwork. Many of the diseases which darken the brain come from the unwise neglect of physical exercise. What is sweeter than the fragrance of the upturned soil? What is more beneficent than the law of labour, which calls forth the exercise of body, mind, and spirit?

III. WORK OF WINNOWING IS A DIVINE WORK ALSO. God uses his *tribulum* in our history, and the tribulation-work produces experience, patience, hope. When we are mourning over some sorrow or loss, it is the bruising flail of God's correction. And this comes at *all seasons* of life, even in the evening of the day. For we shall need chastisement even unto the end. What a doom is *that* "without chastisement."—W. M. S.

Ver. 11.—*Above rubies*. "A virtuous woman." Here is the crown of all beauty. What a renown is this of Ruth's. No jewelled necklet, no Eastern retinue, can give such attraction as this. We may have women of genius, and we admire genius; we may have women of scientific attainment, and God has given no lack of intellectual endowments to women, but we *must* have virtue. Let the history of later Rome tell us what the loss of this is.

I. NO LIFE IS HIDDEN. "All the city of my people doth know that thou art a virtuous woman." Every history stands revealed. Concerning Nehemiah, we read of the testimony given in time of national trouble: "There is a man in thy kingdom in whose heart is the fear of the holy God." And so this simple-hearted Ruth, who had not tried to make herself attractive to the young men, poor or rich, who had been modest in manner and heroic in conduct, left the impress of her character on the city.

II. NO LIFE CAN BE RELIGIOUS THAT IS NOT VIRTUOUS. We may, indeed, have virtue of a kind, a morality of respectability, without religion; but we cannot be religious without morality, for religion does not consist in ceremonies however impressive, or days however sacred, or opinions however sound; but in a life of consecration to God, and of obedience to all the sanctities of the moral law. There may be a religion of emotionalism merely; but blessed as it is to feel the true, we must live it out as well in common life.

III. NO POWER IS SO PERMANENT AS THAT OF HOLY LIFE. Character lives in others. We do not die when we pass from earth. Ruth lives to-day. It would be interesting to know how many have been led even in this age to devoutness and decision by the remembrance of her conduct and the exquisite pathos of her words. The little "city" of which our text speaks has passed away, but wherever the word of God is known and read, there Ruth reproduces herself in the history of others. The very name has become a family name, and is honoured by constant use in every generation.—W. M. S.

Ver. 12.—*Woman's influence*. In all history woman has held a place of regal influence. Not by intruding on the sphere of man, not by acting as if there were no Divine providence in the more delicate physical constitution of woman which incapacitates her for the strain of hardest toil; but in the ideal of "home," in which she is to be the "abiding" one, filling it with the charm of quiet influence and the sacredness of self-sacrificing love.

I. HERE IS A STRANGE CONJUNCTION OF TERMS. "Virtuous" comes from the Latin *vir*, which means a man. What then? Is a woman to be like a man? Does it mean a manly woman? In one sense it does. For "the man" is taken in the

Scripture as the type of humanity in its best estate. "Show thyself a man," says David to Solomon. It means all that is pure, and brave, and true, and good. Thus "abominable" means something *ab homo,* to be designated as "away from a man; " something altogether alien to his nature. A virtuous woman is a woman who has strength of resistance to evil, strength of devotion to God, strength of patience and endurance in the path of obedience.

II. HERE IS THE POWER OF INFLUENCE. "All the people of my city (or, at the gate) doth know that thou art a virtuous woman." Certainly. "They that be otherwise cannot be hid." What a lesson that is! Character tells everywhere. You may not note the current running, but place your boat upon it, and you soon *see* it. So it is with a good life—it bears others in its current. We are all known. Men and women are judged at their true worth even in this world, and even the wicked respect the upright and the just. It was said of Nehemiah to the king in a time of trouble, "There is a man in thy kingdom in whose heart is the fear of the holy God."

III. HERE IS THE SECRET OF NATIONAL GLORY. It was so in Rome when they could speak with pride of the Roman matron, and it has been so in every nation under heaven. A Divine judgment was needed to purify this nation after the days of Charles II. Had it not been a time of judgment, the nation, as Charles Kingsley says, would have perished. Let the young be taught modesty even in dress and demeanour. Let all that is "fast" be frowned upon and made unfashionable. The grace that Christ gives is humility with the fear of the Lord.—W. M. S.

EXPOSITION.

CHAPTER IV.

Ver. 1.—**And Boaz went up to the gate, and sat there.** He "went up," for the city stood, as it still stands, on a ridge (see on ch. i. 1; iii. 6). "And sat there," on one of the stones, or stone benches, that were set for the accommodation of the townsfolk. The gateway in the East often corresponded, as a place of meeting, to the forum, or the market-place, in the West. Boaz had reason to believe that his kinsman would be either passing out to his fields, or passing in from his threshing-floor, through the one gate of the city. **And lo, the kinsman of whom Boaz had spoken was passing; and he said, Ho, such a one! turn hither and sit here. And he turned and sat down.** Boaz called his kinsman by his name; but the writer does not name him, either because he could not, or because he would not. The phrase " such a one," or " so and so," is a purely idiomatic English equivalent for the purely idiomatic Hebrew phrase פְּלֹנִי אַלְמֹנִי. A literal translation is impossible. The Latin *N. N.* corresponds.

Ver. 2.—**And he took ten men of the elderly inhabitants of the city, and he said, Sit ye here; and they sat down.** Boaz wished to have a full complement of witnesses to the important transaction which he contemplated.

Ver. 3.—**And he said to the kinsman, Naomi, who has returned from the land of Moab, has resolved to sell the portion of land which belonged to our brother Elimelech.** Boaz, it is evident, had talked over with Ruth the entire details of Naomi's plans, and could thus speak authoritatively. Naomi, we must suppose, had previously taken Ruth into full confidence, so that Boaz could learn at second - hand what in other circumstances he would have learned from Naomi herself. The verb which we have rendered " has resolved to sell," is literally "has sold," and has been so rendered by many expositors, inclusive of Riegler and Wright. The Syriac translator gives the expression thus, "has sold to me." The subsequent context, however, makes it evident that the property had not been sold to any one, and consequently not to Boaz. The perfect verb is to be accounted for on the principle explained by Driver when he says, "The perfect is employed to indicate actions, the accomplishment of which lies indeed in the future, but is regarded as dependent upon such an unalterable determination of the will that it may be spoken of as having actually taken place : thus a resolution, promise, or decree, especially a Divine one, is very frequently announced in the perfect tense. A striking instance is afforded by Ruth (iv. 3) when Boaz, speaking of Naomi's determination to sell her land, says מָכְרָה נָעֳמִי, literally, ' has sold ' (has resolved to sell. The English idiom would be ' is selling ')" ('Treatise on the Use of the Tenses in Hebrew,' pp. 13, 14). In King James's English version the verb is thus freely rendered " selleth." Luther's version is equivalent—*beut feil,* " offers for sale;" or, as Coverdale renders it, " offereth to sell." Vatable freely renders it as we have done, "has determined to sell" (*vendere decrevit*): so Drusius (*vendere instituit*). The kind family feeling of Boaz, shining out in the expression, "our *brother* Elimelech," is noteworthy. "Brother" was to him a homely and gracious term for "near kinsman."

Ver. 4.—**And I said (to myself).** There is little likelihood in the opinion of those who maintain, with Rosenmuller, that the expression, "I said," refers to a promise which Boaz had made to Ruth (see ch. iii. 13). It is a primitive phrase to denote internal resolution. There is a point where thought and speech coalesce. Our words are thoughts, and our thoughts are words. **I will uncover thine ear,** that is, "I will lift the locks of hair that may be covering the ear, so as to communicate something in confidence." But here the phrase is employed with the specific import of secresy dropt out. It is thus somewhat equivalent to "I will give thee notice;" only the following expression לֵאמֹר, *i. e.* **to say,** must be read in the light of the undiluted original phrase, "I will uncover thine ear to say." The whole expression furnishes the most beautiful instance imaginable of the primary meaning of לֵאמֹר. The thing that was to be said follows immediately, viz., **Acquire it, or Buy it.** It is as if he had said, "Now you have a chance which may not occur again." It is added, **in the presence of the inhabitants.** This, rather than "the assessors," is the natural interpretation of the participle (הַיֹּשְׁבִים). It is the translation which the word generally receives in the very numerous instances in which it occurs. There was, so to speak, a fair representation of the inhabitants of the city in the casual company that had assembled in the gateway. **And in presence of the elders of my people.** The natural "aldermen," or unofficial "senators," whose presence extemporised for the occasion a sufficient court of testators. **If thou wilt perform the part of a kinsman, perform it.** The translation in King James's English version, and in many other versions, viz., "If thou wilt redeem *it*, redeem *it*," is somewhat out of harmony with the nature of the case. Naomi was not wishing Elimelech's estate to be redeemed. It was not yet in a position to be redeemed. It had not been alienated or sold. She wished for it not a redeemer, but a purchaser. And as it was the *right* of a גֹּאֵל or kinsman to redeem for a reduced brother, if he was able and willing, the estate which had been sold to an alien (Levit. xxv. 25), so it was the *privilege* of the same גֹּאֵל or kinsman to get, if the reduced brother was wishing to sell, the first

offer of the estate. It would, in particular, be at variance with the prerogative of the nearest of kin if some other one in the circle of the kindred, but not so near, were to be offered on sale the usufructuary possession of the family estate (Levit. xxv. 23, 27). Hence Boaz recognised the prior prerogative of his anonymous relative and friend, and said to him, "If thou wilt perform the part of a kinsman, and buy the property, then buy it." It is added, **and if he will not.** Note the use of the third person *he*, instead of the second *thou*. If the reading be correct, then Boaz, in thus speaking, must for the moment have turned to the witnesses so as to address them. That the reading is correct, notwithstanding that some MSS. and all the ancient versions exhibit the verb in the second person, is rendered probable by the very fact that *it is the difficult reading.* There could be no temptation for a transcriber to substitute the third person for the second ; there would be temptation to substitute the second for the third. The unanimity of the ancient versions is probably attributable to the habit of neglecting absolute literality, and translating according to the sense, when the sense was clear. Boaz, turning back instantaneously to his relative, says, **Make thou known to me, that I may know, for there is none besides thee to act the kinsman's part (with the exception of myself), and I come after thee.** The little clause, "with the exception of myself," lies in the sense, or spirit, although not in the letter of Boaz's address, as reported in the text. **And he said, I will act the kinsman's part.** He was glad to get the opportunity of adding to his own patrimonial possession the property that had belonged to Elimelech, and which Naomi, in her reduced condition, wished to dispose of. So far all seemed to go straight against the interests of Ruth.

Ver. 5.—**And Boaz said, In the day when thou acquirest the land from the hand of Naomi, and from Ruth the Moabitess, (in that day) thou hast acquired the wife of the deceased, to establish the name of the deceased upon his inheritance.** So we would punctuate and render this verse. Boaz distinctly informed his relative that if the land was acquired at all by a kinsman, it must be acquired with its living appurtenance, Ruth the Moabitess, so that, by the blessing of God, the Fountain of families, there might be the opportunity of retaining the possession of the property in the line of her deceased husband, that line coalescing in the line of her second husband. It was the pleasure of Naomi and Ruth, in offering their property for sale, to burden its acquisition, on the part of a kinsman, with the condition specified. If there should be fruit after the marriage, the child would be heir of the property, just as if he had been Machlon's son, even though the father should have other and older sons by another wife.

Ver. 6. — **And the kinsman said, I am not able to perform, for myself, the kinsman's part, lest I should destroy my inheritance. Perform thou, for thyself, the kinsman's part devolving on me, for I am not able to perform it.** The moment that Ruth was referred to, as the inseparable appurtenance of Elimelech's estate, a total change came over the feelings of the anonymous relative and the spirit of his dream. He "could not," so he strongly put it, perform the kinsman's part. The probability is that he already had a family, but was a widower. This being the state of the case, it followed that if he should acquire Ruth along with her father-in-law's property, there might be an addition, perhaps a numerous addition, to his family; and if so, then there would be more to provide for during his lifetime, and at his death an increased subdivision of his patrimony. This, as he strongly put it, would be to "destroy" his patrimony, inasmuch as it might be frittered into insignificant fractions. There can be no reference, as the Chaldee Targumist imagined, to his fear of domestic dissensions. Or, if he did indeed think of such a casualty, he certainly did not give the idea expression to Boaz and the assessors. Cassel takes another view. "It must be," he says, "her Moabitish nationality that forms the ground, such as it is, of the kinsman's refusal. Elimelech's misfortunes had been popularly ascribed to his emigration to Moab; the death of Chilion and Machlon to their marriage with Moabitish women. This it was that had endangered their inheritance. The *goël* fears a similar fate. He thinks that he ought not to take into his house a woman, marriage with whom has already been visited with the extinguishment of a family in Israel." But if this had been what he referred to when he spoke of the "destruction" of his inheritance, it was not much in harmony with the benevolence which he owed to Boaz, and to which he so far gives expression in the courtesy of his address, that he should have gratuitously urged upon his relative what he declined as dangerous for himself. The expressions "for myself" and "for thyself" (לִי and לָךְ) are significant. The anonymous relative does not conceal the idea that it would be only on the ground of doing what would be *for his own interest* that he could entertain for consideration the proposal of Naomi. He likewise assumed that if Boaz should be willing to act the kinsman's part, it would be simply because it could be turned to account *for his own*

interest. He did not know that there was in Boaz's heart a love that truly "seeketh not her own," but in honour prefers the things of another.

Ver. 7.—**And this was formerly a custom in Israel, on occasion of surrendering rights of kinship, or of selling and buying land, in order to confirm any matter; a man drew off his shoe and gave it to the other contracting party. This was attestation in Israel.** We give a free translation. The custom was significant enough. He who sold land, or surrendered his right to act as a kinsman in buying land, intimated by the symbolical act of taking off his shoe, and handing it to his friend, that he freely gave up his right to walk upon the soil, in favour of the person who had acquired the possession. Corresponding symbolical acts, in connection with the transfer of lands, have been common, and probably still are, in many countries. No doubt the shoe, after being received, would be immediately returned.

Ver. 8.—**And the kinsman said to Boaz, Acquire for thyself; and drew off his shoe.** On the instant that he said, "Acquire for thyself," viz., the land with its living appurtenant, he drew off his shoe and presented it. Josephus allowed his imagination to run off with his memory when, mixing up the historical case before us with the details of the ancient Levirate law (Deut. xxv. 7—9), which were, in later times at all events, more honoured in the breach than in the observance, he represents Boaz as "bidding the woman loose the man's shoe and spit in his face." The actual ceremony was not an insult, but a graphic and inoffensive attestation. Yet it gradually wore out and was superseded. No vestige of it remained in the days of the writer, and the Chaldee Targumist seems to have been scarcely able to realise that such a custom could ever have existed. He represents the anonymous kinsman as drawing off his "right-hand glove" and handing it to Boaz. But take note of the German word for "glove," viz., *Handschuh* (a *hand-shoe*).

Ver. 9.—**And Boaz said to the elders and all the people, Ye are witnesses this day that I have acquired the whole estate of Elimelech, and the whole estate of Chilion and Machlon, from the hand of Naomi.** It is absolutely necessary that, at this part of the narrative, as well as in several other portions, we read "between the verses." Naomi, either personally or by representative, must have appeared on the scene, to surrender her territorial rights and receive the value of the estate that had belonged to her husband. But the writer merges in his account these coincidents, and hastens on to the consummation of his story. In the twofold expression, "the whole estate of Elimelech, and the whole estate of Chilion and Machlon," there is a kind of legal particularity. There was of course but one estate, but there was a succession in the proprietorship.

Ver. 10.—And likewise Ruth the Moabitess, wife of Machlon, have I acquired to myself to wife, to establish the name of the deceased upon his inheritance, so that the name of the deceased may not be out off from among his brethren, and from the gate of his place: ye are witnesses this day. This, to Boaz, would be by far the most delightful part of the day's proceedings. His heart would swell with manly pride and devout gratitude when he realised, amid all the cumbrous technicalities of old Hebrew law, that Ruth was his. And he would rejoice all the more, as, in virtue of her connection with Machlon and Elimelech, both of their names would still be encircled with honour, and might, by the blessing of Yahveh, be linked on distinguishingly and lovingly to future generations. Note the expression, "that the name of the deceased may not be cut off from among his brethren, *and from the gate of his place.*" The people who assembled at the gate might on some future day be able to say, "This boy is the heir of Machlon and Elimelech, who once migrated to Moab."

Ver. 11.—And all the people who were in the gateway, and the elders, said, Witnesses! May Yahveh grant that the wife who has come into thy house may be as Rachel and Leah, who built, the two of them, the house of Israel! The people of the city in general, and the venerable elders in particular, were pleased with every step that Boaz had taken. They felt that he had acted a truly honourable part, at once in reference to Naomi, and to Ruth, and to the nearest kinsman, and likewise in reference to themselves as the representatives of the general population. Blessings rose up within their hearts, ascended into heaven, and came down—charged with something Divine as well as something human and humane—in showers upon his head, and upon the head of his bride. When they prayed that the woman who was the choice of their fellow-citizen's heart should be as Rachel and Leah, they simply gave expression to the intensest desire that Israelites could cherish in reference to an esteemed sister. When they spoke of Rachel and Leah—the mothers of Israel—as "building up the house of Israel," they first of all compared the people to a household, and then they passed over from the idea of a household to the idea of a house as containing the household. They added, more particularly in reference to Boaz himself, Do thou manfully in Ephratah. The expression is somewhat

peculiar, ringing changes on the peculiar and remarkable term that occurs both in ch. ii. 1 and in ch. iii. 11. The expression is עֲשֵׂה־חָיִל. The people meant, "Act thou the part of a strong, substantial, worthy man." They added, in a kind of enthusiastic exclamation, Proclaim thy name in Bethlehem. They had, however, no reference to any verbal proclamation, or tribute of self-applause. The spirit of ideality had seized them. They meant, "Act the noble part—the part that will without voice proclaim in Bethlehem its own intrinsic nobleness."

Ver. 12.—And may thy house be as the house of Pharez, whom Tamar bare to Judah, (springing) from the seed which Yahveh will give to thee of this young woman! Pharez's descendants, the Pharzites, were particularly numerous, and hence the good wishes of Boaz's fellow-townsmen (see Num. xxvi. 20, 21).

Ver. 13.—And Boaz took Ruth, and she became to him his wife; and he went in to her, and Yahveh gave her conception, and she bore a son.

Ver. 14.—And the women said to Naomi, Blessed be Yahveh, who has given thee a kinsman this day! May his name become famous in Israel. Of course it is Ruth's son who is the kinsman referred to, the nearest kinsman, still nearer than Boaz. The kinsman was given, said the women, "this day," the day when the child was born. The expression which we have rendered, "who has given thee a kinsman," is, literally, "who has not caused to fail to thee a kinsman." The sympathetic women who had gathered together in Boaz's house were sanguine, or at least enthusiastically desirous, that a son so auspiciously given, after most peculiar antecedents, would yet become a famous name in Israel. Canon Cook supposes that the kinsman referred to by the women was not the child, but his father, Boaz ('Speaker's Commentary, *in loc.*). Yet it is obvious that the kinsman specified was the one who, as they said, had been given, or had not been caused to fail, "that day." He was, moreover, the one of whom they went on to say, "May his name become famous in Israel, and may he be to thee a restorer of life, and for the support of thine old age," &c. Dr. Cook's objections are founded on a too narrow view of the functions devolving on, and of the privileges accruing to, a *goël*.

Ver. 15.—And may he be to thee a restorer of life, and for the support of thine old age: for thy daughter - in - law, who loved thee, hath borne him, and she is better to thee than seven sons. The number *seven* suggested an idea of fulness, completeness, perfection. The whole inhabitants of the city knew that Ruth's love to her mother-in-law had been indeed transcendent, and also that it had been transcendently returned.

Ver. 16.—**And Naomi took the boy, and placed him in her bosom, and she became his foster-mother.** She became his nurse in chief.

Ver. 17.—**And the women, her neighbours, named the child, saying, A son has been born to Naomi ; and they called his name Obed. He was the father of Jesse, the father of David.** "Obed," if a participle of the Hebrew verb עָבַד, naturally means *serving* or *servant*. No other derivation, apparently, can at present be assumed (but see Raabe's 'Glossar.'). Josephus gives the participial interpretation as a matter of course, and Jerome too. If the objective correlate of the servitude referred to were Yahveh, then the word might be equivalent to *worshipper*. If the name, however, as seems to be the case, was imposed first of all by the matronly neighbours who had come to mingle their joys with those of the mother, and of the grandmother in particular, then it is not likely that there would be an overshadowing reference, either on the one hand to servitude in relation to Yahveh, or on the other to servitude in the abstract. Something simpler would be in harmony with their unsophisticated, impressible, and purely matronly minds. It is not at all unlikely that, in fondling the welcome "Newcome," and congratulating the overjoyed grandmother, they would, with Oriental luxuriance of speech and Oriental overflow of demonstrativeness, speak of the 'lad' as come home to be a faithful *little servant* to his most excellent grandmother. The infirmities of advancing age, aggravated by anxieties many, griefs many, bereavements many, toils many, privations many, disappointments many, had been one after another accumulating on "the dear old lady." But now a sealed fountain of reviving waters had been opened in the wilderness. Might it for many years overflow ! Might the oasis around it widen and still widen, till the whole solitary place should be blossoming as the rose ! Might the lively little child be spared to minister, with bright activity and devotedness, to the aged pilgrim for the little remainder of her journey ! The word which the sympathetic neighbours, with not the least intention to propose a real name, had been affectionately bandying

about, while fondling the child, was accepted by Boaz and Ruth. They would say to one another, "Yes, just let him be little *Obed* to his loving grandmother." Naomi, soothed in all her motherly and grandmotherly longings and aspirations, would seem to have yielded, resolving, we may suppose, to train the child up to be *a servant of Yahveh.*

Vers. 18—22.—**And these are the lineal descendants of Pharez. Pharez begat Hezron, and Hezron begat Ram, and Ram begat Amminadab, and Amminadab begat Nahshon, and Nahshon begat Salmon, and Salmon begat Boaz, and Boaz begat Obed, and Obed begat Jesse, and Jesse begat David.** This is the genealogy of King David, and it is therefore an integral part of the genealogy of King David's great descendant, his "Lord" and ours. As such it is incorporated entire in the two tables that are contained respectively in the first chapter of the Gospel according to Matthew, and the third of the Gospel according to Luke. Some of the names are somewhat Grecised and otherwise modified in those New Testament tables. Instead of Hezron we have Esrom ; instead of Ram we have Aram ; instead of Nahshon we have Naason ; instead of Boaz we have Boos ; in 1 Chron. ii. 11 we have Salma instead of Salmon. It has been keenly debated by chronologists and genealogists whether we should regard the list of David's lineal ancestors, given here and in 1 Chron. ii. 10—12, as also in Matt. i. 3—5, and Luke iii. 31—33, as complete. It is a thorny question to handle, and one not ready to be finally settled till the whole Old Testament chronology be adjusted. It is certain that in the larger tables of our Lord's genealogy there was, apparently for mnemonic purposes (Matt. i. 17), the mergence of certain inconspicuous links (see Matt. i. 8) ; and it would not need to be matter of wonder or concern if in that section of these tables which contains the genealogy of King David there should be a similar lifting up into the light, on the one hand, of the more prominent ancestors, and a shading off into the dark, on the other, of some who were less conspicuous. It lies on the surface of the genealogy that the loving-kindness and tender mercies of Yahveh stretch far beyond the confines of the Hebrews, highly favoured though that people was. "Is he," asks St. Paul, "the God of the Jews only ? Is he not also of the Gentiles ? Yes," the same apostle answers, "of the Gentiles also" (Rom. iii. 29).

HOMILETICS.

Vers. 1—12.—*The bridal of Boaz and Ruth.* I. There were some obstacles in the way. There were none, indeed, in Boaz's heart; it was full of pure esteem and love for Ruth. There were none in his financial circumstances; he was able to provide amply for her comfort, and for all his own necessities and conveniences. There were none in his physical condition; he had been temperate in all things, and was in the enjoyment of health and strength. Neither were there any obstacles in Ruth's heart. It had already sought for refuge under the wings of Boaz's protection and sympathy. Nor were there any in her physical, intellectual, or moral condition. She was exceptionally "capable" in every respect, and eminently virtuous and good. She was filled, and had for long been filled, with the love "that seeketh not her own things." Although reduced in circumstances, she really belonged to the very class in society in which Boaz himself was moving. Nor were there obstacles on the part of Boaz's friends on the one hand, nor on the part of Ruth's one precious friend on the other. The obstacles were technical, arising out of the legal prerogative of a third party. Boaz set himself, in full concert with Ruth and Ruth's mother-in-law, to deal with these obstacles.

II. He did not loiter over the matter, or protract the proceedings unfeelingly from day to day, week to week, month to month, and even year to year, until "hope deferred" ate out every atom of enthusiasm from his own spirit, and made the heart of Ruth grow "sick." He took steps, without a single day's delay, to get his prospects and the prospects of Ruth righteously settled (see vers. 1—4).

III. Yes, "righteously settled." For it was not so much the simple settlement as the righteousness of it that he longed for. He would not gratify his desire to obtain Ruth—greatly as he esteemed, prized, and desired her—if he could not get her righteously and honourably. Hence the forensic scene in the gateway of the city.

IV. It is an old world picture that is drawn in the narrative, unveiling to view the grave, solemn manners of primitive but well-mannered times. The city had but one gate, through which, therefore, every one who went out or came in must needs pass. It would hence become the principal place of concourse for the townsfolk. It was the place of primitive marketing and bartering. It was the place of primitive judicature. It was, as it were, the senate-hall or parliament-house of the town. The elders and fathers "did congregate" there, in the presence of the casual public, to discuss the incidents that were transpiring, or the topics that were interesting the public mind. It was the place of morning and evening lounge. Boaz was careful to be early in the morning at this gateway, and immediately on arrival he took steps to secure a judicial settlement, if needed, and, at all events, a complete attestation of the facts of any nuptial arrangement that might be made. The people would begin to assemble leisurely. They would salute one another courteously. Every one would be of staid demeanour. There would be no rush, or push, or panting haste. The true Oriental likes to be self-possessed and leisurely. Some would be passing out, some passing in; but all would be ready to pause and hail one another respectfully. Kindly salutations would be directed to Boaz, and returned. It would be manifest from his countenance, from the tones of his voice, from his entire demeanour and manner, that he *meant business* that morning. See him as he moved about, stable, yet elastic, and wound up. He invites certain venerated fathers to be seated on the stone benches set in a row at the base of the city wall, as he had an affair to transact which he wished them by their presence to attest. Other citizens, meanwhile, one by one, would be arriving on the scene, some of them younger men and some older. They are grouped about. They feel that something unusual is in the air. At length there is a full conclave, and Boaz opens his case with his kinsman. It was this:—Naomi, who had so recently returned from the land of Moab, was now unfortunately in such reduced circumstances that she had resolved to sell the property which had belonged to her deceased husband. Now then was the opportunity of the nearest kinsman. In virtue of being the nearest in kinship, he was entitled to the first offer of the property. "Buy it, therefore," said Boaz, "before the inhabitants, and before the elders of my people. If thou wilt act the part of the nearest kinsman (as thou art entitled to do), then act it, and buy the property" (ver. 4). The kinsman seemed glad that he should have such an opportunity of adding to his patrimonial estate, and accordingly, in presence of the elders and other inhabitants, he heartily said, "I will act the kinsman's part." As he thus spoke there would, in all likelihood, be murmurs of applause round and round. Who could object to the kinsman getting the estate if he should offer to pay a liberal price to the reduced widow? It was, in its own little sphere of things, quite a crisis. Deep-drawing interests, affections, and desires were trembling in the balance. Boaz looked grave. But it was evident to perceptive eyes that he had not yet unfolded the whole case to view. After the briefest possible pause he resumed, and said, in the presence of the judicial conclave, "In the day when thou buyest the land from Naomi, thou must buy it not from her only, but from Ruth also, as prospective heiress; and more, thou must buy it *with Ruth at present upon it, as its inalienable appurtenant,* in order that the name of her deceased husband may, by the blessing of the God of Israel, descend with it in the line of her posterity (ver. 5). It was only for a moment that the fate of the gentle Moabitess trembled in its scale. The kinsman was not prepared to accept the property on Naomi's terms. He feared that new interests would spring up to fritter into insignificant patches the property which he already possessed. Hence he said to Boaz, in the presence of the elders and the other citizens, "I cannot act the part of the nearest kinsman; do thou it, Boaz, in my room" (ver. 6). Boaz would triumph in his heart; and so, when she became informed of the decision, would Naomi; and so would Ruth. But some legal formalities required to be observed ere the renunciation of the prerogative attaching to the nearest kinsman became absolutely binding in law. "This," says the writer, "was formerly a custom in Israel on occasion of surrendering rights of kinship, or selling and buying land, in order to confirm every matter. A man drew off his shoe and gave it to the contracting party. This was attestation in Israel" (ver. 7). Accordingly, the nearest kinsman in the case before us drew off his shoe and tendered it to Boaz, in testimony that he therewith resigned all right to walk upon the ground in question (ver. 8). After this formality had been completed, and Boaz had courteously, in presence of the assembled witnesses, returned the symbolic shoe, he seems to have sent for Naomi and Ruth, and to have finished with them, in the presence of the people, the arrangement which was the most momentous into which he had ever entered, and which promised to be big with blessing to others as well as to himself. It was not only a marriage settlement; it was a bridal ceremony. The antique benisons of the elders and the other citizens fell round him thick and fast (vers. 9—12), and that blessing which maketh rich, and to which no sorrow is added, the blessing of the God of families and of all family love, descended and crowned the union.

V. It is infinitely becoming that all things in marriage should be done "DECENTLY," "IN ORDER," and ABOVE-BOARD. Let everything clandestine be sensitively avoided. Whenever there is anything in marriage or its preliminaries that needs smothering up, the wind is sown, and the whirlwind will need to be reaped.

VI. If stable HAPPINESS AFTER MARRIAGE be desired, care should be taken to have all preliminaries duly, clearly, and righteously pre-arranged, more particularly such as have reference to possessions, money, rights, or prerogatives. There should be also, especially in these modern times, distinct preliminary arrangements regarding the chief manners and customs of the home, and the relationship that is to be sustained to Churches, and Church assemblies and ordinances. Much indeed must be left to future and incidental adjustment; but great regulative principles should be mutually settled.

VII. If, in "the estate of marriage," there be, as there should be and might be, on both sides a continual aim after whatsoever things are true, honest, seemly, honourable, just, pure, lovely, virtuous, and praiseworthy, then the light of life will shine in the home and in the heart with inexpressible sweetness and brightness. But if there be suspicion, jealousy, hard authority, tyranny, a dictatorial spirit, or any grossness, or secret faithlessness, or the neglect of courtesy, or the extinguishment of kindness and daily benevolence, if there be hard selfishness, however glitteringly glozed over with a semblance of good manners, then the light of life will be not only partially, but totally eclipsed. When the selfishness unmasks itself to the full, the last feeble flame, flickering in the socket, will die out, and be succeeded by a darkness that is the very " blackness of darkness." The true ideal of conjugal relationship is presented by St. Paul in his Epistle to the Ephesians (ch. v. 25—33). The husband's love should be as the love of Jesus to his Church. The love of the wife should be as the love of the Church to Jesus. Then the marriage is " in the Lord ; " and, what is better still, the life after the marriage is life " in the Lord," and life *to the Lord*. It was from ages and generations " a great mystery," but now it is made manifest in every Christian home that is Christian indeed.

Vers. 13—22.—*Little Obed.* A birth, and in particular a first birth, in the homes of the " excellent of the earth " is always an interesting and exciting event. What multitudes of beginnings there are in childhood ! What multitudes of buds and beautiful rose-buddings ! What possibilities and uncertainties ! What wonderful littlenesses of hands and feet, and other organs, all so marvellously harmonised and complete ! What wondrous and wondering eyes, looking, and still looking, as if they would really read your very heart ! What winsome smiles and early recognitions !

I. LITTLE OBED WAS A FORTUNATE CHILD. He had three great privileges. He had a good father, a good mother, and a good grandmother. What a blessing ! His father was one of the most upright, most honourable, most gracious of men. His mother was " one among a thousand." She had a large heart, full of singular affection and self-denying devotedness. His grandmother was a woman with bold outline of character, but with a capability of yearning and attachment unfathomably deep.

II. If little Obed grew up, as is likely, IN THE FEAR AND FAVOUR OF GOD, then what was long afterwards said of Timothy might by some one be said of him, " I call to remembrance the unfeigned faith that is in thee, which dwelt at first in thy grandmother Lois, and thy mother Eunice, and I am persuaded in thee also " (2 Tim. i. 5).

III. FROM HIS VERY BIRTH HE WOULD BE CRADLED IN LOVE, the threefold love of Ruth, Boaz, and Naomi, intertwined into a delightful unity of affection.

IV. GREAT WOULD BE THE REJOICINGS OVER HIS ADVENT. 1. Ruth would think of Machlon, and rejoice. 2. Naomi would think of Elimelech, and rejoice. 3. Boaz would think of both the deceased, and rejoice that their names were not to be cut off from among their brethren. Then again (1) Ruth would rejoice for her husband's sake, whose home would be brighter now than ever. And she would have peculiar joy for Naomi's sake, whose fondest wishes and hopes and plans had been so happily consummated. (2) Boaz would rejoice over the joy and consolation of Ruth and Naomi ; and he would drink from another fountain of joy as he realised that he himself, instead of being the terminal link in the genealogical chain, might now have a place in the line of future generations. (3) Naomi would rejoice because her deepest desires had been brought up into the light, and crowned with the blessing of the Almighty. No longer was He the embitterer of her lot (ch. i. 20). Her name was true, and not to be exchanged for Mara. She was herself again " Naomi," for " sweet is Jah." His character is " sweet," his thoughts, his feelings, his plans, his ways, all are " sweet."

V. In another respect would there be peculiar rejoicings over Obed's advent. HE WAS THE MUCH LONGED-FOR HEIR OF TWO DISTINCT ESTATES. Let us hope that he would be trained up to think of the responsibilities as well as of the privileges that would come to him in virtue of being born into a good position in society.

VI. HIS NAME WOULD BE BEAUTIFULLY SIGNIFICANT TO HIM IN PROPORTION AS HIS MIND UNFOLDED AND EXPANDED. He would have various ministries to fulfil. A ministry to his grandmother. A ministry to his mother. A ministry to his father. A ministry to his dependents. A ministry to his friends and neighbours, and countrymen in general. Above all, he would have a ministry to the God of his fathers and of their children's children. It would be his business to be OBED in all relations. Even Jesus, out of all compare the greatest of his descendants, became OBED, and took upon himself "the form of a SERVANT," and took far more than the form ; he came " not to be ministered unto, but to minister."

VII. It was the hope of the congratulatory matrons who fondled the welcome child, that he would be to his grandmother " a restorer of life " and " a nourisher of her old age " (ver. 15). High is the privilege of children and grand-children thus to brighten to the aged the evening of life, when the long shadows are stretching far away. Happy they who count this a privilege !

VIII. What a charm is thrown over infant life by the action of Obed's great descendant in reference to children. He said, "Suffer the little children to come unto me, and forbid them not, for of such is the kingdom of heaven." He took them up in his arms, laid his hand upon their heads, and blessed them (Matt. xix. 14 ; Mark x. 14—16). At another time he called a little child to him and set him in the midst of his ambitious disciples, and said, " Except ye be converted, and become as little children, ye shall not enter into the kingdom of heaven" (Matt. xviii. 2, 3). In this love for little children Jesus, as in so many other respects, was "the image of the invisible God." He shows us exactly what is the heart, and what are the heart affections, of God. *Such as was the visible Jesus in feelings and character, such is the invisible God.* He, therefore, he, even he, is a lover of little children, without distinction or exception.

HOMILIES BY VARIOUS AUTHORS.

Vers. 1, 2.—*A primitive council.* The writer of this book depicts for us in this passage a very picturesque scene. We observe—1. *The place of judgment and public business.* "Judges and officers shalt thou make thee in all thy *gates* . . . throughout thy tribes, and they shall judge the people with just judgment." The parents of the disobedient son were to "bring him out unto the elders of his city, and unto the *gate* of his place." Absalom, when plotting against his father's authority, "stood beside the way of the *gate*," and intercepted those that came to the king for judgment. 2. The court in whose presence important business was transacted—"the *elders* of the city." Such elders were prescribed, as is evident from several passages in Deuteronomy ; and the early books of the Old Testament contain frequent references to them and to their duties. Allusion is made to the elders of Succoth, of Jezreel, and of this same Bethlehem in the time of Samuel. Ten seems to have been what we should call a quorum. There is wisdom, gravity, deliberation, dignity, in the proceedings here recorded.

I. HUMAN SOCIETY REQUIRES INSTITUTIONS OF LAW AND JUSTICE. The relations between man and man must not be determined by chance, or left to the decision of force or fraud. " Order is Heaven's first law."

II. LAW AND JUSTICE SHOULD BE SANCTIONED BY RELIGION. Religion cannot approve of all actions done by all in authority ; but it acknowledges and respects government as a Divine institution, and awakens conscience to support justice.

III. THERE ARE CERTAIN CONDITIONS IN CONFORMITY WITH WHICH PUBLIC BUSINESS SHOULD BE TRANSACTED. 1. Openness and publicity. 2. Solemn and formal ratification and record of important acts. 3. Equality of citizens before the law. 4. As much liberty as is compatible with public rights. 5. Integrity and incorruptness on the part of those who administer the law.—T.

Vers. 3—8.—*The goël.* Every nation has its own domestic and social usages. Among those prevalent in Israel was the relationship of the *goël.* He was the redeemer, or the next kinsman of one deceased, whose duty it was to purchase an inheritance in danger of lapsing, or to redeem one lapsed. The duties were defined in the Levitical law. According to the custom and regulation known as Levirate, he was expected to marry the widow of the deceased, and to raise up seed unto the dead, in case no issue were left of the marriage dissolved by death. From this Book of Ruth it is clear that the two duties, that with regard to property and that respecting marriage, centered in the same person. Failing the unnamed kinsman, it fell to the lot of Boaz to act the part of the near relative of Ruth's deceased husband. Usages and laws differ, but the fact of kindred remains, and involves many duties.

I. HUMAN KINDRED IS A DIVINE APPOINTMENT.

II. AND IS BOTH SUGGESTIVE AND ILLUSTRATIVE OF RELIGIOUS, OF CHRISTIAN TRUTH. *E. g.* of the fatherhood of God ; of the brotherhood of man ; based upon that of Christ.

III. KINDRED IS AT THE FOUNDATION OF HUMAN LIFE, AS SOCIAL AND POLITICAL.

IV. KINDRED INVOLVES CONSIDERATION AND REGARD.

V. AND, WHERE CIRCUMSTANCES RENDER IT EXPEDIENT, PRACTICAL HELP.

Appeal :—Do we recognise the just claims of kindred ? If we do not, is not our failure traceable to an imperfect apprehension of spiritual relationships ?—T.

Vers. 4, 6.—*Our own inheritance.* "Lest I mar mine own inheritance." How many do this ? They have noble inheritances, but in a multitude of ways they mar them.

I. THERE IS THE INHERITANCE OF PHYSICAL HEALTH. Most precious ; not to be gotten for fine gold. Yet how often it is injured by sloth and sin, by intemperance and lust, or by the overtaxed brain, and neglect of the simple economy of health.

II. THERE IS THE INHERITANCE OF A GOOD NAME. This too is a priceless gift. More to be desired than gold, yea, than fine gold. Character. It *takes years to win*—whether for a commercial house or for a personal reputation ; but it takes only *a moment to lose*. How many a son has marred his inheritance ! The "good name" is irrecoverable in the highest sense. Forgiveness may ensue, but the memory of evil lives after.

III. THERE IS THE INHERITANCE OF A RELIGIOUS FAITH. "My father's God." Then my father *had* a God ! There had been a generation to serve him before I was born ! Am I to be the first to break the glorious chain, to sever the great procession ? "One generation shall praise thy works to another." How beautiful ! Is *my* voice to be silent, my thought to be idle, my heart to be cold and dead to God my Saviour ? Let me think of the unfeigned faith of my grandmother Lois and my mother Eunice, and not mar the inheritance through unbelief.—W. M. S.

Vers. 9—11.—*Honourable conduct honourably witnessed.* By the "shoe" in the context is meant, no doubt, the sandal, which in the East was, and is, the ordinary covering of the foot, fastened by means of a thong of leather. Although in a house, or in a temple, the sandal was dispensed with, it was always used in walking and upon a journey. It was taken off at meals, in every sacred place, and in the presence of every sacred person, and on occasion of mourning. The context brings before us a symbolical use of the sandal. In early times—for even when this book was written the custom was obsolete—it was the usage of the men of Israel, in taking possession of any landed property, to pluck off the shoe. This was the survival of a still older custom—the planting the foot upon the newly-acquired soil, outwardly and visibly to express the taking possession of it, and asserting a right to it as one's own. Having, by the permission and at the suggestion of the unnamed kinsman, performed this simple symbolical act, Boaz proceeded to address the assembled elders of the city, calling them to witness two facts: his purchase of the field of Elimelech, and his resolve to take Ruth, the widow of Elimelech's son, as his own wife. The elders, in presence of one another, formally and solemnly declared, We are witnesses.

I. A RELIGIOUS MAN SHOULD BE SCRUPULOUSLY HONOURABLE IN THE TRANSACTIONS OF LIFE.

II. IN NOTHING IS THIS RULE MORE IMPORTANT THAN IN QUESTIONS AFFECTING PROPERTY AND IN MARRIAGE.

III. PUBLICITY, THE PRESENCE OF COMPETENT AND VERACIOUS, HONOURABLE WITNESSES, MAY BE REGARDED AS OF THE HIGHEST IMPORTANCE. Secret marriages and underhand proceedings with regard to property are to be avoided.

IV. A PUBLIC PROFESSION OF CHRISTIANITY IN THE PRESENCE OF WITNESSES IS WISE, RIGHT, AND EXPEDIENT.—T.

Ver. 10.—*The name of the dead.* Elimelech was dead, Mahlon was dead. But to Naomi and to Ruth, who survived, and even to Boaz, the kinsmen of the deceased, the dead were sacred. Not only was their memory treasured in the hearts of the survivors ; the fact that they had lived exercised an influence, and a very marked influence, over the conduct of those still living. This was human, admirable, and right.

I. THE NAME OF THE DEAD SHOULD BE SACRED IN EVERY FAMILY. We were theirs, and they are still ours—ours whilst we live. To forget them would be brutish and inhuman. Their memory should be cherished. Their wishes, within reasonable limits, should be fulfilled. Their example, if good, should be reverently studied and diligently copied.

II. THE NAME OF THE DEAD IS A NATIONAL POSSESSION AND POWER. "One generation passeth away, and another generation cometh." But each generation inherits from its predecessor. Patriotism is fostered by the traditions of the great men who have gone, and whose memory is the national pride and glory. To us in England what inspiration does "the name of the dead" afford! The heroes, statesmen, patriots, saints, discoverers, &c. have left behind them imperishable names. "Let us now," says the apocryphal writer, "let us now praise famous men and our fathers which begat us."

III. THE NAME OF THE DEAD IS THE INSPIRATION OF THE WORLD'S LABOURS AND HOPES. All great names, save One, are names of the dead, or of those who soon will be such. One was dead, but lives again, and for evermore. His undying life gives true life and power to the great names of those whom he causes to live again; for he teaches us that nothing he has sanctified can ever die.

Query :—What shall our name be when we are with the dead ?—T.

Vers. 11, 12.—*Good wishes.* When the marriage of Boaz with Ruth was resolved upon, the elders of the city, the bridegroom's neighbours and friends, expressed with cordiality their congratulations and good wishes. They wished well to himself, to his wife, to his house or family, to his offspring, his seed.

I. KIND WISHES ARE FOUNDED IN A PRINCIPLE DIVINELY PLANTED IN HUMAN NATURE. Sympathy is a principle of human nature. Benevolence is as natural as selfishness, though less powerful over most minds. And we should "rejoice with those who do rejoice."

II. IT IS RIGHT THAT KIND WISHES SHOULD BE EXPRESSED IN WORDS. There is no doubt danger lest insincerity should creep into the customary salutations and benedictions of life ; many compliments are utterly insincere. Yet even the most scrupulous and veracious may legitimately utter good wishes. It is churlish to withhold such utterances.

III. CHRISTIANITY GIVES A RICH, FULL MEANING TO THE KIND WISHES OF FRIENDSHIP. For our religion teaches us to turn every wish into a prayer. It is a sufficient condemnation of a wish that it cannot take this form. With Christians, "God bless you ! " should be a hearty and fervent intercession.—T.

Ver. 13.—*The birth of a son.* With true piety as well as justice the author of this book refers the blessings of domestic life to him who setteth his people in families, and of whom it is said, " Lo, children are an heritage of the Lord, and the fruit of the womb is his reward." Whenever a child is born into the world the Spirit of wisdom teaches us, as Christians, lessons of the most practical and valuable kind.

I. GRATITUDE TO GOD FOR A PRECIOUS GIFT. Christian parents feel that they receive no gifts so valuable, so dear as the children bestowed upon them by the goodness of God. Thanks are ever due for the Divine favour thus shown.

II. A SENSE OF PARENTAL RESPONSIBILITY. He must be stolid and insensible indeed who, when his firstborn is placed in his arms, has no thought of the sacred charge laid upon him. Gifts are trusts. The parent's desire and prayer should be for grace to fulfil solemn responsibilities.

III. RESOLUTIONS REGARDING EDUCATION. Remembering that for the first years of life a child is almost entirely under the parents' influence, fathers and mothers will not only at the first seriously and prayerfully dedicate their offspring to God, but will consider how they may train them up in the way they should go, that when they are old they may not depart from it.

IV. A SPIRIT OF DEPENDENCE UPON " THE FATHER OF THE SPIRITS OF ALL FLESH " FOR A BLESSING. We cannot too much connect our children with the throne of grace. Private and family prayer will be the means of domestic happiness, and will assist parents in exercising a watchful care and faithful guidance, and children in using aright the opportunities of improvement with which they are favoured.—T.

Ver. 13.—*The birth-hour.* " And she bare a son." Memorable day that! Read to the end of the chapter: " There was a son born to Naomi; and they called his name Obed: he is the father of Jesse, the father of DAVID." The old divines used to consider that Ruth the Moabitess becoming an ancestor of David was a prefigurement of the admission of the Gentiles into the Christian Church. Certain it is that the Jews did think this a dishonour to David, and Shimei in his revilings is supposed to taunt David with his descent from Ruth. But the descent of the same true spirit is the real descent of honour.

I. THE CHILD'S NAME. Obed, a servant. It may be a remembrancer of duty. Just as the motto of the Prince of Wales is—" Ich dien," I serve. Any way it is beautiful never to despise *service.* A Christian is to be " meet for the Master's use." How many there are who are of no *use* in the world! Some dislike all service, and prefer the dainty hand that is never soiled, and the life that is never separated from selfishness.

II. THE BENEDICTION ON NAOMI. Naomi was there to receive congratulations. What a time for the mother in Israel to be with the new mother! There is sacred anxiety in such hours in the household. Why should the name of mother-in-law be the butt for satire? Many can testify how precious her care and kindness is in such a season. It is easy, but wicked as easy, to satirise a relationship which, if it creates responsibilities, confers also kindness which cannot be bought.

III. THE PROPHECY CONCERNING THE BABE. How soon infancy merges into youth and manhood. In a few years Naomi will be bent and bowed. The white winter of age is coming, and then this child shall be a nourisher of Naomi's old age. A desolate time indeed for those who have no children's children to brighten their declining days, and, if needful, to succour them when friend and helper are gone. But all here is traced, as in Hebrew history all is ever traced, to the good hand of God. " Blessed be the Lord, which hath not left thee this day without a kinsman."—W. M. S.

Vers. 14—17.—*The benevolent happiness of old age.* The story of Ruth closes amidst domestic prosperity and happiness, and amidst neighbourly congratulations. And it is observable that Naomi, whose trials and sorrows interest us so deeply at the commencement of this book, appears at its close radiant with renewed happiness: her daughter-in-law a mother, she herself a grand-parent, surrounded by rejoicing neighbours, expressing their congratulations, and invoking blessing upon her and those dear to her. The narrative loses sight of Ruth in picturing the felicity of her mother-in-law. The neighbours who before had asked, " Is this Naomi?" now exclaim, " There is a son born to Naomi: blessed be the Lord, which hath not left thee this day without a kinsman." She is encompassed with the blessings which, in the language of our poet, " should accompany old age "—" honour, love, obedience, troops of friends."

I. UNSELFISHNESS IS REWARDED. Naomi had all along thought more of Ruth's sorrows and of Ruth's happiness than of her own. And now this very Ruth is made the means of her prosperity, comfort, and joy in declining years.

II. HOPES are FULFILLED. It was Naomi's desire that Ruth might attain to " rest," and her counsels had been directed to this end. Now she sees the Moabitess a happy wife, a happy mother.

III. A JOYOUS PROSPECT is OPENED UP. The day has been cloudy and stormy, but how brightly does the sun shine out at eventide! " A restorer of her life," " a nourisher of her old age," is given her. The child Obed becomes her delight, and her imaginations picture his manhood, and his position in an honourable line of descent.

IV. SYMPATHY ENHANCES HAPPINESS. There is mutual reaction here; Ruth, Naomi, and the neighbours, with unselfish congratulations, rejoicings, and prayers, contribute to one another's welfare.—T.

Vers. 18—22.—*The lineage of David.* This book closes with a genealogy. Readers of the Scriptures may sometimes have felt perplexed at the frequency with which genealogical tables occur both in the Old Testament and in the New. There is a sufficient reason for this.

I. SCRIPTURE SANCTIONS THE INTEREST HUMAN NATURE FEELS IN GENEALOGY. No one is insensible to his own ancestry, especially if among his progenitors have been men of eminence. Interest in ancestry may be carried too far, and may spring from, and minister to, a foolish vanity, but in itself it is good. It is a witness to the dignity of human nature; it may be an inspiration to worthy deeds; it may be an incentive to transmit influences of character and culture to posterity.

II. SCRIPTURE ATTACHES SPECIAL IMPORTANCE TO THE GENEALOGY OF THE DESCENDANTS OF ABRAHAM. Israel was the chosen people, and the lineage of the tribes of Israel, and especially of Judah, was a matter of national and local, but also of worldwide, importance.

III. SCRIPTURE CAREFULLY RECORDS THE GENEALOGY OF CHRIST JESUS. He was the Son of man, the Son of David, as well as the Son of God. By evincing this, provision was made for commending Jesus to the reverence of the Hebrew people; for making manifest the fulfilment of prophecy, which was thus authenticated; for presenting the Saviour in all the power of his true humanity before the human race, as the object of faith, attachment, and devotion.

Lessons:—1. The obligations under which we individually may be laid by a pious ancestry. 2. Our debt to posterity. 3. The claims of the Son of man upon our hearts.—T.

HOMILETICAL INDEX

TO

THE BOOK OF RUTH

1 SAMUEL

EXPOSITION BY

R. PAYNE SMITH

HOMILETICS BY

C. CHAPMAN

HOMILIES BY VARIOUS AUTHORS

D. FRASER   B. DALE

THE
BOOKS OF SAMUEL

◇

INTRODUCTION

THE Books of Samuel are so called not because they were written by Samuel, though possibly some of the materials may claim him as their author, but because they describe his work for Israel ; and it is not too much to say of him, that as Moses was the founder, so it was Samuel who reorganised and developed the political constitution of the Jewish nation, and enriched it with institutions which made it capable of taking the high place among the families of mankind to which the providence of God was calling it.

Its training was in every way remarkable. It had spent its childhood in Egypt, and owed a great deal to that progress in mental culture in which Egypt had outstripped the world. But it was in the wilderness, surrounded by the bracing desert, and under the command of one who had mastered all Egyptian learning, that Israel was formed into a high-souled people. And there Moses endowed it with a law, which, if valuable to us chiefly in its typical aspect, contains nevertheless so perfect a re-enactment of the fundamental principles of morality that its "Ten Words" still hold their place as the best summary of the rules that should guide and control human life. In its civil and administrative aspect confessedly there was much in the Mosaic law conceded because of "the hardness of the people's hearts," or, in other words, because of their imperfect state of civilisation ; but even this was intended to lead them onwards. Confessedly preparatory and educational, the institutions of Moses were but as a stage or scaffolding to aid in the erection of a more perfect building. But they pointed out what that building was to be, and can equitably be judged only in their relation to it. For we must not suppose that the mass of the people had attained to that high level on which Moses stood. Great as was the impress made upon them by his master mind, and noble as were the qualities of the Israelites themselves, yet as soon as the generation had passed away which had personally known Moses, the nation hurried back into barbarism. Instead of developing and realising the grand ideal which their lawgiver had sketched for them, they perpetually sank lower and lower. In the narratives contained in the Book of Judges we find them wild, rough, lawless, generous often, but oftener cruel; disgraced by fearful crimes, and punishing them with atrocious barbarity. The priests and Levites appear powerless and apathetic; the judges are brave soldiers, but with little administrative capacity. Even with them Gideon, an early judge, is far superior in character to Samson. Who would have thought that a nation, which seemed fast degenerating into a loose aggregate of Bedouin tribes, contained in it the germ of all that is best and noblest in modern culture, and of that pure and spiritual religion which alone has been found capable of satisfying the wants and longings of the human heart! And it was Samuel who arrested Israel's decay, and placed it upon the pathway which led it, though by an uphill and tangled route, to its high destiny of being the teacher of religion to mankind.

Never did time seem more hopeless than when Samuel arose. The Philistines, strengthened not merely by a constant influx of immigrants, but by the importation of arms from Greece, were fast reducing Israel to the condition of a subject race. It might contend on equal terms with Moab and Ammon, but the same superiority of weapons which had given Greece the victory at Marathon and Platæa made the Philistines more than a match for the rude levies of Israel. Samson with a bone might slay of the enemy heaps upon heaps, but the nation which had helmets and shields, and coats of mail, and swords and spears, must in the long run prevail. When the Assyrians had broken up Egypt into a number of petty districts, Psammetichus united them together again by means of his "brazen men;" for the cuirass made its wearer practically invulnerable. And so the loss of the sea-coast, or the neglect to conquer and secure it in the days of Judah's strength (Judges i. 18, 19), nearly lost Israel her independence, and made her forfeit her noble calling. Content with those rolling downs on which they found abundant pasture for their cattle, the princes of Judah forgot, or had never learned, that the empire of the sea carries with it the mastery of the land.

But just when it seemed that Israel must be crushed out from among the nations Samuel arose. There had been a gleam of comfort under his predecessor Eli. Of the early life of this remarkable man we know nothing. He was the head of the inferior house of Ithamar, the younger of Aaron's sons; but as the chiefs of both the priestly houses held a high place in the commonwealth of Israel, it may not after all be so extraordinary that we should find him at the commencement of the Books of Samuel possessed not only of the supreme civil power, but also of the high priesthood. We so carry back our modern notions into ancient times that any deviation from succession by right of primogeniture seems to us to require explanation. In ancient times it was the family, and not the individual, to whom the succession belonged. The more powerful of the kin, or the father's favourite, a Solomon, and not an Adonijah, took the father's place. It was this probably which led to that wholesale slaughter of relatives which usually accompanied the accession of an Oriental king. What is really remarkable is that Eli should be Israel's civil ruler. If he was strong enough to take this, no one would dispute with him the priesthood. And here Scripture is absolutely silent.

The whole tone, nevertheless, of the history sets Israel before us as enjoying under Eli a period of greater ease and prosperity than had been its lot under Samson. The hill land of Israel was so easy of defence, and the people so valiant, that under an able leader it repeatedly held its ground against the mail-clad Philistines, and in Eli's days they had lost the supremacy which made even Judah during Samson's judgeship obey their commands. It was only after a long period of slow decay, of which Eli's worthless sons were the cause, that Israel lost its independence and had to submit to vassalage. It is an indication of the greatness of the reverse, that the minds of the people were so embittered against him that they have struck his name and the names of his race out of the genealogies, and have put the worst construction upon the prophecies to which the broken-spirited old man submitted with such touching humility. To this cause perhaps is also due the suppression of all account of his earlier doings. What we have is taken probably from "the Acts of Samuel;" for there is a curious humour and play upon words running through all Eli's sayings such as none but a contemporary would record. Samuel, we may be sure, had a loving regard for Eli, but the people remembered him only in connection with the Philistine invasion and the cruelties which accompanied it, and of which the memory filled them with an intense horror. It was a calamity too great to be fully narrated in history, but the Psalmist speaks of it as the climax of Israel's degradation (Ps. lxxviii. 59—64), when God "greatly abhorred" them, and the mention of it by Jeremiah (ch. xxvi.) roused all Jerusalem to fury. It was thus from its deepest fall that Samuel raised the nation to a new life, and from its shattered ruins built it up into an orderly and progressive kingdom.

The foundation of all his reforms was the restoration of the moral and religious life of the people. Without this nothing was possible. But in spite of all its faults, Israel was still sound at heart, simple-minded and primitive; backward indeed in culture, but free from those debasing and effeminate vices which too often make sensuality the companion of refinement. It was no sickly, sentimental people among whom Samuel preached; and when his words had brought conviction to them, with strong heart they followed him; and so he won for them an alleviation of the Philistine yoke, and prepared the way for its final destruction. In a year when the elements were greatly disturbed—for there was lightning during wheat-harvest—a violent thunder-storm enabled the Israelites, rushing down the steep hill of Mizpeh, to break the terrified ranks of the Philistines, and God by the great deliverance wrought that day set his seal to the prophet's work.

But as long as a man's work depends upon his personal energy it has no enduring existence. Many men who in life have been all powerful have left behind them nothing more lasting than a Jonah's gourd. Samuel was too wise to trust to mere personal influence. If Israel was to be saved, it must be by institutions which would daily exercise their pressure, and push the people upward to a higher level. He seems to have studied the past history of his nation carefully, and to have clearly seen where its weakness lay. And so he set himself earnestly to the task of giving it mental culture and orderly government; externally security from danger, internally progressive development. The means he employed for the nation's internal growth was the founding of schools, and here the honour of the initiative belongs to him, as well as of the wise development of his institutions. What Walter de Merton long afterwards did for Oxford and England, that Samuel effected for Israel. But as regards the kingdom he was rather the regulator than the initiator of the movement. Still his wise mind saw the ripeness of the times for it, and to him is due its greatness and success.

Thus then, in prophecy and the kingdom, Samuel gave to Israel first education, and secondly constitutional monarchy. Samuel was the first founder of schools, and as the great and primary object of his life had been the internal reformation of the Jewish people, we can well understand how his personal work had led onwards to this attempt to redeem his countrymen from ignorance. In those long years which he spent in perpetual wanderings up and down the land he must have constantly found that a chief obstacle to his work was the low mental state of the people. He had been brought up himself amidst whatever learning the nation had imported with it from Egypt; but Shiloh's sun had set. Was learning to perish with it? Nowhere in Israel were men to be found fit to bear office or administer justice. The decisive failure of one so highly gifted by nature as Saul, and who started with so much in his favour, and under Samuel's guidance, but who seems to have had no ideas beyond fighting, proves that Samuel was right in his hesitation about creating a king. The fitting man was nowhere to be found. Schools were the primary necessity. Through them the whole mental state of the people would be raised, and men be trained to serve God in Church and State. From these schools came forth a David. Without them the brave warrior, but fierce despot, Saul was all that was possible.

At the Naioth, or Students' Lodgings, for so the word means, near Ramah, his own patrimonial inheritance, Samuel gathered the young men who were to lift up Israel from its debasement. He taught them reading, writing, and music; he also impressed their minds with solemn religious services, and apparently made history and psalmody their two chief studies. These schools were termed Schools of the Prophets not only because Samuel was a prophet, and the teachers bore the same honoured name, but because the young men were trained expressly for the service of Jehovah. Of course Samuel did not expect his students to receive the gift of inspiration. That was the most rare and precious of gifts, to be obtained by no education, but bestowed directly by

God ; from whom it might come to a herdman, with only such learning as could be picked up in a country town (Amos vii. 14, 15), but was never given except for high purposes, and where there was a special internal fitness on the part of the receiver.   But the word has a wide meaning in Holy Scripture.   Any religious uninspired service, especially if musical, was called prophecy , David's trained singers prophesied with harps and other instruments (1 Chron. xxv. 1—3). But all of them, inspired and uninspired, went forth to do work for Jehovah ; not as priests, not necessarily as teachers, or as musicians, though they were Israel's bards.   The institution was essentially free, was open to all comers, and when educated the prophet might return to his farm, or to some avocation of town life.   But he was first of all an educated man, and, secondly, he had been taught the nature of Jehovah, how he was to be worshipped, and what was the life which every member of a covenant nation ought to lead.

Thus Samuel's schools not only raised Israel to a higher mental level, but were the great means for maintaining the worship of Jehovah, and teaching the people true and spiritual notions of the nature of God.   As such we find future prophets earnest in maintaining them.   Incidentally we learn that Elijah's last earthly work was the visitation of the prophetic schools at Gilgal, at Bethel, and at Jericho.   He must have restored these schools, for Jezebel had done her utmost to exterminate the prophets.   He must also have laboured with masterly energy ; for within ten years after Elijah's great victory at Mount Carmel, Ahab, at Jehoshaphat's request, was able to collect at Samaria no less than 400 men who claimed to be "prophets of Jehovah."   Of Elisha we have abundant evidence that the main business of his life was to foster these schools, and even personally teach in them (2 Kings iv. 38).   What we read of these two men was probably true of all the great prophets.   At suitable places there were schools in which they gathered the young men of Israel, and the learning which at Shiloh had been confined within the sacred priestly enclosure was made by them general and national.   It ceased to be a special prerogative, and became the inheritance of the whole race.   Apparently it culminated in the time of Heze-kiah, and then came the Assyrian invasions, and with them the destruction of a high and noble civilisation.   But under Ezra and the men of the great synagogue it revived, and Israel became again, and continued to be, a learned and intellectual nation.

This then was one part of the labours of Samuel.   He laid the foundation and fostered the rapid growth of a grand system of national education.   At Ramah he trained men to be Israel's teachers ; but he did not confine himself to this.   Most of the great ornaments of David's court were his disciples, and it is probable that large numbers of the wealthy and more promising youth of the kingdom went to his schools simply to learn something of those wonderful arts of reading and writing, which opened so new a world to the youth of a race always distinguished for its intellectual aptitudes.   And through them Samuel raised the whole people mentally and morally.   Trained men henceforward were never wanting for high service both at court and throughout the land. Other results followed of which the whole world reaps the benefit. The gift of a series of inspired men would have been impossible had Israel continued in the state of barbarous ignorance into which it had sunk in the time of the Judges. Brave fighting men there might have been plenty; occasionally a man of witty jest and proverb like Samson; an Isaiah never. He and his compeers were educated men, speaking to an educated people, and themselves foremost in the rank of teachers. When inspired prophecy ceased, gradually the scribes took the prophets' place; so much so that in the Chaldee Targum "prophet" is often translated "scribe;" and however inferior their work, yet they kept learning alive. The Old Testament was the fruit of Samuel's schools, and so also was the New. The noble tree which he had planted was still vigorous when our Lord traversed the land of Israel; for none but an educated people could have understood his teaching, and retained it in their memories, and taught it to mankind. If St. Paul added to the teaching of Gamaliel the intellectual train-ing of a Greek university, it was in order that he might give to Christian teaching that many-sidedness which was necessary for its reception by Greek and barbarian as well as by Jew. But side by side with him in equal perfect-ness stands the Jewish St. John. Who will say which of the two shall carry off the palm? And it was Samuel who laid the broad foundations of that culture which, carried on first by prophets and then by scribes, made the Jews capable of writing the Bible, of translating the Old Testament into Greek, of teaching its principles in most of the cities of Greece, and finally of going forth as missionaries, carrying with them the gospel of our Lord Jesus Christ.

The other great labour of Samuel was concerned with the establishment of the kingdom, as an external necessity for Israel's orderly development. And here again we find a man far in advance of his age; for his great aim and purpose was to found a limited, or, as we might even call it, a constitutional, monarchy. To a certain extent he was an unwilling agent; for he saw that the times were not ripe. A limited monarchy is only possible among an educated people, and Samuel's Book of the Kingdom (1 Sam. x. 25) could have had but little influence upon a Saul, who could neither read nor write. Perhaps anarchy is inevitably followed by despotism, and certainly Saul became too like what Samuel feared the king would be. It was only after he had trained David that there was a Jewish Alfred ready to sit upon the throne; and when we read so emphatically that he was a king after God's own heart, we must bear in mind that, with all his private faults, David never attempted to set himself above God's law, or even to pervert it to his own use. He strictly confined himself within the limits of a theocratic king, and his crimes were personal, and as such repented of, and the punishment humbly borne.

But the term theocracy is ambiguous, or at least has two sides according to the nature of its administration. As administered by the high priest it was a failure. The appeal to Jehovah by Urim and Thummim was seldom made, and then only under exceptional circumstances, and there was no orderly method of carrying out its commands. Those commands themselves were of the most general kind, confined apparently to a simple affirmative or negative. It was thus irregular, fitful, in abeyance in all calm and peaceful epochs, and when called into exercise was liable to terrible abuse, which it even seemed to sanction. When Israel set itself to exterminate the tribe of Benjamin, the people may have supposed that they had a sort of religious approval of their extreme measures in the fact that the oracle had encouraged them to make the third attack (Judg. xx. 28). Really the ferocity was their own, and the priest who had given an affirmative answer to their question may and ought to have been horrified at the cruelty which followed upon the victory, and which he was absolutely powerless to prevent. A theocracy has been tried again in the Papacy, with much the same result, of being actually one of the worst possible forms of government; and, like the theocracy of the time of the Judges, it must necessarily be a snare to the conscience, as claiming or appearing to give a religious sanction to deeds that offend the moral sense.

The theocracy which Samuel endeavoured to establish was that of kingly power in the hands of a layman, but acting in obedience to the written law of God, or to his will as declared from time to time by the living voice of prophecy. It was a monarchy limited by the priest and the prophet, the former taking his stand upon the Mosaic law, the latter with a more free and active force giving a direct command in God's name, appealing to the king's moral sense, and usually representing also the popular feeling. To the old theocracy there had practically been no check, and, what was almost as bad, no person responsible for carrying out its commands. But it seems soon to have fallen into abeyance, and the judges were men raised up irregularly under the pressure of some extreme peril. Usually they did well, chiefly in expelling invaders from the land, but the priest with the ephod took in their exploits little or no share. Under so irregular a form of government there was small chance for the orderly development of the powers that lay dormant within Israel, and which were to make it a blessing to all the nations of the earth.

Samuel's object was to found a monarchy active and powerful for the maintenance at all times of order, but controlled by such checks as would prevent it from becoming a despotism. And here we have the key to his struggle with Saul. Samuel had a hearty detestation of mere arbitrary power, as we know from his own words to the elders (1 Sam. viii. 11—18); but Saul with his body-guard of 3000 men had both the will and the means of making himself absolute. Perhaps all minds of great military ability have a natural tendency to arbitrariness. Unqualified obedience is a soldier's duty, and a general knows that in discipline lies his strength. It is otherwise with a king. He is the best ruler who trains his people to habits of self-reliance, and to do what is right not because he orders it, but because they choose it. A nation drilled to obedience, a Church made orthodox by having its creed forced upon it, loses thereby all moral strength, because, alike in national and religious life, it is only by the exercise of a moral choice that human nature can advance upward. Samuel was labouring for Israel's growth in all that was good, and the only king of whom he could approve was one under whom Israel would be free to work out its own destiny; and such a king would be no tyrant, but one who would rule in submission to the same law as that which governed the people. The two particulars in which Saul set his own will above the command of Samuel may have been matters of no great primary importance. But the one happened soon after Saul's appointment, and thus showed a very early tendency on his part to make his own judgment supreme; the other was an express order, backed by Israel's past history; and both were given by the man who had called Saul to the throne. But the real point at issue was that Saul was moving so quickly towards despotism, and that when a second trial of him was made he had advanced a long way towards it; and never was despot more thorough than Saul when he stained his hands with the blood of the priests at Nob, and of their innocent wives and children, on the mere supposition of their complicity with David's escape. Possibly, if we knew the particulars, the slaughter of the Gibeonites was a crime of the same deep dye. It is at least significant that the cause of the famine was said to be " Saul and his bloody house." People in those days were not so tender-hearted as to have troubled much about putting a few men of a subject race to death, unless the deed had been done barbarously. The manner of it must have shocked them, or it would not have remained imprinted so deeply upon the conscience of the nation.

In David, trained by Samuel from his youth, we have a noble example of a theocratic king, and that notable fact, which I have already pointed out, that David, in spite of his terrible personal crimes, never set himself above the law, was due we may feel sure to Samuel's early teaching. He had in Joab the very man to be the willing tool of a despot. He would have delighted in playing a Doeg's part. David valued his faithfulness, appreciated his bravery and skill, nay, even used him for his crimes, but he shrank from his lawlessness. God was always in David's eyes greater than himself. His law, often violated in hours of lust, was nevertheless to be bowed before as supreme. And so as regards his subjects, there seems to have been no intentional oppression of them. The idea of law was ever a ruling one in David's mind, and thus he approached Samuel's ideal of " the anointed one," though his fierce passions brought upon him personally deep and terrible stains.

It was thus Samuel's lot to sketch out two of the main lines of thought which converge in Christ. The idea of the prophet and the idea of the king gain under him their shape and proportion. This is especially true as regards the latter. The king is ever in Samuel's eyes " the Messiah," Jehovah's anointed one. Again and again the word occurs with marked prominence. And it was the pregnant germ of a great future with the Jew. He never lost the idea, but carried it onward and forward, with David's portrait for its centre, as of one in whom Messiah's lineaments were marked in outline, feebly indeed and imperfectly, but with the certainty that a Messiah would come who would fill up with glorious beauty that faint, blurred sketch.

Such then is a brief summary of Samuel's work, and it justifies us in claiming especial importance for this portion of Jewish history, independently of the interest connected with the development of two such extraordinary characters as Saul and David, and with the many remarkable persons grouped around them, such as Eli and Jonathan, and the brave soldiers who formed the court of the two kings.

As regards the external history and description of the Books of Samuel, the following are the points most worthy of notice :—

§ 1. NAME.

In Hebrew manuscripts the two Books form but one ; it is in the Septuagint that we find them divided, and called the First and Second Books of the Kingdoms. The Vulgate has followed the Septuagint in its division, but calls them the First and Second Books of Kings. Finally, Daniel Bomberg, in the great Hebrew Bible published by him at Venice early in the sixteenth century, adopted this arrangement, and most modern Hebrew Bibles follow his example. But the division is most awkward. Saul's death is separated from David's pathetic lamentation over the fallen monarch, and the break in the narrative prevents the reader from following easily the development of David's character and history. In these days, when no matters of convenience require the disruption of the Book, a great advantage would be gained by once again arranging it as a whole, instead of following the Septuagint in its unphilosophical division. The name there, "Books of the Kingdoms," refers to the two monarchies of Israel and Judah, and is carried on through the two following Books of Kings.

§ 2. AUTHOR.

Who was the compiler of the Book of Samuel is absolutely unknown, and we are left also to gather our conclusions as to the date and character of its composition from incidental facts and allusions scattered through the history. One such conclusion forced upon us is that the Book is made up of a number of detached narratives, each of which is complete in itself, and carries the history down into its remoter consequences. Of these narratives we have five or six grouped together in 2 Sam. xxi.—xxiv. without any attempt at arrangement. The execution of Saul's seven sons or grandsons, the list of victories over the Philistines, David's psalm of thanksgiving, his last words, the names of his heroes, and the numbering of the people seem placed thus at the end because the compiler had no means of knowing what was their proper place in the history. The "last words" might fitly form the conclusion of the whole, but the other narratives are entirely out of place, and conceal from the reader how little we know of David's conduct after he had returned to Jerusalem, penitent and saddened by the death of his beloved but unfilial son. The question thus arises as to what were the materials at the disposal of the compiler of these Books.

§ 3. Materials.

First then and foremost there were the Acts or Memoirs of Samuel himself. For the words of 1 Chron. xxix. 29 literally are, "And the Acts (or matters) of David the king, behold, they are written upon the Acts of Samuel the Roëh, and upon the Acts of Nathan the Nabi, and upon the Acts of Gad the Chozeh." It is interesting to find in these words the archaic title of Roëh (see 1 Sam. ix. 9) still clinging to Samuel, but still more so to find that records were kept apparently by himself. He had been educated at Shiloh among all the learning of the priesthood, and the place, protected by the powerful tribe of Ephraim, had remained unravaged by war, so that whatever records had been laid up with the ark, or written since the days of Joshua, himself no mean scribe, had accumulated there. We may well believe that a youth with such great natural abilities as Samuel had made no ordinary use of such opportunities, and whatever was saved for the use of future times from the wreck of Shiloh was most probably removed through his exertions and wise forethought.

In 1 Chron. xxvii. 24 we also read of "the Chronicles of King David," or, more literally, "the Acts of the Days of King David," i. e. a digest of his acts arranged in chronological order. But when we read in 2 Sam. viii. 16, 17 of two officers of David's court, of whom one, Jehoshaphat, was recorder, the other, Seraiah, was scribe, we must not rashly conclude that their duties were historical. The recorder, or, as the word means, remembrancer, was more probably a judge, whose business it was to enrol and publish royal decrees; while the scribe was a state secretary, concerned with the army and with the king's exchequer. It seems to have fallen to the lot of the prophets to write histories, probably for the use of the prophetic schools, and certainly as the result of the bent given to their minds by their studies in those institutions.

Thus henceforward the prophets, and not the priests, became the custodians of Israel's literature. In the Books of Chronicles a numerous list of authors is given, who almost to a man are expressly said to have been prophets or seers. At every prophetic college there would be gathered stores of such writings, and also of psalms and poems. David probably arranged the ritual of the temple after the fashion of Samuel's services (1 Sam. xix. 20), for which reason doubtless psalmody, as we have seen, was called prophesying, and consequently the temple would also have its library of hymns and musical compositions. Moreover, the prophet Gad is also supposed by many to have made the collection of songs and ballads called the Book of Jasher, i. e. the Upright, whence was taken David's spirited elegy over Saul and Jonathan. As Gad was David's companion in his wanderings from the time he took refuge in Moab (1 Sam. xxii. 5) till his death, his Acts must have contained full information of all the more important events of David's life.

But it is easy to over-estimate the completeness and extent of these contemporary records. Literature depends very much upon the nature of the materials available for writing. Printing followed at once upon the discovery of paper. The copious materials now being brought to Europe illustrative of Assyrian history are the result of the use that people made of cheap tablets of clay. The materials most frequently referred to in the Bible are tablets of metal. With no cheaper or more convenient writing materials Gad's records would be but scanty, and David's psalms must have been for several years chiefly preserved by memory. The Canaanites had certainly known how to prepare skins for writing, and when Samuel's schools had caused a revival of learning, the art was probably restored. Perhaps it had never been entirely lost, and Samuel may have obtained such skins for writing his book upon "the manner of the kingdom" (1 Sam. x. 25); but we can hardly imagine that writing materials were easy to procure until the prosperous days of David's kingdom.

With skins of animals or plates of metal still used in Isaiah's days (Isa. viii. 1, where *tablet* is wrongly translated *roll*), the narratives would be short and each complete in itself. This fact has often been noticed in the Commentary. Thus the narrative in 1 Sam. vii. carries the history down to Samuel's death. The narrative in ch. xiv. carries Saul's history down to the end of his victorious wars. That in ch. xvi. gives us David's history up to the time when Saul began to envy and hate him. We may safely conclude that the Acts of Samuel, of Nathan, of Gad, and even the Chronicles of King David, were not well-digested histories, but a series of brief stories each complete in itself. These the compiler, in days when they had not merely skins, but even rolls made of many skins sewn together, seems to have arranged, adding a note here and there, blending perhaps occasionally several narratives into one, but never attempting to form out of them a consecutive history, such as a Thucydides or a modern writer, formed upon classical models, would have done.

§ 4. Date.

The next question refers to the compiler's date, and here some of our materials are sufficiently decisive. When we are told that "Ziklag pertaineth unto the kings of Judah unto this day" (1 Sam. xxvii. 6), it is plain that he lived after the disruption of Solomon's kingdom. When he thinks it necessary to apologise for Samuel being called a roëh, it is plain that the name had ceased to be honourable, and, by that degradation which happens to so many titles of office or sex, had become a term of dubious respectability. There is too the frequent recurrence of the phrase "unto this day;" the change of the name of Saul's successor from Ishbaal to Ishbosheth; the distinction between Israel and Judah in passages like 1 Sam. xviii. 16, where nothing but subsequent usage would have made a writer so express himself; the note that even princesses wore the same dress as men (the meïl) in 2 Sam. xiii. 18, and so on. But besides these there are one or two other facts not so generally referred to, and which may be worth noting.

Thus, then, we have seen that the compiler places six narratives at the end of the second Book because, excepting David's "last words," there was nothing in them to show to what period of his reign they belonged. Evidently a considerable interval must have elapsed before tradition had so completely died out as to leave no trace behind for the historian's guidance. The same conclusion follows from his uncertainty as to the chronology of Saul's reign. The compiler uses the formula common in the Books of Kings, but he cannot fill it up. Literally he says, "Saul was one year old when he began to reign, and he reigned two years over Israel." Evidently the numbers *one* and *two* answer to our formula M and N. The compiler plainly knew neither Saul's age nor the length of his reign. St. Paul (Acts xiii. 21) says that Saul reigned forty years; but not only is forty with Hebrew writers a most indefinite number, signifying a "good long time," but it is very uncertain when these forty years begin and end. They certainly include the seven and a half years during which the house of Saul maintained a show of ruling, and possibly also several years during which Samuel was judge. Some think that as Saul is described as a "young man" (ch. ix. 2) when Samuel anointed him, but had a grown-up son when he was made king, there was a long abeyance, either before he was chosen by lot as king, or possibly between that and his defeat of the Ammonites. But what was hard for the compiler is still harder for us, and the chronology of Saul's reign is beset with difficulties.

On the other hand, the style of the Hebrew is more pure and free from Aramaisms than that of the Books of Kings. Local worship, moreover, and sacrifices are spoken of without any doubt of their propriety, whereas in the Books of Kings they are condemned. It is a further note of antiquity that the compiler never refers to his authorities, nor are there any hints or allusions to late Jewish history. While then we can at best only give a conjectural date, yet we may feel sure that the compiler must have lived at some period between the reign of Rehoboam and the upgrowth of the strong disapproval of worship anywhere except at Jerusalem. The reign of Jehoshaphat is a not improbable era, for "the high places were not taken away" (2 Chron. xx. 33), though idolatry was sternly repressed. Had the compiler lived nearer to David's reign, he would probably have been able to give us more definite information as to Saul's age and the duration of his kingdom.

§ 5. Books of Samuel classed among the "Early Prophets."

The Books of Samuel are classed by the Jews among the "Early Prophets" for the reason given above, that history was their especial study, and the compiler we may feel sure belonged to their order as well as did the writers of the various "books of acts" used by him. The "Early Prophets" comprise the Books of Joshua, Judges, Samuel, and Kings, and all these works were most probably written for the use of the prophetic schools, and certainly were the result of the mental activity awakened in Israel by Samuel, and maintained by those who after his decease presided over the colleges which he had called into existence.

§ 6. ARRANGEMENT.

The Books of Samuel naturally arrange themselves into four parts according to the chief actors. In Part I., consisting of chs. i.—vii., we have the history of Samuel as the restorer of Israel. This again divides itself into two portions, of which the former, consisting of chs. i.—iii., gives us the details of Samuel's birth and early life up to the time when he was acknowledged by all Israel as a prophet; while the latter, chs. iv.—vii., gives us Samuel as judge. With this the period of the Judges closes, and in Part II., chs. viii.—xv., we have the history of the first king, Saul, including the preparation for his appointment, his establishment as king, and his final rejection.

In Part III., chs. xvi.—xxxi., David is the chief actor, but side by side with Saul, and we see the one daily declining in moral worth and external prosperity, while the other is ripening into the full stature of a theocratic king. During most of this period Samuel lived on no unconcerned spectator of the development of Jehovah's purpose, though devoting his own time to the training of the young men who came to his schools. Finally Saul falls so low as to become the dupe of a wicked charlatan, and dies by his own hand in battle.

In Part IV., 2 Sam. i.—xxiv., David is the sole hero of the narrative. In the first section, chs. i.—x., we see him made king, and reigning in glory. In the second, chs. xi.—xvii., his glory is tarnished by personal vices, imitated too readily by his sons; upon these follow bloodshed in his family, rebellion, and the loss of the royal power. In the third section, chs. xix., xx., we see him restored to his throne. In the last, chs. xxi.—xxiv., we have an appendix, the contents of which have been already described. Naturally we long to know how David reigned after so severe a punishment, and would gladly have seen how he retrieved in his later years the crimes of his passion-fraught manhood. But the ways of God are not as the ways of man. A veil is thrown over this portion of David's reign, but we may gather from his last words, and from his psalm of thanksgiving, that he returned to Jerusalem a changed man, and that his last years rivalled in piety his early promise.

7. LITERATURE.

The most important modern works upon the Books of Samuel are, in German, the commentaries of O. Thenius, 'Kurzgef. Handbuch z A. Test.,' 2te Auflage, Leipzig, 1864; C. F. Keil, 'Bibl. Com. ü. das A. Test.,' Leipzig, 1864; C. F. D. Erdmann, in Lange's 'Theol. Hom. Bibelwerk,' Bielefeld, 1873; and Bunsen, 'Bibelwerk, die Propheten.'

On the text of the Books of Samuel there is a useful treatise by L. J. Wellhausen, Göttingen, 1871.

In English the most important commentaries are that in the 'Speaker's Commentary' by the Bishop of Bath and Wells; Bishop Wordsworth's; and the translations of Keil and Erdmann, the latter in Dr. Schaff's edition of Lange, Clark, Edinburgh, 1877.

Other illustrative works are Ewald's 'History of Israel;' Stanley's 'Lectures on the Jewish Church;' Robinson's 'Biblical Researches;' Wilson's 'Lands of the Bible;' Thomson's 'The Land and the Book;' and Conder's 'Tent Work in Palestine,' a most valuable addition to our knowledge of the Holy Land.

THE FIRST
BOOK OF SAMUEL

THE EARLY LIFE OF SAMUEL.

EXPOSITION.

CHAPTER I.

THE GENEALOGY AND BIRTHPLACE OF SAMUEL (vers. 1—8). Ver. 1.—**There was a certain man of Ramathaim-Zophim.** Though Samuel belonged to the tribe of Levi, yet no special mention is made of the fact, because he owed his importance and rank as a judge not to his Levitical origin, but to the gift of prophecy, which was independent of the accidents of birth and station. In the First Book of Chronicles, ch. vi., his parentage is twice given, that in vers. 22—28 being apparently the family genealogy, while that in vers. 33—38 was probably taken from the records of the temple singers, sprung from Heman, Samuel's grandson (1 Chron. vi. 33). His name there appears as Shemuel, our translators not having perceived that it is the same as that for which elsewhere they give the familiar rendering, Samuel. The variations Elkanah, Jeroham, Elihu, Tohu, Zuph (1 Sam. i. 1); Elkanah, Jeroham, Eliab, Nahath, Zophai (1 Chron. vi. 26, 27); Elkanah, Jeroham, Eliel, Toah, Zuph (*ibid.* vers. 34, 35), are interesting as showing that the genealogies in Chronicles were compiled from family documents, in which, as was usual in the case of proper names, there was much diversity of spelling, or possibly of interpreting the cumbrous signs used for letters in those early days. The variations, however, in Elihu (God is he), Eliab (God is Father), and Eliel (God is God) were probably intentional, as were certainly other changes in names, such as that of Ishbaal into Ishbosheth. The name of Samuel's father, *Elkanah* (God is owner),

is a common one among the Kohathites, to which division of the sons of Levi Samuel belonged.

The prophet's birthplace was **Ramathaim-Zophim,** no doubt the Ramah which was Samuel's own head-quarters (1 Sam. vii. 17; xv. 34; xvi. 13; xix. 18—23; xxv. 1); the place where he dwelt, wrought, died, and was buried, and the Arimathæa of the Gospels. The Septuagint generally gives the name in full, but this is the only place where it is so written in the Hebrew. Ramah signifies a *height*, and the dual Ramathaim the *double height*, the town being situated on a hill ending in two peaks. But which it was of the many Ramahs, or hill towns, in the Holy Land, is hotly contested; probably it was the Ramah in Benjamin, about two hours' journey north-west of Jerusalem. Its second name, Zophim, is taken from Zuph, Samuel's remote ancestor, with whom the genealogy here begins. Zuph had apparently emigrated from Ephraim, one of the three tribes (Ephraim, Manasseh, Dan) to which the Kohathites were attached, and was a person of sufficient power and energy to give his name to the whole district; called the land of Zuph in 1 Sam. ix. 5. His descendants, the Zophim, had Ramah as their centre, and Elkanah, as their head, would be a man of wealth and influence. Though actually belonging to the tribe of Benjamin, Ramah is said to be upon Mount Ephraim, because this limestone range extended and kept its name almost up to Jerusalem (see Judges iv. 5, and 2 Chron. xiii. 4; xv. 8, compared with xiii. 19). Elkanah too is called an Ephrathite, *i. e.*

an Ephraimite, no doubt because before Zuph emigrated the family had belonged to Ephraim, it being apparently the practice to reckon Levites as pertaining to the tribes to which they were attached (Judges xvii. 7). The Heb. Ephrathite is rightly rendered Ephraimite in Judges xii. 5, and should be so translated here, and in 1 Kings xi. 26. In Ruth i. 2 ; 1 Sam. xvii. 12 it means Bethlehemite, that town being also called Ephratah, *the fruitful;* Ephraim has the same meaning, but being a dual, no adjective can be formed from it.

Ver. 2.—As a wealthy man, Elkanah **had two wives, Hannah**—the Anna of Virgil, who very properly gives this name to the sister of the Phœnician Dido, the language of Phœnicia being identical with Hebrew— **and Peninnah.** The word Hannah signifies *gracefulness,* while Peninnah is the *red pearl,* translated coral in Job xxviii. 18, but ruby in Prov. iii. 15, &c. Its ruddy colour is vouched for in Lam. iv. 7. The Hebrew names for women generally bear witness to the affection and respect felt for them ; while those for men are usually religious. Though polygamy was a licence permitted to the Jews, it does not seem to have been generally indulged in, except by the kings. Here, as elsewhere, it was the ruin of family life. In Christianity it was marked for final extinction by the rule that no polygamist should be admitted even to the diaconate, and much less to higher office (1 Tim. iii. 2, 12).

Ver. 3.—**This man went up out of his city yearly.** Once in the year Elkanah went up to offer sacrifice before the ark. The original command had required this thrice a year of all Israelites ; but though a Levite and a religious man, Elkanah went up but once ; and such apparently was the rule in our Lord's time (Luke ii. 41), the season preferred being naturally the passover, while the other feasts gave opportunities for the performance of this duty to those unable to leave their homes at so early a period of the year. The ark was now at Shiloh, a town in Ephraim, about ten miles south of Shechem ; for Joshua had removed it from Gilgal (Josh. xviii. 1), not merely because Shiloh occupied a more central position, but as marking the primary rank of his own tribe (1 Chron. v. 1, 2). Its destruction by the Philistines after the capture of the ark (1 Sam. v. 1) was so complete, and attended apparently by such barbarous cruelties (Ps. lxxviii. 60—64), that it never recovered its importance, and Jeroboam passed it by when seeking for places where to set up his calves.

To sacrifice unto the LORD of hosts. This title of the Deity, " LORD (in capitals, *i. e.* Jehovah) of Hosts," is a remarkable one. Fully it would be " Jehovah God of Hosts," and the omission of the word God shows that the phrase was one of long standing shortened down by constant use. And yet, though found 260 times in the Bible, this is the first place where it occurs. " Lord of Hosts" (Lord not in capitals, and meaning *master, ruler*) occurs only once, in Isa. x. 16. " God of Hosts," Elohim-Sabaoth, though rare, occurs four times in Ps. lxxx. 4, 7, 14, 19. The word Sabaoth, hosts, does not mean *armies,* inasmuch as it refers to numbers, and not to order and arrangement. It is usually employed of the heavenly bodies (Gen. ii. 1 ; Deut. iv. 19 ; xvii. 3), which seem countless in multitude as they are spread over the vast expanse of an Oriental sky (Gen. xv. 5) ; and as their worship was one of the oldest and most natural forms of idolatry (Deut. iv. 19 ; Job xxxi. 26—28), so this title is a protest against it, and claims for the one God dominion over the world of stars as well as in this lower sphere. Its origin then is to be sought at some time when there was a struggle between the worship of the sun and stars and the pure monotheism of the Hebrews. Occasionally the angels are called " the host of heaven" (1 Kings xxii. 19 ; Ps. ciii. 21 ; cxlviii. 2), whenever the allusion is to their number, but when the idea is that of orderly arrangement they are called God's armies (Gen. xxxii. 2).

The two sons of Eli . . . were there. The right translation of the Hebrew is, " And there (at Shiloh) the two sons of Eli . . . were priests." Eli apparently had devolved upon his sons his priestly functions, while he discharged the duties only of a judge. His position is remarkable. In the Book of Judges we find a state of anarchy. The people are rude, untutored, doing much as they pleased, committing often atrocious crimes, yet withal full of generous impulses, brave, and even heroic. There is little regular government among them, but whenever a great man stands forth, the people in his district submit themselves to him. The last judge, Samson, a man of pungent wit and vast personal prowess, seems to have been entirely destitute of all those qualities which make a man fit to be a ruler, but he kept the patriotism of the people alive and nerved them to resistance by the fame of his exploits. In Eli we find a ruler possessed of statesmanlike qualities. The country under him is prosperous ; the Philistines, no longer dominant as in Samson's time, have so felt his power that when they gain a victory the Israelites are astonished at it (ch. iv. 3). Moreover, he is not only judge, he is also high priest ; but instead of belonging to the family of Phinehas, the dominant house in the time of the Judges, he belongs to that of Ithamar. When, to solve the problem, we turn to the genealogies in the Chronicles, we find Eli's house omitted, though, even after the massacres at Shiloh and Nob, his grandson Ahimelech was still powerful (1 Chron. xxiv. 3), and one of his descendants returned from Babylon as jointly high priest with a descendant of Phinehas (Ezra viii. 2). How long a space of time elapsed between the rude heroism of Samson's days and Eli's orderly government in Church and State we do not know, but the difference in the condition of things is vast. Nor do we know the steps by which Eli rose to power, but he must have been a man of no common ability. Warrior as well as statesman, he had delivered the people from the danger of becoming enslaved to the Philistines. In his own family alone he failed. His sons, allowed to riot in licentiousness, ruined the stately edifice of the father's fortunes, and the Philistines, taking advantage of the general discontent caused by their vices, succeeded in once again putting the yoke on Israel's neck.

Ver. 5.—**A worthy portion.** This rendering is based upon the idea that the Hebrew, which is literally " one portion of two faces," may mean "one portion enough for two persons." But for this there is no sufficient authority, and though the word is a dual, it really signifies the two sides of the face, or more exactly "the two nostrils," and so simply the countenance. The Syriac translation, " a double portion," is based upon an accidental resemblance between the words. As the term sometimes signifies anger from the swelling of the nostrils of an enraged person, the Vulgate translates, "And Elkanah was sad when he gave Hannah her portion; for . . ." The Septuagint has a different reading, *epes* for *apaim*, and though the words look different in our writing, they are nearly identical in Hebrew. This is probably the true reading, and the translation would then be, "*And to Hannah he gave one portion only* (because she had no child, while Peninnah had many portions, as each son and daughter had a share); *for he loved Hannah* (and did not

leave her without this mark of affection), *though Jehovah had shut up her womb.*" These portions were of course taken from those parts of the victim which formed a feast for the offerers, after Jehovah and the priests had had their dues. It is plain from this feast that Elkanah's annual sacrifice was a peace offering, for the law of which see Lev. vii. 11—21.

Vers. 6, 7, 8.—**Her adversary also provoked her sore.** The pleasure of this domestic festival was spoiled by the discord of the wives. Peninnah, triumphant in her fruitfulness, is yet Hannah's adversary, because, in spite of her barrenness, she has the larger portion of the husband's love; while Hannah is so sorely vexed at the taunts of her rival, that she weeps from sheer vexation. In vain Elkanah tries to give her comfort. The husband really is not " better than ten sons," for the joy of motherhood is quite distinct from that of conjugal affection, and especially to a Hebrew woman, who had special hopes from which she was cut off by barrenness. In ver. 7 there is a strange confusion of subject, owing to the first verb having been read as an active instead of a passive. It should be, "And so it happened year by year; when she (Hannah) went up to the house of Jehovah she (Peninnah) thus provoked her, and she wept and did not eat." It must be remembered that the Hebrews had no written vowels, but only consonants; the vowels were added in Christian times, many centuries after the coming of our Lord, and represent the traditional manner of reading of one great Jewish school. They are to be treated with the greatest respect, because as a rule they give us a sense confirmed by the best authorities; but they are human, and form no part of Holy Scripture. The ancient versions, the Septuagint, the Syriac, and the Vulgate, which are all three older than the Masoretic vowels, translate, "And so she (Peninnah) did year by year;" but this requires a slight change of the consonants.

HOMILETICS.

Vers. 1—3.—*Transitions.* The main facts implied or expressed in this section are—1. A state of national degeneracy. 2. A scarcity of spiritual illumination. 3. A family morally imperfect and troubled, yet rigidly observant of religious duties. 4. A Divine will using that family for the further unfolding of Messianic purposes.

I. An UNBROKEN CONTINUITY runs through the revelations of the Old Testament, analogous to that of the physical order and the education of the individual. It is only ignorance of the Bible that can suppose it to be destitute of the unity in variety which is known to characterise the material creation. Separate books, like diverse strata in the crust of the earth, are preliminary to what is to follow; and the character of the events recorded, and the condition of morality and religious light referred to, must be considered as related to the one general purpose. Sometimes the transition seems to be sudden and abrupt, and a totally new set of subjects appears; but, as in the reference here to a "certain man," whose life was chiefly spent during the era covered by the latter part of the Book of Judges, so generally connecting links may be found.

II. The CONSERVATION AND DISCIPLINE OF THE CHOSEN RACE are subservient to the development of the Divine purpose in Christ. History is the basis of revelation. Man is not to be saved by abstract truth, but by an historical Christ. The historical Christ is to appear in the "fulness of time," not from the skies, but from a human line well authenticated. Human factors are the transitory element in the Divine unfolding of salvation in Christ. That God should use men, during a long succession of ages, as the channel through which his mercy should embrace all the world, is as natural and reasonable as that he should perfect his will in the beautiful order of the earth by a long series of changes in crude material elements. God did not make imperfect men perfect in order to use them; but showed his wisdom in training and holding together the chosen race just as they were. Degenerate as they were during the period of the Judges, they were not cut off for ever, but chastened and quickened. Thus the process was continued, until the purpose was ripe for the appearing of the Christ, and his proper identification, by the combination of history and prophecy.

III. The FORM AND DEGREE OF REVELATION vouchsafed to an age are largely dependent on the ideas and moral character previously attained to. Man at first entered on life devoid of ancestral literature; and so Adam's descendants, in succeeding ages, inherited less of knowledge and experience in proportion as they were nearer to the founder of the race. It is not wise to import our modern ideas into the minds of those who, in the days of Jacob, Moses, and the Judges, had not been fashioned by our inheritance of knowledge. The devout men and women of Elkanah's time, having acquired knowledge of the existence of hosts of intelligent beings, took a wider conception of God's sovereignty (vers. 3, 11) than was possible to men of an earlier age. God conveyed truth in so far as men were able to bear it. It would be as unnatural for Isaiah's lofty teachings to follow at once on the scanty illumination of the era of the Judges, as for philosophical conceptions to be set before children. Divine wisdom shines through the graduated teaching of Israel's history (Matt. xix. 7, 8).

IV. The EDUCATION OF A PEOPLE, with ulterior view to the world's instruction, by provisional, not final truth, necessitates eras of transition. All through the ages God was educating a race for the benefit of the world; and, as education means steady development, widening vision, the elements of things would form the staple of early teaching. Times came when a new feature had to be introduced, and early arrangements to give place to something more suited to the wider truth to be taught. The occasional vision and message, suited to patriarchal life, were followed by the systematic symbolism and rigid rules appropriate to national consolidation under Moses. The casual illumination of the Judgeship, also, yields to the more steady teaching and guidance of the prophetic schools inaugurated by Samuel. Later on, the early dawn of the prophetic ages gives place to the "dayspring" which reveals the Sun of righteousness. As in nature, so in revelation, stage succeeds stage; transitions are according to law.

V. The INSTRUMENTS FOR EFFECTING A TRANSITION are duly chosen, and are silently, unconsciously prepared for their work. The world little knew of the germinal Divine purpose working out in an obscure home of Mount Ephraim; nor did the "certain man" know how the conflicting elements in his home were being graciously over-ruled to the development of a piety not surpassed in Old Testament history, and the sending forth of one who should be a blessed forerunner of One greater still. Germs of future good lie in undreamed-of places and persons. Out of the vast storehouse of the universe the all-gracious God is constantly preparing some new channel of good to his creatures. In the scattered villages and towns of the land there are being nurtured, unconsciously, the lives that in days hence shall be foremost in the Redeemer's host. "Little Bethlehem," and the lowly Joseph and Mary, were in reserve for the greatest of events. Any new advances to be made by the Church in the future are sure to be provided for by chosen men, possibly unknown to the world, and silently trained by Providence for their work.

VI. PERSONS, PLACES, AND EVENTS, IN THEMSELVES OBSCURE, BECOME IMPORTANT when associated with the unfolding of high spiritual purposes. It was the connection of Samuel with Christ's glorious kingdom that linked a "certain man" and his wife with the same, and so raised them from obscurity. Spiritual uses give real value to things. The frail and insignificant becomes enduring and important when blended with the interests of the "kingdom that cannot be moved." Every member of Christ's body is precious to him. Names are recorded in heaven which enter on no earthly roll. The life and spirit of every lowly Christian are known by God to exercise a widespread, abiding influence in the invisible sphere. As the kingdom is to be eternal, so, whatever part each one may take in its unfolding, that item will be saved from the transitoriness and oblivion of other toil. Fame in the world is not the criterion and measure of real usefulness. The chief concern should be so to live as to be, in some form, useable by God for advancing the glory of Christ. All are morally great when employed in his service to the full extent of their capacities.

VII. A DILIGENT USE OF SUCH LIGHT AS IS BESTOWED, especially in degenerate times, may qualify even obscure men for rendering important service. The family religion of a "certain man" bore its fruit. The moral ground of usefulness lies in character, and character is spiritually strong in so far as improvement is daily made of privileges, however few they may be. Men's fitness to confer benefits on the world is more connected with a wise use of what they have and know, than with the absolute possession of knowledge. A little goodness, and a humble routine of devotion in a dark age, shines the brighter because of the surrounding gloom. From the ranks of pious men in modern times, who cared for piety at home, there have gone forth many sons distinguished for service in the Church of God. It is worthy of note how fixed ordinances and seasons of Divine worship nourish whatever of piety may be struggling here and there against degenerate manners and official corruption. The usual services of the tabernacle and the recurring festivals, though despised and profaned by many, furnished comfort and cheer to the faithful few. In spite of unworthy priests, God is found in his courts by all who seek him.

Vers. 4—8.—*Domestic troubles.* The facts given in this section are—1. Hannah's grief and disappointment. 2. Peninnah's cruel jealousy. 3. Elkanah's efforts to console.

I. PROVIDENCE sometimes seems to RUN COUNTER TO WHAT IS MOST DESIRABLE, in withholding gifts where they would be devoutly valued and wisely used. Humanly speaking, Hannah was the most fit person to be blessed with offspring to be nurtured. The course of nature which finds expression in family life is of God. Though the free element of human action plays a part, yet God is supreme. Providence is over the home of the pious. Poverty and riches, new life and bereavement, are of the Lord. Looked at in its early stages, and tested by our range of vision, the course of Providence is often the reverse of what makes for the joy of the home and the good of the world. Often the illiberal spirit holds wealth, while the loving heart has only good wishes. Many a good, Christlike heart laments that it has not the means of clothing the poor, and sending forth messengers of the cross. Men of very slender abilities and lowly position, but of intense enthusiasm for Christ, may wonder why they have not been endowed with the intellectual and social qualities which would enable them to stem the tide of scepticism, and gain over to Christianity persons now inaccessible to them.

II. PROVIDENCE, for reasons not obvious, sometimes SEEMS TO FAVOUR INFERIOR CHARACTERS, bestowing gifts where there is not the purest spirit to improve them. Peninnah was immensely inferior to Hannah in all that makes character to be admired. If judged by the benefits conferred on some persons, and the disposition to use them, Providence would be said to have erred. The writer of Psalms xxxvii. and lxxiii. had once bitter reflections on this subject. The causes of the Divine conduct lie deep in hidden counsels. The inequalities and disproportions of life clearly show that we see only the beginning of things, and that there is a future where every man shall receive according to his work. It is enough to know, that in the abundant blessings which often fall to the lot of the inferior and the bad, they have experienced goodness and mercy, so as to be without excuse for ingratitude, and that the Judge of all the earth cannot but do right.

III. INTENSE GRIEF IS NATURAL ON THE BLIGHTING OF A SUPREME HOPE. Every one must see the naturalness of Hannah's grief. The ordinary course of nature fosters hope; it is the basis of reasonable expectations. A well-balanced mind lives in strong sympathy with nature's ways, for they are of God, and always beneficent in final issue. God is not displeased with grief, not discontent, when it comes in the order of Providence, even though the grief rise from a wish that he had ordered otherwise. Tears have been consecrated by Christ. The wail over Jerusalem was not unconnected with blighted hope. But so far as men are concerned, the roots of their sorrow frequently lie in their ignorance of God's times and methods. He doth not willingly afflict or grieve the children of men. There is some undeveloped purpose for their good which will yet vindicate his goodness.

IV. To have a deep and SACRED GRIEF INTENSIFIED BY UNMERITED AND CONTINUOUS REPROACH is the climax of domestic suffering. The griefs of private life are sacred. The wounded spirit shuns the inquisitive eye. Sorrow often seeks sad comfort in self-isolation. The cruel jibes of her rival were agony to Hannah's gentle spirit. So the Man of sorrows felt the bitter reproach of his own people as a most painful addition to that secret sorrow he ever carried in his heart. In many an unhappy home there is yet to be found a meek, loving soul grieving over deferred hope of a husband or children saved, and compelled also to bear scorn, and perhaps ill-treatment, from those most dear. A patient, Christlike spirit is the Divine counterpoise of such suffering.

V. LONG YEARS OF MEEKLY-ENDURED TRIAL MAY BE THE DIVINE TRAINING for subordinating natural gratification to high spiritual ends. Completed history gives the clue to the enigmas of its early stages. Posterity has seen that the long trial of Hannah was not without its blessed uses in sublimating her hopes, and deepening her piety. It is a first principle that trial to the devout is essentially a good. The spirit of the sufferer has to grow up to the Divine intent by meek submission. Like many mothers, Hannah might have rested in the simple joy of bearing offspring had not a merciful God prepared means for directing her desires to a higher good. When sympathy with the holy purposes of Christ is developed in the soul, natural desires will fall into harmony with his will, and be laid at his feet. And the deepened piety of a mother tells most powerfully on the subsequent nurture of her child.

VI. It is possible for HIGH RELIGIOUS FESTIVALS TO BE (1) embittered by the presence of wicked jealousies, (2) marred by an outburst of pent-up grief. The holy sanctuary is frequented by the devout and the profane, and the longing heart of a Hannah is fretted by the unkind expressions of a Peninnah. Side by side before the holy throne may be found men and women embittered by the very presence of each other. Divine worship and hallowed festivities should be the occasion when all animosities and vexations of spirit are lost in the calm, holy joy of God's favour. But when the wounded heart is pierced afresh in the house of God, or amidst Zion's rejoicings, the very joyousness of the occasion makes sorrow more sorrowful. Many are the tears shed in the sanctuary! The heart speaks its woes the more that joy becomes the place.

VII. INDISCREET FAVOURS IN A HOME ONLY ADD TO TROUBLE. Monogamy is the dictate of religion and of philosophy. Trouble must arise in society by departure from the prime law. Elkanah's troubles were his own seeking, and no amount of affection ostentatiously bestowed availed to cover the original error, or to lessen the inconveniences of it. Persons committed to conflicting domestic obligations, and beset with difficulty, need to exercise more than ordinary discretion in the expression of their feelings. Even in properly-constituted homes, unwise preferences lay the foundation for alienation and strife.

VIII. MEN OF TENDEREST AFFECTION AND ORDINARY GOODNESS MAY BE INCAPABLE OF FULLY APPRECIATING THE GREAT SORROW OF THEIR HOME. With all his kindness, Elkanah was unable to enter fully into the grief of his wife. Natures move in diverse spheres. Some lack responsiveness to the deepest experiences of their kindred and friends, or they have not the spiritual insight to recognise more than secular elements in trouble. The full bliss of one is not a standard for another. There are incommensurable joys, and joys inconceivable. A husband's love is a perfect, beautiful thing. A wife's joy in holy offspring is also perfect and beautiful. The presence of the one blessing may console, but cannot compensate for the absence of the other. The "woman of sorrowful spirit" yearned to be the means of advancing Messiah's kingdom, and mourned that the joy was not hers; no assurance of affection could satisfy such an unrealised yearning. And so, good as the love of friends may be, it can never give full rest to the souls that peer into the future, and long to have the bliss of contributing their best to the Redeemer's glory.

Hence the *Practical suggestions :*—1. Be not hasty in forming a judgment on the course of Providence. 2. Cherish sympathy with those whose hopes are deferred. 3. Be careful and sow not in the home, by some irrevocable action, the seeds of permanent discord. 4. Avoid partiality where vows and relationships demand equal treatment. 5. Adore the wisdom that can out of our failings and errors elicit a future blessing.

HOMILIES BY VARIOUS AUTHORS.

Vers. 1—8. (RAMAH.)—*A Hebrew family.* The family is a Divine institution. It is the most ancient, most needful, and most enduring form of society; and, in proportion as it accords with the plan of its original constitution, it is productive of most beneficent effects, both temporal and spiritual, to the individual and the community. In times of general laxity and anarchy it has been, in many instances, a little sacred islet of purity, order, and peace, and nurtured the elements out of which a better age has grown. The real strength of a nation lies in its domestic life, and Israel was in this respect eminent above all other ancient nations. Even in the days of the judges, when "there was no king in Israel," and "every man did that which was right in his own eyes" (Judges xxi. 25), there were many godly families scattered through the land. One of these was that which gave birth to SAMUEL, the last of the series of the judges, the first of the order of the prophets, and the founder of the Hebrew monarchy. *This* family is introduced with a brief description (vers. 1, 2). The *residence* of the family was Ramah (the Height), or, more fully described, Ramathaim (the Two Heights). Here Samuel was born and nurtured; had his permanent abode during the latter portion of his life; died, and was buried. There is not a more sacred spot on earth than the home which is endeared by tender association and religious communion.

> "A spot of earth supremely blest;
> A dearer, sweeter spot than all the rest."

"Things are not to be valued on account of places, but places for the good things which they contain" (Bede). "God chooses any common spot for a mighty incident or the home of a mighty spirit." Consider the family as—

I. ORDERED BY A GODLY HEAD (ver. 3). His piety was shown—1. By his regular attendance on *Divine ordinances.* He worshipped "the Lord of hosts," not Baalim and Ashtaroth (ch. vii. 4); in the way of his appointment, at the tabernacle in Shiloh, at the proper season, and with the prescribed sacrifices; not according to his own reason or inclination merely, a will-worship which is not acceptable to God. 2. By his sincere and *spiritual service,* in contrast to the formal, worthless, and hypocritical service of others, especially the sons of Eli, Hophni and Phinehas (ch. ii. 12), and undeterred by their evil conduct in the priestly office. 3. By his faithful performance of his *vows* (ver. 21). 4. By his conversation and *prayer* in his own house (ver. 23). 5. *By his conducting all the members of his family to "the house of the Lord"* (ver. 7), in the exercise of his parental authority, accompanied by instruction and example. The words of the Law of Moses were evidently familiar to him (Deut. vi. 6—9), and happy is the family in which they are obeyed.

II. UNITING IN SOCIAL FESTIVITY (vers. 4, 5). Once a year he took his journey, in company with his family, from Ramah to the central sanctuary of the Divine King of Israel, for the twofold purpose of worshipping (lit., bowing down) and sacrificing before Jehovah. The sacrifice he offered was a peace offering (Deut. xxvii. 7), in which, when the animal was killed, the priest received its breast and right shoulder as his lawful portion, whilst the rest was given back to the worshipper that he and his family might feast on it before the Lord. Their festivity was—1. *Religious.* It was the festivity of those who were received into communion with God. They were guests at his table, and overshadowed by his presence. It is said of the elders of Israel that they "saw God, and did eat and drink" (Exod. xxiv. 11). And if no such visible sign of his glory now appeared, yet their consciousness of his presence (according to his promise, and symbolised by the ark of the covenant) would give solemnity to their repast, and prevent improper indulgence and revelry, which were but too common in this corrupt time (ver. 14 ; Judges xxi. 19, 21). It should ever be the same when Christians join in social festivity. 2. *Joyous* (Deut. xii. 12 ; xvi. 11). Its religiousness did not detract from its gladness, but made it pure, elevating, and refreshing. "The joy of the Lord is your strength." 3. Participated in by the *whole family,* children as well as adults. As the fathers the women and the children took part in idol feasts (Jer. vi. 18), so they should take part in "feasting before the Lord." 4. It also called forth expressions of *affection* (ver. 4). The kindness of God to all should lead to kindness one toward another, and the example of kindness set by the head of the family should be followed by all its members. Even the ordinary family meal may and ought to be such a scene of sacred festivity, but the highest realisation of it on earth is in "the Lord's Supper" (1 Cor. xi. 20). And how great is the blessing which rests upon the family, all the members of which partake together of the "cup of blessing," and are "all partakers of that one Bread."

III. Disquieted by domestic trouble (vers. 5—8). It was natural that Hannah should feel disappointed at being childless. Her condition was deemed a reproach, and a sign of Divine displeasure. But her grief arose chiefly from the conduct of her rival, Peninnah. There was thus an element of discord and trouble in the family. This trouble—1. Existed where it might have been *least expected.* The family was distinguished by earthly prosperity and genuine piety. But what home is there on earth wholly free from trouble? Beneath the fairest appearances there is seldom wanting a cause of disquiet, to check self-complacency and teach the soul its true rest. 2. Was occasioned by *want of conformity to a Divine ordinance.* The introduction of a second wife by Elkanah was not according to the Divine appointment "in the beginning" (Gen. ii. 24 ; Mal. ii. 15 ; Matt. xix. 4). The violation of that appointment had taken place at an early period (Gen. iv. 19) ; it was sanctioned by long usage ; and it was permitted under the Law "for the hardness of their hearts," and until they should be educated up to a higher moral condition. But it was followed by pernicious consequences (Gen. iv. 23 ; xxx. 8), as it always is in those families and nations where it obtains. Ignorance of the laws of God may mitigate or exempt from guilt ; but it does not do away with all the evil consequences of their violation ; for those laws are rooted in the fixed relations and tendencies of things. 3. Was immediately caused by the indulgence of improper feeling and *unseemly speech.* Peninnah may have been jealous of the special love shown to Hannah by her husband (ver. 5). She was proud and haughty on account of her own sons and daughters, and, instead of sympathising with her who had none, she made her defect a ground of insult ; and trials ordained by Divine providence are peculiarly severe when they become an occasion of human reproach. Finally, she gave free play to "an unruly evil" (James iii. 8), especially at those seasons when it should have been held under restraint. Such things are the bane of domestic life. 4. *Disturbed* the proper performance of sacred duties. Peninnah could have little peace in her own breast, and be little prepared for Divine worship or sacred festivity. As for Hannah, although she did not angrily retaliate, but patiently endured the reproaches cast upon her (affording an admirable example of meekness), yet "she wept and did not eat" (ver. 7), and her joy was turned into mourning. Domestic disturbances tend greatly to hinder prayers (1 Pet. iii. 7). 5. Was *alleviated* by affectionate expostulation (ver. 8). "In Elkanah we have an example of a most excellent husband, who patiently tolerated the insulting humour of Peninnah, and comforted dejected Hannah with words full of tender affection, which was truly, in St. Peter's words, to dwell with them according to knowledge" (Patrick). Let each member of the family endeavour to soothe and alleviate the sorrows of the rest, and all learn to find their own happiness in promoting the happiness of others. 6. Was *over-ruled* by Divine providence for great good. In her trouble Hannah was led to pray fervently, and her prayer was answered; sorrowing gave place to rejoicing; the family was benefited; and the people of God were greatly blessed. So, in his wonderful working, God "turned the curse into a blessing" (Neh. xiii. 2).—D.

Ver. 3. (SHILOH.)—*Public worship.* Worship is worth-ship, the honour paid to superior worth; more especially it is the reverence and homage paid to God in religious exercises. Public worship (as distinguished from private and family worship) is designed to give an open expression, before men, of the praise and honour which are his due (Ps. cxlv. 10—12); a purpose which is not fulfilled by those who neglect it, and is forgotten by those who observe it only as a means of obtaining their own spiritual benefit. It is often enjoined in the word of God, and is commended by the example of good men. The conduct of Elkanah is suggestive of useful hints concerning—

I. GOING TO WORSHIP. Persuaded of the obligation and privilege, "he went up out of his city" and home. He did "not forsake the house of the Lord" (Neh. x. 39; Heb. x. 25). Neither the distance, nor the trouble involved, prevented him; nor did the unworthy conduct of many of the worshippers keep him away. He took all his family with him, except when any of them were hindered by sickness or necessary duties (ver. 20). He thought of the purpose for which he went, and made the needful preparation for "worshipping and sacrificing unto the Lord." He was careful to be in time; and, doubtless, sought the blessing of God on his service, entertained the journey with profitable conversation, and came with reverence and self-restraint (Eccles. v. 1).

II. THE OBJECT OF WORSHIP. "The Lord of hosts." He did not worship an "unknown God." Man must worship because he is a man; but he will worship a false or unworthy object, as well as in a wrong manner, unless he be Divinely taught, because he is a sinner. He "knew what he worshipped," even the living and true God, who had revealed himself to his people; Creator, Redeemer, Ruler; holy, just, and merciful (Exod. xxxiv. 6, 7). Our knowledge of God is necessarily imperfect (Job xi. 7); but it may be true as far as it goes, and the true idea of God is "the root of all absolute grandeur, of all truth and moral perfection" (John xvii. 3).

III. THE PLACE OF WORSHIP. He went to worship in Shiloh (Deut. xvi. 15), where the tabernacle, made in the wilderness, having been first pitched at Gilgal, had now been standing 300 years. It was the palace of the great King. Here his servants the priests ministered, and offerings were presented by his subjects at his altar in the outer court (ch. ii. 33); the lamp of God (ch. iii. 3), the altar of incense (ch. ii. 28), and the table of shew-bread (ch. xxi. 4) stood in the holy place; and the ark of the covenant (ch. iv. 3) in the holiest of all (Heb. ix. 25). These were symbols of spiritual truth and means of Divine communion (Exod. xxix. 43; Deut. xvi. 11). The ideas that underlay them are fully realised in Christ and his Church, and the symbols are no longer needed; nor is there any more one central and sacred spot "where men ought to worship" (John iv. 20, 23). God draws nigh to us, and we can call upon him "in every place." The presence of holy souls makes all places holy, in so far as any place can be so called.

> "What's hallowed ground? 'Tis what gives birth
> To sacred thoughts in souls of worth."

Common worship, however, renders necessary special places of worship, the declared purpose and holy associations of which make them dear to good men and helpful to their devotions, so that they are sometimes constrained to say with Jacob, "How dreadful is this place," &c. (Gen. xxviii. 17). "A fearful place, indeed, and worthy of all reverence, is that which saints inhabit, holy angels frequent, and God himself graces with his own presence."

IV. THE TIME OF WORSHIP. "He went up yearly," or from year to year, and continued several days. The Law required that the tribes should assemble at the sanctuary three times a year; but in those unsettled times it appears to have been the custom for them to attend only once, probably at the passover. What acts of worship he performed, or what times he observed at Ramah, we are not told. The

Sabbath (though not mentioned in the Books of Samuel) we may be sure was not neglected by him, nor should it be by us. The spirit of continual Sabbath keeping (Heb. iv. 9) is, indeed, of greater importance than the observance of one day in seven; but its observance, with reference to the higher truths which the first day of the week commemorates, is most needful and beneficial.

V. THE MANNER OF WORSHIP. "He went up to worship and sacrifice." His worship consisted of adoration, confession, petition, thanksgiving. It was connected with and embodied in sacrifices of various kinds, and of different significance : expiatory (sin offerings), self-dedicatory (burnt offerings), and eucharistic (peace offerings). They had a real and deep relation to the sacrifice of Christ. From it they derived their worth, and by it they have been done away. Our worship demands *spiritual sacrifices*, the broken and contrite heart, the "presenting of our bodies as a living sacrifice," prayer, thanksgiving, holy and benevolent dispositions and conduct. "By him, therefore (who brings us nigh to God, and makes us capable of serving him aright), let us offer the sacrifice of praise to God continually," &c. (Heb. xiii. 16.)

VI. RETURNING FROM WORSHIP. After the sacred feast was over, he and his family "rose up in the morning early, and worshipped before the Lord, and returned" (ch. i. 19). Morning is a most favourable season for devotion (Ps. v. 3) ; and those who are about to take a journey or enter on a new enterprise do well to rise up early and seek the Divine guidance and help. Elkanah showed that he was not weary of his devotions, but desired to avail himself to the utmost of the opportunities afforded him ; and, by doing so, he obtained the greatest permanent benefit from his visit to the sanctuary. The manner in which we return from public worship greatly influences its permanent results (Matt. xiii. 4, 19 ; Luke xi. 28). And our aim and endeavour, when we return, should be to sanctify all places, all times, all occupations by the spirit of unceasing prayer and thanksgiving, and so make the whole of life a preparation for the services of the heavenly temple.—D.

Vers. 3, 11. (SHILOH.)—*The Lord of hosts.* There is no subject more worthy of study than the nature and character of God. His perfections are often called his Name, and his Name is expressed by various words, all of which are significant. They are not merely designations, but also descriptions. The word *God* is commonly supposed to mean *the Good One*, but it probably denotes "he on whom one calls," or "he to whom one sacrifices ;" the word *Lord* = Giver or Distributor of bread ; *Deity* (Sanscrit, *Dyaus*) = the Resplendent, Light-giving Heaven, the Shining One, showing the pure conception which the ancient Aryans (the ancestors of the Indo-European nations) entertained of the Divine Being. But the Bible mentions other names of God, which were either in common use among the Semitic nations, or given by special revelation to the Hebrews ; and of these one of the most noteworthy is that of "the Lord of hosts" (Jehovah Sabaoth), which occurs no less than 260 times, this being the first instance of its use (see Max Müller, 'Science of Language,' p. 172 ; Fairbairn, 'Studies in Philosophy ;' Plumptre, 'Biblical Studies '). Observe—

I. ITS HISTORICAL USE. 1. Founded on what had been previously known or revealed. Jehovah Sabaoth = Jehovah, Elohe (God of) Sabaoth (Keil ; 2 Sam. v. 10). El (Beth-*El*, Isra-*El*, *El*-kanah, Samu-*El*) = the Strong or Mighty One ; used in the plural as "comprehending in himself the fulness of all power, and uniting in himself all the attributes which the heathen ascribe to their divinities." Jehovah (Yahveh) = he who is, or he who will be, the Being, the Absolute One, the Cause and Support of all other beings, the Eternal, the Unchangeable ; employed with special reference to his personality, unity, his close relationship to his people, and his promise to be their God ; the Proper Name of Israel's God (Exod. iii. 14 ; vi. 3). Sabaoth (hosts) = the heaven and the earth (Gen. ii. 1 ; Deut. iv. 19), the angels (Gen. xxxii. 2, where, however, another word of similar import is used ; Ps. ciii. 21), and more commonly armies of men (Gen. xxi. 22 ; Exod. vi. 26 ; Josh. v. 14). The whole name = "Jehovah, the God of the armies of Israel, the Giver of the victory in battle, of the stars and of the angels." 2. First used when he was about to make a fresh display of his power and grace to his people under their anointed king (ch. iv. 4 ; xvii. 45 ; 2 Sam. vi. 27). By Hannah, the most spiritually-minded person of that age (see Wordsworth's 'Com.'). 3. "Rose into new prominence in proportion as the people came into contact with the Assyrian and Chaldæan races, by whom the worship of the heavenly bodies was systematised into a national religion, and was therefore perpetually on the lips of Isaiah and Jeremiah as a protest against it" (Isa. vi. ; Jer. xlvi. 18 ; xlviii. 15). 4. Most frequently used by the later prophets, "who doubtless sought to counteract by this means the fear which the Jews, as a poor, despised people, had of the power of the Gentiles, and to prove to them that the God in whom they believed had hosts enough to protect them, though they should be devoid of all earthly might wherewith to defend themselves against their enemies" (Roos). 5. Only once employed, in direct statement, in the New Testament (James v. 4) ; other and still higher revelations of his character being made by Jesus Christ.

II. Its SUBLIME IMPORT. "God alone is great." 1. *His personality and unity,* as opposed to "the gods many and lords many" worshipped by the heathen ; the key-stone of the faith of Israel being, "The Lord our God is one Lord." This is not contradictory to the Christian doctrine of the Trinity, which signifies a threefold distinction in the One God. 2. *His supremacy.* He is higher than the highest, the great King and Law-giver, whose will all must obey (Ps. xxiv. 10 ; Mal. i. 14). 3. *His immensity.* He fills all space ; rules over sun, moon, and stars ; myriads of angels ; nations, families, and individual men. "All are thy servants." 4. *His omnipotence.* "Lord God Almighty." "Power belongeth unto God." "It is the flower of his crown imperial, which he will suffer none to usurp. If the proudest of creatures go beyond the bounds and limits of his present permission, he will send worms to eat them up, as he did Herod" (Owen). "Thine omnipotence is not far from us when we are far from thee" (Augustine). Other revelations have now been given. "God is spirit." "God is light." "God is love." "Our Father which art in heaven." But his name as the Lord of hosts ought often to be an object of devout contemplation.

III. Its PRACTICAL INFLUENCE. It is adapted—1. *To correct error:* atheism, polytheism, pantheism, positivism, scepticism, secularism, &c. 2. *To elevate our conceptions of him,* and fill us with humility, reverence, and adoration. 3. *To encourage us to pray to him, with strong confidence that we shall be heard* (ch. i. 11 ; Zech. viii. 21 ; Matt. xxvi. 53 ; Eph. iii. 20). 4. *To strengthen us in labour.* "Work: for I am with you, saith the Lord of hosts" (Haggai ii. 4). 5. *To incite us to contend against his foes,* to "fight the good fight of faith." "I come to thee in the name of the Lord of hosts" (ch. xvii. 45). 6. *To console us in trouble.* "The Lord will protect his own" (Ps. xxxiv. 7 ; Isa. viii. 13). He is the Protector and Avenger of the oppressed (James v. 4). "He calls God the Lord of hosts in order to strike terror into those who think that the poor have no protector" (Bede). 7. *To warn all who disobey his voice, and set themselves in opposition to him and his people.* "Beware, therefore."—D.

EXPOSITION.

HANNAH'S PRAYER FOR A SON (vers. 9—18). Ver. 9.– **After they had eaten . . . after they had drunk.** The Hebrew favours the translation, "After she had eaten in Shiloh, and after she had drunk;" the somewhat forced rendering of the A. V. having arisen from a supposed discrepancy between this verse and ver. 7. Really there is none. The words simply mean that Hannah took part in the sacrificial banquet, though she did so without appetite or pleasure ; and thus they connect her visit to the temple and her prayer with the most solemn religious service of the year. To take part in this banquet was a duty, but as soon as she had fulfilled it she withdrew to the temple to pour out her grief before God. There Eli, **the priest,** *i. e.* the high priest, as in Num. xxvi. 1 ; xxvii. 2, was seated upon, not *a* seat, but *the* pontifical throne, placed at the entrance leading into the inner court of the tabernacle, so that all who came to worship must pass before him. It is remarkable that the tabernacle is called the *temple* (so 1 Sam. iii. 3 ; Ps. v. 7), or, more literally, the "palace" of Jehovah, his royal residence; and it thus appears that the name had come into use before Solomon's building was erected. The curtains (Exod. xxvi. 1) also had given place to a *mezuzah,* translated *a post,* but really a sort of porch, with doors, as appears from ch. iii. 15 (comp. Exod. xxi. 6 ; 1 Kings vii. 5).

As the tabernacle remained stationary at Shiloh for 300 years, naturally numerous buildings of a more solid nature grew up around it.

Vers. 10, 11.—**She . . . prayed unto the LORD.** Kneeling down in the inner court, but within sight of Eli, whose throne in the porch probably overlooked the whole inner space, Hannah prays unto "Jehovah of Sabaoth" for a male child. Her humility appears in her thrice calling herself Jehovah's handmaid ; her earnestness in the threefold repetition of the entreaty that Jehovah would look on her, and remember her, and not forget her. With her prayer she also makes a twofold vow in case her request is granted. The son given her is, first, to serve not for a stipulated number of years, as was the law with the Levites (Num. iv. 3), but for life ; and, secondly, he is to be a Nazarite. We gather from Num. vi. 2 that Moses found this singular institution in existence, and only regulated it, and admitted it into the circle of established and legalised ordinances. Essentially it was a consecration to God, a holy priesthood, but not a sacrificing priesthood, nor one by right of birth, as the Aaronic, but personal, and either for a limited period, or for life. During the continuance of the vow, a Nazarite might (1) partake of no produce of the vine, signifying thereby abstinence from self-indulgence and carnal pleasure. He might (2) take no part in mourning for the dead, even though they were his nearest relatives, because his holier duties raised him above the ordinary joys and sorrows, the cares and occupations of every-day life. Lastly, no razor might come upon his head, the free growing hair being at once the distinctive mark by which all men would recognise his sacred calling, and also a sign that he was not bound by the usual customs of life. By Hannah's first vow Samuel was devoted to service in the sanctuary, by the second to a holy consecrated life. This institution remained in existence unto our Lord's days ; for John the Baptist was also consecrated to God as a Nazarite by his mother, though not as Samuel, also given to minister in the temple.

Vers. 12—18. — **She continued praying.** Hannah's prayer was long and earnest, but in silence. She spake not in, but "to her heart," to herself. It was an inward supplication, which only her own heart and God heard. Eli watched, and was displeased. Possibly silent prayer was something unusual. It requires a certain advance in civilisation and refinement to enable a supplicant to separate the petition from the outward expression of it in spoken words, and a strong faith before any one can feel that God hears and knows the silent utterances of the heart

(comp. Matt. viii. 8—10). Naturally men think that they shall be heard for their much speaking, and for speaking aloud. Unused then to such real prayer, Eli, as he marked the quivering lips, the prostrate form, the face flushed with earnestness, came to the coarse conclusion that she was drunken, and with equal coarseness bids her "put away her wine from her," that is, go and sleep off the effects of her debauch. Hannah answers indignantly, "No, my lord." She is "a woman hard of spirit" (see marg.), heavy-hearted, as we should say, and she had been lightening her heart by pouring out her troubles before Jehovah. She is no "worthless woman ;" for Belial is not a proper name, though gradually it became one (2 Cor. vi. 15), but means *worthlessness*, and "a daughter of worthlessness" means a bad woman. "Grief" is rather *provocation, vexation.* Hannah cannot forget the triumph of her rival, exulting over her many portions, while for her there had been only one. Convinced by the modesty and earnestness of her answer, Eli retracts his accusation, gives her his blessing, and prays that her petition may be granted. And Hannah, comforted by such words spoken by the high priest (John xi. 51), returned to the sacrificial feast, which apparently was not yet finished, and joined in it, for "she did eat, and her countenance was to her no more," that is, the grieved and depressed look which she had so long borne had now departed from her. There is no reason for the insertion of the word *sad.*

HANNAH'S PRAYER ANSWERED (vers. 19, 20). Vers. 19, 20.—**They rose up.** After solemn worship early the next morning Elkanah returned to his home at Ramah, and God answered Hannah's prayer, and gave her the wished-for son. She calls him Samuel, lit. Shemuel (Num. xxxiv. 20 ; 1 Chron. vii. 2), which was an ordinary Hebrew name, and means "heard of God," not "asked of God," as in the margin of the A. V. It seems to have been the mother's right to give names to her children (Luke i. 60), and Hannah saw in Samuel, whom she had asked of God, a living proof that she had been heard by him. The name, therefore, is of fuller significance than the reason given for it. Ishmael has virtually the same meaning, signifying "God heareth."

THE VOW FULFILLED (vers. 21 — 28). Ver. 21.—**Elkanah . . . went up.** When at the return of the year Elkanah went up as usual to Shiloh, Hannah remained at home, purposing to wait there till her son was old enough to be given to the Lord. This followed soon after his weaning, which in the East is delayed much longer than with us. In 2 Macc. vii. 27 we find three years mentioned as the usual period of lactation, but the chief Jewish authorities make the time one year shorter. At three years old a child in the East would cease to be troublesome ; but besides this, there was an order of women attached to the sanctuary (see on ch. ii. 22), and probably regulations for the training of children devoted to the temple service. **The yearly sacrifice**, lit. "sacrifice of days," would include among its duties the carrying to Shiloh of the tithes which were to be consumed before the Lord (Deut. xii. 17, 18), and the payment of those portions of the produce which belonged to Jehovah and the priests, and had become due during the year. **His vow** shows that Elkanah had ratified Hannah's words, by adding thereto a thank-offering from himself.

At Shiloh Samuel was to **abide for ever** ; his dedication was to be for his whole life. And when Elkanah prays, **Only the Lord establish his word**, it is evident that he and Hannah expected that a child born under such special circumstances would, like so many children of mothers long barren, be intended for some extraordinary work. The word of Jehovah referred to is that spoken by Eli in ver. 17, which contained not merely the assurance of the birth of a son, but a general confirmation and approval of all that Hannah had prayed for. In ver. 24 the Septuagint reads, "a bullock of three years old," probably on account of the one bullock mentioned in ver. 25 ; but as three-tenths of an ephah of flour formed the appointed meat offering for one bullock (Num. xv. 8—10), the mention of a whole ephah confirms the reading **three bullocks**. Probably the one bullock in ver. 25 was the special burnt offering accompanying the

solemn dedication of Samuel to Jehovah's service, while the other two were for Elkanah's usual yearly sacrifice, and the thank offering which he had vowed. At the end of the verse the Heb. reads, "And the child was a child," the word in both places being *na'ar*, which may mean anything up to fifteen years of age. The child really was about three years old, and the Sept. is probably right in reading, "And the child was with them." Both the Vulgate, however, and the Syriac agree with the Hebrew.

Ver. 28.—**I have lent him**. The word *lent* spoils the meaning. Hannah really in these two verses uses the same verb four times, though in different conjugations, and the same sense must be maintained throughout. Her words are, "For this child I prayed, and Jehovah hath given me my *asking* which I *asked* of him : and I also have *given back what was asked* to Jehovah ; as long as he liveth he is *asked* for Jehovah." The conjugation translated *to give back what was asked* literally means *to make to ask*, and so to give or lend anything asked. The sense here requires the restoration by Hannah of what she had prayed for (comp. Exod. xii. 35, 36), but which she had asked not for herself, but that she might devote it to Jehovah's service. At the end of ver. 28 the sing. "he worshipped" is rendered in the pl. by all the versions except the Sept., which omits it. But *he*, i. c. Elkanah, includes all his household, and it may be correctly translated in the pl., because the sense so requires, without altering the reading of the Hebrew. In the sing. it puts an unnecessary difficulty in the way of the ordinary reader.

HOMILETICS.

Vers. 9—18.—*Trial sanctified.* The main facts are—1. Hannah, impelled by trouble, goes to the sanctuary and records her wish in a vow. 2. Eli misjudges her character, but hearkens to her self-defence. 3. Eli discovers therefrom her real piety, and helps to create within her heart an assurance of answer to prayer. 4. Hannah enters on a brighter path.

I. IT BRINGS THE SOUL DIRECT TO GOD. It was doubtless good for Hannah to join the family worship, and derive all possible comfort from the festivals which to the devout mind told of a "mercy" which "endureth for ever ; " but when sorrow is of the godly sort, when the gentle or heavy hand of God has been duly recognised in trial, the soul needs more than the prayers of others. Heart and flesh then cry out for the living God. There are clearly traceable stages in trial before this result ensues. In the case of Hannah, which is typical of many others, it began with a fond hope deferred, awakening only the anxiety common to such domestic incidents. Then, as time wore on, grief was generated, wearing away the strength of the spirit. Years of silent waiting on Providence followed—wonder, doubt, occasional hope, and corresponding despair filling up the experience. The weary heart would turn sometimes to God, and social worship would be valued as a means of grace, but without relief. Sadder and sadder, increasingly sensible of dependence on God, and impelled by the discovery that not even a husband's love can enter into the deepest sorrow, a strong resolve is taken to seek refuge in God by an act of urgent appeal to him.

Such is the proper issue of all trials when sanctified. There is no morose repining, no internal war against the Supreme Will, no utter abandonment to despair, no resting in the sympathy and counsel, or even prayers, of the Church; the soul wants God, and, as never before, carries its load straight to him.

II. IT LEADS TO THE MERCY-SEAT. There is all the difference between fleeing to God in ignorant desperation, and recognising his covenant mercies in Christ. No doubt there is compassion for every poor dark creature who under the impulse of trouble cries out to the invisible God; but it was not without a reason that the devout Hebrew preferred to retire to the place where the ark of the covenant and the mercy-seat were kept. She knew, as the most enlightened of her people knew, that there was a way to God, and drawing nigh towards the mercy-seat was a distinct recognition of One in whom the troubled might expect to be blessed. Trial still leads us to God, not trusting in our righteousness, but by the " new and living way " consecrated by Christ. And though that invisible mercy-seat is ever near, it is the wont of those who are being blessed by trial to seek the house of God, and there, pleading his mercy, find relief and lay off their burdens.

III. IT MAKES NATURAL DESIRES FOR AN EARTHLY GOOD SUBORDINATE TO HIGH RELIGIOUS FEELING. It is not certain at what stage in the providential discipline the event occurred, but the fact is clear that there was a time in the process when a natural love of offspring, *per se*, became absorbed in a passion for devoting the most precious of gifts to God. It is difficult to trace the purifying process by which pure and lofty spiritual feeling emerges out of the fires, but experience in all ages attests the fact that it does. It is an evidence that trouble is blessed when one can say, "There is none on the earth that I desire beside thee." All good things are intended to be helpful to our higher spiritual life, and it is a sign of spiritual health when the possession of them is sought primarily for the furtherance of religious ends, either in self or in the world. Religion is not in antagonism with nature. It rather purifies and ennobles it. Personal endowments, reasonable desires for family, or influence, or wealth, are laid at the cross when self is lost in zeal for God. There were a *few features in Hannah's experience which correspond with the action of sanctified trial on others*. 1. She learnt the vanity of life apart from God's blessing. Unless he made life rich with the desired good, there was no sense of joy or perfection in life. It is a great gain to learn the lesson of our need of God in order to feel life to be a daily bliss. 2. She, by the action of long trial, was being weaned from dependence on earthly good for the joy of life, and hence was more free to cherish awakening sympathy with the enduring kingdom of God. Disappointment in temporal affairs has often been blessed to a deepened interest in the unseen realities of Christ's kingdom. 3. Her religious sensibilities, being gradually quickened and refined, rendered her increasingly sensitive to the terrible abominations of the age, and hence opened her eyes to see the need of some great reformer of the nation. Thus would the natural desire for offspring merge into the hope that she might send forth *the man*. It is when souls are more alive to their own spiritual condition that they long also for means by which to check prevailing sin.

IV. IT ISSUES IN THE HIGHEST FORM OF PERSONAL CONSECRATION. Solemn vows are the strongest expression of self-surrender. In Hannah's case a mother gives up her body and soul, her present powers and future possessions and influence, specifically to God. It was not possible for female service to go further. The routine service of the Levite, to be entered on at a definite age, was not enough for the now sanctified woman. Her heart was not satisfied even with the prospect of a son who should grow up in blamelessness of life. It was not the personal comfort of the presence in the house of a loving, pious child that stirred the soul to pray : a vision, given of God, of the coming Messiah imparted spiritual tone to her nature, and nothing would, therefore, give satisfaction short of the consecration from infancy, to the service of the sanctuary, of a son, to be thus prepared for holy labours among the degenerate people, and to be a faint type and useful forerunner of a still more blessed Child. Thus, the limits set by nature, the requirements of an emergency, and the prospective honour of Christ are recognised in an intelligent consecration brought about by the all-wise discipline of him who knows how to qualify for noble service. The exalted ideal of life attained to by this "sorrowful woman" bespeaks the thoroughness of the discipline through which she passed. A young life habituated to the calm and elevating influences of the sanctuary, separated from the sad and sorrow-producing evils of the age, untouched by the artificial appliances of man, and nourished in health without the man-created stimulants which give so much unreality to conduct —a very Nazarite in spirit and in body—this rose before the mind as an object of fond desire, and was laid lovingly at the throne of God; doubtless, also, in prediction of the One true and perfect life.

V. IT QUALIFIES FOR RENDERING CONTINUOUSLY IMPORTANT SERVICE TO THE CHURCH. No better service can be rendered to the Church than to nurture a life in such a way as to impart to it a tone far above the average of spirituality, and while doing that to pour forth from the heart sentiments that shall act as an inspiration to the wise and good in all ages. It was worth while for Hannah to spend years of sorrow, to issue, under the blessing of God, in the superbly beautiful nurture of a son like Samuel, and in the lofty strains of her celebrated song. Sanctified affliction enriches the soul with qualities permanent in value. The invalid gains spiritual power which in daily prayer brings down blessings on those nigh and afar off. The devout mother who has quietly borne reproach for Christ's sake, sweetens home all the rest of her days by her calm faith in God and ever-present gentleness. The merchant who has endured adversity as befits a child of God, gathers from the deep sorrows of his life power to pray and live for imperishable good far in excess of his former capacity. It is *good* to be afflicted.

If these things be so, there arise several *Practical questions* deserving conscientious replies:—1. Is desire for temporal good toned and regulated by regard for spiritual usefulness? 2. Do the private unspeakable sorrows of life draw us nearer to God, or render us sullen and bitter? 3. In our approaches to God do we sufficiently recognise the mercy-seat of the New Testament? 4. Have we ever consecrated ourselves or our belongings to God by deliberate vow, and as far as nature permits, and the claims of religion require? 5. Does our personal consecration, or the devotion of our offspring to God, approach toward the Nazarite ideal consecration of perfect freedom of life from all that is artificial and unwholesome—a holy simplicity?

Vers. 9—18.—*Character misjudged.*—I. A RARE FORM OF WORSHIP. It was a rare thing for a solitary woman to be seen offering prayer without audible words and with a semblance of folly. The vicinity of the sanctuary was the scene of many strange and painful events in those days; but here was singularity combined with and expressive of the deepest piety. Prayer, though not in form of set phrase, is true worship when characterised by the features seen in that of the "sorrowful" woman: such as longing of the heart for a definite object, intense fervour of spirit, reverent submission to the will of God, profound regard in what is sought for the Divine glory, and directed to the Source of all power through the mercy-seat in Christ. The question of set forms of utterance for public worship must be settled by considerations covering the range of history, and the order and welfare of the Church. The heart of the true Christian will contain petitions which no words can anticipate or express. It is not just to prescribe how individuals shall pray, for a living piety must grow according to its inner laws, which partake of our own individuality. Sometimes the Church may witness the spectacle of unusual acts of worship, and it is good for the world when they arise. Spurious worship, eccentricity in the name of religion, can be readily detected. Deviation from ordinary forms where piety is sincere may occur when intense feeling precludes or subdues utterance. Sighs, tears, groans may be prayers. Or the privacy of the request, though it be made under the eye of worshippers in the house of God, is unsuited to the public ear. Many a secret vow is made on the Sabbath in the sanctuary. And sometimes the spirit may know its want, but cannot speak to God for very awe of the Divine presence.

II. A MISTAKEN JUDGMENT. Eli erred in judgment when he classed among the vile the most devout and holy of the age. Here was an instance of the guardian of the sanctuary, and the chief authority in law and religion, judging from appearance, and not from the heart. The causes of the error were probably such as frequently act among men. 1. Natural inability of man to read the real character by casual outward appearances. The heart is too deep to be penetrated by aid of occasional signs, for the same outward action may proceed from diverse internal motions. 2. Strong tendency in some persons to estimate others by the standard of their own experience. The area of one man's life may be much broader than that of another. The form, therefore, of religion in the one may be far beyond the appreciation of the other. 3. The strong hold on some good men of conventional modes of worship. Religion in some instances has been trained to find outward expression for itself by rule, and hence whatever expression deviates from the conventional type is liable to be regarded with suspicion. 4. In some cases men hold office in connection with public worship whose sympathies are not broad enough for the varieties of character and want that come under their observation.

III. A NOBLE SELF-VINDICATION. The "sorrowful spirit" of the worshipper shrinks from the very thought of being counted vile and a defamer of the place she loved. The cruel pang of the accusation only developed the strength and beauty of her piety. The depth of her sorrow and the utter absorption of her spirit in the one longing of her life, coupled with a sense of her unworthiness to be used in the high service of Messiah, checked any tendency to anger and recrimination. True self-vindication can dispense with passion. Its qualities are calm self-possession even under cruel wrong, a gentleness of spirit which knows how to be firm, a respectful deference to authority when confronting it, a delicate reference to self and the private sorrows that may have occasioned the misapprehension, an abstention from all that would exasperate, and a plain and fearless assertion of innocence. The comfort of the misjudged lies much in the conviction that God knows all. Religion gains much when the injured exhibit the spirit inculcated and exemplified by Christ. It requires much grace to be a Christian indeed. The world is slow to practise what it always in its heart admires, when the misjudged vindicate themselves after the Saviour's example.

IV. A LIGHTENED HEART. It was a morn of joy after the long night of sorrow, when, giving a true interpretation to the official words of the high priest, Hannah rose from prayer and went her way. The free, joyful heart shone forth in the countenance, and gave ease to every common duty of life. When God makes us glad, new energy enters into our nature. Hence, true religion, bringing to men elasticity of spirit, increases a man's power as a citizen, improves his capacity for business, lends lustre to the home, and, in fact, becomes an important element in the material wealth of nations. And what is most important is, the joy which God gives is real, permanent, resting on foundations which abide amid all change. In so far as the really devout are concerned, the lightened heart is the result of—1. The relief natural to true prayer. Even when specific answers are not obtained, the believer is rested and relieved by laying the burden before the mercy-seat. 2. Clear indications of God's acceptance. These vary with the age and circumstances. The high priest was endowed under special conditions with the power of indicating the Divine approval. External channels may convey unmistakably the will of God. The immediate course of events may be seen to correspond to the request. God is at no loss to convey outward intimations that the prayer of faith is not in vain. 3. The inward witness may be given, clear and strong, when God has important ends to accomplish thereby. The Spirit of God is in direct contact with the human, and can make known a truth. Christ's people know his voice. As the Spirit moved St. Paul to go to definite places, so he moves the true heart to believe in coming answer to prayer.

Practical suggestions:—1. Much prayer may be offered when forms of worship are lacking, in the sanctuary, in the city, on the open sea, and at daily toil. 2. Encouragement may be found in remembering that God understands our thoughts "afar off," and when words fail. 3. We should not estimate the value of prayer in others by what we can ascertain of it by our observation. 4. The guardians of pure worship have much need of charity and a discriminating spirit. 5. Errors of judgment should be freely admitted when ascertained. 6. The quiet dignity of truth befits all acts of self-defence. 7. The joy coming from God is the real strength and beautifier of life.

Vers. 19—28.—*Conjugal sympathy.* The facts are—1. Hannah, having independently fixed the future of her offspring, reveals the vow to her husband.

2. Elkanah acquiesces in her vow, and allows her will in respect of time and method of perfecting it. 3. A united and solemn surrender of Samuel to his life work.

I. QUALIFIED WIFELY INDEPENDENCE. Although Elkanah knew his wife's great sorrow, yet in the matters connected with its removal and in the subsequent transactions she evidently followed her own course. It was a great decision to fix a child's lot in life apart from consultation and consent. The spontaneous choice of a name, though harmonious with a mother's secret knowledge of past experiences, was in any case, and more so in Hebrew instances, a bold undertaking. The event of naming furnished, most probably, the occasion for explanation and revelation of the anterior vow, and was faced with the most perfect composure. The mother's feelings are ever to be considered in parting with children as they enter on life's work; but here the time and method appear to have been fixed by the mother taking the initiative, and, contrary to rule, the wife is the prominent figure in the religious ceremonial of dedication, whose set purpose throughout therein attains its goal. No *law of social and domestic life* is more clearly laid down in Scripture than the *subordination of the wife* to the husband, and though there are principles which limit the subordination, and sentiments which convert it into blissful freedom, yet independence of action where offspring are concerned, is as rare as it is, *per se*, undesirable. The high intellectual and moral qualities which render wifely action free and firm within the sphere of private affairs, are perverted when applied to the independent determination of the destiny of a son. The spirit of self-assertion will have no place in a well-ordered home. The grace and the moral power of woman vanish or become enfeebled when deeds are done in secret, and the natural authority of the head of the house is anticipated. Yet there are *conditions* which render such *independence* for a season *both necessary and even religious*. 1. Hannah's conduct was connected with an event in her religious experience too sacred even for a loving husband to be acquainted with. One cannot unbosom, even to the dearest earthly friend, the deep and passionate longings of the soul after God. The child of promise belongs primarily to the one to whom the promise is made, and so a special proprietorship is created which gives right to choice as to the use to be made of the gift. 2. Confidence in a husband's sympathy with lofty religious aims will justify wifely freedom, when that freedom is employed to perfect holy purposes. There are great and noble deeds within the proper right of a husband which he would only rejoice to see independently performed by a confiding wife. Where mutual confidence is fortified by years of common sorrow, no great error will be committed in interpreting religious wishes. 3. The soul that is bent on the realisation of a great religious hope, and has pondered it for years, best knows the means by which it may be secured. None but Hannah could see clearly the need of winning over the assistance of Eli, and the previous interview of the woman of "sorrowful spirit" with the high priest required that she should figure in the great ceremonial of devoting a child to God.

II. WISE HUSBANDLY CONSIDERATION. The legal rights secured by Divine law (Num. xxx. 6—8) are at once surrendered by acquiescence in a holy, God-honouring vow; acceptance of a memorial name; deference to wishes in matters of detail, and cheerful co-operation in completing the vow. Piety and prudence combine in making concessions where pure motives have influenced conduct, and where the ends sought are wise and useful. Exacting men never enjoy the full love and confidence of their home. It would be blessed for many homes were the holy daring of Hannah and the wise, gentle bearing of Elkanah more frequent. The key to such conduct lies not in rigid conformity to excellent rules prescribing spheres of action, nor in mutual watchfulness, but in pure affection for a loving, faithful wife; a quick perception of the special providence which over-rules earthly trials; sympathy with the noble piety that could so spontaneously and cheerfully surrender the realised hope of many a weary year; a conviction that a devout soul so evidently led on by God is by far the safest guide in matters pertaining to completed vows, and an unexpressed joy in the honour of being permitted to join in offering to God the precious treasure he had given. Hence we may learn a few

General lessons :—1. Personal and private decisions based on a supreme regard for the glory of God, and free from selfishness, are sure to be appreciated in a pious

home.   2. A loving recognition of individuality and force of character is essential to
perfect domestic harmony.   3. Personal influence in the sphere of home becomes
powerful when holy discipline has purged selfishness and brought the spirit into deep
sympathy with the kingdom of God.   4. There is no pain, but joy, in sacrifice when
our possessions are recognised as truly God's, and we perceive the honour of their
being employed in his name.   5. It is a blessed thing for children to be spontaneously
consecrated to God by the prayers of self-sacrificing parents.   6. Those who by
reason of circumstances cannot serve in the sanctuary, may perhaps be permitted to
nurture children for the ministry of the word.

HOMILIES BY VARIOUS AUTHORS.

Ver. 9 (iii. 3). (SHILOH.)—*The temple of the Lord.*   Most of the religious ideas and
expressions with which we are familiar had their origin far back in distant ages ; and
it is interesting and instructive to trace them to their source, and mark their
alteration and expansion in the progressive course of Divine revelation.   This is
the first instance in which the expression " the temple of the Lord " occurs.   Notice—
I. ITS SCRIPTURAL APPLICATIONS.   1. *A material structure.*   " In the earliest ages
God was worshipped without any distinction at any time and at any place, whenever
and wherever the promptings of devotion moved in the hearts of his creatures ; more
especially, however, under the shadow of embowering trees, on hills and mountains,
and in places where they had experienced some special manifestations of his favour "
(Jahn).   The first erection (with the exception of altars) was (1) the tabernacle or
tent (Exod. xxv. 8), here called the temple or (more literally) the *palace* of Jehovah,
as the royal residence of the king of Israel.   Afterwards (2) the temple of Solomon ;
(3) of Zerubbabel ; and (4) of Herod.   2. *The incarnate Word* (John i. 14 ; ii. 21 ;
Col. ii. 19).   3. *Christian men.*   The body of each (1 Cor. vi. 19).   The whole
assembly (1 Cor. iii. 16 ; 2 Cor. vi. 16 ; Eph. ii. 20—22 ; 1 Pet. ii. 5).   Observe the
progress :—God *for* us, *with* us, *in* us ; Father, Son, Spirit.   4. *The heavenly world.*
Although there is no temple *therein* (Rev. xxi. 22), yet heaven is altogether a temple
(Rev. vii. 15).
II. ITS MAIN SIGNIFICANCE in all these applications.   It is—1. *Set apart for the
Lord.*   Selected, separated, and consecrated as his possession, and for his use.   2.
Inhabited by him.   His throne is there.   He dwells between the cherubim, in
fellowship with the redeemed.   3. *Manifests him* in his holiness and love.   His
glory appears, his voice is heard, his will is declared (Exod. xxv. 22 ; Heb. iv. 16).
4. *In it service is rendered to him.*   At first it was chiefly in outward symbolical
acts ; afterwards of the man himself, " body, soul, and spirit " (Rom. xii. 1 ; 1 Pet.
ii. 9 ; Rev. i. 6).   In each of these particulars we see the principle of progress, from
the natural to the spiritual (1 Cor. xv. 46).
III. ITS SPIRITUAL SUGGESTIONS.   1. *That the place in which man worships is of
far less importance than man himself and his possession of a holy character.*   No
place or building can be *holy* in the full sense of the word.   For holiness implies
intelligence, affection, freedom ; and these make him unspeakably greater than all
"the gorgeous palaces and solemn temples" which the earth contains.   "To this
man will I look," &c. (Isa. lvii. 15 ; lxvii. 1, 2 ; Matt. xii. 6).   "Let more regard
be paid to the promotion of religion than the decoration of churches ; for although
it is a good thing that churches should be beautiful edifices, yet virtue forms their
best crown and ornament.   It seems to us that the building of handsome churches
pertains rather to the Old Testament, whilst the improvement of character and life
is the more peculiar work of the Christian dispensation " (Charlemagne, Capitulary
of the year 811).   2. *That the pattern to which the character of man must be conformed is Jesus Christ.*   He is not only the Living Stone to whom every one must
come that he may be built up into the " spiritual house," the Chief Corner-stone on
which the whole building rests, but also the perfect Model according to which each
and all must be fashioned (Rom. viii. 29).   3. That the character of man is conformed to its Divine pattern *by the indwelling of the Holy Ghost.*   4. *That only
those in whom God dwells here will be fit to dwell with God hereafter,* and constitute

the heavenly tabernacle and temple (Rev. xxi. 3). Above all things, *seek to be in the building* which God is rearing for his habitation, and for an everlasting monument to his praise.—D.

Vers. 9—13. (SHILOH.)—*Effectual prayer.* Prayer is converse with God. The general principles which are necessary that it may be acceptable and effectual were exemplified by Hannah in the prayer which she offered at the porch of the tabernacle in Shiloh, whilst other and more special principles were contained therein. She was possessed of great intelligence, sensibility, meekness, and spirituality of mind, and embodied the noblest spiritual element existing amongst her people, even as she was a type of their history (ever rising out of weakness and distress through humiliation, faith, and prayer, into strength, and joy, and triumph). Consider her prayer as—

I. BORN OF DEEP SORROW. " She was in bitterness of soul, and wept sore " (ver. 10). Seemingly forgotten of God, an object of reproach and scorn, without indulging feelings of resentment, unable to tell her trouble to any one else, she betook herself to him who is " a Refuge for the oppressed in times of trouble." Prayer is the best resource at such times ; and grief of heart, together with the loneliness which it usually causes, often lead to "the pouring out of the soul before the Lord." What a beneficent power is sorrow in a world like this ! And how blessed are the fruits which, through Divine grace, it produces ! (Ps. lv. 22 ; Hosea ii. 15 ; 1 Pet. v. 7).

II. UTTERED ONLY IN THE HEART (ver. 13). The first recorded instance of silent or mental prayer. The ordinary worshippers at the tabernacle prayed with audible words, and significant gestures ; and in the East to this day the people pray in the same manner, and have little or no idea of praying only in the mind. They are more demonstrative than ourselves. " Mental prayer is a lifting up of the mind to God in actual or virtual supplication for what we desire." It is—1. Frequently a *necessity ;* inasmuch as it would not be always proper to express in the presence of others the desires of the heart. 2. Presumptively *sincere ;* inasmuch as it consists of direct intercourse with the Invisible and Omniscient One, and cannot spring from a desire to be seen or heard of men. 3. Highly *beneficial ;* inasmuch as it serves to strengthen the spirit of prayer, and is heard of God (Neh. ii. 4). Even when it does not shape itself in words within the mind, but consists of aspirations and "groanings which cannot be uttered," " he that searcheth the hearts knoweth what is the mind of the spirit" therein (Rom. viii. 27).

III. EXPRESSIVE OF FERVENT DESIRE. Desire is the soul of prayer. It arises from, and is proportionate to, the sense of need. Its intensity is not always manifested by audible words ; for sometimes its strength is dispersed and exhausted thereby ; whereas silence condenses and increases it. " Deepest waters stillest flow." Our desires cannot be too fervent, or our requests too importunate, provided they be for things which are according to the will of God (Rom. xii. 12 ; 1 John v. 14, 15).

> " Fervent love
> And lively hope with violence assail
> The kingdom of the heavens, and overcome
> The will of the Most High ; not in such sort
> As man prevails o'er man ; but conquers it
> Beeause 'tis willing to be conquer'd ; still,
> Though conquer'd, by its mercy conquering."
>
> Dante, 'Div. Com.,' Par. xx.

IV. EXHIBITING GENUINE FAITH. " O Lord of hosts," &c. (ver. 11). Like Abraham, she "believed in the Lord " (Gen. xv. 6) ; trusted, leant on him, as a child rests on the bosom of a parent. She had exalted conceptions of his character ; believed in (1) his living personality, supreme dominion, power, goodness, faithfulness (Heb. xi. 6) ; relied on (2) his promises, summed up in the assurance, " I will be your God " (Exod. vi. 7 ; Levit. xxvi. 12) ; and (3) although she had no express promise of the particular blessing which she desired, yet, inwardly taught, she applied the general promise to herself, and had " confidence respecting things hoped for " (Heb. xi. 1). When express promises are wanting, it behoves us to seek particular blessings with the utmost dependence and submission ; but, so far from being prohibited from seeking them, we are encouraged to do so by the unlimited range of such directions as this : " *What things soever* ye desire, when ye pray," &c. (Mark xi. 24).

V. DISTINGUISHED BY ENTIRE SELF-SURRENDER. Once and again she called herself the " handmaid " of the Lord, as belonging to him, and wholly devoted to his service. Her will she freely offered up in sacrifice to his, and made a fresh surrender of herself in her solemn engagement to render back to him the gift he might bestow. She sought not her own gratification, but his glory and the welfare of his people. " The vow of the Nazarite embodied the yearning of the better part of the nation for a moral and religious reformation, as the only hope of Israel. It symbolised Israel's perfect calling of voluntary self-surrender to God " (Edersheim). When we seek not our own, but make it subservient to higher and larger good, we place ourselves in a line with the Divine purposes, and may entertain sure and steadfast hope of success.

VI. OFFERED WITH STEADFAST PERSEVERANCE. " She continued praying before the Lord " (ver. 12). It was not a momentary ebullition of feeling, but the fixed direction of her whole soul (Gen. xxxii. 26 ; Luke xi. 8 ; xviii. 1 ; Eph. vi. 18).

VII. FOLLOWED BY AN ABUNDANT BLESSING. The benediction of the high priest (ver. 17) was to her an oracle of God, to be in due time fulfilled ; whilst the immediate effect on her heart was peace and gladness, and " she went away, and did eat, and her countenance was no more sad." " Prayer is heart's ease to the gracious soul."—D.

> " Lord, what a change within us one short hour,
>   Spent in thy presence, will prevail to make ;
>   What heavy burdens from our bosoms take ;
>   What parched grounds refresh as with a shower ! " (Trench).

Vers. 11 (21, 23, 28). (SHILOH.)—*Vows.* "And she vowed a vow." The first recorded instance of a religious vow is that of Jacob (Gen. xxviii. 20 ; xxxi. 13). Under a sense of obligation to God, he entered into a spontaneous and solemn engagement before him to do what he believed would be pleasing in his sight, joining with it the desire of obtaining certain benefits at his hand. He did not, as it has been said, make a bargain with God ; but gratefully repeated what had been virtually promised (" if " or " since God will be with me," &c.), and simply desired those blessings, without which it would be impossible for him to fulfil his purpose. Directions concerning the practice of making vows were given in the Law (Levit. xxvii. ; Num. vi., xxx.). The age of the judges was an age of vows. " Then appears a new power of the age, the binding vow—a spasmodic impulse, dangerous to many, yet in the greatest emergencies of life indispensable ; bracing up the deepest energies, and working the greatest marvels ; often renovating, or else entirely transforming, whole nations and religions ; assuming a thousand forms, and in all, while the first fidelity endures, exercising an indomitable power " (Ewald). Jephthah — Samson — Samuel. Vows are seldom alluded to in the New Testament (Luke i. 15 ; Acts xviii. 18 ; xxi. 23). In some of their forms, and in so far as they might embody a *legal* spirit, they are done away. But they are not prohibited ; and, understood as denoting a solemn binding of ourselves to the service of God, or resolutions and engagements made before him to perform or omit certain definite acts, they are often needful and beneficial. Consider that—

I. THERE ARE CERTAIN THINGS TO WHICH THEY MAY LAWFULLY PERTAIN. 1. *Things over which we possess a rightful authority.* We may not vow what does not belong to us. 2. *Things which ought to be done, independently of vows ;* but the obligation of which is felt for the first time, or with unusual force. 3. *Things which are in themselves indifferent ;* being right or wrong according to the individual conscience, but with reference to which a vow creates a new obligation. The vow of a Nazarite to abstain from wine, &c. 4. Things, more particularly, that relate to the use of (1) *property* (Gen. xxviii. 22 ; 1 Cor. xvi. 2) ; (2) *time ;* (3) *influence* over others, especially in the training of children ; (4) the *various powers of body and soul* (Rom. xii. 1).

II. THERE ARE SPECIAL OCCASIONS ON WHICH THEY ARE APPROPRIATELY MADE. 1. *Severe trouble*—personal affliction, nearness to death, bereavement ; bringing the invisible and eternal nigh, teaching dependence on God, and exciting desire for his help (Isa. lxvi. 13, 14). 2. *Singular prosperity*—unexpected recovery from illness, extraordinary deliverance from danger, unwonted providential and spiritual benefits, temporal success. 3. *Spiritual exercises*—in public worship, private meditation, religious profession. 4. *Starting-points of life*—a birthday, the first day of a new year, the commencement of a fresh enterprise. These things are often occasions of spiritual illumination and impression, mountain heights that rise above the mists of ordinary life ; and it is well to embody the views and feelings then entertained in fixed purposes, definite resolutions, solemn vows for future guidance and help. "Vow, and pay unto the Lord your God" (Ps. lxxvi. 11).

III. THEY SHOULD ALWAYS BE MADE IN A PROPER SPIRIT. With—1. *Due delibera-tion* (Eccles. v. 2), so as to ascertain "what the will of the Lord is," and what we may reasonably hope to accomplish, lest they should become a burden and tempta-tion. 2. *A sense of dependence on Divine grace ;* and not in a self-righteous spirit, as if our service were exceedingly meritorious, and deserved to be richly rewarded. 3. *Humble and earnest prayer for the aid of the Divine Spirit.* Vows made in our own strength are "as the morning cloud and the early dew." 4. *Faith in Christ,* the perfect pattern of self-surrender and self-sacrifice, the way of approach to God, the medium of Divine blessing. "Bind the sacrifice with cords, even unto the horns of the altar" (Ps. cxviii. 27).

IV. WHEN MADE THEY OUGHT TO BE STRICTLY FULFILLED. Their making is optional, voluntary ; not so their performance. Their obligation — 1. *Changes not with a change of feeling,* even with respect to those things which are, in themselves, indifferent.

> "The things which are in insight willed
> Must be in hours of gloom fulfilled."

2. *Rests upon the same ground as that of the obligation of promises generally,* and is specially strong because of their sacred character. 3. *Is enforced by the conse-quences of their observance or neglect.* Their fulfilment is a means of grace. Broken vows undermine the foundations of character, interfere with Divine fellowship, and pave the way to destruction (Eccles. v. 4—6). 4. *Requires their performance with sincerity* (in the sense intended, not by the substitution of something else, not in part merely), *cheerfulness* (Ps. cxvi. 17, 18), and *promptitude.* "Defer not." "There is a Greek mythical story of the treatment of the goddess Juno by Mandra-bulus the Samian. This man had, under her auspices, and by her directions, dis-covered a golden mine. In the first flush of gratitude he vowed to her a golden ram ; however, he presently exchanged that for a silver one, and again that for a very small brass one, and that for nothing at all" (Trench). "It is storied of a merchant that in a great storm at sea vowed to Jupiter, if he would save him and his vessel, to give him a hecatomb. The storm ceaseth, and he bethinks that a hecatomb was unreasonable ; he resolves on seven oxen. Another tempest comes, and now again he vows the seven at least. Delivered, then also he thought that seven were too many, and one ox would serve his turn. Yet another peril comes, and now he vows solemnly to fall no lower ; if he might be rescued, an ox Jupiter shall have. Again freed, the ox sticks in his stomach, and he would fain draw his devotion to a lower rate ; a sheep was sufficient. But at last, being set ashore, he thought a sheep too much, and purposeth to carry to the altar only a few dates. But by the way he eats up the dates, and lays on the altar only the shells. After this manner do many perform their vows" (Adams, vol. i. p. 112).—D.

Vers. 13—18. (SHILOH.)—*Undeserved rebuke.* The duty of rebuking others when they do evil is often enjoined (Levit. xix. 17 ; 1 Thess. v. 14), and is especially incumbent on those who occupy positions of authority. But how seldom is rebuke given or received aright ! Eli, the aged judge and high priest, sitting on the judg-ment-seat, "by a post of the temple of the Lord," and observing a woman exhibiting signs of excited feeling, severely rebuked her for being intoxicated with wine. In his words, and what followed, we have rebuke—

I. UTTERED WITHOUT JUSTICE (vers. 13, 14). There was certainly apparent ground for the judgment he formed ; for excitement caused by wine was probably no uncommon thing at the tabernacle in those corrupt times. But he did not "judge righteously" (John vii. 24). Learn—1. That apparent ground for censure is often found on inquiry to be really groundless. Therefore there should be proof before reproof. 2. That the most excellent are often the most misjudged, especially in religious matters. Whilst sensual excitement was often seen, spiritual excitement was rare. Religious services were formal, cold, and dead ; and holy fervour was naturally misunderstood and misinterpreted by superficial observers. So they who were filled with the Spirit on the day of Pentecost were accused of being filled with new wine. And men of large views, disinterested motives, and exalted aims are often condemned by the ignorant, selfish, and unspiritual. 3. That the highest in authority are liable to err in judgment. Infallibility belongs to God alone. The assumption of it by men is rebuked by their own manifest mistakes and failings, and is an insult to heaven. 4. That persons who think that they see clearly the faults of others are commonly blind to their own transgressions (Matt. vii. 3 ; Rom. ii. 1). Eli was unconscious of his own easily besetting sin, which consisted in his indulgent treatment of his children and their vices. 5. That those who censure others should themselves be undeserving of censure. 6. That our own exposure to judgment should make us cautious in passing judgment on others (Matt. vii. 1—5). 7. That it is the part of charity to put the best construction on their conduct. "Believeth all things ; hopeth all things." Eli exhibited a want of knowledge, consideration, charity, and tenderness. How different the High Priest and Judge "with whom we have to do"!

II. BORNE WITH MEEKNESS. Hannah was not only innocent of the vice for which she was rebuked, but was at the time uttering a vow that if the Lord would give her a son he should be a Nazarite, and a life-long protest against that vice and other prevailing evils. Her fervour of spirit was equalled by her calmness, self-control, and discreet answer to the reproach of Eli (vers. 15, 16). Learn—1. That resentment and retaliation toward unjust accusers afford no evidence of innocence. Some persons when rebuked fly into a passion, and utter worse judgments on others than have been pronounced on themselves. 2. That a good conscience can be calm under accusation. 3. That appearances which seem to justify censure should be as fully as possible explained. 4. That those who say they are not guilty of sin should show their abhorrence of sin. "Call not thine handmaid a daughter of Belial" ('a worthless woman'). In her view intoxication was a great sin, and deserving of severe condemnation. 5. How beautiful is "the ornament of a meek and quiet spirit." 6. To look to Christ as the perfect pattern of the spirit here exhibited, and the source of the grace which is needed for its exercise (1 Pet. ii. 20—23). "Let me find grace in thy sight."

III. TURNED INTO BENEDICTION (vers. 17, 18). Learn—1. That those who see that they have erred in judgment should be ready to acknowledge their error. 2. That meekness and patience are adapted to change a severe reprover into a kind friend. 3. That the endurance of rebuke in a right spirit is often a means of obtaining a favourable answer to prayer. God himself spoke through the voice of the high priest (ver. 17; John xi. 51). 4. That it also causes perturbation and sorrow to give place to peace and joy (Matt. v. 5, 11). "Strive to rejoice when others use towards thee words of injury or rebuke, or despise thee. For a rich treasure lies hid beneath this dust ; and, if thou take it willingly, thou wilt soon find thyself rich unperceived by those who have bestowed this gift upon thee" (Scupoli).—D.

Vers. 13—18.—*Harsh judgment meekly answered.* We hear much of the mothers of eminent men, and it is easy to see whence Samuel derived his elevation of mind, his religious temperament, and the natural aptitude to be a seer and prophet of God. It was from his mother—the sensitive, poetical, devout, unselfish Hannah. Her prayer at the house of the Lord in Shiloh shows her in a noble light. She asked for no vengeance on her adversary Peninnah, who had so often taunted her, but only for a son whom she might devote as a pure Nazarite to Jehovah's service. Her thought recurred to the last great judge of Israel—the Nazarite Samson. The work which he might have performed had been very imperfectly done ; and Hannah's devout and patriotic wish was to give birth to one who might repair the failure of Samson, as well as remedy the evil wrought by the sons of Eli, and work a great deliverance for Israel.

I. PIOUS EMOTION HARSHLY CENSURED. If Hannah's prayer had been mocked by the profane, it had not surprised her; but this was her trial, that the venerable priest, whose duty it was to recognise and encourage religious aspiration, cruelly miscon-strued her agitation, and charged her with wickedness. Eli was weak towards men, stern to a woman. He could not restrain his own sons, but he could speak sharply and severely to Hannah. The only palliation of his readiness to impute evil to her lies in the fact that, through his weakness, there had come to be a great license of manners at the time, and women of Israel misconducted themselves at the very seat of worship. Eli took Hannah for one of these, and her holy ardour for the agitation of one unduly excited by wine. Religious emotion, especially in persons of a sensi-tive and pensive nature, may resemble the effect of "wine wherein is excess" in the eyes of a careless or unsympathetic observer. And this applies to the joyful as well as to the sorrowful in spirit. On the day of Pentecost, when the power of the Spirit descended on the disciples of our Lord, and joy in the Holy Ghost expressed itself in their looks and words, some of the bystanders began to mock and say, "These men are full of new wine." That religious fervour should be unappreciated by worldly minds need cause no wonder. That tears and prayers poured forth before the unseen God should be despised as drivelling superstition, or the flush of spiritual gladness derided as irrational frenzy, by persons of a cold, unbelieving temper, is what may be expected. But it is hard to bear misconstruction from men like Eli, who ought to understand that the spirit of man or woman sometimes faints, sometimes leaps for joy before the Lord.

II. THE EQUANIMITY OF A GOOD CONSCIENCE. When one is quite conscious of innocence he can meet accusations with calmness, and repel them without passion or bitterness. If Hannah had been unguarded in eating or drinking at the feast after the sacrifice in Shiloh, she would probably have given a sharp answer to Eli, and exonerated herself from his charge with some heat of temper. But her conscience was quite clear in the matter. From her vow to make the son for whose birth she prayed a Nazarite, we infer that she was strongly sensible of the evils which indulg-ence in wine, and consequent licentious excess, had brought on the nation. So her answer to the priest, while firm, was calm, and even meek: "No, my Lord, I am a woman of a sorrowful spirit."

III. THE TRUE RESOURCE OF THE SORROWFUL. "I have poured out my soul before the Lord." Hannah abhorred the kind of evil of which Eli accused her. "Count not thine handmaid for a daughter of Belial." Alas, how many, because they are in low spirits, or vexed with their lot, seek exhilaration in wine or strong drink! It is a gross and dangerous consolation, fit for children of Belial, not for children of God. "Is any afflicted? Let him pray." Is any anxious? Let him by prayer and supplication, with thanksgiving, make his request known to God. To be excited with wine is to have the imagination and passions fired through the flesh and the senses. For a time care or grief may be forgotten, and the mind may seem to become gay and brilliant; but as the appetite grows, and the fallacious pleasure beguiles, there ensues degradation and sorrow upon sorrow; the mind is clouded and enfeebled, and the heart made selfish and gross. How different from the excitement of the praying heart that is "filled with the Spirit!" This takes hold of the best and highest part of our nature, and from this acts on the whole man—sub-dues sensual passion, scatters delusion, and while it may for a time agitate the frame, as Hannah's was agitated, never disturbs or unhinges the regulative principles of reason and conscience within.

IV. THE COMFORT AFTER PRAYER. Whatever the worth of Eli's personal character, his office gave weight to his words; and when he invoked from the God of Israel an answer to Hannah's petition, she received his words with reverence, and went home with a glad assurance in her heart. Have not we a great High Priest who mis-understands no one, requires no corrective explanation, discourages no suppliant; and is it not he who has said, "What things soever ye desire, when ye pray, believe that ye receive them, and ye shall have them"? Look to Jesus, and where is your burden? It is gone. Where are your tears? They are wiped away. Where is your desired thing, your Samuel? It is at hand. Go your way when you have poured out your prayer, for he has heard you, and "let your countenance be no more sad."—F.

Vers. 19—28. (RAMAH and SHILOH.)—*Samuel's birth and infancy.* (*References*— 1 Chron. xxix. 29, "the seer;" Ps. xcix. 9; Jer. xv. 1; Acts iii. 24; xiii. 20; Heb. xii. 32; Apoc. Ecclus. xlvi. 13—20.) Consolation and hope were from the first associated with the birth of children (Gen. iii. 15; iv. 1, 25; v. 29; xxi. 6). More than ordinary joy (John xvi. 24) was felt at the birth of Samuel by his mother, because of the peculiar circumstances connected therewith, and the expectations entertained by her of the good which he might effect for Israel. Often as she looked upon her God-given infant she would think, "What manner of child shall this be?" (Luke i. 66), and ask, "How shall we order the child, and how shall we do unto him?" (Judges xiii. 12). Nor did she fail to do her utmost towards the fulfil-ment of her exalted hopes. The child was—

I. REGARDED AS A DIVINE GIFT (Ps. cxxvii. 4). Every little infant bears the impress of the "Father of spirits" (James iii. 9).

> "Trailing clouds of glory do we come
> From God, who is our home."

The gift of a fresh, new, mysterious human life, with its vast capabilities, is a *great gift,* and demands *grateful acknowledgment* of the Divine goodness; but it is not an *absolute gift;* it is rather a *trust* which involves serious responsibilities on the part of those into whose hands it is placed. God says in effect, "Take this child," &c. (Exod. ii. 9).

II. DESIGNATED BY AN APPROPRIATE NAME (ver. 20). Samuel = heard of God. "The mother names, the father assents, God approves, and time confirms the nomina-tion" (Hunter). Like other personal names in the Bible, it was full of significance; being a *grateful memorial* of the goodness and faithfulness of God in the past, and a *constant incentive* to faith and prayer in the future. "Our very names should mind us of our duty." The name "Samuel" was uttered by the Lord as mindful of his history, and recognising his special relation to himself (ch. iii. 10). The name of a child is not an unimportant matter, and it should be given with due consideration. When parents give their children names borne by excellent men, they should train them to follow in the footsteps of such men.

III. NURTURED WITH MOTHERLY TENDERNESS (vers. 22—25). His mother was herself his nurse (ver. 23), not intrusting him to others, and not neglecting him, whereby many young lives are sacrificed; but thoughtfully, carefully, and constantly ministering to his physical needs, praying over him, and directing his thoughts, with the earliest dawn of reason, toward the Lord of hosts. That she might the more perfectly fulfil her trust, she remained at home, and went not up to Shiloh until he was weaned. Her absence from the sanctuary was justifiable, her worship at home was acceptable, and the service which she rendered to her child was a service rendered to God and to his people. "A mother's teachings have a marvellous vitality in them; there is a strange living power in that good seed which is sown by a mother's hand in her child's heart in the early dawn of the child's being, when they two are alone together, and the mother's soul gushes forth on her child, and the child listens to his mother as a God; and there is a deathless potency in a mother's prayers and tears for those whom she has borne which only God can estimate" (W. L. Alexander). "Who is best taught? He that is taught of his mother" ('Talmud').

IV. PRAYED OVER WITH FATHERLY SOLICITUDE. Elkanah consented to the vow of his wife (Num. xxx. 6, 7), and appears to have made it his own (ver. 21). He was zealous for its performance, and whilst he agreed with her in the desire of its post-ponement for a brief period, he expressed the wish in prayer, "Only the Lord establish his word" (ver. 23). "*Word,* that is, May he fulfil what he designs with him, and has promised by his birth (vers. 11, 20). The words refer, therefore, to *the boy's destination to the service of God,* which the Eternal has in fact acknowledged by the partial fulfilment of the mother's wish" (Bunsen). HIS PRAYER indicates, with respect to the Divine word—1. *Confidence in its truth.* He believed (1) that it was *his* word which had been uttered by the high priest (ver. 17); (2) that its Divine origin and faithfulness had been in part confirmed by his own act (ver. 20); and (3) that it would be completely established by his bringing about the end designed. 2. *Desire of its fulfilment.* (1) As a matter of great importance. (2) Deeply felt. "Only." (3) Through the continued and gracious operation of God. "*The Lord* establish his word." 3. *Obedience to its requirements.* In order to its establishment, co-operation on their part was—(1) Necessary. God's purposes and promises are fulfilled in connection with human endeavour, and not independently of it. (2) Obligatory. It had been solemnly promised by them, and was a condition of the bestowment of the Divine blessing. (3) Fully resolved upon. "His father used to open his breast when he was asleep and kiss it in prayer over him, as it is said of Origen's father, that the Holy Ghost would take possession thereof." ('Life of Sir Thomas Browne').

V. CONDUCTED TO THE HOUSE OF THE LORD. As soon as he was weaned (the first step of separate, independent life) "she took him up with her" (ver. 24), and "they brought the child to Eli" (ver. 25). Children are in their right place in the temple (Matt. xxi. 15, 16), and their praises are acceptable to the Lord. Even infants (sucklings) belong to the kingdom of heaven, and are capable of being blessed by him (Matt. xix. 13). Therefore the "little ones" should be brought unto him (Matt. xviii. 14).

VI. DEDICATED TO A LIFE-LONG SERVICE (vers. 25—28), *i. e.* a continual (and not a limited or periodical) service at the sanctuary as a Levite, and an entire (and not a partial) service as a Nazarite. It was done (1) with a burnt offering, (2) accompanied by a thankful acknowledgment of the goodness of God in answer to prayer offered on the same spot several years previously, and (3) in a full surrender of the child. "My child shall be entirely and absolutely thy servant. I give up all my maternal rights. I desire to be his mother only in so far as that he shall owe his existence to me; after that I give him up to thee" (Chrysostom). "For this child I prayed, and the Lord hath granted me my request which I asked of him; therefore I also make him one asked of the Lord all the days that he liveth; he is asked of the Lord" (Keil). So the vow was performed. And in the spirit of this dedication all parents should give back to God "the children which he hath given them."

VII. FOLLOWED BY PARENTAL PRAYERS AND THANKSGIVINGS. "He (Elkanah) worshipped the Lord there" (ver. 28). "And Hannah prayed, and said, My heart rejoiceth in the Lord" (ch. ii. 1). "And Elkanah went to Ramah to his house" (ch. ii. 11). The sacrifice made in leaving the child behind was great, but it was attended, through Divine grace, with great joy. The more any one gives to God, the more God gives back to him in spiritual blessing. Hannah felt little anxiety or fear for the safety of her child, for she believed that he would "keep the feet of his saints" (ch. ii. 9). What holy influences ever rest on children whose parents pray for them "without ceasing!" and what multitudes have by such means been eternally saved!—D.

> "The boy was vowed
> Unto the temple service. By the hand
> She led him, and her silent soul, the while,
> Oft as the dewy laughter of his eye
> Met her sweet serious glance, rejoiced to think
> That aught so pure, so beautiful, was hers,
> To bring before her God.
>
> I give thee to thy God—the God that gave thee,
> A well-spring of deep gladness to my heart!
> And precious as thou art,
> And pure as dew of Hermon, he shall have thee,
> My own, my beautiful, my undefiled!
> And thou shalt be his child.
>
> Therefore, farewell!—I go, my soul may fail me,
> As the stag panteth for the water brooks,
> Yearning for thy sweet looks.—

But thou, my first-born, droop not, nor bewail me !
Thou in the Shadow of the Rock shalt dwell,
The Rock of Strength.—Farewell ! ” (Mrs. Hemans).

EXPOSITION.

CHAPTER II.

HANNAH'S SONG OF PRAISE (vers. 1—
10). Ver. 1.—**And Hannah prayed and
said.** Like the Magnificat, Hannah's hymn
of thanksgiving begins with the temporal
mercies accorded to herself, but rises immediately into the realms of prophecy, foretelling Christ's kingdom and the triumphs
of the Church. From this prophetic element,
common more or less to all the hymns of the
Bible, most of them have been used in Christian worship, and still merit a place in it,
though we in the liturgy of the Church of
England now use only two, taken both from
the New Testament. In ver. 1, in four strophes
of equal length, Hannah declares how, first,
her *heart*, the centre with the Hebrews, not
merely of the physical, but also of the moral
and intellectual life, rejoices in Jehovah ;
while the exaltation of her *horn*, the symbol
of strength and vigour, signifies that this
inward joy is accompanied, or even occasioned, by the changed circumstances of her
outward lot. Her *mouth*, therefore, is opened
wide over her enemies, yet not for cursing
and in bitterness, but for joyful praise of the
God who has answered her prayers. It is
his salvation, the being delivered by him,
that makes her thus burst forth into thanksgiving. It is a proof too of her faith and
spirituality that she thus refers all to
Jehovah.

In ver. 2 she gives her reasons for this
holy joy. The first is God's absolute holiness ;
the second his absolute existence, in which
she finds the proof of his holiness. Hannah
may have meant to express only the language
of piety, but she also stated a primary
philosophical truth, which was early grasped
by the deeply religious instinct of the Hebrews, that outside of God is no existence.
Many necessary deductions follow from this
fundamental truth, that God alone absolutely exists, and that all other existence is
secondary and derived ; but no deduction is
more certain than Hannah's own, that such
a Being must be absolutely holy. In calling
him a **rock** she assigns to him strength,
calm, immovable, enduring, but a strength
which avails for the safety of his people
(comp. Deut. xxxii. 4, 15 ; Ps. xviii. 2).
For rocks, as being capable of easy defence,
formed the nucleus of most ancient towns,
and continued to serve as their citadels.
In ver. 3 she appeals to God's omniscience,
"for Jehovah is a God of knowledges," the

pl. being intensive, and signifying every
kind of knowledge. As too he weighs and
judges human actions, how can men venture
to talk so arrogantly before him, lit. *so
proudly, proudly.* The last clause is one of
those numerous places in which there is a
doubt whether the Hebrew word *lo* means
not, or *by him.* If the negative sense be
taken, which the Hebrew spelling favours,
the rendering will be "though actions be
not weighed." Though wicked actions be
not immediately punished, yet Jehovah is
cognisant of them, and in due time will
requite.

In vers. 4—8 Hannah illustrates the
working of this attribute of the Deity by enumerating the vicissitudes of human events,
which are not the result of chance, but of
that omniscience combined with holiness
which she has claimed for Jehovah in vers.
2, 3. She begins with the vicissitudes of
war ; but these are not more remarkable than
those of peace, by which the **full**, the rich
and wealthy, have to descend to the position
of a hireling ; while those previously hungry
have ceased, *i. e.* from labour, and keep
holiday. In a nation of small proprietors,
where the land was tilled by the owner
and those "born in his house," the position
of the hireling, the "mean white" of the
southern States of America, was lower than
that of the slave, especially in Judæa, where
the slave was more in the position of a vassal
than of a serf or forced labourer. In the next
clause the translation may either be, "She
that was long barren hath borne seven," or,
"Until the barren" &c. ; *i. e.* these vicissitudes may even reach so far as to make a
barren woman the mother of seven, *i. e.* of
a perfect number of children, happily generalised in Ps. cxiii. 9 into "a joyful mothei
of children." But see Ruth iv. 15 ; Jer. xv.
9. In this there is also a typical reference
to the long barrenness of the Gentile world,
to be followed by a fruitfulness far exceeding
that of the Jewish Church, while it, prolific
once in patriarchs, and prophets, and saints,
is now comparatively sterile. In ver. 6 "the
grave," Heb. *Sheol*, is "the pit," the hollow
vault underground, which is the dwelling of
the dead. Lit., therefore, Hannah's words
might seem to imply a belief in the resurrection ; but her meaning rather was that God
brings a man to the very brink of the grave,
and then, when all hope seems past, raises him
up again. In ver. 8 **beggar** is simply *needy*,
but the expressions *dust* and *dunghill* add

dishonour to his poverty. **To set** might more correctly be translated *to make them sit ;* sitting, especially on a raised seat, being a mark of honour among Orientals, who generally squat on mats on the ground. In the next clause the A. V. particularises what in the Heb. is quite general. "He will make them possess (or enjoy) a glorious throne." Their seat among the princes is not inherited, but acquired ; and though promoted thus to a place among men of hereditary rank, and given an honourable position among them, yet it was not necessarily "the throne of glory," the highest seat. Still even this was quite possible ; for while the tribal chiefs and heads of fathers'-houses obtained their rank by inheritance, nevertheless, in early days the judges, and among them Eli and Samuel, acquired rank and power for themselves. Subsequently, under the kings, the great officers of state took their place along with the hereditary princes, but were dependent upon royal favour. In the last clause the word rendered *pillars* is rare, being found only here and in ch. xiv. 4. In both places the ancient versions are uncertain as to its signification, but in the latter it can only mean a crag, or mass of rock. If then the rock-masses of the earth are Jehovah's, and he can lift up and poise upon them the inhabited world (Heb. *tebol*), how much more easily can he raise up a man !

Ver. 9. — **The feet of his saints.** The Heb. written text (*ch'tib*) has *his saint*, sing. ; but the word really means not *saint*, i. e. one sanctified and holy, but *pious*, i. e. one lovingly disposed towards God. The sense, therefore, is not affected by the number, but the sing. is more forcible. "He will guard the steps, the earthly course, of each one that loveth him ;" while over against this watchful providence, ever exerted for the safe-keeping of all who love the light, stands God's punitive justice, whereby the wicked are finally brought down to the dark silence of the grave. For they had only human strength and prowess upon which to depend, and no man can sustain himself in the manifold conflict of life without help from above.

Ver. 10.—**The adversaries.** In the Heb. the nouns are again sing., though the verb is pl., showing that they are to be taken collectively. Lit. the translation is, "Jehovah—they shall be broken in pieces, whoever it be that contendeth with him ;" the word having reference to contentions in a court of law, and the whole verse keeping the administration of justice in view. It proceeds, "Upon him he shall thunder in heaven ;" i. e. Jehovah, seated on his throne in heaven, shall, as the supreme Judge, utter the sentence ; and thunder was to the Hebrew God's voice. **He shall judge the ends of the earth,** i. e. the whole earth up to its remotest quarters. The last distich is remarkable. It is a distinct prophecy of David's kingdom, and of the king as the anointed one, but looking onwards to the Messiah, David's greater Son. So distinct a reference to a king before a king existed has made Ewald and others regard the whole hymn as an interpolation of later times. But already Hannah's thoughts had risen to a higher level than the fortunes of the literal Israel. In claiming for Jehovah, her covenant God, the righteous government of the whole world, she prepares our minds for the corresponding thought of Jehovah being the universal Saviour. Very probably the whole national mind was set upon having a king to enable them to make head against the Philistines long before, under Samuel, the desire became so strong as to be irresistible. The thought of a king was in no respect alien from the Jewish commonwealth (Deut. xvii. 14). They had wished Gideon to hold this office (Judges viii. 22) ; Jotham's parable in Judges ix. described the nation as eager to be thus governed, but the better minds as bent on declining so dangerous a pre-eminence. There is very much to prove that the nation had come to regard the appointment of a king as an eventual necessity, however long delayed. But not here only, but everywhere, the Jewish mind constantly brooding upon the future. Hannah does no more than every patriarch and saint and prophet of the old dispensation. Prophecies such as that in Gen. xlix. 10 filled the hearts of all alike. And though the present longings of the nation for a king make Hannah's words not unnatural even in their lower sense, yet the truer exposition is that which acknowledges in Israel a people raised up for a special purpose, and the bestowal by God upon its seers for the carrying out of this purpose of the gift of prophecy. And it was this extraordinary gift which bent and shaped the mind of the nation, and filled it with future aspirations ; and not a causeless state of the national mind which, excited by vague hopes, made men from time to time give utterance to anticipations which by some strange coincidence always came true.

HOMILETICS.

Vers. 1—10.—*Salvation.* The facts implied and indicated in the song are—1. Hannah's deliverance from grief and realisation of desire are perfected. 2. God is recognised as the author of the great salvation.   3. Under Divine inspiration Hannah sees in her own personal experience a type of various triumphs which God achieves for his people.   4. She is conscious of an overwhelming joy in her own deliverance, and in the prevision of future triumphs of the Church.   5. A clear and joyous recognition of Christ's final triumph as the climax of all.   The burden of this glorious song is the salvation wrought by God, and this may be considered as—

I. TYPICAL.   The term "salvation" is very common in the Old Testament, and its application is "exceeding broad," being inclusive of deliverance from evils and a realisation of positive good.   It may be applied to an episode in personal experience, as in the case of Hannah, David, and others; a soul's restoration to God through Christ; a nation's rescue from calamity and elevation to relative influence, as when Israel was delivered from the waters of the Red Sea, and later, from the Assyrian hosts; the deliverance of the Church from persecution, as in apostolic days and subsequently; and especially the completion of Christ's triumph over all enemies and the gathering into one of the redeemed children of God (Titus ii. 13; Heb. ix. 28; Rev. vii. 9—17).   The episode in the life of Hannah was *typical of all other salvations* to be wrought by the same merciful God.   As in the physical world the trained eye can detect what are called "typical forms," so in the records of God's dealings with the saints the spiritually enlightened can see in the personal experience of individuals a foreshadowing of numerous instances yet to occur in human experience.   *Omnia in Uno* will hold true here.   The elements of all salvations are found in the blessing vouchsafed to the "woman of sorrowful spirit."   For there is in her case, as in all, a deep *human need*, arising from a pressure of a heavy burden, and the *non*-realisation of the very end for which life was supposed to be given; utter *despair of human* resources for the removal of the evil and the acquisition of the good; *Divine energy graciously acting* directly on the hidden forces by which sorrow or joy are governed and produced; *Divine patience in working out* the processes by which the want and sorrow shall be made to pass away; *completeness of result* in the bestowment of the very boon so long desired and waited for; *connection of the result* attained with some *ulterior issue* of still wider blessing; and *employment* throughout of *visible and invisible second causes* in working out the purposes of mercy.   Each item found reality in Hannah's experience, and has its counterpart in our deliverance from trouble; in the restoration of the lost soul; in the rescue of a nation or Church from destruction; and in the completion of the desire of him who from the travail of his soul looked on through the ages, saw, and was satisfied.   Every deliverance of every saint now is a shadowing forth and a prediction sure and certain of the great salvation, in the bliss of which Christ, and angels, and men shall share.

II. OCCASION OF JOY.   Naturally salvation in every form brings joy.   It is *the* great event of the life.   It means freedom, rest, enrichment, full, sunny favour of God.   Hannah could not but sing.   Moses led the joy of Israel on the shores of the Red Sea.   When Saul became Paul the Churches enjoyed "comfort of the Holy Ghost."   The fatted calf and dance awaited the restored prodigal son.   The very advent of the one true Saviour awoke the chorus of the skies, and heaven will resound with the joyous acclaim of innumerable hosts when the woes of earth are past, and all power submits to Christ (Rev. xix. 1).   It is noteworthy that the *joy awakened* by accomplished salvation is *not a mere selfish delight* in one's own happiness.   It is *joy in God*.   In "*thy* salvation" do I rejoice.   "In the Lord" is my "horn exalted."   "The heart" is not set on the bliss of a Samuel's love, it "rejoiceth *in the Lord*."   Again, it is joy in God *saving through his Anointed*.   The "promised seed," the foreordained Messiah, was the spring of all inspired Hebrew expectation of blessing.   The birth of a son called forth Hannah's song.   It is curiously sweet to notice how like the echo of some distant melody is this song, reminding us of a Child more holy than even Samuel.   Surely in the invisible spheres angels recognised here the substance of that hymn they on a later day sang over the plains of Bethlehem.   In that severe but blessed discipline of years the spirit of Hannah had been trained to pass over in vision to a salvation more perfect than what Samuel would effect for Israel, and by a Child more truly given of God. The songs of faith and of fulfilment find alike their inspiration in "his King" and "my Saviour." But the relationship to his chosen One grows closer and dearer as the ages roll on. What shall it be at last! And what joy will it awaken! Also, the *condition of sharing in this joy is twofold*, being personally a saved one, and cherishing full sympathy with "his King." Hannah, blessed with a great deliverance from sorrow and desolation, could sing and, laying all at the feet of God in holy sympathy with the coming kingdom, she found inspiration for song beyond the range of her own experience. A "new song" is learnt on earth, in so far as its first notes, by all who have known in their personal experience *the* salvation of God; and it becomes sweeter and more inspired as the freed spirit sees by faith the blessed day when the ends of the earth shall also see the King in his beauty.

III. REVELATION OF DIVINE PERFECTIONS. In some sense all God's acts are revelations. Nature, as we call the beautiful system around us, is but the shadow of the Eternal Presence. The Eternal Power and Godhead are clearly seen through the visible creation. In the Incarnation of God in Christ we have, therefore, a higher expression of a general truth; so that in one respect the most stupendous and mysterious of all supernatural facts is in keeping with Nature. Especially is every instance of salvation, whether typical or antitypical, individual or national, a revelation to the universe of the ever-blessed One. From Hannah's deliverance from sorrow and desolation, on through the ages of mercy, to Christ's final victory over death and sin, the same attributes are revealed in the deeds and processes by which the salvation in each instance is effected. 1. *Mercy*, as seen in compassion shown to the sorrowful and helpless. 2. *Holiness*, inasmuch as the salvation is wrought out *against* evil powers and persons, *for* only good and pure issues, *by* exacting and nourishing into maturity holy, unselfish motives, and ordaining suffering and deferred good only for pure and blissful ends. 3. *Power*, demonstrating that "beside" him "there is none," as seen in complete control over the hidden forces of Nature, and full realisation of all that is promised. 4. *Wisdom*, counteracting the devices of the proud, and causing the bitterest grief and protracted suffering to contribute at last to depth and fulness of joy. 5. *Faithfulness*, unshaken and firm as a "rock," insuring that all the strength and wisdom of the Divine nature shall be exercised for the final bestowment of the covenanted blessings. The *retrospect of a personal history* was to Hannah the means of *reading the outlines of the manifestation of the Divine glory*, especially in the salvation of the Church. She, like us, saw only the beginnings of things. The remote glory shone through a glass darkly. It was for St. Paul and St. John to declare the same truth in fuller and more precise terms, as the one tells of the "manifold wisdom of God" being made known "by the Church" unto "principalities and powers in heavenly places," and the other, of him who by virtue of what he has wrought out for his redeemed is "worthy" of all that is due to the only Lord of glory. Men are now intent on studying the material framework of the universe; the day will come when the best minds will study with unbounded delight the perfections of God as seen in the restoration of spiritual order, beauty, and joy out of the chaos of sin and sorrow.

IV. INSTRUCTIVE TO THE WICKED. There was a time when the jealous and cruel Peninnah was proud in her strength and abundance. Also Pharaoh, and other oppressors of Israel, could boast of their power and resources. The infant Church in primitive times was as nothing in comparison with the numerical and social power of her enemy. The exceeding proud talk and arrogancy of men who proclaim their vast superiority in secular knowledge to the mass of Christians, is in keeping with the conduct of the kings and princes who "take counsel against the Lord and against his Anointed." But as Hannah's fear and trembling yielded to confidence and joy, consequent on the casting down of her proud enemy and the lifting up of the sorrowful spirit, so the same ever-recurring triumphs of the Redeemer, awakening in his people the song of salvation, reads out in clear and forcible terms the instructive lesson to the proud to "talk" no more, and to the arrogant to "shut their mouth," and to the seemingly prosperous that all "actions are weighed" by him who is a "God of knowledge." It is ever true that no weapon formed against God's children can prosper. In what God has effected for the lowly pious in time past, the proud, the wise, the strong may find instruction; and, if they will, learn both how vain it is to curse in heart or mouth whom God has blessed, and how important for themselves that they "kiss the Son," lest they perish, "while his wrath is kindled but a little."

V. INVOLVING GREAT REVERSIONS. Providence vindicated itself for former apparently unequal and undesirable distributions of favour by breaking the bows of the strong and giving strength to the feeble; by causing the self-satisfied Peninnah to feel the lack of a satisfaction not to be obtained by the cruel, and the yearning Hannah to want for nothing more. The once proud mother of many children, from causes in the home life, fails in her joys, while the unfruitful attains to the perfection of earthly bliss. In the one case hopes and joys are smitten; in the other, created. The rich in home delights becomes poor, by possibly erring sons, or enfeebled health; the poor and sorrowful is enriched with a treasure for the use of all ages. Thus does Hannah see in outline the reversions ever occurring in the working out of God's salvation in the individual, the nation, or the Church. 1. In the *human soul* saved by Christ, forces of evil once strong and self-satisfied, lacking nothing, and usurping authority, are brought low, enfeebled, made conscious of their impotence, and finally killed; while the poor, faint, struggling spirit of love and faith is, when once "made alive," girded with strength, satisfied with good, and made finally dominant over the entire nature. Doubts, fears, and mighty temptations are laid low. Hopes, joys, and victories of faith are called forth; and, as a final issue, the once outcast, unhappy soul is enriched with the full bliss of a child of God. 2. In *national affairs.* The strength of Egypt sinks in the sea; the helplessness of Israel puts on the strength of God. The boastful nations that in pride of their resources set aside the practice of righteousness, one by one are brought low by the corruption concealed beneath their material splendour; while the feeble people who live in the fear of God go from strength to strength, and "delight themselves in the abundance of peace." 3. In the *Church.* The wealth, power, and wisdom of Rome and Greece fell before the rising power and spiritual knowledge of poor fishermen. The mighty evils of an age are at length brought down, and the despised "things that are not" are caused to be the most potent and blessed of all agencies.

VI. TRACEABLE TO GOD. Well did Hannah know that her deliverance was of God, and not of man. In all the second causes co-operating towards the completion of her desire she, with true spiritual instinct, saw the work of the First Cause. "The Lord" it was who "killed and made alive." "The Lord" "brought low" the proud rival, and "lifted up" "the woman of sorrowful spirit." He it is who "keeps the feet of his saints," and causes the wicked at length "to be silent." So through the unfolding ages it is "the Lord" who works to destroy the evils of the soul, and to create and nourish the good. All the triumphs of the Church over political scheming, pseudo-learning, violent persecution, and satanic opposition are by the might and power of him who raiseth up the wise and good, checks the rage of man, and in the invisible sphere frustrates the "gates of hell." All things are of God, who worketh all and in all. It is not *crude anthropomorphism* that refers all the processes of individual, national, and Church salvation to the energy of God. It is the most *penetrating philosophy*, born of the inspiring Spirit of God. There are "pillars" or foundations, or bases, of all terrestrial things. We may call this a cause, and that an effect. We may clothe matter with qualities, and point out their uniform and necessary interaction. But still they are all traceable down to some original constitution inherent in the elemental forces and materials; and that constitution, that firm and grand arrangement of invisible "pillars" or bases, is what it is because God made it so, and for no other reason. Wisely and beautifully, therefore, does the prophetess anticipate the philosophies of the coming ages by referring all the agencies and powers involved in the accomplishing of salvation for men to "the Lord." Not unto us, but to thy name be the glory.

VII. CULMINATING IN CHRIST'S PERFECT REIGN. The prophetic eye looks on through the material disorder of Eli's day to a typical King in Zion. The order and prosperity of a David's reign are but the temporal shadow of the enduring order and unfading prosperity of the "Anointed," who is in the highest spiritual sense to "exalt" his "horn," and "judge the ends of the earth." What though, meanwhile, "adversaries" may combine, and the occasional "strength" of the wicked threaten to cast down "the saints;" he that sitteth in the heavens has in reserve his swift and awe-inspiring forces (Ps. ii.) to shatter all opposition, and ultimately insure a peaceful reign over mankind. It was some years before Peninnah's ground of annoyance to Hannah was removed, and the lowly one was raised to joy and full satisfaction ; so, proportionately to the vaster deliverance to be wrought out for mankind, it may require many centuries to cast down all foes and create and perfect the bliss of the redeemed. But the " strength " of the " King " will bring it to pass by a combination of invisible and visible forces more subtle and intricate, but not less obedient to his will, than those which brought a mother's joy to Hannah. Here we see the beautiful unity of all Scripture reference to the final triumph of Messiah. The "serpent's head " is to be " bruised " was consolation to our weeping ancestors, bereft of Eden. In him " all nations shall be blessed " was the grand assurance that made Abraham's life one of large sympathy with the future. " To him shall the gathering of the people be " was the solace of Jacob's dying hour. And thus, aided by Hannah's joyous song of victory, as though already real, the holy, blessed succession ran on, telling of the " kingdom " that " shall have no end," and the day when to the Name that is " above every name " every knee shall bow, and every tongue confess that he is Lord and Christ.

From this survey of truth concerning " salvation " note a few important *Practical truths :*—1. See here a beautiful instance of how *a single life's experience*, when under the holy discipline of God, may be rich *in instruction and inspiration for men in all ages.* This is brought about not by mere natural genius, but by a woman's pure and full consecration to Christ, and passionate desire to accelerate the advent of his kingdom. Happy they who can live so as to inspire and help posterity ! Let our life become a song of thanksgiving to our successors. This is possible to all in some degree. 2. An underlying current of *faith in Christ's complete triumph* runs through the ancient Church, and this should embolden us. True saints live much in the future, while not careless of present duties. There may be much inspiration for work from the prospect of what is to be. 3. The *effect of true faith* is to *enlarge the vision* and *broaden the sympathies.* Hannah's faith in a coming Christ caused her spirit to be open to those inspirations which carried the vision over the weary ages to the true golden age, and she felt with all the saints in all time. Religion of this kind becomes an expansive power in whatever nature it dwells. 4. The *proper unity of the Church* lies in the *one faith* which holds the life to Christ, whether to come, or having come ; and this will insure sympathy with his kingdom and with purity of life, as well as consecration of what is most precious to its realisation.

HOMILIES BY VARIOUS AUTHORS.

Vers. 1—10. (SHILOH.)—*Rejoicing in the Lord.* " My heart rejoiceth in the Lord." The song of Hannah, " the Magnificat of the Old Testament Church," was the outburst of her deep and holy joy in the Lord. Whilst watching over the infant Samuel at Ramah, she had silently pondered the ways of God, and the condition and prospects of his people and kingdom. After several years of absence from the central sanctuary at Shiloh, she appears once more at its entrance ; and, standing on the well-remembered spot where she had prayed in her distress, she fulfils her vow, and gives back to God the sacred treasure intrusted to her care. The trouble of former years recalled, provocations and inward conflicts ended, the sunshine of Divine favour experienced, cause her full heart to " bubble up like a fountain," and pour itself out in lofty poetic strains (ver. 1). What a contrast does this language indicate between her condition at the time of the previous visit and her condition now ! 1. Then her heart was full of grief ; now it " rejoiceth in the Lord." 2. Then her " horn " (*strength*, a figure taken from animals whose strength is in their horns, and here first employed. 2 Sam. xxii. 3 ; Luke i. 69) was trampled in the dust ; now it is " exalted," and she is endued with strength and honour " by the Lord." 3. Then her mouth was shut, in silent endurance, beneath the provocation of her adversary (ch. i. 6) ; now it is " enlarged," or opened in holy exultation, " above her enemies." 4. Then she was petitioning for the help of the Lord · now she " rejoices in his salvation," or the deliverance which he has wrought on her behalf; and it is "because" of this that she utters aloud her thanksgiving and praise. Her soul with all its powers, like a harp of many strings, touched by the Divine Spirit, gives forth exquisite music. "The Divinely-inspired song of Hannah is like a golden key for the interpretation of the whole book" (Wordsworth's 'Com.'). Compare this song with the song of Miriam and of Deborah. "Those compositions are grand, indeed, and elevated, and worthy of that inspiration which produced them; but they have not that tenderness of spirit, that personality of devotion, and that eucharistic anticipation of good things to come which characterise the hymn of Hannah" (Jebb, 'Sac. Lit.,' p. 395). It is the model after which the song of the Virgin Mary was formed, though there are notable points of difference between them. Considered in relation to the circumstances, and in its general nature, her song was a song of—1. *Gratitude.* Her prayer had been answered in the gift of a son; and, unlike those who look no further than the blessings bestowed upon them, she looked from the gift to the Giver, and praised him with joyful lips. Her heart rejoiced not in Samuel, but in the Lord. 2. *Dedication.* She had given back her child to God, and with him herself afresh. The more we give to God, the more our heart is enlarged, by the shedding abroad of his love therein, and filled with exceeding joy. 3. *Triumph;* remembering how she had been delivered from her adversaries in the past. 4. *Faith* in his continued help. 5. *Patriotism.* She sympathised with her people in their oppression by the Philistines; and, identifying herself with them, she almost lost sight of what God had done for her in the contemplation of what he would do for them. "From this particular mercy she had received from God she takes occasion, with an elevated and enlarged heart, to speak of the glorious things of God, and of his government of the world for the good of the Church." "She discerned in her own individual experience the general laws of the Divine economy, and its signification in relation to the whole history of the kingdom of God" (Auberlen). 6. *Prophetic hope.* She beheld the dawn of a new day, and was glad. In all and above all—7. *Joy in the Lord.* "My heart rejoiceth in the Lord;" not merely *before* him (Deut. xii. 12); but *in* him, as the Object and Source of its joy; in communion with and contemplation of him, and in the admiration, affection, and delight thereby excited. "My meditation of him shall be sweet: I will be glad in the Lord" (Ps. civ. 34). "When I think of God," said Haydn (on being asked the reason why the style of his music was so cheerful), "my soul is so full of joy that the notes come leaping and dancing from my pen." More especially observe that Hannah rejoiced in—

I. THE PERFECTIONS OF HIS CHARACTER (vers. 2, 3). Such perfections must not, indeed, be thought of as existing in God separate and distinct from each other; they are essential attributes of his living personality, and are all really present in his every purpose and act. What is here declared of God is, that—1. *He alone is "holy."* (1) *Supremely* excellent; whatever excellence exists in any other being falls infinitely short of his (Isa. vi. 3). (2) *Morally* perfect; invariably willing what is right and good; transcendently glorious in the view of conscience (Levit. xi. 44). (3) *Absolutely* existent, which is the ground of his excellence and perfection. "For there is none except thee." "God is the most perfect Being, and the cause of all other beings." His moral perfection is a peculiar distinction of the revelation which he made to his chosen people, needs to be specially magnified in times of corruption, and can only be rejoiced in by his saints. The conception which men form of God is an evidence of their own character, and exerts a powerful influence upon it (Luke i. 49). 2. *He alone is strong.* "A Rock." (1) Firm, unchanging, enduring; a sure foundation for confidence. (2) None can be compared unto him. They may not be trusted in, and they need not be feared. (3) Happy are those who can say, He is "our God." That which is a terror to others is a consolation to them. "The children of a king do not fear what their father has in his arsenal." "Let the inhabitant of the rock sing." But men often speak proudly and arrogantly (ver. 3), as if they were independent of him, and could do whatever they pleased. Let them not boast any more; for—3. *He is the All-wise;* a "God of knowledge" (lit., knowledges), of all knowledge. "The Lord knoweth the thoughts of man, that they are vanity" (Ps. xciv. 11; cxxxviii. 6). His knowledge is (1) immediate, (2) perfect, and (3) universal. And, 4. *He is the Judge of human actions.* He determines how far they may go before they are effectually checked by the manifestation of his power and wisdom (Thenius). "By strength shall no man prevail." He also forms a just estimate of their moral worth, and gives to every man his due reward. His righteousness and justice, as well as his strength and wisdom, when contemplated by the good, fill them with great joy.

II. The operations of his providence (vers. 4—8). The operations of Providence are the operations of God in the natural world, the laws of which are the uniform methods of his activity, and more especially in human affairs; wherein, whilst there is room for human freedom and prudence, and the use of means, his will encircles and overrules all things, and his hand moves in and through those events which are commonly attributed to chance or accident, and directs and controls them for the good of those who love him (Rom. viii. 28). In and by these operations—1. *He manifests the perfections of his character:* his holiness, power, wisdom, and justice. "The Lord is righteous in all his ways" (Ps. xcvii. 2; cxlv. 17). 2. He apportions the *different conditions* of men, and accomplishes the *varied changes* of their condition. (1) Makes the strong weak and the weak strong (ver. 4). (2) The full empty and the empty full (ver. 5). (3) Increases the lonely and diminishes the numerous family. (4) Brings into great distress, even to the verge of the grave, and again restores to health and prosperity (ver. 6). (5) Makes poor and makes rich. (6) Brings low and raises up. Prosperity and adversity alike, when received from the hand of God and used aright, become occasions of joy; and the changes of life are morally beneficial (Ps. lv. 19; Jer. xlviii. 11; James i. 9, 10). 3. He does great things, especially for the *lowly* (ver. 8). Stooping to them in their utmost need and shame (Ps. cxiii. 7, 8), and raising them to the highest honour and glory. "God does nothing else," said an ancient philosopher, "but humble the proud and exalt the lowly." "Set thyself in the lowest place, and the highest shall be given thee; for the more elevated the building is designed to be, the deeper must the foundations be laid. The greatest saints in the sight of God are the least in their own esteem; and the height of their glory is always in proportion to the depth of their humility" (Thomas à Kempis). 4. He *supports the earth* and all that is upon it. His dominion is supreme; and he has therefore the power, as he has the right, to do whatever may please him. An unfaltering trust in Providence is a cure of undue anxiety and a cause of abounding peace and joy. "Certainly it is heaven on earth to have a man's mind move in charity, rest in Providence, and turn upon the poles of truth" (Bacon). "The prophets of the Old Testament inculcate with a remarkable perspicuity and decision the overruling agency of God's providence in the affairs of the world. Their whole prophecy is more or less a commentary on this doctrine. . . . . . What a basis is laid by it of peace and tranquillity to every thoughtful and most feeling mind; and how different the aspect of the world becomes when we have reason to know that all things in it, and every combination of them, whether in the fortunes of kingdoms or in a more private state, are under the control of an intelligent and gracious Ruler. Were we in the chains of chance, how gloomy would our case be. Were we in the hands of men, too often how fearful, how humiliating, how conflicting. But the impression of the scene is changed when we admit into it the direction of an all-wise and perfect Being, in whose rectitude and goodness we may acquiesce through the whole course of his providential dispensation" (Davison 'on Prophecy,' p. 59).

> "One adequate support
> For the calamities of mortal life
> Exists, one only ;—an assured belief
> That the procession of our fate, howe'er
> Sad or disturb'd, is order'd by a Being
> Of infinite benevolence and power,
> Whose everlasting purposes embrace
> All accidents, converting them to good" (Wordsworth).

III. The establishment of his kingdom (vers. 9, 10). God is a moral governor, and directs his providential operations with a view to the setting up of a kingdom of righteousness upon earth. This kingdom existed from the first, was more fully exhibited in the theocracy of Israel, and culminated in the rule of Christ, who "must reign until he hath put all enemies under his feet." In every stage of development it involves conflict. But—1. *He will protect its subjects;* his saints (lit., pious, those who *love* God), against whom the wicked will contend in vain (ver. 9). 2. *He will overthrow its adversaries* (ver. 10); their overthrow being (1) certain, (2) unexpected, (3) complete— "broken to pieces," — and (4) signally indicative of the interposition of heaven (ch. vii. 10). 3. He will *extend its borders* to the ends of the earth. 4. *And he will clothe with strength,* honour, and majesty the king whom he appoints and anoints for the accomplishment of his purposes. Hannah commenced her song with rejoicing on account of the strength and honour conferred upon herself, and she closes it with rejoicing on account of the strength and honour which would be conferred on him who should be "higher than the kings of the earth." "Let the children of Zion be joyful in their king." "The anointed of the Lord, of whom Hannah prophesies in the spirit, is not one single king in Israel, either David or Christ, but an ideal king, though not a mere personification of the throne about to be established, but the actual king whom Israel received in David and the race, which culminated in the Messiah. The exaltation of the horn of the anointed of Jehovah commenced with the victorious and splendid expansion of the power of David, was repeated with every victory over the enemies of God and his kingdom gained by the successive kings of David's house, goes on in the advancing spread of the kingdom of Christ, and will eventually attain to its eternal consummation in the judgment of the last day, through which all the enemies of Christ will be made his footstool " (Keil).—D.

Vers. 1—10.—*The prayer-song of Hannah.* In her prayer of asking Hannah was intent not merely on having a child, but on giving to the service of God a priest, and to the government of Israel a judge, very different from the sons of Eli—a Nazarite, a second and a better Samson. No wonder, then, that when she brought her son to the sanctuary, her prayer of thanksgiving took a large scope, and revealed even a prophetic fervour. What religious poetess has made such an impression as Hannah with one ode ? Reproduced in Ps. cxiii., and yet again in the song of the blessed Virgin Mary, commonly called the Magnificat, it may be said to have continued in devout minds, Hebrew and Gentile, for about 3000 years. The first verse is the introduction, and strikes the key in which all that follows is pitched—a tone of warm and grateful confidence in God. Then follow the praises of the Lord, with some anticipation of better days to come.

I. PRAISE OF JEHOVAH (vers. 2—8). 1. Because of his sublime attributes (vers. 2, 3). "There is none *holy* as Jehovah." The root idea of holiness is always that of separateness from what is evil or profane. The God of Israel was the Holy One, absolutely unique, immaculate, inviolate, and inviolable. None among the gods of the nations might be likened to him. So he called and required Israel to be a holy nation, *i. e.* separate from the nations of the world, who are idolatrous and unclean. So under the New Testament the saints are the separated ones who touch not the unclean thing. "Neither any rock like our God." His protection cannot be invaded. His purpose does not vacillate. His power does not fail. He is the Rock of Ages. This was what made Israel unconquerable so long as faithful to God. The "rocks" of the nations, *i. e.* the gods in whom they trusted, were not as Israel's Rock. "Jehovah is a God of knowledge." Let not the wicked boast proudly. No word of scorn cast at the humble, no haughty glance of the eye, is unobserved by the Lord ; and nothing is more certain than that, sooner or later, he will abase the proud. "And by him actions are weighed." In his estimate of human conduct he holds the balances of a perfect equity. 2. Because of his mighty works (vers. 4—8). Ruling in holy sovereignty, God often reverses the conditions of men, lowering the exalted and exalting the lowly. He even kills and makes alive, leads down into Hades, and leads up from it again. Sheol or Hades was no mere pit of extinction from which there could be no uprising. God was able to raise even the dead. Such being his power, what could the boastful effect against Jehovah ? What might not the humble hope from him ? This is the central thought of Hannah's song, and it is still more finely expressed in that of the blessed Virgin. "He hath showed strength," &c. (Luke i.

51—53). Of the elevation of the despised, celebrated here and in Ps. cxiii., how many illustrations in sacred story! Joseph, Moses, Gideon, before the time of Hannah; and afterwards, David, and the great Son of David, the Man Christ Jesus, and his Galilean apostles. This fact is not to encourage contempt of, or impatience under, earthly dignities; but it is to cheer those who are or may be depressed by worldly disadvantage of poverty or obscurity. God's grace is no appanage of the rich or powerful. Was not Martin Luther a poor miner's son? David Brainerd a small farmer's son? John Bunyan a tinker's son, brought up to follow the same craft? Were not the good missionaries Carey and Knibb apprentices, the one bound to a cobbler, the other to a printer? And are not such men among the princes of God's people? The house of Elkanah was of no eminence in Israel; but thence God was raising up this child Samuel, whom Hannah brought to his courts, to be, if not king, king-maker, and to stand at the head of a line of prophets who should be the guides of the kings and the people so long as the kingdom stood.

II. Anticipation of better things to come. The end of this prayer-song has a prophetic strain (vers. 9, 10). Hannah was confident of God's preservation of his saints, and of the correlative truth of the perdition of ungodly men. Not that he has any pleasure in their death; but that if men will fight against eternal order and righteousness, they must fail in the struggle, they must perish. "As for Jehovah, those who contend against him are broken." The prophetic element shows itself in the closing expressions of the song. The government of Israel at the time may be described as that of a commonwealth, so far as concerns human administration. It was a theocracy, as it had been from the time of the exodus; but the actual administration was carried on through leaders, or judges. The eye of Hannah opened on a new epoch, foresaw a king to whom Jehovah would give strength as his Anointed. It is the first mention of a Messiah in Holy Writ. No doubt Hannah's words are a prediction of David, whose horn of power the Lord was to exalt, giving him a career of victory over all his enemies. But whether or not it was clear to Hannah's mind, the Spirit who rested on her signified a King greater than David, and a more illustrious kingdom. It is he of whom the angel said to Mary, "He shall be great," &c. (Luke i. 32, 33). We see not yet his kingdom. We see not all things put under him. But we see Jesus crowned with glory and honour; and we wait for his appearing and his kingdom. The longings of many generations, the hopes of many Hannahs, the visions of many seers and prophets, O may they come to pass speedily!—F.

Ver. 2. (Shiloh.)—*The Rock of Israel.* "Neither is there any rock like our God." The figurative representations of God which are given in his word enable us to attain exalted, varied, and most impressive views of his character. They are derived from objects with which the lands of the Bible abounded; and no other lands on earth were equally adapted to be the theatre of a Divine revelation for men universally. Of these representations, this is one of the most common. It was first employed by Jacob (Gen. xlix. 24—stone, *eben*, or rock), with allusion, perhaps, to Gen. xxviii. 11, 22; afterwards by Moses (Deut. xxxii. 4, 18, &c.—rock, *tzur* = what is solid, firm, enduring; a support, foundation, as in the text), who was so familiar with the rocks and mountains of Sinai; frequently by David (2 Sam. xxii. 3—rock, *sela* = height, cliff or crag, resorted to as a refuge) and the prophets. Notice—

I. His character in itself. 1. *His power.* "To know thy power is the root of immortality." 2. *His unchangeableness* and faithfulness. "I change not" (Mal. iii. 6), with reference to his merciful covenant. 3. *His eternity.* "From everlasting to everlasting." These attributes are ascribed to Christ: "all power" (Matt. xxviii. 18); "the same yesterday, and to-day, and for ever" (Heb. i. 8—12; xiii. 8). "That Rock was Christ" (1 Cor. x. 4). He is the highest and the only perfect manifestation of God. "Jesus is that Divine Being to whom we can draw near without pride, and before whom we can be abased without despair" (Pascal).

II. His superiority to others. They are—1. *Weak.* Their very strength is weakness compared with His infinite power. 2. *Changeable.* "All men are liars," false, unworthy, and disappointing objects of trust. 3. *Transitory.* They and their works pass away, whilst the rock endures for ever (see Swinnock,—"the incomparableness of God, —'Works,' vol. iv.). Expect not true or lasting satisfaction from any created object. "Cease ye from man" (Isa. ii. 22). Fear him not (Isa. li. 12, 13).

III. HIS RELATION TO HIS PEOPLE. "Our God." His people are those who live in direct fellowship with him, and show the reality of their fellowship by walking in the light and keeping his commandments. To them he has promised to be all that their true welfare requires. 1. A *support;* "the immovable foundation on which they may stand firm, impregnable, secure." 2. A *defence,* protecting them against their enemies; "a shadow from the heat, a refuge from the storm;" bearing on himself the tempest that would have fallen on them. "He that believeth shall not make haste," or be terrified. 3. A *source* of strength, of peace, and of consolation. "Rabbi Maimon has observed that the word *tzur,* which we translate rock, signifies, when applied to Jehovah, fountain, source, spring. There is no source whence continual help and salvation can arise but our God" (A. Clarke).

IV. HIS CLAIMS UPON ALL. 1. To *trust* in him. 2. Abide in him; not merely fleeing to him in a time of trouble and danger (as a traveller may seek shelter in a hovel while the storm lasts, and immediately afterwards leave it), but making him our habitation and home. 3. To make him our portion and "exceeding joy." "Trust ye in the Lord for ever; for the Lord Jehovah is the Rock of Ages" (Isa. xxvi. 4).

> "Rock of Ages, cleft for me;
> Let me hide myself in thee."   D.

Ver. 3.—*The Divine judgment of human actions.* "By him actions are weighed." It is customary to determine the worth of many things by weighing them. For this purpose a fixed standard is used, and a comparison is made with it by means of a balance and scales or other instrument. Nothing can be more natural than to speak of determining the moral worth of actions in the same manner, and Justice is commonly represented as a woman holding in her hand a pair of scales in which "actions are weighed." In this sense the above expression is employed; not, however, of men, whose judgment is often mistaken or unjust; but of "God, the Judge of all." His judgment is—

I. A PRESENT JUDGMENT. They *are* (now) weighed. According to the ancient Egyptians, there was erected at the entrance of the unseen world a balance or scales, over which the Judge of the dead presided, and by it the character of every man was tested as soon as he died. In one of the scales the figure or emblem of truth was placed, and in the other the heart of the deceased; and the result determined his destiny. This is not an unworthy conception of the judgment to come. But their religion pertained chiefly to what would be in the future, rather than to what exists in the present. And there are many at the present day who never think that they have anything to do with God or his judgment except when they come to die. They forget that the living and all-seeing God "pondereth their goings" (Prov. v. 21), "judgeth according to every man's work" (1 Pet. i. 17), and that to him they stand responsible (Heb. iv. 13—"with whom is the account").

II. ACCORDING TO A PERFECT STANDARD. The estimate which men form of themselves and others is often false, because it is not formed by means of such a standard. As "weights and measures" need to be examined and to be rectified by an imperial standard, so the human judgment and conscience need to be examined and to be rectified by the righteousness of God as declared in the Law and the Prophets and the Gospel of Christ. What is our relation to this standard?

III. ACCORDING TO MOTIVES. The moral worth of actions does not depend upon their "outward appearance," but upon the heart. In the sight of God, who sees hearts as we see faces, the inward motives, principles, and intentions are in reality the actions which are weighed (Prov. xvi. 2; xxi. 2; xxiv. 11, 12; Isa. xxvi. 7). Our ignorance of these necessarily makes our judgment imperfect, even in relation to ourselves. But "he is a God of knowledge," "searches the heart," and perceives the motives which underlie all actions, and which are often so different from what they are thought to be (Ps. cxxxix. 33).

IV. UNIVERSAL. "The Judge of all the earth." It pertains to all actions that have in them a moral element; to the actions of every individual soul (for each soul stands before him in its separate personality, bearing its own burden of responsibility and of sin, and is dealt with by him as though there were no other) ; and to every one of its actions, however apparently insignificant, though it cannot be really such because of its relation to God, and its bearing upon character and destiny.

V. EXERCISED WITH A VIEW TO REWARDING EVERY MAN ACCORDING TO HIS WORKS. It is not useless and ineffective; but is attended with important consequences (Jer. xvii. 10). This life is not simply one of probation; it is also, in part, one of retribution. The approbation or disapprobation of God is always followed by corresponding effects in the mind and heart and conscience of men, and often by startling providential occurrences; as when it was said, "Thou art weighed in the balances, and art found wanting" (Dan. v. 27, 30) ; "The world's history is the world's judgment;" and, "We must all appear before the judgment seat of Christ" (Rom. xiv. 12; 2 Cor. v. 10). Application:—1. "Let a man examine himself." 2. Seek forgiveness of the sins that are past. 3. "Walk before me, and be thou perfect."—D.

Ver. 9. (SHILOH.)—*God's guardianship of his saints.* "He will keep the feet of his saints." Who are his saints? 1. The term is sometimes used as one of reproach, by persons who are destitute of religious life, concerning those who bear the Christian name. Pointing to the inconsistency of some of the latter, they would thereby fain persuade themselves and others that there is no such thing as true godliness to be found in the world. There are, doubtless, many who "profess to know God, but in works deny him." But there would be no counterfeit money unless there were some genuine coin. 2. The word is also used to designate those who have been "canonised;" and who, having gone into heaven, are supposed to have influence with God in the granting of petitions presented on earth. But such a use of it is unscriptural, and the doctrine is false and injurious. 3. The saints of God are those who have been accepted by him through faith in Christ, who do his will and walk in the way to heaven. Their way, indeed, is often difficult and painful, like the uneven, intricate, and stony paths of Palestine, and beset by numerous dangers. But, for their consolation and encouragement, it is promised that "he that keepeth Israel" will "keep their feet" firm and safe, so that they may not fall and perish. The promise is directly of preservation from temporal calamity, but it may be regarded as including also preservation from spiritual failure and destruction. Consider—

I. THE DANGER FROM WHICH HE WILL KEEP THEM. 1. *From wandering out of the way.* Obscurity may gather over it. Other ways may appear plainer, easier, and more pleasant, and tempt them to leave it. Or they may seem more direct and shorter than the circuitous and wearisome path they have to pursue. But kept by him they will not go astray. 2. *From stumbling in the way.* "It must needs be that offences (or occasions of stumbling) come." Some of them consist of (1) The difficulties of Divine revelation : "things hard to be understood." (2) The mysteries of Divine providence, which have led many to say, "As for me," &c. (Ps. lxxiii. 2). (3) Direct solicitations to evil. (4) "Afflictions and persecutions that arise for the word, whereby many are offended." But "great peace have they that love thy law, and nothing shall cause them to stumble" (Ps. cxix. 165). 3. *From failing to reach the end of the way.* Some start with bright hopes which are not afterwards altogether fulfilled in their experience : storms gather, enemies threaten, severe conflict must be waged ; and they become weary and desponding, and ready to halt. "But the righteous shall hold on his way" (Job xvii. 19; Isa. xl. 31).

II. THE MANNER IN WHICH HE WILL KEEP THEM. By—1. *Providing means of help for them :* the *word,* which is an instrument of guidance, refreshment, and defence ; *prayer ;* the *fellowship* of those who are travelling in the same way ; the ministration of *angels* (Ps. xci. 11 ; Heb. i. 14). 2. *Watching over them at every step.* They are not alone ; but he is with them ; and they are "kept by the power of God" (1 Pet. i. 5). 3. *Imparting grace and strength* to them according to their need. "As thy day," &c. It matters not how great the need if "the supply of the Spirit" (Phil. i. 19) be equal to it. And, "My grace," he says, "is sufficient for thee."

III. THE CERTAINTY WITH WHICH HE WILL KEEP THEM. 1. He has a special *interest* in them, for they are "*his*" saints," "the portion of his inheritance." 2. He has *already done much* for them, which is an earnest of continued preservation. 3. He has *high purposes* to accomplish in them and through them. And, 4. He has solemnly *promised* "never to leave them" (Heb. xiii. 5), and "he is faithful that promised" (Heb. x. 23).

1. Rely upon the promise. 2. Presume not upon your security, nor think that without fulfilling his commandments you can receive his promises. 3. Use the appointed means of grace with all diligence.—D.

Ver. 10. (SHILOH.)—*The King Messiah.* The last word of the song of Hannah is the first mention of the Lord's Anointed, Messiah, Christ. 1. Her language was a direct prediction of the appointment of a theocratic king, for which Samuel prepared the way, and which, under Divine direction, he was the chief agent in effecting. 2. It was an indirect prediction of One who had been long expected (Gen. iii. 14, 15; xii. 1—3; xxii. 17, 18; xlix. 10; Num. xxiv. 17—19; Deut. xviii. 15—19), and in whom the *idea* of such a king would be completely realised. 3. It marks the dawn of a splendid series of prophecies founded on the reign of David, and ever brightening to the perfect day (2 Sam. vii.; xxiii. 1—7; Ps. ii.; cx.; Isa. ix. 9; Dan. ix. 25; Micah v. 1; Mal. iv. 2. Fairbairn, 'Typology,' i. 111; Pye Smith, 'Script. Test.,' i. 169). Consider—

I. HIS REGAL OFFICE. Its general purpose was—1. To *unite* a divided people (Gen. xlix. 10). Nothing was more needed in the days of the judges. 2. To *save* them from their enemies. "Thy salvation" (ch. ii. 1; Ps. xviii. 50; xcv. 1; Matt. i. 21). 3. To *rule* over them, *judge* them in righteousness, and establish among them order, peace, and happiness. "The regal office of our Saviour consisteth partly in the ruling, protecting, and rewarding of his people; partly in the coercing, condemning, and destroying of his enemies" (Pearson 'on the Creed,' Art. ii.). It was the fatal mistake of Israel in all ages to look for an outward, worldly, and imposing, rather than an inward, moral, and spiritual fulfilment of this purpose. The same mistake has, to some extent, pervaded Christendom. "My kingdom is not of this world." "The kingdom of God is righteousness, peace, and joy in the Holy Ghost." "Alexander, Cæsar, Charlemagne, and myself have founded empires. But upon what did we rest the creations of our genius? Upon force. Jesus Christ alone founded his empire upon love; and at this moment millions would die for him" ('Table Talk and Opinions of Napoleon Buonaparte').

II. HIS DIVINE APPOINTMENT. "*His* King." "*His* Anointed" (Ps. ii. 6; xviii. 50). 1. The choice was *of God.* "Chosen out of the people" (Ps. lxxxix. 19). Even Saul, a man after the people's heart rather than after God's heart, was selected and appointed by him. The invisible King of Israel did not relinquish his authority. 2. Founded on *personal eminence.* David. The ancient Persians believed that their ruler was an incarnation of the eternal light, the object of their worship, and therefore rendered him Divine honour. This was a reality in Christ. 3. Confirmed and manifested by the *anointing of his Spirit* (ch. x. 1; xvi. 13; 2 Sam. ii. 4); the outward act being a symbol of the inward endowment (Matt. iii. 16; Luke iv. 18). "God giveth not the Spirit by measure unto him" (John iii. 34; Heb. i. 9).

III. HIS GLORIOUS EXALTATION. 1. After a state of *humiliation;* implied in the language here used; also indicated in ver. 8; and typified by the lowly origin of David and his course to the throne. 2. By the *right hand of God.* "He will give strength;" "All power is given unto me in heaven and in earth" (Matt. xxviii. 18); exhibited in his resurrection, ascension, and possession of supreme honour, authority, and power. 3. To a kingdom *universal* and eternal. "The Lord shall judge the ends of the earth" (Ps. ii. 8; lxxii. 2—5; cxxxii. 18; Luke i. 31—33, 69). Whilst Jesus lives and reigns in heaven, he also lives and reigns on earth. He does so by the continued and ever-increasing power of his example and teachings, his wondrous life, and still more wondrous death. The truths and principles which he declared and embodied are, at this moment, accepted by the loftiest intellects, the purest consciences, and the tenderest hearts amongst men. Who now reverses a single judgment which he pronounced upon men or things? Who can conceive any character more worthy of reverence and affection than his? The lapse of time has only served to invest his words and character with fresh interest and power.   Other kings and conquerors are fading away amidst the shadows of the past ; but he is ever rising before the view of mankind more distinctly, and living in their thoughts, their consciences, and their hearts more mightily.   Yea, more, he lives and reigns on earth by his Divine presence, his providential working, and the power of his Spirit.   Just as the sun, shining in mid-heaven, sheds down his rays upon the earth ; so Christ, the Sun of righteousness (though no longer seen by mortal eye), pours down the beams of his influence upon us continually, and rules over all things for the complete establishment of his kingdom.—D.

EXPOSITION.

SAMUEL'S MINISTRATIONS AT SHILOH (vers. 11—21).   Ver. 11.—**The child did minister.**   Left by his parents at Shiloh, Samuel ministered unto the Lord ; that is, certain duties were allotted him to perform suited to his age ; but few at first, when he was but three years old, but increasing in importance as time went on ; for the words refer to the whole period of his service, until Eli's death. At first Samuel would be but a scholar, for, as we have mentioned on ch. i. 21, there were, no doubt, regulations for the training of children devoted to the service of the sanctuary.   The peculiarity about Samuel was that he was devoted for life, for possibly it was a not uncommon practice for young persons to receive some training at Shiloh ; just as we find that Samuel himself subsequently gathered youths round him at Naioth in Ramah for educational purposes.   Learning practically was confined to the priesthood, and we can scarcely imagine that the knowledge which Phinehas and the family of Aaron brought with them out of Egypt would be allowed to perish.   Samuel certainly had himself received careful instruction (see on ch. x. 25), and this could scarcely have happened if the training of young persons had not been part of the priests' duties at Shiloh.   This then explains why Samuel was brought to Eli at so tender an age, and why the charge of so young a child was undertaken without a murmur.   **Before Eli** means under his general superintendence. Everything done at Shiloh was done *before Eli*, as being the chief ruler there.

Ver. 12.—**Now the sons of Eli were sons of Belial,** *i. e.* worthless men (see on ch. i. 16).   **They knew not Jehovah.**   He had never been revealed to their consciences, and so his fear had no influence upon their lives.   The next words, in ver. 13, are difficult, but lit. mean, " The legal right of the priests towards, or as respects, the people."   On this account the Vulgate and several commentators couple the sentence with what precedes : "they knew neither Jehovah, nor their own legal rights."   But the word *also* in ver. 15 is incompatible with this rendering ; for if what is mentioned there be illegal, so must also the practice be which is recorded here.

But neither does *custom* give the sense ; for the Heb. has not priest's (sing.) as the A. V., but *of the priests,* of all priests generally, and not of Eli merely and his sons.   The right translation is that given by the Sept., Syriac, and Chaldee, namely, " the due of the priests from the people," on which see Lev. vii. 31—35.   In the original this is put absolutely " And as to the priests' due from the people, when," &c., but our language requires some insertion to make it read more smoothly. " And as to the due of the priests from the people, the manner of its exaction was as follows : When," &c.   But besides the due and legal portion, which, nevertheless, they took in an illegal way, they demanded a part of the flesh reserved for the feast of the offerer, and to which they had absolutely no right (see Lev. viii. 31 ; 2 Chron. xxxv. 13).

The legal due of the priest was the right shoulder and the wave breast ; but before he took them they were to be consecrated to God by the burning of the fat upon the altar (Lev. iii. 5 ; vii. 31, 34).   It is worth observing that the people seem well acquainted with the words of the Law, and are indignant because the priests, its proper guardians, do not abide literally by them.   This contempt of the Law distressed their religious susceptibilites, while the cupidity of Eli's sons offended their moral nature.   And so **men abhorred the offering of Jehovah.**   Lit. it is the *minchah,* the unbloody sacrifice, or meat offering, but it is put here for every kind of sacrificial offering.

Ver. 18.—**But Samuel ministered.**   While the misconduct of Eli's sons was thus bringing religion into contempt, and sapping the nation's morals, Samuel was advancing in years and piety, and was gaining that education which made him fit to retrieve the evil of their doings.   He is still styled *na'ar,* a boy ; for the word, according to the Rabbins, may be used up to fifteen years (ch. i. 24).   In the sense of servant there is no limit of age ; and as it is the word translated "young men " in ver. 17, it probably means there not Eli's sons, but the servants by whose instrumentality their orders were actually carried out.   Samuel's dress, an ephod of white linen, was probably that worn by the Levites in their ordinary ministrations ; for the ephod of the priests was richer both in material and colour (Exod. xxviii. 6—8). As being thus the simplest ministerial garment, it was apparently worn also by laymen when taking part in any religious service, as by David when he danced before the ark (2 Sam. vi. 14).

Ver. 19.—**His mother made him a little coat.** The coat, *meïl*, was worn by priests (Lev. viii. 7), by kings and their sons (1 Sam. xviii. 4), by prophets (*ibid.* xxviii. 14), and even by women (2 Sam. xiii. 18). It was an under garment of wool, woven throughout without seam, with holes for the head and arms, and reaching nearly to the ground : when used by women it had sleeves (*ibid.*). Under it they had a tunic or shirt fitting so closely that a man simply so clad was considered naked (1 Sam. xix. 24), and over it priests and Levites wore the ephod, and so also David on the occasion mentioned above (1 Chron. xv. 27). The *meïl* seems, moreover, to have often been a handsome dress, as that of the priests was of purple-blue, with embroidery of pomegranates in three colours, and golden bells (Exod. xxviii. 31—34); and when made of delicate materials for the use of the rich, it and the tunic are the soft luxurious clothing spoken of in Matt. xi. 8. As the *meïl* was the ordinary dress of all classes of people, it was made for Samuel at home, and can have no special meaning; but the ephod shows that he was brought up in the daily practice of holy duties. This annual present, however, of clothing made by the mother's hands proves that the dedication of her son to God was not allowed to interfere with home affections, and both parents and child must have looked forward with joy to happy meetings at each recurrence of the family visit to the sanctuary.

Vers. 20, 21.—**The Lord give thee seed,** &c. The manner in which Eli blesses Elkanah shows that this surrender of a very young child to religious service was not looked upon as imposing a burden upon the sanctuary, but as the bestowal of a valued gift. *Loan* and *lent* by no means give the whole sense, which is in fact beyond the power of our language to express ; for the Hebrew is remarkable for its manner of saying a great deal in a few words, by using them indefinitely. Besides the sense, then, of lending the child to God, the Heb. also conveys the idea of Samuel having been obtained by prayer, but by prayer *for Jehovah*. Hannah had not asked simply for a son, but for a son whom she might dedicate to God. And now Eli prays that Jehovah will give her children to be her own (see on ch. i. 28).

ELI'S COMPLICITY IN THE SINS OF HIS SONS (vers. 22—26). Ver. 22. — **Eli . . . heard all that his sons did.** To the profanity and greed described in vers. 12—17 the sons of Eli added unchastity ; and their sin was the greater because the women whom they corrupted were those dedicated to religious service (see Exod. xxxviii. 8). The order of ministering women instituted by Moses probably lasted down to the destruction of the temple, and Anna may have belonged to it (Luke ii. 37); afterwards it appeared again in a more spiritual form in the widows and deaconesses of the Christian Church. The word rendered **assembled** means "arranged in bands," and shows not merely that they were numerous, but that they had regular duties assigned them, and each one her proper place and office. The frequent sacrifices, with the feasts which followed, must have provided occupation for a large number of hands in the cleaning of the utensils and the cooking of the food. But though Eli heard of the depraved conduct of his sons in thus defiling those who ministered in the tabernacle, he gives them but the faintest rebuke, and that apparently only because their misdeeds were in everybody's mouth ; for the last clause of ver. 23 really is, "For I hear of your evil doings from all this people." Eli's old age may have increased his indifference, but his religious character could never have had much depth or earnestness, to allow him to regard such heinous sins so lightly. It seems even as if he chiefly felt the annoyance occasioned to himself by the expostulations urged upon him "from all this people." Still all that he says is wise and thoughtful. The sins of men in high station do not end with themselves ; they make others also to transgress. And as Eli's sons were Jehovah's ministers, and they had led into wickedness those who also were bound to holy service, their misconduct was a sin against Jehovah himself.

Vers. 24, 25.—**Ye make,** &c. Eli's words are very obscure, but "Ye make Jehovah's people to transgress" is upon the whole the best rendering of the clause. Both the Sept. and Syriac have a different reading : "Ye make Jehovah's people cease to worship him." In the next verse there is no sufficient reason for supposing that Elohim, God, here means a **judge.** Elohim was the head of the theocracy, the ruler of Israel in all things, and he would set to rights these delinquencies of "one man against another" by the ordinary exercise of his judicial functions. So far all is easy, and we must translate, "If one man sin against another, God shall judge him." But in the last clause there is one of those plays upon words to which the Hebrew language, with its numerous conjugations, so readily lends itself (see on ch. i. 28) ; and it is rarely possible to transfer to another language the force of passages in which the sense depends upon the terms in the original having a double meaning. The verb rendered *shall judge* in the first clause is used again by Eli in the second, but in a different conjugation, in which its usual meaning is to *pray*. According to the lexicon, therefore, we must translate : " If a man sin against Jehovah, who shall pray for him ? " But surely it was just the occasion in which the only remedy left was intercessory prayer. Bearing then in remembrance the use made by Eli of the verb in the first clause, we must translate : " Who shall act as judge for him ? " " Who shall interpose as arbitrator between him and Jehovah to settle the quarrel ? " The verb itself, moreover, is a rare and old-fashioned one, and apparently means to *settle a dispute.* So it is used of Phinehas, who by his righteous zeal put an end to the rebellion against God's laws ; and accordingly in Ps. cvi. 30, where our version renders " executed judgment," the Vulgate has *placavit, appeased* Jehovah's anger.

The sense then is, In case of wrong done between man and man, God as the supreme Arbitrator settles the dispute ; but where the two parties are God and man, what third power is there which can interfere ? The quarrel must go on to the bitter end, and God,

who is your opponent, will also punish you. The same idea is found in Job ix. 33. Naturally to so mild a remonstrance, and founded upon so low a view of the Divine nature, the sons of Eli paid but slight attention, and by thus hardening themselves in sin they made their punishment inevitable, " because it pleased Jehovah to slay them." Man can bring upon himself neither good nor evil except by the working of God's will, and the punishment of sin is as thoroughly a part of God's will as the rewarding of righteousness. An intense conviction of the personality of God was the very foundation of the religious life of the Israelites, and lies at the root of the words of Eli here and of those of Job ; and it was this which made them ascribe to God that hardening of the wicked in sin which is the sure means of their punishment. We ascribe it to the working of natural laws, which after all is but saying the same thing in a round-about way ; for the laws of nature, in things moral as well as in the physical world, are the laws of God. In ver. 26, in contrast with Eli's sons ripening for punishment, and daily more abhorred of God and man, we have Samuel set before us advancing in age and "in favour with Jehovah and also with men," like him of whom in so many respects he was a type (Luke ii. 52), our blessed Lord.

HOMILETICS.

Vers. 11—19.—*Degenerate sons.* The facts given are—1. Eli's sons manifest their extreme wickedness by profaning the worship of God. 2. As a consequence, a grievous scandal is caused, and Divine worship comes into disrepute. 3. In spite of many evil surroundings, Samuel grows up in the blameless discharge of religious duties. 4. Hannah continues to visit and take a deep interest in her son's spiritual life. The sorrowful experience of Eli in old age is sometimes repeated in modern times. Many a good man is bowed down even to the grave by the irreligion of sons of whom better things had been expected. No more painful condition can a father be in than when he scarcely dare name his children to those who ask after their welfare. The world and the Church look on with wonder and pain at the spectacle of vile children issuing from a pious home. The feeling of surprise with which men read of the family of the high priest of Israel becoming so utterly wicked is attended with the conviction that desperately bad youths ought never to issue from Christian homes. Such an event is contrary to all just expectations. The *presumption* that the *offspring of pious parents* would *be holy* is based on various considerations, which for the most part apply to the case of Eli. 1. There are various *promises and statements* to encourage the belief that the *children of the pious* will share in *special mercies* (e. g. Deut. xxx. 2, 6 ; Prov. xxii. 6 ; Isa. xliv. 7 ; Mal. ii. 15 ; 1 Cor. vii. 14). 2. In so far as *susceptibility to religious impressions* is affected by *inherited qualities,* they have an advantage over others. 3. The *means of grace,* instruction, example, and prayer are *more employed* for them than for the majority. 4. The *power of early habit,* which plays so important a part in the formation of character, is likely to *be on the side of godliness* where religious influences early operate. The *causes* which account for the *ungodliness of the children of the pious* are diverse, intricate, and partly inscrutable. A broad margin must be left for the mysterious action of a free being, even under the most favourable conditions. It is not possible to trace the lines and say where parental responsibility ends and the responsibility of the child begins. The two factors are to be recognised. Moreover, anterior physical causes, operating perniciously through ancestors, may act detrimentally on the mental and moral condition. But allowing for these and other untraceable elements of the case, there are causes of this sad feature of domestic life—

I. IN THE CHILDREN. The *natural depravity* of the heart is a grave fact. It is the first foe to be encountered in seeking a child's salvation. Its subtle power is beyond all knowledge. There may not be the complications of wickedness which exist in the full-grown nature of the adult after years of developed sin, but the power is persistent and insinuating. Eli's children shared this tendency in common with others. The *special propensities inherited* are sometimes very strong, and seem to partake of the force of the old habits of the ancestors from whom they were derived. It is also a fact that where a malformation, or unequal development of the physical system, supervenes on the inheritance of special evil propensities, these latter gain immensely in force. A line of pious ancestors, as a rule, would guarantee freedom from such abnormal developments, because continuous piety tends to the symmetrical development of the entire man ; but occasionally there are backward leaps in nature, and old elements reappear. Possibly some of Eli's blood-relatives were not so good as they ought to have been. No doubt grace can subdue even the worst natures, but the elements referred to must be considered in connection with other causes.

II. IN THE TRAINING. It cannot be supposed that Eli was perfect in this respect. Few persons consider how much of care, of wisdom, of forethought, of yearning sympathy, of specific, well-adapted guidance, and of prayer is involved in the "nurture and admonition" required in training children for God. There may be a fatal lack of faith in the very possibility of infant piety ; an expectation that, as a matter of course, a child will grow up in sin till an age for conversion arrives ; a cold, cruel casting of the spiritual welfare of a child on teachers, attendants, official aids—the parent, under pressure of business, declining to bear his offspring ever on his heart before God ; or a lack of discretion in dealing with each soul according to its temperament. Absence of a mother's deep and tender interest tells most prejudicially. An unwise method of instilling religious truth ; an assertion of mere authority in severe tones ; a lack of discipline to check wrong tendencies ; a constant appeal to a sense of fear ; an avoidance of the essential truths of the gospel, or a low, grovelling representation of them, may create aversion, awake silent resistance, and finally set the entire nature against what is falsely supposed to be religion. Perhaps there is *no department of religious obligation so little studied as this*. The tender, susceptible nature of children cannot be safely treated without much thought and prayer. No wonder if the promise which hangs on a faithful discharge of most delicate and solemn duties carried on year by year should sometimes not be fulfilled. Parents have need to pray, "Search me and try me."

III. IN EXAMPLE. This is part of training, but, as exercising a perpetual and unconscious influence, it may be regarded as distinct from direct efforts. Children learn more of religion from what they observe in parents than by any other means. The life they see lived is their daily book of lessons. If it is selfish, hard, formal, worldly, no amount of verbal teaching or professed interest will avail. There is no surer encouragement for a child to despise all religion than a discovery of insincerity in the professions of a parent. Real character comes into clear view in the home, and those who, under influence of public considerations, restrain themselves in the world, but give freedom to unhallowed feelings in private, cannot wonder if children do not covet the piety they witness.

IV. IN ASSOCIATIONS. Associations out of the home circle, both in youth and early manhood, exercise much influence over character. It is not every youth that is solely formative on others. Most young people receive more from companions than they impart. The good of home may be largely neutralised by the tone of society outside the home. Eli's sons were not strong enough to counteract the evil tendencies of the age, and their father erred in not taking precautions adequate to the occasion. Probably one reason why the sons of good and eminent men sometimes become notoriously godless is, that the utter absorption of the parent in public affairs, albeit religious, gradually issues in alienation of sons from home interests and committal to friendships evil in tendency. The charm of novelty is powerful where home life is rendered dull through inattention to the tastes and enjoyments of the young, and hence consent is given to enticing sinners. If, in any instance, there are in *operation* causes, either singly or combined, of the nature referred to, it is *inevitable* that a home, though in some degree pious, should be distressed by the *presence of ungodly sons.* So far as man's conduct determines religion or irreligion in offspring, it would be contrary to the action of natural laws for pious sons to be the product of efforts inadequate to the end in view. If sons are godly in spite of errors and bad influence at home, it is because God in his mercy has brought other and more blessed influences to bear. Even defective training may be ultimately remedied by a more true use of prayer for mercy.

Great sinners. The sons of Eli were the greatest sinners of their degenerate age. From the most favoured home the worst men came forth. All sin is a great evil. It is the curse of man, the abomination of God. In its essence it is rebellion against the All-wise and Holy One. For all lack of conformity to his will implies a will supposed to be a more desirable guide than his, which is insult and insubordination. But the Bible represents some sins as of deeper dye than others. There are beings deserving to be "beaten with many stripes." The tests by which the enormity of sins is estimated are, after reference of all to the perfect purity of God—

I. THE CHARACTER OF THE DEEDS. The deeds perpetrated by the sons of Eli were of the vilest kind. In themselves they were calculated to awaken the intensest disgust and abhorrence of every pure and reverent mind. It is hard to conceive how men blessed with early privileges could sink so low, were it not that modern Christian times have produced the darkest sins in the professedly religious. The sins of open profanation of the sanctuary, of despite to the solemn sacrifice, of pollution in guiltiest lust, were but the outward expression of a state of soul foul, reckless, defiant beyond all description. So, generally, the dark, horrid deeds on which men look are but the indicators of a very hell of iniquity deep down in the soul. There are—

II. THE PRIVILEGES ENJOYED. It added guilt to the sin of the young men that they were the *sons of the priest of God.* It is a grave responsibility to be born of parents endued with any degree of piety. Especially are they under strong obligation to avoid sin who are, by virtue of their connection with the ordinances of worship, taught out of the law of the Lord, and surrounded by the hallowed influences of the sanctuary. Every wise book read, every kind influence exercised, every prayer offered in public, or by parents at home, gives additional light and power wherewith to avoid the paths of sin. It requires a long and hard inward struggle to keep down conscience so as to become a desperate sinner. Men do not sink to lowest depths of vice suddenly. Every successive step is taken against clear light and restraining powers, and when the final surrender to guilty deeds is made, the whole privileges of the past speak out the greatness of the evil. The poor idolater ignorantly causing his sons to pass through the fire to Moloch is less guilty than the sons of Israel's high priest, when, crushing every sacred feeling, they turn from all the light of years to profane the sanctuary by violence and lust. Sodom was vile, but decorous Capernaum viler. The sin of despising a holier Sacrifice than of bulls and lambs is often committed by men blessed with faithful teaching.

III. THE POSITION OCCUPIED. To the eye of the Hebrew the office of priest was most sacred. The reverence cherished for the office was transferred in some degree to the person who filled it. Hence, perhaps, the patience and submission with which the worshippers endured the greed and violence of the guilty sons of Eli. In itself, being a consecration of life to the holiest of employments, and considered, also, as a type of the one perfect Priesthood, there was solid reason for the common sentiment. No position is morally higher than that of him who stands between man and God for the performance of most solemn duties. Hence in all ages it has been recognised that the ministers of the sanctuary, whether priests, as anciently, or pastors and teachers, do exercise an influence which, while increasing the force of goodness, also aggravates their guilt when sin is committed. Power, when used sinfully, means magnified sin. A professed Christian sinks relatively very low when he does what other men do. A pastor by one act may come under a condemnation from which on earth he will never recover. A judge who sells justice is the most despised of men. A statesman who barters truth and peace for personal greed is worse than a common forger. Holiness is to be loved and sought for its own sake, yet it is helpful to ask, "What manner of persons ought we to be," who stand out in society as rulers, magistrates, pastors, teachers, parents? If the ordinary sinner cannot escape the swift judgment of God, where shall they appear who by virtue of exalted position become intensely and grievously sinful when they sin?

IV. THE NATURE OF THE EFFECTS. Some sins, like the falling of heavy bodies in still water, produce wider and more violent effects than do others. The effect is always pernicious, but when prominent men and professed servants of God sin, the consequences are painfully and conspicuously injurious. The sons of Eli by their crimes not only debased their own nature and *fell* to lower depths of shame, but they brought the holiest services into disrepute, alienated from the sanctuary the feelings of the people, caused intense anguish in the minds of the pious Jews, gave encouragement to wicked men more freely to transgress, and thus did more than others could do to exterminate morality and religion from the land. It is a serious question for every one, and especially ministers and all persons in positions of influence, *how far the neglect of religion* by multitudes is the *natural effect of their own short-comings.* It is a mark of a great sinner when, by reason of his conduct, the "wicked blaspheme." Also, our Lord has branded those as great sinners who wantonly cause offence to "one" of his "little ones." If scepticism and antagonism to Christianity are most lamentable evils, it is a matter of grave consideration how far the presence of these evils is due to the formality, the greed, the gross inconsistencies of those professing to exhibit and love the religion of Christ. It behoves all to see to it that they lift up "holy hands," and speak a "pure language." Otherwise the terrible woes pronounced by the Saviour over would-be religious men may find an application to modern great sinners. Arising from this subject we may notice certain

Practical lessons.—1. The extreme importance of every one forming, by the aid of Scripture and of conscience, a *proper estimate* of the *responsibility* of his position as a professed Christian, a parent, a minister of the gospel, a teacher, or civil ruler. 2. The possibility of undergoing a process of *spiritual decay* by which the *finer sensibilities* of earlier days shall become *almost annihilated*, and deeds be done with impunity which once were most abhorrent. 3. The need of frequent *self-examination*, to ascertain whether the elements of religious degeneracy may be *unconsciously at work* in the soul ; the more so as it is characteristic of spiritual declension to make us blind to the fact of declension. 4. The necessity of much prayer, lest, trusting to early privileges and official services, the elements of decay should enter the spiritual life, and, consequently, the duties of self-scrutiny and watchfulness be shunned.

Youthful piety. It is not without significance that the sacred historian breaks the thread of his ordinary narrative by frequent references to the child Samuel (vers. 11, 18, 21, 26 ; cf. iii. 1, 18). The contrast with ungodly priests is striking. "*But* Samuel ministered before the Lord, being a *child*." "The child was *young*." "The child *grew* before the Lord." Beautiful progression ! "Following on" to "know the Lord." "The path of the just" grows brighter. Here in face of evil is the "perseverance of the saints." The case of Samuel may be regarded as a *typical instance of youthful piety*. The frequent allusions to him, combined with the tenor of his subsequent life, go to prove that he was a religious child from earliest days. Humanly his piety was the product of his mother's intense earnestness. Hannah had faith to believe that a child may be God's from the very dawn of life. In essential features his piety was the same as that of all God's people. There were special reasons for its assuming the form it did in that entire and early separation from home. 1. A mother's *prevision* had respect to a *new and higher* office to be created and duly authenticated. 2. *Extraordinary preparation* was needful for the great work to be finally entered on, and such as separation to the hallowed service of the sanctuary would secure.   3. The mother could thus evince her *freedom from mere selfish gratification* in seeking a child from the Lord, and at the same time do all within her power to advance the coming kingdom.   4. There was a *secret providence* in this *preparing the way* for the *first great step* in the reformation of the people, namely, the authoritative announcement of national disaster (ch. iii. 11, 20).   Taking, then, Samuel's as an instance of *typical youthful piety*, we may notice—

I. That YOUTHFUL PIETY IS A POSSIBILITY.   Evidently it was in Samuel's case.   Since all children are psychologically alike ; are born under the same covenanted mercies ; and are, therefore, open to the same Divine regenerating influence, the position might be considered as established.   But the Church has been slow to believe the truth ; and much of the nurture of families seems to proceed on the supposition that, as a rule, at least early manhood must be reached ere piety be regarded as trustworthy.   The causes of this unfortunate distrust of child piety are varied.   They may be indicated as—1. The habit of *estimating all piety* by the forms and manifestations appropriate to *adult life*, which habit is based on—2. A *misconception* of what constitutes the *essence* of all true religion.   3. The long *continued neglect of the Church*, as a consequence of this misconception, issuing in a *scarcity of youthful piety*.   But the possibility of it is seen in—1. The *nature of a child* being *capable* of the *essentials* of true piety.   In Samuel, and so in every child, there was a capability of recognising the Great Unseen and Holy One; of cherishing *pure love* for the living, ever-present Friend ; of *trusting* on Almighty care with an unusual absoluteness ; of *learning* the truth concerning the works and ways of God, both by witnessing and sharing in acts of worship, and listening to special instruction ; and of *obedience* to a sovereign Will.   Indeed, in some respects the nature of a child, being free from the carking cares of life and the unhappy suspicions of mature years, is much more susceptible of holy, elevating influences than is that of men.   2. The remarkable *welcome to children given by Christ*.   The child Samuel was welcome in the house of Jehovah.   He "*grew up* before the Lord," and was in "*favour* with God."   Thus in his case we see a beautiful congruity with, and may we not say prophetic of, the loving welcome given later on by the blessed Saviour himself, in terms never to be forgotten.   Possibly some officious priests might deem the presence of the child clad in sacred ephod an innovation and a nuisance in the tabernacle, just as some in excessive but erring zeal would not have Christ troubled with little ones who could not be supposed to understand his profound teaching.   The only recorded instance of Christ being "*much* displeased" is when it was supposed that he was indifferent to the spiritual condition of little children.   3. The *harmony of Hannah's conduct and Samuel's piety with the general tone of Scripture*.   Hannah both consecrated and nurtured her son for the Lord, thus exemplifying the precepts, "Train up a child in the way he should go," "Bring them up in the nurture and admonition of the Lord," and also illustrating the just expectation of the apostle, who seemed to take for granted that pious parents rightly conforming to all their covenanted duties and privileges would have "*holy*" children (1 Cor. vii. 14).

II. That YOUTHFUL PIETY IS VERY DEPENDENT ON CAREFUL NURTURE.   All religion needs culture.   It is the most delicate as also the most precious of our treasures.   The production of piety in children, though of God, as the Source of all grace, is intimately connected with the prayers and faith of parents.   Hannah travailed in spirit for a holy child long before Samuel was born, and the succeeding nurture was only an expression of the same earnestness.   There is no warrant to think that the world would have been blessed with a pious Samuel apart from the deep piety of a Hannah ; and so the presence and growth of piety in our children rests with the Church of God.   The very condition of children in a sinful world suggests a care on their behalf most wise, tender, and constant.   The *elements of true nurture* are seen in Hannah's care of Samuel.   There was—1. The *one* and *perpetual devotement* of the child *to the Lord*—the absolute giving up to the grace of God with a faith that would take no denial.   This act was repeated in spirit day by day for years.   When leaving him in Shiloh ; when silently bowing before God at home ; when engaged in making the little ephod ; when refitting it, as year by year he grew : when with joyous heart visiting Shiloh at the annual festivals—the mother carried Samuel on her heart before God, and gave him up to be blessed.   This is what mothers can ever do for their loved ones, and they sorely need such care in this sinful world. 2. The *impressive teaching imparted.* Surely Samuel was not placed in the house of the Lord without much teaching suited to his capacity as to the holy life he was to live. It is something to make a child believe that he is the Lord's, to see the beauty and joy of being given up to his service. With exquisite delicacy did Hannah teach her son that he must for ever be holy. The girding with the ephod meant to him, "Thou art a servant of God, a child of the sanctuary, *thou* canst not do any unworthy deeds or speak unholy words. Remember thou belongest to the Lord, my son." Happy they who know the art of showing their sons the beauty of holiness, and the manner of persons they ought ever to be. 3. *Association with the sanctuary.* The hallowed associations of the house of God exercised power over the tender child; and so the principle is set forth that in our nurture of youthful piety we must seek to encourage a love for the worship of the Lord and of all pertaining to his service. It is a great gain when our youth can rejoice in the Sabbath services, feel that in the sanctuary they have a much-loved spiritual home. 4. *Engagement in useful religious work.* It was a wise choice of this mother to divert the child's attention from the evil habits of the age by absorption in works suited to his little powers, and under the immediate eye of a venerable man of God. Whatever love to God may dwell in the heart of a child is strengthened and guarded by being exercised in deeds pertaining to his service. And the service of God is very wide and varied. There are many ways in which youthful piety may be exercised. Let children be caused to feel that they by life, by simple prayers, and by sympathy can bless the sorrowing world, and their piety will grow and the world will be enriched. The momentous interests involved in the presence or absence of youthful piety should awaken deep concern on several

Practical questions :—1. To what extent does it prevail in Church and home ? 2. How far the lack of early piety is due to parental neglect, erroneous views, defective Church organisations, or unhealthy literature ? 3. In what form can the existing piety of children be more utilised for their own benefit and for the good of the world? 4. How is it possible to render the services of the sanctuary more interesting and helpful to the young ? 5. How can the missing link between the youthful and more mature piety of the Church be restored ? 6. By what means can Christian parents be led to manifest an all-absorbing concern for the development of piety in their offspring ? 7. What would be the effect on the ultimate conversion of the world if the Church could be so wrought upon to exercise faith in the possibility of early piety as to save the need of employing agencies to convert in adult age any who have passed through its hands ?

Faith's symbols. Judged by the customs of the age, it was a *daring thing* for Hannah to *clothe her child* with the *ephod,* the every-day robe of the priest, seeing that her son was only a Levite (1 Chron. vi. 19, 23 ; cf. Ex. xxxix. 27 ; 1 Sam. xxii. 18). She clearly intended him to be invested with the prerogatives of the priest. The holy daring went further in her making for him the "little coat," which properly was part of the dress of the high priest, and sometimes of princes and nobles. The act is in perfect keeping with the first deed of consecration, and with the tenor of the inspired song. To her prophetic vision this child was from birth ordained to be an extraordinary servant of God, for the reformation of that age and the advancement of that kingdom the glories of which she saw afar. It is not likely that a woman of such strong and exalted hope would be ready to speak out in detail what was in her heart, and yet the force of her faith would demand adequate expression. Some natures are not demonstrative by words, but prefer silent acts to both indicate their thoughts and to nourish their faith and hope. Therefore the clothing of Samuel with the pure " ephod " and the " little coat " was the creation of permanent symbols of faith for his instruction and impressment, and her own satisfaction and support. It is not for mere notice of casual incident that the sacred writer refers to the event. but evidently to set forth valuable truth.

I. FAITH SEES GERMS OF FUTURE GOOD WHERE UNBELIEF WOULD SEE NOTHING. It is probable that neighbours reflected on the eccentric conduct of the mother who so unnecessarily parted with her child. To them he was as other children. The spiritual travail of his birth was hidden from them. But Hannah, being in sympathy with God's merciful purposes to mankind, saw in her son the man of the future, the defender of the faith, the restorer of pure worship, the consecrated spirit which has spiritual right to do priestly work, and it was rest to her soul to express this faith not by words which might be contradicted, but by a solemn act full of instruction to the child, and a permanent record of what she knew would be. So is it ever. The eye of faith sees in the infant Church of God the promise of a " glorious Church." Simeon saw in a babe the " Salvation " of God. A few poor men saw in the " Man of sorrows " the coming " King of glory." The true believer now sees in the occasional triumphs of the gospel the earnest of a world's subjugation to Christ.

11. FAITH HOLDS MORE THAN CAN BE PUT INTO WORDS. There was no one to whom Hannah could unfold in words all that was grasped by her faith. To her the presence of this holy child in the house of God, serving him in the minor details of daily routine, was virtually the realisation of the prophet's office, and the enhancement of Messiah's glory. " Faith is the *substance* of things hoped for." The essential reality of the remote is already in the heart. The future is as though it were present. Prevision and accomplishment become subjectively one. This holy mysticism of the highest spiritual life is foolishness to the unspiritual, but is a profound and blessed fact in the experience of the true children of God. God's word given is as good as fulfilled, and the soul finds more in the consciousness of this truth than can ever be indicated in language. There is always a vast reserve of religious feeling that can never find expression. Life is more than the forms of life. The " ephod " and " little robe," and the annual visits to the child, were outward signs—symbolical forms—of a something which was too great for utterance. They were the shadows of a great reality too sacred, too rich, too varied in its issues to be set forth in ordinary terms. So likewise our faith holds a Christ more glorious and precious than any terms can utter. He is " *formed* in the heart." He is the " *unspeakable* gift." Eye hath not seen, nor ear heard, nor heart conceived what is grasped by the Christian's faith as an ever-present treasure. Human speech, in prose or song, falls below the soul's sense of blessedness in Christ.

111. FAITH IS VENTURESOME IN ADOPTING FORMS OF EXPRESSING ITSELF. Holding converse with realities which lie beyond the ordinary mind, it deviates from routine, and carves out new and rare modes of indicating its existence. Hannah could not rest content with telling Elkanah, Eli, and Samuel, in casual conversation and fleeting words, what she knew this ministering child was to be in days to come, and what she knew of the coming kingdom. Jacob made a coat of many colours to gratify a questionable feeling of partiality. Jochebed made a covering of bulrushes to save a precious life, possibly with a trust in a wise Providence. But Hannah had a faith in God, in the revival of religion, in the Messiah's glory, which not only sought vent for itself, but dared to create new and, to the eye of man, questionable forms of expression. Persistently, year by year, as the sacred ephod required readjustment to varying stature, did the faith reassert itself in every stitch and every trial of approval. Innovation it might be, but it was true to faith, and faith loves reality, and seeks congruity between itself and its outward forms. The apostle writing to the Hebrews on the triumphs of faith recognises its heroism, *its superiority to conventional forms, its intense energy in asserting itself* (Heb. xi.). There are modern instances of the same holy daring. Symbolism may, like other things, sometimes be the resort of weak minds and superstitious tendencies, yet it may be a legitimate outgrowth of strong faith. The stately sanctuary ; the hushed feeling in listening to the word of God ; the surrender of fortune to the propagation of the gospel ; the adoption of righteous usages against the current of opinion and custom, are only some of the symbols of a faith that longs and dares to indicate its presence. As feelings grow in power when exercised, so faith nourishes itself by fit permanent expressions, especially when in some bold and truthful deed.

Practical considerations :—1. How far the faith of these times is a reality as distinguished from a formal consent to what is commonly believed. 2. Whether the Church of Christ sufficiently lays hold of the fruition of all future toil in the acquired results of present toil. 3 To what extent the individuality of a powerful religious life proves itself by deeds of daring devotion. 4. The distinction to be drawn between a safe or unsafe symbolism in stated forms of worship, and the natural spontaneous symbolism of an energetic personal faith. 5. The possibility of a masterful faith in degenerate times, rightfully deviating from established practices, and being used by God as preliminary to great reformations.

Vers. 20, 21. — *Solid character.* The facts are—1. Eli forms a favourable estimate of the conduct and character of Elkanah and Hannah. 2. God enriches them with several children. 3. Samuel advances in years and gains in repute. 4. The sons of Eli, becoming more dissolute, are rebuked by their father. Time had gradually brought out to the view of Eli the solid character of Elkanah and his wife. Their regular attendance on worship at the appointed seasons, and their reverent spirit, were in striking contrast with the degenerate habits with which Eli was too familiar. Their quiet, unassuming conduct harmonised with Hannah's early professions of piety, and the child which they had presented to assist Eli in his ministrations had fully answered his expectations. Here, then, we have solid character :—

I. APPRECIATED BY MAN. The opportunities given through a succession of years had enabled Eli to form a favourable estimate of these obscure dwellers on Mount Ephraim. He was the more glad to give them his priestly benediction because of the rash words with which he once (ch. i. 13, 14) wounded a " sorrowful spirit." It is a blessed thing to enjoy the approval of the good. A good name is a precious treasure. There is a sweet reward for years of toil, and possibly under misapprehension and neglect, in being at last fairly appreciated for what one is and has done. Although there are proud ungodly men who will despise the godly poor, yet the conditions of character being appreciated by the better sections of society are within the reach of the most lowly. These conditions are—1. *Constancy in the discharge of religious duties.* Observance year by year of public worship and of all the ordinances of God is a good sign of a religious spirit. Eli was not wrong in supposing that there must be solid worth in a family that kept to the ways of the Lord when so many neglected religious duties. A man cannot claim a reputation by asking for it. The testimony of faithfulness in religious worship is admitted by all. Fluctuations in religious zeal always awaken distrust. Constancy is an element always honoured. 2. *Manifestation of an unostentatious spirit.* This must have impressed Eli very strongly. The quiet, unpretending spirit of the Levite and his wife gained on the venerable man year by year. And so always the quiet, even tenor of life tells an irresistible story. All sensible men shrink from the egotism and ostentation which sometimes assume the garb of religion. The proper thing for all is an earnest, lowly mind, more concerned with quietly doing what is right and pleasing to God than with making an impression on man. Those who think much of what men will say and think, and make corresponding demonstrations of zeal, are sure to fall into the snare of " eye service." Like the steady influence of light and dew, quiet goodness at home and in the Church and world is a real power. There are thousands of such lives in Christian homes. 3. *Self-denial in God's service.* Though Hannah's joy in giving her heart to God took off the edge of self-denial, yet Eli could not but be deeply impressed with the unusual self-sacrifice of both husband and wife. The true religious spirit of a man comes out in spontaneous offerings to the efficiency of the services of the sanctuary and the advancement of Christ's kingdom. Character expressed in free, unconstrained surrender of money, or time, or sons for religious purposes cannot but be appreciated. It is in the power of all to perform some acts of self-denial for God, and apart from such acts, no professions will establish a reputation in the true Church of God. The *intrinsic value of self-denial* lies much in its freeness, its timeliness, its form. The surrender of a Samuel at such a time, in such a spirit, is an example to all ages. Are there no other Hannahs ? Is all the " precious ointment " of the Christian Church exhausted ?

II. HONOURED BY GOD. God does not save by virtue of human merit, but through Christ ; yet he honours fidelity by his special favour and greater blessing. Hannah had been honoured variously ; *e. g.* in being heard, in having a son according to promise, in being permitted to consecrate him to the special service of God, in receiving grace to part with him from home if not from heart, and in being enabled to enjoy a blessed vision of One greater and more holy than Samuel. But the fidelity wherewith she and her husband had, during the period covered, served God in home and in public life, as also by the general tenor of their lives, was crowned with a great increase of domestic joy. The home of Hannah emptied for God became full. The surrendered child was returned in fivefold form. The long, pining years of early life were followed by old age of blessed satisfaction. Thus do all ages show that " there is that scattereth and yet increaseth." " I sent you forth ; " " lacked ye anything ? " There is a promise of a " hundredfold " for all that has been forsaken for Christ. In one way or another God will prove that he is not unrighteous to forget the work of faith and labour of love. " Them that honour me I will honour."

Practical lessons :—1. Let the lowly be patient in their endeavour to follow out the light they enjoy in worship and in service. 2. Many individuals and families can win for themselves the precious treasure of human and Divine favour, even though the wealth and fame coveted in the world fall not to their lot. 3. The multiplication of quiet, unostentatious religious characters is an end earnestly to be sought, as adding in every sense to the welfare of the world. 4. The severity of our trials in the cause of Christ, if entered into rightly, is sure to be crowned with blessing.

Vers. 22—26.—*Abandoned.* The facts are—1. Eli in advancing years hears of the abominable deeds of his sons. 2. He remonstrates with them, pointing out the consequences of their conduct. 3. Heedless of the warning, they persist in sin, being abandoned by God. The narrative of the sacred historian seems to take in two extremes—two elements working on in moral antagonism till the one passes away and the other becomes ascendant. The abominations and profanations of Eli's sons, and Samuel's purity and entire devotion to God, are placed in striking contrast. The history of the former is sketched as explaining the course of Providence in the deliverance wrought by Samuel's subsequent conduct. The stage in the course of the dissolute priests here indicated brings into view—

I. FEARFUL PROGRESSION IN SIN. The iniquity of years culminates in the most abominable crimes men could commit. The descent to shamelessness and utter corruption becomes very rapid. One can hardly imagine these vile sons of Belial as once having been gentle youths taught to revere Jehovah's name, and to tread his courts with awe. The *momentum* gained by evil desires when once let loose is among the most fearful features of human experience. It is the same sad story as often told now to the hearts of wailing parents :—disobedience, aversion to holy things, formal observances, secret associations of evil, seared conscience, loss of self-respect, profanation of sacred places, contempt for religion, self-abandonment to lust, defiance of God. What tears fall to earth nightly over erring ones ! What blasted hopes lie on life's pathway ! What cruel triumphs of sin over all that is fair and strong in human nature ! Holy Saviour, many of thy followers share in thy tears once shed over sin finished in righteous doom ! (James i. 15). When, when shall the mighty power come in answer to the cry of thy Church to turn back the tide of woe, and drive the curse from the heart and home of man ? " How long, O Lord, how long ? "

II. DEFECTIVE DISCIPLINE. No doubt Eli, as a good man, deplored the vices of the age, and above all the crimes of his sons, and he performed a father's part in remonstrating with them on account of their deeds, warning them of the dangers to which they were exposed at the hand of the invisible Judge. But the day for warning and remonstrance was past, and the day for swift, unsparing punishment had come. As judge in civil capacity, and as high priest in spiritual capacity, the course of Eli was clear—*immediate banishment* from office and *capital punishment* (Lev. xviii. 6, 20, 29 ; xx. 10 ; xxi. 6, 7, 17, 23). We see how a *man good in many respects*, may *recognise duty* and *not perform it*. Eli knew that the sin of contempt for the ordinance of sacrifice, utter disregard of the honour due to God, prostitution of the holiest office to the vilest uses, was past condoning, past covering even by sacrifice. For God, as Eli puts it, makes no provision to pardon and save those who wantonly scorn the means of pardon and salvation. No sacrifice ! no intercessor ! Yet the appointed judge in Israel is content with a bare declaration of truth, refraining from an exercise of the powers wherewith he is invested for the vindication of justice and the maintenance of order. *Moral weakness* was the sin of Eli. The imperious claims of God, of public welfare, of religious purity, appealed to the sense of duty in vain, because of some personal sentiment or lack of resolution. Cases often arise in national affairs, Church discipline, home life, where duty comes into collision with private sentiments and personal affection. Sometimes, as with Nathan in accusing David, and Ambrose in placing Theodosius under the ban, moral strength is conspicuous. Often, as with Eli, Jonah, and David in one instance, sense of duty yields to inferior impulses. *True moral courage* is a *quality of high order.* It confers great honour on those in whom it appears, and is a most important element in securing the welfare of the individual, the home, and the public. Its presence in *most perfect Christian* form may be ascribed to the combination of various elements. (*a*) A *natural sense of justice*—a psychological condition in which moral perceptions have more prompt influence than transitory emotions. (*b*) A *careful culture of the conscience* through early years, and in relation to the minutiæ of life. (*c*) *Intelligent faith* in the *inviolability* of *moral law.* (*d*) Formation of the *habit of immediate submission* to *moral dictates,* on the general principle that in morals first thoughts are truest. (*e*) *Strength of will* to *endure present suffering,* as not being the worst of evils. (*f*) A nature *brought fully under* the *quickening influence* of *practical Christianity,* as consisting in radical renewal, obedience to the precepts of Christ, fellowship with a holy God, and perpetual aspiration after holiness. There are *instances still* in which failure in moral courage is the *one great blot* on an otherwise excellent life. Where such occur sin flourishes, and the righteous mourn. The severe hand of justice is frequently the hand of true kindness. Favouritism and subordination of righteousness to personal ends, in public and domestic life, cause iniquity to abound, and sooner or later these will be visited by the judgment of God.

III. DIVINE ABANDONMENT. The sons of Eli were given up by God to their deserved doom. They heeded not remonstrance, for they had gone so far into sin as to be left destitute of that gracious influence from God, without which the soul is held fast in the cords of its iniquity. The outward fact of despising the father's warning was evidence to the historian that God had judicially abandoned them. "They hearkened not, *because the Lord would slay them.*" The solemn truth is clear that *men may persist in sin* so utterly as to be *given up by God* without mercy to *all its consequences.* 1. The *evidence* of this is full. (*a*) Men are sometimes *smitten with death* as a consequence of persistent sin, as in case of Sodom, and the rebellion of Korah, all means of repentance being judicially cut off. (*b*) The New Testament references to the sin against the Holy Ghost, and the apostasy of counting the blood of Christ an "unclean thing." (*c*) The fact that at the end of life the impenitent are given over to look for "tribulation and anguish." 2. The *rationale of this is partly discoverable.* It is not mere arbitrariness, nor is it the effect of imperfect benevolence. (*a*) It is consonant with the *working of natural law.* Physiology and psychology prove that there is a tendency to permanence of character in all. This is especially true of those who persist in strong unhallowed desires. (*b*) There are *transgressions even in society* which admit of *no restoration* to society. (*c*) In a wise and endlessly *ramified moral government* which rests on an eternal right, there can be no proof that a moral Ruler, whose existence is bound up with right and order, is *obliged to cover the past* of free beings who *have deliberately persisted in evil,* by giving them a new power which shall make them different from what they prefer to be. (*d*) The *judicial abandonment* of the intensely sinful acts as a *wholesome deterrent* on the moral universe, by vindicating the holiness of God, and the claim of universal society on the pure, loving life of each of its constituents, and this too while giving to free beings only what they prefer.

Practical lessons:—1. The importance of *guarding against first tendencies* to deviate from the path of purity and truth. 2. The value of early *habits* of devotion, regard for right and purity, as a *preventive* of *habits* of a reverse character. 3. The extreme danger to the Church of a *professional religion* in alliance with a tendency to *sensual indulgence,* and the need of watching closely against such a possible combination. 4. The value of an early *training of the moral sense,* and its constant culture, as against the *inferior elements* of our life. 5. The use of the lessons of history, as illustrating the terrible power of sin, and the damage done to society and the Church by defective discipline.

HOMILIES BY VARIOUS AUTHORS.

Ver. 11. (SHILOH.)—*Samuel's childhood and growth.* "And the child did minister unto the Lord before Eli the priest." "And the child Samuel grew on, and was in favour both with the Lord, and also with men" (ver. 26). (Ch. i. 24; ii. 18, 19, 21; iii. 1.) "Great is the reverence due to children." It is said of an eccentric schoolmaster in Germany, who lived about 300 years ago, John Trebonius, that he never appeared before his boys without taking off his hat and bowing very humbly before them. "Who can tell," said he, "what may not rise up amid these youths? There may be among them those who shall be learned doctors, sage legislators, nay, princes of the empire." Even then there was among them "the solitary monk that shook the world." But a much greater than Luther (with whom he has been compared— *Ewald*) was the little Nazarite, who with unshorn locks ministered in the tabernacle at Shiloh; and at a very early age he gave signs of his future eminence. "Even a child is known by his doings" (Prov. xx. 11). "The child is father to the man." But what he will be depends greatly on his early training; for "the new vessel takes a lasting tincture from the liquor which is first poured in" (Horace); "the soft clay is easily fashioned into what form you please" (Persius); and "the young plant may be bent with a gentle hand, and the characters engraved on the tender bark grow deeper with the advancing tree" (Quinctilian). Consider—

I. HIS EDUCATION, or the influences to which he was subject, consisting of—1. *Impressions under the parental roof.* He did not leave his home at an age too early to prevent his receiving deep and permanent impressions from the example, prayers, and instructions of his parents. His destination would be explained to him by his mother, and made attractive and desirable; so that when the time came for the fulfilment of her vow he might readily make it his own. The memory of those early days must have been always pleasant to him; and the sacred bond of filial affection would be renewed and strengthened by the annual visit of his parents, and by the yearly present which his mother brought to him (ver. 19). The making of the "little coat" was a work of love, and served to keep her absent boy in mind, whilst the possession of it was to him a constant memorial of her pure affection. The first impressions which he thus received were a powerful means of preserving him from evil, and inciting him to good. "Every first thing continues for ever with the child; the first colour, the first music, the first flower paint the foreground of life; every new educator affects less than its predecessor, until at last, if we regard all life as an educational institution, the circumnavigator of the world is less influenced by all nations he has seen than by his nurse" (Locke). 2. *Association with holy things.* Everything in the tabernacle was to his childish view beautiful and impressive, and overshadowed by the mysterious presence of the Lord of hosts. "Heaven lies about us in our infancy." And the veil which separates the invisible from the visible is then very attenuated. When he afterwards saw how much beneath the outward form was hollow and corrupt, he was strong enough to endure the shock, and distinguished between "the precious and the vile." Association with sacred things either makes men better than others, or else very much worse. 3. *Occupation in lowly services.* Even when very young he could perform many little services in such a place as the tabernacle, and in personal attendance on Eli, who was very old and partially blind. A part of his occupation we know was to open the doors (ch. iii. 15). By means of such things he was trained for a higher ministry. 4. *Instruction in sacred truth,* given by his kind-hearted guardian in explanation of the various objects and services in the tabernacle, and, still more, gained by the perusal of the religious records stored up therein (ch. x. 25). 5. *Familiarity with public life.* "There at the centre of government, he must early have become conversant with the weightiest concerns of the people." 6. *Observation of the odious practices of many,* especially Hophni and Phinehas. For this also must be mentioned among the influences that went to form his character. It is impossible to keep a child altogether from the sight of vice. External safeguards are no protection without internal purity. On the other hand, outward circumstances which are naturally perilous have often no effect on internal purity, except to make it more decided and robust. "The jarring contrast which he had before his eyes in the evil example of Eli's children could but force more strongly upon his mind the conviction of the great necessity of the age, and impel to still more unflinching rigour to act up to this conviction" (Ewald). But this could only take place by—7. *The power of Divine grace*, which is the greatest and only effectual teacher (Titus ii. 11, 12). The atmosphere of prayer which he breathed from earliest life was the atmosphere of grace. The Holy Spirit rested upon him in an eminent degree, and he grew up under his influence, "like a tree planted by the rivers of water," gradually and surely to perfection.

II. HIS CHARACTER, or the dispositions which he developed under these influences. He "grew on" not only physically and intellectually, but also morally and spiritually, manifesting the dispositions which properly belong to a child, and make him a pattern to men (Matt. xviii. 3). 1. *Humble submission*. 2. *Great docility*, or readiness to learn what he was taught. 3. *Ready obedience* to what he was told to do. How promptly did he respond to the voice of Eli, who, as he thought, called him from his slumber (ch. iii. 5). The watchword of childhood and youth should be "Obey." And it is only those that learn to obey who will be fit to command. 4. *Profound reverence*. For "he ministered before the Lord," as if under his eye, and with a growing sense of his presence. "He was to receive his training at the sanctuary, that at the very earliest waking up of his spiritual susceptibilities he might receive the impression of the sacred presence of God" (Keil). 5. *Transparent truthfulness* and guilelessness. 6. *Purity* and self-control (1 Tim. iv. 12; 2 Tim. ii. 22). 7. *Sincere devotion* to the purpose of his dedication to the Lord. In this manner he gradually grew into the possession of a holy character, and needed not, like many others, any sudden or conscious "conversion" from the ways of sin to the ways of God. Like John the Baptist, "he grew and waxed strong in spirit" (Luke i. 80); and his childhood is described in the very words employed to describe the childhood of our Lord:. "And Jesus increased in favour with God and man" (Luke ii. 40, 51, 52).

III. HIS ACCEPTANCE, or the favour he obtained (Prov. iii. 4). 1. *With God*, who looked down upon him with delight, beholding in him the effect of his grace, and a reflection of his light and love. For "the Lord taketh pleasure in his people' (Ps. cxlix. 4). 2. *With men*. The gratification which Eli felt in his presence and service appears in the benediction he uttered on his parents when they visited the tabernacle, and in accordance with which they were compensated with three sons and two daughters for "the gift which they gave unto the Lord" (ch. ii. 20, 21). Even Hophni and Phinehas must have regarded the young Nazarite with respect. And the people who brought their offerings to the tabernacle looked upon him with admiration and hope. So he was prepared for the work that lay before him.—D.

Vers. 12—17. (SHILOH.)—*A degenerate priesthood*. "The best things when corrupted become the worst." It is thus with official positions such as were held by the priests of old. Their positions were an hereditary right, and their duties consisted largely of a prescribed routine of services. It was required, however, that their personal character should accord with their sacred work (Mal. ii. 7); and their influence was great for good or evil. Whilst they reflected in their character and conduct the moral condition of the times, they also contributed in no small degree to produce it. The sons of Eli employed their high office not for the welfare of men and the glory of God, but for their own selfish and corrupt purposes, and afford an example of "great and instructive wickedness." Concerning them the following things are recorded:—

I. CULPABLE IGNORANCE OF GOD (ver. 12). They had no proper conception of him as holy and just, and they did not consider that he observed and hated sin by whomsoever it was committed, and would surely punish it. They had no communion with him, no sympathy with his purposes, and no sense of their own obligations to him. They were unspiritual men, and practically infidel. And they were such notwithstanding the instructions they received, the opportunities they possessed, and the services they rendered. Although the servants of God, "they knew not God," and were "without excuse." Amidst a blaze of light men may be dark within. "And if the light within thee be darkness, how great is that darkness ! "

II. OFFICIAL ROBBERY OF MEN (vers. 13, 14). Not satisfied with the liberal portions of the peace offerings which were legally assigned to them (the breast and shoulder), they claimed other and larger portions, to which they were not entitled, and robbed the people for the gratification of their own appetites. What they would have fiercely denounced in others they deemed venial offences in privileged men like themselves. How often do official positions and selfish indulgences blind men to the injustice of their conduct, and harden them in iniquity.

III. WILFUL VIOLATION OF THE LAW (ver. 15). It was required by the Levitical law that the fat should be burnt on the altar before the offering was divided between the priest and the offerer ; but instead of doing this, the priest sent his servant beforehand to demand his portion with the fat, that it might be better fitted for roasting than boiling, which was not to his taste. He thus appropriated to his private use what belonged to the Lord, and "robbed God " of his due. It was a gross act of disobedience, sacrilege, and profanity, prompted by the same pampered appetite as his dishonesty toward men ; and, in addition, it hindered the people from fulfilling their religious purposes, and made his own servant a partner in his sin.

IV. DESPOTIC EXERCISE OF AUTHORITY (ver. 16). When the people gently remonstrated, and promised to give up their own portion if the fat were first burnt on the altar, it was said to them, "Nay, but thou shalt give it me now, or else I will come and take it by force." · Reason as well as right was overridden. Instead of regarding himself as a servant of God for the good of men, the priest made himself a "lord over God's heritage " (1 Pet. v. 3). Having cast aside the authority of God, he made his own arbitrary dictum the law of others, and urged obedience to it by the threatening of force. By the same means, backed by spiritual terrors, he has often sought to accomplish his wishes in every age.

V. INJURIOUS INFLUENCE ON RELIGION (vers. 17, 24). Men abstained from presenting as many offerings as they would have given, or even from presenting them at all, being repelled from the service of God by the evil conduct of his ministers. "Ye make the Lord's people to transgress " (ver. 24). One unworthy priest has often made many unbelievers. Instead of strengthening what is noblest and best in men, he has destroyed it, and made its restoration impossible. And, generally, ungodly conduct on the part of professed servants of God is a great hindrance to the spread of truth and righteousness, and a powerful influence in extending error and evil in the world. "One sinner destroyeth much good." To complete the picture, two other things must be added, viz.—

VI. SHAMELESS INDULGENCE IN VICE (ver. 22). They knew nothing of self-control, gave the rein to their lusts, and indulged in vices which the heathen commonly associated with their idol worship, and which made that worship so terrible a temptation to Israel. The idol feasts at Shiloh were doubtless scenes of gross sensuality ; and the sons of Eli scarcely cared to disguise their participation in similar indulgences, and made the tabernacle of the Lord like a heathen temple.

VII. SUPERSTITIOUS USE OF SACRED THINGS (ch. iv. 11). Having become insensible to the presence of the invisible King, they treated his services as a mere outward ritual, which may be performed without any felt inconsistency between it and any amount of immorality. Why should they observe it at all ? From self-interest and from superstition. They still supposed that there was some mysterious benefit inseparably connected with the ark, and enjoyed by those who possessed it, apart from their moral and spiritual state. Their religion had become a superstition, like that of the heathen. And hence they took the ark into the battle-field, in sure confidence of their safety, and were deprived of it by the heathen, and they themselves destroyed. 1. It is possible for men to possess the highest privileges, and yet sink into the deepest degradation. 2. The patience of Heaven toward sinners. is wonderful, and designed to lead them to repentance. 3. When men despise the goodness of God, and persist in transgression, they are certain to meet with signal punishment.—D

Vers. 22—25. (Shiloh.)—*Ineffective reproof.* A man may possess many amiable qualities, and be, on the whole, a good man, and yet be marked by some defect which mars his character, prevents his usefulness, and makes him the unintentional cause of much mischief. Such a man was Eli. Of his early life nothing is recorded. He was a descendant of Ithamar, the youngest son of Aaron, and held the office of high priest, which formerly belonged to the elder branch of the Aaronic family, that of Eleazar (Num. xx. 26), but which was now transferred to the younger, from some unknown cause, and which continued therein until the time of Solomon. At the age of fifty-eight he became judge, and " judged Israel forty years " (ch. iv. 18). When first mentioned he must have been at least seventy years old. His sons were children of his old age; for some time afterwards they were spoken of as young men (ch. ii. 17), and, as is not uncommon in such cases, he treated them with undue indulgence. He was hasty and severe in reproving Hannah, but slow and mild in reproving them. The inefficiency of his REPROOF appears in that—

I. IT WAS NOT ADMINISTERED IN PROPER TIME. The tendency to go wrong generally appears at an early age; and it must have been seen by him in his sons long before the rumour of their flagrant transgressions reached him, if he had not been blind to their faults. But he had no adequate sense of his parental responsibility, was old and weak, of a gentle and easy-going temperament, and omitted to reprove them (1 Kings i. 6) until they had become too strongly devoted to their evil ways to be amenable to expostulation. A little plant may be easily rooted up, but when it has grown into a tree it can only be removed by extraordinary efforts. If some children are " discouraged " (Col. iii. 21) by too much strictness, far more are spoiled by too much indulgence. " Indulgence never produces gratitude or love in the heart of a child."

II. IT WAS NOT GIVEN WITH SUFFICIENT EARNESTNESS (vers. 23, 24). Gentle reproof may sometimes be most effective, but here it was out of place. 1. It was not *sufficiently pointed* in its application; being given to them *collectively* rather than individually, in *indefinite* terms, by way of *question*, and concerning things which he had *heard*, but into the certainty of which he had not troubled himself to inquire. 2. It exhibited no sufficient sense of the *evil of sin* (ver. 25). He spoke of the consequences rather than of the nature, the " exceeding sinfulness " of sin, and spoke of them in a way which indicated little deep personal conviction. 3. It showed *no sufficient determination* to correct it. He did not say that he would judge them for their injustice toward men; and with reference to their sin against the Lord, which was their chief offence, he simply confessed that he could do nothing but leave them to the judgment of a higher tribunal. " In the case where the rebuke should have descended like a bolt from heaven we hear nothing but low and feeble murmurings, coming, as it were, out of the dust. Cruel indeed are the tenderest mercies of parental weakness and indulgence. And the fate of Eli shows that by such tender mercies the father may become the minister of vengeance unto his whole house " (Le Bas).

III. IT WAS NOT FOLLOWED BY ADEQUATE CHASTISEMENT. The law of Moses in the case of disobedient children was very severe (Deut. xxi. 18—21). But Eli neither observed this law " when they hearkened not to his voice " (ver. 25), nor took any further steps to prevent the continuance of the evil which he reproved. He had none of the zeal for which Phinehas the son of Eleazar was approved (Num. xxv. 11—13); but as a father, a high priest, and a judge he was guilty of culpable infirmity and wilful disobedience (ch. iii. 13). " Osiers," says an old writer, " can never be pillars in the State or in the Church."

IV. IT DID NOT RESULT IN ANY IMPROVEMENT (ver. 25). Their contempt of reproof showed that they were already infatuated, hardened, and abandoned to destruction; or (reading for = therefore), it filled up the measure of their iniquities, and exposed them to inevitable judgment. " He that hateth reproof shall die " (Prov. xv. 10). 1. Reproof is often a solemn obligation. 2. It should be given in an effective manner. 3. When not so given it does more harm than good. 4. When justly given it should be humbly and obediently received.—D.

EXPOSITION.

THE DIVINE JUDGMENT UPON ELI AND HIS HOUSE (vers. 27—36). Ver. 27.—**There came a man of God.** The title *man of God* is the usual appellation of a prophet in the books of Judges, Samuel, and Kings, and as such is applied by Manoah to the angel who appeared to him (Judges xiii. 6, 8). Though the recorded interpositions of the Deity in those times were generally by angels, still the readiness with which Manoah gave his visitant this title makes it probable that prophets did appear from time to time; and the mission of one, though, as here, without a name, is recorded in Judges vi. 8. As regards the date of this visitation of the man of God, we find that Eli was ninety-eight years of age when the ark was captured (ch. iv. 15). At that time Samuel was not merely a man, but one whose reputation was established throughout the whole land, and who was probably regarded not merely as a prophet, but as Eli's successor in the office of judge (ch. iii. 19, 20). But Eli was "very old" (ch. ii. 22) when he rebuked his sons, probably between seventy and eighty, for Samuel is then called a child (ver. 26); whereas he can scarcely have been much less than thirty years of age when the Philistines destroyed Shiloh. In ch. viii. 1—3, when the misconduct of Samuel's own sons led to the revival of the agitation for a king, he is himself described as already "old;" but as he lived on till nearly the end of Saul's reign, he could not at that time have been much more than sixty. Even when God spake by him to Eli he is still described as a boy, *na'ar* (ch. iii. 1), though the higher position to which he had attained, as is proved by his duties, would lead to the conclusion that he was then verging on manhood. As some time would naturally elapse between two such solemn warnings, we may feel sure that the visit of the man of God occurred shortly after Samuel's dedication. Then, as Eli neglected the warning, and the wickedness of his sons grew more inveterate, some eight or ten years afterwards the warning was repeated in sharper tones by the voice of his own youthful attendant. Meanwhile Eli seems himself to have grown in personal piety, but he could do nothing now for his sons. Past eighty years of age, the time of activity had gone by, and resignation was the sole virtue that was left for him to practise. And so the warning given by the mouth of Samuel is stern and final. Ten or fifteen more years must elapse before the ruin came. But the gloom was deepening; the Philistines were increasing in power, and the valour of Israel was decaying as its morality declined; then there was a short violent crash, and the house of Eli met its doom.

The prophet begins by enumerating Jehovah's mercies to "the house of thy father," that is, the whole family of Aaron, in selecting them for the priesthood (on the choice of the house of Aaron, see Exod. xxviii., xxix.), and in richly endowing the office with so large a portion of every sacrifice. These portions are termed literally *firings*, or fire-sacrifices, but the term soon became general, and in Lev. xxiv. 7, 9 is applied even to the shew-bread. Added then to the tithes, and to the cities with their suburbs given them to inhabit, this share of every sacrifice gave the house of Aaron great wealth, and with it they had also high rank. There was no one above them in Israel except the kings. In Sparta we find that one of the endowments of the kings was the skins of animals offered in sacrifice (Herod., vi. 56). Why then do Eli and his sons, who benefit so greatly by them, "kick at Jehovah's sacrifices and offerings?" The word is taken from Deut. xxxii. 15, and refers to the efforts of a pampered steer violently to shake off the yoke. Eli's sons treat the ordinances which have raised them to rank, and given them wealth and power, as if they were an injury and wrong. And Eli, instead of removing them from the office which they disgraced, preferred the ties of relationship to his duty to God and the moral welfare of the people.

Ver. 30.—**I said indeed.** By thus acting Eli became an accomplice in the irreligion of his sons, and God therefore revokes his grant of a perpetual priesthood. The promise had been made to Aaron's family as a whole (Exod. xxix. 9), and had then been renewed to the house of Eleazar (Num. xxv. 13). But the house of Ithamar was now in the ascendant, probably owing to Eli's own ability, who during the anarchical times of the Judges had won for himself, first, the civil power, and then, upon some fitting opportunity, the high priesthood also, though I suppose the heads of the houses of Eleazar and Ithamar were always persons of great importance, and high priests in a certain sense. Eli had now the priority, and had he and his family proved worthy, the possession of this high station might have been confirmed to them. Like Saul in the kingdom, they proved unworthy of it, and so they lost it for ever. Their names, as we have seen above, do not even occur in the genealogies.

I said . . . . but now Jehovah saith. Can then a promise of God be withdrawn?

Yes, assuredly. Not from mankind as a whole, nor from the Church as a whole, but from each particular nation, or Church, or individual. To each separate person God's promises are conditional, and human action everywhere is a co-worker with the Divine volition, though only within a limited sphere, and so as that the Divine purposes must finally be accomplished. Eli then and his sons may suffer forfeit of the promise by not fulfilling the obligations which, whether expressed or implied, are an essential condition of every promise made by God to man. But the high priesthood will continue, and will perform its allotted task of preparing for the priesthood of Christ. "Them that honour me I will honour," states one of these conditions essential on man's part to secure the fulfilment of God's promises.

Ver. 31. — **I will cut off thine arm.** The *arm* is the usual metaphor for strength. As Eli had preferred the exaltation of his sons to God's honour, he is condemned to see the strength of his house broken. Nay, more ; there is not to be an "old man in his house." The young men full of energy and vigour perish by the sword ; the survivors fade away by disease. The Jews say that the house of Ithamar was peculiarly short-lived, but the prophecy was amply fulfilled in the slaughter of Eli's house, first at Shiloh, and then at Nob by Doeg the Edomite at the command of Saul. There is nothing to warrant an abiding curse upon his family. The third or fourth generation is the limit of the visitation of the sins of the fathers upon the children.

Ver. 32. — **Thou shalt see an enemy.** The translation of ver. 32 is very difficult, but is probably as follows : "And thou shalt behold, *i. e.* see with wonder and astonishment, narrowness of habitation in all the wealth which shall be given unto Israel." The word translated *narrowness* often means an "enemy," but as that for *habitation* is the most general term in the Heb. language for a dwelling, being used even of the dens of wild beasts (Jer. ix. 10 ; Nahum ii. 12), the rendering an "enemy of dwelling" gives no sense. Hence the violent insertion of the pronoun *my*, for which no valid excuse can be given. But *narrowness of dwelling* means distress, especially in a man's domestic relations, and this is the sense required. In the growing public and national prosperity which was to be Israel's lot under Samuel, Saul, David, and Solomon, Eli was to see, not in person, but prophetically, calamity attaching itself to his own family. His house was to decay in the midst of the progress of all the rest. Upon this denunciation of private distress naturally follows the repetition of the threat that the house of Ithamar

should be left without an old man to guide its course onward to renewed prosperity.

Ver. 33. — **The man of thine,&c.** The meaning of the Heb. is here again changed by the insertion of words not in the original. Translated literally the sense is good, but merciful, and this the A. V. has so rendered as to make it the most bitter of all denunciations. The Heb. is, "Yet I will not cut off every one of thine from my altar, to consume thine eyes and to grieve thy soul ;" that is, thy punishment shall not be so utter as to leave thee with no consolation ; for thy descendants, though diminished in numbers, and deprived of the highest rank, shall still minister as priests at mine altar. "But the majority of thy house—lit. the multitude of thy house—shall die as men." This is very well rendered in the A. V. "in the flower of their age," only we must not explain this of dying of disease. They were to die in their vigour, not, like children and old men, in their beds, but by violent deaths, such as actually befell them at Shiloh and at Nob.

Ver. 34. — With this the sign here given exactly agrees. Hophni and Phinehas died fighting valiantly in battle, and then came the sacking of Shiloh, and the slaughter of the ministering priests (Ps. lxxviii. 64). Upon this followed a long delay. For first Eli's grandson, Ahitub, the son of Phinehas, was high priest, and then his two sons, Ahiah and Ahimelech, and then Abiathar, the son of Ahimelech. It was in Ahimelech's days that the slaughter took place at Nob, from which the house of Ithamar seems never to have fully recovered.

Ver. 35. — **I will raise me up a faithful priest.** This prophecy is explained in three several ways, of Samuel, of Zadok, and of Christ. St. Augustine, who considers the whole passage at length in his 'De Civ. Dei,' xvii. 5, argues that it cannot be reasonably said that a change in the priesthood foretold with so great circumstance was fulfilled in Samuel. But while we grant that it was an essential characteristic of Jewish prophecy to be ever larger than the immediate fulfilment, yet its primary meaning must never be slurred over, as if it were a question of slight importance. By the largeness of its terms, the grandeur of the hopes it inspired, and the incompleteness of their immediate accomplishment, the Jews were taught to look ever onward, and so became a Messianic people. Granting then that Christ and his Church are the object and end of this and of all prophecy, the question narrows itself to this—In whom was this prediction of a faithful priest primarily fulfilled ? We answer, Not in Zadok, but in Samuel. Zadok was a commonplace personage, of whom little or nothing is said after the time that he joined David with a powerful contingent (1 Chron. xii. 28). Samuel is the one person in Jewish history who approaches the high rank of Moses, Israel's founder (Jer. xv. 1). The argument that he was a Levite, and not a priest, takes too narrow and technical a view of the matter; for the essence of the priesthood lies not in the offering of sacrifice, but in mediation. Sacrifice is but an accident, being the appointed method by which the priest was to mediate between God and man. As a matter of fact, Samuel often did discharge priestly functions (1 Sam. vii. 9, 17; xiii. 8, where we find Saul reproved for invading Samuel's office; xvi. 2), and it is a point to be kept in mind that the regular priests disappear from Jewish history for about fifty years after the slaughter of themselves, their wives, and families at Shiloh; for it is not until Saul's time that Ahiah, the great-grandson of Eli, appears, as once again ministering at the altar (1 Sam. xiv. 3). The calamity that overtook the nation at the end of Eli's reign was so terrible that all ordinary ministrations seem to have been in abeyance. We are even expressly told that after the recovery of the ark it was placed in the house of Abinadab at Kirjath-jearim in Judæa, and that for twenty years his son Eleazar, though a Levite only, ministered there before it by no regular consecration, but by the appointment of the men of that town. During this time, though Ahitub, Ahiah's father, was probably high priest nominally, yet nothing is said of him, and all the higher functions of the office were exercised by Samuel. Instead of the Urim and Thummim, he as prophet was the direct representative of the theocratic king. Subsequently this great duty was once again discharged by Abiathar as priest, and then a mighty change was made, and the prophets with the living voice of inspiration took the place of the priest with the ephod. For this is a far more important matter than even the fact that Samuel performed the higher functions of the priesthood. With him a new order of things began. Prophecy, from being spasmodic and irregular, became an established institution, and took its place side by side with the priesthood in preparing for Christ's advent, and in forming the Jewish nation to be the evangelisers of the world. The prediction of this organic change followed the rule of all prophecy in taking its verbal form and expression from what was then existent. Just as the gospel dispensation is always described under figures taken from the Jewish Church and commonwealth, so Samuel, as the founder of the prophetic schools, and of the new order of things which resulted from them, is described to Eli under terms taken from his priestly office. He was a "faithful priest," and much more, just as our Lord was a "prophet like unto Moses" (Deut. xviii. 15), and a "King set upon the holy hill of Zion" (Ps. ii. 6), but in a far higher sense than any would have supposed at the time when these prophecies were spoken.

As regards the specific terms of the prophecy, "the building of a sure house" (1 Sam. xxv. 28; 2 Sam. vii. 11; 1 Kings ii. 24, xi. 38; Isa. xxxii. 18) is a metaphor expressive of assured prosperity. The mass of the Israelites dwelt in tents (2 Sam. xi. 11; xx. 1, &c.; 1 Kings xii. 16), and to have a fixed and permanent dwelling was a mark of greatness. From such passages as 1 Kings ii. 24; xi. 38, it is plain that the idea of founding a family is not contained in the expression. As a matter of fact, Samuel's family was prosperous, and his grandson Heman had high rank in David's court and numerous issue (1 Chron. xxv. 5). Probably too the men of Ramah, who with the men of the Levite town of Gaba made up a total of 621 persons (Neh. vii. 30), represented the descendants of Samuel at the return from Babylon. Nevertheless, the contrast is between the migratory life in tents and the ease and security of a solid and firm abode, and the terms of the promise are abundantly fulfilled in Samuel's personal greatness.

In the promise, "he shall walk before mine anointed for ever," there is the same outlook upon the office of king, as if already in existence, which we observed in Hannah's hymn (ch. ii. 10). Apparently the expectation that Jehovah was about to anoint, i. e. consecrate, for them some one to represent him in civil matters and war, as the high priest represented him in things spiritual, had taken possession of the minds of the people. It had been clearly promised them, and regulations for the office made (Deut. xvii. 14—20); and it was to be Samuel's office to fulfil this wish, and all his life through he held a post of high dignity in the kingdom.

But the promise has also a definite meaning as regards the prophets, in whom Samuel lived on. For St. Augustine's error was in taking Samuel simply in his personal relations, whereas he is the representative of the whole prophetic order (Acts iii. 24). They were his successors in his work, and continued to be the recognised mediators to declare to king and people the will of Jehovah, who was the supreme authority in both Church and state; and in political matters they were the appointed check upon the otherwise absolute power of the kings, with whose appointment their own formal organisation exactly coincided. From Samuel's time prophet and king walked together till the waiting period began which immediately preceded the nativity of Christ.

Ver. 36.—**Piece of silver** is lit. a small silver coin got by begging, and the word marks the extreme penury into which the race of Eli fell. Gathered round the sanctuary at Shiloh, they were the chief sufferers by its ruin, and we have noticed how for a time they fall entirely out of view. During the miserable period of Philistine domination which followed, Samuel became to the oppressed nation a centre of hope, and by his wise government he first reformed the people internally, and then gave them freedom from foreign rule. During this period we may be sure that he did much to raise from their misery the descendants of Eli, and finally Ahiah, Eli's grandson, ministers as high priest before Saul. Though his grandson, Abiathar, was deposed from the office by Solomon, there is no reason for imagining that the family ever again fell into distress, nor do the terms of the prophecy warrant such a supposition.

HOMILETICS.

Vers. 27—36.—*Impending retribution.* The facts in this section are—1. A Divine message declares to Eli the coming doom of his house. 2. The justice of the judgment is brought home to him by a reference to past privileges enjoyed and sins committed. 3. A painful sign of the certainty of the whole prediction being ultimately fulfilled is given in a reference to the sudden death of his two sons, in due time to be realised. 4. Another faithful servant of God is to be raised up to vindicate the honour which has been despised. The patience of God in allowing men free scope to develope what is in them has its limits. Eli and his sons, though differing in kind and degree of sin, alike are amenable to a law which must be maintained. Although the sons were in the ordinary sense the most guilty, it is significant that the weight of the doom here indicated is intended to fall on the aged parent, thus showing to all ages the solemn responsibility attached to *public* conduct, and the certainty of terrible chastisement of official transgressors, even though they be not cut off from the covenant mercies that cover sin and save the soul.

I. DUTY NEGLECTED AND TROUBLE EVADED ARE SURE TO REASSERT THEMSELVES. Eli got rid of the pressing duty of punishing his sons by substituting a paternal remonstrance, and thus for the time evaded the pain of suppressing the urgency of personal affection and the distress of a family exposure. But "duty" never dies ; and the trouble it entails, always passing away when duty is done, continues in aggravated form when duty is neglected. No safer rule in life than to *do* duty when it is due. The demands of justice will be asserted sooner or later, and they gather in force the more they are shunned. The whole visible and invisible forces of nature, the undeveloped resources that lie in the womb of the future, are on the side of *right*, and will converge some day on its maintenance. The first trouble in the path of duty is the least. Embarrassments are born of procrastination ; for the rule applicable to imperfect knowledge in the midst of difficult circumstances does not apply to the clear decisions of conscience. No time should ever be lost in vindicating the honour of God, the purity of the sanctuary, and the claims of national righteousness. If *we* do not execute God's will because of the personal inconvenience and pain it may cause, *he will* execute it by other means, and nameless griefs shall follow us. History shows how true this is in national, Church, domestic, and private life.

II. Clear INDICATIONS OF COMING RETRIBUTION are sometimes given, and THEY BECOME in their immediate effects PART OF THE RETRIBUTION. Many are the "servants" of God that come visibly or invisibly to the disobedient with intimations of what is in store for them. The "man of God" who came to Eli is representative of the forms of the Divine voice which comes to the guilty to disturb the ease they had hoped for in neglecting onerous duties. To the fraudulent, the sensual, the unrighteous ruler, the unfaithful parent and pastor, conscience, leading events, and converging circumstances tell the sad tale of coming woe. The lines of justice are straight, and the wicked are compelled to look along them far ahead. *Two important elements* enter into the forebodings of coming retribution. 1. *A revived power of conscience.* The privileges and favours conferred on the house of Eli are brought home to the dormant conscience in contrast with his personal and official conduct. So likewise, by the interaction of the laws of thought, or by converging of painful events, or by some strong passage of Scripture, or by a faithful friend, or by the silent, reflected light of some holy Christian life, the privileges and favours of bygone years are flashed before the spirit, to the sudden terror and quickened action of conscience. Past mercies cannot be thought of in isolation ; by a well-known mental law they raise up the ghosts of former sins committed in the face of mercies. As the aged Eli saw the truth of the words of the " man of God," so do others see their former selves, and feel their inward condemnation. 2. *A conviction of the fixed character of coming events.* " Behold, the days COME." The guilty man sees the dismal train of events, and knows, on highest authority, that the decree is fixed. To the prophetic eye the future is as the present ; events that are to be are recorded on the spirit as done, with all their natural effects realised by the discerning mind. Nature, with her usual quiet certainty, was at work elaborating events out of the sins perpetrated by father and sons ; and therefore to the Hebrew mind that recognises nature only as the dumb instrument of the Eternal, the coming disasters are recognised properly as the fixed elements of the deserved retribution. There is the *same conviction* in others who have sinned. The human mind, in spite of its sins, answers to the course of nature. It mirrors in its conviction of certain punishment the regularity and fixity with which the laws of nature are at work. In the instance of many a man, powers have been set at work by his sins in virtue of the operation of which family reputation will fade and perish ; premature decay will fall to the lot of descendants ; sorrow and trouble will cast shadows over their pathway ; and life generally will be marred. Yes ; and he *knows it now.* The committal of sin is as the unloosing of forces of ill which enter of necessity into all the ramifications of subsequent life. The sorrow and pain consequent on this certain knowledge is no slight element in the retribution experienced.

III. RETRIBUTION AFFECTS THE LIVING THROUGH THE UNBORN, AND THE UNBORN THROUGH THE LIVING. Sin injures and degrades the sinner, but does not end in himself. Every being is related to every other being. Interactions are as real and constant in the moral sphere as in the sphere of physics. An act of sin is an act of will, and therefore the production of a wave of influence which moves on and modifies the totality of life. Wisely and beautifully, then, does the Bible teach truth in harmony with the usual order of things when it represents Eli's sin as cutting off the arm (strength) of his father's house, shortening the days of his children, lowering their position in the world, and causing them to bear the sorrow of seeing a culmination of their ancestor's sin in the " presence of an enemy " to mar the wealth of blessing properly enjoyed by Israel. 1. *A general law* is exemplified in Eli's punishment. The Bible teaches that the sins of the fathers bring woe on children. The course of nature establishes the fact. No man can give out from himself any influence above what his real constitution and character are fitted to produce. A defective moral courage works detrimentally on descendants by example as truly as do imperfect manners. Social laws insure that a lost reputation modifies the relative position of offspring. The degenerate habits of a Hophni and a Phinehas cannot but lessen the years and enfeeble the moral and physical vigour of several generations. God's laws are uniform in all ages and climes. The experience of Eli's family is repeated in the home of the drunkard, the sensual, the educationally neglected, the morally weak, and in the effects of wicked statesmanship. But the law has *two aspects.* The living affect the unborn, but also the known future condition of the unborn affects the condition of the living. Wisely men are constituted so as to be deeply affected by what may happen to their future reputation and their descendants. That the good fame of his house should perish ; that his descendants should be reduced in social position, and variously injured in consequence of the guilt of himself and sons, was a bitter element in Eli's punishment. Nor is this a rare case, for as a rule men are more influenced by what comes to their children than by what personal pain they themselves suffer. In his descendants man sees himself repeated in multiplied form. 2. *The general law is subject to limitations.* The evil that comes to posterity through sin of ancestors does not shut out from the mercy that saves the soul. Disgrace, loss of health, early death, poverty may be part of the curse of a father's sin ; but through the mercy of God in Christ these sufferers may find renewal of spirit, pardon, and eternal life. " By one man's disobedience" we all have suffered physically and spiritually; but by one Redeemer we may find power to become the true children of God. It is true Eli's descendants, if renewed, would not become so good and physically perfect men as though the ancestors had not sinned; and we on earth, though saved in Christ, cannot be so physically perfect as though the curse had never fallen on us; yet the spirit will at length be set free from the bondage of corruption, and be perfect before God. 3. *This law is a great and beneficent power in life.* Those who rail against these Biblical announcements of retribution, because they affect descendants, are profoundly ignorant or perverse. The Bible tells only what is in nature, with the additional information that God vindicates his holiness by what occurs in nature. Any objection to the Biblical doctrine is therefore, this fact being admitted, the result of a perverse spirit. Human experience testifies how beneficially the law of retribution works in ordinary affairs. No arithmetic can calculate the amount of woe escaped by the restraining action of a knowledge of this law on human tendencies. On the other hand, the reverse side of the law—the reward of goodness in the happiness of a posterity—is one of the most healthful stimulants and guides of human exertion. It is only the morally-indisposed that do not like law. Did we but know the whole intricate relationships of a moral universe stretching through all time, even the severest laws would then be seen to be an expression of broadest benevolence.

IV. RETRIBUTION ON THE INSTRUMENTS OF ACCOMPLISHING AN ULTIMATE PURPOSE IS COMPATIBLE WITH THE REALISATION OF THAT PURPOSE. As factors in the development of the Jewish economy, both Eli and his sons were instruments in preparing the way for the coming Messiah and the final supremacy of his kingdom. The house of Ithamar inherited, in common with others, the promise made to the Aaronic house. As long as there was need for an earthly high priest to shadow forth the enduring high priesthood of Christ, the promise (ver. 30) to Aaron would hold good. But the completion of that purpose was not frustrated by the disgrace and displacement of the section of the house represented by Eli in consequence of unfaithfulness. God has, in his foreknowledge of what will be required, as also in his resources to provide for the erratic action of human wills according to that foreknowledge, legions awaiting his creative call to come forth and prepare the way for the Christ. He who could "of these stones raise up children to Abraham" was at no loss to dispense with the leadership in his ancient Church of a degenerate family. If the old injured instruments are judicially confined to lower forms of service, as in the case of Ahiah, grandson of Phinehas (ch. xiv. 3), a holy Samuel is raised up for the emergency till a Zadok assumes the orderly high priestly functions; thus teaching us that in spite of all sins and their punishment the kingdom of God must advance. Men may rise and fall, dark seasons of priestly corruption may afflict the Church, apostates may spread consternation; but, foreseeing all, the Eternal has in reserve, and is quietly sending forth, men like Samuel and David and Paul and Luther, men who shall not cease to be employed in the high service of the "Anointed" even when they cease to speak by words.

General suggestions:—1. It is worth considering how much is lost to the world of mental and physical power by the indwelling of sin, and what a valuable contribution to the sum total of a nation's welfare is a righteous life, by conserving and improving and making the most of all the powers of body and mind. 2. The essential folly of all sin is capable of being illustrated in what it entails, fails to avoid, and also takes away from the elements of individual and public well-being. 3. There is a philosophical argument in support of the claims of Christianity in the fact that, as it seeks, and is proved by numerous facts to have the power of perfecting, the moral life, it thereby contains the solution of all our physical and economical difficulties, and needs only to become actual in individual life to constitute a real millennium. 4. There is ample ground in history for confidence in the vindication of right, even though rulers may for a season avoid disaster. 5. In the lives of most men there must be seasons when they are visited by a messenger from God; and it is a question whether, if that messenger be disregarded, another may not come bringing tidings of more terrible things. 6. In any case, where by former sins physical and social evils have come on others, it is an encouragement to know that we may labour to bring those so suffering to the great Physician for spiritual healing, and that the spiritual health will in some measure counteract the inherited evils. 7. The comforting aspect of retribution lies in that for every one who suffers from it, possibly thousands and millions indirectly gain permanent good in the influence it exerts on existing evils and on otherwise forthcoming evils; and also that the same purpose which thus works out deserved judgment insures the fulfilment of all the promises.

HOMILIES BY VARIOUS AUTHORS.

Vers. 27—36. (Shiloh.)—*A message of approaching judgment* 1. This message came from God, who observed, as he ever does, the sins of his people, and especially his ministers, with much displeasure, and after long forbearance resolved to punish them (Amos iii. 2; 1 Pet. iv. 17). 2. It came through a man whose name has not been recorded, and who was probably unknown to him to whom he was sent. When God sends a message it matters little by whom it is brought. He often makes his most important communications in a way the world does not expect, and by men who are unknown to fame. The authority of the Lord invests his messengers with dignity and power. And their best credentials are that they "commend themselves to the conscience" (2 Cor. iv. 2). 3. It came through a "man of God," a seer, a prophet, and not directly from God to Eli, the high priest. He chooses for special service men who live near to him, and are in sympathy with his purposes, in preference to those who occupy official positions, but are possessed of little personal worth. For a long season no prophet had spoken (Judges iv. 4; vi. 8; xiii. 6); and when the silence of heaven is suddenly broken, it is an intimation that great changes are impending. 4. It came some time before the events which it announced actually transpired. "The Lord is slow to anger" (Nahum i. 3), and executes judgment only after repeated warnings. Predictions which are absolute in form must often be understood as in their fulfilment conditioned by the moral state of those whom they concern (Jer. xviii. 7; Jonah iii. 4, 9, 10). The purpose for which this message was sent was to lead to repentance, and it was not until all hope of it had disappeared that the blow fell. In substance the message contains—

I. A REMINDER OF SPECIAL PRIVILEGES bestowed by the favour of God, and shown— 1. By the *revelation of himself to those* who were in a condition of abject servitude (ver. 27). 2. By his *selection of some*, in preference to others, for exalted and honourable service (ver. 28). 3. By his liberal *provision* for them out of the offerings made by the people to himself. Religious privileges always involve responsibilities, and should be faithfully used out of gratitude for their bestowment.

II. A CHARGE OF GROSS UNFAITHFULNESS (ver. 29). The purpose for which the priests were endowed with these privileges was not the promotion of their own honour and interest, but the honour of God and the welfare of his people. But they acted in opposition to that purpose. 1. By *irreverence* and self-will in his service. "Wherefore do ye trample under foot my sacrifice?" 2. By *disobedience* to his will. "Which I have commanded." 3. By *pleasing others* in preference to him. "And honourest thy sons above me." Eli's toleration of the conduct of his sons, from regard to their interest and his own ease, involved him in their guilt. 4. By *self-enrichment* out of the religious offerings of the people. "The idol which man in sin sets up in the place of God can be none other than himself. He makes self and self-satisfaction the highest aim of life. To self his efforts ultimately tend, however the modes and directions of sin may vary. The innermost essence of sin, the ruling and penetrating principle, in all its forms, is selfishness" (Müller, 'Christian Doctrine of Sin'). When men use the gifts of God for selfish ends they render themselves liable to be deprived of those gifts, and to be punished for their misuse.

III. A STATEMENT OF AN EQUITABLE PRINCIPLE, according to which God acts in his procedure with men (ver. 30). They have been apt to suppose that privileges bestowed upon themselves or inherited from their ancestors were absolutely their own, and would be certainly continued. But it is far otherwise; for—1. The fulfilment of the promises of God and the continuance of religious privileges depend on the *ethical relation* in which men stand toward him. His covenant with Levi was "for the fear with which he feared me" (Mal. ii. 6, 7); but when his descendants lost that fear they "corrupted the covenant," and ceased to have any claim upon its promised blessings. It was the same with the Jews who in after ages vainly boasted that they were "the children of Abraham." In the sight of the Holy One righteousness is everything, hereditary descent nothing, except in so far as it is promotive of righteousness. 2. *Faithful service is rewarded.* HONOUR FOR HONOUR. "Them that honour me I will honour." Consider—(1) The *ground :* not merely his relationship as moral Governor, but his beneficence in bestowing the gifts of nature, providence, and grace. (2) The *method :* in thought, word, and deed. (3) The *reward :* his approbation, continued service, extended usefulness, &c. 3. *Unfaithful conduct is punished.* "Promises and threatenings are made to individuals because they are in a particular state of character; but they belong to all who are in that state, for 'God is no respecter of persons'" (Robertson). "He will give to every man according to his works."

IV. A PROCLAMATION OF SEVERE RETRIBUTION upon the house of Eli (vers. 31—34). Consisting of—1. The deprivation of *strength*, which had been abused. Their power would be broken (Zech. xi. 17). 2. The shortening of *life*, the prolonging of which in the case of Eli had been an occasion of evil rather than of good. "There shall not be an old man in thine house for ever;" the result of weakness; repeated in ver. 32. 3. The loss of *prosperity ;* the temporal benefits that would otherwise have been received. "Thou shalt see distress of dwelling in all that brings prosperity to Israel" (Ed. of Erdmann). 4. The infliction of *misery* on those who continue, for a while, to minister at the altar, and of violent death (ver. 33 ; xxii. 18). 5. Although these things would not take place at once, their commencement, as a sign of what would follow, would be witnessed by Eli himself in the sudden death of the two chief offenders "in one day" (ch. iv. 11). If anything could rouse the house of Eli to "flee from the wrath to come," surely such a fearful message as this was adapted to do so. Fear of coming wrath, although it never makes men truly religious, may, and often does, arouse and restrain them, and bring them under the influence of other and higher motives. The closing sentences contain—

V. A PREDICTION OF A FAITHFUL PRIESTHOOD in the place of that which had proved faithless (vers. 35, 36). "I will raise up a faithful priest," &c., *i. e.* a line of faithful men to accomplish the work for which the priesthood has been appointed, and to enjoy the privileges which the house of Eli has forfeited. In contrast with that house, it will do my will, and I will cause it to endure; and it will continue to live in intimate fellowship and co-operation with the anointed kings of Israel. It will also be so exalted, that the surviving members of the fallen house will be entirely dependent upon it for a "piece of bread." The prediction was first of all fulfilled in Samuel, who by express commission from God acted habitually as a priest; and afterwards in Zadok, in whom the line of Eleazar was restored; but the true underlying *idea* of a priest, like that of a king, has its full realisation in Jesus Christ alone. The gloomiest of prophetic messages generally conclude with words of promise and hope.—D.

Ver. 30.—*Honour and dishonour.* Concerning the *moral attitude* assumed by men toward God, which is here described, observe—

I. THAT IT IS PLAINLY OF THE UTMOST IMPORTANCE. "*Me.*" Our relation to others is a light thing compared with what it is to him. This is everything; and knowledge, power, riches, reputation, &c. nothing. 1. Because of his *nature* ("There is none holy as the Lord"), his government (moral, supreme, universal), and his claims. 2. It is *the effectual* test of our character, what we are really and essentially. 3. It is the *principal means* of forming and strengthening it. What are we in his sight? What does he think of *me ?*

II. THAT IT IS NECESSARILY ONE OR OTHER OF TWO KINDS. "*Honour* me." "*Despise* me." 1. *Honour ;* by reverence (the fundamental principle of the religious life), trust, prayer, obedience, fidelity, living to his glory. 2. *Despise ;* by forgetfulnesss, unbelief, self-will, pride, selfishness, disobedience, sin of every kind. 3.

There is *no other alternative.* "For me or against me" (Exod. xxxii. 26; Jer. viii. 1; Matt. vi. 24; vii. 13, 14; xii. 30).

III. THAT IT IS ALWAYS FOLLOWED BY CORRESPONDING CONSEQUENCES. "I will honour." "Shall be lightly esteemed." 1. *Honour;* by his friendship, appointment to honourable service, giving success therein, open acknowledgment before men here and hereafter. "Enter thou into the joy of thy Lord." 2. *Lightly esteemed;* by himself, men, angels, despised even by themselves, and cast away among the vile. "He that saveth his life shall lose it." 3. There is a *strict correspondence* between character and consequences, both generally and particularly, in kind and measure. And the joy and misery of the future will be the consummation and the ripened fruit of what now exists (Gal. vi. 7).

IV. THAT ITS CONNECTION WITH ITS CONSEQUENCES IS ABSOLUTELY CERTAIN. Men often think otherwise. But "be not deceived." Consider—1. The *natural constitution* and tendencies of things, as ordained by him who is "above all, and in all, and through all." 2. The recorded and observed *facts* of life. 3. The *express declarations* of him "who cannot lie." "*I will* honour." "*They shall be* lightly esteemed."—D.

Ver. 30.—*Office nothing without character.* The worthlessness of rank or hereditary position without corresponding wisdom or virtue is a commonplace of moral reflection. But it is startling to find how strongly it is affirmed in Holy Writ of those who hold high office in the house of God. The priesthood in Israel was hereditary, though in point of fact the regularity of the succession was often broken; but such hereditary office was never meant to protect unworthy men like the sons of Eli. Their position was forfeited by their misconduct, and their priestly functions were transferred to other hands. The principle is for all time, and for general application. Does one reach and occupy a high station in the Church? No matter what his line of "holy orders" may be, or who laid hands of ordination on his head, or what functions he is held competent to perform, he must be judged by this test—Does he honour God in his office, or honour and serve himself? Does he so live and act as to commend and glorify Christ? And the same test must be applied to the man professing himself a Christian who occupies a throne on the earth, or who holds high dignity in the state, or who has power as a writer or an orator over the minds of men, or who as a capitalist has great means and opportunities of usefulness. Does he in his station glorify God? If not, his rank, or office, or grand position avails him nothing.

I. THE PIOUS DIVINELY HONOURED. To honour God; think what this implies. To know him truly, to reverence and love him. In vain any verbal or formal homage without the honour rendered by the heart (see Matt. xv. 8). He whose heart cleaves to God will show it in his daily conduct. He will be careful to consult God's word for direction, and observe his statutes. He will openly respect God's ordinances, and give cheerfully for their maintenance, and for the furtherance of righteous and charitable objects. He will honour the Lord with his substance, and with the first-fruits of all his increase. He will worship God with his family, and teach his children "the fear of the Lord." In his place or station he will make it his aim, and hold it his chief end, to glorify God. And, without any vaunting or ostentation, he will show his colours—avow his faith and hope openly. The boy-king, Edward VI., showed his colours when he sat—alas! for how short a time—on the English throne. So did Sir Matthew Hale on the bench, and Robert Boyle in the Royal Society, and William Wilberforce in the highest circles of political life. So did Dr. Arnold among the boys at Rugby, and Dr. Abercrombie and Sir James Simpson among their patients in Edinburgh; Samuel Budgett in his counting-house at Bristol, and General Havelock among his troops in India. These men were not in what are called religious offices; but, in such offices or positions as Providence assigned to them, they bore themselves as religious, God-fearing men. And others there are in places and callings more obscure who are quite as worthy of esteem; those who, in houses of business among scoffing companions, in servants' halls, in workshops, in barrack-rooms, in ships' forecastles, meekly but firmly honour the Lord, and ennoble a lowly calling by fidelity to conscience and to God. The Lord sees and remembers all who honour him. Nay, he honours them; but after his own manner, not after the fashion of the world. He honours faithful servants in this world by giving them more work to do. He honours true witnesses by extending the range for their testimony. Sometimes he honours those with whom he is well pleased by appointing them to suffer for his cause. St. Paul evidently deemed this a high honour. Witness his words to the Philippians: "Unto you it is given in the behalf of Christ, not only to believe in his name, but also to suffer for his sake." Some he calls away in early years out of the world, but they leave behind a fragrant honoured name, and they go to "glory, honour, and immortality" in a better land. It is right to value the good opinion of our fellow-men; but there are always drawbacks and dangers in connection with honour which comes from man. In seeking it one is tempted to tarnish his simplicity of character, and weaken his self-respect. There is a risk of envying more successful, or exulting over less successful competitors for distinction. But it need never be so in seeking "the honour which comes from God only." We seek it best not when we push ourselves forward, but when we deny ourselves, honour him, and by love serve the brethren. And then in our utmost success we have no ground of self-glorying, for all is of grace. Nor is there room for grudging or envying. With the Lord there is grace enough to help all who would serve him, and glory enough to reward all who serve him faithfully.

II. THE IMPIOUS DESPISED. "And they that despise me shall be lightly esteemed." Despise the Lord God Almighty! Amazing insolence of the human heart, yet not infrequent. The sons of Eli openly slighted Jehovah by their rapacity in the priest's office, and their profaning the precincts of his house with their debauchery. Long after this, priests of Judah are reproved by the prophet Malachi for despising the name of the Lord of hosts, making his table contemptible by laying on it polluted bread, and dishonouring his altar by offering maimed animals in sacrifice. The warning then, in the first instance, is to those who bear themselves profanely or carelessly in sacred offices, and in familiar contact with religious service. But the sin is one which soon spreads among the people Ezekiel charged the people of Jerusalem with having "despised God's holy things, and profaned his sabbaths" (ch. xxii. 8). This sin is a common thing in Christendom. Men do not in terms deny God's existence, but make light of him; never read his word with any seriousness; never pray unless they are ill or afraid; count Church service and instruction a weariness. The base gods of the heathen receive more respect and consideration from their votaries. Allah has far more reverence from the Moslem than the great God of heaven and earth obtains from multitudes who pass as Christians. They live as if he had no right to command them, and no power to judge them. They lift their own will and pleasure to the throne, and despise the Lord of hosts. With what result? They shall be lightly esteemed. Even in this world, and this life, the ungodly miss the best distinctions. They are not the men who gather about them the highest confidence or most lasting influence and esteem. After they leave the world, a few are remembered who had rare force of character or an unusually eventful career; but how the rest are forgotten! A few natural tears from their nearest kindred, a few inquiries among friends about the amount and disposal of their property, a decorous silence about themselves on the principle that nothing but what is good should be said of the dead, and so their memory perishes. But all is not over. A terrible hereafter awaits the despisers of the Lord. "As a dream when one awaketh; so, O Lord, when thou awakest, thou shalt despise their image." The clear alternative in this text is one that cannot be evaded. One may try to assume a negative attitude, and allege that he remains in a state of suspense, and does not find the recognition of a Divine Being to be an imperative necessity; but this is practically to despise the Lord—making light of his word, and pronouncing his very existence to be a matter of doubtful truth and of secondary importance. Reject not wisdom's counsel; despise not her reproof. "To-day, if ye will hear the voice of the Lord, harden not your hearts."—F.

Ver. 35.—*A faithful priest.* In the strictest sense Christ alone is now a Priest. In himself assuming the office, he has for ever abolished it in others. Hence none are called priests in the New Testament, except in the modified sense in which all who believe in him are so called (1 Pet. ii. 9 ; Rev. i. 6).   But taking the expression as equivalent to " a faithful ministry," consisting of men appointed by Christ to a special service for him (Mal. ii. 6, 7 ; Acts vi. 4 ; Ephes. iv. 11 ; Col. i. 7 ; 2 Tim. ii. 2), and faithfully fulfilling the purpose of their appointment, it leads us to notice—

I. WHENCE IT IS DERIVED.   " I will raise up."   1. He alone *can* do it.   From him come natural gifts and, still more, spiritual graces, eminent faith and patience, humility, courage, meekness, tender compassion " on the ignorant and on them that are out of the way," &c.   2. He has *promised* and made provision for it (Jer. iii. 15).   " I will build him a sure (enduring) house."   " The death of Christ hath a great influence unto this gift of the ministry.   It is a branch that grew out of the grave of Christ ; let it be esteemed as lightly as men please, had not Christ died for it we had not had a ministry in the world " (Owen, vol. ix. p. 441).   He " will be *inquired of* " for it.   If Churches would have " good ministers of Jesus Christ," they must seek them from God (Matt. ix. 38).

II. WHEREIN IT APPEARS.   " Shall do according to that which is in my heart and in my mind."   1. *Supreme regard* to his will as the rule of character and labour. 2. *Clear insight* into his mind in relation to the special requirements of the time, place, and circumstances.   3. Practical, earnest, and constant *devotion* to it in all things, the least as well as the greatest.   Even as " Christ himself."   " I have given you an example."

III. WHEREBY IT IS HONOURED.   " And he shall walk before mine anointed for ever."   1. Enjoyment of the King's *favour* (Prov. xvi. 15).   2. Employment in the King's *service ;* in continued, honourable, beneficent, and increasing co-operation with him.   3. Participation in the King's *glory* for ever.   " Be thou faithful," &c. (Rev. ii. 10).   " To him that overcometh will I grant to sit with me in my throne " (Rev. iii. 21).—D.

EXPOSITION.

CHAPTER III.

THE CALL OF SAMUEL (vers. 1—10).   Ver. 1.—**The word of the Lord was precious in those days.**   Or rather *rare ;* it came but seldom, and there was no proper order of persons from whose ranks the "speakers for God" would naturally step forth.   It was this which made the revelation of Jehovah's will to Samuel an event so memorable both for the Jewish nation and for the Church ; for he was called by the providence of God to be the founder of prophecy as an established institution, and henceforward, side by side with the king and priest, the prophet took his place as one of the three factors in the preparation for the coming of him who is a King to rule, a Priest to make atonement, and also a Prophet to teach his people and guide them into all the truth.   **There was no open vision.**   Literally, "no vision that broke forth" (see 2 Chron. xxxi. 5, where it is used of the publication of a decree).   The meaning is, that though prophecy was an essential condition of the spiritual life of Israel, yet that hitherto it had not been promulgated and established as a fact.   The gift had not absolutely been withheld, but neither had it been permanently granted as a settled ordinance.   There are in Hebrew two words for **vision** : the one used here, *hazon*, refers to such sights as are revealed

to the tranced eye of the seer when in a state of ecstasy ; while the other, *mareh*, is a vision seen by the natural eye.   From the days, however, of Isaiah onward, *hazon* became the generic term for all prophecy.

Ver. 2.—**Eli . . . could not see.**   *I. e.* clearly.   His sight was fast failing him, and Samuel, still called a **child**, *na'ar*, but probably, as Josephus states ('Antiq.,' v. 10, 4), now fully twelve years old, was in constant attendance upon him because of his increasing infirmities.   Both were sleeping in the temple ; for literally the words are, *And Samuel was sleeping in the temple of Jehovah, where the ark of God was.*   Of course neither Eli nor Samuel were in the holy place ; but, as in ch. i. 9, the word *temple* is used in its proper sense of the whole palace of Israel's spiritual King, in which were chambers provided for the use of the high priest and those in attendance upon him.

In ver. 3 the **lamp** is mentioned as fixing the exact time.   Though it is said that the seven-branched candelabrum was "to burn always" (Exod. xxvii. 20), yet this apparently was to be by perpetually relighting it (*ibid.* xxx. 7, 8) ; and as Aaron was commanded to dress and light it every morning and evening, and supply it with oil, the night would be far advanced and morning near before it **went out.**   In the stillness then of the late night Samuel, sunk in heavy

sleep, hears a voice calling him, and springing up, naturally hurries to Eli, supposing
that he needed his services. Eli had not
heard the voice, and concluding that it was
a mistake, bids Samuel return to his bed.
Again the voice rings upon his ear, and again
he hastens to Eli, only to be told to lie down
again.

In ver. 7 the reason is given why Samuel
was thus thrice mistaken. **Samuel did not
yet know Jehovah, neither was the word of
Jehovah yet revealed unto him.** Doubtless
he knew Jehovah in the way in which the
sons of Eli did not know him (ch. ii. 12),
i. e. in his conscience and spiritual life, but
he did not know him as one who reveals his
will unto men. Prophecy had long been a
rare thing, and though Samuel had often
heard God's voice in the recesses of his heart,
speaking to him of right and wrong, he knew
nothing of God as a living Person, giving
commands for men to obey, and bestowing
knowledge to guide them in doing his will.

Ver. 8.—But Eli was neither so inexperienced, nor so lost to all sense of Jehovah
being the immediate ruler of Israel, as not
to perceive, when Samuel came to him the
third time, that the matter was Divine.
Possibly he recalled to mind the visit of the
man of God, and had some presage of what
the message might be. At all events he bade
Samuel lie calmly down again, because the
best preparation for hearing God's voice is
obedience and trustful submission.

Ver. 10.—**And Jehovah came, and stood,
and called as at other times.** It is something more than a voice; there was an
objective presence; and so in ver. 15 it is
called, not *hazon*, a sight seen when in a
state of ecstasy, but *mareh*, something seen
when wide awake, and in the full, calm possession of every faculty. **As at other times**
simply means *as before*, as on the two previous occasions. But now, instead of hurrying to Eli, Samuel obediently waits for the
revelation of the Divine will, saying, "Speak;
for thy servant heareth."

THE MESSAGE TO ELI (vers. 11—18). Ver.
11.—**Behold, I will do.** Rather, *I do*, I am
now doing. Though the threatened ruin may
be delayed for a few years, yet is it already
in actual progress, and the fall of Eli's house
will be but the consummation of causes
already now at work. **At which both the
ears of every one that heareth it shall
tingle.** This implies the announcement of
some event so frightful and unlooked for
that the news shall, as it were, slap both ears
at once, and make them smart with pain.
And such an event was the capture of the
ark, and the barbarous destruction of the
priests and sanctuary at Shiloh. The phrase
is again used of the destruction of Jerusalem
by Nebuchadnezzar (2 Kings xxi. 12; Jer.

xix. 3), a calamity which Jeremiah compares
to the fall of Shiloh (Jer. vii. 12, 14; xxvi.
6, 9), inasmuch as both of these events involved the ruin of the central seat of the
Jewish religion, and were both accompanied
by revolting cruelties.

Ver. 12.—**I will perform.** Literally, "I
will raise up," *i. e.* I will excite and stir up
into active energy all the denunciations of
the man of God (ch. ii. 27), which hitherto
have been as it were asleep and at rest. **All
things which.** Better, quite literally, *all that
I have spoken.* **When I begin, I will also
make an end.** In the Hebrew two infinitives
used as gerunds, "beginning and ending,"
i. e. from beginning to end. The Hebrew
language constantly thus uses infinitives with
great force; as, for instance, in Jer. vii. 9:
"What! stealing, murdering, committing
adultery," &c.

Ver. 13.—**For I have told him,** &c. These
words may be translated, with the Septuagint
and Vulgate, "For I have told him that I
would judge his house," referring back to the
message of the man of God; or, with the
Syriac, "And I will show him that I do judge
his house." **For ever.** *I. e.* finally; his house
shall pass away. **His sons made themselves
vile.** The verb used here invariably means
to curse; but "they cursed themselves" does
not, without straining, give a good sense.
The Septuagint for "themselves" reads *God,*
and the Syriac *the people.* Buxtorf says
('Lex. Rab.,' sub תִּקוּן) that the right reading
is *me,* and that this is one of eighteen places
where the scribes have changed *me* into
themselves or *them.* But while thus there is
much uncertainty about the right text, the
evidence is too uncertain to act upon, and it
is best to translate, "His sons have brought
a curse upon themselves," while acknowledging that the ordinary rendering would
be "have cursed themselves." **And he restrained them not.** The Versions generally
take the verb used here as equivalent to one
differing only in having a softer medial consonant, כהה = כאה, and translate *rebuked;*
but that really found in the Hebrew text
signifies "to weaken, humble, reduce to
powerlessness." The A. V. takes neither one
verb nor the other in the rendering *restrained.* Eli ought to have prevented his
sons from persisting in bringing disgrace upon
God's service by stripping them of their office.
Their wickedness was great, and required a
stern and decisive remedy.

Ver. 14.—**Sacrifice nor offering.** The first
of these is *zebach,* the sacrifice of an animal
by the shedding of its blood; the second is
the *minchah,* or unbloody sacrifice. The
guilt of Eli's sons could be **purged,** *i. e.* expiated, by none of the appointed offerings for
sin, because they had hardened themselves
in their wrong-doing even after the solemn

warning in ch. ii. 27—36. Hence the marked repetition of the denunciation of finality in their doom. Again it is said that it is **for ever.** It has, however, been well noticed that though the message of Samuel confirms all that had been threatened by the man of God, yet that no bitter or painful words are put into the mouth of one who was still a child. For this there may also be a further reason. The first message was intended to give Eli and his sons a final opportunity of repentance, and, that it might produce its full effect, the severity of the doom impending upon them was clearly set before their eyes. They did not repent. Eli hardened himself in his weakness, and took no steps to vindicate God's service from the slur cast upon it by an unworthy priesthood. His sons hardened themselves in crime, and made their office a reproach. It was enough, therefore, to repeat and confirm generally the terms of the former prophecy, as no moral object would be gained by calling attention to the severity of the coming judgment.

Ver. 15.—**Samuel . . . opened the doors.** In Exod. xxvi. 36 : xxxvi. 37, the word used, though translated *door*, really means an opening, protected by a hanging curtain. The word used here means *double* or *folding doors* of wood, and we must therefore conclude that solid buildings had grown up round the tabernacle (see on ch. i. 9), and a wall for its defence in case of invasion, or the assault of predatory tribes. The confiding the keys of these enclosures to Samuel shows that he was no longer a mere child, or he would have been incapable of holding a position of such high trust (on the key as an emblem of authority see Isa. xxii. 22). **Vision,** as noticed above on ver. 10, means something seen by a person awake and in full possession of his senses.

Vers. 16, 17, 18.—**God do so to thee,** &c. This adjuration shows how great had been the agony of Eli's suspense, yet, true to his sluggish nature, he had waited patiently till the morning came. Then he summons Samuel to him, calling him lovingly **my son,** and everything tends to show that there was a real affection between the two. He next asks, **What is the thing that he hath said unto thee?** The A. V. greatly weakens this by inserting the words "The Lord." The original is far more suggestive. Put quite indefinitely, it says, "Whoever or whatsoever be thy visitor, yet tell me all." Then, when Eli has heard the message, he says, **It is Jehovah.** Though he had not had the courage to do what was right, yet his sub-

mission to God, and the humility of his resignation, prove that the Holy Ghost had in these years of waiting being doing its work upon the old man's heart. Eli's adjuration, we must further note, was equivalent to putting Samuel upon his oath, so that any concealment on his part would have involved the sin of perjury.

ESTABLISHMENT OF SAMUEL IN THE OFFICE OF PROPHET (ver. 19—iv. 1). Ver. 19.—**And Samuel grew.** His childhood up to this time has been carefully kept before our view ; now he passes from youth to manhood. **And Jehovah was with him.** By special gifts, but especially by establishing his words. Spoken by Divine inspiration, they were all fulfilled. So in Eccles. xii. 11 the words of the wise are compared to "nails fastened" securely, and which may therefore be depended upon. But in their case it is experience and sound judgment that makes them foresee what is likely to happen ; it was a higher gift which made Samuel's words remain safe and sure, and capable of firmly holding up all enterprises that were hung upon them.

Ver. 20.—**From Dan,** upon the north, **to Beer-sheba,** upon the south, means "throughout the whole country." The phrase is interesting, as showing that, in spite of the virtual independence of the tribes, and the general anarchy which prevailed during the time of the judges, there was nevertheless a feeling that they all formed one people. **Was established.** The same word used in Num. xii. 7 of Moses, and there translated *was faithful.* It is one of those pregnant words common in Hebrew, containing two cognate meanings. It says, first, that Samuel was faithful in his office ; and, secondly, that because he was found trustworthy he was confirmed and strengthened in the possession of it.

Ver. 21.—**And Jehovah appeared again.** Literally, "added to appear," *i. e.* revealed himself from time to time on all fit occasions. *To appear,* literally, "to be seen," is the verb used of waking vision (see on ver. 15). **By the word of Jehovah.** Many of the old commentators refer this to the second person of the Holy Trinity, but he is himself Jehovah, as we affirm in the Te Deum : "We believe thee to be the Lord," *i. e.* the Jehovah of the Old Testament, usually translated, in deference to a Jewish superstition, "the LORD." As the Word, Christ is "the Word of God." The phrase really means, "by prophetic inspiration" revealing to Samuel the truth (comp. Isa. li. 16 ; Jer. i. 9).

HOMILETICS.

Vers. 1—10.—*Light withheld.* The facts given are—1. A lack of the manifest revelations of the Divine will to which Israel had been accustomed. 2. A consciousness of this want on the part of the few pious in Israel.   3. The continued service of Samuel in the ordinary routine of the sanctuary.   4. The resumption of the manifest revelation by the call of Samuel to receive it.   5. Samuel experiences difficulty in recognising the call of God.   6. Eli renders to him the assistance by which he becomes recipient of the Divine communication.   The statement concerning Samuel's continued service in the sanctuary is evidently to prepare the way for the new prophet's summons to important duties.   The historian's mind rests primarily on a dreary period during which a valued privilege was not enjoyed.

I. A PROGRESSION OF LIGHT IS NEEDED IN THE CHURCH OF GOD.   The ancient Jewish Church was very dependent for its growth in knowledge, in direction for present duty, and in advancing joy in life, upon well-ascertained communications from God.   The fragmentary history from patriarchal times onwards acquaints us with many specific instances in which " open vision," as distinguished from individual enlightenment for private uses, was vouchsafed.   It is probable that much other light was given than we have record of, as truly as that the apostles received more from Christ than is explicitly contained in the Gospels.   The clear light of God was necessary in successive years to enable Israel to do the work required in paving the way for Messiah.   Therefore men looked for " vision " through some chosen instrument, and felt that the normal course of Providence was interrupted when, through long and weary years, none was granted.   *Substantially* the light has now been given to the modern Church.   No one is to " add to or take away from the words of the book " which God has given for the instruction and guidance of his people.   But *relatively*, to the perception of the Church and of the individual, there *is still a progression* in what is made known to us.   *All* the truth was in Christ before it gradually came forth " in divers manners to the fathers ; " and all the truth requisite for salvation is in the word of God.   But as occasional manifestations in ancient times brought successive beams of light from the original Source to supply the need of men, so now out of the word of God much light has to break forth for the instruction, guidance, and comfort of the Church.   There is all the difference imaginable between adding to the sum of truth by traditions of men or superior " light of reason," and having the things of Christ revealed to us by the Spirit.   Our growth in knowledge is consequent on clearer " visions " from God's word.

II. SPIRITUAL RECEPTIVITY IS A CONDITION OF RECEIVING FURTHER LIGHT FROM GOD.   The absence of " open visions " in the days of Eli is implicitly accounted for by the circumstance that the official persons through whom the communications usually came were not in a state of mind to be so honoured by God.   There seems to be a beautiful adaptation between the fitness of the instrument and the fulness of the truth conveyed.   Isaiah's intense spirituality of mind made him a fit instrument for conveying to men the more advanced truth revealed to him.   The tone of the Apostle John's nature qualified him for the special quality and degree of truth characteristic of his writings.   There seem to be high regulative laws by which God sends forth his light to the spiritual man corresponding to those in the lower sphere of intellect and moral perception.   The *application of this principle* is seen in the *history of the Church and of the individual*.   When the leaders of the Church have been intent on earthly things, no advance has been made in the understanding of the Scriptures.   As protoplastic life must pre-exist in order to the assimilation of protoplasm, so a certain spiritual light and love must dwell in man in order to the absorption into self of light from God's word.   No wonder if irreligious men cannot know the mysteries of the kingdom.   The highest spiritual truth is not intellectually, but " spiritually discerned."   Christ may have many things to say to us, but we, through deficient receptivity, " cannot bear them now."   Hence the wisdom of God is often foolishness to men, or the darkness is real because the eye that should see is dim.

III. It is a GREAT CALAMITY FOR ANY PEOPLE TO BE DEPRIVED OF THE LIGHT which ordinarily comes from God for human use.   The historian indicates the sad loss from which the people were suffering in this withholding of " open vision."   All light is good, only good.   It is the chief means of life.   It means cheer, safety, development.   To be without it in any measure is, in that degree, to be practically blind, and to suffer all the evils of blindness.   We mourn over those who cannot see the sweet, beautiful light of day. Agony enters us when we gaze on men devoid of the light of reason. The wisest grope as in perpetual fear when the pillar of fire and Divine silence show not the way to take. Worst of all when the Church has no guidance suited to its need. There have been periods when the written word has been almost lost to the mass of Christians. There are souls dark, sad, hopeless because no " vision " points to the Refuge from sin and the rest to come. If one could speak out the secret miseries of some who, dazed by exclusive gaze on the light of reason, feel that life is hopeless, the world would scarcely credit the story.

IV. The LACK OF RECEPTIVITY BY WHICH this calamity is experienced is often THE RESULT OF A DEGENERATE, CORRUPT STATE OF MIND SELF-INDUCED AND LOVED. The spiritual unfitness of people and leaders in Eli's day to receive more and frequent " visions " was the creation of their own wicked wills. The calamity of being left for a while was the fruit of their doings. Sin is a blinding power, as also a creator of positive aversion. The natural effect of religious declension is to render men *indifferent* to the value of God's truth for its own sake and for its elevating influence ; *incapable of appreciating* and even discerning it in its purity ; prone to *set a wrong interpretation* upon it when in any degree it is given ; and even, in many instances, *disposed to refer* that which professes to be from God to *any other than the true* source. It is a fair question how much of the professed *rejection of Christianity on reasonable grounds* is really traceable to the pure exercise of the reason under the guidance of an undefiled love of truth. Is not zeal to be free from such holy restraints as Christ imposes often an important element in the case ? The finer and most convincing evidences of the truth of Christianity lie in the spiritual beauty and glory of the Christ, and this is a factor which mere intellectual processes cannot assess. How is it that the *unholy* always *welcome* objections to Christianity ? It is ever true, " sin lieth at the door." " Ye *will* not come unto me." " Out of the *heart* are the issues of life."

V. The CAUSE OF THE DEGENERACY which issues in a calamitous loss of spiritual light LIES IN A NEGLECT OF SUCH LIGHT AS IS ALREADY GIVEN. The inaptitude of Eli to receive " visions," and of the people to profit by them, was the fruit of a religious decay brought on by inattention to the instructions given by Moses, and a heedless performance of acts of worship. Thus calamity came of abuse or neglect of existing privileges. The principle holds good over a wide sphere. Unfaithfulness in some Churches of Asia led to the dire calamity of a removal of the " candlestick." Apostles sometimes turned from cities that failed to use the opportunities they afforded them. Those who, seeing the " Eternal Power and Godhead " in the " things that are made," glorified not God, had their " foolish heart darkened." An exclusive fondness for one side of intellectual nature, to the habitual neglect of the secret and subtle moral elements in conscience, often results in the folly and wickedness of finding not even a trace of God in the universe. Of many it may still be true, " Hadst thou known, even thou, at least in this thy day, the things which belong unto thy peace ! but now they are hid from thine eyes."

VI. The CORRUPTION OF AN AGE and consequent WITHHOLDMENT OF DIVINE LIGHT is NO PERMANENT BAR TO THE DEVELOPMENT OF TRUTH. Israel's degeneracy brought its chastisement ; yet God had a holy servant in reserve both to remove the impeding corruption and to continue the declarations of God's will. Waters held back by a barrier retain and multiply their force, and in course of time will first sweep away the opposition and then flow peacefully on. God's purposes are an eternal force pressing on into the future. In ancient times a measure of truth was given to the world to make ready a fit time and condition for the Christ to come ; and this was done, if not by one unwilling instrument, yet by another when that was swept away. Likewise the Church is to get more truth from the Bible for the " perfecting of the saints ; " and in spite of dark seasons it *will rise to a clearer vision* of the truth in Christ by the providential removal of obstructions and the introduction of a more holy and teachable order of men. Man lives and toils, and opposes and dies. God ever lives in full resistless energy.

Practical considerations :—1. It is a question how far errors and theological conflicts are to be associated with a defective spirituality arising from either overabsorption in purely philosophical pursuits, external Church order, or political and party arrangements.   2. To what extent is it possible to remedy the absence of Divine truth in much of the literature of modern times.   3. By what means the Church and the individual may secure more of that holy, teachable spirit by which alone a fuller vision of truth shall be enjoyed.   4. How far the conduct of controversies of the day respecting Divine truth is defective by not sufficiently taking into account the spiritual condition of men opposed to religion, and whether there is a proper dependence on the power of the Holy Spirit to give eyes to the blind.   5. To what extent, in personal seasons of darkness, the cause lies in our personal indulgence in secret or open sin.

Lowly instruments.   The transition from the employment of Eli, as the messenger of God to the people, to Samuel, brings into view important truths concerning the instrumentality by which God effects his purposes concerning man.

I. God always has IN RESERVE AND TRAINING SUITABLE INSTRUMENTS for promoting the ends to be sought in connection with Christ's kingdom.   Judged from the outward aspect of things, all around appeared dark and hopeless.   There was no one able to cope with the difficulties of the position.   A similar condition of things has been found in certain countries during the history of the Christian Church.   Some desponding minds would find a correspondence in the prevailing unbelief and daring atheism of modern times.   There are also conditions of the individual spiritual life when decay has apparently gone on to utter hopelessness.   Missionaries have now and then felt almost the horror of despair in view of nameless barbarities.   But two or three saw a little beneath the surface.   Hannah was sure of coming deliverance.   Elkanah in some degree shared her confidence, and Eli surmised a purpose of the Lord in the presence of the holy child of the sanctuary.   And, answering to these better spirits of a corrupt age, there are always a few—" a remnant "—who know and are comforted in the assurance that God has instruments in reserve.   As in the case of Samuel, they are *chosen*, in *training*, and *biding their time*.   There are instances of this general truth—1. In the *preparation of the earth for man*.   From remote times there were already chosen, and qualified, and retained in other forms till fit season, the agencies by which, in spite of catastrophes of fire and convulsion and deluge, the beautiful earth would come forth in material realisation of the thought and purpose of God.   2. In the *infant Christian Church*.   The end of Christ's earthly life seemed most disastrous to his kingdom.   The corruption and craft of the wicked were dominant, and the removal of the Saviour seemed to human judgment to be the climax of disaster.   Yet God had chosen, was training and holding in reserve, the men by whom the evils of the age were to be overcome, and truth and righteousness and love asserted as never before.   3. In *definite periods of the Church's history*.   The scholastic subtleties of the middle ages on the one side, the deplorable decay of morals and the prostitution of Church ordinances to gain on the other, caused the earth to mourn.   Nevertheless, in the seraphic devotion of here and there a devout monk, in the inquiring spirit of Erasmus, the clear intelligence of Melancthon, and the courage and firm grip of truth by Luther, God had his chosen instruments for producing a wonderful advance in all that pertains to freedom, purity, and Christian knowledge.   4. In the *midst of the evils indicated by modern antagonism to Christianity*.   Doubtless the principles advocated, logically wrought out, as they are sure to be when the mass embrace them, contain the seeds of immorality, anarchy, and decay of noblest sentiments ; and often there is an eagerness in adopting them which may well cause some to tremble.   But *God is alive*, not dead.   He has his agencies, fitted, and, so to speak, under restraint.   They will be found to consist in the practical futility of all endeavour to get substitutes for a holy religion ; the hopeless miseries into which individuals will be plunged ; the horror created by the very violence of vice ; the natural, never-to-be-quenched instinct which compels man to " cry out for the living God ; " the calling forth of wise men of saintly life who are masters in secular knowledge ; the silent force of Christian lives in health, sickness, and sorrow ; and the aroused prayerfulness of the Church.   Men like Samuel are in existence— 5. In the *conflict of the individual Christian life*.   The dire evils of latent sin, weak resolutions, stains of early years, seem to be a " body of sin and death " from which there is no escape.   But God has in reserve the truth, the afflictions, the tenderness, the quickening power of the Holy Spirit, by which all these shall pass away, and a restored life shall result.

II. The CHARACTERISTICS OF THE MOST EFFECTIVE INSTRUMENTS in working out God's will are, SO FAR AS PERSONS ARE CONCERNED, WELL ASCERTAINED. There is great advantage in having the child-life of Samuel sketched in contrast with the habits and principles of those no longer worthy to be the instruments for doing the highest work in the world. The qualities in Samuel that fitted him for his work were purity of life, deep love for God and his sanctuary, personal consecration to any service in which it might please God to employ him, and the humility that disdains not even menial work if God would thus have it. These qualities are really embraced in the one supreme quality—*conformity of will to the Divine will*. In this respect all *human instruments* are *alike* when thoroughly effective. In so far as it is our "meat and drink" to do the Father's will, our nature becomes a fit channel for the Divine energy to work through for spiritual ends. The failure of moral agents lies in the condition of the will. The power of Christian life in prayer, in work, in silent influence, is in proportion as the consecration takes the form of, "Not *my* will, but *thine* be done."

III. The EFFECTIVENESS OF THE INSTRUMENTS used lies essentially in THE POWER WHICH WORKS THROUGH THEM. The excellent qualities of Samuel no doubt exercised a power appropriate to their own nature; but the real work he did was more than the mere natural influence of what he was. It was God who worked, not only within him to will and to do, but also with and by him. Everywhere in Scripture stress is laid on the unseen energy of God acting on the visible and invisible elements of things, and at last bringing all into subjection. The *reality of the Divine power* in the human instrument is *often conspicuous*. The child Samuel did not secure of himself the submission of the people or the deference of Eli. God wrought on their spirits and made them willing to take him as prophet. Saul was the stronger man, but God *used* David to slay Goliath. God, in the case of apostles, had chosen the "weak things of the world to confound the mighty." His grace was sufficient for them. "Not by might, nor by power, but by my Spirit."

General lessons:—1. There is the most perfect ground for confidence that agencies will be found for doing any work really essential to the salvation of men. 2. It is important for all so to live and labour that they may be available for any service requisite in seasons of trial. 3. The fitness of each Christian for doing greatest possible good in the world rests with his own diligent self-culture and entireness of consecration. 4. It is essentially necessary that in all effort God be recognised as the Author of all good.

Call to higher service. The service of God is very wide and varied. Every true heart may find some employment therein. "They serve who wait," as also those who simply exhibit a holy life. The weary Christian invalid conveys many an impressive lesson to the strong and vigorous. The patient endurance of adversity may do more good than the enjoyment of prosperity. In making distinctions in the value of service rendered, we are not always in a position to pass perfect judgment. In one respect a lowly Christian may be "greater than John the Baptist." In reference to public functions there are gradations, and in this respect Samuel was called to a higher form of service.

I. There ARE CALLS TO A SERVICE RELATIVELY HIGHER. In the estimation of Hannah and Eli, the early occupation of Samuel in the tabernacle was the initiatory stage of a life-work. Except so far as a pure, simple life in contrast with vileness can teach, Samuel's service was confined to attendance on the venerable high priest. The position for which he was finally called was more conspicuous, of wider influence, and involving the display of superior qualities. The narrative relating the call to this higher service is a *record in spirit* of what has *often transpired in the course of history,* and is *being realised every day.* Abraham, Moses, and David served God, each in his own restricted sphere, when they obeyed the Divine call. As Christ once summoned fishermen to leave their occupation to be fishers of men, so now others hear his voice urging them to leave the ship, the desk, the farm, to do his will in preaching the gospel. To the attentive ear of the devout there are frequent calls to rise to more arduous positions in the Church, or to enter on some line of private Christian endeavour that shall more truly bless mankind. Let devout men not forget that the Divine call to higher work is not confined to public functionaries. All kinds of workers are engaged on the spiritual temple.

II. There is A SPECIAL FITNESS REQUIRED FOR HIGHER SERVICE. Obviously, only a Samuel trained by a devout mother, accustomed to the hallowed associations of the sanctuary, was suited for the work that had henceforth to be done. The chief elements that qualify for entrance on higher service are—1. *Deep piety;* for as piety is a requisite to all useful spiritual work, so deep piety is required for the more trying forms of usefulness. 2. *Fidelity* in lower forms. He that is faithful in that which is least becomes fitted for superior responsibilities. "Come up higher" is the voice which crowns earthly toil. 3. *Natural aptitude* for new emergencies. God never puts a man in a position for which natural powers when sanctified are unsuited. The wondrous adaptations in the material world find their analogies in the spiritual. 4. *Readiness to endure* what is unknown. God's servants have to enter an untraversed ground, and their qualification for a call to this must embrace a spirit that says, "Here am I." "Speak, Lord." "What wouldst thou have me to do?" The representation given of Samuel, and of others in the Bible, shows that they were endowed with these qualifications. This, also, may be a test by which good men may now judge of themselves. No one ought to think of departing from any useful sphere of labour without severe scrutiny as to capabilities for heavier duties.

III. The FITNESS FOR HIGHER SERVICE IS, IN SOME INSTANCES, UNCONSCIOUSLY ACQUIRED. Growth is not felt while in process, and only when attention is called to it is the fact recognised. Samuel became month by month more pious and true; his aptitudes enlarged, and his courage rose with every discharge of inconvenient duty. He became spiritually wealthy without being aware of it—sure evidence of vital godliness. The disposition sometimes found to complain of one's lot, to hanker after some more showy occupation in God's service, and to watch and plan for personal advancement, is not a good sign. The humble deeds of opening the door, lighting the lamps of the house of God, when done out of pure love for the Lord of the sanctuary, are means of raising the tone of the entire life. To do the smallest deed *for Christ* is blessed, and years of such fond service is an education, the results of which are only brought out to view when a perhaps sudden demand is made for some difficult duty. By his bitter repentance, and the all-absorbing love for Christ consequent on full restoration, Peter little knew that he was becoming the man to lead the Church on to great triumphs.

IV. The MEANS OF CALLING TO HIGHER SERVICE ARE WONDERFULLY SUITED TO THE CIRCUMSTANCE. The miraculous manifestation of the Divine Being was in harmony with the method by which, as Samuel knew from history of the past, God conveyed his will to men. No terror would arise in his spirit, for he was accustomed to reverence the *house* of God, and to feel that God was nigh. A pure, loving heart does not dread God. The more childlike the piety, the more welcome the thought and presence of the eternal Friend. If Samuel was to become a prophet, and the emergency required that a prophet should speak at that juncture; and if, for authentication, Eli must be used, it is difficult to conceive how these ends could be more naturally secured than by the manner in which the call was made. The objections men raise to what they call the *anthropomorphism* of such a portion of Scripture as this are utterly baseless. Does not God reveal himself in the material world by the visible things which are the outward expressions of his mind? Does it make any real difference to him whether he form them by a slow or by a more swift process? Was the first expression, in an act of creation, *slow?* Who, then, shall say that in expressing his moral purposes for men he must not and cannot adopt an outward visible form, by which the mind to be taught shall be surely arrested? Given a revelation to be made, will men prescribe *à priori* and infallibly *how* God is to act in making it? If so, do they not draw on their human views, and create a God of their own? And what is this but *anthropomorphism* of deepest dye? All God's acts are perfect. The call of his servants is by means suited to time, purpose, and condition. Abraham and others after him each heard the Divine voice differently, but naturally, so far as special conditions determine events. There are "diversities of operations," but "one Spirit." So now it may be by "still small voice," or by suggestion of the wise, or by pressure of circumstances, that his servants receive the assurance that God would have them enter on enlarged responsibilities.

V. It is POSSIBLE THAT A CALL MAY NOT BE CLEARLY DISTINGUISHED AT FIRST. It was not wonderful that Samuel mistook the voice of God for the voice of man. It was Divine tenderness gradually to prepare his mind, through the suggestion of Eli, for a great event. God accommodates his voice of majesty to mortal ears. A spirit like Samuel's, satisfied with the honour of doing anything in the house of God, would scarcely suppose that the greatest of honours was at hand. We are *not sure* that calls to higher service are in *any case immediately clear*. Scripture tells of the fact in many instances without reference to the mental history of the individuals. Abraham's *strong* faith implies special difficulties, and possibly conflicts. Isaiah could scarcely believe that God would use him. Though the disciples knew that Jesus of Nazareth called them to be his servants, doubts subsequently came over them, for they "trusted that it had been he which should have redeemed Israel." Good men become so habituated to lines of action, ruling of impulses, and guidance of common events, that at first they cannot recognise a superior will in new openings, new gentle longings, and pressure from without. It is by the use *of ordinary faculties and means* that the *call to duty* is ascertained. Samuel inquired of Eli, and followed the suggestions of the experienced. The great lines of duty are close to all who will take the trouble to know them. Wise men, passing events, openness of spirit, willingness to be led, these are the means by which every perplexed Samuel will be sure to solve his doubts. To know the possibility that God has some unknown duty to indicate, to be saying in heart, when attention is aroused, "Speak, Lord, for thy servant heareth "—this is often the first step to a new career of usefulness.

Vers. 11—14.—*Privileges and cares.* The one great fact here set forth is that God reveals to Samuel—1. The judgment impending over the house of Eli, and its reasons. 2. That Eli had been already informed of its nature. 3. That the judgment when it comes will cause the most intense consternation in Israel.

I. An ENTRANCE ON SUPERIOR PRIVILEGES. Hitherto Samuel had waited on man. Now he is honoured to hear the voice of God, and wait directly on the Divine presence. His acquaintance with the history of his race—acquired from his mother, and the conversation of Eli, and possibly records in the tabernacle—must have caused him to know that, in being thus called to listen to the voice of God, he was about to take rank among the distinguished in Israel. The honour would be esteemed in proportion to the purity of his nature and sense of unworthiness in the sight of God. The question as to *why God* should *raise a mere child to a position of such importance* may admit of partial answer in this instance, though there is always in the Divine choice an element of wisdom which we cannot unfold. If the regular officials of Israel are unfaithful, God may teach men by using the feeblest of instruments, and out of the ordinary course. And it might be important for the new prophet to be properly installed and authenticated before the aged judge passed away, and the ark of God fell into the hand of the foe. It is always a season of solemn importance when a servant of God enters on higher privileges, and becomes a special medium for reaching the world with Divine truth. It may be, as in this case, in quietude, without the knowledge of the restless world. In any instance is it a marked era in a personal life.

II. An UNWELCOME DISCOVERY. Throughout the ten or twelve years of Samuel's service in the sanctuary he had been to Eli as a loving, dutiful, reverent son. To his awakening piety and simple nature the aged high priest would be the most august personage in the world, the representative of the Most High. The quiet good-nature of Eli in relation to himself would impress the youthful mind very favourably. There would be in Samuel's deportment a tenderness and deference suited to age. It would therefore be a *terrible discovery to learn* from the mouth of God that this revered man *was so guilty* as to deserve chastisement *most severe.* The surface of life was removed, and the object of love and reverence stood condemned. The shock to a child's sensibilities could not but be great at first. When honoured character is found to be blasted, the first impulse of the heart is to give up faith in men and things. But well-balanced holy minds, as was Samuel's, soon recover themselves. He *felt* that God must do right. His horror of sin was in proportion to his purity of life. Therefore, with all the awe, silent and loving, of a true child of God, he would grieve, yet feel that God was wise and good. In *more ordinary forms* the *same discovery is sometimes made.* Children have to learn now and then all at once that the father is discovered to have lived a life of secret sin. The Church is occasionally astounded by discoveries of character not suspected. Even the disciples were unaware of the presence of a thief and traitor as their friend and companion. How many characters have yet to be unveiled !

III. A PREMONITION OF COMING CARES. If we search further for reasons why so terrible a revelation was made to the child-prophet, one might be found in the preparation it gave him for future anxieties. It is well for youth and men to go forth to their career remembering that troubles will come. Samuel's knowledge that disasters of most painful character were close at hand would be morally good and useful. For when cares gather around the soul flees more earnestly to God. The same thing occurred in the instance of the apostles. The honour conferred on them in receiving the truth was weighted with the knowledge that "in the world" they would "have tribulation." Every one who enters on a new course of service must look for cares as part of the lot assigned ; and the prospect will not daunt the true heart, but bring it more into contact with the Source of strength.

IV. A REVELATION OF DIVINE PROCEDURE. Samuel, if at all reflective, must have been struck with the *exceeding deliberateness of the Divine judgments.* Here was a case of vile conduct long manifested, and wicked irresolution to put it down ; yet, instead of sudden and swift punishment coming on father and sons, there is first a declaration to the father that the judgment is coming, and that all is in train for it ; then a lapse of some little time, and a declaration to Samuel that the judgment is fixed and sure ; and after that a succession of events that must have occupied a considerable time before the execution of the judgment (ch. iv. 1—11). This calm deliberateness of God is an awful thing for the guilty, and may inspire the patience and hope of the righteous. It is to be seen in the predictions and preparations for the destruction of Jerusalem ; in the steady wave of desolation and woe he in due time causes to sweep over apostate nations ; in the slow and sure approach of disaster on all who make wealth by fraud, or barter his truth for gain ; as, also, in the calm, orderly arrangement of laws by which all who have despised the only Saviour reap the fruit of their ways.

Vers. 15—21.—*Diverse experiences.* The principal facts are—1. Samuel, on entering upon his daily duties, fears to relate to Eli what had been told him. 2. Eli, under the action of conscience, and convinced that something important has been communicated, employs strong pressure to obtain it from Samuel. 3. Eli, hearing the account, recognises the righteousness of the judgment. 4. Samuel's position as prophet is established through the land. Samuel rose a new youth. During one night events had transpired which gave him a new position, wrought a change in his views and feelings, and tinged his life with a great sorrow. Weary with nervous exhaustion, and haunted by the thought of a sad discovery, it was no wonder if he moved more languidly than usual. The brief narrative sets before us a group of facts resulting from the communications made to him during the night.

I. THE TRIUMPH OF DUTY OVER FEELING. Samuel had *an onerous duty to discharge.* The old man, weak with weight of years and sorrowful in heart, has to be informed of the seal put on his doom. "No prophecy is of private interpretation" applies here in the sense that Samuel's increased knowledge was not intended as a mere secret for himself. Duties are real though not imposed in form of words, and the sensitive spirit quickly recognises them. The eagerness of Eli to learn all that had been communicated left Samuel no option. Thus duties spring up as soon as increased knowledge is a fact ; and when God puts honour on us we must be prepared to face fresh obligations. But duty arising naturally out of new relations is sometimes *counter to legitimate feelings.* "Samuel feared to show Eli the vision." His quick sense saw, as soon as he awoke that day, that he would have to relate a painful story. The natural shrinking of a kindly heart from the infliction of a wound would become more marked as an eager request was made for information.   He knew that Eli would be filled with anguish, both because of the coming doom and the present virtual substitution of another in his place as medium of Divine communication.   It is human to dread the infliction of humiliation and pain.   There is a lawful sympathy with suffering and pity for disgrace.   The judge may weep in passing sentence of death, and yet be a perfect judge.   A parent's heart may righteously bleed at the thought of administering severe chastisement.   Duty is not confronted by feeling as a foe.   Even Christ shrank from taking the cup which a Father's will ordained.   But *disagreeable duty is met fully* by the *supremacy of sense of right*.   Feeling is suppressed, regard for truth is strong, and immediate and future consequences are left to God.   Samuel kept nothing back.   Herein lies the triumph of duty.   The moral victories of life may be won by the young and inexperienced; for the secret lies not in vast knowledge and critical skill, but in a sound heart, swayed by supreme regard for God.

II.   The BODINGS OF A RESTLESS CONSCIENCE.   It was more than curiosity that induced the inquiry of Eli.   His strong language, almost amounting to a threat, revealed an internal conflict.   Conscience is quick in arousing suspicions.   Did the aged man half hope that some relaxation of the sentence already passed would come?   Did the alternate feeling arise that the specific hour of punishment had been announced?   The presence of an *uneasy conscience* is a *fearful bane* in life.   No age, no past reputation, no external honours, no official dignity, no formal employment in religious duties, can give exemption from it where sin has been deliberately indulged.   It is as an enemy in the home, a spoiler in a city, a ghost along one's pathway.   What a power for misery lies in some men!   How easily it is aroused by passing events!   How it makes men quiver even in the presence of children!   How possible it is for even good men to embitter old age by pangs which God will not assuage on this side the grave!   How unspeakably blessed they who keep a clean conscience, or have found cleansing and *rest* in Christ!

III.   SUBMISSION TO THE INEVITABLE.   If Eli had now and then cherished a faint hope that the execution of the sentence against him, already deferred, would be either set aside or modified, all hope vanished as he listened to the simple narrative of Samuel. The terrible tension of his spirit was at once relaxed, and with a reverence and awe which revealed that the religious life, though sadly injured, was true, he could only say, " It is the Lord: let him do what seemeth him good."   Poor old man !   A study for others in responsible positions in the Church of God.   It was well for him that he could thus speak, and give to the saints of all time a form of words exactly suited to them when adversity falls and the heart sinks within.   God is merciful even in the chastisement of his erring people, giving them grace to bow submissively to his righteous will.   Well is it when men can kiss the rod that smites them !   There are, at least, *four characteristics* in a *true submission* to the inevitable.   1. A *distinct recognition of God's acts*.   " It is the *Lord*."   No mere blind working of laws, though forces do sweep on bringing desolation to the soul.   The true spirit sees God in all the trouble.   2. An *absence of all complaint*.   " It is the *Lord*."   That is enough. " The Lord " known in Israel, who made all things, who is the same in all ages, who visited Lot for his covetousness, who kept Moses out of the promised land for his rashness; " the Lord " who raises to honour and crowns life with good, and has only been known as faithful, holy, just, and good.   Not a murmur, not a bitter word or resentful feeling, finds place in true submission.   3. *Conformity to the stroke*.   " Let him do."   The back is bared to the rod.   It is duty and privilege to wish none other than the execution of his purpose.   4. *Belief that all is for good*.   " Let him do what seemeth him good."   " Though he slay me, yet will I trust him."   Chastisement of the good, and also direct punishment of the wicked, are in the judgment of God *good*. True submission acquiesces in that judgment.   Such has been the submission of the saints in ancient and modern times ; and pre-eminently, and with reference to special sorrows, of him who, when bearing a burden which others deserved, said, " Father, not my will, but thine be done."

IV.   A GROWING REPUTATION.   Samuel's fidelity in discharging a painful duty was a good beginning of an official life.   He was furnished with the special knowledge requisite to the emergency of the time.   The repeated secret vision in Shiloh, and the outward confirmation of his words before the people, gave him courage, and secured his recognition in the place of Eli. Thus *three elements* enter into the *gradual acquisition of a reputation*. 1. *Fidelity* in discharge of *known duty*. This gives power to the soul for any further duty, however unpleasant. Temptations overcome in one instance lose force afterwards. Sense of right gains energy in action by each exercise. The basis of substantial character is laid in acts of righteousness. 2. *Continuous help from God*. We cannot go on to new conquests by the mere force of what we have become by previous deeds. As Samuel needed and enjoyed aid from God for his position in life, so every one can only acquire a solid reputation by looking for and using such aid as God may see fit to bestow day by day. 3. *Continued verification of profession by deeds corresponding thereto*. A character attained to by faithful deeds in the past, aided by Divine grace, becomes practically a profession. It is the exponent of principles supposed to be dominant in the life, and men give a certain value to it. But if reputation is to grow and become broader in its base and wider in its influence, the profession of principles of conduct must be verified constantly by actions appropriate to them.

Practical lessons :—1. It is of extreme importance for young and old to cultivate a rigid regard for truth, combined with a tender consideration of human feeling. 2. The discharge of disagreeable duties is greatly helped by the remembrance that they arise out of the circumstances in which God himself has placed us. 3. We should distinguish between wise submission to what God lays on us for discipline, and indolent acquiescence in circumstances self-created, and largely removable by our efforts.

HOMILIES BY VARIOUS AUTHORS.

Vers. 1—18.—*The old priest and the child-prophet.* Every imagination must be struck by the contrast between the old man and the child. The more so, that the natural order of things is reversed. Instead of admonition to the child coming through the lips of age, admonition to the aged came through the lips of childhood.

1. The character of Eli illustrated. 1. His good points. The Lord had ceased to speak to or by Eli ; but when the old priest perceived that the Lord had spoken to the child, he showed no personal or official jealousy. On the contrary, he kindly encouraged Samuel, and directed him how to receive the heavenly message. He did not attempt to interpose on the ground that he, as the chief priest, was the official organ of Divine communications, but bade the child lie still and hearken to the voice. Nor did he claim any preference on the ground of his venerable age. It is not easy to look with complacency on one much younger than ourselves who is evidently on the way to excel us in our own special province. But Eli did so, and threw no hindrance whatever in the way of the young child. Let God use as his seer or prophet whom he would. Eli was anxious to know the truth, and the whole truth, from the mouth of the child. He had been previously warned by a man of God of the disaster which his own weakness and his sons' wickedness would bring on the priestly line (ch. ii. 27—36). But the evil of the time was too strong for him ; and having effected no reform in consequence of that previous warning, the old man must have foreboded some message of reproof and judgment when the voice in the night came not to himself, but to the child. Yet he was not false to God, and would not shrink from hearing truth, however painful. "I pray thee hide it not from me." He meekly acquiesced in the condemnation of his house. Eli had no sufficient force of character or vigour of purpose to put away the evil which had grown to such enormity under his indulgent rule, but he was ready with a sort of plaintive surrender to Divine justice. It was not a high style of character, but at all events it was vastly better than a self-justifying, God-resisting mood of mind. 2. His faults. No meek language, no pious acquiescence in his sentence, can extenuate the grievous injury which, through indecision and infirmity, Eli had brought on Israel at large, and on the priestly order in particular. His virtues may almost be said to have sprung out of his faults. He was benevolent, submissive, and free from jealousy because he had no force, no intensity. He could lament and suffer well because he had no energy. So he commanded little respect because, instead of checking evil, he had connived at it for a quiet life. " There are persons who go through life sinning and sorrowing, sorrowing and sinning. No experience teaches them. Torrents of tears flow from

their eyes. They are full of eloquent regrets. But all in vain. When they have done wrong once they do wrong again. What are such persons to be in the next life? Where will the Elis of this world be? God only knows" (Robertson).

II. THE CHILD CALLED TO BE A PROPHET. We may discern even in "little Samuel" the beginnings of a great character, prognostics of an illustrious career. The child was courageous, not afraid to sleep in one of the priest's chambers alone, no father or mother near. And he was dutiful to the aged Eli, hastening to him when he thought that he had called in the night; and considerate to his feelings, reluctant to tell him in the morning the heavy judgments of which God had spoken. From that night he began to be a prophet. Very soon were the hopes of Hannah for her son fulfilled, nay, surpassed. "Samuel grew, and the Lord was with him, and did let none of his words fall to the ground." The nature of the first communication made through Samuel gave some indication of the future strain of his prophetic life and testimony. He was not to be one of those, like Isaiah, Daniel, and Zechariah, whose prophecies and visions reached far forward into future times. His function was more like that of Moses, Elijah, or Jeremiah, as a teacher of private and public righteousness. He was destined to maintain the law and authority of God, to rebuke iniquity, to check and even sentence transgressors in high places, to withstand the current of national degeneracy, and insist on the separation of Israel from the heathen nations and their customs. The pith of his life-ministry lay in his urgency for moral obedience.

III. LIGHT THROWN ON THE EARLY TRAINING OF GOD'S PUBLIC SERVANTS. It is acknowledged that some who have been eminently useful in Christian times have been converted in manhood, and their earlier life may seem to have been lost. Paul was so converted. So was Augustine. But these really form no exception to the rule that God directs the training of his servants from childhood. Paul had a good Jewish Rabbinical education, and, besides this, an acquaintance with Greek literature and forms of thought. Having been brought up a Pharisee, he was the more fitted after his conversion to estimate at its full force that Jewish resistance to Christianity on the ground of law-righteousness which he above all men combatted. At the same time, knowing the world, and being from his youth up cultivated and intelligent according to the Greek standard, he was prepared to be, after his conversion, a most suitable apostle of Christ to the Gentiles. A similar process of preparation may be traced in Augustine. His early studies in logic and rhetoric prepared him, though he knew it not, to become a great Christian dialectician; and even the years in which he served his own youthful passions were not without yielding some profit, inasmuch as they intensified his knowledge of the power of sin, and ultimately of the sin-vanquishing power of grace. By far the greater number of those who have served the Lord as prophets, preachers, or pastors of his flock, have been nourished up for such service from early years, though they knew it not. Some of them went first to other callings. John Chrysostom was at the bar; Ambrose in the civil service, rising to be prefect of Liguria; Cyprian was a teacher of rhetoric; Melancthon, a professor of Greek. Moses himself grew up a scholar and a soldier, and no one who saw him in the court of Egypt could have guessed his future career. But in such cases God guided his servants in youth through paths of knowledge and experience which were of utmost value to them when they found at last their real life-work for his name. There is danger, however, in sudden transitions from one walk of life to another, and from one mould of character to another. It is the danger of extravagance. There is a proverb about the excessive zeal of sudden converts; and there is this measure of truth in it, that persons who rapidly change their views or their position need some lapse of time, and some inward discipline, before they learn calmness, religious self-possession, and meekness of wisdom. It is therefore worthy of our notice that God gave Moses a long pause in the land of Midian, and Paul also in Arabia. We return to the fact that the great majority of God's servants in the gospel have grown up with religious sentiments and desires from their very childhood. So it was with John the Baptist, with Timothy, with Basil, with Jerome, with Bernard of Clairvaux, with Columba, with Usher, with Zinzendorf, with Bengel, and many more. So it was with Samuel. His first lessons were from the devout and gifted Hannah in the quiet home at Ramah. From his earliest consciousness he knew that he was to be the Lord's, and a specially consecrated servant or Nazarite. Then he was taken to Shiloh, and his special training for a grand and difficult career began. Early in his life he had to see evil among those who ought to have shown the best example. He had to see what mischief is wrought by relaxation of morals among the rulers of what we should call Church and State, so that an abhorrence of such misconduct might be deeply engraved on his untainted soul. But at the same time Samuel grew up in daily contact with holy things. The sacred ritual, which was no more than a form to the wicked priests, had an elevating and purifying influence on the serious spirit of this child. And so it was that Samuel, conversant day by day with holy names and symbols, took a mould of character in harmony with these—took it gradually, firmly, unalterably. It gave steadiness to his future ministry ; for he was to retrieve losses, assuage excitements, re-establish justice, reprove, rebuke, and exhort the people and their first king. Such a ministry needed a character of steady growth, and the personal influence which attends a consistent life. So the Lord called Samuel when a child, and he answered, "Speak ; for thy servant heareth." May God raise up young children among us to quit themselves hereafter as men—-to redress wrongs, establish truth and right, heal divisions, reform the Church, and pave the way for the coming King and the kingdom !—F.

Vers. 1—18. (SHILOH.)—*Samuel's call to the prophetic office.* "The Lord called Samuel" (ver. 4).

> "In Israel's fane, by silent night,
> The lamp of God was burning bright ;
> And there, by viewless angels kept,
> Samuel, the child, securely slept.
>
> A voice unknown the stillness broke,
> 'Samuel !' it called, and thrice it spoke.
> He rose—he asked whence came the word.
> From Eli ? No ; it was the Lord.
>
> Thus early called to serve his God,
> In paths of righteousness he trod ;
> Prophetic visions fired his breast,
> And all the chosen tribes were blessed " (Cawood).

Introductory.—1. This call to the prophetic office took place at a time of great moral and spiritual darkness. "The word of the Lord " (the revelation of his mind and will to men) " was rare in those days ; for " (*therefore*, as the effect ; or *becau e*, as the evidence of the absence of such revelation) " there was no vision " (prophetic communication) " spread abroad " among the people (ver. 1 ; 2 Chron. xxxi. 5). (1) The word of God is *needed* by man because of his ignorance of the highest truths, and his inability to attain the knowledge of them by his own efforts. (2) Its *possession* is hindered by prevailing indifference and corruption. (3) Its *absence* is worse than a famine of bread (Ps. lxxiv. 9 ; Amos viii. 11), and most destructive (Prov. xxix. 18). 2. It was the commencement of a fresh series of Divine communications, which culminated in the teaching of the great Prophet, " who spake as never man spake " (Acts iii. 24 ; Heb. i. 1). This is the chief general significance of the event. "The call of Samuel to be the prophet and judge of Israel formed a turning-point in the history of the Old Testament kingdom of God." 3. It was given to one who was very young (twelve years old, according to Josephus, when childhood merges into youth ; Luke ii. 42), and who held the lowest place in the tabernacle, where Eli held the highest, but who was specially prepared for the work to which he was called. "Shadows of impenitent guilt were the dark background of the picture from which the beams of Divine love which guided that child of grace shone forth in brighter relief " (Anderson). 4. It came in a manner most adapted to convince Eli and Samuel that it was indeed from the Lord (ver. 8), and to answer its immediate purpose in regard to both. Notice—
I. THE VOICE of the Lord. 1. It was heard in the *temple* (vers. 2, 3), or palace of the invisible King of Israel, proceeding from his throne in the innermost sanctuary (Exod. xxv. 22 ; 1 Sam. iv. 4 ; Heb. ix. 5) ; not now, however, addressing the

high priest, but a child, as a more loyal subject, and more susceptible to Divine teaching (Matt. xi. 25, 26). 2. It broke suddenly on the silence and slumbers of the *night;* "ere the lamp of God went out," *i. e.* toward the morning—a season suitable to deep and solemn impression. "Untroubled night, they say, gives counsel best." The light of Israel before God, represented by the golden candelabrum, with its "seven lamps of fire," was burning dimly, and the dawn of a new day was at hand. 3. It called Samuel by *name,* not merely as a means of arousing him, but as indicating the Lord's intimate knowledge of his history and character (John x. 3), and his claims upon his special service. The All-seeing has a perfect knowledge of each individual soul, and deals with it accordingly. 4. It was often *repeated,* with ever-increasing impressiveness. Natural dulness in the discernment of spiritual things renders necessary the repetition of God's call to men, and his patience is wonderfully shown in such repetition. 5. It was in the last instance accompanied by an *appearance.* "Jehovah came, and *stood,* and called" (ver. 10). Probably in glorious human form, as in former days. "Allied to our nature by engagement and anticipation, the eternal Word occasionally assumed its prophetic semblance before he dwelt on earth in actual incarnate life." There could now be no doubt whence the voice proceeded; and even the delay which had occurred must have served to waken up all the faculties of the child into greater activity, and prepare him for the main communication he was about to receive.

II. THE RESPONSE of Samuel. 1. He did not *at first* recognise the voice as God's, but thought it was Eli's (vers. 4—6). For "he did not yet know the Lord" by direct and conscious revelation, "neither was the Word of the Lord *revealed* to him" (literally, made bare, disclosed; as a secret told in the ear, which has been uncovered by turning back the hair—Gen. xxv. 7; 1 Sam. ix. 15; Job xxxiii. 16) as it was afterwards (ver. 21). "We must not think that Samuel was then ignorant of the true God, but that he knew not the manner of that voice by which the prophetical spirit was wont to awaken the attention of the prophets" (John Smith's 'Sel. Discourses,' p. 208). "God speaketh once, yea twice, yet man perceiveth it not" (Job xxxiii. 14). How often is *his* voice deemed to be only the voice of man! 2. He *acted up to the light* he had (vers. 7, 8). Three times his rest was broken by what he thought was the voice of Eli; three times he ran to him obediently, uncomplainingly, promptly; and three times he "went and lay down in his place" as he was bidden. The spirit which he thus displayed prepared him for higher instruction. 3. He obeyed the *direction* given him by the high priest (ver. 9). Although Eli could not himself hear the voice, yet he perceived that it was heard by another, showed no indignation or envy at the preference shown toward him, and taught him to listen to the Lord for himself, and what he should say in response. "He showed himself a better tutor than he was a parent" (Hall). 4. He responded in a spirit of *reverence, humility,* and *obedience* to the voice that now uttered his name twice (ver. 10). "Speak; for thy servant heareth." His omission of the name "Jehovah" was perhaps due to his overwhelming astonishment and reverence But he confessed himself to be his servant, virtually ratifying of his own accord his dedication to his service, and testified his readiness to "hear and obey." Oh, what an hour is that in which the presence of the Lord is first manifested in living force to the soul! and what a change does it produce in all the prospects and purposes of life! (Gen. xviii. 16, 17). "We were like them that sleep, them that dream, before we entered into communion with God."

III. THE COMMUNICATION of God to Samuel. 1. It *differed* from the message of the "man of God," which had come some time previously, in that it was more brief, simple, and severe; and was given to Samuel alone, without any express direction to make it known to Eli, who seems to have paid no regard to the warning he previously received. 2. It was an announcement of *judgment on the house of Eli* which would be—(1) Very startling and horrifying to men (ver. 11). (2) The fulfilment of the word which had been already spoken (ver. 12). (3) Complete. "When I begin, I will also make an end." (4) Righteously deserved, inasmuch as his sons had grievously sinned, and *he knew it* as well as the approaching judgment, and restrained them not (ver. 13; James iv. 17). "Sinners make themselves vile (literally, curse themselves), and those who do not reprove them make themselves accessaries" (M. Henry). (5) Permanent and irrevocable. "For ever." "I have sworn," &c. (ver. 14). 3. It was very *painful* to Samuel because it was directed "against Eli" (ver. 12—as well as his house), for whom he entertained a deep and tender affection. The "burden of the Lord" was heavy for a child to bear. It was his first experience of the prophet's cross, but it prepared him for his future work. "Woe to the man who receives a message from the gods." 4. It put his character to a *severe test*, by leaving to his discretion the use which he should make of so terrible a communication. Wisdom and grace are as much needed in using God's communications as in receiving and responding to his voice.

IV. The disclosure by Samuel to Eli. 1. It was *not* made *hastily* or rashly (ver. 15). "He lay down till the morning," pondering the communication ; he suffered it not to interfere with the duty that lay immediately before him, but rose and "opened the doors of the house" as usual, though with a heavy heart ; and exhibited great calmness, self-control, discretion, and considerate reserve. He "feared to show Eli the vision" lest he should be grieved, or take it in a wrong manner. 2. It was only made under strong *pressure* (vers. 16, 17). "Samuel, *my son*" (B'ni), said Eli ; and "how much is expressed by this one word!" (Thenius). He asked, he demanded, he adjured. 3. It was made *truthfully*, faithfully, and without any reserve (ver. 18). 4. It was followed by a *beneficial effect*. Not, indeed, in rousing the high priest to strenuous efforts for the reformation of his house, which he probably deemed impossible, but in leading him to acknowledge that it was the Lord who had spoken, and to resign himself to his will. No such effect followed the warning previously addressed to him. A similar spirit was shown by Aaron (Levit. x. 3), by Job (i. 21), by David (2 Sam. xviii. 14, 15, 32, 33), by Hezekiah (2 Kings xx. 19), and, above all, by the great High Priest himself (Matt. xxvi. 42). No other Divine message came apparently to Eli or his house. Henceforth there was only the silence that precedes the thunderstorm and the earthquake.—D.

Ver. 10.—*The faithful servant.* "Speak ; for thy servant heareth." The well-known picture by Sir Joshua Reynolds, representing the child Samuel in the attitude of prayer, aptly expresses the spirit of his whole life. His own language in response to the call of God does this still more perfectly, and "contains the secret of his strength." It also teaches us how we should respond to the Divine call which is addressed to us, and what is the spirit which we ought ever to possess. For God speaks to us as truly as he spoke to Samuel, though in a somewhat different manner. He speaks to us often, and calls each of us to special service for him; and there cannot be a nobler aim than that of possessing the mind, disposition, and character of a "faithful servant" (Matt. xxv. 21) here portrayed. This implies—

I. Consciousness of the Master's presence. 1. *Peculiar ;* not merely a general belief in his omnipresence, such as most persons have, but a realisation of his presence *here ;* not as in a dream, but in full waking thought; not as if he were at a distance from us, but "face to face." "Thou God seest me." 2. *Intense ;* filling the soul with the light of his glory and with profound reverence (Job xlii. 6). 3. *Habitual ;* abiding with us at all times, carried with us into every place, and pervading and influencing all our thoughts, words, and actions.

II. Acknowledgment of the Master's claims. "Thy servant." His claims are —1. *Just ;* because of—(1) What he has *done* for us. He has given us our being, and all that makes it a blessing (ch. i. 11). He has purchased us at a great price (1 Pet. i. 18). "Ye are not your own" (1 Cor. vi. 19, 20). (2) Our *consecration* to him (ch. i. 28). "I am the Lord's" (Isa. xliv. 5). (3) Our *acceptance* by him. 2. *Supreme.* All other claims are inferior to his, and must be regarded as subordinate to them. 3. *Universal ;* extending to all our faculties, possessions, &c.

> "My gracious Lord, I own thy right
> To every service I can pay,
> And call it my supreme delight
> To hear thy dictates and obey.
>
> What is my being but for thee,
> Its sure support, its noblest end ;

> Thy ever-smiling face to see,
> And serve the cause of such a Friend ? " (Doddridge).

III. Listening to the Master's directions. "Speak." "I am waiting to hear thy commands, and desire to know thy will." "What saith my Lord unto his servant?" (Josh. v. 14). "What wilt thou have me to do?" (Acts ix. 6). His directions are given by—1. His *word*, in the law and the gospel. 2. His *providence*, in the various events of life, affording fresh opportunities, bringing new responsibilities, indicating special methods of service. "New occasions teach new duties." "There are so many kinds of voices in the world, and none of them is without signification" (1 Cor. xiv. 10). 3. His *Spirit;* teaching the meaning and application of the word, suggesting thoughts and activities in accordance with his revealed will, filling the heart with holy and benevolent impulses. "It is written in the prophets, And they shall be all taught of God" (John vi. 45). "Behold, as the eyes of servants look unto the hand of their masters" (watching with the utmost attention for every indication of their will), "so our eyes wait upon the Lord our God" (Ps. lxxxv. 8; cxxiii. 2; Hab. ii. 1).

IV. Readiness for the Master's work. "Thy servant heareth;" stands ready to obey—1. *Whatever* thou mayest direct. 2. With my *utmost* strength. 3. *Promptly;* without delay. "When it pleased God to reveal his Son in me, *immediately* I conferred not with flesh and blood, but went" (Gal. i. 15—17). When Ledyard (whose life was the first of many sacrificed to African discovery) closed with the proposal of the Association for Promoting the Discovery of the Inland Parts of Africa to undertake a journey in that region, and was asked how soon he would be ready to set out, he replied, "To-morrow morning." The like promptitude should be exhibited by every "good and faithful servant."—D.

Ver. 13.—*Parental restraint.* "And he restrained them not." The parental relation was universally regarded in ancient times as one which involved a closer identity between parents and children, and a more absolute authority on the part of the former over the latter, than would now be deemed just. This fact explains many occurrences in the sacred history. It also makes more apparent the inexcusable conduct of Eli in omitting to restrain his sons from their evil way. To every head of a family, however, belongs a certain measure of authority, and he is responsible for its exercise in "commanding his children and his household" (Gen. xviii. 19) to do what is right, and restraining them from doing what is wrong. Concerning PARENTAL RESTRAINT, observe that—

I. Its need is urgent. 1. Because of the strong *tendency* to evil which exists in children. However it may be accounted for or explained, there can be no doubt of the fact. If it be simply, as some say, a desire of self-gratification, and dislike of everything that hinders it—self-will, it is necessary that it should be checked; for those who are trained to deny themselves in very early life, and submit to the will of their parents, are far more likely than others to accept and submit to the will of God when they become conscious of it. "In order to form the minds of children, the first thing to be done is to conquer their will and bring them to an obedient temper. This is the only strong and rational foundation of a religious education, without which both precept and example will be ineffectual. As self-will is the root of all sin and misery, so whatever cherishes this in children insures their after wretchedness and irreligion; whatever checks and mortifies it promotes their future happiness and piety" (The mother of the Wesleys). 2. Because of the evil *examples* by which they are surrounded, and which act so powerfully on their susceptibility to impression and their propensity to imitation. 3. Because of the manifold *temptations* to which they are exposed. However guarded, they cannot be altogether kept from their influence.

II. Its obligation is imperative. 1. It is obviously a part of parental *duty.* 2. It is often enjoined in the word of God (Deut. xxi. 15- 21; Prov. xix. 18; xxiii. 13, 14; xxix. 15, 17). 3. It is clearly adapted to accomplish beneficial results (Prov. xxii. 6). It is thus a duty which parents owe not only to their children, but also to the great Parent of all, who, by the manner in which he deals with his earthly children, has himself set them an example.

II. ITS METHOD IS IMPORTANT. It should be—1. *Timely ;* commenced at an early age (Prov. xiii. 24). 2. *Firm* and *just.* 3. With *consideration, kindness,* and *patience* (Eph. vi. 4 ; Col. iii. 21).

> " O'er wayward childhood wouldst thou hold firm rule,
>   And sun thee in the light of happy faces,
>   Love, hope, and patience, these must be thy graces,
> And in thine own heart let them first keep school ;
>   For as old Atlas on his broad neck places
>   Heaven's starry globe, and there sustains it ; so
> Do these bear up the little world below
>   Of education—patience, love, and hope " (Coleridge).

IV. ITS OMISSION IS RUINOUS. 1. To *children* (ch. iv. 11). 2. To *parents* (ch. iv. 18). 3. To the *nation* (ch. iv. 22). " Indulgent parents are cruel to themselves and their posterity " (Hall). How numerous are the facts which justify these statements ! " As in individuals, so in nations, unbridled indulgence of the passions must produce, and does produce, frivolity, effeminacy, slavery to the appetite of the moment ; a brutalised and reckless temper, before which prudence, energy, national feeling, any and every feeling which is not centred in self, perishes utterly. The old French noblesse gave a proof of this law which will last as a warning beacon to the end of time. The Spanish population of America, I am told, gives now a fearful proof of this same terrible penalty. Has not Italy proved it likewise for centuries past ? It must be so. For national life is grounded on, is *the development of, the life of the family.* And where the root is corrupt the tree must be corrupt likewise " (Kingsley, ' The Roman and the Teuton,' Lect. ii.). Therefore (1) let parents exercise due restraint over their children ; and (2) let children submit to the restraint of their parents (Exod. xx. 12 ; Levit. xix. 3 ; Prov. xxx. 17 ; Jer. xxxv. 18, 19).—D.

Ver. 18.—*Resignation.* " It is the Lord : let him do what seemeth him good." The sentence which was pronounced on Eli and his house was almost as severe as can be conceived. But the manner in which it was received by him shows that, notwithstanding the defects of his character, he possessed the " spirit of faith," which shone like a spark of fire amidst the ashes and gloom of his closing days. He did not refuse to admit its Divine Author, did not question its justice, did not rebel against it and seek to reverse it, did not fret and murmur and give himself up to despair. His language expresses a spirit the exact opposite of all this. " When Samuel had told him every whit, Eli replied, It is the Lord. The highest religion could say no more. What more can there be than surrender to the will of God ? In that one brave sentence you forget all Eli's vacillation. Free from envy, free from priestcraft, earnest, humbly submissive ; that is the bright side of Eli's character, and the side least known or thought of " (F. W. Robertson).

I. HE RECOGNISES THE APPOINTMENT OF GOD. " It is the Lord," or " he is the Lord," who has spoken. He believed that the voice was really his, notwithstanding (1) it came to him *indirectly*—through the agency of another ; (2) it came in an *unexpected* manner ; and (3) it announced what he naturally *disliked* to hear, and what was most grievous. These things sometimes dispose men to doubt " the word of the Lord," and are made excuses for rejecting it. It is not, in its mode of communication or in its contents, " according to their mind." But the spirit of faith ventures not to dictate to God how or what he shall say, and it perceives the Divine voice when those who are destitute of it perceive only what is purely natural and human.

II. HE JUSTIFIES THE RECTITUDE OF GOD. Such justification (Ps. li. 4)—1. Is *implied* in the acknowledgment that it comes from Jehovah, who alone is holy (ch. ii. 2). " Shall not the Judge of all the earth do right ? " (Gen. xviii. 25). 2. *Proceeds* from the conviction that it is deserved on account of the iniquity of his sons, and his own sins of omission (Lam. iii. 39 ; Micah vii. 9). They who have a due sense of the evil of sin are not disposed to complain of the severity of the sentence pronounced against it. 3. Is not the less *real* because not fully expressed, for *silence* itself is often the most genuine testimony to the perfect equity of the Divine procedure. " Aaron held his peace " (Lev. x. 3 ; Ps. xxxix. 9, 11).

III. He submits to the sovereignty of God. "Let him do what seemeth him good." 1. Very *reverently and humbly* (1 Pet. v. 6). It is vain to contend against him. 2. *Freely and cheerfully;* not because he cannot be effectually resisted, but because what he does is right and good; the spontaneous surrender and sacrifice of the will. 3. *Entirely.* "The will of the Lord be done" (Acts xxi. 14).

IV. He confides in the goodness of God. "Good." "Good is the word of the Lord" (2 Kings xx. 19). Eli could not have spoken as he did unless he believed that—(1) God is merciful and gracious; (2) in wrath remembers mercy, mitigating the force of the storm to all who seek shelter in his bosom; and (3) "out of evil still educes good" (Rom. viii. 28). Let us be thankful for the surpassing motives and influences afforded to us under the gospel (2 Cor. iv. 17; Heb. iv. 15; xii. 10, 11; Rev. xxi. 4; xxii. 3).—D.

Ver. 19—iv. 1. (Shiloh.)—*Samuel the prophet.* "A prophet of the Lord" (ver. 20). "A prophet was a man who drew aside the curtain from the secret counsels of Heaven. He declared or made public the previously hidden truths of God; and, because future events might chance to involve Divine truth, therefore a revealer of future events might happen to be a prophet. Yet, still, small was the part of a prophet's functions which contained the foreshadowing of events, and not necessarily any part of it" (De Quincey, 'Confessions,' p. 27). The greatest of prophets, and more than a prophet, was Moses (Num. xii. 6—8; Deut. xviii. 15; xxxiv. 9). After him a prophet arose at rare intervals. With Samuel, who was second only to Moses, a new prophetic era began. He was called to a permanent prophetic work; a type of the future line of the prophets which he virtually founded, and "set for all time the great example of the office of a prophet of the Lord." "In Samuel—Levite, Nazarite, at the sanctuary of Shiloh, prophet, and destined founder of a mightier prophetic power—were united from the first all spiritual gifts most potent for the welfare of the people, and under his powerful control stood the wheels on which the age revolved. . . . He was truly the father of all the great prophets who worked such wonders in the ensuing centuries" (Ewald. See 'Davison on Prophecy;' 'Fairbairn on Prophecy;' 'Prophecy a Preparation for Christ,' by the Dean of Canterbury). The summary of his prophetic activity here given leads us to consider—

I. His qualification. "And Samuel grew, and the Lord was with him" (ver. 19). "And the Lord appeared again in Shiloh (ver. 10): for the Lord revealed himself to Samuel in Shiloh by the word of the Lord" (ver. 21). 1. *The possession of a holy character*, which was the general condition of prophetic endowment. At the time of his call Samuel entered into a higher knowledge of God, and a closer fellowship with him than he had before; he gradually advanced therein, and his character became more and more perfect. "Equable progression from the beginning to the end was the special characteristic of his life." "The qualifications which the Jewish doctors suppose necessarily antecedent to render any one *habilem ad prophetandum* are truly *probity* and *piety;* and this was the constant sense and opinion of them all universally, not excluding the vulgar themselves" (John Smith, 'Sel. Disc.' p. 250). 2. *The revelation to him of the Divine word*—by voices, visions, insight, intuition, inspiration (ver. 7). "For the prophecy came not in old time by the will of man; but holy men of God spake as they were moved (borne along as a ship by the wind) by the Holy Ghost" (2 Pet. i. 21). The communications of God to men have been made in many ways (by dreams, by Urim, by prophecy), and one communication faithfully received and used has prepared the way for another. How long after the Lord first appeared to Samuel he "appeared again" to him is not stated. 3. *The conviction of its Divine origin,* amounting to absolute certainty, and impelling him to speak and act in accordance with the revelation he received.

II. His vocation. "And the word of Samuel came to all Israel" (ch. iv. 1). He had not only to receive the word from God, but also to utter it to men. He was a spokesman for God, a messenger or interpreter of the Divine will. 1. *The nature and purpose* of his vocation were—(1) *The communication of doctrine;* the teaching of moral and spiritual truth; the declaration of the mind and will of the invisible and eternal King, with special reference to the requirements of the time in which he lived. He was a witness of the presence and government of Jehovah, his nature and character, his hatred of sin and love of righteousness, his dissatisfaction with merely formal and ceremonial services, his opposition to idolatry, his gifts, claims, and purposes with respect to his people. "The prophetic order in its highest signification was nothing else than a living witness for those eternal principles of righteousness which previous revelation had implanted in the Hebrew race, and through them in the life of humanity" (Tulloch). (2) *The enforcement of practice,* by urgent appeals to the conscience, and presenting powerful motives of gratitude for past benefits, hope of future good, and fear of future evil. "The prophets, beside their communication of doctrine, had another and a direct office to discharge as pastors and ministerial monitors of the people of God. Their work was to admonish and reprove, to arraign for every ruling sin, to blow the trumpet of repentance, and shake the terrors of the Divine judgment over a guilty land. Often they bore the message of consolation or pardon ; rarely, if ever, of public approbation or praise" (Davison). (3) *The prediction of things to come;* not simply general results of good or evil conduct, but specific events that could not have been known except by Divine inspiration (ch. vii. 4 ; x. 2 ; xii. 17 ; xiii. 14) ; an element which became more prominent in subsequent times—the things to come having relation to the setting up of a kingdom of heaven on earth. We need not here dwell upon other matters connected with and growing out of the prophetic vocation of Samuel, viz., (4) his offering sacrifice ; (5) his civil magistracy ; (6) his presiding over the "school of the prophets ; " (7) his recording the events of his time (1 Chron. xxix. 29). 2. *The persons whom his vocation immediately concerned.* (1) The people and the elders of Israel—directing them what to do, exhorting them to forsake their sins, sometimes opposing and condemning their wishes. "His business was to keep all Israel true to the Divine purpose for which they had been made a nation" (' Expositor,' vol. iii. p. 344). (2) The priesthood, as in the case of Eli and his sons. (3) The *king*—teaching him that he was a servant of Jehovah, appointed by him, and bound to obey his laws, and when he departed from them denouncing his disobedience. "Under the protection generally, though not always effectual, of their sacred character the prophets were a power in the nation often more than a match for kings and priests, and kept up in that little corner in the earth the antagonism of influences which is the only real security for continued progress . . . . The remark of a distinguished Hebrew, that the prophets were in Church and State equivalent to the modern liberty of the press, gives a just but not an inadequate conception of the part fulfilled in national and universal history by this great element of Jewish life" (J. S. Mill, ' Representative Government,' p. 41). 3. *The manner in which it was fulfilled :* diligently (Jer. xxiii. 28 ; xlviii. 10 = negligently), faithfully (not according to his own natural wishes, but God's will) ; fearlessly ; established=found trustworthy—Num. xii. 7 ; 1 Sam. ii. 35), fully (not shunning to declare all the counsel of God—Deut. iv. 2 ; Acts xx. 27).

III. HIS CONFIRMATION. "The Lord was with him, and did let none of his words fall to the ground" (but made them stand firmly, or attain their aim like an arrow which hits the mark—ver. 19). He attested, sealed him as his messenger—1. By bringing to pass the good or evil foretold by him (Num. xxii. 6). 2. By providential and even miraculous occurrences, indicating his approval (ch. vii. 10 ; xii. 18). 3. By clothing his word with power, so that it was felt by those to whom it was addressed to be the word of the Lord ; for there is something Divine within which responds to the Divine without, and every one who is truthful perceives and obeys the voice of eternal truth (John xviii. 37).

IV. HIS RECOGNITION. "And all Israel from Dan even to Beer-sheba knew that Samuel was established to be a prophet of the Lord" (ver. 20). The Divine word was no more rare (ch. iii. 1). 1. His *authority* was universally admitted. It was familiarly known throughout the land that he had been appointed as a regular medium of communication between Jehovah and his people. 2. His *utterances* were widely disseminated, and regarded with reverence. "The word of Samuel came to all Israel." 3. His *work* thereby became highly effective. Its full effect appeared long afterwards. But even before the blow of judgment, which he predicted, fell (some ten years after his call), he doubtless laboured not in vain ; and during the succeeding twenty years (ch. vii. 2) he "spent his time in a slow but resolute work of kindling the almost extinguished flame of a higher life in Israel."—D.

EXPOSITION.

CHAPTER IV.

Ver. 1.—**And the word of Samuel . . . all Israel.** This clause is rightly connected with the foregoing verse of the previous chapter in the Syriac and Vulgate. Attached to the fourth chapter, it gives a wrong sense, namely, that Samuel gave the command for the assembling of all Israel for battle with the Philistines. This is so plainly erroneous that the A. V. dissents from it by translating the *and* in the next clause by *now*. Joined to the previous chapter, it gives the true meaning. Because Samuel spake *by the word of Jehovah*, therefore *his word came to all Israel*, that is, it was a binding and authoritative command throughout the whole land ; or, in other words, when Samuel was acknowledged to be Jehovah's prophet he also became the virtual judge of Israel, though probably he did not act with full authority until after Eli's death.

DEFEAT OF ISRAEL AND CAPTURE OF THE ARK (vers. 1—11). **Now Israel**—rather, And Israel — **went out against the Philistines.** During the declining years of Eli, the yoke of the Philistines, which apparently had been shaken off in his manhood, began once again to press heavily upon the neck of Israel. But Israel was still strong enough to make valiant resistance, provoked apparently by the Philistines invading the land, as we find that they had **pitched,** *i. e.* encamped, **in Aphek.** As Aphek means *a fortress*, many places bear the name ; but the position of the Philistine camp is fixed by its being near both to Eben-ezer and to Mizpah, and probably, therefore, it was the Aphek in Judah (Josh. xii. 18). Eben-ezer, *the stone of help*, had not as yet received this name (see ch. vii. 12) ; and apparently it was not a town, but a monument set up in an open plain fit for the purposes of war, and which up to this time had no specific appellation.

Ver. 2.—**In the field** means "in the open country." By a gradual change of language it now signifies cultivated ground, and even an enclosure, whereas in the A. V. it retains its old meaning of unenclosed and uncultivated land (see 2 Kings iv. 39).

Ver. 3.—**When the people were come into the camp.** Before the battle Israel had entrenched itself, so that upon its defeat it had a place capable of defence into which to retire. We find also that their communications were open, so that they could send to Shiloh. The army is called *the people* because battles were not fought in those days by men specially trained, but by all the inhabitants of the country of the proper age. The question, **Wherefore hath Jehovah smitten us ?** expresses surprise. The elders had evidently expected victory, and therefore the domination of the Philistines could not have been so complete as it certainly was in the days of Samson. There must have been an intermediate period of successful warfare during which Eli had been their leader. **Let us fetch the ark of the covenant of Jehovah.** This, the remedy suggested by the elders, was to employ their God as a talisman or charm. The ark was the symbol of Jehovah's presence among them, and of their being his especial people, and by exposing it to danger they supposed that they would compel their God to interfere in their behalf. They would have done right in appealing to their covenant relation to Jehovah ; and had they repented of the sins which had grown up among them, fostered by the evil example of Eli's sons, he would have shown them mercy. But for God to have given Israel the victory because of the presence of his ark in their camp would have been to overthrow all moral government, and would have insured their spiritual ruin as inevitably as would the granting to any order of men now the power of working miracles or of infallibly declaring the truth.

Ver. 4.—**Which dwelleth between the cherubims.** Literally, "which sitteth, *i.e.* is enthroned, upon the cherubim." The idea is not that of Jehovah's habitation, but of his seat in state as Israel's King. In bringing the ark they brought to the camp the throne of Jehovah, as their theocratic Ruler ; but **the two sons of Eli, Hophni and Phinehas, were there with the ark,** representing the immorality of the nation, whose very priests were abandoned men. We are not to suppose that there was any fault in the manner of bringing, because it is said **that the people sent that they might bring the ark** from Shiloh. Levites may have carried it, and priests with the Urim and Thummim have had the charge of every detail. But there was the ill-omened conjuncture of personal immorality with superstitious reverence for mere material symbols, and thereby the presence of the ark only insured, in the moral government of God, Israel's defeat.

Ver. 6.—But they, sure of its talismanic influence, shout for joy as they see its approach, and the Philistines ask the meaning of the **great shout in the camp of the Hebrews.** This name is constantly given to the Israelites by those not belonging to them, and probably has a certain amount of animosity in it, as showing that they were foreigners ; literally, *passers over*, people who in the person of Abraham had come from the other side of the Euphrates, and having began as feeble immigrants, had ended in obtaining possession of the land, and ousting the rightful inhabitants.

Ver. 8.—**These mighty Gods.** In Hebrew *Elohim*, though plural, is used of the one true God, but in this sense has always the verb or adjective belonging to it in the singular. In ver. 7 the Philistines conform to this rule, and say, **Elohim is come** ; but here the verb, pronoun, and adjective are all plural, *i. e.* they speak as heathen, to whom polytheism was natural (comp. 1 Kings xii. 28). **With all the plagues.** Rather, "with every plague," *i. e.* with every kind of plague. **In the wilderness.** God did not really smite the Egyptians in the wilderness. The plagues, including the destruction of Pharaoh and his host in the Red Sea, had all happened before the Israelites had entered it. But probably the Philistines confused together the plagues of Egypt and the miracles in the wilderness, and even the conquest of Canaan, in one grand but vague whole, and so were ready to give way to despair, as they called to mind the traditions they had heard of these mighty interpositions of God for his people.

Ver. 9.—**Be strong.** But, as is often the case, despair served only to nerve them to bitter determination. The greatness of the danger—for as heathen the Philistines fully believed that the ark would act as a charm—and the fearful alternative of being **servants**, *i. e.* slaves to those who not so very long ago had been slaves to them, made them resolve to do their very utmost. The result was a complete victory.

Ver. 10.—**Israel fled every man into**— better *to*—**his tent.** Their camp stood them this time in no stead. It was stormed by the Philistines, and the whole army fled in confusion. In those days the Israelites dwelt in tents, and to flee "every man to his tent" means that they fled away in every direction, each to his own home. It is in this indiscriminate flight that an army suffers most. As long as men keep together the loss is comparatively slight. But now, thus utterly broken, **there fell of Israel thirty thousand footmen**—a terrible slaughter. They are called footmen because the Israelites had neither cavalry nor chariots.

Ver. 11.—Moreover, **the ark of God was taken, and the two sons of Eli, Hophni and Phinehas, were slain**, according to the prediction of the man of God. Probably the last resistance was made round the ark, and the sons of Eli at least died "as men" (ch. ii. 33).

THE OVERTHROW OF ELI'S HOUSE (vers. 12—22). Ver. 12.—**There ran a man of Benjamin.** The whole story is told with so much vividness, and is so full of exact particulars, that it must have come from an eye-witness, probably from Samuel himself. According to Jewish tradition, this Benjamite

was no other than Saul, but the chronology is at variance with this supposition. The importance in old time, when even roads did not exist, of men capable of running long distances to carry news in war is evident, and many instances are recorded showing the high appreciation in which their services were held. Thus the running of the Cushite and of Ahimaaz forms an interesting episode in the pathetic history of Absalom's death (2 Sam. xviii. 19—31). So Herodotus mentions that Pheidippides, when sent to urge the people of Sparta to come to the help of the Athenians against the Persians, arrived there on the second day after his departure from Athens (Herod., vi. 105, 106). Shiloh, apparently, was but a comparatively short distance from Eben-ezer, as the runner arrived there on the evening of the very day on which the battle was fought. The rent clothes and the earth upon the head were the usual signs in token that some great calamity had taken place (2 Sam. i. 2).

Ver. 13.—**Upon a seat** — literally, "the throne "—**by the wayside**, whither his official chair had been removed to some spot near the gate of the city (see ver. 18), and probably commanding a view of the pathway by which a messenger would arrive. There probably for hours he had sat, anxiously awaiting tidings of the ark, which, we may feel sure, he had very unwillingly allowed to be carried away into the camp. **When the man came into the city.** Literally the words are, " And the man came to tell it in the city, and all the city cried out." We are not to suppose with some that Eli, being old and now blind, let the messenger slip by unobserved. A man of his high rank would not be alone, and the mention of his throne suggests that he was seated there in somewhat of official dignity. And so, as the runner drew near, with the symbols of disaster upon his person, the priests and Levites in attendance upon Eli would begin the cry of sorrow, and soon it would spread throughout all Shiloh.

Ver. 14.—**And when Eli heard the noise of the crying**, he asked the meaning of **this tumult.** The word signifies any confused noise, as the splashing of rain (1 Kings xviii. 41), but especially the din made by a multitude of people (Job xxxix. 7). It exactly expresses here the Babel of voices, all asking news at once, which at the coming of the messenger surged around the high priest's throne. He demands the reason, and the uproar is quelled, while "the man hasted, and came and told Eli." Not **came in,** for Eli was without on the wayside, but simply *came to Eli,* being summoned thither by one of the Levites in attendance. Eli, as the chief ruler, was, of course, the person whom he sought, and immediately that he knew where he was, he hasted to him.

Ver. 15.—**Eli was ninety and eight years old.** Until the invention by the Arabs of the present system of numerals, all ancient nations had a most cumbrous system of expressing numbers. The Hebrew method was to attach a value to each of the letters of the alphabet, and then add them together, and thus the eighth and nineteenth letters would between them make up ninety-eight. Such a system led to constant mistakes in copying, and thus the numerals in the earlier parts of the Old Testament are beset with uncertainty. Here the Septuagint has *ninety*, and the Syriac *seventy-eight*. But as Eli was described already as "very old" in ch. ii. 22, the Hebrew text is the most probable. Instead of **dim** the Hebrew has *set*, i. e. Eli was now absolutely blind, as the word expresses the motionless state of the eye when obscured by cataract. In ch. iii. 2 a different word is used, rightly there translated "dim," as the disease is one which comes on gradually. In 1 Kings xiv. 4 we read that Ahijah was blind from the same cause, and the word is there correctly rendered "set."

Vers. 16, 17.—**What is there done, my son?** Literally, What is the thing? Or, as the phrase is translated in 2 Sam. i. 4, "How went the matter?" Eli must have gathered from the words of the messenger that Israel had been defeated; for he expressly says, **I fled,** and his haste, as testified by the added words to day, showed that the defeat was a severe one. Eli, therefore, anxiously asks what has happened, and the answer piles misery upon misery, rapidly heaping together four crushing catastrophes. For **Israel** had **fled before the Philistines; there** had **been a great slaughter;** among the slain were Eli's two sons; and, worst of all, **the ark of God** was **taken.**

Ver. 18.—At this last sad news the old man's spirit failed; and though it was his own want of a firm sense of duty that had prepared the way for this sad ruin of his country, yet we cannot but respect his deep attachment and reverent love for the symbol of his faith. The rest he could have borne; but that the ark of God, especially intrusted to his care, was now captive in heathen hands was a calamity that broke his heart.

He had judged Israel forty years. The Septuagint reads *twenty*, but these differences in numbers occur constantly. In either case he would have been well advanced in years before he reached the judgeship, and probably he attained to it slowly; not by one great act, but by the qualities of a statesman, by which he lightened the yoke of the Philistines, and rendered the people for a long time a match for them in war. His character is not that of a hero, but of a wise, patient, and prudent ruler, but one whose good qualities were spoiled at last by his weak partiality for his unworthy sons.

Vers. 19—21.—**His daughter-in-law.** The death of Eli's daughter-in-law is equally tragic with his own. The news of the terrible calamity that had befallen the ark of God brought on a premature delivery; but when she had given birth to a son, the attendant women naturally hoped that the good tidings would cheer the mother's heart. They haste, therefore, to tell her; **but she answered not, neither did she regard it.** This does not mean that she was already dead; if so, the women would not have told her. It means that no private joy could compensate her for the loss of the outward sign and proof that the covenant of Jehovah was with her and her people. The loss of the ark seemed to her to signify the overthrow of her national religion. But she heard, for immediately **she named the child I-chabod.** There is some doubt as to the exact meaning of the word. It may mean *Alas! the glory;* but more probably it signifies *No-glory* — the glory of Israel is no more. In the reason given by the narrator for her sorrow, as summed up in the name given to her child, the deaths of Eli and of Phinehas are included, but her own words refer only to the ark. Literally they are, "The glory is gone into captivity from Israel." There is possibly a reference to this in Ps. lxxviii. 64, where, speaking of the fall of Shiloh, the Psalmist says, "Their priests fell by the sword, and their widows made no lamentation." Others, it may be, like the wife of Phinehas, felt that there was no room for private grief at a time of so great national distress and humiliation.

HOMILETICS.

Vers. 1—11.—*Moral causes of disaster.* Assuming that the first sentence properly belongs to the third chapter, and refers generally to the acceptance of Samuel as prophet by the whole nation, the section (vers. 1—11) sets forth the following facts:—1. Israel, suffering from subjection to the Philistines, enters on war for the recovery of freedom and suffers defeat. 2. Ordinary means failing, recourse is had to the ark of God in order to insure success. 3. The visible presence of the ark at once raises the courage and hope of Israel and fills the Philistines with fear. 4. As a counter-stimulus to conflict, the Philistines stir up their own love of freedom. 5. The battle issues in the heavy defeat of Israel, the death of

Eli's sons, and the capture by the Philistines of the ark of God. There can be no doubt but that the will of God is being wrought out in the triumphs and disasters of national life through all time. The laws by which men are governed are uniform. They are often slow and subtle in operation, and it requires that the whole life of a people be known before we can see the sure working out of the laws that determine success or ruin. It is an advantage to the world that in sacred history we have revealed to us, in concrete form, the principles on which God rules men. The disasters that fell upon Israel in the early years of Samuel's life furnish us with much instruction. We learn that—

I. There is for a PEOPLE A STATE OF PROSPERITY FOR WHICH THEY ARE ORIGINALLY DESIGNED, AND AFTER WHICH IT IS NATURAL FOR THEM TO ASPIRE. Israel, as a people, was constitutionally fitted to enjoy a high degree of national well-being. There are material blessings proper to all nationalities, and especially were these included in the lot promised to Israel through Moses (Deut. xxviii. 1—13). It was quite natural, therefore, for the people in Samuel's time to seek freedom from a foreign yoke, and to strive to regain political influence and internal prosperity. There stands, more or less clear, before the mind of nations and individuals, an ideal of what they ought to attain to. The vision of good, though remote, is a powerful influence in life. Before every State, Church, and home there lies a condition of freedom, peace, and influence for which it is designed by Providence, and which should ever be the goal of effort.

II. The DIVINE FAVOUR IS REQUISITE FOR TRUE SUCCESS IN THE EFFORT TO ATTAIN TO THE GOAL. Israel could not obtain the national blessings so eagerly sought unless the favour of God be secured. This is the record of their entire history. It is the "blessing of the Lord that maketh rich." The life of a nation extends possibly over centuries ; and as during the few years of a man's life he may be allowed to strive on without God to the end before disaster is apparent, so the course of centuries alone may reveal whether it is possible for *true*, enduring success to be realised apart from the favour of God. The favour of God means a co-working of the Divine energy with his creatures, so as to secure a convergence of all physical, mental, and social forces towards their welfare. That he should do this without dislocations of nature is as reasonable as that our spirit should, in its measure and mode, strike in on the external forces of matter, and, without violating their laws, cause them to subserve its purposes.

III. The REVEALED CONDITION OF INSURING GOD'S FAVOUR IS CONFORMITY TO HIS WILL. Israel could not expect that God would, as a matter of course, prosper their endeavours after the goal of life. The evils from which the nation suffered were the result of *non*-conformity to the will of God. It is clear that God discriminates between men, and although it may be that God's energy works along lines fixed and uniform, yet, inasmuch as all the lines are his creation, and are coincident with his great law of blessing the good and chastising the bad, it turns out, in every case, that his favour, in specific acts and issues, goes with conformity to his will. Moreover, is there not a very true sense in which it may be said that the whole being of God is in immediate and constant contact with every subtle element in existence ? They are all ministers that do his pleasure. God has not banished himself from all spheres of action, so as to be the only powerless Power in the universe.

IV. CONFORMITY TO THE WILL OF GOD LIES IN TWO THINGS:—1. EXERTION. 2. MORAL CHARACTER. The natural craving of Israel for national prosperity could only be satisfied by making strenuous efforts to shake off the Philistines' yoke and develop all the resources of the land, and, further, by the possession of a moral character such as God delights in. It is the will of God that if men will enjoy whatever enters into the conception of a well-developed, prosperous life, they must work for it. But that is only *one side of duty*. We are not only bound to *act*, to *work*, but are bound to BE ; and it depends on the kind of persons we are as to the direction and force of our acts. Israel in Samuel's time had a moral character, but not according to the will of God. Every nation and every individual bears a moral character before the eye of God. It is only when our moral condition is a reflex of the righteousness of God that we can be said to have the conformity to his will which is essential to the favour that insures real success to life's effort.

V. Reliance solely on physical and mental exertion for the attainment of a desired good is sure to end in final disaster. Israel put forth physical and mental effort to attain to freedom and former prosperity. In this respect there was conformity to the will of God, and an observance, therefore, of the laws of success. But the radical defect in the case was that of an utter carelessness concerning the possession of the character which alone can be acceptable with God. The people lacked all the force which lies in being right with God. Those who strive for the masteries must, we are told (2 Tim. ii. 5), "strive lawfully"—in harmony with all the moral as well as physical laws which govern the enterprise, whatever it be, public or private, relating to commerce, education, or religion. The great practical truth here exhibited is *that it is possible for a people to set heart on the achievement of a purpose* good in itself, to devise means, combine forces, and arouse enthusiasm likely to issue in the desired result; but yet there may be in the *daily life some irreligious, unholy spirit*, which, being known to God, has the effect of causing the *hidden wheels of Providence* so to move as to *render useless efforts otherwise sufficient. Righteousness is the most important factor in life.* Unrighteousness will in the end neutralise all exertion. The seeming prosperity of the wicked is short, and "shall destroy them." Sin saps the foundations of public and private good. True godliness alone makes the most of men.

VI. Distinguished goodness of individuals and regard for religious symbols are no substitutes for righteousness of life. Samuel had become known in Israel. The long lost "open vision" was restored. The people knew that he was a prophet. There was, therefore, so the people reasoned, an evident sign that the favour of God was returning. Their own character was bad enough; but had they not a holy man of God, a superior character, in the sanctuary at Shiloh? Encouraged by this trust and heedless of repentance and reformation, they sought freedom and prosperity by the exertion of their own physical powers. The moral element of conformity to the will of God was despised. Disaster came. In like manner it is in vain for a nation to leave goodness to officials in the Church, and for men of business to leave goodness to their wives and children. God will take no substitute for personal holiness. Not even is the perfect righteousness of the Redeemer of any avail to the man who *will* live in unrighteousness. He is "our righteousness" when our faith in him brings forth the fruits of the Spirit. But the ingenuity of the heart in evil is marvellous. Israel, finding that vicarious goodness is of no avail, has *recourse to a new expedient—outward regard for the symbols of religion.* Men remember historical facts, though they may have lost a perception of their spiritual significance. Had not the waters of Jordan and the walls of Jericho recognised the presence of the "ark of God"? Did it not go before the people to "search out a resting-place" for them? If the presence of a Samuel in the land was not a guarantee of victory, surely all power must submit to this ancient and renowned worker of wonders? And thus the unholy heart imagines that an outward exhibition of the sacred things pertaining to Divine worship will be a practical substitute for the character not possessed. "History repeats itself." Yes; men still trust in the symbols of the Church—creeds more or less orthodox, outward forms of worship, and much else—in vain hope that these will prove a charm by which the crushing power of sin will be avoided and life end prosperously. The most sacred of forms and symbols are a poor refuge for a soul that loves unrighteousness (Ps. xxiv. 3—5).

Practical lessons:—1. Study well *all* the laws of permanent success in secular government, religious organisations, commercial transactions, domestic life, and spiritual culture. 2. Let personal conduct be influenced by the fact that even the salvation of the soul is according to *law* (cf. Matt. xi. 28, 29; Acts iv. 12; x. 43; 1 Cor. ix. 25; 2 Tim. ii. 5). 3. The comparative failure of religious efforts outwardly suitable may be remedied by a revival of the spiritual power. 4. In times of depression and religious weakness in the Church, look not so much to the adoption of new expedients for subduing the world to Christ, as to the spiritual condition of his professed servants.

Unexpected coincidences. It was declared to Eli that a sign of coming judgment on him and his house should be found in the death of his two sons in one day (ch.

ii. 34), and also that an event should occur at which "both the ears of every one that heareth it shall tingle" (ch. iii. 11). The fulfilment of this prediction was, to the mind of Eli, certain, but the means and occasion were uncertain. It was difficult for the old man to conjecture how God would keep his word. The narrative reveals the unlooked-for coincidences which established the veracity of God.

I. MEN ARE INDUCED TO ADOPT A COURSE OF CONDUCT AT VARIANCE WITH THEIR USUAL PRACTICE. The recent history of Israel proved them to be utterly indifferent to religion. The vile conduct of the priests caused them to abhor the sacrifices of the Lord. In their conflicts with foes they had gone forth at first without the presence of symbols of religion; but now these same people, being *left judicially to the blind guidance* of their corrupt hearts, lead forth to war the "ark of God," and the priests in charge of it. In like manner the ordinary course of the Philistines would be to yield to the force of their knowledge of what wonders had been achieved by the "ark of God" (vers. 6—8), and either refrain from fighting or flee at the first onset. But instead of that, by, doubtless, the subtle, secret action of God on their spirits, the ordinary course was deviated from, and the strongest sentiments of religious superstition were overborne by an urgent appeal to weaker sentiments. The last thing men do is to go in face of religious fears and historic facts. History furnishes parallel instances. The Jews, in their desire to get rid of Christ, although disgusted with Roman supremacy, took the strange course of pleading their loyalty as against his treason. In ordinary affairs, also, men are often found acting on new lines which perplex their opponents.

II. GOD SOMETIMES DOES THINGS THAT ARE NOT ANTICIPATED. The Israelites little thought that God, whose symbols they paraded, would so act on the spirits of their foes as to counteract the natural effect of their own expedient. Man is a very imperfect judge of the ways of God. There are no doubt immutable laws of righteousness on which all his actions are based, and in many spheres we are enabled by a careful study of things to say what is sure to happen. But we see only "parts of his ways." His "thoughts are not as our thoughts." He sometimes does "a new thing." Precedents are being created. An ordinary observer would not have thought that the eternal God would suffer his covenant people to endure serfdom. It was foolishness to the Greeks that a crucified One should be the Divinely-appointed Saviour of the world.

III. BY THE COINCIDENCE OF UNEXPECTED HUMAN AND DIVINE ACTIONS THE PURPOSES OF GOD ARE SOMETIMES ACCOMPLISHED. Had not Israel deviated from their usual course in demanding the ark, the sons of Eli would have remained in Shiloh. Had not the Philistines striven hard to overcome religious fears, no defeat would have fallen on Israel. Had God exercised his power as in former times, the ark would not have been captured. But the reverse of these events occurred, and therefore, in accordance with prediction, Eli's sons were on the battle-field, and perished in one day, and "both the ears" of all the people were made "to tingle" with the awful tidings that the "ark of God" was taken. So is it true in other instances that, by the concurrence of events not anticipated, and by the secret action of God along with the human events, his purposes are realised in judgment or in mercy.

General lessons:—1. God holds a complete mastery over the spirits of men, and can, when it pleases him, so act on them as to secure the realisation of his designs without destroying their freedom. 2. The Church may look on with confidence to the fulfilment of all that is said of Christ's kingdom, since God can bring about the desired conjunction of events. 3. Wicked men, emboldened by deferred judgments, may well tremble at the thought that the "day of the Lord" may come as a "thief in the night."

Vers. 12—18.— *Victory in defeat.* The facts given are—1. Eli, aware of the absence of the ark on the battle-field, awaits with anxiety the earliest tidings of the issue of the conflict. 2. A fugitive relates to him and to the people of Shiloh the nature of the disaster that had befallen Israel. 3. The effect of the news on the city is a wailing cry of despair, and on Eli sudden death. By record and tradition the people were familiar with the disasters and sufferings occasionally experienced by ancestors. Influenced by the prediction of the "man of God" (ch. ii. 27), Eli, while sitting by the wayside, feared the worst. But even he was not prepared for such a climax of calamity. Defeat would bring sorrow, not surprise ; for were not the people godless ? Slaughter would be regarded with pain as retribution for national sins. Was it not his own fault that his sons had not suffered capital punishment long ago? All that was most sacred and revered in the history of the chosen race, the very glory of God—this to be wrested from the hands of Israel and borne off in triumph by the heathen, who can hear it and live ! There is nothing now to live for.

I. To THE EYE OF MAN GOD SUFFERS DEFEAT. The men of Shiloh may be taken as a type of the worldly, unspiritual mind. They had been instructed to believe that Jehovah was engaged on their side in conflict with the wicked idolatrous nations. The ark had become with them almost synonymous with the Almighty himself. Hence the sudden wail of the city when they, hearing the sad tidings, leapt to the sudden conclusion that now at least the Vanquisher was vanquished. The disaster was a check to his purposes proceeding from his declared enemies. There are *occasions when the surface of events suggests such a thought.* The introduction of sin into the world by an evil power appeared to mar the work of God and defeat his purpose in creating a pure and beautiful world. In the days of Noah the power of evil seemed to triumph, inasmuch as the earth became utterly corrupt. The destruction of the holy hill of Zion, and desecration of the courts of the Lord by the declared enemies of Israel's God, was regarded by the heathen as a proof of his inability to guard his own. To the terror-stricken disciples of Christ it seemed for a while that the "gates of hell" were prevailing against him, and that the kingdom of which prophets wrote and poets sang was prematurely annihilated.

II. The APPEARANCE OF DEFEAT IS OWING TO THE CONDITIONS UNDER WHICH GOD IS PLEASED TO CARRY OUT HIS DESIGNS. God does not govern in the moral world by hard mechanical laws, but realises his purposes under the conditions involved in the existence of creatures endowed with freedom and accountability. He adapted his exercise of power to the spiritual condition of Israel. Hence, what is defeat to the human eye may really be fore ordained and reasonable restraint. Symbol and chastisement were suited to the imperfect state of the religious thought and feeling. If the surrender of the symbol shall issue in better results than its retention, then what seems defeat arises out of the peculiar conditions under which God works his will. The *principle has wide application.* It is a condition of the possible existence of free moral creatures that their life may or may not be marred by sin. If, then, sin mars the world, God's purpose is not really defeated. The forces of evil in the antediluvian age might have been crushed out by the Spirit had God reversed the conditions under which he governed men, and *forced* them to be holy. The visible, transitory life of Christ and his liability to death were, from "the foundation of the world," Divinely-recognised conditions of accomplishing human redemption. The occasional obliteration of religious ordinances and of personal piety often results from the fact that the Church is amenable to the law, " From him that hath not shall be taken away even that which he hath." Finally, so far as we can see, the happiness of a world is reasonably made conditional on the free, responsible action of the world as an interrelated community, in which the good or evil of one is wisely made to affect all the rest.

III. WHAT SEEMS DEFEAT TURNS OUT TO BE A STEP TO FINAL VICTORY. It is the perfection of wisdom to snatch victory from defeat. This is seen in the first effect of the capture of the ark. The dormant conscience of the people was aroused. Righteousness, not charms and ceremonials, must be the antecedent of victory. It will be found that all other apparent defeats of God's designs prove to be *stages toward a higher good.* The curse of sin was the occasion of the "seed of the woman" being promised to "*bruise* the serpent's *head.*" The men of Noah's time procured a sweeter earth and a most weighty warning and encouragement for the use of all future generations. The sighs and tears of desponding disciples yielded to the exultant joy and abounding hope of the kingdom won with his blood who now liveth evermore. And however much sin may now mar the life of the world, there is reason to believe that, under the control of him who is " able to subdue all things to himself," the issue of all will be the vindication of right and the more glorious assertion of God's majesty.

*General lessons:—*1. It is proper to avoid haste in expressing unfavourable judgment on events that seem adverse to the final success of Christianity.   2. When great calamities come on the Church, the first effect should be great searching of heart. 3. There is every encouragement, from the history of the past, for strongest confidence in the final triumph of Christ over every foe.   *Rejoice not against me, O mine enemy* (Micah vii. 8).   *Cast down, but not destroyed* (2 Cor. iv. 9).   *Surely the wrath of man shall praise thee* (Ps. lxxvi. 10).   *He must reign till he hath put all enemies under his feet* (1 Cor. xv. 25).

Neutralised usefulness.   There is deep pathos and much instruction in the words of the sacred historian as he closes the references to Eli: "And he had judged Israel forty years."   A man eligible for so honourable a position, having rendered varied service to his people, dies in a state of blended consternation, grief, shame, and remorse.   Not the calm, joyous end of the righteous ; not the end cheered by views from Pisgah's peak of a glorious inheritance ; but an end amidst a horror of great darkness.   "*And he had judged Israel forty years!*"   Oh, the exquisite pathos of the Bible !

I. The POSITIVE GOOD OF A MAN'S LIFE MAY BE LARGELY NEUTRALISED BY HIS WEAK-NESSES.   The tenor of the narrative suggests that as a whole Eli's life was good. Forty years' discharge of important functions indicates a long series of holy desires and beneficent acts.   The natural effect of this would be only for the formation of a sound national character.   For in those times, as seen in the instance of Moses and Joshua and others, the moral and material welfare of a people was more entirely dependent ou force of individual character in the leader and ruler than on the mani-fold influences which prevail in modern times.   But negative qualities hindered the effect of the good.   Thus it is *not enough* for a man—ruler, pastor, or parent—to be *religious at heart,* attentive to routine duties, and "harmless" in conduct.   These may fail in their desired issue unless accompanied with the energy and resoluteness of a will that rests only in seeing right done, God feared, and life made holy.   The good that some men do with one hand they undo with another.   A little sin destroys much good.

II. It MAY BE A LONG TIME BEFORE THIS NEUTRALISATION OF POSITIVE GOOD IS FULLY DISCOVERED.   Eli was not blind to the fact that for years past the condition of the people and priests had degenerated ; but some men are slow in detecting their own part in a given result.   As he gave more heed to causes outside his own conduct and bearing, so do men still overlook their own contributions of a negative character to the formation of opinion and habit in their too exclusive thought of what proceeds from others.   A weak ruler wonders how it is the people are dissatisfied, and perhaps rebellious.   A weak parent deplores that his words and deeds are so little heeded at home.   Each of these is conscious of sincere motive, upright purpose, and actual toil ; but it is only by slow degrees that he comes to see the neutralising process.

III. The ISSUE THAT REVEALS THE NEUTRALISATION MAY BE OF THE NATURE OF A JUDGMENT.   In Eli's case the catastrophe which fell upon the nation and himself was the means of revealing to him, in unmistakable terms, the truth that the element of indecision and moral cowardice in his character had rendered comparatively useless his "forty years" of office.   The death of sons and desolation of the Church of God tell of years of honourable care and toil spoiled by irresolution to visit the guilty with punishment and purge the sanctuary of the vile.   There are *crises* in the *lives of communities and individuals.*   The effect of these is to bring into clearer light the causes of failure.   "The day shall declare" "every man's work," "because it shall be revealed by fire."   The ruin which comes to a business, a Church organisation, a home, or a reputation, exposes the weak parts of an elaborate superstructure. Although the catastrophe may come about in a natural way, it nevertheless is under Divinely-ordained law, and therefore is the judgment of God.

IV. The POSITIVE GOOD IN PERSONAL CHARACTER MAY SURVIVE DISASTER TO LIFE'S WORK.   The last act of Eli's life was one of homage to religion.   The better side of his character asserted itself in his dying moments.   His horror and shame and grief on the mention of the capture of the ark of God revealed his loyalty of heart to spiritual religion.   The poor old man reaped in pain and death the reward of his sinful weakness; but while gathering the bitter fruit, he showed his profound interest in the honour and glory of Jehovah by being so sensitive to the reproach brought on the sacred name. We must distinguish between the *ruin of a man's work* and the *ruin of his soul*. In the former there is a grievous chastisement for carelessness and avoidable ignorance; in the latter there is an abandonment to the essential and preferred wickedness of the heart. Eli's heart was right with God, but his will was weak to work as he ought. Those who by faith are on the one Foundation are safe. They may build up a superstructure in personal qualities and in deeds for others, much of which may perish in the fire which tries every man's work, while they may be "saved yet so as by fire" (1 Cor. iii. 11—15).

Practical lessons:—1. We should seek self-knowledge if we would avoid errors in conduct and make the best use of a Christian life. 2. When the results of effort are not satisfactory, strict attention should be given to causes within self. 3. When constitutional or acquired weakness is discovered, it may be counteracted by a care to exercise as much as possible the opposite positive virtue.

Vers. 19—22.—*Ichabod.* The facts given are—1. The wife of Phinehas, hearing the sad tidings of Israel's disaster and of the death of her husband and of Eli, suffers premature labour. 2. The loss of the ark of God contributes more to her anguish of spirit than does the sudden death of her nearest relatives. 3. She deliberately refuses the most natural of all consolations. 4. When dying she gives a name to her child that shall express her sense of the calamity fallen on Israel. The record furnishes us with three typical references to persons greatly affected by the tidings brought from the field of battle. 1. The superstitious populace of the city, who utter a cry of consternation and despair. 2. The public functionary, good but blameworthy, who sees in the event a just judgment, and, being sensible of his personal offence, pays dying homage to the sacred cause with which his life had been identified. 3. A very spiritually-minded individual in private life, whose dying words manifest her extraordinary piety. In the brief reference to the wife of Phinehas we see—

I. The NATURE OF SUPREME CALAMITY. Opinions of men differ with respect to what it is that constitutes the greatest calamity that can fall to the lot of nations, Churches, and individuals. The dying experience of the pious Hebrew mother throws useful light on this question. The ark of God was gone; and also, as its moral cause, the righteousness of the people. Hence, as a people's "glory" lies in the enjoyment of the highest distinction God confers, and the happiness resulting therefrom, it follows that the greatest calamity falls on a people when that distinction and consequent happiness are taken away. The *nature of the supreme distinction enjoyed* depends on the *capacities and vocations* of those concerned. 1. *Israel.* The supreme distinction of Israel was the enjoyment of all that was suggested by the presence of the ark of God. By virtue of its structure, its contents, and uses, the ark was the outward sign of an inestimable good. It meant that Israel was chosen above all people for a holy and far-reaching purpose, in which all nations should be blessed, and that great covenanted blessings were theirs. To them the ark was favour, noble destiny, protection and enrichment, knowledge, holy influence, fellowship with the Eternal. And, in so far as its continued presence was connected with their possession of a character conformable in some degree to its purpose and their own destiny, its abode among them would suggest that they had not become utterly corrupt and unfit for the end for which they were chosen. When, then, the ark of God was allowed to be taken away, there happened, so far as the outward sign was still a correct index to its original and ordinary intent, the direst calamity conceivable. The evidence of being the people of Jehovah was gone! The tables of covenant were lost! The mercy-seat was inaccessible by the appointed means! And, also, the righteousness of life appropriate to the continuance of such blessings and honours was lacking! Marvel not that a wail of woe arose from at least one true heart—"Ichabod!" Loss of men, of commerce, of political influence, of home, of health, of all, was not to be compared with this. For what is *Israel* worth, what *Israel's* function in the world, without Divine favour and blessing? 2. *Nations.* Taking nations generally in their relation to God and one another, their crowning distinction lies in *righteousness of spirit and conduct*. Population, trade, armies, fleets, science, art, have no permanence, no real value, apart from a healthy national conscience and right doing. If by any means this righteousness disappears, then the greatest calamity has come ; and it is only a question of time with respect to the passing away of greatness. God never allows an unrighteous people to attain to the best a nation is capable of. 3. *Churches*. The Christian Church is the body of Christ. It exists as a body to exhibit the spirit and do the work of Christ, the Head. Its highest honour is in doing what Christ would have done in the world. But if a Church, professing to be part of the One Body, so far loses love for Christ and true holiness of life as to fail to answer the practical ends for which it exists, then it suffers a calamity far more serious than depletion of numbers, loss of social status, the pains of poverty, and the fiercest persecution. " Ichabod " was once appropriate to Laodicea (Rev. iii. 15—18). 4. *Individuals*. The highest distinction and bliss of a human being is to be conformed in nature to the holy nature of Christ. This is the permanent crown of life. It could be shown that a soul so blessed will find the most perfect development. This is that for which Christ came, lived, died, and rose again. And it is obvious that *not thus to be saved* is to suffer the greatest loss ever possible to a human being. " What shall it profit a man if he gain the whole world and lose his own soul ? " Then, indeed, " Ichabod " is fearfully true. 5. *The ministry of the gospel*. A true ministry must embrace all the teaching requisite for the " perfecting of the saints." A full and perfect gospel means *all* that Christ and his apostles have left us. An examination of the apostolic ministry will show that the great theme on which the inspired preachers chiefly dwelt was the *cross of Christ*. This is the peculiar distinction of the New Testament teaching, and it is a truth which enters directly or indirectly into everything pertaining to Christian life. A ministry is good in proportion as it gives due place to this dominating truth. An aversion to the cross as the apostles preached it is an unhappy sign, as, also, is a mere parade of the term or the symbol. History proves that a Christless ministry is always a failure. " Ichabod " may be affirmed of it. Generally, then, " Ichabod " is true whenever the crowning characteristic has departed ; in that lies a supreme calamity.

II. HOW A JUST APPRECIATION OF A SUPREME CALAMITY REVEALS ITSELF. The wife of Phinehas was a study to her attendants. They, in common with the mass of Israel, felt that a sad disaster had befallen them, but *her* extreme anguish and singular conduct were perplexing. The fact was, she formed a just appreciation of what had occurred, and her feelings, words, and conduct were the natural expression of it. The appreciation appears in—1. *All-absorbing concern*. A more striking instance of this is perhaps not to be found in the entire range of sacred history. This unnamed person was passing through the most momentous personal crisis possible to woman ; the anguish of nature was enough to absorb every thought and power. Birth of a son was a new demand on attention and care, and the death of a husband was, at such a season, a special occasion of sorrow. Yet all these most important and pressing matters were entirely lost sight of in her soul's utter absorption in the interests of that Divine kingdom which lay so near to her heart. We have read of widows dying under the shock caused by a husband's death, and with his name on the tongue as the last sign of affection and interest ; but here the one word is " *Ichabod*." The cause of God was the *one thought*. In like manner will a just appreciation of calamity show itself when *nations have lost the righteousness which exalts*, when Churches have failed in their holy design and have become a reproach, when souls cared and watched for are lost, when a ministry professedly of the gospel leaves out the cross. The whole soul will be filled with anguish and care. 2. *Refusal to accept any substitute*. The highest and most welcome comfort nature can afford to a sorrowing widowed mother is to give her a son. In the love of offspring the heart finds some healing and solace. But, marvel of devotion to the Spiritual and Eternal, this mother refuses to derive compensation from the new-born child ! " She answered not, neither did she regard it." The mother's conduct was right and natural ; for the cause of God is first and highest. Nature sanctified will not accept a lower transitory good in the place of the higher eternal good. Jerusalem is to be preferred above our " chief joy." No wealth and fame will comfort the statesman who mourns the departure of national righteousness. Eloquence, logic, and elevation of taste are as nothing to one who glories in preaching Christ crucified, if *he* be not preached. 3. *Tremendous effort to awaken regard for the spiritual.* The dying woman made a great effort to think and speak. She loved the dear child, but loved the holy kingdom more ; and therefore, to do the utmost in her power to arouse regard for what was too little regarded, she even imposed on her child a name associated with sorrow, shame, and trouble. Thus by this dying exertion did she (1) impress her attendants with her sense of what calamity is, and what should be sought first and chief ; (2) direct her countrymen, through her son, to the great need of a radical reformation ; and (3) leave him a reminder of what was dearest to his mother's heart. Noble woman ! "She hath done what she could." Love of God stronger than love of husband, child, national fame, and even of personal comfort. In times of spiritual calamity the faithful, in proportion to faithfulness, put forth extraordinary efforts. Moses could wish himself blotted out of the book of God (Exod. xxxii. 32).

General lessons :—1. In darkest times God has in reserve a "holy remnant" (cf. 1 Kings xix. 10, 18 ; John x. 14). 2. The deepest piety may exist where least expected. The wife of the vilest of men (cf. Matt. viii. 10). 3. Adverse circumstances, when met with a determined spirit, may even conduce to exalted piety. The vile husband became the occasion of a more entire and constant trust in God (cf. Ps. ix. 9, 10 ; xxvii. 10). 4. How truly the requirements of Christ to love him and his cause above all finds response in the most devoted souls (cf. Matt. x. 37 ; Phil. iii. 8). 5. The piety must be very profound, and wide in its spiritual vision, that can bring all the claims of nature into subordination to the kingdom of God, and feel assured of the essentially rational character of the subordination. 6. The Saviour is a *unique* instance of absorption in the spiritual, and exertion to realise it ; and the experience of his people is a fellowship with his sufferings (cf. Matt. iv. 9 ; xvi. 21, 22 ; xx. 28 ; xxiii. 37 ; xxvi. 38, 39 ; Luke xxiv. 21—26 ; John iv. 32 ; vi. 15 ; x. 11 ; Phil. iii. 10). "The zeal of thine house hath eaten me up."

HOMILIES BY VARIOUS AUTHORS.

Vers. 1—11. (EBEN-EZER and APHEK.)—*Judgment inflicted on Israel.* "Israel was smitten, . . . and the ark of God was taken ; and the two sons of Eli, Hophni and Phinehas, were slain" (vers. 10, 11). The law of retribution which prevails in the world is, more especially in the outward life, often slow in its operation, inexplicable, and sometimes apparently partial and imperfect. But in many instances it is manifested in a sudden, clear, and most equitable manner. One of these instances is here described. Hophni and Phinehas were warned in vain, and pursued their evil way. The influence which they exerted on others was pernicious, and their sin was largely shared in by the people. At length the hour of judgment struck. "Israel went out against the Philistines to battle "—not, probably, according to the counsel of Samuel, but according to their own will, and to repel a fresh attack of their most powerful foes and oppressors (ver. 9). They were defeated with a loss of about 4000 men ; but instead of humbling themselves before God, the elders expressed their surprise and disappointment at the result. They were blinded by sin, and assumed (as others have often done) that because they were the acknowledged people of Jehovah they would necessarily receive his help according to his covenant, whether they fulfilled their part of the covenant and obeyed his commandments or not. To insure his help more effectually, they sent to Shiloh for "the ark of the covenant of the Lord of hosts, which dwelleth between (is enthroned upon) the cherubim." They looked for deliverance from the ark of the Lord rather than from the Lord of the ark. Hophni and Phinehas, its appointed guardians, readily consented to go with it, not knowing that they were going to their doom ; and the aged high priest was too weak to oppose the presumptuous enterprise. The exultation of Israel was speedily turned into humiliation, and the fear of their enemies into triumph ; and one of the greatest calamities Israel ever experienced occurred. These events suggest the following reflections :—

I. HOW OFTEN ARE THE UNGODLY EMPLOYED BY GOD FOR THE CHASTISEMENT OF HIS PEOPLE (vers. 1, 2). 1. When those who have been chosen to be separate from and superior to the ungodly have learnt their ways, it is *just* and appropriate that they should be given up to chastisement at their hands. 2. The chastisement which is thus inflicted upon them is the most *severe* they can experience. " Let us not fall into the hand of man " (2 Sam. xxiv. 14). " The tender mercies of the wicked are cruel " (Prov. xii. 10). 3. In fulfilling their own purposes the wicked are subject to the *control* of God ; they can go no further than he pleases, their designs are overruled for good, and when they have done their work they are broken and cast aside like useless saws and axes (Isa. xxvii. 7, 8 ; Acts v. 28). This is the case with Satan himself. " Satan is a very important element in the Divine economy. God needs him, and he therefore keeps him until he shall have no more use for him. Then will he be banished to his own place. The Scriptures call the wicked heathen tyrant Nebuchadnezzar a servant of God. They might give Satan the same name " (Hengstenberg).

II. HOW VAIN IS THE POSSESSION OF THE FORM OF RELIGION WITHOUT ITS SPIRIT (vers. 3, 4). Israel had a great though superstitious reverence for the ark, and expected that it would " save them out of the hand of their enemies." 1. Excessive devotion to the outward forms and ceremonies, and dependence upon them, is commonly associated with the absence of spiritual life (Matt. v. 20 ; 2 Tim. iii. 5). 2. Reliance upon such forms arises from the *delusion* that they insure the presence and working of God apart from the spirit in which they are employed. They are, however, neither the *necessary* nor the *exclusive* channels of Divine grace (John vi. 63), and no benefit *formerly* received through them (Num. x. 35) is to be expected, unless there be a right relation to him who has appointed them. 3. The vanity of it is clearly shown in the day of *trial*. " If progress to perfection is placed only in external observances, our religion, having no Divine life, will quickly perish, with the things on which it subsists ; but the axe must be laid at the root of the tree, that, being separated and freed from the restless desires of nature and self, we may possess our souls in the peace of God " (À Kempis).

III. HOW NEAR ARE THOSE WHO ARE ELATED IN FALSE CONFIDENCE TO THEIR SIGNAL DOWNFALL (ver. 5). There was a shout in the camp at the arrival of the ark. It struck consternation into the Philistines, who had heard of the wonders wrought by Jehovah in former times (ch. vi. 6), and who, like Israel, supposed that his presence was inseparably connected with the symbol thereof (vers. 6—8). But they speedily regained courage, and obtained a second and greater victory (ver. 9). 1. False confidence is *blind* to its own weakness and danger. 2. It is generally associated with *neglect* of the proper means of safety. 3. Nothing is more *displeasing to God* than pride and presumption ; nothing more frequently condemned or more severely punished (ch. ii. 3 ; Prov. xvi. 18 ; Isa. ii. 11). " By that sin fell the angels." " We must therefore bear this in mind throughout our whole life, every day, every hour, and every moment, that we never indulge so much as a thought of confidence in self " (Scupoli).

IV. HOW SURE IS THE FULFILMENT OF THE DIVINE THREATENINGS AGAINST THE IMPENITENT (vers. 10, 11 ; ch. ii. 30, 34). In mercy it may be long delayed ; but mercy has its limits, and judgment comes at last (Prov. xxix. 1 ; Rom. ii. 5). 1. The *priests*, who had so grossly abused their power in many ways, and now exposed the ark of the Lord in battle, were struck down by the sword of his enemies.

> " Wisdom supreme ! how wonderful the art
> Which thou dost manifest in heaven, in earth,
> And in the evil world, how just a meed
> Allotting by thy virtue unto all " (Dante, ' Inferno ').

2. The *elders and people,* who " asked not counsel at the mouth of the Lord," were abandoned to their own devices, and 30,000 of them were slain. 3. The whole *nation*, which had forsaken the Lord, was deprived of the sign of his presence (ver. 11) ; the place of the sanctuary, which had been defiled, was made a perpetual desolation (Ps. lxxviii. 59—64 ; Jer. vii. 11, 12, 14 ; xxvi. 6) ; and they who would not serve the Lord with gladness were compelled to wear the heavy yoke of their oppressors (Deut. xxviii. 47, 48 ; 1 Sam. vii. 2, 14).

> " The mills of God grind slowly, but they grind exceeding small ;
> Though he stands and waits with patience, with exactness grinds he all."

" God's judgments are the expressions of his opinion about our guilt. . . . But there is this difference between man and God in this matter:—A human judge gives his opinion in words; God gives his in events. And God always pays sinners back in *kind*, that he may not merely punish them, but correct them; so that by the kind of their punishment they may know the kind of their sin" (C. Kingsley).—D.

The inquiry of the afflicted. "Wherefore hath the Lord smitten us?" (ver. 3). Men are accustomed to meet affliction in various ways. 1. Some meet it *lightly*, and endeavour to laugh at it. But this is possible only when it is not very severe. 2. Others exaggerate it, lose their self-possession, and sink under it into despondency and despair. 3. Others quarrel with it as with an enemy, become embittered and cynical. 4. Others, still, endure it with philosophical (stoical) fortitude, accounting it not an evil, and resolving not to feel it. But this method breaks down in actual experience, and leaves the character unimproved. The truly wise, whilst fully sensitive to its natural influence, and confessing it to be an evil, seek to understand its meaning and purpose, and act in accordance therewith. They adopt this inquiry of the elders of Israel, though in a somewhat different spirit. The inquiry pertains to—

I. THE HAND FROM WHICH IT COMES. "Wherefore hath *the Lord* smitten us?" 1. His dominion is *supreme* and *universal*. 2. His operations are often *indirect*, and to our view intricate and perplexing. Adversity is not the less under his direction and control because it comes by the hand of man. 3. All he does is done in perfect *wisdom, justice,* and *benevolence*. It must be so, even when it appears otherwise (Ps. lxxvii. 19, 20). The mystery which beclouds his ways is itself adapted to beget in us proper feelings toward him. The first necessity in affliction is to settle it in our hearts that "it is the Lord."

II. THE CAUSE TO WHICH IT IS DUE. Whence? Suffering is the result and penalty of violating the natural or moral order which God has established in the world. 1. It may be often traced to the transgression of the sufferer, but not always. Those who are greater sufferers than others are not necessarily greater sinners (Luke xiii. 1—5). 2. It is often due to the transgressions of others with whom we are intimately associated, and in the effects of whose conduct we necessarily have part. 3. It is connected with the sinfulness of the heart, and implies participation in the fallen and corrupt nature of humanity. "This is the key both to the sufferings of the righteous and to many other secrets." Human suffering points, as with the finger of God, to human sin, and should ever lead to self-examination and profound humiliation.

III. THE PURPOSES FOR WHICH IT IS SENT. Herein the fatherly love of God appears; and to those who love him *punishment* is transformed into *chastisement* and a means of blessing (Heb. xii. 11). It is designed—1. To *manifest* the presence and evil of sin, which would not be otherwise properly felt. The consequences of transgression often quicken the conscience to its "exceeding sinfulness," and lead to godly sorrow (Isa. xxvii. 9). 2. To *restrain,* and *prevent* future disobedience (Ps. cxix. 67). 3. To *educate* and *improve* the character—by instructing the soul in spiritual truth, working in it submission and patience, disposing it to sympathy, &c. (Ps. xciv. 12; Rom. v. 3; 2 Cor. i. 4). "All things work together for *good*," i. e. for the perfecting of the character in conformity to "the image of his Son" (Rom. viii. 29). 4. To *prepare* for the experience of higher joy, here and hereafter (2 Cor iv. 17). 5. To promote the holiness and happiness of *others* in many ways. 6. To bring glory to God (John ix. 3; xi. 4). What is naturally a curse has thus hidden within it a priceless blessing; which, however, is not attained without human co-operation and Divine grace. Affliction has not in itself the power to purify, strengthen, and save.

IV. THE MEANS BY WHICH THESE PURPOSES ARE ACCOMPLISHED. 1. Humility and *penitence* (Job xl. 4; xlii. 6). 2. Filial *trust;* entering into fellowship with Christ in his sufferings, and receiving his Spirit according to his promise. 3. The hope of heaven, where there shall be "no more pain" (Rom. viii. 18).

> " Whatever thou dost hate,
> Whatever thou wouldst cast away and scorn
> As profitless—Affliction never lose;
> Affliction never cease to venerate.

> "For sorrow sanctified bears fruit to God,
> Which, in his heavenly garner treasured up,
> Shall feed his own to all eternity."   D.

Ver. 11.—*Symbol and spiritual truth.* "And the ark of God was taken." The ark was a Divinely-appointed symbol or material sign of spiritual truth, and especially of the presence and majesty, the holiness, mercy, and protection, of the invisible King of Israel. It was a part of a system of symbolical worship which was adapted to an early stage of human culture, and formed an important element in a dispensation introductory and preparatory to "the ministration of the Spirit" (2 Cor. iii. 8). But even under the new dispensation symbolism is not absolutely done away, for Baptism and the Lord's Supper are both symbolic. With special, though not exclusive, reference to the ancient symbol, notice that—

I. The symbol serves important purposes in relation to the truth or spiritual reality which it represents. Its need arises from our being constituted of body and soul, the dependence of thought and feeling on sensible impressions, and the necessary influence of imagination in religion ; and it serves—1. To make its nature more *conceivable.* "In the symbol proper, what we can call a symbol, there is ever, more or less distinctly and directly, some embodiment and revelation of the infinite ; the infinite is made to blend itself with the finite, to stand visible and, as it were, attainable there" (Sartor Resartus). 2. To make its presence more *certain ;* not, indeed, in itself, but in the convictions of the soul. 3. To make its influence more *powerful,* constant, and universal. It should, however, be observed that only the symbols which have been appointed by God may be *authoritatively* used in his worship ; that these should be regarded with due reverence ; not improperly exalted, not altered, not despised, not handled by unworthy hands ; and that no others should be introduced, or only such as do not inculcate error, and do not conduce to superstition or formalism.

II. The symbol may be possessed whilst the truth is partially or wholly lost. This comes to pass—1. When the symbol receives an undue share of *attention* in comparison with the truth, which is distinct from it and incomparably more important ; when it centres thought upon itself, and hinders rather than helps the soul in its spiritual aspirations. 2. When there is a *moral indisposition* and dislike, on the part of those who possess the symbol, toward the truth. 3. When, in consequence of such dislike, and the lowering of the idea of the truth, the sign is confounded with the thing signified, *identified with it,* and substituted for it. This is ever the chief danger attending the use of symbols in Divine worship.

III. The retention of the symbol without the truth is worthless and injurious. 1. It fails of its purpose ; is a means of grace no more ; an empty cistern ; a meaningless, unreal, and hollow form. Nehushtan (a piece of brass—2 Kings xviii. 4). 2. It fills men with false confidence, and increases their error, formality, and corruption. 3. It woefully disappoints the trust which is reposed in it, and often leaves them to despair (Gal. v. 1, 2).

IV. The removal of the symbol is sometimes necessary to the recovery of the truth. And this effect is accomplished by—1. Its *correction* of fatal error. In the case of Israel, teaching that the ark was not the same as the Divine presence, and did not necessarily insure it. 2. Causing deep *humiliation.* 3. Leading to earnest inquiry and *prayer.* "They lamented after the Lord" (ch. vii. 2), not after the ark, which had long been restored, and lay in a private dwelling without public honour, and appears to have exerted no influence whatever in the revival of spiritual truth and life that followed.

Conclusion :—1. Symbols are useful when rightly used and held in subordination to spiritual truth. 2. The course of the Divine dealings with men (like that of men with children) is less and less symbolical, more and more spiritual. "They shall say no more, The ark of the covenant," &c. (Jer. iii. 16 ; Col. ii. 17 ; Heb. ix. 23). 3. Symbols will completely vanish away in the light of perfect knowledge (1 Cor. xiii. 10—12).—D.

Ver. 11.—*The ark misplaced and lost.* The elders of Israel were chagrined at the defeat suffered by the national army in its attempt to throw off the yoke of the

Philistines. But, instead of seeking the Lord by repentance, they fell on a device to compel him, as they supposed, to give them a victory. Had not the ark been carried round the walls of Jericho, when Israel had no engines of siege to bring against a fortified city; and had not the walls fallen flat to the ground? Why not try its power again? "Let us fetch the ark of the covenant of Jehovah unto us, that, when it cometh among us, it may save us out of the hand of our enemies."

I. A SACRED SYMBOL MISUSED. Forthwith the ark was brought into the camp, and the people in their foolish confidence shouted till the earth rang again. A superstitious fear ran through the ranks of the Philistines, but it did not unnerve them for the battle. They gained a signal victory, "and the ark of God was taken." At such a cost had Israel to learn that the ark ought not to be used as a charm or talisman, and that, if so regarded and employed, it could not save them, could not save itself, while the face of God was turned away from the wicked priests and the degenerate nation. It is a lesson for all times. Men are often tempted to rely on religious symbols and appointments, not so much to glorify God therewith as to protect themselves. It is much easier to shout over these than to break off sins by righteousness. So the cross has been worn in many an evil enterprise, and carried into many battles, to defend cruel and rapacious men. So, also, men shout over their Church, their English Bible, their prayer-book, or their sabbath, in a vain confidence that their relation to one of them, or to all of them, will secure the Divine favour, or, at all events, Divine defence, though in character and life they be no better than others who boast of none of these things. But it is all delusion, and they who go into some hard battle of life with no better security are destined to a thorough defeat. The ark of God itself could do nothing for men who by their sins had driven away the God of the ark. What a selfish man wants in religion is to have God bound to take his part and fight on his side, instead of his studying to be on God's side, which is the side of righteousness. Such was the thought of the heathen nations of the East. Each of them had its guardian deity or deities, who were worshipped and propitiated at any cost, in order that they might befriend that particular nation or tribe, and injure its enemies. The gods were expected to give strength and victory to their own people, taking their part whether their cause were just or unjust. The Hebrews sometimes fell into the same way of thinking of Jehovah. He was their national God, and bound as such to fight for them. He was to be praised if they succeeded, to be reproached if they failed in whatever enterprise they undertook. Have not many Christians similar thoughts of God? Almost every great act of rapine has been perpetrated, and every war, however unjust, has been waged, with grave appeal to heaven, and gross usurpers and tyrants have had "Te Deum" sung for their infamous victories. But in vain do unrighteous men claim religious sanctions. God defends the right, and his face is against the wrong-doer. The ark of his covenant, brought into the din and dust of battle by those who were full of sin unrepented of, went into the enemy's hand, and the priests who stood beside it were slain.

II. FOREBODING OF EVIL. The aged Eli sat in his chair of office by the gate of Shiloh, watching the road, eager for early tidings from the army, his heart trembling for the ark of God. The natural fearfulness of old age was aggravated in this case by a reproaching conscience, which told Eli that he ought not to have permitted the ark to be taken without any warrant from the Lord into the turmoil of battle. So he sat foreboding calamity; and when the heavy tidings came to him of the discomfiture of Israel, the death of his sons, and the capture of the ark by the Philistines, Eli fell to the earth without a word, and died. We do not present the pathetic figure of the old priest trembling for the ark as a model for servants of God. The right and noble thing for Eli to have done would have been to resist the desecration of the sacred ark, and to call the people to repentance, that so they might be strong in God before they encountered the Philistines. But he had governed so weakly that he had no moral influence or authority; and his great age, which ought to have brought him reverence, only brought him feebleness; so Eli could but tremble and die. We have seen such feeble saints in our own time; they are always foreboding evil; they are in great alarm about the dangers which beset Christian truth; they sit trembling for the ark. Popery is about to swallow us up! Or, Infidelity is carrying all before it! Alas for the ark of God! So they wail and lament, and spread misgivings among all who listen to them. But they do little else; they have no vigour in counsel or action to prevent or to remedy spiritual disaster. It is a poor-spirited, ineffective style of Christian character. We want something much firmer and bolder for the defence and propagation of the gospel. We want repentance insisted on, righteousness preached and practised, wrongs redressed, abuses cast out of the Church, and then we need not fear the Philistines. Granted that the times are perilous; there is cause of anxiety, and there is need of prayer. But prayer itself will not gain any victory for those whose hearts and lives are not right with God. Hophni and Phinehas went to the battle-field reeking from their sins. How could God fight by or for them? And the people of Israel, following the bad example in high places, were quite demoralised. Why should they have a victory? Let repentance begin at the house of God. Let iniquity be abhorred and forsaken. So God will be with us, and we need not fear the foe. We shall tremble at his word, but we shall not tremble because of the Philistines. "Though an host should encamp against me, my heart shall not fear."—F.

Vers. 12—18. (SHILOH.)—*The judgment of God on the judge of Israel.* "And he had judged Israel forty years" (ver. 18). The life of Eli was lengthened out to ninety-eight years, during the last forty of which he judged Israel. In him we see that—1. The highest official position may be held by one who is destitute of the qualities which it demands. 2. Much excellence is sometimes associated with grave defects. 3. Sins of omission have a ruinous effect on others—the family, the Church, the nation. 4. A good man is not spared when he is guilty of disobedience. The judgment of Heaven is impartial. The last hour of his long life has now come, and in it we see the old man—

I. WATCHING WITH ANXIETY FOR THE ARK (ver. 13). Why does his heart tremble? He has truly an affectionate regard for it. But—1. He has been accessory to its exposure in the battle-field. 2. He is doubtful about its safety. 3. He dreads the consequences of its loss. Already he experiences the evil effects of his sin.

II. RECEIVING THE TIDINGS OF DISASTER (vers. 12, 14—17). "Woe upon woe." 1. The defeat of Israel with a great slaughter. 2. The death of his two sons. 3. The capture of the ark. "With the surrender of the earthly throne of his glory the Lord appeared to have abolished his covenant of grace with Israel; for the ark, with the tables of the law and the Capporeth, was the visible pledge of the covenant of grace which Jehovah had made with Israel" (Keil).

III. SMITTEN WITH THE STROKE OF DEATH (ver. 18). 1. After long and merciful delay. 2. Directly connected with his sin. 3. "Suddenly, and without remedy." Nevertheless, it was his dismay at the loss of the ark that caused his trembling heart to cease to beat; and his love for the sacred symbol lightens up the gloom of his melancholy end.—D.

Vers. 19—22. (SHILOH.)—*Ichabod.* "The glory is departed' (ver. 22). Ichabod = (1) Where is thy glory? (It is departed); (2) The Inglorious; or, (3) Alas! the glory. The last words of the wife of Phinehas. Her piety was—1. *Genuine.* She called the ark "the glory," and, doubtless, had regard not merely to the symbol, but also and chiefly to the Divine presence which it represented. 2. *Peculiar.* Living in corrupt times, the wife of an ungodly man, yet truly devout; a pearl among pebbles, a rose among thorns, a grain of wheat in a heap of chaff. 3. *Eminent.* Her grief at the loss of the ark surpassed her sorrow at the death of her husband and her father-in-law, and swallowed up her joy at the birth of a son. 4. *Early perfected* by death amidst the righteous judgments of Heaven. From her dying utterance learn that—

I. THE PRESENCE OF GOD IS THE TRUE GLORY OF A PEOPLE. It is the source of—1. Their real dignity. 2. Their internal prosperity. 3. Their external influence. In vain do we look elsewhere for these things. "Thy God" (shall be) "thy glory" (Isa. lx. 19; lxii. 2).

II. THE TRUE GLORY OF A PEOPLE MAY DEPART. This takes place when the presence (*i. e.* the favour and protection) of God is withdrawn. 1. It is *caused* by human sin of various kinds. He is not desirous of leaving men, but they are unwilling to fulfil the conditions according to which alone he can dwell among them.   2. It is often held out as a *warning*.   3. It has actually *occurred* (Ezek. x. 18). " Moreover, at that feast which we call Pentecost, as the priests were going by night into the inner temple, as their custom was, to perform their sacred ministrations, they said that in the first place they felt a quaking and heard a great noise, and after that they heard a sound as of a great multitude, saying, 'Let us depart hence.'" (Joseph., 'Wars,' vi. 5, 3).   The warnings given to the seven Churches of Asia (Rev. ii., iii.) were neglected, and the evils predicted came to pass.   The candlestick was removed out of its place (Rev. ii. 5), and darkness and desolation succeeded.   "But though particular Churches may fall, our Lord's promise will never fail the Catholic Church : 'Lo, I am with you alway, even to the end of the world'" ('Sp. Com.').

Conclusion :—1. The presence of God should be accounted by us the greatest blessing, and his departure dreaded as the greatest calamity.   2. Whatever contributes to his departure must be zealously renounced or corrected (Lam. iii. 40). 3. No condition is altogether hopeless.   "If from *thence* thou shalt seek the Lord thy God, thou shalt find him," &c. (Deut. iv. 29).   The glory of Israel, which, it was thought, had gone for ever, was restored ; and out of the night of sorrow a new day was born.—D.

EXPOSITION.

CHAPTER V.

THE ARK OF GOD IN PHILISTIA (vers. 1—12). Ver. 1.—**The Philistines took the ark of God.** The silence of Scripture is often as remarkable as what it tells us. From Ps. lxxviii. 60—64 ; Jer. vii. 12 ; xxvi. 9, we gather that from Aphek the Philistines marched upon Shiloh, and having captured it, put all whom they found there to the sword, and levelled the buildings to the ground. Especially their wrath fell upon the priests, in revenge for the bringing of the ark to the camp, by which the war was made a religious one, and the worst feelings of fanaticism aroused. Of all this the history says nothing, nor of the measures taken by Samuel under these trying circumstances. From his previous eminence, the government would naturally devolve upon him, especially as Eli's sons were both slain ; and evidently he must have managed in some way to save the sacred vessels of the sanctuary, and the numerous records of the past history of the nation laid up at Shiloh. Whatever learning there was in Israel had its seat there ; it was probably the only school wherein men were initiated in the knowledge brought out of Egypt ; and it is one of the worst and most barbarous results of war that it destroys so much connected with human progress and civilisation, overthrowing with its violent hand as well the means of a nation's culture as the results thereof. Samuel evidently did all that was possible to counteract these evils ; and as the Philistine army withdrew into its own country immediately after the destruction of Shiloh, probably to carry home the rich spoils obtained there, he was apparently able to ward off the worst effects of the Philistine invasion, and by rapidly reorganising the government to save the

people from utter demoralisation. But upon all this Scripture is silent, because it concerns the history of Israel on its temporal side, and not as it exemplifies God's spiritual dealings with nations and men. **From Eben-ezer** (see on ch. iv. 1) **unto Ashdod.** This town, the Azotus of Acts viii. 40, was with Ekron and other Philistine cities, assigned to the tribe of Judah (Josh. xv. 47), but never actually conquered. It lay near the sea, about thirty-two miles north of Gaza, and is now an unimportant village, still bearing the name of Esdud. Of the five Philistine capitals Ashdod and Gaza were of the most importance, as being the keys of Egypt, and the former was also enriched by the sale of the produce of Arabia, of which it was the emporium.

Ver. 2.—**When the Philistines**, &c. The words are exactly the same as those in ver. 1, viz. "And the Philistines took the ark of God, and brought it," marking the simplicity of ancient narrative. **Dagon** is derived by Philo from *dagan*, "corn," and is explained by him as an emblem of the earth's fertility ; but as the shape of this national deity of the Philistines was certainly that of a man to the waist, ending in the body and tail of a fish, the true derivation is doubtless that from *dag*, "a fish." It represented, however, not so much the sea, on which the Philistines trafficked, as the fruitfulness of water, which in the East is looked upon as the active principle of life (comp. Gen. i. 20). In one of the sculptures brought from Khorsabad there is a representation of a battle between the Assyrians and the inhabitants of the Syrian sea-coast, and in it there is a figure, the upper part of which is a bearded man with a crown, while from the waist downwards it has the shape of a fish (Layard's 'Nineveh,' ii. 466). Moreover, it is swimming in the sea, and is surrounded by a multitude of marine creatures. Doubtless this figure represents Dagon, who, nevertheless, is not to be regarded as a sea-god, like Neptune; but as the fish is the product of water, he is the symbol of nature's reproductive energy. Together with Dagon a female deity was commonly worshipped, called Atergatis, half woman and half fish, whose temple is mentioned in 2 Macc. xii. 26. In the margin there she is explained as being *Venus;* but the ideas have only this in common—that Venus also, as rising out of the sea, symbolises life as springing out of water. As Dagon had a temple also at Gaza (Judges xvi. 23), and at the other cities of Philistia (Jerome on Isa. xlvi. 1), he was evidently the chief deity of the nation, and the solemn depositing of the ark in his temple, and **by Dagon,** — literally, "at his side,"—was intended as a public demonstration that the God of the Israelites was inferior to, and had been vanquished by, the national deity of the Philistines.

Vers. 3, 4.—**On the morrow, behold, Dagon was fallen upon his face to the earth before the ark of** Jehovah. *I. e.* he was in the attitude of adoration, and instead of triumphing over Jehovah, he was prostrate, as if compelled to worship. But his priests perhaps thought that it was an accident, and so they set the image in its place again. They also, we may be sure, took due precaution against any one entering his temple by stealth; but when early on the second morning they came with anxious minds to see whether any new prodigy had happened, they found their god not only prostrate, as before, but mutilated, and **his head and both the palms of his hands were cut off**—not broken off by the fall of the image from its place, but severed with deliberate care, and placed contemptuously **upon the threshold,** *i. e.* upon the door-sill, the place where all must tread. **Only Dagon was left to him.** We cannot in English render the full contemptuousness of this phrase, because Dagon is to us a mere proper name, with no significance. In the original it conveys the idea that the head, the emblem of reason, and the human hands, the emblems of intellectual activity, were no real parts of Dagon, but falsely assumed by him; and, deprived of them, he lay there in his true ugliness, a mere misshapen fish; for *dag,* as we have seen, means a fish, and Dagon is here a diminutive of contempt. In spite of his discomfiture the Philistines were true to their allegiance to their god, because, believing as they did in "gods many," he was still their own national deity, even though he had been proved inferior to the God of Israel, and would probably be rendered more particular and exacting as regards the homage due to him from his own subjects by

so humiliating a defeat. For the gods of the heathen were jealous, fickle, and very ill-tempered if any slight was put upon them. After all, perhaps they thought, he had done his best, and though worsted in the personal conflict, he had managed so cleverly that they had gained in fair fight a great victory.

Ver. 5. — Henceforward, therefore, his priests and other worshippers carefully abstained from treading on the door-sill, where his nobler members had lain, **unto this day.** Apparently the Books of Samuel were written some time after the events recorded in them took place, and we have remarkable evidence of the permanence of the custom in Zeph. i. 9, where the Philistines are described as "those that leap on," or more correctly *over,* "the threshold." The custom, so curious in itself and so long continued, bears strong testimony to the historical truth of the narrative.

Ver. 6.—**But the hand of Jehovah was heavy upon them of Ashdod.** *I. e.* his power and might were exercised in smiting them with severe plagues. A question here arises whether, as the Septuagint affirms, besides the scourge of emerods, their land was desolated by swarms of field-mice. It is certain that they sent as votive offerings golden images of "the mice that mar the land" (ch. vi. 5); but the translators of the Septuagint too often attempt to make all things easy by unauthorised additions, suggested by the context; and so probably here it was the wish to explain why mice were sent which made them add, "and mice were produced in the land." Really the mouse was a symbol of pestilence (Herod., ii. 141), and appears as such in hieroglyphics; and by sending golden mice with golden emerods the lords of the Philistines expressed very clearly that the emerods had been epidemic. This word, more correctly spelt hæmorrhoids, has this in its favour, that the noun used here, *ophalim,* is never read in the synagogue. Wherever the word occurs the reader was instructed to say *tehorim,* the vowels of which are actually attached to the consonants of *ophalim* in the text of our Hebrew Bibles. In Deut. xxviii. 27 *tehorim* is mentioned as one of the loathsome skin diseases of Egypt, and though rendered "emerods" in the A. V., is possibly, as translated by Aquila, "an eating ulcer." *Ophalim* need only mean *tumours, swellings,* its original signification being "a hill" (2 Chron. xxvii. 3); yet as the word was not thought fit for public reading in the synagogue, we may feel sure that it means some such tumours as the A. V. describes.

Ver. 7.—**His hand is sore upon us.** The epidemic was evidently very painful, and, as appears from ver. 11, fatal in numerous instances. Connecting this outbreak with the prostrate condition and subsequent mutilation of their god, the people of Ashdod recognised in their affliction **the hand,** *i. e.* the power, of Jehovah, and determined to send away the ark, the symbol of his ill-omened presence among them.

Ver. 8.—**The lords of the Philistines.** Philistia was governed by a council of five princes, but whether they were elective or hereditary in the several towns is by no means clear. They are called "seranim," from *seren*, " a hinge," just as the cardinals of the Church of Rome take their name from the Latin word *cardo*, which has the same meaning. There is no ground for connecting the word with *sar*, " a prince." When Ewald did so he probably forgot that the two words begin with different letters — seren with *samech*, and sar with *shin*. Seranim is the word constantly used of the lords of the Philistines (Josh. xiii. 3 ; Judges iii. 3 ; xvi. 5, 8, &c. ; 1 Chron. xii. 9), though after being correctly so styled in 1 Sam. xxix. 2, they are popularly called in vers. 3, 4, 9, *sarim*, " princes." **Let the ark of the God of Israel be carried about unto Gath.** Unwilling to part with so signal a proof of their victory, the lords of the Philistines determine to remove the ark to another locality, but thereby only made the miraculous nature of what was taking place more evident to all. Of Gath but little is known ; but Jerome describes it as still a large village in his days, and as situated near the border of Judæa, on the road from Eleutheropolis to Gaza.

Ver. 9.—**And they had emerods in their secret parts.** The verb used here, *sathar*, is found in Hebrew only in this place, but is of common occurrence in Syriac and Arabic. Its ordinary meaning in both these languages is to " cover," " conceal," and the A. V., taking it in this sense, supposes that the boils were hidden, and translates as above. But the root has a double meaning, and signifies also " to destroy," though in this sense the Arabic has a slight difference in spelling, namely, *shatara* instead of *satara*. The old versions were evidently at a loss in understanding the meaning, though their renderings are suggestive, except the Syriac, which translates quite literally, but leaves thereby the difficulty untouched of the twofold meaning of the word, and the Syro-Arabic

lexicons are uncertain which to choose. Some give, "and the emerods hid themselves in them," in the sense of gnawing and burrowing into the flesh, *i. e.* they became cancerous. Others take the alternative sense, and render, "and the emerods were burst upon them," *i. e.* became fissured and rent, and turned into open sores. Another translation has been proposed, namely, "the tumours or emerods brake out upon them;" but as the verb, both in the Hebrew and the Syriac, is passive, this rendering can scarcely be defended. Upon the whole, the most probable sense is that the tumours buried themselves deep in the flesh, and becoming thus incurable, ended in causing the death of the sufferers.

Vers. 10, 11.—**The Ekronites cried out.** Convinced by this second and more fatal plague that the ark was the cause of their punishment, the people of Ekron, when it was passed on to them from Gath, protested loudly against its presence. Compelled to receive it until the lords of the Philistines could be convened in council to decide upon its ultimate destination, the plague broke out so heavily among them that they were in utter dismay. For the rendering **deadly destruction** is untenable. Literally the words are, "a dismay of death ;" but in Hebrew *death* added to a word of this sort simply means " very great." So " terrors of death " in Ps. lv. 4 are very great terrors. In the next verse we learn that many did die, but the words used here describe the mental agony and despair of the people as they saw the ark, which had wrought elsewhere so great misery, brought unto them.

Ver. 12.—**The cry of the city went up to heaven.** Not the word used in ver. 10, where it is an outcry of indignation, but a cry for help, a cry of sorrow and distress. Though in ver. 10 Ekronites is in the plural, yet in all that follows the singular is used. "They have brought about the ark to me, to slay me and my people. . . . That it slay me not and my people." It is the prince of Ekron who, as the representative of the people, expostulates with his fellow-rulers for the wrong they are doing him. But finally all join in his lamentation, and the whole city, smitten by God's hand sends up its prayer to heaven for mercy.

HOMILETICS.

Vers. 1—5.—*Foreshadowings.* The facts given are—1. The Philistines, acting on polytheistic principles, place the ark in their heathen temple, thus ascribing to it Divine honour, and yet indicating its inferiority to Dagon. 2. During the night their god Dagon falls to the ground. 3. Supposing the fall to be the result of some unaccountable accident, they replace their god, and on the next day find him even broken to pieces. 4. The event is memorialised by the establishment of a superstitious custom. The supernatural and ordinary events connected with Israel's history have a prophetic significance for future ages. The record is "for our admonition, on whom the ends of the world have come." There is another bondage than that of Egypt, another conflict than that of Dagon and the ark. Here are two powers in collision, and we have given us—

I. A FORESHADOWING OF THE FALL OF HEATHENISM. 1. The *fact is established* that heathenism is *doomed to perish*. The occurrence in the house of Dagon is a single instance, in palpable form, of what has taken place in many lands, and will recur till every idol is abolished. No prediction in Scripture is more clear than that the day will come when paganism will cease to exist (Ps. ii. 8 ; Isa. ii. 18 ; xi. 9). Events daily point on to it. Dagons fall in many lands. History is really but the completion of processes set in operation by God in ages past. Destruction is inherent in the essential falsehood of heathenism. The truth of God cannot be converted into a permanent lie (Rom. i. 25). It is a mercy that God has so ordained things that only true worship can endure. 2. *Heathenism is doomed to perish by contact with God's truth.* Dagon might stand erect and receive the homage of men when he and they are left to themselves ; but in presence of the ark, the visible manifestation of God's will to the world, he must fall on his face to the earth. Doubtless corruption in men, if left long enough on earth, would cause them to become extinct, because in the nature of things it tends to utter ruin of morals, society, health, and life. It is, however, the purpose of God to extinguish it without extinguishing the race of men, and that too by his revealed truth. Events prove that this has been the process. Britain ceased to be idolatrous when the light of life came to her shores. Hence the missionary enterprise ; hence the need of " holding forth the word of life." 3. The *downfall of heathenism is brought about by the secret, silent power of God exercised through his truth.* There is suggestiveness in the hint that the fall of Dagon occurred during the silence of night. The fall was through the unseen power of God, operating by ways men could not trace, and that revealed its existence in its effects. The conquests of the gospel are instrumental. It is not history, though pure and impressive ; nor precept clear and useful ; nor sublime thought for the intellect ; nor mere influence of character, though holy and elevating ; but the quickening Spirit, who, in the depths of human nature working by means of the instrument, turns men to God. There is a profound secrecy and mystery in every soul's regeneration. 4. The *final downfall of heathenism* by means of the truth is *brought about after repeated efforts to revive it.* They placed Dagon on his seat again, and rejoiced once more in his sufficiency ; but the Unseen Power wrought on with greater energy, till the head and hands, the seat and instruments of power, were cut off. Beautifully does Scripture thus indicate the ebbs and flows of the stream of truth in process of subjugating every principality and power to Christ. A thousand years with God are as one day. He gives free scope to men and principles. Yet the truth will prevail until the earth is "filled with the knowledge of the Lord as the waters cover the deep."

II. The FRUSTRATION OF ALL EFFORTS TO DISHONOUR GOD'S REVELATION OF HIMSELF. The placing of the ark in the presence of Dagon was intended to indicate a belief in it as *a* power among men, but as a power *inferior* to that exercised by the Philistines' god. Jehovah was a deity, but yet a conquered deity. Hence the glory due to Dagon. Now the ark represented at that time the specific revelation which God had given for bringing to pass his purpose in the deliverance of the world from the curse of sin. The practical effect, therefore, of the Philistines' conduct was to rob revelation of its supremacy. The tendencies of human nature are constant ; and now that the full revelation has been given in Christianity, there is the same effort to dishonour and discredit it before men by placing it in unwarrantable positions. 1. *The insult offered to Christianity.* There are *two forms of insult.* (1) That offered by persons who simply *recognise Christianity as one among the many and equally authorised powers* for promoting the good of mankind. Human society is regarded as a whole, needing, for its intellectual, moral, and material development, a wise use of various educational appliances which God has provided. Religions, philosophies, statecraft, productions of men of genius, are all of God, and equally demand the respect and deference of men. An inspiration from the Almighty ru s through them all, since they are his agents. Hence Christianity is just *one* of the religions of the world, doing its part in common with them.   As a philosophy it may have a place among other systems.   As useful in the management of peoples, statesmen may lay hold of it in support of other agencies.   Christ may adorn the Pantheon in company with other heroes in thought and action.   (2) That offered by persons who *regard Christianity as a power inferior to other agencies for influencing human destiny.*   There are few who would esteem it inferior *as a religion,* when compared with prevailing forms in *non*-Christian lands ; but by some it is held to be inferior as compared with a pure theism and the higher philosophies.   Its supernaturalism is branded as the crude product of unphilosophical minds.   Its cardinal doctrine of atonement is declared to be at variance with first principles in morality.   Unless divested of its outward garb, it is supposed to be unsuited to the higher order of intellect.   Its power as a supreme authority is said to be on the wane, and pride is felt in placing its pretensions side by side with those of the modern Dagon.   2. The *rebuke of those who offer the insult.*   Without dwelling on the sure disappointment and sorrow which come on those who dishonour Christianity by regarding it as merely one of the various powers equally deserving of respect, it may suffice to point out how—(1) Facts show that *all systems in rivalry* with Christianity *lose their vaunted pre-eminence ;* and this too, on the one hand, by the loss of their influence, and on the other by the permanent and growing power of Christianity. The wisdom of the Greek ceased to be a ruling force, while the truth of Christ won for him the Roman empire.   The cold theism of the eighteenth century sank into obscurity as the great evangelical impulse of the Church of God developed its force. The men who pride themselves in antagonism to Christ have never done anything to regenerate the savage, to make the dying-bed peaceful.   (2) It is in the *nature of the case* that such a *result should always ensue.*   No other religion is so fully attested as Divine.   Every other system partakes of the imperfection of its authors ; fails in motive power ; is more of a criticism on man and his position in the world than a solvent of the deep spiritual cravings of the soul ; and is liable to pass out of influence under the analysis of succeeding minds.   The policy that would suggest to a statesman the use of Christianity as a tool for government thereby proves its moral instability.   The unseen power of the " jealous God " will work in silence, and cause the " Name that is above every name " to have " in all things the pre-eminence."   A refuge of lies means trouble and anguish.

General lessons :—1. History confirms faith in the sufficiency of the gospel for the conquest of heathenism.   2. In all use of means the power of the Holy Spirit should be recognised.   3. We must seek proof of the pre-eminence of Christianity in deeds such as no rivals can produce.   4. We may yet expect many boastful claims from human systems before men learn fully the lessons of history.

Vers. 6—12.—*Coercive providences.*   The facts given are—1. God visits the men of Ashdod with severe affliction.   2. In their perplexity they remove the ark to another locality.   3. The device proving a failure, and the men of Ekron refusing to receive the unwelcome symbol, a council of authorities decides to return it to Israel.   Providence had so ordered events for high moral ends as to bring the ark into captivity. The influences were at work in Israel to issue in the result desired.   Hence there arose a need for a turn in the course of Providence.

I. The NEED FOR COERCIVE PROVIDENCES ARISES CHIEFLY FROM TWO CAUSES.   1. *Imperfect acquaintance with the Divine will.*   These men had some knowledge of the Divine power in the ark, but could not learn the precise will of the strange god. One of the first things, therefore, is to prompt to an inquiry as to what is desired. But man, especially when grossly ignorant, is indisposed to search for light, and cannot bear very clear light.   If men will not act because they do not know, they must be aroused to learn, or to do without knowing ; for God's great ways must not be barred and blocked by man.   2. *Unwillingness to be convinced of the Divine will.*   The fall of Dagon on the first night aroused the thought of a superior power, and the danger of keeping it from its natural place.   This first gleam of light was extinguished by a new trial of Dagon's power to stand.   A second failure brought more light, but the expedient of change of abode was adopted to evade the new and clearer suggestion.   Men often do not like to know the path of duty.   There is much ingenuity spent in evading the force of Divine teaching. If they will not follow increasing light when their doing so is necessary to the realisation of a Divine purpose, pressure must be brought to bear. Pharaoh, Balaam, and Jonah are instances of this.

II. The KIND OF COERCION EMPLOYED WILL DEPEND ON THE MENTAL AND SOCIAL CONDITION OF THE PEOPLE. Men are influenced strongly by events which touch their interests, and which come in such shape as to be adapted to their ordinary modes of thought and views of things. The people of Ashdod were highly susceptible to religious impressions, and their religious associations were entirely with the honour of their god. Philosophical arguments and high-toned reasons suited to pure Hebraism or Christianity would not have touched them. Moreover, by education and inheritance they were governed by the habit of associating bodily sufferings, when great, with a positive Divine purpose. Now, God governs men according to their capabilities, and reveals his will in ways conformable to their ruling ideas. Whether by miracle or natural coincidences, there is always adaptation to the minds to be influenced. This principle solves many events in Old Testament history, and shows the perfect reasonableness and even propriety of the pressure brought to bear on the benighted Philistines. God fits every rod to the back of the fools he smites, and speaks to every ear in accents suited to its delicacy or obtuseness.

III. The COERCION IS PROGRESSIVE IN INTENSITY. The select body of priests of Dagon first feel the hand of God, then the people as individuals, and then the entire community as such. Also, there was first a rude blow to the religious prejudices of the priestly body, and through them of the people; then an assault on the physical condition of multitudes; and finally a disastrous blow on the prosperity of the state. Men will answer religious arguments by religious arguments, and evade truth if possible; but touch their bodies and their fields, and some earnest inquiry as to the cause and intent will be evoked. Especially does material disaster induce effort to learn the truth when authorities are compelled to deliberate on possible remedies. In national providences the pressure at last reaches the rulers.

General lessons :—1. God uses pressure on each of us when our inclination runs against our true interest and his glory. Lot was led urgently out of Sodom. 2. The pressure used never crushes the will, but develops thought, and opens out lines of conduct for adoption. 3. It is important to study the meaning of events in our lives which are inevitable and disagreeable. 4. The coercive action of Providence will become less or more according as we turn from sin or harden our hearts. "The way of transgressors is hard."

HOMILIES BY VARIOUS AUTHORS.

Ch. v., vi. 1—9. (ASHDOD, GATH, EKRON.)—*The ark among the heathen.* "And the ark of the Lord was in the country of the Philistines seven months" (ch. vi. 1). The scene is now changed. Whilst there arises in every household in Israel a cry of mourning for the dead, Shiloh is ravaged and burnt with fire, and the yoke of oppression made heavier than before, the hosts of the Philistines return to their own country elated with victory. They carry with them the ark of the Lord, which had never before been touched by unconsecrated hands, or for ages exposed to the gaze of any but the priests; and the interest centres on the sacred symbol amidst its new and strange surroundings. It is first of all taken to Ashdod, three miles from the sea-coast, the chief seat of the worship of Dagon, the national god of the Philistines (1 Chron. x. 10); afterwards to Gath, ten miles distant (the native place of Goliath, and twice the temporary residence of David); and then to Ekron (ch. vii. 14), the most northerly of their cities. Although the other two cities of the Philistine Pentapolis, Gaza, the scene of Samson's death (Judges xvi. 21—30), and Askelon (ch. xxxi. 10; 2 Sam. i. 20), were deeply concerned in the events which attended its presence (ch. v. 8; vi. 17), it does not appear to have visited them. 1. The time of its abode among the Philistines was for them a time of *judgment*. Although the ark when among the people of Israel seemed to be abandoned by God and destitute of power, it was now defended by him and clothed with might. The difference arose from the different circumstances in which it was placed; and in both cases it was shown that the possession of institutions appointed by God does not profit those who refuse to stand in a right relation to God himself, but rather serves to increase their condemnation. Judgment also is executed in many ways. 2. Judgment was mingled with *mercy*. The afflictions which they endured were "less than their iniquity deserved" (Job xi. 6), and were "established for the correction" (Hab. i. 12) of their sins and the prevention of their ruin (Ezek. xviii. 30). The God of Israel has supreme dominion over the heathen, "chastises" them (Ps. xciv. 10) for their good, and never leaves himself "without witness" (Acts xiv. 17). 3 The *design* of the whole was the furtherance of the purpose for which Israel was called, viz. to bear witness to the living and true God, and to preserve his religion separate and distinct from the idolatry and superstition of the heathen. 4. The *effect* of the display of his power in connection with the presence of the ark among them appears here and in their subsequent history. Consider these Philistines as—

I. TRIUMPHING IN THE CAPTURE OF THE ARK (vers. 1, 2). "They brought it into the house (or temple) of Dagon, and set it by Dagon," as a trophy or a votive offering, ascribing their victory to him, and magnifying him as superior to Jehovah. The process described by the Apostle Paul (Rom. i. 18—23) had taken place in them. Their worship was a nature-worship, joined with the embodiment of their "foolish" imaginations in an image with which their god was identified. Dagon was "the god of natural power—of all the life-giving forces of which water is the instrument; and his fish-like body, with head and arms of man, would appear a striking embodiment of his rule to those who dwelt near the sea." When men have fallen away from the knowledge of the true God they—1. *Do honour to a false god;* impelled by the religiousness of their nature, which will not let them rest without an object of worship. 2. *Dishonour the true God*, by declaring him inferior and subject to the false, and by "despising his holy things." The Philistines did not deny the existence of Jehovah; they were willing to account him one among "lords many and gods many," and regarded him as having a local and limited dominion. But the fundamental idea of the religion of Israel was that Jehovah is God alone, and demands the supreme and entire affection of man (Isa. xlii. 8). "Thou shalt have no other gods before me," *i. e.* in my presence. 3. *Give glory to themselves;* are proud and boastful of their wisdom, power, and success. Self is really the idol of all who forsake the Lord. But the triumph of the ungodly is short.

II. SMITTEN BEFORE THE PRESENCE OF THE ARK (vers. 2—4). Almost as soon as they obtained possession of it, the victory which they thought they had obtained over him whose presence it represented was turned into disastrous defeat. 1. Their *god* was cast down and broken in pieces. (1) *Mysteriously*. In the night. (2) *Significantly*. "Fallen upon his face to the ground before the ark of the Lord," as if in subjection, or rendering worship to the Lord of all. (3) *Irresistibly*. Unwilling to lay the lesson to heart, they "set him in his place again," but only to prove that their efforts on his behalf were abortive (Isa. xlv. 9). (4) *More and more signally*. Their very efforts affording occasion for a greater manifestation of Divine power, and one which could not be, as the first may possibly have been, attributed to accident. "The face, as a sign of its worthless glory and vain beauty, struck down to the earth; the head also, as the seat of the wisdom which is alienated from God and opposed to God; the hands, as a symbol of the powers of darkness which work therein, cut off" (Lange). (5) *Contemptuously*. "Upon the threshhold," as if fit only to be trodden under-foot. Such, however, was the blindness of his votaries, that they henceforth accounted the spot as peculiarly sacred (ver. 3). (6) *Completely*. "Only the fish-stump was left." "Thus the kingdom of Satan will certainly fall before the kingdom of Christ, error before truth, profaneness before godliness, corruption before grace in the hearts of the faithful." 2. Their *sustenance* was wasted and destroyed (ver. 6; vi. 4, 5). "Mice were produced in the land, and there arose a great and deadly confusion in the city" (Septuagint). The corn-fields, the chief means of their subsistence and the source of their prosperity, rendered fertile, as they deemed, by the power and favour of Dagon, were wasted by a plague of field-mice (not unknown in the history of other lands) under the special arrangement of Divine providence, that they might learn the vanity of their idol and the supremacy of Jehovah. 3. Their *persons* were afflicted with disease. "The hand of the Lord was heavy upon them of Ashdod" and "the coasts (territory) thereof," and "smote them with emerods" (vers. 9, 12; either boils or hemorrhoids, bleeding piles —Ps. lxxviii. 66). (1) Painful. (2) Reproachful, because of the moral corruption sanctioned in connection with idolatrous worship (Rom. i. 24—32). (3) Instructive— concerning the self-control and moral purity which the true God requires in men. These things were adapted to show the folly of idolatry, the majesty of God, and the necessity of humiliation before him. Nor were they wholly without effect.

III. INSPIRED WITH DREAD OF THE ARK (ver. 7), for such was evidently the pre-vailing feeling of the men of Ashdod, and of others subsequently, as more fully expressed in vers. 11, 12. They attributed their afflictions to its presence—"His hand is sore upon us, and upon Dagon our god;" and feared a continuance of them. Hence they wished to get rid of it, as the Gergesenes desired Jesus to "depart out of their coasts" (Matt. viii. 34). 1. The religion of the heathen is a religion of fear. 2. The fear of man in the presence of the supernatural bears witness to the sinfulness of his nature, or of his disturbed relations with the Divine. 3. It springs from a conviction or instinct of retribution, which, however, is often mistaken in its applications. 4. A servile, selfish fear drives away the soul from God instead of drawing it near to him, and is contrary to the reverential, filial fear in which true religion has its root (2 Tim. i. 7).

IV. STRIVING FOR THE RETENTION OF THE ARK (vers. 8—12). The effect of their sufferings on the people of Ashdod was to lead them to resolve, "The ark of the God of Israel shall not abide with us;" but its removal was deemed a matter of such importance that they called a council of the lords (or princes) of the confederacy to determine what should be done with it. Whilst they may have felt toward Jehovah a like fear to that with which they regarded Dagon, they were unwilling to render honour to him by "letting it go again to its own place" (ver. 11), still less to renounce their idolatry. They wished to retain the ark for their own honour and glory; and so indisposed were they to desist from their attempt, and acknowledge their fault, that even their own priests found it necessary to admonish them against "hardening their hearts as the Egyptians and Pharaoh" (ver. 6; ch. iv. 8). They sought to effect their purpose by sending it to Gath; and it was only when both Gath and Ekron were still more severely afflicted than Ashdod, many died, and the cry of distress "went up to heaven" (ver. 12), that in a second council they consented to let it go. 1. The devices of men against the Lord are foolish and vain (Prov. xxi. 30). 2. Their continued resistance to his will causes increased misery to themselves and others. 3. Their efforts against him afford opportunities for a wider and more signal display of his power. 4. What they are unwilling to do in the beginning they are, after much suffering, constrained to do in the end.

V. INQUIRING ABOUT THE RETURN OF THE ARK (ch. vi. 2—9). The Philistine princes, having resolved to send it back, called "the priests and soothsayers" to-gether, to show them in what manner it should be done; and the answer they received, though not unmingled with the caution generally exhibited by heathen priests, was wise and good. 1. Men in all ages have had need of special guidance in Divine things. The very existence of a priesthood is a confession of such need. 2. Conviction often forces itself upon the most reluctant. 3. There is in men generally a deep feeling of the necessity of a propitiatory offering in order to avert Divine wrath—"trespass offering" (ver. 3). 4. Even the light which shines upon the heathen indicates the need of the higher light of revelation. Their wisest advisers exhibit uncertainty and doubt (vers. 5, 9).

VI. RENDERING HOMAGE TO THE GOD OF THE ARK. 1. By sending it back to its own place. 2. By the open acknowledgment of their transgression in the trespass offerings they present on behalf of the whole nation. "Give glory unto the God of Israel" (ver. 5). 3. By providing the most appropriate and worthy means of making their offerings. "A *new* cart" (2 Sam. vi. 3). "Two milch kine on which there hath come no yoke" (Num. xix. 2). 4. By the humble attendance of their chief men (vers. 12, 16). 5. By confessing the incompatibility of the worship of Jehovah with the worship of Dagon. "And from this time we hear no more of the attempts of the Gentile nations to join any part of the Jewish worship with their own" (Warburton). Imperfect as their homage was, it was not unacceptable to him "who is a gracious

God and merciful, slow to anger, and of great kindness, and repents him of the evil" (Jonah iv. 2; Acts xvii. 27, 30).

VII. Persisting in their attachment to idols. We know not all the beneficial effect of the presence of the ark among them, in restraining them from evil and inciting them to good; but we know that—1. They did not renounce their idolatry. 2. They did not cease from their oppression of Israel. And, 3. Were not permanently deterred from making fresh attacks upon them (ch. vii. 7), and by their opposition to the God of Israel "bringing upon themselves swift destruction."—D.

Ver. 3. (Ashdod.)—*The overthrow of idolatry.* "Behold, Dagon was fallen upon his face to the earth before the ark of the Lord." Idolatry still prevails over by far the larger portion of the earth. It is an ancient, persistent, and enormous evil. And we, like Israel of old, are called to be witnesses to the heathen of the living and true God; not, indeed, by keeping outwardly separate from them, nor for that purpose, and the preservation of the truth intrusted to us, by contending against them with the sword; but by going into all the world, and preaching the gospel to every creature. Our only weapons are those of truth, righteousness, and love.

> "Nor do we need
> Beside the gospel other sword or shield
> To aid us in the warfare for the faith."—(Dante.)

When the ark was defended with carnal weapons, it was carried away by the heathen, and placed in the temple of Dagon; but he whom the sacred symbol represented smote the idol to the ground (vers. 1—5). "Wherever he comes with the ark and the testimony, there he smites the idols to the ground. Idolatry must fall where the gospel finds a place." Concerning idolatry, notice—

I. The nature of the evil. 1. False and unworthy conceptions of *God.* The instinct of worship was possessed by the Philistines; but their worship was rendered to a monstrous image, which was wholly destitute of, and opposed to, the perfections of the true God. It is the same with other idolatrous nations. Of the innumerable gods of India it has been said, "What a lie against his supreme majesty! Their number is a lie against his unity; their corporeal nature is a lie against his pure, invisible spirituality; their confined and local residence a lie against his omnipresence and immensity; their limited and subdivided departments of operation a lie against his universal proprietorship and dominion; their follies and weaknesses a lie against his infinite wisdom; their defects, vices, and crimes a lie against his unsullied purity and perfection." "Having no hope, and without God in the world" (Ephes. ii. 12). 2. Great *corruption* of life and manners; gross sensuality, incessant strife, oppression, cruelty, &c. (Ps. lxxiv. 20). "The land is defiled, and vomiteth out her inhabitants" (Levit. xviii. 25). 3. A *downward tendency* towards still greater darkness, corruption, and misery. "The true evil of idolatry is this. There is one sole idea of God which corresponds adequately to his whole nature. Of this idea two things may be affirmed, the first being that it is the root of all absolute grandeur, of all truth, and all moral perfections; the second, that, natural and easy as it seems when once unfolded, it could only have been unfolded by revelation; and to all eternity he that started with a false conception of God could not through any effort of his own have exchanged it for the true one. All idolatries alike, though not all in equal degrees, by intercepting the idea of God through the prism of some representative creature that *partially* resembles God, refract, and splinter, and distort that idea. And all experience shows that the tendency of man, left to his own imaginations, is *downwards.* Many things check and disturb this tendency for a time; but finally, and under that intense civilisation to which man intellectually is always hurrying, under the eternal evolution of physical knowledge, such a degradation of God's idea, ruinous to the *moral* capacities of man, would undoubtedly perfect itself, were it not for the kindling of a purer standard by revelation. Idolatry, therefore, is not *an* evil, and one utterly beyond the power of social institutions to redress; but, in fact, it is the fountain of all other evil that seriously menaces the destiny of the human race" (De Quincey, 'Leaders in Lit.,' p. 308).

II. The means of its overthrow. 1. The proclamation of *Divine truth,* of

which the ark may be accounted a symbol ; the revelation of the righteous and merciful purposes of God toward men in his Son Jesus Christ.   2. The operations of
Divine providence, by which heathen lands are rendered accessible, and their inhabitants disposed to pay attention to the truth ; not only those which are afflictive, but
also those which are benign (ver. 6).   3. The influences of the *Divine Spirit*, by
which false systems are shaken as by a " mighty rushing wind," and consumed as
with fire, and lost souls are enlightened, purified, and saved.   " By my Spirit, saith
the Lord of hosts " (Zech. iv. 6).   He works in silence and secrecy ; but the effects
of his working become manifest to all.   The light of the morning reveals them.
III. THE CERTAINTY OF ITS DOOM ; from—1. The *adaptation* of the means.   2.
The *work* which has been already accomplished, and which is an earnest of and
preparation for "greater things than these."   3. The *predictions* of the word (Num.
xiv. 21 ; Isa. ii. 18 ; Jer. x. 11 ; Mal. ii. 11).
Conclusion :—1. Pity the heathen "in the compassion of Jesus Christ."   2. " Go
ye."   " Give ye."   " Pray ye."   3. Do all in faith and hope.—D.

Ver. 3.—*Infatuation.*   I. OF THE HEATHEN.   Samson, calling on the name of Jehovah God, pulled down the temple of Dagon at Gaza, and showed the weakness of the
idol.   When the Philistines got possession of the ark of Jehovah, they placed it in
another temple of Dagon at Ashdod, in order to re-establish the credit of their god.
Great must have been their chagrin when they found the god of the victors prostrate
before a sacred symbol connected with the God of the vanquished.   But it was no
easy thing to break their confidence in their own god.   They set the idol up again,
trying to persuade themselves, perhaps, that the fall had been accidental.   The restoration of Dagon, however, only prepared for him and his worshippers a greater
discomfiture.   As the Philistines would learn nothing from the humiliation of their
god, they had to behold with horror his mutilation and destruction.   A plague fell at
the same time on the people of Ashdod, like the plague of boils that smote the
Egyptians in the days of Moses.   They were filled with dismay, yet they would not
restore to its place in Shiloh that ark which, as they owned, had brought such distress
upon them (ver. 7).   They carried it from city to city, though in each place the Lord
punished them.   For some months they continued in this infatuated course.   The
lesson of the weakness of their own gods they learned very slowly, very reluctantly ;
indeed, they never turned from their idols.   Dreading the judgments of Jehovah, they
at last sent back the ark to the land of Israel ; but their minds and hearts were not
changed.   All that they cared for was to be free of this terrible ark, that they might
cleave undisturbed to their own gods and their own heathen usages.
II. OF UNGODLY MEN IN ALL NATIONS.   An evil habit is reproved, an error refuted,
or a vain hope in religion exposed ; yet men will not abandon it.   They have some
excuse for it, and after it has been thrown down they " set it up again in its place."
The lesson is repeated with emphasis more than once, and yet it is not learned.
Ungodly and self-willed men fall on one excuse after another, rather than give up
errors which suit their minds and evils to which they are addicted.   They have no
objection to keep religion as a talisman ; but rather than be called to account concerning it, or compelled to choose between it and their own devices, they will send it
away.   They prefer even a weak Dagon, who lets them sin, to the holy God, who
requires his people to be holy too.   The Philistines continued to be heathens, notwithstanding the reproof and humiliation inflicted upon them, just as the Egyptians
remained in heathen blindness after all the proofs given to them of the power of
Jehovah over their gods and their Pharaoh.   Alas ! many persons in Christendom
have solemn reproofs from God and exposures of their helplessness when he rises up
to judgment, yet never turn to him.   In their infatuation they first treat the ark with
disrespect, then send it away.   They dismiss God from their thoughts, and are as mad
as ever on their idols.
[" This chapter, with the following, strikingly illustrates the non-missionary character of the Old Dispensation.   For centuries the Israelites were near neighbours of
the Philistines, and yet the Philistines had no particular knowledge of the religion of
the Israelites, and only a garbled and distorted account of their history.   This religious isolation was, no doubt, a part of the Divine plan for the development of the

theocratic kingdom; but if we look for the natural causes, we shall find one in the narrowness of ancient civilisation, when the absence of means of social and literary communication fostered mutual ignorance, and made sympathy almost impossible; and another in the national local nature of the religion of Israel, with its central sanctuary, and its whole system grounded in the past history of the nation, thus presenting great obstacles to a foreigner who wished to become a worshipper of Jehovah."— Dr. Broadus].—F.

EXPOSITION.

CHAPTER VI.

RESTORATION OF THE ARK TO THE IS-RAELITES (vers. 1—12). Vers. 1, 2.—**The ark of Jehovah was in the country**—literally, the field, *i. e.* the territory—**of the Philistines seven months**, during which long time the people wherever the ark was deposited were afflicted in their persons with a most painful malady. The princes determined, therefore, to restore it to Israel, and convened **the priests and the diviners**, that they might advise them as to the manner in which this purpose should be best carried out, lest some error or want of due reverence might only serve to increase their sufferings. It would be the duty of the priests to see that the proper ceremonial was observed in moving the ark, while the diviners would decide what day and hour and special method would be lucky. The importance of the diviner, *qosem*, is shown by his being mentioned in Isa. iii. 2 in an enumeration of the leading orders in the state. He is placed there between the prophet and the elder or senator; but the A.V., displeased perhaps at finding one who practised a forbidden art nevertheless described as practically so valued, translates the word *prudent*. Literally it means a *divider* or *partitioner*, because it was his office to separate things into the two classes of lucky and unlucky. **Tell us wherewith**, &c. Though this translation is tenable, the right rendering is probably *how*. The princes did not assume that gifts must accompany the ark, but inquired generally as to the best method of restoring it. So the answer of the priests and diviners is not merely that expiatory offerings are to be made, but that the ark is to be sent back in such a way as to give proof that Jehovah had intervened, or the contrary (vers. 7, 8, 9).

Vers. 3, 4.—**A trespass offering.** The offering that was to be made when the offence had been unintentional (Levit. v. 15). **Why his hand is not removed from you.** A euphemism for "why your punishment continues to be so severe, without sign of abatement." If healing follows the gift, you will know that the malady was Jehovah's doing. The trespass offering was to consist of **five golden emerods, and five golden mice**, it being an

old heathen custom, still constantly practised abroad, of presenting to the deity tokens representing the deliverance wrought for such as had implored his aid. Thus Horace ('Carm.,' i. 5) speaks of the custom of hanging up in the temple of Neptune the clothes in which a man had escaped from shipwreck. Slaves when manumitted offered their chains to the Lares; and the idea is so natural that we cannot wonder at its prevalence. **One plague was on you all.** Rather, "is on you all." It did not cease until the ark had been restored. The Hebrew has *on them all;* but as all the versions and several MSS. read *you all*, the substitution of *them* is probably the mistake of some transcriber.

Ver. 5.—**Mice that mar the land.** The idea of a plague of field-mice is, as we have seen, due to one of those many unauthorised insertions of the Septuagint by which they supposed that they removed difficulties from the way of their readers. As the ancients use the names of animals in a very generic way, any rodent may be meant from the jerboa downwards; but probably it was the common field-mouse, *arvicola arvensis*, still common in Syria, which multiplies with great rapidity, and is very destructive to the crops, and so became the symbol of devastation and pestilence (see on ch. v. 6). When, as Herodotus relates (Book ii. 141), the Assyrian army of Sennacherib had been defeated, because a vast multitude of field-mice had overrun his camp and gnawed asunder the bow-strings of his troops, the Egyptians raised a statue to Hephæstus, holding in his hand a mouse. But very probably this is but the literal explanation by Herodotus of what he saw, while to a well-instructed Egyptian it represented their god of healing, holding in his hand the mouse, as the symbol either of the devastation which he had averted, or of the pestilence with which he had smitten the Assyrian army (see on ch. v. 6).

Ver. 6.—**Wherefore do you harden your hearts, as the Egyptians and Pharaoh?** On this reference to Egypt see on ch. iv. 8. It is remarkable that they so correctly point out that it was the obduracy of the Egyptians which made their punishment so severe. Yet finally even they, in spite of their determined opposition were compelled to let

Israel go. So now the question is whether the Philistines will restore the ark on the warning of one plague, or whether they will hold out till they have been smitten with ten.

Ver. 7.—**Make a new cart, and take**, &c. The Hebrew is, "Now take and make you a new cart, and two milch kine." The transposition of the A. V. throws undue stress upon the verb *make*, whereas the Hebrew simply means that both the cart was to be new, and the heifers untrained and unbroken to the yoke. Both these were marks of reverence. Nothing was to be employed in God's service which had been previously used for baser purposes (comp. Mark xi. 2). No animal was deemed fit for sacrifice which had laboured in the field. The separation of the kine from their calves was for the purpose of demonstrating whether the plague after all was supernatural, and it is remarkable what great care the Philistine priests take against confounding the extraordinary with the Divine. If, however, the kine act in a manner contrary to nature, their last doubt will be removed.

Ver. 8.—**Put the jewels of gold . . . in a coffer**. Instead of jewels the Hebrew word signifies any article of workmanship, and so figures, images wrought in gold. They were to be placed reverentially at the side of the ark, for it had wrought them so great evil that they had learned to look upon it with awe.

Ver. 9.—**His own coast**, or "border." The ark throughout this verse is spoken of as if it were itself a deity. **Beth-shemesh** — *i. e.* "the house of the sun," also called Irshemesh, "city of the sun" (Josh. xix. 41) —had evidently been in the time of the Canaanites the seat of this popular idolatry. It was now a city of the priests, situated in the tribe of Judah, on its north-eastern border, next the tribe of Dan, and was the nearest Israelite town to Ekron. If, then, the kine, albeit unused to the yoke, left their calves behind, and drew the cart by the most direct route unto the land of Judah, they would give the required proof that the Philistines were smitten by the hand of Jehovah, and that it was no chance that had happened unto them.

Ver. 12.—**The kine took the straight way**. The Hebrew brings out the directness with which the heifers took the route to Bethshemesh very forcibly. It says, "And the kine went straight in the way upon the way to Beth-shemesh; they went along one highway, lowing as they went," *i. e.* they went in one direct course, without deviating from it. Nevertheless, their continual lowing showed the great stress that was laid upon their nature in being thus compelled to separate themselves from their calves. **And the lords of the Philistines went after them.**

I. e. behind them, leaving the kine free to go where they chose. The usual position of the driver of an ox-cart in the East is in front. Conder ('Tent Work,' i. 274) describes the view up the great corn valley of Sorek to the high and rugged hills above as extremely picturesque, and this it is, he adds, which was spread before the eyes of the five lords of the Philistines as they followed the lowing oxen which bore the ark on the "straight way" from Ekron to Bethshemesh. The ruins of the latter place, he says, lie on a knoll surrounded by olive trees, near the junction of the valley of Sorek with the great gorge which bounded Judah on the north.

THE ARK AT BETH-SHEMESH (vers. 13— 20). Ver. 13. **And they of Beth-shemesh**. More exactly, "And Beth-shemesh was reaping its wheat-harvest," the whole population being in the fields. Though a priestly city, we find in ver. 15 the Levites distinguished from the ordinary inhabitants, as though they and the priests formed only the ruling class. **In the valley**. Now called the Wady Surar, branching off into another valley on the south. Robinson ('Later Bibl. Res.,' 153) speaks of the site of Beth-shemesh as a very noble one, being "a low plateau at the junction of two fine plains." The wheat-harvest takes place in Palestine in May, and consequently the disastrous battle of Eben-ezer must have been fought in the previous October.

Ver. 14.—**Stood there, where there was a great stone**. Probably a mass of natural rock rising through the soil. This they used as an altar, breaking up the cart for wood, and sacrificing the kine. In this joyful work all the people seem to have joined, though the sacrifice would be offered only by the priests.

Ver. 15.—**The Levites took down the ark**. Naturally, in a city of which priests formed the ruling caste, the people would be acquainted with the general nature of the regulations of the law. Apparently it was only after the sacrificial feast that they forgot the reverence due to the symbol of Jehovah's presence among them.

Ver. 16.—**They returned to Ekron the same day**. The lords of the Philistines would of course take no part in this rejoicing, but, having seen the ark restored, and the people busied in making preparations for the sacrifice, returned immediately home.

Vers. 17, 18.—**The golden emerods**. We have here and in ver. 18 an enumeration of the gifts differing from, without being at variance with, that in ver. 4. They are still five golden emerods, for which the name here is not *ophalim*, but *tehorim*, the word always read in the synagogue (see ch. v. 6). From its use in the cognate languages it is pretty certain that it is rightly translated in our version. But besides these there were **golden mice, according to the number of all the cities**, &c. The priests had named only five mice, one for each of the lords of the Philistines ; but the eagerness of the people outran their suggestion, and not only the fenced towns, but even the unwalled villages sent their offering, lest they should still be chastised. **Country villages.** Literally, "the village" or "hamlet of the Perazi.' The Septuagint, a trustworthy authority in such matters, makes the Perazi the same as the Perizzite. Both words really signify "the inhabitant of the lowland," i. e. of the plain country of Phœnicia ; but from Zech. ii. 4, where Perazoth is translated "towns without walls," and from Ezek. xxxviii. 11, where it is rendered "unwalled villages," we may conclude that it had come popularly to mean an open village, though literally, in both these places, it means "the hamlets of the lowland." **Even unto the great stone of Abel**, &c. All this part of the verse is exceedingly corrupt, and requires large interpolations to obtain from it any meaning. Both the Vulgate and the Syriac retain the unmeaning word Abel ; but the Septuagint gives us what is probably the true reading : "and the great stone whereon they set the ark of Jehovah, which is in the field of Joshua the Beth-shemeshite, is a witness unto this day" (comp. Gen. xxxi. 52 ; Isa. xxx. 8).

Ver. 19. — **He smote the men of Beth-shemesh**, &c. In this verse also the text is undoubtedly corrupt. The Septuagint ascribes the sin not to all the people, but to "the sons of Jeconiah, who were not glad when they saw the ark, and he smote them." But as this reading is not supported by the other versions we may pass it by. The numbers, however, are evidently wrong. Fifty thousand men would imply a population of 250,000 people, whereas Jerusalem itself in its palmiest days never had a population of even 70,000. There were no large cities among the Israelites, but a scattered population living upon their fields, and with a few small walled towns here and there to protect them and their cattle in any sudden emergency. Kennicott, however, has satisfactorily explained the mistake. In the old way of denoting numbers by the letters of the alphabet an *'ain* = 70 had been mistaken for a *nun* with two dots = 50,000. The Syriac has 5000, that is, a *nun* with one dot. We must add that the Hebrew is not **fifty**

thousand and threescore and ten men, but "seventy men, fifty thousand men," without any article between, and with the smaller number first, contrary to Hebrew rule. The occasion of the calamity was probably as follows :—As the news of the return of the ark spread from mouth to mouth, the people flocked together to take part in the sacrifice, which would of course be followed by a feast. Heated thereat by wine, perhaps, and merriment, they lost all sense of reverence, and encouraged one another to look into the ark and examine its contents, though the words need not absolutely mean more than that "they looked at the ark." Even so the men of Beth-shemesh, as a city of priests, must have known that death was the penalty of unhallowed gazing at holy things (Num. iv. 20), and it is more than probable that those who were smitten were priests, because in them it would be a heinous sin ; for it was a repetition of that contempt for religion and its symbols which had been condemned so sternly in Eli's sons. The mere seeing of the ark was no sin, and had given the people only joy (ver. 13), but as soon as they had received it the priests ought to have covered it with a vail (Num. iv. 5). To leave it without a vail was neglectful, to pry into it was sacrilege. **Because Jehovah had smitten many of the people**, &c. This clause should be translated, "because Jehovah had smitten the people with a great smiting." The sudden death even of seventy men in an agricultural district, especially if they were the heads of the priestly families there, would be a great and terrible calamity, enough to fill the whole place with grief.

Vers. 20, 21.—**Who is able**, &c. Literally, "Who is able to stand before Jehovah, this holy God ?" A punishment so severe following upon their unhallowed temerity made the inhabitants of this city of priests eager to pass the ark on to others. They therefore **sent messengers to the inhabitants of Kirjath-jearim** to request them to fetch it away. Kiryath-yarim—for so it ought to be pronounced—means *the city of forests*—Wood-town, softened among us into Wooton. It was chosen apparently simply because it was the nearest town of any importance, and was therefore identified in early Christian times with the modern Kuriet-el-'anab, *grape-town*, the woods having given way to vines, and which is about ten miles off, on the road to Mizpah. Conder, however, doubts the correctness of this view, and places Kirjath-jearim at Sôba (see 'Tent Work,' i. 18 — 22).

HOMILETICS.

Vers. 1—9.—*Seeking light*. The facts are—1. The Philistines, oppressed by Providence, are uncertain what to do with the ark. 2. They, consulting the priests and diviners, are advised to send the ark away with all due honours and safeguards in case it is sent at all. 3. They are instructed how to carry out the advice, and warned not to refuse so to do. 4. Having done their best, they are to learn the truth from the issue. The incidents recorded furnish an instance of men seeking light. The events of the past few months had clashed with their material interests, and a series of observations had given rise to the opinion that these events were traceable to a restlessness on the part of the Hebrew Divinity. They did not wish to send back the ark. At the same time, there might be some error in the observations already made ; and if so, the troubles of the land and the presence of the ark would be a mere coincidence. This then was more than an ordinary case of perplexity. The Philistines knew the ark to be a superior power. Their doubt was whether it was indicating its mind by the events which troubled the land, and if so, what should be their conduct in relation to it. Thus the crude ideas and superstitious conduct of heathens embrace truths which find expression in modern experience.

I. There ARE IN HUMAN LIFE SEASONS OF DEEP PERPLEXITY, WHEN MEN WANT TO KNOW THE TRUTH CONCERNING GOD. More intelligently than the Philistines, we believe in God as *the* Lord of all, and the ever-present Worker in human affairs. Although events move on in well-defined lines of natural order, we know that God uses them to indicate his will, in conjunction with the intimations furnished by his word and Spirit. "The steps of a good man are ordered by the Lord." But amidst the voices that fall on the ear, and owing to dulness of perception, the soul sometimes is in great doubt concerning the mind of God, and what course should be pursued. This is especially true when events run counter to our desires and apparent interests, and when pride of spirit is cherished. Home may be wrecked. Business may bode disaster. Great decisions have to be taken. In each God has a will of his own, and conduct must have primary regard to him. The desire to do right is out of proportion to the perception of what in the particular instance *is* right.

II. The COURSE TO BE ADOPTED FOR THE REMOVAL OF PERPLEXITY. The Philistines proved themselves to be men of good sense by the course they took. The particular methods of obtaining more light will always depend on the spiritual state and previous attainments of those seeking it ; yet the main lines pursued will be the same. Summarising then the reference here to men of experience, and the advice given by them, we see a course available for all. 1. *To act on the experience of the past.* The priests and diviners were the embodiments of generations of experience in matters pertaining to the gods. Their advice, therefore, was the product of experience. Likewise for every man there is a rich store of wisdom in the events of his own life, in the records of history, in the judgment of contemporaries. Experience is a process which gradually enkindles and feeds a lamp within the spirit of a man. It is one of God's ways of making our path plain. Especially should the experience of others both show us the line of duty and warn us of the risk of shutting our eyes to the light. The reference to the experience of Pharaoh, under circumstances in some respects similar to theirs, was extremely judicious on the part of the Philistine priests. 2. *To fulfil all known religious obligations.* The advice to send back the ark intact, with due honours and with emblems of confession of sin, was based on the best religious knowledge of the people. The only way of ascertaining the real mind of the Hebrew Divinity was to honour and propitiate it. In this crude conception we have a great principle. Our escape from many perplexities depends largely on our careful performance of such religious duties as are imposed by our present knowledge. No man can know the will of God as he ought unless he obey that will as far as he knows it, and at any cost. If prayer is a clear duty, pray ; if confession of sin, confess ; if some great act of self-denial, perform it. The perceptive powers are clearer when calmed by true practical religion. The discharge of high duties fits for discerning others. A sound spiritual condition, conserved by daily observance of religious obligations, is a powerful solvent of doubts. "If any man will do the will of God, he shall know of the doctrine whether it be of God." 3. *To supplement these means by watching carefully for new indications.* The Philistines were to do all in their power to enable them to judge the *significance of coming events.* We cannot always make occasions for Providence to reveal itself; but we can fulfil all conditions for observing clearly, and then can watch the indications of the will which we know does speak to us in daily life, in the word and in the "still small voice." Then, acting in a reverent spirit, straitness will yield to a "large place," and darkness will be made light before us.

General lessons:—1. God has means of helping even the most ignorant to a fuller knowledge of his will. 2. By what wise and unlooked-for methods God accomplishes the realisation of his purpose among men who do not love him! 3. How superior the privileges of those who in mental darkness can cry direct for more light to the Father of light!

Vers. 10—15.—*Restored blessings.* The facts are—1. The kine bearing the ark, contrary to their instincts, go away from their home to Beth-shemesh. 2. The men of Beth-shemesh, seeing the returning ark, leave their occupations, and express their joy in sacrificial worship. 3. The Levites, exceeding their privileges, open the ark and examine its sacred contents. 4. The representatives of the Philistines observe the issue of their experiment and return. The rapid succession of incidents connected with the restoration of the ark illustrates several important truths.

I. The SUPREMACY OF GOD OVER HIS CREATURES. As a human device, the means for ascertaining the will of the God of Israel were excellent; and it is a mark of condescension that God should thus use imperfect men to effect his purpose. The men argued that he who commands disease and the ravages of vermin can, if disposed, effect his will through the agency of other creatures. God is not indisposed to exert his great power, should moral cause exist, even through the actions of men who act up to the measure of light attained to. The departure of the kine from their home and young to a strange land was a remarkable instance of the control of God over the strongest instincts. The seeming unnaturalness of the event is owing to our one-sided views of God's purposes and methods. It was contrary to their nature, as ordinarily exercised, to go from home. It was not contrary to the nature of things for them to do the will of their Maker. 1. It is a *reality in every case of animal life* that God's will is done. All creatures are " HIS." He formed their powers and gave them tendencies. Therefore every creature, in following its ordinary course, is actually carrying out a Divine intent. In this the kine were one with all cattle. Animals exist not for themselves. The end of their existence is moral and spiritual. The fabric of the universe and the lower creatures are for the development of the spiritual and eternal. In the case of the kine a great spiritual end was subserved—the restoration of the ark and consequent development of the " kingdom which cannot be moved." The original appointment of instinct and the specific control of it are acts identical in kind—supernatural. 2. There are *other instances of special control.* Balaam's ass was used to reprove the prophet. The lions were restrained from touching Daniel. In either case, as here, the event was connected with a manifest spiritual purpose; and who shall say that he who governs men and calms the sea shall not be free to control the movements of kine, as truly as when on his way to Jerusalem he guided the ass on which he sat? 3. It is a *means of teaching important truth.* This subordination of the most powerful impulses to the high purposes of God sets forth the truth that the most powerful natural attachments must yield to the requirements of the kingdom of God; as well perhaps as that, in coming years, the inferior creatures will subserve the advance of Christ's kingdom as certainly as that they will share in its blessings (Isa. xi. 6, 7; Matt. xiii. 32).

II. The JOY OF RESTORED BLESSINGS. The men of Beth-shemesh were the first honoured with a sight of the ark, and with the instinct of the true Israelite they appreciated the boon. 1. The *blessing now received was very great.* The significance of the ark to Israel cannot be fully expressed. Its return from captivity meant to the people a reinstatement in the favour of God. Their cry of anguish and the intercession of Samuel had been heard. Likewise the Church, after seasons of chastisement and loss of privilege, knows the greatness of the boon when God makes "the place of his feet glorious," and comforts Zion with the light of his countenance. 2. The *restoration was unexpected*. Both as to the fact and the means there was no anticipation of what occurred. Men were called from common toils to share in a great spiritual joy. Thus does God in his mercy break in on the cares and sorrows of common life with blessings in excess of our hopes. Israel was not able to devise means of delivery from Egypt, and surprise filled their minds when they saw the salvation of God. Christ's appearance after death even took away the power of utterance (Luke xxiv. 36—41). "For a small moment have I forsaken thee, but with great mercies will I gather thee." 3. The *expression of joy was natural*. It was most proper for a nature toned by recent chastisement to rush from the occupations of life to bid welcome to the long-wept-for ark of God. The recovery of property, the return of a lost son, nothing, could stir such deep feelings as the sign of the restored favour of Jehovah. The sacrifice of the kine was a form of penitence, homage, and gratitude culminating in highest joy. There is no joy like that of God's assured presence and favour. It is a gladness beyond that of the time when corn and wine increase. "Then was our mouth filled with laughter, and our tongue with singing."

III. Unlawful curiosity. A debased condition is not recovered from suddenly. Despite the repentance for past sin and gratitude for return of God's favour, the low tone of life consequent on former practices remained. As a consequence of the singular combination of good and bad qualities at this hopeful turn in affairs, the joy of the day was marred by a wicked, profane curiosity. This was the more culpable because the inhabitants were chiefly Levites, who must have been acquainted with the very strict prohibition to manifest any rude curiosity in reference to the sacred symbols (Exod. iii. 5; xix. 21; Num. iv. 20). 1. *Curiosity, though useful in the acquisition of knowledge, is sometimes wicked*. (1) In *human affairs*, as when it consists in an idle intrusion into the secret business or sorrows of others, or endeavour to obtain information with malicious intent. (2) In *Divine things*, as when it consists in a restless craving to know the secret purposes of God; or an endeavour to subject the Divine nature to the same kind of criticism and analysis as the work of his hand; or a fruitless endeavour to solve the mystery of his sovereignty in relation to the existence of evil; or a rude, irreverent attempt to penetrate into the great "mystery of godliness," the person of Christ. 2. The *wickedness of such curiosity is evident*, because of—(1) The *relation of man to God*. God is the infinite, eternal, holy One, of whom all that is is but the dim shadow. No ideas, no beings, not even the totality of the material and spiritual universe, are commensurate with him. On the other hand, man is only one among many creatures, limited in power, defective in nature, and incapable even of knowing the mysteries within his own breast. The moral evil in man unfits him for the vision of God even so far as that is possible to holy beings. The reverence due to God is due also in measure to man from man when justice and fellow-feeling bar the way to secret things. (2) The *habit is destructive to all that is good*. In no instance is evil better known by its fruits than in that of curiosity carried into Divine and human things. It is the ruin of reverence, which is the essence of worship, the guardian of all that is good in life, the crowning grace of conduct, and the spring of manifold virtues. It, when prevalent, renders man distrustful of his fellows, and loosens the bonds of home. No society can exist where all reverence is dead, and unbridled curiosity *is* its death.

IV. An important discovery. The five lords of the Philistines witnessed the restoration of the ark and the joy of the men of Beth-shemesh, and they became wiser men. They carried back the information that Jehovah was indeed the Destroyer of Dagon, the Controller of disease, the Lord of the brute creation, and unchanged Friend of Israel. Thus in defeat there was a triumph. Thus have we an indication of what will yet be. The foes of the Church of Christ will learn that he does hold the mastery over all. Ebbs there may be in the prosperity of the Church, but the *power* will reassert itself, and men will marvel both at the means and the fact. A great discovery will be made to all creatures when, after the conflict of ages with the *world-power*, the true Israel of God shall rejoice in the perfect and everlasting presence of their Lord,

Vers. 17—21.—*Trophies and chastisement.* The facts are—1. An enumeration by the Israelites of the golden images sent with the ark. 2. A terrible chastisement on the men of Beth-shemesh for their profane curiosity. 3. An effort to send the ark away, consequent on the terror created. These closing incidents of the restoration introduce for consideration—

I. The TROPHIES WON IN THE CONFLICT WITH foes of the Church of God. The golden emerods and mice were expressions of pagan superstition, and yet of submission to the superior power of Jehovah. In so far as they represented the five lords of the country, they were, in the eyes of Israel, evidence of the extent to which the might of Jehovah had been recognised. As the pot of manna and Aaron's rod were kept as memorials of what God had done, and prophetic of what he would do, so these images were noted in the annals of the time as signs of the same power in conquest. The remembrance of them would inspire courage, and also suggest due fear. The *Church of Christ has won many trophies.* Christ himself has led "captivity captive." He has in many instances snatched learning, science, art, statesmanship, and literature from the hand of the enemy, and made them contribute to the splendour of his kingdom. The extent to which trophies have been gathered deserves a register as truly as that given of the offerings of the Philistine lords. A calm reflection on this subject will inspire the Church for new efforts, and awaken gratitude for the past.

II. CHASTISEMENT FOR SINS OF PROFANITY. The joy of restoration was soon beclouded by the sorrow of death. The death of seventy men for the sin of treating the ark of God profanely raises the question of what there can be in such sins to merit so severe a chastisement. A general answer to such a question is that we are not in a position to determine for God the form, time, or extent of punishment due to sin. None can adjudge sin correctly but the perfectly holy One. There may be far more in an act than comes to the surface. Hence a reverent spirit is mostly concerned to know the fact. But there are a *few considerations* which may throw a little *light on the apparent severity of the chastisement.* 1. The *essential evil of the sin.* Much difficulty arises from not considering that some sins, and this especially, are a most virulent moral poison. They are at the very antipodes to the true spirit of love and obedience. Hence the dire consequences of their prevalence come more sharply into view when we remember the special contagion of example in such cases as these; for profanity of spirit is easily caught from example, and at once lowers the entire nature of a man. 2. The *liability to fall into it.* Not only is the sin heinous, and spread by example, but there is a predisposition to it which gives to the slightest encouragement from without double power. The evil already in man is good soil for such seed. If a sinful nature means aversion to a holy God, then it requires only a small encouragement to turn that aversion into the positive form of disregard of the Divine presence. 3. The *privileges of the transgressors.* Punishment is always proportionate to privilege abused. As officials in the service of God, the Levites were doubly criminal. Those who grow up amidst the sanctities and quiet reverence of the sanctuary or pious home commit deadly sin when they think or act towards God profanely. Had we all the details of the behaviour of the men of Beth-shemesh, no doubt the grossness of their conduct would stand out in fearful contrast with the privileges they had enjoyed as servants of the altar. 4. The *bearing on ages to come.* Every sin bears on the future, and so does its punishment. The deterrent effect of punishment is important; and its infliction with this reference is equitable, seeing that the sin acts on others and in ages to come. The effect of the death of the men at Beth-shemesh was seen in the salutary fear that came on all. "*This holy Lord God!*" It was a great gain to the world to have driven home this great truth. Nor would the effect end there. God has taught the entire world by the terrible things in righteousness which have been recorded. Here is *one* of the means of the education of the future race. Men are more reverent for what they read in the Old Testament. 5. The *infliction of death is a prerogative of God.* God sets the appointed time. Temporal death is not less of God when it comes gradually. Its direct infliction is the form in which he marks his disfavour and impresses his creatures. If seventy men sin, and commit in the civil-religious state of Israel a capital crime (Num. iv. 5, 15, 20), they of course must pay the prescribed penalty. It is an awful thing to die by the sudden stroke of God, but a more awful thing to be in a state of mind to deserve it.

Practical lessons:—1. Let us keep watch over the first risings of a spirit of levity. 2. Cultivate in young and old, by all conceivable means, reverence for all things connected with the worship of God. 3. Remember that the severity of God is really mercy to his creatures as a whole.

HOMILIES BY VARIOUS AUTHORS.

Ver. 10—ch. vii. 1. (BETH-SHEMESH and KIRJATH-JEARIM.)—*The return of the ark.* On the taking of the ark Israel sank to the lowest point of degradation. But " when the night is darkest then dawn is nearest." And the return of the sacred symbol was the first gleam of returning day. It was—

I. RESTORED BY DIVINE FAVOUR (vers. 10—12), which was—1. Exceeding *abundant* (1 Tim. i. 14). The people of Israel do not appear to have made any effort for its restoration, but God remembered them, and for their sake constrained their enemies to send back the precious treasure. " That is free love which never has been desired, never has been deserved, and never can be requited." 2. Shown in an *extraordinary* manner. It was brought by creatures acting contrary to their natural instincts, under a Divine impulse, in a direct line to the nearest border-city of Israel—Beth-shemesh (the house of the sun) ; a sign to Israel as well as the heathen. " Two kine knew their owner as (Isa. i. 3) Hophni and Phinehas knew him not " (Lightfoot). God's favour often comes by the most unlikely agencies and means. His power is universal, and all things serve him. 3. *Unexpected and surprising* (ver. 13). It was the time of harvest, and the men of Beth-shemesh were pursuing their ordinary secular occupations, thinking nothing of the ark, when they suddenly lifted up their eyes and beheld it approaching. It was found by them like " the treasure hid in the field." 4. *Distinguishing.* Shown toward Beth-shemesh beyond other cities, and toward Joshua beyond any other man ; for some reason, perchance, in the people as well as in the locality. The city we know was a priestly city (Josh. xxi. 10). " We shall probably be doing them no wrong if we suppose that they regarded its presence as an honour to themselves. It distinguished their township above all the cities of Israel."

II. RECEIVED WITH GREAT JOY (vers. 13—18). We can imagine how promptly they put aside their harvest work and gathered with one accord around the sacred object. Their joy was the joy of—1. *Gratitude* for the favour shown toward them (1 Kings viii. 62—66 ; Ezra vi. 16, 17). 2. *Devotion* (vers. 14, 15). " They offered burnt offerings and sacrificed sacrifices (peace offerings) unto the Lord." 3. *Hope ;* for in it they saw a proof of the power of God over the heathen, and a promise of their own freedom and prosperity. 4. And the day of their abounding joy was *commemorated* by means of the *great stone* on which the ark and the coffer containing the jewels of gold were set, " which remaineth unto this day."

III. REGARDED WITH IRREVERENT CURIOSITY (vers. 19, 20). 1. Their *conduct* consisted of " looking into (or upon) the ark." Whether they actually pried into it is uncertain. Whatever may have been the precise nature of their conduct, the spirit in which they acted was their chief offence in the sight of him who " looketh at the heart." There may be much sin in a look. 2. Their *sin* was great ; exhibiting want of reverence and godly fear, presumption, perhaps rationalism, recklessness, profanity (Levit. x. 3). A spirit of intelligent curiosity and inquiry is of unspeakable worth, being the principal means of discovering truth and promoting human progress ; but it should be ever joined with humility and reverence, as it has been in the greatest minds. " Fools rush in where angels fear to tread." The fact that Beth-shemesh was a city of the priests would lead us to expect better things of its inhabitants. " It is not improbable that in their festive rejoicing they may have fallen into intemperance, and hence into presumptuous irreverence, as it is thought was the case with Nadab and Abihu " ('Sp. Com.'). 3. Their *punishment* was severe ; for " of fifty thousand men, seventy died a sudden death " (Hengstenberg ; ver. 19). What is sent as a blessing is often turned by men themselves into a curse. 4. The effect was *morally beneficial* on the people generally. " Who is able to stand before this holy

Lord God?" &c. (ver. 20). (1) A conviction of his transcendent and awful *holiness*. "Our God is a consuming fire" (Heb. xii. 29). (2) A feeling of their own deep *sinfulness*, which the former never fails to produce (Isa. vi. 5; Luke v. 8). (3) A persuasion of the necessity of "righteousness and true *holiness*" in those among whom he dwells; for their request to the inhabitants of Kirjath-jearim, "Come ye down, and fetch it up to you," was the expression of something more than selfish dread (ch. v. 7), being caused by the belief that it would be more worthily honoured by others than by themselves. The conduct of a single city sometimes reveals the moral condition of a whole nation. And Israel was evidently not prepared to receive openly and fully the sign of God's presence among them, nor, until they should have passed through long and painful discipline, any further signal manifestation of his favour.

IV. REINSTATED IN RESPECTFUL BUT IMPERFECT HONOUR (ver. 21; ch. vii. 1). From Beth-shemesh it was taken (not to Shiloh, which had been rendered unworthy, and was now perhaps in ruins, but) to Kirjath-jearim (city of forests or woods, Ps. cxxxii. 6), where it was—1. Settled among a *willing people*, and in the house of a devout man—Abinadab, "on the hill." "God will find out a resting-place for the ark." When one people prove themselves unworthy of it, and wish to part with it, he will provide another people of greater worth, and ready to welcome it. "It is no new thing for the ark to be in a private dwelling-house." 2. Placed under special and proper *guardianship*. "Sanctified (consecrated) Eleazar his son to keep the ark from profane intrusion." Even in the most corrupt times there are individual instances of true piety. These are honoured of God, and for their sakes others are spared (Isa. i. 9). 3. *Disassociated* from the tabernacle and its services. After the capture of the ark the desecrated tabernacle appears to have been removed from Shiloh to Nob, where we find it long afterwards (ch. xxi. 6), attended by more than eighty priests, and subsequently to Gibeon (1 Kings iii. 4; 1 Chron. xvi. 39; xxi. 29; 2 Chron. i. 3, 6, 7), where it finally fell into decay and perished; the ark itself remained in Kirjath-jearim about seventy years, when it was removed to the house of Obed-edom (2 Sam. vi. 3, 11. Gibeah = the hill), and shortly afterwards to Jerusalem, where it abode "in curtains" until deposited in the temple of Solomon. The separation was anomalous, preventive of the full observance of the prescribed order of Levitical services, and indicative of the imperfect moral relations which subsisted between the people of Israel and their Divine King. 4. *Long disregarded* by the nation. No public assemblies appear to have met at the place where it stood; no sacrifices to have been offered there, no festivities held, as previously at Shiloh. It is not even mentioned again until the time of David, when it was said, "We inquired not at (or for) the ark in the days of Saul" (1 Chron. xiii. 3). Its neglect was permitted because its proper use was impossible until a thorough internal reformation and more complete union of the nation should be effected. "It was made evident that the nation was not yet worthy to receive the perfect fulfilment of the promise, 'I will dwell in your midst.' They endeavoured to dispose of the ark in the best possible way. It was *buried*, as it were, in Kirjath-jearim until the time when God would bring about its joyful resurrection" (Hengstenberg).—D.

Ver. 13. (BETH-SHEMESH.)—*The ark in harvest*. It was in the time of harvest that the ark was restored to Israel. Whilst the cornfields of the Philistines were wasted by an extraordinary plague, the valley of Beth-shemesh was covered with golden grain, and the men of that city were busily occupied in gathering it in (Ruth i. 6). But at the sight of the sacred symbol they left their secular occupation, gathered around it with great joy, and spent the day in "offering burnt offerings and sacrificing sacrifices to the Lord" (ver. 15). We may regard the harvest as representing *material* blessings, which are more richly bestowed at this season of the year than any other; the ark as representing *spiritual* blessings: "the law which came by Moses," and "the grace and truth which came by Jesus Christ;" the throne of grace, and the mercy and grace which are there obtained. And the fact just mentioned suggests a comparison between the former and the latter. Both come from the same hand; but spiritual are *superior* to material blessings, inasmuch as they—

I. REVEAL MORE OF THE DIVINE GOODNESS. Consider them—1. In the *principle* from which they proceed. The one class of benefits from benevolence in general;

the other from benevolence in the form of mercy. "According to his mercy he saved us" (Titus iii. 5). 2. In the *mode* by which they are communicated. The operation of the laws of nature (Gen. viii. 22 ; Jer. v. 21) ; the gift and sacrifice of his only begotten Son. "Through Jesus Christ." 3. In the *nearness* with which the great Benefactor comes to us. "Thou visitest the earth " (Ps. lxv. 9) ; but "blessed is the man whom thou choosest and causest to approach unto thee " (Ps. lxv. 4), in that closer fellowship which those who are reconciled in Christ enjoy, and whose hearts are the temple of thine abode, the habitation of thy Spirit. "Revelation is the voluntary approximation of the infinite Being to the ways and thoughts of finite humanity ; and until this step has been taken by Almighty grace, how should man have a warrant for loving him with all his mind, and heart, and strength ? " (A. H. Hallam).

II. INVOLVE MORE VALUABLE GOOD. 1. The one pertains to the *body*, the other to the *soul.* 2. The one to man considered simply as a *creature*, needing support ; the other as a *sinner*, needing forgiveness, renewal, salvation. 3. The one pertains to *time*, the other to *eternity ;* "bread that perisheth," "bread that endureth to ever-lasting life " (John vi. 27, 51) ; "that good part which cannot be taken away " (Luke x. 42).

III. PRODUCE MORE EXALTED JOY. "Rejoiced." "The joy in harvest " (Isa. ix. 3). 1. In its relation to *God.* The one is felt less and the other more directly in him. The difference is very much the same as that which exists between the joy felt at receiving a present from a friend at a distance, and that of seeing his face and holding personal intercourse with him. And what are all the harvests which the earth ever produced compared with one smile of the Father's countenance, one whisper of Divine love ? (Ps. iv. 6, 7). 2. In its influence on the *heart ;* elevating, purifying, enlarging, strengthening, satisfying it. 3. In its power over *circumstances.* The joy of our harvest may be speedily turned into sorrow by bereavement (ver. 19) and other afflictions ; but the joy which is felt in God is independent of outward circum-stances, lifts the soul above them (Hab. iii. 17, 18), lives in death, and is perfected in heavenly bliss.

IV. INCITE TO MORE COMPLETE CONSECRATION. 1. With respect to the *Giver.* His bestowment of " fruitful seasons, filling our heart with food and gladness," incites to *some* return to him (Exod. xxiii. 14—17) ; but his bestowment of mercy and grace, to the " whole burnt offering " of the man himself (Rom. xii. 1). 2. With respect to our *fellow-men.* The one incites to the giving of " those things which are necessary for the body " (Exod. xxiii. 11) ; the other incites (and effectually constrains) to the giving of what is good for the whole man, body and soul ; to self-sacrifice, and the " peace offerings " of brotherly kindness, and of charity toward all men. 3. The *whole course* of life ; not in one or two acts merely, but in a continued service of love to be completed in eternity.

Conclusion.—1. If God has bestowed upon you temporal good, rejoice not in it so much as in spiritual. 2. If he has withheld it, rejoice in the higher good which is yours. 3. "Seek first the kingdom of God," &c. (Matt. vi. 33).—D.

Vers. 19, 20.—*Irreverence.* I. THE OFFENCE. The Philistines are not blamed for sending away the ark of God on a wooden car. They did not know, or, if they knew, they had no means of observing, the mode of carriage by Levites which had been prescribed in the Mosaic law. In placing the ark on a new car never before used, and drawn by young cows that had never before worn a yoke, the Philistines meant to show respect. But the men of Beth-shemesh, being Israelites, and having Levites among them, knew, or ought to have known, the laws regarding the sacred ark. So they were more severely judged. Their familiar handling of the ark was a pre-sumptuous sin. Irreverence had grown during the years of misgovernment and license through which Israel had passed. It is evident that before the people would have dared to send for the ark to Shiloh, and take it into the field of battle, they must have lost much of the veneration with which their fathers had regarded the symbol of Jehovah's presence. And now the men of Beth-shemesh actually presumed to look into the ark, perhaps to ascertain whether the Philistines had put any gold into it, besides the golden offerings which they had placed in a separate coffer. So doing, they forgot, or wilfully broke, the law which allowed none of the people at large so much as to approach the ark, and required that the priests should cover it with a veil, before the Kohathites might carry it; and in carrying it those Levites might not lay their hands upon it, but were commanded to bear it on gilt staves passing through golden rings in the four corners of the sacred chest. Indeed the Kohathites, though thus honoured as the bearers of the ark, were forbidden not only to touch it, but even to go into the most holy place to see it covered under pain of death.

11. THE PENALTY. The Lord saw it needful to restore reverence for his law and for the ark of his testimony by striking a blow at presumption which would not be soon forgotten. Accordingly, seventy of the country people at Beth-shemesh were smitten with death. On the same ground, a few years later, was Uzzah the Levite stricken dead because he put his hand on the ark of God. What a warning against irreverence! For this cause men may die close to the ark of the covenant, perish beside the mercy-seat. Nay, that which is the greatest blessing may be turned by presumption into the greatest disaster. The savour of life may be turned into a savour of death. It is especially a warning to those who "name the name of the Lord." The ignorant and profane are judged, but not so strictly as those who "profess and call themselves Christians;" just as the Philistines were afflicted with boils, but the Israelites were visited with death. God is much displeased with listless minds, irreverent postures, and heedless spirits in his Church. No doubt it may be pleaded that such faults come of want of thought, and not of any evil intent; but want of thought is itself a very grave offence in such a matter as the service of God. Even levity is inexcusable; for, at all events in adult persons, it comes of hardness of heart, ingratitude to Christ, neglect of reflection on sacred themes and objects, engrossment of thought and affection with the things which are seen, and an indifference to the presence and purpose of the Holy Spirit. Let us study reverence. "God is greatly to be feared in the assembly of the holy ones, and to be had in reverence of all that are round about him."—F.

EXPOSITION.

CHAPTER VII.

Ver. 1.—At Kirjath-jearim the people reverently undertook the charge of the ark, and carried out their arrangements so carefully that no further calamity occurred. On its arrival they placed it in **the house of Abinadab in the hill**. More probably *at Gibeah*, as it is translated in 2 Sam. vi. 3, 4. In Josh. xv. 57 a village of this name is mentioned in the tribe of Judah not far from Kirjath-jearim (*ibid*. ver. 60), and probably Abinadab, who lived there, was a Levite, and so his house was chosen, and his son Eleazar **sanctified to keep the ark**. The names of both father and son are common in the Levitical genealogies, and none but a member of this tribe would have been selected for so holy a duty. If, however, the translation *in the hill* be preferred, we may suppose that it was because lofty heights were still considered fit places for Jehovah's worship, or there may even have been a "high place" there, of which Abinadab was the keeper. What exactly were the duties of Eleazar we cannot tell, as the word *to keep* is very indefinite; but probably, after the fearful ruin at Shiloh, all regular services and sacrifices were in abeyance until the re-

turn of happier times. Even here it was the men of the city who sanctified Eleazar, and not a priest.

THE REFORMATION OF ISRAEL (vers. 2—6). Ver. 2. — **While the ark,** &c. The literal translation of this verse is, "And it came to pass, from the day that the ark rested at Kirjath-jearim, that the time was long; for it was twenty years." The words dwell wearily upon the length of this mournful period, during which Israel was in a state of subjection to the Philistines, with its national life crushed to the ground, and its strength wasted by unjust exactions and misrule. For though the Philistines gave up the ark, there was no restoration of the national worship, nor did they abandon the political fruits of their victory at Eben-ezer. But quietly and calmly Samuel was labouring to put all things right. It was the principle of the theocracy that Jehovah punished his subjects for their sins by withdrawing his protection, and that on their repentance he took again his place at their head as their king, and delivered them. Samuel's whole effort, therefore, was directed to bringing the people to repentance. What means he used we are not told, nor what was his mode of life; but probably it was that of a fugitive, going stealthily from place to place that he might teach and preach, hiding in the caverns in the limestone range of Judæa, emerging thence to visit now one quarter of the country and now another, ever in danger, but gradually awakening, not merely those districts which were contiguous to the Philistines, but all Israel to a sense of the greatness of their sins, and the necessity of renewed trust and love to their God. And so a fresh spiritual life sprang up among the people, and with it came the certainty of the restoration of their national independence. **All the house of Israel lamented after Jehovah**. The word used here is rare, and the versions all differ in their translation of it. Really it is a happy one, embracing the two ideas of sorrow for sin, and also of returning to and gathering themselves round Jehovah. The Syriac alone retains this double meaning, by saying that " they all cast themselves down after Jehovah," *i. e.* that they sought him with deep humility. Gradually, then, a change of heart came over the people ; but the removal of the ark to a more fit place, and the restoration of Divine service with ministering priests and Levites, could take place only after the Philistine yoke had been broken. From ch. xiii. 19 — 22 we learn how vigilant and oppressive that tyranny was ; and the heart of the writer, in inditing this verse, was full of sorrow at the thought that the repentance of Israel was so slow and unready, and that therefore it had to wait twenty years before deliverance came.

Ver. 3.—**If ye do return,** &c. At length everything was ripe for a change, and the reformation wrought privately in their hearts was followed by public action. Samuel's secret addresses had no doubt been watched with anger by the Philistines, but he now ventures upon open resistance ; for this public summons to Israel to put away its idols by a national act was a summons also to an uprise against foreign domination. We must suppose that the people had often assured Samuel in his wanderings of the reality of their repentance, and of their readiness to stake everything upon the issue of war. As a statesman, he now judges that the time has come, and convenes a national assembly. But everything would depend upon their earnestness. They were virtually unarmed ; they would have to deal with an enemy long victorious, and who held the most important posts in their country with garrisons. Terrible suffering would follow upon defeat. Was their faith strong enough, their courage desperate enough, for so fearful a risk ? Especially as Samuel is never described to us as a warrior or military hero. He could inspire no confidence as a general. He himself makes everything depend upon their

faith, and all he can promise is, " I will pray for you unto Jehovah" (ver. 5).

Ver. 4.—**Then the children of Israel did put away** [the] **Baalim and** [the] **Ashtaroth**. This must have been done by a public act, by which at some time previously arranged the images of their Baals and Astartes were torn from their shrines, thrown down, and broken in pieces. Of course this was an overt act of rebellion, for these deities were especially Phœnician idols, and subsequently it was the Phœnician Jezebel who tried so fanatically to introduce their worship into Israel in Ahab's time. To cast off the Philistine deities was equivalent to a rebellion generally against Philistine supremacy. Baal and Astarte, the husband and the wife, represented the reproductive powers of nature, and under various names were worshipped throughout the East, and usually with lewd and wanton orgies.

Ver. 5.—**Gather all Israel to Mizpeh**. Mizpah, for so the place should be spelt, means a *watch-tower* (Gen. xxxi. 49), and so is a not uncommon name for spots among the hills commanding an extensive outlook. This was probably the Mizpah in the tribe of Benjamin, distant about five miles from Jerusalem (see Conder, ' Tent Work,' i. 25) ; and though Samuel may have partly chosen it as a holy place (Judges xi. 11 ; xx. 1), yet the chief reason was probably its lofty situation, 500 feet above the neighbouring tableau, which itself was 2000 feet above the sea level. It was thus difficult to surprise, and admirably adapted for warlike purposes. The gathering of the people at Mizpah was the necessary result of the public insult offered to the Philistine gods, and virtually a declaration of war, as being an assertion of national independence.

Ver. 6.—**They . . . drew water, and poured it out before Jehovah**. While the drawing of water was a joyful act (Isa. xii. 3 ; John vii. 37, 38), as symbolising the winning from the depths below of the source of life and health, the pouring it out before Jehovah expressed sorrow for sin, and so it is explained by the Chaldee Paraphrast : " They poured out their heart in penitence like water before the Lord" (comp. Ps. xxii. 14). It might here also signify weakness and powerlessness, the being " as water spilt upon the ground, which cannot be gathered up again " (2 Sam. xiv. 14). They further expressed their sorrow by fasting, enjoined " for the afflicting of their souls " upon the great day of atonement (Levit. xvi. 29, 31 ; xxiii. 27, 32 ; Num. xxix. 7). And to these symbolical acts they joined the confession of the mouth, acknowledging that "they had sinned against Jehovah."

And Samuel judged the children of Israel in Mizpeh. That is, he now became the acknowledged ruler of Israel in things temporal, both civil and military, as he had previously been in things spiritual by virtue of his office as prophet. This was, of course, the result of the decisive action he had taken in summoning this national convention; but the words strongly suggest that there was some direct appointment, or at the very least a national acknowledgment of Samuel's authority, especially as they precede the history of the defeat of the Philistines. He had summoned the people together as Nabi, prophet, and when he said, "I will pray for you unto Jehovah," there was the implied meaning that he would be with them only in that capacity. But when the time came to appoint a general, who would act under him as Barak had acted under Deborah, the great chiefs, probably, who saw in him the prime mover of all that was being done, urged him also to take the command, and upon his consent he became also Shophet or judge.

ISRAEL'S DELIVERANCE FROM THE TYRANNY OF THE PHILISTINES (vers. 7—14). Vers. 7, 8.—**When the children of Israel heard it, they were afraid of the Philistines.** This was perfectly natural, and implied no intention on the part of the Israelites not to fight it out. No dominant nation would permit a subject race to hold such a meeting as Samuel's at Mizpah without having recourse to arms; but the Philistines acted with such promptness and vigour as brought home to the assembled Israelites not merely the conviction that they would have to fight, but that they must do it at once, and with the combined forces of the enemy. In spite, nevertheless, of their fears, they determine to await the attack, and that this decision was taken in faith their own words prove. For they say, **Cease not to cry unto Jehovah our God for us, that he will save us out of the hand of the Philistines.** The words literally are, "Be not silent from crying," &c. Let him mediate for them with God, and they will await the onslaught of the foe.

Ver. 9.—**And Samuel took a sucking lamb.** Samuel now appears as priest, and makes intercession and atonement for them. The lamb was at least seven days old, for so the law required (Levit. xxii. 27), but probably not much older; for the word, a rare one, occurring elsewhere only in Isa. lxv. 25, means something small and tender: this then **he offered for a burnt offering wholly unto Jehovah.** The A. V. translates in this way because *chalil*, "whole," is masculine, while *'olah*, "a burnt offering," is feminine; but *chalil* had in course of time come to be used as a substantive (Levit. vi. 23; Deut. xiii. 16; xxxiii. 10), and is really here in opposition to *'olah*, and so the two together signify "a whole burnt offering," and clearly indicate that the lamb was entirely consumed by fire. *'Olah* means *that which ascends*, and symbolised devotion and consecration to God. *Chalil* intensified this signification, and showed that all was God's, and no part whatsoever reserved for the priest or the offerer. And thus then Samuel's burnt offering implied that the people gave themselves unreservedly to Jehovah. **And Jehovah heard him.** Really, "Jehovah answered him," by the thunder mentioned in ver. 10. For thunder was regarded as God's voice (ch. ii. 10), and in Ps. xxix. we have a poetic description of its majesty and power. Express mention is also made in Ps. xcix. 6 of Jehovah having thus answered the prayers of Moses (Exod. xix. 19), and of Samuel.

Vers. 10, 11.—**As Samuel was offering,** &c. We have here a detailed and lively description of the whole event. The lamb is still burning upon the altar, and Samuel still kneeling before it, when the Philistine hosts appear upon the lofty plateau just below the hill of Mizpah, and marshal themselves for battle. It seemed as if Israel's case were hopeless, and many a heart, no doubt, was bravely struggling against its fears, and scarcely could keep them down. But as the enemy drew near the electric cloud formed in the heavens, and **Jehovah thundered with a great voice** (so the Hebrew) **on that day upon the Philistines.** Alarmed at so unusual a phenomenon, the Philistines hesitate in their advance, and Samuel, seeing their consternation, gives the signal for the charge, and Israel, inspirited by the voice of Jehovah, rushes down the hill upon the foe. Full of enthusiasm, they forget the poorness of their weapons, and the weight of their impetuous rush breaks through the opposing line. And now a panic seizes the Philistines; they attempt no further resistance, but flee in dismay from the pursuing Israelites. Their course would lead them down a huge valley 1000 feet deep, at the bottom of which was a torrent rushing over a rocky bed; nor was their flight stayed **until they came under Beth-car.** Of this place we know nothing, but probably it was a fastness where the Philistines could protect themselves from further attack.

Ver. 12.—**Then Samuel took a stone, and . . . . called the name of it Eben-ezer.** We saw on ch. iv. 1 that the place where Israel then suffered defeat, but which now received a more happy name, was an open plain, over which the people now chased their then victorious enemies. Here, then, Samuel set up a memorial, according to Jewish custom, and called its name *Help-stone*. In giving his reason for it, **hitherto hath Jehovah helped us,** there is a plain indication of the need of further assistance. There was a long struggle before them, and Jehovah, who had aided them so mightily at its beginning, would also help them unto the end. The memorial stood halfway **between Mizpeh and Shen,** both which names have the article in Hebrew, because one signifies *the watch-tower*, the other *the tooth*. It was a steep, pointed rock, but is not mentioned elsewhere. *Dent*, the French for tooth, is a common name for mountains in the Alps and Pyrenees.

Ver. 13.—**So the Philistines were subdued.** Not completely, for we find that they had garrisons in Israel when Saul was made king; but it was a thorough victory for the time, and was followed up, moreover, by an invasion of Philistia, in which Samuel recovered the towns which had been wrested from Israel upon the western borders of Judah and Benjamin. Moreover, the enemy **came no more into the coast of Israel.** That is, all invasions ceased. **And the hand of Jehovah was against the Philistines all the days of Samuel.** This, of course, includes the reign of Saul, till within four years of his death; for Samuel continued to be prophet, and to a certain extent shophet, even when Saul was king. The words, moreover, imply a struggle, during which there was a gradual growth in strength on Israel's part, and a gradual enfeeblement on the part of the Philistines, until David completely vanquished them, though they appear again as powerful enemies in the days of King Jehoram (2 Chron. xxi. 16). It is certain, however, that fifteen or twenty years after this battle the Philistines were again in the ascendant (ch. xiii. 19—23), and it was this which made the Israelites demand a king (ch. ix. 16). But it is the method of the Divine historians to include the ultimate results, however distant, in their account of an event (see on ch. xvi. 21; xvii. 55—58); and Israel's freedom and the final subjugation of the Philistines were both contained in Samuel's victory at Mizpah.

Ver. 14.—**From Ekron even unto Gath.** Not that Israel captured these two towns, but they mark the limits upon the borders, within which the Philistines had previously seized towns and villages belonging to Israel, and which Samuel now recovered. **There was peace between Israel and the Amorites.** In Israel's weakness the remains of this once powerful Canaanitish stock had probably made many a marauding expedition into the land, and carried off cattle and other plunder; now they sue for peace, and unite with Israel against the Philistines.

SAMUEL'S CONDUCT AS JUDGE (vers. 15—17). Vers. 15, 16.—**And Samuel judged Israel all the days of his life.** As long as Samuel lived there was no clear limitation of his powers as shophet compared with those of Saul as king. In putting Agag to death (ch. xv. 33) he even claimed a higher authority, and though he voluntarily left as a rule all civil and military matters to the king, yet he never actually resigned the supreme control, and on fitting occasions even exercised it. It was, however, practically within narrow limits that he personally exercised his functions as judge in settling the causes of the people; for **Bethel, and Gilgal, and Mizpeh** were all situated in the tribe of Benjamin. Both Bethel and Mizpah were holy spots, and so also, probably, was Gilgal; and therefore we may conclude that it was the famous sanctuary of that name (see ch. xi. 14), and not the Gilgal mentioned, in 2 Kings ii. 1; iv. 38. For this latter, situated to the south-west of Shiloh, near the road to Jerusalem, had no religious importance, and would not, therefore, attract so many people to it as one that was frequented for sacrifice. Probably, too, it was upon the occasion of religious solemnities that Samuel visited these places, and heard the people's suits.

Ver. 17.—**His return was to Ramah.** We have seen that Elkanah was a large landholder there, and Samuel had now apparently succeeded to his father's place. **And there he built an altar unto Jehovah.** This old patriarchal custom (Gen. xii. 7) long continued, and it was only gradually that local shrines and worship on high places were superseded by attendance upon the temple services at Jerusalem. At this time there was especial need for such altars. The established worship at Shiloh had been swept away, the town destroyed, the priests put to the sword, and the ark, though restored, was resting in a private dwelling. Probably Samuel had saved the sacred vessels, and much even of the tabernacle, but no mention of them is here made. We see, however, both in the erection of this altar and all through Samuel's life, that the Aaronic priesthood was in abeyance, and that he was not only prophet and judge, but also priest. In thus restoring the priesthood in his own person he was justified not merely by his powers as prophet, but by necessity. Gradually, with more prosperous times, matters returned to their regular channel; but even when Ahiah, the grandson of Eli, was with Saul (ch. xiv. 3), he was employed not for the offering of sacrifice, but for divining with the Urim and Thummim. On a most important occasion the offering of sacrifice is spoken of as undoubtedly Samuel's right, and when he delayed his coming no mention is made of a priest, but Saul is said to have offered the victim himself (ch. xiii. 9). It is plain, therefore, that we must not tie down the priesthood too tightly to the house of Aaron; for throughout there lies in the background the idea of a higher priesthood, and with this Samuel was invested, as being a type of him who is a Priest for ever after the order of Melchisedek (comp. ch. ii. 35).

HOMILETICS.

Vers. 1, 2.—*Fitness for service.* The facts are—1. At the request of the terrified men of Beth-shemesh the men of Kirjath-jearim bring the ark to their high place. 2. Arrangements are made in the house of Abinadab for the due care of the ark. 3. The time of the sojourn of the ark in this place, up to the date of Samuel's test of repentance, was twenty years. 4. Towards the close of this period the people long for the full restoration of the Divine favour. A new stage was being entered on in the process of restoration to full privileges, and God must have men fitted to the occasion. The ark could not go to Shiloh for evident reasons; so far as the Divine will could be gathered from the controlled action of the kine, Beth-shemesh was the place for it in which to rest. But the profane conduct of the officials proved that the privilege must be forfeited, and the unmitigated terror of the survivors indicated that they possessed not the spiritual qualifications for the respectful, loving guardianship of Israel's glory. For some reason the men of Kirjath-jearim had a reputation which justified the belief that they dared and could safely convey and keep what their neighbours dare not touch. Their actions justified this belief.

I. NEW FORMS OF SERVICE ARE CONSTANTLY ARISING IN THE UNFOLDING OF GOD'S PURPOSES. There was once a need of workmen to build the ark, of men to bear it, of kine to bring it back, and now of men to carry and keep it in all decency and order. Emergencies are inherent in the outworking of the Church's mission. Ages bring their demands. Education, national affairs, assaults on truth, openings for the gospel in foreign lands, and many other things, call for new lines of action or modifications of old. And thus it will be till the world is brought to Christ.

II. THERE ARE ALWAYS IN RESERVE THE MEN FITTED FOR THE WORK GOD HAS TO BE DONE. If Beth-shemesh cannot supply the men who know how to behave properly towards the sacred symbol, there are others elsewhere. The qualities are being acquired parallel with the providential processes that evolve the new demand. God takes care of all sides of his holy cause. Those disqualified must yield the privilege of new and important service to the qualified, and God knows where these are. In every age he has his chosen, secret methods of laying hold of ability, learning, strength of purpose, and whatsoever else may be required to do his will.

III. THE FUNDAMENTAL FITNESS FOR GOD'S SERVICE ON NEW OCCASIONS IS TRUE REVERENCE AND INTEREST. Many minor qualities were requisite to the bringing and caring for the ark, but the primary was that of proper reverence for the ark of God and due interest in its sanctity and use. The men of Beth-shemesh lacked this; for they lost true reverence in terror and dread, and they were distrustful of their ability to keep the ark with due honour to it and benefit to themselves. Here we have in *incidental contrast a religion* characterised by *dread, and a religion of true reverence.* 1. The *religion of dread* is a sense of infinite holiness and power unrelieved by a recognition of other Divine attributes. The men of Beth-shemesh had been struck with the awful holiness of Jehovah, and of his mighty power expressing holiness in acts of swift judgment. Thus, generally, when religion consists mainly in this there is a shrinking from God's presence; attention to ordinances under the sheer force of conscience. In so far as Christian men—so called—know only such a religion they approximate towards paganism. The *religion of true reverence is a sense of infinite holiness and power toned by a trustful love.* The men of Kirjath-jearim were not perfect, but they had as correct views as their neighbours of the holiness and power of Jehovah; and yet it is obvious, from the quiet, interested manner in which they received and provided for the ark, that they in some degree loved and trusted their God. In true reverence the awe created by ineffable holiness and almighty power is mitigated by the remembrance that HE is merciful and gracious, and cares for his people, even in their self-brought sorrows. When this reverence is perfected in Christian life by a due appreciation of the august majesty and love seen in the sacrificial work of Christ, the heart rests in God with all the reverential love of a child. Duty and privilege then are coincident.

General lessons :—1. We should be on the look-out for any new work God may have for us to do. 2. Never despair of God finding agents for the various enterprises opened up by his own providence. 3. Cultivate every possible quality, and hold it in readiness for any use which God may make clear. 4. Court the honour and bliss of welcoming to city or home the treasures dear to God, be they ordinances of worship or those commissioned to do his will; for such bring blessings with them— "angels unawares."

Divine reserve. The return of the ark was an outward sign of the returning favour of God, and was so understood by the men of Beth-shemesh. But the full service of the tabernacle, with the ark as its centre and glory, was not established. Nor were the Philistines deprived of their hold on Israel. The Divine power was held in reserve. The set time to favour Zion in plenitude had not arrived. The reasons for this are clear. The people were too degraded to enjoy the full benefit of the services and festivals. A degenerate priesthood, steeped in vice, cannot at once pass on to the holy duties of Jehovah's worship. A regenerative process requires time, and twenty years was not too long for the old generation of priests to die off and give way to men brought up under better influences. The *general truth here set forth is,* that it is in *the heart of God to do great things for his people, but that for good reasons he holds himself,* so to speak, *in reserve*—veiling his glory, bestowing his blessing sparsely. Indeed, there is even a wider application of the truth than in relation to the Church. Take a few illustrations.

I. CREATION. The material and spiritual universe is the outcome of the power and wisdom of God. But vast and intricate as it is, no one can suppose that it is coextensive with all that is in his nature. There are not two infinites. The power and wisdom of God are in excess of what are traceable in the works he has formed. There is a vast *reserve,* which for aught we know may some time come out in an order of things not now conceived or deemed possible. It is a crude philosophy which teaches that God has done all he intends to do in the way of positive creation. Every new spirit that comes into being is an evidence of the Divine reserve.

II. REVELATION. There is a varied revelation of God, but in each case it may be said that, supposing we have learnt all they teach, we "know only in part." For as there is more in God than in his works and word, there is a reserve of truth which may yet be drawn upon. In the gradual bestowment of revelation we see how God keeps back from one age what he gives to another. Christ had many things to say once which his disciples could not then bear to hear. There must be deep and far-reaching principles of the Divine government which underlie the at present revealed facts of the Trinity, atonement, human responsibility, and future punishment; and these are kept out of full view till, perhaps, we become free from the flesh.

III. NATIONAL PROSPERITY. All *true* national prosperity is of God. If it comes not to men, it is because he withholds the blessings desired. The absence of prosperity has a practical side; it means that God reserves good because conduct and motive are not what he approves. There was nigh at hand all the power and wisdom by which Israel should cease to depend on Philistines for axes and coulters, but it came not forth. Had Israel in earlier or later times been more true to God, he would have "fed them also with the finest of the wheat" (Ps. lxxxi. 13—16).

IV. CHURCH PRIVILEGES AND USEFULNESS. "Glorious things" are spoken of Zion. The Church inherits a wondrous destiny. She is to be the envy of the world. Her "feet" are to be "beautiful;" her garments "white;" her influence as the "light" and "salt." And all this not by virtue of what may be in the Church of herself, but because of the power and grace of God within her. If she is "in the dust," we ask the cause; the first answer is, because God stays his hand, keeps the residue of the Spirit, holds himself in reserve. The second answer is, that this Divine reserve is in consequence of the Church having backslidden from her God and disqualified herself from being a vehicle for the full flow of the blessing that is to enrich mankind. The Divine light is to shine from "*golden* candlesticks."

V. PERSONAL RELIGIOUS EXPERIENCE. Personal religion is, in one sense, the passing into and dwelling within the soul of the power and love of God—by the Holy Spirit. It is the proper heritage of a believer to enjoy a sense of the Divine favour not known to the unbelieving. A vision of God sweet and blessed comes to the pure in heart. Christ manifests himself as he does not to the world. But the backsliding soul does not share in the full bliss. "Why art thou cast down?" is often asked. The answer is, there is not the spiritual fitness for *perfect* fellowship. Some "idols" have been cherished. Divine reserve is a discipline to cause the heart to lament after God.

　　General lessons :—1. There is ample ground for believing that all things shall be subdued unto Christ. His *great* power is yet to be put forth. 2. Inquiry should be made as to the existence of anything in motive, conduct, or spirit which keeps the Church from enjoying the full exercise of the power of God. 3. We may profitably reflect on what might be ours in private life if by our devotedness to God we secured more of the "residue of the Spirit."

　　Vers. 3—12.—*Ebenezer.* The facts are—1. Samuel calls on the people to prove their desire to return to God by putting away idols and preparing their hearts for a blessing. 2. A response to the call is followed by a summons to Mizpah for prayer and humiliation. 3. A rumoured approach of the Philistines excites fear, and an urgent request for Samuel's intercession with God. 4. While Samuel is engaged in worship God discomfits the assailing Philistines by thunder. 5. The victory is commemorated by raising the stone Ebenezer. This paragraph is to be considered in relation to Israel's true goal in life—to fulfil the Messianic purposes of their existence as a chosen people. Associated with this ulterior object, and subservient to it, was the full favour and blessing of God. This, again, was to be indicated by the restoration in developed form of the holy services and festivals connected with the ark and the sanctuary. The turning-point in the degeneracy had come in a sense of desolation and misery consequent on the recent defeat and the capture of the ark. The return of the ark gently fanned the flickering flame of hope, but as yet the goal was far distant, and the conditions of attaining to it were very unsatisfactory. The narrative sketches, in the instance of Israel, an outline of *true effort towards the goal of life,* and the encouragements to persevere in the effort. The *Christian Church and the individual soul have each* an issue of life to attain to. It is also true of them that they start from a relatively low and unsatisfactory position, and will succeed in their endeavour only as they observe conditions inseparable from their position.

　　I. The MEANS AND CONDITIONS OF REALISING LIFE'S PURPOSE. Confining attention to those involved in this portion of history, we find them to be—1. *A hearty renunciation of all that is alien to the mind of God.* Idols had to be put aside. Man is attached to idols. They may be feelings entertained, passions gratified, favourite motives cherished, customs cultivated, aims kept in view, objects unduly loved. The "covetousness" which clings to forbidden things is "idolatry." In so far as these things absorb our feeling and receive our attention after that God has indicated that they ought not, so far do we set them up as deserving regard and love in preference to himself. The Church and the individual must search and cast aside all that is alien to the mind of God. 2. *Confession of sin and humiliation of spirit.* No soul can attain to its goal, no Church can do its work and acquire purity and freedom, apart from sincere confession and deep humiliation for what is past. Israel's gathering at Mizpah to acknowledge their guilt and bow before God, as though they were "like water spilt on the ground" (ver. 6; cf. 2 Sam. xiv. 14), was a great step towards recovery of strength and joy. Seasons may arise when special services shall alone give due expression to the sense of shame and sorrow for the past; but daily sin needs to be confessed and the spirit to be chastened before the holy One whom we serve. Power for holy deeds grows out of true penitence. 3. *Adaptation of the mind to a better course in the future.* The "preparing" of "the heart" unto the Lord implies a self-control, a searching of the seat of feeling, a cleansing process by such spiritual helps as God may give, a fitting one's self internally for a higher mode of life than yet has been known. Internal, carefully-sought reformation is a guarantee of improved external acts. Most of us are not in a mood adapted to the grand future which God has in reserve. We are to seek it. Fellowship with God more pure, and close, and constant is not the result of accident, but is the issue of an earnest endeavour. 4. *Special prayer for power to live a better life.* The cry of Israel's heart was a prayer for more than human aid to help them to perfect the renunciation of false gods and the contrition due for sin. And the aid of the prophet's powerful intercession was to give more effect to their own cry. Life, to be blessed in issue, must be one of prayer—an incessant cry for help to live. And, also, recourse must be had to the true Intercessor, who is "touched with the feeling of our infirmities." The Church has not duly appreciated this means of accomplishing its purpose in the world. In so far as the individual Christian is a man of prayer, and looks daily to the Intercessor, will he press on till he attains to "the mark and prize of his high calling." 5. *A due recognition of the atonement of Christ.* Not without reason was the "sucking lamb" offered when Israel sought the Lord. The "way to God" was clearly recognised. And the life of man will be right and will press on to a safe and blessed issue only so far as the Lamb of God is recognised as the "way." The Church can fulfil her mission in the world only by faithfully exhibiting the cross of Christ to the guilty and desponding. 6. *Determined conflict with the natural enemies of God and man.* Israel had to fight Philistines. Only on condition of supplementary acts of confession and worship, by earnest conflict with the foe, could they secure peace in their borders, and finally answer their Messianic purpose of existence. In like manner the Church and the individual must "war a good warfare." The militant character should be maintained as long as there is an enemy to Christ in the heart as in the world.

II. The ENCOURAGEMENT TO PERSEVERE TO THE END. The raising of the stone "Ebenezer" was an act retrospective and prospective. The hopes inspired in the mind of Samuel when first he undertook the work of reformation were being justified by events, and he desired the people to share in his expectations. In so far as fidelity has been shown by the Christian Church or by the individual in complying with the requirements of life's true issue, so far is there in every instance a ground of confident expectation. For consider — 1. *The primary basis of confidence.* In Israel's case the return of the ark within their borders was a pledge of mercy for the penitent. They were not lost without remedy. And in the more glorious manifestation of God in Christ we have the pledge that there is mercy for all, and that all energy spent conformably to the object of his presence among men will be crowned with success. 2. *The consciousness of being on the side of right.* There is in even the fallen a remnant of the original sense of right which furnishes a ground of appeal, and assures of responsibility. The guiltiest man in Israel knew that to forsake Jehovah was wrong. In turning unto the Lord and seeking his favour the people were sustained by the deep conviction of right in hope of attaining the desired good. The moral support of such a consciousness is great to every one. The soul that seeks holiness and eternal life may look on with hope. A voice within declares that, being on the side of eternal right, we must, so far, win. The struggling Church of Christ feels the force of the same conviction which gives the foretaste of victory. 3. *The manifest improvement in one's condition proportionate to desire and effort.* In so far as Israel's desire and effort were sincere and carried through, to that degree did the personal, domestic, and national life rise above the baneful circumstances resulting from former sins. Every good feeling, every tear of penitence, every casting away of idols, left its mark on the surface of society, and indicated what might be expected if only the reformation be carried through. God gives according to our work. Likewise all Christian desire and effort succeed so far as they are genuine. The acquired results of fidelity to God confirm the truth that everything promised shall in due time be realised. Each step in the ascent heavenwards is to a clearer view of the summit of our ambition. 4. *The assured sympathy of the great Intercessor.* Perhaps nothing gave downcast Israel so much encouragement of final restoration to God, with its ulterior consequences, as the effort of Samuel, the chosen prophet, to assure them of his full sympathy. He was their friend, and in him they found solace and hope. As a prefigurement of the one true Intercessor, we see here what reason we have for boldness. The pains which Christ has taken to assure every earnest soul personally, and the Church collectively, of his deep sympathy are most extraordinary. By word, deed, tears, sorrow, death, yes, by resumed life and outpouring of the Spirit, he would have us know that we are not *alone.* The past may be black and full of sadness, but with him as Helper and Friend who may not hope on? 5. *The co-operation of Providence.* Providence works for men in forms adapted to their mental and spiritual condition. Whether the thunder which discomfited the Philistines was a special exertion of Divine power out of the ordinary course of atmospheric changes, or a coincidence brought about by him who, in the primary settlement of nature, foresees his own relations to his people, and harmonises physical and moral lines, the result abides. God fights for those who fight for righteousness. Providence does not always favour the search after wealth, or pleasure, or ease, but it *does* always favour the Christian in his conflict with sin. A "besom of destruction" is being formed for use against the forces of evil. Never in the history of the world has a case arisen in which defeat has come on any soul that has sincerely trusted in God and conformed to his requirements. They that "trust in the Lord are as Mount Zion, which cannot be moved." The battle is not to the strong, but to those who are under the cover of the Almighty hand.

III. The GROUNDS OF ENCOURAGEMENT, WHEN FAIRLY BROUGHT BEFORE THE MIND, OPERATE IN TWO WAYS. 1. *Retrospectively.* The retrospective survey, which brings the mind in view of facts bearing on the future, also awakens gratitude for what has been already accomplished. It was with no formal thankfulness that Samuel inscribed "Ebenezer;" and the poor wayward people, whose sins had borne such bitter fruit, caught his spirit as they reflected on the mercy that was proved, by recent events, not to be clean gone for ever. Sinful hearts, when penitent, love to look back on even the slightest sign of God's love and care. The development of gratitude itself is the introduction of a new and helpful power in the sore conflict with sin and sorrow. If only men would consider, by careful retrospection, what God has done for them! Men too often dwell on their own deeds and failings, and so nourish despondency. "Be ye thankful" is apostolic exhortation. And, despite all defections, blunders, and disasters of the Church, how tenderly and wisely he has led, chastened, and worked with the people called after his holy name. Powerful reasons still exist for the contending hosts to raise their cheerful, grateful "Ebenezer." 2. *Prospectively.* "Hitherto" is relative. There is a future term in the thought; and its use, as the result of a survey of grounds of encouragement, means that *the heart is bracing itself for new exertions.* Samuel would work on, devising in cheerful spirit new means of further raising the people, while they would avail themselves of his assistance to regain lost joys and honours. A higher tone, a more vigorous effort, would mark the coming years.

Practical lessons:—1. It is very useful in private, domestic, and Church life occasionally to take a solemn review, with appropriate religious exercise, of progress made, and of what God has done for us. 2. We should study more carefully the formative power of a frequent consideration of the mercies of God. 3. When engaged in actual religious work and worship to which God has clearly called us, we may be certain that our general interests will not be allowed to suffer from the hand of enemies, seen or unseen. 4. If we honour God to the extent of our spiritual attainments, power will come for doing him still greater honour.

Vers. 13—17.—*First-fruits of repentance.* The facts are—1. Israel enjoy freedom from the oppression of the Philistines and regain lost cities. 2. Their restless ancestral enemy the Amorite is quiet. 3. Samuel quietly and happily attends to his civil functions. 4. Ramah, the home of Samuel, is blessed with an altar to Jehovah. The mention of these suggestive facts immediately after the reference to the call to repentance and its response exhibit the natural results of the efforts of prophet and people. A fruitful theme is given.

I. In RELATION TO ISRAEL THESE FRUITS WERE MOST IMPORTANT; just such as a nation might well prize. An active, powerful foe was held in restraint. Territory and cities were restored to the government and general influence of a true man of God. Their fathers' foe, who disputed the march of Joshua, and ever lay as a savage beast by their side, was controlled by an unseen hand. An orderly and beneficent civil administration, diligently maintained on religious principles, was enjoyed by the various districts, and the residence of the ruler of the people was conspicuously a centre of religious influence. Blessed fruits of national repentance! When will nations learn the clear lessons of this precious book of God?

II. IN RELATION TO THE RELIGIOUS LIFE OF CHRISTIANS THESE FACTS ARE FULL OF SIGNIFICANCE. It is not wise to seek out spiritual meanings from every simple historic fact in the Old Testament. Plain history is not given as a religious enigma to be solved by some transcendental insight. Yet there are analogies between national and individual life, and principles of holiness and righteousness work in the same directions in both. As there is a Babylon both spiritual and historical, so there is the Philistine and Amorite of our great warfare. As treasures change hands in Israel's conflict, so there are valuable possessions in man which may be dominated by opposing powers. Thus, then, we may consider some of the *first-fruits of repentance in Christian life*. 1. The *great world-power is largely subdued and cast off*. The man who in his life has passed through what Israel did in answer to Samuel's call finds that the evil influences of the world around have less hold on him. They are repressed. Their force has been weakened, if not annihilated. 2. *Faculties once governed by unhallowed tendencies are restored to the rightful ruler*. There are, so to speak, cities—seats of power and resource—in every man's nature. While in a sinful course of life these are dominated largely by principles alien to God, and adverse to true self-interest: true repentance brings every faculty, thought, and desire into a willing subordination to him whose right it is to reign. The soul is a " holy land " in which Christ is King. 3. *Deep-seated, corrupt passions are quieted*. There are ancient, very corrupt passions of a fleshly character embedded in human nature. These Amorites of our experience are unusually powerful during a life of sinful indulgence. They grow fat and flourish. One of the first consequences of the new life is to tone them down. The causes of their extreme activity and restlessness are partially removed. A strong hand holds them down in comparative quietude. Their destiny, like that of Israel's cruel foe, is to be utterly destroyed ; but even now, compared with former almost irresistible aggressions, there is peace with them. 4. A *considerable degree of prosperity and order is maintained*. The reformed soul has law administered within itself. Every interest, every claim of striving powers and tendencies, is considered and decided in harmony with the law of Christ. The intellect does not absorb the time and energy due to the culture of the emotions, and *vice versâ*. To some degree the inner man is in an orderly, prosperous condition. He is an improved being. 5. The *holy, elevating power of devotion is cherished at the centre of influence*. Samuel's home was the centre of influence in Israel, and it was made by express arrangement conspicuously devout. There is in our nature a seat of supreme influence. The faculties and tendencies of the soul act in subordination to the commanding affection of life. True repentance issues in the heart becoming the seat of a powerful influence dominating all else. There is an *altar there* on which the inextinguishable fire burns, filling with its heavenly glory the entire man. " Old things have passed away ; all things are become new." Are these fruits found in all lives called Christian ? They ought to be, and are, if " Christian " is more than a name.

HOMILIES BY VARIOUS AUTHORS.

Vers. 1—12.—*Steps of return to God*. The whole interest of this passage is moral. No stress is laid on the forms, or even the authorised appurtenances, of religion. The ark, of which we have heard so much, and which had been treated with a singular mixture of superstition and profanity, plays no part in the history. It is left for years in a quiet retreat. Israel had backslidden from the Lord. The steps of their return have a meaning and a moral lesson for all generations.

I. THE FEELING OF A GREAT MORAL AND SPIRITUAL WANT. " The house of Israel lamented after the Lord." For twenty years the ark had been withdrawn, and under the yoke of the Philistines the spirit of Israel seemed to be quelled and stupefied. Even Samuel appears to have held himself in reserve till a time should arrive more favourable for the moral suasion and admonition of a prophet. And heathen worship crept over the land. But at last conscience began to stir, the soul of the people was weary, and there rose a wistful, sorrowful cry after the God of their fathers. This surely is always the beginning of a backslider's restoration. He wearies, and is ashamed of his own ways ; feels his folly and wickedness, and then sighs after a forfeited blessedness—laments after the Lord.

II. REPENTANCE PREACHED AND PRACTISED. When the time came for the people to hear him with an awakened conscience, Samuel addressed all the tribes with a voice of moral authority that recalls the admonitions of Moses and the last words of Joshua (ver. 3). And the people obeyed his word, showing their repentance in the most thorough and practical way by " putting away Baalim and Ashtaroth." So must every true prophet or preacher of righteousness summon men to repentance, and testify to them that God will not take their part while their hearts are disloyal to him. It is useless to lament after the Lord and still retain false gods. Our God is not mocked, nor can his favour be gained by mere words and empty sighs.

III. A NEW ORDER BEGUN. At Mizpah, after solemn public confession of sin against Jehovah, " Samuel judged the people of Israel." He seized the opportunity to institute a more authoritative and vigorous administration of public affairs. He knew well the need of establishing order and discipline under the sacred law. And the people consented. So when there is sincere repentance a new order begins. The authority of the law of the Lord over conscience and life is acknowledged, and there is evinced a new obedience.

IV. A FIGHT FOR HOLY LIBERTY. The Philistines had no objection to the Israelite worship of Baal and Astarte ; but so soon as they heard of their return to the service of Jehovah and of the increased authority of Samuel, they mustered their forces to attack them. And the faith of the penitent tribes was not yet sufficiently established or assured to prevent their being " afraid of the Philistines." They stood their ground, however, and asked Samuel to pray for them to the Lord. So they got the victory. When a backslider returns to God, endeavouring to regain his self-respect, and to resume his place as a well-doer, he finds that evil rises up within him and fights hard for the mastery. As Pharaoh would not let the people go, and the Philistines would not let them restore religion or regain national independence without a struggle to keep them down, so does sin strive to retain under its yoke the sinner who is escaping through repentance. But let faith appeal to God along with the burnt offering of entire consecration to him. He gives the victory to the weak.

V. GRATEFUL ACKNOWLEDGMENT OF HELP FROM GOD. Samuel knew the value to a nation of inspiriting recollections, and therefore set up a stone or pillar to commemorate the great victory. But he was careful to make it a witness not to Israel's prowess, but to Jehovah's timely help. It was Ebenezer, the stone of help. It said " Te Deum Laudamus." The spiritual life has its Ebenezers,—many of them. Nations are ready enough to raise proud pillars and triumphal arches to celebrate their feats in war. Europe has ever so many columns, streets, squares, and boulevards, and bridges named after battles. Let us remember the battles of principle, the fights with temptation through which we have passed. When we have failed, ours is the shame. When we have overcome, to God be the glory. We recommend not remembrance only, but some stone of remembrance. It is a true and wise impulse which has often led Christians to commemorate a great deliverance or consolation vouchsafed to themselves by building a church, an hospital, or an almshouse, or by founding a mission, or some institution of learning or benevolence. Such a stone of remembrance helps him who rears it to resist the tendency to let religious impressions and memories fade from the mind, and it proclaims to others that some men, at all events, have proved God as the Hearer of prayer and the Helper of the needy.—F.

Vers. 2—6. (MIZPAH.)—*A national revival.* The history of religion in the world is largely a history of a series of declensions and revivals ; the former being due to the downward tendency of human nature, the latter to the gracious interposition of God. Of this fact the period of the judges affords an illustration. The revival which took place at its commencement (Judges ii. 1—5) is specially worthy of notice ; another, and more important, occurring toward its close, is here described. It was—1. *Needed* on account of the condition of the people of Israel. The great defeat which they suffered twenty years before (ver. 1 ; ch. iv. 1 ; vi. 1) checked their prevailing sin, especially as manifested in sacerdotalism, formalism, superstition, and presumption ; but it by no means cured it. Superstitious veneration for sacred objects passed rapidly, as commonly happens, into unbelieving irreverence (ch. vi. 19) and spiritual indifference ; whilst participation in the false worship and corrupt practices of the heathen continued, and even increased (ver. 4). The law of God was made void, and his presence withdrawn.   2. *Effected*, under God, by the influence of one man—Samuel.   Nothing is expressly said concerning him during these twenty years; but he appears to have retired from Shiloh to Ramah, his native place, and it is not likely that he remained there altogether inactive for so long a time.   The statement of ch. iii. 20, 21; iv. 1, must be considered as, to some extent, prospective.   The oppression of the Philistines was not such as to interfere with him, nor was his activity of such a kind as to cause them much concern.   His holy example and quiet labours doubtless contributed greatly to the keeping alive of true piety in the hearts of a faithful few; and when the time came for more public effort he stood ready—in the full maturity of his powers, above forty years of age—to utter the word of the Lord, and to take the leadership of the nation.   "During the long oppression of a stormy time the nation at last gathered more and more unanimously around Samuel, like terrified chickens around the parent hen" (Ewald).   3. *Marked* by features of a peculiar nature.   Every great religious revival that has been recorded in sacred history or has occurred in the Christian Church has had a character of its own, determined by the wants of the age.   And this revival was characterised by the restoration of the moral law to commanding influence on the conscience of the people by means of the prophetic ministry.   The office of hereditary priest became secondary to that of inspired prophet, and was even absorbed in it for a while; for Samuel, although not a priest, acted constantly as such in offering sacrifice; and the Levitical law lay in abeyance, or was modified in practice under his direction.   "As Moses established the theocracy, Samuel restored its fundamental principles to the supreme place in the national life, and thus in a true and noble sense was its second founder."   The revival he was the chief instrument in effecting involved a more complete separation from idolatry, laid the basis of higher internal unity, and was followed by prosperity and independence.   In the description of it we observe—

I. A GENERAL CONCERN ABOUT THE PRESENCE OF THE LORD.   "And all the house of Israel lamented after the Lord" (ver. 2).   1. Occasioned by the experience of the long and bitter *effects of transgression*.   2. Implying a sense of *misery in the absence of God*.   The idols to which men give their affections cannot satisfy the heart (Hosea ii. 7, 8; v. 15, vi. 1).   "It is well to feel worn and fatigued with the fruitless search after happiness, that we may welcome our Deliverer" (Pascal).   3. Consisting of an intense *longing after his favour and fellowship*.   "The phrase, 'lamented after the Lord,' is taken from human affairs, when one follows after another and entreats him with lamentations until he assents.   An example of this is the Syrophenician woman" Matt. xv. (S. Schmid).   The sorrow thus felt was a "godly sorrow;" a sorrow which comes from God, is felt for God, and tends to God, and which works genuine repentance, effectual deliverance, and lasting satisfaction (2 Cor. vii. 10).   4. Felt by the *nation as a whole*.   "All the house of Israel."   And wherever such concern is felt it is a sure sign of God's returning favour.   "They inclined after the Lord; they groaned, complained, bemoaned themselves in their following the Lord, as a child followeth his departing parent; they called, cried, and lifted up their voice after the Lord by earnest prayer and supplication.   Why?   (1) Because God is infinitely more worthy than all ordinances; his presence is valuable in itself.   (2) God purposely withdraws, that men may lament after him; as when a mother steps out of a child's sight, and when she seems to be gone the child raises a cry after her.   (3) Because sincere lamenting after the Lord may occasion his return" (O. Heywood, iii. 419).

II. AN EARNEST ATTENTION TO THE WORD OF THE LORD (ver. 3).   The word was—1. *Revealed* in former days, and included in the law of Moses (Deut. vi. 14).   There is not generally so much need of new truth as that the old should be vitalised.   How much of dead truth lies in the mind of every man!   2. *Spoken* with new power; opportunely, faithfully, and with holy zeal, by the prophet who had been commissioned to utter it.   The preaching of the word is necessary and important in every genuine revival of religion.   That word is a fire, a hammer, and a two-edged sword (Heb. iv. 12).   3. *Adapted* to the condition of the people.   (1) To *test* the sincerity of their desires and purposes.   "If," &c.   (2) To *instruct* them in their duty.   "Put away the strange gods," &c.   Prepare your hearts = "*Fix* your hearts towards, or in trust in, God" (Heb. xiii. 9).   (3) To *encourage* them to hope for deliverance.   "And he will deliver you out of the hand of the Philstiines." 4. *Listened* to in a right spirit ; with fresh interest, reverence, self-application, and a determination to put it into practice. When the heart is prepared the truth is invested with new meaning and power ; as words written on paper with invisible ink are clearly perceived when held to the fire. " Faith cometh by hearing, and hearing by the word of God " (Rom. x. 17).

III. A SINCERE RENUNCIATION OF SIN AGAINST THE LORD (ver. 4), which was—1. A *proof* of their genuine repentance ; " a heart broken *for* sin, and *from* sin." 2. *Shown* with respect to the transgressions to which they were specially addicted—the worship of Baalim (images or modifications of Baal, the principal male divinity of the Phœnician and Canaanitish nations—the sun-god) and Ashtaroth (images of their supreme female divinity, " the queen of heaven," the Syrian Venus—*Astarte*), and the corrupt practices connected therewith (Judges ii. 11, 13). 3. *Combined* with positive acts of obedience and piety. They not only ceased to worship false gods, but also " served the Lord alone " (Matt. vi. 24). Sin is most effectually broken off " by righteousness " (Dan. iv. 27) ; an old affection most effectually expelled by a new one. The heart cannot rest without some object of love and trust. And if, " when the unclean spirit is gone out of a man," it be not immediately replaced by a pure spirit, it is sure to return " with seven other spirits more wicked than himself " (Matt. xii. 43). 4. Made by men *individually* and in private ; whereby they become prepared to make a national profession, and to receive the Divine blessing. God can bless men only by " turning every one of them from *his* iniquities" (Acts iii. 26).

IV. A PUBLIC CONSECRATION TO THE SERVICE OF THE LORD (vers. 5, 6). At the word of Samuel a national assembly was gathered together at Mizpah for the purpose of openly expressing and confirming the general feeling ; and there under the open sky they " yielded themselves to the Lord" (2 Chron. xxx. 8) with—1. Solemn *vows* of obedience to the law of their God. " They drew water and poured it out before the Lord." " We take this act to have been a sign and symbol, or rather confirmation of an oath—a solemn vow. To pour out water on the ground is in the East an ancient way of taking a solemn oath—the words and promises that had gone forth from their mouth being as water spilt upon the ground that cannot be gathered up again " (Kitto). 2. Sincere *humiliation* on account of former disobedience. The symbol just mentioned is interpreted by some as denoting the pouring out of their hearts in penitence. They also " fasted on that day, and said there, We have sinned against the Lord." 3. *Prayers* and supplications for Divine mercy and help. " I will pray for you." " Cease not to cry unto the Lord our God for us," implying that Samuel had already prayed for them. He gave expression to their desires, and made intercession on their behalf. " So Moses prayed for the people at Rephidim and for Miriam, so Elijah prayed at Carmel, so Ezra prayed at the evening sacrifice, so the high priest prayed for the house of Israel on the day of atonement, and so does our Lord Jesus Christ ever live at God's right hand to make intercession for us " (' Sp. Com.'). 4. Devout *acknowledgment* of the prophet of the Lord as their leader and judge. " And Samuel judged the children of Israel in Mizpah." On that day he commenced his public labours as judge, and a great moral and spiritual reformation was inaugurated. It was a day long remembered (2 Chron. xxxv. 18 : " There was no passover like to that kept in Israel from the days of Samuel the prophet "), and such a day as every godly man desires to see in this land (Ps. lxxxv. 6 ; Hos. xiv. 1—3 ; Hab. iii. 2).—D.

Ver. 6. (MIZPAH.)—*Confession of sin.* " We have sinned against the Lord." When any one has done wrong to another he ought to make acknowledgment and reparation to him (Matt. v. 23, 24). We are directed to " confess our faults one to another " (James v. 16) ; and there are cases in which we may derive benefit from confessing our sins against the Lord to a godly man. The passage just referred to, however, affords no ground for " auricular confession " to a priest ; nor does the commission given to the apostles (John xx. 23), since (in addition to other reasons) it simply conferred authority to declare the ordinances of the kingdom of heaven, and especially the terms or conditions according to which sins are remitted or retained ; and the practice of such confession is most injurious. But we ought all to confess our sins to God. Every wrong done to men is a sin against God, and there are multitudes of sins against him that do not directly affect our fellow-men. " In many things we all offend." And the word of God often enjoins the confession of all our offences before him, and declares it to be the necessary condition of obtaining forgiveness. Consider—

I. WHAT IT IMPLIES. 1. That we see the *essential evil* of sin. "Sin is the transgression of the law" (1 John iii. 4). More generally, it is whatever is contrary to the character and will of God. As he is the only perfect Being, and deserves and claims the supreme love of men, so the root of sin consists in the absence of such love, and the departure of the heart from its true rest; and whenever man departs from God he falls into selfishness, vanity, and misery. Sin is aversion to God and devotion to self (see Tulloch, 'Christian Doctrine of Sin'). "Against thee, thee only, have I sinned," &c. (Ps. li. 4). 2. That we are convinced of the *just desert* of sin. "Howbeit, thou art just in all that is brought upon us," &c. (Neh. ix. 33). 3. That we are resolved upon an *entire renunciation* of sin. This determination springs from a real hatred towards it, and is associated with "hunger and thirst after righteousness." Confession is of the nature of a solemn oath of abjuration. "Whoso confesseth and forsaketh his sins shall find mercy" (Prov. xxviii. 13).

II. HOW IT SHOULD BE MADE. 1. Under a *due impression* of the greatness of our sin. (1) In order to this we must contemplate the holy love of God, his just requirements, his merciful blessings and boundless claims; above all, we must stand before the cross and behold that great sight (Luke xxiii. 48). "There is no better way to obtain the gift of tears for having offended God than meditation on the greatness of God's goodness and of his love which he has shown to man." (2) We must, in the light that shines upon us, consider the particular transgressions we have committed in thought, word, and deed against God, our neighbour, and ourselves,—sins of omission and commission,—and the sinful disposition revealed by them and pervading our whole life (Luke xviii. 13). General confessions of sin without personal and particular application are of little worth. "Usually, the more particular we are in the confession of sin, the more comfort we have in the sense of pardon" (M. Henry). (3) In this manner we shall, by Divine grace, be filled with self-abasement, godly sorrow, and true repentance. "That which makes manifest is light;" and in proportion to the brightness with which the light of truth shines upon us will it manifest our sin (1 John i. 8); just as a sunbeam darting across a room shows us the floating dust that was not seen before (Job xlii. 5, 6). 2. In *sincere, frank*, and *unreserved* acknowledgment of our sin; without any attempt to cover, excuse, or palliate it. "Pardon my iniquity, *for it is great*" (Ps. xxv. 11; xxxii. 3—5). 3. With a *turning of the heart to God* in faith and prayer and acts of obedience. "For thou, Lord, art good, and ready to forgive; and plenteous in mercy unto all them that call upon thee" (Ps. lxxxvi. 5).

"Repentance is heart's sorrow
And a clear life ensuing" (Shakespeare).

III. BY WHOM. 1. Each individual (Luke xv. 21). "God be merciful to me a sinner" (Luke xviii. 13). 2. Each family. "Every family apart" (Zech. xii. 14). 3. The whole people. Those who have united in sinning must unite in confessing their sin (ch. xii. 19; Ezra ix. 6—15; Dan. ix. 4—19). "We have all sinned and come short of the glory of God."

IV. WHY IT IS NECESSARY. 1. That we may give glory to God. By it we act in accordance with his will, justify him in his dealings with us, and give to him the honour which is his due. "Give glory to God, and make confession unto him" (Josh. vii. 19). 2. That we may be prepared to receive pardon, peace, and salvation. Until we open our hearts to God he will not open his heart to us. We must cease to have fellowship with idols in order that we may have fellowship with the holy One, and become the habitation of his Spirit (2 Cor. vi. 16). 3. That we may have confidence in the fulfilment of his promises. This is conditioned by our fulfilment of his requirements, without which our confidence is vain. "If we confess our sins," &c. (1 John i. 9). "And if any man sin, we have an Advocate with the Father, Jesus Christ the righteous" (1 John ii. 1).—D.

Vers. 7—14. (EBENEZER.)—*The victory of Ebenezer.* Whenever a people is set right in its relation to God and purified from its sin, it is certain to obtain victory over its enemies and enjoy prosperity and peace. Israel was now restored from its apostasy, and on the very spot where it experienced an overwhelming defeat twenty years before it gained a signal triumph. We have here—

I. THE GATHERING OF THE ENEMY (ver. 7). 1. So long as the yoke of the ungodly is patiently borne they remain quiet, and do not deem it needful to harass the victims of their oppression. 2. The revival of piety and activity seldom fails to call forth the fierce opposition of evil men. The spirit of good and the spirit of evil are contrary the one to the other, and the more intense the former becomes, the more intense also becomes the latter. The "prince of this world" dislikes to be deprived of his captives, and therefore seeks to prevent sinners from coming to the Lord (Luke ix. 42), and hinders saints from working for him (1 Thess ii. 18). 3. The purpose for which the pious assemble is not always understood by their enemies; their meeting for prayer is sometimes mistaken for an organising of a political or military attack upon them ; and their union for any purpose whatever is instinctively felt to bode them no good, and regarded as a sufficient ground for their dispersion. "Now we see here—(1) How evil sometimes seems to come out of good. (2) How good is sometimes brought out of that evil. Israel could never be threatened more seasonably than at this time, when they were repenting and praying ; nor could the Philistines have acted more impoliticly for themselves than to make war upon Israel at this time, when they were making their peace with God " (Matthew Henry).

II. THE PREPARATION FOR THE CONFLICT (vers. 7, 8, 9). 1. *Mistrust of self.* "They were afraid of the Philistines." Their experience of defeat and oppression had taught them their own weakness and cured their presumption. The consciousness of human weakness is the condition of receiving Divine strength (2 Cor. xii. 10; Heb. xi. 34). 2. *Trust in God.* "Cease not to cry unto the Lord our God for us," &c. (ver. 8). Their need impelled them to look to God, whom they called *their* God, with reference to his covenant, and from whom they expected deliverance according to the promise previously given to them (ver. 3). "They have found their God again, after whom they had till now sighed and mourned" (Erdmann). Their urgent request of Samuel was an evidence of their reliance on Jehovah and the proper way of seeking his aid, for Samuel was not only a spokesman for God to men, but also a spokesman for men to God, and he proceeded to exercise the priestly function of mediation by offering sacrifice and making intercession. 3. *Self-dedication,* of which the whole burnt offering was the expression and appointed means, "the sign of complete consecration of the whole man, and here of the whole people ; " the sucking lamb being a symbol of their new life now freely devoted to God. Samuel acted as priest at Mizpah and elsewhere by Divine commission under peculiar circumstances ; the regular priesthood being in abeyance, the ark separated from the tabernacle, Shiloh desolate, and no other place chosen by God "to put his name there ; " and as preparatory to the time " when in every place incense shall be offered to my name, and a pure offering " (Mal. i. 11). "A most important part of the prophetic office was to maintain the spiritual character of the Hebrew worship, and to prevent the degeneracy of the people into such ritualism as they had fallen into at the time our Lord appeared " (Kitto). " Let, then, thy oblation be without earthly affection or self-will of any kind. Look neither to earthly nor heavenly blessings, but only to the will and order of God, to which thou shouldst submit and sacrifice thyself wholly as a perpetual burnt offering, and, forgetting all created things, say, ' Behold, my Lord and Creator, each and all of my desires I give into the hand of thy will and thine eternal providence. Do with me as seemeth good to thee in life and death, and after death ; as in time, so in eternity " (Scupoli). 4. *Prayer.* "And Samuel cried unto the Lord for Israel " with a piercing and prolonged cry. And with his prayer their own rose up to heaven. " By prayer (if thou use it well) thou wilt put a sword into the hand of God, that he may fight and conquer for thee." A praying army is irresistible. What victories have been achieved by prayer ! " The forty years' domination of the Philistines over Israel (Judges xiii. 1) could not be overthrown by the supernatural strength of Samson, but was terminated by the prayers of Samuel " (Wordsworth). Samson only *began* to deliver Israel (Judges xiii. 5) ; Samuel completed the work.

III. THE RECEPTION OF HELP (vers. 9, 10). 1. It came in *answer to prayer*. "And the Lord answered him." 2. It came at the moment of their greatest *extremity*. "And as Samuel was offering up the burnt offering, the Philistines drew near to battle against Israel." But man's extremity is God's opportunity (Gen. xxii. 11—14). 3. It came in an *extraordinary* manner. "The Lord thundered with a great thunder on that day." It was, as it were, his voice in answer to prayer. The ordinary forces of nature operated in such a manner as to make it plainly appear that they were directed by his hand (1 Sam. ii. 10). 4. It was most *effectual*. "They were discomfited and smitten before Israel" (Job xl. 9; Ps. lxxvii. 18).

IV. THE PURSUIT OF THE FOE (ver. 11). 1. The sense of the presence of God inspires his people with fresh confidence and courage, and without it they can do nothing. 2. The help of God does not render their *co-operation* unnecessary. It rather calls for the putting forth of their strength. He gives them strength that it may be employed against the enemy, and in the faithful and zealous use of it he gives them more strength, and crowns their efforts with success. 3. Victory over the enemy should be *followed up* to the utmost (Judges viii. 4). "They smote them until they came to Beth-car." How often from not following up a victory are its advantages lost!

V. THE MEMORIAL OF THE VICTORY (ver. 12). 1. The help which is derived from God should be gratefully *ascribed* to him. 2. Thanksgiving to God should be expressed in a *definite* and *permanent* form. 3. One deliverance is an *earnest* of another. 4. The memorial of past deliverance should incite to future confidence, and the continued use of the means in connection with which it was achieved. "Hitherto; for all Jehovah's help is only hitherto—from day to day, and from place to place; not unconditionally, not wholly, not once for all, irrespective of our bearing" (Edersheim). More conflicts have to be waged, and it is only in mistrust of self, trust in God, self-dedication, and prayer that they can be waged successfully. "The life of man is nothing else but a continual warfare with temptation. And this is a battle from which, as it ends only with life, there is no escape; and he who fights not in it is of necessity either taken captive or slain. Because of this warfare thou must watch always, and keep a guard upon thy heart, so that it be ever peaceful and quiet" (Scupoli).

VI. THE MAGNITUDE OF THE RESULT (vers. 13, 14). A true revival is always followed by beneficial and lasting effects. 1. The power of the enemy is broken. "The Philistines were subdued, and came no more into the coasts of Israel." 2. A sure defence is afforded against every attempt they may make to regain their dominion. "The hand of the Lord was against them all the days of Samuel." 3. Lost territory is restored (ver. 14). Along the whole line, extending north and south, from Ekron to Gath. 4. Far-reaching peace is established. "And there was peace between Israel and the Amorites." "When a man's ways please the Lord he maketh even his enemies to be at peace with him" (Prov. xvi. 7). The battle of Ebenezer may be considered one of the decisive battles of the world, inasmuch as it introduced a new order of things in Israel, and contributed in an eminent degree to its subsequent prosperity and power. "The revival of religion has ever had a most important bearing on social and moral improvement. The return of man to God restores him to his brother. Restoration to the earnest and hearty performance of religious duties towards God leads to a corresponding reformation in relative and political duties. Those countries in Europe which have had the greatest religious reforms have advanced most in liberty, civilisation, and commerce. They are not trodden by the iron heel of despotism, and they possess the greatest amount of domestic quiet. It was the revival of religion which secured the Protestant succession to England, and many of the liberties which we now enjoy. It was the revival of religion that gave such a martyr-roll to the Scottish Covenanters, and led to the revolution settlement of 1688. In Israel every revival of religion was succeeded by national prosperity and political independence" (R. Steel).—D.

Ver. 12. (Between MIZPAH and SHEN—the tooth or crag.)— *The stone of help*. The setting up of memorial stones was one of the earliest methods adopted for the purpose of recording interesting and important events. These memorials consisted of a single block or of a heap of stones; they generally received some significant name, or were marked with a brief inscription, and they sometimes became centres around which the people gathered, and were replaced by more imposing structures. The earliest instance mentioned in the Bible was at Bethel (Gen. xxviii. 8). Other instances, Gen. xxxi. 45; Exod. xvii. 15; Josh. iv. 9, 21, 22; xxiv. 26. This memorial was set up—

I. ON THE OPPORTUNE RECEPTION OF DIVINE HELP. Looking backward on the past, let us remember—1. How much that help has been *needed* by us—in sorrow, labour, conflict, danger, which our own strength was wholly inadequate to meet. 2. How often it has been afforded when we were at the point of *despair*. But why, it may be asked, should God have allowed us to arrive at such a point? (1) To teach us the very truth concerning ourselves, and deliver us from a vain confidence in ourselves. "This unfortunate self-reliance forms within us a little favourite sanctuary, which our jealous pride keeps closed against God, whom we receive as our last resource. But when we become really weak and despair of ourselves, the power of God expands itself through all our inner man, even to the most secret recesses, filling us with all the fulness of God" (A. Monod). (2) To produce in us humility and submission, to excite us to fervent prayer, and to strengthen and perfect our faith. (3) To afford occasion for a more impressive manifestation of his power and grace. 3. How completely it has been *adapted* to our need and accomplished our deliverance. Here we are this day, after the trouble and conflict, ourselves monuments of his mercy! "We went through fire and through water: but thou broughtest us out into a wealthy place" (Deut. viii. 2; Ps. lxvi. 12; lxxvii. 10; Acts xxvi. 22).

II. IN GRATEFUL RECOGNITION OF DIVINE HELP. Looking upward to heaven, let us reflect—1. How *plainly* the Source of our deliverance now appears. "Hitherto hath the *Lord* helped us." "Not with thy sword, nor with thy bow" (Josh. xxiv. 12). His arm alone has brought salvation nigh. We see it now more clearly than we did before, and as we meditate upon it our hearts overflow with thankfulness. We have not always recognised the Source of our mercies, and therefore often omitted to be thankful; but who can fail to see these signal tokens of his power? "Not unto us," &c. (Ps. cxv. 1). 2. How much we *owe* to the God of our salvation. Everything. 3. How we can best *testify* the gratitude of our hearts. "What shall I render unto the Lord?" (Ps. cxvi. 12). Loud songs of praise. Renewed vows of consecration. Earnest written or spoken words for God. Large gifts of what he has given. Fresh acts of piety and beneficence. These shall be the memorial we now set up.

III. AS A PERMANENT RECORD OF DIVINE HELP. Looking forward to the future, let us consider—1. How helpful the record may be to ourselves in times of conflict and trial. For such times will come; we are liable to forget what has occurred; and it will remind us of him who changes not, and incite us to faith and prayer. 2. How useful it may be to others in similar circumstances. What he has done for us he can do for them, and seeing it they "may take heart again." 3. How conducive it may be to the glory of God. As often as we behold it we shall be stirred to fresh thanksgiving. When we are gone it will still endure. Others will gather around it, and ask the meaning of the "great stone which remaineth unto this day" (ch. vi. 18), and, on being told, will give glory to God. So his praise shall be perpetuated from generation to generation, until it merge into the anthem of heaven.

Conclusion.—1. Let us be thankful for the memorials of Divine help which others have left for our benefit. They are among the greatest treasures the earth contains, and meet our view wherever we turn. 2. Let us do something to add to these treasures, and further enrich the earth. 3. Above all, let us seek to be ourselves the everlasting monuments of the Divine power and grace.—D.

Vers. 15—17. (RAMAH, BETHEL, GILGAL, MIZPAH.)—*Samuel the judge.* The "judges" of Israel were deliverers from oppression, leaders in war, perpetual dictators in national affairs, and supreme arbiters in judicial matters. "All that was greatest in those times was certainly due to them, and some of their names shine eternally like bright stars in the long night of a troubled age" (Ewald, 'History'). Of these judges Samuel was the last and greatest. His superiority appears in — 1. The *character* he possessed. He was free from the vices into which some of the most

distinguished amongst them fell, and surpassed them in the virtues they exhibited.
He had higher conceptions of God and his law, held more intimate communion with
him, and was altogether of a nobler type of human excellence. His constant aim
was to do the will of God; he was upright in heart and life, humble, patient, generous, and full of disinterested zeal and holy energy in seeking the true welfare of men.
In these respects he approached as nearly, perhaps, as any of the servants of God
under the old covenant the perfection of him who was "without sin." 2. The
method he pursued. As he effected the deliverance of Israel not by the sword,
but by "the word of God and prayer," so he continued to make use of the same
means as the most effective in preserving their liberty and increasing their strength
and happiness. His method was moral rather than physical. He taught them "to
do justly, love mercy, and walk humbly with their God" (Micah vi. 8). His policy
was one of peace, and he relied on God to restrain the aggression of surrounding
nations, and afford protection against their attacks. Nor was his trust misplaced.
3. The *work* he accomplished. Idolatry, which was rebellion against the Divine
King, was banished. The principles of the theocracy were confirmed. Order, justice,
and peace were established; and closer unity prevailed among the tribes, based
upon their common loyalty to their King. "This was the great achievement and
crowning point of his service to Israel and the God of Israel; the scattered and disunited tribes became again a nation. The rival tribes Ephraim and Judah make
common cause against the common enemy, and the more distant tribes do not seem
to withhold their allegiance" (Milman). The labours of Samuel as judge are here
summed up in a few sentences, suggestive of some things wherein he was an instructive example to rulers, statesmen, magistrates, and "all that are in authority."
Notice—

I. HIS SUPREME CONCERN FOR RELIGION. Samuel was first a prophet, then a "faithful priest," finally a ruler and judge. "His judicial work not only proceeded from
the prophetical, but was constantly guided by it. For we may presume not only
that he gave legal decisions with prophetical wisdom, but also that, in general, he
conducted the affairs of the people as a man who had the Spirit of the Lord"
(Nägelsbach). At the different places to which "he went from year to year in
circuit"—Bethel, Gilgal, and Mizpah—he probably taught the word of God and offered
sacrifice, combining his prophetic and priestly with his judicial work. At Ramah
he built an altar to the Lord, "testifying thereby the power from which alone he
could receive either the authority or wisdom to judge." The position of Samuel
was peculiar, and his work unusually comprehensive; but it may be observed of
every good civil magistrate that—1. He is qualified for his office by his possession of
reverence for God. "He that ruleth over men must be just, ruling in the fear of
God" (2 Sam. xxiii. 3). He feels his responsibility to the supreme King and Judge,
by whose providence he has been placed in authority, and has constant regard to his
will. 2. His personal piety pervades his public activity. The one is not separated
from the other, but is its animating spirit, and thereby he seeks to afford in his judgments a reflection of the perfect judgments of God. 3. His highest desire, knowing
that "righteousness exalteth a nation," is to see the people all righteous. That end,
he is persuaded, cannot be attained by force; but, as a godly man, he ever seeks it
by moral means; and, in his public capacity, he endeavours to do something towards
it by restraining the violence of the wicked and protecting the good in their labours
"unto the kingdom of God."

II. HIS FAITHFUL ADMINISTRATION OF JUSTICE. In the theocracy the laws were
already given, and Samuel's judicial work consisted in arranging for their proper
administration, in which he doubtless availed himself of the method formerly
appointed (Deut. xvi. 18—20), reserving to himself the proper interpretation and
application of them in more difficult and important cases. For this purpose he went
to different centres of the land at stated times, and "judged Israel in all those places."
He has been not inappropriately called the Hebrew Aristides. Like him, the faithful
magistrate—1. Strives to bring justice within easy reach of every man. 2. Administers it wisely, impartially, fearlessly, without respect of persons (Exod. xviii. 21, 22;
2 Chron. xix. 5—7; Jer. xxii. 3). 3. Devotes himself disinterestedly and diligently
to the common weal (ch. xii. 3). "The Hebrew judges were not only simple in their

manners, moderate in their desires, and free from avarice and ambition, but they were noble and magnanimous men, who felt that whatever they did for their country was above all reward, and could not be recompensed ; who desired merely to be public benefactors, and chose rather to deserve well of their country than to be enriched by its wealth " (Jahn, ' Heb. Com.,' sect. 22).

III. HIS WISE PROVISION FOR EDUCATION. During the period of his judgeship Samuel appears to have established one or more " schools of the prophets," in which he taught young men sacred knowledge, and, in connection with it, reading, writing, and music, thus preparing them to give instruction to the people, which the Levites had failed to do (ch. x. 10 ; xix. 20). So a wise statesman, seeing that " for the soul to be without knowledge is not good," and that " the people are destroyed for lack of knowledge," adopts proper means for the education of the young, the diffusion of knowledge, and the advancement of the race (Ps. lxxviii. 5—8). " Education is the debt which one generation owes to another " (J. S. Mill). The schools of the prophets " were hearths of spiritual life to Israel. Their aim was not to encourage a contemplative life (like the cloisters), but to arouse the nation to activity. Every prophetic disciple was a missionary " (Hengstenberg).

IV. HIS CONSISTENT CONDUCT AT HOME. " And his return was to Ramah ; for there was his house; and there he built an altar unto the Lord " (ver. 17). There, also, he continued his judicial labours. The faithful magistrate, whilst he does not allow his public duty to interfere with proper attention to his duty to his own household, seeks to make the latter helpful to the former. He exemplifies in his private life the conduct he openly commends to others, and " walks in his house with a perfect heart " (Ps. ci. 2). Though he be not a Nazarite, he is simple, self-denying, and unostentatious in his habits ; and though he be not wealthy, he is kind to the poor, hospitable to friends (ch. ix. 24), and liberal towards the Lord (1 Chron. xxvi. 28 : " all that Samuel the seer had dedicated "). He recognises the presence and claims of God in his home, sanctifies it by prayer (Job i. 5), endeavours to make it a centre whence holy influences emanate to all, and does all things to the glory of God (1 Cor. x. 31). " The indispensable basis afforded by the home and its eternal sanctity no superior religion and legislation should seek to destroy, or even to disturb ; and, on a comprehensive survey, we cannot fail to recognise that there is no other ancient nation in which, during the days of external power, domestic life remained for a long period so vigorous ; and, secondly, during the gradual decline of the external power, became so little weakened and corrupted as was the case with Israel " (Ewald, ' Antiquities ').

V. HIS LONG CONTINUANCE IN OFFICE. " And Samuel judged Israel all the days of his life " (ver. 15). " Simple words, but what a volume of tried faithfulness is unrolled by them ! " He pursued his course till he was " old and gray-headed " (ch. xii. 2)—nearly twenty years from the victory of Ebenezer. The appointment of a king relieved him of a portion of the burden ; but he still continued to exercise his prophetic office, and, " as last judge, he held in his hands the highest control of the theocracy and the kingdom." He devoted his last years to the training of youthful disciples for future service ; and when at length he died, " all the Israelites were gathered together, and lamented him, and buried him in his house at Ramah " (ch. xxv. 1). His protracted labour was an evidence of his public spirit, indomitable energy, and efficient service, and the principal means of raising the nation to its subsequent power and glory.—D.

EXPOSITION.

SAUL (CHS. VIII.—XXXI.).

CHAPTER VIII.

THE great interest of the First Book of Samuel lies in the fact that we have in it the orderly consolidation of two of the main factors in the preparation for the manifest-

ation of our Lord, namely, prophecy and the kingdom. The first seven chapters give us the history of Samuel's birth, and of the gradual development in him of those spiritual powers which finally made him not merely a prophet, but the founder of prophecy as a permanent and regularly-organised institution of the Jewish Church. The whole of the rest of the book, while adding many interesting particulars about Samuel, is occupied with the establishment of the kingdom and with Saul. We have in him, both in his uprise and his fall, one of the most remarkable personages of the Old Testament. But his character for good and for evil will develop itself as we proceed. Before, however, we can appreciate his history, it is necessary for us to understand something of the vast issues that depended upon the change of government effected in his person. With Samuel, then, and Saul we have come to the time when the prophet and the king take their due place in the development of Israel. They were both essential to its progress, and the accomplishment of its Divine mission, and in Deut. xvii. 14—20, and again *ibid.* xxviii. 36, the establishment of the monarchy is spoken of as a virtual necessity. It was not Israel's highest ideal, far from it. Had religion been as far advanced as in the days of Hezekiah and Isaiah, the theocracy might have existed in such a form as would have insured the national safety. But such as the people were in the centuries which followed the conquest of Canaan, it was rather a high and glorious idea than a fact capable of being realised. It was one of those magnificent thoughts which raised the Israelites so high above the level of ordinary nations, and gave such grandeur and nobleness to the long struggle of their history ; but it was a thought, the value of which lay in its giving them a future, towards which their faces were ever turned, and which, by the sublimity of its conception, ever drew them onwards and upwards to all that was best and most Divine.

To be then Jehovah's own subjects, ruled directly by him, a republic with Jehovah for its chief, and its officers speaking at his command, and under his direct influence and control—this was Israel's grand ideal. As a matter of fact, it did not give them peace at home nor security from foreign invasion. It did not even enable them to advance in the path of culture or morality, nor did it so work as to bind the twelve tribes together into a harmonious whole. Throughout the Book of Judges we find the record of a desperate struggle in which Israel again and again is in danger of being utterly destroyed from among the nations, and at the end of this period the Philistines are the dominant power, and Israel is disarmed and virtually at their mercy. The cause of this was that somehow or other the priests and Levites were unable to prevent the people from lapsing into idolatry, and though upon their repentance Jehovah, as their King, did on every emergency raise men to be their saviours, yet the system was too cumbrous and exceptional for ordinary times. It was only in times of trouble that the nation roused itself to the conviction that it was Jehovah's realm, and fought with the heroism which so grand a thought must give it ; at other times it sank down each day to a lower level, till all that the last judge, Samson, could do was to arouse the national spirit to a prolonged resistance and a last effort against the dangers and difficulties that were threatening Israel with gradual extinction (see on ch. i. 3).

This powerlessness in war was the inevitable result of having no settled ordinary ruler, whose business it was to convoke the national forces, and provide for the general safety ; but it was by no means the worst evil attendant in practice upon the theocracy. In the three last chapters of the Book of Judges we have the history of a fearful crime, punished with equally fearful cruelty. What makes it the more remarkable is that it took place in the days of Phinehas, the grandson of Aaron, at a time when the public morality still stood high, and religion had great influence over the people. Now, had there been a king he would have punished the malefactors, as a matter of course ; but when it had to be done by an extraordinary gathering of the people in arms, the Benjamites, always a high-spirited tribe, imagined themselves bound in honour to resist an invasion of their territory, and a violent civil war was the result. So embittered did the feelings of the Israelites become at the brave defence of the Benjamites, that when at last they had overpowered them, they burned their cities with fire, and put men, women, children, and cattle to an indiscriminate slaughter. Repenting soon afterwards of their revolting cruelty, they treated the men of Jabesh-Gilead with almost equal violence, on the pretence of their not having taken part in the war, but really to provide the remaining Benjamites with wives. Now, both at the beginning and end of this narrative, it is carefully pointed out that all this crime and cruelty was the result of the state of anarchy which everywhere prevailed. " In those days there was no king in Israel : every man did that which was right in his own eyes " (Judges xxi. 25). There was no regular administration of justice, no person whose business it was to maintain law and order, no one whose authority kept malefactors in awe, and who, when a crime had been committed, would punish it in a regular manner, and with the general approval of all parties ; and so every species of villainy could be practised with impunity, until the patience of the community was exhausted, and it visited the offenders with a violence so summary as to make it repent afterwards of its own cruelty.

The position of these three chapters, immediately preceding in the Hebrew the Books of Samuel (for the insertion of the Book of Ruth is a modern attempt at a chronological arrangement), seems intended to point out that the king was as absolutely necessary for the well-being of the Hebrew commonwealth as he was essential for the perfecting of the Messianic idea. It is in Christ's kingdom that the theocracy becomes a realised fact, and Christ is above all things a King. Now in Israel the King was emphatically the Anointed One, *i. e.* the Messiah or Christ (ch. ii. 10, 35 ; x. 1 ; xii. 3, &c.). True it is that in Christ all offices must be united, and he must be a Priest to make atonement and a Prophet to teach as well as a King to rule ; yet we find in Israel, as the type of Christ's kingdom, that priest and prophet stood at the king's beck. In Solomon we have the delineation of Israel's king in his full power and glory ; and we find him thrusting out Abiathar from being high priest (1 Kings ii. 27), appointing the order of service for the priests and Levites (2 Chron. viii. 14), and having the prophets in attendance upon him to record his noble deeds (*ibid.* ix. 29). To Solomon's reign the Israelites ever looked back as giving the ideal of what their "anointed one" should be, and onward they looked to the coming of One who should perfect this ideal, and instead of staining it with sin, as Solomon did, should raise it to the full and vast dimensions of Israelite thought. Most painful must it have been to the nation that each one of its first three kings, though rising every one far above the level of ordinary men, yet fell so very far short of their ideal. And then came the rent in the kingdom, and an ideal king was possible no longer.

But the prophets kept the thought ever alive in the hearts of the people, and in the fulness of time the Messiah came. Meanwhile the establishment of the earthly monarchy was an essential condition for the security, the continuance, and the development of Israel. Without a king Israel could never have performed its work of preparing for Christ. Even the organisation of prophecy was delayed till there was a king, because when a nation has to fight for its very existence there is no room for a literary and educated order of men. Learning would have died out in the middle ages had there not been cloisters into which men who loved mental culture might retire. Still it was not this which made the people cling so tenaciously to the hope held out to them by Moses, but the daily vexation of Philistine misrule. And what the Philistines were to them now all the neighbouring nations had previously been in turn. Throughout the Book of Judges we find a state of things described from which all thoughtful men must have desired deliverance, and the few exceptions, as when they flourished for a time under the strong hand of Gideon, only served to bring out the contrast more clearly between times when they had a ruler and times when they had none. We need not wonder, therefore, at the persistency with which the people urged their demand, even after the dark pictures which Samuel had drawn of what a king might become if he degenerated into a tyrant. But our admiration is due to the patriotism and generosity which made this noble-minded man grant their request, though he knew that he thereby limited his own powers, and gave his sons an inferior place. So also had Moses done before. While he gave Aaron high and perpetual office, he let his own family fall back into the position of ordinary Israelites. And, moreover, the king whom Samuel chose was a grand hero, though, like so many men gifted with great powers of command, he fell through that self-will which is the be-setting sin of ruling natures. Few men can endure the trial of the possession of absolute power, and least of all those endowed with an energetic and resolute temperament. It is a noble testimony that David bears to

Saul and his heroic son in the "Song of the Bow" (2 Sam. i. 19—27): "mighty" they were, and "the beauty of Israel," though Saul marred his glory by great and ruinous faults. With Saul, then, the rest of the book is occupied, and it divides itself into two parts—(1) the founding and establishment of Saul's kingdom (chs. viii.—xv.); and (2) its gradual decay and final fall (chs. xvi.—xxxi.).

The Establishment of Saul's Kingdom (chs. VIII.—XV.).

REJECTION OF SAMUEL'S SONS (vers. 1—5). Ver. 1.—**When Samuel was old.** As Samuel lived for very many years after this time, till towards the close of Saul's reign, he was probably not more than sixty when this happened. The dates are all very uncertain, but he was probably between twenty and thirty when Shiloh was captured, and no doubt, according to Israelite custom, had married as soon as he arrived at manhood. Then came the most important and active period of his life, during which the ark rested for twenty years in the house of Abinadab, and Samuel was traversing every part of the country, preaching repentance, and preparing the people for a revolt from the tyranny of the Philistines. Upon this followed the victory at Mizpah, and the establishment of Samuel as judge. Now some considerable time would elapse before Samuel so felt the weight of increasing years as to delegate a part of his authority to his sons, and more again before the national dis-content at their covetousness became general. The Talmud, however, represents Samuel as being at this time only fifty-two years of age, while Abravanel says seventy, and the latter number is by no means impossible; for as a Nazarite Samuel would lead a life of perfect temperance, and his predecessor Eli lived to be ninety-eight, and died then by an accident. Still, probably, Abravanel's calculation is too high, and we must remem-ber that besides the misconduct of Samuel's sons, there was the growing danger of the re-establishment of the domination of the Philistines to quicken the people's move-ments. They had garrisons again in Israel when Saul was chosen king, and it was this which made the nation long for a change, but their choice would probably have fallen upon one of Samuel's sons had either of them been worthy. A king they had long wished for; it is only when they saw that none of Samuel's race would give them internal peace and security that they took public action for the appointment of some one else. Ver. 2.—**The name of his firstborn was Joel.** The names of Samuel's sons are pledges

of his faith—Joel meaning *Jehovah is God*, and Abiah *Jah is Father.* The name given in 1 Chron. vi. 28, *Vashni*, is a mistake. It means, "and the second," the name of Joel the firstborn having somehow been omitted. The names of Saul's sons, and even of Jonathan's, unlike those in Samuel's family, bear witness to their religion having been of a curiously mixed character. **In Beer-sheba.** Not, therefore, in any of the places to which Samuel went in person, and which were all near Ramah, his home. Beer-sheba was in the extreme south of the tribe of Judah (see on Gen. xxi. 31), on the Philis-tine border, and his being able to place his sons there in authority proves, not merely that his rule was acknowledged throughout the whole country, but also that the Philis-tines did not interfere much with the internal arrangements of the Israelites. Josephus ('Antiq.,' vi. 3, 2) represents only one son as placed at Beer-sheba, and says that the other was judge at Dan, but it may be doubted whether the northern tribes were sufficiently under control to submit to be governed by a southern judge. Ver. 3.—**His sons . . . took bribes.** This sin was expressly forbidden in Exod. xxiii. 6, 8; Deut. xvi. 19, and it marks the high spirit of the nation that it was so indignant at justice being thus perverted. They **walked not in his way** (singular—so the written text); for Samuel's own administration of justice had been most upright (ch. xii. 4), nor is it laid to his charge that he connived at the misconduct of his sons. On the con-trary, after remonstrance indeed, not for his sons' sake, but for the honour of the theo-cracy, and that the people might be on their guard against a despotic exercise of the power with which they were about to intrust a single man, he superseded not them only, but also himself. His conduct in this trying conjuncture was most admirable, and few commentators have done justice to the man, who, possessed of what was virtually kingly power, yet gave it over for the nation's good into the hands of another. Vers. 4, 5.—**The elders of Israel.** Here, as elsewhere (1 Sam. xv. 30 : 2 Sam. v. 3 ; 1 Kings viii. 3, &c.), we have traces of a popular assembly, representing the Israelite nation, and composed probably of the chiefs and heads of fathers-houses. Already in Egypt (Exod. iii. 16, &c.) we find some such body in existence, and it seems to have lasted throughout the whole history of the nation ; for it outlived the monarchy, gained increased power after the exile, and continued down to New Testament times. The demand, therefore, for a king, though a sort of revolt against Samuel's authority, was at least made in a constitutional manner, and came before him with all the weight of a formal decision on the part of the representatives of the nation. They put it also in the form of a request, for which they give two reasons. First, the decay of his physical powers — **Behold, thou art old.** Wise and vigorous as his rule had been, yet with increasing years there was less of energy ; and the events recorded as having occurred at the beginning of Saul's reign show, that in order to check the increasing power of the Philistines, a leader was needed who was at once daring, resolute, and skilful in war. But there was a further reason—**Thy sons walk not in thy ways.** These words show that the elders had the most perfect confidence in Samuel. They felt that he would not connive at the wickedness of his sons, but would do what was right by the nation. Thus they had everything to hope from the father's justice, while if they waited till his death the sons might resist what was virtually their deposition. That the sons of a judge possessed considerable power see Judges ix. 2. **Make us a king to judge us like all the nations.** *I. e.* just as all the heathen nations have a king. The words are those of Deut. xvii. 14, and were probably intended to remind Samuel that the nation was only asking what had virtually been promised.

Ver. 6.—**But the thing displeased Samuel,** and justly so. For, in the first place, they had determined to have a king without consulting the will of God. Granting that it would give them the security necessary for the nation's welfare and progress, yet so weighty a matter ought not to have been decided without an appeal to Jehovah. Samuel did make it a matter of prayer ; the elders were actuated solely by political motives. And, secondly, they undervalued their own religious privileges. They wanted a king such as the heathen had, whereas something far better and higher was possible for them, namely, a king who would be the representative of Jehovah, as the shophet had hitherto been. The nation's real need was not a new power, but the permanent organisation of what up to this time had

been a casual authority. And it was Samuel's high office to give the nation this, while he also changed the outward form of prophecy, and made it too into an orderly institution. **A king to judge us.** *I. e.* to govern us, as the shophet or judge had done, only in a more regularly - constituted manner. **And Samuel prayed unto Jehovah.** There had been no such submission to the will of God on the part of the elders ; but deeply as Samuel must have been hurt by this determination of the nation to take the government out of the hands of himself and his sons, yet he leaves the decision to Jehovah. Moreover, we must note that it was as prophet that he thus acted as mediator between the people and God ; and he gave them his services in this his highest capacity as faithfully when the question was one injurious to himself as he had ever done on more pleasing occasions.

Ver. 7.—In prayer then the answer came to him that the request of the people must be granted, however wrongly it had been urged. In itself it was wrong ; **for they have not rejected thee, but they have rejected me, that I should not reign over them.** As we saw above, they wanted no theocratic king, whose first duty would be to maintain the Mosaic law (Deut. xvii. 18, 19), and protect the priest and prophet in the discharge of their legitimate functions ; all they wanted was a soldier who would put an end to their state of anarchy, and enable them to cultivate their fields without the danger of seeing the produce swept off by marauders.

Vers. 8, 9.—**According to all the works,** &c. They showed in this the same want of respect and affection for their own institutions and religious privileges which had marked all their history since the day when Jehovah brought them up out of Egypt. And therefore Samuel was to **protest solemnly unto them, and show them.** The two verbs do not mean different things, but the same. "To protest" is to testify, to bear witness, and warn them of the danger they were incurring. And as they were asking not for the development and perfecting of their own institutions, but for a government modelled upon the institutions of the heathen round them, Samuel shows what are the dangers inherent in the establishment of a despot such as the kings of the heathen were. As a rule the kings of Judæa did not resemble the picture drawn by Samuel, but -in spite of many blemishes remained true to their allegiance to Jehovah as the supreme Ruler of the nation, and confined themselves within the limits marked out for them by the Mosaic law. **Now therefore**, at the beginning of the verse, is in the Hebrew simply "And now." There is no inference implied in it.

Ver. 11.—**This will be the manner of the king**. On the meaning of this word see ch. ii. 13. Here also it signifies not so much the legal right itself, as the way in which that right was exercised. **His chariots.** The word is singular, both here and at the end of the verse, and though it may be taken, as in the A. V., for a collective noun, "his chariotry," yet the singular is better, because this verse does not refer to war, but to the personal magnificence and grandeur of the king. Instead of the old simplicity in which the judges had lived, he would have a state chariot (see 2 Kings ix. 21), and go forth escorted by horsemen and runners on foot. **To be his horsemen.** Rather, "upon his horses." The whole clause should be translated, "And he will set them for him (*i. e.* for his service) upon his chariot and on his horses; and they will run before his chariot."

Ver. 12.—**Captains over thousands, and captains over fifties.** The largest and smallest divisions respectively of an Israelite army. However objectionable the king's personal state might be, this would fall in with the people's wishes, for it would give them the promise of a well-organised army. Not so the next clause, **to ear**—*i. e.* to plough—**his ground.** Forced labour was one of the most unjust, oppressive, and wasteful exactions of absolute governments, and was the chief cause of the revolt of the ten tribes from Rehoboam (comp. 1 Kings v. 13—16; xii. 4). And yet it was the universal rule in ancient times, and in some countries it has continued even to the present day to be the law that the peasants must at certain seasons give their labour unpaid either to the proprietors or to the state. Naturally, for a nation of agriculturists to have to leave their own fields just when their presence at home was most needed to plough the king's ground and reap his harvest would be a bitter annoyance, because to the loss would be added a sense of wrong. How determinately a high-spirited nation like the Jews did resist this injustice we gather not merely from the indignation felt against Solomon's levies, but also from the reproach cast in Jehoiakim's teeth by Jeremiah, that "he used his neighbour's service without wages, and gave him not for his work" (Jer. xxii. 13). **To make his instruments of war.** Such work must be done; but in well-organised states it is paid for by means of taxes, *i. e.* by a money compensation in place of personal service. In semi-barbarous states forced labour is used, and the national arsenals furnished at the greatest possible expense and vexation to those compelled to labour, and loss to the national resources.

Ver. 13.—**Confectionaries.** Rather, "perfumers," makers of ointments and scents, of which Orientals are excessively fond. It is remarkable that Samuel does not mention the far worse use to which Solomon put their daughters (1 Kings xi. 3), and to a less extent David and some other kings.

Ver. 14.—**Your fields.** The history of the seizure of Naboth's vineyard shows that the kings were not able to exercise this arbitrary power. Jezebel had to use great art and falsehood before she could get possession of the coveted plot of ground. But throughout Samuel describes a despot ruling after the fashion of heathen kings such as the people had desired.

Ver. 15.—**The tenth.** *I. e.* the king will cost you as much as all the ordinances of religion. Still national security would be cheaply purchased at this, or even a greater cost, if the money were well spent; but Samuel says that the king would lavish it not on **his officers**, but on his *eunuchs*, those miserable creatures, so cruelly wronged, and generally so hateful, who ministered to the pleasures of Oriental kings.

Ver. 16.—**He will . . . put them to his work.** Again the hateful forced service, but here not, as in ver. 12, of themselves, but of their households. Instead of **your goodliest young men** the Septuagint reads, "your best *oxen*," which requires only the change of one letter, and is in agreement with the rest of the verse. Samuel would scarcely place their choicest young men between the female slaves and the asses. But while the ass was used chiefly for riding, the ox was, as he still continues to be upon the Continent, man's most faithful and valued friend and fellow-labourer.

Ver. 17.—**His servants.** Literally, "his slaves." Under an absolute monarchy no one is free.

Ver. 18.—**Ye shall cry.** In despair at this cruel oppression ye shall appeal to Jehovah, but in vain. The king was given them at their own request, persisted in even after warning, and they must abide by their choice. It is worth noting that in the northern kingdom a majority of the kings more or less fulfilled Samuel's evil forebodings, and there they were much more completely the product of the temper condemned by the prophet than they were in Judah. The ten tribes roughly snapped the tie which bound them to Jehovah; they discarded the ark and all the services of the sanctuary, and were content with so poor an imitation of them that all piously-disposed men were compelled to abandon their lands and migrate into Judæa (2 Chron. xi. 16); and so the majority of their kings, not being held in check by religious influences, were tyrants. At Jerusalem, on the contrary, most of them were content to remain within the limits of the Mosaic law, and were upon the whole a series of men far superior, not merely to the judges and the monarchs in old time, but to any European dynasty.

Vers. 19, 20.—**The people refused to obey**—literally, to hearken to—**the voice of Samuel.** The words of Samuel were no doubt formally considered by the elders, and we may be sure that there would not be wanting men to urge attention and obedience to his warning; but when the decision had to be made, whether by vote or acclamation, the majority persisted in their choice, and for a reason which completely justified Samuel's displeasure; for they say— **That we also may be like all the nations.** Their wish was not to develop and perfect their own institutions, but to revolt from them, and escape from the rigour of the Mosaic law. It is remarkable that their nearest neighbours and most inveterate enemies, the Philistines, had no king, but an oligarchy of five princes. Probably it had been argued, in the assembly of the elders, that if the whole power of Israel were gathered into one hand it would be more than a match for the Philistines, whose energy must often have been diminished by discords among its rulers. **That our king may judge**—*i. e.* govern (ch. vii. 17)—**us, and fight our battles.** Here the people had reason on their side. Both the internal administration of justice and the defence of the country would be better managed under a permanent and regular authority than under the judges, whose rule was extemporised to meet difficulties, and had no inherent stability.

Ver. 21.—**All the words.** The elders had of course reported to Samuel all the arguments used in the assembly, and just as previously he had carried his own distress at the national discontent with his government to Jehovah's footstool in prayer (ver. 6), so now, in his mediatorial office as prophet, he carries thither the nation's petition.

Ver. 22.—**Hearken unto their voice.** The Divine consent is now given for the third time to their request (see vers. 7, 9). For the will of God ever leaves the will of man free, even when overruling it to the carrying out of some higher and fore-ordained purpose. Everything was ripe in Israel for the change, but it was due to the moderation and disinterestedness of Samuel that the revolution was made without bloodshed or armed struggle. Ordinary rulers too often resist a popular demand, and stem back the flowing current of thought till it breaks through the opposing barrier, and sweeps with resistless violence all opposition away. Samuel yielded, and the nation trusted him so thoroughly that they left the choice of the king entirely to him, permitted him to settle the terms and limits of the monarchy, or, as we should say, to give the nation a constitution (ch. x. 25), and treated him throughout the rest of his life with the deepest respect. He was deprived neither of his prophetic rank nor of his judicial functions, for "Samuel judged Israel all the days of his life" (ch. vii. 15), *i. e.* he remained to the last a co-ordinate power by the side of a king so self-willed and energetic even as Saul. **Go ye every man unto his city.** Prudence forbade a hasty choice. It would be well to let the agitation subside, or otherwise some busy intriguer among the elders might have managed to get himself selected by the popular voice. We gather from ch. x. 27 that there were leading men who felt aggrieved when the choice fell on none of them. But how wonderful is the confidence reposed in Samuel by the nation, when thus it left to the ruler whom virtually it was setting aside the choice of the person to whom he should cede his powers.

HOMILETICS.

Vers. 1—9.—*Discontent with God's methods.* The facts are—1. In Samuel's old age his sons, being judges over Israel, abuse their office by accepting bribes. 2. This fact is adduced by the people as a reason for asking Samuel to make them a king. 3. Samuel in his grief seeks counsel of God. 4. Samuel is instructed to yield to their request, while protesting against it. 5. The conduct of the people is declared to be an expression of the perverse tendency characteristic of their history. The order of government under which Israel was living had received the special sanction of God, and had, also, grown naturally out of their circumstances. Though often sinful and foolish, it had never before entered into their minds to seek, apart from God, a change in the political settlement inherited from the times of Moses. The deputation which waited on Samuel, asking for a king, was not the expression of a sagacious patriotism, or of profound concern for the spiritual interests of the commonwealth, and ultimately of the world; but of a restless desire for what God would give in his own time, mingled with a dissatisfaction with the system which God then was sanctioning (ch. v. 20, 21). Practically, to Samuel, it meant, *We* can suggest and we demand now a course more agreeable to our views of life and our aspirations than that *you* represent.

Samuel's pain was acute and natural, and the concession made to the discontented, though apparently a breach in the Divine order, was in keeping with God's usual treatment of men.

I. DISCONTENT WITH GOD'S METHODS AND TIMES IS VARIOUSLY SHOWN. Men can detect and condemn faults in others which they either do not see or condone in themselves. It is possible for us, in the light of history, to dilate on the sin and folly of Israel while the same temper may be manifested by us in other forms. Discontent with God's methods and times may appear in various relations. 1. *The general government of the world.* It is not often *said* that God has made a mistake in constituting the moral and material universe in such a way that so much sin and suffering should be possible ; but the *feeling* is often entertained that it would have been well if some other course had been instituted. There is more of this feeling lurking in some hearts than is supposed. Men dare not face certain of their mental operations. How far the feeling affects theology, philosophical theories, personal rest in God, and fitness for doing the best Christian work, demands serious consideration. 2. *The manner and form in which revelation has been conveyed to man.* Many attacks on the Bible proceed from a discontent with what is conceived to be inadequate to the wants of the world ; and in some this feeling has generated the supposed discovery of reasons for discarding the book as a revelation from God at all. The very primitive biographical notices ; outlines of tribal history interblended with singular personal experiences ; genealogies of uninteresting names ; crude ideas and antique customs of strange people—all this in connection with a favoured people, and relieved by streaks of light suited to men of later times, does not seem to be a mode of revelation most likely to survive the advancing intelligence of the world. It is also not the most satisfactory thing for so precious a boon as a revelation to be given in detached portions, to be conveyed originally to men of one country, and to be characterised by a series of supernatural events. Men feel that God has imposed a hard task on them to have to defend and justify what seems open to assault from so many sides. They wish it had been his will to have given his light so unmixed with an ancient human history that the most keen antagonist would be compelled to recognise its presence. To some it really seems as though the form and origin of the contents of the Bible were a misfortune. Of course *this discontent,* silent or expressed, *springs from an imperfect consideration of the real nature and purport of the revelation given,* as well as of the inevitable conditions of *any* revelation that has to be coextensive with the wants of both the first and last ages of the world ; and that, moreover, has to be concentrated and verified in a Divine person duly attested by a contemporary evidence harmonious with a chain of antecedent proof. It would be useful to the Church if some one, dissatisfied with the way in which God is affirmed to have made known his will to succeeding ages, would prescribe the right way. 3. *The method of saving men by atonement.* That God does save souls by means of an atonement bearing, in some way, an objective relation to his government, as well as a moral relation to men's lives, is so clearly the *natural* teaching of the Bible that it can only be eliminated by the adoption of a *forced, non-*natural interpretation of fact and statement. The discontent which some feel with the atonement is the reason for what is manifestly a *forced* interpretation of language. Entertaining the crude notion that the atonement is a transaction affecting *three distinct beings,* forgetful of the pregnant fact that it was *God in Christ* who, by sacrifice, effects redemption, and not considering well that all the pain and suffering, supposed to be imposed for the benefit of another, *abide on any theory for the benefit of some one,* they prefer a system in which pardon is based on the merits of a moral change brought on by a display of love in the shame and agonies of the cross ! 4. *The means of perfecting holiness in character.* The long and tedious process by which often the soul advances from one degree of purity to another awakens dissatisfaction and fretfulness. Why should so blessed an issue as sanctification be insured by sometimes loss of property, friends, and health ? Is it not possible to secure elevation of character apart from tribulation ? 5. *The means used for the conversion of the world.* There is not a more common form of discontent than this. The Apostle Peter had to contend with it when he reminded his readers of the thousand years being with God as one day. That a religion demonstrably Divine, destined to be supreme, so entirely conducive to the temporal as also spiritual interests of all men, should be slow in progress and skill is a puzzle to many. Indolence, wild interpretations of prophecy, and latent scepticism are often but indications of a wish that God had not so ordained the constitution of things.

II. The PLEA FOR DISCONTENT IS PLAUSIBLE. The plea of the Israelites was that Samuel's sons were untrustworthy—the sources of justice were corrupt. The argument urged seemed to indicate a love of purity, concern for the moral welfare of the state, a fine sense of national honour, a real advance from the degradation which had acquiesced in the vices of Eli's sons, and an appreciation of Samuel's own character. But men often pay homage to conscience by creating delusive arguments wherewith to set aside the behests of conscience. This reference to the sons of Samuel was only a pretext ; for the evil could have been remedied by demanding their removal. It is clear that the plea was only a cover for a deep aversion, a predetermined plan to get rid of the present system, whether the prophet of God approved or not. Nor is *the discontent of men* with other of the methods of God *without apparent reason*. As in Samuel's time, so now, men who cherish or express uneasiness with respect to God's ways in the government of the world and revelation seize hold of some incident, some human aspect, some partial truth that really does not touch the main issue, and make it the cover for an aversion of deeper moral origin. An everlasting universal government has only had time to exhibit its first principles, and yet some transitory phenomenal inequalities are seized on as grounds of dissatisfaction with what must be of immeasurable range and ceaseless development. From scattered incidents of which the circumstances are not fully known, and from forms of representation suited to men not blessed with full gospel light, the discontented draw a plea for a revelation to the individual man apart from Scripture. To a plain, unbiassed mind an objective revelation and an objective atonement are as truly *facts* as was God's government by judges, and as is his present government of the world in spite of apparent inequalities ; but earnest desire to see the world blessed with " true ideas " and " beneficent influences " are pleas for explaining away what is very clear. The plea sounds well ; but if men will look deeper it may be found to cover a settled aversion to submit to a ruling not chosen by self. No revealed truth is in moral antagonism with our *true* nature.

III. The EFFECT OF THIS DISCONTENT ON THE LOYAL IS TO AWAKEN THEIR DEEP SYMPATHY WITH GOD. Samuel was deeply wounded, not by the allusion to his sons, but by the people's evident aversion to God's ways and time. That any one should dare to suggest a variation from what God had approved was to him incomprehensible. He felt that God's method and time must be wisest, best, safest, because they were his. As a true man of God, he naturally seeks counsel from on high. In Samuel's displeasure there was an element of surprise, but his dominant feeling was sympathy with all that was of God. *Sympathy with God is one of the natural fruits of piety.* It was seen in Caleb and Joshua when the people were averse to the Divine procedure. Jeremiah knew it when wishing that his head were waters and his eyes a fountain of tears. In " Not my will, but thine be done " it received its highest expression. In *proportion as it is strong* does the resistance of men to the ways of God *cause wonder, shame, and anguish.* To such a soul all the works of God are excellent; they shine with supernal glory. Providences dark and painful are even welcomed as parts of the Father's blessed discipline. What men call imperfections are felt to be only dim intimations of some glorious, loving purpose. " Whatever is is right," comes from the heart when the intellect is baffled. This blessed sympathy with God ! This belief which no argument can shake ! This glorious optimism resting on the fact that the all-wise and loving One cannot but do right ! It is not any so-called Christian that attains to it. Yet it is the truest philosophy ; for it is rest in God, content with his will. " Just and true are thy ways, thou King of saints."

IV. The DIVINE TREATMENT OF DISCONTENT IS CHARACTERISED BY WONDERFUL PATIENCE. No sudden vengeance came on the rejecters of God. Consolation is poured into the heart of the sorrowing prophet ; a reference of their conduct to their ineradicable perversity is made, and they are to have their way under protest (vers. 7—9). This patience is in keeping with the record of God's treatment of Israel in the seventy-eighth Psalm. " He remembered that they were but flesh ; a wind that passeth away, and cometh not again" (Ps. lxxviii. 39). The *same is seen still.* As Christ once "endured the contradiction of sinners," so does God constantly suffer men to raise their voice against his appointments. He is "slow to anger." Calmly he allows men even to deny his existence, to criticise his government, to reject the light of his revelation, to invent ways of their own for securing future blessedness, and to murmur at his means of subduing the curse of sin. In their folly men interpret this patience of God as evidence of the correctness of their position, forgetting that "the day of the Lord" is coming, when men shall reap the fruit of their ways. To the *successors of the prophet* there is still *consolation* in the assurance that their prayer *is* heard, and their honour covered by the honour of their God. Hence the calmness, "the patience of the saints." They often can do little more than "protest" against the unbelief and waywardness of the world. A whole nation on one side and a Samuel on the other does not convert error into truth and folly into wisdom. But none of these things shake the confidence of the few who, in critical seasons, are in deep sympathy with God; for they know, by a varied experience, his vast patience, and are assured that some day feeble men will learn the lesson, perhaps bitterly, that his ways are best.

General lessons:—1. The inconsistencies of men in office furnish occasion for developing the latent evils of their fellows (vers. 3, 4). 2. The deceitfulness of the heart is seen in the eagerness with which men endeavour to justify what dare not be plainly avowed (ver. 5). 3. Human history shows how utterly incompetent man is to form a correct estimate of the ways of God (vers. 5, 8). 4. It is possible for our theologies to be framed more after what we prefer than after what is actually the fact. 5. When the Church of God is distressed because of the aversion to what is revealed, patience and prayer should be combined. 6. The most sore trial to those in deep sympathy with what Christ has approved is to witness, on the part of his professed people, a desire to escape his appointments for something more congenial to unsanctified ambition. 7. Every heresy and departure from God's ways is plausible to many, and may seem to be unchecked, but God never vacates his seat of authority.

Vers. 10—22.—*Permitted, not approved.* The facts are—1. Samuel points out to the people that their desired king will aggrandise himself at their expense, and that, once entering on their course, there will be no deliverance. 2. The people, nevertheless, decide to have a king, and assign the motive of their preference. 3. Samuel, on laying the matter before God, receives a command to make them a king. The question at issue was not whether this or that form of government was intrinsically best, nor whether at some time in the near future God might or might not cause judgeship gradually to develop into kingship; but whether, at this juncture, it was God's will to introduce a monarchy. The references in Deut. xvii. 14—20 were probably a forecast of the events now brought to pass. At all events, God's time for monarchy in Israel was not yet come; the people's had come. The historian sets forth the bearings and result of the controversy. The instance is *unique,* but the principle involved is of frequent exemplification in human affairs.

I. There are spheres of action in which God allows men to take their choice of the methods by which his purposes are to be wrought out. Israel was a nation working out a spiritual issue. The day must come when in the "*seed of Abraham*" all nations shall be blessed. Thus far, politically, this issue was being reached by a peculiar arrangement with as much success as the perverse spirit of the people would allow to any system. When "Samuel told all the words of the Lord unto the people that asked of him a king" (ver. 10), it was understood that, though they were not at liberty to set aside recognition of Jehovah, the institutions of worship, and the moral law, they were free, if they so willed, to adopt political methods of their own. They would not cease to be Messianic in purpose, but they would work toward the goal by a new method unusually characterised by human frailty. There is a *marked distinction in the accomplishment of Divine purposes* through *irrational* and *rational agents.* The one is a channel of necessity; the other the free organ of controllable actions. Every stone falls because it must; every will acts because it wills. The marvel and mystery is that the eternal Will should in the end get its own through, or in spite of, the free action of other wills.

Yet so it is. Likewise there are *differences* in the *ruling of rational creatures*. In one sense every free being can, and is left to, take what course he pleases. He may sin or not sin ; he may love God or not ; and this, too, while the obligation is most binding. But, nevertheless, God enforces some things and in others allows option. It is *essential* that God be loved ; that Christ be the Medium through which saving mercy comes to all, infant and adult ; that repentance and faith be exercised by all who hear the gospel call ; and that certain duties to man be discharged. These are conditions of safety, purity, and bliss. But it is *not essential to the same degree and in the same sense* that men should pursue their calling in one way only. There is an option left as to how men shall obtain and use their knowledge ; what methods shall be followed in pursuit of life's calling ; what means taken to promote spiritual culture and material advantage ; what social and national arrangements may best subserve the common good. Having laid down the *broad lines* of faith in Christ and righteousness of principle in all things, God seems to *have left a margin* for the exercise of our discretion. It is as though the Eternal would thus mark his estimate of the great prerogative of freedom. He educates the individual and the race by the accumulation of varied experiences, the outgrowth of freedom.

II. Any CHOICE OF MEN, AS TO METHODS of pursuing their course, is ATTENDED WITH INCONVENIENCE IN SO FAR AS IT DEVIATES FROM THAT WHICH GOD CLEARLY APPROVES. Samuel declares to the people that the choice of a monarchy would impose on them inconvenient burdens, and rob them of much of the happiness they enjoyed under the form of government already approved of God (vers. 11—18). Personal pomp and splendour would mean taxation and regal aggrandisement. The sense, therefore, of this warning is that Israel might yet be God's chosen people, subject to Mosaic law, guided in great affairs by prophets, and working to a Messianic goal ; but the form of government chosen by man would be more costly and hindering than that at present approved by God. *The teaching is true generally.* There are clear lines of conduct laid down by Providence indicative of the way in which God would have us fulfil our purpose in the world. The man of business will not realise the end in view in so far as his methods are precisely contrary to the teachings of Providence. Statesmen may take a course of their own, heedless of what God prefers ; their troubles will be proportionate. It is God's method of developing the full manhood of Christian life that, while walking humbly with him in private, we do not " forsake the assembling of ourselves together." Men who chose a different course may do so, but must bear the consequences of a dwarfed Christianity.

III. NOTWITHSTANDING A CLEAR STATEMENT OF THE PERILS OF DEVIATING FROM GOD'S METHODS, MEN, UNDER THE INFLUENCE OF A MASTERFUL PASSION, WILL SOMETIMES TAKE THEIR OWN COURSE. In vain did Samuel warn the people of the disapproval of God, and the costs of their desired monarchy ; they refused to obey his voice, and said, " Nay ; but *we will have a king* to reign over us " (ver. 19). It was not whether God approved or not ; it was not a question of promoting righteousness ; it was not a desire to see the Messianic purposes more speedily realised ; but *a longing to be like other nations*, and consequently a desire to be less in direct connection with God as Ruler. The *strength of this passion* is obvious ; for it disregards personal loss, the prophet's aversion, and the declared disapproval of God.   1. The *overpowering influence of a passion* may be felt by the *individual Christian*. It is possible for Christian men, when piety is at low ebb, to hanker after the mode of life pursued by the Christless. The prayer of Christ that his people may " not be of the world " is sometimes either forgotten or freely interpreted. " Come out from among them, and be ye separate " may be admitted as a general duty, while its execution is sadly deficient. It is only when the soul has, in unguarded hours, come under the spell of the *worldpassion* that the clear lessons of Scripture and of experience are set aside for the paltry gratification of being like other men.   2. The *same passion may lay hold of the Church.* History shows that the Church has not been free from the spell which once laid hold of Israel. The simplicity of Christ has sometimes perished in the attempt to reproduce in the Church the formalities and pomp of the Philistines. " How far the Church can safely conform to the world " is a dangerous question, and should be substituted by " How may the Church best fashion the world to its own pure and lofty standard ? "

IV. MEN DEGRADE THEMSELVES in so far as the METHODS THEY ADOPT DO NOT HAR-MONISE WITH THE SUPREME OBJECT FOR WHICH THEY LIVE. The ordinary reader feels that Israel was self-degraded in preferring to live like heathen nations when another course was open. The ends of Israel's existence were highly moral ; the mere love of pomp and splendour had no congruity with this end. What had grand military and regal parade to do with the righteousness which alone exalts a nation, and which was *the* peculiar qualification for advancing Messianic issues ? It would not save them from the disasters consequent on loss of righteousness—rather it would aggra-vate them (ver. 18) ; nor would it make the practice of righteousness more easy. There is an *intellectual and moral debasement in choice of means for an end not con-gruous with it,* and in face of warning. The individual Christian and the Church profess to live for spiritual purposes. They degenerate when, from sheer self-will and hankering after the outwardly sensational, they seek to promote private or public ends pertaining to their Christian calling by anything not spiritual in character and tendency.

V. The CHOICE OF METHODS NOT APPROVED BY GOD IS NO BAR TO THE FINAL REALISA-TION OF THE DIVINE PURPOSE. As when men from discontent with God's provision sought flesh, he sent them quails in abundance, so now he allows their freedom and gives a king. The quails and manna were only means of subsistence. "The life was more than meat." So the government by judges or kings was only method of training the people for their ultimate purpose in life. Men might sicken and die with excess of flesh, but the nation would live on. Trouble and sorrow might arise from a change of form of government, and the people might morally sink in the choice, yet God would overrule all and effect his purpose. The *Church may suffer much from her perverseness,* and comparatively tedious advance will be made in the world ; yet Christ will at last subdue all to himself, albeit his foolish people have to learn many a bitter lesson. Likewise *personally* the image of Christ will some day be more perfect in the soul, though late in life, and after many a sorrow induced by our own self-will in deviating from his methods of perfecting character.

HOMILIES BY VARIOUS AUTHORS.

Vers. 1—3. (BEERSHEBA.)—*Ignoble sons of an honoured father.* Nearly all that is known of Samuel's household is here stated. He had at least two sons, Joel (Jehovah is God) and Abiah (my father is Jah), whose names were indicative of the de-vout spirit in which they were given (1 Chron. vi. 28: "And the sons of Samuel, the firstborn, and the second Abiah ; " ver. 33 : " Heman a singer, the son of Joel ; " ch. xv. 17 ; xxv. 5 : "Heman, the king's seer "). During the period of his judgeship they grew to maturity, and toward its close he made them " judges over Israel," and sent them to administer justice in Beersheba, in the southern limit of the land. His influence as judge as well as prophet extended "from Dan even to Beersheba" (ch. iii. 20), and with advancing age he needed assistance in his labours. "It may be doubted whether Samuel acted wisely in making this appointment, especially if, as seems to have been understood, the nomination in his lifetime of his sons to fulfil the functions he had hitherto discharged alone was an intimation that he meant them to be regarded as his successors in such government as he exercised. Nothing of this kind had been done before. And thus, almost unconsciously, perhaps, he was led to give a kind of sanction to the hereditary principle of government which was soon to be turned against himself " (Kitto). He acted according to his judgment of what was best, and doubtless with disinterestedness. There is no reason to suppose that he failed to train his sons in the right way, or that he was aware of their conduct at Beersheba "and restrained them not." He is not, therefore, to be blamed. No man is infallible. The plans of the wisest men are often marred by the misconduct of others. And this appointment was, in its result, disastrous.

I. THEIR ADVANTAGES WERE GREAT. They were sons of one of the most faithful and eminent servants of God, had the benefit of his instruction and example in private and public, studied perhaps in a school of the prophets, were well acquainted with the law, held in honour for their father's sake, placed in responsible positions. All these things, we might have expected, would have made them circumspect, just, and devout; and they should have done so. How, then, can we account for their defection? 1. Goodness is not hereditary. "The sinner begets a sinner, but a saint doth not beget a saint" (M. Henry). Hereditary relationship exerts a powerful influence on the mind and disposition, but nothing but Divine grace can change the heart.

> " Rarely into the branches of the tree
>   Doth human worth mount up : and so ordains
> He who bestows it, that as his free gift
>   It may be called " (Dante, 'Purg.' vii.).

2. Education is not omnipotent. When children of a good man turn out badly, it may generally be traced to some defect of training, through attention to other duties, absence from home, inconsistency at home, unwise methods, excessive strictness, unjust partiality, undue indulgence, maternal carelessness, intimate association with evil companions (in some cases unknown and unpreventable). We do not know enough of Samuel's household to say that it was wholly free from such influences. But the most perfect education is limited in its power over character. 3. Power is a perilous trust. It presents temptations which are sometimes too strong for men who under other circumstances might not have fallen. It is a severe test, and a sure revealer, of character (Luke xii. 45). Power shows the man. 4. Each man is responsible for his own conduct. He is endowed with the power of choosing or refusing good and evil, and no external circumstances can fully account for the choice he makes. "Every man shall bear his own burden" (Gal. vi. 5). "As the soul of the father, so also the soul of the son," &c. (Ezek. xviii. 4).

II. THEIR CONDUCT WAS BASE. "His sons walked not in his ways" of truth, integrity, self-denial, and true godliness; but "turned aside" from them to—1. Covetousness, or the undue love of earthly possessions. "The love of money is a root of all kinds of evil" (1 Tim. vi. 17—19). "Covetousness is idolatry" (Luke xii. 15; Col. iii. 5). "It is the idolatry of the heart, where, as in a temple, a miserable wretch excludes God, sets up gold instead of him, and places that confidence in it which belongs to the great Supreme alone." It was one of the necessary qualifications of judges that they should be "men of truth, hating covetousness" (Exod. xviii. 21). Nothing is more corrupting than "the narrowing lust of gold." 2. Bribery (Exod. xxiii. 6, 8; Deut. xvi. 18, 19). 3. Perversion of justice (Prov. xvii. 15). 4. Their conduct in all these things was so persistent and flagrant that it was known to "all the elders of Israel." They openly abused their power for selfish ends, trampled on the law which they were appointed to "magnify and make honourable," and wrought against the purpose which Samuel spent his life in effecting.

III. THEIR INFLUENCE WAS PERNICIOUS. Not only did they bring misery upon themselves, and occasion bitter sorrow to their aged father; but they also—1. Inflicted grievous injury on those with reference to whom they "took bribes and perverted judgment." 2. Set a bad example to all men (Ps. xii. 8). 3. Brought their high office into contempt. 4. Contributed directly to a national revolution. How true it is that "one sinner destroyeth much good!"—D.

Vers. 4—22. (RAMAH.)—*Israel's desire for a king.*

> " The old order changeth, giving place to new
>   And God fulfils himself in many ways,
> Lest one good custom should corrupt the world " (Tennyson).

Introductory.—The desire of Israel for a king, as expressed by their elders to Samuel, was a turning-point in their history. 1. This desire was *not new.* It existed long before (Judges viii. 22; ix. 9). But new circumstances had arisen,—the greater order and unity resulting from the labours of Samuel, the misconduct of his sons, the threatening attitude of surrounding nations,—causing it to become stronger and more general, and to issue in a definite and fixed determination. The elders simply gave expression to what the heart of the people was set upon. 2. The object of their desire was *not essentially wrong.* It had been foretold that kings should arise in

Israel (Gen. xvii. 6, 16; xxxv. 11; Num. xxiv. 17). Provision had been made in the law of Moses for the choice of a king, and directions given concerning the manner in which he should govern (Deut. xvii. 15—20); and, more recently, intimations had been afforded that the time for his election was at hand (ch. ii. 10, 35). His appointment was only in *apparent* contradiction to the fundamental principle of the theocracy, that " God was their King," for it was not intended to supersede the Divine authority; he was to be the viceroy or deputy of Jehovah, as the judges had been; and he might be better adapted than they to the present condition of the people. Nevertheless, the transition was in one aspect from a higher to a lower order of things, from a *direct* to a *mediate* theocracy; it tended to set the invisible Ruler in the background, and it was fraught with imminent peril. 3. The *sinfulness* of their desire consisted in the sort of king they sought and the spirit they manifested; whereby they, in effect, rejected the Lord as their King. " If they had simply desired a king to be given them according to the law of God (Deut. xvii. 15), that should govern them in equity, and such an one as feared God, they then had not offended; but now they do ask a king of a preposterous desire only that they might be like unto other nations; yet God, having purposed to erect among his people a kingly throne, and to raise unto them a king of whose seed Messiah should come, took this occasion to accomplish his purpose, so turning their evil and inordinate desire unto a good end, as God can convert the evil thoughts and actions of men to serve for his own glory " (Willet). 4. Their desire was *fulfilled*, and the transition peaceably effected through the agency of Samuel, who yielded to their request because he perceived the good which was hidden therein, and that in the providence of God the time was come for a king to be appointed (ch. ix. 16). " Israel was in the position of a boat which has been borne down in a swift stream into the very suction of the rapids. The best would be that she should put back; but if it be too late for this, then the best is that there should be in her a strong arm and a steady eye to keep her head straight. And thus it was with Israel. She plunged down the fall madly, rashly, wickedly, but under Samuel's control steadily " (Robertson). " He had to guide the difficult transition of Israel's political organisation from a Divinely-ruled republic into a regularly-constituted monarchy." " To mediate between the old and the new was, indeed, the peculiar position of Samuel. He was at once the last of the judges, and the inaugurator of the first of the kings. Take the whole of the narrative together—take the story first of his opposition, and then of his acquiescence, in the establishment of the monarchy. Both together bring us to a just impression of the double aspect in which he appears; of the two-sided sympathy which enabled him to unite together the passing and the coming epoch " (Stanley). His calmness, moderation, breadth of view, practical adaptation, and lofty devotion to God and his people were herein exhibited in an eminent degree. " Samuel is one of the few great men in history who, in critical times, by sheer force of character and invincible energy terminate the previous form of a great existing system—at first against their own will, but afterwards, when convinced of the necessity, with all the force and eagerness of their nature; and who then initiate a better form with the happiest results, though amidst much personal suffering and persecution " (Ewald, ' History ').—D.

Vers. 4—22. (RAMAH.)—*The popular desire for a king.* " Make us a king to judge us like all the nations " (ver. 5). This narrative teaches us—

I. THAT THE POPULAR DESIRE, ALTHOUGH IT MAY BE PLAUSIBLE, IS OFTEN REPREHENSIBLE (vers. 4, 5). 1. *Its alleged grounds were insufficient.* (1) The old age of Samuel. But due respect to him and gratitude for his past services should have prevented their desire to set him aside; and the prosperity that attended his rule during many years should have led them to wish for its continuance as long as possible. They were inconsiderate, forgetful, unthankful, hasty, and unjust. (2) The misgovernment of his sons. But they might have been removed from their office without the office itself being abolished. It is better to try to mend an institution than to destroy it. (3) To be like other nations. But Israel was designed to be unlike them, and superior to them (Levit. xx. 26); and most of the miseries they had suffered arose from conformity to their ways. The wish *to be like others* is a fruitful source of sin and woe. The cause of truth and righteousness in the world is greatly damaged when those who should be the guides of the ignorant and the wicked become their servile followers. " Palestine in ancient times was pre-eminently a land of kings. Every district, nay, every considerable city, had its king and its court. In most cases the king was an autocrat, absolute and irresponsible, lawgiver, judge, and executor, the source of all honours, offices, and emoluments, the commander of the army, the dispenser of favours, the awarder of punishment. The rights, claims, and pre-rogatives of royalty extended to every person, and to every relation of life. The king was the master, the people were his subjects, nay, slaves—his property. In a better sense he was the common father of the community, they his children, with all the kindlier duties and obligations implied and included in this most sacred of human relations. Royalty thus constituted and administered was selected by Jehovah as the synonym and exemplar of his special relation to the Hebrew people " (Thomson, ' Bibliotheca Sacra,' vol. xxx.). (4) The threatening attitude of the Philistines (ch. ix. 16) and the Ammonites (ch. xii. 12), which was doubtless referred to in the inter-view of the elders with Samuel. But the Lord of hosts, who had hitherto delivered them, was able to do so still ; and to rely upon a new institution for safety instead of upon him was to lean upon a broken reed. " Instead of seeking for the cause of the misfortunes which had hitherto befallen them in their own sin and want of fidelity toward Jehovah, they searched for it in the faulty constitution of the nation itself " (Keil). 2. *Its real grounds were blameworthy.* (1) Dissatisfaction with the govern-ment which had been Divinely appointed and sanctioned. When the hearts of men are right with God they are not disposed to complain of his ordinances. (2) Dis-trust of the presence and might of their invisible King. " God was not sufficient for them without a creature prop." " Their demand of a visible earthly sovereign was in disparagement of that extraordinary Providence which had distinguished them from the nations of the earth, and taken them by a privilege under an immediate theocracy. Their sin was founded in a revolt from God, in the abdication of a perfect trust and reliance upon his providential government in that method in which with respect to them he had ordered it. But their fault, though uncommon in its form, is not at all in its principle. Something to *see* and nothing to *believe* is the wish and propensity of more than the Israelites " (Davison ' on Prophecy '). (3) Impatience, presumption, and self-will. " God gave them judges, . . . and afterwards they desired a king " (Acts xiii. 20, 21). Instead of first seeking to know the will of God, and then wait-ing his time for a change, if it should seem good in his sight, they thought that they knew what was best, took counsel of their own hearts, and, having chosen their course independently of him, proceeded forthwith to follow it up, and resolved to have their own way. They were thus disloyal to their Divine King, to whose direction and con-trol they were bound to submit. (4) The love of worldly pleasure, power, and glory. They desired a king not merely (*a*) that he might judge them without interruption, by the law of hereditary descent; but also (*b*) that " he might go out before them and fight their battles " (ver. 20) ; and, still further (*c*), that he might hold a splendid court, and gratify their ambition and lust of shining or making a boastful display. They wished to be thought in no respect inferior to the surround-ing nations. It was a result to which prosperity too often leads. The worldliness from which the misconduct of Samuel's sons proceeded was but a symptom of a widespread evil. " The secret spring of their rebellion was the ambition of their leaders, who could live no longer without the splendour of a regal court and house-hold. 'Give me' (say they, as the prophet Hosea makes them speak, ch. xiii. 10) ' a king and princes,' where every one of them might shine a distinguished officer of state. They could get nothing, when their affairs led them to their judge's poor residence in the schools of the prophets, but the gift of the Holy Ghost (ch. x. 10 ; xix.), which a courtier, I suppose, would not prize even at the rate of Simon Magus, or think it worth the bribing for a piece of money. This it was, and only this, that made their demand criminal" (Warburton, ' Div. Leg.,' Book V.). How often has their sin been repeated in the history of nations ! " All the tragical wars of the Greeks or barbarians, whether civil or foreign, have flowed from one fountain—from the desire either of riches, or of glory, or of pleasure ; for in pursuit of these things the human race brings on its own destruction " (Philo Jud., ' In Decal g.).

II. That the popular desire is not unfrequently an occasion of great trouble to a godly man (vers. 6—9). "The thing was evil in the eyes of Samuel." He saw that it was wrong, felt disappointed and grieved, and was at first altogether opposed to it, and disinclined to listen to those by whom it was expressed, "because," says Josephus, "of his inborn sense of justice, because of his hatred of kings, as so far inferior to the aristocratic form of government which conferred a godlike character on those who lived under it." "For kings are many, and the good are few" (Dante). 1. As a good man has no greater joy than to see the people seeking what is right and good, so he has no greater sorrow than to see them "going after vain things which cannot profit nor deliver; for they are vain" (ch. xii. 21). Abraham (Gen. xviii. 23), Moses (Exod. xxxii. 18, 31), Elijah (1 Kings xix. 10). The Psalmist (Ps. cxix. 158), Jeremiah (Jer. ix. 1), Paul at Athens (Acts xvii. 16). 2. The grief he feels is of the noblest kind. (1) Unselfish. Samuel did not resent or complain of what was said concerning his old age or his sons' misgovernment; and if he was not absolutely indifferent to the injustice done to himself, yet his trouble arose chiefly from other and higher considerations. (2) Patriotic. (3) Divine. He was concerned, above all things, for the honour and glory of God. His own loyalty to him made him quick to resent the disloyalty of others, and his sympathy with his purposes filled him with holy jealousy lest they should be defeated or in any way hindered. He felt in some degree as God himself feels. 3. His resource in trouble is prayer to God. "And Samuel prayed to the Lord" (ver. 6); probably all night, as on a subsequent occasion (ch. xv. 11). Such had been the resource of his devout mother in her distress. Nor is there any other so effectual (Ps. lv. 22; Phil. iv. 6). 4. In communion with God he finds abundant consolation and help. God takes upon himself the burden of his servant who has laboured and suffered for his sake (Ps. lxix. 7). "They have not rejected thee, but they have rejected me." He assures him that it is "no strange thing that has happened unto him." "According to all the works which they have done," &c. (ver. 8). He removes his perplexity, tells him what to do, and gives him strength to do it. "Hearken unto their voice," &c. (ver. 9). All questionings cease when the Divine voice speaks, and, with the morning light, Samuel goes forth humbly, fearlessly, and cheerfully to deliver his message to the elders.

III. That the popular desire, when it is wrong, should be rebuked, and its evil effects declared (vers. 10—18). It may not be allowed to pursue its course without warning on the part of those who feel that it is wrong, and to whom a Divine message comes. 1. This message *consists* of—(1) A testimony against its sinfulness. "Hearken unto their voice: howbeit yet protest solemnly (testify) unto them" their sin, and the displeasure of Heaven. (2) A declaration of the evils involved in its fulfilment. "Show them the manner (*mishpat*) of the king that shall reign over them," *i. e.* his regal rights, claims, privileges, and prerogatives; not what might be *de jure*, according to "the manner of the kingdom" (ch. x. 25; Deut. xvii. 14), but would be *de facto*, according to the custom of the kings of the heathen nations whom they wished to resemble. We have here a picture of "the dark side of the institution" in contrast with the theocracy:—(*a*) Its ruling motive—personal aggrandisement and indulgence. "He will take for *himself, his* chariots, *his* horses," &c., whilst for *your* welfare he will care nothing. (*b*) Its arbitrary and oppressive character. "He will take your sons" to be his personal attendants (ver. 11) for military and agricultural service (ver. 12), your daughters for domestic service (ver. 13), your land to give to his attendants (ver. 14), a tenth of your corn and wine to reward his officers (imposing heavy taxation—ver. 15), your servants and cattle "to put them to his work" (ver. 16), and a tenth of your sheep; "a great retinue, a great table, a standing army, great favourites, great revenues" (M. Henry); and you yourselves will lose your political and social liberty, and become his slaves (ver. 17). (*c*) Its helpless and hopeless misery (ver. 18)—brought upon yourselves, causing you to cry out to God for help, "and the Lord will not hear you in that day." "The yoke once assumed you must bear for ever" (1 Kings xii. 4). 2. The message must be *declared* faithfully and fully, whether men will bear or forbear. "And Samuel told all the words of the Lord to the people" (ver. 10). 3. The *purpose* of such declaration being to lead them to consideration and repentance, and, if they still persist, to throw the responsibility for the result upon themselves alone. The watchman who warns the wicked, even if they turn not from their way, "hath delivered his soul" (Ezek. xxxiii. 9); and the faithful minister is "unto God a sweet savour of Christ, in them that are saved, and in them that perish" (2 Cor. ii. 15).

IV. THAT THE POPULAR DESIRE IS SOMETIMES EFFECTUALLY CORRECTED BY BEING GRATIFIED (vers. 19—22). 1. In spite of every admonition, men can and do *persist* in their sinful desire. "Nay; but *we will* have a king over us." Their self-will appears more plainly than before. Expostulation only makes it stronger. They will have their way. And God, who coerces not whom he has endowed with moral freedom, permits them to do so. 2. By their persistency they even *obtain* of him the fulfilment of their request. "Make them a king," is his final response to Samuel, who "rehearsed the words in his ears," and now dismisses them "every man unto his city," to await the speedy accomplishment of their desire. The evil which would have resulted from its refusal is thus averted. The principle of the theocracy is preserved. Jehovah continues to rule over Israel; and they recognise his authority in so far, at least, as to leave the selection and appointment of a king in his hands. His sovereign will encircles and controls their purposes. But he does not, by granting their request, sanction their sin. On the contrary—3. In its fulfilment he inflicts upon them a just *chastisement*, and teaches them, by the experience of its legitimate results, the folly of their devices. Their first king is a man after their own heart, reflects their sin, and brings overwhelming calamity on himself and them. "I gave thee a king in mine anger" (Hosea xiii. 11; Ps. cvi. 15). "God, when he is asked for aught amiss, showeth displeasure when he giveth, hath mercy when he giveth not. The devil was heard in asking to enter the swine, the apostle was not heard when he prayed that the messenger of Satan might depart from him." 4. He *prepares* them thereby to receive as their ruler "a man after his own heart" (ch. xiii. 14), who shall conduct them to power and honour, and foreshadow him who is higher than the kings of the earth. How wonderfully are the Divine purposes fulfilled in and through the errors and sins of men! "In a very remarkable sense the *vox populi* was the *vox Dei*, even when the two voices seemed most utterly out of harmony. . . . The Jews were asking for heavy punishment, without which the evil which was in them could not have been brought to light or cured. But they were asking also for something besides punishment, for that in which lay the seeds of a higher blessing. Beneath this dark counterfeit image was hidden the image of a true King reigning in righteousness; the assertor of truth, order, unity in the land; the Helper of the poor, who would not judge after the sight of his eyes, nor reprove after the hearing of his ears; but would smite the earth with the rod of his mouth, and with the breath of his lips would slay the wicked" (Maurice).—D.

Ver. 6.—*The benefit of prayer.* "And Samuel prayed unto the Lord." The blessings obtained in answer to prayer are real and manifold. Some of them are outward and material—daily bread, health, safety, life. God is "in all, above all, and through all," the personal and free Ruler of the universe, and able to grant our petitions for temporal good in harmony with the established order of nature. The mind and will of man can produce changes in the material world without disturbing that order; much more can the eternal mind and will do the same. Other blessings are inward and spiritual—wisdom, righteousness, peace, and joy. The "Father of spirits" has access to the human spirit, interpenetrates it as light the atmosphere, holds communion with it, and disposes it to holiness. Spiritual blessings are incomparably more valuable than material. What we *are* determines our relation to surrounding objects. And beneficial changes wrought *within* are followed by similar changes in the world without. "In prayer we make the nearest approaches unto God, and lie open to the influences of Heaven. Then it is that the Sun of righteousness doth visit us with his directest rays, and dissipateth our darkness, and imprinteth his image on our souls" (Scougal).

"Speak to him, thou, for he hears, and spirit with spirit can meet.
Closer is he than breathing, and nearer than hands and feet" (Tennyson).

In illustration of the spiritual benefit of prayer let us consider how Samuel, who "prayed unto the Lord" in his trouble, and "rehearsed all the words of the people in the ears of the Lord" (ver. 21), was comforted and helped in time of need. What a different man he was when he came forth from communion with his Almighty Friend to speak to the elders of Israel from what he was when he went from them, "displeased" (ver. 6) and distressed, to pour out his heart before the Lord! "What profit shall we have if we pray unto him?" 1. *Relief* for a burdened heart. It is often a great relief to tell our trouble to an earthly friend; much more is it to pour it forth into the bosom of God. "No other God but the God of the Bible is *heart to heart*" (Niebuhr). "They went and told Jesus" (Matt. xiv. 12). 2. *Sympathy* under bitter disappointment. Samuel seemed to have "laboured in vain and spent his strength for nought." But God sanctioned his work, identified himself with him, shared his disappointment, and took his burden on himself. In rejecting his faithful servants men reject the Lord. "Why persecutest thou me?" (Acts ix. 5). He sympathises with them (Heb. iv. 5); and one smile of his more than compensates for apparent failure and the frowns of the whole world. "By degrees two thoughts calmed him. The first was the feeling of *identification* with God's cause. The other element of consolation was the Divine *sympathy*. Atheism and revolution here, as elsewhere, went hand in hand. We do not know how this sentence was impressed by the infinite mind on Samuel's mind; all we know is, he had a conviction that God was a fellow-sufferer" (Robertson). 3. *Guidance* in great perplexity. The will of the Lord, it may be, is at first hidden or obscure, but in fellowship with him the mists and clouds that prevent our seeing it are cleared away, the sun shines forth, and our way is made plain. We see "the light of this world" (John xi. 9). "The vocation of man is the sun in the heavens of his life." "The secret of the Lord" (the counsel or advice, such as a man gives to his friend) "is with them that fear him" (Ps. xxv. 14). God tells his secrets only to his friends. "The meek will he guide in judgment: the meek will he teach his way" (Ps. xxv. 9). "He will guide you into all the truth" (John xvi. 13). 4. *Submission* to the supreme will. That will is always wisest and best; it cannot be altered or made to bend to ours; and one of the chief benefits of prayer is that thereby we receive grace which disposes us to accept humbly and cheerfully what at first appears evil in our sight. We are made of one mind with God. 5. *Strength* for painful duty. It may be to "protest solemnly" (ver. 9) against the course resolved upon by others, to alter our own course and expose ourselves to the charge of inconsistency, to face opposition, danger, and death. But God never appoints us a duty without giving us strength to perform it. "Habitual prayer constantly confers decision on the wavering, and energy on the listless, and calmness on the excitable, and disinterestedness on the selfish" (Liddon). 6. *Composure* amidst general excitement. Whilst the elders clamour, "Nay; but we will have a king over us," Samuel is unmoved. He calmly listens to their decision, takes it back to God in secret prayer, and then comes forth and says, "Go ye every man to his own city." "Thou wilt keep him in perfect peace, whose mind is stayed on thee: because he trusteth in thee" (Isa. xxvi. 3). Hurricanes revolve around a centre of perfect calm. Outside the charmed circle the tempest may rage furiously; within it all is peace. Such is the heart and mind kept (garrisoned) by the peace of God (Phil. iv. 7). 7. *Confidence* in a glorious future. "The Lord will not forsake his people for his great name's sake" (ch. xii. 22). He works out his purposes by unexpected methods, overrules human perversity, and makes the wrath of man to praise him (Ps. lxxvi. 10). "What will the end be?" it was said at a time of great and general anxiety to an eminent servant of God (Dr. A. Clarke), who replied, with a beaming countenance, "Glory to God in the highest, and on earth peace, good-will toward men."—D.

Ver. 22.—*The unwise demand granted.* The government by judges fell into discredit. Samuel, indeed, was without reproach; but when advancing age made the burden of public affairs too heavy for him, his sons, to whom he naturally delegated his authority, proved unrighteous rulers. They do not seem to have been licentious, like the sons of Eli, but they were covetous, and corrupted the fountains of justice by taking bribes. What a persistent thing sin is! How it repeats itself! How hard it is to eradicate it! Samuel's lifelong example of integrity was lost upon his sons. The terrible fate of Eli's family was lost on them too. To the dignity of justice, to the honour of truth, they were indifferent for filthy lucre's sake. Then the elders of Israel asked Samuel to set a king over them.

I. THE IMPROPRIETY OF THE REQUEST. 1. It followed a bad precedent. The experiment had been tried about 150 years before. The people asked Gideon to be their hereditary prince, and that hero declined the proposal, as inconsistent with a pure theocracy. After his death Abimelech was king for three years; but his career began in cruelty, ended soon in disaster and death, and no one from that time had sought the royal dignity. 2. It proceeded on a wrong principle. The desire to be as the other nations round about was in flat contradiction to the revealed purpose of God that Israel should be separate as a people unto him. The wish to have a king to lead them out to battle betrayed a thirst for war unworthy of a holy nation, and a mistrust of the Lord's power to defend them. Here, indeed, is the point in which they departed from the permissive law regarding a king recorded in the seventeenth chapter of Deuteronomy. A regal government was not to be reckoned inconsistent with the theocracy, provided the king was not a foreigner, and was chosen by Jehovah, whose vicegerent he should be. The elders asked for a king not after the mind of the Lord, but after the pattern of the heathen round about.

II. REASONS OF THE DIVINE CONSENT. 1. A headstrong people must learn by experience. The elders and people of Israel were warned of the risk they ran. A king such as they desired would restrain their ancient liberties, and subordinate all their rights and interests to the maintenance of his court and army. They heard Samuel's warning, and persisted in their demand. So the Lord bade his servant make them a king. If men will not take advice, let them have their way. Wisdom seldom comes to wilful men but through sharp lessons of the results of folly. 2. The way must be prepared for the king and the kingdom that God would choose. It is important to remember that Divine purposes are accomplished on earth not by direct fiats of authority or exertions of power, but through long and complex processes of human action and counteraction, by the corrections of experience, the smart of suffering, and the recoil from danger. It was God's design to constitute Israel into a kingdom under a sure covenant—a kingdom which should furnish the basis for glowing prophetic visions of the kingdom of Christ; but this design was not to be fulfilled abruptly, or by a sudden assertion of the Divine will. The way was prepared by the failure of all other devices for holding together the Hebrew people. First the government by judges lost credit; then the kingdom as set up by popular desire failed; so that the tribes, seeing the ruin of their own devices, might be ready to receive the kingdom as God would have it, and the man whom he would choose to "feed Jacob his people and Israel his inheritance."

III. ILLUSTRATIONS OF THE SAME PROCESS. 1. Men have set up their own devices in the administration of the Church; and with what result? They have not been content with an unseen Lord and King. The early patriarchates may be described as a government by judges; but men were not content therewith, and Latin Christianity set up an ecclesiastical and spiritual supremacy on earth, a Saul-like kingship at Rome. Those parts of the Western Church which broke away from this doomed kingdom at the Reformation, for the most part gave power to secular princes in exchange for their protection. All such arrangements are temporary devices; but they are witnesses and preludes to something higher and more Divine. They prepare the way for the reign of Jesus Christ, as the broken, confused reign of Saul prepared for the strong kingdom of David. 2. Inward Christian experience can tell a similar tale. What plans have to be tried and found wanting, what thrones of confusion in the heart to be subverted, before the Lord alone is exalted! We are permitted to have our own way that we may learn how small our wisdom is, how vain are our devices. We exalt our own righteousness, our own will, our own religious confidence. It is our Saul; and the issue is confusion and disorder, till we renounce our pride and vainglory, and receive the Son of David, Jehovah's true Anointed, to reign over and rule in us. Self-religion starts thus—"Nay; but we will have a king." The religion which is taught of God says, "Blessed be the king that cometh in the name of the Lord!"—F.

EXPOSITION.

CHAPTER IX.

SELECTION OF SAUL AS KING BY THE VOICE OF PROPHECY. GENEALOGY OF SAUL (vers. 1—27). Ver. 1.—**A man . . . whose name was Kish.** The genealogy of Saul is rendered obscure by the Hebrew custom of abbreviating such records by the omission of names. The family documents were no doubt kept in full, but when transcribed, as here and in the First Book of Chronicles, only a summary is given, and as the omitted links are not always the same, great difficulty is necessarily the result. The most satisfactory genealogy is that given by Schaff from a comparison of Gen. xlvi. 21 ; 1 Sam. ix. 1 ; xiv. 51 ; 1 Chron. vii. 6—8 ; viii. 29—33 ; ix. 35—39, and is as follows : 1. Benjamin ; 2. Becher ; 3. Aphiah, perhaps same as Abiah ; 4. Bechorath ; 5. Zeror, or Zur ; 6. Abiel ; 7. Ner ; 8. Kish ; 9. Saul. Very many links, however, are omitted, among whom must be placed Matri, mentioned in 1 Sam. x. 21 ; and Jehiel, mentioned in 1 Chron. ix. 35 (and see *ibid.* viii. 29). He is described as the first settler and coloniser of Gibeon, and as husband of Maachah, a daughter or granddaughter of Caleb. The spelling of his name with an *'ain* forbids our confounding him with Abiel, as is done by Schaff and most commentators, and whom, apparently, he preceded by many generations. In the two places referred to above a large family of sons is ascribed to him ; but as, first of all, the lists do not agree, as, moreover, they are said to dwell with their brethren in Jerusalem (1 Chron. viii. 32), and as Ner, the father of Kish, is mentioned in the second list, it is pretty certain that we are not to regard them as his actual children, but as the leading names among his posterity. The fearful cruelty recorded in Judges xx. 48 may well account for the hopeless entanglement of Benjamite genealogies. An ancestor of Saul must, of course, have been among the 600 who escaped to the rock Rimmon, but he could have saved only his own life. **A mighty man of power.** Really, "of wealth." Saul, like David afterwards, was sprung from an affluent family, whose landed property was situated at Gibeah, about four miles north of Jerusalem, afterwards known as Gibeah of Saul.

Ver. 2.—**He had a son, whose name was Saul.** I. e. *asked*, a name usually given to a firstborn son. **A choice young man.** This is a double translation of the Hebrew word, and consequently one half or other must be wrong. It may either be a participle, *elect* or *choice*, and is so rendered by the Syriac and Vulgate ; or an adjective, *young*, the

rendering of the Chaldee, and virtually of the Septuagint, which gives *well-grown*. This is the preferable translation ; for the word constantly occurs coupled with virgin (Deut. xxxii. 25 ; Isa. lxii. 5, &c.), for one in the full flower of manhood. Saul could not, therefore, have been the runner of ch. v. 12, though, as we read that Jonathan his son was a grown man two or three years afterwards (ch. xiii. 2), he must have been at least thirty-five years of age, after making allowance for the early period at which the Jews married. His noble appearance and gigantic stature were well fitted to impress and overawe a semi-barbarous people, who were better able to form an estimate of his physical qualities than of the high mental and moral gifts possessed by Samuel.

Ver. 3.—**The asses of Kish . . . were lost.** So strangely is the trivial ever united with events most solemn and weighty, that Saul set out upon this journey, in which he was to find a kingdom, with no other object than to look for some lost asses—Hebrew, "she-asses." As used for riding (Judges x. 4), the ass was valuable, and as these were probably kept for breeding, they were allowed more liberty than the males, and so strayed away.

Ver. 4.—**Mount Ephraim.** Though Gibeah, Saul's home, was in Benjamin, it was situated on this long mountain range (ch. i. 1). **The land of Shalisha.** I. e. *Three-land*, and probably, therefore, the region round Baal-shalisha. It takes its name from the three valleys which there converge in the great Wady Kurawa. **The land of Shalim.** *I. e.* of jackals ; probably the same as the land of Shual, also = jackal-land (ch. xiii. 17). The very name shows that it was a wild, uninhabited region. The derivation *hollow-land* is untenable.

Ver. 5.—**The land of Zuph.** See on ch. i. 1. This Levite ancestor of Samuel had probably occupied and colonised this district after the disasters recorded in the last chapters of the Book of Judges. **Lest my father, &c.** A mark of good feeling on Saul's part, and a proof of the affectionate terms on which Kish and his family lived.

Ver. 6.—**In this city.** Probably Ramathaim-zophim, *i. e.* Ramah, Samuel's dwelling-place and property. Confessedly, however, Saul's route hither and thither in search of lost cattle is very obscure, and it is difficult to reconcile this identification with the statement in ch. x. 2, that Rachel's sepulchre lay on the route between this city and Gibeah of Saul. Nevertheless, Ramah was certainly in the land of Zuph, whence too it took its longer name (see on ch. i. 1) ; and it is remarkable that Jeremiah (ch. xxxi. 15) describes Rachel's weeping as being heard in Ramah. It seems extraordinary that Saul should have known nothing of Israel's chief ruler, and that his servant was acquainted with him only in his lower capacity as a person to be consulted in private difficulties. He describes him, nevertheless, as **an honourable man,** or, more literally, an honoured man, one held in honour.

Ver. 7 —**The bread is spent in our vessels.** In the East a great man is always approached with a present, and offerings of food were no doubt the most usual gifts (ch. xvi. 20). Those made to the false prophets are contemptuously described in Ezek. xiii. 19 as "handfuls of barley and pieces of bread." **A present.** The word is rare, and apparently is the technical name for a fee of this kind, half payment and half gift.

Ver. 8.—**The fourth part of a shekel.** Apparently the shekel, roughly stamped, was divided into four quarters by a cross, and broken when needed. What was its proportionate value in Samuel's days we cannot tell, for silver was rare ; but in size it would be somewhat bigger than a sixpence, and would be a very large fee, while the bread would have been a small one. It very well marks the eagerness of the servant that he is ready to part with the considerable sum of money in his possession in order to consult the seer. The whole conversation is given in a very lively and natural manner.

Ver. 9.—**Beforetime, &c.** This verse is evidently a gloss, written originally by some later hand in the margin, in order to explain the word used for seer in vers. 11, 18, 19. Inserted here in the text it interrupts the narrative, and is itself somewhat incomprehensible. The Septuagint offers a very probable reading, namely, "for the people in old time used to call the prophet a seer," *i. e.* it was a word used chiefly by the common people. Prophet, *nabi*, is really the older and established word from the beginning of the Old Testament to the end. The word *roëh*, used in this place for seer, is comparatively rare, as a popular word would be in written compositions. It refers to that which is seen by the ordinary sight, to waking vision (see on ch. iii. 1, 10), whereas the other word for seer, *chozeh*, refers to ecstatic vision. *Roëh* is used by Isaiah, ch. xxx. 10, apparently in much the same sense as here, of those whom the people consulted in their difficulties, and they might be true prophets as Samuel was, or mere pretenders to occult powers. The present narrative makes it plain that *roëh* was used in a good sense in Samuel's days ; but gradually it became degraded, and while *chozeh* became the respectful word for a prophet, *roëh* became the contrary. Another conclusion also follows. We have seen that there are various indications

that the Books of Samuel in their present state are later than his days. Here, on the contrary, we have a narrative couched in the very language of his times ; for the writer of the gloss contained in this verse was displeased at Samuel being called a *roëh*, but did not dare to alter it, though taking care to note that it was equivalent in those days to calling him a *nabi*.

Vers. 11, 12.—**As they went up.** Ramah was situated on a double hill, whence its name Ramathaim (ch. i. 1). As, then, *they go up the ascent* — so the Hebrew, literally — they meet maidens on the way to the well, and ask them, **Is the seer**—the *roëh*—**here ?** They answer, Yes ; **behold, he is before you.** *I. e.* they are to go straightforward, and farther on in the town they will find him. **He came to-day to the city.** As Saul's servant knew that this city was Samuel's abode, the words must mean that he had just returned from visiting one of those places, probably, to which he was in the habit of going as judge. From ch. xvi. 2 we learn that Samuel went occasionally even to distant places to perform priestly duties. **In the high place.** Hebrew, Bamah. Samuel, we read, had built an altar at Ramah (ch. vii. 17), and probably the present sacrifice was to be offered upon it. Such altars, and the worship of the true God upon high places, were at this time recognised as right, and were, in fact, in accordance with, and were even the remains of, the old patriarchal religion. But gradually they were condemned, partly because of the growing sanctity of the temple, but chiefly because of the tendency of religious rites celebrated in such places to degenerate into nature-worship, and orgies such as the heathen were in the habit of holding on the tops of mountains and hills. We thus find in the Bible an illustration of the principle that rites and ceremonies (as not being of the essentials of religion) may be changed, or even abolished, if they are abused, or lead on to evil consequences.

Ver. 13.—**As soon as . . . straightway.** This is too forcible a rendering of the Hebrew particles, and makes the talk of these water-carriers even more garrulous than it is in the original. The latter word should be omitted, as they simply say that on entering the city Saul and his servant would easily find Samuel ; for he would not go up to the feast till all was ready, nor would the people begin till he had arrived, because it was his office to bless the sacrificial banquet. The pious custom of asking a blessing on meals, our Lord's "giving of thanks," is inherited by us from the Jews.

Ver. 14.—**When they were come into.** More correctly, "As they were going into the city." This agrees with what is said in ver. 18, that Saul and Samuel met in the gateway. As Ramah occupied two hills, the Bamah would be on the summit of one, while the city probably nestled between them.

Ver. 15.—**Now Jehovah had told Samuel in his ear.** Literally, "had uncovered his ear," as in Ruth iv. 4; 2 Sam. vii. 27. The phrase is taken from the pushing aside of the head-dress in order to whisper, and therefore means that Jehovah had secretly told Samuel.

Ver. 16.—**That he may save my people out of the hand of the Philistines.** Though Samuel had lightened the yoke of the Philistines by his victory at Mizpah, yet he had by no means altogether broken their power. It is so constantly the habit of the historical books of the Bible to include the distant and ultimate results of an act in their account of it, that we must not conclude that what is said in ch. vii. 13—15 was the immediate consequence of Samuel's victory. Especially, when it said that "the hand of Jehovah was against the Philistines all the days of Samuel," it is plain that Saul's successful wars are included in the writer's summary of events, inasmuch as Samuel's life was prolonged until nearly the close of that monarch's reign. The words further show that Saul's office was essentially military, though this is too much emphasised in the A. V., which renders by **captain** a word which really means *prince, chief.* Saul, as a Benjamite, belonged to the bravest and most warlike tribe of Israel, and one whose country was the seat of perpetual combat with the Philistines. **Their cry is come unto me.** Plainly, therefore, Israel was again suffering from Philistine domination.

Ver. 17.—**Jehovah said unto him.** Literally, "Jehovah answered him." When Samuel saw the young stranger, struck by his towering height, he wondered within himself whether this were the destined hero who was to win freedom for Israel. The affirmation, therefore, came in answer to the question asked by his heart. **The same shall reign over my people.** More literally, the margin, "restrain in," *i. e.* coerce, control. The A. V., preferring as usual a general to an exact rendering, loses this plain indication that Saul's would be a strict and stern rule.

Ver. 18.—**In the gate.** The same preposition is used here as that translated "*into* the city" in ver. 14. The contradiction which many commentators suppose that they find between the two verses arises from their not remembering that prepositions constantly lose their original meaning. Literally the preposition means *in the middle,* but its common meaning is simply *within.* So with us *immediately* has lost all reference to the middle, though derived from that word, and signifies *directly, at once.* Saul, then, and his servant were just going (it is a present participle) *within* the city when they meet

Samuel coming out, and accost him in the very portal.

Vers. 19, 20.—**Go up before me.** Addressed in the singular to Saul, to whom, as the future king, Samuel pays every mark of honour. The next words, **Ye shall eat,** include Saul's servant. **I will tell thee all,** &c. Intended not merely to set Saul's mind at rest, but also to prepare him for the great news he was to hear. So, too, the information that the asses were found, given to him before he had even hinted at the object of his visit, would convince him of the reality of Samuel's prophetic powers. **On whom is all the desire of Israel?** Rather, "To whom belongs all that is desirable in Israel? Is it not for thee, and for thy father's house?" The words were intended to indicate to Saul, though in an obscure manner, that the supreme power in Israel would be his. Why trouble about she-asses? They might be beautiful, and a valuable property for a husbandman; but he was about to become a king, to whom would belong everything that was best and most precious.

Ver. 21.—**Wherefore then speakest thou so to me?** Though Samuel's words contained the promise of supreme power,—for to whom less than a king could all that was desirable in Israel belong?—yet Saul probably regarded them as a high-flown compliment, such as Orientals love to use, and gave a modest and proper answer. Benjamin, already the smallest tribe, had been so crushed that its power must have been very small, and Saul's house, though opulent, was not a leading one; how then could one of its members expect so high a dignity? For **families of the tribe of Benjamin** the Hebrew has "tribes," probably owing to some confusion with the words "tribes of Israel" just before.

Vers. 22, 23.—**Into the parlour.** Strictly the cell or room attached to the chapel of the high place, now used as the *guest-chamber,* wherein the thirty chief men, who came as invited guests, were to dine. The rest of the people would be in the open air. There Samuel not only placed Saul in the seat of honour, but also his servant, and representing the king's officers of state, and commanded the cook to set before him a **portion** that had been reserved. This was the shoulder; but whether it was the left shoulder, of which the laity might eat, or the right shoulder, which was sacred, as belonging to the priest (Levit. vii. 32), is not mentioned. If the latter, it was Samuel's own share, and he may by his prophetic authority have assigned it to Saul, in token that the priesthood would be subject to the royal power. Be this, however, as it may, it was the portion of honour, and it seems that Samuel, on receiving intimation the previous day of Saul's visit (ver 16), had given orders that it should be carefully reserved for him (ver. 24). He now orders it to be set before Saul, with **that which was upon it**, *i. e.* all the flesh and the fat not appointed to be burnt upon the altar.

Ver. 24.— **And Samuel said.** Samuel's name is not given in the Hebrew, and though inserted by the Septuagint and Vulgate, it is so only by a manifest error. The Syriac and Chaldee, like the Hebrew, make the cook the speaker. The right translation is, "And the cook lifted up the shoulder with that which was upon it, and set it before Saul, and said, ' Behold, that which hath been reserved is set (a participle, and not the imperative) before thee ; eat, for it hath been kept for thee unto the appointed time of which he (*i. e.* Samuel) spake, saying, I have invited the people.' " The word translated in the A. V. *since I said* is one which means *saying*, and nothing else ; and as what goes before contains no verb to which *saying* can refer, it is plain that there is an ellipse. But if the cook be the speaker, the meaning is plain, as follows :—When on the previous day the revelation was made to Samuel that Israel's future king would present himself on the morrow, the prophet at once made preparations to receive him with due solemnity, and for this purpose arranged a sacrifice, and invited thirty of the chief citizens of Ramah to assemble at the high place, and sit at the banquet with him. And then it was, when telling the cook of his invitation, that he gave orders that the portion of honour should be carefully reserved, to be set at the fitting time before the stranger. The chat of the cook is entirely after the manner of ancient times, and would show Saul how completely his coming had been foreseen and provided for.

Ver. 25.—When the feast was over they went down from the high place, and having entered the city, proceeded to Samuel's dwelling, where he **communed with Saul upon the top of the house.** The Septuagint has a very probable reading, namely, "And they spread a bed for Saul upon the roof, and he lay down ; " but the Syriac and Chaldee agree with the Hebrew. Without communicating to Saul that he was to be king, which was not revealed to him till the next day (ch. x, 1), Samuel might be anxious to impress on Saul's mind the great principles of the theocratic government, and also the nature of the remedies necessary for Israel's recovery from its present misery.

Vers. 26, 27.—**It came to pass about the spring of the day.** This is not a separate act from **they arose early** ; for the A. V. is wrong in translating the next clause, " Samuel called Saul to the top of the house." Saul had slept there, and, wearied out with his long wanderings and the excitement of the previous day, was fast asleep when Samuel came to him. The Hebrew is, "And they rose early ; for at the spring of the day Samuel called to Saul upon the house-top, saying," &c. And no sooner had Saul risen than they started upon his journey home, and as soon as they had left the city, at some fitting spot, Samuel bade the servant go forward, and as soon as he and Saul were alone he spake unto him **the word of God.** And by that Divine word he who had left his father's house in search of lost asses was summoned to a post which, if one of the greatest dignity, was full also of danger, and burdened with solemn responsibility. And while on the human side Saul proved not unworthy of a royal crown, in his relation towards God he failed, because he let self-will and earthly policy prevail in his heart over obedience and trust in God.

HOMILETICS.

Vers. 1—10.—*Divine consideration.* The facts are—1. Saul the son of Kish, a wealthy Benjamite, and remarkable for stature and goodliness, seeks his father's asses. 2. Not finding them, he fears lest his father should be anxious about his own safety, and suggests a return home. 3. His servant advises a recourse to a distinguished man of God then in those parts. 4. Obtaining a small present, Saul resolves to consult the man of God concerning the lost asses. A great crisis has come in which the dangerous elements at work in Israel's heart might lead to much mischief. The chief motive for desiring a king being a craving for outward display, and a corresponding distrust and dislike of God's more unseen and immediate direction of national affairs, it was evidently possible for steps to be taken which would ruin Israel's prosperity. The narrative relates to us a series of Divinely-governed events, apparently trivial, which prevented that calamity and insured the national safety.

I. GOD'S REGULATION OF IMPERFECT DESIRES AND DANGEROUS ASPIRATIONS. There is no harm in desire for monarchy *per se ;* but the form it assumed in this instance was defective, and it revealed a moral tendency which, if fed by appropriate nourishment, would lead to a frustration of Israel's true work in the world. The saving feature in their conduct was their deference to Samuel. The instruction conveyed to him to select a king was consistent with the fact that God was displeased with their request (ch. viii. 7 ; cf. Hosea xiii. 11). The solution of the apparent discrepancy lies in the circumstance that God does not leave his people to the full bent of their own heart. He mercifully regarded their condition, and governed their tendencies in such a way as to make the best of a bad case. *This is true*, more or less, *of all men not yet judicially abandoned*. There is a force of evil in men enough to destroy them speedily but for the restraining power of God. The mental operations of sinners are governed by an unseen hand, and often directed to their advantage, when, otherwise, evil would ensue. *There have been ages in the history of the Church when conspicuously unhallowed desires and worldly aspirations* have not been left to work ruin, but *have been chastened, controlled, directed* to objects better than they, left to themselves, would have chosen. The age of Constantine would have been more calamitous for religion had not the Head of the Church governed rising tendencies and provided moderating influences.

II. GOD'S CARE IN MEETING MAN'S WEAKNESS. Not any man would suit Israel as king at that time. There were conditions in the state of the people which needed to be wisely met. The people were impressible by the outward physical aspect of things ; they required a leader of social position to command respect ; and their own hankering after likeness to other nations rendered it important that their king should have some moral character ; at the same time, being their choice, he must be a representative of the weaknesses and wisdom of the age. Hence the care of God in directing Samuel to Saul, a man of commanding appearance (ver. 2), of wealthy family (vers. 1—3), of quiet, plodding, God-fearing disposition,—as seen in occupation, in his concern for his father, and in his deference to the prophet,—and yet of no deep, intelligent piety. This *Divine care is no novelty in history*. 1. *It is constant*—coextensive with the history of the race. Even fallen Adam was cared for in temporal things. The order of Providence, the adaptation of his Word to varying exigencies of life, the appointments in his Church for the perfecting of the saints, are only some instances of a care that never faileth. 2. *It is secret*. Israel little knew, while those asses were wandering from home, that their God was caring so wisely and tenderly for them. Silent as the light is the voice that orders our path ; more subtle than either is the hand that guards our spirit. By day and night his hand leads, even to the uttermost parts of the earth. 3. *It is beyond all desert*. Even when Israel was in spirit rejecting him he cared for them. "How shall I give thee up?" is the feeling of the Father's heart. He rewards us "not according to our iniquities." The daily mercies of God are more than can be numbered, and they come because he delighteth in mercy, not because we earn them by obedience and love.

III. GOD'S LEADING BY UNKNOWN WAYS. While restraining and regulating Israel's tendencies, an unseen hand is leading the son of Kish by a way he knew not. In the straying of asses and in the following their track we first see natural events ; but behind and in them all we soon learn to see God gently leading Saul from a quiet, rural life to undertake a great and honourable responsibility. It is *not strange for God to lead by unknown paths* those whom he chooses for his service. Abraham did not know the full meaning of the secret impulse to leave Ur of the Chaldees. Joseph's imprisonment was not man's sole doing. Egyptians in the court of Pharaoh saw not the hand guiding Moses into a knowledge of their legislation and their learning. Likewise is it *true in the bringing of men to a knowledge of Christ*. Many a simple circumstance has brought a wanderer to a greater than Samuel. And in *the Christian life* we are led by circuitous, untrodden paths to duties, privileges, joys, and eternal rest. God is Guide and Counsellor—by monitions of conscience, by word of truth, by voice of friends, by barred pathways of life, by yearnings created within, by events great and small.

General lessons :—1. Let us have faith in God's mastery over all that is in man. 2. Let us believe that he will provide for his people suitably to their need. 3. Let us keep our heart and eye open to the guidance of the unseen Power, and not despise events that seem trifling in themselves.

Vers. 11—17.—*Man's accidents God's ordinations.* The facts are—1. On entering the city Saul inquires for the seer, and is informed that he is present for a special religious service. 2. Following the directions given, he meets Samuel ascending to the high place. 3. Samuel is already instructed by God to expect during the day the man whom he is to anoint as king. 4. On seeing Saul, an intimation is given from God that he is the chosen man. In some respects this narrative of events resembles what is occurring every day in every land, for we have here a set of independent actions converging on a common result. No single meeting of men occurs in society without a variety of acts and movements having directly or indirectly preceded it as links in the chain of causation. But the speciality in this instance is the information that the meeting of Saul and Samuel was pre-ordained of God. Hence the incident is an illustration of the double side of what to men may appear to be only ordinary human occurrences. An uninformed person would have said that it was accidental that the asses went astray, and that maidens directed Saul to their city, where Samuel happened to be. To Saul it so appeared ; but, guided by the inspired narrative, we know that the " accident " was " fore-ordained " without destroying its really accidental character. We may notice what light the record before us throws on the general question of special providences.

I. We SEE HERE THE FREE ACTION OF MANY INDEPENDENT WILLS. In so far as asses exercise will, those were free in straying from home on that day. The action of Kish in selecting Saul rather than any one else to seek them was quite his own. The readiness of Saul to obey his father and not find a substitute in the toil was unconstrained. The mental and emotional antecedents of the citizens prompting their will to arrange for Samuel to visit their city were natural, and operated on wills perfectly independent. The suggestion of the servant that Saul should not return, but go to this very city, arose spontaneously ; and Saul's concern for his father was relieved by considerations which he freely yielded to. The action of Samuel, amidst his many public engagements, was free in deciding to offer sacrifice, and, so far as we can see, not exclusively connected with an expectation of meeting the coming king in that particular place. In addition to all these free and independent acts, there were events which tended to turn the free acts in the one direction. Lack of pasture in certain places may have influenced the asses to take the course they did. The distance to be traversed was just such as to bring Saul to the vicinity of Samuel where persons were at hand to answer his questions. The difficulty of approaching the prophet with a proper token of respect was overcome by the casual possession of a small coin. *This analysis of fact accords with what may be affirmed of thousands of incidents every day.* Independent lines of force converge on one point and issue in an historical resultant. In no case recorded in Scripture does any supreme power take away freedom of action.

II. The FREE ACTION OF MANY IS ATTENDED BY THE UNRECOGNISED ACTION OF GOD. In the instance before us this is obvious, for it was ordained that Samuel should meet with Saul on that very day, though they were so far apart (vers. 15, 16). Whether it was " chance " that took Saul to that city or some influence exerted on him is easily answered by the fact that it was God's purpose for Samuel to see and anoint him. God's fore-ordination does not wait on " chance." The same reasoning would show that even the course taken by the asses, though free, was not without God's action. The inspiration of Samuel's conduct is a primary fact of the prophetic office. It is *possible to start difficulties* in relation to this subject ; but *they are difficulties of ignorance, not of knowledge,* and therefore lose much of their force. We do not even *know what* the free act of will is, though we know the *fact.* We know that our actions are free, and yet that we *are* influenced by others. The point of junction between the external influence and the free act of our will has never been detected ; therefore, any difficulties which men raise against these narratives in the Bible lie equally against all interaction of free natures. The *Scripture doctrine is that God does act on man without destroying his freedom.* God is not a *latent* energy. He assures us that he is a real Power, working in some " mightily to will and to do," and striving with others. The highest government is only possible on this supposition. The *possibility of what are called special providences* resolves itself into the *free action of a supreme Spirit on created spirits,* so as to secure their free and independent action, and at the same time cause that action to converge on given points. We even can do that in some degree with children and feebler natures. Why do men wish to banish the eternal energy from all participation in human affairs? Do not these events with their issue stand out as a microcosm of the great converging lines which in the far-distant future are to issue in one glorious resultant—the realisation of a holy will through the free and independent action of created wills?

III. The RECOGNITION OF GOD'S ACTION COMES OUT IN THE RESULT. The Divine action is silent, unobserved, often unknown while in process. Samuel saw it as a reality when Saul stood before him. The story of the asses and of the search then had another meaning. Men see not one half of the realities of life. The true, real world is the unseen. The great transactions are wrought in the inner man. We are often led by a hand we do not see, and drawn on by a sweet influence we cannot define. Only the more spiritual, saintly souls discern God. But as Samuel saw what God had been doing, so we at last come to see what God hath wrought. That will be a wondrous recognition of the all-working Spirit when a vast redeemed race shall, in review of life's chequered course, sing the new song, and exclaim with deep significance, "Not unto us, O Lord, not unto us, but unto *thy name* give glory."

IV. The DIVINE REASON FOR THE EXERCISE OF THIS SILENT POWER. The compassion of God for his wayward people (ver. 16) was the spring of the particular direction he gave on this day to the course of Saul and Samuel. Every small series of events affecting individuals and families is, so far as relates to the action of God in them, governed by some Divine reason. Though trouble be brought on, the reason is still one of mercy. The retributions of Providence are in mercy to the universe he governs. And it may certainly be said of the sum-total of events, that when the great result shall be attained, it will be known then, if not before, that all was the expression of a compassion which sought to save the erring world from its own miseries.

General lessons:—1. The perfect government of God is secured by his mastery of every detail in the action and willing of his creatures. 2. There is consolation for his people in the fact that he directeth the spirit of man, and can subdue *all* things to himself. 3. It is blessed to go forth daily with the assurance that God works with us, in us, and for us, and will therefore perfect that which concerneth us.

Vers. 18—24.—*Shadows of coming events.* The facts are—1. Saul, on accosting Samuel, is invited to stay with him, is assured of the safety of the asses, and is caused to know that great honour is in store for him. 2. Saul, taken by surprise, desires to have further explanations of the language used. 3. Samuel entertains Saul with all the honours due to a distinguished guest. The position of Samuel was one of relative advantage, for Saul was ignorant of the Divine intent, while he knew the purpose of God. The course taken by Samuel was as follows:—First he intimated to Saul that it would be well to accept his proffered hospitality, as he had a communication to make which would draw out his interest (ver. 19). Then he relieves his care about his father's property, and awakens more curiosity by the further intimation that the choice things of Israel were in reserve for him and his father's house. To prevent hasty explanations, he next induces him to take his place in an entertainment as chief guest; thus by a significant act preparing him and the people for something more definite. And with all the kindliness and courtesy due to distinction, he threw a gleam of light on the strange proceeding by reminding him that though his presence there seemed accidental, it was not quite so, as he was the person for whom the dish of honour had been reserved (ver. 24). Thus was the nomination of Saul as the king shadowed forth. In all this the prophet acted in his official capacity as representative of God. May we not see here how God prepares us for disclosures of his will?

I. The FULL TRUTH GOD WOULD HAVE US KNOW IS BROKEN UP AND MADE CLEAR BY DEGREES. The prophet here was slightly opening the veil before the eyes of Saul; he was qualifying his sight for dazzling splendour. And that is just what all the prophets of God have done and are doing for us. They intimate to us that there are great truths in reserve, and so speak to us by the way as to indicate in dim outline what some day will stand out in eternal clearness. The figures, the types, the allusions to the "unspeakable," the reminders that we are but disciples, children—all are foreshadowings of great realities on which the mind will in future gaze. "We know in part." It is true *the Bible is all we need* for salvation, and contains more spiritual truth than elsewhere to be found ; but in one sense it is to men a treasure, and we are only fitted to receive out of it a dim intimation of *the* truth, as Saul was fitted only to receive from the mind of the prophet a portion of what was there for him. The *process by which God's truth* was given to the world—by allusion, dim prophecy, type, historical examples foreshadowing *the* Christ, till at last the full announcement came—is another illustration of the gentleness and wisdom wherewith God has "spoken" to men.

II. The FULL HONOURS GOD HAS IN RESERVE FOR HIS PEOPLE ARE GRADUALLY REVEALED. Saul wondered what distinction was awaiting him. He felt unworthy of such language as that used by the prophet. His wonder was not satisfied at once. Men have been known to die under the sudden declarations of bliss awaiting them. Equally so God has in reserve for all who are one with Christ a crown, a glory, an honour, which though we know by name, we know not in reality. "We know not what we shall be." There is a joy and glory unspeakable. There are things which an apostle could not utter. Future realities are only dimly shadowed forth by earthly words and symbols. A full vision of coming honours might paralyse the strongest frame.

General lessons :—1. Deep interest in the welfare of the Church of God will suppress all feelings of personal jealousy. 2. A good man will enter heartily into new methods recognised by God, even though at first they were distressing to his own heart. 3. The qualities of gentleness and courtesy towards God's servants have the highest sanction, and do much to facilitate private and public business. 4. The keenest sense of unworthiness is that experienced when God confers on us the choice honours and treasures of his kingdom. 5. The transition to the full glory of the future will be natural and easy in so far as we avail ourselves of the shadowings forth of the reality contained in God's word.

Vers. 25—27.—*Interest in public affairs.* The facts are—1. After the public intimation of Saul's coming distinction Samuel converses with him in private. 2. On sending him away on the next day Samuel will have no one present at the moment of parting. Saul is passive. Samuel is still the most important. As yet all had been public. Enough had been said to call up from Saul's heart feelings and aspirations which in his quiet life had lain dormant (ver. 19). He now felt that God had *something* for him to do in Israel, and his heart revealed sentiments answering to the shadowed honour. It was fit, therefore, to commence privately on topics connected with the condition and prospects of Israel. The invitation to the privacy of the house-top for this purpose was thus in keeping with Samuel's wise procedure, and a good illustration of his deep interest in the public welfare. The most probable explanation of the conduct of Samuel certainly is, that his concern for the welfare of the nation and of the coming king irresistibly prompted him to converse on the wants of the age, and the responsibilities of Saul's new position as a chosen servant.

I. IT IS THE DUTY OF A RELIGIOUS MAN, AND IN KEEPING WITH HIS CHARACTER AND PROFESSION, TO TAKE A DEEP INTEREST IN PUBLIC AFFAIRS. Samuel's interest in affairs was, it is true, official, as head of the state, but the official acts had their root in a deep personal longing for the prosperity of Israel. "Pray for the peace of Jerusalem." "They shall prosper that love thee," was the feeling which every true descendant of Abraham was supposed to entertain. The best days of Israel's history show that the pious were proud of their country, its institutions, its rulers, its laws, and the order and purity of its administration. 1. *The state claims our interest.* (1) *The law of benevolence* supports this claim. Every man in the state is our neighbour ; his comfort and peace and safety depend on the administration of affairs ; we can only reach the individuals by doing our part to render affairs useful to all. (2) The *principles of religion are applicable to state affairs.* Faith in Christ and repentance toward God are not the whole of practical religion, though they are the spring and support of many other feelings and principles. Righteousness, purity, supreme regard for the Unseen, kindliness and generosity, unselfishness and truth, can find expression in laws, in commercial arrangements, and in foreign and domestic policy. Loyalty to these religious principles requires that we see that they are recognised everywhere. (3) The *adaptation of Christianity to the entire life of man* is one of the *most commanding evidences of its Divine character*. It professes to make *all* things new. It forms the true, perfect manhood. A religion which is seen practically to enter into every sphere of human activity, as the conserving "salt," carries with it the proof that it comes from the Creator of man and of society. He, then, who loves his Christianity, and would advance its conquests, must show by his interest in the State that it is "profitable unto all things," even to public affairs. (4) The *great calamities brought on communities* have resulted from the *predominance in state affairs of irreligious principles*. When "rulers of Sodom," men of godless lives, are left to have charge of affairs, when the holy and conscientious leave their country's business to persons with whom they would not leave their own private affairs, disaster has come, and will ever come. There can be nothing in such a line of conduct at variance with Christian character or profession. The enforcement of righteousness all over the world must be right. To love Christ supremely, and to labour that souls may be converted to him, is no more inconsistent with promoting righteousness in state affairs, and watching its progress there with keen interest, than with seeing that our private business is honestly transacted.

II. Emergencies will arise when interest in public affairs may find distinct expression. The emergency which developed Samuel's deep interest did not create it. There is a fountain of strong feeling and righteous thought in a truly good man's nature. Crises in a people's history bring out the latent feeling, and shape it into word or deed. There should not be a day on which a Christian does not bear all the interests of his country on his heart, and give them some direct or indirect support. But in the changes of human affairs, and in the incessant struggle between the good and evil forces of society, there arise now and then opportunities for every righteous man to do his best towards securing a righteousness in the State.

III. The manner in which interest is shown will depend on position and opportunities. Samuel showed his interest by discussing with Saul the general question of the people's welfare, and by fitting his mind for coming responsibilities. Every Christian can express his interest intelligently, faithfully, kindly, and prayerfully by seizing the opportunities appropriate to his situation in life. But prayer for kings and rulers, personal observance of the course of events, acquaintance with the real needs of the country, encouragement of a sound, righteous, political literature, support to men of tested character, exercise of powers conferred by law, infusion into controversies of a generous, truth-loving spirit—these are means within reach of most, and cannot but issue in blessing to all. The *interest thus due to public state affairs* is also due by the Christian to the *general affairs of the Church of God*. Every one should bear on his heart the welfare of the body of Christ, and do all he can to heal its wounds, cleanse its spirit, and insure its highest happiness and prosperity. Do men sufficiently identify their personal religious interests with those of the one Church? Is the oneness of the body of Christ properly appreciated? Do our prayers and tears flow forth as they ought for the *kingdom of God?*

General considerations:—1. The causes of so little interest in public affairs by many Christian people. 2. How Christian people can manifest a proper interest apart from the painful contentions to which they are perhaps constitutionally unfitted. 3. The degree of sympathy due to good men who from sense of duty enter into the perils and annoyances of public life, and how it can be expressed. 4. The question of how much of national trouble, sorrow, and poverty is connected with neglect on the part of the morally powerful sections of society. 5. How far Christian men are really making love of righteousness and truth and peace superior to social customs and party ties.

HOMILIES BY VARIOUS AUTHORS.

Vers. 1—25. (Gibeah, Ramah.)—*The king desired by the people.* 1. The *choice* of the first king of Israel was made by Samuel, prophet and judge, as the highest authority under God in the nation; and it was afterwards confirmed by lot, wherein the Divine will was openly expressed (ch. x. 21). "The history of the world cannot produce another instance in which a public determination was formed to appoint a king, and yet no one proposed either himself or any other person to be king, but referred the determination entirely to God " (Scott). 2. In *making choice* of Saul, Samuel believed that he would be acceptable to the people, and fulfil the purpose for which they had desired a king, in saving them out of the hand of the Philistines (ch. ix. 17) and the children of Ammon (ch. xii. 12); and he appears to have expected that he would be faithful to the principle of the theocracy, and rule in obedience to the Divine will. He did all that lay in his power that this expectation might be realised; he entertained a strong affection for Saul; and it was only when the latter proved utterly unfaithful to his trust that he reluctantly and sorrowfully abandoned him to his fate. 3. His choice was *directed* by a higher wisdom than his own, which saw the end from the beginning. Whilst the Divine King of Israel sanctioned what was good in their desire, he fulfilled it in such a manner as to convince them of what was evil in it, and to accomplish far-reaching purposes which the prophet himself did not foresee.

> " The ken your world is gifted with descends
> In the everlasting justice as low down
> As eye doth in the sea, which though it mark
> The bottom from the shore, in the wide main
> Discerns it not; and, nevertheless, it is,
> But hidden by its deepness" (Dante, ' Purg.').

" Saul is not selected by them, but given to them; whom they adopt and embrace they know not why; and who, whether or not he is able to guide and govern them, proves to be a faithful representative of their own state of mind, a very type and embodiment of that character and those habits of mind which they themselves are exhibiting " (Maurice). " The theocratic principle was more fully developed in the reaction than could have happened had the king been truly pious, so that we may say that Saul was chosen by God, because in his omniscience he foresaw that he would not turn to him with his whole heart. Saul and David are in necessary connection. On the threshhold of royalty God first shows in Saul what the king of Israel is without him; then in David what the king is with him. Both are types or representatives. The events which befell them are actual prophecies, which first of all passed into fulfilment in the history of the Israelitish monarchy, and then through the whole history of the world " (Hengstenberg). The following chapters record the development of the successive stages of the Divine method according to which the popular desire was gratified and corrected. The man destined for king was—

I. FITTED BY PECULIAR QUALIFICATIONS (vers. 1, 2). Notice—1. *His family relationship.* He was the son of Kish, of the family of Matri (ch. x. 21), of the tribe of Benjamin; his cousin (or perhaps uncle—1 Chron. viii. 33) being Abner, afterwards " the captain of his host " (ch. xiv. 51); his name—Saul = asked—being " an omen of his history." Kish was a man of wealth and good social position, a fact which would gain for his son general respect; he appears to have been an affectionate father (ver. 5; ch. x. 2); and he resided at Gibeah (ch. x. 26), " a hill," formerly a place of notorious profligacy (Judges xix.), and subsequently the seat of Saul's government, but was buried at Zelah (2 Sam. xxi. 14). Of him nothing more is known. Benjamin was the smallest of the tribes of Israel (ver. 21), but the most warlike of them (Gen. xlix. 27). The selection of a king from it, therefore, would not be likely to excite the jealousy of the other tribes, whilst he would doubtless prove an able leader of their armies. There was in Saul " the strange union of fierceness and of gentleness which run, as hereditary qualities do often run, through the whole history of that frontier clan " (Stanley). 2. *His personal appearance.* He was in the prime of manhood, and of lofty stature and great warlike beauty (ver. 2; ch. x. 23, 24). " Great stress is laid upon this, because his distinguished stature, with the impression of bodily prowess which it conveyed, helped much to recommend him to the choice of the people. When, after a long peace, there was no man of distinguished renown among them, and when in battle much less depended upon the military skill than upon the bodily prowess of the chief in single combats, or in the partial actions with which most battles commenced, it was natural enough that the people should take pride in the gigantic proportions of their leader, as calculated to strike terror into the enemy and to inspire confidence in his followers ; besides that, it was no mean advantage that the crest of the leader should, from his tallness, be seen from afar by the people " (Kitto). 3. *His mental and moral characteristics.* He was possessed of little mental culture. He had not been instructed in the schools of the prophets (ch. x. 11). His life had been spent in retired, rustic occupation, in which he was so absorbed that he was less acquainted with the political and religious movements of his time than his own servant (ver. 6). He was obedient to his father (ver. 4), tenderly concerned about his feelings (ver. 5), persevering in labour, and ready to take advice even from one beneath him (ver. 10). He exhibited a courteous, modest, and humble bearing (ver. 21 ; ch. x. 21). He was, in his earlier career, capable of prudent reserve (ch. x. 16, 27) ; patriotic, zealous, fearless, energetic (ch. xi. 6), resolute, and magnanimous (ch. xi. 13); and he had a strong sense of the value of religion and religious institutions. But underneath these qualities there lay others of a different nature, which his subsequent course revealed, viz., waywardness, rash and fiery impulses, impatience, the love of display, pride and self-will, and morbid tendencies to distrust and jealousy ; and instead of overcoming them by the aid of Divine grace, he yielded to them, until they gained the entire mastery over him, choked the good seed which was sown in his heart (Matt. xiii. 22), and caused his ruin. God sees the latent as well as the manifest dispositions of men, and adapts his dealings toward them accordingly.

II. GUIDED BY SPECIAL PROVIDENCE (vers. 3—14). These verses furnish a practical commentary on what was said by Hannah concerning the operations of Providence (ch. ii. 7, 8). In leaving his home in Gibeah, at the direction of his father, in search of the lost asses, travelling through the hill country of Ephraim, the land of Shalisha, of Shalim, and of the Benjamites, to the land of Zuph (ch. i. 1), and going in search of the " seer " (*roëh*), Saul acted freely, and according to his best judgment ; but his three days' journey and all connected with it—his lack of success, his desire to return, his servant's advice, his destitution of food, his servant's possession of a coin for a present, his meeting with " young maidens going out to draw water," his presence in the city at a certain time—were ordered by God to the attainment of an end of which he had no conception. "All these incidents and wanderings were only preparations and mediate causes by which God accomplished his design concerning Saul." His providence—1. Often makes *insignificant* events productive of important results. It is truly astonishing how the very greatest things depend upon events which are generally regarded at the time of their occurrence as of little account. Of this the lives of individuals and the history of nations afford innumerable illustrations. "What is it that we dare call insignificant ? The least of all things may be as a seed cast into the seed-field of time, to grow there and bear fruits, which shall be multiplying when time shall be no more. We cannot always trace the connections of things ; we do not ponder those we can trace, or we should tremble to call anything beneath the notice of God. It has been eloquently said that where we see a trifle hovering unconnected in space, higher spirits can discern its fibres stretching through the whole expanse of the system of the world, and hanging on the remotest limits of the future and the past " (Kitto, ' Cyc. of Bib. Lit.,' first ed., Art. ' Providence ; ' Knapp's ' Theology '). 2. Makes *accidental* circumstances subservient to a pre-arranged plan. "The thread of every life is entangled with other threads beyond all reach of calculation. Those unforeseen accidents which so often control the lot of men constitute a *superstratum* in the system of human affairs, wherein, peculiarly, the Divine providence holds empire for the accomplishment of its special purposes. It is from this hidden and inexhaustible mine of chances—chances, as we must call them—that the Governor of the world draws, with unfathomable skill, the materials of his dispensations towards each individual of mankind " (Isaac Taylor, ' Nat. Hist. of Enthusiasm '). 3. Overrules *human plans*, in harmony with human freedom, for the fulfilment of Divine purposes (Prov. xvi. 9, 33).

III. INDICATED BY DIVINE REVELATION (vers. 15—25). Such revelation—1. *Was primarily and directly given* to one who lived in closest fellowship with God. Samuel was like the lofty mountain peak, which catches the rays of the morning sun long ere they reach the valleys below. On the day before Saul came to the city (of Ramah), the prophet, ever watching and listening for the indications of the Divine will concerning the future king, was fully instructed therein by "the word of the Lord" (ch. iii. 21), which contained (1) a promise of *sending* him (ver. 16), (2) a direction to *anoint* him, (3) a statement of the *purpose* of his appointment, and (4) an expression of *commiseration* for the need of the people. Nothwithstanding they had rejected God, he had not rejected them, but still calls them "my people," and in wrath remembers mercy. The long-suffering of God toward transgressors should teach his servants forbearance, and incite them to renewed efforts for their welfare. It appears to have been after Samuel had received the Divine message that he invited the people (perhaps the elders who had formerly waited upon him) to a sacrificial feast, and arranged for the worthy entertainment of his chief guest (ver. 24). The displeasure which he previously felt at their request (ch. viii. 6) has now given place to disinterested and earnest desire for its fulfilment. 2. *Harmonised with, and was confirmed by,* the operations of Providence. Samuel is expecting the fulfilment of the promise given to him, and already is on the way from his own house in the city to offer sacrifice on the height (the loftier of the two hills on which Ramah was situated), when he sees the towering form of Saul, a stranger to the place, who has come up into the midst of the city according to the direction of the maidens at the foot of the hill, and the inner voice with which he is so familiar says to him, "Behold the man," &c. (ver. 17). There is nothing in the simple dress of the prophet to indicate his dignity; and as he passes onward Saul "draws near to him in the gate," and in reply to his inquiry concerning the seer's residence, receives the answer, "I am the seer." Seldom has the meeting of two persons shown more clearly the co-operation of the revealed word with the guiding providence of God or the unity of the purpose by which both are pervaded, or been followed by more momentous results. 3. And its communication required a *gradual preparation* on the part of him to whom it chiefly pertained, in order that it might be received aright. This Samuel sought to effect—(1) By awakening in Saul new and elevated thoughts and hopes (vers. 19, 20); directing him to go up before him, as a mark of respect, inviting him to be his guest, telling him that he would "reveal to him his innermost thoughts," setting his mind at rest from lower cares, and assuring him of the highest dignity. "For whom is every desirable thing in Israel?" (ver. 20). (2) By giving him honour in the presence of others (vers. 22—24); appointing to him the chief place among his thirty guests, appropriating to him the best portion of the meal, and intimating that the honour had been reserved for him in foreknowledge of his arrival. (3) By holding confidential and prolonged conversation with him (ver. 25), pertaining "not to the royal dignity, but surely to the deep religious and political decline of the people of God, the opposition of the heathen, the causes of the impotency to oppose these enemies, the necessity of a religious change in the people, and of a leader thoroughly obedient to the Lord" (O. von Gerlach). In this manner Saul was prepared for the more definite indication given on the following morning. A gradual preparation of a somewhat similar kind is often needed by men when about to receive a Divine commission.—D.

Ver. 9. (RAMAH.)—*Perplexity.* "Peradventure he can show us our way." Here is a picture of a young man perplexed about his way. Consider—

I. THE OBJECT OF HIS PERPLEXITY. It is a common thing for a young man to be uncertain and anxious with reference to—1. The *ordinary business* of life. He knows not, it may be, the particular vocation for which he is most fitted, or which affords the best prospect of success. Leaving his father's house,

> "The world is all before him, where to choose
> His place of rest, and Providence his guide."

But he is doubtful whither to direct his steps. He meets with disappointment in his endeavours. "The bread is spent" (ver. 7), and he has no money in his purse. Under such circumstances many a one has first awoke to a sense of his dependence on God, and his need of his guidance, or has sought him with a fervour he has never displayed before. His loneliness and distress have been the occasion of spiritual thought and high resolve (Gen. xxviii. 16, 20; Luke xv. 18). 2. The *chief purpose* of life. As each vocation has its proper end, so has life generally. It is something higher than the finding of strayed asses, the recovery of lost property, or "buying and selling and getting gain." Even the dullest soul has often a feeling that it was made for a nobler end than the gratification of bodily appetites, or the supply of earthly needs. But "what is the chief end of man?" Alas, how many know not what it is, nor the means of attaining it; miss their way, and wander on "in endless mazes lost!" 3. The *true Guide* of life. Who shall tell thee "all that is in thine heart" (ver. 19)—declare its aspirations, and direct them to their goal? Where is he to be found, and by what means may his favour be obtained? Books and teachers abound, and to them the young man naturally turns for instruction; but how often do they leave him in greater perplexity than ever. "Where shall wisdom be found?" (Job xxviii. 12). "To whom should we go?" "We must wait patiently [said Socrates] until some one, either a god or some inspired man, teach us our moral and religious duties, and, as Pallas in Homer did to Diomede, remove the darkness from our eyes" (Plato). "I know that Messias cometh, which is called Christ: when he is come, he will tell us all things" (John iv. 25). "Sir, we would see Jesus" (John xii. 21).

II. THE METHOD OF HIS PROCEDURE. The course which it behoves him to take is that of—1. *Diligent inquiry* concerning the object of his desire. It exists, and a firm belief in its existence is the first condition of such inquiry. There may be healthy doubt about its nature, but absolute scepticism is destruction. Inquiry is the way to truth. It must be pursued with quenchless zeal and ceaseless perseverance. And if so pursued it will not be vain (Prov. ii. 4, 5). 2. *Ready reception of light*, from whatever quarter it may come. Truth often comes from unexpected sources. The true inquirer is reverent and humble, and willing to receive information from the most despised (vers. 10, 11).

> "Seize upon truth, where'er tis found,
>   Amongst your friends, amongst your foes,
>   On Christian or on heathen ground;
>   The flower's Divine, where'er it grows.'

3. *Faithfully acting up to the light he possesses.* "Well said; come, let us go." Inquiry alone is insufficient. The duty that lies plainly and immediately before us must be performed.

III. THE SUCCESS OF HIS ENDEAVOUR. 1. *He is brought face to face with the best Guide.* "I am the seer" (ver. 19). The best service that men and books, including the Scriptures themselves (John v. 39, 40), can render is to bring us into direct communion with the Prophet of Nazareth, "the Way, the Truth, and the Life." Our perplexity ends only when he manifests himself to us and says, "I that speak unto thee am he." "Master, where dwellest thou? Come and see" (John i. 38).

> "And what delights can equal those
>   That stir the spirit's inner deeps,
>   When one that loves, but knows not, reaps
> A truth from one that loves and knows?" (Tennyson).

2. He rises into a *higher region* of thought and feeling, and receives all the direction that he really needs. His anxiety about earthly affairs is relieved (Matt. vi. 32). The true purpose of life is shown him (Matt. vi. 33). He has "an unction from the Holy One, and knows all things" (1 John ii. 20). He is "turned into another man," and "God is with him" (ch. x. 6, 7). 3. He attains great *honour and power*. Saul is not the only one who has gone forth in the performance of lowly duty and found a kingdom, or to whom a temporary loss has been an occasion of permanent and invaluable gain. "Be thou faithful unto death, and I will give thee a crown of life."—D.

(A SACRAMENTAL ADDRESS.)

Ver. 13. (RAMAH.)—*Guests at a sacred feast.*—"For the people will not eat until he come, because he doth bless the sacrifice; and afterwards they eat that be bidden." This language refers to a feast provided on the high place of the city where Samuel dwelt. 1. It was a sacrificial feast. The victim (a thank offering) having been slain, and its blood sprinkled about the altar, a portion of it was burnt in the sacred fire, and the rest reserved for food. "The thank or praise offering was the expression of the worshipper's feelings of adoring gratitude on account of having received some spontaneous tokens of the Lord's goodness. This was the highest form (of the peace offering), as here the grace of God shone prominently forth" (Fairbairn, 'Typology'). 2. It was attended by numerous guests—thirty persons—distinguished in some way from others, and specially invited by Samuel. "The participation by the offerer and his friends—this family feast upon the sacrifice—may be regarded as the most distinctive characteristic of the peace offering. It denoted that the offerer was admitted to a state of near fellowship and enjoyment with God, shared part and part with Jehovah and his priests, had a standing in his house and a seat at his table. It was, therefore, the symbol of established friendship with God, and near communion with him in the blessings of his kingdom; and was associated in the minds of the worshippers with feelings of peculiar joy and gladness" (Fairbairn). 3. It required the presence of Samuel himself in order that the guests might properly partake thereof. "The blessing of the sacrifice must mean the asking of a blessing upon the food before the meal. This was done at every common meal, and much more at a solemn festival like this. The present, however, is the only *recorded* example of the custom" (Kitto). "It refers to the thanksgiving and prayer offered before the sacrificial meal" (Keil). Now this feast may be regarded as a foreshadowing of the Lord's Supper. A greater than Samuel is the Master of the feast (Matt. xxvi. 18; John xiii. 13, 14). Our Lord has provided it by the sacrifice of himself — of which the ancient sacrifices were a type, and the Holy Supper is a memorial. And he himself comes to preside at his own table. As his guests—

I. WE AWAIT HIS PRESENCE. "The people will not eat until he come." His presence is—1. Necessary to the feast. The bread and wine are not simply memorials, they are also symbols; and in order to partake of them aright we must "discern the Lord's body." "Without me ye can do nothing." 2. Promised by himself. "There am I in the midst of them" (Matt. xviii. 20). "I will see you again, and your heart shall rejoice" (John xvi. 22). "Lo, I am with you alway" (Matt. xxviii. 20). The sacred ordinance itself is a permanent assurance of his presence. 3. Realised in the heart. We look not for his *real presence* in the material emblems, but in the believing heart. "I in them" (John xvii. 26; xiv. 21; Ephes. iii. 17). In a different spirit from that in which the words were originally spoken, we ask, "What think ye, that he will not come to the feast?" (John xi. 56). We await his coming with reverence and humility, contrition, and faith, and ardent desire. O that he may appear to each of us, saying, "Peace be unto you," and be "known in breaking of bread." "Blessed are they that wait for him" (Isa. xxx. 8; John xx. 29).

II. WE DESIRE HIS BLESSING. "He doth bless the sacrifice," and in doing so he also doth bless his guests. 1. As of *old*, when he often gave thanks before the meal (Matt. xiv. 19; xv. 36; Mark xiv. 22; Luke xxiv. 30; John vi. 23; 1 Cor. xi. 24). 2. As the ever-living Intercessor, representing his people, and rendering their prayers and praises acceptable to God. "I will declare thy name unto my brethren, in the midst of the Church will I sing praises unto thee" (Heb. ii. 12). 3. As when he went away, still stretching forth his hands in benediction toward his disciples, and enabling them to be "continually praising and blessing God" (Luke xxiv. 51—53). "Stretch forth, O Lord, in blessing toward us thy hands, that were nailed for our redemption to the bitter cross!"

III. WE PARTAKE OF HIS PROVISION. "And afterwards they eat that be bidden." We do not merely look upon the emblems of his body and blood, but we eat and drink, and thereby signify—1. Our participation in the benefits of his death—forgiveness, peace, and righteousness. 2. Our fellowship with him in his sufferings and death, his spirit and life, his strength and joy (John vi. 53). "And truly our fellowship is with the Father, and with his Son Jesus Christ" (1 John i. 3). 3. And our union and communion with each other, through fellowship with him, in love and gladness. "For we being many are one bread, and one body" (1 Cor. x. 17). Let us, then, "rejoice before the Lord." The cup is "a cup of blessing" (thanksgiving). The service is intended to be a service of joy—joy in the Lord; in the contemplation

of his glorious character, in the reception of his manifold benefits, and in the anticipation of "the marriage supper of the Lamb."—D.

Vers. 26, 27; ch. x. 1—8. (RAMAH.) — *Saul privately anointed king.* "And
Samuel took a vial of oil, and poured it upon his head." There is in the life of almost
every man some day beyond all others, the events of which serve to determine his
future course. Such a day was that which is here described in the life of Saul. On
the preceding day he had been guided by Providence to Samuel, and led by means
of his conversation to entertain exalted expectations concerning his future destiny.
"And when they were come down from the high place into the city, Samuel communed with Saul upon the top of the house" (ver. 25). "And a bed was spread
for Saul on the roof, and he lay down" (LXX., Vulg.). "The roofs in Judæa were
flat, with a parapet around them. To be lodged there was considered an honour.
In fine weather it was not unusual to sleep in the open air, but the place might occasionally be covered with a tent" (Geddes). Strange thoughts must have passed
through his mind as he rested there under the silent stars. He rose early to prepare
for his journey, and watched the morning dawn over the distant hills, ushering in the
most eventful day of his life. Then the voice of Samuel called to him from below,
saying, "Arise, and I will send thee away." The prophet accompanied him, as a
mark of respect, along the street, toward the end of the city (Ramah). But before
parting from him he directed him to send his servant forward, that he might communicate to him alone "the word of God." And in this private interview Saul was—

I. APPOINTED TO THE HIGHEST DIGNITY (ver. 1). 1. *By a rite of consecration.*
"Taking a vial, he anointed Saul, thus placing the institution of royalty on the same
footing as that of the sanctuary and the priesthood (Exod. xxx. 33; Levit. viii. 10),
as appointed and consecrated by God and to God, and intended to be the medium for
receiving and transmitting blessing to the people" (Edersheim). "Anointing with
oil was a symbol of endowment with the Spirit of God; as the oil itself, by virtue of
the strength which it gives to the vital spirits, was a symbol of the Spirit of God as
the principle of Divine and spiritual power" (Keil). "Two very good reasons they
(the Jews) render why God did command the use of such anointing oil as in respect
of the action. First, that it did signify the Divine election of that person and
designation to that office; from whence it was necessary that it should be performed
by a prophet who understood the will of God. Secondly, that by it the person
anointed might be made fit to receive the Divine influx." "In respect to the matter
they give two reasons why it was *oil*, and not any other liquor. First, because, of
all other, it signifies the greatest glory and excellency. Secondly, they tell us that
oil continueth uncorrupted longer than any other liquor. ·And, indeed, it hath been
observed to preserve not only itself but other things from corruption; hence they
conclude it fit their kings and priests, whose succession was to continue for ever,
should be anointed with oil, the most proper emblem of eternity. Beside, they
observe that simple oil without any mixture was sufficient for the candlestick; but
that which was designed for unction must be compounded with principal spices,
which signify a good name, always to be acquired by those in places of greatest
dignity by the most laudable and honourable actions" ('Pearson on the Creed,' Art.
ii.). 2. Accompanied with *an act of homage.* "And kissed him." The kiss was
given on the mouth, the hand, the feet, or the garment, and was a token of friendship, affection, and, in the case of princes, of reverence and homage (1 Kings xviii.
19; Ps. ii. 12; Hosea xiii. 3). 3. And with *a statement of its significance.* "Is
it not?" &c. "Hath not the Lord anointed thee to be ruler over his people, over
Israel? And thou shalt rule over the people of the Lord, and thou shalt save them
out of the hand of their enemies" (LXX.). His appointment was of God, and the
purpose of it was the deliverance of his people. The manner in which he received
it shows the change which had already taken place in his feelings (ch. ix. 21).
When God has work for a man to do, he has power to dispose and prepare him to
do it.

II. ASSURED OF CONFIRMATORY SIGNS (vers. 2—6). The events which Samuel
predicted were *proofs* of the Divine interposition, *means* of Saul's further preparation,
and *emblems* of his future dignity and power. 1. *First sign*—his royalty was an

appointment made by God.   By it he would be convinced that it was not made by Samuel merely, but by God, who fulfilled his words (ch. ix. 20); at the same time he would be taught to leave lower cares, and aspire after the highest things. "Inwardly free, and consecrated to the Lord alone, he is to pursue his way *upward*." 2. *Second sign*—his royalty was an honour shared with God, and held in subordination to him (vers. 3, 4). A part of the offerings that were about to be presented before Jehovah in Bethel would be presented to Saul, but only a part of them; the greater portion would be given to Jehovah as a sign of the supreme homage due to the invisible King of Israel, while he was to accept the lesser portion as a sign of his subordinate position under him. "That this surprising prelude to all future royal gifts is taken from bread of offering points to the fact that in future some of the wealth of the land, which has hitherto gone undivided to the sanctuary, will go to the king" (Ewald).   God commands us to "honour the king" (1 Pet. ii. 17), but the honour which is due to himself may not be usurped by man (Matt. xxii. 21; Acts xii. 23).   3. *Third sign* — his royalty was an endowment dependent upon God, and effectually administered only through his grace.   Coming to the hill (Gibeah) of God, near the city (Gibeah, his home), where there stood a garrison of the Philistines (or perhaps a pillar erected by them as a sign of their authority), which could hardly fail to impress upon him with great force the main purpose for which he had been appointed king, he would meet a band of prophets descending from the high place (of sacrifice), playing instruments of music and prophesying (speaking and singing in ecstatic utterances the praises of Jehovah, declaring his greatness, and his victory over his adversaries), and—(1) He would be imbued with a Divine power. "The Spirit of Jehovah will come upon thee."   (2) He would catch the spirit of the prophets, and join them in their ecstatic utterances.   "Thou wilt prophesy with them."   (3) He would undergo a surprising transformation.   "And will be turned into another man."   When he had turned his back to go from Samuel, "God gave him another heart" (ver. 9), but the prediction of the prophet was more completely fulfilled afterwards (ver. 10).   The fulfilment of these predictions shows that apparently accidental events are clearly foreseen by God, human affairs are under his direction and control, and "the king's heart is in the hand of the Lord, as the rivers of water: he turneth it whithersoever he will" (Prov. xxi. 1), and that "the teachings of Providence unite with the teachings of revelation and of the Holy Spirit to show men their duty and their destiny."

III. ADMONISHED OF FUTURE DUTY (vers. 7, 8).   In relation to—1. *Circumstances.* "Do thou what thy hand findeth," *i. e.* what circumstances indicate to be thy duty. His own judgment would have to be exercised, but he would not be left to it alone. 2. *God.*   "For God is with thee," to observe, direct, and aid thee.   The firm belief in his presence is a mighty preservative from the neglect of duty, and a powerful incentive and encouragement to its performance.   3. *The prophet*, through whom he would receive "the word of God," in obedience to which he was bound always to act.   "Gilgal, on the south-western bank of the Jordan, was then, from all indications, one of the most holy places in Israel, and the true centre of the whole people; it had a like importance before, and much more then, because the Philistine control reached so far eastward that the middle point of the kingdom must have been pressed back to the bank of the Jordan.   There the people must have assembled for all general political questions, and thence, after offering and consecration, have marched forth armed to war" (Ewald).   Thither he was to gather the people; not, indeed, immediately, but when circumstances indicated that it was the proper time to prepare for war with the Philistines, which was the main object of his appointment. Samuel promised to meet him there, offer burnt offerings (dedicatory) and peace offerings (eucharistic), and tell him what to do; and directed him to wait seven days, and to do nothing without him.   The direction was explicit, it set a limit to his authority, and its neglect was the first step in his disobedience (ch. xiii. 13).   When God places men in positions of authority, he teaches them the obligations which they involve; and if they fail it is not from want of knowing them.—D.

Ver. 17.—*The man, yet not the man.* I. THE SANCTION GIVEN BY THE LORD TO SAUL'S ELEVATION.   Instances may easily be adduced in which the writers of the

Old Testament ascribed to the Lord directly what was only indirectly recognised or permitted by him; but in the present case there is obviously more than Divine allowance. Jehovah pointed out Saul to the prophet Samuel, and commanded that he should be anointed captain, or king. We account for this on that principle of Divine government which allows to men that which they most wish for, in order that they may learn wisdom from the result. The people of Israel had not asked the Lord for such a king as he might see fit to choose and appoint. They had asked the prophet for a warlike chief like the kings of the nations and tribes around them, and the Lord saw meet to let them have what they desired; the young giant Saul was just the style of man they sought, cast in the very mould they admired, and one that would teach them some painful lessons through experience. Therefore, though the Lord foresaw the disappointing career of Saul, he authorised Samuel to anoint him privately, and afterwards sanctioned his public selection and elevation to the royal dignity. Here was a leader to suit the fancy of the people—strong, impetuous, valiant. Let them have Saul for their king. Such is the way of the Lord to this day, and in individual as well as national life. He admonishes and corrects us by letting us have our own way and be filled with our own devices. We are apt to complain in our disappointment at the result, that God himself sanctioned our course. No. We did not ask him to show us his way, that we might do his will; but took our own way, did our own pleasure; and he allowed, nay, facilitated our desire. Let the issue teach us to be more wary and more humble in time to come.

II. EARLY PROGNOSTICS OF SAUL'S FAILURE. 1. The manner of his entrance on the page of history. How different from the first mention of David, faithfully keeping the sheep before he was anointed to be the royal shepherd of Israel, is the first appearance of the son of Kish in search of his father's stray asses, and visiting the venerable prophet Samuel with no higher thought in his mind than to learn, if possible, where those asses were! He did not even know Samuel by sight, though he lived but at a short distance. He seems to have been an unreflecting rustic youth, with none of those premonitions of greatness which come early to the wise, and tend to give them seriousness of purpose and elevation of aim. 2. Indications of a fitful mind. We read nothing of Saul's bearing before Samuel when informed of the destiny before him. Probably he was stunned with surprise. But so soon as he left the prophet new currents of thought and feeling began to flow through his heart. A mood of mind fell on him more grave and earnest than had appeared in him before. The Old Testament way of saying it is, that "God gave him another heart;" for the change which passes on a man under the consciousness of a high vocation suddenly received is none the less of God than it is evidently born of the occasion. He sees things in a new light, feels new responsibilities; new springs of feeling and new capacities of speech and action reveal themselves in him. But Saul took every influence by fits and starts. He quickly gained, and as quickly lost. There was in him no steady growth of conviction or principle. When he fell in with men of religious fervour he was fervent too When he met the prophets chanting Jehovah's praise he caught their rapture, and, joining their procession, lifted up his voice also in the sacred song. But it was a mere fit of piety. Of course Saul had been educated in the religion of his fathers, and in that sense knew the God of Israel; but it seems evident, from the surprise occasioned by his appearance among the prophets, that he had never shown any zeal for the glory and worship of Jehovah; and the sudden ecstasy at Gibeah, having no foundation of spiritual principle, came to nought. Alas! men may sing spiritual songs with emotion who have no enduring spiritual life. Men may catch the infection of religious enthusiasm, yet have no moral health or soundness. Men's faces may glow with a fine ardour, and yet soon after be darkened by wicked passion. Pulses of high feeling and moods of noble desire may visit minds that yet are never moved by Divine grace, and therefore are liable to be mastered, after all, by evil temper and base envy. Occasional impulses are not sufficient. "Ye must be born again."—F.

EXPOSITION.

CHAPTER X.

SAUL ANOINTED TO BE KING, AND SIGNS
GIVEN HIM CONVINCING HIM OF THE TRUTH
OF HIS APPOINTMENT (vers. 1—16). Ver. 1.
—**A vial of oil.** Hebrew, "the vial of oil,"
because it was that same holy oil with which
the priests were anointed (Exod. xxix. 7).
Throughout Holy Scripture the office of king
appears as one most sacred, and it is the
king, and not the priest, who is especially
called Messiah, Jehovah's anointed (ch. ii.
10, 35 ; xii. 3, 5 ; xvi. 6, &c.), because he
represented the authority and power of God.
And kissed him. *I. e.* did homage to him,
and gave him the symbol and token of allegiance (see Ps. ii. 12). **Is it not ?** . . . A
strong affirmation often takes the form of a
question, especially when, as probably was
the case here, surprise is manifested. Saul,
on whom the occurrences of the previous
day must have come as strange and unintelligible marvels, was no doubt still more
embarrassed when one so old and venerable,
both in person and office, as Samuel solemnly
consecrated him to be Israel's prince (see
ch. ix. 16), and gave him the kiss of fealty
and allegiance. Samuel, therefore, answers
Saul's inquiring looks with this question,
and, further, gives him three signs to quiet
his doubts, and convince him that his appointment is from God.

Ver. 2.—The first sign—**Thou shalt find
two men by Rachel's sepulchre.** In Jer.
xxxi. 15 (quoted in Matt. ii. 18) Rachel's
sepulchre is connected with Ramah, but
in Gen. xxxv. 19 it is placed near Bethlehem. The whole of the geography of Saul's
wanderings is very obscure, but Wilson
('Lands of the Bible,' i. 401) places **Zelzah**
at Beit-jala, to the west of Bethlehem, in
the neighbourhood of the Kabbet Rahil, or
Tomb of Rachel. Though both are now in
the tribe of Judah, yet by a slight rectifi-
cation of the frontier, in conformity with
Josh. xviii. 11—28, Zelzah would be on the
border of Benjamin, and there may have
been local reasons for Saul and his companion
not taking the most direct route for Gibeah.
The news given by these men, that the asses
were found, would set Saul's mind at rest,
and, freed from lower cares, he would be
able to give his thoughts entirely to preparation for the higher duties that were before
him. For an interesting note upon the
journey of Saul home see Wilson, ii. 36.

Ver. 3.—The second sign was to be the
presenting of an offering to him out of their
sacrificial gifts by three men going on a
pilgrimage to Bethel. He would meet them
not **in the plain of Tabor,** but at the oak,
ēlon, of Tabor. Many attempt to connect
this *ēlon-Tabor* with the *allon,* or oak, under
which Deborah, Rachel's nurse, was buried
(Gen. xxxv. 8), and suppose that Tabor is a
corruption of the name Deborah. This is
scarcely possible, and it is better to acknowledge that we know nothing of the site of
this tree, except that it was on the road to
Bethel. This was one of the places which
Samuel used to visit as judge (ch. vii. 16) ;
but these men were on a pilgrimage thither
because since the days of Jacob it had been
a sacred spot, and a chief seat of the old
patriarchal worship, for which see ch. ix. 12.

Ver. 4. — These pilgrims would **salute**
Saul, *i. e.* give him the usual friendly greeting of travellers, and would then present to
him, a stranger, two loaves of the bread
intended for their offering at Bethel. By so
doing, in the first place, they acknowledged
him as their lord (see ch. ix. 7 ; xvi. 20),
and, secondly, they indicated that the king
would henceforth share with the sanctuary
the offerings of the people. And Saul was
to **receive of their hands** the present, as
being now his due, for by anointing him
Samuel had designated him as king.

Ver. 5.—The third sign was to be his
taking part with the prophets in their religious exercises in **the hill of God**—really
Gibeah, his own home. Gibeah is strictly
a rounded hill, while Ramah is a height.
This *Gibeah ha-Elohim* was probably that
part of the hill on which the "high place"
was situated, and which was evidently outside the city ; for Saul, on his route homeward, met the troop of prophets descending
from it. For "Gibeah of Saul" see ch. ix.
1 ; but, as Conder remarks, this name is
given to a district as well as to a town, inasmuch as Ramah is described as situated
within it—ch. xxii. 6 ('Tent Work,' ii. 111).
The garrison of the Philistines was probably
on some height in this district, and, coupled
with the mention of similar military posts
elsewhere (ch. xiii. 3; xiv. 4), shows that
most of the tribe of Benjamin was subject to
that nation, and disarmed (ch. xiii. 19); but
probably, as long as the tribute was paid, its
internal administration was not interfered
with **A company of the prophets.** At
Gibeah Samuel had established one of his
"schools of the prophets," by means of
which he did so much to elevate the whole
mental and moral state of the Israelites.
The word rendered *company* literally means
a cord or line, and so a *band* of people.
These prophets were descending from the
Bamah (see on ch. ix. 12), where they had
been engaged in some religious exercise, and
were chanting a psalm or hymn to the

music of various instruments. Music was one of the great means employed by Samuel in training his young men ; and not only is its effect at all times elevating and refining, but in semi-barbarous times, united, as it is sure to be, with poetry, it is the chief educational lever for raising men's minds, and giving them a taste for culture and intellectual pleasures. The musical instruments mentioned are the **psaltery**, Hebrew, *nebel*, a sort of harp with ten strings stretched across a triangle, the longest string being at its base, and the shortest towards its apex ; the **tabret**, Hebrew *toph*, a tambourine struck by the hand ; the **pipe**, Hebrew, *chalil*, i. e. "bored" or "pierced," so called from the holes bored in it to make the notes, and being probably a sort of flute ; and, lastly, the **harp**, Hebrew, *cinnor*, a sort of guitar, chiefly used for accompanying the voice, and sometimes played with the fingers, and sometimes with a plectrum or quill. There is nothing to indicate that there was only one of each of these instruments, so that the articles would be better omitted. No doubt every prophet was playing some one or other of them. **And they shall prophesy**. The conjugation used here is not that employed for the prediction of future events, but means, literally, and " they will be acting the prophet," the right word for men who were in training for the prophetic office (see ' Prophecy a Preparation for Christ,' 2nd ed. p. 50). They were really engaged in chanting God's praises with fervour, and this was no doubt one of the methods employed by Samuel to refine and spiritualise their minds. Years afterwards David was thus educated, and learned at one of Samuel's schools that skill in metre and psalmody which, added to his natural gifts, made him " the sweet singer of Israel." For *prophesying* in the sense of playing instruments of music see 1 Chron. xxv. 1—3, and in the sense of chanting, 1 Kings xviii. 29.

Ver. 6.—**The spirit of Jehovah will come upon thee**. The Hebrew means, will come mightily upon thee, will come upon thee so as to overpower thee. **And thou shalt prophesy**. Shalt act as a prophet (see above). Albeit untrained, thou shalt be carried away by religious fervour, and join in their singing and psalmody. **And be turned into another man**. New thoughts, new emotions shall take possession of thee, and in addition to the bodily strength for which hitherto thou hast been famous, thou shalt be filled with mental power, making thee eager for action, and capable of taking the lead among all men, and in all emergencies. We have an instance of this enlarged capacity in the vigour with which Saul acted against the Ammonites.

Ver. 7. - **Do as occasion serve thee.**

Literally, " do for thyself as thy hand shall find," *i. e.* follow the 'ead of circumstances, and do thy best. This is the flood-time of thy fortunes ; press onward, and the kingdom is thine own, for **God is with thee**, and success is sure.

Ver. 8.—**Thou shalt go down before me to Gilgal.** We find in ch. xiii. 8—13 a meeting at Gilgal so exactly parallel to what is arranged here that we cannot help looking upon this, again, as a sort of sign to be fulfilled at a later period. It is no argument against it that Gilgal was the place where in the mean while Saul was solemnly inaugurated king ; for he was appointed in order that he might deliver Israel from the Philistines (ch. ix. 16), and we may feel sure that this grand purpose would form the subject of conversation between the prophet and the soldier, either on the house-top or the next morning. In this conversation Gilgal would be selected as the place where Saul would assemble Israel for the war of independence (so Rashi and other Jewish interpreters) ; and so great an enterprise must necessarily be begun with religious rites, and Saul was to wait a full week for the prophet's coming, both to try his faith, which ought to have been confirmed by the fulfilment of the three appointed signs, and in order that the war might be undertaken under the same holy auspices as his own election to the kingdom. The two years' interval, were it really so long, would give time for Saul's character to develop under the forcing influences of royalty, and it would then be proved, when he felt himself every inch a king, whether he was still as amenable to the Divine authority as when he was first summoned from obscurity to mount a kingly throne. But, really, the words in ch. xiii. 1 do not justify this conclusion, and most probably the occurrences mentioned in that chapter followed immediately upon Saul's confirmation as king.

Ver. 9.—**God gave him another heart.** The Hebrew is remarkable : " When he turned his shoulder to go from Samuel, God also turned for him another heart," *i. e.* God turned him round by giving him a changed heart. He grew internally up to the level of his changed circumstances. No longer had he the feelings of a husbandman, concerned only about corn and cattle ; he had become a statesman, a general, and a prince. No man could have gone through such marvellous events, and experienced such varied emotions, without a vast inward change. But it might have been only to vanity and self-complacency. Saul's change was into a hero.

Vers. 10, 11.—**To the hill.** Hebrew, "to Gibeah," his home. **He prophesied.** Took part in prophetic exercises (see on ver. 5).

On seeing this, the people of Gibeah, who **knew him beforetime,**—Hebrew, "from yesterday and the day before," but equivalent to our phrase "for years,"—asked in surprise, **What is this that is come unto the son of Kish?** What makes him thus act in a manner unlike all our long past experience of him? **Is Saul also among the prophets?** From this question two things are evident: the first, that the schools founded by Samuel already held a high place in the estimation of the Israelites; the second, that Saul had not shared in that education which so raised the prophets as a class above the mass of the people. Probably also Saul's character was not such as would have made him care for education. A young man who, while living in his neighbourhood, knew so little about Samuel (ch. ix. 6), could not have had a very inquiring or intellectual frame of mind. Of course Samuel could not, by gathering young men together, and giving them the best education the times afforded, gain for them also the highest and rarest of gifts, that of direct inspiration. Even when Elisha, the friend and attendant upon Elijah, asked his master for an elder son's portion of the Divine spirit, Elijah told him that he had asked a hard thing (2 Kings ii. 10). The disparity then that the people remarked between Saul and the prophets was that between a rich young farmer's son, who had been brought up at home, and cared only for rustic things, and these young collegians, who were enjoying a careful education (comp. John vii. 15). How good that education was is proved by the fact that at David's court all posts which required literary skill were held by prophets. No man could found schools of inspired men; but Samuel founded great educational institutions, which ended by making the Israelites a highly-trained and literary people. Saul's prophesying was not the result of training, but came to him by a Divine influence, rousing the slumbering enthusiasm of an energetic but fitful nature.

Ver. 12.—**One of the same place**—*i. e.* Gibeah—**answered and said, But who is their father?** The Septuagint, Syriac, and Vulgate read, *But who is his father?* But this would be a foolish reply to the question, "What has happened to the son of Kish?" The meaning rather must be, You ask about the son of Kish; but what has birth to do with prophecy? None of these young men have inherited these gifts, and if Saul can take part in their prophesyings, why should he not? Kish, his father, is no worse than theirs. **Is Saul also among the prophets?** Under very different circumstances Saul once again took part in the exercises of these youthful prophets (ch. xix. 24), and evidently on both occasions with such skill and success as prove the readiness of his genius; and so struck were the people at the strange power which he thus evinced, that their expression of wonder became fixed in the national mind as a proverb. Saul was a man of great natural ability, and yet not the sort of person whom the people expected would be made king. He probably could neither read nor write, and from his extreme height was perhaps awkward and bashful; as he suffered afterwards from fits of insanity (ch. xvi. 14), he may always have been flighty and wilful; and altogether, though possessed of marvellous gifts, was certainly the very opposite of Samuel's well-trained and orderly scholars.

Ver. 13.—**He came to the high place.** Saul had met the prophets coming down from the Bamah; but the same religious fervour, which had made him take so earnest a part in the prophesyings of the young men, urged him now, after parting from their company, himself to go up to the high place, there to offer his prayers and praises to God.

Vers. 14—16.—**Saul's uncle.** According to ch. xiv. 50, 51; 1 Chron. viii. 33, this would be Abner. The conversation probably took place after Saul had returned from the Bamah and gone to his own home, for in so brief a summary much necessarily is omitted. It is curious that the conversation should have taken place with the uncle, and not with the father; but possibly the latter was too well pleased to have his son back again to be very particular in his inquiries. Not so Abner. He was evidently excited by his nephew's visit to the prophet, and struck perhaps by the change in Saul himself, and would gladly have heard more. But Saul does not gratify his curiosity. **Of the matter of the kingdom . . . he told him not.** It was not merely prudent, but right to keep the matter secret. An able man like Abner would probably have begun to scheme for so great an end. Saul's silence left the fulfilment of the prophet's words entirely to God.

HOMILETICS.

Vers. 1—8.—*Supports to faith and duty.* The facts are—1. Samuel privately anoints Saul as the chosen of God. 2. He gives him four signs of the Divine sanction of the act of anointing. (1) The safety of the asses, and his father's sorrow. (2) The spontaneous gift of sacrificial bread near Bethel. (3) A welcome by the prophets at Gibeah. (4) An inspiration from God to prophesy. 3. He instructs him on the completion of the signs to act on his own judgment, with the assurance that God is his helper. 4. He finally directs him to wait at Gilgal for himself, there to receive further guidance. The course taken by Samuel was the natural completion of his protracted intercourse with Saul. The hour had come in which the symbolism of the recent feast and the foreshadowings of suggestive language must receive definite form in word and deed. As one chosen of God to high office in his government of Israel, Saul is anointed with oil; and Samuel voluntarily gives him what he must have valued above all price, the kiss of homage and of congratulation, thus indicating his perfect readiness to fall in with the new order, and his tender interest in the king's prosperity. A new era of responsibility opened up to Saul. He had to go forth, believing himself to be God's chosen servant, ready for the onerous duties attaching to great honours. But a man could not thus have his faith taxed without craving for encouragement. There were, in the circumstances of Israel and of Saul, obvious reasons for this private announcement and anointing. The deliberate act of such a man as Samuel must go far to banish doubt. But still human nature needs many supports, and God is very considerate of our frame. The day might come when difficulties and disappointments would recall the primary misgivings of the reality of the Divine call. Hence the provision made by Samuel for the encouragement of Saul.

I. THERE IS ALWAYS IN GOD'S SERVICE A NEED OF SUPPORT TO FAITH AND DUTY. Others have been summoned to a life requiring strong faith and unfailing courage in duty. 1. *There is a call to special service.* Abraham was called to be a pilgrim in a strange land, and to thereby secure a seed in whom all should be blessed. Moses was called to surrender the wealth of Egypt, and to lead God's people to freedom. The apostles were bidden to leave house and business for Christ's sake. Every true pastor and Christian worker recognises a voice which, in commanding separation to his service, puts honour on the servant. The instrument by which each is called may be human, as truly as it was a human hand and voice that set apart Saul. The evidence of the call may be clear. But tedious toils have to be borne. Events will not realise the expectations of a too sanguine temperament. Abraham needed the support of occasional manifestations, as well as of fulfilled predictions. Moses could not go without "signs." Christ promised proofs that he was sending forth his disciples. 2. *There is a call to Christian life.* This is the most blessed summons to privilege, honour, and obligation. The call to Christian life is endless in its form and manner and seasons. It may come in infancy, when we are unconsciously made new creatures in Christ; or in mature years, by the preacher's voice, the written word, the loss of friends, and the adversities of life, or the still small voice in the heart. There may be instances in which it is as clear as was Samuel's voice and hand to Saul; and a wonder and sense of unworthiness may arise as sincere and deep as was his. But times will come when a horror of great darkness falls on the spirit; the difficulties of one's path will raise the question as to the reality of that call which once seemed so clear, and the possibility of maintaining the distinct line of duty once entered on. A man cannot find support simply in retrospect of what was a marked change in his life; he needs something else to convince him that all is right, that the past change was not an illusion.

II. The SUPPORT GIVEN IS VARIED—ADAPTED TO THE ENTIRE NEED. Saul needed to be assured of the *fact* that it was God, and not merely man, who appointed him; he had it in the *fourfold fulfilled prediction* (vers. 2, 3, 5, 6). He needed the sympathy and concurrence of the religious portion of Israel; he was assured of it symbolically by the *worshippers* spontaneously offering him nourishment. He needed the *co-operation* of the most important *educators of the age;* he was assured of it in the symbolical welcome given to him by the company of prophets, the then rising power, which in years hence was to exert so great an influence on the national life. He needed, moreover, a power and wisdom in excess of that inherited from his father, and acquired during years of private life; he had it given when the spirit of the Lord made him another man. Wisely, therefore, were these arrangements made for the servant of God. They are beautifully congruous with the position of Saul, and the age in which he was called to act. An examination of the lives of Abraham,

Moses, and the apostles will show that an equally wise arrangement was made for the support of their faith and duty. So modern servants of God can point to promises fulfilled, in a blessing on their toil, as evidence that they were not mistaken in the call to work; and their once distrustful heart becomes strong in the consciousness of a power not their own. In a different, though not less real, way the individual Christian finds varied support to his belief that God has called him into the kingdom, and made him a "king and a priest;" as also to his discharge of the duties appropriate to his high and holy calling.

III. The REALISATION OF THE PROVIDED SUPPORT ENSUES ON THE EFFORT TO EXERCISE THE FAITH AND TO DISCHARGE THE DUTY. When Saul acted on the belief that Samuel was a true prophet speaking and acting for God, he found all to turn out as he had been promised. The exercise of such faith as he had, in the first instance, put him in possession of the supports to faith for future times; and the discharge of duty, so far as made clear, led to a discovery of the supports to duty that would be his in the more conspicuous acts of life. So was it with Abraham, and Moses, and the apostles. Every true servant gets encouragement, not by waiting, but while "going on his way," and doing the deeds appointed. The Saviour said to the palsied, "Put forth thy hand." In the attempting of the impossible act the faith came and grew. Faith finds nourishment for itself, and waxes strong in proportion as it is exercised.

General lessons:—1. We may render valuable service by timely sympathy and co-operation with those called to occupy difficult positions. 2. The most unassailable Christian evidence is that to be gained in a life of entire devotion to Christ. 3. Full confirmation of our hopes and beliefs will come in so far as we are faithful to carry into action what confidence we already have.

Another man. The mind of Saul was evidently overcharged with the great things which had so unexpectedly been brought before his attention. His imagination must have been filled with those pictures of royal state and lofty duties which are ever in Eastern minds associated with kingship. But he was scarcely able to frame an adequate conception of what Samuel meant by saying, "Thou shalt be turned into another man." There are several grades of transformation brought before us by ordinary life and by Scripture.

I. "ANOTHER MAN" IS SOMETIMES MADE BY TOTAL CHANGE OF CIRCUMSTANCES. We all are partly subject to our surroundings; but some natures happen to be in circumstances which appear to be quite alien to the development of what is in them. They are repressed; the strong forces of their life refuse to come forth; they are comparative nonentities; if no change occurs in their relative position they will pass away from life unknown and almost useless. There are in some persons mental faculties which, being predominant, but not drawn out by appropriate nutriment and exercise, give to the individual an appearance of stupidity and vacuity. A poet's soul encompassed by everything antagonistic to its development will be miserable as a lark that cannot rise. But when the unnatural restraints are removed, and the dispositions and faculties of individuals are placed amidst circumstances favourable to their proper development, there comes a change as rapid, as fresh, and striking as when the light and rain of spring call forth the bulb from under the dull earth into a form of beauty and sweetness. An observer of life cannot but have met with many cases of this.

II. "ANOTHER MAN" IS SOMETIMES MADE BY SPECIAL ENDOWMENTS FOR OFFICIAL DUTIES. This was the case with Saul. It is the teaching of Scripture that "every good and perfect gift" cometh from God. He gave wisdom and cunning to the men who framed the choice work of the tabernacle (Exod. xxxi. 2—6). Reason is his gift, though too often used against him. The Old Testament speaks of special gifts for men called to lead on the people of God. The endowment of Saul was in harmony with that of Moses and Joshua. The contrast of the men as *not* endowed and endowed is striking. The figure of Moses after he went forth in the *name of Jehovah* dwarfs the Moses feeding Jethro's sheep. The timid, questioning, spiritually ignorant men who followed Christ as long as they dared, and "thought" that he "would have redeemed Israel," can scarcely be recognised as the men who, when endowed with power from on high, stood forth on the day of Pentecost, and, with calmness and fearlessness, expounded the spiritual nature of his kingdom who was crucified.   Spiritual power works marvels in men.

III. "ANOTHER MAN" IS MADE WHEN THE SOUL IS RENEWED BY THE SPIRIT OF GOD.   This is the most radical of all changes; it is more than an enlargement of the ordinary powers, more than the gift of discrimination by which ordinary duties can be discharged; it is the renovation of that deep, subtle spring of feeling and willing which determines the character of the entire life.   The will of a man is supposed to be the key to his destiny; but the change wrought by the Holy Spirit seems even to penetrate into the mysterious rear of the will, and insure that it shall issue in acts of repentance; of faith in Christ, of supreme love for God, of delight in holiness.   The *reality of the transformation* is seen in the new aims, the new joys, the new acts of the soul, the new outward form of life, the new spiritual discernment of the spiritual and unseen, the new hidden secret which no words can reveal, the new absorption in Christ.

IV. "ANOTHER MAN" IS MADE WHEN WE ATTAIN TO THE COMPLETE REDEMPTION FOR WHICH CHRIST DIED.   Relatively to a life of sin, the regenerate life of the Christian on earth is a new creation, he is "another man;" and likewise, relatively to the imperfect, struggling life we spend on earth, that which awaits us beyond is a new creation. When the full stature of a man in Christ is attained, and becomes clothed upon with a body "like unto his own glorious body," then may it be most truly said of each, he is "turned into a new man."   How unlike our former selves will be that perfectly holy, tearless, strong, joyous, unwearied life, exercised in a "spiritual body," created in special adaptation for the new activities and joys of the kingdom of heaven.

General considerations:—1. Reflect on what the world may lose by careless disregard in our social life of the adaptation of circumstances to aptitudes and abilities. 2. There is room for every man to examine himself and see whether his religion is really the product of a radical renewal by the Holy Spirit.   3. With so lofty a destiny before us as Christians, the inquiry should arise, how it is that we are so little affected by the prospect, and by what means we can more fully live under the inspiring "powers of the world to come."

Limitations of prerogative.   Saul was told that when the promised "signs" came upon him he might do as occasion required, and for the assigned reason that God was with him (ver. 7).   This great freedom immediately receives a limitation in the command to wait at Gilgal till Samuel came and offered sacrifice, and gave further instructions.   The royal prerogative was to be exercised under limitations.   Here the question of civil and spiritual power is brought into distinct concrete form as the natural outcome of Israel's history.   The analogy between Israel and all other nations cannot be established in detail with respect to this question; but, nevertheless, there are a few truths of general application illustrated in the restrictions put by the prophet of God on the actions of Israel's king.

I. The ULTIMATE ENDS FOR WHICH GOVERNMENTS EXIST ARE SPIRITUAL.   There is a difference between the immediate concern of a government—namely, with protection of life and property, the repression of crime; scope for the free action of citizens, and for the development of national resources—and the ultimate end for which Providence designs it and all other institutious.   Man's body exists for his spirit.   Society, in the mind of God, exists for the spiritual welfare of individuals. There is an evolution progressing towards a world-wide righteousness, and governments are one of the agencies which are to subserve this issue.   Attention to the material and intellectual interests of a people may be to rulers an end in itself, but not to God.   Governments may subserve this spiritual end without consciously entering into questions pertaining to its nature and varied means for securing it. A faithful discharge of definite functions, on approved principles, cannot but help on the purpose for which God is himself governing mankind.

II. The CHURCH OF GOD IS THE TRUE WITNESS-BEARER AND THE MEANS OF ACCOMPLISHING THESE SPIRITUAL ENDS.   Samuel was the representative of the spiritual power.   He had authority to assert the Messianic truth, to educate the people in harmony with that truth, and to demand that the king should govern in such a way as to allow free scope to the spiritual work.   He and the religious community were one in this respect.   And the living Church of Christ is the assertor of Messianic truth—claiming to hold what Christ has given, pointing to the spiritual reign of Christ over every heart and home as the goal of all effort and the hope of the world ; and the witness-bearer, calling upon rulers to observe in their administration the principles of righteousness, truth, and benevolent regard, which God alone will honour with his blessing.

III. CIVIL RULERS ARE BOUND TO ACT IN HARMONY WITH THE WITNESS-BEARING OF THE CHURCH.   Saul was bound, morally, and as a condition of stability to his throne, to recognise Samuel in his capacity as prophet of God, working, with all the devout, for Messianic purposes.   He must not ignore the spiritual power, and thus dishonour God (ver. 8 ; cf. ch. xiii. 8—10) ; nor must he arrogate its functions.   His duty lay in administering government on the principles of righteousness, and so as not to bar the way to the realisation of the Messianic purpose.   And knowing as we do that in the truth given by Christ, and borne witness to by the living Church, there are all the sound principles of human progress as well as of personal salvation, every government is morally bound to act on them, and is guilty of fearful presumption if it professes to supplant them by creations of its own.   As surely as decay at the root of a tree will issue in its fall, so surely will every government perish which acts on other principles than those asserted by the living Church of God.   No government can successfully wage war with the one living Church, which, by example, word, and deed, preaches righteousness, and claims the right to do so.

IV. The CHURCH IS BOUND TO CONFINE ATTENTION TO HER OWN PROPER FUNCTIONS. Samuel left Saul to "do as occasion" might "serve" (ver. 7).   He simply claimed that there was another power in the development of Israel's life beside the civil, and that Saul must recognise this.   The exercise of the power had reference to general principles of conduct, and the securing of Messianic purposes.   The Church of Christ is bound to avoid everything that would be inharmonious with her spiritual nature and uses.   To be the educator of the state conscience, to assert her own independence as a spiritual community for spiritual purposes, this is the function of the Church in relation to the civil power, as illustrated in the conduct of Samuel, involved in the spiritual nature of Christ's body, and confirmed by the adversities and prosperities of history.

General considerations :—1. How far the controversies connected with spiritual supremacy are the result of a deviation from the simplicity of purpose characteristic of apostolic times.   2. To what extent calamities have befallen the world by the professing Church being more concerned for the assertion of power than for the preaching and practising of righteousness.   3. Whether history does not show that an earnest Church, solely bent on preaching the gospel, and enforcing it by example, exercises more real power over the destinies of nations than a Church ever watchful to limit the powers of civil rulers.

Vers. 9—17.—*The reasonableness of incongruities.*   The facts are—1. Saul experiences the truth of all that Samuel had told him.   2. Being met by a company of prophets, Saul, under an inspiration from God, also prophesies.   3. The people remark on the incongruity of Saul's being among the prophets.   4. Saul's uncle, being too inquisitive in the matter of Samuel's intercourse with him, is not gratified.   The general reader of the Bible is struck with the incongruity between Saul's antecedents and his sudden participation in the gifts of prophecy ; and men generally have sympathised with the surprise which expressed itself in the proverb, "Is Saul among the prophets?"   Too frequently the event here recorded is left as one of the strange, unaccountable things scattered over the page of sacred history, furnishing to the mind more of perplexity and embarrassment than of instruction and aid to faith.   It will, however, be found that in the course of Providence the seeming incongruities play an important part, that they are not essentially unreasonable, and are all reducible to a common principle.

I. The COURSE OF PROVIDENCE PRESENTS NUMEROUS INSTANCES OF STRIKING INCONGRUITY.   Whatever the precise definition of incongruity, the thing itself may be found in the form of conduct, association, relation, and means.   Leaving out all instances resulting from human folly and eccentricity, we may notice a few in the order of

Providence as seen in—1. *Conduct.* Saul's is a case in point. He was an instrument in the hand of God of producing the strange impression indicated by the familiar proverb. To the Jews in Jerusalem on the day of Pentecost there was an unaccountable incongruity in the speech and bearing of men who, up to that time, had been timid, obscure followers of the Crucified. Considering the reputed character of Peter as a rash, impulsive man, it was, in the judgment of his companions and in the light of his denial, scarcely congruous to commit to him the "key" of the kingdom. And the joyful songs which rose from the apostles when in the stocks were strange music to their warders. Modern history is not without its notable instances. 2. *Associations.* For Saul to be associated with a prophetic order was a marvel. That a glorious star should lead wise men from afar only to a babe in a manger, and that the hosts of heaven should sing on the birth of a helpless child, was an association rare and astonishing. The most perplexing incongruity to many is that the Eternal One should for a term of years be in association with a frail body, with all the sorrowful incidents inseparable therefrom. 3. *Relations.* We find this in Saul's case; for men can see no congruity between his ecstatic excitement as prophet and the office of king to which he was being called. The relation of John the Baptist, an austere, unsociable ascetic, as forerunner to the mild, approachable Christ, struck men as remarkable, and needed the vindication that "wisdom is justified of her children" (Matt. xi. 16—19). It also occurred to John as a most incongruous thing that he should have to baptize the holy Saviour (Matt. iii. 13—15). 4. *Means.* As a means of qualifying Saul for the discharge of kingly functions this prophetic excitement seemed to be most unsuitable. So, likewise, to many there is no propriety in the uplifting of a brazen serpent as a means of restoring health to the poisoned. Naaman could not think the Jordan better than the rivers of his own country. The cross of Christ was despised by the Greeks as foolishness—a most incongruous means for the subjugation of the world to him who died thereon.

II. The SEEMING INCONGRUITIES IN THE COURSE OF PROVIDENCE ARE RELATIVE TO OUR IGNORANCE. That is incongruous only which is not understood. "Things are not what they seem." Our surprises and astonishments are often the index of our lack of knowledge. It may not be possible in every instance to find a complete solution, but some clue may be found if we will consider all the events of Providence as interrelated, and throwing light on one another. The reasonableness of incongruities may be illustrated by taking as a typical instance *the conduct of Saul.* The appearance of a prophetic order at that juncture, under the direction of Samuel, was a necessary feature in the moral elevation of the people. The stagnant indifference of men could be best aroused by urgent zeal. The reasonableness of Saul's excitement resolves itself into that of the order. We are to remember that a *coming good* in Messiah's reign was *the* hope of the true Israel. In so far as their conviction was deep, and was attended by a corresponding pity for present degradation, it, when full on the spirit, would not unnaturally produce an excitement proportionate to the susceptibility of the temperament and the external occasion, and the utterance of the truth would be measured by the degree of excitement. Therefore the educational value of these men was great, and they were obedient, in their extravagance, to the laws of mind and the urgency of religious conviction. Now it was reasonable for Saul to share in this gift—1. *For the people.* It would call their attention to him, and prepare them for the subsequent action of Samuel. 2. *For Saul himself.* He was to be king, and the people imagined that their king would be after the pattern of other kings. But Israel's king must rule in harmony with the spiritual destiny of the nation. He must be in sympathy with prophets. 3. *For the order of prophets.* This order was one of the great powers in fashioning the future of the people of God. It therefore was interested in the character and aspirations of whatever king might be chosen. Saul's endowment with their own gift would assure them that he was worthy of their support, and would not be as the kings of the nations. The incongruity was most reasonable.

III. The TRUE SOLUTION OF ANY INCONGRUITY IN THE COURSE OF PROVIDENCE IS TO BE FOUND IN THE SERIES OF WHICH THE EVENT IS BUT ONE. Saul's conduct, regarded in relation to the antecedents of Israel's life, and the gradual preparation of the world for Christ, stands out as most fit and useful; therefore, natural. No one can rightly judge of Scripture events who does not consider the course of Providence as a development from the imperfect to the more perfect. The place and power of every molecule in the universe are relative to the antecedent and subsequent movements of the whole. Astronomers have met with perturbations and irregularities which seemed incongruous with all they knew, but in time they discovered the place of these so-called irregularities in the mechanism of the heavens, and they became at once beautiful regularities. The issue of redemptive methods will throw light on the process.

*General lessons :—*1. The most unlikely of men may be called to do God's will in forms unlooked for. 2. The varied gifts requisite to an office will be forthcoming to all whom God calls to the office. 3. We should be careful to keep our mind free from prejudice against methods which, though unusual, may be of God. 4. A deep and patient study of the Bible as a whole is the only means of learning the beauty and harmony of his ways. 5. A true philosophy will induce us to suspend our judgment on some subjects until we can see more clearly the relation of the past to the future.

Wise reticence. The notice taken of an inquiry by Saul's uncle is evidently for the purpose of bringing in bold relief Saul's wisdom in being reticent on the important matters concerning the kingdom. It is probable that the bearing of Saul indicated that something unusual had transpired, and the prophesying would only confirm the suspicion. Saul's replies do not make clear whether the uncle was designedly prying into what he knew were secrets, or was simply seeking general information. But in either case Saul formed a proper estimate of his own position, and manifested a proper reserve.

I. A DEGREE OF RETICENCE IS ESSENTIAL TO A WISE LIFE. "There is a time to speak, and a time to be silent." Reticence, however, is more than silence ; it is deliberate silence where speech is possible and sought. It may be considered with reference to—1. *Its source.* In every case its source is in the will acting freely in the form of a negative judgment. But still this judgment may in some persons be connected more with temperament than with an enlightened estimate of what is proper. The wise reticence is that which comes from a just estimate of what is due to the occasion and the subject-matter. 2. *Its proper subject-matter.* This must be determined by a calm judgment on the right of others to know what we know, and the utility of unveiling our knowledge. But taking a general view of human life, we may say that reticence is due to—(1) *Our deepest religious experience.* There are depths in the soul which no eye but God's can penetrate, and there are experiences there so sacred, tender, and awful that it would be a species of profanity to endeavour to unfold them in form of speech. If, for purpose of seeking assistance, reference is made to secret experiences, the surface only is to be touched. No one who reveres the sacredness of religious life will attempt to pry into what is secret between the soul and God, or to probe wounds which " shame would hide." (2) *Private and domestic affairs.* There are in every life interests which belong to no one else ; and in home there are solemn secrets on which the cold, critical eye of the world must not be allowed to gaze. Much of the sweet, binding influence of home lies in the unforced reticence of its members. (3) *Secrets pertaining to office.* Office in Church, State, or commerce implies knowledge to be used only for specific purposes in relation thereto. No one is fit for office who cannot control his tongue and resist temptation to speak. 3. *Its value.* As a *habit of mind*, when distinguished from sullen reserve, the result of mere temperament, it gives power to the possessor. It reveals a sober, discriminating judgment, a strength of purpose that can resist inducement, and a profound regard for the sanctities of life. In *society* it, wisely exercised, insures confidence, renders transaction of affairs easy, and promotes respectful, courteous bearing. In *religious associations* it tends to reverence, devoutness of spirit, and sincerity. 4. *Its dangers.* It is, if not carefully guarded, likely to degenerate into a love of secrecy, an unnaturally close, reserved habit of mind. In religious life its excess may put a check on the free utterance of life's sorrows and cares even to God, and also deprive the Church of the benefits of a rich experience.

II. WISE RETICENCE WILL ALWAYS BE CONSISTENT WITH TRUTHFULNESS. It is possible to state partial truth in such a way as virtually to lie, and to be silent when silence may be designed to convey a false impression. Saul was truthful in his reticence. He answered questions; he did not volunteer information. Had he been pressed he most likely would have declined to answer. Christ was reticent when pressed on the question of John's baptism, and when examined by Pilate, but no false impression was conveyed. In cases of difficulty it is better point blank to refuse information than incur the risk of suspected prevarication. Inquisitive men should be plainly rebuked rather than put off with questionable answers.

HOMILIES BY VARIOUS AUTHORS.

Ver. 10. (GIBEAH.) — *A company of prophets.* This is the first mention of "a company (cord, chain, or band) of prophets" (Nabhis). There were previously individual prophets. And on one occasion the seventy elders prophesied (Num. xi. 25), and Moses said, "Would God that all the Lord's people were prophets, and that the Lord would put his Spirit upon them." But until the time of Samuel there was no association or community, college or school, of prophets.   1. His language shows his intimate relation to this "company," of which he was doubtless the founder, and appears subsequently as president (ch. xix. 20); for it is not likely that there were now several such "companies," as in later times (1 Kings xx. 35; 2 Kings ii. 3, 16; iv. 38).   2. Its formation was due to a newly-awakened religious life among the people, and intended as a means of deepening and extending it.   3. It arose about the same time as the establishment of the monarchy, and furnished a regular succession of prophets, by whom the word of the Lord was spoken for the guidance and restraint of the king. "Samuel saw the need of providing a new system of training for those who should be his successors in the prophetic office, and formed into fixed societies the sharers of the mystic gift, which was plainly capable of cultivation and enlargement. As it was a leading crisis of the dealings of God with men, unusual operations of the Spirit marked the time of Samuel; but they were not confined to him, though he is far the most conspicuous figure" ('Heroes of Heb. Hist.'). Notice their—

I. SPIRITUAL CALLING. They are called prophets with reference to their vocation or profession. But this was founded upon an individual and inner call by the Divine Spirit. Dwelling on the high ground of Divine contemplation, they were often visited by breezes of spiritual influence to which others were strangers, borne along in an ecstasy beyond their own control, and impelled to give utterance to the overflowing feeling of their hearts; and some of their number were chosen by God to be the recipients of the gift of prophecy in the highest sense. Their calling represents that of the Christian ministry, and more generally the vocation of all Christians (Acts ii. 17; Ephes. v. 18, 19).

II. FRATERNAL UNION. They formed a "company," a voluntary, organised society, apparently dwelling together in the same place, and pursuing the same mode of life. The bond of their union was the common spirit they possessed; and their association contributed to their preservation and prosperity, and their power over others. "They presented the unifying, associative power of the prophetic spirit over against the disruption of the theocratic life, which was a legacy of the time of the judges" (Erdmann). Of Christian union the like, and much more, may be said (John xvii. 21; Acts ii. 46; iv. 23).

III. MUSICAL SKILL. "And before them a psaltery (cithara), and a tabret (tambourine), and a pipe (flute), and a harp (guitar);" stringed, percussion, and wind instruments of music (ver. 5; Gen. iv. 21; xxxi. 27; Exod. xv. 20). They made a religious use of music, and cultivated it with great care. It prepared them for high and holy emotion (2 Kings iii. 15), and gave appropriate expression to it. It strengthened the feeling to which it gave expression, regulated it, and stirred in others a similar feeling. Their sacred music was the germ of the splendid choral service of the temple in subsequent time.

> " What passion cannot music raise and quell ?
>   When Jubal struck the chorded shell,
>   His listening brethren stood around,
>   And wonder on their faces fell,
>   To worship that celestial sound ;
>   Less than a god they thought there could not dwell
>   Within the hollow of that shell,
>   That spoke so sweetly and so well.
>   What passion cannot music raise and quell ? " (Dryden)

IV. PROPHETIC UTTERANCE. "And they shall prophesy." Poetry, like music, is the natural vehicle of strong emotion. And in it they recited and sang in an impassioned manner the praises of God, and the wonders which he had wrought on behalf of his people (1 Chron. xxv. 1, 3).

V. POPULAR REPUTATION. The manner in which they were spoken of by the people generally (ver. 11) shows the important position they occupied, and the high estimation in which they were held. When the professed servants of God are so regarded—1. It is an evidence of their worth and consistency. They commend themselves to "every man's conscience." If, being faithful to their vocation, they are despised, it only reveals the evil character of their despisers ; and it is not honour, but shame, to be commended by foolish and wicked men (Luke vi. 26). 2. It indicates the prevalence of a right sentiment in society. 3. It affords a favourable condition of bearing witness for God and successful spiritual labour.—D.

Vers. 11—13. (GIBEAH.)—*Saul among the prophets.* "Is Saul also among the prophets ? " Of the three signs of which Saul was assured, the occurrence of the last alone is particularly described. "And the Spirit of God came upon him, and he prophesied among them." "Turned into another man" (ver. 6). It was "the most important for his inner life." "Through this sign his anointing as king was to be inwardly sealed." In what is here recorded we see an instance of—

I. SURPRISING TRANSFORMATION. The question was mainly one of surprise. The change was—1. *Sudden.* In what are called "sudden conversions," indeed, there is often a secret preparation of mind and heart. Even in the case of Saul the surprise would not have been so great if his recent interview with Samuel and its effect upon him had been known. 2. In extraordinary *contrast* to his previous life, wherein he had exhibited little interest in or aptitude for spiritual exercises. Four or five days ago among them wholly occupied with the care of oxen and asses—dull, moody, and silent ; now in a transport of religious emotion, and "speaking in a new tongue ! " 3. *Supernatural.* It was plainly due to the "Spirit of God," *i. e.* (in the Hebrew conception) the direct, invisible, operative energy of God, whether put forth in nature or in man, in imparting mental or physical force for great enterprises, in promoting moral improvement, in producing exalted states of feeling, or in acts of the highest inspiration (Gen. i. 2 ; Exod. xxxi. 3 ; Num. xxiv. 2 ; Judges xiii. 25 ; 2 Sam. xxiii. 2 ; Isa. xi. 2) ; and (according to the fuller revelation of the New Testament) the holy, personal, Divine Spirit of God and of Christ. The expression (here used in this book for the first time) is not employed with respect to Samuel, whose intercourse with God is represented as more voluntary, self-conscious, intimate, and continuous than that which it here denotes.

II. SYMPATHETIC ENTHUSIASM. Saul was drawn into sympathy with the Divine enthusiasm of the "company of prophets." 1. The links which unite men are secret, subtle, and mysterious, and the influence which some men exert over others is extraordinary. 2. Human influence is a common condition of Divine. 3. The contagious power of strong emotion is often seen in religious revivals, and to some extent also in other public movements. "Ecstatic states have something infectious about them. The excitement spreads involuntarily, as in the American revivals and the preaching mania in Sweden, even to persons in whose state of mind there is no affinity to anything of the kind " (Tholuck). "As one coal kindles another, so it happens that where good is taught and heard hearts do not remain unmoved—Acts xvi. 13, 14 " (Hall).

III. SPIRITUAL ENDOWMENT. "And one of the same place answered," in reply to the question (asked somewhat contemptuously and sceptically), " What has happened to the son of Kish ? Is Saul also " (whose relationship and antecedents are so different) " among the prophets ? and said, But who is *their* father ? " " Who is he that teacheth these prophets, and causeth the spirit of prophecy to rest on them ? Nor is there any cause for astonishment in this ; for the same holy, blessed One who teacheth these prophets teacheth also this one " (Kimchi). " Prophetical perfection is not a matter that is conveyed from father to son. Under these circumstances the son may be a prophet, though the father is not so " (R. Levi Ben Gersom, quoted by Ed. of Smith's ' Sel. Dis.'). 1. Spiritual gifts are not the result of natural relationship. 2. They are due to the free and sovereign operation of the Divine Spirit, " dividing to every man severally as he will." 3. When they are bestowed on ourselves they should be received with humility, and when they are observed in others they should be regarded without envy, and with admiration and thankfulness.

IV. PARTIAL CONVERSION. " And when he had made an end of prophesying, he came to the high place " (ver. 13). His inspiration was transitory, and the change which he had undergone, great as it was, and in the direction of a renewal of his heart in righteousness, did not involve such renewal. " This transformation is not to be regarded as regeneration in the Christian sense, but as a change resembling regeneration which affected the entire disposition of mind, and by which Saul was lifted out of his former modes of thought and feeling, which were confined within a narrow, earthly sphere, into a far higher sphere of his new royal calling, was filled with kingly thoughts in relation to the service of God, and received another heart—ver. 9 " (Keil). 1. Great spiritual gifts may be possessed without the possession of a new heart (Num. xxiv. 35 ; xxxi. 8 ; Matt. vii. 22 ; 1 Cor. xiii. 2). 2. There may be considerable moral reformation, much spiritual feeling, correct orthodox beliefs, outward profession of piety, and strict observance of religious ordinances, whilst the supreme affection or ruling purpose of the soul remains unchanged (Matt. xiii.). 3. A real renewal of the heart is manifested by its permanent fruits (Matt. vii. 20 ; John xv. 16 ; Heb. iii. 14). " If Samuel is the great example of an ancient saint growing up from childhood to old age without a sudden conversion, Saul is the first direct example of the mixed character often produced by such a conversion. . . . He became ' another man,' yet not entirely. He was, as is so often the case, half converted, half roused. . . . His religion was never blended with his moral nature " (Stanley)

> " Let not the people be too swift to judge;
> As one who reckons on the blades in field
> Or e'er the crop be ripe. For I have seen
> The thorn frown rudely all the winter long,
> And after bear the rose upon its top ;
> And bark, that all her way across the sea
> Ran straight and speedy, perish at the last
> E'en in the haven's mouth. Seeing one steal,
> Another bring his offering to the priest,
> Let not Dame Birtha and Sir Martin thence
> Into Heaven's counsels deem that they can pry ;
> For one of these may rise, the other fall " (Dante, Par. xiii.).—D.

Vers. 14—16. (GIBEAH.)—*Inquisitiveness.* Inquiry after truth is a necessary and invaluable exercise. But inquiry, when it is directed to matters in which we have no proper concern, degenerates into vain curiosity, or mere inquisitiveness. And this often appears both in relation to Divine affairs (Gen. iii. 6 ; Deut. xxix. 29 ; 1 Sam. vi. 19 ; Luke xiii. 23 ; Acts i. 6) and human affairs (John xxi. 21). Of the latter we have here an illustration. Saul, having reached his home, was asked by his uncle concerning his journey and interview with Samuel. " Whither went ye ? " " Tell me, I pray thee, what Samuel said to you." This man was doubtless acquainted with the popular agitation about a king, but what his precise motives were we are not told. Such inquisitiveness as he displayed—

I. MANIFESTS A WRONG DISPOSITION. 1. An unrestrained desire of knowledge. There must be self-restraint in this desire, as in every other ; else it leads to recklessness, irreverence, and pride. 2. An unjust disregard of the rights of others. The claims of family relationship are sometimes exaggerated so as to ignore or interfere with those rights. It is imagined that they justify the expectation of an answer to any inquiry, however little it affects the inquirer. 3. Uncharitable and suspicious thoughts about the conduct of others, expressed in impertinent and annoying questions, which naturally cause resentment and discord. It may be added, that persons who are "busybodies in other men's matters" (1 Pet. iv. 15) are seldom so diligent and faithful in their own as they ought to be. The proper province of every man affords plenty of scope for his attention and effort (2 Thess. iii. 11 ; 1 Tim. v. 13).

II. REQUIRES TO BE PROMPTLY CHECKED. 1. Out of *due regard to higher claims.* What Samuel said to Saul was intended for him alone, and to divulge it would be a breach of duty. 2. Lest the information given should be used to the *disadvantage* of him who gives it. Who knows how Saul's uncle would have employed the knowledge of his having been appointed king by the prophet ? He might have done irreparable mischief. Many excellent projects have been frustrated by an untimely disclosure of them. 3. For the *good* of the inquirer himself. The gratification of his curiosity tends to increase his inquisitiveness, the mortification thereof to its cure. It was for the benefit of the Apostle Peter that the Lord said, "What is that to thee ? Follow thou me."

III. SHOULD BE CHECKED IN A RIGHT MANNER. Judiciously, discreetly, and, more particularly—1. With *strict truthfulness.* "He told us plainly that the asses were found" (ver. 16). Saul spoke the truth, but not the whole truth ; nor was he in the circumstances described under any obligation to do so. "A fool uttereth all his mind ; but a wise man keepeth it till afterwards" (Prov. xxix. 11). 2. With *due courtesy.* By a blunt refusal and rude repulsion Saul might have alienated his uncle, and turned him into an enemy. "Honour all men." "Be courteous." 3. With *few words* or *resolute silence.* "But of the matter of the kingdom whereof Samuel spake he told him not." There is a "time to keep silence" (Eccles. iii. 7 ; Amos v. 13). "Then he (Herod) questioned him with many words ; but he answered him nothing" (Luke xxiii. 9). Our Lord himself is thus an example of silence to us when addressed with questions which it would not be prudent or beneficial to answer. "Silence is golden."

Conclusion.—1. Check the tendency to curiosity in yourselves, so that it may not be checked, disappointed, and reproved by others. 2. In checking it in others seek their improvement rather than your own dignity and honour.—D.

EXPOSITION.

PUBLIC SELECTION OF SAUL AS KING (vers. 17—24). Ver. 17. — **Samuel called the people together unto Jehovah to Mizpeh.** For the reason why Mizpah (so the name should be spelt) was chosen as the place of meeting see ch. vii. 15. **Unto Jehovah.** Because in some way the Divine presence there was indicated ; possibly by the high priest having been summoned thither with the Urim and Thummim.

Ver. 18.—**And said . . .** Samuel first points out in his address to the assembled people that Jehovah always had done for them the very thing for which they desired a king. They wished for deliverance from the Philistines, and **Jehovah had delivered them out of the hand of the Egyptians, and out of the hand of all kingdoms that oppressed them** (the A. V. wrongly inserts "and of them "). But their deliverance by Jehovah had been made dependent upon their own conduct ; they were required to repent them of their sins, and purge the land from idolatry, before victory could be

theirs. What they wanted was national independence freed from this condition, and secured by an organisation of their military resources.

Ver. 19.—Samuel, therefore, protests unto them, **Ye have this day rejected your God,** because what you want is a divorce of your national well-being from religion. Nevertheless, God granted their request, it being a law of his providence to leave men free to choose. The king was, however, to be appointed by him, the selection being by lot. **By your thousands.** The natural subdivision of a tribe is into families ; but when Moses distributed the people into thousands, hundreds, fifties, and tens (Exod. xviii. 25), the numerical arrangement was probably made to yield as far as possible to the natural, so that about a thousand men more or less of the same kin should be classed as a family. Hence the terms are synonymous here, and in Num. i. 16 · x. 4 ; Josh. xxii. 14, &c.

Ver. 21.—**The family of Matri, or of the**

Matrites. Matri is not mentioned anywhere else ; and numerous as are the omissions in the genealogies, we can scarcely suppose that the name of the head of one of the main subdivisions of a tribe could be passed over. The conjecture, therefore, is probable that Matri is a corruption of Bikri, *i. e.* a descendant of Becher, for whom see 1 Chron. vii. 8. After the lot had fallen upon this family they would next cast lots upon its smaller subdivisions, as in Josh. vii. 17, 18, until at last they came to households, when first Kish, and finally Saul was taken. The latter, foreseeing that this would happen, had concealed himself. For though a noble change had taken place in him (ver. 9), yet no really worthy man was ever promoted to high office without having to overcome his own unwillingness, and no one probably ever worthily discharged solemn duties without having felt oppressed and humbled with the consciousness of his own unfitness to undertake them. As a matter of fact, Saul was now called to a most weighty responsibility, and he failed and was rejected, though not without proving that he was a man of extraordinary genius and power. And it never can be said of him that presumption was the cause of his fall, or that he hastily undertook serious duties in the spirit of light-hearted levity.

Ver. 22. — **They inquired of Jehovah further, if the man should yet come thither.** More correctly, "Is any one as yet come hither?" The Septuagint and Vulgate translate as if there were an article before "any one" (Hebrew, *a man*), and give, "Is the man coming hither?" But the Hebrew text is the more satisfactory. For the object of the inquiry, made by the Urim and Thummim, was to find Saul, wherever he might be ; and the enigmatical way of putting the question, Is any one as yet come? was regarded as more reverential than asking directly, Is Saul come? **Among the stuff.** *I. e.* the baggage, as in ch. xvii. 22, where it is translated "carriage." The people, collected from all Israel, would come with wagons and provisions, and such arms as they could procure ; for very probably the Philistines would interrupt such a meeting, as they had that convened formerly by Samuel (ch. vii. 7). Naturally, therefore, they would follow the regulations of an army, and so arrange their baggage as to form a place of defence in case of attack. See on ch. xvii. 20.

Vers. 23, 24.—**And when he stood.** This rendering spoils the poetic force of the original, where the rapidity of their action is expressed by three preterites following hard upon one another. The Hebrew is, "And they ran, and took him thence, and he stood forth (see ch. xii. 7) among the people, and **he was taller,**" &c. And now Samuel pre-

sents him to the multitude as "the chosen of Jehovah," and the people shout their assent by saying, "Let the king live." For this the A. V. puts our English phrase, but the Hebrew exactly answers to the French *Vive le roi!*

THE EVENTS WHICH FOLLOWED IMMEDIATELY UPON SAUL'S ELECTION (vers. 25—27). Ver. 25.—**The manner.** The difficult word already discussed in ch. ii. 13 ; viii. 11. Here, however, it is not used for rights so exercised as to become wrongs, but in a good sense, for what we should call a *constitution.* The heathen kings were despots, subject to no higher law, and Samuel, in ch. viii. 11— 18, speaks with merited abhorrence of their violation of the natural rights of their subjects ; but under the theocracy the king's power was limited by laws which protected, in the enjoyment of their privileges, the people, the priests, and the prophets. The latter class especially, as being the mouthpiece of Jehovah, formed a powerful check upon the development of despotic tendencies. In sketching Saul's kingly rights Samuel would be guided by Deut. xvii. 14—20, and would give the king his true position as the representative of Jehovah both in all matters of internal administration and of war. **And laid it up before Jehovah.** Probably by the side of the ark. We are not to suppose that Samuel wrote this at Mizpah. He would fully explain to Saul and the people there what a theocratic king ought to be, and would afterwards draw up a formal document both as a memorial of what had been done, and for the use of future sovereigns, and place it within the sanctuary. It is noteworthy that this is the first notice of writing since the days of the illustrious scribe Eleazar.

Vers. 26, 27.—Saul did not at once enter upon his duties, but **went home to Gibeah, and there went with him,** not **a band of men,** but *the host,* or *the force,* i. e. those brave men **whose hearts God had touched.** Whatever was noble and valiant accompanied him, to take counsel for the nation's good ; **but the children of Belial,** *i. e.* worthless, good-for-nothing creatures (see ch. i. 16 ; ii. 12), **despised him.** In the A. V. the antithesis between *the force,* the strength and bravery that went with Saul, and the *worthlessness* which rejected him, is lost by the mistranslation of both words. The Septuagint, on the contrary, strengthens it by rendering "sons of strength" and "pestilent sons." As there was a garrison in the district of Gibeah, this proceeding was likely to embroil Saul with the Philistines, and probably was so intended. They **brought him no presents.** Apparently, therefore, the people did bring him presents ; and as these would chiefly consist of food, they would be useful only for maintaining a body of men. This, too, would scarcely escape the notice of so watchful an enemy, and yet until Saul smote one of their garrisons they did nothing; but then, forthwith, they invaded Israel so promptly, and with such overwhelming numbers, as seems to prove that they had been busily making preparations meanwhile to maintain their empire. **He held his peace.** Literally, "was as one that is deaf." Had Saul not controlled his anger, a civil war would have been the result, and the lordly tribes of Ephraim and Judah might

have refused a king chosen from the little tribe of Benjamin. In fact, Judah never does seem to have given a hearty allegiance to Saul. The Septuagint, followed by Josephus, offers a not improbable different reading, which involves but a very slight change in the Hebrew. Uniting the words with the next chapter, they translate, "And it came to pass, after about a month, that Nahash the Ammonite," &c. The Vulgate has both readings.

HOMILETICS

Vers. 17—25.—*Casting the lot in life.* The facts are—1. Samuel, in calling the people together to exercise their choice, reminds them of their sin. 2. Proceeding to a choice by lot, Saul is taken. 3. For reasons secret to himself, Saul is not forthcoming when sought. 4. By acclamation the people recognise him as their king, and thereupon receive from Samuel instructions relating to the new form of government. During the intercourse of Samuel with Saul the people were waiting for the fulfilment of the promise implied in the prophet's words (ch. viii. 10). In this section we have the consummation of their desire for change in the form of government. Its details are essentially Hebrew, but its teaching is world-wide.

I. MEN FINALLY COMMITTING THEMSELVES TO A SELF-WILLED COURSE ARE FURNISHED WITH OPPORTUNITY FOR CONSIDERING THEIR RESPONSIBILITY. The self-willed character of Israel's conduct had been emphatically marked and denounced by the prophet in the first instance (ch. viii. 6—10). Had they received his rebuke in a becoming spirit, they would, during the interim, have repented of their decision, and have entreated that the old order might continue until such time as it might please God to alter it. Sometimes, as here, God takes men at their word, and yet, before an irreversible committal to their choice is made, another chance is given to retreat if they so willed. It was thus that Pharaoh was dealt with when it was in his mind to prefer self-will to the will of God. Nineveh had an opportunity of persisting in sin or turning from it. To erring Christians in Asia a chance of retracing their steps was given (Rev. ii. 21). Providence raises up for us all some voice or circumstance which, before a final step is taken, sounds the last warning, and creates a definite consciousness of unfettered responsibility.

II. EVERY REVIEW OF GOD'S DEALINGS WITH HIS PEOPLE ONLY CONFIRMS THE UNREASONABLENESS OF SELF-WILL. The reference to God's all-sufficing care in the past, and the magnitude of the deliverances effected (vers. 18, 19), was both a justification of Samuel's former remonstrance, and a new demonstration of the sinful folly of the resolve to have a king. It was considerate on the part of Samuel to draw their attention to the past before translating their resolve into accomplished fact; for in the impetuosity of life the will is apt to be misled by delusive reasons, which in calmer moments vanish before the light of history. The axiom that God's way and time are best shines in full lustre whenever we consider the works he has wrought. If ever blind self-will urges on to a course agreeable to taste, and apparently sustained by reason, we cannot do better than take a survey of what God has done for us when we were obedient to his will. There are deliverances in the life of every one, and a quiet reflection of these when we are under the temptation to embark on some questionable career will prove a wholesome check, at least it will vindicate the ways of God when judgment overtakes our folly.

III. MEN IN CARRYING OUT THEIR PURPOSE FALL INTO PERPLEXITY WITH RESPECT TO WHAT IS BEST. To desire a king is one thing, to select one another. In Israel there were diversities of opinion concerning the qualities requisite to their regal representative. As they took their own way in having a monarch, there was a fitness in his being, with respect to culture, morality, patriotism, and religion, an embodiment of the average attainments of the nation. The choice was thrown upon the people as a whole, and they were conscious of the difficulty. Sinners must take the consequences of self-will, as did Balaam when his path was hedged with obstacles, and Jonah when he preferred to go to sea. The difficulty in case of Israel was incidental, and soon removed by the mercy of God; but the principle holds good that the very first step of a self-willed course is attended with embarrassment. All nature is at war with wrong. Sin is a condition of disorganisation.

IV. WHEN GOD PERMITS ACTION TO MEET SELF-CREATED DIFFICULTIES, IT IS WISE TO USE MEANS MOST APPROPRIATE TO THE END IN VIEW. Although the difficulty of finding a king truly representative of the age was self-created, God permitted action in reference to it as truly as though he had originated the resolve for a king; and under such circumstances, guided by Samuel, the wisest means were adopted for overcoming the difficulties of the case. As the nation willed a king, every one had equal choice, and was, theoretically, in the absence of precedents, equally eligible. Abstractedly there was as much reason against one being chosen as against another. The jealousies and envies consequent on a preferential choice might prove a source of perpetual intrigue. The "lot" was believed to meet these requirements of the case, and therefore was adopted. In *this particular the conduct of Israel* under Samuel's guidance is *worthy of imitation in many seasons of difficulty independent of self-will.* In every life there are emergencies when men are at their wits' end. Home has to be provided for, business improved, sons placed out in the world, embarrassments in the Church removed. Our wisdom lies in considering all the facts, and then deliberately adopting those means which seem to us to be most suited for the occasion. And if, in a spirit of prayer, we are able to consult the "lively oracles," there is no doubt that in the main the right steps will be taken, as in the case of the disciples (Acts i. 13—26). We in our way "cast the lot" when we take a choice of possible means and commit our way to the Lord.

V. THERE IS REASON TO BELIEVE THAT IN USING THE BEST MEANS AT OUR DISPOSAL IN A RIGHT SPIRIT GOD WILL DIRECT THE MEANS TO THE BEST RESULT. God approved of Israel's use of the "lot" as just to a community where political equality was recognised, and as least likely to engender jealousies and strifes; and *because he approved,* and because the people believed that, though the lot was "cast into the lap, the whole disposing thereof was of the Lord" (Prov. xvi. 33), he graciously so controlled the intricacies of the free actions of men as to insure the result which, in relation to Israel's conduct and aspirations, was best. The deep conviction dwelt even in the heart of imperfect Israel that God exercises complete and constant control over all the subtle and intricate actions and movements of men. When it is said of Christ that he is "Lord of all," the language is not that of courtesy, but of fact. It means *power* to act, to direct, to control. If there is any sense in Scripture on this subject, and any congruity in our primary notions of the *almighty, ever-present, free, living God,* we must believe that he can and does hold a mastery over every atom, every resolve, in all time and circumstances. Unbelief in his supremacy over will and action and matter and force is most irrational. The *real energy* of God is the most philosophical of all beliefs; and therefore we see that he can direct the "lot" while allowing fullest, most conscious freedom. Let men but have *faith in God.* This is the great lack. "O ye of little faith!"

VI. IT BECOMES MEN TO REJOICE IN THE RESULT OF THE USE OF MEANS APPROVED BY GOD IN SO FAR AS IT IS EXPRESSIVE OF HIS WILL. In the shout, "God save the king," the people no doubt expressed their gratification in seeing their self-will realised; but blended with this there was a distinct recognition of God as the Disposer of the lot. Saul's self-concealment seems to indicate that his sense of responsibility, and perhaps feeling of awkwardness in handling public affairs, may have moderated his joy, yet he must have felt that God's will was being done as well as man's. Realised preference may carry its own chastisement with it; yet in so far as God has enabled us to obtain something better than would have been possible had we been left alone without his kind control, we may heartily rejoice. Leaving out the weakness and sin of man in this transaction, are we not reminded of a time when the true King, the King of the spiritual Israel, shall be welcomed with a joy unspeakable? The "King in his beauty" shall be glorified in all who believe, and by every heart and tongue of the purified, perfected kingdom.

General lessons:—1. It is useful to obtain seasons, free from strong impulse, for calmly considering the wisdom and justice of our main lines of conduct. 2. One of the great helps in battling with sinful propensities lies in occasional studies of the mercies of God. 3. It will add strength to purpose and comfort in trouble to remember that God always works with those who use means approved by him. 4. One of the cures for modern unbelief is to be found in a more frequent and reasonable exposition of what is contained in the primary and necessary beliefs of men. 5. If the heart remains true we need never fear undertaking responsibilities put on us by Providence.

Vers. 26, 27.—*Sympathy and disparagement.* The facts are—1. Saul is followed by a band of men brought into sympathy with him by the Spirit of God. 2. He is despised by a depraved section of the people. 3. He takes no notice of the disparagement.

I. The SIMPLE FACTS GIVEN ARE EXCEEDINGLY NATURAL. For in Israel there were men anxious for a king, and pledged to sustain one; and men, as in all communities, corrupt, unreasonable, prone to disapprove of anything not done solely by themselves. Equally natural was it that he who had graciously regulated Israel's self-will should incline some, by voluntary personal attendance, to assure the monarch of sympathy in seeking honourably to discharge the duties of his onerous office. The principal facts here recorded are of constant recurrence. Chosen ones enter on grave responsibilities; they need the support which flows from hearty sympathy; God provides it by his secret action on human hearts; the entrance on duty renders them objects of criticism, and men of depraved natures assail them with reproach and abuse; having confidence in their appointment, they move on, relying on coming events for their self-vindication.

II. The MOST ILLUSTRIOUS INSTANCE ON RECORD OF THE TRUTH HERE EXPRESSED IS THAT OF OUR SAVIOUR. The parallel is remarkable in the most prominent features. 1. *He was* the true, perfect, *anointed One,* chosen of God to rule over the true Israel, and introduced into publicity by a control of intricacies more lasting and complicated than those of the lot at Mizpah. 2. His *rulership* was to be *coextensive with the whole of God's people*—over a holy nation more complete and united even than was Israel before the dispersion of the ten tribes; and a rulership conducted on principles of righteousness more sweeping in their range and fruitful in consequences than those embodied by Samuel in the book laid up before the Lord (ver. 25). 3. *He,* as bone of our bone and flesh of our flesh, *was in need of the sympathy of true, loving hearts* in bearing the burdens and cares of his exalted position; and such hearts were drawn to him both from the human and the angelic spheres. 4. *His appearance among men* was the occasion of *the most severe and relentless criticism* ever issuing from suspicious, captious minds. His social connections, his habits of life, his requirements of obedience, his claim to save all mankind, were assailed from the first to the last. 5. *He "held his peace."* He did "not strive nor cry," nor "lift up his voice in the streets." He was "meek and lowly in heart," and bided his time. What though hated and scorned? He knew what was coming. He saw "from the travail of his soul, and was satisfied."

III. WHAT IS TRUE OF CHRIST IS in a measure TRUE OF ALL WHOSE LIVES ARE CONFORMABLE TO THE OBJECT OF HIS SUFFERINGS. Every disciple is a chosen one, sustained by God-created sympathy, laden with responsibilities as well as honours, criticised and despised by "men of Belial," and confident that, in due time, his righteousness will come forth as the light, and his judgment be established as the noonday.

General lessons:—1. Let our concern be that we are among the chosen ones called to be kings and priests unto God. 2. Let us accept and yield sympathy from and to all who are doing God's work in the world. 3. Let not disparagement shake our confidence, as though some strange thing had befallen us. 4. Cherish faith in the slow but sure triumph of all that is Christly.

HOMILIES BY VARIOUS AUTHORS.

Vers. 17—25. (MIZPAH.)—*Saul publicly chosen.* There are critical days in the history of nations as well as in the life of individuals. One of these days in the history of Israel was that which is here described. What had taken place hitherto was only private and preparatory. The people themselves must now take their part in relation to the choice of a king; yet in such a way as to recognise the fact that he was really chosen by God, "the only difference between God's appointment of the judges and Saul being this, that they were chosen by internal influence; he by lots, or external designation" (Warburton). For this purpose Samuel summoned a national assembly to Mizpah, the site of an altar to Jehovah, and the scene of signal victory over the Philistines (ch. vii.). Thither the chief men of the tribes repaired in great numbers, and, collecting their travelling baggage in one place (ver. 22), presented themselves before him for his instructions. He was desirous of correcting the wrong state of mind which they had exhibited in requesting a king; of showing them that Saul was appointed by the Lord, and not by himself merely (ch. viii. 5); of securing their united and hearty acceptance of "him whom the Lord chose," so that the purpose of his appointment might be effected; and of guarding as far as possible against the abuse of the royal power. With these ends in view he spoke and acted on that eventful day. The choice of Saul was—

I. PRECEDED BY A SALUTARY REPROOF OF SIN (vers. 18, 19). 1. Based upon the *gracious help* which their Divine Ruler had afforded them. He brought them out of Egypt, delivered them from the hand of Pharaoh and his hosts, and saved them from all who afterwards fought against them and oppressed them. Remembrance of the compassion, faithfulness, and aid of God, so great, so long-continued, and so effectual, should lead men to cleave to him with all their heart (Josh. xxiii. 11), even more than fear of the consequences of disobedience (ch. viii. 11). The goodness of God, as displayed in "his wonderful works to the children of men," is the mightiest incentive to repentance of sin and the practice of righteousness. 2. Consisting of a charge of *flagrant disloyalty.* "And ye have this day rejected your God," &c. Their conduct was *unreasonable,* inasmuch as no other could do for them what he had done; *ungrateful,* viewed in the light of the past; and *wilful,* because, in spite of expostulation, they had said, "Nay, but a king thou shalt set over us" (ver. 19). It was, therefore, inexcusable, and deserving of severest reprobation. And it must be plainly set before them, that they might be convinced of their guilt, humble themselves before the Lord, and seek his pardon. "Therefore will the Lord wait, that he may be gracious unto you" (Isa. xxx. 18). "The Lord will not forsake his people for his great name's sake" (ch. xii. 22). 3. Associated with instruction concerning the *proper course* they should pursue. "And now present yourselves before the Lord," &c., at his altar, where your relation to him may be set right, and his guidance may be afforded. Although sinful requests may be granted by God, yet the spirit in which they are made must be renounced. And the ready submission of the people to the direction of Samuel shows that his reproof was not without effect.

II. CONDUCTED UNDER THE SPECIAL DIRECTION OF GOD (vers. 20—22). 1. He determined, by means of the sacred "lot," *who should be their king.* "As the result of the lot was regarded as a Divine decision, not only was Saul to be accredited by this act in the sight of the whole nation as the king appointed by the Lord, but he himself was also to be more fully assured of the certainty of his own election on the part of God" (Keil). "The lot is cast into the lap (bosom of a garment), but from Jehovah is all its decision" (judgment) (Josh. vii. 19; 1 Sam. xiv. 37; Prov. xvi. 33). "A lot is properly a casual event, purposely applied to the determination of some doubtful thing. As all contingencies are comprehended by a certain Divine knowledge, so they are governed by as certain and steady a providence. God's hand is as steady as his eye. Now God may be said to bring the greatest casualties under his providence upon a twofold account:—(1) That he directs them to a certain end; (2) oftentimes to very weighty and great ends" (South, i. 61). 2. He indicated, in answer to special inquiry, *where he was to be found.* Assured beforehand of what the result would be, and out of the same diffidence, modesty, and humility as he had previously exhibited (ch. ix. 21), Saul "preferred to be absent when the lots were cast." Hence inquiry was made (apparently by *Urim* and *Thummim*) concerning him (ch. xxii. 10; xxiii. 2), and the response of the oracle was definite and conclusive. God mercifully adapts his modes of communication with men to their common modes of thought, their capacity and need; and those who humbly and sincerely seek his guidance are not long left in uncertainty. His communications to men, moreover, carry in themselves the evidence of their Divine origin to those who truly receive them, and are further verified by the events to which they lead (ver. 23). 3. He presented him before them, through his recognised servant, as *chosen by himself*. "See ye him whom the Lord hath chosen, that there is none like him among all the people?" (ver. 24). The conduct of Samuel herein was singularly generous and noble. He did not exhibit the slightest trace of jealousy or distrust of the king into whose hands his own power as civil magistrate was just about to be transferred. "No man ever resigned the first power in the state into other hands with so much courtesy, tenderness, dignity, and grace." Having ascertained the will of the Lord concerning his people, he aimed at nothing else but to carry it into effect.

III. Confirmed by the general approbation of the people (vers. 23, 24). Although the choice was of God, it was necessary that it should be recognised and accepted by them; and their approbation—1. *Accorded* with the commendation of Samuel. 2. Was *influenced* by Saul's outward appearance: "higher than any of the people from his shoulders upward"—just such a man as they wished "to go out before them and fight their battles." 3. And was *expressed* in the acclamation, "God save the king" (literally, May the king live). The people had now the object of their desire; but the Divine providence which had guided Saul guided them to the result. Nations, as well as individuals, are subject to the direction and control of him "who stilleth the noise of the sea and the tumult of the people." "Every act of every man, however it may have been against God in intention, falls exactly into the even rhythm of God's world-plan."

IV. Followed by permanent regulations for the monarchy (ver. 25). "The manner (*mishpat*) of the kingdom" = "the laws and rules by which the kingly government was to be managed" (Poole), and differs from "the manner (*mishpat*) of the king" (ch. viii. 11); being designed by the wisdom and forethought of Samuel to guard against the evils incident to royalty. "Thus under the Divine sanction, and amidst the despotism of the East, arose the earliest example of a constitutional monarchy" (Kitto). But there was no stipulation or compact between the people and the king. His rights and duties were prescribed by the will of God, whose servant he was. His power was restrained by the living voice of prophecy, and sometimes justly opposed by the people themselves (ch. xiv. 45). "This much, however, is clear upon the whole, that the king of Israel was not an unlimited monarch, as the defenders of the Divine right of kings and of the passive obedience of subjects are wont to represent him" (Michaelis, 'Laws of Moses,' i. 286). The regulations for the monarchy were—1. *Founded* upon the existing law of Moses (Deut. xvii. 14—20), although, doubtless, not entirely confined to it. The king must not be *ambitious*, occupied in military preparations and aggressive wars, vying with heathen despots, relying on "an arm of flesh" rather than on God. He must not be given to *sensual indulgence*, forming a large harem and luxurious court; nor to the accumulation of *wealth*, taxing and oppressing the people for that purpose. But he must make himself familiar with "the law," and humbly obey it like his brethren (2 Kings xi. 12). His work was not to make new laws, but to administer those which Jehovah had given, and "do all his pleasure." "Then must he constantly bear in mind that above him there abides another King—the Eternal; and that only in as far as he works together with God, and consequently with all spiritual truth, can any earthly monarch be a king after the heart of the King of kings" (Ewald). O that Saul had borne these things in mind! 2. *Expounded* in the hearing of the people. 3. *Recorded* and carefully preserved for future reference. "That the law of the king should not be a dead letter, that royal self-will should be kept within bounds, was to be the care, not of a representative popular assembly, but of prophecy, which stood as theocratic watchman by the side of royalty" (Oehler).—D.

Ver. 24. (MIZPAH.)—*God save the king.* For the first time in the history of Israel there now arose the cry of "Long live the king" (*Vive le roi*), which was to be so often repeated in subsequent ages (2 Sam. xvi. 16; 2 Kings i. 19; xi. 12). The nations of the earth have since undergone vast and varied changes. Great empires have arisen and disappeared. The theocratic kingdom of Israel, in its outward form, has long ago passed away; and the kingdom of Christ, in which its spiritual *idea* has been realised, has grown up amidst the kingdoms of the world. But the old acclamation is still often heard at the accession of a monarch, and in it Christians as well as others may and ought to join. The acclamation is expressive of—

I. CHEERFUL RECOGNITION OF HIS DIGNITY. 1. As *appointed* by Divine providence. The invisible and eternal Ruler of the universe is the Source of all law and order, and is ever working in the world for the purpose of bringing out of the evil and confusion that prevail a state of things in which "righteousness, peace, and joy" shall abound. And in connection with and subserviency to this design he has ordained civil government (Dan. iv. 32; John xix. 11). "The powers that be are ordained of God" (Rom. xiii. 1), *i. e.* human government generally is appointed by him, although no judgment is expressed by the apostle concerning the Divine right of any one form of government or particular office beyond others. When a ruler is directly chosen by the people he is still a "minister of God." 2. As *representing* the supreme authority and power of "the Most High, who ruleth in the kingdom of men." There is in every government an element which is Divine; a reflection, however dim and distorted, of that Divine power which is above all. But that government is most Divine which is the fairest exhibition of wisdom and truth, righteousness and justice, mercy and loving-kindness;" "for in these things I delight, saith the Lord" (Jer. ix. 24). "By me (wisdom) kings reign and princes decree justice" (Prov. xviii. 15). Reverence for God should be expressed in giving honour to those who, in their high office, represent God, and "to whom honour is due." "Fear God. Honour the king. Submit yourselves to every ordinance of men for the Lord's sake, whether it be to the king as supreme," &c. (1 Pet. ii. 13, 14)—*supreme*, i. e., not in all things, but in those over which he has legitimate authority. In a theocracy, where the laws of God were identical with those of the state, the sphere over which that authority extended was larger than that which properly belongs to any existing government. 3. As *ministering* to human good. Even the absolute rule of a Cæsar or a Czar is unspeakably better than anarchy. "He is a minister of God to thee for *good*" (Rom. xiii. 4). He exists for the good of the community; and although the good which he is able to effect and ought to aim at is necessarily limited, he "does not bear the sword in vain." He bears it for the protection of the good against the bad. And under his sway, when he uses his power aright, his subjects are able to "lead a peaceable and quiet life, in all godliness and gravity."

II. FERVENT DESIRE FOR HIS WELFARE. "May the king prosper" ('Targum'). 1. The preservation of *his life*, which is of great importance to the well-being of the nation, and is often exposed to imminent danger from the exalted position he occupies. 2. The possession of *strength and wisdom*, justice and the fear of God (2 Sam. xxiii. 3). Adequate sympathy is not always felt with "kings and those who are in authority" in their arduous duties and extraordinary difficulties. 3. The *prosperity* of his reign. The desire thus felt should be expressed in prayer to the supreme Ruler and the Giver of every good and perfect gift (1 Tim. ii. 1, 2). "We (Christians) do intercede for all our emperors without ceasing, that their lives may be prolonged, their government secured to them, their families preserved in safety, their armies brave, their senates faithful to them, the people virtuous, and the whole empire at peace, and for whatever, as man or Cæsar, an emperor would wish" (Tertullian, 'Apology,' ch. xxx.).

III. LOYAL DEVOTION TO HIS GOVERNMENT. 1. *Personal obedience* to its laws. "Put them in mind to be subject to principalities and powers, to obey magistrates" (Titus iii. 1). "Ye must needs be subject." (Acts iv. 19; v. 29; Matt. xxii. 21.) 2. *Strenuous opposition* to its enemies. 3. *Faithful endeavour* to promote its efficiency and prosperity. This is plainly our duty as citizens; and whilst, under the protection afforded us, we also seek as Christians in various ways to extend the kingdom of Christ, we thereby make the work of good government easier, and secure the wisest and most just and honourable men for its accomplishment.   So far from being contrary to each other, the Christian religion and civil government are mutually helpful, and each has its part under Divine providence, the one more and the other less directly, in bringing about the time when "the people shall be all righteous."

> "When all men's good (shall)
> Be each man's rule, and universal peace
> Lie like a shaft of light across the land,
> And like a lane of beams athwart the sea,
> Through all the circle of the Golden Year" (Tennyson).—D

Vers. 26, 27. (MIZPAH and GIBEAH.)—*Friends and opponents in godly enterprise.* It was a saying of Socrates that every man in this life has need of a faithful friend and a bitter enemy—the one to advise him, the other to make him look around him.   This saying was more than fulfilled in Saul, who, on being chosen king, was followed by a band of faithful friends, and despised and opposed by "certain worthless men."   The same thing often happens, under different circumstances, to other men, and especially to the servants of God when they enter upon some new enterprise which has for its aim the furtherance of his kingdom, and deeply affects men's interests and passions.   In relation to such an enterprise we have here an illustration of—

I. THE DIVERSE DISPOSITIONS OF MEN, as—1. Often *existing* when not suspected, and notwithstanding all that is done to harmonise them.   When the people shouted, "Long live the king," the dissatisfaction that lurked in many breasts was little surmised.   Samuel did all that lay in his power to bring about a complete union of the tribes ; but his efforts did not altogether succeed.   Reason and persuasion, though they ought to be employed to the utmost, frequently fail to conciliate men because of the different disposition of their hearts.   2. Commonly *manifested* by special events. The honour conferred upon the leader of a new movement, or the decisive action taken by him, serves to "reveal the thoughts of many hearts."   A single circumstance sometimes, like a flash of lightning in the darkness, suddenly lays bare to the view what was previously hidden.   3. Clearly *distinguished* as belonging to one or other of two classes: "the host" (sons of strength, LXX.) "whose hearts God had touched," and "sons of worthlessness."   "He that is not with me is against me" (Matt. xii. 30).   The demands of certain enterprises, like those of Christ himself, render neutrality impossible.

> "Once to every man and nation comes the moment to decide,
> In the strife of truth with falsehood, for the good or evil side ;
> Some great cause, God's new Messiah, offering each the bloom or blight,
> Parts the goats upon the left hand, and the sheep upon the right,
> And the choice goes by for ever 'twixt that darkness and that light" (Lowell).

II. THE INESTIMABLE WORTH OF FRIENDS.   Their worth is always great ; but it is especially so in a time of *need,* when new and responsible positions have to be occupied, arduous duties to be performed, numerous enemies to be encountered. Their *counsel* and *support* are indispensable ; their very *presence* is a mighty encouragement.   "Whom when Paul saw, he thanked God, and took courage " (Acts xxviii. 15).   Their worth depends upon—1. Their *hearty sympathy* in spirit and aim. A merely formal adherence is of little value ; and if there be an inward and ardent devotion, it is "from the Lord " (Ps. cx. 3).   And when God impels a man to useful service he does not leave him without those who sympathise with him.   2. Their *perfect unanimity* in arrangement and method.   3. Their *practical co-operation* in labour and conflict.   They "went with him," formed his body-guard, and stood ready to defend and help him.   In this manner their sympathy proved itself to be genuine, and rendered most effectual service.   Would that all who are favourable to noble enterprises, and all members of Christian Churches, rallied thus around their "leaders !" (Phil. i. 27).

III. THE PRUDENT TREATMENT OF OPPONENTS. " How shall this man save us ? " " Shall Saul reign over us ? " (ch. xi. 12). It is not improbable that they who thus spoke belonged to the princes of Judah and Ephraim, and were *envious* at his election. They were certainly *unbelieving*, neither recognising the hand of God therein, nor looking further than man for deliverance. They were *contemptuous*, deeming him unfit to rule over them. " This man." And they were *disloyal and disobedient*. The law said, " Thou shalt not revile the gods (= God, or the judges), nor curse the ruler of thy people " (Exod. xxii. 28) ; but they " despised him, and brought him no presents," like others, as an expression of their submission. They might, therefore, have been justly punished as traitors. Yet " he was as though he were deaf ; " although he heard them, he did not retaliate, but went on his way in silence. This is often the best way of treating opponents, and it displays—1. *Great self-control.* 2. *Much wisdom and foresight.* To attempt at this time to punish these men might have produced civil war. It is sometimes necessary that gainsayers should be answered, but in most cases they do least mischief by being let alone, and are soonest silenced by silence. 3. *Strong confidence* in Divine help, and the success which it insures. In contending against those whom God calls to do his work men contend against him, and faith calmly leaves them in his hands, to be dealt with as he may think fit (Acts v. 39 ; Rom. xii. 19).

Conclusion.—1. Expect to find opposition in the way of duty. 2. Let the forbearance of God toward his enemies teach you forbearance towards yours. 3. Be thankful for the sympathy and help of earthly friends, and still more for the sympathy and help of the Lord.—D.

Vers. 26, 27.—*Illusive Presages.* A mild, clear morning may be followed by a stormy day. A prince may begin to reign with gentleness who afterwards becomes proud, ruthless, impatient, even harsh and bloodthirsty. There are few instances of this in history so pathetic as the case of Saul, who began his reign with every indication of a magnanimous character, yet was soon deteriorated by the possession of power, and made himself and all around him most unhappy. In him we see how good impulses may be overcome by evil passion, and what fair promise may come to nought. In order to catch the lessons of warning and admonition which come from the tragic story of Saul, it is necessary to do full justice to the bright beginning of his career.

I. HIS RELIGIOUS SENSIBILITY. We know that his prophesying left little trace behind ; but that Saul was quickly susceptible of religious impressions is plain enough, and this in his early days must have awakened fond hopes regarding him in the breasts of those who were zealous for the Lord of hosts.

II. HIS ATTRACTION FOR THE FERVENT SPIRITS OF THE NATION. We are told, with a sort of *naïveté*, how his height impressed the people at large, and was pointed to even by Samuel. So the Greeks gloried in the huge Ajax, and in the towering form of Achilles. It is not said or implied, however, that Saul himself showed any pride in the admiration which his grand appearance won. The significant thing is, that he drew after him " a band of men whose hearts God had touched." They saw in his eye, or supposed they saw, the fire of a kindred enthusiasm. Here was one, they thought, worthy to be king of a holy nation. So they formed a body-guard round him as the Lord's anointed. Their mistake is not at all an isolated one. Ardent young men often fail in discernment of character, and attach themselves to questionable leaders. Let no one count it enough that some good people think well of him, and assume his warmth of spirit as sufficient evidence of his being " born again." A man is what he is in the enduring habits and controlling principles of his character and life. Value the good opinion of the wise, if they have opportunity to see the unexcited tenor of your conduct ; but do not count it a sure mark of grace that you have at some time felt a glow of religious ardour, and that others in the same mood have hailed you as brother, or even leader, in the Church of God. After all the attraction exerted by Saul over the fervent spirits of his time, he hardened his own heart, and the Lord departed from him.

III. HIS PATIENCE AND MAGNANIMITY. There were exceptions to the general approval with which Saul was raised to the throne. Some held aloof, and scoffed at the confidence which was placed so rashly in the tall Benjamite. They disliked him all the more that the devout rallied about him; for they themselves were "sons of Belial," men whose hearts the Lord had not touched. It was a serious risk for the young king to have a disloyal faction, treating his authority with open contempt. Yet Saul bore it quietly. He "held his peace." Nor was this a mere politic delay till he should be strong enough to crush the malcontents, for there is no mention of his ever having called these sons of Belial to account. Surely this was a fine point of character—to bear obstruction so patiently, and be content to earn public confidence by his kingly bearing and exploits. It was a virtue beyond the expectations, and even the wishes, of his people. Who that saw that young king could have imagined that he who was so patient would grow so restless as he did; and he who was so magnanimous would become almost insane with envy, and chase his own son-in-law among the hills of Judæa, thirsting for his blood? So hard is it for a man to be known! Virtue may leap to the front, and show itself on some auspicious day; but vice lurks in the rear, and may prove the stronger. When its day comes it will take the mastery, and then the fair promise of youth is succeeded by a wilful, selfish, ignoble manhood. You meet a man with bloated face and reckless bearing, a companion of fools, half a rogue and half a sot. Yet, could you have seen him twenty years ago, you would have looked on a healthy, happy, kindly boy, the hope of his father's house, the pride of his mother's heart. But there was a weak point in him, and strong drink found it out. So it has come to this degradation. Virtue is laughed at; self-respect is gone; the boy is sunk and lost in this gross and shameless man. Or you see one who is hard and mercenary, inexorable to those who fall into his power, indifferent to the works of genius and to the efforts of philanthropy, occupied always with his own moneyed interest. Yet, could you have seen him thirty years ago, you would have looked on a young man who loved art, or letters, or religion, and seemed likely to develop into a cultured and useful citizen. But in an evil hour the passion of worldly acquisition seized him; or, rather, that which had long been dormant and unperceived began to rule over him, as his opportunities for acquisition widened, and so his bright beginning has resulted in this sordid and ignoble character. Human deterioration, the disappointment of youthful presages of goodness—it is a painful subject, but one which moral teachers may not neglect. It is difficult to stop the evil process once it has begun; and the beginning may be so quiet, so little suspected! It is difficult to know one's self, or any one else, and to say whether it be only a good impulse one has in his youth, or a rooted principle. Some men certainly turn out much better than they promised, but some turn out much worse. Let us watch and pray.—F.

EXPOSITION.

CONFIRMATION OF SAUL IN THE KINGDOM (CHS. XI., XII.).

CHAPTER XI.

THE DEFEAT OF THE AMMONITES (vers. 1—13). Vers. 1, 2.—**Nahash the Ammonite.** The same name is found in 2 Sam. x. 2 as that of the father of Hanun, who treated David's ambassadors so shamefully, and probably they mean the same person. He is there said to have shown kindness to David; and as we read in 2 Sam. xvii. 25 that Abigal (so the Hebrew, not Abigail as the A. V., who was David's wife), Amasa's mother, was the daughter of Nahash, and as Abigal was the sister or half-sister of Zeruiah, David's aunt, there seems to have been some relationship between them. The Ammonites were old enemies of the Israelites, alleging that Israel had taken possession of territory east of the Jordan which rightfully belonged to them (Judges xi. 13); but after their defeat by Jephthah their power was so broken that they allowed a century to elapse before they ventured again to assert their claim. Nahash, apparently after other invasions (ch. xii. 12), now attacks Jabesh-Gilead, a city in the half-tribe of Manasseh, which had been cruelly treated by the Israelites (Judges xxi. 10), but apparently had risen again from its ruins. Its inhabitants were willing humbly to submit to Ammonite rule; but Nahash will grant them no other terms than that they should let him **thrust out**—Hebrew, bore through—**all their right eyes**, not from any special spite against them, but as an insult to all Israel. No better proof could be given of the disorganisation of the nation than that a petty despot should venture to show his contempt for it in so offensive a way.

Ver. 3.—The elders who govern the town know nothing of a king having been appointed, nor do they send to Samuel to ask him, as the judge, to protect them; but they request a seven days' respite, that they **may send messengers unto all the coasts of Israel**, and Nahash, feeling sure that no combined action would be the result, grants their request, that so Israel far and wide might know of his triumph.

Vers. 4, 5.—Among other places **the messengers came to Gibeah of Saul**, where they make no appeal to him, but tell their sad **tidings in the ears of all the people**. Powerless to help, they can only weep; but in the midst of their lamentation **Saul came after the herd** (Hebrew, following the oxen) **out of the field**. Saul was not driving a herd of cattle home, but had been ploughing, and, labour being over, was returning with the team of oxen.

Ver. 6.—**And the Spirit of God came upon Saul**. Rather, *descended mightily* upon Saul (see ch. x. 6). No miraculous influence is here meant; far more full of meaning and piety is the lesson so constantly taught in the Book of Judges, that all mighty and noble acts are from God (Judges iii. 10; vi. 34; xi. 29; xiii. 25; xiv. 6; xv. 14, &c.). Even the heathen saw in enthusiasm something Divine, for it means the having God within. The energy with which Saul acted was strictly natural, but yet as truly Divine; and it is a sign of the irreligion of modern days that it can see and hear of great and heroic achievements and assign no part in them to God. In the days of Samuel and the judges the whole glory of such acts was ascribed to God. But equally now, whenever men are moved to noble acts, it is "the breath of God" that descends upon them and inspires them.

Ver. 7.—Acting then with Divine enthusiasm, Saul cut into pieces a yoke of oxen, **and sent them throughout all the coasts of Israel by the hands of messengers**. For a similar act see Judges xix. 29. Probably Saul cut the oxen into twelve pieces, and sent one to each tribe, with the threat that in case of disobedience their oxen would be similarly treated. The threat was moderate in that it did not touch their persons, but severe as regards their property, the labouring ox being man's faithful friend and servant. It is important also to notice that Saul speaks not only in his own name, but also in that of Samuel. It was as the man chosen of Jehovah to be king by the voice of his prophet that he acted, and so as one possessed of legitimate authority; and it seems also that Samuel went with him in person to

the war (ver. 12). And the result answered to the energy with which Saul acted, for **the fear of Jehovah**—or, rather, "a terror from Jehovah"—**fell on the people, and they came out with one consent**, or, as it is rendered far more correctly and forcibly in the margin, "as one man." United by the kingly power, it was a nation that rose to defend one of its injured members.

Ver. 8. — **He numbered them in Bezek**. This place was in the tribe of Issachar, and must be distinguished from that mentioned in Judges i. 3, 4, which was in Judah, and too remote from the scene of operations. And here Saul appears as the commander-in-chief; for the numbering included the forming of battalions, arranged in thousands, hundreds, and fifties, and the setting officers over them. These, naturally, were the chief men in each district. The result would be that, coming to Bezek, the appointed rendezvous, a disorderly multitude, they would leave it as an army arranged in order, and Saul, in the many difficulties that would arise, would have his first opportunity of showing his powers of command. **Children of Israel, . . . men of Judah**—the distinction which ended in the disruption of the nation. Judah, too, with its 30,000 men, is but poorly represented, nor is it a sufficient explanation of the small number who came that the tribe had enough to do at home in making head against the Philistines. As a matter of fact, Judah always stood apart until there was a king who belonged to itself. Then, in David's time, it first took an active interest in the national welfare, and it was its vast power and numbers which made him so powerful. Had it been so nearly overpowered by the Philistines, it could not so suddenly have sprung forth with a might which made it well-nigh a match for all the rest.

Ver. 9.—**To-morrow, by that time the sun be hot**. As Bezek is about twenty miles distant from Jabesh-Gilead, Saul would probably march most of the way that evening, and then, halting for food and sleep, would continue his advance early the next morning.

Ver. 10.—**To-morrow we will come out unto you**. This was apparently intended to throw the Ammonites off their guard, as they would suppose that the men of Jabesh-Gilead had given up all hopes of deliverance.

Ver. 11.—**They came . . . in the morning watch**. By a forced march Saul came upon the unsuspecting Ammonites just before daybreak, when sleep is deepest; and as his host was unwieldy, he arranged it in three divisions, assigning to each a different route, that they might not impede one another on the way, and might also cut off the retreat of the enemy. As the fighting went on for five or six hours, **until the heat of the day**, the Ammonites must at first have made some resistance ; but when all three divisions of Saul's army had come up, they were so utterly routed that "no two of them were left together."

Vers. 12, 13. — **The people said unto Samuel.** Even after this glorious victory the people turn to Samuel, and doubtless his presence and influence had had great weight in gaining obedience to Saul's command (ver. 7). They now, with the old tumultuous violence, demand that those who had opposed Saul's election should be put to death. Probably the ringleaders of Saul's opponents were some of the elders disappointed at not being chosen themselves (see on ch. x. 27). But Saul displays, first, the kingly virtue of clemency, saying, **There shall not a man be put to death this day**—a decision politic as well as generous, for bloodshed would have led only to future feuds; and, secondly, piety, in so humbly ascribing to Jehovah the salvation that had been wrought in Israel.

SAUL SOLEMNLY CONSECRATED AS KING (vers. 14, 15). Ver. 14.—**Let us go to**

Gilgal. The famous sanctuary (ch. vii. 16) of that name, situated lower down, in the Jordan valley, near Jericho. It was not far from Jabesh-Gilead, and naturally the victorious host would move from the field of battle to the nearest religious spot to consecrate their king.

Ver. 15.—**They made Saul king.** This is not to be interpreted, with the Septuagint, of a second anointing of Saul, but of his confirmation in the kingdom by the unanimous voice of the nation, whereas the first election of him at Mizpah had met with opposition. **Before Jehovah.** *I. e.* with religious ceremonies conducted by Samuel and the high priest. The difference between Saul's election at Mizpah and the confirmation of it at Gilgal is much the same as between the first proclamation of a king and his coronation. The latter is the nation's acknowledgment of his sovereignty, and the solemn consecration of him to his high office. **Peace offerings** were tokens of joy and gratitude, and were followed by a feast. At this there was great rejoicing, because the king whom they had desired had so quickly proved himself worthy to be their head.

HOMILETICS.

Vers. 1—3.—*The relative power of evil and good.* The facts are—1. The Ammonites, in pursuit of the enterprise previously arranged for (see ch. xii. 12 ; cf. viii. 5), threaten Jabesh-Gilead. 2. The inhabitants in terror seek to make a covenant with their enemy. 3. This being insolently refused, a respite of seven days is granted, during which external aid is to be sought. The narrative is evidently designed to trace the circumstances under which the discontent and base insinuations of "men of Belial" (ch. x. 27) were practically shown to be baseless. This was a war of revenge undertaken by the strong against the weak, and the facts as a whole set forth three important truths of general interest.

I. EVIL IS STRONG RELATIVELY TO THE FAITHFULNESS OR UNFAITHFULNESS OF GOD'S PEOPLE. Ammon was Israel's ancestral foe (Deut. xxiii. 4 ; Judges xi. 4). The prosperity of one seemed incompatible with that of the other. When, under the inspiring leadership of Jephthah, the Ammonites were utterly smitten, their strength was brought down to its proper proportions. Had Israel continued faithful in the improvement of privileges enjoyed as the chosen race, their moral and political strength would have proportionately advanced in harmony with the promises given through Moses (Deut. xxviii. 1—14). The relative position of the representatives of good and evil had entirely changed when Nahash in pride of strength threatened Jabesh-Gilead. Even the partial reformation effected through Samuel had not yet placed Israel beyond the fear of well-organised foes. God's people are strong when holy, true, and diligent in use of the advantages of their position. The truth thus taught is *exemplified in Church history, in modern society, in private and domestic life.* 1. *Church history* testifies that *the energy of evil and its range have been proportionate to the faithfulness of the Church* to its lofty mission as conserver of God's truth and witness for Christ among men. The Ammonites have multiplied, become insolent, and have awakened fear only when the Christian Israel have lost their first love and failed to keep their solemn vows. 2. *Modern society feels that the growth of evil is another form of weakened spiritual grace.* There may be, in the unseen sphere of spiritual "principalities and powers," seasons when energetic spontaneous exertions are made to overcome the influence of the gospel. But to speak of the portentous growth of spiritual ignorance, disregard of religion, infidelity, and open vice, especially in large centres of population, is but another way of saying that the professed followers of Christ have not been as earnest and united in effort as he would have them to be. It is in the nature of light to get rid of darkness, of salt to remove corruption. The grave problem of the age may require many elements—social, sanitary, educational, political—for its solution, but men feel that *the* chief requirement is higher spiritual power in Christians. 3. *In private and domestic life* the power of evil depends on personal fidelity to what God has given and imposed. The remnants of sin in our nature lose force in so far as we faithfully seek cleansing by the indwelling of the Spirit, and keep a strong hand on the first uprising of unholiness. The force of external temptation diminishes in so far as our cultured holiness of disposition furnishes it with no affinity within. And as domestic life is but the first social form of the life cultured in private, its spiritual evils become formidable or feeble in so far as the soul is true to its God.

II. DANGERS IMPENDING FROM THE GROWTH OF EVIL MAY INDUCE RECOURSE TO THE TRUE SOURCE OF DELIVERANCE. The dangers threatening Jabesh-Gilead sprang from the action of a spiritual law. Israel *never* had been in real peril during any seasons of obedience to God. In the present instance the danger, which was brought on by a train of sad defections in years gone by, was very real, and became so pressing that, in utter desperation, the people turn their thoughts towards the king. The miseries consequent on past sins aroused a cry for the lawful deliverer. This was one of the results of the partial reformation. Much is gained when men are impelled to have recourse to the agencies and sources of power which God has specifically ordained for their help. There are illustrations of this in life. 1. *The soul is often driven, in desperation, to Christ for help.* Men do awake to the fact that destruction awaits them. The jailor's cry to the Apostle Paul has been repeated by thousands. Sin and judgment are terrible realities. But often men, when oppressed with fear of coming doom, endeavour to find relief by various expedients. At last, half in despair and half in hope, they turn to him who is *the* Anointed One to secure redemption to Israel. 2. *In the spiritual conflict a sense of need impels to a use of Divine aids.* Some men, trusting too freely to merely human wisdom, find that disaster comes in the Christian conflict. Principles become gradually weaker, and there is a risk of a loss of place in the commonwealth of Israel ; but after a bitter experience they remember and recognise the means of defence and freedom. Weary, sad, conscious of inability to cope with the foe, they seek closer fellowship with Christ, and a more earnest use of the sword of the Spirit. 3. *The modern Church is driven by the sheer magnitude of social dangers to have recourse more fully to the radical cure of all ills—the gospel.* Thoughtful Christians see that no mere social reforms and sanitary arrangements, or scientific discoveries, will avail to arrest the real dangers of human nature. The evil is great, the risks desperate ; the full gospel, presented with all the energy and self-denial and love which the Christian spirit can call forth, is the only means of spiritual deliverance. The material and social will follow. Whatever others may do, the Church must betake herself with apostolic zeal to the ancient lines of action.

III. EVENTS IN THE NATURAL ORDER OF PROVIDENCE AFFORD OPPORTUNITY FOR THE VINDICATION OF GOD'S SERVANTS. It is instructive to notice how long lines of intricate events, and working out collateral purposes, converge in securing for the anointed king an opportunity of answering by deeds the aspersions and insinuations of disaffected men. The growth of Ammon's power for evil consequent on Israel's religious defection, and the gradual reformation that had for some years been progressing in Israel,—these with all their subsidiary events,—created occasion for an appeal to Saul. He "held his peace" when "men of Belial" reviled, but Providence was working in his behalf. There are "wheels within wheels." *The same order is ever going on.* The Saviour's earthly life and subsequent resurrection is a case in point. Righteous men, whose motives have been misinterpreted and characters maligned, have committed themselves in silence to God, and he has brought forth their "righteousness as the light," and their "judgment as the noonday." And, also, all events are converging to the vindication of Christ's claim to be King of kings and Lord of lords.

General considerations :—1. What may be the *special* causes of the relative progress of irreligion in different localities? 2. To what extent the prevalence of irreligion and of influences adverse to the gospel are traceable to the unfaithfulness of the Church in generations gone by, and how best to counteract the effect of such historic unfaithfulness on the public mind. 3. In how many ways do professing Christians sometimes endeavour to compromise with their natural enemy? 4. What opportunites does Providence naturally open for the vindication of our personal claim to be true servants of Christ?

Vers. 4—11.—*The perfecting gift.* The facts are—1. The message brought to Gibeah throws the inhabitants into grief and consternation. 2. Saul, on hearing the tidings, is aroused by the Spirit of God to summon the nation to follow him and Samuel. 3. The people responding to the call, help is assured to the men of Jabesh. 4. The result is the utter defeat of the Ammonites. The effect of the appeal of the men of Jabesh on the people of Gibeah, on Saul, and subsequently on the conflict with the foe, brings out three truths of wider range than the particular instance recorded.

I. AN IMPERFECT APPRECIATION OF THE RESOURCES PLACED WITHIN THEIR REACH ACCOUNTS FOR SOME OF THE TROUBLES OF MEN. "The people lifted up their voices and wept." Their hearts sank within them; the boding ruin of Jabesh was the precursor of their own. This conduct was the effect of a non-appreciation of the position they then held under the care of God. Had they duly considered the significance of the return of the ark, the value of the reformation already inaugurated, and the lessons of history (Judges vii. 7), they must have seen that an appeal to their God-approved king, in humble dependence on God, would have in some way saved their brethren of Jabesh. *Men in all ages have lost much good and brought on much misery by not adequately considering the resources put within their power.* 1. *The earth, air, and sea* have been for ages full of God's hid treasures for the use of man; there lie powers to heal, to accomplish work, to promote the material and domestic good of all. Neglect or forgetfulness of their presence for generations deprived men of physical blessings now enjoyed by rich and poor. Doubtless other resources are close at hand, if only we duly appreciated them, and sought them in the right way. 2. In *the human constitution* there are valuable powers which, in numberless instances, are not duly considered and developed. Faculties lie dormant which might contribute to the wealth, culture, and comfort of the possessor and society. The material and intellectual loss to the world of undeveloped powers is enormous. The occasional results of education only reveal the extent of our deprivation of possible good. 3. In *the Christian there are gifts of the Spirit* not sufficiently stirred up. In the ordinary gifts of the Spirit there is generally a reserve of power in excess of the exertion put forth. In maintaining the conflict with sin and in doing deeds of love more might be accomplished by a proper estimate and use of what already dwells in the renewed soul. 4. In *the reserved power of God, dependent for its exercise on the prayer of faith, there is a vast store of blessing not often touched.* The Divine energy has not all been expended. Largely, in connection with the progress of Christ's kingdom, it is dependent for its outflow on the effectual fervent prayers of his servants. We are to prove him, whether he will not open the windows of heaven and pour out a blessing. 5. In *the provision for the renewal and forgiveness of the most guilty* there is a resource not always appreciated. Many men continue to carry their guilt and yield to the impulses of a depraved nature because they forget or do not duly consider WHO stands by them mighty to save. Did they but truly "*know* the gift of God, and who it is" that speaks to them of salvation, they would not go hither and thither, sad, and weary, and tearful, but would ask of him, and he would give them "living water."

II. THERE IS A PERFECTING GIFT FROM GOD REQUISITE TO DEVELOP AND TURN TO BEST ACCOUNT MUCH ELSE BESTOWED BY GOD. Saul was already a powerful man, chosen by the nation, and recognised by God as king. He was endowed with prerogative and latent capabilities. The tidings which caused wailing among the men of Gibeah because of their non-appreciation of their true position were the occasion of a remarkable display of courage and energy on the part of Saul, and that because "the Spirit of God" came upon him. Whatever the precise nature of this higher gift, its practical effect was to draw out all that was in the man and the king, and to enable the powers already bestowed to act for the benefit of Israel. It perfected all else done for Saul. *There is a relation of dependence in the blessings God bestows on us.* Some come to full development only when allied with another, which, therefore, may be called a higher good. The physical energy for defeat of Ammon lay in Israel. The gift of Saul turned it all into victory. The same relation is seen amongst us; *e. g.* material wealth is a boon not to be despised, often the gift of God; but for its full development and enjoyment it needs another gift—health of body and generosity of spirit. Great mental abilities are of God; the additional gift of a devout, lowly spirit insures their most perfect use. Home adorned and enriched by all that wealth, art, and domestic affection can contribute is a precious blessing; yet its joys are more full and varied, its affections more pure, and its sorrows more endurable, when the higher blessing of personal religion is supreme there. The external privileges of religion, free use of the word of God, instruction and care of pious parents, associations of the sanctuary, entreaties of pastors and friends, are among the greatest mercies enjoyed by men; yet even these are raised to their highest value only when the Holy Spirit comes down, like "upper and nether springs" to water the "south land."

III. GOD SOMETIMES EFFECTS HIS PURPOSES AMONG MEN BY INDIRECT ACTION UPON THEM. In the accomplishment of Divine purposes, in the physical, mental, or spiritual spheres, a variety of combinations are often requisite. To the deliverance of Jabesh-Gilead it was needful to arouse the people as well as the king. It was by the tremendous energy of the king, aroused by the direct action of the Spirit of God, that their instant co-operation was secured. The *law of indirect action widely prevails.* That the Eternal is in direct, constant, energetic contact with each being is certain. He "*upholds*" all things by the word of his power." Yet, if language may be so used to indicate a mystery, the import of his energy on men is not always immediate. The energy of one spirit acting on another is, so to speak, a refraction of a force originally in God, and coloured by the character of the medium through which it passes. There are many illustrations of the general truth of indirect action. 1. In *the sphere of mind* much is accomplished by powerful intellects affecting a few with their ideas and feelings, who, being more in contact with the masses, give forth the truth or the emotion tinged by their own peculiarities. 2. In *the sphere of spirit*, religiously considered, a large proportion of what we call *influence* is of this character. Not only do superior Christians act on a wide area by means of the few who come under their personal attention, but much of the action of God on the world is through his people. *His light* is not seen by many except mediately in the beautiful lives of the holy. *His love* acts on the hard heart of man through the compassion he directly produces in the followers of Christ. Men see by holy deeds and spiritual achievements that "God is with" his people, and are thus influenced by God to submit to his blessed sway.

General lessons:—1. It behoves every one to search and see what talents, and means of becoming holy, and of advancing Christ's kingdom, lie unused. 2. It should be a matter of serious inquiry how much of our wailing and fear are the result of a guilty forgetfulness or distrust of God's readiness to bless our endeavours. 3. If we are in possession of valuable blessings, and they do not yield all the joy and satisfaction reasonably to be looked for, we should find out what is that higher gift not yet sought from God. 4. The Church and the Christian have need to inquire how much of the non-success of endeavour is due to lack of receptivity for the highest gift of all, the rich outpouring of the Holy Spirit. 5. Every one should so live as to be a fit and perfect vehicle for the transmission of the healing, saving power of God on mankind.

Vers. 12—15.—*The concurrence of human and Divine action.* The facts are—1. On the completion of the victory over the Ammonites, the supporters of Saul desire the punishment by death of the "men of Belial" who had reviled him. 2. Saul, recognising the merciful help of God, refuses to mar the joy of victory by personal retaliation. 3. At the invitation of Samuel the people assembled in Gilgal for the recognition of Saul as victorious king, coupled with thanksgiving to God. To an ordinary observer looking on the conflict between Israel and Ammon, it would seem to be simply a struggle of men with men. The preceding verses (6—11) show that an element more than human entered into the conflict, and Saul gratefully refers to this in saying, "To-day *the Lord* hath wrought salvation in Israel." The subsequent celebration of worship by Samuel was a recognition of the same fact.

I. It is THE CONCURRENCE OF GOD'S ACTION WITH THAT OF MAN WHICH BRINGS ABOUT RESULTS OF A JOYOUS CHARACTER. The personal will and muscular and mental energy of Saul, aided by the co-operating powers of the people, led to the defeat of the Ammonites. That was the visible human element. But these powers were set at work and sustained by the action *directly* on the nature of Saul by the Spirit of God (ver. 6), and *indirectly* through the awe inspired thereby on the minds and bodies of the people. The issue, therefore, is to be ascribed to concurrent action of the human and Divine, the latter partly direct and partly indirect. In a general way it may be said that all effects realised by man are by this concurrence of action. For even when they exercise their power of willing and devising in a wrong direction, it is only possible in consequence of the energy of God sustaining those powers of volition and thought. But the more specific sense in which the concurrence is true may be seen by taking instances. 1. In *the realisation of Messianic purposes.* The appearance of Christ on earth was the result of a long double line of action. The descendants of Abraham freely cherished the hope of Messiah, and by effort of their own will they contributed, as described in the Old Testament, the human line of action towards this issue. But all this time, and along with all these acts, the Spirit of God was at work, making them willing to be a separate people, controlling events to secure their isolation, inspiring their prophets with rapt vision of the future, and at last coming on the one honoured among women for the perfecting of all that had been hoped and laboured for (Luke i. 27—35). 2. In *the production of the Bible.* In revelation, as a whole, we have a long train of human events intertwined with a successive manifestation of the Divine will. The Bible is the record of the combination. This holy Book itself is what it is, in its historical portions, because human hands gathered out the selected facts in pursuance of a principle given of God. Moreover, the devout exercises of human spirits in such portions as the Psalms were free, yet concurrent with a Divine influence in their initiation ; and as also in the selection of them subsequently for the benefit of mankind. 3. In *the victories achieved by Christianity.* The victories of Christianity have come about by the free effort of individual minds combining under forms of Church organisation. Men have spoken, written, entreated, sympathised, prayed. Some critics ascribe all success in heathen lands to sheer force of superior intelligence and moral influence ; and in civilised lands to what of moral excellence there may be in connection with a great superstition, enforced as this is by a zeal that takes captive the uncritical. But *the* solution is that God is a co-worker with the Church. The human and Divine action are concurrent, the one being the vehicle through which the other operates. 4. In *the sanctification of the soul.* The work to be done before the human soul can rise to the highest form of life is enormous. Few men consider what is involved in "*entering into the kingdom of heaven*" even on earth. To rise to the life of the "kingdom" means work, conflict, suppression, elevation, excision, nurture, self-denial, aspiration, ambition, persistence within a sphere into which only the eye of God can penetrate. Yet all the expenditure of energy the greatest mind can command is of itself inadequate. We are conquerors and "more than conquerors through Christ," who helpeth us. He "worketh within us to will and to do." In this subtle concurrence of the Divine and human the highest form of life is realised for the " whole body, soul, and spirit."

II. It is BEFITTING TO SEIZE OCCASION FOR RECOGNISING GOD'S CONCURRENT ACTION WITH US IN BRINGING GOOD ISSUES TO PASS. It was fit that Saul should publicly recognise the hand of God in his first victory. The spontaneity of the act, and the magnanimous spirit that would not mar the joy of the victory by personal retaliation on his despisers, indicate that at this period of his history he possessed some excellent moral qualities, which certainly were strengthened by this public expression of them. Samuel's participation in the common joy was also proof of the good feelings of Saul. 1. It is *good to pause in life's struggles and consider gratefully our personal indebtedness to God's power working with us.* There are dangers in activity. Absorption in the outgoing of our own energy may unconsciously induce the belief that by "our own arm" have we gotten the victory. Occasional reflection of the need and fact of the Power that "worketh all in all," with deeper dependence on God, awaken gratitude, give tone to our own exertions, and sustain hope of final triumph. 2. It is *good in families to seize opportunities for recognising God's help.* The parent whose business has prospered, whose children are being happily settled in life, whose home has been kept free from great calamities, or who has come out of severe trials with honour, will do well to remember who giveth power to be rich, ordereth right paths, sheltereth from "the destruction that wasteth at noonday," and raiseth the needy from the dust, and not be ashamed to let his household know how much he owes to God. Such conduct will bear blessed fruit. 3. It is *good for nations to recognise God in signal deliverances.* God works with and for every nation that loves and seeks righteousness. National homage is as proper as individual worship. Thanksgiving services are of Scriptural authority. The precedents are numerous in the Old Testament. It is no doubt owing solely to the fact that Christianity had not permeated nations as a whole, when the New Testament was written, that no precedents are found in its records. Yet the Church as such held special services for prayer and thanksgiving (Acts iv. 23—33). Those who contend that vigorous human action is the true and only form of homage to God overlook the fact that there is in good results *more than human action,* and that positive acts of worship, in recognition of dependence and in expression of gratitude, not only pay honour to whom honour is due, but exercise a beneficial reflex influence on the worshippers. Such acts quicken the public conscience, raise thought to a higher level, nourish the religious feeling, offer excellent occasions and topics for instruction, strengthen the national sentiment, awaken the kindly interest of class for class, call forth the more generous and restrain the harsher impulses of life.

General lessons:—1. It should be a question with individuals and nations as to whether they in their aims and spirit fulfil the conditions on which alone the concurrent action of God can proceed. 2. Much of the non-success of effort may arise from an insufficient recognition of God as a co-worker with us. 3. Things and private persons rise in honour and influence as they display a generous magnanimity. 4. The joy of great salvation should be undiminished by the intrusion of any bitter human feeling.

HOMILIES BY VARIOUS AUTHORS.

Vers. 1—15. (GIBEAH, BEZEK, JABESH.)—*Saul's first victory.* Although Saul had been privately anointed and publicly chosen king, he did not immediately assume royal state. Guided, doubtless, by the counsel of Samuel, and perceiving from the disaffection of certain men (ch. x. 27) that the nation was not yet quite prepared for the change, he did not deem it prudent to do so. Returning to his former mode of life at Gibeah (ver. 5), he awaited some further indication of his call to be "captain over the Lord's inheritance." "Nothing but true, royal action for the welfare of the state, alike bravely undertaken and firmly carried out at the right moment, could win for him that real deference, that joyful, voluntary co-operation for state purposes from all his subjects, without which his sovereignty must ever remain most feeble and equivocal" (Ewald). It was not long ("a month," LXX.) before the opportunity for such action occurred. He proved himself equal to the occasion, and his patience was justified and rewarded. His position as a *military leader* was fully vindicated by the result, and his sovereignty was heartily recognised by all the people. This is the chief historical significance of his warlike enterprise or *campaign* against the Ammonites for the relief of Jabesh-Gilead. Observe that it was—

I. UNDERTAKEN IN A RIGHTEOUS CAUSE (vers. 1—4). If ever war is justifiable (and it seems impossible that it should be altogether avoided), it is when undertaken, as in this case—1. *To repel hostile aggression.* The Ammonites were old enemies (Deut. ii. 19; xxiii. 3, 4; Judges iii. 13; x. 7; xi. 5). They were a nomadic, predatory, cruel, and idolatrous people. For some time Nahash, animated by the desire of war and conquest, "the malady of princes," had assumed a threatening attitude (ch. xii. 12), and now laid siege to the capital of Gilead, a part of the Israelitish territory belonging to the half-tribe of Manasseh, beyond the Jordan. His aggression was—(1) Without adequate ground. He probably revived a claim previously asserted and refuted (Judges xi. 12—15). But men readily find pretexts for a course to which they are disposed. "From whence come wars?" (James iv. 1). (2) Revengeful. He wished to avenge the defeat long before inflicted by Jephthah. Hatred between nations tends to perpetuate itself, and to become intensified; and successes in war often sow "dragon's teeth" that produce a subsequent harvest of strife and misery. (3) Proud, boastful, and cruel (ver. 2). 2. *To aid imperilled brethren.* Between the people of Jabesh and the Benjamites, especially, there was an intimate connection (Judges xxi. 12—14). Their condition was now degraded, fearful, wretched; and although it was due to their want of patriotism, faith, and courage, yet it did not deprive them of a claim upon the sympathy of their brethren, but was a powerful appeal to their compassion. The appeal of the poor, the oppressed, the slave cannot be unheeded without sin (Prov. xxiv. 11, 12). 3. *To avert a common danger.* The siege of Jabesh was evidently intended as the first step in an attack upon all Israel. The distress of the people of Gibeah arose not merely from sympathy with their brethren, but also from fear for themselves, and a sense of helplessness against so powerful an adversary. Saul's enterprise was thus one of self-defence. 4. *To maintain the Divine honour.* The Ammonites worshipped Moloch (Molech, or Milcom), "the abomination of the children of Ammon" (1 Kings xi. 7), and sought his honour in opposition to that of Jehovah. It was a part of the calling of Israel to extirpate idolatry, and it was commanded them concerning the Ammonites, "Thou shalt not seek their peace nor their prosperity all thy days for ever" (Deut. xxiii. 6). In their wars with the heathen they acted under a Divine commission. The religious wars which have been waged under the Christian dispensation have sometimes been undertaken from lofty motives, but they have not had the same justification, and the honour of God ought to be sought by other and more effectual means.

II. WAGED WITH HOLY ENTHUSIASM (vers. 5—11). Enthusiasm = God in us. It was—1. *Inspired by the Divine Spirit.* On returning from the field, and learning the cause of the people's distress, "the Spirit of God came upon Saul, and his anger was kindled greatly." There is an anger which is not sinful (Mark iii. 5; Ephes. iv. 26). The feeling of resentment is a weapon put into our hands by God against injury, injustice, and cruelty of every kind. (1) The anger of Saul was incited by the same spirit as previously constrained him to utter Divine praises. (2) It was a feeling of wrath and burning zeal against wrong. (3) It was directed towards the welfare of his people and the honour of God. (4) It qualified him for a great enterprise; led him to assume the leadership of the nation to which he had been appointed, and to summon the tribes to rally around him. The gifts of the Spirit of God are various, and adapted to the requirements of the age. 2. *Shared in by all the people.* (1) "The fear of Jehovah fell on the people," *i. e.* a fear inspired by him. "In Saul's energetic appeal the people discerned the power of Jehovah, which inspired them with fear and impelled them to immediate obedience" (Keil). That power is able to fill a whole nation, as well as an individual, with new emotions and impulses. (2) Under its influence "they came out as one man" (with one consent). (3) Mustered under the leadership of Saul in Bezek, near to Bethshan. A common danger often draws men into closer union and co-operation than peace and prosperity. 3. *Expressed in a confident assurance of help.* "To-morrow, by the time the sun be hot, ye shall have help" (ver. 9). Faith looks upon that which is believed as if it were already an accomplished fact. 4. *Manifested in energetic action.* His promise was not in words merely, but was followed up by deeds (ver. 11). "It was night when Saul and the armed multitude which followed him broke up from Bezek. Little did he know how well the brave men of Jabesh would requite the service (ch. xxxi. 8—13). Strange that Saul's first march should have been by night from Bethshan to

Jabesh, the same route by which at the last they carried his dead body at night"
(Edersheim).

III. ATTENDED WITH EXTRAORDINARY SUCCESS.   1. The *defeat* of the enemy—
sudden, unexpected, and complete.   "Two of them were not left together," and their
king, Nahash, was slain (Josephus).   " Those that walk in pride he is able to abase "
(Dan. iv. 37).   2. The *deliverance* of the oppressed, who were not afterwards wanting in gratitude or courage.   3. The *cessation* of disaffection (vers. 12, 13).   4. The
united and joyful *devotion* of all Israel (vers. 14, 15).

Observe—1. We have other enemies to encounter than those of flesh and blood
(Ephes. vi. 12).   2. We must contend against them not simply for our own safety,
but for the good of our fellow-men.   3. It is only by the help of the Lord that we
can prevail.—D.

Vers. 12, 13.—*Generosity toward enemies.* Some men are subject to noble impulses,
under which they rise to a higher level of thought and feeling than that which they
ordinarily occupy.   The difference is sometimes so great that they do not seem to
be the same persons.   But the change is transient, and they speedily relapse into
their former state.   Their character is one of varying, wayward, and uncertain moods
rather than high, steadfast, and consistent principle.   Such a man was Saul.   The
impulse under which he spared his enemies after his victory over the Ammonites
(probably due, as other impulses were, to the influence of Samuel, who may have
accompanied him to the battle—vers. 7, 12) displayed extraordinary magnanimity.
The act is the noblest recorded of him, and stands out in strong relief against the
dark background of his subsequent career.   "Saul herein showeth his piety, humanity, wisdom.   Hitherto he declareth himself an innocent man and a good prince ; but
afterward he forgot his own rule, when he would have killed Jonathan (ch. xiv. 45).
This mutability in Saul and changeable nature, in falling from clemency to cruelty,
from piety to profanity, from a good governor to become a tyrant, doth show that
these virtues were not thoroughly grounded in him, but only superficially infused "
(Willet).   Let us regard him as a pattern of a principle which ought always to be
exhibited.   His generosity toward his enemies was shown—

I. UNDER STRONG PROVOCATION, arising from—1. The recollection of their *past
conduct* towards himself (ch. x. 27).   He could not altogether forget it, and when
he was disposed to put it away from his thoughts, he was reminded of it by others.
Nothing is more provocative of wrath than brooding over the wrongs that have
been received.   On the other hand, the surest way to forgive is to forget.   2. The
feeling of *natural resentment* toward them.   " Revenge is sweet," say men who
are not restrained by Divine wisdom and grace ; and they are especially apt to say
it when they have the *power* to avenge themselves, and when they persuade
themselves that *justice* and *prudence* require that the wrong should not go
unpunished.   They *do* require it, doubtless, in some cases ; but how large a place
does the desire of gratifying personal animosity hold in most instances in which
men seek to inflict punishment on others.   " Say not, I will do so to him as
he hath done to me : I will render to the man according to his work " (Prov. xxiv.
29 ; xx. 22).   3. The *urgency* of others.   Men are only too prone to indulge wrath
without such an incitement, but they are often led by it to go beyond their own
judgment and feeling, and he who, like Saul, overcomes it gains a double victory.
" Thereby he gained another victory—(1) over himself—he restrains himself in the
exercise of a right ; (2) over the anger of those who demanded that justice be
executed ; (3) over his former opponents, who now clearly see that which, under
the influence of haughty contempt, they had doubted ; and (4) over the whole people,
who must have been carried along by him in the path of noble moral conduct, and
lifted above themselves to the height on which he stood " (Erdmann).

II. IN A ROYAL MANNER.   " There shall not a man be put to death this day."
1. *Promptly.*   If he had waited till the morrow his purpose might have changed.
When a generous emotion fills the heart it should be at once translated into word and
deed.   First thoughts in things moral, unlike first thoughts in things intellectual, are
always best.   Hesitation and delay dim their brightness and weaken their power.
2. *Decisively.*   Saul spoke like a king.   He refused to stain his laurels with blood.

And whilst he resolved not to punish his enemies, he declared his determination that none other should punish them. "Where the word of a king is there is power." **3.** *Completely.* "Not a man." Not a single example was to be made, but his clemency was to extend to all. In the same royal manner we may and ought to show mercy. "Blessed are the merciful, for they shall obtain mercy."

III. FROM A PROPER MOTIVE. "For to-day the Lord hath wrought salvation in Israel." "Not only signifying that the public rejoicing should not be interrupted, but reminding them of the clemency of God, and urging that since Jehovah had shown such clemency upon that day, that he had overlooked their sins and given them a glorious victory, it was only right that they should follow his example and forgive their neighbours' sins without bloodshed" (Seb. Schmid). Saul showed— 1. Regard for the *transcendent excellence of mercy.* Nothing is more beautiful or more pleasing to God, and its exercise is necessary that we may obtain mercy (Matt. vi. 15). He is "merciful and gracious." "Mercy rejoiceth against judgment." (Prov. xxv. 21; Rom. xii. 19, 20; James ii. 13.)

> "It becomes
> The throned monarch better than his crown;
> His sceptre shows the force of temporal power,
> The attribute to awe and majesty,
> Wherein doth sit the dread and fear of kings;
> But mercy is above this sceptred sway;
> It is enthroned in the heart of kings,
> It is an attribute to God himself,
> And earthly power doth then show likest God's
> When mercy seasons justice" ('Merchant of Venice').

To return good for good and evil for evil is natural, to return evil for good is devilish, but to return good for evil is Divine. 2. Gratitude for the *abounding goodness of God.* His hand was fully recognised in recent victory and deliverance. His kindness to us should constrain us to be kind to others, and his forgiveness is shown to have been experienced only when it leads us to forgive (Matt. xviii. 35). 3. Desire for the *welfare of men.* "The Lord hath wrought salvation in *Israel*," to whom these "worthless men" belonged. Even such men are objects of his forbearance and benevolence. "He maketh his sun to rise on the evil and on the good" (Matt. v. 45). He does them good, and thereby seeks to subdue their hostility toward himself (Ezek. xxxiii. 11). We ought to exhibit the same spirit, and by doing so we shall promote the general peace and happiness. "Be ye therefore merciful, even as your Father also is merciful" (Luke vi. 36).—D.

Vers. 11—13.—*Saul at his best.* Self-control, promptitude, courage, capacity, ascription of praise to God, forbearance towards men, these are all exhibited by the young king. Alas, that from such heights he fell!

I. SELF-CONTROL. Though hailed as king at Mizpah, Saul was in no haste to assume regal state. He resumed his country life at Gibeah, waiting till the Lord should call him forth in some emergency to take command of the army of Israel. In this he followed the example of the judges, who, so to speak, won their spurs before they wore them—first wrought some deliverance for their country, and then assumed the government.

II. PROMPTITUDE. News of the doom which threatened the town of Jabesh reached Saul as he returned home from the field, following his oxen with a farmer's slow and heavy step. In a moment he was another man, no more a seeker of asses, or a follower of oxen; but a leader of men, prompt and resolute. And such energy did he show that in a few days he had rallied a large army to his standard.

III. COURAGE AND CAPACITY. Saul had no time to train or discipline his forces, but he managed to gain an advantage for them. He lulled the enemy to security, and then, surprising their camp by night, fell on them with impetuous fury. So completely were they dispersed that, as the graphic historian says, "two of them were not left together."

IV. ASCRIPTION OF PRAISE TO GOD.   After the victory Saul showed no disposition to vain boasting.   Nothing could be better than his *Te Deum laudamus*—"To-day Jehovah hath wrought salvation in Israel."

V. FORBEARANCE TOWARDS MEN.   Saul was urged by the exultant people to put to death those who had opposed his elevation ; but he would not have the lustre of his victory darkened by such a deed of vengeance, and, not only ruling his own spirit well, but checking the intolerance of others, he said, " There shall not a man be put to death this day."

Yet from this moral elevation Saul miserably fell.   He who seemed to be the rising hope of Israel became one of the most hapless and tragical personages in all his nation's history.   He who showed at first patience and self-control became a restless, jealous king.   His great fault was wilfulness, leading to the most foolish impatience, and wretched envy.   He who executed his first military exploit so skilfully, and with such complete success, became notorious for his failures.   And, at last, he who had shown such fearless readiness to set upon the Ammonites was afraid to encounter the Philistines (ch. xxviii. 5).   Not that his natural courage had died out of him, but the sustaining faith in God was gone.   "God is departed from me, and answereth me no more."   He who was so averse to shed the blood of disaffected subjects shed the blood of many faithful men, as of the priests of the Lord, and hurled the javelin from his own hand again and again at the worthiest of all his subjects, hating him without a cause.   1. The true character of a man will show itself.   No veil will cover it ; no prudential consideration can bind it.   Sooner or later it will have its way.   2. The higher the promise of virtue, the greater the momentum of him who falls from his integrity, the farther he goes into evil.   3. The path of the wilful and proud is one of waning light and thickening darkness ; but " the path of the just is as the shining light, which shines more and more until the perfect day."—F.

EXPOSITION.

CHAPTER XII.

SAMUEL'S EXHORTATION TO THE PEOPLE AT GILGAL.   This speech of Samuel is not to be regarded as a farewell address made upon his resignation of his office ; for though a new power had been introduced, and Samuel's sons excluded from the succession, yet it was only gradually that a change was made in his own position.   He was still judge (ch. vii. 15), and on extraordinary occasions came forward with decisive authority (ch. xv. 33).   But as Saul gathered men of war round him (ch. xiv. 52), the moral power possessed by Samuel would be overshadowed by the physical force which was at Saul's command.   But no formal change was made.   It had been the weakness of the office of the judges that their power was irregular, and exercised fitfully on special occasions.   Such a power must fall into abeyance in the presence of the regular authority of a king surrounded by armed men.   Without any direct deposition, therefore, or even still retaining the form of his office, Samuel would henceforward chiefly

act as the prophet, and Saul as Jehovah's king.

The address divides itself into three parts : —1. The testimony to Samuel's integrity as judge (vers. 1—5). 2. The reproof of the people for their disobedience and ingratitude (vers. 6—17). 3. The Divine testimony to Samuel's uprightness and teaching (vers. 18—25).

SAMUEL'S INTEGRITY (vers. 1—5).   Ver. 1.—**I have hearkened unto your voice.**   See ch. viii. 7, 9, 22.

Ver. 2.—**The king walketh before you.** *I. e.* you have now one to protect and lead the nation, whereas my business was to raise its religious and moral life.   The metaphor is taken from the position of the shepherd in the East, where he goes before his flock to guide and guard them.   On this account the word shepherd or pastor is used in the Bible of the temporal ruler (Jer. ii. 8 ; xxiii. 4, &c.), and not, as with us, of the spiritual guide.   **My sons are with you.**   This is no mere confirmation of the fact just stated that he was old, but a direct challenge of their dissatisfaction with his sons' conduct, as far at least as concerns any connivance on his part, or support of them in their covetousness. Samuel says, You know all about my sons; I do not profess to be ignorant that charges have been brought against them. Give full weight to them, and to everything said against them and me, and then give judgment.

Vers. 3, 4, 5.—**Witness against me.** Literally, "answer," as in a court of justice to the formal question of the judge. **His anointed.** *I. e.* the king (see on ch. ii. 10, 35; x. 1). **Whose ox, . . . whose ass?** See on ch. viii. 16. **Of whose hand have I received any bribe to blind mine eyes therewith?** Bribe should be rendered *ransom.* Literally it signifies a covering, and was used of money given by a guilty person to induce the judge to close or "blind his eyes," and not see his sin. It does not mean, therefore, any bribe, but only that given to buy off a guilty person. Such persons are generally powerful men who have oppressed and wronged others; and the knowledge that they can cover their offence by sharing their gains with the judge is to this day in the East the most fruitful source of bad government. The people all bear witness to Samuel's uprightness, nor is there any contradiction between this and their desire to have a king. His internal administration was just and righteous, but they were oppressed by the nations round them, and needed a leader in war. And in Samuel's sons they had men, not vicious or licentious, but too fond of money, and so neither fit to be their generals in war nor their judges in peace. We gather from ch. xxii. 2 that though Saul proved a competent leader in war, he was not successful in the government of the country in peace.

SAMUEL'S REPROOF OF THE PEOPLE (vers. 6—17). Ver. 6.—**It is Jehovah that,** &c. In the Hebrew Jehovah is put absolutely, without any government, and the Septuagint rightly supplies *is witness.* Samuel had said, "Jehovah is witness against you;" the people in answer shouted the last word, "Witness" (see end of ver. 5, where *He is* is supplied). Then Samuel solemnly repeats Jehovah's name, saying, "Even Jehovah that advanced Moses and Aaron." This rapid interchange of words brings the whole scene vividly before us, whereas nothing could be tamer than the A. V. **Out of the land of Egypt.** Samuel begins with this as the first act of Jehovah as Israel's King; for the theocracy began with the deliverance from Egypt.

Vers. 7, 8.—**Stand still.** Literally, *station yourselves, take your places, stand forth* (see ch. x. 23). **That I may reason with you.** Literally, "that I may deal as judge," *i. e.* that with all the authority of my office I may declare that Jehovah has acted justly by you, and that you have dealt unjustly

with him. **Righteous acts.** The margin, *benefits,* is wrong. Samuel vindicates God's dealings with them against the charge of his having failed to protect them implied in their demand for a king.

Ver. 9.—**When they forgat Jehovah their God.** The theocracy, as we have seen (ch. x. 18), was a moral government, under which idolatry and the immorality attendant upon it, as being rebellion, were punished by Jehovah's withdrawing his protection, and the consequent subjection of the nation to foreign rule. It was the repeated sin, therefore, of the people which made Israel's history so chequered. Sisera (Judges iv. 2), the Philistines (*ibid.* iii. 31), and Eglon, king of Moab (*ibid.* iii. 12), are mentioned as three of the earlier oppressors of Israel, but are given here in the reverse order to that found in the Book of Judges.

Ver. 10.—**We have served** [the] **Baalim and** [the] **Ashtaroth.** *I. e.* the numerous Baals and Astartes, which were worshipped under various titles by the heathen. For though representing the same power, each people had their own epithets for their own particular personification of the god (see on ch. vii. 4).

Ver. 11.—**Bedan.** Numerous ingenious explanations of this name have been given, but the only probable account is that Bedan is a misreading for Barak. The two names are very similar in the Hebrew, and the two most ancient versions, the Septuagint and the Syriac, actually have Barak. **And Samuel.** This is even more puzzling than Bedan. We cannot suppose that Samuel, who hitherto had confined himself to the old deliverances, would thus suddenly introduce his own name. In mentioning only them he had avoided everything that would grate upon the ears of the people, but this would look like giving way to personal vexation. Some, therefore, would read Samson; but this, though found in the Syriac, is supported by no other version. Possibly some scribe, mindful of Samuel's recent achievement at Mizpah, wrote his name in the margin, whence it was admitted into the text. **And ye dwelled safe.** Literally, "in confidence," in security. With sin came danger and unquiet; upon repentance, not only was their country free from danger, but their minds were at rest.

Ver. 12.—**Nahash the king of the children of Ammon.** This makes it probable that there had been threats of war, and even incursions into the Israelite territory, by Nahash before his attack on Jabesh-Gilead. We thus, too, should be able to account for the rancour displayed in his wish so to treat the men of that town as to make them a reproach to all Israel; for his hatred of Israel may have grown in intensity in the course of a harassing war, or he may have learnt to despise a people incapable of offering a regular resistance. At all events, Samuel describes Nahash as giving the final impetus to the desire of the nation for a king. **When Jehovah your God was your king.** See Judges viii. 23.

Ver. 13.—**Behold the king whom ye have chosen!** . . . **behold, Jehovah hath set a king over you.** We have here the two sides of the transaction. The people had desired a king, chosen and appointed by themselves, to represent the nation in temporal matters ; Jehovah gave them a king to represent himself, with authority coming from God, and limited by God. Most, too, of the kings of Judah were as truly representatives of Jehovah as any of the judges had been, and David even more so. **Desired** is rather "demanded," "required." They had done much more than desire a king.

Ver. 14.—**If ye will fear,** &c. This verse, like Luke xix. 42, is left unfinished, and we must supply *well*, as in Exod. xxxii. 32. For the verse cannot be translated as in the A. V., but is as follows: "If ye will fear Jehovah, and serve him, and obey his voice, and not rebel against the commandment (Hebrew, the mouth) of Jehovah, and if both ye and the king that reigneth over you will follow Jehovah your God, *it shall be well.*" Samuel piles up one upon another the conditions of their happiness, and then from the depth of his emotion breaks off, leaving the blessed consequences of their obedience unsaid. "To follow Jehovah" implies willing and active service as his attendants, going with him where he will, and being ever ready to obey his voice.

Ver. 15.—**Against you, as it was against your fathers.** The Hebrew has "against you and your fathers," and so the Vulgate, for which the Septuagint reads, "against you and your king," as in ver. 25. The text is probably corrupt, and to make sense requires the insertion of some such words as those given in the A. V., with which the Syriac also agrees.

Ver. 16.—**Stand.** Better *stand forth*, as in ver. 7 ; take your places in solemn order.

Ver. 17.—**Wheat harvest.** Barley was fit for reaping at the Passover, and wheat at Pentecost, *i. e.* between the middle of May and the middle of June. Jerome, on Amos iv. 7, testifies that during his long residence in Palestine he had never seen rain there during June and July ; but Conder ('Handbook of Bible,' p. 221), says, "Storms still occur occasionally in harvest-time." **He shall send thunder.** Hebrew, *voices*, and so in ver. 18 (see ch. ii. 10 ; vii. 9).

DIVINE TESTIMONY TO SAMUEL'S INTEGRITY (vers. 18—25). Ver. 18.—**Jehovah sent thunder and rain** Rain in Palestine

falls usually only at the autumnal and vernal equinox, and though thunder-storms are not unknown at other times, yet, by the general testimony of travellers, they are very rare. Naturally, therefore, this storm deeply impressed the minds of the people. Though not in itself miraculous, the circumstances made it so.

Ver. 19. — **Pray for thy servants.** On Samuel's mediatorial office see ch. vii. 5, 8.

Ver. 20.—**Ye have done all this wickedness.** The *ye* is emphatic, and to give its force we should translate, "Ye have indeed done all this evil." **From following Jehovah.** See on ver. 15.

Ver. 21.—**For then should ye go after vain things.** The word *for* is omitted in all the ancient versions, and the sense is complete without it : "And turn ye not aside after *tohu*," the word used in Gen. i. 1, and there translated "without form." It means anything *empty, void*, and so is often used, as here, for "an idol," because, as St. Paul says, "an idol is nothing in the world" (1 Cor. viii. 4). So Isaiah (ch. xliv. 9) calls the makers of idols vanity, Hebrew, *tohu*, i. e. empty people, with no sense in them. The word is used again at the end of the verse — **which** idols **cannot profit nor deliver; for they are** *tohu*, emptiness.

Ver. 22. — **For his great name's sake.** Though Samuel in ver. 14 had described their well-being as dependent upon their own conduct, yet in a higher light it depended upon God's will. He had chosen Israel not for its own sake (Deut. vii. 7, 8), but for a special purpose, to minister to the Divine plan for the redemption of all mankind, and so, though individuals might sin to their own ruin, and the nation bring upon itself severe chastisements, yet it must continue according to the tenor of God's promises (see on ch. ii. 30), and through weal and woe discharge the duty imposed upon it.

Ver. 23.—**God forbid,** Hebrew, "Far be it from me." **That I should sin . . . in ceasing to pray for you.** In no character of the Old Testament does this duty of intercessory prayer stand forward so prominently as in Samuel (see ver. 19) ; nor does he rest content with this, but adds, **I will teach you the good and the right way.** This was a far higher office than that of ruler ; and not only was Samuel earnest in discharging this prophetic office of teaching, but he made provision for a supply of teachers and preachers for all future time by founding the schools of the prophets.

Ver. 42.—**For consider,** &c. Samuel concludes his address by appealing to the mighty deeds wrought in old time by Jehovah for his people ; literally, it is, "For consider how grandly he hath wrought with you."

HOMILETICS.

Vers. 1—5.—*Character a power*. The facts are—1. Samuel reminds the people that he (*a*) has carried out their wishes in setting a king over them, (*b*) is now a very old man, and (*c*) has spent the whole of his life among them. 2. He appeals to God in asserting that the whole of his official life has been free from self-seeking. 3. The people freely admit that his public conduct has been honest, considerate, and free from greed. The meaning of Samuel's reference to himself is to be sought not in egotism, but in a desire to find a basis for his intended argument and appeal. The actual weight of counsel depends not on the abstract wisdom of the language used, but on the readiness of the hearers to give heed to the speaker and their conviction of his integrity of purpose. Samuel appeals to character in order to secure moral power in argument. He availed himself of the privilege of honoured age.

I. CHARACTER IS A GROWTH. A human being is mutable in purpose and disposition, and time is requisite in order to insure fixity of either. Character lies in determinateness, permanent fixity. Morally it is the form, style, and expression the life eventually assumes. It remains a long unsettled question as to what determinateness some men's nature is to come. In so far as instability itself is an undesirable quality, its presence is the sign of permanent badness. But even in the absence of instability, men suspend their judgment of their fellow-men because all good qualities in them are regarded as only tentatively established in the soul. The true progress of a life is secured when holiness of disposition becomes so gradually master of every faculty as to be the distinctive, invariable mark of the man. Obviously, this character is a passing of an inner silent force into all the avenues of thought, feeling, and action, repeating its self-manifestations in these day by day, till those who know the individual are compelled to see that such is the natural, fixed, reliable style of his life.

II. The CONDITIONS OF ITS POWER ARE TWOFOLD—one in the individual himself, and the other in observers. 1. *Constancy and steadiness of growth* is one condition. It is this which creates a belief that the man is true. There is a strong belief that fluctuations in conduct and opinion are signs of either weakness or actual badness. Those who watch the steady, early growth of a doubtful plant, and observe how by the action of a powerful law it at length assumes a given type of leaf and bud, know then what they have in sight, and treat it accordingly. So a quiet advance in goodness is essential to the acquisition of power in character. 2. The *existence in observers of a sense of right is another condition*. The power which a holy, consistent character has over all grades of men implies that there is something in them which, in virtue of its own nature, pays homage to goodness. Men *know and inwardly revere the right*. In this moral necessity of judgment we have a clue to the deference often paid by bad men to the good; the uneasiness of the vile and unjust in presence of purity; and the strong hold which the holy gospel of Christ has secretly over even the most daring of its opponents.

III. The POWER OF CHARACTER IS SOMETIMES DEVELOPED BY UNUSUAL CIRCUMSTANCES. It may exist as the result of a growing, unconscious influence over observers. Neither party may be aware of its real force. Many a man exercises more power on society than either he or others contemplate. The degree to which the present condition of the world is owing to this silent, unconscious influence of holy, consistent characters is beyond all conception. The fact should be a comfort to those whose lives seem to be barren of usefulness because no great deeds are chronicled. But now and then events transpire which bring out the depth of reverence and respect cherished for, it may be, an ordinary quiet Christian man.

IV. It is ALLOWABLE TO USE CHARACTER AS A MEANS OF URGING IMPORTANT CLAIMS. Samuel was right in referring to his long consistent life. He could honestly, and without self-glorying, speak of his having never enriched himself by his office. He was within the limits of modesty in claiming some credit for consistency, for his object was to enforce the claims of God. Thus the Apostle Paul referred to his manner of life, his self-denying labours, in order to win among Corinthians attention

to the message he delivered, and counteract the insinuations of false brethren (2 Cor·
xi.).   There are occasions when a pastor, a teacher, and parent may fitly refer to
their general character as furnishing a reason for attention to their appeals.

Practical lessons:—1. It is of supreme importance to be well established in strong
religious principles early in life; roots set in virgin soil strike deep and thrive
steadily.   2. We should watch carefully against tendencies to instability, and at the
same time not think over much about what men think of us.   3. No man who is
ambitious to obtain power of character will get it: it comes to those who are concerned to *be* good rather than to have the power which goodness confers.   4. We
honour God when we pay honour to those who bear his image.   5. The quality of
holy self-sacrifice is that in official persons which most impresses observers, and should,
after the Saviour's example, be cultivated by all persons in things small and great.

Vers. 6—15.—*The immutable condition of well-being.*   The facts are—1. Samuel,
having shown his right to be heard, calls on the people to hearken to his argument.
2. He refers to historic instances to show that trouble always came with unfaithfulness to God, and prosperity with a return to fidelity.   3. He reminds them that their
desire for a king implied distrust of God.   4. Recognising the new order of things,
he insists that the adversity or prosperity of the nation rested where it always had—
on their own disobedience or obedience to God.   Samuel, having gained a respectful
hearing, proceeds to urge his argument with the view to convince Israel that constant
obedience to God will be in future, on their part, the only rational conduct.   The
principles involved are universal, and they imply what some have recklessly denied
or questioned, namely, the essential reasonableness of religion.   Changing the historic allusions for corresponding facts in modern experience, the identical argument
could be urged with equal force upon many who fain would escape the yoke of
Christ as being inconsistent with the claims of human reason.

I. CONFORMITY TO THE WILL OF GOD IS THE SUPREME CONDITION OF WELL-BEING.
Israel would, as a people, dwell in safety, be rich, prosperous, and, in fact, realise all
the best ends of national existence, in proportion as they obeyed the Lord God.   The
interactions of material agencies, and the habits of irrational beings, in so far as
they flow from necessary physiological laws, are conformed to the Divine will.   The
possession by man of moral freedom renders it possible for him to be resolutely and
knowingly out of accord with the same.   *The will of God is variously expressed,
though always one.*   In external nature, in constitution of mind, in moral relations,
in social laws, in Scripture there are harmonious expressions of will varying according to the subject-matter and occasions.   It being in the power of man, as free, to
conform in feeling, in purpose, and actual outward movement of will to what God
reveals of himself, perfect life, personal, social, and national, lies in that conformity,
and that alone.   *The continuous act of obedience is conformity.*   Observing physical,
mental, and moral laws in every detail of life; acting in harmony with the revealed
requirements of repentance and effort after holiness; constant exercise of faith in
Christ as the revealed means of the highest spiritual life—this course of action is a
fulfilment of the conditions of blessedness, the prelude to final likeness to Christ.

II. THAT SUCH CONFORMITY IS THE CONDITION OF WELL-BEING IS A TRUTH ATTESTED
BY HISTORY.   It could be shown by independent lines of proof that religion, as consisting in true conformity to God's will, is essentially reasonable, and that, conversely,
sinful men are most irrational.   But Samuel knows human nature, and, therefore, he
deals with the concrete facts of history, and points out how the past records of Israel's
national life establish his contention.   GOD gave them freedom from Egypt by Moses
and Aaron.   Disobedience and neglect entailed subjection to Sisera and the Philistines.
A return to God brought deliverance once more.   Therefore history connected prosperity with due recognition of God, adversity with disobedience.   *Every sinful
nation and individual is deluded by fallacy.*   There is induced, by the blinding
effect of moral corruption on the intellect, a belief that the miseries endured are not
connected with moral causes.   But a fair induction of the facts of public and private
life will demonstrate Samuel's position, that when the soul or the nation has been
true to God it has enjoyed the truest prosperity.   The very prosperity of fools is in
the long run their destruction.   The merriment of the impious, like the brilliant

glare of a rocket, yields to a more conspicuous reverse. Pious men may not in some instances be equal, in power and general social usefulness, to men not pious ; yet, given men of equal natural abilities, the pious will do more and better than the *not* pious. Every-day life is full of cases in which men, by conforming to the gospel law of repentance and faith, at once place themselves and their homes in a new and better relation to all material and mental laws ; and rise from poverty, disease, ignorance, and shame to comfort, health, fair attainments, and honour. A nation of *true Christians* would be a model to the world in all excellence and acquisitions and happiness.

III. ALL ATTEMPTS TO EVADE THE CONDITION OF WELL-BEING ARE FRUITLESS. Samuel's reference to Israel's desire for a king, in connection with his argument and closing appeal, evidently means that the people were under the delusive impression that their troubles and dangers were in some way associated with the external form of government under which they had hitherto lived. But Samuel points out the sin involved in this thought—it was distrust of God's all-sufficiency ; and he also indicates that the attempted substitution of a form of government for the practice of righteousness is utterly vain. *Human nature is constant in its self-revelations.* This attempted substitution of what is formal and outward for what is moral and inward is of common occurrence. Nations often cry out for changes of form of government when the real need is a change in disposition and conduct. Nominal Christians present an outward, and, in emergencies, a more elaborate, form of worship in place of the sacrifice of the penitent and contrite heart. It is *hard to learn the lessons of history ;* but all its testimony confirms what could be, *à priori,* shown to be true—that however good external arrangements may be *per se,* they are as fruitless to secure a nation's highest good, a Church's truest prosperity, and an individual's most vigorous and joyous piety, in the absence of a faithful conformity to the whole will of God, as was Israel's acquisition of a king fruitless to insure, apart from righteousness of life, safety from danger and internal prosperity. "Abide in me." "For *without me ye can do nothing.*"

IV. THE TRUTH THUS VINDICATED CAN BE VERIFIED IN SPITE OF PAST SINS AND ERRORS. Samuel admits the existence of the king as a fact, though having its origin in sin and folly. He does not cut Israel off from the hope of proving the truth of his contention, that well-being depends on conformity to the will of God. Under their new and, as he thinks, unjustifiable arrangements they may, if they will, verify the correctness of his teaching ; and hence the urgent appeal. The *sins and errors of men in the past have had the natural effect of placing them in disadvantageous circumstances* for the fullest development of piety. Even in so-called Christian countries the social arrangements and customs, the habits of thought, the methods and principles of commerce, the form and spirit of legislation, and the attitude of class toward class, are the expression of the faults as well as of the virtues of our ancestors. They to that extent impede the full expression of the gospel spirit. The same holds good of antecedents in private and Church life. *Nevertheless, God gives* to nations, Churches, and individuals *opportunities for testing the value of conformity to his will,* and each may prove its sufficiency by new acts of obedience. Here we have a philosophy of life which each may experimentally establish.

General lessons :—1. Conformity to the will of God being the immutable maxim of life, care should be taken to ascertain that will as distinct from our own wishes ; and, when ascertained, all the force of our nature should be bent on insuring its observance. 2. It is well to fortify conduct by an appeal to the reasonableness of a religious life, since in a struggle reason and faith are both helpful. 3. In all times of restlessness and dissatisfaction deeper search should be made than into the outward forms of life, for the outward change is no sure cure for the inward unrighteousness. 4. Gratitude to God for permission to recover lost prosperity best shows itself in renewed consecration to him.

Vers. 16—25.—*The outward sign.* The facts are—1. Samuel, to confirm his argument, calls for thunder and rain during the wheat harvest, thus imperilling their property. 2. The people, awed by the event, entreat for his intercession. 3. Samuel encourages hope on the ground of God's mercy, and promises to pray for and instruct them.   4. He makes a final appeal, setting forth the blessed and sad alternative consequences.   Samuel knew well with whom he had to deal ; and, therefore, besides securing a deferential hearing in virtue of age and character, and enforcing the reasonableness of conformity to God's will, he now calls attention to a display of Divine power in a form suggestive of the material disasters that may come if they should, by disobedience, come into collision with that power.   Men soon feel the force of an argument that touches their property.   The natural force of his previous statements would compel the assent of reason, and secure the echo of conscience. But in morally weak men the clear light of reason is apt to become eclipsed by the uprising of wilful desires, and the voice of conscience dies away amid the clamours of passion.   It was, therefore, great kindness, an act of beautiful, Divine consideration, to introduce another means of insuring the impressment of the lessons conveyed

I. Outward signs are helpful to religion.   Manifestations of God's presence and power in impressive forms, in some instances miraculous, are aids to faith and practice.   There is a modern tendency to dispute this.   Even some Christian apologists speak of the miraculous events recorded in Scripture as rather a hindrance than an aid to faith.   The difficulty proceeds from a defective comprehension of all the facts that enter into a consideration of the question.   No doubt moral truth is its own witness ; no doubt reason recognises what lies within the range of her vision.   The whole sum of truth we have in Christ, and in the records associated with his name, enables us to say, "This is the Son of God."   The personal experience of the man who is one in life with Christ is superior to all "external evidences."   But obviously all this applies to men in the full light of Christian truth, and can have no appreciable bearing on the gradual education of the world by a chosen nation, through "here a little and there a little," as men were morally and intellectually fit to receive it.   Observe more specifically—1. *General education by outward signs is universal.*   By education we mean development of the entire nature, rational and moral.   We have to regulate life and unfold its capabilities by means other than the mere subjective effect of what is perceived and appreciated as rational or moral.   (1) In *childhood* the mind accepts truth on external authority.   Its movements, its receptivity, and its resistance to certain influences are often determined by the appearance of an external power, which either awakens fear or insures unquestioning submission.   (2) In *mature life* we are influenced not by subjective truth alone, but by external authority in form of testimony on matters of importance.   This testimony has sometimes sufficient force to compel conduct against inclination, and create fear as determinant in action.   Also in government the exercise of external power insures on the part of many a respect in practice for moral truth which otherwise would not exist.   (3) In *the formation of opinion* we are constantly looking out for an external confirmation.   That is, we do not live intellectually even by the sheer light that is within. In so far as external confirmations are necessary for some of our opinions, we are dependent on powers outside us for the direction our own thought, and, consequently, conduct, will take.   That these powers, human it may be, do not act suddenly and miraculously is not to the point, for the *principle contended for* is education by outward signs.   2. *Spiritual education of men by appropriate outward signs is a fact recognised throughout all time.*   The three means, irrespective of inspiration of the heart by the Holy Spirit, of spiritual education—presentation of truth to the moral perception, the convincing of the judgment by reasons, and the suggestive power of outward signs—are found in the whole course of history, from the day when Adam's conscience recognised the moral force of the Divine command because Divine, appreciated the argument of life or death as the alternative of obedience or disobedience, and looked on the "tree" as a visible sign of a power worthy to be feared, unto the latest observance of the Lord's Supper, affording an outward sign of a power merciful in its almightiness.   (1) The *entire dispensation covered by the Old and New Testament was characterised by the outward sign in a miraculous manner.* Abraham desired to know by some means that he should inherit the land (Gen. xv. 8), and the sign was given.   Moses had granted to him a sign of his delegation (Exod. iv. 1—5).   The blackness and darkness around Sinai were visible demonstrations to inspire the too rash people with becoming awe.   Signs and wonders were one means by which Nicodemus recognised the "Teacher come from God" (John iii. 1, 2 ; cf.

Acts ii. 29).   The excision of the miraculous element may be consistent for those who exclude God from direct action in the education of mankind, but it is an illogical act when done by believers in a personal "living God."   The Bible is a very consistent book.   (2) In *so far as the Bible record is an education of mankind, it*, containing a faithful account of the visible signs of the past, *causes those signs to be a formative influence still.*   The visible manifestations during the ages covered by Biblical records not only made people then know and feel the reality of God's presence and power to a degree that otherwise would not have been possible, but they cause the "ends of the earth" to be more thoroughly convinced of it.   It takes much effort to shake men out of their indifference to the Unseen, to strengthen faith in an ever-ruling Power.   The Bible comes to the aid of our reason and conscience, and by these recorded facts helps us to live as though we saw him who is invisible.   Those who object to the reality of miracles in the past because, forsooth, similar do not occur now, and are not needed, forget how much of their present faith in God is due to the combination of these ancient miracles with the spiritual element that abides. We may have a spiritual appreciation of the truth of Christianity which amply satisfies us; but that spiritual Christianity so appreciated is impossible apart from the stupendous "outward sign" of an Incarnation and Resurrection.   (3) The *facts consequent on the establishment of Christianity are outward signs* which continue to furnish aid to faith.   The indirect result, in the continued existence of the Jews as an essentially separate people, is impressive.   The direct effects, in the salvation of souls, the pure, elevating spirit, and the social ameliorations naturally flowing from Christianity, are signs and wonders which indicate the mighty power of God.   3. *Spiritual education by outward signs is very reasonable.*   This will be admitted so far as relates to our children, and also the formation of character by outward signs of power that are not miraculous.   Therefore the controversy is limited to the reasonableness of the outward miraculous signs related in the Bible.   Here observe, those who admit that the Incarnation, "God manifest in the flesh," was a reality, and not a figure of speech, have conceded the principle; and if it was the Divine intention by this miracle to save men in Christ, where is the difficulty of admitting that by miracle God wrought the way for Christ, and educated the world for the event?   If the escape is sought in the supposed number of miracles in Old Testament times, then who is to tell God how *many* he shall work?   Where do wisdom and propriety begin and end?   Let any one try and settle what and how often God shall work. Moreover, it is all a delusion as to the vast number of miracles.   Genesis covers at least 2800 years, and yet not over twenty-two miracles, or strictly open manifestations, are recorded during that period, giving an average of one in 127 years. Further, what more reasonable than, *e. g.*, this of the "thunder"?   The people have had the truth, and reason has been appealed to; but they are weak, as history proves. God is the supreme Power, but they evidently need to be impressed, so that the lessons just given may abide.   Fear thus produced will act with consciousness of moral truth and force of reason, and consequently it is an act of great mercy to render them this additional aid, just as it is an act of kindness to enforce lessons on children by an authority which they can appreciate.

II. THERE ARE SPECIAL ENCOURAGEMENTS TO CONFORMITY TO GOD'S WILL set forth by his prophets, justified by reason and conscience, and supported by outward signs. It is instructive to note how God's methods have respect to the whole man.   Moral obligation is placed before the conscience (vers. 13—15), reason is appealed to (vers. 7—11), fear of disobedience is aroused by outward sign of supreme power, and now the hopes of the soul are to be sustained by appropriate considerations.   Would that men who sneer at the Old Testament records had the heart to study its spiritual teaching!   They would see how beautifully the terrible and the mild blend to meet the needs of the real man.   The encouragement is threefold.   1. *An assurance of God's great mercy.*   "Fear not."   He "will not forsake his people."   This "fear not" comes to the sinful soul still.   It came with the angels' song over the plains of Bethlehem; it was heard by the "little flock;" and the conscience-smitten jailor heard the same.   God "hath not forsaken" mankind.   Not for what virtue he sees in perverse, ungrateful men, but "for his own sake" he saves the penitent.   As Israel had "for his own sake" been made his people, with prospective reference to the introduction of the Messiah and the future education of the world, so in the redemption wrought by Christ every man on earth is embraced in a covenant of mercy, sealed with the "blood that cleanseth from all sin." To know that God is merciful and gracious, that all his terrible displays of power are in love, this brings cheer to the entire race of man. If only despisers of the gospel knew the richness of its mercy for all men, they would surely not seek to hinder its acceptance by this sorrowing world. 2. *The prayer and sympathy of the faithful.* Samuel assures Israel that he will bear them on his heart. His affection for them and his spiritual duty to them were such that not to continue to pray would be sin (ver. 23). This encouragement has every one who is called on to conform to the will of God. The Church pleads "for all men." The penitent and struggling are especially on the heart of God's faithful children. In thousands of homes daily prayer is made for persons never seen and unknown by name. 3. *Continuous instruction.* As long as Samuel lived he would teach them "the good and the right way." No doubt, like the Apostle Peter, he would also devise means so that they should have his wise words "after" his "decease." It requires "line upon line, precept upon precept," to keep men in the safe and blessed pathway; and how fully is this secured to us in the "lively oracles"! By the written word, by the suggestions of the Holy Spirit, by the wise counsel of friends, God teaches us the way in which we should go. We are not left to wander at our will, or to follow the contradictory voices of men. There is "a sure word of prophecy which shineth as a light in a dark place."

General lessons:—1. A study of the signs of God's presence in human affairs will prove a salutary restraint on sinful tendencies. 2. It becomes the true Christian to manifest tender sympathy for men who are spiritually weak and erring. 3. Great influence is gained over men when we can convince them that, though they are very sinful, God is merciful and waiting to bless. 4. The element of fear in religion, to be healthful, must be supplemented by that of hope and confidence.

HOMILIES BY VARIOUS AUTHORS

Vers. 1—25. (GILGAL.)—*Samuel's admonitions to Israel.* 1. The *occasion* of his admonitions was the full recognition of the first king of Israel ·by the national assembly, and his retirement from the more active duties of his office as judge. He was not mortified at parting with power, nor did he wish to reverse the change which had been effected. He cheerfully acquiesced in the will of God, and cordially united with the people in giving honour to the "Lord's anointed" (vers. 3, 5). Yet he might not allow them to suppose that there was nothing blameworthy in their desire for a king, as they were apt to do, or enter upon their new career in perilous self-complacency, without warning them of the rocks ahead. He spoke not merely as judge, but also as a prophet and "faithful priest" (ver. 19). 2. The *form* which they assumed is varied. They consist generally of a *dialogue* between him and the elders; partly of an *apology*, or defence of his official conduct; partly of a *narration* of the dealings of God with Israel; and partly of exhortations, warnings, and promises closely connected together. The whole may be conceived of as a judicial scene occurring before the invisible Judge, in which Samuel, having vindicated himself as against the people, sets forth their sin against God, who himself confirms his words in the thunderstorm (Job xxxviii. 1), which leads them to confess their transgression and seek the intercession of the prophet, who consoles and admonishes them, and assures them of his continued help. The language is direct and rugged and full of force. 3. The main *subject* is the course of sinful perversity which Israel had pursued in desiring a king; the chief *aim* to produce a humble and penitent state of mind, and lead to the maintenance of a proper relation to the invisible King. His former words may be compared (ch. iii. 11—14; vii. 3—6; viii. 10—18; x. 17—19); also the words of Moses (Num. xvi. 25—30; Deut. xxix.), and of Joshua (Josh. xxiv.). He speaks of *their course* as—

I. ADOPTED WITHOUT SUFFICIENT REASON (vers. 3—6) in the light of his just administration. He sets himself, as it were, before the tribunal of the invisible Judge, and before the king,—himself, "old and grey-headed," on the one hand, Israel on the other,—and seeks an open vindication (as public men are often under the necessity of doing); not, however, so much from regard to his own dignity as to their welfare and the honour of God. We have here—1. *A challenge*, on the part of Samuel, to bear witness against him. "Behold, here I am," &c. (ver. 3). It is a common temptation for men in authority and power to use their position for selfish and unjust purposes, such as (1) appropriating wrongfully what belongs to others, (2) defrauding them of what is their due, (3) oppressing the poor and weak, and (4) perverting the proper course of justice, especially in the case of the rich and strong, for the sake of "a gift," or bribe. How have these evils prevailed in every age ! But Samuel had consciously wronged no one, and if any can show that he has done so, he stands ready to make restitution (Luke xix. 8). His conscience is "as the noontide clear." "No doubt he found himself guilty before God of many private infirmities; but for his public carriage he appeals to men. A man's heart can best judge of himself; others can best judge of his actions. Happy is that man that can be acquitted by himself in private, in public by others, by God in both " (Hall). 2. *A testimony*, on the part of the elders, to his integrity (ver. 4) ; ready, explicit, and with one voice. It is almost impossible for men in public office to be faithful without making enemies. If Samuel had any, they now nowhere appear; and his character shines forth "as the sun when he goeth forth in his might" (Judges v. 31). 3. *An invocation*, on the part of both, to the Lord and his anointed to confirm the testimony (ver. 5) ; thereby making it more solemn and memorable. Why, then, seeing his government was so unblamable, did they wish to set it aside? Their testimony to him was a sentence of condemnation on themselves for their inconsideration, ingratitude, and discontent. The force of the testimony was increased by his further invocation of the Lord as he who had "appointed Moses and Aaron, and brought their fathers out of the land of Egypt" (ver. 6). As the appointed and faithful leader of Israel, even as they, no other was necessary, and his rejection was the rejection of the Lord. With this he passes on to speak of their course as—

II. MARKED BY AGGRAVATED TRANSGRESSION (vers. 7—12) in the light of the righteous dealings of God in past time. "Now therefore stand forth," &c. (ver. 7). He and they now change places ; he becomes their accuser, and *reasons* or contends with them (in order to convict them of sin) "concerning the righteous acts of Jehovah," who had acted justly in his covenant relation with them throughout their whole history, faithfully fulfilled his promises, inflicted punishment only when it was deserved, and bestowed upon them the greatest benefits (Ezek. xxxiii. 17 ; Micah vi. 2). These acts include—1. *A wonderful deliverance* (ver. 8) from a crushing oppression, in compassion to the cry of the needy, through the instrumentality of men raised up for the purpose, with "a mighty hand and an outstretched arm," and completed in their possession of the land of promise. This deliverance is always regarded as the foundation of their history. "History was born in that night in which Moses, with the law of God, moral and spiritual, in his heart, led the people of Israel out of Egypt" (Bunsen). 2. *Repeated chastisements* (ver. 9), rendered necessary by forgetfulness of God, varied (the Canaanites, the Philistines, the Moabites), and with a view to their moral improvement. "Notice here Samuel's prudence in reproof. (1) By his reproof of their ancestors he prepares their minds to receive reproof ; (2) he shows that their ingratitude is old, and so worse, and they should take care that it grow no stronger ; (3) he chooses a very mild word, 'forget,' to express their offence " (Pool). 3. *Continued help* (vers. 10, 11), through penitence and prayer, by means of successive "saviours," — Jerubbaal (Gideon), Bedan (Barak), Jephthah, Samuel (ch. vii. 10 ; referring to himself in the third person, because now speaking as the advocate of Jehovah),—against their "enemies on every side," and in their safe preservation unto the present time. "And ye dwelled safe." But what return did they make for all his benefits ? As soon as they saw the threatening attitude of Nahash (ver. 12), they forgot the lessons of the past, lost their confidence in God, trusted in an arm of flesh, and recklessly and persistently demanded a king, virtually rejecting the Lord as their king. Former experience of the goodness and severity of God greatly aggravates present transgression (ver. 19).

III. INVOLVING PERILOUS RESPONSIBILITY (vers. 13—15) in the light of present circumstances. "Now therefore behold the king whom ye have chosen," &c. Although they had taken the initiative in the matter, he had reserved to himself the authority of appointing him, and abides the supreme Ruler over both people and king (ver. 12). In the new order of things—1. *They are specially liable to forget* this primary truth, and to trust in man, and hence he impresses upon them once and again the fact that "the Lord God is their king." No earthly monarch can release them from their responsibility to him, and no human help can save them apart from him. "It is better to trust in the Lord than to put confidence in princes" (Ps. cxviii. 9). 2. *They can prosper only by being faithful to him.* "If ye will fear the Lord," &c., it will be well with you and your king. But—3. *If unfaithful, they will expose themselves to heavy judgments,* as their fathers had done before them. Wherein, then, have they improved their condition? What a perilous course have they entered upon! And how can they hope to avoid its consequences except by profound humiliation, and seeking the Lord "with full purpose of heart"?

IV. NECESSITATING SINCERE REPENTANCE (vers. 16—18) in the light of approaching judgment. "Now therefore stand and see this great thing," &c. Hitherto the words of Samuel appear to have produced little effect; something further was necessary that they might not be spoken in vain; and, in response to his prayer, the thunder crashed above the heads of the great assembly, and the rain fell in torrents around them—things "incomprehensible to a Hebrew" in time of harvest. The miraculous sign—1. *Corroborates* the word of truth as well as the Divine commission of him who uttered it, and confirms the testimony borne to his integrity. The voice of the supreme Judge answers the appeal which had been made to him (ver. 5), and there is "an end of all controversy" (Heb. vi. 16). 2. *Is significant* of the Divine displeasure at their sin, and of terrible judgments (Exod. ix. 28). "Hereby the Lord showed his power, and the people their foolishness in not being contented to have such a mighty God for their protector, who could with thunder and rain fight for them against their enemies, as he did for Israel against the host of Pharaoh, and not long before this against the Philistines. And, beside, it appeared with what small reason they should be weary of Samuel's government, who by his prayer could fetch down rain and thunder from heaven" (Willet). "God had granted their desire; but upon them and their king's bearing toward the Lord, not upon the fact that they had now a king, would the future of Israel depend; and this truth, so difficult for them to learn, God would, as it were, prove before them in a symbol. Did they think it unlikely, nay, well-nigh impossible, to fail in their present circumstances? God would bring the unlikely and seemingly incredible to pass in a manner patent to all. Was it not the time of wheat harvest, when in the East not a cloud darkens the clear sky? God would send thunder and rain to convince them, by making the unlikely real, of the folly and sin of their thoughts in demanding a king" (Edersheim). 3. *Is designed* to effect a moral end, in filling them with salutary fear. "That ye may perceive that your wickedness is great" (ver. 17). And it is not in vain; for "all the people greatly feared the Lord and Samuel" (ver. 18), thus solemnly avouched to be his prophet. God is never at a loss for means to accomplish his purposes, and goes beyond his usual method of operations when the occasion demands it. The end of his dealings with men is to bring them to repentance and make them holy.

V. NOT EXCLUDING CONSOLATION AND HOPE (vers. 19—25) in the light of the great name and merciful purposes of God. By means of repentance and faith men place themselves within the circle where the "consuming fire" of Divine wrath (Rom. i. 18; Heb. xii. 29) is transformed into the genial beams of Divine grace; and "he is faithful and just to forgive us our sins" (1 John i. 9). We have here—1. *A description of a penitent people* (ver. 19), overwhelmed with fear, freely and fully confessing their sin, rendering honour where they had formerly shown ingratitude and disrespect, and seeking Divine mercy in the way in which they had reason to believe it might be obtained. 2. *An exhortation to an amended course of life* (vers. 20, 21). (1) A consoling word. "Fear not." (2) A reminding and humbling word. "Ye have done all this wickedness." (3) A restraining word. "Turn not aside from following the Lord" (as ye have done in your distrust and self-will). (4) A directive word. "But serve the Lord with all your heart" (in faith, and love, and entire consecration). (5) A warning word. "And turn ye not aside" (from God to any false object of trust, idols). (6) An instructive word. "For they are vain" (utterly empty and disappointing). 3. *An assurance of mercy and grace* (ver. 22), resting on—(1) His relationship. They are still "his people." (2) His name—his revelations of power and salvation to his people, and his honour and glory before all the nations. (3) His good-will. "Because" (he will not forsake his people, because) "it hath pleased the Lord to make you his people." Whatever benefits he has conferred have proceeded from his pure benevolence, and are a pledge of further benefits (Jer. xxxi. 3). His free and unmerited love is the sinner's chief hope. 4. *A promise of continued aid*, on the part of Samuel, in intercession and instruction (ver. 23). "In this he sets a glorious example to all rulers, showing them that they should not be led astray by the ingratitude of their subordinates or subjects, and give up on that account all interest in their welfare; but should further persevere all the more in their anxiety for them." 5. *A final admonition to steadfast obedience* (vers. 24, 25), without which both people and king will be overwhelmed in destruction. In keeping with the tone which pervades these admonitions, and as in foresight of coming evils, they end with a warning.—D.

Ver. 2. (GILGAL.)—*Piety in old age.* "Old and grey-headed." On speaking of himself as "old and grey-headed," Samuel immediately afterwards made reference to his childhood. "I have walked before you from my childhood unto this day." He loved to linger (as old men are wont) over his early days; and in his case there was every reason for doing so, for they were surpassingly pure and beautiful. One of the chief lessons of his life is that a well-spent childhood and youth conduces greatly to a happy and honoured age. Consider him as an eminent illustration of piety in old age.

I. OLD AGE IS PRESUMPTIVE OF PIETY, inasmuch as—1. Piety *prevents* indulgence in vices that tend to shorten life. How many are brought by such vices to a premature grave! When, therefore, we see an old man we naturally infer that he has been a good man, nor can there be any doubt that he has exercised much self-control. Samuel was a Nazarite. 2. It has a *direct tendency* to prolong life by producing healthful virtues. "The fear of the Lord prolongeth days" (Prov. x. 27). 3. It has the *promise* of many days. "With long life will I satisfy him" (Ps. xci. 16). "Even to old age I am; and even to hoar hairs will I carry you" (Isa. xlvi. 4). "A good old age" (Gen. xv. 15). "Thou shalt come to thy grave in a full age, like as a shock of corn cometh in his season" (Job v. 26). 4. It is *commonly* associated with long life. There are, doubtless, exceptions, the causes of which are not far to seek, but this is the rule.

II. OLD AGE IS MADE HONOURABLE BY PIETY, because of—1. Its maintaining the *respect* which is naturally felt for the aged. Among the Spartans, when a hoary-headed man entered their assemblies, they all immediately rose, and remained standing till he had taken his place; and it is enjoined in the law of Moses: "Thou shalt rise up before the hoary head, and honour the face of the old man" (Levit. xix. 32). But this injunction assumes the possession of godliness, without which old age neither deserves nor receives appropriate reverence. 2. The beauty and *perfection* of character which it develops. There is beauty in the fresh-springing corn, but there is still greater beauty in "the full corn in the ear," bending under its golden burden. A good old man, matured in character by long growth, and abounding in "the fruit of the Spirit," is one of the noblest sights on earth. He is a king amongst men. "The hoary head is a crown of glory if it be found in the way of righteousness" (Prov. xvi. 31; xx. 29). 3. The *conflicts* and perils that have been passed. "An old disciple" (Acts xxi. 16), or "such an one as Paul the aged" (Philem. 9), is like a veteran soldier bearing on him the scars of many a hard-fought battle, and wearing the honours conferred by a grateful country. He is like a giant of the forest, standing erect when the storm has laid his companions in the dust. 4. The *good* that has been done in past time, and lives to bear witness to the doer, and "praise him in the gates." We value the young for the good they may hereafter effect, the old for the good they have already accomplished. "Them that honour me I will honour."

III. OLD AGE IS RENDERED USEFUL BY PIETY, for thereby it—1. Furnishes a convincing *evidence* of the truth and power of religion. When faith survives doubts, temptations, difficulties, its very existence is an argument for the reality of that which is believed, a proof of the practicability of a religious life, and a commendation of its unspeakable worth. 2. Sets forth an impressive *example* of the spirit of religion—humility, trustfulness, calmness, patience, resignation, cheerfulness (Gen. xlviii. 21 ; Deut. xxxiii. 1 ; Josh. xiv. 10, 12 ; xxiii. 14 ; 2 Sam. xix. 32). 3. Bears valuable *testimony* for God, and continues in prayer and labour on behalf of men. "They shall still bring forth fruit in old age," &c. (Ps. xcii. 14, 15 ; lxxi. 14, 17, 18). Although some services are no longer possible, others, often more valuable, may, and ought to, be rendered till the close of life. 4. Affords wise *counsel* to the younger and less experienced. Wisdom is proverbially associated with age. Those who have seen and heard much of the world, and had long experience of life, may be expected to know more than those who are just starting out in their course. Their judgment is less influenced by passion and impulse ; they look at things in a clearer light, and in a calmer frame of mind, and are more likely to perceive the truth concerning them.

> " Whose ripe experience doth attain
> To somewhat of prophetic strain."

Much of the inspired wisdom of the Scriptures is based upon the sanctified experience of the aged. "Moreover I will endeavour that ye may be able after my decease to have these things always in remembrance" (2 Pet. i. 15, 12—14 ; 1 Pet. v. 1, 5). "My little children, let us not love in word, neither in tongue ; but in deed and in truth" (1 John iii. 18). "Little children, love one another."

IV. OLD AGE IS GREATLY COMFORTED BY PIETY. It has its drawbacks and troubles. Bodily infirmities increase, the mental powers lose their vigour, and friends become fewer (Eccles. xii.). It is also liable to moral failings, such as irritability, fretfulness, despondency, and excessive carefulness, which need to be guarded against. "When I consider in my mind, I find four causes why old age is thought miserable : one, that it calls us away from the transactions of affairs ; the second, that it renders the body more feeble ; the third, that it deprives us of almost all pleasures; the fourth, that it is not very far from death" (Cicero ' on Old Age '). But notwithstanding such things, it has, "with godliness," abundant compensations, consisting of—1. Pleasant *recollections* of the past, especially of the Divine benefits that have been received. "Surely I will remember thy wonders of old" (Ps. lxxvii. 11). 2. Wide *observation* of the works and ways of God. "I have been young, and now am old," &c. (Ps. xxxvii. 25). 3. Inward support and *consolation* derived from communion with God. "Though our outward man perish, yet the inward man is renewed day by day" (2 Cor. iv. 16). "The glory of the old age of the godly consists in this, that while the faculties for the sensible no less than mental enjoyments gradually decline, and the hearth of life gets thus deprived of its fuel, the blessings of godliness not only continue to refresh the soul in old age, but are not until then most thoroughly enjoyed. The sun of piety rises the warmer in proportion as the sun of life declines." 4. Bright *prospects* of the heavenly home—"a house not made with hands," the vision of God, perpetual youth, reunion with parted friends, perfect and endless blessedness. As the world of light draws near, some of its rays seem to shine through the crevices of the earthly tabernacle that is falling into decay (Gen. xlix. 18 ; Luke ii. 29, 30). "The state in which I am now is so delightful, that the nearer I approach to death, I seem, as it were, to get sight of land ; and at length, after a long voyage, to be getting into the harbour. O glorious day ! when I shall depart to that Divine company and assemblage of spirits, and quit this troubled and polluted scene" (Cicero). "If the mere conception of the reunion of good men in a future state infused a momentary rapture into the mind of Tully ; if an airy speculation—for there is reason to fear it had little hold on his convictions—could inspire him with such delight, what may we be expected to feel who are assured of such an event by the true sayings of God" (R. Hall). "I have a desire to depart and to be with Christ, which is far better" (Phil. i. 23 ; 2 Tim. iv. 6—8)

Observations :—1. Let us be thankful for the consolations of religion in "the time of old age." 2. Let the aged cherish the dispositions by which it is made beautiful and useful. 3. Let the young honour the aged, and not forsake "the counsel of the old men" (1 Kings xii. 8). 4. Let them also remember that they will grow old, and so live that they may then be honoured and happy.—D.

Vers. 3—5. (GILGAL.)—*Integrity in public office.* "Behold, here I am : witness against me before the Lord." It is a noble thing for a man in any position of life, but especially in exalted, public, and responsible office, to "do justly and love mercy" as well as to "walk humbly with his God ; " to continue for many years in the fulfilment of his duty with strictest integrity and unselfish devotion to the public good. Of this Samuel was an illustrious pattern. Concerning integrity in public office, observe that—

I. It is generally, and not improperly, EXPECTED, because of—1. The superior knowledge which one who fills such an office is assumed to possess (Ezra vii. 25). 2. The important trust which is reposed in him. "Moreover, it is required in stewards that a man be found faithful" (1 Cor. iv. 2). 3. The powerful influence which he exerts over others, for good or evil (Prov. xxix. 2).

II. It is beset by numerous TEMPTATIONS, such as—1. To prefer his ease and pleasure to laborious and self-denying duty (Rom. xii. 8). 2. To use his power for the enrichment of himself and his family, to the disregard of the general welfare, and even by means of extortion, fraud, and oppression (Acts xvi. 22 ; xxiv. 26). 3. To seek the praise of men more than the praise of God, and to yield to the evil wishes of the multitude for the sake of personal advantage (John xix. 13).

III. It lies open to public CRITICISM, for—1. The conduct of a public man cannot be wholly hidden from view. 2. His responsible position invites men, and gives them a certain right, to judge concerning the course he pursues ; and, in many instances, his actions directly affect their persons, property, or reputation. 3. As it is impossible to restrain their criticism, so it is, on the whole, beneficial that it should be exercised as a salutary restraint upon those "who are in authority." Happy is he in whom "none occasion nor fault can be found, forasmuch as he is faithful" (Dan. vi. 4).

IV. It is NOT always duly APPRECIATED, but is sometimes despised and suspected. 1. The reasons of the conduct of one in public office are not always fully understood, nor the difficulties of his position properly considered, nor the motives of his actions rightly interpreted. 2. Evil-doers, to whom he is "a terror," may be expected to hate and speak ill of him. "What evil have I done ? " said Aristides, when told that he had *every one's* good word. 3. Men are apt to be envious of those who are exalted above them, and to forget their past services if they do not favour the gratification of the present popular feeling. Samuel was not the only judge who experienced ingratitude. "Neither showed they kindness to the house of Jerubbaal, namely, Gideon, according to all the goodness which he showed unto Israel " (Judges viii. 35).

V. It sometimes requires to be openly VINDICATED, for the sake of—1. Personal character and reputation. " I have not taken one ass from them, neither have I hurt one of them " (Num. xvi. 5). 2. Truth, and righteousness, and the honour of God. How often, on this account, did the Apostle Paul vindicate himself, in his epistles, from the accusations that were made against him ! 3. The welfare of the people themselves, on whom misrepresentation and unfounded suspicions exert an injurious influence.

VI. It is certain, sooner or later, to be fully RECOGNISED. 1. Time and circumstances bring real worth to the light. 2. There is in men a sense of truth and justice which constrains them to acknowledge and honour the good. 3. God takes care of the reputation of those who take care of his honour. There comes a " resurrection of reputations." The judgment of one generation concerning public men is often reversed by the next. "There is nothing hidden that shall not be made manifest." "And the righteous shall be had in everlasting remembrance."—D.

Vers. 8—12. (GILGAL.)—*Doctrine in history.* This is an important chapter in the history of Israel. In it are set forth certain truths of universal import, which are also illustrated, though less distinctly, in the history of other nations. They are such as follows :—

1. The sovereignty of God (ver. 8). "It hath pleased the Lord to make you his people" (ver. 22). Of his own free and gracious will, always founded in perfect wisdom, he raises up a people from the lowest condition, confers upon them special blessings and privileges, and exalts them to the most eminent place among the nations of the earth (Deut. xxxii. 8; Acts xvii. 26, 27). As it was with Israel, so has it been with other peoples. His right so to deal with men cannot be questioned, his power therein is manifested, his undeserved goodness should be acknowledged, and the gifts bestowed employed not for selfish ends, but for his glory and the welfare of mankind.

II. The sinfulness of men. "They forgat the Lord their God" (ver. 9). So constantly and universally have men departed from God and goodness as to make it evident that there is in human nature an inherited tendency to sin. "It is that tendency to sinful passions or unlawful propensities which is perceived in man whenever objects of desire are placed before him, and laws laid upon him." As often as God in his great goodness has exalted him to honour, so often has he fallen away from his service; and left to himself, without the continual help of Divine grace, his course is downward. "In times past the Divine nature flourished in men, but at length, being mixed with mortal custom, it fell into ruin; hence an inundation of evils in the race" (Plato. See other testimonies quoted by Bushnell in 'Nature and the Supernatural'). "There is nothing in the whole earth that does not prove either the misery of man or the compassion of God; either his powerlessness without, or his power with God" (Pascal).

III. The certainty of retribution. "He sold them into the hand of Sisera," &c. (ver. 9).

> "The sword of Heaven is not in haste to smite,
> Nor yet doth linger, save unto his seeming
> Who, in desire or fear, doth look for it."—(Dante, 'Par.' xxii.).

"Morning by morning doth he bring his judgment to light; he faileth not" (Zeph. iii. 5). "History is a voice for ever sounding across the centuries the laws of right and wrong. Opinions alter, manners change, creeds rise and fall, but the moral law is written on the tablets of eternity. For every false word or unrighteous deed, for cruelty and oppression, for lust or vanity, the price has to be paid at last; not always by the chief offenders, but paid by some one. Justice and truth alone endure and live. Injustice and falsehood may be long-lived, but doomsday comes at last to them in French revolutions and other terrible woes" (Froude, 'Short Studies').

IV. The beneficence of suffering. "And they cried unto the Lord, and said, We have sinned," &c. (ver. 10). Underneath what is in itself an evil, and a result of the violation of law, physical or moral, there is ever working a Divine power which makes it the means of convincing men of sin, turning them from it, and improving their character and condition. A state of deepest humiliation often precedes one of highest honour. It is only those who refuse to submit to discipline (Job xxxvi. 10) and harden themselves in iniquity that sink into hopeless ruin.

V. The efficacy of prayer. "And the Lord sent . . . and delivered you," &c. (ver. 11). "Then they cried unto the Lord in their trouble, and he delivered them out of their distresses" (Ps. cvii. 6, 13, 19, 28). As it was with Israel throughout their history, so has it been with others, even those who have had but little knowledge of "the Hearer of prayer."

> "In even savage bosoms
> There are longings, yearnings, strivings·
> For the good they comprehend not,
> And the feeble hands and helpless,
> Groping blindly in the darkness,
> Touch God's right hand in that darkness,
> And are lifted up and strengthened" ('The Song of Hiawatha').

VI. The prevalence of mediation. "Then the Lord sent Moses and Aaron" (ver. 8). "And the Lord sent Jerubbaal, and Bedan, and Jephthah, and Samuel" (ver. 11). He sent help by men specially raised up and appointed, and deliverance came through their labours, conflicts, and sufferings. One people also has been often made the medium of blessing to others. And herein we see a shadowing forth of the work of the great Mediator and Deliverer, and (in an inferior manner) of his people on behalf of the world.

VII. THE INCREASE OF RESPONSIBILITY on the part of those who have had the experience of former generations to profit by, and who have received higher privileges than they (vers. 12, 19). "Now all these things were written for our admonition," &c. (1 Cor. x. 11). "Two things we ought to learn from history: one, that we are not in ourselves superior to our fathers; another, that we are shamefully and monstrously inferior to them if we do not advance beyond them" (Froude).—D.

Ver. 23. (GILGAL.)—*Intercessory prayer.* "God forbid that I should sin against the Lord in ceasing to pray for you." "I bless God," said Mr. Flavel, the Puritan, on the death of his father, "for a religious and tender father, who often poured out his soul to God for me; and this stock of prayers I esteem the fairest inheritance on earth." And another eminent man said that he "set a greater worth upon the intercessions of the good than upon all the wealth of the Indies." The people of Israel esteemed the prayers of Samuel on their behalf in like manner. They had experience of their amazing power and worth (ch. vii. 8, 9); they were in great need of them; they appear to have thought that he might cease to offer them on account of their past treatment of him, and they entreated him, saying, "Pray for thy servants," &c. (ver. 19). His reply was, "Moreover as for me," &c. Every true Christian, as "a priest unto God," an intercessor with God for his fellow-men, ought to adopt this language as his own. It expresses—

I. AN ACKNOWLEDGED OBLIGATION, which—1. Arises out of the fact that it is *one of the principal means of doing good* to others—obtaining invaluable blessings for them. Of the fact there can be no doubt (James v. 16). Why it should have been ordained as such a means we cannot fully tell; but it is plainly in accordance with the intimate relationship and mutual dependence of men; teaches them to feel a deeper interest in each other, and puts signal honour upon eminent piety. The principle of mediation pervades all things, human and Divine. 2. Is *an essential part of the duty of love* which we owe to others; the force of the obligation being determined by the nearness of their relationship, and the extent of their claims upon our love and service—our kindred and friends, our country, mankind. 3. Is *often expressly enjoined in the word of God.* "Pray one for another" (Luke xi. 5; 1 Tim. ii. 1). "If any man see his brother sin a sin which is not unto death, he shall ask (of God), and he shall give him life for them that sin not unto death" (1 John v. 16). 4. Is *inculcated by the example of the best men*—Abraham, Moses, Job (Job xlii. 8, 10), Samuel and all the prophets; above all, by the example of our Lord himself, who has prayed for us all, and through whose intercession we present our prayers and hope for their acceptance.

II. A POSSIBLE OMISSION. Intercessory prayer may *cease* to be offered. It is sometimes omitted from—1. *Want of consideration* of others; the worth of their souls, their lost condition, the love of God to them, the ransom that has been given for them. Attention is so absorbed in other objects that they are uncared for. The more we think of them, the more we shall feel and pray for them. "Love for souls *as* souls is not a passion of earthly growth. It is a holy fire from heaven. But how can we have it; how can it be begotten in our hard hearts? The only true method is to draw near to them, and to look at them—to look on them in the light of reason and revelation, of immortality and of God" (C. Morris). 2. *Deficiency of love* and desire for their salvation. 3. *Unbelief.* 4. *Delay* in the fulfilment of our requests, and apparent denial of them. But remember that sincere prayer is never offered in vain, and "pray without ceasing." God knows best when and how to answer our petitions.

III. A DEPRECATED SIN. "God forbid that I should" (far be it from me to) "sin against the Lord," &c. The sin of its omission is spoken of in direct relation to *him*, and consists in—1. *Disregarding his benevolent designs concerning others.* "The Lord will not forsake his people," &c. (ver. 22). If he loves them and seeks their

welfare, we should do the same.   2. *Disobeying his declared will concerning ourselves.*   He has not only commanded us to intercede for others, but the very position
in which he has placed us is a plain indication of his will.   "Ye who remember
Jehovah, leave yourselves no rest, and give him no rest," &c. (Isa. lxii. 6, 7).
3. *Burying in the earth the greatest talent that he has intrusted to us.*   4. *Grieving
the Holy Spirit,* who is ever inciting those in whom he dwells to "cry unto God day
and night."   "Quench not the Spirit."   Whilst the devout should be urged by these
considerations to "continue instant in prayer," others should remember that it is
possible to place an improper reliance on the intercessions of the good, especially in
expecting to obtain benefit from their prayers whilst they neglect to pray for themselves or walk in "the good and right way."—D.

Ver. 24. (GILGAL.)—*The good and right way.*   "Only fear the Lord," &c.   Samuel
assured the people that (as a priest) he would continue to pray for them, and (as a
prophet) to show them the way of happiness and righteousness (Acts vii. 4).   Of
this way the text may be taken as a further explanation, and gives—
I. ITS DESCRIPTION.   1. *Filial reverence.*   Fear not (be not terrified—vers. 17,
18, 20) ; but fear (with a lowly, affectionate, trustful reverence), implying a knowledge of his character and saving purposes, in so far as he has revealed them to men ;
in our case, of him who is "the Way, the Truth, and the Life."   2. *Practical obedience.*
"And serve him."   Recognise yourselves as servants, his servants, and act accordingly.   "Fear God, and keep his commandments" (the practical expression of the
principle) : "for this is the whole of man" (Eccles. xii. 13).   The two may not be disjoined (Josh. xxiv. 14 ; Ps. ii. 11).   "The life of service is work ; the work of a
Christian is obedience to the law of God" (Hall).   3. *Thorough sincerity and whole-
heartedness.*   "In truth, with all your heart."   Do not suppose that it is sufficient to
render an outward and formal service ; or a partial service, in which the love of
idols may be united with the love of God.   "Serve him only" (ch. vii. 3).   "God
will put up with many things in the human heart ; but there is one thing he will *not*
put up with in it—a second place.   He who offers God a second place offers him
no place ; and he who makes religion his first object makes it his whole object"
(Ruskin).
II. ITS NECESSITY.   "Only."   You *must* walk in it, whatever else you do ; for it is
only by doing so that you can—1. *Avoid walking in the evil and wrong way.*   The
"vision of life" which the great Teacher saw and described contained only two ways,
the broad and the narrow, and there is no other.   2. *Escape the destructive consequences of that way.*   You have already entered on a perilous course, *only* (in order
that you may escape the end to which it naturally conducts), "fear the Lord," &c.
"If ye still do wickedly, ye shall be consumed, both you and your king" (ver. 25).
"The way of transgressors is hard."   "It leadeth to destruction."   3. *Receive, and
continue to receive, the blessings that have been promised.*   "The Lord will not forsake
his people," *only* (in order that you may enjoy his favour), "fear," &c.   "I will pray
for you, and teach you," *only* (in order that you may be really benefited thereby),
"fear," &c. (Jer. vi. 16 ; Isa. i. 19).
III. ITS INCENTIVE.   "For consider how great things he hath done for you."
The motive here is not fear of punishment, nor hope of reward, nor even the sense
of right, but *gratitude* and love.   1. *What benefits ;* so great, so numerous, so long
continued—temporal and spiritual (vers. 6—11).   2. *Toward you,* in comparison with
others (ver. 22).   3. *He hath wrought.*   He, and no other ; freely and graciously.
"Free love is that which has never been deserved, which has never been desired, and
which never can be requited."   "We have known and believed the love that God
hath to us.   God is love" (1 John iv. 17).   But in order that his love may be perceived and its influence felt, in awakening love, we must *consider,* fix attention
upon it, especially as manifested in "his unspeakable gift" (1 John iv. 10).   Our
responsibility in regard to "salvation" depends directly on the power we possess of
directing attention to Divine truth, and considering it with a real and earnest desire
to know it, and live according to it ; and by this means, as ice is melted by the sun-
beams, so the heart is softened, renewed, and sanctified by the Spirit of truth.   "O
that they would consider !"—D.

Ver. 23.—*The good man's weapons.* There was a vein of misgiving evident in the words of Samuel. Perhaps the new king and his triumphant soldiers ascribed it to the timorousness of old age ; but the seer looked further into the future than they, and if he felt bound to warn them of the danger they would incur by rebelling against the commandment of the Lord, he gave them at the same time an assurance that he would do all in his power to preserve them from such wickedness and its inevitable consequences. The man of God could never forget Israel. But what could he do in old age for this intractable people? The reins of government had been taken out of his hands ; and it had never been his duty, now less than ever, to go out to battle. What remained for him to do? Must he not let king and people take their own course—sow as they pleased, and then reap what they sowed? Nay. Samuel would not, under a plea of helplessness, withdraw himself from all care for Israel's future. There remained to him the two greatest weapons for moral effect— prayer and teaching. The one points to God in heaven, the other to men on the earth. Such are a prophet's weapons, and they are mightier than a king's sceptre or a warrior's sword. That the intellectual and the moral are the highest forms of greatness and usefulness is a truth which has established itself throughout all history. The most illustrious and influential of the Hebrew race were the prophets. Moses, Samuel, Elijah, Elisha, Isaiah, Jeremiah, and Ezekiel, none of the kings compare with these, except David and Solomon, and they because they had qualities resembling those of the prophets—the one of them a poet, and the other a sage. In like manner the greatest of the Greeks were not their warriors or rulers, but such as Socrates, Plato, and Aristotle—the men who thought and who taught. That unique and ancient people, the Chinese, regard as by far their most important man the sage Confucius. Their most powerful emperors have been comparatively little men. Our modern nations too have had their characters moulded by their thinkers and teachers far more than by their princes and soldiers ; and a nation's character makes its history as much as its history shapes its character. There is a supreme illustration of this truth. Unspeakably the greatest effect ever produced by one personality on the human race has been exerted by the man Christ Jesus. The widest, deepest, and most beneficial influence has issued from him ; and he began that mighty movement, which has outlasted many governments, and shows no symptom of weakness or decay, by the very instruments or weapons which were named and used by the prophet Samuel, viz., prayer and instruction. Jesus prayed ; Jesus taught. How weak in comparison were the men of the sword—Herod, and Pontius Pilate, and Pilate's imperial master at Rome! Jesus had no worldly title, and used no carnal weapon. If he was a king, it was to bear witness to the truth. The weapons by which he overcame were these—he prayed, and so prevailed with God ; he taught, and so prevailed with men. In the same manner he continues to animate and strengthen the Church. He makes continual intercession in heaven ; and by the abiding of his words and the living guidance of his Spirit he gives continual instruction on earth. In the very beginning of the Church the apostles showed their deep appreciation of this truth, and refused to be drawn aside from that way of highest usefulness which their Master had shown to them. They would concentrate their energies on moral and spiritual work. "We will give ourselves to the word of God and to prayer." Paul was of the same mind in his apostolate. He relied on weapons "not carnal, but mighty through God." He foresaw, and it is evident from the writings of Peter and John that they too in old age foreboded, evil days, as Samuel did in his declining years ; but those apostles knew no better course to recommend to the faithful than that which Samuel followed—to pray always, and to teach sound doctrine. Evil might come, even apostasy might ensue ; but the elect would be proved and purified, and after troubled days the kingdom would ultimately be set up in "the sure mercies of David," and the confusion of the time of Saul would be past for ever. No emphasis is laid on rite or ceremony. Samuel was a priest, and lived in a dispensation of religion which gave great scope for ritual. But we are left to assume that the rites prescribed through Moses were observed at this period. We hear wonderfully little about them. Samuel was intent on teaching that "to obey is better than sacrifice, and to hearken than the fat of rams." How weak and puerile to lay the stress of our religion on the observance of ritual, or the performances of a priesthood! The way to make and keep a people Christian is not to sing masses for them, or multiply altar ceremonies and celebrations, but to pray, and to " teach the good and the right way," of obedience to conscience and to God. Whoso would serve his own generation well, let him pray, and let him by example, and persuasive speech or writing, preach righteousness. These are the good man's weapons, and these through God are mighty. Mischief may go on, as Saul went on to distress the people of God ; but prayer and teaching quietly counteract the mischief, and prepare the way for a revival of piety and the reign of the " King of kings and Lord of lords."—F.

EXPOSITION.

SAUL'S PROBATION AND FAILURE (CHS. XIII.—XV.).

CHAPTER XIII.

WAR AGAINST THE PHILISTINES (ver. 1— ch. xiv. 46). Ver. 1.—Saul's age and length of reign. **Saul reigned one year.** This verse literally translated is, " Saul was one year old when he began to reign, and he reigned two years over Israel." In its form it exactly follows the usual statement prefixed to each king's reign, of his age at his accession, and the years of his kingdom (2 Sam. ii. 10 ; v. 4 ; 1 Kings xiv. 21 ; xxii. 42, &c.). The rendering of the A. V. is too forced and untenable to be worth discussing. As we have seen before, the numerals in the Books of Samuel are not trustworthy ; but the difficulty here is an old one. The Vulgate translates the Hebrew literally, as we have given it ; the Septuagint omits the verse, and the Syriac paraphrases as boldly as the A. V. : " When Saul had reigned one or two years." The Chaldee renders, " Saul was as innocent as a one-year-old child when he began to reign." In the Hexaplar version some anonymous writer has inserted the word *thirty*, rashly enough ; for as Jonathan was old enough to have an important command (ver. 2), and was capable of the acts of a strong man (ch. xiv. 14), his father's age must have been at least thirty-five, and perhaps was even more. As regards the length of Saul's reign, St. Paul makes it forty years (Acts xiii. 21), exactly the same as that of David (1 Kings ii. 11) and of Solomon (*ibid.* xi. 42) ; and Josephus testifies that such was the traditional belief of the Jews ('Antiq.,' vi. 14, 9). On the other hand, it is remarkable that the word here for *years* is that used where the whole number is less than ten. The events, however, recorded in the rest of the book seem to require a longer period than ten years for the duration of Saul's reign ; thirty-two would be a more probable number, and, added to the seven and a half years' reign of Ishbosheth (see 2 Sam. v. 5), they would make up the whole sum of forty years ascribed by St. Paul to Saul's dynasty. It is quite possible, however, that these forty years may even include the fifteen or sixteen years of Samuel's judgeship. But the two facts, that

all the three sons of Saul mentioned in ch. xiv. 49 were old enough to go with him to the battle of Mount Gilboa, where they were slain ; and that Ishbosheth, his successor, was forty years of age when his father died, effectually dispose of the idea that Saul's was a very short reign.

OCCASION OF THE FIRST WAR AGAINST THE PHILISTINES (vers. 2—7). Ver. 2.—**Saul chose him.** Literally, "And Saul chose him," the usual way of commencing the narrative of a king's reign. He probably selected these 3000 men at the end of the war with the Ammonites, to strengthen the small body-guard which he had gathered round him at Gibeah (ch. x. 26). As being always in arms, they would become highly disciplined, and form the nucleus and centre of all future military operations (see on ch. xiv. 52). He stationed these on either side of the defile in the mountain range of Bethel, so exactly described in Isa. x. 28, 29, where Sennacherib, as we read, leaves his carriage, *i. e.* his baggage, at Michmash, and after defiling through the pass, arrives at Geba. Gibeah, where Jonathan was posted with 1000 of these picked warriors, was Saul's home, and his son would have the benefit there of the aid of Kish and Abner, while Michmash was the more exposed place, situate about seven miles north-east of Jerusalem. Conder ('Tent Work,' ii. 110) describes this defile as "a narrow gorge with vertical precipices some 800 feet high—a great crack or fissure in the country, which is peculiar in this respect, that you only become aware of its existence when close to the brink ; for on the north the narrow spur of hills hides it, and on the south a flat plateau extends to the top of the crags. On the south side of this great chasm stands Geba of Benjamin, on a rocky knoll, with caverns beneath the houses, and arable land to the east ; and on the opposite side, considerably lower than Geba, is the little village of Michmash, on a sort of saddle, backed by an open and fertile corn valley." This valley was famous for producing excellent barley. **Every man to his tent**. This with us would be a warlike phrase ; but as the mass of the Israelites then dwelt in tents, it means simply their dispersion homewards ; and so the Syriac translates, "He dismissed them each to his house " (see Ps. lxix. 25).

Ver. 3.—**In Geba.** By this garrison the Philistines commanded the further end of the defile, and they had also another outpost beyond it near Gibeah itself (ch. x. 5). Probably neither of these garrisons was very strong, and Saul may have intended that Jonathan should attack them while he held the northern end of the pass, which would be the first place assailed by the Philistines in force. As regards the word translated *garrison*, attempts have been made to render it *pillar*, and to represent it as a token of Philistine supremacy which Jonathan threw down, while others, with the Septuagint, take it as a proper name ; but the word *smote* is strongly in favour of the rendering of the A. V. **Let the Hebrews hear.** Saul must have intended war when he thus posted himself and Jonathan in such commanding spots, and probably all this had been sketched out by Samuel (see on ch. x. 8). He now summons all Israel to the war. It is strange that he should call the people "Hebrews," the Philistine title of contempt ; but it is used again in ver. 7, and of course in ver. 19. The Septuagint reads, "Let the slaves revolt," but though followed by Josephus, the change of text is not probable.

Ver. 4.—**That Saul had smitten.** Though the achievement was actually Jonathan's, yet it belonged to Saul as the commander-in-chief, and probably had been done under his instructions. **Israel was had in abomination with the Philistines.** They must have viewed with grave displeasure Israel's gathering together to choose a king, and Saul's subsequent defeat of the Ammonites, and retention with him of a large body of men, and so probably they had been for some time making preparations for war. Saul, therefore, knowing that they were collecting their forces, does the same, **and the people were called together after Saul.** Literally, "were cried after him," *i. e.* were summoned by proclamation (comp. Judges vii. 23, 24 ; x. 17, where see margin). For **Gilgal** see ch. vii. 16 ; xi. 14. This place had been selected because, as the valley opens there into the plain of Jordan, it was a fit spot for the assembling of a large host. For its identification see Conder, 'Tent Work,' ii. 7—12.

Ver. 5.—Long before Saul could gather Israel the Philistines had completed their preparations, and invaded the country in overwhelming numbers ; but **thirty thousand chariots** compared with **six thousand horsemen** is out of all proportion. Possibly the final *l* in Israel has been taken by some copyist for a numeral, and as it signifies thirty, it has changed 1000 into 30,000. Or, simpler

still, *shin*, the numeral for 300, has been read with two dots, and so changed into 30,000. **They came up, and pitched in Michmash.** Saul had withdrawn eastward to Gilgal, and the Philistines had thus placed themselves between him and Jonathan. There is a difficulty, however, in the words **eastward from Beth-aven ;** for as this, again, was east of Bethel, it puts the Philistines' camp too much to the east. As it is not, however, the regular phrase for eastward, some commentators render, "in front of Beth-aven." "It means 'the house of naught,' and was the name originally given to the desert east of Bethel, because of its barren character " (Conder, 'Tent Work,' ii. 108). The Philistines, however, had come in such numbers that their camp must have occupied a large extent of ground.

Ver. 6.—**The people were distressed.** Literally, were squeezed, pressed together, were in difficulties. The Philistines had so promptly answered Saul's challenge, that the Israelites, forgetting their victory over Nahash, whose men, however, had probably very inferior arms to those worn by the Philistines, lost courage ; and even the picked band of 2000 men dwindled to 600. As for the mass of the people, they acted with the most abject cowardice, hiding themselves **in caves,** of which there are very many in the limestone ranges of Palestine. David subsequently found safety in them when hunted by Saul. Also **in thickets.** The word as spelt here occurs nowhere else, nor do the versions agree as to its meaning. Most probably it signifies *clefts*, rifts or fissures in the rocks. The next word, **rocks,** certainly means precipitous *cliffs ;* and thickets or thornbushes would scarcely be placed between caverns and cliffs, both of which belong to mountains. **In high places.** This word occurs elsewhere only in Judges ix. 46, 49, where it is rendered *hold*. But this meaning is not supported by the ancient versions, and it more probably signifies a vault or crypt, which better suits the hiding-place next mentioned, **pits,** *i. e.* tanks, artificial reservoirs for water, with which most districts were well supplied in Palestine, even before its conquest by Israel. They were absolutely necessary, as the rains fall only at stated periods, and the chalky soil will not hold water ; when dry they would form fit places for concealment.

Ver. 7.—**Some of the Hebrews.** A contemptuous name for Israel (see ver. 3). If the reading is correct, it must be used here of a cowardly portion of the people (as in ch. xiv. 21), for the insertion of **some of** in the A. V. is unjustifiable. But by a very slight change, simply lengthening the stalk of one letter, we get a very good sense : "And they went over *the fords of* the Jordan **to the land** of Gad and Gilead," *i. e.* to the mountainous district in which the Jordan rises.

SAUL'S RASH SACRIFICE (vers. 8 — 14). Ver. 8.—**Seven days, according to the set time.** See on ch. x. 8. The lapse of time between Samuel's appointment of the seven days during which Saul was to wait for him to inaugurate the war of independence, and the present occasion, was probably not so great as many commentators suppose; for ch. xiii. 1 is, as we have seen, wrongly translated, and everything else leads to the conclusion that the defeat of the Ammonites, the choice of the 3000, and Jonathan's attack on the garrison at Geba followed rapidly upon one another. As the Philistines would rightly regard Israel's choice of a king as an act of rebellion, we cannot suppose them to have been so supine and negligent as not at once to have prepared for war. **Had appointed.** The Hebrew word for this has been omitted by some accident. It is given in the Septuagint and Chaldee and some MSS. The whole importance of the occurrence arose out of its having been appointed by Samuel on his selection of Saul as king.

Ver. 9.—**A burnt offering,** &c. The Hebrew has the definite article, *the burnt offering and the peace offerings,* which were there ready for Samuel to offer. **He offered.** Not with his own hand, but by the hand of the attendant priest, Ahiah, who was, we know, with him. Possibly, nevertheless, the Levitical law was not at this period strictly observed.

Ver. 10. — **That he might salute him.** Literally, "bless him," but the word is often used of a solemn salutation (2 Kings iv. 29). It is evident that Samuel came on the seventh day, and that Saul in his impetuosity could not stay the whole day out.

Ver. 11.—**What hast thou done?** The question implies rebuke, which Saul answers by pleading his danger. Each day's delay made his small force dwindle rapidly away, and the Philistines might at any hour move down from Michmash upon him at Gilgal and destroy him. But it was the reality of the danger which put his faith and obedience to the trial.

Ver. 12.—**I have not made supplication unto Jehovah.** Literally, "I have not stroked the face of Jehovah," but used of making him propitious by prayer (Exod. xxxii. 11; Jer. xxvi. 19). **I forced myself.** Saul pleads in his justification the imminence of the danger, and perhaps there are few who have faith enough to "stand still and see the salvation of Jehovah" (Exod. xiv. 13).

Ver. 13.—**Thou hast done foolishly.** Saul had not only received an express command to wait seven days, but it had been given him under special circumstances, and confirmed by the fulfilment of the appointed

signs. He knew, moreover, how much depended upon his waiting, and that obedience to the prophet's command was an essential condition of his appointment. Nevertheless, in his impatience and distrust of Jehovah, he cannot bide the set time; not really because of any wish to propitiate God, but because of the effect to be produced upon the mind of the people. It was tedious to remain inactive; his position in the plains was untenable; at any moment his retreat to the mountains might be cut off; and so he prefers the part of a prudent general to that of an obedient and trustful servant of God. And we may notice that there is no confession of wrong on his part. His mind rather seems entirely occupied with his duty as a king, without having regard to the higher King, whom it ought to have been his first duty to obey.

Ver. 14.—**Jehovah hath sought him a man after his own heart.** The language of prophecy constantly describes that as already done which is but just determined upon. As David was but twenty-three years of age at Saul's death, he must now have been a mere child, even if he was born, (see ver. 1). But the Divine choice of Saul, which upon his obedience would that day have been confirmed, was now annulled, and the succession transferred elsewhere. Years might elapse before the first earthly step was taken to appoint his successor (ch. xvi. 13); nay, had Saul repented, we gather from ch. xv. 26 that he might have been forgiven: for God's threatenings, like his promises, are conditional. There is no fatalism in the Bible, but a loving discipline for man's recovery. But behind it stands the Divine foreknowledge and omnipotence; and so to the prophetic view Saul's refusal to repent, his repeated disobedience, and the succession of David were all revealed as accomplished facts.

CONTINUANCE OF THE WAR (vers. 15—18). Ver. 15.—**Samuel . . . gat him up from Gilgal to Gibeah of Benjamin.** Samuel would pass by Gibeah on his way to his own home at Ramah; but he seems to have tarried there to encourage the people; and probably he carried instructions from Saul to Jonathan to unite his forces with him, as we next find the father and son there in company. Even if this be not so, yet friendly relations must have continued between Saul and Samuel, as the latter would otherwise certainly not have chosen Saul's home for his halting-place; nor would he go thither without seeing Jonathan, and giving him aid and counsel. **Saul numbered.** See on ch. xi. 8. After summoning the whole nation there did not remain with him even as many as a third of his selected band.

Ver. 16.—**In Gibeah of Benjamin.** This

is an arbitrary change of the A. V. (in company with the Septuagint and Vulgate) for *Geba*, which is the word in the Hebrew text. Our translators no doubt considered that as *Gibeah of Benjamin* occurs in the previous verse, this must be the same place. But our greater knowledge of the geography of the Holy Land enables us to say that Geba is right ; for, as we have seen, it was at one end of the defile, at the other end of which was Michmash ; and here alone could the small army of Saul have any chance of defending itself against the vast host of the Philistines. However much we may blame Saul's disobedience, he was a skilful soldier and a brave man, and his going with his little band to the end of the pass to make a last desperate stand was an act worthy of a king.

Vers. 17, 18 — **The spoilers.** The conduct of the Philistines is that of men over-confident in their strength. They ought to have pounced at once upon Saul in the plain of Jordan, where their cavalry would have secured for them the victory, and then, following Samuel's and Saul's route, have seized the other end of the defile, and overpowered Jonathan. But they despised them both, and regarding the country as conquered, proceed to punish it, as probably they had done on previous occasions, when no one had dared to make resistance. Leaving then the main army to guard the camp at Michmash, they sent out light-armed troops to plunder the whole land. **One company turned unto the way . . . to Ophrah, unto the land of Shual.** This company went northward, towards Ophrah, a place five miles east of Bethel. The land of Shual, *i. e.* fox-land, was probably the same as the land of Shalim in ch. ix. 4. **Another company,** &c. This went eastward, towards Beth - horon, for which see Josh. x. 11. The third went to the south - east, towards the wilderness of Judæa. Zeboim, and all the places mentioned, are in the tribe of Benjamin, which had committed the offence of making for itself a king. To the south Saul held the mountain fastnesses towards Jerusalem.

DESCRIPTION OF ISRAEL'S EXTREME STATE OF OPPRESSION (vers. 19—23). Ver. 19.— **There was no smith.** This accounts for the contemptuous disregard of Saul by the Philistines. The people were disarmed, and resistance impossible. Apparently this policy had been long followed ; but we need fuller information of what had happened between Samuel's victory at Mizpah and Saul's appointment as king, to enable us to understand the evident weakness of Israel at this time. But probably this description applies fully only to the districts of Benjamin, near the Philistines. The people further away had arms with which they defeated the Ammonites,

and Saul and his men would have secured all the weapons which the enemy then threw away. But evidently no manufacture of weapons was allowed, and no one as far as possible permitted either to wear or possess arms.

Ver. 20.—**The Israelites went down to the Philistines.** *I. e.* to their land. This could only have applied to the districts near the Philistines, unless we suppose that they set up forges also at their garrisons. **To sharpen.** The verb chiefly refers to such work as required an anvil and hammer. As regards the implements, not only do the versions disagree in their renderings, but the Septuagint has a very curious different reading, to the effect that at harvest-time the Israelites had to pay the Philistines three shekels for repairing and whetting their tools. The **share** is more probably a *sickle*. The **coulter** is certainly a *ploughshare*, as rendered in Isa. ii. 4 ; Joel iii. 10. Of the **ax** there is no doubt ; and the **mattock** is a heavy hoe for turning up the ground, as spades for that purpose are scarcely anywhere used, except in our own country.

Ver. 21. — **A file.** Margin, *a file with mouths.* The word only occurs here, and is translated a file on the authority of Rashi. Almost all modern commentators agree that it means *bluntness*, and that this verse should be joined on to the preceding, and the two be translated, " But all the Israelites went down to the Philistines to sharpen his sickle, and his ploughshare, and his axe, and his mattock, whenever the edges of the mattocks, and the ploughshares, and the forks, and the axes were blunt, and also to set (so the margin rightly) the goads." The Israelites were thus in a state of complete dependence upon the Philistines, even for carrying on their agriculture, and probably retained only the hill country, while their enemies were masters of the plains.

Ver. 22.—**There was neither sword,** &c. Armed only with clubs and their farming implements, it is no wonder that the people were afraid of fighting the Philistines, who, as we gather from the description of Goliath's armour, were clad in mail ; nor is it surprising that they despised and neglected Saul and his few men, whom probably they regarded as an unarmed mob of rustics. The Ammonites probably were far less efficiently armed than the Philistines, who, as commanding the sea-coast, could import weapons from Greece.

Ver. 23.—**And the garrison,** &c. When the Philistines heard that Saul with his six hundred men had joined the small force already at Geba with Jonathan, they sent a body of men to occupy an eminence higher up in the defile which lay between Geba and Michmash (see on ch. xiii. 2). The purpose of this was to keep the route open, that so, when they pleased, they might send a larger body of troops up the defile in order to attack Saul. It would also keep a watch upon his movements, though they could have had no expectation that he would venture to attack them. It was this garrison which Jonathan so bravely attacked, and by his success prepared the way for the utter defeat of the enemy.

HOMILETICS.

Vers. 1—7.—*The great antagonism.* The facts are—1. Saul, entering on the military organisation of his kingdom, forms a select force under the command of himself and Jonathan. 2. The defeat of the Philistine garrison by Jonathan is announced to all Israel. 3. This first success arouses the hostility of the Philistines, who threaten Israel with overwhelming numbers. 4. The effect of this display of force is to dishearten the followers of Saul who waited at Gilgal. The presence of the Philistines within the borders of Israel was inconsistent with the privileges originally granted, and was a perpetual source of danger and annoyance. One of the ends contemplated in seeking a king was to clear the promised land of foes. The normal state of the people of God was only realised when the land was the exclusive home of the descendants of Abraham. The reformation, in slow yet steady progress, created the ambition and effort to cast out the enemy. Saul's movements, therefore, were a correct expression of national feeling, and in harmony with the high purpose of Israel's existence. In this attempt to subdue the great enemy of the kingdom we have an historic representation of the great conflict which is ever being waged between the spiritual kingdom and the evils which largely hold possession of the world; and in the varying experience of Israel we see shadows of truths that find expression in Christian times.

I. The EXISTENCE OF THE KINGDOM OF CHRIST INVOLVES A CONFLICT WITH A WATCHFUL, POWERFUL FOE FOR THE POSSESSION OF THE EARTH. The separate existence of Israel, combined with the promise made to Abraham (Gen. xv. 7), and the spiritual purpose to be wrought out for the glory of God, rendered war with the Philistines at this time inevitable. The existence of Christ's kingdom in the actual separation to himself of those who form his Church, combined with his right to be King of every land and heart, and the prediction that he shall have the uttermost parts of the earth for his possession, involves ceaseless strife with men, spirits, customs, laws, principles, purposes, and all else, visible and invisible, that is incompatible with his full and blessed sway. Light is not more opposed to darkness, life to death, purity to corruption, than Christ and his holy rule are opposed to much that now governs human society.

II. The EARLY EFFORTS OF THE FAITHFUL ARE ENSAMPLES FOR FUTURE CONDUCT, AND THE TRIUMPHS WON ARE AN EARNEST OF WHAT MAY BE ON A LARGER SCALE. The early efforts of Saul and his followers were characterised by faith in their mission as people of God, loyalty to the Divine cause they represented, courage and self-denial for the good of the land, unity of aim and concentration of strength. They had a right to believe in success, because the promised land was for Israel, and not for the idolatrous Philistine. The victory at Geba was a pledge of coming events. The war against sin has been carried on ever since the first promise cheered the heart of our fallen ancestor. But we may regard the exertions of the early Christian Church as the first organised effort, under the laws of the kingdom of Christ, for the extirpation of all sin and evil. The early Christians were fine examples of clear and deep conviction that they were the servants of Christ, and had a Divine mission to work out in an antagonistic world. And the splendid triumphs won, though, compared with the area of sin, as small as was the capture of Geba relatively to the whole possessions of the Philistines, are an indication of what awaits the Church if only, laying aside internal strifes, worldly policies, self-indulgence, she will but brace her energies to the perfecting of the conquests already made. Novelties we need not; the old weapons, the old spirit, the old consecration, the old singleness of aim, will pull down strongholds still.

III. The ANTAGONISM MAY GROW IN INTENSITY AS A CONSEQUENCE OF SUCCESS. Up to a given point success in war arouses more thoroughly the energies of the defeated. The acquisition of Geba made Israel more than ever detestable to the Philistines, and developed their resources. The same effect was produced by the triumphs of Pentecost (Acts iv.). Subsequently rulers took counsel, being afraid "whereunto this would grow" (Acts v. 24), unless more severe measures were taken to suppress it. It was the necessarily aggressive spirit of Christianity, combined with its growing influence, that aroused the fierce, persecuting spirit of ancient Rome. The more a pure Christianity is urged on men, the more do evil passions arise in resistance. It is probable that there are seasons when the "principalities and powers" of the unseen world combine in all fierceness to arouse human antagonism to the gospel. The bitter hostility and outspoken defiance of the present day are in instructive coexistence with Christian efforts and triumphs surpassing in range any recorded in history.

IV. HOPE OF FINAL VICTORY DEPENDS MORE ON OUR FAITH IN GOD THAN ON THE WEAKNESS OF THE FOE. The followers of Saul became disheartened when they heard of the tremendous efforts of the Philistines. As Peter on the sea looked away from Christ at the waves, and began to sink, so these men lost hope when, forgetting the "mighty God of Jacob," they fixed attention on the forces of the enemy. It was not a question of few or many Philistines, but of faith in their God. The *faint-heartedness of Israel finds its counterpart in modern times.* The vast area over which evil reigns, the desperate vices that enchain thousands, the extent to which society is impregnated with principles alien to the gospel, the utter absorption of millions in matters purely material, the fierce assaults made on the supernatural character of Christianity, and the growing positiveness and intellectual licence of many who fight under the stolen banner of "science"—these signs of power are brooded over, and the heart sinks for fear. This *faint-heartedness is as irrational as it is sinful.* Is Christ a living Saviour? Is he *the Lord of all?* It is a simple question of *fact.* If *not,* then our Christianity is a delusion; we are without hope in the world, and life is an insoluble, awful, heart piercing enigma. But *if he is,* then *who* are men, or *what* are their resources? They are but creatures of a day, and their strength perishes. He *must* reign. On his own head his crown shall flourish.

General lessons:—1. Every Christian should inquire how far he, in loyalty to Christ and full conviction of his triumph, is doing his part in the common work of the Church. 2. It is a matter of inquiry how far we may be impeding the progress of Christianity by compromising with the world in hope of lessening antagonism. 3. It should guide our conduct to remember that the severest holiness of life, blended with the tenderest love, has ever accomplished the most enduring spiritual work. 4. It will tend to nourish faith in the sufficiency of God if we, by thought and prayerfulness, habituate ourselves to actual fellowship with him.

Vers. 8—16.—*Representative temptations.* The facts are—1. Saul, waiting at Gilgal for Samuel, gives orders for the observance of sacrificial worship. 2. Towards the close of the ceremony, and before the full time was expired, Samuel makes his appearance. 3. In reply to Samuel's remonstrance, Saul assigns the reasons for his conduct—the discouragement of the people, the non-arrival of Samuel, and the threatening attitude of the foe. 4. Samuel charges Saul with having failed to keep the commandment of God, and declares that his family shall not succeed to the throne. 5. Samuel retires to Gibeah, whither Saul and his son also go with their followers. Whether the appointment to meet at Gilgal was that mentioned in ch. x. 8, or a subsequent arrangement, does not affect the fact that, in view of measures to be taken conjointly, Saul had been distinctly *commanded by God,* through the prophet, to wait seven days till Samuel came. Evidently it was a distinct understanding that in the coming effort to rid the land of the Philistines the *spiritual power,* represented by the prophet of God, was to be prominent. Thus would the "manner of the kingdom" (ch. x. 25) be recognised, and Israel's ruler, though a king, would still be the agent for working out a spiritual destiny. It was of immense importance that, having a king like unto other nations, Israel and the monarch should still be made to feel that, not the form of government, but the blessing of God granted in answer to prayer, and on due recognition of the spiritual institutions, was the most important thing. And the command to wait for the *spiritual* guide and ruler was eminently fitted to impress Saul and the people with the undiminished authority and value of the spiritual head. There is no evidence that the *end* of the seven days had come, only that it was nigh. Even had it come, the Author of the command was responsible for consequences, not Saul. The first duty of a subject is to obey law. Saul had no right to break the commandment of his King. The assumption of the control of spiritual functions violated a great principle in the eyes of the people. It would mean, the prophet of God can be dispensed with; the king can invent ways other than God's of meeting pressing dangers; rigid obedience to God's command is not expedient at all times; the religious arrangements in the recent settlement of the kingdom, impeding as they do the military movements, are defective; all must, by pressure of events, come into the monarch's hands. Thus the very essence of the constitution, as approved by God and explained in act and word by Samuel (ch. ix. 26, 27; x. 1, 8, 25; xii. 13, 14), was set aside.

I. LIFE INEVITABLY BRINGS WITH IT TEMPTATIONS TO SACRIFICE CLEAR DUTY TO SINFUL EXPEDIENCY. The difficulties surrounding Saul seemed to rise from the natural course of events. The defection of many of his followers was as readily accounted for, by the overwhelming force of the enemy and the inactivity enforced by the absence of Samuel, as it was, from a heathen point of view, pregnant with disaster. The military power of the nation, in being thus subject to spiritual arrangements, was less an arm of strength than a monarch might desire. The first operation of the subordination of man's skill and force to the religious element of the national life was by no means promising. Was it not expedient to act without the spiritual authority as at present constituted? Now this temptation was no "strange thing." It was just an early and sharply-defined form of what Saul would be liable to all his days; for events and his own imperfect nature would constantly conspire to raise the question as to whether he would not better hold his own in war if he were not troubled by *non*-military considerations. The spiritual character of the kingdom would continually test his loyalty to God. His case was not singular. 1. *Moral life on earth involves trial*. Created moral existence is not possible apart from liability to the rival claims of duty to God and regard for self, in some form supposed to be more or less expedient. Temptation grows out of the conditions under which we live. 2. *Every special course of life is attended with temptations peculiar to its nature*. Saul as king would feel the pressure of what, as a man living in obscurity, he would not have known. Israel chosen of God to traverse the desert and attain to freedom and rest in Canaan were open to trials of faith which, as bondmen in Egypt, would not have come to them. Our Saviour himself endured temptations in virtue of his *unique* position as Founder of a spiritual kingdom.

II. IT IS A MERCIFUL PROVIDENCE WHEN REPRESENTATIVE TEMPTATIONS COMING EARLY IN LIFE'S CAREER ARE UNDER CIRCUMSTANCES MOST FAVOURABLE TO RESISTANCE. The circumstances of a temptation tell wonderfully in the act of resisting. Should it find the mind predisposed by dallying with evil, or should it come in the absence of clear and recent indications of duty, with a sudden impulse, or insinuating itself into intricate considerations and engagements, the chances of its success would be increased as compared with opposite conditions. This temptation to sin came on Saul when he was free from the entanglements of a court and domestic politics; it was in sharp contrast *with a most explicit command;* it was counter to the recent instance of God's help in presence of a great danger (ch. xi. 4—14); and it came when his moral sense was at its best. Inasmuch as during coming years Saul would inevitably feel the force of temptations to assert his own methods and will as being apparently better than those indicated by the spiritual requirements of the kingdom, it *was really a mercy that this representative temptation came when it did, and in a form most easy to resist*. If resisted, a principle would assume an incipient form of habit. The moral strength of the man would be developed by exercise. Success over the foe, consequent on the first triumph *of faith in God and submission to his spiritual order*, would be a memorial for future inspiration. We *have here a clue to the solution of other trials*. It is too often imagined that the trial of Adam, of the Israelites at the Red Sea, of Christ in the desert, and of the apostles during the dark days of the crucifixion and death, were arbitrary, severe, and, at least, without a clear trace of kindness. But consider—1. *Life in each case was liable to many temptations.* It was inseparable from Adam's existence as a man on earth, from Israel's march to and occupation of Canaan, from our Saviour's position among men and the evil spirits who would act upon his soul, and from the apostolic career in face of Jewish and Gentile antagonism, that temptation again and again, in forms peculiar to each, would arise. So, also, with every man's life. 2. In each case the *conditions for resisting representative temptation of what was coming were most favourable at the entrance on the career.* Man in Eden was pure, free from bad impulse, independent of entangle- ments and want, familiar with the emphatic and recent command. Israel at the Red Sea had just seen marvellous and repeated tokens of the sufficiency of God to shelter them and ward off danger, and the command to go forward to the sea was explicit. Our Saviour when tempted of the devil was fresh from the baptism of the Holy Spirit, as yet not worn down by ingratitude and scorn, filled with the call to enter on his work in founding a *spiritual* kingdom. So, likewise, when a monarch, or pastor, or Church, or any individual first enters on an office or work, there is a freedom from the entanglements which spring from mixed relationships, an *éclat* which inspires hope, a sense of responsibility which makes the spirit sober and watchful, and a fame to win which appeals to the noblest sentiments of duty and honour. 3. *Resistance in each case would impart a moral force which would be of great advantage in all subsequent conflicts.* Had Adam said a final "nay" to the tempter, his moral con- quest over all other temptations would have been comparatively insured. Imperfect as Israel were in the desert, their moral power was greatly strengthened both by the act of faith at the Red Sea and the consequent victory over Pharaoh. As One who had conquered in the desert, our Lord would doubtless confront the later temptations to exchange poverty and want and spiritual rulership for the pomp and outward splen- dour of an earthly kingdom with a more equable spirit. And the endurance of the apostles during those dark and harrowing hours prior to the resurrection would only render their faith a mightier power wherewith to face the persecution of men and the seeming tardiness of the world's subjugation to Christ. So, likewise, those who are brought by Providence to bear temptation under favourable conditions when entering on a career actually receive a great mercy. They are enabled thereby, if they will, *to gain power for life and to qualify for higher service.* This will find illustration also with the young. Their early trials, under good conditions, make them more competent to cope with all that is sure to follow.

III. Sin committed under conditions favourable to the resistance of tempt- ation becomes thereby aggravated in character. *Saul's sin was great.* It was marked by deliberation and yet by extreme folly. He "forced himself." The com- mand was so clear, the risks of disobedience so palpable, that only a perverse ingenuity could persuade him to disobey. The effort to silence the conscience always aggravates a crime. Prompt, unquestioning obedience is due to clear commands. Man is not responsible for anything but duty. *The folly was conspicuous.* To break a clear command in order to offer an act of worship is the perfection of foolishness. Only a "lying spirit" could induce a man to honour God by dishonouring him. The blind reasoning of the heart when once clear duty is trifled with is extraordinary. It would be a wonderful revelation of perverted intellect if we could read the processes of thought by which men are led to force themselves to deliberate acts of sin.

IV. The punishment following on sin includes the loss of that for which the sin was committed. Two consequences ensued on Samuel's exposure of Saul's sin—the forfeiture of his family's permanent possession of the throne of Israel, and the withholding of immediate interposition on behalf of the nation. Now it is obvious that Saul had yielded to the temptation in hope thereby of inspiring his fol- lowers to action, and of insuring the stability of his throne for himself and family in the subjugation of his foes. There was an eminent propriety in Saul's sin being visited by a loss of the kingdom to his family. He was the people's king—chosen because they desired a monarch. Therefore it was in harmony with the usual course of Providence that, though he sinned, he should be allowed to rule, and thus by his infirmities be the rod for their chastisement. Although representing in his virtues and failings the people who demanded a king, he was afforded by the recent trial a good opportunity of conforming to the higher spiritual order, and of thus becoming by degrees educated into the loftier spiritual aims of the national life. Therefore, failing to rise to the level essential to the Messianic conception of the kingdom, he proved the moral unfitness of his principles and methods for transmittal to successors. Have we not here *a truth of constant recurrence?* Sin is committed to realise a purpose, and the purpose is not realised, but is missed by the very act of sin. Our first parents sought the rest of satisfaction in taking the forbidden fruit ; but whatever rest they had before was lost in the act of disobedience, as also the kind of rest sought by the deed. The unhappy man who, under pressure of circumstances as trying to him as the hosts of Philistia were to Saul, forces himself to commit a fraud in order to insure relief and final success in his enterprise, learns to his cost, when once the act is committed, that mental relief is further off than ever, and a remorseless course of events ultimately brings on ruin to the enterprise. "He that seeketh his life shall lose it."

General lessons :—1. When pursuing a path of duty, impatience with God's ways should be strictly suppressed, or it will lay us open to the pressure of strong temptations.   2. In the high service of God we may be placed in circumstances of extreme peril, but these should never shake confidence in his all-sufficiency. 3. Sometimes the loftiest path of duty is "to be still," and pray for grace "to enter not into temptation."   4. The Christian is warranted, by the fact of the existence of "the kingdom," as also by the experiences of the past, to believe that above all the forces that threaten the Church there is a Power that sometimes restrains its manifestation for purposes of discipline.   5. It is a profitable study for the Church to consider how far prayer is not effectual in consequence of the constant breach of plain commands.   6. It is the sign of a guilty conscience, and of the hardening effect of even one sin, that plausible reasons are ready at hand to justify conduct.   7. If we prove ourselves unfit for service by our lack of spirituality, Providence will sooner or later remove us for others more spiritual.

Vers. 17—23.—*The ramifications of evil.* The facts are—1. In the absence of Divine interposition, and consequent on Saul's inability to resist advance, the Philistines develop their forces and plunder certain districts of country.   2. As a matter of policy on their part, and as one result of Saul's transgression, the Philistines deprive the people of the ordinary means of conducting warfare.   3. This state of things necessitates Saul's protracted inactivity, and inflicts considerable inconvenience on the people with respect to their daily pursuits in agriculture.   Although we cannot say precisely what course events would have taken had Saul, in loyalty to God, awaited the arrival of Samuel (vers. 8—10), yet the whole history of Israel and the recent promises made through Samuel (ch. xii. 20—25) lead to the belief that, as when Jabesh-Gilead was in danger help came from God (ch. xi. 6), so now the Philistines would have been scattered by a Power more than human. The facts given in this paragraph appear to be designed to prepare the way for the narrative of Jonathan's heroism in the following chapter ; at the same time they illustrate, in themselves, some truths of wider range than Israel's political and social condition. We have here an instance of—

I. THE DEPRESSING INFLUENCE OF A SENSE OF GUILT ON THE CONDUCT OF AFFAIRS. The military inactivity and general helplessness of Saul after Samuel's interview with him (vers. 11—14) are in striking contrast with his energy at other times, and are not altogether to be ascribed to the absence of special Divine interposition. The explanation is to be sought in his personal conviction of sin. There was no joy, no hope, no spring in his soul, no eagerness for a close conflict with the foe ; and that, too, because a sense of sin brought moral paralysis upon his entire nature. The sense of guilt is not always present in men, but *when it is brought home to a man it exercises a depressing influence on his entire life,* and seriously affects the transaction of affairs. Conscience, when guilty, not only "makes cowards of us all," but it robs life of brightness, drains the springs of hope, fetters the operation of the faculties, and impairs the sum total of energy. No man's life is made the most of as long as some unrepented and unforgiven sin haunts his spirit. This is the reverse side of another fact, namely, that the soul possessed of the peace and joy of the reconciled is in a condition to render its best service to the world, and to attain to the most perfect development of its powers. The wisdom of every one oppressed with a sense of guilt is to humble himself before God, and seek in Christ forgiveness and power for a truer life in future.

II. THE MANIFOLD RAMIFICATIONS OF EVIL. The sin of Saul did not begin and end with himself. His failure in duty affected the general interests of his kingdom. Even the brief narrative before us enables us to see how directly and indirectly the following circumstances were connected with his disobedience—namely, the inability of Israel to assail the threatening host; the depredations of the three divisions of the Philistine army; the private and social misery over a considerable area inseparable from the raids of the invader; the cutting off of the ordinary means for waging successful war; the impediments to the pursuits of trade and agriculture; the general humiliation and dread brought on the *non*-combatants of the land; and the withdrawal for a while of the counsels and encouragements of the prophet of God. The truth thus exemplified in the instance of a monarch's sin *finds expression also in every sin, and especially in sins of persons in responsible positions.* No sin can end in the act or in the person of the sinner. It impairs the tone and force of the entire man; it adds another item to the germs of future sorrow and shame; it further disqualifies for conferring on the world spiritual good; it gives a stronger taint of evil to the current of thought and feeling which flows out from the inner man to the world. Sin in us is as a wave of influence that spreads out, by laws of association and impulse, over the whole area of the spirit, and modifies all conduct for the worse. Especially is this true of persons in office and of parents. A monarch's official acts reach all classes. A parent's sin ramifies through the home— inducing, it may be, loss of peace, certainly loss of hallowed influence over children, and possibly ruin to health in offspring.

III. UNFAITHFULNESS IN THE SERVICE OF GOD DEPRIVES US OF A MOST IMPORTANT MEANS OF ACCOMPLISHING OUR MISSION AS CHRISTIANS IN THE WORLD. The scarcity of smiths and weapons of war is evidently associated by the historian with the disobedience of Saul. · It is possible for Christian men engaged in the endeavour to maintain and extend the kingdom of Christ to be brought into an analogous condition as a consequence of their manifest unfaithfulness. In our conflict with the world it is of supreme importance that we make use of the ever available and potent instrument—*influence of character*. With this as a weapon we can accomplish much, by the blessing of God. If this be lost, if by our manifest inconsistencies before the world we virtually place this instrument of war at the feet of the men whom we seek to bring to Christ, then we shall be as powerless with them as was Saul and his people when the Philistines had control of their smiths and weapons of war.

General lessons:—1. The general spiritual power of our life will be in proportion as we keep pure, or, in case of falling into sin, at once humble ourselves before God and seek for pardon and a right spirit (Ps. li. 6—13). 2. It is an encouragement to holiness and obedience to know that the ramifications of righteousness may become as wide as are those of sin. 3. It is a mercy to know that, though the enemy may sometimes triumph over the servants of Christ because of their weakness of character, yet the eternal Source of strength is in reserve, and will manifest himself.

HOMILIES BY VARIOUS AUTHORS.

Vers. 1—7. (MICHMASH, GIBEAH, GEBA, GILGAL.)—*The trumpet sounded.* "And Saul blew the trumpet throughout all the land, saying, Let the Hebrews hear." 1. The great conflict between good and evil which has been waged from the first (Gen. iii. 15) has been concentrated in every age on some particular issue. At this time it was whether Israel and the worship of the true God or the Philistines and the worship of idols should prevail. It was thus of the highest importance in relation to the kingdom of God upon earth. 2. The Philistines were old enemies and powerful oppressors (Judges iii. 3; x. 7; xiii. 1; 1 Sam. vii. 2). During the administration of Samuel they were held in check (ch. vii. 13), although they appear to have had military posts or garrisons in the land (ch. x. 5; ver. 3), and the overthrow of one of these by Jonathan (at Geba, four miles north of Gibeah, and opposite Michmash) gave the signal for renewed conflict. Having evacuated Michmash, where he had stationed himself with an army of 2000, Saul summoned all the men of Israel to gather to him at Gilgal; but the advancing hosts of the enemy filled the country with terror, so that he was left with only 600 followers, and found it necessary, after his interview with Samuel, to join his son Jonathan at Gibeah (Geba) (vers. 2, 16; ch. xiv. 2). Meanwhile the enemy occupied Michmash, whence three companies of spoilers issued, plundering the plains and valleys. A second and greater exploit of Jonathan, however, drove them out of Michmash, and it was followed by a general engagement, in which large numbers of them were slain, and the rest "went to their own place" (ch. xiv. 23, 31, 46). 3. The conflict to which Israel was summoned represents that to which Christians are called. It is a conflict with physical and moral evil, with the world, the flesh, and the devil (John xv. 19; 2 Cor. x. 4; Ephes. vi. 12; 1 Pet. ii. 11; 2 Pet. v. 8; 1 John ii. 16), and with men only in so far as they are ruled by sin, and in order to their salvation; a conflict which is good ("the good fight of faith"—1 Tim. vi. 12) and necessary, and affords full scope for whatever warlike instincts and energies are possessed. What does the sound of the trumpet signify? (1 Cor. xiv. 8).

I. A BLOW HAS BEEN STRUCK AGAINST THE FOE. The greatest blow that was ever inflicted upon the "power of darkness" was struck by "the Captain of our salvation" in his life and death and glorious resurrection (John xii. 31; xvi. 33; 1 John iii. 8); and in the spirit and power of his victory his followers carry on the conflict (Matt. x. 34). At times there seems to be something like a truce, but it never lasts long; and when a fresh blow is struck by "a good soldier of Jesus Christ" it—1. *Reveals* the essential difference between the spirit that is in "the Israel of God" and "the spirit that is in the world." 2. *Intensifies* their antagonism (ver. 4). 3. *Commits* them to more definite and decisive action. And to this end the fact should be proclaimed. "When Saul the king of the Hebrews was informed of this (ver. 3), he went down to the city of Gilgal, and made proclamation of it over all the country, summoning them to freedom" (Josephus).

II. THE ENEMY IS MUSTERING HIS FORCES (ver. 5), which are—1. Exceedingly *numerous*, "as the sand which is on the sea-shore." 2. *Skilful*, crafty, and deceitful (2 Cor. xi. 14). 3. Very *powerful*. There is at the present day an extraordinary combination of anti-christian agencies (2 Tim. iii. 1—9; Rev. xiii. 11—18), threatening Christian faith and practice, which might well fill us with fear, did we not believe that "they that be with us are more than they that be with them" (2 Kings vi. 16). "The spirits of the unseen world seem to be approaching us. Times of trouble there have been before; but such a time, in which everything, everywhere, tends in one direction to one mighty struggle of one sort—of faith with infidelity, lawlessness with rule, Christ with antichrist—there seems never to have been till now" (Pusey).

III. THE FAITHFUL MUST RALLY AROUND THEIR LEADER. The gathering forces of the enemy should constrain us to closer union, and the proper centre of union is he of whom the greatest kings and heroes were feeble types and shadows. 1. He has been Divinely *appointed*, and claims our obedience and co-operation. 2. He is fully *qualified* as "a Leader and Commander of the people." 3. He is the only *hope* of safety and success. "God is with him" (ch. x. 7).

> "With force of arms we nothing can,
> Full soon were we down-ridden,
> But for us fights the proper man,
> Whom God himself hath bidden.
> Ask ye, Who is this same?
> Christ Jesus is his name;
> The Lord Sabaoth's Son;
> He, and no other one,
> Shall conquer in the battle" (Luther).

IV. THE SUCCESS ALREADY ACHIEVED GIVES ASSURANCE OF VICTORY (ch. xi. 11; ver. 3). 1. What triumphs has he gained in former days! 2. They are an earnest of "still greater things than these." 3. And they should inspire us with the confidence and courage which are needful to participation in his victory and glory (Rev. xvii. 14; xix. 11). "This is the victory that overcometh the world, even our faith."—D.

Vers. 8—15. (GILGAL.)—*The first wrong step.* All men are subjected in life to various tests which prove "what spirit they are of." These tests may appear insignificant in themselves (like that which was applied to Adam and Eve—Gen. ii. 17), but they involve important principles, and the manner in which they are endured is followed by serious consequences. The position of Saul necessitated a trial of his fidelity to the fundamental principle of the theocratic kingdom, viz., unconditional obedience on the part of the king to the will of God as declared by his prophets. He was directed (1) to wait for Samuel seven days, and (2) to attempt nothing till he came (ch. x. 8). He omitted the former and did the latter, and thus took his *first wrong step*—a step never retraced, and leading to a course which ended on the fatal field of Gilboa. Observe—

I. ITS APPARENT EXPEDIENCY. His conscience told him that it was not right, as he virtually acknowledged in the defence he offered for his conduct (vers. 11, 12). Yet he persuaded himself (as others are accustomed to do) that it was venial, expedient, and even necessary, because of—1. *The pressure of worldly circumstances.* "Because I saw that the people were scattered from me," &c. Resources diminish, and danger is imminent. When they are considered in themselves alone, anxiety and fear increase, and temptation becomes strong to make use of any means of relief that may be presented. How often are men tempted by the plea of necessity to disobey the voice of conscience! The tempter says, "It is better to steal than starve, better to sin than perish." 2. *The disappointment of religious expectations.* "And that thou camest not at the appointed time." "Help has been long waited for, but it comes not; nor is it likely, now that the seventh day is drawing to a close, that it will come at all. The promise has not been fulfilled. The time for action has arrived, and the long delay indicates that the most expedient course must be taken. Nothing else remains. If there be any blame, it cannot be attributed to one who has waited so long, has been left in such extremity, and acts for the best." 3. *The efficacy of ceremonial observances.* "And I forced myself, and offered a burnt offering." Inasmuch as such an offering was required on entering upon his enterprise against the Philistines, he could not hope to succeed without it, and he had at all times great regard for the external ceremonies enjoined by the law (ch. xiv. 33, 35). A doubtful or wrong act is often supposed to be blameless when performed in connection with sacred rites, or with a righteous end in view (John xvi. 2); and disobedience is sometimes clothed in a religious guise, its real nature being thereby obscured to the view of conscience, and its commission rendered easy. 4. *The prospect of immediate advantages.* Apparent and immediate good is the first and last and most powerful incentive to departure from the path of duty. "The tree was good for food, and pleasant to the eyes," &c. (Gen. iii. 6). "And the history of Adam is as ancient as the world, but is fresh in practice, and is still revived in the sons of Adam."

II. ITS REAL CULPABILITY. "What hast thou done?" said Samuel, speaking as with the voice of God, and seeking to arouse his conscience and lead him to repentance. He had been guilty of—1. *Disobedience to a plain commandment.* "Thou hast not kept the commandment of the Lord thy God" (ver. 13). The fact could not be denied. He had not waited *all* the appointed time, and he had acted without Divine direction. He had rejected the supreme authority of the Divine King, and no excuse that might be made could do away with his guilt. "Sin is not estimated by God according to its outward form, but according to the amount and extent of the principle of evil embodied in that form." 2. *Distrust of promised help.* Men sometimes wait long for the fulfilment of Divine promises, but not long enough; and their lack of perseverance shows weakness or absence of faith. The force of adverse circumstances is exaggerated by being exclusively dwelt upon; doubt of the power of God prevails through disregard of preservation from harm hitherto afforded; and as faith unites the soul to God, so unbelief severs it from him, leaves it a prey to disquiet and impatience, and leads it to adopt worldly and godless expedients. Unbelief was the root of the transgression of Saul, as it is of the transgression of men generally. 3. *Formality in religious service.* A burnt offering was a symbol and expression of consecration, and when offered aright, in a spirit of obedience, it honoured God and obtained his blessing ; but when wrongly offered it was worthless, dishonoured him, and was abomination in his sight (ch. xv. 22 ; Prov. xxi. 27 ; Isa. i. 13). It is the same with other outward forms of service. "Saul is a specimen of that class of persons who show a certain reverence and zeal for the *outward forms* of religion, and even a superstitious reliance on them, but are not careful to cherish the *inner spirit* of vital religion" (Wordsworth's 'Com.'). 4. *Self-will, pride, and presumption.* In disobeying the will of God he set up his own will as supreme, and was guilty of pride, "by which sin fell the angels." It is not said that he offered sacrifice with his own hand, and he may have simply directed it to be done by the priest who was with him (ch. xiv. 18) ; nor is it certain that if he had done so he would have gone beyond the privilege and prerogative possessed by other kings. His sin did not consist of intrusion into the priestly office. It was nevertheless very great. "He had cast away his obedience to God. The crown he thought was his own. From that moment he fell ; for all our good qualities retain their ascendancy over our evil passions by the presence and power of God claiming them as his." "Samuel, according to modern expositors of the story, was angry because he felt that he was losing his own influence over the mind of the king. No ; he was angry because the king was so much the slave of his influence, or of any influence that was exerted over him for a moment ; because he was losing the sense of responsibility to One higher than a prophet, to One who had appointed him to rule not in his own name, but as the minister and executor of the Divine righteousness" (Maurice).

III. ITS EXCEEDING FOLLY. "Thou hast done foolishly" (ver. 13). The folly of the sinner appears in his—1. *Being deceived by the appearances of things*—the magnitude of danger, the false promises of advantage, the specious arguments of expediency. He is like the foolish man who built his house upon the sand, instead of "digging deep and laying the foundation on a rock" (Luke vi. 48). He is infatuated, fascinated, and under a glamour cast over his mind by his own evil desires and the spell of the tempter. 2. *Making light of the enormous evil of sin.* It is the only real evil. But he is thoughtless, ignorant, and foolish enough to account it a trivial thing, which may be easily excused and passed by. As he who says in his heart "No God" is called a "fool," so he who deems it a little matter to offend him is appropriately designated by the same name. "Fools make a mock at sin" (Prov. xiv. 9) ; and he who makes light of sin makes light of God. 3. *Leaving the only path of safety and honour.* "For now" (if thou hadst obeyed his commandment) "the Lord would have established thy sovereignty over Israel for ever." 4. *Entering on a course of certain loss and misery.* (1) *Inward*—weakened moral power, increased tendency to sin, unsteadiness, rashness, &c. What a man does once he is almost certain under similar circumstances to do again. Saul's subsequent course was a continuation and complete development of the same kind of transgression as he now committed. He was already so blinded by sin as not to repent. (2) *Outward.* "But now thy sovereignty shall not continue," &c. (ver. 14). The sentence "embodied the principle that no monarchy could be enduring in Israel which did not own the supreme authority of God," and it declared that Saul's crown would not be transmitted to his descendants ; but not until afterwards was he personally rejected from being king (ch. xv. 23). Having failed to endure the trial to which he was subjected, he was left by Samuel (ver. 15), and nothing is further recorded of his intercourse with the prophet for some years. "He had not even accomplished the object of his unseasonable sacrifice, viz., to prevent the dispersion of the people" (Keil). O that he had waited a little longer ! "Saul lost his kingdom for want of two or three hours' patience."

1. Beware of the first wrong step. "It is always marked by a peculiarity of evil which does not attach to any subsequent offences" (Miller). *Principiis obsta.* 2. If you have taken such a step, instantly repent of it. "It is not sinning that ruins men, but sinning and not repenting, falling and not getting up again."—D.

Ver. 14. (GILGAL.)—*A man after God's own heart.* This expression occurs only here and in the quotation (Acts xiii. 22), " I have found David the son of Jesse (Ps. lxxxix. 20), a man after mine own heart, which shall fulfil all my will." 1. It was uttered by Samuel on the occasion of his *reproving Saul* for not obeying the commandment of the Lord (ver. 13). 2. It formed a part of the announcement of the *purpose of God* to appoint another man to be " captain over his people " in consequence thereof. The time of its fulfilment was not defined, nor was it known to the prophet who he should be; it is uncertain even whether David was yet born. 3. It was descriptive of *his character in contrast to that of Saul,* and it had respect to him in his public official capacity as theocratic sovereign rather than in his private moral life, although it is impossible wholly to separate the one from the other. He would obey the commandment of the Lord, and, as it was predicted of " a faithful priest " (ch. ii. 35 ; iii. 10), " do according to that which was in his heart and in his mind ; " he would " serve the will of God in his lifetime " (Acts xiii. 36), and second and carry out his purposes concerning his people (Isa. xliv. 28) ; he would be truly " his servant," and therefore his throne would continue and (in the full realisation of the theocratic idea it represented) be established for ever (Ps. lxxxix. 19—37). In " a man after God's own heart " (such as David was) there is—

I. THE RECOGNITION OF THE WILL OF GOD as supreme. His will is above that of king and people ; declared in manifold ways, it is the rule of human life ; and he who perceives it most clearly and observes it most humbly and constantly approaches nearest to perfection. Saul paid but little regard to it, and, when it was opposed to his own inclination or judgment, set it aside and went his own way. With David it was otherwise. In his royal office especially he embodied the spirit of loyalty to the invisible King of Israel, and of zeal for his law and ordinances. "The vain cavils of infidels appear to have arisen from not considering that the phrase to which they object may be interpreted with equal propriety as referring to the Divine *purpose,* design, or intention as to designate peculiar *favour* and affection. The latter undoubtedly was true, yet the former is most clearly the meaning intended here " (Poole).

II. THE CONVICTION OF THE CALL OF GOD to his service. Unlike Saul, he felt deeply and constantly that he was individually an object of Divine regard, and appointed to do a certain work from which he neither desired nor dared to shrink. And a similar feeling exists in every true servant of God. "The life of David is the life neither of a mere official fulfilling a purpose in which he has no interest, nor of a hero without fear and without reproach ; but of a man inspired by a Divine purpose under the guidance of a Divine teacher " (Maurice).

III. DEVOTION TO THE HONOUR OF GOD from the heart. Although Saul possessed many admirable qualties, he sought to honour God by outward sacrifices rather than real obedience, his noblest deeds were the offspring of sudden and transient impulses, and his predominant motive was his own honour and glory. "He had none of the work of Divine grace upon the heart, turning impulses into principles, ruling all actions by the law of an unseen Judge. He never experienced what the apostle calls the powers of the world to come, that is to say, the sense of God, of another world, smiting upon his soul through the veil of visible things, and making him feel the presence and the real, awful personality of his Maker. His soul was not like David's, a harp touched by the hand of the Almighty, and attuned to celestial melodies. It was only an instrument over which the wind swept wildly, waking a fitful and irregular music which soon died away into the confused murmurs of a harsh and tuneless discord " (A. Blomfield).

IV. DEPENDENCE ON THE HELP OF GOD for success. Saul was proud of his own strength, and both in ruling the people and contending against their enemies he relied on his own skill and prudence, and " an arm of flesh." David trusted in God for everything. " He never represents himself as a compound of strength and weakness. He represents himself as weakness itself — as incapacity utter and complete. The Lord is his strength. He has faith in God as his physical Inspirer or Protector. He has a deeper, a far deeper instinct than even that—the instinct of a communion, personal, practical, loving, between God, the Fount of light and goodness, and his own soul, with its capacity of darkness as well as light, of evil as well as good.   In one word, David is a man of faith and a man of prayer" (Kingsley, 'Four Sermons').

V. REPENTANCE AT THE REPROOF OF GOD on account of sin.   The heart of Saul trembled not at the word of the Lord.   When the prophet said, "What hast thou done?" he offered excuses for his conduct, and when on a subsequent occasion he was constrained to say, "I have sinned," his confession was insincere and hypocritical. How different was it with David when Nathan said to him, "Thou art the man." "Never was repentance more severe, or sorrow more sincere; so that he may justly be said (his repentance included, though not his fall) to be a man after God's own heart" (Yonge).

VI. SYMPATHY WITH THE PEOPLE OF GOD in their experience.   He identified himself with them, made their varied joys and sorrows his own, and thereby (as well as by other means) promoted their highest good.   His character "gathered into itself—so far as might be—all the various workings of the heart of man.   This is the special attribute of the life and character of the son of Jesse.   There is a hard, narrow separateness of soul marked in every line of the character of Saul.   He is a wayward, wilful, self-determined man, well-nigh incapable of any real sympathy with others.   Such an one could learn little of the workings of the human heart, which is so immeasurable in the multitude and compassion of its tones.   Deep as were his sorrows, he never knew the grace of contrition.   Thus his dark heart is full of sullenness and suspicion, inviting the entrance of the evil one, who came at his bidding, and closed with yet sterner bars all the avenues of his soul.   In every one of these particulars David is the most complete contrast to Saul" (Wilberforce, 'Heroes of Heb. Hist.').

VII. SINCERITY IN HIS WHOLE RELATION TO GOD and in the main course of his life. "What are faults—what are the outward details of life, if the inner spirit of it, the remorse, temptations, true, often-baffled, never-ended struggle of it be forgotten? . . . David's life and history, as written for us in those Psalms of his, I consider to be the truest emblem ever given of a man's moral progress and warfare here below. All earnest souls will ever discern in it the faithful struggle of an earnest human soul towards what is good and best; struggle often baffled, down as into entire wreck, yet a struggle never ended; ever with tears, repentance, true, unconquerable purpose begun anew" (Carlyle, 'Heroes').—D.

Vers. 16—23. (MICHMASH.)—*Under the heel of the oppressor.*   "Now there was no smith found throughout all the land of Israel" (ver. 19).   The invasion of the Philistines produced great fear and distress among the people.   Many hid themselves in caves, and thickets, and cliffs, and vaults, and pits; others fled across the Jordan; those who followed Saul did so with trembling (vers. 6, 7); his army melted away— some deserted to the enemy, or were pressed into their service (ch. xiv. 21); their homes and fields were plundered by marauding bands (ver. 17; ch. xiv. 22), which went forth from Michmash without fear of resistance, for the people had been disarmed and deprived of the means of making weapons of war, and even of sharpening their implements of husbandry (2 Kings xxiv. 14) when they became *blunt* (literally, "there was bluntness of edges;" A. V., "they had a *file*"), except at the pleasure of their oppressors (ver. 21).   "The result of the burdensome necessity of going to the Philistines was, that many tools became useless by dulness, so that even this poorer sort of arms did the Israelites not much service at the breaking out of the war" (Bunsen).   How long this state of things continued is not recorded; but it was sufficiently long for those who remained with Saul and Jonathan (ver. 22) to be left without "sword or spear," or any regular armament.   Their condition was thus one of helplessness, dependence, and wretchedness, and affords a picture of that to which men are reduced by error and sin.   In it we see—

I. THE MANIFEST FAILURE of a self-chosen way.   "Nay; but we will have a king over us" (ch. viii. 19).   They have a king self-willed like themselves; but their way fails, as the way of those who prefer their own plans to the guidance of God must ever fail.   1. In delivering them from the evils of which they complain (ch. viii. 5), or which they fear (ch. ix. 16).   2. In preserving to them the advantages which they possess.   "Ye dwelled safe" (ch. xii. 11).   Where is their safety now?

3. In procuring for them the good which they desire—liberty, power, victory, prosperity, honour, and glory (John xi. 47, 48; Rom. x. 2, 3). How completely do the prospects that lure men onward in their self-chosen way vanish before them as they advance!

II. THE MISERABLE SUBJECTION of those who forsake God. "They have rejected me" (ch. viii. 7). With what result? They are "delivered unto the will of them that hate them" (Ezek. xvi. 27; Deut. xxviii. 48), and endure—1. Oppression that cannot be effectually resisted. "Of whom a man is overcome, of the same is he brought in bondage" (2 Pet. ii. 19), and without the means of freeing himself. 2. Increased difficulty, toil, and trouble in the necessary pursuits of life. Life itself without the friendship of God is a burden too heavy to be borne. 3. Shame and contempt continually (ver. 4). "Is this the grandeur and power which they fondly expected under their king? Was it for this they rejected the Shield of their help and the Sword of their excellency?"

III. THE MERCIFUL PURPOSE to which trial is subservient. "The Lord will not forsake his people" (ch. xii. 22). Their distress has some alleviation, and it is designed (in his abounding goodness)—1. To convince them of the evil of their way. 2. To teach them to put their trust in God, and serve him in truth (ch. xiv. 6). 3. To prepare them for help and salvation.

Learn that 1. The highest wisdom of man is to submit to the wisdom of God. 2. The service of God is the only true freedom; the way of honour and happiness. "To serve God is to reign." 3. They who refuse the free service of God fall into the forced service of their enemies. 4. In the greatest of earthly calamities there is no room for despair. "If from thence thou shalt seek the Lord thy God, thou shalt find him" (Deut. iv. 29).—D.

Ver. 13.—*Tried and found wanting.* I. THE STORY. Saul's bright morning was a very short one, and his sky soon gathered blackness. Beginning with popular acclamation, succeeded after the exploit in Gilead by popular enthusiasm, he lost in a very short time the respect of his subjects. Beginning with a Divine sanction signified through the prophet Samuel, and with appearances of religious fervour, he quickly forfeited the favour of the Lord and the good opinion of the prophet. The ship of his fortunes had hardly left the harbour, with sails set and flags flying, before it ran aground on a rock of wilfulness, and though it kept afloat for years, it ever afterwards laboured uneasily in a troubled sea. The critical question for Saul was whether or not he would be content to act simply as executant of the Divine will. Samuel had pressed this upon him again and again. Would he wait on God, and act for him; or would he act for and from himself? Would he lead the people still to look up to Jehovah as their real King and Lawgiver; or would he imitate the heathen kings, who themselves took the initiative, and then called on their gods to be propitious to them, giving them success in their expeditions and victory in their combats? Would Saul do his own will, expecting the Lord to follow and favour him; or would he set the Lord always before him, follow and obey his voice? It is a great mistake to think that Saul was hardly dealt with on a point of small importance. The principle at stake was great, was fundamental. The test was definite, and was applied in the most public manner before all the army of Israel. The courage which had been roused against the Ammonite invaders of Gilead was now turned against the still more formidable Philistines. The gallant Jonathan struck the first blow, and then his royal father, knowing that the Philistine army could and would be very soon mobilised (as the modern phrase is) and hurled against Israel, summoned his people to arms. But, alas, the greater part of them were afraid to come, and in the threatened districts hid themselves. So the king found himself at Gilgal in a terrible plight, at the head of a small and dispirited force. He must have known that, unless Jehovah came to their help, all was lost. Let it not be said that it was unreasonable to judge and punish a man for anything done by him in such an emergency. Saul had received long notice of this week of patience. On the morning when Samuel anointed him three signs were given him, all of which had been exactly fulfilled. Then he had been told that he would have to tarry seven days at Gilgal for the coming of Samuel to offer sacrifice. But he had forgotten this. The word of the prophet had made no lasting impression on his mind. There was nothing profound about the man. He had no controlling reverence for God, no abiding faith. So he acted from himself, only calling on God to help him in what he was going to do, instead of waiting to know what the Lord would have him to do, and acting as his servant. He bore the strain of anxiety for days, but not till the end of the time appointed. The troops (if one may give such a designation to hastily-collected and ill-armed levies) were faint-hearted, and but loosely attached to the standard of their king. They wondered why the sacrifice was delayed. They feared that God would be displeased, and not fight for them. Then Saul, impulsive and unwise, ordered that the sacrifice should proceed. Rather than wait a few hours more, he violated the direction he had received from the prophet of the Lord, and betrayed once for all an unreliable character and presumptuous heart.

II. THE LESSONS. 1. God rules men on large principles, but proves them by specific tests. His law is great and equitable; the trial of obedience to it is sometimes quite minute. In the garden within the land of Eden man and woman were put under a rule of universal obedience to the voice of the Lord, and they were tested by this specific requirement, to abstain from the fruit of one of the trees in the garden. Lot, his wife, and daughters were rescued by angels from a doomed city, and enjoined to flee to the mountains; "but his wife looked back from behind him, and she became a pillar of salt." Hezekiah, devoutly referring everything to God, had great deliverances, and a prosperous reign; but failing to consult the Lord when a flattering embassy came to him from Babylon, he revealed vain-glory lurking in his heart, and broke down the wall of defence which his previous piety had reared round his throne. Saul was tested more than once, but this one trial at Gilgal was enough to prove his unfitness to rule over God's heritage. The fact is, that one act may show character as clearly and decisively as a score or a hundred could do; not, indeed, an incidental act of inadvertence or error, but a thing done after explicit instruction and warning. He who breaks through the line of obedience at one point, out of self-will, is not to be depended on at any point. He disentitles himself to confidence by one instance of misconduct, not because of its intrinsic importance, but on account of the key which it gives to his inward tone of character. 2. One action, hastily performed, may carry irremediable consequences. Adam ate of the forbidden fruit, and he could never reverse that fatal act. Cain struck down his brother, and was from that day a wanderer and an outlaw on the earth. Esau sold his birthright, and never could recover it. Moses erred once at the rock in Kadesh, and forfeited his entrance into the promised land. The sins of those who are penitent are forgiven; but there are consequences of sinful habits, nay, even of one sinful act, which have no cure or corrective. It is well that this should be kept sternly before the eyes of men; for the moral nature of many is slippery and self-excusing, and they are too ready to count on impunity, or on finding some easy corrective for what they do amiss. The truth is, that one action may spoil a whole life, and, indeed, may hurt not oneself only, but many others also; just as Saul's impatience at Gilgal injured not himself alone, but the nation of Israel during all his unhappy reign. 3. He whom God will exalt must first learn patience. For want of this was Saul rejected from being king. By means of this was David educated for the throne. The son of Jesse was privately anointed by Samuel, as the son of Kish had been. Thereafter he came into public notice by his promptitude and bravery against Goliath, just as Saul had come into public favour by similar qualities against Nahash. So far their paths may be said to have corresponded; but then they quite diverged. Saul, impatient, behaved foolishly, and fell. David, when tried, "behaved himself wisely," made no haste to grasp the sceptre, waited patiently till God should lift him up. So when the time at last came for his elevation, he knew how to reign as God's king on the hill of Zion. How beautiful is this in the Son of David, the meek and lowly One, who, because he patiently observed the will of God, has now a name above every name! Jesus pleased not himself. He always spoke and acted as in behalf and by direction of his Father in heaven. Therefore has God highly exalted him. 4. It is a dangerous thing to ask for, or accept, a vicegerent of God on earth. It betrays unbelief rather than faith, and it entails tyranny and confusion. What a calamity it has been to the Latin Church to have an alleged vicar of Christ on earth! The arrangement quite falls in with the craving for a spiritual ruler who may be seen, and the uneasiness of really unspiritual men under the control of One who is invisible. So there is a Popedom, which began indeed with good intentions and impulses, as did the monarchy of Saul, but has long ago fallen under God's displeasure through arrogance, and brought nothing but confusion and oppression on Christendom. We are a hundred times better without any such vicegerent. Enough in the spiritual sphere that the Lord is King. Our Divine Saviour, now unseen, but in due time to appear in his glory, is the only as well as the blessed Potentate, Head of the Church, Captain of the host, Lord of all.—F.

EXPOSITION.

CHAPTER XIV.

JONATHAN SMITES THE PHILISTINE GARRISON (vers. 1—15). Ver. 1.—**Now it came to pass upon a day.** Literally, "And there was a day, and Jonathan," &c.; or, as we should say, And it happened one day that Jonathan. The phrase means that Jonathan's brave feat took place not many days after the garrison had occupied the cliff, probably only two or three, but without definitely stating how many. **He told not his father.** Not only because Saul would have forbidden so rash an enterprise, but because secrecy was essential to any chance of success : probably too the purpose came upon him as an inspiration from above.

Ver. 2. **Saul tarried in the uttermost part of Gibeah.** I. e. the part nearest Geba. **Under,** not a, but *the* **pomegranate tree,** the well-known tree at Migron. Saul evidently shared to the full in the love of trees common among the Israelites (see ch. xxii. 6). The Hebrew word for pomegranate is Rimmon, but there is no doubt that the tree is here meant, and not the rock Rimmon (Judges xx. 45, 47), so called probably from a fancied resemblance to the fruit. **Migron,** said to mean a *cliff*, was apparently a common name for localities in this mountainous district, as in Isa. x. 28 we read of one lying to the north of Michmash, whereas this is to the south.

Ver. 3.—**Ahiah, the son of Ahitub.** (See on ch. xiii. 9.) It is interesting to find the house of Eli recovering at last from its disaster, and one of its members duly ministering in his office before the king. It has been debated whether he was the same person as Ahimelech, mentioned in ch. xxi. 1, &c., the supposition being grounded on the fact that Ahiah is never spoken of again. But he may have died ; and with regard to the argument drawn from the similarity of the names, we must notice that names compounded with *Ah* (or *Ach*), brother, were common in Eli's family, while compounds with *Ab*, father, were most in use among Saul's relatives. Ahiah or Ahijah means *Jah is brother;* his father is Ahitub, *the brother is*

good; why should he not call another son Ahimelech, *the brother is king?* **Jehovah's priest in Shiloh.** This refers to Eli, the regular rule in Hebrew being that all such statements belong, not to the son, but to the father. **Wearing an ephod.** Literally, ephod-bearing. The ephod, as we have seen on ch. ii. 18, was the usual ministerial garment ; but what is meant here is not an ordinary ephod of linen, but that described in Levit. viii. 7, 8, wherein was the breastplate, by which Jehovah's will was made known to his people, until prophecy took its place. All this, the former part of the verse, must be regarded as a parenthesis.

Ver. 4.—**Between the passages.** *I. e.* the passes. **A sharp rock.** Literally, "a tooth of rock." Conder ('Tent Work,' ii. 112) says, "The site of the Philistine camp at Michmash, which Jonathan and his armourbearer attacked, is very minutely described by Josephus. It was, he says, a precipice with three tops, ending in a long, sharp tongue, and protected by surrounding cliffs. Exactly such a natural fortress exists immediately east of the village of Michmash, and is still called 'the fort' by the peasantry. It is a ridge rising in three rounded knolls above a perpendicular crag, ending in a narrow tongue to the east, with cliffs below, and having an open valley behind it, and a saddle towards the west, on which Michmash itself is situate. Opposite this fortress, on the south, there is a crag of equal height, and seemingly impassable. Thus the description of the Old Testament is fully borne out—'a sharp rock on one side, and a sharp rock on the other.' The southern cliff was called **Seneh,** or 'the acacia,' and the same name still applies to the modern valley, due to the acacia-trees which dot its course. The northern cliff was called **Bozez,** or 'shining,' and the true explanation of the name only presents itself on the spot." Conder then describes how, "treading perhaps almost in the steps of Jonathan," after arriving on the brink of the chasm, or defile of Michmash, they were able to descend Seneh, even with horses and mules. "I noticed," he says, "that the dip of the strata down eastward gave hopes that by one of the long ledges we might be able to slide, as it were, towards the bottom. It is not likely that horses had ever before been led along this ledge, or will perhaps ever again cross the pathless chasm, but it was just possible, and by jumping them down one or two steps some three feet high, we succeeded in making the passage. . . . Though we got down Seneh, we did not attempt to climb up Bozez. . . . Horses could scarcely find a footing anywhere on the sides of the northern precipice ; but judging from the descent, it seems possible that Jonathan, with immense labour, could have ‘ climbed up upon his hands and upon his feet, and his armour-bearer after him’ (ver. 13). That a man exhausted by such an effort could have fought successfully on arriving at the top can only be accounted for on the supposition of a sudden panic among the Philistines, when they found the enemy actually within their apparently impregnable fortress.”

Ver. 5.—**Was situate,** &c. The word thus translated is that rendered *pillar* in ch. ii. 8, and the verse should possibly be translated, “And the one tooth (or crag) was a rocky mass on the north over against Michmash, and the other was on the south over against Geba” (not *Gibeah*, as the A. V. ; see ch. xiii. 16). But the word is omitted in the versions, and may be an interpolation.

Ver. 6.—**Uncircumcised.** An epithet of dislike almost confined to the Philistines. But underneath the whole speech of Jonathan lies the conviction of the covenant relation of Israel to Jehovah, of which circumcision was the outward sign. Notice also Jonathan’s humble reliance upon God. **It may be that Jehovah will work for us,** &c.

Ver. 7.—**Turn thee.** The Hebrew seems to have preserved the very words of the young man, and the difficulty in rendering this phrase arises from its being a colloquial expression. “ Face about” would be our phrase ; but the sense is, “On with you ; I will follow.”

Ver. 9. — **Tarry.** Hebrew, “ be still,” “ stand still,” the word used by Joshua of the sun (Josh. x. 12, 13) ; but not the word rendered **stand still** just below, where the Hebrew has, “ We will stand under us,” *i. e.* we will stop just where we were.

Ver. 10. — **A sign.** The waiting of the garrison for Jonathan and his armour-bearer to mount up to them would be a sign of great indifference and supineness on their part ; but what he rather meant was that they were to regard it as an omen. Kim’hi has a long digression in his commentary on this place to show that there was nothing superstitious in their looking for a prognostic to encourage them in their hazardous under-

taking. God, he says, bade Gideon go to the camp of the Midianites to obtain such a sign as Jonathan looked for here (see Judges vii. 11).

Ver. 11.—**Both of them discovered themselves.** They had crept up the precipice unseen, but at some convenient spot near the top they so placed themselves that the garrison must see them, and waited there till their presence was observed. **Behold, the Hebrews.** There is no article in the Hebrew. What the Philistines say is, See ! Hebrews come out of the holes wherein they had hid themselves.

Ver. 12.—**Come up to us, and we will show you a thing.** The Philistines thus give Jonathan the very omen he had desired. The last clause is a popular phrase, and expresses a sort of amused contempt for the two adventurers. Raillery of this sort is not at all uncommon between the outposts of two armies.

Ver. 13.—**Upon his hands and upon his feet.** Of course a single stone rolled down upon them while thus clambering up the precipitous side of the cliff would have sent them to the bottom ; but the Philistines, apparently considering the ascent impossible, seem entirely to have neglected them. The youthful appearance of the two no doubt contributed to throw them off their guard. **And they fell before Jonathan.** The brevity of the Hebrew very well expresses the rapidity of Jonathan’s action. Used to mountaineering, he was ready, as soon as he had reached the summit, to commence the attack, and the Philistines, little expecting so vigorous an onslaught from so feeble a force, were surprised, and made but a slight resistance. The armour-bearer also behaved with a bravery like his master’s.

Ver. 14.—**Within as it were an half acre of land, which a yoke of oxen might plow.** The Hebrew for this long circumlocution is, “ within about a half furrow of a yoke of land.” The Septuagint translates, “ with darts and slings and stones of the field,” but the other versions give no support to this rendering. The Israelites, like most ancient nations, were accustomed to measure land by the quantity which a yoke of oxen could plough in a day,—something really less than an acre,—so that the A. V. gives the right sense. When Jonathan made his attack, the garrison probably, not knowing how few their assailants were, ran in confusion to the narrow tongue of land where the exit was, and getting in one another’s way, were soon panic-stricken and helpless.

Ver. 15. — **Trembling.** *I. e.* “ terror,” “ fright.” **In the host.** Hebrew, “ in the camp,” *i. e.* the main camp at Michmash, contrasted with **the field,** *i. e.* the open country, in which the soldiers were foraging for supplies. **The people.** *I. e.* the camp followers, as opposed to the soldiers. All these were terrified by **the garrison** rushing down the pass, with tidings of the attack magnified by their fears, and who communicated the alarm to **the spoilers,** who, having now for a fortnight met with no resistance, had probably discontinued all measures of precaution. **The earth quaked.** This may be taken literally, but is more probably a poetical description of the widespread terror and confusion which prevailed far and near. **So it was a very great trembling.** Literally, "and it became a terror of God;" but the name of the deity (Elohim, not Jehovah) is constantly used in Hebrew to express vastness.

DEFEAT OF THE PHILISTINES (vers. 16—23). Ver. 16.—**The watchmen,** &c. Conder says ('Tent Work,' ii. 115), "The watchmen of Saul in Gibeah of Benjamin must have seen clearly across the chasm the extraordinary conflict of two men against a host, as the 'multitude melted away, and they went on beating down one another.' The noise in the host was also, no doubt, clearly heard at the distance of only two miles, and the army would have crossed the passage with comparatively little difficulty by the narrow path which leads down direct from Geba to Michmash, west of the Philistine camp. Thence the pursuit was towards Bethel, across the watershed, and headlong down the steep descent of Aijalon — that same pass where the first great victory of Joshua had been gained, and where the valiant Judas was once more, in later times, to drive back the enemies of Israel to the plains." **The multitude.** The Hebrew is, "And behold the tumult (the word is so rendered in ver. 19, margin) was reeling and going . . . and thither." Of course *hither* has dropped out of the text before *and thither* (comp. ch. xiii. 8). The Septuagint and Vulgate both read "hither and thither." Tumult means the din made by a confused mass of people, and so the crowd itself. **Melted away** does not give the exact meaning. The Philistines were not dispersing, but were *reeling,* moving to and fro purposeless, and in confusion. It may mean, however, to˙ *shake* or *melt with terror,* as in Isa. xiv. 31, where it is rendered *art dissolved.*

Vers. 17, 18.—**Number now.** On hearing from the watchmen that fighting was seen on the other side of the ravine, Saul commands the roll to be called, that he may learn who has made the attack, and finds only his son and the armour-bearer missing. Uncertain what their absence might mean, **he said unto Ahiah, Bring hither the ark of God.** The Syriac, Vulgate, and Chaldee support this reading, but the Septuagint has *ephod,* and there can be no doubt that this is the right

reading; for the verb rendered *Bring hither* is never used of the ark, but only of the ephod; nor was the ark used for making inquiry of God, but the ephod with the breastplate inserted in it. The rest of the verse is a gloss added by some scribe struck at this strange mention of the ark, which we know was still at Kirjath-jearim. It is itself corrupt and ungrammatical, being, "For the ark of God was in that day and the children of Israel." Still both the reading *ark* and the gloss are very ancient, being found in the versions, except the Septuagint, as above.

Ver. 19.—**Withdraw thine hand.** Saul, impatient of delay, cannot wait till the will of God is made known to him. There would have been no real loss of time, and he might have been saved from the errors which marred the happiness of the deliverance. But this precipitancy very well shows the state of Saul's mind.

Ver. 20.—**Saul and all the people . . . assembled themselves.** Margin, *were cried together,* i. e. summoned by trumpet-note. The Syriac and Vulgate, however, make the verb active, and translate, "And Saul and all the people with him shouted and advanced to the battle." **Discomfiture.** Rather, "dismay," "consternation," as in ch. v. 9.

Vers. 21, 22.—**Round about, even.** All the versions by a very slight alteration change this into *turned,* which the A. V. is forced to supply. With this necessary correction the translation is easy: "And the Hebrews who were previously with the Philistines, and had gone up with them into the camp, turned to be with the Israelites who were with Saul and Jonathan." It appears, therefore, that certain districts of the Israelite territory were so completely in the power of the Philistines that they could compel the men to go with them, not perhaps as soldiers, as is our custom in India, but as drivers and servants. These now turned upon their masters, and were reinforced by the Israelites who had taken refuge in Mount Ephraim. It is noteworthy that these subject "Hebrews" retain the name of contempt given them by their masters.

Ver. 23.—**Over unto Beth-aven.** Hebrew, "the battle passed Beth-aven," *i. e.* no rally was made there. In ver. 31 we read that the pursuit continued as far as Aijalon. For Beth-aven see on ch. xiii. 5.

SAUL'S RASH COMMAND (vers. 24—35). Ver. 24.—**The men of Israel were distressed that day.** The word is that used in ch. xiii. 6 of the state of terror and alarm to which the Israelites were reduced by the Philistine invasion; here it refers to their weariness and faintness for want of food. **For Saul had adjured the people.** Hebrew, "had made the people swear." He had recited before them the words of the curse, and made them shout their consent. His object was to prevent any delay in the pursuit; but in his eagerness he forgot that the strength of his men would fail if their bodily wants were not supplied. But though worn out and fainting, the people faithfully keep the oath put to them.

Ver. 25.—**And all they of the land.** Hebrew, "the whole land," or, as we should say, *the whole country*, which had risen to join in the pursuit. **Honey upon the ground.** The wild bees in Palestine fill fissures in the rocks (Deut. xxxii. 13 ; Ps. lxxxi. 16) and hollow trees with honey, till the combs, breaking with the weight, let it run down upon the ground. A similar abundance of honey was found by the early settlers in America.

Ver. 26.—**The honey dropped.** More correctly, "Behold, a stream (or a flowing) of honey."

Ver. 27.—Jonathan, who had not been present when his father **charged the people with the oath,**—literally, "made the people swear,"—dipped the end of his staff hastily, so as not to hinder the pursuit, **in an honeycomb**—Hebrew, "into the honey wood," *i. e.* into the hollow branch or trunk out of which the honey was flowing (but see Cant. v. 1). **His eyes were enlightened.** *I. e.* made bright and clear, the dimness caused by excessive weariness having passed away. But this is a correction made by the Jews (*kri*), and the written text (*c'tib*) has "his eyes saw," which is more forcible and poetic. When the A. V. was made the *kri* was supposed to be authoritative, but most modern commentators have come to the opposite conclusion.

Ver. 28. — **And the people were faint.** There is great diversity of opinion whether this be part or not of the speech of the man who informed Jonathan of the oath forced on the people by Saul. It makes, perhaps, the better sense if regarded as the continuation of the history, and inserted to justify Jonathan's disapproval of his father's hasty command. The right rendering is *were weary*, as in the margin and Judges iv. 21.

Ver. 29.—**My father hath troubled the land.** *I. e.* hath brought disaster upon it (see Gen. xxxiv. 30 ; Josh. vii. 25). This disaster was the incompleteness of the victory, owing to the people being too exhausted to continue the pursuit.

Vers. 30, 31.—**For had there not been now a much greater slaughter?** This clause is really an indicative : "For now the slaughter of the Philistines is not very great." Never-

theless, the pursuit was continued as far as the pass of Aijalon, and though, owing to the increasing weariness of the people, but few of the Philistines were overtaken, nevertheless it would compel them to throw away their arms, and abandon all the booty which they had collected. For **very faint** the Hebrew has *very weary*, as in ver. 28.

Ver. 32.—**The people flew upon the spoil.** The written text has, "And the people set to work upon the spoil, and took sheep," &c., but as the sentence is not very grammatical the *kri* has corrected it from ch. xv. 19. The versions have either "greedily desired," or "turned themselves unto." The people who had waited until evening, when the oath forced upon them by Saul was over, then in their hunger broke the law doubly : first in killing calves with their dams on the same day (Levit. xxii. 28), and secondly, more seriously, in so killing them "on the ground" that the blood remained in the carcase. The law enjoined the utmost care in this respect (*ibid.* xvii. 10—14), but the people were too weary and hungry to trouble about it.

Vers. 33, 34. — **Ye have transgressed.** Better as in the margin, "dealt treacherously," *i. e.* faithlessly, to the covenant between Israel and Jehovah. **Roll a great stone unto me this day.** Or, as we should say, *this minute ;* but the Hebrew uses "this day" for anything to be done at once (see on ch. ii. 16). The purpose of this stone was to raise up the carcases of the slaughtered animals from the ground, so that the blood might drain away from them. On tidings of this arrangement being dispersed throughout the army, the people obey Saul with the same unquestioning devotion as they had shown to his command to abstain from food.

Ver. 35.—**And Saul built an altar unto Jehovah** as a thank offering for the Divine favour in gaining so great a victory. **The same was the first altar,** &c. Literally, "As to it he began to build an altar unto Jehovah." On these words the question has arisen whether the meaning be that Saul began to build an altar, but with characteristic impetuosity left off before he had completed it ; or whether on that occasion he commenced the custom followed by David (2 Sam. xxiv. 25) of erecting altars as the patriarchs had done in old time. The latter interpretation is more in accordance with the usage of the Hebrew language, and is approved by the translations of the Septuagint and Vulgate.

HOMILETICS.

Vers. 1—12.—*Inspiration in Christian enterprise.* The facts are—1. Jonathan, on his own responsibility, and without his father's knowledge, resolves on an attack upon the Philistine garrison.   2. He expresses to his armour-bearer his hope that God will help, and also the ground of that hope.   3. He proposes to regard the first encouragement from the enemy to ascend the cliff as a sign of coming success. 4. The sign appearing, Jonathan advances in confidence of victory.   The recent transgression of Saul was now bearing some bitter fruit in his comparative inactivity and helplessness.   It is not likely that Jonathan was ignorant of the displeasure of the prophet of God, or was surprised at the embarrassment which had come upon his father's affairs.   In seasons of disaster and wrong there are select men of God who mourn the sins of their superiors and the woes of their country.   Being one of this class, Jonathan may be regarded as exhibiting some of the highest results of the instruction and influence of Samuel during the slow reformation subsequent to the victory at Ebenezer.   It is in God's heart to have pity on his people and to deliver them ; but at this juncture can we not discern a wise propriety, not unmixed with retribution on the king, in conferring the honour of deliverance upon a man of piety, whose heart evidently yearned for the highest good of Israel ? Thus do we see here, as in many other instances, how readily, and where not looked for, God raises up instruments to effect his purposes when the ordinary instruments fail through sin. Private enterprise can often accomplish what, in consequence of a loss of the right spirit, organised and official effort is utterly powerless to perform.   The enforced inactivity of Saul, the desolations of the spoilers, and the multitudes of refugees in the caves of the mountains, must have produced a most depressing effect on the king and his followers.   In their extremity, under an inspiration most pure and noble, help came in the daring enterprise of Jonathan, as recorded by the historian.   It is possible that a secular mind on reading the narrative may regard the story as just one of those records of military adventure that are to be found in the annals of all warlike nations.   But we are to form our estimate of the event by the light of Scripture ; and when we consider it in connection with God's revealed purpose to work out the Messianic covenant through a chosen race, the tenor of Jonathan's life, and especially his words declaring his faith in God (ver. 6), we must then see here not a wild freak of a daring soldier, nor even a clever device for achieving merely military distinction, but a true and noble inspiration to accomplish a great work in the name of God, and for the ultimate realisation of the Divine purposes.   It may be assumed that, under the present conditions of the kingdom of Christ in the world, there is frequent and full scope for endeavours corresponding, in their relation to the organised efforts of the Church and in their chief characteristics, to the effort of Jonathan in its relation to the monarchy.   Likewise the same inspiration is needed for the more perfect development and successful use of the organised forces of the Church. While nations live in sin, fearful evils fester in our crowded towns, debasing and dangerous customs hold multitudes in bondage, avenues to the human mind lie untraversed by Christian men, and possibly propriety degenerates into a rigid, obstructive conservatism, there is room for men and women who dare to go and do what seems impossible, and for a fresh baptism on the hosts of God to inspire them to deeds of valour and self-denial.   It is possible that spurious forms of enthusiasm may arise, and may pass for heaven-created zeal.   Contagion of sentiment may obtain the force of a torrent.   The emotional element in religion may be abnormally developed, and incline, under stimulus, to deeds which no sound judgment will justify.   But grant all this, and more, and yet it is true that there is a pure inspiration in the service of Christ much to be coveted.   Let us consider the *characteristics of such a true inspiration.*

I.   It is distinguished by individuality.   Whether it be found in private action or in the combined effort of the Church, it does not appear as the mere product of organisation, nor as a revival of stereotyped custom.   Jonathan's inspiration began in his own heart.   It was, in the shape it took, the natural outcome of the man. Considerations of the position of affairs aroused his nature, but he was no copyist, no waiter upon other men's deeds.   Keeping the secret from his father was essential to the more perfect individuality of his feelings and his enterprise.   Ideas grow in power over us when we nourish them. Sometimes, like the Apostle Paul and Jonathan, we do better not to " confer with flesh and blood," but brood over our thought and purpose, by the aid of the Spirit of God, till they become a power which must work outwards in forms true to our own personality.   There is far more individuality in the Christian Church than is at present developed.   When a Christian is, as the result of brooding over things, so permeated with a conviction of his obligation to Christ, a yearning to save men from sin, and a spirit of self-sacrifice, as to be mastered by these forces, he will find out some way in which his natural aptitudes and capabilities may be turned to account in Christ's service.   All great and beneficial movements have borne the stamp of individuality, from the labours of the Apostle Paul on, by Luther, up to the latest endeavours to save the waifs of our city population.

II. IT CONTEMPLATES AN END CONFORMABLE TO THE END FOR WHICH CHRIST DIED. Jonathan reveals his piety and his intelligence in using language to his armour-bearer to the effect that he thought it probable that the Lord might save through his instrumentality.   He sought the salvation which God loves to accomplish, and for which the order of Providence was working.   It is our privilege to take a wider and more spiritual view than even a devout Hebrew.   There is an end contemplated by God, and being wrought out by the great sacrifice on the cross, with its concomitant influences—a multitude that no man can number redeemed out of every nation, kindred, and tribe from the bondage and pollution of sin.   Whoever sets his heart on any good work, conformable, and therefore tributary, to that issue,—be it social amelioration, rescue of lost ones from vice, sanitary improvements, diffusion of knowledge,—is so far sharer in the true inspiration.   But especially is that a true and noble inspiration which not only aims at ends which, being good and moral, are so far conformable and helpful to the end for which Christ died, but aims at that spiritual salvation on which the heart of Christ was supremely set when he gave himself a ransom for us.   This is the longed-for issue of all those noble workers at home or abroad who visit the abodes of sin, and seek, as though they cannot refrain from it, to gather the poor degraded ones into the Saviour's blessed fold.

III. IT IS CHARACTERISED BY FREEDOM FROM PERSONAL VANITY.   Jonathan's motives were transparently pure.   There was none of the restlessness of the inactive soldier craving for opportunity to display prowess; no regard for self in his self-denial and risks.   His references to the Lord and the saving of the people he loved reveal a true, generous, self-sacrificing spirit.   It is when works of benevolence, and especially works strictly spiritual, are devised and carried through in this spirit that we are under the influence of a true inspiration.   A love of praise, a desire for prominence, fondness for being counted a great and successful worker, an unreasonable sensitiveness to apparent neglect, and kindred feelings, are the " little foxes " that steal the grapes.

IV. IT IS MARKED BY IMPLICIT DEPENDENCE ON THE POWER OF GOD.   Jonathan showed prudence and skill in the ascent of the precipice and in the encouragement he sought for advancing by means of the " sign ; " but the feat passes out of the category of " reckless," or even, in the common usage of the term, " daring," when we note that, having the sign as a kind of answer to the prayer of his heart, he rested his success not on his skill or strength, but on the Lord, with whom there " is no restraint to save by many or by few."   He was inspired every step of the way up the rocks by trust in the ever-present Power which shields the faithful and works the wonders of redemption for his people.   Here lies the *secret of the true inspiration* that has wrought so powerfully in the Church of God in its purest and most successful eras.   The apostles felt that it was not of man, but of God, to save.   A few feeble Jews were mighty, *through God*, to the pulling down of many a stronghold. It is this which enables the missionary to toil on amidst the loathsome vices of the savage, and the friend of the outcast at home to attempt what none others dare.

V. IT IS MARKED ALSO BY THE BUOYANCY OF HOPE.   When Jonathan said, " It may be that the Lord will work for us," it was not to express uncertainty, but to cheer a man of less faith, and to indicate the belief that God was about to use him in his service.   He rightly interpreted his yearning to be used as an inspiration of God, and when the " sign " came that assured him that his heart's desire was accepted, he moved on with a cheerful spirit.   " Come up after me : for the Lord hath delivered them into the hand of Israel."   The modesty of the assurance !   "The hand of *Israel ;* " not "*my* hand."   This buoyant spirit that looks on in hope founded on deep conviction of God's faithfulness inspires every one who is truly called to labour for Christ. The tone of the apostles all through their toils is one of cheer. The golden gates of the eternal city seem ever to shine before them, and they hear already the new song. Every one on whom this true apostolic succession has come enters into sympathy with them, and no longer toils with dejected brow and despairing heart.

General lessons :—1. There is abundant encouragement for Christian work in the historically illustrated fact that God does accomplish great results through feeble and varied means. 2. It is a question with each of us whether we really believe that there " is no restraint with the Lord," and whether lack of faith in this great truth does not explain much in our life and labour which we deplore. 3. We may ask ourselves whether there is anything in the present state of the Church and the world affording scope for our special exertion after the manner of Jonathan's. 4. It should be an inquiry as to whether we are open to receive and welcome an inspiration from the Lord to enter on some work involving self-denial and difficulty. 5. If we think we are inspired to undertake some difficult work for Christ, we should discriminate between sudden impulse and mature irresistible longing; and, seeking counsel of God, follow the signs of Providence.

Vers. 13—23.—*God's faithfulness to his own.* The facts are—1. Jonathan and his servant ascend the precipice and slay, on a narrow strip of land, about twenty men. 2. A panic arising, from a combination of causes, the commotion attracts the attention of Saul's sentinels. 3. It being ascertained that Jonathan was engaged against the Philistines, inquiry is sought of God, by Saul, through the priest Ahiah. 4. The tumult among the Philistines increasing, Saul abruptly stops the inquiry and leads on his followers to battle. 5. The deserters and the fugitives fall on the rear of the retreating Philistines. The historian sums up the narrative of events in this section by the suggestive words, " So the Lord saved Israel that day." It was "the Lord," working through the instrumentality of a noble-hearted man and the events concurrent with his action—not withholding the reward of fidelity, notwithstanding the questionable conduct of the king. "It is the Lord," must be the verdict of history, not only of their deliverance, but of many others in all time.

I. GOD'S FAITHFULNESS IS SEEN IN PERFECTING THE WORK WHICH HE INSPIRES. There can be no doubt but that Jonathan received this "good and perfect gift" of inspiration, to seek the salvation of his country, from God. We have seen that it could not have been a mere human, earth-born impulse. There may be a point at which the human free aspiration becomes touched with a Divine power; but, as a whole, the impulse is of God. The narrative tells us how certainly God wrought for the perfecting of that which he saw in the heart. Not a step of his way did Jonathan find to be a practical denial of the truth of his inward prompting. Thus the life of the true man of God is crowded with evidences of the Divine faithfulness. He who begins a "good work" within us will carry it through. He is "not unrighteous to forget our work of faith and labour of love." He will "perfect that which concerneth us." "Loving his own," he loves "to the end." Abraham, under an inspiration from God, went forth, and all through his pilgrimage he found Jehovah to be a covenant-keeping God. In our painful and protracted endeavours, in obedience to an aspiration born from above to rise to the heights of holiness and to bless others, we shall find him faithful who hath promised never to leave nor forsake us.

II. IN MAINTAINING HIS FAITHFULNESS TO HIS PEOPLE GOD CAUSES VARIED INFLUENCES TO CONVERGE ON THE DESIRED RESULT OF EFFORT. The Divine faithfulness is not arbitrarily and absolutely manifested. It is seen in realising the desired end by a succession of events naturally connected. Jonathan's exertions were put forth as though all rested on the courage of his own heart and the strength of his own arm. The narrative shows us how an unseen hand upheld the brave soldier, and caused diverse things to converge on the one issue: *e. g.* the young soldier's skill, tact, and courage ; the folly of the defenders in allowing him a footing on the narrow pathway of the upper part of the precipice ; the fear aroused through ignorance of the full facts of the assault ; the panic spread from post to post—strengthened, possibly, by a slight shock of earthquake ; the onward movement of Saul's troop ; and the opportunity created for the rallying of fugitives and deserters (vers. 21, 22).

Such an historical episode is of great value to us, as indicating in distinct, traceable incidents *the reality of that Divine wisdom and power* which ever *presides over all the efforts of Christians* to rid themselves and the world of sin. It illustrates as on a picture the great formula of faith—"All things *work together* for good to them that love God." As "the stars in their courses fought against Sisera," and as even holy angels are "ministering spirits sent forth to minister to those who shall be heirs of salvation," so may it be said, in the case of every one who strives to purify himself from all sin, or seeks by some bold or ordinary endeavour to win the world over to Christ, "all things are yours,"—are being governed by the Lord of all so as to subserve the one holy end to the attainment of which your hearts are inspired.

III. IN MANIFESTING HIS FAITHFULNESS TO HIS PEOPLE GOD PERMITS THE IMPER-FECT TO SHARE IN THE BLESSINGS PROCURED BY THE MORE PERFECT. Primarily, it was God's compassion for Israel and his covenant with Abraham that must account for this new deliverance. Secondarily, it was a reward to Jonathan's fidelity and self-consecration. Saul had shut himself out of the honour and privilege of obtaining deliverance for the nation. Even now his old folly and rashness reappear, in religiously beginning to seek counsel, thus honouring God, and then in irreverently discontinuing to seek that counsel, through his impetuous haste to join in the pursuit, thus preferring the impulse of his heart to the declared will of God. Nevertheless, even Saul derives great advantage from the prowess of the good and devout Jonathan. God, in his mercy, does not sacrifice the final interests of his people to the folly of a leader. Thus, also, Joseph's brethren shared in the prosperity won by their holy and wise brother. The inferior Christians of to-day participate in some of the outward blessings accruing to the faithful as the result of their fidelity.

General lessons:—1. It would be a profitable study to note in detail, over the field of sacred and Church history, and in the sphere of private Christian enterprise, to what a large extent the world is indebted for spiritual, material, and educational good to the honour God has put on the labours of the most faithful of his servants. 2. We may be perfectly sure in the pursuit of any holy enterprise, to which person-ally we may feel inadequate, that God, with whom is "no restraint," will develop helping circumstances. 3. The helping circumstances desiderated will arise, not at first, but only as we faithfully press along the line of duty. 4. The cumulating record of God's faithfulness to his people through the long ages should make us calm, strong, and immovable in the most perilous of enterprises undertaken for Christ.

Vers. 24—35.—*Unwise zeal and moral obtuseness.* The facts are—1. Saul by a rash vow causes great distress among the people and diminishes the fruits of victory. 2. Jonathan, unawares, takes food contrary to his father's prohibition, and on being informed of the truth, deplores the unwisdom of the vow. 3. As a consequence of the enforced exhaustion, the people at the close of the day violate the ceremonial law by a voracious meal of flesh unduly prepared. 4. Saul, professing to be shocked at their sin, provides means by which the offence may be avoided, and raises an altar unto the Lord. The turn in affairs brought on by Jonathan's heroism was most wel-come to Saul, as it seemed to be the return of the prosperity which had received a check in his own sin at Gilgal. There had been no expressions of sincere penitence, nor, as far as the narrative gives light, any effort to regain former relationships to Samuel. The impulsive rush from the inquiring priest to join in the pursuit revealed a state of mind which at once accounts for the curse pronounced on any one who should dare to take food. The facts included in the section before us furnish a conspicuous instance of unwise zeal and moral obtuseness.

I. UNWISE ZEAL. The zeal of Saul was conspicuous enough. As in the case of Joshua (Josh. viii. 8—13), there was an intense desire to put into a single day all the exertion possible in order to make the victory over God's enemies more complete. There was clearly in his mind an idea that he was doing God service (ver. 33). But the unwisdom of the zeal is equally conspicuous; for it prevented, by the physical weakness induced, the very end designed (vers. 29, 30): it caused pain and annoy-ance to an obedient people, who, while submissive, must have lost some respect for their monarch's judgment; it exposed the best man of the day to a great peril, and the people to a strong temptation to commit excess. *Unwise zeal may be considered variously.* 1. *As to form.* It assumes diverse forms according to the circumstances of the case. (1) Sometimes the *aim may be wrong*, as when the Jews in apostolic times, in their zeal, not according to knowledge, sought most energetically to perpetuate a decaying ceremonial. The same is true of all who compass sea and land to make mere proselytes to their order or sect, or to bring modern feeling and usage back, in matters of minor significance, to the style of the past. (2) Often the *method is wrong*, as in the case of Saul. Men have not always the wisdom to conserve or develop, as the occasion may demand, their energy suitably to the end in view. There is an enormous waste in the world from this cause. Perhaps no man, in his daily calling, is free from this form of unwise zeal. We see illustrations of this in the untiring effort of some to be justified before God by their own deeds of righteousness; in the constant and painful flow of penitential tears and self-inflicted sorrows as means of the forgiveness which comes only by calm trust in Christ; and in the wild and ill-considered agencies sometimes used to win careless men to Christ. (3) Sometimes the end is good and the method, but the *time is unsuited.* It might be good for Israel to chase the foe with full energy, and also good to fast, but the time was not suitable for the conjunction of the two. It is mistaken zeal to concentrate all strength on the edification of a Church when multitudes are living outside the fold of Christ. Wisdom lies much in doing work at the right season. 2. *As to origin.* Saul's unwise zeal arose from his impulsive temperament not being chastened and regulated by a diligent use of the counsel which was always available to him as king from God. This radical error accounts for the ill-balanced judgment which could not see the effect of a long fast on physical energy, for the rash utterance, for the eager springing at the first chance to escape from the helpless position consequent on recent transgression, and for the egotistical reference to avenging *his own* enemies. The origin of unwise zeal in most instances is connected with deficient waiting upon God. The knowledge of men may be defective, their temperament may be impulsive, their prevision of a low grade, their self-regulation a matter of emotional pressure rather than of reason; and yet if such men would, remembering their obvious imperfections, devoutly wait on God for his guidance, and seek daily grace to govern themselves, they would avoid many blunders in practice. Imperfectly-balanced men will never do work in life perfectly. We must lay to our account a large proportion of foolish deeds in Christian and secular enterprise. The calming, enlightening power of devotion is not fully recognised. 3. *As to consequences.* In Saul's case, as already indicated, it induced trouble and pain to his people, interfered with the most perfect success of Jonathan's effort (vers. 29, 30), lowered himself in the eyes of his subjects as a king deficient in judgment, and, by exercise, intensified the defective qualities which gave rise to it. We have here a summary of what always attends unwise zeal. Every foolish display of energy, even in a good cause, brings distress to those who have the interests of religion and humanity at heart. Being a waste of power, and therefore a violation of the moral and social laws by which God brings the highest results to pass, it impedes the subjugation of evil to good, and the final triumph of God's kingdom. The world is suffering still from erratic courses, destitute of sound judgment, pursued in the name of religion; from a concentration of energy on superficial instead of on radical evils; and from an undue application of resources to the curative methods, in frequent oversight of the preventive.

II. MORAL OBTUSENESS. The moral obtuseness of Saul's character had manifested itself in his evident inability to see at Gilgal (ch. xiii. 8—10) the stupidity of seeking to please God by an act of worship which itself was a violation of his explicit commands. Character becomes more fixed as time passes on; and here we see Saul so morally obtuse as not to perceive that, while condemning a ceremonial offence on the part of the people (ver. 33), he was unconscious of the folly of his own conduct, and of the moral offence both of laying on the people a serious hindrance to victory and of preferring his own wild impulse to the counsel of Jehovah. *Moral obtuseness* may be regarded in reference to—1. Its *causes*—e. g. inherited dulness of conscience, imperfectly-formed moral discrimination in early years, growing habituation to formal religious acts, the influence of a low state of public morality, and postponement of sincere repentance after known transgressions. 2. Its *manifestation*—e. g. in rigid external observances to the neglect of spiritual culture, combination of religious zeal with positive indulgence in immoral feelings, ease in detecting palpable offences in others with self-complacent views of one's own condition, insensibility to the truth which awakens the finer spiritual feelings of other men, and coarse treatment of the sensitive. 3. Its *danger*—e. g. in being inaccessible to many of the most elevating influences, rendered more dense by every repeated exercise, and productive of a delusive self-righteousness which becomes more self-assertive in proportion as inward unholiness prevails. 4. Its *treatment*—e. g. by distinct personal teaching of the most discriminating and pungent character, placing the individuals in close association with persons of fine spiritual discernment and delicacy of character as a striking foil, prompting to acts that will tend to reveal the inward incompetency, and special prayer for the quickening of the life-giving Spirit.

General lessons:—1. Cultivate a refined moral sensibility in youth as a basis for life. 2. Men in office need prayer for special spiritual wisdom. 3. When sin has been committed it should be repented of at once, and special prayer made lest its inward influence be to lower the tone of feeling.

HOMILIES BY VARIOUS AUTHORS.

Vers. 1—15. (GEBA, MICHMASH.)—*The heroism of Jonathan.* "Come, and let us go over unto the garrison of these uncircumcised," &c. (ver. 6). The character of Jonathan is one of the bravest, most generous, devout, and blameless in history. Of his earliest years nothing is recorded. When first mentioned he was in command of a thousand soldiers (ch. xiii. 2), and his overthrow of the Philistine garrison in Geba was "the first act of the war of independence;" but (as in the case of Moses—Acts vii. 25) it failed to deliver his people from oppression. His attack upon the enemy's camp at Michmash, which is here described, resulted in victory. He inherited the physical strength and courage of Saul; but in other respects presented a contrast to his father; exemplified the best, as the latter exemplified some of the worst features of the age, and set a pattern of *true heroism* for all time.

> "What makes a hero ? an heroic mind
> Expressed in action, in endurance proved."

I. EXALTED ASPIRATIONS (ver. 1) which—1. *Are cherished in adverse circumstances* (ch. xiii. 22; ver. 2). Instead of being crushed by adversity, "an heroic mind" bears it patiently, rises above it, and aspires to higher things (Acts xxi. 13). In its midst it shines all the more brightly, like gold purified by the fire. 2. *Lead to courageous projects.* Jonathan often looks across the ravine between Bozez and Seneh (vers. 4, 5), and revolves in his mind how he can strike a blow at the apparently inaccessible fortress of the enemy; and at length goes forth secretly in the night or at early dawn, attended only by his armour-bearer. To communicate his project to others, even if it were as yet clear to himself, would be to hinder or defeat its accomplishment. He feels called to attempt something great, and "confers not with flesh and blood." 3. *Are inspired by the Divine Spirit.* More of "the mind of the Lord" was doubtless made known to Jonathan than to the king, notwithstanding the presence of the priest with him (ver. 3). What appears presumption to others is often to one Divinely taught the simple path of duty.

II. EMINENT FAITH (ver. 6), including—1. *A firm conviction of the covenant relation of God* to his people. "These uncircumcised" in opposition to Israel. Jonathan's thought was not of himself, but of his people, and of the promises and purposes of God concerning them. 2. *A lofty conception of the unlimited power of God* to save them. "There is no restraint to the Lord to save by many or by few" (2 Chron. xiv. 11; Micah ii. 7). In comparison with his might the strength of man, whether much or little, is nothing. He has often used "the weak things of the world to confound the things that are mighty" (1 Cor. i. 27, 28), and he can do so again. Faith is shown in contemplating the power of God, and is thereby greatly increased. 3. *Humble reliance on the gracious co-operation of God* on their behalf. "It may be that the Lord will work for us." He is ready and able to afford help, but whether it will be given in connection with a particular course of action is, without express direction or promise, uncertain; and the indications of his will should be followed with humility, hopefulness, and confidence. "The measure of faith is the measure of God's help." "All things are possible to him that believeth."

III. PRUDENT WATCHFULNESS (vers. 9, 10). 1. *In contrast to reckless adventure.* Faith in God gives insight into the hidden principles and tendencies of things, teaches the adoption of appropriate means, and makes men calm as well as fearless when others lose self-control, and adopt foolish and dangerous expedients (Acts xxvii. 25, 30). 2. *In ascertaining the prospects of success.* If the enemy are on the alert and exhibit courage, it will be vain to expect to take them by surprise (ver. 9); but if they feel themselves secure in their position, are careless and slack, and blinded by self-confidence, "the Lord hath delivered them into the hand of Israel" (ver. 12). 3. *In working wisely with a view to that end.* God works by means, and not without them, and the wisest means are the most successful.

IV. DARING ENERGY (vers. 11—14) in—1. Enduring great *risk.* 2. Putting forth immense *effort.* "Jonathan climbed up on his hands and knees." It is a severe as well as a dangerous climb to reach the point where the conflict begins. 3. Following up every *advantage* to the utmost. "When he came in full view of the enemy they both discharged such a flight of arrows, stones, and pebbles from their bows, crossbows, and slings that twenty men fell at the first onset, and the garrison fled in a panic."

V. INSPIRING SYMPATHY (vers. 7, 13). A believing and heroic spirit begets the same spirit in others. 1. At first those with whom it comes into closest contact—it may be a *single individual.* 2. Afterwards a *host* (vers. 21, 22). 3. And their aid *contributes to the general result.* "The history of battles should teach us the mighty power of sympathetic relations."

VI. DIVINE APPROVAL. 1. *Expressed in the overthrow of the enemy*—bringing them into confusion (ver. 15), turning them against one another (ver. 16), and saving Israel from their oppression, as well as in the Providential ordering of all things that contributed to it. 2. *In commendation of "the spirit of faith"* in which the enterprise was undertaken and carried out. 3. *Recognised by all the people.* "He hath wrought with God this day" (ver. 45)—wrought effectually through his favour and power. The day was won by Jonathan; still more by God. "So the Lord saved Israel that day" (ver. 23). And to him the glory must be ascribed.—D.

Vers. 16—23. (GIBEAH.)—*Impatience in seeking Divine counsel.* "Withdraw thine hand" (ver. 19). In order to ascertain the will of God two things are necessary:—1. A special method of communication. In ancient days it was "by dreams, Urim, and prophets" (ch. xxviii. 6). The Urim (light, illumination) and Thummim (perfection, completeness, truth) were symbols of some kind or other attached to or placed within the folded breastplate connected with the ephod of the high priest (Exod. xxviii. 30; Num. xxvii. 21). "The question brought was one affecting the well-being of the nation, or its army, or its king. The inquirer spoke in a low whisper, asking one question only at a time. The high priest, fixing his gaze on the 'gems oracular' that 'lay on his heart,' fixed his thoughts on the light and perfection which they symbolised, on the holy name inscribed on them. The act was itself a prayer, and, like other prayers, it might be answered. After a time he passed into the new, mysterious, half ecstatic state. All disturbing elements—selfishness, prejudice, the fear of man—were eliminated. He received the insight he craved. Men trusted in his decisions, as with us men trust the judgment which has been purified by prayer for the help of the eternal Spirit more than that which grows only out of debate and policy and calculation" (Smith's 'Dic.'). "When at length a visible king reigned by Divine appointment, the counsel of the Urim and Thummim passed into the public ministry of the prophets, which modified and controlled the political organisations of the kings" ('Bible Educ.,' iv. 37). We have now the written word and the guidance of the Holy Spirit. 2. A proper spirit of inquiry—humility, sincerity, faith, patience, and perseverance. Saul "inquired of the Lord" (Judges i. 1; xx. 27; ch. x. 22), but not in a right manner, impatiently breaking off his inquiry before the answer came, and commanding the priest to desist from pursuing it. In like manner many persons begin to pray, and forthwith cease, instead of "continuing instant in prayer;" ask, and wait not to receive; call upon God under the pressure of trouble, and neglect to do so when it has passed away.   Such impatience in seeking to "understand what *the will of the Lord* is "—

I. ARISES FROM UNDUE CONCERN ABOUT SECONDARY MATTERS.   1. *The need of human effort,* as if nothing else were necessary to success (Ps. xxiii. 16, 17 ; cxxvii. 1, 2). 2. *The gain of earthly honour or other advantages.*   Saul was eager to obtain, beyond everything else, the glory of a victory over his enemies.   3. *The loss of a favourable opportunity.*   But "there is no time lost while we are waiting God's time. It is as acceptable a piece of submission to the will of God to sit still contentedly when our Lord requires it as to work for him when we are called to do it " (M. Henry).

II. PROVES SINFUL INDIFFERENCE TO THE HIGHEST OBJECT.   1. *Inappreciation of its worth.*   Men often imagine that their own wisdom and strength are sufficient, and that it can be done without.   2. *Indisposition to bow to its authority.*   They love to have their own way.   3. *Incredulity as to its communication* at the right time and in the right manner.   They disbelieve the promises as well as reject the conditions of obtaining them.

III. EXHIBITS RECKLESS DISREGARD OF THE LORD HIMSELF.   By—1. *Seeking him in an insincere, inconsistent, and hypocritical manner,* which the cessation of prayer plainly shows (Job xxvii. 10).   2. *Preferring personal and immediate convenience to his honour,* and desiring his help only in so far as it may be conducive to self-interest.   3. *Disobedience to his will ;* for to act without the knowledge of that will when it may be obtained is a manifest act of disobedience (Isa. xxx. 1).

IV. INVOLVES DISASTROUS CONSEQUENCES.   1. Destitution of the highest counsel and aid.   2. Unpreparedness for duty and conflict.   3. A course of recklessness, sin, trouble, and humiliation (vers. 24, 37, 39, 44, 45).   "Therefore turn thou to thy God: keep mercy and judgment, and wait on thy God continually" (Hosea xii. 6). "I will *hear* what God the Lord will speak," &c. (Ps. lxxxv. 8).—D.

Vers. 24—46. (MICHMASH, AJALON.)—*Rashness.*   "Cursed be the man that eateth any food until evening," &c. (ver. 24).   Rashness is often a cause of trouble ; and some persons might profitably ponder the advice once given by the town-clerk of Ephesus, "Do nothing rashly" (Acts xix. 36).   It is also, sometimes, very sinful, as it was in Saul.   Whilst pursuing the Philistines, and wishing to exterminate them, he imposed a solemn oath upon the people not to take food until the evening under penalty of death.   This rash oath was followed by two others of a similar nature (vers. 39, 44), all indicating the recklessness and wilfulness of his course.   His concern for the law (vers. 33, 34), his erection of an altar (ver. 35), his asking counsel of God before going to spoil the enemy by night (ver. 37), his eagerness to ascertain by lot the cause of the silence of the oracle (ver. 41), were not an exhibition of genuine piety ; they were rather a substitute for it, and the fruits of an unsanctified, blind, and passionate zeal ; and the death of the noble Jonathan, if it had taken place, would have completed his folly and sin.   Consider his rashness as—

I. REVEALING A WRONG STATE OF MIND.   1. *Inconsideration.*   His oath was uttered without deliberation (Eccles. v. 2).   He did not consider whether it was according to the will of God, nor what its consequences might be.   He did not afterwards reflect how far the transgressions of others and the silence of Heaven might be due to his own fault, and he did not apparently recognise his fault when plainly set before him.   2. *Insincerity.*   "It did not proceed from a proper attitude toward God, but was an act of false zeal in which he had more regard to himself and his own kingly power than to the cause of the kingdom of Jehovah" (Keil).   3. *Vainglory.*   "That I may be avenged on *mine* enemies."   "In this prohibition there was a secret pride and misuse of power, for he desired to force, as it were, a complete victory, and then appropriate the glory of it to himself."

II. IMPOSING A NEEDLESS BURDEN upon others.   Once and again it is said "the people were faint" (vers. 28, 31).   They were exhausted with severe and prolonged exertion, famished with hunger, and unable to continue the pursuit.   Their suffering was great, their power diminished, their temptation strong.   But Saul had thought only of himself.   Rulers should seek the welfare of their subjects rather than their own glory ; and all men should consider the effect of their resolutions, promises, and commands on other people, and use their influence over them for their good.

III. OCCASIONING GRIEVOUS SIN in them (vers. 32—35). They avoided one offence only to commit another with a rashness equal to that of Saul himself (Gen. ix. 4; Deut. xii. 16; Levit. iii. 17; vii. 27). He censured and checked them. Would that he had also censured and checked himself! But men who severely condemn the faults of others are often blind to their own, even when the former reflect and are occasioned by the latter (Ps. xix. 12, 13). The altar, erected doubtless with a view to the presentation upon it of thank offerings for the victory, was still more needed for the sin offerings (expiatory) which ought to have been offered on behalf both of ruler and people (Levit. iv. 13, 22).

IV. IMPERILLING INNOCENT LIFE. Not having heard the oath, Jonathan, in unconsciously violating it (ver. 27), was morally blameless. Yet his act could not be passed by with due regard to the great name in which the people had been adjured. It interrupted Divine communications (ver. 37), and resulted in his being chosen by the lot (ver. 42). Again Saul should have been led to consider his own error as its cause, and a trespass or guilt offering might have sufficed (Levit. v. 4). To inflict the "curse" would be wholly unjust, as is implied in Jonathan's simple, mild, and submissive remonstrance (ver. 43). But Saul's last oath was more reckless than his first; it was ignorant and wilful, showed more concern about the literal fulfilment of his word than humble and faithful obedience to a higher will, and brought him to the brink of a great crime.

> "Take then no vow at random: ta'en in faith
> Preserve it; yet not bent, as Jephthah once,
> Blindly to execute a rash resolve,
> Whom better it had suited to exclaim,
> 'I have done ill,' than to redeem his pledge
> By doing worse" (Dante, 'Par.' v.).

V. BRINGING DEEP HUMILIATION (ver. 45). The ominous silence of the people (ver. 39) is followed by their unanimous and resolute voice, in which reason and justice, conscience and God, speak with irresistible might. They set their will in opposition to his, and he is compelled to submit. His purpose is frustrated. "The son is raised above the father, and the people above the king." But although his sin is now forced home upon him, of voluntary submission there is no sign. Rashness and self-will are sure to meet with a check, and happy is he who lays to heart the lesson which it teaches.

VI. DEFEATING ITS OWN AIMS (ver. 46). "My father hath brought disaster on the land," &c. (vers. 29, 30; Josh. vii. 25). The completeness of the overthrow of the enemy is marred. The opportunity of inflicting a fatal blow upon them is lost. "And there was sore war against the Philistines all the days of Saul" (ver. 52). That which begins in rashness ends in disappointment and grief.—D.

EXPOSITION.

JONATHAN'S DANGER AND DELIVERANCE (vers. 36—46). Ver. 36.—**Let us go down after the Philistines by night.** Saul, conscious that he had prevented the victory from being so decisive as it would otherwise have been, proposes to repair his fault, now that the people have taken food, by continuing the pursuit during the night. The people render the same unquestioning obedience as before, but Ahiah gives counsel that they should first ask the approval of God. **Let us draw near hither.** I. e. to the altar which Saul had just set up. Ahiah may have done this because he disapproved of Saul's project, or because generally God ought to be consulted before undertaking anything of importance. Already the neg-lect of this had led to no good results (see ver. 19).

Vers. 37, 38.—**He answered him not.** From this silence Saul concludes that some sin has been committed, and therefore calls together **all the chief of the people**—literally, "the corner stones" (Judges xx. 2)—to inquire who was the guilty person, and wherein he had sinned.

Ver. 39.—**He shall surely die.** With despotic violence, without waiting to learn what the offence was, and judging simply by consequences, because he was delayed in following up the pursuit, he takes a solemn oath that the offending person shall be put to death. Thus twice in the same day he was guilty of the sin of rash swearing. The people condemn him by their silence. They had obeyed him with ready devotion ; but now they listen in terror to the rash and violent words which condemn to death the young hero by whom God had that day wrought deliverance for them.

Vers. 40, 41.—As God also condemned Saul by his silence, the Urim and Thummim giving no answer, he places himself and Jonathan on one side, and the people on the other, and determines to cast lots. He then prays, **Give a perfect lot**, or, as in the margin, "Show" (literally, give) "the innocent." This is undoubtedly the meaning of the Hebrew, while the rendering of the text is taken from Kimchi. There are few mistranslations of the A. V. which have not some good Jewish authority for them, as King James's translators were singularly well versed in Jewish literature, while they seem strangely to have neglected the still higher authority of the ancient versions. These generally translate "Give holiness," a phrase equivalent to "Show the truth." The Septuagint and Vulgate add explanations, which, however, throw no light upon the passage.

Ver. 44. — **God do so**, &c. Again Saul takes an oath to put Jonathan to death, supposing himself bound by his former words. But he must have been pained beyond measure at the miserable consequences of his rashness, and have bitterly reproached himself for thus twice marring the happiness of the day by unhallowed oaths. Jonathan's trespass, committed unwittingly, required nothing more than a trespass offering for its expiation, nor did the silence of the Urim and Thummim imply any fault in him. The fault lay in Saul having imposed an oath upon the army ; that oath had been broken, and a formal expiation must be made. But Saul was by nature a despot, and could endure nothing that seemed even for the moment to stand in his way.

Ver. 45.—**The people said.** They had hitherto shown their disapproval of Saul's conduct by their silence ; now they decide that Jonathan shall not die, and their decision was right and godly. Saul might feel bound by his rash oath, but the consciences of the people told them that an oath to commit a crime is an oath to be repented of as a sin, and not to be performed as a duty. They do not say, however, **God forbid**, but "Far be it." The name of the Deity is constantly taken in vain in the A. V. without adding either beauty or energy to the word of God. But even if it did, what right have translators to add energy to the word of God ? **He hath wrought with God this day.** The argument of the people is wise and good. Jonathan's whole conduct on that day proved an especial presence of God with him. It would be

morally wrong and an offence against religion to condemn that which God approved, and the people therefore set their oath against the king's oath, and prevail.

Ver. 46.—**Saul went up,** &c. Thus, as the final result of his self-will, Saul had to discontinue his pursuit of the Philistines, and their power, though weakened by the overthrow, remained unbroken.

SUMMARY OF SAUL'S WARS, AND ACCOUNT OF HIS FAMILY (vers. 47—52). Ver. 47.— **So Saul took the kingdom.** Instead of *so* the Hebrew has *and*, rightly ; for this is no result or consequence of Saul's victory over the Philistines, but a mere historical introduction to the summary of his wars. The more correct translation would be, "When Saul had taken the kingdom over Israel, he fought," &c. Saul's reign was valiant and full of military glory. He was, in fact, in war all that the people had longed for, and not only did he gain independence for Israel, but laid the foundation of the vast empire of David and Solomon. But it is not the purpose of Holy Scripture to give us the history of all Saul's valiant exploits, but only of his moral probation and failure. Of wars we read more than enough in profane history ; here we read of the formation of character, and how a hero in the midst of noble and worthy feats of arms may yet lose something nobler and worthier—the favour of God. **On every side.** Moab and Ammon were on the east, Edom on the south, Zobah on the north-east, and the Philistines on the west. Zobah lay beyond Damascus, and, from the accounts given in 2 Sam. viii. 3—8 ; x. 6, must have been a powerful state. **He vexed them.** The verb is a judicial one, used of punishing the guilty, and might be translated "he chastised them." The Syriac and Vulgate give the real sense—"he was victorious."

Ver. 48.—**He gathered a host.** So the Syriac and Vulgate, but the margin is probably the true meaning, "He wrought mightily," or valiantly.

Ver. 49. — Saul's family and kindred. Three sons only of Saul are here mentioned, apparently those slain at the battle of Mount Gilboa, where, however, Ishui is named Abinadab (ch. xxxi. 2, as also in 1 Chron. viii. 33 ; ix. 39). A fourth son, Esh-baal, subsequently called Ishbosheth, is omitted. The daughters, Merab and Michal, are mentioned because of the history in ch. xviii. 17—21.

Ver. 50.—**Saul's wife was Ahinoam, the daughter of Ahimaaz.** We have noticed on ver. 3 the fondness of the family of Eli for names beginning with *Ah*, "brother." It does not justify us in concluding that Ahinoam was a descendant of Eli, but she may possibly have been so. **Abner,** whose name is here given in its strictly proper form,

Abiner, was Saul's first cousin, both Kish and Ner being sons of Abiel (comp. ch. ix. 1).

Ver. 51.—**The son of Abiel.** There can be little doubt that the right reading is *sons*, and not *son*. We thus get an intelligible statement—"And Kish the father of Saul, and Ner the father of Abner, were sons of Abiel."

Ver. 52.—The summary ends with two important particulars respecting Saul's kingdom—the first, that the Philistines were powerful and dangerous enemies to Israel all his days ; the second, that in order to carry on the war with them he ever kept around him the nucleus of a standing army. In thus forming a "school of heroes" he raised the whole spirit of the people, and took an essential and necessary step for maintaining Israel's freedom. With much of the despot in him, Saul had grand qualities as a soldier, and for many years admirably fulfilled the primary object for which he was chosen. And while he was thus giving the nation internal security, Samuel was teaching it how to use its growing prosperity, and was raising it in the scale of intellectual worth. If in the time of the judges we have Israel in its boyhood, as in the Sinaitic desert we have it in its infancy, under Saul and Samuel it reached its manhood, and became a powerful, vigorous, and well-ordered community, able to maintain its freedom, and with means for its internal development in the schools of the prophets, which ended in making it not merely enlightened itself, but the giver of light to the rest of mankind.

HOMILETICS.

Vers. 36—46.—*Seeking counsel of God and keeping one's word.* The facts are— 1. Saul, following his own impulse, desires to pursue the Philistines during the night, but is restrained by the priest advising to seek counsel of God. 2. No answer coming from God, Saul concludes that sin has been committed, and resolves that the sinner when discovered shall die. 3. A lot being taken, it falls on Jonathan, who admits having tasted honey, and submits to the sentence. 4. Saul, again solemnly consigning his son to death, is confronted by the people, who claim and rescue Jonathan's life on the ground that he was doing God's work that day. Rash impulse was the besetting sin of Saul. Being by Divine arrangement more than a military leader, it was his duty to seek guidance from God in times of uncertainty. Men of cooler judgment doubted whether it was wise to urge on all through the night men who had been worn down by fasting all day, and were scarcely free from their evening meal. The priest evidently saw that Saul's haste and the unexpressed hesitation of the people could be best dealt with by consulting the Urim. The Divine silence at once indicated that something was wrong, and according to precedent it was necessary to ascertain where it lay. The ceremonial wrong was Jonathan's, the moral Saul's. The moral degeneracy of Saul was not only seen in his impulsive neglect of God's counsel, but also in the self-complacent zeal with which he sought out the breach of his own rash command, and in the unnatural harshness of his sentence. People are sometimes better than their rulers, and hence the popular sense of justice demanded that in this instance royal authority and national custom should give way before the manifest will of God. Jonathan must not die, even though a king's word be broken. The three prominent matters of the narrative are seeking counsel, keeping one's word, and safety in God.

I. SEEKING COUNSEL. It is the part of wisdom in life's affairs to seek counsel of God ; and although sometimes no counsel is given, its absence is very instructive, and the causes of it are ascertainable. In the case of Saul both duty and privilege demanded a frequent appeal to God. On the occasion before us the need was real, the method was at hand, and response was possible, and a lack of response was itself of value. Our common human relation to God is not unlike that of Israel's king. 1. *There is for every one frequent need of Divine counsel.* Life; even under the direction of the clearest reason and purest natural impulses, is not safe ; for sin has disturbed the nature of the best of men. It is not always that that which at first seems good and safe turns out in the end to be so. What to do in private, domestic, and public affairs, and what proportion of time and strength to give to various claims, are questions pressing on every conscientious mind. In matters pertaining to religious belief, culture, and enterprise, we each, if life be not stagnant, require more than earthly wisdom. The heart of man is sensible that it is not in him infallibly and safely to "direct his steps," and hence in all lands it instinctively though often in ignorance, cries out for the living God (Prov. xvi. 9 ; Jer. x. 23). 2. *There is a method at hand.* The Urim was not far from Saul. By a study of God's will as seen in his word, his providence, the yearnings of a sanctified heart, and the voice of his people, we may gain guidance in addition to that private illu- mination which unquestionably comes in answer to true prayer. No rule can be laid down for individuals. Each day's circumstances must suggest the means we use to ascertain the will of God. 3. *There is reason for looking for a response to our seeking.* It was a tacit understanding with Saul on the settlement of the kingdom (ch. ix. 25—27 ; x. 24, 25) that he might count on the guidance of God. Samuel's exhortations and instructions all through proceeded on this assumption. Nor was God's silence on the present occasion contrary to this ; for it was of itself a signifi- cant indication of the mind of God. Saul knew its meaning. The exhortations to us to " seek the Lord," the distinct promises that he will " hear," the many instances on record in which men sought and followed the Lord, raise an assurance that the seed of Jacob shall not seek his face in vain (Isa. xix. 1). The answer may come in unlooked-for forms,—in the clearing of our moral perceptions, the secret bent given to the purified heart, the opening up of courses of action, or a concurrence of events and influences,—but come it will some time if we are sincere and earnest. 4. *The absence of response is often accountable.* We know why Saul's seeking for counsel was in vain. There are frequent instances in which the silence of God is conspicuous. He was silent when the Psalmist cried unto him to " awake " (Ps. xxxv. 22—24) ; when defiled men cried unto him (Isa. i. 12—15) ; when amidst the storm men were in fear (Matt. viii. 24—26) ; when in presence of a wounded heart he would not heed captious men (John viii. 6, 7) ; and when questioned by one who had no right to assume a tone of authority (John xix. 9). Even though our holiness of life, or at least consistency, be real, and our supposed need be urgent, it is possible that the discipline of faith and patience is the reason for no response.

II. KEEPING ONE'S WORD. Saul felt bound in honour to keep his word, even at the cost of his son's life. He found himself in an awkward position, for it would reveal an irresolution unfavourable to authority if he should overlook his son's deed under a plea of ignorance which any one might make ; and, on the other hand, as the people did believe Jonathan's plea, and held him to be the real victor of the day, it would expose Saul's folly and injustice if he should take away so valuable a life. Such was Saul's sense of the importance of keeping his word, that all must be sacri- ficed to it. 1. *There is a fictitious truthfulness.* The bare doing as he had said, and merely because he had said it, was Saul's ideal of truthfulness. Here, then, was a vague apprehension of a grand virtue, and a crude presentation of moral obliquity as being identical with it. Truth is a virtue entering into the depths of life ; and had Saul been really a man of truth, he would have considered Jonathan's case on its own merits, have honestly admitted the folly and sin of his own rash declaration, and have sacrificed his own repute to the general interests of righteousness. There is *much fictitious truthfulness in the world.* Some men, by sheer obstinacy of dispo- sition, will do as they say simply because they said it, heedless of the injury it may do. To keep to what one has acknowledged to be binding is supposed to be truth- fulness in act, and yet many will be rigorous in the observance of some moral obligations and careless of others. To avoid theft and murder is coincident with deeds of lying and selfishness. A similar fictitious truthfulness is seen in the careful outward observance of days without cherishing the spirit in accordance with them, and in the performance of acts of worship as a substitute for the homage of the soul. 2. *Real truthfulness is a quality of extreme importance.* Saul confessed this in his zeal for the fictitious ; as do all men in their devices to secure an appearance of it, and their instinctive homage to the reality when presented in word or deed. Real truthfulness does not apply merely to correspondence of statement with occurrence. It is another name for *reality* in thought, feeling, *life ;* and it applies to our relation both to man and God. The conformity of our nature with what is befitting a crea- ture of the Holy One is the real truthfulness. Hence, nothing enters the New Jerusalem that " maketh a lie." Hence, regeneration is a renewal " in the image of him " who created us. Hence, also, in so far as we are like unto him who is " the Truth," all our relations to men are pure, lovely, honest—the natural outcome of "truth in the inward parts." This quality is essential to the most perfect social confidence; for it renders fraud, deceit, selfishness, dissimulation, distrust impossible, and the reverse virtues real, whenever it is dominant in human nature. Attention to this in education is supremely important.

III. SAFETY IN GOD. Jonathan's life was safe in God's care in spite of zeal for a fictitious regard for truth on the part of his father. The voice of the people demanding his release was the voice of God, and the honour put on Jonathan during the previous day was evidence to all but the obstinate king of a favour much to be desired. He who had gone forth in the service of the Lord with true, honest heart, and had been shielded in the dangerous enterprise, was not forsaken by his God when now the rashness of man encompassed his life with peril. Thus, the custom of Eastern rulers keeping their word when once uttered (Judges xi. 30—39; Matt. xiv. 9), personal consistency, and royal authority must give place where God makes manifest his approval. Does not the position of Jonathan lead our thoughts on to our own in a greater day of trial? We are not to be tried by the variable impulse of man or established custom, but by impartial justice. What God declares shall be done when our day's battle is over will be done in truth. If he acquits us then, who is he that condemneth? His favour will save from a worse calamity than any that threatened Jonathan; and the practical question is how to come into such relation to God that the universal demand of justice shall be for our not perishing. The answer is—"There is no condemnation to them that are in Christ Jesus" (Rom. viii. 1); "Who shall lay anything to the charge of God's elect? It is God that justifieth" (Rom. viii. 33).

General lessons:—1. We are consistent with our privileges when not only our calamities and great affairs, but our ordinary actions, are made subject to Divine guidance (Phil. iv. 6). 2. It is especially desirable to seek counsel of God when we are conscious of restlessness and ill-regulated impulse. 3. Faithfulness requires that, a promise or engagement being made, we keep our word even at much personal cost; but when such loss would occur, generosity requires of the gainer that it be not wholly insisted on (Ps. xv. 4; Luke vi. 31; Ephes. iv. 32). 4. Truthfulness in character is the opposite of sinfulness, for sin is a practical lie (Gen. iii. 1—5; 1 John ii. 4). 5. Our final safety rests not on the past untarnished purity of life (Rom. iii. 10; 1 John i. 8), but on our being identified with Messiah's life and purpose (John xiv. 19; Rom. viii. 35—39).

Vers. 47—52.—*Gradation in service.* The facts are—1. Saul's warlike efforts issue in the general discomfiture of his enemies. 2. The domestic relations of Saul are incorporated in the record of facts pertaining to gradual unfolding of the Divine purpose. 3. During all his conflicts with the Philistines Saul shows prudence in strengthening his military position. The section gives a summary of the military operations of Saul's reign and of the success of his efforts, and also places on the page of sacred history the names of the members of his family. Judged by rules applicable to ordinary historical records, the brief reference to his wars may appear to have little or no moral significance, and the allusion to his father, his wife, and children to be merely a matter of Jewish antiquarian interest. But the Bible was composed under the guidance of a higher than human wisdom; and both in what it includes and omits there is a relation to the higher spiritual issues in which the events of Jewish history culminated. There had been given to Saul the opportunity of rendering service to Israel, both by setting them free from the oppression of enemies and by inspiring the nation with a spirit conformable to the great Messianic purpose for which they existed. He failed to enter into the high spiritual aspirations suitable to a ruler of the chosen race, and therefore history simply records the fact that his life was spent in the rendering of the lower kind of service. Repression of the foe was service, but of an inferior type. He missed a chance of doing a more glorious and enduring work.

I. THERE IS A GRADUATED SERVICE POSSIBLE TO MEN. The possibilities of Saul's life when entering on his public career are manifest. They were not realised, though he, using certain natural abilities, succeeded in rendering valuable service as a warrior. Of every human being it may be said, as he enters on life, there is a possibility of conferring few or many, small or great, benefits on his kind. The conditions of rising to the higher grade of service are the possession of appropriate natural abilities and an occasion for employing them. These conditions being given, it rests with his will to rise to the higher level or to be content with the lower. Secular and spiritual are not always good terms to indicate spheres of activity, because every act can and ought to be spiritual in its tone and principle. But for our present purpose we may use the terms in the common acceptation. There are grades of service—1. *In the secular sphere.* It may not be easy to construct a scale that shall in detail exhibit the relative value of labour, but there are broad outlines which are always recognised in civilised society. Manual toil is not comparable with mental. That service which relates to the material condition of mankind is inferior to that which bears on the moral. Whatever produces temporary effects is of less value than that which issues in the enduring. There are men who remain all their days on the lowest level, and there have been some who rose from that position to almost, if not quite, the highest in the scale. No man's contribution to the common weal is to be despised, but every man is bound to rise as high as possible in the scale of valuable service. 2. *In the spiritual sphere.* As in ancient times there were "hewers of wood and drawers of water," subordinate, in the common work of the chosen race, to men of loftier aspiration and more refined occupation, so in the Christian Church there are diversities in gifts and service. Generically all true Christians are equal in privilege of position and in function as witness-bearers for Christ. And there is no room for boasting or invidious comparisons, as it is the "grace of God" which worketh all in all. Yet as a matter of fact, arising partly from great diversity in natural capacity and partly from causes in the individual will, there are distinct gradations in kind and value of service rendered, as tested by the strength of principle involved and the enduring character of the effect. There are men who devote time and means only to the preservation of the outward organisations of the Church. Others, nourishing their own piety with care, minister consolation and instruction to the sick and ignorant. Others, again, by a wonderfully holy and beautiful life at home, as well as quiet zeal outside, train souls for Christ, and leave an imperishable impress on the world.

II. The GRADE OF SERVICE ATTAINED TO DEPENDS CHIEFLY ON A WISE USE OF EARLY OPPORTUNITIES. Had Saul cherished the spirit awakened by his converse with Samuel and the subsequent inspiration from God (ch. ix. 25—27 ; x. 9), and strengthened it by obedience in the hour of trial (ch. xiii. 13), far nobler service would have been recorded of him than that he made war with the Philistines all the days of his life. His successor David entered on a higher sphere. Of course both in the secular and spiritual spheres natural capacity and education are important determinants, as also the occurrence of favourable opportunities. But, as a rule, the position we occupy depends on our disposition to improve such opportunities as now and then fall to the lot of most persons. Hundreds are "hewers of wood and drawers of water" all their days because in early life they failed to seize the chance of developing their own powers. In science and literature there are men who, when raw youths of meagre education, laid hold of some passing opportunity for self-improvement which opened the way to still higher advantages. In the Church there are and have been noble men who, carefully nourishing the sacred gift of a new spirit and availing themselves of some chance of doing good, rose from obscurity to the distinction of ambassadors for Christ, "whose praise is in all the Churches." There are Sauls and Davids still.

General lessons :—1. While thankful for being permitted to render the smallest service to the Church and the world, we should "covet earnestly the best gifts" (1 Cor. xii. 31). 2. Youths and persons young in the Christian life should be impressed with the importance of the due improvement of their position. 3. Whenever possible we should look favourably upon any effort to enter on a wider range of usefulness. 4. The standard of service, as to aim, method, and spirit, by which our aspirations should be regulated, is the life of Christ.

HOMILIES BY VARIOUS AUTHORS.

Vers. 36, 37. (AJALON.)—*Drawing near to God.* Of the fallen house of Eli, one at least, Ahiah (Ahimelech—ch. xxi. 1), the grandson of Phinehas, appears to have been a faithful servant of God. When the people, having ended their pursuit of the Philistines and satisfied their hunger, rested around their gleaming camp-fires, and Saul proposed a nocturnal expedition against the enemy so as "not to leave a man of them," he devoutly and courageously interposed with the words, "Let us draw near hither unto God." He had already witnessed the effects of the king's rashness, feared its further results, and felt that "it was dangerous to undertake anything without asking counsel of God" (see ver. 19). His language is suggestive of—

I. THE EXERCISE OF A RELIGIOUS PEOPLE in prayer. It is—1. *A possibility.* For God is "nigh at hand, and not afar off" (Deut. iv. 7; Ps. cxlv. 18; Jer. xxiii. 23). He has provided a way of access—an altar (Heb. xiii. 10), a sacrifice, and a high priest (Heb. vii. 19; x. 20—22; Ephes. ii. 18). The throne of God is not only a throne of glory and of judgment, but also a throne of *grace.* "The Lamb is in the midst of the throne." 2. *A privilege.* What higher privilege or honour can be conferred than to hold intercourse with so glorious a Being? What greater benefit than his fellowship, counsel, and aid? (Ps. lxxiii. 28). 3. *An obligation,* arising out of his relationship to men, and indicated by his word, by conscience, and the deepest needs and impulses of the soul. "Draw nigh to God, and he will draw nigh to you" (James iv. 8; Ps. xliii. 4). "Ye people, pour out your heart before him" (Ps. lxii. 8).

II. THE VOCATION OF A FAITHFUL MINISTER with respect to this exercise. It is—1. *To bear a fearless testimony concerning it before the people:* setting forth the supreme claims of God upon their homage, reminding them of their want, reproving their forgetfulness, and teaching them the good and right way (ch. xii. 23). 2. *To exhibit a devotional spirit in his intercourse with them.* He who exhorts others to pray should be himself a man of prayer, and speak to them by his example as well as by his words. Exhortation to them is often less beneficial than intercession for them. "We will give ourselves continually to prayer" (Acts vi. 4). 3. *To invite them to sincere union with him* in seeking the face of God. "Let *us* draw near." "Let us pray"—not merely with the lips or in outward form, not regarding iniquity in the heart; but humbly and sincerely, with one accord, with a true heart, and in full assurance of faith (Ps. lxvi. 18; 1 Tim. ii. 8).

III. THE INFLUENCE OF TIMELY INTERVENTION on the part of a good man. "*Then*" (when both king and people were about to set forth without seeking Divine counsel) said the priest," &c.; and he did not speak in vain (ver. 37). Such advice and prayer are generally effectual—1. In *restraining* from the pursuit of a wrong course—a doubtful or dangerous enterprise, devotion to worldly objects, following selfish and revengeful inclinations, &c. A single "word in season" sometimes prevents much mischief. 2. In *constraining* to the performance of neglected duty. The inquiry which Saul had broken off was now formally resumed, though not on his part in a right spirit. 3. In *obtaining* the possession of needful good. It is not always what is sought. There may be delay or refusal in granting a definite answer; but the experience thereby gained is itself beneficial, and the necessary condition of obtaining the highest good.

IV. THE INSTRUCTIVENESS OF UNANSWERED PRAYER. "He answered him not that day" (ch. xxviii. 6, 15). The silence of God is significant. It indicates—1. *The presence of sin,* which hinders the communications of Heaven, as a cloud intercepts the beams of the sun (Isa. lix. 2; Lam. iii. 44; Hosea v. 15; James iv. 2, 3). 2. *The duty of its discovery,* by means of diligent inquiry and self-examination (Josh. vii. 13; Ps. cxxxix. 23, 24; Lam. iii. 40). 3. *The necessity of humiliation,* removing "the accursed thing," and turning to God with full purpose of heart, so that he may cause his face to shine upon us. "Praying will either make a man leave off sinning or sinning will make him leave off praying." In the former case his path is upward into the light, in the latter it is downward into darkness and despair.—D.

Ver. 45. (AJALON.)—*Remonstrance with rulers.* The obedience which subjects owe to the commands of a ruler is not absolute, but limited by their obligation to a higher law. When he determines on measures which are not good they have a right to remonstrate, and are sometimes bound to do so. Concerning the remonstrance of the people with Saul (after yielding notable obedience in other things—vers. 26, 34, 36), observe that it was—

I. JUST ; in opposition to an unreasonable, arbitrary, and cruel decision (ver. 44), in defence of the innocent, and impelled by " an enlightened conscience and generous enthusiasm."

II. DEVOUT ; recognising the hand of God in the victory of Jonathan, testifying their gratitude for the deliverance wrought through him, and obeying a higher will, thereby indicated, in preference to that of the king.

III. RESOLUTE ; whilst stating the ground of their determination, manifesting a disposition to carry it into effect, and binding themselves by a united and solemn oath to do so.

IV. SUCCESSFUL. They prevailed, Jonathan was rescued, a great crime was prevented, and Saul was checked and warned in his despotic career. When the people remonstrate in the same manner they may expect the same success.—D.

Ver. 45. (AJALON.)—*Co-operation with God.* " He hath wrought with God this day." Apart from the power of God man can do nothing. In opposition to it he is defeated and crushed. Only in co-operation with it can he accomplish anything great or good. As in the material, so in the moral and spiritual world it is our wisdom, strength, and dignity to be " labourers together with God " (1 Cor. iii. 9 ; 2 Cor. vi. 1). Notice—

THE AIM of this co-operation. 1. To overcome sin and misery amongst men. 2. To promote righteousness and happiness in ourselves and others. 3. To extend the kingdom and glory of God.

II. THE MEANS. 1. Studying the laws or modes of God's working (Eccles. iii. 14) and the manifold intimations of his will. 2. Trusting in him, firmly resting on his promises, and patiently waiting their fulfilment. Oftentimes " our strength is to sit still." 3. Using with diligence the strength he gives, still depending on him " who worketh all in all " (1 Cor. xii. 6 ; Phil. ii. 13 ; Isa. xxvi. 12).

III. THE RESULT. 1. Conscious approbation of God. 2. Effectual aid. 3. Certain achievement. " In due season we shall *reap* if we faint not."—D.

Vers. 47—52. (GIBEAH.)—*Saul's sovereignty and wars, his army and family.* From this summary observe that—

I. THE PEOPLE OF GOD ARE BESET BY NUMEROUS ADVERSARIES. Moab, Ammon, &c.—" on every side," of varied character, imbued with the same enmity, and threatening their existence. Conflict is necessary to self-preservation.

II. THE CHASTISEMENT OF THE WICKED IS INFLICTED BY SUITABLE AGENTS. " And Saul took the kingdom," &c. " Whithersoever he turned himself he chastised them. For this work he was well qualified by warlike courage and skill, indomitable energy and zeal, and in it he met with success. God often employs men to carry out his purposes who possess little of the spirit of obedience.

III. DIVERSITY OF CHARACTER IS OFTEN MANIFESTED IN THE SAME CIRCUMSTANCES. " Now the sons of Saul were Jonathan, and Ishui (Abinadab), and Melchishua." The fourth, Esh-baal (Ishbosheth), is not here mentioned. " And the names of his two daughters were Merab and Michal," &c. (vers. 49—51). What a contrast of character is presented in this family—*e. g.* between Jonathan and his father and sister (Michal). Hidden hereditary influences and special associations may have contributed to the difference, but much more the voluntary use or abuse of preliminary conditions, outward circumstances, and spiritual gifts.

IV. THE MISUSE OF POWER IS THE RUIN OF ITS POSSESSOR. " He gathered a host " (ver. 48), or acquired power. He formed a standing army, as it had been predicted (ch. viii. 11, 16 ; xxii. 7). He employed his power for his own aggrandisement. " If he could have done as he wished, there would have been an end to the supremacy of God in Israel. Rude despotism would have usurped its place " (Hengstenberg).

Samuel's antagonistic working preserved the principle of the theocracy, and Saul's kingdom departed from him (Dan. iv. 31).

V. The perversity of men involves them in sore distress. "There was sore war," &c. (ver. 52). "Very different had been the state of things when Samuel ruled Israel (ch. vii. 13). And the people who looked for protection to an arm of flesh rather than to God, who was their King, were punished by that instrument— Saul—which they had chosen for themselves in order that they might be saved by it" (Wordsworth's 'Com.').

VI. The kingdom of God must prevail over all opposition, whether from open adversaries or disloyal adherents. That which seems to hinder it is often made a means of its furtherance. The Divine purpose concerning it cannot be defeated. It endured, wrought, and was developed amidst all the vicissitudes of Israel's history until the advent of "the King Messiah," and it is still advancing toward its perfect and eternal consummation (1 Cor. xv. 24, 25).—D.

Vers. 47, 48.—*The restless king.* When a locomotive engine slips off the rails, it would do little harm if it could stop at once; but its momentum carries it forward. It ploughs up the way, it dashes over an embankment, and drags ever so many carriages and passengers to destruction. So is it with the deflection of a man of force and influence from the right course. If he would stop at once, or if he should soon die, the mischief might be small. But the momentum of his character and position drives him on; he goes further and further from the straight lines of righteousness, and in the end not only hurls himself on ruin, but pulls many after him to their hurt. It was so with king Saul. He sinned, and the prophet Samuel intimated to him the Lord's displeasure. Had the king stopped there, no great damage might have been done; but he could not stop. The vehemence of his nature, and what seemed to be the necessities of his position, drove him on. He became more and more arbitrary. So we see him in this chapter of the history issuing the most unreasonable restrictions and commands, lenient when he should have been strict, and severe when he should have been lenient. By his rashness he very nearly turned to mourning the signal·triumph over the Philistines which crowned the faith and valour of Prince Jonathan, and from that day he fell even below his own subjects in his perception of right and wrong, forfeited their respect, and became more and more wayward and unreasonable. Yet he had successes—great successes as a warrior. His martial temper and skill did not leave him, and all the surrounding nations felt his heavy hand. Not content with defending the territory, Saul organised and disciplined the army of Israel, so as to be able to use it in aggressive war, and smite the nations which had at various periods oppressed his country. Whithersoever he turned himself he was victorious. And yet Saul did not conduct those wars or win those victories in a manner worthy of a servant of Jehovah. There is no trace of his having command or counsel from God. There is no reference to the fulness of Divine promise regarding the land such as one sees in the thoughts of David when he enlarged the territory of Israel till they possessed all that the Lord had assigned to the posterity of Abraham. Saul struck right and left as the mood seized him, and "whithersoever he turned himself" he conquered. This is worth noting. A man may have many successes in life; nay, may have them in the Church, and in vindication of sacred truth, yet not have them as a Christian ought, and so not please God. Especially may this be the case in ecclesiastical and theological controversy. One may be quite on the right side, and may strike heavy blows at errorists and heretics all round, just as he "turns himself," and yet have no communion with the God of truth whom he seems to serve, obey motives unworthy of a servant of Christ, and indulge a harsh and wilful temper such as God cannot approve. Restlessness indicates an undisciplined, unhallowed energy. Restfulness belongs to those who submit all their plans to God, and lay all their energies at his feet. No men are so deaf to expostulation and so hard of recovery as those who try to keep an accusing conscience quiet by ceaseless activity. They turn hither and smite, thither and smite again. Perhaps they attack what deserves to be smitten; but it is a bad sign of themselves that they are never still before the Lord, letting his word search them. Under ever so much noise of debate and controversy, what hollowness may lurk, what degeneracy! Alas, it is so easy to go wrong, and having gone wrong once, easier to do it again. And then it is so hard to accept blame before God or man, and to submit to correction. Why not brandish our swords, and show ourselves brave Christian soldiers? Will not this compensate for our faults? O foolish Saul! O more foolish followers of the restless, haughty king! Lord, keep us back from all presumptuous sin!—F.

EXPOSITION.

FINAL REJECTION OF SAUL (CH. XV).

CHAPTER XV.

DIVINE COMMAND TO PUNISH THE AMA-LEKITES, AND ITS EXECUTION BY SAUL (vers. 1—9). Ver. 1.—**Samuel also said.** Better literally, "And Samuel said." There is no note of time, but probably a consider-able interval elapsed before this second trial of Saul was made. God does not finally reject a man until, after repeated oppor-tunities for repentance, he finally proves obdurate. David committed worse crimes than Saul, but he had a tender conscience, and each fall was followed by deep and earnest sorrow. Saul sinned and repented not. Just, then, as Eli had a first warning, which, though apparently unconditional in its terms (ch. ii. 27—36), was really a call to repentance, and was only made irrevocable by his persistence for many years in the same sins (ch. iii. 11—14), so was it with Saul. The prophet's words in ch. xiii. 13, 14 were a stern warning, and had Saul taken them to heart, God would have forgiven him his sin. He repented not, but repeated the offence, and so the sentence was confirmed. When, then, critics say that we have two accounts of Saul's rejection, and that he is represented as having been set aside first for one reason and then for another, their ob-jection arises entirely from a false view of God's dealings with mankind. Alike pro-mises and threatenings, blessings and pun-ishments are conditional; for there is no heathen fatalism in Holy Scripture, but mercy waiting to triumph over justice. God, then, was not willing lightly to cast away so noble an instrument as Saul. His first sin too had been committed when he was new in the kingdom, and in a position of danger and difficulty. He waits, therefore, till Saul has had some years of success and power, and his character has developed itself, and is taking its permanent form; and then again gives him a trial in order to test his fitness to be a theocratic king. The interest, then, of this chapter lies in the unfolding of Saul's character, and so it follows immediately upon ch. xiv., which was occupied with the same subject, without any note of chronology, because the historical narrative is subserv-ient to the personal. Hence, too, Samuel's

solemn address, reminding Saul that he was Jehovah's anointed one, and therefore had special duties towards him; that he had also been anointed by Samuel's instrumentality, and after earnest instruction as to his duties; and, finally, that Israel was Jehovah's people, and their king, therefore, bound to obey Jehovah's commands.

Ver. 2.—**Amalek.** The Amalekites were a fierce race of nomads who inhabited the desert to the south of Judæa towards Egypt. They were, and still continue to be in their descendants, the Bedouins, an untamable race of savages, whose delight is in robbery and plunder. Between them and Israel there was bitter hostility occasioned by their having attacked the people immediately after the Exodus (Exod. xvii. 8—16), and the command there given to exterminate them is repeated now, probably in conse-quence of their raids having become more numerous and sanguinary under their present king, as we gather from ver. 33. The refer-ence to a war with the Amalektes in ch. xiv. 48 no doubt refers to this expedition, as we have there a mere summary of Saul's military enterprises. **I remember.** Literally, "I have visited;" but the sense of *remembering* seems confirmed by such passages as Gen. xxi. 1; l. 24; Isa. xxiii. 17; xxvi. 16. The Septuagint, however, and Aquila give a very good sense: "I have considered," "thought over." **How he laid wait for him in the way.** There is no idea in the Hebrew of ambuscade or treachery. It is simply, "How he set himself in the way against him," *i. e.* opposed, withstood him, tried to bar his progress.

Ver. 3.—**Utterly destroy.** Hebrew, "put under the ban." The word *herem*, ban, properly signifies a thing set apart, especially one devoted to God; and whatever was so devoted could not be redeemed, but must be slain. When a country was put under the ban, all living things, men and cattle, were to be killed; no spoil might be taken, but it was to be burnt, and things indestructible by fire, as silver and gold, were to be brought into the treasury. Everything, in short, belonging to such a nation was looked upon as accursed (see Num. xxi. 2, 3).

Ver. 4.—**Telaim.** Kimchi identifies this

with Telem (Josh. xv. 24), a place on the southern border of Judah near the country of the Amalekites. But as *telaim* means "lambs," more probably *beth*, "house," is to be understood; and so it was no town, but the "place of lambs," *i. e.* some open spot where at the proper season the lambs were collected from the pastures in the wilderness. **Ten thousand men of Judah.** A very small number compared with the hosts of Israel, especially as Judah was most exposed to the Amalekite, raids (but see on ch. xi. 8. A large army was necessary, because the Bedouin race, though offering little direct resistance, would be very difficult to overtake.

Ver. 5.—**A city of Amalek.** More probably *Ir-Amalek*, the name of their one town. **Laid wait.** Many commentators follow the Syriac in rendering this verb *contended, strove;* others, like the A. V., with the Septuagint and Vulgate, regard it as a contracted form of a verb signifying *to lay an ambuscade.* It is not, however, a **valley,** but a "torrent-bed," which was more fit for an ambush than for a strife or dispute. Rashi explains the verb as signifying "contended with himself," and quotes from the Talmud an opinion that when Saul reached the torrent he called to mind the command in Deut. xxi. 4, to slay a heifer at a torrent in expiation of a murder, and had misgivings whether a slaughter so indiscriminate as that on which he was engaged could be justified. The law of the Herem was soon softened down, but we find David in several of his wars guilty of fearful cruelty. The translation of the A. V. is the more probable.

Ver. 6.—**Saul said unto the Kenites.** Not while he was lying in ambush in the torrent-bed, but after smiting Ir-Amalek. The Kenites were always friendly to the Israelites, but seem, like the Amalekites, to have been a Bedouin nation, ever wandering about without a settled home. In Abraham's time they were a powerful people (Gen. xv. 19), but, for some reason or other, broke up into small tribes, some, as those here spoken of, choosing the wilderness of Judah for their home (Judges i. 16), others living far to the north in Naphtali (*ibid.* iv. 11, 17), others among the rocks of Arabia Petræa. Of these last we know but little, but the rest continued to be on friendly terms with David (1 Sam. xxx. 29).

Ver. 7.—**From Havilah until thou comest to Shur.** Hebrew, "from Havilah as thou goest towards Shur." It seems impossible that this Havilah can be the north-western portion of Yemen, called Chawlan, and identified with the Havilah of Gen. x. 7, 29, as this would make Saul smite them from south-east to north-west. **Shur,** which means *wall,* is, as Wellhausen (Text Sam. 97) observes,

originally the name of the wall which ran from Pelusium past Migdol to Hero, and which gave to Egypt, as Ebers thinks, its name Mizraim, the *enclosed* or *fortified.* Shur is again mentioned in ch. xxvii. 8 as indicating the direction towards Egypt of the region occupied by the Amalekites. Havilah, which means *circle,* must have been some spot on the route to the isthmus of Suez, lying on the edge of the wilderness to the south of Judah, where Saul commenced his foray. Beginning thus upon the borders of Judæa, Saul continued his devastations up to the limits of Egypt.

Ver. 8.—**He took Agag.** This was the official name of the Amalekite kings (see Num. xxiv. 7), as Pharaoh was that of the kings of Egypt. For its meaning we must wait till we know more about the language of this race. Agag, however, from ver. 32, seems to have been able to speak Hebrew. **He utterly destroyed** — *i. e.* put under the ban—**all the people.** They appear, however, again in ch. xxvii. 8, and with so vast a wilderness in which to take refuge, it would be impossible really to exterminate a people used to lead a wandering life. Moreover, as soon as Israel began to lay hands on the spoil the pursuit would flag, as the cattle would be killed by over-driving.

Ver. 9.—**The fatlings.** So the Syriac and Chaldee render the word, but the Hebrew literally means "the second best." Kimchi and Tanchum give perhaps a preferable rendering, "the second-born," such animals being considered superior to the first-born, as the dams had by that time arrived at their full strength.

REJECTION OF SAUL AND HIS DYNASTY (vers. 10—23). Ver. 11.—**It repenteth me.** By the law of man's free will his concurrence is necessary in carrying out the Divine purpose, and consequently every man called to the execution of any such purpose undergoes a probation. God's purpose will be finally carried out, but each special instrument, if it prove unworthy, will be laid aside. This change of administration is always described in Scriptural language as God's repentance, possibly because the phrase contains also the idea of the Divine grief over the rebellious sinner. But though Saul and his dynasty were thus put aside, and no longer represented Jehovah, still Saul remained the actual king, because God works slowly by the natural sequence of cause and effect. Saul's ill-governed temper, and his hatred and malice towards David, were the means of bringing about his ruin. **It grieved Samuel.** Hebrew, "it burned to Samuel," *i. e.* he was angry and displeased. The same phrase occurs in Jonah iv. 1, where it is rendered "he was very angry." But with whom was Samuel vexed? Generally at the whole course of events, but especially with Saul. In choosing him he had hoped that, in addition to high military qualities, he would possess a religious and obedient heart. He had now obtained for him a second trial, and if, warned by his earlier failure, he had proved trustworthy all might have been well. Saul had too many noble gifts for Samuel to feel indifferent at the perversion of so great an intellect and so heroic a heart. But he was of a despotic temperament, and would bend to no will but his own ; and so he had saved the best of the plunder to enrich the people, and Agag possibly as a proof of his personal triumph. **And he cried unto Jehovah all night.** *I. e.* he offered an earnest prayer for forgiveness for Saul, and for a change in his heart. As Abravanel says, Samuel no doubt loved Saul for his beauty and heroism, and therefore prayed for him ; but no change came in answer to his prayer, and as forgiveness is conditional upon man's repentance, Saul was not forgiven. It is remarkable how often Samuel is represented as "crying" unto God (see ch. vii. 8, 9 ; xii. 18).

Ver. 12.—**Samuel rose early.** If Samuel was at home at Ramah, he would have a journey of several days before reaching Carmel, the city mentioned in Josh. xv. 55, on the road from Arad, on the borders of the wilderness of Judah, about ten miles south-east of Hebron. The words **in the morning** should be joined with **rose early.** Before setting out, however, Samuel learned that Saul had already marched northward towards Gilgal, having first **set him up a place** —Hebrew, "a hand," *i. e.* a monument, something to call attention to his victory. In 2 Sam. xviii. 18 Absalom's pillar is styled "Absalom's hand." A Hebrew trophy in honour of a victory possibly had a hand carved upon it. **Gilgal** was the city in the Jordan valley near Jericho, whither Samuel now followed Saul.

Ver. 13.—**Blessed be thou of Jehovah.** Saul meets Samuel with all external respect, and seems even to expect his approval, saying, **I have performed the commandment of Jehovah.** And so he had in the half-way in which men generally keep God's commandments, doing that part which is agreeable to themselves, and leaving that part undone which gives them neither pleasure nor profit. Saul probably had thought very little about the exact terms of the command given him, and having successfully accomplished the main point of carrying out a vast foray against the Amalekites, regarded the captive king and the plundered cattle as proofs of his victory. The trophy at Carmel is a token of his own self-satisfaction.

Ver. 14.—**What meaneth then this bleating ?** &c. Literally, "What is this voice of sheep in my ears, and the voice of oxen ?"

While Saul's own conscience was silent they were proclaiming his disobedience.

Ver. 15.—**They have brought them.** No doubt this was verbally true, and very probably the excuse of holding a great sacrifice to Jehovah had been put prominently forward. But reasons are never wanting when men have made up their minds, and the people who so readily obeyed Saul before (ch. xiv. 24, 34, 40) would have obeyed him now, had he really wished it. For a king so wilful and imperious as Saul thus to seek for excuses, and try to throw the blame on others, marks, as has been well observed, a thorough break-down of his moral character.

Ver. 16.—**Stay.** Samuel will hear no more. Long as he had striven for him in prayer (ver. 11), he now feels that Saul has fallen too low for recovery to be possible. **This night.** It is plain from this that Samuel had not gone to meet Saul at Carmel, but on receiving information of his movements had proceeded straight to Gilgal, distant from Ramah about fifteen miles.

Ver. 17.—**When**—rather, Though—**thou wast little in thine own sight.** Before his elevation to the royal dignity Saul had deemed himself altogether unequal to so heavy a task (ch. ix. 21) ; now, after great military successes, he is filled with arrogance, and will rule in open defiance of the conditions upon which Jehovah had appointed him to the office

Ver. 18.—**The sinners.** The Amalekites were a race of robbers, and the command "to devote them" was the consequence of the robbery and murder practised by them on the Israelite borders.

Vers. 20, 21.—Saul's justification of himself is remarkable, as he seems entirely unconscious of having done anything wrong. His education had no doubt been defective (ch. x. 12), and his knowledge of the law was probably very small ; but he must have listened to Samuel's injunctions in a very off-hand way, and have troubled himself about very little more than that he was to make war upon the Amalekites. There may even have been the wish in his mind to let Samuel know that he was now king, and would carry on affairs after his own fashion. The very form of his answer requires notice ; for the word rendered **yea** is literally *in that,* or *because,* and may be paraphrased as follows : Do you reproach me thus because I have obeyed you ? See, there is Agag in proof of our victory ; and if the people have spared the cattle, it was with the best of intentions. The next clause, **the chief of the things which should have been utterly destroyed,** reads in the A. V. like an ironical parenthesis. It is not so, but an important part of Saul's defence. These sheep and oxen were "the best of the devoted things," selected as the first-fruits for sacrifice. Saul may not have known that such a sacrifice was forbidden (Deut. xiii. 15 — 17). The words, **to sacrifice unto Jehovah thy God,** imply that Samuel ought to be pleased at the victorious army doing this public homage to the Deity whose prophet he was. It was virtually a compliment to himself, and is very much in accordance with the notions of the generality of people now, who consider that attendance at a place of worship, or sending their children to school, is a favour to the clergyman.

Vers. 22, 23.—The rebuke of Samuel contains one of those pregnant sayings which mark the high moral tone of the teaching of the prophets, and soon became a fundamental principle with them. **To obey is better than sacrifice** is a dictum reproduced by Hosea (ch. vi. 6), the most ancient of those prophets of Israel whose lessons have been preserved in writing; it is referred to in still earlier psalms (see Ps. l. 8—14 ; li. 16, 17) ; by other prophets (Isa. i. 11 ; Jer. vi. 20 ; Micah vi. 6, 8) ; and finally received our Lord's special approbation (Matt. ix. 13 ; xii. 7). It asserts in the clearest terms the superiority of moral to ritual worship, and that God can only be really served with the heart. **Witchcraft** is in the Hebrew *divinution*, a sin always strongly condemned in the Old Testament. **Iniquity** literally means *nothingness*, and so is constantly used for "an idol ;" and this must be its signification here, as the word coupled with it, and rendered **idolatry**, is really *teraphim*. These were the Hebrew household gods, answering to the Roman *Lares*, and were supposed to bring good luck. Their worship, we see from this place, was strictly forbidden. The verse, therefore, means, "For rebellion is the sin of divination (*i. e.* is equal to it in wickedness), and obstinacy (*i. e.* intractableness) is an idol and teraphim." Samuel thus accuses Saul of resistance to Jehovah's will, and of the determination at all hazards to be his own master. With this temper of mind he could be no fit representative of Jehovah, and therefore Samuel dethrones him. Henceforward he reigns only as a temporal, and no longer as the theocratic, king.

SAUL'S PROFESSION OF REPENTANCE AND FINAL REJECTION (vers. 24—35). Ver. 24.— The words of Samuel struck Saul with terror. The same authority which had first given him the kingdom now withdraws it from him, and pronounces his offence as equal in God's sight to crimes which Saul himself held in great abhorrence. He humbles himself, therefore, before Samuel, acknowledges his sin, and frankly confesses that the cause of it had been his unwillingness to act in a manner contrary to the wishes of the people ; and we must fairly conclude that the sparing of the

spoil had been the people's doing. But was it not the king's duty to make the people obedient to Jehovah's voice ? As the theocratic king, he was Jehovah's minister, and in preferring popularity to duty he showed himself unworthy of his position. Nor can we suppose that his confession of sin arose from penitence. It was the result simply of vexation at having his victory crossed by reproaches and disapproval from the only power capable of holding him in check. It seems, too, as if it were Samuel whom he feared more than Jehovah ; for he speaks of **thy words,** and asks Samuel to pardon his sin, and to grant him the favour of his public presence with him at the sacrifice which was about to be celebrated in honour of their triumph.

Vers. 26, 27, 28.—At first the prophet refuses the king's request. Saul had dishonoured God, and, therefore, had no claim to public homage from God's minister. He turns, therefore, to go away, and Saul in his eagerness seizes hold of Samuel's **mantle.** The A. V. is very careless about the exact rendering of words of this description, and seems guided in its choice of terms simply by the ear. Now the mantle, *addereth*, though used of the Shinar shawl stolen by Achan (Josh. vii. 21, 24), was the distinctive dress of the prophets, but naturally was never worn by Samuel himself. Special dresses come into use only gradually, and Elijah is the first person described as being thus clad. Long before his time the schools of the prophets had grown into a national institution, and a loose wrapper of coarse cloth made of camel's hair, fastened round the body at the waist by a leathern girdle, had become the usual prophetic dress, and continued so to be until the arrival of Israel's last prophet, John the Baptist (Matt. iii. 4). The garment here spoken of is the *meïl*, on which see ch. ii. 19, where it was shown to be the ordinary dress of people of various classes in easy circumstances. Now the *meïl* was not a loosely-flowing garment, but fitted rather closely to the body, and, therefore, the tearing of it implies a considerable amount of violence on Saul's part. **Skirt**, moreover, gives a wrong idea. What Saul took hold of was the *hem*, the outer border of the garment, probably at Samuel's neck or shoulder, as he turned to go away. He seized him, as we should say, by the collar, and endeavoured by main force to retain him, and in the struggle the hem rent. And Samuel, using it as an omen, said, **Jehovah hath rent the kingdom of Israel from thee this day, and hath given it to a neighbour of thine, that is better than thou.** *Neighbour* is used in Hebrew in a very indefinite manner, and here means generally "some one, whoever it may be," but one who will discharge the duties of thy office better than thou hast done (comp. Luke x. 36).

Ver. 29.—**The Strength**—better, as in the margin, the Victory or Triumph—**of Israel**. He who is Israel's Victory, or He in whom Israel has victory, will not repent. In ver. 11 God was said to repent, because there was what appeared to be a change in the Divine counsels. "God gave Israel a king in his anger, and took him away in his wrath" (Hosea xiii. 11). But such modes of speaking are in condescension to human weakness. Absolutely with God there is no change. He is the Eternal Present, with whom all things that were, and are, and shall be are one. But even looked at from below, as this finite creature man looks at his Maker's acts, there is no change in the Divine counsels, because, amidst all the vicissitudes of human events, God's will moves calmly forward without let or hindrance. No lower or secondary motives influence him, no rival power thwarts him. One instrument may be laid aside, and another chosen, because God ordains that the instruments by which he works shall be beings endowed with free will. Saul was the very counterpart of the Jewish people— highly endowed with noble qualities, but head-strong, self-willed, disobedient. Nevertheless, he laid the foundation for the throne of David, who in so many points was the ideal of the theocratic king; and Israel in like manner prepared the way for the coming of the true Messianic King, and gave mankind the one Catholic, *i. e.* universal, religion. "He who is Israel's Victory does not repent."

Vers. 30, 31. — **Then he said, I have sinned.** We have here no real confession of guilt. Even in ver. 24 the words were rather an expression of vexation at the strictness with which he was held to the letter of the command, than an acknowledgment that he really had done wrong. Here Saul's meaning seems to be, Well, granting that I have sinned, and that this sentence of exclusion from the kingdom is passed upon me, yet at least pay me the honour due to the rank which I still continue to hold. And to this request Samuel accedes. Saul was *de facto* king, and would continue to be so during his lifetime. The anointing, once bestowed, was a consecration for life, and so generally it was in the days of the son that the consequences of the father's sin came fully to pass (1 Kings xi. 34, 35; xiv. 13, &c.). Had Samuel refused the public honour due to Saul's rank, it would have given an occasion for intrigue and resistance to all who were disaffected with Saul's government, and been a step towards bringing back the old anarchy. **Jehovah thy God.** See on ver. 13.

Ver. 32. — **Delicately.** The Septuagint and Vulgate translate this word *trembling*,

and the Syriac omits, probably from inability to give its meaning. Most commentators render *cheerfully, joyfully*, forming it from the same root as Eden, the garden of joy (comp. Ps. xxxvi. 8, where Eden is translated *pleasure*). The very word, however, occurs in Job xxxviii. 31, where the A. V. renders it *bands*, and this seems the right sense: "Agag came unto him in fetters." The idea that Agag came cheerfully is contradicted by the next clause—**Surely the bitterness of death is passed.** Though put affirmatively, there is underlying doubt. It is no expression of heroic contempt for death, nor of real confidence that, as Saul had spared him hitherto, his life was in no danger. He had been brought to the national sanctuary, and a great festival in honour of the success of the army was to be held. It was entirely in accordance with the customs of ancient times that his execution should be the central feature of the spectacle. Agag's words show that this fear was present in his mind, though they are put in such a form as to be a protest against his life being taken after so long delay. Samuel's reply treats Agag's assertion as being thus at once a question and a protest. The bitterness of death has still to be borne, and the cruelty of Agag's past life makes the shedding of his own blood just. The Syriac translates, "Surely death is bitter;" the Septuagint, "If death be so bitter," with which the Vulgate agrees. Thus they all understood that Agag came trembling for his life.

Ver. 33.—**As thy sword hath made women childless.** Agag's life had been spent in freebooting expeditions, in which he had shed blood ruthlessly, and so justice required his execution in requital of his deeds to others. **Samuel hewed Agag in pieces.** The verb occurs only here, and probably refers to some particular method of execution, like the quartering of the middle ages. Being in the Piel conjugation, it would mean not so much that Samuel put Agag to death himself as that he commanded it to be done.

Ver. 35.—**Samuel came no more to see Saul.** The friendly intercourse which had previously existed was now broken off, and though they met again (ch. xix. 24), it was neither in an amicable manner, nor was their interview of Samuel's seeking. But the words have a higher meaning than the mere seeing or meeting one with the other. They involve the cessation of that relation in which Samuel and Saul had previously stood to one another as respectively the prophet and king of the same Jehovah Saul was no longer the representative of Jehovah, and consequently Samuel no more came to him, bearing messages and commands, and giving him counsel and guidance from God. **Nevertheless Samuel mourned for Saul.**

There was so much in him that was good and admirable, and he had wrought such brave services in delivering Israel from its many enemies, that Samuel loved him. Now he saw all his high qualities perverted, the man fallen, his powers of usefulness destroyed. Already, too, there was probably the beginning of that darkening of Saul's intellect which filled so many of his future years with melancholy, bursting out from time to time into fits of madness. All this would end in the expulsion of himself and his dynasty from the throne, for **Jehovah repented that he had made Saul king over Israel.** See on ver. 11

HOMILETICS.

Vers. 1—7.—*God's terrible acts.* The facts are—1. Saul is reminded that though a king he is but the servant of God, and bound to carry out his declared will. 2. Saul is commanded to utterly destroy Amalek in retribution for former sins. 3. In prosecuting his duty Saul discriminates in favour of the Kenites, then resident among the Amalekites, in consequence of their former kindness to Israel. It appears from xiv. 48 that, although the sin of Amalek in bygone times (Exod. xvii. 8—16) was the primary ground of the judgment about to be inflicted, the recent annoyance and injury caused to Saul's subjects was the occasion for the execution of the ancient sentence at this juncture. Those living under the mild and beneficent influences of the Christian dispensation are conscious of a shock to their sensibilities in reading the account of wholesale destruction brought by human instrumentality on an entire people; and the emotional disturbance is supplemented by intellectual perplexity on observing that the transaction was in obedience to a most explicit command of God. It is sometimes the practice, very easy for all who will not take pains to enter carefully into the subject, to get rid of the emotion and the perplexity by rejecting the inspiration of the entire record, or else by saying that Samuel and Saul sincerely but ignorantly mistook their own views of policy and dispositions of heart for the voice of God. The question at issue is a large one, but as it embraces in principle the whole of what in the Psalms are called his " terrible acts," which, whenever occurring or read, tax our feelings and perplex our intellects, we may notice a few points applicable more or less to all God's righteous judgments.

I. THE SPIRIT WITH WHICH WE SHOULD APPROACH THE CONSIDERATION OF GOD'S "TERRIBLE ACTS." It is not improbable that an unteachable, self-assertive spirit—a spirit that will not repose in a higher wisdom and goodness than its own, or that chafes under its inability to square human views of sin and its relations with God's—is the moral cause of man's quarrel with some of the records of Old Testament history. Our present contention is not with atheists, who to get rid of one difficulty create many others, but with those who believe in an almighty, all-wise, and merciful God, who is the Author of the moral and physical laws, by the action of which the world finds bliss or woe. We cannot help finding ourselves face to face with events bringing sorrow and shame, material and moral desolation to multitudes, because God so willed one creature's condition to be affected by the conduct of another. Apart from all human conduct, there are awful events in which, so to speak, the reputation of God for goodness and tenderness seems to be at stake. This circumstance should make the rejecter of Old Testament records pause ere he yields to the spirit of unbelief. There are " clouds and darkness" round about the throne; and he who would flee from mystery may well seek to flee from the universe. The judgment that condemns everything of which it does not see the reason is not qualified to exercise itself on the acts of an infinite Being. The cherubim and seraphim cover their faces, not presuming to attempt to pierce even with their clear and strong vision the ineffable glory; and so when a great burden of fear rests on our heart because of the terrible things of God, it is for us to bow in lowliness and trustfulness, saying for our comfort, because of what we know him to be, and not because we can solve the awful problems of existence, " Just and true are thy ways, thou King of saints. Who shall not fear thee, O Lord, and glorify thy name?" (Rev. xv. 3, 4; cf. Ps. xxxvi. 6).

II. FACTS AND PRINCIPLES THAT SHOULD WEIGH WITH US IN OUR THOUGHTS UPON GOD'S "TERRIBLE ACTS." It is not possible to find a perfect solution of all the acts ascribed to God, or even those known, without question, to result from his appointments. But some light shines around the "clouds and darkness," and here and there a rift in the awful covering appears. 1. *There is an awful as well as a mild aspect of the Divine nature.* Christianity is no doubt mildness, tenderness, peace, love— all that is precious to the sorrowing, perplexed spirit. The tendency of some, however, is to overlook the significant fact that all this becomes real to us in virtue of the awful sufferings and death of the Son of God. The fact, and the evident necessity of the fact, for otherwise it would not occur, of his unutterable woes is perhaps the most stupendous of all terrible acts known by man. There was the love that gave him for man ; yes, and the awful righteousness which had so originally constituted the moral relations of men to a holy God that love could only effect its work through a catastrophe, on which angels must have gazed with perplexity, and possibly pain, greater than any we know when contemplating a ruined Amalek or a world swept by deluge. It is an imperfect Christianity which eliminates the majesty of righteousness in Law. He who said, "Come unto me, all ye that labour, and are heavy laden, and I will give you rest," is the same who one day will say, "Depart." "These shall go away into everlasting punishment." The "wrath of the Lamb" is as real as his love. 2. *The events which confound our thought are not confined to the Scripture record.* Who shall estimate the pains of death experienced during the succession of catastrophes incident to the history of our globe ? It is probable that the number of Amalekites who fell under the judgment of God was less than the sum of young and old who in one day experience the "pains of death" by the ordination of God. The destruction caused by the deluge, the fire on Sodom, the waters on the Egyptians, is not greater in the number of lives cut off than what befell the thousands cut off by events not mentioned in the Bible. What though the events—the sweeping calamities of famine, plague, earthquake, and flood, and the daily sufferings and death of thousands of young and old—be the outcome of law ! God is the Author of that law, and, therefore, the events are in a significant sense his, as truly as were the ruin of Sodom and the doom of the Amalekites. No doubt the sum of enjoyment in the lives of creatures cut off by catastrophes was far in excess of the sum of misery experienced in the cutting of them off, and so a philosopher can still rest in the benevolence of God. Sudden destruction is not identical with a whole existence given up only to anguish. 3. *So far as we can see, the great woes that come by ordinary law and by special command are alike subordinate to an ulterior issue.* Although we speak of some events occurring by the action of natural law,—*e. g.* earthquakes, floods, famines, and plagues,—yet those in which the specific command appears are also according to law. The difference lies in the fact of the Divine origin of the arrangement which issues in destruction being brought out and emphasised. The laws that work ruin in fire and tempest and flood are subordinate to the higher laws involved in the perfect economy of the world. Laws involving incidental disasters subserve the conservation of the whole system of which they are a part. The laws which bring destruction to men who have sinned, and because they have sinned, are subordinate to the moral laws that govern man's relation to God. They are so inter-related, in these instances, as to be parts of one great system, and to subserve the final supremacy of the law of righteousness on which the health and well-being of the world depend. It is a Divine ordination, and is incorporated with the physical and mental constitution of man, that the sin of the fathers shall be visited, not to the exclusion from woe of the parent, but intensifying it, on the third and fourth generation. We see this law at work every day. Awful as it is, we can even now see its value as subservient to the righteousness which alone makes men blessed ; for it is a most potent check to vice. Irrespective of their own immoral condition, the cutting off of the Amalekites for the sin of their ancestors is analogous to the shortened lives, the wretched health, the filthy poverty, and other miseries which are the inevitable lot of the offspring of the desperately vicious ; and this for ulterior issues. 4. *Nations have no posthumous existence.* For individuals judgment is often reserved till another life. Nations, if visited with judgment at all, must suffer here. In the instruction of the individual, the fact of the coming punishment of the individual sinner bears an important part as a deterrent. In the instruction of nations as such, the signal and conspicuous punishment of a people also plays an important part. This use of national judgments is constantly recognised in the language of Scripture. "The Lord hath made bare his holy arm in the eyes of all the nations" (Isa. lii. 10). "Put them in fear, O Lord, that the nations may know themselves to be but men" (Ps. ix. 20). At the same time the judgments which on earth come on nations *as such* do not necessarily foreclose hope to the young and innocent among them of a personal salvation from the woe due to the personally guilty in another life. 5. *God is the only true Judge of the actual demerits of a guilty nation.* We cannot rightly estimate the intrinsic evil even of our own personal sins. "The Judge of all the earth" must decide what is appropriate punishment for national crime; for he only knows the degree of enmity in the minds of Sodomites and Amalekites. None but he can see the intricate bearings of their sin and of their continued existence as a people. He also knows best what blessed deterrent influence will arise to mankind from the conspicuous character of the judgment executed. 6. *The means by which judgment is executed appear to be determined by conditions known to God.* Judgment works inwardly through the conscience and the mental faculties in general. They bear the curse of the sin committed. It also works externally by the pressure against the sinner of the order of nature, which is in league with righteousness, and ultimately makes "the way of transgressors hard." Nations have not a very lively conscience. The force of Divine judgments usually comes from without. The instrumentality used is evidently connected with the actual presence of forces which, acting in a natural way under the preordained direction of the Omniscient, become "his arm." Doubtless there were physical conditions of earth and atmosphere which rendered destruction by a deluge both natural and yet conspicuously of God. The Sodomites were destroyed not by water, nor slow plague, nor famine, but by the natural combustible materials close at hand. The Amalekites were not left to die out by internal anarchy, or famine, or pestilence, but were given up to the action of that international hostility which was as real an element of destruction close at hand as was the volcanic force at Sodom. He who in his vast prevision, seeing the co-existence of the vices of antediluvians with certain fluvial conditions of a portion of the earth, and the co-existence of the sin of Sodom with certain volcanic conditions, used them for this purpose, may have also given full freedom to the play of national sentiment in the minds of Israel co-existing at that juncture with the fit time for the execution of a purpose to obliterate a guilty nation. Had pestilence or earthquake carried them off, it would have been God's act as truly as when the soldiers of Saul were the executioners of a decree. The employment of an executioner gives no right, but the reverse, to others to go and do the same. 7. *The form of punishment on communities under the Old Testament dispensation is evidently suggestive of the danger of antagonism to Christ.* The sin of Amalek was that of deliberate attempt to destroy the people of God (Exod. xvii. 8—16; Deut. xxv. 17—19). That means to prevent the realisation of salvation in the "seed of Abraham." If Amalek knew, as is certainly possible, the lofty claims of Israel, the crime was most fearful. That in the mind of God and of Israel such was the nature of the sin is seen in the discrimination made in favour of the Kenites because they showed kindness to Israel (ver. 6). It is at all events clear that God would have men learn that it was the sin of obstructing his purposes of mercy for mankind that was so obnoxious in his sight. The terrible *national* destruction which this sin brought on is a clear intimation of the "destruction from the presence of the Lord" which must come on the *individuals* who set themselves in antagonism to Christ and his purposes of mercy to the world. A more terrible sin than that cannot be conceived; a more terrible act of judgment cannot be imagined than that which will come when Christ shall say, "Depart from me, ye cursed" (Matt. xxv. 41). "It is a fearful thing," even under the gospel dispensation, "to fall into the hands of the living God" after a life of deliberate antagonism to the very Saviour he has sent to redeem us. Although, therefore, there may be much in the recorded "terrible acts" of God which weighs on our spirit and demands of us reverence and humility, still we are not without some gleams of light to sustain our faith both in the sacred records and the righteousness which never fails.

*General lessons:—*1. We see how judgment does surely come, though for generations it seems to linger. 2. It becomes us to inquire whether we by any conduct of ours are impeding the march of God's people. 3. We see how God remembers, and causes his servants to remember, acts of kindness rendered to the weary on their way to the promised rest. 4. It is a painful duty to have to be executors of God's judgments; yet when men in national and domestic affairs are really called to it, let them subordinate personal sentiment to solemn duty. 5. In all our painful thoughts over the woes that come on the universe, involving the young and old, let us seek grace to "be still," and to wait for the passing away of the night and the coming of the light that shall turn weeping into joy; for it will come.

Vers. 8—11.—*The limits of patience.* The facts are—1. Saul, in disobedience to the command of God, spares Agag and the best of the spoil. 2. God declares to Samuel that he can endure with Saul as king no longer. 3. Samuel, in his grief, cries unto God all night. It is never said that God changes his purpose absolutely. Where promises are given conditional on conduct they are revoked when conduct fails. We cannot ascribe human feelings to God; yet it is only by the analogy of human feelings that we can know anything of the mind of God. The setting aside from kingly office of Saul was an act of the Divine mind conformable with the original purpose of making him king, since the condition of permanence had not been fulfilled. Saul had been borne with so long; now he is to be borne with no longer. Patience yields to judgment.

I. THERE IS A LIMIT TO DIVINE PATIENCE. Patience bears relation to wrong-doing, or the sufferance of ill. In God it relates to the restraint he puts on himself in the presence of that which merits his displeasure. That there is such a limit to Divine patience is clear. 1. *The language of Scripture indicates it.* The heart of God is represented as being under pressure of a moral force which can scarcely be resisted. "How shall I give thee up, Ephraim?" (Hosea xi. 8). The retrospect of the past brings into view the overpowering considerations which withheld good and allowed calamity to come. "He should have fed them with the finest of the wheat" (Ps. lxxxi. 16). "O that my people had hearkened unto me!" (*ibid.* ver. 13). The persistence of men in sin, despite all counsel and mercy, raises the question of the length of time during which the hand of justice can be stayed. "How long shall I bear with this evil congregation?" (Num. xiv. 27). A reference to love, tenderness, and care is set in sad contrast with the doom which the ingratitude so long endured is about to bring (Matt. xxiii. 37, 38). 2. *Recorded facts illustrate it.* The vices of the antediluvians were long endured, and it was after the Spirit had striven long with men, and they had refused the warnings of Noah, that patience yielded to the execution of judgment (1 Pet. iii. 20). The repeated warnings given to Pharaoh reveal a patience which terminated in the overthrow in the Red Sea. Patience was "grieved" with the perverse generation in the wilderness, but grief gave place to a "wrath" which barred their entrance into rest (Heb. iii. 9—12). God endured long with some of the seven Churches in Asia, but at last judgment came, and the candlesticks were removed from their place. 3. The *close of the Christian dispensation in a day of judgment* is the most awful illustration of the limit to God's patience. The plain teaching of that great event is that here men have time to repent and obtain through Christ all that will qualify for a perfect life —that for the term of our earthly life God bears with our sins and provocations, and proves by thousands of favours that he "is slow to anger;" but that the end of all this must come, and judgment on the whole life ensue. His long-suffering is great. But "it is appointed to men once to die, and after this the judgment" (Heb. ix. 27).

II. THE GROUND OF THE LIMIT OF GOD'S PATIENCE. The yielding of patience to judgment in the case of Saul was on the occasion of his clear and deliberate breach of the command (vers. 1—3, 8, 9), and this too after other opportunities of obedience had been abused. But the question arises how it is that a certain degree or persistence in wrong is the occasion of the cessation of patience. There is a vague impression in some minds that because God is perfectly tender and loving his patience need and ought never to fail. This kind of thinking springs from very defective views of the character of God and of his relation to a moral order. It may not be possible for us to give a perfect *rationale* of Divine procedure; but there is perhaps light enough to indicate the wisdom and goodness of even a limit to God's patience. 1. The *privileges of responsible beings imply a probation for their use.* The primary notion of a responsible being is one blessed with privilege, and able to use or abuse it at will. But men are constituted so as to derive much wisdom from experience, and hence failure in the use of privilege, in a few instances, may possibly create an experience that will constrain to a more careful observance of duty when newly imposed. Life is full of helps to obedience as well as of hindrances. But as time is required for the development of responsibility, so it is obvious that the possession of privilege involves a limit to the period for use or abuse. Government without a reckoning would be no government. Everlasting patience is inconsistent with responsibility attendant on privilege. 2. In a *moral order, where beings are closely inter-related, breach of duty affects others.* Saul's conduct could not end in himself. He, as fount of authority and influence, would damage his people by every act of disobedience to the Divine command. The repeated sins of men are so many attacks on the common welfare of the universe. God " desireth not the death of a sinner," but that he should "turn and live ; " but he is the Guardian of right, of good, of peace, and of all that enters into the true welfare of the entire universe, and hence there is a love most deep and a wisdom unsearchable in not allowing the wilful sinner any longer to be exempt from the restraints which judgment imposes. 3. *Repeated acts of disobedience reveal to God a state of mind which will not benefit by further favours.* Every act of sin brings man lower in the moral scale. But while mercy and gentleness afford the sinner every possible chance to recover what is lost, it is possible for the habit of sin to gain such power over the entire man that to the eye of the Eternal his last chance of improving additional opportunities is clean gone. Samuel's distress at the abandonment of Saul (ver. 11) was natural, and if his cry all night was intercession, it was only what might be expected of a good man who knows only in part. The intercession of Moses (Num. xiv. 15—23) was for pardon, and was partially successful. Samuel's would appear to have been for pardon in the form of Saul's continuance in the kingly office with the usual Divine sanctions. It is, however, obvious that the judgment of God was based on his perfect knowledge that the heart of Saul was too far gone to be trusted any further. It is an awful fact that a man may, by transgression, work himself into such a condition that all is lost on him, and will be lost. God, knowing this, may cease to be long-suffering, and reject him as " nigh unto cursing " (Heb. vi. 6—8). 4. *The holiness of God requires vindication.* Every pang which followed Saul's earlier sins and every rebuke from Samuel was some vindication of the holiness of God. The private and subjective recognition by the sinner of an insulted holiness is not all that the government of God requires. He is a jealous God ; he will be honoured in the eyes of all people. Continued long-suffering followed by judgment renders holiness more conspicuous than when judgment forestalls long-suffering.

General lessons: — 1. We should never forget that every day affords us new opportunities of keeping God's commands. 2. It will repay the effort if we endeavour to form an estimate of the privileges conferred on us in the past, and the extent to which we have drawn on the patience of God. 3. If we are deliberately disobedient in any office of trust, we may some day look for a grave judgment. 4. We are not always competent to see the wisdom of God's severity, and may possibly pray for what is not to be granted.

Vers. 12—23.—*The sin of rebellion.* The facts are—1. Saul, having raised a monument in honour of his victory, meets Samuel with a pious salutation, as though all were well. 2. On being reminded of the presence of spoil, Saul explains by saying that it was spared for the worship of God in sacrifice. 3. Samuel, referring to the instructions received from God, presses home upon him the fact of his guilt in disobeying the Lord. 4. Saul, in response, maintains that substantially he has obeyed the voice of the Lord, but that the people spared the spoil for a religious purpose. 5. Samuel, therefore, urges the great truth that rigid obedience to God is the primary and essential duty, without which all else is sinful, and that rebellion is a sin as heinous as those which men admit to be most vile. 6. Samuel declares to Saul his rejection of God. The important interview between the disobedient king and the prophet of God brings out several great truths.

I. MAN'S PREFERENCE OF HIS OWN WILL TO THE CLEARLY-DECLARED WILL OF GOD IS POSITIVE REBELLION AGAINST THE SUPREME AUTHORITY. Saul's sin was known to himself as a preference of his own course in dealing with the Amalekites. He thought it best to modify the command in its detailed execution. No doubt there were reasons which seemed to render such a course useful. It is clear that he did not realise all that it involved, though that was his own fault. To him as a king, whose word was supposed to be law to his subjects, there is something very appropriate in the prophet assuring him that this preference of his own will, however plausible the reasons for it, was not a simple weakness or fault, but nothing less than *rebellion*—a term of fearful significance under a properly-constituted government. The preference was virtually a setting up a counter-authority, impeaching the wisdom of God. Saul is not the only one to whom God has plainly declared his will. More or less he has spoken to all men (Rom. i. 20). To those blessed with the revealed will as contained in the Scriptures he has given commandments as precise and emphatic as that to Saul to destroy the Amalekites. Every believer in Christianity knows as well as he knows anything that God *commands* him to repent of sin (Acts xvii. 30); to believe in the Lord Jesus Christ for salvation from the curse of sin (John xx. 31; Acts xvi. 30, 31; 1 John v. 10—13); to exterminate all evil—all Amalekites—from the soul (Rom. viii. 13; 1 Thess. iv. 3; 1 Pet. i. 16); and to submit heart, will, and intellect to the authority of Christ (Matt. xi. 29; John v. 23; Acts x. 36; Phil. ii. 10, 11). Now is it not a fact that men often prefer not to do this? They do not dispute in formal terms the authority of God, any more than did Saul; yet for reasons known to themselves they prefer *not* to repent of sin, *not* to commit themselves to Christ, *not* to cast out sinful desires, *not* to bow in all things to the yoke of the Saviour. It is possible that reasons may be forthcoming to, at least, show that there is no violent antagonism. But when carefully looked at it is nothing but the positive setting up of man's will as a better, more-to-be-desired will than God's; it is positive rebellion of a subject against a king—a setting at nought of the supreme authority of the universe.

II. MAN'S ESTIMATE OF THE SIN OF REBELLION IS IN STRIKING CONTRAST WITH GOD'S. Whether Saul was self-persuaded that he had not committed any sin (ver. 13) is, as we shall yet see, doubtful. The probability is that he was conscious of uneasiness, but had no true conception of the enormity of his sin. His feeling was that he had no wish to disown the authority of God, that it was a mere matter of detail, that his general conduct was exemplary, and that he followed the inner light which seemed just then to indicate another way of ultimately and substantially carrying out the command. So do men tone down their sins and regard them as venial. The prophet's words reveal God's estimate of the sin of disobedience. It is *the cardinal sin* (vers. 22, 23). It cuts at the root of all authority. It is the assertion of a power and a wisdom over against the power and wisdom of the Eternal. It makes man a worshipper of himself rather than of God. It ignores the solemn truth that we "cannot serve two masters." It does dishonour to him whose commandments are holy, just, and good. It sows in the moral sphere seeds of evil, which, taking root, must widen the aberration of man from God. It claims for the desires and dim light of a sinful creature a higher value in the determination of actions than is to be attached to the purposes of the All-Perfect. To render its heinous character more clear, the prophet asserts that it *renders useless and even wicked the most solemn acts of worship* (ver. 22; cf. Isa. i. 11—15). No profession of religion; no self-denial in surrender of choice property; no conformity with venerable customs, or obedience in other particulars, will for a moment be accepted in lieu of full and implicit obedience to the clear commands which God lays on man both in relation to himself and mankind. God will have no reserve of our will. Again, to make it more impressive, the prophet assures Saul that this rebellion is in its evil nature *equal to the sins which men are led* by education and custom *to regard as the most abominable and indefensible.* "As the sin of witchcraft, ... as iniquity and idolatry." There are men still who shrink in horror at heathenism and vile arts. Are they prepared to believe that *not* to obey the clear command to repent, to believe on Christ, to become pure, and to submit in all things to the yoke of Christ, is as dreadful in the sight of God as being an idolater or a vile deceiver? It is this Divine estimate of sin which alone explains the "many stripes" with which they will be punished who, knowing the Lord's will with respect to these matters, nevertheless prefer their own. It will be more tolerable in the day of judgment for Sodom than for some of our day (Matt. xi. 20—24).

III. MAN'S CONDITION AND CONDUCT AFTER DELIBERATE REBELLION IS A REVELATION OF ITS EVIL NATURE. All sin degrades and debases; it prevents clear vision of one's own condition and a true estimate of conduct. Sin is always self-apologetic. It enslaves its victims. The opinion of a morally fallen being on matters of high spiritual import must always be discounted. Men in internal opposition to God are not safe guides in dealing with the loftiest problems of human existence. This general effect of sin is more manifest when a man has, after enjoying great advantages, deliberately preferred his own will to the clear will of God. He then enters into darkness most dense, and the fountain of moral thought and feeling becomes more corrupt. We see this in Saul's subsequent conduct and perverse reasoning with Samuel (vers. 20, 21). Even when conscience began to be aroused by the impressive language of the prophet, he found a subtle evasion in that, as a king, he had done his part in placing Agag at the disposal of Samuel, but that the people were to blame in the matter of the spoil. Thus it is ever. Sin does not end in itself. It by its evil power induces self-complacency, creates ingenious excuses, prompts to observance of outward religious acts, throws blame on circumstances over which there is no control, and even emboldens the soul to argue with the messengers of God.

IV. ONE SERIOUS CONSEQUENCE OF REBELLION IS TO DISQUALIFY FOR SERVICE IN THE KINGDOM OF GOD. Apart from the personal effects of Saul's sin, the relative effect was to unfit him for performing the part to which he had been called in the service of God. He was rejected from being king (ver. 23). God's sanction and blessing were henceforth to be withheld. He was to be king in name only. The life once promising good to Israel was to be unblest and fruitful in sorrows. This result follows from every preference of our own will. We cease to hold the position and exercise the influence of God-made kings (Rev. i. 4, 5) in so far as we fail in perfect execution of the will of the King of kings. It is possible for a man to proceed from step to step in deliberate rebellion till, both on account of his inward moral decay and his pernicious influence, God sets him aside altogether. A pastor, a parent, a professed Christian may thus be practically disowned by Providence. However he may continue to labour in some lower departments, the higher spiritual service of God will cease to be his.

General lessons :—1. It is very dangerous to begin to compare our wishes and plans with the clear will of God; every thought should at once be brought into subjection. 2. Sudden and unusual outbursts of pious zeal may be a sign of an uneasy conscience; steady growth is the proof of reality. 3. The folly of excuses for sin is seen by all except the sinner himself. 4. Sin, when we are exalted to privileges, is doubly base (ver. 17). 5. We must never subordinate what we may call *general* obedience for actual literal obedience to God's will (ver. 20). 6. Participation of others in our sin is no palliation of ours (ver. 21). 7. Property obtained by unholy means is not acceptable to God when laid on his altar for professedly religious purposes (ver. 22). 8. Obedience in matters outside acts of worship is a condition of acceptable worship, but not the ground of our salvation. 9. Deceitfulness, depravity, and idolatry are the true and ruinous characteristics of every act of doing our own pleasure when professedly engaged in doing only the will of God (ver. 23).

Vers. 24—31.—*Conviction of sin not repentance.* The facts are—1. Saul, alleging fear of the people, admits his sin, and seeks Samuel's presence while he worships the Lord. 2. On Samuel refusing and turning away, Saul seizes and rends his garment, which circumstance is used as a sign that so the Lord had rent the kingdom from Saul and given it to another. 3. On being assured that God's purpose was irrevocable, Saul entreats, for the sake of his credit among the people, that Samuel would join him in an act of worship, to which Samuel complies. The decisive language of the prophet, given in a tone which admitted of no mistake, aroused the slumbering conscience of Saul, and brought about his remarkable pleading for pity and help. We have here the case of a man guilty of a great sin, concerned for its forgiveness, but sternly assured that he shall not have it. The apparent severity of the prophet is not based on any arbitrary decree of God, nor on an unchangeableness in the "Strength of Israel" irrespective of human character and conduct, but upon God's knowledge of Saul's actual condition. The repentance which Saul thinks to be adequate, and which many men would recognise, is known by the Searcher of hearts not to be true repentance, but only a bare conviction of sin, attended with a consequent dread of the outward temporal consequences attached to it, as just indicated by Samuel. *Bare conviction of sin is not true repentance.* Consider—

I. ITS REAL NATURE. Conviction of sin is a matter only of an aroused conscience, brought about by the evidence of facts being set before the understanding and the presence of penalties consequent on the evidence. There was no resisting Samuel's argument. The common understanding saw that a human will in opposition to a Divine was necessarily sin, and the uneasiness of conscience thus naturally aroused was aggravated by the emphatic announcement of a great penalty—loss of the kingdom. The mental operation was that of a pure logical progression from admitted premises to an irresistible conclusion. Conscience does not disturb a man in working out a syllogism in formal logic or a demonstration in mathematics; but it does when the question reasoned on is the man's own conduct. This is the general nature of the conviction of sin which many experience. Here, observe, is an absence of all that fine spiritual discernment which sees in sin essential unholiness, and that corresponding feeling which loathes it because of what it is in the sight of God. There is no change in the spirit towards sin itself, no detestation of the self-preference which rose against the supreme will.

II. ITS MANIFESTATIONS. The manifestation of Saul's conviction of sin is a remarkable illustration of the enormous difference between bare conviction and true repentance. The force of evidence and pressure of penalty extorted the admission, "I have sinned:" yet, owing to the lack of the spirit of repentance, the mere generality of that admission was revealed by the immediate palliation, "I feared the people." Pardon, consisting in the removal of penalty, was the only pardon cared for, and even this was sought by a superstitious trust in the prayers of another. A zealous and prompt observance of some outward act of worship was thought to be a sure means of recovering lost favour. The slightest movement of Samuel indicative of the non-reversal of the penalty only excited a spasmodic dread, without the slightest trace of any changed sentiment towards sin itself. And when no hope of avoiding the penalty remains, the only thought is to break his fall before his elders, and so save some civil advantage. This analysis, expressed in terms suitable to our times, will be found to hold good of multitudes whose conviction of sin is unattended with the spirit of a true repentance. How different the conviction that accompanies true repentance! Then, "I have sinned" has a deep, unutterable meaning. Forgiveness is then not the mere release of life from suffering and loss, but a restoration of the soul to the joy of personal reconciliation with a holy Father. No thought of excuse is ever entertained, but "against thee, and thee only, have I sinned and done this evil," is the sincere confession of a broken and contrite heart. The soul is so filled with self-loathing, and so agonised in being far from God, that it thinks not of punishment and position among men, and can only go direct to God and plead, "Create in me a clean heart, O God, and renew a right spirit within me." Contrast Simon Magus (Acts viii. 24) and Felix (Acts xxiv. 25; Ps. li.; Luke xv.).

III. ITS CONSEQUENCES. Saul, though convinced of sin, was practically an unchanged man. He was, after his pleading with Samuel, and after Samuel's kindly act of consoling his poor blind heart by joining in worship, as fond of his own self-will as before. No spiritual change being wrought, no remission of penalty was ever possible. On his knowledge of what was Saul's radical evil—a heart out of all sympathy with God's holiness—and of its continuance, did God resolve to provide for Israel another king. The Strength of Israel is not dependent on existing arrangements or human beings for the maintenance of his authority and accomplishment of his purposes. Saul as a king was ruined. His defective conviction was of no avail. It should be urged on all that a mere admission of sin and effort to be free from its punishment are of no avail. Loss of all that is deemed precious *must* ensue. Only repentance of the heart will serve. This is sure to lead away from all false means of deliverance to him who is exalted to give remission of sins.

General lessons:—1. A spirit of blended firmness and kindness should influence us in the discharge of unwelcome duties. 2. We should be careful not to encourage men in their self-delusions. 3. Respect for an office and consideration for social relations should enter into our treatment of offenders.

Vers. 32—35.—*Painful duties.* The facts are—1. Samuel summons Agag into his presence and hews him in pieces. 2. Samuel departs from Saul, and though mourning for him, no longer holds any official connection with him. The effect of Saul's disobedience on the people would have been disastrous were the original command to be in any way evaded; and, therefore, though it was no part of the prophet's ordinary functions to act as executioner, Samuel so far deviated from his usual course, and put his feelings under restraint, as to slay the captive king. There could be no mistake of the imperativeness of the Divine command when the people saw Samuel perform on the body of the king an act symbolical of the utter destruction of the enemies of God. The act itself, as also the occasion of it, must have given pain to the prophet's mind. The subsequent suspension of relations with Saul was the natural result and formal expression of God's rejection of him. Any other line of conduct would be open to serious misinterpretation. Samuel naturally was grieved in thus setting his ban on one for whom he had taken such pains, and in whose successful career he himself was deeply interested. But duty is above personal feeling.

I. HUMAN IMPERFECTION GIVES OCCASION FOR THE DISCHARGE OF PAINFUL DUTIES. Samuel is not the only one who has had to discharge solemn duties with a sorrowful heart. 1. *There are instances recorded in Scripture.* (1) *Of men.* It was not without pain that Moses broke away from the associations of the home of Pharaoh's daughter, where he had from childhood been treated with consideration and kindness. Nathan could not but put constraint on his feelings when he exposed the sin of one for whom he had cherished the profoundest respect (2 Sam. xii. 7—14). See the case of the apostles (Acts v. 1—10; ix. 23—29; Rom. ix. 1—3; Phil. iii. 5—8). (2) *Of Christ.* It was as much beside his usual course as for Samuel to slay Agag when the gentle Saviour made a scourge and drove the money-changers from the temple (John ii. 15). There was evident sorrow of heart running through the terrible denunciations and forebodings which duty required him to utter over Capernaum, Jerusalem, and the scribes and Pharisees. His leaving Nazareth and never returning, after the cruel rejection of his word, must have been, considering his associations with the place, a duty as painful almost as the revelation to his disciples that one of their number would betray him (Luke iv. 28—30; xxii. 21—23). And may we not say that it will not be without a tone of sadness, more marked than any that entered into Samuel's demand for Agag, that Christ, the great Judge, will on the day of judgment say to those who once heard his call of mercy and scorned it, "Depart from me." 2. *There are instances recurring in modern life.* On some is imposed the sorrowful duty of rebuking friends for disgraceful deeds, or of administering chastisements which cause more pain to the chastiser than to the chastised, or of enforcing with bleeding heart the rigorous rules of Church discipline upon persons once honoured and beloved. Samuel is but one of a host who have to assert Divine authority, moral order, and the interests of the community at the cost of much personal suffering.

II. SUCH DISCHARGE OF PAINFUL DUTIES IS AN ILLUSTRATION OF THE SUPREMACY OF RIGHTEOUSNESS. The emotional element is strong in life. Personal considerations have, wisely and usefully, great weight in regulating actions. But it was profound regard for right that enabled Samuel to rule every feeling of his nature and subordinate it to the ends of justice, and therefore of benevolence. The same is seen in every kindred instance. It is indicative of a healthful moral condition where regard for right is dominant. Love, tenderness, pity are useful, powerful elements in a moral character; but they cease to be strictly moral when they operate as mere feelings apart from the guidance and control of righteousness. This looking high above personal relations to the requirements of a universal equity is the sublimest form of conduct.

HOMILIES BY VARIOUS AUTHORS.

Vers. 1—9. (GIBEAH.)—*A probationary commission.* 1. *The fidelity of Saul* to the principle of his appointment, viz. obedience to the will of Jehovah, was once and again put to the test. He had been tried by inaction, delay, and distress, which became the occasion of his being tempted to distrust, and the use of his power for his own safety, in opposition to the word of God (ch. xiii. 11). He had been tried by enterprise, encouragement, and the expectation of brilliant success, which became the occasion of his being tempted to presumption in entering rashly upon his own ways, and adopting "foolish and hurtful devices" for conquest and glory, independently of the counsel of God (ch. xiv. 19, 24). He must now be tried by victory, power, and prosperity. Having chastised his enemies on every side (ch. xiv. 47), his assured success becomes the final test of his character and fitness to rule over Israel. 2. *The temptations of Saul* may be compared with those of others, and especially with the three temptations of Christ (Matt. iv. 1—10; Luke iv. 1—12), which are "an epitome of all the temptations, moral and spiritual, which the devil has contrived for man from the day of his first sin unto this very hour." The antecedents in both cases, the circumstances under which the temptations occurred, the principles to which they appealed, the inducements which they presented, the means afforded for their resistance, and their result, are all suggestive. Where the first king of Israel failed the last King of Israel prevailed, and whilst Saul was rejected, Jesus was perfected, and "crowned with glory and honour" (Luke xxii. 28, 29; Heb. ii. 10, 18). 3. *The commission of Saul* to execute judgment upon the Amalekites was brought to him by Samuel, whose authority as the prophet of the Lord he never called in question, however much he may have acted contrary to his directions. After Saul exhibited a determination to have his own way, Samuel seems to have exerted little influence over him. At the battle of Michmash the high priest Ahiah was his only spiritual counsellor. It became more and more evident that he wished to establish a "kingdom of this world," like the surrounding heathen kingdoms, in opposition to the design of God concerning Israel, which the prophet represented and sought to carry into effect; and it was inevitable that, with such contrary aims, a conflict should arise between them. "The great prophet's voice brings him a new commission from his God, and preludes it by a note of very special warning: 'The Lord sent me,' &c. This tone of adjuration surely tells all. It speaks the prophet's judgment of his character, of prayers and intercessions, of days of watching and nights of grief for one he loved so well, as he saw growing on that darkening countenance the deepening lines of wilfulness. The prophet sees that it will be a crisis in that life-history with which by God's own hand his own had been so strangely entwined." The commission was—

I. DIVINELY APPOINTED (ver. 1). 1. When a communication enjoining the performance of any action comes *unquestionably* from God. it should be unhesitatingly obeyed. His authority is supreme, his power is infinite, and his commands are right and good. It does not follow that everything he directs men to do in one age is obligatory on all others in every age. But some things he has undoubtedly enjoined upon us all. 2. When such a communication is made with *peculiar directness* and solemnity, it should be obeyed with peculiar attention and circumspection, for important issues are involved in its faithful or faithless observance. "If thou hast failed in other things, take heed that thou fail not in this." 3. When *special privilege* and honour have been bestowed upon men by God they are placed under special obligations of obedience to him. "Though thou wast little in thine own sight," &c. (ver. 17).

II. JUSTLY DESERVED by those against whom it was directed (ver. 2)—"the sinners the Amalekites" (ver. 18). 1. Some sins are marked by an unusual degree of criminality and *guilt.* Like the people of Israel, the Amalekites were descendants of Abraham (Amalek being the grandson of Esau—Gen. xxxvi. 12, 16); but they attacked them at Rephidim on their way through the desert, and strove to annihilate them (Exod. xvii. 8—16); they lay in wait for them secretly and subtly, and smote the hindermost, the feeble, the faint and weary, and "feared not God" (Deut. xxv. 17—19). Their conduct was ungenerous, unprovoked, cruel, and utterly godless. 2. Special sins are *perpetuated* in families and nations and increase in intensity. The Amalekites were hereditary, open, and deadly foes of Israel (Num. xiv. 45; Judges iii. 13; vi. 3). They lived by plunder, and were guilty of unsparing bloodshed (ver. 33). Some fresh act of cruelty may have shown that they were "ripe for the judgment of extermination." 3. Sinners long spared and persisting in flagrant transgression bring upon themselves sudden, signal, and overwhelming *destruction*. If judgment is pervaded and limited by mercy, mercy has also limits beyond which it does not pass, and they who despise it must perish. Men may forget what God has spoken (Exod. xvii. 14); but he remembers it, and fulfils his word at the proper time. "Injuries done to the people of God will sooner or later be reckoned for." Impenitent sinners "treasure up unto themselves wrath against the day of wrath" (Rom. ii. 5). It accumulates like a gathering thunder-cloud or an Alpine avalanche (Luke xi. 50, 51), and it frequently comes upon them by ways and means such as they themselves have chosen. The Amalekites put others to the sword and spared not; they must themselves be put to the sword and not be spared. The moral improvement of inveterate sinners by their continuance on earth is sometimes hopeless, and their removal by Divine judgment is necessary for the moral improvement and general welfare of other people with whom they are connected, and teaches valuable lessons to succeeding ages.

III. FULLY EXPRESSED (vers. 3, 18). The will of God is made known in different forms and with various degrees of clearness, and some men, whilst acknowledging their obligation to obey it, have sought to justify themselves in the neglect of particular duties on the ground of their not having been fully directed. But this could not be the case with Saul, whose commission was—1. *Imperative;* so that there could be no excuse for evasion. "Go and smite Amalek." 2. *Plain;* so that its meaning could not be mistaken, except by the most inattentive and negligent of men. "Utterly destroy (devote to destruction). Fight against them until they be consumed." 3. *Minute;* so that no room was left for the exercise of discretion as to the manner or extent of its fulfilment. It required simple, literal obedience, such as is now required in many things. "Whatsoever he saith unto you, do it."

IV. ZEALOUSLY COMMENCED (vers. 4, 5, 7). The "journey on which he was sent" (ver. 18) was entered upon by Saul with something of the same energy and zeal which he had formerly displayed against the Ammonites, but the deterioration which had since taken place in his character by the possession of power soon appeared. 1. The work to which men are called in the way of duty sometimes bears a close affinity to their *natural temperament* and disposition. 2. Men may *appear* to others, and even to themselves, to be very *zealous for the Lord* whilst they are only doing what is naturally agreeable to themselves. "Come with me," said Jehu, "and see my zeal for the Lord" (2 Kings x. 16, 31). "But Jehu took no heed to walk in the law of the Lord God of Israel." Saul of Tarsus, like Saul of Gibeah, appeared to be fighting for God when he was really fighting against him. 3. *The real nature of their zeal* is manifested when the requirements of God come into collision with their convenience, pleasure, ambition, or self-interest. Then the hidden spring is laid bare.

V. UNFAITHFULLY EXECUTED (vers. 8, 9). "Spared Agag, and the best of the sheep," &c., "and would not destroy them." "He hath turned back from following me, and hath not performed my commandments" (ver. 11). 1. There may be *the performance of many things* along with the neglect or refusal to perform others of equal or of greater importance. Saul was "a type of those who are willing to do something as against the world and on behalf of Christ, but by no means willing to do all that they ought to do." Herod "did many things, and heard John gladly" (Mark vi. 20), but he would not give up his ruling passion. 2. Disobedience in one thing often manifests *the spirit of disobedience* in all things. It shows that the heart and will are not surrendered to the Lord, and without such a surrender all else is worthless. In Saul's sparing Agag and the best of the sheep, &c, we have "a melancholy example of sparing sins and evils that should be slain, and sheltering and harbouring them under false pretences by unworthy pleas and excuses." 3. *The love of self* is the supreme motive of those who refuse to obey God. Saul was actuated by covetousness (ver. 19), worldly-mindedness (Matt. iv. 9 ; 1 John ii. 15, 16), and vainglorious pride, which are only different forms of the love of self. "Behold, he set him up a monument, and is gone about (as in a triumphal procession), and passed on, and gone down to Gilgal " (ver. 12), intending probably to make a display of the royal captive for his own glory ; perhaps to make him a tributary prince and a source of profit. "Pride arising from the consciousness of his own strength led him astray to break the command of God. His sin was open rebellion against the sovereignty of the God of Israel ; for he no longer desired to be the medium of the sovereignty of Jehovah, or the executor of the commands of the God-king, but simply wanted to reign according to his own arbitrary will" (Keil).—D.

Vers. 5, 6. (THE WILDERNESS OF JUDAH.) — *Come out from among them.* The Kenites were descendants of Abraham (Gen. xxv. 2 ; Num. x. 29 ; Judges i. 16) like the Amalekites, but they were unlike the latter in character and conduct. Many of them were incorporated with Israel ; others, whilst standing in friendly relationship to them, lived in close contact with "the sinners the Amalekites." They may be regarded as representing those who are "not far from the kingdom of God," but imperil their salvation by evil companionship. In this message (sent by Saul, perhaps, according to the direction of Samuel) we notice—

I. THE PERIL OF UNGODLY ASSOCIATION. It is not every association with irreligious persons indeed that is to be deprecated (1 Cor. v. 10), but only such as is unnecessary, voluntary, very intimate, and formed with a view to personal convenience, profit, or pleasure rather than to their improvement (Gen. xiii. 12). This—1. Destroys the good which is possessed. 2. Conforms to the evil which prevails (Ps. i. 1 ; Rev. xviii. 4). 3. Involves in the doom which is predicted—certain, terrible, and imminent. The *ban* has been pronounced (1 Cor. xvi. 22 ; 2 Thess. i. 9), and it will ere long be executed. "A companion of fools shall be destroyed" (Prov. xiii. 20).

II. THE OPPORTUNITY OF EFFECTUAL ESCAPE, which—1. Is afforded by the mercy of God, of which the message spoken by man is the expression. 2. Shows the value which he sets upon even the least measure of kindness and piety. "Ye showed kindness," &c. (ver. 6). Moral goodness, like moral evil (ver. 2), tends to perpetuate itself. God honours it by the blessing which he causes to follow in its track. He desires its preservation and perfection, and hence he says, "Destroy it not" (Isa. lxv. 8). 3. Offers a certain, great, and immediate benefit. "Come out from among them and be separate, saith the Lord, and I will receive you" (2 Cor. vi. 14—18).

III. THE NECESSITY OF IMMEDIATE SEPARATION. 1. This requires decision, self-denial, sacrifice, and effort. 2. Nothing else can avail (Ephes. v. 11). 3. And every moment's delay increases danger. "Escape for thy life ; look not behind thee, neither stay thou in all the plain " (Gen. xix. 17). "Be wise to-day, 'tis madness to defer."—D.

Vers. 10, 11. (RAMAH.)—*Samuel's intercession for Saul.* The recorded instances of Samuel's praying are of an intercessory character (ch. vii. 9 ; viii. 6, 21 ; xii. 18, 23). The last of them is his intercession for Saul. He appears to have been told by God in a dream of the result of the probationary commission which had been given to the king. Agitated and distressed, and not yet clearly perceiving it to be the fixed purpose of God (ver. 29) that Saul should no longer reign over Israel as his recognised servant and vicegerent, Samuel gave himself unto prayer, if thereby he might avert the calamity. Respecting his intercession, consider—

I. ON WHOSE BEHALF IT WAS MADE. Chiefly, doubtless, on behalf of Saul, though not without regard to the nation, on which his rejection seemed likely to produce a disastrous effect. Intercession should be made for *individuals* as well as communities. "Satan hath desired to have you," said he who is the perfect example of intercessory prayer, "but I have prayed for *thee*" (Luke xxii. 32). There were many things in Saul calculated to call it forth. 1. *His good qualities*, exalted position, and intimate relationship to the prophet. 2. *His grievous sin* (vers. 11, 19, 23), exceeding his previous transgressions. 3. *His great danger*—falling from his high dignity, failing to accomplish the purpose of his appointment, losing the favour and help of Jehovah, and sinking into confirmed rebellion and complete ruin. "It repenteth me that I have made Saul king; *for* he is turned back from following me" (vers. 11, 35). When a change takes place in the conduct of man toward God, as from obedience to disobedience, it necessitates a *change* of God's dealings toward him (otherwise he would not be unchangeably holy), and this "change of his dispensation" or economy (Theodoret) is called his repentance. It is not, however, the same in all respects as repentance in men. No change in him can arise, as in them, from unforeseen events or more perfect knowledge, seeing that "his understanding is infinite;" yet, on the other hand, as in their repentance there is sorrow, so also in his—sorrow over those who turn from him, oppose his gracious purposes, and bring misery upon themselves (Gen. vi. 6; Judges x. 16); and of this Divine sorrow the tears and agonies of Christ are the most affecting revelation.

II. IN WHAT SPIRIT IT WAS MADE. 1. *Holy anger* against sin, and against the sinner in so far as he has yielded himself to its power, arising from sympathy with God and zeal for his honour (Ps. cxix. 126, 136, 158). 2. *Deep sorrow* over the sinner, in his essential personality, his loss and ruin; not unmingled with disappointment at the failure of the hopes entertained concerning him. Sorrow over sinners is a proof of love to them. 3. *Intense desire* for the sinner's repentance, forgiveness, and salvation. "And he cried unto the Lord all night" with a loud and piercing cry, and in prolonged entreaty. The old home at Ramah, which had been sanctified by parental prayers and his own incessant supplications, never witnessed greater fervour. Wonderful was the spirit of intercession which he possessed. Well might the Psalmist, in calling upon men to worship the Lord, single him out as pre-eminent among them that "call upon his name" (Ps. xcix. 6). But still more wonderful was the spirit which was displayed by the great Intercessor, who often spent the night in prayer, and whose whole life was a continued act of intercession, closing with the cry, "Father, forgive them, for they know not what they do." Would that more of the same spirit were possessed by all his disciples!

> "We are told
> How much the prayers of righteous men avail;
> And yet 'tis strange how very few believe
> These blessed words, or act as were they true."

III. TO WHAT EXTENT IT AVAILED. 1. *Not to the full extent he desired.* Saul did not repent, neither was he exempted from the sentence of rejection. The relation of the sovereignty of God to the will of men is inexplicable. How far the Almighty may, by special and extraordinary grace, subdue its opposition we cannot tell. But he has conditioned the general exercise of his power by the gift of freedom and responsibility. He does not destroy or recall the gift; and the power of human resistance to the Divine will is a fearful endowment. There are stages of human guilt which would be followed by the wrath of God "though Moses and Samuel stood before him" (Jer. xv. 1). "There is a sin unto death; I do not say that he shall pray for it" (1 John v. 16). "The sin, namely, of a wilful, obstinate, Heaven-daring opposition to the ways of God and the demands of righteousness, and which, under a dispensation of grace, can usually belong only to such as have grieved the Spirit of God till he has finally left them—a sin, therefore, which lies beyond the province of forgiveness" (Fairbairn, 'Typology,' ii. 341). 2. *Yet, doubtless, to obtain many benefits* for the transgressor, in affording him space for repentance and motives to it. Who shall say how many blessings came upon Saul in answer to Samuel's intercession for him? 3. *And to calm the soul* of him who prays, to make known the will of God to him more clearly, to bring him into more perfect acquiescence with it, and to strengthen him for the duty that lies before him. "And he arose early to meet Saul in the morning" (ver. 12).

1. How great is the privilege and honour of intercessory prayer. 2. Since we know not who are beyond the reach of Divine grace, we should never cease to intercede

for any.   3. If intercession does not avail to obtain all that it seeks, it does not fail to obtain invaluable blessings.—D.

Vers. 12—21. (GILGAL.)—*Excuses for disobedience.*   1. Samuel met Saul at *Gilgal.* It was a sacred spot, and a well-known scene of important events in former time and in more recent years. There the kingdom had been established (ch. xi. 15), and Saul "had solemnly pledged him and the people to unconditional obedience." There also he had been previously rebuked and warned (ch. xiii. 13). And thither he repaired ostensibly to offer the sacrifices of thanksgiving for victory, really to make a boastful display and confirm his worldly power. How strangely and intimately are particular places associated with the moral life of individuals and nations! 2. The interview (like the former) appears to have been held in *private.* The sentence of rejection was heard by Saul alone, and long kept by him as a dreadful secret. Yet it was probably surmised by many from his breach with Samuel, and was gradually revealed by the course of events. The sacred history was written from a theocratic point of view, and indicates the principles of which those events were the outcome.   3. The *appearance* of Samuel was an arraignment of the disobedient king before the tribunal of Divine justice. Blinded in part and self-deceived, he made an ostentatious profession of regard for the prophet (ver. 13), and with the assumption of perfect innocence and praiseworthy obedience uttered "the Pharisee's boast"—"I have performed the commandment of Jehovah." His subsequent confession proved the insincerity of his declaration. His disobedience was crowned with *falsehood* and *hypocrisy.* When formally called to account (ver. 14), he forthwith began to justify himself and make excuses for his conduct, such as transgressors are commonly accustomed to make. They were—

I. EXCEEDINGLY VARIED. He—1. Attributes to *other persons* what cannot be denied to have occurred, and seeks to transfer to them the blame which is due to himself. "*They* have brought them from the Amalekites: for the people spared the best of the sheep and of the oxen" (ver. 15). So spoke Adam and Eve at the commencement of human transgression and human excuses (Gen. iii. 13). On a former occasion, when desirous of having his own way, he had not been so considerate of their wishes or so compliant (ch. xiv. 24, 39, 45). "If this excuse were false, where was the integrity and honour of the monarch? If it were true, where was his devotion and obedience? And whether true or false, how utterly unworthy did it prove him of continuing the servant and viceroy of the King of Israel" (Le Bas). 2. Protests *good intentions,* and even religious and commendable motives. "The people spared the best to sacrifice unto the Lord *thy* God;" whereby he seeks to gain the approval of the prophet, but betrays his own inward alienation from the Lord, for he cannot truly say "my God" (Matt. xxiii. 14); and whilst he has regard to the outward ceremonies of the law, he knows not (or wilfully disregards it) that by the law the sacrifices of "devoted" things were altogether prohibited (Deut. xiii. 15; Num. xxxi. 48).   3. *Professes his faithful obedience.* "And the rest we have utterly destroyed." Again and again he declares his innocence (vers. 20, 21), and insinuates, that instead of being reproved by the prophet, he ought to be commended by him for his zeal.   4. *Asserts complete readiness to meet* whatever charge may be preferred against him. "Say on" (ver. 16). "See how sin is multiplied by sin. The transgressor of God's command stands forth as the accuser of the people, the speaker of gross falsehood. The spirit of disobedience evoked as with the rod of an enchanter those other agents of iniquity from their lurking-place; and lo! they sprang forth to do his bidding. Verily their name was legion, for they were many" (Anderson, 'Cloud of Witnesses,' ii. 350).

II. FAITHFULLY EXPOSED. Samuel's fidelity, moral courage, and dignity, mingled with something of bitter disappointment and sorrowful resentment, are specially noteworthy. He—1. *Points to incontestable fact.* "What is this bleating of sheep in mine ears, and the lowing of oxen which I hear?" (ver. 14). It flatly contradicts thy statement, reveals thy sin, and exposes thy excuses. Between it and thy duty there is a contradiction which no explanation can remove. Sin cannot be wholly concealed. "God knows how to bring it to light, however great the care with which it may be cloaked." He was convicted of it by the voices of the animals which he had spared. And "it is no new thing for the plausible pretensions and protestations of hypocrites to be contradicted and disproved by the most plain and undeniable evidences." 2. *Checks the multiplication of vain excuses.* "Stay" (ver. 16); proceed no further in thy endeavour to justify thyself. "And I will tell thee," &c. When the voice of truth, of conscience, and of God speaks, it must perforce silence all other voices. 3. *Recalls the requirements* of the Divine commission (ver. 18), which had been kept out of sight and evaded in the attempts made in self-defence. "Go and *utterly destroy* the sinners the Amalekites" (see ver. 3). 4. *Reveals the motives* of outward conduct (ver. 19), viz. self-will, pride (ch. ix. 21), avarice, rapacity, "love of the world" (Col. iii. 5; 2 Tim. iv. 10), rebellious opposition to the will of Jehovah, and daring ambition to reign independently of him. In all this Samuel sought to rouse the slumbering conscience of the king, and lead him to see his sin and repent. If even yet he had fallen upon his face and given glory to God, there might have been hope. But the reiteration of his previous assertions, his repudiation of what was laid to his charge, and his blindly pointing to his main offence ("and have brought Agag the king of Amalek") as an evidence of his fidelity and zeal, showed that he was insensible to reproof. What should have humbled him served only to harden him in rebellion and obstinacy. And nothing was left but his rejection. His excuses were—

III. UTTERLY FUTILE, sinful, and injurious. They—1. Failed of their intended effect. 2. Increased his delusion, and prevented the light of truth from shining into his mind. 3. Deepened his guilt in the sight of Heaven. 4. Brought upon him heavier condemnation. "As he returned with his victorious troops the prophet met him. That sorrow-stricken countenance, round which hung the long Nazarite locks, now whitened by the snows of ninety years, pale and worn with the long night's unbroken but ungranted intercession, might have told all. Now the thunder-cloud, which began to gather fourteen years before, breaks and peals over the sinner's head. 'Stay,' is the sad and terrible voice as it breaks through the cobweb limits of self deception and excuse, 'and I will tell thee what the Lord said to me this night,' &c. . . . . 'The people took of the spoil,' &c.—the very utterance of dark superstition and mean equivocation. Then the lightning came. The prophet's voice, gathering itself up into one of those magnificent utterances which, belonging to another and a later dispensation, antedate the coming revelation, and are evidently launched forth from the open ark of the testimony of the Highest, said, 'Hath the Lord,'" &c. ('Heroes of Heb. Hist.').—D.

Vers. 22, 23. (GILGAL.)—*The sentence of rejection.*

> " Hath Jehovah (as much) delight in burnt offerings and sacrifices,
>   As in obeying the voice of Jehovah?
> Behold, to obey is better than sacrifice,
>   And to give heed than the fat of rams.
> For (like) the sin of divination is rebellion,
>   And (like) an idol and teraphim is obstinacy.
> Because thou hast rejected the word of Jehovah,
>   He hath rejected thee from being king."

The crisis has now fully arrived. The aged prophet confronts the self-deceived king, whom he looks upon as no longer reigning as servant of Jehovah, in consequence of his endeavour to rule according to his own will and pleasure, though in connection with the outward forms of the religion of Israel. He has striven in vain to turn him from his way, and can henceforth only regard him as a rebel against the supreme Ruler. Inasmuch as Saul, in seeking to justify himself, showed that he estimated moral obedience lightly in comparison with ritual worship, Samuel first of all asserts the incomparable superiority of the former to the latter. He then declares that disobedience is equivalent to heathenism and idolatry, against which Saul, in offering sacrifices to Jehovah and other ways, exhibited such zeal. And, finally, he pronounces, as a judge upon a criminal, the sentence of his rejection. "There is a poetical rhythm in the original which gives it the tone of a Divine oracle uttered by the Spirit of God, imparting to it an awful solemnity, and making it sink deep into the memory of the hearers in all generations" (Wordsworth). Notice—

I. THE PARAMOUNT WORTH OF OBEDIENCE, considered in relation to offerings and sacrifices and other external forms of worship (ver. 22). 1. It is often *less regarded* by men than such forms. They mistake the proper meaning and purpose of them, entertain false and superstitious notions concerning them, and find it easier and more according to their sinful dispositions to serve God (since they must serve him somehow) by them than in self-denial and submission to his will. It is indeed by no means an uncommon thing for those who are consciously leading a sinful life to be diligent and zealous in outward religious worship, and make use of the fruit of their disobedience " to sacrifice unto the Lord," imagining that it will be pleasing to him, and make compensation for their defects in other things. 2. It is *absolutely necessary* in order that they may be acceptable to God. The spirit of obedience and love is the soul of external services of every kind, and without it they are worthless. " To love him with all the heart is more than all whole burnt offerings and sacrifices " (Mark xii. 33). The one ought never to be disjoined from the other, but it is often done ; and they are set in *contrast* to each other. " If we were to say charity is better than church-going, we should be understood to mean that it is better than such church-going as is severed from charity. For if they were united they would not be contrasted. The soul is of more value than the body. But it is not contrasted unless they come into competition with one another, and their interests (although they cannot in truth be so) seem to be separated " (Pusey, ' Minor Prophets,' Hosea vi. 6). " The sacrifice of the wicked is abomination" (Prov. xxi. 27). 3. It is *incomparably superior* to them, considered as needful and appointed modes of serving God (apart from the "wicked mind" with which they are sometimes observed). Because—(1) The one is *universal;* the other is *partial*, and really included in it. (2) The one is *moral*, the other *ceremonial*. It is a "weightier matter of the law." (3) The one is of a *man himself*, the willing sacrifice of his own will ; the other of only a *portion* of his powers or possessions. And "how much better is a man than a sheep ! " (4) The one is *essential*, being founded upon the natural relation of man to God ; the other is *circumstantial*, arising from man's earthly and sinful condition. "Angels obey, but do not sacrifice." (5) The one is the *reality*, the other the *symbol*. (6) The one is the *end*, the other the *means*. Sacrifice is the way of the sinner back to obedience, and the means of his preservation therein. Even the one perfect sacrifice of Christ would not have been needed if man had been obedient. Its design is not merely to afford a sufficient reason for the remission of punishment in a system of moral government, but also to restore to obedience (Titus ii. 14). (7) The one is *temporary*, the other is *eternal*. The sacrifices of the former dispensation have now been abolished ; and how much of the present form of Divine service will vanish away when we behold the face of God ! But love and obedience will " never fail." Since obedience is thus the one thing, the essential, more important than anything else, it should hold the supreme place in our hearts and lives.

II. THE IDOLATROUS CHARACTER OF DISOBEDIENCE (ver. 22). In proportion to the excellence of obedience is the wickedness of disobedience. 1. It is a common thing for men to *make light* of it, especially in actions to which they are disposed, or which they have committed, being blinded by their evil desires and passions. 2. In the sight of God every act of disobedience is *exceedingly hateful*. "Thou art of purer eyes than to behold evil " (Hab. i. 13) without punishing it. 3. In the light of truth it is seen to be *the same in principle* as those transgressions on which the severest condemnation is pronounced, and which are acknowledged to be deserving of the strongest reprobation. It is probable that Saul had already taken measures to put down the "sin of divination" (ch. xxviii. 9), and prided himself upon his zeal against idolatry ; but he was acting in the spirit of that which he condemned, and was an idolater at heart. For he was turning away from God, resisting and rejecting him, and making an idol of self, which is done by all who (in selfish and superstitious fear or desire) seek divination (witchcraft) and trust in an idol (" which is nothing in the world ") and teraphim (household gods—ch. xix. 13). " The declinations from religion, besides the privative, which is atheism, and the branches thereof, are three—heresies, idolatry, and witchcraft. Heresies when we serve the true God with a false worship ; idolatry when we worship false gods, supposing them to be true ; and witchcraft when we adore false gods, knowing them to be wicked and false—the height of idolatry.   And yet we see, though these be true degrees, Samuel teacheth us that they are all of a nature, when there is once a receding from the word of God " (Bacon, 'Advancement of Learning').   "All conscious disobedience is actual idolatry, because it makes self-will, the human I, into a god " (Keil). " Little children, keep yourselves from idols " (1 John v. 21).

III. THE JUST CONDEMNATION OF THE DISOBEDIENT (ch. xxviii. 18).   1. The punishment of the disobedient is the *appropriate fruit* of his disobedience.   " Because thou hast rejected me," &c.   Saul wished to reign without God, and have his own way ; what he sought as a blessing he obtains as a curse.   Sinners say, " Depart from us," &c. (Job xxi. 14) ; and the most terrible sentence that can be pronounced upon them is, " Depart from me, ye that work iniquity " (Ps. vi. 8 ; Matt. vii. 23). "God rejects no one unless he is before rejected by him."   2. It involves *grievous loss and misery*—the loss of power, honour, blessedness ; the experience of weakness, reproach, unhappiness, which cannot be wholly avoided, even though mercy be afterwards found.   3. Judgment is mingled with *mercy*.   Although Saul was discrowned as theocratic king, he did not cease to live or to reign as " legal king."   He was not personally and entirely abandoned.   God sought his salvation to the last.   " His rejection involved only this—(1) That God would henceforth leave him, and withdraw from him the (special) gifts of his Spirit, his counsel through the Urim and Thummim and by his servant Samuel ; and (2) that in a short time the real deposition would be followed by tangible consequences—the kingly ruins would be destroyed, and the kingdom would not pass to his descendants" (Hengstenberg, 'Kingdom of God,' ii. 89).—D.

Vers. 24—31. (GILGAL.)—*Insincere confession of sin.*   " I have sinned " (vers. 24, 30).   On hearing the sentence of his rejection, Saul at length confesses his sin.   The words of Samuel have some effect upon him, but not the full effect they should have had.   For his confession does not proceed from a truly penitent heart (see ch. vii. 6), and it is not followed either by the reversal of his sentence or the forgiveness of his sin.   It was like that of Pharaoh (Exod. ix. 27), of Balaam (Num. xxii. 34), and of Judas (Matt. xxvii. 4)—springing from "the sorrow of the world, which worketh death " (2 Cor. vii. 10).   Notice—
I. ITS CHARACTERISTICS.   It was made—1. *Under the pressure of circumstances,* rather than as the free expression of conviction.   Confession comes too late when it is extorted by the demonstration of sin which can no longer be denied.   Some men, like Saul, conceal their sin so long as they can, and confess it only when they are compelled.   2. *From the fear of consequences* (vers. 23, 26), and not from a sense of the essential evil of sin.   This is the most common characteristic of insincerity.   As Saul confessed his sin from the fear of losing his kingdom, so do multitudes from fear of death, and live to prove their insincerity by their return to disobedience. " There are two views of sin : in one it is looked upon as a wrong ; in the other as producing loss—loss, for example, of character.   In such cases, if character could be preserved before the world, grief would not come ; but the paroxysms of misery fall upon our proud spirit when our guilt is made public.   The most distinct instance we have of this is in the life of Saul.   In the midst of his apparent grief, the thing still uppermost was that he had forfeited his kingly character ; almost the only longing was that Samuel should honour him before the people.   And hence it comes to pass that often remorse and anguish only begin with exposure " (Robertson).   3. *To the servant of God,* and to gain his approval, and not to God, and to obtain his favour.   " Thy words " (ver. 24).   " Now therefore " (as if on the ground of his confession he could justly claim pardon), " I pray thee, pardon my sin " (ver. 25).   Many confess their sin to men without confessing it to God, and attach to their confession a worth that does not belong to it.   4. *With an extenuation of guilt,* rather than with a full acknowledgment of its enormity.   " I feared the people, and obeyed their voice " (vers. 24, 15).   He returns to his first excuse, which he puts in a different form.   If what he said was true, what he had done was wrong (Exod. xxiii. 2).   There is a higher law than the clamour of a multitude.   True penitents do not seek to palliate their sin, but make mention of its greatness as a plea for Divine mercy (Ps. xxv. 11).

5. *With an entreaty for public honour*, rather than in deep humiliation before God and man. " Honour me now, I pray thee, before the elders of the people, and before Israel " (ver. 30). " If Saul had been really penitent, he would have prayed to be humbled rather than to be honoured" (Gregory). 6. *With repeated promises of rendering worship* before the Lord, rather than a serious purpose to obey his voice (vers. 25, 30). He does not seem even yet to have laid to heart the truth which had been declared by the prophet; and he probably looked upon public worship by sacrifice as something peculiarly praiseworthy, and sought, by urging Samuel to remain and offer it, to promote his own honour in the sight of the people, and not as the expression of penitence and the means of forgiveness " The most prominent feature in the character of Saul was his insincerity." And yet, in his repeated promises to worship the Lord, and his urgent entreaties of Samuel, there was doubtless an element of good that might not be despised (1 Kings xxi. 29).

> "The blackest night that veils the sky,
>   Of beauty hath a share ;
> The darkest heart hath signs to tell
>   That God still lingers there."

II. Its consequences. In the language and conduct of Samuel there was—1. *A reiteration of the sentence* of rejection. Thrice it was declared that Jehovah had determined that Saul should no longer reign under his sanction and by his aid (vers. 26, 28). Although he may not have known all that the sentence involved, he felt that its import was alarming. An insincere confession of sin darkens the gathering cloud instead of dispersing it. 2. *A confirmation of it by an impressive sign*, the occasion of which is afforded by the sinner himself (ver. 27). Thereby it comes home to him with greater force. 3. *An intimation of the transfer to a better man* of the dignity which has been forfeited by sin. This was the second time that an announcement of a truly theocratic king was given (ch. xii. 14); and whilst it showed that the Divine purpose could not be defeated, however it might be striven against, it must have been peculiarly painful to Saul. The dreadful secret was a constant burden to him, and when he recognised the man in whom the prediction was about to be fulfilled, it excited his envy and hatred toward him. When any one is not right with God, every favour shown to another fills him with grief and wrath (Gen. iv. 5). 4. *A declaration of the unchangeable purpose of God.* "The Strength " (Perpetuity, Confidence, Refuge, Victory) " of Israel will not lie nor repent," &c. (ver. 29). Saul evidently thought of him as capable of acting in an arbitrary, capricious, and inconstant manner, like himself ; but, inasmuch as he formed his purposes with perfect knowledge, and acted on immutable principles, and there was no real change in the heart of the transgressor, there could be no reversal of his sentence. " He cannot deny himself " (2 Tim. ii. 12). If in some things his purposes toward men appear to change because men alter their relative position toward him (as the sun appears to change by the rotation of the earth, causing day and night), in others they abide the same for ever, and he who sets himself against them must be overthrown. It is now certain that he cannot again be a theocratic king ; but his renewed importunity, in which, perchance, notwithstanding its apparent selfishness, the prophet sees a gleam of hope, is followed by—5. *An indication of pity* toward the foolish and fallen king. "And Samuel returned after Saul ; and Saul worshipped Jehovah " (ver. 31). May he not even yet be led to true repentance ? Although the birthright is given to another, there is a blessing for him who weeps and prays (Gen. xxvii. 38—40). His request is granted. He has what he desires and is prepared to receive. He is still the king after the people's heart. He shall continue such. The sentence shall not be published, nor any special effort be put forth for his dethronement. It would result in general confusion. The just and merciful purposes of God toward the people in giving him for their king are not yet fulfilled, and they will slowly ripen to their accomplishment. 6. *An exhibition of judgment* upon an obstinate offender (ver. 32). One of the reasons, doubtless, why Samuel "turned again after Saul " was that he might execute on Agag the Divine sentence which he had faithlessly remitted. "The terrible vengeance executed on the fallen monarch by Samuel is a measure of Saul's delinquency." It is also a solemn warning to him of the doom which sooner or later comes upon every impenitent and persistent transgressor.

Observations:—1. It is not confession of sin, but the spirit in which it is made, that renders it acceptable to God. 2. Sincerity is the foundation of a truly religious character. 3. Though mercy long lingers over the sinner, yet if it be despised doom comes at last.—D.

Ver. 29. (GILGAL.)—*The unchangeable One of Israel.*

> "And also the Strength of Israel will not lie nor repent :
> For he is not a man, that he should repent."

The word rendered Strength. in the A. V. (*netsach*, here used for the first time) has a varied signification (splendour, victory, truth, confidence, perpetuity, &c.), but is used in this place in the sense of steadfastness, constancy, and unchangeableness. Jehovah, the prophet says, is the Immutability, or unchangeable One, of Israel. He is not like man, inconstant, unreliable, changeable. He is not such an one as Saul imagined him to be ; does not vacillate in his thoughts, feelings, or purposes ; but acts on immutable principles, and performs the word which he has spoken ; and hence the sentence of rejection cannot be reversed. *His unchangeableness* is often declared in the Scriptures. It is implied in the name of Jehovah. It was dwelt upon by Moses (Deut. xxxii. 4, 18, 31), perceived by Balaam (Num. xxiii. 19), and asserted by Hannah in her song of praise (ch. ii. 2). And although it is often disbelieved or misinterpreted, it is a source of strength and consolation to all by whom it is properly understood and realised. Observe that it—

I. ACCORDS WITH APPARENT CHANGEABLENESS in—1. *The creation of the world and the varied operations of his hand.* It is not stoical indifference (without affection) nor absolute quiescence (without activity). He is the living God, and freely exercises his boundless power in producing infinite changes "Over all things, animate and inanimate, flows the silent and resistless tide of change." But whilst he is "in all, above all, and through all," he is separate and distinct from all ; and the creation of the world and all the mutations of matter and force are only expressions of his eternal and unchangeable thought. The physical universe is the garment in which the Invisible clothes himself and manifests himself to our apprehension (Ps. cii. 25—27 ; civ. 2). 2. *The revelations of his character and the successive dispensations of his grace.* These are not contrary to one another. They are simply the clearer and more perfect manifestations of him who is always "the same ;" adapted to the need and capacity of men. God deals with them as a parent with his children, affording them instruction as they are able to bear it. 3. *The relations in which he stands to men, and his diversified dealings with them.* They sometimes appear the opposite of each other. At one time he approves of individuals and nations, and promises them manifold blessings, whereas at another he condemns and punishes them. Hence he is said to *repent.* But the change arises from a change in men themselves. The Glory of Israel always shines with undimmed lustre ; but they shut their eyes and turn their backs upon the light, so that to them it becomes darkness. And it is his unchangeable holiness that necessitates this result ; for if he were "altogether such an one as themselves," they might expect (like Saul) to enjoy his favour whilst they continued in sin. "With the pure thou wilt show thyself pure ; and with the froward thou wilt show thyself froward " (Ps. xviii 26).

II. DENOTES REAL UNCHANGEABLENESS in—1. *The perfections of his character.* Change is an element of imperfection, and no such element can exist in the absolutely perfect One. With him "there is no variableness, neither shadow caused by turning " (James i. 17). "In him there is no darkness at all " (1 John i. 5). And it is "impossible for God to lie " (Heb. vi. 18). 2. *The principles of his government :* wisdom, truth, equity, goodness, &c. In these things he delights, and from them he never departs. They stand like rocks amidst a sea of perpetual change. They are more immutable than the laws of nature, being the foundation on which those laws rest, and inseparable from the Divine character. "The word of our God " (in which they are expressed) "shall stand for ever " (Isa. xl. 8 ; li. 6). "Till heaven and earth pass," &c. (Matt. v. 18). 3. *The purposes of his heart,* formed in perfect knowledge of all that will take place, and effected in harmony with the principles before mentioned. Some of these purposes are hidden (Deut. xxix. 29). Others are revealed, and include the general conditions of peace and happiness, and the results of their observance or neglect (promises and threatenings), also particular events, occurring either independently of the free action of men, or in connection with it, whether in the way of opposition or co-operation, as, *e. g.*, the setting up of a theocratic kingdom, the advent and death of the Messiah (Acts iv. 27, 28), and his universal reign. " The counsel of the Lord standeth for ever " (Ps. xxxiii. 10, 11 ; Prov. xix. 21 ; Isa. xlvi. 10 ; Jer. iv. 28). " I am Jehovah, I change not ; therefore ye sons of Jacob are not consumed " (Mal. iii. 6). " When we find predictions in Scripture not executed, we must consider them not as absolute, but conditional, or, as the civil law calls it, an interlocutory sentence. God declared what would follow by natural causes, or by the demerit of man, not what he would absolutely do himself. And though in many of these predictions the condition is not expressed, it is understood " (see Jer. xviii. 7, 8 ; Ezek. xxxiii. 13, 14 ; Jonah iii. 4 ; iv. 2).

III. INCITES TO HUMAN CONSTANCY in—1. *Faith.* He never disappoints the trust that is reposed in him. His covenant with his people is firm and sure ; "for the mountains shall depart, and the hills be removed," &c. (Isa. liv. 10). " All the promises of God in him are yea, and in him Amen " (2 Cor. i. 20). What an incentive is thus afforded to each believer, and the whole Church, to " abide in him " ! " Whose *faith* follow, &c. Jesus Christ (is) the same yesterday, and to-day, and for ever ; (therefore) be not carried about (like a ship driven by varying winds) with divers and strange doctrines ; for it is a good thing that the heart be *established* with grace " (Heb. xiii. 7—9). 2. *Love.* Only the unchangeable One can be a true, satisfying, and enduring rest of the affections ; for all earthly objects change and pass away, and must leave the immortal spirit desolate. His unchanging love should keep our love to him and to each other burning with a steady flame (John xiii. 1, 34 ; Jude 21). 3. *Righteousness.* (1) Which consists in conformity to the constant obedience of Christ to the righteous and unalterable will of the Father. (2) Which is faithfully assured of enduring blessedness (Rev. xxii. 14). " He that doeth the will of God abideth for ever " (1 John ii. 17). (3) But without which there will be an irrevocable loss of the most glorious crown and kingdom. The persistently rebellious dash themselves to pieces against the unchangeable holiness and justice of God.—D.

Vers. 32, 33. (GILGAL.)—*The execution of Agag.* Agag was put to death, perhaps, by the hand of Samuel ; more probably by other hands under his order, for it is common to speak of official persons doing what they simply command to be done (John xix. 1). " In ancient time persons of the highest rank were employed to execute the sentence of the law (Jether, the eldest son of Gideon, Doeg, Benaiah). Sometimes the chief magistrate executed the sentence of the law with his own hands " (Paxton's ' Illustrations,' iv. 171). The act was one of great severity. It should, however, be remembered that—1. The Amalekite king had committed great atrocities (ver. 33), and was the chief representative of cruel and irreconcilable enemies of Israel. 2. Amalek lay under *a ban of extermination* which had been pronounced by Jehovah (Exod. xvii. 14 ; Num. xxiv. 20), and was now required to be fully carried into effect. Samuel acted in obedience to a higher will than his own ; not from personal revenge, but in his public capacity, doing what Saul (from no feelings of humanity) had failed to do, and giving honour to Jehovah before his altar. " There must indeed have been inadequate ideas of the *individuality of man* and of the rights of human life before a dispensation could have been received which enforced wars of extermination—wars which would now be contrary to morality ; for the reason that our ideas on the subject of human individuality and the rights of life are completely changed, and that we have been enlightened on these subjects, upon which the early ages of mankind were in the dark " (Mozley, ' Ruling Ideas in Early Ages,' p. 161). 3. The peculiar circumstances of the case necessitated some such exhibition of the authority and justice of Jehovah for the maintenance of the theocracy, and the reproof and warning of the people who had shared in the sin of their king. "Such a sinking age could be saved from imminent dissolution only by extreme severity. He who, however kindly disposed in other respects, was most direct and inexorable in carrying out what seemed urgently needed, he alone could now become the true physician of the times, and the successful founder of a better age" (Ewald). We have here—

I. A NOTORIOUS OFFENDER MEETING HIS JUST DOOM. 1. Although sentence upon an evil work is not speedily executed, it is not reversed. The long-suffering of God waits, "as in the days of Noah" (2 Pet. iii. 20), when judgment was suspended for 120 years; but "he spared not the old world" (2 Pet. ii. 5). 2. Justice requires that incorrigible sinners should be punished with significant severity. "As" (in the same manner as) "thy sword," &c. 3. Death is naturally bitter to men, and especially to those who have heavy guilt upon their consciences. The last words of Agag were, "Surely the bitterness of death is past." 4. When sinners deem themselves most secure, then "sudden destruction cometh upon them." Having been spared so long, he imagined that the danger was over, and little thought that the venerable prophet was the messenger of wrath. "The feet of the avenging deities are shod with wool, but they strike with iron hands."

II. AN AMIABLE PROPHET CLOTHED WITH HOLY SEVERITY. 1. The more a man loves righteousness, the more intensely does he hate sin. "Ye that love the Lord, hate evil." What woes were ever so terrible as those that fell from the lips of Christ? 2. A good man may inflict punishment on the wicked without feelings of personal revenge against them. "Our Lord declared the inferiority of the legal position of the Old Testament not because the desire of retribution ought to be excluded from the religion of reconciliation, but because it ought not to predominate in it" (Tholuck). 3. When some fail to carry out the purposes of God, others are bound to make up for their defect, and sometimes to do things for which they do not seem well adapted, and which do not harmonise with their general character (1 Kings xviii. 40). "When kings abandoned their duty God often executed his law by the prophets" (Grotius). 4. That which is severity to one must often be done, provided it be not contrary to justice, for the good of all.

III. AN OBSTINATE PEOPLE TAUGHT A SALUTARY LESSON. 1. No excuse can justify disobedience to the commands of God. Doubtless the people, if called to account, would have been as ready as Saul to offer excuses for the part they took in sparing Agag and the best of the sheep, &c. 2. They who fail to obey these commands deprive themselves of invaluable blessings. The sunshine of heaven is beclouded, and the sentence of rejection on their king, although at present little known, will ere long produce disastrous effects in them. 3. God's work must be done, and if one refuses to do it, another is raised up for the purpose. As with individuals, so with nations (Num. xiv. 21; Rom. xi. 22). 4. Those who, although the professed people of God, contend against his purposes must share the fate of his open enemies. "If ye shall still do wickedly ye shall be consumed, both you and your king" (ch. xii. 25).—D.

Vers. 34, 35. (GILGAL.)—*A melancholy parting.* The interview between Samuel and Saul was now ended. "It was a fearful meeting; it was followed by a lifelong parting." The earlier course of Saul (from the time the prophet met him in the gate at Ramah) was marked by modesty, prudence, generosity, and lofty spiritual impulses, and was one of brilliant promise. His subsequent course (from his first wrong step before the war of Michmash), although distinguished by external prosperity, was marked by self-will, presumption, disobedience, and selfishness, and was one of rapid degeneracy. "How must the prophet have lamented as he saw the wreck of that early brightened life!" On his part, more especially, the separation was—

I. NEEDFUL. A good man is compelled to separate from those to whom he has given his counsel and aid—1. When from lack of sympathy and opposition of aim he can no longer effectively co-operate with them. 2. When he cannot hope to exert a beneficial influence upon them. 3. When his continuance with them affords a sanction to a course which he cannot approve. His parting is a condemnation of it, and is rendered necessary by truth and righteousness. "God's ambassador was recalled from him; the intercourse of the God of Israel came to an end because Saul, sinking step by step away from God, had by continued disobedience and increasing impenitence given up communion with God" (Erdmann). "Had he spared this spiritual child, when to spare him would have been contrary to the fundamental law of the theocracy, the worst possible precedent would have been afforded for future ages by this first king" (Ewald).

II. RESPECTFUL. Samuel acceded to the request of Saul to honour him before the people; and although it is not stated how far he participated with him in worship, yet he evidently avoided an open and violent rupture with him, and gave him honour, as civil ruler, to the last. Respect is due "not only to the good and gentle, but also to the froward," on account of—1. The authority and power that may be intrusted to them in the providence of God (Rom. xiii. 1). 2. The natural dignity of man— great in ruin, capable of restoration, and susceptible to the influence of kindness or contempt. Jesus did not resent the kiss with which Judas betrayed him, but said, "*Friend,* wherefore comest thou hither?" 3. The requirements of social order and peace. Saul was even yet the best king the people were fit to receive, and the conduct of Samuel indicated the duty of submission, which, in the spirit of their king, they were not always disposed to render (ver. 24; ch. xiv. 45).

III. SORROWFUL. "Nevertheless Samuel mourned for Saul." With heavy heart and weary feet the old prophet took his way up from Gilgal to Ramah, and mourned for Saul, who, on the opposite hill of Gibeah, pursued his wilful way, bringing upon himself and Israel inevitable and overwhelming woe; alive, yet dead; so near, yet so completely lost. 1. What object is more mournful than a soul "going astray" from God? 2. What sorrow is too great at such a sight? 3. How vast is that Divine sorrow of which the human is the product and reflection! "And the Lord repented," &c. The prophetic spirit is one of wide and deep sympathy at once with God and man, and it was perfectly possessed by "the Man of sorrows." "Samuel mourned for Saul, but we do not hear that Saul mourned for himself."

IV. FINAL. He "came no more to see Saul"—gave him counsel no more as aforetime, which indeed was not desired; and he only saw him once again, when he forced himself into his presence (ch. xix. 24). When good men are compelled by the conduct of the wicked to separate from them, the parting—1. Deprives the latter of incalculable benefits, however lightly they may be estimated at the time. 2. Tends to increase the moral distance between them, and render the restoration of their intercourse more and more impossible. 3. Is certain to be hereafter bitterly but vainly regretted (ch. xxviii. 15, 18). Oh, the sad and perpetual separations that are caused by sin! The paths of Samuel and Saul (like those of Moses and Pharaoh, Paul and Demas) may be compared to the courses of two ships that meet on the ocean, and sail near each other for a season, not without danger of collision, and then part asunder, the one to reach a "desired haven," the other to make shipwreck and become a castaway.—D.

Ver. 25; xvi. 1—4. (RAMAH.)—*Recalled to the path of duty.* "Go, I will send thee to Jesse the Bethlehemite." 1. The greatest and best of men experience seasons of sorrow, depression, and doubt, and sometimes fail in the fulfilment of duty. It was thus with Abraham, Moses, and Elijah, and with others in later ages. It was the same with Samuel, though to a less extent than almost any other. His grief for Saul was excessive. He surrendered himself to it without seeking the consolation and help by which it might be mitigated, and suffered it to interfere with the work which he might yet accomplish on behalf of Israel; and hence he was reproved by God. "The excellent prophet here displays something of human weakness. Samuel here looked on the vessel, made by the invisible hand of God himself, utterly broken and minished, and his emotion thereat shows his pious and holy affection; yet he is not without sin" (Calvin). 2. The failure of good men often appears in those things in which they are pre-eminently excellent. Samuel exhibited extraordinary sympathy with the purposes of God concerning his people, unquestioning obedience to every indication of his will, and strong faith, and hope, and dauntless courage in its fulfilment. Yet here we find him a prey to "the grief that saps the mind," apparently hopeless and desponding, and smitten with fear like Elijah when "he arose and went for his life" on hearing the threat of Jezebel. "Such things would seem designed by God to stain the pride of all flesh, and to check all dependence upon the most eminent or confirmed habits of godliness" (A. Fuller). The strongest are as dependent on God as the feeblest. 3. A higher voice than that of their own troubled and fearful hearts speaks to men of sincerity, and in communing with it they are led into a clearer perception of duty and to gird themselves afresh for its performance. The "spirit of faith" regains its ascendancy over them. And in going forth to active service they find new strength and hope at every step. The night gives place to the morning dawn, and

> "They feel, although no tongue can prove,
> That every cloud that spreads above
> And veileth love, itself is love" (Tennyson, 'The Two Voices').

Consider the way of duty, trodden by the good man, as—

I. PRESCRIBED BY GOD, whose will is the rule of human life, and is—1. Indicated in many ways—the word of truth, providential circumstances, reason, and conscience, and "that awful interior light which the dying Saviour promised, and which the ascending Saviour bestowed—the Spirit of God." 2. Sometimes obscured by frustrated effort, grievous disappointment, immoderate grief, desponding and doubtful thoughts (Matt. xi. 2, 3; Acts xviii. 9; xxiii. 11). 3. Never long hidden from those who are sincerely desirous of doing it, and seek for the knowledge of it with a view to that end (vers. 2, 3; 1 Kings xix. 15).

II. BESET BY DANGER. "How can I go? If Saul hear of it, he will kill me." The question was not simply an inquiry for direction, but also an expression of fear; and it may possibly have arisen from indications of Saul's wilfulness such as afterwards appeared (ch. xix. 22). 1. Danger is sometimes formidable, even to the bravest of men. 2. It is exaggerated by despondency, doubt, and fear.

> "Thy soul is by vile fear assailed, which oft
> So overcasts a man, that he recoils
> From noblest resolution, like a beast
> At some false semblance in the twilight gloom" (Dante).

3. No danger in the way of duty is equal to that which will be certainly found in departing from it. "In the way of righteousness there is life, and in the pathway thereof there is no death."

III. PURSUED WITH FIDELITY. "And Samuel did that which the Lord spake" (ver. 4). His hesitation was only for a moment, and with further light his faith revived and was displayed in fearless devotion. Fidelity to duty—1. Demands the renunciation of self and many cherished plans and purposes. 2. Appears in trustful, practical, and unreserved obedience. Samuel went in dependence upon the promise, "I will show thee what thou shalt do," &c. 3. Sometimes necessitates a prudent reserve. There was no deception in withholding a reason for the action directed, beyond that which lay on the surface of the action itself. To reveal it would be to defeat the end designed. And fidelity is sometimes best shown by silence.

IV. TERMINATING IN SAFETY AND HOPE. 1. Threatened danger is averted. 2. Promised guidance is obtained. 3. A brighter day dawns, and

> "God's purposes will ripen fast,
> Unfolding every hour."

Samuel returns to Ramah in peace, and with renewed zeal devotes his remaining days to the work of training a body of younger prophets (ch. xix. 20), whose influence, together with a change of dynasty, will save the nation and promote the establishment of the kingdom of God. "Let us ask ourselves whether the Jewish nation would have played any part as a 'main propelling agency of modern cultivation,' if its monarchy had been allowed to take the form which Saul would have given it, if he had made religion a creature of the kingly power, and war an instrument of rapine, and not of justice, and we shall see that Samuel's view of the matter was the true one, and in accordance with the proper vocation of a prophet" (Strachey, 'Jewish Hist. and Politics ').—D.

Ver. 35. (RAMAH.)—*Samuel a man of sorrows.* "Nevertheless Samuel mourned for Saul." There are many kinds of sorrow in the world. One is *natural*, such as is felt by men in temporal affliction. Another is *spiritual*, such as is felt by a penitent for his sin. A third is *sympathetic*, benevolent, Divine, such as is felt by a godly man over the ungodly. "I beheld the transgressors, and was grieved." Of this last Samuel had experience throughout his life (ch. iii. 15; iv. 11; vii. 2; viii. 3, 6), and more especially at the persistent transgression and irrevocable rejection of Saul. Observe of such sorrow, that—

I. IT IS OCCASIONED BY A DEPLORABLE SIGHT. Look at it. A soul—1. Failing to fulfil the purpose for which it was made, and "coming short of the glory of God." 2. Falling into degradation, misery, and woe. A ruined temple! A wandering star! (Jude 13). A discrowned monarch! A despairing spirit! Oh, what a contrast between what it might have been and what it is here and will be hereafter! 3. Inciting others to pursue the same path.

II. IT IS AN EVIDENCE OF EXALTED PIETY, inasmuch as it shows—1. Genuine zeal for the honour of God, whose law is "made void," whose goodness is despised, and whose claims are trampled in the dust. 2. Tender compassion toward men. "Charity to the soul is the soul of charity." 3. Intense sympathy with the noblest of men, with the Son of God, and with the eternal Father himself. "I have great heaviness and continual sorrow in my heart," &c. (Rom. ix. 1—3). "O that thou hadst known," &c. (Luke xix. 42). "O that thou hadst hearkened to my commandments!" (Isa. xlviii. 18).

III. IT IS SOMETIMES IMPROPERLY INDULGED (ch. xvi. 1), as—1. When it is mingled with feelings of personal disappointment and mortification, and of dissatisfaction with the ways of God. 2. When it is allowed to become a prolonged and all-absorbing emotion, to the exclusion of those considerations and feelings by which it ought to be modified and regulated. 3. When it produces despondency and fear (ch. xvi. 2), weakens faith, and hinders exertion.

IV. ITS IMPROPER INDULGENCE IS DIVINELY CORRECTED. By means of—1. Gentle rebuke, indicating that it is useless, unreasonable, and reprehensible. 2. Clear and deep conviction of the over-ruling purpose of God, and unreserved submission to it. "*At that time* Jesus answered and said, I thank thee, O Father," &c. (Matt. xi. 25). 3. Renewed, benevolent, and hopeful activity.—D.

Ver. 31.—*Tried again and rejected.* God proves his servants, and does not show them the fulness of his favour and confidence till they have been tested. Abraham was tried and found faithful; so was Moses; so was David; so was Daniel. Abraham, indeed, was not without fault, nor Moses either. David once sinned grievously. But all of these were proved true at heart and trustworthy. Saul is the conspicuous instance in the Old Testament of one who, when called to a high post in Jehovah's service, and tested therein again and again, offended the Lord again and again, and was therefore rejected and disowned. 1. The question on which the king was tested was the same as before. Would he obey the voice of the Lord, and rule as his lieutenant, or would he be as the kings of the neighbouring nations and tribes, and use the power with which he was invested according to his own will and pleasure? On this critical question the prophet Samuel had exhorted both Saul and the people when the monarchy was instituted. If the king erred, he could not plead that he had not been forewarned. The accepted principle of modern constitutional government is that the ruler exists and is bound to act for the public good, and not for his own aggrandisement or pleasure. At root this is the very principle which Samuel inculcated 3000 years ago. The Old Testament required a king to reign in the fear of the Lord, and loyally execute his will. The New Testament describes the ruler as a "minister of God for good." Now the Divine will and the public weal are really the same, and the most advanced political principle of modern intelligence is no other than the old doctrine of the Bible. There is no Divine right of kings to rule as they think proper. That doctrine of base political subservience is opposed to both the spirit and the letter of the sacred writings. The king is for God, not God for the king. The king is for the people, not the people for the king. The voice of the people may not always be the voice of God, but the good of the people is always the will of God. 2. The test to which the king was now subjected was, like the former one, specific, and publicly applied. Would he obey the Lord in the extermination of Amalek or no? And he disobeyed. If there was one of all the Amalekite race who deserved to forfeit his life, it was the king, Agag, a ruthless chief, whose sword, as Samuel expressed it, had "made women childless;" yet him Saul spared when he showed no mercy to others. It was not at all from a feeling of humanity or pity. To have scrupled about shedding the blood of a hereditary foe would not have occurred to any Oriental warrior of the period. But Saul would reserve the royal captive to grace his triumph, and be a household slave of the king of Israel. It was the pride of the chiefs and kings of that age to reduce the princes whom they had conquered to slavery in their courts. Adonibezek is said to have kept seventy such captives, whose hands and feet he had mutilated to unfit them for war, and who, as slaves, gathered from his table. Besides Agag, the best of the sheep and cattle belonging to Amalek were spared by Saul and his army. They used their success to enrich themselves, and forgot that the sentence of God against that nation was the only justification of the war. 3. The Divine censure on the disobedient king was pronounced by Samuel. The prophet was deeply grieved. He had loved the young man on whose lofty head he had poured the sacred oil, and whose failure to fulfil the early promise of his reign had already caused him, if not much surprise, distress unfeigned. And Samuel was concerned for the nation. If the new government was so soon discredited, and Saul forfeited his kingly seat, what but anarchy could come upon Israel, and with anarchy, subjection, as before, to the Philistines or some other warlike nation of the heathen? The prophet fulfilled his commission, however painful; gravely reproved the king, brushed aside his excuses and evasions, and refused, not without a touch of scorn, his offered bribe of animals for sacrifice. 4. Samuel took occasion to declare that "to obey is better than sacrifice, and to hearken than the fat of rams." These words contain the very quintessence of the testimony of the prophets; not Samuel only, but Hosea, Micah, Isaiah, Jeremiah, and in fact all the great teachers whom Jehovah sent to his ancient people. Sacrificial oblations could never be accepted in lieu of practical obedience, and a rebellious, wilful temper was as offensive to the Lord as any kind of idolatry. Priests and Levites were appointed for religious ceremonial, but the great function of the prophets was to maintain the supremacy of what is moral over what is ceremonial, and to lift up fearless voices for mercy and truth, judgment and righteousness, integrity and probity, reverence for Jehovah, and obedience to his revealed will. Such was the testimony of the Lord Jesus himself, as the greatest of prophets. He recognised and respected the sacrifices appointed in the law, but did not in his conversations or discourses dwell on them. His aim was to cause men to hear the word of God, and do it. And such is the message or burden of all New Testament prophets, and of those who know how to guide and teach Christians. To be lax and indulgent on questions of moral conduct, while strict about services and offerings to God and the Church, is the part of a false prophet. The true prophet, while witnessing to free forgiveness in the blood of Christ, will enjoin all who seek that forgiveness to cease to do evil and learn to do well, will faithfully declare to them that they cannot be kept in the love of God if they are not obedient to his word. 5. The behaviour of Saul under reproof betrayed a shifty, superficial character. He showed no real sense of sin, or desire of Divine forgiveness. David, during his reign, committed a more heinous offence against domestic and social morality than anything that Saul as yet had done; but he was pardoned and restored because when charged with the sin—"Thou art the man"—he confessed it, and excused not himself. And then he cried to God, "Purge me with hyssop, and I shall be clean." But Saul, when charged with disobedience, showed no shame or sorrow on its account. He at once put himself in a defensive attitude, stooped to subterfuge, laid the blame on others, had no feeling but a desire to escape consequences. He would propitiate the Lord and his prophet by sacrifices; but his former religious sensibility was now almost quite gone from him, and he was becoming, like Esau, a "profane person," hard and godless. It is pitiful to see that the king looked no higher than to Samuel, and asked no more than that the prophet would pardon him, and favour him so far as to join with him while he publicly worshipped the Lord. Evidently his object was to have his credit upheld by the venerated presence of Samuel; and, on his repeating the request, the prophet thought fit to yield to his wish, probably to avoid the weakening of the royal influence, and the premature fall of the monarchy. 6. The rejection of Saul took no sudden effect. Gravely and sadly it was pronounced by Samuel; but it brought about no immediate catastrophe. None the less was it a sure and fatal sentence. We know that Saul was not dethroned. He had a long reign, and died on the battle-field. But the process was already begun which led him to dark Gilboa, which led one better than him to Hebron and to Jerusalem; and the remainder of this book is occupied in showing how the Divine rejection of Saul took effect, and how the Lord brought forward and trained the son of Jesse for the kingdom. It is a thought full of solemnity, that a man may long keep his place and hold his own in Christian society who yet is rejected by the Lord, and is growing at heart more and more profane, till at last the evil spirit rules him instead of the good, and he dies as one troubled and God-forsaken. The process may be long, but it is none the less tragical. May God keep us from the beginnings of declension, and from all excusing of our sins, or laying of the fault upon others! Lord, take not thy Holy Spirit from us!—F.

CHOICE OF DAVID TO BE ISRAEL'S KING, AND DECLINE OF SAUL'S KINGDOM.
(CHS. XVI.—XXXI.)

EXPOSITION.

DAVID ANOINTED AS THE FUTURE KING, AND HIS FIRST INTRODUCTION TO SAUL.
(CH. XVI.)

CHAPTER XVI.

CHOICE OF DAVID AS SUCCESSOR TO SAUL (vers. 1—13). Ver. 1.—**How long wilt thou mourn?** The grief of Samuel was prolonged almost to a sinful extent, nor can we wonder at it. We who see Saul's whole career, and know how deeply he fell, are in danger of discrediting his high qualities; but those who were witnesses of his military skill and prowess, and saw him and his heroic son raising the nation from its feebleness and thraldom to might and empire, must have given him an ungrudging admiration. Both David's dirge (2 Sam. i. 19—27) and Samuel's long mourning, and the unqualified obedience which he was able so quickly to extort from a high-spirited people unused to being governed, bear decisive testimony to his powers as a ruler and commander in war. But God now warns Samuel to mourn no longer. Saul's rejection has become final, and God's prophet must sacrifice his personal feelings, and prepare to carry out the purpose indicated in ch. xiii. 14; xv. 28. We must not, however, conclude that Samuel's sorrow had only been for Saul personally; there was danger for the whole nation in his conduct. If wilfulness and passion gained in him the upper hand, the band of authority would be loosed, and the old feebleness and anarchy would return, and Israel become even more hopelessly a prey to its former troubles. Samuel, therefore, is to go to Bethlehem and anoint there a son of Jesse. As this place lay at some distance from Ramah, and out of the circuit habitually traversed by Samuel as judge, he probably had but a general knowledge of the family. Evidently he had no acquaintance with David (vers. 11, 12); but as Jesse was a man of wealth and importance, his reputation had probably reached the prophet's ears.

Ver. 2.—**And Samuel said, How can I go? if Saul hear it, he will kill me.** Saul was actually king, and the anointing of another in his stead would be regarded as an act of open treason, and the stirring up of civil war. This was not indeed intended. The anointing of David was a prophetic indication of the man whom God, in his own way and at his own time, would place upon Saul's throne, without either scheming or action thereto on the part either of Samuel or of David. Its value would chiefly lie in the careful training he would receive from Samuel; but when David was king, it would also greatly strengthen his position; for it would be known that from his boyhood he had been marked out for his high office. Never did man mount a throne with purer hands than David; and if Saul would have permitted it, he would have been a faithful and loyal servant to the last. It was Saul really who thrust the kingdom upon David. As regards Samuel's fears, headstrong as Saul was, he owed too much to the prophet to have put him to death ; but he would have visited the act upon Jesse and his family with revengeful violence, and Samuel would henceforward have lost all freedom of action, even if he were not cast into prison, or banished from the land. God therefore commands him to **take an heifer with** him, **and say, I am come to sacrifice to Jehovah.** The question has been asked, Was there in this any duplicity ? In answer we may ask another question : Is it always necessary, or even right, to tell in all cases the whole truth ? If so, quarrels and ill-feeling would be multiplied to such an extent that social life would be unendurable. All charitable, well-disposed persons suppress much, and keep a guard over their lips, lest they should stir up strife and hatred. Now here there was to be no treason, no inciting to civil war. David, still a child, was to be set apart for a high destiny, possibly without at the time fully knowing what the anointing meant, and certainly with the obligation to take no step whatsoever towards winning the crown that was to descend upon his head. This was his probation, and he bore the trial nobly. And what right would Samuel have had, not merely to compel David to be a traitor, but to place Jesse and his family in a position of danger and difficulty ? To have anointed David publicly would have forced Jesse to an open rupture with the king, and he must have sought safety either by fighting for his life, or by breaking up his home, and fleeing into a foreign land. David in course of time had thus to seek an asylum for his parents (ch. xxii. 3, 4), but it was through no fault of his own, for he always remained true to his allegiance. Even when David was being hunted for his life, he made no appeal to Samuel's anointing, but it remained, what it was ever intended to be, a secret sign and declaration to him of God's preordained purpose, but of one as to which he was to take no step to bring about its fulfilment. It was a pledge to David, and nothing but misery would have resulted from its being prematurely made known to those who had no right to know it. God wraps up the flower, which is in due time to open and bear fruit, within many a covering ; and to rend these open prematurely is to destroy the flower and the fruit that is to spring from it. And so to have anointed David openly, and to have made him understand the meaning of the act, would have been to destroy David and frustrate the Divine purpose.

Vers. 3—5.—**Call Jesse to the sacrifice.** The word used is *zebach*, and means a sacrifice followed by a feast, at which all the elders of

the town, and with them Jesse and his elder sons, would be present by the prophet's invitation. It is plain that such sacrifices were not unusual, or Saul would have demanded a reason for Samuel's conduct. As the ark remained so long in obscurity at Kirjath-jearim, and the solemn services of the tabernacle were not restored until Saul at some period of his reign removed it to Nob, possibly Samuel may have instituted this practice of occasionally holding sacrifices, now at one place and now at another, to keep alive a sense of religion in the hearts of the people ; and probably on such occasions he taught them the great truths of the law, thus combining in his person the offices of prophet and priest. Nevertheless, **the elders of the town trembled at his coming.** More literally, "went with trembling to meet him." Very probably such visitations often took place because some crime had been committed into which Samuel wished to inquire, or because the people had been negligent in some duty. And though conscious of no such fault, yet at the coming of one of such high rank their minds foreboded evil. He quiets, however, their fears and bids them **sanctify** themselves ; *i. e.* they were to wash and purify themselves, and abstain from everything unclean, and put on their festal garments (Exod. xix. 10 ; and comp. 1 Sam. xxi. 5). It is added, **He sanctified Jesse and his sons,** *i. e.* he took especial care that no legal impurity on their part should stand in the way of the execution of his errand.

Vers. 6—10.—**When they were come.** *I. e.* to the house of Jesse, apparently in the interval between the sacrifice and the feast. The latter we learn in ver. 11 did not take place until after David had been sent for. But many hours would elapse between the sacrifice and the feast, as the victim had to be skinned and prepared for roasting, and finally cooked. This interval was spent in Jesse's house ; and when he saw there Eliab, the first-born, and observed his tall stature and handsome face, qualities which Samuel had admired in Saul, he **said**, *i. e.* in himself, felt sure, that the goodly youth was **Jehovah's anointed** (see on ch. ii. 10, 35 ; x. 1, &c.), but is warned that these external advantages do not necessarily imply real worth of heart ; and as **Jehovah looketh on the heart,** his judgment depends, not on appearances, but on reality. As Eliab is thus rejected, Jesse makes his other sons pass before the prophet. Next **Abinadab,** who has the same name as a son of Saul (ch. xxxi. 2) ; then **Shammah,** so called again in ch. xvii. 13, but Shimeah in 2 Sam. xiii. 3, and Shimma in 1 Chron. ii. 13, where, however, the Hebrew is exactly the same as in 2 Sam. xiii. 3. After these four other sons follow, of whom one apparently died young, as only seven are recorded in 1 Chron. ii. 13—15, whereas these with David make eight. To all these seven the Divine voice within Samuel gave no response, and he said unto Jesse, **Jehovah hath not chosen these.**

Vers. 11, 12.—**Are here all thy children?** The word literally is lads, *na'arim*. The elder sons must have been nearly or quite grown up, but David was probably a mere boy, and as such had not been thought worthy of an invitation, but had been left with the servants keeping the sheep. The prophet now orders him to be summoned, and marks his value in God's sight by saying, **We will not sit down till he come hither.** The verb literally means, *we will not surround*, i. e. the table, though at this time the Jews did sit at meals, instead of reclining on couches, as in the days of Amos and our Lord. We gather, moreover, from Samuel's words that the selection of the son that was to be anointed took place while the preparations were being made for the feast. At the prophet's command David is fetched from the flock, which was probably near the house, and on his arrival the prophet sees a **ruddy** boy, *i. e.* red-haired, correctly rendered in the Vulgate *rufus*, the colour loved by all painters of manly beauty, and, from the delicacy of complexion which accompanies it, especially admired in the East, where men are generally dark-haired and sallow-faced. Moreover, he was **of a beautiful countenance.** The Hebrew says, "with beautiful eyes," and so the Syriac and Septuagint rightly. He was also **goodly to look to,** *i. e.* to look at. These last words give the general idea of the beauty of his face and person, while his bright hair and delicate complexion and the beauty of his eyes are specially noticed in the Hebrew.

Ver. 13.—**Then Samuel took the horn of oil, and anointed him in the midst of his brethren.** Did he or they understand the meaning of the act? We think not. Certainly Eliab (ch. xvii. 28) had no idea of any special greatness being in store for his brother. Most probably both Jesse and his sons regarded David as simply selected to be trained in Samuel's schools; and there can be little doubt that he was so trained. Samuel gave unto David that which Saul had not received —long and careful training; and David profited by it, and at Naioth in Ramah perfected his skill, not only in reading and writing, but in poetry and music. Saul and David were both men of extraordinary natural ability; but the one is always shy, awkward, and with all the defects of an uneducated man; while David is altogether the contrary. But Samuel gave his youthful pupil something better than accomplishments—he carefully educated him in the law of God, and led his mind onward to all that was good. It was Samuel's last and crowning work. Prophecy and monarchy

were both of his institution, as orderly elements of the Jewish state; he also trained the man who more nearly than any other approached unto the ideal of the theocratic king, and was to Israel the type of their coming Messiah. It was Samuel's wisdom in teaching his young men music which gave David the skill to be the sweet singer of the sanctuary; and we may feel sure also that when David arranged the service of the house of God, and gave priests and Levites their appointed duties (1 Chron. xxiii.—xxvi.), the model which he set before him was that in which he had so often taken part with Samuel at Ramah. As Eliab, Abinadab, and Shammah were but lads (ver. 11), David must have been very young, and many years have elapsed between his anointing and his summons to Saul's presence and combat with Goliath; and they were thus well spent in the prophet's company, whence at proper intervals he would return to his father's house and resume his ordinary duties. **The Spirit of Jehovah came upon David from that day forward** (comp. ch. x. 6, 9). In modern language we should say that David's character grew and developed nobly, both intellectually and morally. With far more ethical truth the Israelites saw in the high qualities which displayed themselves in David's acts and words the presence and working of a Divine Spirit. It was a "breathing of Jehovah" which moved David onward, and fostered in him all that was morally great and good, just as it was "the breath of God" which at the creation moved upon the face of the waters to call this earth into being (Gen. i. 2). **Samuel rose up and went to Ramah.** His mission was over, and he returned to his ordinary duties; but, doubtless, first he made arrangements that David should in due time follow him thither, that he might be trained for his high office under Samuel's direct influence and control.

DAVID'S INTRODUCTION TO KING SAUL (vers. 14—23). Vers. 14, 15.—From this time forward David is the central figure of the history. Saul has been rejected, and though, as being the actual king, he must still play his part, more especially as his decline goes on side by side with David's growth in every kingly quality, yet the record of it is no longer given on Saul's account. Interesting, then, as may be the information concerning the mental malady with which Saul was visited, yet the object of this section is to acquaint us with the manner in which David was first brought into connection with him. From the description given of David in ver. 18 it is evident that there has been a considerable interval of time between this and the previous section. David is no longer a child, but a "mighty valiant man." The connection is ethical, and lies in the contrasted moral state of the two men, as shown in the two parallel statements: "the Spirit of Jehovah came upon David;" "the Spirit of Jehovah departed from Saul." There was a gradual decline and debasement of his character; and as David grew from a child into a hero in war and a scholar in peace, so Saul, from being a hero, degenerated into a moody and resentful tyrant. **An evil spirit from Jehovah troubled him.** Really, as in the margin, *terrified him;* that is, Saul became subject to fits of intense mental agony, under which his reason gave way, and temporary insanity, accompanied by outbreaks of violence, came on. It is very difficult for us with our richer language to give the exact force of the Hebrew; for the word rendered *spirit* is literally *wind, air, breath.* A student of Hebrew can trace the word *ruach* through all its modifications, from its physical signification as the material wind, to its metaphysical meaning as an influence from God; and then still onward up to the beings who minister before God, and of whom the Psalmist says, " He maketh his angels to be winds" (Ps. civ. 4); till finally we reach up unto the third person of the blessed Trinity: and then, as with this full knowledge of the Divine nature we read backward, we find the presence of the Holy Ghost indicated, where to the Israelite probably there was mention only of a material agency. Jost, in his ' History of the Jews since the time of the Maccabees,' vol. i. p. 12, says that Saul suffered under that form of madness called *hypochondria,* and that the Jews gave this the name of *bad air,* the words translated here " evil spirit ; " for they held, he says, that " the devil inhabited the air." So St. Paul speaks of the " wicked spiritual beings that are in high places," *i. e.* in the loftier regions of the atmosphere (Ephes. vi. 12). A study of Saul's character makes it probable that, as is often the case with men of brilliant genius, there was always a touch of insanity in his mental constitution. His joining in the exercises of the prophets (ch. x. 10—12) was an outburst of eccentric enthusiasm ; and the excitement of his behaviour in the occurrences narrated in ch. xiv. indicate a mind that might easily be thrown off its balance. And now he seems to have brooded over his deposition by Samuel, and instead of repenting to have regarded himself as an ill-used man, and given himself up to despondency, until he became a prey to melancholy, and his mind was overclouded. His servants rightly regarded this as a Divine punishment, but their words are remarkable. **Behold, an evil spirit from God** terrifieth thee. And so again, in ver. 16, **the evil spirit from God,** as if they were unwilling to ascribe to Jehovah, their covenant Deity, the sending of this evil "influence," while

rightly they saw that evil as well as good must come from the Almighty, inasmuch as all things are in his hand, and whatever is must be by his permission. The writer of the book has no such scruples ; he calls it "an evil spirit from Jehovah," because it was Jehovah, their own theocratic King, who had dethroned Saul, and withdrawn from him his blessing and protection.

Vers. 16—18.—**A cunning player on an harp.** Literally, one skilful in striking the chords on the harp. In Saul's case music would have a soothing influence, and turn the current of his thoughts. His officers suggest, therefore, that search should be made for an expert musician, and Saul consents ; whereupon one of **the servants** recommended the son of Jesse. The word used here is not the same as that found in vers. 15, 16, 17. There we have Saul's *officers;* here it is *na'arim,* "young men." Thus it was a youth of David's own age, who had probably been with him at Naioth in Ramah, that described him to Saul. The description is full and interesting, but it has its difficulties. David is not only skilful in music, of which art he would have had ample scope to manifest his powers in the service of the sanctuary at Ramah, but he is also **a mighty valiant man, and a man of war, and prudent in matters,** or, rather, *intelligent in speech* (see margin), as well as handsome and successful. Nevertheless, in ch. xvii. 33—36 David appears as a youth about to make his first essay in fighting ; and though the two exploits mentioned there, of killing the lion and the bear, might justify his friend in calling him **a mighty valiant man,** literally, "a hero of valour," they do not justify the words **a man of war.** It is strange, moreover, that Saul should be so entirely ignorant of David's person and lineage as he is represented in the narrative in ch. xvii., if thus David was court musician, though reference is made there to this visit of David to Saul in ver. 15. Possibly, however, David and this youth may have served together in repelling some marauding expedition of the Philistines, and though David may not have actually done much,—nothing, at all events, so well worth repeating to Saul as the combats with the wild beasts, — yet he may have achieved enough to convince his friend that he had in him the qualities of **a man of war,** *i. e.* of a good soldier. For the rest, we must conclude that this first visit of David was a very short one, and that after playing before Saul and being approved of, he then returned home, ready to come again whenever summoned, but that Saul's malady did not immediately return, and so a sufficient interval elapsed for Saul not to recognise him when he saw him under altered circumstances. Saul's question, "Whose son is this stripling?" (ch. xvii. 56) seems to imply that he had a sort of confused idea about him, without being able exactly to recall who he was. The ultimate consequences of this introduction to Saul, as well as its immediate effect, are all narrated here after the usual manner of Old Testament history (see ch. vii. 13).

Vers. 19, 20.—**Saul sent messengers** to fetch David, the description of him as a brave soldier being even more to the king's liking (see ch. xiv. 52) than his skill in music. As a great man might not be approached without a present (ch. ix. 7 ; x. 4), Jesse sends one consisting of produce from his farm. It consisted of **an ass of bread**—a strange expression ; but there is little doubt that a word has been omitted, and that we should read, with the Syriac, "And Jesse took an ass, and laded it with bread, and a skin of wine, and a kid." It was not **an ass laden with bread,** as in the A. V., but all three things were placed upon the animal.

Vers. 21 — 23. — **David came to Saul, and stood before him**. The latter phrase means, "became one of his regular attend-

ants." This, and his being appointed one of Saul's armour-bearers, happened only after the lapse of some time. The armour-bearer, like the esquire in the middle ages, had to carry his lord's lance, and sword, and shield, and was always a tried soldier, and one whom the king trusted. It was apparently after the combat with Goliath that Saul sent to Jesse, and asked that David might be always with him ; and until his jealousy burst forth David was very dear to him, and his music exercised a soothing influence upon his melancholy. At first, probably, these fits of insanity came upon Saul only at distant intervals, but afterwards more frequently, and with such loss of self-control that he more than once tried to murder David, and even Jonathan, his own son. We have, then, here a summary of the relations of Saul to David until the unfortunate day when the king heard the women ascribe to the youthful soldier the higher honour (ch. xviii. 7); and thenceforward these friendly feelings gave way to a growing dislike which deprived Saul of a faithful servant, and finally cost him his crown and life on Mount Gilboa.

HOMILETICS.

Vers. 1—5.—*The progression of Providence*. The facts are—1. Samuel is aroused from his sorrow for Saul by a command from God to anoint a son of Jesse. 2. Being in fear, he is directed to go and offer sacrifice and await further instructions. 3. Arriving at Bethlehem, he quiets the trembling elders and makes preparation for the sacrifice. It was natural for Samuel in his retirement to cherish sorrow for Saul ; and his brooding over disappointment would become more habitual as no active measures were as yet taken to provide a successor. The section before us introduces a new phase in the development of God's purposes. The part which Samuel was called on to play, and the spirit in which he set about it, bring out some truths of general import.

I. PROVIDENCE PROCEEDS IN ITS ORDERLY COURSE IRRESPECTIVE OF PERSONAL DISAPPOINTMENTS AND FAILURES. Saul was a failure ; Samuel was disappointed ; and to human appearance a pause of very uncertain duration must be made in the progress of events. The attitude of Samuel was one of sorrowful waiting. He could only nurse his grief. To man it was as though a break had occurred in the continuous unfolding of the Divine purposes in relation to the Messianic kingdom. But this was only in appearance. God will not have his great purpose in Christ arrested in realisation by the failure of one or the brooding grief of another. During the separation of Samuel from Saul the unseen hand had been guarding and guiding a youth at Bethlehem, and now that his age and the circumstances of the family were ripening for action, the sorrowing prophet must rouse himself to share actively in the coming order of events. In *every age God has his purposes to fulfil, and they continue to unfold* notwithstanding the unfaithfulness of some and the complaining voice of others. The changes experienced by men are only incidents of a moment ; the providence of God is one and continuous. In the process of establishing the Messianic kingdom, one by one men and kingdoms rose and disappeared,—the people raged and submitted, wept and rejoiced, were now true and now false,—but all the while the one Will was working on to the setting of the true King in Zion. In the history of the Christian Church, men of the type of Saul have been discarded and others of Samuel's spirit have wept in solitude ; but neither the failure nor the protracted sorrow have been allowed to arrest the silent, sure progression towards the goal of human existence. A careful survey shows, that as the wholesome economy of the globe is preserved and its ultimate issue being attained amidst and even by the storms of life, so there is a wise and merciful Providence working on in unbroken lines towards the realisation of the promise made to Abraham : " In thy seed shall all the nations of the earth be blessed."

II. GOD'S SERVANTS SHOULD ADAPT THEMSELVES TO THE PROGRESSION OF HIS PROVIDENCE. Men of Samuel's type must rouse themselves and join freely and confidently in the blessed progression. New conditions are daily arising. The instruments for the realising of the Divine purpose are limited only by his creative power. The earth is his, and he raises up a David when a David can best furnish the next link in the unbroken chain. Faculties and aptitudes need only circumstances to develop them into direct forces in the Messianic line. Samuel must brace himself to this aspect of things, and share in the honour and the toil of covering the failures of some by drawing out the better qualities of others. We *must guard against the tendency to settle down into a mournful, inactive mood* because, forsooth, the lines of Providence seem to us to be involved and past all disentanglement. There are men whose delight it is always to sing in the minor key. They overlook the fact that God's will is being wrought out in spite of necessarily imperfect creatures. There is a voice calling on all such to arise, to cease to feed their soul on regrets, to believe that the " covenant is ordered in all things, and is sure."

III. WE SHOULD AVOID A PREJUDGMENT OF GOD'S WAYS BASED ON PARTIAL KNOWLEDGE. The fear of Samuel finds its counterpart in the fear of many when called to undertake arduous duties. In his case it was based on partial information, and, therefore, while natural, was unreasonable. He appears to have concluded beforehand that he was to go and at once set up an actual king, and summon Israel to turn their allegiance from Saul to the new monarch. No doubt this would be exasperating to Saul, and by many might be regarded as treason. His reference to Saul's killing him would not, therefore, express mere fear of death so much as his view of consequences which it was desirable to avoid by a less obtrusive policy. Samuel had no right to prejudge the appointment of God. He was simply told to go to Bethlehem with his horn of oil, for that a king was to be forthcoming from the sons of Jesse. We *possess only partial information* concerning many of the purposes and methods of God. We are not justified in forming a judgment of all his acts by what is made known to us. The morality of all he commands is ever the same, whatever the future developments may be. Every day will bring its light. We must not put more into God's words than he intends. If he says, " Fill thine horn with oil and go to Jesse," we must not make that mean that we are to raise a standard of rebellion and place ourselves in peril. Men do put into Scripture what is not there, and then see consequences which arouse anxiety.

IV. DUTY REQUIRES THAT WE PLACE OURSELVES IN A POSITION TO OBTAIN FURTHER LIGHT. Samuel, instead of dwelling on his fear, arising from an unwise prejudgment of God's acts, was directed to go and do the one thing, and then look out for what next to do (ver. 3). He was to obey, and so be in a position to learn whether the next step was to raise publicly a standard of rebellion around a new king, or privately to anoint the coming man and let him await the removal by death of the people's leader. We have *here an important practical rule.* By doing each duty fully as it comes we qualify for more light and greater aptitude for succeeding duties. When bent on the performance of duty, which in its issues may involve consequences serious and untraceable, it is well to associate religious exercises with them. It is as true for us as for Samuel that, in our sphere, the Lord will show us what next to do. Faithfulness day by day in small things will make us keen to recognise the Divine voice with reference to greater things.

Vers. 6 — 13. — *Human and Divine judgments contrasted.* The facts are—1. Samuel, being impressed with the appearance of Eliab, concludes that he is the coming king. 2. An intimation is given that Eliab is not the man, and the reason assigned for the imperfect judgment of Samuel is, that man looks on the outward appearance, but God on the heart. 3. It being found that the other sons were not

chosen of God, inquiry is made concerning the absent one.   4. On the youngest
being brought, Samuel at once recognises him as the chosen of God, and, in obedience
to the voice of God, anoints him in the midst of the family.   5. Henceforth the
Spirit of the Lord rests on David.   We have here the introduction of an entirely
new feature in the development of Israel's mission in the world.   The former choice
of a king was virtually man's.   The initiation of the choice was taken in the desire
to have a king to embody their idea of government (ch. viii. 5, 19, 20).   In this case
the people are not consulted or heeded.   God selects the man according to his
knowledge of what is best.   The human device had failed; the Divine choice can
now come in with impressiveness.   Yet human instrumentality brings to pass God's
purpose.   Samuel, however, is influenced by the appearance of things, and has to
learn that even the judgment of the wise and good is liable to err.   The essential
imperfection of man's judgment as compared with God's is explained by the fact
that man's knowledge does not enter into the realities of things as does God's.

I. Life is a series of judgments.   In every act of perception there is involved
an intuitive judgment; and in every comparison of different objects, as also in every
course of silent reasoning, a decision is arrived at which helps to form the stock of
ideas constituting our knowledge.   Thus do we acquire opinions respecting the value
of men and things.   In some persons there is a tendency to criticise human actions
and words, and to proceed from what is clear to the senses to a deliberate judgment
on the invisible; but in all there is a necessity of nature by which, apart from
criticism, some estimate is formed of every one coming under our observation.   This
necessity of our nature is full of advantage.   It is the means of enrichment to the
mind; it furnishes a basis for friendship; it preserves from treachery; it facilitates
the intercourse of life; and when the series of judgments is formed, under the guidance of such light as Christ gives, it constitutes an imperishable fount of enjoyment
when this life is past.

II. God also has his judgment of things.   It is not correct to speak of God's
knowledge in the terms applicable to man; for he does not pass from the small to
the great, the obscure to the clear, the sensible to the invisible.   Yet it may be said
of God that there is in his mind a clear judgment respecting each, as to what it
essentially is, and what its value in the great economy of the universe.   To say that
God knows us altogether is another way of saying that he has a judgment of our
character and position.   It is a solemn fact for us that the Eternal adjudges our
actions and thoughts one by one as they arise (Rev. xx. 12), and the day of judgment will be a summary of the judgments passed on our actions one by one as they
occur.   If men only had more faith in God, and did but let a knowledge of his
estimate of actions influence their lives, what wonders we should see!

III. Man's judgment and God's judgment are often very different.   Possibly,
while the distinction between infinite and finite exists, there can never be a perfect
coincidence of the human and Divine judgment, in the strictest sense of the term.
But apart from this there are several aspects of the truth affirmed and illustrated in
the case of Samuel.   1. *The constitution of things.*   We know and judge only of
the appearance of things.   The material universe, even when subjected to the
scrutiny of the most correct scientific appliances, and reduced to the last analysis
of elements, is only known on *the outside.*   What the ultimate relation of the
primary forces to the one almighty Power, and why they work in certain observed
lines to which we give the name "laws," we know not.   The same is true of mind.
It is a vast world, on the outer fringe only of which we at present can gaze.   Not
so God's.   As Author and Upholder of all, he has an estimate of the internal, essential
constitution of things more perfect than our estimate of the outward appearance.
Hence the folly of men professing to say what cannot be; or that the universe, as
seen by us in operation, is to be and has been always thus.   Hence the wisdom of
submitting to the revealed truth of God when it touches on his relation to the order
of things and the mysteries of his own ineffable Being (Matt. xxviii. 19; John vii.
28).   2. *The worth of lines of action.*   Man's judgment is freely expressed in reference to certain lines of action pursued by what are called the "great."   The heroes
of the world have often won admiration for deeds which, had man's judgment
been based on a finer perception of what constitutes greatness, would have been

buried in oblivion. Have not the most costly monuments been raised to warriors?
Is not the world's idea of "glory" that of conquering by force of arms, or the enjoyment of wealth and splendour? The judgment of God is not thus. He looks on
the heart of things. True greatness lies in saving, healing, curing, elevating, purifying, binding in bonds of peace and good-will. Imagine Jesus Christ raising an *Arc
de Triomphe!* Imagine him conferring highest honours on men of great and bloody
victories! Imagine him pointing to wealth as the goal of a youth's ambition! The
noblest men are those who best reproduce the spirit and deeds of the Son of God.
3. *Human character.* Man's judgment of character is necessarily imperfect; for
words are not always a revelation of the inner man, but the reverse, and the seat of
motive is not pierced by the human eye. There is often a worse heart than appears
on the surface of a man's conduct, and, also, a better heart than a man sometimes
gets credit for. We are too apt to be influenced by prejudice, social considerations,
personal interests, and to estimate the principles of others by the narrow standard of
our own. Some men are suspicious, or self-righteous, or limited in their area of
observation, and therefore they can never be sure of their judgment of other men.
Others are easily caught by what is fair and conformable to custom, and, like
Samuel, they spring to hasty conclusions. It is better often to fall into the hands
of God than of man. On the other hand, *God's judgment of us is perfect.* The
most secret avenue of thought and feeling is naked and open to his eye. He reads
us entirely. His knowledge is not inferential from words and actions, but is that of
the disposition and hidden motive (Ps. cxxxix.). 4. *Fitness for position.* Samuel
was in error in supposing that the qualities which might be inferred from his outward appearance to exist in Eliab would enable him to perform the part required of
a true king in Israel. God alone knew the high spiritual work to be done by the
coming king, and he alone could see the latent qualities in David by which it could
be performed. At best our judgment is guess-work. We especially feel this in
seeking to fill up secular offices, and more so when making appointments to spiritual
duties (Acts i. 24; 1 Tim. v. 22).

General lessons :—1. There is abundant scope in life for caution, patience, charity
in our estimate of others. 2. The best qualities of life are not always those which
come to the surface on first acquaintance. 3. It should be an effort to be inwardly
such as God will approve, and then all else will follow in due course. 4. Reticence
in reference to the character of others is the sign of a proper estimate of our powers.
5. It should be a spring of comfort to the sincere that God knows them and approves
when man errs in judgment.

Vers. 12, 13.—*The coming king.* The facts are—1. The personal appearance of
David is pleasing. 2. Samuel is instructed to anoint him as the chosen of God. 3.
Subsequent to the anointing the Spirit of God rests on David. 4. Samuel, having
performed this important duty, retires to Ramah. Samuel, like many a servant of
God in public affairs, carried in his heart a great secret. He sought the coming
king, but not a word was said to indicate to the family of Jesse the specific object
of his mission. For anything they knew, the selection of one of the family might
be designed for some purpose connected with Samuel's work not yet made plain.
The command to anoint was based, not on any discovery of qualities from mere
outward appearance, though these were not unfavourable, but on God's knowledge
of the inner life. Man's king had been chosen because of his being an average
representative of the age, and an embodiment of the physical and mental qualities
agreeable to the people. The coming king was chosen because God knew him to be
the best representative of the spiritual vocation of Israel in the world. The coming
king may be regarded as—

I. A TYPE. Events under the Old Testament dispensation were so ordered of
God as to shadow forth the Christ, and both Old and New Testaments especially speak
of David as the type of the true King in Zion. This is seen in several respects.
1. *In qualities.* Of course no man, no words, no institutions can adequately set
forth the qualities of the "express image" of the Father's person. But, in comparison with others, David certainly shadowed forth more than any one some of the
features of character so prominent in Christ. *Negatively,* there was an absence of

the qualities on which men were accustomed to depend. Great physical strength, lofty stature, overpowering physique were not his. And so in Christ there was an absence of the outward form which men of low type count powerful. He was not apparently competent to subdue the world by the only force which men take count of. But, *positively*, there was in this coming king an adumbration of the higher spiritual qualities which shone so brightly in Christ. The allusions to his personal appearance are both to indicate that he was not the embodiment of mere physical force, and that he did possess what was of more value, namely, vigour and freshness, capable of buoyant effort in any good endeavour ; grace of spirit—gentle, approachable, one of whom the poor and needy need not be afraid ; sincerity and ingenuousness of mind, free from double motives and self-seeking ; love of what is right and good because right and good, uncorrupted by long and dubious association with the world's business ; sympathy with God that finds joy in quiet fellowship with him by prayer or holy psalm ; aspirations after the future elevation of mankind to a holier life ; subordination of spirit to a higher will, for the working out of the covenant made with his people. He who sees not as man sees knew that these qualities were actually or germinally in the youngest son of Jesse. How fully the same were in Christ is evident from his life and words and sacrificial work. 2. *In object*. Saul's reign was a failure in so far as concerned the elevation of the nation to its proper position. The object for which the coming king was anointed was to deliver Israel from thraldom, fear, and degradation, and enable them to more worthily subserve the ulterior spiritual ends of their existence as a nation. In large measure David did this. In this he was certainly a type of him who was chosen for the deliverance of a larger community from worse evils ; and that, too, with reference to a permanent order of things stretching beyond the day of judgment (John xvii. ; 1 Cor. xv.). 3. *In call and preparation*. Leaving out the fact that Bethlehem was the place of birth to David and Christ, we may notice two or three correspondences. This youth was specially chosen of God irrespective of popular voice ; he grew up in quietude, awaiting the opening of events before entering on his predestined work ; and was anointed with the abiding presence of the Holy Spirit, and so gradually became qualified for his important duties. Emphatically, Christ was "the Chosen One," "Elect," "Precious ; " in youth he grew in wisdom and stature, far removed from the worries of public business, and received the anointing of the Spirit "without measure."

II. A MODEL. Confining attention to the qualities of this coming king, and the objects that in due course he set before himself, he may be regarded as the model king. It had been well for Israel had all subsequent kings shared these qualities and kept before them the same lofty spiritual ends. And although civilisation in the West differs from that of the East in David's age, yet it would be a great boon to the nations if all kings and queens would adopt and manifest the same principles, and seek to harmonise all the people's habits and aspirations with Messiah's kingdom. Likewise, as each Christian is to be a "king" unto God (Rev. i. 5), we may see in the qualities and aspirations of this model king what manner of persons we ought to be.

III. A CONTRAST. This is obvious. Saul was man's man ; David was God's. Saul was man's device for saving the people (ch. viii. 5, 19, 20) ; David was God's provision for raising them to the Messianic standard. Man's device failed—the instrument partook too largely of the weaknesses of the people to be raised ; God's provision succeeded, in so far as related to national freedom, higher spiritual elevation, and actual furtherance of Messianic purposes. The *contrast is suggestive of a wider expedient and a more blessed provision*. Mankind was in need of deliverance from the evils consequent on sin. During long ages the human expedient of "wisdom" was tried, but in vain. But "after that in the wisdom of God the world by wisdom knew not God, it pleased God by the foolishness of preaching to save them that believe." The CHRIST has become the Deliverer. His gospel is the power of God unto salvation. By him the highest and most blessed issues are wrought out for mankind. The contrast may be traced, also, in respect to our personal deliverance and elevation to the loftiest position attainable by human nature. Our bare human reason, human morality, human force of will must issue in trouble. We need the Anointed One, the God-given Saviour.   He, transfusing our natural powers with his glorious energy, will make us "more than conquerors."

General lessons :—1. Great natures may be nurtured in lowly places while engaged in quiet pursuits.   2. Amidst the intricacies of life God keeps his eye on his loved ones, and calls them forth in due time.   3. Aspirations are awakened, but insight into the future is not perfected at once.   David was stimulated, but knew not all at first.   4. Full confidence is felt when God reveals his call: then the "horn," not the vial (ch. x. 1), may be used.   5. To God's true servants the Holy Spirit comes as abiding Helper, to teach, sanctify, comfort, and elevate.

Vers. 14—23.—*Disquietude caused by sin.*   The facts are—1. Saul, being left to himself, is troubled by an evil spirit from the Lord.   2. His servants, in their concern for his peace, suggest music as an alleviation, and obtain permission to provide it.   3. David, being famed for music, is sent for, and finds favour with Saul.   4. The music of David brings relief to Saul's troubled spirit.   The narrative relates the effect of God's judicial abandonment of Saul to the impenitent spirit he had deliberately cherished (ch. xv. 23—29).   The transaction between him and Samuel in reference to his sin and rejection had been private, and during the interval from the departure to Ramah (ch. xv. 34) up to the date of the reference in ch. xvi. 14, the secret knowledge of this fact had wrought its subjective effect on the mind of Saul.   The secrecy of the business is a clue to much that follows.   It matters not to our purpose what sense be put on "an evil spirit from the Lord;" the fact is clear that disquietude of mind follows on transgression duly brought home to conscience yet not repented of, and that this disquietude is aggravated by secrecy.

I. THE CAUSES OF MENTAL DISQUIETUDE.   There are instances of mental disquietude (Ps. xlii. 5; John xii. 27; xiv. 1) differing in character and cause from that before us.   In the case of Saul there was a strange blending of sullen remorse, despondency, instability, passion, fear, and desperation.   He was sometimes beyond self control, and his outbursts aroused the apprehensions of his attendants.   The manifestations of a disquieted spirit will be partly determined by natural temperament, and partly by external conditions, and partly by bodily health.   But of the class of which Saul's is an example, the general causes are akin to those which operated in him.   1. *A secret consciousness of sin.*   That Saul had done wrong in the matter of the sacrifice (ch. xiii. 13), the rash vow (ch. xiv. 45), and the Amalekites (ch. xv. 18, 19) he knew full well; that the people knew that something was amiss with him is evident from their deliverance of Jonathan and Samuel's slaying of Agag; but that their knowledge of Saul's conduct was co-extensive with his own is not probable.   The more private interviews with Samuel had brought him face to face with sin as it appeared to the Lord.   His admission, "I have sinned" (ch. xv. 24), being a conviction without true repentance, remained in his memory after his final separation from Samuel.   The fact that his people did not know all only served to make the sad secret of guilt more distressing.   Now it is impossible for a man's spirit to be at ease when he carries with him at home and abroad a thorough conviction of being guilty before God.   His sin haunts him as a ghost.   It creates a desire to flee from himself.   It causes him to feel that he is a disgraced, degraded being, the bearer of a dark secret, the subject of a remorse that will not die.   2. *Knowledge of loss of a goodly heritage.*   Saul's mind dwelt much in the past.   He remembered the comparative innocence of rural life, when seeking his father's asses; the unexpected honour shadowed forth by the prophet; the private anointing; the bestowment of special gifts that won the confidence of the sons of the prophets; the high and elevating intercourse concerning the manner of the kingdom, and the solemn proclamation of his kingship over the chosen race.   Now all that was gone.   It was of the past in a double sense.   The splendid prospects had faded; the rejection by God had been privately announced by one whose word never failed.   But the future had to be feared, and Saul, when daring to look into it, saw and felt that Providence was against him.   The same elements of disappointment, bitter regret, and fearful foreboding enter into the life of others.   How many a man in crowded cities is forced by conscious secret guilt to look back on a splendid heritage of good gone for ever!   How many feel that, though friends and the world may flatter, God has turned away his face, and that, being bent on their secret guilty way, the whole force of Providence is against them in the future! 3. *Fear of exposure.* Samuel took no steps to dethrone Saul or to alienate the people from him. He kept the secret of rejection, and expressed the Divine will only in ceasing to hold official intercourse with Saul, and in quietly selecting David as one favoured of God. Saul knew his coming doom in rough outline. The dread of this was foreshadowed in the prayer that Samuel would not openly dishonour him before the people (ch. xv. 30). A moody temperament, naturally subject to impulse, would easily be urged, under this dread, now to desponding and melancholy, and now to the sudden grasping at a shadow of hope; and the alternations of hope and despair could not but induce a nervous condition which, while a guilty secret was covered, might express itself in painful irritability. *The fear of exposure drives men in upon themselves,* and induces an abnormal condition of mind and nerve. Guilty men, who will not sincerely repent and seek rest in Christ, know that judgment is coming, but they take care to hide that truth from others, and often bear a terrible strain on their spirits. 4. *Secret persistence in wrong.* Saul had said, "I have sinned," but he never repented. No doubt he regretted the consequences that flowed from his preference of self to the will of God; but he still loved to have his own way. The spirit that prompted to set aside God's command for his own choice was unchanged. It in itself was a state of war; but still it was restive, unsubdued; it chafed under restraint and conviction of rejection, and sometimes would break out in fury that its preferences should thus be chastised. "As a bullock unaccustomed to the yoke." It is this element of cherished sin, this persistent continuance in the original state of mind that contracted guilt, which poisons the entire life. It sets the whole man at war with God, and renders irksome what to a penitent, lowly heart would be meekly borne. Truly when men sin, and "will have it so," they are so far left to themselves as to work out in their life all manner of miseries.

II. Temporary alleviations of mental disquietude. The servants of Saul were true philosophers in seeking *diversion* for their master. In cases of trouble, diversion from self and the causes of trouble always affords relief. This is recognised by guilty men, who seek diversion in business, or pleasure, or public affairs. It is a rule with some wicked men to plunge more deeply into public or private business in proportion as conscience has to be quieted. The *diversion* was of a nature to *soothe* the nervous system. Music has in it something refined and pure and remote from the turmoil and confusion of sinful life. As a curative or alleviative element in certain sicknesses its power has not been sufficiently developed. Saul felt the charm, and for a while the irritation consequent on internal conflict was toned down. The *diversion* would have *increased effect* if associated with spiritual song. There is evidence that David cultivated psalmody in his early years; and who can tell the subduing influence on the restless Saul as David poured forth to his harp strains of love and trust and hope in God! We see constantly that even the boldest of impenitent sinners are touched by sweet, simple hymns, which seem to call back a lost purity, and open up a gleam of hope for the most depraved. The songs of Zion are as the echo to many of long-lost music. Their power over men should be diligently used. But in all cases of mere diversion the *benefit* is *transitory*. The old enmity remains. The old fears come back in force. The true remedy has not been sought.

III. The radical cure is one and constant. What would have been the course of Providence had he truly repented we know not. But looking at his sin and the rejection from the kingdom in the light of Scripture, we can see what would have been the safe and happy course. Had Saul been true to the passing impulse of tenderness, he would have ceased in his persistence in sin, and have humbled himself before God, and sought mercy in the appointed way. Retirement to private life would then have been no great burden, but rather a willing, loving homage to the holiness of God. The troubled spirit would have found rest. The cure for the internal miseries of men lies in self-renunciation and placing the soul at the mercy of the great Saviour. We must cease to seek rest and peace apart from his loving embrace.

General lessons :—1. We should faithfully search out how much of our restlessness in daily life is due to unforgiven sin. 2. In all our efforts to alleviate mental distress we should pay due regard to moral causes.   3. The longer the delay in repenting of sin, the more difficult it becomes.

HOMILIES BY VARIOUS AUTHORS.

Ver. 1. (BETHLEHEM.)—*David's parentage and education.* (*References :*—Family register—1 Chron. i.—iii.   I. *Early life :* shepherd, harper, champion—chs. xvi., xvii.   II. *Courtier and outlaw life*—chs. xviii.—xxxi. ; 2 Sam. i.   III. *Royal life* in Hebron and Jerusalem—2 Sam. ii.—xxiv. ; 1 Kings i., ii. ; 1 Chron. x.—xxix.) While Saul pursued his own way at Gibeah, and Samuel mourned for him at Ramah, there dwelt at Bethlehem (twelve miles from the latter place) *a shepherd youth* who was destined to attain peerless renown as " a man of war," a ruler over men, an inspired poet and prophet, and (because of his fulfilling the idea of a truly theocratic king more perfectly than any other) a type of One to whom is given " a name which is above every name."   Once and again the prophet had declared that Saul would be replaced by a worthier successor (ch. xiii. 14 ; xv. 28) ; but who that successor should be he knew not until the inner voice said, "Arise, anoint him : for this is he " (ver. 12).   DAVID (the beloved) was sixteen or eighteen years of age.   His personal appearance is minutely described.   In comparison with the gigantic Saul, and even his eldest brother, he was of short stature (ver. 7).   He had reddish or auburn hair, and a fresh, florid complexion, which were rare among his black-locked and swarthy countrymen ; a pleasing countenance, keen, bright eyes, and a graceful form.   He also possessed great physical strength, courage, intelligence, sagacity, and power of expression (ver. 18) ; above all, a firm trust in God and ardent love toward him. Many influences combined to make him what he was, and to develop his extra-ordinary gifts ; which, after his anointing, advanced rapidly towards perfection. " It is impossible to draw a line of distinction between his life before and after his designation by Samuel ; but we may well believe that those elements of character were already forming which began to shine forth when the Spirit of Jehovah came upon him."   " Royalty was inborn in him."   Among the *formative influences* referred to were those of—

I. FAMILY RELATIONSHIP.   1. He belonged to one of the most *honourable families* in Judah, the foremost tribe of Israel.   His ancestor, Nahshon, was prince of the tribe (Num. ii. 3 ; vii. 12) ; another, Salmon, married Rahab, " who received the spies in peace " (Matt. i. 5) ; another, Boaz (great-grandfather of David), married Ruth the Moabitess, " a truly consecrated flower of heathendom turning longingly to the light of Divine revelation in Israel " (Ruth iv. 17).   His father, Jesse (Isa. xi. 1), who would often speak of them, had attained " a good old age " (ch. xvii. 12), was in pros-perous circumstances, had eight sons, of whom David was the youngest, and two daughters-in-law (2 Sam. xvii. 25), whose children—Abishai, Joab, and Asahel (sons of Zeruiah), and Amasa (son of Abigail)—were old enough to be his companions. Peculiar physical, mental, and moral qualities often characterise certain families, are transmitted from one generation to another, and are sometimes concentrated in a single individual ; and great family traditions tend to excite noble impulses and aspirations.   2. He was connected (through Tamar, Rahab, Ruth) with several *Gen-tile races.*   This served to enlarge his sympathies, and accounts for his friendly intercourse with them (ch. xxii. 3 ; 1 Kings v. 1).   " No prince of Israel was ever on such friendly, intimate terms with the heathen about him " ('Expositor,' ii. 9).   3. He received a *godly training.*   Jesse was a man of simple piety (vers. 1, 5 ; ch. xx. 6) ; his mother (whose name has not been recorded) was a " handmaid of Jehovah " (Ps. lxxxvi. 16 ; cxvi. 16).   " How much David owed to her we cannot doubt.   The memory of it abode with him through all the trials and all the splendours of his sub-sequent career ; and hence, whilst nowhere does he mention his father, he seems in these passages to appeal to the memory of his mother's goodness, as at once a special token of the Divine favour to himself, and an additional reason that he should prove himself the servant of God " (W. L. Alexander).

II. ORDINARY OCCUPATION.   Whilst his brothers cultivated fields and vineyards on the slopes of Bethlehem, he kept his father's sheep "in the wilderness " of Judah (ch. xvii. 28), and his lowly occupation—1. Was adapted to nurture *physical strength*, agility, and endurance ; to call forth energy, self-reliance, and courage amidst numerous perils in a wild country, from beasts of prey and hill robbers (1 Chron. vii. 21) ; to make him expert in the use of the sling, like the neighbouring Benjamites (Judges xx. 16 ; 1 Sam. xvii. 50 ; 1 Chron. xii. 2) ; and to prepare him to rule over men by developing a sense of responsibility, and leading him to seek the welfare and study the increase and improvement of the flock (Ps. lxxviii. 70—72). 2. Left him much alone, and afforded him leisure for meditation and the cultivation of a *taste for music*, by playing on the hand-harp, which he could easily carry with him when he " followed the flock," and the rare gift of song, in both of which he may have greatly improved, after his anointing, by attendance at the school of the prophets at Ramah (ch. xix. 18). To his musical skill he owed his first introduction to the court of Saul, and by its means he became " the sweet singer of Israel." " With his whole heart he sang songs, and loved him that made him " (Ecclus. xlvii. 8). 3. Furnished him with the *suggestive imagery* of many of his psalms, especially Ps. xxiii.—' The Divine Shepherd.' " It is the echo of his shepherd life, and breathes the very spirit of sunny confidence and of perfect rest in God."

III. THE NATURAL CREATION. To him the visible universe was a manifestation of the glory of the invisible, immanent, ever-operating God (Ps. civ.). He regarded nature " not as an independent and self-subsisting power, but rather as the outer chamber of an unseen Presence—a garment, a veil, which the eternal One is ever ready to break through " (Shairp, ' Poetic Inter. of Nature '). Brought into direct and constant communion with it, he felt a boundless delight in contemplating

> " The silence that is in the starry sky,
> The sleep that is among the lonely hills ; "

in listening to its mysterious voices, and watching its ever-varying aspects ; and poured forth the thought and feeling of his heart in songs of adoration and praise ; as in Ps. xix. 1—13—' The heavens by day ;' Ps. viii.—' The heavens by night ;' Ps. xxix.—' The thunder-storm.' " What we call the love of nature is in fact the love and admiration of the Deity (so far forth as he is perceived in external nature). The enthusiasm with which men survey the endless vicissitudes which the spectacle of the universe exhibits is nothing else than the devotional temper, moderated and repressed by the slight veil which sensible objects interpose between us and their author " (D. Stewart).

IV. HISTORIC REVELATION. He was instructed in " the law of the Lord " (Ps. xix. 7—14—' The moral law'), and in the wonderful works which he had wrought on behalf of his people in past time (Ps. cv.) ; whilst the scenes amidst which his life was spent formed a pictorial Bible, by which they were more deeply impressed on his memory. His acquaintance with the contents of the sacred records then existing would be greatly increased under the teaching of Samuel. " Thy creatures have been my books, but thy Scriptures much more " (Bacon).

V. PROVIDENTIAL PRESERVATION. The same special care which had been exercised by Jehovah over Israel he was taught to recognise in the lowly course of his own individual life. Once and again he was preserved in imminent danger (ch. xvii. 37), and thus his faith in the ever-watchful presence and providence of the Great Shepherd grew strong. " Every Hebrew might consider himself alone in the presence of God ; the single being to whom a great revelation had been made, and over whose head an exceeding weight of glory was suspended. His personal welfare was infinitely concerned with every event that had taken place in the miraculous order of Providence. . . . . His belief in him could not exist without producing, as a necessary effect, that profound impression of passionate individual attachment which in the Hebrew authors always mingles with and vivifies their faith in the Invisible " (A. H. Hallam).

VI. RELIGIOUS INSPIRATION. Led by Divine grace from his earliest years into direct and loving communion with Jehovah, he was endowed with unusual spiritual power, which, as he faithfully surrendered himself to it, wrought in him more and more mightily, and prepared him for his high destiny. And all true spiritual life, as well as the peculiar endowments of the prophets and apostles, is a Divine inspiration

(John iii. 8; Acts ii. 17). "The morning of his day this extraordinary man spent not in colleges nor camps nor courts, but in following the sheep among the pastures of Bethlehem. There, under the breathings of spring and the blasts of winter; there, in fellowship with fields and flocks and silent stars; there, with the spirit of nature and of God fresh upon him; there, in the land of vision, miracle, and angels—there it was that his character was formed, a character which afterwards exhibited so rare a combination of simplicity and grandeur, sensibility and power" (C. Morris).

Application (to the young):—1. The morning of life is the appropriate season for education—physical, mental, moral. If neglected, the evil cannot be repaired. 2. No educational advantages can be of service without your own diligent co-operation. 3. All circumstances—adverse as well as propitious, solitude and society, work and recreation—may be helpful to your highest progress. 4. "Have faith in God," the secret of all David's greatness.—D.

Vers. 4—13. (BETHLEHEM.)—*David chosen and anointed*. "Arise, anoint him: for this is he" (ver. 12). In the exercise of his prophetic office Samuel appears to have been accustomed to visit one place or another, rebuking crime and sin. Hence his presence at Bethlehem (clad in a mantle, his white hair flowing over his shoulders, holding a horn of consecrated oil in his hand, and attended, perhaps, by a servant), driving before him a heifer for sacrifice, filled the elders with consternation. Having quieted their fears, he showed special honour to Jesse and his sons by inviting them to be his principal guests at a sacrificial feast. By the express direction of God he allowed his seven sons, who were introduced to him, to pass by without any mark of distinction; and, having delayed the feast until his youngest son came, poured upon his head the sacred oil, and "anointed him from amongst his brethren." "As far as outward appearances go he simply chooses him as his closest companion and friend in the sacrifice" (Ewald). The act may have been regarded as "somehow connected with admission to the schools of the prophets, or more probably with some work for God in the future, which at the proper time would be pointed out." Its main significance was known only to the prophet, and was not revealed by him at the time to any one else. Consider *the Divine choice of David* (representing that of others) to eminent spiritual service and honour, as—

I. DIFFERING FROM THE NATURAL JUDGMENT OF MEN (vers. 6, 7). They are accustomed—1. *To judge according to the "outward appearance,"* which alone is clearly perceived, which is often deemed of greater worth than properly belongs to it, and which is erroneously supposed to be united with corresponding inward reality. On this account Saul suited the popular desire. 2. *To prefer the eldest before the youngest;* an arrangement which is an imperfect one, and often set aside by the choice of God, who thus exhibits his superior knowledge and maintains his sovereign right. 3. *Even the oldest and wisest* of men fall into error when left to themselves. Not only did Jesse and the brethren of David look upon him as unfit for anything but the lowliest occupation (ch. xvii. 28), and unworthy to be called to the sacred feast, but Samuel himself thought at first that in Eliab the Lord's anointed was before him. The stone which the builders refuse becomes (by the operation of God, and to the surprise of men) "the head stone of the corner."

II. DETERMINED BY A RIGHT STATE OF HEART, which—1. In the sight of God is of greater *value* than anything else, and essential to the worth of everything else. 2. *Implies* such qualities as sincerity, humility, trust, fidelity, courage, purity, and unselfish, generous, entire devotion, which were eminently displayed by David. 3. *Renders capable of noble service*, prompts to it, and prepares for the highest honour. "Is thy heart right?" (2 Kings x. 15). Whatever great things may lie in the future, right-heartedness is the first condition of attaining them. "My son, give me thine heart."

III. DISTINGUISHING ITS OBJECT IN A SPECIAL MANNER (vers. 11, 12). 1. *By his separation from others*, and by directing their attention to his worth, which had been previously unrecognised. "We will not sit down till he come hither." Circumstances often constrain attention to those who have been despised. "The stone which is fit for the building will not be left in the road." 2. *By indications of* his being providentially destined to *future eminence.*   David did not himself understand the chief purpose of his anointing, but he must have inferred from it that he was not always to continue in "the sheep-folds" (Ps. lxviii. 70), and have been impelled to look forward to a higher service on behalf of Israel.   Possibly it was afterwards explained to him by Samuel in more familiar intercourse.   3. *By communications of Divine grace* and strength to his inner life.   "And the Spirit of Jehovah came upon David from that day forward."   It is recorded of Samson that "the Spirit of Jehovah began to move him at times in the camp of Dan;" it was the same in the case of David (ch. xvii. 34), and in a much higher manner (see ch. x. 1, 10; xi. 6).   "The natural basis for this symbolism of oil is its power to dispense light and life, joy and healing; by which it sets forth the Spirit's dispensation of light and life, and the gifts and powers therein contained" (Bähr).

IV. DELAYED IN THE FULFILMENT OF ITS ULTIMATE AIM.   Many years must sometimes elapse before one who is chosen by God for a special work is fully called to its performance.   Why such delay?   For—1. *The removal of obstacles* that lie in his path.   Saul must be suffered to go to the natural termination of his melancholy career.   2. *The occurrence of circumstances* that make it necessary and cause it to be generally desired.   The people must learn by experience the folly of their former choice, and their need of another and different kind of ruler.   3. *His own instruction,* discipline, and preparation.   The proper course for him who is impelled to higher service is patiently to bide his time in the humble and faithful discharge of the duty that lies immediately before him.   "David's peculiar excellence is that of *fidelity to the trust committed to him;* a firm, uncompromising, single-hearted devotion to the cause of God, and a burning zeal for his honour.   This characteristic virtue is especially illustrated in the early years of his life.   Having borne his trial of obedience well, in which Saul had failed, then at length he was intrusted with a sort of discretionary power to use in his Master's service" (J. H. Newman).—D.

Ver. 7. (BETHLEHEM.)—*God's regard to the heart.*   "The heart is the centre of (1) the *bodily* life; (2) the *spiritual-psychical* life—will and desire, thought and conception, the feelings and the affections; and (3) the *moral* life, so that all moral conditions—from the highest mystical love of God to the self-deifying pride and the darkening and hardening—are concentrated in the heart as the innermost life-circle of humanity" (Delitzsch, 'Bib. Psychology,' p. 295).   The declaration that "Jehovah looketh on the heart" is profitable for—

I. THE CORRECTION OF ERRORS into which we too commonly fall in relation to others.   1. The adoption of *an imperfect standard* of human worth:—"the outward appearance," personal strength and beauty; wealth and social position; cleverness, education, and refinement of manners; external morality, ceremonial observances, and religious zeal.   These things are not to be despised, but they may exist whilst the chief thing is wanting—a right state of heart.   "One thing thou lackest."   2. The assumption that we are *competent judges* of the character and worth of others. But we cannot look into their hearts; and what we see is an imperfect index to them, and liable to mislead us.   3. The formation of *false judgments* concerning them.   How common this is our Lord's words indicate (Matt. vii. 1).

II. THE INCULCATION OF TRUTHS which are often forgotten in relation to ourselves. 1. That we are *liable to be deceived* concerning the real state of our hearts, and to think of ourselves "more highly than we ought to think" (Rom. xii. 3).   2. That the heart of each of us *lies open to the inspection of God:* certainly, directly, completely, and constantly.   He beholds its deepest motive, its supreme affection and ruling purpose.   However we may deceive ourselves or others, we cannot deceive him (1 Chron. xxviii. 9; Ps. xliv. 21; Prov. xv. 11; Jer. xvii. 9, 10; Luke xvi. 15; Rev. ii. 23).   3. That *only a right state of heart* can meet with his approval.   It is the effect of his grace, and he cannot but take pleasure in his own work; but "the heart of the wicked is little worth" (Prov. x. 20).

III. THE ENFORCEMENT OF DUTIES which ought to be diligently fulfilled in relation both to ourselves and others.   1. To seek supremely that *our own hearts* be set right and kept right—by self-examination, self-restraint, and fervent prayer to him "who searcheth the reins and the hearts" (Ps. li. 10; cxxxix. 23, 24; Jer. xxxi. 33).

2. To *endure patiently* the wrong judgments that others may form and utter concerning us. If we sometimes judge wrongly of them, need we wonder that they should judge wrongly of us? "Unto God would I commit my cause" (Job v. 8). 3. To *judge charitably* of their motives, character, and worth. A judgment must sometimes be formed (Matt. vii. 15—20); but "let all your things be done with charity" (1 Cor. xvi. 14).—D.

Vers. 14—16. (GIBEAH.)—*Mental and moral effects of transgression.* The soul is an arena where light and darkness, good and evil, heaven and hell, strive for mastery. But it is not an unconscious scene or passive prize of the conflict. It is endowed with the power of freely choosing right or wrong, and, with every exercise of this power, comes more or less under the dominion of the one or the other. Saul was highly exalted, but by his wilful disobedience sank to the lowest point of degradation. His sin was followed by lamentable effects in his mental and moral nature, and (since soul and body are intimately connected, and mutually affect each other) doubtless also in his physical constitution. His *malady* has been said to be "the first example of what has been called in after times religious madness" (Stanley). His condition was, in many respects, peculiar; but it vividly illustrates the mental and moral effects which always, in greater or less degree, flow from persistent transgression, viz. :—

I. THE WITHDRAWAL OF THE DIVINE SPIRIT. "And the Spirit of Jehovah departed from Saul" (ver. 14; ch. x. 10). 1. His *presence* in men is the source of their highest excellence. What a change is wrought in Saul, turning him into "another man." It imparts enlightenment, strength, courage, order, harmony, and peace; restrains and protects; and, in the full measure of its influence, quickens, sanctifies, and saves (Isa. xi. 2; Gal. v. 22; Ephes. v. 9). 2. His *continuance* in them depends on the observance of appropriate conditions. He is often compared with the *wind, water*, and *fire*, the most powerful forces of the natural world; and as there are conditions according to which they operate, so there are conditions according to which he puts forth his might. These are, humble and earnest attention to the word of the Lord, sincere endeavour to be true, just, and good, and believing and persevering prayer. 3. His *departure* is rendered necessary by the neglect of those conditions. "They rebelled and vexed his Holy Spirit," &c. (Isa. lxiii. 10; Acts vii. 51; Ephes. iv. 10; 1 Thess. v. 19). And with his departure the effects of his gracious influence also depart. Hence David prayed so fervently, "Take not thy Holy Spirit from me."

II. SUBJECTION TO AN EVIL INFLUENCE. "And an evil spirit *from* Jehovah troubled him." The expression is only used once before (Judges ix. 23),—"God sent an evil spirit between the men of Abimelech and the men of Shechem" (producing discord, treachery, and strife), — and denotes a breath, influence, agency, or messenger (1 Kings xxii. 22) which—1. Prevails only *after the withdrawal of the Divine Spirit.* When the soul ceases to be governed by God, it lies open to the power of evil, and comes under its dominion. 2. Is sent in just *retribution* for sin. "No man living needs a heavier chastisement from the Almighty than the letting his own passions loose upon him" (Delany). But the expression means more than this. "It is a spiritual agency of God, which brings to bear upon Saul the dark and fiery powers of Divine wrath which he has aroused by sin" (Delitzsch). Even that which is in itself good becomes evil to those who cherish an evil disposition. As the same rays of the sun which melt the ice harden the clay, so the same gospel which is "a savour of life unto life" in some is "a savour of death unto death" in others (2 Cor. ii. 16). And it is God who appoints and effectuates the forces of retribution. "The punitive justice of God is a great fact. It is stamped on all the darker phenomena of human life—disease, insanity, and death. It is in the nature of sin to entail suffering, and work itself, as an element of punishment, into all the complicated web of human existence" (Tulloch). 3. Implies the domination of the *kingdom of darkness.* Josephus, speaking according to the common belief of a later age, attributes the malady of Saul to demoniacal agency. "It was probably a kind of possession, at least at times, and in its highest stage. As a punishment for having given himself willingly into the power of the kingdom of darkness, he was also abandoned physically to this power" (Henstenberg). How fearful is that realm of rebellion, evil, and disorder to which men become allied and subject by their sin !

III. THE EXPERIENCE OF UNCONTROLLABLE FEAR; "troubled him" — terrified, choked him. 1. In connection with *the working of peculiar and painful thoughts:* brooding over the secret of rejection, which might not be revealed to any one ; the sense of disturbed relationship with God, and of his displeasure, the removal of which there was no disposition to seek by humble penitence and prayer. 2. In *the darkening aspect* of present circumstances and future prospects; suspicion and "royal jealousy, before which vanish at last all consistent action, all wise and moderate rule" (Ewald). 3. In *occasional melancholy,* despondency, and distress, irrational imaginations and terrors (Job vi. 4), and fits of violent and ungovernable passion (ch. xviii. 10, 11). "There are few more difficult questions in the case of minds utterly distempered and disordered as his was than to determine where sin or moral disease has ended, and madness or mental disease has begun" (Trench). Sin not only disturbs the moral balance of the soul, but also disorders the whole nature of man. It is itself a kind of madness, from which the sinner needs to "come to himself" (Luke xv. 17). "Madness is in their hearts," &c. (Eccles. ix. 3 ; 2 Pet. ii. 6).

IV. THE TENDENCY TO RAPID DETERIORATION. 1. In the case of the malady occasioned by sin there is *no self-healing power* in man, as in many bodily diseases, but it tends to become worse and worse. 2. Its *fatal course* may often be distinctly marked. "These attacks of madness gave place to hatred, which developed itself in full consciousness to a most deliberately-planned hostility" (Keil). His courage gave place to weakness and cowardice ; general fear and suspicion fixed on a particular object in envy and hatred, displayed at first privately, afterwards publicly, and becoming an all-absorbing passion. "The evil spirit that came upon him from or by permission of the Lord was the evil spirit of melancholy, jealousy, suspicion, hatred, envy, malice, and cruelty, that governed him all the after part of his life ; to which he gave himself up, and sacrificed every consideration of honour, duty, and interest whatsoever" (Chandler). 3. It is, nevertheless, *amenable to the remedial influences* which God, in his infinite mercy, has provided.

> "All cures were tried : philosophy talked long
> Of lofty reason's self-controlling power ;
> He frowned, but spake not. Friendship's silver tongue
> Poured mild persuasions on his calmer hour :
> He wept ; alas ! it was a bootless shower
> As ever slaked the desert. Priests would call
> On Heaven for aid ; but then his brow would lower
> With treble gloom. Peace ! Heaven is good to all ;
> To all, he sighed, but one,—God hears no prayer for Saul.
> At length one spake of *Music*" (Hankinson).

—D.

Vers. 19, 20. (BETHLEHEM.)—*Setting out in life.* David, setting out from his father's house at Bethlehem to go to the court of Saul at Gibeah (a distance of about ten miles), presents a picture of many a youth leaving home for more public life—to enter a profession, learn a business, or occupy a responsible position. Notice—

I. THE PECULIAR CHARACTER of the step. 1. Some such step is *necessary*. A young man cannot always continue under the paternal roof. He must go forth into the world, be thrown on his own resources, and make his own way. 2. Its nature and direction are commonly determined by his ability and tastes, and the use he makes of early advantages (ver. 18). 3. It is also greatly influenced by the wishes of others. David was sent for by Saul, and sent to him by his father. 4. It is ordered by Divine providence. This was plainly the case with David. And we are as truly the children of providence as he was. God has a purpose concerning each of us.

> "There's a Divinity that shapes our ends,
> Rough-hew them as we will."

5. It opens a wider field for the exercise of natural or acquired abilities, and the attainment of desired objects.   6. It determines in most instances, the subsequent course of life.   It is like the commencement of a river; or like the rolling of a stone down the mountain-side, the course of which is determined by the direction and impulse which it first receives.

II. THE PROPER SPIRIT in which it should be taken.   1. Due consideration; not thoughtlessly or rashly.   2. Lowly and loyal obedience to rightful claims.   3. Cheerful anticipation of new scenes, duties, and enjoyments.   4. Not unmingled with misgiving and self-distrust at the prospect of new difficulties and trials, and watchfulness against new and strong temptations.   5. Simple trust in God and fervent prayer for his guidance.   6. Firm determination to be true to oneself faithful to God, and useful to men.

> "Now needs thy best of man;
> For not on downy plumes, nor under shade
> Of canopy reposing, fame is won;
> Without which whosoe'er consumes his days
> Leaveth such vestige of himself on earth
> As smoke in air, or foam upon the wave" (Dante, 'Inferno,' xxiv.).

Consider—1. That life itself is a setting out in a course which will never terminate.   2. That the manner in which this step is taken will decide your future destiny.—D.

Ver. 23. (GIBEAH.)—*The soothing influence of music.*   All men, with rare exceptions, are susceptible to the influence of music; some men peculiarly so.   It was thus with Saul (ch. x. 10; xix. 23); and on this account, perhaps, his servants suggested the sending for a skilful musician to soothe his melancholy.   The visit of David had the desired effect, and he "went and returned" (was going and returning) "to feed his father's sheep at Bethlehem" (ch. xvii. 15, 55—58; xvi. 21, 22—a general, and to some extent prospective, summary of his early relations with Saul). Consider the soothing influence of music as—

I. PROVIDED BY DIVINE PROVIDENCE.   It is one of the manifold indications of the goodness of God in the adaptation of man to his surroundings so as to derive enjoyment from them.   The world is full of music.   In trouble and agitation especially it soothes and cheers.   "It brings a tone out of the higher worlds into the spirit of the hearer" (Köster).   Its direct influence is exerted upon the nervous system, which is intimately connected with all mental activity.   As the condition of the brain and nerves is affected by it, so also it affects the state of the mind.

> "There is in souls a sympathy with sounds;
> Some chord in unison with what we hear
> Is touched within us, and the heart replies" (Cowper).

"Pythagoras quieted the perturbations of the mind with a harp" (Seneca, 'On Anger').   Elisha, when chafed and disturbed in spirit, called for a minstrel, and was prepared by the soothing strains of his harp for prophetic inspiration (2 Kings iii. 5). Divine providence ordered the visit of David to Saul, over whom mercy still lingered. He was not only freed from the immediate pressure of fear and despondency, but also restored to a mental condition which was favourable to repentance and return to God.   Music is a means of grace, and when rightly used conveys much spiritual benefit to men.   It is "one of the fairest and most glorious gifts of God, to which Satan is a bitter enemy; for it removes from the heart the weight of sorrow and the fascination of evil thoughts" (Luther).   "It is a language by itself, just as perfect in its way as speech, as words; just as Divine, just as blessed.   All melody and all harmony, all music upon earth, is beautiful in as far as it is a pattern and type of the everlasting music which is in heaven" (C. Kingsley).

II. PRODUCTIVE OF EXTRAORDINARY EFFECTS.   "Saul was refreshed, and was well, and the evil spirit departed from him."   "The music was more than a mere palliative. It brought back for the time the sense of a true order, a secret, inward harmony, an assurance that it is near every man, and that he may enter into it" (Maurice).

" He is Saul, ye remember in glory,—ere error had bent
    The broad brow from the daily communion ; and still, though much spent
    Be the life and the bearing that front you, the same, God did choose,
    To receive what a man may waste, desecrate, never quite lose " (Browning, 'Saul').

Many other instances of a similar nature, both in ancient and modern times, have
been recorded.   One of the most noteworthy is that of Philip V. of Spain, who was
restored from profoundest melancholy by the magical voice of Farinelli (see Bochart ;
Burton, 'Anat. of Mel. ;' Kitto, 'D. B. Illus. ;' Jacox, 'Script. Texts Illus. ;' Bate, 'Cyc.
of Illus.').   "Psalmody is the calm of the soul, the repose of the spirit, the arbiter
of peace.   It silences the wave and conciliates the whirlwind of our passions.   It
is an engenderer of friendship, a healer of dissension, a reconciler of enemies.   It
repels the demons, lures the ministry of angels, shields us from nightly terrors, and
refreshes us in daily toil " (Basil).

III. Perfected by special endowments possessed by the musician.   David's
harp was the accompaniment of his voice as he sang "psalms and hymns and
spiritual songs " (see Josephus), expressive of the sympathy, confidence, hope, and
joy of his soul ; "the prelude to the harpings and songs which flowed from the harp
of the future royal singer."   His musical and poetic gifts were great, and they were
consecrated (as all such gifts should be) to the glory of God and the good of men.
"Did the music banish the demon?   Not so.   But the high frame of mind into
which the king was brought by it sufficed to limit at least the sphere of the operation of the evil spirit within him ; while the full, clear, conscious life of faith on the
part of Saul would have altogether destroyed the power of the wicked one.   Besides,
the silent intercessions of David sent up to heaven on the wings of the music of his
harp must have contributed not a little to the results with which his melodies were
crowned " (Krummacher).   "The Lord was with him " (ver. 18).

IV. Partial and temporary in its wholesome power.   Saul was not completely
cured of his malady.   A breathing-space was afforded him for seeking God, and
if he had faithfully availed himself of it he might have been permanently preserved
from its return.   But he failed to do so.   On the indulgence of envy, "the evil spirit
from God came upon him" again (ch. xviii. 10 ; xix. 10) with greater power than
before (Matt. xii. 45), and that which formerly calmed and gladdened him now excited him to demoniacal frenzy and murderous passion.   "It is said that the evil
spirit departed, but not that the good spirit returned.   Saul's trouble was alleviated,
but not removed.   The disease was still there.   The results of David's harp were
negative and superficial.   So is it with the sinner still.   There are many outward
applications which act like spiritual chloroform upon the soul.   They soothe and
calm and please, but that is all ; they do not go below the surface, nor touch the deep-
seated malady within.   Our age is full of such appliances, literary and religious, all
got up for the purpose of soothing the troubled spirits of men.   Excitement, gaiety,
balls, theatres, operas, concerts, ecclesiastical music, dresses, performances, what are
all these but man's appliances for casting out the evil spirit and healing the soul's
hurt without having recourse to God's remedy" (Bonar, 'Thoughts and Themes').

Learn—1. That the excellent gift of music should excite our admiration of the
Giver, "the First Composer," and our devout thankfulness to him.   2. That it ought
not to be perverted from its proper intention, and employed, as it too frequently is, in
the service of sin (Isa. v. 12 ; Amos vi. 5).   3. That the soothing and elevating
effect of a "concord of sweet sounds " must not be mistaken for the peace and joy
of true religion.   4. That nothing but the gospel of Christ and the power of his
Spirit can effect the moral and spiritual renewal of man, and restore him to "his right
mind " (Mark v. 15).—D.

Vers. 12, 13.—*The chosen one.*   The Lord is never without resource.   If Saul fail,
the God of Israel has another and a better man in training for the post which Saul
discredited.   This new personage now appears on the page of history, and he will
occupy many pages.   It is David, the hero, the musician, the poet, the warrior, the
ruler, a many-sided man, a star of the first magnitude.   1. *Not chosen according to
the thoughts of men.*   Samuel, who at first hesitated to go to Bethlehem on so

dangerous an errand as the Lord prescribed to him, when he did go was inclined to be over-hasty. Assuming that a new king who should supplant Saul ought to be not inferior to him in stature and strength, the prophet at once fixed on Eliab, the eldest son in Jesse's family, as the one who should be the Lord's anointed. Here was a man able to cope with, or worthy to succeed, the almost gigantic son of Kish. But the Lord corrected his servant's mistake. The time was past for choosing a leader on the score of "outward appearance." The Lord sought for the regal position a man whose heart would be true and obedient. Now Eliab's heart, as the next chapter shows, was small, though his body was large; his temper was vain and overbearing. So he had to pass; and all his brothers who were present at the feast had to pass. Not one of them had such a heart as the Lord required; and it is a significant fact that we never read of any of these men in after years as playing any honourable or memorable part in the history of their country, unless the Septuagint reading of 1 Chron. xxvii. 18 be right, and the Eliab here mentioned held the office of a tribal chief under his royal brother. 2. *Chosen according to the thoughts of God.* When the young shepherd, being sent for by his father, entered the chamber with his bright hair and fair countenance, fresh from the fields, the Lord bade Samuel anoint him. "This is he." The selection of the youngest son is in keeping with what we find in many Bible stories. Divine choice traversed the line of natural precedence. The Lord had respect to Abel, not to Cain; to Jacob rather than to Esau; to Joseph above his elder brethren. Ephraim was blessed above Manasseh; Moses was set over Aaron; Gideon was the youngest in his father's house. In this there is something so pleasing to the imagination that it has passed into the tales and legends of many nations. Of three brothers, or seven brothers, it is always the youngest who surpasses every one, accomplishes the difficult task, and rises to be a king. David's superiority to his brothers was intrinsic, and the result not of luck, but of grace. The Lord had drawn his heart to himself in the days of youth. Accordingly, where such men as Saul and Eliab were weak David was strong. He revered and loved the Lord, and could therefore be depended on to do God's will. "To whom also," says Stephen, "he gave testimony, and said, I have found David the son of Jesse, a man after mine own heart, who shall fulfil all my will." The last clause in this extract shows what is intended by the one which goes before. David was a man after the Lord's heart in loyally doing his will. He was not without fault; he certainly displeased God more than once; but he thoroughly apprehended what Saul never could understand—that a king of Israel must not be an autocrat, but should without question or murmur carry out the paramount will of God. In this respect David never failed. He had many trials and temptations, afflictions that might have made him discontented, and successes that might have made him proud; but he continued steadfast in his purpose of heart to be the Lord's, to consult the Lord about everything, and carry out his revealed will. 3. *Prepared in retirement for future eminence.* There is a sort of augury of his career in his father's words, "Behold, he keepeth the sheep." Saul first came before us going hither and thither in search of asses that were astray, and not finding them. So, as a king, he went up and down, restless and disappointed. But David kept the flock intrusted to him, and, as a king, he shepherded the flock of God. "So he fed them according to the integrity of his heart, and guided them by the skilfulness of his hands." (1) As a shepherd David formed habits of vigilance. He had to think for the flock, lead the sheep to pasture, see that they were regularly watered, watch that none strayed or were lost, and look well after the ewes and the tender lambs. All this served to make him in public life wary, prudent, thoughtful for others, a chieftain who deserved the confidence of his followers. Saul had little or none of this. He went to and fro, and fought bravely, but evinced none of that unselfish consideration for his people which marks a kingly shepherd. David showed it all through his career. He watched over his subjects, thought for them, instructed and led them. Near the end of his reign he committed an error which brought disaster on Israel; and it is touching to see how the true shepherd's heart was grieved that the flock should suffer through his fault. He cried to the Lord, "Lo, I have sinned, and have done wickedly; but these sheep, what have they done?" (2) As a shepherd David proved and improved his courage. Shepherds in Palestine, in those days, were obliged to protect their flocks from prowling beasts of prey. How many encounters of this kind David may have had we do not know ; but we learn from himself that, while yet a stripling, he had fought and slain both a lion and a bear rather than give up one lamb or kid of the flock. His was the best sort of courage—natural intrepidity of a true and brave spirit, sustained and elevated by unquestioning trust in God. While encountering the wild beasts in defence of his flock David was being fitted, though he knew it not, to face an armed giant in behalf of Israel, and in many battles afterwards to beat down the enemies of his country. The springs of his courage were in God. "Jehovah is my light and my salvation: whom shall I fear ? Jehovah is the strength of my life : of whom shall I be afraid ? " (3) As a shepherd David had leisure for music and poetry. As he kept the sheep he learned to play on his harp with a skill which was the occasion of his first rise from obscurity ; and he composed and sang sweet lyrics, pious and patriotic. Whether he looked up to the sky, or looked round on the hills and valleys, or recalled to mind famous passages of his nation's history, everything gave him a song to Jehovah. Every poet writes juvenile pieces, which, though defective, show the bent of his genius ; and in after years, if he has not rashly published them, he is able to recast them into new and more perfect forms as his mind grows and his skill improves. So, doubtless, the son of Jesse, in the pastoral solitude at Bethlehem, began to compose lyrics which in more mature life, under the guidance of the Holy Spirit, he threw into the forms of those Psalms which carry down his fame to the end of time. What a contrast to the unhappy son of Kish ! Saul had the impulse of music and song upon him more than once ; but he had to be acted on by others, and his own spirit had no inward harmony. As the years advanced his life became more and more unmelodious and out of tune ; whereas David's early addiction to devout song and minstrelsy prepared him to be something better than a gruff warrior in his manhood. Born with genius and sensibility, he grew up a man of some accomplishment, and when called to the throne, elevated the mental and spiritual tone of the nation, and was, through a long reign, himself a very fountain of musical culture and sweet poetic thought. 4. *Anointed without and within.* Samuel anointed the youth outwardly, pouring oil over his head ; Jehovah anointed him inwardly, for "the Spirit of the Lord came upon David from that day forward." The old prophet is a figure of John the Baptist, another Nazarene, and one who came to prepare the way of the King. David suggests Another, a descendant of his own, born in the same Bethlehem, and, like himself, lightly esteemed. As Samuel poured oil on the head of David, so John poured water on the head of Jesus, the Good Shepherd. Then Samuel retired from view. So John too retired, and made way for him whom he had baptized. "He must increase, but I must decrease." The parallel goes still further. David had been a child of grace, but on that day the Spirit of the Lord came upon him, and he got what Samuel could not impart—a Divine qualification for the work and dignity to which he was destined. Jesus had been holy, harmless, and undefiled from his mother's womb ; but on the day of his baptism the Spirit, as a dove, descended and rested upon him, and he got what John could not impart—the Divine qualification of his humanity for the work and dignity to which he was destined as the Christ, the Lord's Anointed. "Now know I that the Lord saveth his anointed." Therefore He will save us who follow the King. Only let the name of the King be our watchword, his righteousness our righteousness, his strength our strength, his mind our mind, his anointing our anointing. So shall we see him and be with him in his kingdom and glory.—F.

Ver. 23.—*The king and the minstrel.* I. THE COMPLICATION OF MENTAL AND MORAL DISORDER. Saul was the victim of cerebral disease, but not an innocent victim. His unhingement of mind was due in large measure to causes for which he was morally responsible. The expression, "an evil spirit from the Lord was upon him," is just an Old Testament way of saying that the state into which he fell, as a result mainly of his own misconduct, bore the character of a Divine retribution. From the beginning there seems to have been a morbid tendency in the mind of Saul. He was at once very impulsive and very obstinate ; and as his troubles and anxieties increased, the original weakness or unhealthiness of his brain became more and more apparent.

He had an evil conscience because of his disobedience to Divine commands, and though faithfully reproved by the prophet Samuel, he does not appear to have ever sought pardon or healing.   Thus the purpose of God to give the kingdom to another and a better man weighed on him as a dreadful secret, and his native melancholy deepened.   The thing preyed on his mind till he became wretchedly suspicious and jealous, and at times gave way to homicidal mania.   For considerable periods, as during the active struggle with the Philistines, this evil spirit left the king ; but he fell back into his passionate gloom.   As we trace his course, the better lines of his character fade away, and the worse become deeper and more obvious.

II. THE REMEDY APPLIED—ITS SUCCESS AND ITS FAILURE.   In so far as there was mental disease, the case called for medical treatment ; in so far as it was complicated with and grounded on moral disorder, it needed a moral corrective.   But even if there had been any scientific treatment of insanity known at the period, it would have been difficult to apply it to King Saul, and it occurred to his attendants to try the soothing charm of music.   This might be the opiate to assuage the anguish of the spirit—

> "The soft insinuating balsam, that
> Can through the body reach the sickly soul."

So David was brought to the court to allay, if he could not cure, the malady of the king by his skilful minstrelsy.   It was a wise experiment.   From the readiness of Saul to catch the fervour and join in the strains of the sons of the prophets, and from the fact that in his frenzy he "prophesied in the midst of the house," we infer that his temperament was peculiarly open to musical impression, and are not surprised that the sounds of David's lyre and voice, especially when chanting some Divine and lofty theme, affected and in some degree controlled the unhappy king.   As he listened his spirit became more tranquil, and wicked thoughts and jealousies lifted from off him, as clouds lift from a mountain for a while, even though they gather again.   The refining and calming effect of music and song no wise man will disparage.   It is not religion, but it may legitimately and powerfully conduce to moral and religious feeling.   Elisha called for a minstrel, that his mind might be attuned and prepared to receive the prophetic impulse.   Martin Luther found the inspiration of courage in the same manner.   "Next to theology," he said, "I give the first place and the greatest honour to music."   Milton, too, delighted in such musical service

> "As may with sweetness, through mine ear,
>   Dissolve me into ecstasies,
>   And bring all heaven before mine eyes."

David sang before the clouded face of Saul, and "played with his hand."   So let sweet and sacred minstrelsy confront the sin and sorrow of the world.   It is better than the fabled power of Orpheus, who, when he touched his lyre, moved the very trees and rocks, and gathered the beasts of the forest to listen to his notes.   Another myth regarding Orpheus has indeed a noble meaning beneath the surface of the story.   When the Argonauts passed the island of the sirens, Orpheus, on board their ship, loudly chanted the praises of gods and heroes, so as to drown the voices from the shore, and so he and his comrades passed the fatal spot in safety.   The moral is obvious.   The sirens represent pleasures of sense, which begin with blandishment, but end in cruel destruction ; and a powerful resistance to sensual temptation is to be found in preoccupation of mind and heart with holy and heroic song.   Yet the moral power thus exerted has its limit, and we see this clearly in the case of Saul.   The king was acutely sensitive to the influence of David's minstrelsy, but he was only charmed, not cured ; and even while the youth played before him he attempted his life in a paroxysm of jealousy.   So is many a man thrilled with delight by sacred music wedded to holy words in an oratorio or in Church service who is not delivered thereby from some evil spirit or base passion that has mastered him.   Alas, how many men of musical taste and sensibility, some of them of poetic capacity also, have been quite unable to shake off the yoke of that most conspicuous evil spirit of our time and nation, the love of strong drink! This infatuation may be quieted or checked for a time, but it is not expelled by music ever so good and true. The harp, even David's harp, cannot subdue the power of sin. This requires the power of David's God. There is need of a prayer of David, such as Saul seems never to have offered up: "Create in me a clean heart; Lord, renew a right spirit within me." There is need to apply to the Son of David, who cast out unclean spirits by his word, and brought men to their right mind, and now in the power of the Holy Spirit not only controls, but corrects and cures all the evils which prey on the mind or defile the heart of man. The blackness of envy, the foulness of hatred, the demons of deceit, avarice, intemperance, and cruelty are expelled by nothing less than the grace of Christ.

> "And his that gentle voice we hear,
> Soft as the breath of even,
> That checks each fault, that calms each fear,
> And speaks of heaven."
>
> —F.

ADVANCE OF DAVID IN REPUTATION BY THE SLAUGHTER OF GOLIATH (CH. XVII.).

EXPOSITION.

CHAPTER XVII.

GOLIATH'S DEFIANCE OF ISRAEL (vers. 1—11). Ver. 1.—**The Philistines gathered together their armies.** As the object of the historian is not to give us an account of the Philistine wars, but only to record the manner of David's ripening for the kingly office, nothing is said as to the space of time which had elapsed between Saul's victory at Michmash and the present invasion. We are, however, briefly told that "there was sore war against the Philistines all the days of Saul" (ch. xiv. 52), and apparently this inroad took place very many years after Saul's establishment upon the throne. The Philistine camp was at **Ephes-dammim,** called Pas-dammim in 1 Chron. xi. 13. The best explanation of the word gives as its meaning *the boundary of blood,* so called from the continual fighting which took place there upon the borders. **Shochoh,** spelt more correctly *Socoh* in Josh. xv. 35, was one of fourteen villages enumerated there as lying in the Shephelah, described by Conder ('Tent Work,' ii. 156) as a region of "low hills of limestone, forming a distinct district between the plain and the watershed mountains." In this district Socoh lay north-east of Eleutheropolis (Beth-jibrin), midway between it and Beth-shemesh, from each of which places it was distant about eight or nine miles. It is now called *Shuweikeh.* For **Azekah** see Josh. x. 10.

Vers, 2, 3.—**The valley of Elah.** *I. e.* of the terebinth tree. **A valley between them.** Conder ('Tent Work,' ii. 160) describes the spot from personal observation thus: "Saul, coming down by the highway from the land of Benjamin, encamped by the valley on one of the low hills; and between the two hosts

was the *gai* or ravine." In the A. V. no exactness of rendering is ever attempted, and both the *emek,* the broad strath or valley of Elah, with gently sloping sides, and the *gai,* the narrow, precipitous ravine, are equally rendered *valley.* Really the *gai* is most remarkable, and fully explains how the two hosts could remain in face of one another so long without fighting; for Conder proceeds, "Two points require to be made clear as to the episode of David's battle with Goliath: one was the meaning of the expression *gai* or ravine; the other was the source whence David took the 'smooth stones.' A visit to the spot explains both. In the middle of the broad, open valley we found a deep trench with vertical sides, impassable except at certain places—a valley in a valley, and a natural barrier between the two hosts. The sides and bed of this trench are strewn with rounded and waterworn pebbles, which would have been well fitted for David's sling. Here, then, we may picture to ourselves the two hosts, covering the low, rocky hills opposite to each other, and half hidden among the lentisk bushes. Between them was the rich expanse of ripening barley, and the red banks of the torrent, with its white, shingly bed. Behind all were the distant blue hill-walls of Judah, whence Saul had just come down. The mail-clad champion advanced from the west through the low corn, with his mighty lance perhaps tufted with feathers, his brazen helmet shining in the sun. From the east a ruddy boy in his white shirt and sandals, armed with a goat's-hair sling, came down to the brook, and, according to the poetic fancy of the Rabbis, the pebbles were given voices, and cried, 'By us shalt thou overcome the giant.' The champion fell from an unseen cause, and the wild

Philistines fled to the mouth of the valley, where Gath stood towering on its white chalk cliff, a frontier fortress, the key to the high road leading to the corn-lands of Judah and to the vineyards of Hebron."

Vers. 4—7. — **A champion.** Literally, "a man of the two middles," *i. e.* one who enters the space between the two armies in order to decide the contest by a single combat. **Of Gath.** In Josh. xi. 21 this town is mentioned, together with Gaza and Ashdod, as still having among its inhabitants men of the race of Anak. **Whose height was six cubits and a span.** In our measure his height was eight feet five and one-third inches ; for the cubit is sixteen inches, and the span (really the hand-breadth) is five and one-third inches. A span, *sit*, is eight inches, but the word used here is *zereth*. See on these measures, Conder, 'Handbook,' p. 79. This height, though very great, has been attained to in modern times. **Armed with a coat of mail.** Literally, "clothed in a shirt of scales," *i. e.* a corselet made of metal scales sewn on cloth so as to overlap one another. It was flexible, and protected the back and sides as well as the front. **Five thousand shekels of brass.** Really copper, as brass was then unknown. Conder gives the shekel as equal to two-thirds of an ounce. This would make the corselet weigh at least two hundred-weight, an enormous load to carry even for a short time. Goliath's other equipments correspond in heaviness, and largely exceed the weight of medieval suits of armour. **Greaves of brass upon his legs.** The thighs were protected by the corselet, so that only the legs required defensive armour. This would account for the weight of the corselet, as it was much longer than the cuirass, as worn by the Greeks and Romans. **A target.** Really, "a javelin." It was carried at the back, ready to be taken in the hand and thrown at the enemy when required. The versions have a different reading—*maqan*, shield, for *chidon*, javelin. The shield was carried before him by an armour-bearer. **The staff.** The written text has a word which usually signifies *shaft*, *arrow*, for which the Kri substitutes *wood*, the noun actually found in 2 Sam. xxi. 19 ; 1 Chron. xx. 5 ; but most probably the word used here is an archaic name for the handle or staff of a spear. **Six hundred shekels.** The weight of the iron head of the spear would be about twenty-five pounds. However tall and strong Goliath may have been, yet with all this vast weight of metal his movements must have been slow and unready. He was got up, in fact, more to tell upon the imagination than for real fighting, and though, like a castle, he might have been invincible if attacked with sword and spear, he was much too encumbered with defensive

armour to be capable of assuming the offensive against a light-armed enemy. To David belongs the credit of seeing that the Philistine champion was a huge imposition.

Vers. 8—11.—**He stood and cried unto the armies.** Literally, "the ranks," the word being the noun formed from the verb translated *set in array*, just below. The same word is used throughout (see vers. 10, 20, 21, 22, 26, 45). **Am not I a Philistine ?** Hebrew, "the Philistine," the champion on their side. **I defy the armies.** Hebrew, "I have cast scorn or insult upon the ranks of Israel this day." The sense is not so much that he defied them as that they were dishonoured by not accepting his challenge. **They were dismayed.** That is, terrified, and made uncertain what to do (comp. Jer. l. 36). We have seen from Mr. Conder's account that each army held an impregnable position on the two sides of the ravine, which neither could cross without the certainty of being defeated in the attempt by the other side. Under such circumstances there seemed no way of deciding the contest except by a single combat. But though Saul and his warriors were too terrified at Goliath's appearance to venture to meet him, still they held their ground for forty days, inasmuch as it was evidently impossible for him to cross the ravine clad in such cumbrous armour, nor did the Philistines venture to make the attempt, as the Israelites would have taken them at a manifest disadvantage.

DAVID'S VISIT TO THE CAMP (vers. 12—31). The Vatican codex of the Septuagint omits the whole of this section, and it was inserted in the Alexandrian copy by Origen. It is found, however, in the other versions ; and possibly this treatment of David's history as of a person unknown, just after the account given of him in ch. xvi., did not seem so strange to readers in old time as it does to us, with whom reading is so much more easy an accomplishment. It is, nevertheless, one of the many indications that the Books of Samuel, though compiled from contemporaneous documents, were not arranged in their present form till long afterwards. It was only gradually that Samuel's schools dispersed throughout the country men trained in reading and writing, and trained up scholars capable of keeping the annals of each king's reign. The Books of Kings were, as we know, compiled from these annals ; but probably at each prophetic school there would be stored up copies of Psalms written for their religious services, ballads such as those in the Book of Jashar, and in the Book

of the Wars of Jehovah, narratives of stirring events like this before us, and histories both of their own chiefs, such as was
Samuel, and afterwards Elijah and Elisha,
and also of the kings. There is nothing
remarkable, therefore, at finding information repeated; and having had in the previous narrative an account of a passing introduction of David to Saul as a musician,
which led to little at the time, though subsequently David stood high in Saul's favour
because of his skill upon the harp, we
here have David's introduction to Saul as a
warrior.

Vers. 12—14.— **Jesse . . . went among
men for an old man in the days of Saul.**
This translation is taken from the Vulgate;
but the Hebrew is, "And the man in the
days of Saul was old, gone among men."
Some explain this as meaning "placed,"
i. e. "reckoned among men of rank;" but
probably an aleph has dropped out in the
word rendered *men*, and we should read
"gone," *i. e.* "advanced in years." *Old* is
used in a very indefinite way in the Books of
Samuel; but as Jesse had eight sons, of
whom the youngest was now grown up, he
must have been nearly sixty. **Went and
followed.** Hebrew, "And there went the
three elder sons of Jesse went after Saul to
the war." Some grammarians consider that
this repetition of the verb is intended to give
it the force of a pluperfect,—they had gone,—
but it is more probably an error, and one of
the two verbs should be omitted.

Ver. 15.—**David went and returned from
Saul.** This is a very important statement,
as it shows that the writer, in spite of what
is said in vers. 55—58, knew that David had
visited Saul at his court, and become personally known to him. Apparently it had been
but a short visit, possibly because after the
fit of melancholy had passed away there was
no return of it for the present; and if David
had been back at Bethlehem for two or three
years, a young man changes so much in appearance at David's time of life that it is no
wonder that neither Saul nor Abner recognised him in his shepherd's dress. For some
reason, then, or other David had not remained with Saul at Gibeah, but had resumed
his pastoral life at Bethlehem, and the statements made in ch. xvi. 21—23 belong to
the time immediately after the combat with
Goliath, and not before.

Vers. 16—19.—**The Philistine . . . . presented himself.** *I. e.* took his stand (see on
ch. x. 23; xii. 7, 16). This verse takes up
the narrative, disturbed by the inserted explanation about David's family relations.
The extraordinary formation of the ground,
as described in ver. 3, shows how it was
possible for this challenge to go on for forty
days without either army advancing or retiring. During this long time it seems to
have been the business of the friends at home
to supply the combatants with food, and so
Jesse sends David with **an ephah**, about three
pecks, **of parched corn**—as the word is spelt
in the Hebrew it means "parched pease."
Also **ten loaves,** and, for the captain of their
thousand, **ten cheeses**—rather, "ten slices of
fresh curd." David was also **to take their
pledge.** Apparently neither Eliab nor his
brethren could write, and therefore they
would send back to their father some token
previously agreed upon to show that they
were in good health, and had received the
supplies sent them. **Now Saul,** &c. This
is a part of Jesse's speech, telling David
where he would find his brethren. For *were*,
the right translation is, "They are in the terebinth valley, fighting with the Philistines."

HOMILETICS.

Vers. 1—11.—*Aggression not defence.* The facts are—1. The armies of Israel
and Philistia are drawn up in array, with a valley between them. 2. A gigantic
champion, heavily armed and proud of his strength, challenges any one of Saul's
army to a personal encounter, and with lofty words defies the armies of Israel.
3. Saul and his men are in great fear. The episode given by the sacred writer is
one of those occurrences likely to arise under the conditions of ancient warfare. It
must be viewed by us as one of the events which Providence overruled for the
gradual introduction of David to the notice of Israel. But in this section we may
confine attention to truths not immediately affecting him.

I. We have here AN EXHIBITION OF THE WAR-SPIRIT. This giant was under the
influence of a mere love of fighting. It was not a question of rightness or wrong-
ness, but of slaying or being slain. The modicum of patriotism was overlaid by the
lust of contention. This *passion dwells* more or less *in all men.* Its mildest form
is a contentious spirit—a quarrelsome temper, a desire to try our strength against
others. It has found wide and pernicious scope in the history of nations. There is
a tendency to foster this unhallowed spirit even in civilised, so-called Christian

countries. The profession of soldier, the pomp of military parade, the zest with which battles are described, the haze of glory thrown around the unutterable horrors of war, and rivalry among men for distinction in action—all show that the war-spirit is fostered. Is it not true that a mere desire to find actual occupation in fighting determines the first choice of multitudes in entering on warlike enterprises? The *evils of this spirit* are patent. *In itself* it is a *debasement of our nature.* The God of peace and love is our Father, and we are to be his children in the spirit that governs us. The execution of law and right is a totally different thing. *The woes it has brought on the world,* in deaths, widows, orphans, poverty, desolations, debts, suspicions, and engendered vices, can never be told. It is the duty of every Christian to strive to crush it out, by careful training of the young, by discouragement of popular passions, by enforcement of the teaching and Spirit of Christ, and by earnest prayer that the Church may be firm in protest against it.

II. We have also AN EXHIBITION OF PRIDE IN HUMAN STRENGTH. This giant thought himself mighty, and he boasted in his strength. Boastfulness in any form is disgraceful. Man is not in a position to magnify himself on any possession, for it is as a shadow, and may quickly vanish. Pride in mere physical strength is the lowest form of boasting, save that in actual vice. A quick, bright, intelligent mind is of more account than height of stature and strength of limb. Yet self-satisfaction in intellectual qualities and powers is evidence of a moral weakness which renders man inferior in the higher realms of life. We have need to learn that man at his best estate is vanity; that it is not by might nor by power that the highest achievements are wrought in the spiritual sphere.

III. We have also A REVERSION OF THE NATURAL ORDER OF THINGS. The natural order is that which follows from the normal constitution and relations of things. By appointment Israel were the possessors of the land. The promise had read thus: Be true and obedient, and ye shall possess the land in peace, and be exalted above all nations (Deut. xxviii. 1—13). Had the conditions been faithfully observed, God long ere the days of David would have subdued their enemies (Ps. lxxxi. 13—16). Or, had new enemies trespassed on their borders, Israel would have assailed in confidence, and not be assailed in great fear. Aggression on the foes of God and man is the work of God's people; there is a reversion of the natural order when they are barely able to hold their own, and tremble at the aggressive onslaughts of the foe. The *attitude and work of the Church in relation to the manifold forms of evil* in the world is not inaptly indicated in Israel's original relation to the abominable nations that once held and begirt the promised land—namely, *aggression till the earth is subdued to Christ.* If there are defiant systems assailing the Church of God and making inroads upon her, it is because she has been unfaithful in her aggressive work. If we do not make aggression on the domain of sin, the forces of evil will gain power and make positive aggression on the domain of religion. Vices of all kinds, and infidelity in brazen forms, flourish and become more than defensive in action when Christians lose faith in their mission and sink to the level of other men. Not even the vilest of men nor the hardiest unbeliever will venture to assail a pure and very devoted spiritual life.

General lessons:—1. The Christian Church should consider how much of the prevalence of the war-spirit is due to her imperfect treatment of the natural tendency to it. 2. Those who despise the low type of life which glories in mere brute force should remember that, from the higher spiritual sphere, glorying in any mere human possession may be regarded in the same light. 3. The earnest cultivation of spiritual life will be proved by the aggression which, as individuals, we make on our besetting sins, and, as communities, on the sins of the world.

Vers. 12—19.—*Co-operation in spiritual warfare.* The facts are—1. Three of Jesse's sons are with the army opposing the Philistines. 2. David, being relieved from attendance on Saul, keeps the flock at Bethlehem. 3. Jesse sends David to the camp with provisions, and instructs him to look after the welfare of his brethren. It is possible that Jesse may have surmised that some considerable developments would soon arise out of Samuel's recent visit to Bethlehem and the wonderful interest taken in young David. At all events, it was providential that he sent him from caring for sheep to care for his brethren on the battle-field. Leaving out of view the moral condition of Israel and its consequences, as dwelt on in the last section, we may regard the army of Saul as being engaged in the service of the living God (vers. 26, 36), virtually against the foes of the kingdom of the Messiah. David's visit to the army with provisions and messages relating to the welfare of his soldier-brothers, therefore, brings out the relation that should subsist between those engaged in open conflict in the service of God and such as are not called to serve in that form.

I. The EXIGENCIES OF THE CHURCH REQUIRE SOME TO BE SPECIALLY ENGAGED IN OPEN CONFLICT WITH SIN. The circumstances of Israel necessitated just then that some of God's people should devote themselves to the campaign as soldiers. Combination under the guidance of skill would effect what isolated private effort could not touch. In the Christian economy every true follower of Christ is a soldier, following the lead of the Captain of our salvation. Nevertheless, the circumstances in which Christians find themselves demand that some should be more emphatically fighting men, to undertake, in combination with others, arduous work which can never be done by Christians in a private and isolated capacity. Hence we have men, separated from various occupations, consecrating all their time and energies not merely in defence of the gospel, but in making war upon the manifold evils which obstruct the triumph of Christ. These sustain a relation to others, whose time is otherwise employed on purely personal pursuits, similar to that of the army at Elah to the Jesses and Davids engaged in domestic and rural occupations.

II. The CONFLICT THUS OPENLY MAINTAINED INVOLVES THE INTERESTS AND CLAIMS THE SUPPORT OF ALL. Obviously every one in Israel was concerned in the issue of the conflict with the Philistines. All that free people hold precious was at stake. If it was in the power of *non*-combatants to render aid, clearly it ought to be forthcoming. In a higher and wider sense is it true that the business of Christ's soldiers at home and abroad is the business of the entire body of believers, irrespective of age, position, or ability. The Church is one body, and the sufferings or pleasures of one member are of moment to all the members. The feeling which suggests that certain efforts to save men are no concern but to those engaged in them is unintelligent and unchristian. The call to hold forth the word of truth is to the one body of the faithful. Our sympathy with Christ's mission is real only as we identify our hopes, and aspirations, and endeavours with those of all who have the "same mind." Consequently, every consideration of humanity, of brotherly regard, of love for Christ, and joy in his advancing conquests, should stimulate aid to those on the high places of the field.

III. THERE ARE AVAILABLE MEANS BY WHICH EVERY ONE MAY RENDER SUBSTANTIAL AID IN THIS WARFARE. Jesse's forethought and David's readiness contributed to the strength and encouragement of the absent warriors. Likewise every one in Israel could aid in the conflict by contributions of food and clothing, and by cherished sympathy and prayer. In modern nations every member of the community renders assistance in war, by payment of taxes, combination of counsel, deep and variously-expressed sympathy, and that quota from each one which makes up the sum of support to be found in public opinion. The means by which the scattered members of Christ's Church can fulfil their duty to their brethren devoted entirely to the campaign against sin are varied and effective. 1. *By loyally bearing the common cause on the heart.* This may become a habit if we will but make an intelligent study of what is due from us. Its value to the distant and near soldiers of the cross is clear to the spiritual eye. Moral natures are knit together by subtle bonds. 2. *By special acts and seasons of prayer.* Emphasis given to our general sympathy by special pleading with God on behalf of his faithful servants is the all-powerful means of taking our share in the one great conflict. Even the greatest of apostles felt that he would do his work better if friends would but respond to his appeal, " Brethren, pray for us." This is an aid which may be rendered by young and old, hale and weak, the rich and poor. Only eternity will reveal how much, among the many concurring causes that issue at last in the full triumph of Christ, is due to the prayers even of the helpless invalids, and poor, unheard-of saints that dwell in cottage homes. 3. *Moral and material support.* We may seize opportunities for assuring our brethren, whose hearts are often faint and weary, that we do carry their cares and sorrows, and do regard their work as ours. We rob devoted men of strength when we are chary of letting them know our deep interest in them. The *material support* is also within the reach of most. To devote a portion of our means to Christ's cause is a great privilege. Had the Church devoted half on Christian enterprise that has been devoted to questionable self-indulgences, the joys of men and angels would ere this have been doubled.

General lessons:—1. We should encourage by example and personal influence in young people an intelligent interest in all Christian work because it is *Christian.* 2. Where true love exists, ingenuity will devise means of cheering those engaged in arduous service. 3. The spiritual unity of the Church may thus be largely realised, notwithstanding diversity of organisations.

HOMILIES BY VARIOUS AUTHORS.

Vers. 1—11. (THE VALLEY OF ELAH.)—*Israel smitten with fear.* "They were dismayed, and greatly afraid" (ver. 11). 1. The renewed attempt of the Philistines to subjugate Israel shows, in comparison with their former invasion, a decrease of power. They did not penetrate into the heart of the land (ch. xiii. 5), but advanced only a short distance from their own border, and "pitched between Shochoh and Azekah, in Ephes-dammim," a dozen miles south-west of Bethlehem. They had been driven back and held in check. 2. It could hardly have been possible, but for the rashness of Saul in "the war of Michmash," by which the opportunity of inflicting a fatal blow was lost. Hearing, perhaps, of his condition, and perceiving signs of the laxity of his rule, they sought to repair their defeat. 3. It found the people of Israel, notwithstanding their previous success, ill-prepared to repel the aggression. Although they went to meet the enemy, and encamped opposite to them, they did nothing more. In the spirit of a better time they would have immediately fallen upon them in reliance upon "the Lord of hosts" (Deut. xxxii. 30); but now they were *paralysed with fear*, especially at the appearance of the gigantic champion who came out against them. The Philistines desired to make the issue depend on a single combat between this man and any Israelitish warrior who might be appointed to meet him; and he "drew near morning and evening, and presented himself forty days" (ver. 16). A similar fear has sometimes pervaded the Christian community in the presence of the enemy.

I. IT IS INSPIRED BY FORMIDABLE OPPONENTS. 1. *Their number is great.* They consist not merely of one or two, but of a host of giants. (1) *Within:* carnal affections, corrupt tendencies, proud thoughts, evil imaginations, and wrathful passions. (2) *Without:* ignorance, error, unbelief, superstition, intemperance, licentiousness, worldliness, and "all ungodliness." (3) In the *background* of all "the prince of the power of the air, the spirit that now worketh in the children of disobedience" (Ephes. ii. 2). 2. *Their appearance is imposing.* They seem to be possessed of extraordinary might, and arrayed in terrible armour, and are of great renown. "Am I not that Philistine" (ver. 8), who has exhibited such prowess and slain so many foes? "He arose, and came, and drew nigh, like a stalking mountain, overlaid with brass and iron" (M. Henry). 3. *Their attitude is proud*, boastful, defiant, contemptuous, and increasingly confident of victory as day after day the challenge is renewed, and no one dares to answer it. "The first challenge to a duel that we ever find came out of the mouth of an uncircumcised Philistine" (Hall). How often has the contemplation of such adversaries filled even good men with dismay! While we measure our natural strength against the forces of evil our case is hopeless. "Who is sufficient for these things?"

II. IT RESULTS FROM PREVIOUS UNFAITHFULNESS. 1. *Distrust of God* and alienation from him. Faith prevents fear. It looks to God, judges of the power of the enemy in the light of his omnipotence, unites to him, and inspires with unbounded courage (ch. xiv. 6; ver. 47); but unbelief is blind and weak and fearful (Matt. viii. 26). And dismay in great emergencies reveals the absence or feebleness of faith in the preceding and ordinary course of life. 2. *Outward acts of disobedience* to the Divine will — diminishing moral power, and producing inward distraction and dread. 3. *Sympathy with a faithless leader*, and participation in the " spirit of fear " (2 Tim. i. 7) which he possesses. Saul had forsaken the Lord. He had not the presence of Samuel with him; nor, apparently, that of the high priest; nor did he seek the Divine counsel as aforetime. He ruled independently of Jehovah; and the people loved too much " to have it so," sharing in his faithlessness and fear. A faithless and fearful leader cannot have faithful and fearless followers.

III. IT INCURS DESERVED REPROACH (vers. 8, 26)—uttered by the enemy, and echoed in the conscience of the people, on account of—1. The *cowardice* of their conduct. 2. The *inconsistency* of their position, as professed servants of the living God: unfaithful to their calling, trembling before the votaries of " gods that were no gods " (ver. 44), and bringing dishonour upon the name of Jehovah. " The name of God is blasphemed among the Gentiles through you " (Rom. ii. 24; Prov. xxv. 26). 3. The likelihood of their *defeat*, of which it is a virtual acknowledgment, and to which it must infallibly conduct, unless a better spirit be infused into them. " How is it that ye have not faith? " (Mark iv. 40).

Learn that—1. The spirit of fear can be expelled only by the spirit of faith. 2. Fearfulness in conflict, difficulty, and danger indicates a lack of faith, and should constrain to renewed trust in God. 3. In their greatest extremity God does not abandon his people to despair, but provides for them " a way of escape."—D.

Vers. 17, 18. (BETHLEHEM.)—*Parental solicitude.* Family life occupies a prominent place in the Books of Samuel, and the affectionate concern of parents for their children is often mentioned (see ch. ii. 24; x. 2). Jesse, who, in consequence of his advanced age (ver. 12), was himself unable to go against the Philistines, had his three elder sons in the army of Israel; and after they had been absent for some weeks, sent their youngest brother with provisions for their need, to make inquiries about their welfare, and " take their token," by which he might be assured thereof. Such solicitude as he displayed is—

I. NATURAL. 1. Arising out of the instinctive affection which is felt by parents. 2. Continuing throughout the whole of life. 3. Commended by the heavenly Father, who puts it into the heart; and often illustrated, directed, and regulated by the teachings of his word (Gen. xviii. 19; xxii. 2; 2 Sam. xviii. 33; Ephes. vi. 4; 1 Tim. v. 8).

II. CONSIDERATE. 1. Of the distance of children from home, and of their deprivation of parental oversight, counsel, and restraint. 2. Of their need: temporal, spiritual, and eternal. 3. Of their peril: from their own tendencies, their intimate associations, and their open enemies.

III. PRACTICAL. Expressed—1. In sending them presents of that which is best adapted to their wants. 2. By the hand of a brother (Gen. xxxvii. 14; xliii. 11). 3. With the request of a token of affectionate regard for the gratification of a heart that desires and seeks their happiness.

IV. ILLUSTRATIVE of " the kindness and love of God our Saviour toward man " (Titus ii. 4). The relation of an earthly father to his children is a shadow of that of the heavenly Father to men; it was doubtless appointed from the first to be such, and the loving care which arises out of it is, in comparison with that of the " Father of spirits," only as a ray of light compared with the sun. This also is—1. Natural and spontaneous, for " God is love." 2. Considerate (Ps. ciii. 13, 14). " In thee the fatherless findeth mercy " (Hosea xiv. 3). 3. Practical. " I have loved you, saith the Lord," &c. (Mal. i. 2; Matt. vii. 11; John iii. 16).

Exhortation:—1. To parents. Let your kindness to your children be such as accords with that of your heavenly Father to you, and as affords a true image of it. 2. To children. Show kindness to your parents in return for their kindness to you (ch. xxii. 3), as your heavenly Father requires. 3. To all. " If I be a father, where is mine honour? " (Mal. i. 6).—D.

EXPOSITION.

Vers. 20—22.—**He came to the trench.** More probably the barricade, or outer circle of defence for their camp, made of their wagons (see on ch. x. 22). Strictly the word means a *wagon-track*, but the primary meaning of the verb is *to be round.* This was the shape of camps in old time, and they were protected against surprise by having the wagons and baggage placed round them. The word occurs again in ch. xxvi. 5, 7. The latter part of the verse is literally, "And he came to the circle of the wagons, and to the host that was going forth to the array ; and they shouted for the battle." If the article be omitted before "going forth," for which there is some authority, the rendering of the A. V. would be right. **David left his carriage.** *I. e.* that which he was carrying. The word is rendered *stuff* in ch. x. 22 ; xxv. 13 ; xxx. 24. Literally the word means *utensils,* and so whatever he had with him for any purpose (comp. Acts xxi. 15). **Ran into the army.** Literally, "to the array," "to the ranks," the place where the troops were drawn up (see ver. 10).

Vers. 23, 24.—**The champion, the Philistine of Gath, Goliath by name.** The Hebrew is, "The champion (see on ver. 4), Goliath the Philistine his name, of Gath," probably the very words of the original record. **Out of the armies,** or *ranks.* This is a very probable correction of the Kri, made by restoring a letter which has apparently dropped out. The word in the written text might mean "the open space between the two armies ;" but it occurs nowhere else, and this space was chiefly occupied by the ravine. **The men of Israel . . . . fled from him.** *I. e.* they drew back in haste from the edge of the ravine, which Goliath could no more have crossed, encased in armour weighing two and a half hundred-weight, than a knight could have done in the middle ages. In ver. 40 we read that it was out of this ravine that David selected his pebbles, and, being encumbered with no armour, it was easy for him to climb up the other side and attack his heavily-armed opponent.

Vers. 25—27.—**To defy Israel.** Rather, "to cast scorn on," "to dishonour Israel" (see on ver. 10). **The king will enrich him with great riches, ... and make his father's house free in Israel.** Many years must have elapsed before Saul could thus have developed the powers of the crown, and the last words show that contributions were levied from all the households in Israel for the support of the king and his retinue. There had manifestly been a great advance since the day when Jesse sent the king a few loaves of bread, a skin of wine, and a kid (ch. xvi. 20).

Still we cannot imagine that Saul had introduced taxes, nor was the political organisation of the State ripe enough for so advanced a state of things. The words more probably refer to freedom from personal service in the army and elsewhere ; though it is quite possible that on special occasions contributions may have been levied, and presents, no doubt, were constantly being made to the king, though on no regular system. **Taketh away the reproach.** The noun formed from the verb rendered *defy* in ver. 10, where see note. **Uncircumcised.** See on ch. xiv. 6. David, like Jonathan, sees a ground of confidence in the uncovenanted relation of the Philistine towards God. **The living God.** A second ground of confidence. The god of the Philistines was a lifeless idol ; Jehovah a Being who proved his existence by his acts. **So shall it be done.** As the people all answer David's inquiries in the same way, Saul had evidently made a proclamation to this effect, which we may suppose he fulfilled, though not in the frankest manner (ch. xviii. 17, 27).

Vers. 28, 29.—**Eliab's anger was kindled against David.** As David, with growing indignation at an uncovenanted heathen thus dishonouring the subjects of the living God, puts eager questions to all around, his elder brother angrily reproaches him with words full of contempt. Between the eldest and youngest of eight sons was a vast interval, and Eliab regards David's talk as mere **pride,** or, rather, "presumption," "impertinence ;" and also as **naughtiness,** or badness, **of heart,** probably because he imagined that David's object was to provoke some one else to fight, that he might **see the battle.** David's answer is gentle and forbearing, but the last words are difficult. **Is there not a cause ?** Have not those whom we are ready to condemn a reason and justification for their conduct ? Such a question put to ourselves might stop much slander and fault-finding. But the Hebrew literally has, *Is it not a word ?* And the ancient versions and the best modern commentators understand by this, "It was but a mere word ;" "I was only talking about this challenge, and was doing no wrong."

Vers. 30, 31.—**Manner.** Literally, *word,* the noun translated *cause* in ver. 29, and meaning in both verses "conversation." It occurs here thrice, the Hebrew being, "And he spake according to this word : and the people returned him a word according to the former word." And as David thus persisted in his indignant remonstrances at the ranks of the living God being thus dishonoured by no man accepting the challenge, **they rehearsed them before Saul,** who thereupon sent for him. And thus David a second time, and under very different circumstances, found himself again standing in the king's presence.

DAVID UNDERTAKES THE COMBAT WITH GOLIATH, AND PREPARES FOR THE ENCOUNTER (vers. 32—40). Vers. 32, 33.—On being brought before the king, David says, **Let no man's heart fail because of him,** *i. e.* "on account of this Philistine." Literally it is "upon him," and some therefore translate "within him." The Septuagint for man reads "my lord"—"Let not my lord's heart fail within him." Probably "within him" is the best rendering of the phrase. **Thou art but a youth.** *I. e.* "a lad" (see on ch. i. 24 ; ii. 18). It is the word applied to David's brethren in ch. xvi. 11, and his friend must have been very enthusiastic when, in ch. xvi. 18, he described him as a "hero of valour and a man of war."

Vers. 34—36.—David does not appeal to any feat of arms. He may have served with credit in repelling some Philistine foray, but these combats with wild beasts, fought without the presence of spectators, and with no urgent necessity (as most shepherds would have been too glad to compound with such enemies by letting them take a lamb without molestation), still more clearly proved David's fearless nature. Lions and bears were both common in ancient times in Palestine, when the country was more densely covered with wood ; and bears are numerous in the mountainous districts now. Lions seem to have been less feared than bears (Amos v. 19) ; but Canon Tristram thinks there were two species of the lion in Palestine—one short-maned, which was not very formidable, the other long-maned, which was more fierce and dangerous ('Nat. Hist. of Bible,' p. 117). The Hebrew literally is, "There came the lion and even the bear," the articles implying that they were the well-known foes of the shepherd. The written text has *zeh*, "this," for *seh*, "a lamb," probably a mere variety of spelling. There can be little doubt that David refers to two different occasions, especially as bears and lions never hunt in company. **By his beard.** Neither the bear nor the lion has a beard, and the word really means "the chin," "the place where the beard grows." The Chaldee translates *the lower jaw*, and the Septuagint *the throat*. It is plain from this description that David slew the beast with his staff. **He arose against me.** This shows that the combat thus particularly described was with the bear, which does thus rise on its hind legs to grapple with its foe, while the lion crouches and then springs. Pliny also says that the weakest part of a bear is its head, and that it can be killed by a smart blow there. The manner in which David killed the lion is not described. **Defied.** See on ver. 10.

Ver. 37.—**Saul said unto David, Go.** The king's consent was necessary before David could act as the champion of the Israelites. It was a courageous act in Saul to give his permission, considering the conditions of the combat (see ver. 9), but the two arguments here given persuaded him : the first, David's strong confidence in Jehovah, insuring his courage ; and, secondly, the coolness and bravery he had shown in these dangerous encounters with savage animals.

Vers. 38—40.—**Saul armed David with his armour.** Rather, "Saul clad David in his war-dress." The word does not mean *arms*, either offensive or defensive ; for in ch. iv. 12, where it is rendered "clothes," we read of its being rent. It occurs again in ch. xviii. 4, and is there rendered "garments." Strictly it was the soldier's coat, worn under his armour, and girt close to the body by the sword-belt. It does not follow that David was as tall as Saul because he thus put on his military coat ; for it would be adjusted to the body by the belt, and its length was not a matter of much consequence. When, then, it is said that **David girded his sword upon his armour,** it means upon this coat, though the corselet of mail would also be worn over it. **He assayed to go.** *I. e.* he made an attempt at going, took a short walk thus arrayed, making trial all the while of his equipments ; and he found them so cumbrous that he felt that he would have no chance against the Philistine except as a light-armed soldier. The agility of his movements would then make him a match for one so heavily overweighted as Goliath. Wearing, therefore, only his shepherd's dress, armed only with a sling, David descended into the ravine which separated the two armies, chose there five pebbles, and, clambering up the other side, advanced towards the Philistine. For **brook** the Hebrew has "torrent bed." Conder speaks of a torrent flowing through the ravine (see on ver. 2).

COMBAT OF DAVID AND GOLIATH (vers. 41—54). Vers. 41—44.—When David had crossed the ravine, Goliath and his armourbearer advanced towards him ; and when he saw that the Israelite champion was but a lad (see ver. 33), with red hair, which added to his youthful appearance, and handsome, but with nothing more than a staff in his hand, he regarded this light equipment as an insult, and asks, **Am I a dog,**—an animal held in great aversion in the East,—**that thou comest to me with staves?** The plural is used as a contemptuous generalisation, but the Septuagint is offended at it, and with amusing matter-of-fact exactness translates, "With a staff and stones." **And the Philistine cursed David by his gods.** The Hebrew is singular, "by his god," *i. e.* the deity whom he had selected to be his especial patron.

Vers. 45—47.—**And with a shield.** Really, "a javelin" (see on ver. 6). David of course mentions only his arms of offence. As Goliath had reviled David by his god, so David now expresses his trust in the God of Israel, even **Jehovah of hosts,** whom the Philistine was dishonouring. **This day.** *I. e.* immediately (see ch. xiv. 33). **Carcases** is singular in the Hebrew, but is rightly translated plural, as it is used collectively. **That all the earth may know,** &c. As we saw on ver. 37, it was David's strong faith in Jehovah, and his conviction that God was fighting for him in proof of his covenant relation to Israel, that not only nerved him to the battle, but made Saul see in him one fit to be Israel's representative in so hazardous a duel.

Vers. 48, 49.—**When the Philistine arose.** Apparently he was seated, as was the rule with armies in ancient times when not engaged in conflict (comp. ver. 52). When, then, he saw David emerge from the ravine, he rose, and, carrying his vast load of armour, moved slowly towards his enemy, trying to frighten him by his curses. David, meanwhile, in his light equipment, **ran towards the army,** Hebrew, "the rank," *i. e.* the Philistine line, in front of which Goliath had been sitting. As the giant's helmet had no visor, that protection not having as yet been invented, and his shield was still carried by his armour-bearer, his face was exposed to David's missiles. And in those days, before firearms were invented, men by constant practice "could sling stones at a hair-breadth, and not miss" (Judges xx. 16). And even if David were not quite as skilful as those Benjamites, yet, as the giant could move only very slowly, the chances were that he would hit him with one or more of his five pebbles. As it was, he struck him at his first attempt upon the forehead with such force that Goliath was stunned, and fell down upon his face to the ground.

Vers. 50, 51.—**So David prevailed over the Philistine with a sling and with a stone.** It is evident that the narrator regarded David's victory as extraordinary; and no doubt it required not only great courage, but also perfect skill, as only the lower portion of the forehead would be exposed, and on no other part of the giant's body would a blow have been of any avail. The narrator also calls attention to the fact that David relied upon his sling alone, for **there was no sword in the hand of David.** Slings probably were regarded as useful only to harass an enemy, while swords, which they had only lately been able to procure (ch. xiii. 22), were regarded as the real weapons of offence. David, therefore, completes his victory by killing Goliath with his own sword as he lay stunned upon the ground. As Ahimelech considered it fit for David's own use (ch. xxi. 9), it was

probably not so monstrous in size as Goliath's other weapons. **Champion** is not the word so rendered in vers. 4, 23, but that used in ch. xvi. 18 for "a *hero* of valour."

Vers. 52, 53.—**To the valley.** Hebrew, *gai.* As we have seen, there was a *gai* or ravine between the two armies, but in the Hebrew there is no article, and the Israelites must also cross this before any fighting began. The panic which struck the Philistines when they saw their champion fall enabled the Israelites to do so, but the pursuit only then commenced. The Septuagint reads Gath, a very probable emendation, for, as we saw in the passage quoted from Conder on ver. 2, Gath was situated at the mouth of the terebinth valley. The Syriac and Vulgate retain *valley,* but the former understands it of the mouth of the valley of Elah. **Shaaraim** was a town assigned to Judah (Josh. xv. 36) in the Shephelah (see on ver. 1), but was now held by the Philistines. **They spoiled their tents.** More correctly, "their camp."

Ver. 54.—**David . . . brought it to Jerusalem.** This is an anticipation of later history. The Jebusites at this time held Jerusalem; but when David had taken it from them, he removed the head of Goliath thither, and the narrator, following the usual custom of Hebrew historians, mentions the ultimate fate of this trophy here (see on ch. xvi. 21). **He put his armour in his tent.** *I. e.* he carried it to his home (see on ch. ii. 35 ; iv. 10 ; xiii. 2, &c.), where it became his private property. The mistranslation of *camp* by *tents* in ver. 53 might lead an English reader to suppose that it meant a tent in the camp of Israel; but most probably the men all slept under their wagons. Abravanel supposes that by David's tent was meant the tabernacle of Jehovah, but this would surely have been stated more fully. Either, however, now, or at some later period, David must have presented the sword as an offering to the tabernacle, as it was laid up at Nob, whence he took it with him in his flight (see ch. xxi. 9).

SAUL'S INQUIRY CONCERNING DAVID'S PARENTAGE (vers. 55—58). Vers. 55—58.— **Abner, whose son is this youth?** Hebrew, "lad," *na'ar.* We have seen that the narrative in ch. xvi. 21—23 carries the history of David's relations with Saul down to a much later period, and that in ver. 15 of this chapter David is represented as not dwelling continuously at Saul's court, but as having returned to Bethlehem and resumed his pastoral occupations there, whence he would be summoned back in case of the recurrence of Saul's malady. It is plain from what is stated here that David had not thus far spent time enough at Gibeah to be personally well known either to Saul or his officers (see note on ver. 15). **Stripling.** Not *na'ar,* but *'elem,* the masculine of the word *'almah,* used in Isa.

vii. 14. It means a young man fully grown, and arrived at the age to marry, and so is more definite than *na'ar*, which Saul uses in ver. 58. **As David returned**, &c. Abner, as captain of the host, would naturally watch the combat, and as soon as it was possible would bring the young warrior into the king's presence. But what is recorded here could have taken place only after the pursuit of the Philistines was over, and really these five verses should be united with ch. xvii., as their object is to introduce the account of the love of Jonathan for David. Starting then with the inquiry made by the king of Abner, asking for fuller information as to the young man's parentage, the historian then tells how after the chase he was brought before Saul, and then, in ch. xviii. 1, that the result of their conversation was the warm love that henceforward knit together these two kindred souls.

HOMILETICS.

Vers. 20—30.—*A religious man's view of things.* The facts are—1. David arrives at the camp just as preparations are being made for battle. 2. While with his brethren he hears the defiance of Goliath, and observes the dismay of Israel. 3. Being informed of the inducement offered by Saul for any one to slay Goliath, he makes particular inquiries as to the facts, and suggests the vanity of the defiance. 4. His inquiries arouse the jealousy of Eliab, who imputes to him unhallowed motives. 5. Nevertheless, David persists in his attention to the matter. The pusillanimity of the entire army seems to have been accepted by Saul as quite reasonable in presence of such a foe. David's converse with the men revealed a remarkable unanimity of sentiment among them. Estimated by the ordinary maxims of war during times when brute force in individual conflict decided the day, there was, indeed, small chance for a dwarf against a giant. The embarrassment was great, natural, and irremovable. But from the moment of David's arrival this condition of things appeared to him unreasonable. Coming fresh from the fold, unfamiliar with the ordinary rules of armed warfare, and interpreting facts by principles acquired elsewhere than in the camp and among pusillanimous men, he marvelled at the dismay of Israel, and dared to be singular in his opinion that the giant was not to be dreaded. Events from a religious point of view assume a different aspect. Notice—

I. An EMINENTLY RELIGIOUS MAN'S IMPRESSIONS OF FORMIDABLE DIFFICULTIES. David was at this time, in comparison with others, eminently religious. The facts of life impress us according to sentiments and views already entertained. When, therefore, this devout, God-fearing youth looked on the conflict, he saw it with eyes full of religious light. He felt that the entire army was wrong in feeling and opinion. The *principle holds good in other applications.* The eminently religious get an impression of the world peculiar to their refined spiritual condition. The most conspicuous instance of this is in the case of the holy Saviour. Coming from the pure, loving sphere of heaven, more sweet and restful than David's rural pastures, how different would the earth, with its conflicts, cares, and woes, appear to him as compared with their impression on men! Holy men see the world with new eyes when they descend from some mount of transfiguration. No wonder if some highly-purified and trustful souls, looking on the fear and inactivity of professed followers of Christ, are disgusted and ashamed at the lack of hope and confidence. If we have the "mind of Christ," fresh, pure, deep in conviction of God's all-wise and mighty will, toned with pity, and elevated by undying hope, we shall often get impressions of our surroundings which may make us singular, but which, nevertheless, will be just.

II. An EMINENTLY RELIGIOUS MAN WILL NOT HESITATE TO INDICATE AND JUSTIFY HIS IMPRESSIONS. The clear, truthful eyes of the shepherd youth saw the world through a Divine medium, and, with all the sincerity of goodness and force of deep conviction, he was not afraid to let it be known that he differed from others. "*Who* is this Philistine?" *He* defy the "armies of the *living God!*" The fire burned; he could not but speak. To him it was a most abhorrent thought that any one could dare to assert his strength against God. It is obvious that David reduced the whole situation to a question of first principles. He remembered *who* the Philistine was in the sight of God, and *what* the meaning of Israel's existence in the great purpose of redemption. The fear of Israel he referred to loss of faith in the people's mission to the world, and in God as the perfecter of that mission. *Illustrations of the same course are elsewhere found.* True religious enlightenment must express itself in some form. The holy cannot look on life and be silent. Our Saviour's words and deeds were largely the expression of the effect of man's condition upon his nature. It is especially important to remember this reference to first principles in their application to—1. The *sorrows and woes of mankind* through sin. We cannot solve the mystery of evil, but can fall back on the primary truth that God is good and wise, and therefore his government in the end will be justified. 2. The *prevalent habits of the world.* We must not fail to trace them to radical alienation from God, and apply the only radical cure, renewal of nature by the Spirit of God. 3. The *obstacles in the way of Christ's triumph.* They are real as facts, but we must justify our faith in their removal by indicating their essentially transitory character in contrast with the "everlasting strength" of our God.

III. A RELIGIOUS MAN IN GIVING EFFECT TO HIS IMPRESSIONS MAY BE MISREPRESENTED. David's pure mind was charged with vanity and idle curiosity (ver. 28). The accusation was the more painful in coming from a brother. Jealousy creates a jaundiced medium through which the holiest and most beautiful things appear hideous. A greater than David was also reviled, and his most holy and blessed words and deeds associated with the most wicked of origins (Mark iii. 22; John x. 20). Pliny and Tacitus, judicious men of the world, could not appreciate the opinions and motives of the early Christians. Even now strong faith in God, and belief that all obstacles to the progress of Christianity will give way because essentially human, is regarded as fanaticism. Even among some *professed* believers in Christ those are held to be too sanguine who feel sure that the most formidable of modern giants is as nothing before the mighty power which somehow will sweep it away. Be it so; time will show.

General lessons:—1. Clearness of vision on religious matters, and indirectly on all, is a result of superior devoutness of spirit. 2. We never need fear being singular when sustained by a clear conscience and the approval of God. 3. The earnest convictions and simple faith of one man may, in the providence of God, work a revolution in popular thought. 4. We give value to our religious convictions when they are indicated with candour and are sustained by simplicity and purity of life. 5. A love of detraction and petty fault-finding, while it does not really injure the devoted who are its object, debases those who indulge in them.

Vers. 31—37.—*Reasonable confidence in God.* The facts are—1. David's words being reported to Saul, he sends for him. 2. David volunteers to go forth and fight the Philistine. 3. In justification of his confidence, he refers to God's deliverance of him from the lion and bear. 4. Saul bids him go, and desires for him the Lord's presence. It was doubtless a relief to Saul to be informed that at least there was one in Israel who dared to accept the Philistine's challenge. His surprise was equal to his relief, and may have lessened his hope, when he saw the stripling. The quiet confidence of David was natural and reasonable to himself, but evidently required some justification before Saul. The story of the lion and bear was adduced, with beautiful simplicity of spirit, to indicate to Saul that the confidence cherished was amply warranted by past experience. To David's mind the logic was unanswerable. It is by tracing the mental process by which David rested in his firm conviction that we shall see the true ground of our confidence in God, when called by his providence to enter upon undertakings of a serious nature.

I. A PRIMARY TRUTH. The power of God is adequate to any human need. This general truth was the basis of David's reasoning. It was involved in his very conception of Jehovah, and found beautiful utterance in his language of later years. The power of the Eternal was not a mere philosophic idea requisite to complete the *notion* of God, but a living energy permeating all things. The ascription of natural changes and events immediately to God (Ps. xviii.) is only the expression of a faith which sees the Divine energy in and through all things. The people at Elah, on seeing Goliath, thought of his strength. The reverse effect produced in the mind of David by Goliath's boast was the thought of the eternal power. The *influence of general truths on our life is great*—greater than some suppose. They lie deep down in the mind, and yet are ever at command to regulate thought and feeling, and to suggest lines of conduct. Hence those in whom they are most fresh and clear are persons of wider range of view, sounder judgment, and deeper convictions. It is *important to have the mind well fortified with those general truths that relate to God;* and, in view of the difficulties and dangers of life, it is well to keep clear the truth that in Jehovah is "everlasting strength."

II. An experience. David referred to the experience he had had of the power of God in delivering him from the lion and bear while in the discharge of his life's calling. The Almighty hand had befriended him at a time when he put forth his own energies to subdue his dangerous enemies. Without having recourse to miracle in these cases, it is enough to notice that David recognises Divine aid in the putting forth of effort, and the primary truth had been translated into the experience of life, and so become strikingly verified. A fact is an unanswerable argument. The logic strengthens. Most of us can *fall back on deliverances from lions and adders* (Ps. xci. 13). The mental record of the past furnishes a premiss on which to build an argument of hope for the future (2 Tim. iv. 17, 18).

III. A revealed fact. David could not cherish the confidence he did without welding with his primary truth and personal experience the fact that the Almighty was always the same, and that, therefore, continuity in aid might be looked for. The unchangeableness of God was an assured fact, not from philosophic speculation on the necessary nature of the Supreme, but because made clear to the mind by the Holy Spirit (2 Pet. i. 21). "From everlasting to everlasting thou art God," keeping covenant for ever (Ps. lxxxix. 34). Therefore the argument from past experience of his power was, so far, available for conflict with a gigantic foe. The *force of this revealed fact concerning the Divine Being is great.* It gives our mind a resting-place amidst the incessant flux of things. It opens up to view a rock on which we can stand calm and secure in face of all changes of earth. The frailty of our life seems a blessing in association with so precious a reality. As the uniformity in the laws of nature furnish a basis of wise calculation and confidence in action, so the unchanging power of God in relation to human need is a ground of hope and confidence in pursuit of legitimate objects.

IV. A present emergency. David found himself in presence of an emergency more trying than when lion and bear were confronted, for the interests were wide. He was too sensible a youth to imagine that the eternal power would be manifested because men desired it, whatever the occasion. But if aid was given formerly in real need, and now a need more pressing was felt, the argument of faith was conclusive. Moreover, the earlier occasions were private and personal; this was public, affecting the interests of Israel; and were not these the interests of him for whose advent Israel lived? The ruddy youth perhaps saw a connection between the overthrow of Goliath and the great kingdom of which he sang in Ps. lxxii. We have here a *safe criterion of the reasonableness of confidence in God's aid.* When an emergency arises which deeply affects the honour and safety of Christ's Church, and the diffusion of the blessings of his reign, we are warranted to cherish fullest confidence that God will help us in our endeavour, by such means as we possess, to meet the peril. Let Churches and individuals act by this rule, and they will never be disappointed. It is involved in the promise, "Lo, I am with you alway, even unto the end of the world."

V. A providence. The previously-noticed elements in the ground of David's confidence were more influential from the fact that he did not force himself into the position, but was there by providential leading, in which he was quite passive. A man may at the last moment shrink from a dangerous work if conscious that he, by contrivance, sought it out; but when we are literally urged by circumstances into difficulties and dangers, and have a good cause in hand, then we may take the providence as an encouragement to go through. Providence led the apostles into conflict with rulers, and, hence, they dared to be confident.

VI. A plea. David could fortify his expectation of help by the plea that his heart was honest in intent. He sought not to fight the giant for love of fighting, for securing renown, for any private end, but for love to his people Israel and the honour of Israel's God.   Purity of motive in ordinary life is no substitute for faith in Christ for acceptance with God ; but it is a condition on which God grants his aid to us in our exertions. If we face gigantic evils, in themselves too great for our wisdom and strength, from an intense desire to conquer them for Christ, cherishing no vain personal ambition, then the highest confidence is justified.   A power equal to our need, unchanged by time, realised in past experience, required for an emergency in which the honour of Christ is at stake, sought by one providentially led to face the difficulty, and desired not for vain reasons, but purely for the glory of God—such a process of thought places confidence in God's help on a most reasonable basis.

General lessons:—1. We should consider whether Providence has really given us arduous work to do for Christ.   2. Our wisdom is to go forth, not under the influence of the opinions of unspiritual men, but under the full force of our own religious convictions.   3. We must not expect to know in what way the power of God will work with us ; the fact that it will is enough.   4. Success or failure in perilous enterprises for Christ depends much on the purity of motive, and this should receive prayerful attention.

Vers. 38—40.—*Naturalness.* The facts are—1. Saul clothes David with his armour. 2. David, distrusting its value, puts it aside.   3. He goes forth to the conflict armed only with a sling and a stone.   There is a curious blending of cowardice, prudence, and folly in Saul's conduct.   Not daring to fight the foe, he hesitates not to accept a youth ; and while providing ordinary armour for his defence, he fails to see that an armed youth would really be at a disadvantage with an armed giant. Apart from higher considerations, David's good sense shows him that free nimbleness would be of more value than limbs stiffened under a coat of mail.   The gentle negation, "I have not proved them," covered a positive faith in other armour often proved.   He would be David in the conflict, and no one else.   The issue was staked on his perfect naturalness.   He knew "in whom he believed," and was true to his own individuality.   The teaching is wide and important in relation to—

I. Education. To be natural is one of the ends of education, and there is a naturalness in the means and process by which alone that and all the ends of education will be secured.   While psychologically the sum of faculties is the same in all, the relative power of them may vary.   Constitutional tendencies and tastes also greatly differ.   The inherent capacity of certain faculties seems likewise to be affected by inheritance.   Discrimination is therefore requisite in education, otherwise we may place a Saul's armour on a David, and encumber his mental movements. No doubt a weak faculty is benefited by being stimulated to work, and a deficient taste may be improved by exercise ; but the apportionment of work to faculties and tastes should be regulated, not by some general average of minds, but by what will make the most of the idiosyncrasies of the individual.   That educational training and equipment is natural which leaves the mind most free and effective.   What is gained on one side by painful drudgery may be lost on another by embitterment and crippled talents.   Especially in *religious education is this important.*   Let us not clothe the mental nature of children with the forms suited to men.   Probably much of the distaste for religious instruction springs from the perfect unsuitability of the form to the receptivity of the mind.

II. Occupation. Success in any calling depends largely on the naturalness of it to the abilities, tastes, and aspirations of the employed.   The Goliath of poverty and disappointment too frequently overpowers really good and able men, because their occupation, though good and useful in itself, is unnatural to them.   In the pressure of life it is hard, no doubt, to find the proper place for each one ; but more forethought on the part of parents and guardians would obviate some of the evils.   The over-crowding and eager race of men, trampling one another down in poverty, raises the thought whether these troubles are not the voice of Providence calling on men to spread abroad and cultivate the rich distant lands waiting for occupants.   *Naturalness of occupation and of manner* is also desirable in *works of charity and religion.* Let not men be armed with powers and prerogatives out of accord with their mental and moral stature.   Let not the youth of the Church, in their enthusiasm for Christ, be fettered by impositions that will nullify their zeal   Nor let the immature assume functions for which ripe experience alone can qualify. The wise Church is that which takes cognisance of all its members, and finds out and encourages some sphere of Christian activity natural to the attainments and social position of each individual. Ministries may differ in style and be most natural—*e. g.* Paul and John.

III. SPIRITUAL CONFLICT. In one respect David's was a spiritual conflict. He discerned the great religious issues at stake, and the fitness of the means by which the battle was to be fought. For sweeping off from the earth a great foe of God's purpose in Israel, and, therefore, in Christ, he had not proved the armour of Saul, the unspiritual king; but he had proved other means of warfare suited to his individuality as a youth full of faith in God and enthusiasm for the golden age of the world. The man after God's own heart will not fight in the attire of the man who had lost faith in God. He must have freedom for such powers as are natural to himself, and that would give scope for his trust in God. 1. Is there not here a *foreshadowing of a greater than David?* Christ, in seeking to rid the earth of the giant foe of God's righteous government, *sin,* knows that men have been accustomed to contend with the evil by various appliances—philosophy, art, social and political organisation, repressive ordinances, commercial intercourse, and other agencies created for the preservation of society. There were men who hoped that he would adopt some of the ordinary appliances (John vi. 15). But Christ worked out his mission on the line of his own individuality. Recognising organisations, and social laws, and ordinary knowledge as useful, he nevertheless struck at the root, not at the ramifications, of sin. "Except a man be born again, he cannot see the kingdom of God." "Make the tree good and his fruit good." And this he effects by the power of his holy life, of his self-sacrifice, and pure truth, brought to bear on the deepest springs of thought and volition by the mighty working of the Holy Spirit (Matt. xi. 29; John iii. 7; x. 16—18; xiii. 15; xvii. 17; 2 Cor. v. 21; Phil. ii. 5; 1 Pet. ii. 21—25; iii. 18). 2. *We may also see here a parallel to our personal conflicts with evil.* There are "carnal" weapons sometimes used for subjugation of evil, but the spiritual man knows of an "armour of God" (Ephes. vii. 11—17), often proved and never known to fail. Both in our own hearts and in the world sin will be most surely overcome if we distrust mere accommodations to its nature and conformities to its methods, and use with all our free energy the spiritual power which comes of God. Christian naturalness lies in using Christian means—faith, prayer, truth, love, hope, and patience.

Vers. 41—51.—*The governing principle of life.* The facts are—1. The Philistine, on observing the youth and simple weapons of David, disdains and curses him, and boasts of soon giving his flesh to bird and beast. 2. David, in reply, declares that he comes in the name of God, and expresses his assurance that, in the speedy death of his foe, all men would learn that the battle is the Lord's. 3. Goliath falls by means of the sling and stone. 4. Seizing his sword, David cuts off his head, whereon the Philistines flee. We may regard Goliath and David as representatives of two very distinct orders of character—the one serving as a foil to the other. The low human purpose, the boastful trust in human strength, and the vanity of gaining personal renown, on the one side, set off in bold relief the execution of a Divine purpose, the quiet trust in Divine strength, and the supreme desire to see God glorified, on the other side. "I come to thee in the name of the Lord of hosts, the God of the armies of Israel, whom thou hast defied"—here is the great principle that governed David's conduct. "*In the name of the Lord*" did the stripling raise his voice, select his stones, and use his sling. Nor was this a mere accident in his life. A crisis may bring out into clear and bold expression the principle which governs a good man's life, but it does not create it. "In the name of the Lord" was his motto when feeding the sheep, slaying the lion and bear, and composing the Psalms. Consider—

I. The NATURE AND RANGE OF THE GOVERNING PRINCIPLE OF A GOOD MAN'S LIFE. There are various mental acts entering into and lying at the spring of conduct—some more original than others. Life cannot be fully understood without an analysis of them and a recognition of their mutual relation. At one time a passion may be regarded as the governing principle—*e. g.* "The love of Christ constraineth us;" at another, supreme regard for right—*e. g.* "Do justly;" at another, obedience to a superior will

—*e. g.* "Not my will, but thine be done." But these and others of kindred nature are in Scripture summarised in the beautiful formula, "In the name of the Lord." David's conduct brings this principle into triple form. 1. *The purpose of life is the purpose of God.* That which God, by the revelations of his mercy and the ordinations of providence, is working out—the cutting off of evil and the establishment of righteousness—is the adopted and cherished purpose of life. In every calling, pursuit, enterprise, alliance, pleasure, secular or spiritual conflict, the true man goes forth "in the name of the Lord" to destroy the foe of God and man. He is conscious of a definite unity of purpose, and wills that it be identical with the one purpose of God. 2. *The power trusted to is the power of God.* The Lord in whose name David went forth "saveth not with sword and spear." The stripling did not expect Goliath to fall down dead while he lay at rest in his tent, but he went forth using those means natural to him as a youth, and this too because of the unseen hand which taught "his fingers to fight." God's strength is not a vast reserve locked up for use on some far distant day, when some new system of worlds has to be created, any more than that it has been all poured forth into laws and forces now acting. The Eternal Spirit is eternally strong, and as a Spirit is in such contact with us that, by placing ourselves in a certain attitude of loving trust, we receive from him according to our need. 3. *The glory sought is that of the Lord.* The motive of David was not to become notorious among men, not to promote some private advantage, but that "all the earth might know that there is a God in Israel." Here the stripling warrior was governed by the same reference to God as was recognised by the Apostle Paul when he said, "Do all to the glory of God" (1 Cor. x. 31). This abnegation of self, this joy in the honour of the holy name, this ambition to see men bowing in reverence to the Lord of all, enters into the private and public, the secular and spiritual, works of the renewed man. See the beautiful and impressive language of saints of different ages (2 Sam. xxii. 33, 35; 2 Chron. xxxii. 7, 8; Ps. xx. 5; lxiii. 4; cxv. 1; 2 Cor. x. 4; Heb. xi. 32—34).

II. The TRUE GOVERNING PRINCIPLE OF LIFE IS NOT UNDERSTOOD BY THOSE WHO ARE NOT UNDER ITS INFLUENCE. Goliath, judging others by the principles that governed his own conduct, disdained David: his abusive language shows that he had no conception of the nature of the inspiration that made the stripling so cool and brave. Some men live in a world not penetrated even by the vision of others. Spheres of life come into collision, but do not intersect. The scorn and contempt of the ungodly is a common fact (Ps. cxxiii. 4; 1 Cor. i. 18; iv. 13). Christ and his apostles were treated with contempt, and their design of subduing the world was, and still is, by some referred to madness. Ridicule of prayer, of missions to savage men, of expectation of Christ's gospel being accepted by all, still abounds. Are not the people "few," the means contemptible—out of harmony with the age, and opposed to the principles of physical science? It is the old story of a boastful Goliath. It is the same revelation of profound ignorance. Verily, if there were no more in Christian men than in their foes, the conflict would soon be settled (2 Cor. iv. 4).

III. The TRIUMPH OF THE OUTWORKING OF THE TRUE GOVERNING PRINCIPLE OF LIFE IS ASSURED. David was sure that on that very day his foe would fall, and so illustrate the supremacy of the good man's principle. Events confirmed the truth. The issue of the great conflict between Christ's Church and opposing forces of evil is thus foreshadowed. We may go forth with the same assurance that at the end of the world's great day of battle we shall be in a position to say, "Now thanks be unto God, who always causeth us to triumph in Christ" (2 Cor. ii. 14; 1 Cor. xv. 57, 58). The same result may be looked for in respect of our own personal conflicts with sin; for though we may be weak, and pained by the scorning of the proud, yet, using our sling and stone in the strength of God, it will be found at last that we are "more than conquerors." And this, which applies to life as a whole, is of equal force in respect to any form of vice or moral evil we contend with day by day (Ps. xliv. 6, 7; Micah vii. 8).

General lessons:—1. The continued boasting of the enemies of Christianity is an illustration of its spiritual nature and the truth of its predictions (2 Pet. iii. 3). 2. The great need for Christians is to rise to the height of their powers and privileges as soldiers of Christ (1 Cor. xvi. 13). 3. Every triumph achieved for Christ over sins, or individuals, or obstacles is a pledge of coming victories.

Vers. 52—58.—*Unknown and yet well known.* The facts are—1. Stimulated by the exploit of David, the people complete their victory over the Philistines. 2. David leaves his weapons in his tent and carries Goliath's head to Jerusalem. 3. During the conflict Saul inquires who David was, but obtains no information, till, on presentation, David declares himself to be the son of Jesse. The summary of events here given brings out incidentally a fair illustration of general truths.

I. MULTITUDES ARE INSPIRED TO VIGOROUS ACTION BY THE INFLUENCE OF INDIVIDUAL HEROISM. The force of David's character passed beyond the death of Goliath: it infused fear into the Philistines and aroused the spirit of his countrymen. In this stimulating power we have one of the prime qualities of true leadership. The value of our actions lies much in this moral force. One of the difficulties of conflict in a good cause is to arouse enthusiasm, nourish courage, and incline men to exchange their lethargy for action. In the cause of Christ we have need to pray that he would raise up men fitted, by their heroic spirit, to arouse the slumbering energies of his people.

II. FORMER FRIENDS REAPPEAR UNDER A NEW GUISE. The stripling who befriended Saul in his military difficulties was the same as comforted him in his private sorrows. The deft fingers that once drew sweet music from the harp now used the stone that brought Saul's enemy to the earth. This was the second of the many acts of kindness rendered by the future to the present king, though Saul recognised not his *quondam* comforter under the new guise of chivalry. It is a happy circumstance when a man can enrich others by the exercise of diverse and unlooked-for gifts, even when not recognised. By such merciful providences does God sometimes mitigate the misfortunes even of the undeserving.

III. THERE IS SOMETIMES IGNORANCE IN HIGH PLACES OF PERSONS AND QUALITIES WORTH KNOWING. For some time David had, next to Samuel, been the most beautiful character in Israel. This is a just inference from his choice and anointing by Samuel, the sweet charm of his music and song, his noble endurance of Eliab's base imputation (vers. 28, 29), the simple story of the lion and bear, the tone of his address to Goliath, and the entire spirit displayed through the day. If moral and high spiritual qualities are of greatest permanent value to a nation, then David was, next to Samuel, Israel's greatest benefactor. And yet Saul and his officers knew him not. Concerned with the arm of flesh and the framework of national life, great authorities are often unaware of the presence of persons most important on account of their elevation of character. This will ever be true until the time comes when moral and spiritual considerations have their proper place in the councils of kings and princes. But though "unknown" in earthly courts, the holy and Christly have their record in the court of heaven, and are held in everlasting remembrance by him who delighteth in his saints and guards them as the apple of his eye.

General lessons:—1. We should pray God that the spirit of his chosen servants may become more prevalent in the Church. 2. If our goodness is real, it will find out new forms of manifestation, and not refrain because men see not the personality that blesses. 3. It may be useful to foster courage and hope for future conflicts in life by a frequent reminder of past victories, for the giant's head in Jerusalem was not without moral intent. 4. It will be an encouragement to constancy in goodness to remember that while "unknown" we are "well known" (2 Cor. v. 9).

HOMILIES BY VARIOUS AUTHORS.

Vers. 19—31. (THE VALLEY OF ELAH.)—*Self-conquest.* "What have I now done? Is there not a cause?" (ver. 29. Was it not a word? or, Was it anything more than a word?). In the conflict of life the first victory which every one should seek to achieve is the victory over himself. Unless he gain this, he is not likely to gain others, or, if he gain them, to improve them aright; but if, on the other hand, he gain it, he is thereby prepared to gain others, and to follow them up with the greatest advantage. Such a victory was David's. 1. He arrived at the wagon-rampart when the host was about to make an advance ; leaving there the things he carried, he ran into the ranks to seek his brethren ; and, while talking with them, there stalked forth, as on previous days, the Philistine champion, at the sight of whom "all the men of Israel fled, and were sore afraid" (ver. 24). The shepherd youth alone was fearless. There was in him more faith than in the whole army. And in conversing with the men around him he intimated the possible overthrow of this boastful giant, and the "taking away of the reproach from Israel," and expressed his amazement at the audacity of the man in "defying the ranks of the living God" (whose presence and power all appear to have forgotten). 2. On hearing his words, and probably surmising that he entertained the thought of encountering the champion, Eliab was filled with envy and anger, and reproached him as being out of his proper place, as only fit to have the charge of a few sheep, and even neglectful of them, and as proud, discontented with his calling, bad-hearted, and delighting in the sight of strife and bloodshed, which, he said, he *knew*, however others might be deceived. Ah, how little did he really know of his brother's heart ! But angry men are more desirous of inflicting pain than of uttering the truth. 3. This language would have excited the fierce wrath of most persons. But David maintained his self-control, and gave the soft answer which "turneth away wrath." He thus obtained a victory which was hardly less noble than that which he shortly afterwards obtained over Goliath. Consider his self-conquest (with respect to the passion of anger) as—

I. ACHIEVED UNDER SEVERE PROVOCATION. 1. *The contemptuous reproach of a brother*. From him at least better things might have been expected. But natural affection often vanishes before envy and anger (Gen. iv. 8), and is transformed into intense hatred. "There is no enemy so ready or so spiteful as the domestical" (Hall). 2. *An ungrateful return for kindness*. David had come with valuable presents and kindly inquiries, and this was his reward. 3. *An unjust impugning of motives*. "Eliab sought for the splinter in his brother's eye, and was not aware of the beam that was in his own ; the very things with which he charged his brother were most apparent in his own scornful reproach" (Keil). 4. *An open attack upon reputation*. His words were intended to damage David in the eyes of others, as unworthy of their confidence and regard. All these things were calculated to exasperate. "Thus David was envied of his own brethren, herein being a type of Christ, who was rejected of the Jews, being as it were the eldest brethren, and was received of the Gentiles" (Willet). The followers of Christ are often exposed to similar provocation. "And the strength of a good soldier of Jesus Christ appears in nothing more than in steadfastly maintaining the holy calm, meekness, sweetness, and benevolence of his mind amidst all the storms, injuries, strange behaviour, and surprising acts and events of this evil and unreasonable world" (J. Edwards).

II. EXHIBITING AN ADMIRABLE SPIRIT. 1. *Extraordinary meekness and forbearance in enduring reproach*. "He that is slow to wrath is of great understanding," &c. (Prov. xiv. 29 ; xv. 18 ; xxv. 28). 2. *Firm and instant repression of angry passion*. For it could hardly be but that a flash of indignation should glance into his breast ; but "anger resteth in the bosom of fools" (Eccles. vii. 9). 3. *Wise and gentle reserve in the language employed*. It is as useless to reason with the wind as with an angry man. "Set a watch, O Lord, before my mouth," &c. (Ps. cxli. 3). 4. *Continued and steadfast adherence to a noble purpose*. David went on talking "after the same manner" (ver. 30). We ought not to suffer ourselves to be turned from the path of duty by the reproach which we may meet therein, but we should rather pursue it more diligently than ever, and prove by our conduct the sincerity and rectitude of our spirit. "He that is slow to anger is better than the mighty, and he that ruleth his spirit than he that taketh a city" (Prov. xvi. 32). "It is better to conquer the deceitful lusts of the heart than to conquer Jerusalem" (St. Bernard).

> "The bravest trophy ever man obtained
> Is that which o'er himself, himself hath gained."

"When thou art offended by others, do not let thy mind dwell upon them, or on such thoughts as these :—that they ought not so to have treated thee ; who they are; or whom they think themselves to be, and the like; for all this is fuel, and a kindling of anger, wrath, and hatred. But in such cases turn instantly to the strength and commands of God, that thou mayest know what thou oughtest to do, and that thine error be not greater than theirs. So shalt thou return into the way of peace" (Scupoli). And of this spirit Christ is the supreme pattern (1 Pet. ii. 21—23).

III. FOLLOWED BY A BENEFICIAL EFFECT. 1. *A sense of peace and Divine approbation.* "Angels came and ministered unto him" (Matt. iv. 11). It is always thus with those who conquer temptation. 2. *The purifying and strengthening of faith,* by means of the trial to which it is subjected (1 Pet. i. 7; James i. 2). 3. *The commendation of character* in the sight of others, who commonly judge of the truth of an accusation by the manner in which it is met, and naturally confide in a man of calmness, firmness, and lofty purpose. "They rehearsed them" (his words) "before Saul: and he sent for him" (ver. 31). 4. *The preparation of the spirit for subsequent conflict.* "Could the second victory have been achieved if he had failed in the first conflict? His combat with Goliath demanded an undimmed eye, a steady arm, and a calm heart, and if he had given way to stormy passion for only a brief season there would have been a lingering feverishness and nervousness, utterly unfitting him for the dread struggle on which the fate of two armies and two nations was depending" (C. Vince).—D.

Vers. 32—37. (THE VALLEY OF ELAH.)—*Faith's argument from experience.* "He will deliver me out of the hand of the Philistine" (ver. 37). Many things tend to hinder the exercise and work of faith. Some of them arise from the heart itself. Others arise from the speech and conduct of other people. Such was the scornful reproach cast upon David by his eldest brother, and such the cold distrust with which he was at first regarded by Saul. But as he had doubtless overcome his own tendency to unbelief by recalling what God had done, so now by the same means he overcame the unbelief of the king, and excited his confidence and hope. "Let no man's heart fail," &c. (ver. 32). "Thou art not able," &c. (ver. 33). But "there was that in the language of this youth which recalled the strength of Israel, which seemed like the dawn of another morning, like the voice from another world" (Edersheim). "And Saul said unto David, Go, and Jehovah be with thee" (ver. 37); thus displaying one of the best features of character he possessed after his rejection. We have here—

I. AN EXPERIENCE of great deliverances. 1. Consisting of *accomplished facts.* "Thy servant kept his father's sheep," &c. (vers. 34, 35). They were not imaginary, but real events. 2. Occurring in *personal history,* and therefore the more certain and deeply impressed on the mind. How full is every individual life of instructive providential occurrences, if we will but observe them. 3. Wrought by *a Divine hand.* "The Lord that delivered me," &c. (ver. 37). Where unbelief perceives nothing but chance and good fortune a devout spirit sees "him who is invisible;" and the extraordinary success which the former attributes to man the latter ascribes to God. 4. Treasured up in a *grateful memory.* "Therefore will I remember thee," &c. (Ps. xlii. 6; lxxvii. 10, 11). "Experience is the collection of many particulars registered in the memory."

II. AN ARGUMENT for strong confidence. The argument—1. Rests upon the *unchangeableness of God,* and the uniform method of his dealings. "The Strength of Israel will not lie nor repent" (ch. xvi. 29). Hence every instance of his help is an instruction and a promise, inasmuch as it shows the manner in which he affords his aid, and gives assurance of it under like conditions. "Because thou hast been my help, therefore in the shadow of thy wings will I rejoice" (Ps. lxiii. 7; xxvii. 9). "This was a favourite argument with David. He was fond of inferring future interpositions from past. And the argument is good, if used cautiously and with just discrimination. It is always good if justly applied. The difficulty is in such application. The unchangeable God will always do the same things in the same circumstances. If we can be certain that cases are alike we may expect a repetition of his conduct" (A. J. Morris). 2. Recognises *similarity between the circumstances* in which Divine help has been received and those in which it is expected · viz., (1) in the path of duty; (2) in conflict with an imposing, powerful, and cruel adversary; (3) in a state of perilous need; (4) in the exercise of simple trust; (5) in the use of appropriate means; (6) and in seeking the honour of God. When there is so close a resemblance the argument is readily applied, and its conclusion irresistible. 3. Regards the help formerly received as a *pledge of personal favour*, and an encouragement to expect not only continued, but still greater, benefits from him whose power and love are measureless. " I was delivered out of the mouth of the lion; and the Lord shall deliver me from *every* evil work," &c. (2 Tim. iv. 17, 18; 2 Cor. i. 10).

> " Man's plea to man is that he never more
> Will beg, and that he never begged before:
> Man's plea to God is that he did obtain
> A former suit, and therefore sues again.
> How good a God we serve, that, when we sue,
> Makes his old gifts the examples of his new" (Quarles).

4. Is *confirmed in practice* as often as it is faithfully tested, and increases in force, depth, and breadth with every fresh experience of Divine help. "Oh, were we but acquainted with this kind of reasoning with God, how undaunted we should be in all troubles! We should be as secure in time to come as for the time past; for all is one with God. We do exceedingly wrong our own souls and weaken our faith by not minding God's favours. How strong in faith might old men be that have had many experiences of God's love if they would take this course! Every former mercy should strengthen our faith for a new, as conquerors whom every former victory encourageth to a new conquest" (Sibbes, 'Works,' i. 320).—D.

Vers. 38—54. (EPHES-DAMMIM.) — *David's conflict with Goliath.* "So David prevailed" (ver. 50). 1. David was *specially prepared* for the conflict by the whole of his previous life, and especially by his successful attack upon the lion and the bear, and his victory over himself. 2. He was *providentially led* into the conflict. "Jesse little thought of sending his son to the army just in the critical juncture; but the wise God orders the time and all the circumstances of actions and affairs so as to serve his designs of securing the interest of Israel and advance the man after his own heart" (M. Henry). 3. He was *inwardly impelled* to the conflict by the Spirit of the Lord that had come upon him (ch. xvi. 13), and had formerly inspired Saul with fiery zeal against the Ammonites (ch. xi. 6). If he had gone into it in any other manner he would doubtless have failed. 4. He rendered *invaluable service* to Israel by the conflict, not only thereby repelling the invasion of the Philistines, but also teaching them the spirit they should cherish, and the kind of king they needed. "It is not too much to assert that this event was a turning-point in the history of the theocracy, and marked David as the true king of Israel, ready to take up the Philistine challenge of God and his people, and kindling in Israel a new spirit, and in the might of the living God bringing the contest to victory" (Edersheim). 5. He became an *appropriate type of Christ* by the conflict. "It is a rehearsal of Christ's temptation and victory a thousand years afterwards" (Wordsworth's 'Com.'). 6. He was also an *eminent pattern for Christians* in the conflict; exhibiting the spirit which they should possess in their warfare with " the world, the flesh, and the devil." " David's contest with Goliath will only be apprehended in its true light if the latter be regarded as a representative of the world, and David the representative of the Church" (Hengstenberg). Notice—

I. THE WEAPONS which he chose (vers. 38—40). 1. *He neglected not the use of weapons altogether.* To have done so would have been rash and presumptuous; for it is God's method to grant success to those who employ the legitimate aids which he has provided for the purpose. Although David did not trust in weapons of war, he did not throw them away, but used them wisely. We must do the same in the spiritual conflict. 2. He *rejected the armour*, defensive and offensive, which seemed to others indispensable. "I cannot go in these; for I have not proved them. And David put them off him" (ver. 39). Some weapons may appear to others, and even to ourselves, at first, to be the best, and yet not be really such. Some weapons may be suitable to others, but not to us. We must learn by experience. We must be simple, genuine, and true to ourselves. And above all, we must look for Divine guidance in the matter. "The weapons of our warfare are not carnal," &c. (2 Cor. x. 4). 3. *He selected the weapons which were most effective.* "And he took his staff in his hand, and chose him five smooth stones," &c. (ver. 40)—selected them carefully, knowing well which were the best for his purpose; and he was not satisfied with one or two merely, but provided a reserve. His weapons were insignificant only in the view of the inconsiderate. They were the most suitable that can be conceived, and gave greatest promise of success; and his genius was shown in their selection. *Intelligence was opposed to brute force.* "It was just because the sling and the stone were not the weapons of Goliath that they were best fitted to David's purpose. They could be used at a distance from the enemy; they made his superior resources of no avail; they virtually reduced him to the dimensions and condition of an ordinary man; they did more, they rendered his extraordinary size a disadvantage; the larger he was, the better for the mark. David, moreover, had been accustomed in his shepherd life to the sling; it had been the amusement of his solitary hours, and had served for his own protection and that of his flock; so that he brought to his encounter with Goliath an accuracy of aim and a strength and steadiness of arm that rendered him a most formidable opponent" (A. J. Morris). The lesson here taught is not that anything will do to fight with, but that there must be in spiritual, as well as in secular, conflicts a proper adaptation of means to ends.

II. THE SPIRIT which he displayed (vers. 41—48). 1. *Humility.* His heart was not haughty and proud (Ps. cxxxi. 1), as Eliab said it was, but humble and lowly. He was conscious of unworthiness before God, of utter weakness and insufficiency in himself, and ready to do and bear whatever might be the will of the Lord concerning him. Humility (from *humus*, the ground) lies in the dust, and is the root out of which true excellence grows. It is the first, the second, and the third thing in religion (Augustine). "Before honour is humility" (Prov. xv. 32). "He giveth grace to the humble." "Be clothed with humility." 2. *Faith.* "I come to thee in the name of the Lord of hosts" (ver. 45; see ch. i. 3). He looked beyond man to God, and relied upon his help. "He did not compare himself with Goliath, but he compared Goliath with Jehovah," who was the Leader and "God of the ranks of Israel." He believed, and therefore he spoke, and fought, and prevailed (2 Cor. iv. 13). "Although unarmed in the estimation of men, he was armed with the Godhead" (St. Ambrose). 3. *Zeal.* He was little concerned about his own honour and renown, but he was "very jealous for the Lord God of hosts" (1 Kings xix. 14). He heard the gods of the heathen extolled (ver. 43), and the name of Jehovah blasphemed, and he was desirous above all things that he should be glorified. "All the earth shall know," &c. (ver. 46). "All this assembly shall know," &c. (ver. 47). When we fight for God we may confidently expect that he will fight for us. "The battle is the Lord's." 4. *Courage*, which stood in contrast to the fear with which Israel was smitten, and was the fruit of his humility, faith, and zeal. It was shown in his calm and dauntless attitude in going forth against his opponent, in the presence of the two armies, in breathless suspense; in his bold and confident answer to the contemptuous challenge of the foe; and in his eagerness and energy in the actual conflict. "David hasted, and ran," &c. (vers. 48, 49, 51). "So David prevailed."

III. THE VICTORY which he achieved. Not only was the boastful Philistine overthrown, speedily, signally, and completely, but also—1. The enemy fled in terror (ver. 51), and their power was broken (ver. 52). 2. Israel was imbued with a new and better spirit (vers. 52, 53). 3. He himself was honoured—by God in giving him the victory and opening before him a wider sphere of activity, by the king (vers. 55—58; ch. xviii. 2), and by all the people. Even the Philistines long afterwards held his name in dread (ch. xxi. 11). "This first heroic deed of David was of the greatest importance to him and all Israel, for it was his first step on the way to the throne to which Jehovah had resolved to raise him" (Keil). "Raised by the nation, he raised and glorified it in return; and, standing at the crowning point of the history of the nation, he concentrates in himself all its brilliance, and becomes the one man of greatest renown in the whole course of its existence" (Ewald).—D.

Ver. 47.—*The battle is the Lord's.* Many of the battles which are waged on earth are not the Lord's. They are unnecessary and unrighteous. The end they seek and the means they adopt to attain it are evil. Other conflicts are only the Lord's in an inferior sense. Although not unnecessary, nor in themselves unrighteous, they are waged with secular aims and carnal weapons. But there is one which is the Lord's in the highest sense. It is a holy war ; a conflict of the kingdom of light with the kingdom of darkness. Observe that—1. *The obligation is imposed by the Lord.* " Fight the good fight of faith." 2. *The adversaries are the adversaries of the Lord.* " Principalities and powers," &c. 3. *The soldiers are the people of the Lord.* Those in whose hearts the principles of the kingdom of God are implanted—" righteousness, peace, and joy in the Holy Ghost." 4. *The Commander is the Anointed of the Lord.* " The Captain of our salvation." " The Leader and Commander of the people." 5. *The weapons are provided by the Lord.* " Put on the whole armour of God "—" the armour of light." 6. *The success is due to the Lord.* He gives the strength which is needed, " teacheth our hands to war, and our fingers to fight," and " he will give you into our hands." 7. *The end is the glory of the Lord.* When it is over God will be " all in all." " Who is on the Lord's side ? "—D.

Vers. 29, 37—39, 45—47.—*Three victories in one day.* Here the history assumes the charm of romance, and David stands forth a hero above all Greek and Roman fame. By the grace of God he won three victories in quick succession. 1. *Over the spirit of anger.* When David, shocked to see all Israel defied and daunted by one Philistine, showed his feeling to the men that stood by him, his eldest brother, Eliab, sneered at him openly, and taunted him with being fit only to keep sheep, or to look at battles which others fought. Probably this ungracious brother had not forgiven David for being preferred before him in the day when Samuel visited the house of Jesse ; probably too he was conscious that it was the duty of some such tall soldier as himself to encounter the Philistine champion, and he was ashamed and irritated because he was afraid to fight. So he vented his ill-humour in a most galling and insulting reproach, hurled at his stripling brother. His words might have provoked a sharp retort. But David was in a mood of feeling too exalted to descend to wrangling. He was forming a purpose, at once patriotic and pious, which he saw that Eliab was unfit to appreciate, and therefore made a calm and mild reply : " What have I now done ? It was only a word ; " *q. d.* " I may surely ask a question." Thus the hero ruled his own spirit ; was master of himself before he mastered others ; had that disinclination and disdain for paltry quarrels which belongs to men who cherish high and arduous aims ; and David's first triumph was the triumph of meekness. 2. *Over the precautions of unbelief.* When the youth was led to the king, and in his presence offered to fight with the Philistine, he was told that he was not old or strong enough for the encounter. When a tried soldier of lofty stature like Saul himself shrank from the combat, how could this stripling attempt it ? It was certain death. David was not shaken from his purpose. He showed the king that his trust was in God, and that the remembrance of past encounters with wild beasts when the Lord delivered him made him confident of victory over the giant. Then Saul said, " Go, and the Lord be with thee." Perhaps he said it from a mere habit of using such phrases, perhaps with a melancholy feeling that from himself the Lord had departed. But he had so much consideration for the brave youth before him as to put his own armour on him, and gird him with his own sword. It may seem strange that he did not assign to him a suit of armour more suited to his size ; but there was little armour of any kind among the Israelites, and none so good as that of the king. It was well meant, but it was a sign of unbelief. Saul could not trust in God to defend this young champion, but would cover him with a brazen helmet and a coat of mail. David, however, happily for himself, put off the armour. It only encumbered his body, taking away his native nimbleness of movement, and it tended to weaken in his mind that total faith in God and sense of dependence on him which was more to him in such a field than even the armour of a king. Thrice was he armed who had his quarrel just, and the living God for his refuge and strength. 3. *Over the proud blasphemer.* Goliath was a terrible opponent in a time when gunpowder as yet was not, and prowess in the field depended on size, strength, and armour. No one dared to accept his challenge; and as he stalked along the valley he scoffed at the men of Israel with impunity. It was a prodigy of courage on the part of a youth like David—however strong and active, not above the customary height of men—to assail that moving tower of brass. But it was no blind fanaticism, such as despises caution and skill, and disowns the use of fit means, as though implying a want of faith. David's faith made him use his utmost care and dexterity, trusting in God to give him a sure aim and a quick victory. It is quite a mistake to dwell on the simplicity of David in going forth to the combat with a weapon so unlikely, so inadequate, as a sling. On the contrary, he would have shown not simplicity only, but folly, if he had trusted to sword and spear. If he were to strike the giant at all, it must be from a distance, and not with weapons held in the hand; for Goliath's long arm and long spear would never have let him near enough to inflict a blow. So David shrewdly took the sling, with which he was familiar, and picked from the bed of the brook a few pebbles which would pass through the air like bullets. The sling was in fact the rifle of the period, and men who practised the art could make their bull's-eyes with this weapon as well as our modern rifle-shooters, though not at so great distances. The giant, seeing the shepherd's staff in David's hand, and probably not perceiving the thong of the sling, demanded whether he was regarded as a dog, that might be beaten with a stick. Then he loudly defied the rash boy who ventured to meet him in combat, and cursed him by his own heathen god. Back across the valley went the noble answer of Jehovah's servant. "I come to thee in the name of the Lord of hosts, the God of the armies of Israel, whom thou hast defied." Then came the terrible moment, and both armies "held their breath for a time." David made the attack. Nimbly he ran forward to be within shot. Goliath had opened the visor of his helmet to look at the foe whom he despised, and to shout defiance. Thus was his forehead exposed. David's quick eye saw the advantage; he slipped a pebble into the sling, and let it fly. A sharp whistle in the air, and the stone sunk into the giant's haughty brow. "He fell on his face to the earth." How the men of Israel shouted as they heard the clang of his heavy armour on the ground, and saw their young champion cut off the boaster's head with his own sword! Then it was the turn of the Philistines to fear and to flee; and the Israelites pursued them, and "spoiled their tents." So one man gained three battles in a day, and thousands reaped the advantage of his victories. Is not this what we have under the gospel? One who was born in Bethlehem, but in whom his own brethren did not believe, is our Deliverer and the Captain of our salvation. Jesus overcame provocation by his meekness and lowliness of heart. He overcame all temptation to unbelief and self-will by his perfect trust in God his Father. He also overcame that strong adversary who had long defied and daunted the people of God, and had lifted up the name of false gods on the earth, blaspheming him who is true. This enemy seemed to stride to and fro in the earth, and boast himself against the Lord with impunity. But the Son of David has bruised the enemy's head, laid low his pride, and now thousands and tens of thousands enter into his victory and shout his praise. To David belonged the honours of the day. Jonathan loved him. All Israel extolled him. So let us love and praise him who has won for us a greater victory and a richer spoil. We thank victorious generals, we decorate valiant soldiers, we raise statues and trophies to national champions. But, in truth, the country which they have saved is their real monument, the nation which they rescue from oppression or danger is the true and lasting pillar of their fame. So is it in regard to the Captain of our salvation. Words and offerings for his cause are insufficient for his praise. The Church of the redeemed is his monument. All whom he has saved out of the enemy's hand are to the praise of his glory. "Hosanna to the Son of David; hosanna in the highest!"—F.

EXPOSITION.

PERSONAL RELATIONS OF SAUL AND DAVID (CHS. XVIII.—XXVII.).
FRIENDSHIP OF DAVID AND JONATHAN (CHS. XVIII.—XX.).

CHAPTER XVIII.

JONATHAN LOVES DAVID (vers 1—5). **Ver. 1.—When he had made an end of speaking.** This conversation took place as soon as the pursuit of the Philistines and the collecting of the spoil were over. There would then be a muster of the Israelites, and Abner would naturally present the youthful champion to the king, who is represented as having virtually forgotten him, and as anxious to learn his history; nor had his stay been long enough for Abner to remember him. As this conversation is narrated as an introduction to the account of Jonathan's friendship for David, the last four verses of ch. xvii. ought to be prefixed to ch. xviii. A new beginning commences with them, in which we are told of the commencement of this friendship, of the growth of Saul's hatred, and of the trials which befell David, proceeding on the king's part from bad to worse, till at last he was driven away and compelled to lead the life of an outlaw. But by his envy, cruelty, and bad government Saul was alienating the minds of the people from him, and preparing the way for his own downfall and David's ultimate triumph. The episode of Jonathan's love is as beautiful as Saul's conduct is dark, and completes our admiration for this generous and noble hero. **The soul of Jonathan was knit with the soul of David.** These kindred spirits had so much in common that, as David with modest manliness answered the king's questions, an intense feeling of admiration grew up in the young warrior's heart, and a friendship was the result which ranks among the purest and noblest examples of true manly affection. The word rendered *knit* literally means *knotted*, tied together firmly by indissoluble bonds.

Vers. 2—4.—Saul took him that day. Bent solely on war, Saul gladly took so promising a young soldier as David to be one of his body-guard (ch. xiv. 52), and henceforward he was constantly with him. Thus in two ways, first as a musician, and now as a soldier, David was forced into those intimate relations with Saul, which ended so tragically. For a while, however, those happier results ensued summed up in ch. xvi. 21. **Jonathan and David made a covenant.** We are not to suppose that this happened immediately. David continued on friendly terms with Saul for a considerable period, during which he went on many expeditions, and grew in military renown (see ver. 5). And thus the love which began with admiration of David's prowess grew deeper and more confirmed by constant intercourse, till this solemn bond of mutual friendship was entered into by the two youthful heroes, by which they bound themselves under all circumstances to be true and faithful to one another. How nobly Jonathan kept the bond the history proceeds immediately to tell us; nor was David subsequently unmindful of it (2 Sam. ix. 1, 7). **Jonathan stripped himself of the robe,** &c. In confirmation of the bond Jonathan gave David first his *robe*, the *meïl*, which, as we have seen on ch. ii. 19, was the ordinary dress of the wealthier classes; and next **his garments,** his military dress (see on ch. xvii. 38, 39), worn over the *meïl*, and which here seems to include his accoutrements,—the bow, sword, and girdle,—though elsewhere distinguished from them (2 Sam. xx. 8). In thus clothing David in his own princely equipments Jonathan was showing his friend the greatest personal honour (Esther vi. 8), and such a gift is still highly esteemed in the East.

Ver. 5.—David went out. *I. e.* went on military expeditions (comp. ver. 30). As the verb has thus a technical signification, it makes a complete sense, and the verse should be translated, "And David went forth (*i. e.* on warlike enterprises); whithersoever Saul sent him he prospered, and Saul set him over the men of war." These expeditions were not upon a very large scale; for it is not until ver. 13 that we read of David being made "captain over a thousand." Still, even while only a centurion in rank, yet, as being in constant attendance upon the king, he would often temporarily have the command of larger bodies of men, or would go on campaigns as one of the king's officers. As it is mentioned that his promotion caused no envy because of his great merits, it follows that it was rapid enough to have given occasion to ill-will under ordinary circumstances. **Behaved himself wisely.** This is the primary meaning of the verb; but as success is the result of wise conduct, it constantly signifies *to prosper.* This verse is a summary of events which may have occupied a very considerable space of time. It was only gradually that David's fame became so great as to rouse all the worst feelings in Saul's mind.

SAUL'S HATRED OF DAVID (vers. 6—16). **Ver. 6.—When David was returned from the slaughter of the Philistine.** Or more probably, as in the margin, "of the Philistines." The allusion is not to the combat with Goliath, but to one of the expeditions referred to in ver. 5, in which David had gained some decisive victory. The women would not have described the slaughter of one champion as the slaying of ten thousand, nor would there have been any contrast between this act and the military enterprises of Saul. Probably he too would have looked with indifference upon this Oriental exaggeration of the daring bravery of a boy; but what galled him was David's continual success in repeated campaigns. **The Philistine** means the whole people of that name; and as the war between them and Saul lasted all the days of Saul's life, and was his main kingly work, he saw with envy the rapid growth of David's reputation; and when, after some noble achievement, the women gave David an ovation, and declared in their songs that he had achieved a success ten times as great as Saul, an outburst of ill-feeling was the result. Saul suddenly became aware that the young captain on whose shoulders he had devolved the chief labours of the war had supplanted him in the popular estimation, and hatred took the place of the good feeling which he had previously entertained towards him. **The women came out of all cities of Israel . . . to meet king Saul.** It is evident that this refers to some grand occasion, and probably to the conclusion of a peace between the two nations. The battle in the valley of Elah was probably followed by several years of warfare, during which David developed those great military qualities which made him subsequently the founder of the wide empire over which Solomon reigned. It was unendurable for Saul, himself a great soldier, to find, when the war at last was over, that the people recognised in his lieutenant higher military qualities than they had discovered in himself. **With tabrets.** See on ch. x. 5. **With joy.** As this is placed between the names of two instruments of music, it must mean some kind of joyous shouting or singing to the sound of their tabrets. **With instruments of music.** Hebrew, with triangles, a very ancient but effective instrument for an outdoor procession accompanied with dancing.

Ver. 7. — **The women answered.** *I. e.* they sang alternately. It was this alternate singing which led to the psalms being composed in parallel sentences, and not in metre; and we from the temple service have inherited our method of chanting antiphonally. **As they played.** The word is ambiguous, and to an English reader would suggest the idea of the women playing upon the musical instruments. It usually refers to merriment, and so in Zech. viii. 5 it is used of the children *playing* in the streets, but especially it refers to dancing. Thus in

2 Sam. ii. 14 it is used of a war-dance ending in a real conflict; and again (2 Sam. vi. 5, 21; 1 Chron. xiii. 8; xv. 29) of David dancing to instruments of music before the ark. Michal probably would not have despised David for playing an instrument of music during a religious ceremony; it was the posturing of the dance which seemed to her beneath the dignity of a king. So these women danced in alternate choruses to the beating of their tambourines and triangles. In Judges xvi. 25, where, however, it is in a different conjugation, the verb is translated "to make sport." Really Samson was compelled to dance Israel's national war-dance before the Philistines.

Vers. 8, 9.—**What can he have more?** &c. Literally, "And there is beside for him only the kingdom." Though many years had passed since Samuel pronounced Saul's deposition, and the choice of another in his place (ch. xv. 28), yet it was not a thing that a king could ever forget. No doubt he had often looked out for signs of the person destined to be his successor; and now, when he had stood powerless before the enemy, a shepherd boy had stepped forth and given him the victory. And this stripling, taken to be his companion in arms, had shown so great qualities that the people reckoned him at ten times Saul's worth. Had Saul been the high-minded man he was when appointed to the kingdom (ch. xi. 13), he would have thrust such thoughts from him. But his mind had become cankered with discontent and brooding thoughts, and so **he eyed David from that day and forward.** In many nations the eye of an envious man is supposed to have great power of injury. Here it means that Saul cast furtive glances at David full of malice and ill-will.

Vers. 10, 11.—**It came to pass on the morrow.** The day had been a time of public triumph, and yet one of the chief actors goes home to a sleepless couch, because he thinks that another has received higher honour than himself. His melancholy deepens till a fit of insanity comes on. For **the evil spirit from God came upon Saul.** Literally, "an evil spirit (breath) of God descended mightily upon Saul" (see ch. xvi. 15). Just as all mighty enthusiasms for good come from God, so do strong influences for evil, but in a different way. In all noble acts men are fellow-workers with God; when evil carries them away it is of God, because he it is who has made and still maintains the laws of our moral nature; but it is by the working of general laws, and not by any special gift or grace bestowed by him. Saul had brooded over his disappointment, and cherished feelings of discontent at his own lot and of envy at the good of others to such an extent that his mind gave way before the diseased workings of his imagination. And so he lost all control over himself, and **prophesied**. The conjugation employed here (Hithpahel) is never used of real, true prophecy (which is always the Niphal), but of a bastard imitation of it. Really Saul was in a state of frenzy, unable to master himself, speaking words of which he knew not the meaning, and acting like a man possessed. In all this there was something akin to the powerful emotions which agitated the true prophet, only it was not a holy influence, but one springing from violent passions and a disturbed state of the mind. In order to soothe him **David played with his hand**, as at other times, but without the desired effect. On the contrary, Saul brandished the javelin, which he carried as a sort of sceptre in his hand, with such violence that David twice had to escape from this threat of injury by flight. It is not certain that Saul actually threw the javelin. Had he done so it would be difficult to account for David escaping from it twice. After such an act of violence he would scarcely have trusted himself a second time in Saul's presence. Instead of **Saul cast the javelin**, the Septuagint in the Alexandrian codex and the Chaldee render *lifted*, i. e. retaining the same consonants, they put vowels which refer the verb to another root. But even with the present vowels it may mean "made as though he would cast," or aimed "the javelin." On a later occasion Saul actually threw the javelin, and struck the wall where David had been sitting (ch. xix. 10).

Vers. 12—16.—**Saul was afraid of David.** A new feeling. To his jealousy succeeded a sense of powerlessness, as knowing that a higher power was with David, while he had lost the Divine protection. This miserable feeling grew upon the unhappy king, till before the battle of Gilboa we find him with all his old heroic spirit gone, a miserable wreck, seeking for comfort at the hands of a woman of the most worthless kind (ch. xxviii. 5, 7, 20). In this despondent state of mind he dismisses David from attendance upon him, but in an honourable manner, giving him the command of a thousand men, at the head of whom **he went out and came in before the people**, i. e. in a public capacity, as an officer of state. As Saul seems entirely to have neglected the internal administration of the kingdom, this would refer to military expeditions (see on ver. 5); and in these **David behaved himself wisely.** Rather, "prospered" (see on ver. 5). His great success only increased Saul's fears; but both **Israel and Judah loved David**, now that in this higher command they had full opportunities for judging of his high qualities. Thus again his removal from his place in Saul's body-guard only served to make him better known. The separate mention of Israel and Judah is an indication of the Books of Samuel having been written at a post-Solomonic date, though the distinction was a very old one (see on ch. xi. 8).

SAUL, UNDER PRETENCE OF A MARRIAGE WITH HIS DAUGHTER, PLOTS DAVID'S DEATH (vers. 17—30). Vers. 17, 18.—**Behold my elder daughter Merab**. Saul had promised that he would give his daughter in marriage to whosoever should slay the giant (ch. xvii. 25); and not only was there in this the honour of a close alliance with the royal house, but, as it was usual to give large presents to the father in return for the daughter's hand, the gift had also a substantial value. After long delay Saul now refers to this promise, not so much with the intention of fulfilling it, as of leading David on to enterprises which might cost him his life. The marriage may have been deferred at first on account of David's youth; the subject is now revived, but with evil intentions. **My elder daughter** is literally "my daughter, the great one," while Michal is "the little one," a way of speaking used only where there are but two daughters. **Be thou valiant**, &c. This exhortation would be natural under the circumstances; but Saul hoped that David, in order to secure so great a prize, would be encouraged to undertake rash adventures. **For Saul said**, *I e* in himself; his purpose was to urge David to perpetual fighting, that so in some rash undertaking he might be slain. Thus Saul's malice grows, and though not prepared as yet to put David to death himself, he would have felt relief if he had died by the fortune of war. David answers modestly and discreetly that he is not worthy of so great an honour. We are not to suppose that he discerned Saul's treachery, which only came to light afterwards. **What is my life**,—*i. e.* my condition, **—or my father's family?** The *or* is not in the Hebrew, and the meaning is, What is my condition, even my father's family? &c. David's condition or rank in life was settled by the rank which his father held.

Ver. 19.—**Merab . . . was given unto Adriel**. A large dower was doubtless offered to Saul in return for his daughter, and, as he had never wished David to have her, he proved untrue to his word. For the unhappy death of the sons of Merab and Adriel see 2 Sam. xxi. 8.

Vers. 20, 21.—**Michal . . . loved David.** Probably there was some short lapse of time between Merab's marriage and the growth of this affection, the news of which pleased Saul. He was not an ungenerous man, and possibly may have felt ashamed at having acted so meanly by David after having exposed him to danger. And yet evil thoughts again are uppermost, and his purposes are selfish; for either way Saul will be the gainer. David will probably be slain, he thinks, in trying to get the dowry asked of him; and if not, at all events he will himself be cleared of the stain of public dishonesty now resting upon him. Therefore **Saul said to David**. Not in person, which accounts for David giving no answer, but through his servants, as is recounted more fully afterwards.

Vers. 22, 23.—**Commune**, &c. This is a more full and exact account of what was said summarily in ver. 21. We cannot suppose that Saul first spoke to David himself, and then told his servants to coax him, as this would also require us to suppose that when offered her by Saul, David refused Michal in marriage. But we may well believe that he was displeased at having been deceived, and that the renewed proposal of marriage with one of the king's daughters had to be made carefully, as he might naturally think that there was danger of his being cajoled a second time. David replies, in fact, very discreetly, saying that to be the king's son-in-law was indeed a great honour, but that he was too poor to provide a sufficient dowry. Strictly the promises given in ch. xvii. 25 bound Saul to give her without dowry; but it appears quite plainly from David's words that he had lost Merab because not able to purchase her as Adriel had done. For the custom of giving large sums to the bride's father see Gen. xxxiv. 12; Exod. xxii. 16, 17.

Vers. 24, 25.—David's answer exactly fell in with Saul's purposes, and he forthwith asked as a dowry proof of David having slain a hundred Philistines. As this slaughter would have to be effected not in regular warfare, but in a sort of private raid, there would be every likelihood of David being overpowered by a rapid gathering of the Philistines and slain in attempting it. It marks the unscrupulous character of ancient warfare that the lives of enemies should thus be taken, without any public provocation, for private purposes (comp. Judges xiv. 19).

Vers. 26, 27.—**It pleased David well to be the king's son-in-law.** Besides the great honour, David, not suspecting any malicious purpose on Saul's part, may have hoped that this relationship would put an end to the miserable state of things which existed between him and Saul. He harboured no treasonable purposes, and would have gladly served Saul faithfully if he had been permitted. The nature also of the dowry fell in with his adventurous and war-loving disposition. **The days were not expired. Wherefore**, &c. A difficulty arises here from the wrong division of the verses, and from our translators having rendered the clauses as if they were independent of each other. The Hebrew is, "And the days were not full, and David arose," &c. The dowry was to be given within a fixed time, and before it had expired David, who had been forming his plans, set out with his men and made an incursion into the Philistine territory, whence he brought back to the king twice as many foreskins as had been stipulated; and thereupon Michal became David's wife.

Vers. 28, 29.—The failure of his evil purpose, and the knowledge that Michal loved her husband, and would protect him against his intrigues, and that the marriage had brought rank and influence to David, made Saul hate him all the more bitterly, because he could not now openly put to death one so closely connected with him.

Ver. 30.—**The princes of the Philistines went forth.** See on ver. 5. This new war was the result of David's raid, but it only led to an increase of his fame and popularity. For **he behaved himself more wisely.** *I. e.* was more successful and skilful than any of Saul's other officers.

HOMILETICS.

Vers. 1—4.—*Religious friendship.* The facts are—1. Jonathan, on becoming acquainted with David, forms a strong attachment for him. 2. Saul, to show his gratitude for David's aid, constrains him into his service. 3. Jonathan and David enter into a solemn covenant of friendship. It is obvious that David desired to retire to the quietude of rural life, thus displaying simplicity of purpose and freedom from the ambition charged on him by Eliab (ver. 28), as also superiority to the temptation of success. Saul's will that he should "go no more home to his father's house" was fraught with a long train of consequences which told on the development of the higher qualities of the coming king. The first of these was the formation of that beautiful friendship with Jonathan, which shines as a welcome light amidst the gloom of the last years of Saul's reign. There are in this section two matters deserving special attention.

I. AN ILLUSTRATION OF THE HARMONIES OF PROVIDENCE. On *à priori* grounds we may conclude that always, in all things, however apparently clashing, there is an interior harmony in the ordinations and unfoldings of Providence. In many instances we seem to hear discord ; faith only enables us to refer the discord to our defective organs of knowledge. But here, as in some other instances, we can trace the exquisite harmony between David's detention by Saul, involving his friendship with Jonathan, and David's subsequent entrance on the duties and dignities foreshadowed by the anointing by Samuel. Unquestionably, as seen in the history and in the Psalms composed during the period, David's trials and the public position arising out of this forced detention by Saul were, in their effects on his character and abilities, wonderfully harmonious with his pre-ordained kingship. Moreover, this providential opportunity for forming personal friendship beautifully harmonises with both the cutting off of Saul's line (ch. xv. 27—29) from the succession and the acquisition by David of the title, in virtue of his religious and general qualities. Such friendship, formed on the purest religious basis, and before developments with respect to the succession were made, would save both David and Jonathan from the possibility of regarding each other as rivals, and would also be a blessed counterpoise to David's unmerited sorrows during Saul's violent persecutions. Jonathan never lived to see the throne taken by another ; but his life was not embittered by the griefs of jealousy, because of the deep love he had for his friend. David, while in the decree of God destined to be king, loved Jonathan too well to think of setting him aside. Beautiful providence that could insure a succession out of the line, and yet sweeten and ennoble the lives of those whose interests were involved in it ! It would be easy for Jonathan to resign to David, should they both survive Saul's decease ; for did he not love him with a love passing that of women ? (2 Sam. i. 26). And it would be far from David's desire to set him aside, seeing the loving esteem in which he was held. Yea, was there not an instinctive homage paid to David's character, as though the pure soul saw in him the coming king, when Jonathan stript himself of his princely attire and placed it on David ? Harmonies of Providence are constant, if only we had the eye to discern them. Paul's early training worked into his life's mission, though at first tending another way. The flight of Mary and Joseph into Egypt no doubt checked a premature notoriety of the child Jesus.

II. AN ILLUSTRATION OF A TRUE RELIGIOUS FRIENDSHIP. Friendship in some degree is a necessity of man's life. A perfectly solitary being, whose feelings cling to no one, and around whom no one clings, is truly lost. Ordinary friendships are based on the existence of natural affinities and contrarieties. That similarity of mind is the basis of friendship is only true in a limited sense, for one is drawn to another not only by the affinity of common tastes and qualities, but because of a recognition and admiration of qualities that are lacking in self. We seek to supplement the deficiencies of our own life by taking into ourselves, as far as possible, the excellences of another life, and friendship is the means to this end. This is not indeed a full *rationale* of friendship, nor must it be inferred that cool calculation of personal profit enters into it. The love, the sympathy, the tender, undefinable interest and absolute trust cannot be disentangled from the perception of qualities supplementary to one's own. The friendship of David and Jonathan embraced all that enters into ordinary friendship,—appreciation, love, confidence, tenderness, fidelity, unsuspicious intercourse,—with an additional religious element. This religious friendship may be considered as to—1. *Its nature*. In David and Jonathan we recognise, besides the usual essentials of friendship, the responsive action of a common faith in God and delight in his service. Each saw in the other, as by a higher spiritual insight, a spiritual kinship. *The circumstances of the age intensified this mutual attraction*. As holy, consecrated young men, they cherished a secret sorrow over the unhappy spiritual condition of their countrymen ; and their joy in the recent victories was joy in God and the holy cause for which Israel was chosen out from among the nations. Among *Christians the same religious feeling operates* in the formation and maintenance of friendships. It is true that all are one in Christ, and each sees in every other a member of the household of faith : religiously there is a common interest in all (1 Cor. xii. 26, 27). So far, therefore, there is a friendship subsisting between each member of Christ's body and every other, as distinguished from his interest in men of the world. But affection needs for its own life concentration ; and while, therefore, we are in general friendship with all Christ's people, and are conscious of a blessed and indestructible bond, the necessities of our life lead to the formation of personal friendships in which all ordinary feelings are intensified and beautified by the infusion of a spiritual element. Some *modification of the view* just given is requisite in considering the *friendship of Christ* for John and the family at Bethany. But although the perfect Saviour saw not in others qualities deficient in himself, he did see in the ardent John and the tender sympathy and fine appreciation of the family at Bethany that which he was so eagerly in quest of in this rough, unspiritual world. His weary heart delighted to rest in such pure love and sympathy, and he returned the affection a hundredfold. 2. *Its maintenance.* The noblest form of friendship needs culture if it is to be permanent. How David and Jonathan nourished theirs is a matter of history, and should be noted. Few things are more sad to reflect on than a broken friendship—it means the embitterment and sad solitariness of two human beings. No detailed rules can be set for nourishing that which in its very nature overleaps all formalities and rigid lines. Ordinarily we may strengthen our friendships by cherishing a conviction of their *sacredness*—not to be rudely handled and lightly thought of; by making it a point to secure sufficient intercourse or interchange of feeling (Prov. xviii. 24); by a studied respect for the minor differences which advancing age and changed circumstances may develop; by prayer for the blessing of God on each other; and, if possible, by sharing in some common work for Christ. Why should not friendships continue through life?

General lessons :—1. Knowing the force of impulse and the growth of interest when once aroused, we should be careful in placing youth in such circumstances as may lead to the formation of true and lasting friendships. 2. It should be a question for each how it is that Christian feeling does not enter so fully as it ought into the friendships of some professedly religious people. 3. It would be an instructive study for young and old to trace out in history some of the achievements in religious work and fidelity promoted by the maintenance of strong personal friendships.

Vers. 5—11.—*Some dangers of persistent sin.* The facts are—1. David, behaving wisely in his public position, wins favour with the people, and in the welcome to him on his return from the battle the women ascribe to him, in their song, higher praise than to Saul. 2. The fact excites Saul's envy henceforth. 3. In a fit of envious rage Saul seeks to smite David. The victory over Goliath brought Saul and David into a proximity highly favourable to the development of their respective characters. Their mutual influence acted powerfully on the main springs of life; and as these were so utterly different in moral quality, so the sequel reveals very diverse conduct, We have in this section an instance of—

I. MISINTERPRETED PROSPERITY. The decisive words of Samuel (ch. xv. 26) and his entire separation from Saul (ch. xv. 34, 35), as also the threatening attitude of the Philistines, were certainly enough to depress the spirit of the king; and his melancholy was but the outward sign to men of his painful secret. But the appearance of David, and the consequent defeat of the enemy, was an unlooked-for gleam of light, and at once raised hopes which of late had been lost. He even set David over his men of war. The old prosperity was returning; the kingdom was saved; Saul was not dishonoured in battle. After all, with such helpers as David, might not the dreaded doom be avoided? Thus do we see a man, conscious of moral degeneracy, and sensible of being rejected, putting an interpretation on events according to his wishes, and not from a perception of their real bearing. The heart, when destitute of the spirit of true repentance, obstinately clings to unwarranted hope, and, by its own perverse ingenuity, obliterates or weakens the force of hard facts and moral laws (ch. xv. 26—29). In the eye of God the recent victory was the public presentation of the "neighbour," as a preliminary to his supplanting Saul; in the eye of Saul it was the postponement, if not the rendering void, of the dreaded doom. The *tendency thus to misinterpret facts is common to sinful men.* An impenitent heart is unwilling to believe in the vindication of justice. Not being in moral sympathy with the purposes of God, it will not, if possible, see those purposes in process of realisation. The very riches of goodness are perverted into an occasion for persistence in sin (Rom. ii. 4), and the temporal prosperity of life, despite the voice of conscience and the clear word of God, is supposed to be a sign that the issue will not be so fearful as was anticipated (Ps. x. 6, 11; Heb. ii. 3).

II. THE SOUNDNESS AND THE DEFECTS OF POPULAR INSTINCTS. The mass of the people were quick in recognising the fact that David was the hero of the day, and only expressed the real truth in ascribing to him his "ten thousands," and to Saul his "thousands." Their instincts led them to honour above the king the man who was proved to be better than the king. But while correct in their appreciation of fact, they had no adequate, if any, perception of the moral bearings of it. Samuel, probably Jesse, and a few other devout men, would trace in David's exaltation of the "name of the Lord" (ch. xvii. 45—47) a spiritual power and a spiritual man destined to work wonders for Israel. It is a good philosophy that *trusts the popular mind in reference to the recognition of the broad facts of life.* It is this faith which lies at the foundation of constitutional governments and the judicial administration of our own country. The common sense of mankind is a safe guide in ordinary matters of fact. But by reason of the low condition of man's spiritual life, and his inveterate proneness to look at the "things that are seen," the mass of men do not recognise quickly the moral and spiritual bearings of facts. There is a moral and spiritual "intention," to use a logical term, in human facts; they carry with them qualities that determine the future; they exhibit to the spiritually enlightened powers that will germinate, and that, too, not always in the form desired by the populace (Matt. xvi. 3).

III. THE LIABILITY OF MEN, WHEN WARRING AGAINST PROVIDENCE, TO FALL INTO NEW SINS. We have seen (ch. xv. 24—31) that Saul cherished impenitent feelings when told of his sin. As a consequence, he tried not to believe that the threatened disaster would come. One of the consequences of this mental condition was, that as soon as he heard the honest, popular approval of David's prowess, he, dreading lest after all the decree might be fulfilled, eyed David as a rival, and fell into the grievous sin of ceaseless and cruel envy. The grievous character of this sin is seen if we notice its manifestation, and the main features are true of all envy. 1. It *blinded him to actual facts.* It was true that David had slain "his ten thousands," as compared with Saul's "thousands;" but to the envious eye this was as though it were not. Its reality must not be tolerated. The Pharisees in like manner were wilfully blind to the fact that Christ *had* opened the eyes of the blind. 2. It *led to the imputation of base motives.* He at once charged David with readiness for treasonous designs on the kingdom. The pure man was deemed impure. This is the common practice of narrow and base men, as appeared in the instance of Joseph (Gen. xxxvii. 8, 11), and of Christ (John vii. 20). 3. It *made himself perfectly wretched.* His life lost all joy and hope, and suspicion and fear entered in. And whoever falls into this sin finds that it slayeth him (Job v. 2), and is as rottenness to the bones (Prov. xiv. 30). 4. It *impelled to deeds of blood.* The thrust of the javelin was virtual murder. The same process wrought in the heart of Cain, of the scribes and Pharisees (Matt. xxvii. 18; Mark xv. 10), and is active in many who are guilty of no overt act (1 John iii. 15). The dark thoughts, the unspoken intents of envious minds; who shall declare them? How true it is that he who hardeneth his heart, not bowing in true penitence, submissive to all God's judgments, falleth into mischief (Prov. xxviii. 14) again and again, till at last he is destroyed suddenly and without remedy (Prov. xxix. 1; cf. 1 Sam. xxxi. 3, 4).

General lessons:—1. All human judgments on the course of Providence are to be discounted in so far as sin is cherished in the life. 2. The key to the future of the individual and national life is to be sought in moral conditions 3. It is important that the popular mind should be trained to estimate things in their moral relations. 4. Christians should strive to be entirely free from the spirit of envy, both in relation to worldly prosperity and to position in the Church of God (Ps. xxxvii. 1; 1 Cor. xiii. 4; 1 Pet. ii. 1). 5. In so far as we indulge in any envy we lay ourselves open to temptations to further sins.

Vers. 12—16.—*The disturbing power of goodness.* The facts are—1. Saul, seeing the signs of God's presence with David, fears him, and removes him to a distance. 2. Increasing wisdom of David adds to Saul's fear, and secures the favour of the people. 3. The departure of God from Saul explains his self-abandonment to the influence of this fear. We have here a statement of the diverse relation of God to

David and Saul,—he was with the one and was departed from the other,—and the consequences ensuing thereon in their respective lives. Each man made his own position, and was answerable for the state he was in and attained to; nevertheless, the presence and absence of God accounted for much. Thus, also, we have the diverse effect of the same wise and holy life upon different persons—the diversity arising from the moral condition of the persons acted upon.

I. The RELATION OF GOD TO MAN IS NOT IN EVERY INSTANCE THE SAME. There are certain natural relationships which God sustains to all men, in all time, irrespective of their character. His power upholds them in life; his equitable rulership is never withdrawn. All this was true in reference to David and Saul, while it was equally true that God was to the one what he was not to the other. There was the relation of moral nearness and support to David, and of moral abandonment and disapproval to Saul. The Lord "knoweth the way of the righteous" (Ps. i. 6). His delight is in his people (Ps. xxii. 8). "The proud he knoweth afar off" (Ps. cxxxviii. 6), and is "angry with the wicked every day" (Ps. vii. 11). The effects of moral nearness and support are seen in the instance of David:—piety was sustained and rendered beautiful in development; abilities, under such favouring influences, were more fully and evenly exercised; the vision being cleared, practical sagacity found wider scope; and the Divine energy acting everywhere in harmony with moral ends, opportunities would be created for usefulness, and the minds of men disposed to favour. On the other hand, moral nearness and support being wanting to Saul, the evils long cherished found more unrestrained exercise; conscience became more remorseful; natural abilities were impaired in their development, and foolish deeds became habitual.

II. The DIVERSE RELATION OF GOD TO MAN ARISES FROM MAN'S PREVIOUS CONDUCT. The recent history of David shows that from a youth he had quietly and consistently followed the measure of light vouchsafed to him; while Saul's course reveals a deliberate and persistent preference of his own will to the revealed will of God. Grace was added to valued grace. Light disregarded had become darkness. In this diverse consequence there is nothing unusual. It is the New Testament law that "to him that hath shall be given, and from him that hath not shall be taken away even that he hath" (Matt. xiii. 12; Hosea xi. 8; Luke xix. 42; John xii. 35—40; 1 Tim. iv. 8).

III. A RECOGNITION OF THE DIVERSE RELATION OF GOD TO MAN IS AN OCCASION OF TROUBLE TO THE DELIBERATELY WICKED. While David won the affection of the mass of the people, his name and presence were disturbing to Saul. "Saul was afraid of David, because the Lord was with him, and was departed from Saul." The reasons for this effect on Saul are obvious. David's holy life and glorying in the name of the Lord (ch. xvii. 45—47) revealed by contrast the spiritual condition of Saul to himself; and, being destitute of the spirit of repentance, he trembled under the silent rebuke. There was also a reminder of joys and privileges once within reach, but now gone for ever; and he could not but associate the rising character of David with the predicted doom of his own monarchy. It is a well-known fact that *goodness does exercise a disturbing influence in the domain of sin.* Goodness in its own nature is a repellant power. It creates a commotion whenever it enters the realms of darkness. The powers of evil know it as their natural foe, and quail in consciousness of its predestined triumph. There appears to have been fear and excitement among the evil spirits when the holy Saviour drew near to their sphere of influence on earth (Matt. iv. 1—11; xvi. 18; Mark v. 7; Luke xxii. 53; Col. ii. 15). While the natural effect of embodied goodness on minds not bent on sin is to soothe, to cheer, and to gladden, as when Christ drew near to the poor and needy, the sick and penitent, and as we all feel when a very wise and holy man enters a home or a sick chamber, yet the effect is the reverse when sin is being deliberately practised. It is in this way that we may understand Herod's fear on mention of the name of John, Ahab's fear of Elijah, and the evident uneasiness of scribes and Pharisees at the presence of Christ.

General lessons :—1. We see the value to the ordinary affairs of life of a consciousness of the favour of God (Ps. xxx.). 2. The development of our powers is intimately connected with our faithfulness in spiritual things. 3. In proportion as we attain to true holiness of life will the power of our presence and actions be recognised. 4. We must expect the actual antagonism of those who have rejected God in so far as we come into contact with them, but this should be regarded as proof of the truth of our religion.

Vers. 17—30.—*The plot and its lessons.* The facts are—1. Saul, in hopes of compassing the death of David, promises him his eldest daughter to wife, on condition that he is valiant against the Philistines. 2. David expresses his unworthiness of so great an honour. 3. Saul, having broken this promise by giving Merab to Adriel, offers David his daughter Michal. 4. On David intimating that, being poor, he was not able to provide a becoming dowry, Saul is content with proof of the death of a hundred enemies of Israel. 5. David presents double the number required, and takes Michal to wife. 6. In spite of his devices, Saul sees the growing prosperity of David, and becomes more than ever afraid of him. This section further unfolds, on the one side, the downward progress of the man who has wilfully sinned under circumstances favourable to obedience, and has consequently been left to the tendencies of his impenitent heart; and, on the other side, the steady advance in wisdom and aptitude for affairs of the man who gloried only in the " name of the Lord of hosts." The narrative relates events as they appeared to observers at the time, and introduces statements of the sacred historian designed to indicate how those events were regarded by God. The outward acts are connected with the hidden motive, and so made to bear their proper moral character.

I. THE CHARACTERISTICS OF THE PLOT. Did we not know Saul's entire history, there is much in the narrative of this section which might suggest to a casual reader no thought of a plot. The addition of statements unveiling the hidden purpose of his words and deeds changes the moral bearing of the whole, and sets forth the triple characteristics of the plot. 1. *Cleverness.* It is said that insane persons often display unusual cunning and skill in compassing their ends; and also the " devices " of the wicked, both in relation to God and to man, are in Scripture proverbial (Job v. 12; Ps. x. 2; xxxiii. 10). The incipient madness and settled wickedness of Saul at this period of his life indicate the truth of these remarks; for consider the plausibility of his conduct. (1) There was a *fair appearance of truthfulness.* He had virtually promised his daughter to the man who should slay Goliath (ch. xvii. 25). To keep one's word was becoming a king and due to a youthful hero. (2) There was an *obvious display of magnanimity.* For the recent violent attempt on the life of David (ver. 11) must have produced an impression of injustice on both David and the people. What then more proper than that a fit of unreasonable anger should be followed by some expression of the wrong done, and some effort to render compensation. (3) *Religious feeling was conspicuous.* Had not David appeared on the arena to fight the battle of the Lord? (ch. xvii. 47). Was it not proper, after the signal victory in the Lord's name, that the king should recognise the conflict with the heathen oppressor in its theocratic aspect, and encourage the valiant youth still to go forth in the same holy name? (4) *Personal interest was natural.* Saul's instructions to the courtiers to endeavour to induce David to accept of Michal had an appearance of naturalness, as it was important to honour so able a man and to ally him with the interests of the monarchy, as also to remove any chagrin on account of Merab having been given, probably for state reasons, to Adriel. (5) There was a *kindly consideration for David's position.* A sense of poverty is hard to bear when it stands in the way to honour and influence. David felt that, despite his services, he was too poor to comply with custom in offering as dowry what became a suitor to a king's daughter. It was, therefore, very thoughtful on the part of Saul to ask as dowry what certainly few men could provide, but what the conqueror of Goliath would, no doubt, readily and with increasing honours secure. A kindly, considerate bearing disarms suspicion. The plot was clever, like all the plots whereby our great adversary, the devil, seeks to ensnare the innocent. A parallel might be developed without much difficulty. 2. *Vileness.* The cleverness is discovered by tracing the course apparent to men; the vileness by the light thrown upon that course by the Searcher of hearts. We are enabled to look beneath the surface, and to estimate words and deeds by their relation to motive. The vileness is seen in—(1) The *deliberate intent to commit murder.* The whole procedure originated in a determination to insure David's death. Blood was shed in intent. The true universe is the unseen, for it is enduring. In that sphere Saul slew, before the clear, searching eye of God, the best friend he ever had next to Samuel. (2) The *covering of murderous intent, with professions of kindness and esteem.* Open hostility is bad enough in an evil cause, but to play the hypocrite for compassing a cruel purpose is the blackest of crimes (Ps. x. 7). To be clothed as an angel of light is not confined to Satan. (3) The *attempt to make Providence subservient to a secret intent.* Saul dare not lay hands on David, but he dare lay a train of circumstances by which Providence should be charged with doing what all men would deplore except himself. Man would make God the servant of his vile designs. Cowards wish Providence to do what they have not the courage to avow. 3. *Foolishness.* It is no uncommon thing for the cunning and skill of the wicked to turn out the veriest foolishness. Such is the force of right and justice, that wicked wisdom is always found in the issue to be mad folly. That it was so in this case is seen by observing—(1) God *knew all from the first.* It is a proof of the utter stupidity of the sinful heart that it acts as though God were not. This unreasonableness enters into all sin. The wicked heart retires into its own darkness, and says, " He will never see it " (Ps. x. 11). (2) The plot *secured to David the special protection promised to the innocent.* God pledges his care to the poor and needy when they walk in innocency. He " saveth the upright in heart " (Ps. vii. 10). The "needy shall not alway be forgotten " (Ps. ix. 18 ; xxxvii. 32, 33). Saul ought to have known that a holy man, one who had been blessed in conflict, would not be left to himself in the day of danger. (3) It *issued in David's advantage.* Saul really fell into a pit prepared for another. The man who was to be put down rose higher, while Saul himself sank in the esteem of all. The scheme brought out in clear and beautiful form David's personal integrity (vers. 18, 23). Its issue gave him greater influence with Israel (ver. 30). He became a greater terror to his enemies (ver. 27), and his marriage with Michal subsequently proved a great help in escaping the snares of Saul (ver. 21 ; cf. xix. 12).

II. THE GENERAL TRUTHS IT TEACHES. Among the many truths set forth in the plot of Saul and escape of David, the following may be specially noticed:—1. The *moral value of conduct is seen when the light of God shines on it.* Saul's conduct, as watched by casual observers ignorant of the secret between him and Samuel (ch. xv. 26—28, 30), would have attached to it a moral value quite inconsistent with real truth. It is the light which God enabled the historian to pour on the inner motive that reveals the whole as vile. Our estimate of conduct is necessarily approximate. A measure of doubt or suspense attends our judgments of character. There is no principle more clearly held than that the secret intent, the private, unexpressed, and often inexpressible motive, is the real determinant of moral character in actions. Yet such are the depths and intricacies of human thought and feeling, that every man is largely an unknown being to his fellows. This uncertainty creates a belief in a future manifestation of character, when every man shall receive from all exactly his due. Otherwise justice is defeated, and moral worth is cheated of its honour. Scripture assures us of the truth that the day will come when the true spring of conduct shall be manifested ; the inner real man will be known. The day is coming on when men shall see themselves and others in that all-revealing light (Eccles. xii. 14; Matt. x. 26; xxv. 31, 32). Hence the good cheer of the upright in heart whose actions are misinterpreted, whose position is obscure, who suffer from the scorning of the proud, and whose outward success in life is not commensurate with the largeness and purity of their desires. Hence, also, the warning for those who cover up a defiled heart beneath an attractive exterior. 2. *Integrity is the best human defence against wicked craft.* The manifest integrity of David in all his relations to Saul and the people was better to him than all possible contrivances to cunningly checkmate the movements of his enemy. There was a moral power in his blameless, unaffected conduct which caused his secret foe to dwell in fear. Looking back on this period, he could say, " I have walked in mine integrity " (Ps. xxvi. 1) ; and doubtless, knowing the value of such defence in the past, he could say, in view of future dangers, " Let integrity and uprightness preserve me " (Ps. xxv. 21). It is ever so. As simple truth is mightier than all ramifications of falsehood, so an upright heart, an innocent life, is, in the issue, more than a match for all cunning combinations of evil. Were men more simple in purpose, less given to mere policy, keeping their hearts free from petty jealousies and ambitions, their foot would be less often caught in a snare, and their reputation would take care of itself. 3. God *takes care of his faithful servants who have a work to do in the world.* David's innocence was an object of interest to God, and received his protection; but David was a chosen servant in course of unconscious preparation for high and important duties. He, therefore, was cared for by God in the midst of unknown dangers. Nor was there anything exceptional in this, for such is the heritage of all who fear the Lord. Bodily suffering, and even death, may come on the innocent and true, but these are not the worst of evils. There is a more fearful fall; and in this respect, such is the care of God, that though a thousand fall at the side of the faithful, the great spiritual evil does not touch him (Ps. xci. 7, 14). Every one has a charmed life in Christ's service as long as his work is not finished. No weapon formed against David could prosper before he became king. No power was allowed to take away our Saviour's life till he had finished the work the Father gave him to do. No stones and lying in wait of wicked men were of any avail against Paul before he had preached the gospel to the Gentiles (Acts ix. 15, 23, 24; 2 Cor. xi. 24—27). 4. The *ulterior object of a sinful course is never attained.* One object of Saul's cunning was to get rid of David. History tells us how this object was frustrated. The Lord was with David. Disappointment, vexation, intenser misery were the result to Saul. It is not too wide an assertion to affirm that the ulterior object is never attained in a sinful course. A careful analysis of the workings of sin in every instance will show that the end in view is to secure a pleasure deemed greater and more welcome than any supposed to result from obedience to God's will. If sin in its origin be self-assertion, as against conformity to a supreme will, the object in view is evidently to attain to a state of being superior to that involved in conformity. It seeks a rise, and, behold, it is itself a *fall*. It is always self-defeated. This can be shown to be true of all who wilfully refuse to have rest in God—they miss the bliss they sought in rebellion; of all who prefer to be saved by other means than by the one Mediator—they never attain to the pardon and purity which alone constitute salvation; of all who sacrifice Christian principle to acquire wealth or power—they get the wealth and power, but not the satisfaction of soul which their possession was believed to insure. It cannot be insisted on too strongly, that not only is sin essentially evil and degrading, however fascinating its form, but is also in its issue a bitter disappointment. "He that sinneth against me wrongeth his own soul" (Prov. viii. 36). The desire, the expectation, the way of the wicked "*shall perish*" (Ps. i. 6; cxii. 10; Prov. x. 28). 5. *Exalted piety and simplicity of life are consistent with pre-eminence in secular affairs.* It is often supposed that a very pious man, and one of simple purpose in life, cannot compete with men less spiritual in character. The language of Christians has sometimes given sanction to this belief. But facts and reason are against it. David, the most pious of men, attained to a capacity for affairs far in advance of others (ver. 30). Newton was not a worse mathematician and astronomer for his deep and simple piety. It is reasonable that a mind pure, devout, calm in sense of God's favour, free from the distraction induced by waywardness of will, and enjoying the promised blessing of God, should, when called by Providence to any sphere of activity, excel those of equal natural powers, but destitute of the spiritual tone. If such men do not attain to highest public stations, it may be because Providence has other work for them to do; or if only a few rise to pre-eminence, it may be because the combination of great piety and great natural aptitude for special pursuits is rare.

HOMILIES BY VARIOUS AUTHORS.

Vers. 1—30. (GIBEAH.)—*David's life at court.* On his victory over Goliath, David was conducted by Abner (ch. xiv. 50) into the presence of Saul, "with the head of the Philistine in his hand." He appears to have been unrecognised by the king, perhaps because of the alteration that had taken place in his personal appearance. Henceforth he resided at Gibeah (ver. 2), where he remained for two or three years. The court of Saul, while unlike that of Solomon, half a century later, was not destitute of worldly show, and was marked by the obsequiousness, self-seeking, emulation, and intrigue which too often prevail in such places, especially when the monarch is capricious, proud, and without the fear of God (ch. xxii. 6, 7). David's connection with it was of great importance in relation to the position which he was destined by Divine providence to occupy; continued his education for it; and afforded (as every promotion to high place does in its measure) a wider scope for—

I. THE EXERCISE OF ABILITY. 1. Outward circumstances, though they may not create eminent ability, serve to *call it forth.* Much excellence doubtless exists, but is never displayed on account of the absence of favourable conditions. 2. Great genius is shown in one who has the *faculty of adapting himself* to varied positions in life and their varied requirements. 3. The proper use of power *strengthens it* and develops it to perfection. 4. The humble, faithful, and efficient discharge of duty in one position *prepares the way* for another and a higher. It was thus with David, who passed from the narrow circle of private life to the wider one of public life, from the sheepfold to the palace, from contending against a lion and a bear to military expeditions (vers. 5, 13, 30) against the enemies of Israel, and ultimately from loyal obedience to royal rule.

II. ACQUAINTANCE WITH MEN, and the knowledge of human nature. David was familiar with "fields, and flocks, and silent stars," but needed training in another school. 1. There are few things more *valuable* than an accurate and extensive knowledge of men: their divers temperaments, tendencies, and capacities; their peculiar excellences and defects; their varied wishes and aims; and underneath all the great principles of humanity that are the same in all. 2. Some circumstances afford *special opportunity* for the attainment of such knowledge. What a field of observation were the court and camp of Saul to one of such mental activity and profound insight as David! 3. The knowledge of men produces in the heart that is sincere, devout, and acquainted with itself a *large sympathy* with them in their sorrows, joys, imperfections, and strivings after higher things. Of this sympathy the psalms of David are a wonderful expression. 4. It is necessary to the knowledge of the most *effectual methods of dealing with them*—one of the most needful and desirable qualifications in a ruler.

III. THE TRIAL OF PRINCIPLE. David, no less than Saul, must be put to the test, and his fidelity to Jehovah tried as silver "in a furnace of earth." 1. Trial is *needful* to prove the reality of principle, and manifest its strength and brightness. 2. One trial is often *followed by another* and a greater. The royal favour into which David was suddenly raised was as suddenly succeeded by royal jealousy, hatred, and craft. Surely no man was ever more fiercely assailed by temptation. 3. When endured aright, in faith and obedience, trial, however painful, is *morally beneficial.* 4. The victory which is gained over one temptation is an *earnest* of a victory over the next. The triumph of humility in David was followed by that of simplicity, patience, and forbearance.

IV. ADVANCEMENT IN POPULAR FAVOUR (vers. 7, 16, 30), which, in the case of David, paved his way to the throne; though he neither coveted nor, during the life of Saul, put forth any effort to gain that object. 1. A course of wise and prosperous action, as it well deserves, so it *generally obtains* the approbation of the people. 2. Such a course of action ought to be aimed at, rather than the popular favour with which it is attended. 3. The favour of the people is to be valued only in *subordination* to the favour of God, and in so far as it accords with it. 4. Popular favour should be regarded not as an end in itself, but as a *means* of promoting the Divine glory and human welfare.—D.

Vers. 1—4. (GIBEAH.)—*True friendship.* (*References:*—ch. xix. 1—5; xx. 1—23; xxiii. 16—18.) 1. Friendship is a mutual affection between persons of congenial minds, arising out of their esteem for each other's excellence, and expressing itself in kindly offices. Attachment to kindred is in some respects surpassed by that which is felt towards the friend "who is even as thine own soul" (Deut. xiii. 6). In allusion to it "Abraham was called the friend of God" (2 Chron. xx. 7; Isa. xli. 8; James ii. 23)—possibly in the first instance by God himself; and "God spake to

Moses as a man to his friend" (Exod. xxxiii. 11). The Book of Proverbs abounds in statements concerning the worth and claims of friendship (Prov. xvii. 17; xviii. 24; xxvii. 6, 9, 10, 17). And Jesus said to his disciples, "I have called you friends" (John xv. 15). 2. Much that is usually called friendship is not worthy of the name. "There are three things that engender friendship—profit, pleasure, virtue. The first two do not beget true friendship, for as soon as the profit or pleasure ceaseth, friendship is gone; but virtue only maketh love and friendship to continue" (Willet). 3. The *true friendship* which subsisted between Jonathan and David "shines for all ages an eternal type." It is "the first Biblical instance of such a dear companionship as was common in Greece, and has been since in Christendom imitated, but never surpassed, in modern works of fiction" (Stanley). The most celebrated of the instances referred to were those of Orestes and Pylades, Damon and Pythias, Nisus and Euryalus. 4. The friendship of Jonathan toward David (the *formation* of which is here described) was Divinely provided as a means of guarding the life of the latter from the attacks of Saul, and of preserving his loyalty to the king and his faith in God. "Thy love to me was wonderful" (2 Sam. i. 26). On the other hand, that of David toward Jonathan exerted an elevating and sanctifying influence upon him. Of true friendship observe that—

I. IT EXISTS ONLY IN NOBLE SOULS. Both Jonathan and David were virtuous, generous, and devout. They were one in "the love of virtue and the fear of God." Persons destitute of these principles can neither esteem the excellence of others nor be esteemed for their own. "We are so formed by nature that there should be a certain social tie among all; stronger, however, as each approaches each. Now friendship is nothing else than a complete union of feeling on all subjects, Divine and human, accompanied by a kindly feeling and attachment. The entire strength of friendship consists in an entire agreement of inclinations, pursuits, and sentiments" (Cicero, 'On Friendship').

> "A generous friendship no cold medium knows,
> Burns with one love, with one resentment glows" (Homer).

"A *good* man is the best friend, and therefore soonest to be chosen, longest to be retained, and, indeed, never to be parted with, unless he ceases to be that for which he was chosen" (Jer. Taylor).

II. IT IS FOUNDED UPON MUTUAL ESTEEM. When David "had made an end of speaking unto Saul," in which he doubtless said much more than is recorded, the soul of Jonathan "was knit (linked or chained) with the soul of David," &c. (ver. 1). Nothing is said of Jonathan at the time of David's conflict with Goliath. He may have been absent; or, if present, not permitted to risk his life in the encounter. Perhaps his faith and courage were not strong enough. But "he loved that which went beyond his own spirit, yet was of the same heroic order. He saw in David a higher and greater Jonathan, the ideal of his own actual life, himself transfigured and perfected. What he had dreamt he might be he beheld in David" (B. Kent). He admired the faith, courage, modesty, and moral excellence which lay beneath the "outward appearance." "Now they are worthy of friendship in whom there exists a reason why they should be loved; a rare class, for in truth all that is excellent is rare" (Cicero).

III. IT CONSISTS OF DISINTERESTED AFFECTION. "Jonathan loved him as his own soul" (vers. 1, 3; ch. xx. 17); with the same kind and the same measure of affection. Hence the sympathy, generosity, fidelity, and constancy which he displayed. A friend is "another self." "Though judgment must collect the materials of the goodly structure of friendship, it is affection that gives the cement" (Melmoth). "It really seems to consist in loving rather than being loved. It is the wishing a person what we think good for his sake, and not for our own, and, as far as is in our power, the exerting ourselves to procure it. And a friend is he who entertains and meets a return of this feeling" (Aristotle, 'Ethics,' viii.; 'Rhetoric,' ii.). "I hope I do not break the fifth commandment if I conceive I may love my friends before the nearest of my blood, even those to whom I owe the principles of life. I have loved my friend as I do virtue, my soul, my God" (Sir T. Browne, 'Religio Medici').

IV. IT UNITES IN A STEADFAST BOND. Knit—sincerely, closely, firmly joined, grappled together "as with hooks of steel." "A friend loveth at all times," in adversity as well as in prosperity; and his friendship endures the strain caused by conflicting interests, misrepresentation, and many imperfections; it may even be said to be "one soul dwelling in two bodies." "Now the foundation of that steadfastness and constancy which we seek in friendship is *sincerity;* for nothing is steadfast which is insincere" (Cicero). "Friendship founded on worldly principles is natural, and, though composed of the best elements of nature, is not exempt from its mutability and frailty; but friendship founded on religion is spiritual, and therefore unchanging and imperishable" (R. Hall, 'Works,' v.).

V. IT IS CONFIRMED BY A SOLEMN COMPACT. "And Jonathan and David made a covenant," &c. (ver. 3; ch. xx. 16, 17). In it they gave and received assurance of affection, agreed to be faithful to each other under all circumstances, and called the Lord in whom they trusted to be witness between them; to it they were impelled by the strength of their love and "a loftier necessity of finding and loving in one another, if possible in a yet higher degree, the purely Divine power already felt within, and thus mutually living under its influence" (Ewald); and by it their friendship was rendered sacred and strong and permanently established. In times when "the love of many waxes cold and iniquity abounds," men of a common faith and love toward God do well to draw closely together and strengthen each other's hearts and hands by sacred vows.

VI. IT IS MANIFESTED IN GENEROUS GIFTS. "And Jonathan stripped himself of the robe that was upon him," &c. (ver. 4). He gave him what best expressed the gift of himself, and what would continually remind David of his friend and increase his confidence and love. It was little that David could give him in return of an outward kind, but he gave him confidence for confidence, love for love, life for life. Friendship is practical, self-sacrificing, and helpful, and gives of its best. "David is seen in Jonathan's clothes that we may take notice he is Jonathan's second self. Our Lord Jesus Christ has thus showed his love to us, that he stripped himself to clothe us, humbled himself to enrich us. Nay, he did more than Jonathan—he clothed himself with our rags, whereas Jonathan did not put on David's" (M. Henry).

Exhortation:—1. Seek friendship only among the wise and good. If you would have a true friend, make a friend of him who is a friend of God. 2. Strive to be as worthy of the friendship of the good as David was of the friendship of Jonathan. 3. Be as sincere and faithful to your friend as Jonathan was to David. 4. Value the friendship of Christ beyond all other.—D.

Ver. 4.—*Divine friendship.* "He loved him as his own soul" (ver. 3). Human friendship is a shadow of Divine. The greatest and best Friend is God in Christ Jesus. Happy is every one who can say from the heart, "This is my beloved, and this is my friend" (Song of Sol. v. 16). Consider—

I. ITS CONDITIONS, on the part of man. 1. *Rationality:* capacity of thought, voluntary choice, moral esteem. "Amidst the ashes of our collapsed nature there slumber certain sparks of celestial fire" (Owen). 2. *Reconciliation;* inasmuch as man is alienated from God, and under condemnation. 3. *Renewal* in righteousness and true holiness, so that we may be "partakers of the Divine nature" (2 Pet. i. 4). "Friendship is a union of souls, and souls can be united only where there is more or less accord" (Amos iii. 3).

II. ITS CHARACTERISTICS, on the part of the Lord. All his perfections render it in every respect transcendently excellent. But notice more particularly — 1. *Its disinterestedness.* "He first loved us," with a pure, free, condescending, self-sacrificing love. "Greater love hath no man," &c. (John xv. 13). 2. *Its faithfulness.* 3. *Its constancy.* "The love of friends of this world is defective in three respects—they begin to love late, cease early, love little. But the love of God is an unequalled love. He loves us without beginning, without intermission, and without end" (Nouet).

III. ITS BENEFITS, or the blessings enjoyed by those who have fellowship with him. 1. *Counsel,* warning, rebuke. Reproofs are "the graver looks of love." 2

Defence, support, and effectual help. 3. *Sympathy,* encouragement, and everlasting consolation. "And now," said Jonathan Edwards, on his death-bed, turning from his earthly friends toward the approaching darkness, "where is Jesus of Nazareth, my true and never-failing Friend ?"

IV. ITS CLAIMS, or the duties of those who enjoy such benefits and desire their continuance. 1. To cherish proper feelings toward him—confidence, affection, and delight in intercourse with him. 2. To do those things that please him. "Ye are my friends if ye do whatsoever I command you." 3. Not to be ashamed of him, but to confess his name before men ; to love and serve his friends for his sake, and to seek in all things his honour and glory.—D.

Vers. 6—16. (GIBEAH.)—*Envy.* "And Saul eyed David from that day forward" (ver. 9). How extraordinary are the moral contrasts which are often presented in human life! The friendship of Jonathan here stands in opposition to the envy of Saul. Hardly had David experienced the one before he was exposed to the other. "His victory had a double issue, Jonathan's love and Saul's envy, which God so mixed that the one was a remedy of the other." (Hall). On the day of public rejoicing the seeds of jealousy, envy, and hatred were sown in his heart. He eyed David not with favour, as before, but with dislike on account of the honour given to him beyond himself. The general suspicion which he entertained in consequence of the intimations of Samuel concerning his successor also seems to have fastened on him as the man ; and henceforth he looked upon him as a dangerous rival. "Mingling with his constitutional malady, it poisoned his whole future relations with David." Of *envy* notice that—

I. IT TAKES ROOT IN AN EVIL HEART. In the case of Saul the soil was congenial and ready prepared by—1. *Alienation* from God and conviction of his disfavour. 2. *Selfishness* and morbid concentration of thought upon himself. 3. *Self-will,* pride, and worldly ambition, still continuing and increasing. 4. *Wrathful passion.* He "was very wroth, and the saying displeased him" (ver. 8). "He who is apt to feel indignation, feels pain at those who are undeservedly successful ; but the envious man, going beyond him, feels pain at every one's success" (Aristotle, 'Ethics').

II. IT GROWS IN THE SHADE OF ANOTHER'S PRE-EMINENCE in—1. *Popular estimation.* "They have ascribed unto David ten thousands," &c. (ver. 8). "What properly occasions envy is the *fruit* of the accomplishments of others ; the pre-eminence which the opinion of the world bestows, or which we dread it will bestow, on their talents above ours" (Blair). 2. *Successful achievements,* from which such preference proceeds. "The bright day brings out the adder." Prosperity is generally attended by envy. 3. *Personal excellences.* David "behaved himself wisely" (ver. 5) ; "very wisely" (ver. 15) ; "more wisely than all" (ver. 30). He acted prudently, cautiously, skilfully, and therefore prosperously.

"Base envy withers at another's joy,
And hates the excellence it cannot reach" (Thomson).

4. *Divine approbation,* which appears in prosperous enterprises. "And Saul was afraid of David, *because* the Lord was with him," &c. (ver. 12). "And Cain was very wroth," &c. (Gen. iv. 5 ; 1 John iii. 2). The envy felt at the favour shown to another by God is peculiarly criminal, because of its opposition to God himself.

III. IT IS MARKED BY MANY ODIOUS FEATURES. 1. *Unreasonableness.* 2. In most cases *ingratitude.* David had conferred a great benefit on Saul and Israel by his victory over Goliath ; he "went out whithersoever Saul sent him," and fought his battles ; and often soothed his melancholy with the music of his harp (ver. 10). 3. *Injustice.* He did him "shame" (ch. xx. 34) by entertaining suspicions of his loyalty and treating him as a traitor. 4. *Ungodliness* and all uncharitableness. "Charity envieth not." "Envy is the worst of all passions, and feedeth upon the spirits, and they again upon the body ; and so much the more because it is perpetual, and, as it is said, keepeth no holidays" (Bacon, 'Essays').

IV. IT IS PRODUCTIVE OF MUCH DEADLY FRUIT, in relation both to others (Prov. xxvii. 4) and to the envious man himself (Prov. xiv. 30) ; partly of *hatred* and partly of *grief*. "As it shows itself in hatred it strikes at the person envied; but as it affects a man in the nature of grief it recoils and does execution upon the envier. It lies at the heart like a worm, always gnawing and corroding and piercing it with a secret, invisible sting and poison" (South, 'Sermons,' lviii.). In Saul it produced unrest of soul, increased subjection to the power of evil—"it came to pass *on the morrow*," &c. (ver. 10); ungovernable rage—"he poised the javelin" twice; craft and hypocrisy; fear (vers. 11, 15); continual enmity (ver. 21); deliberate avowal of murderous intentions (ch. xix. 1); open and unceasing persecution; despair and self-destruction. "When in the last judgment envy is placed at the bar of God, what an indictment will be laid against the evil spirit! The insulting anger of Eliab, the cruelty of Joseph's brethren, the murderous wrath of Cain, and the greatest share in the greatest crime in the world—the crucifying of the Lord of glory—will be charged upon him. To cast this demon out of our bosoms before that final condemnation is one purpose of Jesus, and with all our hearts we should pray for his complete and speedy victory" (C. Vince).

Conclusion :—In order to the cure or prevention of this evil passion, seek a renewed heart; dwell much on the Divine love "that spurns all envying in its bounty;" estimate aright temporal advantages; entertain lowly thoughts of self; learn to admire excellence in others, and regard it as if it were your own; check the first impulse of jealous or envious feeling; and "commit thy way unto the Lord."

> "O man! why place thy heart where there doth need
> Exclusion of participants in good?
> > Heaven calls,
> And, round about you wheeling, courts your gaze
> With everlasting beauties. Yet your eye
> Turns with fond doting still upon the earth.
> Therefore he smites you who discerneth all" (Dante, 'Purg.' xiv.).—D.

Vers. 17—30. (GIBEAH.)—*Simplicity*. There is a simplicity which springs from ignorance, and is displayed in folly and presumption (Prov. xxii. 3). There is also a simplicity which is the fruit of innocence, truthfulness, and goodness, and appears in an ingenuous mind, a guileless disposition, and straightforward speech and conduct. In its best sense (*simplicitas*—without fold or twist) it is opposed to duplicity, deception, and "cunning craftiness" (Rom. xii. 8; xvi. 19; 2 Cor. i. 12; xi. 3); and it was exemplified, in an eminent degree, by David, especially in his earlier intercourse with Saul; for, through familiarity with court life, and much more in consequence of the straits to which he was reduced by the craft and persecution of the king, the simple-minded, open-hearted shepherd youth once and again turned aside from the right path (ch. xxi. 2). Consider simplicity as—

I. BESET BY THE WORKING OF CRAFT. Having given way to envy, and in a violent fit of madness threatened the life of David, Saul continued to hate and fear him (Mark xi. 18), and sought to get rid of him, though indirectly from restraint of conscience and secretly from fear of the people (Mark vi. 20; Luke xxii. 2). Sin works in the dark. Malicious craft often—1. Seeks to accomplish *ends* which it may not dare to avow. Springing from jealousy for personal position and renown, it aims at the depreciation of every one by whom they seem to be endangered; and at his removal, whether accidentally by the hands of others, or by his committing some overt act which may justify his open punishment (vers. 17, 21, 25). And toward these ends it works with ever greater directness and less concealment; for that which is hidden in the heart must sooner or later come to light. 2. Makes use of *fair professions*, and uses pretexts which are specious, false, and hypocritical. David was assured that no harm was really meant him, and made "captain over a thousand" (ver. 13); whereas he was removed from the presence of the king because he was hated and feared, and that he might be exposed to greater danger. His not receiving the fulfilment of Saul's promise (ch. xvii. 25) was probably accounted for by his lack of wealth and social status (ver. 25); but the promise was repeated insincerely. "Only be thou *valiant for me*" (expose thyself to every hazard), "and *fight the Lord's battles*" (with zeal for Jehovah, which I know thou hast), and (*sub voce*) "let not my hand be upon him," &c. (ver. 17). On the loss of Merab he was consoled by the promise of Michal (ver. 21), but only as "a snare," and her love was made use of for the purpose. And at length (when the king had formed his plan, and felt sure of its success), he was told by his servants (as if in confidential communication), "Behold, the king hath delight in thee," &c. (ver. 22), "desireth not any dowry," &c. (ver. 25) ; "but Saul thought to make David fall by the hand of the Philistines." 3. Adopts *means* which are unworthy, base, and godless. Scheming, plotting, murderous attempts on life under the sanctities of affection and religion ; at heart, infatuated opposition to the will of God. If it were not the Divine purpose that David should be king, why fear him ? if it were, of what avail would resistance be ?

II. Displayed in the midst of craft. The snares that were woven around David seem plain enough to us ; but there is no reason to suppose that they were at first observed by him. The simple-hearted man—1. Is accustomed to *look upon others as sincere* like himself, regards their statements and assurances as truthful, and is slow to suspect their evil intentions. Even to the last David could hardly believe that Saul, of his own accord, sought his life (ch. xxvi. 19). He is "simple concerning evil." Large experience makes men cautious ; but it is better to be deceived a hundred times than to lead a life of continual suspicion. 2. Entertains modest and *lowly views of himself*, takes contempt and disappointment without complaint, and accepts humbly and cheerfully whatever honour may be conferred upon him (vers. 18, 23). "Seekest thou great things for thyself? seek them not" (Jer. xlv. 5). "A pious man is even in prosperity humble in heart." 3. Is intent upon the honest, faithful, and efficient *discharge of the duty* that lies before him, and fears danger little because he fears God much (vers. 5, 14, 27). "David's calm indifference to outward circumstances affecting himself were very strikingly expressed in his conduct. Partly from his poetic temperament, partly from his sweet, natural unselfishness, and chiefly from his loving trust in God, he accepts whatever happens with equanimity, and makes no effort to alter it" (Maclaren). It has been remarked that "*genius* is simply the carrying into the maturity of our powers the simplicity and ardour of childhood."

III. Preserved from the devices of craft. It is the best means of preservation, inasmuch as—1. It affords the *least occasion* for an adversary to take an advantage. Although the ingenuous man may appear to lie open to attack, yet he is really most effectually guarded against it. 2. It attracts the *respect* of other men (ver. 16), gains the love of those who warn and help him (ver. 28 ; ch. xix. 11), and makes it difficult for his enemies to prevail over him. 3. It insures the *favour of God.* "The Lord was with him" (vers. 12, 14, 28) to guide, defend, and help him (Ps. xxxvii. 24, 33). "In thee do I trust."

IV. Resulting in an end opposed to that of craft. 1. Instead of returning no more from the conflict, he returns in triumph, and receives an unwilling honour from the hand that was lifted up against him (vers. 27, 28 ; Rev. iii. 9). 2. Instead of being less an object of terror to the wicked, he is more so (ver. 29). 3. Instead of being deprived of the love of the people of God (ver. 16: "All Israel and Judah loved David"), he is more completely enthroned in their hearts (ver. 30).

Remark—1. How ineffectual are the devices of the wicked against "the upright in heart." 2. How beneficial may even their devices become when met with " simplicity and godly sincerity." 3. How inexpressibly beautiful is the character of the Son of David—"meek and lowly in heart." 4. How necessary is the " anointing of the holy One," that we may become like unto him.—D.

Vers. 1—9.—*Love and jealousy.* One great exploit performed in the sight of two armies took David at once and for ever out of obscurity. Thenceforth he was a man much observed. The quiet pastoral life at Bethlehem was ended, and could never be resumed. Sudden success brings rapid distinction, but also brings trials and risks from which the obscure are free. David leaped at a bound into honour and fame, but for that very reason he found himself at the beginning of his troubles. Well that, before those troubles began to press him, he knew the Lord as his refuge ; well, too, that he won to himself in the very sphere of danger a loving and faithful friend.

I. JONATHAN'S LOVE. If there was a man in Israel who had reason to be jealous of David, it was the Prince Jonathan. He was a gallant soldier, and here was a greater hero to eclipse him. He had by personal valour gained a signal victory over the Philistines, and here was a personal courage still more brilliant, and a discomfiture of the enemy more easy and more complete. He was the heir to the throne, and if this youth should aspire to rule as well as deliver Israel, it was Jonathan whom he would supplant. Yet in this generous prince there appeared not even a shade of envy. He saw in the young shepherd a congenial spirit—a temper adventurous as his own, with a faith in God firm and ardent as his own. The soul of Jonathan was knit to the soul of David. It was good for Jonathan to find a friend who could evoke an admiration and affection so intense. He could no longer look up to his own father with respect or confidence. In the circle or court about the king the finer qualities of Jonathan's nature found no harmony, no encouragement. But here was one who could understand him, and in whom he could see and admire what a leader in Israel ought to be. It was good for David, too, to find that he was cared for, that his pure and devout patriotism was appreciated, and that he had the fraternal sympathy of at least one in that higher grade of life on which he was now so suddenly to enter. The time was at hand when such strong and faithful love would be very precious.

II. SAUL'S JEALOUSY. At first it appeared as though David was to have nothing but honour. The king obeyed his good impulse, and gave the young hero high promotion among his officers, with the evident approval of the soldiers and all the people. But a black cloud of jealousy soon gathered. Saul could not bear to hear this new champion praised more than himself; and he began to brood over the thought that this might be the man at whom Samuel hinted, to whom the Lord would give the kingdom. "What can he have more but the kingdom? And Saul eyed David from that day forward." We soon read of the jealous king trying to take David's life. Oh, cruel envy! No worthiness, no goodness is a defence against it. The sight of good excites it to evil. It is the passion of a mean spirit; or, if it fastens on a character which has some great qualities, it tends to weaken and degrade it. Indeed, no more wretched fate can befall any man than to be filled with envy, and so to chafe and jibe at all who surpass him; to become a prey to jealousy, and mistrust or disparage all who seem to please God or man more than he. How fatal for Saul himself was this jealous passion! By the help of David the king might have recovered something of his lost health and happiness, and repaired some of the errors of his reign. But once jealousy took possession of him all this was impossible. Saul became gloomy, crafty, and cruel; and the more David did for the kingdom, bearing himself wisely in camp and court, the more was he watched with envious eyes, and pursued with sullen hatred. "Wrath is cruel, and anger is outrageous; but who is able to stand before envy?" This seemed an ominous beginning for David; but it served its purpose in the training through which God meant him to pass. After Saul was anointed he was put through no such ordeal. The slight opposition which was made to his sudden elevation was soon surmounted, and the son of Kish stepped up to the throne of Israel with very little difficulty. But this was really ominous. It was a sign that God was to have little service or glory from King Saul. The son of Jesse had a higher destiny, and therefore he was tried and proved. His faith was tested as by fire; his discretion was ripened by the knowledge that jealous eyes were watching him; his patience was perfected; his staying power developed through an experience hard and harassing.

III. SUGGESTIONS OF JESUS CHRIST, LOVED AND HATED. As David in his youth, and on the threshold of his public career, overcame the strong enemy of Israel in single combat, so Jesus in youth, and on the threshold of his public life, encountered the adversary of the people of God, and overcame the tempter in the wilderness. Then, as David endured much before he reached the throne, so Jesus Christ endured much before God raised him up and gave him glory. And during that time of his lowly suffering Jesus was, like his human ancestor David, solaced by love and pursued by envy. 1. *Loved.* The Son of David had the applause of the multitude, and bore himself so wisely that the keenest observers could find no fault in him. Withal he had the power of knitting souls to himself, so as to make them willing to forsake all for his sake. Now this was always a strong characteristic of David—a charm of character and bearing which attached to him many lovers and friends. Jonathan loved him in youth as his own soul. His warriors were so devoted to him, that he had but to wish for water from the well of Bethlehem, and three heroes dashed through the ranks of the Philistines to draw water and bring it to their chief. Ittai the Gittite and others are evidences that David retained this attaching power even in old age. And did not the Son of David, with an attraction which we cannot analyse or define, draw to himself the sons of Zebedee, and the sons of Jonas, the brother and sisters at Bethany, Mary of Magdala, and many more who found in his companionship and favour all that their hearts desired? Did he not afterwards draw to himself the persecutor, Saul of Tarsus, and engage the all-enduring loyalty and love of Paul? And are there not thousands on thousands who, though they have not seen him, love him, and in whose eyes he is never more worthy of love than when contemplated as One despised and rejected of men, "a Man of sorrows, and acquainted with grief"? It was a solace to Jesus in his deepest suffering that they who knew him best loved him. How often he dwelt on it, on the night in which he was betrayed! "If ye love me, keep my commandments." "He that loveth me shall be loved of my Father." "The Father himself loveth you, because ye have loved me." Just as it comforted David when hunted and proscribed to know that Jonathan loved him truly and well, so it comforted the Son of David, that though men might hate and kill him, there were those who loved him truly and well, and whom neither death nor life could separate from his love. 2. *Hated.* We have seen how David's courage and discretion stirred Saul's jealousy. A man so rare in his qualities, so evidently fitted for greatness, drew after him eyes of cruel envy. So it befell the Son of David. Because Jesus drew to him disciples and friends, the priests and rabbis hated him. Because he was followed by multitudes, the rulers took counsel together against him. Because he answered and acted wisely, the scribes and Pharisees were filled with malice against him. Wherever he went, jealous eyes watched him, and crafty questions laid wait for him. The Scripture was fulfilled: "They hated me without a cause." Pontius Pilate easily detected the motive (no just cause) which led the Jewish Council to arraign the Son of David at his judgment-seat. "He knew that for envy they had delivered him." So it is to-day. Jesus Christ is proclaimed as mighty to save. The world is being filled with his name, and everywhere cries ascend of "Hosanna to the Son of David." And how is it taken? Some love, but some also hate. Some feel as Jonathan did. They are quite drawn out of themselves to the Lord Jesus. He is, he must be, their Beloved and their Friend. And how significant of his greatness it is that he, now unseen, awakens in human hearts a faith as strong, an attachment as ardent, as thrilled the breasts of apostles who accompanied him and women who ministered to him in Galilee! Paul, who had not seen him in the flesh, loved him as truly and served him as enthusiastically as Peter and John, who had. Christians of the eleventh century, like Bernard of Clairvaux, or of the fifteenth, like him who wrote as Thomas à Kempis, clave to him as devoutly as the Fathers who lived within a few generations of the apostles. And comparative moderns, like Herbert, Bengel, Rutherford, Madame Guyon, Brainerd, Whitefield, the Wesleys, Toplady, Hervey, Henry Martyn, McCheyne, Adolph Monod, have held him as precious as did the most fervent spirits of earlier times. Jesus Christ has always known how to draw men to himself, and hold them by cords of spiritual attraction, so that they have loved him as their own souls. Others, however, eye him as Saul eyed David, in order to find fault with him. Oh, what a triumph it would give to a certain class of men if they could only find a blot in the Lord Jesus; if they could show him to have been no better or higher than other men! But it cannot be done. His way is perfect. His character, however closely scrutinised, reveals no flaw. It comes to this, that men hate him because he is so good. They love the darkness rather than the light, because their deeds are evil.—F.

Vers. 29, 30.—*David proved and tried.* I. EXEMPLARY CONDUCT UNDER TRIAL. One can hardly imagine a course of events more likely to turn a young man's head and make him giddy with elation than the rapid promotion of the youthful David. Brought at once from comparative obscurity into the full blaze of public admiration as a national hero, appointed as an officer of high rank in the army, made son-in-law to the king, and at the same time trusted and honoured by the people, the son of Jesse had much to tempt him to self-complacence. It is a sign that the Lord was with him that he bore himself meekly, circumspectly, and with "sublime repression of himself." A man who is conscious of fitness for a great position can afford to wait. It must come to him, if he lives long enough ; and if he is not to live, why should he fret his few years with an idle ambition ? David had something better than such a consciousness ; he knew himself to be anointed and ordained of God to fill an eminent place in his service. True, that nothing seems to have been said about the kingship at the private anointing in Bethlehem ; and David's gift of sacred song seemed to point him out as successor of Samuel rather than of Saul. But kings, not prophets, were anointed ; and the thought of being king, especially after the exploit at Elah, must have passed and repassed through the young hero's mind. Yet because he believed God he did not make haste. If the high and perilous seat of a king of Israel was destined for him, let it come ; but he would not grasp it, or climb into it by dispossessing its first occupant. Not by him would Saul be dethroned, or any dishonour done to a head which had received a holy anointing. God would give what he pleased, as and when he might see fit. Enough that David should act wisely and justly in the station to which he was assigned. This was no fatalism. The history shows that David used all lawful (and some rather questionable) endeavours to preserve his own life, and that he missed no opportunity to advance his public interest. He was far from inferring that, as God had marked out for him a destiny, he must not give any heed to his way or to his safety, because God would bring his own purpose to pass. On the contrary, he knew that the fulfilment of the destiny must be through his own discretion, valour, and proved fitness for the royal dignity. Therefore, while David would not push his way ambitiously to the throne, he was careful to do nothing that would make such promotion impossible. In fact David took the course which may be recommended to every young man who desires to rise in the esteem and confidence of others. He did well whatever was given him to do. He behaved himself wisely as a minstrel, as a soldier, as a prince. The historian marks the steps of his advance—"wisely," "very wisely," "more wisely than all the servants of Saul " (vers. 14, 15, 30). If we read " prospered," " prospered exceedingly," " prospered more," the lesson remains the same. We are reminded of the youthful Joseph, always prosperous in administration, whether in Potiphar's house, in charge of the prison, or in the government of Egypt. It was because the Lord was with him (Gen. xxxix. 2, 23). Yet the promotion of Joseph was through his well-approved discretion and fidelity winning for him more and more confidence (Gen. xxxix. 39—41). So David prospered ; every step of his elevation bringing out more clearly to view his fine combination of boldness and discretion, and his consequent fitness to rise yet higher, and to be the leader and ruler of all Israel. Happy the nation where such proved fitness counts for more than the highest birth or the strongest interest ! If survival of the fittest be a rule in nature, selection of the fittest is the true principle for the public service. Not that every one who holds an inferior position well is fit to hold a higher and rise toward the highest. Men have their range, beyond which they are ill at ease and incapable. But this is certain, that men who are fit for a leading position will reveal their capacity while serving in a subordinate place. Only in judging of this account must be taken not of brain power and acquired knowledge merely, but of character, and that moral influence which character and conduct give. Is it not on this principle that God promotes the heirs of glory ? All who have received his grace are anointed ones ; but they have to serve before they rule, and to be tested in labours and patience before they can reign with Christ. Has not our Saviour taught in parables that his people must be servants till he returns, and that only good and faithful servants are to enter into the joy of their Lord ? Has not St. Paul spoken of eternal life as given to those " who by patient continuance in well-doing seek for glory, honour, and immortality " ? Behold the way to " the honour that comes from God only." Behave wisely in the present sphere of duty. Do well, and do it with patience. Make not your advancement in this world, or even in the world to come, a matter of passionate anxiety. Foster and obey the sense of duty, attend conscientiously to the obligations of your present station, and fear not but the Lord will give you as much elevation as is good for you in this present time, and in the age to come a place and a portion with the King and with his saints.

II. THE IMPRESSION WHICH DAVID PRODUCED. 1. *On the people.* They were captivated by his gallantry and his discretion. Both in martial skill and in civil administration he surpassed all the public men of his country, and was fast becoming a popular idol. It is too true that, notwithstanding this, Saul was able to drive him into exile, and found soldiers enough to pursue him for his life. Popular favour did not protect him from such outrage. Yet two facts are worth noting. (1) That David gave clear evidence of a man who could, and therefore should, sooner or later, lead his countrymen. This early approval of himself to all observers, however obscured or disparaged during the days of his persecution, was not forgotten by the people, and helped his ultimate elevation to the throne. (2) That, though many turned against him at the bidding of Saul, David from this very time drew to himself friends that would not forsake him, for they saw in him the hope of Israel; and, following him to the caves among the rocks of Judah, and even to the land of the Philistines, were the companions, first of his tribulation, and then of his kingdom and glory. 2. *On the king.* The effect of David's well-doing on Saul was sinister and shameful. The good points which had once appeared in this unhappy man now recede from view, and the bad points of his character come out in strong relief under the baleful influence of jealousy. When he was himself the sole hero, and the eyes of all Israel turned to him, he could be gracious and even humble in his bearing. But elevation had made him proud; power had made him wilful; and a bad conscience made him hate and fear a well-doer near the throne. He felt that this youth from Bethlehem was far the better man, and he suspected that the nation thought so too. Envy completed the moral ruin of Saul. As the worm seeks out the best fruit to eat the heart of it, so envy fastens on the best and noblest persons to hate and hurt them. It goes by quick steps to injury—even to murder. "Saul spake to Jonathan his son, and to all his servants, that they should kill David." O cursed envy! O hideous ingratitude! O foul and furious jealousy!

III. THE TREATMENT OF JESUS CHRIST FORESHADOWED. The Son of David lived unblamably, answered discreetly, behaved himself wisely. The people gathered to him in multitudes, with eyes and ears of admiration. They judged him worthy to be made their king. It is true that the fickle populace took part with their rulers against our Lord, just as the fickle subjects of Saul took part with him against the son of Jesse. But, in the one case as in the other, some hearts clave to the persecuted One. And as all the malice that pursued David failed to keep him from the kingdom to which God had destined him and for which God had fitted him, so the rejection, betrayal, and crucifixion of Jesus could not keep him from the throne far above all principality and power which was his in virtue of an eternal covenant. The rulers hated him without a cause; his very wisdom and goodness irritated them, and they took counsel together how they might slay him. For envy they delivered him up to judgment, and demanded that he should be crucified. At the period described in our text a crisis had arrived in Israel. Men were forced to choose between Saul and David, for these were contrary the one to the other, and could not live in unity. We know what side such a man as Doeg took. But David had his friends, who dared everything rather than renounce his cause. Better, in their opinion, to be exiles and pilgrims with him than to remain with the moody tyrant from whom the Lord had departed. So, in the days of his showing to Israel, many refused Jesus, but some clave to him. Better, in their opinion, to be cast out of the synagogues, to go forth without the gate, bearing his reproach, than to take part with the world that hated him, especially with that hard and gloomy Judaism from which the Lord had departed. The crisis continues. Before all men the alternative lies—for Christ, or against him. Oh, receive him whom the world has rejected; give him your hearts; identify and associate yourselves with the "once despised Jesus."—F.

EXPOSITION.

SUCCESSIVE ATTEMPTS UPON DAVID'S LIFE FRUSTRATED BY THE LOVE OF JONATHAN AND MICHAL, AND FINALLY BY FLIGHT (CH. XIX.).

CHAPTER XIX.

JONATHAN'S LOVE FOR DAVID (vers. 1—7). Ver. 1.—**Saul spake to Jonathan his son . . . that they should kill David.** The translation of the last clause is untenable ; it really means "about killing David," and so both the Septuagint and the Syriac render it. The descent of men once full of noble impulses, as was the case with Saul, into open crime is gradual, and with many halts on the way. Saul first gave way to envy, and instead of struggling against his bad feelings, nourished them. Then, when scarcely accountable for his actions, he threatened David's life ; and next, with growing malice, encouraged him in dangerous undertakings, in the hope that in one of them he might be slain. And now he goes one step farther. He talks to Jonathan and his officers concerning the many reasons there were for David's death ; argues that without it there will be no security for himself and his dynasty ; represents David probably as a traitor, with secret purposes of usurping the throne ; and reveals what hitherto had been but the half-formed wishes of his heart. But even now, probably, he still spoke of David's death as a painful necessity, and had many misgivings in his own mind. But he was really encouraging himself in crime, and by cherishing thoughts of murder he was gradually descending towards the dark abyss into which he finally fell.

Vers. 2, 3.—**Until the morning.** Rather, "in the morning." Saul's purpose was taking shape, and as there are always men too ready to commit crime at the bidding of a king, there was the danger that secret murder might be the quick result of Saul's open communication of his wishes to his men of war. Jonathan, therefore, warns David of the king's malice, and urges him to hide himself until he has made a last entreaty for him. This was to take place **in the field**, the open common land. There was no idea of David overhearing the conversation, but when the king took his usual walk Jonathan was to join him, and hold a conference with him apart in the unenclosed hill pastures. After probing his father's real feelings he would continue his walk, and, without awakening any suspicions, would meet David and communicate to him the result. **What I see, that I will tell thee.** More exactly, "I will see what (he says), and will tell thee."

Vers. 4—7.—In the field Jonathan intercedes for David, assures his father of his friend's innocence, reminds him of his noble exploit, and of Saul's own joy at it, and beseeches him not to shed innocent blood. And Saul, fickle and selfish, yet not destitute of noble feelings, repents of his purpose, and with characteristic impetuosity takes an oath that David's life shall be spared. Whereupon a reconciliation takes place, and David resumes his attendance upon the king's person.

RENEWED ATTEMPT TO SLAY DAVID FRUSTRATED BY MICHAL (vers. 8—17). Vers. 8, 9.—**The**—more correctly *an*—**evil spirit from Jehovah.** The friendly relations between Saul and David continued for some time ; but when at length war broke out again, David acquitted himself with his usual ability and success, whereupon Saul's envy and jealousy returned, and fits of melancholy, deepening into insanity, once again overclouded his reason. It is no longer called "an evil spirit from God," as in ch. xviii. 10, but **from Jehovah,** as in ch. xvi. 14, suggesting that it was no longer a natural influence, but that Saul, having broken his covenant relations with Jehovah, was now punished by him. While in this moody state the same temptation to slay David with his javelin came over him, but with such violence that he was no longer able to restrain his evil intent.

Vers. 10—12.—**Saul sought to smite David.** The verb used here is not that rendered *cast* in ch. xviii. 11, where probably we had the record of a purpose threatened, but not carried out. Here Saul actually threw his javelin at David with such violence that it was fixed into the wall. But David, though playing some instrument of music at the time, was on his guard, and slipped away. **And David fled, and escaped that night.** As usual, the historian gives the ultimate results of Saul's violence first, and then returns and gives the particulars ; for plainly David first went home, and it was only when he found that the house was surrounded by Saul's emissaries that he fled away to find refuge with Samuel. **Saul also sent messengers.** As is often the case, this outbreak of violence on Saul's part broke down all the former restraints of upright feeling and conscience. He had lost his self-respect, was openly a murderer as regards everything but the success of his attempt, and he determined that that should not be long wanting. He sends persons, therefore, to watch David's house, with orders that when in the morning he came out, suspecting no danger, they should fall upon him and slay him. But Michal in some way or other became aware of her husband's danger. Possibly she had been at her father's house in the afternoon, and with quick observation had noticed that more than usual was going on, and seeing that her own house was the object of these preparations, had divined their intent; or possibly Jonathan may have given her information, and so she warned David of his danger. As the entrance was guarded, he was let down through a window, like St. Paul afterwards, and so began the weary life of wandering which lasted through so many troubled years.

Ver. 13.—**Michal took an image.** Literally, "the teraphim," a plural word, but used here as a singular. Probably, like the corresponding Latin word *penates*, it had no singular in common use. It was a wooden block with head and shoulders roughly shaped to represent a human figure. Laban's teraphim were so small that Rachel could hide them under the camel's furniture (Gen. xxxi. 34), but Michal's seems to have been large enough to pass in the bed for a man. Though the worship of them is described as iniquity (ch. xv. 23), yet the superstitious belief that they brought good luck to the house over which they presided, in return for kind treatment, seems to have been proof against the teaching of the prophets; and Hosea describes the absence of them as on the same level as the absence of the ephod (Hosea iii. 4). **A pillow of goats' hair for his bolster.** More correctly, "a goat's skin about its head." So the Syriac and Vulgate. The object of it would be to look at a distance like a man's hair. The Septuagint has a goat's liver, because this was supposed to palpitate long after the animal's death, and so would produce the appearance of a person's breathing. But this involves a different reading, for which there is no authority; nor was Michal's deception intended for close observation. She would of course not let any one disturb David, and all she wanted was just enough likeness to a man to make a person at a distance suppose that David was there. Soon or later her artifice would be found out, but her husband would have had the intervening time for effecting his escape. As the word rendered **pillow,** and which is found only here, comes from a root signifying "to knot together," "to intertwine," some commentators think that it means a network of goats' hair, perhaps to keep off flies. But this is a mere guess, and not to be set against the combined authority of the two versions. **With a cloth.** Hebrew, *beged.* This *beged* was David's every-day dress, and would greatly aid Michal in her pious arti-

fice. It was a loose mantle, worn over the close-fitting *meïl* (see ch. ii. 19). Thus Ezra (ch. ix. 3, 5) says, "I rent my *beged* and my *meïl,*" which the A. V. with characteristic inexactness translates "my garment and my mantle." In Gen. xxviii. 20, where it is rendered *raiment,* Jacob speaks of it as the most indispensable article of dress; and in Gen. xxxix. 12, where it is rendered *garment,* we find that it was a loose plaid or wrapper. In those simple days it was used for warmth by night as well as for protection by day, and it is interesting to find David in his old age still covered up for warmth in bed by his *beged* (1 Kings i. 1), where it is translated *clothes.*

Vers. 14—17.—When, after waiting till the usual hour for David's appearance, he came not, the watchers send and inform Saul, who now orders his open arrest. But Michal despatches a messenger to tell her father that he is sick. Upon this Saul orders bed and all to be brought, that he may slay him. As an Oriental bed is usually a mere strip of carpet, this would be easy enough. But when the messengers force their way through, in spite of every obstruction which Michal can devise to waste time, and come up close to the sleeping figure, "Lo, teraphim in the bed, and a goatskin at its head." They carry the news to Saul, who sends for Michal, and reproaches her for letting his enemy go. And she, afraid of bringing her father's anger upon herself, answers with a falsehood, such as we find David also too readily having resort to; for she tells Saul that his flight was David's own doing, and that she had taken part in it only to save her life. **Why should I kill thee?** She pretends that David had told her not to force him to kill her by refusing to give her aid in his escape. Saul, no doubt, saw that she had been a willing agent; but as she professed to have been driven to do what she had done by David's threats, he could say no more.

DAVID'S FLIGHT TO SAMUEL AT RAMAH (vers. 18—24). Ver. 18.—**David . . . came to Samuel.** We have seen that there is every reason to believe that David had been taught and trained by Samuel among the sons of the prophets, and now, conscious of his innocence, he flees for refuge to his old master, trusting that Saul would reverence God's prophet, and give credence to his intercession and his pledge that David was guiltless. **He and Samuel went and dwelt in Naioth.** Rather in *Nevayoth,* as in the written text. This is not the name of a place, but signifies "dwellings," "lodgings," and is always translated in the Chaldee "house of study," *i. e.* student's lodgings. Somewhere near to Ramah Samuel had erected buildings to receive his young men, who were called "sons of the prophets," not because their fathers were prophets, but because they were under prophetic training, with prophets for their teachers, though not necessarily intended to be prophets themselves. At first Samuel, we may suppose, built one *nevath*, one simple hospice for his students, and then, as their numbers grew, another, and yet another, and so the plural, *nevayoth*, came into vogue as the name of the students' quarters.

Vers. 19, 20.—On hearing where David was, Saul sends messengers to arrest him, and we thus incidentally gain a most interesting account of the inner condition of Samuel's schools. Evidently after Saul had become king Samuel devoted his main energies to this noble effort to raise Israel from the barbarous depths into which it had sunk ; and when the messengers arrive they enter some hall, where they find a regularly organised choir, consisting not of "sons of the prophets," young men still under training, but **of prophets**, men who had finished their preparatory studies, and arrived at a higher elevation. The Chaldee Paraphrast calls them *scribes ;* and doubtless those educated in Samuel's schools held an analogous position to that of the scribes in later days. And **Samuel** himself was **standing**— not **as appointed over them ;** he was the founder and originator of these schools, and all authority was derived from him. What the Hebrew says is that he was "standing as chief over them," and they, full of Divine enthusiasm, were chanting psalms to God's glory. So noble was the sight, that Saul's messengers on entering were seized with a like enthusiasm, and, laying aside their murderous purpose, joined in the hearty service of the prophetic sanctuary. Instead of **they saw** the Hebrew has "he saw," but as all the versions have the plural, it is probably a mere mistake. The Hebrew word for **company** is found only here. By transposing the letters we have the ordinary word for *congregation,* but possibly it was their own technical name for some peculiar arrangement of the choir.

Vers. 21—24.—Saul sends messengers a second and even a third time with the same result, and finally determines to go in person. Having set out, **he came to a**—more correctly *the*—**great well that is in Sechu**—more probably the cistern or tank there. From the value of water it was no doubt a well-known spot at the time, but in the present ruined state of the country all such works have perished. Sechu, according to Conder ('Handbook'), was probably on the site of the present ruin of Suweikeh, immediately south of Beeroth. Having there made inquiries whether Samuel and David were still at Ramah, courageously awaiting his coming, he proceeds on his way. But even before arriving in Samuel's presence, with that extraordinary susceptibility to external impressions which is so marked a feature in his character, he begins singing psalms, and no sooner had he entered the Nevayoth than **he stripped off his clothes**— his *beged* and *meïl*—**and lay down naked**— *i. e.* with only his tunic upon him—**all that day and all that night.** His excitement had evidently been intense, and probably to the chanting he had added violent gesticulation. But it was not this so much as the tempest of his emotions which had exhausted him, and made him thus throw himself down as one dead. And once again the people wondered at so strange an occurrence, and called back to mind the proverb, **Is Saul also among the prophets ?** When first used (ch. x. 11) Saul's enthusiasm was an outburst of piety, genuine but evanescent, and which had long since passed away. What was it now ? The Chaldee, as explained by Rashi, says he was mad. More probably, in the violent state of excitement under which Saul had for some time been labouring, the thought of seeing Samuel, from whom he had been so long separated, brought back to his mind the old days when the prophet had loved and counselled him, and made him king, and been his true and faithful friend. And the remembrance overpowered him. What would he not have given to have continued such as he then was ! And for a time he became once again the old Saul of Ramah ; but the change was transient and fitful ; and after these twenty-four hours of agony Saul rose up, full perhaps of good intentions, but with a heart unchanged, and certain, therefore, very quickly to disappoint all hopes of real amendment, and to become a still more moody and relentless tyrant.

HOMILETICS.

Vers. 1—7.—*Open enmity and open friendship.* The facts are—1. Saul reveals his purpose to kill David. 2. This being made known to Jonathan, he arranges with David to let him learn the result of an effort to turn Saul from his purpose. 3. He pleads with Saul David's good services and personal risks, God's approval, and the king's own joy therein. 4. Saul yields to persuasion, resolves not to shed "innocent blood," and recalls David into his personal service. The historian traces the progress of Saul to ruin, and of David to royal honours, and here brings out the aroused hostility of Saul on the one side, and the open services of Jonathan's friendship on the other. Father and son are at cross purposes concerning the life of one who in the providence of God is to supplant both. Each performs his part with perfect natural-ness; and in the progress of the conflict between enmity and friendship there is a revelation not only of the individual characteristics of the men, but also of principles in constant operation. We have here an instance of—

I. THE INEVITABLE GROWTH OF SECRET SIN. Except in occasional seasons of moodiness, Saul's conduct towards David had not found formal expression. His servants probably set down his violence (ch. xviii. 11) to irritability, and we have seen how cleverly Saul had striven to throw on Providence the slaying of David while he was doing him honour (ch. xviii. 17—30). The frustration of these secret schemes brought out the fact that the sin so long cherished in the heart, and for very shame concealed, had, by that very nurture, gained such power over the entire man as to force its way into open day, regardless of all considerations of prudence and self-respect. The murder in intent became murder avowed. The ruling passion of the inner life now became the acknowledged master, and a public avowal of servitude to it is therefore voluntarily made. Saul's experience is but an *instance of the experience of multitudes.* Progress in wickedness is from within outwards. Lust, when it hath conceived, brings forth sin (James i. 15). Every deliberate murder, theft, deed of adultery, fraud, and rebellion against Christ's authority was at first germinal in the heart. Each stage of internal growth lessened the power of the will over its progress, till at last it revealed its evil nature in open acts. This psycho-logical genesis of sin is an awful fact, and may well cause those to tremble whose dalliance with secret evil becomes habitual. Truly he who committeth sin is "the servant of sin," and every consideration of duty and interest should urge us to cry daily for a "clean heart," and that sin may have "no more dominion" over us (Ps. cxxxix. 23; Rom. vi. 14).

II. THE STUPIDITY CONSEQUENT ON THE DOMINION OF SIN. Facts prove that all sin is a species of madness. Adam and Eve imagined that a thicket would hide them from God. Saul's clearness of intellect suffered by his first public disobedience; and now that the evil passion had gained ascendancy, extreme stupidity appears in his soliciting the aid, in the execution of his cruel purpose, of Jonathan, David's bosom friend (ch. xviii. 1—4; xix. 1). If he knew nothing of their friendship, which is very improbable, he ought to have known enough of so good and devout a son as to be sure that he would be no party to a base and villanous deed. If he imagined that Jonathan was likely to be actuated by jealousy of a rival, he per-formed the stupid act, common to base men, of thinking that reasons which have force with themselves have force with others. In proportion to the power of sin over the will is the effect of it on the intellect. Even the most clever sinners, when seeking to cover their sin from man, manifest some infatuation or folly which affords the clue to their crime. But it is especially in relation to God and the future issues of sin that this stupefying effect appears. It is only this blinded spirit that explains the ease with which men read of the coming "terrors of the Lord" (2 Cor. v. 10, 11; iv. 3, 4; Heb. ii. 3).

III. THE DOMESTIC SORROWS CREATED BY SIN. It was with a sad, heavy heart that Jonathan had witnessed the gradual decay of his father's character, but the saddest blow was when the father sought to make the son partaker in his sin. The grief of the son would be proportionate to his piety. To be tempted by a father, to have filial obedience tested in deeds of evil, to see the utter ruin of a parent's moral character, was a bitter trial; and, as a true son, Jonathan could not but bear these sorrows as a fearful secret. In how many families are there sorrows of this kind! How many a child has to watch the decay of a father's reputation, to bear induce-ments to sin, and to hide deeds and intentions of evil! A parent is far gone when children are prompted to wrong. A child is indeed a "child of sorrow" when com-pelled to carry on a pure heart the secrets of a sinful home.

IV. THE TRIUMPH OF RELIGIOUS FRIENDSHIP. It is scarcely likely that Saul would speak to Jonathan about killing David without pointing out how dangerous a rival he was to both father and son. It raised in Jonathan's mind the conflict of worldly interest and fidelity to a friend. Not a few have yielded to such temptations. But

Jonathan's pure soul was equal to the occasion. His conduct was marked by exquisite delicacy of feeling and wisdom. He would not so degrade his father as to tell David that he had been asked to slay his friend, while he assured David of his real danger. While not assuming the tone of an advocate, he skilfully handled facts so as to achieve the end in view. The point of the temptation was to sacrifice friendship to private and public interests. There are persons still subject to the same trial. May we not also see something analogous to the common temptations of Christians to renounce the "anointed One" for reasons pertaining to earthly wealth and glory? Where there is real oneness of heart with Christ, no blandishments of sin, no prospect of greater worldly distinction, avail to break the sacred bond.

V. THE FORCE OF TRUTH ON THE CONSCIENCE. Jonathan simply, in a kindly, gentle way, conversed with his father on the matter, and called his attention to a few facts, —David's risks, services, and evident approval by God, and Saul's own joy in his victories,—and then asks whether such innocent blood should be shed. The effect even on the impenitent Saul is to soften his hard heart and draw forth the declaration that he shall be spared. Happy the son who has such influence with an unhappy, wicked father! In dealing with hardened sinners *three things are necessary*. 1. *Truth to present to the conscience*. That David was innocent Saul knew; but ordinarily passion blinded him to the due recognition of it. If we can hold forth "the word of life," the actual truth concerning Christ, so that it shall shine straight in upon the conscience, men cannot but acknowledge its power, and it will exercise some restraint on their conduct. 2. *A kindly, unaffected manner*. It was the manner of Jonathan that secured an attentive hearing and disarmed Saul's suspicion. Harsh language tends to arouse antagonism. The secret of success lies in so presenting the truth that it stands forth alone, unmixed with disturbing elements from our personality. "He that winneth souls is wise" (Prov. xi. 30). 3. *Prayerfulness of spirit*. We may be sure that Jonathan as well as David prayed in spirit on this occasion. The tone of our mind is wonderfully affected by prayerfulness. We then speak for God and man with a gentle force which guilty men cannot but feel.

General lessons:—1. More attention should be called to the importance of crushing out sinful feelings on their first appearance, and means suggested for so doing. 2. Parents and persons in positions of influence should be earnestly warned of the fearful crime of seeking to induce young persons to violate their sense of right and truth. 3. The good that is in us may be much more utilised if we strive to act with the "wisdom of the serpent and the harmlessness of the dove."

Vers. 8—17.—*Revived sins and troubles*. The facts are—1. The fresh fame of David arouses the latent ill-will of Saul, who seeks in vain to smite him with a javelin. 2. David fleeing to his house, Saul sends men to lie in wait for and slay him. 3. Michal warns him of danger, and during the night aids his escape. 4. By a clever device she diverts his enemies from an immediate pursuit, and on being accused of aiding her father's enemy, she pleads self-preservation. The troubles of life are but temporarily overcome. It was destined for David to smite the national enemy, since he went forth as none other did, strong in the "name of the Lord." The fame of his exploits no sooner reached the ears of Saul than the effect of Jonathan's recent endeavour to reconcile him to David was utterly lost; and hence arose a series of new troubles for persecutor and the persecuted. We see here—

I. That A RADICAL CHANGE OF DISPOSITION IS THE ONLY GUARANTEE OF CONDUCT AND CHARACTER. The change wrought in Saul by Jonathan's recent presentation of truth was only superficial. The old sin was loved and unrepented of. The nature of the man was alienated from the life of God; and hence on the slightest approach of temptation the old spirit broke forth. It is *universally true* that no *intellectual recognition of truth*, no acquiescence of conscience in the injustice of a course, no reformation consequent on human influence over the feelings or the intelligence, *will make man, or enable him to be, what he ought to be*. The fundamental disposition must be renewed. There are instances of this in Christian history. The lion becomes a lamb. A Saul of Tarsus becomes an apostle of Christ. It is in the nature of things that so it should be. For in the ordained subordination of the powers of the mind there is a ruling disposition to which all bend: if it be pure all will move in a holy direction; if it be impure the whole life will be stained. Out of the heart are the issues of life. It is the weakness of all systems of morality that they exalt virtue and teach the evils of vice, but furnish no adequate power to render the life virtuous in the highest sense of the term. Moralists may be immoral. The doing of truth is not involved in a knowledge of it. Here it is that the New Testament comes in to supplement man's knowledge, and to perfect codes of morality. By the gift of the Holy Spirit it builds up outward character from within, and insures that at last sin shall have no dominion over us. There is *danger of men overlooking this truth*, especially when "many run to and fro, and knowledge is increased." Civilisation, by securing a presentable exterior, diverts attention from the "hidden man of the heart." The indirect effect of Christianity is to incorporate with the ordinary character many of the virtues nourished only by itself, and hence men imagine that society would be what it is without Christianity. It is extremely important, therefore, to insist on the New Testament teaching of the need of a radical change by the power of the Holy Spirit; to seek to bring our children early under his renewing power, and to pray constantly that men may be renewed and become new creatures in Christ Jesus.

II. That THE AFFLICTIONS OFTEN BEFALLING THE SERVANTS OF GOD PUT A SEVERE STRAIN ON THEIR FAITH. If Ps. lix. was written in reference to this persecution, we can see the propriety of the assertion, "Not for my transgression, and not for any sin of mine" (Ps. lix. 3), do they "set themselves." To a young man conscious of his integrity, and not without hope of being accepted of God, it must have seemed a strange providence which allowed his life to be so troubled. Could Samuel's anointing really have a Divine significance? (ch. xvi. 13). Was it not a mistake to have left the quiet sheepfold for the scene of conflict? (ch. xvii. 20). Would it not be well even now to retire into private life? Why should an innocent, sincere soul have such constant reason to cry, "Awake to help me, and behold?" (Ps. lix. 4). The *experience is not confined to David*. One greater than David, when in pursuit of his higher work in the world, was a "Man of sorrows, and acquainted with grief." And likewise for many a year his Church, when pursuing her holy and beneficent course, was exposed to relentless persecution. It is still true that "many are the afflictions of the righteous," and that "through much tribulation" we enter the kingdom. But all this is *not a matter of chance*, nor an indication of imperfect wisdom and love. The world is evil, and goodness can only live in it by conflict. It is part of the great battle of the universe that sin shall be exterminated by endured sorrows. History proves that the purest lives and most beautiful virtues have flourished in times and by means of severe trial. Every sufferer knows how blessed it is to be driven nearer to God. The tribulation is only for a brief space, and works out a far more exceeding and eternal weight of glory. Hence faith can bear the strain; the more so as God does succour and delight the soul with his comforts (Ps. lix. 17; xciv. 19).

III. That THOSE WHO DEVISE EVIL AGAINST THE SERVANTS OF GOD ARE SOMETIMES CAUGHT IN THEIR OWN DEVICES. In the exercise of his low cunning Saul gave Michal to David that she might be a snare to him (ch. xviii. 21), her character and tendencies being such as might in his judgment bring him into trouble. It now turned out that the snare for David became a snare for Saul (Ps. vii. 14, 15). Wicked men cannot always reckon safely on their instruments. Men laid snares for Christ, but were entangled in their own talk (Matt. xxii. 15—22). Pharaoh thought he would find Israel "entangled in the land" (Exod. xiv. 3), and he found himself ensnared therein to his own destruction. Snares are laid for the Church of God in modern times, and some of these will doubtless prove the reverse of the original intent. We are invited with persuasive voice to enter the pathway of severe historical criticism and of physical science, and it is hoped thereby to disenchant us of the fascination of a supernatural Christianity. Men are as confident of the result as was Saul when he gave Michal to David (ch. xviii. 21); but we have nothing to fear, for criticism and science thus far only bring out the truth that the CHRIST is unexplainable on any hypothesis but that of the supernatural; and hence, on the ordinary principles of scientific research, men are bound to accept that hypothesis, or else declare themselves unscientific. "He must reign till he hath put all enemies under his feet" (1 Cor. xv. 25),

IV. That ALTHOUGH IMPERFECT MORAL CONDUCT MAY SUBSERVE THE INTERESTS OF GOD'S SERVANTS, IT NEVERTHELESS IS DISHONOURING TO THEM. Michal acted a lie, and also told deliberate lies, in order to shield David and then herself. The issue was advantageous to David, as it put a wide distance between him and his pursuers. The statement of the facts in Scripture is by no means identical with approval of them. God's purposes have sometimes been furthered by the actions of imperfect men, but the actions have been their own, and never have had Divine approval. It is true still that many a defective "earthen vessel" is the instrument of good. Indeed, were God to refrain from working out his blessed purposes of mercy till we were all pure as the angels, the prospects of the world would be dark enough. The safe rule is "not to do evil that good may come." Good does come often in spite of evil, as when God's truth is diffused in spite of the mixed motives and strifes of those engaged in his service, and when comfort and joy flow to the poor from money given even for purposes far from benevolent. The command of God is "Lie not one to another" (Levit. xix. 11). It is not for us to say that dangers will be avoided by occasional lies. The principle involved in truth-speaking is of vast importance in all times and places, and is worth the sacrifice of much for its vindication. Suppose a man is slain rather than utter a lie, does not his martyrdom for truth, in the enduring moral sphere, bring greater good to moral beings and himself than could have come from trampling on a sacred principle for a present advantage? God, moreover, does not leave his servants when they do right. Had Michal stated the facts she would have saved her husband from slander, and there were ten thousand ways by which God could have frustrated the purpose of the men and shielded David. Our duty is to be true and leave consequences to God. God does not lie— we are children of God; Christ did not lie—we are followers of Christ. We may be sure that permanent good must ensue on our being conformed to Christ, the image of God. There is a gain which is loss, and a loss which is gain (Ps. xxxvii. 3—8, 27, 28; Mark viii. 36; Ephes. v. 9; vi. 14).

General lessons:—1. The influence of Christians may restrain the development of sin in some of its grosser forms, but it is an imperfect Christianity which rests in that. 2. The "wrath of man" is made to praise God, in that persecutions issue in greater spirituality of mind and fitness for permanent service (Rom. v. 3—5). 3. We need not fret and be uneasy about the snares of the wicked if only we are in God's service, as time is on our side (Ps. xxxvii.). 4. Christians should strive to put down all practical forms of falsehood prevalent in society, and train children in a severe love of truth at any cost.

Vers. 18—24.—*Saintly refuge and spiritual restraint.* The facts are—1. David takes refuge with Samuel at Naioth in Ramah. 2. The messengers sent by Saul to take David are restrained in the presence of Samuel and the prophets, and themselves begin to prophesy. 3. Other messengers come under the same influence. 4. Venturing to go himself, he, on approaching the place, also falls under the prophetic influence, and is utterly overcome by it in the presence of Samuel. Human wisdom may be almost confounded by the prominent facts of this section, but this must not be taken as proof of our infallibility, nor of the unfitness of the event with the order of Divine providence. Had it been left to man to invent and regulate the process by which the earth and life upon it arrived at the forms now familiar to us, would he have introduced some of those ancient physical conditions and changes which must have been so utterly unlike what now prevail? The convulsions, the transformations, the climatic conditions, the huge forms of life of some past ages are as much unlike the present facts as the spiritual manifestations of the prophetic schools are unlike the orderly course of Christian influence. It is only of late years that men have in some degree traced the naturalness of the physical process, and even now there is diversity of opinion on the subject. It is not to be wondered at, therefore, if, in man's comparative ignorance of the unseen spiritual sphere in which the great development of God's purpose in Christ really occurs, he should not be able to supply all the links connecting the spiritual manifestations of the era of Samuel with the rigid legal era of Moses and the more calm and orderly methods of the Christian dispensation.

> " Blind unbelief is sure to err,
> And scan his work in vain ;
> God is his own interpreter,
> And he will make it plain."

Looking at the teaching of the section, we see—

I. An important spiritual power being nourished amidst the turmoil of public affairs. While battles were being fought, and the kingdom was troubled with the unsatisfactory condition of the court, Samuel was quietly gathering around himself a band of men who, devoting attention to the records of Israel's history, the exercise of psalmody and music, and the spiritual interests of men, were becoming a power to influence the national life in days to come. The extent and strength of that influence cannot be minutely traced, because of its spiritual nature ; but the higher tone of national life during the reigns of David and Solomon was doubtless largely due to it. *Centres of spiritual influence are formed* when the great political world is intent on its wars and intrigues. Notably, Christianity arose and found its first nourishment amidst the quiet valleys and hills of Palestine while Roman imperialism was intent on conquests and ignorant almost of its existence. The band of men and women who met for prayer in an upper room (Acts i. 13, 14) cultivated there the power which afterwards penetrated into all parts of the Roman empire. The quiet retreats and colleges of the middle ages in some respects were the seats of an influence which the world could ill spare. During the close of the last century small bodies of Christians nourished here and there the missionary spirit which has since affected the destinies of millions in the East and South. Amidst all the conflicts of politics and controversies of science and worry of commerce there are quiet fellowships of Christians devoted to the nourishment of a life destined to conserve and elevate the national life. The *Christian Church has need to form and sustain* "*schools of the prophets*" to meet the demands of the age. Samuel's course and the injunctions of Paul to Timothy (1 Tim. iii. 1—7 ; v. 21, 22 ; 2 Tim. ii 4 ; cf Ephes. iv. 11—15) suggest that it is the duty of the Church as a whole, and not to be left as a private enterprise to a few zealous individuals, to provide for the training of men for spiritual service. Had more care been devoted to this in years past it had been well for the world.

II. The sorrowful soul seeks refuge from the cares and troubles of life in fellowship with the devout. It was a spiritual instinct that drew David to Samuel. The penalties of public life had already fallen heavily upon him. He had found, even in the beginning of his career of service to mankind, that " offences must needs come." The whole tone of life around the throne was out of accord with his most cherished aspirations. He was conscious of being misunderstood and misrepresented. The earlier days of quiet service and holy communion with God were now but sweet memories, bringing the bitter realities of daily life into stronger relief. With bounding heart and rapid flight, therefore, did he seek consolation, counsel, and rest with the honoured man who once anointed him to some unexplained service. Many have been, and still are, *in full sympathy with the troubled David*. The devout heart is brave, and dares not shun to fight the holy battles of the Lord in daily life. Religion is to flourish in face of evil and care, and not away in solitude. The business of life must not be left to the greedy and the vile. The great prayer was not that the disciples should be taken from the world, but that they should be kept from its evil (John xvii. 15 ; cf. 1 Cor. v. 10). Yet human nature cries out under the strain ; the spiritual mind is disgusted with the sins it witnesses ; the sense of belonging to a higher citizenship rises in force ; sympathy with kindred spirits is longed for ; the support of stronger natures is a pressing need ; and opportunities for prayer and for contemplation on the loftier aims of life are earnestly desired. Under this common inspiration, Jacob and Moses and Elijah sought each his " Bethel," and found strength for the coming trials and relief from present cares. It was in the same participation in human infirmities and sorrows that Christ loved to retire from the alien world to seek solace with his Father and with his people (Matt. xiv. 23 ; xvii. 1 ; Mark vi. 31 ; John xi. 3, 32—36 ; xii. 1, 2 ; Heb. v. 7). For the same reason we love to retire from the turmoil of life to the fellowship of a pious home, a meeting for prayer and counsel, and the service of the sanctuary. It is helpful to court occasional retirement. The "communion of saints" should be more than an article in our creed.

III. A DIVINE RESTRAINT IS PUT ON THE ENEMIES OF GOD'S SERVANTS. Saul's wicked desperation was great when he sent to Naioth to take David, and at its highest pitch when, after three despatches of men, he ventured to go to the abode of Samuel on a cruel errand. Hitherto Saul appeared to be fighting solely against David; but now that the mysterious spirit of prophecy came upon his messengers and rendered them harmless, it ought to have been obvious to him that in persecuting David he was at war with God. The knowledge of this mysterious restraint on them could not but add to his mental confusion, though it was not sufficient to the subjugation of his wild passion. Yet Saul was not bereft of reason; and could he have travelled to Ramah on such an errand without passing in review events prior and subsequent to his last intercourse with Samuel? (ch. xv. 26—35). Must he not have gone back in thought to the fearful day when the prophet declared the doom of his reign; the earlier days when as king he received the cheers of the people and the instructions of the prophet (ch. x. 24, 25); and the still earlier time when, fresh from his anointing, on meeting a band of prophets, the spirit of prophecy came on him and turned him into another man? (ch. x. 5—9). And now, after long separation, he was drawing near to that revered man of God and the company of the prophets, not the former Saul, full of hope and courage, but a man sinking deeper and deeper in sin, and with only the courage bred of remorse. If he was to be restrained and rendered harmless, what more natural method—more in harmony with the characteristics of the age and locality, and the psychological facts—than that for a season the old prophetic excitement should come upon him? It is no solitary fact that the mental and moral atmosphere of a place exercises power over men. The *main truth, however, is that God restrains.* Divine restraint enters into all things. The *nature* of things is but their limit assigned by God. The original relation of forces in the physical world is so settled by God that their interaction shall be bounded by definite results. To every effect wrought out in the development of the material universe it has been virtually said, "Thus far shalt thou go, and no farther." Scripture makes known the restraint which God puts on hearts and on moral beings. Lions dare not touch a Daniel. Evil spirits beg permission of Christ before they can go forth. Men sent to seize the Saviour were unable to fulfil their mission (John vii. 46), and soldiers were powerless in his presence (John xviii. 3—6). The history of the Church and of individual Christian life brings out instances of the restraining power which silently lays hold of man and renders his enmity innocuous. "It shall not come nigh thee" (Ps. xci. 7) has often been verified. In all these instances we have but glimpses of that unseen Power by which in due time all principalities and powers, and whatever opposeth itself to God and his Church, shall be either turned unto him or deprived of their power of injury (Isa. xi. 9; xxxv. 9, 10; 1 Cor. xv. 24—26; Phil. ii. 9—11; Col. i. 19, 20; Rev. xxi. 22—27).

HOMILIES BY VARIOUS AUTHORS.

Vers. 1—7. (GIBEAH.)—*The proof of true friendship.* Adversity is the touchstone of friendship, as of many other things; and its experience, sooner or later, is certain. Notwithstanding the secret jealousy and plotting of Saul, the prosperity of David continued to increase; and at length, unable to endure the sight of it, he "spoke to Jonathan his son, and to all his servants, about killing David." Persons in high places are generally attended by some men who, like Doeg (ch. xxi. 7; xxii. 22) and Cush (Ps. vii., inscription), are ready to carry out their evil wishes. The danger of David was now imminent. And with the revelation of it to him by Jonathan his troubles began. Whilst adversity shows the insincerity and worthlessness of false friends, it also shows the sincerity and worth of true. "In adverse hours the friendship of the good shines most." The proof of true friendship appears in—

I. THE STEADFASTNESS OF ITS ATTACHMENT. "Jonathan delighted much in David." Notwithstanding—1. *Misrepresentation* on the part of enemies. There can be no doubt that Saul spoke of David as treacherously aiming at the throne. The mouths of others were full of detraction and calumny, by which they sought to destroy him as with sharp swords (Ps. lix. 7). 2. *Urgent claims* on the part of friends and kindred. A father's wishes are sometimes opposed to a friend's welfare. 3. *Self-interest*. If David were spared Jonathan's accession to the throne would be jeopardised (ch. xxi. 13). But true friendship stands the test. It "thinketh no evil" of a friend, will do him no wrong, nor admit the least feeling of jealousy or envy. The wintry storm only serves to strengthen its attachment. "Yet these two charges of inconstancy and of weakness condemn most men : either in their prosperity they despise a friend, or in his troubles they desert him" (Cicero).

II. The FAITHFULNESS OF ITS COMMUNICATIONS. "And Jonathan told David," &c. (vers. 2, 3). 1. It reveals the *whole truth* and conceals nothing. "If you think any one your friend in whom you do not put the same confidence as in yourself you know not the real power of friendship" (Seneca). 2. It gives the *best counsel* in its power. 3. It *promises aid* as it may be needed.

III. The SELF-DEVOTION OF ITS ENDEAVOURS. "And Jonathan spake good of David," &c. (vers. 4, 5). 1. It undergoes *personal risk* in undertaking the cause of a friend. 2. It makes *earnest entreaty* on behalf of the absent one ; asserting his innocence, enumerating his services, setting forth his claims upon gratitude and esteem, and remonstrating against his being injured "without cause" (ver. 5; John xv. 25). 3. It shows a *prudent and respectful regard* for those whom it wishes to influence. In Jonathan prudence and principle were combined. "Prudence did not go so far as to make him silent about the sin which Saul was purposing to commit ; principle was not so asserted as to arouse his father's indignation" (W. M. Taylor).

IV. The VALUE OF ITS ACHIEVEMENTS. "And Saul hearkened," &c. (vers. 6, 7). "How forcible are right words !" Even the heart of Saul is moved, and his better feelings gain the ascendancy. How often by a generous and prudent attempt at peace-making is—1. A threatening *evil* averted. 2. A *reconciliation* of the alienated effected. 3. *Intercourse* between friends renewed, " as in times past." " Blessed are the peacemakers," &c. (Matt. v. 9). " There are four, young man " (says an Eastern sage), " who, seeming to be friends, are enemies in disguise—the rapacious friend, the man of much profession, the flatterer, and the dissolute companion. These four, young man, are true friends—the *watchful* friend, the friend who is *the same in prosperity and adversity*, the friend who gives *good advice*, and the *sympathising* friend" ('Contem. Rev.,' xxvii. 421).—D.

Vers. 8—18. (GIBEAH.)—*David's escape from court*. "And David fled, and escaped that night" (ver. 10). "There was war again" (ch. xvii. ; xviii. 5, 30), victory by David again, an evil spirit upon Saul again (ch. xvi. 23 ; xviii. 10) ; and, as David once more sat in the palace, "playing with his hand," the king not merely brandished his spear as before, but hurled it at him. It was his last attempt of the kind. After what had taken place he might not be trusted again ; and David fled, first to his own house, and during the night from the city. It is one of the *memorable nights* of the Bible. 1. That night was the commencement of his *open persecution by Saul*, and of the long and varied troubles he experienced as an outlaw. He had been at court some three or four years, and now at three-and-twenty went forth to his seven years' wanderings (2 Sam. v. 5: "He lived seventy years"—Josephus). 2. That night was, as is commonly thought, the occasion of the composition of *the first of David's psalms*. PSALM LIX., 'the refuge of the persecuted,' "is perhaps the oldest of the Davidic psalms that have come down to us" (Delitzsch). It is not necessary to suppose that it was actually written on the night of his escape. The thoughts and feelings then entertained may have been penned subsequently ; perhaps while he continued at Ramah with Samuel and "the prophets" (vers. 18, 20). Other psalms have been referred by some to the same occasion—viz., Ps. vi., vii., xi. "His harp was his companion in his flight, and even in the midst of peril the poet's nature appears which regards all life as materials for song, and the devout spirit appears which regards all trials as occasions of praise" (Maclaren). How wide and deep was the stream of sacred song of which this was the commencement ! 3. That night afforded one of the most remarkable instances of the protecting and guiding *providence of God* by which the life of David was manifestly ordered. Notice—

I. His DANGER, and the anxiety and distress by which it was naturally attended (vers. 11, 14, 17, compared with Ps. lix.). Adversity—1. Often follows closely upon *prosperity*. In the morning David occupied a position of high honour as the king's son-in-law, the successful general, the popular hero; at night he was hiding in secret and fleeing for his life. Vicissitude is the law of life; and none, however exalted, may boast of their security or continuance (Job xxix. 18). 2. Appears sometimes to fall most heavily upon *the godly man*. "Not for my transgression nor for my sin" (Ps. lix. 3). Why should it be permitted? To test, manifest, strengthen, and perfect his character. David had been tried by prosperity, he must also be tried by adversity. 3. Is due, in great measure, to the opposition and persecution of *the ungodly*. What a picture is here presented of the enemies of David, "when Saul sent messengers, and they watched the house to kill him"! (Ps. lix. 3, 6, 14). And what a revelation does it make of the wickedness of the human heart, which was consummated in the crucifying of the Lord of glory! "As then he that was born after the flesh," &c. (Gal. iv. 29). The conflict is renewed in every age and in every individual life. "All that will live godly," &c. (2 Tim. iii. 12). 4. Leads the good man to *more entire trust* in God and more earnest prayer. This is one of its chief purposes.

> "Deliver me from mine enemies, O my God!...
> *O Jehovah, God of hosts*, God of Israel!....
> O my Strength, on thee will I wait,
> For God is my Fortress."

5. Is never so bitter to him as trouble to the wicked, for he has *peace within* and undying hope. How different was it with David in this respect from what it was with Saul! 6. However long the good man may suffer from the persecution of the wicked, his deliverance is *certain;* for "God is Ruler in Jacob," &c. (Ps. lix. 13). "By him actions are weighed."

II. His DELIVERANCE (vers. 11, 12, 17, 18). The interposition of Providence, to which it was due—1. Is not made without the watchful and diligent use of appropriate *means*. David did not presumptuously wait in the palace or his own house, but availed himself of the opportunity of escaping. "When they persecute you," &c. (Matt. x. 23). 2. Is shown in *turning to good* what was meant for evil. The snare that was woven for his soul (ch. xvii. 21; ver. 11; Ps. lix. 3) aided his escape. 3. Often fills the wicked with *disappointment* and confusion when most confident of success (ver. 17). 4. Provides a *home* for the good man when driven out of their society. "Came to Samuel and told him all," &c. That night he was received by his revered friend, to whose instructions he had doubtless often listened; and with whom else could he have found such sympathy and shelter? 5. Causes him to *render praise* to God.

> "But, as for me, I will sing of thy strength,
> Yea, I will shout aloud of thy mercy in the morning;
> For thou hast been a Fortress to me,
> And a Refuge in the day when I was in distress:
> O my Strength, unto thee will I harp,
> For God is my Fortress, my merciful God."

6. Conduces to the *benefit* of many. These Psalms of David—the result (under "an unction from the Holy One") of his distresses and deliverances—are among our greatest spiritual treasures. "They are for all time. They never can be outgrown. No dispensation while the world lasts and continues what it is can ever raise us above the reach or the need of them. They describe every spiritual vicissitude, they speak to all classes of minds, they command every natural emotion. They are penitential, jubilant, adorative, deprecatory;—they are tender, mournful, joyous, majestic;—soft as the descent of dew; low as the whisper of love; loud as the voice of thunder; terrible as the almightiness of God!" (Binney, 'Service of Song in the House of the Lord').—D.

Vers. 11—17. (GIBEAH.)—*Michal*. The women mentioned in the Books of Samuel are, for the most part, distinguished for their eminent piety. But what shall be said of Michal, the wife of David? She was a daughter of Saul, inherited much of his temperament and disposition, and (unlike Jonathan) was without the religious principle by which they might have been controlled and sanctified. She was—1. *Impressionable and impulsive.* Fascinated by his personal appearance and popularity, the young princess "loved David," and made no secret of her affection; but she does not appear to have perceived anything of his highest qualities. The relation of husband and wife, no less than that of friends, is firmest when sanctified by common faith and love toward God. 2. *Capable of a noble action.* Under the influence of strong feeling she warned David of his danger and aided his escape, at the risk of her own life. 3. *Designing and deceptive.* Her quick-wittedness devised the means of escape, deceived the messengers of Saul to gain time, and invented a ready story to disarm her father's wrath. Her fear of her father was greater than her love for truth; and her love for her husband greater than her hatred of sin. "She could tell lies for David, but she had not the courage and the faith to go with him into suffering, or to tell the truth for him" (W. M. Taylor). 4. *Superstitious.* Teraphim (ch. xv. 23). See Bible Dictionaries. It is not said that David knew of her possession of these idolatrous objects. 5. *Changeable and wayward.* During the wanderings of David she was given in marriage to Phalti, apparently without reluctance (ch. xxv. 44); and (as appears when restored to David) "she had evidently gained his affections; he most likely had won hers" (2 Sam. iii. 16). 6. *Proud, jealous, and scornful.* Proud of her birth and rank, jealous of her rivals, Abigail and Ahinoam (2 Sam. vi. 16, 20—23; Blunt, 'Script. Coincidences,' p. 126), and scornful toward her husband. "She despised him in her heart."

> "Preceding the blest vessel, onward came,
> With light dance leaping, girt in humble guise,
> Israel's sweet harper; in that hap he seemed
> Less and yet more kingly. Opposite
> At a great palace, from the lattice forth
> Looked Michal, like a lady full of scorn
> And sorrow" (Dante, 'Purg.' x.).

7. *Unspiritual, and destitute of sympathy* with the feelings of boundless gratitude, joy, and adoration expressed before the Lord.—D.

Ver. 20. (RAMAH.)—*Samuel the president.* Of Samuel one more glimpse is afforded before his life closes. After his separation from Saul he appears to have devoted himself to the training of a body of younger men to carry on his prophetic work. The flight of David to him shows that an intimate relationship had previously subsisted between them. He went to him for counsel and sanctuary, and the intercourse of the young hero with the old prophet is full of suggestion. Samuel might have advised him to make armed resistance against the godless tyranny of Saul; in which, with his great popularity, he might have succeeded, but only at the cost of a long and ruinous civil war. As at the rejection of Saul he avoided violent measures in support of the theocracy, so now he counselled the same course, and took David with him from his own house to Naioth (dwellings), or the common residence of "the company of the prophets" (ch. x. 10), in the neighbourhood of Ramah. It was the chief home of order, light, and religion; the centre of spiritual influence. "He found there only temporary safety, indeed, from Saul's persecution, but abiding consolation and strength in the inspired prophetic word, in the blessings of the fraternal community, and in the consoling and elevating power of the holy poetic art, whereby he doubtless stood in peculiarly intimate connection with the community" (Erdmann). "God intended to make David not a warrior and a king only, but a prophet too. As the field fitted him for the first and the court for the second, so Naioth shall fit him for the third" (Hall). How long he continued is not stated; but, on hearing of his refuge, Saul sent three times to take him by force, and ultimately went himself for the purpose. The messengers found an assembly (*lahak*, used here only, probably by a transposition of letters, i. q. *kahal*—Gesenius) of prophets engaged in religious exercises under the presidency of Samuel. It is not necessary to suppose that the service, which may have had a special character, was conducted in a large hall, though there may have been such ; it was probably in the open air, and capable of being seen and heard from a distance (ver. 22). With respect more particularly to Samuel, notice—

I. HIS HONOURED POSITION—"standing as appointed over them," or as leader ; not probably appointed by any official act of theirs, but generally recognised and honoured, and directing their holy exercises. The honour in which he was held was due to—1. The pre-eminent *authority* he possessed as a prophet of the Lord (ch. iii. 19). 2. The high *character* he had so long sustained in that office, and the course of labour he had pursued. 3. The *special work* he had accomplished in gathering around him such young men as seemed to be qualified by their gifts and piety to act as prophets in Israel, and forming them into a school or college of prophets. He was the venerable founder of their order, and reaped the reward of his labours in their reverence and affection, and still more in their devotion to Jehovah and their zeal for his honour.

II. HIS PROPHETIC ASSOCIATES. They were "prophets," not "sons" or disciples "of the prophets" (2 Kings ii. 3), who seem to have occupied in later times a more dependent and inferior position. They were a union or free association of men "endowed with the Spirit of God for the purpose of carrying on their work, the feeble powers of junior members being directed and strengthened by those of a higher class" (Kitto, 'Cyc. of Bib. Lit.'). Among them probably were Gad (ch. xxii. 5 ; 2 Sam. xxiv. 11), Nathan (2 Sam. vii. 2 ; xii. 1), and Heman, the grandson of Samuel (1 Chron. vi. 33 ; xxv. 5 ; "the king's seer," &c.). 1. They had been under his *instruction* in the knowledge of God and his law, and, as subservient to this, in reading and writing, poetry, music, and singing. "Education is not a panacea for all human ills, but it is an indispensable condition both of individual and of national progress" ('Expositor,' iii. 344). 2. They were in sympathy with his *purposes* concerning the true welfare of the people of Israel, and strove to carry them into effect. They formed "a compact phalanx to stand against the corruption which had penetrated so deeply into the nation, and to bring back the rebellious to the law and the testimony" (Keil). 3. They were endowed, like Samuel himself, with a peculiar measure of the *Divine Spirit* for the accomplishment of their work. By his influence they were drawn together, variously gifted, and sometimes impelled to ecstatic utterances.

III. HIS DEVOUT OCCUPATION. He presided over the prophets, and took part with them in "prophesying," or uttering with a loud voice the praises of God. His last recorded act was one of worship, and under his influence David's intense love for public worship was probably acquired. The service was—1. Accompanied with *music* (as in ch. x. 10). "A principal part of their occupation consisted—under the guidance of some prophet of superior authority, and more peculiarly under the Divine influence, as moderator and preceptor—in celebrating the praises of Almighty God, in hymns and poetry, with choral chaunts, accompanied by stringed instruments and pipes" (Lowth). 2. *Edifying*. Whilst their utterance expressed their inward feeling, it was also the means of teaching and exhorting one another, and of "awakening holy susceptibilities and emotions in the soul, and of lifting up the spirit to God, and so preparing it for the reception of Divine revelations." 3. *United*. which tends by the power of sympathy to intensify feeling, strengthen faith, enlarge desire, and perfect those dispositions in connection with which worship is acceptable to God.

IV. HIS POWERFUL INFLUENCE. "The Spirit of God came upon the messengers," &c. The immediate effect was to transform these men, to protect David from their power, and to afford a sign of the opposition of God to the designs of Saul. More generally, the influence of Samuel was put forth in and through the "company of prophets" for—1. The maintenance of the principle of the *theocracy*, which was imperilled by the conduct of Saul. The prophets were its true representatives and upholders in every subsequent age. 2. The elevation of the *people* in wisdom and righteousness. Their work was to teach, reprove, and exhort those with whom they came into contact ; and "through such a diffusion of prophetic training the higher truths of prophecy must have been most rapidly diffused among the people, and a new and higher life formed in the nation" (Ewald). 3. The *preparation* of men for a better time—the advent of Christ, the outpouring of the Spirit, and the proclamation of the gospel. The prophets, not the priests, were the true forerunners of the gospel ministry.—D.

Vers. 22—24. (RAMAH.)—*The meeting of three remarkable men.* This appears to have been the only occasion on which Samuel, Saul, and David were present at the same time and place. The meeting was a notable one, and may be compared with others (Exod. x. 16; 1 Kings xviii. 16; Acts xxv. 24). Besides the three men just mentioned, there was also present One infinitely greater, and, although invisible, his power was displayed in a marvellous manner. Considered in relation to the *Divine power*, the narrative sets before us—

I. AN AGED PROPHET IMBUED WITH FEARLESS DIGNITY. His danger was great. What Saul might do may be judged from the fear which Samuel expressed on a former occasion (ch. xvi. 2), and from what he actually did not long afterwards (ch. xxii. 18, 19). But the prophet went on with his holy service calm and undismayed. He was inwardly sustained by Divine power, as others have since been in danger and suffering (Acts xvi. 25). Such fearlessness is possessed by God's servants in connection with—1. A firm persuasion that they are in *the path of duty.* They have within "a peace above all earthly dignities, a still and quiet conscience." If conscience "does make cowards of us all," it also makes us heroes. And

> " He that hath light within his own clear breast
> May sit in the centre and enjoy bright day;
> But he that hides a dark soul and foul thoughts
> Benighted walks under the midday sun " (Milton, 'Comus').

2. A vivid realisation of the *presence and might of the Lord.* Faith "sees him who is invisible" and "the mountain full of horses and chariots of fire" (2 Kings vi. 17). 3. A strong assurance of *deliverance* from their adversaries.

II. A PERSECUTING MONARCH TURNED INTO A HARMLESS ENTHUSIAST. The Divine power was exerted first upon Saul's messengers and then upon himself. In a somewhat similar manner, if not to the same extent, it is often exerted upon evil and persecuting men—1. In connection with the utterances of *the praises of God* by his servants (2 Chron. xx. 22; Ps. cxlix. 6). Instances are not unknown in which "one that believeth not" has come into their assembly, and, hearing their praises, has fallen down on his face and worshipped God (1 Cor. xiv. 24, 25). This was not the first time that Saul was so affected, and the recollection of his earlier experience had probably some influence upon him. But *then* it was a sign that the power of God was for him, *now* that it was against him. 2. In order to *restrain* the wicked from carrying out their evil designs. He who holds the hearts of men in his hand thereby says, "Do my prophets no harm" (1 Chron. xvi. 22). 3. In order to *restore* them to the right way. It was to Saul more than a warning that he was fighting against God. "He was seized by this mighty influence of the Spirit of God in a more powerful manner than his servants were, both because he had most obstinately resisted the leadings of Divine grace, and also in order that, if it were possible, *his hard heart might be broken* and subdued by the power of grace. If, however, he should nevertheless continue obstinately in his rebellion against God, he would then fall under the judgment of hardening, which would be speedily followed by his destruction" (Keil).

III. AN INNOCENT FUGITIVE RESCUED FROM IMPENDING DESTRUCTION. David was saved from the hand of Saul, and even (as it would appear) formally reconciled to him (ch. xx. 18, 27). The putting forth of the power of God was to him—1. An indication of the varied and abundant *resources of God* to protect in the greatest peril. 2. An assurance of *Divine approbation* in the way of trust and obedience. 3. An encouragement to *patient endurance.* He might be tempted to reach the goal for which, as he was now probably fully aware, he was destined (ch. xx. 15; xxiii. 17) by violent measures; but ever as he thought on this scene, together with the counsel and the whole course of the venerable prophet, he would feel that "the way of order is the best."

"The way of order, though it lead through windings,
Is the best. Right forward goes the lightning
And the cannon-ball ; quick, by the nearest path,
They come, opening with murderous crash their way
To blast and ruin ! My son, the quiet road
Which men frequent, where peace and blessings travel,
Follows the river's course, the valley's bendings ;
Modestly skirts the corn-field and the vineyard,
Revering property's appointed bounds,
And leading safe, though slower, to the mark" (Schiller, 'Wallenstein').
D.

Vers. 18—24.—*Religious consolation and religious excitement.* The consolation was tasted by David ; the excitement was shown by Saul.

I. CONSOLATION. We are not surprised to learn that David, when driven from his house by the deadly malice of the king, betook himself to the prophet Samuel at his residence in Ramah. In reporting the treatment he had received to the venerable prophet, he reported it to God, whose authority was represented by Samuel. The path of his life seemed to be blocked by the undeserved ill-will of Saul. Was there any further instruction for him from the Lord ? There is no evidence that Samuel had held any communication with David from the time of his visit to Bethlehem to anoint the young shepherd ; but it may be assumed that he had kept a watchful eye on his career, and prayed much for a youth with so great a destiny. Some painter ought to show us their meeting: the aged prophet, his countenance traced with sorrow for his own unworthy sons, and not less for the untoward career of Saul, receiving with outstretched arms and ready sympathy the fugitive David, in the very perfection of his gallant youth, yet coming with weary steps and dejected visage. The old man took the young chief to shelter with him in Naioth, where was a settlement of prophets—a group of dwellings where servants of God lived in retreat and cultivated sacred song and fraternal fellowship. David was not to tarry long in such a refuge, but it was good for him to visit it. It solaced and strengthened his spirit in God. Undisturbed by the jealousies of the court and the dangerous frenzy of the king, surrounded by an atmosphere of devotion, mingling not merely with aged seers like Samuel, but also with young men of his own age whose time was spent in sacred study and brightened with music and song, David must have been in his best element. He was a good soldier, and happy at the head of his troops, charging the Philistines. But he was still more a thinker, a poet, a minstrel, a prophet, a man of fervent spirit toward God, and so must have been happier in the goodly fellowship of the prophets at Naioth than in the rush of battle and the pride of victory. There is no record of the words of consolation and counsel which Samuel spoke to him ; but doubtless we have traces and echoes of them in those psalms in which David has discussed the afflictions of the servants of Jehovah, and sung of their ultimate deliverance and reward. Ps. lix. is traditionally ascribed to the period when the armed men sent by Saul surrounded David's house to put him to death. As it is highly artificial in structure, it can hardly have been composed on the spur of the moment. Very probably it was written at Naioth while the impression of the danger was fresh, and was sung among the prophets there. In the case of David we read of no agitation or excitement. It would be little surprising if he, fleeing for his life, had been overcome by emotion when he found himself in safeguard. But all we read of his bearing is rational and calm.

II. EXCITEMENT. It was in the servants of Saul, and subsequently in Saul himself, that a religious excitement appeared. Three successive bands were despatched by the king to seize his son-in-law, but with a strange result. As each band saw the venerated Samuel stand forth at the head of the prophets, they feared to do violence to one under such august protection. Nay, more ; the spiritual enthusiasm of the prophets communicated itself to them and overmastered them, so that they forgot their errand and joined in the burst of holy song. King Saul himself, provoked by the failure of his emissaries, went to Naioth, and he was more completely overpowered than they. We have seen already that his temperament was exceedingly amenable to the impressions of music and song. We remember how he had flung himself among the prophets in the very outset of his history; and although sadly deteriorated in character, he still retained his early sensibilities. Indeed, through the very disorder of his faculties he had become more susceptible than ever of religious excitement; so when he reached Naioth he was quite beyond himself. The spiritual electricity of the place was too much for him, and he fell into a very paroxysm of enthusiasm. At first when, on the way to Naioth, he lifted his voice in some sacred chant, it was well, and the historian does not hesitate to say that "the Spirit of God was upon him." But at Naioth he behaved like a fanatical devotee of some heathen god, or a wild dervish of the East. He threw off his royal tunic, and after long and exhausting exercise of body and spirit lay in nothing but his under-dress, prone and probably motionless, on the ground for "all that day and all that night." But though "among the prophets," he was not of them. It was a mere fit of fervour soon to pass away. The heart of Saul was by this time hopelessly "jangled and out of tune." The subject of temporary religious excitement needs to be carefully thought out and discreetly handled. But it can never be fully explained—at all events not till more is known of the action of the nervous system, and till more light falls on the mysterious question of contagious emotion and imitative cerebral stimulation. One or two things, however, are plain enough, and deserve to be noted; e. g.— 1. *There is a religious excitation which carries with it no moral influence whatever.* It is not feigned or insincere. He who is the subject of it is really lifted up or carried along as with a rush of earnest feeling. He cries for mercy; he prays with strong supplication; or he sings of pardon and of unutterable joys. His emotions are all aglow, and his brain is stirred to unusual activity. This occurs the more easily if one who is constitutionally accessible to such gusts of feeling falls among others who are much in earnest. He finds himself where prayers burst forth from importunate souls, and hymns are sung with a swing of enthusiasm. At once he feels as those around him do. Yet there is no change of his moral nature; he is merely a person of susceptible or imitative constitution, who has caught the contagion of religion from others, yet has not come, and may never come, to repentance. It is not for a moment to be denied that in many cases a real moral and spiritual change is produced in the midst of much excitement; but the excitement is only an accompaniment of the change—perhaps necessary for some minds, but always fraught with some degree of danger. The only thing of lasting value is the exercise of conscience, and the turning of the affections and will to God in Christ. 2. *The degree in which new religious emotion overpowers the body is generally proportioned to the previous ignorance of the mind, or its estrangement from God.* David at Naioth fell into no frenzy, lay in no swoon, because he was a man of God, and devout feeling flowed through him unimpeded, found in him a congenial heart. But Saul had been in an evil mood; envy and murder were in his breast. So, when a pure and sacred impulse came upon him, it met resistance; and there were bodily manifestations which, far from being marks of grace, were signs of a moral state at variance with the Spirit of God. This case should teach caution in ascribing any religious value to prostrations, trances, and long fasts. These things most frequently occur in cases of a morbid hysterical temperament, or in very ignorant persons who are disturbed and terrified, or in instances where religious feeling, suddenly flowing in on unprepared minds, encounters obstinate obstruction. When the mind is thoughtful and refined, or when the heart is gentle and open to any good influx, religious fervour seldom causes any disorder in the nervous system or the physical constitution. We may be reminded here that David could show no small excitement, for he danced before the ark in the sight of all Israel (2 Sam. vi. 14). True; but in all the enthusiasm of that great occasion King David was sober-minded and self-possessed. He had good reasons for leading the sacred processional dance, as may afterwards be shown; but, far from giving way to excitement, or losing his senses like Saul, he went calmly through the duties of an eventful and fatiguing day. He offered burnt offerings and peace offerings. Then he blessed the people, causing provisions to be distributed among them. And after all this "David returned to bless his house." Such is the enthusiasm we desire. To be full of joy before the Lord, but at the same time to be of a healthy mind, ready for public or private duty hour by hour. But we see no good in nervous excitement or hysterical ecstasy. When we consider that the Bible is a collection of

Eastern books, and that the East has always been the home of strange religious extravagances, we recognise in the well-balanced sobriety of mind which pervades the Bible a new proof of its Divine inspiration. It takes notice of the varied phenomenal effects of strong religious feeling on the human frame; it tells of long prostrations, excited movements, and prophetic trances; but it always attaches moral significance and value not to such abnormal conditions, but to the effects which appear and remain in character and life. The greatest of all, the Man Christ Jesus, the Lord whom we are to love and follow, is shown to us full of a sublime enthusiasm, but full at the same time of meekness and of wisdom. The Scriptures teach us to be calm and fervent, fervent and calm. If rushes of devout emotion come upon us, be it so. If men who have no faith call us fanatical and mad, be it so. Such men said of our Master, "He rageth, and hath a demon;" and of Paul, "Thou art beside thyself." But let the evidence of our Christian faith and principle be found not in any moods of excitement, but in the moral excellence we exhibit, the fruit of the Spirit we bring forth. So shall we find consolation and strength when others only expose their weakness; and every pause at Naioth, or the place of prayer and holy fellowship, will brace our spirits for the trials that must yet befall us before we are perfected.—F

EXPOSITION.

JONATHAN ENDEAVOURS TO RECONCILE SAUL TO DAVID (CH. XX.).

CHAPTER XX.

JONATHAN'S COVENANT WITH DAVID RE-NEWED (vers. 1—23). Ver. 1.—**David fled from Naioth**. While Saul was under the influence of the prophetic enthusiasm David escaped; but it is evident that this visit to Samuel, and the extraordinary occurrences which attended it, were not without a good influence for the time upon Saul's mind. Some sort of reconciliation must have been patched up, probably by the mediation of Samuel; for David assumed that at the new moon he would be expected to dine at the king's table (ver. 5), and that Saul would look for him as a matter of course (ver. 6). We find, moreover, that his place was made ready, not only on the new moon (ver. 25), but also on the following day (ver. 26). But whatever professions Saul may have made to Samuel, it is evident that no promise had been made personally to David, and taught by past experience that the intention of slay-ing him had grown more and more fixed in the king's mind, he feels that his position is full of danger, and takes counsel with Jonathan, with the view of learning whether he might venture once again to take his place as a member of Saul's family.

Ver. 2.—**God forbid.** An exclamation of horror; literally, "Far be it" (see on ch. ix. 45). In spite of the many proofs of Saul's bitter hatred, Jonathan cannot believe that after all that had taken place at Ramah his father would still persist in his murderous purpose. He further assures David that Saul would do nothing without telling him; literally, without uncovering his ear, with-out telling it him privately (see on ch. ix.

15). The phrase is used again in ver. 12. For **will do nothing** the written text reads "has done for himself," which the Kri properly corrects. The rashness of Saul's temper, and his frank talk about killing David recorded in ch. xix. 1, confirm Jona-than's statement about the openness of his father's ways, and he therefore assures David that he may take his place in safety.

Vers. 3, 4.—**Thy father certainly knoweth,** &c. Though Saul did not know the entire-ness of Jonathan's love for David, yet he was aware of the friendship that existed between them, and consequently might keep his pur-pose a secret from Jonathan, especially if he considered that his frankness in speaking openly to his son and servants on a previous occasion had led to David's escape. David, therefore, urges upon his friend a different course, to which he assents. But how are we to explain the entirely different views taken of Saul's conduct by the two. When David tells his fears Jonathan utters an exclamation of horror, and says, "Thou shalt not die." Yet he knew that his father had talked to him and his officers about putting David to death; that he had tried to kill him with his own hand, and on his escape had set people to watch his house with orders to slay him; and on David's flight to the prophet had thrice sent emissaries to bring him away by force. The explanation probably lies in Saul's insanity. When he threw his javelin at David and during the subsequent proceed-ings he was out of his mind. The violent fit at Naioth had for the time cleared his reason, and he had come back sane. Jona-than regarded all that had taken place as the effect of a mind diseased, and concluded, therefore, that David might now return to his home and wife, and resume his duties and take his place at the royal table. Should the old craze come back about David being his rival and destined successor, Saul would be sure to talk about it, and then Jonathan would give him timely warning. But David was convinced that it was no craze, but that Saul, sane or insane, had determined upon his death.

Vers. 5—7.—**To-morrow is the new moon.** The first day of the new moon was a joyful festival, its appearance being greeted with the sounding of trumpets, and celebrated by a burnt offering and a sin offering. It was, moreover, kept by Saul as a family festival, at which David, as his son-in-law, was expected to be present. As, moreover, David was to hide **unto the third day at even**, counting from the time when he was arranging his plans with Jonathan, it is plain that it was the rule to prolong the feasting unto the second day. When then Jonathan, convinced by David's pleading, had consented to aid him in his own way, they arrange that he shall absent himself from this festival, and remain during it hidden out of sight. In case Saul missed him and asked the reason of his absence, Jonathan was to offer as an excuse for him that he had earnestly requested leave to pay a hurried visit to Bethlehem, in order to be present at an annual festival : and if Saul took the excuse in good part it would be a sign that he had no malicious purposes towards David, whereas if he fell into a rage it would be a proof of a settled evil design. **A yearly sacrifice for all the family.** For all the *mishpachah*, i. e. not for all Jesse's household, but for all that subdivision of the tribe of Judah to which Jesse belonged ; for a tribe was divided into families, and these again into fathers' houses (Josh. vii. 16, 17). The occasion would thus be a grand one. In ch. xvi. 2 we have an instance of a special sacrifice at Bethlehem, but this feast of the *mishpachah* was held every year ; and evidently before the temple was built at Jerusalem these local sacrifices were the rule. We may well believe that there was such a festival, and that the fictitious part of Jonathan's story was that David had been summoned to it.

Ver. 8.—**Thou hast brought thy servant into a covenant of Jehovah with thee.** As the friendship between Jonathan and David had been cemented by the invocation of the name of Jehovah, it was one firm and assured, and David might look not merely for one act of kindness, but for constant truth and help. It was, moreover, Jonathan's own doing ; and yet, **if there be in me**, David says, **iniquity**, *i. e.* treason against Saul, if I have not been a faithful and true servant to him, but, on the contrary, have plotted

evil against him, or now entertain any evil designs, then let the covenant be abrogated. David refuses to shelter himself under it if he has incurred guilt, and only asks that Jonathan, by the authority which he exercised as the king's son, should himself put him to death, and not deliver him up to Saul.

Ver. 9.—**Far be it**, the word rendered *God forbid* in ver. 2. It indignantly rejects the idea of David having committed any crime. The rest of the verse is an incomplete sentence : " If I knew certainly that evil were determined by my father to come upon thee, and did not tell thee—— " These broken sentences have great force in the original, as signs of intense feeling (comp. Luke xix. 42). We must complete the sentence mentally in some such way as the Syriac : "then Jehovah do so to me, and more also."

Ver. 10.—**Who shall tell me ? or what if,** &c. The *if* is an insertion of the A. V. Really David's question is very involved and ungrammatical, as was natural in his excited state. It may be translated, "Who will tell me (or, how shall I know) what rough answer thy father will give thee ?" But some Jewish authorities render, "Who will tell me if so be that thy father give thee a rough answer ?"

Vers. 11–13.—**Let us go out into the field.** David's question had shown Jonathan that there were grave difficulties in their way, and so he proposes that they should walk into the country, to be able to talk with one another more freely, and concert measures for the future. And there Jonathan binds himself with a solemn oath, if Saul's intentions be good, to send a trusty messenger to inform David, but if there be danger, then to come and tell David himself. **O Lord God.** With a few MSS. we must supply the usual formula of an oath : "As Jehovah the God of Israel liveth." **About to-morrow any time, or the third day.** This cumbrous translation arose out of the mistaken idea that the word rendered **to-morrow** could only be used in that limited sense. Strictly it signifies the *morning*, and is applicable to any morrow. Jonathan fixes one time, and one only, and the passage should be rendered, " By this time on the third morrow." The meeting was to be on the morrow after the second day of the festival, and so on the third morrow after the conversation. The whole may be translated, " As Jehovah the God of Israel liveth, when by this time on the third morrow I have searched my father, and, behold, there be good for David, if then I send not to thee, and uncover thy ear, Jehovah do so and much more to Jonathan." The alternative case is then put, and if the news be evil, Jonathan undertakes himself to be the messenger, and David is to provide for his safety by flight. The concluding prayer that Jehovah might be with David as he had been with Saul contains the same presentiment of David attaining to great power and dignity which is more directly expressed in the following verses.

Vers. 14, 15.—The construction of this passage is very difficult if we retain the three negatives of the Masoretic text; but most commentators, following the reading of the Syriac as regards at least one of them, consider that the Masorites have been mistaken in the vowels which they have attached to the consonants (see on ch. i. 7). Read with other vowels, two of these negatives become interjections of desire—*O that;* and the whole may be translated, "And O that, while I still live, yea, O that thou wouldst show me the kindness of Jehovah,—*i. e.* great unfailing kindness, such as was that of Jehovah to Israel,—that I die not, nor shalt thou cut off thy kindness from my house for ever." It was the sanguinary custom in the East on a change of dynasty to put all the seed royal to death (1 Kings xv. 29; xvi. 11, &c., and comp. 2 Sam. xix. 28). As then Jonathan foresaw that it was Jehovah's will to transfer the kingdom to David, he binds him by the memory of his own true love to him to show mercy to his race.

Ver. 16.—This verse also is very difficult, but it is probably to be taken as an insertion of the narrator: "So Jonathan made a covenant with the house of David"—that is, so as to bind his descendants—"saying, Let Jehovah require it at the hand of David's enemies." These last words probably are a euphemism, and mean David himself. So Rashi explains the words. The courtesy of an Oriental forbade his saying, May Jehovah punish David for it, but he prays that God would requite it on some one. But if the Divine anger visits even David's enemies for it, how much more the guilty perjurer himself.

Ver. 17.—**Jonathan caused David to swear again.** So strong was his conviction in David's future kingdom, and his wish that there should be an unbroken bond of love between the two families, that he makes David solemnly repeat his promise. The Septuagint and Vulgate, by altering the vowels, read, "And Jonathan sware again to David." At first sight this interpretation seems most in accordance with the reason given for the renewal of the oath, namely,

Jonathan's own love; but the Masoretic text agrees better with what has gone before, and with his wish that their covenant under no change of circumstances should be broken.

Vers. 18, 19.—Jonathan now arranges his plan for communicating the result to David. For **when thou hast stayed three days**, at which all the versions stumble, a slight alteration gives the right sense: "And on the third day." David on the third day was to **go down quickly**—Hebrew, "greatly," *i. e.* he was to go a long way down into the valley. The rendering *quickly* is taken from the Vulgate, but makes no sense. It did not matter whether David went fast or slow, as he was to hide there for some time, but it was important that David should be far away, so that no prying eye might chance to catch sight of him. **When the business was in hand.** Literally, "the day of the business," probably that narrated in ch. xix. 2—7. The Septuagint, Vulgate, and Chaldee all understand "a working day," in opposition to a feast day; but "where thou didst hide thyself on a week day" gives no intelligible meaning. **By the stone Ezel.** As the name Ezel is formed from a verb signifying *to go*, some understand by it a *road-stone*, a stone to mark the way.

Vers. 20—23.—The two friends now agree upon the sign. Jonathan was to shoot three arrows at this stone, Ezel, as his mark, and was then to send his servant to gather them up. When he had gone some distance Jonathan was to shout to him, loud enough for David to hear. If Jonathan said that the arrows were on that side the mark, *i. e.* between it and Jonathan, David was to come forth boldly, as all was well. But if Jonathan said that the arrows were further on, then David must understand that he was to seek safety in flight. For **there is peace to thee, and no hurt**, the Hebrew has "there is peace to thee, and it is nothing," a simpler and more idiomatic rendering. **As touching the matter**, &c. Rather, "As for the word that we have spoken, I and thou, behold, Jehovah is between me and thee for ever." The *word* was the bond and covenant by which they had pledged their truth to one another. Though separated, their love was to continue, and Jehovah was to be their eternal centre of union, and the witness to their covenant.

HOMILETICS.

Vers. 1 — 10. — *Endangered life and reputation.* The facts are — 1. David, believing in Saul's purpose to kill him, flees to Jonathan, and inquires into the cause of this persecution. 2. Jonathan quiets him by the assurance that Saul would not hide any purpose from him. 3. On David referring to Saul's knowledge of their friendship and its effect on his methods, Jonathan expresses readiness to do whatever David may suggest. 4. Thereupon David suggests a means by which Saul's disposition towards him can be ascertained. 5. He further pleads, on the ground of their strong friendship, that Jonathan should slay or aid to deliver him. It is not improbable that the coming of the prophetic spirit on Saul was, among other reasons, designed to help him once more to a due consideration of his course. But by this time David appears to have awakened to the conviction that the recent attempts on his life were not to be ascribed to fitful outbursts of madness, but to a fixed purpose, for reasons he could not surmise. As then he had sought refuge with Samuel from the hand of passionate violence, so now he naturally turns to his beloved friend Jonathan to ascertain from one presumably in his father's secrets the causes of this persistent attempt on his life, and to demand of him the offices of true friendship. A triple consciousness pervades this appeal of David: namely, of integrity, of danger, of duty of self-preservation.

I. A MAN CONSCIOUS OF INTEGRITY OF LIFE. It would appear that David was quite unaware of the secret of Saul's conduct. It is probable that he knew nothing of that fearful doom pronounced by Samuel (ch. xv. 26—29) which had operated so disastrously on the guilty mind of Saul. With the innocence of an unworldly man, he could not imagine that a monarch reigning over the people of God could ever devise destruction against a subject unless he believed that subject to have committed some crime worthy of death. Possibly the king might be under an unfounded impression; and as Jonathan was heir to the throne and in his father's confidence, he would surely inform his friend. At all events, so far as he knew his own heart, he was conscious only of integrity. "What have I done? What is mine iniquity?" In dealing with the important matter involved in these questions, let us observe that —1. *Integrity is to be sought in every man.* David was correct in the assumption underlying his inquiry—that every one ought to be characterised by integrity of life, and that on its existence alone can we justly claim exemption from scorn, suffering, abandonment, and a right to respect, enjoyment of life, and personal protection. There is in every man a voice unceasingly demanding of him uprightness, moral soundness. The eye with which we look on one another is guided by this conviction. And it is in the universal recognition of the truth that integrity is to be sought in every one that we find a basis of appeal in the name of righteousness, and a rational place for the doctrines of atonement and regeneration. 2. *Integrity is to be regarded in a twofold aspect.* It will be observed that David simply raises the question as to what he had done in relation to Saul or his kingdom. He distinguished between integrity in his relations to man and integrity in his relations to God. All moral relations to man involve moral relations to God, but the reverse is not true. Man's relations to God are wider than those to his fellow-men. Religious morality is not identical with secular morality. The spiritual embraces obligations transcending the humanly moral. Integrity in relation to man lies in the faithful discharge of all obligations due to man, under the influence of pure motives in detail, and a supreme sense of justice in general. But integrity in relation to God means perfect rightness of spirit, manifesting itself in perfect love of God, perfect obedience to God, perfect purity of thought—in fact, conformity in every secret and open movement of will with the holy will of God. This soundness, this health, is certain to insure integrity in relation to man, but the reverse is not true. This distinction is of great importance to the understanding of Scripture and the regulation of life (cf. 2 Chron. vi. 36—39; Job xv. 14; Ps. xv.; Isa. xxxiii. 15, 16; Rom. iii. 23—28; James v. 16; 1 John i. 8). 3. *Integrity in its human relation is, in ordinary life, maintained without self-assertion.* During the months of David's service, from the day he entered into conflict with Goliath till his flight to Naioth, he had been a true, sincere man, doing his duty. But all this time he was not conscious of anything remarkable. The beauty of integrity of life lies in the naturalness which suggests no reflection upon itself. True virtue excludes self-admiration, and, when in exercise, self-consciousness. Our Saviour never refers to his goodness as a praise to himself. The sun needs only to shine, the truth only to be (Matt. vi. 1—4; Luke xviii. 12). 4. *Integrity may be asserted when challenged by detractors, or when wrong is done to one's interests.* David's uprightness of life would have gone on without self-introspection and self-assertion were it not that he was subject to a treatment not explicable on ordinary principles. It was time for him to affirm his innocence, and bring his natural integrity into distinct consciousness. He often does this in the Psalms, not to claim righteousness in relation to God, but to rebut accusations in reference to his conduct amongst men. It was the same sense of injustice which led Job to assert his innocence of many of the charges of his friends. "I will maintain mine own ways before him" (Job xv. 13—16). The Apostle Paul also vindicated his own life against the insinuations of false brethren (2 Cor. x. 8—11; xi. 6—10, 21—30). Our Saviour also, when persecuted by malicious men, could ask, "Which of you convinceth me of sin?" (John viii. 46). Only a stern sense of duty—a protest against wrong—will break a righteous man's silence in relation to himself. 5. *Integrity before man must never be a substitute for integrity before God.* David's object was simply vindication from supposed charges of wrong deliberately done to Saul. He had a deep consciousness at the same time that in the sight of God, as a spiritual being, he was unworthy and in need of *mercy.* Only such a man, sensible of sinfulness before God, would dwell so much on mercy (Ps. lii. 8; lxii. 12; lxxxvi. 5), and at the same time on "integrity" and "uprightness" (Ps. vii. 8; xxv. 21; xxvi. 1; xli. 42). Men take a very superficial view of things when they imagine that goodness which passes among men, and is a fulfilment of our earthly obligations, "extendeth" unto God (Ps. xvi. 2, 3). This was one of the deadly errors of the Pharisees, and it was exposed by the whole tenor of our Saviour's teaching (Luke xviii. 9—14; John iii. 1—11). As we have not integrity before God, we must be born again, repent, seek forgiveness and acceptance, not because of what we are and have done, but because of Christ having loved us and *given himself for us* (Acts iv. 12; Rom. iii. 24—28; iv. 5, 6; v. 1, 2; Phil. iii. 8, 9).

II. A MAN SENSIBLE OF GREAT PERIL. Two perils beset David. He feared death at the hand of Saul, and, most of all, loss of reputation. He rightly judged that if the king of Israel sought his life and chased him with that end in view, the impression would be conveyed to many that he had been guilty of some act of wrong well known to Saul, though unknown to the people. An upright man, although able to commit himself to God, dreads to be thought a wrong-doer, and to die as though he were such. Hence his pleading with Jonathan, his pain at the suspicion of want of integrity, his desire to learn whether the king's mind was more placable. *These two perils beset us all.* In one sense we are safe from death till our appointed time has come, for God's care fails not; yet in relation to the forces at work around us we know not what a day or an hour may bring forth. Life is begirt with powers of destruction. There is but a "step" between us and death. "In the midst of life we are in death." The *proper effect of this sense of peril is wholesome.* It leads to such an estimate of life as renders it wiser, more sober, earnest, and devout (Ps. xxxix. 4—7; xc. 12; Eccles. ix. 10; xi. 9; xii. 13; 1 Cor. vii. 29—31). But to a sincerely good man *danger to reputation is more serious.* Many would rather die than either actually lose character or be deemed to have lost it. They can sympathise with David's wish that Jonathan would slay him if really moral cause existed. Our Saviour's pain was great because of the effort to ruin his character. But though all are exposed to these two perils in common with David, there is *one other peril of life* which often is an occasion of loss of reputation. We are *exposed to the wiles of the devil.* As Saul sought the life of David, so Satan goeth about seeking whom he may devour (1 Pet. v. 8). Every day the adversary destroys by "his strong ones." The language of the Psalmist (Ps. x. 8—10) will apply with wonderful precision to the destroyer of souls, the "murderer from the beginning" (John viii. 44). The *proper effect of this sense of peril* is to *induce watchfulness,* avoidance of the haunts of iniquity, prayer for strength, and such consecration to work as shall leave no time or thought for dalliance with the tempter (Matt. vii. 13; xxvi. 41; Ephes. vi. 11, 12, 18).

III. A MAN INTENT ON SELF-PRESERVATION. While in conflict with Goliath, amidst the regular duties of his public course, David seems to have been under no concern for his life or reputation. He did his duty and trusted in God. But when he suspected attempts in the dark on his life and character, he felt bound to devise means of securing himself, and rightly manifested much anxiety in relation thereto. It is possible that character may be so defamed during life that only death will prove its vindication, as in case of our Saviour; nevertheless, no means should be left unused to assert our innocence and if possible prove it. The *subtle powers which threaten our life may be often avoided* by observance of laws of health and abstention from unnecessary risks. Many men commit slow suicide by wilful neglect of fresh air, good and moderate food, and by excessive toil for gain. The *preservation of character* may often be secured by abstaining from the "appearance of evil," though we shall never rid ourselves of uncharitable defamers.

General lessons:—1. We should strive to be free from the narrow suspicions and uncharitable thoughts which tend to injure excellent reputations (1 Cor. xiii. 4—7). 2. If we cannot vindicate our reputation before men, let us have comfort in God's knowledge of us (Ps. xxxvii. 5, 6; cxxxix. 1—4). 3. Like Jonathan, we should manifest great sympathy with those whose honourable character is defamed or in peril. 4. Our supreme concern should be to live in spirit so as to find acceptance with the holy, all-seeing God.

Vers. 11—23.—*The spring of self-sacrifice.* The facts are—1. Jonathan and David retire from observation to confer further. 2. Jonathan undertakes to do all that David requires, and solemnly pledges himself to let him know the mind of Saul. 3. He pleads with David, in prospect of his elevation to power, that he and his house may receive mercy. 4. In his eagerness he seeks a renewal of David's promise. 5. They then arrange that, after consulting with Saul, an arrow before or beyond a certain mark shall reveal safety or danger. This beautiful narrative brings out the love and confidence of these young men in such a way that one is constrained to ask whether there is not here, not only an exquisite instance of what all our religious friendship should be in spirit and expression, but an historical foreshadowing of the relation of the loving, confiding soul to the true Anointed of the Lord. We know that in the New Testament the promised land is a shadow of the "better country," the "rock" in the wilderness a figure of Christ (1 Cor. x. 4), Zion and Jerusalem a type of the city of God, and David, the king after God's own heart, a pattern of another David, the only begotten of the Father, the eternal King in Zion (Isa. ix. 7; Acts ii. 25—36). Also in the Psalms (Ps. xlv.) and in Isaiah there are references to the deep interest of the Church in Christ and of Christ in the Church. It is not, then, unwarrantable to regard the devotion of Jonathan to the coming king, and because he was beloved as the coming king, as, at all events, suggestive of an analogous devotion of the true believer to Christ. The most striking feature of the narrative before us is the utter self-sacrifice of Jonathan and the deep love from which it sprang. We may notice the main features of the story, and in doing so point out their truth in Christian life.

I. There IS A FULL ACQUIESCENCE IN DAVID'S DESIRES SO FAR AS THEY ARE EXPLICITLY KNOWN. Some might regard the retirement of the two into the seclusion of "the field" as suggestive of the private and sacred communion of a believer and Christ; but, without dwelling on that, it may be noticed that as soon as privacy was secured Jonathan at once, with solemn and pathetic earnestness, pledges himself to all that David had so far required. How true this is of a believer in Christ! When the "Anointed of the Lord" makes known his request, whether it be to bear witness for him, to remember his death, or to feed and clothe the little ones, the true heart responds with all zeal and delight. It is a mark of a true Christian, that of delighting to do his will. His yoke is easy and his burden light. It was a very delicate and difficult business to find out Saul's mind, and involved no little risk to Jonathan; and it is possible that much in which we have to acquiesce involves a strain and tension of feeling, a firmness and endurance, a risk of worldly loss, and a certainty of personal inconvenience; but nevertheless all is welcome, because it is for him who has won our love and is worthy of the best service we can ever render.

II. There IS A DISTINCT RECOGNITION OF HIS ENDURING SUPREMACY, AND A CORRESPONDING SENSE OF PERSONAL UNWORTHINESS OF SUCH DISTINGUISHED FRIENDSHIP. It is hard to say in words how refined spiritual minds obtain all their knowledge. They seem to possess an insight, a supersensual instinct, which takes them straight through the present external conditions to the abiding reality. At all events, Jonathan was convinced that his beloved friend was destined to be king in Israel, and he speaks as one not worthy of such honour; and yet, with all this reverence and awe of the coming majesty and power, there was the tender love "passing that of women." Faith saw through the loneliness and oppressed state of David, and recognised the king in Zion. *This was the real feeling of the apostles,* in their better moods, during the Saviour's humiliation. They knew that, though men were divided in judgment, he was "the Christ, the Son of the living God" (Matt. xvi. 13—16). The deep love of John when reclining on his bosom, and the sense of unworthiness of Peter when he cried, "Depart from me, for I am a sinful man, O Lord" (Luke v. 8), were only instances of the feeling which usually pervaded their minds. And it is *this recognition and the feeling accompanying it which enters into every believer's life.* He is *the* King, the Hope of the afflicted nations, the "Restorer of paths to dwell in" (Isa. lviii. 12). As Jonathan with passionate love and strong confidence gazed on the beautiful face of David, so do we look with intense interest on Christ and feel sure, in spite of the slow ages and the present antagonisms, that he "must reign," that on his own head an imperishable crown shall flourish (Ps. lxxii.). And while admiration, joy, and satisfaction attend this prevision of the coming glory, the heart is filled with wonder and gratitude in being permitted to call that Chosen One a Friend.

III. There IS A FREE SURRENDER OF ALL THAT IS DEAREST TO THE REALISATION OF HIS SUPREMACY. Nothing, humanly speaking, was more precious to Jonathan than his right to the succession, and the prospects of power and distinction involved therein. Nothing in history is more beautiful than the spontaneity and heartiness with which he laid aside all this, and found joy and satisfaction in the coming supremacy of David (vers. 14—17). What noble self-sacrifice for high spiritual purposes! This was more than "houses and lands," more than "father and mother" (Matt. xix. 29). Only the true spiritual vision of the kingdom of God will account for such deviation from the selfish ways of the world. "The Lord" was in the mind of Jonathan, and "the Name" (ch. xvii. 45) which David had exalted was the "Name" to be still more honoured in his coming reign. And in this is the essence of our Christian life. Surrender of all for Christ: sacrifice of every power, prospect, hope, and wish to the holy purposes for which the "Anointed One" lives. In this there is no exaction and no constraint. Christ does not demand something for his mere personal gratification, and we do not yield to a loss because a more powerful One claims what we have. Jonathan and David were as one (ver. 17). They had but one interest, and lived for one object. Loss and gain were inadequate terms. The surrender to one was as a surrender to self. Loss was gain, and gain was loss. So is it in the mystical union of our lives with Christ. Though we give up all, and perform what men call self-sacrifice, we yet give up nothing. For us "to live is Christ." Blessed oneness! Always giving, always receiving; ever denying self, ever enriching self! The glory of the King is our glory; the sorrows of our heart are his sorrows; deeds to his are deeds to him (Matt. xxv. 34—40; John xvii. 24; Heb. iv. 15).

IV. LOVE, CONSTANT AND MASTERFUL, IS THE SPRING OF ALL THIS SELF-SACRIFICE. Jonathan's love was the master passion—"passing that of women"—pure, steady, unaffected by public opinion and private influence (vers. 30, 31), illumined and regulated by spiritual insight, prompt in expression, giving joy and satisfaction to every deed and word that might bring future honour to David or present comfort in trouble. This undying love, this regnant force, so pure, so sweet, so strong, so gentle, ennobled its possessor, and was regarded by its object as the most beautiful and precious thing on earth. Events show that it was reciprocal (ver. 41; 2 Sam. i. 25, 26). It is this strong master passion that lies at the spring of all our true Christian service. "We love him because he first loved us." "The love of Christ constraineth us." We do his will, lay our talents, possessions, prospects, all we inherit or can acquire, at his feet because we love to do so, and would not do otherwise if we could. No box of ointment is too costly for those dear feet that have trodden the sorrowful paths of life for us! No crown too glorious for that brow that once was pierced and pained for us! No joy too excessive in final enthronement over all principality and power of him who once did battle for us, and destroyed the gigantic foe of God's people! To measure out our service, to reckon how little we can spare or do, to shut him out

from any section of our life—this were debasement and shame indeed. Love—
"passing that of women"—seeks satisfaction in living for Christ and glorying only
in him.

General lessons:—1. We should inquire whether any of Christ's requirements
have as yet been disregarded. 2. It is a matter of doubt whether the professing
Christian Church fully enters into the joy of Christ's coming glory, and is sufficiently
identified in hope and feeling with it. 3. Each one may ask, Have I surrendered all
that is precious to Christ? Is there any reserve? 4. The due culture of love for
Christ as the supreme affection of life demands thought and care. 5. The cure of
many of the sorrows and ills of Christians and Churches lies in the quickening of
this personal interest in Christ.

HOMILIES BY VARIOUS AUTHORS.

Vers. 1—10. (GIBEAH.)—*The intercourse of friends.* The regard which true
friends have for each other prompts to much communion. In it they find an exalted
pleasure, and a sure resource of help and comfort in adversity. Hence David, in
his continued distrust and fear of Saul, hastened to his friend Jonathan. Concerning their intercourse, notice—1. *Its entire freedom.* They tell each other, without
reserve, all that is in their hearts. Such freedom can be wisely indulged only in the
presence of a friend. "A *principal* fruit of friendship is the ease and discharge of
the fulness and swellings of the heart which passions of all kinds do cause and
induce. No receipt openeth the heart but a true friend, to whom you may impart
griefs, joys, fears, hopes, suspicions, counsel, and whatsoever lieth upon the heart
to oppress it, in a kind of civil shrift or confession. It redoubleth joys, and cutteth
griefs in halves" (Bacon, 'Essays'). 2. *Its gentle expostulations* and reproofs. When
David said, "Thy father seeketh my life" (an expression often used in the Psalms),
Jonathan reproved his distrust—"It is not so;" and only after a solemn oath could
be induced to share it (ver. 9). Rebuke is a duty and evidence of true friendship;
and "where a man's ears are shut against the truth so that he cannot hear it from a
friend, the welfare of such a one is to be despaired of." "As many as I love I
rebuke." 3. *Its kindly assurances.* "Whatsoever thy soul desireth, I will do it for
thee." Such assurances he gave generously, sincerely, solemnly, and repeatedly, and
they imparted encouragement and increased confidence. How "exceeding great and
precious" are the promises which the heavenly Friend has given for this purpose to
his friends! 4. *Its anxious consultations* and intelligent counsels. "The *second*
fruit of friendship is healthful and sovereign for the understanding, as the first is
for the affections; for friendship maketh indeed a fair day in the affections from
storm and tempests, but it maketh daylight in the understanding out of darkness
and confusion of thoughts; neither is this to be understood *only* of faithful counsel.
The last fruit is aid, and bearing a part in all actions and occasions" (Bacon). 5.
Its earnest requests of aid (ver. 8). Although it is the part of friendship to grant
help to a friend rather than to beg it of him, yet it shows itself by reliance upon him
in great emergencies, and confidently claims the fulfilment of former assurances;
nor will it look for aid to a true friend in vain. 6. *Its manifest imperfection.* For,
like all things earthly, human friendship is imperfect. Its communion is liable to
interruption (vers. 10, 41). It often entertains thoughts, devises plans, and makes
requests which are mistaken and injurious. The statement of David (though founded
upon a measure of truth) was a mere pretext, and through failing faith in God he
fell into "foolish and hurtful devices." It also omits reproof when it should be
given, complies with doubtful requests, and promises what it is not able to perform.
But all the defects which are found in the highest human friendship are absent from,
and all the excellences which it possesses, and infinitely more, are present in, the
friendship of Christ.—D.

Ver. 3. (GIBEAH.)—*Only a step.* Our path in life lies along the brink of a river
or the edge of a cliff; and we may by a step—a single step—at any moment meet
our fate. The asseveration of David may be regarded as the expression of a strong
conviction ("As Jehovah liveth," &c.) of—

I. THE SOLEMNITY OF DEATH. The event is a serious one. To leave familiar scenes and beloved friends, to "be missed" from our accustomed place is a saddening thought. But what gives solemnity to death as well as life is its moral aspect, its spiritual and Divine relations. 1. *It terminates our earthly probation*—severs our immediate connection with the privileges, means, and opportunities by which character is proved and the soul prepared for another state. When this step is taken, all these things belong to the past. 2. *It ushers us into the Divine presence;* no longer partially concealed by the veil of material things, but fully revealed in light, which reveals the moral attitude of every human spirit and judges it "in righteousness." "After death" (and following close upon it) "the judgment" (Heb. ix. 28). "We must all be manifest before the judgment-seat of Christ," &c. (2 Cor. v. 10). 3. *It fixes our future destiny,* in weal or woe. "What is a man profited," &c.

II. THE UNCERTAINTY OF LIFE. The step *must* be taken, but *when* we know not. That we may be duly impressed by a truth which all admit, but few adequately realise, consider—1. *The frailty of the body,* and the innumerable dangers to which it is exposed. "Between us and hell or heaven there is nothing but life, the most fragile thing in existence" (Pascal). 2. *The facts of daily observation.* What occurs to others so often, so suddenly and unexpectedly, may occur to ourselves. We have no guarantee that it will not. "Man's uncertain life is like a raindrop on the bough, amid ten thousand of its sparkling kindred, and at any moment it may fall." 3. *The declarations of the Divine word.* "Man knoweth not his time," &c. (Eccles. ix. 12). "Ye know not what shall be on the morrow. For what is your life?" &c. (James iv. 14). Why should we be left in such uncertainty? (1) To teach us the sovereignty of God and our dependence upon him. (2) To accord with our present probationary position, which necessitates the proper adjustment of motives to our freedom and responsibility. (3) To enable us properly to perform the ordinary duties of life, in connection with which we are appointed to serve God here and prepare for his service hereafter. (4) To check presumption in devoting undue attention to the affairs of this life and neglecting those of the life to come. (5) To lead us not to put the event out of our minds altogether, but rather to constant preparation for it and for the life that lies beyond. "The last day is kept secret that every day may be watched" (Augustine). "Take ye heed, watch and pray: *for* ye know not when the time is" (Mark xiii. 33). "Be ye therefore ready also," &c. (Luke xii. 40).

III. THE NECESSITY OF WATCHFUL PREPARATION. Seeing that at any instant the step may be taken, it plainly behoves us to be *always ready.* 1. By seeking and maintaining *a right state of heart* (John iii. 2, 14). 2. By diligent, faithful, and persevering *performance of duty.* 3. By constant and prayerful *committal of our souls into the hands of God.* So, whenever the step is taken, it will be "only a step" out of the shadows and sorrows of earth into the glory and joy of heaven.—D.

Vers. 11—23. (THE OPEN COUNTRY, NEAR GIBEAH.)—*A covenant of friendship.* "And Jonathan made a covenant with the house of David" (ver. 16). The friendship of Jonathan and David was expressed and confirmed by a sacred covenant (ch. xviii. 3). The covenant now made differed from the former. 1. It was made at a time of trial. Their friendship was put to a severe test; for it had become clear to the mind of Jonathan that David was destined to be king (ver. 13), as he afterwards stated more fully (ch. xxiii. 17). "Jonathan caused David to swear again" (ver. 17), not because he distrusted him, but "because he loved him: for he loved him as he loved his own soul;" and in times of special danger such repeated and solemn assurances may be needful and beneficial. 2. It included the obligation to show kindness to the house of Jonathan as well as himself. Consider it as—

I. CONFIRMED BY AN APPEAL TO GOD. It was customary in making a covenant (contract or agreement) to take an oath in which God was appealed to as a witness and an avenger of its violation (Gen. xxvi. 28; xxxi. 45—53). Even when no such appeal is expressly made it should be remembered—1. That he observes the promises and engagements which men make to one another, and keeps a faithful record thereof (Mal. iii. 16). 2. That he loves to see truth and faithfulness in their speech and conduct (Deut. vii. 9; xxxii. 4). 3. That he manifests his displeasure toward those who neglect or violate their engagements (Ezek. xvii. 9). 4.

That he shows favour and affords help to those who strive to keep them faithfully. "Who hath not lifted up his soul unto vanity, nor sworn deceitfully. He shall receive the blessing from the Lord" (Ps. xxiv. 4; xv. 4; Ephes. iv. 25).

II. DEEPENING THE SENSE OF OBLIGATION. In some cases a covenant creates a new obligation; in others (like that of friendship) it intensifies the force and feeling of it—1. By the solemn manner in which it is made. 2. By the greater definiteness in which the obligation is expressed. 3. By the permanent record which is formed of it in the memory, often associated with particular places and objects (Josh. xxiv. 27). 4. And this is important as an incentive to faithfulness in temptation arising from self-interest and strong passion to set it aside. As often as Jonathan and David remembered their sacred covenant they would be impelled to ever higher love and faithfulness.

III. CONTRIBUTING TO THE BENEFIT OF BOTH. "By Jehovah," &c. (ver. 12). "And O that thou wouldst while I live show me kindness," &c. (ver. 14). Each received as well as gave assurances of kindness, which served—1. To afford a claim that might be confidently urged in difficulty and danger (ver. 8). 2. To enrich the soul with a permanent feeling of pure and elevating joy. "Very pleasant hast thou been to me" (2 Sam. i. 26). 3. To preserve it from despondency in hours of darkness and trouble. 4. To increase its aspiration and endeavour after all that is excellent. The continued loyalty of David to Saul and his acts of kindness to him were doubtless greatly incited by the love of Jonathan; and the latter was not less morally strengthened and blessed by the love of David. "There is no influence on a feeling mind stronger than the sense of being loved; nothing more elevating, more securing to the inner life."

IV. INVOLVING THE WELFARE OF OTHERS. "And that thou wouldst not cut off thy kindness from my house for ever," &c. (vers. 15, 23). "His request that his house may be excepted from this judgment, as executor of which he regards David, is founded on and justified by his position outside the circle of 'enemies' (since he recognises God's will concerning David, and bends to it as David's friend), so that, though a member of Saul's house, he does not belong to it as concerns the judgment of extermination" (Erdmann). 1. A parent naturally desires and ought to seek the welfare of his family. 2. He may by his faithful conduct do much to promote it. 3. For the sake of one many are frequently and justly spared and blessed. "Is there yet any that is left of the house of Saul, that I may show him kindness *for Jonathan's sake*" (2 Sam. ix. 1). 4. The memory of the good is a perpetual incitement to goodness.

Learn—1. The wonderful condescension of God in making with men a friendly covenant (arrangement, constitution, dispensation), according to which he graciously assures them of unspeakable privileges and blessings (Gen. ix. 14; Jer. xxxi. 33; Gal. iii. 15—18). 2. The sure ground which is thereby afforded for confidence and "strong consolation." 3. The necessity of observing the appointed conditions thereof. 4. To look to God for all good through "Jesus, the Mediator of the new covenant" (Heb. xii. 24), and "for Christ's sake" (Ephes. iv. 32).—D.

Ver. 3.—*Mortal peril.* Brave men have their times of depression, and believing men have their fits of discouragement. Of David's courage there could be no question. He had faced death without flinching, both in defence of his flock from beasts of prey, and for the deliverance of Israel from the boastful Philistine. Yet he now recoiled, saying, "There is but a step between me and death." He felt as on the edge of a precipice. One push, and he was gone. We need not wonder at this; for it is one thing to meet an enemy in the open field, another thing to feel that one's steps are dogged by treacherous malice, and not know but one may be attacked in his sleep, or struck from behind, or entrapped by some cruel stratagem. Of David's faith in God there could be just as little question as of his bravery. All the successes he had gained had been triumphs of faith. But temperament goes for something too, and the son of Jesse had the sensitive nature which goes with poetic genius. He was capable of great exultation, but just as capable of sudden discouragement; and when he gave way to a foreboding, melancholy mood, his faith looked like unbelief. The young and healthy cannot, should not, wish to die. We can feel for

Henry Kirke White, though his tone was too gloomy, when he wrote, deprecating his early fate—

> " It is hard
> To feel the hand of Death arrest one's steps
> Throw a chill blight o'er all one's budding hopes,
> And hurl one's soul untimely to the shades."

Poets, both heathen and Christian, have often deplored the disease and violence which cast young lives headlong from the precipice. And we regard the youthful David's recoil from the cruel death which Saul designed for him as quite natural, and in no sense discreditable to his manhood. But there is more than this in his melancholy.

I. THE OLD TESTAMENT WAY OF REGARDING DEATH. In the days before Christ, dimness overhung the doctrine of a future existence. "Life and incorruption" had not been brought to light. It was therefore reckoned a blessing to live long in Palestine. It was a sore calamity to die in one's youth. The soldiers of Israel would encounter death in the excitement of battle; and such prophets as Elijah and Jonah could even wish for death in a hurt and discouraged mood of mind; but, as a rule, even the most devout Hebrews regarded death with sadness and reluctance. No wonder that David, brought up in the ideas of his own age, not of ours, should shrink from the cutting short of his days by violence, just when he had won distinction, and begun to be of service to his nation. The horror of it hung above him for many a day; for even after many wonderful escapes we hear him say, "I shall now perish one day by the hand of Saul." This sadness or reluctance in view of death never left an Old Testament worthy like David except in the hour of battle, or under some such strong emotion as once made him cry, "Would God I had died for thee, O Absalom, my son, my son!" At the end of his career he made express mention in his song of thanksgiving of his deliverance from the "sorrows" and the "snares of death" (2 Sam. xxii.). And when we see him in old age, anxiously nursed that his days might be prolonged, we catch no sign of a spirit longing to be free and assured of being with the Lord, such as one expects to find in the latter days of almost any eminent Christian. "Now the days of David drew nigh that he should die, and he charged Solomon his son, saying, I go the way of all the earth." Compare the language in Ps. xiii. 3; xxx. 9; lxxxviii. 11; and that of Hezekiah in Isa. xxxviii. Contrast with this the contempt of death which was admired and often exhibited by the heathen. But the Hebrew feeling on the subject was really the more exalted, as having a perception of the connection of death with sin, and a value for communion with the living God in the land which was his, and therefore theirs, of which the heathen mind knew nothing.

II. BRIGHTER VIEW OF DEATH IN THE NEW TESTAMENT. 1. Contrast with the case of David in youth that of Stephen at Jerusalem, evidently young, or in the prime of life. His powers were at the full, and a distinguished career of usefulness among the Hellenist Jews opened before him. Those who entered into controversy with him "were not able to resist the wisdom and the spirit by which he spake." Suddenly the enraged Jews seized him, and dragged him before the Sanhedrim on the capital charge of blasphemy. Well did Stephen know that there was but a step between him and death; but no melancholy fell upon his spirit. "All that sat in the council, looking steadfastly on him, saw his face as it had been the face of an angel." 2. Contrast with the case of David in old age that of "such an one as Paul the aged," and his feeling when he was "ready to be offered," and the time of his departure was at hand. He too was a man of sensitive temperament, and suffered keenly at times from dejection. He too was careful not to throw his life away. But when there seemed but a step between him and death, what an access of light, what an advance of consolation and hope, had the servant of God in the New Testament over the servant of God in the Old! David said, "I go the way of all the earth." But Paul, "We are confident, and willing rather to be absent from the body and present with the Lord." O happy ending of this troubled life! O welcome escape from fleshly impediment, weariness, temptation, insufficiency, and sorrow!

III. CHRIST'S CONTEMPLATION OF HIS OWN DECEASE. He who is the Son of David, and the Lord of Stephen and of Paul, saw in the very prime of youthful manhood that there was but a step between him and death, and that too a death of harsh violence such as his ancestor had feared. There was, however, this difference between "the Man Christ Jesus" and all other men—that he knew when, where, and how he should die. It was to be at Jerusalem, and at the time of the feast. He foretold the very day on which he should "be perfected," and indicated that it would be by crucifixion in saying that the Son of man would be "lifted up from the earth." From such knowledge it is well that we are exempt. To know the place, time, and manner of our death would tempt, perhaps, at first to carelessness; and then, as the date came near, would put a strain on our spirits very hard to be borne. Such a strain was upon Christ, and, as the bitter death approached, his spirit was "exceeding sorrowful." As David had his friend Jonathan to show him sympathy and endeavour to drive from his mind the presentiment of death, so Jesus Christ had his disciples, who, as lovers and friends, besought him not to think of dying; but he could not take comfort from them. The cup which his Father had given him to drink, should he not drink it? To him death was gain. He finished all his work and travail, then left the world and went to the Father. "Father, into thy hands I commit my spirit." We have much to learn from David, more from Stephen and Paul, most of all from our Lord Jesus. What if there be but a step between us and death? It is a step which cannot be taken but as, and when, and where our Lord appoints. "Lord Jesus, into thy hands I commit my spirit!" "Absent from the body, present with the Lord."—F.

EXPOSITION.

OPEN HATRED OF SAUL AGAINST DAVID (vers. 24—34). Vers. 24—26.—**The king sat him down to eat meat.** Hebrew, "the king sat down at the bread to eat." On sitting at table see ch. xvi. 11. **And Jonathan arose.** When the king had taken his usual place, that of honour, next the wall, and therefore farthest from the door, Jonathan arose and took his place on one side of the king, while Abner sat on the other. David's place below them was left empty. The omission of the statement that Jonathan *sat down* makes the passage obscure, and the versions bungle in rendering it, but there can be little doubt that these words ought to be supplied. **He is not clean.** Saul supposed that some ceremonial defilement (see Levit. xv. 2—16) had befallen David, and as the new moon was a religious festival, this would necessarily prevent his attendance.

Vers. 27—29.—**On the morrow, which was the second day of the month.** Hebrew, "on the morrow of the new moon, the second day." David's absence on the second day made Saul aware that it was no accident, and he demands of Jonathan the reason; whereupon he gives the excuse previously arranged, adding that it was David's brother who had required his attendance. The Septuagint has *brothers*, being offended at the singular, because Jesse was still alive. But as the festival was not confined to Jesse's household, his brother might very properly be the convener, without usurping his father's place. **Let me get away.** Literally, "let me escape," "let me get off," a light, half

jocose way of speaking adopted by Jonathan, as if the matter were a mere trifle.

Vers. 30, 31.—**Thou son of the perverse rebellious woman.** Literally, "thou son of one perverse in rebellion." In the East it is the greatest possible insult to a man to call his mother names; but the word rendered *perverse*, instead of being a feminine adjective, is probably an abstract noun, and "son of perversity of rebellion" would mean one who was thoroughly perverse in his resistance to his father's will. **Unto the confusion of thy mother's nakedness.** *I. e.* thy mother will feel ashamed and disgraced at having borne such a son. **He shall surely die.** Hebrew, "he is a son of death," *son* being constantly used in Hebrew to express qualities, or, as here, the fate to which a man is destined.

Vers. 32—34.—When Jonathan pleaded mildly for his friend, Saul did not **cast**, but "brandished" (see on ch. xviii. 11) his **javelin at him**, threatening **to smite him.** This fierce behaviour of his father filled Jonathan also with anger, and he arose, refused to partake of the meal, and went away in wrath. His indignation was roused not merely at his father having thus brandished his javelin in his face, for he was sitting close to Saul, but because he had cast shameful aspersions upon David in saying that he was a rebel, and deserved death.

JONATHAN'S LAST MEETING WITH DAVID (vers. 35—42). Vers. 35—38.—The next morning **Jonathan went out into the field,** not **at the time**, but "to the place" **appointed**, taking with him a **little lad**, as less likely to suspect a reason. Having shot at the mark, he sends him to pick up the arrows, and as he runs to do so he shoots one beyond him, and, calling aloud, gives David the sign that there was no hope. To keep the boy's attention engaged he gives him hurried commands — **Make speed, haste, stay not.** Instead of **the arrows** the written text has "Jonathan's lad gathered up the arrow," *i. e.* that one especially which Jonathan had shot beyond him, and to which his rapid commands referred.

Vers. 40 — 42.—**His artillery.** *I. e.* his weapons. To get rid of the boy Jonathan sends him home with his bow and arrows, and then **David arose out of a place toward the south,** or "from the south side" of the stone Ezel, and while not forgetting in his repeated obeisance the honour due to Jona-

than's dignity, yet friendship prevailed, and they kissed one another and wept sore, **until David exceeded,** *i. e.* broke down, and was completely mastered by his grief. And so they parted, David to begin a life of danger and wandering, while Jonathan returned to the city to be a dutiful son to Saul. Phillipson remarks, "The scenes in this chapter are some of the most affecting presented to us in history, whether in old or modern times, and we may well wonder at the delicacy of feeling and the gentleness of the sentiments which these two men in those old rough times entertained for one another. No ancient writer has set before us so noble an example of a heart-felt, unselfish, and thoroughly human state of feeling, and none has described friendship with such entire truth in all its relations, and with such complete and profound knowledge of the human heart."

HOMILETICS.

Vers. 24—34.—*Wasted influences, muffled thoughts, and conflicting interests.* The facts are—1. While David lies hidden, Saul notices his absence from the feast on the first day, and refers it to some ceremonial defilement. 2. On the second day he calls Jonathan's attention to the fact, and inquires the cause. 3. On his explaining the reason, Saul, in a fit of anger, accuses him of friendship with David, and points out the injury which he thinks will arise therefrom. 4. On Jonathan reasoning against the command to fetch David that he may be slain, Saul, in his rage, casts a javelin at him. 5. Jonathan, indignant at the injustice and cruelty of his father, leaves the court and spends the day in fasting and sorrow. The chief interest of this section turns on the conduct of Jonathan and Saul in the absence of David. The event proved the sagacity of David in keeping at a safe distance from his declared enemy. The facts of this narrative may be best dealt with as furnishing suggestions of realities common even in modern life.

I. THE COMMINGLED CHARACTERS OF LIFE. Here was a festive board, a court banquet, and a blending in it of characters most dissimilar. First there was Saul, sullen, morose, charged to the full with envy and malice, ready for deeds of blood, and fearful of a doom of which he dared not speak. Then there was Jonathan, pure, bright, the very soul of chivalry and honour, carrying on his heart a tender secret, and bound by holy bonds to the interests of a coming king. By him was Abner in a seat of honour, just coming into distinction, a warrior destined to play an important part in the future affairs of Israel. Others, not named, were there— men of influence, varying in temper and diversely influenced by the strange events of the age. And, in spirit, holding his right to a vacant place, David, who in sympathy sustained the heart of his beloved friend in face of a perilous undertaking. A motley assembly in a moral point of view! Representative of many a banquet and social gathering! Society is strangely formed. The necessities of life, sustained by custom, bring into contact elements most dissimilar, each being toned down by the presence of the other, and the powers that lie in the heart being systematically repressed out of deference to the proprieties of life. The contending forces of sin and holiness, modified by diversities in education and association, issue in shades of character in endless variety. Take any assembly, around the festive board or in a wider circle; what passions, hopes, fears, terrors, joys, aspirations, motives, designs lie concealed in each breast! Each one there is a distinct world; carries in himself a special destiny; is a sepulchre of buried joys, or a garden of germinating seeds. How little we know of those sitting by our side! What tragedies are to be wrought out by some we meet! (Matt. x. 26; 1 Cor. ii. 11).

II. Wasted influences. Saul's spirit and conduct at this time were evidence that all the efforts to bring him to a right state of mind were in vain. During his career Providence had wrought through trouble and joy, prophet and people, threatening and encouragement, and lately through the wise and gentle persuasions of his eldest son and the awe-inspiring presence of the prophetic company (ch. xix. 21—24). But it all proved to be as the " morning cloud and early dew." Indeed, the coarse language and foul abuse and increased violence on this occasion remind us of the unclean spirit returning with other spirits to make the last state worse than the first (Matt. xii. 45). This necessarily raises the thought of the *extent and lessons of the wasted influences of life.* That vast and varied influences are brought to bear on human beings, which, so far as we can trace in this life, do not issue in their legitimate results is obvious. "Seed on stony ground." is a fact in the moral as in the physical world. "How often would I have gathered thee!" is repeated by hundreds of parents and teachers after the example of the sorrowing Lord. The bitter tears of broken-hearted parents and the lamentations of our true Jeremiahs over degenerate nationalities raise the question of Why such wasted energy for good? It does not, indeed, follow that all is lost which seems to be lost on the immediate object. The waste of life which Butler refers to in his 'Analogy' is, we know, not really such in the economy of the universe. And so even the fruitless expenditure of moral influence on our reckless souls is wrought up into useful expenditure, for moral instruction and maintenance of justice, in the whole circle of moral existence. Our Saviour's appeals issued in rejection by the Pharisees, but the two together will form an element in the discipline and instruction of untold ages which will be highly useful. It suggests thought as to the mystery of the human will, and the relation of present to future existence. It suggests inquiries for all Christian workers—whether their methods are wisest, are sustained in a right spirit, and are sufficiently varied in kind. It brings grave questions to the conscience of those who enjoy privileges—as to what account they will render, and whether they shall ever be more than awful monuments in the universe for the warning of other beings.

III. Muffled thoughts. "Saul *spake* not anything that day: for *he thought*" (ver. 26). As the monarch sat at the head of his table the guests saw his stately form and heard his voice when he conversed on the ordinary topics of the day; but also "*he thought*"—thoughts of David, his past honours, his possible future, his absence to-day, and his appearance on the morrow, and then his speedy death, passed swifter than lightning through the dark mind, indicating their existence in the low, muffled tones which only the ear of God could discern. Thought is constantly tending to expression in words, and there are gradations in its movement. From simple definiteness of existence up to loud exclamations, Saul's thoughts, like muffled bells, were ringing within in subdued tones, their language being distinct to himself and to God. It is often forgotten that thought is language in the world of mind; and it is a solemn fact that our real life lies in the thoughts we allow to pass through our mind. Many are under the delusion that what is said audibly and done visibly constitutes the material of which character is built and on which judgment will one day be pronounced. We are spiritual, invisible beings. And while thus our thoughts are the real forms of our life, it is worthy of remark that not one thousandth part of what we think ever finds expression in distinct, audible tones. The vast preponderance of our thoughts beat in muffled tones because we dare not or cannot utter them. What God must hear beating in the hearts of men daily! It was muffled thought which Christ detected saying, "This man blasphemeth" (Matt. ix. 3; Luke vi. 7, 8), and which said, "There is no God." The same is true of the "groaning of the prisoner" which cometh up before God, and the dumb prayers of the children of God all over the earth. "Keep thy heart with all diligence."

IV. Conflicting interests. Jonathan appears to have been an authority with his father in all matters pertaining to the court and government (vers. 2, 27). The muffled thoughts which all along had muttered vengeance against David now found audible and violent expression in the abuse poured on Jonathan and the villanous attempt on his life. He set before Jonathan as conflicting interests, between which he was to make a choice, his friendship for David and his succession to the kingdom.

If Jonathan kept the one he must lose the other. Saul assumed that policy and prudence would dictate the choice of the succession, for, with the swift logic of the cruel, he wound up his argument by, " Therefore now send and fetch him unto me, for he shall surely die " (ver. 31). It is easy to show that Saul's logic, like that of all the wicked, was faulty; for if David was really the "neighbour" to whom God had decreed to give the kingdom (ch. xv. 28), no breaking of friendship would prevent his having it ; and if David was a friend of Jonathan he would never rob him of his right should the friendship be maintained. Jonathan's love and spiritual insight enabled him to see through the fallacy and to make his choice. There are *alternatives open to most men in the course of years* which bring material and spiritual considerations into sharp contrast. Here it was selfish grasping at power *versus* joy in God's purposes for Israel and mankind. Moses had to say whether the probability of becoming prime-minister of Egypt was more attractive than identifying himself with the despised slaves in prosecution of a spiritual enterprise. The same contrast arose, though the choice was different, when the young rich man was required to evince his supreme love for God and all that that implies by giving up the wealth on which his heart was set (Matt. xix. 20—22). The possession of wealth and acquisition of honour in public life are not inconsistent with true piety, but it makes all the difference when parents say to young men, " Give up your religion if you are to make your way in the world ; " " Surrender the Greater than David, and grasp the honours of this life." Every one is called on to decide between Christ and the supremacy of material, earthly interests. In which lies wisdom is evident (Matt. x. 37 ; xix. 27—29).

V. VIRTUE VICTORIOUS. Jonathan was proof against parental influence, material considerations delusively presented, and even threatening of death. He pleaded for right and innocence. He mourned the debasement of a father. He was indignant at the base insinuations against the noblest and purest of men. He dared to let the court know his preference for the spiritual over the material (ver. 34). This is heroism requiring far more courage than to go amidst the cheers of men and the pageantry of war to the cannon's mouth. Here is the power of faith, the sufficiency of God's grace, the victory that overcometh the world (Heb. xi. 32—38). The world is short-sighted. Jonathan now wears a crown which will never fade (2 Tim. ii. 12 ; iv. 7, 8 ; Rev. iii. 21).

General lessons :—1. Seeing that such varied characters are around us, let us be in every place as the " salt of the earth " and " light of the world." 2. It is our duty to exercise the holiest influence and to work unweariedly, whatever be the issue (Eccles. xi. 6). 3. We should cultivate such an inner life that if all our thoughts found audible expression we need not be ashamed (Ps. li. 6, 10). 4. Every one is tempted to reject Christ, and so every one has to determine his own destiny. 5. Fidelity in seasons of great trial depends much on previously-cultivated friendship with Christ.

Vers. 35—42.—*Warning in danger.* The facts are—1. In accordance with arrangement, Jonathan, on the next day, goes out into the field, and, on shooting the arrow beyond the lad with him, he cries out the signal of danger. 2. David recognises the sign, and the lad is sent away to the city. 3. Thereupon David and Jonathan embrace each other, and take a sorrowful farewell—Jonathan giving him his benediction, and reminding him for his comfort of the sacred covenant between them both. A crisis had come in the life of David which demanded prompt action. He had passed from a quiet pastoral occupation to the full glory of a victor's triumph, and from thence through the chequered scenes of public service in the army and the court. Meanwhile the hidden purposes of God were fast developing ; and now the " anointed " has to take a painful step in order to insure the preservation of life essential to the realisation of the end for which Samuel had chosen him in the name of God. The manner in which Jonathan performed his part is a beautiful instance of wise and faithful friendship under most perilous circumstances. We see here—

I. HOW WE MAY COME INTO CIRCUMSTANCES OF GREAT DANGER WHICH AT ONE TIME WOULD NOT BE ANTICIPATED. The life of the anointed of the Lord was in real peril by reason of the fixed purpose of an enraged and envious king. No one would have supposed such a condition of things when the ruddy youth went forth to meet the giant, and subsequently received favours at the hand of Saul. But the possibilities of human experience transcend all our effort to foresee. What the web of life will embrace as the weaving goes on who can tell? It is true one stage prepares the way for another according to fixed laws, but we know not what new external condition a day or an hour may bring forth to modify an existing stage. Who less than Divine could have supposed that Adam, pure and blessed, would soon be exposed to so deadly a peril in Eden? or that he who received the homage of wise men and was the subject of angelic praise would be sought by a murderous Herod? The *great lines of human experience are still the same.* In business affairs the once prosperous come sometimes into risks of property, reputation, and all that is dear. By associations not looked for, characters once without suspicion are in danger of a fatal compromise. The tender, happy youth of a pious home, encircled by all that love can provide, is found far from home on the verge of a moral precipice. No position of privilege or service sets us above the possibility of grave dangers. Even David, the chosen servant, was nigh unto death, and the holy apostle was anxious lest, having preached to others, he himself should at last be a "castaway" (1 Cor. ix. 27).

II. PROVIDENCE ALWAYS PROVIDES KINDLY WARNINGS OF DANGER AND INCENTIVES TO ESCAPE. In the service of God David came into this great peril, but by the offices of friendship God mercifully provided for his need. The signal was given, and he recognised its meaning. It said to him, "Flee; escape." Perhaps it may be safely said that there is no circumstance of moral—and often of material—danger into which we may be brought in the unfolding of events but that God makes known our position and opens a way of escape. Even in ordinary affairs the voice of a sober judgment, if not of some personal friend, may warn the merchant of his risks, and suggest a speedy retreat from entanglements. Often a man, gradually forming undesirable associations, is warned by relatives and those who love him best of the peril of his reputation. The *quondam* youth of purity hears a voice as from a mother's heart saying, as he in later years stands on the brink of ruin, "Flee!" Providence has many a Jonathan to shoot the arrow and cry "Beyond."

III. It is REASONABLE THAT IN ALL TIMES OF DANGER WE SHOULD PROMPTLY ACT ON THE WARNING AT ANY COST. In David's case we see the reasonableness of his noting the sign, acting on its significance, even though in so doing it cost him the bitter pang of parting from the dearest friend of his life, and becoming a beggar and a fugitive. Only thus could he ultimately fulfil the end of his existence. It was reasonable, for Jonathan knew the danger to be real, and would not deceive. So in any case of our peril, whether of health, business, reputation, Christian profession, or future salvation, it is important at once to heed the voice of warning; for Providence never lies. It is a *fact that many are ruined in spite of warning.* The reason is, they either will not cultivate the habit of discerning the "signs of the times" in moral and spiritual matters (Matt. xvi. 3); or, discerning them, they fall under the delusion that somehow they shall escape, even though they remain as they are; or else they refuse to believe the signs. Many reject the testimony of the faithful Jonathan. They prefer their own speculations to the declared testimony of Christ (Rev. i. 18). Verily unbelief is folly, and those who pride themselves on reason are most unreasonable. It *often costs much to act promptly on the voice of warning.* We may not have to endure a separation from a holy friend as did David; but a temporary loss may be sustained of serious character. The ruin threatening from a man's entangled business affairs may be escaped by a prompt surrender of luxurious habits and home comforts. To save reputation friends may have to be abandoned. A soul can only be saved from death sometimes by a resolute plucking out of a right eye (Matt. v. 29). Lot lost all in Sodom but saved himself.

General lessons:—1. Knowing the perilous possibilities of life, let us go forward cautiously, yet quietly trusting in God. 2. Whenever it is in our power, let us prove ourselves friends by warning others of their material or spiritual dangers. 3. We should give careful heed to the first promptings of conscience, remembering that in moral questions the first motions of conscience are safest for action. 4. We may make a useful study of the partings of life—of, *e. g.*, Lot and Abraham, Moses and Pharaoh, Paul and the Ephesians, Christ and his disciples.

HOMILIES BY VARIOUS AUTHORS.

Vers. 24—34. (GIBEAH.)—*Anger.* " Saul's anger was kindled against Jonathan "
(ver. 30). " And Jonathan arose from the table in fierce anger " (ver. 34). Anger
is not necessarily sinful. " It is in itself, and in its original, no more than indignation against injury and wickedness " (Butler, on ' Resentment'). But it is too
frequently sinful because of the manner in which it is indulged. How different was
the anger of Saul now from what it was on a former occasion (ch. xi. 6). Consider
that—

I. IT MAY BE UNINTENTIONALLY EXCITED (vers. 24—29). The reason which Jonathan
gave why " David's place was empty " was doubtless a mere pretext (ver. 12), harmless as he thought, and not designed to provoke wrath ; but Saul saw through it at once,
and his " anger was kindled against Jonathan " on account of it and his taking part
with one whom he regarded as his enemy. Care should be exercised, even when no
harm is meant, to furnish no occasion for offence, especially in intercourse with
those who are of an irritable and passionate temper, and to avoid " all appearance
(every kind) of evil." Deception practised for a good end is not good, and sometimes
produces much mischief.

II. IT IS OFTEN UNRIGHTEOUSLY INDULGED (vers. 30—33), as—1. *When it springs from
selfishness* and pride, and is associated with malice and revenge. Saul's anger against
Jonathan was the offspring of the envy toward " the son of Jesse " which slumbered
in his breast, if indeed he had not now formed the deliberate purpose of putting him
to death at the first opportunity. It is not said that " the evil spirit from Jehovah
came upon him " again. Hatred of David had become the pervading spirit of his
life, and it gave a colouring to everything. " Anger is an agitation of the mind
that proceeds to the resolution of a revenge, the mind assenting to it " (Seneca, on
' Anger '). 2. *When it is felt without just or adequate cause.* The questions of
Jonathan (ver. 32) did not, any more than the reason he had previously given, justify
his father's wrath, and his jealousy of David was groundless and wicked. " Whosoever is angry with his brother without a cause," &c. (Matt. v. 22). 3. *When it
becomes excessive,* and ceases to be under the control of right reason. " Be master of
thine anger." 4. *When it issues in bitter words, and violent and unjust acts.*
" Whosoever hateth his brother is a murderer," &c. (1 John iii. 15). He has within
him the principle of murder, the germ from which the outward act naturally grows.
" Cease from anger and forsake wrath " (Ps. xxxvii. 8). " Where envy and strife
are there is confusion and every evil work " (James iii. 16). " Sinful anger destroys
our own peace of mind, hurts the unity of spirit among brethren, blocks up the way
to the Divine throne, exposes us to danger, makes work for bitter repentance, fires
the minds of others, makes us unlike the meek and lowly Jesus, causes us to resemble
madmen and devils, and is cruel and murderous " (Fawcett, ' Essay on Anger').

III. IT CAN BE UNBLAMABLY ENTERTAINED (ver. 34). It may in certain circumstances be a Christian virtue. But in order to this—1. *It must be directed, out of love
to righteousness, against the wrong* which is done or intended rather than against
the wrong-doer, and be associated with sorrow for him and good-will toward him.
" Resentment is not inconsistent with good-will. These contrary passions, though
they may lessen, do not necessarily destroy each other. We may therefore love our
enemy and yet have resentment against him for his injurious behaviour toward us "
(Butler, on ' Forgiveness of Injuries'). " And when he had looked round about on
them with anger, being *grieved* for the hardness of their hearts," &c. (Mark iii. 5).
2. *It must be felt from love to others* rather than ourselves, especially to those who
love God, and from zeal for his honour. " He was grieved for David, because
his father had done him shame." 3. *It must be kept under proper control.* Jonathan
did not retaliate. He " arose from the table," and went out ; to fast, not to raise a
rebellion against his father, as Absalom did at a subsequent period. 4. *It must not
be suffered to continue too long.* " Wise anger is like fire from flint ; there is a
great ado to bring it out ; and when it does come, it is out again immediately " (M.
Henry). " Be ye angry and sin not ; let not the sun go down upon your wrath,
neither give place to the devil."

IV. It must be unceasingly guarded against and duly suppressed by the use of proper means, such as consideration of the effects of sinful anger on others and on ourselves, of the allowance which ought to be made for others, of our own faults, and of the patience and gentleness of Christ; the realisation of the presence and love of God; the cultivation of the opposite principles of humility, charity, and meekness; and continual prayer for the Holy Spirit.—D.

Vers. 35—40. (The stone Ezel.)—*An obedient lad.* (A word to-the young.) Prince Jonathan went out into the country, by the stone Ezel, to practise archery on his famous bow (2 Sam. i. 18, 22), and took with him a lad, "a little lad" (ver. 35), to carry his arrows and gather them up after they had been shot at the mark. This lad—1. *Had learnt a great lesson,* the first and most important lesson of life— obedience. He was a young soldier, and had learnt a soldier's chief duty. "Children, *obey* your parents" (Ephes. vi. 1). "Servants, *obey* your masters" (Col. iii. 22). "*Obey*" your teachers (Heb. xiii. 17). "*Obey* magistrates" (Titus iii. 1). 2. *Had learnt his lesson well.* He did what he was told to do willingly, cheerfully, quickly ("make speed, haste, stay not"), fully, "without asking any questions." 3. *Was very useful to his master.* Though but a little lad, he could be of service to a prince and great hero. 4. *Did a greater service than he was aware of.* He was seen by David from his hiding-place in the rock, and was useful to him as well as to Jonathan. "And the lad knew not anything" (ver. 39). In doing our duty One sees us whom we see not, and regards it as done to him. 5. *Did not go unrewarded.* He pleased his master, and would be more highly valued for this service and promoted to a higher position, for which it helped to prepare him. 6. *Set a pattern* of the kind of service we should render to God. "We ought to obey God" (Acts v. 29) above all. "Speak, Lord; for thy servant heareth."—D.

Ver. 41. (The stone Ezel.)—*The parting of friends.* Friends sometimes part because they cease to esteem each other. They also sometimes part not in feeling, but only in space; not willingly, but under the constraint of a higher necessity; and their separation is one of the most painful trials of life. Such was the parting of Jonathan and David. "This is the culminating point in the mutual relations of the two friends who furnish the eternal type of the perfection of noble friendship; and, moreover, in these last hours before their separation, all the threads of their destinies, henceforth so widely different, are secretly woven together. It is also at this point, consequently, that the clearest anticipation of the whole subsequent history already shines through. As Jonathan here foresees, David afterwards obtains the kingdom; and, in accordance with his oath to his friend, he afterwards, when a powerful king, always spares the descendants of Jonathan, in grateful remembrance of his dearly-loved friend, and never loses an opportunity of showing them kindness" (Ewald). In their parting we observe—
I. Courtesy. David "fell on his face to the ground, and bowed himself three times." He did so not merely in external and courtier-like obeisance to the prince, but also in heartfelt esteem and homage to the friend, who had shown his fidelity in a great crisis, virtually renounced the prospect of a kingdom for his sake and in obedience to what he saw to be the Divine purpose, and was worthy of the highest honour. True courtesy—1. *Has its seat in the heart,* and expresses itself in appropriate speech and conduct in intercourse with others, according to the custom of the time and place and the relative position they occupy. The outward bearing, of itself, is morally worthless. It may be superficial and hypocritical. Yet "courtesy of feeling is very much acquired and promoted by cultivating courtesy of manner. Gentleness of manner has some influence on gentleness of life." 2. Is the *opposite* of selfishness and pride (the chief causes of its absence); unsociableness, austerity, and moroseness; coldness, reserve, and neglect; contemptuous demeanour, rudeness, and undue familiarity. And it by no means implies obsequiousness or want of self-respect. 3. *Consists* of humility, benevolent regard for others, kindly consideration for their feelings even in little things, gentleness, and frankness. 4. Is *attended* with many advantages; commended by the examples recorded in the word of God, and enjoined by its

precepts (Gen. xxiii. 12 ; Luke vii. 44 ; Acts xxviii. 7 ; Philemon). "Whatsoever things are lovely," &c. (Phil. iv. 8). "Be courteous" (1 Pet. iii. 8).

II. TENDERNESS. "And they kissed one another, and wept with one another, until David exceeded" (LXX., "wept one with another with great lamentation "). The tenderness of their affection and grief was "wonderful." Something of the same tenderness—1. Is commonly possessed by men of a *brave and noble type* of character. "There is in David (as there is said to be in all great geniuses) a feminine as well as a masculine vein ; a passionate tenderness, a keen sensibility, a vast capacity of sympathy, sadness, and suffering which makes him truly a type of the Man of sorrows " (Kingsley). 2. Is revealed in them by *special circumstances*, and is in such circumstances worthy of them. 3. Is shown in *sympathy with the trouble of others*, rather than in grief occasioned by the deprivation of their friendship and aid. The loss which David and Jonathan were each about to suffer by the separation was great ; but they were chiefly affected by the thought of the trouble which awaited each other: the one to become an outlaw and to be pursued with relentless malice ; the other to bear the frowns of his royal father, and witness his ruinous career, without any consolation but that derived from the prospect of a better time under the rule of his chosen friend. 4. Appears in the *restraint* which is put upon the indulgence of personal feeling, from concern for others' welfare. The interview might not be prolonged. There was danger in delay. And Jonathan hastened the departure of his friend, saying, "Go in peace." Equal tenderness appears in none save those whose hearts are softened and pervaded by Divine grace (Acts xx. 37, 38 ; xxi. 13), or in "the Friend of sinners."

III. PIETY. "Go in peace, forasmuch," &c. Their souls were "knit" to God before they were knit to each other ; the one was the cause of the other ; their covenant was made "in the name of Jehovah," and he would still be with them when they parted. The piety which is possessed in common alleviates and sanctifies the grief occasioned by the separation of friends. It appears in—1. The *fellowship* which is held with the eternal Friend and abides amidst all earthly changes. 2. *Submission* to his sovereign will, which appoints the lot of each and all (Acts xxi. 13). 3. *Faith* in his overruling power and goodness, according to which "all things work together for good "—the welfare of his people, the establishment of his kingdom. 4. The wish and *prayer* for his continued presence and blessing. In him parted friends may still meet, continue of "one heart and one soul," and obtain by their prayers invaluable benefits for one another.

IV. HOPEFULNESS. They did not part without the hope of meeting again in this life (which was fulfilled—ch. xxiii. 16), and doubtless also in the eternal home to which God gathers his people. "Let it be considered what a melancholy thing any friendship would be that should be destined to expire with all its pleasures and advantages at death. That is the worthy and happy friendship, and that alone, where the parties are zealously preparing and have a good hope to meet in a nobler scene " (J. Foster). The friendship which is formed and cherished in God is not dissolved by death, but is renewed in "a life beyond life," and perpetuated for ever.

> "As for my friends, they are not lost ;
> The several vessels of thy fleet,
> Though parted now, by tempest tossed,
> Shall safely in the haven meet."   D.

EXPOSITION.

DAVID'S FLIGHT TO NOB, AND SUBSEQUENTLY TO THE PHILISTINES (CH. XXI.).

CHAPTER XXI.

DAVID'S FLIGHT TO NOB (vers. 1—9). Ver. 1.—**Then came David to Nob.** Nob means a *knoll* or *hill*, and apparently was situated a little to the north of Jerusalem on the road leading to Gath. The ark had evidently been removed thither by Saul early in his reign, after it had remained for twenty years in the house of Abinadab ; and as eighty-five priests wearing an ephod were murdered there by Doeg at Saul's command (ch. xxii. 18, 19), it is plain that the worship of Jehovah had been restored by him with something of its old splendour. And · this agrees with Saul's character. At the commencement of his reign we find Ahiah with him as high priest, and even when he fell his excuse was the necessity for performing the public rites of religion (ch. xv. 15). But with him the king's will was first, the will of Jehovah second; and while he restores God's public worship as part of the glory of his reign, he ruthlessly puts the priests with their wives and families to death when he supposes that they have given aid to his enemy. **Ahimelech was afraid at the meeting of David.** More literally, "went trembling to meet David." Ahiah, described as high priest in ch. xiv. 3, was either dead or, more probably, was a younger brother, who, while Ahimelech remained with the ark, acted as high priest at the camp for Saul, especially in consulting God for him by means of the ephod with the breastplate. **Why art thou alone?** Nevertheless, in Mark ii. 26 our Lord speaks of those "who were with David," and the "young men" are mentioned in vers. 4, 5. While David went alone to consult Ahimelech, that his visit might be kept quite secret, he had taken a few of his servants with him, and had left them somewhere in the neighbourhood, or even, more probably, had instructed some one to meet him with such men as he could collect. The arrival of the king's son-in-law without an escort would naturally strike the high priest as strange, and therefore as alarming.

Ver. 2.—**The king hath commanded me a business.** This pretence of a private commission from the king was a mere invention, but his "appointing his servants to meet him at such and such a place" was probably the exact truth. After parting with Jonathan, David probably did not venture to show himself at home, but, while Saul still supposed him to be at Bethlehem, gave orders to some trusty officer to gather together a few of his most faithful men, and await him with them at some fit place. Meanwhile alone he sets out on his flight, and, having as yet no settled plan, goes to Nob, because it was out of the way of the road to Bethlehem, whither Saul would send to arrest him. Naturally such a visit would seem strange to Ahimelech; but David needed food and arms, and probably counsel; and but for the chance of the presence of Doeg, no harm might have ensued. As it was, this visit of David completed the ruin of Eli's house.

Vers. 3, 4.—**What is under thine hand?** This does not mean that Ahimelech was himself carrying the shewbread out of the tabernacle, but simply, "What hast thou?" The sense of the whole verse is, "Now, therefore, what hast thou at hand? Give me five loaves, or whatever there may be." Ahimelech answers, "There is no common bread at hand." I have no ordinary food; there is only **hallowed bread**, that is, the shewbread, which, after remaining in Jehovah's presence from sabbath to sabbath, was then to be eaten by the priests in the holy place (Levit. xxiv. 8, 9). As Ahimelech could not venture to refuse David's request, he asks if his attendants are at least ceremonially clean, as in that case the urgency of the king's business might excuse the breach of the letter of the commandment. Our Lord in Matt. xii. 3 cites this as a case in which the inward spirit of the law was kept, and the violation of its literal precept thereby justified.

Vers. 5, 6.—**About these three days since I came out.** This exactly agrees with the time during which David had lain concealed (ch. xx. 24, 27, 35), and explains the hunger under which he was suffering, as he had no doubt taken with him only food sufficient for his immediate wants. He wishes, however, the high priest to believe that he had been engaged with his men during this time on public business, whereas they had been at home, and some of them possibly were unclean. The whole chapter sets David before us in a very humiliating light. Just as some books of Homer are styled "the prowess" of some hero, so this chapter might be called David's degradation. The determined hatred of Saul seems to have thrown him off his balance, and it was not till he got among the hills of Judah, wherein was the cave of Adullam, that he recovered his serenity. **The vessels of the young men.** Their scrips, in which they would carry the bread, and their baggage generally. **The bread is in a manner common,** &c. The word *bread* is supplied by the translators, to give some sense to this most difficult passage. Literally translated, the two last clauses are, "And the way is profane, although it be sanctified to-day in the vessel." Among the numerous interpretations of these words the following seems the best: "And though our journey be not connected with a religious object, yet it (the bread) will be kept holy in the vessel (in which it will be carried)." There is no difficulty in supplying *bread* in the last clause, as the shewbread was the subject of the conversation, and a nominative is constantly supplied by the mind from the principal matter that is occupying the thoughts of the speakers. David's argument, therefore, is that both his attendants and their wallets were free from legal defilement, and that though their expedition was on some secular business, yet that at all events the bread would be secure from pollution. **The shewbread that was taken from before Jehovah.** The Talmud ('Menach.,' 92, 2) points out that this bread was not newly taken out of the sanctuary, but, as the last clause shows, had been removed on some previous day. As after a week's exposure it was stale and dry, the priests, we are told, ate but little of it, and the rest was left (see Talmud, 'Tract. Yom.,' 39, 1). It also points out that, had such violations of the Levitical law been common, so much importance would not have been attached to this incident.

Ver. 7.—David's visit to Nob had probably been dictated simply by a desire to get food while a few attendants were being collected for him, and under ordinary circumstances would have remained unknown to Saul. Unfortunately there chanced to be a person present there who informed the king of it, and brought a second terrible catastrophe upon the house of Eli (see on ch. ii. 33); by working too upon his jealousy he caused Saul to commit a crime which sets him before us as a hateful and remorseless tyrant. This man was **Doeg, an Edomite**, who had, it seems, long been in Saul's service, as he was his chief herdsman. According to the Septuagint he had charge of the king's mules, but the other versions agree with the Hebrew. As herds would form the main part of Saul's wealth, his chief herdsman would be a person of importance. He was **detained before Jehovah**. *I. e.* shut up in close seclusion within the precincts of the tabernacle, either for some vow, or for purification, or perhaps as suspected of leprosy (Levit. xiii. 4), or, as some think, as a proselyte. Ephrem Syrus thinks he had committed some trespass, and was detained till' he had offered the appointed sacrifice. David at once felt that Doeg's presence boded much ill (ch. xxii. 22), and it probably was the cause of his taking the rash resolution to flee for refuge to Gath.

Vers. 8, 9.—**Is there not here under thine hand spear or sword?** The sight of Doeg made David feel how helpless he was in case of attack, and he excuses his request for weapons by saying that he had left home unarmed because of the urgency of the king's business. The whole matter must have seemed very suspicious to Ahimelech, but he was powerless, and answers that the only weapon in the sanctuary was David's own votive offering, the sword of Goliath, carefully deposited in a place of honour behind the ephod with the Urim and Thummim, and **wrapped in a cloth** for its protection. As the word is used in Isa. ix. 5 of military attire, it may mean Goliath's war-mantle, but more probably it was a covering to preserve it from rust and damp. In ch. xvii. 54 it is said that Goliath's armour became David's private property, and nothing could be more natural than that he should thus lay up the sword in the tabernacle, as a thank offering to God. He now takes it with pleasure, saying, **There is none like**

that; for it was a memorial of his greatest achievement, and might be the presage of good fortune again.

DAVID SEEKS REFUGE WITH THE KING OF GATH (vers. 10—15). Ver. 10.—**David arose and fled that day**. The presence of Doeg at Nob was a most untoward circumstance; and though David could never have anticipated that Saul would visit upon the priests the unwitting assistance they had given him with such barbarous ferocity, yet he must have felt sure that an active pursuit would be at once instituted against himself. He therefore took a most unwise and precipitate step, but one which clearly shows the greatness of the danger to which he was exposed. For he flees to Achish, king of Gath, the first town upon the Philistine border, at the mouth of the valley of Elah (see on ch. xvii. 3). Achish is called Abimelech in the title of Ps. xxxiv., written by David in grateful commemoration of his escape, that being the official title of the kings of Gath handed down through many successive centuries (see Gen. xxvi. 1). It has been objected that nothing could be more improbable than that David, the conqueror of Goliath, should seek refuge with a Philistine lord, and that this is nothing more than a popular tale, which has grown out of the real fact recorded in ch. xxvii. But when men are in desperate straits they take wild resolutions, and this meeting with Doeg, just after he had broken down with grief (ch. xx. 41), evidently put David to his wits' end. As, moreover, Saul was degenerating into a cruel tyrant, desertions may have become not uncommon, and though only three or four years can have elapsed since the battle of Elah, as David was only about twenty-four years of age at Saul's death, yet the change from a boyish stripling to a bearded man was enough to make it possible that David might not be recognised. As for Goliath's sword, we have seen that it was not remarkable for its size, and was probably of the ordinary pattern imported from Greece. Even if recognised, Achish might welcome him as a deserter from Saul, the great enemy of the Philistines; for as a deserter never received pardon or mercy, he must now use his prowess to the very utmost against Saul. Finally, the historical truth of the narrative is vouched for by Ps. xxxiv., and the details are all different from those in ch. xxvii. David there is a powerful chieftain with a large following of trained soldiers, and feels so secure that he takes his wives with him; he asks for some place in which to reside, and occupies himself in continual forays. Here he is in the utmost distress, has no trained band of soldiers, and goes well-nigh mad with mental anguish. And this is in exact keeping with that extreme excitement to which David was a prey in his last interview with Jonathan (ch. xx. 41); and only in his first grief at Saul's cruel bitterness would his mind have been so affected, and his conduct so rash.

Ver. 11.—**David the king of the land.** The servants of Achish use the title of *king* in a very general way. Thus Achish, though really a *seren* (see on ch. v. 11), is called king of Gath ; and they meant nothing more as regards David than that he was Israel's great man, though in accepting Goliath's challenge he had undertaken what in old time was regarded as the king's especial duty. **Did they not sing one to another of him in dances?** The Hebrew method of singing was by choruses, who sang and danced in turns to the music of their tambours (see on ch. xviii. 7). David evidently had hoped not to be recognised, but to be admitted to serve as a soldier, or in some other capacity, without many questions being asked. As we find an Edomite in Saul's service, Cushites, Maachathites, and other foreigners in the employment of David, there was probably much of this desertion of one service for another, especially as kings in those days had absolute authority and their displeasure was death.

Ver. 13. — **He changed his behaviour.** The same word is used in the title of Ps. xxxiv. Literally it means "his taste," and, like the Latin word *sapientia*, is derived from the action of the palate, and so from the faculty of discriminating flavours it came to signify the power of discrimination generally. Thus "to change his taste" means to act as if he had lost the power of distinguishing between

objects. **Feigned himself mad.** Literally, "he roamed hither and thither" restlessly and in terror. **In their hands.** *I. e.* before them, in their presence. **Scrabbled on the doors of the gate.** The Vulgate and Septuagint read *drummed* upon them. Literally the verb means "to make the mark of a Tau," the last letter of the Hebrew alphabet, and which anciently was in the form of a cross. The gate, on the leaves of which David scrawled, was probably that of the court or waiting-room, in which the servants of Achish passed their time when in attendance upon him. Possibly David had witnessed these symptoms of madness in Saul's case during his fits of insanity. The idea of some of the older commentators, that David really for a time went out of his mind, is opposed to the general sense of the narrative.

Vers. 14, 15.—**The man is mad.** Achish supposes that David's madness was real, and "drove him away" (Ps. xxxiv., title). Here we have only his contemptuous words, declaring that he had madmen enough of his own, and needed no more. As madmen were looked upon in old time as possessed by the Deity, and therefore as persons who must not be interfered with, they probably presumed upon the liberty granted them, and gave much annoyance. **In my presence.** Rather, "against me." Achish feared personal injury. **Shall this fellow come into my house?** A strong negative taking the form of a question. It means, David shall not enter into my service (comp. Ps. xxxiv., title). The whole psalm bears witness to the deep perturbation of David's spirit, and helps to explain his strange conduct.

HOMILETICS.

Vers. 1—7.—*Weakness in embarrassment.* The facts are—1. Arriving at Nob, David quiets the suspicions of Ahimelech by stating that he was on the king's secret business.   2. On this ground he asks for and obtains hallowed bread to appease his hunger, and the sword of Goliath.   3. Doeg the Edomite, being detained there that day, is observant of David's proceedings.   Hitherto David had held position as an officer in Saul's household or in the army, and therefore, despite Saul's private jealousy, had a right to the respect and protection of every man. Henceforth loyalty to Saul meant death to David.   Therefore the paternal home at Bethlehem was out of the question, and there were reasons for not compromising Samuel with any appearance of open revolt.   To a devout mind it was natural under these circumstances to flee to the sanctuary, and there seek solace and aid.   The narrative relates how good and evil were blended in the conduct of the man of God at this critical juncture, and it suggests for consideration several important truths.

I. THE HIGHER LAWS OF LIFE.   David desired the shewbread to appease his hunger, and the priest in charge at first objected to the request on the plea that it was contrary to the ceremonial law to give it to him.   The fact that David, a devout and reasonable man, ventured to ask for it, combined with his argument on the priest's own ceremonial principles (ver. 5), shows that he perceived the existence of a law which rose above the ceremonial.   Some would perhaps regard David's action as typical of the prerogatives of the real King and Priest of Zion, and even interpret his statement about the "king's business" as a spiritual enigma, pointing to the

"Father's business" which Christ was commissioned to accomplish (Luke ii. 49; John xvii. 4—9). But, at all events, it is certain that our Saviour regarded David's request and the response of the priest as indicative of the subordination of a lower to a higher law (Mark ii. 24—28). To save and sustain the life of a man, though a fugitive, was more important than the observance of a ritual. This *subordination of law runs through all things*, till we come up to the highest—that of supreme love of God. Health, and even life, may have to be set aside for the assertion of a moral principle. Hence the paradox (Matt. x. 39). Class distinctions, official relations, domestic claims, and private rights may be, in seasons of extreme national peril, entirely ignored for the maintenance of public safety. On this principle it is that attention to the affairs of this life, though right and good, is to yield to the higher obligation of regard to eternal things; and deference to self—one of the most important of laws—must give way when Christ claims submission to his yoke, the submission of love. Thus it could be shown how entirely in harmony with the scientific principle of interaction and subordination of laws is the cardinal teaching of the gospel.

II. WEAKNESS IN EMBARRASSMENT. The embarrassment of David was great, and not unlike what many fall into when called to high service for God. He was evidently under the impression that he was being led by God to some service for Israel not yet explicitly revealed (cf. ch. xvi. 13; xvii. 26, 45; xix. 18—24; xx. 13—15). At the same time he had neither the will nor the thought to rise in revolt, nor would Samuel or Jesse encourage it; yet, without home, friend, or covering, whither could he flee, and what do? To aid him would be deemed by the enraged king as treason. Under these circumstances, as a devout man, he naturally fled from his hiding-place to the sanctuary at Nob. But the considerations which hindered him from compromising Samuel, Jesse, and Jonathan also operated with him to save Ahimelech from the cruel suspicion of Saul. Hence, for covering the priest as well as for saving life, he fabricated the falsehood. 1. *God's service and approval afford us no exemption from embarrassment.* No man was ever more truly called to service and more distinctly approved than was David, and it is difficult to find in history a case of more undeserved and painful embarrassment. The Psalms, especially vii., x., xiii., xxxv., lii., liv., reveal how keenly he felt his position. Those who think that the service of God is free from cares and trials know little of history and life. The Apostle Paul had his full share, though chief of apostles (2 Cor. xi. 23—28). The purifying fires easily enkindle in this world. There are materials for them in domestic affairs, in business, in the developments of private experience. 2. The *causes of weakness in embarrassment are often traceable.* If we fall, as did David, it is because of either—(1) *Partial consideration of the facts of our position.* We may dwell too much on the difficulties, too little on the Unseen Hand. Peter looked at the waves, and not at Christ, and then began to sink. "Man does not live by bread alone" (Deut. viii. 3). (2) *Physical exhaustion conduces to this partial consideration*, and also *renders the action of the mind less steady.* David was suffering mentally by the recent suspense, parting from his friend, and long abstinence from food. The inception of many a sin takes place when the flesh is literally weak. Our Saviour recognises this (Matt. xxvi. 40, 42). 3. *Education may have impaired our moral perception* in reference to some actions. Custom does in one age tolerate what in another is abominated. Good men have bought and sold slaves. In David's time the tongue that lied for bread may have committed only a venial offence. 4. There *may be too much inventiveness in seeking an outlet from embarrassment.* It is possible to think and scheme too much, not leaving to God that which in our desperate need always belongs to him. In this state of mind evil suggestions are sure to arise, and they lay hold of the spirit just in proportion as, in extreme self-reliance, we lose trust in God. Our Saviour seems to have this in view in Matt. vi. 25—34. 5. It is *possible that amidst the pressure of life we do not keep near enough to God.* Possibly David had been too hurried and worried by the purely human aspect of affairs to have strengthened his faith by fellowship with God. The soul, as in the case of Peter, is weak if it fasts too long, as is the body when bread fails.

III. THE PRESENCE OF AN UNFRIENDLY EYE. Doeg the Edomite was present, and David's conduct was noted. Little sympathy had this proselyte with the lofty aspirations of the " anointed ; " great his pleasure in revealing to Saul anything gratifying to his wicked malice. The lesson is obvious. The servants of God live in the midst of a " perverse generation," and any inconsistencies in their conduct are sure to be used against them. Some men take unusual delight in detecting the frailties of professing Christians, as though these were an excuse for their own habits. Deeds which attract no attention in other men become conspicuous in Christians, because of the utter contrast with their holy profession (1 Tim. vi. 1 ; Titus ii. 4—8).

IV. A PARALLEL AND A CONTRAST. There is a singular *parallel* in many of the circumstances of David's life at this period and those of our Saviour's. David, the anointed, was destined to work out a great issue for Israel, but for years carried the secret in his own breast, and was now despised, persecuted, unsustained openly by any in authority, without food, shelter, and visible means of defence, and, moreover, exposed to strong temptations arising out of his sorrows. And so the "Anointed of the Lord," later on, kept for a long while the purpose of his life in his own heart, and only by degrees unfolded it to men. He also was despised and rejected of men ; unrecognised by the authorities ; cruelly persecuted, being charged with motives and intentions most base ; not knowing " where to lay his head ; " without means of defence against physical injury ; and not unacquainted with hunger and weariness. No wonder if the Psalms which assert the " righteousness " of David (Acts ii. 29—31 ; 2 Pet. i. 21) shadow forth the " righteousness " of the " Holy One " (Acts ii. 27) and his more glorious triumph. But the *contrast* is manifest. David in poverty and distress trusts in God, but not perfectly. He proves his frailty in common with all others. He knows the shame and bitterness of sin. Not so the Christ. He would have no recourse to expedients for obtaining bread or relief from apprehension (Matt. iv. 2—4 ; xxvi. 38, 39, 50). " Of the people there was none with him." " He trod the winepress alone." But in all things he was " holy, harmless, undefiled, and separate from sinners." In the deepest sense, therefore, do we see the appropriateness of the reference of the Psalms to him in all ascriptions of right and dominion by virtue of purity and righteousness (Ps. xxiv. 3—10). Not in David, but in Christ is the solution of the grandest language of the Psalms. How impossible of solution are the problems when men eliminate the inspiration of the Holy Ghost from the Old Testament !

General lessons :—1. We should be careful to avoid such a rigid adherence to useful and approved ordinances and arrangements as might deprive the poor and needy of spiritual nourishment. This danger attends some Church regulations. 2. It should be laid down as a rigid rule that no embarrassment, no perils from men, should ever justify even the thought of deception or wrong. Such a principle engrained into the soul will be a " breastplate of righteousness." 3. The prime consideration in times of peril is to commit our way to God, and be willing if need be to suffer and die. 4. We are justly indebted even to the failures of good men ; for, out of the bitter review of their sins, they have borne testimony to the value of righteousness and the blessedness of trusting in God. Hence many of the Psalms. 5. We should guard against partiality in judging of the weakness of good men ; for an occasional falsehood may be shocking to a man who thinks little of his own habit of backbiting or self-righteous censoriousness. 6. It requires many righteous deeds to remove the bad impression created on unfriendly observers by one indiscretion.

Vers. 10—15.—*Uncertain light.* The facts are—1. In continued fear of Saul, David flees to the king of Gath. 2. Being recognised as the conqueror of Goliath, he fears the consequences. 3. To escape vengeance he feigns madness. 4. Achish the king thereupon refuses to have him in his service. There is no evidence that David received any Divine direction through the high priest, but the reverse (ch. xxii. 15). He appears to have been left to the exercise of his own judgment as to a future place of refuge. To be alone, unable to remain in one's own land, a hunted fugitive, on religious principle averse to resistance by sword or concerted revolt (ch. xxiv. 6), with no guide but such as the judgment unhinged by conflicting thoughts could afford—this was certainly being " desolate " and " afflicted." The result was a determination to seek shelter among the enemies of his God and country, a step most perilous, and of very doubtful character, and which involved farther recourse to a most humiliating expedient.

I. THERE ARE TIMES WHEN GOD'S SERVANTS ARE APPARENTLY LEFT TO THEIR OWN USE OF PREVIOUS TEACHING, which they find difficult to apply to new and dangerous circumstances. David was placed in great peril, with no other guidance than what his own spirit might gather from a consideration of his calling by Samuel, and the general signs of God's past favour. There is, as a rule, a difficulty to the inexperienced in applying general principles to novel conditions ; and under the physical and mental exhaustion of this crisis David found it hard to extract from the past sufficient light to guide his present steps. He walked in comparative darkness. "Thou hast laid me in the lowest pit, in darkness, in the deeps" (Ps. lxxxviii. 6). The *supposition that it is reserved only to the deliberately wicked to walk in darkness is not correct.* The present life of the righteous in a sinful world is one of discipline, in which they both reap some of the fruits of former imperfections and become trained to higher service. Our Christian course is a campaign in which dark nights of watching and groping and trembling are to be expected as well as bright days of onslaught and victory. The degree of clearness in which the pillar of fire and cloud may stand before us may be affected by our disordered vision—the result of imperfect health, or distraction, or sheer exhaustion. The disciples of Christ, during those dark and dreadful hours of his passion and death, were left to the guidance and cheer of such of the truths as he had taught them in the days of prosperity as their judgment might deem appropriate to their present need. To the young man from home, tossed and torn by the adversities of life, unable to find means of sustenance, and destitute of friends, there is left the lessons of his childhood and such truth as may have been gathered from a brief experience of life. In his agitation he sees no clear light. A "horror of great darkness" comes over the soul, and the servant of God asks why his God is so "far from helping" him (Ps. xxii. 1).

II. THE SERVANTS OF GOD, ACTING ON THEIR OWN JUDGMENT AT SUCH TIMES, MAY COMMIT THEMSELVES TO INCREASING DANGERS AND HUMILIATING DEVICES. Exercising his judgment both on his present circumstances and his past experience of God's dealings with him, David thought he saw amidst the gloom a hand pointing to Gath as a place of refuge. No voice from heaven said, "Go not thither," and no light led elsewhere. Men would say he did the best under the circumstances, and in all sincerity of purpose. Nevertheless, the step was a false one, apart from his motive, both in itself and in its results. For it was shocking for a pious Hebrew—the assertor of the "name of the Lord" (ch. xvii. 45), and the victor of Elah—to enter the abode and seek the service of the "uncircumcised Philistine," and the event proved that safety was not secured, but was so imperilled as to suggest the adoption of a most humiliating expedient. Oh, the bitter anguish of those who, having lived in the light of God's countenance, find themselves sinking deeper and deeper into helplessness and sorrow ! *Thus may it be with us all in our "dark and cloudy day."* Every new step we take only makes our path more painful, and taxes more severely our ingenuity. Peter's "following afar off" led him amidst scoffing men and women, and their words (ch. xxi. 11; cf. Matt. xxvi. 58, 69—75) made a demand on his ingenuity more serious in its success than David's feigned madness. And this has been the experience of multitudes. There are *two great dangers of the "hour of darkness"* which David's experience indicates. 1. *The danger of causing scandal among the enemies of religion.* If the servants of Achish suspected David of the low cunning (ver. 11) which seeks to slay by stealth, then his brave, chivalrous character as a defender of the honour of Jehovah's name (ch. xvii. 45) is gone ; and if they regard him as a fugitive fleeing from his king and country, then he reveals to the "uncircumcised" the woes and troubles of the people of God. It is a sacred duty in all our times of adversity to avoid whatever would cause irreligious men to think that we can do their base deeds, and not to expose to the eye of the unsympathetic the internal sorrows of the Church of God. 2. *The danger of appearing to be what we are not.* It may have been a harmless and successful device to simulate madness ; but self-respect was gone, and a "more excellent way" of escape might have been sought of God. This is the great peril of us all both in prosperity and adversity. The guise under which the simulation appears is varied.

An appearance of wealth covers real poverty ; a geniality of manner is adopted when real aversion lies in the heart ; a pretence of ill-health secures escape from obligations ; ambiguous words and evasions are employed to suggest our ignorance of matters when we know them well.   To be real, to be known to be just what we are, is the only safe and wise course for a true Christian.

III. The moral value of these seasons of darkness cannot be appreciated at the time.   David was doubtless confounded at the providence that should have him "anointed" to a special service and yet allow him to be hunted as an outcast. He saw not the good of being bereft of friend and counsellor.   But God deals with his servants in view of their actual need and the future service they are to render. Unchecked prosperity might have been the greatest curse to such a young man.   We do not know what subtle dangers were lurking in his heart, and how necessary it was to cause him to feel his utter helplessness when left to himself.   Facts prove that out of this bitter experience he rose a more devout, and humble, and trustful man, and was thereby enabled to be a better king, and to enrich the world for ever with psalms expressive of the deepest experience of the human soul. *Time is essential to the interpretation of the ways of God.*   The cruel wrongs of Joseph and the anguish of Jacob proved among the good things of life.   The forty years' trial in the desert was a blessing to Israel.   "No chastening for the present seemeth to be joyous, but grievous ; " but history proves how blessed it is.   The absolute trust expressed in the Psalms could only have been stated by one who had been very poor, desolate, and afflicted.   Even the life of the Apostle Peter was the better for the bitterness and shame of his deed.   Many on earth can say that they are grateful for their adversities, for through them they have got nearer to God, have found Christ's love more precious, and have set their affections more intently on things unseen and eternal. Who can adequately praise the unsearchable wisdom and love that can thus turn our darkness into light, and convert our sorrows into joys, and even build up holy characters out of the ruins of our own actions and follies ? (Rom. xi. 36—39).

HOMILIES BY VARIOUS AUTHORS.

Vers. 1—8. (Nob.)—*Deceit.*   1. As in the outward life, so in the inward experience of men great exaltation is often followed by great depression.   Whilst David was with Samuel and the prophets his faith in God appears to have been strong, and it was justified by the extraordinary manner in which he was preserved.   But soon afterwards (some events which are not recorded having taken place in the interval) he was in mortal fear for his life, and resorted to an unworthy pretext in order to obtain an assurance of safety, and now took another false step.   "There seems ground for suspecting that from the time of his parting with Jonathan—if not, indeed, from the time of his leaving Naioth—David had *lost some of his trust in God*" (Kitto).   2. The intention to deceive constitutes the essence of lying.   Truth is the representation of things as they are, and it may be departed from in many ways without such an intention.   But veracity is always obligatory.   Even if intentional deception be ever justifiable, as some have supposed, it clearly was not in the case of David.   The sacred historian records the fact without approval, and without comment, except as the mention of its disastrous consequences may be so regarded (ch. xxii. 2).   "Whoso thinketh that there is any kind of lie which is not sin deceiveth himself" (Augustine).   3. The amount of guilt involved in lying depends upon its circumstances, nature, and motives.   The forms which it assumes are endlessly varied (direct, equivocation, suppression of truth, for advantage, pious frauds, malicious, &c.) ; but that which is marked by hatred and malice is the most reprehensible.   This element was absent from the deception practised by David. The age in which he lived, too, was one in which a "lie of necessity" was deemed comparatively venial ; and it was borne with, though not approved, by the "God of truth" until men should be trained to a higher moral state.   Concerning *deceit* observe that—

I. It is usually urged by special inducements ; such as—1. *The pressure of circumstances.*   When David presented himself alone before the high priest at the commencement of the sabbath (the evening of Friday) he was pressed by hunger and fear, and thereby tempted to invent a falsehood. If he had steadfastly set his face against the temptation his need would probably have been met in some other way. There is, strictly speaking, no such thing as a lie of necessity. A man may die of necessity, but not lie. 2. *The promise of advantage.* He thought that no harm could possibly come of his deceit. But how little do men know, when they enter upon a false way, to what end it may lead! 3. *The possession of a natural tendency* or susceptibility to such a temptation. There was in him (notwithstanding he abhorred lying from his heart) "a natural disposition which rendered him peculiarly open to this temptation: a quick, impulsive genius fertile in conceiving, and a versatile cleverness skilful in colouring things different from the actual fact. And does it not read a most striking lesson to those who are in any way similarly constituted?" (J. Wright, 'David, King of Israel').

"Ever to the truth
Which but the semblance of a falsehood wears
A man, if possible, should bar his lip,
Since, although blameless, he incurs reproach" (Dante).

II. IT IS ALWAYS DESERVING OF STRONG REPROBATION, inasmuch as—1. It is a violation of the *bond by which society is held together.* Without confidence in each other's truthfulness men could not live together in social union. It is a sin against the justice and the love which we owe to our neighbour. What the apostle says with reference to the Christian community applies to all: "Wherefore putting away lying," &c.: "for we are members one of another" (Ephes. iv. 25). 2. It is contrary to the dictates of an *enlightened conscience.* 3. It is prohibited and condemned by the *word of truth.* "Ye shall not lie one to another" (Levit. xix. 11). "Keep thy tongue from evil, and thy lips from speaking guile" (Ps. xxiv. 13; cxix. 29; Prov. xii. 22; Col. iii. 9; Rev. xxi. 8). "Lying is a base, unworthy vice; a vice that one of the ancients portrays in the most odious colours, when he says that 'it is to manifest a contempt of God, and withal a fear of man.' It is not possible more excellently to represent the horror, baseness, and irregularity of it; for what can a man imagine more hateful and contemptible than to be a coward toward men and valiant against his Maker?" (Montaigne).

III. IT IS OFTEN DETECTED BY UNEXPECTED MEANS (ver. 8). Little did David think of seeing Doeg the Edomite detained (literally, shut up) in the tabernacle, to witness his deception with quick eyes and ears, and ready to reveal it with a tongue "like a sharp razor, working deceitfully" (Ps. lii. 2). But—1. However cautious men may be in practising deceit, they can *never calculate upon all the means* by which it may be discovered. "A bird of the air shall carry the voice, and that which hath wings shall tell the matter" (Eccles. x. 20). 2. Even its *temporary success* often leads to inquiry and discovery (ch. xxii. 6). 3. God, before whom "all things are naked and open," causes *the whole course of things* to work together for its exposure (2 Sam. xii. 12), in order to teach men to avoid "the way of lying," and "speak the truth in their heart." It was through the operation of his providence that Doeg was there that day. Human history and individual life afford innumerable instances of the exposure of deceit in unexpected ways (Eccles. xii. 14).

"Lie not; but let thy heart be true to God,
Thy tongue to it, thy actions to them both.
Dare to be true! Nothing can need a lie;
The fault that needs it most grows two thereby" (Herbert).

IV. IT INVARIABLY PRODUCES PERNICIOUS CONSEQUENCES. 1. In those who deceive —by their moral deterioration, encouragement in deception when they are successful, and filling them sooner or later with bitter regret (ch. xxii. 22). 2. In those who are deceived, to an extent which cannot be anticipated. 3. In other men, by lessening their confidence in one another, and giving "occasion to the enemies of the Lord to blaspheme" (2 Sam. xii. 14).

Learn—1. That we may not "do evil that good may come." 2. To judge charitably of others, inasmuch as we know not the strength of their temptations.

3. To watch against the least approach to deception in ourselves. 4. To seek preservation from it by firmly trusting in God.—D.

Ver. 2. (NOB.)—*The sins of good men.* Some of the most eminent servants of God mentioned in the Bible fell into grievous sins. This has often been to some a ground of objection to the Bible, and to others a subject of perplexity. But there is little reason for either. Consider it in relation to—

I. THE TRUTH OF SCRIPTURE. If men had been described therein as wholly free from sin there would have been much more reason for doubt or perplexity concerning its truth than now exists; for its representation of them—1. Proves the *impartiality* of the writers, who record the failings of good men as well as their excellencies, concealing nothing. It shows that the sacred writers were influenced by the highest principles, and even guided by a higher wisdom than their own. 2. Accords with the *results of observation* and experience, which teach that men are sinful, that those who are unquestionably good men are liable to fall, and that the most eminently pious are not perfect. Much of the Bible is chiefly a faithful picture of human nature, which (both without and under the power of Divine grace) is essentially the same in all ages. 3. Confirms the *doctrines* it contains : such as that man is fallen, sinful, and helpless; that his elevation, righteousness, and strength are of God; that he can attain these blessings only through faith and prayer and conflict; that he can continue to possess them only by the same means; and that when he ceases to rely on Divine strength he utterly fails.

II. THE CHARACTER OF GOD. They were accepted and blessed by him notwithstanding their sins. Is he, therefore, unholy, unjust, or partial? Let it be remembered—1. That their sins were not sanctioned by him. 2. That they were forbidden by him. 3. That they were punished by him. 4. That they were forgiven only when repented of. 5. That they were in some cases mercifully borne with for a time because of the good which he saw in his servants, and in order to the ultimate removal of the evil. 6. That if such endurance of some things in them appears strange to us, under the higher light and grace vouchsafed, there are probably some things in ourselves, the evil of which we scarcely perceive, but which will appear hereafter in a different light to others. 7. That the principle on which God deals with the individual and the race is that of a gradual education, the aim of which is that we should be "holy as he is holy."

III. THE WORTH OF SUCH MEN. If they had continued in conscious and persistent transgression they could not have been held in honour or regarded as really good (1 John iii. 6); but though their sins may not be excused, their names are worthy of being had in everlasting remembrance, because of—1. The surpassing virtues which distinguished their character. 2. The main current of their life—so contrary to isolated instances of transgression. 3. Their deep sorrow for sin, their lofty aspirations after holiness, and their sure progress toward perfection.

IV. THE EFFECT ON OTHERS. This has doubtless been injurious in some directions. But, on the other hand, it has been, as it must be when the subject is rightly viewed, beneficial in—1. Making others more watchful against falling. If such eminent servants of God fell, much more may we. "Let him that thinketh he standeth," &c. 2. Preventing despair when they have fallen. If those who fell could be restored, so can we. 3. Teaching them to look to Jesus Christ as the one perfect example, the only propitiation for our sins, the all-sufficient source of "wisdom, righteousness, sanctification, and redemption." "Nothing can be an excuse or apology for sin; yet by God's mercy it may be turned to account, and made to produce the opposite to itself. To some men's errors the world has been indebted for their richest lessons and ripest fruit. . . . To the lamentable lapse, the penitence and the punishment of David, we owe some of the most subduing, the most spiritually instructive and consolatory of his psalms—psalms that have taught despair to trust, and have turned the heart of flint into a fountain of tears" (Binney).—D.

Vers. 3—6. (NOB.)—*The letter and the spirit.* "So the priest gave him hallowed bread" (ver. 6). More than half a century had elapsed since the destruction of Shiloh. The remaining members of the family of Eli had greatly increased, so that eighty-five priests now dwelt at Nob, where the tabernacle (and possibly the ark—ch. vii. 1) had been placed. But the condition of the priesthood was very different from what it once was. The spiritual power of the nation lay in the "company of the prophets;" and Saul, rejected of God and ruling according to his own will, "assumed the power of giving the high priest orders at all times through his messengers (ch. xxi. 2); so far had the theocracy sunk from that state in which the people used to stand before the tabernacle to receive the sole behests of Jehovah their King, through the prophet and priest " (Smith, 'O. T. History'). Nevertheless Ahimelech (Ahiah, ch. xiv. 36) appears to have been a man of high character (ch. xxii. 14, 15); and when David, in his necessity, requested "five loaves," he gave them to him from the shewbread which had just been removed from the holy place. He may have been influenced by sympathy with David's character and position (of which he could not fail to know something), as well as by compassion for his need and by loyalty to the king, or by the advice of Abiathar (his son and successor, afterwards friend and companion of David—ch. xxii. 20—23; 1 Kings ii. 26; and removed from the priesthood by Solomon, giving place to Zadok, of the elder branch of the Aaronic family). The shewbread (literally, "bread of the presence") "set forth Israel's permanent consecration in obedience and in producing the fruit of good works" (see Fairbairn, 'Typology,' ii. 324), and was permitted to be eaten only by the priests (Levit. xxiv. 9); but he departed, with some reserve (ver. 4), from the strict *letter* in observance of the *spirit* of the law. And our Lord "selected this act of Ahimelech as the one incident in David's life on which to bestow his especial commendation, because it contained—however tremulously and guardedly expressed—the great evangelical truth that the ceremonial law, however rigid, must give way before the claims of suffering humanity " (Stanley). Observe that—

I. THE LETTER IS DISTINCT FROM THE SPIRIT. To the former belong particular customs, maxims, rules, rites, and ceremonies; to the latter, general principles, and essential moral and spiritual obligations. As a simple illustration—Christ said to his disciples, "Ye also ought to wash one another's feet " (here is the rule); "Love one another " (here is the principle). 1. The letter *rests upon the spirit* as its foundation. The whole Mosaic law, *as law* (moral, ceremonial, political), was a "letter" based upon great principles, springing directly out of the relation of God to men—granite foundations on which more recent strata rest, and which often crop through them into distinct view (Levit. xviii. 18; Deut. vi. 5). "There is a 'letter' and 'spirit' in everything. Every statement, every law, every institution is the form of an essence, the body of a soul, the instrument of a power. These two things are quite distinct—they may be quite different " (A. J. Morris, 'Christ the Spirit of Christianity'). 2. The letter is a *means* to an end, the spirit is the end itself. The shewbread was set apart for a particular purpose, and permitted to be eaten only by the priests, in order to represent and promote the consecration, good works, and true welfare of the whole people. So "the sabbath was made for man" (Mark ii. 27). 3. The letter is *restricted* in its application to certain persons, places, and times; the spirit is universal and abiding. 4. The letter (as such) is in its requirement *outward*, formal, mechanical, and in its effect conservative, constraining, and preparatory; the spirit necessarily demands thoughtfulness, affection, moral choice, and is productive of liberty, energy, perfection. "The words that I speak unto you, they are spirit and they are life " (John vi. 63).

II. THE LETTER MAY BE CONTRARY TO THE SPIRIT. It is not essentially so; it is not always so when men imagine it to be, as, *e. g.*, when it is a restraint only upon their selfish convenience and sinful propensities. The fact that it is such a restraint shows that they still need the discipline of the law and the letter. If they were truly spiritual and free it would not be felt. But generally—1. When it is applied to *cases not contemplated by it*,—to inappropriate times and circumstances,—and when it hinders rather than promotes its chief end. 2. More particularly when it prevents the meeting of the real and *urgent necessities* of men, and the accomplishment of their true welfare—the satisfaction of hunger, the removal of sickness, the preservation of life, the salvation of the soul (Matt. xii. 1, 12). On this principle David "entered into the house of God, and did eat the shewbread," &c. 3. When it is opposed to the proper exercise of *benevolence*. On this principle Ahimelech gave him the bread, and our Lord acted (Luke vi. 10). "I desired mercy, and not sacrifice" (Hosea vi. 6). 4. When it hinders the *highest service of God*. In all such instances the strict observance of the letter "works mischief and misery, and not only kills, but kills the spirit itself from which it came" (2 Cor. iii. 6).

III. THE LETTER MUST BE SUBORDINATED TO THE SPIRIT. It should not be despised or arbitrarily set aside; but the lower obligation (in so far as the "letter" is obligatory) ought to be secondary and subservient, and give place to the higher. And we learn that—1. In the order of God's dealings with men it was necessary that the *dispensation of the letter* should be superseded by that of the spirit. This incident affords a glimpse of their predominant elements. "The law was like a book of first lessons—lessons for children. Christianity is like a book for men." 2. In the *Christian dispensation* what is ceremonial, regulative, temporary (however important) must be deemed of less consequence than what is moral, essential, enduring; and devotion to the former should be surpassed by devotion to the latter. Unduly to exalt external rites or special forms of worship is to return to the bondage of the letter; whilst zealously to contend about them without brotherly love and charity is to lose the substance for the sake of shadows. "Redeemed and sanctified man stands no longer under the disciplinary form of the law, but stands above and controls the form of the requirement" (Erdmann). He is a king and priest. "Pure religion" (literally, outward ceremonial service), &c. (James i. 27). It is charity and purity. 3. In the *individual life*—renewed and sanctified—the chief endeavour should ever be to "live in the spirit," and exhibit " charity out of a pure heart" (1 Tim. i. 5).

> " I'm apt to think the man
> That could surround the sum of things, and spy
> The heart of God and secrets of his empire,
> Would speak but *love;* with him the bright result
> Would change the hue of intermediate scenes
> And make one thing of all theology."

4. In everything *Christ must be regarded as supreme,* the perfect embodiment and only source of the spirit, Redeemer, Lord, "all and in all" (Col. iii. 11; 2 Cor. iii. 17, 18).—D.

Vers. 8—10. (NOB.)—*The sword of Goliath.* "There is none like that; give it me" (ver. 9). When David slew Goliath "he put his armour in his tent" ("the ancient word for *dwelling*"). But he appears to have afterwards deposited his sword in the tabernacle at Nob as a sacred relic, dedicatory offering, memorial, and sign; and on seeking for means of defence during his flight "from the face of Saul" (ver. 10) it was still there, carefully "wrapped in a cloth behind the ephod," and was handed over to him by the priest. It was of special significance for him, and (as other memorials often do to others) it must have spoken to him with an almost oracular voice in the way of—

I. REMEMBRANCE of the help of God; afforded—1. In the gaining of a notable victory over the enemies of the Lord and his people. 2. At a time of imminent peril and utmost extremity. 3. Through faith "in the name of the Lord of hosts." David's deliverance, as he then acknowledged, was accomplished not by the sling and stone, nor yet by the sword, but by the Lord on whom he relied; and he much needed to be reminded of it now.

II. ENCOURAGEMENT to trust in God. 1. In his service, in conflict with his enemies and obedience to his directions, the Lord is with his servants. They are not "alone" (ver. 1), but he is on their side (Ps. cxviii. 6). 2. In the greatest extremity, when ordinary means seem unavailing, he is able to deliver them by those which are extraordinary. 3. The confidence which they place in him he never disappoints. "Fear not." "It is better to trust in the Lord than to put confidence in princes."

III. WARNING against confidence in man. Overwhelmed with fear, he was about to take the daring step of leaving his people and seeking shelter with the Philistines, and eagerly grasped the weapon as an omen of the success of his scheme. But if he had reflected it would surely have taught him that—1. There is no safety for a servant of God in dependence upon or in alliance with his enemies. None might

be like " the sword of Goliath " when used in " the Lord's battles," but in no other.
2. His own wisdom and strength avail nothing "without the Lord." And he
was now evidently venturing on an erroneous and presumptuous course, in which
he had no assurance of Divine guidance and help. 3. The weapon which has been
powerful by faith is powerless without it, and may even be turned against him who
employs it. Ancient memorials, institutions, methods are valueless apart from the
spirit which they represent. It is probable that David was discovered in the native
place of Goliath by the sword he bore ; and the next thing we hear is that he and
the renowned weapon he so highly prized were in the hands of the Philistines.—D.

Vers. 10—15. (GATH.)—*The fear of man.* " And David laid up these words in his
heart, and was sore afraid " (ver. 12). The fear of man is not always sinful. As in
certain cases, and within certain limits, the approbation of others is a natural and
proper object of desire, so the disapprobation of others is a like object of dread ; and
it often restrains from temptation and impels to virtuous conduct. But it is sinful
when it exists where it ought not, or in an undue measure ; when it hinders us from
doing right lest we should incur their displeasure, or incites us to do wrong in order
to avoid it. Such fear has often possessed the servants of God (Gen. xii. 12 ; Exod.
xxx. 11, 22 ; 1 Sam. xvi. 2 ; Matt. xxvi. 72). It was felt by David when he fled
from Saul ; and still more when recognised by the servants of Achish, king of Gath,
and brought before him. To avoid what appeared to him inevitable death he
feigned madness, and his dissimulation (though no more reprehensible than the
stratagems which many others have devised in great straits) was unworthy of his
high character. Notice—
I. ITS PRINCIPAL CAUSES. 1. *Distrust of Divine protection,* which he had already
exhibited. If he had not, to some extent, " cast away his confidence," he would
hardly have come to Gath at all ; for God could assuredly protect him in his own
land. And now, deprived of " the shield of faith," he became victim to a fear as
great as the courage he had formerly displayed. 2. *The failure of worldly policy,*
which, through lack of faith, he had adopted. Like Peter, he went whither he was
not called to go ; and when his folly and presumption were suddenly revealed he
was overwhelmed with dismay. His failure was, in its ultimate result, good ; for,
although he had no intention of turning his sword against his people, it prevented
further entanglements arising out of his relation with his enemies, humbled him, and
constrained him to cry to God for deliverance. It is better for a good man to be
driven forth from the wicked in contempt than to be retained amongst them in honour.
3. *The presence of personal danger ;* doubtless great, but exaggerated, as it always
is, by fear. " He that seeketh his life shall lose it." How common is the fear of
man, arising from similar causes, in social, political, and religious life !
II. ITS INJURIOUS INFLUENCE (ver. 13). The intercourse of David with Saul may
possibly have suggested the device ; which, moreover, was not an inappropriate
expression of his inward agitation and misery. Fear—1. *Fills the mind with distracting anxiety and distress.* He whose faith fails is no longer himself. He is
driven hither and thither, like a ship upon the open sea (Luke xii. 29). 2. *Incites
to the adoption of deceitful expedients.* " The fear of man bringeth a snare " (Prov.
xxix. 25). 3. *Exposes to ignominious contempt* (ver. 15). " Signally did David
show on this occasion that he possessed two of the powers most essential to genius
—powers without which he could never have become the great poet he was—the
power of *observation* and the power of *imitation.* He must previously have noticed
with artistic accuracy all the disgusting details of madness ; and now he is able to
reproduce them with a startling fidelity. And in the possession of these powers we
may, I think, find not an excuse for, but certainly an explanation of, that tendency
to deceit, which otherwise it would be hard to account for in so holy a person.
When a man finds it an easy and pleasurable exercise of ability to throw himself
into existences alien to his own, he is tempted to a course of unreality and consequent untruthfulness which can hardly be conceived by a more self-bound nature.
But if genius has its greater temptations, it also has greater strength to resist them.
And the more godlike a genius is, the more unworthy and humiliating are its
lapses. What more debasing sight can be imagined than that which David presented

in the king's palace at Gath! Fingers which have struck the celestial lyre now scribble on the doors of the gate. From lips which have poured forth divinest song now drops the slaver of madness. The soul which has delighted in communion with God now emulates the riot of a fiend. And all this not brought on by the stroke of Heaven, which awes us while it saddens, but devised by a faithless craft" (J. Wright).

III. Its EFFECTUAL REMOVAL by—1. *The overruling goodness of God*, which often delivers his servants from the snares they have made for themselves, and sometimes mercifully controls their devices to that end; and (as we learn from the psalms which refer to the event) in connection with—2. *Earnest prayer for his help*, and— 3. *Restored confidence in his presence and favour.* Faith is the antidote of fear.

"The following is an approximation to the chronological order of the eight psalms which are assigned by their inscriptions to the time of David's persecution by Saul: vii. (Cush), lix., lvi., xxxiv., lii., lvii., cxlii., liv." (Delitzsch). See also the inscriptions of Ps. lxiii. and xviii. Ps. LVI., 'The prayer of a fugitive' (see inscription):—

> "Be gracious unto me, O God. . . .
> In the day that I fear, in thee do I put my trust,
> In God do I praise his word.
> In God have I put my trust; I do not fear.
> What can flesh do unto me?" (vers. 1, 4, 9, 12).

Ps. xxxiv., 'Thanksgiving for deliverance' (see inscription):—

> "I will bless Jehovah at all times. . . .
> I sought Jehovah, and he answered me,
> And out of all my fears did he deliver me.
> This afflicted one cried, and Jehovah heard,
> And saved him out of all his troubles" (vers. 1, 3, 7, 12—16).

"When David sang these two songs God's grace had already dried his tears. Their fundamental tone is thanksgiving for favour and deliverance. But he who has an eye, therefore, will observe that they are still wet with tears, and cannot fail to see in the singer's outpourings of heart the sorrowfulest recollections of former sins and errors" (Krummacher).—D.

Ver. 6.—*The letter of the law violated.* How did David, being neither priest nor Levite, venture to eat the presence-bread from the sanctuary? How did Ahimelech venture to give it to him?

I. THERE WAS THE PLEA OF NECESSITY. An ox or an ass which had fallen into a pit might be lifted out on the sabbath, notwithstanding the commandment to do no manner of work on the seventh day. The need of the poor animal, and the mercy due to it in its mishap, were justification enough for a breach of the letter of the law. When the disciples of Christ, walking with him along the edge of a cornfield, pulled some ears to relieve their hunger, they were blameless, for what they did was expressly permitted by the Mosaic law (Deut. xxiii. 25). But they did it on the sabbath, and this the Pharisees challenged as unlawful. The Lord Jesus, however, held it quite lawful. It was necessary that his followers should relieve their hunger and recruit their strength, and the greater object must be put above the less. "The sabbath was made for man, and not man for the sabbath." Our Lord brought out this truth into stronger relief than any other Jewish teacher had done; but it was not new doctrine. We see that while the Mosaic ritual was in the full force of its obligation the priest at Nob felt warranted to suspend one of its most minute regulations in order to relieve pressing human want. Perhaps the tendency in modern Churches is to take too much liberty with rules and ordinances of religion under pleas of necessity which are little more than pleas of convenience or self-will. But there is a golden mean between rigidity and laxity; and it must be left to the judgment and conscience of those who fear the Lord to determine for their own guidance what does or does not constitute a sufficient ground for setting aside regulations or restrictions which are ordinarily entitled to respect. Yet it is only the letter of the law, or the *minutiæ* of religious observance, that may be thus dealt with. There are supreme obligations which not even a question of life and death may overrule. Nehemiah would not flee into the temple to save his life when his duty was to build up Jerusalem. Shadrach, Meshach, and Abednego would not worship the golden image at Babylon to save their bodies from the furnace ; nor would Daniel desist from prayer to Jehovah to escape the lions' den. Paul insisted on his right of protection as a Roman citizen, but he would not for a moment compromise or conceal the gospel to evade persecution. No bonds or afflictions moved him ; neither did he count his life dear to himself, so that he might finish his course with joy. It is true that not all the followers of Christ have had such fortitude. In days of persecution some faltered and apostatised, excusing themselves under a plea of necessity. They could not suffer ; they dared not to die. But the noble army of martyrs consists of those who felt it the supreme necessity to be true to conscience, to the truth of the gospel, and the Christ of God. Not everything, then, must yield to necessity. David thought his hunger a sufficient warrant for taking from the priest's hand the sacred bread ; but when Goliath blasphemed the God of Israel and defied his army, David had shown that his own life was not so dear to him as the glory of God and the honour and safety of his people.

II. THERE WAS A PROFOUND INSIGHT INTO THE TRUE MEANING OF PRIESTHOOD IN ISRAEL. No doubt the priests formed a hereditary order, wearing a distinctive dress, and having special provision made by statute for their position and maintenance. But they were never intended to be a caste of holy intercessors standing between God and an unholy nation. Neither they nor the Levites, their assistants, were isolated from the common life of their countrymen, as by separate charter of privilege or vows of celibacy. They were just the concentrated expression of the truth that all Israel was called to be "a kingdom of priests and a holy nation." The rule was that the priests only should eat the bread which was withdrawn weekly from the table in the sanctuary ; but it was no breach of the essence and spirit of the law if other Israelites, faithful to God, should on an emergency eat of this bread. David was as truly a servant of Jehovah as Ahimelech. Though all the Lord's people never were prophets, they always were, and now are, priests. Knowing this, David took and ate ; not at all in a wilful mood, like Esau in his ravenous hunger eating Jacob's pottage, but with reverential feeling and a good conscience, under sanction of the fact that he was one of a priestly nation, and with confidence that God would not condemn him for exceeding in such a strait the letter of the law, so long as he honoured and obeyed its spirit. The leaders and rulers of the Church, according to the New Testament, are not *sacerdots* invested with a mystic sanctity and intrusted with a religious monopoly. They are simply the intensified expression of the holy calling of all the members of Christ, all the children of God. All these have a right to worship in the holiest ; and as all of them may offer spiritual sacrifices, so all may "eat of the holy things." Order, indeed, is needful in the Church, and no man may assume a leading place or charge therein until duly called and appointed to the same. If David had for a light cause, or frequently, taken the presence-bread, it would have been a sign of irreverence or arrogance. And in like manner if a Christian not intrusted with office in any constituted Church pushes forward when there is no emergency, and assumes to lead the Divine service, or to appoint or conduct the observance of the Lord's Supper, he steps out of his place, and may be designated "unruly." But there are places and occasions which do not admit of the usual regulations being observed ; and in such cases a private or unofficial Christian may take upon himself any religious function rather than that any soul should suffer damage, and this under the general principle that all Christians form a "royal priesthood." The teaching of this passage is against religious pedantry and ecclesiastical *hauteur*. Count form subordinate to life. Value order, and reverence ordinances that are really of God. Play no "fantastic tricks" with sacred things "before high heaven ;" but do not reduce religion to a question of meats and drinks, and do not count any one a serious offender who in a strait has violated prescription or usage. One who breaks the letter of the law may keep the law itself better than another who knows nothing but the letter. We are called to liberty ; not licence, indeed, but order and liberty. If we are true to God and to our consciences we need not dread that, for a formality or an informality, Christ will cast us off. The Son of man is Lord of the sabbath and of the table, "Minister of the sanctuary and the true tabernacle," Lord of all the ordinances that are binding on his followers. And there is a freedom—not from order, but in God's order—with which the Son of man, being Son of God, has made his people free.—F.

Vers. 8—15.—*The hero unheroic.*   I. A WEAPON WAS GIVEN TO DAVID AT NOB THAT SHOULD HAVE STIRRED ALL THE HEROIC ELEMENT IN HIM AND RESTORED HIS FALTERING FAITH. Had he forgotten that the sword of Goliath was in custody of the priests? Or did he remember it, and was it for a sight and a grasp of this mighty weapon that he longed? Who can tell? The priest reminded him of the day when, with that very sword, he beheaded the prostrate giant in the valley of Elah. The words must have sent a thrill through David's heart, and touched some chord of shame. Why was he now so much afraid? Why could he not trust the Lord who had saved him in that dreadful combat to protect him now? He was all eagerness to have the sword in his hand again—"There is none like it; give it me." It may have been too ponderous for a man of ordinary size and strength to wield with any freedom, but its associations and memories made it more to David than many weapons of war. He ought to have been of good cheer when in one day he got both bread and sword out of the sanctuary. Is not this suggestive of a way of help and encouragement for all who know the Lord? In new emergencies let them recall past deliverances. As Matthew Henry says, "experiences are great encouragements." The God who helped us in some past time of need is able to help us again. The grace which gained one victory is strong enough to gain another. But—

II. RECOLLECTION WITHOUT ACTIVE FAITH AVAILS LITTLE. The courage which must have leaped up in David's breast at the sight and touch of Goliath's sword soon ebbed away. His mood of despondency returned as he neared the frontier, and he relapsed into shifts unworthy both of his past and of his future. It must be owned that his position was very critical. To cross the western frontier was to expose himself to suspicion and obloquy in Israel, and to run great risk of his life among the Philistines. He was between two fires: enraged Saul behind him, and before him the king of Gath, who might very probably avenge upon him the humiliation and death of the great champion of Gath, Goliath. When the latter of these risks actually threatened him, David, always quick to scent danger, perceived his extreme predicament; and, equally quick in suggestion and resource, fell on an ingenious plan to save his life. It was not dignified—it was not worthy of a devout and upright man; but it was clever and successful. David had often seen Saul in his frenzy, and knew how to counterfeit the symptoms. So he feigned insanity, and was allowed to leave the Philistine town unmolested, and to escape to his native land. (Illustrate from the stories of Ulysses and of Lucius Junius Brutus.) What may pass without censure in heathen Greeks and Romans may not so pass in a Hebrew like David, who knew the true God; and though we should not judge severely the action of a man under imminent mortal peril, we are disappointed to see the son of Jesse betake himself to stratagem and deceit. We are vexed to find the hero unheroic, the saint unsaintly. But—

III. ALL THE WHILE THERE WAS A DEEP VEIN OF DEVOUT FEELING IN DAVID'S MIND. Two of his psalms are said to refer to this time of trouble at Gath. The first of these is the thirty-fourth. It makes no definite allusion to the events related here, but we see no reason to disregard the old tradition embodied in its title, which refers its origin to the time of David's narrow escape from the Philistines. Not that he composed it on the spur of the moment, for the elaborate acrostic structure of the ode forbids that supposition. But the sweet singer, recalling his escape, recalled the devout feeling which it awakened. He did not introduce into his song any of the actual incidents at Gath, for he must have felt that, so far as his own behaviour was concerned, the incidents were not worthy of celebration; but he recorded his experience of Divine succour for the consolation of others in their extremity, ending with "Jehovah redeemeth the soul of his servants: and none of them that trust in him shall be desolate." The other psalm to which we allude is the fifty-sixth. This, too, is ascribed to "David when the Philistines laid hold on him in Gath." It vividly describes his condition and his alarm, and tells where his hope of deliverance really lay. God knew his wanderings and regarded his tears; and thoughts of God were in David's heart even when he was playing the part of a maniac to delude the Philistines. " In God I put my trust : I am not afraid : what can man do unto me ? " We do not palliate anything in David's conduct at Nob or at Gath that was unbecoming a servant of God. We must go to the great Son of David to learn a faultless morality, so that no guile may proceed out of our mouths, and we may use no pretexts to gain our objects, but count the keeping of a good conscience superior to all considerations of comfort and even of life, and have no fear of them who can kill the body, " but are not able to kill the soul." But the Psalms come in well to prevent our doing David any injustice. All through this painful passage of his life—in his flight, his grief, his mortal peril—his heart was crying out for God. So he was saved out of the hands of enemies. Goliath could not hurt him, nor Saul, nor Achish either. Not that God sanctioned any shift or subterfuge ; but God heard him, and saved him out of all his distresses.—F.

EXPOSITION.

CHAPTER XXII.

COMMENCEMENT OF DAVID'S LIFE AS AN OUTLAW. Ver. 1.—**The cave Adullam.** According to Josephus this was situated near a city of the same name ('Ant.,' vi. 12, 3), which formed one of a group of fifteen in the Shephelah (see on ch. xvii. 1), and its site has now been recovered by Mr. Conder (see ' Tent Work,' ii. 156—160). " The great valley," he says, " of Elah, which forms the highway from Philistia to Hebron, runs down northwards past Keilah and Hareth, dividing the low hills of the Shephelah from the rocky mountains of Judah. Eight miles from the valley head stands Shochoh, . . . and two and a half miles south of this is a very large and ancient terebinth." This stands on " the west side of the vale, just where a small tributary ravine joins the main valley ; and on the south of this ravine is a high rounded hill, almost isolated by valleys, and covered with ruins, a natural fortress," the site of the city Adullam. David's cave, he considers, would not be one of the larger caverns, as these are seldom used for habitations ; but " the sides of the tributary valley are lined with rows of caves, and these we found inhabited, and full of flocks and herds ; but still more interesting was the discovery of a separate cave on the hill itself, a low, smoke-blackened burrow, which was the home of a single family. We could not but suppose, as we entered this gloomy abode, that our feet were standing in the very footprints of the shepherd king, who here, encamped between the Philistines and the Jews, covered the line of advance on the cornfields of Keilah, and was but three miles distant from the thickets of Hareth." After describing the fine view from this hill, which is about 500 feet high, he adds, " There is ample room to have accommodated David's 400 men in the caves, and they are, as we have seen, still inhabited." Thus then David's cave was one of many in the Terebinth valley and the ravine opening into it, and was not far from Gath, though over the border. Here **his brethren and all his father's house** joined him through fear of Saul. Among these would be Joab, Abishai, and Asahel, his cousins ; and we learn how great was the love and enthusiasm which David was able to inspire among them from the feat of the three heroes, of whom Abishai was one, who, while he was in the cave of Adullam, and a garrison of the Philistines at Bethlehem, broke through them to bring David water from the well there (2 Sam. xxiii. 13—17). As Bethlehem was thus held by the Philistines, there was double reason for the flight of Jesse's family ; and it is a proof how thoroughly Saul's government had broken down that, while Samuel could maintain a son at Beersheba as judge (ch. viii. 2), Saul was unable to defend places so much more distant from the Philistine border.

Ver. 2.—**Every one that was in distress,** . . . **in debt,** or **discontented** (Hebrew, bitter of soul), **gathered themselves unto him.** Had Saul's government been just and upright David would have had no followers ; but he never rose above the level of a soldier, had developed all that arbitrariness which military command fosters in self-willed minds, and seems entirely unaware of its being his duty to attend to the righteous administration of the law. The Israelites had in him the very king they had desired, but they found that a brave general might at home be a ruthless tyrant. Debt was one of the worst evils of ancient times. The rate of usury was so exorbitant that a loan was sure to end in utter ruin, and not only the debtor, but his children might be made slaves to repay the debt (2 Kings iv. 1). It was one of the first duties of an upright governor to enforce the Mosaic law against usury (Levit. xxv. 36) ; but all such cares Saul despised, and there were probably many in the land impoverished by Saul's own exactions and favouritism (ver. 7), and made bitter of soul by his cruelty and injustice. All such were glad to join in what seemed to them the banner of revolt. Afterwards at Ziklag David was joined by nobler followers (see on ch. xxvii. 6). With David we may compare Jephthah's case in the old days of anarchy (Judges xi. 3—6), and note that bad government leads to lawlessness just as surely as no government.

Vers. 3, 4.—**David went thence to Mizpeh of Moab.** The position of this place is unknown, but as the word means a *watch-tower*, it was no doubt some beacon-hill in the highlands of Moab on the east of the Dead Sea, and probably in the mountains of Abarim or Pisgah. Here David placed his father and mother under the care of the king of Moab. They had fled from Bethlehem under the combined fear of Saul and the Philistines, but were too old to bear the fatigues of David's life. He therefore asks for a refuge for them with the king of Moab, probably on the ground that Jesse's grandmother, Ruth, was a Moabitess. But as Saul had waged war on Moab (ch. xiv. 47), the king was probably glad to help one who would keep Saul employed at home. The language of David is remarkable, and is literally, "Let, I pray, my father and my mother come forth with you" (pl.); but no better interpretation has been suggested than that in the A. V.: "Let them come forth, *i. e.* from the hold in Mizpeh, to be or dwell with you." **While David was in the hold.** Not merely that in the land of Moab, but up to the time when David was settled in Hebron. During all this period David was wandering from one natural fortress to another. **Till I know what God will do for** (or to) **me.** These words show that David had recovered his composure, and was willing calmly to leave everything to the wise disposal of God.

Ver. 5.—**The prophet Gad.** This sudden appearance of the prophet suggests Stähelin's question, How came he among such people? But, in the first place, David's followers were not all of the sort described in ver. 2; and, next, this must be regarded as a declaration of the prophetic order in his favour. As we have a summary of David's proceedings in ver. 4, extending over some time, during which the massacre of the priests at Nob took place, we may well suppose that Saul had alienated from him the minds of all religious people, and that Gad, probably by Samuel's command, came to be David's counsellor. The advice he gives is most important —**Abide not in the hold.** I. e. do not remain in the land of Moab. Had David done so he probably would never have become king. By remaining in Judah, and protecting the people from the Philistines, which Saul could no longer do, David grew in reputation and

power, and from the list of those who joined him at Ziklag (1 Chron. xii. 1—22) it is evident not only that such was the case, but that there was a strong enthusiasm for him throughout not merely Judah, but all Israel. In the happier times which followed Gad became David's seer (2 Sam. xxiv. 11), was God's messenger to punish David for numbering the people (*ibid.* ver. 13), and finally wrote a history of his life (1 Chron. xxix. 29). As he thus survived David, he must have been a young man when he joined him, and possibly had been a companion of David in the prophetic schools at Naioth in Ramah. **The forest of Hareth.** Or, rather, Hereth. "This lay on the edge of the mountain-chain (of Hebron), where Kharas now stands, surrounded by the thickets which properly represent the Hebrew *yar*, a word wrongly supposed to mean a woodland of timber trees" (Conder, 'Tent Work,' ii. 88). *Yar* is translated **forest** here. Hereth was about three miles from Adullam (see on ver. 1).

MASSACRE OF THE PRIESTS AT NOB (vers. 6—19). Ver. 6.—**When Saul heard that David was discovered.** Hebrew, "was known." The meaning is easy enough, though rendered obscure by the involved translation of the A. V., and is as follows: When Saul heard that there was information concerning David and his men, he held a solemn council, in which we see how simple was the dignity of his court, but how great the ferocity to which he was now a prey. There is no parenthesis, but the account of Saul taking his seat, surrounded by his officers, follows directly upon the narration of the fact that news of David had reached him, and should be translated thus: "And Saul takes his seat in Gibeah under the tamarisk tree on the height, holding his javelin (as a sceptre) in his hand, and all his officers stand in order by him." For Saul's fondness for trees see ch. xiv. 2; but at a time when there were no large buildings a branching tree formed a fit place for a numerous meeting. **A tree.** Really a tamarisk tree, which "sometimes reaches such a size as to afford dense shade. . . . It is a very graceful tree, with long feathery branches and tufts, closely clad with the minutest of leaves, and surmounted in spring with spikes of beautiful pink blossom" (Tristram, 'Nat. Hist. of Bible,' p. 357). It grows abundantly on the seashore of England, but requires a warmer climate to develope into a tree. In Spain beautiful specimens may be seen, as for instance at Pampeluna. **In Ramah.** Conder (Handbook) thinks that Gibeah was the name of a district, which included Ramah; others take the word in its original signification, and render "on the height." **Standing.** The word means that they took each their proper posts around him (see on ch. x. 23; xii.

7, 16 ; xvii. 16). Saul was holding a formal court, to decide what steps should be taken now that David had openly revolted from him.

Vers. 7, 8.—**Ye Benjamites.** Saul had evidently failed in blending the twelve tribes into one nation. He had begun well, and his great feat of delivering Jabesh Gilead by summoning the militia of all Israel together must have given them something of a corporate feeling, and taught them their power when united. Yet now we find him isolated, and this address to his officers seems to show that he had aggrandised his own tribe at the expense of the rest. Moreover, he appeals to the worst passions of these men, and asks whether they can expect David to continue this favouritism, which had given them riches and all posts of power. And then he turns upon them, and fiercely accuses them of banding together in a conspiracy against him, to conceal from him the private understanding which existed between his own son and his enemy. **Hath made a league.** Hebrew, "hath cut." This use of the formal phrase for making a covenant seems to show that Saul was at length aware of the solemn bond of friendship entered into by Jonathan with David. **To lie in wait.** To Saul's mind, diseased with that suspicion which is the scourge of tyrants, David is secretly plotting his murder. **As at this day.** *I. e.* as to-day is manifest (see ver. 13).

Vers. 9, 10.—**Doeg the Edomite, which was set over the servants of Saul.** This translation is entirely wrong, nor would Saul's Benjamites have endured to have an Edomite set over them. The verb is that used in ver. 6, and refers simply to Doeg's place in the circle of attendants standing round Saul. The words mean, "Doeg the Edomite, who stood then with the servants of Saul." As chief herdsman he was present as a person of some importance, but far below " the captains of thousands and the captains of hundreds." **I saw the son of Jesse,** &c. As Saul was in a dangerous state of excitement, bordering on insanity, Doeg's statement was probably made with the evil intent of turning the king's suspicions from the courtiers to the priests. His assertion that the high priest **enquired of Jehovah for** David was possibly true (see on ver. 15).

Vers. 11—13. — **All his father's house.** Doeg's suggestion that the priests were David's allies at once arouses all Saul's worst passions. As if he had determined from the first upon the massacre of the whole body, he sends not merely for Ahimelech, but for every priest at Nob. Shortly afterwards they arrived, for Nob was close to Gibeah, and Saul himself arraigns them before the court for treason, and recapitulates the three points mentioned by Doeg as conclusive proofs of their guilt.

Vers. 14—16.—Ahimelech's answers are those of an innocent man who had supposed that what he did was a matter of course. But his enumeration of David's privileges of rank and station probably only embittered the king. In his eyes David was of all Saul's officers the most **faithful**, both trusty and trusted (see on ch. ii. 35). He was, moreover, the **king's son-in-law**; but the next words, he **goeth at thy bidding**, more probably mean, "has admission to thy audience," *i. e.* is thy privy councillor, with the right of entering unbidden the royal presence (comp. 2 Sam. xxiii. 23, margin; 1 Chron. xi. 25). **Did I then begin to enquire of God for him ?** Though the meaning of these words is disputed, yet there seems no sufficient reason for taking them in any other than their natural sense. It was probably usual to consult God by the Urim and Thummim on all matters of importance, and David, as a high officer of Saul's court, must often have done so before starting on such expeditions as are referred to in ch. xviii. 13. But the Bible is singularly reticent in such matters, and it is only incidentally that we learn how fully the Mosaic law entered into the daily life of the people. But for this frightful crime we should not even have known that Saul had brought the ark into his own neighbourhood, and restored the services of the sanctuary. But just as he took care to have Ahiah in attendance upon him in war, so we cannot doubt but that his main object in placing the priests at Nob was to have the benefit of the Divine counsel in his wars. It would be quite unreasonable to suppose that such consultations required the king's personal attendance. **Thy servant knew nothing of all this, less or more.** Whatever Ahimelech had done had been in perfect good faith, and though David's conduct must have seemed to him suspicious, yet there was nothing that would have justified him in acting differently. Nevertheless, in spite of his transparent innocence, Saul orders the slaughter not only of God's high priest, but of the whole body of the priesthood whom he had placed at Nob, and now had summoned for this ferocious purpose into his presence.

Vers. 17—19.—**Footmen.** Hebrew, "runners." They were the men who ran by the side of the king's horse or chariot as his escort (see on ch. viii. 11). In constant training, they were capable of maintaining a great speed for a very long time. Here they were present at the king's council as his bodyguard, but when commanded to commit this horrid deed not one of them stirred from his place. Saul might have seen by this that he was alienating the hearts of all right-minded men from him; but, unabashed, he next orders Doeg to slay the priests, and he, aided probably by his servants, **slew in that day four-score and five persons that did wear a linen ephod.** The fact that they were thus clad in their official dress added not to the wickedness, but to the impiety of this revolting act. And, not satisfied with thus wreaking his rage on innocent men, he next destroyed the city of the priests, barbarously massacring their whole families, both men and women, children and sucklings, and even their oxen, asses, and sheep, as if Nob was a city placed under the ban. It is a deed in strange contrast with the pretended mercy that spared Agag and the best of the Amalekite spoil on the pretext of religion. Only once before had so terrible a calamity befallen the descendants of Aaron, and that was when the Philistines destroyed Shiloh. But they were enemies, and provoked by the people bringing the ark to the battle, and even then women and children escaped. It was left to the anointed king, who had himself settled the priests at Nob and restored Jehovah's worship there, to perpetrate an act unparalleled in Jewish history for its barbarity. Nor was it an act of barbarity only, but also of insane and wanton stupidity. The heart of every thoughtful person must now have turned away in horror from the king whom they had desired ; and no wonder that when, two or three years afterwards, war came Saul found himself a king without an army, and fell into that deep, despondent melancholy which drove him, in need of some human sympathy, to seek it from a reputed witch.

ESCAPE OF ABIATHAR TO DAVID (vers. 20—

23). Vers. 20—23.—**Abiathar escaped.** Probably he was left in charge of the sanctuary when Ahimelech and the rest were summoned into the king's presence, and on news being brought of Saul's violence, at once made his escape. Naturally, as representing a family who, though originally Saul's friends, had suffered so much for David, he was kindly received, and a friendship commenced which lasted all David's life ; but, taking at last Adonijah's side, he was deprived by Solomon of the high priesthood, and sent into honourable banishment at Anathoth (1 Kings ii. 26). On hearing of the terrible tragedy from which Abiathar had escaped, David, with characteristic tenderness of conscience, accuses himself of being the cause of all this bloodshed. Perhaps he felt that when he saw Doeg at Nob he ought at once to have gone away, without implicating Ahimelech in his cause ; but he could never have imagined that Saul would have treated innocent men so barbarously, and may have supposed that their sacred character as well as their guiltlessness would have secured them from more than temporary displeasure. David now warmly promises Abiathar safety and friendship, and possibly the inversion of the natural order, **he that seeketh my life seeketh thy life** (where the *my* and *thy* are transposed by the Septuagint in one of its usual improvements of the Hebrew text), is meant to express this entire oneness and close union henceforward of the two friends. As to the question when and where Abiathar joined David, see on ch. xxiii. 6.

HOMILETICS.

Vers. 1—5.—*Difficult circumstances.* The facts are—1. David, escaping from Gath, takes refuge in the cave of Adullam. 2. Here he is joined by his kindred and a miscellaneous band of men, over whom he exercises authority as captain. 3. Anxious for the comfort of his father and mother, he desires and obtains of the king of Moab permission for them to dwell at Mizpeh. 4. On being advised by the prophet Gad, he returns to Judah. This section covers the conduct of David up to the point when the "walking in darkness" terminated in a merciful Divine intervention. Four leading characters are here set before us : David, his adherents, his parents, and the seer ; and the teaching of the passage may be arranged by making each of these in succession the prominent figure.

I. PRUDENCE IN DIFFICULTY. The line of action taken by David after his escape from the dangers of Gath is a remarkable instance of prudence, when regard is had to the utterly hopeless condition to which he was apparently reduced, and that no light was afforded him from any prophetic source. Lonely and hunted, he sought an impregnable cave for shelter, abstaining from any publicity to attract men into revolt against Saul. Being, apart from his choice, surrounded by men who for various private reasons were in sympathy with him, he simply organised them for defence in case of need. Knowing the peril of parents advancing in years, he sought out a place of safety where they would be free from possibility of annoyance. To secure this, and also to betake himself as far as possible from collision with Saul, he availed himself of the advantage of a kinship through Ruth, and yet, after having made the best disposition of affairs his judgment could suggest, he at once yielded to the superior wisdom of the prophet of God.   In all this we get traces of the qualities which subsequently made David a wise king.   Herein are *lines of conduct worthy of our imitation* amidst the perplexities which sometimes fall to our lot in private, domestic, and public life.   Amidst the fears and gloom of our position let us cherish that faith in God's purpose concerning us which, in spite of fears and sorrows, underlies all David's procedure (Ps. vii., xxiv.), and then exercise our best judgment on the avoidance of evil, the discharge of daily duty, and the measures most conducive to the end in view.   To avoid all occasions of annoyance, to avail ourselves of such aid as Providence may bring to us, to lay hold of and control any unsatisfactory surroundings so as to divest them of possible mischief and convert them into useful agents, to see to it that others shall not if possible come to grief by being associated with our movements, to go on steadily awaiting God's time for action, and to welcome any clear intimations of his will, however contrary to our own arrangements—this will prove our wisdom.

II. UNSATISFACTORY ADHERENTS.   The men who flocked to David were of miscellaneous characters, and were swayed by diverse motives; not such perhaps as David would have chosen.   The manifestly unjust treatment of the young deliverer of Israel, and the increasingly irritable and impulsive temper of the king, accompanied with misgovernment in matters of detail, could not but make brave and chivalrous men "discontented;" and it was no wonder if at such a time many were brought to poverty.   It is certain, however, that many of them did not enter into the lofty spiritual aims of David, and, in so far as their principles were not identical with his, they were a questionable support.   *Yet the fact is instructive.*   Persons of high character and lofty aims exercise an attractive influence over many who cannot enter fully into their conceptions.   The assertors of great principles do sometimes find adherents very inferior to themselves.   The adherents of a just cause are not always to be credited with an intelligent appreciation of its nature.   It is therefore wrong to judge leaders of important movements by the crude notions and imperfect character of their followers.   In the case of our Saviour it was the force of his personal character that drew disciples of diverse tastes and degrees of intelligence around him.   But just as David disciplined and educated his followers till they became valiant, loyal men in the kingdom (1 Chron. xi.), so Christ in due time endowed his disciples with power to enter into the spirit of his mission.   Neither in the Church nor in social and political affairs can we dispense with men who, though drawn to leaders, are not yet in perfect harmony of intelligence and character.

III. FILIAL PIETY.   Amidst the gravest anxieties of his life David manifested concern for the welfare of his parents.   Indeed all his private and public movements for a time seem to have been subordinated to securing their freedom from danger and distress.   If ever a man could plead inability he could just then.   This tenderness of character is very prominent in his entire life.   Filial piety is strongly enjoined in the Bible.   The "commandment with promise" relates to duty to parents.   Our Saviour's example is conspicuous (Luke ii. 50—52; John xix. 26, 27).   It is impossible to lay claim to religion without this love, care, tender interest, self-denial, and reverence for parents (Ephes. vi. 1—3).   There are manifold ways in which it may be displayed: by sympathy in sorrow and sickness, by reverence and affection in health, by deference to their wishes whenever consistent with holiness and right, by forecasting their needs and providing for them, by insuring support and comfort in old age, and by the cherished love which ever causes them to thank God for the gift of children.

IV. OPPORTUNE COUNSEL.   During the long season of darkness David had groped his way from place to place, exercising his judgment, and doubtless lifting up his heart for more light.   He stumbled at Nob; he fell into a net at Gath; he showed prudence at Adullam; and now in the land of Moab, where perhaps he mourned in being so far from the sanctuary of God, he is remembered on high, and the prophet Gad brings to him the first Divine and official communication he, as far as we can learn, ever received.   This circumstance was full of meaning.   The prophetic order was recognising him.   The dayspring had come.   Henceforth he was to be instructed more openly in the way in which he should go (vers. 20—23; ch. xxiii. 2).   *There is, also, a limit to our seasons of darkness.*   We have not a prophet Gad; but when patience has had her "perfect work," and discipline has brought us nearer to God, a "more sure word of prophecy," which "shineth as a light in a dark place," will make clear to us the perfect will of God.   Like as Christ found an end to the "hour of darkness," so all who share in his sorrows will find darkness made light before them. The resurrection morn was an end to the gloom and uncertainty of the apostles. Many an anxious soul, troubled with dark doubts and on the borders of despair, has found at last a light which has turned doubt into confidence and made the path of submission to Christ the path of joy.   "I will not leave you comfortless, but will come unto you."

General lessons :—1. We should not despise or discourage persons seeking to be identified with a good cause on account of their inferiority to those who lead.   2. There may be many waiting for action if men of energy and attractiveness would afford them facility.   3. The experience of the Church in all ages justifies faith in the guidance of God when we have work to do for him.

Vers. 6—16.—*Resistance to God's purposes.*   The facts are—1. Saul, hearing at Gibeah of David's movements, makes an appeal to his Benjamite attendants.   2. He insinuates the existence of secret designs against himself, connivance at David's supposed purpose, and lack of pity for his condition.   3. Thereupon Doeg the Edomite relates what he saw at Nob, and makes the statement that the high priest inquired of the Lord for David.   4. Saul sends for Ahimelech and charges him with conspiracy. 5. Notwithstanding the high priest's denial of the charge, and his conviction of David's innocence, Saul condemns him and his house to death.   The conduct of Saul is increasingly devoid of reason, and this gradual failure of intelligence has its root in moral decay.   The key to his infatuation is to be found in the obstinate impenitence of his heart in relation to the sins of his probationary career, and the consequent fight of his entire nature against the settled purposes of God (ch. xi. 24, 25 ; xii. 24, 25 ; xiii. 11—14 ; xv. 26—29).   The events recorded in the section before us reveal a more fatal advance in this course of mental and moral degeneration.

I. RESISTANCE TO GOD'S PURPOSES FORCES ON INCREASED DANGERS.   Had Saul with penitent spirit bowed to the will of God, as expressed in ch. xv. 26—29, and at once retired into private life, the rest of his days might have been at least devout and quiet.   But, persisting in rebellion, he soon saw in the innocent son of Jesse a personal enemy.   And the resistance to God's purposes which induced personal envy and ill-will prompted also to open deeds of violence, and these deeds, designed by the perverted judgment to negative the Divine decree (ch. xv. 26—29), had the triple effect of cementing the bond between David and Jonathan, of developing the sympathy of the prophets and of all just men with the persecuted one, and of making David the leader of a band of 400 men.   Thus the very devices of a guilty, hardened heart to prevent the fulfilment of the purposes of God were conducive to a reverse issue.   Saul's dangers multiplied just as he sought their removal.   The *only safe course* for guilty men, guilty Churches and nations, *is to bow at once before God,* and place themselves unreservedly at his mercy.   The laws of providence are in incessant movement toward the realisation of God's purpose against sin.   Every effort to set them aside, or to avoid their inevitable issue, only tends to multiply the agencies by which they at last shall be vindicated.   The man who, having committed secret sin, seeks, in the exercise of an impenitent spirit, to cover it up, or brave it out, creates by every thought of his mind a new cord by which he is bound fast to his fate.   Nations that seek to ward off the judgments due to past sins by guilty acts for strengthening their position in the world, rather than by sincere repentance and newness of life, are only heaping up wrath for the day of wrath.   Penitence, submission, righteousness, these are the "way everlasting."   Practical godliness is the soundest philosophy for individuals and communities.

II. IT INDUCES A STATE OF MIND WHICH CREATES GREAT FEARS OUT OF SLIGHT CIRCUMSTANCES.   Three circumstances were the occasion of much fear to Saul—the existence of David, his friendship with Jonathan, and his holding a cave with 400 men.   External events are to us what the medium through which we view them makes them appear to be, and this medium is often the creation of our moral nature. With all his daring resistance to the purposes of God, Saul could not lose the consciousness that he was a guilty man, that the judgment pronounced was just, and that, in spite of all wishes, hopes, and efforts to the contrary, the dreaded doom would come. In such a state of mind he saw messengers of justice and supplanters of his position where others saw only blessings to Israel. A prudent act for purposes of self-defence against cruel persecution became to him a formidable attack on his throne. The secrets of a holy friendship were the plottings of unfaithful men, and the want of sympathy on the part of upright men with his malicious designs against an honourable man and public benefactor, he construed into conspiracy against himself. This *tendency of the mind to clothe all things with its own moral colouring is universal.* As the holy and the wise see occasions for joy and confidence in everything except the sins of men and their natural effects, so the guilty and foolish see occasions for trouble and fear in what to others is the expression of goodness and of righteousness. It is a slight circumstance for a policeman to walk the street, but there are men who quail at the sight. The bare mention of a name or incidental reference to a transaction will cause agitation in the minds of evil-doers. The appearance among men of the holy Saviour caused trembling in the heart of the guilty Herod (Matt. ii. 3 ; xiv. 1—3). A man like Saul carries within him all the elements of a hell. Small things become instruments of self-inflicted torture. In such a moral mood a man becomes an Ishmaelite indeed by reason of the quickness of his fears and the strength of his suspicions. If, beyond this life, this state of mind is intensified in the wicked by the complete dominion of sin and absence of present mitigations, it is not difficult to conceive the imperfection of language to indicate the future of the lost.

III. IT PROMPTS TO NEW EXPEDIENTS FOR RELIEF FROM SELF-CREATED DIFFICULTIES. The circumstances which caused fear to Saul were the product of his transgression ; for had he not disobeyed there would have been no need for a David to be brought out from the sheepfold as a conqueror of Goliath and chosen supplanter of his line, and hence no suspicious friendship and no cave of Adullam ; but now that the fears bred of these circumstances were heavily upon him, the old resistance to God manifests itself in fresh contrivances to extricate himself from trouble. He addresses the leading men of Benjamin, seeking for loyal support. He works on the feeling of clanship. He appeals to their lust for promotion and wealth. He claims their pity in his sorrows, and suggests that they, as loyal men, should avoid the suspicion of conniving at a conspiracy between his son and the son of Jesse. There is here a strange blending of hardihood and cowardice, defiance of God's will and sense of weakness, distrust of his friends and hope of assistance from them—a fair index of the mental confusion out of which spring all devices for warding off the certain doom which the guilty conscience sees to be approaching. *Generally very much energy and skill are spent by men in seeking to avert the necessary consequences of their past lives.* No mental operation is more universal than that which associates evil consequences, remote or near, with wrong-doing. But a guilty man's repugnance to suffering, combined with a determined spirit of rebellion against the moral order, induces an incessant strain of energy and skill to evade the inevitable. It is possible for men to look on Saul's appeals to Benjamites, and his stratagems for nullifying the words of Samuel (ch. xv. 28, 29), as vain and foolish as would be an attempt to prevent the action of the law of gravity, while in their own sphere they may be pursuing a similar course. All who live in hopes of a future blessedness while not laying a foundation for it in purity of nature and personal fellowship with Christ are practically like Saul ; for no law is more unchangeable than that the pure in heart alone can see God. History relates how men of abandoned lives have, in later years, under a dread of future consequences, become precise in formal acts of worship, and bountiful in use of wealth, without the slightest perception of the need of a radical love of holiness, hoping by such external means to break open the door that bars the entrance into the kingdom of God of whatever defileth. A salvation from uneasiness and pain men are eager for, not a salvation which consists in holiness of nature and joy in God.

IV. IT IS SURE TO FIND SOME ABETTORS OF ITS STRIFE WITH GOD. It is probable that the more sober of the Benjamites had begun to distrust their king, and although they may not have known all his dread secret (ch. xv. 28, 29), they could not but see that he had lost the moral support of Samuel, and was bent on a reckless course in hunting the life of David. But one man was ready to strengthen his hate and urge him on in the fatal conflict. Doeg the Edomite, a man of low spiritual tastes, an alien to Israel, maliciously added fuel to the raging evils of the unhappy king. There are several suggestive items in this brief account of the dark deed of Doeg. 1. He was *not a true Israelite*. By education, habit, and taste he could not have sympathy with the lofty, Messianic aims of a David or a Samuel. He is the type of a formal professor, who bears the name, but has none of the spirit, of the true religion. 2. He had *material interests at stake* in the continued reign of Saul (ch. xxi. 7; xxii. 9). The psalm supposed to refer to him represents him as bent on the acquisition of wealth (Ps. lii.). He is the ideal of a man whose main thought is business, and who therefore forms a judgment of religious, social, and political claims according to their presumed bearing on worldly advancement. 3. He was *cruelly cool in his plans and conduct*. The simulated tone of ingenuousness in his reference to what he had seen at Nob, his abstention from personal invective, and the matter-of-fact way in which he welded his lie about the priest inquiring of the Lord for David with the other part of the story, reveal a cruelly cool scheme for destroying one whose pure life and lofty aspirations must have mirrored too painfully his own vileness. The readiness with which he could subsequently shed the blood of God's priests fully bears out all the severe language of Ps. lii. He reminds us of the many vile men who, under cloak of attachment to a religion too pure for them, pursue this cruel course, seeking to heap up treasure by any means, and ready by word or deed to blight fair reputations and pander to the passions of the powerful. It only requires a little knowledge of the facts of David's life to enable every just and pure mind to sympathise with his strong denunciation of such men (Ps. xxxv. 4—9; lii. 2—5; lvii. 4; lviii. 4—11). There are affinities of evil. Sauls yearn for Doegs, and Doegs are ever ready to blend interest with the Sauls. Satan is not the only one lying in wait to destroy the poor and needy. Hand joins hand in wickedness, and base heart encourages base heart in the mad endeavour to destroy a greater than David.

V. IT WILL PROCEED TILL IT SETS AT NOUGHT THE MOST SACRED THINGS. Bad men are often checked in their antagonism to God's purposes by the wholesome influence on their remaining religious instincts of spiritual institutions and characters. The priesthood was revered by Saul at one time. The spiritual power had been prominent in his installation to the kingdom. All the influence of early Hebrew training conspired to make him look up with reverence to the high priest as in some sense the representative of all that is holy and Divine. Common prudence, religious prepossessions, every sentiment of tenderness and awe ought to have discounted the assertion of Doeg in the presence of the high priest's emphatic denial of having inquired of the Lord for David. It was therefore an evidence of the utter suppression of all that hitherto had acted as a beneficial restraint when, in the desperate violence of his strife with God, Saul dared to sentence the innocent high priest to death. He now sank to a deeper deep. The spiritual powers became the object of his deadly hate. The warfare must now be urged against the most sacred things of God. *Facilis descensus Averni. Spiritual deterioration is nearly complete when men set themselves in antagonism to the institutions of religion.* It argues a terrible power of evil when a soul can accept the suggestions of bad characters and cast aside all the reverence fostered by years of education and discipline. Yet there is a reason in the madness; for, no doubt, as the spiritual in Israel was at this time the most formidable, though not conspicuously active, force against Saul's permanence in the kingdom, so it is the spiritual, as embodied in a pure Christianity, which bars the way most surely to the permanent prosperity of the man who persistently lives in impenitence, and, therefore, from his mistaken point of view, it is essential if possible to doom it to destruction. It is the old tragedy again when men, for love of their own sinful will, trample underfoot the Son of God, and count the "blood of the covenant an unholy thing" (Heb. x. 29). The bold defiance of religion is too often simply an effort to cast away the cords of a holy restraint (Ps. ii. 3).

General lessons:—1. It is well to consider the force of habit in its bearing on unwillingness to submit to God's judgments. 2. Whenever slight circumstances create great fears it should be regarded as instant proof of the existence of a perilous spiritual condition, and a demand for great searching of heart. 3. Remembering how much all our judgments are coloured by our imperfect moral state, we should pray much that God would open our eyes to see things in his light and lead us in the "way everlasting." 4. History and personal experience should teach us that the shortest and indeed only way to extricate ourselves from difficulties induced by our sins is to shun every evil way and submit ourselves entirely to God. 5. Reputations are to be held sacred, and all gain at the cost of others' ruin brings a curse with it. 6. One of the best safeguards against the dangerous allurements of wealth and the love of worldly power is a lofty spiritual aspiration—sympathy with the Lord's Anointed. 7. It is in vain to spend arguments on men who in self-abandonment to their sinful will seek to destroy the institutions of religion; for it is not a question of reason, but of perverted, degraded nature. 8. We should avoid the slightest approach to evil, seeing that when indulged in the impetus downwards is so fearful.

Vers. 17—23.—*The tragedy at Nob.* The facts are—1. Saul commands his guards to slay the priests of Nob, but they refuse. 2. Thereupon he commands Doeg to effect their death, who slays eighty-five priests, and procures the destruction of the entire city. 3. Abiathar, escaping to David, makes known to him what has happened. 4. David perceives that his presence at Nob was the occasion of this sad calamity, and admits that he feared the course Doeg would take. 5. He encourages Abiathar to remain with him, and assures him of safety. This section sets forth Saul's conduct in the darkest characters, and brings out a turn in the course of events of great consequence to David, while at the same time illustrating several important truths.

I. SINFUL MEN ARE SOMETIMES THE INSTRUMENTS OF FULFILLING DIVINE PREDICTIONS OF JUDGMENT. It had been declared as a judgment on the house of Eli that terrible things should befall his descendants (ch. ii. 31—36; iii. 11—14). In the fearful destruction at Nob this prediction was partly fulfilled. The sins of Saul brought on retribution for the sins of Eli and his sons. In this we have an instance of frequent occurrence in human history, both of nations and individuals. The savage ambition of Rome realised the truth of our Saviour's words concerning the judgment due to impenitent Jerusalem (Matt. xxiii. 34—38; Luke xxi. 20—24). The untruthful conduct of Jacob was most severely chastised by the lying tongues of his sons who conspired against his favourite Joseph; just as now the judgment due to a parent for irreligious example in the home is often realised in the open vices of his children, which perhaps ruin his health and fortune. In all these cases we have to distinguish between the just purpose of God to visit sin by future retribution, and the free action of the men who are the means of bringing it to pass. Had pestilence, or plagues, or earthquakes been more in the line of natural order just then, these would have conserved the Divine purpose. But man's sinful action, free, responsible, was the agency used, thus illustrating the statement which sometimes perplexes superficial students of the Bible—"the wicked, which is thy sword" (Ps. xvii. 13). The metaphysical question, involved in this conjunction of a righteous retribution with the free agency of man in the perpetration of crimes for which alone they are responsible, may be beyond present solution, but the fact is plain. Philosophical difficulties are inherent in common facts, and are not peculiar to theological truth.

II. IN ORDINARY MEN RELIGIOUS INSTINCTS ARE STRONGER THAN POLITICAL AND SOCIAL CONSIDERATIONS. We need not be surprised that Saul's Hebrew guards declined to obey his command to slay the "priests of the Lord." No doubt strong reasons were present to prove their loyalty to their king. Not only is loyalty a first principle of action with good subjects, but the fact that he was of their own tribe, and had been their choice out of all Israel (ch. x. 19—24), must have made them anxious to sustain his authority against all comers. Even the very weaknesses of a monarch will induce some men to put down with strong hand all charged with conspiracy against him, whether or not the charge be fully established. Yet these men had been wont to recognise a higher authority than Saul's. They belonged to a race whose vocation in the world was of God. All the sanctities of religious worship and ritual, all the rich instruction of their marvellous history, strengthened and purified

the instinct that leads man to fear God.   To them the high priest and his subordinates were representatives of a sacred order, the exponents of a spiritual power, and
it would therefore be violence to all that was sacred, inexpressible, and most influential in their nature were they, out of loyalty to the king or from tribal considerations, to touch the "priests of the Lord." The *religious instincts of men are a great
power*.   They not only prompt to actions more or less good according to the degree
of enlightenment, but we cannot calculate the vast benefits resulting to mankind by
their restraining power.   The fact is worthy of much study, and the wide world
furnishes ample illustrations of its importance.   On the nation, the family, and the
individual it acts as a conservator of good and a represser of much that would
destroy.   It is often the only barrier against the tide of passion and ignorance.   The
wise know how to appeal to it and turn it to their own uses.   It is this in men,
among other things, which renders null and void all efforts to exterminate Christianity.   Men may call reverence for sacred persons and offices superstition, and in
extravagant forms the term is fitly applied, yet it is the indication of a governing
influence in human affairs superior to all the advances of civilisation.   Man must be
remade if his life is permanently to be regulated by any principles or opinions at
variance with the natural religiousness of his spirit.

   III. ACTIONS INNOCENT IN INTENTION MAY BE FRAUGHT WITH SERIOUS CONSEQUENCES
TO OTHERS.   It can scarcely be charged on David that he was guilty of sin in visiting
the tabernacle at Nob, seeking there food and shelter, though it may have been an
indiscretion.   The false representation by reason of which Ahimelech was induced to
give him bread and a sword was the real wrong.   On a wider survey of facts, and
with a juster estimate of the risks of compromising the officials of the sanctuary, he
would probably have sought food in some other quarter, or have cried out to God for
special deliverance.   As it was, his device of being on Saul's business was evidently
intended to save the high priest from the political sin of aiding one outlawed by the
king.   But his good motives were entirely useless because the overt act was witnessed by an enemy, who, David felt sure, would put on it a construction inconsistent
with his own wishes and the knowledge of the high priest.   His conduct, therefore,
pure in intentions and fenced with precaution, did compromise a band of innocent
men, and was, owing to the wickedness of the parties he had to contend with, and not
to the natural justice of the case, the occasion of the fearful slaughter of the priests
and entire population of the city.   The guilt of the slaughter rested on Saul; the
occasion for the exercise of the murderous malice was unwittingly created by
David.   With a sorrowful heart he admits the great woe to have had its origin
incidentally in his own action.   It is a truism that *every action carries with it consequences into the future*, in which we ourselves and others are concerned.   One of
the effects of our action is to prompt the action of other men, or to modify the
course which otherwise they would have taken.   And as the interests of many may
depend not on what we do directly, but on the conduct of others whom we directly
affect, it is obvious that it is often possible for us to perform deeds or pursue courses
which shall give occasion for other men to perpetrate great wrongs on those we
would gladly shield.   In that case we are not responsible for their crimes or follies,
but we are responsible for any indiscretions which may have given plausible ground
for their procedure, or have rendered it possible.   But it is only *where indiscretions are possible that blame really rests*.   The wise men from the East, inquiring
with all simplicity of purpose for the new-born king, were the occasion of the
slaughter of the children of Bethlehem; but though they no doubt were pained, if
ever they knew the fact, they were not guilty of any wrong.   We cannot always
refuse to act because evil men exist.   Indiscretion is chargeable where a knowledge
of facts and of the probable uses men will make of our deeds is presumably possible.
The practical bearing of the risks attendant on our actions is to induce extreme
caution, to awaken watchfulness, lest by our well-intentioned deeds we should compromise others, or give an appearance of reason for wicked men to manifest their
wickedness.   In the memory of many a man there are records of deeds unwise and
out of season, which have left a fatal mark on the world in spite of subsequent
efforts of wisdom and goodness.   Like David men can say, "I have occasioned" all
this.

IV. THE DESIGNS OF THE WICKED DEFEAT THEMSELVES. The conflict waged by Saul was, as we have seen, really against the decree of God, but its ostensible object was a plot on the part of David against the throne. Whatever fears Saul may have had concerning Samuel's sympathy with David, there was no public ground for them in any positive action taken by the prophet in concert with David. What he dreaded most of all was the open espousal of David's cause by the spiritual power; for the priesthood had immense influence with the people. It was to crush out by one terrible blow any supposed concert that he caused the slaughter at Nob; and it is instructive to observe how this very attempt to deprive David of the official support of the spiritual power really put it on his side. The deeds of bad men are never complete enough for insuring a final triumph; some oversight, some weakness, some so-called accident gives occasion for the ultimate frustration of their purpose. By some chance, as men say, Abiathar escaped and went over to David. Saul fell into the pit he had prepared for David (Ps. lii. 6). There is now a *Christian spiritual power*, and the truth thus exemplified is especially seen in the great conflict of men against it. The same interests in higher form are still in conflict with opposing forces. Every effort to subvert or crush out the kingdom of God, though it should be a great "slaughter" either of bodies or of characters, develops more life, leads to closer union, throws the Church more on the power and guidance of God, and so prepares the way for a new movement of a higher spiritual character before which the powers of evil must yield. Give time, and the spiritual will triumph.

General lessons:—1. In matters of doubt, where evil consequences may possibly ensue from our conduct it is best to abstain from action; for it is a good rule to bar the way to evil by every possible contrivance. 2. Where the reputation of others is affected by our conduct we should either seek their consent or avoid a possible compromise of their character. 3. Any false step in life is greatly embittered in review if it has been attended with untruthfulness. 4. We may confidently appeal to the religious feelings of men in our defence of Christian truth even when by bare argument we cannot touch them. 5. In the frequent historical illustrations of the impossibility of men crushing out the spiritual power, whether in Jewish or Christian form, we see a prophecy of the time when Christ shall have "put down all rule and all authority and power" (1 Cor. xv. 24).

HOMILIES BY VARIOUS AUTHORS.

Vers. 1, 2. (THE CAVE OF ADULLAM.)—*David's refuge and following.* David's escape from Gath to the cave of Adullam marks a fresh starting-point in his career. Henceforth he led the life of an independent outlaw at the head of a band of armed men. He was openly and continually persecuted by Saul, under the illusion that he was aiming at the crown, although he neither rebelled nor encouraged rebellion against his authority. He was thereby kept prominently before the minds of the people, and must have fixed the attention of the most observant and devout upon him, as, in contrast to Saul (whose government became more and more arbitrary, inefficient, and ungodly), the man who alone was worthy to be "captain over the Lord's inheritance;" and the experience through which he passed served to prepare him for his destination. "This very period of his deepest sufferings becomes the decisive turning-point of his whole history, at which it enters upon a true upward course, thence to rise ever higher and higher; while his real destiny, viz., to rule, is now for the first time not only foreshadowed, but already begun, though only on the smallest scale; and the clearest proof that this actually is his destiny is found in the fact that he begins to work it out without consciously exerting himself to do so" (Ewald). He may be considered as representing, in some respects, *the good man under persecution*, and as—

I. PROTECTED FROM THE VIOLENCE OF PERSECUTORS, with which the servants of God have been threatened in every age. 1. Underneath the personal and ostensible grounds of such violence lie *the opposition of "the kingdom of darkness"* to the kingdom of God, and the enmity of the evil heart against righteousness and goodness. David was "the representative of the theocratic principle for which he suffers and endures; Saul of the anti-theocratic principle." Like Moses, David bore "the reproach of Christ," who was in him and suffered with him (Acts ix. 4; Col. i. 24; Heb. xi. 26, 32—38). 2. It is *limited* in its power, and is always ultimately defeated. "Be not afraid of them that kill the body," &c. (Luke xii. 4). 3. God himself is *the Refuge of the persecuted*, and provides varied, wonderful, and effectual means for their deliverance. "Thou art my refuge" (Ps. cxlii. 5). "Thou hast delivered my soul from death," &c. (Ps. lvi. 13). The operation of Divine providence was displayed in a remarkable manner in the preservation of David throughout the whole course of his persecution by Saul.

II. SYMPATHISING WITH THE MISERY OF THE OPPRESSED. "His brethren and all his father's house," endangered by Saul's jealousy as well as by the Philistine garrison at Bethlehem (2 Sam. xxiii. 13, 14), "and every one that was in distress" (outwardly impoverished and harassed), "and in debt" (to avaricious usurers, and not necessarily through any fault of his own), "and discontented" (inwardly embittered and dissatisfied with the existing state of things), owing to bad government. "Surely oppression maketh a wise man mad" (Eccles. vii. 7), and incites and justifies the adoption of a course which, under other circumstances, would be highly culpable. They did not gather to David in vain. 1. Sympathy with suffering is usually *felt in an eminent degree* by those who have themselves suffered (Heb. ii. 18). 2. It is always shown, when it is genuine, in *practical effort* for its alleviation (2 Cor. i. 4). 3. It generally produces in those toward whom it is shown a peculiarly strong and enduring *attachment*. "Pain is the deepest thing we have in our nature, and union through pain has always seemed more real and more holy than any other" (A. H. Hallam). "I do not know where a better home could have been provided for David than among those men in distress, in debt, in discontent. If it behoved a ruler to know the heart of his subjects, their sorrows, their wrongs, their crimes,—to know them and to sympathise with them,—this was surely as precious a part of his schooling as the solitude of his boyhood, or as any intercourse he had with men who had never faced the misery of the world, and never had any motive to quarrel with its laws. Through oppression, confusion, lawlessness he was learning the eternal, essential righteousness of God" (Maurice).

III. ASSUMING THE LEADERSHIP OF THE FAITHFUL. "He became captain over them: and there were with him about four hundred men"—afterwards six hundred (ch. xxiii. 13); including his nephews, Abishai (ch. xxvi. 6), Joab, Asahel, and Amasa, Ahimelech the Hittite, the "three mighty men" who "broke through the host of the Philistines and drew water out of the well of Bethlehem" (2 Sam. xxiii. 16), many of those whose names are recorded in the list of David's heroes (1 Chron. xi. 10—47), Gadites "whose faces were like the faces of lions, and were as swift as the roes upon the mountains," Benjamites and men of Judah, under Amasai, on whom "the Spirit came, and he said, Thine are we," &c.; "for thy God helpeth thee" (1 Chron. xii. 8—18). Some of them possessed, perhaps, little religious principle, and were ready for any adventurous enterprise; but most of them were young, free, noble spirits, resenting the tyranny of Saul, and sympathising with all that was best in the nation—"the unconscious materials out of which a new world was to be formed." David's leadership was —1. Exercised by virtue of his peculiar position, eminent godliness, and *surpassing ability*. 2. Accepted by them *voluntarily*, and followed with fidelity and enthusiasm. 3. Contributed to their discipline, *improvement* (Ps. xxxiv. 11), and future service against the common enemy, as well as his own moral force and power of organisation and rule. "The effect of such a life on his spiritual nature was to deepen his unconditional dependence on God; by the alternations of heat and cold, fear and hope, danger and safety, to temper his soul and make it flexible, tough, and bright as steel. It evolved the qualities of a leader of men, teaching him command and forbearance, promptitude and patience, valour and gentleness. It won for him a name as a founder of a nation, and it gathered around him a force of men devoted to him by an enthusiastic attachment, bred by long years of common dangers and the hearty friendships of many a march by day and nightly encampment round the glimmering watchfires beneath the lucid stars" (Maclaren).

IV. DEVOTED TO THE SERVICE OF GOD. The effect of persecution on a good man is to cause him to draw nigh to God in—1. Renewed *confidence* and hope. 2. Intense *desire for the manifestation of his glory* in "bringing the wickedness of the wicked to an end and establishing the just" (Ps. vii. 9). He wishes above all things and strives for the setting up of the kingdom of God upon earth. 3. Earnest *prayers* and thanksgivings, such as are expressed in the "cave songs" of David. Ps. CXLII., 'A cry of the persecuted to God' (see inscription):—

> "With my voice to Jehovah do I cry,
> With my voice to Jehovah do I make supplication.
> Deliver me from my persecutors,
> For they are stronger than I."

Ps. LVII., 'Trusting in the protection of God' (see inscription):—

> "Be gracious unto me, O God, be gracious unto me,
> For in thee hath my soul found refuge ;
> And in the shadow of thy wings will I find refuge
> Until the destruction passeth by.
> Be thou exalted above the heavens, O God,
> Thy glory above all the earth."

"When his companions in arms were carousing or asleep, he sat by his lamp in some still retreat, or 'considered the heavens' as they spread above him, or meditated on the law, or engaged in prayer, or held intimate communion with God, and composed and wrote (though he thought not so) what shall sound in the Church and echo through the world to all time" (Binney).—D.

Vers. 3, 4. (MOAB.)—*Filial kindness.* To honour parents is the earliest obligation of life, the foundation of human duties and a stepping-stone to Divine. It applies to children not only when they dwell at home and depend on their parents, but also when they leave home and become independent of them. The manner in which it should be shown in the latter case differs in some respects from that in the former ; but such kindness as David exhibited towards his aged father and mother ought never to be neglected. It was—

I. NEEDFUL. In early life we need the care of parents, in old age that of children. 1. Bodily *weakness* and failing health often render parents dependent for physical comforts and even necessaries (Gen. xlvii. 12). 2. Increasing *loneliness* makes them desirous of the cheering presence and intercourse of their children ; and much pain is naturally given by lack of respect, affection, confidence, and gentle ministrations. 3. Special *emergencies*, like those here alluded to, sometimes demand unusual efforts for their safety and happiness. Their condition appeals to the tenderest and best feelings of the heart, though, alas, it sometimes appeals in vain.

II. OBLIGATORY. 1. Arising out of *natural relationship*, the duties of which on the part of children, however imperfectly they may have been fulfilled on the part of parents, cannot be cancelled. 2. Required by the claims of *gratitude* for innumerable benefits received. 3. Enjoined by the *Divine word* in many precepts to which great promises are annexed. "The fifth commandment is the centre of all the others ; for upwards it is the point of departure for Divine, and downwards for human duties" (Ephes. vi. 1). "Despise not thy mother when she is old" (Prov. xxiii. 22). "God commanded, saying, Honour thy father," &c. (Matt. xv. 4—9). "Let them learn first to show (filial) reverence to their own household, and to requite their parents," &c. (1 Tim. v. 4). 4. Commended by the *example* of the good. "Because ye have obeyed the commandment of Jonadab your father," &c. (Jer. xxxv. 18, 19). Jesus Christ himself (John xix. 26).

III. EXEMPLARY in the way in which it was displayed. 1. *Thoughtful*, affectionate, and tender. 2. *Self-denying* and self-sacrificing, with much effort and risk, and as was best suited to the circumstances of the case. 3. *Religious :* "Till I know what God will do to me ;" where there is a recognition of his will as supreme, faith in his wise and gracious disposal (Ps. xxvii. 10), and hope of his enabling him to see again his parents, from whom he parted with regret, and provide for their permanent welfare.

Exhortation:—1. To children. Be kind to your parents, though you no longer need their care, if you would not have your children be unkind to you. 2. To parents. Seek to gain the respect and affection of your children, and teach them to honour God, if you would have them to honour you. 3. To all. Be not like those of whom the heavenly Father said of old, "I have nourished and brought up children, and they have rebelled against me" (Isa. i. 2).—D.

Ver. 4. (MOAB.)—*Awaiting the future.* "Till I know what God will do to me." There are times when our thoughts naturally turn toward the future: the commencement of a fresh enterprise or a new season, suspense in sickness, the approach of critical events, especially when they lie beyond our control or even our probable conjecture. At such times this is the appropriate language of a good man. He awaits it in—

I. UNCERTAINTY about the events of the future—new positions, opportunities, advantages, trials, duties. "We know not with what we must serve the Lord until we come thither" (Exod. x. 26). "Ye have not passed this way heretofore" (Josh. iii. 4), and cannot tell what may befall you therein. "Shadows, clouds, and darkness rest upon it." But the good man is not distracted by curiosity or anxiety, inasmuch as—1. Neither is of any avail. 2. The Father has reserved the times and the seasons "in his own power" (Acts i. 7). 3. And he has done so wisely and *for our good.* "The veil that hides the future is woven by the hand of mercy."

II. CONFIDENCE in the care of God. "My times are in thy hand" (Ps. xxxi. 15). "I will cry unto God that performeth all things for me" (Ps. lvii. 2). Such confidence respects—1. His perfect knowledge, almighty power, and *supreme control* of all things, including the thoughts and purposes of men (ch. xix. 23). 2. His *individual observation.* 3. His *beneficent operation.* "Being well assured of the justice of his cause as contrasted with the insane persecutions of Saul, David confidently hoped that God would bring his flight to an end" (Keil).

> "O Lord, how happy should we be,
> If we could cast our care on thee,
> If we from self could rest,
> And feel at heart that One above,
> In perfect wisdom, perfect love,
> Is working for the best" (Keble).

III. READINESS for whatever may take place. 1. By *watchful attention* to every indication of the will of God, looking out for it as a watchman for the dawn of the morning. "I will stand upon my watch," &c. (Hab. ii. 1). 2. By cherishing a spirit of *humble submissiveness* to what he may think fit to do and fixed determination to do what he may require. 3. By faithful fulfilment of the plain and *immediate duty* of the present time. "Let my father and mother come forth" (from the hold in Mizpeh) "and be with you, till," &c. Its performance is the best preparation for the events and duties of the future.—D.

Ver. 5. (MIZPEH OF MOAB.)—*A summons to duty.* The prophet Gad was probably sent at the instance of Samuel to David, who was now "in the hold" in Moab, and with whom he may have become acquainted at Ramah. His message was important in relation to the future course of David (ver. 3). "According to the counsels of God he was not to seek for refuge outside the land; not only that he might not be estranged from his fatherland and the people of Israel, which would have been opposed to his calling to be king of Israel, but also that he might learn to trust entirely in the Lord as his only refuge and fortress" (Keil). There was also a special reason why he should be recalled in the incursions of the Philistines, which Saul failed to repel (ch. xxiii. 1). And the message furnished a test of his obedience to the will of God as declared by the prophets. "Immediately he conferred not with flesh and blood," but did as he was directed, and thereby afforded an instructive example to others. Consider the *message* as—

I. COMMUNICATED BY THE PROPHETIC WORD. This word is, for us, contained in 'the Scriptures of truth." 1. It speaks with *authority.* 2. It speaks *plainly,* "in

divers manners," according to our need, and "for our good always." 3. It speaks
in the reading of the Scriptures, in the voice of preachers and teachers, parents and
friends, in the recollections of the memory, and often comes to the heart and conscience with peculiar force. "Believe his prophets, so shall ye prosper" (2 Chron.
xx. 20).

II. CALLING TO UNEXPECTED DUTY; unexpected, inasmuch as, not unfrequently—
1. It is such as we should not naturally have supposed. 2. It differs from the
course which we have chosen for ourselves. "Abide not in the hold." 3. It requires
us to meet unusual *difficulties and dangers.* "Depart, and get thee into the land of
Judah" (into the very presence of a deadly foe). "Master, the Jews of late sought
to stone thee; and goest thou thither again?" (John xi. 8—10; Luke ix. 51).

"Do thy duty; that is best;
Leave unto thy Lord the rest."

III. COMPLIED WITH IN A RIGHT MANNER. "And David departed," &c. 1.
Without question, like a good soldier at the word of command. 2. Without hesitation or delay. 3. Without fear. How different was it with Saul! (ch. xiii. 11;
xv. 11). "Whosoever will save his life," &c. (Matt. xvi. 25).

IV. CONDUCTING TO SAFETY, USEFULNESS, AND HONOUR. 1. Safety; for he was
"kept by the power of God." 2. Usefulness; for he "saved the inhabitants of
Keilah" (ch. xxiii. 5). 3. Honour; for he was more fully recognised as the true
defender of Israel against their enemies, and his heroic band was largely increased
(ch. xxiii. 13).

"Stern Lawgiver! yet thou dost wear
The Godhead's most benignant grace;
Nor know we anything so fair
As is the smile upon thy face:
Flowers laugh before thee on their beds,
And fragrance in thy footing treads;
Thou dost preserve the stars from wrong:
And the most ancient heavens through thee are fresh and strong.
Give unto me, made lowly wise,
The spirit of self-sacrifice;
The confidence of reason give,
And in the light of truth thy bondman let me live."

(Wordsworth, 'Ode to Duty.')—D.

Vers. 6—19. (GIBEAH.)—*The tyranny of Saul.* With his spear-sceptre in his
hand, Saul, now considerably past the meridian of life, sat in the midst of his
council of officers and magnates, under the tamarisk tree on the height, in Gibeah.
The description of what took place in this assembly—"a kind of parliament in the
open air"—casts a lurid light upon his character and rule. In it we see—1. The
fulfilment of the *prediction* of Samuel concerning the course which would be
pursued by a king such as the people desired (ch. viii. 11—18). 2. The moral
deterioration of Saul since the day when they shouted "God save the king" in
Mizpeh (ch. x. 24), and "made him king before the Lord in Gilgal" (ch. xi. 15);
and even since his rejection (ch. xv. 26). 3. The working out of the law of
retribution in their chastisement through the king chosen by themselves and reflecting their own sin. The early brilliance of his reign had been long overcast, and the
thunder-storm was approaching. Saul had ceased to be a servant of Jehovah. His
government was the reverse of what it ought to have been. Although it had respect
to the outward forms of religion, and displayed much zeal against irreligious practices, yet it did not really recognise the invisible King of Israel, obey his will, or
observe "the manner of the kingdom" which had been ordained of old (Deut. xvii.
14—20), and formally recorded as a permanent law and testimony (ch. x. 25). It
was essentially anti-theocratic. The true theocracy was represented by Samuel and
the prophets at Ramah, and David and his band at Adullam; and through them
(in the wonderful working of Divine providence) the nation would be raised to power
and glory, and the purposes of God concerning it accomplished. His character and
rule were marked by—

I. Morbid selfishness. By constantly directing his thoughts toward himself, instead of toward God and his people, Saul had come to think of nothing else but his own safety, power, and honour. Selfishness appears in—1. *Pride* and vainglory. Of this he had previously exhibited unmistakable signs (ch. xv. 12). Yet it was expressly required that his heart should not be "lifted up above his brethren" (Deut xvii. 20). 2. The use of power for *personal ends*. In contrast to charity, it seeketh its own. The king exists for the good of the people, not the people for the glory of the king. "Behold, I am against thee, Pharaoh king of Egypt, the great dragon that lieth in the midst of his rivers, which hath said, My river is my own, and I have made it for myself" (Ezek. xxix. 3). 3. The *neglect* of the performance of duty to others. Unlike Samuel, when he was judge, Saul had evidently, in his concern for himself, omitted to maintain law and order (ver. 2), and even to resist the encroachments of the Philistines, against whom he had formerly rendered signal service.

II. Avowed misgovernment (vers. 7—9). 1. *Partisanship*. He placed men of his own tribe in the chief offices of state, and this would not be conducive to the unity of the nation. "Hear now, ye Benjamites." 2. *Mercenariness*. He sought to attach them to his interest by the lowest motives. "He boasts that he has given fields and vineyards to all his Benjamite servants and accomplices; and what he gave to them he must have taken away from others" (Hengstenberg). His reign was oppressive, as it had been predicted. 3. *Suspicion* of disloyalty, and reproach for want of gratitude and sympathy. "All of you have conspired against me," &c. A man is apt to suspect in others the evil which exists in his own heart. 4. *Falsehood*. Having heard that a number of men had gathered around David, he said, "My son hath stirred up my servant against me," &c. "There is herein a twofold false accusation: as to David, that he was lying in wait to take his throne and his life; and as to Jonathan, that he was the cause of this insurrectionary and insidious conduct of David."

III. Flagrant injustice (vers. 9—16). The people desired a king that he might judge them (ch. viii. 20). But Saul abused his judicial office by—1. Receiving and relying upon *insufficient testimony*. The law required the evidence of at least two witnesses; but he was satisfied with the information of one of his creatures—Doeg the Edomite. 2. A prejudiced *prejudgment* of the guilt of the accused. He sent for Ahimelech "and all his father's house," having already resolved, apparently, upon their destruction. 3. Utter disregard of the plainest *proofs of innocence*. The priest gave his evidence in a dignified, simple, and straightforward manner. In what he had done he was fully justified. And he had not done all that was attributed to him. "The force of the word *begin* lies in this, that it would have been his first act of allegiance to David and defection from Saul. This he strenuously repudiates" (Speaker's 'Com.') He was ignorant of any treason in others, guiltless of it himself, and had done no wrong. 4. A rash, precipitate, revengeful, and disproportionate *sentence*. "Thou shalt surely die, Ahimelech, thou, and all thy father's house" (ver. 16).

IV. Persistent wilfulness (ver. 17). "Never was the command of a prince more barbarously given, never was the command of a prince more honourably disobeyed" (M. Henry). "We ought to obey God rather than man." The besetting sin of Saul received another check; and another merciful warning was given him, which should have made him pause and desist from his evil purpose. But, blinded by passion, and probably thinking (being turned aside by a deceived heart) that his course was justifiable, he heeded it not, outraged the public conscience, as expressed in the refusal of his own body-guard, and gave the order for immediate execution to one of his vilest servants and accomplices. Wicked men generally find appropriate instruments for the accomplishment of their wickedness.

V. Atrocious cruelty (vers. 18, 19). Impelled by the same self-will as formerly led him to spare Agag, he not only destroyed eighty-five "priests of the Lord," but also gave to the sword "the city of priests, both men and women, children and sucklings, and oxen, and asses, and sheep;" nor was he, as in his attack upon the prophets, restrained by the hand of God. 1. In fulfilling their own purposes evil men often unconsciously execute the *predicted and righteous judgments of Heaven* (ch. ii.

31—36; iii. 11—14). 2. Those judgments, though startling in their immediate occasion, are *connected with their main cause*. If the house of Eli had not been reduced to a dependent and despised condition by notorious transgression, Saul would hardly have dared to commit this act. 3. The evil which men do *lives after them* in its effects, and one generation suffers for the preceding (Exod. xx. 5). 4. Although men in doing wrong may execute the will of God, they are *responsible* for their own acts, and must sooner or later suffer the penalty due to them. Saul's reckless cruelty alienated the best of his subjects and hastened his doom. This was not the only instance in which it was displayed (see 2 Sam. xxi. 1—6).

VI. IMPIOUS REBELLION. In destroying the servants of God for imaginary rebellion against himself Saul was guilty of real rebellion against the Divine King of Israel. More fully than ever he renewed a conflict which could end only in his defeat. "Woe to him that striveth with his Maker."

Reflections:—1. How vast is the mischief which self-will works in the world! 2. How base do men sometimes become under its dominion! 3. How fearfully is the possession of power frequently misused! 4. "How unsearchable are his judgments, and his ways past finding out!"—D.

Vers. 18, 19. (GIBEAH.)—*Doeg the Edomite.* Wicked men, especially when they occupy positions of authority and possess wealth and influence, attract to themselves others of like character, and become more wicked by association with them. Of the latter Doeg the Edomite was one. He belonged to a people between whom and Israel the bitterest enmity existed. But he had apparently become a proselyte, and, being a man of some ability, was made overseer of the herdsmen of Saul and one of his council. His real character seems to have been perceived by David before he fled from court (ver. 22); and it is very probable that he gave secret information to the king of what took place at the tabernacle at Nob previous to bearing open testimony in the council. He was—

I. A HEARTLESS WORSHIPPER; "detained before Jehovah" (ch. xxi. 7). Whatever may have been the reason of his detention, there can be no doubt that he was present in the sacred place either unwillingly and by constraint, or offering a formal and hypocritical worship. "He concealed his heathen heart under Israelitish forms." He was more observant of the conduct of others in the house of God than careful to correct his own. He cherished "a wicked mind," and perhaps revolved therein how he could turn what he saw to his own advantage, or employ it for the gratification of his hatred and enmity. All who join in the outward forms of worship do not "lift up holy hands without wrath and disputation."

II. A MALICIOUS INFORMER (vers. 9, 10). His immediate purpose in giving information may have been to avert the reproaches of the king from his courtiers; but he must have known what its effect would be with respect to the high priest, and doubtless deliberately aimed at producing it. He also appears to have gone beyond the truth; perchance supposing that when he saw the priest take "the sword of Goliath" from behind the ephod, he used the latter for the purpose of "inquiring of the Lord." "Thou lovest evil more than good; and lying rather than to speak righteousness. Thou lovest all devouring words, O thou deceitful tongue" (Ps. lii. 3, 4).

III. A RUTHLESS EXECUTIONER (vers. 18, 19). What others, whose consciences were not hardened, refused to do he willingly and readily accomplished, and probably found therein a gratification of the enmity of his race against Israel. The command of the king could not relieve him of his responsibility for his deed of blood. "Louis XIV., who had sanctioned the Dragonades, died declaring to the cardinals Rohan and Bissy, and to his confessor, that, being himself altogether ignorant of ecclesiastical questions, he had acted under their guidance and as their agent in all that he had done against the Jansenists or the Protestant heretics, and on those his spiritual advisers he devolved the responsibility to the supreme Judge" (Stephen, 'Lect. on the Hist. of France').

IV. A RETRIBUTORY INSTRUMENT (see last homily). When the great wickedness of men like Doeg is considered, it is not surprising that David (living under the former dispensation) should predict and desire their due punishment as public enemies; "not in a spirit of revenge, but rather in a spirit of zeal for the glory of God, desire for the vindication of right, and regard for the peace and purity of society" ('Expositor,' iv. 56), as he does in Ps. LII., "The punishment of an evil tongue" (see inscription) :—

> "Why boastest thou thyself in wickedness, O mighty man?
> The mercy of God endureth continually.
> Destruction doth thy tongue devise,
> Like a sharp razor, working guile.
> Thus then God will smite thee down for ever.
> He will seize thee and pluck thee out of thy tent,
> And root thee out of the land of the living."

Other psalms have been supposed by some to refer to Doeg and the massacre of the priests, viz., xvii., xxxv., lxiv., cix., cxl.—D.

Vers. 20—22. (THE FOREST OF HARETH.) — *Conscience.*   Conscience is the consciousness a man has of himself in relation to the standard of right which he recognises. It is at once a judgment of his conformity or otherwise to that standard, and a corresponding feeling of approbation or disapprobation. It is the crowning faculty of the soul. "The whole world is under a solemn economy of government and judgment. A mighty spirit of judgment is in sovereign exercise over all; discerning, estimating, approving or condemning. And it is the office of conscience to recognise this authority and to represent it in the soul. It communicates with something mysteriously great without the soul, and above it, and everywhere. It is the sense (more explicit or obscure) of standing in judgment before the Almighty" (J. Foster). Its operation appears in what is here said of David as—1. *Uttering a warning against sin.* "I knew it that day," &c. Conscience is not only reflective, but prospective in its operations. The sight of Doeg led him to see and feel that the course which he was about to take in deceiving Ahimelech was wrong, and would be productive of evil consequences. But under the pressure of urgent need he neglected the premonition. 2. *Inflicting remorse on account of sin.* "I am guilty as to every soul (life) of the house of thy father." The information he received called his conscience into the highest activity. He judged himself strictly. He felt his sin deeply. And most gladly would he recall the evil he had done if he could. But that was impossible. "The lie had gone forth from him; and having done so, it was no longer under his control, but would go on producing its diabolical fruits" (W. M. Taylor). 3. *Constraining to the confession of sin.* He did not (as Saul had done) seek to conceal or palliate his transgression, but freely and fully acknowledged it, renounced it, and sought its forgiveness (Ps. xxxii. 5). 4. *Inciting to reparation for sin.* "Abide thou with me," &c. It was little that he could do for this purpose, but what was in his power he did. It is evident that, notwithstanding he had yielded to temptation, he possessed a *tender conscience* (Acts xxiv. 16). "And wouldst thou be faithful to that work which God hath appointed thee to do in this world for his name? Then make much of a trembling heart and conscience; for although the *word* be the line and rule whereby we must govern and order all our actions, yet a breaking heart and tender conscience is of absolute necessity for so doing. A hard heart can do nothing with the word of Jesus Christ. Keep then thy conscience awake with wrath and grace, with heaven and hell. But let grace and heaven bear sway" (Bunyan).

> "O clear conscience and upright!
> How doth a little failing wound thee sore."   D.

Ver. 23. (HARETH.)—*The defender of the persecuted.*   As David afforded protection to Abiathar, so Christ affords protection to those who betake themselves to him. This is not a mere resemblance, but is directly involved in that (his royal office) wherein David was a type or Divine foreshadowing of "the King of kings." They—

I. ENDURE PERSECUTION FOR HIS SAKE. "He that seeketh my life seeketh thy life." They do so—1. Because of their *union* with him, and partaking of his life and righteousness, to which "this present evil world" is opposed. 2. Because of their *love* to him, which will not suffer them to leave him, or be unfaithful to him for the sake of gaining the favour of the world. 3. Because it has been thus *ordained*. "Unto you it is given," &c. (Phil. i. 29). "With persecutions" (Mark x. 30), which are an occasion of spiritual blessing (Matt. v. 10).

II. MUST ABIDE IN HIS FELLOWSHIP. "Abide thou with me." 1. By unwavering *reliance* upon him (John xv. 4—7; 1 John ii. 28). 2. By intimate *intercourse* with him. 3. By constant *obedience* to him.

III. FIND SAFETY UNDER HIS PROTECTION. "Fear not; with me thou art in safeguard." "David spoke thus in the firm belief that the Lord would deliver him from his foe and give him the kingdom" (Keil). Christ has "all power in heaven and in earth," and he will assuredly be "a hiding-place from the wind and a covert from the tempest." 1. Because of *his love* to them. 2. Because of his regard for *his kingdom*, to which they belong, and which they represent. 3. Because of his express and *faithful promise*. "Fear not." If the worst that can befall them should happen, even then

> "Thou, Saviour, art their charmèd Bower,
> Their magic Ring, their Rock, their Tower."   D.

Vers. 1, 2.—*The cave of Adullam.* David knew well that he could nevermore live in safety at the court of Saul. He would not raise a hand against his king and father-in-law, but he would not place himself again within his reach. Better a free life even in deserts and caves of the earth than a life in constant peril in ceiled houses. Behold him then in the cave of Adullam.

I. THE CAPTAIN OF THE REFUGEES. No question arises here respecting the right of revolt against a perverse, tyrannical king. We entirely believe in such a right, because the king exists for the good of the people, not the people for the service of the king. We have no misgiving as to the right of the British nation to rid itself of King James II., or that of the people in the kingdom of the Two Sicilies to drive away King Francis II. But the case of Saul's royalty over Israel was unique. The people had chosen him by acclamation, and there was no proof as yet that the mass of the people wished to dethrone him. Even if they had so wished, David was not the man to lead their revolt; for it was one of the tests of his fitness for the succession that he should not snatch at the honour to which he was destined, but wait the evolution of the Divine purpose, recognising God only as the true and absolute King of Israel. Therefore, what he did at this period was simply for preservation of himself and his relatives. The times were "out of joint," and he had no protection of law or civil order against the mad suspicions of the king. So he took refuge in a cavern, waiting for God and hoping in his word. The hero raised no standard of revolt, and drew no followers by prospect of plunder or revenge. Yet he did draw hundreds of the men of Israel to his place of refuge. These must not be likened to the riotous and desperate followers of Catiline, or even to the "empty persons" who attached themselves to Jephthah. Doubtless there may have been among the young men some who were more adventurous than devout, and cared for their leader's sword and spear more than for his psalms; but they were in general young men of patriotic temper who had suffered damage through the misrule of the time, and found the public disorder and tyranny intolerable. They turned their wistful eyes towards one who had borne himself wisely in the station he had occupied, and from whom they hoped for a just and prudent administration of public affairs. There are parallels to this position in the history of other nations; but most worthy of our thought is the parallel of the great Son of David, our Lord Jesus Christ. When he was a young man in Galilee the people were distressed under their rulers. The civil government was oppressive; the religious *surveillance* by the chief priests and elders was worse. Heavy burdens were imposed without pity, and grievous abuses of power and office were committed. The eyes of many had failed them, looking long for a deliverer who should be the Consolation of Israel. Then appeared Jesus of Nazareth, raising no standard of revolt, indeed refusing to be made a king by the voice of the multitude, while himself under the evident displeasure of the authorities, and exposed to frequent risks of arrest and death. But to him followers repaired, and they were welcome. Jesus called to him the labouring and heavy-laden. He had powerful attraction for all who were distressed. And from the day when he took up a position apart from the rulers of the Jews, though he headed no movement of resistance, it became more and more obvious that those rulers had lost the favour of Jehovah, and had nothing before them but thickening disaster and a final collapse of their power like that of Saul on Mount Gilboa. The only hope of Israel thenceforth was with and in the despised and rejected One who had been born in David's city and of David's line. So it is still. It is Jesus Christ, as rejected of men, humbled, crucified, who appeals to human hearts. Who will go out to him, "without the camp, bearing his reproach"? Who will repair to him at the cave of Adullam? Not the proud, nor the thoughtless, nor the self-satisfied; but the distressed, the ruined, and the bereaved will go; and over such he is willing to be Captain. Let them come to him, and his life is thenceforward bound up with theirs, and theirs with his. With him they are "in safeguard" till the end of the tribulation; and when the King appears in his great power these will appear with him in glory; the trials of Adullam more than recompensed by the joys of New Jerusalem.

II. THE POSITION OF SEPARATION. When is it justified? David and his followers went apart from the common life of their countrymen, and renounced all idea of rendering service or occupying any post of honour under Saul. Jesus Christ and his disciples broke with the course of the Jewish and Galilean world in which they lived, and took up a position quite aloof from the priests, elders, and scribes. What is the duty of modern Christians towards the society around them? Are they to come out and be separate? Some persons have almost a craze for separation, and support it on this story of Adullam. They hold it to be the duty of Christians to stand aloof from all the existing order of things, and all the plans and occupations of society; to accept no office in the State, and be subject to the powers that be only in the sense in which David continued subject to Saul; and to come out from all organised historical Churches, on the ground that they contain worldly elements and principles, and are therefore impure and ready to perish. All this seems to us extravagant in theory and uncharitable in spirit. Separation from evil does not mean alienation from every place and every institution in which a fault can be found. For good men to hold aloof from public affairs is simply to play into the hands of evil-doers; and to separate from every Church that has a faulty element in it is to disintegrate Christian society, and miserably embitter it in the process. But we must hold the balance true. It may be one's duty to separate himself from institutions of both Church and State under which he was born. As to civil institutions, this is plain enough. As to ecclesiastical relations, there are critical times when, as it was right for Israelites to separate from Saul and go over to David, so it has been and is right for Christians to withdraw from positions which they could not correct or amend, and go over to some simpler and purer expression of their faith and hope. On this ground we justify without hesitation the erection of reformed Churches in the sixteenth century apart from the unreformed. The Papal system had a long trial, and was found wanting. Such men as Wickliffe, Savonarola, and Huss tried to correct its errors and rouse a new spirit within its pale, just as David played on his harp to cure the mania of King Saul. It was labour lost. That which was evil grew worse. The tyranny which hung over Western Christendom became intolerable. Then they did wisely and well who threw off the yoke and began afresh, with the word of God for their directory, and the Son of God, who became Son of David, for their Captain. On the same ground we justify those who now-a-days break away from the same Papal infallible, and therefore incurable, system to join or to organise a reformed Church. And we add that those who do so in a Roman Catholic country, like Spain or Italy, to worship with some small evangelical congregation in a hall, mocked and despised, show a courage not at all inferior to that of the four hundred who defied the power of Saul, and flocked around David in the cave of Adullam. Those men did not lift their swords against Saul. David did not desire them to do so. He saw something still to honour in that king, and knew that the throne would be vacated without any assistance from him. So, in that system of infatuation and spiritual tyranny which centres at Rome, there is something of that common Christianity which we must reverence, and against which we may not fight.

While we expose its errors, let us always acknowledge whatever of the truth of God it contains, and be patient. Ultimately that system must perish. As the Philistines, and not the followers of David, made an end of Saul, so the democratic infidelity, not the reformed Church, is likely to make an end of the Papacy, and all the religious delusion and oppression of the Latin Church. Happy they who are in a fellowship which gives them direct access to the Lord Jesus, and has in him the living centre and the joy of all. O Saviour, draw us to thyself, and be thou a Captain over us!—F.

Vers. 18—23.—*Massacre and safeguard.* The tragic interest of this passage groups itself about four men: (1) the furious king; (2) the cruel officer; (3) the innocent priest; (4) the self-reproaching hero.

I. SAUL AND HIS MAD TYRANNY. How much allowance may be made for actual insanity in the king God only knows. But it must not be forgotten that the disorder of his mind was largely due to his own indulgence of fierce and arrogant passions, and his wilful refusal to obey the commands of the Lord and the guidance of his prophet. He had now become quite furious in his jealousy of David and in his suspicion of all around him as plotting his downfall. Unable to capture David, he turned fiercely on those whom he supposed to be aiding and abetting him in rebellion; and the homicidal mania which he had already betrayed in hurling his javelin at David, and even at Jonathan, now broke out against the innocent priests. When one begins to indulge a bad passion, how little he can tell the length to which it may carry him! We remember how Saul at the outset of his reign would not have a man in Israel put to death on his account. But now he had no pity on the innocent. Nothing can be more shocking than the hardness of heart which disregarded the noble defence of the priests against unjust accusation, and condemned them and their families to immediate death. By this Saul forfeits all claim to our sympathy. He is a bloodstained tyrant. Nero on his accession to the imperial dignity at Rome showed a similar reluctance to sign a legal sentence of death on a criminal, and yet broke forth into horrid cruelty at the age of seventeen. Saul was not so precocious in cruelty, and seems to have been free from other vices that made Nero infamous. But it should be considered, on the other hand, that Saul had knowledge of Jehovah, while Nero knew only the gods of Rome; and that though Nero had a great teacher in Seneca, Saul had a still greater in Samuel. There is no palliation of his conduct admissible unless on the plea of disease of the brain—an excuse which may also be advanced in behalf of such wretches as Antiochus Epiphanes and the Emperor Caligula. The lesson of admonition is that wickedness has horrible abysses unseen at first. Stop short at the beginnings of evil. Check your peril, calm your anger, correct your suspicions, hold back your hasty javelin; for if you lose self-control and a good conscience there is hardly any depth of injustice and infatuation to which you may not fall.

II. DOEG AND HIS RUTHLESS SWORD. Cruel masters make cruel servants. Tyrants never lack convenient instruments. Caligula, Nero, and Domitian had favourites and freed-men ready to stimulate their jealous passions and carry out their merciless commands. At Saul's elbow stood such a wretch, Doeg the Edomite. The repeated mention of this officer's extraction seems to imply that he was actuated by the hereditary jealousy of Israel which filled the descendants of Esau, and took a malicious pleasure in widening the gulf between Saul and David and slaying the priests of Israel's God. With his own hand he cut them down, when the Israelite officers shrank from the bloody deed; and no doubt it was he who executed the inhuman sentence against the women and children at Nob, and smote the very "oxen, asses, and sheep with the edge of the sword." Doeg has had many followers in those who have with fiendish relish tortured and slain the servants of our Lord and of his Christ. And indeed all who, without raising the hand of violence, take part with malicious purpose against servants of God, who misrepresent them and stab their reputations, are of one spirit with this Edomite whose memory is cursed.

III. AHIMELECH IN HIS INTEGRITY. How fine the contrast between the calm bearing of the chief priest on the one hand, and the unreasoning fury of Saul and truculent temper of Doeg on the other! How straightforward was the vindication of Ahimelech! If Saul had not been blind with passion he must have seen its transparent truth and noble candour.   When it became known through the land that Ahimelech and the priests had been killed by the king's order on a mere suspicion of disaffection which was false, a thrill of horror must have run through many bosoms, and those who feared the Lord must have had sore misgiving that he had forsaken his people and his land.   Under such mishaps in later times similar fears have been awakened.   Indeed men have been tempted to question whether there be any God of righteousness and truth actually governing the world ; for the virtuous suffer, the innocent are crushed, might overrules right, victory seems to be to the proud and not the lowly.   It is useless to deny that there are strange defeats of goodness and truth, and that blows fall on heads that seem least to deserve them.   All that we can do is to cleave to our belief, firm on its own grounds, that God is, and to say that the calamities complained of have his permission for some good ends in his far-reaching purpose.   At all events we can go no further into the mystery on a survey of this present life.   But there is another, and in it lies the abundant recompense for present wrongs.   It seems strange that a life so precious as that of Paul should have been assailed, bruised, and finally taken by violence for no crime, but for the name of Jesus.   But Paul himself has given us some clue to the compensation : " our light affliction, which is but for a moment, worketh for us a far more exceeding and eternal weight of glory."   Ahimelech and the priests, we may be sure, though they suffered not directly for Christ, but on account of his human ancestor, lost nothing, but gained much, by forfeiting their lives in innocence.

IV. DAVID AND HIS SELF-REPROACH.   News of this massacre must have shocked all thoughtful men in Israel, and deepened the distrust with which Saul was now regarded. David, when he heard of it, felt, besides horror and indignation, a bitter pang of self-reproach.   It was he who had played on the simplicity of the priests at Nob, and so had given occasion to Doeg to accuse them.   Would that he had gone without bread, whatever the consequence to himself, rather than have exposed so many innocent persons to such a cruel fate !   And now the horrid deed was done, and quite past remedy.   What a lesson against crafty strokes and plausible pretexts !   One may gain his point at the time by such devices, but after consequences little expected may fall on some innocent head ; and surely there is no sting so sharp in the conscience of an honourable man as the feeling that, for his own safety or interest, he has misled his own friends, and unwittingly brought disaster on them.   We can believe that David, on hearing what Abiathar told him, was bowed down with shame such as he never yet had needed to feel.   In this respect he failed to typify Christ.   Our Lord had no *self-reproach* to bear.   He never had recourse to subterfuge, and no guile was found in his mouth.   Those who have suffered for his sake have not been led into the risk of death unwittingly.   It was of some comfort to David that he could give protection to Abiathar.   " He that seeketh my life seeketh thy life."   We have a common enemy.   Thy life is in peril on my account ; therefore stay with me ; " thou shalt be in safeguard."   Here we do seem to hear the voice of Christ in a figure.   " If the world hate you, ye know," &c. (John xv. 18—20).   Our Lord gives his people safeguard with himself.   " Abide in me."   " Continue in my love." Such words are dear to mourners.   As David gave to Abiathar immediate and sympathetic attention, so the Son of David hearkens at once to those who repair to him with the tale of their mishap and grief.   He will take them all under the guarantee of his faithful safeguard.   Whatever solace it is possible to have in this world they have who abide with him.   And no one can pluck them out of his hand.—F.

EXPOSITION.

ADVENTURES OF DAVID AT KEILAH AND IN THE WILDERNESS OF ZIPH (CH. XXIII.).

CHAPTER XXIII.

DAVID RESCUES KEILAH, BUT HAS TO ESCAPE FROM THE TREACHERY OF ITS IN-HABITANTS (vers. 1—13).   Ver. 1.—**They told David**, &c.   The return of David into

his own land was quickly followed by exploits which not only increased his power, but turned the eyes of all the people towards him as their protector.   His first success was the deliverance of the city of **Keilah** from a body of Philistines who were plundering it of the produce of its harvest. This place lay a few miles south of the stronghold of Adullam, and itself occupied a defensible position, being perched on a steep hill overlooking the valley of Elah, not far from the thickets of Hareth (Conder, 'Tent Work,' ii. 88). Being thus at no great distance from the Philistine border, a band of men started thence on a foray for the purpose of robbing the **threshing-floors**. As no rain falls in Palestine in the harvest season (ch. xii. 17), the corn is threshed out in the open air by a heavy wooden sledge made of two boards, and curved up in front, with pieces of basalt inserted for teeth, drawn over it by horses, or it is trampled out by cattle. Conder ('Tent Work,' ii. 259) describes the threshing-floor as "a broad flat space on open ground, generally high. Sometimes the floor is on a flat rocky hill-top, and occasionally it is in an open valley, down which there is a current of air; but it is always situated where most wind can be found, because at the threshing season high winds never occur, and the grain is safely stored before the autumn storms commence." As the grain after winnowing is made into heaps until it can be carried home, there is always a period when the threshing-floors have to be watched to guard them from depredation, and this was the time chosen by the Philistines for a foray in force.

Vers. 2—5.—**David enquired of Jehovah**. This seems to show that Abiathar was already with David, as the prophet Gad had no ephod, and at this time, and for a considerable period subsequently, the usual way of consulting God was by the Urim and Thummim (see ver. 6). Though the answer was a command to go, yet David's men hesitated; not that they had any doubt of the immediate result, but, regarding Saul as their most dangerous enemy, they were unwilling to embroil themselves also with the Philistines. They argue, **We be afraid here in Judah**: why then should we close the Philistine territory against us by attacking their **armies**? Hebrew, "ranks," men disciplined and drawn up in array (see ch. xvii. 22). In order to remove these prudential doubts, David again consults God, and being a second time encouraged to undertake the rescue of Keilah, proceeds thither with his men. This attack, being unexpected, was entirely successful. The Philistines were driven back with great slaughter, and David **brought away their cattle**. The word signifies "small cattle," such as sheep and goats. Besides robbing the threshing-floors, the Philistines apparently had been driving off the flocks from the neighbouring pastures. Both Hareth, where David and his men had lain hid in the thickets (ch. xxii. 5), and Keilah were in the tribe of Judah, in the

southern portion of the Shephelah (Josh. xv. 44).

Ver. 6.—**When Abiathar . . . fled to David to Keilah, he came down with an ephod in his hand**. Literally, "an ephod came down in his hand," and so, word for word, the Syriac. The object of this verse is to explain how it was that David (in vers. 2 and 4) was able to inquire of Jehovah. The words **to Keilah** — Hebrew, Ke lah-wards—do not mean that it was at Keilah that Abiathar joined David, but that he came in time to go thither with him. In ch. xxii. 20 it seems as if Abiathar must have joined David even at an earlier date, for he is represented as fleeing to him immediately after the massacre of the priests at Nob. Now, granting that David's stay at Gath with Achish was very brief, he must have remained at Adullam a considerable time, inasmuch as men joined him there in large numbers (ch. xxii. 2), which seems to show that his hiding-place had become generally known. It was probably this concourse of men to him that was "discovered," i. e. made known, to Saul, and, as being an act of formal revolt, so raised his ire. As being supposed to be in league with David, Saul put the priests to death, and Abiathar fled; but probably the news of this terrible act had already reached David, and, in anxiety about his father and mother, he had gone to find refuge for them in Moab. Thither Gad follows him, bringing prophetic approval of his conduct, but ordering him to return into the territory of his own tribe. If then David was on his way to Moab when Abiathar reached Adullam, he may have remained in hiding there till David's return to the thickets of Hareth. But, possibly, even before Abiathar joined him the news may have arrived of the Philistine foray, and David's mind was set Keilah-wards. But there were those who doubted of the prudence of this proceeding, and Abiathar's arrival with the ephod enabled him to consult Jehovah's will. By his presence also David had now the approval of the priesthood.

Vers. 7, 8.—It was well-nigh a hopeless matter to hunt David as long as he remained on the borders of the desert of Judah, but once shut up in a town his capture was inevitable. When Saul, therefore, heard that David was at Keilah, he said, **God hath delivered him into my hand**. The Syriac, Chaldee, and Vulgate translate in the same way, probably as the nearest equivalent to the Hebrew, while the Septuagint has a different reading—*sold*. The Hebrew phrase is a very strong one; literally, "God hath ignored him," hath treated him as a stranger, and so let him fall "into my hand." Possibly Saul's metaphor was taken from the popular language, and no attempt should be made to get rid of unusual expressions, as if they were false readings. **By entering into a town that hath gates and bars.** Either the people of a walled town would give up David rather than expose themselves to the horrors of a siege (2 Sam. xx. 21, 22), or, if they stood by him, its capture would be a mere matter of time, David, it seems, would have run the risk, but happily was prevented.

Vers. 9 — 13. — **Saul secretly practised mischief.** This phrase is correctly translated "devised evil" in Prov. iii. 29; xiv. 22. There is no idea of secrecy in the Hebrew verb, which literally means "to work in metals," "to forge." Saul's purpose was open enough, and when David heard of it he tells Abiathar to bring the ephod, and then offers earnest prayer to God for counsel and advice. In his prayer his two questions are put inversely to the logical order, but in accordance with their relative importance in David's mind, and no ground exists for altering the text. But when the ephod was brought forward the questions were of course put in their logical sequence. To the first question, "Will Saul come down to besiege Keilah?" the answer was, "He will." To the second, "Will the citizens of Keilah deliver me and my men into the hand of Saul?" the answer also was, "They will." Whereupon he and his followers, now increased to 600 men, withdrew, **and went whithersoever they could go.** Literally. "they went about whither they went about," *i. e.* without any fixed plan, as chance or their necessities dictated. As David was once again at large, Saul had no longer any reason for besieging Keilah, especially as its citizens had preferred his side, as that of the more powerful, to gratitude for the safety of their lives and property.

HOMILETICS.

Vers. 1—5.—*Deference to the Divine will.* The facts are—1. David, being informed of the inroads of the Philistines against Keilah, seeks counsel of God. 2. Being directed to go against them, he finds his men in doubt of the safety of the enterprise. 3. Hence, to satisfy them he makes further inquiry of the Lord, and is again directed to go, with promise of victory. Acting on these instructions, he saves Keilah. The moral degeneracy of Saul seems to have been accompanied with some degree of inefficiency of government, by reason of which portions of the country were still exposed to incursions of the Philistines. The subsequent conduct of Keilah, bad enough as it was in itself (ver. 12), would lead us to infer that the people who sought David's interposition were patriotic men not resident in the city. Possibly David's reputation for energy and courage had been sustained of late by the manner in which he had developed his few resources in defence against the wiles and force of his personal foe, and hence it would be natural for oppressed neighbours to seek his aid on an emergency. The narrative relates how he met the demand on his intervention, and with what result. It brings out a fine truth bearing on both public and private life.

I. The habit of deference to the Divine will is a necessary and valuable element in life. It is remarkable how, without choice of his own, David had been forced into a position of isolation and danger. There perhaps never was a life, except that of our Saviour, in which habitual submission to a supreme will was more conspicuous. The critical position in which he found himself when urged to make war on Philistine plunderers brought out into more public view a condition of mind habitual in private life. His unwillingness to take the step without being sure of the will of God was a revelation to those who sought his services of what was constant in his experience. The question was not, Can I gain wider reputation, or win Israel to my standard? Is it the will of God, was the first and last thought. *David's conception of life was that which becomes every Christian.* Whether our lot be kingly or lowly, our calling public or private, it should be a primary thought with us that God has a will of his own as to what manner of persons we ought to be, and what line of conduct we should adopt in the most common affairs of our life; for every action, and word, and spirit possesses in God's sight a moral character derived from the motive in which it originates and the final result to which it is made subservient. Our great business is to form an estimate, by a study of God's character and providence and of our own position and capabilities, of what he would regard as a pure and righteous course, and then strive, as demands are made on us, to translate that

into our actual deeds and temper.   There is abundant scope for this habitual deference to God's will in the demands which come upon us from all quarters.   By reason
of the strong interaction of various tendencies within us, and the opposing claims of
what seem to be benevolence and prudence, we may, like David, find ourselves in an
ambiguous position, and it is at such junctures especially that the habitual deference
will manifest its valuable presence.   The difference between a really good man and
one of formal godliness comes out in this, that the one always feels as though
another and higher will was present and supreme over his own, while the other only
thinks of that superior will on special occasions when painful events fill him with
fear.   This habitual deference is partly owing to the fact that a correct view is taken
of life.   David understood his vocation in the world.   He had a part to perform in
the great Messianic purpose.   Although his vision of the future unfoldings of that
purpose, varying in distinctness at different periods (Ps. ii. ; cf. Ps. lxxii.), was not
of details, yet he had faith enough in its reality and grandeur to induce the conviction that every step of his daily course was in some way associated with its
realisation.   And in like manner the humblest Christian is permitted to believe that
he has a similar vocation in the world, as a member of Christ's mystical body.
Hence we, as members of Christ's body, have no *raison d'être* apart from habitual
deference to the will of Christ.   And as, by the varied experience of life, this deference deepens, so its effect on our general character is more conspicuous.   It induces
a sobriety of judgment, for haste and rashness are due to self-will ; it creates a
refined susceptibility of spirit by which moral perfections are quickened and the
existence of evil is discerned from afar ; and it gives zest and carefulness in use of
means to ascertain, in cases of difficulty, what is the perfect will of God.

II. The manifest approval of God in any case of difficulty or peril is an all-
sufficient encouragement to a sincere man.   David's position was still one of
embarrassment and danger.   He was potentially king, but could not avow it.   He
was loyal to Saul, though strongly tempted by his persecutions to rise in open
rebellion.   He was assured by the anointing and by Samuel's sanction and
encouragement that a great future was awaiting him, and yet, like many since
his time, he had to bear all the pains and sorrows of the outcast.   The agony
of feeling expressed in the Psalms can be understood only as we remember his
call to a holy work and the consciousness of innocence.   The recent experience
at Nob caused him to feel how incidentally others might be compromised in
his procedure, even when undertaking useful service.   But all fear, all sorrow,
every feeling of uneasiness as to consequences, disappeared when God recognised
him by an answer to the official inquiry of Gad or Abiathar.   The fact of the
inquiry on his behalf is very important (Num. xxvii. 18—21 ; Judges xx. 26—28).
That one or both of these after the slaughter of Nob sought counsel for David was a
declaration in most emphatic form that he was the coming king.   God thus by his
servants openly sanctioned him, and hence his soul was encouraged to brave any
danger, to bear any consequences, so long as God approved (Ps. lvi. 11).   It is the
assured approval of God, obtained in diverse ways according to the nature of the
case, that emboldens Christians in courses of extreme difficulty and peril.   The
apostles feared not Jewish or Roman power when they had, after the ascension of
Christ, received the inward and outward testimony of the Holy Spirit of the Divine
character of the cause they professed.   The same spirit is created in others when
called to go forth to heathen lands, or to wage war with fearful evils at home.   Let
the youth, the sire, the statesman, the parent, the merchant, and the pastor only hear
the word " go," at once the soul may take courage and assert its strength.

III. The means by which God affords guidance to his people vary in different
ages.   David now is guided in his public capacity as the coming king by prophet or
by priest using the ephod.   As a private man he depended for the ordinary course
of life on the more private and unexpressed guidance which God insures to all his
faithful children.   The means by which his public course was directed were unlike
the more ancient and the more modern.   From the beginning of human history we have
to distinguish between the communications which God may have given to men for
their personal comfort and use and that which was designed to reveal the fact of his
purposes of mercy to the world and gradually unfold their scope, although in some

instances, as in the case of Abraham (Gen. xv. 1), the personal and general might coincide. The guidance granted to the patriarchs for the unfolding of the redemptive purposes was chiefly in form of visible or audible manifestations, a method well suited to a primitive life without religious literature, precedents, fixed regulations, and official teachers, and needing greatly, in the midst of visible surroundings and material tendencies, to be impressed with the reality of the unseen power. To Israel in the desert the guidance and spiritual impressment was given by the visible pillar of cloud and of fire, and by the stupendous signs on Mount Sinai which accompanied the communications to Moses for their benefit. The Urim and Thummim of the high priest were chiefly employed during the years subsequent to Moses, thus largely dispensing with the irregular visible display. In the prophets Samuel, Gad, and others after them a more spiritual method came into use, God making known his will to the people by some spiritual manifestation to or elevation of the prophet's spirit. In Christian times the personal prophetic medium reached its culmination in Christ and his apostles, who, out of the fulness of the Spirit that dwelt in them, gave forth such teaching and guidance in action as the Church required. Thus in divers manners God has spoken for the guidance of the Church. We have to consult the "living oracles" (2 Tim. iii. 16) for our guidance as a Church of Christ in reference to the general principles and the manifold details involved in establishing "the kingdom" (Isa. viii. 20 ; John v. 20 ; Acts xvii. 11). As individual Christians, besides acting in unison as a Church for the common objects of the kingdom of Christ, we may seek guidance daily by private use of the same means as those enjoyed privately by David.

IV. THE HIGHEST QUALITIES OF THE RELIGIOUS CHARACTER may be associated with THE MORE ORDINARY AND PRACTICAL, and when so associated THEY GIVE VALUE AND COMPLETENESS to them. It is a too frequent belief in the world that a man absorbed in the pursuit of the highest religious vocation and distinguished by the loftiest spiritual aspirations, such as are revealed in the Psalms and in David's life, becomes thereby one-sided in development, and falls by neglect in the detailed and minor moralities of life. A saint is synonymous with a moody, unpractical man, too much occupied with spiritual realities to be careful of little things. David's conduct in the affairs of Keilah is a refutation of this false conception. The narrative brings out his full-orbed religion, and in this he may be considered as a fit representative of the well-developed Christian. 1. The *line of conduct pursued with reference to Keilah,* taken in historic connection with his call to service, *brings out a remarkable combination of high and ordinary qualities.* With his consciousness of high mission was joined a patient endurance of bitter trials as a consequence of the very position to which Providence was calling him. Not a word of complaint and distrust escapes his lips during this weary hiding from his foe, although in his agony he was constrained to cry, "How long, O Lord!" Then there was that beautiful self-reserve, lest by any impetuous act he should seem to forestall the ways of God and force on the final issue—as seen in his unwillingness to annoy or embarrass Saul and press him to a conflict by an attack, without royal commission, on the Philistines. This following and not going before appears also in his using the official means of guidance only when Providence had placed them clearly in his way, and not by privately enticing Gad and Abiathar to join his company. But while intent on these high spiritual objects, there was a generous disinterestedness in relieving the troubles of others, even at a time when his own sorrows were multiplied, for he spared not himself when Keilah was oppressed. Nor did he feel for them alone, since the second inquiry of the Lord (ver. 4) was evidently dictated by a tender consideration for men whose faith was unequal to his own. And, finally, all this also associated with a wonderful tenderness for his personal enemy, based on a recognition of his kingly office, and more so on pity for a character once hopeful, but now fast on the way to ruin. Never, perhaps, were the precepts of the New Testament with respect to personal enemies (Matt. v. 38—44) more truly exemplified in combination with so utter a detestation of the sins that tended to frustrate the spiritual ends for which Israel existed in the world. 2. Taking, then, the conduct of David and the special qualities indicated therein as a basis, we may *summarise the qualities* which seem to *enter into a well-developed religious character,*

(1) *Recognition* of a *high vocation in life*, associated with God's merciful purposes toward mankind. No man is great whose energies do not in their results aim at something beyond himself; nor is that a high style of character which is governed by aspirations terminating with the material and temporal wants of mankind. As David was conscious of a vocation in life which linked his whole existence with the advancement of the highest spiritual interests of the world, and with the highest material as naturally included in the spiritual, so every truly religious man believes and rejoices to know that his business in life lies outside his fleeting earthly occupation and possessions, and in fact coincides with that for which Christ came into the world. What tone and power the Church would have in the world if all her members duly realised for what end Christians exist! A lofty ideal always gives power and elevation to actual life; and no higher ideal can be set before us than that which is the normal vocation of every one of Christ's disciples. (2) *Submission to God's ways and times.* The realisation of the ideal before David was by a process which seemed to run counter to the dictates of human wisdom. The great scope of a religious ideal, while it expands the intellect and fills the imagination with the glowing colours of future good, also makes a present demand on the more sober and less brilliant qualities of the soul. The course of nature and the progress of spiritual forces are determined by primary principles of government and a combination of incidental and final issues which in their entirety are comprehensible alone to God, as, indeed, they received their co-ordination from him. A mind that forms a just estimate of itself, and regards the outworking of the powers of the kingdom of God as the visible index of an infinite secret, will bow in loving submission to all the methods and seasons appointed by God in bringing on the setting of his King on the holy hill of Zion. (3) *Confidence in God* in spite of adverse events. The key to David's life when fleeing from cave to cave, and through all the lowly submission to years of waiting, was, as so often expressed in the Psalms, *trust in the Lord.* The trusting power of our nature is large, but unfortunately has been injured in its development by the suspicions created in our intercourse with untruthful, selfish men. There is a danger of importing this impaired confidence from the secular to the spiritual sphere, and practically treating God as though he were one of us (Jer. xv. 18). There is a spiritual heroism in believing in God against hope (Rom. iv. 17—21; Heb. xi.). The religious trust is not founded on knowledge of things, either as to their intrinsic nature or their correlation, but on the fact that God is over all and is *true* to his word. What some would call unreasoning fanaticism is the soul's rational, loving homage to the wisdom that never errs, the goodness that ever blesses, and the power that works all things to its own ends. History justifies the faith of God's people. "They are *dead* which sought the young child's life" (Matt. ii. 20). "He shall live," and "upon himself shall his crown flourish," was predicted of the most despised and reviled (Ps. lxxii. 15; cxxxii. 18; Isa. liii. 3); and, in a modified sense, it will hold true of all who endure and are faithful to the end (Rev. iii. 21). (4) *Kindliness towards the weak and the oppressed.* The kindly feeling which prompted an effort to save Keilah, although not personally interested, and which sought support for the weak faith of doubting men by a second inquiry of the Lord (vers. 2—4), is but an illustration of the humane spirit of true religion when properly developed. The virtues of submission and confidence, which find exercise toward God as their object, are supplemented by those which bear on the sorrows of men. The loftiest spiritual aspirations—of the severest purity, of the widest range of vision, and of intensest gaze on the realisation of a spiritual salvation for man—were combined in Christ with the tenderest and the most considerate regard for the weaknesses and woes of men, and did, directly or indirectly, during a brief sojourn on earth, more than anything else to alleviate temporal sufferings and finally break the bonds of social and political oppression (Luke iv. 18). 3. *The attainment of this well-developed personal religion is within reach of all.* The character of David was not supernatural, but the outgrowth of a mental and moral constitution, under the carefully-cherished influences of such religious privileges as fell to his lot. The position of each one of us is in the main that of David: we have our natural temperament, which may determine the prominence of this over that virtue; we, as Christians, have received our solemn call by One greater than

Samuel; we, in our private or public sphere, have, as the business of our life, the maintenance of a theocracy more blessed and wide in its influence than that for which David lived; the Divine truth for our instruction and admonition embraces more than he was wont to meditate on by day and night; and it is our privilege to wait on the Lord daily for both strength and wisdom.   A nature less capacious than that of David's, and called to a department of service for God less conspicuous to the public eye, may, by corresponding diligence in self-culture, attain to a symmetry of Christian excellence akin to that of David, and embracing all the qualities we have just sketched.   Every man is a well-developed Christian when such a nature as he happens to possess is brought, in all its tendencies and developments, entirely under the sway of the Christian spirit.   A knowledge of our constitutional tendencies should be accompanied by special guarding of those forms of temperament which imperil symmetry of character.   Occasional reviews of our vows and of the goodness and mercy of our God will prompt to a renewed and fuller consecration, which will not fail to develop patience in worse trials possibly than those of David, and confidence in God despite the most adverse of circumstances.

Ver. 6—12.—*Misinterpretation and miscalculation.*   The facts are—1. The moral position of David at Keilah is strengthened by the presence of Abiathar with the ephod.   2. Saul, believing David to be shut up in the city, prepares a force to lay siege to Keilah.   3. David, aware of this, has recourse to the ephod, and asks through Abiathar whether Saul was really coming, and whether, in case he came, the men of Keilah would give him up to Saul.   4. He receives an affirmative reply to each inquiry.   We have here two men moving in opposite lines and under totally diverse principles, yet each making reference to God in relation to his own conduct—a fair illustration of the intelligent and the ignorant use made of religious language and sentiments in human affairs.   And while David in the deep earnestness of his soul seeks through the appointed means to know the will of God, and Saul in his infatuation concludes God to be on his side, the Eternal reveals his knowledge of the secret tendencies of men and his tender regard for the upright in heart.   The actual conduct of Saul and the hypothetical conduct of the men of Keilah suggest the misinterpretation of conduct and the miscalculation consequent thereon.   No doubt the action of an energetic man at the head of a band of followers might cause uneasiness to a monarch whose hold on the people was not very strong, and consequently the movement of David, viewed at a distance and considered irrespective of his known character, might suggest the thought of an attempt to ingratiate himself with the nation, and gain a position from which a blow might, with greater chance of success, be struck at the throne.   Saul's interpretation of the attack on the Philistines, and consequent entry into Keilah, was either that David was carrying on a freebooting expedition from mere love of plunder and exploit, or that, under cover of aiding the oppressed, he was entering upon active hostilities against himself.   He could not conceive of such an act as compatible with friendliness to himself, and called forth by pure regard for the honour and freedom of Israel, patriotic hostility to the national foe, generous sympathy for the weak, and readiness to benefit sufferers, even though in so doing a man should pursue a course open to the possibility of being misunderstood.   The Saul of this date was not the Saul who once (ch. xi. 1—8), with large-hearted patriotism and generous impulse, rescued the men of Jabesh from the power of Nahash the Ammonite.   Hence his misinterpretation of David's conduct. But thought and action are closely allied, and a false view of things is the basis of a miscalculation of the results of action when we proceed to carry out a purpose. So reversely did Saul now read all the lessons of the past few years in the life of David and himself as to comfort himself with the belief that God, in the order of his providence, was now shutting up David in a city in order that Saul might take and slay him.   This phenomenon of a morally diseased nature is worthy the study of Christian men, and may well make the resolutely impenitent to stand aghast at their possible madness.   *Quem Deus vult perdere.*   Miserably did Saul miscalculate the course of events.   God does not act for men because their wishes are made a substitute for knowledge.   Generalising the truth involved in the case of Saul and David, we may notice—

I. That MISINTERPRETATION AND MISCALCULATION ARE COMMON IN THE AFFAIRS OF MEN. It is a truism that men make mistakes; but making mistakes is not always identical with misinterpretation of human conduct, and the false reckoning proceeding therefrom. There is a too prevalent opinion among certain classes of men that they do understand their fellows, and, by the exercise of keen observation, can avoid the error of referring actions to wrong motives. On the other hand, there are ingenuous minds that imagine that no one will ever think of referring their conduct to an origin other than that which is so clear and pure to their own conscience. Such persons need to be instructed. The question may be raised whether, even in the most holy and blessed society of intelligent beings, there is ever a sufficient capacity in one mind to unravel and ascertain perfectly the secret springs of action in others. We each, some time or other, have to bear the frown and condemnation of our fellow-creatures, because what we do is not associated, in their judgment, with the motives which are clear in our consciousness; and in so far as they have to calculate on the issue of the conduct misjudged, error is inevitable. The Bible affords notable instances of misinterpretation and miscalculation. We have seen how Hannah's heart was misread by Eli (ch. i. 14). The Apostle Paul was supposed by false brethren to display zeal for Christ for reasons utterly alien to his nature. The rejection of Christ by the Pharisees was the practical form of their interpretation of his words and deeds. Some of the bitterest trials of private life consist in generous, true hearts having to bear the consciousness that suspicion and distrust are meted out to them when, were all known, love and confidence would abound. In like manner *the false reckonings of men are manifold.* Every one calculates amiss when he has laid a false foundation in a partial or wrong reading of character. True prophecy, in relation to what will come of the conduct of those we criticise, can only proceed from a just estimate of their moral position. Saul was a false prophet when he predicted that God would now deliver David into his hand. No laws exist for bringing events to pass so that they shall harmonise with our estimate of men. "God hath forsaken him," may be said of a David; but the false judgment of his desert will not destroy the loving-kindness which endureth for ever. On the basis of their interpretation of Christ's character and conduct men esteemed him "smitten of God and afflicted," and calculated that the silent tomb would put an end to his influence in the world. Those who contend with a holy, Christ-loving people, whose spiritual principles are not appreciated, forget that they are embarked in a war against the mightiest forces that operate in the universe.

II. That MOST OF THE MISINTERPRETATIONS AND MISCALCULATIONS OF LIFE ARE TO BE REFERRED TO A DOUBLE ORIGIN. The source of these evils is partly intellectual and partly moral. Saul understood not David and miscalculated the issue of his entering Keilah because of his defective knowledge of human nature and of the order of Providence. In his case, however, apart from radical narrowness of mental range, his mind was injured, with respect to the normal exercise of his intellect, by the moral disturbance consequent on his dreadful alienation from God. He furnishes a typical instance of what may be regarded as the power of the moral state over the intellectual faculties—fearfully suggestive of what demented, shrivelled beings men may become should they in another life still be under the domination of a masterful aversion to God. The liability of every man to fall into the evils of misinterpretation should induce attention to the twofold cause in ourselves. The *intellectual cause* is often seen in a radically defective knowledge of human nature and its possibilities; in a structure in the mind of rigid lines of conduct, based on a narrow experience; and in a partial acquaintance with the actual facts connected with the case on which judgment is exercised and reckonings are made. The *moral cause* is often more subtle in operation, and therefore more difficult of detection; but frequently it appears in the morally wrong act of applying our limited power to questions not fairly within their reach, in the obstinate tendency to make the possibly imperfect governing principles of our own life the infallible tests by which all conduct is estimated, in the embittered spirit with which we contemplate the course of events, and in the active presence of envy, jealousy, suspicion, and selfishness. As a rule, moral causes have more influence in determining our judgments of conduct and character, and in calculating the issues of action, than intellectual. It is easy to believe what we wish, and to see evil where we cherish ill-will. A very pure, loving soul will avoid errors where others of superior intellect will fail ; for purity and love will hold the will back from judgment on uncertain *data*, and will also, by a sort of moral intuition, recognise goodness where less spiritual natures would not discriminate.

III. That THE EVILS INCIDENT TO MISINTERPRETATIONS AND MISCALCULATIONS ARE OF BOTH SHORT AND LONG DURATION. The evils are twofold—those affecting the injured and those attaching to the wrong-doer. David and Saul suffered by Saul's errors. It is true some of the evils affect both for the same time, such as the mutual distrusts, the alienations, the loss of co-operation which inevitably attend the misreading of character and conduct ; and it is impossible to estimate the grievous loss to the world arising from this source. But in instances such as that of David and our Saviour, and of all truly good, the injury on their side is soon removed ; for Providence so orders events that what was hidden becomes revealed, and their righteousness shines forth as the light, and their judgment as the noon-day (Ps. xxxvii. 28—40). The day of judgment will, to many, be a day for lifting up their head with joy. On the other hand, in so far as we are governed by the tendencies which induce wrong judgments, so far and so long our whole nature is impaired and debased. Indeed, the sum total of our mental and moral wealth is lessened for ever by the indulgence in wrong habits of this class ; for we can never become the intellectually and morally perfect beings we should be had no energy, no faculty been perverted and abused. No amount of growth and development, after years of defective mental action, can overtake the position due to a healthful advance from the first. But especially will the evils be of long duration in the case of those who, by persistent, persecuting, false judgments, seek to harass and wound the children of God. The shame and the remorse of having bruised a tender heart or misjudged a holy character cannot easily die out. Saul's anguish of spirit consequent on his sin against David survived David's injury.

General lessons:—1. If we would escape undesirable judgments we should avoid, as much as possible, ambiguous actions and the appearance of evil. 2. Nevertheless, in the cause of humanity we ought to be ready to act, even though men, not knowing our feelings, may misinterpret us. 3. We should hold our judgment in strong reserve when but partial knowledge is within reach, even though plausible reasons appear to urge a criticism. 4. Proper weight should always be allowed for the modifying influences of education, habit, and range of experience. 5. We may take consolation in the knowledge that God weighs conduct in reference to its intention, and that he rules events so as to vindicate the just. 6. If ever we have wronged another by harsh and wicked judgment, we are bound to make some amend by word or deed.

Undeveloped tendencies. The second topic suggested by this section is evidently that involved in the predicted conduct of the men of Keilah under the circumstances specified in the inquiry of David. The service rendered by David to Keilah was such as gave him a just claim to their gratitude. No doubt zeal was abundant in expressing their obligation to him, and judging from appearances one might suppose that the men would be quite prepared to befriend him in case of need. In the early overflowings of gratitude for favours received men are wont to be strong and lavish in the expression of personal attachment and readiness to return kindness for kindness ; and most certainly the men of Keilah, had they then been questioned as to the possibility of their ever casting aside one who had so generously befriended them in a time of sore distress, would each have felt inclined to say, "Is thy servant a dog, that he should do this thing?" But there was more in their complex human nature than they themselves imagined, and the sentiments ruling their will just then and creating agreeable words and kind intentions might, under new conditions, subside and give scope for the play of a different set of tendencies, kept by the present auspicious events in abeyance. David appears to have surmised the existence within their hearts of weaknesses which would not bear the strain of the tests that must be created by his sojourn in their city, and hence, not to be misled in so important a matter, he calls for the priest and makes special inquiry as to whether, in case Saul should come against the city, these men, now so grateful and devoted, would deliver him up. The answer which David received from the Searcher of hearts was to the effect that, should they be brought to the test, they would develop tendencies which gave no sign of present existence, and which if charged on them would probably be emphatically repudiated. Thus do we see how there may dwell in men, unconsciously to themselves, latent tendencies which, though repressed and rendered by present surroundings inoperative, are so real and patent as, under conditions yet to be created, to become the determinant powers in regulating conduct.

I. THE EXISTENCE OF UNDEVELOPED TENDENCIES IS A GENERAL FACT IN HUMAN LIFE. It is a truth that as we find ourselves in daily life we each possess a complex nature in which an inextricable interweaving of thought and feeling is the prominent feature. Every idea and feeling that has become an item stored in memory becomes a power in the subsequent course of our inner experience, even though not distinctly traceable. There are certain fundamental dispositions by which the great lines of action are decided, and minor feelings or sentiments which are tributary to them as servants and prompters. But experience proves that all contained within our nature cannot operate at once, and which of the inner forms of activity may be brought into exercise at any given moment depends on the influences brought to bear and the laws of association thereby set in operation. The tendency to shrink from pain and conflict found no occasion to indicate its presence when the entry of a victorious David into Keilah aroused sentiments of joy and gratitude. It is possible for a tendency to be apparently annihilated by the constant demand on a feeling or sentiment antagonistic with its nature. Hence men may often carry within them possibilities of action while ignorant of their reality, and they may, therefore, be induced to make professions and undertake obligations without reckoning on what may be aroused within when circumstances require the fulfilment of the obligations. Theories of conduct are held which may be belied by the hidden man of the heart when his unhappy hour for development comes. Are we not all now and then startled by the uprising from the unfathomed deeps of our nature of a hideous form which lets us see just enough of its unholy self to create distrust and fear that other powers of evil are there waiting to appear in actual life? The precautions employed in educating youth and the care bestowed on enforcing public sentiment proceed on the belief that the germs of ruin in young and old only await nourishment in order to gain a destructive ascendancy. Nor is the fact confined to what is evil. There are latent tendencies to good—to truthfulness, gentleness, generosity, chivalrous consideration, kindliness, and kindred virtues—which by reason of circumstances do not always find expression. There is a tender place in the hardest heart, though not often touched. Have we not seen a word, an allusion, draw out feelings not supposed to have existence? And in many a Christian there is much more germinal goodness than is developed in outer life. Christ shocked the complacent Pharisees by assuring them of the latent wickedness of their hearts (Matt. xxiii. 25—28; Mark vii. 21—23), and the Apostle Paul urged Timothy to "stir up the gift" bestowed on him (2 Tim. i. 6).

II. THE RECOGNITION OF THE EXISTENCE OF LATENT TENDENCIES IS OF PRACTICAL IMPORTANCE IN ALL DEPARTMENTS OF LIFE. Our course through life is not regulated simply by what is known. A recognition of the unknown or at least undeveloped forces of our own nature ought to exercise considerable influence in the conduct we daily pursue. 1. *In our association with men.* David clearly recognised the fact of certain undeveloped tendencies in the men of Keilah, and he discreetly dealt with that unknown factor by endeavouring to find out whether it would come into ascendancy. It should be a maxim with us that there is far more in the men we have to do with than appears in overt act and uttered sentiment, and this, without degenerating into a painful suspicion and cruel distrust, will enable us often to escape being placed within their power; and also, if our intention is to draw out their better qualities, will stimulate to that end. 2. *In our professed allegiance to Christ.* It should be our rule to watch and govern ourselves in his name on the supposition that there lie within us on the one hand secret tendencies which, under favourable conditions of temptation, may, at least, embitter our life by a fearful struggle for the mastery, and possibly, in consequence of lack of resolution and forethought, for the time mar our character; and on the other hand tendencies germinal repressed, and scarcely conscious, which, if we bring to bear on our heart the warm light of his truth, will expand and assume in our outward life permanent forms of usefulness and beauty. 3. *In our work for Christ.* Both the kind and character of Christian work are influenced by our recognition of the less manifest tendencies of human nature. It is noticeable how constantly Christ spake to the hidden thoughts and feelings of men rather than to the questions they raised and the attitude they professed to assume. A preacher may often effect most by directing his effort toward some unuttered and even deliberately-suppressed sentiment of his hearers. In so far as our persistence in Christian work is concerned we have to consider not merely the value of the impulses and principles that make us earnest during the day of prosperity, but what weaknesses are inherent in us that may develop themselves in unwelcome proportions when trials and adversities threaten. The men of Keilah could sympathise with and swear by the "anointed" when no thought of Nob was present. We may count on this undeveloped factor as one of our best allies in Christian work. Beneath all the vices and superstitions of heathenism and all the shams and scepticism of modern civilisation there lies the hidden, slumbering sense of God and immortality.

III. IT IS GOD'S PERFECT KNOWLEDGE OF ALL THE UNDEVELOPED TENDENCIES OF LIFE THAT RENDERS HIS GOVERNMENT SO STRONG AND HIS PROVISION FOR MAN'S REDEMPTION SO WISE. This is included in the broad truth that there is nothing hidden from his sight. According to Ps. cxxxix. every incipient force—chemical and mechanical, moral and spiritual—in every point of space, through all the ages, has been and still is as clear to the eye of the Eternal, and as traceable in all its endless and intricate developments, as is the mighty sun that sheds its light on our earth. It is this knowledge of the undeveloped which lies at the foundation of prophecy, and renders it possible that, notwithstanding the developments resulting from adverse human wills, the great end for which Christ lived and died shall at last be attained. The warnings and admonitions, "here a little and there a little," for the guidance of our conduct; the form and variety of the promises; the ordinances of religion; the special features of the redemptive work effected by Christ—all these are adapted to the possibilities, and not merely to the present actualities, of human life. "He knoweth our frame." Hence the reasonableness of submitting our reason to his revelations.

IV. IT IS OUR WISDOM, IN ALL TIMES OF DOUBT, TO HAVE RECOURSE TO THE MEANS OF ASCERTAINING GOD'S KNOWLEDGE OF THINGS. No doubt David speculated on the probable course of the men of Keilah should they ever be brought to decide between grateful attachment to him and the frown of Saul, and his general acquaintance with human nature may have inclined him to believe in their treachery when under the influence of fear. But as it was a question of his personal safety, and involved in that a question also of ultimately realising the great purposes of a Messianic kingdom, he wisely sought a solution of all doubts by a recourse to the available means of putting himself in possession of God's knowledge with reference to this particular matter. The knowledge which God has of the secret powers of the universe does in effect become ours when in any instance he condescends to make us acquainted with the result in which they will issue. A really wise man in seasons of uncertainty, when important interests are at stake, whether temporal or spiritual, will not rest with speculations on what may be; but will, like David, inquire of the Lord, so as to regulate his present action according to God's knowledge of what is inevitable. The means of ascertaining God's knowledge may vary with the case in hand; it may be by laying the candid mind open to direct Divine illumination, or by devoting special attention to the monitions of Providence, or by consulting the "lively oracles" which are to us the voice of God on great moral and religious matters. In one respect we are all in a position analogous to that of David; for there are intricate and hidden powers at work within and without which, when fully developed by the new circumstances that may arise, may have the effect of delivering us bound to a condemnation far more terrible than any Saul could pass on a captive David. Now it is a serious question to each whether this one enemy will ever gain power over us, and by what means its dominion can be escaped. In a case of such importance we cannot afford to trust to speculation and humanly-grounded hope. We are permitted to inquire of God, who in his word and in the redemption provided in Christ has put us in possession of his knowledge of the undeveloped tendencies of sin in human nature, by assuring us that under certain conditions—our following our own independent course—we shall come into condemnation on the day of judgment, and that under other conditions—our self-surrender to Christ for pardon and renewal —we shall be not only free from that woe, but shall rise to sit on thrones of honour and power (2 Tim. ii. 10—12).

Practical lessons:—1. Inasmuch as the great issues of life are determined by the mastery of one set of principles over another, it is very important to seek the expulsion or entire suppression of latent evil tendencies by the careful nurture of tendencies of opposite character, for the strength of principles is in proportion to their exercise.   2. In so far as tendencies to evil lie within us, we should avoid unnecessary exposure to influences that may draw them into activity ; and, reversely, we should seek those conditions of life that will aid the development of the good.   3. Caution should be exercised lest we be misled in our estimate of what we can do in resisting evil inclinations by basing our calculation on circumstances hitherto helpful ; for the men of Keilah, in the flush of David's achievement, and not yet threatened by Saul, were like Peter, who could fearlessly avow fidelity to Christ while he was present to inspire and cheer.   4. The fact that in the emergencies of their life God gave specific replies to the inquiry of his chosen servants, because they were instruments of working out the great Messianic purpose, is encouragement to believe that he will give heed to every one whose life is devoted to the same issue, and who is equally sincere in prayer.

HOMILIES BY VARIOUS AUTHORS.

Vers. 1—6. (HARETH, KEILAH.)—*Public spirit.* "So David saved the inhabitants of Keilah " (ver. 5).   Another step in advance was now made by David.   Whilst Saul (in addition to alienating the prophets, and well-nigh exterminating the priests) failed to afford adequate protection to his subjects, David was called to defend them against the incursions of the Philistines.   This was doubtless the chief purpose for which he was recalled from Moab to Judah.   And he fulfilled it, in obedience to the direction of God, which he sought and received through Abiathar, who had come down to him "with an ephod in his hand."   "For his conscience and his assurance of faith, as well as for the certainty and success of the whole undertaking, he needed the Divine authorisation ; if he had not the sanction of the theocratic king, he must have that of God himself, since the question was of a matter important for the people of God and for the affairs of God's kingdom in Israel—war against Israel's hereditary foe " (Erdmann).   His *public spirit* was—

I. INDICATIVE OF A NOBLE DISPOSITION.   Some men are unduly concerned about their own convenience, safety, interest, and refuse to look beyond them.   Others render public services from selfish motives.   But the truly public-spirited man, like David, possesses—1. *An intense desire for the welfare of the people,* to whom by Divine providence he is united by special ties, not contrary to, but closer and more immediately affecting him than those which unite him to all mankind.   2. *Genuine sympathy with the distresses of the weak,* the injured, and the imperilled (ver. 1). Their condition fills his heart with generous impulses, and makes him forget his own troubles.   3. *Supreme concern for* "*God's kingdom and righteousness,*" which inspires him with zeal against evil-doers, and (along with his unselfish regard for his people) makes him willing to undergo labour, conflict, sacrifice, suffering, and death. "Be of good courage, and let us play the men for our people," &c. (2 Sam. x. 12).

II. DIRECTED BY THE DIVINE WORD (vers. 2, 4) in—1. *General principles,* such as are contained in the commandment, "Thou shalt love thy neighbour as thyself" (Levit. xix. 18), and others of a similar nature (Gal. vi. 10 ; Phil. ii. 4).   In order that our love to the whole human race (included in the commandment in its widest sense) may be real and effectual, it must begin by the exercise of love toward those who are nearest to us and have the first claim upon us (Ps. cxxii. 6—9 ; cxxxvii. 5, 6 ; Luke xiii. 34 ; xxiv. 47 ; Rom. ix. 3).   2. *Particular precepts* pertaining to the varied relationships, capabilities, and needs of men, as rulers, subjects, &c.   3. Joined with *numerous promises* and encouragements to the performance of duty.   If public spirit in the form of *patriotism* is not expressly enjoined in the New Testament, it is not without reason. "It was worthy of the wisdom of our great Legislator to decline the express inculcation of a principle so liable to degenerate into excess, and to content himself with prescribing the virtues which are sure to develop it, as far as is consistent with the dictates of universal benevolence" (R. Hall).

III. OPPOSED BY PRUDENTIAL FEARS. "David's men said unto him, Behold, we are afraid here in Judah," &c. (ver. 3). They were not of the same mind as himself, had not a proper sense of their obligation, were unduly concerned about their own safety, and full of doubt and fear. But he was not disheartened nor deterred. And on a further revelation of the Divine will they were (as others often are)—1. Persuaded that their opposition was wrong. 2. Convinced that their fears were groundless. 3. Induced to accompany their leader in a brave and generous enterprise (ver. 5). One man imbued with strong faith and public spirit thus overcomes the opposition of many, and converts them into zealous helpers.

IV. PRODUCTIVE OF IMPORTANT CONSEQUENCES. The hand of God was with them, and—1. Injustice was punished, the public enemy defeated, and the prey taken from the mighty. 2. Those who were in the utmost peril were saved. 3. All the people were taught where to look for their deliverer. In seeking the good of others David found his own honour, and received a Divine testimony to his royal destination.—D.

Vers. 1—12. (HARETH, KEILAH.)—*Answers to prayer.* Inquiry of the Lord by Urim and Thummim really meant prayer in which Divine direction was sought in a particular manner (see ch. xiv. 19, 36). It was made by David soon after the arrival of Abiathar, on three several occasions (vers. 2, 4, 10),—on the last of them by two separate questions,—and in each case a definite answer was received. "God shows great care for David, instructing him now by prophets (ch. xxii. 5), and now by Urim and Thummim" (Grotius). "That which in the olden Jewish times was the prerogative of a few becomes in Christian days the privilege of the many. Christ makes all his faithful followers 'kings and priests unto God.' And much of the sacred symbolism that gathered around the ancient priesthood now gathers in another form around the believer in Christ. Mere symbols have given place to true spiritual power. The Spirit of God which once underlay the symbols, and spake through them to the devout mind, now communicates directly with the heart, and needs no material intervention" ('Bible Educ.,' iv. 38). Those who seek guidance of God in a right spirit never fail to obtain it, especially in—

I. PERPLEXITY concerning the knowledge of duty. Asking, "Shall I go?" (ver. 2) they receive, perchance, the definite answer, "Go;" not, indeed, by an audible voice, but by means of—1. The elevating, calming, and enlightening of their minds through communion with God, and more particularly by *the purifying of their moral nature* from carnal and selfish affections by his indwelling Spirit, which enables them to see "what the will of the Lord is." "Our notions resemble the index and hand of the dial; our feelings are the hidden springs which impel the machine; with this difference, that notions and feelings react on each other reciprocally" (Coleridge). "The understanding resembles not a dry light, but admits a tincture of the will and the passions, which generate their own system of truth accordingly" (Bacon). And when the heart (which is the soul's eye) is pure we see God (Prov. xxviii. 5; Matt. v. 8; John vii. 17). 2. A *clear understanding* of the meaning of the *written word,* and of its application to the circumstances in which they are placed. As by that word thoughts, impressions, and purposes are tried, in order that it may be proved whether they are of God, so by the same word they are formed and directed (Isa. viii. 20; John xvi. 13). 3. A *correct judgment* of what is right and most expedient, accompanied by an inward assurance of the Divine approbation. "If any of you lack wisdom, let him ask of God," &c. (James i. 5; Ps. xxv. 9).

II. DIFFICULTY arising from hindrances to the performance of duty. "David inquired of the Lord yet again" (ver. 4). The obstacles placed in the way of duty, especially by friends, ought to lead to renewed consideration and prayer, and these are often followed by—1. Strong *confirmation* of the conviction previously entertained. "Arise, go down to Keilah." 2. Increased *confidence* of success. "I will give the Philistines into thine hand." 3. Entire *removal* of the difficulty. "David and his men went." It appears to have been chiefly for their satisfaction that the second inquiry was made. Whilst we should endeavour to persuade men to adopt a right course, we ought above all things to look to God to dispose them to walk therein.

III. DANGER, which sometimes occurs on the fulfilment of duty (vers. 7—12). "In the deed of deliverance itself lies the seed of new suffering." Saul misinterprets events (ver. 7), like other men blinded by sin and "using the name of God when God is farthest off from them," confidently calculates on seizing David, levies war, and openly devotes himself to the execution of his wicked purpose. But David is warned; he has also, probably, reason to suspect the fidelity of the citizens of Keilah, and again inquires of the Lord. He does so with much fervour, calling him the "Lord God of Israel," and humbly acknowledging himself to be his servant; and the answers he obtains afford him—1. *Foresight* of the perilous events of the future. "He will come down." 2. *Insight* into the hidden purposes of men. "They will deliver thee up." We may often ascertain more of the secret thoughts of men by communion with God than by consultation with men themselves. 3. *Guidance* for the frustration of ungrateful and evil intentions, and escape from every danger. "David and his men, &c." (ver. 13). How perfect is the knowledge which God possesses of all things! How sure is the guidance which he affords to those who seek him! How safe are they who make him their Rock and their Fortress! In the midst of all his troubles David can sing of "his marvellous loving-kindness in a fenced city;" as he does in Ps. xxxi.: "In thee, O Jehovah, have I found refuge."

> "See Judah's promised king bereft of all;
> Driven out an exile from the face of Saul.
> To distant caves the lonely wanderer flies,
> To seek that peace a tyrant's frown denies.
> His soul exults; hope animates his lays;
> The sense of mercy kindles into praise;
> And wilds familiar with the lion's roar
> Ring with ecstatic sounds unheard before" (Cowper).　　　　D.

EXPOSITION.

SAUL'S PURSUIT OF DAVID IN THE WILDERNESS OF ZIPH (vers. 14—28). Vers. 14, 15.—**Strong holds**. Natural fortresses in the woods and mountains are meant, and places difficult of access. **The wilderness of Ziph**. This lay to the south of Hebron, upon the edge of the great desert of Judah (Josh. xv. 55). **Saul sought him every day**. The pursuit was maintained constantly, with men always spying David's movements, and ready to report to Saul any opportunity of seizing him; but apparently there was no body of men at present perpetually in quest of him. **In a wood**. Many rightly regard this as a proper name, *Horesh*, and as the same place as the **mountain** mentioned in ver. 14; for, as Conder remarks ('Tent Work,' ii. 89), "a moment's reflection will convince any traveller that, as the dry, porous formation of the plateau must be unchanged since David's time, no wood of trees can then have flourished over this unwatered and sun-scorched region."

Vers. 16—18.—**Jonathan . . . went to David into the wood**. To Horesh, as in ver. 15. This visit suggests two things: the first, that, after the scene in ch. xxii. 8, Saul was estranged from his son, and treated him harshly, regarding him as a fellow-conspirator with David; the second, that there was a growing conviction, not only in Jonathan's mind, but generally, that Jehovah had transferred the kingdom from Saul to David, and that consequently David's final success was inevitable. He **strengthened his** (David's) **hand in God**. Such a visit, and the expression of Jonathan's strong conviction that Jehovah was with David, must necessarily have had a powerful moral effect upon his mind. Under such trying circumstances David must often have been tempted to despair; but the assurance of Jonathan's unbroken love for him, and the knowledge that he and many more regarded him as chosen by God to be Israel's king, would revive his courage and make him content to bear the hardships of his present lot. **I shall be next unto thee**. Had he not been killed in Mount Gilboa, it seems that, unlike Ishbosheth, Jonathan would have resigned all claim to the crown. But the feeling must often have distressed David, that the kingdom could become his only by dispossessing his true and unselfish friend. Nor would such a regret be altogether removed by Jonathan's ready acquiescence in it as God's will, though, as next to him, and beloved as he deserved, his position as the king's friend would have been a not unenviable one. Still, to be second where by right of inheritance he should have been first would have been a very trying lot, and it was better for Jonathan that he should die a soldier's death, even granting that he would have felt a lively joy in David's success and the glory of his empire. But their love was to be exposed to no vicissitudes, and the two friends parted never to meet again—David remaining at Horesh, while Jonathan returned to his home at Gibeah.

Vers. 19, 20.—**The Ziphites.** Rather, "some Ziphites," or "people of Ziph," as there is no article. They tell Saul that David was hiding in the fastnesses of the wild region in their neighbourhood, and especially in **the hill of Hachilah**, a ridge that ran along eastward of Maon. Conder recognises it in the long ridge called El Kôlah, running out of the Ziph plateau towards the Dead Sea desert. It lay **on the south of Jeshimon**, or rather "on the right hand of the desert." Jeshimon is not a proper name, but means any desert (Ps. cvii. 4; Isa. xliii. 19), though it is used specially of the desert of Sinai in Deut. xxxii. 10, and of that of Judah here and in Num. xxi. 20; xxiii. 28. Conder ('Handbook,' p. 213) calls it "the dreary desert which extends between the Dead Sea and the Hebron mountains. It is called Jeshimon, or 'Solitude,' in the Old Testament, and 'wilderness of Judea' in the New (Matt. iii. 1). It is a plateau of white chalk, 2000 feet lower than the watershed, and terminated on the east by cliffs which rise vertically from the Dead Sea shore to a height of about 2000 feet. The scenery is barren and wild beyond all description. The chalky ridges are scored by innumerable torrents, and their narrow crests are separated by broad flat valleys. Peaks and knolls of fantastic forms rise suddenly from the swelling downs, and magnificent precipices of ruddy limestone stand up like fortress-walls above the sea. Not a tree nor a spring is visible in the waste, and only the desert partridge and the ibex are found ranging the solitude. It was in this pathless desert that David found refuge from Saul's persecution, and the same has been a place of retreat from the days of Christ to the present time." The Ziphites assure Saul that from their knowledge of this region they shall be able, if he come in force, so to guide him as that David must fall into his hands.

Vers. 21—23.—**Ye have compassion on me.** There is something pitiable in Saul's answer. He had brooded over his rejection from being king, and the many indications that David was to be his successor, till he had become the prey of abject melancholy. He evidently regarded himself as a wronged and injured man, while David to his diseased imagination was ever conspiring against him and plotting his murder. With much pro-

lixity he encourages them still to keep a close watch upon all David's movements, so as to know **his place where his haunt is.** Literally, "his place where his foot will be," the place whither he goes for rest and refuge. The reason he gives for this long and close observation of David's doings is that **it is told** him **that he dealeth very subtilly.** That is, according to Saul's information, he behaved with the utmost prudence, ever keeping a careful look-out against surprise, and using much skill to conceal his movements and to provide for his escape from danger. Finally, they are to return **with the certainty**—with trustworthy and accurate information, and then Saul will gather his forces and **search** David **out throughout all the thousands of Judah.** These are the larger divisions of the territory of the tribe (Num. i. 16; x. 4), throughout which Saul will hunt for him till he has got him into his power.

Ver. 24.—While the Ziphites were conferring with Saul and gathering information David had moved about six miles to the south of Ziph, and was **in the wilderness of Maon.** This town is still called Main, and occupies a conical hill, whence Robinson ('Bibl. Res.,' ii. 433) counted no less than nine cities belonging to the hill country of Judah. Conder ('Tent Work,' ii. 90) calls it a great hump of rock. **In the plain on the south of Jeshimon.** Literally, "in the 'Arabah to the right of the desert." The 'Arabah was the name of the low-lying desert tract extending along the valley of the Jordan from the lake of Gennesareth to the Dead Sea. Maon lay upon the edge of this depression, in the southern portion of the Jeshimon or Solitude.

Vers. 25, 26.—**He came down into a rock.** Hebrew, *sela'*, a cliff or precipice. In the next verse it is described as a mountain, on one side of which was David and his men, in full view of Saul and his army on the other. But as Saul's forces were much more numerous, they were preparing to separate, and so enclose David, while he **made haste.** The word expresses anxiety and fear, and may be translated, "And David sought anxiously to go from before the face of Saul." Conder's description of the spot ('Tent Work,' ii. 91) sets the whole scene most vividly before us. It is as follows:— "Between the ridge of El Kôlah (the ancient hill of Hachilah) and the neighbourhood of Maon there is a great gorge called 'the Valley of Rocks,' a narrow but deep chasm, impassable except by a detour of many miles, so that Saul might have stood within sight of David, yet quite unable to overtake his enemy; and to this "cliff of division" the name Malâky now applies, a word closely approaching the Hebrew *Mahlekoth.* The neighbourhood is seamed with many torrent beds, but there is no other place near Maon where cliffs such as are to be inferred from the word *sela'* can be found. It seems to me pretty safe, therefore, to look on this gorge as the scene of the wonderful escape of David, due to a sudden Philistine invasion, which terminated the history of his hair-breadth escapes in the south country." This cliff in ver. 28 is called Sela-Hammahlekoth, "the cliff of divisions," or "of separations," *ham* representing the Hebrew article. Many other derivations have been suggested, but the above, which alone agrees with the ordinary meaning of the Hebrew verb, is proved to be right by Mr. Conder's researches. They enable us also to correct some small errors. Thus David did not come down into a rock, but "to the cliff," the *sela* or precipitous gorge described above. Nor did he "descend the rock" (Erdmann) "in order to conceal himself in the low land, or in the caves at its base," but he went to it as being an impassable barrier between him and his pursuers. But "he hasted anxiously to get away" (ver. 26), because Saul would divide his army into two parts, and so David would only have the advantage of the few miles of detour which Saul must make. But for the news of the Philistine invasion his final escape would have been almost hopeless. The ordinary notion that David and his men were concealed from the sight of Saul by an intervening mountain is disproved, not only by no such mountain existing, but also by the clause, "Saul and his men were surrounding David and his men" (ver. 28). They had them in sight, and were forming in two divisions, so as to pass the gorge at the two ends and close upon the flanks of David's small band of followers.

Verse 29 belongs to the next chapter.

HOMILETICS.

Vers. 13—18.—*Deepening sorrows and new encouragement.* The facts are—1. David, deeming it unsafe to remain in Keilah, goes forth with his men in uncertainty as to their destination. 2. Saul, forbearing to march against Keilah, seeks in vain to capture David in the wilderness of Ziph. 3. While David, fully aware of Saul's evil intent, remains in the wilderness, he is comforted by a visit from Jonathan, who expresses his confidence in David's future supremacy and renews with him a covenant of friendship. It is one of the most beautiful features in David's life that he never hesitated to follow the indications of the will of God, however humiliating to himself, and apparently adverse to the attainment of the objects dearest to his heart. This obedience is the natural outcome of the full trust in the Lord so amply expressed in the Psalms. To exchange the comforts of an anticipated sojourn in Keilah for a rough and unsettled life in the mountainous district of Ziph was a new trial to the faith already highly strained. But the obedience was speedily followed by the occurrence of an event full of interest and encouragement, and the narrative of this section thus furnishes us with one of the most suggestive instances on record of the providential alleviation of sorrows incident to the path of duty. The connected truths here conveyed may be set forth as follows:—

I. Deepening sorrows may follow on manifest tokens of God's favour and tender care. No one could doubt but that the response given to David's inquiry at Keilah was clear evidence to himself and others that he was the chosen servant of God, and the character of the reply to his prayer was proof that the tender care of Jehovah was keeping him from the rage and cruelty of Saul. We can thus understand the strong expressions of confidence in God and gratitude for his mercy to be found in the psalms of this period; and yet the anguish of spirit and heaviness of heart which also are manifest in portions of those psalms are to be accounted for only by the fact that the loving-kindness thus shown was accompanied by the permission of continued and almost unendurable sorrows. No sooner had David been delivered from the hand of Saul at Keilah than he found himself, if possible, worse off than before entering Keilah, an outcast and fugitive, hiding daily for his life amidst the wilds of the rugged wilderness of Ziph. It is a riddle which the unspiritual mind can never solve, but which becomes increasingly simple and beautiful to those who enter into the spirit of our Saviour's mission on earth—that the sorrows of life often deepen when God is putting honour on his servants by preparing them for a more pure and blissful fellowship with himself, and for a higher grade of spiritual service. Our Saviour was the "beloved Son," the object of the Father's complacent love, and his work for the benefit of mankind was one of suffering, shame, and death. In his case we see how the higher the service, the wider its range, and the more pure and blissful its issue, the deeper were its sorrows. To him there was no contrariety between the bitterness of the cup provided and the love unspeakable and unmeasured. Not every one is fitted to enter fully into the higher form of service. Many sons of Zebedee long for the honour apart from the cost. The loftier views of the Apostle Paul enabled him to regard the manifold sorrows of his life as an honourable and to-be-coveted participation of the sufferings of Christ. The power of spiritual service lies not in knowledge, not in culture of mere intellect, but in more perfect purity of spirit and a high development of the spiritual powers of faith, love, and free, cheerful absorption of will in the will of God; and such is human nature at its best, that only tribulation, it may be increasing tribulation, can so check our unspiritual tendencies as to enable us to serve God on the highest plane. A rough and rugged wilderness may fall to our lot not only while God loves and cares for us, but possibly as a further means of developing in us those high spiritual qualities which in days to come will fit us to minister psalms of comfort and cheer to the saints of God, and occupy positions of influence in the invisible Church corresponding in the spiritual sphere to that held by David in Israel when he swayed a royal sceptre over the land.

II. PROVIDENCE BRINGS SPECIAL SOLACE IN SEASONS OF INCREASING SORROWS. What though David exchange the prospective comfort of a stay in Keilah for a fugitive life in the wilderness, what though his heart for the moment find it "too hard" to solve the strange problem of his chequered course; just then that same Providence which directed his steps from Keilah was mercifully operating in the heart of the noblest man at the court of Saul to bring him sweetest consolation. There are many lines of influence at work under the unifying hand of God for the defence and guidance of his people; and though in his first feeling of disappointment on leaving Keilah David could only see one line, the subsequent appearance of Jonathan where he least expected him made it clear that others were in existence and found their centre in God. God never really impoverishes those who trust and serve him. Our course when faithful is one of progressive enrichment, and will be till we enter on the perfected inheritance above. It is contrary to the laws of a spiritual life for a true servant of God to be worse off to-day than yesterday. The ordinary springs of comfort open to David—meditation on God's past faithfulness, the conviction that he was working out a high and Divine purpose, and the pouring out of his heart in prayer—were now supplemented by the presence and love of his dearest earthly friend. And so God never takes away what seems to be a good, and never lays any new burden on us but that he gives us a corresponding blessing. Abraham sorrowed for kindred in a distant home, but had God for his portion and exceeding great reward. Our health fails, our material possessions vanish, or our loved ones die, and we turn our hearts more truly and passionately toward him who never fails, who is an everlasting portion, and who "gathers into one" the living and dead. Oh, blessed discipline! How tenderly the great Father cares for his sorrowing ones! With what precision does he follow them "whithersoever" in the order of duty they go, to raise up streams in the desert and cause them to feel, as the Apostle Paul in his sorrows felt, that God is able to supply all their need and never does forsake his saints.

III. In the unfolding of the GENERAL PURPOSES OF GOD'S KINGDOM there is a SUBORDINATION OF SERVICE in which, however, the HIGHER IS DEPENDENT FOR COMPLETEST EFFECTIVENESS ON THE LOWER. In Israel at that time God's merciful purposes toward mankind were being wrought out through the agency of servants occupying in the execution of the Divine will positions of relative subordination. Samuel, David, Jonathan were each working out the same results. But the part which Jonathan played in the sum of events comprised in the period covered by the history was inferior to that of David. As a spiritual man he had his work to do, and it was as important in its place as was that of Samuel and of David; yet we can see how wisely he formed an estimate of his position and service for the one great end, when he regarded David as superior in calling and in the honours and responsibilities he would have to bear. Jonathan by visiting David and ministering to his comfort recognised this unity and diversity of service. And it is instructive to notice how in the spiritual service which unites us those who are supposed to hold inferior positions, and certainly do not carry so heavy responsibilities, are able to render most important aid to others above them in these respects. David was relatively the greater man, and yet David needed the spiritual encouragement and support which Jonathan was able to afford; and Jonathan, by strengthening "his hand in God," was for the time so far the benefactor and the superior. The *unity and subordination of spiritual service* is a truth applicable to the world as a whole, and to the part taken by any of us at particular stages of its history. There is to be at last "a glorious Church, not having spot, or wrinkle, or any such thing" (Ephes. v. 27), and things are to be gathered together in one in Christ (*ibid.* i. 10). This unity of result is to be the product of all the manifold influences and agencies which God is pleased to employ through the whole course of time,—from the first to the last man,—as truly as the complete temple is the product not of the more prominent toilers, but of the totality of workers, from the highest to the lowest, first to last. As every separate ray of light and drop of dew is necessary, and therefore of value, in the totality of vegetation we witness—as the vegetation would be less perfect were any one of these to be absent from the process, so there is need, in converting the Divine idea of salvation into the grand reality indicated in the New Testament, for every small as well as great spiritual influence, and the most perfect fruition of the great thus becomes dependent on the action of other influence inferior to itself. Abraham, Moses, David, Isaiah, and Paul were respectively great in faithfulness, wisdom, devotion, fervour, and zeal, yet the educating influence of their lives is in the same line, and is ultimately strengthened by association with the holy patience of a despised Lazarus and the large liberality of a poor widow. Men *do not see the interlacings of spiritual agencies.* The influence exerted by Jonathan's counsel and friendship on the man chosen to do so wonderful a work for all time raises the thought whether in the main the great results achieved by some whose names are prominent may not be closely allied to the influences exerted by others unknown to fame. There are doubtless great revelations yet to be made in reference to the interdependence of the forces of the spiritual world. We do not as yet see the full bearings of the prayers of the lowly on the raising up of distinguished workers and their enrichment with spiritual power. The devoted missionary, the successful pastor, the great teacher and leader of men, may therefore owe much of their peculiar spiritual usefulness to the untraceable influence of prayers offered by the obscure. This principle helps to explain the great stress laid in the Bible on the prayers of ordinary Christians, and thus enables us to see how after all a poor afflicted child of God may be an unconscious strengthener of persons unknown by name.

IV. A TRUE SPIRITUAL PERCEPTION RECOGNISES THIS UNITY AND SUBORDINATION, AND SEEKS TO GIVE EFFECT TO IT. The actions and words of Jonathan sprang from his distinct recognition of the fact that David, though greater than himself, was inspired by the same aim, and longed for the realisation of Israel's glory. He could not bless Israel by a virtuous reign; it was denied him to be in Zion a king typical of the Messiah; but he could strengthen the heart of him who was destined to that honour; and with unparalleled magnanimity and self-denial, with utter absorption in Israel's good, and cheerful submission to the manifest will of God, he contributed his part toward the final issue. It is a question whether amidst our modern religious parties we sufficiently realise the unity and subordination of our work for Christ. The narrowness of our *isms* is not healthful in itself, and it tends to rob the great body of workers of much of the sympathy and large-hearted prayer that would unconsciously to themselves make them strong in God. What elevation of thought and grandeur of life should we more uniformly attain to could we, like Jonathan, put into practice the feeling that our prayers and sympathies, in going forth for all who labour for Christ, and especially for those who are called to bear the strain of high and perilous service, are our contribution to the one great enterprise which from first to last has filled the heart of Christ and is absorbing the best energies of his Church!

V. THE BEST FORM OF SERVICE WE sometimes can RENDER TO GOD IS TO INSPIRE WITH COURAGE the hearts of those who DO A WORK TO WHICH WE ARE NOT CALLED. Jonathan was not called to be a king, but he served God by inspiring the heart of

David with courage amidst his sorrows and cares. The narrative implies that the friends conversed freely on the situation and prospects of David. Doubtless Jonathan, besides assuring David of his own belief in God's purposes and his personal allegiance, would also press upon him the fact of Israel's need, the past care of God, the anointing by Samuel and its significance, the historic trials of patriarchs, the high purposes of sorrow and patience, the honour of being chosen to serve and to wait, and the grand issue when, in some as yet unknown manner, the best Messianic hopes of the nation would be realised. He knew that David's need was quiet trust in God, and with the tenderness and love of a true friend he diverted his thoughts away from Saul and the sorrows of a fugitive life to the everlasting Refuge. "Strengthened his hand in God." Noble man! noble service! There are in the lives of many of God's servants seasons when their wisdom, strength, courage, and patience are taxed almost beyond endurance. "Heart and flesh fail." What they need is faith in God. To move on in the dark, to toil when success seems hopeless, to hold on though dangers thicken, to hope when events are adverse—this was the case of David, and often that of missionaries, pastors, parents, and others called to high and arduous service. How such men long for the inspiring word, the significant sign of sympathy, the reminder of the truth well known! The history of the Church is full of such instances. "Who is sufficient for these things?" "Could ye not watch with me one hour?" Angels came and cheered the heart which men left to bear the unutterable burden. Following the example of Jonathan and of the angels, we each may do something to inspire with new faith and hope those who feel the pressure of care and toil for Christ; we may do it by our words of cheer, by our assured sympathy, by our fervent prayer, and by hearty, free co-operation in the enterprise which absorbs their energy.

Practical lessons:—1. We should seek the evidence of our being blessed with the favour of God in the unquestionable spiritual blessings he has conferred on us in the past, in the fact of our being led by him and not by our own choice, and in the answer of a good conscience to his claim on our obedience and love, and not in the presence or absence of easy circumstances. God's chosen ones have often known the pains of wilderness life. 2. We may be sure that before troubles become so manifold as to destroy the end for which God has called us into his service some appropriate aid will come, not to relieve us of all care, but to fortify us for duty; for he will not suffer us to be tempted above that we are able to bear. 3. It should inspire every Christian worker amidst his toils that he is daily borne on the heart of many who, though unseen and unknown by name, are friends in Christ. 4. Honour is due to every one who by prayer or kindly word contributes to the sum of Christian effort. 5. True religious sympathy will lead us to rejoice in the superior service to which others are called, and will devise new means of aiding their progress. 6. There are seasons in the religious life when calm trust in God, in the absence of favouring circumstances, is almost our sole duty; and when we are strengthened in this respect we shall be able to possess our souls in patience till the desire of our heart is attained (Luke xxi. 14—19).

Vers. 19—29.—*The unobserved side of life.* The facts are—1. The Ziphites send to Saul, offering their services to secure David if only he will come to their country in pursuit of him. 2. Saul, indulging in pious language, thanks the Ziphites for their sympathy, and promises to comply with their request when properly informed of David's movements. 3. Going in pursuit of David in the wilderness of Maon, Saul encompasses him with his men. 4. At this critical juncture Saul is called away to repel an invasion of the Philistines, whereupon David seeks refuge in Engedi. This brief narrative is full of suggestion of profitable topics, such as the intense zeal of men in sinful courses, its reasons and its issue; the pernicious influence of local jealousy in determining the bearing of men towards others; the blindness and folly of combinations of men against the quietly-developing purposes of God; the power of the love of gain, leading, as it does, men to adopt a course of evil from which others shrink; the causes of the indifference or aversion of sections of the community to the governing and advancing sentiment of a nation, as seen in the attitude of the Ziphites contrasted with the general feeling in relation to Saul and

David; the moral causes of disregard for the signs of the times; the tendency to cover up deeds of wrong under the plea of patriotism and loyalty; the degree to which religious forms of speech and professions of sanctity may survive the utter decay of vital godliness; and the moral uses of protracted trouble to the children of God. But leaving these, we may generalise the most prominent teaching in the following way :—

I. THERE IS AN IMPORTANT UNOBSERVED SIDE OF LIFE WHICH MUST BE TAKEN INTO ACCOUNT IN FORMING A PROPER ESTIMATE OF CONDUCT. In this section we have a record of facts as they appeared to an observer. The acts of the Ziphites are recorded, and not the reasons from which they proceeded. Our knowledge of men compels us to believe that there were intellectual and moral causes of the active zeal against David which they alone of all Israel manifested; but, so far as the narrative itself informs us, their conduct may have been inspired by loyalty to a recognised king. Thus, also, Saul's conduct as here described is only that which appears to the casual observer. There is nothing wrong in a monarch endeavouring to capture a subject who holds a strong position by the aid of armed men; nor is there anything but an appearance of piety in imploring the Divine blessing on men who express in tangible form their sympathy with his troubles. Again, the conduct of David as here recorded embraces only that side of life on which men can gaze, for he here appears as one acting as though his entire safety depended alone on his exertions, and not on any other power. The inner, religious side of his life is not noticed. And, finally, the acts of the Philistines are narrated as they would appear to a historian—simply as the movements of men bent on some of the ends common to the warlike and restless, no reference being made to the over-ruling power which silently worked on the inner side of life, causing their action to synchronise with the perilous position of David. What is thus true of the Ziphites, Saul, David, and the Philistines, as their acts are set forth in the history, is also true of all men whose deeds are recorded in history, and of every individual in the prosecution of his daily course. The main purpose of history is to state fact in such a connection as to show the dependence of one on the other. There is always presupposed a vast area of life, which furnishes the immediate moral causes of what appears in the field of human observation. In so far as historians profess to trace actions back to their governing principles, and thus reveal the other and inner side of life, they become philosophers, and must not expect the same deference for their conclusions as for their statements of fact. The Ziphites would have Saul think that their zeal was the offspring of a cherished patriotism and loyalty, whereas there is reason for believing that other causes were chiefly in operation. It is the characteristic of sacred history that sometimes it gives an authoritative record of the inner life, assigning the true causes of the actions described. The practical use of the fact that there is an unobserved side of life is—1. To *induce more care with respect to our unobserved life.* When we believe that there is more real life lived within than without, that the causes and germs of things are all nurtured beyond human observation, that the moral value of what is observed is determined by the quality of what is unobserved, and that though, like the Ziphites, we may seem to do only what may possibly proceed from worthy motives, God looks at the actual spring of conduct—then shall we be more earnest in seeking a pure heart, an unobserved life which shall be acceptable to God. 2. To *regulate our judgment of human actions.* The knowledge that there is an unobserved side of conduct cannot but induce caution in our estimate of character. The apparent loyalty of a Ziphite and the pious language of a Saul may be the expression of a good or of an evil condition of the unobserved life. Our own deceitful hearts tell us how possible it is to appropriate virtues to ourselves before others when in our deepest consciousness we know that no just claim can be made to them. On the other hand, as it would be unjust to infer that because in this historical section there is simply a record of David's exertions to escape Saul, therefore he was destitute of the pious trust which seeks refuge in God (Ps. liv.), so, in viewing the outward life of men, we must not conclude that that is all; for in the unobserved life, spent concurrently with the observed, there may be a devout, holy trust in God which, beyond all human view, sustains and strengthens the entire man. There is a vast demand on our pity and sympathy in the life which underlies many a calm and brave endurance of toil and care; and beneath many a fair exterior there is a secret second life deserving scorn and indignation.

II. ANTAGONISM TO RELIGION IS USUALLY TRACEABLE TO MORAL CAUSES. Although the record does not state the reasons for the conduct of the Ziphites, we, taking it in connection with the entire history of the period, may approximately arrive at their real nature. Remembering that these men belonged to a nation whose very existence was due to the predominance in public affairs of religious considerations, that government with them was a question of allegiance to God as well as to man, that the national life of their own period had been one in which religious principles had become increasingly prominent in public affairs, that they were well aware of Saul's recognition as king on the understanding that he acted in subordination to the higher principles of which Samuel was the assertor, that it was within their knowledge that Samuel and the high priest Abiathar had disowned Saul and favoured David, and that David's prowess had been distinctly approved of God and beneficial to the nation, while his holy, beautiful life was in striking contrast with the life which had secured the slaughter of the priests at Nob, alienated the head men of his own tribe, and become an occasion of sorrow to the land — it follows from all this that these men could not have set themselves against the most renowned and honoured man of their own tribe unless they were under the influence of motives sufficiently strong to overbear the evidence, on the one side, of David's integrity and recognition by God, and, on the other, of Saul's debasement and rejection. That they did not reason and act in harmony with facts admitted arose from two circumstances. 1. That David was now, and for some time had been, an outlaw, isolated and sorrowful, a fact seemingly inconsistent with the previous honours conferred upon him by God, and with the continued sanction of Samuel and Abiathar. 2. That lack of sympathy with the holy aspirations of David and jealousy against one of their own tribe induced them to take his present unfortunate position as disproof of any value to be attached to the earlier evidences of his being a chosen servant of God. We have in this case an *illustration of the antagonism of men towards Christ* while he was on earth, and *towards Christianity in the present age*. In the case of our Saviour there was the most clear and convincing evidence that he was the Anointed, resembling that of David's call. Only resort to the absurd supposition that he was influenced by Beelzebub could afford an appearance of logical consistency in disputing his Messiahship. But a further point of resemblance arises; for the Pharisees construed the lowly life, the unostentatious bearing, the manifest sorrows, in fact, the strange delay in rising to complete dominion, as inconsistent with their idea of what became an Anointed of the Lord. Moreover, as with the Ziphites, so with the Pharisees; there was a moral offence because of Christ's insistence on internal holiness, and they were averse to the kind of government over men which he alone cared to establish. But as aversion to holiness and jealousy of distinction are strong principles of action, the Pharisees, like the Ziphites, could not await the development of events; they must needs take active measures to capture and destroy One who had proved by his deeds of power the greatest benefactor of the age. In the case of *modern antagonism to Christianity* we find the *same causes at work* under analogous conditions. Given the existence of a Supreme Being, interested in the spiritual condition of his creatures and free to act for their welfare, and given, also, as can be well established to every mind free from preconceived ideas on the impossibility of the supernatural, the veracity of the evangelical records, we have then a body of evidence concerning the supernatural origin and character of Christianity as clear as, and much fuller than, the evidence to the Hebrews of David's selection through Samuel and distinct approval by God; and this becomes overwhelming when taken in conjunction with that wondrous life which no other hypothesis can possibly explain. Yet men seek to set aside this evidence because, forsooth, it does not fall in with their conception of what a revelation from God to man should be; much after the model of the Ziphites, who could not believe a wandering, sorrowful outlaw to be the coming king, notwithstanding that some earlier events seemed to point in that direction. No doubt in many theoretical objectors to Christianity there is a positive aversion more or less pronounced to the inward holiness and entire submission of heart and intellect and will which

Christ makes the invariable condition of being his subjects, and this perverts the judgment.

III. STRONG FAITH IN GOD IS THE PROPER COMPLEMENT OF THE MOST EARNEST EXERTION, AND IS A POWER IN BRINGING ABOUT THE DESIRED RESULT. Confining our attention to this narrative, we should conclude that David not only strove with all his energy to avoid a conflict with Saul, but that he was conscious that success rested entirely on his exertions. But there was an unobserved side of David's conduct of which the narrative says not a word. The fifty-fourth Psalm reveals that other side, and we there learn that though he strove to escape as though everything depended on his skill and discretion, yet he trusted in God as though hope were alone to be found in him. This double life is well known to every child of God. Whatever metaphysical questions may be started concerning it, as a fact it is unquestionable. Faith is a power acting in the unseen, spiritual sphere concurrently with our exertions in the visible, material sphere. Both are real powers in God's government of man. We are apt to under-estimate faith because we do not see its incidence ; or we are disposed to doubt its utility because we cannot trace the intricate operations by which events are brought to pass. It is some aid to our faith to remember that the Divine energy is immanent in every mind and in every ultimate force, and can carry out millions of lines of action concurrently for definite ends as readily as we by concentration can carry out one to a single end. God does rule among the armies of heaven and the inhabitants of the earth. His control of men's movements is evidently not a mere general survey of hard, rigid lines of force originally set in motion, but the free exercise of his personal energy on the deepest springs of human action, so as to insure a concurrence of events at such times and places as may subserve some advantage to those whose lives are moving in harmony with his holy purposes. God becomes a reality to us in so far as we believe this and act on the belief. Our Christian enterprises, private conflicts with sin and sorrow, and daily occupations should be pursued with all zeal, and yet with all faith in the need and certainty of God's help. If we wish men to be moved, money to be raised for Christ's service, hindrances to religion to be overcome, and events to be brought about for which we have not the adequate means, there is no presumption, but rather there is profound wisdom and piety, in asking God to exercise his boundless power for the glory of his name. "When the Son of man cometh" to visit his Churches, as when once he walked among the seven golden candlesticks (Rev. i. 13—17), "*shall he find faith on the earth*"? (Luke xviii. 8).

*General considerations :—*1. It is worthy of consideration how far the outward life observed by men is a genuine expression of the inner, and to what extent our secrets are holy and lawful. 2. A study of the intellectual and moral causes of unbelief, as manifested by various grades of intellect and during many centuries, would furnish instruction and warning to the tempted. 3. It is to be feared that the extreme development of man's activity in all departments of life and the insistence on personal effort have withdrawn the attention of Christians too much from the great part which faith in God is ordained to play in the government of the world and salvation of men.

HOMILIES BY VARIOUS AUTHORS.

Vers. 13, 14.—*David's wanderings in the wilderness.* "And Saul sought him every day, but God delivered him not into his hand" (ver. 14). From the time of his leaving Gath till his return (ch. xxvii. 2) David dwelt in the following places successively—1. The cave of Adullam. 2. Mizpeh of Moab. 3. The forest of Hareth. 4. Keilah. 5. The wilderness of Ziph (Hachilah, Horesh). 6. The wilderness of Maon. 7. En-gedi. 8. "The hold" (ch. xxiv. 22). 9. The wilderness of Paran (ch. xxv. 2). 10. The wilderness of Ziph again. The period over which his wanderings in these places extended is not stated, but it was probably upwards of five years ; "and the time that David dwelt in the country of the Philistines was a year and four months" (ch. xxvii. 7). Like the journeyings of the people of Israel (the events of which "were written for our admonition"), they resemble, in some respects, the course of all God's servants through the present world to "the everlasting kingdom of our Lord and Saviour Jesus Christ." "Thou tellest my wanderings : put thou my tears into thy bottle: are they not in thy book?" (Ps. lvi. 8).   Regarded generally they were a scene of—1. *Bitter hostility.*   "Saul sought him every day."   And so long as the servants of the great King are "in the world" they are objects of the hatred and opposition of "the prince of this world" and "the children of disobedience" (Ephes. ii. 2; Gal. i. 4), because "they are not of the world."   The hostility which is directed against them is unreasonable and unrighteous, but real and deep; sometimes fierce and violent, and never ceases.   2. *Outward distress.* David was hunted like "a partridge on the mountains" (ch. xxvi. 20), "wandered in deserts and mountains and caves of the earth," sometimes (like the Son of man) "had not where to lay his head," suffered hunger and thirst and continual hardship, was separated from "lover and friend," and lived in the midst of extreme peril. Others are more highly favoured, but none can escape the ordinary sorrows of life; some are "greatly afflicted," and not a few suffer reproach and persecution for Christ's sake.   "We must through much tribulation enter into the kingdom of God" (Acts xiv. 22).   3. *Inward conflict,* temptation, care, depression, grief, and fear, such as are described in the psalms which refer to David's wanderings, and are full of imagery derived therefrom.   "His sanctified genius did not give forth its perfect fragrance till it was bruised in God's chastening hand.   It was the storm of affliction that awoke the full harmonies of David's harp" (Binnie).   And these are echoed in the experience of the servants of God in every age.   4. *Divine protection* and instruction, by means of providential occurrences, the prophetic word, and the inward teaching of the Holy Spirit.   "God delivered him not into his hand."   "Out of these great experiences in David's sorrowful life of the grace and power, wisdom and justice, mercy and goodness of God, was developed in him, and through him in his people, that intelligence of faith and theological knowledge which we see in the Psalms and the prophetical writings" (Erdmann).   And still higher privileges than of old are now conferred on the people of God.   5. *Sacred devotion.*   His harp was his constant companion in his wanderings, and mingling with its tones in every place, his voice rose up to God in prayer and praise, making every place a temple.

> "Serene he sits and sweeps the golden lyre,
> And blends the prophet's with the poet's fire.
> See with what art he strikes the vocal strings,
> The God, his theme, inspiring what he sings" (Lowth).

"Whether it be the Divine excellences, or the deep-toned voice of penitence, or the longing of the soul after God, the rejoicing in the light of his countenance, or thanksgiving for his mercies, in short, every emotion of the renewed heart finds adequate expression in the Book of Psalms" (J. Duncan).   It is "the poetry of friendship between God and man" (Herder).   6. *Active service.*   For during his wanderings he was called to render special service (ver. 2), and in the latter part of them continually afforded protection to his people (ch. xxv. 16).   "None of us liveth to himself."   We are the Lord's servants, and must serve him in faithful and diligent labour on behalf of others.   7. *Necessary preparation* for future service, honour, and joy.

> "Oh spread thy covering wings around,
> Till all our wanderings cease,
> And at our Father's loved abode
> Our souls arrive in peace."   D.

Vers. 15—18. (HORESH, in the wilderness of Ziph.)—*The benefit of true friendship.* "And Jonathan . . . strengthened his hand in God" (ver. 16).   The friendship of Jonathan for David here stands in contrast not only to the hatred of Saul, but also to the ingratitude of the citizens of Keilah, and the treachery of the Ziphites (ver. 19).   The benefit of it, which had been long enjoyed by David, was even more fully than ever experienced by him now, when he left Keilah with his 600 men, wandered hither and thither, and "abode in a mountain (Hachilah) in the wilderness of Ziph."   He was exposed to the persecution of Saul, who sought to destroy him by every means in his power (ver. 14), driven from one stronghold to another, able to procure only a precarious subsistence, anxious, fearful, and sometimes ready to sink in doubt and despondency.   "Just at this moment Jonathan, as though led by

God, made his way to him in the thickets of the forest (literally, Horesh), and consoled him as if with words and promises from God himself" (Ewald). He did not accompany the force in pursuit of David (ver. 15), but came from Gibeah. His peculiar and trying position made it impossible for him to do more for his friend than hold this secret interview with him, without altogether breaking with his royal father, and openly incurring the charge of disobedience and rebellion. Never was friendship more faithfully shown ; never did it render more valuable service. Well might the blind man, when asked what he thought the *sun* was like, reply, "Like friendship." Its benefit, as received by David, was—

I. OPPORTUNE. "A friend loveth at all times ;" but his kindly offices are peculiarly grateful and beneficial in a *time of need ;* as, *e. g.*, in—1. Physical distress, affliction, homelessness, privation, peril of liberty or life. 2. Mental anxiety, loneliness, discouragement, depression, when the

> "Light is low,
> When the blood creeps, and the nerves prick
> And tingle ; and the heart is sick,
> And all the wheels of Being slow."

3. Spiritual trial, temptation, failing faith hope and patience ; in view of the prosperity of the wicked, the patience of Heaven, the delay of promised good. At such a time how unspeakably precious is a true friend ! His countenance is like sunshine breaking through thick clouds. "Friendship is the only point in human affairs concerning the benefit of which all with one voice agree. There is nothing so suited to our nature, so well adapted to prosperity or adversity. I am not aware whether, with the exception of wisdom, anything better has been bestowed on man by the immortal gods. And they seem to take away the sun from the world who withdraw friendship from life" (Cicero). "Refuge failed," &c. (Ps. cxlii. 4 ; Matt. xxvi. 40, 56).

II. ADAPTED to the most pressing need. "And strengthened his hand in God, *i. e.* strengthened his heart not by supplies, or by money, or any subsidy of that kind, but by consolation drawn from his innocence and the promises of God" (Keil). "Exhorted him to put confidence in God" (Dathe). He strengthened him by—1. *His genial presence,* especially since his visit was expressive of his fidelity, confidence, and sympathy, and made with much effort, self-denial, and risk. "They that fear thee will be glad when they see me" (Ps. cxix. 74 ; Prov. xxvii. 17). "Whom when Paul saw," &c. (Acts xxviii. 15 ; 2 Cor. vii. 7). "When I ask myself whence it is that I feel this joy, this ease, this serenity when I see him—it is because it is he, it is because it is I, I answer; and that is all that I can say" (Montaigne). 2. *His encouraging words.* "Fear not" ("the keynote of Jonathan's address"), &c., in which he assured him of—(1) Preservation from threatening danger, doubtless pointing him to the Divine protection. (2) Exaltation to the highest dignity : "Thou wilt be king over Israel;" pointing him to the Divine purpose, which had been plainly declared, and could not fail to be fulfilled. He had already intimated (ch. xx. 15), and now explicitly asserted, his faith in that purpose. What ground was there for David's fear ? (3) His anticipation of continued and intimate association with him when he should sit on the throne, all claim to which he willingly renounced for his sake, and in obedience to the will of God. (4) The conviction of Saul himself that he would prevail. If Saul believed it, why should David doubt ? What more he said is not recorded. But this was admirably adapted to strengthen his heart and hand. "It is difficult to form an adequate conception of the courage, the spiritual faith, and the moral grandeur of this act. Never did man more completely clear himself from all complicity in guilt than Jonathan from that of his father. And yet not an undutiful word escaped the lips of this brave man" (Edersheim). 3. *His renewed covenant with him* (ch. xviii. 3 ; xx. 16, 17, 42), in which, whilst he pledged his own faithful love and service, he drew forth the expression of his faith in his future destiny as well as of his fidelity to himself and his house ; and both appealed to God as witness. The intercourse of friends is peculiarly beneficial when it is sanctified by their common recognition of the presence of God, and their common devotion to his will. "Next to the immediate guidance of God by his Spirit, the counsel and encouragement of virtuous and enlightened friends afford the most powerful aid in the encounter of temptation and in the career of duty." It was the last time David and Jonathan met.

> " O heart of fire ! misjudged by wilful man,
>   Thou flower of Jesse's race !
> What woe was thine, when thou and Jonathan
>   Last greeted face to face !
> He doomed to die, thou on us to impress
>   The portent of a bloodstained holiness " (' Lyra Apostolica ').

III. ENDURING. The influence of their meeting continued long afterwards, and produced abundant fruit (ch. xxiv. 7 ; xxvi. 9). " The pleasures resulting from the mutual attachment of kindred spirits are by no means confined to the moments of personal intercourse ; they diffuse their odours, though more faintly, through the seasons of absence, refreshing and exhilarating the mind by the remembrance of the past and the anticipation of the future. It is a treasure possessed when it is not employed ; a reserve of strength, ready to be called into action when most needed ; a fountain of sweets, to which we may continually repair, whose waters are inexhaustible " (R. Hall). " If the converse of one friend, at one interview, gives comfort and strengthens our hearts, what may not be expected from the continual supports, daily visits, and powerful love of the Saviour of sinners, the covenanted Friend of believers ! " (Scott).—D.

Vers. 19—23. (THE HILL OF HACHILAH.)—*Treachery.* One of the most painful of the afflictions of David (suspicion, hatred, calumny, ingratitude, &c.) was treachery, such as he experienced at the hands of some of the people of Ziph. They were men of his own tribe, had witnessed his deliverance of Keilah from the common enemy, were acquainted with his character and relations with Saul, and might have been expected to sympathise with him when he sought refuge in their territory. But " those who should have rallied around him were his enemies and betrayers." They had " a panoramic view of the country from Tell-Zif, and could see from thence David's men moving about in the desert ; " went and informed the king that he was hiding himself " in strongholds in the wood (Horesh), in the hill of Hachilah (south of Tell-Zif, which is four miles south-east of Hebron), on the right hand of the desert ; " urged him to come down and accomplish his desire, and promised to deliver David into his hand. This new affliction came upon him almost immediately after he had been encouraged by the visit of Jonathan, and in it we see—

I. AN EXHIBITION OF HUMAN DEPRAVITY. There can be no doubt, after what had taken place, about the motives by which they were actuated. Underneath their apparent " compassion " for Saul (ver. 21) lay hatred of David, aversion to his principles, and the " evil heart of unbelief, departing from the living God," which exists in all ages, and manifests itself in an endless variety of ways (Ps. xiv. ; Rom. iii. 10 ; Heb. iii. 12). It appears in—1. *Unfeeling faithlessness ;* indifference to the claims of close relationship, superior worth, and valuable service ; deficiency of compassion for the needy and unjustly persecuted ; voluntary misuse of advantages, and abuse of trust. 2. *Subtle selfishness,* making some temporal good its chief aim ; for its sake doing injury to others, eagerly seeking the favour of the wealthy and powerful, and disguising itself under professions of loyalty and public service ; running " greedily after the error of Balaam for reward " (Jude 11 ; Matt. xxvi. 14, 15). 3. *Ungodly zeal.* " Any one at that time in Israel who feared God more than man could not lend himself to be made a tool of Saul's blind fury. God had already manifestly enough acknowledged David " (Delitzsch). Saul knew that it was the purpose of God that David should be king (ver. 17), notwithstanding his pious language (ver. 21), and the men of Ziph participated with him in his endeavour to defeat that purpose. Their character is described in Ps. LIV., ' The Divine Helper against ungodly adversaries ' (see inscription) :—

> " O God, by thy name save me,
>   And in thy might judge my cause.

> For strangers have risen up against me,
> And violent men have sought after my life;
> They have not set God before them."

They were *strangers* " not by birth or nation, but as to religion, virtue, compassion, and humanity " (Chandler) ; and in calling them such " there is a bitter emphasis as well as a gleam of insight into the spiritual character of the true Israel " (Rom. ii. 28, 29 ; ix. 6).

II. AN EXPERIENCE OF SEVERE TRIAL often endured by good men, who " for righteousness' sake " are betrayed by false friends, and even those " of their own household " (Matt. x. 36), in whom they have put confidence. The trial—1. *Causes intense suffering ;* grieves more than the loss of earthly possessions, and inflicts a deeper wound than a sword (Ps. lv. 12). 2. *Becomes an occasion of strong temptation ;* to indulge a spirit of revenge, to doubt the sincerity of others, to refrain from endeavour for the general good as undeserved and vain (Ps. cxvi. 11). But when regarded aright—3. *Constrains to fervent prayer* and renewed confidence in the eternal and faithful Friend.

> " O God, hear my prayer ;
> Give ear to the words of my mouth.
> Behold, God is my Helper,
> The Lord is the Upholder of my soul" (Ps. liv. 2, 4).

III. A FORESHADOWING OF MESSIAH'S SUFFERINGS, for the afflictions of David on the way to the throne of Israel were ordained to be a type of " the sufferings of Christ, and the glory that should follow." " He came unto his own, and his own received him not," was persecuted by the rulers of the nation, and, after escaping many treacherous designs of his enemies, was betrayed by Judas (the only Judæan among the twelve) " into the hands of sinners." And his betrayal was necessary to—1. *The completeness of his experience* as the chief of sufferers. 2. *The setting forth of his example* of spotless holiness and quenchless love. 3. *The perfection of his sympathy* as the Succourer of the tempted. " It became him," &c. (Heb. ii. 10, 18). " The end of Christ's incarnation was that he might draw up into his own experience all the woes and temptations of humanity, to draw around him all the swathings of our imperfect nature, and make our wants his own, till not a cry could go up from it which had not first come into his own consciousness " (Sears).—D.

Vers. 24—28. (THE WILDERNESS OF MAON.)—*A marvellous escape.* " Therefore they called that place Sela-hammahlekoth "—the cliff of separations (ver. 28). It seemed as if at length Saul was about to accomplish his purpose. Led by the treacherous Ziphites, he went down to the hill of Hachilah, from which David had withdrawn to " the wilderness of Maon, in the plain on the south of the desert." In his further pursuit (ver. 25) there was but a short distance between them—Saul standing on a ridge of Hachilah, David on a rock or precipice in Maon ; but a deep chasm separated them from each other. And when " Saul and his men were encircling David and his men to seize them, and David was sore troubled to escape " (ver. 26), " there came a messenger unto Saul, saying, Haste thee, and come ; for the Philistines have invaded the land." Thus his purpose was suddenly and effectually defeated. The escape of David suggests, concerning *the dealings of God with his servants*, that—

I. HE SOMETIMES SUFFERS THEM TO BE REDUCED TO SEVERE STRAITS. Danger is imminent, the enemy exults, their own wisdom and strength are unavailing, and they are full of anxiety and dread. They have no resource but to betake themselves to " the Rock of Israel ; " if he should fail them they are lost ; and it is to constrain them to seek refuge in him that they are beaten off from every other (see ch. vii. 12).

II. HE NEVER SUFFERS THEM TO CONTINUE THEREIN WITHOUT HELP. Although the space that separates them from destruction be narrow, it is impassable ; for the invisible hand of God is there, and the enemy cannot go a step further than he permits. " He shall cover thee with his feathers," &c. (Ps. xci. 4). Sometimes nothing more can be done than to " stand still and see the salvation of the Lord ; " if an effort to escape must be made, it is still he who saves, and to him we must ever look in faith and prayer. "What doth not prayer overcome and conquer? What doth not resistance drive back when accompanied by distrust of self and trust in God? And in what battle can he be conquered who stands in the presence of God with an earnest resolve to please him?" (Scupoli). "When I cry unto thee, then shall mine enemies turn back," &c. (Ps. lvi. 9).

III. HE OFTEN DELIVERS THEM AT THE MOMENT OF THEIR GREATEST PERIL. He does so both in temporal calamity and in spiritual trouble, labour and conflict. At the point of despair deliverance comes (Micah vii. 8). And thereby his interposition is rendered more apparent, the designs of the enemy are more signally frustrated, and the gratitude of his servants is more fully excited. "David was delivered at the last hour, it is true; but this never strikes too late for the Lord to furnish in it a proof to those that trust in him that his word is yea and amen when it says, 'I will never leave thee nor forsake thee'" (Krummacher).

IV. HE MAKES USE OF VARIOUS AND UNEXPECTED MEANS FOR THEIR DELIVERANCE (ver. 27). Who could have predicted the arrival of such a message? The incursion of the Philistines was the natural result of the course pursued by Saul in levying war (ver. 8), going out to seek the life of David (ver. 15), and leaving the country unprotected; but the message came at the opportune moment by the overruling providence of God. His resources are boundless; he employs his enemies for the preservation of his friends, diverts their attention to other objects, and impels them to spend their strength in conflict with each other. "The Lord knoweth how to deliver the godly out of temptations" (2 Pet. ii. 9).

V. HIS INTERPOSITION ON THEIR BEHALF SHOULD BE GRATEFULLY RECORDED; as it was in the name which was given to the spot, and still more fully in the psalm ending

> "With willing mind will I sacrifice unto thee;
> I will give thanks to thy name, O Jehovah, for it is good.
> For out of all distress hath he delivered me,
> And upon mine enemies hath mine eye seen its desire" (Ps. liv. 8, 9).   **D.**

Vers. 16—18.—*Sweet counsel in time of need.*   I. THE DISCOURAGEMENT OF DAVID. The citizens of Keilah, after he had with his good sword delivered them from the Philistine marauders, were so ungrateful, perhaps so much afraid of sharing the fate of the city of Nob at the hand of Saul, that they were ready to betray the son of Jesse and surrender him to the king. From this danger he no sooner escaped than the people of Ziph—though he did not compromise them by entering their town, but encamped in a wood—were not only willing, but eager, to reveal his hiding-place. And the pursuit was hot. "Saul sought him every day." To add to the danger, David had with him 600 armed men—too many to be easily concealed, but too few to encounter the force which Saul led against him, and which was numbered by thousands. It was therefore a critical time for David; and his poetic, sensitive nature felt the ingratitude and injustice more keenly than he dreaded the actual peril, so that he began to be quite chagrined and disheartened. The Apostle Paul had a similar tendency to depression. He felt ingratitude and calumny most acutely, and was more cast down by these than by any of the physical sufferings and mortal risks that befell him. But Paul was like David too in his quick susceptibility to words of kindness, and in drawing strength from fellowship with congenial minds.

II. THE FRIEND IN TIME OF NEED. St. Paul tells, "When we were come into Macedonia, our flesh had no rest, but we were troubled on every side; without were fightings, within were fears. Nevertheless God, who comforteth those that are cast down, comforted us by the coming of Titus." In like manner did God comfort David amidst fightings and fears by the coming of Jonathan. This noble-minded prince cheered the fugitive in the forest of Ziph—1. *By showing to him a generous human affection.* This was love indeed, which clave to David in exile as closely as ever it had done when he was in the sunshine of public favour, and which was willing to run great risks for the delight of clasping hand in hand and talking face to face. Here was genuine friendship, which is perhaps more rare than love. Cynics point out that the celebrated friendships, as of David and Jonathan in the Bible, and Damon and Pythias the Pythagoreans in Greek story, belong to "the heroic and simple period of the world;" and they allege that these cannot be reproduced in the sophisticated society of modern times. There is something in this, though it is not absolutely true. The tone of "In Memoriam" may be too intense for most of us, but it is not incomprehensible. That is a rare and lofty friendship which prefers another in honour above ourselves. From the early days of David's promotion Jonathan augured his advancement to the throne, and took generous delight in the prospect. He still retained and openly expressed the same feeling. David would be king, and he, his friend and brother, would share his joy and stand at his right hand. It was not to be so. But we see David, when established on the throne, looking, if we may so speak, for Jonathan. "And David said, Is there yet any that is left of the house of Saul, that I may show him kindness for Jonathan's sake?" (2 Sam. ix. 1). 2. *By lifting his thoughts to God.* It was not possible or proper for Jonathan to levy troops and lead them to the help of his friend against the king his father. But he did what he could, and did the best thing possible in such a case, when he animated the faith and hope of David in the promise and providence of God. He referred to the Divine purpose as no secret, but revealed, and known to Saul himself, though he struggled against it. The counsel of the Lord must stand. How could David doubt it? But David did sometimes doubt and fear, and he is not alone in the weakness. Sarah had the promise of God that her son should be Abraham's heir and successor, and yet she was uneasy lest he should be dispossessed or hurt by the son of Hagar. Jacob at Bethel got a promise that he and his posterity would possess the land on which he lay, yet when he returned to it he was quite alarmed lest Esau should destroy his family and himself. And so also many persons who have eternal life in the gospel and in the sure provision of grace by Christ Jesus grow faint and raise foreboding questions: What if God forget me? What if I perish after all? The best thing that a friend can do for such a doubter is to show him that God cannot lie and cannot be defeated. For his name's sake he will do as he has said. So one may strengthen the weak hands of another in God.

III. THOUGHTS SUGGESTED BY THE MEETING IN THE WOOD. 1. *The value of an early friendship in the fear of God.* It is in youth that the strongest friendships are formed, and permit interchanges of criticism and correction that are not so palatable when years have increased our reserve, and perhaps our obstinacy. This is especially true of the moral and religious aspect and use of friendship. Old men, even when they are on terms of cordial personal regard, do not easily exchange spiritual confidences. But young friends can do so; and never do they put the bond between them to better use than when they warn each other of moral risks and snares, and encourage one another to trust in God. 2. *The great part which secondary personages in history may play.* David takes a primary or front place in sacred story; but he was much indebted to the kindly help of others who take a less conspicuous rank—*e. g.*, Jonathan encouraging him in the wood, and Abigail turning him back from hasty bloodshedding. Again we pass on in thought to the Apostle Paul, who fills a very high place in the Christian annals, but was much helped by men and women in quite a secondary position. Himself tells us so, joyfully acknowledging his obligation to such as Aquila and Priscilla, Mary, Urbane, Timothy, Epaphroditus, John Mark, Luke, and Aristarchus. These Christians did direct work for the Lord; but perhaps did their best piece of service when they helped Paul, and encouraged his hand in God. So is it at all times with the greatest men in both Church and State. They owe much to others who are far less known than themselves, if known at all. A sympathetic wife, a faithful friend, a humble helper, quite incapable of taking the conspicuous position or doing the public work, supplies a strengthening, restoring element in hours of discouragement or weariness, and so does much to preserve a notable career from failure. In fact every great man draws up into his thought and work the cogitations of many minds, the desire of many hearts, the faith or fortitude of many spirits; and the efforts and sympathies of many combine in the results which are associated with his name. 3. *The uncertainty that friends who part will meet again on earth.* "They two made a covenant before the Lord," and parted, little knowing that each was taking the last look of his friend. Their thoughts were of days to come, when they should not need to meet by stealth. They would be always together by and by—take counsel together fight side by side against the enemies of Israel, do exploits for their nation, and re-establish the worship of Jehovah and the honour of his sanctuary. The elevation of one would be the elevation of both; and the spirit of jealousy which now darkened the court and the kingdom would give place to generous confidence and love. So they proposed; but God disposed otherwise. Jonathan never saw David again. Death broke their "fair companionship," and the elevation of David was bedewed with tender sorrow for his friend, "the comrade of his choice, the human-hearted man he loved." There is one Friend, only one, from whom we cannot be severed. Oh, what a Friend we have in Jesus! especially helpful to us in cloudy days and seasons of distress. He comes to us when we are in the wood, perplexed, embarrassed, cast down. Let us tell all our straits and misgivings to him. This Friend will never die. And not even our death can break the friendship or separate us from the love of Christ.—F.

EXPOSITION.

DAVID IN THE WILDERNESS OF ENGEDI (CH. XXIII. 29—XXIV.).

CHAPTER XXIV.

DAVID SPARES SAUL'S LIFE IN A CAVE (vers. 1—7). Ver. 1.—**The wilderness of En-gedi.** Finding no safety on the western side of the desert of Judah, where the Ziphites were ever watching his movements, David now boldly crossed this arid waste, and sought shelter in the remarkable oasis of En-gedi, on the shore of the Dead Sea. The word may signify either the Fountain of Luck or the Kid's Spring, the latter being the meaning of the name Ain-Jadi, which it still bears. In 2 Chron. xx. 2 it is identified with Hazazon-Tamar, the Palm-Wood, an ancient seat of the Amorites, and evidently famous from of old for its fertility (Gen. xiv. 7). Conder ('Tent Work,' ii. 126) describes the country over which David would have to travel as almost impassable, so that in four and a half hours of hard riding he and his party advanced only six miles, so deep were the valleys which they were obliged to cross. From a lofty peak on their way the view was most extraordinary. On every side were other ridges, equally white, steep, and narrow; their sides seamed by innumerable torrent-beds, their summits sharp and rugged in outline. Not a tree was visible, and the whole region was like the dry basin of a former sea, scoured by the rains, and washed down in places to the hard foundation of metamorphic limestone which underlies the whole district. But the desert once crossed, "there is no scene," he says, "more vividly impressed on my memory than that of this magnificently rocky and savage pass, and the view from the spring below." He had encamped on a plateau upon the top of the cliffs, which rise to a height of 2000 feet above the Dead Sea; and 1340 feet below him the warm spring of En-gedi, 83° F., rises from under a great boulder, and dashing down the rest of the descent, flows across the plain at the foot of the cliffs, which is about

half a mile square. All around are the ruins of ancient gardens and thickets, among which he saw the beautiful black grackles with gold-tipped wings, bulbuls, and thrushes. Solomon seems to have delighted in the spot, and to have covered the hills with vines; for he compares his beloved to a "cluster of camphire in the vineyards of En-gedi" (Cant. i. 14). Neither palm nor vine is to be found there now, but there is still a rich vegetation, and groves of trees. According to Thomson ('The Land and the Book,' p. 602) the sides of the ravines leading to En-gedi are full of natural and artificial caves and sepulchres.

Ver. 2.—**Chosen.** See on this word ch. ix. 2. **The rocks of the wild goats.** Apparently this was the proper name of some cliffs near En-gedi, so called from their being frequented by the ibex, or Syrian chamois, an animal which, according to Thomson (p. 603) is still found there. It shows Saul's pertinacious hatred of David, that no sooner was the war with the Philistines over, than he pursues him with 3000 picked warriors into these lonely fastnesses. Comp. Ps. lvii. 4, written, according to the title, upon the occasion recorded in this chapter.

Ver. 3. — **He came to the sheepcotes.** Rather, "to sheepcotes," there being no article in the Hebrew. Such sheepcotes were common in Palestine; for Thomson (p. 603) says, "I have seen hundreds of these sheepcotes around the mouth of caverns, and indeed there is scarcely a cave in the land, whose location will admit of being thus occupied (i. e. by the flocks), but has such a "cote" in front of it, generally made by piling up loose stones into a circular wall, which is covered with thorns, as a further protection against robbers and wild beasts. During cold storms, and in the night, the flocks retreat into the cave, but at other times they remain in this enclosed cote. . . . These caverns are as dark as mid night, and the keenest eye cannot see five paces *inward;* but one who has been long within, and is looking *outward* toward the entrance, can observe with perfect distinctness all that takes place in that direction. David, therefore, could watch Saul as he came in, and notice the exact place where he " covered his feet," while Saul could see nothing but impenetrable darkness." **To cover his feet.** The Syriac understands this of sleeping ; more correctly the Vulgate and Chaldee take it as in Judges iii. 24, margin.

Vers. 4, 5.—**Behold the day of which Jehovah said unto thee,** &c. David's men regard this deliverance of Saul into their hand as providential, and the fulfilment of the promises made in David's favour, with which, no doubt, they were well acquainted. But with a noble self-control he refuses to take the matter into his own hand, and leaves unto God in trusting faith the execution of his purposes. To prove, nevertheless, to Saul his innocence, to soften his bitterness, and refute the suspicion that he was lying in wait to murder him, he cuts off the corner—Hebrew, wing—of his *meïl* (see ch. ii. 19). Even for this his **heart smote him.** So tender was his conscience that he condemned himself for even deviating so slightly from the respect due to the anointed king.

Vers. 6, 7.—**Seeing he is the anointed of Jehovah.** David bases his allegiance to Saul on religious grounds. He was Jehovah's Messiah, and as such his person was sacred. To this principle David steadfastly adhered (see ch. xxvi. 9 ; 2 Sam. i. 16). **The Lord forbid.** Hebrew, " Far be it from me from Jehovah," *i. e.* for Jehovah's sake. **So David stayed his servants.** The verb is a strong one, and means *to crush down.* It shows that David had to use all his authority to keep his men, vexed by Saul's pursuit, from killing him.

TEMPORARY RECONCILIATION OF SAUL AND DAVID (vers. 8—22). Ver. 8. — Saul apparently had withdrawn from his men, and David seizes the opportunity of proving to him his innocence, and quieting the king's fears. He goes out, therefore, and calls after him, saying, **My lord the king,** addressing him thus as his *master,* to whom his obedience was due. He also pays him the utmost reverence, bowing his face to the earth and making obeisance. By this lowly bearing David showed that, so far from being a rebel, he still acknowledged Saul's lawful authority, and was true to his allegiance.

Vers. 9, 10.—In his address David complained of Saul's listening to **men's words,** which slanderously represented him as lying in wait to kill the king (comp. ch. xxii. 8). In answer to their calumnies he now pleads Saul's own experience of his deeds. **Some**

bade me kill thee. Hebrew, "he bade to kill thee." The literal rendering is, "Jehovah delivered thee to-day into my hand, and bade kill thee." The A. V. supplies *some,* or, more exactly, "*one* said." This is supported by the Syriac and Chaldee, but the literal rendering is probably the right one. Had David killed Saul, it would have seemed as if it were ordered by Providence so to be, and as if by putting Saul into his power God had intended his death. But what seem to us to be the leadings of Providence are not to be blindly followed. Possibly David's first thought was that God intended Saul to die, and so the Vulgate, "I thought to kill thee." But immediately a truer feeling came over his mind, and he recognised that opportunities, such as that just given him, may be temptations to be overcome. The highest principles of religion and morality do not bend to external circumstances, but override them.

Vers. 11—13.—**My father.** David thus salutes Saul not because he was actually his father-in-law, but as a title indicative of the respect due from an inferior to his superior (2 Kings v. 13). So David calls himself Nabal's son (ch. xxv. 8). In the rest of the verse he contrasts his refusal to slay Saul, when it might have seemed as if it were Providence that had put him into his power, with Saul's determined pursuit of him. **Thou huntest my soul to take it.** Thou perpetually usest every artifice and stratagem against me for the confessed purpose of killing me, and pursuest me as eagerly as the hunter pursues his game. Hence David commits his cause to Jehovah, in the sure confidence that he will avenge him, and with the firm determination never himself to raise his hand against one who, though his enemy, was also the king. In proof of the impossibility of his ever seeking the king's hurt, he quotes an ancient proverb, " From the wicked goeth out wickedness." Had David harboured evil intentions he would have executed them when so fair an opportunity offered, but as he has no such purposes " his hand will never be" upon Saul.

Vers. 14, 15.—Finally, David makes a pathetic appeal to Saul, contrasting him in his grandeur as **the king of Israel** with the fugitive whom he so relentlessly persecuted. In calling himself a **dead dog** he implies that he was at once despicable and powerless. Even more insignificant is **a flea,** Hebrew, " one flea," "a single flea." The point is lost by omitting the numeral. David means that it is unworthy of a king to go forth with 3000 men to hunt a single flea. As the king's conduct is thus both unjust and foolish, David **therefore** appeals to Jehovah to be judge and **plead his cause,** *i. e.* be his advocate, and state the proofs of his innocence. For **de-**

liver me out of thy hand, the Hebrew is, "will judge me out of thy hand," *i. e.* will judge me, and by doing so justly will deliver me from thy power.

Ver. 16.—This address of David produced a lively effect upon Saul. Philippson says of it, "The speech of David has so much natural eloquence, such warmth and persuasiveness, that it can be read by no one who has any feeling for the simple beauties of the Bible without emotion. The whole situation, moreover, has much of sublimity about it. We see David, standing on the summit of some rock in the wilderness, raising on high the trophy of his magnanimity, while addressing the melancholy Saul, whom he loved as a father, obeyed as king, and honoured as the Lord's anointed, but who nevertheless hated him without reason, and followed him with unremitting energy to put him to death ; using his opportunity of touching the heart of his enemy with words hurried, but expressive of his innermost feelings, and showing himself full of humility, oppressed by unutterable sorrows, bowed down by the feeling of his powerlessness, yet inspirited by the consciousness of a noble deed." So affected is Saul by David's words that he breaks into tears, affectionately addresses David as his son, and acknowledges his innocence and the uprightness of his cause.

Ver. 19.—Will he let him go well away? Hebrew, "will he let him go on a good way?" *i. e.* will he let him go on his way in peace, unhurt? As David, nevertheless, had let his enemy go unharmed, Saul, touched momentarily by his generosity, prays that Jehovah will reward him for what he had done.

Vers. 20—22.—I know well that thou shalt surely be king. Jonathan had expressed a similar conviction (ch. xxiii. 17), and probably there was a growing popular belief that David was the person in whom Samuel's prophetic words (ch. xv. 28) were to be fulfilled. Something may even have been known of the selection of David and his anointing at Bethlehem ; not perhaps by the king, but in an indistinct way by the people. As for Saul himself, he must long have felt that God's blessing had departed from him, and, brooding perpetually over Samuel's words, it required but little discernment on his part to make him see that the kingdom which he had forfeited was to be bestowed upon one so worthy of it, and so manifestly protected and blessed by God. He therefore makes David swear that he will not cut off his seed after him (see on ch. xx. 15); and so they part. Saul returns to Gibeah, while David and his men gat them up unto the hold. The word *gat up, mounted,* suggests that *the hold,* or fastness, was their previous haunt at Hachilah. They would go down to En-gedi, and the difficulty of obtaining food there for 600 men would be insurmountable, except for a very short period. On the other side of the desert they were in a pastoral country, and the large flock-masters there probably from time to time sent them supplies. The position of David was thus improved for the present by Saul's reconciliation with him.

HOMILETICS.

Vers. 1—7.—*Instruction in caves.* The facts are—1. Saul, having repelled the incursion of the Philistines, returns to pursue David in the wilderness of Engedi. 2. Saul, entering privately into a cave while David and his men lie concealed there, comes unwittingly within the power of David. 3. David's men, referring to a Divine prediction, urge him to slay Saul. 4. Apparently to indicate how entirely Saul was within his power, David stealthily cuts off the skirt of his coat. 5. Reproaching himself for the levity thus displayed in treating the Lord's anointed, he at once justifies his refusal to touch Saul's life, and also restrains his men. It is observable how the sacred narrative of this period is entirely occupied with the conflict between Saul and David ; not a word being said of the social and spiritual state of the nation, its commerce and agriculture, its hopes and fears, or even of the nature and degree of influence being exerted by Samuel and the prophetic schools. The specialty of sacred history lies in the concentration of all thought in the development of the chain of events by which the original promise to Adam and Abraham is traceable to fulfilment in Christ. This principle will account for countless omissions of fact which might reasonably be expected in a nation's annals, and for the prominence given to persons and circumstances otherwise of no public significance. It is because men do not consider the spiritual principle on which the Old Testament is evidently constructed that they mistake much of its meaning, fail to see its exquisite teaching, and regard as heterogeneous what is pervaded by a marvellous unity. The incidents of this stage in the history not only reveal the gradual process by

which Providence was working out great issues for Israel and all mankind, but also
suggest several topics of far wider range than the individual life of David. *Caves,*
from Machpelah, the centre of solemn and tender interests (Gen. xxiii. 1—9; xxv. 9;
xxxv. 29; l. 13), on to the hiding-place of a weary-hearted prophet (1 Kings xix 9),
to Plato's imaginary scene for illustrating the limitations of human knowledge and the
hiding-places of persecuted saints (Heb. xii. 38), have figured in human affairs, and
the cave of Engedi certainly merits attention. It reminds us of—

I. THE DOMINANCE OF AN EVIL PASSION. In reply to the inquiry, How is it that the
king of Israel is here away from his ordinary seat of government, and exposed to
peril of life? the answer must be, Because the passion of cruel envy has gained
dominion over his entire nature. Any considerations of policy or prudence wherewith he may have sought to justify his conduct in pursuing David were mere fictions
created by a perverted will under the control of a masterful envy of one better than
himself. The history traces the growth of this feeling. The dire evil, like a
repressed torrent, seemed to gain force by the check given by Samuel and the prophets (ch. xix. 18—24), until at last it gained such ascendancy over Saul's life that
the entire energy of his mind and the ordinary administration of his kingdom were
made subordinate to its expression. He was the slave of an evil once consisting in a
sudden feeling of ill-will, which, had it been dealt with as every unhallowed feeling
should the moment it appears, might have been crushed in the germ. *The case of
Saul is not unlike that of many men,* although the governing feeling may be
different. Men are more entirely dominated by some powerful disposition than they,
in their neglect of introspection and consequent lack of self-knowledge, imagine.
The reality is seen in the instance of persons given up to intemperance, dissolute-
ness of life, and cruelty; and ordinary observers may be able to trace the process
from slight indulgence in the sin to its complete mastery over the life. Others, who
look at life more closely and estimate its value by the Scriptural standard, can also
see the same enslavement, brought on by degrees, in the instance of persons who
pursue wealth, worldly fame, or personal enjoyment as the chief end of life. The
Pharisees thought it shocking to have killed the prophets, and were not disposed to
admit their own enslavement to evil feelings deadly in character. The positive
antagonism of men to Christ means the gradual growth in them of aversion to his
holy restraints until they become its slaves. There is a proud but delusive sense of
independence attaching to this enslavement to evil. "We were never in bondage to
any man" (John viii. 33). It is a device of the devil to make his captives content
with their chains or to blind them to their reality. "Are we blind also?" (John ix.
40). And as in the case of Saul the domination of the evil only drew him on and
on to deeper trouble, till at last all was lost, so, unless our ruling evils are destroyed
by prompt submission of will to Christ's yoke, and consequent subjection of the life
to his purifying grace, sin will "bring forth death."

II. THE INFLUENCE OF HUMAN FEELING IN THE INTERPRETATION WHICH MEN PUT
UPON REVELATION AND PROVIDENCE. Different opinions may be entertained as to
the sense attached to the words of David's men (ver. 4), and accordingly the practical lessons deducible will vary with the choice we make. (1) On the supposition
that they were here quoting a specific communication conveyed to David through
Samuel or Gad, and probably divulged in course of conversation with them, we have
raised the question of the fact of revelations having been made in past ages to holy
men which, serving for their personal guidance and comfort, have not been incorporated in the ordinary records, which conserve only what has been deemed necessary to the connected history of redemption and the general instruction of mankind.
If this be so, it is obvious obscurities might cease to be obscurities to us did we
but know what those immediately concerned in the events recorded may have been
familiar with. (2) On the supposition that the language of these men was the interpretation which they put upon the predictions contained in ch. xv. 28; xvi. 1, 12,
and on the avowed beliefs of Jonathan (ch. xx. 15; xxiii. 17), which by this time
may have become current, we have raised the question of the influence of a cherished
state of feeling—its extent and legitimacy—on the interpretation which men put
upon the teachings of Scripture in reference to doctrine, history, and worship. (3)
On the supposition that their words were simply intended to be the sense they put

upon the indications of Providence as then working out in favour of David's cause, we have the question of the proneness of men to view passing events in the light of their own tendencies, and, therefore, to make Providence mean what it was never designed to suggest.   Apart from controversy on the fore-mentioned points, it is possible to generalise the teaching of the passage by saying that there is a prevailing tendency in men to prejudice the interpretation both of Divine words and providential events by undue regard to their own wishes.   It is clear that these men wanted David to slay Saul.   Being less spiritual and generous than he, not having risen to his lofty conception of the kingdom of God, and restive under the restraints which kept them from positions of power under the coming king, they easily believed it was God's will that David should force on the issue by the death of his enemy. Passing event or spoken word in the past would have no other meaning for them. 1. *This fact should be remembered* in relation to controversies and *diversities of opinion on matters of sacred history, doctrine, and worship*.   The existence of such diversities is no evidence against a revealed religion, as some suppose, but just the reverse ; for in the nature of the case men view the truth through the medium created by their own cherished moral condition.   The final supremacy of truth is not to be attained in violation of laws which govern the operations of the human mind, but by means of them.   That men so diverse in opinion and in worship should nevertheless have so much in common that is fundamental, and should be under the mighty influence of it, is a sign that the truth is one and of God, while the error is of man and is manifold.   No student of human nature can be surprised that men should seek to eliminate the supernatural from Scripture history ; for only let a desire be cherished to see a revelation harmonise with what a man thinks would be a proper way of giving it to the world,—namely, by just such an absence of supernatural manifestations as characterises an era when no new revelation is longer needed,—and it will be as easy for him to see only naturalism in Scripture events as for David's men to see in words and events an authorisation to slay Saul.   It is a suggestive circumstance that men of diverse temperaments and emotional or æsthetic tendencies gravitate towards certain ecclesiastical organisations ; nor can we overlook the fact that it is rare for men to pass over from a system in which their tastes have been formed to another, the advocates of which claim to represent the truth.   2. *The fact should variously affect our conduct in relation to our fellow-men and to the truth.*   It should induce a *distrust of our own judgment* in so far as, on severe self-examination, it is *seen to be associated with our wishes*.   Every one is bound to "search the Scriptures," to "see whether these things are so," and to "hold fast what is true."   No surrender of this great duty and privilege to an order of men can be pleaded on the ground that possibly feeling may distort the vision of truth in the private individual ; for men acting for others are men still, and cannot escape the conditions of human nature, while the aid of the Holy Spirit is as available for one sincere heart as for another.   Our duty is to bring the most vigorous powers we can command to bear on our understanding of the will of God, and in so far as we do so in dependence on the Holy Spirit we may calmly rest in our conclusions, with the proviso that they, however good, are not coextensive with truth, and that we have purged our hearts of all human preference and prejudice.   *It should induce charity towards others*.   The exercise of charity in matters of opinion is not identical with a surrender of our own judgment to a superior, nor a denial of the importance of fundamental truth and the possibility of its attainment, nor a blindness to the serious consequences resulting from error, but an exercise of kindly consideration for those who differ from us, proceeding from the consciousness that our own views may be in some degree affected by our subjective moral condition, and that our superiority to others depends on the belief we have in the comparative freedom of our judgment from personal bias.   It is a characteristic of the interaction of feeling with thought that in so far as feeling has become habitual we are, by a well-known psychological law, less conscious of its presence as an element in the formation of judgment ; and consequently we may, as may others, be very sincere though in error.   This by no means justifies error, or renders men safe from its consequences ; but it does demand mutual consideration, and imposes on every man the solemn responsibility of so guarding the beginnings of his life that no unholy feeling or form of self-will shall gain ascendancy in his nature. They are wise who in a kind and tender spirit seek to bring men to a higher form of spiritual life. It is in love—the pure love of God—that truth is to be seen. It should induce us *to seek for ourselves and others* more of the *purifying grace of the Holy Spirit*. Possibly while on earth men will not entirely rise above the disturbing or perverting influence of tastes and sentiments inwrought with their early education, and unconsciously fostered as years advance ; for by the mental law of association we are, while in the body, in some measure subject to bondage. Yet the truth is clear that in so far as we do become pure in heart and like as a little child—with a nature open to receive what God may teach, and not furnished with wishes by which truth is to be judged—we shall rise to a correct view of God's word and providence. Pure souls are quick in spiritual perception and responsive to all that is Divine, and, on the other hand, sensitive to the faint appearance of evil. The more fully the Church becomes sanctified, the more unity will be created in a discernment of all that constitutes fundamental truth. The eras in which men have paraded opinions alien to the faith once delivered to the saints, priding themselves on their skill and ability, have not been distinguished by extreme dependence on the sanctifying power of the Holy Spirit ; nor perhaps has the Church ever, since apostolic days, sufficiently associated growth in spiritual knowledge with his blessed indwelling.

III. THE MEANS OF SUCCESS AS VIEWED BY MEN OF DIVERSE CHARACTER. All the men in the cave were one with David in the cause on which he was embarked. But followers do not always enter into the lofty aspirations of their leaders, or share equally with them the responsibility of the position assumed, while they often outstrip them in apparent zeal for the completion of their work. Hitherto the chief obstacle in the way of success was Saul, and now that Providence had manifestly put him within the power of David, what more conclusive evidence to ardent followers of the true road to success could be forthcoming? Let David smite his persecuting foe, and the cause is won ! Such was the road to success suggested by policy, self-interest, usages of Eastern warfare, and restless impatience of the ways of God. Against this David protests. It is his duty to abide God's time for entrance on his royal dignities. Even the slight liberty which David, on the impulse of the moment, took with the king in spoiling his garment became on reflection an occasion of self-reproach. Respect for office is a power in social life, being one form of reverence for law and order, and contributing to the easy maintenance of lawful authority ; and therefore the levity of finding amusement for himself and others at a king's expense was inconsistent with the true Hebrew culture which indicates its regard for the finer sentiments of life by such prohibitions as, " Thou shalt not seethe a kid in its mother's milk ;" "Thou shalt not speak evil of the ruler of thy people." It should be remembered generally that there is a *seeming way to rapid success* which is *not the true way*, and, *vice versâ, a tedious, painful way which is the right*. David's superior discernment was fortunate for him, though doubtless his adherents were annoyed at his apparent timidity and, as they supposed, fastidiousness. Lot ungenerously made choice of the richest district in haste to be rich, but his uncle eventually was most successful (Gen. xiii. 8—11 ; xiv. 11, 12). On the other hand, Moses refused the temptation to become possessed of the honours and riches of Egypt, and finally was raised to the highest position a servant of God could occupy (Heb. xi. 24—26). Our Saviour might have gained a vast following and been regarded by the authorities of Jerusalem as their Messiah had he only accommodated his standard a little to their wishes ; but now he is Lord of millions. The apostles constantly resisted inducements to achieve an immediate success by lowering their standard of preaching to the tastes of men, and so lost some (Gal. iii. 1—4) disciples ; but the result has been most blessed. In Church organisation, modes of worship, and methods of labour it is possible to devise means by which at first a large accession shall be made to the ranks of nominal Christians, yet at the same time wrong may be done to the claims of order, purity, reverence, and truth, which wrong will be avenged in years to come by corruption of manners, low spiritual tastes, and possibly apostasy from the truth. In matters of business men often see an easy way by which wealth may be speedily won, and, in preference to the slow and steady process of honest toil, it may be chosen to the ruin of the soul. Simple, earnest waiting on

Providence, doing daily work as it comes, not seeking to force matters by any act that conscience would condemn, is the course suggested by the conduct of David and all who fear God.

Vers. 8—15.—*Discrimination in relation to men, truth, and vocation.* The facts are—1. David follows Saul out of the cave and pays him homage. 2. He remonstrates against Saul heeding the lies of slanderers, and declares to him how he had just spared his life. 3. Exhibiting the skirt of the robe in evidence of his words, and appealing to God, he protests his innocence of purpose. 4. He, while admitting his own insignificance, commends his cause to the justice of God, and prays for deliverance. If we take into account what human nature is under provocation, and the rough and painful life of David at this period, we shall not fail to admire the generous, highly spiritual tone of his conduct on this occasion. It is a remarkable instance of real conformity of spirit with Christian requirements among those in ancient times not blessed with our advantages. It is also a remarkable testimony to the value of these virtues that men, without dissent, admire the beautiful spirit of David, even though in many instances they have not the will to act likewise in analogous situations. But the general teaching of the section may be arranged in the following order :—

I. DISCRIMINATION OF CHARACTER IS A PRODUCT OF TRUE GOODNESS, and is ESSENTIAL TO SUCCESS IN DEALING WITH MEN amidst the difficulties of life. David was a man of valour, of deep piety, and of keen discernment. His intense love of righteousness was not attended by a hasty and harsh condemnation of Saul's conduct, evil as it was. While keenly alive to the wrong Saul was doing him, and recognising that One above visits every evil-doer, he nevertheless in his first words to Saul recognises the fact, which doubtless through Jonathan and others he had ascertained, that there were greater sinners in this sad business than Saul. "Wherefore hearest thou men's words, saying, Behold, David seeketh thy hurt?" He knew how the unhappy king had departed from God, and subsequently had become melancholy, and at times almost insane, and he understood how the original wicked envy was associated with this sad fall from God's favour; and hence, apart from the reverence cherished for the office of king, he could not but commiserate his persecutor. Saul, in the judgment of David, was now but a mere tool in the hands of cunning, unscrupulous men at court, who basely roused the enmity of the unfortunate monarch by inventing lies concerning the intentions of David. *Discrimination of character may find abundant scope* in every man's life. How much it is lacking is obvious when we reflect on the wholesale condemnation often passed on individuals and communities. Accidental association in public life is frequently the sole basis of a common judgment. Much of the faulty training of families and imperfect education in schools is to be ascribed to this source, while errors in this particular are the cause of manifold mistakes and disastrous failures in private life. It is due to others, as also safe for ourselves, that we act on our Saviour's exhortation, "Judge righteous judgment." David was just to Saul in regarding him as the weak instrument of stronger wills; as was our Saviour just to a misled people when he charged the scribes and Pharisees with hindering them from obeying the gospel (Matt. xxiii. 13). A certain development and balance of the intellectual faculties are requisite to discriminate character. It is to be feared that very little attention is paid to this kind of culture in many homes and schools, and consequently there are thousands in a far worse position for the great conflict of life than they need be. But where ordinary capacities for discernment exist, true piety will insure their right and just exercise; for religion raises the whole moral tone of a man, and gives a superior moral element to our judgments on the motives and conduct of men. The gift of "discerning spirits" is of much value still in the Church of God and in daily affairs.

II. OUR JUDGMENT ON THE LANGUAGE OF THE BIBLE SHOULD BE REGULATED BY REGARD TO THE SPECIFIC KNOWLEDGE ON WHICH IT IS BASED. David discriminates between the weak and sinful Saul and the cunning, determined men who used him as a tool for their wicked schemes. The language employed by him here in reference to Saul is mild and tender—recognising wrong, but expressive of the conviction that his actions were now not responsible in the same degree as when he disobeyed the command of God through Samuel. In the Psalms we have other language—strong, severe, withering—intended for "men set on fire, sons of men whose teeth are spears and arrows, and their *tongue* a sharp sword" (Ps. lvii. 4). "Deceit," "fraud," "lying lips," "poison of adders," tongues "set on fire," that "wrest words" and "love all devouring words," are the terms used to indicate the motives and purposes of the men prompting the action of Saul. .Now as we find the explanation of the mild language in the intimate knowledge which he had of the weakness of his enemy, and the use which stronger wills were making of him, so, by the same rule of interpretation, ought we to allow an appropriateness of other and more severe language to men so utterly vile as these were known to be, and to whom he alludes in ver. 9 and ch. xxvi. 19. Too often Christian men, and especially unbelievers, read the strong language of the Psalms as though it were expressive of sentiments ordinarily entertained towards any who might differ from David ; and it is viewed as in contrast with his address to Saul and the precepts of Christ. The unreasonableness of this judgment is evident when we only consider what David knew these men to be, and to be aiming at. They were deliberate, calculating liars, knowing by his deeds, by Samuel's approval, and by his pure and useful life, that he was a chosen man of God, and yet endeavouring by false representations to blast his reputation, to incite a moody king to slay him on account of his vileness of intention, and, in fact, to frustrate the purpose which God had announced through Samuel, and of which Jonathan, Gad, Abiathar, and others were aware. A baser, more cruel and cowardly conspiracy against character, life, and *national welfare* can hardly be imagined. The knowledge of these specific facts renders David's wrath and indignation most holy, and, in view of what would be the calamity to Israel should they succeed in annulling the purpose of God as declared to Samuel and made known to David and others, the Church can say Amen to the Psalms. This *principle of interpretation is wider than the case before us.* None of us dare use towards others the severe language of Christ's denunciation of the scribes and Pharisees, because we have not the minute knowledge of motive and internal, irreclaimable deceitfulness which was clear to his eye ; but his view of what is hidden from us rendered his words just and good. Also, the language used with reference to the necessity of atonement, the manner in which it is made, and the conditions on which it becomes available for those made acquainted with it, should be considered reverently, as being founded on an intimate knowledge on the part of God of very many facts pertaining to moral existence, the inter-relation of all moral beings, and the administration of a government stretching through all time and place, which necessarily at present escape our observation. The same principle may apply to much of the language in reference to the future condition of the wicked. Even the right interpretation of historical matter in many dubious cases may depend on facts which to the writers were well known, but to us are unknown. It would be useful to direct attention to the conditions of a right understanding of the Bible, embracing in the purview moral health, attained by the quickening of the Holy Spirit, caution, reverence, regard to its spiritual aims, its fragmentary character, its progressive teaching— especially sympathy with its purpose.

III. A MAN'S VOCATION IN LIFE EXERCISES A POWERFUL INFLUENCE IN DETERMINING HIS MORAL QUALITIES. The moral qualities of consideration, forbearance, magnanimity, and candour so prominent in David during this interview with Saul met with little sympathy among his followers at the time, though subsequently they would see the wisdom of his conduct. Like others, they judged of what should be done by what from their lower moral position they were inclined to do. The superior conduct of David was not due simply to tenderness of natural disposition, nor to the presence of piety considered *per se*, but largely to the educating influence on his generally pious character of his *calling in life.* He perfectly understood that, as servant of God, he was called to be future ruler of Israel, and meanwhile so to live and act that no deed of his should touch his personal reputation in Israel or create the impression on the mind of Saul that he sought his removal from the throne to gratify private ambition. Virtually he was already a royal personage. His actions and words were therefore public property. The building up of national character and development of national resources were matters of deepest concern. The consciousness of this drew him nearer to God, attached responsibility to his deeds, imparted dignity and grace to his bearing, put a restraint on the flow of private feelings, and, though uncrowned, made him royal in his magnanimity. David as a coming king was morally a more developed man than would have been David as a simple citizen. *A consideration of the influence of calling on character would afford much instruction* in relation to social habits, mental and moral development, Christian excellence and degeneracies, national and provincial characteristics and tendencies, domestic comfort and discomfort, personal antagonisms and aversions, and the need for a large charity in estimating conduct different from our own, as also for profound thought in reference to the best means of remedying some evils incident to a highly-developed civilisation, in which the comforts and luxuries of one class are procured by avocations of another class that tell perniciously on their mental and moral development. Christians are especially exhorted to walk worthy of their high calling ; and, apart from direct influence of the Holy Spirit in the formation of character, it would be helpful to all to study the natural influence over the entire man of a calling to be " kings and priests unto God." " What manner of persons ought ye to be ? " " As he which hath called you is holy, so be ye holy in all manner of conversation" (1 Pet. i. 15).

IV. The COMMITTAL OF OUR INTERESTS TO GOD IS THE PROPER SEQUEL TO A CONSCIENTIOUS DISCHARGE OF DUTY. David had done all an honest man could do to clear himself of guilt and to pacify Saul, and with strong faith in an over-ruling Providence he leaves his cause with God. Personal retaliation for injuries done is no part of our duty. " Vengeance is mine, I will repay, saith the Lord." Whether we succeed in a difficult work is not our business. To have done right is the chief concern. Our Saviour has set us an example of fulfilling all righteousness and then committing himself and his cause to the " righteous Father." There is that in the conscience of men which bows before such appeals to the " Judge of all the earth." The name of God is a power over men because they are moral beings. It is a refuge for the oppressed and a terror to the wicked.

General lessons :—1. The real guilt of men is to be estimated both by the intrinsic evil of their intentions and the influence they seek to exercise over others. 2. Men who desire to find the Bible faulty in its language can have their desire easily gratified by reasoning as though they knew all concerning its production and contents ; while a different disposition will lead to suspension of judgment or minute search for hidden facts. 3. The moral influence of a calling on character should guide us in our arrangements for our sons and daughters. 4. Deeds are the tests and signs of principles ; for as wickedness is the natural outcome of the wicked man, good actions, as in the generous sparing of Saul's life, are the product of a righteous soul (ver. 13).

Vers. 16—22.—*Tenderness transitory and truth suppressed.* The facts are—1. Saul, subdued by the magnanimity of David, weeps and admits his own wrong in contrast with David's kindness. 2. Acknowledging his belief that David is to be king, he pleads with him to be merciful to his seed. 3. David, granting the request, returns to his stronghold, and Saul to his home. Good actions soon begin to authenticate their Divine mission in the world. The noble self-vindication from the calumnies of slanderers and the rare display of generosity to a persistent foe told at once even on the obdurate nature of Saul, and in the effect produced we have an instance of two facts often observable among men and of some significance in their experience.

I. The TRANSITORY TENDERNESS OF SINFUL MEN. Saul's heart was softened, and he wept. Words of tenderness and of frank confession of guilt came forth with all sincerity. The terrible encrustation formed by years of transgression and disobedience seemed to be broken, and the true man reasserted itself from within. The power of kindness received a conspicuous illustration. Wickedness could no longer confront goodness. And yet, as we know from the subsequent care of David to escape from Saul, the tenderness was only as " the morning cloud and early dew." 1. *There are seasons of tenderness even in the lives of the most impenitent of men.* This might be inferred from our necessary knowledge of the conflicting principles at work in all moral beings, and from our observation that it requires enormous effort to kill outright all the better qualities of our humanity ; but the fact comes before us in history, biographical confessions, and in the intercourse of daily life. Who has not seen a hardened sinner subdued by a reminder of a mother's prayers, or the mention in gentle tones of the Saviour's name, or the kindly gaze of a Christian eye ? In the vilest abodes of sin, and among the proudest sceptics, there are those who sometimes weep in secret or relent in their rebellion against God. 2. *The causes of this tenderness are often ascertainable.* In the case of Saul we see a combination of causes. The display of magnanimity was impressive because of its very rarity ; it came home to his sense of right ; it was in vivid contrast with his own conduct ; it was in its logic so conclusive as to the goodness of the man he was persecuting ; it brought out the fact that all along he had known David to be good, but had forced the fact out of thought ; it was a revelation of his bondage to vile men, to whose character he could not be quite blind ; and it could not but call up to memory days once bright and happy, when he was a young man unburdened by present guilt and care. Varied are the causes which enable the remnant of good in men to assert itself for awhile ; some lie deep in the hidden processes of thought, where the association of ideas is made subservient to the force of Scriptural truth learnt in early years and to the unconscious influence of the Spirit of God ; while others arise in the events of daily life, such as sickness, casual words of kindness, presence of a beautifully holy life that suggests a contrast, mention of the words of Jesus, or the open grave. 3. *The import of these seasons of tenderness deserves consideration.* Is there not some hope for such men in spite of their past and present surroundings ? Is there not a basis on which Christians may work in wisdom ? Have we not here the secret on the human side of the mighty power of the truth of God ? Is it not important to make such men believe that there is some germ worth caring for in their otherwise sad and wretched life ? Does not the transitoriness of the tenderness often arise from the absence of some wise friend to encompass the self-condemned heart with love ? Ought not Christians to go among men with the conviction that they are all reclaimable, and that it is largely a question of gaining access to the tender place in their nature and caring for them as a wise physician would for a patient desperately ill ? There are many ways in which the Church may apply the thoughts thus awakened in our endeavours to win to Christ even the most abandoned. Immense power is gained over men when they know us to be cognizant of any transitory feeling of tenderness ; and half the battle is won when they begin to look on us as friends to be trusted.

II. THE FORCED SUPPRESSION OF TRUTH. Saul was evidently sincere in saying, " Now, behold, I know that thou shalt surely be king ; " but the confession was also a revelation of the fact that all through these persecutions he had more than surmised that David was the coming king. Had he been anxious to know the actual truth before as surely as he professed now to have attained it, the course was clear enough. But these words confirm the teaching of the entire history—that he was aware not only of his own rejection, but that this slayer of the lion and bear, and conqueror of Goliath, and *protégé* of Samuel, and friend of Jonathan, was the chosen servant of· God. The course adopted by Saul can only be explained on the supposition that he suppressed the truth. It is in the nature of truth to assert its power over the life by convincing the understanding and constraining the will, and only the rebellious spirit that refused to submit to the sad punishment announced by Samuel, sustained by cherished envy of David, and wrought upon by cunning slanderers, could have rendered the facts clear to Saul so nugatory in their influence over his life. Well would it have been if this were a solitary instance of suppression of truth ! Every man persisting in a sinful course has to force out truth from thought. The internal war consists partly in crushing the free evidence of knowledge. Men know more than they like to admit and act upon ; and all kinds of devices are resorted to, to explain away or to divert attention from what is manifestly true. The suppressions of truth in controversy are denounced as very wicked, but in relation to personal moral conduct and religion it is possible for the advocates of candour to shut their eyes to much that is out of harmony with their wishes. It is a truth that self is sinful before God, that efforts to find true rest apart from Christ are unavailing, that the chosen life of sin is " hard," that the holy are happier than the sinful, and that

Christ is waiting to be gracious, and yet this truth is constantly put away from view as unwelcome, troublesome. Doubtless, also, many who under the influence of stronger wills are bold in their denial of Christ's authority know in their secret heart that he *is* Lord and will establish his kingdom. Sin makes men dishonest to themselves; under its power they are not of the truth. They prefer darkness because their deeds are evil.

General lessons:—1. In the issue goodness will be recognised by those who despise it, and generosity is always influential. 2. The anguish of wrong-doing occasionally felt is fearfully suggestive of the future experience of the unrepenting. 3. The occasional triumphs of the good over all their slanderers and oppressors are intimations of the final triumph of Christ in the establishment of his kingdom. 4. Vows and promises in reference to future acts in so far as they embrace the quality of mercy may be freely and at all times made (ver. 21).

HOMILIES BY VARIOUS AUTHORS.

Vers. 1—7. (ENGEDI.)—*David's forbearance toward Saul.* "Would it not be manly to resent it?" said one, on receiving an affront. "Yes," was the reply, "but it would be Godlike to forgive it." In the spirit of this answer David acted when he spared Saul in the cave at Engedi, and thereby proved that he was guiltless of the design which the latter in his delusion attributed to him—of aiming at his throne and his life (ch. xxii. 8). Saul himself had shown generosity toward enemies in the earlier part of his career (ch. xi. 12); but his character had fearfully deteriorated since that time, and his generosity toward others was far surpassed by that of David toward him. "Generosity toward his enemies was a part of David's very being. And he alone is the true hero who, like David, forces involuntary recognition and friendship even from his bitterest foe" (Ewald). Observe that—

I. HE WAS STRONGLY TEMPTED TO AVENGE HIMSELF. He had been bitterly hated and grievously wronged; "was a man of like passions with ourselves;" and the temptation came to him, as it comes to others, in—1. *A favourable opportunity* to take revenge. His enemy was entirely in his power, and his life might be taken away at a stroke.

> "O, Opportunity! thy guilt is great;
> 'Tis thou that execut'st the traitor's treason;
> Thou set'st the wolf where he the lamb may get;
> Whoever plots the sin, thou point'st the season;
> 'Tis thou that spurn'st at right, at law, at reason;
> And in thy shady cell, where none may spy him,
> Sits sin, to seize the souls that wander by him" (Shakespeare).

2. *A plausible argument* used by others. David's men not only desired to see the deed done and sought permission to do it (vers. 7, 10), but also said, "See, this is the day of which Jehovah hath said to thee, Behold, I give thine enemy into thine hand," &c. "The speakers regarded the leadings of Providence by which Saul had been brought into David's power as a Divine intimation to David himself to take this opportunity of slaying his deadly enemy, and called the intimation a word of Jehovah" (Keil). Men are apt to interpret the Divine purpose of events according to their own interests and inclinations (ch. xxiii. 7), and it is often the exact reverse of what they imagine it to be. It was not that David should slay Saul, but (among other things) that he should be *tried*, and by sparing him vindicated, blessed and made a blessing. What is meant for good is by a deceived heart turned to evil. "And those temptations are most powerful which fetch their force from the pretence of a religious obedience" (Hall). 3. *A sudden thought* tending in the direction of revenge (ver. 10, Vulgate: 'And I thought to kill thee'). He did not cherish it or form a distinct purpose to carry it into effect, but came perilously near doing so in the indignity he offered to the king. "He does not seem to have been quite free from the temptation to kill Saul. The words (ver. 5) are only intelligible on the supposition that, on cutting off Saul's skirt, his thoughts were not directed only to the use which he afterwards made of it, at least in the beginning, but that his object was

rather to prove the goodness of his thoughts at the first weak beginning he made to carry them into effect. But his better self soon awoke; all impure thoughts fled; his eye became clear; with horror he put the temptation from him" (Hengstenberg). "Blessed is the man that endureth temptation," &c. (James i. 12).

II. HE COMPLETELY OVERCAME THE TEMPTATION. By—1. *The possession of a tender conscience*, which enabled him to perceive the will of God, shrank from sin, and smote him for his "thought of foolishness" (Prov. xxiv. 9) and irreverent act. "It is a good thing to have a heart within us smiting us for sins that seem little; it is a sign conscience is awake and tender, and will be a means to prevent greater sins" (M. Henry). 2. *Regard to the Divine will*, which directed him not to avenge himself, but to leave vengeance with the Lord; to honour the king, and love his neighbour as himself. His regard for it was lowly, reverent, and supreme. The purpose of providential events must be interpreted in harmony with conscience and the moral law. How often do the Scriptures enjoin forbearance and forgiveness toward enemies! (Prov. xx. 22; xxv. 21, 22; Matt. v. 44; Rom. xii. 19—21; Col. iii. 13). 3. *Repression of evil thought* and impulse; immediate, firm, and entire. "The better to know how to guard against the wiles of the enemy, take it for a certain rule that every thought which discourages and removes thee from growing in love and trust towards God is a messenger of hell; and, as such, thou must drive him away, and neither admit him nor give him a hearing" (Scupoli). David repressed such a thought in himself and in his men, became the protector of Saul, was not overcome of evil, but overcame evil with good, and was made by means of temptation stronger and more illustrious. "Temptation is the greatest occasioner of a Christian's honour; indeed, like an enemy, it threatens and endeavours to ruin him, but in conquest of it consists his crown and triumph" (Hales, 'Golden Remains').

As aids to the practice of forbearance—1. Consider the "goodness, forbearance, and long-suffering of God." 2. Contemplate the example of Christ. 3. Watch against the first thought of evil. 4. Pray for the spirit of patience, forgiveness, and love.—D.

Vers. 8—12. (ENGEDI.)—*Calumny.* "Wherefore hearest thou men's words, saying, David seeketh thy hurt?" (ver. 9). Saul's hatred and persecution of David were stirred up by slanderers; and, in vindication of himself from the charge of seeking his hurt, David referred to them on this and on a subsequent occasion (ch. xxvi. 19). One of them seems to have been Cush the Benjamite (see Kitto, 'D. B. Illus.'), on account of the calumnies of whom he wrote Ps. VII., 'The righteous judgment of God' (see inscription):—

> "Jehovah my God, in thee have I found refuge;
> Save me from my persecutors and deliver me!"

How much he felt the wrong which they had done him, and how intensely his zeal burned against their sin against God and man, appears in many of his psalms (Ps. xxiv. 13; xxxv. 11; lii. 2; lvi. 5; lvii. 4; lix. 7, &c.). Good men are often exposed to the calumnious attacks of men of similar character.

> "Be thou as chaste as ice, as pure as snow,
> Thou shalt not escape calumny."

I. IT IS ONE OF THE MOST ODIOUS OF VICES. It is "the uttering of false (or equivalent to false, morally false) speech against our neighbour in prejudice to his fame, his safety, his welfare, or concernment in any kind, out of malignity, vanity, rashness, ill nature, or bad design" (Barrow, Ser. xviii.); and it is exhibited in an endless variety of ways. 1. It is *marked* by falsehood, folly, injustice, malice, and impiety. 2. It exerts a most pernicious *influence*. The tongue on which it dwells is like a fire, which (though at first but a single spark) may set a whole forest in a blaze (James iii. 5); is "full of deadly poison," and sends forth "arrows, firebrands, and death." In private reputations, domestic life, social intercourse, the Church and the world, what mischief it works! 3. It is frequently forbidden and condemned in the word of God (Levit. xix. 16; Prov. x. 31; 1 Cor. vi. 9). "I say unto you that every idle (empty, insincere, wicked, and injurious) word," &c. (Matt. xii. 36, 37). "God is angry (with the wicked) every day" (Ps. vii. 11).

II. IT OUGHT NEVER TO BE COUNTENANCED. "Wherefore hearest thou?" No one should listen to it; for by doing so—1. He *encourages* the wicked in their wickedness (Prov. xxv. 23). "When will talkers refrain from evil speaking? When listeners refrain from evil hearing" (Hare). 2. He *injures himself;* becomes a tool of designing men, and is led to do things which his better nature cannot approve; whilst, at the same time, he manifests his own unreasonableness and sinful disposition. 3. He makes himself "*partaker* of their evil deeds," and exposes himself to the same condemnation. Although incited by others, Saul was not guiltless in "hunting after" the soul of David "to take it" (ver. 11).

III. IT SHOULD ALWAYS BE MET IN A RIGHT MANNER by those who are calumniated; as by—1. An *open assertion* of innocence, direct denial and rebuke of false statements, and faithful remonstrance against their being entertained. "Whose mouths" (says Paul concerning unruly and vain talkers and deceivers) "must be stopped" (Titus i. 11). 2. A *clear proof* of innocence afforded by becoming, righteous, and merciful actions (vers. 10, 11; compare Ps. vii. 3, 4). 3. A *sincere appeal* to God as the Vindicator of the innocent; lowly submission to his will and firm confidence in the manifestation of his righteous judgment. "The justice of God is a refuge and comfort to oppressed innocency" (M. Henry). "The Lord judge between me and thee," &c. (ver. 12).

> "Jehovah judgeth the people.
> Judge me, O Jehovah, according to my righteousness,
> And according to my integrity be it done to me.
> Oh let the wickedness of the wicked come to an end,
> And establish thou the righteous;
> For thou that triest the hearts and reins art a righteous God.
> My shield is with God,
> Who delivers the upright in heart" (Ps. vii. 8, 9, 10).

Learn—1. To use the gift of speech in speaking well, and not ill, of others. 2. To rely on God more than on your own efforts for your vindication when evil spoken of. 3. The blessedness of those against whom men "say all manner of evil falsely" for Christ's sake.—D.

Vers. 13—15. (ENGEDI.)—*A proverb of the ancients.* "Wickedness proceedeth from the wicked" (ver. 13). Proverbs are brief and apt sayings expressive of the general experience of men. They have been described as "the wisdom of many and the wit of one" (Russell); and, more poetically, "jewels five words long, which on the stretched forefinger of time sparkle for ever" (Tennyson). The most valuable of "the words of the wise" were uttered by Solomon, and are contained in the Book of Proverbs. But this saying was already ancient in the days of David. It is also "true and faithful" and very instructive. Consider—

I. ITS MEANING. "Ill men do ill things." "Actions usually correspond to the quality of the mind" (Grotius). 1. *An evil disposition is possessed by some men.* The ancients noticed the distinction between evil *actions* (as well as good) and evil *character* (as well as good). There is in some men, in contrast to others, a selfish and bad disposition. All men, it is true, are sinful; but some, instead of striving against sin and overcoming it, are the slaves of sin; their supreme affection is set upon unworthy objects, and the ruling principle of their life is wrong. This is due to many causes—previous voluntary acts, wilful neglect of Divine aid, &c.; but the fact is certain. Their *nature* differs from that of good men just as (though not so necessarily or to the same extent) the serpent from the dove, and the thistle from the vine. 2. *An evil disposition expresses itself in corresponding actions.* It uses power and opportunity according to its nature (ver. 19), and turns to evil the same circumstances which a good disposition turns to good (ver. 6). This is in harmony with the established order of things in the world. "A good tree bringeth not forth corrupt fruit; neither doth a corrupt tree bring forth good fruit" (Luke vi. 43). "Do men gather grapes of thorns?" &c. (Matt. vi. 16—20; xii. 35). "Doth a fountain send forth at the same place sweet water and bitter?" &c. (James iii. 11—13;

Prov. xiii. 16).   3. *An evil disposition is plainly proved by evil actions.*   It is so especially when they are performed deliberately, habitually, and on occasions of decisive trial.   "By their fruits ye shall know them."   The proof is perfectly reliable, easily perceivable, and generally applicable.

II. Its application (ver. 11).   "But my hand shall not be upon thee" (vers. 12, 13).   "David means to say that if he had been guilty of conspiracy against the king he would not have neglected this favourable opportunity to kill him, since men usually indulge their feelings, and from a mind guilty of conspiracy nothing but corresponding deeds could come forth" (Clericus).   The application may be made to the conduct of *others*, but it should be made first and chiefly to our *own ;* and it should lead us—1. *To test our character* by our actions, and to prove to others when it is suspected and calumniated that it is good, and not evil.   As wickedness proceedeth from the wicked, so goodness proceedeth from the good.   2. *To feel increased aversion to evil*, to act according to the integrity we assert of ourselves, to resolve to do nothing wrong, and to endeavour to prevent others from doing wrong (ver. 14).   3. *To appeal to God*, who searches the heart, and, in the consciousness of sincerity and innocence, to put confidence in his righteous and merciful aid (ver. 15).   "Beloved, if our heart condemn us not, then have we confidence toward God " (1 John iii. 21).

In the review of the subject let us bear in mind that—1. Men are responsible for the character they possess.   2. An evil character may be transformed into a good one by the power of Divine grace and the use of proper means.   "I will give you a new heart."   "Make you a new heart."   3. We ought to strive continually to attain the highest degree of virtue and goodness possible.

> "Such is this steep ascent,
> That it is ever difficult at first,
> But more a man proceeds less evil grows.
> When pleasant it shall seem to thee, so much
> That upward going shall be easy to thee,
> As in a vessel to go down the tide,
> Then of this path thou wilt have reached this end.
> There hope to rest thee from thy toil" ('Purg.' iv.).   D.

Vers. 16—22.   (Engedi.)—*The goodness of bad men.*   "And Saul lifted up his voice and wept" (ver. 17).   The opportunity given to David to avenge himself on Saul was a severe test of principle, but by the use he made thereof it became a means of his further advancement.   His forbearance was also another test of the character of Saul, over whom Divine mercy still lingered, and toward whom it was in such forbearance shown afresh.   Nor was it without effect.   The heart of the man who had ordered the massacre of eighty-five priests and was bent on the destruction of his most faithful servant relented at the words addressed to him ; his voice trembled with emotion, tears flowed down his cheeks, he wept aloud, acknowledged his guilt, and turned from his purpose.   It seemed as if he had undergone a sudden transformation and become a new man.   But his heart remained unchanged.   And his goodness, as on former occasions, was like that of those to whom the prophet said, "Your goodness " (fits of piety) " is as the morning cloud, and as the early dew it goeth away " (Hosea vi. 4).   Concerning such goodness, notice that—

I. It is not unfrequently displayed.   There is in the worst of men some capacity of moral and spiritual impression ; and those who might be least expected to be moved are often most powerfully affected by—1. *The force of a powerful appeal*, in which the truth is set before their minds and brought home to their hearts and consciences (vers. 9—15).   They walk in the darkness of error and illusion, and the light breaks suddenly upon them, revealing what they could not or would not see before.   It is made so plain that they are unable to deny its reality or resist its impression.   2. *The exhibition of unusual generosity* and superior excellence, which shows by contrast their own defects, shames and subdues them, overcomes not only them, but also, in some degree, the evil that is in them—their envy, hatred, and sin.   "The simple self-presentation and self-witness of moral purity and truth has a great missionary power, and often makes a mighty impression on spiritually darkened and morally perverted natures, in such wise that the Divine in them is freed from the binding power of evil, and the religious moral element of the conscience, which is concealed deep under religious moral corruption, breaks freely forth, at least in some bright and good moments, in order to point to the way of salvation and show the possibility of deliverance, provided the man is *willing* to be saved and renewed" (Erdmann). 3. *The apprehension of an extraordinary escape* from danger and death (ver. 18). Saul had been placed by the hand of God within reach of the stroke of death, and if David had acted as men would ordinarily have done he would not have been now alive (ver. 19). The heart must be hard indeed if it be not melted by such things as these.

II. IT IS APPARENTLY GENUINE; the proof of a radical change of disposition. In tears and words and actions there is—1. *The presence of strong emotion.* It is evidently not simulated, but real. 2. *The operation of an awakened conscience* (ver. 17), which produces the recognition of what is right, the vindication of one who has been wronged, the confession of sin, and prayer for the blessing of God on one who has been regarded as an enemy (ver. 19). 3. *The conviction of the Divine purpose.* "And now, behold, I know well," &c. (ver. 20). That purpose had been indicated to Saul by Samuel and by the course of events; but he refused to recognise it, sought to change it, and fought against it. Now he acknowledges its inevitable fulfilment on the ground of the superior worth of David (ch. xv. 28), submits to it without complaint, and even seeks a solemn pledge of forbearance toward his house on its accomplishment (ver. 21). He says in effect, "The will of the Lord be done." 4. *The abandonment of evil designs.* His amendment goes beyond good resolutions, and appears in his actually leaving off the pursuit of David and returning home to Gibeah (ver. 22). When good actions follow good words, what more can be needed? Yet Saul among the saints, like Saul among the prophets, was Saul still.

III. IT IS REALLY WORTHLESS. Although the signs of repentance and reformation in Saul were greatly valued, they were not absolutely relied upon by David, who had experience of his impulsive and changeable nature, and "knew what was in man." The most promising signs may be, and often are, connected with a goodness which is—1. *Superficial;* the depth of the heart being still hard and stony. 2. *Defective,* in hatred of sin, renunciation of self, return to God, surrender of the will, true faith, inward renewal, and spiritual strength to resist temptation. 3. *Transient.* "They *soon* forgat his works," &c. (Ps. cvi. 13). Not long afterwards Saul was again in pursuit of David, and his heart was more obdurate than ever (ch. xxvi. 1). Transient goodness issues in permanent destruction. "Water that riseth and floweth from a living spring runneth equally and constantly, unless it be obstructed or diverted by some violent opposition; but that which is from *thunder-showers* runs furiously for a season, but is quickly dried up. So are those spiritual thoughts which arise from a prevalent internal principle of grace in the heart; they are even and constant unless an interruption be put upon them for a season by temptations. But those which are excited by *the thunder of convictions,* however their streams may be filled for a season, they quickly dry up and utterly decay" (Owen, 'Spiritual-Mindedness').

Consider that—1. Men may be near the kingdom of God and yet never enter into it. 2. We are liable to be deceived by the appearance of goodness in others, and even in ourselves. 3. Whilst we should "search and try our hearts," we should also pray, "Search me, O God," &c. (Ps. cxxxix. 23, 24). "Create in me a clean heart," &c. (Ps. li. 10).—D.

Vers. 16, 17.—*Evil overcome by good.* Recent passages of this history have shown more of David's weakness than of his strength. But here he is again a hero. The fine points of his character shine out—his self-control, his magnanimity, and his reliance on the justice of God to vindicate his integrity. To this period is ascribed the seventh Psalm, in which the son of Jesse appeals against the slanders with which he was assailed, and looks to God for solace and deliverance. The situation strikes both the imagination and the heart. The young chief stands at the mouth of the cavern, holding up the proof of his generous forbearance, and protesting with picturesque eloquence against Saul's hot pursuit. The king amazed, ashamed, and subdued; the sternness fading from his face, the haughty anger in his eyes drowned in tears. So evil was for the time overcome by good. David was helped to this noble behaviour at Engedi by his recent meeting with Jonathan in the forest of Ziph. At and through that meeting he had been encouraged in God. So in the hour of temptation he abstained from revenge, confided to God the vindication of his innocence and the preservation of his life, would not lift a hand, or let one of his officers lift hand, against the king. With what thankfulness and joy must Jonathan have heard of the sparing of his father's life by his friend! Their meeting had borne fruit very soon. Their prayers were heard. Perhaps we have a happy meeting with a friend, or a strengthening and refreshing service at church, and the reason why is not at once apparent; but soon we fall into some temptation or danger, and then we are helped by the recent confirmation of our faith to endure with patience. Our "good time" in the wood of Ziph is meant to prepare us for the hour of temptation in the cave of Engedi.

I. MARK THE RESTRAINT OF GOD UPON THE PERSECUTOR. Saul seemed to have every facility for gaining his object. No one disputed his will. Armed men by thousands followed him in pursuit of David; and Saul knew how to lead men, and how to fight. He had spies to track out the fugitive. The country was small, and the inhabitants, both at Keilah and at Ziph, showed their readiness to help the king. Yet he could never reach David to arrest or to smite him. More than once he had thrown the javelin at him, but missed. In the highlands of Judah he was more than once close upon his steps, but still missed him. He went on one side of a hill while David moved round the other side. He had almost caught him when he was called off to repel a sudden inroad by the Philistines. He actually entered the cave in which David and his men lay hid, and did not see them. This was no mere luck. It was God who preserved David and baffled the malice of Saul. And in the tragical history of persecution the restraining hand of God has often been shown. As Saul was allowed to kill the priests but not to kill David, so has the Lord allowed many a tyrant to go so far, but no farther. Jezebel could make away with Naboth, but not with Elijah. Herod could kill St. James, but not St. Peter. The Roman Catholic persecutors could burn Huss, but not Wickliffe; George Wishart, but not John Knox. There has been a cord of Divine control round every oppressor, and whenever God saw meet he has simply drawn that cord, and so has restrained the remainder of wrath, defeated the devices of cruelty.

II. DISTINGUISH BETWEEN A RELENTING MOOD AND A REPENTING HEART. An evildoer may be thrown into a fit of shame and grief over his own misconduct, promise amendment with tears, and yet never truly repent. The generous conduct and appeal of his son-in-law overwhelmed the king with confusion, and woke lingering echoes of good feeling in his troubled breast. He even wept before all, and, with the hot tears pouring from his eyes, confessed that he was in the wrong, praised the noble forbearance of David, acknowledged that the young captain was destined to fill the throne, and even asked him to swear that on his accession he would not exterminate the royal family. David swore, and they parted. Saul went home, but David did not attend him, for he was too shrewd to trust to the altered mood of the king. Well for him that he was so cautious, for Saul had only relented for a little while, not really repented of his malignant purpose. Softened feeling is one thing, repentance in mind and purpose another thing. This is familiar to those who try to reclaim criminals. They find them melt under kind words, bewail their misconduct, promise to lead lives of honesty and sobriety, and yet after all this fall very soon under temptation, and not only renew, but increase, their wickedness. It is because they have only a gush of feeling, not a grasp of principle, and are sorry for themselves, but not penitent towards God. It is often illustrated in persons who have succumbed to the infatuation for strong drink. One has allowed this vice to grow insensibly, and does not know how far it has mastered him, till at last there comes an exposure of drunkenness which covers him with shame. A friend speaks to him about it seriously and kindly, and tears come promptly to his eyes, expressions of poignant regret and promises of the utmost caution flow from his lips. He is quite surprised that he should have been so foolish, hopes that no more will be said about it, and is quite sure that nothing of the kind will ever happen again. But there is little disturbance of conscience, no grave sense of sin, no humbling of self before God with petitions for pardon and for help to cease from this insidious vice. So in a little while the shame is gone, the good promises are forgotten, the friend who spoke so kindly is hated for his pains, and the perverse man succumbs to temptation, and goes on to a drunkard's disgrace, goes down to a drunkard's grave. There are many other instances of this folly without descending to gross vice. Men have twinges of compunction and gusts of admirable feeling, and so resolve to lead better lives. But there it ends. They mean well, but somehow cannot carry out their intention. It is for want of repentance toward God.

III. RECOGNISE THE SUPERIOR STRENGTH OF MORAL WEAPONS. Whatever good is done to those who are going astray is effected by moral means and weapons only. David might have fought Saul and beaten him, but that would not have brought even a temporary relenting to his heart. It would probably have hardened him. David smote him with the moral power of truth and love, and so disarmed him for the time, and subdued him to unwonted tenderness. So now we can best benefit our fellow-men by using the moral influences of probity and kindness. So may our nation influence other nations as a Christian people ought to do, not by vaunting our power to go where we like and kill whom we please, but by showing righteousness and good-will towards all mankind. Physical weapons of destruction are not worthy to be compared with the moral weapons that reach the conscience and the heart.

IV. RISE TO THE THOUGHT OF GOD'S MAGNANIMITY TO US. Though we have conceived in our minds enmity against him, he does not crush us by the might of his arm, or willingly slay us as with the edge of a glittering sword. The gospel conveys to us the sublime appeal of his truth, righteousness, and pardoning love. We enter no cave where God is not. We are never beyond his reach ; and if he should smite, who is there that could deliver out of his hand ? But he has no pleasure in our death. Much as we have provoked him, he has compassion, he spares, he even pleads with us to be reconciled to him. Let us consent to his proposals of grace not with mere evanescent feeling, but with inward repentance and cordial faith. Then we shall not part from our God, as did Saul from David, but abide and "walk together as those that are agreed."—F.

EXPOSITION.

CHAPTER XXV.

DEATH OF SAMUEL (ver. 1). Ver. 1.— **And Samuel died.** According to Josephus, Samuel had for eighteen years been contemporaneous with Saul's kingdom. If this calculation, which probably rests upon some Jewish tradition, be at all correct, we must include the years of Samuel's judgeship in the sum total of Saul's reign (see on ch. xiii. 1), as evidently his fall was now fast approaching. Samuel's life marked the beginning of the second age of Israelite history (Acts iii. 24). Moses had given the people their law, but Samuel in the schools of the prophets provided for them that education without which a written law was powerless, and called forth also and regulated that living energy in the prophetic order which, claiming an all but equal authority, modified and developed it, and continually increased its breadth and force, until the last prophet, Jesus of Nazareth, with supreme and Divine power re-enacted it as the religion of the whole world. And as neither his educational institutions nor the prophetic order, whose ordinary duties were closely connected with these schools, could have flourished without

internal quietness and security, Samuel also established the Jewish monarchy, which was ideally also necessary, because the Messiah must not only be priest and prophet, but before all things a king (Matt. ii. 1, 6 ; John xviii. 37). And side by side with the kingdom he lived on to see the military successes of the first king, and the firm establishment of the royal power ; but to witness also the development of that king into a despot, the overclouding of his mind with fits of madness, the designation of his successor, the probation of that successor by manifold trials, his ripening fitness under them to be the model of a theocratic king, and his growth in power so as practically to be now safe from all Saul's evil purposes. And so in the fulness of time Samel died, and all Israel gathered together and made lamentation for him (see Gen. l. 10), **and buried him in his house.** The tomb at present shown as that of Samuel is situated upon a lofty hill, the identification of which with Ramah is very uncertain. Probably he was buried not actually in his house, as that would lead to perpetual ceremonial defilement (Num. xix. 16 ; Luke xi. 44), but in some open spot in his garden (comp. 2 Kings xxi. 18 ; 2

Chron. xxxiii. 20). So Joab was buried in his own house (1 Kings ii. 34). **At Ramah.** Thenius thinks that the prophets shared with the kings the right of intramural burial. DAVID IN THE WILDERNESS OF PARAN (vers. 1—42). DAVID ASKS A GIFT OF THE WEALTHY NABAL AND IS REFUSED (vers. 1— 13). Ver. 1.—**David arose.** This is not to be connected with the death of Samuel, as though David had now lost a protector. But as he had fully 600 men with him, and his force was continually increasing, it was necessary for him to roam over a wide extent of country in order to obtain supplies of food. **The wilderness of Paran.** Paran strictly is a place in the southernmost part of the peninsula of Arabia, a little to the west of Mount Sinai ; but there can be little doubt that it gave its name to the vast extent of pasture and barren land now known as the desert of El-Tih (see 1 Kings xi. 18). Of this the wildernesses of Judah and Beer-sheba would virtually form parts without the borders being strictly defined. We need not therefore read " the wilderness of Maon," with the Septuagint and many comment-ators. On the contrary, we have seen that **the hold** in ch. xxiv. 22 was the hill Hachilah in that neighbourhood, and David now moved southward towards the edge of this vast wilderness.

Ver. 2.—**A man in Maon.** Though strictly by descent belonging to Maon (for which see on ch. xxiii. 24), his **possessions**—rather, " his business," " occupation " (see Gen. xlvii. 3, and Eccles. iv. 3, where it is translated *work*)—**were in Carmel**, the small town just north of Maon, where Saul set up a trophy at the end of the Amalekite war (ch. xv. 12), and to which Abigail belonged (ch. xxvii. 3). He is described as **very great** because of his wealth arising from his large flocks of sheep and goats, which fed upon the pasture land which forms the elevated plateau of Carmel, where **he was shearing his sheep**, usually a time of lavish hospitality (2 Sam. xiii. 23, 24).

Ver. 3.—**Nabal**, the word rendered *fool* in Ps. xiv. 1 ; literally, " flat," " vapid." **Abi-gail** means " one who is the cause (father) of joy," *i. e.* one who gives joy. She, with her bright understanding and beautiful per-son (the Hebrew word takes in much more than the **countenance**; see ch. xvi. 18, where it is rendered *comely person*), is in contrast with the coarse, churlish man who was her husband. His name was either one which he had acquired by his conduct, or if given him by his parents shows that they were clownish people. **He was of the house of Caleb.** The written text has, " he was according to his heart," *celibbo*, i. e. a self-willed man, or one whose rude exterior answered to his inner nature ; but there are linguistic diffi-

culties in the way of this reading, and the Kri is probably right in correcting *calibbi*, a Calebite, a descendant of Caleb, who had large possessions assigned him in the neigh-bourhood of Hebron (Josh. xv. 13—19), which is only ten miles north-west of Car-mel. The versions support the Kri, though the Syriac and Septuagint render *doglike*—one who, like a dog, though he has plenty, yet grudges others. The meaning of the name Caleb is literally " a dog."

Vers. 4, 5.—Though David had gone some distance southward of Carmel, yet it was worth his while to send men to Nabal's sheep-shearing, as the maintenance of his numerous force must have been a continual difficulty. The large number, **ten**, also shows that he expected a liberal gift of food. Pro-bably such missions were not uncommon, and the large sheep-masters were glad to supply the wants of one who guarded their flocks and defended them from the incur-sions of the desert tribes.

Vers. 6—8.—**Say to him that liveth in prosperity.** The Hebrew is obscure, but the rendering of the A. V. is untenable, and also very tame. Literally it is, " Ye shall say to him, For life ! " Probably it was a colloquial form of greeting, and equivalent to " good luck," " success," *life* in Hebrew being sometimes used for prosperity. So Luther translates it, and Rashi and the Babylonian Talmud are also in its favour. The reading of the Vulgate, " To thy bro-thers " (be peace), is to be altogether rejected. **We hurt them not.** Literally, " we caused them no shame" (see Judges xviii. 7), we did nothing to vex and injure them. Really the words mean that David had protected them, and enabled them to feed their flocks in safety. The fact that David waited till the sheep-shearing, when hospitality was the rule, proves that he did not levy black-mail upon his countrymen, though necessarily he must have depended upon them for the food indispensable for the support of his men. **A good day.** *I. e.* a festive day, which should bring us a share in thy prosperity. **Thy son David.** A title expressive of the reverence due from the youthful David to his senior, and an acknowledgment of Nabal's superiority over his fugitive neighbour.

Ver. 9.—**They . . . ceased.** Literally, " they rested ; " *i. e.* either they remained quiet awaiting Nabal's answer, or sat down, as is the custom in the East, for the same purpose.

Vers. 10, 11.—**There be many servants,** &c. Nabal would scarcely have ventured to speak in so insulting a manner if David had been at Maon, but as he had moved with his men a long distance towards the south, he gave free vent to his rude feelings without restraint. David was to him a **mere slave** who had run away from his master, Saul. **My bread, . . . my water.** These are the necessaries of life, while the flesh was the special luxury provided for the festival. David's ten young men would not literally carry water to him at so great a distance, nor did Nabal mean more than our phrase "meat and drink." The use, nevertheless, of *water* as equivalent to *drink* marks the value of water in the hill country, and also the abstemious habits of the people.

Vers. 12, 13.—**Gird ye on,** &c. David's determination was fierce and violent. No doubt Nabal's insult irritated him, and possibly also the rude outlaws round him would have protested against any other course ; but Nabal's words, rude though they were, would not justify David in the rough vengeance which he meditated. Abigail throughout her speech argues that David was taking too violent a course, and one for which he would afterwards have been sorry.

ABIGAIL PACIFIES DAVID (vers. 14—35). Vers. 14—17. — **One of the young men.** Hebrew, "a lad of the lads," *i. e.* one of the servants (see on the word ch. i. 24) ; when used in this sense it has no reference to age (see ch. ii. 17). This man was probably some old and confidential servitor. **To salute.** Hebrew, "to bless" (see ch. xiii. 10 ; 2 Kings iv. 29). **He railed on them.** Literally, "flew upon them like a bird of prey." **We were not hurt.** Literally, "not put to shame" (see on ver. 7). The language of a people always bears witness to their character, and it is a mark of the high spirit of the Israelites that they thought less of the loss than of the disgrace of an injury. **As long as we were conversant with them.** Hebrew, "as long as we went about with them." **In the fields.** Really, "in the field," the wilderness, the common pasture land. **A wall.** *I. e.* a sure protection both against wild beasts and Amalekite and other plunderers. **A son of Belial.** A worthless, bad man (see on ch. i. 16), so coarse and violent that it is hopeless to expostulate with him.

Vers. 18—20.—**Five measures of parched corn.** The measure named here, the seah, contains about a peck and a half. As this seems little, Ewald reads 500 seahs, but probably it was regarded as a delicacy. **Clusters of raisins.** Rather, as in the margin, lumps of raisins. The bunches of grapes when dried were pressed into cakes. Sending her servants in front leading the asses which carried the present, she followed behind, and met David as she was coming down **by the covert of the hill.** Hebrew, "in secret of the hill," under cover of the hill, *i. e.* she met him as she was descending into some glen into which he had entered from the other end.

Vers. 21, 22.—David justifies his fierce anger by referring to the services he had rendered Nabal, and which had been requited so shabbily. For the phrase **so do God unto the enemies of David** see on ch. xx. 16. A superstitious feeling probably lay at the root of this substitution of David's enemies for himself when thus invoking a curse.

Vers. 23—25.—**Abigail . . . fell before David on her face.** This very abject obeisance may have been grounded on her belief in David's future kingship, or it may simply mark the inferior position held by women in those days (see ver. 41). Her whole address is couched in very humble terms. David (ch. xxiv. 8) only stooped with his face to the ground before Saul. **Upon me.** Abigail represents herself as the person really guilty, on whom the **iniquity,** *i. e.* the punishment of the offence, must fall. Nabal is a mere **son of Belial,** a worthless, bad man, whose name Nabal, *i. e.* fool, is a sign that folly is with him, and accompanies all his acts. As a fool he is scarcely accountable for his doings, and Abigail, whose wont and business it was to set things to rights, **saw not the young men,** and so was unable to save them from her husband's rudeness.

Vers. 26, 27.—Abigail begins her appeal by affirming that it was Jehovah who thus made her come to prevent bloodshed ; she next propitiates David with the prayer that his enemies may be as Nabal, insignificant fools ; and finally asks him to accept her present, not for himself,—that would be too great an honour,—but as good enough only for his followers. The first of these affirmations is obscured by the rendering in the A. V., and should be translated, "And now, my lord (an ordinary title of respect, like our *sir*), as Jehovah liveth, and as thy soul liveth, so true is it that Jehovah hath withholden thee from blood-guiltiness, and from saving thyself with thine own hand ; and now let thine enemies," &c. The same words recur in vers. 31, 33. **Blessing.** *I. e.* gift, present (see ch. xxx. 26). This beautiful term shows the deep religiousness of the Hebrew mind. The gift is something that comes not from the donor, but from God, in answer to the donor's prayer.

Ver. 28.—**Forgive the trespass of thine handmaid.** Reverting to her words in ver. 24, that the blame and punishment must rest on her, she now prays for forgiveness ; but the intermediate words in ver. 26, emphasised in ver. 31, have raised her request to a higher level. Her prayer rests on the ground that she was saving David from a sin, and that in his thirst for vengeance he was bringing upon himself guilt. If the form of Abigail's address was most humble, the matter of it was brave and noble. **A sure house.** *I. e.* permanent prosperity (see on ch. ii. 35). **Because my lord fighteth.** Hebrew, "will fight." David was not fighting these battles now because he was not yet enthroned as the theocratic king. It was Saul's business at present to fight "Jehovah's battles," either in person or by his officers (ch. xviii. 17). The words, therefore, distinctly look forward to the time when David as king will have the duty imposed upon him of protecting Jehovah's covenant people. **Evil hath not been found in thee.** Hebrew, "shall not be found in thee," *i. e.* when the time comes for thee to take the kingdom no one shall be able to allege against thee any offence by which thou hast lost thy title to the kingly office ; nor afterwards as king shalt thou be guilty of any breach of thy duty to Jehovah, Israel's supreme Ruler, so as to incur rejection as Saul has done.

Vers. 29—31.—**Yet a man is risen.** Rather, "And should any one arise to pursue thee," &c. The reference is of course to Saul, but put with due reserve, and also made general, so as to include all possible injury attempted against David. **Bound in the bundle of life.** Hebrew, "of the living." The metaphor is taken from the habit of packing up in a bundle articles of great value or of indispensable use, so that the owner may carry them about his person. In India the phrase is common ; thus, a just judge is said to be bound up in the bundle of righteousness ; a lover in the bundle of love. Abigail prays, therefore, that David may, with others whose life is precious in God's sight, be securely kept under Jehovah's personal care and protection. In modern times the two words signifying "in the bundle of the living" form a common inscription on Jewish gravestones, the phrase having been interpreted in the Talmud, as also by Abravanel and other Jewish authorities, of a future life. **Shall he sling out,** &c. In forcible contrast with this careful preservation of David's life, she prays that his enemies may be cast away as violently and to as great a distance as a stone is cast out of a sling. The **middle** is the hollow in which the stone was placed. **Ruler.** *I. e.* prince. It is the word rendered *captain* in ch. ix. 16 ; x. 1, but its meaning is more correctly given here. **Grief.** The word really means much the same as stumbling-block, something which makes a person stagger by his striking against it unawares. Abigail prays, therefore, that when David has become prince, and so has to administer justice, this violent and revengeful act which he was purposing might not prove a cause of stumbling and an offence of heart to himself, by his conscience reproaching him for having himself done that which he had to condemn in others.

Vers. 32—35. — David, in his thankful acknowledgment of Abigail's remonstrance, sees in it the hand of **Jehovah the God of Israel,** who had **sent** her, *i. e.* stirred her up to come. He commends also her **advice,** literally, her "taste," *i. e.* wisdom, discretion. It is the word rendered *behaviour* in ch. xxi. 13. But for this prudent conduct on her part in thus coming to meet him on the way, he solemnly assures her on oath that nothing could have saved Nabal and every male in his household from death. Finally, he accepts her present and dismisses her with the assurance that all was forgiven.

DEATH OF NABAL AND MARRIAGE OF DAVID AND ABIGAIL (vers. 36—42). Vers. 36—38.—**For he was very drunken.** Hebrew, "and he was very drunken." This was not the cause of his heart being merry, but the result ; he gave himself up to enjoyment till he became drunken, and then his merriment was over. When Abigail came back he was stupefied by drink, and it was not until the next day, when his debauch was passing off, that he was capable of being told what his wife had done. And when Abigail recounted to him David's fierce resolve, and how she had pacified him, he seems to have given way. to a fit of violent indignation, flying out possibly at her as he had at David's messengers (ver. 14), the result of which was an attack of apoplexy, and after lying in a state of insensibility for ten days, he died.

Vers. 39—42.—**Hath pleaded the cause of my reproach.** In the causes tried at the gate of an Israelite city the friends of the accused both pleaded his cause, defended him from wrong, and punished any who had wronged him. So God had avenged David, while preventing him by Abigail's interference from avenging himself (see ch. xxiv. 13). As a widow's legal mourning seems to have lasted only seven days, David, on hearing of Nabal's death, sent messengers to Abigail at Carmel to ask her in marriage. He was probably moved to this not merely by her sensible conduct, but also by the news that Michal had been given to another. She expresses her willingness in true Oriental fashion by saying she was ready to perform the most abject menial duties, even for his servants, and at once with five maidens proceeds to join him. It is a proof that David considered himself practically secure against Saul's attempts that he thus married and allowed women to accompany his small force, as their presence would not only impede the rapidity of his movements, but also implies a certain amount of ease and comfort for their maintenance.

ADDITIONAL PARTICULARS RESPECTING DAVID'S MARRIED LIFE (vers. 43, 44). Vers. 43, 44.—Besides Abigail, David also took to wife **Ahinoam of Jezreel,** a small village among the hills of Judah (Josh. xv. 56), and not the better known town of that name in the tribe of Issachar. Ahinoam was the name also of Saul's wife (ch. xiv. 50). **They were also . . . his wives.** *I. e.* besides Michal. She had been given by Saul to **Phalti the son of Laish,** called Phaltiel in

2 Sam. iii. 15, where we read of his lamentation at her being torn from him by Ishbosheth in order that she might be restored to David. **Gallim** is described in Isa. x. 30 as being situated between Gibeah of Saul and Jerusalem.

HOMILETICS.

Vers. 1—12.—*Honour to the dead and insult to the living.* The facts are 1. Samuel dies, and is buried at Ramah amidst the sorrow of Israel. 2. David, returning to the wilderness, sends a greeting to Nabal, a wealthy man at Carmel, and asks for some favour to his young men on account of the friendly aid recently rendered to Nabal's shepherds. 3. Nabal, in a churlish spirit, sends an insulting reply, and refuses the request. 4. Whereupon David resolves on taking revenge for the insult. The allusion here to the death of Samuel, while a necessary part of the history of the age, seems to be introduced to prepare the way for the continuance of the narrative concerning David, who now has become the principal figure in the national life. We have to consider the teaching of the *good man's death and the churlish man's insult.*

Honour to the dead. The various points brought out in the brief reference are, the brevity of the notice compared with the length of service, the ground of the public homage, the loss and gain to Israel, the extent of influence revealed, and the temporary subsidence of party conflicts. Formulating the truths thus suggested, we see—

I. That THE SCANTY REFERENCE IN THE BIBLE TO THE PERSONAL WORK AND DEATH OF GOD'S BEST SERVANTS is in instructive CONTRAST WITH THE RECORDS CONCERNING CHRIST. Samuel's life was long and immensely useful to the world by the reformation wrought in Israel by the force of his character, and the preparation made for prophetic teaching and stable government. A holier and more devoted man was not found, and yet one verse tells us all about his death and burial. The same reticence is true concerning Abraham, Moses, Isaiah, and indeed all the most distinguished of men. They during life spoke little of themselves, and referred little to their ancestors. The apostles also live, labour, and die, and no stress is laid on their work and death, a circumstance in keeping with the self-abnegation which never made themselves prominent objects of faith. The contrast with Christ is impressive. He is all and everything. His self-reference is perfect egotism if he be a mere human being ordained only in higher degree than others to execute a Divine purpose. The exaltation of his name, work, and death by the apostles is most natural and harmonious with the silence of the Bible in relation to all others if he be really Divine. The question of his personality cannot be settled by mere verbal discussions. Broad facts must be considered, and these clearly determine the verbal sense where exegetes may be supposed to differ. This kind of argument appeals to the common sense of men, and accords also with the instinct of the Christian heart to worship Christ.

II. That THE HONOUR PAID TO THE DEAD, so far as referred to in Scripture, is THAT DUE TO HOLY CHARACTER AND SERVICE. The allusion here and elsewhere to a proper homage to the dead is clearly associated with the holy life and conduct previously recorded in the sacred narrative. There is a singular silence in the Bible with respect to any honours paid to men, on account of the greatness supposed to consist in warlike exploits. True greatness lies in good abilities being pervaded by a spirit of piety, and consequently consecrated to the advancement of the kingdom of God on earth. The value of a man's life is to be sought in the contribution he makes to the spiritual impulse by which the world is brought nearer to God. The supreme honours often paid to mere titular rank, to wealth, to military prowess, and even to bare learning, are expressive of a human judgment which is discounted by the language of the Bible, and will be reversed when, adjudged by the lofty standard of Christ, every man shall receive according to the deeds done in the body.

III. That THE DEATH OF TRULY GOOD MEN is both a LOSS AND A GAIN TO THE WORLD. Israel properly mourned because the "godly man" failed, for the activity and personal influence of the greatest man of the age henceforth would cease. We cannot say whether a good man's activity of spirit no longer operates as a power on men after his death—probably it does if there be any truth in the conservation and persistence of spiritual forces; but so far as survivors are concerned they are unconscious of it, and, on the other hand, are henceforth more open to the action of other visible influences. We lose much when good men die; yet we gain something. The whole life becomes more impressive in death than during its continuance. The germinal good sown in the heart by silent goodness and actual effort is quickened around the grave into healthy growth. The sobering, elevating influence of a sainted memory is a permanent treasure. Many have to bless God for the death of his saints. Heaven becomes more real to those whose beloved ones have gone before, and the levities of life are subdued by the thought of our temporary separation from the "general assembly."

IV. That THE REALITY AND EXTENT OF A GOOD MAN'S INFLUENCE OVER OTHERS IS BROUGHT OUT IN DEATH MORE THAN IN LIFE. The public homage paid to Samuel was the nation's response to his life's appeal to the heart and conscience. Like Elijah, he no doubt often deplored the degeneracy of the age, and questioned whether he was doing any substantial good. This doubt is the common experience of all God's servants. They cannot see the incidence of the rays of light as they silently fall on the dull heart of the people, though in theory they know that every ray performs its part in the great spiritual economy of the universe. But the subjects of holy influence do receive in some degree all that comes forth from a consecrated life, and it often requires the removal of a good man from this world to make manifest how strong a hold he has had on the thought and feeling of others. There are many instances of this in all grades of society. Churches and families reveal the power of a character when that character ceases to exercise its wonted energies. This should induce calmness and confidence in all who strive to bless the world by a devoted life. Those who exercise moral power are not always the best judges of its force and extent. God mercifully keeps from our view some of the good we are doing, lest we fall into the snare of the devil.

V. That MAN'S CONSCIOUSNESS OF THE SACREDNESS AND MYSTERY OF HUMAN EXISTENCE, when aroused, is SUPREME OVER EVERY THOUGHT AND FEELING. All Israel, embracing Saul, David, the prophets, and the slanderers and conspirators at the court, assembled around the grave of Samuel and wept. The strifes and rivalries of parties, the deadly feuds and cruel animosities of life, the most urgent of human passions, were for the time set aside under the influence of that deep, all-mastering feeling that human existence on earth is a sacred mystery. The holiest and most honoured are seen to succumb to the strong hand which carries off the most worthless. Each asks, Is this the end? Is there nothing beyond? If there is, what? Thus it is man's reflectiveness, awakened by the death of the great, which causes him to recognise at the same time both his littleness and his greatness. The solemnity of having a rational existence comes on all in presence of death. That we are made for something far above what now engages our attention is forced on the spirit, and our connection with an invisible sphere and final tribunal rises into awful distinctness. This frequently-recurring sense of the sacredness and mystery of existence is a check on sinful tendencies, and furnishes occasions for the application of the gospel to the hearts of men. Gospel truth learnt in early years will often assert its power in men as, leaving awhile the contentions and sins of life, they stand by the open grave.

Insult to the living. The question arises, Why is it that this narrative of Nabal's churlishness occupies so prominent a place in the sacred records, seeing that so adventurous a life as that of David must have abounded in striking incident? Among, then, the topics suggested by the account of the churlish man's insult we may notice—

I. THE PRINCIPLE ON WHICH EVENTS ARE RECORDED IN SCRIPTURE. Is this principle ascertainable? Can any hypothesis concerning it be verified by an induction of facts? Granting an affirmative reply to these questions, do we here get a harmony of Scripture superior to that of literal agreement in details? Now, in dealing with such questions we have to be guided by a few broad facts, such as, the order of Providence among men is subservient to the working out of the redemptive purpose in Christ; the redemptive purpose is wrought out through the instrumentality of chosen servants, succeeding one another by Divine arrangement; events touching the lives of these men affected the performance of their part in the accomplishing of the purpose, in so far as they developed character or brought the great principles for which they lived into conflict with opposing principles; the Bible is designed to be a record of the events which advanced the unfolding of the redemptive purpose, either directly, or by indirectly shaping the character and conduct of those engaged in its outworking, and forcing the Divine idea into sharp contrast with various forms of evil. The attempt to find the principle of selection of facts for incorporation in God's record of the history of redemption in any other direction must fail. The great thought of this Book of Samuel is the conflict of the Messianic hope with opposing evils. Hence all through the life of David we see that the "salvation of the Lord," *i. e.* the great spiritual reformation to be wrought as a prelude to a future and more blessed one, was the issue at stake; and those events are evidently related which helped it on, and such as were opposed to it. Principles are embodied in each of these instances, and thus the relation of events to the unfolding purpose of God is that quality in them which accounts for their insertion in the Scriptures. The verification of this is an interesting study. It may suffice here to note that when we consider the great influence on the life of David of such a woman as Abigail, and therefore on his work for the world, we can see the propriety of some account of her in relation to him, and we shall see directly how completely Nabal's churlishness was an illustration of the grovelling spirit which scorns such lofty spiritual aspirations as are involved in working out the Divine purpose for mankind.

II. The causes and cure of domestic infelicity. The home life of Nabal was evidently not happy, arising partly from utter diversity of taste, temperament, and culture, and partly from dissimilarity of moral conduct and religious principle. A low, grovelling disposition, revelling in sensual indulgence and proud of wealth, could not but embitter the life of a "woman of good understanding," and of such fine spiritual perceptions as are indicated by her words to David (vers. 27—31). There are unfortunately many such homes. Wise and holy women are held to the humiliation and sorrow of a lifelong bondage. In modern times the causes of domestic infelicity are various—fashion, that considers station before happiness; love of wealth, that lays beauty, sweetness, and culture at the feet of mammon; inconsiderate haste, acting on partial knowledge of character; concern for a livelihood irrespective of moral qualities; incompatible religious sentiments; selfishness on the one side, seeking inordinate attention, and neglect on the other, heedless of the sacred bond. In many cases the release is only in death, so utter is the desolation. So far as Abigail was concerned, her discretion and self-command mitigated the evils of her home; but the radical remedy is a renewal of the spirit, a turning of the life to God.

III. The obligations of wealth. That every talent imposes on its possessor corresponding obligation is a first principle of morals and religion. No man holds material wealth for himself. He is a member of society, and bound to exercise his gifts for the welfare of others. The common responsibilities attached to wealth therefore devolved on Nabal, and no narrow, private views or acquired greed of gain could release him from the laws of God, however irksome they might make obedience to it. But there were special reasons why he was bound to allow David to share in his plenty; for was he not known to be a man persecuted for righteousness' sake, of the same tribe as Nabal, admitted by the popular voice to have been a benefactor by his prowess on behalf of the nation, the guardian, by means of his men, of Nabal's servants in a recent season of peril, and regarded in Nabal's house (vers. 27—31) and elsewhere as the coming king, well fitted by his qualities to raise the spiritual and social condition of the people? The modest request of David was just, and the duty of the rich man was clear. The question of the obligations attaching to the possession of wealth needs to be pressed home with earnestness and elucidated with intelligence. The "love of money" is so strong in some as to blind the intellect and harden the heart against a recognition of the proper uses of it. No fixed standard can be set up for the distribution of wealth, for the duties of giving and spending are relative to position and surroundings. The first thing to recognise is that wealth is not for self-indulgence or aggrandisement, but for the enrichment of all around. The next is the cultivation of a kindly, generous spirit that looks tenderly on the more needy, combined with a sound judgment as to the best means of enabling many to enjoy the distribution of wealth as the recompense of labour and skill. Above all, every man should, in a spirit of love and gratitude, lay all on the altar of God, and see to it that a good proportion be devoted to the cause of Christ. None have ever regretted consecrating wealth to God. But that is not consecration to God which appropriates to religious uses when dependent ones are lacking means of support (Mark vii. 11). It would work a revolution in the social condition of our country, and that of the mildest and most beneficent kind, as well as give an immense impulse to the cause of religion, did men of wealth but conscientiously estimate their obligations to God and man, and act accordingly.

IV. CONTEMPT FOR SPIRITUAL ASPIRATIONS. "Who is David? and who is the son of Jesse? there be many servants now-a-days that break away from their masters." Thus did Nabal, knowing well who David was, what course he had pursued, what trials had befallen him, and what high spiritual anticipations were associated with his chequered life, express his contempt for the coming king and his supposed mission in Israel. This was clearly the case of a rich man, fond of sensual indulgence, boastful of his possessions, indifferent to the culture, moral elevation, and spiritual prosperity of his countrymen, and looking with scorn on the men who long for a higher form of life in which purity, knowledge, and joy in God are prominent features. He wanted to have nothing to do with "theorists," "fanatics," and men of that type. The country was well enough, and the son of Jesse was not wanted. The insult to the living was insult to man. Men are often only the exponents of principles that survive when they are gone. Samuel during his early labours was the energetic exponent of the spiritual idea of God's kingdom as against the grovelling conceptions of Israel's function entertained by the degenerate nation. Later David became its chosen representative, and in this his anointing as a more worthy man than Saul had its significance. Those who, like Jonathan, Gad, and Abiathar, identified themselves with David became a party in the State devoted to the assertion of the higher hope, while the men who prompted Saul to evil, the Ziphites, and now Nabal, were the supporters of the low, earthly ideal of Israel's life. Their antagonism to David was, therefore, deeper than at first appears; it was based on lack of sympathy with, and in fact positive dislike of, the spiritual aspirations cherished by David, and which he in the providence of God was destined largely to enunciate and realise. What is meant by "*such as love thy salvation*"? (Ps. xl. 16). Evidently those who are yearning for that great deliverance from evil which God was then working out for Israel—typical of the wider deliverance which the true King of Zion is now working out for men. And as men like Nabal despised the holy aspirations of David, so do the same men now despise the aspirations of those who think not their work done till spiritual religion is universal. The Saviour heard men say, "Is not this the carpenter's son?" The pure and lofty aspirations of his life met with the reverse of a response in grovelling minds. Men do not object to a religion, but they do dislike a holy religion.

Practical lessons:—1. Let it be our effort so to live that men may remember us with feelings of loving interest. 2. The tone of our daily life may often be raised, and a shield against temptation may be found, by occasionally communing in spirit with the honoured dead whom we have known. 3. In all arrangements for life we should allow moral and religious considerations to have chief influence. 4. Conscientious regard for the teaching of God's word in reference to wealth, and special prayer for guidance in its use, cannot but make it a blessing to the possessor and to others. 5. It requires careful thought to trace out the connection between growing riches and distaste for spiritual religion (Mark x. 23—27).

Vers. 13—17.—*Creed and practice.* The facts are—1. David, stung by the insult, prepares to take summary vengeance on Nabal. 2. A servant, overhearing his intention, reports it to Abigail. 3. He also relates to her the circumstances of David's kindness to Nabal's men, and appeals to her for intervention, as he has no faith in Nabal's wisdom or generosity. The course taken by David would ordinarily be termed natural for an Eastern chieftain; that of the servant was more considerate than usually is found among men of his class when placed in personal peril.   Regarding the two causes separately, we may express the teaching thus :—

I. THERE IS AT TIMES A SAD DISPROPORTION BETWEEN THE BELIEFS AND THE PRACTICE OF EVEN THE BEST OF MEN.   David was undoubtedly the most spiritually enlightened, patient, and devout man then living.   The psalms of the period indicate a wonderful faith in the care and goodness of God, and his recent conduct had illustrated his patience, generosity, and forbearance.   The elevated tone of his language to Saul (ch. xxiv. 11—15), in which he commits his personal wrongs to God, is worthy of New Testament times.   The common faith of his life could not but have been strengthened by the solemnities of the funeral from which he had lately returned.   Nevertheless David could not bear an insult and ingratitude, but must in unholy zeal cease to trust his cause to God, and avenge evil with his own hand.   Sons of Zebedee live in every age, who cannot wait the calm purpose of God to vindicate his saints, while at the same time professing to be of a spirit born of heaven, and akin to that of him "who when he was reviled, reviled not again."   This falling below our ideal is a too common calamity in individual and Church life.   The question may rise whether we really believe what we say we do when conduct does not harmonise therewith, for is not real faith influential?   The great verities of our Christian Scriptures, respecting Christ's love, our destiny, the world's spiritual need, and the unspeakable importance of eternal things, are enough to enchain every soul to holy consecration that knows no reserve.   It is well that we estimate the disparity between creed and conduct; the dishonour it brings, the harm to religion it entails, and the effect of it on our prayers (James v. 16).

II. OUR STANDARD OF CONDUCT IS TO BE TAKEN NOT FROM GOOD MEN, but from the EXPLICIT TEACHING OF SCRIPTURE AND THE EXAMPLE OF CHRIST.   As we read the books of men with reserve, and accept only that which accords with a standard of truth apart from them, so our reading of the conduct of saints is to be discriminating.   They are often illustrious examples of good, but not our models.   Our conduct under analogous circumstances is not to be regulated by that of David, but by the teaching which tells us not to "avenge" ourselves, but to return good for evil, and even love our enemies.   If men ask what this *non*-personal retaliation means, the answer is, *the life of Christ*.   That it is alien to human tendencies and often regarded as unmanly does not make it less Christian.   Very few persons "enter into the kingdom of God" in the sense of behaving in the world as Christ did.   Even Christian men sometimes speak as though it were madness to display just the spirit of meekness, love, and compassion which marked his career under provocation.   Who dare say in the truest sense, "We have the mind of Christ"?

III. DISCRIMINATION AND PROMPTITUDE ARE VALUABLE QUALITIES IN AVERTING EVILS INCIDENT TO HUMAN WRONG-DOING.   The evil consequences of one great sin on the part of a good man may be very serious, and, as in this case, calling for exceeding care if they are to be averted.   The conduct of the servant (vers. 14—17) is worthy of imitation in many departments of life.   He did not selfishly flee to secure himself, but, reading well the purpose of David, thought of the safety of all, formed a just estimate of Abigail's tact and courage, and of Nabal's stupidity, and without delay laid before his mistress the provocation offered to David.   A wise and prompt servant is a blessing in a home.   These qualities go far to render men successful in life ; and if more attention were paid in early years to the development of them, many an one would be saved from disaster, and the whole machinery of saints would move more smoothly.   May we not also see an analogy here to the case of a man who, foreseeing spiritual calamity to others, promptly devises means of delivering them from it?

Practical lessons :—1. We should be on the watch against sudden provocations of our unholy tendencies, and we shall find an habitually prayerful spirit one of the best aids to the immediate suppression of passion.   2. It is worth considering how much the Church and world have lost by failure on the part of Christians to live out the spirit and precepts of Christ.   3. It is a question whether sufficient attention is paid to the suppression of the love of fighting and taking of revenge in children, and how far literature and customs foster these evils.   4. In cases of moral conduct prompt action is always best.

Vers. 18—31.—*Wise persuasiveness*. The facts are—1. Abigail, aware of the danger, provides an ample present, and secretly sends on her servants to prepare the mind of David for an interview.   2. On seeing David she humbly seeks an audience, and intimates that Nabal was not to be regarded as of importance.   3. She pleads her cause by reminding David of the kind restraint of Providence in keeping him from wrong, of Nabal's utter unworthiness of his notice, of the provision made for the young men, of his own integrity and coming distinction, of his spiritual safety amidst trials, of the future satisfaction of not having causelessly shed blood, and then begs that she may not be forgotten in coming days of power.   This narrative may be considered in relation to Abigail and to David.   In the former it affords—

I. AN ILLUSTRATION OF THE ART OF PERSUASION.   The course pursued by Abigail was creditable to her courage, tact, piety, and loyalty to truth.   A more beautiful instance of the art of persuasion in the sphere of private life is not found in the Bible.   It may be considered in two ways.   1. *In relation to the method adopted*. This may be seen by noticing the line of argument.   David is, after a respectful act of obeisance, informed that the omission of which he complained was without the knowledge of the person who was largely responsible for acts of hospitality (ver. 25).   Then, with exquisite delicacy, he is reminded of the sin of avenging self, and of the goodness of God in restraining from it (ver. 26).   This appeal to the moral sense is strengthened by an assurance that the offending person was far beneath the notice of one so distinguished, and that dignity could well afford to let him alone (ver. 24).   Moreover, the occasion which properly roused his generous concern for hungry and deserving servants was passed, as ample provision was at hand for them (ver. 27).   Passing from others, David is assured of confidence in his Divine call and the integrity of his life, despite all slanders (ver. 28).   And though persecution is hard to be borne, yet he is reminded that full compensation is made in being securely kept by God, and thus blessed with the spiritual life embraced in the everlasting covenant (ver. 29)—a blessing which wicked foes cannot share.   To crown all, he is led to think of the not distant day when, as king of God's people, he will enjoy the highest honours ; and it is gently suggested that it would be a pity to mar the joys of such a time by reflection on an act of personal revenge by deeds of blood. A beautiful instance of what a wise, holy woman can do when emergency arises.   2. *In relation to the general principles involved*.   Persuasion is required in the pulpit, the home, and the common intercourse of life ; and observation proves how much depends on the adoption of right principles in using it.   Some never succeed.   The human soul can be successfully approached by certain avenues only.   To be successful there ought to be—(1) A tone and manner befitting the persons and the circumstances.   (2) A clear but delicate reference to the governing sense of right ; for conscience properly addressed is sure to become an internal advocate for us.   (3) A readiness to meet every lawful claim and satisfy every generous instinct ; for heed is given to those who are zealous in doing right.   (4) An evident appreciation of the actual position in which those are whom we address ; for confidence in our judgment and professed sympathy is then awakened.   (5) A gentle appeal to the most sacred religious hopes and aspirations which, though unexpressed, may exercise a controlling power over life.   (6) Regard to the principle of self-interest as a force in life supplementary to higher considerations.   It is worth a study to become "wise to win souls."

II. AN ILLUSTRATION OF THE INFLUENCE ON TEMPER AND CONDUCT OF RELIGIOUS CONSIDERATIONS.   There was power in Abigail's argument derived from her appeal to David's sense of the wrong of revenge, and the assurance that his generous concern for his young men was now unnecessary.   But that which evidently touched David most was her reference to his being the object of God's love and care.   To be restrained by a loving God, to be in favour with him amidst the wrongs of evil men, to have an interest in the higher spiritual life which is nourished and guarded by God was more than all beside.   How could one so richly and undeservedly blessed be revengeful or act in any way unworthy of the name of God ?   The apostle adopts the same line of argument when he, enjoining a spirit of forgiveness, reminds his readers of the forgiveness they have received (Ephes. v. 32).   If we would be humble, gentle, forgiving, and grateful, let us consider what it is to have our "names written in heaven" (Luke x. 20), and to be objects of a love from which nothing can separate us (Rom. viii. 38, 39). A judicious use of such reflections and considerations is extremely important in spiritual culture. Men are deeply touched by the thought of what God has done for them. A little religious retrospect would save many a man from yielding to violent impulses. The same result is secured by cherishing due regard to our lofty aspirations. Those who are to be raised to thrones will not do mean and wrongful deeds. Who can estimate the influence of Christian anticipations on present conduct?

III. An illustration of deepening faith in Messianic purposes. Men like Doeg, Cush, and the Ziphites might combine and by slander seek to destroy faith in David's integrity, and so seem to put back the realisation of the purposes for which he had been anointed; and the Psalms reveal how these things sometimes depressed his spirit. But all this time the more intelligent and devout saw clearly that he was the man to build up the kingdom, and Abigail, by this beautiful revelation of her confidence in his coming elevation to power, was only a revelation to him of advancing faith. The strength thus brought to his heart reminds us of the comfort evidently conveyed to the Saviour's heart by Peter's explicit avowal (Matt. xvi. 16, 17). And as time advances there will arise, as a cheering set-off to the scorners and detractors, superior minds bearing witness to the Divine truth and coming triumph of Christ's kingdom. Equally so will confirmations rise up of the call of the Christian to share in the higher service of the future.

General lessons:—1. A wise man will bring his impulses to the light of religious truth and allow it to tone them down. 2. In cases of difficulty, where temper is concerned, a quiet, fervent spirit is of great importance. 3. To have a place in the Lamb's book of life is full compensation for the ills we may suffer at the hands of men. 4. It is beneath the dignity of a Christian man to contend with the mean and base. 5. It is a sound maxim to suffer inconvenience rather than do anything that will tend to mar the enjoyment of the success we hope to win.

Vers. 32—35.—*Restraining mercy.* The facts are—1. David, recognising the hand of God, expresses his sense of his mercy and blesses Abigail for her advice. 2. He perceives, in the light of her remonstrance, the terrible evil of the passion that had swayed him. 3. Accepting her present, he dismisses her in peace. The success of Abigail's wise conduct was now assured in a good man being saved the guilt and shame of acting at variance with his professed trust in God; and while duly honouring the instrument of deliverance, God's restraining mercy is fully brought into prominence. Notice—

I. Restraining mercy is a fact in every life. This instance was conspicuous, but David elsewhere acknowledges the constant keeping of his God (Ps. xix. 13; cxli. 9). We owe much to God for what we are not and do not, as also for what we are and do. "By the grace of God I am what I am" applies to prevention as well as endowment. Every man is conscious of carrying within him a power of evil in excess of what finds outlet in deeds, and its repression is due not only to human wisdom and strength. The conditions of social life that check the development of inward sinfulness are of God as truly as the truth we cherish that we may not sin against him (Ps. cxix. 11). The friends who counsel and warn, the ordinances that tend to weaken the force of evil and nourish holiness, are the agencies of the same gracious God who endowed us with the helping conscience to which they appeal. If occasional providences, be they disasters or personal interventions, draw special attention to the unseen hand, they do not render the restraint at other times less real because they are more steady and gentle. There is a spirit that strives silently with man and holds him back from ruin.

II. Our recognition of restraining mercy is more pronounced when we have passed through unusual temptations. Temptations are common experience, but sometimes they come in "like a flood." The admission of God's kindly and constant restraint is an item of daily belief, attended with more or less gratitude; but when the soul has been brought face to face with a terrible sin by the force of violent impulses, and kept from committing it by what is called a narrow chance, then the good hand of God is distinctly recognised. In the lull of the storm we see clearly the rocks on which character well-nigh made shipwreck. The light of truth reveals whither we were going, and the soul is aghast at the spectacle. In the lives of most there have been occasions when we were on the very verge of destruction, or, like David, were about to mar our consistency and usefulness by a sad transgression. The refined spirit of a Christian shrinking in horror at the very thought of what might have been cannot but say, "Blessed be the Lord God;" and where human instruments have been employed, a benediction falls on them for their kindly aid. These acts of recognition, so full of gratitude and joy, are but faint indications of that inexpressible joy and gratitude when, in survey of all life's dangers, the soul will praise the "mercy that endureth for ever."

III. A PROPER RECOGNITION OF RESTRAINING MERCY IS ATTENDED WITH A CALM AND STEADY ATTENTION TO THE DUTIES OF OUR SPIRITUAL POSITION. David, as chosen servant of God, quietly accepts the gift of Abigail, and, dismissing her, reverts to the normal course of trusting in God and biding his time. He lived out his true character all the better for this narrow escape. It is the natural effect of mercy, when recognised, to render us more true to our holy calling in God's service. We go on our way with stronger determination to submit to his will, whatever it may bring, and to live in closer fellowship with him.

General lessons:—1. It is good to place our stormy passions in the clear light of God's truth. 2. Our spiritual life acquires more elevation and tone by occasionally reflecting on God's restraining mercy. 3. The sin of indulging in violent passions must not be overlooked in the deliverance from their overt expression. 4. From an experience of deliverance from fearful moral perils we may enlarge our knowledge of the possibilities of life, and find increased reasons for habitual watchfulness.

Vers. 36—44.—*Contrasts, patience, and domestic ties.* The facts are—1. Abigail, finding Nabal in the midst of a drunken revel, refrains from speaking of her inter-view with David. 2. In the morning, on her relating what had transpired, he became insensible, and soon after dies. 3. On hearing of his death David recognises afresh the mercy that had restrained him, and sees the wisdom of leaving judgment to the Lord. 4. David, deprived of his wife Michal, though possessed of Ahinoam, seeks to take Abigail to wife, and she, accepting his advances, consents. The sacred narrative is wonderfully effective in making David the central figure amidst the diversity of detail alluded to, and thus indicates the unity of principle on which it is framed, as well as foreshadows the higher presentation of Christ as the one figure, discernible by the eye of faith, amidst the varied teachings of Scripture. The manifold teaching of this section, while associated with David as the central figure, may be most conveniently represented under three heads. We have here—

I. CONTRASTS OF CHARACTER. Nabal may be regarded as an instance of a type of character well known in every age—low in taste, devoted to material gains, in-sensible to lofty spiritual aspirations, the miserable victim of disgusting habits, exercising a pernicious influence, and coming to an end dishonourable and ruinous. Grades of this character may be found, but the essential features of it are sensuality, irreverence, and earthliness. The chapter presents us with three characters agree-ing in a common contrast to this—Abigail's, David's, Samuel's. Each of these, in the sphere allotted by Providence, stands out as the very opposite of Nabal. That which formed the inspiring power in them was intelligent devotion to the higher interests of life and strong faith in the Divine purpose that was being worked out in Israel. The reference in ver. 1 to the honourable burial of Samuel, and in vers. 36—38 to the disgraceful end of Nabal, as well as the intermediate references to David and Abigail, show that the contrast of characters lies in *four* things—*spirit, aims, influence,* and *end.* All characters may be tested by these *criteria.* The *spirit* is either devout, reverent, trustful, and obedient, or grovelling, profane, alien to God. The *aim* in life is the creation of the spirit, and is either to promote individual and public righteousness in association with God's purpose in the Messiah, or to gather wealth and find transitory gratification. The *influence* is either to elevate, inspire, and enrich the world with what is best and enduring, or to drag down, embitter, and brutalise mankind. The *end,* as in the case of Samuel, is either peace, honour, and future blessedness, or wretchedness, dishonour, and future woe. In every age and locality where truth is loved and rejected these opposite tendencies and issues are found, and it would be instructive and impressive to develop with illustrations from history the gradations of contrast. The clue to contrasts in taste, habit, and final condition is to be sought in the state of the spirit in its relation to God. "The carnal mind is enmity against God." "You hath he quickened who were dead."

II. THE JUSTIFICATION OF PATIENCE. It is possible to take David's words (ver. 39) as expressing thanks for preservation from sin, and at the same time pleasure that his churlish enemy was now smitten; but the sense more congruous with the circumstances seems to be that he was, on reflection, more and more grateful for Divine restraint; and the fact that God had, without his agency, done what seemed to him best was evidence that man need never hasten to vindicate himself by violent measures, but may be patient under wrong. He was glad that God, and not he, had vindicated right. Events in the course of Providence will justify abstention from evil even under strong provocation. Many a man, patiently repressing violent passions, and content to endure rather than savagely avenge wrong, has lived to see the day when God, in some unlooked-for way, has visited the wrong-doer with chastisement, and then, while thankful for restraint, he is able to see in the Divine conduct a justification of the patience once so hard to exercise, and that seemed to men of the world so inexpedient and weak. And here comes out the great truth that the meek and quiet virtues enjoined by Christ are always justified by Providence, though at the time they are exercised they seem to be contrary to human nature. This is but a branch of a still wider truth, that all holiness of feeling and conduct is in the issue coincident with self-interest. Utility may not be the basis of morality, but in its broadest sense, taking in endless existence and future relations, it is exemplified in the effects. A few observations may suffice on this subject. 1. *It often requires much effort to be truly virtuous.* David felt it harder to abstain from avenging wrong than to avenge it. The positive side of his virtue was patient trust in the justice of God, and the impulses of the old man are against this. Very often personal losses and social disadvantages attend our patient endurance of evil, and these set into operation our strong feelings of resentment, our estimate of profit and loss, and our professed love of right. 2. *All such virtue has the promise of success.* To trust in God, to be patient in tribulation, and kindred qualities are pregnant with victory. Right feeling and conduct *per se* have a tendency, as Butler has shown, to ultimate happiness; and the ordinations of Providence are all subordinate to the vindication of right. 3. *Personal and general history show that patient trust in God's justice is honoured.* Martyrs have found it better to leave their cause to God. The results of their endurance are perpetual, and most blessed and powerful. Every Christian can see in his own life that God does not forsake his saints, but turns their patient trust to his honour and glory, and the higher education of the individual and the race. Events will justify religious feeling in any form. It answers in every way to be like Christ.

III. THE DOMESTIC FACTOR IN LIFE. The details concerning Nabal are given because of David's place in the history of redemption, and for the same reason we have an account of David's domestic relationships. It is well known that the domestic tie is of extreme importance in every life. Men are helped or hindered, blessed or cursed, by the kind of influence that sways the home. Considering how much the general character is affected by the development of the tender and pure feelings proper to home life, the loss to the world arising from domestic miseries is incalculable. What a change in society were our toilers blessed in the person of their wives with the love, the refinement of feeling, and the intelligent Christianity which knows how to make home a welcome, cheery place! Men like Nabal would be much worse were it not for the restraining influence of an Abigail. David's public and private career was necessarily the better for the presence in his home of such a woman, though the elevating influence of her character was impaired by his adoption of polygamy. Many are the counteracting influences under which the best of men develope, and Scripture, by thus calling attention to David's domestic affairs, gives us a clue to some of the circumstances amidst which his virtues and failings appeared. The extreme importance of the domestic factor in life should urge to care in contracting alliances, in the maintenance of a spirit at home in harmony with the sacred character of the marriage bond, and in rendering home life subservient to a faithful and efficient discharge of one's calling in life (Ephes. v. 22—33; 1 Pet. iii. 1—7). The question of marriage is a delicate one, and needs to be handled with great care, but it is doubtful whether the Church has in her pastors and teachers done as much for the education of the people on the subject as is required. A wise pastor will know how to incorporate earnest Scripture teaching with his ordinary ministrations without intruding into the privacies of life, and wise parents have it in their power to save their sons and daughters from many troubles by first winning confidence, and then judiciously aiding to right decisions.

General lessons :—1. In order to form a correct estimate of a life we must take into account the end, and the bearing of the principles cherished on the endless existence beyond the grave. 2. The practical exhibition of the Christian spirit in our dealings with bad men is often more difficult than the maintenance of a devout spirit in relation to God. 3. The cure for some of the ills of modern life is in making home more attractive to those now seeking unhallowed joys elsewhere. 4. A nation careful of the purity and fulness of domestic life will survive those making light of these qualities.

HOMILIES BY VARIOUS AUTHORS.

Ver. 1. (RAMAH.)—*Samuel's death and burial.* "And Samuel died." 1. The end of the great prophet's life is recorded in brief and simple words. This is according to the manner in which the death of men is usually spoken of in the Scriptures. Whilst their life is narrated at length, their death is either passed over in silence or mentioned only in a sentence, as of comparatively little consequence in relation to their character, work, and influence. There is one significant exception, viz., that of him " who once suffered for sins, the just for the unjust, that he might bring us to God." 2. In the last glimpse afforded of him *before his decease* he is described as " standing as one appointed over the company of the prophets," and occupied with them in celebrating the praises of God (ch. xix. 20). During the years that had since elapsed he was left unmolested by Saul; and it is hardly likely that David ever ventured to Ramah again, although he probably kept up indirect intercourse with his aged and revered friend (ch. xxii. 5), and was often in his thoughts. 3. In *connection with* the mention of his death it is stated that " David arose and went down " (from " the hold " in the hill of Hachilah, to which he had returned from Engedi) " to the wilderness of Paran." He may have done so for reasons independent of this event, or without the knowledge of it; or possibly because he feared that with the removal of Samuel's restraining influence Saul might renew his persecution. However it may have been, the melancholy intelligence would speedily reach him. 4. " Samuel died." Good and great as he was, he could not escape the common lot of men. " One event happeneth to them all." But that which comes as a judgment to " the fool " (ver. 38) comes as a blessing to the wise. " Precious in the sight of the Lord is the death of his saints." The news of it came upon the people as a surprise and filled them with grief. " It was as if from that noble star, so long as it shone in the heaven of the holy land, though veiled by clouds, there streamed a mild beneficent light over all Israel. Now this star in Israel was extinguished " (Krummacher). " Another mighty one had passed away. The very heart of the nation sighed out its loving, weeping requiem. But who among them all mourned as that son of Jesse, on whose head he had at God's command poured the anointing oil, as he arose and went down to the wilderness of Paran ? Doubtless in those waste places he heard again in living memory the echoes of the prevailing cry of him who was so great among those that call upon the name of the Lord. Doubtless his own discipline was perfected in this new sorrow, but he learnt in losing Samuel to lean more simply and alone on Samuel's God " (' Heroes of Heb. Hist.'). We have here—

I. THE DECEASE OF AN ILLUSTRIOUS MAN : saint, prophet, intercessor, judge, restorer of the theocracy, founder of the monarchy. " He was a righteous man, and gentle in his nature ; and on that account he was very dear to God " (Josephus). " Samuel, the prophet of the Lord, beloved of the Lord, established a kingdom and anointed princes over his people. And before his long sleep he made protestations in the sight of the Lord, &c. And after his death he prophesied, and showed the king his end" (Eccles. xlvi. 13—20). He died—1. *In a good old age.* At what age we know not; but long ago he spoke of himself as "old and grayheaded" (ch. xii. 2). His protracted life was an evidence of his self-control and piety, a mark of Divine favour, and a means of extended usefulness. He was cut down not like "the flower of the field," which blooms for a day and is gone, nor like the spreading forest tree smitten by a sudden blast; but rather like the ripe corn, bending down beneath its golden burden and falling under the sickle of the reaper; and "as shocks of corn are brought in in their season," so was he "gathered to his people." 2. *At the proper time.* When his appointed work was done, the new order of things firmly established, and, he could by his continuance do little more for Israel, he was "taken away from the evil to come" through which the nation was to attain its highest glory. "He was the link which connected two very different periods, being the last representative of a past which could never come back, and seemed almost centuries behind, and also marking the commencement of a new period intended to develop into Israel's ideal future" (Edersheim). "If David's visible deeds were greater and more dazzling than Samuel's, there can be no doubt that David's blaze of glory would have been impossible without Samuel's less conspicuous but far more influential career, and that all the greatness of which the following century boasts goes back to him as its real author" (Ewald). 3. *In peaceful retirement;* removed from public strife, under Divine protection, surrounded by prophetic associates, reviewing the past, contemplating the present, and awaiting the final change. A holy and useful life is crowned with a peaceful and happy death. 4. *In Divine communion,* which constitutes the highest life of the good. In God (with whom he had walked from his childhood, and whose inward voice he had so often heard) he found his chief delight, to his will he cheerfully submitted, and into his hands he committed his spirit in hope of continued, perfect, and eternal fellowship. The ancient covenant to be "the God" of his people overshadowed the present and the future; nor did they suppose (however dim their views of another life) that he would suffer them to be deprived by death of his presence and love "All live unto him" and in him. He "died in faith." His decease was like a peaceful summer sunset.

> "Not the last struggle of the sun
> Precipitated from his golden throne
> Holds, dazzling, mortals in sublime suspense;
> But the calm exode of a man,
> Nearer, but far above, who ran
> The race we run, when Heaven recalls him hence" (W. S. Landor).

II. The mourning of a whole people. "And *all* Israel" (represented by their elders) "were gathered together" (out of common veneration and love), "and lamented him" (whom all knew and none would see again), "and buried him in his house at Ramah" ("the ancient and the manor house," so long his residence, and endeared to him by so many tender associations). It was "a grievous mourning," as when Jacob was buried at Machpelah (Gen. l. 11; Acts viii. 2). The honour rendered to his memory was simple and sincere, very different from that which, it is said, was paid to his dust in later times, when "his remains were removed with incredible pomp and almost one continued train of attendants from Ramah to Constantinople by the Emperor Arcadius, A.D. 401" (Delany, i. 148). But "of Samuel, as of Moses, it may be said, 'No man knoweth of his sepulchre unto this day'" (Stanley). The national mourning was an indication of—1. *The high esteem* in which he was held, on account of his great ability, eminent piety, and beneficent activity—his integrity, firmness, gentleness, consistency, disinterestedness, adaptability, and living communion with God (ch. ii. 30; Ps. cxii. 6). "A true Christian may travel in life under troubles and contempts; but mark his end, and you shall find (as peace, so) honour. Life is death's seed-time; death life's harvest. As here we sow, so there we reap. He that spends himself upon God and man shall at last have all the honour that heaven and earth can cast upon him" (R. Harris). 2. *The deplorable loss* which had been sustained. "The men who had once rejected Samuel now lamented him; when the light of his presence was departed they felt the darkness which remained; when the actual energy of his example had ceased to act they remembered the strength of his principles, the consistency of its operation. There was a feeling common to man. Whilst we enjoy the gift we ofttimes forget the Giver, and are awakened only to the full consciousness of the value of that which we once possessed by finding that we possess it no longer" (Anderson). 3. *The unjust treatment* which he had received, and which was now regretted. His predictions had proved true (ch. viii. 11), and his course was fully vindicated. "The sorrow at his decease was the deeper, the more heavily the yoke of Saul's misgovernment pressed on them." 4. *The continued influence* he exerted upon the nation. "The holy expression stamped by him on the tribes of Benjamin and Judah remained for centuries uneffaced. Never was a single man more instrumental in sowing the soil of a district with the enduring seeds of goodness. It seems to have been mainly through his influence that piety found a home in Judah and Benjamin when it was banished from the rest of the country. Humanly speaking David could never have been king if Samuel had not prepared the way. He was to King David what John the Baptist was to Christ. Unquestionably he is to be ranked among the very greatest and best of the Hebrew worthies" (Blaikie). "And he being dead yet speaketh."

> "O good gray head which all men knew,
> O voice from which their omens all men drew,
> O iron nerve to true occasion true,
> O fall'n at length that tower of strength
> Which stood four-square to all the winds that blew !" (Tennyson).

Learn to—1. Honour the memory of the good. 2. Praise God for their lives. 3. Imitate their example. 4. Carry out their purposes.—D.

Vers. 1—44. (THE WILDERNESS OF PARAN.)—*David's activity and advancement.* "And David arose, and went down to the wilderness of Paran" (ver. 1). Samuel was dead. Saul was becoming more and more incapable of fulfilling the duties of his high office. Meanwhile David was being prepared by Divine providence to grasp the sceptre when it fell from his hand and wield it in a nobler manner. He was the rising sun of the new era. And we see in this chapter numerous signs of his peculiar qualification for his future rule and of his gradual progress towards it ; such as, *e. g.* —1. *The strict discipline* which he exercised among his men. Those 600 warriors dwelt in the neighbourhood of Nabal's shepherds, and could easily have supplied their wants from the flocks kept by the latter ; but "the men were very good to us," said one of them, "and we were not hurt, neither missed we anything," &c. (ver. 15). "He was bringing his wild followers under a loving discipline and government which they had never experienced ; he was teaching them to confess a law which no tyrant had created, no anarchy could set aside" (Maurice). 2. *The valuable service* which he rendered to his people. "They were a wall unto us both by night and day" (ver. 16). He employed his followers (whom he could not lead against Saul without incurring the charge of rebellion) in protecting those who were occupied in honest industry against the plundering Bedouin, and thus doing the work which had been left undone by the king. There is no place or position but affords opportunity for useful work. Even an outlaw may be serviceable to his country. 3. *The perfect equity* of the claim he made. His defence of the sheep gave him a right to some share in them ; and he was justified in voluntarily undertaking it by the condition of society at the time and his own peculiar position. The reply of Nabal, in its application to David, was destitute of justice, truth, and charity (vers. 10, 11). 4. *The respectful consideration* he showed in urging his claim. He did not make it unseasonably, but waited till "a good day" (a festive occasion on which men were usually disposed to be generous), and then sent ten young men to offer him a courteous greeting, state the case, and humbly seek as a favour what might have been demanded as a right (vers. 6—8). He appealed to what was noblest and best in the man. 5. *The conscious power* which he displayed. "Greet him in my name"—a name well known in Israel as that of a faithful, though persecuted, servant of Jehovah. Not a word escaped his lips, indeed, on this or any other occasion concerning his royal destiny. But he knew the strength of his position (see ch. xxvi.), which was very different now from what it was at the beginning of his wanderings, was manifested in his whole bearing, and especially in the marriage relationships into which he entered (vers. 42—44). 6. *The increased renown* which he had acquired. The words of Abigail (vers. 28—31) expressed the growing conviction of the godly in Israel that David was destined to be their theocratic ruler. She may also have "received certain information of his anointing and destination through Samuel, or one of the pupils of the prophets" (Keil). 7. *The Divine restraint* by which he was kept from doing what would have imperilled or interfered with his future honour and happiness (ver. 26). When God has an important place for a man to fill, he prepares the way to it and prepares him for it, and a part of his preparation consists in his being taught faithful co-operation with the Divine purposes.—D.

Vers. 2—39. (MAON, CARMEL.)—*The prosperous fool.* "Now the name of the man was Nabal" (ver. 3; "a son of Belial," ver. 17; "Nabal is his name, and folly is with him," ver. 25). This chapter is like a picture gallery in which are exhibited the portraits of Samuel and the elders of Israel, David and his men, with the Bedouin marauders in the background; Nabal, the wealthy sheep-owner, his sheep-shearers and boon companions, Abigail and her maidens, and Ahinoam of Jezreel (mother of Amnon, the eldest son of David). Let us pause and look at one of them—Nabal. "As his name is, so is he;" a fool, *i. e.* a stupid, wicked, and godless man. "According to the Old Testament representation folly is a correlate of ungodliness which inevitably brings down punishment" (Keil). He is such an one as is described by the Psalmist (Ps. xiv. 1), often mentioned by the wise man (Prov. xvii. 16; xix. 1; xxi. 24), called a churl by the prophet (Isa. xxxii. 5—7), and referred to by our Lord in the parable (Luke xii. 13—21). What a contrast between his appearance and that of Samuel!

I. HIS ADVANTAGES WERE GREAT. 1. *He belonged to a good family.* "He was of the house of Caleb," who "wholly followed Jehovah God of Israel," and had "a part among the children of Judah." But he inherited none of the better qualities of his illustrious ancestor. "A good extraction is a reproach to him who degenerates from it." Religious privileges also (such as he enjoyed from his connection with Israel), unless rightly used, only serve to increase condemnation. 2. *He possessed an excellent wife;* "a woman of good understanding and of a beautiful countenance," prudent, generous, and devout. "A prudent wife is from the Lord" (Prov. xix. 14). But many a man is little benefited by the gift. His worldly prosperity may be increased by her skilful management of his household (vers. 14, 25), whilst his spiritual condition is not improved by her example, counsel, and prayers. The persistently bad are hardened by their intimate intercourse with the good. 3. *He enjoyed immense prosperity.* "The man was very great (wealthy), and he had three thousand sheep, and a thousand goats," a palatial residence in Maon, and a house at Carmel (Kurmul), where his business lay (vers. 2, 36). He may have inherited his wealth, or he may have had wisdom enough to know how to make and keep it, industrious himself, and profiting by the industry of others; it is not improbable from his language concerning slaves (ver. 10) that he was one of those usurers and oppressors from whose exactions many of David's men sought to free themselves by flight (ch. xxii. 2). "Here we may see the fickle and uncertain state of the world" (Willet); "the wicked in great power" (Ps. xxxvii. 35), and the good oppressed (Ps. lxxiii. 10). But "a man's life consisteth not in the abundance of the things which he possesseth" (Luke xii. 15). His abundance should make him thankful to God and generous to men. It has often, however, the reverse effect, and "the prosperity of fools shall destroy them" (Deut. viii. 10—20; Prov. i. 32).

II. HIS CHARACTER WAS WORTHLESS. "The man was churlish" (hard and harsh) "and evil in his doings" (ver. 3). 1. *He had evidently no thought of God* as the living, ever-present One, the true King of Israel, the Author and Preserver of his life, the Giver of all his blessings, the moral Ruler to whom he was responsible for their proper employment. What was material and sensible was to him the only reality. He recognised in practice no will superior to his own, and lived "without God in the world." 2. *He was regardless of the claims of other people;* despising those who were beneath him in social position, headstrong, and resentful of every word which his servants might say to him in opposition to his way and for his good (ver. 17); illiberal toward the needy, unjust and ungrateful, "requiting evil for good" (ver. 21); disparaging the character and conduct of others (vers. 10—12), and railing upon them (ver. 14) in coarse and insulting language. "His wealth had not endowed him with common sense; but, like many in our own day, he imagined that because he was in affluent circumstances he might with impunity indulge in rude, ill-mannered sneers at all who were around him" (W. M. Taylor). 3. *He lived for himself alone;* regarding his wealth as his own ("*my* bread and *my* water," &c.), using it only for himself; making an ostentatious display ("the feast of a king"), and indulging in intemperance, "the voluntary extinction of reason." "So is he that layeth up treasure for himself, and is not *rich toward God.*"

III. HIS END WAS MISERABLE (vers. 36—39). 1. *He was overtaken by death very suddenly* and unexpectedly, and when he was unprepared for it. "Thou fool, this night thy soul shall be required of thee," &c. 2. *He suffered the natural penalty* of the course which he had pursued. 3. *He was consigned to his grave without honour.* Whilst "all Israel mourned" for Samuel, none lamented him.

Learn that—1. The worth of a man consists not in what he has, but in what he is. 2. Wealth entails on its possessor a serious responsibility for its proper use. 3. The inequalities of men's earthly position disappear in the light of truth and eternity.—D.

Ver. 10. (CARMEL.)—*Masters and servants.* "There are many servants now-a-days that break away every man from his master." What Nabal said was probably the fact. Many servants did in that unsettled time break away from their masters, preferring independence with its risk and privation to servitude with its protection and provision. But the imputation which he intended to cast upon them was either wholly unjust, as in the case of David, or partially so, as in the case of many others. He omitted to state that their conduct toward their masters was due to the conduct of their masters toward them. People are never so ready to see and condemn the faults of the class to which they belong as those of the opposite class. Concerning masters and servants, consider—

I. THE NATURE OF THE RELATION. It has been aptly illustrated in the following language:—"A party of friends, setting out together upon a journey, soon find it to be the best for all sides that while they are upon the road one of the company should wait upon the rest, another ride forward to seek out lodging and entertainment, a third to carry the portmanteau, a fourth take charge of the horses, a fifth bear the purse, conduct, and direct the route; not forgetting, however, that as they were equal and independent when they set out, so they are all to return to a level again at the journey's end" (Paley, 'Mor. Phil.,' book iii.). The relation is confined to life's journey alone. 1. It is, in some form or other, *necessary and mutually beneficial.* The benefit received is really greater on the part of masters than servants. 2. It must of necessity *vary with the circumstances* of those among whom it exists. Hence the Mosaic law tolerated and regulated a species of slavery (though no Hebrew could become other than a "hired servant" for a specified time); but "no other ancient religion was ever so emphatically opposed to it, or at least to all inhumanity connected with it, or made such sure preparations for its abolition" (Ewald, 'Antiquities'). 3. It always involves *mutual obligations.* These "now-a-days" are often neglected. The tie between master and servant (mistress and maid, employer and employed) is not what it once was. There is less dependence on the one hand, and less authority on the other. Each complains of the other: "servants are careless and too independent;" "masters are too exacting and selfish." And the relation can only be what it ought to be by their common submission to "the law of Christ" (Gal. vi. 2).

II. THE DUTY OF SERVANTS (Ephes. vi. 5—8; Col. iii. 22—25; 1 Tim. vi. 1, 2; Titus ii. 9, 10; 1 Pet. ii. 18). 1. *Obedience*—lowly, respectful, cheerful; always in subordination to the supreme will of God. This is the first duty of a servant. 2. *Diligence* in performing the work given them to do, with attention and earnestness, and in the best possible manner. "And be content with your wages" (Luke iii. 14). 3. *Faithfulness* to the trust committed to them, seeking their masters' interests as their own ; honesty, thorough sincerity, " as the servants of Christ, doing the will of God from the heart."

III. THE DUTY OF MASTERS (Ephes. vi. 9 ; Col. iv. 1). 1. *Equity ;* giving to them " that which is just and equal," and imposing upon them no unnecessary burdens (Mal. iii. 5 ; James v. 4). 2. *Consideration,* respect, courtesy, kindness, seeking their physical, moral, and spiritual welfare. "Thou shalt not rule over thy servant with rigour " (Levit. xxv. 43). And a mere money payment is not all that a fellow-creature is entitled to expect, or an adequate compensation for his services. 3. *Consistency ;* acting in accordance with their position, reproving wrong-doing, setting a good example, exercising their authority and influence as a trust committed to them by God and in obedience to his will. Those who expect to receive honour must seek to make themselves worthy of it.

Let both learn—1. To be less observant of the faults of others than of their own. 2. To be more concerned about fulfilling their duties than insisting on their rights. 3. To look for their chief reward in the approbation of God.—D.

Vers. 14—42. (CARMEL.)—*Abigail.* Of her family and early life nothing is recorded. When first mentioned she was the wife of the wealthy and churlish Nabal. It was an ill-assorted union, probably due (like most Oriental marriages) to parental arrangement. She was distinguished by a beautiful countenance and form, and (what is not always associated therewith) by a beautiful mind and character, embodying the ideal of womanhood (Prov. xxxi. 10—31). "Where do we find in all the heathen world a woman comparable with Abigail, the daughter of the wilderness ? " She was a woman of—1. *Superior intelligence,* practical wisdom, prudence, tact, and good management. "Of good understanding " (ver. 3). The part she took in the affairs of her husband is evident from the servants telling her of the threatening danger (ver. 17), and her apology (ver. 25). Her discretion was also shown in her reserve (ver. 19). 2. *Prompt decision,* energy, and activity. "Abigail made haste," &c. (ver. 18). Not a moment was lost, and she was promptly obeyed. 3. *Unaffected humility,* meekness, modesty, and self-devotion. "She fell before David on her face," &c. (vers. 23, 41). Her meekness and patience must have been greatly tried by the temper of Nabal, and had doubtless previously averted many a disaster. 4. *Noble generosity* and sacrifice. "Two hundred loaves," &c. (ver. 18). She felt that no sacrifice was too great to save her husband and his household. " David's men and David felt that these were not the gifts of a sordid calculation, but the offerings of a generous heart. And it won them, their gratitude, their enthusiasm, their unfeigned homage" (Robertson). 5. *Conciliatory, faithful, eloquent speech,* and pacifying, beneficent influence (vers. 24—31). Having taken the blame upon herself (as intercessor), and referred to her husband " with that union of playfulness and seriousness which above all things turns away wrath" (Stanley), she directed the thoughts of David to God, by the leadings of whose providence she had been sent to divert him from his purpose, utters the wish that he to whom vengeance belongs would avenge him, humbly begs the acceptance of her offering for his young men, and beseeches his forgiveness. Then (assuming her prayer to be granted) she assures him of the brilliant future that awaited him, inasmuch as he would fulfil the purposes of Jehovah, and not his own ; that, should any one seek to do him harm, Jehovah would preserve him in safety, and punish his adversaries ; and that when he should be "ruler over Israel" it would be a source of comfort, and not of trouble, to him that he had not shed blood causelessly, nor taken vengeance into his own hand. Finally she says, " And Jehovah will do good to my lord, and thou wilt remember thine handmaid " (for good)—" remember the things which I have spoken " (Dathe). No dissuasions from revenge could be more effective.

> " When a world of men
> Could not prevail with all their oratory,
> Yet hath a woman's kindness overruled."

" Doubtless she had not studied eloquence in the schools, but the Spirit of God alone made her such an orator. God put wisdom into her heart, and it flowed out in wise discourse " (Roos). 6. *Exalted piety ;* faith in the righteousness and goodness of

God, his overruling providence, and the establishment of his kingdom (see the song of Hannah), devotion, spiritual insight, manifested in this appeal, and in her whole conduct (Prov. xxxi. 26, 30). It is not surprising that, after the death of Nabal, "David sent and communed with Abigail, to take her to him to wife" (ver. 39).—D.

Ver. 29. (CARMEL.)—*The bundle of life.* 1. The bundle of life, or the living (the word bundle, *tseror*, being used once before of the bag or purse of money which each of Joseph's brethren found in his sack of corn, Gen. xlii. 35), signifies the society or *congregation of the living* out of which men are taken and cut off by death (Barrett, 'Synopsis of Criticisms'). It contains those who possess life, continued and prosperous life, in the present world in the midst of the dangers to which they are exposed, and by which others are taken away from "the land of the living" (Isa. iv. 3). Life is a gift of God, and its continuance is presumptive of his favour. 2. What is here desired and predicted concerning them is based upon their *moral distinction* from other men. They are, like David, servants of God, and differ from others, as David from Saul and Nabal, in their character and conduct. They constitute the community of the godly in "this present evil world," and "their names are written in heaven." 3. They are of *inestimable worth* in the sight of God. He values all men because of their *capacity* for goodness, but much more some on account of their actual *possession* of it. Their worth surpasses all earthly possessions and distinctions. "The whole system of bodies (the firmament, the stars, the earth, and the kingdoms of it) and spirits together is unequal to the least emotion of charity" (Pascal). 4. They are his *special possession ;* belong to him in a peculiar manner, because of what he has done for them "above all people," and their own voluntary devotion to him. "Know that the Lord hath set apart him that is godly for himself." "The Lord taketh pleasure in his people," and calls them "my jewels" (Mal. iii. 17). 5. They live in *intimate communion* with him. "A people near unto him" (Ps. cxlviii. 14) ; "bound up in the bundle of life *with* the Lord thy God." 6. They are *preserved safely* from the malicious designs of their enemies, and from all evil. "Should a man arise to pursue thee and seek thy soul," &c. The expression is derived from the common usage of men, who put valuable things together and keep them near their persons to prevent their being lost or injured. "Your life is hid with Christ in God" (Col. iii. 3). 7. They have a *common participation* in the strength and blessedness afforded by his presence and favour. Their life is of the highest kind—life in the truest, fullest sense, directly derived from him who is "the Fountain of life," and involving all real good. "In thy presence," &c. (Ps. xvi. 11.) The life of others is but "a race to death," and they are "dead while they live." 8. They are designed for *useful service ;* not merely to be looked upon and admired, but employed according to the will of the owner. It is for this that they are preserved. 9. They have "the promise of *eternal life.*" Their spiritual fellowship with God and with each other in this life is an earnest of its continuance and perfection in the life to come. "God is not the God of the dead, but of the living." The pious Jew dies with the words of the text upon his lips, and has them inscribed upon his tomb. "Whosoever is so hidden in the gracious fellowship of the Lord in this life that no enemy can harm him or injure his life, the Lord will not allow to perish, even though temporal death should come, but will then receive him into eternal life" (Keil). "And so shall we ever be with the Lord." 10. Their destiny (like their character) is the *opposite* of that of the ungodly. "Concerning the bodies of the righteous it is said, 'He shall enter into peace; they shall rest in their beds' (Isa. lvii. 21) ; and of their souls it is said, 'And the soul of my lord shall be bound in the bundle of life with the Lord thy God.' But concerning the bodies of the wicked it is said, 'There is no peace, saith God, to the wicked.' And of their souls it is said, 'And the souls of thine enemies, them shall he sling out, as out of the middle of a sling '" (Talmud, quoted by Hurwitz).—D.

Vers. 32, 33. (CARMEL.)—*Moral restraints.* 1. Between the purpose to transgress and the intended act of transgression there is usually an interval, and in that interval there may occur *physical* restraints, rendering the act impossible but not affecting the purpose or disposition ; or *moral* restraints, affecting the purpose, and often altering it and thereby preventing the act.   The latter alone truly tests and reveals the character.   And of this nature was the restraint put upon David when he was on his way to inflict vengeance on Nabal and his household for the affront which he had received.   2. His terrible purpose seems surprising after his forbearance toward Saul (ch. xxiv. 7, 22).   But the conquest of temptation is not unfrequently the occasion of subsequently succumbing to it.   This happens when any one supposes that he is no longer in danger from it, and ceases to watch against it, and depend on God for his safe-keeping.   "David was not secure against the temptation to personal vengeance and to self-help, although he had previously resisted it.   The lesson of his own weakness in that respect was all the more needed that this was one of the most obvious dangers to an ordinary Oriental ruler (ch. xxiv. 21).   But David was not to be such, and when God in his good providence restrained him as he had almost fallen, he showed him the need of inward as well as of outward deliverance, and the sufficiency of his grace to preserve him from spiritual as from temporal dangers" (Edersheim).   Consider special moral restraints as—

I. MUCH NEEDED EVEN BY A GOOD MAN, because of—1. *External incentives to sin.* The language of Nabal was adapted to excite anger and revenge, as his servant plainly perceived (ver. 17).   2. *Sudden impulses of passion,* under which one of ardent temperament especially is in danger of taking a rash oath (ver. 22), and rushing towards its accomplishment without fully considering what he does, or "inquiring of the Lord" whether it is right.   3. *Natural deficiency of strength* to resist temptation, and natural liability to self-deception.   Reason and conscience should always hold the rein, but how often is it torn from their grasp by fiery passions ! David probably also thought for the moment that it was right to avenge the wrong which had been done ; but even if Nabal's offence were the greatest conceivable, he was not yet constituted king and judge of the people, much less ought he to inflict so fearful a vengeance for a private offence.   "Lord, what is man ?   What need have we to pray, Lord, lead us not into temptation ! "

II. VARIOUSLY VOUCHSAFED ACCORDING TO HIS NEED.   What is most needed is the restoration of reason and conscience to their proper place and power, and this is often brought about by—1. *Providential circumstances,* leading to reflection and the recognition of the will of God.   2. *Wise and faithful counsel* (vers. 26—31), indicating that will, addressed to conscience, and persuading to the adoption of a worthier course.   3. *Inward influence,* exerted by the Spirit of God, giving the inclination and strength to walk in "the good and right way."   "Lo, all these things worketh God oftentimes with man," &c. (Job xxxiii. 29).   And with him whose heart is not "fully set to do evil" he worketh not in vain.

III. GRATEFULLY ASCRIBED BY HIM TO GOD.   "Blessed be the Lord God of Israel," &c.   He is grateful to the messenger of God, but first and chiefly to God himself ; and his gratitude is sincere and fervent on account of—1. The *evil* which has been prevented.   2. The *good* which has been conferred.   3. The *abounding mercy* which has been experienced.   "Do you think that any one will praise God in heaven with so loud a voice as I shall ? " said one (who had been speaking of the course of flagrant transgression from which by Divine mercy he had been reclaimed).   "Yes," was the reply, "I hope to do so, because by Divine mercy I have been kept from it." "It is not a converting, but a crowning grace ; such an one as irradiates and puts a circle of glory about the head of him upon whom it descends ; it is the Holy Ghost coming down upon him in the 'form of a dove,' and setting him triumphant above the necessity of tears and sorrow, mourning and repentance, the sad after-games of a lost innocence " (South, 'Prevention of Sin an Invaluable Mercy ').—D.

Ver. 29.—*The bundle of life and the sling.*   The appeal of Abigail had all the more persuasiveness that she avowed her sympathy with David's cause, and her faith in the Divine purpose to make him king.   Such a conviction was by this time widely diffused in the land among those who feared Jehovah and honoured the prophet Samuel.   We have seen that it was confessed by Saul himself, and by Jonathan it was cherished with generous pleasure.   But Nabal would not have it mentioned in his presence.   In his eyes David was a mere runaway servant of the king who had turned freebooter.   His wife showed the vigour of her mind, the clearness of her judgment, and the strength of her faith in not fearing the displeasure of Nabal or the wrath of King Saul, but declaring her confident belief that the Lord would raise David to be ruler over Israel. On this ground she entreated him not to burden his conscience or sully his name with a hasty deed of blood. What a power of figurative expression those Eastern believers had; and not least those devout women whose spirits were stirred by urgent occasions to ardent utterance —Deborah in her triumph, Hannah in her song, Abigail in her appeal!

I. THE FIGURE OF SAFETY. A soul bound up in the bundle of life with Jehovah. What could a Nabal's churlishness, or even a Saul's pursuit, avail against a man whose life God guarded by night and day? If we use Abigail's phrase we extend its meaning. The question with her was of David's preservation to fill the throne of Israel; but it is not for us under the New Testament to set our hearts on earthly rank. Our treasure is in heaven. Our inheritance is reserved for us till our Lord's return. Our days are few and uncertain. But we have an eternal life, freely given to us in Christ Jesus; and the bundle of life means for us the unity of all the living ones in Christ, the totality of the life which " is hid with Christ in God." They who are bound up therein have been taken out of the bundles of sin and death, extricated from what is evil and therefore doomed to destruction, and have been by the power of the Holy Ghost joined to Christ and the Church. Happy day that sees this done! Strong security that follows! Who is he that can harm us if we are Christ's, bound up in the bundle of life with God our Saviour?

II. THE FIGURE OF REJECTION. Abigail made no further reference to Nabal. He was her husband, and in no case could he be formidable to David. All she asked was that the son of Jesse would magnanimously overlook his churlishness. But the whole country rang with reports of the angry pursuit of David by the king, and Abigail predicted that his enemies would have discomfiture and rejection from the Lord his God. With rare felicity of allusion she spoke of their souls as flung away, as a stone is cast " out of the middle of a sling." The very mention of the weapon with which David had gained his first great success must have stirred his faith and courage. The figure, as the history shows, was remarkably appropriate to the career of David's chief enemy, Saul. "As he that bindeth a stone in a sling, so is he that giveth honour to a fool" (Prov. xxvi. 8). Now honour had been given to Saul. He was anointed and exalted to the throne, and yet was at heart unwise and disobedient. So was the stone laid in the pan of a sling. After a while we see the stone whirled round in the sling, i. e. we see Saul troubled and tossed—wayward, disturbed, passionate, insanely jealous. The end was now drawing near, and the stone was about to be cast out of the sling in despair and death on Mount Gilboa.

On vers. 32, 33 Dr. South has left us a sermon entitled, 'Prevention of sin an invaluable blessing.' In the " application " of it the preacher shows that a much higher satisfaction is to be found from a conquered than from a conquering passion. " Revenge is certainly the most luxurious morsel that the devil can put into a sinner's mouth. But do we think that David could have found half the pleasure in the execution of his revenge that he expresses here upon the disappointment of it? Possibly it might have pleased him in the present heat and hurry of his rage, but must have displeased him infinitely more in the cool, sedate reflections of his mind." Another point which South enforces is that the temper with which we receive providential prevention of sin is a criterion of the gracious or ungracious condition of our hearts. " Whosoever has anything of David's piety will be perpetually plying the throne of grace with such like acknowledgments as—Blessed be that Providence which delivered me from such a lewd company or such a vicious acquaintance! And blessed be that God who cast stops and hindrances in my way when I was attempting the commission of such and such a sin; who took me out of such a course of life, such a place, or such an employment, which was a continual snare and temptation to me! And blessed be such a preacher and such a friend whom God made use of to speak a word in season to my wicked heart, and so turned me out of the paths of death and destruction, and saved me in spite of the world, the devil, and myself!"—F.

EXPOSITION.

DAVID A SECOND TIME SPARES SAUL'S LIFE (CH. XXVI.).

CHAPTER XXVI.

SAUL, ON INFORMATION FROM THE ZIPH-ITES, AGAIN SEEKS TO DESTROY DAVID (vers. 1—3). Ver. 1.—**The Ziphites came unto Saul.** There are so many points of similarity between this narrative and that contained in ch. xxiii. 19—24 ; xxiv. 1—22, that it has been argued that in these two accounts we have substantially the same fact, only modified by two different popular traditions, and not recorded until a late subsequent period, at which the narrator, unable to decide which was the true form of the story, determined upon giving both. The main points of similarity are—(1) The treachery of the Ziphites (ch. xxvi. 1 ; xxiii. 19). (2) David's position in the hill Hachilah (ch. xxvi. 1, 3 ; xxiii. 19). (3) Saul's march with 3000 men (ch. xxvi. 2 ; xxiv. 2). (4) The speech of David's men (ch. xxiv. 4 ; xxvi. 8). (5) David's refusal to lay hands on the anointed of Jehovah (ch. xxiv. 6 ; xxvi. 9, 11). (6) Saul's recognition of David's voice (ch. xxiv. 16 ; xxvi 17). (7) David's comparison of himself to a flea (ch. xxiv. 14 ; xxvi. 20). Besides these there are several remarkable verbal coincidences ; but some other matters which have been enumerated are either such as must have happened, supposing the two events to have occurred, or are even points of difference. Of these there are many. Thus the first occasion on which David spared Saul's life was in a cave at En-gedi; the latter was in Saul's entrenched camp. In this second narrative David's return to Maon was the natural result of his marriage with Abigail, and when the Ziphites report his presence there to Saul, which they were sure to do for fear of David's vengeance for their former betrayal of him, he awaits Saul's attack, whereas before he fled in haste, and was saved for the moment by the wonderful ravine which Conder has so unmistakably verified (see on ch. xxiii. 26), and finally by an invasion of the Philistines. Mr. Conder's visit to the ground, and the way in which the difficulties in the previous narrative are cleared up by what he saw, sets the historical credibility of that account above all reasonable doubt. Had there been a mountain between David and his pursuers, he would have been safe enough ; but as it was he was in full sight of his enemies, and the ravine alone enabled him to escape from Saul's vengeance. The number of Saul's army, 3000, was the number of the chosen men whom he always had in attendance upon him (ch. xiii. 2) ; and it is Saul who encamps on the hill Hachilah, while David, instead of being all but caught as before, had scouts to watch Saul's movements, and was himself safe in the wilderness on the south. On the previous occasion Saul had withdrawn from his men, but here he lies in his camp surrounded by them, when David, accompanied only by Abishai, undertakes this bold enterprise, which was entirely in accordance with his growing sense of security. The argument, moreover, that Saul must have been a "moral monster" thus to seek David's life after his generous conduct towards him keeps out of view the fact that Saul was scarcely accountable for his actions. We have seen that he was subject to fits of madness, and that the form which it took was that of deadly hatred against David. Even this was but a form of the ruling passion which underlies all Saul's actions, namely, an extreme jealousy of everything that in the slightest degree seemed to trench upon his royal prerogative and supremacy. To what an extreme length his ferocity was capable of proceeding in punishing what he regarded as an overt act of resistance to his authority we have seen in the account of the massacre of the priests at Nob with their wives and children (ch. xxii. 18, 19). No worse act is recorded of any man in history, and we may hope that Saul would not have committed such a crime had not his mental faculties been disturbed. Nor was Saul alone in his estimate of what was due to him as Jehovah's Messiah ; David had equally high views of Saul's rights and position, and regarded them as fenced in by religious sanctions. But in Saul's case the passion had grown till it had become a monomania, and as he brooded over his relations to David, and thought of him as one that was to usurp his crown, and was already a rebel and an outlaw, the sure result was the return of his hatred against David, and when news was brought him that his enemy was so near, he gladly welcomed another opportunity of getting him into his power. **On the hill of Hachilah.** See ch. xxiii. 19. It is there said to be "on the right hand," but here "over against," i. e. facing the desert which lies on the north-eastern coast of the Dead Sea.

Vers. 2—4.—**Three thousand chosen men.** Not chosen for this expedition, but the force which Saul always kept under arms (ch. xiii. 2). **By the way.** The high road which led down to Arad. **David abode in the wilderness.** Hebrew, "abides." Instead of fleeing in haste as before, he remains apparently on the higher ground, as he speaks in ver. 6 of *going down* to Saul's camp. **And he saw.** *I. e.* learned, was told. It was only when his scouts brought him their report that he knew that Saul was come **in very deed,** or "for a certainty" (see ch. xxiii. 23).

Ver. 5. — **David arose.** It seems as if David could scarcely believe that Saul would thus a second time pursue him ; but when the scouts informed him that it was really so, he went in person to reconnoitre Saul's camp. From the opposite hill he was able to see that **he lay in the trench,** *i. e.* the barricade formed by the wagons. At night Saul's place would be in the centre, with Abner near him, while the rest would lie sleeping around, but all of them within the rampart. When David reconnoitred them they would probably be arranging their wagons to form this barricade.

Ver. 6.—**Ahimelech the Hittite.** Though a portion of this once powerful people (Gen. xv. 20 ; Judges i. 26) was reduced to the position of bondmen (1 Kings ix. 20), yet others had retained their independence, and their kings even are spoken of (*ibid.* x. 29 ; 2 Kings vii. 6). As Ahimelech is mentioned before Abishai, he must have held an honourable place with David, as did subsequently another Hittite, Uriah (2 Sam. xi. 3). **Abishai the son of Zeruiah.** Zeruiah is described in 1 Chron. ii. 16 as sister to Jesse's sons, but apparently only by adoption, as both she and Abigail seem to have been daughters of the king of Ammon (2 Sam. xvii. 25), whence probably the absence of any direct reference to their father. Abishai, who was probably about David's age, and his two brothers were high in rank among David's heroes (1 Chron. xi. 6, 20, 26), and apparently he was one of the three captains who, when David was in the cave of Adullam, broke through the host of the Philistines to fetch him water from the well of Bethlehem. **Who will go down?** It is evident that David and his men remained upon the mountains, which extend from Maon far to the south-west. Saul's camp, being "by the way," *i. e.* near the road, would be on the lower ground. David having personally examined it, and seen that the watches were ill kept, asks which of the two will accompany him for the more hazardous enterprise of penetrating into it. Ahimelech seems prudently to have declined, but Abishai at once offers his services.

Vers. 7, 8.—The two accordingly go **by night,** or "at night," as soon as night came on, and find Saul asleep **within the trench,** *i. e.* inside the wagon-rampart, as in ver. 5, and **his spear,** the sign of his royal authority, stuck in the ground ; not **at his bolster,** but "at his head ;" and so in vers. 11, 12, 16. The word literally signifies "the place where

the head is." Like David's men in ch. xxiv. 4, Abishai sees in Saul's defenceless condition a proof that it was God's will that he should die, but there is a difference of language in the Hebrew which the A. V. does not represent. There the word rendered *deliver* is really *give;* here it is "hath locked up." **At once.** Hebrew, "once." Abishai would pierce him through with a single stroke so thoroughly that no second blow would be necessary. The purpose of this would be to prevent an outcry.

Vers. 9 -- 11. — David forbids the deed as before (ch. xxiv. 6), because of Saul's office. As we there saw, this was an ingrained principle in David's mind on which he constantly acted. Present with equal strength in Saul's mind, it was the cause of moral ruin to the one, and of a noble forbearance and self-control to the other. David therefore leaves him in Jehovah's hand, saying, **As Jehovah liveth, Jehovah shall smite him ; or his day,** &c. Literally, "As Jehovah liveth (I will not smite him), but Jehovah shall smite him ; either his day shall come and he shall die ; or he shall go down into battle and perish." Whenever he falls, it shall be Jehovah's doing, whether he die a natural death, or a violent one in battle. "The smiting of Jehovah" does not imply a sudden death. God smites men with disease (2 Kings xv. 5) and other troubles. What David means is that he will leave the matter entirely to God, but that if Saul's death is to be a violent one, he must fall honourably, not by the hand of a subject, but in battle with Israel's enemies. **Jehovah forbid.** The same phrase as in ch. xxiv. 6. **Cruse of water.** *I. e.* water-bottle, as in 1 Kings xix. 6.

Ver. 12.—**And no man saw it,** &c. The Hebrew text describes the occurrence in a much more lively manner : "And none saw, and none knew, and none awaked." **A deep sleep from Jehovah,** &c. So surprising a fact as that two men could penetrate into the very centre of a considerable army, and remove the king's sceptre and water-bottle from his side, could only be accounted for by the interference of Providence in their behalf.

Vers. 13—16.—**The top of a hill.** Hebrew, "the top of the hill," the particular mountain from which David had reconnoitred Saul's camp (ver. 5). **A great space being between them.** At En-gedi Saul was alone, and had placed himself in David's power ; he therefore had followed him closely. Here Saul had his army round him, and David had entered his camp by stealth. It is not, therefore, till he had placed an ample interval between them that he calls to **Abner,** and asks in derision, **Art thou not a man?** The irony is enfeebled by the insertion of the word *valiant* (comp. ch. iv. 9). No special valour was needed; any one worthy of the name of man ought to have guarded his master better. **Who is like to thee—** Hebrew, "who is as thou"—**in Israel?** Among all Saul's subjects there was no one so powerful and highly placed as the commander-in-chief, and he ought to have shown himself worthy of his pre-eminence. Justly, therefore, for neglecting his duty and exposing the king to danger, he and his people were **worthy to die.** Hebrew, "sons of death" (see on ch. xx. 31). Finally David bids him search for the king's spear and water-bottle, that he may understand how completely Saul had been in his power. It has been suggested that Abner was probably a personal enemy of David, with whom he could never have held the high position which he occupied with his near relative Saul. Possibly instead of dissuading Saul from persecuting David, he stirred up his ill feelings. Still absolutely there is nothing in this banter which was not justified by Abner's official position.

Vers. 17—19.- **Is this thy voice?** So ch. xxiv. 16. In the darkness the only way of recognising David was by his voice. **If Jehovah have stirred thee up,** &c. This is one of the many passages indicative of the intensity with which the Israelites had grasped the idea of the omnipresence of the Deity, and of his being the one power by whose energy all things exist and all acts are done (see on ch. ii. 2). Alike evil and good come from God, for he alone is the source of all; but it does not therefore follow that everything which he makes possible, or to which his providence seems to lead, is therefore right for man to do (ch. xxiv. 4, 6). On the contrary, all leadings of providence are to be judged by God's immutable law, and the conduct of a Shimei may be absolutely wrong and unjustifiable, even though "Jehovah had bidden him do it" (2 Sam. xvi. 11). If, indeed, an external command come by the hand of a properly accredited person, it may take the same high position as the published law of God, and so over-ride the conscience; but Shimei's bidding came through the working of his own passions, and was no more binding than the moving of David's mind by Jehovah to number Israel (2 Sam. xxiv. 1). David, then, here sets forth the two only possible cases: first, Saul may be stirred up by Jehovah to persecute David, *i. e.* the temptation may come by the working of his own mind under those strong impulses which to the Israelite had in them always something Divine. But this was an impulse to break God's law, and was therefore to be resisted; and just as in modern phrase we should bid a person when strongly moved to some act

to carry it to God's throne in prayer, so David urges Saul to seek for the quieting of his emotions in religion. Under holy influences these fierce passions would pass away, and Jehovah would **accept an offering.** Hebrew, "would smell it," because the offering, *minchah*, consisting of flour and frankincense, was burnt for a sweet odour before God. But, secondly, Saul might be stirred up by the calumnies of wicked men, in which case David prays that they may be **cursed before Jehovah;** because by forcing him to leave the covenant land of Israel they virtually say to him, **Go, serve other gods.** To a mind so intensely religious as David's, not only was the private devotion of the heart a necessity, but also the taking part in the public worship of the Deity (Ps. xlii. 2; lxiii. 2; lxxxiv. 2); and, therefore, to deprive him of this privilege and expel him from **the inheritance of Jehovah,** *i. e.* the earthly limits of Jehovah's Church, was to force him, as far as his enemies could do so, to be a heathen and a worshipper of strange gods.

Ver. 20.—**Let not my blood fall to the earth before the face of Jehovah.** Hebrew, "far from the presence of Jehovah." The point of David's appeal is not that his life may be spared, but that he may not thus be driven far away from the land where Jehovah manifests himself; nor does he seem so much to contemplate Saul's putting him to death as the probability that sooner or later the life of an exile will be cut short by one or other of the many dangers by which he is surrounded. **A flea.** Hebrew, "a single flea," as in ch. xxiv. 14. **A partridge.** Many emendations of the text have been proposed on the supposition that partridges are only to be found in plains. But Mr. Conder tells us that partridges are among the few living creatures which still tenant these wilds; and, speaking of the precipitous cliffs which overhang the Dead Sea, he says, Here, among "the rocks of the wild goats, the herds of ibex may be seen bounding, and the partridge is still chased on the mountains, as David was followed by the stealthy hunter Saul" ('Tent Work,' ii. 90; see also ch. xxiii. 19).

Ver. 21.—**I have sinned.** Saul's answer here is very different from that in ch. xxiv. 17—21, where the main idea was wonder that David should with such magnanimity spare the life of an enemy so manifestly delivered into his hand. Here a sense of vexation seems uppermost, and of annoyance, not merely because his purpose was **frustrated,** but because his own military arrangements had been so unsoldierlike. **I have played the fool.** His first enterprise had ended in placing his life in David's power, and it was folly indeed a second time to repeat the attempt. But though the words of Saul convey the idea rather of vexation with himself than of sorrow for his maliciousness, yet in one point there is a sign of better things. He bids David return, evidently with reference to the grief expressed with such genuine feeling by David at being driven away from Jehovah's land. It was of course impossible, as Saul had given David's wife to another, and David had himself married two other women, but at least it expressed a right and kindly feeling.

Vers. 22—24.—**Behold the king's spear.** Rather, "Behold the spear, O king." The other is an unnecessary correction of the Kri. Having restored to Saul this ensign of his authority, David prays that **Jehovah** may **render to every man his righteousness,** *i. e.* may requite David for his upright conduct towards Saul, and by implication punish Saul himself for his unjust conduct. And also **his faithfulness,** his fidelity, and steady allegiance. This refers exclusively to David, who gives as proof of his faithfulness to his king that he had spared his life when it was delivered into his power. In return for which act God, he affirms, will protect his life. Ver. 24 would be better translated, "And behold, as thy life was great (in value) in my sight this day, so shall my life be great (in value) in the sight of Jehovah, and he shall deliver me out of every strait," every narrowness and difficulty into which Saul's persecution might drive him.

Ver. 25.—**Thou shalt both do,** &c. Better, "Thou shalt both do mightily, and thou shalt surely prevail." The words are very general as compared with those in ch. xxiv. 20, 21, where Saul expressed his conviction that David would be king, and intrusted his family to his care. The poverty of sentiment here, and the mere vexation expressed in ver. 21, justify Keil's remark that Saul's character had deteriorated in the interval, and that he was more hardened now than on the previous occasion. And so they parted—David still leading the life of a fugitive, for Saul's *return* in ver. 21 was the most evanescent of good purposes, while the king went back **to his place,** his home at Gibeah.

HOMILETICS.

Vers. 1—12.—*The moral use of Biblical difficulties.* The facts are—1. At the request of the Ziphites, Saul goes out in pursuit of David, who by spies ascertains his true position. 2. David, observing Saul's camp, goes to it by night with Abishai while all are asleep. 3. Abishai urges David to seize the opportunity to slay Saul, but is rebuked by the declaration that if Saul dies it shall be in such way as God may ordain, and not by the self-chosen hand of David. 4. David carries off Saul's spear and cruse of water. Expositors raise the question as to whether this narrative is identical in point of time and main circumstance with that of ch. xxiii. 19—26 ; xxiv. 1—15. That question is dealt with elsewhere. Our business is with the fact of the difficulty and with the teaching it involves. We may therefore consider—

I. THE MORAL USE OF BIBLICAL DIFFICULTIES. The difficulty raised in reference to this section is only one of a class on which for ages much ingenuity and learning have been spent, and which have been the occasion of no little trouble and anxiety to certain minds in consequence of their supposed bearing on the reality of revelation and the authority of Scripture. The enemies of Christianity have not been slow to take advantage of any apparent discrepancies or confused statements. The following considerations may be of service from a practical point of view :—1. These various difficulties *teach us the vanity of our wisdom* in relation to the unfolding of the purposes of God. God has certainly revealed his will to mankind, and wrought out a merciful purpose in Christ. None but those who reject plainest evidence can doubt that he has been pleased to give this revelation concerning his merciful purpose in the Bible as we have it. The presence of variations in narrative, as here and in Gen. i. and ii., and in the Gospels, is the fact which causes great perplexity. Now had *we* the construction of a vehicle of revelation intended for man, our wisdom would have suggested its freedom from all such difficulties to its reception. Is not this the real feeling of many ? Man would have left no room for hesitation. All should have been so clear that no adverse criticism should be possible. Facts, however, are against this wisdom. It is shown to be inadequate to deal with the vast problems of universal life. God's ways are not our ways. 2. These difficulties *enable us to believe in the honesty of the writers of the sacred history*. As soon as our wisdom is assessed we discern in the variations and free representations of the same or similar events clear evidence that the book could not have been the work of cunning men intent on making out a consistent theory of their own.   For such men would have made each document to square in detail with the one preceding, and compilers intent on furthering a theory handed down by tradition would have been careful to exclude all separate documents not manifestly coherent with others.   3. *We can use the Bible*, with these variations in it, *with deeper interest because of the intensely human character of its narratives.*   Had all been so sifted and reduced to such mathematical precision and sameness of statement as to eliminate any possible appearance of discrepancy, we should have felt the *non*-human character of the historic record.   As it is, we see human life in its pages, and trace human idiosyncracies in its varieties of representation, and as " one touch of nature makes the whole world kin," so this human element in the Bible lays hold of men, and excites in them a greater interest in its narratives.   4. The careful reader also, by means of these variations, *sees in stronger light the one spiritual purpose running through the whole.*   The great revelation of God in Christ is more conspicuous in its oneness and continuity by reason of the very diversities and sometimes irreconcilable differences of the narrative.   Our appreciation of the spiritual is the higher because we see that not one great truth is in the slightest degree affected by any verbal, chronological, or historical difficulties.   Admit them all, if need be, and the real saving truth is as clear as the sun at noonday.   5. The *difficulties in question are a means of wholesome discipline.*   All historic studies furnish scope for the exercise of caution, discrimination, patience, reticence, and suspended judgment because of the necessary incompleteness of all historic records.   This is especially true of the Bible, the more so as we do not always know the particular reason of the selection or omission of items, while we do know that we have not a thousandth part of the actual events associated with the unfolding in the long line of human history of the great purpose of God in Christ.   The light thrown on obscure passages by advancing discoveries is an additional reason for the exercise of patience and cautious reserve. God is educating us by the intricate lessons, written often with an appearance of confusion, in the rocks that form the crust of the globe ; and likewise in the peculiar manner in which he has been pleased to allow his revelation to man to be incorporated by human hands with narratives of events.

II. The special truth embodied in the facts which constitute the difficulty of this section.   The object of the narrative is evidently to point out that David was under a strong temptation to forestall the order of Providence by forcing events with his own hand, and that he, with true spiritual heroism, resisted the suggestions of expediency.   As we have dwelt on this topic in treating of ch. xxiv. 1—8, and xxv. 36— 44, it may suffice here to note how, in this triple reference to the same form of trial, the historian was impressed with the persistence of this peculiar temptation during this period of David's life.   Doubtless other unrecorded instances of the same, in one form or another, occurred during the period of his persecution, but these three representations are enough to indicate the fact.   The persistence of the temptation to desire the disposal of events to be in our own hands, by wishing something to be done which God does not do, or to take the disposal into our hands by actually doing what is not warranted by religious principle, but only by the rules of a contracted expediency, is real in the lives of many of God's servants.   Our Saviour himself was tempted to it again and again.   There is an hypothesis that even Judas was induced to betray Christ to force him to assert his power, and so hasten the establishment of his kingdom.   The trials of the persecuted Church suggested the expediency of rising in armed endeavour to defend and extend their principles.   The slow progress of Christianity suggests to some the adoption of methods other than apostolic.   The safe rule for us is that of David—God carries on his cause on earth according to laws which he himself has ordained, and no improvement can be made on them, even though their working appears to us to be too slow and painful.   Saul was anointed by God's command ; David was chosen to succeed Saul.   He who appointed Saul had power to end his life ; till he did this of his own will, and in his own way, David must wait as the coming king.   So the laws of the human mind, of the social forces at work in the world, and of the spiritual agencies that operate on the soul of man are of God ; the cause of Christ among men is to be established by action in harmony with these ; we are to resist any temptation to seek to set them aside by the introduction of agencies not spiritual, and are not to wish that other agencies operating according to other laws were in existence. The principle of living and acting according to *law* will also apply to private life and enterprise.

General lessons :—1. A reverent spirit will prove a good solvent of many Biblical difficulties, and will extract many lessons from them. 2. Where there is not concern for spiritual life the verbal and historical difficulties of the Bible will not assume great importance. 3. It is a matter of gratitude that the way of life is clear to the most unlettered of men (Isa. xxxv. 8). 4. While we are waiting and doing our best as God's servants, his providence is quietly at work to realise the purpose of our life. 5. In dealing with men who urge expediency, it is safe to appeal to God's word and his unceasing government of men. 6. No man ever regretted fidelity to principle ; many have mourned over the bitter fruits of expediency.

Vers. 13—25.—*Afflictions and righteousness.* The facts are—1. David seeks to arouse the attention of Saul by an appeal to Abner, blended with reproof of his negligence. 2. Saul, on recognising David's voice, is answered by him in terms expressive of loyal homage. 3. David appeals to Saul with respect to his conduct, pointing out its harshness and unreasonableness. 4. Saul, valuing his own life just spared, admits the force of the plea, and promises to desist from persecution. 5. David reasserts his integrity, and expresses the hope that God would accept his motives and actions. 6. Saul acknowledges the moral superiority of David, and professes to foresee his success in life. As the persistence of trial is set forth by the various items of the history, so the integrity of David is also variously illustrated. Afflictions and righteousness are most conspicuous features of his experience during the period prior to his accession to power ; beautifully suggestive to us of the conditions of our attaining to fitness for the higher service of Christ (Acts xiv. 22). The general teaching of the section may be arranged under the following statements :—

I. That IT IS CONSISTENT WITH SUBMISSION TO THE WILL OF GOD TO ENDEAVOUR TO REMOVE THE HUMAN CAUSES OF TROUBLE. The life and writings of David prove his trust in God and acquiescence in his appointments ; at the same time he spared no pains to get rid of the troubles of his life by removing the causes of them as existing in the mind of Saul. In this fresh appeal he declares to Saul that if God be the mover of his spirit to do these things (ver. 19), he has no more to say, only let it be proved. His appeal to Abner was an additional effort to remove the trouble, since not Saul only, but the general and army would now see in his abstinence from violence the purity of his motives. The same course is proper for all in tribulation. Trials are permitted, and are blessed in their effects when rightly received (Heb. xii. 6—11) ; but we have to do with preventible causes, and may seek to remove them. Even the failure of effort to remove causes of trouble which, being human, ought not to operate, in becoming itself a trial is the more blessed in its effects because of our having done our duty. God's secret purposes and methods are not the rules of our action, and any fruitless action of ours performed in reverent submission to his unsearchable will is itself a means of grace, because of his turning it to spiritual profit.

II. That THERE IS A DOUBLE BASIS OF APPEAL TO MEN BENT ON A WRONG COURSE which should regulate our dealings with them. David addresses himself to Saul's sense of right and to his reasoning powers. "What have I done?" The answer was clear in Saul's conscience. "Now, therefore, I pray thee, let my lord the king *hear the words* of his servant." The reasoning powers of Saul gave heed and were convinced by the subsequent argument. In our private controversies, in our efforts to win men over to Christ, and in our treatment of the young, we are on safe ground when we address the moral and rational nature. A wise appeal to the two cannot be wholly lost. Man is compelled by force of his nature to recognise right when placed before the eye of conscience, and the laws of thought insure the acquiescence of reason when the argument is intrinsically as well as formally sound. It is this necessary recognition of truth and right which forms the philosophical ground for faith in the final triumph of Christianity, and wise teachers as well as private Christians may labour on in confidence as long as they present the truth of God in an earnest and prayerful spirit.

III. That THE DEFECTIVE MORAL CONDITION OF WEAK MINDS LAYS THEM OPEN TO THE PERNICIOUS CONTROL OF BASE MEN OF STRONGER MIND. David hit the mark when he said, "If they be the children of men." The strong-willed men at the court of Saul, and referred to in the Psalms, had obtained influence over him, and by lies and slanders had embittered his spirit against David. But it was the decayed piety and persistently impenitent spirit in Saul which exposed him to this danger; for even a weaker intellect will resist the stronger in matters of moral conduct when the heart is sound in its spiritual tendencies. A man's moral condition has more to do with his superiority to the devices and urgencies of the strong and crafty than his knowledge or force of intellect. Moral affinities are powerful for good or evil, and moral repulsions are life's safeguards for the good. Hence the supreme importance of a new heart and a right spirit. Hence, also, the profound wisdom of the New Testament teaching and the mercy of the provision for our renewal. The bearing of this on our education of youth, on personal resistance of temptation, and on the means for counteracting the influence of powerful but unholy men, is obvious.

IV. That a RECOGNITION OF RIGHT AND WRONG IN CONDUCT MAY BE PERFECTLY SINCERE, BUT DESTITUTE OF GOVERNING POWER OVER THE LIFE. Under the appeal to conscience and reason Saul admitted his wrong and folly, and David's right and wisdom. Being just then keenly alive to the value of deliverance from death, he was prompted to let right and reason exercise a legitimate sway over his thoughts, and thus was honest in his declaration. Yet the recognition was, so to speak, intellectual, and not moral. It was admission of truth, not response to its power over the life. Men are not governed in conduct by thoughts, or propositions, or formal confessions of right and propriety, but by positive tendencies of their moral nature. And as Saul's tendencies were not altered by the interview with David, his recognition of right failed to become a power over his conduct in days hence. We often see how men delude themselves by regarding a recognition of right as tantamount to a healthy moral condition for the time being. Here again we come upon the fundamental truth that a radical change of nature is the only hope of salvation and safeguard of daily life.

V. That THE PAIN OF SEPARATION FROM THE PRIVILEGES OF WORSHIP IS ONE OF THE SEVEREST TRIALS OF GODLY MEN. Of hunger and thirst David said nothing, nor of loss of social position; but he dwelt with emphatic language on the grievous wrong of driving him from "the inheritance of the Lord," virtually saying, "Go, serve other gods." As the hart panteth after the water-brooks, so did his soul pant after God (Ps. xli. 1—4). As the patriot feels the anguish of exile, so more keenly does a servant of God feel banishment by man from the fellowship and hallowed joys of the sanctuary. Those in authority should be very careful lest by harsh conduct they drive away into godless regions of thought and association men of noble, reverent spirit. Origen, Luther, and others have shared the bitterness of David; and even our Lord was cast out from the Jewish Church, and was taunted with the suggestion of going to "teach the Gentiles" (John vii. 35). Our love to the house of the Lord and for the communion of saints is a test of the reality of our piety.

VI. That INTEGRITY OF CONDUCT IS A CONDITION OF RECEIVING GOD'S BLESSING, AND MAY WITH ALL HUMILITY BE ASSERTED. David was most deeply conscious of being a loyal, loving subject, free from ambition or desire to do other than good to his king. He referred to his sparing Saul in evidence of this, and now, as in the presence of God, affirms that, so far as his conduct toward Saul was concerned, he was quite prepared to abide by the Divine rule of rendering to every man "his righteousness and his faithfulness." So far as his own personal deliverance from tribulation was to be measured to him according to his treatment of Saul, he was quite satisfied that it would be complete. Here is no trusting to personal goodness for pardon and eternal life, no glorying in his own virtues; but a strong assertion of his integrity of conduct in one particular, and a belief that, so far as integrity in this case was a condition of being blessed, he would not come short of the blessing. The Old Testament is one with the New in the conditions of pardon and eternal life, and also in the condition of godly men being prospered in their way. When challenged with reference to a particular deed, it is legitimate to affirm our righteousness with all solemnity, and with a deep sense of our general unworthiness before God.

VII. That MEN WHOSE LIVES ARE CONSCIOUSLY WRONG AND UNSATISFACTORY INWARDLY RECOGNISE THE SUPERIORITY OF THOSE THEY OPPOSE, and discern the signs of coming success. Saul felt David to be the nobler man, and under the transitory influence of truth he openly avowed what was always felt (ver. 25). Much of the resentment cherished against him had arisen from the conviction, so unwelcome to the envious, of his being endowed with qualities that would justify the anointing by Samuel. The silent homage to goodness is universal. Instances have occurred in biographies testifying that while in former antagonism to Christian truth and Christian men the writer was sensible of the beauty and power of Christian character, and saw in it elements of future happiness not in his own. The tone of the opposition to Christ and his apostles reveals the same fact. The character built up by a true piety is a creation of God, and is among his noblest works, as it is also most permanent. The more we can present such a character before men, the more shall we multiply the evidences of Christianity, and reveal to mankind in what lies the germ of permanent success.

HOMILIES BY VARIOUS AUTHORS.

Vers. 1—12. (THE HILL OF HACHILAH.)—*The man worthy of the sceptre.* " And David took the spear and the cruse of water from Saul's bolster" (ver. 12). 1. David's *innocence* with respect to any evil design against Saul was fully vindicated at their previous meeting. Saul himself was melted to tears, confessed, "Thou art more righteous than I," &c., prayed that the Lord might reward his preserver, and declared, "I know well that thou shalt surely be king" (ch. xxiv. 17—20); but his insincerity, instability, and perversity were such that as soon as he was informed by the treacherous Ziphites that David was again in the hill of Hachilah (ch. xxiii. 19), he started in pursuit with his 3000 men (ch. xiii. 2). His sin was now greater than before because of its opposition to his clearer conviction of the integrity of David and the purpose of God, and there are indications in this interview of the increased obduracy of his heart. 2. The aim of David is not so much to afford a further vindication of himself as to *stay the persecution* of Saul, and induce him to act in accordance with his former confession (ver. 18). For this purpose he proves to him that although he might have the power to deprive him of his authority and life, he has no wish to do so, and is his most faithful guardian (ver. 16); appeals to his best feelings, and warns him that he is fighting against God and exposing himself to his righteous judgment. He takes away his spear-sceptre (an emblem of royal authority—Gen. xlix. 10; Num. xxiv. 17; Ps. xlv. 6) and his cruse of water (a necessary sustenance of life—ch. xxv. 11), but only to restore them into his hand (ver. 22). 3. In acting thus David shows his incomparable *superiority* to Saul, and that he alone is worthy to reign over Israel, even as he has been ordained to succeed to that exalted dignity. "Behold now, once more, our David, as he goes away with Saul's spear, the emblem of his sovereign power. At that moment he presents a symbolically significant appearance. Unconsciously he prophesied of his own future, while he stands before us as the projected shadow of that form in which we must one day behold him. In the counsel of the invisible Watcher it was indeed irrevocably concluded that the Bethlehemite should inherit Saul's sceptre, and here we see before us a dim pre-intimation of that fact" (Krummacher). As the man most worthy to rule, and furnishing in some respects a pattern to others, he was distinguished (see ch. xiii. 14) by—

I. PRE-EMINENT ABILITY (vers. 4—7). In the enterprise which he undertook during the night (either with the express intention of doing what he did, or from some internal impulse) he displayed those qualities for which Saul and his ablest general, Abner, were noted, and in a higher degree than they, viz.—1. *Sagacity*, skill (Ps. lxxviii. 72), and practical wisdom; perceiving what was defective in the condition of his adversaries and how to take advantage of it. Tact, although by no means one of the highest mental endowments, is an indispensable qualification in a successful ruler. 2. *Vigilance.* His experiences in the desert had taught him to be ever on the alert, and he watched while others slept (vers. 4, 16). 3. *Courage.* "Who will go down with me to Saul to the camp?" (ver. 6). Even the brave Hittite dared not accept the challenge, and only Abishai (afterwards David's preserver—2 Sam. xxi. 17) would accompany him. They went fearlessly (like Jonathan and his armour-bearer) right into the midst of danger. 4. *Energy* and activity, by which alone he could achieve success. Mental and physical strength is of God, should be ascribed to him and employed for him.

> "For by thee I can scatter a troop,
> And by my God do I break down walls;
> Who maketh my feet like hinds' feet,
> And setteth me on my high places;
> Who traineth my hands for war,
> So that mine arms can bend a bow of brass"
> (Perowne, Ps. xviii. 29, 33, 34).

II. LOWLY REVERENCE, submission, and obedience. "The Lord forbid that I should stretch forth mine hand against the Lord's anointed" (ver. 11; ch. xxiv. 6). There was in David (as there should be in others)—1. An unbounded reverence for *God* as the source of power, justice, order, and all excellence. This was the principle from which his conduct toward Saul proceeded. 2. Profound respect for every *authority* ordained by God. Saul had been anointed king, and was still openly reigning by Divine permission (his rejection having been only privately declared to him); his person was therefore regarded by David as sacred. "Liable as the Israelite kings were to interference on the part of priest and prophet, they were, by the same Divine power, shielded from the unholy hands of the profane vulgar; and it was at once impiety and rebellion to do injury to the Lord's anointed" (Kitto, 'Cyc. of Bib. Lit.'). "He gives two reasons why he would not destroy Saul, nor permit another to do it:— (1) It would be a sinful affront to God's ordinance. (2) It would be a sinful anticipation of God's providence" (M. Henry). 3. Due subordination of the *claims* of every such authority to the claims of God; which both rulers and subjects, who have proper reverence for him, must observe. 4. Entire subjection of *personal impulses*, purposes, and aims to the will of God, in the assurance that he will "render to every man his righteousness and his faithfulness" (ver. 23). "Commit thy way unto the Lord," &c. (Ps. xxxvii. 5—9).

III. NOBLE GENEROSITY. "Destroy him not," &c. (vers. 8—11; Ps. lvii., inscription, Altaschith = Destroy not; see Hengstenberg). The opportunity of slaying his enemy was again placed in his hands, and in sparing him a second time David showed still greater forbearance than before, because of—1. The renewed persecution to which he was subjected, and the increased hopelessness of turning Saul from his purpose. "I say not unto thee, Until seven times," &c. (Matt. xviii. 22—35). 2. The peculiar circumstances of the case. He was there *alone* with Abishai in the night, and his companion entreated that he might be permitted to give but one stroke (ver. 8). None else would witness the deed. Moral restraint alone prevented his permission of it. 3. His not entertaining the temptation for a moment; even the thought of it could find no place in his breast. Recent experience had evidently strengthened his spirit (ch. xxv. 32). 4. His fixed determination to leave the matter entirely with God (ver. 10). "It is evident that David's faith in God was one of the great roots out of which all these fruits of forbearance and compassion grew. He was confident that God would in his own way and in his own time fulfil the promises which had been made, and, therefore, instead of taking the matter into his own hands, he could rest in the Lord and wait patiently for him" (C. Vince). And he alone who will exercise power in mercy as well as in justice is worthy to have it intrusted to him.

IV. DIVINE APPROVAL. "A deep sleep from the Lord was fallen upon them" (ver. 12), indicative of the fact that the Lord "favoured David's enterprise." He was providentially preserved from harm, and this, along with many other circumstances (all concurring with his eminent personal qualifications), manifested it to be the will of God that he should rule over his people. The sceptre which he had no desire to wrest from the hand of Saul would be given to him by the hand of God, and be "a sceptre of uprightness." The highest realisation of these principles appears in One greater than David, and alone "worthy to receive" the sceptre of universal dominion (ch. ii. 10; 2 Sam. xxiii. 2; Phil. ii. 9; Heb. i. 8; Rev. v. 5, 12).—D.

Vers. 13—16. (THE HILL OF HACHILAH.)—*Manliness.* "Art not thou a man?" (ver. 15). A man should prove worthy of himself; his nature, power, dignity, and responsibility. Every man should do so (not only every one who, like Abner, occupies an exceptional position), for every man (fallen though he be) is great. "Let us not disparage that nature which is common to all men; for no thought can measure its grandeur. It is the image of God, the image of his infinity; for no limits can be set to its unfolding. He who possesses the Divine powers of the soul is a great being, be his place what it may. You may clothe him with rags, may immure him in a dungeon, may chain him to slavish tasks; but he is still great. Man is a greater name than president or king" (Channing, 'Self-culture').

> "A beam ethereal, sullied and absorpt;
> Though sullied and dishonoured, still Divine!" (Young).

In order that he may act according to his true nature, and not unworthily of it—1. *The body must be the servant of the soul.* It was designed, with its various passions, to obey, and not to rule; and to keep it "in subjection' (1 Cor. ix. 27) requires watchfulness, self-control, and manly strength.

> "Call to mind from whence ye sprang;
> Ye were not form'd to live the life of brutes,
> But virtue to pursue and knowledge high" (Dante, 'Inferno').

2. *The mind must be faithful to the truth;* esteeming it as more precious than gold, searching for it as for hid treasure, receiving it on proper evidence, cleaving to it when discovered, and confessing it without fear. Here is room for the exercise of the highest *virtue* or martial courage. "In understanding be men" (1 Cor. xiv. 20). 3. *The heart must be set on the supreme good;* resisting and overcoming the temptation to set its affections on wealth, pleasure, fame, that "satisfy not" (Ps. iv. 6).

> "Let thy heels spurn the earth, and thy raised ken
> Fix on the lure which heaven's eternal King
> Whirls in the rolling spheres.
>   O ye misguided souls!
> Infatuate, who from such a good estrange
> Your hearts, and bend your gaze on vanity,
> Alas for you!" (Dante).

4. *The conscience must be reverenced as the king;* its integrity defended against all foes, its voice obeyed at all risks, and its favour desired above all earthly dignities. "Reverence thyself" (ch. xxii. 22). 5. *The will must be fixed on doing the will of God*—resolutely, firmly, and constantly; in striving against sin, advancing in holiness, and promoting his kingdom. "Watch ye, stand fast in the faith, quit you like men, be strong" (1 Cor. xvi. 13).

> "Be as the tower that, firmly set,
> Shakes not its top for any blast that blows."

6. *The character must be conformed to that of "the man Christ Jesus,"* the highest and only perfect pattern of true manhood (John xiii. 15; Ephes. iv. 13; Phil. ii. 5), and the Saviour and Helper of all who endeavour to be like him. 7. *The present life must be a preparation for the future.* Man is made to live for ever, and it is not manly to live only for the passing moment. He who sleeps at his post of duty and neglects to watch and pray is surely "worthy to die" (ver. 16). "Look up to heaven, look down to hell, live for eternity!"—D.

Vers. 13—25. (THE HILL OF HACHILAH.)—*David's last meeting with Saul.* 1. This meeting took place *at night.* The encampment of Saul was over against the desert by the way (ver. 3). The light of the stars, or of the moon, and the flickering camp-fires, together with the intense silence of the place, would enable the quick eye and ear of David to perceive its position and defenceless condition. And it may have been early morning when, on his return from his adventurous and successful enterprise, the voice of David rang across the ravine which separated him from it. "Answerest thou not, Abner?' 2. The conversation that followed occurred in the presence of the *followers of Saul*, and was doubtless heard by them, on awaking, like Abner, out of the deep sleep that had fallen upon them (ver. 12). At the former interview Saul was alone with David and his men, and, having no reason for concern about the manner in which his royal dignity, of which he was always so jealous, might be regarded by others, his feelings were less restrained and his expressions more explicit. What was now said must have shown them the evil of the course he pursued; it was a public testimony against the wickedness of the men who incited him to it (ver. 19), and could not but convince them of David's integrity and future success (ver. 25). 3. It took place under circumstances which made it *impossible* for Saul to do him harm. David's distrust of him was such that he took care to gain a safe position before speaking. The temptation to get him into his power was always too strong for Saul to resist. He was not morally, but physically, restrained from effecting his purpose (ch. xxv. 32). David could have destroyed Saul, but he would not; Saul would have destroyed David, but he could not; he was under the dominion of a depraved will, even when he expressed his determination to abandon his evil designs, and seemed to himself and others sincerely penitent. In this interview then we see—

I. THE CONSCIOUS INTEGRITY OF AN UPRIGHT HEART. After asking, "Wherefore doth my lord pursue after his servant?" &c., David said, "If the Lord have stirred thee up against me," &c. (vers. 19, 20); and again, "The Lord render to every man his righteousness," &c. (vers. 23, 24). His conscious integrity appears in—1. *Earnestly urging the adoption of proper means to overcome temptation.* "Pray to God that he take the temptation from thee" (Bunsen). "Let no man say when he is tempted, I am tempted of God," &c. (James i. 13, 14). But God often affords him opportunity to manifest the evil that is in his heart, with a view to his conviction of sin and turning from it; and "if he does not repent, the *forms* in which sin exhibits itself are no longer under his control, but under God's dispensation, who determines them as pleases him, as accords with the plan of his government of the world, for his own honour, and, so long as he is not absolutely rejected, for the good of the sinner" (Hengstenberg). And he has respect to the offering that is presented to him in righteousness (Gen. iv. 7). The meat offering (*minchah*) here meant "was appended to the burnt and peace offerings to show that the object of such offerings was the sanctification of the people by fruitfulness in well-doing, and that without this the end aimed at never could be attained" (Fairbairn). David spoke from his deep experience of temptation, his faithful endeavour after holiness, his exalted estimation of the Divine favour and help, and was as desirous that Saul should stand in a right relation to God as of his own deliverance from persecution (Ps. cxli. 2). "The way in which he addresses Saul is so humble, so gentle, and so reverent that we may sufficiently thence recognise the goodness of his heart." 2. *Solemn invocation of Divine judgment on wicked men who incite to wickedness.* "If it be the children of men," &c. (ver. 19). This is in accordance with the tone which pervades the imprecatory psalms, and should be interpreted in the light of his personal conduct toward Saul, his zeal for the kingdom and righteousness of God, the facts of the Divine treatment of evil men, similar expressions in the New Testament (Matt. xi. 21; xxiii. 13—39; Acts viii. 20; 1 Cor. v. 5; 2 Tim. iv. 4), and the inferior position occupied by saints under the Old Testament dispensation (see commentaries on the Psalms by Tholuck, Perowne, and others). "When David's whole career is intelligently and fairly viewed, it leaves on the mind the impression of a man of as meek and placable a temper as was ever associated with so great strength of will and such strong passions" (Binnie, 'The Psalms'). "David is the Old Testament type of the inviolable majesty of Christ, and therefore his imprecations are prophetic of the final doom of the hardened enemies of Christ and his Church. As such they are simply an expansion of the prayer, 'Thy kingdom come.' For the kingdom of God comes not only by the showing of mercy to the penitent, but also by the executing of judgment on the impenitent" (Kurtz). 3. *Fervent entreaty of an enemy to abandon his unjust, unpitying, and unworthy designs.* "Now, therefore," &c. (ver. 20). "This speech of David was thoroughly suited to sharpen Saul's conscience and lead him to give up his enmity, if he still had an ear for the voice of truth" (Keil). 4. *Confidently appealing to the perfect justice of God and his merciful interposition on his behalf.* "The Lord render to every man," &c. (vers. 23, 24). This is not the language of boastfulness or self-righteousness, but "the answer of a good conscience toward God." He desired that God would deal with him as he had dealt with others (Ps. vii. 4, 5), and fully vindicate his "righteousness and faithfulness" by delivering him "out of all tribulation." Only one who was consciously upright in heart could speak thus; and similar expressions often occur in the Psalms (Ps. xvii. 1—5). "The Psalmist is not asserting his freedom from sin, but the uprightness and guilelessness of his heart toward God. He is no hypocrite, no dissembler; he is not consciously doing wrong" (Perowne). In addition to the eight psalms previously mentioned as referred by their inscriptions to the time of Saul's persecution, there are two others, viz., Ps. LXIII., 'Longing in the wilderness for the presence of God in the sanctuary' (see inscription; vers. 19, 20):—

> "O God, thou art my God; early will I seek thee.
> My soul thirsteth for thee, my flesh pineth for thee,
> In a dry and weary land where no water is."

Ps. XVIII., 'An idealised representation of the experience of Divine deliverances' (see inscription; 2 Sam. xxii.). Other psalms have also been referred by many to the same period as "the fruitful soil of David's psalm poetry," viz., Ps. vi., xi., xii., xiii., xvii., xxii., xxvii., xxxi., xxxv., xl., lvi., lviii., lix., lxiv., lxix., cix., cxx., cxl., cxli.

II. THE UNCONSCIOUS INSINCERITY OF AN EVIL HEART. "And Saul said, I have sinned," &c. (vers. 21, 25). He acknowledged the sin and folly of his past conduct (though not with tears, as before), invited David to return, and promised no more to do him harm, uttered a benediction upon him, and predicted that he would "do great things and prevail" (omitting, however, any allusion to his royal dignity, as on the former occasion)—"at once a vindication of David's conduct in the past, and a forecast of his glory in the future." He doubtless meant at the time what he said, but it is to be observed that—1. *The most corrupt heart is capable of good impressions, emotions, and purposes.* History and observation afford innumerable instances of the fact. 2. *It is apt to be the subject of them under special circumstances* (ch. xxiv. 16—22), and particularly when convinced of the futility of sinful endeavours, and restrained by a power which cannot be effectually resisted. "Behold, thou hast spoken and done evil things as thou couldest" (Jer. iii. 5). So long as the power to do evil things is possessed, it is exercised; but when it is taken away men often seem sincerely penitent and fully determined to do good. But how seldom does the "goodness" exhibited in such circumstances prove really sincere and enduring! 3. *The experience of them is no certain evidence* to a man himself or others of a right state of heart. They are liable to deceive, and can only be depended upon when expressed and confirmed by corresponding and continuous acts. Strong feeling is often temporary and never transformed into settled principle. 4. *The removal of the influences* by which they are produced, and the occurrence of favourable opportunities for the manifestation of the true character, commonly prove its utter *insincerity.* It was thus with Saul. He did not repent in deeds of righteousness, nor "bring forth fruits meet for repentance." On the contrary, he soon afterwards renewed his persecution, and ceased not until David was wholly beyond his power (ch. xxvii. 1). "They return, but not to the most High: they are like a deceitful bow" (Hosea vii. 16). He was under the dominion of an evil disposition and depraved will, and with every broken promise of amendment his moral condition became worse, until he sank into despair. "The only good thing in the world is a good will" (Kant).

> "But ill for him who, bettering not with time,
> Corrupts the strength of heaven-descended Will,
> And ever weaker grows through acted crime,
> Or seeming genial venial fault,
> Recurring and suggesting still!

He seems as one whose footsteps halt,
Toiling in immeasurable sand,
And o'er a weary, sultry land,
Far beneath a blazing vault,
Sown in a wrinkle of the monstrous hill,
The city sparkles like a grain of salt" (Tennyson).   **D.**

Ver. 21. (THE HILL OF HACHILAH.)—*Playing the fool.* "Behold, I have played the fool, and have erred exceedingly." At his first wrong step it was said to Saul by Samuel, "Thou hast done foolishly" (ch. xiii. 13); and now (a man of about sixty years of age), looking back upon a long course of disobedience and self-will, and more especially upon his recent persecution of David, he himself said, "I have sinned. . . Behold, I have done foolishly, and have erred exceedingly." "There is no sinner so hardened but that God gives him now and then a ray of illumination to show him all his error." And under its influence many a man, in reviewing the past, has been constrained to make a similar confession. With reference to the case of Saul, a man plays the fool—1. *When he suffers illusive thoughts and sinful passions to find a place within him.* This was the root of Saul's wasted and miserable life. How different would it have been if he had adopted proper means to expel such thoughts and passions from his breast, and prevent their return! " How long shall thy vain thoughts lodge within thee?" (Jer. iv. 14). 2. *When he listens to the false representations of wicked men,* insinuating, it may be, suspicions of his best friend, and urging him to regard him as his worst enemy (ch. xxiv. 9). 3. *When he acts in opposition to what he knows to be right.* Saul had done so continually, following the impulses of "an evil heart of unbelief," instead of the dictates of reason and conscience. "Therefore to him that knoweth to do good, and doeth it not, to him it is sin" (James iv. 17). 4. *When he rests in feelings merely, and does not translate them into deeds* (ch. xxiv. 17). They are "dead without works." Every delay to act in accordance with them weakens their power, renders it less likely that they will ever be acted upon, and prepares the way for the return of the "evil spirit." 5. *When he makes good resolutions and immediately breaks them* (ver. 21), thereby destroying his moral power, and hardening himself in sin. 6. *When he contends against the Divine purposes in the vain hope of succeeding* (ver. 25). Sooner or later he must be crushed. "Who hath hardened himself against him and prospered?" (Job ix. 4). 7. *When he expects to find happiness except in connection with holiness.* The illusion is dispelled, if not before, at the hour of death and the dawn of eternity, and he has to confess his folly when it is too late to repair it.—D.

Ver. 21.—*A fool returns to his folly.* I. THE BIBLE IS FULL OF REDUPLICATION. It teaches by line upon line, precept upon precept, and narrative upon narrative. There are repetitions of the same story or song. There are also separate and independent narratives which go over similar ground, and teach the same lessons, the second confirming the first. Joseph is described as having had duplicate dreams with one and the same meaning. So also Pharaoh. Nebuchadnezzar's dream of empires is followed by Daniel's dream of the same. And there are duplicate parables of Jesus Christ. Then actual events described are followed by other events so closely resembling them that they might almost be taken for the same—*e. g.* Abraham's weakness, Sarah's danger, and Pharaoh's respect for the sanctity of marriage (Gen. xii.) seem to be all repeated (Gen. xx.), with the Abimelech of Gerar substituted for the Pharaoh of Egypt. And then all the incidents are told again of Isaac and Rebekah, and the Abimelech of their time (Gen. xxvi.). We have Moses fetching water from the rock in Horeb, and the same prophet fetching water from a rock at Kadesh Barnea; Jesus Christ anointed by a woman in the house of Simon the Pharisee, and the same Divine Master anointed by a woman in the house of Simon the leper. Again, we have Jesus feeding 5000 men, besides women and children, from a small stock of bread and fish, and then the same Lord feeding 4000, besides women and children, from a similar inadequate supply. The similarity of the story in this chapter to that which we have read in the twenty-fourth chapter of this book need not surprise us, or raise a suspicion that they are independent reports of the same adventure admitted into the pages of the history by a clumsy compiler. The reduplication is in harmony with Biblical usage; nay, more, it is in harmony with historical truth.

II. HISTORY IS FULL OF REPETITION. In private life the same conditions recur with startling precision; and in public affairs the same emergencies occur again and again, and lead to the same line of action, the same remedies, and even the same blunders. Why should it be thought incredible, or even improbable, that Saul fell back into his former mood of hostility to David? Alas, what is more common than that fools forget admonition, and return to their folly; sinners, after promises of amendment, relapse into their old sins? The amendment goes against secret inclination, whereas the sin indulges some constitutional propensity or passion. So it is that a man who has grown too fond of strong drink, after abstaining from it for a time, goes back to his bottle. A libertine, after a short attempt to live purely, goes back to his intrigues. And in like manner Saul, being passionately jealous, forbore from the pursuit of David only for a season, and then, at the first offer of help from the Ziphites, went back to his cruel pursuit of the son of Jesse. There are cases in which history repeats itself on the favourable side, in a return to goodness; but such is man, that the more frequent experience is of a return to evil courses, obliterating the very traces of a short-lived, superficial repentance.

III. SUPERFICIAL REPENTANCE MAY BE EXPECTED TO END IN RELAPSE. We mean by superficial repentance a mere emotional effect, while the root of sin lies undisturbed in the unrenewed will. A man of impulsive constitution can repent in this fashion again and again, with no conscious insincerity, and yet remain at heart the same; nay, grow worse in the very habit of lamenting without abandoning his besetting sin. There is some indication of such a falling off in Saul. On the first occasion, when his life was spared at Engedi, he shed tears over David's magnanimity and his own folly, and he openly confessed that the man whom he had sought to kill was more righteous than himself, and was destined to fill the throne. On the second occasion, at Hachilah, he was ready again to confess his fault and to promise abandonment of his unnatural and unjust pursuit of David, but we hear nothing of tears. There is a ring of vexation rather than of contrition about his confession: "I have sinned. I have played the fool." Cases of superficial repentance leading to relapse and deterioration are not rare. Emotion fades away; and some temptation is sure to come, as the Ziphites came to Saul and induced him to resume what he had renounced. So it happens that converts from among the heathen, who are changed only on the surface, and not in heart, but are baptized and endure well for a while, relapse under temptation into their old customs. Criminals in our own country, who have to all appearance sincerely repented, and have, after undergoing punishment, begun a new course of life, relapse after a while into the old roguery, tired of honest industry. In fact, it is not so difficult to induce men to turn over a new leaf as to keep them, after turning it, from turning back again.

IV. ONE MAY MUCH ADMIRE NOBLE CONDUCT AND YET NEVER IMITATE IT. Saul retained enough of his early magnanimity to feel the moral superiority of David's behaviour—his grand forbearance and chivalrous loyalty. He acknowledged the contrast between David's conduct and his own, and yet he never imitated what he admired. He turned back from the pursuit, as he had done before, but he did not reinstate his son-in-law in the honour to which he was entitled, or relieve him of the harassing sense of insecurity. So we often see that it is one thing to recognise and applaud what is good, another thing to do it. How many admire great and generous characters in history, poetry, and romance, and yet themselves remain small-minded and ungenerous! How many applaud good men and kind actions, and yet continue in their own bad habits and selfish lines of conduct, without any vigorous effort to follow what they praise! After all, a man is himself, and not another, and as his heart is, so will his action be. Unless the tree be made good from the root, it is vain to expect good fruit on its branches.

V. A SELF-ACCUSER MAY BE PROUDER THAN ONE WHO PROTESTS HIS INNOCENCE. A careless reader might think better of Saul confessing his folly so frankly than of David appealing to God for his integrity. But he who appeared so humble was still proud and obstinate, and he who maintained his rectitude was of a lowly and tender heart. A certain amount of self-reproach is quite easy to a pliant nature, which takes emotion quickly on its surface, and yet is quite unchanged beneath. Such was Saul's confession, which did not for a moment change his character or delay his fate. On the other hand, self-vindication against misrepresentation and unjust treatment may issue from a man who entirely abhors self-righteousness and self-praise. It is this which we trace in David and the prophets; in the Apostle Paul, and in the greatest and lowliest, the man Christ Jesus. A servant of God breaks no rule of humility when he repels calumny, and asserts his innocence or his integrity. In this view read the seventeenth and eighteenth Psalms, the latter of which has a significant title—"Of David, the servant of God." All the Psalms are for the servants of the Lord. Sometimes, alas, they can chant none but those which are penitential, because sin has prevailed against them and defiled them. But in their experience of the mercies and deliverances of the Lord they can sing praises; and in the consciousness of the cleanness of their hands, their innocence and integrity of purpose and action towards their fellow-men, they may even venture to go through the hundred and nineteenth Psalm in all that wonderful strain of devout feeling which combines with cries for Divine pardon and direction, assertions of loyal obedience and entire sincerity.—F.

EXPOSITION.

DAVID FINDS A REFUGE AT ZIKLAG (CH. XXVII.).

CHAPTER XXVII.

DAVID AGAIN SEEKS PROTECTION AT GATH (vers. 1—4). Ver. 1.—**David said in his heart.** Hebrew, "to his heart," to himself (see ch. i. 13). **I shall perish by the hand.** The verb is that used in ch. xii. 25; xxvi. 10, but instead of *by the hand* the Hebrew has *into the hand.* Hence the versions generally render it, "I shall some day fall into the hand." Really it is a *prægnans construction:* "I shall perish by falling into the hand of Saul." It was the second treachery of the Ziphites which made David feel that, surrounded as he was by spies, there was no safety for him but in taking that course to which, as he so sorrowfully complained to Saul, his enemies were driving him (ch. xxvi. 19). His words there show that the thought of quitting Judæa was already in his mind, so that this chapter follows naturally on ch.xxvi., and not, as some have argued, upon ch. xxiv.

Vers. 2—4.—**Achish, the son of Maoch.** No doubt the Achish of ch. xxi. 10; but if the same as **Achish, son of Maachah,** in 1 Kings ii. 39, as is probably the case, he must have lived to a good old age. As it is said in 1 Chron. xviii. 1 that David conquered the Philistines, and took from them Gath and other towns, it would seem that he still permitted Achish to remain there as a tributary king, while Ziklag he kept as his private property (ver. 6). On the former occasion, when David was alone, Achish had paid him but scant courtesy; but now that he came with 600 warriors, each **with his household,** and, therefore, with numerous followers, he shows him every respect, and for the time David and his men settle at Gath, and Saul gives over his pursuit, knowing that if he followed him into Philistine territory he would provoke a war, for which he was not now prepared. It has been pointed out that David probably introduced from Gath the style of music called Gittith (Ps. viii., lxxxi., lxxxiv., titles).

ACHISH ASSIGNS ZIKLAG TO DAVID AS A RESIDENCE (vers. 5—7). Vers. 5, 6.—**If I have now found grace in thine eyes.** *Now* is not an adverb of time, but means "I pray," *i. e.* If verily I have found favour with thee. David's position was one of difficulty. The fame of his exploits, and of Saul's vain pursuit of him, made Achish no doubt regard him as a bitter foe of the Israelite king, and expect valuable assistance from him; whereas David was unwilling to take up arms even against Saul, and much less against his own countrymen. He is anxious, therefore, to get away from a too close observation of his acts, and requests Achish to give him **a place in some town in the country.** Hebrew, "a place in one of the cities in the field." **Why should thy servant,** &c. David's presence with so large a following must in many ways have been inconvenient as well as expensive to Achish. In some small country town David and his men would maintain themselves. Achish accordingly gives him **Ziklag,** a small place assigned first of all to Judah (Josh. xv. 31), but subsequently to Simeon (*ibid.* xix. 5). Its exact position is not known. It seems to have been valued by David's successors, as it is noted that it still belonged **unto the kings of Judah.** This phrase proves that the Book of Samuel must have been compiled at a date subsequent to the revolt of Jeroboam, while the concluding words, **unto this day,** equally plainly indicate a date prior to the Babylonian exile.

Ver. 7.—**A full year.** Hebrew, "days." Rashi argues in favour of its meaning *some days*, and Josephus says the time of David's stay in Philistia was "four months and twenty days;" but already in ch. i. 3; ii. 19, we have had the phrase "from days day-ward" in the sense of *yearly*, and comp. Levit. xxv. 29; Judges xvii. 10; also *ibid.* xix. 2, where the A. V. translates the Hebrew *days four months* as meaning "four months" only. Probably, as here, it is a year and four months, though the omission of the conjunction is a difficulty. So too for "after a time" (*ibid.* xiv. 8) it should be "after a year"—Hebrew, *after days.*

EXPEDITIONS OF DAVID FROM ZIKLAG (vers. 8—12). Ver. 8.—**Went up.** The Geshurites inhabited the high table-land which forms the north-eastern portion of the wilderness of Paran. Like the Kenites, they seem to have broken up into scattered tribes, as we find one portion of them in the neighbourhood of Bashan (Deut. iii. 14), and another in Syria (2 Sam. xv. 8). Probably, like the Amalekites, they were a Bedouin race, and so great wanderers. Hence the verb translated **invaded** is literally "spread themselves out" like a fan, so as to enclose these nomads, whose safety lay in flight. **Gezrites.** The written text has *Girzites*, which the Kri has changed into Gezrites, probably from a wish to connect a name never mentioned elsewhere with the town of Gezer. But Gezer lay far away in the west of Ephraim, and the connection suggested in modern times of the Girzites with Mount Gerizim in Central Palestine is more probable. They would thus be the remains of a once more powerful people, dispossessed by the Amorites, but who were now probably a very feeble remnant. **For those nations,** &c. The grammar and translation of this clause are both full of difficulties, but the following rendering is perhaps the least objectionable: "For these were (the families) inhabiting the land, which were of old, as thou goest towards Shur," &c. *Families* must be supplied because the participle *inhabiting* is feminine. What, then, the narrator means to say is that these three Bedouin tribes were the aboriginal inhabitants of the north-western portion of the desert between Egypt and South Palestine. On the **Amalekites** see ch. xv. 2. We need not wonder at finding them mentioned again so soon after Saul's expedition. A race of nomads would sustain no great harm from an expedition which soon began to occupy itself with capturing cattle. On **Shur** see ch. xv. 7.

Vers. 9, 10.—**David smote the land.** These expeditions were made partly to occupy his men, but chiefly to obtain the means of subsistence. They also seem to have brought

David great renown, for in 1 Chron. xii. 1—22 we read of warriors from far distant tribes coming to him to swell his forces, and the enthusiasm for him was even such that a band of men swam across the Jordan to join him (*ibid.* ver. 15); while others from Manasseh deserted to him from Saul's army before the battle of Mount Gilboa, so that at last he had with him "a great host, like the host of God" (*ibid.* vers. 19—21). **He came to Achish.** To give him a portion of the spoil. **And Achish said.** Like the verb *went up* in ver. 8, the word indicates repeated action. David made many expeditions against these wild tribes, and on each occasion, when presenting himself at Gath, Achish would inquire, **Whither have ye made a road**—*i. e.* an inroad, or a raid—**to-day?** As it stands the Hebrew means, "Do not make an inroad to-day;" but the correction of the text given in the A. V. has considerable authority from the versions. **The Jerahmeelites,** mentioned again in ch. xxx. 29, were the descendants of Hezron, the firstborn of Pharez, the son of Judah (1 Chron. ii. 9), and so were one of the great families into which the tribe of Judah was divided. Apparently they occupied the most southerly position of its territory. **The Kenites** (see on ch. xv. 6) are here described as being in close alliance with the men of Judah. Probably they lived under their protection, and paid them tribute. **The south** is literally "the Negeb," the dry land, so called from the absence of streams (comp. Ps. cxxvi. 4), which formed not only the southernmost part of the territory of Judah, but extended far into the Arabian desert. Achish naturally understood it as the proper name for that part of the Negeb which belonged to Judah, whereas David meant it as it is translated in the A. V., where there is no obscurity as to its meaning.

Vers. 11, 12.—**To bring tidings.** The A. V. is wrong in adding the word *tidings*, as the Hebrew means "to bring them to Gath." Prisoners to be sold as slaves formed an important part of the spoil of war in ancient times. But David, acting in accordance with the cruel customs of warfare in his days, and which he practised even when he had no urgent necessity as here (see 2 Sam. viii. 2), put all his prisoners to death, lest, if taken to Gath and sold, they should betray him. The A. V. makes his conduct even more sanguinary, and supposes that he suffered none to escape. **And so will be his manner all the while he dwelleth.** The Hebrew is "he dwelt," and thus the rendering of the A. V., though supported by the Masoretic punctuation, is untenable. But this punctuation is of comparatively recent date, and of moderate authority. The words really belong to the narrator, and should be translated, "And so was his manner all the days that he dwelt in the field of the Philistines." It seems that Achish was completely deceived by David, and supposing that his conduct would make him hateful for ever to his own tribesmen of Judah, and so preclude his return home, he rejoiced in him as one who would always remain his faithful vassal and adherent.

HOMILETICS.

Vers. 1—4.—*Loss of faith.* The facts are—1. David, fearing lest he should fall by the hand of Saul, deems it better to go to the land of the Philistines. 2. He and his family and attendants are received by Achish at Gath. 3. Saul, hearing of this, seeks him no more. There is a latent thought in many minds that the great and good men of whom the Bible speaks ought to figure in Scripture as only models of excellence, and hence a sense of disappointment is experienced when, in its fidelity to facts, the Bible relates their failings and sins. Here we have David in despair of preserving his life by the means hitherto adopted; and in his evidently long and painful meditations on the path of prudence (ch. xxvi. 19; cf. xxvii. 1) he comes to the conclusion to avoid collision with Saul by fleeing to an enemy's country. This is not absolute despair, but despair of preserving life for the realising of one's vocation by the means consistent with that vocation and the character suited to it. Loss of faith in righteous means is, so far, loss of faith in God.

I. PROTRACTED AND PAINFUL CONFLICTS MAY BE INVOLVED IN ATTAINING TO THE HIGHEST PURPOSE IN LIFE. To become king in Israel and bless the world with wise rulership was the high purpose revealed to David; and for moral reasons the long discipline of trial was inevitable. The position into which he was often brought seemed to render the accomplishment of life's purpose impossible, and the nearer the goal the more severe the risks of life. The more numerous his men and able his captains, the greater difficulty in preventing collision with Saul, and the more impossible to find food apart from trespass on property. A righteous cause was therefore a suffering cause. This is the case with us. Often Christians have been evidently called to a work for God, and yet become so beset with perils that the end for which they live seems impossible of realisation. How the heart becomes pained and oppressed with incessant struggle with evils that stand in the way of a rise to perfect holiness! The enemy is ever upon us, and humanly speaking it seems as though we some day shall fall by his hand in spite of all endeavours of the past.

II. THERE ARE RECOGNISED MEANS BY WHICH THE HIGHEST PURPOSE OF LIFE IS TO BE ATTAINED. David was to wait God's time, and not force the hand of providence. To make such movements as to avoid collision with Saul, to look up to God for promised or implied help when, in spite of care, life is threatened, and to seize occasions for softening the heart of his foe, even if for a season only—these means hitherto had been honoured with success, and, so far as we can see, were the only lawful means. In attaining to our ultimate position as Christians we have to follow the spiritual methods of the New Testament in humble dependence on God—watchfulness, abstention from evil, evasion of deadly arrows and poison of adders, and whatever will keep the soul holy and true for Christ. In doing our work in the world we have to avoid falling into the power of the great enemy by severe simplicity, love of truth, spirituality of mind, and prayerful use of the gospel. So, in reference to any specific holy end in view, the means used are to be in harmony with the goodness of the end. We are not to do evil that good may come.

III. UNDER THE PRESSURE AND PAIN OF LONG CONFLICT WE BECOME EXPOSED TO THE TEMPTATION TO SEEK RELIEF BY NEW METHODS. Probably some degree of mental and physical exhaustion, accompanied with increasing worries of providing for a large following, laid David open to the thought of fighting the battle with his difficulties on new ground. There is a risk to the cultivation of our spiritual life arising from the weariness consequent on long trial. The tension may seem to justify and necessitate diminished watchfulness and prayer—virtually a departure to new ground. In work for Christ, good men, when oppressed and worn down, and not attaining to their goal, are induced to think of expedients hitherto not approved, and apparently more easy in application. This temptation gains force when, amidst the mental confusion incident to weakness and disappointment, the value of the securities given us by God is not duly assessed. More consideration on the part of David of what security was implied in his being the anointed, and in the repeated assurance of God's intention to raise him to the throne, would have induced the conviction that, using ordinary means in Judah, he *must* be safe from Saul. Temptations gain power when we fail to consider that the promises of salvation and of blessing on our toil are yea and amen in Christ Jesus.

IV. A SLIGHT DALLYING WITH TEMPTATION DURING A LONG CONFLICT MAY ISSUE IN A NEGLECT OF PRAYER FOR GUIDANCE AND SUPPORT. The fall of good men is seen, but the real causes are not. The probability is that during his absorption in details he may have lost the spirit of devotion which hitherto had distinguished him, and hence his decision in this case without seeking counsel by the Urim. The secret departure of the heart from God is fraught with mischief and trouble. We then devise means of our own and distrust those which God has blessed. Then it is that we become faint and despondent and impatient, and, while not renouncing our life's calling of God, yet we pursue it in a manner inconsistent with our profession. Near to God in private life, humble dependence on his daily strength and guidance, this alone fosters faith in his wisdom and protection, and saves from recourse to expedients that reflect on his care.

General lessons :—1. Temporary ease in a righteous cause may mean loss of spiritual power and a beginning of disaster. 2. A course of duty hitherto successful for the specific purpose in view, though very painful, ought never to be exchanged for another line of conduct. 3. If we would endure hardness as good soldiers we must be one in fellowship with the Captain of our salvation. 4. In the service of God the weight of evidence is in favour of confidence and against fear, and we misread God's word and discipline when fear prevails.

Vers. 5—12.—*The perils of expediency.* The facts are—1. David, being unwilling to live in the royal city, seeks and obtains Ziklag as his place of abode. 2. During his stay there he makes war on neighbouring tribes. 3. He gives Achish the impression that he was acting in hostility to Judah, and so creates the belief that henceforth he must be an ally of the Philistine. The painful backsliding of David is a reminder of the frailty of the best of men, and should induce great watchfulness over the subtle springs of thought and feeling. The prominent teaching of this section may be arranged thus :—

I. THE PERILS OF SELF-CHOSEN MEANS OF SAFETY. David's passing over the border was a step unwillingly taken, originating in the proper belief that when possible dangers ought to be avoided, but chiefly in the fear that the oft-experienced help in Judah would not be continued there. The imperfect spiritual condition which rendered groundless fear possible also induced a self-choice of means of safety irrespective of guidance of prophet or Urim. But no sooner is the step taken than dangers thicken. A sojourn with Achish meant dependence for support, exposure to treachery, increasing obligations to serve a heathen king, the evils to religious life of association with idolaters, and consciousness of self-debasement. We have to learn that the path of duty may be encompassed with difficulties, but is always better than any course we may from love of ease strike out for ourselves. The Church has never gained anything but ultimate loss and dishonour in evading the pains and sorrows of high spiritual service by a spirit of conformity to the world. The merchant beset with risks incurs worse dangers by passing over the line of truthfulness and fraud. The soul sensible of its spiritual dangers and annoyed by restless temptations finds no real relief in leaving the " way everlasting " for the expedients suggested by a deceitful heart.

II. THE SHAME OF SUPPRESSING OUR TRUE CHARACTER AND THE OBJECT FOR WHICH WE LIVE. Obviously David was careful not to let Achish know that he was the anointed, and was living in hope of rising to the throne of Israel. For as Israel was the declared and natural enemy of Philistia, this would be to foster the means of his future overthrow. It was impossible for a man of fine sensibilities to thus suppress his real character and objects without constant sense of shame, and even dread lest by some means he should be detected and suddenly assailed. Occasionally for political reasons men have adopted a policy of concealment, though even in this department of life it is attended with loss of self-respect and considerable peril. There are temptations for religious men to hide their religion, to pass unknown as professors, to assume for a while the habits and enter into too intimate associations with the irreligious.   In festive scenes, in plans of business, in converse with strangers, there may arise a feeling of shame, or a thought of inexpediency, which not merely restrains from a natural expression of Christian feeling consonant to the occasion, but even prompts to an effort to give the impression that we are not religious.   The sin of this suppression of our Christianity, this hiding of the great end for which we profess to live, cannot but bring most grievous trouble to the soul, as it so manifestly dishonours the name by which we are called.

III. The futility of all expedients for courting the favour of the irreligious.   David's scheme was to live in favour with the Philistines, and to this end he represented himself as their friend and the foe of their foe.   Not only did he produce the false impression of having attacked Judah,—an act of untruthfulness,—but he did himself and brethren the cruel wrong of representing himself as alien to them.   For awhile Achish was misled, but his people were suspicious (ch. xxix. 3), and the result was a loss of reputation to David.   Good men cannot compromise their position with irreligious men and secure or confer any permanent advantage thereby. The consideration and interest they manifest for a season, resting on false representations, will soon yield to suspicions, distrust, and contempt.   If it be thought that accommodations of life to the standard of the unspiritual will tend to benefit them, events will prove the thought to be delusive.   "Be not conformed to the world" is the wise policy, as it is the solemn duty, of the Christian.

IV. A compromise with the irreligious may involve the contraction of very unwelcome obligations.   From the day that David sought the friendly protection of Achish to the outbreak of war with Israel, David was becoming involved in obligations which could only be set aside at the cost of a reputation for deceit and ingratitude.   He had to play a double part to save his own life and to avoid the fearful sin of raising his hand against his own countrymen (cf. vers. 11, 12; xxviii. 1, 2).   There is here warning for the Church and the individual.   Christian action should always be so free and truly based on righteous principles as to raise no claim for service or friendship inconsistent with the holy vows of consecration to Christ.   He who by suppression of his religious principles puts himself in the power of irreligious companions or associates will find his position to be one of increasing embarrassment ; and after a painful and tortuous line of conduct it will be necessary to lose all respect by breaking away from the wicked alliance or retain friendship by a shipwreck of faith.   "The friendship of the world is enmity with God" (James iv. 4).   Young persons who are thrown much among the irreligious should take to heart the lessons of David's experience.

HOMILIES BY VARIOUS AUTHORS.

Ver. 1.—*Unbelief and its unworthy device.*   This history metes out equal justice, and, having shown to us the perversity of Saul, immediately exposes to us the fault of David, for he also, though no fool, returned to folly.   In both cases equity and charity allow some plea of extenuation.   Saul's hostility to David was due in some measure to an unsound brain, unable to shake off morbid suspicion.   And David's mistrust of the Divine protection was the result of a very sensitive temperament tried beyond measure, a chafed and weary spirit.   How far such pleas may be considered in weighing actions is a question for the Divine justice rather than for our sentence.   Enough for us to recognise them, that we may the better understand how Saul could renew a pursuit which he had abandoned with tears, and how David could return to the land of the Philistines, from which he had formerly escaped only by simulating madness.

I. The fault of David was unbelief.   It was not his habit ; but it came upon him as a fit or mood, and, while it lasted, led him into actions unworthy and unwise. 1. *He broke down at a strong point, as men often do.*   His faith rose to a heroic pitch in the valley of Elah, when the stripling, as a believer, encountered the blaspheming giant.   But when he was put among princes his faith failed under apprehensions of mortal peril, and he fled to Nob, and thence to the Philistine town of Gath. He recovered his faith in God, and, assured of Divine protection, refused to injure Saul when the king on two occasions was within his power. But again his faith failed, and he was afraid. There is no mention of his having prayed, or consulted God through the priest as at other times. In his unworthy fear he took counsel with himself, and " said in his heart " that he would surely perish. Such is man. He falls at a strong point. Noah stood in his integrity against a whole world of sinners, but when he had no world to stand against he fell, and disgraced himself by intemperance. Moses was the meekest of men and most observant of the word of the Lord, and yet he erred at Kadesh in respect of self-control and fidelity to the Divine command, so forfeiting his entrance into Canaan. Hezekiah was eminent for prayerfulness and humility, and yet he fell in not spreading a matter before the Lord, but giving way to vain boasting. Simon Peter was all ardour and devotion to his Master, and yet, just after honest protestations of attachment, he lost courage, and denied his Lord. In like manner strong believers may fall into a fit of unbelief, in which past blessings are forgotten, promises are doubted or let slip, dangers are exaggerated, and the heart, instead of asking counsel of the Lord, takes counsel with itself, and suggests all sorts of folly. 2. *Unbelief seems to have been the sin to which David was most tempted in his youth.* We infer this both from this history and from the Psalter. The former tells how he more than once despaired of his life, and how Jonathan exerted himself to reassure his desponding mind. The latter reveals to us with touching candour the apprehensions of his youth in those psalms which plainly refer to his wanderings and hairbreadth escapes. The sorrows of death had compassed him, and the floods of the ungodly made him afraid. He saw his enemies ready to swallow him up. And though he was naturally brave, unbelief enfeebled and distracted him, so that his " heart was sore pained " within him. Indeed David's cries to God in the Psalms, and his way of repeating to himself that God was on his side, and was able to defend and deliver him, indicate not obscurely his inward struggle. If he had felt no fear he would not have thought of writing, " I will not fear what man can do to me." If he had known no failure of faith he would not have said so much as he has of crying after God and putting his trust in him. We read of Abraham simply that he believed. He fell on his face and listened to the voice of God ; then he acted, journeyed, obeyed in faith ; but we do not find him speak of his believing. David had a struggle to hold fast his confidence, and therefore has he given so much expression to the life of faith and its conflict with doubt and fear.

II. UNBELIEF LEADS A SERVANT OF GOD TO UNWORTHY DEVICES. " Nothing better for me than that I should escape to the land of the Philistines." Now we know that God did order and overrule this flight for the good of David and of Israel ; but none the less was it, on the part of his servant, an unworthy action springing from unbelief. Better surely to have lived by faith in the forests and caves of Judæa than live by sight and behave like a freebooter in the land of the heathen Philistines. His stay at Ziklag, the town assigned to him by the king Achish, marks a bad period in the life of David. His incursion into the territory of certain southern tribes was most unjust and cruel. The injustice, indeed, may not have been apparent to his mind ; for David and his men had, of course, been educated in the ideas of their own age and country, and had no scruple about invading and laying waste any territory of the heathen. They had also little, if any, respect for the lives of the heathen. Yet David must have sinned against his conscience in the cruel massacre of the southern tribes. One sin leads to another. And the son of Jesse added deceit to cruelty, and exulted in covering the first sin by the second, leaving no man or woman alive to contradict the tale he told to the Philistine king. Lord, what is man ? When thou didst not hold up the goings of thy servant, into what miry places did he stray, into what a ditch did he fall ! When his faith failed, what a break-down of his character and conduct ! Restraint of prayer, self-direction, then rapine, bloodshedding, and falsehood ! What are we that we should have immunity from similar deterioration of character, if we give way to unbelief ? A Christian in good repute takes some course that we should have thought incredible and impossible. We ask in amazement, What infatuation seized him ? or, Can it be that he was always insincere, and wicked at

heart under a cloak of seeming goodness ? The real clue to his misconduct lies here—
that he lost hold of God and fell through unbelief, allowed himself to doubt whether
God would or could keep him in some strait, and took to trusting and keeping himself.
So he fell into unworthy company, or betook himself to unworthy devices ; and the
end is what you see—dishonesty, duplicity, prevarication. Remember that nothing
is so hard to be extirpated from the heart as unbelief. In his book of the Holy War
Bunyan shows that when the town of Mansoul was in the devil's power, Incredulity
was first made alderman, then lord mayor. When Immanuel took the town, Incredulity (unbelief) was doomed to execution, but managed to break out of prison, and
lurked in hiding-places where he could not be found. When the devil assaulted the
town in hopes to retake it, "Old Incredulity" reappeared, and was made general of
the army. After the assailing army was defeated, and many of the officers and
soldiers in it were put to death, Unbelief still evaded capture. He did yet dwell in
Mansoul, though he "hid in dens and holes."

Application :—1. Let believers beware. It is easy to slip off the way of faith,
and it may seem to answer well for a time. You may get your Ziklag to dwell in,
and find it more comfortable than the hold at Engedi or the hill of Hachilah, but
you are in a state of declension from God, and on the way, as David was, to commit
presumptuous sin. Matthew Henry remarks in his sententious way, "Unbelief is a
sin that easily besets even good men. When without are fightings and within are
fears, it is a hard matter to get over them. Lord, increase our faith !" 2. Let unbelievers be warned. If unbelief be so damaging when it prevails even temporarily
over a servant of God, what ruin must it work in those who lie always under its
power ! "He that believeth not in the Son of God shall not see life ; but the wrath
of God abideth on him."—F.

Vers. 1, 2. (THE WILDERNESS OF ZIPH.)—*Despondency.* "I shall now perish one
day by the hand of Saul" (ver. 1). It is seldom (at least in a climate like ours)
that a day passes in sunshine without clouds. And human life is as varied as the
aspects of the sky. The best of men are liable not only to adversity as well as
prosperity, but also to seasons of spiritual depression as well as of spiritual elation ;
and the one often follows the other very closely. These seasons of depression ought
not, indeed, to be attributed to a Divine, sovereign, and uncontrollable influence.
They are due to certain causes in men themselves which ought to be watched
against. Yet who resists them constantly, effectually, and completely ? Here is
David, who recently said, "Let the Lord deliver me out of all tribulation," and heard
Saul say, "Blessed be thou, my son David," &c. (ch. xxvi. 24, 25), talking to
himself in a desponding mood, and coming to the conclusion that there is nothing
better for him than to flee into the land of the Philistines. It may be preferable for
a man to "commune with his own heart" of his fears and doubts, rather than pour
them indiscriminately into the ears of other people ; but his proper course is not to
continue brooding over them, or surrender himself to their power, but to "inquire of
the Lord," and "hope in God" (Ps. xlii. 11). "More of these no man hath known
than myself, which I confess I conquered not in a martial posture, but on my knees"
(Sir T. Browne). Concerning the state of mind which this language expresses,
consider—

I. WHEREIN IT CONSISTS. 1. *Fear of approaching danger.* Saul had renewed his
persecution, and David thought that he should be "consumed." There was apparently
no more reason why he should think so now than there had been before ; but the
desponding mind projects its shadow over all things, and magnifies ordinary into
extraordinary peril. Imaginary evils are often occasions of greater trouble and
temptation than real evils, and more difficult to overcome. 2. *Distrust of Divine
care.* This is its chief element. If his faith had been in vigorous exercise he
would have said, "Whom shall I fear?" (Ps. xxvii. 1). But it seems to have completely failed, leaving him a prey to overwhelming anxiety and fear. "My way is
hid from the Lord, and my judgment is passed over from my God" (Isa. xl. 27).
"Our bones are dried, and our hope is lost" (Ezek. xxxvii. 11). 3. *Depression of
personal energy.* He has lost heart, and thinks it impossible to continue safely in
the land of Judah, to which the prophet had formerly recalled him, and where

Divine providence has appointed his lot. The fearful and faithless shrink from difficulties which in a better state of mind they encountered boldly.

II. WHEREBY IT IS OCCASIONED. The influences productive of it are partly—1. *External and physical.* Numerous perils, long hardship, constant watchfulness, great exertions, bodily exhaustion and suffering. "There are hours in which physical derangement darkens the windows of the soul; days in which shattered nerves make life simply endurance." Much of this may be removed by the adoption of proper methods, and where its removal is impossible, special grace should be sought that it may be borne cheerfully and patiently. 2. *Mental and emotional.* Perplexing thoughts, conflicting arguments, unjust and ungenerous treatment, want of sympathy, deferred hope, reaction from excited feeling. "Something of it might be due to those alternations of emotion which seem to be incidental to our human constitution. We have ebbings and flowings within us like the tides ; and just as in nature the lowest ebb is after the highest spring-tide, so you frequently see, even in the best of men, after some lofty experience of spiritual elevation and noble self-command, an ebbing down to the lowest depth of fear and flight " (W. M. Taylor). 3. *Moral and spiritual.* Omission of duty, parleying with temptation, contemplating doubtful expedients (ch. xxvi. 19), intimate association with persons of little or no piety, self-confidence, bedimmed spiritual vision, loss of spiritual fervour, "restraining prayer before God." It is significant that nothing is said about David's asking counsel of the Lord concerning the step which he was contemplating, as he did on other occasions. "Josephus tells us that he advised with his friends, but no writer informs us that he advised with God" (Delany). His state of mind appears to have been unfavourable to his doing so ; and it is probable that if he had done so the course on which he had half resolved would have been forbidden. Communion with God prevents or cures despondency and averts many a disastrous step.

III. WHEREFORE IT IS BLAMEWORTHY. For that it is so there can be no doubt. In it—1. *Past deliverances effected by God are ungratefully forgotten.* Of these David had experienced many ; they were assurances of continued help, and in better hours he regarded them as such (ch. xvii. 37). But now his remembrance of them is clouded with fear, and produces neither thankfulness nor confidence. He speaks to his heart, but says not, "Bless the Lord, O my soul, and forget not all his benefits." 2. *The faithful promises of God are faithlessly ignored.* He who doubts them despises the Giver, deprives himself of the treasures of wisdom, strength, and blessedness which they contain, and "forsakes his own mercy." 3. *The great name of God is greatly dishonoured.* It is a "strong tower," and not to "run into it," but to continue in despondency, as if it were inaccessible or incapable of affording adequate protection, is to oppose the purpose for which it is made known, to act unworthily of the knowledge of it, and to incur just reproach. "Who art thou, that thou shouldst be afraid of a man that shall die, and forgettest the Lord thy Maker ?" (Isa. li. 13). Surely nothing dishonours him more.

IV. WHERETO IT LEADS. "And David arose," &c. (ver. 2). He thought nothing could be better for him ; but, in reality, nothing could be worse. "For by this step he would alienate the affections of the Israelites from him, justify the reproaches of the enemy, deprive himself of the means of grace and the ordinances of religion, grieve his soul with the vice and idolatry of the heathen, put himself out of the warrant of Divine protection, and lay himself under peculiar obligation to those whom he could not serve without betraying the cause of God." He escaped from one danger only to rush into another and much greater. Unbelieving and desponding fears commonly—1. Incite to unwise and foolish courses of action. 2. Conduce to temptation and transgression (ver. 10). 3. Involve in embarrassment and great distress (ch. xxviii. 1 ; xxx. 1—5).

> "Beware of desperate steps. The darkest day,
> Live till to-morrow, will have passed away."
>   (Cowper, 'The Needless Alarm.')

Exhortation :—1. Guard against the causes of despondency. 2. At its first approach turn instantly to God in faith and prayer. 3. Take no new step under its influence, nor until the will of God is clearly seen. 4. "Be strong in the Lord and in the power of his might."—D.

Vers. 3—12. (GATH, ZIKLAG.)—*David's residence among the Philistines.* David had taken the decisive step, crossed the border, and passed with his 600 men and their families ("a little ambulant kingdom") into the Philistine territory. His position was very different now from what it had been five or six years before, when he came to Gath as a lonely fugitive (ch. xxi. 10); and he was gladly received by Achish, who regarded him as in open revolt against Saul and Israel, and expected to obtain from him valuable assistance in his future conflicts with them. And here and at Ziklag he continued sixteen months (ver. 7). His condition (like that of other good men who enter into intimate association with the ungodly, voluntarily, unnecessarily, and for the sake of worldly advantage; see ch. xv. 6) was marked by—

I. TEMPORARY SECURITY (ver. 4). By placing himself under the protection of Achish, David gained his end; for Saul dared not follow him lest he should excite another Philistine war, and (*physically* restrained, though still retaining an evil will) "sought no more again for him." His outward circumstances were completely changed. Instead of the uncertain, anxious, hazardous, and despised life which he had led in the wilderness, he enjoyed repose, comfort, safety, and respect in a royal city. To obtain advantages such as these men often swerve from the appointed path of duty, especially in times of persecution, not considering at what a cost they are obtained, how brief is their duration, or how great the trouble by which they may be followed.

II. CONSCIOUS INCONSISTENCY (vers. 5—7). In open alliance with the enemies of Israel, silently witnessing their idolatrous practices, looked upon as a traitor to his country, and ready to aid them against it, David must have felt what a contradiction there was between his apparent and real character. Yet he might not declare himself by a single word or act, for thousands of watchful eyes were always on him. He did not feel at home, and requested (under the plea of the unsuitableness and expensiveness of his residence with his large retinue at Gath) that the king would give him "a place in some town in the country," his real motive being that ho might be "out of the way of observation, so as to play the part of Saul's enemy without acting against him." At Ziklag he would be less under restraint, and his real sentiments less likely to be discovered, though even there he might still be suspected. No outward advantages that good men may gain by their alliance with the ungodly can afford adequate compensation for the insincerity, distraction, restlessness, and vexation of soul which it involves (2 Pet. ii. 8).

III. SUCCESSFUL ENTERPRISE (vers. 8, 9). As soon as he was settled at Ziklag he made warlike expeditions against the Amalekites, Geshurites, and Gezrites, "of old the inhabitants of the land" (unlike the Philistines); and from the rich booty which he procured he supplied the wants of his men, and gave valuable presents to Achish (ver. 9). His setting forth on these expeditions, and the cruel severity with which he executed them, must be judged of in the light of "the circumstances of those times, and the constant practices of nations one to another, especially of the neighbouring nations towards the Hebrews" (Chandler), and of the ban under which some of them had been placed (see ch. xv. 1, 32, 33). He was doubtless animated therein by public spirit and religious zeal (ch. xxx. 26), but his motives were not altogether unmixed, and his successes brought him a doubtful honour (ver. 12).

IV. CRAFTY POLICY (vers. 10, 11). To retain the confidence of Achish, he gave him the impression that his expeditions were directed against his own countrymen and their allies, instead of against Amalek and other neighbouring tribes; and he was thus, through distrust of God, again guilty of deceit (ch. xxi. 1, 10). "If a man will put himself among Philistines, he cannot promise to come forth innocent" (Hall). "David might perhaps seek in some way to justify himself by the thought that in his ambiguous manner of speech he made use only of an allowable stratagem, and that he was a *heathen* to whom he veiled the truth. But he will yet be made to experience that God will weigh those who would be his in the balances of the sanctuary, in which, among others, that inviolable word is found as one of the weights, 'Thou shalt not bear false witness'" (Krummacher).

V. INCREASING POWER and importance. While at Ziklag he received large reinforcements (ch. xxii. 1, 2; 1 Chron. xii. 1—22), some of whom were "of Saul's brethren of Benjamin''—evidently from dissatisfaction with the turn which things had taken (see also 2 Sam. xv. 16—23). "As a matter of fact, David in this city laid the foundation of all his kingdom. Here he could already rule with greater freedom and independence, collect fugitives and deserters around him in larger and larger numbers, send or receive embassies like a prince (ch. xxx. 26—31), and, as a ruler over soldiers and over peaceable citizens, rehearse, on a small scale, those arts by which he afterwards acquired and maintained his great kingdom" (Ewald). Notwithstanding all this, his condition was one of—

VI. Spiritual disadvantage, and even spiritual deterioration. That which he had dreaded as the worst of evils (ch. xxvi. 19) had come about by his own voluntary act. Although he was not forbidden the exercise of his religion under Achish (ch. xxix. 6), yet his circumstances were unfavourable to it; he was absent from the land and the sanctuary where God manifested his gracious presence to his people (ch. xxvi. 20; Ps. xlii. 2, 3), and his whole course of life is indicative of a lower tone of piety than before. "Being a genuine poet and lover of art, he took advantage of all his opportunities in this direction, and exercised himself as a musician in the Gittite and the Philistine style (Ps. viii., inscription), which he afterwards transferred from there to Jerusalem" (Ewald); but not a single psalm of his can be referred to this period.

VII. Dangerous entanglements, intense suffering, and probably also serious delay in the attainment of his high destiny (ch. xxviii. 1, 2; xxx. 3). The evils that sprang from his want of faith and patience were truly great. "His presence in Judah would have given an opportunity which Saul could hardly have refused, for calling him forth as the champion of Israel. At all events he would have been at hand to relieve the disaster, and would doubtless have been hailed as king by the united voice of Israel. As it was, his nation suffered a terrible defeat, which, instead of doing his best to avert, he narrowly escaped taking a share in inflicting; his recognition as king of Israel was postponed for seven years and a half at the cost of a civil war and a permanent alienation of Judah from the rest of Israel; and meanwhile he was involved in a course of pitiable deceit" (Smith, 'Old Testament Hist.'). Nevertheless the overruling hand of God must be recognised in all, and by Divine mercy he was delivered "out of all tribulation."

> "Ay me, how many perils do unfold
> The righteous man, to make him daily fall,
> Were not that heavenly grace doth him uphold,
> And steadfast truth acquit him out of all!
> Her love is firm, her care continual,
> So oft as he, through his own foolish pride
> Or weakness, is to sinful bands made thrall" (Spenser). D.

EXPOSITION.

Downfall and Death of Saul (Chs. XXVIII.—XXXI.)

The Philistines gather together for War. Distress of Saul, and Visit to the Witch of Endor (Ch. XXVIII.).

CHAPTER XXVIII.

Achish summons David to join him in the war against Israel (vers. 1—2). Ver. 1.—In those days. I. e. while David was dwelling at Ziklag. The Philistines gathered their armies together. This was, as Josephus has observed, a war upon a much larger scale than any that had been carried on since the defeat of the Philistines in the valley of Elah; for we find that the invasion was made from the north, and the decisive battle fought not in the usual field of operations, but in the territory of the tribe of Issachar, in the neighbourhood of Jezreel. We are not indeed to suppose from this that the Philistines had conquered all the central districts of the land, and, driving Saul before them, at last brought him to bay, and slew him in the north; for though Ishbosheth was compelled to withdraw to Mahanaim, a city on the eastern side of the Jordan, yet Abner is said to have made him king there not only over the trans-Jordanic tribes, but also "over Jezreel, and over Ephraim, and over Benjamin" (2 Sam. ii. 9). It may be said, however, that these were but titular claims; but the Philistine conquests, as described in ch.

xxxi. 7, if not confined to the valley of Esdraelon, as in 1 Chron. x. 7, were nevertheless all of them to the north of Mount Gilboa, thus leaving Ephraim, Benjamin, and Judah untouched. Nor do we find the Philistines encamped between David at Hebron and Ishbosheth at Mahanaim, or interfering in their contests; and it is only when David was made king over the whole of Israel that they again assembled their forces to dispute the empire with him, and twice suffered defeat (2 Sam. v. 20, 25). More probably, therefore, they marched northward through their own territory, raising the whole of the military population as they went, and then, turning eastward, broke into the Israelite territory by the valley of Jezreel. It was probably the rapid decline of Saul's power which encouraged the Philistines to attempt once again to place their yoke upon the neck of Israel; and Saul, conscious that God's blessing had departed from him, in pitiable agony sought for unholy aid, but finally, with his sons, made a last brave defence, and died a soldier's death. **Achish said unto David.** As a vassal David was bound to accompany his lord to the field; and Achish, supposing that David had of his own accord made war upon Judah, probably assumed that the invitation was one which he himself desired. **To battle.** Hebrew, "in the army."

Ver. 2.—**Surely thou shalt know.** Hebrew, "Therefore thou shalt know," *i. e.* if the case be so, thou shalt know, &c. The rendering of the A. V. makes David repeat the words of Achish, which literally are, "knowing thou shalt know," the Hebrew way of making a strong affirmation. David's reply is really ambiguous, but is understood by Achish as a boastful assent, and he thereupon promises, **Therefore will I make thee keeper of mine head,** *i. e.* captain of my body-guard, **for ever.** **Therefore** is exactly the same word as that used by David, and has just the same meaning, namely, "If the case be so," if thou provest thy valour, then I, &c.

SAUL AND THE WITCH OF ENDOR (vers. 3—25). Ver. 3.—**Samuel was dead.** A repetition of ch. xxv. 1, inserted to explain Saul's conduct, as is the other fact, that **Saul had put away those that had familiar spirits,** &c. We are not told when Saul did this; but at the commencement of his reign, when he brought the ark to Nob, he was probably earnest generally in his observance of the precepts of the Mosaic law. **Familiar spirits.** Hebrew, *ôboth*, the plural of *ôb*, a leathern bottle. It is generally taken to refer to the distended belly of the conjurer, into which the summoned spirit of the dead was supposed to enter, and thence speak; for which reason the Septuagint renders the

word "ventriloquist," and is followed by most modern commentators. **Wizards.** Hebrew, "knowing ones," from the verb *to know;* just as *wizard* comes from the old verb *to wiss.* With ignorant people unusual knowledge is always looked upon with suspicion; but these supposed magicians professed a knowledge to which they had no claim.

Ver. 4. **The Philistines . . . pitched in Shunem.** Having collected their forces, the Philistines entered Palestine as we have seen, by the valley of Jezreel, also called Esdraelon, and, marching eastward, encamped at Shunem. This was a village in the tribe of Issachar (Josh. xix. 18), rendered famous as the abode of the woman who made a little chamber for Elisha (2 Kings iv. 8); and from thence also came Abishag (1 Kings i. 3). Conder describes it as being at present only a mud hamlet, with cactus hedges and a spring, but the view extends, he says, as far as to Mount Carmel, fifteen miles away ('Tent-Work,' i. 123). It is now called Sûlem, a name given to it also by Eusebius, and lies upon the slopes of the little Hermon, opposite Mount Gilboa, from which it is separated by the valley of Jezreel. This broad plain "is bounded on the east by the range of Gilboa, rising 1500 feet above the sea, and consisting of white chalk; while on the west a long spur runs out at about the same average elevation with Gilboa, and wends north-west to the ridge of Carmel (Conder, 'Handbook,' p. 209). As the valley is about 250 feet above the sea level, Saul, from an elevation of 1200 feet, would easily see the camp of the Philistines pitched upon the slopes of the opposite range at a distance of about four miles.

Vers. 5, 6.—**When Saul saw,** &c. It is plain from this that the Philistines had not forced their way up through the Israelite territory; for this was evidently Saul's first sight of their forces, and his alarm was caused by finding them so much larger than he had expected. He therefore in his anxiety **enquired of Jehovah,** but received no answer, **neither by dreams.** He had expected these to be vouchsafed, possibly to himself, but more probably to some class of prophets (see Jer. xxiii. 25, where false prophets claim to have dreamed, in imitation no doubt of true prophets); but though dreams were thus recognised as a means for communicating God's will to man, yet, as Erdmann well remarks, "a subordinate position is certainly assigned in the Old Testament to the *dream* as the medium of the Divine influence on the inner life, which in sleep sinks into a state of passiveness." **Nor by Urim.** Though Abiathar after the massacre of his family had fled to David with the ephod, it is quite possible that Saul may have had another ephod made, and have set up a fresh sanctuary, perhaps at Gibeon, with Zadok, of the family of Eleazar, as high priest. This would account for Zadok being joined with Ahimelech, the son of Abiathar, as one of two high priests early in David's reign (2 Sam. viii. 17). It is remarkable, however, that Saul does not mention the Urim himself in ver. 15, and very probably it is named here not because the ephod was actually used, but as enumerating all the various ways by which men inquired of Jehovah. **Nor by prophets.** In his despair Saul may have turned to some reputed soothsayer present with the host, but his wilful life had alienated both priest and prophet from him. And this is the meaning of the passage in 1 Chron. x. 14 : "Saul enquired not of Jehovah; therefore he slew him." He may have gone through the form of inquiring, and certainly now would have been glad of an answer, but his whole mind was determinately set upon carrying out his own purposes, and he would never permit, after the first year or two of his reign, the royal prerogative to bend to the will of God.

Vers. 7, 8.—**Seek me a woman that hath a familiar spirit.** Hebrew, "owner of an ôb" (see on ver. 3). This determination of Saul proves how obstinate was his self-will. He wanted an answer simply that he might know what was about to happen, not that he might receive guidance and counsel from God. From his bidding them seek him out "a woman mistress of an ôb," we gather that women were the usual claimants to these occult powers, just as now they are the most successful clairvoyantes. **Endor**—"the spring of the round," i. e. perhaps of the dwelling, houses being originally circular in shape, like tents — lay a little to the north-east of Shunem, and it was therefore a hazardous matter for Saul to visit it. Conder ('Tent-Work,' i. 122) says, "East of Nain is a village of mud huts, with hedges of prickly pear. This is Endor, famous in connection with the tragic history of the death of Saul. The adventurous character of Saul's night journey is very striking when we consider that the Philistines pitched in Shunem on the southern slopes of the mountain, and that Saul's army was at Jezreel ; thus, to arrive at Endor he had to pass the hostile camp, and would probably creep round the eastern shoulder of the hill, hidden by the undulations of the plain, as an Arab will often now advance unseen close by you in a fold of the ground." He proceeds to speculate upon the cave in which the sorceress may have lived, dismissing those in the town as too modern, but suggesting one on the hill-side. But there is nothing in the narrative to suggest that she lived in a cave, but rather the contrary, and the idea may be

dismissed as due to the imagination of painters. As the journey was very dangerous, Saul **disguised himself,** and went **by night,** accompanied only by two men ; and nothing could more plainly set before us his mental anguish, and also his intense desire to pry into the secrets of futurity, than this strange journey. All faith and hope are gone, and a feverish excitement, ready to catch at any aid, however lawless and untrustworthy, had taken their place. In this state of mind he arrives at the woman's dwelling, and says, **Divine unto me by the** ôb. Though divination was strictly forbidden (Deut. xviii. 10, 14), yet we find the *diviner* (A. V. prudent) in high popular estimation in Isa. iii. 2 ; and it was probably a lucrative profession, or this woman would not have been willing to incur so great a danger as was involved in its practice. **Bring me him up,** &c. The fancy that we can see the spirits of the dead is a most natural and enduring superstition, and it seems generally assumed that they must have some knowledge not accessible to the living. It must be said for Saul that he did not become the victim of this folly until after his reason was disturbed, and as a punishment for heinous sins.

Vers. 9, 10.—**Thou knowest what Saul hath done.** Not only had Saul in the earlier part of his reign been earnest in his zeal for the Mosaic law, but even now it seems as if a witch was in danger of death ; for he has to take an oath before she will acknowledge that she practises any illicit art.

Ver. 11.—**Whom shall I bring up to thee ?** Assured by Saul's oath, the woman now asserts her ability to call up the spirits of the dead, and asks, just as would happen now with those who claim similar powers, who it is to be. We need not suppose that she possessed either greater or less powers than those claimed or even exercised now ; for many of the phenomena of clairvoyance, though undoubtedly natural, still belong to an unscientific, and therefore vague and illusory, region. Perhaps on this very account these arts have always had an extraordinary fascination for men, and been practised in all ages and among all people with considerable skill. **Bring me up Samuel.** Samuel had been Saul's friend in his youth, and his guide and counsellor in those happy days when the young king walked uprightly, and all went well with him. But gradually the light yoke of respect for one who loved him became too heavy for a despotic temperament, which would brook no will but its own. Now that self-will is broken ; it had brought the warrior king to a hopeless despair, and in his distress his mind once again returns to its old channels. Intense as was the degradation for one so haughty, in disguise by night, at the risk of his life, to seek help from a sorceress, he bears it all that he may at least for a few minutes see the spirit of the true though stern monitor, whose memory once again filled his whole heart.

Ver. 12.— **When the woman saw Samuel, she cried with a loud voice.** Evidently the last thing that she had expected was that anything else should happen than the usual illusion by which she imposed upon her victims ; nor is it certain that anything else did happen. Her assertion that she saw Samuel was probably false ; and it was in feigned excitement that she cried out, **Why hast thou deceived me ? for thou art Saul.** She could not but have noticed the tall stature, the dignified manner, and also the intense excitement of her strange visitor ; and when he bade her call up the spirit of Samuel, she must have been dull indeed not to know who the stranger was.

Ver. 13.—**What sawest thou ?** Thus far Saul had seen nothing ; and as the words literally are *What seest thou?* it is plain that she had not gone into another room, as some have supposed. The vision was entirely unsubstantial, and Saul, hearing her cry, and observing her excitement, and her steady gaze upon some object, asked what that object was. Probably she was at some distance from him, as was no doubt her custom when performing her incantations, in order that what she did might not be too closely observed ; probably, too, she burnt odours, and surrounded herself with the smoke of incense. In answer to Saul she says, " I see Elohim ascending out of the earth." As the participle is plural, she does not mean God ; nor, as it was a single appearance, is the rendering **gods** correct. What she means is that she saw some grand supernatural appearance rising out of the ground, which she calls *a god* in a general way, without attaching any very exact meaning to the term.

Ver. 14.—**What form is he of?** Rather, "What is his aspect?" *i. e.* his look. As the term *a god* conveyed no other idea than that she had seen something majestic, Saul asks for a more exact description. She answers that it was an old man clad in a robe, *meïl* (see on ch. ii. 19). Samuel seems never to have worn the prophetic mantle (see on ch. xv. 27), but always the *meïl*. There was nothing, therefore, distinctive in the dress ; but as she says that she has seen an old man, Saul concludes that he for whom he had asked had appeared to him. Instead of **Saul perceived,** the Hebrew has "Saul knew." There is nothing to prove that Saul really saw anything ; all that is said is that by the woman's description " Saul recognised that what she had seen was Samuel, and he bowed himself to the ground, and made obeisance."

Vers. 15, 16.—**Why hast thou disquieted me ?** *I. e.* Why hast thou caused me to be disturbed by the incantations of this woman ? **Neither by prophets nor by dreams.** It is suggested in the Talmud (Berach xii. 2) that Saul omitted all mention of the Urim from shame at having murdered the priests. **Is become thine enemy.** By a slight difference of reading the Septuagint have, "is on the side of thy neighbour."

Vers. 17—19.—**Jehovah hath done to him.** Rather, "hath wrought for himself;" but the LXX., Vulgate, and some MSS. read "hath done *to thee*," as in ver. 18. **As he spake by me.** See ch. xv. 28. Saul's rebellion is there said, in ver. 23, to be a crime as great as the witchcraft which he was at that time so zealously punishing ; here, where the sentence is being carried into execution, Saul has himself become guilty of what in his better hours he so abominated. **Jehovah will also deliver Israel with thee.** Rather, " will deliver Israel also with thee," *i. e.* the nation is to share thy punishment. **To-morrow shalt thou and thy sons be with me.** *I. e.* shall be dead. Whence this voice came it is difficult to say. St. Augustine thought that the woman really conjured up a demon, who took the form of Samuel. Maimonides treats the whole as the effect of Saul's diseased imagination ; while many modern commentators regard it as a well-played piece of jugglery on the part of the woman, who recognised Saul at once on his entrance, but professed not to know him till his name was revealed to her by the pretended apparition, in whose name she reproached him for his crimes, announced to him, what now all were convinced of, that David was to be his successor, and foretold his defeat and death. In the face of such a passage as Deut. xviii. 10 —12 we cannot believe that the Bible would set before us an instance of witchcraft employed with the Divine sanction for holy purposes ; but we can easily believe that the woman would gladly take a bitter revenge on the man who had cruelly put to death all persons reputed to have such powers as those to which she laid claim. The object of the narrative is plainly to set before us the completeness of Saul's moral downfall and debasement. Here is the man endowed with so many and so great gifts of genius, and who in so many things started so well and behaved so nobly, the victim of a despairing melancholy ; his conscience is blackened with the wholesale massacre of the priesthood, his imagination is ever brooding over the sick fancy of treason plotted by his son-in-law, whom now he supposes to be in the Philistine camp ; his enemies have invaded his territory in extraordinary numbers and upon new ground ; to him it seems as if they have come to dethrone him and place his crown on

David's head. In this dire extremity his one wish is to pry into futurity and learn his fate. There is no submission to God, no sorrow for disobedience, no sign of even a wish for amendment ; it is to unholy arts that he looks, simply that he may know what a few more hours will make known to all. Neglecting his duties as a general and king, instead of making wise preparation for the coming fight, he disguises himself, takes a dangerous and wearisome journey round the enemies' camp, arrives at his destination by night, and, exhausted with hunger and mental agitation, seeks there for the knowledge unattainable in any upright manner from a reputed witch. He has rejected God, lost all the strength and comfort of true religion, and is become the victim of abject superstition. Whether he were the victim also of the woman's arts, or of his own sick fantasy, is not a matter of much consequence ; the interest of the narrative lies in the revelation it makes to us of Saul's mental and moral state ; and scarcely is there in the whole of Scripture anything more tragic than this narrative, or any more intense picture of the depth of degradation to which a noble but perverse intellect is capable of falling.

Vers. 20—25.—**Saul fell straightway all along,** *i. e.* at full length, **on the earth.** He fainted, partly from mental distress, partly from bodily exhaustion, as he had gone **all the day** and **all the night** without food. It was this long-continued violent emotion of feeling which had driven Saul to this rash enterprise ; but fasting and agony of mind were the worst possible preparation for a visit to one used to cajole her victims by pretended magical arts, and gifted, as people of her class usually are, with great shrewdness. But practised as she was in deceit, yet even in her triumph over her enemy she felt, when she saw him swoon away, a natural sympathy for his misery and weakness, and urged him to take food. Perhaps she saw that without it he could never have got back to the Israelite camp. At first he refused, but the necessity of it was so plain, that when the two men with him also urged it, he at last consented. **So he arose from the earth, and sat upon the bed.** During this colloquy he had remained prostrate upon the ground, but now he seated himself, not on a *bed,* but upon the raised bank, or divan, which runs along the wall of an Oriental house, and is furnished with carpets and cushions for men to sit or lie upon. There he rested, a prey, we may well believe, to bitter thoughts, while the woman hastily prepared a meal, killing a calf and baking unleavened cakes, as there was no time to leaven the dough. And so "they ate, and rose up, and departed that night."

HOMILETICS.

Vers. 1—5.—*The operation of moral causes.* The facts are—1. On war arising between the Philistines and Israel, Achish reminds David of his obligation to assist him in battle. 2. David, although answering ambiguously, is trusted by Achish, who promises him promotion. 3. On the opposing forces being assembled, Saul's heart faints for fear of his enemy. The narrative shows that both David and Saul were at the same time in embarrassed circumstances, and each as the consequence of his sin. They were bent on totally diverse objects, but neither of them was in a position of safety. The penalties of transgression were being paid. We see here an instance of—

I. THE QUESTIONABLE AMBIGUITIES OF LIFE. David's false step in yielding to unwarrantable fear, followed as it was by actions unworthy of his fair fame, was now developing to a crisis in which the principles of his entire life would be put to an unavoidable test. His heathen friend and protector naturally claimed his help in the coming struggle with Israel. Painfully must David have winced as Achish, trusting to his honour and gratitude, reminded him of his obligations. Although he had simulated hostility to Israel for his own selfish purposes, and had done himself and his countrymen a wrong by allowing it to be supposed that he could ever be their enemy, yet there was enough of fidelity in his heart to save him from so dire an evil as was suggested by Achish. To escape from the awkward position, recourse was had to the craft of an ambiguous statement, to which he and Achish attached different meanings. The common judgment on David's conduct will be adverse. Even though some would apologise for it under the plea of danger, yet they must condemn its essential falsehood. It is not lawful to palliate our deceit by reference to difficulties created by our own misconduct. Plain, straightforward words and conduct, even in times of perplexity, are not only morally best, but, even from a utilitarian point of view, are most conducive to permanent welfare. It is to be feared that ambiguities abound in life more than becomes a Christian profession. There is conduct as well as language admitting of double interpretation. We should always aim to be and to speak so as not to be objects of suspicion. To say exactly what we mean and to act with singleness of purpose is to approximate towards the "simplicity that is in Christ" (cf. Rom. xii. 8; 2 Cor. i. 12; xi. 3).

II. UNTIMELY TROUBLES. Troubles are in the way at any time, but there are seasons when their presence is most inconvenient. It was annoying to David that war should break out between Israel and the Philistines just when he was, according to the ordinary judgment of men, under obligation to assist Achish; and it was especially inconvenient to Saul that this trouble of war should occur when, by reason of Samuel's long discountenance of his reign, the gradual alienation of able men, the loss to the kingdom of David's prowess, and his own private sorrows, it was not possible to gather adequate forces and act with wonted energy. Providence has a manifest tendency to allow troubles to cross the path of the wrong-doer just when, for his own purposes, it is desirable to have it quite clear. "Behold, I will hedge up thy way with thorns," is a prediction likely to be fulfilled in the lives of rulers and nations bent on a crooked course of conduct; nor can individuals escape the law of providential vexation when they practise deceit or, like Saul, cherish an impenitent spirit. It is thus that the delusiveness of sin appears; for the ease and pleasure anticipated in doing one's sinful will vanish before events, which, like mists around a mountain, seem to come from we know not where. A man's sin will be sure to find rebuke in forms he could not foresee. It is very inconvenient to be on the wrong side in the moral conflicts of life. Good men can bear trouble in patience, knowing that it is as truly helpful to their highest interests as is joy; wicked men not only lose the support of a clear conscience, but have to learn that the end for which they have striven will be frustrated (cf. Ps. vii. 9; xxxvii. 38; cxii. 10).

III. THE OPERATION OF MORAL CAUSES. The troubles which thus came on David and Saul, producing in the one a questionable ambiguity of conduct, and in the other a sense of helplessness, were connected with a set of moral causes that had been in steady operation for a considerable period, and had interacted with the physical in producing the crisis. Taking the case of Saul, we see how his sin in the early part of his reign, being unrepented, induced the line of conduct which drove David from the land, alienated the spiritual power and many of the ablest men, gradually drew around himself evil men, and created uneasiness and distrust in the nation. Whatever reluctance on the part of the people to assemble in full force, and whatever want of nerve on the part of Saul to lead them on, might have been the immediate cause of his fear—these were the result of the moral defection which had slowly worked on all departments of life. Besides this, the sin of Saul had had the effect of so withdrawing the Divine favour that Providence, by not restraining their will, permitted the attack of the Philistines. For moral reasons Saul's predicted doom was preparing, in spite of all his efforts to avoid it. It is one of the most striking characteristics of the Bible, as compared with other books, that it brings into prominence the moral causes that affect the present and future position of men. Assuming the orderly action of physical laws, it impresses us with the truth that the mental and moral are above the physical, and that man by his conduct sets in motion moral forces which, by a subtle interaction, ultimately govern the bearing of the physical upon his condition. Moral causes are *primary*. In so far as we may imagine the Divine action in creation having a beginning, the moral cause of action was antecedent. The reason of the exercise of power was moral. In our world's sad history moral causes have been primary. The same is true of our personal life. They lie at the spring of our joy or woe. They are also *silent and slow*. Saul's sin and impenitence were not uttered, and they worked on in silent, slow course all through his life. It seems to require time for the higher moral laws to work out their legitimate consequences in the sphere of the physical. There are many illustrations of this in the lives of evil men, as also of good. They are also *invincible*. No energy or cunning on the part of Saul could obviate the political and military weakness of his kingdom. No power can check the tendency to physical and political decay consequent on the sins of statesmen and peoples. The whole universe submits to the action of the moral forces that are tending to bring men into judgment. The sea even will obey and give up its dead.

General lessons:—1. In embarrassments brought on by our sins it is honouring to God to speak the plain truth and trust to his care. 2. The affairs of life will be

easily conducted in proportion as men are honest and simple in word and deed.   3.
Those only who learn the lessons of trouble in their early stage will escape later evils.
4. We should be thankful to God for hedging our erring steps with difficulties.   5. It
is a comfort to the holy that the principles ruling in their souls are destined to finally
subdue all things to their truest welfare.

Vers. 6—14.—*Man's appeal from God to man.*   The facts are—1. Saul in his
trouble seeks in vain guidance from God.   2. In despair he has recourse to the witch
of Endor, promising her that no harm should come to her for assisting him with her
incantations.   3. Saul desires of her to bring up Samuel.   4. On Samuel coming forth
the woman is in terror, and also discovers Saul's identity.   5. By the aid of the woman
Saul recognises Samuel, and bows himself to the earth.   The strange events here
narrated awaken feelings of wonder, and, in minds not acquiescent in God's methods
of developing his purpose in connection with the Hebrew race, some degree of incredulity ; but the important spiritual teaching is obvious, and the difficulties of the
subject, also, are not without their practical value.   We have here an instance of—

I. A MAN RIGHTEOUSLY LEFT OF GOD IN TIME OF DISTRESS.   The triple reference
to dreams, prophets, and Urim indicates the intense desire of Saul to obtain some
intimation of the Divine will ; and this renders the futility of his endeavour the
more impressive.   Outwardly he conformed to the usages of a ruler in Israel, and,
were he judged by men who have regard only or chiefly to the zeal which meets the
eye, he would be regarded as, so far, a religious man, and within the range of blessing.
To those who are unfamiliar with Scripture it may seem painfully strange that a
man presumably in earnest should be so utterly left of God ; but, as in other instances,
a little more knowledge will afford a solution of the fact and justify the ways of God.
1. *It is a fact that men are left to themselves.*   Divine guidance had been withheld
from Saul from the day of his rebellion (ch. xv. 20—23) up to the date of this event.
The antediluvians and, at one stage of history, Israel were abandoned to their
devices (Gen. vi. 1—3 ; Isa. i. 15).   Pharisees were left to the blindness of their
hearts notwithstanding their many prayers.   When men deliberately darken the light
that is in them God does not enable them to see the "Light of the world."   2. *There
are moral reasons for such abandonment.*   In Saul's case there was an absence of
that state of mind which alone would render attention to his cry for help honourable
to God and blessed to mankind.   There was no penitential recognition of his former
sin, nor of the years of persistent impenitence, nor of his cruelty to David ; his desire
for God's guidance and help sprang entirely from fear of military disaster, of loss
of influence, and of the fulfilment of the prediction outstanding against him (ch. xv.
28, 29).   The response of God to man's cry is based on law as beautiful in its
orderliness as anything in the physical world.   The notion that God *must* help every
one in trouble is based on sheer ignorance, and is profoundly unscientific.   Even in
home and society we recognise the necessity of moral conditions of receiving attention and favour.   Divine mercy is free, but is righteous in its flow.   It never sets a
premium on selfishness and impenitence ; it is never exercised in such a way as to do
violence to our radical sense of right and moral propriety.   This will account for the
deaf ear which God is represented as turning to bad men when, in desperation, they
cry to him in adversity, and when, at the end of life, they seek him in vain ; for they
do not care for God, for holiness, for anything but selfish deliverance from uncom-
fortable circumstances and great danger.   Hence—3. *The abandonment is in harmony with the current of God's promises.*   Again and again we are encouraged to seek
the Lord.   Nothing is more certain than that God delights to answer our cry for help.
The appeal of David later on in life, and the dumb pleading of the Magdalene, were
freely answered ; but the fifty-first Psalm reveals the contrast of David's spirit with
that of Saul, and the tears of the unholy woman told of a heart altogether turned
toward God.

II. THE SUPERHUMAN CHARACTER OF GOD'S WAYS.   There is in some minds a feeling
of surprise that such a narrative as this should find a place in a book supposed to be
written or compiled under Divine inspiration for the instruction of the world in
spiritual truth ; and, assuming that its fitness in such a book can be made out, it is
deemed incredible that God should allow his servant to come from the invisible world

at the request of such a man as Saul, and through an agency condemned in the Bible. Now on this difficult subject it may suffice for our purpose to observe—1. A *revelation of God's purpose* towards mankind in connection with and by means of the history of a race is *natural only in so far as it embraces what the chief figures of the history actually did,* and especially in their relation to him, be it good or bad. That Saul actually did as here recorded is evident on the face of the whole narrative, for never was there a more perfect air of truthfulness on a record. The very unreasonableness of his conduct in applying to a witch for such a purpose, and after executing the law against witchcraft, is quite reasonable when we reflect on the utter mental and moral confusion involved in his despair. Compare his unreasonable act of seeking a blessing through a sinful act (ch. xiii. 8—14; xv. 21—23). The record, therefore, of such a transaction is reasonable in an inspired book. 2. There *are cases in which God allows bad men to have their desire* without the advantage they expect from its being granted. Quails were given to men to their grief. A king was desired contrary to God's will, and one was given, much to the affliction of the nation. There is so far a similarity in this instance, that the granting of the desire to see Samuel was only to seal Saul's doom, not to give the guidance anticipated, and which had been hitherto refused (ver. 6). 3. There was *a manifest fitness in Samuel being permitted to declare the fixity of Saul's fate and its equity.* He had instructed and warned Saul at first in private (ch. ix. 25, 26), and subsequently (ch. xv. 26—31). All through he had looked with sorrowful pity on this poor wayward, sinning man. With Saul's belief in the existence of the spirits of good men after death, it was the most natural thing to wish, if possible, to see this wise, kind, and faithful friend, and in his utter despair appeal to his pity; and considering that there evidently still lurked in his mind a last hope that the old, long-deferred prediction of downfall might yet be averted, with a feeling that it was very hard, and perhaps unjust, for him to be thus left in misery, there seems to be a blending of Divine tenderness and judgment in this kind and faithful friend being permitted once more to be seen and heard, and at the same time to vindicate the justice of God in the doom about to be accomplished. The Divine tenderness and judgment which had borne with and chastised Saul all through his perverse life were now conspicuous in the irrevocable sealing of his doom. He would rather hear his sentence from Samuel than any other being, if it is to be pronounced. 4. There is *no evidence that the woman had anything to do with the appearance of Samuel.* He came forth before she called, and hence her wild shriek. That she subsequently played her part as a witch was consistent with the character of such persons. That Saul should suppose her to be the cause of the appearance does not touch the question. He was not in a mental condition to discriminate. That God should allow an invisible being to become visible under such conditions is to be settled by history, for—5. There is *no moral principle violated in God allowing a being from the invisible world to become visible.* There is here no sanction of witchcraft, no admission of its powers. Kindness and judgment only are displayed in relation to Saul. The whole difficulty, therefore, resolves itself in a visible appearance of a dead man. Will any one say that God *cannot* cause a Samuel to appear as truly as a Moses and Elijah? Does the incredulity lie in the fact that *we* never see the departed, or that God does not cause them to appear to others? By what law is God bound to make a specific exercise of his power common? Will the case be improved by saying it is such an exercise of power as *we* should not deem wise and useful? What is that but saying we make our method of government a standard by which God's reported acts shall be judged? Is it not wiser to submit to the force of historical testimony, and admit that his ways are not our ways? God does strange things in the earth, at which men marvel, but never unholy things. There is nothing incredible in the existence of departed spirits, nor in their employment when God has a fit purpose to accomplish through them.

III. The permanence of religious sentiments. It is noteworthy that although Saul had lived so long in impenitence, and had become even hardened in his sinful course, he still retained an awe and reverence for the supernatural and invisible. His very folly and sin in having recourse to a witch revealed the strength of the feeling which could not rest without some help from the unseen world. If God cannot be found men will seek out a substitute. Idolatry and all forms of religious superstition are evidence of the power of the religious sentiment in man. Thousands of men have done much to crush it out, but it has reasserted itself in seasons of distress. Because man is formed for religion, and carries within him feelings which crave for the unseen and eternal, therefore he often becomes the slave of false systems of belief and worship. The permanence of this sentiment gives hope to the missionary, and adds to the remorse of the finally impenitent.

IV. THE POWER OF RELIGIOUS INFLUENCE. The influence of Samuel over Saul appears in this bitter cry for his presence in the hour of misery. The foundation of this influence was laid in Samuel's character, and in the kind and wise interest he took in Saul when entering on his public duties as king. Holy example, faithful warning, wise instruction, tender forbearance, and pitiful concern had not been altogether lost on this erring, self-willed man, although in the perversity of his heart he had for years gone counter to Samuel's guidance. In the dark and painful hour of despair the thought of the wise counsellor and sincere friend came over the soul with memories rich in homage to him. How often does the poor prodigal, when sinking in misery, feel the spell of a mother's piety! How many a man after years of neglected instruction thinks of the faithful pastor, and perchance takes to heart the lessons of his words and life!

General lessons:—1. The climax of trouble is reached when God refuses to hear our prayer, for "What can I do?" then admits of no satisfactory answer. 2. We ought to search our hearts, to see whether we so "regard iniquity" therein as to be in an unfit moral condition to receive a blessing from God (Ps. lxvi. 18). 3. God has methods by which he can vindicate the justice of his judgments, even when we are craving for relief from them. 4. It is important to exercise religious influence over others as early and constantly as possible, since we know that it will be a power even when we are gone.

Vers. 15—25.—*The last fruitless effort.* The facts of this section are—1. Saul, in reply to Samuel's question, declares, as the reason of seeking him, his deep distress and desire to know what to do. 2. Samuel intimates that the inquiry is vain, as he cannot go against God; that the event causing so much distress was simply the perfecting of what had long before been declared; that David was the coming king, and that all this was the consequence of deliberate disobedience. 3. He also declares that the morrow should witness the overthrow of Saul's power and the death of himself and sons. 4. The effect of the message on Saul is to prostrate him in terror on the ground. 5. Out of compassion the woman seeks in vain to rouse Saul from his helpless despair, but by the aid of his attendants he is at last constrained to rise and partake of the meal she had prepared. Among the many truths suggested by this impressive scene we may notice a few.

I. THE DARING OF DESPERATION. Ordinarily men shrink in dread from all thought of contact with visitants from the unseen world, and bad men especially tremble at the possible presence, seen or unseen, of the ghosts of the departed. The experience of all ages testifies to this. And yet here we have an instance of a man, not usually distinguished by calm self-possession, deliberately seeking, and actually holding, converse with one from the dead. The solution of this reversal of the course of human feeling and conduct lies in the desperation of despair, which so overpowers all thought and feeling as to dare to do what at other times would be impossible. Such the urgency of conscience, the pressure of misery, the violent struggle of a will caught in the coils of its own perversity. The same occurs in other circumstances, as when, to extricate themselves from self-brought miseries, men dare to perpetrate deeds of honour or shame, or even commit suicide. Is there not a similar feeling implied in the cry to the rocks, "Fall on us and hide us from the wrath of the Lamb"?

II. AN UNANSWERABLE QUESTION. One question had agitated Saul for some days. He appealed to God, and no answer came; and now Samuel is told that the object for which he was summoned into the visible sphere was to reply to this one question, "What shall I do?" The silence of God and the words of Samuel show that practically this was a question for which no answer was possible. The day for doing was in the past, when Samuel delivered instructions in the name of God. Years of persistent impenitence for disobedience and of self-willed warring against the purposes of God had brought the unhappy man to a time and position in which no action on his part could reverse the judgment impending. Too late! So is it in human life still. Men may persist in evil ways at home or in business till ruin of domestic peace and of prospects is inevitable, and no course is open for retrieval. The question of the jailor, "What must I do to be saved?" was opportune, and then, as generally, it admitted of a blessed answer; but it is possible for men to scorn and despise Christ so long that the other question may arise, "How shall we escape if we neglect so great salvation?" (cf. Heb. ii. 3; vi. 3—7; x. 26—31).

III. THE UNALTERABLE LAW OF LIFE. The whole of Saul's conduct during these closing days of his life was based on the ignorant supposition that by some device he could be sustained in the kingdom notwithstanding his former disobedience and continued impenitence. Conformity in act and spirit to the mind of God is the law of true prosperity in life. Israel's king rises or falls according to this law. As a servant called to perform an important part in unfolding Messianic purposes, Saul's hold on the kingdom was made to *depend on character*. No plea, no consideration of personal misery, no device suggested by the living or the dead, could avail to give to a self-willed, impenitent man what is due to the obedient and holy. In all his misery and desire for guidance there was not a trace of the broken or contrite heart which God accepts; there was only and always a blind effort to avert the passing away of the power which sin had forfeited. This law of life is never changed. Men struggle against it, seek to evade its action, crave for some relaxation of its pressure, but it is unbending, unrelenting. Character determines destiny. The lines of experience in the future are the outcome of the present, and not disconnected. As we sow we reap.

IV. THE MORAL INTERPRETATION OF EVENTS. No doubt there were hours when the revival of conscience would enable Saul to read the meaning of the troubles that had long befallen him; but generally, and especially at this juncture, he appears to have wondered at the miseries of his position. Men do bring on themselves manifold troubles, and then, forgetful of the conduct which gave rise to them, or not tracing them carefully back to their own former moral condition, they marvel at, and perhaps complain of, the sufferings endured. The visitant from the unseen world threw light on Saul's position by reference to conduct and character. Here was an interpretation, from a moral point of view, of a long succession of events in the political, physical, and mental spheres. We never estimate events in our life aright if we leave out the moral element. A vast accumulation of disasters in the history of nations and individuals, Churches and homes, is understandable in the light of what men have been and have done. Hence the value of the Bible, which comes as a visitant from the spiritual sphere, casting light on the matters that worry and distress the heart of man. Sinful men need a voice to tell them how to estimate the experiences of their life.

V. THE VINDICATION OF GOD'S SEVERITY. It seemed hard to Saul to be thus left of God, the mere wreck of his former self, and now exposed to a great disaster as commander of an army. Had casual observers, unacquainted with antecedent moral facts, looked on his miseries, they might pronounce the treatment severe. There is, however, in the conscience of even the most self-willed sinner that which recognises the majesty of right and echoes the voice of judgment. It was only for Samuel to refer to the deliberate disobedience of former days, and Saul saw at once the connection of all his woes with the depraved moral condition then manifested and subsequently cherished. Divine patience had borne with him during years of rebellion, content to let the natural outgrowth of his own acts bring on the judgment predicted, and, now that it was falling on him with crushing force, this reminder of great and continuous sin was even to the suffering king a full vindication of the course of Providence. Here is *warning* and *instruction* for us. Let us never suppose that we or others bear more than we deserve. We should avoid the bare thought that God deals harshly with any of his creatures. The bitterest element in the cup of suffering is that *we* put into it by our transgressions; for facts prove that overwhelming material disasters, with a good conscience, are not the worst of evils, and become not only endurable, but means of spiritual good. The hour may come to each when, by a voice full of truth, we shall be made to see how just are God's judgments on ourselves. The escape from so awful a position is by fleeing now for refuge to Christ our Righteousness. The dumb consent of Saul to the truth of Samuel's words is in keeping with the acquiescent silence wherewith, in the future life, the wicked are represented as bowing to the sentence of the Judge (cf. Matt. vii. 21—23; xxv. 11, 12, 31—46; Luke xvi. 23—25; xix. 22—26).

VI. The great disappointment of life. Saul certainly cherished hope to the last that by some contrivance, some casual aid, he should avert the evil due to his sins. With all the unreasoning energy of desperation he sought Samuel as a final resource; but instead of the hoped-for guidance of what he shall do, he meets with a declaration of his doom. Sentence of death is passed by the very friend whose counsel is sought. This doubtless was the most grievous disappointment of his earthly life, and might well lay him low in the dust. Not instruction, but judicial utterance. Not deliverance, but destruction. There are bitter disappointments during the life of most men, and the heart sinks in pain and dismay, but *the* great disappointment of some is at the end of their earthly course. Christ represents some as expecting to be received into heaven, and all the hopes of years are blasted by the awful words, " Depart from me, ye that work iniquity." The parable of the Pharisee and publican points to the same fearful issue. Would that men did but " ponder the path " of their feet, and by timely penitence and renewal of soul obviate that most calamitous of all disappointments!

VII. Sympathy with fallen greatness. There is an awful and instructive contrast in this closing scene of Saul's career—between the calm, measured, though evidently tender words of Samuel, followed by his return to the invisible world, leaving the wretched king prostrate and helpless on the ground, and the active compassion of this evil woman for the distinguished sufferer at her feet. Samuel was still the true, loving man as of old; but in the invisible sphere he saw things in a clear moral light, and was restrained by his judicial commission from manifesting in action sympathy for the fallen king. It is a question how far a perfect perception of the enormity of sin, such as must be attained by the " spirits of the just made perfect," diminishes what we ordinarily understand as sympathy for those who receive " according to the deeds done in the body." Be that as it may, we cannot but note how even those addicted to a life of sin, as was this woman, are touched by the presence of a great sorrow. There is something exquisitely beautiful in her conduct. For a time the old cunning and moral insensibility and cynicism are set aside, and the humane feelings of her soul find free exercise, as perhaps in the days of her youth—suggestive to us of the germ of true humanity that underlies the accretions of a guilty life, and of the power that may be exercised over even the worst, if only we knew the art of touching the hidden spring. Every reader of the narrative must enter into her gentle and respectful feelings towards the fallen monarch; and we feel that had we been there we also should have sought to raise him from the earth, and provide generous nourishment for his exhausted frame. For sympathy with the righteous judgments of God does not extinguish pity for those who fall under them. In fallen greatness we see the majesty and the dishonour, the possibilities and the actualities, of our common humanity. It is as though a large part of ourselves had come to grief; and though we cannot but deplore the sin, we feel disposed to weep over the lost one, and to render the last offices of kindness with a tender hand. So did our blessed Lord, the *perfect Man*, weep over the lost city when proclaiming with full acquiescence its righteous doom (Matt. xxiii. 37, 38; Luke xix. 41—44).

General lessons:—1. The only safe course when sin has been committed is at once, after the example of David and Peter, to return to the Lord and cast ourselves entirely on his mercy. Saul's neglect of this was the secret of his subsequent miseries. 2. There is great probability of cherished sin issuing in a state of mind such that men shall imagine they are seeking good of God when in reality they are seeking only the evasion of his righteous judgments. 3. It cannot be too earnestly and frequently impressed on young and old that moral character is the governing element in the determination of their present and future condition. 4. The occasional justification of God's apparently severe judgments recorded in Scripture may be regarded as foreshadowing the future moral solution of the dark and painful events connected with the history of the intelligent universe. **5.** If we would be prepared to end life with a realisation of our hopes we must give heed to the reality of our oneness with the mind of God.

HOMILIES BY VARIOUS AUTHORS.

Vers. 1—6. (GILBOA.)—*Darkening shadows of retribution.* "And when Saul saw the host of the Philistines, he was afraid, and his heart greatly trembled" (ver. 5). **1.** The *end of Saul* was now approaching. How long he reigned is not stated ("forty years," Acts xiii. 21; perhaps a round number, including the judgeship of Samuel). But his course from his first wrong step (ch. xiii. 8—15) had been a downward one, broken only by brief seasons of amendment. His mental malady may account in part for some of his actions in his later years. During his persecution of David the enemies of Israel became more powerful and aggressive, and, in retribution for unfaithfulness to Jehovah, he was about to be delivered with the host of Israel "into the hand of the Philistines," from whom he had been chosen to effect deliverance (ch. ix. 16). **2.** The *Philistine invasion* was on a larger scale than any that had recently occurred (ch. xiii. 5; xvii. 1), and in a different part of the country. It was evidently planned with a view to inflict a fatal blow on Israel. The enemy marched northward, entered the plain of Esdraelon (Jezreel), the battlefield of Palestine (stretching out eastward in three branches, like fingers from the hand), and encamped at Shunem (at the base of Little Hermon, north of the central and principal branch). "And the Israelites pitched by the fountain which is in Jezreel" (ch. xxix. 1), on a spur of Mount Gilboa (south of the central branch), from which they could see the Philistines, three miles distant across the plain, where on the morrow the conflict must be waged. **3.** What *the issue of the conflict* was likely to be Saul's heart told him only too plainly. He felt that what he had so long dreaded was about to come upon him; that the sentence of rejection formerly uttered by Samuel (ch. xvi. 14—16), now gone to his rest (ver. 3), was to be fully executed, and that he would be deprived of his crown, and probably of his life. David, who had once saved Israel in similar peril, had gone over to the Philistines (ch. xxvii. 4), was now (as he thought) among them, and would "surely be king" (ch. xxiv. 20). The night of retribution is setting in. The ministers of vengeance are gathering, like vultures to the prey,

> " From the invisible ether ;
> First a speck, and then a vulture,
> Till the air is dark with pinions."

The experience of Saul is shared by many a persistent transgressor in the presence of imminent danger and approaching death, when "the terrors of God do set themselves in array against" him (Job vi. 4; xxiv. 17). He is—

I. BESET BY IRRESISTIBLE FEAR. The sight of superior hostile forces is calculated to produce such fear, but its power to do so depends chiefly upon the inward state of a man himself, more or less conscious of his condition; **1.** *The remembrance of past transgressions,* and of the punishment threatened against them, and already in some measure experienced. Circumstances often quicken the memory and open its secret records, so that former actions and events reappear, are seen in their true character, and fill the soul with consternation. "I will reprove thee, and set them in order before thine eyes" (Ps. l. 21). **2.** *The consciousness of Divine displeasure* in consequence of disobedience, and the heart not being right with God. Although conscience may slumber long, the hour of awakening comes, and when it asserts its power "its frown is more to be dreaded than the frowns of kings or the approach of armies. It is a fire in the bones, burning when no man suspects" (South). "A wounded spirit who can bear?" (Prov. xviii. 14).

> " O conscience, conscience, man's most faithful friend,
> How canst thou comfort, ease, relieve, defend !
> But if he will thy friendly checks forego,
> Thou art, oh, woe for me ! his deadliest foe" (Crabbe).

3. *The foreboding of approaching doom.* Conscience "exerts itself magisterially, and approves or condemns, . . . and if not forcibly stopped, naturally and always, of course, goes on to anticipate a higher and more effectual sentence, which shall hereafter second and affirm its own" (Butler).

II. IMPELLED TO SEEK DIVINE COUNSEL. "And Saul inquired of Jehovah" (ver. 6). It is not recorded that he had ever done so since he "asked counsel of God" and "he answered him not" (ch. xiv. 37). His communication with Heaven had evidently been long interrupted. But under the influence of fear he felt the urgent need of it, as other men who have neglected to seek God often do in times of danger, and he expected that it would come at his bidding, as a matter of course, when he made use of the recognised means of obtaining it, apart from a proper state of heart, therein exhibiting the same blindness as of old (ch. xiii. 9). Cherishing a spirit of envy and hatred, how could it be expected that he should be visited by the Divine Spirit in *dreams* of good? Having slain the high priest, and compelled his son to flee to David "with the ephod" and the *Urim,* how could it be expected that he should obtain counsel through another whom he had appointed in his stead, or, having alienated the *prophets,* that he should gain it through them? Divine aid is often sought through proper channels in vain because—1. *It is not sought at the right time,*—"When thou mayest be found" (Ps. xxxii. 6). "Then shall they call upon me, but I will not answer" (Prov. i. 24—33),—which takes place not merely as a just punishment for long neglect, but also on account of the increased hardness of their hearts thereby induced, and rendering them incapable and utterly unworthy of holding communion with God. "If we do not hear God's voice when it goes well with us, God can and will refuse to hear our voice when it goes ill with us" (Starke). 2. *It is not sought in a right spirit*—with humility, penitence, self-renunciation, and faith. Of these principles there is no trace in the inquiry of Saul. 3. *It is not sought with a right purpose,* but with some earthly and selfish end in view, rather than the Divine honour. "As the event proved, Saul did not really inquire of the Lord in the sense of seeking direction from him, and of being willing to be guided by it. Rather did he, if we may so express it, wish to use the Lord as the means by which to attain his object. But that was essentially the heathen view, and differed only in detail, not in principle, from the inquiry of the familiar spirit, to which he afterwards resorted" (Edersheim). "Ye ask, and receive not, because ye ask amiss," &c. (James iv. 3; Ps. lxvi. 18; Isa. lxvi. 4; Ezek. xiv. 4; xx. 31).

III. DENIED THE DESIRED RESPONSE. "Jehovah answered him not," &c. (ver. 6). "I am sore distressed; for the Philistines make war against me, and God is departed from me, and answereth me no more" (ver. 15). "Saul received from God no answer more, except for judgment." 1. What dreadful *silence* and *loneliness* are here revealed! "We read of the silence of the desert, the silence of midnight, the silence of the churchyard and the grave; but this is something more profound and appalling —the silence of God when appealed to by the sinner in his extremity. It is not the silence of indifference, nor of inability to hear, nor of weakness, nor of perplexity; but of refusal, of rejection, of displeasure, of abandonment" (Bonar, 'Bible Thoughts'). "Ephraim is joined to idols: let him alone" (Hosea iv. 17). 2. What utter *helplessness!* 3. What intolerable *darkness* and *distress!* (Heb. x. 27).

Consider—1. That if "inquiry of the Lord" be left unanswered, the reason of it is to be sought in the moral condition of the inquirer. 2. That nothing but the offering of the sacrifice of "a broken and a contrite heart" can prevent despair. 3. That the boundless mercy of God should awaken hope even at "the eleventh hour."—D.

Vers. 7—10. (GILBOA, ENDOR).—*Resorting to superstitious practices.* "Seek me a woman that hath a familiar spirit, that I may go to her, and inquire of her" (ver. 7). 1. The religion of Saul (like that of many others in Israel) was largely pervaded by *superstition.* He regarded Jehovah as an object of dread rather than of trust and love, and observed the outward forms of his service not in a spirit of willing and hearty obedience, but because he thought that they would of themselves procure for him the Divine favour. Hence his zeal in putting away "those that had familiar spirits" (*Oboth*=spirits of the departed, supposed to be called up from the unseen world to make disclosures concerning the future, and dwelling in them and speaking through them in hollow tones of voice, Isa. viii. 19 ; xxix. 4; ventriloquists, LXX. ; necromancers) "and wizards" (sorcerers). And when his inquiry of the Lord was not answered, he resorted to one of these, in the expectation of being told what he must do (ver. 15) to avert the wrath which he feared. In like manner the heathen resorted to their priests and diviners (ch. vi. 2). He was an embodiment of the heathen mind in Israel. "There were three courses open to him : he might sit down in quiet hopelessness, and let the evil come; or he might in faith and penitent submission commit the whole matter to God, even amid the awful silence ; or he might betake himself to hell for counsel, since heaven was deaf. He chooses the last ! 'God has cast me off; I will betake myself to Satan. Heaven's door is shut ; I will see if hell's be open' " (Bonar). He had about him *servants* who pandered to his superstitious propensities (ch. xvi. 15), and informed him of a practitioner of the heathen art residing at Endor, eight miles distant (north of Little Hermon) ; and thither two of them conducted him " by night." (Another of the *night scenes* of this book—ch. iii. 3 ; v. 3 ; ix. 25 ; xv. 11 ; xix. 10 ; xxv. 36 ; xxvi. 7 ; xxx. 17). It was "a dreadful journey, a terrible night ; both symbols of Saul's condition, lost on the way of inner self-hardening and thorough self-darkening " (Erdmann). The readiness with which he was directed to the sorceress shows the secret prevalence of superstition in Israel. **3.** He *failed* to obtain the aid he desired, committed his crowning act of apostasy, and hastened his doom. "So Saul died for . . . asking counsel of one that had a familiar spirit, to inquire of it " (1 Chron. x. 13). "There is no wisdom, nor understanding, nor counsel against the Lord " (Prov. xxi. 30). There may have been "an objective reality, a dark background of magical agency " (Delitzsch, ' Bib. Psychology,' p. 363) ; but, on the other hand, "the actual references to magic in Scripture do not involve its reality. The mischiefs resulting from the *pretension*, under the theocracy, to an act which involved idolatry justified the statute which denounced it with death " (Kitto, ' Cyc.,' art. Witchcraft). " In the doctrinal Scriptures magic is passed by with contempt ; in the historical Scriptures the reasonableness of this contempt is shown. Whenever the practisers of magic attempt to combat the servants of God they conspicuously fail " (Smith's ' Dict.,' art. Magic). Resorting to superstitious practices of various kinds (the selection of " lucky " days, fortune-telling, spirit-rapping, psychography, necromancy, and, in more direct connection with the Christian religion, image-worship, prayers to the dead, superstitious rites and ceremonies of various kinds) is not unknown at the present day. Notice—

I. ITS INDUCEMENTS. Among them are—1. *Unbelieving fear.* "Superstition is the restless effort of a guilty but blind conscience to find rest and peace and good by unauthorised propitiations and ceremonies " (R. Watson). " The true cause and rise of superstition is indeed nothing else but a false opinion of the Deity, that renders him terrible and dreadful, as being rigorous and imperious ; that which represents him as austere and apt to be angry, but yet impotent and easy to be appeased again by some flattering devotions, especially if performed with sanctimonious shows and a solemn sadness of mind " (Smith, ' Sel. Dis. Superstition '). "The human heart needs something to cling to, something to which it may hold fast, a prop which its tendrils may firmly clasp ; therefore when it leaves him for whom it was made, when it sinks into unbelief, then it clings to superstition and darkness " (Schlier). 2. *Unhallowed curiosity,* which is not satisfied with what has been revealed in the word of God, and wishes to become acquainted with the secrets of the unseen world and the future, designedly concealed. Such curiosity " is a flattering serpent, which promises us the wisdom of God, and cheats us out of a blessed paradise of happier, childlike waiting." " Let no man beguile you," &c. (Col. ii. 18). 3. *Foolish presumption,* which fancies that it can attain the knowledge and help of the supernatural by other ways and means than God has appointed. " He who, in respect of supersensual things and of the mysterious background of sensible things, regards as true, and allows impressions to be made on himself by thoughts or occurrences whose reality has neither the warranty of undoubtedly credible tradition nor the warranty of internal force of conviction in their favour, is rightly called superstitious " (Delitzsch).

II. ITS DEVICES. They usually—1. *Involve artifice,* effort, trouble, and sacrifice (vers. 7, 8). What extraordinary pains do men sometimes undergo in the practice of superstition! (1 Kings xviii. 28). 2. *Affect darkness* and secrecy, and necessitate the adoption of undignified, mean, and shameful courses. They are carried out under the cover of night, which is favourable to deception. Saul disguised himself not to escape the Philistines, but to elude the observation of his own people, and to impose upon the sorceress (ver. 9). 3. *Involve mental blindness* and credulity, so that those who yield to them become the ready dupes of others who traffic on their gloomy fears and illusory hopes, "deceiving and being deceived." " It was a shame that the king who had expelled all sorcerers must himself at last fall into the hands of a sorceress " (Winer).

III. ITS SINFULNESS. 1. *It casts contempt upon the sufficiency of Divine revelation.* "Wilt thou have light for all the riddles and dark questions of this life? betake thyself to God's word, there enough is revealed, and what goes beyond that comes of evil." 2. *It chooses evil instead of good*, disregards the moral dispositions which God requires, and violates the sense of goodness, righteousness, and truth. Saul took an oath " by the Lord " to protect what he knew was displeasing to the Lord, and was guilty of connivance at what he himself had condemned as worthy of death (ver. 10). 3. *It does what the word of God prohibits*, and in its worst forms, casts off allegiance to God, and makes alliance with his enemies (Levit. xix. 31; xx. 6, 27; Deut. xviii. 10; 2 Kings xxiii. 24; Gal. v. 20; Rev. xxii. 15). " Knowing that the act of divination co-operates in no slight degree with the errors of the lives of the multitude, so as to lead them out of the right way, Moses did not suffer his disciples to use any species of it whatever. All these things are but the furniture of impiety. How so? Because he who attends to them and who allows himself to be influenced by them disregards the cause of all things, looking upon those things alone as the causes of all things, whether good or evil " (Philo, ' On Monarchy ').

IV. ITS INJURIOUSNESS. 1. It fills the votaries of superstition with miserable disappointment. 2. It makes them the victims of delusion, and further estranges them from the way of truth. 3. It increases their guilt, hardens their heart, and quickens their pace to final ruin. Saul's night-visit was an ill preparation for the coming conflict. It extinguished every ray of hope, and turned his fear into despair.—D.

Ver. 11. (ENDOR.)—*Samuel's counsel vainly desired.* " Bring me up Samuel." The character of Samuel was so great, his life had been so long-continued, his appearance so familiar to all, his influence so powerful and extensive, that after his departure his form must have seemed still to brood over the land. What the thoughts of Saul were at his death we know not. Perhaps he was glad of his removal. Although dwelling near him, he was altogether estranged from him, and entirely neglected to seek his counsel. But the time came—the threatening hosts of the Philistines, his overwhelming fear, the silence of Heaven—when he urgently needed it, and earnestly but vainly desired the benefit of it. Whether he went to the sorceress with the deliberate purpose of seeking an interview with his old and faithful counsellor, or sought it under the impulse of the moment, is not stated. The former is the more probable. He was certainly persuaded of the power which she professed to have (ver. 11) of raising up the spirits of the departed, and (after her expression of surprise, and her description of his well-known appearance) of the actual presence of Samuel in consequence of his request ("I have called thee," ver. 15). The result of the interview, however, proved that his hope of obtaining good from it was vain. It is not unusual for those who have neglected the advice of a teacher or friend to desire, when he is gone, that he might come back and again grant it to them. In such a desire we see—

I. THE VALUE OF FAITHFUL COUNSEL, to which it is a testimony. The reproofs and warnings which a faithful counsellor gives are not always agreeable. They are often deemed unnecessary, regarded with contempt, and cause him to be accounted an enemy. But they are justified by events; and then their worth is felt, and they are longed for, when perchance it is too late. The sore distress which Saul now suffered would have been averted if he had listened to the counsel of Samuel. He is your best friend who tells you the truth, and seeks your welfare rather than your favour. Give heed to what he says while it may conduce to your profit.

II. THE FOLLY OF FAITHLESS NEGLECT, of which it is a confession. "How have I hated instruction, and my heart despised reproof; and have not obeyed the voice of my teachers, nor inclined mine ear to them that instructed me!" (Prov. v. 12, 13). "How many who have despised the advice of a father or a mother, and grieved their parents by opposition and disobedience, long bitterly to bring them back when they have gone down to the grave, that they may have the benefit of the counsel which they once slighted and scorned! If they could go to the necromancer in the hour of their distress, it would not be, 'Bring me up the companion who cheered me in my gaieties, who was with me at the revel and the dance and the public show;' but, 'Bring me up the father with his gray hairs, who solemnly told me that the way of transgressors was hard; or the mother who with weeping eyes and broken voice admonished me against sinful indulgences.' . . . And yet, if you neglect the Lord and continue to resist the strivings of his Spirit, so that at length he departs from you as he departed from Saul, what would it avail that the grave could give up its inhabitant—if the parent, the friend, or the minister should return at your bidding?" (H. Melvill).

III. THE WORTHLESSNESS OF PIOUS WISHES in those who persist in transgression. Saul was deeply humbled. His self-will and pride were broken down into pitiable abasement, and he seemed willing to receive and obey the counsel which he had previously slighted. Yet his motive was doubtless the same as in inquiring of the Lord (vers. 1—6); he looked upon Samuel as more merciful than the Lord, relied upon him to effect a change in the Divine purpose (ch. xv. 29), and expected his aid at the very moment he was committing a capital offence. He was more blinded and self-deceived than ever. Men often abase themselves deeply in affliction while they remain wholly destitute of the spirit of obedience. "Let no man deceive himself." What value can there be in a religious desire which is combined with the violation of the plainest religious duty?

IV. THE USELESSNESS OF EXTRAORDINARY COMMUNICATIONS, such as have been sometimes desired from the dead. Saul had what to him was the fulfilment of his desire; but he was told only what he already knew or feared, he was not led to repentance and faith, and sank into despair. Is it supposed that benefit would be derived from the reappearance and counsel of the departed? Consider that—1. The light which might be brought would only be a confirmation of the truth which has been already revealed. If even future events, as, *e. g.*, the time of death, should be declared, the knowledge thereof would probably be useless and injurious. Should death be distant, it would be a strong temptation to sloth and continued sin; should it be very near, whilst it might arouse some to make preparation for it simply from a selfish dread of threatening evil, it would lead others to feel that it was too late to avert the danger, and resign themselves to reckless indulgence or blank despair (see ch. xx. 3). 2. Those who are not improved by existing inducements to faith and obedience would be proof against such as might be thereby presented, and would in most cases be hardened in sin (John xii. 10). "If they hear not Moses and the prophets, neither will they be persuaded, though one rose from the dead" (Luke xvi. 31). 3. God has given to men the knowledge and inducements which are best adapted to their probationary condition and sufficient for every practical purpose, and has wisely determined that no more shall be afforded. "He that is unjust," &c. (Rev. xxii. 11). "As no additional dissuasions from sin and inducements to holiness would be presented, they who, notwithstanding these disclosures, remained impenitent and unbelieving must continue in irreclaimable wickedness." "Say not in thine heart," &c. (Rom. x. 6—11). Crave not for "secret things"—the mysterious, the supernatural, the miraculous, the speculative, the impossible. "If thou shalt confess with thy mouth the Lord Jesus, and shalt believe in thine heart that God hath raised him from the dead, thou shalt be saved."—D.

Vers. 12—20. (ENDOR.) — *The sentence of rejection confirmed.* "And Jehovah hath done for himself, as he spake by me" (ver. 17). 1. The *narrative* of Saul's interview with the sorceress is graphic, but brief, incomplete, and in many respects, as might be expected, indefinite. Whether on his request, "Bring me up Samuel," she employed her illicit art is not expressly stated, nor whether any supernatural agency was concerned in what took place. "The woman saw Samuel," and she *alone* (ver. 14), "and she cried out" (in real or feigned surprise and fear), "Why hast thou deceived me? for thou art Saul." There is no intimation that the name of Samuel or the distinguished stature of her visitor had previously suggested who he was; nor of any "gestures of fearful menace such as he could only show towards a deadly enemy, *i. e.* towards Saul" (Ewald, Stanley). It was from her description of "gods ascending out of the earth," and of the well-known appearance of the venerable judge and prophet, that "he perceived that it was Samuel," and prostrated himself in abject homage before him whom he had formerly moved by his importunity to comply with his request (ch. xv. 30); and while "stooping with his face to the ground" he heard a voice which he was persuaded was the voice of Samuel. The evidence of an apparition or vision (for there can be no question concerning anything else) depended solely on the testimony of the woman; of the hearing of an unearthly voice on that of Saul, from whom also (unless his two servants were present at the time, which is not likely) the whole account must have been primarily derived. 2. It has been *explained* in various ways, *e. g.*, that there was—(1) *A real apparition* of the prophet (Ecclus. xlvi. 20), either evoked by the conjurations of the woman (LXX., Josephus, Talmud), or effected by Divine power without her aid, and contrary to her expectation (see, for authorities and arguments, Wordsworth, 'Com.;' Waterland, Delany, Sir W. Scott, 'Demonology;' Kitto, 'D. B. Illus.;' Lindsay, Hengstenberg, Keil). (2) *An illusory appearance* produced by demoniacal (or angelic) agency, and, according to some, employed as a medium of Divine revelation (Luther, Calvin, Grotius, Gilpin, 'Dæmonologia Sacra;' Hall, Patrick, M. Henry). (3) *A mental impression* or representation produced by Divine influence. (4) *A superstitious self-deception* on the part of the woman, combined with a psychological *identifying* of herself with the deceased prophet (Erdmann). (5) *A conscious deception* practised by her (perhaps not entirely without illusion) on the fearful and superstitious mind of the king, fasting, wearied, terrified, and in the dark (Chandler, W. Scott, 'Existence of Evil Spirits;' Thenius); little other than a dream, though *terribly real to him.* The circumstances of the case were such that the almost dramatic language of the historian may be fairly understood as descriptive of what seemed to Saul, and was afterwards popularly believed, rather than of the actual reality. All that occurred may be accounted for more satisfactorily on this hypothesis than any other. Almost every other involves assumptions concerning the power of necromancy, the reappearance of the dead, evil spirits, &c., which are unsupported by Scripture and exceedingly improbable. A Divine interposition would have been unmistakably indicated in the narrative (which is not the case, ver. 21), inconsistent with the Divine refusal to answer Saul's inquiry, unnecessary in order to reprove him further for the past (for there is no expressed reproof of his present crime), without adequate theocratic purpose, contrary to the holiness of God, and a confirmation (not a punishment) of "the anti-godly attempt of the sorceress." 3. Its *chief significance* (however it may be explained) lies in the revelation which it makes of the depth of degradation to which Saul had sunk and the effect of his apostasy. His "sin of divination" (ch. xv. 23) led to despair, and was speedily followed by the full execution of the sentence of his rejection. The silence of God was the silence that precedes the thunderstorm and the earthquake. Observe that—

I. THERE IS NO APPEAL FROM THE DIVINE JUDGMENT TO ANY OTHER (vers. 16, 17). Saul appears to have clung to the delusion that the sentence of Divine judgment uttered against him might be effectually resisted and entirely revoked; refused to acknowledge and submit to it, and hoped to succeed in his conflict with it when success was plainly perceived by others to be impossible. Hence (and not merely to gratify his curiosity concerning his fate) he sought the counsel of Samuel. In answer to the voice (asking reproachfully the reason why he had "disquieted" the dead, and drawing forth the expression of his feelings and wishes), he pathetically described his distress in consequence of the attack of the Philistines and his abandonment by God, and appealed for aid in his perplexity. Without supposing a desire of revenge on the part of the sorceress, hardly any other reply could be more accordant with his state of mind and deepest convictions than that which came to him. Since (by his own confession) he was abandoned by the Lord, it was useless to expect effectual help from the prophet of the Lord, who was the exponent and executor of his will. No direction was given "what he must do," and no ground of hope afforded that he might find mercy with the Lord himself if he sought it in a right spirit. "The belief that Samuel had come to revisit him from the dead so worked upon Saul's mind as to suggest to his conscience what seemed to be spoken in his ear" (Smith's 'Old Testament History').

II. THE DIVINE JUDGMENT IS SOMETIMES FELT TO BE IRREVOCABLE. Of this he had occasionally caught a glimpse, but it was now brought home to him with over-whelming force in connection with—1. *The consciousness of his present condition*, as an object of Divine displeasure, and destined to be replaced in the kingdom by David, to whom he had long ago applied the words of the prophet (ch. xiii. 14 ; xv. 28): "The Lord hath rent," &c. (ver. 17). "The perfects express the purpose of God which had already been formed, and was now about to be fulfilled" (Keil). 2. *The remembrance of his past transgression.* "Because," &c. (ver. 18). The sparing of Amalek was the well-known cause of his estrangement from Samuel and his rejection ; and how vividly does some former act of disobedience sometimes rise before the mind of the sinner, increasing his burden of guilt and justifying his condemnation! 3. *The fear of his future fate,* now foreseen to be approaching (ver. 19). Israel would share his defeat, he and his sons would be on the morrow numbered with the dead, and the camp spoiled by the enemy. It was a terrible message, an inward realisation and confirmation of the Divine sentence. How little had he profited by resorting to divination! "The Strength of Israel will not lie nor repent."

III. THE CONVICTION THAT THE DIVINE JUDGMENT CANNOT BE ALTERED PRODUCES DESPAIR. "And Saul fell straightway all along on the earth," &c. (ver. 20). Up to this moment some hope lingered in his breast.

> "The wretch condemned with life to part
>   Still, still on hope relies ;
> And every pang that rends the heart
>   Bids expectation rise.

> "Hope, like the glimmering taper's light,
>   Adorns and cheers the way ;
> And still, as darker grows the night,
>   Emits a brighter ray" (Goldsmith).

But now it was quite extinguished. "Whilst evil is expected we fear, but when it is certain we despair." "Saul was too hardened in his sin to express any grief or pain, either on his own account, or because of the fate of his sons and his people. In stolid desperation he went to meet his fate. This was the terrible end of a man whom the spirit of God had once taken possession of and turned into another man, and whom he had endowed with gifts to be leader of the people of God" (O. von Gerlach). "All human history has failed to record a despair deeper or more tragic than his. Over the close of this life broods a thick and comfortless darkness, even the darkness of a night without a star" (Trench, 'Shipwrecks').

Remark that—1. If men are forsaken by God, it is only because he has been forsaken by them. 2. Their only effectual resource in distress is the mercy of God, against whom they have sinned. 3. Persistent transgression infallibly ends in misery and despair.—D.

Vers. 20—25. (ENDOR.)—*The witch of Endor.* According to Jewish tradition she was the mother of Abner, on which account perhaps she escaped when others were "put away ; " and the two attendants of Saul, in his visit to her, were Abner and Amasa. She dwelt at Endor (the fountain of habitation), a village four miles south of Mount Tabor (Josh. xvii. 11 ; Ps. lxxxiii. 10). "The calcareous cliffs around are filled with wide caverns, and some of the modern habitations are formed of front walls shutting in these caves," in one of which she may have dwelt and practised her forbidden art. This possessor or mistress of Ob (see vers. 7—10), although differing much from those who were accounted "witches," greatly abhorred and severely punished in more recent times, was a representative of many of them in—1. *Perverted religiousness.* Her history might have shown that she possessed a more than ordinary measure of the religious sentiment prevalent in women, and that it had been (as it often is) misdirected by the influences under which she fell. She was at first a victim of superstition, and afterwards, finding herself perhaps endowed with peculiar and mysterious susceptibilities, and looked up to by others on account of her superior "wisdom," practised on their superstitious fears, in part deceived and in part deceiving. The mischief of the perversion of the religious sentiment (in deception, bigotry, cruelty, &c.) is incalculable. 2. *Secret criminality.* If she had lived among the heathen from whom her art was derived, she might have been held in general repute, like the oracles of Greece. But in Israel necromancy was condemned as treason against the Divine King, an abomination associated with and promotive of the worship of idols, and she displayed a daring impiety in practising it even in secret. "The Hebrew witch, or she who communicated or attempted to communicate with an evil spirit, was justly punished with death, though her communication with the spiritual world might either not exist at all, or be of a nature much less intimate than has been ascribed to the witches of later days ; nor does the existence of the law against the witches of the Old Testament sanction in any respect the severity of similar enactments, subsequent to the Christian revelation, against a different class of persons accused of a very different species of crime " (Sir W. Scott). 3. *Unholy cupidity.* The desire of gain, to which she may have been urged by necessitous circumstances, was probably her principal motive in practising her art at the risk of life. The same desire leads to the basest actions, and even turns godliness into ungodliness. It is "a root of all evil." 4. *Perpetual fear* of discovery and suspicion of deception on the part of those to whose wishes she ministered, and of whose weaknesses she made traffic (ver. 9). The sword of justice hangs over the head of secret transgressors, and suffers them not to enjoy a moment's peace. 5. *Skilful deception.* Saul thought to deceive her, but was himself deceived by her, and fatally deluded. Whatever may have been her power in magic, clairvoyance (Keil), and ventriloquism (Isa. xxix. 4), she certainly professed what she did not possess (ver. 11) ; employed it in "cunning craftiness," and became (whether designedly or undesignedly) accessory to his ruin (1 Chron. x. 14). How much of the power which is now abused and made a curse might if properly used become a blessing ! 6. *Kindly sympathy* and ministration. On observing his heavy fall (for she was apparently in the same room) she came to his side, and seeing that he was "sore troubled," felt a woman's pity, spoke to him in soothing tones as to a wilful child, requested him to gratify her wishes in eating " a morsel of bread " to strengthen him, in return for her obeying his voice (with " a talkativeness characteristic of this class of women, and a certain humour"), perhaps called his servants, and with them constrained him. Her heart was not dead. "She had one calf that she was very fond of, and one that she took a great deal of care of, and fed it herself ; for she was a woman that got her living by the labour of her own hands, and had no other possession but that one calf ; this she killed, and made ready its flesh, and set it before his servants and himself. Now it is but just to recommend the generosity of this woman " (Josephus). 7. *Pitiable desolation.* Saul is gone forth into the night to meet his fate. Left to herself, distrusted and distrustful, feared and fearful, without the consolations of religion, she is as much an object of pity as of blame. "We take leave of her, as she took leave of the ruined king, with a pitying heart."—D.

Vers. 11—15.—*A God-forsaken man.* I. FOREBODING BEFORE THE BATTLE. As the clouds gather blackness before a storm, so the mind of King Saul became more than ever dejected and gloomy before his defeat and death on Mount Gilboa. He who in the beginning of his reign struck so boldly at the Philistines, and threw off their yoke from the neck of Israel, was now afraid at the approach of their host, and "his heart greatly trembled." Not that his natural courage had deserted him, but, amidst all the disorder of his brain, this one thing he knew, that it was the God of Israel who had given him success against the Philistines, and now he found himself without God. There was no priest with the army to obtain Divine direction by the Urim and Thummim. Saul had slain the priests. There was no prophet to bring messages from God. By his breach with Samuel Saul had alienated from his cause all those who had any measure of prophetic gift. We hear the wail of a perturbed spirit—" I am sore distressed ;" but no confession of sin, no accent of repentance. This is an ominous characteristic of Saul, that he never fairly faces the question of his own misconduct, always palliates his sin, always evades self-judgment and self-reproach. What breaks from him in his extremity is only the cry of hurt pride, the bitter vexation of a man who saw that his career was a failure, and that he had brought himself to disappointment and defeat. His foreboding before the battle was only too well grounded. So Shakespeare describes Richard III. gloomy and desperate before the battle of Bosworth Field :—

> " I have not that alacrity of spirit
> Nor cheer of mind that I was wont to have."

And shadows in the night struck yet deeper terror into the soul of Richard. In like manner Macbeth at Dunsinane, expecting the attack, has dark foreboding :—

> " There is no flying hence, nor tarrying here.
> I 'gin to be aweary of the sun."

II. Recourse to forbidden arts. The troubled thoughts of the king went after that great prophet who had anointed him to be king, and had been to him as the voice of God. All his mishaps had come from inattention to Samuel's instructions and warnings. And it seemed to him that his fortune might still be retrieved if only he could have once more the advice of Samuel. The prophet was dead and buried, and there was no way to communicate with him except through the forbidden art of necromancy. Saul had in his zeal against heathen practices expelled from his dominions those who plied this art for gain ; but now he fell in this, as in so many other respects, below his own former level, and repaired to a female necromancer at Endor. As to what occurred at Endor it is not necessary or perhaps possible to pronounce a very decided opinion. It was no mere piece of jugglery. To the perception of the woman there really was an apparition ; but there is room for much question whether this was the actual appearance of a departed spirit, or a sort of waking vision dependent on the ecstatic and clairvoyant state of the necromancer. If there was a real presence, it was that of Samuel, or possibly that of an evil spirit personating Samuel. Neither of these suppositions commends itself to our judgment. No doubt the historian says, " Samuel said to Saul." But he describes the scene merely according to appearance, and so as to account for the effect produced on the mind of the king. He does not analyse appearances at all, or look under them for possible elements of illusion or delusion. But if it be possible to account for the apparition any otherwise, we shrink from the belief that Samuel was actually brought into this scene of gloom and wickedness, and, coming into it, spoke to poor distracted Saul without any tone of pity or exhortation to repentance, grimly telling him that to-morrow he would be defeated, and he and his sons would join the ghosts in Sheol. The moral improbability of this is very great. As to an evil spirit personating Samuel in order to drive the king to despair, there is no moral unlikelihood in the conjecture, and it has been the opinion of Tertullian, of Luther, of Grotius, and many more ; but it supposes a greater marvel than the phenomena require to account for them, and therefore we reject it. Our view is that the apparition was real, but was no more than an apparition. The old man in the mantle had no existence whatever but to the morbid mind of the woman, who had fallen into a clairvoyantic trance. It is perfectly well known that women of a certain constitution have extraordinary aptitude for such trances and visions, and there is good reason to believe that the female necromancers and sorcerers of antiquity were persons of the same class with the nervous, crazy creatures who are now-a-days spoken of as " powerful mediums." Such persons in our own time see apparitions of the dead, and if they add some elements of trick and imposture the better to establish their reputation, it is only what such unhappy beings have done in the past, and what the woman at Endor very likely did also. The voice that Saul heard may easily have proceeded from her as a practised ventriloquist (see Isa. xxix. 4). Saul had fallen with his face to the ground before the apparition, which was invisible to him. So the ventriloquism was easy enough, and there was nothing in the words ascribed to Samuel which it was beyond the power of the necromancer to say, well aware as she must have been of the king's unfitness to encounter the great Philistine army, and the strong probability that the battle on the morrow would go against him. The wretched conclusion of the whole matter was that Saul was bereft of all hope, and "was sore afraid."

III. COMMUNION WITH THE DEAD. Necromancy, unfortunately, is not a lost art among ourselves. Men and women of education are not ashamed or afraid to practise arts and consult "mediums" that are referred to in the Old Testament as abhorrent to God and utterly forbidden to his people. In the communication with the dead which is said to be established there may be an element of trickery, there may be an element of power of some evil sort that no one can define; but the process all in all is one of base delusion, its whole tendency is crazy, and its issues are in gloom and madness. Above all, it tends to draw men away from God, or it is an attempt to obtain preternatural direction for souls that have fallen out of communion with him, like the soul of Saul, and it cannot come to good. But we do not say to the children of God, "Have nothing to do with the dead." In the communion of saints we are bound to those who have departed, as much as to those who are in the body. How they may help us even now is one of the things of which we have no certain knowledge. But we pay them most honour when we refrain from any attempt to disturb their sacred repose, and endeavour to remember their counsels, to walk in their steps, to live as they would wish us to live before God and man.

"How pure in heart and sound in head,
      With what Divine affection bold,
      Should be the man whose thought would hold
An hour's communion with the dead.

"In vain shalt thou or any call
      The spirits from their golden day,
      Except, like them, thou too canst say,
My spirit is at peace with all.

"They haunt the silence of the breast,
      Imaginations calm and fair,
      The memory like a cloudless air,
The conscience as a sea at rest" (Tennyson).   F.

EXPOSITION.

DAVID'S DISMISSAL FROM THE PHILISTINE CAMP (CH. XXIX.).

CHAPTER XXIX.

MARCH OF THE PHILISTINE ARMY (vers. 1—5). Ver. 1.—**The Philistines gathered**, &c. The narrative, broken off for the description of Saul's abasement, is again resumed from ch. xxviii. 1. **Aphek.** As we saw on ch. iv. 1, this word, signifying a *fortress*, is a very common name for places. If it was the Aphek in Judah there mentioned, David's dismissal would have taken place near Gath, and so soon after Achish joined the Philistine army. Mr. Conder thinks it was the place represented by the modern village *Fuku'a*, near Mount Gilboa, in the tribe of Issachar ; but as this was distant from Ziklag eighty or ninety miles, it would not have been possible for David to have reached home thence on the third day (ch. xxx. 1), nor was it probable that his presence with his little army would remain long unnoticed. **A fountain which is in Jezreel.** Hebrew, "the fountain." Conder says, "Crossing the valley we see

before us the site of Jezreel, on a knoll 500 feet high. The position is very peculiar, for whilst on the north and north-east the slopes are steep and rugged, on the south the ascent is very gradual, and the traveller coming northward is astonished to look down suddenly on the valley with its two springs : one, 'Ain Jâlûd, welling out from a conglomerate cliff, and forming a pool 100 yards long with muddy borders ; the other, the Crusaders' fountain of Tubania " ('Tent-Work,' i. 124). The former is the fountain mentioned here ; and it is evident that even now Saul had chosen a strong position for his army. The reading of the Septuagint, *En-dor* instead of " the fountain " (Hebrew, '*En*, or '*Ain*), is indefensible, as the Israelites were many miles to the southward.

Vers. 2, 3.—**The lords of the Philistines passed on.** Evidently they were on their march northward, with their troops arranged in divisions, when David's presence in the rearward with the contingent of Achish was noticed. **The princes**—not the strict word for the Philistine lords (see on ch. v. 8), but a loose, general term used again in ver. 4—on having it reported to them in the course of a day or two that there was a body of strange troops in the army of Gath, asked, **What do these Hebrews here?** Hebrew, " What these Hebrews?" *i. e.* What mean these Hebrews? using of them the ordinary Philistine term of contempt. Achish answers that these men were the followers of David, who, having deserted from Saul, had been with him **these days or these years,** *i. e.* an indefinitely long time, during which he had conducted himself with the utmost fidelity to his new master.

Vers. 4—6.—Angrily rejecting the testimony of Achish in David's favour, they say, **Make this fellow** (Hebrew, "the man") **return, that he may go again to his place,** *i. e.* to Ziklag. **He shall not go down with us to battle** Though the Philistines marched *up* into the Israelite territory, yet they speak naturally of *going down* into battle, because while armies usually encamped on opposite ranges of hills, they descended into the plain between for the encounter. **An adversary.** Hebrew, "a satan," without the article, and so in 1 Chron. xxi. 1. As a proper name it has the article, as in the books of Job and Zechariah. **Should he reconcile himself.** The verb means, "to make himself pleasing," "to commend himself." **The heads of these men,** pointing to the Philistine ranks. **David of whom they sang,** &c. The song of the Jewish maidens seems to have been as well known in Philistia as in the land of Israel. On the former occasion it had made the Philistines drive him away from the court of Achish (ch. xxi. 11—15) ; here, too, it made them drive him from their army, but he was thereby saved from the painful necessity of making war on his own country, and returned just in time to rescue his wives and property.

ACHISH SENDS DAVID AWAY (vers. 6—11). Vers. 6, 7.—**As Jehovah liveth.** These words are strange in the mouth of a Philistine, nor can we suppose that out of respect to David he would thus swear by David's God. Probably they are the equivalent of the oath which Achish really used. He sends, however, David away with the utmost courtesy, assuring him that his own wish had been that he should remain with him, because all his conduct had been upright since he had come to him at Gath.

Ver. 8.—David's answer is subtle and prevaricating ; he pretends that his honour has been attacked, when really he had tricked the unsuspecting Achish. But truth is a modern virtue, and though David extols it in the Psalms (Ps. xv. 2 ; li. 6), we too often find him practising falsehood.

Ver. 9.—**I know that,** &c. Rather, "I know it, for thou art good in my sight," *i. e.* I know all that thou wouldst say as to thy trustworthiness, and assent to it. **As an angel of God.** *I. e.* as a messenger of God, as one set to me by God.

Vers. 10, 11.—**With thy master's servants.** It has been well remarked that while this would be a strange description of David's own men, it would exactly describe that band of deserters belonging to the tribe of Manasseh who, instead of obeying Saul's summons to the war with the Philistines, joined David about this time (see 1 Chron. xii. 19—21). **As soon as ye be up early in the morning,** &c. If it was on the second day's march that the Philistine lords objected to David's continuance with them, he would be back at Gath in two days, and on the third day reach Ziklag, as is said in ch. xxx. 1. However difficult David's position may have been, still every one must condemn his conduct towards Achish as dishonourable ; but God, who often deals with men more mercifully than they deserve, nevertheless rescued him from his state of perplexity, and saved him from the necessity of either fighting against his own countrymen or of still more dishonourably breaking his word to Achish by deserting in the battle. He also sent him home just in time to rescue from a miserable fate those whom he loved.

HOMILETICS.

Vers. 1- -5.—*The counteractions of Providence.* The facts are—1. The Philistines make preparations for battle, and David and his men form the rear. 2. On the princes complaining of the presence of the Hebrews, Achish pleads the faithfulness of David. 3. The princes insist on the dismissal of David and his men to a safe quarter, being suspicious that he might in battle turn against them. The conduct of David, as recorded in chapter xxvii., now began to be embarrassing both to himself and his Philistine protectors ; and had events gone on as once appeared probable, David would have been put in inextricable difficulties. It was only the quarrel between Achish and the leaders of his forces that solved the ambiguity of his position.

I. THE COURSE OF HUMAN EVENTS, regarded in isolated sections, OFTEN SEEMS TO

RENDER THE REALISATION OF GOD'S PURPOSE UNCERTAIN, IF NOT IMPOSSIBLE. The prophet Samuel had declared it to be God's purpose to bring David to the throne, as a man worthy of the confidence of the nation. The arrangement that had been made on the accession of Saul to power had been modified in harmony with this fact. Yet in the ambiguous position in which David was now placed by his own erring conduct it seemed as though events were tending in a different direction. The very man on whom the hope of the pious was set was now allied with Israel's foe, and on the way to fight against his own people. Already dissimulation had injured his reputation, and should he now engage against his own countrymen, how could he ever be worthy of confidence as a loyal Hebrew? This is not an isolated instance. The readiness with which the descendants of Jacob seemed to settle in Egypt after his death gave no promise of the fulfilment of God's purpose concerning them. The scattering of the disciples by the first persecution appeared to run counter to Church consolidation, and therefore to power of Christian effort. There are ebbs in the individual Christian life which while in progress suggest the uncertainty of final salvation. Even the long course of evils subsequent to the creation of man, considered in their earthly development, may give rise to the doubt whether the benevolent purpose of a good Creator can ever be attained. It should not be forgotten, however, that we see only sections of life's course, and we must not draw a conclusion from partial knowledge. God allows freedom of action, and trains his creatures by the dearly-purchased lessons of a painful experience, and, moreover, calmly awaits the issue of the whole.

II. THE ERRORS OF MEN OF SINCERE PIETY ARE VERY TENDERLY TREATED BY GOD. We cannot but be struck with the great difference between the conduct for which Saul was so heavily punished and that of David which did not issue in his rejection. Saul's sin was radical—it was "rebellion" (ch. xv. 23). It indicated that self-will ruled his conduct. David's sin in dissembling and in settling without Divine direction as an ally of Achish was the sin of backsliding and neglect. He was radically sincere in his piety, but in an hour of weakness lost his full faith in God, and so yielded to the influence of fear. Hence he was chastised by sorrow, by increasing fears, by self-humiliation, loss of reputation, and that secret sense of Divine displeasure which the erring soul of the devout knows too well. Though the sincere servant of God falls, he shall not be utterly cast down. God remembers that he is dust. In David's case the troubles created by his actions produce regret that he ever put himself in such a false position, and quicken the spirit of true repentance. Our Saviour's treatment of hardened, self-willed men and those whose spirits were struggling to do right and to be right was very different. It is a consolation to us all to know that he is touched with the feeling of our infirmities, and does not cast off those who, not being able to "watch one hour," fall into temptation.

III. GOD NEVER FAILS TO EXERCISE CONTROL OVER THE SET OF EVENTS WHICH SEEM TO RUN COUNTER TO HIS PURPOSES, and when the fit time arrives HE BRINGS NEW ELEMENTS INTO OPERATION. David erred and sinned; but David was restrained and inwardly humbled. This dangerous alliance, though bringing him to the verge of a precipice, was limited, in the pressure of its obligations, by a new set of influences being brought into operation. So far as the bond between David and Achish was working, David's hand must soon be raised in battle against Israel; but the inscrutable Providence which ordained him to be future king, and allowed him, for hidden reasons, to come into perilous and damaging relationships, also held sway over the spirits of Philistine princes, and just when the sin of the man of God was about to bear its cruellest fruit, moved them to protest against his entering into the conflict. Thus tenderly does God deal with his erring servant, and, in a manner unknown and unexpected, counteract the course of events which recently had tended to the frustration of his own purposes. How often would God's servants ruin their own reputation and the very cause dear to their hearts did he not raise up means of checking the tendency of their conduct. It is of the Lord's mercies that we are not consumed.

IV. IN THUS COUNTERACTING THE EFFECTS OF OUR MISCONDUCT GOD CAUSES CHASTISEMENT TO COME ON THE ERRING. David was mercifully saved from the peril of smiting his own people, and the pressure of any obligation which human friendships and customs may have laid upon him was removed, and the prospects of his being welcomed as king in Israel were brightened; yet in his own heart he was made to feel all the pain and shame of being regarded as a man of treacherous character. He could not but smart under the contempt of heathen princes if, as is likely, he knew of their language concerning himself. "Make this fellow return," and for the reason "lest in the battle he be an adversary to us." To profess to be true and faithful, and yet to be scorned and treated as one whose word and profession are worthless, this was one means by which Providence caused the erring one to suffer from the fruit of his own deeds.

General lessons :—1. Let us not be allured into questionable courses by a prospect of present ease, seeing that a perilous crisis may arise out of the very means we take for securing ease. 2. Whatever troubles beset the Church by reason of the imperfect conduct of God's servants, let us still cherish faith in his wisdom and power to counteract the natural effects of their conduct. 3. It is of great importance so to act as never to merit the scorn and distrust of irreligious men, for we thereby dishonour the name of God and destroy our proper influence in the world.

Vers. 6—11.—*Escape from danger.* The facts are—1. Achish informs David of the remonstrance of the princes, and at the same time expresses confidence in his integrity. 2. On Achish urging his return from the scene of conflict, David professes to be surprised that he should be distrusted, and appeals to his past fidelity. 3. Being reassured of the confidence of Achish, and of the determination of the princes, David returns with his men. The relations of Achish and David appear to have been most honourable to both, and there is something beautiful in the respect and consideration with which this heathen ruler treats the refugee. He does his best to lessen the pain which he presumes the communication of the resolve of the princes will cause him, and sends him away with the strongest assurances of interest and confidence. On the other hand, while keenly feeling the implication of the princes, David displays in his self-vindication the art of a skilled diplomatist. He does not say that he wishes to go against Israel, or that he regrets not being permitted to go, but shrewdly asks whether, so far as concerns his past conduct while with Achish, he might not be trusted in conflict with a foe. There are several topics suggested by this discussion between the heathen king and the Hebrew refugee.

I. The STING OF SUSPICION. David was hurt by the imputation of possible treachery. His sojourn among the Philistines had been marked by carefulness not to abuse their hospitality, and to fulfil the obligations incident to his position as a protected refugee. Also, as a pious Hebrew, he claimed to be far above the uncircumcised in all that makes character noble and trustworthy. Moreover, the probability is he did not entertain thoughts of treachery, but rather in his conscious embarrassment was secretly praying to God for some escape from the dilemma of his position. Although, as a man of the world, he must have seen the legitimacy of their conclusion from their premises, yet this did not remove or lessen the sting of the suspicion of the princes. He was reaping the bitter fruit of his former act; and we have noticed under vers. 1—6 the element of chastisement in this pain. To every upright mind it is most distressing to be an object of suspicion, and especially among persons with whom friendship has been maintained. It eats away the joy and strength of the heart, and destroys much of our power with men. Happy is it for us if a good conscience is a private solace; but we should see to it that the suspicion is not warranted by any puzzling ambiguities in our words or deeds.

II. FIDELITY IN ENGAGEMENTS. Achish, in strong language, testifies to the fidelity with which David had kept every engagement involved in his position in the country, and David himself appears to have been honestly conscious that in this matter he was upright. He had done his duty, and that is much to say in a world where so many temptations arise to induce selfish action, regardless of relative claims. It is of great importance in the social order that men understand their position to rulers, to neighbours, and to home, and with careful exactitude discharge the varied obligations resting on them with religious scrupulosity. It is hard to say what material loss, moral injury, and social and commercial disorganisation arise from laxity in keeping engagements. The ease with which some, even professing Christians, can disregard the obligations of their position in society and the Church, and also fail to meet undertakings deliberately made, is very painful to contemplate. We honour God when we "fulfil *all* righteousness." Our supposed fidelity in great things is deprived of much of its honour and glory by neglect of what are deemed the "minor moralities." Our Lord has taught us the connection between the two. "He that is faithful in the least is faithful also in much."

III. THE INFLUENCE OF SUPERIOR CHARACTER. There is evident sincerity in the words of Achish when he says of David, "Thou hast been upright. . . I know that thou art good in my sight as an angel of God." The fact is, the force of David's superior character as an enlightened Hebrew and a God-fearing man was duly recognised by this heathen king. The disparity between the two men in point of spiritual enlightenment and holy aspiration was enormous. The peaceful, kindly disposition of Achish enabled him to live on such terms of intimacy with David as to feel the full force of his superiority. The highest form of character on earth is realised when great natural powers are fully permeated with the light and love of the Christian spirit; and in any case of moderate powers, elevation is attained in so far as the pure, loving mind of Christ rules the life. Such character is a silent formative power in society. Men who speak not of it consciously recognise its beauty and force. They feel its charm, its restraining power, its elevating tendency, its quickening and soothing effects. How blessed the influence of a missionary among degraded heathen! What power for good is exercised by many a devout pastor in village and city! Who can estimate the value of holy character in the master of workmen, the teacher of the young, the mother of a family, the statesman at the head of affairs?

IV. CONCEALMENT OF THOUGHT. David complained to Achish of the suspicions of his lords, and was prepared to prove that nothing in his conduct since he had been amongst them gave the slightest ground for their imputation; but his defence was so carefully worded as to conceal from Achish the real thought of his heart. He simply reasoned from his known conduct to a general conclusion of fidelity to his protector; he said nothing of the private wish that he may not have to fight Israel, or of any hope that he shall escape the test of fidelity, or of his secret pleasure that a door of escape was opening. The form of the language, to one not keen in detecting shades of thought under general terms, might lead to the belief that he was referring to the impending battle, and so far perhaps David's words may be challenged. Yet he only said what was generally true. He concealed the sentiments pertinent to the coming contest. This practice of concealing thought requires much watchfulness. We are not bound to let out all we think, nor are we to give faculties to men to understand what others would see at once, but we are bound not to *design to give a wrong impression*. Truthfulness lies in intent as also does falsehood.

V. DOORS OF ESCAPE. After the fearful strain that must have been put on David's feelings by the ambiguous position in which he had placed himself, it must have been an immense relief to see the door open for an honourable retreat. The Bible does not tell us all that God's servants thought and felt and did; but judging from David's usual conduct when in great straits, and from the references in the Psalms to times of trial, we may infer that during this painful and self-caused season of peril he cried from the depths of his heart for deliverance. It came, and the "salvation" was of the Lord. How this suggests to us the many escapes which God secures for us during our earthly course! What instances there are of the same Providence in the records of the Bible and the history of the Christian Church! And above all, there is now "an open door" set before us by which, if we will, we may escape from the degradation and woe of sin, and walk in the liberty of the children of God. "Escape for thy life," was once said to Lot. He gave heed, and was saved. He that hath an ear to hear, let him now hear what the Spirit saith to the Churches.

HOMILIES BY VARIOUS AUTHORS.

Vers. 1—11. (ON THE MARCH TO APHEK.)—*A good man in bad company.* "What do these Hebrews here?" (ver. 3). The results of the wrong step which David had taken in going into the country of the Philistines now became manifest. In the war against Israel Achish naturally looked to him and his men to go out with him to battle. What was he to do? He might refuse to go. This would have been his straightforward course. But he would thereby forfeit the friendship of Achish, and expose himself to imminent danger. He might go and fight against Israel. This would be to incur the greatest guilt, and imperil his accession to the throne. He might go and turn traitor on the battle-field. This was what the Philistines expected (ver. 4), but it would have covered his name with infamy. He determined for the present to continue his prevarication with Achish, who said he should be captain of his body-guard for the future (ch. xxviii. 1, 2), and went, probably with a troubled conscience, and hoping that he might in some way be relieved from his inconsistent and perplexing position. He was clearly out of his proper place in the Philistine army. His condition represents that of a good man—

I. IMPROPERLY ASSOCIATED WITH THE UNGODLY. It is by no means uncommon for a good man to yield to the temptation to join the wicked in their pursuits, unnecessarily, and from an unjustifiable motive; such as the desire of personal safety, convenience, information, pleasure, or profit—like Lot in Sodom, Jonah going to Tarshish, Peter in the palace of the high priest (see ch. xv. 6). The relation into which he thus enters is inconsistent with—1. *Truth;* inasmuch as it usually requires him to deceive others concerning his real character and purposes, by pretending to be what he is not, and concealing what he is. 2. *Piety;* inasmuch as he is thereby hindered in his devotions (ch. xxvi. 19), exposes himself to fresh temptations, sanctions sinful or doubtful conduct, strengthens the ranks of the enemy, violates his duty to God and "his own company" and people. "Those that would be kept from sin must not go on the devil's ground" (M. Henry). "What doest thou here, Elijah?" David—Hebrew—Christian? 3. *His own real welfare;* inasmuch as he involves himself in unforeseen but certain trouble, places himself beyond the promised protection of God, and exposes himself to the threatened fate of his enemies.

II. SHREWDLY SUSPECTED BY HIS ASSOCIATES. He may endeavour to escape their suspicion, and for a time succeed, but it is sooner or later excited by—1. *Something in himself*—his name, appearance, relation to past events ("Is not this David?" &c., vers. 3, 5), peculiar behaviour, faltering and ambiguous explanations. "Thy speech bewrayeth thee." "Did I not see thee in the garden with him?" 2. *The occurrence of new circumstances,* which quicken perception, call for decision, test and manifest the character, and its congruity or otherwise with present associations. 3. *The general instinct of the ungodly.* Although some of their number may be deceived, and exhibit unbounded confidence in him (ver. 3), let no one think to escape. "There is nothing hidden that shall not be revealed."

III. DEEPLY HUMILIATED BY HIS TREATMENT. 1. *Outwardly.* In the eyes of others. "Make this fellow return," &c. (ver. 4). He is compelled to leave the society which he has chosen; expelled from it publicly and ignominiously, as one unworthy to be trusted. 2. *Inwardly.* In his own eyes. The heathen king of Gath appears to have been a faithful and honourable man; and his expression of confidence in David (vers. 3, 6), in contrast to the dishonourable prevarication of the latter (ver. 8), must have put him to shame. "The flattering commendations of worldly people are almost always purchased by improper compliances, or some measure of deception, and commonly may cover us with confusion" (Scott).

IV. PROVIDENTIALLY EXTRICATED FROM HIS EMBARRASSMENT. He may not be able to extricate himself from the net in which he has become entangled. But God does not readily abandon him to all the natural consequences of his conduct. He has many ways of working out his deliverance, and effects it—1. From regard to the good that is in him, and in pity toward him in his perplexity and distress. 2. For the honour of his name, that his merciful care over his servants may be seen, and his glory promoted by them. 3. Not without testifying his disapproval of his sin. "David returned the next morning to Ziklag no doubt very light of heart, and praising God for having so graciously rescued him out of the disastrous situation into which he had been brought" (Keil). "The snare is broken, and we are escaped" (Ps. cxxiv. 7). But on the third day he found Ziklag in ashes, was overwhelmed with grief, and more deeply humbled than ever before. The folly and guilt of the course which he had pursued were at length brought home to him with irresistible force.

Remarks :—1. There are associations with the ungodly which are not sinful, but right and beneficial to a good man himself, as well as to them. 2. No one should place himself in the way of temptation, and then expect that God will preserve him from falling or extricate him from the consequences of his presumption. 3. If any one finds that he has improperly associated himself with the wicked, he ought to adopt all proper methods to effect his speedy separation from them. 4. When he has found deliverance from his perplexity and peril he should give the glory of it to God alone.—D.

Vers. 1—11.—*Achish.* David had, in the course of his life, friendly relations with several heathen princes. One of these was Achish (elsewhere called Abimelech, Ps. xxxiv., inscription), son of Maoch, and king of Gath, one of the five royal cities, the seats of the princes of the Philistine confederacy. What is recorded of him shows that he was a remarkable man. Whilst Saul persecuted David, Achish protected him ; and whilst the former, in the midst of Israel, "with the law" of Moses, committed atrocious crime, and sank into heathen superstition, the latter, in the midst of heathenism, "without the law" (Rom. ii. 11—16), exhibited much moral excellence, and approached the faith of Israel (ver. 6). He may have profited in religious knowledge by his intercourse with David ; on the other hand, his example was in some respects worthy of imitation by him. We must not attribute to him virtues which he did not possess ; but we see in him a man much better than we might have expected to find from the disadvantages under which he lived. He was distinguished by—1. *Self-interested policy.* Although he may have felt some sympathy with David in his persecution by Saul, yet he appears to have received him under his protection chiefly because of the aid he hoped to obtain from him for himself and his people (ch. xxvii. 12). 2. *Unsuspecting confidence.* He had much reason to be suspicious of David from his knowledge of his victory over the champion of Gath, and his recollection of his former visit ; but he put an unreserved trust in his representations (ch. xxviii. 2), and even when others suspected him did not withdraw it. A trustful disposition is liable to be imposed upon, but it is always worthy of admiration. 3. *Royal generosity*, in permitting David to dwell in Gath, making him a present of Ziklag, and appointing him to an honourable post in his army. He was without envy or jealousy, and acted toward him in a manner worthy of a king. 4. *Discriminating appreciation ;* admiring the military bravery of David and the still higher qualities which he possessed. "I have found no fault in him," &c. (vers. 3, 6, 9). There must have been much in common between these two men to have enabled them to live on such friendly terms with each other for so long a period. Excellence perceives and appreciates excellence. 5. *Honourable fidelity*, both in testifying to the worth of David and in submitting to "the lords of the Philistines," with whom he was associated (ver. 7). 6. *Courteous consideration.* "And now return, and go in peace," &c. (ver. 7). "Rise up early in the morning with thy master's servants," &c. (ver. 10 ; 1 Chron. xii. 19—22). He was frank and commendatory even to flattery, and desirous not to hurt his feelings by the manner of his dismissal. 7. *Devout sentiment.* "As Jehovah liveth," &c. (ver. 6). How much he meant by this expression we know not. But we may believe that, notwithstanding he was united with others in conflict with Israel, there was in him (as the effect of that Divine mercy and grace which wrought in all nations) "some good thing toward the Lord God of Israel." And "in every nation he that feareth God, and worketh righteousness, is accepted with him" (Acts x. 35).—D.

Ver. 2.—*A false position.* What a dilemma for David ! He could not refuse the confidence he had sought from Achish. He could not renounce the allegiance he had so recently pledged. If he should disobey the king of Gath, he could look for nothing but indignant reproach and a traitor's doom. If he should obey him, he would, in course of a few days, be fighting against his own nation, and bringing them again under the yoke of the Philistines; and this would be worse than death. Perplexed and reluctant, he marched in the rear of the invading army, suffering inwardly all the more that he was obliged to hide his unwillingness, and to affect a zeal against Israel which his heart disowned. See in this story—

I. THE ILLUSTRATION OF DIVINE PROVIDENCE. While David wrought himself into a most critical position, and an apparently fatal embroilment with the Philistines, the Lord wrought wonderfully through the very errors of his servant, so as to preserve him in safety, and open his way to a higher destiny. It was well appointed that he should be out of the land of Israel at this time, so that he should neither hasten nor hinder the discomfiture of Saul, and that the Philistines should give him shelter, and yet not involve him in the crime of desolating and enslaving his native land. How to escape from the dilemma in which he was caught baffled even David's ready mind ; but the Lord always knows how to deliver. He does so through means and agencies that are natural ; in this case through the very natural jealousy of the Philistine lords, and their proper military prudence, objecting to have the person of the king intrusted to the keeping of a band of Israelites, and that band commanded by a skilful and daring captain in the rear of their army, where their defection would be most dangerous. " The lords favour thee not," said Achish. And, like our kings in old times, who durst not disregard the voice of the barons, Achish intimated to David that it was best for him to retire from the army. David was quite acute enough to see the advantage which the Philistine chiefs were unwittingly conferring upon him. They, as his enemies, helped him out of the dilemma in which he had been placed by Achish, his friend. Such things are not infrequent in the providence of God. Often a man's enemies open to him the way out of great difficulty. Disfavour is shown, or a sharp word spoken, and it turns out a great advantage. The wrath of opponents or rivals may act as so much dynamite to explode a rock of obstruction which friendly hands cannot remove, and so to clear the path of deliverance.

II. THE ILLUSTRATION OF HUMAN LIFE. See how a man may fall through want of moral firmness into a false position utterly unworthy of his character. It was, as respects David's integrity, unfortunate that he found such favour with the Philistine king. It is always a misfortune to be successful in the beginning of wrong-doing, for it soothes the conscience and leads one on to compromise himself more deeply. And one false step leads to another. David's unbelief led him into a course of deceit and dissimulation from which he saw no way of escape, and every day drew him further into a position which was false and unworthy. It is a story full of admonition and warning. One may easily let himself into a trap from which he cannot let himself out. One may take a false step, which involves another and another, till there is a course of deflection. An object is gained, but in the success the conscience is soiled ; and then the penalty is that one is compelled to act out the part he has assumed, to go on in the way on which he only meant to venture for a time and for a purpose. He thought to do a questionable thing and then return to his integrity ; but lo ! he is in a maze, and cannot find the way out. The gain which he sought turns out to be a loss ; the favour which he craftily won proves to be a burden and a danger ; and there is no remedy. It is very unsafe to possess great powers of deception. David had them, and they nearly ruined him. But the experience through which he passed taught him to abhor deceit, and to desire, what God desires, truth in the inward parts. For proof of this see Ps. xv. 1, 2 ; xxxiv. 12, 13 ; li. 6. Mark, too, how he appeals to the God of truth, and, ashamed of his own unveracity in certain passages of his early life, puts all his dependence in his later years on the veracity and faithfulness of God, who has made with him an " everlasting covenant, ordered in all things and sure " (see 2 Sam. xxiii. 5 ; Ps. xxv. 10 ; xxxi. 5). The security of our salvation rests not on our tenacity of faith, but on the truth of God our Saviour. He cannot lie. The Son of David, our Prince of life, is faithful and true ; and he who is our God in Christ Jesus will never fail those who rely on his word. " Yet he abideth faithful ; he cannot deny himself."—F.

EXPOSITION.

DAVID RESCUES HIS WIVES FROM THE AMALEKITES (CH. XXX.).

CHAPTER XXX.

DAVID UPON HIS RETURN FINDS ZIKLAG BURNT BY THE AMALEKITES (vers. 1—6). **Ver. 1.—On the third day.** David evidently could not have gone with the Philistines as far as to Shunem ; for, as noticed in the previous chapter, it would have been impossible to march back to Ziklag in so short a time. But as he had gone first to Gath, where no doubt Achish collected his vassals, and then marched northwards with the army for two days, he must altogether have been absent from Ziklag for some little time. **The Amalekites.** Doubtless they were glad to retaliate upon David for his cruel treatment of them ; but, besides, they lived by rapine, and when the fighting men of Philistia and of Judæa were marching away to war, it was just the opportunity which they wished of spoiling the defenceless country. **The south.** *I. e.* the Negeb, for which see ch. xxvii. 10. It was the name especially given to the southern district of Judah, whence these freebooters turned westwards towards Ziklag. They would probably not dare to penetrate far into either territory. The word for **invaded** is the same as in ch. xxvii. 8, and implies that they spread themselves over the country to drive off cattle and booty, but with no intention of fighting battles.

Vers. 2—5.—**They slew not any.** No resistance was made, as the men of war were all away. It was probably for thus leaving their wives and families absolutely defenceless that David's people were so angry with him. As we are told in ch. xxvii. 3 that the refugees with David had brought each his household with him into the Philistine territory, the number o women must have been large. The Amalekites spared their lives, not because they were more merciful than David, but because women and children were valuable as slaves. All the best would be picked out, and sent probably to Egypt for sale. **Ver. 6.—The soul of all the people was grieved.** Hebrew, "was bitter." Their great sorrow is pathetically described in ver. 4. But, as is often the case with those in distress, from grief they turned to anger, and sought relief for their feelings by venting their rage upon the innocent. Possibly David had not taken precautions against a danger which he had not apprehended ; but, left almost friendless in the angry crowd who were calling out to stone him, **he encouraged himself in Jehovah his God.** Literally, "strengthened himself" in Jehovah, and summoned the

priest to ask counsel and guidance of God by the ephod.

DAVID'S PURSUIT OF THE AMALEKITES (vers. 7—16). Vers. 7, 8.—Looking only to Jehovah for aid, David sends for **Abiathar**, who seems to have remained constantly with him, and bids him consult Jehovah by the Urim. In strong contrast to the silence which surrounds Saul (ch. xxviii. 6), the answer is most encouraging. Literally it is, "Pursue ; for overtaking thou shalt overtake, and delivering thou shalt deliver." Vers. 9, 10.—Having obtained this favourable answer, David starts in pursuit with his old band of 600 men. So rapid was his march that one third of these dropped out of the ranks, so that the new-comers from Manasseh would have been useless, nor had they lost wives or children. The **brook** (or rather "torrent") **Besor** practically remains unidentified, as the site of Ziklag is unknown ; but possibly it is the Wady-es-Sheriâh, which runs into the sea a little to the south of Gaza. As there was water here, **those that were left behind stayed.** Hebrew, "the stragglers stayed." It seems also to have been wide enough to cause some difficulty in crossing, as it is said that these 200 were too **faint**, or tired, **to go over the** torrent **Besor.** From ver. 24 we find that David also left with them as much as possible of his baggage. Stragglers had no doubt been falling out for some time, but would here be rallied, and obtain rest and refreshment.

Vers. 11, 12.—**An Egyptian,** the slave, as we read in ver. 13, of some Amalekite, left **in the field,** in the open common, to perish. He had become faint and could not travel as fast as they did, and so was left behind with no supplies of food, for he had eaten nothing for three days and three nights. The Amalekites had thus a start of at least this time, or even more, as this slave would probably have carried some food away with him from Ziklag. **Ver. 13.—To whom belongest thou ?** As he was probably unarmed, and his garb that of a slave, David asks who is his owner and what his country. He learns from him besides that he was left behind three days ago because he **fell sick.** The word does not imply more than temporary faintness, and is that translated *sorry* in ch. xxii. 8. But his life was of too little value for them to mount him on a camel, or even to leave with him supplies of food, and so their inhumanity led to their destruction. **Ver. 14.—The Cherethites.** The interest in this people arises from David's body-guard having been composed of foreigners bearing the name of Cherethim and Pelethim. We here find the Cherethim inhabiting the southern portion of the land of the Philistines, and such was still the case in the days of Zephaniah (Zeph. ii. 5, and compare Ezek. xxv. 16). As David retained Ziklag (ch. xxvii. 6), he appears to have chosen the men who were to guard his person from this neighbourhood, having probably been struck by their stature and martial bearing when dwelling among them. Hence it is probable that the Pelethim were also a Philistine race. Whether the Cherethim and the Philistines generally came from Crete to Palestine is a very disputed question, but they were certainly not indigenous, but immigrants into Canaan. **Caleb.** Upon the settlement of the Israelites in Canaan, Hebron with a large district in the south of Judah was assigned to Caleb the Kenezite, who with his clan had been incorporated into the tribe of Judah. Though the town was afterwards assigned to the priests, the whole country round remained subject to Caleb (Josh. xxi. 11, 12), and continued to bear his name. Evidently the Amalekites, beginning on the east, had swept the whole southern district of Judah before entering the country of the Philistines, where they no doubt burnt Ziklag in revenge for David's cruel treatment of them.

Ver. 15. — **To this company.** Better, "troop." The word signifies a band of soldiers, robbers, or the like. Required by David to act as his guide, the Egyptian consents upon condition that David bind himself neither to kill him, it being one of the unscrupulous customs of ancient warfare to put deserters, persons forced to act as guides, and even noncombatants, to death to save trouble; nor give him up to his master, who would treat him in the same way.

Ver. 16.—**When he had brought them down.** Though left behind, the Egyptian knew the course which the Amalekites intended to take, and was thus able to bring David quickly up to them, as they would move slowly because of their large booty of cattle. On overtaking them David found them dispersed in scattered groups **abroad upon all the earth** (literally, "over the face of all the land"), **eating and drinking, and dancing.** More probably, "feasting." The word literally means *keeping festival;* but though they had solemn dances at festivals, yet, as is the case with our word *feasting,* good eating was probably the uppermost idea; still the word may have only the general sense of "enjoying themselves as on a festival."

DEFEAT OF THE AMALEKITES AND RECOVERY OF THE WOMEN AND SPOIL (vers. 17 —20). Ver. 17.—**From the twilight.** It has been debated whether this means the evening or the morning twilight; but the words which follow, "unto the evening of the next day," literally, "of (or *for*) their morrow," seem to prove that it was in the evening that David arrived. Moreover, in the morning they would not have been feasting, but sleeping. David probably attacked them at once, and slew all within reach until nightfall. The next morning the battle was renewed; but as David had but 400 men, and the Amalekites covered a large extent of country, and probably tried to defend themselves and their booty, it was not till towards the next evening that the combat and the pursuit were over. As they would need pasture and water for their cattle, they had evidently broken up into detachments, which had gone each into a different place with their herds. The pursuit must have been prolonged to a considerable distance, as no more than 400 young men escaped, and even they only by the aid of their camels.

Vers. 18, 19. — **Recovered.** Hebrew, "rescued," or "delivered." The word occurs again in the second clause of the verse, and is there translated "rescued." **Had carried away.** Hebrew, "had taken." In ver. 19 **recovered** is literally "caused to return," *i. e.* restored.

Ver. 20.—This verse, which is made unintelligible in the A. V. by the insertion of the unauthorised word *which,* is really free from difficulty. After David, as related in vers. 18, 19, had recovered the cattle carried off by the Amalekites, he also took all the flocks and herds belonging to them; and his own men "made these go in front of that body of cattle, and said, This is David's spoil," *i. e.* they presented it to him by acclamation. It was this large booty which he distributed among his friends (vers. 26—31).

DAVID ENACTS A LAW FOR THE DIVISION OF THE SPOIL (vers. 21—25). Vers. 21, 22. —On returning David finds the 200 stragglers, **whom they had made to abide at the brook Besor.** Rather, "whom he had made to abide," as it was David's office to give such a command. The singular is supported by all the versions except the Chaldee, and by some MSS. David had made such men as were growing weary halt at the torrent, because it was a fit place where to collect the stragglers, and also, perhaps, because it would have required time and labour to get the baggage across. All the more wicked and worthless (see on ch. i. 16) members of the force now propose to give the 200, only their wives and children, and send them away with no share of the spoil. Besides the sheep and oxen given to David, there would be camels and other animals, arms, gold and silver, clothing, and other personal property.

Ver. 23, 24.—**Ye shall not do so, my brethren.** David rejects their unjust proposal kindly, but firmly. **With that which.** *I. e.* in respect of that which, &c. **Who will** hearken **unto you in this matter?** Literally, "this word," this proposal of yours. David then enacts that those left to guard the baggage are to share in the booty equally with the combatants. Patrick in his commentary quotes a similar rule enacted by Publius Scipio after the capture of New Carthage (Polybius, x., xv. 5).

Ver. 25.—**That he made it.** *I. e.* David. Having been thus enacted by him and practised during his life, no king henceforward would venture to change it. In the war with the Midianites Moses had ordered that half the spoil should belong to the combatants and half to the congregation who remained in the camp (Numb. xxxi. 27). This enactment of David was in the same spirit.

DAVID PROPITIATES HIS FRIENDS BY SHARING WITH THEM HIS BOOTY (vers. 26—31). Ver. 26.—**The elders of Judah.** The spoil taken from the Amalekites and assigned to David must have been very large, as it was worth distributing so widely. He did not, however, send to all the elders of Judah, but to such only as were his friends. **A present.** Hebrew, "a blessing" (see on ch. xxv. 27).

Ver. 27.—**Bethel** cannot be the famous city of that name, but is probably the *Bethul* of Josh. xix. 4, where it is mentioned as lying near Hormah and Ziklag. **South Ramoth.** Hebrew, "Ramoth-Negeb," called Ramath-Negeb in Josh. xix. 8. Like Bethul, it was a Simeonite village. **Jattir** belonged to Judah (Josh. xv. 48), and was one of the cities assigned to the priests (*ibid.* xxi. 14).

Ver. 28.—**Aroer,** a different place from that on the eastern side of the Jordan, mentioned in Josh. xii. 2, is probably the ruin 'Ar'arah, twelve miles east of Beer-sheba. **Siphmoth.** Some village in the Negeb, but unknown. **Eshtemoa** (Josh. xv. 50), the present village Semu'ah, south of Hebron.

Ver. 29.—**Rachal.** Rather Racal, unknown. The supposition that it may be Carmel is untenable. **The Jerahmeelites;** see on ch. xxvii. 10, as also for **the Kenites.**

Ver. 30. — **Hormah.** Anciently called Zephath. For the reason of the change of name see Judges i. 17. **Chor-ashan.** More correctly Cor-ashan, the same place as Ashan (Josh. xv. 42), a Simeonite town (1 Chron. iv. 32) assigned to the priests (*ibid.* vi. 59). **Athach,** never mentioned elsewhere, may be a false reading for *Ether* (Josh. xix. 7).

Ver. 31.—**Hebron,** destined soon to become David's capital (2 Sam. ii. 1), lay about fourteen miles south of Jerusalem. For an account of it see Conder, 'Tent Work,' ii. 79, *sqq.* In comparing the list of David's heroes (1 Chron. xi. 26—47) with this catalogue of friendly towns, it will be found that several of them came from them, and had probably shared his exile at Ziklag. Such were Ira and Gareb, Ithrites from Jattir, Shama and Jehiel from Aroer; perhaps also Zabdi the Shiphmite (1 Chron. xxvii. 27) came from Siphmoth. We find David in this narrative acting justly as a soldier, generously to those who had been kind to him in his wanderings, and forming friendships which he retained and cherished long afterwards, when from being a fugitive he had become a king.

HOMILETICS.

Vers. 1—10.—*The spiritual uses of calamity.* The facts are—1. David, on returning to Ziklag with his men, discovers that the Amalekites had smitten it and carried off the families as captives. 2. In their deep distress David and his men weep bitterly. 3. On a mutiny arising among his men, threatening his life, David betakes himself to God for comfort and guidance. 4. Inquiring of God through the high priest, he receives assurance of success in pursuing the Amalekites, and therefore, leaving the faint at Besor, he presses on with the rest of his force. The sojourn of David in the country of the Philistines had thus far been conducive to his safety, and events had seemed to justify the step taken when, from fear of being slain by Saul, he without positive Divine direction left his native land. It is true the ambiguous position into which he had brought himself exposed him for a while to a danger of being treacherous to his protector or hostile to his countrymen, but this peril had at last been providentially obviated by the opening of a door of escape. It must, therefore, have been intensely mortifying, and, as the event proved, impressively instructive, to learn, just when the joy of escape was at its height, that his self-chosen course had issued in a terrible disaster. A great calamity had come, but religiously it proved a blessing, which fact may be generalised by saying that *calamities brought on by the mistakes of good men have important religious uses.*

I. THE AVOIDANCE OF ONE CALAMITY by the adoption of our own policy of distrust of God's care IS NO GUARANTEE FOR FREEDOM FROM ANOTHER. David, without good reason distrusting the care of God, thought he should one day perish by the hand of Saul (ch. xxvii. 1), and therefore, taking his own course, sought safety under the protection of Achish. We know how groundless was his fear; but, apart from that, events proved that though the dreaded evil was escaped, another most terrible one came. Nor is there much defence for the self-chosen policy in saying that his own life *was* secure, for escape from Saul gave no immunity from death by the hands of other men, and there are calamities even worse than death. We are too often influenced by present dangers, forgetful that though we avoid them we have no security in that avoidance from others equally fearful. The Israelites feared the giants reported to occupy the promised land, and escaped being, as they groundlessly thought, slain by them; but they saw not the physical miseries and the exclusion from the promised land consequent on choosing thus to escape. David ought to have profited by their example, as also should we from his. The application of this to common life is obvious.

II. Our self-chosen policy may be long before it reveals its character in any positive disaster. The ambiguous position of David rendered the months during which he was with Achish a season for verifying the wisdom of his policy. Although slight inconveniences arose which necessitated minor expedients, as when he sought a separate city and made raids apparently on the south of Judah (ch. xxvii. 5, 10), yet no event transpired to awaken manifest regret for the course pursued. It was only toward the end of the sojourn in the land of the Philistines that his policy bore the bitter fruit referred to in this section. Trouble came at last in addition to the mental embarrassments which had been a secret in his own breast. So long as moral laws have force will every false policy tend to disaster, the form and degree of it being determined by the nature of the case. Men may go on hoping for exemption from trouble, concealing the occasional fears and embarrassments of their own heart, successful escape may be well nigh assured, there may be even joy at the thought of providential deliverance from impending perils; but just then, from unexpected quarters, a blow may fall which confirms the truth that it is better to trust in the Lord than to listen to the fears of a wayward heart. Lot's ungenerous policy toward Abraham, successful at first, issued in loss of all in Sodom. Jonah's timid policy avoided the scorn and stones of the Ninevites, and bid fair to secure life and peace; but the storm arose, and a trouble quite unforeseen sprang forth. In commerce, in Church action, and domestic arrangements, distrust of God and self-seeking cannot but issue in evil, though the evil seem to tarry and be beyond calculation.

III. The form of calamity may prove to be a near approach to that which self-chosen policy was designed to avoid. David lost his family and his property, the next best things to his own life, and also was put in as much danger of being slain by his own men as ever he had been by Saul. He virtually found himself as he was when the distrust of God's care suggested a flight from Judah. The same was true of the Israelites, who, avoiding the "giants" of the promised land, encountered the physical giants, famine and plague, and at last left their carcases in the wilderness. A merchant, by irreligious policy, may for a season avoid ruin, and yet by the means devised ultimately bring on an event equally disastrous.

IV. The first effect on a good man of the pressure of calamity is to reveal to him the folly and evil of his self-chosen policy. It often requires a heavy blow to awaken us from our complacent belief in our own wisdom. Such a blow fell on David in the desolation of his city, the loss of his wives, the injury to his adherents, and the mutiny of his own friends and admirers. The well-woven veil of expediency which imagination and reason had fabricated during the past sixteen months was thus rudely rent, and he saw at once how much better it would have been for him and his people to have continued trusting to the care of God in Judah, till, at least, specific directions were given to depart. The reference to David encouraging himself in God (ver. 6) implies the prostration of his spirit in the new light which had broken in upon him. He had not sought the Lord on leaving Judah, and now he sees the mistake. Here notice the diverse effect of calamity on men of real piety and men of no vital religion. David is humbled before God, sees his error, is bitterly penitent; whereas Saul in all his calamities persists in his self-will, and hardens his heart against God. The truly religious spirit may err, may become wretched in its wanderings from God, may for a long season cleave to its self-produced miseries, but when brought face to face with great calamity that bespeaks the judgment of God, at once bows in sorrow and shame, recognising what an evil and bitter thing it is to depart from the living God. How many a backslider and erring man has had occasion to bless the disaster that rent the delusion of their life and revealed their sin !

V. THE SUBSEQUENT EFFECT OF SUCH CALAMITY IS TO THROW A GOOD MAN MORE ENTIRELY UPON GOD FOR HELP AND GUIDANCE. David, humiliated, self-condemned, looking on to the future not knowing what best to do, took heart by casting his burden on the Lord, and seeking through the appointed channel specific directions as to the future. Affliction worked the fruit of righteousness. This is the proper religious use of all calamity, whether in the nation, the Church, our business, our domestic affairs, or the unrecorded events of private life. Jacob's trouble consequent on his falsehood brought him nearer to God at Bethel. The sorrows that came on Israel in the days of Nehemiah developed a trust in God and earnest looking for his guidance not known in former days. There is good reason for all who are smitten with sorrow brought on by folly and sin to encourage themselves in God ; for, as to David so to all his children, he is a covenant-keeping God, having prepared for us a kingdom that cannot be moved. He it is who allows the trial to fall not for our injury, but for our profit, that we may be partakers of his holiness ; the abandonment to ourselves and to the suffering of trouble is all in mercy, and specially intended to remind us of the security and rest to be found in him ; and he is willing to hear our cry, and to cover all the sins of the past, as well as to vouchsafe the aid necessary to escape from the present anguish, and even to make it issue in some permanent spiritual advantage. We may therefore " hope in God " when all help fails (cf. Ps. xlii. 5 ; lvi. 13 ; Isa. liv. 8 ; Jer. iii. 12 ; Heb. xii. 5—12).

Vers. 11—20.—*The consequences of kindness.* The facts are—1. Pursuing the Amalekites, David finds an Egyptian slave in distress, and administers to him food and drink. 2. On being questioned, the man states that his master, who was one of the force destroying Ziklag, had left him there three days before. 3. On promise of not being delivered up to his master, he engages to act as guide to the rendezvous of the Amalekites. 4. On coming upon them in the midst of their revels, David smites them, and recovers all that his force had lost, and acquires also much spoil. 5. David keeps the captured flocks and herds as his portion of the spoil. The incidents of this section suggest—

I. THE UNKNOWN RESULTS OF KINDNESS. Here was a case of a sick, starving foreigner, a poor waif nigh unto death ; and the kind attentions of David and his men not only were appreciated by a fellow-creature, but issued in important results which, prior to the act of kindness, were not, perhaps, deemed possible. The feeble man, well used, led on to victory. At the close of that eventful day David must have felt how useful as well as how holy a thing it is to act the part of a good Samaritan. Men are often under temptation to be indifferent to the sorrows of others ; but good always comes out of an exhibition of the law of kindness. No man ever lost anything by binding up the wounds of another ; and often the healer has obtained an inward blessing as a pledge of some still further good that is to flow from his deed. The blessing of those ready to perish is worth more than the applause and favour of the rich and strong. By single acts of kindness hard hearts have been touched, and a new and blessed course of life has been entered on. Many a waif, fed and nourished by Christian benevolence, has become an honourable and holy member of society, aiding to overthrow an evil power worse than that of the ancient Amalekites. Who can tell the vast and blissful consequences that may ensue if only Christians would care more constantly and wisely for the outcast and degraded ?

II. THE VALUE OF DETAIL IN SCRIPTURE HISTORY. The historian is specific in the account of what was given to this poor slave—" bread," " water," " a *piece* of a cake of figs," and "*two* clusters of raisins." This occasional detail indicates the pure historic character of the Biblical narrative, and invests the Bible with a human interest. This circumstantial character of narrative is especially seen in the Gospel by St. Mark, and more or less in every writer. As a book designed for all degrees of culture, and in all ages and climes, the Bible wins its way to the heart and commends itself to the common sense of mankind by the air of reality with which its great facts are incorporated with an incidental setting of circumstances; and it is singular that its occasional detail is never contradicted by well-established fact, but, on the other hand, is being constantly confirmed by discoveries concerning manners, customs, natural productions, and international relations.

III. THE BARBARITIES OF SLAVERY AND OF WAR. This unfortunate man had a master, but longed not to be restored to him. The barbarous manner in which he had been left to die justified his horror of his former owner. Slavery necessarily hardens the heart and debases the entire nature of all who promote it. The horrors that have been perpetrated under its influence more befit a hell than an earth like this. Christianity has proved its beneficent character in removing from many a fair region this accursed evil; and it enjoins on masters of the free to manifest towards their servants a kind, generous spirit, worthy of the Saviour they profess to follow. It is well when servants care to return to employers, and there is something wrong where there is aversion and reproach. The *barbarities of war*, which in this section and elsewhere are conspicuous, are among the foulest blots on human nature. In nothing as in war do the vilest passions of men break forth in wild licence. The ease and complacency with which many so-called Christians speak and read of war is really shocking to one who enters deeply into the spirit of Christ. More care ought to be taken in preventing our children from imbibing a love of war and its literature, and in the Christian state its manifold, incipient, and actual evils ought to be removed or avoided by the most energetic measures. It is doubtful whether the Church rises to a due sense of its solemn obligations in this respect.

IV. THE RESTORATION SUBSEQUENT TO REPENTANCE AND OBEDIENCE. David had repented of the course to which he had committed himself, and, encouraging himself in God, he had followed the direction conveyed through the high priest. The result was a restoration of all he had lost by his folly and an acquisition of much besides. Of course this was a case of material loss, through misconduct, attended with much anguish of spirit, and the restoration was of the same character; but have we not here something analogous with the result of our repentance and renewal of life? The loss and damage occasioned by our sins are removed when we turn to God and follow the guidance of our High Priest. In due time we recover purity, peace with God, most blessed joys, varied spiritual treasures, and even convert the weapons of our great enemy into means of moral advancement. Much has been ruined by our sins, and the whole race has suffered from the curse; but the effect of our restoration of soul to God through Christ is a recovery of the lost position and blessedness, with also an attainment of a bliss surpassing anything known by our first parent in his state of innocence. The promise reads, "I will restore to you the years that the locust hath eaten, the canker-worm, and the caterpillar, and the palmer-worm, my great army which I sent among you" (Joel ii. 25).

V. PRUDENT FORESIGHT IN ANTICIPATION OF COMING EVENTS. David's consideration for his followers in allowing them a large share in the spoil was attended also with a wise prevision of what was soon to take place, and no doubt it was on this account that he kept for himself the cattle taken from the enemy. Having repented of his former self-choosing, and having drawn nearer to his God (ver. 6), his soul rose to the old confidence in his call to the kingdom, and, calm in the fresh assurance of God's care, he saw from impending events that the end of Saul's reign was nigh at hand. Hence, to pave the way for an easy and prosperous return to Judah, he selected what would prove suitable gifts to elders and friends (ver. 20; cf. ver. 26). Thus we see how recovery from backsliding tends to a healthy tone and balance of ordinary mental operations, and how prudent anticipation of requirements becomes one called to high service in the kingdom of God. Faith in God's purposes concerning us should be accompanied with wise effort to obviate difficulties in the realisation of that purpose. Our elevation in the service of Christ's kingdom is to be secured on our part by the vigorous use of our best powers in dependence on God.

General lessons:—1. Amidst the hurry and excitement of our life we, like David, should turn aside to care for the poor and destitute, and shall find in so doing a blessing for ourselves. 2. As slavery was put down by the energetic assertion of the principles and spirit of the gospel, so may not the Church, if in earnest, equally suppress the war spirit which too largely prevails in so-called Christian lands? 3.

After the pattern of David in temporal matters we ought to strive with all zeal and constancy to recover the blessed inheritance of good lost to us individually and as a race through sin. 4. In so far as men are convinced of the certainty and glory of Christ's kingdom will they exercise all their utmost powers to hasten it on and win men over to it. Indifferent action is a sure sign of spiritual decay.

Vers. 21—31.—*The law of service.* The facts are—1. On returning to the men who had remained at Besor, some of David's followers oppose his intention to give them a share of the spoil, and are even desirous of sending them away. 2. David resists this spirit as being inconsistent with gratitude to God for his care and aid, and with strict justice to those who serve in humble form according to their strength. 3. David's decision becomes a standing ordinance in Israel's future national life. 4. He sends presents to the elders of cities that had befriended him during the days of his persecution. David's course all through was wonderfully chequered. He had good reason for saying, "Many are the afflictions of the righteous." No sooner had he rejoiced in the triumph of victory, and was devising in his heart kind and generous deeds, than he has to experience the annoyance and pain of contending with a murmuring and mutinous spirit among his own followers. As we look at him, the "man after God's own heart," bent on a noble mission for Israel, generous in spirit to all around, rising high above others in integrity of purpose and spiritual aspiration, and surrounded by a motley group of men, hard to control, and often low in tendency, we cannot but think of One greater, who later on stood among wayward, ignorant men, the Holy One, intent on establishing a throne never to be shaken, and wearied and wounded by the incessant "contradiction of sinners." But God teaches mankind through lessons evolved from the varied and often painful experience of his servants, and it is a consolation to them that the fires which try them should also emit light for the benefit of coming generations. There are three truths practical in bearing brought out by this part of David's experience.

I. THE DIVERSE CHARACTER OF MEN IS SEEN IN THE EFFECT OF SUCCESS UPON THEIR SPIRIT AND CONDUCT. David and his men had achieved a great success, and were returning full of the joy of victory. The record tells us nothing of the bearing of the leader and of the men on the first flush of success ; no doubt the wild excitement over the spoil of many of his followers was in striking contrast with the tremulous joy which found vent in his private thanksgiving to God. But on their return to Besor, the depraved, irreligious spirit of those termed " men of Belial " appeared in the love of greed and the cruel indifference to the wants of the weary which drew forth David's remonstrance. Success revealed the iniquity of their hearts, while it drew forth the grateful, tender qualities of David's character. Prosperity is as real a test of what men are as is adversity. It draws forth a different set of qualities, but is not the less a means of proving and intensifying a man's character, be it good or bad. When we say that sometimes success in commerce, literature, science, or military skill makes a man vain and scornful of others, or humble and considerate, we really mean that it has developed hidden weakness in the one case, and moral strength in the other. When the character deteriorates or improves under the influence of prosperity, it depends on casual circumstances as to how the deterioration or improvement will manifest itself. Here the presence of feeble men unable to engage in conflict happened to be the occasion of an outburst of selfish feeling. The same occasion furnished a manifestation of kindly consideration and love of justice. While few things create in generous hearts more disgust and sorrow than the selfishness, luxurious indulgence, and purse-proud bearing of men whose struggles in life have brought material success, few qualities are more admired than those of large-hearted benevolence, simplicity of habit, compassion for the destitute, and the grateful, lowly spirit which ascribes all good to God, and proves the sincerity of the ascription by deeds of self-denial on behalf of others. He who can conquer prosperity is often a greater man than the conqueror of adversity. Only the spirit of him who " made himself of no reputation," who " became poor " that we " might be rich," will enable us to subdue *all things* to his glory (cf. Ps. lxxiii. 3—12 ; Prov. i. 32 ; Mark x. 23— 25 ; Phil. iii. 7, 8).

II. THE LAW OF SERVICE IN THE KINGDOM OF GOD. The selfish spirit of some of

David's men gave occasion for the exercise of his authority in a right royal manner, and issued in the establishment of an ordinance in relation to service in his cause which became a law in Israel, and fitly foreshadows the principle on which all service in Messiah's kingdom is based. David would not allow the men who, through exhaustion in the hasty march, had remained at Besor to care for the baggage to be deprived of their share of the spoil through the greed of the actual combatants. His principle was that they were all engaged in one enterprise, that their position had been determined by the circumstances of the case, and that all honour should be done them. The ruling faculty in David was beginning to bear good fruit for the poor and needy—beautifully typical of One who is the Refuge and Defender of the oppressed! Considering the passage in its bearing on service in Christ's kingdom, we may notice—1. *That all his people are equally his servants, and have their proper work.* The equality in Christ's kingdom is that of oneness of spirit, aim, and relationship to him. All true Christians are zealous for his supremacy, eager to see him triumph over powers of evil, and on the same level as servants of one Lord and Leader. They are all workers, warriors, contending in accordance with their power and position for a common issue. Every member of the body has its function in securing the purposes of the head (1 Cor. xii. 12—14). 2. *That diversity of employment is necessary to the execution of his purposes.* The care of the "stuff" was as necessary in so dangerous a country as the pursuit and attack on the foe. In accomplishing the purposes of Christ on earth there are diversities of operations. The analogy of the body is used by the Apostle Paul to enforce this truth on the Church (1 Cor. xii. 12—31). It is an instructive study to notice how the manifold agencies and gifts of the Church and of individual Christians have worked together in producing the complex result we witness in the present advanced position of Christ's kingdom. The recognition of diversity should stimulate and encourage all, whatever their powers and opportunities. 3. *That incapacity for rendering conspicuous service is compatible with quiet yet important service.* Those who by Providence are hindered from fighting in the high places of the field have good work to do in a quieter form. Missionaries, popular preachers, diligent pastors, and men of high literary culture may be in the forefront; but the mothers who train children in the fear of God, fathers who live godly lives in the world, quiet, wise men who conduct religious movements, widows who cast in their mite, and even sick and weary ones who in the solitude of their chamber offer daily prayers for the hosts of God—render most valuable service in the common enterprise. 4. *Where there is loyalty in service, whatever its lowly form, there is to be honourable recognition.* David would not overlook the claims of the feeble men in charge of the "stuff." In this he was true to the principles and precedents of Israel's greatest leaders (Num. xxxi. 27; Josh. xxii. 8). In Christ's kingdom there is to be, after his great example in the case of the widow's mite and the hosannas of children, a recognition by all of the need and value of services apparently insignificant. This is further taught in the blessing pronounced on the giver of a cup of cold water, the mention in the day of judgment of the care bestowed on the sick and needy, and also in the equal welcome which the Lord declares he will give to the gainer of ten and two talents. The rewards of the advancing kingdom are shared in the joy and satisfaction which all true workers experience, and in the material improvement of the world consequent on its advance; and while he makes all "kings and priests" now, he will at last honour them with a vision of the glory he had with the Father before the world was (John xvii. 24).

III. There is a wise policy in the expression of gratitude. The tenor of David's life shows that the sending presents from the spoil taken to those who had befriended him in his time of need was the genuine expression of a grateful heart. At the same time this was coincident with a wise policy, and, in his mind, distinctly blended with it. Had the gifts been the product of a mere calculation of results, the act would only command the respect due to expediency, but having its root in feeling, it rises to a higher value. The recompense of kindnesses when occasion offers is the suggestion of a true heart, and though utilitarian ideas may not enter into the recompense, yet it is always useful in view of future contingencies. A prudent man called to a great work, is bound to prepare the

way for its realisation by securing as far as possible the good will and co-operation
of others.

General lessons:—1. It behoves us to be on our guard against the perils of success,
and to remember that as God is a refuge from the storm, so he is a shade upon our
right hand to tone down the light of prosperity (Ps. cxxi. 5, 6). 2. A degree of
suspicion is always proper concerning ourselves, as there are latent evils which
events may draw forth. 3. We should be careful not to disparage the services of
persons seeking in a humble way to promote the glory of Christ (Matt. xviii. 6).
4. The chief question for each is the existence within of a spirit of loyalty to Christ;
the form of service is a matter of opportunity (John xxi. 15—17). 5. Those who
render aid to the people of God in their time of distress are sure to be recompensed
on earth as in heaven (Luke vi. 31—38; xiv. 13, 14).

HOMILIES BY VARIOUS AUTHORS.

Vers. 1—10. (ZIKLAG.)—*Confidence in God.* "But David encouraged himself in
the Lord his God" (ver. 6). Delivered from their embarrassing position in the
Philistine army, David and his men set out early in the morning, and by forced
marches (evident from the exhaustion of one third of them, ver. 10) arrived at
Ziklag on the third day. Instead of being welcomed by their wives and children,
they found the city a smoking and desolate ruin. "When we go abroad we cannot
foresee what evil tidings may meet us when we come home again. The going out
may be very cheerful, and yet the coming in very doleful" (M. Henry). The
Amalekites (whom Saul had failed to exterminate, and David often attacked) had
been there, and, in revenge for what they had suffered, had carried off the undefended people and property, and given the place to the flames. Deeming their
recovery hopeless, the strong men wept like children "until they had no more power
to weep." Then their grief turned to exasperation, and seeking a victim on which
to expend their wrath, they fixed on David, and "spake of stoning him" as the cause
of all their misery. He was reduced to the utmost extremity, and could not fail to
see in his trouble a just chastisement for his unbelief, prevarication, and cruelty.
Possibly the reinforcements that "fell to him as he went to Ziklag" (1 Chron. xii.
20) rendered him valuable service. But his hope was not in man; and instead of
resigning himself to despair (like Saul), he was impelled by his distress and deprivation of human help to seek help in God alone. "The long misery of the first stage
of his public career seems to have reached its culminating point. When things are
at the worst, as the common proverb says, they must mend. And from that moment
when he believingly cast all his dependence upon the Lord his God only, whom he
had found faithful in all his promises, and whose providence had never failed him in
his deepest dangers, from that moment he was safe, from that moment he was prosperous" (Kitto). Concerning the confidence in God which he exhibited (therein
setting an eminent example to others), observe that—

I. IT SPRINGS OUT OF CONSCIOUS HELPLESSNESS. Few men have an adequate conviction of their own helplessness; and one aim of the Divine discipline is to produce it. "When I am weak," said Paul, "then am I strong"—when I feel my
utter weakness under the pressure of trial, then I am constrained to depend on the
Lord, and become imbued with his strength (2 Cor. xii. 10). In the exercise of "the
same spirit of faith" others "out of weakness were made strong, waxed valiant in
fight, turned to flight the armies of the aliens" (Heb. xi 34). True faith and
spiritual power have their foundation amidst the "dust and ashes" of self-abasement and self-distrust. Confidence in God began to revive in David when Ziklag
was reduced to ashes. The same thing is often occasioned in others by means of—
1. Sudden and severe bereavement; wife and children, it may be, taken away with a
stroke. 2. The failure of cherished plans and purposes; the loss of property through
robbery by men or accidents by fire or flood, the break-down of health, the disappointment of long expectation. 3. The falling away of friends; their unreasonable anger and bitter reproaches. It must have been peculiarly painful to David to
bear the mutiny of his own men, to witness the selfishness of many of them (ver.

22), and to learn what little confidence could be put in man (Ps. cxlvi. 3).   He was left almost alone.   4. The upbraiding of conscience for past sin.   Trouble is a powerful means of bringing sin to remembrance (1 Kings xvii. 18).   5. The threatening of danger; the presence of "the king of terrors" (Job xviii. 14).   6. The lack of wisdom and power to deliver from distress.   When we become fully aware of our utter helplessness, two courses lie open before us—either to sink into despair or to cast ourselves wholly upon God.   That the latter may be taken trial is sent; it is taken by him whose heart is in the main right with God, and it is never taken in vain.

II. IT LAYS HOLD OF ALL-SUFFICIENT HELP.   "When David could not comfort himself in his wives, nor his children, nor his goods, nor in anything under the sun, he could in something above the sun.   And the reason is at hand: God is the God of all consolation, the spring of comfort; if any water, it is in the sea; if any light, it is in the sun; if any comfort, it is in God—there it rests, there it is when nowhere else.   God is all-sufficient; there the heart finds every want supplied, every good thing lodged.   As God is all-sufficient to furnish us with all necessaries, so infinite in power, wisdom, goodness to help us against all evils feared or felt" (R. Harris).   Faith strengthens the soul by uniting it to God and making it partaker of his strength.   It has respect to—1. *His great name* (see ch. i. 3).   "Hope thou in God" (Ps. xlii. 5; ix. 10; cxxiv. 8).

> " Hope, said I,
> Is of the joy to come a sure expectance,
> The effect of grace Divine and merit preceding.
> This light from many a star visits my heart;
> But flow'd to me, the first, from him who sang
> The songs of the Supreme; himself supreme
> Among his tuneful brethren. 'Let all hope
> In thee,' so spake his anthem, 'who have known
> Thy name'" (Dante, 'Par.' xxv.).

2. *His intimate relationship* to his people.   "Jehovah his God."   3. *His past doings* on their behalf.   When David formerly fell into despondency (ch. xxvii.) he seems to have forgotten all these, and failed to receive the encouragement which they were adapted to impart.   But now he remembered them and "took courage."   4. *His faithful promises.*   "The free expressions of his goodness and beneficence," the unchangeable assurances of his almighty help in time of need.   "The mistake we make is to look for a source of consolation in ourselves; self-contemplation instead of gazing upon God.   He is not affected by our mutability, our changes do not alter him.   When we are restless he remains serene and calm; when we are low, selfish, mean, or dispirited he is still the unalterable I AM.   What God is in himself, not what we may chance to feel him in this or that moment to be, that is our hope" (Robertson).

III. IT MAKES USE OF APPROPRIATE MEANS.   "He encouraged (strengthened) himself," &c. by—1. *Repressing fear* and unbelief.   "Why art thou cast down, O my soul?"   2. *Directing the thoughts* toward God, the ever-present, invisible, eternal Protector of his servants, and stirring up the heart to renewed trust in him.   "The Lord is on my side; I will not fear: what can man do unto me?" (Ps. cxviii. 6; cxxi. 1).   3. *Inquiring of the Lord.*   "And David said to Abiathar," &c. (vers. 7, 8).   He sought him as he had not done on the previous occasion; sought him in a right spirit, and therefore (unlike Saul) received an answer:—"Pursue, for thou shalt surely overtake and deliver."   He was thereby further strengthened.   His confidence, moreover, was expressed and perfected in—4 *Obeying the will of the Lord* (vers. 9, 10), and co-operating toward the fulfilment of his promise.   Despondency led him to flee from difficulty and danger, but faith and hope incited him to go into their midst, and made him "as bold as a lion."   "I will fear no evil, for thou art with me."

IV. IT IS CROWNED WITH COMPLETE SUCCESS.   By the help obtained of God fear is removed, strength renewed, and confidence inspired (ver. 9).   After a brief delay and some untoward events by which faith is still further tested (ver. 10)—1. The object which is sought is providentially discovered (ver. 11).   2. The enemy is completely defeated (ver. 17). 3. That which has been lost is recovered (ver. 19). 4. Much more than has been expected is gained (ver. 20). "A few days after David's own people were about to stone him on the ruins of Ziklag the royal crown was laid at his feet."

Observations:—1. When good men transgress they must expect to be " chastened of the Lord," and wicked men are sometimes used as a rod for the purpose. 2. The wickedness of the wicked is mercifully restrained (ver. 2), often turns to the benefit of those whom they seek to injure, and returns upon their own heads. 3, The chief purpose of chastisement is to bring men to God in humility, penitence, submission, and trust, and prepare them for future service and exaltation. 4. The difference in the effects of calamity upon men (as upon Saul and David) manifests the difference of their character. 5. The more heavily trouble presses upon men, the more closely should they cling to God, that it may be rightly borne and accomplish its intended moral end. 6. God never disappoints the confidence of his children, but fulfils his promises to them more richly than they dare to hope.—D.

Vers. 11—20. (SOUTH OF THE BROOK BESOR.)—*An Egyptian slave.* " I was reminded of the poor Egyptian whom David found half dead, and brought to life again by giving him 'a piece of cake of figs and two clusters of raisins' to eat, and water to drink, by an incident which occurred to me when crossing the plain of Askelon. Far from any village, a sick Egyptian was lying by the road-side in the burning sun, and apparently almost dead with a terrible fever. He wanted nothing but ' water ! water ! ' which we were fortunately able to give him from our travelling-bottle ; but we were obliged to pass on and leave him to his fate, whatever that might be" (Thomson, 'The Land and the Book'). How the "young man of Egypt" became "slave to an Amalekite" is not stated, but it is probable that he fell into his hands in some marauding expedition, like the Hebrew women and children in the raid on Ziklag. His condition was an involuntary, hard, and degrading one. He was—

I. ABANDONED BY HIS MASTER with—1. *Indifference* and contempt. His worth as a man created in the image of God was disregarded (as is generally the case in the odious institution of slavery). He was treated as the absolute property of his master, "an animated tool " (Aristotle), and when deemed no longer useful, thrown away. 2. *Injustice.* Every claim in return for his services was ignored. He was entirely at the mercy of his master, and unprotected by any law (such as existed among the Hebrews). 3. *Inhumanity.* "My master left me three days agone because I fell sick" (ver. 13). He might have been easily carried forward on one of the camels (ver. 17), but the Amalekites were hard and cruel, and he was left to perish with hunger or to be devoured by wild beasts. "He that is higher than the highest regardeth " (Eccles. v. 8), and the meanest slave cannot be despised and neglected with impunity.

II. BEFRIENDED BY STRANGERS (vers. 11, 12). 1. *Out of compassion* and desire to save his life by every means in their power. 2. *In fulfilment of the law of God,* which required that kindness should be shown to the poor, the stranger, and the slave. "Love ye therefore the stranger, for ye were strangers in the land of Egypt" (Deut. x. 19 ; xxiii. 7, 15, 16). 3. *With appreciation of the service* he might render (ver. 15). The more helpless any one is, the more urgent his claim to assistance ; yet no one is so helpless but that he may be capable of requiting the kindness shown to him. Slavery among the Hebrews differed widely from slavery among other ancient and modern peoples (ch. xxv. 10 ; Ewald, Ginsburg, 'Ecclesiastes,' p. 283 ; ' Ecce Homo '). " By Christianising the master the gospel enfranchised the slave. It did not legislate about mere names and forms, but it went to the root of the evil, it spoke to the heart of man. When the heart of the master was filled with Divine grace and was warmed with the love of Christ the rest would soon follow. The lips would speak kind words, the hands would do liberal things " (Wordsworth, 'Com. on Philemon ').

III. SERVICEABLE TO HIS BENEFACTORS. 1. *From gratitude* for the benefit received. No human heart is wholly insensible to the power of kindness. 2. *Under a solemn assurance* of protection. After his abandonment by his master he could have no scruple concerning his right to his continued service, if any such right ever existed;

but experience had made him fearful and suspicious of men, and therefore he said, "Swear unto me by God," &c. (ver. 15). He had a sense of religion, and believed that Divine justice would avenge the violation of an oath, though it should be taken to a slave. 3. *With efficient and faithful performance* of his engagements. He not only gave David the information he sought, but guided him to the camp of the enemy, and contributed to a result which repaid him a hundred-fold (ver. 18). IV. PRESERVED AND EMPLOYED BY DIVINE PROVIDENCE, which—1. Cares for the lowliest. "Behold, God is mighty, and despiseth not any" (Job xxxvi. 5). "Neither doth God respect any person" (2 Sam. xiv. 14). 2. Often makes use of the feeblest instrumentality for the chastisement of the "wicked in great power." 3. And for the promotion of the welfare of the people of God, and the establishment of his kingdom. What a rich harvest may spring from a single act of kindness toward even the most despised !

> " He prayeth well who loveth well
> Both man and bird and beast.
> He prayeth best who loveth best
> All things both great and small :
> For the dear God who loveth us
> He made and loveth all " (Coleridge).　　　　D.

Vers. 21—31. (THE BROOK BESOR, ZIKLAG.)—*The fruits of victory.* When David overtook the Amalekites in the evening twilight he found them given up to riotous indulgence, undefended, and little thinking how near they were to destruction. He forthwith fell upon them, and after a severe conflict, which lasted till the evening of the next day, gained a complete victory. He "recovered all" that had been carried away. In addition he obtained much spoil, consisting of flocks and herds, and of "arms, ornaments, jewels, money, clothes, camels, accoutrements, and so on." The former were assigned to David (according to his wish, and as better adapted to the end he had in view), and driven in front of the recovered flock with the exclamation, "This is David's spoil." The latter were carried away for distribution among his men. By his victory a crushing blow was inflicted on a bitter enemy of the people of Israel, and a great deliverance wrought for them. He evidently regarded himself as (not merely engaged in a private enterprise, but as) acting on their behalf, and carrying out God's purpose ; and his conduct after the battle was marked by—1. *Considerate sympathy* with the faint and weary who had been disabled from taking an active part in the conflict. "He saluted them" (ver. 21). As he had not previously urged them beyond their strength, so now he exhibited a kindly interest in them, and a marked respect toward them. His heart was not lifted up by success. They had "done what they could," and formed part of his following. "They also serve who only stand and wait." 2. *Strenuous resistance* to the arrogant, selfish, and unjust procedure of some of his followers (ver. 22). " Rough, wild men were many among them, equally depressed in the day of adversity, and recklessly elated and insolent in prosperity. Nor is it merely the discipline which David knew how to maintain in such a band that shows us ' the skilfulness of his hands' in guiding them, but the gentleness with which he dealt with them, and above all the earnest piety with which he knew how to tame their wild passions, prove the spiritual 'integrity' or 'perfectness of his heart ' " (Edersheim). The spirit which these " wicked and worthless men" displayed is sometimes found even in the Church of Christ, and requires to be met with firm and uncompromising opposition (1 Pet. v. 9). 3. *Devout recognition* of the hand of God, in bestowing whatever good is possessed, preserving from harm, and delivering from dangerous adversaries. " Ye shall not do so, my brethren, with that which the Lord hath given us," &c. (ver. 23). " Man could not boast of his own merit in obtaining these possessions " (Ewald). They were a gift of God, and should be used for his honour and the good of all. There is a higher law than that of self-interest. Men are only " stewards " (not absolute owners) of property, ability, time, influence, &c., and as such it behoves them to "be found faithful." "Freely ye have received, freely give." 4. *Equitable distribution.* " And who will hearken unto you in this matter ? " &c. (vers. 24, 25). The course proposed was as contrary to the common convictions of men concerning what is reasonable and just as to the benevolent purpose of God. "The equity of this law appears from hence—that by common consent these 200 men were left behind to look after the baggage ; were part of the same body of men, linked together in the same common society; hindered by mere weariness from going to fight, which otherwise they would have done; their will was accepted for the deed ; and they were in the same common danger, for if the 400 had been routed their enemies would have soon cut them off" (Patrick). "The members should have the same care one for another" (1 Cor. xii. 25). 5. *Grateful acknowledgment* of friendly aid during his "wanderings in the wilderness." "He sent of the spoil unto the elders of Judah, his friends," &c. (vers. 26—31). They had suffered from Amalekite raids, but it was not to make restitution for their losses so much as to testify his gratitude and strengthen their attachment. His victory enabled him to display a princely munificence. "It is a remarkable proof of the grateful nature of David, and his fidelity to his early friendships, as well as a curious instance of undesigned coincidence, that we find among those employed by David in offices of trust in the height of his power so many inhabitants of those obscure places where he found friends in the days of his early difficulties" ('Sp. Com.'). 6. *Commendable policy*—wise, generous, patriotic, and religious. "Behold a present" (blessing, gift) "for you of the spoil of the enemies of Jehovah." The elders of Judah and others looked to him as their future theocratic ruler. He himself felt that the time of patient waiting was nearly gone, and the time of active effort for the fulfilment of the Divine purpose concerning him well-nigh come, if, indeed, the tidings of the death of Saul had not already reached him. He also foresaw that he must look for his chief support in his own tribe, and adopted the best method of securing it. "Piety without policy is too simple to be safe ; policy without piety is too subtle to be good." "This was already a royal act in vivid anticipation of his impending accession to the throne. Already the crown of Israel was unmistakably though dimly visible above his head" (Krummacher). "Whilst Saul's star sinks in the north, the star of David rises in the south, and there begins the long line of fulfilments of the prophecy concerning the Star that should come out of Jacob" (Num. xxiv. 17) (Erdmann).—D.

Ver. 6.—*Faith reviving in distress.* I. CORRECTION. David, being a true but faulty child of God, was corrected by the rod. Quickly fell stroke after stroke. First he had to bear the galling scorn and suspicion of the Philistine lords. This was all he had gained by cajoling their king. Next he had to see Ziklag plundered and burnt. This was all he had gained by attacking the Amalekites and concealing the deed. Next, and in some respects most trying of all, he saw the loyalty of his own followers swept away in their passionate grief. "The people spake of stoning him." This was all he had gained by all his unworthy devices to save his own life. All refuge failed him. So God in loving-kindness scourges his children now when they have faltered in faith, and, mistrusting his defence, have betaken themselves to some Ziklag, some position unworthy of them. Their new confidences reject them, and they have to sit like David in dust and ashes.
II. ITS HAPPY ISSUE. Faith revived. When all refuge failed him, David returned to his Divine stronghold. "He encouraged himself in Jehovah his God." Mark the contrast with Saul. When that unhappy king was stricken he departed from God more and more, hardened his heart in pride, found no place of repentance, and at last betook himself to unhallowed and forbidden arts. So we find Saul passing from gloom into thicker and blacker shadow, while David emerges into the sunshine. Such is the happy experience of many of the children of God. Faith revives in distress, and darkness turns to light. This, too, as the New Testament teaches us, always by the gracious operation of the Holy Spirit, reviving childlike trust, rekindling holy courage. The way in which David's recovered faith wrought in him is full of instruction for us. 1. *Revived faith rests on the Divine word of promise.* David had let the promise of the kingdom made to him through Samuel slip from his mind when he began to despair of his life ; and it is remarkable that he gave way to this fear at a time when there was a lull in the persecution directed against him. But when real danger was upon him, when he had lost all, and his own followers turned against him, his faith again caught hold of the Divine promise. He could not die then and there,

for the purpose of the Lord must stand, the word of the Lord must be fulfilled. Now those who believe in Christ have the promise of eternal life in him. In hours of relaxed diligence they perhaps let it slip; but under real pressure faith revives and grasps the promise again. They shall not perish. They may be humbled and distressed, and they will acknowledge that they have brought this on themselves; but they are persuaded that he is faithful who promised, and so will not cast them off. He has said, "I will never leave thee nor forsake thee;" so that we may boldly say, "The Lord is my helper." 2. *Revived faith takes to prayer and to diligent effort.* The first thing which David did was to inquire of God. Faith restored always acts thus. Rising against discouragement, it is sure that God can turn darkness into light, loss into gain, death into life, and simply asks for direction. "What shall I do? Shall I sit still, or shall I move? Shall I pursue?" There are trials and dangers in which the only wise course is to be quite patient and passive; the "strength is to sit still." When Daniel was cast to the lions his faith was shown in not struggling with the wild beasts, but sitting among them calm and still till rescue came at break of day. So may a Christian fall into a den of troubles out of which no effort of his own can bring him up; and his faith is shown in prayer and waiting on God, who is able to send his angel to minister to the weak and protect the helpless. Those whose faith has not failed at all may do more than pray—may sing praises, as Paul and Silas did in the dark dungeon. Other cases there are, and more frequent, in which prayer should be promptly followed by active exertion. David did not ask the Lord to work a miracle, or send angels, to restore to him what the Amalekites had taken. It was possible for him and his men to pursue, overtake, and defeat the spoilers. So he asked the Lord whether he should pursue; and receiving the Divine command to do so, he addressed himself at once to the pursuit, and obtained a splendid success. Such is the energetic action of revived faith. Difficulties go down before its resolutions, and lost things come back to him who boldly pursues. Tears of defeat are turned into songs of victory. The troubles that afflict the people of God are to a large extent chastisements for unbelief or unfaithfulness. At the time they are not joyous, but grievous; nevertheless, afterward they yield the peaceable fruit of righteousness to those who are exercised thereby. Such are sufferings in sympathy with David. But to some extent those troubles are in sympathy with and for the sake of the Son of David, the Lord Jesus Christ. In such a case we have the comfort that

> "Christ leads us through no darker rooms
> Than he went through before."

He is touched with a feeling of our infirmities. He has wept and he has loved. So if we are despoiled, he is our present help, and through him we may do valiantly and recover all. If messengers of Satan buffet us, his grace is sufficient for us, for his "strength is made perfect in weakness."—F.

EXPOSITION.

DEFEAT AND DEATH OF SAUL (CH. XXXI.).

CHAPTER XXXI.

SAUL AND HIS SONS SLAIN (vers. 1—7). Vers. 1, 2.—**The Philistines fought.** Literally it is a participle present, "the Philistines are warring," as if it were a mere resumption of ch. xxviii. 1. In the battle fought on the day following Saul's visit to the witch the Israelites were defeated, and fell in large numbers **slain in Mount Gilboa,** either because the Philistines had attacked them there, or because, after fighting in the valley of Jezreel, they had made on its steep ridges their last defence. Among those thus slain were the three sons of Saul mentioned in ch. xiv. 49, where see note.

Vers. 3, 4.—**The archers.** Literally, as in the margin, "shooters, men with bows." As the first word would equally apply to men who threw javelins, the explanation is added to make the meaning clear. **Hit him.** Literally, "found him," *i. e.* found out his position, and came up to where he was. **He was sore wounded.** Rather, "he was sore distressed." In Deut. ii. 25 the verb is rendered "be in anguish." The meaning is that Saul, finding himself surrounded by these archers, and that he could neither escape nor come to close quarters with them, and die fighting, ordered his armour-bearer to kill him, that he might be spared the degradation of being slain by "uncircumcised" heathen. **Abuse me.** This verb is translated *mock* in Jer. xxxviii. 19. "Maltreat" would be a better rendering in both places, and also in Judges xix. 25, where, too, the word occurs. Its exact meaning is to practise upon another all that passion, lust, anger, or malice dictate. Probably Saul thought that they would treat him as they had previously treated Samson (Judges xvi. 21—25).

Vers. 5, 6. — **His armour-bearer.** The Jewish tradition says that he was Doeg the Edomite, and that the sword on which Saul fell was that with which he had massacred the priests. This is not very probable; but whoever he was, his horror on being asked to slay his master, and his devotion to him, are deserving of admiration. **All his men.** In 1 Chron. x. 6 " all his house." But Ishbosheth and Abner survived, and the meaning probably is not that his whole army, but that his personal attendants, all those posted round him, fell to a man, fighting bravely for their king, as the Scots fought round King James V. at Flodden Field. As suicide was very rare among the Israelites, the death of Saul is made more intensely tragic by the anguish which drove him thus to die by his own hand.

POLITICAL RESULT OF THE BATTLE (ver. 7). Ver. 7.—**The men of Israel.** The term is here applied to non-combatants, while in ver. 1 it meant those following Saul in arms. **On the other side of the valley.** *I. e.* of Jezreel, and so all the Israelites inhabiting the tribes of Issachar, Zabulon, and Naphthali, and the region generally to the north. In 1 Chron. x. 7 this flight is confined to the inhabitants of the valley, one of the most fertile districts of Palestine; but probably the statement made here, that a very large extent of country was the prize of victory, is the more correct. **On the other side Jordan.** This phrase constantly means the eastern side of the Jordan, nor need we doubt but that the people living near it abandoned their homes and fled; for the river would form but a' slight protection for them in this northerly part of its course. Still the conquests on the eastern bank of the Jordan must have been confined to a small district near the lake of Tiberias, as Abner was able to place Ishbosheth as king at Mahanaim, a town about twenty miles to the east of the river, and not far from Jabez-Gilead. South of Jezreel the Philistines made no conquests, and thus Ephraim, Benjamin, and Judah remained free, and of course Gilead, and the most part of the region beyond Jordan (see 2 Sam. ii. 8—11).

MALTREATMENT OF THE BODIES OF SAUL AND HIS SONS (vers. 8—10). Ver. 8.—**It came to pass on the morrow.** The previous verse gave us the results of the victory as they were in course of time developed. We now return to the narrative of the battle and its immediate consequences. As the spoiling was deferred till the morrow, the struggle must have been obstinately contested, and decided only just before nightfall.

Vers. 9, 10.—**They cut off his head.** This was probably done not simply in retaliation for what had happened to their champion Goliath, but in accordance with the customs of ancient warfare. The fierce joy of the Philistines over the fallen Saul proves how great had been their fear of him, and how successful he had been in breaking their yoke off Israel's neck. Had he still had David with him the victory would assuredly have remained on his side. **They put his armour in the house of Ashtaroth.** Hebrew, " of the Ashtaroth." Whether it was divided among the various shrines of Astarte, or whether it was all placed in her famous temple at Askelon, described by Herodotus (i. 105) as the most ancient of the fanes of the Syrian Venus, is uncertain. The former view agrees best with the Hebrew text and with what is said in 1 Chron. x. 10, where we have the additional information that they suspended Saul's head in the temple of Dagon. **They fastened his body to the wall of Beth-shan,** as also the bodies of his sons (ver. 12). Beth-shan or Scythopolis lies about four miles from the Jordan on the west, and twelve miles south of the lake of Tiberias. It is almost in a straight line to the west of Mahanaim, and must have been at once occupied by the Philistines, and as they hung the bodies of the fallen king and his sons on its wall, they evidently intended to retain it.

RECOVERY OF THE BODIES OF SAUL AND HIS SONS (vers. 11—13). Ver. 11.—**Jabesh-Gilead.** Eusebius describes this place as situated on the road from Pella to Gerasa, and therefore it would be much nearer the Jordan than Mahanaim, and probably was not more than twelve or fourteen miles distant from Beth-shan. The people there had not forgotten how bravely Saul had saved them, and now showed their gratitude by rescuing his remains from disgrace.

Vers. 12, 13.—**They burnt them.** Cremation, though highly honourable among classical nations, is here mentioned for the first time in Holy Scripture, and was probably resorted to on this occasion to insure the bodies of Saul and his sons against further maltreatment, as, if buried, the Philistines might have made the attempt to get them again into their power. Some suppose that the burning of the dead was afterwards practised by the Jews, and quote in its favour 2 Chron. xvi. 14; Isa. xxxiii. 12; Jer. xxxi. 40; xxxiv. 5; Amos vi. 10, but these passages bear a different interpretation. After the exile, interment was the sole method of disposing of the dead among the Jews, and in the Talmud cremation is condemned as a heathen practice. The burial of the bones of Saul and his sons proves that their bodies here were really burnt. **Under a tree.** Hebrew, "under the tamarisk," the famous tree of that species at Jabesh. It was under one tamarisk that Saul commanded the massacre of the priests (ch. xxii. 6), and now his bones are placed in rest beneath another. Perhaps the people remembered the king's fondness for trees. For the final fate of these relics see 2 Sam. xxi. 12—14. They **fasted seven days** (see Gen. l. 10). The time of mourning was thirty days for Aaron (Numb. xx. 29) and for Moses (Deut. xxxiv. 8). The Talmudic rule is strict mourning for seven days, less strict for the next twenty-three, in all thirty ; and for a father or mother mourning was continued for a year. The fasting was mourning of the strictest kind, and proves that the people of Jabesh-Gilead honoured to the utmost their deliverer.

HOMILETICS.

Vers. 1—6.—*Judgment at last.* The facts are—1. In the battle at Gilboa the men of Israel suffer a defeat from the Philistines. 2. His sons being slain, the conflict presses hard on Saul. 3. Dreading to fall by the hand of a Philistine, and failing to find death through the hand of his armour-bearer, he falls on his own sword, his example being followed by his armour-bearer. Here we have the closing scene in the tragedy of Saul's life, verifying the prediction of Samuel. Our heart mourns over an end so sad, and as we read the narrative we are sensible of a strange pity for this once promising but now ruined man. Notice—

I. THE PRESSURE OF EVENTS WORKING OUT A RIGHTEOUS JUDGMENT. Connecting this defeat and death of Saul with the early prediction of Samuel (ch. xv. 23, 28, 29) and the recent solemn declaration in the cave at Endor (ch. xxviii. 16—20), we see how, as by an unseen hand, Saul was urged on to his doom. For instead of making terms with the enemy, or fleeing from the scene of conflict, he, knowing his doom, drew up his men, pressed on to the thickest battle, became a conspicuous mark for archers, and drew around himself and heirs to the throne the fiercest of the assault. We cannot but observe how the Philistine force was unrestrained by the power which checked Pharaoh's army at the Red Sea, weakened Amalek when the hands of Moses were raised (Exod. xvii. 11—13), inspired terror in the army opposed to Jonathan (ch. xiv. 15—23), and generally put fear in the hearts of Israel's foes. Samuel's words make clear to us that Providence was leaving Saul to the impulses which led him to death, and withholding from the Philistines all that would otherwise have impeded their way to victory. It is a fearful thing thus to fall into the hands of the living God. The truth brought out here is, that though judgment is often for unrevealed reasons long deferred, yet events are so disposed as to concentrate irresistibly on the enforcement of the penalty of sin. Men pursue a crooked and unholy course for years, during which time justice seems to linger ; but the time comes on when, as by infatuation, they go straight into the concurrences of events which Providence has permitted for their downfall. So also fell Babylon, Rome, and other nations, made drunk with the wine of the wrath of God (Isa. lxiii. 6). So likewise, under the pressure of Providence, will the sea give up its dead, and all that are in their graves come forth, to receive according to the deeds done in the body (John v. 28, 29 ; 2 Cor. v. 10 ; Rev. xx. 13).

II. THE SINS OF PARENTS CUT OFF THE HOPES OF SONS. We feel deep sympathy with Jonathan that he, the brightest and best of Israel's manhood, should perish in the calamity brought on by his father's persistent impenitence. Brave, gallant son, knowing and lamenting the failings of his parent, and the woes his conduct was bringing on the kingdom, with true filial piety he stands by him and the kingdom to the end ! It was better to die, if so God willed it, than to live and share in the joys of even a David's friendship. The fond hopes of seeing David enthroned over a happy and prosperous people after his father's natural decease (ch. xx. 12—17 ; xxiii. 16—18) were rudely blighted. It is the old sad story of the sin of one bringing sorrow and suffering to many innocent. The fearful havoc made by sin ! The awful responsibility of our conduct ! Millions die before their proper time, and a wail of woe rises daily from myriads of hearts because of the transgression of parents.

III. A SAD END OF LIFE IN KEEPING WITH ITS ORDINARY COURSE. There is a singular blending of diverse thought and motive in the last utterances and acts of Saul. He knew his doom was at hand; and yet, partly under a sense of utter wretchedness which made him willing to die, and partly from the patriotic feeling that his unwillingness to face his country's foe should not be added to his crimes, he goes forth to battle. Then, also, when pressed in battle and in great straits, was there not a sense of misery, a consciousness of Divine abandonment, which made the continuance of life a burden no longer to be endured, blended with the thought precious to the Hebrew, that he was one of the chosen race, allied by nationality with the great Messianic purpose, and that, as such, it must never be said that Israel's king was abused by the touch of the "uncircumcised" alien? In this commingling of light and darkness, moral quickenings and mad infatuation, we have an analogue to his conduct all through his sad career. It is not for us to say whether there was not in those last sad moments, as he lay on the earth, a melting of that heart which had so long striven against God. As in many other instances, there is no light thrown on the inner experience of the soul in its most sacred relations to God. The case of the thief on the cross may suggest the possibility of a cry from the heart to which the mercy that endureth for ever responds. But it is for us to stand in awe, and take to ourselves the solemn lesson of this sad and perverted life.

IV. A QUESTION AS TO THE MORAL CHARACTER OF SUICIDE. Willet, in his 'Harmonie upon the first Booke of Samuel,' quotes authorities *pro* and *con* on the general question and on Saul's act; but without entering on a wide subject, it may suffice to note that *moral cowardice* is ordinarily the cause of suicide, and that it is a violation of the prerogatives of God. As we have indicated, there may have been considerations of a semi-religious character which influenced Saul in desiring not to be slain by the "uncircumcised," and to him it was *certain* that death was at hand. Nevertheless, no private feeling, no relief from dishonour, can justify a forestalling, in the matter of life and death, of the course of Providence. The principle involved is most vital, and when once the door for its violation is opened, the whole fabric of society is sapped at its foundation.

General lessons:—1. It is instructive to contrast the beginning and end of lives, and note how by the action of a deceitful heart the fatal turn is taken toward disgrace and despair. 2. Although some parents ruin their sons by their sins, yet we all do them wrong and damage in so far as sin taints our life. 3. Although God cuts off the hopes of the good by the calamities which come through the sins of others, yet in his mercy he raises them to a purer and safer joy. 4. Whatever judgments God brings should be submitted to with resignation.

Vers. 7—13.—*The final issues of life a criterion of worth.* The facts are—1. The defeat of Saul is followed by the general flight of the men of Israel from the neighbouring cities, and the occupation of these by the Philistines. 2. The bodies of Saul and of his sons being found, the Philistines strip the king's of his armour, publish the fact in the houses of idols, and dishonour him on the wall of Beth-shan. 3. The men of Jabesh-Gilead, hearing of this, rescue the bodies and bury them at Jabesh amidst much mourning. The historian closes the narrative concerning Saul's reign by a reference to the immediate result of the defeat on the adjacent cities, and to the barbarous treatment of Saul's body. The people who had demanded a king, and who were proud of his powerful bodily presence, were now to learn in saddest form how much better it is to wait the time of God, and to trust rather to righteousness of national life than to physical force and martial display. The people and the king were at fault, and the judgment falls on both. We here see—

I. THAT LIFE'S WORTH IS TESTED BY ITS FINAL RESULT. The public life of Saul at one time promised well for himself and Israel. Every aid which wise advice and holy influence could render had been freely bestowed by Samuel, the man of God, and the promise of Divine help was given on condition of obedience to the Divine voice. Although troubles came in consequence of disobedience, and thus indicated that his life was proving a failure, there were doubtless men so blind to the signs of the times as to refer the troubles to accidents and unforeseen circumstances, and to hope still that there would be a turn in the tide of affairs which would insure a prosperous reign. But the panic which came on Israel on Saul's death and the occupation of cities by the detested Philistine must have made clear to the most prejudiced that his public career was disastrous and unrighteous. The issue of a monarch's reign should be the moral and material elevation of the people, the improved administration of law, the greater security of life and property, a prevalence of the blessings of internal peace and freedom from foreign oppression, and a higher degree of national influence. The reverse of this was the outcome of Saul's life. By thus looking at the result of life's labours we may form an estimate of the worth of monarchs, statesmen, merchants, and professed Christians. Have men blessed their fellow-creatures with permanent good? Is the great enemy, *sin*, more in occupation of country, home, and the soul at the end than at the beginning? The day is coming when every man's work will be tried of "what sort it is" (1 Cor. iii. 13). Can we face that test? Will the end be better than the beginning? Dare some men try to answer this question in relation to their spiritual condition and the spiritual effect of their personal influence.

II. That the apparent triumph of the wicked is one of the saddest consequences of the sins of God's people. The triumph of the "uncircumcised" was complete when, stripping the body of Israel's king, they carried his head in savage delight to the house of Dagon (1 Chron. x. 10), nailed his corpse to the wall of Beth-shan, and proclaimed their victory in honour of their gods. It was this result following on the death of Saul and defeat of Israel that seemed to be an occasion of so much sorrow and dread to David (2 Sam. i. 20). The fond hopes cherished by the pious on the solemn day of repentance and consecration at Mizpeh and Ebenezer (ch. vii. 9—12) were now rudely destroyed. Heathenism gloried in its strength; while Israel, smitten with fear, mourned in bitterness of soul. Ignorance, barbarity, idolatry took a new lease of power, and Jehovah's name was dishonoured in the eyes of the nations. The death of a king is comparatively a small matter, the wasting sweep of war over fair fields and flourishing cities is a material calamity; but for irreligion to flourish, debasing religious rites to manifest all their vileness, and the cause of purity, truth, and righteousness to be made to suffer even apparent defeat, this was the most fearful consequence of Saul's unhappy reign. All actions in public and private individuals are to be judged by their bearing on the honour of God's name and the extension of the kingdom of Christ. Does a monarch's or a statesman's policy give greater scope for whatever is alien to the supremacy of Christ in heart, conduct, and home? If so it is very criminal. Does our private life give occasion for the enemies of the cross to blaspheme? He who so lives and dies as to strengthen the hold of ignorance, superstition, immorality, and anti-Christian principles on the world is the enemy of his country and of God. When men professedly in the Church of God, as Saul was in Israel, so become unfaithful to their privileges as to give an apparent triumph to the irreligious and profane, they, in whatever degree this is true, perpetrate an injury, the spiritual issues of which are beyond all calculation.

III. That the most terrible trials may give rise to occasional deeds of heroism. Various were the effects of Saul's death on Israel. On all there must have come that inexpressible anguish which in some degree David sought to express in his beautiful "song of the bow" (2 Sam. i. 18—27). But there were faithful men who could not yield to inaction while God's name was being dishonoured and Israel, in the person of the king, covered with ignominy. The men of Jabesh-Gilead had not forgotten the day when, in the prime of his strength, and bidding fair to defend his country in the fear of God, Saul had come to their rescue and had aroused the patriotism of the nation (ch. xi. 4—11). To them he was more than king; he was hero and friend, and doubtless their children had used his name as a household word. And now dead, forsaken, mutilated, the tall, majestic form exposed to heathen scorn—should they suffer it? Never! "All the valiant men arose." With set purpose, at risk of life, they bring away the mangled remains, and sorrowfully lay them low in the place that witnessed his early heroism. Thus do we see how misfortune, sorrow, and death call forth the nobler qualities of men, and bring to light hidden sympathies and secret friends. There was some hope for Israel yet. The terrible disasters of life stir up the energies of the faithful few, and though they cannot at once redeem all that others have lost, they can reassert the supremacy of love and the nobler sentiments of life, and so pave the way for a better order of things.   Men in Israel revived a little from despair when they heard of this heroism and affection.   Was there not a darker night and more complete apparent defeat of Israel's high purpose in the world when another and more sacred body was exposed "a spectacle to angels and to men"?   Then also one was found who dared to identify his reputation and all that was dear with respect and love for that holy body.   Joseph of Arimathea was morally more heroic than the men of Jabesh-Gilead.   In similar ways the disasters of life have drawn forth the heroism of many who could not endure to see the "uncircumcised" triumph.   Thus light shines forth in darkness, assuring us that in the long conflict with evil the morning of an endless day full of the joy of the ransomed will dawn on the sorrowful earth.

General lessons:—1. To form a just estimate of our life we should not regard our personal enjoyments as pain, but have chief respect to the ultimate effect of it on our home and country.   2. Wicked men find encouragement to believe in their false principles when men professing opposite principles are untrue to them.   3. We ought to consider how much of the power of irreligious principles and practices over men is due to our want of consistency.   4. It will be blessed for us and our survivors if friends are able to commit our body to the grave with affection and gratitude unalloyed with painful memories.

HOMILIES BY VARIOUS AUTHORS.

Vers. 1—6. (GILBOA.)—*The death of Saul.*   "So Saul died" (ver. 6; 2 Sam. i. 1—16; 1 Chron. x.).   While the events mentioned in the preceding chapter were taking place in the south, and even before their occurrence, "the great drama so closely connected with them was being played out" in the north.   On the morrow of Saul's consultation of "the witch of Endor" the Philistines marched across the plain, with their archers, chariots, and horsemen (2 Sam. i. 6), and attacked the army of Israel.   The issue appears to have been soon decided.   "The men of Israel fled from before the Philistines, and fell down slain in Gilboa," up the slopes of which they had been pursued.   "And the Philistines followed hard upon Saul and his sons," who fell fighting around him.   Hard pressed and found by the archers, he trembled ("was sore wounded," A. V.) before them, seeing no way to escape falling into their hands; and (as the night set in), with the reckless courage of despair with which he had fought, his armour-bearer having refused to slay him, he "took the sword and fell upon it."   His armour-bearer followed his example.   "At that moment a wild Amalekite, lured probably to the field by the hope of spoil, came up and finished the work which the arrows of the Philistines and the sword of Saul himself had all but accomplished" (Stanley).   "A remarkable dispensation.   As the curse on Amalek was accomplished by Saul, so that on Saul was accomplished by Amalek" (Hengstenberg).   Or, perhaps, the story of the Amalekite was false, and told to ingratiate himself with David and obtain a reward for the diadem and bracelet of which he had stripped the fallen king.   In either case, self-willed to the last, scorning "these uncircumcised," and more concerned about his own honour than the honour of God, he rushed upon his own destruction.

> "O Saul!
> How ghastly didst thou look, on thine own sword
> Expiring in Gilboa, from that hour
> Ne'er visited with rain from heaven nor dew" (Dante, 'Purg.' xii.).

Observe that—

I. RETRIBUTION SURELY OVERTAKES THE IMPENITENT TRANSGRESSOR.   1. The full desert of sin might be justly inflicted immediately on its commission.   But in a state of probation space is allowed for repentance and motives afforded to induce it.   Yet, if sin be persisted in, guilt increases and judgment becomes more inevitable and severe.   "He, that being often reproved hardeneth his neck, shall suddenly be destroyed, and that without remedy" (Prov. xxix. 1).   "The wages of sin is death" (Rom. vi. 23).   "The wages may be deferred or may not be consciously received, but they are paid without stint sooner or later; the fatal consequences may not always equally appear, but they never fail in some form or other." 2. Although inflicted by the free act of man, it is not less the result of the operation of retributive justice. "Saul took the sword and fell upon it;" but he "died for his transgression which he committed against the Lord; therefore *the Lord slew him,* and turned the kingdom unto David, the son of Jesse" (1 Chron. x. 14). 3. The operation of the law of retribution, so manifest in history and to observation, shows the evil of sin in the sight of God, and is a solemn warning against its indulgence. Even repentance may come too late to avert its consequences in this life.

> "Look to thyself then, deal with sin no more,
> Lest he that saves, against thee shuts the door" (Bunyan).

II. SELF-WILL NATURALLY CULMINATES IN SELF-DESTRUCTION. All self-will, in opposition to the will of God, is a self-injury (Prov. viii. 36); and not less so because the sinner seeks what he falsely imagines to be for his good. Its tendency is ever towards destruction, and, unless checked in its course, it infallibly conducts to that end. It is a special and aggravated form of it when, in order to escape the misery and shame which are experienced or expected, he directly and voluntarily takes away his own life. *Suicide* is—1. *Contrary to the natural instinct* of self-preservation and a properly enlightened and regulated self-love. 2. An act of *unfaithfulness to the trust* that is committed to man by God in the bestowment of life, and of refusal to fulfil the duties that he has ordained in life, which cannot be rightly surrendered or left without his consent nor until the time he has appointed. "Pythagoras forbids us to abandon the station or post of life without the orders of our commander, that is, of God" (Cicero). "'Why do I tarry on earth, and not hasten hence to come to you?' 'Not so, my son,' he replied; 'unless that God, whose temple is all this which you behold, shall liberate you from the imprisonment of the body, you can have no admission to this place'" ('Scipio's Dream'). 3. An act of *cowardice* in the presence of real or imaginary evils, whatever reckless bravery it may exhibit with respect to death and that which lies beyond. "To die and thus avoid poverty, or love, or anything painful is not the part of a brave man, but rather of a coward; for it is cowardice to avoid trouble; and the suicide does not undergo death because it is honourable, but in order to avoid evil" (Aristotle, 'Ethics,' book vii. ch. 7). In Saul it was "the act of completed despair." 4. Expressly *prohibited by the Divine command:* "Thou shalt not kill." In accordance with this Paul said to the Philippian gaoler, when "he would have killed himself," "Do thyself no harm" (Acts xvi. 28). 5. Virtually *forbidden by all the exhortations* of the New Testament to endure affliction with patience and submission to the will of God. "Suicide is the result of impatience" (see Paley, 'Mor. Phil.,' book iv. ch. 3). 6. *Injurious to others* in many ways: inflicting much distress, teaching pernicious lessons, setting a bad example. It is "as unfavourable to human *talents* and resources as it is to human *virtues.* We should never have dreamt of the latent power and energy of our nature but for the struggle of great minds with great afflictions, nor known the limits of ourselves nor man's dominion over fortune. What would the world now have been if it had always been said, Because the archers smite me sore, and the battle goeth against me, I will die?" (Sydney Smith). 7. *Condemned by the example* of good men, who have borne the heaviest calamities with holy courage, and sanctioned only by evil men, like Ahithophel and Judas. How far, indeed, Saul was in full possession of his faculties and responsible for his act, or what was his final destiny, is not stated. "It is evident that more arguments may be gathered of his condemnation than of his salvation; yet because nothing is expressly set down touching his state before God, it is better to leave it" (Willet).

> "O mortal men! be wary how ye judge:
> For we, who see our Maker, know not yet
> The number of the chosen" ('Par.' xx.).

"There appears to be but one efficient means by which the mind can be armed against the temptations to suicide, because there is but one that can support it against *every* evil of life—practical religion, belief in the providence of God, confidence in his wisdom, hope in his goodness" (Dymond, ' Essays ').

> " Nor love thy life, nor hate ; but what thou liv'st
> Live well, how long or short, permit to Heaven " (' Par. Lost,' bk. x.).

III. THE EVIL EXAMPLE OF MEN IN HIGH STATION IS ONLY TOO FAITHFULLY IMITATED. "And when his armour-bearer," &c. (ver. 5). He had faithfully fought by his side to the last, and feared to take away his life (of which he was appointed guardian) ; perhaps out of reverence for his sacred person; doubtless, also, he dreaded to fall alive into the hands of the Philistines and to be put to a shameful death by them ; and now, incited by his example, "dares to do that to himself which to his king he durst not." Example is proverbially powerful. No one, especially if he occupy a position of power and influence, can do wrong without thereby inducing others to follow, who thus share his guilt and may not have equal excuse for their transgression. According to Jewish tradition the armour-bearer was Doeg the Edomite (ch. xxii. 18, 19), "a partner before of his master's crimes, and now of his punishment." "That Saul and his armour-bearer died by the same sword is, I think, sufficiently evident. ' Draw thy sword,' says he to him, ' and thrust me through;' which when he refused, ' Saul took *the* sword and fell upon it.' What sword ? (Not his own, for then the text would have said so.) Why, in the plain, natural, grammatical construction, the sword before mentioned must be the sword now referred to, that is, the armour-bearer's. Saul and his executioner both fell by that very weapon with which they had before massacred the priests of God " (Delany).

IV. THE INNOCENT OFTEN SUFFER ALONG WITH THE GUILTY. "And the Philistines slew Jonathan," &c. (vers. 2—6). It is impossible not to lament the untimely fate of the friend of David and of God. The sins of the father were visited upon the son. But let it be considered that—1. God is the supreme Proprietor of every human life, and has a right to dispose of it as it pleases him. Moreover, "death passed upon all men, for that all have sinned " (Rom. v. 12). 2. He has united men to each other in relations more or less intimate, whereby they necessarily affect each other for good as well as for evil. 3. The sufferings of the godly, in consequence of their connection with the wicked, serve many beneficent purposes. The death of Jonathan would deepen the impression of the severity of the Divine judgment on the house of Saul for disobedience, and be a perpetual warning. It also made David's accession to the throne clearer and more indisputable. 4. The godly cannot experience the worst sufferings of the wicked—remorse, fearfulness, despair ; and if some are called to an early death in the path of duty, they are only called a little earlier than others to their inheritance in " a better country, that is, a heavenly," an eternal kingdom.

> " Joy past compare ; gladness unutterable ;
> Imperishable life of peace and love ;
> Exhaustless riches and unmeasured bliss."   D.

Vers. 7—10. (GILBOA.)—*The chastisement of Israel.* The thunderstorm of which they were long ago warned (ch. xii. 18, 25) had now burst upon the people of Israel. Since the capture of the ark they had not experienced so great a calamity, and in it the fatal results of their demand for a king were made manifest. Although the demand was evil, it contained an element of good, and was complied with by God in judgment mingled with mercy. "As no people can show a visible theocracy, so no monarchy can be accused, simply as such, of usurping the Divine prerogative. But still the transaction does involve a moral lesson, which lies at the foundation of all sound policy, condemning the abandonment of principle on the plea of expediency, and pointing by the example of Israel the doom of every nation that seeks safety and power in a course known to be wrong " (P. Smith, ' Ancient History'). They had their own way, yet the purpose of God was not defeated, but accomplished less directly, and in such a manner as to convince them of the folly of their devices, and exhibit his over-ruling wisdom and power. Whilst they pursued their course under a king " according to the will of man," their Divine King was preparing " a man after his own heart to be captain over his people " (ch. xiii. 14 ; Acts xii . 22).

When the end came David stood ready to occupy the throne, and, after a brief period of conflict and confusion, the whole nation, taught by experience, gladly received him as its ruler. This is the theocratic "argument" of the greater portion of the Book. In the terrible defeat of Israel we see—

I. THEIR IDOL BROKEN IN PIECES. "So Saul died," &c. "The men of Israel fled, and Saul and his sons were dead," &c. (vers. 6, 7). Men are apt to imagine that something else beyond what God has ordained is necessary to their welfare, to be impatient of his time, to attach an undue value to the expedients which in their imperfect knowledge and sinful desires they devise, to set their hearts upon earthly and visible objects, and depend upon them rather than upon "him who is invisible." This tendency finds expression in many ways, and embodies itself in many forms. And although God may permit such *idols* to continue for a time, he always overthrows them. When Israel made an idol of the ark it was given into the hands of the Philistines, and when they made an idol of "a king" (ch. viii. 5) he was slain. Their hope in him was bitterly disappointed, and inasmuch as he was (according to Divine prescience, though not by absolute necessity nor without personal guilt) a representation and reflection of their sin (worldliness, formalism, self-will), they were severely punished in him and by his instrumentality. How little did they gain, how much did they lose, by having their own way! "I gave thee a king in mine anger, and took him away in my wrath" (Hosea xiii. 11). "Cease ye from man," &c.

II. THEIR CITIES FORSAKEN. "And when the men of Israel that were by the side of the plain" (west of the central branch of the valley of Jezreel, "opposite to the place of conflict, which the writer assumed as his standpoint"—Keil), "and by the side of the Jordan" (east of the plain, between Gilboa and the Jordan), "saw that the men of Israel" (who were engaged in the battle) "fled," &c. "they forsook the cities; and the Philistines came" (from that time onward) "and dwelt in them" (so that the whole of the northern part of the land fell into their hands). Instead of overcoming their enemies, they were overcome by them, driven from their homes, reduced to the most abject condition, and without any prospect of regaining by their own strength their lost possessions. "Your country is desolate," &c. (Isa. i. 7). The peaceful government of Samuel gave them prosperity (ch. vii. 13, 14); but the warlike rule of Saul, which they preferred, ended in their overthrow. "Sore distressed," like him (ch. xxviii. 15), whither should they turn for help? Men are deprived of all hope in themselves that they may "set their hope in God."

III. THEIR ENEMIES TRIUMPHANT. "And it came to pass on the morrow" (after the battle, which ended at nightfall) "when the Philistines came," &c. "And they cut off his *head* (as in the case of Goliath of Gath, and afterwards deposited it in the temple of Dagon, in Ashdod, 1 Chron. x. 10; ch. v. 1), and sent (messengers bearing his head and armour) into the land of the Philistines round about, to proclaim the good tidings in their idol temples (to their idols) and among the people (2 Sam. i. 20). And they put his *armour* in the house of Ashtaroth (in Askelon), and they fastened his *body* to the wall of Bethshan" (Judges i. 27). It has been remarked of the Philistines that "so implacable was their enmity to the Israelites, that one would be almost tempted to think that they had been created on purpose to be a thorn in their sides" (Russell, 'Connection,' History of the Philistines). Their victory was the victory of their gods; the defeat of Israel the dishonour of Jehovah. Rather than sanction sin in his people, God not only suffers them to be overthrown by their enemies, but even his own name to be for a while despised and "blasphemed among the heathen." But the triumph of the wicked is short (2 Sam. v. 17—25).

IV. THEIR TRUE STRENGTH UNDESTROYED. It consisted in the presence and power of their Divine and invisible King; his benevolent and unchangeable purpose concerning them (ch. xii. 22); his faithful, praying, obedient subjects in their midst, who had been long looking to David as his chosen "servant," and were now rallying round him daily until his following became "a great host like the host of God" (1 Chron. xii. 22). There was an "Israel after the flesh" (constituting the State), and there was an Israel "after the spirit" (constituting the Church); and in the latter lay "the power of an endless life." Judgment might sweep over the nation like a destroying hailstorm, and leave it like a tree bereft of all its leaves, and even "cut it down" to the ground. But its true life would be spared, would be tried and purified by affliction, and become a source of renewed power and greater glory. "As a teil tree, and as an oak, whose substance is in them, when they cast their leaves: so the holy seed shall be the *substance* thereof" (Isa. vi. 13; i. 9; lxv. 8).

Observations:—1. That which is wrongly desired as an instrument of good becomes when obtained an instrument of evil. 2. Men may have their own way apparently in opposition to the way of God, but his purpose does not change, and he knows how to carry it into effect. 3. The people who sanction the sins of their rulers justly share their punishment. 4. When the people of God expect to prevail against their enemies by adopting their sinful policy (ch. viii. 20), they are certain to be ultimately defeated. 5. The suffering and humiliation that follow sin are the most effectual means of its correction. 6. The hope of a nation in the day of trouble lies in its praying, believing, godly men. 7. God over-rules all things, including the sins and sorrows of his people, for the establishment of his kingdom upon earth (ch. ii. 10).—D.

Vers. 11—13. (BETHSHAN, JABESH-GILEAD.)—*Gratitude.* The first victory of Saul (ch. xi.) is connected with his death by the noble exploit of the men of Jabesh. It was due partly to loyalty and patriotism; chiefly to gratitude for benefits formerly conferred upon them. It is seldom that any one closes his earthly course without some token of grateful remembrance. Of one of the worst tyrants that ever held the reins of power in Rome (Nero), it is recorded that on the morning after he was buried amidst general execration fresh flowers were found strewn by an unknown hand upon his grave. Saul had done many generous deeds, and they were not forgotten. The gratitude of the men of Jabesh was marked by many admirable features. It was—1. *Unexpected.* Who would have thought that the city which was so faithless and cowardly as to say to Nahash, "Make a covenant with us, and we will serve thee," could have furnished such an instance of devotion? The noblest qualities sometimes appear in association with the meanest, and where men expect to find no good thing. Let us not despise our nature, nor think that at its worst it is wholly incapable of generous acts. 2. *Long-cherished.* It was many years previously that Jabesh had been saved by Saul; but its grateful feeling had not (as is sometimes the case) grown cold with the lapse of time. When a philosopher was asked, "what doth soonest grow cold?" he replied, "Thanks." 3. *Spontaneous.* No special appeal was made to them; but perceiving that they could do something to testify their gratitude to their benefactor by rescuing his remains from the indignity to which they were subjected, "all the valiant men arose" of their own accord, "and went all night" (a distance of ten miles, across the Jordan) and accomplished it. Gratitude loses its proper character and ceases to be gratitude when it requires to be solicited and urged. 4. *Disinterested.* Saul and his sons were dead, and no reward for their daring effort might be expected. It was performed in somewhat of the same spirit as that with which Saul himself formerly acted; what was best in his life was remembered and admired by them (as it was by David, 2 Sam. i. 23), and it served to stir them to similar excellence. Disinterested conduct begets its like.

> " Good deeds immortal are—they cannot die ;
> Unscathed by envious blight or withering frost,
> They live, and bud, and bloom ; and men partake
> Still of their freshness, and are strong thereby" (Aytoun).

5. *Heroic* and self-sacrificing; exhibited practically and at the risk of life, and displaying great energy and valour. "The pillars of fire of genuine human heroism are the noble lights of history, which make us feel at ease while sojourning among spectres, and horrors, and graves" (Lange). 6. *Complete.* It did not stop short of doing its best. "They took their bones, and buried them under the tamarisk at Jabesh, and fasted seven days" (ver. 13; 2 Sam. xxi. 14). They could do no more; and what they did was done tenderly, mournfully, reverently, and in fulfilment of a sacred custom and religious duty.

Exhortation:—1. Endeavour so to live that when you are gone you may be remembered with gratitude, and leave behind the recollection of good deeds which may incite others to the like. 2. Fail not to render gratitude to every one who has conferred a benefit upon you in the best way you can; be thankful, especially to God, for all his benefits towards you. "Nothing more detestable does the earth produce. than an ungrateful man" (Ausonius). 3. Seek above all things to obtain in life and death the honour that comes from God. "This Book began with Samuel's birth, and now ends with Saul's burial, the comparing of which together will teach us to prefer the honour which comes from God before any honours of which this world pretends to dispose" (M. Henry).—D.

Ch. xxxi.—*Saul of Gibeah, and Saul of Tarsus.* It is instructive to compare the characters of different men with each other. This is done by Plutarch in his Lives of celebrated Greeks and Romans; and it may be done with advantage in the case of some of the characters described in the Scriptures. There was an interval of a thousand years between Saul of Gibeah and Saul of Tarsus, "who also is called Paul" (Acts xiii. 9). But if we look at them attentively, "and examine the several parts of their lives distinctly, as we do a poem or a picture" (Plutarch), we shall find in these two illustrious Hebrews, the one under the Old Covenant, the other under the New—

I. RESEMBLANCE in their—1. *Ancestral relation,* religious privileges, and outward circumstances. Both belonged to "the tribe of Benjamin" (Acts xiii. 21; Phil. iii. 5), received the name of Saul when " circumcised the eighth day," were brought up "under the law," after early years of obscure diligence held important public positions,—the one as first king of Israel, the other as a "chosen vessel" unto the Lord, to bear his name "before the Gentiles, and kings, and the people of Israel" (Acts ix. 15),—lived a long life (over sixty years), and died a sudden and violent death. 2. *Natural qualities:* passionate, impulsive, warlike, zealous, daring even to rashness, resolute, persistent; inherited from their common ancestor, of whom it was said, "Benjamin as a wolf shall ravin," &c. (Gen. xlix. 27); and characteristic of their tribe, as appears in Ehud (Judges iii. 15). The Apostle of the Gentiles, "in the prompt audacities of his apostolic career, does not allow us to forget of what tribe he was." 3. *Sudden conversion:* the one on the way to Gibeah, on beholding "a company of the prophets" (ch. x.); the other on the way to Damascus, overcome by the glorious revelation of the Lord (Acts ix.), whose followers he was persecuting; a startling surprise to all, and the commencement of a different course of life. "Is Saul also among the prophets?" "They were all afraid of him, and believed not that he was a disciple." 4. *Energetic enterprises,* to which they were called by the Divine Spirit, on behalf of the kingdom of God against its adversaries; in the one case with the sword, in the other with the word (ch. xi.; Acts xii. 25; xiii. 1—3).

II. CONTRAST in still more numerous particulars. They were the opposite of each other; as in physical appearance and mental culture, so also in their—1. Extraordinary change, which in the one was *partial,* superficial, and temporary; in the other *complete,* deep, and enduring. 2. Real character. The one *lived unto himself,* and did not freely and fully surrender himself to the Divine will; the other *lived unto the Lord,* not being disobedient to the heavenly vision (Acts xxvi. 19; Gal. i. 16; Phil. i. 21). 3. Gradual progress: in the one case, after brilliant promise, *downward,* in "pride, caprice, jealousy, cruelty, excusive avenging of himself, and at last open contempt and defiance of God;" in the other *upward,* in heavenly-mindedness, spiritual power, and higher usefulness. 4. Fierce persecution. "The second Saul for a while followed only too faithfully in the footsteps of the first. If the one persecuted David, the other, with an energy of hate that did not fall short of his, David's greater Son. Presently, however, their lives divide, and one is the Saul of reprobation, the other of election" (Trench). The latter began where the former ended (Gal. i. 23), and became himself an object of the persecution in which he once shared. 5. Representative relation. The one represented, embodied, and promoted what was *worst* in his tribe and nation, the other what was *best.* 6. Tragical end: the one in *despair* by his own hand, the other in glorious *hope* as a martyr of Christ (2 Tim. iv. 6—8). 7. Lasting memorial: the one is a *warning,* the other is a *pattern* (1 Tim. i. 16; Phil. iii. 17). The second Saul was "the likeness in the Christian Church" not so much of what the first was as of "what he might have been—the true David, restorer and enlarger of the true kingdom of God upon earth" (Stanley).

III. INSTRUCTION. 1. Religious advantages and eminent positions are of no real benefit unless they be rightly used. 2. The natural qualities which make one man a power for evil, make another, when sanctified, a power for good. 3. The heart must be right with God in order to a proper use of his gifts and a worthy course of life. "If the heart be not upright, whatever favourable beginnings there may be, there cannot be a uniform perseverance in goodness or any happy conclusion" (Robinson). 4. Divine grace when persistently resisted is withdrawn, leaving the soul a prey to the "evil spirit;" when humbly and faithfully received, is followed by more grace. 5. In proportion as a man lives to himself or to God he becomes weak, sinful, and miserable, or strong, holy, and happy. 6. There is no standing still in moral life; if men do not become better they infallibly become worse. 7. As a man lives so he dies. "Think of the end of Saul of Gibeah, and learn in time to be wise." Think of the end of Saul of Tarsus, and "be faithful unto death."—D.

Vers. 3—6.—*The bitter end.* The tragic element, so conspicuous in this history, is intense in the last scene of all.

I. SAUL'S DEATH. 1. *His despair.* When the battle went against him, and the Philistines, keeping beyond reach of his long arm and terrible sword, hit him from a distance with their arrows, the king's spirit suddenly failed and died within him. "He trembled sore because of the archers." Always fitful in his moods, liable to sudden elation and sudden depression, he gave up all for lost. He would not flee, but he would fight no more. Probably the horrible recollection of the words spoken to him by the spectre at Endor increased his despair, and he thought only how to die. 2. *His pride.* Saul had never shown much regard for the sacredness of human life, but he cherished a most exalted sense of the sacredness of his own person as the Lord's anointed. No descendant of a long line of so-styled Christian or Catholic sovereigns has held a loftier claim of personal inviolability. So he resolved that no heathen should cut him down in battle. Anything rather than this. If his armour-bearer would not kill him, he would kill himself. 3. *His suicide.* With all his horror of being slain by a heathen, Saul died like a heathen—dismissed himself from life after the manner of the pagan heroes; not with any sanction from the word of God or the history of his servants. (Illustrate from the stories of Brutus and Cassius and the younger Cato.) The only instance of what can be called self-destruction among the men of Israel prior to the days of Saul was that of Samson, and his was a self-devotion for the destruction of his country's enemies which ranks with the heroism of one dying in battle rather than with cases of despairing suicide. There is a case after the days of Saul, viz., that of Ahithophel, who, in a fit of deep chagrin, deliberately hanged himself. To the servants of God suicide must always appear as a form of murder, and one that implies more cowardice than courage. English law regards it as a very grave crime, and to mark this our old statutes, unable to punish the self-murderer, assigned to his body ignominious burial. It is, however, the charitable custom of our times to assume that one who kills himself must be bereft of reason, and so to hold him morally irresponsible. Apology of this kind may be pleaded for King Saul, and pity for his disordered brain takes away the sharpness from our censure. Still we must not overlook—4. *The admonition which his death conveys.* Saul had really prepared for himself this wretched death. He had disregarded the prophet, and so was without consolation. He had killed the priests, and so was without sacrifice or intercession. He had driven away David, and so was without the help of the best soldier in the nation, a leader of 600 men inured to service and familiar with danger. He had lived, in his later years at least, like a madman; and, like a madman, he threw himself on his sword and died. Here lies admonition for us. As a man sows he reaps. As a life is shaped, so is the death determined. We speak of the penalty on evil-doers, but it is no mere arbitrary infliction; it is the natural fruit and necessary result of the misconduct. One leads a sensual life, and the penalty on him is that of exhaustion, disease, and premature decay. One leads a selfish life, hardening his heart against appeal or reproach, and his doom is to lose all power and experience of sympathy, to pass through the world winning no love, and pass out of the world drawing after him no regret.

II. JONATHAN'S DEATH. 1. *Its innocence.* Look at the pious, generous prince, as well as the proud and wilful king, slain on that woeful day. A man who loves God and whom God loves may be innocently involved in a cause which is bound to fail. It may be by ties of family, or by official position which he cannot renounce; and, unable to check the fatal course of his comrades, he is dragged down in the common catastrophe. Jonathan died in the same battle with his father, but not as his father died. Let us remember that men are so involved with one another in the world, in ways quite defensible, sometimes unavoidable, that as one may share the success of another without deserving any part of the praise, so also may one share the downfall of others without being at all to blame for the courses or transactions which brought about the disastrous issue. 2. *Its timeliness.* The death of Jonathan, occurring when it did, brought more advantage to the nation than his continued life could possibly have rendered. It opened the way for David's succession to the throne. Had Jonathan survived his father, he might have been willing to cede the succession to David, but it is not at all probable that the people would have allowed his obvious claim to be set aside, and any conflict between the partisans of two such devoted friends would have been most painful to both. So it was well ordered and well timed that Jonathan died as a brave soldier in the field. He missed an earthly throne indeed, but he gained all the sooner a heavenly home. So is it with many a death which seems to be sad and untimely. A man of God cannot lose by dying. To die is gain. But he may by dying advance the cause of God more than he could by living. His departure may clear the ground for other arrangements under Divine providence, for which the time is ripe, or open the way for some one who is chosen and called to do a work for God and man that must no longer be delayed.—F.

HOMILETICAL INDEX TO

THE FIRST BOOK OF SAMUEL

II SAMUEL

EXPOSITION BY

R. PAYNE SMITH

HOMILETICS BY

C. CHAPMAN

HOMILIES BY VARIOUS AUTHORS

B. DALE   G. WOOD

THE SECOND
BOOK OF SAMUEL

INTRODUCTION

THE Second Book of Samuel is virtually the history of David's reign, while the First had comprised a twofold narrative, that, namely, of Samuel's reformation of Israel, followed by the account of the uprise and fall of Saul. And never had king a more pathetic history than Israel's first monarch. Full of hope and vigour, yet modest, brave, and generous, he had entered in a most praiseworthy spirit upon the duties of his high but difficult office. Unhappily, there was a flaw in a character otherwise so noble. Throughout the history of Israel one great principle is never forgotten, and that is the presence of a higher than any human power, ever ruling in the affairs of men, and making right and justice prevail. And Saul could not bring himself into accord with this power, and again and again crossed the boundary which lay between the king's authority and that of God. It might seem a small matter, that at a time of great urgency Saul could not wait till the expiry of the seven days appointed for Samuel's coming to Gilgal (1 Sam. xiii. 13); and to lose a kingdom for such hastiness seems to many modern commentators a hard measure. Nor are excuses wanting for his leniency towards the Amalekites, and Saul himself could see in it at first no violation of God's command (1 Sam. xv. 20). But in both cases there was present the same spirit which made him murder in cruel haste the high priests at Nob, and put even their women and babes at the breast to death for the supposed violation of his royal authority. Saul could not submit to the Power that is higher than man, nor consent to make his own will bend to that of God; and this wilfulness was rebellion as hateful and contrary to right as open dealings with unclean spirits, or the actual abandonment of Jehovah for idols (1 Sam. xv. 23). It is easy to see its hatefulness in such deeds as the murder of the priests and the repeated attempts to slay David. The unerring judgment of God condemned it at its first outbreak, and before it had ended in crime; and this condemnation was in mercy. Had Saul repented and humbled himself in heart, his course would have been one ever brightening into light. But he was stubborn and rebellious, and the gloom deepened round him till all was dark.

Saul was not prepared to do right because it was right; and when Samuel and those who loved the right for its own sake drew away from him, his vanity was wounded, and jealousy took possession of his heart. Undoubtedly he was a man possessed of great mental and bodily gifts, and his achievement in so rapidly raising the militia of Israel and crushing Nahash the Ammonite gave him just reason for exultation. It was a deed in which he gave proof of high courage, strong will, and great military capacity. He must have been himself surprised at the rapidity and completeness of his success. And in that hour of gratified self-love he could be generous and noble-minded (1 Sam. xi. 13). But it was largely vanity as well as fanaticism which led to the rash vow which nearly cost Jonathan his life; and when he heard the women sing of David having slain his ten thousands, this wrong done to his self-love filled him with a mean spite against one who would have been the truest of his friends, and his strong bulwark against the evils which filled his latter years with distress. And it was this brooding jealousy which disturbed the balance of Saul's mind, and made him subject to fits of mania, marked generally by intense depression, but breaking out occasionally into deeds of fierce violence.

Saul, in the midst of his violent acts, had never ceased to be a religious man, though there was none of that personal love and loyalty to Jehovah which so distinguished David. It was the national religion to which he gave his allegiance; and it was as a statesman and patriot that he respected it, though doubtless he never shook off the influence of Samuel. But there was little genuine piety in his heart, and no trust in God, nor any feeling of union with him. In domestic life he retained his simple manners, and did not give way to that voluptuousness which disgraced David, and filled the last twenty years of his life with shame and sorrow. But as a ruler he had failed. It had seemed at first as if the hope of Israel, that under a king the nation might dwell safely, would be fulfilled in him. For many years he was a vigorous and successful chieftain, and a hero in war. And Israel under him was rapidly advancing in the arts also of peace. Protected by the military successes of the king, Samuel was able in tranquillity to carry on his schools, and through the sons of the prophets to promote the great work of internal reform. Justice was administered (1 Sam. vii. 15), and the rudiments of learning were being generally acquired. When the younger son of a farmer, evidently little thought of at home, and in his brother's estimation fit only to look after a few sheep, could read and write, education must have been a thing not uncommon. For David thus taught was but a mere drudge at home. His elegy over Saul and Jonathan tells us of domestic refinement; of women clad in scarlet, and with jewels of gold.

Saul had done much; but in his last years he brought all to ruin, and at his death he left his country in abject thraldom, and with all its national liberties trampled underfoot.

In his fall Saul involved in equal ruin his son Jonathan, one of the most generous and beautiful characters that ever the world saw. And his death at Gilboa was but the ending of a path wrapped in deepening shadow and leading inevitably to misery and disaster. In 1 Sam. xiv. we see Saul in almost as bad a light as when he murdered Ahimelech and his brethren. The youthful Jonathan and his armour-bearer had wrought one of those feats of desperate valour which are not uncommon in the history of the Israelites. And their bravery had stricken the raw levies of the Philistines with panic, increased by the action of a body of Hebrews drawn from the districts conquered by the Philistines, and forced to serve in their army. They were posted in the rear to guard the camp, and their defection placed revengeful enemies in the very pathway of flight. Saul meanwhile concludes from the absence of Jonathan and his armour-bearer that it was some brave exploit of theirs which was causing this confusion in the Philistine host; but when the priest asks counsel of God, with just the same absence of self-control as had made him refuse to wait for Samuel at Gilgal, Saul bids him withdraw his hand from the ephod and desist. He needs no counsel from above. He will act for himself, and with extraordinary rashness and absence of good sense he commands the people under a solemn curse to abstain from food until all is over. They must fight the battle and pursue fasting. Had he given himself time for reflection, he would have felt that the slight loss of time spent in taking refreshment would be more than compensated by increased vigour of body and power of endurance. The pursuit, too, had come suddenly, and his men were not prepared; and to have partaken of the provisions cast aside by the runaways would have kept up their strength. They must at last stop from sheer exhaustion, and then the whole army would be in a state of ravenous hunger. Worst of all, he was laying a trap for those who had gained the victory. Saul's body-guard would hear his orders, and obey with grumbling. Jonathan and all who joined in the pursuit from a distance, rushing from caves and from the hills of Ephraim, would be in danger unwittingly of bringing upon themselves a curse.

The results were most disastrous. When they reached Aijalon the people were so faint with hunger that they began slaying sheep and oxen, and eating them without observing the command of the Law, that they must carefully free the flesh from the blood. And Saul, aghast at this violation of a solemn ceremonial ordinance, bids his body-guard disperse themselves among the people, and compel them to bring their oxen to a large stone, and there slay them in the manner prescribed. There was thus long delay before the wants of the troops could be supplied, and when at last they had taken a hurried meal, and Saul was eager to resume the pursuit, they gave him so sulky an answer as to be virtually a refusal. And now the priest, mediating between king and people, purposes to ask counsel of God, and Saul consents. But no answer comes. Saul had refused God's counsel in the morning, and now the oracle is silent.

But Saul sees no fault in himself. Fault he assumes there is, and he will find it out by drawing lots. He bids the people stand on one side, and himself and Jonathan on the other; and again, with a sulky answer, the people assent. Again and again the lot falls, till Jonathan is left, and Saul, nothing doubting that he is guilty, asks for confession; whereupon Jonathan tells him how, unwitting of his command, he had tasted almost by chance a little honey. Never was man more innocent than Jonathan, and God by him that day had wrought a great deliverance for Israel. Yet his guilty father, with dark fanaticism, condemns him to death. The people indeed rescue him, but all his legal rights were gone. In the eye of the Law he was a dead man, and henceforward Jonathan ever acts as if there was a bar between him and the kingdom. He never once speaks as if it were possible for him to inherit Saul's throne, or as if he were ceding to David anything to which he had a claim. His father's curse, his father's condemnation, still rested upon him. The people had saved him by force, but the legal act remained, and the father had destroyed the son.

From first to last Saul was the destroyer of himself, his family, and his kingdom. Samuel foretold his fall, but the warning was given personally to the king to move him to repentance. Repentance would have saved him, and Samuel allowed him ample time; for, during four or five years, he did absolutely nothing to help on his words to their accomplishment. Only after this long delay, spent by Samuel in mourning (1 Sam. xv. 35), at God's express command he arose and anointed David; but neither of them, either openly or by secret conspiracy, took any steps to compass Saul's ruin. All that David did he was driven to do. To the last he was loyal to his king. And when in an evil hour he deserted his country, and entered the service of the Philistine king of Gath, it was almost a renunciation of his anointing. He seems himself to have given up all idea of ever becoming king, and, in a fit of desperation, to have thought only of saving his life. To his countrymen this open alliance with their enemies put him entirely in the wrong, and sorely he was punished for it by a seven years' delay. Yet slowly both predictions were moving on to their fulfilment, and if the purpose was Divine, the human agency was that of the self-willed Saul.

There is thus a tragic interest in the First Book of Samuel. Unrepentant, stubborn, wilful even in his deepest depression, the king struggles against his fate, but each effort only entangles him in fresh difficulties, and burdens his conscience with darker crimes. The one pathway of safety which David tried, and not in vain, in his season of terrible sin, Saul will not try. He sees his doom; is driven by it to melancholy, is unhinged in mind; but the prophet's words, " rebellion," " stubbornness," indicate the unyielding elements of his nature, and stubbornly he died in the lost battle-field. Like Prometheus, he defied the Almighty, in deeds if not in words, but the heroism was gone, and in that last sad scene, when, in mental and moral degradation, the despairing monarch sought the witch's cave, stubbornness alone remained. And, meanwhile, the other purpose of God was growing in strength, and, through strange scenes of heroism and feebleness, the shepherd-boy becomes the nation's champion, the king's son-in-law, an outlaw and a deserter, before finally he becomes a king.

In the two Books of Samuel, David's uprising and reign, his sins and his terrible punishment, are given us in great detail, not merely because of their intrinsic interest and the clearness with which they teach the great lesson that sin is ever punished—not merely this, but even more because he was a most important factor in the development of Israel as the Messianic nation. There is in this respect a parallel between the Book of Genesis and the Books of Samuel. The great business of the one is the selection of the man from whom was to spring the nation predestinated to be the depository of God's revealed truth. In the Books of Samuel we have the choice of the man who, next to Moses, was to form that nation for its high office, and to be the ancestor of Christ. In David the great purpose of Israel's existence was to advance a great step onwards. Eight hundred years had passed since the choice of Abraham, and four hundred since Moses gave laws and political unity to those sprung from him; and it had often seemed as if the folk were too tiny to be of any real service to mankind, and as if it must be crushed out of existence by the more powerful kingdoms that surrounded it. It was a territory so small, was placed in so dangerous a position on the very battle-ground of Egypt and Assyria, and the constitution of the realm was so little adapted to purposes of war, that it seemed impossible for it to have more than a short-lived endurance. But small as was Israel, God had chosen it to light a torch that should illuminate the whole world, and God's Word, which is the light of men, received through David a most precious addition to its contents.

As a preparation for the selection of David, the work of both Saul and Samuel was necessary. Saul had given Israel a sense of unity and, at least, a taste of the blessings of independence. The wish for a united Israel was as strong an influence in the uprise of David's empire as it has proved in modern times in the endowment of Europe with a united Italy. This right feeling had begun in Samuel's time, brought about probably by the tyranny of the Philistines; and Samuel, who saw in it a tacit reproach to himself, who had done so much, for not having done more, withstood it in vain. Saul's victory over the Ammonite Nahash, won by united Israel, made this feeling so strong, that David's election to the crown came as an inevitable necessity, though long delayed by his relations with the Philistines; and, when elected, he had not to build up the kingdom from the foundations—Saul had done that, but to retrieve the evil results of one terrible disaster. But the moral and mental development wrought by Samuel was a condition even more indispensable to David's kingdom than

Saul's restoration of the nation to political life. David's empire was a matter of vast importance to Israel as the Messianic nation, and Saul prepared the way for it. But it was a matter, after all, of only secondary importance, and Samuel's reforms had kindled again into brightness the nation's inner life. He purified Israel's morals, fanned its decaying faith into heroic confidence in Jehovah, and enriched it with a high civilization. The learning which had always had a home in the sanctuary, and which was for a time trampled out when Shiloh was destroyed, found a new dwelling in the Naioth at Ramah. Reading, writing, music, history, not merely existed there, but were taught to an ever-increasing number of the choicest spirits of Israel. Ramah was the centre of an active propaganda, and the sons of the prophets went back to their homes as missionaries, bound to teach and to elevate and to indoctrinate with Samuel's views all the inhabitants of their villages or towns. And these views had a strong practical bearing both upon the political and the spiritual life of the nation. The eighth psalm, composed by David to be sung to a melody learnt by him when in the service of Achish, King of Gath, is testimony enough to the refinement both of thought and of language that followed upon Samuel's reforms. For David, the youngest of a large family of sons of a yeoman at Bethlehem, could have gained only in Samuel's schools that acquaintance with literary arts, and that knowledge of the history of his country, which undoubtedly he had acquired somewhere. To suppose that he could have obtained them elsewhere is to suppose, what probably became true in course of time, that Samuel's scholars had already set themselves to teach in all parts of the country. Among a race of farmers learning would not advance with such extreme rapidity; but the Israelites were no common people, and their progress was sure and steady. It is probable that Gad, David's friend throughout his life, joined him at the very beginning of his wanderings as an outcast, from a personal affection which began when they were school-friends together at Ramah. For Gad, who is expressly said to have been a prophet (1 Sam. xxii. 5), is by the name certified to have been one of Samuel's scholars. He chose a very hard life when he went to be chaplain to a band of men composed of such dangerous elements as David's freebooters; but he loved David, was confident in his power of governing them, and deep in his heart was the conviction that Samuel's prophecy would surely be fulfilled.

And this captain of a band of wild outlaws was destined in course of time to remodel the temple service, to teach men to "prophesy," *i.e.* to testify to Divine truth, on harp and cymbal and psaltery (1 Chron. xxv. 1), and to give to the national worship its most spiritual element. Not only did David write psalms himself, but his temple service gave them a use, made them the common property of all, and caused others also to give expression to their devotion in the same way, as occasion called their feelings forth. The psalms were not mere lyric compositions, the result of poetic genius and fervour; no doubt many psalms at first were simply so; but they soon became the voice of the nation's worship, the expression of its faith and love and trust in its God. In this there was a distinct advance, and a most pure and ennobling and spiritual element was added, not merely to the ritual of the temple, but to the worship of God in the homes of the people. The sacrifice was full of teaching, but its details were coarse, and to us would be revolting. In the psalms sung to bright melodies in the temple, we have a form of worship so perfect, that it has lasted from David's day unto our own time; and the similar use of hymns in our services has enriched our Church with a body of spiritual poetry almost as precious as David's psalms. And like hymns in our own days, the psalms would be learnt by the people, and sung in their homes; and the worship of Israel would consist not merely of stately services in the temple, but of the voice of prayer and praise chanted throughout the land to the tunes of Asaph and his brethren, and in David's words.

In this respect we reap the benefit of David's varied experiences. Had he been a man of unblemished morality, his psalms would have struck no deeper note than those of Korah, or Asaph, or Jeduthun. In Jeremiah alone we should have had a psalmist whose words were the outpouring of a troubled heart. As it is, the passion-fraught nature of David hurried him into sins so terrible as to cover his character with disgrace, and bring upon him twenty years of severe punishment, ever following blow upon blow, and darkening even his death-bed with the fate of his eldest son, of the nephew who had been the pillar of his safety in every danger, and of the priest who, having alone escaped from the slaughter of his family at Nob, had been David's faithful companion all the days of his life. No regal splendour, no greatness of glory, could compensate for the lurid gloom of that death-bed. But God overruled all this misery for lasting good; for David has been for all ages the psalmist of sorrow and of repentance. Myriads of sinners have found in the fifty-first psalm the best expression of feelings that were rending their hearts. Nor does this psalm stand alone. When we read utterances such as those in Ps. xxxi. 9, 10; xxxviii. 4; xl. 12, etc., the words would seem overstrained did we not know the greatness of David's sin, the depth of his penitence, and the stern righteousness which punished him not once only, but with ever-recurring severity.

The words quoted by St. Paul from 1 Sam. xiii. 14, that David was a man after God's heart, often trouble the minds of believers, because they take them as the Divine verdict upon his whole character. Really they are spoken of him such as he was when Samuel anointed him, and when his youthful piety was still unstained. Yet to the very last he manifests such tenderness, such spirituality, and so devout and personal a trust in God as still to justify, though with large exceptions, this high estimate of him. And almost all his psalms belong to the days when trouble and anguish had stirred depths in his soul which otherwise would have remained stagnant. There are but few which belong to the days of his pure innocence. His poems then would have celebrated the beauties of nature, the Creator's goodness, the brave exploits of his countrymen, and the like. It was after his terrible fall that the contrite and humbled David poured forth from the inmost recesses of a struggling breast the words of earnest penitence, of deep humiliation, and withal of intense trust in the God who was punishing him so sternly, and of unwavering faith in the Divine goodness, which was manifesting itself to him as justice that could by no means clear the guilty.

The Second Book of Samuel is thus the basis and the justification of the Book of Psalms. The intensity of feeling manifested there is proved to be no mere poetry, but the cry of real distress. And because of the reality of his repentance David was forgiven; but his forgiveness did not save him from punishment. Never was history more sad than David's from the day when Nathan said, "Thou art the man!" unto that last death-bed scene, when, troubled by the cry of rebellion, he was forced to condemn old friends in order to prevent civil war and save the throne of his chosen son. And as David's sin was the violation of domestic chastity, so all his sorrows sprang from the same source, and not only were his own sons the workers of his misery, but it was in and by his children that he was punished.

Yet amidst it all, David was a man after God's heart in this respect at least, that there was neither rebellion nor stubbornness in his character. His sins were greater than those of Saul, but they were not persisted in. David humbled himself before God, and bore his chastisement not only meekly, but with a clinging love to the hand that was scourging him. Let but God deliver him from blood-guiltiness, and amid the ruin of his earthly happiness he would sing aloud of Jehovah's righteousness (Ps. li. 14).

But besides the interest inseparable from the study of a character such as David's, the Second Book of Samuel gives us the history of the founding of Israel's empire. War is a dreadful thing, and involves a terrible amount of material loss and injury; but it is at once God's penalty upon national debasement, and his remedy against national meanness and selfishness. Nations rise to moral greatness through war, and when they have been sinking through social corruption and private immorality, it is generally war which reveals to them the gangrene in their midst, and either forces them by repeated disaster to humble themselves for it, or displaces them in order that a worthier people may fill their room.

So Israel had displaced the Canaanite tribes in Palestine. And with all their faults, the repeated acts of heroism of which we have the record in the Book of Judges prove them to have been a race of sterling worth. No commonplace people could have produced such men as Saul and Jonathan, to say nothing of Samuel, whose wisdom and goodness and ability as the restorer of a crushed nation, and the founder of institutions which enriched it with intellectual and moral and religious life, raise him to an extraordinary pre-eminence. Yet the extraordinary men of a nation always hold some relation to its ordinary level, and Samuel did not stand alone. He was followed by David and the numerous worthies of his court. But Israel could not have maintained its heroism and nobleness by the mere memory of the feats recorded in the Book of Judges. Even then the nation was sinking downwards. Jephthah and Samson were men of lower worth than Barak and Gideon. The ruinous defeat at Aphek, followed by the capture of the ark and the destruction of the national sanctuary at Shiloh, convinced Israel of its degradation, and made it ready to yield to Samuel's exhortations. Then followed a period of struggle, and then came the empire of David and the splendour of Solomon's court. It was a short-lived glory. Christ's kingdom was not to have much of earthly magnificence about it. But the Messianic people before his advent had a tremendous work to do, and needed some noble memories to strengthen them as well as grand hopes bidding them ever move onwards. And David's grandeur and the splendour of Solomon, who to this day holds a unique position in the imagination of Oriental nations, gave them what they needed. Throughout a checkered history they continued to be a firm, strong, and heroic people, and with powers of endurance which have enabled them to remain a miracle and a wonder to the present day.

David's wars and conquests had thus a great importance for Israel, and therefore for mankind. But his empire was also a symbol of the Christian Church, and David is the representative of sin-stained fallen man finding forgiveness through repentance. And there is thus a reason for the restriction to him of the promise that the Messiah should be his Son. It is never renewed to any of his successors. Solomon was the glory of the East for his wisdom; Hezekiah and Josiah emulated David's piety, and were unstained by his sins; but no prophet hails them as the inheritors of David's promise. The seed of Judah's kings were to serve as "eunuchs in the palace of the king of Babylon" (Isa. xxxix. 7). It was from Nathan, a son uncrowned, and scarcely mentioned in the history, lost quickly to view among the crowd of ordinary citizens, that *he* was to spring who is the Church's King, but who nationally was but a sucker from the cut-down stem of Jesse (Isa. xi. 1). We have given the reason above. David is the type of fallen man, sternly chastised for his iniquity, but finding forgiveness, rest, peace, strength, in "the God of his salvation" (Ps. li. 14).

We have thus in the Second Book of Samuel a history essential to Holy Scripture, and of profound and even painful interest. For never had human soul a more checkered record of sin and sorrow, of discord in its relations with itself, of intense contrition and earnest pleading for forgiveness, and of genuine faith, than that which is set before us here. But without the Psalms, which disclose to us the inner working of David's heart, we should lose much of its significance. For here, chiefly, we have David's sin and his lifelong punishment; while there we have the struggle of his soul wending its way through darkness and sorrow upwards to forgiveness, to light, and to joyful communion with God.

The book is composed of three separate parts, of which the first ends with the list of David's chief officers (ch. i.—viii.). This narrative probably included a good deal of the latter part of the First Book of Samuel, the division of the history into two portions being unauthoritative. It gives the history of David in its noblest aspect, and if we include in it the victory over the giant, it might be called in Homeric phrase the Ἀριστεία τοῦ Δαυίδ, the prowess and brave achievements of a hero. It traces him step by step till from the sheepcote he becomes the sovereign of all Israel, whereupon immediately he brings the ark to Jerusalem, and is appointed (ch. viii.) the Messianic king, whose office it is to build the temple, to ordain a spiritual worship for Jehovah, and, as Messiah's representative, to take the heathen for his inheritance. It was probably a contemporary document, as was also the next, which forms ch. ix.—xx. In it we have the record of David's sin and its terrible consequences. Beginning abruptly with his kindness to Mephibosheth, but of which we see the reason when we come to the details of the flight from Jerusalem and sorrowful return, it next gives us fuller details of David's conquests, but only to lead up to the history of David's sin, committed when his heart was turned away from God by the glory of earthly victories. All that follows is the painful record of God's just severity. This narrative also ends with a catalogue of David's chief officers, but there is now a touching difference. At the end of ch. viii. we read that David's sons were his *cohanim*, his confidential ministers. His family was then happy and united, and his children were the chief stay of his throne. At the end of ch. xx. it is a stranger, Ira the Jairite, who is *cohen*, David's private counsellor. His sons have all lost their father's respect, and the numerous children who had once been his pride are now a terror to him and a cause of unhappiness. Perhaps in this mention of Ira as David's *cohen* we may find an explanation of the fact that all David's elder children were passed by, and the succession to the throne given to Solomon, who at this time was but eleven or twelve years old. For if no one was any longer fit to be entrusted with the office of *cohen*, still less was he fit to be king. But we also see the fitting punishment of the king's polygamy. David had set a bad example in multiplying unto himself wives, and he reaped from it an evil harvest. His son and successor was even more sensual, and his many wives wrought also his ruin.

The remaining four chapters have no internal connection with one another, nor are they placed in chronological order. For ch. xxii., which is virtually identical with Ps. xviii., was written shortly after Toi's embassy (ch. viii. 10); the "last words" in ch. xxiii. belong to the very close of David's reign; while the execution of Saul's descendants, the battles with the Philistines, and the numbering of the people record events which happened in the earlier years of the kingdom. The "last words" give us the assurance that David's closing years were tranquil, and spent in an unbroken walk with God. The storms of his life were over, and so also was his enjoyment of the pleasures of victorious war and of royal state and magnificence. But his sin had been forgiven him. There was peace in his own heart and undiminished trust in God. Time would never quite heal his sorrow at the death of son after son, caused alike by his own sin and theirs. If Saul had wrought the ruin of his kingdom, David had wrought the ruin of his family and home. But the one was stubborn in his perverseness, the other was humbled and penitent, and his sin was taken away. And now, calm and thankful, he was approaching the haven of eternal rest in Jehovah, and the enjoyment of that " everlasting covenant, ordered in all things and sure, which was all his salvation and all his desire " (ch. xxiii. 5). It was the peaceful end of a troubled life; and it makes us confident that he had been accepted, and that the words of his penitential psalms came from his heart. And we, when we recite them, may feel sure that we are using the words of one who, if he had sinned much, had also been forgiven much, because he had a large love for God, warm genuine piety, and deep and earnest penitence.

THE SECOND
BOOK OF SAMUEL

—◆◆—

EXPOSITION

CHAPTER I.

Ver. 1.—Now it came to pass. During the last few days events had been crowding fast upon one another. Living as fugitives at Ziklag, in the land of the Philistines, David and his men, unfit for the peaceful occupations of agriculture, had been driven to seek their maintenance by raids upon the wild tribes in the desert. Of these the chief were the Amalekites, whose home was the bare region lying between the south of Judah and Egypt. We have ample proof that this race was utterly hostile to all order and quietness; it lived by the plunder of others, and, sheltering itself in the recesses of the wilderness, broke out thence on every opportunity to carry ravage and ruin into all the neighbouring districts. The Amalekite was thus every man's enemy, and the object of universal dislike; and the cruelty which he habitually practised would justify to David's mind the barbarity with which he put to death all whom he found, man and woman alike. But his object was not justice. His cruelty was the result of selfish motives. For it was necessary for him to keep tidings of his real doings from the ears of Achish, who naturally would not approve of David's military activity. He very probably had put him there upon the borders to protect his realm from incursions; but David in the Amalekite war was the assailant, and was, moreover, practising his men for ulterior objects. Achish most probably received a share of the captured cattle; but his inquiries were met with an equivocation (1 Sam. xxvii. 10—12), which made him suppose that David, with the usual bitterness of a renegade, had been harrying his own tribesmen. And the falsehood soon entangled David in most painful consequences; for Achish, nothing doubting of his fidelity, and of his bitter hatred of Saul, determined

to take him with him in the grand army of the Philistines, which was slowly moving northward for the conquest of the land of Israel. David had God's promise of ultimate safety, and he ought not to have deserted his country. As a deserter to the Philistines, he had to descend to falsehood, and now treason seemed inevitable. His only choice lay between betraying his country or the king who had given him so hospitable a refuge. The jealousy, or rather the good sense, of the Philistine lords (1 Sam. xxix. 4) saved him from this dreadful alternative, and he was sent back, to his great joy, to Ziklag. But it was a dreadful sight which there met his view. With strange mismanagement, he had left no portion of his men to guard his little city, and the Amalekites had made reprisals. The news of the Philistine army upon its march upwards would be quickly carried through the desert, and the wild tribes would be sure to take the opportunity for gathering plunder far and wide. So undefended was the whole country, that they met nowhere with resistance. And David saw, on his return, only the smoking ruins of the little city where for many months he had dwelt. His wives, Ahinoam and Abigail, the wives and children of his men, had all been carried away for the Egyptian slave-market. So secure were the Amalekites, that they had no fear about encumbering their march with a vast multitude of children and cattle. And to add to his distress, his men, indignant, and not without reason, at David's want of precaution, were threatening to stone him as an alleviation for their distress. Never had David's fortunes fallen so low as at that moment; but quickly they were to rise again. By energetic action he not only recovered the spoil and the captives taken from Ziklag, but also won the immense wealth gathered by the Amalekites in a wide raid made at a time when there was no one to resist them. His own share of the spoil was so large that he was able to send valuable presents of sheep, oxen, and camels to his friends in Judæa, probably not without some prescience that the way to his return might be opened by the events of the war between the Philistines and Saul. The dangerous issues of that war could not be hidden from him; but he would find solace for his anxieties in the active work of restoring order at Ziklag, and in providing hasty shelter for the women and children whom he had brought back to their desolated homes. But his suspense did not last long. For when **David had abode two days in Ziklag**, news came which confirmed his worst fears. The battle had been fought; Israel had been routed; and Saul and Jonathan, the friend who had been to him more than a brother, lay among the slain.

Ver. 2.—**On the third day.** This means the third day after David's return with the spoil and captives recovered from the Amalekites. If we study the data, we find that David had marched with Achish as far as Aphek in the plain of Jezreel (1 Sam. xxix. 1), opposite to which, on the rising ground near Gilboa, Saul had posted his army. A march of three days had brought him back to Ziklag (1 Sam. xxx. 1), and after the shortest possible delay he had started in pursuit of the Amalekites. The rapidity of his movements is proved by so large a proportion of his hardy men falling out of the ranks at the brook Besor; but nevertheless some time must have been lost at Ziklag in discovering the greatness of their disaster, in searching for any who might possibly have escaped, in getting food, and in mustering again together for the pursuit. Near the brook they seem to have found the Egyptian slave who became their guide, and who had been abandoned three days before David found him. It follows, therefore, that the Amalekites were then three days' march in advance, and however rapidly the pursuit was urged on, we cannot allow less than five days for it, and one for the battle (vers. 12, 13, 17). The march homeward would take a longer time, as David was now encumbered with flocks and herds, women and children. If it took eight days, the time occupied in it by the Amalekites, the whole period that had elapsed since David was sent away from Aphek by the Philistine lords would be eighteen or nineteen days; and it is thus evident that the Amalekites were plundering Ziklag at the very time when he was being dismissed, half angry, half rejoicing, at the slight put upon him, but little thinking of the sad need there was for his presence elsewhere. Now, the messenger from Gilboa, if an active runner, would easily traverse in two days the dis-

tance which David and his men had travelled in three. And thus it follows that the battle at Gilboa was fought on the very day of David's happy return from the pursuit, and about nineteen days after the review at Aphek. If the word "to-morrow" in 1 Sam. xxviii. 19 seems to imply a more rapid march of events, we must remember that the meaning of the word in Hebrew is more indefinite than with us (comp. Gen. xxx. 33; Exod. xiii. 14). **With his clothes rent, and earth upon his head.** Though the Amalekite came **out of the camp**, yet we are not to suppose that he had been one of the combatants. Every army is followed by a vast number of vagabonds, intent upon gain, purchasing of the troops their booty, plundering wherever they have the chance, and carrying on a lucrative but illicit trade. He was more probably a sort of gipsy sutler than, as many suppose, the slave of some Israelite. He professes, however, to be upon Israel's side, and appears with the usual marks of sorrow. By so doing he hoped to commend himself to David, whom he knew to be too patriotic to rejoice at the defeat of his countrymen, though he doubted not that he would hear with joy of the death of so inveterate a personal enemy as Saul. On this account, and because the way would now stand open to David's ambition, he evidently felt sure of receiving a large guerdon for his news. There is, moreover, a further interest in his conduct; for it demonstrates the existence of a widespread popular feeling that David was destined to be Israel's king. It was this conviction which made him give David kingly honour; for **he fell to the earth, and did obeisance.** And all Israel, on the morrow after the defeat, would probably have done the same, but for David's own conduct. Israel was too high-spirited a nation to take at once for a king a man who had marched with their enemies to fight against them, even though they knew that the voice of prophecy had appointed him to inherit Saul's throne.

Ver. 3.—**Out of the camp of Israel am I escaped.** Non-combatants would hang about the army, watching, as soon as the battle had begun, the fortunes of the day, and immediately that they saw the impending defeat of their own side, would think chiefly of their personal safety. But for an active young man the opportunity would then have come for booty. The Philistines, in pursuit of the enemy, would soon leave the battlefield in their rear, and multitudes would quickly prowl about it to plunder the dead. While so busied, the Amalekite falsely represents himself as having come by chance upon the wounded, but still living, Saul.

Ver. 6.—**As I happened by chance upon**

Mount Gilboa. The story of the Amalekite is at variance with the account of Saul's death given in the last chapter of the preceding book. There, sore pressed and wounded by archers, hopeless of escape, and unable to make any further resistance, in sore distress at the death of his sons and the loss of the battle, Saul and his armour-bearer fall upon their own swords. Here, closely pursued by chariots and horsemen, the king is so utterly deserted by all his body-guard that he calls to a vagabond prowling about for booty to slay him. Naturally, Ewald and his followers, who regard the books of the Bible as mere patchwork, find here the marks of different narrators, whose stories the compiler of the Book of Samuel pieced together without having the shrewdness to observe that they were utterly irreconcilable. Some modern commentators have, however, attempted to harmonize them with little success. Really, the story of the Amalekite is a most improbable fiction, and utterly untrue. He knew nothing as to the manner of Saul's death, but found the body, probably some time after the king had fallen; and he was able to strip it because the pursuing Philistines were hurrying forward to make their victory complete, without being aware of what was the crowning glory of their success. As the pursuit advanced it would soon become safe for the Amalekite and others like him to try and secure some of the booty before the Philistines returned. Archers shooting from a distance might easily so distress Saul as to make him despair of escape—and it appears from the first narrative that they had not recognized him; for Saul is afraid lest they should do so, and, having taken him alive, should "abuse," or make a mock of him. Here chariots and horsemen are in close pursuit, and the king faces them grimly; nevertheless, they allow a stranger, who would not have dared to mix himself up with the battle, to rob them of their prize. We may feel sure that it was not until the tide of battle had moved onward in pursuit that the Amalekite ventured upon the field to rob the dead. When so occupied he came upon a corpse, now for some brief space dead, and at once recognized the tall form of the king, whose identity was made more plain by the golden circlet upon his helmet. At once he saw the chance of larger gains, and hastily tearing off the royal crown and the bracelet from the fallen monarch, without a thought of rescuing the remains from the indignities which the Philistines were sure to inflict upon them, he hurried away with his tidings. Of course, he knew nothing of David's recent conduct, nor that for some time he had accompanied the invading army, nor that Ziklag had just experienced rough treatment from his own countrymen. Still, if he had told the truth, he would have fared well; for he brought news of great importance. But truth was not a virtue much practised in those days, and, fancying that the treatment he had met with from Saul would fill David's heart with bitter rancour against him, the Amalekite invented this story of his having slain the king with his own hands, in the expectation that it would win for him a double reward.

Ver. 9.—**Anguish.** This word, which occurs only in this place, comes from a root signifying to entwine or knot together. On this account Jewish commentators explain it of cramp, which often follows upon loss of blood; but it is equally possible that it means vertigo, or giddiness, when things seem to dance or interweave themselves together before the eyes. The next words signify, **For yet is my life whole within me,** and give the reason why Saul asked the Amalekite to slay him. The story is at least plausible. It represents the king as deserted by his army, even to the last man, and with the Philistine cavalry and chariots in close pursuit. He is not mortally wounded, but, as giddiness prevents his escape, there is danger of his falling alive into the enemy's hand; and as they would probably not have killed him, but carried him in triumph through their cities, the way would still have been blocked against David's succession. The fear of this indignity would account for Saul's earnest appeal to the Amalekite to slay him, and, so requested, it seemed right to put him to death, instead of trying to carry him off to a place of safety. But all this was merely to keep up appearances, and in his heart he doubted not that David would regard it as a signal service that his enemy was put out of the way.

Ver. 10.—**After that he was fallen;** Hebrew, *after his fall;* that is, his defeat; for Saul was standing and supporting himself with his spear. The **crown,** probably, was a narrow band of gold encircling the royal helmet. **Bracelet.** We read of "bracelets" in Numb. xxxi. 50, in the enumeration of the spoil taken from the Midianites, and there too apparently they were the ornaments of warriors. In the Assyrian monuments chiefs are generally represented with ornaments upon their wrists and arms (see Layard, 'Nineveh,' etc., pl. 18).

Ver. 12.—**They mourned, and wept, and fasted.** The sight of Saul's royal insignia was clear proof of Israel's disaster; and this sorrow of David and his men shows how true their hearts were to their country, and how unbearable would have been their position had not the prudence of the Philistine lords extricated them from the difficulty in which they had been placed by David's want of faith. But David had other reasons besides patriotism for sorrow. Personally he had lost the truest of friends, and even Saul had a place in his heart. For he would contrast with his terrible death the early glories of his reign, when all Israel honoured him as its deliverer from the crushing yoke of foreign bondage, and when David was himself one of the most trusty of his captains. Otto von Gerlach compares David thus weeping over the fall of his implacable enemy with David's Son weeping over Jerusalem, the city whose inhabitants were his bitter foes, and who not only sought his death, but delivered him up to the Romans, to be scourged and spitefully intreated, and slain upon the cross.

Ver. 15.—**Go near, and fall upon him.** This was no hasty sentence, for they had "fasted until even." And before pronouncing it David asks, "Whence art thou?" that is, he makes more full inquiry into his condition and previous doings. He knew that he was an Amalekite, and most probably had seen clearly enough that his whole story was false; but before deciding upon his fate, he desired fuller information as to the man's previous life. His question elicits from him that he was a subject of Saul. For the word "stranger" means a settler, who had withdrawn from his own country and joined himself to Israel. Moreover, it was the Amalekite's father who had done this, and probably he was one of many, who, finding their old nomad life too dangerous, had sought a home in the southern districts of Judah; but when the war broke out, the old instinct of these Bedaween made them follow the army for pilfer and trade in spoil. But as the son of a settler, the Amalekite owed by birth allegiance to Saul, and, should the occasion arise, was bound to render him loyal aid. Now, according to his own account, he had found Saul in no immediate danger of death, "for his life was still whole within him." Escape was at least possible with the Amalekite's aid, but he is eager to kill him. And David's question, "How wast thou not afraid . . . to destroy the Lord's anointed?" virtually means, "How wast thou not afraid to kill thy own king?" The Lord, that is, Jehovah, was no name of power to any outside 'the covenant people, nor in settling in Judæa did the Amalekites accept the national religion. But the words would show even to a stranger that Saul was Israel's lawful and consecrated king. Commentators, with strange perverseness, have found in these words an outbreak of selfishness on David's part, and have supposed that he wished to guard his own person against future treason by making a wholesome example. But this is both to

misunderstand the examination of the culprit summed up in vers. 13, 14, and also to put aside all account of the deep and agonizing sorrow which was rending David's heart. What would have been an Englishman's feelings if news had come that we had lost, for instance, the battle of Waterloo, and if the fugitive who brought the information had said that he had killed the wounded commander-in-chief? In David's case, besides deep distress at the disaster which had befallen his country, there was personal grief for the death of Jonathan and of Saul's other sons, who were David's brothers-in-law; and the words really prove his loyalty to Saul himself. He was still Jehovah's anointed, whatever his conduct might have been; and we have found David on previous occasions actuated by the same generous respect for duty when clearly it was contrary to his own interests (see, for instance, 1 Sam. xxvi. 9). David put the wretch justly to death for meanly murdering one whom he might possibly have saved. And the man's very purpose was to suggest to David, in a covert way, that escape really was possible, but that he had made all things sure, and so deserved a large reward. As a matter of fact, he had not killed Saul, but had invented the story because, judging David by his own immoral standard, he had supposed that he would regard the crime as a valuable service.

Ver. 17.—**David lamented with this lamentation.** The Hebrew word for "lamentation" is *kinah*, a technical term for an elegy or poem commemorative of the dead. Thus Jeremiah wrote a *kinah* in memory of King Josiah (2 Chron. xxxv. 25); and there is little doubt that the "lamentations" there spoken of were a collection of dirges, in which probably this ode written by David held an honoured place. In ch. iii. 33, 34 we have a short *kinah* in Abner's honour, which possibly formed part of a longer poem, of which those two verses only are quoted as sufficing to prove, not only David's innocence, but also his indignation at Joab's foul deed. In both these places we have remains of David's secular poetry, and find it marked by the same strong emotion and the same sublimity of thought as distinguish his psalms. We observe also the nobleness of David's nature in his total silence concerning himself, and 'his generous eulogy, not of Jonathan only, but also of Saul. The mean envy and the implacable jealousy of the latter are no more remembered, and he sees in him, not the personal foe, but the brave king who has fallen in his country's cause.

Ver. 18.—**Also he bade them teach the children of Judah** [the use of] **the bow.** The old view is that given by the inserted words, and is well put by Ephrem Syrus in his commentary upon the passage. He says that, as Israel's defeat at Gilboa was the presage of a long struggle, and as the Philistines had gained the victory there by their skill in archery, David used his utmost authority with his own tribe to get them to practise this art for their protection in future wars. This explanation would be plausible were it not that we have reason for believing that the Israelites were already skilful in the use both of the sling and the bow, in both of which the Benjamites especially excelled (1 Chron xii. 2). The modern view is that given in the Revised Version, where the inserted words are "the song of" the bow. "The Bow" is thus the name of the elegy, taken from the allusion to Jonathan's skill in the use of that weapon (ver. 22; comp. 1 Sam. xviii. 4; xx. 36); and the meaning is that David made his own tribesmen, who were probably ill disposed to Saul and his family, learn this dirge, not so much for its preservation, as to make them give the fallen king due honour. Similarly Exod. iii. is called "The Bush" in Mark xii. 26. **The book of Jasher.** See on this book Josh. x. 13, where the Syriac Version calls it "The Book of Canticles," and understands by it a collection of national ballads commemorative of the brave deeds of Israelite heroes. Jasher literally means "upright," and the Book of Jasher would be equivalent to "Hero-book," the Hebrews always looking to the moral rather than the physical prowess of their great men.

Ver. 19.—**The beauty of Israel.** The word *zebi* means both "beauty" and also "the gazelle." Ewald takes it in the second sense, and explains it of Jonathan. "everywhere the first in courage, in activity, and speed; slender also and of well-made figure, and whose personal beauty and swiftness of foot in attack or retreat gained for him among the troops the name of 'the gazelle.' The Syriac Version also translates 'gazelle,'" but Ephrem says that the whole Israelite nation is meant, the flower of whose manhood lay slaughtered on Mount Gilboa. Which signification we take must really depend upon the meaning we attach to the words, "thy high place;" and these in the Authorized Version have nothing to refer to, and so become unmeaning. The Revised Version follows the Vulgate in taking Israel as a vocative, and renders, "Thy glory, O Israel, is slain upon thy high places." The sense would thus be that given by Ephrem, Israel's glory being its "mighty" men or heroes, its warriors slain upon Mount Gilboa with their king. But ver. 25 makes it plain that the "high places" are Jonathan's, and not those of the nation; and the more correct rendering is "O beauty [or, 'gazelle'] of Israel, slain upon thy high places! how

are the heroes fallen!" Thus Jonathan is certainly meant, and the heroes are the young prince and his father; and as the hunted antelope is said to return to its lair in the mountains, and there await its death, "gazelle" is probably the right rendering. In a dirge in honour of Saul and Jonathan we may be pretty sure that Jonathan would be referred to in its opening words, and the camp-name of his friend would bring back to David's mind many a brave feat wrought together, and many a pleasant hour of companionship in past years.

Ver. 20.—**Gath . . . Askelon.** By thus localizing the triumph, and bringing before the mind the thought of multitudes in these well-known places rejoicing with dance and song over the news of their victory, a more affecting picture is produced by the contrast with Israel's distress than could have been effected by mere generalizations. Probably, too, there was present in David's mind the remembrance of scenes which he had witnessed in these towns. In course of time, "Tell it not in Gath" became a proverb (Micah i. 10). **The daughters.** It is the custom in the East for the women to celebrate the prowess of the nation's warriors (Exod. xv. 20; 1 Sam. xviii. 6; Ps. lxviii. 11 Revised Version). **Uncircumcised.** For some unknown reason, this word is used as a term of reproach, especially of the Philistines (1 Sam. xiv. 6; xvii. 26).

Ver. 21.—**Fields of offerings;** Hebrew, *fields of terumoth.* The terumoth were heave offerings (Lev. vii. 14, 32), and .the Vulgate, regarding these as thank offerings, translates, "Fields of firstfruits." The sense would thus be, "Fields of corn such as was used for heave offerings." Still, this gives us no suitable meaning; for Gilboa was not a place fit for the growth of corn; and Theodoret, in his version, has preserved a different reading, which is probably right, namely, "Ye fields and mountains of death." **The shield . . . is vilely cast away.** This rendering contains a classical idea derived from the Greeks and Romans, among whom it was a disgrace for a soldier to return without his shield. But this imputes personal cowardice to Saul—a reproach which is entirely undeserved; for he did not cast away his shield, but remained steadfast unto death. The right translation is, "For there the shield of heroes, yea, the shield of Saul, was defiled," stained, that is, with blood. We have no proof whatsoever that the Israelites had the same notion as the Greeks, and if they had, David would certainly not have put such a stigma upon the fallen king. [As though he had] not [been] **anointed with oil.** By rejecting the inserted words, we get the original, with all its simplicity, but with all its difficulty.

"There the shield of the heroes was defiled:
The shield of Saul not anointed with oil."

The interpretation put upon these words
in the Authorized Version is taken from the
Vulgate, no mean authority, but it is one
which cannot be reconciled with the Hebrew,
where it is not Saul, but his shield, which is
referred to. It was a Jewish custom to
anoint the shield with oil before a battle
(Isa. xxi. 5), in order probably to make the
missiles of the enemy glance off from it without injury. And bearing this in mind, David
now contrasts the sad issue of the battle
with the hopes with which the warrior had
in old times gone forth to war. Then his
shield glistened brightly; now it was defiled
with blood. In the Revised Version the
rendering, "vilely cast away," is retained,
the Revisers not having perceived that
"defiled," which they have placed in the
margin, is absolutely required for the text
by the contrast with "the shield not
anointed with oil."

Ver. 22.—**From the blood of the slain.** In
old time, Saul and Jonathan had been victorious warriors, who had returned from the
battle-field stained with the blood of their
enemies: from this battle they return no
more, and their weapons have lost their old
renown.

Ver. 23.—**Lovely and pleasant.** The words
of the Authorized Version contain a beautiful antithesis, which, however, does not exist
in the Hebrew, which celebrates the close
union of father and son in life as well as in
death.

"Saul and Jonathan, the lovely and pleasant,
Neither in their lives nor in their death
were they divided."

Notwithstanding Saul's rash vow, Jonathan
had ever been his father's faithful friend
and companion, nor had his affection for
David made him untrue to the ties of natural
affection. And David generously commends
his friend for thus acting.

Ver. 24.—**Ye daughters of Israel.** In old
time, the women of Israel had celebrated
Saul's triumphs (ver. 20), but now it is
their sad office to bewail his death. And a
touching reason is given for their sorrow.
During Saul's reign the condition of the

women had greatly improved. When a
nation is in the miserable plight described
in 1 Sam. xiii. 19—22, there is neither
safety nor comfort for the weak; but when
the strong arm of Saul had won freedom for
Israel, the women were the first to reap the
benefit, and "their scarlet clothing with
delights," that is, their delightful or delicate
clothing of bright colours and their golden
ornaments, prove that the nation had made
a great advance in prosperity and culture
during the happier years of Saul's reign.

Ver. 26.—**Thy love to me was wonderful.**
Never was there a purer friendship than that
of Jonathan for David. It began just after
the combat with Goliath, when the young
prince, instead of seeing in David a rival,
who had equalled his own feat of valour,
took him to his heart, put upon him his
own robe and armour, and thus presented
him to the army as his friend and brother.
Nor did his father's hatred of David, nor
the knowledge that David was to inherit
the kingdom, interfere with his love. He
remained a dutiful son to his father, and
accepted his inferior position with magnanimity, without once seeing in David cause
for blame; and it surpassed the love of
women, because, to requite their devotion,
they look for protection and homage, the
more delightful because it is paid by the
strong to the weak. But here the lives of
the two friends could not combine in one
happy fusion of mutual union. Their hearts
were bound together, but a hard fate, of
which they were fully aware, made the ruin
of the one the certain result of the happiness
of the other. Nevertheless, Jonathan, with
everything to lose, and David with everything to gain, remained true and loyal
friends.

Ver. 27.—**How are the mighty fallen!**
This lament, which occurs three times, is
the central thought of the elegy. Glorious
and noble in their past lives, the heroes had
now fallen, not as Wolfe fell at Quebec, with
the shout of victory in his ears, but in the
lost battle. And David seeks relief for his
distress in dwelling upon the sad contrast
between the splendid victories which Saul
had won for Israel when first chosen to be
king, and the terrible defeat by which life
and kingdom had now been lost.

HOMILETICS.

Vers. 1—10.—The facts of this section may be stated thus: 1. David having retired
to Ziklag during the conflict between Israel and the Philistines, a messenger from the
seat of war comes to pay him homage. 2. David, being as yet in ignorance of the event
on Gilboa, and being impressed by the signs of mourning on the stranger, is prompted
to ask whence he came. 3. Eager to ascertain further information, he learns from the
Amalekite, not only that Saul and Jonathan were dead, but that, according to the

stranger's story, the former had been killed by the hand of the narrator.   4. In evidence of the truth of his story, the man produces Saul's crown and bracelet.

Waiting on Providence.   David's retirement at Ziklag is to be regarded in connection with his well-established conviction that he was the chosen servant destined to occupy a foremost place in establishing the kingdom of God, and his persistent resolve not to take a single step of his own devising that would seem to force on the removal of Saul from the throne, in order to secure thereby his own elevation.   Events had forced him into a quasi-public position as the rival of Saul, much as he disclaimed all rivalry; and now, in a foreign land, with a following not of his own seeking, and sensible that a crisis was at hand, he felt that he could do nothing but maintain a resolute inactivity, leaving the issue of impending events to Providence.   A belief in Providence is very common; in word men express their dependence on it, and there are seasons in human life when, perhaps, all we can do is to wait on Providence.   There is, however, a false, even wicked, waiting, which is but another name for idleness or fatalism, or vague looking for some lucky chance.   Considering the case of David, we can trace some of the features of a true waiting on Providence.   There is—

I. DEEP CONVICTION OF BEING DEVOTED TO A HOLY CAUSE.   Life is devoted to a Divine, not a merely human, purpose.   This was pre-eminently characteristic of David at this time.   He was conscious of being personally identified with the working out of God's holy purpose towards mankind.   He had passed out of the realm of self-seeking into the kingdom of God, and in public and private lived for God.   Here lies the beginning of our right and privilege to wait on Providence.   As our Lord's life was a nobler instance of consecration to a holy cause than was David's, so now ours may be an instance less conspicuous than his, though in our measure as real.   It is possible for us to be one with Christ and his kingdom—absorbed, amidst even private and domestic life, with the purpose dear to his heart.   Our life gains power and glory only in proportion as we are enabled to cherish a well-founded conviction that we are not living for merely temporal and material considerations, but for God, and in that sense are his chosen servants for specific purposes, as truly as was David when, in retirement at Ziklag, he knew he was the chosen King of Israel.

II. FREEDOM FROM SELFISH AND MALEVOLENT DESIRES.   David desired not elevation for the sake of personal gratification; nor did he desire disaster for Saul that a great obstacle to his own advance might be put aside.   Men consecrated to God are open to the subtle temptation of desiring events to move on so as to promote their own personal ease at the cost of much that is sacred.   Under plea of greater usefulness, we may long for Providence to open a pathway for us, when, if motives are severely scrutinized, there is discovered a secret longing for personal gratification.   The interlacings of human life are such that the displacement of one may be a pre-requisite to the freer action and wider usefulness of another; and one whose course is hampered by obstacles may almost unconsciously cherish the wish that some event may happen which, by the trouble and loss it brings to another, will promote his own interests.   No one truly waits on Providence who cherishes this spirit.   The man of business who, amidst difficulties, looks out eagerly for the downfall of others as a means of his own improved chance in competition, must not flatter himself that all along he has been quietly waiting on Providence.   It often requires very high religious principle to labour on in obscurity, blessed by apparently few results, with a calm trust in God untainted by the desire that others, possibly less worthy in character, may be swept away by resistless events to make more room for ourselves.   David's sentiments towards Saul, who stood in his pathway, are full of instruction to all.

III. RECOGNITION OF GOD'S CEASELESS CONTROL OVER OBSTACLES, AND OF HIS STEADILY UNFOLDING PURPOSES.   Most probably David's followers, knowing as they did that Saul stood between him and the throne, often marvelled at his patient inactivity.   But by a keener spiritual vision than they possessed, he recognized the perfect control of the God he served, and had amazing faith in the sure though slow unfolding of his purposes.   Hence he could wait and be still.   This quality has always entered largely into the character of those who have done great service in the interests of truth and righteousness.   Our Saviour, during his earthly life, was a conspicuous instance.   He was despised, rejected, of the people there were none with him, and events seemed to the minds of his disciples (John xiv. 1; xvi. 19—22; Luke xxiv. 21) to be disastrous to his cause; and yet all through he never distrusted the Father, and in fulness of confidence could anticipate the results of a steady unfolding of the Divine purpose (John x. 16). So likewise we in secular and spiritual affairs may be said to wait on Providence when, in spite of difficulties that almost crush out our life, we, being conscious of oneness with Christ, stagger not in our belief in the all-controlling wisdom and power, and rest in the certainty of an order of things which is being directed towards the realization of the Divine purposes with which our entire life is identified. "Have faith in God." He slumbers not; he sleeps not; he works, and who shall let?

IV. READINESS FOR ACTION, REGULATED BY RESOLVE ONLY TO ACT IN HARMONY WITH HIGHEST LAW. David was ready to act whenever occasion offered; but he would not create occasion, and that because he saw that, in the continuance of Saul's life and reign, there was involved a great principle. For had he not been chosen by God? and was not God now allowing him to work out his own chastisement in harmony with far-reaching moral laws? David could only act in harmony with the Divine law which seemed to be expressed in Saul's sad life—namely, the removal of the unworthy by a natural process. There was a reserve of power in Christ during his life among men which could have accomplished startling results had he put it forth—just as David could have precipitated events by putting forth his strength against Saul—but he restrained himself. He was patient, and abstained from any action that would run counter to the moral and physical laws by which God was then governing mankind. On the same principle he now carries on his work in the world. Men do not understand him when they look for an extension of Christianity in violation of the laws of moral and social life which God has ordained. We are entrusted with more power than it is fit to put forth. Its exercise is to be regulated by regard to law. Especially in embarrassed circumstances, when it seems as though, in our business, our domestic affairs, or Church action, we could make marked advance by a vigorous effort in a given direction, does it become us to ask whether such action would be in harmony with the law of righteousness. During the sorrows of the Church (Luke xxi. 9—21), when it seemed as though active resistance by the sword was essential to self-preservation, the disciples were to be patient, and not run counter to the law of the gospel by endeavouring to maintain a kingdom of peace by carnal weapons. We must wait for God, be ready to act when action will harmonize with the holy laws of God's government.

V. JUDICIOUS USE OF TIME, AS JUSTIFIED BY THE CIRCUMSTANCES OF OUR POSITION. David could not act against Saul; he could not benefit Israel by seeking to rid them of an unworthy ruler; but he could seek to remedy the evils caused by the Amalekites at Ziklag (1 Sam. xxx. 1, 26), and also discipline and organize his adherents (1 Chron. xii.), and so put himself and his men in a position to move towards Palestine when God opened the way. The disciples of Christ were powerless to act on the world for some weeks after his death, but they cherished faith in their Lord, and, till the time appointed by Providence came, they wisely kept together for prayer and mutual encouragement (Acts i. 14; cf. ii. 1—13). The Christian Church may believe itself called to enter on a great missionary enterprise in an at-present inaccessible country. It must not violate the laws of God by rushing into disaster under plea of promoting a good cause, but must gather up materials and become ready to enter in when a higher power opens the way. The same principle applies to our extension of business, our entering on new or wider professions, and especially if we are ambitious to consecrate ourselves to the work of the Christian ministry. Those who, after the example of David, wait on Providence, will find in the end that the ways of God, though apparently slow and often trying to patience, are indicated by the issue.

A subtle temptation. The Amalekite who came to David may be regarded as an instance of a quick-witted cunning man, observant of facts affecting the interests of others, and swiftly ingenious to work them up into a plausible form, ostensibly for the advantage of strangers, but really for his own advancement and material gain. He knew just enough of the outward development of the kingdom of God to see in events an opportunity for making them subservient to his own purposes. Like some of the present day, who are aliens to the spiritual Christian commonwealth, but who scruple not to make a profession of some interest in it a means of attaining to social position and material prosperity, so did he pay honour to the chosen servant of God for what he could gain thereby. But the main point in his conduct centres on David. He came practically in the form of a tempter to one who had long been under the force of strong temptation to desire and seek the removal from position, if not from life, of one who had been both an ungrateful enemy and an obstacle to the carrying out of his life's mission. We have seen in our comments on the First Book of Samuel how bravely David had withstood all the influences which urged to action against Saul. He had triumphed, and was now calmly waiting on Providence at Ziklag. But now the hand of Providence was being manifested without any action of his own. For does not this stranger declare the great news that the miserable king was fallen; that by an act of his own he had saved Israel from the shame of his dying directly under Philistine hands; and that the crown—the symbol of authority—was now within David's own camp? Is there not here, then, release from the severe tension of self-restraint which for years had been put on thought and deed? Now surely David may breathe freely, and even bless God and take courage! Gratitude to such a newsbearer was surely due, and a sobered gladness may legitimately be cherished! Let us, then, consider the nature of subtle temptations.

I. THEY MAY SPRING FROM UNLOOKED-FOR SOURCES, AND SO TAKE US OFF OUR GUARD. Who would have supposed that an Amalekite—a man whose tribe had been in conflict with David—would have appeared before him as bearer of news most momentous as affecting his future career? The apparent disinterestedness of one who could not be a partisan would render David open to the natural effect of the tidings on an ordinary heart. So in our life subtle temptations, calling us to no ostensible act of wrong, spring up we know not how, and take us by surprise. It may be an evil thought is suddenly obtruded in a line of ordinary thought; or a friend hints at a possibility without suggesting a deed or a feeling; or a set of facts start before the observing faculty, conveying, by their convergence on a matter of special interest to us, an impulse to cherish a definite class of feelings which, when examined in cool moments, is found to be essentially unholy. "Watch and pray, lest ye enter into temptation," was an exhortation based on a profound knowledge of the manifold avenues along which subtle promptings to evil may enter into and possess the soul.

II. THEY MAY NOT CALL TO ANY DEFINITE ACTION. In this case David was even relieved, by the fact of the tidings, from the pressure that had so long been on him to take action for his own advancement. Whatever appeal there was in the temptation was simply to the seat of feeling. The constitutional weakness of man is to feel satisfaction when an enemy is removed, and, though conventional custom may lead us to say that that satisfaction is tempered by sadness, it is to be feared that in this there is more of form than reality. Many men would not see any temptation in this narrative. They cannot see that character lies in feeling cherished, more than in acts that manifestly violate some law of God or man. Incitements to deeds of open vice do not form the most dangerous evils of our lot. Satan ruins more by undermining than by direct assault. The weakening of the inner seat of purity and kindliness alone need not involve any deed or word known to our fellow-creatures.

III. THEY MAY PRESENT THEMSELVES UNDER COVER OF CONSIDERATIONS OF EXPEDIENCY. Judging from the standard that governs the lives of most men, the Amalekite imagined that his story would gratify David for two reasons—one, that hopes long cherished of being of service to Israel were soon to be realized; the other, that Saul was set aside by other hands than his own. There can be no doubt but that, in proportion to the strength of his hope of some day being the means of raising Israel from the sorrows which had come by the misrule of Saul, so would be the tendency to rejoice in its speedy realization; and this he knew would be legitimate. Hence, although, as a kindly good man, he might well abstain from cherishing any secret satisfaction at the disaster which had befallen Saul, yet, in view of the beneficial issues about to flow from the event, would there not be valid ground for so doing? Was not the welfare of the nation of more importance than sentiment for an individual? And could he not distinguish between malicious joy, and satisfaction in the rising of public good out of personal disaster? It is thus easy for one nation to find, by a swift process of thought, plausible pretext for satisfaction in the calamities of another nation. Possibly our

Church life is not free from the subtle temptation, when we observe, in the decay of rival parties or denominations, a probable increase to the strength of our own. Business men may argue that benefits to society arise from the downfall of houses trading on an insecure basis, and so cover the real character of the personal satisfaction entertained. We need to be much on our guard when the reasoning powers are stimulated to justify sentiments which in their simple nakedness would be instinctively abhorred by a very holy and loving nature. In moral matters the first judgments are safest.

IV. THEY DO NOT REVEAL OR SUGGEST THE IMMEDIATE AND REMOTE CONSEQUENCES OF YIELDING. The point of the temptation, as it fell on David's nature, was simply to develop a certain feeling of satisfaction that, as he could not and would not raise a hand against Saul, some one else, in a natural course of events, had been permitted by Providence to do so, and thus had secured the opening of the door for which he had been waiting. Now, this feeling, so natural to many men, so commonly cherished under kindred circumstances, even though a human weakness, was simply a private transitory sentiment passing over the inner life, and forming no feature in conduct. It seemed to begin and end there and then. Its presence, if permitted, was a trifle, and inflicted no injury on society. Thus, while other temptations on presentation startle the ordinary mind by being associated at once with damage to social position, or to family or nation, temptations of this class do not reveal or suggest at the time their consequences. Of course, evil is to be resisted as evil apart from effects; and a pure mind will immediately detect the essentially immoral nature of any internal incitement to transitory impurity of sentiment. But it is easier to many to detect and resist temptations of the other class. No doubt every deterioration of feeling does issue in disastrous consequences, as surely as do open acts of vice, only the subtle process escapes notice. Consequently many good men, forgetting this, often entertain suggested transitory feelings of evil, which, did they but duly consider the necessary deterioration of their entire life which thereupon sets in, they would carefully watch against and resist.

PRACTICAL LESSONS. 1. We ought to act at all times under the influence of the fact that at no hour are we free from the possibility of being subjected to very subtle temptations. 2. The more cultivated and tried our piety, the more likely is it that the trials of our religious purity will come in forms not suggestive of open acts of transgression. 3. Whenever the reasonings of expediency come in to justify the indulgence of sentiments of which doubt may have arisen as to their moral quality, we may safely be suspicious of fallacy, and so should close the debate at once. 4. It is very possible that a long season of persistent temptation to actual wrong, as in the case of David for years past, may culminate in a temptation more severe, because more difficult of detection, and which, if yielded to, would virtually undo the work of years of resistance. Therefore we need to be specially watchful when the end of our trials is near.

Vers. 11—27.—The facts of the section are: 1. Having become assured, through the testimony of the Amalekite, of the defeat of Israel in the death of Saul and Jonathan, David and his men spent the rest of the day in mourning. 2. On the morrow David examines the Amalekite as to the particulars of Saul's death, and being shocked at the sin and shame of slaying the Lord's anointed, he condemns the man to death. 3. Being left to his own reflections on the sad event which had happened to Israel, he composes an elegy, as an expression of his own feelings and for the use of Israel, in which he refers in impassioned language to (1) the greatness of the calamity; (2) its possible humiliation and shame to Israel should it become freely known in Philistine cities, and its future mournful associations with the locality in which it occurred; (3) the better qualities of Saul and Jonathan in their relation to their country and to each other; (4) the reason for sorrow even among the *non*-fighting members of the community, as they reflect on the improved personal comforts incident to Saul's reign; and (5) his special friendship with Jonathan, as the joy and solace of bygone years. The teaching of these facts and expressions of feeling may be summarized by embracing the public act of mourning for Saul and the poetic lament under one conception, and unfolding the various truths thus contained. But, in order to secure more consecution in dealing with those two items, we may consider first the teaching embodied in the conduct of the Amalekite in its contrast with that of David; and this can perhaps be best expressed by setting forth a contrast of states of mind. Hence notice—

Secularity and spirituality of mind in contrast. The conduct of the Amalekite was very natural, as we find men in general. So far as he had a policy, it would have commended itself to multitudes. Observant, shrewd, and on the alert for an advantage, he evidently was well aware of the feud between Saul and David; and knowing how of late David had smitten his own countrymen, he judged it more prudent to conciliate him by performing an act conducive to his elevation to a throne, than by simply purloining jewels on a battle-field. The story concocted about his actually slaying Saul was told with the utmost self-complacence, as though no one could doubt the mercifulness and the utility of the act; and no one could have been more amazed than himself when David represented the act as most shocking, and condemned him to die for such wicked temerity. On the other hand, David's conduct is the reverse of what would have been generally pursued. For Saul had been a most bitter and unrelenting enemy; had charged him with crimes most heinous; had driven him into a painful exile; had returned generosity by increased hatred; and was, as David knew, the only living obstacle to his return to Israel and elevation to the throne. And yet, not only had David been unwilling to do a single deed that might be construed as tending to weaken Saul's legitimate authority, but he now even deplores the reported action of this his would-be foreign helper, and charges him with having committed, on his own showing, a most shocking crime. Now, the contrast of the conduct and views of the two men is to be found in the utter dissimilarity of their respective habitual states of mind. The one was *intensely secular,* and the other *intensely spiritual.* Consider—

I. IN WHAT SECULARITY AND SPIRITUALITY OF MIND RESPECTIVELY CONSIST, AND HOW THEY EXPRESS THEMSELVES. 1. *The one consists mainly in the tendency to look at things out of their spiritual relations, and the other to look at them in those relations.* As a matter of fact, we know that, consequent on the existence of a supreme Being and a moral government which he exercises over spiritual beings, the whole universe is comprised of two distinct yet inter-related spheres—the material and perishable on the one hand, and the spiritual and imperishable on the other. As men necessitated to work out the first lines of our destiny under material conditions, and therefore in incessant contact with the perishable, we are, through the bluntness of our superior perceptions, superinduced by sin, prone to regard all events as pertaining to our fleeting earthly experience. This is secularity of mind—the mind that sees only the lower side of man's life, and takes no note of the higher destiny of which he is capable. On the other hand, spirituality of mind, while recognizing the value and Divine source of our common lot as creatures of struggle under material conditions, perceives the reality of the higher invisible sphere, and estimates all things in the lower according to its relation to the great facts and dominating laws of the higher. The Amalekite looked on Saul as simply a man belonging to a mundane order of things, in which other men were striving for the mastery with him. David saw the existence, alongside the mundane order, of an invisible kingdom, and he recognized in Saul an embodiment of a Divine principle—an institution of Divine authorization. For was he not the Lord's anointed? Was there not more in his existence than was comprised in range of Amalekite vision? Here lies the dividing line between the two great classes of men. The one sees a passing age, with its wants and struggles appropriate to that age; the other sees an invisible and enduring spiritual order, and that man is to be viewed in relation to that order. The one, therefore, is carnal, restricted in range, utilitarian, and in league with practices that "pay;" the other is religious, wide as infinity in range, pervaded by conscious supremacy of holy principles, and in alliance with only what is pure and pleasing before God. 2. In accordance with their essential nature, they will respectively manifest themselves at times, *the one in a use of sacred things for personal gain, and the other in self-abnegation out of reverence for what is Divine.* It was the purely secular mind of the Amalekite that led to his endeavour to make gain out of the death of the Lord's anointed, and that, too, without supposing that he was doing anything remarkable. It was David's high-toned spirituality that led him to ignore all the wrongs he had experienced at the hand of Saul, and to pass by the faults and follies of the unhappy monarch, and, instead of finding pleasure in prospect of his own coming promotion, to feel as though in the act done by the Amalekite a violence had been perpetrated against the most holy of institutions. So has it been in all ages, and is still. Men can barter religious professions for gain; or calmly and irreverently handle sacred subjects as though of common import; or behave in the presence of sacred realities as though treading on unhallowed ground. Judas, Simon Magus, the revilers at the cross, have their counterparts in those who seek gain by complying with the will of godless authorities, professional zealots for Christianity, and cynics who make sport of sacred things. 3. But, also, *it is a tendency which in each case gives colour to the entire life.* It was not a new thing for the Amalekite thus to think and feel concerning Saul and his relation to Israel and David; for all along Saul had been to him simply one of many rulers among men, and the conflict of the past years had been only a trial of human strength and skill. And, also, David's profound reverence for the Divine idea in Saul's kingship, and his faith in the reality of a Divine purpose for men being incorporated with it, had permeated his life during the weary days of exile. The two men were always governed by their respective tendencies. The one life was narrowed, rendered gross and hard by persistent secularity; the other was broadened, refined, and beautified by constant communion with the unseen and eternal. The whole domestic and private as well as public life of men is affected for the worse or better as they are secular or spiritual in tone. Spirituality is favourable to every phase of human experience. Secularity means debasement. Were society pervaded by so pure, unselfish, and spiritually perceptive a temper as was David's, and more so, David's greater Son, how smoothly would the machinery of life move on, and what music would there be in its roll!

II. THE FINAL RESULT OF INDULGING IN THESE OPPOSITE STATES OF MIND. As a fact, the Amalekite's zeal brought him disappointment—death. David's fine perception of the sanctities of life, his habitual reverence for Divine institutions as seen in all his relations to Saul, his consciousness that God was establishing his own kingdom in his own way,—all this issued in elevation to a position where spirituality of mind could be exercised for the greater good of Israel. Prophetic is this of the end of all secularity and spirituality. The one must end in disappointment—in loss of those things which it was thought would be gained, and even in judicial separation from the pure in heart (Matt. xvi. 26; vii. 21—23). The other is an education by which we become qualified to rise in the kingdom of God, to exercise over others a higher and wider influence than otherwise could be obtained (1 John iii. 2, 3; Matt. xxv. 23; 1 Tim. vi. 11, 12; Rom. iii. 21).

GENERAL LESSONS. 1. It is a dangerous thing to form our estimate of what others may do from the ideas and feelings that govern our own actions. The Amalekite could not conceive of any one not rejoicing in the death of a foe. 2. Dull perception of spiritual realities is a real impoverishment of life, as truly as is an affliction of blindness or deafness. 3. Regard for Divine institutions is to be cultivated irrespective of the imperfect character of men who act in connection with them. 4. The exposure of a base spirit is sure to be the result of a direct judgment of the Son of David when we are called to stand before him. 5. Any attempt to court the favour of the chosen King in Zion by deeds and spirit not in harmony with the holy laws of his kingdom, will inevitably end in banishment from his presence (Luke vi. 46; xiii. 25—27).

Sorrow for the miscarriage of life's great purpose. Contrary to what ordinary men would have imagined, the news of the death of Saul at once diverted David's thoughts from his own personal advantage accruing therefrom, and at once developed an extraordinary sorrow. It must not be concluded that the setting apart of the rest of the day for purposes of mourning (vers. 11, 12) was simply compliance with custom in paying outward respect for the memory of a deceased monarch and his son. No doubt such an act could be decently performed by one who saw in the disaster an occasion of personal joy; indeed, a heartless rival, who cared alone for his own elevation to the throne, would, as a matter of mere policy, encourage the observance of tokens of public sorrow; for history testifies to the presence of a large element of hypocrisy in the elaborate manifestations of grief that have characterized the obsequies of rival rulers. But David was not a man of ceremony; and the elegy penned for the expression of his own anguish of spirit—so tender and pathetic as it is—must be accepted as the interpreter of the act of public mourning in David's camp. None but a deeply earnest and sincere man could thus write of the woe which came to men on the heights of Gilboa. Tested by the principles that govern the secular mind, the elegy is perfectly unaccountable, especially considering Saul's long-continued persecution of David and the open pathway to the throne which the defeat at Gilboa laid open to him. But there was a wonderful spiritual unity in David's life; and to those who have followed our interpretation of his conduct and motives as set forth elsewhere (see 'Pulpit Commentary,' 1 Samuel, Homiletics, pp. 365, 415, 482, 513), there can be no difficulty in perceiving in this public act, and in the elegy, a culmination of the intense and painfully loving interest with which he all along had watched the downward course of the unhappy monarch. There were, indeed, several items entering into his sorrow. He thought of the kingless nation, and mourned for the bereaved "house of Israel" (ver. 12). He thought of the chosen people, distinguished above all nations as the channels of a great and merciful Divine purpose to the world, and he mourned for "the people of the Lord." He could not forget the man whose love to him had been "wonderful, passing the love of women," and he wept for Jonathan (vers. 12, 26). But, most of all, he thought of one great in position, great in responsibilities, who once had set before him the possibilities of a grand destiny in connection with the unfolding of God's merciful purpose to mankind; and he mourned with an overwhelming sorrow that he had fallen on the field a defeated, ruined man, covered with the shame and misfortunes of a woeful miscarriage of his life's mission.

I. FAILURE IN LIFE'S MISSION IS THE GREAT DISASTER OF LIFE. David knew that death came to all men, and that the removal from earth of one who has figured before our vision disturbs the whole current of feeling. Had Saul died under some circumstances David would have sorrowed, but the pang of this his sorrow would not have been experienced. He had known Saul as the chosen of God, equipped for high enterprise in the kingdom of God, and in a position to prepare the pathway for the coming of a mightier king. Splendid opportunities arose; strong influences were brought to bear; but all in vain. Life's mission failed. The noble work was not done. Fine abilities were wasted. Dishonoured, abandoned by God, covered with shame— the shame of an abortive life—he passed away. Simple death would have been glory and blessing as compared with this. What was true of Saul may be true of others and, unhappily, is too often the fact. God has a purpose in the life of every human being, and our business in this world is to comprehend the nature of that purpose and realize it in our experience. It is an unutterable disaster if, knowing why we are here, and possessing all the appliances and means of carrying out God's will, we nevertheless pass away as unprofitable servants (Matt. xxv. 26—30). There are instances of frequent occurrence in which splendid abilities, robust health, excellent social position, fine openings for usefulness, are all wasted by the dominance of unholy passions, and men have to witness the sad spectacle of early promise issuing in a dishonoured name and premature grave. Those who believe that all who are born amidst Christian influences are sent into the world to work out for themselves and others a pure and blessed destiny, and that this can only be secured by our personally falling in the line of Christ's purpose and becoming one with him in the deepest spiritual sense, as Saul was expected to fall in the line of God's great purpose to man through Israel, and live in its spirit,—such persons recognize a terrible miscarriage of life when men live, it may be, in ease and wealth and respectability, but alien in heart to Christ, and then die in the same condition. They have not laid up treasure for the future. Nations and communities are also charged with their respective life-work, and it is a fearful thing when, through unfaithfulness, their mission is abortive. Jeremiah's wail over Judah (Jer. ix.), our Saviour's lamentation over Jerusalem, and his prospective sorrow over the Church at Laodicea (Rev. iii. 14—20), were based on the same view of miscarriage of life's purpose as was David's lament over Saul.

II. The sorrow felt for a miscarriage of life's purpose is DEEPENED BY THE APPREHENSION OF ITS EFFECT ON THE REPUTATION AND PROGRESS OF THE KINGDOM OF GOD. Saul was not simply a monarch maintaining his own special interests as one among the many kings of the earth; he was regarded by David as, and in fact was, the official representative of the theocracy—the kingdom of God in its early stage of development.

It was the pride and joy of devout men that Israel's king governed a people chosen of God for the assertion and exposition of principles superior to those which obtained in the heathen nations. The pledge of prosperity had been given to the chosen people, and their history had demonstrated to the heathen again and again that the God of Israel was indeed supreme. The uncircumcised Philistines could not know, or if they knew could not appreciate, the spiritual conditions on which national prosperity was guaranteed; but they would be quick to boast over Israel's adversity, and to magnify their idols to the detriment of Jehovah's fame. "Tell it not in Gath" was David's spontaneous expression of the increased anguish of his spirit on account of the failure of Saul's life and work. The possibility of the holy kingdom of God among men being a subject of ridicule and blasphemy—the thought of God's honour being for a moment treated with scorn by the ignorant heathen—this was trouble upon trouble. A kindred sorrow falls on all true hearts when, by the wrecked character and abortive lives of professors of religion, or workers in connection with God's holy kingdom, there arises the possibility of the scoffing world bringing the name and interests of Christianity into reproach; for every blasphemous word and triumph of joy against Christ is regarded by the loving soul as another thrust into his side. Irreligious men can little know the anguish of true Christians whenever occasion is given, by the inconsistencies and apostasies of life, to dishonour the sacred Name.

III. The due recognition of the magnitude of this disaster depends on a spiritual perception of the gravity of our earthly life. No doubt many astute men regarded David's great sorrow as a sheer extravagance. Nothing in the event, from their point of view, could justify such a wail over a bitter foe and ostensible rival. The answer to that reflection on the reasonableness of David's sorrow lies in this—that he looked on Saul's life upon its Godward side, and saw beneath the political and merely terrene aspect a spiritual issue, which issue, affecting as it did all that is most great and momentous in man, threw all else into the background. It is only a spiritual perception—a penetration beneath the temporal and material interests to the invisible and eternal relations and possibilities of human existence—that can enable one thus to judge, feel, and act (1 Cor. ii. 15). Habitual contact with the visible and perishable unfits men for recognizing the true solemnity of life, and the subtle elements that enter into the determination of human destiny. Nominally many may adopt our Lord's view of the bearing of man's present spiritual state upon his future condition (Matt. xx, 1—16; xxv. 1—13, 31—46), and yet practically place a successful issue of life in the acquisition of knowledge and wealth, and the development of humanly related virtues. Such persons are disposed to think Christ rather hard and unreasonable in pronouncing the man to be a "fool" (Luke xii. 20) who congratulated himself on the fact of his social and material prosperity. For the same reason they deem Christians narrow and uncharitable when they indicate great anxiety for the future condition of those who, while outwardly prosperous and, on the man-ward side, virtuous, pass away without affording evidence of that renewal of nature by which alone they can come into absorbing sympathy with Christ, and cause the whole tenor of their life to flow in the line of Christ's mission to the world. Saul's failure on the spiritual side was seen by David to lie at the root of his general failure; and those only who estimate modern issues of life by the supreme test of the spiritual, can see in many lives, otherwise excellent, a woeful miscarriage of life's main purpose and consequent irretrievable disaster (1 Cor. i. 18, 19; ii. 6—10; 2 Cor. v. 17, 20, 21; Phil. iii. 8, 9, 18, 19).

The incidental teachings of a great disaster. All events have a teaching function in the Divine economy, and we are exhorted to extract good out of evil. It is possible that in the general evolution of human interests the immediate, if not remote, effects of disastrous events are counterbalanced by the contribution they make to the sum total of instruction, by means of which God ultimately elevates the world in purity and peace. The sad issue of Saul's life was doubtless a blessing to David, in that its solemn lessons gave a tone to his subsequent course, which enabled him to withstand many of the perils of position; and we, studying the words of David when the sorrow was fresh upon him, may, in addition to what has already been noticed, gain instruction on several matters which, in its helpfulness to our life, shall illustrate the truth that under the all-controlling hand of God "all things work together for good."

I. As there is a disposition on the part of irreligious men to find delight in the sins and frailties of Christians, and also to find therein excuse for their own impiety, it BEHOVES ALL WHO HAVE THE NAME AND CAUSE OF CHRIST AT HEART TO BE VERY GUARDED IN THEIR REFERENCES TO THE SINS AND MISERIES OF BACKSLIDERS AND THE ERRING. The sins of professors are to be the subject of silent sorrow, and, when possible, of Church discipline; not to be paraded before the world, as though such free publicity were a due chastisement for their unfaithfulness. The spirit that can readily go and "tell it in Gath" is not the spirit of Christ. The evident pleasure which some feel in making known the shortcomings of professedly religious men, can only spring from a desire to excuse their own indifference, or from a wicked Phariseeism, or from a defective sense of the sacredness of the Name of Christ. Where there is sincere sorrow there will be tenderness, and the family instinct will avoid the publicity of family misfortunes. Christians! weep and pray, but "tell it not in Gath" (Jer. ix. 1—3, 17—19).

II. THE HISTORY OF THE CHURCH REVEALS WHAT SERIOUS INJURY HAS BEEN CAUSED TO RELIGION BY THE IMPERFECT LIVES OF ITS PROFESSED FRIENDS. The "uncircumcised" did know of Saul's disaster, and it made them strong in hostility to the chosen race, and at the same time weakened the hearts of the men of Israel. Saul damaged the cause of righteousness and mercy as well as his own personal reputation. Too often has Christ been wounded in the house of his friends (Zech. xiii. 6). Considering the many miscarriages of those who were professedly engaged in the furtherance of the kingdom of God on earth, it is a marvel that the progress of Christianity has been what it has. They little think how much they retard the final supremacy of Christ who, by a Saul-like unfaithfulness and degeneracy, encourage antagonism among his foes, and produce paralysis among his friends.

III. MOMENTOUS EVENTS BRING OUT THE FACT THAT CULTURE IS OF SECONDARY IMPORTANCE TO RELIGION. David, as is seen from his varied compositions in the Psalms, and also from this elegy, was a man of fine æsthetic taste. He rejoiced in the exquisite beauties of nature. The dewy slopes of Gilboa, and the fat pastures of its valleys, teemed with objects of delight to his cultured taste; but now that his spiritual yearnings were unsatisfied, now that the holy Name of God was being dishonoured, all considerations of beauty in nature, and joy in the higher culture of life, must be utterly set aside. Let Gilboa become a waste, let the joy of local associations perish, since the religious side of life is languishing! The scenes amidst which our loved ones die are often cherished in the memory with mournful pleasure, and we seem to invest them with a more tender loneliness because there the joy of our life fell asleep. But when the smitten heart bleeds over a shipwrecked character—a life failing in its noblest purpose—then the local associations have no charm; blight and desolation are felt to be the most appropriate accompaniments of an unrelieved sorrow. So truly do great tragic events in life bring out the fact that our religious nature will assert itself as above all mere culture and æsthetic refinement.

IV. A WISE AND TENDER HEART CAN, while overwhelmed with sorrow because of spiritual disaster, APPRECIATE THE VALUE OF HUMANLY RELATED VIRTUES. We have made a distinction between virtues that have simply a human aspect, and those qualities which enter into the essence of religion and are Godward in aspect. David's great grief was that, so far as his religious life and work were concerned, Saul was degenerate and practically ruined. But, as a relief to his anguish on this account, he turns toward the manly virtues of the deceased king, and with exquisite tenderness dwells on them. His courage, his love for Jonathan, and his benefactions to his subjects (vers. 22—24), afford some solace for a heart that can find none in contemplating the spiritual mission of the king. Nil mortuis nisi bonum. He could not, from very sorrow and reverence for the most sacred things, speak of the sad miscarriage of his life's work; and this reference to the good of his life was really an expression of deep affection, and at the same time an indication of a sorrow secret and unutterable. Christians who, with the light that Christ gives, see spiritual ruin where others see only, and rejoice in, humanly related virtues, are not blind to the manifest virtues of men; and often, in their silent sorrow for the absence of spiritual saving qualities, they can speak with subdued emotion of the charms and attractions of personal character.

V. THERE IS A WONDERFUL CHARM IN FILIAL PIETY MAINTAINED UNDER MOST ADVERSE

CIRCUMSTANCES. "Saul and Jonathan were lovely and pleasant in their lives, and in their death they were not divided" (ver. 23). Yes; every heart says "yes." We feel the charm of Jonathan's fidelity to his poor erring father even to the bitter end. David's appreciation of this is, under the circumstances (1 Sam. xx. 1—4), most beautiful. Jonathan knew that David was a holy man, vilely treated by his own father, and destined to ascend the throne; he loved him with a tenderness passing the love of women, and was under provocation again and again to revolt from his father's rule; but with patience, tenderness, and faithfulness, he stood by him to the end, lamenting his sins, restraining his evil propensities, and variously striving to lessen the evils of his government. The filial instinct prevailed. Piety purified and strengthened it. A lesson here for sons—the more valuable in proportion as parents may be irreligious or imperfect. It is a noble thing for a son to watch over, care for, and tenderly restrain the tendencies of an erring father. To some it is given to have that for their special work. Remember Jonathan.

VI. IT IS POSSIBLE TO CHERISH VERY TENDER AND HELPFUL FRIENDSHIPS EVEN AMIDST THE PRESSURE OF LIFE. The friendship of David and Jonathan, begun in days of peace, ceased not during all the subsequent seasons of toil and separation. Doubtless David had often been comforted in his solitude and wanderings by the remembrance of that true heart which beat in sympathy with his own, and Jonathan would be upheld in his delicate and painful task of helping and restraining an errant parent by the assurance that David was not unmindful of him before the mercy-seat. The tendency of the hurry and pressure of daily business is to crush out the finer and more tender susceptibilities of the heart, and rob men of the consolations and elevating influence of wise and holy personal friendships. For self-culture, for solace, for spiritual fellowship, and for the acquisition of moral strength, it is well for all men to cherish a few well-selected friendships.

VII. THERE IS A BLESSED INFLUENCE ATTENDING THE CHERISHING OF HALLOWED MEMORIES. David's hallowed memories of Jonathan were to him for years to come a means of blessing. His life was more sober and tender and spiritual for the sweet memory of one so lovable and dear. The language of vers. 25, 26 was the indication of a permanent element in David's subsequent life. We suffer loss when beautiful characters are taken away, and we find a gain. For though visible communion is no more, the tender memories are more constant, and touch more closely the deeper springs of life.

HOMILIES BY VARIOUS AUTHORS.

The Hebrew monarchy. (Introductory.) The Hebrew monarchy holds a prominent place in the development of the purpose of God to establish his kingdom upon earth. In accordance with this purpose Abraham became the father of a *family*, distinguished beyond others by the knowledge of the true God and the hope of his promised salvation; the family grew into a *nation*, and its government was constituted, by the agency of Moses, a *theocracy* (a word first used by Josephus, 'Contra Apion,' ii. 17); and the theocracy (impaired in its practical influence during the period of the judges) was united with a *monarchy*, which commenced with Saul, acquired strength and splendour under David, culminated in the glory of Solomon, and soon afterwards declined to its fall; leaving behind it, when it fell, the undying hope of its restoration under "the King Messiah" (1 Sam. ii. 10). Consider—

I. ITS THEOCRATIC FOUNDATION. Although a king was sought in a wrong spirit, his appointment was not incompatible with the principles of the theocracy. What were these principles? 1. *Its supreme Head,* Lawgiver, and Judge was JEHOVAH; its *subjects* were his chosen people Israel. Having revealed himself to them as the one living and true God, and redeemed them out of bondage, he made a covenant with them, and became to them all, and more than all, that a human king was to other nations (Exod. xv. 18; 1 Sam. xii. 12; Zeph. iii. 15). "He raised and consolidated his universal rule into one of a special nature" (Kurtz, 'Hist. of the Old Covenant,' iii. 107). The *personal relation* thus formed between him and his people was designed to maintain among them his exclusive worship, to keep them separate from the idolatrous and corrupt nations around them, and to make them "a kingdom of priests and a holy nation." 2. *Its laws* were his revealed will, pertaining to the entire circle of civil and religious life. "The commonwealth of the Jews, different in that from all others, was an absolute theocracy; nor was there, nor could there be, any difference between the commonwealth and the Church" (Locke). 3. *Its sanctions* were his favour and displeasure, blessing and curse; reward or punishment of a *temporal* nature following obedience or disobedience, and administered by properly constituted authorities or a special and extraordinary providence. 4. *Its officers* were his appointed servants, whose part it was to declare his will and administer his laws, and who (whether priests, prophets, judges, elders, or princes) were themselves subject to them (Michaelis, 'Laws of Moses,' i. 190; Warburton, 'Div. Leg.,' v. 3; Fairbairn, 'Typology,' ii. 443). In harmony with these principles a human king was appointed (as already provided for, Deut. xvii. 15—20); not, indeed, to reign independently of the Divine King, or according to his own will and pleasure, but as his viceroy and minister. "To the theocracy was added the monarchy, not to subvert or gradually supersede it, but to fulfil the wants of the age by its side. The pure theocracy became a Basileotheocracy" (Ewald). "The Hebrews under the reign of David clearly recognized the theocratic nature of their constitution" (Jahn).

II. Its PRACTICAL EFFICIENCY. The condition of the people rendered the regal office necessary; and it served (especially during the reign of David) to: 1. Gather them into *closer union*, and so consolidate and increase their strength. Nothing was more urgently needed. Their common faith (or rather unbelief) and the previously existing officers of the theocracy were insufficient to maintain the practical union and co-operation of the tribes. 2. *Defend* them against their adversaries, by whose attacks their very existence was imperilled. It secured their safety and independence, and it extended their dominion "from the river of Egypt unto the great river, the river Euphrates," as it had been promised of old (Gen. xv. 18). 3. Establish *order* and the more regular and impartial administration of *justice*. In the days of the judges "every man did that which was right in his own eyes," being subject to no proper restraint by a king, as responsible "minister of God and avenger to execute wrath upon him that doeth evil" (Rom. xiii. 4). 4. Promote the *main purpose* of their national calling, viz. to receive and conserve "the oracles of God" (Rom. iii. 2) for the ultimate benefit of mankind. "By the constitution of the Hebrew government the civil and municipal statutes of the nation were not only founded upon their *religious belief*, but they were also so framed as to have the support of that belief for their main object" (Russell, 'Connection,' bk. xviii.). And this object was more effectually accomplished under the circumstances by means of the monarchy than it would otherwise have been.

III. Its MANIFEST IMPERFECTION. Like other institutions dependent for their worth upon the conduct of weak and sinful men, it was marked, in its actual working, by numerous defects; being: 1. Administered in a manner that did *not fully accord with its nature and design*. "Whate'er is best administered is best." The authority and power entrusted to the king were frequently used in self-will and for self-exaltation. Hence the misery in which the reign of Saul (really an autocracy) terminated. And even the administration of David, although distinguished by surpassing ability and fidelity, was by no means faultless. 2. Weakened and marred by the *personal crimes* of the monarch. David's transgressions exerted an injurious influence, not only upon himself and his family, but also upon his government. They sowed the seeds of insubordination and rebellion. 3. Often employed for *the oppression and corruption of the people*. "Its tendency was to absolutism." The magnificence of Solomon was largely based upon oppressive taxation and forced labour; and, instead of opposing and excluding, he suffered and indulged idolatrous practices—most fatal of all things to the throne and nation. 4. Liable to *frequent changes and gradual deterioration*. Even a good monarch could not hold his office long "by reason of death;" and the hereditary principle did not insure a successor of like character. With the secession of the ten tribes the early splendour of the monarchy became dim; and its course, with intervals of glorious revival, was downward. It virtually terminated with the Captivity (Hos. iii. 4, 5); after which the civil government was subject to a foreign heathen power, and the theocracy survived chiefly as a political hierarchy; at length "the Romans came and took away their place and nation."

IV. Its TYPICAL SIGNIFICANCE. It was not only a stage of preparation for the kingdom of the Messiah, but also a *type* or divinely ordained foreshadowing of it. 1. It rendered the conception thereof *more definite and vivid.* "With the establishment of the kingly power, a new class of ideas was brought into view and developed, which for want of the requisite material groundwork could not be previously illustrated; and it now became possible to descry from a distance and to announce in appropriate and intelligible terms the coming kingdom of the Messiah." 2. It was associated with *express promises and predictions* (ch. vii. 12—16; xxiii. 3—5). "When mankind was limited to a single family, the Hope of the future had lain in the seed of the woman; the patriarchal age had looked forward to a descendant of Abraham; the Mosaic to a Prophet and a Legislator. In like manner the age of the Jewish monarchy in its bloom of youth and prowess was bidden to fix its eye upon an ideal David, who was to be the King of the future of the world" (Liddon, 'Bampton Lectures,' p. 79). "The establishment of the kingdom was in the truest sense a defection from God, and yet, humanly speaking, it was a necessary defection. An earthly king fell infinitely short of the type of Divine government represented by Moses, or Joshua, or Samuel; but he was at once a definite centre, and a clear sign of something greater than himself. If he presented the spiritual idea in a fixed and limited form, he also gave distinctness to the conception of the present moral sovereignty of God, and furnished imagery under which the prophets could construct a more glorious picture of the future" (Westcott. 'The Gospel of the Resurrection,' p. 68). 3. Even its defects and failure *intensified and exalted* the expectation. With every disappointment hope sprang up afresh, and found its purest expression in the utterances of the prophets (Isa. ix. 6, 7; liii.; Micah v. 2). "What was earthly and carnal in the theocracy was made to fall into comparative abeyance, that the glory of its spiritual excellence might be brought more prominently into view" (Fairbairn). Whilst the general expectation immediately before the advent of Christ was of a temporal kingdom, many "waited" with lofty, spiritual hope "for the Consolation of Israel." 4. It was (as a type) *fulfilled* in a higher and more *spiritual* manner in the kingdom of Christ. In this kingdom the principles of the theocracy are preserved and exhibited in perfection. It is the *real* theocracy. Its supreme Head (Eph. i. 22) is at once Divine and human. Its subjects consist of those who are inwardly renewed, and serve him from the heart. It is spiritual, righteous, peaceful, and blessed. Although in the world, it is not of the world. It can coexist in time and place (as the ancient theocracy could not) with every form of civil government; and, without any formal connection or *concordat* therewith, it can exert a sovereign influence over it. It claims the submission of every individual and every nation, and it is destined to fill the earth and endure for ever.

REMARKS. 1. The purpose of God to set up on earth a kingdom of heaven is the key of history. "The grand idea of a kingdom of God is the connecting thread that runs through the entire course of Divine revelation." 2. The methods which God adopts in his dealings with men are adapted to their actual condition, and the accomplishment of immediate and beneficent ends; his revelations of himself are accommodated to their capacity for apprehending and profiting by them. 3. He allows men a large liberty of choice; and, when they use it wrongly, patiently bears with their imperfections and sins, and overrules them for their correction and improvement. 4. His procedure is marked by a progressive development; and the facts and truths involved therein contain the promise and prefigurement of later and greater realities. "The Old Testament, when rightly understood, is one great prophecy of the New" (Augustine). "Christianity lay in Judaism, as leaves and fruit do in the seed; although it certainly required the Divine sun to bring them forth" (De Wette). 5. What is expedient in one age may not be so in another, which has received a higher revelation of the Divine will. The relative worth of institutions and men must be judged of according to their circumstances and the measure of light possessed, their absolute worth according to the highest conceptions of truth and righteousness. 6. God selects and exalts one nation, not for its own good merely, but for the good of others and the fulfilment of his benevolent purposes toward mankind. 7. As the people of God in ancient time were taught to look forward to the coming of the Messiah, so we are now taught to look forward to his coming again, and the complete establishment of his kingdom.—D.

David's reign: B.C. 1051—1011. (References: 1 Chron. x.—xxix.; 1 Kings i., ii.; Psalms. For his earlier life, as shepherd at Bethlehem, servant of Saul at Gibeah, outlaw in the wilderness of Judah and elsewhere, see 1 Sam. xvi.—xxxiv.) When Saul fell on Gilboa, David was about *thirty years old;* the age at which Joseph stood before Pharaoh, the Levites entered on their official duties, and Jesus began his public ministry. The Second Book of Samuel describes the steps by which he became king over Judah, and (after seven years and a half) king over all Israel, the consolidation and victorious expansion of his kingdom (ch. i.—x.); his deplorable fall (when about fifty years of age), his repentance, the consequences of his transgression, and the restoration of his impaired authority (ch. xi.—xx.); and (in an appendix, ch. xxi.—xxiv.) among other things some events and utterances of his last days (his life ending at three score years and ten). "He most happily combined all the qualifications for becoming the true support of the extraordinary efforts of this period; and he thus succeeded in winning, not only a name unequalled in glory by any other king of Israel, but also a halo of kingly fame as ruler of the community of the true God, unattainable by a king of any other nation of antiquity" (Ewald). "The reign of David is the great critical era in the history of the Hebrews." In it we see—

I. THE PURPOSE OF THE DIVINE KING OF ISRAEL FULFILLED. That purpose (subordinate to the larger purpose mentioned in the preceding homily), to make David ruler instead of Saul, was: 1. *Previously indicated.* It was first announced by Samuel, in indefinite terms (1 Sam. xiii. 14; xv. 28), symbolized in the anointing of David (when about sixteen years old), afterwards doubtless plainly declared to him by the prophet, and clearly manifested by the course of events. It was also more and more generally recognized (1 Sam. xxiv. 20; xxv. 30; ch. iii. 17, 18). 2. *Vainly opposed,* at first by Saul, and, after he had been made King of Judah, by Abner and "the house of Saul." It was impossible for them to succeed. "There is no wisdom nor understanding nor counsel against the Lord" (Prov. xxi. 30). 3. Gradually, surely, and fully *wrought out.* There were times in which it seemed to fail, but only to become more apparent and effectual; like a stream disappearing beneath the surface of the earth, and after a short distance bursting forth with renewed strength. 4. Its fulfilment shows the power and faithfulness of God, and should *confirm our faith* in the fulfilment of all his promises. "Wait on the Lord." "There hath not failed one word of all his good promise," etc. (1 Kings viii. 56). "The Davidic age, with those that lie immediately around it, towers by its special glory like a giant mountain above a wide tract of more level periods. It was, moreover, soon afterwards recognized by the nation itself as a period of unique glory in the fortunes of the monarchy; and its memory has therefore been preserved in the historical narrative with the most exuberant fulness of detail" (Ewald).

II. THE CHARACTER OF THE HUMAN KING OF HIS CHOICE PORTRAYED. The interest of David's reign centres in David himself; his activities, achievements, experiences, utterances, so fully recorded, not only in the history, but also in his psalms. His character (more completely revealed than that of any other man) was the growth of a noble and gifted nature under the influence of Divine grace. 1. It was matured by long and varied *discipline.* While keeping his father's flock, in the court and camp of Saul, as an exile at the head of his heroic band, by persecution, calumny, hardship, meditation, temptation, prayer, and during his "apprenticeship to monarchy" in Hebron, his natural endowments and moral qualities were strengthened, developed, and perfected. 2. It was marked by a many-sided *excellence.* His insight, skill, prescient sagacity, tender sensibility, sympathy, imagination, fervour, versatility, courage, magnanimity, power of leadership, and of winning the passionate attachment of others, were never surpassed. He was "one of the greatest men in the world" (Bayle). "The most daring courage was combined in him with tender susceptibility; even after he had ascended the throne he continued to retain the charm of a pre-eminent and at the same time childlike personality" (Wellhausen).

> "Great, valiant, pious, good, and clean,
>   Sublime, contemplative, serene,
>   Strong, constant, pleasant, wise!
>   Bright effluence of exceeding grace;
>   Best man! the swiftness and the race,
>   The peril and the prize!" (Christopher Smart.)

"There never was a specimen of manhood so rich and ennobled as David, the son of Jesse, whom other saints haply may have equalled in single features of his character; but such a combination of manly, heroic qualities, such a flush of generous, godlike excellences, hath never yet been seen embodied in a single man" (Edward Irving). "The most thoroughly human figure, as it seems to me, which had appeared upon the earth before the coming of that perfect Son of man, who is over all, God blessed for ever. Amen" (Charles Kingsley). (1) In relation to *God* he was eminent in faith, hope, and love; loyal obedience, fervid zeal, holy aspiration, enthusiastic devotion, lowly submission, and thankfulness (Neh. xii. 36). (2) In relation to *men* he was tenderly affectionate toward his family; considerate and grateful toward his friends; generous and forgiving toward his enemies; faithful and just, self-denying and self-sacrificing toward his people. (3) Beyond any other monarch of Israel he was a truly *theocratic king.* His heart was perfect with the Lord his God (1 Kings xi. 4). "David did that which was right in the eyes of the Lord, and turned not aside from anything that he commanded him all the days of his life, save only in the matter of Uriah the Hittite" (1 Kings xv. 5). 3. It was marred by *grave defects* and aggravated transgressions. Although these were in great measure due to the spirit of his age, the effect of temptation incident to his position, contrary to the general course of his life, and deeply repented of, yet they incurred heavy guilt, and were followed by severe chastisements. 4. It thus affords a *warning* as well as an *example.* "In this history we have the pattern of a pious and prudent prince. Its utility and profit for example of life appears in the prudence, piety, zeal, humility, equity, and good government of David, and all other his heroic and godly virtues worthy of imitation. As also are set down David's infirmities and falls, as examples of the weakness of the best when they watch not over themselves, or are left to themselves, proponed to be eschewed, *ut majorum ruina sit minorum cautela,* as likewise his repentance to be imitated, and the sharp corrections notwithstanding, as medicinal corrasives wherewith he was chastised; as we see in the Lord's dealing with his dearest sons and servants (Heb. xii. 6, 7)" (W. Guild, 'The Throne of David:' 1659).

III. THE MAJESTY OF THE DIVINE-HUMAN KING MESSIAH FORESHADOWED. David is to be regarded, not simply as an individual, but as a noble, though imperfect, representation of the *idea* of a theocratic king, and therefore also as an adumbration of One in whom that idea would be perfectly realized (Luke i. 32). "His relation to the history of redemption is most peculiar and remarkable. The aim and import of the Old Testament history to prefigure, prophesy, and testify of Christ concentrated in him as in a focus" (Kurtz). "As we have a great increase of the prophetic light breaking forth, and encompassing the family and kingdom of David so subsequent prophecy reverts often to the same subjects, insomuch that there is no individual, king or other person, one only excepted, of whom more is said by the prophets than of this king and his throne" (Davison, 'On Prophecy'). "It is David who, without intending it, supplies the personal foundation of all the Messianic hopes, which from this time contribute with increasing power to determine Israel's career; and so he stands at the turning-point in the history of two thousand years and separates it into two great halves" (Ewald). High above him, in the dim and distant future, rose the majestic form of "the King of kings, and Lord of lords." "A person, as such, can never be a symbol. It was not David, or Manasseh, or Ahab, that was the type of Christ as King of Zion; it was the *royal office* with which these were invested, symbolical as that was of the theocracy, which was typical of the kingly dignity of the Redeemer" (W. L. Alexander, 'Connection of the Old and New Testaments,' 315, 418). The kingly dignity of the Messiah appears in: 1. His Divine appointment (Ps. ii. 6, 7) founded on the Incarnation. "In Jesus the Christ, Jehovah and the Son of David become one. Heaven and earth interpenetrate, that they may unite in him and be united by him" (Delitzsch). 2. His glorious exaltation after deep humiliation and patient endurance. 3. His righteous administration (Ps. lxxii. 1, 2). 4. His advancing triumph over the enemies of his kingdom and our salvation—"the devil with all his retinue, the world, the flesh, sin, death, and hell; whatever doth oppose his glory, his truth, his service; whatever consequently by open violence or fraudulent practice doth hinder our salvation" (Barrow). 5. His munificent gifts and the blessings of his reign; refuge, refreshment, repose (Isa. xxxii. 1, 2); "righteousness, peace, and joy in the Holy Ghost." As a King he gathers, governs, protects, and perfects his people. 6. His wide dominion. 7. His endless continuance. "His Name shall endure for ever."

EXHORTATION. 1. Submit to his rule. "Kiss the Son," etc. (Ps. ii. 12). 2. Rejoice in his salvation. 3. Co-operate with his purposes. 4. Look forward to his final triumph.—D.

Vers. 1, 2.—(ZIKLAG.) *A change of dynasty.* "When he came to David he fell to the earth, and did obeisance" (ver. 2). The title of David to the throne was primarily conferred upon him by the will of God, as declared by Samuel. But it remained in abeyance while Saul lived, and began to take effect only at his decease. On returning to Ziklag from his pursuit of the Amalekites, David occupied himself in repairing its ruins, and awaited tidings from the field of battle. On the morning of the third day there came a young man, "the son of a stranger, an Amalekite," bringing news of the defeat of Israel and the death of Saul and Jonathan. In proof of his statement he brought the king's *diadem*, "a small metallic cap or wreath which encircled the temples, serving the purpose of a helmet, with a very small horn projecting in front, as an emblem of power" (Jamieson), and *bracelet* (or armlet worn above the elbow), and laid them at the feet of David, as the future king (ver. 10). His conduct reminds us of a well-known custom, according to which, whenever a French monarch departed this life, an official of the royal household appeared at the window, broke his staff, and cried, *Le roi est mort!* ("The king is dead!"); then took a new staff and shouted, *Vive le roi!* ("Long live the king!"). The change that occurred was—

I. OCCASIONED BY THE FALL OF AN UNFAITHFUL RULER. "After the death of Saul" (ver. 1). 1. Men are entrusted with power by God that they may employ it, not according to their own will and for their own honour, but according to his will and for his glory. This Saul failed to recognize. 2. Whenever a man misuses his trust he is sooner or later deprived thereof, and suffers the penalty of his sin (1 Sam. xv. 23). 3. No man can fall into sin and destruction without involving others in his ruin. How often has a monarch's unfaithfulness caused the downfall of his dynasty! 4. The place from which he falls is thereby prepared for a more faithful man, and such a man is seldom wanting for the place. "Take therefore the talent," etc. (Matt. xxv. 28). "Saul's elevation was a first experiment in monarchy doomed to failure from the beginning; it was only when the people had been trampled down by his tyranny and involved in his fatal defeat that a lasting monarch was set according to the Divine will in the person and family of David, who was in this sense the man after God's own heart" (P. Smith, 'Ancient History,' i. 168).

II. AWAITED WITH PATIENCE BY A RIGHTFUL SUCCESSOR. "David abode in Ziklag." He was long ago assured of his royal destination. But: 1. The purpose of God is often slow in its accomplishment; which requires to be waited for in faith and patience. 2. Its slow accomplishment presents a strong temptation to impatience, and the adoption of rash and unworthy expedients that hinder rather than promote the desired end. David was subject to such a temptation, and for the most part overcame it. In so far as he yielded to it he suffered the consequences of his imprudence (1 Sam. xxvii. 1). 3. By patient continuance in well-doing men are best prepared for what God has prepared for them. David did not deem the crown "a thing to be grasped at." "What God has destined for him, he would not have until God gave it to him" (Hengstenberg). "Endurance is the crowning quality." *Qui dura vince* ("He conquers who endures"). 4. To those who await the accomplishment of the Divine purpose in a right spirit, it comes surely and at the right time, often suddenly and by unexpected means. "By degrees doth the Lord perform his works to exercise the faith, the hope, the patience, and constancy of his chosen, but at last to the full he accomplisheth whatsoever he promiseth" (Guild).

III. RECOGNIZED AS INEVITABLE BY A SELF-SEEKING OBSERVER. It is remarkable that one of an alien and hostile race should be the first to perceive and acknowledge the speedy and certain transfer of the crown. He was a watchful observer of the course of events; acquainted, probably, with the general opinion concerning David, and with his present position; and, although possessing little love for his character and expecting little good to the Amalekites from his accession, he was desirous of using the occasion for the furtherance of his personal ends. 1. The tendency of human affairs is often so apparent that its result may be easily anticipated by all but the most obtuse. 2. A stranger or an enemy frequently perceives the destination of a man of ability more clearly than those who are intimately connected with him. 3. One who is supremely concerned about his own interest is quick to see anything that may be made conducive to it, however blind and unfeeling he may be in other respects. 4. His attempt to turn it to his own advantage sometimes turns only to the advantage of another, and to his own disappointment and ruin. " David had been long waiting for the crown, and now it is brought to him by an Amalekite. See how God can serve his own purpose of kindness to his people, even by designing men who aim at nothing but to set up themselves" (Matthew Henry).

IV. EFFECTED BY THE OPERATION OF DIVINE PROVIDENCE. "The Lord slew him, and turned the kingdom unto David the son of Jesse" (1 Chron. x. 14). "God is the Judge; he putteth down one and setteth up another" (Ps. lxxv. 7; 1 Sam. ii. 1—10). By his providential working: 1. His purposes are fulfilled and the truth of his Word is confirmed. "By a series of events following in the ordinary course of Providence, without any miracle interposed, this prediction (given by Samuel and exhibited in the act of anointing) was brought to pass. David was raised to his divinely appointed station, when his shepherd's staff became a sceptre, and his flock a great people; none contributing more to the preparation of this event than Saul himself. . . . The complicated narrative is the exposition of the prophetic prescience" (Davison). 2. Those who oppose his purposes are overthrown. 3. He who humbly waits their fulfilment in the way of obedience is promoted. 4. Individuals and nations are constrained to turn from their own way, and submit to his plans as the wisest and best (ch. ii. 4; iii. 9; v. 2). " The secret springs of revolutions are unaccountable, and must be resolved into that Providence which turns all hearts as the rivers of water" (Matthew Henry). "Notwithstanding those appearances which obscure the providence of God, it often makes itself conspicuous in the midst of them all. When we have allowed to human agency, to human wisdom and human power, a large circle of events imputed to nothing else, we see the Divine wisdom frequently disencumber itself from all communication with second causes, and stretch itself out in the face of all men, in defeating and confounding the plans of human wisdom, in the failure of the deepest schemes" (R. Hall).—D.

Vers. 2—10.—(ZIKLAG.) *Selfish craft.* Beyond the assertion of the Amalekite that Israel was defeated and Saul and Jonathan were dead, of which the diadem and bracelet afforded proof, it is uncertain how far his story was true. His statement concerning his own conduct cannot be satisfactorily reconciled with that of 1 Sam. xxxi.; and, although credited by David, it was probably a fabrication, his motive therein being the desire of reward, as David himself clearly perceived (ch. iv. 16). In him we have a picture of what sometimes appears in others under higher moral influences, viz.: 1. *Dominant selfishness.* He is supremely concerned about his own interest. Self-love is an original principle of our nature, and, when properly regulated, points in the direction of virtue and happiness. But it easily degenerates into selfishness, "the source of all the sins of omission and commission which are found in the world." And when a man comes under the dominion of the latter, he may sink into any depth of meanness. 2. *Subtle scheming.* Amidst the dying and the dead, after the battle, his only thought is of gain; and, having plundered the fallen king of the regalia, he coolly calculates how he may dispose thereof to the greatest advantage; and then hastens a long distance across the country to one whom he expects to find ready to welcome the prospect of his own elevation by an enemy's death, and to pay him "the wages of unrighteousness." 3. *Feigned sympathy.* He comes into the presence of David "with the marks of distress and dismay—dust and clay smeared over his face, and his clothes torn"—on account of the disaster which has befallen Israel (1 Sam. iv. 12). But how little does his appearance correspond with the feelings of his heart! "Self-love sometimes borrows the face of honest zeal" (Hall). 4. *Obsequious homage.* "He fell to the earth, and did obeisance;" prostrating himself before the rising sun of the new era with abject, insincere, and wicked mind. "To those who are distinguished in the kingdom of God as specially called and favoured instruments of grace, falsehood and hypocrisy draw near most pressingly and corruptingly in the guise of humility and self-abasement" (Erdmann). 5. *Plausible lying.* (Vers. 6—9.) He artfully mingles falsehood with the truth he utters, for the sake of enhancing the value of his good offices. If he had been satisfied with simply telling the tidings of the death of Saul, all would have been well with him; but by his gratuitous inventions he entangles himself in a dangerous snare. 6. *Unconscious self-accusation.* " I stood upon him, and slew him, because I was sure that he could not live after that he was fallen " (ver. 10). He accuses himself in the excuses he makes for his conduct. *Qui s'excuse s'accuse.* Even the request of Saul would not have justified his act or absolved him from responsibility. And how could he be sure that the wounded king could not live? Even the most hardened villain deems it needful to endeavour to palliate his offence. And he who is solely intent upon his own interest often makes admissions that clearly reveal his guilt. 7. *Fatal miscalculation.* He judges of the character of another by his own, meets with a generosity, loyalty, and justice which he cannot understand, fails of his purpose, and receives a reward which he did not anticipate. "The incident gives us the opportunity of marking the immense difference in the order of mind and character which may subsist between two individuals brought together by one event, and having their attention occupied by one and the same object" (J. A. Miller, ' Saul '). " He taketh the wise in their own craftiness " (Job v. 13). " The wicked is snared in the work of his own hands " (Ps. ix. 16; Prov. vi. 15; xviii. 7).—D.

Vers. 11, 12.—(ZIKLAG.) *Unselfish grief.* " They mourned, and wept " (ver. 12). Few things are more remarkable in the character of David than the generosity which he displayed with respect to Saul. He once and again spared his life ; and, instead of rejoicing, he was overwhelmed with grief at his death. He entirely lost sight of any advantage which it promised to himself, in his sorrow over the disaster which befell the king, his sons, and the people of Israel. We have here—

I. THE NEWS OF A GREAT CALAMITY, now only too fully confirmed (vers. 5—11). A calamity is deeply affecting when, as in this case, it : 1. Consists of a combination of mournful events (ver. 12). 2. Falls on those who are intimately connected with us. 3. Occurs suddenly and unexpectedly. 4. Involves irreparable loss, and affords little prospect of alleviation. And the cloud of affliction is peculiarly dark when it is pervaded by Divine wrath (Hos. xiii. 11). " Lover and friend hast thou put far from me, and my acquaintance into darkness " (Ps. lxxxviii. 18).

II. THE SCENE OF A GRIEVOUS MOURNING. The sincerity and intensity of David's grief, in which his six hundred men shared, were shown by (1) rending the garments; (2) wailing aloud; (3) fasting; (4) until the evening ; common signs of sorrow in the East, as genuine as any other, and relieving as well as indicating a burdened heart. What a "day of trouble" was that on which David and his heroes sat there watching the sinking sun ! (For other days of a like nature, see ch. ii. 24; iii. 32; vi. 9; xii. 1, 16; xiii. 21, 30; xv. 13; xviii. 33; xx. 4; xxi. 1; xxiv. 13, 17.)

III. THE PROOF OF AN EXCELLENT DISPOSITION. Sorrow is an evidence of love. David's disposition was : 1. Forgiving toward an enemy. " For Saul." 2. Faithful toward a friend. " For Jonathan his son." 3. Patriotic. " For the house of Israel." 4. Devout. " For the people of the Lord." " The uprightness of his heart and the sincerity of his feelings cannot for a moment be doubted by those who read his lament over Saul and Jonathan with an unprejudiced mind. Pretended sorrow never could speak thus " (Hengstenberg). " The only deep mourning for Saul, with the exception of the Jabeshites, proceeded from the man whom he had hated and persecuted for so many years, even to the time of his death ; just as David's Successor wept over the fate of Jerusalem even when it was about to destroy himself " (O. von Gerlach).

Observe : 1. That the most generous grief requires to be restrained within due bounds. Its excessive indulgence is injurious and wrong. 2. That the beneficial effect of trouble is not usually experienced at " the present," but " afterward " by means of reflection and submission (Heb. xii. 11). 3. That to the eye of faith the darkest cloud is illumined by Divine goodness and mercy. " At eventide weeping cometh in to tarry for a night ; but with the morning cometh a shout of joy " (Ps. xxx. 5).—D.

Vers. 13—16.—(ZIKLAG.) *Capital punishment.* " Thy blood be upon thy head " (ver. 16). The grief of David at the death of Saul was associated with indignation at the conduct of the Amalekite, who, according to his own confession, had taken part in its infliction. At sunset he recalled the unhappy messenger, and having further questioned him, testified his abhorrence of his deed, and ordered his execution. Notice—

I. THE CRIME which was laid to his charge, viz. the intentional and unjustifiable taking away of the life of another: 1. Proceeding, like every act of murder, from indifference to the sacredness of human life and the dignity of human nature, created in the image of God. 2. Aggravated in guilt by irreverence toward the person of the king, "the Lord's anointed," who ought, on account of his high position, to have been held in special honour (1 Sam. xxiv. 6; xxvi. 11; xxxi. 5). "When the Israelites were under royal authority, it would appear to have been a maxim of their law that the person of the king was inviolable, even though he might be tyrannical and unjust; and, in fact, this maxim is necessary, not only to the security of the king, but also to the welfare of the subject; for it is the dread of assassination and treacheries that usually makes kings tyrants, and novices in tyranny absolute despots" (Michaelis). 3. Exhibiting disobedience to the command of God. "Thou shalt not kill" (Exod. xx. 13), i.e. do no murder (Exod. xxi. 12). With this law the Amalekite was probably acquainted. He knew, at least, that it was wrong to take away life without adequate reason. Hence he sought to justify the act by pleading the request of Saul (ver. 9), and his suffering condition, which it was mercy to terminate. But how could Saul authorize another to do to him what he had no right to do to himself? Genuine loyalty and mercy would have prompted a different course of conduct; and malice and selfishness were clearly the motives of the deed. There was in it nothing praiseworthy, but everything to be abhorred and condemned (ver. 14).

II. THE EVIDENCE on which he was convicted. "Thy mouth hath testified against thee," etc. (ver. 16). His confession was: 1. Voluntarily made; not extorted from him by the infliction or threatening of suffering, or the promise of reward. 2. Confirmed by the signs of his connection with the death of the king (ver. 10). 3. A sufficient ground, under the circumstances, for judgment, without further inquiry. Even if, as is probable, he did not actually commit the deed, he took upon himself the responsibility, and justly incurred the consequences thereof. But why did he not retract and repudiate his confession? Perhaps he thought that it would be of no avail; and he would thereby have acknowledged his falsehood and mercenariness. Possibly he did retract, and was not believed. For "a liar is not believed though he speak the truth." Considered in relation to his times, the evidence on which David acted was sufficient; but the incident affords an illustration of the uncertainty which often pertains to the crime of murder and the fallibility of human judgment.

III. THE AUTHORITY by which he was condemned. Although David was not yet publicly recognized as civil ruler, to whom the right of judging properly belonged, yet he was fully justified in assuming the office, inasmuch as: 1. It had been virtually conferred upon him by the appointment of the Divine King of Israel. 2. The chief hindrance to its exercise was removed by the death of Saul. There was no higher authority than his in the land, and it had been acknowledged by the Amalekite himself (ver. 10). 3. Its assumption was necessary to the fulfilment of the purpose of his appointment, the manifestation of the justice of God, and the promotion of the welfare of the people. He may have wished to clear himself from the suspicion of complicity in the king's death, to show that he entertained no feeling of revenge against him, and to gain the esteem of the people of Israel; but his main motive was of a higher nature. He acted on theocratic principles, as on a subsequent occasion (ch. iv. 9—12).

IV. THE PUNISHMENT which he suffered (ver. 15). "When the sentence of death was pronounced by the king, it was executed by his body-guard" (ch. xv. 18; xx. 23). *Capital punishment* may be upheld on the ground of: 1. *The claims of justice.* It has been generally felt, even from the most ancient period (Gen. iv. 10, 14), that the murderer deserves to die. 2. *The teaching of Scripture.* "Whoso sheddeth man's blood," etc. (Gen. ix. 6). "This was the first command having reference to the temporal sword. By these words temporal government was established, and the sword placed in its hand by God" (Luther). It gave the *right* and imposed the *duty* of inflicting death; and it is of permanent obligation (Lev. xxiv. 17; John xix. 11; Acts xxv. 11; Rom. xiii. 4). 3. *The welfare of society.* It exalts the principle of justice; declares the dignity of man in the most impressive manner; effectually prevents the offender from repeating his offence; powerfully deters others from following his example; and thus conduces to the security of human life. Severity to one is mercy to many. On the other hand, it may be said that : 1. The claims of justice are adequately satisfied by a lifelong penal servitude. 2. Scripture, rightly interpreted, does not justify the infliction of death. The Noachic precept (if it be such) was adapted only to an early stage of society, its literal fulfilment is no longer required, and the principle on which it rests (the dignity of man) is preserved and more fully maintained by the revelations and influences of Christianity. The whole spirit of the New Testament is in favour of seeking the reformation rather than effecting the destruction of the offender. "Mercy glorieth against judgment." Even the fratricide Cain was spared (Gen. iv. 5), as if to show the possibility and propriety of sparing the life of the criminal. 3. The welfare of society is more fully promoted by sparing his life than by taking it away. Hardened criminals and persons under the influence of strong passion are not deterred by the fear of death ; other persons are more powerfully affected by other motives. The possibility of the innocent suffering a penalty which is irreversible causes hesitation in its infliction where there is the least doubt, and so the guilty often escape, punishment becomes uncertain, and men are tempted to commit crime in the hope of impunity. As a matter of fact, crime does not increase in those countries where capital punishment is abolished. "After the Divine permission to inflict capital punishment which had been given for a considerable period of time, had displayed itself as the most extreme madness in the execution of Christ, the question of its abolition has become only a question of time. The question is whether Christ may not have done enough for this" (Ewald, 'Antiquities,' p. 174).—D.

Vers. 17, 18.—(ZIKLAG.) *The song of the bow.* I. THE OCCASION of this lament, threnody, elegy, or funeral dirge, was the arrival of fatal tidings from Gilboa. "There were only two in that great slaughter concerning whose fate David was eager to know the truth—his enemy and his friend. 'How knowest thou that Saul and Jonathan his son be dead ?' (ver. 5). When the news was fully established, he immediately went through all the signs of Eastern grief. He and his six hundred heroes sat with their clothes rent, uttering the loud Oriental wail, observing the rigid Eastern fast until the sunset of the fatal day released them. Then David roused himself to action. The first vent to his grief was in the stern exaction of the life of the unhappy messenger, according to the hard temper of those fierce times. The second vent was in the touching dirge, which, according to the tender spirit of the sweet psalmist of Israel, he poured forth over the two departed chiefs" ('The Songs of Israel,' *Good Words*, 1863). It was probably accompanied by his harp, that had long been silent, but was now taken up afresh and struck to a song of sorrow which for tenderness and intensity has never been surpassed. "The genius and origin of the elegy among the Hebrews may be clearly traced to their manner of celebrating their funeral rites" (Lowth). "If you attend to David's harp, you shall hear as many hearse-like airs as carols" (Bacon). II. THE TITLE of "The Bow" (*Kesheth*), which it appears to have received, may have been derived from the mention of the bow in ver. 22, as the favourite weapon of Jonathan (1 Sam. xviii. 4 ; xx. 20), as it was of his tribesmen (1 Chron. xii. 2); or "because it was a martial ode" (Keil). It is improbable that David introduced "the *use* of the bow" (Authorized Version) into the tribe of Judah, either as a tribute to the memory of his friend, or as a means of repairing the recent disaster ; for that had been long familiar. But he "bade them teach the children of Judah" the *song* of "the bow" (possibly that his youthful warriors might sing it in their military practice with the bow)—a title given to it in the Book of Jashar (Josh. x. 13), or collection of national songs, in which it was preserved. "When the writer of 2 Samuel transferred the dirge to his own pages, he transferred it, as we might do any of the psalms, with its title, which was as follows : 'For the children of Israel to learn by heart. Kasheth from the Book of Jasher'" ('Speaker's Commentary'). III. ITS FORM is that of a *lyrical* composition, the oldest as well as the most common species of Hebrew poetry ; and (like the rest) it is distinguished by *parallelism* or rhythm, "the measured rise and fall of feeling and utterance, in which the poet's effort to become fully master of his poetic inspiration finds harmonious expression, and the external rhythm of sound is properly subordinated to the rhythmic pulsation of thought" (*British Quarterly Review*, January, 1877). It contains a refrain or *chorus*, twice repeated; and falls into three *strophic divisions* marked by its recurrence, either at their commencement (Keil) or their close (Kitto, 'Cyclopædia of Biblical Literature'); or, according to more common arrangement, into five or six stanzas. "The putting of lamentations into poems made them the more moving and affecting, and the more lasting" (Matthew Henry).

IV. IN SUBSTANCE and general character it is an outburst of natural grief (as the song of Hannah was of spiritual gladness) over the fallen heroes, and a celebration of their worth. "We can hardly call it religious poetry. It is not a psalm or hymn. The name of God never occurs in it. It is a war-song which sums up the national feelings of every age over the graves of its departed heroes" (Stanley). Yet it is instinct with most generous and devout feeling. "As in view of the remains of a friend all the pain which he caused us while living is forgotten in the remembrance of his excellences and the kindness which he showed us, so David no longer has a memory for the period of persecution now past. He is a man, and not the judge of the dead. Therefore Saul stands before him only in his virtues, and he celebrates not only Jonathan, but also Saul, as loved ones who can never be forgotten. We see in this case that anger belongs only to the accidental utterances of noble souls, whose constant motive is love" (Delitzsch, 'Old Test. Hist. of Redemption'). "Though God often reproved his ancient people for paying religious homage to the idols of the heathen, yet we never find that he reproved them for paying funeral honours to departed men of superior merit among their own nation. Their example in this respect, therefore, seems to have a Divine sanction, and plainly teaches us the propriety of lamenting the death and commemorating the virtues of those who have been eminently useful in life" (N. Emmons).—D.

Vers. 19—27.—*David's lamentation over Saul and Jonathan.* In this lamentation there is—

I. A DECLARATION OF THE CAUSE OF MOURNING.

> "O pride of Israel, on thy high places slain!
> *Alas! fallen are the heroes.*"
>
> (Ver. 19.)

This is the key-note. It contains "the theme of the entire ode." 1. Men of rich endowments are the ornament, beauty, and glory of a people. 2. Such men are sometimes stricken down suddenly and under unexpected circumstances. "Not on the level plains where defeat from the chariots and horses of the enemy might have been expected and had been before encountered, but on the high places where victory seemed the rightful prize of the mountain chiefs and the indomitable infantry of the Israelitish hosts"—there the towering form of Saul was "hit by the archers," (1 Sam. xxxi. 3), the heroic heart of Jonathan thrust through, the splendour of Israel eclipsed. "All flesh is grass, and all the goodliness thereof is as the flower of the field," etc. (Isa. xl. 6, 7; Jer. ix. 23, 24). 3. Their loss is a great calamity, and a source of bitter grief to those who form a proper estimate of their worth, and possess a genuine concern for the public good (ver. 12).

II. A DEPRECATION OF THE TRIUMPH OF THE ENEMY.

> "Tell it not in Gath,
> Publish not the tidings in the streets of Askelon;
> Lest the daughters of the Philistines rejoice,
> Lest the daughters of the uncircumcised exult."
>
> (Ver. 20.)

In imagination the poet sees the swift-footed messengers bearing the tidings to the nearest cities of the Philistines—to Gath and Askelon; hears their songs of victory; and, in sympathy with his people, he utters the wish, "Oh that it might not have been!" 1. The fall of men of eminence among the people of God causes exultation among their adversaries. 2. The triumph of the wicked (the "uncircumcised") increases the suffering and shame of the godly in their misfortunes (Ps. xliv. 9—26; cxxiii. 4). 3. Whatever contributes to this result should be earnestly deprecated by all who have a sincere regard for the reputation of the great, the welfare of the good, and the honour of God. That which makes the ungodly rejoice should often make the faithful weep.

III. An imprecation on the scene of disaster.

> " O mountains in Gilboa, nor dew nor rain (be) upon you,
>   Nor fields of sacred offerings !
>   For there lies rusting the shield of heroes,
>   The shield of Saul unanointed with oil."
>
> (Ver. 21.)

"Over against the exultant joy of victory of Israel's enemies, which he would be gladly spared, David sets the attitude of mourning, in which he would behold the mountains of Gilboa, the scene of the heroes' death-struggle" (Erdmann). As that scene presents itself to his imagination, its beauty and fertility appear incongruous with the degradation of the slain, the misery of Israel, and his own absorbing grief. Has it no sympathy with them in their woe? He impatiently resents its indifference to his sorrow, and says in effect, "Oh that it might no more enjoy the favour of Heaven, nor produce the oblations by which its wrath is propitiated, but be a perpetual memorial of the mournful event!" (Ezek. xxxi. 15). 1. It is the tendency of grief to dwell upon the objects that are associated with its cause, and by the contemplation of them it becomes intensified. 2. Under the influence of strong emotion the mind seeks sympathy with itself even in material and inanimate objects, and is apt to indulge in wishes that are incapable of literal fulfilment. 3. The aspects of nature correspond in greater or less degree with the mental mood in which they are regarded. Sorrow projects its shadow over the external world, and clothes the fairest scenes with gloom. 4. The language of poetic inspiration must not be interpreted in its literal, prosaic sense, but in the light of the feeling and imagination of the poet. David's imprecation was no more intended to have an actual effect on the fields of Gilboa than Job's (Job iii. 1) on the day of his birth.

IV. A celebration of the virtues of the fallen.

> " From blood of slain,
>   From fat of heroes
>   The bow of Jonathan turned not backward,
>   And the sword of Saul returned not unsatisfied.
>   Saul and Jonathan ! the beloved and lovely !
>   In their lives and in their death they were not parted ;
>   Than eagles fleeter,
>   Than lions stronger."
>
> (Vers. 22, 23.)

The poet turns away from the melancholy scene to contemplate the heroes as he had known them, and describes their warlike prowess, their amiable dispositions, their mutual affection and faithful companionship, their agility and strength. Sincere sorrow over the dead: 1. Imposes a becoming silence concerning their imperfections, is forgetful of personal injuries, and puts out of sight everything that is contrary to itself (vers. 11, 12). *De mortuis nil nisi bonum.* 2. Delights to dwell upon the special aspects of their character which are worthy of admiration. 3. Sees in their extraordinary virtues a measure of the loss that has been experienced. "The nobility of Jonathan's character cannot easily be over-estimated. The rival claims of friendship and of nature, of David and Saul, were adjusted with admirable delicacy. He strengthened his friend's hands (1 Sam. xxii. 16) and saved his life; but he clung to his father. The shadows were falling on Saul, yet he did not join David's party, though he knew that he would succeed to the throne. With a gallant loyalty and a true-hearted despair, he followed his doomed sire to Gilboa" (B. Kent).

V. An enumeration of the gifts of a benefactor.

> " O daughters of Israel, wail for Saul !
>   He clothed you in scarlet with loveliness ;
>   He put jewels of gold upon your apparel.
>   *Alas! fallen are the heroes*
>   In the midst of the battle."
>
> (Vers. 24, 25.)

"The stream of sorrow, which down to this point has been united, here divides." David calls upon the daughters of Israel to wail, while the daughters of the Philistines triumph; and reminds them of the beneficence of Saul in distributing among them the spoils of war gained in his former victories. 1. The benefits conferred by an able and successful ruler upon his people are great, and deserve a grateful recognition. 2. The value of those benefits is seldom fully appreciated until they can be no longer bestowed. 3. Public mourning is as appropriate in its season as public rejoicing (1 Sam. xiii. 7). It expresses and deepens the general sorrow, and is a testimony to departed worth. The chorus is here repeated. "This recurrence of the same idea is perfectly congenial to the nature of elegy, since grief is fond of dwelling upon the particular objects of the passion, and frequently repeating them" (Lowth).

VI. A COMMEMORATION OF THE LOVE OF A FRIEND.

> " O Jonathan, on thy high places slain!
> Woe is me for thee, my brother Jonathan!
> Lovely wast thou to me-exceedingly,
> Marvellous (was) thy love to me beyond the love of woman.
> *Alas ! fallen are the heroes,*
> And perished the instruments of battle."
>
> (Vers. 26, 27.)

"At this culmination of grief the lament again sounds the key-note of the whole, and returns in conclusion to its chief object, the sorrow for the hero-glory of Israel destroyed in Saul and Jonathan." David's expression of sorrow manifests his deep love to his friend; still more, commemorates the "wonderful" love of his friend to him. "And in that love which he had borne towards him, there was something 'separate from all beside,' 'miraculous,' like a special work of God (this is the force of the word), more singular, undivided, and devoted than the love of women—even of Michal, of Ahinoam, of Abigail" (Stanley). 1. Pure, fervent, self-denying love is the chief excellence of human character. It is the greatest of all great things (1 Cor. xiii. 13; Col. iii. 14; Jas. ii. 8; 1 Pet. i. 22). 2. It is exalted and glorified in our view by means of death. 3. The memory of those in whom it dwells in an eminent degree is worthy of being perpetuated to all ages. (For translations and paraphrases of this lament see Lowth; Horsley, 'Bibl. Crit.;' Geo. Sandys: 1636; J. Oldham: 1677.)—D.

Ver. 19.—"*How are the mighty fallen!*" This expression suggests numerous reflections on—

I. THE VANITY OF MAN in the glory of his might. He is proud of his exalted state, his wisdom, strength, or riches; and he is admired and envied by others. But: 1. How precarious his *position!* He stands on "slippery places." All his grandeur rests on life, than which nothing is more unsubstantial or uncertain. 2. How futile his *purposes!* Formed in ignorance, weakness, and presumption, they are defeated and "broken off." "There is no king saved by the multitude of a host," etc. (Ps. xxxiii. 16). 3. How unsatisfying his *possessions!* They afford no solid peace in life or death. "Vanity of vanities," etc. (Eccles. i. 1). 4. How transient his *duration!* "Man is like to vanity; his days are as a shadow that passeth away" (Ps. cxliv. 4). 5. How signal his *downfall!* "How are they brought into desolation as in a moment!" (Ps. lxxiii. 19). 6. How evanescent his *fame!*

> " Your renown
> Is as the herb, whose hue doth come and go;
> And his might withers it, by whom it sprang
> Crude from the lap of earth."
>
> (Dante, ' Purg.,' xi.)

7. How complete his *humiliation!* The sword of Saul is cast away, his shield covered with blood and rust, his sceptre broken, his diadem and bracelet pilfered, his head placed in the temple of Dagon, his body fastened on the wall of Bethshan, his sons slain, and his dynasty destroyed. "Man that is in honour, and understandeth not, is like the beasts that perish" (Ps. xlix. 20; xxxix. 5; Dan. iv. 31; Acts xii. 23). "The last act is sanguinary, beautiful as is all the rest of the play. Dust is cast upon the head, and there is an end and for ever" (Pascal).

> "Farewell, a long farewell, to all my greatness!
> This is the state of man : To-day he putteth forth

> The tender leaves of hope; to-morrow blossoms,
> And bears his blushing honours thick upon him :
> The third day comes a frost, a killing frost;
> And,—when he thinks, good easy man, full surely
> His greatness is a-ripening,—nips his root,
> And then he falls, as I do."
>
> (Shakespeare, 'Henry VIII.')

II. THE PROVIDENCE OF GOD in the fall of the mighty. "If there be a God, the world must be *governed* by Providence" (1 Sam. ii. 1—10; ix. 1—25). 1. How evident its *existence!* "The Lord reigneth." It is not only declared in the Scriptures, but also plainly shown by the facts of history and daily observation. Of Saul it is said, "The Lord slew him" (1 Chron. x. 14). 2. How great its *power!* "He bringeth the princes to nothing; he maketh the judges of the earth as vanity" (Isa. xl. 23; Dan. iv. 25). 3. How vast its *domain!* All space, all time, all orders of being and all events, the least as well as the greatest (Matt. x. 29). Even the actions of free and responsible creatures, of individuals and nations, the Philistines as well as the Israelites, the evil as well as the good, are encircled and pervaded by it; foreseen, permitted, directed, controlled, restrained, or overruled. The course of Saul was foreseen at his appointment; yet he was not thereby placed under the *necessity* of acting as he did

> "Contingency, whose verge extendeth not
> Beyond the tablet of your mortal mold,
> Is all depictured in the eternal sight;
> But hence deriveth not necessity,
> More than the tall ship, hurried down the flood,
> Is driven by the eye that looks on it."
>
> ('Par.,' xvii.)

4. How manifold its *operations!* What skilful adaptations it makes! What endless instrumentalities it employs! What varied issues it evolves! 5. How mysterious its *methods!* The fact is certain, the mode unknown. Its ways are obscure, perplexing, completely hidden for a while, and then made apparent and fully justified. "We know in part." 6. How righteous its *administration!* (Ps. xxxi. 23; xxxvii. 1—11; xcvii. 2). "Saul died for his transgression," and Israel (whose self-will he reflected) was chastised through the man of their own choice. 7. How beneficent its *aims!* The repression of sin, the salvation of men, the glory of God. The fall of Israel's first king was overruled for the good of the nation; the fall of Israel, in subsequent ages, was "the riches of the world." "Oh the depth," etc.! (Rom. xi. 33—36).

IMPROVEMENT. 1. Glory not in any earthly good, but only in the Lord. 2. Be ambitious to serve rather than to rule. 3. "Rest in the Lord, and wait patiently for him." 4. Strive for the crown and kingdom that will endure for ever.—D.

Ver. 26.— *Wonderful love.* Human love is, in proportion to its purity and strength, a gift of Divine love. It also illustrates the love from which it proceeds, by reflecting its image as in a mirror. It is of a twofold nature—viz. benevolence or charity towards all, even the unworthy; and complacency towards those in whom it perceives the signs of excellence, or resemblance to itself. Of the latter kind was the love of Jonathan to David; and it was *wonderful*, considered in the light of (1) the selfishness that prevails among men, (2) the hindrances that stood in the way of its exercise, (3) the Divine grace by which it was produced and maintained, (4) the admirable qualities that distinguished it, and (5) the services and sacrifices in which it was evinced. It may be regarded as a representation of *the unspeakable love of Christ* towards his friends (John xv. 15) and brethren (John xx. 17); which is: 1. *Appreciative* of their worth (see 1 Sam. xviii. 1—4). It sets a special value upon them, however they may be despised by others; looks at them in relation not merely to what they actually are, but to what they may become; and singles them out as objects of its individual concern. "Thy love to *me* was wonderful." "He calleth his own sheep by name" (John x. 3). 2. *Sincere* and thoroughly disinterested (1 Sam. xix. 1—7). It seeks their welfare rather than its own; is trustful, unsuspecting, and watchful over their interests; freely communicates its thoughts and feelings; counsels and reproves; faithfully performs its promises; and affords protection and aid according to their need. 3. *Sympathetic.*

(1 Sam. xx. 1—9.) It finds delight in their society; holds familiar intercourse with them; desires a return of its affection; makes their joys and sorrows its own; and is considerate, gentle, tender, and kind. "Behold, how he loved him!" (John xi. 36). 4. *Intense*. (1 Sam. xx. 10—42.) "More wonderful than woman's love." "No less ardent, sincere, and sweet than the highest conjugal affection; which ought to be (as Strigelius here glosses) ardent without simulation, sincere without any suspicions, and sweet without morosity or disdain" (Patrick). Its intensity is shown in its utterances, efforts, tears; courage, forbearance, forgiveness, and unwearied patience. 5. *Self-denying* and self-sacrificing. Jonathan identified himself with his friend, whose life was in imminent peril; renounced a crown and suffered shame for his sake: but who shall tell what Christ renounced and suffered for us (Phil. ii. 7, 8)? 6. *Enduring*. "Having loved his own which were in the world, he loved them unto the end" (John xiii. 1); and gave them, on the eve of his departure, a proof of his condescending, pure, undying affection. His love is still the same; and it "passeth knowledge" (Eph. iii. 19). 7. *Influential* (1 Sam. xxiii. 16—18) in attracting love and constraining devotion; strengthening, preserving, comforting, purifying those in whom it dwells; perfecting its image in them and preparing them to enter into its eternal joy. "Unto him that loved us," etc. (Rev. i. 5).—D.

Vers. 6—10.—*A sad end of a perverse life*. We have here an Amalekite's account of the death of Saul. Whether it presents the truth, and can therefore be harmonized with the account in 1 Sam. xxxi., is doubtful. Possibly Saul did not die at once when he fell upon his sword, and being in anguish, and fearing to fall into the hands of the Philistines, begged the Amalekite to despatch him. But it is more probable that the account was false. In either case Saul committed suicide. It was a tragic end of a tragic life—a life full of the interest which arises from remarkable events, contrasted characters, the working of powerful passions, etc. But we have to view it in the aspects which tend to our moral and spiritual profit.

I. IT WAS THE END OF A LIFE WHOSE BEGINNING WAS FULL OF PROMISE. Arising from: 1. *His personal qualities*. Those of body—tall and commanding, fitting him in such times to be a leader of men. Those of moral nature. Character is the most powerful factor in a life; and if we see a youth of good character we hope well of him. Saul comes before us as a modest, humble, unassuming youth, diligently discharging his duty as a son, and affectionately concerned not to give pain to his father (1 Sam. ix. 5, where "take thought" means "fear," "be anxious"). Still even then, judging from the silence of the narrative, he was without decided piety. 2. *Divine calls and gifts*. Chosen of God to be king, he was anointed by Samuel, and received unmistakable signs that the prophet was the representative of God in the matter. Chosen also by lot, although some were disaffected, he was soon able to secure general acceptance by his prowess and able leadership in war; and was solemnly set apart as sovereign. Moreover, a change passed over himself which fitted him for his post. "God gave him another heart" (1 Sam. x. 9). He became also a partaker of the spirit of prophecy. (1 Sam. x. 10.) 3. *Great opportunities*. The career opened to Saul was one of peculiar dignity and honour. Called to be the first king of God's nation, he might have been also the father of a race of such kings, and have thus occupied no mean place in the development of God's plans for the redemption of mankind. And his immediate work, that of leading the people to victory over their heathen oppressors and clearing the land of them, and then of drawing the tribes of Israel more closely into unity and framing them into a "kingdom of God," was worthy of the highest powers and the strenuous labours of a long life. 4. *Early achievements*. Those, for instance, recorded in 1 Sam. xi., in which he manifested both courage and capacity, and which obtained for him the general consent of the people to his appointment.

II. IT WAS THE END OF A LIFE WHICH HAD BEEN A CONSPICUOUS FAILURE. He lost his opportunity, forfeited his throne, and deprived his family of the honour of succeeding him. He was tried, found wanting, and rejected. He had shown that he possessed some kingly qualities. Did he possess the most essential quality for the king of such a people—a king under God as supreme Monarch—that of faith in God, showing itself by ready and hearty obedience even under difficulties? It was peculiarly important that the first king should not fail in such qualities. Twice especially he was put to the proof and failed ; in the first instance (1 Sam. xiii.) by doing what he ought not to have done, and in the second (1 Sam. xv.) by leaving undone what he ought to have done. Twice his doom was pronounced by Samuel, who then sorrowfully retired, and left him to his own self-will and certain fate. But though he thus failed in securing the great prize set before him, he had space and opportunity for repentance and its fruits. He became after a time aware who was to secure the honour which he had forfeited, and had he been humbled in spirit and penitent, he might have shown by his conduct to David that he acquiesced in the Divine will, and was prepared to be a co-worker with God in its accomplishment. He might have cherished the spirit of John the Baptist, and said with resignation, if not joy, " He must increase, but I must decrease." Instead of this he cherished envy, which ripened into hatred, and would have culminated in murder but for the special providence which guarded David's life. Baffled in his repeated attempts on his life, he sought to kill his own son, because he pleaded for David; and actually slew eighty-five priests, their wives, children, and cattle, because one of them had shown kindness to David, in ignorance of the real state of affairs. Meanwhile David acted towards him with the utmost forbearance, sparing him when once and again he could easily have taken his life ; the subsequent know-ledge of which softened the king, but only for a little while. Yet he was not without some zeal for the Law of God, and, besides his sacrificial offerings, " had put away those that had familiar spirits, and the wizards, out of the land " (1 Sam. xxviii. 3). In the extremity, however, of his distress and perplexity, he sought the help of a woman that had a familiar spirit, but only to have his doom once more pronounced.

III. IT WAS THE END OF A LIFE IN WHICH THE DISPLEASURE OF GOD HAD BEEN MADE SIGNALLY MANIFEST. 1. *By the sentences of rejection pronounced upon Saul by Samuel.* (1 Sam. xiii. 14 ; xv. 23.) 2. *By the sorrowful abandonment of him by Samuel.* (1 Sam. xv. 35.) 3. *By the departure of the Spirit of the Lord from him, and the entrance into him of "an evil spirit from the Lord."* The Spirit which had fitted him for the dis-charge of his duties forsook him, and an evil spirit troubled him—an habitual melan-choly, most likely, and depression. He felt he was not the same man. He was continually haunted with the sense of his being condemned and rejected, of the inevitableness of his fate, the certainty that, however long he might continue sovereign, he could not transmit the dignity to his son. And this gloom sometimes passed over into frenzy. He was, as we should say, subject to fits of insanity. This, doubtless, furnishes some excuse for the madness of his conduct. 4. *By the refusal of God to answer his prayers in the depth of his distress.* (1 Sam. xxviii. 6.) That had come upon him which is described in Prov. i. 24—31. 5. *By his miserable end.* Nothing, surely, can be more affecting than the circumstances of his death, as recorded in 1 Sam. xxxi. 3—6, supplemented by our text.

CONCLUSION. 1. *Every man has a Divine mission.* Not only kings and great men. God has assigned us our post, and expects us to fill it as under him. In doing so he gives the opportunity of great distinction and honour, even the attainment of an everlasting crown of glory. 2. *Habitual regard to the Divine will is essential to the fulfilment of our mission.* And how shall we ascertain it ? We have no inspired Samuel by our side. But we have a greater than he, even the Lord Jesus Christ—the Word he has given us, the Spirit he bestows, the principles of godliness, holiness, and love which he implants. We need not seriously err. 3. *Disobedience will be surely followed by punishment.* 4. *One serious failure in obedience to God may blight and ruin the whole life.* 5. *Persistent rebellion issues in utter rejection of God.* And the final doom may be foreshadowed by the withdrawment of God's Spirit, and entire abandonment to the spirit of evil. 6. *Let not the young trust to their good moral qualities.* Let them seek at once through Christ that change of heart which will turn their virtues into holiness, render them loving and loyal to God, and ensure for them his favour now and evermore.—G. W.

Ver. 14.—*A weighty question.* David could consistently ask this question, for he had throughout acted with devout regard to the Divine anointing which Saul. had received. When the opportunity was afforded him of slaying Saul, and he was urged to do so, he again and again steadily refused, notwithstanding all the provocation he received, and although he knew that Saul would have no scruple in putting him to death. Yet the person to whom this question was addressed could, perhaps, hardly appreciate its significance. Supposing his narrative truthful, he may have been actuated by compassion in what he did; and he hoped for reward from David, in whom he saw the coming king of Israel. But, however this may be, the question may be used as applicable to those who assail with deadly intention him who is pre-eminently the anointed (the Christ) of God. First, to those who actually slew him, or took part in his death; and then to all who become sharers in their guilt by endeavouring to destroy his authority and sway amongst men.

I. WHO MAY BE THUS ADDRESSED. 1. *Those who assail the gospel of Christ.* 2. *Those who endeavour to destroy his work in the souls of men.* Such as resolutely resist and suppress the thoughts and emotions he produces in themselves, resisting his Spirit. Such also as set themselves to prevent or destroy his influence over others; endeavouring to undermine their faith, to corrupt their morals, to entice them from the paths of piety and goodness (see Matt. xviii. 6, 7). 3. *Those who persecute his people.* "Saul, Saul, why persecutest thou *me*?"

II. WHY THEY ARE NOT AFRAID. 1. *Ignorance, in some, of what they are doing.* As seems to have been the case with this Amalekite. This palliation of guilt is admitted in the case of those who put our Lord to death (Acts iii. 17; 1 Cor. ii. 8). And he told his disciples that their persecutors even unto death would think they were "doing God service" (John xvi. 2). But ignorance itself may be guiltiness, though not so great as sinning against the light, knowing it to be light and hating it on that account. 2. *Disbelief as to the truth of Christianity, as to God himself, or even as to the reality and worth of godliness and goodness.* 3. *Moral insensibility.* Which may spring from disbelief, or from habits of godlessness and wickedness, or of mere worldliness. 4. *Expectation of impunity.* Because of the seeming weakness of him whom they assail (Matt. xxvii. 42, 43), or his delay in punishing (Eccles. viii. 11), or from false notions of the goodness of God. All these reasons cannot exist in the same person; but some in one, some in another.

III. WHY THEY OUGHT TO BE AFRAID. 1. *Because Jesus is the Lord's Anointed— the Christ of God.* He comes to men with Divine authority, appointed to be their King and Saviour. There is sufficient proof of this. "This is my beloved Son" was not only uttered from heaven; it appears in the whole character, teaching, miracles, in the life, death, and resurrection of Jesus Christ; in the correspondence of prophecy and history; in the testimony of the apostles and the miracles which attested their mission; in the birth, growth, and perpetuation of the Church; in the mighty beneficial influence of Christianity in the world; in its effects on individual character and happiness, on family life and national life. It is echoed in the hearts and consciences of men; in the happy consciousness of every Christian. It is fashionable now to apologize for unbelief, and treat sceptics very tenderly, as if their love of truth made them sceptics. But compare the sayings of our Lord, "He that is of the truth heareth my voice," and "If any man willeth to do his will, he shall know of the teaching, whether it be of God." If, then, Jesus be God's Anointed, to fight against him is to fight against God, which is both impious and perilous. 2. *Because of the penalties incurred by opposition to Christ.* The injury they do to themselves now, the judgment which will come upon them hereafter. Him whom they assail they will one day see coming in the clouds of heaven, to take vengeance on his foes. "Those mine enemies . . . bring hither and slay them before me." 3. *Because of the injury they do to others.* Men with any regard to the welfare of others may well be asked to pause before they endeavour to rob them of their faith, and all that springs out of it, in sound moral principles, right character, happiness, comfort under the troubles and burdens of life, and hope in death; especially as avowedly they have no adequate substitute to offer. They ought to be afraid of taking a course which, if successful, would deprive the lowly and the poor of their chief consolation, leave unrestrained by any sufficient check the passions of men, and so demoralize and disorganize society.

IV. THE EXPOSTULATIONS WHICH SHOULD BE ADDRESSED TO THEM. "How is it that thou art not afraid," etc.? Christian speakers and writers sometimes oppose those who are opposing Christ in a style suitable to the discussion of some abstract question. The conflict is conducted as if it were one of mere opinion. But surely those to whom Christ is dear ought to make it felt that they regard the question of his position and claims as one of life and death—one in which all that is most valued by them for the sake of themselves, their families, and society at large is involved. And it is due to the foes of Christ themselves that this should be done. Their consciences should be addressed as well as their reasoning faculty. Remonstrance should be employed, and warning, as well as argument. Only let the warmth shown be that of love and intense desire for the salvation of men.

Finally, let the Christian rejoice that all opposition to "the Lord's Anointed" is, and must be, vain. It cannot injure him; it cannot seriously or permanently injure his cause. It can only recoil on those who engage in it (see Ps. ii.; Luke xx. 17, 18).—G. W.

Ver. 20.—*Joy amongst the enemies of the Church.* "Tell it not in Gath," etc. A poetical deprecation; for already had it been told among the Philistines, and triumphed over; and yet would be. The language expresses David's sorrow at the joy of the Philistines, and its cause. The words have often been used to express the concern of good men when Christians give occasion to the enemies of Christ's kingdom to rejoice. I. THE OCCASIONS OF SUCH JOY. 1. In general, *the misfortunes of the Church*, whatever hinders its advancement or causes reversal. 2. In particular, *the inconsistencies of professing Christians*. It is amazing how men will gloat over the occasional lapses of Christians into sins which they are themselves habitually committing. Still it is a serious enhancement of the guilt of such lapses that they cause "the enemies of the Lord to blaspheme" (ch. xii. 14). 3. *Contentions and divisions among Christians.* When these are rife, the world is apt to exclaim in scorn, "See how these Christians love one another!" 4. *Failures in their work.* II. THE CAUSES OF SUCH JOY. 1. *Hatred of God and goodness.* To "rejoice in iniquity" is a sure sign of this; and to rejoice in the enfeebling of the power which most of all tends to its subjugation—the power of Christian life and teaching—is scarcely less so. It is a diabolical joy. 2. *The encouragement in sin which is derived from the faults of good men.* Sinners feel as if justified in their own sins when Christians fall into them; their guilty consciences are relieved. As if sin in themselves were less sinful because practised by those who profess to have renounced it; or as if the Law of God, which condemns the Christian's occasional sins, did not at least equally condemn the habitual sins of others. Rather should they remember that the knowledge of the evil of sin by which they condemn others is to their own condemnation (Rom. ii. 1, 3). They ought, therefore, to take warning instead of indulging satisfaction. III. How CHRISTIANS SHOULD BE AFFECTED BY IT. 1. *They should be careful not needlessly to publish that which will produce it.* "Tell it not," etc. Not *needlessly;* for ofttimes secrecy is impossible, sometimes it would be injurious. We must not deny facts, nor palliate sin, to prevent the triumph of enemies. But we ought not to eagerly announce to the world the occurrences which tend to our humiliation and their exultation. (1) For the sake of those who would exult. That they may not add to their sins by their unholy joy, nor become more hardened in them. (2) Lest we should put stumbling-blocks in the way of feeble Christians; or (3) discourage our brethren in their conflicts with evil; or (4) lessen the power of the testimony of the Church on the side of Christ and holiness. 2. *They should be still more careful so to live as to give no occasion for such exultation.* "That by well-doing ye may put to silence the ignorance of foolish men" (1 Pet. ii. 15). 3. *They should in no degree imitate it.* Which they do when they rejoice at any scandal which arises in another Church that they regard as a rival, or at failure on its part in efforts to do good. Christian love "rejoiceth not in iniquity, but rejoiceth in the truth," and will be grieved at sin wherever it may be found, and at the failure of Christian work by whomsoever it may be done.—G. W.

Ver. 26.—*A beloved friend's death lamented.* David's lamentation over Saul was genuine. He saw now the good in him, and passed over the evil. He remembered his early kindnesses to himself, and thought not of his later enmity. He associated him with Jonathan, and was softened towards him on that account. He mourned sincerely that his death should have been caused, though not directly inflicted, by the enemies of his nation, the Philistines. He sympathized with the people in their loss, and in the troubles which would surely spring from his death. But his lament over Jonathan was of another order. It was the outburst of a passionate grief at the tragical death of an affectionate and faithful friend, whom he tenderly loved, whose life had been lovely, and to David most kind and helpful.

I. JONATHAN'S FRIENDSHIP WITH DAVID. 1. *It seems to have originated in admiration.* The qualities of David, as they were displayed in the conflict with Goliath, found an echo in Jonathan's own soul, which became "knit with the soul of David," so that "Jonathan loved him as his own soul" (1 Sam. xviii. 1, 3). There were natural affinities—youth, courage, faith in God. But there was, doubtless, also that subtle something, undiscoverable by analysis, which specially adapts one soul for closest union with another. 2. *It was very warm and passionate.* See the above quotation, and David's words in the text, "Thy love to me was wonderful, passing the love of women." 3. *It was cemented and confirmed by pledges and compacts.* (1 Sam. xviii. 3, 4; xx. 16, 17, 41, 42; xxiii. 18.) Note especially 1 Sam. xx. 17, "Jonathan caused David to swear again," etc. His love was so strong and passionate that it was never weary of pouring itself out in vows and protests and covenants. 4. *It was more than disinterested.* For Jonathan soon saw that David would succeed his father on the throne, and the prospect was strongly represented to him by Saul (1 Sam. xx. 31). But no jealousy sprang up in his heart; he was content to be second where David was first (1 Sam. xxiii. 17). 5. *It was shown by practical services.* He interceded with his father repeatedly for David, and exposed himself thereby to death from his father's rage. He warned David of his father's deadly purpose, and repeated the warning when, contrary to his hope, he found how implacable that purpose was. He visited his friend when banished from court and pursued by his relentless enemy. He "strengthened his hands in God." In all ways he proved himself a "brother;" yea, "a friend that sticketh closer than a brother" (Prov. xviii. 24). 6. *It was associated with strict loyalty to his father.* He had a difficult part to play, but he played it well. He was loving and devoted to Saul, while maintaining so warm a friendship with him whose life the father sought. David would only the more admire and love him on this account, for he was equally loyal to the unhappy king, and would have served him as devotedly if he had been permitted; and so, when both were slain on one battle-field, he united their memories in his elegy. "Saul and Jonathan were lovely and pleasant in their lives, and in death they were not divided."

II. HIS DEATH. The dearest friends must be parted by death; and the pleasure they have enjoyed in each other's love and society will make the pain the more severe.

> "There is no union here of hearts
> Which finds not here an end."

Yet this is not strictly true. Christian friendships are immortal.

III. DAVID'S LAMENTATION. A worthy tribute of friendship—tender, sublime, and sincere. David would feel his loss irreparable. No friendship equal to this was it possible to form. Happily, while lamenting his loss, his sorrow was not embittered by the memory of any unkindness or unfaithfulness on his part. It is, however, singular that even in such a composition no reference to future life and reunion should find place. The consolations so natural to a Christian are unnoticed. They were not ordinarily known with sufficient distinctness to be of much service. "Our Saviour Jesus Christ . . . brought life and immortality to light through the gospel" (2 Tim. i. 10).

We may regard the friendship of Jonathan for David as a picture of—

I. THE FRIENDSHIP OF JESUS FOR US. This is "wonderful" indeed, in its condescension, its spontaneousness, its disinterestedness, its sacrifices, its services and bestowments. And it never ends. This Friend never dies, never changes in love or power.

II. WHAT OUR FRIENDSHIP TO HIM SHOULD BE. It cannot be purely disinterested; we owe so much to him, and expect so much from him. Yet may our love be far more than gratitude; we may love him for his own sake, and shall do so if we are his. Nor let us restrain our affection, but lavish it upon him—ardent, tender, even passionate. He requires and deserves to be loved more than our dearest earthly relatives and friends. But ever let us remember that he values most our obedient and self-denying service, and our practical love for his sake of those whom he loves and for whom he gave his life.

III. WHAT OUR FRIENDSHIP WITH EACH OTHER SHOULD BE. Our Lord came to found in the world a sacred friendship, a brotherhood, based on faith in him and love to him, and kept alive by regard for his love to us all. In Jonathan, and still more in Jesus, we see what this friendship ought to be.—G. W.

EXPOSITION.

CHAPTER II.

Ver. 1.—Unto Hebron. As soon as David had assuaged his grief, his thoughts would naturally turn towards his country. Fuller news would reach him every day respecting the movements of the Philistines, who, after so decisive a victory, would quickly overrun all the central districts of Palestine, where the battle had been fought. And very bitter must David's feelings have been. Had he continued in Israel, he and his six hundred men would now have hastened to the rescue, and all the braver warriors of the land would have gathered round them. As it was, he was too entangled with the Philistines, and too much distrusted by the northern tribes, to be of much use. Still, we learn from 1 Chron. xii., that brave men did continually swell the number of his followers. Detachments of the tribes of Gad and Manasseh, instead of joining Saul at Gilboa, went to David as he withdrew to Ziklag. And while he remained there a considerable body of men from Benjamin and Judah came to him under the command of Amasa, David's nephew. So numerous were they as to alarm David, who went out to meet them, fearing lest they had come to betray him; and glad was he to hear their answer, "Thine are we, David, and on thy side, thou son of Jesse." Thus even as it was, his forces daily grew more numerous; for "from day to day there came to David to help him, until it was a great host, like the host of God" (1 Chron. xii. 22). But there was no national acknowledgment. With his numbers thus continually increasing, David was encouraged to make some attempt for the deliverance of Israel; but his position was one of serious danger. Great was the risk, but he knew where to go for guidance, and determines, therefore, to put the matter into God's hand. He summons Abiathar with the ephod, and, in the presence of his captains, asks for permission to go up to some city of his own tribe. The answer is favourable, and Hebron is the city selected. It was a place of ancient sanctity, was well situated in the mountains of Judah for defence, and as the Philistines had not yet invaded that region, but probably would soon try to ravage it, the people would be sure to welcome the presence of one who brought with him a powerful body of trained men.

Ver. 3.—They dwelt in the cities of Hebron. Not only had David wives, whom he took with him to Hebron, but many of his warriors were married, and thus they and their households formed a numerous body of people, for whom Hebron could scarcely find accommodation. Moreover they had flocks and herds captured from the Amalekites, for which they needed pasturage. And therefore David dispersed them in the towns and villages of which Hebron was the capital, posting them in such a manner as to render it easy for him to summon them together, while taking care that they did not injure his tribesmen, or dispossess them of their lands. We may feel sure that he consulted the chief men of Hebron as to these arrangements, and obtained their approval.

Ver. 4.—They anointed David. Samuel's anointing (1 Sam. xvi. 13) had been private, and, if we may judge by the manner in which Eliab treated David (1 Sam. xvii. 28), even his own family had not attached much importance to it. It was nevertheless the indication of Jehovah's purpose, and now the anointing of David by the elders of Judah was the first step towards its accomplishment. And this was an independent act, though the knowledge of Samuel's anointing had prepared the way for it; and David thus acquired a legal right and authority by the nation's will, which Samuel could not have given him. So Saul's anointing by Samuel, and his election to be king at Gilgal, were independent acts; and while the former gave the king his sacredness, the latter conferred upon him jurisdiction and power. **King over the house of Judah.** How came the Philistines to allow this? When subsequently he was again anointed, and became King of all Israel, the Philistines gathered their hosts at once; not because he captured Jerusalem, which was then a mere hill-fort belonging to the Jebusites, but evidently because they thought him dangerous. But why did they not crush him now? One reason, probably, was that Judæa was a difficult country for military operations. The tribe, too, had stood aloof from Saul, and its strength was unbroken. But the chief reason apparently was that David maintained friendly relations with Achish, and paid him tribute. This explains the curious fact that Ziklag continued to be the private property of the house of David (1 Sam. xxvii. 6). The doings of a vassal of the King of Gath were regarded as of little importance. Had he not even marched with them to Aphek, as one of the servants of Achish? But when he endeavoured to restore the kingdom of Saul, they first made a hasty rush upon him, and, when repelled, they gathered their forces for as formidable an invasion as that which had ended in their victory at Gilboa.

Ver. 5.—**David sent messengers unto the men of Jabesh-Gilead.** This was David's first act as king, and it was worthy of him. Some suppose that when David was told of their deed, it was with a view of prejudicing him against them. But this is not credible. By this time all men knew how loyal and affectionate were David's feelings towards his former king; and moreover the men of Jabesh were bound to Saul by no ordinary ties of gratitude (1 Sam. xi.). Nor could David wish that Saul's remains, and those of Jonathan, should be subject to indignity. We may well feel sure that information respecting Saul was eagerly welcomed at Hebron, and the valiant men there would all rejoice at finding that the high spirit of the nation was not quenched. But in sending to thank them, in promising to requite them, and in bidding them persevere in similar conduct, David was acting as the head of the nation; and, to justify his action, he informs them that the men of Judah had made him their king.

Ver. 8.—**Abner.** This hero had been present at the battle of Gilboa, and probably had rallied many of the defeated Israelites, and made as much resistance as was possible to the onward march of the Philistines. And as soon as he had effected his retreat into the region beyond the Jordan, his power would be supreme. There was no one there to oppose the commander-in-chief of what remained of Saul's army. Certainly all that remained of Saul's body-guard of three thousand men would gather round Abner, and as the Philistines did not push their pursuit further than the Jordan, he was free to do as he chose. Nor would there be any opposition. Abner was bound to do his best for Saul's family, and the people would feel this, and approve of his conduct in standing up for the children of their king. Moreover, David by his conduct had made himself an object of suspicion to all the valiant men who had formed Saul's army, and these would be the more embittered against him by their defeat. **Ishbosheth.** This name signifies "man of shame," that is, "man of the shameful thing," the

idol. Originally he was named Eshbaal (1 Chron. viii. 33; ix. 39), that is, "man of Baal," the word *esh* being merely a dialectic variation for *ish*, equivalent to "man." At this early date Baal was not the specific name of any idol, but simply meant "lord," "master," "husband." In the earlier books of the Bible we find the word used of many local deities, who were lords of this or that, but had nothing in common with the Phœnician Baal, whose worship Ahab attempted to introduce into Israel. From that time Baal became a term of reproach, and Bosheth, "the shame," was substituted for it in the old names of which it had formed part. Thus Gideon is still called Jerubbaal in 1 Sam. xii. 11, but the title is transformed into Jerubbesheth, or more correctly, Jerubbosheth, "let the shame plead," in ch. xi. 21. Originally, therefore, the name Ishbaal had no discreditable meaning, but signified, "man of the Lord," or, as Ewald supposes, "lordly man." It was not till long afterwards, when Israel had been horrified by Jezebel's doings, that Baal, except in the sense of "husband," became an ill-omened word. Jonathan, whose own name, "Jehovah's gift," in Greek Theodore, is proof sufficient that Saul's family were worshippers of the true God, called his son's name Meribbaal, "the Lord's strife" (1 Chron. viii. 34). In some strange way this was altered into Mephibosheth, that is, "from the face of the shameful thing" (ch. iv. 4. etc.). Possibly it is a corruption of Meribbosheth, but it is remarkable that a son of Saul by his concubine Rizpah also bore the name (ch. xxi. 8). Among the ancestors of Saul, the simple name Baal, "Lord," occurs (1 Chron. viii. 30). **Mahanaim.** Abner chose this town because it was on the eastern side of the Jordan, and so beyond the range of the Philistines, who never seem to have crossed the river. It was situated on the borders of the tribe of Gad and the half-tribe of Manasseh, from both of which valiant warriors had joined David; but the people generally were not ill affected to the house of Saul. As having been assigned to the Levites (Josh. xxi. 38), it had a quasi-religious character, inherited from the vision of angels seen there by Jacob (Gen. xxxii. 2). As a safe, out-of-the-way place, David subsequently took refuge there (ch. xvii. 24). (On its exact site, see Conder's 'Heth and Moab,' pp. 177—181.)

Ver. 9.—**Make him king over.** A different preposition is used with the first three names from that employed afterwards, as though Ishbosheth's reign over Gilead and Jezreel was a reality, but that he had only a shadowy claim to dominion over Ephraim, Benjamin, and all Israel. **Gilead.** As Mahanaim lay upon the borders of Gad and Manasseh, Abner would easily control these two tribes, and Reuben, which was never an active or enterprising tribe, would follow their lead. Of the **Ashurites** nothing is known, and the reading is uncertain, as the LXX. has "Thasir," and the Vulgate and Syriac "Geshur." The Chaldee paraphrase boldly gives "the house of Asher;" but this tribe lay close to Phœnicia, on the extreme north-west. There are two places called Geshur (see on ch. iii. 3), but neither of them seems meant, and more probably it was some place the name of which was uncommon, and so was wrongly copied by scribes until the present confusion arose. **Jezreel.** The name of this place, as specially subject to Ishbosheth, is surprising; for the town, at this time of no importance, lay in the wide plain between the mountains of Gilboa and the little Hermon. But this district was the prize won by the Philistines, and was a region where their cavalry and chariots gave them a great advantage. For Ishbosheth to have had even a nominal dominion over Jezreel, he must either have become a tributary, or Abner must have maintained a not unsuccessful struggle there after the battle of Gilboa. The latter is the more probable. In safe possession of all the country east of the Jordan, Abner was not likely to consent to anything so humiliating as submission to the Philistines; while David's connection with Achish made it neither so galling to him nor so disadvantageous. As the Transjordanic tribes assembled at Hebron to make David king to the number of one hundred and twenty thousand men (1 Chron. xii. 37), Abner plainly had large resources at his command, and, though the people were not very earnest in the cause of Saul's house, yet they would probably assemble in considerable numbers after the battle of Gilboa, to prevent any irruption of the victors into their country. At their head Abner probably gained some advantages over the Philistines, and thus became powerful enough to proclaim Ishbosheth king, and as Ephraim and Benjamin acquiesced, he became nominally ruler over all Israel.

Vers. 10, 11.—**Ishbosheth . . . two years . . . David . . . seven years and six months.** Where are we to place the five years and a half of difference? The usual assumption is that David was made King of Israel immediately upon Ishbosheth's murder; but this is wrong. We cannot believe that Abner would allow so long a period as five years to elapse before asserting the claims of Saul's family, especially as David was already made King of Judah at Hebron. Still, as the war with the Philistines was the first object of his care, and as some form of

popular ratification was necessary, some months may have passed before Ishbosheth was publicly installed as king, though Abner must have acted in his name from the first. The main interval of five years before David's accession must have been after Ishbosheth's death. That murder, and still more so the murder of Abner, must have made David an object of great suspicion to all Israel. Shimei, when he called him "a bloody man" (ch. xvi. 8), was but uttering a slander commonly current among the people. Gradually most of them would become convinced of his innocence; and all, as they contrasted the anarchy which prevailed in their country with the peace and security won by David for Judah, would regard his election as the best course under the circumstances. As the Philistines immediately resented their action, and endeavoured to crush the king before he could concentrate his power, it is probable that during these five years they had again obtained practical command of the more fertile districts of Palestine. **Ishbosheth . . . was forty years old.** In the previous narrative Jonathan always appears as the most important of Saul's sons, and naturally it is assumed that he was the firstborn; yet his child was but five years old at his father's death, while Ishbosheth, his uncle, a younger brother of Jonathan, is described as a man of forty. Some think that Ishbosheth was the eldest son, but in 1 Chron. viii. 33 he is placed last, and, though a weak man, was not so feeble as to have been set aside from the succession. But confessedly the chronology of Saul's reign is so full of difficulties, that it is impossible altogether to explain it (see note on 1 Sam. xiii. 1).

Ver. 12.—**Abner . . . went out.** This is a further proof of considerable success on Abner's side. Encouraged by the result of numerous skirmishes with the Philistines, and the gradual restoration of the king's authority in Ephraim and Benjamin, Abner determined to make the attempt to win back Judah also. There David had been content with protecting Judah, and establishing good order; and, following his constant custom, had taken no steps to obtain for himself the kingdom "over all Israel." The war was of Abner's choosing, and shows him to us in the character of an able but ambitious and restless man.

Ver. 13.—**The pool of Gibeon.** As Gibeon, which lay about six miles north-west from Jerusalem, was twenty-six miles distant from Hebron, and about the same distance from Mahanaim, it is plain that David knew of Abner's march. Possibly he had been summoned to yield his kingdom up to Ishbosheth as the rightful lord, but, while taking no measures to extend his rule, he felt himself justified in defending his election to be king over Judah. *The pool of Gibeon* is described by Robinson (' Researches,' ii. 136) as " an open tank about a hundred and twenty feet in length and a hundred in breadth, surrounded by a grove of olive trees. Above it, excavated in the rock, is a subterranean reservoir, to receive the water from a copious spring, from which the overflow descends into the tank below." As neither party was willing to shed the first blood in a civil war, of which the Philistines would reap the benefit, they both halted in sight of one another on opposite sides of the hill, with the tank below them in the middle.

Ver. 14.—**Let the young men now arise.** " Now " is not an adverb of time, but is hortative, and therefore rightly translated in the Revised Version, " I pray thee." It is by no means certain that Abner meant that this single combat should decide the war; for similar preludes before a battle are not uncommon among the Arabians, and serve, as this did, to put an end to the mutual unwillingness to begin the onslaught. So, too, games often preceded outbreaks of Scandinavian blood-feuds. And this was probably Abner's object. He was the assailant, but now found that his men shrank from mortal combat with their brethren. There is thus no comparison between this combat and that of the Curiatii and Horatii described in Livy, i. x. 25. **Let them play.** The word is grim enough, though intended to gloss over the cruel reality. On each side twelve of the most skilful champions were to be selected, who were to fight in stern earnest with one another, while the rest gazed upon the fierce spectacle. The sight of the conflict would whet their appetite for blood, and their reluctance would give place to thirst for revenge. The request was too thoroughly in accordance with Joab's temper for him to refuse, and his immediate answer was, **Let them arise.**

Ver. 16.—**His sword in his fellow's side.** The absence of the verb in the original sets powerfully before us the rapidity of the whole action. But what an action! Twenty-four experienced men each take the other by the head, and, without any attempt at self-defence, thrust their swords into their opponents' side, and leave their own sides exposed to a similar thrust. Were they, then, unskilful in the use of weapons? Impossible. Were they blinded by hatred of one another? But no rancour would make a man forget his skill in defence. Here there is no variety, no checkered fortune of the combatants, but all twenty-four do and suffer just the same; and it is remarkable that they had swords only, and no shields. With shields on their arms, they could not have seized one another by

the hair. It seems certain, therefore, that this mutual butchery was the " play ; " nor can we conceive of a more murderous and savage proceeding. Abner, at the head of his fierce Benjamites, thought, perhaps, that Joab had no men among his followers willing to throw life away in so senseless a manner. But Joab was as ready as Abner, and possibly some code of false honour, such as used to make men practise duelling, required the acceptance of the challenge. And so, with their appetite for blood whetted by the sight of twenty-four murders, they hastened to begin the fight. **Helkath-hazzurim.** Literally this means " the field of flints ; " but as the flint is constantly used for any hard rock (Ps. lxxviii. 20), the Authorized Version has admitted into the margin a paraphrase taken from the Vulgate, which supposes that by flints are meant " strong men," and renders, " the field of strong men." So in Isa. xxvi. 4 " the flint," or rock, " of ages," is even translated " everlasting strength." Flints, however, were constantly used by the Israelites for knives whenever extreme sharpness was required. Thus for the circumcising of Israel, Jehovah commanded Joshua to prepare knives of flint (Josh. v. 2) ; and in course of time the sharp or whetted edge of a weapon was called its flint. Thus in Ps. lxxxix. 43 we read, " Thou hast turned back the flint of his sword." The name therefore probably means " the field of the sharp knives " (see margin of the Revised Version), and refers to the short swords with which they murdered one another.

Ver. 17.—**A very sore battle.** The purpose of Abner was thus gained. Excited by the spectacle of merciless slaughter, the armies manœuvred no longer, but rushed fiercely to the attack, and fought with fury. But the mighty men of David were irresistible. Only nineteen of his warriors fell, while Abner lost three hundred and sixty, and was forced to flee.

Ver. 19.—**Asahel pursued after Abner.** This episode is fully narrated, both because of Asahel's rank as David's nephew, and also because of its tragical consequences to Abner himself. Asahel was a son of Zeruiah, David's sister, and, while his own brothers were of little use to him, his nephews, Joab, Abishai, and Asahel, were the mainstays of David's throne. As their father's name is never mentioned, but only the mother's, Zeruiah was probably a woman of great ability, and her sons inherited it from her. Possibly she had married beneath her station, or her husband had died early ; but certainly her sons, thinking more of her than of their father, had soon thrown in their lot with David her brother (but see note on ver. 32). The youngest of the three, Asahel, was remarkable for his personal accomplishments, and especially for swiftness of foot, for which he was compared to the Zebi, the camp-name of Jonathan (ch. i. 19). It now caused his death. For conscious that Abner was the sole support of Ishbosheth's party, and indignant at his challenge to useless slaughter, he pursued after him, allowing nothing to divert him from his object, and hoping to end the war by slaying the veteran commander. But though he had the fleetness of an Achilles, he had not his robust strength, and Abner, knowing that the combat was unequal, remonstrated with him, and bade him turn aside, and be content with winning the spoils of some meaner warrior. It is evident from this that Abner saw in this defeat in a battle of his own choosing, the certainty of the near downfall of the house of Saul, and, as he would then be in Joab's power, he was unwilling to have a blood-feud with a man of such determined character. "How," he asks, "should I hold up my face to Joab thy brother?" It would be his duty, as the avenger of blood, to slay me. Apparently, during this conference, he was standing with the butt end of his lance held towards Asahel, to ward off his blows, but, as the spear-head was turned the other way, Asahel forgot that even so it might be used for offence. For it was pointed, that it might be stuck in the ground at night (1 Sam. xxvi. 7), and possibly shod with iron, though it is more likely that it was only hardened by being thrust into the fire. So when he saw that his words had no avail, and that Asahel was not on his guard, he suddenly struck him with it so violent a blow that it pierced his body right through, and Asahel fell down dead. It is probable, from the merciless force used, that there was a sudden outburst of anger on Abner's part.

Ver. 23.—**The fifth rib.** This rendering here and in other places arises from the derivation of the word from the numeral *five*, but this notion has long been abandoned, and the word is now known to be formed from a verb signifying "to be fat or stout." Really it means the abdomen, and is so translated in the LXX. and Vulgate, while the Syriac gives only the general sense, and renders "the breast." **In the same place**; Hebrew, *under him;* that is, immediately. So violent was the blow that Asahel dropped down dead without a struggle. So tragic was his fate, and so great the affection of David's men for the young warrior, that the pursuit ceased, and all, as they came up, remained standing by the side of the corpse.

Ver. 24.—**Joab also and Abishai pursued after Abner**; really, *but Joab and Abishai*

pursued, and so the Revised Version. The sight of their slaughtered brother made them only the more determined in the pursuit, and doubtless, at their command, the soldiers would leave Asahel and follow their commanders. Of the "hill of Ammah" and Giah we know nothing; but it is evident that no halt was made until sunset.

Ver. 25.—**The children of Benjamin . . . became one troop.** Benjamin was probably the only tribe that entered keenly into Ishbosheth's cause; for the maintenance of the kingdom in the family of Saul meant the continuance of that favouritism which had enriched them at the expense of the community (1 Sam. xxii. 7). They were, too, a very warlike tribe, and Abner was one of themselves, and probably, therefore, the main body of his army, and certainly his most trustworthy men, were Benjamites. Profiting by the delay caused by the halting of David's soldiers round the body of the fallen Asahel, Abner had rallied his men, and posted them on the top of the hill, where they were prepared now to fight on more equal terms.

Ver. 26.—**Knowest thou not that it will be bitterness in the latter end?** The Vulgate renders this, "Art thou not aware that desperation is dangerous?" This is a very obvious truth, but probably Abner had in his mind something more statesmanlike. The struggle was for the empire over all Israel, and whoever won would be king over both sides. But every man slain meant a blood-feud, which would continue even after the kingdom was united; and Abner probably felt that his own slaughter of Asahel that day would render his position in David's realm difficult and dangerous. Among the Arab tribes quarrels are very common, but bloodshed rare, because of the blood-feud which follows. Moderation was thus necessary on both sides, while cruelty and the immoderate use of victory would sow the seeds of future trouble.

Ver. 27.—**Unless thou hadst spoken, surely then in the morning the people had gone up;** or as the Revised Version renders, *had gone away, nor followed every man his brother.* The Revised Version makes the sense more plain. Joab throws the whole blame, and rightly so, on Abner. David would under no circumstances have attacked Ishbosheth, and Joab with his men had marched to the tank of Gibeon simply to repel an invading force. When there, Joab, doubtless by David's orders, had remained strictly on the defensive, and so unwilling were both armies to fight, that Abner had to resort to a most cruel scene of butchery in order to inflame their passions and force them to begin a conflict of brother against brother. But for Abner's challenge, both armies would have separated as friends. And Joab still acts upon the same principle of forbearance, and gives the signal for stopping the pursuit. He was not a man of a tender heart, but he was wise and sensible, and fully aware that the slaughter of Abner and his men, even if he could have destroyed them all, would only have rankled in the minds of all Israel, and set them against David and his rule.

Ver. 29.—**And Abner and his men walked all that night.** At the end of the chapter we learn that Joab did the same. Each army had about twenty-six miles to march, and the night was less exhausting for a long walk than the day. As soon, then, as Abner saw Joab and his men occupied with the removal of Asahel's body, he withdrew from the hill of Ammah, and, passing through the Arabah, or plain of Jordan, crossed the river by the same ford which he had used when starting on his unfortunate errand, and so returned home. The phrase, **all Bithron,** shows that this was a district, but nothing more of it is known.

Vers. 30, 31.—**Nineteen men . . . three hundred and three score men.** Though David's "mighties," as they were called, ex-

celled in the use of arms, yet the disparity of numbers is remarkable; for the Benjamites were also famous warriors. We can only account for it by the superiority of the tactics of Joab, who was a man of consummate military skill, and who knew both how to gain a victory and how to use the advantage which the pursuers have over the pursued to the full. If we sometimes wonder that David endured Joab so long, we ought to remember how much he owed to his nephew's genius, and that Joab was always faithful to himself.

Ver. 32.—**The sepulchre of his father, which** was in Bethlehem. The name of Zeruiah's husband is never mentioned, but he was evidently of the same town as his wife, and at his death, when probably still young, he had received honourable sepulture. As Bethlehem is about eleven miles distant from Gibeon, Joab probably marched thither straight from the battle-field, and spent the next day in paying the last tribute of respect to his brother, and in refreshing his men. At nightfall he resumed his march to Hebron, which was fifteen miles further to the south, and where he would arrive on the morning following that on which Abner reached Mahanaim.

HOMILETICS.

Vers. 1—7.—The facts are: 1. David, knowing that time was come for action, and being in doubt as to what movement would further the end in view, seeks guidance of God. 2. Not only does he obtain sanction to enter Judah, but is even instructed to make Hebron his head-quarters. 3. Entering the district around Hebron with his family and attendants, he is anointed by the men of Judah over the tribe of Judah. 4. Being informed of the kind and valiant act of the men of Jabesh-Gilead (1 Sam. xxxi. 11—13), David sends them a message of thanks, and assures them of the Divine blessing and of his own grateful remembrance. 5. He also reminds them that the crisis in the affairs of the nation, in the death of Saul on the one hand, and his own elevation by the men of Judah on the other, required of them to be true to their reputation as men of courage. There are several themes suggested by these facts. Among them, consider—

The beginnings of prosperity. As the Second Book of Samuel introduces a turn of affairs in the national experience, so this second chapter introduces a turn in the personal experience of David. He passes from the bitter trials of the past, through the anguish depicted in the first chapter, into the more prosperous and easy circumstances of free public activity. Undoubtedly he was conscious of a sense of relief from burdens almost more than he could bear (1 Sam. xxvii. 1); and being naturally buoyant and hopeful in spirit, the hitherto restrained powers of his nature were now eager to manifest their energy. His day had come after a long night of waiting. The promises of the past were about to be fulfilled. Jonathan's dream of his beloved friend being a more worthy successor than himself ('Pulpit Commentary,' 1 Samuel, pp. 381, 382) was coming true. In one sense David had always, even during his exile and sufferings, been a prosperous man, for he was God's chosen servant, blessed with a good conscience and the favour of the Eternal; but now he was all that with the additional circumstance of being about to enter on a position of commanding influence among the people of God. We have a counterpart to David's position at this juncture in some of the circumstances of our life; for in youth, in business, in Church work, and in national affairs we sometimes meet with a similar beginning of prosperity. In so far as the passage before us affords teaching on this subject, observe—

I. THE BEGINNING OF PROSPERITY IS A TIME OF PECULIAR DANGER. In reading the narrative of David's trials on the one side, and of his prosperous circumstances on the other, we feel at once that in' so far as his religious life is concerned there was far more hope of him under the former. The spiritual uses of adversity are very valuable, while on the other hand the spiritual dangers of prosperity are subtile and manifold. And likewise the transition from the one to the other is a time of peculiar danger. For David the occasion for dependence on God was not so obvious; and the demand for action would lay him open to' mistakes and sacrifices of principle new in his experience. The dangers of such a time may perhaps be summarized thus. There arises a new and fascinating diversion of thought and feeling from God; a corresponding absorption of mental energy in the externals of life. The self-culture which consists in the watchful and constrained subordination of every feeling and motive to the will of God becomes somewhat relaxed. The free play of a much greater variety of feeling, passing out toward the attractive objects present in an opening success, lays us open to the insinuating flatteries of events, and the consequent encouragement to substitute expediency for stern principle. The presence or the prospect of a more abundant supply of material comforts cannot but give vitality to whatever of latent power there may be in the lusts of the flesh. The conscious elevation which awaits us is sure to appeal to that deeply seated human pride which, when developed, looks on others with more or less of disdain, and in proportion as the human lot is now or prospectively free from care does the heart care less for the blessings of a future life. The youth passing from the restraints and discipline of years into the wider sphere of life, and so enjoying the first taste of freedom and of manly dignity, stands in a slippery place. Churches passing from the trials of persecution into the ease of toleration cannot be sure of the old fidelity. Nations springing into prominence may contract habits of indulgence and arrogance in strange contrast with their former self-control and devotion to duty. Private Christians when emerging from the struggles of their early convictions may cease to watch and pray as heretofore, and soon lose the vigour of their former faith.

II. THE MORAL STRENGTH ACQUIRED DURING SEASONS OF PREPARATION WILL SHOW ITSELF IN CONTINUED DEPENDENCE ON THE GUIDANCE AND BLESSING OF GOD. Unquestionably David was a much stronger man, as a consequence of the protracted trials of past years, than he would have been had there been no waiting for the realization of hopes enkindled by the promise of God (1 Sam. xvi. 13). In the spiritual sphere, as in the material, reserves of force are gathered, by the action of special laws, in view of a demand to be made at a later stage of development. David in the wilderness and caves, Paul in the retirement of Arabia (Gal. i. 17, 18), other good men during seasons of discipline and culture, fulfilled the Divine law of acquisition of moral power prior to expenditure. And the reality of this acquisition in the case of David appeared at once in the promptitude with which, under all the distracting and diverting influence of a sudden elevation to importance, he acknowledges his need of the guidance and blessing of God. There is a natural necessity, not identical with true godliness, which causes men to turn to God in their troubles. It is the instinct of a genuine piety alone which prompts towards God when troubles cease and success begins. It is a blessed omen when men, on the dawning of their prosperity, and when flushed with the prospect of realizing long-cherished hopes, go straight to God, and in prayer both acknowledge his goodness and seek his special help for the occasion. Thus the subtile temptations and perils of the new circumstances are met by a wise use of that spiritual strength which had been stored amidst the trying influences of adversity or deferred hope. No doubt the apostles during their early ministry, on and after the Day of Pentecost, were giving out some of the spiritual power gathered into their nature during the three years of discipline and restraint under their visible Lord; in like manner men who go forth to successful encounter with evil owe much to the spirit trained to honour God in all things.

III. THE HOPE OF COMING PROSPERITY, WHEN MODERATED BY PIETY, INDUCES CAUTION AND CONSIDERATION FOR OTHERS. Not only is continuous prosperity very perilous to man's higher life, but the prospect of it, after a season of trial, is likely to be charged with elements of danger which only a well-nourished piety can neutralize. David could not but think much of himself now as a free man, an object of public interest, on the high-road to affluence, and about to enter on activities that would render him the chief object of interest. There would thus arise a new and perilous self-consciousness. The sobrieties, caution, and self-restraint acquired in adversity might now seem to be virtues suited to a bygone time. A profound knowledge of the world and of self would correct this judgment; but still the risk would be considerable, for man at his best estate is morally weak. It is just here that a sincere, well-cultured godliness comes in as a support to the dictates of a purely moral judgment and the suggestions of expediency. The man after God's own heart, because of being such a man, looks out on his opening prospects with a careful eye, and moves with as much caution and deference to a higher will as in the former days of trouble; and the comfort of his household, as well as the advancement to comparative ease and plenty of the men who had shared his sufferings, engage his thought, and they become the first partakers of the fruits of his improving fortunes (vers. 2, 3). The same moderating influence of piety is seen in the life of Joseph. The principle involved is taught by our Lord in his perfect freedom, even amidst growing honours, from self-absorption. With the measured step of sobriety he marches on to full dominion, and with tender regard for the welfare of all who have known the "fellowship of his sufferings." The same mind in us will tone down the dangerous excitement of successes, and induce a broad and generous consideration of the claims and requirements of others.

The following GENERAL LESSONS naturally flow from this subject as exhibited in the life of David : 1. The consciousness of our being God's servants, living supremely to effect his purpose in the world, gives great moral power to our conduct. David lived and moved as a "man of God." Blessed is he who can go forth daily with that conviction ! 2. The assurance that God has a definite will in reference to our daily movements is warranted, not only by philosophic considerations, but also by the record of his actual dealings with his servants. David, the "sparrow," and the "hairs" of our head are means of illustrating that nothing in our life is too insignificant for Divine care, and therefore for matter of supplication (Matt. x. 29—31). 3. The true policy of man is another name for what is the will of God. No doubt in this case it was humanly expedient to go first up to Hebron; and because God knew it was best under the circumstances, he willed David to go. In the higher moral sphere, God's will is not a judgment based on knowledge of circumstances; but, though absolute, yet it always coincides with true policy. 4. The means of ascertaining the main lines of right action are within reach of a good man. God speaks in providence, conscience, and his Word. 5. There is immense moral support to our action when we have deliberately sought and have learnt the will of God. Firm is the step of such men, steady is their eye.

The uses of partial success. David's advancement to the throne of Judah was a great step towards the realization of the ideal which, ever since the day of his anointing, had drawn him on in the path of patient endurance; but it was far from being all that he wished. As compared with the understanding arrived at, and encouraged by all that God had said and done during the past years of exile, it fell below what he had a right to expect, for he was chosen of God to be ruler over the whole of the people; but, at the same time, it so far was satisfying that it became a pledge of still further advances till the original promise should be literally and in its entirety fulfilled. There is no indication here or elsewhere in the Psalms that David was vexed and fretful because he did not all at once succeed Saul as king of the entire nation. There were doubtless in the circumstances of the case sufficient pleas for an unfilial spirit to indulge in the language of disappointment; but the past discipline of this true child of God had manifestly wrought in him such confidence in the order of Providence, and such breadth of view with respect to Divine methods, as to render him deaf and indifferent to unhallowed suggestions. His cheerful acceptance of an instalment of fulfilled promise is in keeping with his former patient endurance of deferred hope.

I. THERE ARE MANY CONVERGING LINES INVOLVED IN OUR SUCCESS IN THE SERVICE OF GOD. The true final success of David's career lay in his becoming the beloved and honoured ruler of the entire chosen race. But a fact of this kind means the adjustment, over a considerable period, of countless subtile human relationships, the kindling of apparently divergent interests, and the physical removal of barriers by the action of natural causes directed by a controlling mind towards a single issue. Not only must Saul be put aside and Jonathan be rendered willing to give place to another, but the mass of the nation must be won. The hand that had won over Jonathan and removed Saul now operates silently on the hearts of the men of Judah—David's own kindred; and their recognition of him as king at Hebron was preliminary, in the order of Providence, to the acquisition on the part of David of the experience that would qualify for sovereignty over the entire nation, and to the gradual creation in the various tribes of confidence in his character and abilities, as also the gradual annihilation by a natural process of the interest which men very properly felt in surviving members of the family of Saul. As many lines converged on his reaching the throne of Judah, so this elevation was the opening up of new lines that would ultimately converge on the complete realization of the Divine purpose in his life. While absorbed in our own individual experience, we do not see how the line we have to follow is what it is because of being one of many terminating in a common issue. Later on we are able to take the position of a geographer, who surveying the watershed of a region, sees the convergence, after all the circuitous windings round rugged mountains and through wild gorges, of various water-courses into one calm and majestic stream. Thus we now interpret the lives of Jacob and Joseph, and, above all, the varied earthly experiences of our Saviour. We thus have warrant for believing that there are more forces working toward the goal of our life of godliness than we can at present trace. We ought to cherish faith in God's silent action on the spirits of men for the furtherance of the ends for which we, as his servants, live and strive. David could obey, be patient and step forward when occasion offered; but meanwhile God could dispose the minds of Judah towards him, and educate the rest to recognize in due time his fitness to be their king also. The courses of nature are on the side of good men. The social world is not a chaos; there is a Power which subdues all things unto itself. This should comfort and strengthen us in all our efforts to see Christ recognized as King of kings.

II. Success partially attained is both a pledge of Divine faithfulness and a call to higher and more difficult service. The elevation to the throne at Hebron was certainly a great success in the long and weary, and, so far as David was concerned with Saul, bloodless conflict. It must have given to the act of anointing by Samuel a fulness of meaning hitherto not realized. The venerable records of God's faithfulness to Abraham and Jacob after many a severe trial, which doubtless he was accustomed, at this period of his history, to read and meditate upon (Ps. i. 2; cf. cxix. 97, 99), were seen to be but counterparts of what he now could write. He had waited long; he had abstained from violent means and forced providences, and so could take heart and believe that the Lord forsaketh not his saints, but bringeth to pass that for which they wait (Ps. xxxviii. 1—4). And yet this partial success was to him the starting-point from which he was to advance still further in the fulfilment of life's purpose; it demanded of him more skill, more watchfulness, more caution, than ever. A new set of qualities would find scope for development; different and more subtile temptations would arise; the final triumph would depend on present use of partial success. Now, the case of David reigning at Hebron over part of the nation is the case of all who, like him, are engaged in maintaining the honour of God in a sinful world. What they have attained to, either in personal self-conquest or in subduing men to the obedience of faith, may be taken as pledge of the faithfulness that remains yet to be proved, while it opens up wider reaches of exertion and exposes to new and very dangerous forms of temptation. The history of the Church up to the fourth century, and its subsequent career till it recovered its tone in the time of the Reformation, furnishes abundant illustration of this double aspect of partial success. Our modern missionary achievements furnish distinct pledges of God's faithfulness, but they impose further and very serious obligations with a view to consolidation, and at the same time expose us to peculiar temptations which find no room in the season of early enthusiasm and sturdy endurance. The same applies to our own personal religion and the bringing of our entire nature into subjection to Christ (Luke x. 17—20; 1 Cor. x. 11, 12).

III. Success partially attained furnishes facilities for greater achievements. The acquisition of Hebron as the seat of government, some twenty miles south of Jerusalem, and situated among hills that rendered both defence and administration more feasible, furnished solid ground for the expectation that some day the more important city would become the centre of a greater kingdom. The memorable historic associations of the place (Gen. xxiii. 2—20; Josh. x. 36; xiv. 6—15; xv. 13, 14; xxi. 11—13) could not but create in the mind of David the feeling that he was succeeding men who were substantially engaged in the same cause as himself, and who prospered therein. The natural position of the city, and the wise measures which thence would go forth for the government of a compact tribe, would naturally consolidate his power, and, in due course, issue in a contrast between his judicious rule and that of rivals in Israel, which would tend to break down prejudices against him, and give force to his claim when an opening occurred for his assumption of sovereignty over the twelve tribes. Using well his moderate gains, he would convert them into agencies for complete triumph. Herein is the law of solid advance. In the organic world higher and more beautiful forms are built up by means of the powers latent in the lower forms already in being. Mental life becomes wide in range and profound in thought by conversion of partial knowledge acquired into means of further development. Social weal may proceed by stages, in which for a time progress may seem to be checked; but the institutions and habits consolidated soon become points from which other, and better, are formed. The growth of the spiritual life of the Christian means the successive attainment of points of advantage, which, though far from satisfying the earnest soul who seeks to subdue all to Christ, yet render the subjugation of the entire man to the Law of Christ more easy and certain. Christian enterprise often lays hold of some Hebron, in the heathen world, or in the midst of our non-Christian civilization, and working thence, with memories of past success to cheer and encourage, gets nearer to the goal of all prayer and effort—the bringing of the entire race into cheerful submission to Christ, the true King in Zion. Therefore, like David in Hebron, we all should gratefully accept what is vouchsafed as the reward of effort and patience, and apply our new resources and acquired position to higher issues.

An instructive episode. The sacred narrative is in the main concerned with the great national events which point on to the coming of the permanent King in Zion; but here and there it introduces a personal incident, which forms a pleasing and instructive episode amidst the public transactions which are the staple of the history. So here, while describing the important facts connected with David's elevation to the throne, and the consequent advance in the unfolding of the process by which at last the Christ should appear, the writer relates a circumstance of a more private character, and that both reveals noble qualities in David and sets forth truths of general interest. Observe, then—

I. THAT, IN A TRUE MAN, AFFAIRS OF STATE DO NOT EXTINGUISH THE MORE TENDER AND REFINED SENTIMENTS OF LIFE. To become monarch by a people's choice and in accordance with Divine purpose involves the pressure of heavy responsibilities, the absorption of energy in onerous duties, and the exposure of the spirit to manifold temptations to selfish aggrandizement. It is to the honour of David that he retained, amidst all these new and perilous conditions, his old tenderness of feeling and noble generosity. He found time and faculty for thinking lovingly of his once relentless but now buried foe, and for cherishing gratitude and respect for the men who had, at much personal risk, striven to pay honour to the dishonoured corpse (vers. 5, 6). He was not spoiled as a man of generous sentiments by becoming a king. He nourished private feelings amidst public cares. He would have the men of Jabesh-Gilead know how fondly he cherished the remembrance of their kindness to one now no more. How unlike many who have gained a throne through the disasters brought on rivals! How free, natural, and simple the expression of feeling as compared with the formal courtesies which sometimes society requires toward even the detested dead! In these respects David is a type of the greater One, who, amidst all the cares of life, cherished in his heart only pure, kindly, generous feelings towards even those who by others would have been forgotten. In like manner it is well that we strive to keep the heart fresh and warm when promotion comes, or public affairs absorb, or temptations arise to be indifferent to the minor claims of life.

II. THAT A TRUE MAN WILL EXHIBIT IN HIS CONDUCT THE SUPREMACY OF HIS LIFE'S SPIRITUAL PURPOSE. There is an obscurity in the exhortation sent to the men of Jabesh-Gilead arising from its laconic character (ver. 7). But, read in the light of what we know to have been David's faith in the coming kingdom of God ever since the anointing by Samuel, it means this: "You are perplexed and anxious about the interests of the people of God and their future. Do not yield to that state of mind. Be true men; do your part as patriots in this time of change; for Saul, your master, is dead, and every man, therefore, should do his best for the common weal. I have been made king over one section of the people of God, and I, therefore, am in a position to do my part. Let us, then, work as brave men for the bringing on of the better time." Thus, in the but partial fulfilment of the prediction by Samuel, and amidst the private affairs of life, David cherishes clear and full faith in the onworking of the Divine purpose towards final realization. His destiny as king over all the chosen race, in God's Name, was still the predominant thought. All along during those bitter days of exile and persecution the thought was uppermost, and nerved him with patient courage; and even now, when more than half the people did not want him to be king, he keeps the thought clearly in view. So was it with our Saviour. He came knowing he was to be Lord of all—Head of a united people. "For the joy that was set before him"—in prospect of this—"he endured the cross, and despised the shame;" and when only partially recognized as Lord by a few, he still had faith in the outworking of Divine purposes, and believed that to him "the gathering of the people" would be, and that there would be "one flock and one Shepherd." Those, also, who enter into the Saviour's Passion likewise keep the spiritual purpose of life clear above all earthly things, and adjust the partial successes, the deferred hopes, and even the private intercourse of life to the one absorbing ideal. Blessed men, who thus see Christ's final triumph before it is realized! What tone, elevation, and patience does it give to life!

III. THAT TRUE MEN IN EXALTED POSITIONS GIVE TONE TO SOCIETY. During exile, David was at the head of a band of men, and now he became the ruler of a people with title of king. As leader and chief his spirit had influenced his followers. Now that he is king, the people told him of the men of Jabesh-Gilead burying Saul. Why? Was it that he might be revenged on men who had done honour to a persecuting enemy? Not thus had they learnt of their leader. They knew him of old as generous to Saul (1 Sam. xxvi. 9—12); they had heard his pathetic lament over Saul (ch. i. 17—27), and they were sure that he would be comforted in knowing how poor Saul's corpse had been cared for. Obviously, the leader had given a nobler, more generous tone to men beneath him. In ordinary life, such men would have rejoiced in the death of a foe. It is doubtless true that the tone of society proceeds largely from the higher to the lower in position. A good monarch affects the peasant and the peer. The lower grades of society get their tone very much from what prevails in ranks above them. If our rulers and persons of position display kindliness, temperance, and piety, they do much thereby to fashion the character of others. The same principle applies to thought. Ideas are wrought out by the highest minds, and gradually permeate the thinking of the undisciplined and uncultured. Hence the serious responsibilities of station!

Vers. 8—17.—*Fanatical patriotism.* The facts are: 1. By degrees, and with the aid of Abner, those parts of the country not subject to David, and which, during the decay of Saul's power, had come under the control of the Philistines, now became consolidated under the rule of Ishbosheth. 2. The jealousy between Israel and Judah, owing mostly to the hostility of Ishbosheth's adherents to David, assumes threatening form, and the leaders on each side, attended by a small army, come together face to face, probably to consider the points in dispute. 3. The political questions not being solved by discussion, Abner proposes (vers. 13, 14; cf. ver. 27) as alternative a settlement by a combat of twelve select men from each side. 4. The combat issuing in mutual destruction, the main forces come into conflict, and Abner suffers defeat. The men who entered into the strife here recorded doubtless prided themselves on the zeal they felt for their country, and were ready to justify in words the deeds of the sword. It is customary to credit people with patriotism, and to that extent condone their savage passions. But too often the plea of patriotism is only a cover for a lack of reason and a domination of inferior impulses.

I. ATTACHMENT TO KING AND COUNTRY IS SUBORDINATE TO A HIGHER LAW. Considered in the abstract, such attachment is worthy only of admiration, and it forms an element in a people's well-being. But human feelings, with their corresponding acts, are parts of a great complex whole, and their worth in any particular concrete instance depends on antecedent and concomitant facts. There is a gradation of obligations, and virtues in name cease to be virtues in reality when they appear in isolation, or consequent on a disregard of a higher law. The men of Israel were bound to love their country, and to show love to it by asserting the rights of their ruler. But at the same time they were bound to follow the guidance of God; to submit to his supreme will; and, making this the standard of feeling and action, to modify the form of expressing love to country and ruler accordingly. Now, the men of Israel, especially the leaders, ought to have known, from the events and words of Samuel's life, and, indeed, from the manifest interposition in favour of David and against Saul, that it *was* the Divine will that they should not oppose David; that, in fact, love of country was to show itself in accepting whom God had chosen. Any personal interest, therefore, which they may have felt in a son of Saul, and any regard for what they deemed the good of their native land, should have shaped its form of expression in harmony with their primary and higher obligation. The principle is of wide range. Any passion for our country and sovereign must be exercised within the limits of a higher love. If so-called patriotism involves hatred of men as men, or injustice to them, or national selfishness, then it is a violation of the second great commandment. If upholding a ruler and seeking to subdue a neighbouring ruler involves a contravention of God's will, revealed in the order of manifest Providence or Scripture, then it is a spurious patriotism. Human feelings are not the tests of truth.

II. BLENDED IGNORANCE AND PASSION ENTAIL SUFFERING AND SLOW PROGRESS IN NATIONAL LIFE. Had Israel been alive to the lessons which God was teaching them all through the life of Saul, by means of Samuel and David and Jonathan, they would never have allowed the sentiment of interest in a monarch's son to have developed into a strong aversion to David and a passionate effort to expel him from Judah. Considering all the facts of the case, there is no valid excuse for their ignorance, and, therefore, none for their feelings, even though patriotism be pleaded. Thus we see how neglect to gather up and use the lessons of Providence, slight an evil as it may seem to be at the) time, really is the seed-sowing of the innumerable miseries of a civil war. If, during those painful years of contention, the energies of men are diverted from industrial channels into the wasting channels of war, and if, consequently, national progress is retarded, the cause is to be found in the domination of ignorance and passion. So has it been again and again. That *vox populi* has always been *vox Dei* is little less than blasphemy. Generations looking back on their ancestors see how wars and strifes took their rise in stupidity; and yet, too often, there is an unwillingness to pause lest the same evil be repeated. The woes that have come upon nations in consequence of war are a dark foil, setting forth in wondrous light the wisdom and sweet reasonableness of the gospel of Christ. If peoples would find the clue to progressive national development, let them accept and put into practice the sober, generous precepts and principles of the New Testament. This harmony of Christ's religion with economic law is no feeble strand in the evidence of its Divine origin.

III. THE GREAT ERROR OF LEADERS TOO OFTEN LIES IN THEIR INDISPOSITION TO TRACE OUT THE LEADINGS OF THE HIGHER LAW. Abner's suggestion that the dispute should be settled by combat of twelve on each side was an appearance of humanity and sobriety as compared with the indiscriminate use of force. But in the light of reason it is absurd; for right cannot be constituted by chance superiority of might. The complication in which he found himself was simply the result of previous indisposition to find out the Divine meaning of Samuel's dealings with Saul and of Jonathan's compact with David (1 Sam. xiii. 11—16; xv. 24—31; xvi. 6—13; xx. 12—17; cf. xvi. 57; xxvi. 3—16). It had been easier to follow the family feeling and official impulse (1 Sam. xiv. 50; ch. ii. 8, 9) than to look at private and public interests in the light of such revelations of God's will as were then available. It is a good maxim in moral questions that first promptings are best. The voice of conscience is quick to speak, even though in low tone. Most probably Abner recognized that voice telling of God's will in David. But where there is an unwillingness, because of personal or other interests, to give heed to that voice, it soon becomes easier to follow the lower impulses; and when once on the slippery incline of lower impulse, every movement adds to the momentum downwards. Herein lies the danger of our public men. They especially need the "light of the Lord." Expediency and wrong principles gain on them unconsciously in so far as they lose the primary sensitiveness of conscience. The contagion of their spirit and conduct affects the lower orders. They will have no difficulty in finding men willing, under the cover of patriotic sentiment, to enter the "field of sharp edges," and kill and be killed. Hence, it behoves preachers and all good men to bring the light of the higher law of life to bear with all its clearness and directness on the minds of those in authority.

Vers. 18—32.—The facts are: 1. Asahel, a younger brother of Joab, taking part in the pursuit, fixes his eye on Abner, and keeps on his track, and, being swift of foot, soon overtakes him. 2. Abner, conscious of superiority in arms, and remembering the high family connections of the rash youth, chivalrously urges Asahel to try his prowess on some one else. 3. The counsel being proudly disdained, Asahel falls under the spear of Abner. 4. At the close of the day the scattered men of Israel concentrate on one spot, and pause, while Abner, perceiving the folly and misery of the civil war, appeals to Joab for a cessation of hostilities. 5. Joab, reproaching Abner for his having brought on the conflict by his own acts and words in the morning, sounds the recall to his men, and henceforth they cease to fight their brethren. 6. Abner and his men retire to the east of Jordan, while Joab and his men bury Asahel, and proceed to David's seat of government.

Instructive youthful imprudence. The historian here gives considerable prominence to the rash conduct of Asahel and its sad consequences. Without at all straining the narrative, or indulging in fantastic methods of interpretation, we may call attention to the following considerations naturally suggested by the narrative.

I. THE PRINCIPLE ON WHICH THE MATERIALS ENTERING INTO THE SACRED HISTORY WERE SELECTED. The Bible is a history formed by a selection of a few materials out of many. The unwritten history of a people is more ample than the written. The question naturally arises—On what principle did the sacred historians proceed in accepting some items of fact, and rejecting others equally true? Many a noble youth besides Asahel must have fallen in the course of the ages traversed by the biblical story, but their name and deeds are unrecorded. The theory that the different writers of the historic fragments which from time to time appeared in Jewish life, and now make up the whole Bible, were literary artists or philosophical historians, is not tenable. There is in the narratives an entire absence of the art and the philosophy which may be traced in such writers as Thucydides, Niebuhr, Macaulay, and Froude; while, running through these fragments, there is a unity equal to anything found elsewhere. The case of Asahel is an illustration of the whole. The somewhat detailed reference to the occasion of his death is obviously connected with the subsequent reference to the occasion of the death of Abner, and the death of Abner is closely connected with the removal of the most influential barrier to David's consolidation of the entire kingdom, and David's life and reign are, we know, important in Hebrew history, because of their bearing on the line of providence by which "David's greater Son" at last came to reign in the true Zion. Here, then, we get a clue to the principle on which, by the unconscious guidance of the Spirit of God, facts were culled from Hebrew annals and incorporated in the sacred history. Direct or indirect bearing on the redemptive purpose in Christ was the criterion of incorporation. Not that everything related to that purpose is incorporated, but only such as is. The same doubtless applies to the principle on which the evangelists were, unconsciously perhaps, guided to select out of the mass of fact connected with the life of Christ such items as we have in the four Gospels.

II. THE WASTE INVOLVED IN THE USE OF VALUABLE POWERS TO UNSUITABLE ENDS. Asahel, the Hebrew Achilles without his skill in arms, was swift of foot—a valuable quality, and, in certain uses, likely to render great service to the state; but, as employed against the superior prowess of Abner in personal conflict, it only proved the occasion of premature unavoidable death. All the latent capacity for service in years to come, all the joys of domestic life, were thrown away by this rash encounter of the fleet-footed youth with a man of war. Looking at his conduct from a distance, we can see its essential folly. Physical and mental qualities, like limbs, are adapted to specific uses, and when applied to cases in which their excellence can turn the scale of advantage, then the utmost zeal may be displayed; but apart from this they may involve us in great trouble. Judgment in the use of small gifts will often achieve better results than can be secured by an indiscreet use of greater gifts. Possibly Asahel remembered the youthful David, skilled with the sling, going forth to fight Goliath; and it may be, also, that he was fully conscious of being on the side of the Lord's anointed. But the case of David was not parallel. Then there was an imminent peril for all Israel, and no other means available for warding it off; while here, whatever peril had existed was gone. No conviction of being on the side of God is a justification for rashness. The fall of Abner as a foe of David was in wiser hands than those of the fleet-footed youth. We have all to learn the lesson of adaptation. The student of purely physical science renders great service where physical facts and conclusions embodying them are alone concerned; but, like Asahel, he applies his powers in a dangerous direction when he presumes to be an authority on super-physical questions. Much of the waste of Christian energy arises from individuals attempting to rid the world of evil by working along lines unsuited to their capacities; and we see daily instances of men and women wasting their mental and physical substance in occupations in which their specialities find no suitable objects. A little wisdom goes a long way in human affairs.

III. THE ENFORCED SUBJUGATION OF POWERFUL SENTIMENTS. With all his faults of lurking ambition and infidelity to conscience, Abner was not destitute of chivalrous qualities. Possibly the conviction that his ill-espoused cause was on the wane may have awakened the prudential desire to obviate as far as possible personal offence to Joab, the rising general; but with this there was evident pity for the rash youth, and a chivalrous wish to take no undue advantage over a noble though impetuous foe. His position was one of extreme difficulty. His own death, or that of his pursuer, seemed to him to be the only alternatives. The thought of surrender, or of simply disabling his foe, appears not to have occurred; and in the choice of death to Asahel there was consequently involved a subjugation of the kindly, generous sentiments, and also of minor expediencies, to the love of self-preservation. Junctures of a similar kind occur in the lives of most men. Contending considerations distress the spirit. Deeds have to be done which any way entail misfortune. Abraham had to part company with his kinsman Lot, or perpetuate painful strifes. Moscow was burnt by the hands of its inhabitants to save themselves from possible subjugation. Commercial men can point to instances in which they have had to subordinate strong impulses to one commanding call to safety and honour.

IV. PUBLIC HOMAGE TO ILL-FATED RANK. The general honours paid to Asahel were in accordance with the custom of the age, which made persons of superior birth the objects of unusual attention. In this case there was conjoined the sentiment of admiration for enthusiasm, rash but real. In so far as man can find a reward for self-sacrifice in the sorrowful attentions to mortal remains of survivors, this young man did not die in vain. The instinct of men which leads them to regard with tender sympathy the death of a young hero in a public cause is very sound; for it means a discernment of noble qualities, a charity toward weaknesses, an unspoken lament over promising gifts prematurely lost to the world, and sympathy with aspirations not realized. The addition of social rank intensifies these feelings, and at the same time infuses over them all the superiority derivable from rank being regarded as the symbol of an ideal life toward which human nature constantly aspires. The hard utilitarianism that would banish sentiment as a mystical superstitious nuisance, and the impossible democracy that would annihilate social differences, will ever find human nature too strong for them. It is a fair subject for study—What are the functions in life of the instincts which find an outlet in acts of homage? How much does society owe to their binding power? In what degrees do they tend to tone down the asperities of the struggle to live? How may they be made subservient to the cultivation of religious feeling?

GENERAL LESSONS. 1. We should endeavour carefully to trace analogies between the structure of the Word of God and the structure of the other works of his hand. 2. It is important to watch against the temptations arising from the possession of qualities developed in a high degree. 3. The more prominent our gifts are in a particular direction, the more need is there for the cultivation of a calm judgment, if we would give the world the full benefit of their exercise. 4. In a choice of what seem to be opposing evils, we should endeavour to be guided by some clear and broad principle irrespective of consequences.

The alternations of passion and reason. The battle between the forces of Abner and Joab was a small affair as compared with many of the conflicts recorded in Jewish history; and this is probably to be ascribed to the conviction which both leaders entertained of the weakness of the cause of Ishbosheth. Abner evidently had not made preparations commensurate with an unchangeable determination to see right done to his nominal master. The gathering of his few broken forces on the brow of a hill, and his appeal in their presence to Joab, were the outward signs of his virtual surrender. In his plea of humanity, " Shall the sword devour for ever? " and in Joab's prompt answer, we get revelations of human character common to every age.

I. IT IS THE LOWER PASSIONS OF MEN THAT LEAD THEM TO SEEK TO ESTABLISH WHAT THEY CALL THE RIGHT BY VIOLENT MEANS. Ostensibly Abner was engaged in establishing the right of Ishbosheth to the rulership over the entire nation. As Joab reminds him, it was his will that led to war that day. In the eye of ordinary men, and judged by the customs of both ancient and modern peoples, Abner was justified in seeking to establish his right by force. But in his case, at least, the use of force was not the result of calm reason and conscience applied to the solution of a question of right. His past acquaintance with all the incidents connected with Samuel's recognition of David, and with the general evidence of the Divine rejection of the house of Saul, must have made him feel that however much personal ambition may have inclined him to identify himself with Ishbosheth, reason and conscience pointed the other way. In the depths of his heart, therefore, he knew that his was not the right side. The same may be said of most of the wars into which men have entered. However much they may have talked about their right, it has been passion—love of domination, selfishness, greed, jealousy, family feuds, or some other low-born feeling—that has darkened the eye of reason and drowned the voice of conscience. Let any one study the words and read the feelings of a people at war, and he will soon see how low and base are the passions that sway their conduct. As when an arm is stretched out to smite an individual, there is a flow of passion that dethrones reason for a while, so is it with communities when they enter into strife. As to the abstract question of right being enforced by might, it may suffice to say that while an orderly government is a terror to evil-doers (Rom. xiii. 2, 3), in the disputes of nations no might can make a right, and if rulers and people will but suppress passion of every kind, and give sole heed to the guidance of a calm reason and to the subtle dictates of conscience, they will not be long in doubt as to what the right is; and seeing it, they will not be able to do in the name of reason and conscience what can only come from the domination of low passions. The fact is Christianity is consistent. In so far as men are Christian they will not bring on war. The *war-spirit* is a disgrace to a people calling themselves Christian, and must be shocking to the Blessed One, whose acts were the outcome of light and love.

II. A DEFEAT OF PLANS AND PURPOSES AFFORDS A NEW CHANCE FOR THE DICTATES OF REASON. The inflaming of some of the worst of passions, which necessarily takes place in carrying on war, is a sad detriment to the finer susceptibilities of human nature. Abner was deaf to reason before and during the turmoil of conflict, when the lust of power and the passion of self-defence were at work within him. The frustration of his schemes by the defeat he encountered toned down these strong feelings, and gave some room for higher influence to come into action. The animal had spent its powers, and reason remained. On the brow of the hill, among his exhausted men, he thinks of peace, and recognizes the barbarity and folly of human slaughter. How truly is he a type of others! How often have nations slain and inflicted miseries, and when the fierce passion has spent itself have begun to speak of peace, and the need of staying the devouring sword! That the defeated are the first to do this makes no difference to the bearing of the fact on the moral question, since before defeat they were as much the slaves of passion as the victors. It is sad to think how little human life is governed by high and holy principle. A similar reassertion of the authority of reason and conscience on the occasion of defeat of purpose is seen in individuals who, having followed in their private life the heat of passion, are at last brought low by disaster or sickness, and constrained, as the fires of passion become slack, to give heed to the higher authority within. Though life may have been wasted, and, as in Abner's case, may have caused much misery, there is hope of a better end. The prodigal son is an extreme case of the kind.

III. IN SEASONS OF FAILURE MEN ARE GLAD TO AVAIL THEMSELVES OF THE HIGHER CONSIDERATIONS THEY ONCE SET ASIDE. Both fools and every man of sense must have admitted the force of Abner's appeal (ver. 26). Now in his defeat he pleaded considerations of humanity, of common tribal interests, and of general expediency. One might have thought that the possibility of the death of three hundred and seventy men and the general miseries of a battle would have been of force with Abner in the morning of the day; but it is only when failure had come that he can use the higher reasons for saving himself and followers from still greater calamities. So is it that men can use moral reasons when it answers their purpose. They pay homage to the superiority of moral reasons by pleading them with emphasis when they have anything to gain thereby. France could appeal to Europe against what were termed hard and ruthless conditions when in defeat, but no question of humanity or common European interests was raised when she entered on the war against Germany. Many an evil-doer, overtaken with the consequences of his deeds, speaks of the desirability of mitigating suffering and remembering the innocent that share the consequences of his actions, who, while in the path of his wrong-doing, was heedless of the pleadings of humanity. In these facts have we not an intimation of the more comprehensive truth that the day will come, the day of the defeat of all the enemies of Zion's King, when every soul shall recognize the righteousness and expediency of the great principles which once they rejected as the spring of conduct and which enter into the essence of Christ's government?

IV. AMIDST THE DIN OF LIFE MEN SOMETIMES OBTAIN A GLIMPSE OF A BETTER ORDER OF THINGS THAN THAT THEY ARE IN. Abner was painfully impressed with the miseries consequent on that day's conflict, and by a stretch of imagination he pictured to himself what would be the issue to his nation if the spirit of war which then prevailed in men's hearts were to move on unrestrained. He saw only "bitterness in the latter end." Then, by a reversion of the picture, he could not but think of the comparative blessedness that would ensue should the sword not continue to devour. Human life as we see it is a spoiled thing. Nationally and personally it is often laid waste. Neither individuals nor communities have attained to the development, physical, intellectual, and moral, which is the ideal of life, and which may, if men will, become real. Artists sometimes have depicted in contrast "War" and "Peace," and so have given form to the ideal, which often steals before the imagination, of a more blessed state of things than that familiar to us. The representations of the Bible encourage us to dwell on the beautiful image of a time when the sword shall no more devour—when men shall learn the art of war no more. Also, out of the dull and beclouded life of many a poor victim of sin there arises, consequent on the revived teaching of early years, a lovely and apparently unattainable image of a pure and blessed life, strangely in contrast with the defiled and restless past. Such a "heavenly vision" has a message to which it behoves us not to be disobedient.

V. A CONVICTION OF BEING ENGAGED IN A RIGHTEOUS CAUSE ENABLES MEN TO ABSTAIN FROM STRIFE. Joab did not seek to carry on the conflict. He contented himself with reminding Abner that had he been wiser in the morning he would not have had occasion to lament the evils of the evening. Most probably he knew the aversion of David to a civil war, and was simply carrying out the wishes of his king when he ordered his men back to Hebron. Moreover, his presence with David during the exile gave him abundant opportunities of knowing the validity of his claim. Subsequent facts show that Joab was not of the highest type of character, but he was sagacious, and could, as a Hebrew, recognize the force of the supernatural claims of David. It was doubtless the assurance that he was on the right side, which so often had been vindicated by God's providence, that induced him to cease from war and abide the issue of events. History proves that too often it is the men who are least conscious of rectitude of motive and justice of claim that press on with the sword, as though time, the healer of strifes, would be sure to work against them. David's calm waiting during all the years of provocation, when Saul was eager for conflict, was here showing itself again in the moderate conduct of his general. In the highest sphere, that of Christ's life and kingdom, we see how assurance of right was conjoined with a spirit that would not strive. It is along the same line that the Church should move to moral conquests, and kings and private persons may also do well to act in the same spirit.

HOMILIES BY VARIOUS AUTHORS.

Vers. 1—4.—(ZIKLAG, HEBRON.) *Divine guidance.* "David inquired of the Lord" (ver. 1). A new chapter in the life of David now opens. By the death of Saul and Jonathan the obstacles to his accession were, in part, removed. The time of patient waiting was gone, and the time for decisive action come. As he had not run before he was sent, so he did not expect, without running, to attain. But he would not take a step without the approval and direction of God. His inquiry pertained to the Divine purpose he was chosen to fulfil, and the Divine guidance he needed for its accomplishment. In this inquiry, as in his subsequent conduct and experience, he was a pattern to us; since *there is for every man a Divine plan and purpose of life,* which he should seek to ascertain and strive to realize. Consider Divine guidance (in the way to a crown) as—

I. URGENTLY NEEDED. We are liable (like travellers in a strange country) to go astray from the right path and fall into danger. 1. This liability arises from *many erroneous paths* presented to our view; their attractive appearance and strong temptations. "There is a way which seemeth right unto a man, but the end thereof are the ways of death" (Prov. xiv. 12). 2. And from the *imperfection of our own nature;* our ignorance, and our disposition to please ourselves rather than deny ourselves and please God. "O Lord, I know that the way of man is not in himself," etc. (Jer. x. 23). 3. It is evident from *experience of past failures.* David had taken many false steps. And there is no man but has reason to feel, in looking back over departed years, that his greatest folly has been to walk in the light of his own wisdom, and his greatest wisdom to depend upon the wisdom of God. 4. The need of it is *specially felt* by us when about to enter upon a new enterprise, or a course of action to which we are impelled by outward circumstances or inward conviction, but the exact nature of which is uncertain, or which is dependent for its success upon the disposition and co-operation of other persons.

II. DILIGENTLY SOUGHT. Although the Urim and Thummim are gone (see 1 Sam. xiv. 16—23; xxiii. 1—12), yet: 1. There are *certain means* which must be employed for a similar purpose—such as considering our own capacities and condition; listening to the voice of conscience; seeking the advice of good men; observing the ways of Providence; studying "the Scriptures of truth;" and, above all, offering prayer to the Father "in the Name" of Christ. 2. And to their proper employment a *right spirit* is essential; viz. sincerity, docility, trustfulness, perseverance. Such was the spirit of David, as it appears in his psalms; and therefore, while Saul exclaimed, "God answereth me no more" (1 Sam. xxviii. 15), he could say, "I sought the Lord, and he heard me" (Ps. xxxiv. 4).

III. GRACIOUSLY AFFORDED. 1. In *various ways,* in accordance with the means just mentioned, and especially by the Holy Spirit, who prepares the heart, teaches the meaning and application of the written Word, and produces impressions and impulses in harmony therewith. "Ye have an unction from the Holy One, and know all things" (1 John ii. 20; John xvi. 13). 2. *Individually,* and in a measure fully adequate to the requirements of the case and the capacity of profiting by it. 3. *Certainly.* As of old, so now. God is as desirous as he is able to lead us in the way wherein we should go, and he has given many faithful promises to this effect. "I will guide thee with mine eye" (Ps. xxxii. 8; xxxvii. 23; xlviii. 14). "Thine ears shall hear a voice behind thee," etc. (Isa. xxx. 21; xlii. 16; Prov. iii. 6).

IV. FAITHFULLY FOLLOWED. "And David went up thither" (ver. 2). 1. With humble obedience and entire dependence, as a child relying on the superior wisdom of his father. 2. Without hesitation, questioning, or delay. 3. With cheerfulness, zeal, and energy. It is always given with a practical end in view.

V. GRADUALLY CONFIRMED in the experience of him who obeys. "And his men . . . and they dwelt in the cities of Hebron" (ver. 3). God went before them and prepared their way, so that they met with a peaceable reception and found "a city of habitation." 1. The operations of Providence concur with the teachings of the Word and the Spirit. 2. A stronger assurance of the Divine leading is possessed. "If any man willeth to do his will," etc. (John vii. 17). 3. More light is given for further advancement. "Then shall we know, shall follow on to know the Lord. His going forth is fixed like the morning dawn" (Hos. vi. 3); and it will brighten on our path into the radiance of perfect day.

VI. WIDELY BENEFICIAL. More especially it contributes to the good of those who are associated with him, and who, having shared his perplexity and distress, now share his prosperity. Those who are guided by God are thereby enabled and disposed to guide and bless others (Numb. x. 39).

VII. GLORIOUSLY TERMINATING. "They anointed David king" (ver. 4). And all who truly fulfil the Divine plan and purpose as David did (Acts xiii. 22) are made "kings unto God," and receive exalted honour among men, increased power over them, and at length a crown of life, of righteousness, and of glory. But, alas! how many go stumbling through life without an aim, or only with one which is unworthy, and contrary to the will of God, and then sink into "the blackness of darkness for ever"! "The wise shall inherit glory; but shame shall be the promotion of fools" (Prov. iii. 35).—D.

Ver. 4.—(HEBRON.) *David anointed King of Judah. Course of events* : 1. David's message to the men of Jabesh (vers. 5—7). 2. Ishbosheth made King of Israel by Abner (vers. 8—11). 3. Civil war, and the death of Asahel (vers. 12—32). 4. Increasing strength of the house of David (ch. iii. 1—5). 5. Dissension between Ishbosheth and Abner. 6. Abner's negotiations with David, restoration of Michal, communication with the tribes, and formal league (ch. iii. 12—21). 7. Abner slain by Joab (ch. iii. 22—28). 8. Lamented by David (ch. iii. 31—39). 9. Ishbosheth murdered (ch. iv. 1—8). 10. His assassins executed (ch. iv. 9—12). It was a great day in Hebron. The ancient city among the hills of Judah (where the remains of the patriarchs had slumbered for centuries) was stirred by the assembling of the elders for the coronation of David. His presence among them, at the head of his six hundred heroes, had been virtually a "public assertion of his claims to sovereignty" on the ground of his Divine consecration by Samuel. His first anointing was essentially of a private nature. "This second one, performed by the elders of Judah, was his public solemn installation (based on that anointment) into the royal office." Then followed the acclamation of the people (1 Sam. x. 24; xi. 15). "Now doth David find the comfort that his extremity sought in the Lord his God ; now are the clouds for a time passed over, and the sun breaks forth; David shall reign after his sufferings" (Hall). It has been supposed that he wrote about this time Ps. xxvii. (inscription, "Before the anointing," LXX.).

> "Jehovah is my Light and my Salvation;
> Whom shall I fear?
> Jehovah is the Strength of my life;
> Of whom shall I be afraid?"

"It is not likely that David's muse went to sleep when the death of Saul at Gilboa opened his way to the throne, or that it produced nothing but such comparatively secular songs as the lament for Saul and Jonathan. It is rather remarkable, however, that there is not a single psalm of which one can affirm with confidence that it was written during the seven years and a half that David reigned at Hebron over the tribe of Judah" (Binnie). Those who took part in his inauguration acted in fulfilment, not only of the Divine purpose concerning him, but also of the Divine predictions concerning themselves; for *the pre-eminence of Judah* had been long foretold (Gen. xlix. 8). "In all great questions the men of Judah are the foremost and the strongest. From the time of David's establishment on the throne, the greatness of the tribe follows in some measure that of his family (1 Chron. v. 2; xxxviii. 4)" (Davison). "And as they had the right to choose their own prince, they might reasonably have expected that the other tribes would have followed their example, and, by uniting in David, have quietly submitted to the appointment of God, as they themselves had done" (Chandler). In their conduct we see—

I. AN EXALTED ESTIMATE OF HIS PERSONAL WORTH. One of themselves (Deut. xvii. 15), "chosen out of the people" (Ps. lxxxix. 19), he could understand and sympathize with them. He possessed eminent military abilities and noble moral qualities; and he had rendered invaluable services to his country, and shown special kindness to the elders of his own tribe (1 Sam. xxx. 26). His previous career was well known to them, and had won their confidence and affection. The character of a people is commonly manifested in that of its chosen ruler. As Saul embodied and reflected the prevailing spirit of Benjamin and Ephraim, so David embodied and reflected what was best in Judah; its independent spirit, lion-like courage, and religious devotion.

II. LOYAL ACCEPTANCE OF HIS DIVINE APPOINTMENT. With that appointment they were familiar. They recognized Jehovah as their King; the Source of authority and of the endowments which were needful for the kingly office. Their condition isolated them in feeling, to some extent, from the other tribes (as afterwards more fully appears); but in acting independently of them they rebelled against no existing and legitimate authority, and they neither aimed at dominion over them nor separation from them. They displayed a truly theocratic spirit. And, in the election of a ruler, a people should always 'recognize the authority and obey the will of God. "Kings derive their kingly majesty immediately from God, but also mediately from their subjects" (J. Lange).

III. VOLUNTARY SUBMISSION TO HIS ROYAL AUTHORITY. He was to them "a minister of God." Their obedience to God required their submission to the king of his choice; whose authority, however, great as it was, was not absolute. It is not said, as on a subsequent occasion (ch. v. 3), that "he made a league with them;" but they doubtless submitted to him on the understanding that he would rule according to the Divine will. The efficiency of a ruler depends upon the free submission of his people; and there is not a nobler exercise of freedom than submission to the highest order.

IV. UNBOUNDED CONFIDENCE IN HIS BENEFICENT RULE. They expected, under the government of "the man worthy of the sceptre," deliverance from their enemies, by whom they were now threatened; the establishment of justice, from the want of which they had long suffered; and the attainment of power and prosperity. Nor were they disappointed. The pre-eminence of this tribe was ordained with reference to the advent and exaltation of Christ, the promised Shiloh, "the Lion of the tribe of Judah" (Rev. v. 5); and the conduct of the men of Judah may be taken as illustrating the free acceptance of "him whom God hath anointed with his Holy Spirit" on the part of his people; their humble obedience to his rule, and their fervent desire for his universal reign. "Thou art worthy."

> "Come, then, and, added to thy many crowns,
> Receive yet one, the crown of all the earth,
> Thou who alone art worthy! It was thine
> By ancient covenant, ere Nature's birth;
> And thou hast made it thine by purchase since,
> And overpaid its value with thy blood.
>   Thy saints proclaim thee King; and in their hearts
> Thy title is engraven with a pen
> Dipped in the fountain of eternal love."
>
>   (Cowper.

                                                              D

Vers. 4—7.—(HEBRON.) *Commendation.* The first recorded act of David after he became king was of a kingly character. It is not improbable that the persons who informed him of what the men of Jabesh had done supposed that he had little love for the memory of Saul, and was apprehensive of opposition from his "house" (ver. 8), and wished to excite his jealousy against them; seeking to insinuate themselves into his confidence by detraction from the good name of others. But, instead of yielding to suspicion, he sent a message of peace and good will. His commendation was—

I. WELL DESERVED by men who had performed a noble deed (see 1 Sam. xxxi.

11—13). Their conduct displayed : 1. *Gratitude* toward their benefactor, whose kindness they returned with kindness. 2. *Fidelity* toward their king, whose faithfulness they repaid with faithfulness. 3. *Reverence* toward their God. "To bury the dead with the Jews was always reckoned an instance of humanity and kindness, and, indeed, of *piety*; an act done in imitation of God, who buried Moses; and so it might be expected the Divine blessing would attend it" (Gill).

II. WORTHILY BESTOWED by a king of royal disposition. 1. *Unsuspecting.* Others might find reason for suspecting their intentions, but he could see only what was deserving of praise. 2. *Generous*, with respect to Saul; appreciating and sympathizing with their kindness to their master, even though he had been his enemy. "Use the memory of thy predecessor fairly and tenderly; for if thou dost not, it is a debt will sure be paid when thou art gone" (Bacon). 3. *Practical.* "David sent messengers," etc. 4. *Devout.* "Blessed be ye of Jehovah," etc. Recognizing God as the Observer and Rewarder of men, he invoked for them his commendation and blessing—kindness for kindness, faithfulness for faithfulness—as the highest good (Ps. xl. 11; lxxxvi. 15; Matt. v. 7; Heb. vi. 10). 5. *Becoming.* "And I also"—as one whose office it becomes to observe and recompense good as well as evil—"requite you this kindness" (send you this message), "because," etc. 6. *Encouraging* and stimulating. "And now," as heretofore, "let your hands be strong, and be ye valiant" in the new circumstances which have arisen through the death of your master. 7. *Candid*, considerate, and dignified. "For me have the house of Judah anointed king over them." He indicated delicately, but not obscurely, his claims to their allegiance, and assured them of his protection and help. "To act nobly is always the best policy."

> "Where'er a noble deed is wrought,
> Where'er is spoken a noble thought,
> Our hearts in glad surprise
> To higher levels rise.
> The tidal wave of deeper souls
> Into our inmost being rolls,
> And lifts us unawares
> Out of all meaner cares.
> Honour to those whose words or deeds
> Thus help us in our daily needs;
> And by their overflow
> Raise us from what is low!"

(Longfellow.)

III. WISELY ADAPTED to effect a laudable end. 1. To confirm good men in a virtuous and praiseworthy course. 2. To win the confidence and support of such men. 3. To secure the benefit of their services to the nation and the kingdom of God. 4. To manifest to all the spirit of a just and generous rule.

OBSERVATIONS. 1. One good action tends to produce another; in performing it one knows not how far its influence may reach, or what blessings it may bring upon himself. 2. Although we ought not to do good simply for the sake of reward, yet the desire of the approval of the good is a proper motive of action. 3. We should be as ready to give commendation as to receive it. 4. We should desire, above all things, the approbation of God.—D.

Vers. 8—12.—(MAHANAIM.) *Opposition to the Divine purpose.* The purpose of God, to make David king over his people, was as yet only in part accomplished; and its fulfilment was opposed by Abner (1 Sam. xiv. 50; xvii. 55; xx. 25; xxvi. 5) on behalf of "the house of Saul." Having escaped from the battle of Gilboa, he "took Ishbosheth, the son of Saul" (a man of feeble character, and fitted to become a tool in his hands), "and brought him over to Mahanaim, and made him king over Gilead," etc. After five years of great exertions (while David reigned peacefully at Hebron) he drove the Philistines out of the country, openly proclaimed Ishbosheth (now forty years old) "king over all Israel," and "went out from Mahanaim to Gibeon" with the view of subjecting Judah to his sway. His principal motive was the desire of maintaining and increasing his own power. "He was angry that this tribe had set up David for their king" (Josephus). His conduct was "not only a continuation of the hostility of Saul towards David, but also an open act of rebellion against Jehovah" (Keil), whose purpose, as well as the wish of the elders of Israel, he well knew, as he afterwards acknowledged (ch. iii. 17, 18). His opposition represents and illustrates that of men to the purposes of God generally, and more especially to *his purpose that Christ shall reign* over them and all mankind; of which observe that—

I. IT IS PLAINLY REVEALED. By the testimony of: 1. The Divine *Word* (1 Sam. xvi. 1). "To him give all the prophets witness," etc. (Acts x. 43; 1 Pet. i. 11). 2. Significant *events*, in confirmation of the Word; the overthrow of adversaries, the exaltation of "his Chosen," the growth of his power (Acts ii. 22—24). 3. The irresistible *convictions* of reason and conscience, and the confessions which even opponents have been constrained to make. Abner was present when Saul said, "Thou shalt both do great things and shalt also still prevail" (1 Sam. xxvi. 25). His opposition was therefore inexcusable. "While men go on in their sins, apparently without concern, they are often conscious that they are fighting against God" (Scott).

II. IT MAY BE WICKEDLY OPPOSED (in virtue of the freedom which, within certain limits, men possess) because of: 1. The delusions of *unbelief*. The tempter whispers as of old, "Yea, hath God said?" (Gen. iii. 1); they "wilfully forget" what has taken place (2 Pet. iii. 5); "neither will they be persuaded" of the truth and obligation of the Word of God (Luke xvi. 31). 2. The plea of present *expediency*, and the expectation that, if they must submit, there will come a "more convenient season" for doing so. Abner thought "that he might be able, upon better terms, to make his peace with David when the time should come that the Lord was to advance him to be ruler over all Israel" (Chandler). 3. *Selfishness*, pride, and ambition; the love of pleasure and power, the habit of self-will, the self-confidence engendered by success, "the mind of the flesh," which "is enmity against God." "Ye do always resist the Holy Ghost" (Acts vii. 51).

III. IT CANNOT BE EFFECTUALLY DEFEATED. "He must reign," in fulfilment of the Divine decree (Ps. ii. 7; cx. 1), which: 1. Changes not. "The Strength of Israel will not lie, nor repent" (1 Sam. xv. 29). 2. Is effected by infinite wisdom and might, against which the skill and strength of men contend in vain. 3. Comes to pass either with or without their will, in mercy or in judgment, in the salvation of the penitent or the destruction of the persistently rebellious. "These mine enemies which would not that I should reign over them bring hither and slay them before me" (Luke xix. 27).—D.

Vers. 13—17.—(GIBEON.) *Fratricidal strife.* "And that place was called Helkath-Hazzurim" (ver. 16). The hostile attitude assumed by Abner appeared to David to render necessary active measures in self-defence. It is not said that he inquired of the Lord. If he had done so the conflict which ensued between brethren might possibly have been averted. As it was, he sent an army of observation under the command of Joab, who (although not mentioned before) had doubtless accompanied him in his exile (1 Sam. xxii. 1), and was now general of his forces. And Joab and "the servants of David" marched to Gibeon and encamped opposite Abner "and the servants of Ishbosheth" (ver. 13). At length Abner, impatient of delay, challenged a conflict between certain picked men on each side, not merely "to see which were best" (Josephus), but either to decide the day by the issue or to draw on a general engagement. Joab readily accepted the challenge, and the conflict commenced. It was—

I. BEGUN RECKLESSLY. "Let the young men arise and play [fight] before us." "Let them arise" (ver. 14). 1. Self-interest, ambition, and envy often quench the love of brethren (vers. 26, 27), and indispose them to seek reconciliation with each other. 2. The indulgence of evil passion blinds men to the consequences of their words and actions. 3. Familiarity with scenes of strife and war tends to produce insensibility to human suffering and slaughter. That a deadly struggle could be spoken of as a pastime shows how lightly life was estimated and how heartlessly it was sacrificed. "Ambitious and bloody men often consider the dire trade of war and the slaughter of their fellow-creatures as a mere diversion" (Scott).

> "Some seek diversion in the tented field,
> And make the sorrows of mankind their sport.
> But war's a game which, were their subjects wise,
> Kings should not play at."   (Cowper.)

II. WAGED FEROCIOUSLY. "And they caught each other by the head," etc. (ver. 16). 1. When the love which should prevail among brethren gives place to wrath, that wrath is generally most intense and cruel. Civil wars are proverbially more bitter than any other. 2. Men are sometimes so intent upon injuring their opponents as to forget to defend themselves, and rush upon their own destruction. 3. The attempt to end strife by means of strife is commonly vain; "it is rather a spur to further effusion of blood than a bridle to hinder the same." "What can war but endless war still breed?" 4. The issue of the conflict does not necessarily prove the justice of the cause. 5. Mutual strife tends to mutual extermination. "All they that take the sword shall perish by the sword" (Matt. xxvi. 52). The "field of sharp blades" was a lasting memorial of destructiveness rather than of courage; a warning rather than a pattern.

III. EXTENDED RAPIDLY. "And there was a very sore battle that day," etc. (ver. 17). 1. The strife of a few excites the wrathful passions of many, by whom it is witnessed. 2. Every injurious word and act furnishes an additional impulse to wrath and retaliation; and the conflict goes on increasing. 3. That which at first may be easily checked passes entirely beyond control. "The beginning of strife is as when one letteth out water," etc. (Prov. xvii. 14; xxvi. 21).

IV. ENDED LAMENTABLY. "Abner was beaten," and three hundred and sixty of his men died; Joab's brother Asahel was slain, with nineteen of David's servants. "In war God punishes the sins of both parties." 1. He who gave the challenge and commenced the conflict was the first to complain of the result (ver. 26), and was bitterly reproached as the cause thereof (ver. 27). 2. He who accepted the challenge was filled with grief and revenge. 3. Both sides experienced heavy loss and sorrow. 4. Even David could not but regret the weakening of the nation in presence of the common foe; or fail to see in the strife of brethren the consequences of his own faithlessness (1 Sam. xxvii. 1, 10, 11). If he had not taken up his abode with the Philistines the conflict would probably never have occurred.

REMARKS. 1. When men commence a quarrel they little know where it will end. 2. Strife should be diligently checked at the beginning. 3. "Let us fight that good fight only whereof the apostle speaks, which is between the flesh and the spirit, which only hath the profitable end, the glorious theatre, the godly armour, and the blessed reward of assured triumph" (Guild).—D.

Vers. 18—23.—(GIBEON.) *The untimely fate of Asahel: to young men.* Asahel was the youngest of three brothers; the others being Joab and Abishai. They were the sons of Zeruiah (half-sister of David) and a Bethlehemite (ver. 32) whose name has not been recorded; and they had much in common. When Asahel fled to David at the cave of Adullam (some ten or twelve years before the events here mentioned) he was probably a mere lad; he shared his uncle's hardships and participated in his exaltation. He was one of the famous thirty (ch. xxiii. 24), "valiant men of the armies" (1 Chron. xi. 26); accompanied Joab and Abishai in their march to Gibeon, and took part in the battle with Abner and "the servants [soldiers] of Ishbosheth." He was: 1. *Possessed of eminent gifts.* "Asahel was as light of foot as a gazelle" (ver. 18); like "swift-footed Achilles," and like Harold I. (son of Canute), surnamed *Hare-foot,* "because he was light and swift of foot" (Rapin). He was also distinguished by enterprise, courage, perseverance, and other admirable qualities. Mental endowments are incomparably superior to physical; but both are gifts of God, and should be recognized as such; they enable those who possess them to render valuable service to his people; and they should be employed in humble obedience to his will. Yet not unfrequently they become an occasion of vain-glory, and are perverted from their proper exercise and end. 2. *Actuated by an unwise ambition.* "And Asahel pursued after Abner," etc. (ver. 19). He sought to take him prisoner or put him to death, and so end the conflict; and doubtless, also, to display his own superior speed and strength, and obtain the glory of the achievement. He was on the right side, and, considering the circumstances of the case, there was something laudable in his attempt. But it is possible, even in connection with the kingdom of God, to entertain an improper desire of worldly honour and power (Matt. xx. 20—23). Those who do so generally set an inordinate value upon the object at which they aim, exhibit an undue confidence in their own abilities, depreciate the difficulties of its attainment, and expose themselves to great risk and peril (Titus ii. 6; 1 Tim. vi. 9).

> "Ah! who can tell how hard it is to climb
> The steep where Fame's proud temple shines afar?"
>
> (Beattie.)

3. *Heedless of salutary warning.* "And Abner looked behind him, and said," etc. (vers. 20—23). "Turn thee aside," etc. "Slay one of the common soldiers and take his accoutrements as booty, if thou art seeking for that kind of fame" (Keil). He cared little about the safety of his men, and was chiefly concerned about his own; but his advice was considerate, wise, and once and again repeated. Asahel, though swifter of foot, was not his equal in experience and skill; and (like many other young men) he despised the warning of the old warrior, was headstrong and over-confident of success, and rushed rashly and blindly upon his fate. "Heat of zeal sometimes, in the indiscreet pursuit of a just adversary, proves mortal to the agent, prejudicial to the service" (Hall). 4. *Struck down in youthful prime.* "And Abner with the hinder end of the spear smote him," etc.; suddenly, unexpectedly, and when he seemed on the point of accomplishing his purpose. With one blow his life was cut short, his hope disappointed, his promise of a brilliant future extinguished. "Often do men fancy themselves about to seize upon happiness, when death stops their career and lays them in the dust. And if they will rush forward in the road to destruction, though plainly warned of their danger, they can blame none but themselves" (Scott).

> "Fame is the spur that the clear spirit doth raise
> (That last infirmity of noble mind)
> To scorn delights, and live laborious days;
> But the fair guerdon when we hope to find,
> And think to burst out into sudden blaze,
> Comes the blind Fury with the abhorred shears,
> And slits the thin-spun life."
>
> (Milton, 'Lycidas.')

5. *Regarded with mournful pity.* "As many as came to the place where Asahel fell down and died stood still" (see ch. xx. 12), overcome with surprise, compassion, and grief; "and they took up Asahel, and buried him," etc. (ver. 32). 6. *Remembered with mischievous resentment.* (Ch. iii. 30.) He left behind him a legacy, not of peace and good will, but of wrath and revenge. Pause at his tomb in Bethlehem, and lay to heart the lessons taught by his untimely fate (Jer. ix. 23). Let your ambition be different from his; to overcome carnal and selfish ambition in your own heart, to save life rather than to destroy it, to follow in the steps of him who was servant of all (Matt. xx. 28). Here is scope for your noblest aspirations and most strenuous efforts. And your hope will not be destroyed, but crowned by death.

> "Fool not; for all may have,
> If they dare try, a glorious life, or grave."
>
> (Herbert.)

D.

Vers. 24—29.—(GIBEON.) *War.* "Shall the sword devour for ever?" (ver. 26; ch. xi. 25). The sword is more destructive than ravenous beasts, famine, pestilence (ch. xxiv. 13; Lev. xxvi. 26), earthquake, tempest, or fire. The history of its ravages constitutes a considerable portion of the history of mankind. Of these we have here a slight but noteworthy instance. Twenty-four brave men of the same nation (half of them chosen from each of the opposing forces) fell, pierced by each other's weapons. In the succeeding battle and flight several hundreds were slain (ver. 31). At sunset the defeated general rallied his scattered troops on the hill of Ammah, and appealed to the commander of the pursuing forces to withdraw them and avert the bitter consequences that would otherwise ensue. "Now the battle is going against him he complains of the devouring sword; and, though it had been employed but a few hours, it seemed long to him—a sort of eternity" (Gill). Joab answered that but for his challenge in the morning there would have been no conflict at all; but (probably as yet unacquainted with the death of his brother Asahel) he sounded a retreat (ver. 28); and Abner and his men forthwith departed, not to Gibeon, but across the Jordan to Mahanaim (ver. 29). Regarding the question not merely as the utterance of Abner, nor from an Old Testament point of view, we may take it as expressive of—

I. A CONVICTION OF THE EVILS OF WAR. "Shall the sword *devour* for ever?" By it: 1. *Numberless lives are consumed.* The immediate and avowed object of war is the destruction of men's lives; and its most effective instruments (to the construction of which the utmost ingenuity is devoted) are those that destroy the greatest number in the shortest possible time. "War is the work, the element, or rather the sport and triumph, of death, who glories not only in the extent of his conquest, but in the richness of his spoil" (R. Hall, 'Reflections on War'). Since its ravages began many times more than the whole number of the present population of the globe have probably been its victims. 2. *Incalculable sufferings are inflicted;* on those who are left to die on the field, or are borne to hospitals and linger out a miserable existence; on the non-combatant population among whom the devourer pursues his way; on whole nations and multitudes of desolate and sorrowing homes far distant from the scene of strife. 3. *Enormous cost is incurred;* in the maintenance of armies and the provision of *materiel*, besides the withdrawal of great numbers from the operations of productive industry and serious interference with commerce; immense national debts are accumulated and burdensome taxes imposed on present and succeeding generations. There are nearly thirteen millions of men in Europe who have been trained for arms, and between four and five millions actually under arms, costing in all ways about five hundred millions sterling a year. The sum total of the national debts of the European nations amounts to nearly five thousand millions of pounds ('Statesman's Year-Book'). 4. *A pernicious influence is exerted, with respect to morality and religion.* "War does more harm to the morals of men than even their property and their persons" (Erasmus). It has its origin in unregulated desire (Jas. iv. 1; 1 John ii. 16), which it excites, manifests, and intensifies. "The causes of all wars may be reduced to five heads: ambition, avarice, revenge, providence (precaution), and defence" (Owen Feltham, 'Resolves'). "If the existence of war always *implies* injustice in one at least of the parties concerned, it is also the fruitful parent of crimes. It reverses, with respect to its objects, all the rules of morality. It is nothing less than a temporary repeal of the principles of virtue. It is a system out of which almost all the virtues are excluded and on which nearly all the vices are incorporated" (R. Hall). What angry feelings does it stir up between nations whom "God hath made of one blood"! What infuriated passions does it arouse in contending armies! What cruel deeds does it commend! What iniquitous courses of conduct does it induce! What false views of glory does it inculcate! What bitter and lasting enmities does it leave behind!

> "One murder makes a villain,
> Millions a hero! Princes were privileged to kill,
> And numbers sanctified the crime!
> Ah! why will kings forget that they are men,
> And men that they are brethren? Why delight
> In human sacrifice? Why burst the ties
> Of nature, that should knit their souls together
> In one soft bond of amity and love?"

(Bishop Porteus.)

Is war, then, under all circumstances, inexpedient and wrong? It is maintained that: (1) The state, like the individual, has a natural right of self-defence, and is bound (in fulfilment of the purpose for which it exists) to protect its citizens by repelling external invasion as well as repressing internal violence (Whewell, 'Elements of Morality;' Paley; Gisborne; Mozley, 'University Sermons'). (2) By means of war national subjection is sometimes prevented, national grievances are redressed, national honour is upheld, aggression checked, pride abased, liberty, peace, and prosperity secured, patriotism kindled, powerful energies and heroic virtues developed. (3) It has often received the Divine sanction (Exod. xvii. 14; Josh. viii. 1; 1 Sam. xi. 6). "Perpetual peace is a dream, and it is not even a beautiful dream. War is an element in the order of the world ordained by God. In it the noblest virtues of mankind are developed—courage and the abnegation of self, faithfulness to duty, and the spirit of sacrifice; the soldier gives his life. Without war the world would stagnate and lose itself in materialism" (Von Moltke). But this is the view of one who has been "a man of war from his youth" and "shed much blood" (1 Chron. xxii. 8). And it may be said that: (1) War is not ordained by God like tempests and earthquakes or even pestilence, but is directly due to the wickedness of men. That which is in itself evil, however, often becomes an occasion of good. (2) "There is at least equal scope for courage and magnanimity in blessing as in destroying mankind. The condition of the human race offers inexhaustible objects for enterprise and fortitude and magnanimity. In relieving the countless wants and sorrows of the world, in exploring unknown regions, in carrying the arts and virtues of civilization to unimproved communities, in extending the bounds of knowledge, in diffusing the spirit of freedom, and especially in spreading the light and influence of Christianity, how much may be dared, how much endured!" (Channing). (3) The right of resistance to evil is limited, and does not justify the taking away of life (Wayland, 'Elements of Moral Science;' Dymond, 'Essays'). (4) No advantages gained by war are an adequate compensation for the miseries inflicted by it; less suffering is experienced and higher honour acquired by enduring wrong than avenging it; the exercise of justice, forbearance, and active benevolence is the most effectual means of averting injury and securing safety and happiness. (5) The Divine sanction given to specific wars in the Old Testament was not given to war in general, and it does not justify the wars which are waged, without the like authority, at the present time. (6) War is virtually forbidden by numerous precepts and the whole spirit of the New Testament (Matt. v. 9, 39, 44; xxvi. 52; Rom. xii. 18—21; 1 Thess. v. 15; 1 Pet. ii. 23; iii. 9—13). The most that can be said is that "any principles upon which the Christian casuist would justify war in certain circumstances would not justify perhaps one in ten of the wars that have been waged" (J. Foster, 'Lectures,' vol. ii.).

II. AN APPEAL FOR THE CESSATION OF STRIFE. "*Shall* the sword devour for ever?" Its ravages may be stayed; and means must be employed for that end, such as: 1. The consideration of the real nature and terrible consequences of war; and the education of the people, especially the young, so that they may cease to admire military glory and to be beguiled by "the pomp and circumstance of war"—may feel an intense aversion to it, and seek in other ways their common interest and true elevation. 2. The adoption of political measures for the settlement of international disputes and the removal of causes of strife; viz. arbitration by friendly powers, the reduction and disbandment of standing armies, etc. 3. The repression of evil passions in ourselves and others. 4. The practice and diffusion of Christian principles; which indispose all in whom they dwell to break the peace themselves, and dispose them to make peace among others. "The sons of peace are the sons of God."

III. AN ANTICIPATION OF THE PREVALENCE OF PEACE. "Shall the sword devour *for ever?*" Surely not. The hope of universal peace is warranted from: 1. The advancing intelligence of men, the growth of popular government (making war less dependent than heretofore on the arbitrary will of rulers), the possession of "nobler modes of life, with sweeter manners, purer laws." 2. The better understanding and more perfect realization of the spirit of Christianity. 3. The overruling Providence and quickening Spirit of "the God of peace." 4. The express predictions of his Word concerning the effects of the reign of "the Prince of Peace" (Isa. ix. 7; Micah iv. 3; v. 2, 5; Ps. lxxii. 7). "It is in war that the power of the beast culminates in the history of the world. This beast will then be destroyed. The true humanity which sin has choked up will gain the mastery, and the world's history will keep sabbath. What the prophetic words affirm is a moral postulate, the goal of sacred history, the predicted counsel of God" (Delitzsch, on Isa. ii. 4).

> "O scenes surpassing fable and yet true;
> Scenes of accomplished bliss; which who can see
> (Though but in distant prospect) and not feel
> His soul refreshed with foretaste and with joy?"
>
> (Cowper.)

D.

Vers. 30—32.—(GIBEON, BETHLEHEM, HEBRON.) *The sorrows of victory.* "What a glorious thing must be a victory, sir!" it was remarked to the Duke of Wellington. "The greatest tragedy in the world," he replied, "except a defeat" ('Recollections,' by

S. Rogers). The rejoicing by which it is attended is usually mingled with weeping and sometimes swallowed up of grief. Various persons are thus affected for various reasons. Think of the sorrows endured : 1. *At the fall of fellow-soldiers.* "Nineteen men and Asahel" (vers. 23, 30) who come not to the muster after sunset (vers. 24, 30), nor answer to the roll-call, but lie in the chill embrace of death. "Alas! fallen are the heroes." 2. *In the burial of the dead.* (Ver. 32.) No opportunity is afforded for seeking out and burying all the slain; but the remains of Asahel are carried across the hills by night (ver. 29) and laid in the tomb of his father in Bethlehem, where the sorrow of the preceding day is renewed. It reminds us of a pathetic scene of recent times described in the familiar lines—

> "We buried him darkly at dead of night,
> The sod with our bayonets turning;
> By the struggling moonbeam's misty light,
> And our lanterns dimly burning."
>
> (Wolfe.)

3. *When the news is conveyed to their homes.* "They came to Hebron at break of day;" a day of bitter grief to many bereaved hearts. "By the slaughter of a war there are thousands who weep in unpitied and unnoticed secrecy whom the world does not see; and thousands who retire in silence to hopeless poverty for whom the world does not care" (Dymond). 4. *For the miseries of fellow-sufferers;* the enemy— defeated, bereaved, and mourning—for they too are "brethren," and cannot but be remembered with sympathy and pity. 5. *Concerning the state of the departed.* A soldier's life is not favourable to piety and preparation for heaven, and the passions by which he is commonly swayed when his earthly probation is suddenly terminated are such that we can seldom contemplate his entrance into the eternal world with feelings of cheerfulness and hope. "After death the judgment." 6. *On account of the animosities of the living,* which are increased by conflict and victory, and are certain to be a source of future trouble (ch. iii. 1, 30, 33). 7. *Because of the dishonour done to the cause of the Lord's Anointed.* Religion suffers, the progress of the kingdom is hindered, and the King himself is "grieved for the misery of Israel." "The victory that day was turned into mourning" (ch. xix. 2). So is every victory gained by "the devouring sword." But there are victories which are bloodless and tearless, sources of unmingled joy; spiritual victories over ignorance and sin won by and through the might of him at whose birth the angels sang upon those hills of Bethlehem, "Glory to God in the highest, and on earth peace, good will toward men."—D.

Ver. 1.—*Inquiring of God.* David had now arrived at a very important point in his career. Saul being dead, his way to the throne was cleared; but the next step to take was doubtful. Under these circumstances he adopted the course usual to him when in difficulty. He "inquired of the Lord," sought directions from him as to what he should do. The high priest, Abiathar, was with him with the ephod (1 Sam. xxx. 7), and by means of the Urim and Thummim could ascertain for him the Divine will. By this method, doubtless, he received directions to go into Judah and settle at Hebron; "and the men of Judah came, and there they anointed David king over the house of Judah." We cannot ask direction from God in the same manner as David, but, using the means available for us, we should imitate him in this respect.

I. UNDER WHAT CIRCUMSTANCES WE SHOULD INQUIRE OF GOD. 1. *It should be a constant practice.* Part of our devotions every day should consist of endeavours to ascertain more fully and accurately the will of God concerning us, seeking of him guidance in all our ways, that we may know what the general commands of God mean for us in our position, in the practical details of our individual life. 2. *The practice should be made special under special doubts and difficulties.* (1) When like David we have to make a choice on which much depends, and there is difficulty in choosing. When proposing to enter on a new enterprise, to form new connections (especially a lifelong alliance), to change our place of abode, etc. There will be reasons for and against, promises of good, possibilities of evil, in each direction. What shall be done? Inquire of the Lord. (2) When we meet with perplexities in the inquiry after truth. It is not by mere logical processes that spiritual truth can be ascertained; from first to last we need guidance from above, and should earnestly seek it.

II. How such inquiry should be conducted. 1. *By what methods.* Where shall we find a Divine oracle to answer our inquiries? (1) Reason and conscience will often (if we allow them free speech) give a response which at once commends itself as a Divine reply. If one course be morally right and the other morally wrong, one in manifest accordance with the laws of Christ, the other in plain opposition to them, there is no room for further question. (2) Holy Scripture is to be consulted. Not in the way of bibliomancy, but by study of its revelations and precepts. The New Testament is especially the Christian's *vade-mecum,* from whence he may obtain all needful instruction as to the will of God. (3) The providence of God. Courses to which we are prompted by the best desires may be seen not to be our duty, because ability and opportunity are wanting to pursue them. (4) The counsels of wise and good men. Consulting them, our course will often become clear. Yet we may not submit blindly and slavishly to our fellow-men. (5) The commands of superiors. For children at home the will of their parents is the will of God; for servants, the commands of their employers; always supposing in both cases that what is enjoined is not clearly sinful. (6) Withal and always, prayer for Divine guidance should be resorted to. "Show me thy ways, O Lord; teach me thy paths" (Ps. xxv. 4). By direct influence on the minds and hearts of those who seek him, God becomes their Guide. His Spirit leads those who are willing to be led by him. 2. *In what spirit.* A simple and sincere desire to know and do the will of God. In opposition to pride and self-will, and double-mindedness. Many seek counsel of God as the advice of men is often sought. They virtually make up their minds before they inquire, and "make it a matter of prayer" in order that they may obtain a feeling of the Divine approval of the course they have chosen. Not avowedly, not consciously, is this done. But "the heart is deceitful," and never shows its deceitfulness more than in such cases (comp. Ezek. xiv. 1—5; 2 Thess. ii. 10—14).

III. Motives to such inquiry. 1. *Our ignorance.* "The way of man is not in himself: it is not in man that walketh to direct his steps" (Jer. x. 23). Human affairs are so complex, appearances so deceitful, men often so untrustworthy, our vision so limited, that we may well desire and shall wisely yield ourselves to the guidance of God. 2. *The right and power of God to direct us.* As supreme Ruler, as perfect in knowledge, wisdom, and goodness. 3. *His promises.* (See Ps. xxv. 12, 14; Jas. i. 5.) Especially the great promise of the Holy Spirit to all who ask of God this unspeakably great and precious gift (Luke xi. 13). 4. *The blessedness of being divinely led.* In present wisdom, holiness, and happiness, and in eternal life. 5. *The certainty of fatal darkness and stumbling to those who do not inquire of God.* (See Jer. xiii. 16; John xii. 35.)—G. W.

Vers. 5—7.—*Gratitude and policy.* David was now king of the tribe of Judah by their own choice, but the rest of the tribes had not declared themselves. Amongst these the tribes beyond the Jordan were of special importance and influence; and David took an opportunity of reminding them of his position and claims. The chief city amongst those tribes was Jabesh-Gilead. Brave men from that city had rescued the bodies of Saul and his sons from the wall of Bethshan, and, after burning them, had buried their bones under the tamarisk tree (Revised Version) at Jabesh. David, being made acquainted with what they had done, sends messengers to assure them of his appreciation of their conduct, and at the same time to hint that, Saul being dead, and he having been appointed king over Judah, the way was clear for them to aid, if so disposed, in promoting his election as king by the other tribes. The message was at once a suitable expression of his gratitude and a politic endeavour to ingratiate himself with them.

I. David's gratitude. 1. *On what account.* Their burial of Saul. He speaks of this as kindness to him. We can show kindness to the dead by suitably interring them. Other ways of doing this would be upholding their reputation, caring for those they leave behind, promoting for their sakes any cause in which they were deeply interested. David could not but highly appreciate the brave deed of these men. His own marvellous courage would impel him to admire theirs. But it was the respect they had thus shown to their departed sovereign which especially moved him to send a message to them. His gratitude for this was quite in accordance with his usual feelings towards Saul, both during his life and after his death. 2. *How he expresses his gratitude.* (1) By sending the messengers and message. "I also will requite," etc., should be (according to Otto Thenius and the 'Speaker's Commentary') "I also show you this goodness," viz. sending the messengers with a kind message. They would value David's message as soldiers distinguishing themselves in the field value a message from the queen. (2) By the terms of the message. In which he invokes upon them the blessing of God, his "kindness and truth," his true, faithful, constant kindness. A phrase common in the Old Testament (Ps. xxv. 10; xl. 11, etc.; Gen. xxiv. 49; xlvii. 29, etc.), and reproduced in the New with some additional meaning (John i. 14). To pray for God's blessing on those to whom we feel grateful is always suitable. When we can do nothing else, we can do this; and when we can show gratitude in other ways, we do well to show it thus also. For God's blessing far surpasses ours, and will render ours more valuable and effectual. Only we should be careful not to substitute prayers for deeds when these are possible. But in some way or other we ought to express as well as cherish gratitude and other kindly feelings to others. It is good for ourselves and good for others. It encourages good and noble deeds. It tends to bind men together in the best bonds. It promotes happiness of a high order. We may enlarge the thought. We are required to confess God and our Saviour, as in other ways so by thanksgiving and praise. It' is meet and right so to do. It promotes our own spiritual good and that of others. It glorifies God.

II. DAVID'S POLICY. He intended by this message not only to give to brave men their due, but to win their favour towards himself. He justly thought that those who had at such hazards honoured their deceased king would be fitting helpers of himself, and likely to become loyal subjects. There was nothing unworthy in the course he took, for there was no flattery in his expressed appreciation of their conduct, and his endeavour to gain their co-operation was not an act of mere selfishness or ambition, but of regard to the will of God who had chosen him to be King of Israel, and to the welfare of the people, which was bound up with his speedy and peaceful recognition as king. We have here an illustration of mixed motives; and we learn that: 1. *We should not hesitate to do what is right because we see that it will also be beneficial to ourselves.* All piety, rectitude, and benevolence tend, and are usually seen to tend, to the good of those who practise them. The promises of God are promises of blessing to those who serve him and their brethren, and are to be received as encouragements in doing so. 2. *We may even in some cases aim to do good to ourselves by doing what is right.* Only we must place first that which is first, or our good deeds will cease to be good, and become only another form of selfishness. Where motives are mixed, we need carefully to guard our hearts lest the lower predominate. 3. *We should be glad of opportunities of showing pure, disinterested kindness.* We thus most closely resemble our heavenly Father and our Lord Jesus Christ, and secure the best evidence of our being the children of God (Luke vi. 32—36; John xiii. 34, 35; Eph. v. 1, 2). 4. *We ought not, without clearest evidence, to suspect of selfish motives those who in doing good secure for themselves present reward.* It is to be hoped that only few are like the contributor to some charity who, being asked whether he wished his gift to be published, replied, "Why do you suppose I gave it to you?" And when the motives are not clearly revealed, it is often as just as it is charitable to give credit for the best.—G. W.

Ver. 26.—*Longing for the cessation of wars.* "Shall the sword devour for ever?" This exclamation of Abner respecting the pursuit of his discomfited troops by the conquering troops of Joab, has often been uttered in respect to war in general. As so employed it expresses horror of war, and impatient longing for its final termination.

I. THE QUESTION. The feelings which it indicates are excited in view of: 1. *The nature of war.* The mutual slaughter of each other by those who are "brethren." This aspect of the slaughter of one part of the chosen people by another presented itself to Abner. But in the light of Christianity all men are brothers, and war is a species of fratricide. They are all children of God, brethren of Christ, redeemed by his blood, and capable of sharing his eternal glory and blessedness. In this view of war, not only the actual conflicts, but all the elaborate preparations made for them, appear very dreadful. 2. *Its causes.* "Whence come wars and fightings among you? come they not hence, even of your lusts?" (Jas. iv. 1). The evil passions of men are their cause—lust of territory, of dominion, of glory, of money; the spirit of revenge and retaliation; even the love of excitement and adventure. Not less, but if possible more hideous, is the cool, calculating policy of rulers, which sets armies in motion with no regard to the lives which it sacrifices or the misery it occasions; or, again, the desire for active service, with its opportunities of distinction, promotion, and other rewards, which springs up amongst the officers, if not the rank-and-file, of standing armies, and which takes no thought of the dreadful evil which "active service" inflicts. 3. *Its effects.* "Shall the sword *devour* for ever?" War is like a huge wild beast which "devours." It eats up human beings by thousands or tens of thousands at a time. It was a small consumption of men which took place in the battle and pursuit of which this question was first used. Only twenty men had fallen on the one side, and three hundred and sixty on the other. Modern wars "devour" on a far greater scale, partly in actual battle, more from wounds received in battle, and from the diseases which the hardships of war produce. War not only devours *men* in vast numbers, and thus occasions incalculable sorrow and misery; it consumes the *substance* of nations, the creation of peaceful industry; it wastes their mental and physical energies. And still more sad to contemplate are the moral effects both on the actual combatants and on those who employ them; the hateful passions excited and strengthened, the deterioration of national character produced. 4. *Its universal prevalence.* Among peoples in every part of the world, in every stage of civilization, and down through every age. However men differ in other respects, they are alike in this practice. Whatever changes take place, this survives. The progress of science and art, of discovery and invention, and of mechanical skill, seems to have no other effect in regard to war than to increase the power of mutual destruction. War lays them all under tribute to enlarge its ability to "devour" and destroy more easily and rapidly, and on a larger scale. In view of all these considerations good men may well sigh and cry, "Shall the sword devour for ever?" There have doubtless been wars on which, in spite of all the evils they occasion, lovers of their kind could look with sympathy and satisfaction so far as one party was concerned. Such are wars of defence against unjust aggression, wars undertaken by a people to obtain liberty as against some crushing tyranny, wars against hordes of barbarians who threaten devastation and destruction to hearths and homes, and all that civilized men value. But even in such cases we may well ask—Will it ever be necessary to use so dreadful an instrument as war in the endeavour to obtain rights or abolish wrongs? Will men never be amenable to reason? Must there ever be retained the power to resort to the violent methods of war?

> "The cause of truth and human weal,
> O God above!
> Transfer it from the sword's appeal
> To peace and love."
>
> (Campbell.)

II. THE REPLY WHICH MAY BE GIVEN TO THIS QUESTION. *No.* The sword shall not devour for ever. Wars will at length come to a final end. 1. *Divine prophecy assures us of this.* (Isa. ii. 4; xi. 6—9; Micah iv. 3, 4; see also Ps. lxxii. 3, 7; Zech. ix. 10.) Not only shall wars cease, but there shall be such a feeling of universal security that the arts of war shall cease to be learnt. 2. *An adequate power for effecting this change is in the world.* Christianity—the gospel of Jesus Christ, with the accompanying might of the Holy Spirit. The revelation of God in Christ, especially of the relation of God to all men and his love to all; the redemption effected for all; the precepts of the gospel, inculcating love even to enemies, and the doing good to all; the example of him who was Love Incarnate; the dignity and worth of men, and their relation to each other, as seen in the light of the gospel; the sacred brotherhood into which faith in Christ brings men of all lands; the prospect of a heaven where all Christians will be united in service and blessedness;—these truths go to the root of the evil in the hearts of men. They cannot be truly received without subduing the passions which lead to war, and implanting the affections which insure peace. 3. *Experience justifies the hope that this peace-producing power will at length be triumphant.* That it will be in operation everywhere, and everywhere effectual.

So far as it has been experienced, it has made its subjects gentle, loving, peaceful, more willing to suffer than to inflict suffering. Multitudes exist in the world so ruled by the gospel and the Spirit of Christ, that it is simply impossible they should on any account take to killing each other. What has transformed them can transform others. Let vital Christianity become universal, and peace must be universal too. It is on the way to become universal, though its advance is slow to our view. The effect of Christianity, so far as it has prevailed, on war itself encourages hope. It has become humane in comparison with wars recorded in this Book and in the pages of general history. And amongst civilized nations there is a growing indisposition to resort to war, an increasing willingness to settle their differences by peaceful methods. This is doubtless partly the result of the tremendous costliness and destructiveness of modern warfare, but partly also of the growth of a spirit of reasonableness, equity, and humanity.

In conclusion : 1. Cherish the spirit and principles of peace, *i.e.* of Christ and Christianity. 2. Endeavour to diffuse them. And do this earnestly and hopefully, with the assurance of a final success in which you will participate joyfully. 3. Use your influence as citizens to discourage war. " And the God of peace shall be with you " (2 Cor. xiii. 11).—G. W.

EXPOSITION.

CHAPTER III.

Ver. 1.—**There was long war.** As Ishbosheth reigned only two years, and as " the house of Saul " is the phrase used, it seems probable that after Ishbosheth's murder, during the five years before David's election to the throne of all Israel, the house of Saul had some puppet representative at Mahanaim, and some commander in Abner's place. But after the death of this able man matters would go from bad to worse, and, though David probably remained on the defensive, yet the contrast between the peace and good government of Judah and the misery in Israel made all the tribes wish to put an end to a harassing civil war. It is plain, too, that the Philistines, repelled at first by Abner's skill, had again gained the ascendant, and regarded themselves so completely as the rulers of the country, that they resented immediately with summary violence the bold act of the northern tribes in choosing David to be their common king.

Ver. 2.—**Unto David were sons born.** This increase of his wives is mentioned as a proof of David's prosperity. For though contrary to the Law (Deut. xvii. 17), it was yet looked upon as part of the state of a king, and as such had been practised by Gideon (Judg. viii. 30), who approached more nearly to the royal dignity than any other of the judges. But it is the rule of the Books of Samuel that they generally abstain alike from praise and blame, and allow facts to speak for themselves. But never did a history more clearly deserve the title of ' A Vindication of the Justice of God.' Alike in Eli, in Saul, and in David, their sufferings were the result of their sins, and to the polygamy and lust of the last

are due both the crimes which stained his character and the distress of the last twenty years of his life. (For **Amnon**, his first-born, see ch. xiii.)

Vers. 3—5.—**Chileab.** The Midrash explains Chileab as meaning " Quite like the father." He is called Daniel in the parallel genealogy in 1 Chron. iii. 1, and this was probably his real name, and Chileab a name of affection. He must have died young, for Adonijah appears as David's eldest son after the death of Amnon and Absalom ; and it is thus natural that he should still be known by the name he bore as a child. **Geshur.** The word signifies " Bridgeland," and is the name of two districts, one of which formed the northern part of the tribe of Manasseh, and extended on both sides of the Jordan, from the little Hermon to the sea of Gennesareth (Deut. iii. 14 ; Josh. xii. 5 ; xiii. 13). The other was in Syria (ch. xv. 8), and probably was situated upon some river, though its exact position is not yet known. Talmai, its king, now gave his daughter to be one of David's wives, and though he was probably only a petty prince, still it is a proof of David's growing power that a potentate living at so great a distance was willing to make an alliance with him. Of the other wives and their sons nothing is known except of Adonijah, who inherited, on the death of Absalom, the dangerous position of firstborn ; and who, after trying to make his rights good, was put to death by Solomon (1 Kings ii. 25). As **Eglah** is especially called **David's wife**, the Jewish interpreters hold that she was the highest in rank in his household, and therefore identical with Michal, who was restored to David while at Hebron. But she was childless ; and more probably the words are to be taken as simply closing the narrative, and as belonging, therefore, equally to each of the six.

Ver. 6.—**Abner made himself strong for the house of Saul.** The Hebrew really means that until this miserable quarrel about Rizpah, Abner had been the mainstay of Ishbosheth's throne and dynasty. She is proved to have been a noble woman, with a warm and devoted heart, by the narrative in ch. xxi. 8—11. But the harem of a deceased king was looked upon as the special inheritance of his successor; and Absalom, by taking David's concubines (ch. xvi. 21, 22), treated his father as a dead man, and committed so overt an act of treason as made reconciliation impossible. So Solomon put his brother Adonijah to death for asking Abishag to wife (1 Kings ii. 23—25). Still, as Bathsheba there saw no impropriety in Adonijah's request, and Solomon deposed Abiathar and put Joab to death for complicity, as we must conclude, in Adonijah's request, it was probably part of some scheme of conspiracy, and that, if granted, it would have been used by Adonijah as a proof that the kingdom really was his. Here there was no plot, and as Rizpah had probably always lived apart from Ishbosheth, Abner may have expected that the king would see no difficulty in the matter.

Ver. 8. **Then was Abner very wroth** This extreme indignation on Abner's part is not easy to understand; for he could scarcely have expected Ishbosheth to endure quietly what at least was a great insult. But probably the question, **Wherefore hast thou gone in unto my father's concubine?** does not mean a mild expostulation on the king's part, but the purpose to degrade Abner and strip him of his office. Probably after the defeat by Joab at Gibeon, the army was less satisfied with its leader, and his detractors may gladly have encouraged the king to use this opportunity for bringing Abner down to his proper place. Weak kings often try to play the strong man; but the attempt here only drove the imperious soldier to put the matter to the proof, and show that the strength was his. We know that David groaned all his life through under Joab's iron will, and, though he tried, yet that he never succeeded in throwing off the yoke. But Joab never behaved unfaithfully to his sovereign as Abner did here, and his crimes were deeds of violence committed in David's cause. **Am I a dog's head, which against Judah,** etc.? The words literally are, *Am I a dog's head that is for Judah?* and are rightly rendered in the Revised Version, *Am I a dog's head that belongeth to Judah?* Am I at once worthless and a traitor, a thing of no account, and on the side of thy enemies? In the words that follow he protests, not so much his innocence as his great deserts.

This day—that is, at this very time—I am showing kindness unto the house of Saul . . . and this day thou wouldest visit upon me—that is, punish me for—**the fault about this woman.** I make and maintain thee as king, and thou wouldst play the king upon me, the kingmaker!

Ver. 9.—**As the Lord hath sworn to David.** This not only shows that the prophetic promise of the kingdom to David was generally known (see note on ch. i. 2), but that Abner regarded it as solemnly ratified. There is no express mention of any such oath, but Abner was a man of strong words, and possibly only meant that Jehovah's purpose was becoming evident by the course of events.

Ver. 11.—**He could not answer Abner.** Though the reply was one of open treason, and was spoken with violence, yet Ishbosheth did not venture to bring the matter to an issue. Perhaps he looked round upon his officers to see if any would take his side, and, when all were silent, he was too feeble to dare to order the arrest and trial of his too-powerful captain.

Ver. 12.—**Abner sent messengers to David on his behalf;** Hebrew, *under him.* The Revised Version renders this "where he was;" but the phrase really means "immediately" (see note on ch. ii. 23). And this agrees with the haughty temper of Abner. Without waiting for advice, or allowing his anger to cool, he at once sent trusty envoys to open negotiations with David. **Whose is the land?** Abner's meaning in these words is plain. You, David, he seems to say, will answer that the land is mine; for Jehovah has promised it to me. But, as a matter of fact, much of the land is mine (Abner's), or at least belongs to the house of Saul, whose prime minister I am. Yours is an abstract right; mine is actual possession. Come, let us make the two agree. Give me fitting assurances of safety and reward, and I will make your claim a reality.

Ver. 13.—**Except thou first bring Michal.** Besides David's affection for Michal, there were political reasons for demanding her restoration. Saul's despotic act in giving her in marriage to another man (1 Sam. xxv. 44) had been a public disavowal of David as the son-in-law of the royal house, and equivalent to a proclamation of outlawry. David's rights were all declared null by such an act. But now Ishbosheth must with equal publicity reverse his father's deed, and restore to David his lost position. It must have been a most painful humiliation to him to be driven thus to cancel his father's decree, and declare thereby to all Israel that he was unable to refuse his assent to whatever his rival demanded.

And for this reason David sent his messengers directly to Ishbosheth, because the importance of Michal's surrender to him lay in its being a public act of the state. For *Michal*, in ch. xxi. 8, we ought to read *Merab* (see note there).

Ver. 14.—**A hundred foreskins.** This was the number which Saul had required (1 Sam. xviii. 25), and David acted rightly in not boasting that he had really given twice as many (1 Sam. xviii. 27). As he had paid her father the stipulated price, Michal, by Oriental law, was David's property.

Ver. 15.—**Phaltiel the son of Laish.** In 1 Sam. xxv. 44 he is called Phalti. This word, in Hebrew lexicons, is usually regarded as a contraction for Phaltiyah, "Jehovah is deliverance," while Phaltiel means "El is deliverance." The substitution of *El* for *Yah* is one of those changes which arose out of the superstitious reverence for the sacred name which to this day causes the word LORD to be read in our Bibles where in the Hebrew are the four consonants Y, H, V, H, which, by attaching to them the vowels belonging to the Hebrew word *edonay* (or, *adonay*, lord) we make into "Jehovah" (*Yehovah*).

Ver. 16.—**Her husband went with her along weeping behind her.** "Along weeping" is a very awkward rendering of the Hebrew phrase, "going and weeping." The Revised Version is far better, "weeping as he went and followed her." Phaltiel had been Michal's husband for eight or nine years, and his sorrow at losing her excites sympathy for them both. They had evidently loved one another, and she was now going to be but one of many wives; and though David may have desired her restoration because he valued her and cherished the remembrance of their youthful affection, yet there was a large admixture of political motive in his conduct. At Gallim she had been Phaltiel's one jewel, and had been loved for her own sake; at Hebron she would have many rivals. But women of royal rank have often to pay the price of sacrificed affections for the ends of statecraft. Near **Bahurim**, on the road from Jerusalem to Gilgal, in the valley of the Jordan, the convoy approached the borders of Judah, and Abner will not allow the weeping husband to enter David's dominions. Painful as was his fate, he had himself done wrong in marrying another man's wife; and if he was weeping now, we may well believe that David had felt equal anguish when Michal was torn from him and sold to another,—for fathers in those days received instead of giving a dowry upon the marriage of their daughters. Saul in this matter was most to blame, and if he had

not committed this wrong, David might never have sought an evil solace in multiplying to himself other wives.

Ver. 17.—**And Abner had communication with the elders of Israel.** Most probably this had taken place before Abner escorted Michal to Hebron, and that he paid David but one visit—that recorded in ver. 20. He would probably not take so decided a step as the surrender of Michal without sounding the elders, that is, the local sheikhs, and finding out how far they were inclined to support David as king of all Israel. When everything was ready he would take Michal to Hebron, and so have the opportunity of arranging with David for future action; and though Ishbosheth would dislike the matter and suspect Abner of ulterior purposes, yet he could not refuse so specious a plea as the escorting of his sister. His previous failure, too, had taught him that Abner was master. We may further be sure that David had everywhere many adherents. All Israel knew that he was marked out by prophecy to be their king, and, moreover, "all Israel and Judah loved him" (1 Sam. xviii. 16). But when Abner says, **Ye sought for David in times past** to be **king over you,** he makes it probable that, at some time after the defeat at Gilboa, the attempt had even been made to elect David king. But Abner had then opposed it, and his success in resisting the Philistines, and David's unfortunate entanglement with those inveterate enemies of Israel, had made the attempt fail. And now Abner's attempt was to be equally unsuccessful.

Ver. 18.—**The Lord hath spoken.** Here again Abner's statements go far beyond the text of anything recorded in Holy Scripture, but probably they give the popular interpretation of the prophecies respecting David. It will be noticed also that Abner endeavours to meet the general prejudice against David by asserting that he was Israel's destined deliverer from Philistine oppression. As Abner's speech is virtually an acknowledgment of failure, we may also be sure that he had found himself unable any longer to make head against the Philistines on the western side of the Jordan, and that Judah was the only tribe there that enjoyed tranquillity. Everywhere else they had once again established their supremacy. Though a brave soldier, Abner was inferior, not only to David, but also to Joab, both as statesman and general; and the weak Ishbosheth was no help to him, but the contrary.

Ver. 19.—**In the ears of Benjamin.** This tribe alone, probably, was really loyal to the house of Saul, their kinsman. But since the withdrawal of the court to Mahanaim, they got but little good from it, and were left to resist the predatory bands of the Philistines as best they could. So warlike a tribe too would despise Ishbosheth, and long for a braver man to aid them in fighting their enemies.

Ver. 20.—Twenty men with him. These, we may feel sure, were not common soldiers, but chieftains selected from those elders who were on David's side; and, though the honourable escort of Michal was the pretext, yet Ishbosheth must have felt sure that more was intended. Most of them, however, would join Abner on the road, especially those who represented Benjamin and the western tribes. On arriving at Hebron they were honourably received, and, after a feast, they settled the conditions on which David was to be made king of all Israel; and Abner then departed in peace, after giving the assurance that all the tribes would now gladly assemble, and by solemn compact and covenant make David their king. The terms of the league, and the conditions agreed upon for Ishbosheth, are not mentioned, because upon Abner's death the whole plan fell to the ground, and David had to wait for many years before his hopes were fulfilled. But we gather from this covenant and ch. v. 3 (where see note) that the early kings of Israel were not absolute monarchs.

Ver. 22.—From pursuing a troop. This gives a wrong idea, as though Joab had been repelling an attack. The Revised Version is right in rendering " came from a foray," *the troop* being a company of men sent out on a predatory excursion. It is not unlikely that David had arranged this expedition in order that his interview with Abner might take place in Joab's absence; and as he returned with "great spoil," he had probably been away for some nine or ten days, during which he had penetrated far into the country of the Amalekites. Had David acted frankly and honourably, Joab would not have stood in the way of his master's exaltation, and the blood-feud between him and Abner might have been arranged. But it is evident that David secretly disliked and chafed under the control of his strong-willed and too-able nephew.

Vers. 24, 25.—What hast thou done? David's secret dealing makes Joab see a personal wrong to himself in the negotiation with Abner. There could be no room, he feels, for both of them in David's army, and David meant, he supposes, to sacrifice himself. In hot haste, therefore, he rushes into the king's presence, and reproaches him for what he has done, but covers his personal feelings with professed zeal for his master's interests. Abner is a mere spy, who has come on a false pretext, and with the real intention of learning David's **going**

out and coming in, that is, his present manner of life and undertakings. **All that thou doest**; literally, *all that thou art doing;* all that is now going on, and thy plans and purposes. Abner would not only judge by what he saw, but in his interview with David would lead him on to talk of his hopes and prospects. David had little time to explain the real object of Abner's coming, nor was Joab in a mood to listen to anything he said. He had detected his master in secret negotiations, and would regard his excuses as tainted with deceit. And after giving vent to his anger in reproaches, he hurried away to thwart David's plans by a deed of most base villainy. Had David acted openly, all would have been done with Joab's consent and approval.

Ver. 26.—The well—Hebrew, *cistern*—of **Sirah.** Josephus ('Ant.,' viii. 1, 5) says that this cistern was situated about two miles and a half north of Hebron. There was probably a caravanserai there, at which Abner halted, intending to continue his march homewards as soon as the coolness of evening set in. Here Joab's messengers overtook him, and, speaking in David's name —for otherwise Abner would not have fallen into the trap—asked him to return for further conference, mentioning, perhaps, Joab's arrival as the reason. In this way Abner's suspicions would be set at rest, and it would seem quite natural for him to find Joab waiting for him at the gate.

Ver. 27.—Joab took him aside in the gate. As we read in ch. xviii. 24 of David sitting " between the two gates," and of " the roof over the gate," and in ver. 33 of " the chamber over the gate," Ewald's idea of there being a roofed inner space, with a guard-room over it, as in the mediæval gate-towers in German towns, is probably right. As the "two gates" would make the space between them gloomy, the spot would just suit Joab's purpose. He meets Abner, therefore, in a friendly manner, and drawing him aside, as if to converse with him apart from the people going in and out, there assassinates him. The place was so public that the deed must have been witnessed by multitudes, though the gloom, felt the more by them from the contrast with the bright glare of sunshine outside, had given Joab the opportunity of drawing his sword without Abner's observing it. **For the blood of Asahel his brother.** Joab's act was in accordance with Oriental feeling; and the duties of the avenger of blood might with some straining be made to cover his retaliation for an act done by Abner in self-defence (Numb. xxxv. 26, 27). It is remarkable that Hebron was itself a city of refuge (Josh. xx. 7), and this may have led Joab to murder him in the gate, before he had actually entered.

Still, Abner did not expect any such retribution, and supposing that Joab knew of the purpose that had brought him to Hebron, he could not suppose that he would be so indifferent to his master's interests as to put a summary stop to the negotiations for uniting the tribes under David. As it was, this deed brought upon David an evil name, and four or five years had to elapse before the tribes could be induced to take him for their king. Even then his hold over them was far less than it would otherwise have been; for though the shock was gradually got over, yet the suspicion still clung to him. And if the deed was Joab's own act, still David had contributed to it by underhand dealings. His very fear of Joab had caused him to wrong his able general, and given him just cause for resentment.

Ver. 28.—**I and my kingdom** are **guiltless.** By this David means, not his royal house, but the people generally, who too often have to pay the penalty for the sins of their rulers (see ch. xxi. 1). Necessarily this is the case, wherever the crime is a state crime; but David protests that Abner's murder was a private crime, for which Joab and Abishai alone ought to suffer.

Ver. 29.—**Let it rest on the head of Joab.** The Hebrew word is very strong, "Let it roll itself," or throw itself upon Joab's head. The force of the expression thus indicates the great excitement under which David was labouring; yet even so it was no slight matter to utter so bitter a curse upon a man so powerful, and whose military skill was so essential to the maintenance of his throne. To a man of David's strong sense of justice, it was a small matter that by Abner's murder the kingdom of the ten tribes was lost perhaps for ever; what he hated was the wickedness of this mean act of personal revenge. And thus his imprecations are all such as would be humiliating to a family so distinguished for great physical as well as mental gifts, as the house of Zeruiah. Nor was David content with this; for we gather from 1 Chron. xi. 6 that during the intervening years Joab was deprived of his office, and that he regained it only by an act of daring bravery. (For the miserable condition of one suffering with an issue, see Lev. xv. 2, etc.; and for that of a leper, Lev., xiii. xiv.) Instead of **one that leaneth on a staff,** some translate "a distaff-holder," that is, a poor effeminate creature, fit only for woman's work. The true sense is probably a cripple—one who needs a crutch. **That falleth on the sword;** more correctly the Revised Version, *that falleth by the sword.* The two last imprecations mean that if any of the race of Joab and Abishai escape these personal blemishes, yet that his fate shall be, in war an inglorious death, and in peace

a life of poverty. This curse of David is regarded in the Talmud ('Sanhedr.,' 48. 2) as very sinful. Undeniably it was uttered in violent anger, and while Joab's act was utterly base and perfidious, yet he had the excuse for it of Asahel's death and David's double-dealing. The latter made him conclude that the man who had killed his brother was also to usurp his place. Possibly this suspicion was not without reason. As David was strong enough to deprive Joab of his command, it is plain that he had nothing to fear from telling him his plans. Joab would have assented, the blood-feud have been appeased by a money payment, and all gone well. But David, it seems, wished to hold Joab in check by giving at least a share in the command to the veteran Abner.

Ver. 30.—**Joab and Abishai his brother.** Nothing is said of Abishai having taken part in the murder, but the words suggest that it was a premeditated act, and that Abishai was privy to it.

Ver. 31.—**David said to Joab.** The excuse of the blood-feud made it impossible for David to punish Joab further than by depriving him of his command; but he made him condemn his own deed by taking part in the public mourning for the man he had murdered. This mourning consisted in going in solemn procession, clad in sackcloth, before Abner's body, carried on a bier to the grave, while David followed as chief mourner; and the emphatic way in which he is called **King David** suggests the thought that he went in royal state, so as to give all possible dignity to the funeral. His tears and lamentations with uplifted voice were so genuine and hearty as to move the people to a similar outburst of grief. But while all those at Hebron had proof that David was innocent, the people generally would know only that, when Abner was escorting the king's wife back to him, and arranging for his election to rule over all Israel, he was treacherously murdered at the gate of Hebron by one who was chief over David's army and also his nephew.

Ver. 33.—**The king lamented.** The word is the same as that used in ch. i. 17. The word rendered "fool" is *nabal* (for which see 1 Sam. xxv. 25). The idea contained in the word is not that of mere silliness, but of worthlessness also; and thus in Ps. xiv. 1 we find that the *nabal* is also an atheist.

Ver. 34.—**Thy hands were not bound.** Abner had been put to death by Joab for killing Asahel. But there had been no legal process. He had not been brought in fetters before a judge to be tried for the crime alleged, but murdered for private ends. And thus, "As a man falleth before the children of iniquity, so had he fallen," that is, by crime, and not by law. These words are probably the refrain of the dirge, like those in ch. i. 19, 25, 27, and were followed by the celebration of Abner's bravery, but they alone are recorded, because they contain the main point. Abner's death was not, like the sentence upon Baanah and Rechab, an act of justice, but one of lawless revenge; and by this poem David proclaimed, not only his innocence, but also his abhorrence of the crime.

Ver. 35.—**The people came to cause David to eat meat.** The Jewish commentators, Philippson, Cahen, etc., consider that the occasion for this was given by the custom of taking food after a funeral (Jer. xvi. 7; Ezek. xxiv. 17), which in time degenerated into the giving of a costly banquet (Josephus, 'Bell. Jud.,' 2. 1). To this day, at a Jewish funeral in Germany, the bearers are regaled with eggs, bread, and wine. While, then, others were partaking of the food that had been provided, David remained apart, and when urged by the assembled multitude to join them in their meal, he protested that he would continue fasting until sunset. He thus proved that his sorrow was genuine, and the people were convinced of his innocence, and pleased at the honour which he thus did to the fallen soldier.

Ver. 36.—**Whatsoever the king did pleased all the people.** This is a tribute to the king's conduct generally. The people would have been grieved and astonished if David had been guilty of this mean murder; but his indignant disavowal of it was in accordance with his usual justice and uprightness, and so it confirmed their high opinion of him. Thus while the more distant tribes condemned David, those who had the best opportunity for forming a judgment gave their verdict in his favour.

Ver. 37.—**All Israel understood.** The twenty men who had accompanied Abner would be witnesses of all that David did, and would carry their report of it home, and of the high estimation in which his character was held at Hebron. And this gradually would be told throughout the tribes, and the final verdict of all well-disposed people would be in David's favour.

Ver. 38.—**A prince and a great man.** David pronounces this high estimate of Abner's worth to **his servants**, that is, to his officers, and especially to the six hundred mighty men. His conduct is bold and open, and must have greatly humiliated Joab and Abishai. But though the six hundred approved of David's conduct, and respected him for it, yet probably, as Abner had killed Asahel, they would not have consented to any further punishment than the disgrace inflicted on Joab by his being deprived of the command of David's warriors.

Ver. 39.—**I am this day weak . . . the sons of Zeruiah be too hard for me.** David would gladly have had Abner as a counterpoise to Joab's too-great power. As it was, though an anointed king, he had but one tribe loyal to him; the rest were the subjects of a rival; and the Philistines were oppressing all alike. Had Abner's enterprise been carried out, all the tribes would have been united under his sway. He could thus have made head against the Philistines, and Abner, in command of the Benjamites and other tribes, would have curbed the fierce self-will of Joab. As it was, the sons of Zeruiah might be reprimanded, and could not treat David as Abner had treated Ishbosheth; but they were indispensable. David had a strange set of men around him in those outlaws (1 Sam. xxii. 2); and Joab, brave, skilful, and unscrupulous, was a man after their own heart. They had just returned with great booty from a foray under his command; and it was a brave and manly thing in David to reprove him so openly, and dismiss him from his command. Had he attempted more, and Joab had stood upon the defence, there were plenty of "men of Belial" (1 Sam. xxx. 22) to side with him, and David might have met with the fate threatened him at Ziklag (1 Sam. xxx. 6). As it was, he proved himself to be king, and Joab, in spite of everything, remained a most faithful officer, and the right-hand man in his kingdom, and one even trusted with perilous and disgraceful secrets (ch. xi. 14).

HOMILETICS.

Vers. 1—11.—*Rival interests.* The facts are: 1. A desultory war is carried on between the house of Saul and the house of David, in which the latter has the advantage. 2. David has six sons born to him while at Hebron. 3. A quarrel arises between Abner and Ishbosheth, consequent on an accusation resented by Abner. 4. Abner charges his master with ingratitude, and threatens to transfer his allegiance to David. 5. In seeking to give emphasis to his threat, Abner indicates his knowledge of the Divine will concerning David. The object of the historian in vers. 1—5 is obviously to give a representation, from a political point of view, of David prior to the action of Abner in his favour ; and in vers. 6—11 to state the circumstance that led to a transfer of Abner's support from one side to the other. The general effect of the war between the two royal houses and the growth of David's domestic establishment are the two prominent items of the situation prior to Abner's change of policy. Judged solely by the standard of the age, they pointed in the direction of advancing influence, but looked at in the light of a higher standard they suggest a qualified prosperity. The general truths embodied in this account of rival interests may be set forth as follows.

I. DEFENSIVE ACTION IN A JUST CAUSE IS SOMETIMES THE BEST POLICY. That the cause of David was just is evident to every believer in the truth of the First Book of Samuel, and, as seen there and in the Psalms, the conviction of this governed his conduct. From a purely human point of view it might seem contrary to natural justice to set aside the son of the late king; and the effort of Ishbosheth to urge, by force of arms, his own claim may be a natural sequence of thought and feeling. But kings have no rights apart from the will of God ; and, as the sequel shows (ver. 10), both the young king and his general were not unacquainted with the Divine purpose. The right being with David, it might seem strange that he did not press his claim to entire dominion by aggressive war. His skill and valour, the coherence of his following, and the enthusiasm created by his personality, to say nothing of the demoralizing effect on Abner of his own infidelity to conscience, could not but have speedily made him master of all Israel. Instead of that, we find David simply authorizing such conflict as would suffice to hold his own and check the aggressive efforts of the house of Saul. It is interesting to see here the same David as of old, who had such faith in God and the gradual unfolding of his purposes that he would never raise a hand against Saul, or do anything, except in necessary self-defence, that could be construed into hostility. Had not Abner's evil counsels prevailed with Ishbosheth, David would have lived in peace at Hebron till a mightier hand than his own cleared the way to the throne of a united people. Statesmen would do well to take such an example in many of the painful contingencies that arise. To a just man it is half the victory to be calm and strong in the conviction of his rectitude and the righteousness of his position. There is a watchful Providence cherishing the good and frustrating the evil. Forces under the direction of an evil genius are sure to wear themselves out if only the objects of their hate can hold their own; and the wasting of their strength means the final triumph of the cause of truth and justice. There are seasons in Church life when this policy of pure defence is wise; for at such times God has ends to effect which work in with the scope of more aggressive endeavours.

II. A RIGHT CONTENTION WILL COME TO A RIGHT ISSUE. "David waxed stronger and stronger." Of course he did. It could not but be so, for he was a chosen servant, not seeking or doing his own will, but simply placing his life in the hands of God, to work out for his people and for future ages, purposes the precise nature of which he could not understand. No weapon formed against him could prosper. He who contended against him fought against God. The forces of nature were on his side. Never did mortal more vainly contend against fate than did Ishbosheth contend against David. The principle involved in this instance is of wide range. Right is sure to prevail in the issue. The disturbing element introduced by sin into the universe causes strife of the most grave character. The whole line of Divine government, so far as we can trace it, seems to be a line of conflict between right and wrong, holiness and sin. The antagonism taken up in Eden runs on and becomes more acute on Calvary, and is apparent now in a "long war" between the children of light and the kingdom of darkness. Time is in favour of righteousness. There is an endurance in truth which cannot be affirmed of error. As perhaps the friends of David thought those years of war very tedious and dispiriting, and sometimes even inconsistent with rightness of claim and purpose, so we may be weary in the greater strife and become disturbed by cruel questionings; yet the issue is sure. "Stronger and stronger" may be affirmed of the kingdom of righteousness on earth. For even the seeming failures and delays only become, in the hands of Providence, the means of acquiring the hardier and more enduring virtues by which at last the final victory shall be won. The same is true of any conflicts in which character is at stake. Our "righteousness shall be brought forth as the light," and our "judgment as the noonday." The parallel may be seen also in the conflict of the "old" and the "new man." The one is on the way to perish; the other is "renewed day by day."

III. THE UNEXPRESSED WOES OF LIFE ARE VERY REAL. "There was long war." The sentence is brief, and understandable by a child. It is repeated with careless ease. As a rule, it connotes to the ordinary reader only a general idea of men seeking to slay one another. But to read history aright we ought to bring the faculty of imagination into full play; and it is only as we exercise the historic imagination that we get a glimpse of the sad facts embodied in this simple form of expression. Subjected to the vitalizing power of this faculty, what unexpressed woes rise up to view! What harsh and fierce dispositions! What weary marchings and watchings! What murderous blows and bleeding wounds and agonizing deaths! What widows' wailings and orphans' tears! What losses to homes and nation of strong men and productive toil! This, which applies to the brief statement of the sacred narrative, is equally true of greater woes. Men read of great battles very much as they read algebraic symbols. The real items indicated are not vivid to the mind. Men read also of the banishment of the wicked to outer darkness in the same mechanical way. The hurry of life leaves no time for the imagination to lay hold of the actual facts connoted. Hence the power over the will of mere visible, present realities. Hence the difficulty of getting the "powers of the world to come" to influence motive. Hence, also, the necessity of each man making an effort to bring his mind into actual view of the facts covered by language, and of the preacher and teacher rendering the aid of well-chosen speech to further this effort.

IV. CONVENTIONAL STRENGTH MAY BE AN OCCASION OF MORAL WEAKNESS. The historian tells us of the growth of David's domestic establishment at Hebron. Estimated by the customs prevalent in the East at that time, this acquisition by David of wives and sons was supposed to add to the splendour and stateliness of his regal position. All the paraphernalia of a court, the wide-reaching influence of family connections, and the imposing show of a large household would lead ordinary men to regard him as among the great ones of the earth. The accidental surroundings of life form a delusively important part of what is deemed to be human greatness. We are all children in so far as we are influenced in our judgments on social position and weight of character by the circumstantials of life. Even the more educated are prone to either identify or associate greatness with large establishments. This kind of conventionalism plays an important part in human affairs; but it is not God's standard. David's polygamous habits were consistent with the conventional morality of the age, and his domestic establishment projected his public position before the eye of the people in a form accordant to princely fashion; but we know that beneath all the signs of wealth and greatness there were influences at work which could not but weaken his moral force and mar the beauty and sweetness of his private life. Oriental splendour and conventional moralities were indulged in at great moral cost. David in Hebron with many wives and their accompaniments could not be as morally robust as was David in earlier days. The same danger attends all who conform to customs not based on strict principles of purity and godliness. Fashion cannot make righteousness. Goodness may live amidst habits essentially alien to the welfare of the individual and to saints, as surely as life may continue in an atmosphere charged with malarious poisons; but the enervation of the one will be as certain as of the other. The insensibility of the man to the subtle action of the evil is only an aggravation of its action and in no wise a palliation. Modern Christians should severely scrutinize the moral quality of the circumstances and habits in which conventional usage allows them to live. This can only be done by making use of tests absolutely given by God apart from the colouring which custom is apt to give even to Divine laws.

V. UNRIGHTEOUS MEN PAY HOMAGE TO RIGHTEOUSNESS. There can be no question but that Ishbosheth knew well the nature and validity of David's claims; for the theocratic rule was a reality in Israel during and subsequent to the life of Samuel. It was, therefore, wrong for him to put forth any personal claim of his own. Jonathan's example had been lost upon him; and yet this man recognized the evil done by Abner in lustful indulgence, and even ventured to protest against it. On the other hand, Abner, while being unrighteous enough to indulge in sinful lust and to abet the invalid claim of Ishbosheth, nevertheless is fired with indignation that the love of gratitude should have been violated by the young monarch. Thus men, pursuing a course which they know to be contrary to the will of God, become, when personal and family matters are involved, zealous, each in his own fashion, for what is right and proper. Truly, man is a strange compound of moral light and darkness. The psychological explanation is a study. It is the habituation to the wrong which renders men so dull to appeals, so insensible to the real demerit of their actions, and it is the latent force of conscience which saves them from being parties to a course on which they have not taken the initial step. Hence our Lord's reference to the "gnat" and the "camel." The prevalence of this state of moral confusion is very wide even in Christian society. In the same individual may be found great sensitiveness and great obtuseness. The holding of slaves and gain by the sale of them has coexisted with a profound regard for religious worship. Licentious men have had a dread of dishonesty. Multitudes who rob God of the love and obedience due to him are indignant if an ordinary business debt is not paid. The Pharisees could conspire to kill Jesus Christ, and yet feel very unhappy if they omitted any of the ceremonials of religion. It is a common thing for men and women to indulge in envy, jealousy, and ill will, while extremely careful to keep up an external conduct conformable to the requirements of the Decalogue. There is much scope for searching of heart on this subject; and in dealing with it the preacher needs to exercise great discrimination and delicacy of reference. Abner must be made to see himself as Ishbosheth sees him, and *vice versâ*. "Man, know thyself," is a maxim of immense importance to every one.

VI. PASSING EVENTS MAY SERVE TO UNVEIL THE WORKINGS OF CONSCIENCE. Viewed from a distance by the people, Abner seemed to be a man who all along was conscientiously and faithfully subordinating his life to the maintenance of a just cause. So far as we can see from the narrative, he had been reticent concerning the mental processes of which he was daily conscious. But the incident of Ishbosheth's accusation of immorality was as the removing of a veil whereby the actual thoughts of Abner stood revealed. "So do God to Abner, and more also, except, as the Lord hath sworn to David, even so I do to him." Thus Abner had known all along that it was God's will to give the kingdom to David. The ideas and compunctions connected with this central fact had evidently been covered up and suppressed. The real inner life of struggle against right and God was now exposed by his own act. In the case of every man there is always an inner life necessarily hidden by himself from ordinary view. It is a necessity of social existence that each man should be more unknown than known to his fellows. Only where there is perfect holiness would perfect knowledge of others be helpful to love and confidence. But in the case of men pursuing a deliberate course which seems to others to be conscientious, but is known to themselves to be contrary to right, there is a rigid and designed concealment of their self-condemnation. They gain the reputation of being upright, though perhaps misguided, men, while their own conscience gives the lie to this public judgment. An incidental reference, an unguarded hasty admission of fact, an effort to justify an action, may be as a sudden rent in the covering of the real life within, exposing to the view of others a guilty violation of truth, a perpetual conflict against the well-ascertained will of God. This frequent concealment of an inner guilty life and its possible unveiling by incidental events should be a guide in forming an estimate of conduct, and a warning to evil-doers. The self-exposure, also, however incidental, is to be taken as a preintimation of the final exposure when God shall bring hidden things into judgment.

Vers. 12—21.—The facts are: 1. Abner, disgusted with Ishbosheth's conduct, opens negotiation with David for the transfer of the kingdom to him. 2. David consents to discuss the question on condition that Abner first of all undertakes to restore unto him Michal, Saul's daughter. 3. Concurrent with Abner's efforts to bring this to pass, David makes a demand on Ishbosheth for the restoration of Michal. 4. Abner, taking charge of Michal on her return to David, effects the final separation from her weeping husband. 5. Reminding Israel and Benjamin of their former preference of David, Abner seeks to bring them over to his cause. 6. Charged with instructions from the people, he proceeds to Hebron as a legate to arrange the business with David. 7. As a result of the interview, it was left to Abner to complete the formal submission of all the people to the authority of David

Faithfulness in small things. The passage here in reference to David and Michal brings out a feature in the character of the king which was prominent from first to last. According to the common estimate of things, the *a priori* belief would be that, when a ruler desires the subjugation of a kingdom, he will readily accept offers of submission and of all powerful aids to bring it to pass. To obtain supremacy over Israel was the one thing above all others on which David's mind was set, and the co-operation of so influential a man as Abner was a virtual realization of the king's purpose. To an astute unprincipled man like Abner it was doubtless a cause of amazement that, when the kingdom was within the king's grasp, he should practically refuse to have it unless a certain private affair was first arranged. The great affairs of the nation were made to wait on the settlement of what seemed to be a mere matter of sentiment and personal interest. Few monarchs in the East would thus have dealt with the chance of gaining the ends of long-cherished political ambition. In David's case the stipulation was consistent with his character. He was ever generously careful of maintaining the rights of individuals and of sacrificing his own ambition to the justice due to others. He was faithful in that which is least.

I. THE CLAIMS OF THAT WHICH IS LEAST ARE VALID AND ARE SUBSTANTIAL PARTS OF A VAST SYSTEM OF OBLIGATIONS. Michal was David's wife, bound to his heart and life by ties sacred and memorable (1 Sam. xviii. 17—30). To political schemers it would seem absurd to set a woman, not seen for many years, and known to be living in forced matrimony with another man, over against a whole kingdom. But wrong done to her (1 Sam. xxv. 44) had not invalidated her claim on David's affection. It was due to her, due to the memory of her father in spite of his follies, due to the force of his own character on others, and due to the old love (1 Sam. xviii. 20—28) which changing fortunes had not changed, that she should have justice done her on the very first opportunity of enforcing it. David's vision was clear enough to see that, if his claim to be king over all Israel was valid because of the appointment of God, so equally the claim of this banished woman on his love and care was also valid, because based on principles which God had ordained for the regulation of domestic life. The same Divine will was in both; and, moreover, they were equally parts of the great system of obligations which covers the whole area of human activity, and which is productive of highest good to man when the different parts are equally held as sacred and are rigidly observed. In human affairs there is often an apparent collision of what are called small and great obligations. In reality there is no such thing. There may be a question of order in which actions shall be done; but obligation, in the moral sense, can never clash with obligation. To love the Lord with all the heart is the prime, the chief duty, but it does not destroy the duty of love to our neighbour. To take part in public affairs may be an obligation, but the care of home is a valid claim which cannot be ignored. There are duties which, entering into the minutiæ of life or pertaining to the home rather than to public affairs, may be regarded as relatively small, but inasmuch as they are not the creation of custom but proceed from the will of God and form parts of the great scheme of life, they are to be regarded as sacred and binding as those which figure more largely before the public eye.

II. THE BRINGING ABOUT OF GREAT EVENTS INVOLVES MORE CHANGES THAN LIE WITHIN OUR OWN ACTION, AND PROVIDENCE TAKES CARE OF THEM. The event of all Israel submitting to David would imply manifold influences brought to bear on the elders of the people, and through them on the masses, and in such a process of change there might arise many a circumstance adverse to the desired issue. It was not in David's power to effect this by any personal action. All he could do was to set agencies at work through Abner, and trust in Providence for disposing the hearts of men aright. It was right doubtless for the people to own him as king, but it was not in his power to establish this right. On the other hand, it was in his power to do justice to a banished woman, and demand, as a prior step, that she be restored to his heart and home. There is always an uncertainty attending our efforts to bring about great issues in the world's affairs, even though those issues be predicted and included in the Divine purpose; for our actions are but a few among myriads of forces for and against the end for which we strive, and for ages the goal may not be reached. It is our duty to do what we can, just as it was David's to use means for winning Israel over to the allegiance which had been predicted and was part of the theocratic purpose; but we have to act in faith that an overruling Providence is at work above us and above all forces, and that the great issue will in some unknown way and time be brought to pass. The statesman cannot make the nation great and strong; he can only set in motion social and material forces which in due course may accomplish the purpose in view. The missionary can but contribute an item of force towards rendering the whole earth submissive to Christ. The parent can contribute but some of the elements which in the end will tend to form the final character of his children. The far-reaching aims of life are binding on us, but their realization is not all in our power. It is absolutely within our power to perform single acts of justice and consideration as occasion offers. As the products of will, they may fill but a small place in the world in comparison with the realization of those other wider aims which are products of many wills; yet they afford opportunities for proving our fidelity to truth and righteousness as surely as do the great events to bring about which we can only contribute our part. David's profound regard for what was right shone forth in his care for a single individual, just as truly as his faith in Providence appeared in subordinating the attainment of his political ambition to this act of justice.

III. HUMAN DUTY IS PLEDGED TO THAT WHICH IS KNOWN AND DISTINCT. David knew that Michal was his wife, that she had been forcibly separated from him in the day of adversity, and that as a good man he was bound to amend her wrongs as soon as occasion offered. Though a king, he saw that domestic were prior to political obligations. There may have been, as a matter of fact, policy in showing his regard in this way for the house of Saul, but the evident motive was to do a right deed as soon as it was seen to be right and scope offered for its performance. In morals, prompt action is homage to righteousness. A known duty and scope for its performance should never be deferred. As air, in obedience to the law of its action, rushes in to fill a vacuum, so does a just mind at once seize opportunity for doing what is clearly known to be right. If men linger and hesitate to do specific acts discerned to be just, it is clear evidence that they are defective in righteousness of principle. Their inner life is *pro tanto* alien to that of God. This explains, in one way at least, how it is that some men do not at once turn from positive sins and surrender themselves to Christ. They see what is the right thing to do, but defer it till some great scheme of their life is completed.

IV. FAITHFULNESS IN THAT WHICH IS LEAST GIVES MORAL POWER FOR OTHER ACTS. Having discharged this more private domestic duty, and so satisfied his conscience in reference to an obvious obligation in which a sufferer was concerned, David was a stronger man for carrying through whatever might be useful for realizing the great purposes of Providence. A good conscience is a moral tonic. The impression produced on Abner and others by this regard for what is right in the more private sphere of life, could not but be favourable to the public interests of the king. Evil men are awed by pronounced goodness, and the halting are won to allegiance. History presents many instances of influence augmented by conscientious attention to duties in private and domestic life. The habit formed by such carefulness to do the right thing in minor matters gives momentum to the action of the will when it is called to act in reference to great questions in the face of strong opposition. Many men become morally enervated by careless inattention to obligations of a private nature, yet lying close at hand and clear as daylight. Their influence on great public questions is weakened by their consciousness of neglect, and by the disgust with which men regard public separated from private righteousness.

Policy without principle. The Bible narratives do not enter into details concerning the inner motives of those whose actions are recorded; they rather state outward facts, and leave them to produce their natural impressions. The strange and apparently irreconcilable procedures of Abner are no doubt resolvable into some one governing feeling which, with unvarying consistency though in varying form, shaped his entire public actions. The whole facts from first to last reveal the operation at the base of his conduct of one master-passion—the love of pre-eminence; and it is in the working out of this powerful feeling that we find a remarkable illustration of a policy in life apart from principle.

I. A LOVE OF PRE-EMINENCE IS OFTEN A CLUE TO MUCH IN LIFE THAT IS OTHER-

WISE UNACCOUNTABLE. It certainly does seem strange that a man of Abner's abilities, brought up in full knowledge of the special relation of David to Samuel and Jonathan, and therefore fully aware of the reason why, after the exile from Palestine, David should assume royal state at Hebron and claim dominion also over the entire house of Israel, should give up his services in favour of David's rival. In the light of mere custom and regal order it would seem to be patriotic and manly on his part to identify his life with the interests of a son of the reigning house, and probably he flattered himself that ordinary men would put this interpretation on his conduct. But the best solution of all the facts of his life is to be found in the hypothesis of his passionate love of pre-eminence. With so strong a man as Joab on David's side, and the reputed zeal of the other sons of Zeruiah, there was little chance of his rising to the position of power which alone would satisfy his ambition. Although his ordinary sense must have assured him, to say nothing of the latent truth recognized by the conscience (vers. 9, 10), that Ishbosheth could never successfully compete with so brave and active a rival as David, yet, on the principle that it is "better to reign in hell than to serve in heaven," he found it more congenial to throw in his lot with a man over whom he could exercise chief influence and in whose cause he would be the principal figure. This policy void of principle ran through, as we shall soon see, the actions of his entire course. There lies, also, at the spring of every man's conduct, be he a public character or only a private individual, some master-passion to which all other feelings and aims are subordinate, and it is good for each one, and necessary to the true interpreter of life, to find out what it is. In public affairs there can be no question that in very many instances it is not fear of God, not pure patriotism, not regard for human interests as such, but open or disguised love of pre-eminence which furnishes the main incentive to conduct. The form of conduct may be such as would result from the action of higher and better feelings, but that is simply the result of policy. This feeling, which finds its scope in the rivalry and struggle of individuals, is but the social form of the generic feeling known as selfishness, or, as modern theologians term it, selfism, which in its essence is sin and probably the metaphysical explanation of sin itself, and which, moreover, is the solution of the fact that men do not recognize the eternal King, but prefer to belong to an inferior order of things. To please self, men will even consent to lose moral rank, and become foes rather than friends of the Righteous One.

II. MORAL HUMILIATIONS MAY MODIFY THE FORM OF POLICY, BUT THEY WILL NOT DESTROY THE MASTER-PASSION. To an aspiring man, as was Abner, it was intensely mortifying to be charged with wrong-doing by one nominally his superior, and the moral sting of the charge probably lay in its truth. This was, on the part of Ishbosheth, a virtual assumption of both moral and legal superiority; and, as such, was a blow at that secret, unexpressed sense of superiority which Abner had all along felt in relation to the weak young man whose cause he had patronizingly advocated. In even bad men the moral sense is strong, if not in leading to right courses, yet in making them wretched for wrong-doing. Inwardly and morally Abner was now weak in the presence of his royal master. The soul that is humiliated does not like to be reminded of its humiliation, and, if possible, the occasions of such reminders must be avoided and punished. The change wrought in Abner lay in the deep region of unexpressed and inexpressible feelings. The old love of pre-eminence was untouched by the collision with Ishbosheth. The masterful springs of human life are not easily dried up or supplanted. The immediate effect was simply to raise up a minor yet strong personal feeling, which came as a dam between the old love of pre-eminence and the interests of Ishbosheth, and caused it to flow with widened channel in another direction. Emotions stimulate thinkings, and personal feelings arouse ingenuity. Swift as lightning Abner saw that he could be a yet more important personage than ever, and, at the same time, qualify his moral humiliation by the sweets of revenge. In spite of Joab and the other son of Zeruiah, he would figure as the means of placing the crown of a united people on David's head. It should be seen that what war could not do Abner had the power to do. The names of David, Israel, and Abner would henceforth be indissolubly associated in the annals of the time. Instead of pre-eminence at the court of Ishbosheth, there would be pre-eminence at the court of David, and in the judgment of a compact nation. There have been other instances of statesmen, under the influence of resentment, changing their course, and apparently, but not in reality, their principles.

The policy in all such cases has been to subordinate public interests to certain cherished feelings. A form of sound principles may be adopted for the very same reason as previously it was rejected. Evil men are prone to do the same in ecclesiastical affairs. In private life men have been known even to assume a form of godliness—to quote the Divine truth (vers. 9, 10)—as a means of better subserving their purpose. It were well if rebuke of sin (vers. 7, 8) always produced the godly sorrow that leads to genuine repentance, and then the adoption of the true principles of the kingdom would be, not as a policy, but as a matter of conviction. The case of Saul of Tarsus in relation to the spiritual kingdom stands out in sharp contrast to that of Abner in relation to the temporal kingdom (cf. Acts ix. 5—20).

III. DURING THE WORKING OUT OF THE MASTER-PASSION THE TRUTH OF GOD ABIDES AS A PERMANENT WITNESS. That Abner should have so explicitly referred to the Divine purpose (ver. 9) cannot be ascribed to information recently received, but must be accounted for on the ground that he had all along had the truth suppressed in his own mind. He here unwittingly unveils his own conscience and condemns his past course as a violation of solemn obligations rising far above social considerations and personal preferences. To the people he, perhaps, seemed to be a man upheld by a sense of right, but to himself he was known as a rebel against God. The Divine truth asserted inwardly its own reality. Its light revealed to himself, whenever he calmly reflected on his conduct, the dark and damaging characters of his public career. And though he was now adopting right principles, and so would in future escape the pain of knowing that his actions were not running counter to their direction, yet, being conscious of adopting them for unprincipled reasons, he could not avoid the conviction that he was doing the right thing for David, not because of a love of God, but for personal ends. The sense of right would thus reveal to him the essential crookedness of ways that were ostensibly straight. The man who does right things from bad motives never knows the blessedness of the just. Probably there is no determinate course of wrong-doing in which the light of truth does not bear some witness more or less distinct. Even those who, following lower passions, change the glory of the incorruptible God into images after their own likeness (Rom. i. 23), at times find within a protest against their conduct (Rom. ii. 15). No man who has heard the claims of Christ to universal dominion as clearly and authoritatively set forth as ever Abner had heard of the Divine right of David, can live opposed to him, or, as a mere matter of policy, fall in formally with his rights, without being sensible at times of a voice which tells him of his dangerous position and worthless character. Many a converted man has borne testimony that, for years previous to his conversion, the truth of God bore faithful witness as to what was the will of God concerning him in his relation to the Anointed One.

IV. THE WORKING OUT OF A POLICY CHANGED IN OUTWARD FORM BUT NOT IN NATURE NECESSITATES AND ENSURES MUCH ZEAL AND INGENUITY. The change of allegiance was, for Abner, a momentous step. For onlookers it meant on his part a judgment, and self-respect demanded that that judgment should be justified by every possible means. His policy being the same along an altered course, he must so act as to make it appear that he had come into the possession of new and true principles, and so get the credit of acting on principle and not on policy void of principle. Of course, a man who sincerely came to the belief that God had purposed David to be king, and loved the doing of the will of God, would at once go and offer his services to David. Abner did this. Of course, he would be eager to fulfil all conditions that might be specified by David in bringing to pass the will of God (vers. 13—16). This was true of Abner. And as to gaining over others to his new view of things, no pains would be spared to show the reasonableness of the course now to be taken. Abner made out a case before the elders of Israel and the more sturdy Benjamites, and was able to report to David complete success (vers. 17—21). What zeal and ingenuity were implied in all this may be imagined by those only who know how hard it is to justify sudden changes of conduct and get one's followers to entertain new ideas. But Abner's love of pre-eminence in national affairs must perish if these efforts were not forthcoming. The same will apply to any one who changes sides in public affairs, and at the same time desires to attain to the distinction formerly obtained or secretly longed for. In fact, fully to gratify the cravings of selfish ambition means toil upon toil.

However gratifying the completion of one's aims may seem, it is a vain and miserable issue when regarded in the clear light of pure principle. In the real moral world—the sphere in which God alone awards the prizes of life—he is not crowned who does not "strive lawfully" (2 Tim. ii. 5), that is, is not observant of all the great and holy principles on which alone God would have men act. It is certain, therefore, that men of the Abner stamp, who are doing the right things, not because they are right and of God, but for personal ends, will one day find that their efforts will, while being used up by God in furtherance of the dominion of Zion's King, bring to themselves none of the glory and honour which alone fall to those who persist in "well-doing" (Rom. ii. 6, 7).

GENERAL LESSONS. 1. It becomes us now and then to search into the mainsprings of life, to ascertain what really are the principles or feelings which dominate our conduct. 2. We may rest assured, in our appeals to men on behalf of Christ, that there is in their conscience, confronting their actual life of rebellion, a witness for him the Divine authority of which they must secretly recognize. 3. Any change from an externally wrong to an externally right course is to be tested by its being or not being the outcome of pure love of what is pleasing to God. 4. There is a day coming when the actions which seem to lie in the direction of the kingdom of Christ, and, in fact, as right actions, are due to him, will be unveiled so as to be seen in their relation to the actual feelings in which they originated, and then those, who during a part of their life were regarded as good workers, will be known as "workers of iniquity" (Matt. vii. 21—23). 5. In the lives of some men one portion is spent in endeavouring to undo the deeds of former misspent days, and not always with clean hands in the sight of God. 6. The secret of every life is to be found in the heart, and hence the need constantly of the prayer that God would create within us a clean heart. 7. It is a right thing for men of influence, when the force of truth is openly admitted by themselves, to do what lies within their power to bring others over to its practical recognition. 8. The great mass of the people are very much influenced in the course they take in public affairs by the reasonings of able leaders; hence the responsibilities of leaderships in the government of God.

Policy with principle. A careful examination of facts will show that David's conduct in this narrative, and indeed all through his early career, was the very reverse of Abner's. His entire course, from the day of his call from the sheepfold to the proffered allegiance of Abner, was one of simple honest desire to do the will of God. Again and again had he resisted temptations to grasp at power; and his conduct in the interview with Abner, and use of his services, proceeded from the same principle, that, in its very nature, excluded selfish motive.

I. ACTION GOVERNED BY DIVINE PURPOSE IS THE NORMAL COURSE FOR A RATIONAL CREATURE. In inanimate and irrational things the Divine purpose is so stamped upon their being or wrought into the texture of their nature that as a matter of course they, in their movements, follow in the line appointed. Their action is necessarily normal. In creatures endowed with a rational will there comes in the prerogative of option. The possibility of an abnormal course belongs to such beings as an essential element of their constitution. The angels that have kept their first estate, and fallen angels and man, illustrate the two sides of the case. In the affairs of ancient Israel the revealed purpose of God was that David should be king (ver. 9). This was the will of the Eternal, by which every man, from Samuel and Saul in the highest ranks to the lowliest descendant of Jacob, was to be guided in his political life. How Samuel and Jonathan conformed to this law is beautifully seen in their respective careers. How David was governed by it is to be seen in the strong faith in his own destiny which ran through his patient endurance of exile; in his firm but restrained opposition to Ishbosheth; and also in his negotiations with Abner. It is this conscious conformity of action with the Divine purpose in relation to public affairs that raises the strong assertions of integrity in the Psalms above the suspicion of being the outgoings of a self-righteous spirit that claims perfect internal holiness in the sight of God. As a rule, our private conduct is normal in so far only as it is the carrying out in action of the definite purpose of God that we should govern self for him. Hence sin is properly said to be a fall (Hos. xiv. 1). Hence our Saviour's was the only true life. He was man as man should be. It was his meat and drink to do his Father's will. The goal of redemption is to raise us to the full stature of men in Christ Jesus. This view of human life, inwrought as a principle into all the operations of heart and mind, will do much to bring about the final harmony of our own lives, and indeed of all things, for discords will cease in proportion as rational created wills move in unison with the Divine.

II. The principle on which life should be conducted being clearly recognized, it serves as a light to the choice and rejection of means by which the attainment of the end may be secured. Between David's revealed predestination to be king over the chosen race, and the realization of the Divine will in the actual facts of history, many acts on his part had to be performed. It would be perplexing to an ordinary mind to prestate the agencies and methods by which the shepherd-boy and exile should at last peacefully ascend the throne and reign over a united people. Had human passion, or bare calculation, or mere politic balancing of advantages been taken as guide and governor of action, there would doubtless have been, in his case, a reproduction of the tragic struggles so often recorded in the history of public affairs. But conformity of self to the holy will of God being the root-principle of life, conjoined with the never-absent conviction that Providence was sure to be on his side in seeking to conform self to the revealed will, this illumined his pathway even amidst the darkest of earth's shadows, and enabled him to see what courses should be avoided and what pursued. Clearly he must not give scope to mere lust of power; for where the need and what the use of that when the Holy One had sworn that he should reign? Clearly, also, he must not use force and conquer the people over whom as king he is to rule; for had not God chosen him to be king over a chosen race, for the realization of high spiritual issues stretching far into a glorious future? Equally plain was it that there is no need to have recourse to the cunning and craft and falsehoods—the policy void of moral principle—which a godless spirit might suggest; for was he not the chosen servant of the Holy One of Israel, who has no need of low-born policies to establish his dominion over men? Hence David's patience in exile, his tender regard for Saul even when others suggested revenge, his merely defensive action at Hebron, and his manifest unwillingness to force Ishbosheth from the throne and to compel Israel to submit to himself. He had faith in God and in God's supremacy over the hearts and destinies of men. In so far as he had a policy it was suggested by his fundamental principle, and embraced three things: (1) Use of peaceful means. (2) Waiting on Providence for some free movement on the part of Israel. (3) A regard for the susceptibilities of the house of Saul and the natural interest of the people in that house. Hence: (1) His abstention from hostilities during Saul's lifetime, and his subsequent non-aggressive action against Ishbosheth, as also his willingness to accept the services of Abner with the elders of the people. (2) His acceptance of the allegiance of Abner, viewing it as simply a fact brought about apart from any bribe or effort on his part, and being in its outward form, with which he was alone concerned, conformable to the revealed purpose (ver. 9), and consistent with his belief in an overruling Providence which reaches to the spirits of men. (3) His laying down the condition (vers. 13—16) on which he would accept the services of Abner; for while personal affection and conjugal duty alike suggested the restoration of Michal from her enforced banishment (1 Sam. xxv. 44), such a course would prove to Ishbosheth and Israel that he still cherished his old regard for the house of Saul, and thus tend to win all parties over to a peaceful settlement. Here, then, was a sound and wise policy grounded on, and in fact issuing out of, the abiding recognition of the main principle that God had a will concerning his life, to effect which was at once his glory and delight. The facts suggest their own application and lessons. They find their highest and truest counterpart in the life of the Son of David, whose advance to universal supremacy proceeds from the declared will of God (Ps. lxxii.), and is secured in patience, by means in nature pure and peaceful, by an unseen action on the spirits of men making them willing, and by a kind and considerate regard for the varied susceptibilities of human nature. They also furnish illustrations of how the Church may combine policy and principle, displaying the wisdom of the serpent with the harmlessness of the dove. We furthermore learn that, in pursuing our individual course through the world, we may, by keeping the main principle of having a holy Divine purpose to work out clearly before the mind, ever have at hand a pure, bright light by which we shall see what means and methods in detail may be safely and honourably used for seeking the end we have in view.

III. A POLICY THUS FOUNDED ON PRINCIPLE IS SURE IN THE COURSE OF TIME TO ISSUE IN THE TRIUMPH OF LIFE. There is evidence in David's early career that he had to endure the blame of eager and less conscientious men for being so very scrupulous in the use of means. The sons of Zeruiah were, also, not satisfied with what they would call his timorous policy (vers. 24, 25, 39). Those years spent in Hebron, merely keeping in check the assaults of Ishbosheth's men (vers. 1, 22), seemed to give a doubtful meaning to the Divine promise which had become the property of both David and the true sections of the nation (vers. 9, 10, 17, 18). But the man of God held on, and would not swerve from the policy founded on clear principle. Events proved that he was right and the over-eager men wrong. In due course, Providence so governed the action of leading forces, that the entire people were brought (vers. 17—21) under influences which at last issued in his realizing the end on which his heart had been so long set. In fact, he allowed God to work where man cannot work, i.e. on the spirits of men beyond the reach of our own hand and voice. Once more we see it illustrated that God's time and methods are best. The same peaceful issue is coming on as the result of "the patience of the saints," and their undying faith in the action of the Spirit of God on the spirits of men. It is when professing Christians lose their faith in God, and have recourse to questionable devices, that, in seeking to hasten on, they really retard the progress of that which they have at heart. Taking a wide view of the government of God in the unfolding of the moral order, we see the same attainment of remote ends by means of righteous and quiet acting through long epochs. What is thus true on a large scale will be found true also of the individual life—the effort to realize the holy will of God in our personal experience. In public and private affairs, in working out our lines of policy founded on principle, we should not forget to leave a very broad margin for the action of God beyond anything we can do or attempt. This has ever been the case with the best men. There are springs which God's hand alone can touch. He can govern the free actions of leaders of men, so that the actual course they freely take, though not most pure in motive, shall, in its form, harmonize with the main purpose of the Eternal. Would that man had more faith in God as the *living* God!

GENERAL LESSONS. 1. The sincere satisfaction of those who, like David, restrain feeling and bad impulse, and wait for God to open the way and change the course of events. 2. The important contribution to the realizing of the purposes of Christ the Anointed One sometimes made by men whose acts are not pervaded by his Spirit. As Abner's acts accelerated God's purposes, so the gains of commerce, of science and art, though not always made in the name of God, become means of advancing his kingdom. 3. The survival of sacred feelings amidst and in spite of the turmoil and commotions of life. The old love for Michal was still alive, as many an old affection cherished in early days reappears and asserts itself when occasion offers. 4. The deep wounds and secret sorrows induced by harsh and arbitrary acts. As the cruel deed of Saul (1 Sam. xxv. 44) left its traces in the lives of David, Michal, and Phaltiel (ver. 15), so it is with other deeds of the same spirit but different in form. 5. The apparent subordination of great public interests to private is, in the case of men of principle, only on the surface; the reverse is really the truth. David's promotion of the unification of the nation, on condition of getting back his wife (ver. 13), was, as seen above, in the real interests of the unification under himself; and so when the acts of really good men are traced down to their principles, they only, in outward form, appear to be too personal. 6. The great extent to which the mass of men are biased even against what is plain truth (vers. 9, 17, 18) by prejudice, and are swayed by able leadership. 7. The completeness with which, in the course of providence, influence slowly gathered and widely exercised against the cause of God, may be suddenly turned to work round in promotion of it (cf. Saul of Tarsus and Abner, vers. 17—21).

Vers. 22—27.—The facts are: 1. Joab, returning from an expedition, finds David at Hebron after Abner's departure. 2. Hearing from the people a general statement of what had transpired between the king and Abner, Joab reproaches David for his peaceful conduct, and insinuates that Abner was simply playing the spy. 3. Sending a messenger, unknown to David, after Abner, he induces him to return to Hebron, and, under pretence of a quiet conference, he leads him aside and assassinates him. 4. Hearing of the affair, David at once repudiates it, and in strong terms desires that heavy judgments may fall on the head of Joab and his house. 5. David orders a general mourning for Abner, attends his funeral, and utters a pathetic lamentation over him. 6. The king's sorrow assumes a solemn and impressive form throughout the day, so as to convince the people of his utter abhorrence of the crime and his sense of the national loss. 7. David causes his servants to know that he cherished a regard for the great abilities and possible services to Israel of Abner, and was pained and enfeebled in his action as anointed king by the perverse conduct of the sons of Zeruiah.

Defective sympathy. The first impression, on reading the account of the conduct of Joab, is that of the most villainous treachery, and one at once enters into the anger and vexation of David. But the treacherous act professedly in the service of David was the outcome of a permanent condition of mind. Ostensibly it is to be ascribed to the resentment cherished on account of the death of Asahel; but the action of a man occupying a responsible position in a great undertaking is not governed merely by the presence of a feeling of this kind. The resentment would have had no positive power to issue in this deed had not the mind of Joab been out of harmony with the mind of David in the views taken of the kingdom, its principles, and methods of consolidation. A public servant will govern his private passions if his mind is in full sympathy with his master's, so as to see that the indulgence of them would be uncongenial to him and injurious to his interests. Joab was deficient in sympathy with the higher qualities and aims of his great master, and consequently the bad qualities found an outlet which otherwise would have either had no existence or would have been suppressed for his sake.

I. The employment of men of defective sympathies is, in the present state of the world, unavoidable. That Joab was not in full sympathy with David's pure and lofty aspirations is seen both in this account and also in the pressure previously put upon David in exile by his chief men to take away the life of Saul, as, again, in the subsequent allusions to his conduct (ch. xix. 7). That such a man should have been at the head of military affairs in David's service is not surprising, for David had from the first to take such men as were disposed to follow his fortunes, and when he set up regal authority in Hebron it was in the nature of things for the man of greatest will-power to push his way to the front. Kings cannot make their ministers; they can only use what the age produces. It was not David's fault; it was the natural condition of things, arising from myriads of concurrent causes, that there was not one man since the death of Samuel and Jonathan that was so spiritual and far-seeing as to enter with full enthusiastic sympathy into his conceptions of the kingdom of God and the holy principles on which it should be established and governed. The evil of having to work out great and glorious issues in conjunction with men who do not enter into the inner spirit of the enterprise is remarkably illustrated in the case of our Saviour. There was not one who could enter into the full depth and breadth of his work in the world. Relatively his blundering disciples, often paining his heart by their worldly notions, were as far removed from him as was Joab, with his crude ideas and low feelings, from David. Nor could it be otherwise unless men were supernaturally transformed. The same holds good now in the instruments Christ has to use in carrying on his work in the world. How defective many labourers and followers are in sympathy with his holy aspirations and methods! Indeed, it is the same in every secular employment. Seldom, if ever, does the servant enter fully into the mind of the master. Ideas and feelings cherished by the directing and originating mind are, of necessity, inadequately appreciated by instrumentalities not perfectly charged with them. The servant, in this sense, is not equal to his lord.

II. The existence of this defective sympathy between servant and master is the occasion of various evils. Because Joab did not really understand the pure and generous spirit of David, his very zeal for him assumed forms not only opposed to the king's wishes, but fraught with evil tendencies for the kingdom. It is obvious from ver. 24 that Joab misapprehended the peaceful, generous policy of David, and ver. 25 reveals the fact that he was in his heart actually opposed to the course which had been taken; for he actually dares to rebuke him for not perceiving the cunning spy in the man of peace. So far was he out of sympathy with the principles and policy of the king, that he stealthily, and with the aid of his brother (ver. 30), even allowed the personal resentment of his heart to issue in an act which was not only unjust and base in itself, but also in direct opposition to the will and measures of David. Here we have, as the outcome of his worldly spirit, displeasure with his king, assumption of superior wisdom, indulgence in personal revenge, murder, and practically assertion, for the time being and in a particular instance, of supreme power. Not one of these evils would have come to the surface of life, but would have been crushed in their most incipient stage, had his nature been more in sympathy with that of his master. Inasmuch as by full sympathy we alone can really understand, appreciate, fall in with, delight in, and surrender every faculty and subdue every errant feeling to the prompt carrying out of our Lord's designs, so, conversely, a lack of sympathy cannot but result in the evils of misapprehension of designs, non-appreciation of motives and methods, discontent with actual deeds, withholding of services, and free scope to passions, in nature and consequences at variance with his superior will. The lives of the apostles during our Saviour's ministry on earth abundantly illustrate this. Bred in an atmosphere of formalism and religious exclusiveness, they entered not into the perfect mind of Christ, and consequently wondered at his methods (Luke ix. 44, 45), desired what was contrary to his Spirit (vers. 46—56), and, in the case of Peter, actually rebuked him for arranging to establish his kingdom by a method which seemed to them to be unnecessary and unbecoming (Matt. xvi. 21—23). The persecutions authorized by the Church in dark ages, the methods introduced by Ignatius Loyola and subsequently adopted by his followers, the bitter spirit cherished towards men differing in minor matters of faith or practice, and the sundry base deeds which grow out of a professedly Christian life because it is not well nourished in fellowship with Christ himself,—these are some of the evils appearing in the course of the establishment of the kingdom of heaven as a consequence of the servants of the Lord not being in full harmony of spirit with him they profess to serve.

III. This DEFECTIVE SYMPATHY, IF NOT GRADUALLY REMEDIED, MAY INVOLVE ACTIONS PERMANENTLY DAMAGING TO THE MOST POWERFUL OF MEN. It is probable that Joab was with David in exile, and, like many others, he may have been drawn over to his side partly because of the intimation given by Samuel and recognized by Jonathan of the Divine choice of David, and partly because of disgust at the misgovernment of Saul. However much he might have failed in the first instance to comprehend and appreciate the holy aims and principles of his leader, he could not have shared so long in David's fortunes and misfortunes without having many opportunities of learning what manner of person he was, and how decidedly spiritual were his aims and purposes. He appears not to have profited by these privileges, and consequently, by the action of a well-known psychological law, the original secularity of his nature gained in power, so that when a contest arose between a private passion and acquiescence in his master's arrangements, there was not sufficient moral force to restrain and destroy the passion, and hence the dark deed which disgraced his name and caused him to be in the future a man distrusted and abhorred (ver. 39). The reverse is seen in the case of the apostles, excepting Judas, who all grew out of their imperfect sympathy with the innermost heart of Christ, and brought forth fruit accordingly. In private life there can be no question but that, when opportunities for getting nearer and nearer to the mind of Christ are neglected, the lower tendencies of human nature gain force, and when temptation to exercise them arises, sad deeds are done and reputations are damaged. Probably, if all things were explained, it would come out that many of the sad crimes perpetrated by persons professedly in the kingdom and service of Christ are connected with failure to maintain and deepen the sympathy of the heart with all that is in Christ and his work. "Without me ye can do nothing;" "Abide in me."

GENERAL LESSONS. 1. The incidental evils arising from imperfect sympathy with the holy and far-reaching purposes of God may be found in course of the historic revelation which God has given us, and should be ascribed to their proper human source, and allowed for in our estimate of the form, matter, and incidents of the revelation. 2. A critical estimate of the degree of the triumphs of early Christianity should be formed on a consideration of the degree, more or less, to which the leading and subordinate servants of Christ understood and entered into his spirit. 3. In a selection of men for any form of Christian work, great stress should be laid on their quick and eager perception of the purely spiritual aspects of his kingdom. Intellectual and other qualities are very subordinate to this. 4. It becomes us to be on our guard lest mere private feelings of the lower order should gain ascendency over the more general considerations that pertain to the kingdom of God. 5. It will be useful if we now and then calmly reflect on the degree to which the cause of God may have suffered through our own defective sympathy with its more spiritual interests. 6. The great need of each one is to cultivate close fellowship with Christ, so as more fully to enter into his mind.

The incidence of guilt. When a great crime has been committed, the first question in the public mind is—Who is guilty? In national affairs, where personal actions are supposed to be connected with public interests, it is not always clear at first whether one or another party is to be charged with blame for what has been done. It was impossible, even judged by the low standard that too often governed the conduct and opinions of Eastern people, but that the death of Abner would be regarded with consternation, and men would be swift in their judgment. It was, therefore, only natural that David should take steps to let it be known that, although Joab was a public servant, the guilt in this case must rest on the individual himself, and not in any sense on the government under which he served.

I. IN EVERY CASE, AS TO THE ACTUAL INCIDENCE OF GUILT, THERE IS NO UNCERTAINTY IN THE MINDS OF THE PARTIES CONCERNED. To men of low moral type in Judah, who may have suspected Abner's zeal and who were disposed to judge of David as they would of themselves, it might be an open question as to whether he did not really connive at the treachery of Joab. To men in Israel, who were mindful of Abner's former antagonism to David and who were themselves of implacable temper, it might be conceivable that David was an inactive partner in the crime. In the absence of any superior court of inquiry, or of any statement from David, disquieting rumours may have gained temporary currency. Meanwhile the real fact would stand clear before the conscience of both Joab and the king. Popular discussion never avails to alter the facts of conscience. Joab knew himself to be solely guilty, with consent of his brother (ver. 30); David knew himself to be entirely innocent. Each carried within himself the judgment of God. It is here that we see the dividing line between the opinions and discussions of the world and the invisible moral sphere, where actual facts are registered in clear and ineffaceable lines so as to admit of no shadow of doubt. What though outsiders cannot ascertain reality, it is there, and it is only a question of time as to its being seen by others besides those now familiar with it. The secrecy of the guilty is only a play with an advantage for a short time. Men charged with public crimes, and men who live in sin against God, know that there is no mistake in the incidence of guilt. They possess exclusive knowledge, perhaps, but there is no consolation in that. Likewise those wrongly charged with complicity in evil are possessors of a secret knowledge which enables them to see that the permanent moral order is on their side, and that it is only a question of time, more or less, when their "righteousness shall be brought forth as the light," and their "judgment as the noonday."

II. A SACRED CAUSE IS NOT RESPONSIBLE FOR THE DEEDS OF ITS PROFESSED SUPPORTERS. A hasty judgment would conclude that, as Joab was a prominent supporter of the Davidic cause, it must bear the shame and guilt of his murderous deed; but the only warrant for that being a true view of the case would be that the general spirit of David's administration favoured treachery, and that the master and servant were in secret collusion,—neither of which suppositions can be for a moment entertained. Kings and their officers, masters and their servants, are to be held jointly responsible only when the service generates the wrong. As a fact, governments and employers do suffer temporary loss of prestige when those in positions of trust act out their own individual wickedness; but in due course men will distinguish the manifestation of the individual baseness from the public interests with which it was associated. The separation of these is important in many relationships of life. The divinely appointed kingdom and just rule of David must not be confounded with Joab's malice. The government of a country should not bear the guilt of men whose position enables them to violate moral laws with impunity. Private vice is not one with public crime. The evil deeds and imperfect character of men whose names are in the records of revelation must not be charged on the revelation of God or his method of educating the world for something better. The foul deeds done during the dark days of the Church's life by some of the leaders of Christianity are not to be ascribed to the holy cause with which they were identified. The personal vices of professors of religion do not really compromise Christ. In all these cases it is the Joab-spirit, and not the spirit of the king, which expresses itself, and it is condemned by the very cause in the interests of which it may at first seem to be manifested. Christ's kingdom is one of unchangeable righteousness and love, in spite of all the injustice and hate of men bearing the blessed Name.

III. WHEN OCCASION OFFERS, DEEDS ALIEN TO THE SPIRIT OF A GOOD CAUSE SHOULD BE DISTINCTLY REPUDIATED. As a matter of duty and policy, David felt bound to take an early opportunity of repudiating any association, either in spirit or action, with the crime of Joab. It was due to himself as an individual and as prospective king of a united Israel, and to that better system of government which on the death of Saul he was called to inaugurate. Suspicions cannot be prevented, the odium of connection with a wrong-doer cannot but arise, malicious foes will be sure to turn every possible event to his detriment; but as soon as the ear of the nation can be reached self-vindication becomes imperative. It is a question of opportunity. Sometimes good men may have to pass years "under a cloud," and even go down to the grave trusting only to the vindication of the just in the day of judgment. David escaped that sorrow. His declaration, his daring to denounce so powerful a man, the severity of his curse on the evil-doer, the evident sincerity of his sorrow for Abner, and the suspension of public duties for an elaborate funeral ceremonial,—all made known as distinctly as possible how alien was the spirit of his life and government from the cruel treachery of Joab. The same course is open to us when individually our fair fame may be compromised by others. Modern governments often have to disown deeds of their officials. Our Lord himself has laid down principles in the New Testament by which he may in all ages have wherewith to repudiate the evil deeds and spirit of some of his professed friends; and in course of history, when danger arises of confounding his holy kingdom with vile actions, his providence brings out the true spirit inculcated in sharp contrast with the evil. As occasion offers, we in our age should be careful to let men see that he is not responsible for the abuses which have sprung out of the imperfections of some of his servants. Never did the world more need to see clearly Christ and his kingdom as they are in contrast with much that is done and maintained in his Name.

IV. TIME FAVOURS THE RIGHT ASSIGNMENT OF GUILT. If any were disposed to doubt the sincerity of David's disclaimer—and there are such suspicious, unfriendly men in every age—he could afford to wait. The true interpreter of our actions in the past is to be found in the tenor of our life. The years to come would reveal the true David and the true Joab. The pure feeling that prompted this quick repudiation would reappear in a life of kindliness and generosity and justice, and every good deed and generous sentiment would only make more clear his freedom from complicity in this crime; and, on the other hand, the hard, stern, vindictive feeling which continued to hold and fashion the life of Joab would only render more clear and emphatic the judgment against him. So of much past Church history; time will only tend to bring out more distinctly the separation between Christianity, as it is in Christ and his teaching, and those actions and feelings which too often were identified with his service. Individual deserts also will become manifest, however obscure the facts may be to present observers. The future is against the wicked and on the side of the just. Evil men may well dread the coming of the day when the hidden things of darkness shall be made manifest, when the exact incidence of guilt will be seen; good men, those who have made their peace with God and have received the Spirit of the kingdom, may lift up their heads in confidence in prospect of that same great day.

GENERAL LESSONS. 1. It adds to the guilt of a man when, knowing that he is solely responsible for certain deeds, he allows others with whom he has been associated to fall under suspicion. Joab ought to have voluntarily cleared David. 2. Good men unavoidably under suspicion may find consolation in that some of the best—Joseph, David, and even *the best*, Christ (Luke xxiii. 2 ; John xix. 12)—were suspected of wrong. 3. Although the "peace of God" is the heritage of the just as a personal boon, yet it is due to the cause dear to their hearts to seek self-vindication, as in the case of David and Paul, and this will be the chief motive for a disclaimer. 4. It behoves Christian people especially to exercise a very calm and sober judgment when any one known as a servant of Christ is accused of or imagined to be in complicity with evil transactions. 5. The general character of a man under suspicion ought to give great weight to any disclaimer he may make, and be to us a set-off against all *primâ facie* evidence.

Deferred punishment. It is natural to ask—If Joab's crime was so base, and David's repudiation of complicity with it so emphatic, why was he not punished as an offender against morality and the principles of the new administration? The answer is nigh at hand. David was averse to signalize the establishment of his supremacy over all the tribes of Israel by the shedding of blood, and a less punishment than death in those times would have been misinterpreted to his injury. His cause at that juncture was in a critical position, and to have cleared off so competent and influential a man would have been perilous. Moreover, the execution of Joab would have tallied best with complicity in his guilt; the sparing of his life and abiding the issue of events was most favourable to the establishment of his own innocence. But most of all he was desirous of leaving the judgment in the hands of God, having in most scathing language stated his own sense of the evil desert of the man (ver. 29). Herein we may trace analogies.

I. THE PRESENT STAGE OF THE GOVERNMENT OF GOD DOES NOT PROVIDE FOR THE IMMEDIATE PUNISHMENT OF ALL SIN. Many a modern Joab does not at once suffer for his sin as conscience and public opinion would demand. There are vile deeds performed, horrible. vices indulged, characters and fortunes ruined, and widespread miseries induced, by persons whose actions are not discovered, or, if discovered, are such as civil authority does not touch. The common judgment of men is that severe punishment is due to such, but it comes not in their life. The betrayer of purity, the licentious liver who hides his vices, the forger who escapes discovery, are but instances of many. They seem to escape any open and public infliction of punishment, and carry no more on their conscience than Joab did on his, which would be little, just in proportion as it was debased. The solution of this apparent anomaly is really to be found in the consideration that the government of God extends over an area wider than this present life, and that for profound reasons, not all revealed, it is not best for judgment to fall all at once and at the time of the committal or even discovery of the sin. Bishop Butler has dwelt on this aspect of the Divine government with great wisdom and sobriety of judgment. With God a thousand years are as one day. His methods of ruling men here evidently proceed on the fact that there is a future and a great day of account, when men shall receive according to the deeds done in the body.

II. ALTHOUGH PUNISHMENT IS DEFERRED, THE PERPETRATORS OF EVIL ARE UNDER THE PERSONAL DISPLEASURE OF GOD. David's mind was averse to Joab. He cherished distrust and displeasure toward him. He had scope for action, and possibly for true repentance, but in his monarch's estimation he was a base and condemned man. No easy, jaunty spirit on the part of Joab could alter this serious fact. There existed in the mind of his king the condition of feeling which was prophetic of a doom one day to be actualized. In like manner " God is angry with the wicked every day." Those who seem to escape present punishment are already condemned in the sure, infallible judgment of God. Merciful and pitiful as he is, and not willing that any should perish, he cannot but regard their secret sins with abhorrence, and see in them, unless they repent and seek newness of life and forgiveness in Christ, a debased form of humanity gradually maturing to receive into themselves the wrath treasured up against the day of wrath (Rom. ii. 4—6). The prosperous wicked seldom reflect on how the Holiest and Wisest of all looks on them. Men great and esteemed in the world are often despised by God because he knows what their true character is.

III. THE MIND OF GOD IS REVEALED TO HIS SERVANTS AS TO THE DESERT OF THE WICKED, AND SOME INTIMATION IS GIVEN OF WHAT WILL COME UPON THEM. The imprecation (ver. 29) of David the king was his way of revealing to all offended by the crime of Joab his sense of desert; and, considering how a distinguished posterity was regarded in the East as the crowning good of a long life, and how evidently ambitious Joab was to figure in history, it was not easy for the king to select terms more indicative of a terrible punishment. The utterance was not that of vindictiveness or malice, but of a mind anxious to show its sense of the desert of the evil-doer; and no doubt it intimated his belief that some such terrible issue would in the course of providence be the reward of the crime. This is analogous to what God has been pleased to do. To remove the fears and perplexities arising from the fact that sin is often long unpunished in this world, he has distinctly made known how he regards it, what terrible issues will come of it, and how just is the outcome of all crime on the perpetrator. The words of David concerning Joab's desert are mild compared with those of Christ and his apostles concerning the desert of those who deliberately reject Christ, pierce him with their sins, and trample on the blood of the everlasting covenant (Matt. xi. 20—24; Heb. x. 26—31).

IV. MEANTIME, GOD DOES MANIFEST MUCH SYMPATHY WITH THOSE WHO SUFFER FROM WRONG-DOING. David's lament over Abner as one noble in position and in some aspects of character, and yet brought to a premature end as though he were a mean, weak, and inferior person; his taking upon his own heart the anguish which he knew must afflict multitudes; his abstention from food and present comforts because of the common calamity; his revulsion of feeling from the "men too hard" for him; and his use of authority for securing for Abner the highest funeral honours; all this, so natural and beautiful in Israel's king, so soothing to the hearts of the troubled people, is strikingly suggestive of the wonderful way in which God, while denouncing sin and foretelling its punishment, manifests his sympathy with a world afflicted with the deeds of evil-doers. This is largely the meaning of our Saviour's life among men. This is one element which enters even into the great transaction on Calvary. This is the explanation of the manifold ministries of comfort and encouragement raised up by the Head of the Church for the relief of those who are bowed down, and the mitigation of many of the calamities which come in consequence of the sins of others.

V. WHILE PROVIDING THUS FOR THE DUE PUNISHMENT OF SIN AND THE MITIGATION OF THE CALAMITIES IT ENTAILS, GOD ALSO EXERCISES A RESTRAINING POWER OVER EVIL TENDENCIES. The continued presence of David, asserting his rightful authority and infusing his own generous spirit into the administration of affairs, could not but have the effect of lessening the influence of Joab and setting a limit to the range of evil he otherwise might do. The king was among his people for their good and the restraint of one who, in spirit, was their calamity. Here, again, do we not get a glimpse of what is true in the spiritual sphere? God does not leave evil men entirely unrestrained to carry out their designs and to afflict the world with their base spirit. As responsible beings, they have their freedom to act for a while, but he "restrains the wrath of man;" he is present in our human affairs, checking and controlling so that other influences less powerful in appearance shall be brought to bear and find full and free scope. It is never to be forgotten that, though there are Joabs amongst us, "hard" in spirit and cruel of purpose, and bearing on their conscience the blood of others, there is amongst us the eternal King, whose love, generous sympathy, and determination to care for the faithful never fail.

GENERAL LESSONS. 1. It is characteristic of a just man that, free from personal ill-will, he will have faith in the retribution of wrong-doing, and will even forecast and acquiesce in its form. 2. A righteous indignation will induce a denunciation of men in power in spite of any resentment that may arise. 3. The guilty conscience is so cowardly that righteous denunciation may even increase the moral power of the just over the unjust man. 4. It is important to cherish strong faith in God's methods of government if we would be calm and strong in assertion of right and awaiting a proper adjustment of rewards. 5. It will be a matter of sincere grief to a generous mind to see men of great abilities come to an ignoble end, even though in the past those abilities have not been used in the desired direction—allowance being made for the strong temptations to which such men are liable. 6. A manifestation of sympathy with the sorrows of a people, and an effort to draw out their more tender feelings, is a sure way to the exercise of a moral influence more potent than the assertion of authority. 7. A man proves his capacity for ruling others when, without sacrifice of principle, he can by generous sentiments win their good will and awaken a prevailing kindly sentiment towards himself.

HOMILIES BY VARIOUS AUTHORS.

Vers. 1—5.—(HEBRON.) " *The house of David.*" 1. The theocracy had its chief support in David and his house. On him also rested the Messianic hope (ch. vii. 13). Hence the importance which attaches to events of his life that would otherwise have been left unrecorded. 2. " The summary narrative of these seven years presents the still youthful king in a very lovable light. The same temper which had marked his first acts after Saul's death is here strikingly brought out. He seems to have left the conduct of the war altogether with Joab, as if he shrank from striking a single blow for his own advancement. When he does interfere, it is on the side of peace, to curb and chastise ferocious vengeance and dastardly assassination. The incidents recorded all go to make up a picture of rare generosity, of patient waiting for God to fulfil his purposes, of longing that the miserable strife between the tribes of God's inheritance should end " (A. Maclaren). 3. In the house of David, at war with the house of Saul, we see an embodiment of the great conflict between good and evil; a representation of " the household of faith " as opposed to the *world*, and the *spirit* as opposed to the *flesh* (Gal. v. 17). Notice—

I. ITS PROTRACTED ANTAGONISM. " And *there was long war*," etc. It: 1. Is rendered necessary by the opposite nature and aims of the contending parties. " These are contrary the one to the other." 2. Implies a state of constant warfare, and involves many a painful struggle. " What grievous tales of distress are folded up in these brief words ! " 3. Is permitted by God for wise and beneficent purposes : to test the principles of his servants; to exercise their faith and patience; to strengthen, purify, and perfect their character. 4. And must go on to the end. " This is a battle, from which, as it ends only with life, there is no escape ; and he who fights not in it is of necessity either taken captive or slain " (Scupoli).

II. ITS INCREASING STRENGTH. " David waxed stronger and stronger," in the number of his followers, the amount of his resources, the unity and vigour of their employment, the stability of his position, the extent of his influence, the assurance of his success. And all who " strive against sin " within and without also " go from strength to strength:" 1. In patiently waiting upon God and faithfully doing his will. " Wait on the Lord, be of good courage, and he shall strengthen thine heart " (Ps. xxvii. 14). 2. By the bestowment of his grace and the co-operation of his providence, directing, protecting, and prospering them, in accordance with his promises. Their strength is not self-derived, but " cometh from the Lord." " And he that is feeble among them at that day shall be as David; and *the house of David* shall be as God," etc. (Zech. xii. 8) ; " Greater is he that is in you than he that is in the world " (1 John iv. 4) ; " I have all strength in him that giveth me power " (Phil. iv. 13). 3. And thereby they show that God is with them, and that his righteous purposes concerning them will be accomplished.

III. ITS DECLINING OPPONENTS. " And the house of Saul waxed weaker and weaker," relatively and proportionately to the growth of David's, and in consequence of the protracted antagonism and increasing strength of the latter. 1. In wilful separation from God, and seeking their own selfish ends in opposition to his will (see ch. ii. 8—12). Those who fall away from God fall into self-division and self-contention (ver. 8) ; " and a house divided against itself cannot stand." 2. By the immovable might of God against whom they set themselves (Ps. ii. 4), and his wrath, which is " revealed from heaven against ' all ungodliness," etc. (Rom. i. 18). They are like a wave that dashes against a rock and is broken and scattered in foam. " The face of the Lord is against them that do evil" (1 Pet. iii. 12). 3. And thereby they prove that God *is* against them, and are taught that their purposes will assuredly fail and they themselves be overthrown. From the time of his defeat (ch. ii. 17), if not from the very first, Abner probably felt that the cause in which he had embarked was hopeless. " He recognized now most distinctly in David the rising star in Israel; and, however haughtily his words might sound, he only sought to conceal behind them his despair of Ishbosheth " (Krummacher).

IV. ITS PERILOUS RELATIONSHIPS. (Vers. 2—5.) " The increasing political strength of David was shown, as usual among Eastern monarchs, by the fresh alliances through marriage into which he now entered" (Edersheim). In addition to his three wives, Michal, Ahinoam (mother of Amnon), and Abigail (mother of Chileab, who appears to have died early), he had "Maacah the daughter of Talmai king of Geshur" (mother of Absalom and Tamar), Haggith (mother of Adonijah), Abital, and Eglah; and he afterwards still further enlarged the royal household (ch. iv. 13—16). "None of his sons here mentioned were eminent for virtue, and some of them were notorious for their sins." *Polygamy* was tolerated by the Law of Moses (1 Sam. i. 2), although the king was forbidden (Deut. xvii. 17) to "*multiply* wives to himself;" and it was practised by David in conformity with ancient and prevalent custom, from political considerations and natural inclinations, without reproof (ch. xii. 8); but (as his subsequent history shows) it fostered in him a sensual tendency, undermined his moral strength, and produced innumerable enmities and other evils in his family. "One deadly element of future woe mingled itself with the establishment of the kingdom of David— he brought into his family the curse of the harem. An utter lack of discipline was one of its first fruits; and it brought yet deeper ill even than that; for it poisoned all the springs of family life, and tainted it with ever-recurring impurity; working in him and all around him its universal fruits of impurity, jealousy, hatred, incest, and blood" ('Heroes of Heb. Hist.'). "It was the immemorial custom in all those countries for the magnificence and power of a ruler to display itself in the multiplication of his establishment, that is, of his wives; for every wife involved a separate establishment. It shows the utmost depravity when Christians seek to shelter their own unjust and shameless lives under an appeal to that of David, and that, too, although none of their other proceedings show the smallest trace of David's noble spirit, and although they are by no means ready to bear as David did the consequences of their shame" (Ewald). "If we want exemplifications of all the miseries and curses which spring from the mixture of families and the degradation of woman in the court and country where polygamy exists, David's history supplies them. No maxims of morality can be half so effectual as a faithful record of terrible effects like these" (Maurice). In view of these effects we learn that no strength or prosperity can be lasting where "the friendship of the *world*" is cherished, and "the lusts of the *flesh*" are suffered to prevail; and that victory over some opponents may be followed by defeat by other more subtle and dangerous foes.—D.

Ver. 6.—(MAHANAIM.) *The character of Abner.* Abner, son of Ner, was first cousin of Saul, probably about the same age, commander-in-chief of his army (1 Sam. xiv. 50), and contributed greatly to his early successes. He introduced David to the king after his victory over Goliath, sat at the royal table (1 Sam. xx. 25), was well acquainted with their relations to each other, took part in the persecution (1 Sam. xxvi. 14), and, after the battle of Gilboa, became the main support of the house of Saul (ch. ii. 8). "'Abner made himself strong for the house of Saul,' but God strengthened David, whom Abner knew to have been designed for the kingdom by God" (Wordsworth). Notice: 1. *His eminent abilities*—military skill, prudence, energy, courage, and perseverance; as shown by the honourable position he so long held in the service of Saul, and his successful efforts after his death (ch. ii. 8—12). "Abner's act was *not an ordinary act of rebellion against the person of David* and his rightful claim to the throne; because Jehovah had not yet caused David to be set before the nation as its king by Samuel or any other prophet, and David had not yet asserted the right to reign over all Israel, which had been secured to him by the Lord, and guaranteed by his anointing as one whom the nation was bound to recognize" (Keil). Nor was he destitute of generous sentiments. If he could not be called a *good* man, he was "a prince and a *great* man" (ver. 38). 2. *His worldly ambition* and carnal selfishness. This was probably the main, if not the only, motive of his opposition to the Divine purpose; and to it Ishbosheth evidently attributed the conduct with which he charged him, regarding his act as an assertion of royal rights (ver. 7). His pride and self-esteem are also apparent in his haughty answer (ver. 8).

> "Ambition's like a circle on the water,
> Which never ceases to enlarge itself,
> Till by broad spreading it disperse to nought."

3. *His passionate resentment*, which, as is commonly the case, was an indication of the truth of the charge brought against him; nor did he deny it, but contemptuously declared that he was too great a man and had rendered too many services to be accused of such a "fault;" and then took an oath to avenge the insult by translating the kingdom to David, "as the Lord had sworn" to him (vers. 9, 10). "This was Abner's arrogancy to boast such great things of himself, as if he had carried a king in his pocket, as that great Earl of Warwick in Edward IV.'s time, is said to have done" (Trapp). "No man ever heard Abner godly till now; neither had he been so at this time if he had not intended a revengeful departure from Ishbosheth. Nothing is more odious than to make religion a stalking-horse to policy" (Hall). 4. *His altered purposes.* The change, although right and good in itself, was due to a passionate impulse and probably the desire of personal advantage; and, in its announcement, Abner betrayed his previous ungodliness and present hypocrisy. "Alas! how eloquently can hypocrites employ the Name of God, and take the sanction of religion, when by such means they think to advance their present interests!" (Lindsay). But, on the other hand, it may be said that his sudden wrath was only the occasion of his open avowal of an irrepressible and growing conviction of duty, and of his taking the decisive step which he had been long contemplating; and that he henceforth faithfully endeavoured to make amends for his former errors and sincerely sought the welfare of the nation. "When an opposer of God's Word honestly turns, we should, without reluctance, give him the hand, without undertaking to pass judgment on the motives that are hidden in his heart" (Erdmann). David, unlike Joab (ver. 25), put the best construction on Abner's conduct. 5. *His energetic action* and extensive influence. He sent messengers "immediately" (LXX.) to David, recognizing his authority, etc. (ver. 12); had communication with the elders of Israel (ver. 18); spake in the ears of Benjamin (ver. 19), who might be jealous of the transfer of sovereignty to Judah; and, having obtained their consent, came himself to Hebron with twenty men, "representatives of Israel, to confirm his overtures by their presence," partook of an entertainment "of the nature of a league," and went away in peace. "David believed that in this offer of Abner a Divine providence was to be observed which would make, as he hoped, a full end to the unhappy civil war" (Krummacher). 6. *His cruel fate.* "Now is Ishbosheth's wrong avenged by an enemy" (Hall). Even though his present course was in fulfilment of the Divine purpose, it averted not the consequences of his former conduct; and retribution came upon him suddenly, unexpectedly, and by a wicked hand. "One wicked man is made to be another's scourge." "Human sin must serve the purposes of God's kingdom" (Ps. lxxvi. 10). "David's kingdom is not promoted by Abner's treason, as David so expected, but rather by the taking away of Abner; thus the Lord, in the promotion of his kingdom, chooseth not the instruments nor alloweth even the means which appear good to men; but, by the contrary, he taketh away the same instruments and means in which men have most confidence, and by others more unlikely, and without men's expectation, he advanceth the cause of the Church and worketh great things" (Guild).—D.

Vers. 7—11.—(MAHANAIM.) *The dissensions of the wicked.* 1. The *union* of wicked men rests only upon regard for their own interests. It is not founded on mutual esteem, and does not constitute true friendship (1 Sam. xviii. 1—4).

> "The friendships of the world are oft
> Confederacies in vice, or leagues in pleasure."
>   (Addison.)

2. When their interests come into collision, their *dissensions* begin. And occasions of such collision are sure to arise. "Let us mark the inherent weakness of a bad cause. Godless men banded together for selfish ends have no firm bond of union. The very passions which they are united to gratify may begin to rage against one another. They fall into the pit which they have dug for others" (Blaikie). 3. Wicked men, engaged in a common enterprise against God, are not indifferent to their *reputation* in the sight of one another. "Am I a dog's head," etc. (ver. 8)? Their conscience, though perverted, is not dead; their self-esteem and love of approbation are fully alive; and they estimate to the full their claims upon the gratitude of others. They would even have

their crimes connived at for the sake of the benefits which they confer. 4. Nothing more surely tests and manifests the character of the wicked than being *reproved* by each other for their faults. " Proud men will not bear to be reproved, especially by those to whom they have been obliged " (M. Henry). It is otherwise with the good (Ps. cxli. 5). 5. The *strong* despise the weak, and passionately resent their complaints, however reasonable and just. 6. The *weak* suspect the strong, and, although they may feel justified in speaking, are put to silence by their fears. "And he could not answer Abner a word again, because he feared him." 7. The dissensions of the wicked are the most effectual means of their *common overthrow*, usually turn out to the advantage of the righteous, and promote the extension of the kingdom of God.—D.

Vers. 12—16.—(BAHURIM.) *A domestic episode.* Michal was the first wife of David (1 Sam. xix. 11—17). Of her he had been deprived when he fled from the court of Saul; she was given to Phaltiel (Phalti), the son of Laish, of Gallim (1 Sam. xxv. 44), by her father, perhaps as a piece of policy, to attach him to his house, and they lived together for many years, apparently in much domestic comfort. We have here—

I. AN INJURED HUSBAND DEMANDING HIS JUST RIGHT. "Well; I will make a league with thee: but one thing I require," etc. (ver. 13). The demand was: 1. Founded upon *justice;* David having been unjustly and contemptuously treated. 2. Reverential toward the *Law,* which had been flagrantly violated. It does not appear that Michal was ever legally divorced from David. 3. Incited by *affection* toward her and the memory of her early love to him. 4. Adapted to *test* the sincerity and fidelity of Abner, and prepare the way for further negotiations. 5. Consistent with his *honour.* He could not suffer his wife to live as the wife of another man without shame. 6. Calculated to *remind* the northern tribes of his former services against the Philistines (vers. 15, 18). 7. And to increase his *influence* over them by the maintenance of his family alliance with the house of Saul and the public recognition of his power. There was policy as well as principle in the condition imposed.

II. A FEEBLE RULER ENFORCING A HUMILIATING REQUIREMENT. "And David sent messengers to Ishbosheth, Saul's son," etc. (ver. 14). "Not to Abner, but to Ishbosheth (for the league between David and Abner was a profound secret), whom David knew must act feebly, as he was at Abner's dictation" ('Speaker's Commentary'), "to demand the restoration of Michal, that her return might take place in duly legal form" (Keil), and that it might be apparent that he "had not taken her by force from her husband." Nothing is said of Ishbosheth's feelings on receiving the message. Like other incapable monarchs, he never exhibited any spirit except on the point of his royal dignity; and, even on this, his wrath was extinguished before the frown of Abner. Under constraint, he sent Abner himself, and took his sister from her husband. And the effect of this concession must have been to discredit him in the eyes of the people and hasten his downfall. Henceforth it was hardly necessary that Abner should disguise his intentions (ver. 17). There is no more pitiful sight than that of a man who holds the royal office without adorning it with royal qualities.

III. A HELPLESS SUBJECT SUBMITTING TO A PAINFUL NECESSITY. (Vers. 15, 16.) The scene is a pathetic one. Michal conducted forth, attended by her husband, "weeping behind her" to Bahurim (ch. xix. 17), on the borders of Judah, where he was compelled to part from her, with the contemptuous order, "Go, return." "And he returned" in bitter disappointment, grief, and shame. Yet he had brought his trouble on himself. How fruitful in domestic misery are imprudence, ambition, and sinful expediency! It may be long delayed, but it surely comes. Men reap as they sow. "Wherefore all Phaltiel's tears move no pity of mine. *Caveat raptor,* let him beware who violently takes another man's wife, seeing shame and sorrow are the issue of such ungodly marriages" (T. Fuller). "His tears ought to have been tears of repentance for his sin against God and against David" (Wordsworth). Perchance there lay hid in the evil he now suffered the seed of future good. But here his history ends.

IV. A HAUGHTY PRINCESS RESTORED TO HER LEGITIMATE LORD. Nothing is said of their meeting. This silence is ominous; and it is to be feared that the reunion was not one of unmingled satisfaction. Time and circumstances may have changed her feelings toward David (1 Sam. xviii. 20), separated her more widely from him in spiritual sympathy, and developed in her heart her father's pride. She was now only one of many wives. At a subsequent meeting (ch. vi. 20) she was scornful, jealous, and unspiritual. And that which David anticipated with pleasure became an occasion of pain and lasting trouble.—D.

Vers. 17, 18.—*An urgent appeal: an evangelistic address.* "Now then do it" (ver. 18). Having resolved to transfer his allegiance, Abner here persuades the elders of Israel *to make David king* over the whole land; as they afterwards did (ch. v. 1—3). A similar appeal may be addressed to others, urging them to submit to the royal authority of Christ, of whom David was a type (1 Sam. ii. 10). Translated into New Testament language, it is, "We beseech you, on behalf of Christ, be ye reconciled to God" (2 Cor. v. 20). Consider—

I. WHAT YOU SHOULD DO. Jesus Christ is King, anointed and exalted to the right hand of God; he reigns in grace and righteousness in many hearts; but his kingdom is not yet fully revealed and universally extended on earth, and it cannot be set up "within you" except by your own consent. You must: 1. *Receive him heartily* as your King and Lord, your absolute Owner and supreme Ruler, as well as your Redeemer and Saviour; by a personal, inward, voluntary act; in the renunciation of whatever is opposed to his will, and the submission and surrender of your whole being to his direction and control. "Now be ye not stiff-necked, as your fathers were, but yield yourselves unto the Lord" (2 Chron. xxx. 8; Rom. vi. 13).

> "Our wills are ours, we know not how;
> Our wills are ours to make them thine."

2. *Confess him openly,* by uniting with his people, testifying your faith in him, and proclaiming his Name before men. "With the heart man believeth," etc. (Rom. x. 10; 2 Cor. viii. 5). "Whosoever therefore shall confess me," etc. (Matt. x. 32). 3. *Serve him loyally,* by obeying his commandments, assisting his friends, resisting his foes, seeking his honour and the spread of his kingdom. "It is not enough that I should love the Lord myself alone; every heart must love him, and every tongue speak forth his praise."

II. WHY YOU SHOULD DO IT. "Now then do it: *for* Jehovah hath spoken," etc. 1. It is *the purpose of God* that he should reign over you. "He must reign," either in mercy or in judgment. 2. It is the *promise of God* that through him you may be saved from your enemies—sin, Satan, death, and hell. "There is none other Name." 3. It has been *your own desire* in times past that he might be your King. "Ye sought for David both yesterday and the day before to be king over you: now then do it." Under the bitter oppression of the ruler chosen by yourselves, in view of the superior worth of "the man of God's choice," in weakness, fear, and misery, you have often said. "Oh for one glorious hour of him who, in the Name of the Lord of hosts, smote Israel's most formidable foe!" But your wishes led to no practical result. "Your goodness was as the morning cloud." And now your reason, conscience, and all that is best within you urge you to accept Christ as your King. Let your feelings be translated into definite and decisive action, without which they are worse than useless. "Now then *do it.*" "Crown him Lord of all."

III. WHEN YOU SHOULD DO IT. Whatever reason exists for doing it at all should induce you to do it *now.* There are not a few who are persuaded of their duty, yet break the force of every appeal by delay and the intention of doing it at a future time. But: 1. The present is *a most favourable opportunity.* The King "waits to be gracious," and sends you the message of reconciliation. "Men and brethren, to you is the word of this salvation sent." "Behold, now is the acceptable time; behold, now is the day of salvation" (2 Cor. ii. 1, 2). 2. If you do it to-day, to-morrow and *all your future days* will be days of peace and happiness. 3. If you wait till to-morrow, it is *probable that you will never do it.* Your susceptibility to Divine influences will be lessened, your indisposition, which is the real cause of delay, will be increased; life is uncertain, probation is brief, the end is nigh. "Our gracious Ahasuerus (Esth. iv. 11) reacheth out the golden sceptre to all that have a hand of faith to lay hold of it; but then he shall take his iron mace or rod in his hand to bruise his enemies and break tnem in pieces like a potter's vessel." Say not, with the procrastinator, "To-morrow" (Exod.

viii. 10); "Go thy way for this time" (Acts xxiv. 25); for "the Holy Ghost saith, To-day" (Heb. iii. 7). "'Cras! cras!' (To-morrow! to-morrow!) is the cry of the raven. This is the thing that destroys many; while they are saying, 'Cras! cras!' suddenly the door is shut" (Augustine). "The man that procrastinates struggles ever with ruin" (Epictetus). "There is a circumscribed space of time appointed thee, which if thou dost not employ in making all calm and serene within, it will pass away and thou wilt pass away, and it never will return" (Marcus Antoninus, ii. 4).

> "Defer not till to-morrow to be wise;
> To-morrow's sun to thee may never rise."

> D.

Vers. 22—30.—(HEBRON.) *The vengeance of Joab*. [*References:* (1) Early life (1 Sam. xxii. 1); (2) conflict with Abner (ch. ii. 13, 24, 30); (3) capture of the strong-hold of Zion (1 Chron. xi. 6); (4) captain of the host (ch. viii. 16; xx. 23); (5) conflicts with the Ammonites and Syrians (ch. x. 7); (6) reduction of the Edomites (1 Kings xi. 15, 16); (7) complicity in the murder of Uriah (ch. xi. 14); (8) capture of Rabbah (ch. xi. 1; xii. 26); (9) relations with Absalom (ch. xiv. 1, 29); (10) defeat and murder of Absalom (ch. xviii. 2, 14); (11) upbraiding the king (ch. xix. 5); (12) replaced by Amasa (ch. xx. 4); (13) murder of Amasa (ch. xx. 10); (14) defeat of Sheba (ch. xx. 22); (15) remonstrance with David (ch. xxiv. 3); (16) defection to Adonijah (1 Kings i. 7); (17) denounced by David (1 Kings ii. 5); (18) put to death by Benaiah at the command of Solomon (1 Kings ii. 28, 34).] 1. Among those who played a prominent part in David's reign the *foremost man* was his nephew Joab. He was possessed of great physical strength and daring, clear judgment and strong will, eminent military skill, and immense power over others; "a bold captain in bad times." With the ruder qualities of activity, courage, and implacable revenge, "he combined something of a more states-manlike character, which brings him more nearly to a level with his youthful uncle; and unquestionably gives him the second place in the whole history of David's reign. In consequence of his successful attempt at the siege of Jebus, he became commander-in-chief, the highest office in the state after the king. In this post he was content, and served the king with undeviating fidelity. In the wide range of wars which David undertook, Joab was the acting general, and he therefore may be considered as the founder, as far as military prowess was concerned, the Marlborough, the Belisarius, of the Jewish empire" (Stanley). His patriotism was unquestionable; nor was he without piety (ch. x. 12). 2. His natural gifts, good qualities, and invaluable services were more than counterbalanced by his *moral defects* and numerous vices. "He ever appears wily, politic, and unscrupulous" ('Speaker's Commentary'). "He is the impersonation of worldly policy, secular expediency, and temporal ambition, eager for his own personal aggrandizement, and especially for the maintenance of his own political ascendency, and practising on the weaknesses of princes for his own interests; but at last the victim of his own Machiavellian shrewdness" (Wordsworth). 3. "Joab was a *type* of the national aspect of Judaism. He was intensely Jewish, in the tribal meaning of the word, not in its higher, world-wide bearing; only Judæan in everything that outwardly marked Judaism, though not regarded in its inward and spiritual reality. Nor is it without deep symbolical meaning, as we have the higher teaching of history, that Joab, the typical Eastern Judæan—may we not say, the type of Israel after the flesh?—should, in carrying out his own purposes and views, have at last compassed his own destruction" (Edersheim).

I. EVIL DEEDS ARE SELDOM WROUGHT WITHOUT PLAUSIBLE PRETEXTS. It is uncertain whether Joab was aware of former negotiations between David and Abner; but on returning to Hebron from a military expedition (against marauding troops, ch. iv. 2), being informed of the league that had just been made, his suspicion was aroused; he hastened to the king with the view of inducing him to share it, probably believing that Abner was not to be trusted; and finding the result doubtful or contrary to his expectation, resolved to take the matter into his own hands, on the ground of: 1. *Guilt* incurred by a public enemy. 2. *Zeal* inspired for the king's safety (ver. 25). 3. *Obligation* imposed by personal injury, according to the custom of *blood-revenge* (Exod. xxi. 13; Numb. xxxv. 9—35; Deut. xix. 1—13). This is twice mentioned by the historian (vers. 27, 30) as the ostensible ground, and was perhaps popularly regarded as a sufficient justification of his deed. "The act of Abner was justifiable homicide; but it was precisely to such cases that the rule applied, not to those of murder, against the penalties of which no sanctuary afforded protection. Besides, unless the right of avengement for blood did apply to such cases as this, whence the deep necessity of Abner to avoid slaying Asahel (ch. ii. 22)? It may be admittted that a case of this nature may have involved some doubt as to the application of the rule to it, and very likely it was not in such cases often enforced. But where any room for doubt existed, Joab and Abishai might interpret it in their own favour as their justification for an act the true motives of which durst not be alleged, and as a ground on which they might claim exemption from the punishment due to murder" (Kitto, 'Daily Bible Illus.').

II. PLAUSIBLE PRETEXTS OFTEN COVER THE BASEST MOTIVES, though they cannot entirely conceal them. 1. *Vindictiveness.* Joab's act, even if it fell within the letter of the Law, which allowed punishment for homicide under certain circumstances (Numb. xxxv. 22), was shown, by the place, the time, and the manner of it, to have been done, not from regard for justice, but from deliberate, unwarrantable, malicious revenge. So David regarded it (ver. 28); denouncing it as the "shedding of the blood of war in peace" (1 Kings ii. 5), and joining it with the murder of Amasa. 2. *Jealousy* and ambition (1 Sam. xviii. 6—16). This was his main motive. He was "afraid of losing his command of the army and his dignity with the king, and lest he should be deprived of those advantages and Abner should obtain the first rank in David's court" (Josephus). Hence his suspicion and slander of Abner (ver. 25). "Through envy of the devil came death into the world" (Wisd. of Sol. ii, 24).

> " Envy at others' good is evermore
> Malignant poison setting on the soul;
> A double woe to him infected by it—
> Of *inward* pain the heavy load he bears,
> At sight of joy *without* he ever mourns."
>   (Æschylus.)

3. *Presumption.* He rudely remonstrated with the king (ver. 24), presuming upon his position; and afterwards, without the king's authority, whilst seeming to act under it, recalled the man who had been sent away under the king's protection; and gratified his private revenge, regardless of the effect of his conduct on the king's dignity and reputation. 4. *Treachery.* Under the pretence of speaking with him in a friendly and confidential manner, he drew his victim aside in the middle of the gate, and smote him there. Possibly Abishai alone was witness of the act. "Cursed be he that smiteth his neighbour *secretly.* And all the people shall say, Amen" (Deut. xxvii. 24).

III. IMPUNITY IN CRIME IS COMMONLY PRODUCTIVE OF DISASTROUS EFFECTS. Under the circumstances, it would hardly have been possible for David to punish Joab and Abishai. "Probably public feeling would not have supported the king, nor could he, at this crisis of his affairs, have afforded the loss of such generals, or brave the people and the army" (Edersheim). Great men often owe their exemption from punishment to their position. But crime, although unpunished by man: 1. *Incurs the righteous displeasure of God.* (Vers. 29, 39.) Human punishment does not and cannot always accord with the Divine. Although David could not punish, he durst not forgive. His words "express his moral horror at this evil deed, and at the same time the everlasting law of God's requiting justice." "The extension of the curse to the descendants clearly refers to the threatenings of the Law; and in both cases the offensive character disappears if we only remember that whoever by true repentance freed himself from connection with the guilt, was also exempted from participation in the punishment" (Hengstenberg). 2. *Incites other men to similar crimes.* It is not improbable that Baanah and Rechab were induced to assassinate Ishbosheth (ch. iv. 6) by the unavenged death of Abner. 3. *Encourages the criminal* to continue his evil course, increases his obduracy, and causes him to " wax worse and worse." "Joab prospered even after his sin. God gave him time for repentance. But he hardened his heart by sin. And in the end he was cut off." "Successful crime is splendid misery." 4. *Escapes not for ever* the retribution which it deserves. "Evil pursueth sinners" (Prov. xiii. 21;

xxix. 1). Joab sinned with a strong and violent hand, and by a strong and violent hand he at length perished (1 Kings ii. 34; Ps. lviii. 11).

> "O blind lust!
> O foolish wrath! who so dost goad us on
> In the brief life, and in the eternal then
> Thus miserably overwhelm us!"
>   (Dante, 'Purg.,' xii.)
>   D.

Vers. 31—35.—(HEBRON.) *David's lament over Abner.*

> "As a fool dies should Abner die?—
> Thy hands unbound,
> Thy feet not set in fetters:
> As one falls before the wicked, thou didst fall!"

On hearing of the death of Abner, David exhibited the same generous spirit as formerly at the death of Saul (ch. i. 11, 12). 1. He *disclaimed* (before his trusted servants, as afterwards, ver. 38) against having had *any part therein;* declaring, "I and my kingdom are guiltless before the Lord," etc. Malicious persons, judging others by themselves, might accuse him of it; and if it had been instigated by him, he would have brought guilt upon his people as well as himself (ch. xxi. 1; xxiv. 1, 17). 2. He *invoked a curse* on the head of the author of the deed; not from a feeling of personal hatred and vindictiveness, but of righteous indignation (1 Sam. xxvi. 19). 3. He ordered a *public mourning* in honour of the deceased. "And David said to Joab," etc. (ver. 38). Although he durst not arrest him, he clearly indicated what he thought of his conduct, and sought to remove the odium which it cast on his own good name. 4. He followed in the procession as chief mourner, *wept at the grave* (John xi. 35), and fasted until sunset. "There is no more beautiful picture in his life than that of his following the bier where lay the bloody corpse of the man who had been his enemy ever since he had known him, and sealing the reconciliation which death ever makes in noble souls by the pathetic dirge he chanted over Abner's grave" (A. Maclaren). "This short poem is not only a dirge; it is also an apology for David and for Abner himself" (Wordsworth). It expresses—

I. ADMIRATION OF EMINENT WORTH. Abner was not a villain (fool) or murderer, deserving of being put in fetters and dying a felon's death; but brave, capable, noble-minded, "great in council, great in war," and worthy of respect and honour. A generous man sees and appreciates what is best in other men. "The generous spirit of David kept down all base and selfish feeling, and added another to those glorious conquests over his own heart which were far higher distinctions than his other victories, and in which he has left us an example which all, from the least to the greatest, should try to emulate" (Blaikie).

II. AFFLICTION FOR A PUBLIC LOSS. A light was quenched *"in Israel"* (ver. 38). His presence and influence would have contributed to the reconciliation of the tribes and the welfare of the nation (ver. 21). David's sorrow was sincere; his tears (in confirmation of his words) evinced the tenderness and sympathy of his heart, moved the people also to tears, and (in contrast with the bearing of Joab) convinced them of his innocence and uprightness.

III. ASTONISHMENT AT AN EXTRAORDINARY FATE. "The point of this indignant, more than sorrowful, lament lies in the *mode* in which Abner was slain" (Kitto, 'Cyc.'). How strange that Abner should have fallen in the full possession of strength to defend himself and liberty to flee from danger; neither as a prisoner taken in battle nor (in allusion to the right of blood-revenge which Joab claimed) as a murderer delivered up in bonds to the avenger by lawful authority, as he would have been if he were guilty! His fall—so different from what might have been expected and from what he merited— could be accounted for only by its having been caused by the treacherous malice and murderous violence of "sons of wickedness."

IV. ABHORRENCE OF A WICKED DEED. (Vers. 29, 39.) The death of Abner was, even more than his life would have been, conducive to David's interests. "It must have seemed to him, from a prudential point of view, that it was a piece of good fortune.

But the strength of his moral indignation does not suffer itself to be assuaged by worldly considerations" (Delitzsch). Hatred of wrong is a sign and measure of the love of right. " Ye that love the Lord, hate evil" (Ps. xcvii. 10). David was as severe toward evil-doers as he was tender and pitiful toward the victims of their wickedness. " He was a man extreme in all his excellences—a man of the highest strain, whether for counsel, for expression, or for action, in peace and in war, in exile and on the throne " (E. Irving).—D.

Vers. 36—38.—(HEBRON.) *Acceptance with the people.* " And all the people took notice of it, and it pleased them," etc. (ver. 36). David's conduct not only freed him from suspicion, but also won the confidence and affection of " all the people " (1 Sam. xii. 3—5).

I. THE CONDUCT OF ONE IN AUTHORITY IS CAREFULLY OBSERVED BY THE PEOPLE. Because of : 1. His *elevated* position, which (like a mountain-peak) attracts their attention, and exposes him to their constant gaze. 2. His *responsible* position, which leads them to compare his actions with the principles according to which he ought to rule. 3. His *influential* position, which makes them watchful of his course, out of concern for their own interests.

II. ACCEPTANCE WITH THE PEOPLE IS AN OBJECT WORTHY OF BEING DILIGENTLY SOUGHT. It is not the highest object, and ought not to be sought supremely. Truth and justice are of greater worth than popularity. The praise of God must be loved more than the praise of men (John xii. 43). But it should not be neglected or despised, because : 1. It conduces to his safety and happiness. 2. It renders his measures less likely to be suspected and opposed; enables him to effect his purposes for their good; increases the measure of his usefulness. 3. It aids him in his endeavours to promote the glory of the supreme Ruler.

III. THERE IS NO WAY TO SECURE IT MORE EFFECTUAL THAN THE EXHIBITION OF AN UPRIGHT AND GENEROUS SPIRIT. 1. Other ways are uncertain and variable, like the changing moods of the people. 2. This appeals to what is noblest and most permanent in them, and secures the sympathies of the most reliable men. 3. It also obtains the favour and help of God, who disposes their hearts to approve, submit, and obey.

IV. ITS ATTAINMENT IS HONOURABLE AND BENEFICIAL TO THE PEOPLE THEMSELVES. 1. It shows a readiness to be pleased, and a disposition to admire genuine excellence. 2. It confirms his devotion to their welfare, and encourages him to persevere in well-doing. 3. It tends to their improvement in virtue, and thus contributes to their peace and unity, power and prosperity.

CONCLUSION. What has been said applies to other relations besides that of ruler and subject. " A good name is better than precious ointment" (Eccles. vii. 1) or "great riches" (Prov. xxii. 1); " Let every one of us please his neighbour for his good to edification" (Rom. xv. 2; 1 Cor. x. 33; Titus ii. 9); " Whatsoever things are of *good report*, think on these things" (Phil. iv. 8).—D.

Ver. 38.—(HEBRON.) *The fall of a prince and a great man.* The world is sometimes startled by the fall of an eminent man in a sudden and violent manner—like that of the Czar of Russia or the President of the United States. Here is the *epitaph* of such a man. Reflect : 1. How uncertain is the continuance of human life! This familiar but little-heeded truth is set forth in an impressive manner by such an event, teaching that no station is exempt from the approach of death, no safeguards effectual against it. " Death is come up into our windows, and is entered into our palaces" (Jer. ix. 24). 2. How unstable is the foundation of earthly greatness! It is built upon the sand, and in a moment crumbles into dust. Goodness alone (the essence of true greatness) endures and goes with the soul into "everlasting habitations." 3. How deplorable is the loss of superior excellence! The world is made poorer by its removal. 4. How dreadful is the prevalence of diabolical wickedness! One assassination begets another. And at times there is abroad in society a spirit of lawlessness, recklessness, and ungodliness, which is full of peril, and calls for the earnest efforts and prayers of good men that it may be overcome. 5. How mysterious are the ways of Divine Providence, in permitting the innocent to perish, the godless to succeed, the guilty to be spared ! 6. How often is evil overruled for the promotion of beneficent ends (ch. iv. 1 ; v. 1)!   7. How profitable is the remembrance of a noble-minded man ! "*Know* ye not," etc. ?   " He being dead, yet speaketh."—D.

Ver. 39.—(HEBRON.)   *The sons of Zeruiah.*   The mental and moral qualities of men are largely traceable to hereditary tendencies. If Joab and Abishai resembled their mother, she must have been a woman of strong mind, and of a suspicious, irascible, and intolerant temper, rather than noted for her simplicity, meekness, and forbearance. And so much may be inferred from the manner in which David associates the name of his sister with her sons (ch. xvi. 10; xix. 22 ; 1 Kings ii. 5).   Their spirit and conduct were different from his, obnoxious to him, and constrained him to make this confession to his confidential servants on the evening of the day of Abner's funeral.   " It was one of those moments in which a king, even with the best intentions, must feel to his own heavy cost the weakness of everything human, and the limits of human supremacy " (Ewald).

I. NO MAN, HOWEVER HIGHLY EXALTED, IS EXEMPT FROM WEAKNESS. " I am this day weak [tender, infirm], and an anointed king." The most absolute monarch cannot do all he would. Truly good men, though anointed and endued with spiritual power, are by no means perfect, but are "compassed with infirmity." The weakness of a strong man is felt : 1. *In contending against the evil* that surrounds him and presses in upon him like " the proud waves." 2. *In performing the duties* that rest upon him, and attaining the ideal of character at which he aims. " I will walk within my house with a perfect heart," etc. (Ps. ci. 2—8). 3. *In effecting the purposes* which he may have formed for the good of others.

II. THE WEAKNESS OF A STRONG MAN IS OFTEN OCCASIONED BY HIS RELATIONSHIP WITH OTHER MEN. " And these men, sons of Zeruiah, are too hard [rough, obstinate, powerful] for me." His relationships with them (formed, it may be, independently of his choice, and conducive, in some respects, to his good) not unfrequently : 1. Enable them to acquire *undue power*, and incite them to pursue a presumptuous, obstinate, unjustifiable course. " A man's foes are they of his own household " (Matt. x. 36 ; Numb. xii. 1). 2. Bring him into *intimate association* with those who have little sympathy with his noblest feelings, and expose him to the influence of their adverse principles (Luke ix. 54; Matt. xvi. 22, 23). 3. Become an *occasion of hindrance, temptation, and peril.* For, unlike him in whom the prince of this world " had nothing " (John xiv. 30), every man possesses an inward, carnal propensity on which outward evil may take hold, and thereby cause him to stumble.

III. THE CONSCIOUSNESS OF HIS CONDITION FILLS HIM WITH DEEP DISTRESS. " I am this day weak," etc., which is a complaint of: 1. *Painful restraint* imposed upon him with respect to conduct he cannot approve. 2. *Necessary endurance* of men whom he cannot punish, and with whom he may not, out of regard to his own position and the common good, enter into open conflict. 3. *Partial and not altogether blameless failure* in the fulfilment of the obligations of his high calling. David has been severely condemned for not punishing the sons of Zeruiah ; but in order to justify such condemnation, we should have a better acquaintance with all the circumstances of the case. He was not without sinful infirmity. Yet whose conviction of what is absolutely right exactly corresponds with his consciousness of actual performance ? " The spirit indeed is willing, but the flesh is weak."

IV. THE CHIEF ALLEVIATION OF HIS TROUBLE IS CONFIDENCE IN THE RIGHTEOUS RETRIBUTION OF GOD. " Jehovah reward the doer of wickedness according to his wickedness." This is expressive of : 1. *Dependence* on the Divine power to accomplish what he himself cannot do. 2. *Faith* in the Divine permission of unrequited evil for a time, for wise and beneficent ends. 3. *Desire* for the maintenance, vindication, and triumph of eternal righteousness in the earth (vers. 22—30). " The Lord will render to him according to his works " (2 Tim. iv. 14). " Jehovah shall reward," etc. This was the text to which Lady F. Cavendish directed attention on the occasion of the lamented death of her husband, Lord Frederic Cavendish; and which was so remarkably fulfilled in the fate that afterwards overtook his assassins. " It is the hope of the oppressed and the patience of the saints."—D.

Vers. 9—12.—*Doing right wrongly.*   Abner knew well that David was appointed by God to be king over all Israel. Yet he set up Ishbosheth as king over the eleven tribes in opposition to David, and thus caused much unnecessary and useless delay and bloodshed. When, however, Ishbosheth (whether rightly or wrongly) remonstrated with him for his conduct towards Rizpah, he calls to mind the purpose and promise of God, and resolves to co-operate with him (!) in placing David over all the nation (ver. 9); and he opens communications with David with this view. The known will of God thus becomes a convenient pretext for the gratification at once of his revenge and his ambition. His own lips convicted him of insincerity and hypocrisy. His tardy obedience to the truth he knew was unreal and unacceptable to God, however useful to David. It was self, and not God, that ruled him throughout. Abner has many imitators—men who, instead of simply and sincerely obeying the truth they know, make it wait on their ambition or covetousness, now neglecting it, now acting according to it, and professing great regard for it, as their selfish aims may prompt. They choose their side in religion or politics, not according to conviction, but according to their supposed interests; and if they change sides it is not because of changed convictions, but because their ambition or avarice has been disappointed—they have not been made enough of, or they have quarrelled with some one, or their pride has been mortified, or they see that they have been on the side of a decaying cause which cannot be of much more service to them. Such men may be *welcomed* to the side they join, and may be of some service; but they will not be *trusted*, and their service will be of doubtful value. In religion especially the adherence of such persons is to be deprecated as wanting in the right spirit, and likely to be injurious rather than beneficial. They tend to corrupt the society in which they are active and influential, and deprive it of its true strength—that of sincere, spiritual, consistent character. Observe : 1. *The importance of simple and uniform obedience to the known will of God.* To obey as it suits our worldly aims is not to obey at all, and the pretence of obedience is hypocritical and hateful to God. Such obedience may have its uses to others ; God may overrule it for good ; but it will bring no blessing to the doer. 2. *The language of Abner may be adopted by us in relation to the kingdom of our Lord Jesus Christ.* " As Jehovah has sworn to his beloved Son, even so I do to him." Our knowledge of the purpose and promise of God to establish Christ's rule over all men should stimulate us to devoted service in his cause. It assures us that to be on his side is to be on God's side, on the side that must succeed. In being thus workers with God we cannot labour in vain ; and labouring not in pretence, but in truth, we shall ultimately share in the glory and power of the great King whose cause we espouse (Rev. iii. 21). —G. W.

Ver. 38.—*Death of a great man.* Abner had great qualities, filled a high position, seemed likely to be of great service to David, who sincerely lamented his untimely end, and the wicked treachery and violence by which he fell.

I. GREAT MEN SHOULD BE HIGHLY VALUED. Great generals and naval commanders. If war must be, it is of vast importance that it should be conducted by able captains. But not only these, men great in the arts of peace,—great statesmen, philosophers, historians, scientists, poets, artists, preachers, etc. Especially when distinguished ability is combined with unselfish devotion to the good of the nation or the race. For selfish ambition belittles the great, and moral corruption renders them powerful for evil instead of good. Abner's greatness was marred by his unscrupulous ambition, and Joab was worse than he. The multitude are very dependent on great leaders, whether in war or peace, and can do little without them. " Thou art worth ten thousand of us " (ch. xviii. 3). Leading and inspiring the many, they make them partners in their own greatness. The influence of their deeds, or (in the case of intellectual leaders) their thoughts, raises others towards their own level. The character as well as the progress of a people depends a good deal on its great men.

II. GREAT MEN MUST DIE. In some conditions of society their lives are more exposed to peril than the lives of others—whether from the assassin, or from fickle monarchs or ambitious rivals, using the forms of law to put them out of their way ; or the cares incident to greatness may shorten their days. " I have said, Ye are gods . . . but ye shall die like men " (Ps. lxxxii. 6, 7)—a truth they should bear in mind to keep them sober and humble, to stimulate their diligence, and preserve in them a sense of responsibility to God; a truth which others should remember, that they may not idolize the great, nor unduly confide in them (see Ps. cxlvi. 3, 4) or dread their anger (Isa. li. 12), nor, to secure their favour, sin against him who lives for ever; and that they may be themselves the more content to die.

III. GREAT MEN SHOULD BE HONOURED AFTER DEATH. By general mourning; by honourable burial; by commemoration of their virtues and services, in elegies (as here), or biographies, or monuments to their memory; by carrying out their unaccomplished purposes for the public good; and withal by praise to God for them and their services. Such honour is due to the men themselves, and tends to the good of society by exciting emulation, etc.

In conclusion: 1. Let Britons bless God for the large number and long succession of great men who have adorned and served their country in all departments; and pray that the succession may be maintained to the latest times. Not only are such men invaluable while they live; their works and memories survive them as a perpetual treasure. The truly great do not die altogether.

> " But strew his ashes to the wind
> Whose sword or voice has served mankind—
> And is he dead whose glorious mind
> Lifts thine on high?
> To live in hearts we leave behind,
> Is not to die."

> (Campbell.)

2. Let us be thankful that it is not necessary to be great in order to be either happy or useful. Goodness is the essential thing. A comfort to the many who can never be distinguished. 3. Yet real greatness is possible to all. Through faith in Christ we become children of God, "heirs of God, and joint-heirs with Christ," to be "glorified together" with him (Rom. viii. 17). In the kingdom of heaven greatness is secured by conscientious obedience to the Divine commandments (Matt. v. 19), humility (Matt. xviii. 4; Luke ix. 48), and self-abasing, self-denying service of others (Mark x. 42—45). Such greatness is substantial and immortal (1 John ii. 17). 4. Let us rejoice that the great "Captain of our salvation" lives for ever, in fulness of power to save and bless all who trust in him.—G. W.

Ver. 39.—*A weak king.* "I am this day weak, though anointed king." David, indignant and distressed on account of the murder of Abner, could not venture to attempt to punish the murderers. They were too powerful for even him. Hence this lamentation. It was hardly wise to express his feeling—it would help to confirm the power of Joab and his brother. Many a monarch has been similarly weak, owing to the power of those who are nominally his servants. This is injurious when it prevents the execution of justice; but as to measures of government it is often best, the servant being wiser and abler than the sovereign. We may take the words as a picture of what has place in human nature. Man has over him rightful kings, which too often are not, in fact, his rulers.

I. THE EVIL. 1. *Objectively.* *Truth*, the expressed will of God, is rightful sovereign of men, but it very partially rules. Many "sons of Zeruiah" are "too hard for" it, silence its utterances, oppose its power, prevent its sway. But it *is* king notwithstanding, and, by the Divine judgments it expresses, will determine men's destiny, though they may refuse to let its precepts regulate their conduct. 2. *Subjectively.* *Conscience*, enlightened by truth, is anointed by God as king. "Had it strength as it had right, had it power as it had manifest authority, it would absolutely govern the world" (Bishop Butler). But in actual government it is often "weak." The lower part of human nature is in rebellion against the higher. Appetite and passion and ill-regulated lawful affections, and all these hardened into habits, are "too hard" for it. Hence come degradation, ruin, misery, now and hereafter.

II. THE REMEDY. The redemption effected by the death of our Lord, realized in the heart by faith through the power of the Holy Spirit, is the only effectual remedy. "Our old man is crucified with him, that the body of sin might be destroyed, that henceforth we should not serve sin." " Sin shall not have dominion over you; for ye are not under law, but under grace" (Rom. vi. 6, 14). The revelation of God and man, of sin and holiness, in the cross of Christ; the deliverance from condemnation secured thereby; the new Divine power which is imparted to the believer; the love to his Redeemer which is planted in his heart; the filial relation into which he is brought to God; the new hopes by which he is inspired;—these rescue him from slavery to sin, and give him freedom and will and power to serve God and righteousness (see Rom. vi. and vii., and viii. 1—4). The rightful Sovereign is replaced on the throne, strong to govern, not yet with absolutely universal and perfect sway, but with the assured prospect of it. Let, then, those who groan under the consciousness of their moral weakness accept the great Deliverer, and submit themselves to his methods of imparting strength to the soul.

III. THE SEEMING RESEMBLANCE BETWEEN DAVID AND HIS DIVINE SON. It might seem as if our Lord Jesus, like David, might say, "I am . . . weak, though anointed King." Long has he been exalted to his throne at the right hand of God, as Lord of all; "from henceforth expecting till his enemies be made his footstool" (Heb. x. 13). Yet how small a portion of mankind is actually under his moral and spiritual sway! and these how imperfectly! How much power have his foes, even where he does really rule! And his open foes and false friends seem to speak and act as they please with impunity. It is not, however, that he is "weak," or that any are "too hard for" him. He is long-suffering, and delays to execute judgment; but let his enemies continue impenitent and incorrigible, and they will learn by experience that he is strong to punish them. "Vengeance has leaden feet, but iron hands." "The mill of God grinds late, but it grinds to powder." Meanwhile he uses his foes as slaves to aid in working out his purposes. And as to the limits of his moral and spiritual rule, we must remember that, in extending and perfecting it, he pays respect to the freedom of men. It is not a matter of mere power, but of instruction and persuasion. He counsels, warns, invites, manifests his own yearning pity and love, stirs the conscience, moves the heart; but he does not *compel*—cannot do so consistently with his own purpose or the nature of man and of the rule he would establish. But let us yield ourselves heartily to him, and we shall find that he is as strong as ever to save and make strong those who trust in him.—G. W.

Ver. 39.—*Sure retribution.* "The Lord shall reward the doer of evil according to his wickedness." In the Revised Version the words are rendered as a wish: "The Lord reward the wicked doer according to his wickedness." The substantial meaning is the same in both translations. "In his impotence to punish Joab himself, David remits him to the just judgment of God" ('Speaker's Commentary'). The words may be taken in respect to all evil-doers. None can escape the judgment of God, even if they escape punishment from men.

I. THE CERTAINTY OF THE DIVINE PUNISHMENT OF EVIL-DOERS. This follows from: 1. *The relations of God to men.* As Ruler, Lawgiver, Judge. He will certainly not fail in the exercise of the functions which belong to these relations. Even if we think of him as Father, we may be equally certain that impenitent sinners will not go unpunished. What would a father be worth who should allow a depraved son to defy himself, and seriously injure other children of the family, with impunity? If he can by any means, gentle or severe, reform him, well,—this he will prefer; but if not, he must banish and abandon him. And to say that Omnipotent love need not and cannot resort to this extremity of punishment is to go beyond our knowledge, and contrary to the plain statements of Holy Writ, where the chastisement which reforms and the punishment which crushes are clearly distinguished. To make Gehenna a purgatory is certainly to add to the teaching of our Lord respecting it. 2. *His threatenings.* Those of conscience and those of Holy Writ. They abound throughout the Bible, and are nowhere more frequent and awful than in the teaching of the tender and loving Christ. 3. *His character.* As holy and just, loving righteousness and hating iniquity; truthful in regard to his threatenings as well as his promises. 4. *His omniscience.* Men often succeed in hiding their evil deeds or themselves from their fellow-men; but it is impossible thus to escape Divine judgments (see Job xxxiv. 21, 22). 5. *His omnipotence.* Criminals may in some states of society be, like Joab, too strong to be punished by those in authority; but God is mightier than the mightiest.

There is, therefore, no possibility of resisting his judgments. 6. *The teachings of experience.* The penalties which follow violations of natural law. The results of wrong-doing upon body, mind, circumstances. The penalties inflicted by society on those who practise certain forms of wickedness.

II. THE SATISFACTION WITH WHICH THIS CERTAINTY IS SOMETIMES REGARDED BY THE RIGHTEOUS. According to the Revised Version the words are a wish, a prayer; but even according to the Authorized Version they are uttered with evident satisfaction. David desired that justice should be executed on Joab; and, feeling his own inability to execute it, was relieved by the assurance he felt that it would not therefore fail of execution. Would such a feeling be wrong in a Christian? St. Paul did not think so. "Alexander the coppersmith did me much evil: the Lord reward [or, 'will reward'] him according to his works" (2 Tim. iv. 14, where there are two readings, as here two renderings). In the case of powerful villains injuring and trampling down the weak, but who cannot be reached by human justice, can any one doubt that the feeling of confidence that the justice of God can and will reach them is a proper feeling to cherish, although it should be associated with the desire that they may, if possible, be converted? In the case of impenitent sinners in general, it is the known purpose of God to punish them according to their works. Shall his children disapprove his conduct, or only silently submit; or not rather acquiesce, approve, and, at times at least, cherish complacency? Does not the prayer divinely taught to them, "Thy will be done," apply to this part of his will? They bear the image of God's righteousness as well as loving-kindness. They have strong regard for his character and honour, as well as for the happiness of his creatures. They cannot but desire that all rebellion against him should be put down by the power of his love on the hearts of the rebels, if it may be; if not, by the severe measures of his justice. In the case of serious wrong done to ourselves, we are doubtless to suppress all emotions of revenge, and to pray for and be ready to forgive the wrong-doer; yet the above-cited expression of St. Paul shows that, in certain circumstances, we may remit the offender to Divine justice; and in another place (Rom. xii. 19) he gives this as a reason for not avenging ourselves: "It is written, Vengeance is mine; I will repay, saith the Lord." The love which is so characteristic of Christianity is not, then, incompatible with hatred of sin and the desire that sin should be punished. The two are identical when the punishment is desired that the sinner may be led thereby to repentance. They are not incompatible, when, the persistence and impenitence of the sinner being supposed, love for others and zeal for the law and government of God produce at least acquiescence in his judgments. It should be observed, however, that such emotions as we have been speaking of are to form but a small part of the inner life of the Christian. Indignation against evil, and desire for its punishment, need rather to be restrained and guided, than inculcated and cherished. The sentiments towards others which should ordinarily predominate are those of pure and direct benevolence. Yet let sinners lay to heart that, unless they repent and seek salvation through Christ, God will certainly render to them according to their wickedness. "Be sure your sin will find you out." "Repent ye therefore, and be converted, that your sins may be blotted out."—G. W.

EXPOSITION.

CHAPTER IV.

Ver. 1.—**When Saul's son heard that Abner was dead.** The news of Abner's death must have had a doubly depressing effect upon Ishbosheth; for he learned, not only that the mainstay of his kingdom was slain, but that even he, in despair of a successful issue, had been engaged in treasonable negotiations with his rival. **All the Israelites were troubled.** Their trouble was caused rather by uncertainty than by fear. Abner's plans had fallen through, and the fact of his murder threw grave suspicions on David. Had he now attacked Israel, the chiefs would most probably have stood loyally by Saul's house. But he did nothing, and his innocence slowly but gradually was made clear. They were thus in a state of suspense, and waiting till some brave man arose to lead them to a decision. Unfortunately, a fresh crime threw everything back into hopeless confusion.

Ver. 2.—**Saul's son had two men captains of bands.** The bands mentioned were light-armed troops, used in forays, such as that mentioned in ch. iii. 22. Their captains would be men of importance with Ishbosheth, who is here described somewhat contemptuously, not as king, nor by his own name, but as "Saul's son." **Beeroth.** This place, literally *the Wells*, was one of the four towns reserved for the Gibeonites (Josh. ix. 17), though nominally belonging to Benjamin (Josh. xviii. 25). The note, that it **was reckoned to Benjamin**, suggests that it had until quite lately been occupied by the Canaanites, whose flight to Gittaim had no doubt been caused by Saul's cruel attack upon them referred to in ch. xxi. 1, 2. It was thus remarkable that the destruction of Saul's dynasty was the work of the Gibeonites of Beeroth. As we find another of these Beerothites, Naharai, holding the office of armour-bearer to Joab (1 Chron. xi. 39), it seems probable that many of them saved themselves from expulsion by becoming soldiers. But among David's worthies a large number were strangers, and some even men of foreign extraction. Beeroth, however, was probably seized in Saul's reign by the Benjamites, by force, and occupied by them, as its citizens returned in large numbers from the exile (Ezra ii. 25), and are counted as genuine Israelites. Moreover, by thus dispossessing the natives, Saul was able to give his tribesmen "fields and vineyards" (1 Sam. xxii. 7), which otherwise would have been in violation of the Mosaic Law.

Ver. 3.—Gittaim. This word is a dual, and means "the two Gaths;" the one being, probably, the acropolis, or upper town, at the foot of which nestled a new Gath, protected by the ancient stronghold. It is mentioned as belonging to Benjamin in Neh. xi. 33; but could not have been an Israelite town at this time, as the Beerothites are described as *sojourners*, that is, dwellers in a foreign country. When expelled from Beeroth, they probably seized Gittaim by force, and, on the reconciliation effected by the execution of Saul's sons, returned to their allegiance to Israel.

Ver. 4.—Jonathan, Saul's son, had a son. This is mentioned to show that Saul's lineage virtually became extinct on Ishbosheth's death. Mephibosheth, the heir, was a cripple, and physically incapable of reigning. Saul had, indeed, sons by a concubine, and grandchildren by his daughter Merab (ch. xxi. 8). But throughout the history there is no hint that any of these were regarded as the representatives of Saul's house. (For the name Mephibosheth, see note on ch. ii. 8.)

Vers. 6, 7.—As though they would have fetched wheat. Not only is the narrative confused, but the versions offer extraordinary varieties of reading. The murder of Ishbosheth is fully described in ver. 7,

and is there in its place, while it is out of place in ver. 6. And that the captains would themselves fetch wheat, instead of having it carried from the granary by their men; and that they would go through the king's chamber to obtain it; are both improbable. The very act of going to get wheat at midday, when everybody was having his siesta, would itself be suspicious. The Syriac says nothing about wheat, but that these "wicked men took and smote him." The Vulgate and LXX. lay the blame on the woman who kept the door, the narrative of the latter being as follows: "They entered into the house of Ishbosheth in the heat of the day, and he was asleep in his midday chamber And behold, the woman that kept the door of the house had been winnowing wheat, and she slumbered and slept. And the brothers Rechab and Baanah entered the house without being noticed, and Ishbosheth was asleep on his bed in his chamber, and they smote him," etc. There is, confessedly, considerable confusion in the text, but the versions do not altogether clear it up; and until we have better materials for forming a judgment, we must be content to wait. In ver. 5, instead of "who lay on a bed at noon," the Hebrew has "as he was taking his noonday rest." In ver. 7 the *bed* is the divan, or raised bank, which in an Oriental house runs along the wall, and is supplied with pieces of carpet, or cushions, on which to sit cross-legged or recline. For sleep, the corners were the favourite places. Even the public rooms had these divans. But Ishbosheth had probably retired for his siesta into a private chamber, where the captains knew that he would be alone. The **plain** through which they fled was the Arabah, or Jordan valley, as in ch. ii. 29.

Ver. 8.—Which sought thy life. Saul had sought David's life, but Ishbosheth was innocent of any such attempts. Still, had he been victorious, David, as his rival, would certainly have been put to death. **Jehovah hath avenged my lord the king.** The ordinary language of the East is so religious that these words imply nothing more than that these wicked men saw in their base act a step towards the carrying out of a Divine purpose. But in thus referring to the common belief that David's kingdom was assured to him by Jehovah, they evidently intended to commend their deed to the really devout mind of the king.

Vers. 9, 10.—And David answered. David's answer is worthy of him. His appeal to Jehovah, as One that had saved him in all time of adversity, was a declaration that he had no need of criminals. And throughout he had carefully abstained from taking any steps to bring about the accomplishment of God's will, and had been upright and forbearing alike to Ishbosheth and Saul. How noble his conduct was we see by the contrast with Macbeth, whose better nature was poisoned and spoiled by the hope that he should be king hereafter. At the end of the verse the force is weakened in the Authorized Version by the insertion of irrelevant words. What David said is, "I slew him in Ziklag, and that was the reward I gave him for his tidings."

Ver. 11.—**A righteous person.** Ishbosheth was probably a weak rather than a wicked man; but David is not speaking of him generally, and, as regards Rechab and Baanah, he was quite guiltless, and their crime was not in revenge for any wrong done them.

Ver. 12.—**They cut off their hands and their feet.** This was not intended for the purpose of mutilation, but to carry out an Eastern idea of retaliation. The hands were cut off because they had committed the murder; the feet, because they had brought the head to Hebron. Still, David was violating the spirit of the Mosaic Law. It ordered that the body of a man who had been put to death should be buried the same day (Deut. xxi. 23). In the face of this humane enactment, it is wonderful that the laws of Christian countries should have allowed the mutilation of the bodies of traitors, and the hanging on gibbets of criminals convicted of smaller crimes. Remembering, therefore, the customs of our fathers, we must not blame David much for suspending the hands and feet of these murderers at the pool of Hebron, that all, when coming for water, might know of their punishment. The head of Ishbosheth was honourably buried in Abner's grave (see ch. iii. 32).

HOMILETICS.

Vers. 1—12.—The facts are : 1. On the death of Abner, consternation seizes Ishbosheth and his friends. 2. The only other representative of the house of Saul was a mere boy, whose age and bodily infirmity rendered his coming to the front out of the question. 3. Two of Ishbosheth's officers, forming a secret design, visit Ishbosheth as though on business connected with their duties, and slay him. 4. Stealing away by night, they carry the head of Ishbosheth to David at Hebron, and think to satisfy thereby his love of revenge. 5. David, eagerly reminding himself that God had always delivered him without his having recourse to bloodshed, reminds his visitors also of the punishment he had inflicted on others in a similar case at Ziklag, and denounces their deed as even more atrocious. 6. Thereupon David causes the murderers to be executed, and their limbs to be exhibited in Hebron as a warning to the wicked, and meanwhile he bestows funereal honours on the head of Ishbosheth.

Worldly blindness the parent of sorrow and wrong. The whole of the events of this chapter proceed from the inability of men to read the high principles that governed the conduct of David. The general truth may be developed as follows.

I. THE BODINGS OF IGNORANCE FILL A LARGE SPACE IN THE LIVES OF SOME MEN. When it is said that Ishbosheth and his people were paralyzed and troubled by the news of the death of Abner, the question comes—Why? Was it because now the healing policy of Abner and David (ch. iii. 17—21) would yield to the more fierce policy of Joab? Did the young king and his followers imagine that now it was simply a question of best terms, and that submission was inevitable? Or were they apprehensive that, although David made terms with Abner for the sake of securing his aid, now, when that aid was no longer available for the consolidation of his power, he would take revenge on all who had supported the cause of Ishbosheth? In any case, their fears were not warranted by the governing facts of the situation. Their safety and welfare rested with David, and had they known him, had they read his principles aright, they might have been quite at ease in allowing events to take their course in his supremacy. Their forebodings of trouble sprang from ignorance of the man they had to deal with. They formed their estimate of his possible future conduct on the standards familiar amongst themselves. His life was too lofty in tone and aspiration for them to understand. How much of human life is spoiled, is charged with sorrows and fears, which would have no place were our vision clearer and our estimate of others more just and true! Men too often judge of the thoughts and ways of God by their own standard, and so apprehend what never need have troubled them. Our ignorance of coming events exercises a larger influence over our feelings than is proper; for though we do not know exactly what will occur, we ought to know that all things are in the wisest and kindest of hands. In human relationships men make troubles by supposing their fellow-men, often, to be otherwise affected than they actually are. Even the disciples were troubled in consequence of their blameworthy ignorance of the wisdom and power of their Master, and they were challenged to get rid of the sorrows bred of ignorance by reposing in him a trust as absolute as they, pious Hebrews, were wont to repose in the Eternal (John xiv. 1, 2).

II. The attachment of men not spiritually enlightened is of doubtful permanence. The attachment of the sons of Rimmon and others to the cause of Ishbosheth was based on anything but enlightened views of the theocracy, or a clear interpretation of the events of the life of Saul and David, which must have been well known. Indeed, as in the days of "David's greater Son" the mark of distinction among men lay in the spiritual recognition of him as Divine amidst his sorrows and trials, so in David's time only true unworldly men, whose eyes were open to see the spiritual element in his life, formed political attachments on superior knowledge. That which is earthly partakes of the instability of earth, and, however outwardly zealous the supporters of Ishbosheth may have been and even sincere according to their light, they were open to the influences to change which are sure to arise in times of trouble, but which could never move a mind that saw the higher principles involved in David's claim. The historian seems to imply this in his reference to the age and infirmity of Mephibosheth, as much as to say there was no one else of the house of Saul around whom men might rally in case Ishbosheth's cause should fail. No resort was left but to abandon the young king in his troubles, and form new and more promising attachments. Imagine a Jonathan slackening his attachment to David in his time of stress! or a Paul losing interest in Christ when persecutions arose! On the other hand, there are many instances in which the *weakened attachment* of the sons of Rimmon, proceeding as that attachment did from low and mere conventional views, finds a counterpart in human life. Companionships based on community of sensual enjoyments are held by bonds which perish in adversity. Friendships are perishable in so far as they are pervaded by a worldly element. Whatever ties are formed on any feelings, interests, or considerations than those which make us all one in Christ, cannot but vanish as we pass from the earthly scene into the world where alone the spiritual bond endures. And in the Church militant the adherence of numbers lacks a permanence to be counted on in proportion as it is based on custom, convenience, fashion, superstition, defective knowledge of Scripture, and dimness of spiritual apprehension. Plato was not far from the truth in saying that knowledge and reality were one. Scripture everywhere gives prominence to the unifying, ennobling power of spiritual perception. The distinction of children of light and of darkness proceeds thereon. The "spiritual man judgeth all things." The rejection of Christ was connected with blindness to the higher and more spiritual qualities of his life (1 Cor. ii. 8—16).

III. Men of unspiritual views are, by reason of their blindness, open to terrible temptations, and may be carried away to evil by the lower passions of their nature. These sons of Rimmon, like others, began to consider what course would be most advantageous to themselves, now that the cause of Ishbosheth seemed to be on the wane. Looking on the position of the two kings as simply the consequence of purely worldly forces coming into competition, and caring most of all to be on the winning side, they asked themselves what conduct on their part would be sure to win the favour of David, the stronger of the two. Had they at that juncture in the process of thought conceived of David as a man of God, of high spiritual aims, destined to work out a Divine purpose on principles of righteousness, and ambitious to translate the purest principles of private life into the affairs of his kingdom, they would only have thought of doing some deed of justice and mercy, such as a man of that character would delight in. But being destitute of these spiritual perceptions, regarding all things on the low base level of a worldly expediency, and judging David to be much such a man as themselves, there arose in their process of thought fair opportunity for the cruellest and basest propensities of their nature, to put forth their strength and suggest the murder of the unfortunate king as an act of present wisdom. It takes many impulses and thoughts of advantage and disadvantage to bring about a great crime, and it is difficult, in analyzing the mental antecedents of the crime, to assign to each its exact influence; but it is obvious in this case that worldliness of view, lack of spiritual apprehension, undue estimate of a lofty character, rendered the crime possible, and even cleared away the barriers of reason against its accomplishment. They judged David to be as themselves, and they acted accordingly. The belief that he would be glad inspired the concoction of the plot, and gave tone of exultation in their approach to him with the head of the murdered man. Their darkness was dense, and in this sense theirs was a deed of darkness. It is often that men fall into the snare of the devil in consequence of their lack of spiritual perception. The false is glossed, the true is veiled. Even disciples, not clearly perceiving the purely spiritual character of their Lord's mission, desired fire from heaven to destroy the unbelieving. During the "dark ages" men perpetrated dreadful deeds to please Christ, not rising to a true appreciation of his character and methods. Low conceptions of the nature of the kingdom of Christ as it is in the world, now induce men professing an interest in it to render service in forms that would never be entertained were his kingdom regarded as he regards it—one of purity, of love, and of righteousness. And as this worldly mindedness was a sore cause of sorrow and trouble to David, and hindered the establishment of his authority, so the same evil militates much against the final triumph of our Lord. Hence the need of teaching and the power of the Holy Spirit to open the eyes of the blind, that they may appreciate and regulate their actions by the high principles embodied in the character and kingdom of Christ.

GENERAL LESSONS. 1. Destitution of the power of spiritual apprehension and appreciation is a radical evil of human nature, and can never be removed by any other means than those which God has provided in his truth and the grace of the Holy Spirit. 2. If we would have men knit in imperishable bonds of affection and common interest, we must seek to get them to see Christ as he is, and enter into relationships on the basis of his kingdom. 3. In all our dealings with men we should be careful not to put forward our own feelings and aims as a standard by which to judge them.

Clustered truths. It is not easy to weave all the teaching of this chapter on one line, and yet the various incidents recorded all centre in the disaster which befell the King of Israel consequent on the secession and death of Abner. It may thus be advantageous, for the sake of securing unity of form, to look at the remaining leading truths of the chapter as clustering around this sad event.

I. THE SMALLER FIGURES OF HISTORY. Mephibosheth here figures as an insignificant person in the narrative of persons and events connected with the gradual unfolding of the purposes of God. A mere boy, lamed by a careless nurse, a son of one who had renounced all claim to the throne! His name and misfortune are mentioned, and the tide of events moves on. Now and then we meet with such incidental references in the Bible history. They are but specimens of multitudes equally insignificant who played a small part in the affairs of the world, and are unknown for ever. Their selection for brief allusion is doubtless part of a vast providential method by which the historians were unconsciously guided to refer to whatever might illustrate the process of elimination by which God at last accomplished his purpose in first raising up David to supreme dominion of his people, and afterwards the true David of the present dispensation. The poor lad little knew that he was an element in the working out of a great purpose, and that, small as was his figure in life, it served as a foil to God's greater characters. Modern science teaches us that nothing is really lost, that all small items are used up in the great development of things towards a future higher condition. So the humbler forms of human life are not all lost. They play their part, and to some extent modify all that comes after them. In the Church of Christ, the little ones, feeble and uninfluential in a worldly sense, have some part to perform in the great spiritual development which God is working out. Our Mephibosheths are not lost to mankind. The smaller figures of life render the totality of life more varied, and develop qualities which uniform greatness could never originate.

II. NOTORIOUS IMMORTALITY. These sons of Rimmon have won for themselves a notorious immortality. Had it not been for their base and cruel deed, their names would never have appeared on the page of history. Their crime has given them a prominent place as compared with wiser and better men. In this case, the reason of it is doubtless to be found in the circumstance that their deed served to bring out into more distinctness the character of the kingdom which God was then establishing by means of David, and so, incidentally, it forms one of the links in that singular chain of events by which at last the Christ found a way prepared for him to dwell among men. There is a base passion in some men for this kind of notoriety. Some criminals have gloried in it, and have seemed to derive some satisfaction from the thought that, at all events, they have created a sensation, and will for a time, and perhaps for ever, figure in history. Miserable consolations of sin! The utter delusiveness of sinful reasoning! The charm and delight could only be for a few days; the anguish and shame would come when the eye saw the world no more and the ear ceased to listen to the hum of the people, and then abide for ever. The curse of the righteous rests on the notoriety, and so it becomes a very occasion of deep and recurring disgrace. In modern times incalculable injury is done by a low literature that feeds this morbid love of notoriety of evil, and in the education of youth too much care cannot be given to secure them from the infection.

III. IMPLICIT ASPERSION OF CHARACTER. When these sons of Rimmon went to David with the head of Ishbosheth, no doubt openly and even boasting before they reached his presence, they by that act implicitly cast on his character the foulest and most painful aspersions. It was in act a declaration to men that David was a man of blood, that he looked on the son of Saul as a foe to be got rid of by any means, and that if only supremacy could be obtained over all the people, he cared not particularly as to the means. To David this was the interpretation of the act, and the people about him could not but regard it in that light. Character may be aspersed by deeds in various forms, and by people who do not see that there is aspersion in their conduct. The flatteries of some men are virtually reflections on purity of life. The requests of some men for a certain line of action are founded sometimes on a supposition of character that would be repudiated and scorned.

IV. RIGHTEOUS INDIGNATION. David at once saw the varied bearings of the conduct of these sons of Rimmon; its base treachery, its cold cruelty, its political treason, its disregard of the claims of misfortune, its foolish policy, and, not least, its false and wicked misrepresentations of his own character. To the man called of God, who had in all his adversities trusted in God, whose mission was to establish a rule more wise and just than that of Saul, and to raise the ideas of the people to a higher level and prepare them to perform a part in opening the way for the great Messiah, this insult must have been agonizing. His quick spiritual sensibilities were at once stirred, and yet his indignation was the more strong and impressive in that he selected words wherewith to show to them the enormity of their guilt, and then delivered them to the execution they deserved. Apart from his natural aversion to "bloody men," and his regard for the sacredness of human life even in the case of those who injured him, he could not but dwell in his own private reflections on the shameful insult offered to himself in the supposition that he could glory in such a deed. A fire burned in his soul. All good men, who regard purity and righteousness of life as above all things, will fully sympathize with David. Have we not here a clue to the Saviour's anguish when evil men supposed that he performed miracles by means of the power of Beelzebub? And was not this, perhaps, the deadly sin against the Holy Ghost (Matt. xii. 24—32)?

V. GENEROSITY TO UNFORTUNATE MEN. David was a man rich in noble feelings. His proud indignation at the insult paid to him was accompanied with immediate regard for the unfortunate king whose life had been brought to so untimely an end. For him he cherished true pity. He regarded him as the son of Saul the anointed of the Lord, a man forced probably into a position of danger by stronger wills, and at least mistaken in his views as to what was best for the tribes on the death of his father; and hence, with the generosity so characteristic of him, he had his few remains buried with all honour in the sepulchre of his distinguished captain. Here comes out the unworldliness of David's character. Success in life and rise to a high position too often render men indifferent to those on whom fortune has not smiled. There are many like Ishbosheth—men who have been pushed into positions for which they were unfitted, or have been swayed by feeble reasons of their own into a course of life not useful, or have striven in vain against great social obstacles, and so have come to disappointment and grief. As our Lord was compassionate and considerate of the lowly, so all who cherish his spirit will find out means of showing kindness to the unfortunate, even though they may have been in the position of opponents.

HOMILIES BY VARIOUS AUTHORS.

Vers. 1—3.—(MAHANAIM.) *The unhappy lot of Ishbosheth.* Of the varied types of character which these chapters furnish, that which appears in Ishbosheth (Eshbaal, 1 Chron. viii. 33) is a most pitiable one. The last surviving son of Saul, he bore little resemblance to his heroic father; owed his life to his incapacity for military enterprise; was the legitimate successor of Saul according to the law of Oriental succession; after the brief suspense in which the elders of Israel seemed disposed to accept David as king (ch. ii. 7; iii. 17), was taken under the patronage of Abner; at the end of five years was fully recognized, being forty years old; and reigned two years (ch. ii. 10). It is uncertain how far he was aware of David's Divine designation to the throne, and consciously opposed its fulfilment; and, since the latter was not chosen by the elders, he was not guilty of usurpation. Although David could not speak of him as king, he called him "a righteous person" (ver. 11)—"a man who had done no one any harm" (Josephus)—in the same magnanimous spirit as he always exhibited toward the house of Saul. He was: 1. *Raised to a position for which he was unfit.* "The Scripture presents in him a living example of how the sacredly held right of legitimate inheritance has no root when it is not ennobled by vigorous personality. When the Divine calling is lacking, no legitimate pretensions help" (Cassel). He was destitute of mental force, courage, and energy; ambitious of royal honour and ease; not of royal service and beneficence. The highest offices should be held by the best men. In an ideal state of society it cannot be otherwise; but in its actual condition we often see "servants upon horses, and princes walking as servants upon the earth" (Eccles. x. 7). He who seeks or consents to occupy a position of influence and responsibility for which he is unfit, and those who seek or accept his appointment to it, inflict a serious injury upon themselves and one another. The rule of the "bramble" results in the destruction of all the trees of the forest (Judg. x. 15). 2. *Deprived of the support on which he relied.* "Abner was dead;" by whom he had been exalted and sustained, and to whom, rather than to God, he looked for counsel and help. Although he had alienated him by imprudent remonstrance (ch. iii. 7), yet "he may have hoped to obtain an honourable satisfaction by his mediation" (Hengstenberg). This hope was now cut off. "Cursed be the man that trusteth in man," etc. (Jer. xvii. 5; Ps. cxliii. 3, 4). 3. *Reduced to a condition of extreme weakness.* "His hands became feeble." Nothing remained but unconditional submission or ineffectual and hopeless resistance. He was prepared for neither, and surrendered himself to despair; suffering the consequences of his own "foolishness" (Prov. xix. 3). 4. *Contributory to the distress of a whole people.* "And all Israel was troubled"—agitated, alarmed, confounded, desponding; having no confidence in his ability, participating in his fears, and, like him, experiencing the effects of former errors. "By his death the treaty with David was broken off; or there was no one to manage it with such authority and prudence as Abner had done" (Patrick). 5. *Exposed to the villainy of unfaithful servants.* "And Saul's son had two men," etc. They belonged to his own tribe, and should have been his protectors; served him in prosperity, when he could reward them; but turned against him in adversity, when he could no longer serve their interests; and, although they had suffered no wrong at his hands (ver. 11), acted toward him unjustly and with "treasonous malice," craft, and cruelty. 6. *Smitten at a season of apparent security.* "At noon, in his own house, upon his bed;" where he sought a brief repose, and slept to wake no more. He was left unguarded, and perished "unawares" (Luke xxi. 34). His head was buried "in the sepulchre of Abner in Hebron;" and the opposition to "the house of David" was at an end. None survived of "the house of Saul" save an afflicted son of Jonathan (ver. 4), who could be supposed to have any claim to the crown. 7. *Removed as the last obstacle to the accession of a worthier man.* And herein the overruling providence of God again appears in bringing to pass "the word of the Lord by Samuel" (ch. i. 1, 2). "It is significant that the destruction of Saul's house and kingdom should have issued from Beeroth, the Gibeonite city (ch. xxi. 1, 2)" ('Speaker's Commentary').—D.

Ver. 4.—(GIBEAH.) *An unfortunate prince: a sermon to children.* Mephibosheth was the only son of Jonathan, the friend of David and eldest son of King Saul. When he was five years old the country was invaded by the Philistines (1 Sam. xxix. 1), his father went forth with the king from Gibeah to fight against them in Jezreel, and he was left at home in the care of a nurse (his mother probably being dead). They waited anxiously for news of the conflict; and at length there came a messenger saying that the battle was lost, the king and Jonathan were dead, and the terrible Philistines were coming to plunder and burn the place. The nurse caught up the child, and carried him away on her shoulder; but in her flight across the hills she stumbled, and the little prince fell, was hurt in both his feet, and became a helpless cripple for the rest of his days.

I. CHILDHOOD IS BESET BY MANY PERILS. No other creature on earth is weaker, more helpless or dependent at the commencement of life, than a child. He is peculiarly liable to accident and susceptible to disease; incapable of defending himself from harm or preserving his own life; and is cast entirely upon the care of others. A little neglect on their part may prove fatal. More than a fourth of all the children that are born die before they are five years old. There is the still greater danger to your souls of being allowed to grow up in ignorance and led into "the way of transgressors," stumbling and perishing therein (Matt. xviii. 6). Be *thankful* to your parents, nurses, and teachers for their care over you; still more to your heavenly Father who has taught them such care, appointed his holy angels to be your guardians, sent his Son to bless you, and himself loves, preserves, watches over you, and seeks your salvation (Matt. xviii. 10—14).

II. EVEN A PRINCE IS NOT FREE FROM MISFORTUNE. You may sometimes wish that you belonged to a royal or wealthy family, lived in a palace, and had numerous servants to wait upon you; supposing that you would be happier than you are. Well, here is a prince; yet motherless, fatherless, homeless, helpless, and hopeless. How much better is your condition than that of this poor little orphan cripple! No condition of life is above the reach of trouble; none beneath the possession of enjoyment. Envy not the lot of others, nor fret and be dissatisfied with your own. Hear a fable of *three little fishes* that dwelt in a beautiful stream. On being asked what they wished for, one said, "Wings," and when these grew he flew away so high and so far that he could not get back, sank exhausted, and breathed his last; another said, "Knowledge," and when he obtained it, became anxious and fearful, and durst not touch a fly or a worm or eat any food, lest it should contain a fatal bait, pined away and died; the third said, "I wish for nothing, but am contented with my lot," and this little fish had a long and happy life. Have you not heard of the apostle who was a prisoner for Jesus' sake, and said, "I have learned in whatsoever state I am therewith to be *content*" (Phil. iv. 11)?

> "There is a cross in every lot,
> And an earnest need for prayer;
> But a lowly heart that leans on thee
> Is happy anywhere."

When a little blind girl was asked the reason of her affliction, she replied, "Even so, Father, for so it seemed good in thy sight."

III. THE UNFORTUNATE ARE NEVER LEFT WITHOUT A FRIEND. And "a friend in need is a friend indeed." What became of Mephibosheth? He was carried beyond the river Jordan, out of the reach of the Philistines; found a home "in the house of Machir, the son of Ammiel, in Lo-debar" (ch. ix. 4; xvii. 27), in the neighbourhood of Mahanaim, among the mountains of Gilead; was treated with kindness; and dwelt in a place of safety until he became a man. Only a few persons knew where he lived, or whether he were alive; and when King David heard of him, he invited him to Jerusalem, that he might show him kindness "for Jonathan's sake." Affliction appeals to our pity, and tends to call forth our sympathy and help. We should never despise the unfortunate nor mock at their misfortune; but always try to do them good. Above all, in our trouble we should *trust in God*, in whom "the fatherless findeth mercy" (Hos. xiv. 3). "When my father and mother forsake me, then the Lord will take me up" (Ps. xxvii. 10).

IV. A GREAT MISFORTUNE OFTEN PROVES A GREAT BLESSING. If Mephibosheth had not been made lame by the accident of his childhood, he would have been tempted to aim at the crown, and might have rushed into ambitious and godless enterprises as others did, and perished in like manner. As it was, he spent his days in quietness and peace. His affliction was the means of making him humble, thankful, patient, and devout. His father's property was restored to him by his father's friend; and he had an honourable place assigned to him at the royal table (ch. ix. 13). How often is an orphan taught by the loss of his father to seek his father's God! The hand of God overrules evil for good. And all earthly trouble, when endured in a right spirit, is a preparation for a heavenly home.—D.

Vers. 5—8.—(MAHANAIM.) *Assassins.* " And they brought the head of Ishbosheth unto David to Hebron" (ver. 8). 1. What useful *purpose* can the record of the atrocious deeds of such men serve? To throw light upon the condition of the age in which they occurred. To confirm inspired testimony concerning human depravity (Ps. xiv.). To exhibit the tendency of the evil principles and passions by which these men were actuated, and incite hatred and abhorrence of them. To show that the wickedness of the wicked is subject to restraint and returns upon their own heads in significant punishment. To make us grateful for our preservation from crime and from calamity; thankful for the improved condition of society, and zealous for its further advancement. 2. The crime of the two brothers, Baanah and Rechab, which has given them an infamous immortality, was *not an ordinary murder.* What their former course had been, and whether they were influenced by any other motive besides the love of gain, we know not. But in taking away the life of the head of their tribe, the ruler under whom they held their position, and in their subsequent conduct, they acted disloyally, ungratefully, deceitfully, basely. Notice their—

I. DELIBERATE TREASON. Having lost the feeling of reverence and obligation, they marked the helplessness of Ishbosheth, and resolved to take advantage of it; consulted together as to the time and means of effecting their design; "went, and came about the heat of the day," etc. (ver. 5); "and behold, the woman who kept the door of the house winnowed wheat, and she slumbered and slept. And the brothers Rechab and Baanah got through unobserved," etc. (LXX.). 1. In proportion to the duty of men to do good to others is their guilt in doing them evil. 2. Premeditated sin greatly aggravates its guilt. 3. Those whose hearts are set on crime are lured on by circumstances to its commission.

II. HEARTLESS CRUELTY. "He lay on his bed in his bed-chamber," taking his midday siesta, "and they smote him" etc. (ver. 7). Men of violence, with more than the ordinary fierceness of their tribe, they "murdered sleep, the innocent sleep," without pity and without compunction, being "past feeling;" escaped with their ghastly trophy; and "gat them away through the plain [of the Jordan] all night" to Hebron (a distance of sixty miles), knowing not that they were swiftly pursued by *nemesis* with unerring aim, and hurrying to their doom (Acts xxviii. 4).

III. HYPOCRITICAL MEANNESS. "Behold the head of Ishbosheth thine enemy," etc. (ver. 8). In order to gain the favour of David they hesitated not to blacken the character of their former master by attributing to him feelings of personal revenge; called him their lord the king; and represented their crime as an act of judgment performed by them under the sanction of Jehovah. How often do ungodly men profanely and hypocritically use the name of God when it suits their purpose; and even paint their shameful villainies as praiseworthy virtues! "Hypocrisy is the homage which vice pays to virtue."

IV. MERCENARY SELFISHNESS. Like the Amalekite (ch. i. 2), they sought, not David's welfare, but their own interest (ver. 10). Hence "their feet were swift to shed blood" (Isa. lix. 7; Rom. iii. 9—18), and "their mouth was full of deceit" (Ps. x. 3—10). "Cursed be he that taketh reward to slay an innocent person" (Deut. xxvii. 26). For thirty pieces of silver Judas betrayed the Lord.

V. SELF-BLINDED MISJUDGMENT. They were probably acquainted with the manner in which Abner had been treated (ch. iii. 20) and with the impunity of his murderer; and not unnaturally supposed that whatever promoted the interests of David would be pleasing to him. The nature of the wicked is ever to measure others by themselves. Their ruling motive gives its colouring to their views of everything, and leads them to attribute to the same motive actions which are due to one entirely different. Their delusion is sometimes suddenly dispelled, and they fall into the pit which they have digged (Ps. vii. 15; xxxvii. 15). "Hell is truth discovered too late."

VI. JUSTLY DESERVED DOOM. (Ver. 12.) " David acted with strict justice in this case also, not only to prove to the people that he had neither commanded nor approved the murder, but from heartfelt abhorrence of such crimes and to keep his conscience void of offence toward God and toward man " (Keil). "Indeed, in a war of five years' continuance, which followed upon Saul's death, David never lifted up his sword against a subject; and at the end of it he punished no rebel; he remembered no offence but the murder of his rival." " Though Mephibosheth (the next avenger of blood) was lame and could not overtake them, yet God's justice followed and punished them when they little expected " (Wordsworth).—D.

Vers. 9—11.—(HEBRON.) *A good man's motto.* " As Jehovah liveth, who hath redeemed my soul out of all adversity," etc. 1. An *oath*, such as David took, is properly an act of worship—a direct and solemn appeal to God as a witness, in confirmation of an assertion or of a promise or expressed obligation. There is implied an imprecation of Divine displeasure if the truth be not spoken or the engagement be not fulfilled. It was customary from ancient times (Gen. xiv. 22; xxi. 23); often enjoined in the Law (Deut. vi. 13; Exod. xxii. 10); and served important purposes (Heb. vi. 16). Nor is it absolutely prohibited under the Christian dispensation (Matt. xxvi. 63; Rom. i. 9; 2 Cor. i. 23; Phil. i. 8). "The Saviour forbids absolutely such oaths only as are hostile to the reverence that is due to God" (Tholuck, 'Serm. on the Mount;' Hodge, 'Syst. Theology,' iii. 307; Paley; Dymond, 'Essays'). 2. Baanah and Rechab virtually claimed the Divine sanction to their deed, which, they said, was an act of judgment on David's enemies, and a means of preserving his life. But David could not admit their claim, and would have no part in their crime, however it might seem to promote his interest; and (lifting up his right hand toward heaven, Deut. xxxii. 40) he appealed to the *living God*, on whom, and not on man, least of all on man's wickedness, the preservation of his life depended, in confirmation of his purpose to inflict upon them the punishment of death, which was more richly deserved by them than by one on whom he formerly inflicted it when he confessed to a similar deed. 3. His appeal, considered with reference to the principles and feelings it involved, may be regarded as a statement of the *motto of his life* and expressive of—

I. BELIEF IN THE LIVING GOD. "Living (is) Jehovah," equivalent to " as surely as Jehovah liveth " (Judg. viii. 19; Ruth iii. 13; 1 Sam. xx. 3; xxv. 34; xxix. 6; Jer. xxxviii. 16, "who has made for us this soul "). " Along with the name of God, the person swearing would at the same time designate his other attributes, his power and greatness, or whatever else of the essence of this God appeared to him at the moment of swearing of special significance " (Ewald, 'Antiquities'). "Jehovah liveth" (ch. xxii. 47; 1 Sam. xvii. 26). A godly man believes in: 1. His actual *existence* and self-originated, personal, independent life. With him "is the fountain of life " (Ps. xxxvi. 9). He " hath life in himself " (John v. 26). He "only hath immortality " (1 Tim. vi. 16). The life of all creatures he gives, sustains, or takes away as it pleases him. 2. His immediate *presence* and accurate observation of everything as it really is, every thought, word, and action; and his approbation or disapprobation of it, according to its moral character. He is "a true and faithful Witness" (Jer. xlii. 3; Isa. lxv. 16). 3. His active *intervention* in human affairs, with wisdom and might, justice and mercy. " He is the living God, and an everlasting King" (Jer. x. 10), and gives to every man his due reward (Heb. xi. 6). Faith is not merely a general persuasion of these sublime truths, but also an intense realization of them, and a personal surrender to their influence. It is "an intelligent conviction of the truth, a hearty affection for the truth, and a practical submission to the truth."

II. GRATITUDE FOR PAST DELIVERANCE. "Who hath redeemed my soul out of all adversity "—an expression often on the lips of David (1 Kings i. 29; Ps. xxv. 22; xxxiv. 22; ciii. 4; cxvi. 8), and never uttered without thankfulness to God. 1. The path of even a good man is beset by many *dangers.* What a scene of peril was David's life from his youth upwards (ch. xix. 7)! 2. He traces his *deliverance* from them to the hand of God, and sees therein an evidence of his loving, constant, and distinguishing care for his " soul." 3. He is wont to cherish the *recollection* of such deliverance; and is incited thereby to "speak the praise of the Lord." Nothing is more becoming or beneficial than a thankful spirit; but it is by no means a common possession.

" Some murmur when their sky is clear
		And wholly bright to view,
	If one small speck of dark appear
		In their great heaven of blue;
	And some with thankful love are filled,
		If but one streak of light,
	One ray of God's good mercy, gild
		The darkness of their night."

							(Trench.)

III. CONSCIOUSNESS OF PRESENT RESPONSIBILITY. A good man feels that he is accountable to God; not impelled by forces over which he has no control, nor liberated from moral law; but, whilst free to act, bound by the highest motives to obey. His faith in the living God quickens his conscience, and shows him plainly the way of duty; his gratitude for past deliverance incites him to walk therein. 1. By abhorring that which is evil, and avoiding it. 2. By sincerity of heart, speaking the truth, and doing what is just and right. 3. By using the authority and power entrusted to him, not according to his own will and for selfish ends, but according to the will of God, and for his honour and the welfare of men. His motto is *Ich dien* (" I serve "). He ever lives under a sense of obligation, and finds in faithful service his strength and joy (John iv. 34). "I *must* work " (John ix. 4). "Remember now and always that life is no idle dream, but a solemn reality; based upon eternity, and encompassed by eternity. Find out your task: stand to it: the night cometh when no man can work" (Carlyle).

IV. CONFIDENCE IN FUTURE PRESERVATION. The path of peril is not yet past. But a good man looks to God rather than to men to protect him against the wrath of men and deliver him from all evil. And his confidence is strong, because of: 1. His conviction of the Divine faithfulness. " Jehovah liveth," to fulfil both his promises and his threatenings. 2. His experience of the Divine favour (see 1 Sam. xvii. 32—37). 3. His obedience to the Divine will, and express assurances of safety and of a "crown of life " to every faithful servant. "The righteous hath hope in his death," "Into thine hand I commit my spirit: thou hast redeemed me, O Lord God of truth" (Ps. xxxi. 5). "The foundation of David's character is a firm unshaken trust in Jehovah, a bright and most spiritual view of creation and the government of the world, a sensitive awe of the Holy One of Israel, a striving ever to be true to him, and a strong desire to return after errors and transgressions" (Ewald).—D.

Ver. 12.—(HEBRON.) *The reward of the wicked.* This book contains an account of many sudden and violent deaths (in addition to those that took place in battle) by assassination, suicide (ch. xvii. 23), the direct judgment of God (ch. vi. 7), the judicial sentence of man. Capital punishment for murder was of old deemed right and necessary and divinely sanctioned (see ch. i. 13—16). In this *execution*, we see that: 1. The *agents* by whom the purposes of God are effected (ver. 8) without his commission and from selfish motives are not entitled to the reward of faithful service, although they sometimes expect to obtain it, being turned aside by " a deceived heart." 2. The *reward* which wicked men obtain for their wickedness is the opposite of that which they expect (ver. 10). Even if they gain their immediate object, they fail to find therein the happiness they anticipated, and sooner or later suffer loss and woe. 3. The *guilt* of the crime which such men commit against a fellow-man is aggravated by his innocence and the circumstances under which the crime is committed. " A righteous person in his own house upon his bed." 4. The *authority* to which they vainly appeal in justification of their conduct surely requires their condemnation. " He will by no means clear the guilty" (Exod. xxxiv. 7). What they did as private persons to Ishbosheth without Divine commission, David, as king and " minister of God," was commissioned to do to them, and "take them away from the land " which the Lord had given, but which they had polluted and were unworthy to enjoy. "Gather not my soul with sinners, nor my life with bloody men" (Ps. xxvi. 9). 5. The *example* afforded by a severe and signal punishment is sometimes necessary to maintain public justice; to manifest the evil of sin and the certainty of retribution; to deter others from wrong-doing. The hands that did the deed and the feet that "ran eagerly for reward " were cut off, and their bodies exposed to open shame.

"He that's merciful
Unto the bad is cruel to the good."

6. The *termination* of strife in a land is usually attended with melancholy circumstances. "And they took the head of Ishbosheth," etc. 7. The saddest events are often succeeded by a season of gladness (1 Chron. xii. 40) and *prosperity*, and even directly conducive to it. With the death of Ishbosheth "the whole resistance to David's power collapses;" and "thus at last, not by his own act, but through circumstances over which he had no control—allowed by him who gives liberty to each man, though he overrules the darkest deeds of the wicked for the evolving of good—David was left undisputed claimant to the throne of Israel. Faith, patience, and integrity were vindicated; the Divine promise to David had come true in the course of natural events; and all this was better far than even if Saul had voluntarily resigned his place or Abner succeeded in his plans" (Edersheim). "Thus God will make all the sins of evil men to be one day ministerial to the extension and final settlement of the universal dominion of Christ" (Wordsworth).—D.

Ver. 4.—*A lifelong affliction.* Wars inflict innumerable evils which find no place in the history of them. This verse affords an illustration. When news reached the household of Saul that he and his sons had been slain in battle, a grandson, a boy of five years, was hurriedly borne away by his nurse, and, falling, was lamed in both feet. His lameness continued throughout life, and involved him in serious disadvantages and troubles. There are many who, like Mephibosheth, are weak and suffering from childhood to death. Either inheriting weakness of constitution, or deriving it from some early attack of disease, or injured through accident or the carelessness of those in charge of them when children, they are permanently disabled more or less. With reference to such troubles, notice—

I. THE EVILS THEY INVOLVE. 1. *Sometimes constant bodily suffering.* 2. *Always many privations.* Incapacity for active *employments* and their emoluments. Yet it is wonderful how far this may be conquered. The writer knew a lady who was one of many pupils who learnt drawing from a teacher born without arms or legs, but who, by indomitable perseverance, became proficient in the art. Such affliction also involves inability to share in many *enjoyments*. 3. *Much dependence on others.* And hence liability to be neglected, ill treated, imposed upon, robbed, etc. Ziba's conduct to Mephibosheth is an instance (ch. xvi. 3, 4; xix. 24—27). 4. *Various temptations.* To despondency, spiritlessness, indolence; to discontent, murmuring, fretfulness; to resentment against those who may have occasioned the affliction; to envy of such as are free from similar trial.

II. THE DUTIES THEY IMPOSE. 1. *Trustful resignation and patience.* However they may have arisen, they are the appointment of the infinitely wise and good Father, who thereby calls for and exercises faith and submission. If active service of God be impossible, the service of patient endurance is not, and may be equally acceptable and useful. 2. *Thankfulness.* For the blessings which remain, and those of which the affliction is a channel; and for the affliction itself, as a sign of God's fatherly love and care. 3. *Watchfulness against the peculiar temptations of such a condition.* 4. *Endeavours after the good which is attainable notwithstanding, or by means of, the affliction.*

III. THE ALLEVIATIONS AND COMPENSATIONS BY WHICH THEY ARE OFTEN ATTENDED. 1. *Larger enjoyment of spiritual blessings.* If the earthly is a good deal closed by such a trouble, the heavenly is all the more open and accessible. The needs of the soul may be the more constantly felt, and their supply the more habitually sought. Reading, reflection, and prayer may be more practised. The grace of God may be more abundantly enjoyed. Constant affliction brings the Christian into fuller communion with the sufferings of Christ, and larger participation of his Spirit and realization of his love and salvation. The consolation received may outweigh the suffering. 2. Hence *a higher Christian life and more beautiful Christian character* are often attained by those who are so afflicted. They become more fully "partakers of God's holiness." 3. *Human sympathy and kindness are usually enjoyed in greater measure and continuance.* A source both of pleasure and profit. 4. Even *the power for good over others is often increased.* The increased Christian intelligence and force and beauty of character, the patience, cheerfulness, and thankfulness displayed, move the hearts of others towards him who is their source. The habitual sufferer might often adopt St. Paul's words in 2 Cor. iv. 10—12; xii. 9, 10. His weakness may be made the occasion of the more powerful manifestation of the living energy of Christ through him for the spiritual profit of relatives and friends.

IV. How THEY SHOULD BE REGARDED AND TREATED BY OTHERS. 1. *With pity and sympathy.* 2. *With practical assistance.* The weak and suffering are especially commended by our Lord to the care and kindness of the strong. His example enforces his words. To minister consolation, and, where necessary and practicable, material assistance, blesses him that gives as well as him that receives. The lifelong affliction of one may thus become a lifelong discipline and blessing to his benefactors. But to treat the feeble with hardness or contempt, or to take advantage of their weakness for our own selfish purposes, is peculiarly base, and will not be forgotten by him who will condemn, in the day of judgment, even the *neglect* of the poor and suffering (Matt. xxv. 41—46).

Finally: 1. *If we enjoy freedom from lifelong afflictions, or at least serious ones* (for few, perhaps, are quite free from them), *thankfulness should impel us to care the more for those who are burdened with them*; and if we suffer from them, our sympathies should be the keener with fellow-sufferers, and such help as we can render be all the more cheerfully given. 2. *Let those who suffer much and long in this life make sure that their life hereafter shall be free from suffering*, and that their afflictions shall work out for them an eternal greater glory (2 Cor. iv. 17). These unspeakable blessings are the portion of those who have faith in the Lord Jesus Christ, receive his teaching, and follow his directions.—G. W.

Ver. 9.—*Redemption from all adversity.* "As the Lord liveth, who hath redeemed my soul out of all adversity." An expansion of the form of oath common with the Hebrews, "As the Lord liveth." By adding the words, "who hath redeemed," etc., David reminded himself of the goodness of God to him, and kept alive and expressed his gratitude. The same form of oath as used by him occurs in 1 Kings i. 29 (where the words of the original are precisely the same). Occurring thus at the beginning and the end of his reign, we may reasonably conclude that it was employed in the intervening years, reminding him, in the height of his prosperity and power, of the days of adversity which had preceded them, and of him who had rescued and exalted him. This representation of God would probably be more helpful to the piety of David than grander but more general conceptions of him. So shall we find it well to include in our thought of God what he has been to us and done for us individually (comp. Gen. xlviii. 15, 16). As to the words : "redeemed" is not to be taken here in the signification suggested by its etymology, "bought back," "ransomed," but simply "delivered." The use of the words, "my soul," must not lead us to suppose that David is thinking of the "redemption of the soul" in the spiritual sense. He refers to his deliverance from the perils, hardships, and anxieties of his previous life, through the enmity of Saul and his attempts to destroy him. The phrase is substantially equivalent to "me," though it may suggest that the seat of all the "distress" that attends adversity is the soul. The words are suitable to be used—

I. IN VIEW OF ACTUAL DELIVERANCE FROM VARIED OR PROLONGED TROUBLES. As David used them. They recognize and call to mind : 1. *The extent of the deliverance.* "From *all* adversity." The reference is to the past. David did not mean that he had done with adversity. Nor can we in this world use the words in that sense; but as from time to time troubles arise out of which we are delivered, be they adversities in the ordinary sense, or troubles of the soul strictly (temptations, conflicts, falls, pangs of remorse, fears, insensibility, gloom), let us mark and record our deliverance. 2. *The Deliverer.* "The Lord," Jehovah, the God who "liveth." Not self, not men, but God. David had employed his own great powers of thought and action, and had been well served by human helpers, but he does not ascribe his deliverance to the one or the other, but to God. He well knew that all power for self-help, and all human helpers, are the gift of God; that they are effectual through his working with them; and that apart from them God operates in ways transcendental and inexplicable. The greatness and variety of his troubles, the imminence of his perils, the wondrous special incidents which had contributed to his deliverance, all rendered conspicuous the hand of God. To him, therefore, he gave the glory. Most of our lives will, if carefully reviewed, furnish similar proofs of the operation of the living God, not merely of matter and dead laws, and of friends. And we should gratefully recognize and confess his goodness. Hence will spring humility, continuance and increase of thankfulness, and also confidence and hope in respect to future adversities (see 2 Cor. i. 10; 2 Tim. iv. 17, 18).

II. IN VIEW OF THE REDEMPTION FROM ALL EVIL EFFECTED FOR US BY OUR LORD JESUS CHRIST. The word "redeem" will in this case have the full signification of "ransom by payment of a price." We have "redemption through his blood, the forgiveness of sins." In redeeming us from our sins, he redeemed us from all kinds and degrees of evil. All who accept him as their Redeemer and Lord are thus assured of complete deliverance from all that now distresses them, and from all in the future world that would have distressed them but for his redeeming work; and, in the certainty that the purposes of his death will be accomplished, may speak of their deliverance as already effected. Nor can they fail to remember with unutterable thankfulness and perpetual thanksgiving the redemption thus wrought for them.

III. BY THOSE WHO HAVE EXPERIENCED FINAL AND COMPLETE DELIVERANCE FROM ALL THE EVILS OF THIS PRESENT WORLD. What a blessed thing it will be to look back on all the evils of this present state, including death itself, as actually *past!* and to look forward to an eternity of complete freedom from evil, of full enjoyment of good! No sin, no want, no sickness, no pain, no sorrow, no peril; but perfect peace, perfect service of God, perfect communion with him, "fulness of joy" and "pleasures for evermore" (Ps. xvi. 11; Rev. vii. 14—17; xxi. 4). And evermore will the "redeemed from the earth" be mindful of their Deliverer, and unite in praise of God and the Lamb. In view of this glorious and complete redemption: 1. Let Christians be patient and thankful while enduring the adversities which belong to their condition on earth. 2. Take heed lest, redemption being effected, you fail to attain to its actual experience. To reject Christ is to reject deliverance from death and misery.—G. W.

EXPOSITION.

CHAPTER V.

Ver. 1.—**Then came all the tribes of Israel.** As Ishbosheth reigned only two years, and David's reign at Hebron lasted for seven years and a half, there is an interval of more than five years to be accounted for; and we have given reason for believing (see note on ch. ii. 10) that it must be placed after the death of Ishbosheth. The treacherous murder of Abner, and the tragic fate of Ishbosheth following upon it so rapidly, must have filled all Israel with horror, and made them look upon David as "a bloody man" (ch. xvi. 8). But gradually his innocence became clear to all except inveterate partisans, and as the prejudice against him passed away, the evident advantage of union under so able a ruler would force itself upon their attention, and their decision would be hastened by the advantage which the Philistines would be sure to take of their anarchy. How much they had profited by it we gather from the haste with which they endeavoured to crush David's kingdom. The enormous gathering at Hebron to anoint David king proves not merely the unanimity of the tribes, but that his election

was the result of long preparation and arrangement. We have fuller details of it in 1 Chron. xii. 23—40, where we learn that the people assembled in large numbers, the total being computed in the 'Speaker's Commentary' at 348,222; and it is remarkable that of this vast array only sixteen thousand nine hundred came from the tribes of Judah, Simeon, and Benjamin, which were situated in the neighbourhood of Hebron. On the other hand, the two and a half trans-Jordanic tribes sent no less than a hundred and twenty thousand men, and the three unimportant tribes of Zebulun, Asher, and Naphtali mustered a hundred and eighteen thousand; while Issachar was content to send only two hundred, who were all, however, "men that had understanding . . . and their brethren were at their commandment." These words suggest the probable explanation of the disparity in the numbers, which to many seems so strange that they think they must be corrupt. Each tribe settled for itself in what way it would be represented, and the more distant sent a large proportion of their men of military age on what would be an enjoyable holiday. As they spent three days at Hebron, the expedition would occupy, even for those most remote, little more than a week; and it was well worth the while of the tribes thus to come together. It made them feel the value of unity, and gave them a knowledge of their strength. Their tribal independence during the time of the judges had made them too weak even to maintain their liberty; but now, welded by the kingly power into a nation, they soon, not only won freedom for themselves, but placed their yoke upon the shoulders of their neighbours. As for the difficulty of supplying them with food, all would bring victuals from home; and the neighbouring tribes showed great hospitality. Especially we read that those who were nigh unto Hebron, "even as far as Issachar and Zebulun and Naphtali, brought bread on asses, and on camels, and on mules, and on oxen, victual of meal, cakes of figs, and clusters of raisins, and wine, and oil, and oxen, and sheep in abundance: for there was joy in Israel" (1 Chron. xii. 40). It was a grand national festival, joyously kept because the people saw in the election of David an end to all their troubles; and so vast a gathering overbore all opposition, and gave both to them and their king the consciousness of their might. But while we find in the Book of Chronicles the account of this mighty multitude, it is here (ver. 3) expressly said that it was the elders who made a league with David, and anointed him king. The people by their presence testified their joyful assent to what was done; but David's election was made legitimate by the decision of the constituted authorities in each tribe. It would be most interesting to know the various steps taken, and how the agitation grew and spread from tribe to tribe, until all hesitation and resistance were overcome. But the object of this book is to show us the great qualities, the sin, the repentance, and the punishment of the man who added to the old routine of sacrifice bright services of song, and who was the author of that book of devotion which to this day best expresses the feelings of the heart, as well in the joys as in the sorrows of life. The manner of his election throws no light upon his character, and is passed over. Enough to know that in those five years after Ishbosheth's murder David won the approval of all Israel, and that his appointment to the kingdom was by the free choice of the tribes, acting in a legitimate manner, and sending each their elders to Hebron to notify to David their consent; and that their decision was ratified by this joyful gathering of a mighty multitude from all parts of the land. Three reasons are given by the elders for David's election, and we may be sure that they represent the arguments used in their popular assemblies.

The first, that they were David's bone and flesh. In other words, the tribes were all of one race, and united by the closest ties of relationship. For the descendants of a common ancestor to be at war with one another was both morally and politically wrong. The second, that David had been their actual leader in war even in Saul's time. His personal qualities, therefore, justified their choice of him to be their deliverer from the evils which had overwhelmed the land after the disastrous defeat at Gilboa, when Saul had no longer the aid of David's presence. The third, that Jehovah had by the mouth of his prophet given the throne to David. It is remarkable that the elders place this last. Their view probably was that the Divine command must be proved by outward circumstances, that so reason might confirm faith. So Saul's public appointment by Samuel was ratified by the people only after he had shown himself worthy to be a king by the defeat of the Ammonites.

Ver. 2.—**Thou shalt feed.** In biblical language the pastoral office is that of the civil and not of the spiritual ruler. **Captain**; Hebrew, *nagid*, prince; so the Revised Version (and see note on 1 Sam. ix. 16). The word refers not to military matters, but to the civil administration. David had proved himself a competent leader in war when Saul was king. What Jehovah now gives is the government of Israel in time of peace. The Authorized Version renders "captain" from not perceiving that the Divine promise ensured to David far more than a military chieftainship.

Ver. 3.—**A league.** The early kings of Israel were not invested with despotic power. Thus, on Saul's appointment, "Samuel wrote in a book the manner of the kingdom" (1 Sam. x. 25, made most emphatic in the Revised Version by the note in the margin, that the Hebrew is "the book"). The revolt against Rehoboam was the result of the too great extension of the royal power in the days of Solomon (1 Kings xii. 4). Though subsequently the kings seemed to have retained their supremacy, yet when the good and patriotic Jehoiada restored the family of David to the throne, he reverted to the old ways, and "made a covenant between the king and the people" (2 Kings xi. 17). Besides personal rights, the tribes, accustomed to their own leaders, and unused to yield obedience to a central authority, would certainly stipulate for a large measure of tribal independence, and the management of local matters by themselves. **They anointed David king.** This was the public ratification of Samuel's anointing, and by it David became *de facto*, as well as *de jure*, king. The prophets could not give any right over the people without the consent of the people themselves. But all religious men would see in the Divine command an obligation upon their conscience to accept as their king the man whom the prophet had anointed; and Saul acted in an irreligious manner in seeking to frustrate God's will. And this impiety culminated in his murder of the priests at Nob, which was the open avowal that he would trample all scruples of conscience underfoot.

Ver. 4.—**David was thirty years old.** As David was probably about eighteen or nineteen years of age at the time of his combat with Goliath, the events recorded in 1 Sam. xvii.—xxxi. must have occupied about ten or eleven years.

Ver. 6.—**The king and his men went to Jerusalem.** This expedition took place immediately after David's coronation, and probably he was moved to it by the presence of so large a number of the warriors of Israel. He had long foreseen the arrival of the time when he would be king of all the tribes, and must have debated in his mind the problem of his future capital. He could not remain in Hebron, as it was too far to the south, nor would haughty tribes such as Ephraim have consented to be merged into Judah. On the other hand, he could not move far away, as Judah was his main strength. But living in its neighbourhood, he must often have noticed the remarkable position of the city of Jebus, and admired its rock-girt strength (Ps. xlviii. 2). Though the Jebusites had been conquered by Joshua (Josh. xi. 3), and Jerusalem captured (Judg. i. 8), yet, as the children of Judah did not occupy it, but "set the city on fire," it seems to have been soon repeopled by its old inhabitants, who there maintained their independence, and, owing to the impregnable nature of its site, could not be treated as Saul treated the Gibeonite inhabitants of Beeroth. Even subsequently, the Jebusite chief who possessed what probably was Mount Moriah, still bore the titular rank of king; for the words in ch. xxiv. 23 literally are, "All this did Araunah the king give unto the king." The explanation of this long independence of the Jebusites is to be found not only in the feebleness of the tribes during the troubled times of the judges, but even more in the conformation of the site of their stronghold. Jerusalem is situated on the edge of the precipitous wall which forms the western boundary of the valley of the Jordan, a i occupies a promontory, on three sides of which are ravines so abrupt and steep that, were it not for their vast depth, they might seem to have been the work of man. On the north side alone it is open to attack, but even there, when the besieger has obtained

an entrance, he finds the city divided by another ravine into two parts; whereof the western portion contains the strong citadel of Mount Zion, while the eastern and smaller portion contains the less elevated mountain of Moriah. Though actually raised above the sea-level several hundred feet less than Hebron, it seems to the eye more emphatically a mountain-city; and being well-nigh encircled by the valleys of Ben-Hinnom and Jehoshaphat, it seems to sit enthroned above the Jordan valley, compared with which it enjoys a cool and refreshing climate. To its inhabitants it was "beautiful in elevation, the joy of the whole earth" (Ps. xlviii. 2, Revised Version); to the exiles it was "the city of God," to which their hearts ever turned; to us Christians it is the type of Christ's Church on earth, and of his kingdom in heaven. It was an act worthy of David's genius to foresee the great future of the place, and to inaugurate his kingdom by its capture. We gather from Ezek. xvi. 45 that at the time when the Hittites were the dominant race in Syria, Jerusalem was one of their fortresses. The name is a dual, literally *Yerushalaim*, and probably the town was so called because it consisted of two parts—the upper and the lower city. *Shalaïm* means the "two Salems," thus carrying our minds back to the city of Melchizedek (Gen. xiv. 18). In Ps. lxxvi. 2 Salem is apparently contrasted with Zion, and so would be the lower town, containing Mount Moriah. Of the other part of the word, *Yeru*, numerous derivations are given, of which the only probable one is that which connects it with "Yehovah-yireh "—" God will see to it," the name given to the spot where Abraham on this mountain offered a vicarious sacrifice for his son. We must, however, bear in mind that towns retain the names which they bore in primitive times, and that the name of a Hittite fortress belongs probably to the language of that people. **Except thou take away the blind and the lame, thou shalt not come in hither.** These words have been a sore puzzle to commentators, and many strange explanations have been given. Rashi says that the *blind* meant Isaac, and the *lame* Jacob, and that the words referred to an old compact by which Abraham gave Jerusalem to the Jebusites, and that Isaac and Jacob had confirmed this agreement. Unless, then, David was prepared to violate this covenant, he must abstain from the attack. We get no help from 1 Chron. xi. 5, as the words are there omitted, probably because they were not supposed to have any important meaning. The Orientals delighted in dark sayings, and possibly there was here some local reference which the people of Jerusalem would understand, but which is lost for us. But evidently it was a boastful defiance, and may mean that the Jebusites pretended that it would be enough to post only their feeblest men, the blind and the lame, for defence, and that David would try in vain to break through them. **Thinking;** Hebrew, *to say;* answering to our phrase "that is." It should be translated, "meaning."

Ver. 7.—The stronghold of Zion : the same is the city of David. Zion was the hill on the south-western side of the city ; but we learn from ver. 9 that the Jebusites had not occupied the whole of it, but a part only, which was their *stronghold,* round which there would be scattered dwellings, as the whole tribe dwelt there. The total area of the hill-top was about sixty acres, and it was now quickly covered with houses, and called "the city of David," after its captor. The view of Dr. Birch and others, that the stronghold of Zion was Ophel, is rendered untenable by the fact that this southern tongue of Mount Moriah is completely commanded by other parts of the hill. According to Gesenius, *Zion* means "sunny;" others render it "the dry hill;" others, "lofty;" and Fürst, "the castle." None of these derivations is of any real value, as the word is probably Hittite.

Ver. 8.—Whosoever getteth up to the gutter. The word rendered "gutter" occurs elsewhere only in Ps. xlii. 7, where it is translated "waterspout." Josephus thinks that it was an underground passage or drain. Ewald argues that it was a precipice, and others that it was a dent or hollow in the rocky face of the ravine, which David had noticed and thought practicable. The view of Josephus, suggested to him probably by his knowledge of the way in which the site of Jerusalem is honeycombed by tunnels, has been wonderfully confirmed by the discoveries made by Sir C. Warren ('Recovery of Jerusalem,' pp. 240, *sqq.*). At the northern end of the Pool of Siloam he found an arched passage gradually narrowing down from a considerable height, till finally there was a passage of only fourteen inches, and as there was a depth of ten inches of water, there were left but four inches of space for breathing. But through this his men struggled, and, at the end of four hours' labour, they reached the light of day at the spring called the Virgin's Fount. Beginning here on a subsequent day, they went along a passage sixty-seven feet in length, and came to a perpendicular shaft leading up through the solid stone of the hill; and, having scaled this, they next came upon a sloping passage, which finally conducted them to a spot on the hill of Ophel within the fortifications. Now, there are reasons for believing that this passage is older than the wall built by

Solomon, and through it, or some such tunnel, Joab and a few men may have worked their way, and so have effected an entrance into the city, which otherwise was impregnable. It was probably the entrance near the Virgin's Fountain which they had observed, and David's words mean, "Whoever will undertake this dangerous enterprise, let him try this underground passage, and when he has entered the fortifications by its means, let him smite the lame and the blind, that are hated of David's soul," because of the boast of the Jebusites, that their cripples were a match for his heroes. It must be noticed, however, that the K'tib, or written text, has "who hate David's soul;" and as this is what the Jewish Massorites found in the manuscripts, it has more authority than their correction. These Jebusites had probably, in their boastful insult, spoken of David with contempt, and even said, like Goliath, that they would give his flesh to the vultures (1 Sam. xvii. 44). We learn from 1 Chron. xi. 6 that David promised the office of commander of the host to the man who undertook this exploit; and when Joab had volunteered and succeeded, he regained thereby the post which he had forfeited by the murder of Abner. **The blind and the lame shall not come into the house.** The proverb is one of contempt for these poor cripples, and forbids the exercise of hospitality to them. Such people, if they took to mendicancy, were to meet with refusal, though at their own homes they were fit objects of charity. This way of describing tramps as "the blind and lame" arose, we are here told, from this Jebusite taunt.

Ver. 9.—David dwelt in the fort. It was the stronghold or citadel of Zion which David took for his abode ; but as he needed space for the dwellings of his mighty men, and for those who would soon flock for trade and security to the capital, David proceeded to fortify the whole of the summit. His works began from "the Millo," rendered "the citadel" by the LXX. Many, deriving the name from a Hebrew root signifying "to fill," think that it was a mound, but Nature had herself supplied fit heights for defence, and it is evident that the place was called "the Millo" when David captured the city. We find "Beth-Millo" also in Judg. ix. 6, 20, where it signifies those who held the citadel of Shechem ; and this Millo at Jerusalem was without doubt the old Jebusite keep, and the explanation of its name must be sought in the Jebusite language. As it formed one of the strongest defences of the city, it was rebuilt by Solomon (1 Kings ix. 24; xi. 27), and repaired by Hezekiah (2 Chron. xxxii. 5) in preparation for the Assyrian attack. Probably it stood at a corner, whence the phrase, "round about from the Millo and inward," or, as it is expressed in 1 Chron. xi. 8, "from the Millo inward," that is, starting from. the Millo, the walls enclosed the space behind it. In the parallel place (1 Chron. xi. 8) we find an interesting addition to the narrative, namely, that "Joab repaired the rest of the city." It appears from this that the Jebusites had occupied a good deal of the ground with their habitations, though probably the number of the tribe was not great ; or possibly there remained old buildings which were the remains of the Hittite city, and which, being of massive construction, were easily made fit once again for human habitation. We see also proof of Joab's great ability in peace as well as in war. He it was who had captured the stronghold, and it was now his office to arrange the streets and plan of the city, and to assign dwellings to David's mighty men. This would be a work sure to cause jealousy and heart-burnings, and no one but Joab, their old commander, could have satisfied them. We find that he assigned to one of them, Uriah the Hittite, a space of ground for a dwelling close to the royal palace. We may suppose, then, that David was now fully reconciled to the "hard sons of Zeruiah " (ch. iii. 39), and in the stern wars which followed David's election, he needed and had the full benefit of their vigour and ability.

Ver. 10.—**David went on, and grew great.** This is the Hebrew phrase for "David grew greater and greater." In this and the six following verses (10—16) we have a summary of David's reign, telling us how he increased in prosperity because of the blessing of "Jehovah God of hosts." The birth of Solomon even is recorded in it, though it took place long afterwards. The insertion in this summary of Hiram's acknowledgment of David proves that this event made a great impression upon the minds of the people.

Ver. 11.—**Hiram King of Tyre.** At first sight it seems as if the Hiram who so greatly aided Solomon in the building of the temple was the same person as David's friend (1 Kings v. 10; 2 Chron. ii. 3), but this identification is disproved by the express statement in 2 Chron. ii. 13, and by the chronology. For granting that this account of Hiram's embassy occurs in a general summary, yet David would not long defer the erection of a palace, and in the history of Bathsheba we find, as a matter of fact, that it was then already built (ch. xi. 2). But as Solomon was grown to manhood at his father's death, David's sin must have been committed not more than nine

or ten years after he became king of all Israel. Now, we are told by Josephus ('Contr. Apion,' i. 18), on the authority of Menander of Ephesus, that Hiram reigned in all thirty years. But in 1 Kings ix. 10—13 we have an account of a transaction with Hiram in Solomon's twentieth year. In another place ('Ant.,' viii. 3. 1) Josephus tells us that Hiram had been King of Tyre eleven years when Solomon, in the fourth year of his reign, began the building of the temple. He would thus have been a contemporary of David for only the last seven or eight years of his reign. But the history of this embassy is given as a proof of David's establishment in his kingdom, and cannot therefore be referred to so late a period in his lifetime, when it would have lost its interest. The improbability of two successive kings having the same name is not, after all, so very great, especially as we do not know what the word *Hiram*, or *Haram*, exactly means. Nor is Menander's statement conclusive against it, where he says that Hiram's father was named Abibal—"Baal is my father." This would probably be an official name, borne by Hiram as the defender of the national religion, or as a priest-king. There is, therefore, no real reason for rejecting the statement in 2 Chron. ii. 13 that Hiram, or as he is there called Huram, David's friend, was the father of the Huram who was Solomon's ally. **Cedar trees.** Cedar wood was greatly valued both for its fragrance and durability, owing to the resin which it contains preserving it from the attacks of insects. Its colour also is soft and pleasing to the eye, as may be seen in the Jerusalem Chamber in Westminster Abbey, the panels of which are of cedar. It did not grow in the Antilibanus, or eastern part of Lebanon, which belonged to Israel, but only in the western part, which belonged to Tyre. Cedar from the time of David became the favourite material at Jerusalem for the interior of houses (Jer. xxii. 14), and Isaiah charges the people of Samaria with pride for not being content with the native sycomores which had satisfied their fathers, but substituting for it this costly foreign timber (Isa. ix. 10). **Carpenters and masons.** The necessity of importing "workers of wood, and workers of stone for walls," as the words literally mean, proves how miserable was the social state of Israel in David's time. Though they had been slaves in Egypt, yet at the Exodus the Israelites had men capable of working in the precious metals and jewellery, in weaving and embroidery, in wood-carving, and even in the cutting of gems (Exod. xxxv. 30—35). During the long anarchy of the judges they had degenerated into a race of agricultural drudges, whom the

Philistines had debarred from the use of even the simplest tools (1 Sam. xiii. 19). Possibly in Saul's time there was a faint restoration of the arts of civilized life (ch. i. 24); but when we find Joab killing Absalom, not with darts, but with pointed stakes (ch. xviii. 14), the weapons probably of most of the foot-soldiers, we see that not much had been done even then in metallurgy; and here earlier in his reign David has to send to Tyre for men who could saw a plank or build a wall. When, then, we call to mind the high state of culture and the magnificence of Solomon's reign, we can form some idea of the vigour with which David raised his subjects from a state of semi-barbarism.

Ver. 12.—**And David perceived.** We may well believe that David had many seasons of despondency and misgiving after he became king. His subjects were brave and energetic, but turbulent, unwilling to obey, and but half-civilized. His election had put an end to civil war at home, but only to arouse the hatred of the enemies who had long oppressed them. The tragical fate, too, of Saul, who, after so many heroic struggles, had seen the earlier glories of his reign fade away, and had sought deliverance from his misery by suicide; all this must have often depressed his spirits. But gradually his fears passed away; and when he had twice defeated the Philistines, and been able to establish his rule, and with it some degree of orderly government throughout the twelve tribes, David saw in all this, and in the embassies from foreign nations, the proof, not of his own ability, but of Jehovah's purpose to **exalt his kingdom for his people Israel's sake.** In this David was still a man after God's own heart, in that he felt himself to be only an instrument for the doing, not his own will, but the purpose of his Divine Master.

Ver. 13.—**David took** him **more concubines.** Thus with increase of power came also the increased gratification of David's weakness and sin. Well for him would it have been if, like Saul, he had been content with one wife. But this enlargement of his harem was gradual, and the list includes all the sons born at Jerusalem. Of these four, namely, Shammuah, Shobab, Nathan, and Solomon, were his children by Bathsheba (see 1 Chron. iii. 5, where the names are differently spelt). Besides a variation in the spelling, two sons are mentioned in Chronicles, Nogah and an earlier Eliphelet, whose names are not given here, perhaps because they died young. From 1 Chron. iii. 9 we learn that only the names of the sons of wives are given in these tables.

Ver. 17.—**But when the Philistines heard.** After the battle of Gilboa the Philistines became the virtual rulers of much of the country west of the Jordan, and probably even David and Judah paid them tribute. On its eastern bank, though Abner kept them from molesting Ishbosheth's kingdom, yet the rule of Saul's house in Ephraim and Benjamin must have been nominal only, and the Philistines would have seen him with pleasure wasting his strength in civil war. After Ishbosheth's death they had tightened their grasp over the central districts of Palestine, though probably content with exacting tribute. They must now have seen with displeasure the consolidation of the tribes under one able ruler. Even in their divided state, the natural strength of the country and the bravery of the people had made it a task too great for the Philistine power entirely to crush Israel's independence. But if they could destroy David before he had had time to establish himself in his kingdom, they would at least prolong indefinitely that feebleness of Israel which had made it so long subject to their dominion. Of this supremacy the Philistines have handed down a token for ever in giving to the whole country the name of Palestine, the Philistines' land. **David ... went down to the hold.** Many commentators identify *the hold* with the cave of Adullam, and certainly the account of the brave deed of three of David's heroes, in breaking through the Philistine garrison of Bethlehem to bring him water thence, gives great probability to this view. For we read there that "the Philistines were encamped in the valley of Rephaim, and that David was then in the hold" (ch. xxiii. 13, 14, where note that the word "hold" has the definite article). There are, however, many difficulties connected with this view; for the cave of Adullam was in the valley of Elah, on the road from Hebron to Philistia (1 Sam. xxii. 1), but the valley of Rephaim is close to Jerusalem (Josh. xv. 8), abutting, in fact, upon the valley of Ben-Hinnom. Baal-Perazim also is in the same neighbourhood, being the rocky height which forms the border of Ben-Hinnom, and bounds the valley of Rephaim on the north. Still, the passage in ch. xxiii. 13, 14 seems too precise to be lightly set aside, and we must suppose, therefore, that the Philistines, alarmed by the gathering of half a million of men and women at Hebron, sent messengers throughout their country to assemble their warriors. It was the weakness of ancient warfare that its vast hosts of people melted away as rapidly as they had gathered. For provisions were soon spent, and the men had to return to their farms and their cattle. Thus David, having used some of that large concourse of strong men for the capture of Jerusalem, was left immediately afterwards with no other protection than that of his "mighty men." Saul had endeavoured to have always round him three thousand trained men (1 Sam. xiii. 2), and David subsequently had probably quite as many (ch. xv. 18); but at this early stage he had probably not many more than he had brought with him from Ziklag to Hebron. He could not, therefore, make head against the Philistines coming with all the militia of their land; but, leaving his wives and the wives of his mighty men in the Jebusite stronghold of Jerusalem, we may well believe that he sped away to gather the warriors of Israel. But what seems strange is that he should have gone to the rear of the Philistines, especially as they had come in such vast numbers as to occupy the whole country—a garrison, for instance, being posted at Bethlehem, and doubtless at other fit spots. Still, this country was well known to David, and he could gather there old friends, whose bravery he had often tried before. And while thus waiting for the mustering of such as God would move to help him, in deep distress at so terrible a reversal following so quickly upon his exaltation, a strange longing for water from the well of his native town seized him. He was suffering apparently from fever of body as well as from distress of mind, and soon there was relief from both. For three of his heroes heard the words burst from his parched lips, and, hastening to Bethlehem, broke through the Philistine garrison, and filled a waterskin from the well at the gate of the city. Such an act naturally made a great impression upon David. What room was there for despair when he had such men around him? Pouring out, then, the water as a drink offering to Jehovah, his heart was now filled with hope, and inquiring of the Lord whether he might attack the Philistines, he received the assurance which he had already gathered from the exploit of his heroes, that God would deliver them into his hand.

Ver. 18.—**The valley of Rephaim.** This fruitful valley (Isa. xvii. 5) is about three miles in length, and two in breadth. Occupying it in vast numbers, the Philistines sent out bodies of men to plunder the whole country, while a sufficient force watched Jerusalem, intending to take it by famine. The Rephaim were an aboriginal race, first mentioned in Gen. xiv. 5, and evidently in early times very widely spread in Palestine. The idea that they were giants has no more to be said in its favour than that they were ghosts—the meaning of the word in Isa. xxvi. 14, 19. No sensible philologist will endeavour to explain the names of these primitive races and of their towns by Hebrew roots, though there has been too much of this

craze in past times. The Rephaim seem, however, to have been physically a well-developed people, and several races of Canaan of great stature are described in Deut. ii. 11 as having belonged to them, as did Og, who was a man of extraordinary dimensions (Deut. iii. 11).

Ver. 20.—**Baal-Perazim**; literally, *possessor of breaches*, that is, the place where the attack burst forth. It is called Mount Perazim, "the hill of breaches," in Ps. xxviii. 21, and as we have seen, it was the rocky height on the north of the valley of Rephaim. David must, therefore, have stolen round the army of the Philistines, creeping, probably by night, up to this ridge of Ben-Hinnom, and thence at the dawn of day have rushed down upon the camp. And his onset was sudden and irresistible, like the rush of the waters of some mountain lake when, swollen with rains, it bursts through the opposing dam, and carries hasty destruction to everything that lies in its way.

Ver. 21.—**They left their images.** This is a further proof of the suddenness of the attack, and the completeness of the Philistine discomfiture. For *images* we find "gods" in the parallel place in 1 Chron. xiv. 12, and the word used here is rendered "idols" in 1 Sam. xxxi. 9. As the Philistines supposed that these images of their deities would ensure their victory, they would set great store by them, as the Israelites did by the ark (1 Sam. iv. 4), and the French by the oriflamme. Their capture, therefore, was a feat as great as the winning of the eagle of a Roman legion. **David and his men burned them;** Hebrew, *took them away.* This translation of the Authorized Version, made to force the words into verbal agreement with 1 Chron. xiv. 12, is utterly indefensible; and, like most wrong things, it is absurd. The Bible cannot be improved by frauds, and really the two narratives complete one another. David and his men carried off these images as trophies, just as the Philistines carried off the ark (1 Sam. iv. 11). But the ark proved mightier than the Philistine gods, and in terror the people restored it to Israel. But no avenging hand interfered to rescue these gods, and, after being paraded in triumph, they were made into a bonfire.

Ver. 22.—**The Philistines came up yet again.** Their first defeat had probably not been accompanied by much slaughter; for David's men were few in number, though brave as lions. Retreating then to some distance, the Philistines called in their garrisons, and waited also for reinforcements from home, and then advanced again to the same spot. And as David was prepared to attack them in front, he also must now have gathered round him the chivalry of Israel.

Ver. 23.—**Thou shalt not go up.** The attack in front is forbidden, and the answer shows that the priest with the ephod did more than give a mere affirmative or negative reply. For David receives full instructions. Taking advantage of the valleys, he is to creep round into the rear of the Philistines, and approach them under cover of a thicket of baca trees. **Mulberry trees;** Hebrew, *baca trees.* This suggests the idea that David's place of attack was the Baca valley (Ps. lxxxiv. 6), and that there was such a valley, though this is not certain. For the Revised Version translates "valley of weeping," concluding that *baca* is not there a proper name. By baca trees the LXX. and Vulgate understand "pear trees," but as *bacah* means "to weep," it is probably some balsamic shrub, from which a resin exudes. The Revised Version puts here in the margin, "balsam trees." Dr. Tristram thinks it was a sort of aspen, but the authority of the Vulgate is great in such matters, as Jerome obtained his information in Palestine itself.

Ver. 24.—**The sound of a going;** Hebrew, *a marching.* Under the cover of this thicket David was to wait until he heard the sound as of the regular tramp of an army in the tops of the baca trees. It would be in the morning that the wind would shake the tree-tops, but the sound was to be something more than the soft whispers of a gentle breeze. A gale was to put them into sudden motion, and then the soldiers would know that their Jehovah had gone forth to battle, and David must immediately *bestir* himself. The enthusiasm of his men must not cool down, but as soon as the wind rustled he must charge the enemy, and his warriors, feeling that they were going with the host of God, would break down all resistance by their impetuous onset.

Ver. 25.—**From Geba until thou come to Gazer.** In 1 Chron. xiv. 16 "Gibeon" is substituted for "Geba," and it is one of those corrections which a commentator is inclined to adopt, because it makes all things easy.

For Gibeon lay directly on the road from the Rephaim valley towards Gazer, and the armies must have passed it in the fight. But if "Geba" be the right reading here, then the battle must have been most sternly contested. For it is the "Gibeah of Benjamin," Hebrew, "Geba of Benjamin," described in 1 Sam. xiii. 16. The Philistines had a garrison there in Saul's time (1 Sam. xiii. 3), and had probably again occupied it as a military post after their victory at Gilboa. To reach it the line of retreat would go nine miles northward over difficult ground; but this was not disadvantageous to a retreating army as long as it remained unbroken, and the Philistines would expect to be able to make a successful defence at a strong citadel like Geba, held by a garrison of their own troops. But when driven by David's "mighty men" from this fortified hill, being hemmed in by the defile of Michmash on the east, they would have no choice but to hurry down the valleys to the west, and, still passing by Gibeon, so flee to Gazer. Thus the reading "Geba" implies a stout and long resistance ending in a most complete victory. And confessedly this was a decisive battle, fought with larger forces, and causing far larger loss to the Philistines than that at Baal-Perazim, where, attacked by only a few men, they were seized with panic, and saved themselves by a headlong flight. *Gazer* lay upon the border of Ephraim, and was one of the royal cities of the Canaanites, and so strong that it was left in the hands of its old possessors (Josh. xvi. 3, 10; Judg. i. 19). Subsequently Solomon fortified it (1 Kings ix. 17), as being the key of the defiles which led from Ekron and the plain of Philistia up to Jerusalem. We also find it mentioned as an important military post in the days of the Maccabees (1 Macc. ix. 52). The pursuit would naturally stop here, as the fugitives would now be in their own country, and succour would be close at hand. Probably, too, the Canaanites who held the fortress were friendly to them, and gave them shelter.

HOMILETICS.

Vers. 1—10.—The facts are: 1. The tribes of Israel come to Hebron to formally acknowledge David as rightful king. 2. They assign three reasons for their united action. (1) That David was of their kindred. (2) That he had rendered valuable services in times of need. (3) That God had expressed his will. 3. A solemn league being made between David and the tribes, they anoint him king over Israel. 4. The question of the crown being settled, David applies himself to the acquisition of Jerusalem as the seat of government. 5. Being proudly defied by the Jebusites, on account of the strength of their position, he challenges his officers to take the lead in the subjugation of the fortress. 6. Acquiring possession, he calls the place after his name, and extends the fortifications. **7.** The continued favour of God ensures to him great prosperity.

The triumph of patient fidelity. The first three verses bring into view the realization of David's most cherished desires, the ripe consummation of all his wearying toils and cares. The goal on which Samuel had directed his eye (1 Sam. x. 1; xvi. 1—13) was now attained. The wisdom of his self-restraint when persecuted, and of his trusting more to Divine care than to human weapons, was now fully justified. The historian places together the human popular view of the situation, and the Divine purpose that had to be effected. The being bone of their bone, and the great services rendered to Israel in days of trial, were the natural and political facts which warranted the great gathering at Hebron on that day; and the treasured-up saying of the Lord that this very man should feed his people and be their captain, was the Divine declaration now seen by them to harmonize with the natural and political facts. There is here the language of expediency, and a kind of apology for past opposition to David; for the fact that God had so spoken ought from the first to have prevented all controversy and rendered the nation one in enthusiasm for the divinely chosen man. The acceptance of the authority of the declaration is not absolute, but because they now see what they profess not hitherto to have seen—that by nature and services he is fit to be the shepherd and captain of Israel.

I. GOD'S APPOINTMENTS ARE BASED ON NATURAL PRINCIPLES. The selection of David out of the sons of Jesse was not a mere arbitrary act warranted by no considerations of propriety and fitness. He was the best of the family and of the nation for the specific purpose to be wrought out. His qualities were not bestowed after the call to the position—though grace would abound for development of what was already possessed; they were in him by nature. God uses up what he has prepared in the working out of ordinary natural processes. When the people said, "We are thy bone and thy flesh," they were referring to one prominent instance of natural fitness for the position of authority then assigned to David; his common kinship with them would ensure the sympathy which ought ever to exist between ruler and ruled. The Divine appointment rested, among other fitnesses, on this natural basis. The formal fitness lay in the fact of kinship; but God saw also that in the case of this man the sympathies natural to the fact of kinship were exceptionally strong and deep and broad. There was also a Divine recognition of those other natural qualities of statesmanship and valour and generosity, which would render a decree that he should be king but the formulation of a natural adaptation *plus* the information to men that the Supreme Being will so regulate affairs that this natural adaptation shall manifest itself. We may be sure that the same holds good of all that God ordains. He uses up what is best in nature for the ends in view. Abraham was the fittest man to be commissioned to found a family through which Messiah should come. The choice of Moses to lead the people out of Egypt, and administer law among a people hitherto without law, was evidently based on his natural and acquired qualities. That which may seem to be an exception to this rule is no exception, namely, the appointment of plain and unlettered men to first establish the kingdom of Christ after his ascension. For looking at the spiritual nature of the kingdom, that it is diffused by the spiritual renovation of men by the power of the Holy Spirit, it was befitting that men who had no brilliant gifts wherewith to dazzle others, and so induce the impression that the new cause was one in which human wisdom prevailed, should become the channels through which the power of God might assert itself (1 Cor. i. 23—31; ii. 4, 5). The most illustrious instance of the truth before us is that in the case of our Saviour. By condescending to become bone of our bone, and flesh of our flesh, made like unto his brethren, there is laid a natural fitness for his becoming the Feeder of his people and the Captain of our salvation. The sympathy of nature thus rendered possible sets forth the wisdom which appointed him to be a Prince and a Saviour. History reveals no exceptions to the rule.

II. THE EVIDENCE TO MEN OF DIVINE APPOINTMENT WILL LIE IN SERVICES ACTUALLY RENDERED. The original Divine appointment of David was prior even to his appearance before Goliath; for God's purposes are not the product of changes in time, and the declaration by Samuel to David was only for his guidance and encouragement in view of the troubles that were. coming. David had to act so as to render the words of Samuel credible to the people; he had to make his "calling and election sure" by a line of conduct that would destroy the supposition that possibly Samuel the prophet, in this instance, was mistaking the surmisings of his own mind for the purpose of God. Those long years from the day he left the sheepfold to the death of Ishbosheth, formed the period in which he was to bring out before men the great wisdom of God in his selection. As the other Anointed One later on lived among men in such a way as to show to them that he was from the Father, that he had a work to do for the people of God, and was, in fact, appointed to be the Redeemer of the race, so David had to justify all that Samuel had said, and all that was implied in the prior Divine choice. It is a noble thing when a man believes that God has ordained him to a work in the world, and strives to so regulate his life that every act shall be a demonstration of the wisdom and fitness of the Divine appointment. How David did this, by sympathy with all classes, by carrying on his heart the sorrows of his people, by deeds of valour which broke asunder the chains of Philistine oppression, by gentle forbearance toward those who sought his life, by abstention from pride and acts of violence to further his interests, also by patient trust in the covenant-keeping God during days of terrible suffering, as by wise administration among his own followers,—the history of his early life fully records. However obstinate, for personal and political reasons, men were in refusing him as successor to Saul, they could not but yield at last to the force of evidence that he was the man for the position, and so far demonstrated to be the chosen of God. By a similar method, Christ is creating history which will be the vindication of his claim to be Lord of all. Likewise the Church, as the body of Christ, answers to her calling and duty only so far as she does deeds and manifests a spirit that will furnish unanswerable evidence of the Divinity of the Christian religion. "By their fruits ye shall know them." The test of salt lies in the presence of its peculiar savour.

III. The realization of God's purpose through the loyalty of his servants is only a question of time. It would have seemed that when Samuel made known the will of God it would have been enough at once to have secured the abdication of Saul and the hearty concurrence of the chosen race. But there was the same free way of dealing with Divine declarations, the same perversity of understanding, as in the days of Christ; so that men did not thoroughly accept and act upon what was said. Jonathan and a few elect souls read aright the Divine intent, and rejoiced therein; but the rest found reasons for doubt, as men always can when the spirit is not thoroughly humble and devout. Occasionally, as we have seen in the case of Abner (ch. iii. 9, 10), there was a recognition of truth generally suppressed. A man of less faith than David would have despaired of witnessing the day when the whole nation would, by a solemn act of coronation, fall in with the purpose of God. But through the loyalty of David and the few devout men who were the companions of his heart, the issue was brought to pass. It was not a question of truth or falsehood, of national policy or individual striving; the word of God had gone forth, true and unchangeable, that so it was to be; whether scheming politicians fell in with it or not, the course of nature was the course of God. Time would prove to be the element for solving all. Faithfulness to God has the power, in a mysterious way, of winning over the forces of nature and society to its side. The hour came when all Israel simply met to do what God all along intended should be done. Herein do we see, on a small scale, what is yet to be illustrated on the grandest scale. It is a question of time. The hour is coming when every knee shall bow to the Anointed of the Lord, and every tongue confess that he is the Christ, to the glory of God the Father. The world will then simply recognize, as a whole, what now the faithful followers of Christ know to be true. In spiritual things the world does not acquire truth; it simply comes to admit to be true what Christ's people all along have affirmed is true. The Church is not outstripped; its conclusions are accepted.

General lessons. 1. We cannot fully estimate the cumulative force of Christian consistency in bringing about the final triumph of Christianity. 2 There is a parallel between our modern religious conflicts with unbelief and the struggle of many in Israel against the revealed purpose of God, and we may rest assured that the truth with us, long resisted, will in the end be accepted. 3. It behoves every Church and private Christian to consider how much the solution of our modern difficulties depends on our own faithfulness in daily life.   4. It is helpful to the observance of obligations that we recognize them with the solemn sanctions of religion, " before the Lord " (ver. 3).

The acquisition and building-up of Zion.   This narrative exhibits David as a new man—free from the old trials and embarrassments, and with a clear course before him to raise up the government which should embody the religious principles of the theocracy, and be prospective of a grand spiritual development in the distant future. As one relieved from great cares and conscious of vast unexpended energy, he at once applies himself to the adoption of the means which at that stage of affairs seemed most conducive to the attainment of ulterior issues.   The principles on which he acted, while excellent for the circumstances of the time, admit of a wider application to human affairs, and with this in view we may indicate the wisdom of his conduct and the bearing of the narrative on other matters by a succession of single terms suggestive of both facts and principles.

I. INITIATION.   All along, even in exile, David had learnt to regard his life as linked in the providence of God with some great events in the far-distant future.   His mission to the world and his own nation was understood to be the raising of his own people to such a position of social order and righteousness as should fit them to be most perfectly instrumental in hastening on the latter-day glory.   Now that he was made king, and had the confidence of the people, he devises those initiatory measures which, being well planned and executed, will render the attainment of remoter ends more probable.   The record tells us of the facts, and we have to fill in the mental processes by which David was led to the particular course recorded.   His work was great, far-reaching, and, full of energy and faith and confidence, he makes a beginning in the work of consolidation and administration.   The first movement was *born of faith in his call* to service—faith in the bearing of his life's work on the destinies of men, faith in the existence of a Divine purpose which had to be wrought out in connection with the chosen race, faith in the value of human labour in relation to Divine purposes, and faith in the presence and help of God in all undertaken in his service.   How wisely and broadly the foundation was now about to be laid we may notice further on ; the fact here to be noted is the laying of a foundation in deeds for subsequent efforts.   All wise rulers and governments, when entering into recognized power, take initiatory measures as their wisdom may suggest.   The first stages of action bear an important relation to what follows. The same holds good of other departments of human activity.   This reminds us of the initiatory work of the kingdom of Christ; how his life, sufferings, death, and resurrection may be regarded as the initiation of that long course of activity by which the king in Zion will wondrously affect the destinies of the world.   We know with what clear prevision, what sense of being sent of God, what faith in the value of human effort and in the presence and blessing of the Eternal, all that was done which constituted the beginning of the reign of the Anointed of the Lord.

II. CLEARANCE.   In making a survey of the inheritance into which, as king, he had come, David saw that the presence of alien Jebusites, defiant of himself and worshippers of blind and lame idols, was an evil which ought at once to be got rid of.   For such an alien element to occupy a stronghold in the very heart of the country was a most galling thought to one intensely patriotic and brave, and could not but have suggested to him the defective courage and faith of his ancestors in Israel, who allowed such a thing to be possible.   It was no mere love of fighting, no desire to create a diversion on acceding to power, that induced him to challenge his best men to seize the position ; it was statesmanship, regard for the purity of the national life, and the honour of him who originally gave the land to Israel for an inheritance.   The people of God must be separate from the heathen.   Powers of darkness must not dwell in the land of light. A beautiful example this to all who have an inheritance to hold for Christ.   Our *nature is a holy land,* in which he alone is to be honoured, and it is a prime duty that we take strenuous measures—call upon the co-operation of our best powers—to cast out the evil elements from the centre of our nature, so that there may be nothing within that defileth, or is an abomination, or that maketh a lie.   The work may be difficult, the forces strong and defiant, and faint-hearted rulers may suffer the evils to remain from sheer lack of courage and confidence ; but their removal at an early stage of life is a condition of a prosperous government, in the name and service of God, of the powers that make up our human nature. In one respect also we see an analogy in our Lord's work. His mission in its widest reach is to gather into one all things in hi .self (Eph. i. 10), to sway a blessed sceptre over a perfected humanity, to maintain a kingdom of peace and righteousness that shall never end (Ps. lxxii.) ; and his first work on ascending the throne is to seek the casting out from the heart and life of humanity of the alien spirit, the Jebusite, that so long has usurped the place of influence, and done serious injury to all. The work is now going on, and the Jebusite will be cast down from his stronghold, and the entire world won at last to the Prince of Peace.

III. CONSTRUCTION. In reformation and restoration there is a negative and a positive side. David had to clear out the foe of his people, and so secure free scope for their activities and their happiness. But a positive work had to follow the removal of the evil forces. Hence, in his sagacity, he resolved to construct on the site cleared of the alien a stronghold that should serve the important ends of commanding the entire country from an impregnable position, of giving local prominence to his seat of government, and of facilitating the administration of affairs. The possession of Zion, and the immediate development of its military advantages, were positive advances in the rearing of the stable state which was to stand out so markedly in contrast with the disintegration and weakness of Saul's time. True wisdom is constructive. Evil is destructive and disintegrating. Men prove their capacity to lead and govern by what they can gradually build up. The aim and effort of David all through his reign evidently was to form a national life on solid foundations, and richly developed in all that constitutes true greatness. How truly typical of the Son of David, who, by supremely wise acts in the establishment of his kingdom, laid the foundation for a superstructure of human good which is ever going on toward perfection ! How suggestive of the true wisdom of missionary enterprise—laying solid foundations, in central positions, with a view to bless whole lands with the peace and blessedness of the gospel, and then gradually adding to the first work by positive developments of the same stable character ! Likewise in education and in individual self-culture in godliness, construction should be ever aimed at, ever going on, proceeding upon definite solid foundations of success, laid with care in the very centre of the heart and intellect. Hereby also do we learn the extreme importance of getting supreme mastery of those powerful central forces of our nature which are to the details and outward aspects of our personal life what the stronghold of Jebus was to the varied hills and valleys of the land of Israel.

IV. INSPIRATION. The step taken by David was the natural outflow of his own enthusiasm. The force was latent in him, and now came the occasion for its manifestation. It was a new thing for the tribes to see a man of spirit, conscious of a high destiny to work out and urged, as by a Divine inspiration, to dare deeds not dreamt of for many generations (Josh. xv. 63; Judg. xix. 10—12). The man rose with his position. The consciousness of new and heavy responsibilities developed heroism. Even the barbarous occupants of the stronghold (ver. 8) seemed surprised that any one should dream of touching them. The strong expression, "hated of David's soul," only reveals the high and all-commanding spirit that could not brook the defilement of the holy land by idolatrous feet. But the infection of an enthusiastic spirit is rapid, and this action of the king at once raised the national tone. It made men feel that, as a people, they were entering on a new era ; the possibilities of a great future opened before them ; an ambition of a lofty kind was enkindled ; the dismemberment of the nation, the low political status of Saul's time, when they could scarcely hold their own against heathen tribes, must cease to be imagined, and the great ideas of Abraham and of Moses once more must become regnant in their minds. Possibly on that day of coronation, when the elders of the tribes would come into close conference with David, he would speak out from his own clearer vision of their function in the world as the people of God and his own strong faith in the presence of Jehovah, so that the deeds on Mount Zion would illustrate in impressive form words of power (Ps. xl. 9, 10). Likewise the inspiration given to the Church in days of the founding of the kingdom of Christ has raised the tone and put a strong and masterful confidence in the heart of man. None can fully estimate the widespread and mighty influence exerted by the lofty spirit displayed by our Lord. It has raised new hopes, developed a bolder courage, fixed men's eyes more steadily on the glorious future, and produced the feeling that the faithful are engaged in an enterprise not only sanctioned by God, but pervaded by the very life-giving presence of the Lord of all power and glory. In so far as we each enter on our appointed work for Christ in the same spirit, we carry on the inspiration and swell the moral forces that are to win the world for God.

V. MEMORIES. David, as we know from his early experience and from the Psalms, was a man of much meditation—one who was well versed in the memorials of his nation and deeply imbued with the spirit of devotion. Was it nothing to him that the seat of Melchizedek's reign as King of Salem was possibly this spot where now the impious Jebusites dwelt? Could he forget that here it was Abraham displayed the marvellous faith which, more than anything, won for him the name ever to be cherished, "father of the faithful"? It was creditable to his religious instincts and to his sagacity that one of the first acts of his reign was to recover a place so sacred to the memory, and to gather the associations of the place around his own seat of government. Piety, poetry, and statesmanship are here combined. Great and hallowed associations tend to beget corresponding deeds; and doubtless it was with the fond hope that as king he might still further consecrate that sacred spot, that he made it the centre of his administration. History tells us how age after age memories clustered more and more richly and often sadly, yet instructively, around that holy hill, until the name of Zion has become, perhaps, more rich in pathetic story and suggestive splendour and bliss than any word in human language—next, of course, to the one "Name that is above every name."

> "Glorious things of thee are spoken,
> Zion, city of our God ;
> He whose Word cannot be broken
> Formed thee for his own abode."

Vers. 11—25.—The facts are: 1. The King of Tyre, being friendly with David, supplies him with means of building his house on Mount Zion. 2. David regards the varied successes of his enterprises as confirmation of his belief that he was indeed appointed by God to reign over Israel. 3. He establishes a court on a larger scale, after Oriental style. 4. The Philistines, hearing of his accession to the throne, prepare for an attack upon him, whereupon he seeks guidance of God, defeats them at Baal-Perazim, and destroys their images. 5. Subsequently the Philistines come to a second attack, but on inquiring of God, David is not allowed to assail them in front. 6. Adopting the strategy recommended him, David secures the overthrow of the enemy unto Gazer.

Divine favour vouchsafed to imperfect men. The Bible teaches that the hearts of kings and people are in the hands of the Lord, and that he turns them so as to advance the great purpose he is working out. The friendly attitude of so important a personage as Hiram must be regarded as a mark of God's favour to David. To us the record makes clear that David was indeed called of God, and had the special help of the Almighty, and yet ver. 12 suggests that there were hours when he himself felt the need of confirmatory signs. Some of the Psalms indicate the same. He is here represented as overcoming any doubts and fears arising from his own deep consciousness of moral imperfection, by considering the unmistakable blessings wherewith his efforts so far were crowned. It was all of the Lord. He was not in error in supposing that he was in the path of duty. And yet the very next verses of the narrative (vers. 13—16) tell us of a weakness in David's character—an inferiority to much that later on was attained to by others—so that we cannot but note this conjunction of great and manifold favours conferred on one whose standard of moral and social life was, relatively to ours, very inferior. To the right understanding of this we have to observe—

I. DOMESTIC RELATIONSHIPS ARE MATTERS OF POSITIVE ENACTMENT. Moralists distinguish rightly between obligations moral in their own nature and obligations created by precept. Obviously there is not the same kind of obligation for a man to have only one wife as there is to love God with all his heart. The one depends on considerations subsequent to the existence of more than one person; the other holds from the very nature of the feeling, and cannot but be the right thing. That it is wisest, best, most conducive to personal moral perfection and to social welfare that men should not have plurality of wives, is certain ; but that arises from the constitution of society and the particular purposes God intends to work out by means of the domestic institution, and consequently the prohibition to have more than one wife partakes of the nature of a positive precept. Had man not been told what he should do, he would not have felt and known absolutely that only one wife must be taken. Had he not been told what he should do, he would nevertheless have felt and known that to love not God, to disobey God, to prefer vileness to purity, was wrong. David, left to himself, would see evil in aversion to God, but he would not so distinctly and certainly see evil in having many wives.

II. THE SOCIAL CONDITIONS OF LIFE IN ANCIENT TIMES WERE INHERITED. Inheritance does not make wrong right, but being over a long series of generations it tends to prevent those who are the subjects of it from seeing the evils which others fresh to the facts might soon discover. This applies especially to those forms of evil which are so in a secondary sense, being the opposite of what is termed good by positive precept. Polygamy was a custom very ancient, running through long generations of good men, and among sheiks and heads of nations it became one of the marks of distinction and an inevitable appendage of wealth. That, of course, does not make it useful or morally right, but it accounts for good men adopting it with as little compunction of conscience as others, in modern times, have bought and sold slaves, or sold drink, which are known to be the occasion of great evils.

III. THE MEANS OF EDUCATING MEN TO MORE PERFECT FORMS OF SOCIAL LIFE ARE GRADUAL IN OPERATION, AND THE FORCE OF PRECEPTS CONCERNING THEM IS NOT AT ONCE RECOGNIZED. No doubt monogamy was the will of God—the common law from the beginning (Matt. xix. 4, 5). The subsequent practice of polygamy by good men was tolerated, but it was the evident design of the Mosaic regulations to moderate and minimize it (Deut. xvii. 17; Exod. xxi. 10, 11; Deut. xxi. 11—17). The elevation of the people above the degrading practice was a slow process, and, according to the Talmudists, even the distinct precept (Deut. xvii. 17) was understood in a non-literal sense. It is possible, therefore, that David, inheriting practices straight from Abraham, should be disposed to anticipate the Talmudic interpretation, and understand "multiply" to refer to an "inordinate number," and the reason assigned to be a matter of discretion. The same difficulty in educating men to rise to the full recognition, in social relations, of some of our Saviour's precepts set forth in Matt. v. and vi., is obvious to us even now. In the case of Oriental polygamy in Old Testament times the difficulty was greater from the circumstance that the wife in chief held her place, and others improperly called in English "concubines" were secondary, and often served in court as "maids of honour" do now.

IV. IT IS THE METHOD OF GOD TO WORK BY IMPERFECT AGENTS UP TO A HIGHER FORM OF LIFE. All things in the earlier stages of constructive work are in an elementary condition, and in that sense inferior. Out of the elemental forms organisms arise, and from the lower organisms higher types have appeared. Out of our own imperfect mental condition there arises, by use of that imperfect condition, a superior form of mental life. The same holds good of our moral habits. By use of the weak and inferior, with a tendency upwards, there comes to pass a moral elevation that can never descend to the old conditions out of which it sprang. Likewise, in constructing a perfect human society on the purest and noblest gospel principles, it is God's way to use men as he finds them, with their inherited notions and tendencies, and by precept and inspiration gradually raise them above themselves, and so make them instruments of raising others to a higher level of life. Had God waited till men became as clear in their conceptions of social proprieties and utilities and as strong in purity as Christ, nothing would have been done for the world. He is a Father who pitieth his children. He remembereth that we are but dust. It is, therefore, in unison with general principles of government that David, though a polygamist, was blessed, and for the same reason many a slave-owner's life has been attended with spiritual blessing. Were it not so, who of us dare hope for favour?

V. THE BLESSING OF GOD IS RESTRICTED BY OUR IMPERFECTIONS. Had David risen to the dignity of true monogamy, and, with clear vision and firm spirit, entered on a domestic life in keeping with gospel principles, he would doubtless have exerted a wider and more powerful spiritual influence. But as it was, the kind and measure of prosperity vouchsafed to him were proportionate to his imperfect domestic life. God's blessing is only restrained by the channel through which it has to flow. The more we can anticipate the more holy and consecrated and enlightened future by our present eleva-tion of life, the more surely will the blessing rest on us and our deeds.   According to our faith and love, as seen in perfect conformity of feeling, perception, and action to the blessed life of Christ, so may we expect the favour and blessing of God.

GENERAL LESSONS.   1. It becomes us every now and then to make careful scrutiny of our lives, to see what elements there are in them derived from an ungodly inheritance and resting on mere fashion and custom.   2. The best light by which we may discover what is merely traditional and perhaps morally defective in our characters is that derived from a close study of the spirit that animated our Saviour and the ideal he set up for our model.   3. In our anxiety to know whether we are really accepted of God and are enjoying his favour, we may safely reckon prosperity in our calling, if only, like David, we are conscious of going forth in his Name and not for personal ends.   4. We may, like David, after seasons of long trial for the sake of Christ, well take courage when the tide of success flows freely in, and should be careful at such times to ascribe all to God. 5. We see how the essence of religion, namely, trust in God, desire to know and do his will, and maintenance of righteousness in all affairs according to the measure of light obtained, is distinguishable from the form of social morality which custom or tradition may have generated.

The renunciation of human strength and wisdom before God.   The historian is here fragmentary in his records.   Having noted David's first efforts towards consolidation of his power and his general prosperity, he refers to the troubles that arose in con-sequence of the assaults of the Philistines.   These natural enemies of Israel had doubtless observed with satisfaction the gradual decay of Israel's power during the reign of Saul, and probably were hopeful that the threatened civil war between the adherents of David at Hebron and the friends of Ishbosheth would still further place the people at their mercy.   The seizure of Jebus was, however, so startling an event as to awaken the fear that the near settlement at Hebron and removal of the court to Jerusalem might be the beginning of trouble for themselves.   The remembrance of the prowess of David in years gone by must have intensified this fear.   It was therefore in accordance with the best human policy that they should bring all their forces together and seek to crush him by a single blow.   It is interesting to observe the conduct of David under those circumstances.

I. THE STRONG AND SAGACIOUS MAN SEEKS THE GUIDANCE AND HELP OF GOD.   That David was a man of courage, brave, hardy, and capable of great endurance, is the record of his life.   Naturally he was capable of great things.   Also his whole conduct revealed a remarkable sagacity, such as fitted him for military leadership and statesmanship. If there was one in Israel who, reckoning on personal qualities and acquired renown, was justified in facing the Philistines in sole dependence on his own gifts, David was the man, and yet, instead of that, he turns at once to his God, and seeks guidance and help of him.   This was not an act of superstition; not the result of sudden change of character, in which fear took the place of courage and mental confusion the place of calmness.   It was the product of enlightened piety—a policy of profound wisdom, a sagacious estimate of all the facts and probabilities of the case.   He was the servant of Jehovah, bound to carry out his purposes and cause his great Name to be reverenced in all human affairs.   Therefore it was due to the ever-present and ruling Lord to honour him by seeking to know his will and trusting in his aid.   Past successes in his Name suggested the same.   It was true then as now that the Eternal Spirit could act on masses of men and their leaders so as to change the course of events; and for aught David knew to the contrary, it might have been the Divine will to force them back by some other agency than by his arms.   Prudence, reason, piety, all sound principles and sentiments, concurred in renunciation of all human powers before the Eternal, that his power might be manifest.   This is the course pursued by every strong and wise man in whom piety is a force.   The Apostle Paul was a notable instance of strong will and great general ability laid prostrate before Christ, that his power might work through human channels (2 Cor. iv. 6, 7).   The more distinguished the man in natural gifts and in grace, the more thoroughly is God sought, as in the case of Augustine.   Men of strong will and great force of intellect who refuse to depend on God are not strong and wise all round; they are morally weak and spiritually blind.

The more perfectly the whole man is developed the more complete will be the turning to God for guidance and help.

II. THE STRONG AND SAGACIOUS MAN FOLLOWS THE LIGHT GIVEN. David learnt that it was God's will that the national foe should be smitten, not by pestilence or sudden terror subjectively produced, but by the national arm; and in the two cases by different methods of procedure. Whatever was the method of learning the will of God, and whatever degree of distinctness the revelation, the fact to be noted is that David was not "disobedient to the heavenly vision." His generalship was regulated thereby. We have no Urim to consult, no high priest to receive special communication for specific emergencies; but in our times of danger to business, domestic interests, Church affairs, and personal religious life—to say nothing of national events—we can seek God by prayer, by reading his will in the pure conscience, in the steady lines of providence, and in the principles of his written Word. It should be a cardinal truth with us that God is interested in our affairs, and has ways of making himself known to the earnest spirit. Especially does it behove each Christian and the Church as a body to seek guidance and help when assaults are being made on our holy faith, and the enemy threatens to deprive us of our goodly heritage. There are ways and methods of meeting the foe which God can reveal, and our success will depend on the care with which we adopt the methods approved of God. Infidelity and atheism are to be confronted or attacked in the rear on principles Divine, not on maxims of human expediency.

III. THE STRONG AND SAGACIOUS MAN IS WILLING TO LET GOD WORK, SO THAT THE HAND OF MAN SHALL NOT BE MOST CONSPICUOUS. David acquiesced in the front attack when enjoined, and equally in the restrained action of himself when (vers. 23, 24) an unseen influence was brought to bear on the foe. In this lies the beauty of true godliness, that it is content, when God wills it, that man should not be seen if only the purposes of God are carried through. David cared not for military distinction if the finger of God could only be seen. His strategy in this case was Divine. He stood aside for Providence to work till the hour for human action arrived. This was the apostolic spirit in the early days of Christianity, based in its exercise on the truth that the living God was the great Worker on the souls of men. The same feeling and belief should ever actuate us in all our endeavours to subdue enemies to the cross. We are only instruments, and a true estimate of ourselves will lead us to rejoice in our being counted as nothing and lost sight of in the display of saving power straight from God. Perhaps there is less success because we want to appear in front of the "mulberry trees."

GENERAL LESSONS. 1. We have to hold our own heart and our Church life against the inroads of our natural enemies, "the world, the flesh, and the devil," and the remembrance of this should always make us watchful. 2. In times of great stress in this conflict we should make special requests to God, and not simply proceed on the prestige of former achievements. 3. In dealing with modern forms of attack on Christianity, we have need to ponder well the methods and principles of procedure; and the entire Church should make it a matter of special thought and prayer.

HOMILIES BY VARIOUS AUTHORS.

Vers. 1—3 (1 Chron. xi. 1—3).—(HEBRON.) *David anointed king of all Israel.* 1. About twenty years had elapsed since David was anointed by Samuel, seven years and a half since he was anointed King of Judah; and at length, at the age of thirty-seven, his faith and patience were rewarded, every obstacle was removed out of his path, and the Divine purpose concerning his royal destination fulfilled. "In the fulness of time, at the right moment, in perfect vigour of mind and body, he grasped the supremacy which was offered to him, having passed through every outward stage of power and honour, and every inward test of heavy trial and varied strife" (Ewald). 2. His anointing (performed by prophet or priest) took place at the instance of the *elders* (ver. 3) as the representatives of all the tribes (ver. 1), in accordance with the former summons of Abner (ch. iii. 17, 19, 21), and doubtless after consultation in their national assembly (1 Sam. viii. 4); now desirous and even eager (after long resistance) to accomplish the purpose of God, having "learnt by experience" the kind of king they needed, and being constrained by the pressure of circumstances. 3. "By his anointing by Samuel he acquired *jus ad regnum,* a right to the kingdom; and by his present anointing he had a *jus in regno,* authority over the kingdom" (A. Clarke). It was not merely a designation, but an inauguration to his office; a recognition and acceptance of his Divine appointment, as well as a symbol of his Divine endowment with all needful gifts (see 1 Sam. x. 1, 10; xvi. 12); and it distinguished his person as sacred (1 Sam. xxiv. 6; xxvi. 11), inasmuch as he represented the authority and power of the Divine King of Israel. His anointing for the third; time marks one of the greatest days of Israel's history (ch. ii. 4; 1 Sam. ix. 28; x. 24; xi. 15); and, in connection with it, observe—

I. THE REASONS ASSIGNED BY THE ELDERS FOR THEIR PROPOSAL. 1. *His personal relationship.* "Behold, we are thy bone and thy flesh" (Gen. xxix. 14), expressive of their claims upon him, and of his qualification to rule over them; to understand their wants, sympathize with their aspirations, and promote their welfare (Deut. xvii. 15). "The elders speak as if they had not been very sure whether they were to regard David as a Hebrew, or as a naturalized Philistine; but now their doubts are gone, they dwell on his blood-relationship to them as a conclusive evidence that he would be out and out a Hebrew—that, therefore, he was worthy of the Hebrew crown" (Blaikie). So "in all things it behoved" the Captain of our salvation "to be made like unto his brethren" (Heb. ii. 17). 2. *His proved ability and eminent services* (ver. 2), indicative of his proper calling and the general esteem in which he was held (1 Sam. xvi. 5); "the bond of fellowship and love which had bound him to them, even under Saul, as leader in their military undertakings." 3. *His previous designation.* "According to the word of the Lord by Samuel" (1 Chron. xi. 3); making it their duty to seek his leadership as well as his to undertake it. "Why should they refer to God's choice of David? (1) Because, although they had known all along that David had been fore-appointed to the throne, they had yet been struggling against that arrangement; and so it was fitting now that they should express their repentance and declare their readiness to receive him in God's name, and as from God's hand. (2) Because they wished to remind him and themselves that the royal king of their nation was Jehovah, and that he and they were in allegiance to him" (W. M. Taylor). He did not "take this honour unto himself" without being "called of God" and desired by the people. It sought him rather than he it. And the grounds of his acceptance of it were (as is not always the case with those who assume royal office) unselfish, patriotic, and devout.

II. THE COVENANT MADE BY THE KING WITH THE ELDERS. "And King David made a covenant with [to] them before the Lord" (ver. 3). This covenant, agreement, or promise (whatever may have been its precise terms): 1. Expressed directly and chiefly an engagement, *on his part,* to rule over them according to the Divine will (Deut. xvii. 16—20; 1 Sam. x. 25). He was by no means to be an absolute and irresponsible monarch, or "a king ruling arbitrarily as in heathen kingdoms, where at most a few nobles, the populace, or an imperfect oracular system limited his power;" but to be subject to the Law and to the voice of prophecy. 2. Involved the obligation, *on their part,* to obey him according to the same will (ch. iii. 21). "The Law of God was the rule and square of his government, whereunto both prince and people are sworn; which was a bridle against his absolute power or their rebellious manners" (Guild). 3. Was ratified *in the most solemn manner*—"in a form in which the theocratic principle is distinctly recognized." "The end and cause why God imprints in the weak and feeble flesh of man the image of his own power and majesty is not to puff up flesh in the opinion of itself; neither yet that he that is exalted above others should be lifted up by presumption and pride, and so despise others; but that he should consider he is appointed lieutenant of One whose eyes continually watch upon him and see and examine how he behaves himself in his office" (John Knox).

III. THE SPIRIT DISPLAYED BY THE PEOPLE, not only by the presence of the elders but also by that of the armed hosts, the flower of the nation, who marched to Hebron from all parts of the country, numbering (in addition to his "mighty men," 1 Chron. xi. 10—47; ch. xxiii. 8—39; and those who had come to him during his exile, 1 Chron. xii. 1—22) 339,600, with two hundred chiefs of Issachar "and all their brethren," one thousand chiefs of Naphtali, and Zadok and twenty-two chiefs (1 Chron. xii.

23—40). "All these men of war that could keep rank came with a perfect heart to Hebron, to make David king over all Israel; and all the rest also of Israel were of one heart to make David king." 1. *Voluntary submission.* "Thy people shall be willing in the day of thy power" (Ps. cx. 3). 2. *National unanimity;* such as is celebrated in Ps. cxxxiii. (written subsequently), 'Brotherly love'—

> "Behold! how good and lovely it is
> That (those who are) brethren should also dwell together!"

3. *Enthusiastic devotion.* "And there they were with David three days, eating and drinking; for their brethren had prepared for them," etc. 4. *Abounding joy.* "For there was joy in Israel." This "gathering of the people" (Gen. xlix. 10) was a most memorable one (vers. 4, 5). In it the good hidden in their reprehensible desire for a king (1 Sam. viii. 4—22) becomes apparent; we see the fruit of past labour, conflict, chastisement, and the seeds of future enterprise, success, advancement. "The kingship, as administered by David, appears neither as a necessary evil nor an improved constitution, but as a new ethic potency" (Oehler, 'Theology of the Old Testament,' sec. 165). "His career constitutes the culmination of that general advancement towards which the people of Israel had been aspiring with increasing energy for more than a century" (Ewald).—D.

Vers. 2, 10, 12 (1 Chron. xi. 2, 9; xiv. 2).—(HEBRON.) *The shepherd-king.* This is the first occasion on which we find the occupation of a shepherd made use of to describe the office of a king. Jacob, who had "fed Laban's flocks," spoke of "the Shepherd, the Stone of Israel" (Gen. xlix. 24; xlviii. 15); Moses, who had "kept the flock of Jethro," prayed that Jehovah would "set a man over the congregation" as his successor, so that they might not be "as sheep having no shepherd" (Numb. xxvii. 7); here the elders declare that Jehovah said (through Samuel) to David, who "fed his father's sheep at Bethlehem," concerning his royal destination, "Thou shalt feed [*ruah*, equivalent to 'tend,' 'act as shepherd towards'] my people Israel" (ch. vii. 7; Ps. lxxviii. 70—72; Isa. xliv. 28; Jer. xxiii.; l. 5; Ezek. xxxiv. 1, 23; Micah v. 4; Zech. xiii. 7, etc.). "The business of a shepherd is a preparation for the office of a king to any one who is destined to preside over that most manageable of all flocks, mankind; for which reason kings are called shepherds of their people, not by way of reproach, but as a most especial and pre-eminent honour" (Philo, 'Life of Moses'). "Shepherds are not owners of the sheep; but their office is to feed and govern: no more are kings proprietaries or owners of the people. 'The nations,' as the Scriptures saith, are 'his inheritance;' but the office of kings is to govern, maintain, and protect people. And that is not without a mystery that the first king that was instituted by God, David (for Saul was but an untimely fruit), was translated from a shepherd" (Bacon). What was said to David applies to every king, ruler, magistrate, master, in the sphere over which he has legitimate authority. Consider—

I. THE DIVINE IDEA OF HIS OFFICE. It is an office in which authority and power: 1. *Are entrusted by the ordination of God,* the Proprietor, Ruler, Chief Shepherd of the people; not self-derived nor unlimited; yet investing every under-shepherd with dignity. 2. *Should be exercised according to the will of God* (Ps. ci.), in affectionate interest in the people; intimate acquaintance with them, guiding them, providing for them, defending them, restoring them, and, generally, seeking their welfare with diligence, considerateness, tenderness, patience, self-denial, and self-sacrifice. "Chrysostom writeth that the shepherds in Cappadocia have such love unto their flock, that sometimes for three days together, in following them, they are overwhelmed with snow, and yet they endure it; and in Lydia, how far they travel with the sheep for a month together in the waste deserts and parching heat of the sun; who herein do teach such as are shepherds of men that they should even not spare their own lives for the common good" (Willet). 3. *Must be accounted for, as to their use, before the presence of God.* "These sheep, what have they done?" (ch. xxiv. 17). "A king is a mortal god on earth, unto whom the living God hath lent his own name as a great honour; but withal told him he should die like a man, lest he should be proud and flatter himself that God hath with his name imparted unto him his nature also" (Bacon).

II. THE DIVINE SOURCE OF HIS PROSPERITY. "And David went on going and growing" after the conquest of the stronghold of Zion, etc. (vers. 6—10), which he achieved as captain, "leader and commander of the people" (as well as their shepherd) "waxed greater and greater" (ch. vii. 9) in power and fame; "and Jehovah the God of hosts" (1 Sam. i. 3) "was with him " (as his Shepherd, Ps. xxiii. 1, and Captain, ch. xxii. 35—37). 1. *Approving of the manner in which he devoted himself to his calling.* Fidelity is the necessary condition of the special favour of God; which is ever testified in the heart and conscience, and often shown by outward events (Gen. xxxix. 2, 21). 2. *Assisting him in the performance of the duties of his calling;* strengthening, upholding, directing, protecting him. 3. *Accomplishing the aim of his endeavours in his calling;* for no skill nor effort, without Divine co-operation, can ensure success. "Except the Lord build the house," etc. (Ps. cxxvii. 1). While God was with him (1 Sam. x. 11) Saul prospered; when left to himself he lost his kingdom and his life.

III. THE DIVINE PURPOSE OF HIS EXALTATION AND ESTABLISHMENT IN HIS OFFICE. "And David perceived," from the friendly aid of Hiram, the erection of his palace (ver. 11), which he appears to have regarded as a pledge of the stability of his kingdom (Ps. xxx., inscription), and his continued prosperity, "that Jehovah had established him," in accordance with his former choice, "king over Israel, and that he had exalted his kingdom" (1 Chron. xiv. 2, 17) "for his people Israel's sake;" because he had chosen them to be his people, "the sheep of his pasture" (Ps. c. 3), and sought their prosperity and exaltation, according to his faithful promises (ch. vii. 23) that through them all nations might be blessed, and the whole earth filled with his glory. A faithful servant recognizes in his successes: 1. *An immediate purpose of good toward himself;* beholding therein the hand of God and "the kindness and truth" by which it is directed; ascribing his prosperity, not to himself, but to the Lord. 2. *An ulterior and larger purpose of good toward others,* for whose benefit rather than his own he is exalted (ch. vii. 8, 16). 3. *A powerful incentive to thankfulness, hopefulness,* and fresh *consecration* to the service of God and his people. "It was the successiveness, the continuity of the steps, in his history, which assured him that God's hand had been directing the whole of it. Had David, instead of maintaining the crown, which circumstances pointed out to him as his, seized violently that which was not his, he would not have perceived that the Lord had made him King of Israel; he would have felt that he had made himself so, and would have acted upon that persuasion. The government which a man wins for himself he uses for himself; that which he inwardly and practically acknowledges as conferred upon him by a righteous Being cannot be intended for himself. And thus it is that the early and mysterious teaching of David while he was in the sheepfold bore so mightily upon his life after he became king. The deepest lesson which he had learnt was that he himself was under government; that his heart and will was the inmost circle of that authority which the winds and the sea, the moon and the stars, obeyed " (Maurice).

REMARKS. 1. The lowliest occupation is often a preparation for the highest; and he who shows fidelity in the least is rewarded with opportunity for its exercise in the greatest. 2. The possession of authority and power severely tests men's characters, and sometimes proves their destruction. 3. It is a good sign when one who is exalted shows more concern about performing the duties than enjoying the honours of his position. 4. God sends good rulers out of his regard for the welfare of the people. 5. The best rulers are those who sympathize most with the Divine purposes, and most humbly and faithfully " serve their generation." 6. Even the best are imperfect, and often fail to attain their loftiest aims or fulfil their early promise. 7. In *One* alone do we behold the perfect Shepherd-King (John x. 14; Heb. xiii. 20; 1 Pet. v. 4; Rev. vii. 17).—D.

Vers. 6—9 (1 Chron. xi. 4—9).—*Jerusalem.* David's first act after his anointing amidst the assembled tribes (1 Chron. xii. 38—40) was to place himself at the head of his army, and march against *Jebus,* the capital of the Jebusites. With this place he was familiar from his boyhood, and often, perhaps, wondered why it was suffered to remain so long unsubdued (Josh. i. 3, 4). He perceived its advantages as a site for the capital of his kingdom, and the necessity of its reduction in order to the establishment and extension thereof. His enterprise, whatever may have been its immediate cause, was completely successful. Henceforth supreme interest centres in Zion, the city of

David, *Jerusalem* (" foundation of peace "), beyond any other city mentioned in sacred history, poetry, or prophecy. " Jerusalem was destined to become the seat of the Hebrew government, and the scene of the most extraordinary events, and more strange and awful vicissitudes, than any other city of the universe, not excepting Rome " (Milman). Note—

I. ITS PECULIAR SITUATION. In the heart of the country, remote from the great roads of communication with the East; on a mountainous table-land, and entrenched on a cluster of hills, the highest of which was crowned with the stronghold, rock-fortress, or acropolis of Zion (ver. 7); on the border-line between Benjamin and Judah, belonging equally to both parts of the now united kingdom. Its selection was a striking proof of David's military ability and political insight, and was probably determined by a higher wisdom (Deut. xii. 5; 2 Chron. vi. 6). " God intended not Jerusalem for a staple of trade, but for a royal exchange of religion, chiefly holding correspondency with heaven itself, daily receiving blessings thence, duly returning praises thither; besides, God would not have his virgin people the Jews wooed with, much less wedded to, outlandish fashions " (Thos. Fuller).

II. ITS PREVIOUS HISTORY. As the city of Melchizedek (Gen. xiv. 18; Ps. lxxvii. 2; Josephus, ' Wars,' vi. 10), traditions of whose ancient greatness may have lingered around the spot, and fired the poet's imagination (Ps. cx. 4); of Adonizedec the Amorite (Josh. x. 1), a man of different character, like Adonibezek (Judg. i. 7); smitten by Judah, occupied by Benjamin conjointly with the Jebusites (not, perhaps, driven out of their citadel), and afterwards entirely by the latter (Josh. xv. 63; Judg. i. 8, 21; iii. 5—7; xix. 10—12). " Joshua, and Deborah, and Samuel, and Saul, and David must have passed and repassed the hills, and gazed on the tower of the city, unconscious of the fate reserved for her in all subsequent time " (Stanley, ' Sinai and Palestine ').

III. ITS HEROIC CONQUEST. David found little resistance in taking the lower city, in contrast with the upper city or citadel (Josephus), the defenders of which, relying on the strength of their position, said, derisively, that " blind and lame " were sufficient to repel his attack. But: 1. *Self-confidence is fraught with danger.* (1 Sam. xiv. 22.) " The enemies of God's people are often very confident of their own strength, and most secure when their day to fall draws nigh " (Matthew Henry). 2. *Scorn is a spur to a resolute spirit.* " And David said on that day—

> " ' Whoso smiteth a Jebusite (first),
>   Let him hurl down the precipice (watercourse)
> Both the lame and blind,
> Who are hateful to David's soul.' "

And " he shall be chief and captain" (1 Chron. xi. 6). 3. *Great inducements procure great achievements.* 4. *The prize is sometimes won by those for whom it is least intended.* " So Joab the son of Zeruiah went first up, and was chief," his power, of which David bitterly complained (ch. iii. 39), being thereby confirmed. 5. *The language of contempt comes back on those who employ it, to their lasting humiliation.* It became a proverb: " The blind and lame [ironically applied to the over-confident] shall not come into the house [succeed in anything]." 6. *Severity should be joined with mercy.* Although a hard fate befell some, yet most of the Jebusite inhabitants were incorporated into Israel (Zech. ix. 7), and one of them (ch. xxiv. 18) dwelt peacefully on an adjacent hill (2 Chron. iii. 1). 7. *One victory is often followed by many.* The capture of a fortress by national and world-wide consequences.

IV. ITS PERMANENT OCCUPATION, STRENGTHENING, AND EXTENSION. " And David dwelt in the stronghold [of Zion], and called it the city of David" (see Conder, 'Handbook,' p. 337). " And David built round about from Millo [' the citadel,' LXX.] and inward " (ver. 9). " And Joab restored the rest of the city " (1 Chron. xi. 9). " The erection of the new capital at Jerusalem introduces us to a new era, not only in the inward hopes of the prophet-king, but in the external history of the monarchy " (Stanley, ' Jewish Church;' Ewald).

V. ITS THEOCRATIC RELATION, WHICH WAS ITS CHIEF DISTINCTION. As the metropolis of the chosen people, the residence of the Lord's Anointed (Messiah), the seat of government, the centre of religion and Divine service, the source of far-reaching influence, it was "the city of the great King" (Matt. v. 35), where he dwelt, reigned, manifested his glory, and "commanded his blessing, even life for evermore." So Jerusalem was described by psalmists and prophets, and won the passionate attachment of her children, in which love of country and home, devotion to God, and hope for the world were inseparably blended. "Glorious things are spoken of thee, O city of God" (Ps. lxxxvi. 3; xlviii.; cxxii.; cxxv. 1, 2; cxxxvii.).

VI. ITS EXTRAORDINARY VICISSITUDES. "In the fifteen centuries which elapsed between those two points (Judg. i. 8; Luke xxi. 20), the city was besieged no fewer than seventeen times; twice it was razed to the ground; and on two occasions its walls were levelled. In this respect it stands without a parallel in any city, ancient or modern" (Smith's 'Dictionary'). What a scene did it present during these ages of military, political, religious strife, of prophetic activity and demoniacal wickedness, of mercy and of judgment (Amos iii. 2)! With its rejection of "the Son of David" its lingering theocratic glory departed, and its walls became a desolate heap. "O Jerusalem!" (Luke xiii. 34; xx. 41—44).

VII. ITS SPIRITUAL FORESHADOWING. "In the progress of the city of God through the ages, David first reigned in the earthly Jerusalem as a shadow of that which was to come" (Augustine, 'City of God,' xvii. 14. 20); "Mount Zion, the city of the living God, the heavenly Jerusalem" (Heb. xii. 22); the spiritual kingdom of which Christ is King, the general assembly and Church of which he is the Head; the lofty, free, mother-city of us all (Gal. iv. 25, 26); "the holy city, new Jerusalem" (Rev. xxi. 1); glorious, unchanging, everlasting (Heb. xi. 10; xiii. 14). "O holy Zion! where all is abiding, and nothing passes away!"

> "O happy harbour of the saints!
> O sweet and pleasant soil!
> In thee no sorrow may be found,
> No grief, no care, no toil."

D.

Ver. 12 (1 Chron. xiv. 1).—*Hiram, King of Tyre.* Hiram was another of those heathen princes with whom David stood in friendly relation (Achish of Gath; the King of Moab, 1 Sam. xxii. 3; Talmai of Geshur, ch. iii. 3; Toi, or Tou, of Hamath, ch. viii. 9; Joram, or Hadoram, his son, 1 Chron. xviii. 10; Nahash, the Ammonite king of Rabbah, ch. x. 1, 2; Shobi, his son, ch. xvii. 27). He was king of "the strong (fortified) city, Tyre" (Josh. xix. 29); chief of those Phœnician cities "whose flag waved at once in Britain and the Indian Ocean" (Humboldt); celebrated alike for its maritime enterprise, commercial activity, and mechanical arts (Isa. xxiii. 8; Ezek. xxvii.). "Hiram, like David, had just established his throne securely upon the ruins of the rule of the *shophetim*, or judges, and raised the country to a position of power and independence which it had not previously enjoyed" (A. S. Wilkins, 'Phœnicia and Israel'). Notice: 1. *His political sagacity.* In seeking to secure a "commercial treaty" with the King of Israel, by means of which his people might receive corn, oil, etc. (Acts xii. 20), in exchange for manufactured goods, Tyrian purple, articles of tin and bronze, weapons of war, jewellery, etc., and might not be prevented from continuing their commercial pursuits along the great caravan lines of traffic with Egypt, Arabia, Babylon, and Assyria, that ran through the country. 2. *His peaceable disposition.* In sending "messengers" with friendly communications, either of his own accord, or in response to an embassy. "How little David resembled the later Assyrian, Chaldean, and Persian disturbers of the world is most immediately and clearly shown by the fact that he did not, like these great conquerors, seize upon the Phœnician maritime towns, but always remained on the best terms with the little Phœnician states, which were entirely occupied in commerce and the productive arts, and readily sought peace with him" (Ewald). 3. *His generous appreciation.* Without jealousy or suspicion of David, of whom, doubtless, he had heard much, on account of his ability, energy, and integrity, confirmed by personal intercourse. "God knows how to incline toward pious rulers the minds of neighbouring princes and kings, that they may show them all friendly good will" (Starke). 4. *His valuable assistance.* With "cedar trees" (from Lebanon, as subsequently,

1 Kings v.), "and carpenters, and masons," in building a "house of cedar" (ch. vii. 2; vi. 16; ix. 13; xi. 2), or stately palace in Zion, the city of David; perhaps in erecting and adorning other houses in the city, and generally promoting the arts and industries of Israel (1 Chron. xxii. 2). The intercourse thus commenced was immensely beneficial, though it ultimately proved an occasion of evil. "Many have excelled in arts and sciences that were strangers to the covenants of promise; yet David's house was never the worse nor the less fitting to be dedicated to God for its being built by the sons of the stranger" (Matthew Henry). 5. *His steadfast friendship* with David during his life, afterwards with Solomon, contributing to the maintenance of peace and the increase of prosperity among both peoples. "Hiram was ever a lover of David" (1 Kings v. 1). 6. *His reverential spirit.* "Blessed be Jehovah," etc. (1 Kings v. 7). Without entirely renouncing the worship of "the Lord Melkarth [king of the city], Baal of Tyre," he was drawn to the faith of Israel; and, to that extent, represented the gathering of the Gentiles to "the Desire of all nations" (Ps. xlv. 12; Matt. xv. 27; Acts xxi. 3—6). He was an extraordinary man, eminent in life, honoured in death (by the erection of "the tomb of Hiram," Robinson, ii. 456); and he will "rise in the judgment and condemn" the unfaithful under higher privileges (Matt. xi. 21).—D.

Vers. 17—20 (1 Chron. xiv. 8—11).—(THE VALLEY OF REPHAIM.) *Victory over the Philistines.* (*References:* ch. viii. 1, 12; xxi. 15, 18, 19; xxiii. 9, 11, 13; 1 Kings ii. 39.) "Therefore he called the name of that place Baal-Perazim" (ver. 20). So long as David reigned over a single tribe and was at war with the house of Saul, he was left unmolested by the Philistines (1 Sam. xxix. 1—11), whose suzerainty he, perhaps, acknowledged; but when they heard that he was chosen king over all Israel, that an immense army had gathered around him not far from their own border, and that the Jebusite "stronghold of Zion" had fallen before him, they took alarm, mustered all their forces, marched up "to seek [attack] David" (the chief object of their suspicion and fear), and "spread themselves in the Valley of Rephaim" (near Jerusalem). In the condition and conduct of David (as representing the servants of God in conflict with their adversaries) we observe—

I. PERILOUS EMERGENCY, which: 1. Often occurs *after unusual success and honour;* being adapted to check undue self-confidence and self-security. "Lest I should be exalted above measure," etc. (2 Cor. xii. 7). 2. Clearly *manifests the spirit* which men possess, whether of faith and courage, or of fear and cowardice (1 Sam. xvii. 11). 3. Makes personal effort *indispensable.* The conflict was forced upon David. It could not be avoided without disobedience (ch. iii. 18), dishonour, and destruction. And it is the same in other cases. "Ye approach this day unto battle against your enemies," etc. (Deut. xx. 3).

II. PRUDENTIAL ACTIVITY. "And David heard of it, and went down to the hold," the stronghold of Zion (ver. 7), from his residence on the highest and safest part of the mountain ridge; or more probably the stronghold in the desert of Judah, where he had formerly found refuge (1 Sam. xxii. 5; xxiv. 22; ch. xxiii. 14). It may be sometimes necessary to "sit still" and quietly wait for Divine deliverance; but we should: 1. Not remain inactive through *sloth,* vain-confidence, or presumption. 2. Nor rush into conflict *rashly,* or enter upon new courses unadvisedly. 3. But after due *consideration* adopt those measures which afford the fairest prospects of safety and success. "A prudent man," etc. (Prov. xxii. 3).

III. PRAYERFUL INQUIRY. "And David inquired of the Lord," etc. (ch. ii. 1; xvi. 23; xxi. 1). 1. After the utmost thought and endeavour of our own, we often find ourselves in *perplexity* as to the course we should pursue. 2. Our best resource in perplexity is to seek *Divine counsel;* and those who have had experience of its efficacy will not fail to do so (1 Sam. xiv. 16—23; xxiii. 1—12). 3. Nor shall we fail to find *adequate directions* and encouraging promises if we seek it in a right manner. "Go up," etc. "David did not seek Divine counsel (by consulting the Urim) whether to attack Jebus, apparently, because his mind was clear that the enterprise was advantageous. But when Ziklag had been burned by the Amalekites, and now when a dangerous army is at hand, he is glad of such advice. It would appear that he regarded it as a Divine aid in times of perplexity, but only to be sought for in such times. He had no idea of abdicating his duties as a military leader, and putting the movements of his army into the control of the priest. Hence, perhaps, it is that, as his confidence in his troops and in his own warlike experience increased, he ceased altogether to consult the sacred Urim, for we hear no more of it in his later wars " (F. W. Newman).

IV. Practical obedience to the word of the Lord. "And David came," etc. When the path of duty is made plain, nothing remains but to walk therein with : 1. *Humility,* simplicity, alacrity ; as a soldier at the word of command. The habit of immediate and absolute obedience to the will of God is essential to "a good soldier of Jesus Christ." 2. *Dependence* on Divine strength and confidence in Divine promises. 3. *Courage,* concentration of purpose and energy in performance. "Do it with thy might." David's attack was made with such impetuosity that it was like the breaking forth of water, a torrent or inundation which bursts through, disperses and sweeps away whatever opposes its course.

V. Public thanksgiving and praise. "Jehovah hath broken forth upon mine enemies . . . Therefore he called the name of that place Baal-Perazim," *i.e.* properly, lord, master, *possessor,* and, tropically, *place* (which possesses or is distinguished by something) of breaches, inundations, dispersions, defeats (Gesenius). 1. The spirit in which success is really sought appears in the manner in which it is used. When sought by and for God it will be ascribed to him. "Not unto us," etc. "His right hand and his holy arm hath gotten him the victory" (Ps. xcviii. 1). 2. The help which is graciously and openly vouchsafed by God should be gratefully and openly acknowledged by men (Ps. l. 14, 15). 3. Of Divine benefits a record should be made by those who receive them, for the instruction of "the generation to come" (Ps. lxxviii. 4); and the place which is distinguished by them should become a permanent memorial of Divine power and goodness. This victory was long remembered. "For Jehovah will rise up as on the mountain of Perazim," etc. (Isa. xxviii. 21). "The *military stamp* of the first part of David's reign is the preindication of the military character of the whole of it. In the Psalms of David we hear the echo of this warlike and victorious theocracy. They are mostly songs of conflict and victory in praise of the God who saved his people from their enemies" (Erdmann).—D.

Ver. 21 (1 Chron. xiv. 12).—(Baal-Perazim.) *The destruction of images.* The religion of the Canaanite people was "an apotheosis of the forces and laws of nature; an adoration of the objects in which those forces were seen and where they appeared most active" (Movers). The Philistines carried (probably on sacred carts) their *images* or *gods* (commonly regarded as identical) into battle, expecting victory by their aid; but so sudden was their defeat, and so hasty their flight, that they were compelled to leave them behind, and "David and his men took them away;" and "David gave a commandment, and they were burned with fire." "When the ark fell into the Philistines' hands it consumed them; but when these images fell into the hands of Israel they could not save themselves from being consumed" (Patrick). In their destruction we see : 1. *A proof of the vanity of idols.* These images (*atsabim,* equivalent to "things fashioned with labour") were only "the work of men's hands" (Ps. cxv. 4—8), and "profitable for nothing" (Isa. xl. 19; xli. 7; xliv. 9—20; xlvi. 6, 7), disappointing completely the confidence reposed in them. Who could henceforth regard them or others with fear or respect ? 2. *A testimony to the power of Jehovah,* the living and true God, the Holy One of Israel. It was against him that the Philistines fought in attacking his people; and by him they and their idols were overthrown, as aforetime (1 Sam. v. 3; vii. 7; xvii. 38—54). Yet how persistent was their opposition (ver. 22)! 3. *An expression of abhorrence of idolatry,* and zeal for the worship of God alone; the *personal fidelity* of David to the fundamental principle of the theocracy (Ps. xvi. 4). During his reign idolatry found no place in Israel. 4. *A fulfilment of the injunctions of the Law.* "Thou shalt utterly overthrow them, and quite break down their images" (Exod. xxiii. 24), "and burn their graven images with fire" (Deut. vii. 5). Idolatry was a direct crime against the state, high treason against the Divine King of Israel, and might not be tolerated in any form. 5. *A precaution against exposure to temptation,* by the influence of their presence, forms, names, associations, on hearts always too prone to go astray. "Thou shalt not desire the silver or gold that is on them, nor take it unto thee, lest thou be snared therein," etc. (Deut. vii. 25, 26). No sacrifice was too great to avoid such a snare (Acts xix. 19). "Here, perhaps, the admirer of ancient sculpture will be ready to drop a tear of regret over the fine statues and other monuments of antiquity that must have been destroyed in consequence of the Mosaic mandate; but he may safely dry it up, for the *chef d'œuvres* of this period were not worth sparing" (Michaelis). Even if they had been the finest specimens of art, their preservation from the flames would have been an ill compensation for the moral evil which it would have induced. 6. *A representation of the design of the true religion.* "To destroy the works of the devil" (1 John iii. 8), and to maintain and extend the knowledge, love, and service of God; not, indeed, by force, but by the truth (2 Cor. x. 4; see 1 Sam. v. 3). 7. *A prophecy and an earnest of the complete demolition of idols* (Isa. ii. 18—20), and the earth being "filled with the glory of the Lord" (Numb. xiv. 21). "Thou hast kept me to be head of the heathen," etc. (ch. xxii. 44, 50).

> "All nations whom thou hast made,
> Shall come and bow themselves down before thee, O Lord;
> And shall give glory to thy Name."
> (Ps. lxxxvi. 9; xxii. 27; xcvii. 7; xcvi. 3, 5, 10.)

Conclusion. Those who are zealous in destroying the idols of others should not spare their own. What is an idol? That object (whatever it may be) which a man sets up before his face or *in his heart*, and which he thinks about, delights in, and relies upon, more than God. "Flee from idolatry!" (1 Cor. x. 14; Col. iii. 5; Phil. iii. 19; 1 John v. 21).—D.

Vers. 22, 23 (1 Chron. xiv. 13, 14).—(THE VALLEY OF REPHAIM.) *Renewed conflict.* 1. The life of a godly man on earth is a warfare which is *perpetually renewed.* Hardly has one conflict been passed through before another awaits him with old or new and more formidable foes: the world, the flesh, the devil; ignorance, idolatries, oppressions, sin and misery of all kinds (1 Sam. xvii. 1—11). Yea, each day the "good warfare" begins afresh. "The approach of duty is as a battle-field" (Essenian maxim). "On awaking in the morning, the first thing to be observed by thine inward sight is the listed field in which thou art enclosed; the law of the combat being that he who fights not must there lie dead for ever" (Scupoli). 2. *Signal success* in one conflict does not ensure the like in the next; and it ought, therefore, to be always associated with humility, watchfulness, and prayer; from lack of which many a victory has been turned into a defeat. It was a motto of King Alfred ("Si modo victor eras," etc.)—

> "If to-day thou be conqueror, beware of the fight of to-morrow;
> If to-day thou be conquered, prepare for the fight of to-morrow."

3. One victory affords ground for the *confident expectation* of another, when the latter is looked for in the same spirit as the former, with dependence on the strength of God, submission to his will, devotion to his glory and the good of his people. "David inquired of the Lord *again.*" 4. The *special means* to be employed in every new conflict must be adapted to the special circumstances of the case; and both the wisdom to perceive them and the might to make them effectual are from the Lord. "Thou shalt *not* go up" (directly, in front of them, as in the former conflict, and as he was about to do again); "go round about them to their rear, and come upon them opposite the mulberry trees" (a spot, probably well known to David and his men, where a cluster or grove of baca trees would favour their attack), etc. "The words teach us that in our own strength, and merely with the human weapons of reason and science, we are not to make war against the adversary. Success can only be calculated upon when the conflict is undertaken under the *influence* of the Holy Spirit of God breathed forth, and in the immediate blessed experience of the gracious presence of the Lord and of the truth of his Word" (Krummacher).—D.

Vers. 24, 25 (1 Chron. xiv. 15—17).—(THE VALLEY OF REPHAIM.) *Signs.* "The sound of a going" (as of footsteps, Judg. v. 4; ch. vi. 13) "in the beginnings" (on the tops or at the entrance of the grove) "of the baca trees," which David heard, was a *sign* appointed by God, occurring, either by his extraordinary and miraculous operation for a special purpose; or by his ordinary operation in nature and providence (the rustling of the leaves in a still season by a fresh breeze, such as, in the East, usually springs up about day-dawn), and made use of by him for that purpose. It is not stated that it was intended for or perceived by any one else but David. To him it was "the sound of his Master's feet" (2 Kings vi. 32); the "going out before him" of "the Captain of the Lord's host" (Josh. v. 14) at the head of legions of angels "to smite the Philistines," and summoning him to follow. And the enemy, wrapped in slumber, and attacked at an unexpected time and place, was surprised and routed. Are there now no signs of a similar nature? 1. They are *needed* at certain seasons—in order to the proper under-standing, enforcement, and application of the truths and duties contained in the written Word; especially when iniquity abounds, love waxes cold, labour is vain, and fear and perplexity prevail; when "we see not our signs" (Ps. lxxiv. 9), nor receive "a token for good" (Ps. lxxxvi. 17). 2. They are *afforded* in various ways—by a striking concur-rence of events with the Word (1 Sam. x. 7) or their peculiar combination; by manifest tendencies, vivid impressions, spiritual suggestions, or an unusual expectancy; some-times with "a still small voice," sometimes with "the sound of a trumpet," "thunder and rain" (1 Sam. xii. 17), or "a rushing mighty wind." They are never wholly absent; but do we hear or see them?

> "Earth's crammed with heaven,
> And every common bush afire with God;
> But only he who sees takes off his shoes."
>   (Mrs. Browning.)

Consider them as—

I. PERCEIVED BY A VIGILANT OBSERVER. "When thou *hearest* the sound of a going," etc. Having "inquired of the Lord," and received the promise of aid, David watched for the sign thereof. "I will stand upon my watch," etc. (Hab. ii. 1). Such a watch-man: 1. Fixes his *attention* on the spiritual realities by which the world of sense is surrounded, supported, pervaded; and becomes conscious of what is hidden from others, whose attention is wholly absorbed in earthly things; hearing a voice they cannot hear, and seeing a hand they cannot see. 2. Relies upon the *promises* which have been graciously spoken by "him who is invisible." 3. Looks for their *fulfilment* with fervent desire and unwearied patience, "more than they that watch for the morning" (Ps. cxxx. 5, 6), until at length the sign and then the reality which it denotes are fully revealed. Everything depends upon a thoughtful, believing, waiting spirit!

> "Signs summon not Faith: but they wait for her call;
> For in her own right she holds nature in thrall.
> Where sense sees a blank space, with nought to inspire;
> She, seer-like, finds horses and chariots of fire.
> Sense ransacks all space for the proofs of a God;
> Faith finds them at home, at the end of her rod.
> And he who complains of no God-prints below
> Will find nothing but sense-prints where'er he may go."

"There are chemical experiments, in which, if a certain condition be wanting, the element sought for cannot be elicited. It is present, waiting, ready to leap into activity the moment the condition is present. But as long as that is wanting, the element is imprisoned, separated by an impassable barrier, and might almost be said to be non-existent. Similarly, the preoccupied mind might sleep at the very gate of heaven—no celestial dreams would visit it. The worldly mind might find itself in the house of God, in the holiest of all; but the cloud of glory would sweep by it unnoticed. A mind keen after earthly objects, and engrossed by the interests of time, might live here three score years and ten, with the powers of the world to come all the time surrounding it, soliciting it, pressing in upon it; and yet never once recognize a single indication of the Divine presence. And he who finds nothing of heaven on earth would find nothing but earth in heaven" (J. Harris).

II. POSSESSING INVALUABLE SIGNIFICANCE. "Then will Jehovah go out before thee," etc. The sign in itself is little; the thing signified, as it is revealed to the waiting soul, is great, inasmuch as it relates to the Lord of hosts, and includes: 1. His *presence* with us in a very special manner (2 Chron. xiv. 11; xx. 12; xxxii. 6—8). If a soldier is inspired with courage and strength by knowing that his commander is near and his eye upon him, much more should we be similarly inspired by the conviction of the Divine presence. 2. His *working* for us and in us. "The Lord is my Helper," etc. (Heb. xiii. 6). 3. His *will* concerning us, with respect, not only to our welfare, but also to our duty, the spirit we should cherish, the conduct we should pursue, the manner, place, and time of our activity. There is no greater joy to a faithful servant of God than to feel assured that he is where God would have him to be, and doing what God would have him to do. And this joy is his strength.

III. REQUIRING PERSONAL EXERTION. "Then bestir thyself; go out to battle. And David did so as Jehovah commanded him." There is a time to work and fight as well as to pray and watch. As it is presumptuous and vain to stir before the signal for action is given, so it is slothful and ruinous to wait after it is received. "Wherefore criest thou unto me? . . . Go forward" (Exod. xiv. 15; Josh. vii. 10). Divine assistance is not meant to supersede our exertion, but to quicken it. Because God works we must work, with a feeling of grateful obligation, reverence, and confidence (Phil. ii. 12). "The Captain of our salvation" goes out before us that we may follow him (Rev. xix. 14) with: 1. Implicit *obedience* to his every direction and movement (see 1 Sam. xiii. 1—7). 2. Strenuous *effort* and whole-hearted devotion. 3. The utmost *promptitude*. Now or never. The opportunity, if allowed to slip, returns no more. "Consider that this day ne'er dawns again" (Dante).

> "'Charge!' was the captain's cry.
> Theirs not to make reply;
> Theirs not to reason why;
> Theirs but to do or die."

IV. CONDUCTING TO IMPORTANT ISSUES. "And he smote the Philistines," etc. By such a victory: 1. The imminent danger that threatened is removed. 2. The final overthrow of the enemy is assured (ch. viii. 1). 3. The firm establishment and wide extension of the kingdom are promoted. It became possible to bring up the ark to Zion (ch. vi. ?) and to subdue surrounding adversaries. "And the fame of David went out into all lands," etc. (1 Chron. xiv. 17). God fails not to fulfil his promises; disappoints not the trust that is placed in him; but makes the faithful "more than conquerors."

APPLICATION. With reference to: 1. The individual. 2. The family. 3. The Church. 4. The nation. "Can ye not discern the *signs* of the times?"—D.

Vers. 1—3.—*Tardy acceptance of a divinely appointed ruler.* Abner and Ishbosheth being dead, and Mephibosheth incapable from his lameness, the eleven tribes that for upwards of seven years had not only held aloof from David, but waged war with him, now come to the conclusion that it is best to become his subjects, and again be united with Judah in one kingdom. They accordingly make their submission to him and solemnly accept him as their sovereign.

I. THE GROUNDS OF THEIR ACCEPTANCE OF HIM. 1. *Close relationship.* "Behold, we are thy bone and thy flesh" (comp. Eph. v. 30). God has given to us a King who is one with us in nature. The Ruler of the Church, yea, of all things, is *a Man*; the throne of the universe is filled by a human form (see Heb. ii. 5, *et seq.*)—a fact which endears the Christ to his willing subjects. 2. *Previous service.* (Ver. 2.) "In time past," etc. In which service David had both displayed and increased his capacities for ruling men. With this may be compared Christ's period of service when on earth, especially during his public ministry and last sufferings. By these he was trained and prepared for his throne (made "perfect through sufferings," Heb. ii. 10); and it is in and by these that he reveals himself and attracts the hearts of men. 3. *Divine appointment.* (Ver. 2.) "The Lord said to thee, Thou shalt feed ['shepherd,' 'be the shepherd of'] my people Israel, and thou shalt be a captain [literally, 'foremost man, leader'] over Israel." A king is to be as a shepherd to his subjects, not only ruling them, but caring for, watching over, protecting, guiding, uniting them; guarding and preserving the weak from violence and oppression, as a shepherd his lambs. The image was natural to the Hebrews, and runs through the Scriptures, extending even to the visions of heaven (Rev. vii. 17). The king was also to be leader in peace or war, ever "to the front," worthy to be followed, first and foremost in all noble deeds, accepting courageously the perils of such a position. David was such a king, imperfectly; Christ is such a King, perfectly. Both were divinely designated to the office of Ruler of God's people, Kings by Divine right in the strictest sense. As such David is here recognized at length by the tribes of Israel, as before by the tribe of Judah. As such the Lord Jesus is recognized by his followers. These reasons had existed and should have been as powerful immediately after Saul's death; but they had not been allowed to operate. But the experience of these tribes whilst holding aloof from David, their present disorganized condition, possibly also their knowledge of the benefits of David's rule to Judah, combined to open their eyes, and so impress these considerations on their hearts as to produce a general willingness to accept him whom they had been rejecting. And thus it is with many in respect to the great King. His claims are known, but other lords are preferred, until, after delay more or less protracted, they become convinced of their sin and folly, and surrender themselves to him. Let those who are thus procrastinating beware lest they become convinced too late.

II. THE SOLEMNITIES BY WHICH THEIR ACCEPTANCE OF DAVID, AND HIS OF THEM, WERE SIGNIFIED. 1. *A mutual covenant.* He engaging to rule them, and they to serve him according to the Law of God (Deut. xvii. 14—20). In like manner, when men receive Christ as their King, promising loyalty and obedience, he on his part promises to be to them all that his gospel represents him. These Israelites, indeed, may have imposed special stipulations not expressed in the Law; but we, in accepting Christ, have simply to submit to the terms of the Divine covenant, as we are not in any degree independent parties. 2. *The anointing of David as king.* The third time he was anointed—once by Samuel, once by the tribe of Judah, and now by the rest of the tribes. For the people could in a measure give him authority over them. But our King Jesus can receive no authority from us. He is the Christ (the Anointed) of God; we have simply to recognize his Divine authority. 3. *The presence of God was recognized.* "Before the Lord." This was fitting, as he was supreme Monarch, to whom both king and people were bound to submit, whose blessing was necessary to render the union happy; and an engagement made as in his sight would be felt as peculiarly binding. So should we, in accepting Christ, place ourselves in the presence of God, first in secret, then in his house, and at the Lord's Table. 4. *A joyful feast concluded the proceedings.* (See 1 Chron. xii. 39, 40.) It was to the whole people a suitable occasion for rejoicing. They were again one nation. Their union would be cemented by eating and drinking together. They would the better retain the feeling of union when they had separated to their various localities and homes, and would be the better prepared to perform their common duties to the king and the nation. Thus also our Lord enjoins his subjects to eat and drink together in his Name, that they may recognize each other as his, rejoice together in their privileges, and be more closely united to him and the whole "Israel of God."

In conclusion: 1. Happy is the nation whose rulers and subjects alike recognize God as the supreme Ruler over them, and his will as their supreme law; act as in his sight, and invoke his blessing. 2. Closer union amongst Christians must spring from more thorough acceptance of the royal authority of Christ. They *are* one in him, and they will become more completely, more consciously, and more manifestly one in proportion as they, all alike, renouncing merely human authorities, come to Christ himself, listen to him, and submit to his authority in all things.—G. W.

Ver. 10.—*Desirable greatness.* "And David went on, and grew great, and the Lord God of hosts was with him." The growing greatness of David was owing to the presence and favour of God, and was accompanied with them. It was, then—

I. GREATNESS WELL-DERIVED. All greatness is in some sense from God; but all does not spring from his favour. "Surely thou didst set them in slippery places; thou castedst them down into destruction" (Ps. lxxiii. 18). He that becomes "a great man" through unjust violence, the oppression and swallowing up of the weak, low cunning, unscrupulous ambition, insatiable avarice, or an absorbing activity of mind and body which excludes God from thought and life, cannot rightly attribute his success to the blessing of God. Such greatness is disastrous, and carries a curse with it. It is reached by serving Satan, and accompanied with slavery to him and participation of his doom. He was not altogether lying when he said (Luke iv. 6, 7) that the power and glory of the world were given by him to those who would worship him. The world abounds in instances of greatness so won. But the greatness which is a gift of God's favour is reached by paths of truth and uprightness and piety; by the strenuous employment of all the powers, indeed, but in harmony with the Divine will; not so much, therefore, with the purpose to grow great as to be of service to others. It is rather accepted as a gift of God than sought; and is accepted "with fear and trembling," lest the strong temptations which accompany all worldly greatness should become victorious. Such greatness is accompanied with a good conscience, and may be without serious peril to the soul. It may foster principles of godliness and benevolence. It qualifies for high service of others, and, so employed, enlarges the heart and elevates instead of degrading the character. It thus ministers to the truest greatness—that which is spiritual and eternal.

II. GREATNESS WELL-ACCOMPANIED. Some, the greater they grow the less of God they enjoy; they gradually forsake him, and he at length abandons them. But there are those of whom it may be said, as they grow great in this world, still "the Lord God of hosts is with them." 1. *How the great may secure this blessing.* By: (1) Humility (Deut. viii. 13, 14; Ps. cxxxviii. 6; Jas. iv. 6). (2) Devotion of their enlarged powers to the service of God and of man. (3) Constant prayer. On the other hand, pride, selfishness, and prayerlessness will separate them from God. 2. *The benefits they will derive from it.* (1) The highest and purest enjoyment to which worldly honours and resources can minister. (2) Preservation from the perils of their position. (3) The power to gain the best kind of good from it. (4) And to do the most good by it. (5) Greatness thus accompanied is likely to be lasting.

Finally, spiritual greatness combines in a pre-eminent degree the two excellences of being God-derived and God-accompanied. It springs from the favour of God, and secures its constant enjoyment. It consists in abundance of spiritual wisdom, holiness, and love, and consequent power for good; in the honour which these bring from God, and in the confidence, affection, and respect with which they inspire men. It has the advantage of being accessible to all, its conditions being, first, faith in Christ and God; and then the fruits of faith, such as love, humility (Matt. xviii. 4), obedience to God (Matt. v. 19), self-control (Prov. xvi. 32), self-denying service (Matt. xx. 20—28). Such greatness is intrinsic and essential. It is best for ourselves and best for others. It is inseparable from the man himself, and, surviving all worldly distinctions, goes with him into eternity, and abides for ever (see 1 John ii. 17).—G. W.

Ver. 12.—*Perception of Divine agency and purpose.* These words are introduced after the narration of the taking of the fortress of Zion, the erection of additional buildings around it, and especially the building of a royal residence for David. It was the establishment of a metropolis for the whole kingdom, and both evidenced and promoted a settled state of things. David's thoughts upon the matter are given in the text. He recognized that it was God who made him king, and that his exaltation was for the sake of God's people Israel.

I. THE FACTS PERCEIVED. 1. *The Divine operation.* God had raised David to the throne and settled him on it. At every step the hand of God was clear; especially clear was that hand as the whole series of steps, their connection and issue, were regarded. 2. *The Divine purpose.* All was "for his people Israel's sake." Not for the sake of David and his family, that they might be rich, luxurious, and honoured; but for the good of others. That the tribes might be united and consolidated as one nation, free, settled, safe, prosperous, and glorious. That the people might be elevated in their moral and religious life; and that they might be better fitted to fulfil the great end of their election as God's people, witnessing for him, maintaining his worship, preserving his truth, showing forth his praise, and promoting his kingdom in the world; and that ultimately from them might come the Saviour and salvation. Similarly, the Son of David is exalted, not for himself alone, but that he may deliver, "gather together in one" (John xi. 52), teach, sanctify, elevate, and eternally save, the people of God. He is "Head over all things to the Church" (Eph. i. 22). In like manner, all power, elevation, authority, etc., with which men are endowed are given to them for the sake of others, and ultimately for the sake of God's people, to whom in Christ all things belong (1 Cor. iii. 21—23), that they may be blessed and be made a blessing to mankind.

II. DAVID'S PERCEPTION OF THESE FACTS. 1. *He recognized that his exaltation was from God.* This would check pride and produce humility and gratitude. 2. *He recognized that his exaltation was for the sake of the people.* This would check selfish ambition and produce cordial devotement to the good of the nation. And thus should we seek to have a clear perception and deep impression of the agency and purpose of God in our lives. We should regard all we have of being, faculty, position, or possessions, temporal and spiritual alike, as from him; and all as given us, not merely or chiefly for ourselves, but for the sake of others, especially for their salvation—that they may become, if they are not, God's people, and that as God's people they may prosper, be united, victorious over all the foes of God and man, and powerful to bless mankind. For this is the Divine purpose, and as we make it our own we become intelligent co-workers with God, and our lives are filled with meaning, dignity, and worth, and a fitting preparation for the world where all are consciously, willingly, and habitually engaged in doing the will of God (Matt. vi. 10).—G. W.

Ver. 19.—*Divine assurance of victory.* The enlargement and establishment of David's kingdom, while a joy to Israel, was a grief to their old and formidable enemies, the Philistines. These came in great numbers into the territory of Israel, hoping to seize David himself (ver. 17), as the shortest way of putting an end to the newly united state. So formidable was the invasion that the king found it desirable to leave his new city and go "down to the hold," the fortress probably of Adullam, with such forces as he could collect; and when the enemy "spread themselves in the Valley of Rephaim," he sought direction and promise of victory from God before attacking them, and received the answer, "Go up," etc. Christians are called to a warfare with powerful enemies, who are the enemies of Christ and his kingdom; and it is their satisfaction that they have received Divine assurance of victory. They have to fight against the world, the flesh, and the devil, as they assail themselves and endanger their salvation, and as they prevail in the world and even invade the Church. They are powerful foes, with many resources at command, and their onset is at times alarming. As the Philistines with David, they may be expected to make specially violent assaults when special prosperity has been attained, but the results are not yet fully established. But it is the joy of Christ's warriors that victory is certain. Each faithful soul shall successfully fight his own way to heaven, and the Church shall gain final and complete success in the battle with evil.

I. How THE ASSURANCE OF VICTORY IS IMPARTED. How does God assure us that we shall be successful in the Christian war? 1. *By the intuitions of the soul.* When we distinctly place before our minds the combatants, we cannot doubt which will ultimately be victorious. It is a conflict between good and evil, truth and error, right and wrong, holiness and sin, God and Satan. Evil is mighty, but good is almighty, because the living, true, and holy God is almighty. 2. *By the promises and prophecies of his Word.* These assure victory to every faithful soul in his own personal contest (see 1 Cor. x. 13; Eph. vi. 10—13; Jas. iv. 7; Matt. xxiv. 13), and triumph to the Church in the conflict with error and sin in the world, notwithstanding the deep and firm hold they have upon men, their extensive prevalence, their long reign. These assurances abound throughout the Scriptures, culminating in the descriptions of the conflict in the Apocalypse, and of the victories of the great Leader and his forces, and summed up in the triumphant shout of the great voices in heaven: "The kingdoms of this world are become the kingdoms of our Lord and of his Christ, and he shall reign for ever and ever" (Rev. xi. 15). 3. *By the mission and work of our Lord Jesus Christ.* He came as our "Leader and Commander" (Isa. lv. 4), and, by his personal conflict, endurance, and conquests, not only led the way for his followers, but secured victory for them. "Be of good cheer," he says, "I have overcome the world" (John xvi. 33; see also Heb. ii. 9, 10, 14—18; 1 Cor. xv. 24, 25). 4. *By the victories already won.* The gift of the Holy Spirit and his mighty operations in apostolic times and all through the Christian centuries. The victories over the old paganism; the Reformation; the revivals of religion at various periods; the successes of modern missions. Every true-hearted Christian has in his own experience not only a pledge of final victory for himself, but an encouragement to seek the salvation of others.

II. THE EFFECT WHICH SUCH ASSURANCE SHOULD HAVE UPON US. "Go up." Engage in the battle with evil; and do so with: 1. *Confidence and courage.* 2. *Resolute zeal and determination.* 3. *Persistency, notwithstanding all delays, discouragements, and partial failures.* 4. *Songs of victory.* Not only for every advantage gained, but for the final and complete victory already to faith as good as won. If the hope of victory in other conflicts produces such effects, much more should the absolute certainty which the soldiers of Christ have. An altogether ill effect is that which the Divine assurances produce on some. They say that, as the battle is the Lord's, and he is sure to conquer, their efforts are needless. As relates to a man's own salvation, such a persuasion is fatal; for victory is promised only to the earnest combatant, and the assurance of Divine operation is made a reason why we should "work out our own salvation" (Luke xiii. 24; 1 Tim. vi. 12; Phil. ii. 12, 13). And as respects the spread and triumph of the kingdom of Christ, such a feeling indicates ignorance, indifference, indolence, and unfaithfulness, rather than faith in God. It is quite inconsistent with both Scripture and reason, and will deprive those who cherish it of all share in the joy of final victory, even if they are not utterly cast away as "wicked, slothful, and unprofitable" (Matt. xxv. 26, 30).—G. W.

Ver. 24.—*Divine omens of coming victory.* "When thou hearest the sound of marching . . . then is the Lord gone out before thee," etc. (Revised Version). The Philistines were a brave and determined people, not easily beaten. Repulsed and scattered "as the breach of waters," they reunite and return. David, inquiring of God, receives directions differing from those given him on the former occasion. He is instructed not to "go up" to the higher ground occupied by the Philistines, but to make a circuit to their rear, where was a plantation, and when he hears a sound as of marching on the tops of the trees, then to attack the foe with spirit and energy, knowing that God was gone before to give him certain victory. The enemies of the Christian and the Church are similarly persistent, and must be assailed and defeated over and over again. Indeed, the conflict is continuous. There are, however, certain times when we are specially to "bestir" ourselves, with assurance of conquest; and these are often indicated by special signs that the supernatural powers are "marching" on to lead us and give us success.

I. IN RESPECT TO THE WHOLE CHRISTIAN WARFARE AND WORK, THE SUPERNATURAL EVENTS BY WHICH OUR RELIGION WAS INAUGURATED MAY BE THUS REGARDED. In the incarnation of the Son of God, his supernatural revelations, the miracles of his life, death, resurrection, and ascension, in the all-sufficient sacrifice he offered for sin, and in the descent and operations of the Holy Spirit, God went before his people to lead them on to victory. They were not for the men of that age only, but for all ages. We, recalling them to mind, may ever take courage in the assurance that we are following where God has led and still leads. Evermore they remain as calls to us to "bestir" ourselves with confidence of success; the eternal motives to energy and hope; the eternal armoury, too, from which we draw the offensive and defensive arms we need in the war.

II. IN RESPECT TO OUR OWN PERSONAL SALVATION, THERE ARE AT TIMES SPECIAL INDICATIONS THAT GOD IS GOING BEFORE US TO GIVE US SPECIAL HELP AND BLESSING. We ought not, indeed, to wait for these. The knowledge of our duty, the memory of Christ, the promise of Divine aid, the experiences of the past, constitute sufficient reasons for habitual diligence, prayer, and hope; and special inspirations may be most confidently expected by such as are thus ever "exercising themselves unto godliness," ever striving against evil and for the attainment of greater good. But there are moments of peculiar sensibility which afford peculiarly favourable opportunities and special calls to "bestir" ourselves that we may secure the blessings which they promise. Startling events which deeply move the conscience and heart; personal afflictions which compel retirement and produce impressions favourable to religious exercises; bereavements which bring face to face with death; losses which make the uncertainty and insufficiency of earthly good felt; sermons which unusually touch the heart; earnest appeals of a friend which produce deep emotion; whatever, in a word, brings God and eternity, Christ and salvation, nearer, and creates a sense of their supreme importance, whatever excites a craving for a higher good, are signs that God is working for us, and calls to "bestir" ourselves by special meditation, prayer, etc. We may at such seasons obtain more spiritual blessing in an hour than at others in a month.

III. IN RESPECT TO THE WARFARE AND WORK OF THE CHURCH FOR THE ADVANCE-

MENT OF THE KINGDOM OF GOD, THERE ARE SIMILAR SIGNS FROM HEAVEN ADAPTED TO STIMULATE AND ENCOURAGE. Such are: 1. *Remarkable openings made for the entrance of the gospel.* The operations of Divine providence preparing a way for the operations of Divine grace. These may be on a small scale, laying open to Christian effort an individual, a family, or a neighbourhood; or on a large scale, opening a continent crowded with scores of millions of the human race. The discoveries of travellers, and the removal of barriers and obstacles by military conquests, are thus to be regarded. India, China, Japan, and Africa furnish instances of God going before his people, and calling on them to "bestir" themselves and follow whither he leads. 2. *Impressions favourable to religion.* In one person, or in a family, a congregation, a town, or a nation. Impressions by sickness, by war, pestilence, or other calamities; or by signal displays of the Divine goodness. By these God goes before, and prepares the way for his people to publish more diligently and earnestly the gospel, with good assurance of success. 3. *Unusual religious earnestness in Christians themselves.* Extraordinary emotions of love and zeal towards God and Christ and the souls of men, and of longing to rescue the perishing and enlarge the Church, however they may have been excited, are to be regarded as the yearnings of God's Spirit in the Christian heart, and as calls and encouragements to exertion. The sign that God is working and leading his people to victory is more conspicuous when these emotions are shared by many. 4. *Successes in the Christian war summon to new efforts and encourage the hope of new successes.* They show that God is working, and assure us that he will continue to work with his faithful servants.—G. W.

EXPOSITION.

CHAPTER VI.

Ver. 1.—And David gathered together. The long subjection to the Philistines was at an end, and David's first care is to bring the ark of Jehovah from Kirjath-jearim to Jerusalem. In this he had a twofold object. For, first, it was an act of piety, testifying David's gratitude to God, who had so quickly raised him from the condition of a despairing fugitive hiding away in the cave of Adullam to that of a victorious king reigning over an independent and free people. But David had also a political purpose. The weakness of Israel in the past was the result of its divisions. He would heal this by giving it a capital, whither the tribes would come up for worship, and where they would feel that they formed one nation. David had seen the evils of a divided sovereignty, when he and Ishbosheth were wasting the strength of Israel in civil war. For more than half a century he remedied this, but before there had been time for the union of the tribes to be cemented by the gradual influence of religion, Solomon's oppressive levies of unpaid workmen, forced to labour in his costly buildings, and the despotic stupidity of Rehoboam, broke up united Israel into two feeble states, which henceforward had to struggle hard for a mere existence. The condition of Israel was very similar to that of the United States of North America before their great civil war; except that their president, elected by all the people, and their Congress at Washington, were far stronger bonds of union than any that were possessed by the Israelites. But when there was danger of even these failing to keep them together as one people, the statesmen of the north put forth their utmost powers, and spared neither life nor treasure, because they saw clearly that the victory of the south meant the breaking up of their empire into a multitude of feeble governments, which, by their mutual jealousies, would paralyze and thwart one another. With equal discernment David endeavoured to counteract the jealousy and separate action of the tribes, which was bringing about the disintegration of Israel, by giving them a point of union. Had he gone further north for his capital, he might, perhaps, have overawed the stubborn tribe of Ephraim, which was always the most unmanageable of the sections of Israel. But the situation of Jerusalem upon the borders of Benjamin and Judah, on a hill-top which neither had really possessed, and which was marked out for noble use by its wonderful natural conformation, fully justified David's choice; and it has had the assent of mankind ever since. David then made this unrivalled spot his capital, and placed there, first of all, his royal residence, whereby it became the centre of all public business and of the administration of law; and, secondly, as a matter of still higher importance, he made it the head-quarters of their national religion and the abode of their God. We see the weight of this religious influence in the anxiety of Jeroboam to counteract it, and in the strength given to Rehoboam by the migration into Judah of those who valued the temple services more than their worldly prosperity. Even Saul had valued the national religion, and had established its head-quarters at Nob; but, giving way to the ungoverned anger of a despot, he had destroyed his own work. It was left to one who to the bravery of a soldier added the discernment of a statesman to consolidate the tribes into a nation by establishing their religion upon a sure and influential basis. For this reason also he made their services full of delight and enjoyment by the institution of choral chants and the use of instruments of music; while the psalms which his singers recited were so spiritual and ennobling that we to this day use them in our solemn worship. Granting that there are expressions in them harsher and more intolerant than a disciple of the loving Jesus would now apply to any earthly enemy, yet, as a whole, the Psalms, written in these rough far-off times, still form our best book of devotion! In the parallel place in the First Book of Chronicles we have the narrative of this re-establishment of the Mosaic Law given as looked at on the Levitical side, and with many interesting additions. Here the narrator looks at it with the eye of a statesman. We must not, however, suppose that the history there given is arranged in chronological order, as, if so, the two victories in the Valley of Rephaim would have both taken place in the three months during which the ark was resting in the house of Obed-Edom. If this were so, then David would first have had more than three hundred and forty thousand warriors with him at Hebron to anoint him, and with their aid would have captured Jerusalem. He would next have assembled thirty thousand picked men to bring the ark up to Zion; and yet would have had only his body-guard of "mighty men" wherewith to fight Israel's battles and win its independence. Most probably the order, both here and in Chronicles, is not chronological, and the course of events was as follows. With the help of the men gathered at Hebron David captures Jerusalem. As soon as it is made safe they withdraw, and leave him occupied with planning out and building his city. Alarmed at the vast concourse at Hebron, and made angry by David's seizure of a strong fortress, the Philistines hastily pounce upon him in numbers too vast for him to resist. He escapes, leaving but a few men to defend Jerusalem, and hides in his old fastness. Encouraged there by finding three of his mighties more than a match for the garrison at Bethlehem, he gathers the more valiant spirits, and makes a sudden attack upon the Philistines, who were engaged in ravaging the country as a punishment for its rebellion. They are defeated,

but with no great loss; and so with unbroken strength they again invade the country, and march up once more to Jerusalem, prepared to fight a pitched battle, and seize that fortress as the prize of victory. Again, David, with far larger forces, surprises them, and, driving them from ridge to ridge, so utterly vanquishes them that the power of Philistia was destroyed for ever. It was after this double victory that Hiram, King of Tyre, whose dominions bordered upon the Philistines', and who had found them disagreeable neighbours, made a close alliance with David; and so at length, free from all fear at home, and honoured abroad, he was able to turn his thoughts to the consolidation of his kingdom and the establishment of Jehovah's worship. And in the Book of Chronicles we have the details of that spiritual service of psalmody which David added to the Levitical routine of sacrifice, and which bears the significant name of "prophecy," as being the expression of the moral and spiritual side of the Mosaic Law (1 Chron. xxv. 1). Instead of "Again David gathered," the words of the Hebrew are "And David gathered together all the chosen men of Israel." The first gathering was at Hebron (ch. v. 1), and before they came David must have given his consent to their wishes, and invited their presence at his anointing. They soon gather together a second time to endow their new kingdom with the safeguards necessary for their spiritual welfare, and the maintenance among them of morality and virtue and the fear of God. **Chosen men.** This usually means picked men fit for war. But doubtless on this occasion the elders and all good men possessed of power and influence would be present to strengthen the king's hand. **Thirty thousand.** A large number, but not too large. David probably chose one of the great feasts for the occasion, and by the presence of a large number of warriors, and the display of much military pomp, he would impress upon the minds of the people the value of religion. They would thus learn also to respect their new capital as being the place where was the presence of their Deity, and where they were to come to worship him.

Ver. 2. **From Baale of Judah.** We learn from Josh. xv. 9, 60 that Baalah, or Kirjath-Baal, "the city of Baal," was the old Canaanite name of Kirjath-jearim, the "city of woods." It lay about eight miles westward from Jerusalem (see 1 Sam. vi. 21; vii. 1, 2). The preposition "from" is very startling, as really David went *to* Baale. Yet all the versions have it, but they put on Baale an incorrect meaning. Baal means "lord," "master," and they render, "David went with all the people that were with him *from* [or, *of*] the citizens of Judah," understanding by "master" a householder, one who was master of a family. The real explanation probably is that the narrator wrote according to the sense, and not according to the grammar. The thought in his mind was the bringing up of the ark from its long resting-place, and not the prior physical necessity of going down to the place where it was. **With all the people.** David had consulted with "the captains of thousands and hundreds, and every leader" (1 Chron. xiii. 1), and it was with their good will that he drew the ark of God out of its long concealment. A select body of these nobles, or sheiks, would accompany the king, while the rest, with their attendants, would be posted along the eight miles of road. **Whose name is called by the name.** In the Hebrew, the word "name" is twice repeated, the words literally being, *the ark of Elohim, whereon is called the Name, the Name of Jehovah of Sabaoth.* Most of the versions omit the second *Name*, and the translators of the Authorized Version also felt it to be a difficulty, which they have tried to escape by inserting words between the two. Really it is a most interesting sign of the existence at this early date of a special reverence for the name "with four consonants" which we call "Jehovah." Subsequently it was never pronounced, but the word "Lord" was read instead. In the Revised Version, the importance of the passage is well brought out by the first Name being written with a capital, of the use of which the Revisers are very chary. With their usual inconsecutiveness, they retain LORD for *Jehovah*, though this is "the Name," and though they have restored the word *Jehovah* in several less important places.

Ver. 3.—**And they set the ark of God** (Hebrew, *made it ride*) **upon a new cart.** This was contrary to the Levitical Law, which required that only Levites should bear the ark, and that it should be veiled even from their eyes (Numb. iv. 15). But this mistake is not surprising. It is easy enough for us to turn to our Bibles, and see what the exact letter of a command was. But such reference was no easy matter when the Law was contained in manuscripts which were rare and costly. We cannot imagine that David or even Abiathar carried a manuscript about with them in their wanderings. David very probably had a considerable knowledge of the Pentateuch, gained in Samuel's schools, and stored up in his memory, as was the custom in old days when books were scarce. But this knowledge would be chiefly of its narratives and doctrines, and would comprise such portions as Samuel thought most fitting to influence the lives of his scholars. Abiathar probably

added to this a knowledge of all such ritual as was in daily use in the sanctuary at Nob. He had fled thence in terror, escaping alone from the cruel destruction of the priests by Saul's decree; but even there the restoration of the Levitical services had been too recent to have given time for much study of the old Law. We can quite believe that the murder of the priests at Nob, following upon the catastrophe at Shiloh, had reduced the knowledge of the priests to a very low ebb. Now, the exact way of bearing the ark was a matter that had long been dismissed from their memories, but they would call to mind that it had been brought to Abinadab's house in a new cart drawn by oxen; and they would take this as a precedent, which would justify them in acting in the same manner a second time. But in so solemn a matter the priests ought to have made diligent search, and have gone for instruction to the copies which they possessed of the Divine Law. David did so subsequently (1 Chron. xv. 2), but possibly there was no such copy at present in Jerusalem, and they would have to go to Ramah, where Samuel would deposit whatever records he had saved from the ruin of Shiloh, and where the great work of the prophets was to study the sacred books, and even copy them. But this want of inquiry and easy assumption, that as the ark was brought in a cart to Abinadab's house, so in a cart it should be carried away, was an act of great irreverence, and all the guilty were punished. The heaviest blow fell on the house of Abinadab, which lost a dear son. Entrusted for seventy years with the care of so sacred a symbol of Jehovah's presence, Abinadab and his family ought to have made a special study of the laws concerning it. Apparently they left it very much to itself; for it is never said that God blessed them for their care of it as he did Obed-Edom. And David also was in fault; for he ought to have commanded the priests to make diligent search. His punishment was the breaking out of the Divine wrath, terrifying the people, and turning the joy of the day to mourning. **The house of Abinadab that was in Gibeah**; really, *that was upon the hill.* Uzzah and Ahio, the sons of Abinadab. "Sons" in Hebrew is used in a large sense, and these two men were probably the grandsons of Eleazar, the son of Abinadab, who had been set apart to keep the ark. For seventy years, as it seems, had passed since the ark was hurriedly put in Abinadab's house, namely, twenty during the Philistine supremacy up to the battle of Ebenezer, forty during the reign of Saul, and about ten since. As Eleazar must have been thirty years of age for his consecration to be legal, he must have died long ago, and his sons would be old and decrepit men. His grandsons would be in the prime of life.

Ver. 4.—**Accompanying** (Hebrew, *with*) **the ark**. The verse is evidently corrupt, and we have no aid from the parallel place in Chronicles, except the fact that it is omitted there. The most probable explanation is that the first half of the verse has been repeated from ver. 3 by the error of some copyist, and that the original words were " Uzzah and Ahio drove the new cart with the ark of God, and Ahio went before the ark." While Uzzah walked at the side, Ahio went before the oxen to guide and manage them, as the Basques may be seen at the present day doing in the south of France.

Ver. 5.—**Played**. The word does not mean "played on a musical instrument," but " danced and rejoiced." **On all manner . . . of fir wood**. The Hebrew literally is, *with all cypress-woods*. In 1 Chron. xiii. 8 we find " with all their might, even with songs," etc. Gesenius, in his ' History of the Hebrew Language,' describes this as a mere guess at a misunderstood text, and Maurer ridicules it as a stupid emendation. More sensibly Thenius regards it as the right reading, and the words here as a corruption of it, caused by some scribe misspelling the words, which are nearly identical. In our version the ambiguous meaning of the word "played" makes the passage less startling. For " they danced with all cypress-woods " is unintelligible. The musical instruments mentioned here are the **harp**, Hebrew *chinnor*, a guitar ; the **psaltery**, Hebrew *nebel*, a kind of harp of a triangular shape, with the point downwards ; the **timbrel**, Hebrew *tof*, a tambourine or small drum ; the **cornet**, Hebrew *mena'na'*, a bar on which were a number of loose metal rings, which were shaken in time to the music, but others think that "castanets " are meant, which are pieces of wood beaten in time. The Revised Version adopts this rendering. And finally **cymbals**. For "cornets" we find in the parallel place " trumpets," whence the translators of the Authorized Version took their rendering ; but the Hebrew word means "things to shake."

Ver. 6.—**Nachon's threshing-floor**. In the parallel place (1 Chron. xiii. 9) we find " the threshing-floor of Chidon," and " Chidon " is proved to have been a proper name by the feebleness of the attempts made to find for it a meaning. We therefore gather that " Nachon " is also a proper name, but otherwise we should certainly have translated it " a fixed threshing-floor." The people did indeed thresh or trample out their corn often on summer threshing-floors (Dan. ii. 35), that is, on fitting spots in the fields themselves. But as a large quantity of earth was sure in this case to be mixed with the corn, they preferred to use places with solid floors or pavements, which lasted for many generations, and often became well-known spots (Gen. l. 10). Even if " Nachon " be a proper name, this would be a permanent floor, paved with stones, the approaches to which would be worn and made rough by the tracks of the carts bringing the corn. Here **the oxen shook it** ; Hebrew, *stumbled*, and so the Revised Version. Nothing is said of the ark being in danger. Uzzah's act was one of precaution. The ground was rough, the oxen stumbled, and he put forth his hand to hold the ark till the cart had reached level ground. If the threshing-floor was formed in the natural rock, those who have been in Spain, and seen how the tracks in the Pyrenees are worn by the native carts into deep ruts in the solid stone, can well understand that the neighbourhood of this much-frequented spot would need very careful driving.

Ver. 7.—**Error**. The word so translated is one quite unknown, and Ewald renders it " unexpectedly." The Revised Version puts "rashness " in the margin. But all three alike are mere guesses, of which "error" is that approved by Keil and others. The Syriac has the same reading here as that found in 1 Chron. xiii. 10, namely, " because he put his hand to the ark." This would require the insertion of four or five letters in the Hebrew. **By the ark**. The word translated " accompanying the ark " in ver. 4.

Ver. 8.—**David was displeased** ; Hebrew, *David was angry*. Neither David nor his people had intended any disrespect, and so severe a punishment for what was at most a thoughtless act seemed to him unjust. Uzzah's death was probably caused by apoplexy, and the sudden effort of stretching forth his hand and seizing the ark had been its immediate cause. So tragic an event spoiled the happiness of the day, filled all present with disappointment, made them break off in haste from the grand ceremonial, and placed David before his subjects in the position of a malefactor. He had prepared a great religious festival, and Jehovah had broken in upon them as an enemy. In his first burst of displeasure he called the place Perez-Uzzah, the word " Perez," or " Breach," conveying to the Hebrews the idea of a great calamity (Judg xxi. 15) or of a sudden attack upon a foe (ch. v. 20). The historian adds that the place bore this name unto his day ; but we cannot tell whether these are the words of the original compiler of the Book of Samuel, or, as is more probably the case, those of some subsequent editor or scribe. Many such remarks are supposed to have been inserted by Ezra and the men of the great synagogue.

Ver. 9.—**David was afraid.** This was his next feeling. Neither he nor Uzzah had offended wilfully, and so severe a punishment for an "error" made him dread the presence of so dangerous a thing as the ark seemed to be. Instead, therefore, of taking it into "the city of David," he turns aside and leaves it in the house of the nearest Levite. In both his anger and his dread David manifests himself to us as one whose ideas about God were somewhat childish. He regards Jehovah as a powerful and capricious Being, who must be appeased. He had attained to juster views in Ps. xvi. and other such trustful hymns.

Ver. 10.—**Obed-Edom.** We find two Levites of this name among David's officials—one belonging to the family of Merari, a singer and doorkeeper for the ark (1 Chron. xv. 18, 21, 24); the other of the family of Korah (1 Chron. xxvi. 4, 5). And as it is there said that "God blessed him," he probably it was into whose house the ark was taken. He is called a Gittite, because he belonged to Gath-Rimmon, a Levitical city in the tribe of Dan (Josh. xix. 45; xxi. 24).

Ver. 11.—**Jehovah blessed Obed-Edom.** So far from there being anything unlucky in the ark, its presence brings with it a manifest blessing, and thus David's fears are allayed. But before he returns to his purpose, he commands that proper inquiry be made. The priests must examine the holy book, and, having learned from it where his former conduct was wrong, he assembles the people once again to carry the ark to its home (1 Chron. xv. 2, 12—15).

Ver. 12.—**With gladness.** The words mean, "in a joyful procession with music and dancing."

Ver. 13.—**When they that bare the ark of Jehovah had gone six paces, he sacrificed oxen and fatlings;** Hebrew, *an ox and a fatling.* Many suppose that David sacrificed an ox and a fatling every six paces along the whole way from the house of Obed-Edom, which was probably near or even in Jerusalem, unto the tent prepared for the ark in Zion. "Evidently the way to the holy city was a way of blood. The stained streets of Zion, the rivers of blood, the slaughtered heaps and the blaze of altar-fires formed a strange contrast to the dancing, the singing, and the harping of the multitudes who crowded the city" (Sime, 'Kingdom of All Israel,' p. 288). It is not necessary to suppose, with some objectors, that the ark waited till each sacrifice was completed, or that the road thus lined with victims was many miles in length. The ark did not remain at Perez-Uzzah, but was carried in silent awe to the house of a Levite; and such a house probably was not to be found until they were inside the city

walls. There were no country houses in a region lately twice ravaged by the Philistines. But there is an objection to this view, namely, that it is not the sense of the Hebrew. What is there said is that at starting, after stepping six paces, David sacrificed an ox and a fatling (by the hands, of course, of the priests), to ask a blessing upon the removal of the ark, and avert all misfortune. In Chronicles we read nothing of this, but of a sacrifice of seven bullocks and seven rams offered by the Levites. The one was David's offering made at the beginning, to consecrate the removal; the other was made at the end, and was a thank offering of the Levites, because they had carried the ark safely (1 Chron. xv. 26). The Vulgate has a remarkable addition to ver. 12, taken doubtless by Jerome from manuscripts which existed in his day. It is as follows: "There were with David seven choruses and a calf as victim." The fact is not in itself improbable, and means that the musicians and dancers were divided into bands which mutually relieved one another. And as a sacrifice was also a feast, each band had a calf provided for it. The LXX. omits the thirteenth verse altogether, and substitutes for it, "And seven choruses accompanied him, bearing the ark, and a calf and lambs as a sacrifice."

Ver. 14.—**And David danced.** The word used means the springing round in half-circles to the sound of music. Conder has given a very interesting account of the dancing of the Malawiyeh, which consisted in turning round in whole circles, resting on the heel of the left foot ('Heth and Moab,' p. 65, etc.). As David danced with all his might, he was evidently strongly excited with religious fervour. We have the expression of his feelings in the psalm composed for this occasion (1 Chron. xvi. 7—36); subsequently it seems to have been rearranged for the temple service, as it is broken up into Ps. xcvi. and cv. 1—15. Dancing was usually the office of the women (Exod. xv. 20; Judg. xi. 34; xxi. 21; 1 Sam. xviii. 6); but men may also have often taken part in it, as Michal's objection was that it was unbefitting a king. **David** was **girded with a linen ephod.** David wore this as a tightly fitting garment, which left him free to exert himself in the dance. So far from the use of it being an assumption of the priestly office, it was regarded by Michal as an act of humiliation, as it was a dress worn even by a child when admitted to service in a priest's family (1 Sam. ii. 18). Probably David did mean to rank himself for the time among the inferior servitors of the ark. He might have claimed more. In the theocracy he was the representative of Jehovah, and his anointing was a solemn consecration to a religious office. To have burned incense or offered sacrifice would have been to invade the priestly office, an office parallel to "the administration of the Word and the sacraments," denied, in the Thirty-Seventh Article of the Church of England, to princes. To wear the garb of a servitor was to do honour both to Jehovah and to his priests.

Ver. 16.—**Michal Saul's daughter.** Possibly these words are merely to identify Michal, but they suggest the thought that, as a king's daughter, she valued her royal dignity. The procession evidently passed near David's palace, and his wives and children would be eager spectators.

Ver. 17.—**In the midst of the tabernacle** (*i.e.* tent). This tent would be arranged as nearly as possible like that erected by Moses in the wilderness. The ark would be placed in the holy of holies, a shrine probably of cedar-wood, and the burnt offerings and peace offerings would then be offered and would consecrate the whole. When it is said that **David offered** them, it means that the sacrifices were at his cost and by his command.

Ver. 18.—**David . . . blessed the people in the name of Jehovah of hosts.** Blessing the people was an important priestly function, for which a special formula was provided (Numb. vi. 22—26). But this did not deprive the king, who was Jehovah's anointed representative, of the right of also blessing them, and Solomon, at the consecration of the temple, followed his father's example in a very solemn manner (2 Chron. vi. 3).

Ver. 19.—**A cake of bread, and a good piece . . . and a flagon.** Of the first of the three gifts there is no doubt. It was the round dough cake baked for sacrificial meals (Lev. viii. 26). So, too, there is no doubt of the third; it means "a cake of raisins" (see Cant. ii. 5; Hos. iii. 1, in which latter place raisins, or dried grapes, are expressly mentioned, boldly rendered in the Authorized Version "wine"). The Revised Version has given the correct rendering of the passage. The second word occurs only here, but the rendering of the Authorized Version is that of the Jews; and as it is some common domestic term not likely to be found in literature, but well known in every kitchen, they are most probably right. On the same sort of local authority Jerome renders it in the Vulgate "a piece of beef for roasting." As it is coupled with the bread and the raisin-cake, we may feel sure that it was a portion of the flesh of the animals which had been killed in sacrifice, and which the people were now permitted to take to their homes.

Ver. 20.—**To bless his household.** David, in the midst of his public duties, was not forgetful of the nearer claims of his own family. Doubtless there also a joyful feast would be prepared, and all be gathered together to praise God and rejoice with one consent. **Who uncovered himself . . . as one of the vain fellows shamelessly uncovereth himself!** David's offence in the eyes of Michal was, not his dancing, but his divesting himself of his royal robes, and appearing before his subjects clad in the dress of an inferior class. The Levites were to occupy a humble social position (see Deut. xiv. 29; xxvi. 12), and Michal's words are a proof that such was in David's time the case. The language of Michal is that of a woman vexed and irritated. After reminding David of his high office as "King of Israel," she reproaches him for appearing on a grand public occasion without the upper and becoming robe in which an Oriental enwraps himself. And this he had done before the female slaves of his own servants, with no more self-respect than that shown by the "vain fellows." "Vain" is the "raca" of Matt. v. 22, and means "empty," void of virtue, void of reputation, and void of worldly means. The Hebrews, when expressing the greatest possible contempt for a man, called him an "empty," and no word could be found better conveying the meaning of thorough worthlessness.

Ver. 21.—**It was before the Lord.** The Hebrew is much more forcible than the confused rendering of our version. "Before Jehovah, who chose me above thy father, and above all his house, to appoint me prince over Jehovah's people, over Israel, yea, before Jehovah I have rejoiced" (Authorized Version, "played;" but see notes on ver. 5). The preference of David over Saul was proof that that king's affectation of royal state, and his self-importance, were not pleasing in God's eyes.

Ver. 22.—**And of the maidservants which thou hast spoken of, of them shall I be had in honour.** These words have been variously interpreted, but their simplest meaning is also the best; that even the most uneducated women, though surprised at first at David's want of stateliness, would, on reflection, be led to a right understanding of the greatness of God; and would then feel that even a king was right in owning himself to be nothing in God's presence.

Ver. 23.—**Therefore Michal.** The Hebrew is, *and Michal had no child.* Michal's barrenness was long antecedent to this outburst of pride, and was not a punishment for it. It is noticed as a proof that the blessing of God did not rest upon her; and as such it was regarded by the people, and doubtless it lessened David's affection for her. We must not, however, suppose that he imposed upon

her any punishment further than this verbal reproof. Nor does the interest lie in
Michal's conduct, but in the glimpse which
the narrative gives us of David's tender
piety towards God, so exactly in agreement
with the feelings which animate very many
of the psalms. To unite with this a harsh
bitterness to the woman who was his first
love, who had so protected him in old time,
and whom he had summoned back at the first
opportunity because of his affection for her,
is a thing abhorrent in itself, and contrary
to David's character. His fault in domestic
matters rather was that he was over-fond,
not that he was unfeeling. A little more
sternness towards Amnon and Absalom
would have saved him much sorrow. As
for Michal, the story sets her before us as
caring a great deal for David, and not much
for Jehovah. She could not have approved
of such a number of rivals in David's household, but she had not lost her love for him.
And the narrative represents her as not
having Jehovah's blessing in a matter so
greatly thought of by Hebrew women, and
as valuing too highly royal state, and forgetting that above the king was God. But
she did David no great wrong, and received
from him nothing worse than a scolding.
In the parallel place (1 Chron. xv. 29) the
matter is very lightly passed over; and the
reason why it holds an important place in
this book is that we have here a history of
David's piety, of his sin and his punishment. In itself a slight matter, it yet makes
us clearly understand the nature of David's
feelings towards Jehovah. It is also most
interesting in itself. For David is the type
of a noble character under the influence of
grace. Michal, too, is a noble character, but
she lacked one thing, and that was " the one
thing needful."

The removal of the ark is a matter so
important as to call for careful consideration. For the time it established two centres
of worship—one with the ark at Zion, the
other at Gibeon. The ark in Saul's days
had been forgotten (1 Chron. xiii. 3). It
had long lain in the house of a simple
Levite in the city of woods, and Saul's
religious ideas were too feeble for him to
be capable of understanding the importance
of establishing a national religion. Still,
such as they were, they made him summon
Ahiah, the grandson of Eli, to be his
domestic priest (1 Sam. xiv. 3); and subsequently he even set up at Nob the
tabernacle with its table of shewbread, and
other holy furniture, saved somehow from
the ruin of Shiloh, with Ahimelech as high

priest (1 Sam. xxi. 1). But when in a fit
of senseless jealousy he destroyed his own
work, the nation was left for a time without
an established religion. Gradually, however, this primary necessity for good government and national morality was supplied—
how we know not; but we find a tabernacle
at Gibeon, with the altar of burnt offerings,
and the morning and evening sacrifice, and
apparently the same service as that erewhile
set up at Nob; only Zadok of the line of
Eleazar is high priest (1 Chron. xvi. 39, 40).
He thus belonged to the senior line, while
the last survivor of the race of Ithamar,
Abiathar, Eli's great-grandson, was with
David. Gibeon was in the centre of the
tribe of Benjamin, some few miles from
Jerusalem, with Nob lying half-way between; and probably Saul had permitted
this restoration of Jehovah's worship at
Gibeon, both because he half repented of
his deed, and because the worship there was
ministered by priests not allied to Ahimelech
and Abiathar. But now the ark, which
was Jehovah's throne, had been brought out
of its obscurity, and solemnly placed in a
tabernacle in Zion, with Abiathar, David's
friend, the representative of the junior line,
as high priest; and probably the only difference in the service was that David's psalms
were sung to music at Zion, while the Mosaic
ritual, with no additions, was closely followed
at Gibeon. There was thus the spectacle of
two high priests (ch. viii. 17), and two rival
services, and yet no thought of schism.
Zadok had been one of those foremost in
making David king of all Israel (1 Chron.
xii. 28); he and Abiathar were the two who
moved Judah to bring David back after
Absalom's revolt (ch. xix. 11). The whole
matter had grown out of historical facts,
and probably David always intended that
Zion should absorb Gibeon, and be the one
centre required by the Levitical Law. But
he was content to wait. Had he acted otherwise a conflict would necessarily have arisen
between the rival lines of the priesthood,
and between Abiathar and Zadok, the two
men who represented them, and who were
both his true friends. We find even Solomon
doing great honour to the tabernacle at
Gibeon (2 Chron. i. 3, etc.), but after the
temple was built it passed away; and the
race of Ithamar, weakened by the calamity

at Shiloh, and still more by the cutting off of so many of its leading members at Nob, never recovered itself after Abiathar was set aside by Solomon for taking part with Adonijah. The line continued to exist, for members of it returned from Babylon (Ezra viii. 2) ; but though it produced a prophet, Jeremiah, it never again produced a high priest, and therefore only the line of Eleazar, to which Ezra himself belonged, is given in 1 Chron. vi.

Thus Abiathar's misconduct and the growing fame of Jerusalem put an end to all fear of schism. We easily trace in the Psalms the increase of the nation's regard for Zion. In Ps. xxiv., written probably by David to celebrate the entry of the ark thither, it is simply " the hill of Jehovah . . . his holy place." In Ps. ix. it is " his dwelling," but in Ps. xx. a higher note is struck. Zion is " the sanctuary" whence Jehovah sends "help" and " strength ;" and in Ps. xlviii., written at a later date, Zion is found installed in the very heart of the people's love. Thus the Divine blessing rested fully upon David's work. To Jehovah's worship he gave a grand and noble centre, which from his day has had no rival, unless it be in some respects Rome. The city of David's choice has been, and continues to this hour to be, the most holy spot upon earth alike to the Jew and to the Christian, though to the latter it is so because of David's Son. At Zion, moreover, David's spiritual addition to the Mosaic ritual has given the Church its best book of devotion and the brightest part of its services ; for every hymn sung to God's glory, and every instrument of music played in God's house, is but the continuance of the prophesying with harp, psaltery, and cymbal (1 Chron. xxv. 1), first instituted by David, though, like all that was best in David personally and in his institutions, it grew out of Samuel's influence and the practices of his schools (1 Sam. xix. 20). Finally, the temple services were doing much to weld the discordant tribes into one nation, and would have succeeded in so doing but for the unhappy degeneracy of Solomon's latter years, and the obstinacy of his son. Yet even so, Jerusalem remains for ever a memorial of the genius and piety of this extraordinary man, and the symbol of "Jerusalem the golden, the home of God's elect."

HOMILETICS.

Vers. 1—11.—The facts are : 1. David, deeming the time to be come for reorganizing the religious services, raises a select force wherewith to bring the ark from its obscurity at Kirjath-jearim. 2. Providing a new cart, the ark is set thereon, and brought out of the house of Abinadab under charge of his two sons. 3. David and the people move in joyous procession before the ark to music from all manner of instruments. 4. Arriving at a certain place, Uzzah, putting forth his hand to steady the ark, is smitten for his rashness, and dies before the ark. 5. Thereupon David's spirit is much troubled, and is filled with dread at the thought of taking charge of so sacred and terrible a treasure. 6. David is restrained by this apprehension from his purpose, and meanwhile leaves the ark in the house of Obed-Edom. 7. The sojourn of the ark in the house of Obed-Edom for three months proves an occasion of great blessing to him and his family. The remarkable events of this section naturally arrange themselves in a threefold order—the bringing up of the ark ; the judgment on Uzzah ; and the suspension of the undertaking. We here find three topics, which we will take in succession.

Religious restorations.   I. RELIGION IS THE FOUNDATION OF NATIONAL PROSPERITY. This is the interpretation of David's action in seeking to bring the ark out of its obscurity to the central seat of government. From the time when the ark was captured by the Philistines (1 Sam. iv.) and its deposit at Kirjath-jearim (1 Sam. vi. 21), all through the reign of Saul, with the exception of the brief revival at Ebenezer, the religion of the nation had been at a low ebb. That so sacred a treasure should have been left in obscurity, without the forms and order of worship enjoined in the Law of Moses, was an indication of spiritual decadence, and goes far to account for the political weakness of the nation during the life of Saul. David saw clearly that the elevation of his people depended chiefly on two things—vigorous, enlightened statesmanship, and fidelity in all things to their covenanted God. The establishment of a strong centre of government at Jerusalem was one step; but he saw that, if the nation was to fulfil its highest destiny, the prosperity he desired must also rest on a strictly religious foundation. Hence the effort to restore religious life by bringing up the ark of the covenant. Leaving out of view the particular form of religion, and the symbolism appropriate to that stage in the development of God's revelation, we can see how profoundly wise David's judgment was. The human activities developed in national civilized life can only be counted on to run into right and safe channels, and to avoid mutual destruction, when they are pervaded by the spirit of true godliness. Wealth, art, science, commerce, military display, free and easy interchange of thought,—these are not self-preservative, these do not give rest to the heart, these do not check the tendencies that carry in themselves the germs of decay and death. Only when the national mind is purified, rendered calm, self-restrained, and God-like in feeling by knowledge and worship of the Holy One is there a guarantee that all will go well and endure. This is taught in the history of Greece, Rome, and other lands where God was not honoured by proper worship, and his Spirit not cherished in daily life; and it is the strenuous teaching of prophets and apostles, and especially of the Saviour, who makes clear what is the light of the world and the healing of the nations.

II. THE RESTORATION OF RELIGION IS AN EVENT OF GREAT JOY. The very idea of a restoration of the piety of former days was to David an inspiration. His calling the chief men from all quarters of the land, his expounding to them his sense of what was due to the symbol of God's presence, his grand processional march, and the exuberant delight with which he sang and danced,—reveal the high appreciation he had of the great turn now coming in the religious life of the nation. The awakening of a new enthusiasm by his influence certainly was a remarkable incident in the national life regarded in contrast with the stolid indifference of the age of Saul. The power of a new and healthy religious emotion over all the faculties, and consequently over all departments of activity, is very great, giving elevation, spring, and purpose to all that is done or attempted. In this case there were special elements entering into the joy. The ark was the symbol of God's presence; it contained the overshadowed mercy-seat, which told of forgiveness and communion; it was the exponent of covenant relationship, and the prophetic indicator to the devout mind of a glory yet to be revealed, and of a covenant on wider basis and embracing vaster blessings. Ezra knew something of this joy of restoration of religion to its proper position. There was joy also when, after centuries of error and wrong, the attention of men was directed once more by Luther and his coadjutors to the mercy-seat where men could find a new and living way of access to the Father. No greater occasion for joy could arise for our own land than a full national enthusiasm for those sacred deposits of truth and holy influence which God has given us in his revelation and in the institutions of his Church. What is thus true of restorations on a large scale holds of our own lives, when, after seasons of dreary separation from our God and cold miserable observance of occasional acts of worship, we go forth with all our soul after the living God, and welcome him afresh to our love and trust as the God of our salvation.

III. INDIRECT PERSONAL INFLUENCE CONDUCES TO A RESTORATION OF RELIGION. It is instructive to see how, in the providence of God, great movements have sprung out of individual consecrations. The soul of David, purified, elevated, and aroused to grasp spiritual realities, was the human spring of this great change. Of course his official position would secure attention to his requests and commands; but it depended on the bent of his mind as to the form and scope of his commands. This reformation proceeded from him, but not entirely by direct personal influence. His tone and manner, his habits of devotion and strict regard for God's will, would tell on those in direct contact with him; but that was not enough. Hence in his sagacity he summoned select men from all parts of the land, and through them sought to act on the thousands who could not leave their homes. This call from all towns and villages would awaken thought there, would lead to explanations, would quicken conscience, would disseminate his ideas and the enthusiasm of his spirit, would create the feeling that a holier and wiser time was at hand; and when, subsequently, the thirty thousand returned home, they would further diffuse the influence caught by contact with the godly king, and contribute elements of good to their respective localities. The great reformations of the world have all been effected thus. Few come into direct personal contact with the originators. The multitude get the secondary influences. Nor can we tell how far our influence may thus be diffused. The wave moves on in proportion to the susceptibility of those who first receive its impact. The question of indirect influence deserves much consideration on the part of Churches and individuals.

IV. A TIME OF REFORMATION IN RELIGION DEVELOPS MUCH FEELING NOT PURELY SPIRITUAL. Although a great interest was awakened by David's zeal in the restoration of the more regular worship of God, yet we must discriminate between such devout feelings and clear views of spiritual things as were true of him, and the vague sentiments of the multitude. If Ps. lxviii. and cxxxii. may be taken as indicative of his real state of mind, we are not to suppose that all the rest who joined in the procession or were stirred to excitement in their homes rose to the same height in the religious life. Men cannot help being roused when powerful religious minds put forth their energies; and in some instances they are awakened to a really new spiritual life; but contagion of thought and sentiment and fervid interest in a great public movement are not the same as vital godliness. They may be better than dull indifference, and may even serve as a step to a higher and more permanent elevation, yet if they be all the reformation is very superficial. Forming an estimate on the general rules that govern human action, we may be sure that many who sang and danced before the ark were only nominal worshippers, and had but slight sympathy with the deep meaning of the words of the psalmist. The same was true of the Protestant Reformation. Multitudes took an interest in doctrinal discussions and in the freedom from priestly domination who knew little of that inner spiritual life which, in the case of Luther and the leaders, found its core in personal union with Christ. Our modern revivals are to be estimated in the same way. We may be thankful that crowds flock to sing and hear and welcome ostensibly the true Ark of the covenant, and many, no doubt, sing with the understanding and rejoice in spirit, but the mass have still to be regarded as relatively strangers to the new and deeper life.

Human judgments on Divine acts of judgment. The part of the narrative referring to the conduct of Uzzah and the consequences to himself always awaken in the reader a feeling of surprise at the apparent disproportion of the punishment to the offence. Sympathy is felt with the feeling of David, who was "displeased," and could no further carry out his project of conveying the ark to Jerusalem. Evil-minded men have not been alone in pointing to this record as an evidence of what they would call the unworthy representations of the Divine Being contained in the Old Testament. It is well to look this difficulty fully in the face, and see, if possible, how far man is warranted to express a judgment at all upon an event so terrible and seemingly inexplicable, on such principles at least as govern human acts of justice. Note here—

I. THE REASONS FOR DIVINE JUDGMENTS ARE NOT ALWAYS APPARENT TO MAN, AND YET MAY BE MOST VALID. It is a first principle that the "Judge of all the earth" cannot but do right. That is the solid rock on which to rest when events occur in providence that do not admit of explanation. It is, further, a sound position that God looks at the inner life of men, and knows exactly the tone and spirit concealed from human view; and it is this condition of the inner man, and not the bare outward act, which constitutes the real character and determines the moral value of the action in the sight of God. Also, incidental actions are incidental in their form because of passing circumstances; but the state of mind out of which they spring is permanent; for given two minds of different spiritual tone and bias, they will, when placed under pressure of the same external circumstances, produce totally different actions. Now, we have a right to assume, *primâ facie*, that, if there are no adequate reasons for the sudden terrible punishment discoverable in the bare and apparently well-disposed act of Uzzah, there must have been, in his habitual state of feeling towards the symbol of God's presence and the whole events of the day, something determinately evil, and of which that which seemed to others to be an innocent act was known by God to be the natural outcome. That was the case in the destruction of Dathan and Abiram. The falsehood of Ananias was outwardly only like other falsehoods, but we are told that

God saw something more than the ordinary antecedent of a lie in common life. There have been judgments on nations and families and individuals, and are still, which do come in the providence of God, but the hidden reasons of which only eternity will reveal. As our Saviour during his earthly life often spoke to the unuttered thoughts of men, and not to meet definite words, so here and in other cases the Divine act was doubtless to meet an unuttered, a permanent, not fully expressed state of mind, of which Uzzah was conscious, but of which men knew little. The same will be true of future judgments of God; they will be based, not on the ostensible act merely, but on the tenor of the whole life (Matt. vii. 22, 23; xxv. 40—46).

II. THE GUILT OF ACTIONS IS DEPENDENT VERY MUCH ON PRIVILEGES ENJOYED. The Philistines had handled the ark (1 Sam. v. 1, 2), and no immediate evil came to them for so doing. Their subsequent affliction seems to have been owing to their detention and mockery of the ark (1 Sam. v. 3—7), not to the fact of touching it. But it was a positive injunction that the Levites should not touch the sacred thing (Numb. iv. 15); and the particular injunction was illustrated and rendered more significant by the regulation that the ark should always be carried on staves, thus not needing the touch of any hand. The Philistines were men "without law;" Uzzah was a man "under law." The whole history of his people in relation to ceremonial had been full of instruction of the same kind. The guilt of a deed depends on previous knowledge or means of obtaining knowledge. Capernaum is not judged by the same rule as the people of Sodom. The Jew is pronounced inexcusable because of his superior light (Rom. ii.). Severer punishment comes on those who, possessing gospel light, do deeds worthy of darkness (John iii. 19; Heb. x. 29). Judgment may fall on the "house of God" which would not come on those not in the house (1 Pet. iv. 17).

III. INDIFFERENCE TO DIVINE LAWS IS PROGRESSIVE. The disregard of the well-known injunction in this case was probably the culmination of an indifference which had been growing for a long time. An evil tendency or mental habit may be in process of formation, and may constitute a state of actual spiritual degeneracy, a long time before an occasion occurs for its manifestation in any overt act that is distinctly in violation of positive law. The degeneracy which was far too common during the reign of Saul doubtless had penetrated to the home of Uzzah, and the neglect of honour paid to the ark during those long years of its stay in his father's abode, together with the kind of familiarity with it bred of its presence as a relic of a former elaborate ritual, could not but have resulted in a rather decided insensibility to the sacredness of minute regulations. The act of touching the ark may have been a consequence of this condition, and the "error," or "rashness," spoken of (ver. 8) may indicate that there was not in him that quickness of spiritual sensibility which would at once have seen that no casual circumstance can set aside a command based on a great and Divine order of things. There is not a more subtle evil of our life than this gradual deepening of indifference arising from neglect of spiritual culture and encouraged by unthoughtful familiarity with sacred things. The conscience passes through stages of degeneration till we come to do things without compunction which once would have caused us anguish of spirit. How far our children are in danger from constant familiarity with religious phrases and usages is a serious question. The same applies also to ordinary worshippers in our sanctuaries.

IV. THERE IS POSITIVE IMPIETY IN DISTRUSTING GOD'S PROVISION FOR THE SAFETY OF HIS OWN GLORY. The ark was the visible symbol of God's presence. His glory was there, so far as it could be manifested in visible form to man at that stage of his religious education. The command that no Levite should ever touch it was among the arrangements made for its stay among the people. All such arrangements of God are made on full prevision of every possibility. To say that circumstances might arise when the command would be inadequate to the maintenance of the ark in its integrity among men, would be an impeachment of the Divine wisdom and power. The command had reference solely to human action, and did not reveal what reserve of power and appliance there might be for securing the safety of the ark at all times. Common sense, to say nothing of religious faith, ought to have taught that the Eternal would take care of his own if he declined the aid of man, or at least that it was his will that his own should suffer temporary injury now and then. It was irrational and impious, therefore, to distrust his provision for securing his own ends. The putting forth of the hand in contravention of the command may have been the expression of this.   The same applies equally to the New Testament manifestation of the glory of God in Christ.   For times of danger and of seeming safety he has enjoined on us certain conduct in relation to the kingdom of Christ, which proceeds on the presupposition that he has means of securing the integrity of that kingdom on the basis of our restricting our conduct to that prescribed order.   By prayer, by truthfulness, by spirituality of mind, by love, by persuasive words, by blameless, meek lives, by quiet faith in the invisible power of the Spirit, we are to do our part in relation to the preservation of the integrity of the kingdom, and to its processional march to final triumph.   If, when supposing it liable to suffer, or when observing a great shock arising from the circumstances of its position in our time, we depart from the order laid down, and trim to the world and become unspiritual and untruthful, or depend less on faith in the invisible power of the Holy Spirit than on mere human science and social influences, then we virtually fall into this view of the sin of Uzzah, we distrust God's provision for securing in the world those interests that are bound up with the work and Person of Christ.   Man is responsible for the observance of what is enjoined, not for imaginary temporary consequences that will ensue from an observance of what is enjoined.   Here is the clue to hosts of failures of duty and wretched expediencies.

V. PROFOUND REVERENCE AS AN ELEMENT OF CHARACTER IS OF PRIME IMPORTANCE IN PERSONAL AND NATIONAL LIFE.   No great character is formed without profound reverence as a chief feature.   Men are mean, weak, morally low, in so far as they are trifling and destitute of awe.   The spirit of levity, which treats all things as common and fit subjects for free and thoughtless handling, never reads the great lessons of existence, and never wins respect.   A reverent man alone forms a true estimate of himself in relation to the vast order of things of which he is but a part.   An irreverent nation lacks the strong, sober qualities which alone grow out of reverence as their root, and which alone can produce noble, strenuous actions.   Now, the whole drift of the Mosaic ritual and commands was to develop and foster reverence in the people.   The solemnities and details in reference to the ark, the sanctuary, the altars, the sacrifices, the cleansings, and assemblies were rational in their specific relations.   The great gathering at the foot of Sinai, and the solemn restrictions there laid down (Exod. xix.), were evidently designed to develop a becoming " fear of the Lord " and profound regard for sacred things.   The judgment on Dathan and Abiram was a check on a tendency to irreverence.   The very hope of the people depended on the due maintenance of this reverent spirit.   All had understood the command not to touch the ark in that light, and the judgment on Uzzah for the violation of that command was only another solemn way of impressing the people with the prime importance of this feeling.   Hence, also, our care to encourage such forms of worship as best foster reverence of spirit, and such styles of teaching as exhibit the facts and principles from the recognition of which reverence will naturally arise.   Hence, again, our appreciation of those providential events, such as sickness, bereavement, and stupendous manifestations of untraceable wisdom and power, which awaken or strengthen the feeling, " Great and holy is the Lord : who shall stand in his presence ? "

VI. THERE IS AN EDUCATIONAL CHARACTER IN JUDGMENTS.   The dull heart of man often needs something more than the still small voice and quiet order of events to arouse it to a sense of what is due to God and what is wisest and best for man.   In every judgment—say of Sodom, of Pharaoh, of Dathan, of Ananias—there is pure justice ; no wrong is done to the individuals concerned ; but the acts have a reference beyond the persons affected thereby.   The contemporaries of Abraham, the Egyptians, Israel in the desert, and the primitive Church, were instructed by what occurred in their midst.   Many judgments are connected with the explicit statement that " the nations may know."   The judgment on Uzzah formed part of the educational process by which God was bringing the people out of their low spiritual condition to the elevation in tone which would render them more effective in carrying out Divine purposes in the world.   We cannot fully estimate how much we owe to the influence over us of the record of God's judgments contained in his Word.   Nor is it enough to say that they are repressive in their influence, and not conducive to the developing of love and filial trust and the free joy of a superior life ; for the repression and restraint of evil tendencies is requisite in creatures strongly under their influence, and, while checking from what would soon be utter, hopeless ruin, they open the way for the action of other gentle, tender influences which do develop the free joyous spirit of the obedient child.

VII. THE SEVERITY AND GOODNESS OF GOD ARE PERFECTLY CONSISTENT AND OFTEN COEXIST. It is bad theology based on defective knowledge of Scripture to represent God in an exclusive aspect of mildness. Though we need not become material in our conceptions, and think of contrary attributes in him as so many quasi-physical forces contending one against the other or finding an outlet at the expense of one another, yet the very conception of love, when just, implies a rigid, severe guardianship of the order of things on which the welfare of the holy depends. This combination shines forth in the death of Uzzah. In case he was a really devout man, and simply in an unguarded moment of unwatchfulness put forth his hand, then his sudden death—though necessary to the maintenance of the ritual which we have seen was based on the principle of inculcating reverence, and useful, as an educational act, for the people—would not include, necessarily, loss and ruin in the next life. He might be saved, though as by fire. This combination of severity and goodness shines forth most conspicuously in the work of our Saviour, in whose life and death the reprobation of sin and the outflow of mercy to sinners form the two elements which render the cross a mystery of justice and mercy.

Distrust a foil to faith and love. It is said that David was displeased, and in his displeasure there arose a fear hitherto unknown to him, and, as a consequence of these, the enterprise on which he had entered with so much joy and confidence was abandoned till, as we shall see further on, the reward which came to Obed-Edom's faith and love, standing in contrast with David's gloomy imaginings, brought him round to a better mind.

I. DISCONTENT WITH THE ORDER OF PROVIDENCE PROCEEDS FROM A COMBINATION OF SELF-WILL AND IGNORANCE. David was dissatisfied and vexed in spirit with what had occurred to interrupt the joyous carrying out of his programme. It was not so much dissatisfaction with what Uzzah had done, or pain that he was dead, but annoyance that for such a deed the great terror of death should have come on them all. Had he spoken out all his feelings and thoughts, he would have said that such an event was undesirable, out of proportion to the deed, and an intrusive disturbance of a great and important ceremonial. Had he been at the head of authority, no such calamity as that should have interfered with a grand national undertaking. Possibly, apart from frustration of his own immediate plans for festivity, he may have been apprehensive of the effect of such a dreadful doom upon the mass of the people whom he was anxious to interest in the restoration of religion. But we can now see how all this was the outcome of self-will and ignorance. He wanted things to go on in his own way; he did not know, as he might have known on more profound reflection, that to maintain the authority of law and inculcate reverence and check national tendencies to levity were for the highest good of the people, and that these could be most assuredly promoted by this sad event. We have here an instance, in conspicuous form, of the very common circumstance of men secretly complaining of the order of events which Providence chooses. A rainy season, a sweeping earthquake, a transmission of evil consequences from parent to child, the destiny of the wicked, and many other things which do come in consequence of the constitution of the physical and moral worlds, often raise within the heart the feeling that some other arrangement would surely have been better, and that had we our way such things would not be possible. This is really self-assertion, love of our own way, ignorance of the innumerable ramifications of single events and acts, and inability to penetrate into the conditions on which alone a permanent and generally beneficial order of things can be secured. The psalmist rose to wiser thoughts and holier feelings (Ps. lxxiii. 13—22; xcii. 4—6; cf. Matt. xi. 25, 26; Rom. xi. 33, 34).

II. STRONG UNHOLY FEELING IMPAIRS THE CONCEPTION OF TRUTH AND DUTY. That David's annoyance with the order of Providence was a decidedly unholy feeling is obvious—it was the opposite of that meek, loving acquiescence in the ways and acts of God, even when they are most painful, which characterizes the truly filial spirit; and that it was strong is seen in the fact that from that moment he failed, under its action, to see the glorious truth enshrined in the symbol before him, and was moved to abandon the work to which he had committed himself and the people. Psychologically it can be proved that all emotion affects more or less the steadiness of intellectual perception. Morally it is a matter of experience that an emotion of anger, distrust, or annoyance always interferes with a clear perception of spiritual truth. Plato was right in affirming that the νοῦς unaffected by the storms of passion and sense alone can see reality. The god of this world, by engaging and exciting feelings, blinds the minds of men, so that they see not the glory which shines in the face of Christ. David's fear of the ark, his dread lest something should happen (ver. 9), was contrary to all he had felt before. Hitherto the ark had been to him the symbol of that blessed presence which had brought joy and comfort to his heart—a reminder of the mercy which endureth for ever. It was not possible to see this precious truth through the mists of unholy feeling that had been permitted to rise in his soul. And this shrinking from what had once been reverently regarded as the spring of purest joy and satisfaction at once weakened the resolve he had formed to bring the blessed symbol to his seat of government and give it there the honour due. Duty gave way to the disgust and disappointment and foolish apprehensions generated by his own proud will. The correlative truths are clear, namely, in so far as we are lowly and absolutely acquiescent in the Divine will is our spirit calm and clear and strong in its recognition of highest spiritual truth, and in so far as this truth is perceived the path of duty is steadily followed. None knew the truth and pursued the path of duty as Christ, because none were so pure and calm and one in will with the Father. Herein is a lesson to teachers and taught; to those who meet with trouble and those who move on in joyful procession.

III. FAITH AND LOVE EXERCISED IN A TIME OF RELIGIOUS BACKSLIDING ARE ABUNDANTLY REWARDED. David's piety was now at fault; he had slipped backwards in the path of godliness; his conduct was an unjust reflection on Providence and on the holy symbol that shadowed forth the presence of the people's real Protector and Friend. Had men followed his example or caught his temper, they would have shrunk from the ark as from the source of death ; and it would have been left in an obscurity and neglect equal to that of Kirjath-jearim. But all this serves as a foil to set forth, in striking beauty, the conduct of Obed-Edom, who, not dreading with slavish fear the Holy One of Israel, but, doubtless, in a quiet way, proud of the privilege, welcomed the ark to his house. Whether he first sought the honour, or whether this was the nearest Levite's house, we know not. In any case we can imagine, from the tenor of the narrative, how with careful haste the house was cleansed and prepared for its holy guest ; the best and fairest chamber made, if it might be, yet more meet for such high honour ; the Levite and his sons purified, that they might fitly bear in the ark to its destined place, venturing, perhaps, as they bore it along, to utter or think of the ancient words, "Return, O Lord, unto the many thousands of Israel!" Honoured, happy Obed-Edom ! What faith in God ! what love for the blessed presence ! Did sleep fall upon him that first night ? Was there not a joy that would make "songs in the night"? The bliss, later on, of Zacchæus was in a sense forestalled by Obed-Edom. The reality of the faith and love, and its continued manifestation in various forms of reverential interest, is proved by the rich blessing that came upon him and all belonging to him. The house became the abode of the higher forms of religious sentiment which in themselves are choicest treasures. Honour fell upon parents, and children felt the blessed charm. Servants began to feel, as never before, that their services were more than attentions paid to man. Providence smiled on field and vineyard. Men saw that somehow this home was now blessed above all homes. What lessons here for all ! Who would dread with slavish fear the Christ, the Manifestation of the glory of the Father ? Who would not welcome him as chief, most cherished Guest ? Who would not subordinate all the arrangements of home life that he may be duly honoured there ? Who would not rejoice that the Holy One does condescend to dwell thus with man, and brighten the fairest scenes of home life ? Blessings abound where he is welcome Guest. No fear of flashing fire to destroy. To faith and love there is only mercy and peace.

> " O happy house, O home supremely blest,
>   Where thou, Lord Jesus Christ, art entertained
> As the most welcome and beloved Guest,
>   With true devotion and with love unfeigned;

> Where all hearts beat in unison with thine;
> Where eyes grow brighter as they look on thee;
> Where all are ready, at the slightest sign,
> To do thy will, and do it heartily!"

GENERAL LESSONS. 1. Times of religious excitement may arise ir the natural progress of religion, but they obviously are not to be regarded as a normal condition of thought and feeling, and they may, by their absorption of one class of feelings, lay us open to peculiar temptations. 2. In every season of apparent and real prosperity in religion we ought to exercise self-control in prospect of the possibility of events arising through the imperfection of men which, from their nature, mar our joy. 3. Secret murmuring against what Providence ordains is a sin to which all are very prone, and therefore it is important to watch against it very closely, especially as it does more damage to our inner life than is often supposed. 4. We ought to ponder carefully the enormous injury done, both by our loss of personal influence and the force of example, when we, out of a feeling of sudden disappointment, throw aside solemn duties. 5. Those who render service to the cause of God in times of urgency may be sure that a rich blessing will come that will cause them to forget any temporary inconvenience experienced.

Vers. 12—23.—The facts are: 1. David, learning the blessing that had come upon the house of Obed-Edom, resolves to bring up the ark to Jerusalem. 2. Having made arrangements in accordance with the Law for the proper bearing of the ark, he inaugurates the procession by a sacrifice. 3. Girded with a linen ephod, he dances before the ark, and with music and shouting it enters Jerusalem. 4. Placing the ark in the tabernacle he had provided for it, he offers burnt offerings and peace offerings before the Lord, pronounces a blessing on the people, and distributes to them meat and drink. 5. Returning to his house, he is met by his wife Michal, who, having witnessed his dancing before the ark, now reproaches him with having demeaned himself in the eyes of the people. 6. With mildness of temper, but great firmness, he not only admits the fact, but glories in it as due unto God, and affirms his readiness to again debase himself in the same manner, being sure of winning the esteem of others less prejudiced. 7. Michal his wife remains childless. We have here a great change in David's religious condition; an event of supreme national interest; and the domestic sorrows of a devout man. The topics suggested may be taken in succession.

Joy restored. There is a marked change in the David mentioned in vers. 13—15 as compared with the David of vers. 8—10, and in general terms it may be expressed as a restoration to the joy of his life. But it is well to notice the process implied.

I. THE SINS AND ERRORS OF A REALLY GOOD MAN CAUSE HIM GREAT SUFFERING. In general terms, all sin entails suffering; but facts prove that the degree of personal suffering consequent on particular sins depends on the actual goodness of the man who sins. David was truly a "man after God's own heart," a man of pure sensitive nature, of enlightened conscience and intense sincerity. In some respect his very sin (ver. 8) was consequent on his noble ambition to see God glorified in a great national demonstration. We may be sure, although the historian says nothing of it, that the days immediately after his return to Jerusalem were full of bitterness. The fact that a great project, in which the nation was concerned, had come to a sudden collapse, that elders and common people throughout the land would be talking of his chagrin, that strange impressions would be conveyed as to the stability of his purposes, and the consciousness that his God was not to him now as he had been in days past, must have robbed him of former peace and embittered all the relationships of life. Peter's life was anguish after his fall, because he was so good a man. Dark days and painful sense of solitariness are the lot of many of the faithful after having turned their heart in distrust from their God.

II. REFLECTION ARISES AND GRADUALLY TONES DOWN THE TUMULT OF FEELING. For a time the passion of discontent and distrust, like a storm, would rage, and, while making David wretched by virtue of their own nature, would throw the reflective powers into confusion. No sinner is perfectly sane when under the stormy influence of his sin. In the case of a really bad man the confusion becomes worse by deliberate indulgence in fresh sins in order to get rid of what slight uneasiness is experienced; but with David the disturbing force of sin would gradually expend itself, and the reflective powers would begin to review the situation and gradually allow the influence of truth and fact to reveal the folly and shame of what had been done. The monarch retired from the cares and toils of the day, and, though fretted and vexed by the bad impression his people might entertain as to his persistency of purpose, he could not but ponder the recent path of his feet, and the great truths on which he had formerly been wont to "meditate day and night" (Ps. i. 2). In good men, though fallen and wretched, the intellectual faculties, as under the action of a magnet, will be sure to concentrate on the truths that help to recovery.

III. THE MIND COMES IN DUE COURSE INTO DIRECT CONTACT WITH ACTUAL FACTS AND THE WORD OF GOD. Reflection would clear away the mists of passion, and David would see in the light of the written Word the error of setting out with the ark on a cart; the exposure, therefore, by his own arrangement or connivance, of the man to the temptation to violate the Law, and the justice of the blow which fell, as also its use in checking a spirit of indifference and inculcating reverence for sacred things. The piety of his nature, thus brought into direct contact with truth, would at once recognize its force, the shamefulness and folly of the discontent and distrust, and the desirability of placing the life once more in its proper relation to the general interests of religion. Penitents and backsliders are not far from restoration when once they gaze with calm and steadfast eye on the actual facts as illumined by the light of God's Word. The revealed truth of God is the material on which the reflective powers act, and so the truly sorrowful spirit does not become the victim of false imaginings.

IV. THERE IS BROUGHT ABOUT A VIVID RECOGNITION OF THE MERCY OF GOD IN CHRIST. As long as the passions engendered by indulgence in sin darken the soul, there is a loss of that clear and restful view of God which is the peculiar privilege of the pure in heart. David's sin (ver. 8) had transformed the all-merciful, covenanted God into an object of dread (ver. 9). But now that passion was subsiding, and the Word was allowed once more to shed its light on the facts of the case, the true character of God, as set forth in the sacred symbol, reappeared; and love, and mercy, and faithfulness, and care were seen to be concentrated in the glory over the mercy-seat. The memory of all that the ark had been to Israel, in the passage of the Jordan and elsewhere, also confirmed the returning conviction of the most precious of all truths. Once more the ark of the covenant of the Lord was, as of old, the revelation of Divine love and mercy. The same spiritual change occurs in men now when, on the subsidence of the passions, the full light of Scripture falls on the soul. God ceases to be full of terrors—an object of dread and avoidance. Christ is seen to be the express Image of the Father's Person, full of grace and truth. The old relation to him as God manifest in the flesh is restored; and the vastness and freeness of the mercy in him outshine all other truth, and shed a radiance on every thought and feeling. There is another transfiguration (Matt. xvii. 2).

V. THE FACTS OF HISTORY ARE SEEN TO ILLUSTRATE THE TRUTH RECOGNIZED. It was told David how the Lord was blessing the house of Obed-Edom. The experience of the godly who loved and trusted the ark as a symbol of the true character of God was thus in accord with the conviction arising from the exercise of reflection and the subsidence of sinful passion. History was in accord with the best thought concerning God, and furnished striking instances of the reality of a love and mercy by no means to be dreaded. Thus wonderfully does God interweave the experiences of his people for the common good of the Church and for the special help and cheer of those who have fallen into the snare of the evil one. Many a lowly Obed-Edom, by means of a love and trust simple and strong, and the blessedness resulting therefrom, has been the instrument of restoring to right views and feelings others whose position and powers were far more distinguished. Nothing is lost in the kingdom of God; small and obscure persons and things are employed for great ends. The bearing of the actual experiences of sincere and humble Christians in the common walks of life upon the formation, by the more gifted and influential, of just conceptions of the revelation of God in Christ, is a subject worthy of much consideration.

VI. THE TRUTH BEING FULLY RECOGNIZED, THE OLD JOY RETURNS. The narrative sets forth the strong abounding joy of David exhibiting itself in forms which, judged by the cool feelings and conventional standards of Western life, seem almost fanatical. The question of form and degree is here really one of naturalness, and of this there can be no doubt. The king gave himself up to the full dominion of the present joy. The spring of that joy lay in his restored perception of what the ark of the covenant really was to himself and his people. It was not now the seat of flaming fire and source of destruction, but was the visible sign of the presence and favour of the God merciful and gracious, slow to anger, and plenteous in redemption. It told of protection, and guidance, and pardon, and holy communion. It was the reconciling meeting-place, where the trembling sinner became the loving, trustful child once more. The Jordan, the walls of Jericho, the restfulness of pious souls on the great Day of Atonement, all told of what a blessed heritage is theirs whose God is the Lord; and could he as a man and a king feel other than boundless joy now that the Refuge and Dwelling-place of all generations was coming to make a permanent abode in the very midst of his people? So it is with us all when, having known the oppression and darkness of sin, we come to see in Christ the Manifestation of the reconciling God, who forgiveth our iniquities, shelters us from condemnation, comes into close sympathetic fellowship with our spirits, and abides with us as Guardian and Friend. There are seasons when this restored joy is so pure and strong that all song and music seem too meagre for its due expression—when the spirit exults inexpressibly in the God of salvation. If dancing, when natural, is the gesticulated expression of what cannot be put into word or tone, then it might be an outlet for a joy unspeakable and full of glory.

Wise religious leadership. The narrative from vers. 13—19 describes David's conduct throughout the great processional march to Jerusalem. He was here acting the part of leader of a great religious movement, and in his spirit and deeds we see the conditions of a wise religious leadership.

I. ABSOLUTE DEFERENCE TO THE AUTHORITY OF GOD. By comparing this account with the fuller record in 1 Chron. xv., it will be seen that David was most anxious that every step taken should be in accordance with the will of God. On the former occasion he seems to have left the people to follow the precedent set by the Philistines (1 Sam. vi. 7—9; cf. ver. 3), and we have seen with what sad consequences. The bitter experience of the past few months had, at all events, issued in the desire to pay deference to the revealed will of God in everything, and no longer adopt the questionable methods of men. This feeling is the first prerequisite to all spiritual success. Leaders whose minds are charged with the feeling that God is supreme, and that his will enters into all things and is first of all to be considered, carry with their own actions and words a force of the highest character. Their work is Divine, and God should fill the whole area of their vision. In so far as the thought of God as supreme dominates our mental life do we ensure action on sound principles, and put force and determination into our words and deeds.

II. MANIFESTATION OF A SPIRIT SUITABLE TO THE OCCASION. Whether the wearing of the linen ephod meant the assumption, by inspiration of God, of priestly functions in combination with the kingly and prophetic—typical of him who is our Prophet, Priest, and King—or whether it was but a garment of royalty used on special sacred occasions, this is clear: that by it David manifested a spirit appropriate to a very holy and blessed occasion. He would have people see that this was a time of consecration to the Lord, a time for purity to be the clothing of all, a time of exceptional sacredness. The impression on the people could not but be serious and elevating. Men who lead others have much in their power by virtue of the general spirit they manifest. It should always be in harmony with the occasion, indicating its special character, and bringing other minds into holy sympathy with the end in view.

III. ACKNOWLEDGMENTS OF GRATITUDE AND DEPENDENCE. There must have been among the people some trepidation on the first movement of the ark, and it was a wise arrangement that, on clearing the house of Obed-Edom, sacrifice should be offered expressing gratitude for mercies vouchsafed, and a sense of dependence on God for pardon and all needful good. The same is true of the offerings at the end of the journey. It was characteristic of the leadership of Moses that he sought to cultivate these sentiments in the minds of Israel all through the desert. We do wrong to ourselves and to God when we fail to recognize our obligations to him on every stage of our life's course. Thankfulness of heart for the past, and trustful submission for all things needed, are the two elements of a cheery, earnest, and lowly service. The preacher, the missionary leader, the teacher, and parent, who knows how to foster these sentiments in others, is in a fair way of carrying through any spiritual work that may be in hand (Phil. iv. 6, 7).

IV. PREVISION FOR COMPLETENESS OF WORK. David not only sought to bring up the ark in a manner agreeable to the will of God, and by such personal bearing and special arrangements as should impress and elevate the people, but he looked on, and, by preparing a tabernacle beforehand, secured a completion of the work befitting its nature. Many a good undertaking is left incomplete for want of this prevision. It is true each man should be intent on the work of the hour, but the work of each hour is to be regarded as having relations to all future time ; and so far as lies in our power we may anticipate the success of the succeeding hours and prepare the crowning work. The architect provides for the cupola while careful of the foundations. The statesman arranges for participation in wider privileges while educating the people up to them. The religious reformer looks on to the need of positive instruction and formation of new institutions on newly recognized principles even before releasing the people from the supposed errors of the past. The evangelist who seeks to arouse the people and bring them up to a better life, if wise, will anticipate the result of his efforts by providing solid instruction. Church leaders who seek to conduct the Church through phases of faith and practice, will forecast what is necessary when the present discipline has done its work.

V. HELPFUL WORDS AND BROAD SYMPATHIES. The people must have felt, when David stood up and blessed them in the name of the Lord, and then sent them home with substantial tokens of his sympathy, that he was indeed a leader of whom they might well be proud. The right choice of words, and the deeds which express a personal interest, are things which give a just and beneficial power over men. Human life is very dependent for its highest welfare on words fitly spoken and on deeds which symbolize affection and interest. A master of words that really convey blessing to human hearts is indeed a great man, a worthy leader. It is not by mere assertion of official authority, or performance of deeds strictly in accord with propriety and law, that hearts are won and characters moulded to a nobler type. The leader who can send his people home thankful for his existence and satisfied with the largeness of his heart, is wise in that he not only blesses men, but also renders them accessible in future to his influence.

Domestic hindrances to piety. A day of high festivities and holy gladness was closed by an event which must have made David feel how imperfect is the best estate at which man can arrive in this world. The reviling of his wife Michal was indeed a bitter element in the cup, and suggests to us a sad subject, too frequently illustrated in the lives of good men, namely, the hindrances to piety in domestic life.

I. THE MOST PERFECT HUMAN CONDITION IS MARRED BY SOME BLEMISH. To an ordinary observer David would seem to have been on that day the happiest and most honoured of men—monarch of the chosen race, in the flush of health and fulness of power and intellect, beloved by his people, and filled with joy in having brought to pass an event of great religious significance. But even for him there was a bitterness most bitter. In his home, where love and joy and full sympathy with all his noble aspirations ought to abound, there awaited him scorn, distrust, and the venom of spite. Truly, royal personages are not free from common woes. The fairest, most beautiful life is shaded by some sorrow. Every heart knoweth its own bitterness. In this we have, doubtless, an illustration of what has been true in all ages of all men. Behind all grandeur there is some destroying moth. The most charming prosperity is attended with some defect. There is " a crook in every lot." Even the great apostle knew the " thorn in the flesh."

II. DOMESTIC OPPOSITION TO PERSONAL PIETY IS AMONG THE MOST BITTER OF TRIALS. Though, as king amongst men of stubborn will and perverse disposition, David carried on his heart many a care, there was, doubtless, no trouble of his life comparable to that of the opposition of his favourite wife to the conduct which he, as a pious man, felt bound to adopt. Such sorrow presses heavily in the home where only joy ought to be found, and attends, as a dark, unwelcome shadow, the pathway of daily duty out of the home. In so far as we believe godliness to be the best of all things, and the particular expression of it we may adopt as the tribute due to God, so must the antagonism of those we love most of all embitter the spirit. This wearies and worries when, after the toil of day, the domestic circle is sought for repose and refreshment of heart. Apart from the pain of being opposed in what is most sacred and binding and precious, there is the oppressive feeling that two human beings abiding under the same roof, and pledged to mutual love and confidence, are pressing towards eternity with no assurance of being one there. This is a tender subject, the very mention of which may open the floodgates of weeping.

III. THE FORMS OF ANTAGONISM MAY VARY, BUT THE AIM IS ONE—TO WIN OR DRIVE FROM HIGH-TONED SERVICE. The sharp tongue of Michal was employed to reproach David for a form of service in which he rejoiced, and which he believed to be due to God and for the good of the people; and the ulterior aim was to hinder his adopting such courses in future. Others may meet with smiles and persuasions and all the engaging arts of the charmer, which in themselves do not assume the form of antagonism, but are designed for the same end. The manifestation of earnest piety is too earnest, too spiritual, too elevated, for the carnal mind; and hence must be brought down to a lower level. There are unspiritual wives who thus strive to despiritualize their husbands, and sometimes, but not so often, husbands strive to despiritualize their wives. Through unfortunate alliances many a godly soul has to experience this dreadful evil.

IV. THE TRUE WAY OF MEETING THIS TRIAL IS BY COMBINED MEEKNESS AND FIRMNESS. The rasping tongue of Michal and her base insinuations only provoked a gentle reply in a firm spirit. David would not increase the trouble by bitter, cutting words. Referring to God's choice of him and the consequent obligations to do all he could to raise the tone of religion, he calmly informed his wife that his purpose was unchangeable, and expressed the belief that some at least would see honour and not disgrace in his conduct. It is a hard fight to hold one's own in such a contest, and many, it is to be feared, gradually yield for the sake of what is called "peace," only to sink down to a formality in religion congenial to the unspiritual companion of the domestic hearth. Those thus tried have need to lift up their hearts to God for the wisdom and grace by which they shall know how to be true to their God and disarm the opposition or else neutralize its power. They have this encouragement, that, while the favour of the world can only tend to spiritual death, fidelity to God is sure to win the respect of all the good, command the silent reverence of even the hostile mind, and gather up daily strength wherewith to bear the burden of sorrow, and at last end one's course as a "good and faithful servant."

HOMILIES BY VARIOUS AUTHORS.

Vers. 1, 2 (1 Chron. xiii. 1—6).—(JERUSALEM.) *The ark sought after long neglect.* 1. The ark was the central point of the religion of Israel. In this sacred chest were deposited the two tables of the *Law* (the testimony, the great document of the covenant); on it rested the *covering (kapporeth)* propitiatory (LXX.), expiatory (Vulgate), or mercy-seat (Authorized Version), "above it cherubim of glory overshadowing the mercy-seat," whereon the invisible King of Israel, the Lord of hosts, was enthroned; and there atonement was made, by the sprinkling of blood, for the sins of the people (Exod. xxv. 10—22). It was a symbol of Jehovah's presence and fellowship, his righteousness and mercy, his protection and blessing; a type of heavenly things. 2. Of the ark nothing is recorded since it was placed, about seventy years previously, on its return from the land of the Philistines, in the house of Abinadab, on the hill, at Kirjathjearim; and Eleazar, his son, was consecrated to keep it (1 Sam. vi. 21, 22). During this long period it continued there, separated from the tabernacle (in Nob, 1 Sam. xxi. 6; xxii. 13, 19; and afterwards in Gibeon, 1 Chron. xxi. 29), unsought and neglected (1 Chron. xiii. 3), "buried in darkness and solitude." The worship and service of God were necessarily incomplete—an effect and evidence of the imperfect relations subsisting between the nation and its Divine King, and of its divided and distracted condition. 3. The time had now come for the restoration of the ark to its proper place as the centre of national worship. The union of all the tribes under "the man of God's choice," the conquest of Jerusalem, the defeat of the Philistines, prepared the way for the great enterprise; and to it David was impelled by a truly theocratic spirit. " This act had its root in David's truly pious feeling, was the living expression of his gratitude to the Lord for his favour, and aimed at the elevation and concentration of the religious life of Israel" (Erdmann). 4. The truths and principles symbolized by the ark are fully embodied in Christ and Christianity (Heb. ix. 11). It may, therefore, be regarded, generally, as representing the true *religion;* and its restoration from " captivity " a *religious reformation* (see 1 Sam. vii. 2—6). In the going forth of the king at the head of "all Israel " from Jerusalem " to Baale, that is, to Kirjath-jearim, which belonged to Judah (twelve miles distant), to bring up thence the ark of God," we observe—

I. AN EXALTED AIM. 1. *The rendering to God of the honour which is his due,* by open acknowledgment of his supremacy, proper reverence for his great Name, cheerful obedience to his requirements. The religious life of a people is not only expressed in a proper regard for the ordinances of *public worship* (1 Sam. i. 3), but also greatly promoted thereby. When these are neglected, corrupted, or negligently performed, there can hardly be a higher aim than to make them attractive and pure, and induce a worthy performance of them. "O worship the Lord in the beauty of holiness ! " (Ps. xcvi. 9). 2. *The realization of closer communion with God,* and the reception of the blessings that flow from such communion—mercy and grace, righteousness and strength, safety and peace. "True religion can never be the affair of the individual alone. A right religious relation to God must include a relation to our fellow-men in God, and solitary acts of devotion can never satisfy the wants of healthy spiritual life, which calls for a visible expression of the fact that we worship God together in the common faith which binds us into a religious community. The necessity for acts of public and united worship is instinctively felt, wherever religion has a social influence, and in Israel it was felt the more strongly because Jehovah was primarily the God and King of the nation, who had to do with the individual Israelite only in virtue of his place in the commonwealth " (J. Robertson Smith, ' The Prophets of Israel '). 3. *The fulfilment of the purpose of God concerning his people*—that they may be holy, united, prosperous, mighty, and "show forth his praise" (Isa. xliii. 21). " O Lord, I beseech thee, send now prosperity" (Ps. cxviii. 25). "The next great step of David (after the conquest of Jerusalem) was the re-establishment of the national religion, the worship of Jehovah, with suitable dignity and magnificence. Had David acted solely from political motives, this measure had been the wisest he could adopt. The solemn assembling of the tribes would not only cement the political union of the monarchy, but also increase the opulence of his capital and promote the internal commerce of the country; while it brought the heads of the tribes, and indeed the whole people, under the cognizance and personal knowledge of the sovereign, it fixed the residence of the more eminent of the priesthood in the metropolis " (Milman).

II. AN ENERGETIC LEADER. The enterprise was initiated, inspired, accomplished, by David, whose anxious thought on the matter is alluded to in Ps. cxxxii. (written subsequently), ' Jehovah's resting-place.'

> " Remember, O Jehovah, to David
> All his harassing cares,
> Who sware to Jehovah,
> Vowed to the Mighty One of Jacob :
> ' I will not come into the tent of my house,
> I will not go up to the couch of my bed,
> I will not give sleep to mine eyes,
> Nor slumber to mine eyelids,
> Until I find a place for Jehovah,
> A dwelling for the Mighty One of Jacob.'
> Lo! we heard of it at Ephratah,
> We found it in the fields of the wood.
> Let us go into his dwelling,
> Let us bow ourselves before his footstool.
> Arise, O Jehovah, to thy rest,
> Thou and the ark of thy strength."

(Ps. cxxxii. 1—8.)

"At Ephratah, at Bethlehem, the idea of making this great transference" (Acts vii. 46) may have first "occurred to David's mind" (Stanley; but see Commentaries on this psalm). "And David consulted with the captains of thousands," etc. (1 Chron. xiii. 1—4); "gathered together all the chosen men [warriors] of Israel;" and "arose and went." 1. Eminent piety in the individual manifests itself in deep and tender concern with respect to a common neglect of Divine worship, and in *wise and diligent effort to repair it.* "David's ruling passion was zeal for the house and worship of God" (Ps. xxvi. 8). 2. Men in *authority* should make use of their position for that purpose; not, indeed, in the way of compulsion, but of example and persuasion. "Where shall we find to-day men whose first concern is for the honour of God; who really believe that the favour of the Highest is the true palladium of their country's welfare?" (Blaikie). 3. Thus *one man* sometimes effects a general and lasting reformation. It was so with Samuel and David, and it has been so with others. How much may be accomplished by one man who is thoroughly in earnest! 4. In this manner such a man fulfils the will of God concerning him, and proves his *Divine calling* (see 1 Sam. xiii. 14). "These things show David to be 'a man after God's own heart,' every way fitted for the purpose for which he was exalted, a prince of the largest capacities and noblest views; and the extensiveness and national utility of the scheme he formed, in which the honour of God and the welfare and advantage of his people were equally consulted, demonstrate the piety and goodness of his heart, and clothe him with a glory in which no prince could ever rival or equal him" (Chandler, 'Life of David,' pp. 236, 320).

III. A SYMPATHETIC PEOPLE. In response to David's appeal, "all the congregation said that they would do so," etc. (1 Chron. xiii. 4). He "went with all the people that were with him," etc. 1. A leader of men, however great, stands in *need* of their sympathy and support, and can do nothing without them. 2. It is by their means that he *achieves success.* The age contributes as much to him as he to it. 3. The union and co-operation of the people with him are a sign of *the favour and blessing of God,* and a condition of further prosperity. "The new enthusiasm and elevation of the community was not the creation of David. It met him as his noblest incentive; but it is the completeness with which he suffered it to take possession of him . . . that constitutes the secret of his peculiar greatness, and the charm which never failed to attach to his struggles and triumphs all the strongest and purest spirits of his age" (Ewald).

IV. A UNITED AND ZEALOUS ENDEAVOUR. Captains of thousands, every leader, brethren everywhere, all Israel from Shihor of Egypt even unto the entering of Hamath, priests and Levites, chosen warriors, numbering thirty thousand (seventy thousand, LXX.), went "to find the lost relic of the ancient religion." They felt the value of the object of their search; were intent on its possession; "of one heart and one soul;" rested not in wishes and prayers merely, but exhibited their concord in practical, appropriate, persevering activity. It was a fresh starting-point for the nation, the commencement of a new religious era. Be it ours now to seek and strive after a still more glorious time!

> "Oh, may the hour
> Soon come when all false gods, false creeds, false prophets,
> Allowed in thy good purpose for a time,
> Demolished,—the great world shall be at last
> The mercy-seat of God, the heritage
> Of Christ, and the possession of the Spirit,
> The Comforter, the Wisdom! shall all be
> One land, one home, one friend, one faith, one law,
> Its ruler God, its practice righteousness,
> Its life peace!"

(Bailey, 'Festus.'

D.

Vers. 3—5 (1 Chron. xiii. 7, 8).—(KIRJATH-JEARIM.) *The ark brought out of deep obscurity.* The enterprise was marked by—

I. A GREAT DISCOVERY. "We found it in the fields of the wood" (Ps. cxxxii. 6). 1. An invaluable *treasure*, long hidden from view; like the "treasure hid in a field," and the "pearl of great price" (Matt. xiii. 44—46). 2. A significant *memorial* of God's mercies in times past. What manifold and mighty events would be brought to remembrance by the sight of the sacred, venerable, and mysterious coffer, when it came forth, as from its grave, into the light of day! 3. A sure *pledge* of the continued favour of God in time to come. "The ark was, as it were, the palladium of Israel, the *moving sacrament* of that rude people; not itself Divine any more than our sacramental bread is Christ's body, or our symbolic water God's grace, but the visible symbol of a presence supposed to be local, or of a power manifested in answer to prayer" (Rowland Williams). Yet it was "not a mere dead, idle shadow to look upon, but what certainly declared God's nearness to his Church" (Calvin).

II. A JOYFUL PROCESSION. "And they set [carried] the ark of God upon a new cart [waggon]; and Uzzah and Ahio, the sons [grandsons] of Abinadab, drave the cart; and Ahio went before [Uzzah going alongside] the ark. And David and all Israel played [sported] before Jehovah with all their might, with songs, and with harps," etc. (1 Sam. x. 10; xix. 20). Already commenced the higher order of Divine service, to be afterwards more fully organized and established. For this occasion (as some have supposed) David wrote Ps. lxviii. 'The ark setting forward in victorious might.'

> " Let God arise, let his enemies be scattered,
>   And let them that hate him flee before his face."

Such language was historically appropriate (Numb. x. 35). The sacred procession served : 1. To express their gratitude, gladness, and triumph. 2. To deepen their devotion, union, and joy. 3. To produce a beneficial and lasting impression on the nation. 4. To exalt the Name of Jehovah among surrounding peoples. "No less than eleven psalms, either in their traditional titles, or in the irresistible evidence of their contents, bear traces of this great festival. The twenty-ninth psalm (by its title in the LXX.), is said to be on the 'going forth of the tabernacle.' The thirtieth (by its title), the fifteenth, and the hundred and first (by their contents), express the feelings of David on his occupation of his new home. The sixty-eighth, at least in part, and the twenty-fourth, seem to have been actually composed for the entrance of the ark into the ancient gates of the heathen fortress (Ps. xcvi., cv., cvi., vi., xlvi., cxxxii.)" (Smith's 'Dictionary'). "The hymns of David excel no less in sublimity and tenderness of expression than in loftiness and purity of religious sentiment. In comparison with them, the sacred poetry of all other nations sinks into mediocrity. They have embodied so exquisitely the universal language of religious emotion, that (a few fierce and vindictive passages excepted, natural in the warrior-poet of a sterner age) they have entered, with unquestioned propriety, into the ritual of the holier and more perfect religion of Christ . . . How many human hearts have they softened, purified, and exalted! Of how many wretched beings have they been the secret of consolation! On how many communities have they drawn down the blessings of Divine providence, by bringing the affections into unison with their deep devotional fervour!" (Milman).

III. AN INEXCUSABLE TRANSGRESSION. "The act of David and of Israel was evidently intended as a return to the Lord and submission to his revealed ordinances; but, if so, obedience must be complete in every particular" (Edersheim). It was ordained that the ark should be borne with staves on the shoulders of *men*, the elect men of the nation (Numb. vii. 9), and, in placing it on a new cart drawn by oxen, after the manner of the heathen (1 Sam. vi. 10, 12), they acted contrary to the Divine ordinance, as David subsequently recognized (1 Chron. xv. 13). Were they fully aware of the nature and importance of that ordinance? Perhaps not; especially after it had been so long in abeyance. Were they altogether ignorant of its existence? This could hardly have been the case with the priests and Levites. Such ignorance, moreover, would have been highly culpable. They were doubtless acquainted with it; but they were forgetful, careless, negligent, and adopted the method which seemed most expedient and to have been previously sanctioned. 1. "All religious reformations which are wrought by men, are blemished by human infirmities" (Wordsworth). 2. Long neglect of Divine ordinances commonly renders the renewed performance of them exceedingly defective. 3. Fresh and fervid zeal is often inconsiderate, self-confident, and rash. 4. Example is apt to mislead; and should be imitated only in so far as it accords with the Word of God. 5. The end sought may be in accordance with the

Divine will, whilst the means employed for the attainment thereof are contrary to it. 6. Good intentions do not justify forbidden actions. "Two things make a good Christian—good actions and good aims. A good aim maketh not a bad action good, as here; and yet a bad aim maketh a good action bad, as we see in Jehu" (Trapp). 7. The conduct which is blameless in some may be sinful in others who have received higher privileges. 8. Although the transgression of God's Law may be borne with for a time, it is sure to be followed by deserved chastisement. 9. If negligence and disobedience in relation to the material symbol were displeasing to God, much more must they be so in relation to the spiritual truth of which it was a shadow (Heb. x. 29). 10. The noblest agents should be chosen for the performance of the noblest services.—D.

Vers. 6—8 (1 Chron. xiii. 9—11).—(GOREN NACHON.) *The ark upheld with irreverent hands.*

> "Read who the Church would cleanse, and mark
>   How stern the warning runs:
> There are two ways to guard her ark—
>   As patrons and as sons."

> ('Lyra Apostolica.')

The fair prospects of a great enterprise are sometimes darkened, as by a *thunderstorm*, in consequence of the improper manner in which it is conducted. The forbearance of God toward those who transgress his ordinances is often unheeded, and becomes an occasion of further transgression, until the occurrence of a signal disaster fills them with fear and trembling. The act of one man, it may be, gives definite expression to the spirit which influences many, and on him falls the lightning-stroke of Heaven, as a punishment for his sin and a chastisement of all who are associated with him; a solemn call to consideration and amendment.

> "Give unto Jehovah, O ye sons of God,
>   Give unto Jehovah glory and strength;
> Give unto Jehovah the glory of his Name;
>   Worship Jehovah in holy attire.
> The voice of Jehovah is upon the waters.
>   The God of glory thundereth."

> (Ps. xxix. 1—3.)

I. A SEEMING EXIGENCY. The ark in danger! "For [at the threshing-floor of Nachon, or Chidon] the oxen shook it [kicked, broke loose, or stumbled]," so that the support of Uzzah was apparently needful to arrest its fall. In like manner religion— the Church, its worship, sacraments, doctrines—sometimes appears in perilous need of human help. But the apparent exigency: 1. Is commonly the result of *previous negligence* and disobedience on the part of those to whom its interests are entrusted, and the false position in which it is placed. If the "due order" (1 Chron. xv. 13) had been observed, the danger would never have arisen. 2. Serves the purpose of testing and *manifesting the character* of men. Will it lead them to consider, perceive their error, and amend; or occasion further aberrations? 3. Can never warrant an interference which is *expressly prohibited*, however great the danger or sincere the desire to avert it. "You must rather leave the ark to shake, if it so please God, than put unworthy hands to hold it up" (Bacon). 4. Is not so great as it appears; for God is able to *prevent* its fall or overrule it for good. "The special moral of this warning is that no one, on the plea of zeal for the ark of God's Church, should resort to doubtful expedients and unlawful means for the attainment of his end" (Wordsworth).

II. A SERIOUS ERROR. "Uzzah reached forth to the ark of God, and took hold of it." The Levites (of whom Uzzah was one) were to carry it on staves; but "not touch any holy thing, lest they die" (Numb. iv. 15). His error was *practical*; though in itself trivial, a direct breach of the legal requirement; and (as is often the case with an apparently insignificant act) indicated an unsanctified mind. He was "a type of all who, with *good intentions*, humanly speaking, yet with unsanctified minds, interfere in the affairs of the kingdom of God from the notion that they are in danger and with the hope of saving them" (O. von Gerlach). 1. He acted "unnecessarily, and from the precipitate *impulse* of human nature" (Ewald), unregulated and unrestrained by proper thought and a higher will. 2. With rashness, *irreverence*, and profanity; begotten of long familiarity with the venerable relic (see 1 Sam. vi. 19). He looked upon it as little other than a piece of sacred furniture. 3. In a spirit of official *pride and presumption*, as its hereditary guardian and immediate conductor. "Perhaps he affected to show before this great assembly how bold he could make with the ark, having been so long acquainted with it" (Matthew Henry). Men of high position, great possessions, and eminent gifts in the Church, sometimes display a similar spirit, and even affect to patronize the worship of God! 4. With improper anxiety about the means of progress and success, and *want of faith* in the Divine presence and might. "In our own days there are not awanting men like Uzzah, who act as if it were all over with Christianity if they did not maintain it against the power of modern negations." Their *zeal* is shown in various ways. But "this zeal, notwithstanding its good intention, is yet unholy, because it is as faint-hearted as it is presumptuous. The Lord needs not such helpers" (Krummacher).

III. A STARTLING JUDGMENT. "And the anger of Jehovah was kindled, . . . and he died there by the ark of God." A flash of lightning, an apoplectic stroke, or other secondary cause, was the instrument thereof; in the presence of all Israel, and even before the mercy-seat, he suffered the penalty of his error ("rashness," ver. 7); and the spot where he fell became a monument of the wrath of God and his power to protect his "holy things" (Ezek. xxii. 8). 1. On those who continue to break the Divine Law "the fiery indignation," though long delayed, breaks forth *suddenly* and "without remedy" (Heb. x. 31). 2. Punishment is most *severe* on those who are most honoured, and who ought to be a pattern to others of reverence and obedience (Numb. iii. 4; 1 Sam. v. 6; vi. 19; 2 Chron. xxvi. 21; Acts v. 5; xii. 23). 3. The consequences of sin reveal the *measure* of its sinfulness. 4. The judgment inflicted on one affects *many*, and represents their desert. The procession was stopped, the enterprise hindered, rejoicing turned into mourning, "and great fear came upon all" (Acts v. 11). "When many have sinned God commonly punishes one or two of the leaders, in order that others may remember their sin and beg forgiveness" (Osiander). Judgment is mingled with mercy. The punishment of one is for the good of many.

IV. A SALUTARY ADMONITION. 1. To consider the awful holiness and majesty of the great King (Mal. i. 11, 14); "for our God is a consuming fire" (Heb. xii. 29). 2. To learn the spiritual meaning and sanctity of his ordinances. 3. To cherish a spirit of profound humility and reverence in his service. 4. To exercise repentance and trust, and new and faithful obedience to his will in all things. Then—

> "Jehovah will give strength to his people;
> Jehovah will bless his people with peace."
> (Ps. xxix. 11.)

> D.

Vers. 9, 10 (1 Chron. xiii. 12, 13).—(PEREZ-UZZAH.) *The ark regarded with a fearful heart.* "And David was afraid of the Lord that day" (ver. 9). By none was "the disaster of Uzzah" more keenly felt than by the king. He was disappointed, grieved, and displeased at the interruption of the enterprise on which he had set his heart; and, clearly perceiving the primary offence that had been committed, he was *angry* with all who were responsible for it, not least with himself (2 Cor. vii. 11). "The burning of David's anger was not directed against God, but referred to the calamity which had befallen Uzzah, or, speaking more correctly, to the cause of the calamity which David attributed to himself or to his undertaking" (Keil). His attitude of soul toward Jehovah "that day" was not, indeed, altogether what it should have been. Conscious of sinfulness and liability to err, he was full of apprehension of a similar judgment on himself, if he should receive the ark; and his *fear* (though springing up in a devout heart) was an oppressive, paralyzing, superstitious terror, like that of the men of Beth-shemesh (1 Sam. vi. 20), rather than an enlightened, submissive, and becoming reverence. "This was his infirmity; though some will have it to be his humility" (Trapp). We thus see wherein *fear* is—

I. NEEDFUL. It is as natural and proper a motive as gratitude, hope, or love; is often enjoined; and, in the sense of unbounded reverence, it constitutes "the religious feeling in its fundamental form" (Martensen). To men in their present condition it is specially needful in order to: 1. *Arrest heedless footsteps* and constrain to serious reflection and self-examination. "Serve the Lord with fear, and rejoice with trembling" (Ps. ii. 11; iv. 4). 2. *Convince of sin,* restrain pride and presumption, and lead to godly sorrow. 3. *Deter from disobedience,* and induce circumspection and diligence (Ps. lxxxix. 7; Prov. xvi. 6; 1 Cor. x. 12; 2 Cor. vii. 1; Phil. ii. 12; 1 Pet. i. 17). "Fear is a great bridle of intemperance, the modesty of the spirit, and the restraint of gaieties and dissolutions; it is the girdle to the soul and the handmaid to repentance; the mother of consideration and the nurse of sober counsels. But this so excellent grace is soon abused in the best and most tender spirits. When it is inordinate, it is never a good counsellor, nor makes a good friend; and he that fears God as his enemy is the most completely miserable person in the world" (Jeremy Taylor, 'Of Godly Fear').

II. SINFUL. It is so when associated with: 1. *Misinterpretation* and false judgments of God's dealings; such false judgments being themselves due to personal disappointment or other self-blinding influence. "In his first excitement and dismay David may not have perceived the real and deeper ground of this Divine judgment;" and thought that God had dealt hardly with him. 2. Suspicion, *distrust,* and "the evil heart of unbelief departing from the living God;" from which even the best of men are not exempt, especially when impressed with his severity and forgetful of his goodness (Rom. xi. 22). 3. *Servile* thoughts of the service of God, as a restraint upon freedom and a source of trouble and danger. "How shall the ark of the Lord come to me?" 4. *Immoderate* and morbid indulgence of the feeling, instead of immediate return to God at "the throne of grace," in penitence, hope, and renewed devotion (1 Sam. xvi. 2; xxviii. 1).

III. HURTFUL. By: 1. Producing inward distraction and despondency. 2. Estranging from the fellowship and service of God, and preventing the accomplishment of holy purposes. How many excellent enterprises are abandoned through unworthy fears! 3. Depriving of invaluable blessings. The loss of David appears by the gain of Obed-Edom (ver. 11), into whose dwelling the ark brought sunshine and prosperity. But with time and reflection his misjudgments were corrected, his faith revived, his fear was sanctified (Ps. ci. 2) and associated with holy and ardent aspiration after the presence of God in his tabernacle, and he wrote Ps. xv., 'The character of the true worshipper and friend of God.'

> "Jehovah, who may sojourn in thy tabernacle?
> Who may dwell in thy holy mountain?
> He that walketh uprightly and worketh righteousness,
> And speaketh truth in his heart. . . .
> He that doeth these things shall never be moved."
>
> (Ps. xv. 1—5.)
>
> D.

Vers. 10, 11 (1 Chron. xiii. 13, 14).—(THE HOUSE OF OBED-EDOM.) *The ark received with a right spirit.* By means of the ark "the thoughts of many hearts" were "revealed." Whilst Uzzah treated it with irreverence, and David regarded it with dread, Obed-Edom the Gittite (of *Gath*-rimmon) received it "with reverence and godly fear." He was a Levite, and (like Samuel) of the sons of Korah, a branch of the Kohathites, whose office it was to "bear upon their shoulders" (Numb. vii. 9); and is subsequently mentioned as porter (musician), and doorkeeper of the ark (1 Chron. xv. 18, 21, 24; xvi. 5, 38; perhaps "the son of Jeduthun"). He did not seek to have the ark placed under his care; but, when requested by the king, he was not afraid to receive it, well knowing "that, although God is a consuming fire to those who treat him with irreverence, he is infinite in mercy to those who obey him." "Oh, the courage of an honest and faithful heart!" (Hall). The ark in the house of Obed-Edom may be considered as representing *religion in the home;* and wherever it truly dwells there is: 1. *A consciousness of the presence of God;* of which the ark was the divinely ordained symbol. As often as he and his household looked upon the sacred vessel, mysteriously veiled with its blue covering, they would be the more deeply impressed with the conviction of that presence. We have no longer the symbol; but we have the spiritual reality which it signified; the one is taken away that the other may be more fully recognized, and its recognition cannot but produce in the home thoughtfulness, reverence, and self-restraint. 2. *Obedience to his commandments;* which were deposited in the ark (2 Chron. ii. 10). The Law must be written on the fleshy tablets of the heart; made the rule of life; and diligently taught to the children (Deut. vi. 4—9). The sins which it forbids will thus be avoided, the virtues which it enjoins practised; "righteousness, goodness, and truth," the foundation on which the home is built; and the will of God being recognized as supreme, order and harmony will prevail. 3. *Confidence in his mercy;* according to the appointed method of reconciliation set forth by the mercy-seat, and fulfilled in Christ (Rom. iii. 25; 2 Cor. v. 19; 1 John ii. 1). The fatherly love of God, being "known and believed," becomes a perpetual incentive to love God and one another (Eph. iv. 32; Rom. xiii. 10). The pervading element of the home should be love. "Jesus Christ—Love; the same." 4. *The enjoyment of his fellowship;* which was assured at the mercy-seat. "There will I commune with thee" (Exod. xxv. 22). "Communion with God is the very innermost essence of all true Christian life;" and it is maintained and perfected in the home by family prayer (ver. 20). 5. *Repose under his protection;* represented by the overshadowing cherubim. While Obed-Edom guarded the ark of God, he was himself guarded by the God of the ark. "The Lord is thy Keeper" (Ps. cxxi. 5). "He shall give his angels charge over thee," etc. (Ps. xci. 1, 11). 6. *The reception of his blessing.* "And Jehovah blessed Obed-Edom, and all his household" (ver. 11), "all that he had" (1 Chron. xiii. 14)—blessed him with spiritual, providential, enduring benefits (1 Chron. xxvi. 4—8). "It paid well for its entertainment. The same hand that punished Uzzah's proud presumption rewarded Obed-Edom's humble boldness, and made the ark to him 'a savour of life unto life'" (Matthew Henry). "A good man leaveth an inheritance to his children's children" (Prov. xiii. 22; Ps. cii. 28). 7. *The promotion of his honour and glory.* "And it was told King David," etc. Religion in the home "cannot be hid;" the fame thereof goes abroad and incites many—perchance a whole nation—to render to God the honour which is his due, "so that glory may dwell in our land."—D.

Vers. 12—15 (1 Chron. xv.).—(JERUSALEM.) *The ark led forth with devout enthusiasm.* A man's ruling passion, although repressed for a season, surely reappears. It was thus with David's affection for the ark of God, and his desire to bring it up to Zion, where he had prepared a new tent, tabernacle, or pavilion (Ps. xxvii. 5), for its reception (ver. 17), in or adjoining his own palace (1 Chron. xiv. 1; xv. 1). His zeal, which had been checked by fear, now revived

> "As florets, by the frosty air of night
> Bent down and closed, when day has blanched their leaves,
> Rise all unfolded on their spiry stems."
>
> (Dante.)

I. A RENEWED PURPOSE is ofttimes: 1. Incited by the *example* of another, and the manifest success attending his conduct. "And it was told King David," etc. (ver. 12); "And David said, I will go and bring back the ark with blessing to my house" (Vulgate). To this also his study of the Law, meditation and prayer, during the preceding three months contributed. 2. Accompanied with the conviction and confession of the *cause* of previous failure (ver. 13; 1 Chron. xv. 2, 13, 15). "Pious men will profit by their own errors, stand the stronger for their falls, and not abate in their zeal and affections, but learn to connect them with humility, and to regulate them according to the precepts of the sacred Scripture" (Scott). 3. Carried out with more careful and diligent *preparation* than before. "David gathered all Israel together"—the priests (Abiathar, 1 Sam. xxx. 7; Zadok, 1 Chron. xii. 28) and the *Levites* (mentioned only once in 2 Samuel, viz. ch. xv. 24); charged them to sanctify themselves to bring up the ark, and directed the chiefs of the latter to appoint singers with musical instruments for the procession (1 Chron. xv. 12—16), among whom he seems to have "found a faculty of song and music already in existence" (Hengstenberg).

II. AN AUSPICIOUS COMMENCEMENT. "When they had gone six paces, he sacrificed oxen and fatlings" ("seven bullocks and seven rams," 1 Chron. xv. 26)—"a thank offering for the happy beginning, and a petition for the prosperous continuation of the undertaking" (Böttcher). 1. The *first steps* of an enterprise are of high importance, and, until they are actually taken, even the best prepared are seldom without misgiving. 2. When taken with the manifest *approval* of Heaven, they afford strong confidence and hope of a successful issue. 3. The *gladness* (ver. 12) of successful effort is all the greater because of previous anxiety and grief (Ps. cxxvi. 6). The procession was led by eight hundred and sixty-two Levites clad in white, in three choirs, playing respectively on cymbals, psalteries, and harps; over the first of which were Heman (grandson of Samuel), Asaph, and Ethan, or Jeduthun. Then followed Chenaiah, "chief" or marshal "of the Levites for bearing;" two doorkeepers; *the ark*, attended by seven priests blowing silver trumpets (Numb. x. 1—10); and two other doorkeepers (of whom Obed-Edom was one). Last of all came the king, with the elders and captains of thousands, and the whole body of the people.

> "Before went the singers, behind the players on stringed instruments;
> In the midst of damsels striking timbrels.
> There is Benjamin the youngest, their ruler;
> The princes of Judah—their motley band,
> The princes of Zebulun, the princes of Naphtali."
>
> (Ps. lxviii. 26, 28.)

III. A FESTAL AND TRIUMPHAL PROGRESS. "With shouting and sound of trumpet" (ver. 15). Again arose the well-known shout, "Let God arise," etc.! (Ps. lxviii.; cxxxii. 8). The king may have composed the hymns sung by the Levites, and himself carried a harp in his hand. His clothing "had a priestly character, and not only the ephod of white, but also the *meil* of white byssos, distinguished him as the head of a priestly people" (Keil, on 1 Chron. xv. 27). And David, having laid aside his royal garment, which would impede his movements, "danced before Jehovah with all his might" (ver. 14).

> "The same who sang
> The Holy Spirit's song, and bare about
> The ark from town to town; now doth he know
> The merit of his soul-impassioned strains
> By their well-fitted guerdon."
>
> (Dante, 'Par.,' xx.)

"Simonides used to say of dancing that it was silent poetry, and of poetry that it was eloquent dancing" (Delany, from Plutarch). There is "a time to dance" (Eccles. iii. 4). David's dancing was a *religious* act (ver. 21); customary among a people of simple and demonstrative habits, on a return from *victory* and in public worship (Exod. xv. 20; Judg. xi. 34; 1 Sam. xviii. 6); rendered familiar to him in the school of the *prophets* (1 Sam. xix. 24); practised only on an extraordinary occasion; a natural expression of personal gratitude and joy (Ps. xxx. 11) in a man of ardent temperament; a sign of humble, avowed, and unreserved devotion to Jehovah (Ps. cl. 4); a means of identifying himself with the people, and of infusing his own spirit into them. Those persons who condemn him as deficient in modesty and dignity should remember these things: those who commend dancing as a social amusement or recreation by his example must find other grounds for their commendation; and those who justify the unseasonable, vain, and indelicate manner in which it is ordinarily performed, by his conduct, either misunderstand or shamelessly pervert it (Job xxi. 7—15).

Of *religious excitement* it may be said that: 1. It does not prevail to such an *extent* as might have been expected from the glorious truths set forth in the Word of God. 2. It is of great *value* in inducing the performance of duty, overcoming obstacles, and leading to a decisive course of action. Reason and conscience are often insufficient of themselves to influence the will effectually. 3. It is fraught with serious *danger*—of not being properly regulated by intelligence, of running into imprudence and excess, of being superficial and transient, and perverted to an unworthy and sinful end. 4. It requires to be *controlled* by an enlightened conscience, transformed into fixed principles, and translated into holy and useful deeds. Unless it be immediately acted upon it is injurious rather than beneficial.—D.

Vers. 17—19 (1 Chron. xvi.).—(ZION.) *The ark established in its chosen resting-*

place. The ascent of the ark into "the city of David" may be regarded as: 1. A *termination* of a state of things that had long prevailed, in which the relation of the people of Israel to their Divine King was interrupted, his service neglected, their power impaired. Even the early military successes of Saul were followed by disaster, dissension, and civil strife, which had been only recently healed. Once more there was rest (1 Chron. xxiii. 25). 2. An *inauguration* of a new era: the more manifest and abiding presence of Jehovah among his people, the more general recognition of his sovereignty, the organization of a worthier and more attractive form of worship, the more complete union of the tribes under the Lord's Anointed (Messiah), and the victorious expansion of his kingdom. "It was the greatest day of David's life. . . . It was felt to be the turning-point in the history of the nation. It recalled the great epoch of the passage through the wilderness. David was on that day the founder, not of freedom only, not of religion only, but of a Church, a commonwealth" (Stanley). 3. A *representation* (a type, or at least an emblem) of the coming of "Messiah the Prince" in his kingdom; either, more generally, in his whole mediatorial course from his first advent to his final triumph, or, more specially, at his ascension "far above all the heavens, that he might fill all things" (Eph. iv. 8—10).

> "Thou hast ascended up on high,
> Thou hast led captives captive," etc.
> (Ps. lxviii. 18.)

I. A GLORIOUS CONSUMMATION. "And they brought in the ark of the Lord, and set it in its place," etc. "This is my rest for ever," etc. (Ps. cxxxii. 13, 14). To this occasion may be referred Ps. xxiv., 'The King of glory entering his sanctuary.'

> "The earth is Jehovah's, and the fulness thereof;
> The world, and they that dwell therein. . . .
> Who shall ascend into the hill of Jehovah?
> And who shall stand in his holy place?"
> (Ps. xxiv. 1—6.)

It is here declared that the proper preparation for communion with God is moral purity, not merely external pomp (vers. 9, 11; Ps. xv.; Isa. xxxiii. 15, 16). The former part of this grand choral hymn was probably sung on the way to Zion; the latter on entering the gates of the venerable fortress and city of Melchizedek.

> "Lift up your heads, O ye gates,
> And be ye lift up, ye everlasting doors,
> That the King of glory may come in.
> *Who is, then, the King of glory?*
> Jehovah strong and mighty,
> Jehovah mighty in battle.

> "Lift up your heads, O ye gates . . .
> *Who is, then, that King of glory?*
> Jehovah of hosts;
> He is the King of glory."
> (Ps. xxiv. 7—10.)

"Amidst the glorious wave of song and praise, the ark was placed in the tabernacle." So Christ (in whom the Divine and human king are one) has entered the heavenly Zion, dwells with men, and prepares those who receive him, in faith and love, to dwell with him for ever (Heb. x. 12, 22).

II. AN ACCEPTABLE SACRIFICE. "And David" (as head and representative of a priestly nation, Exod. xix. 6) "offered burnt offerings and peace offerings before Jehovah;" the former expressive of self-dedication, the latter of thanksgiving, praise, and joyous fellowship with God and one another. At the close of the service of dedication he instituted a regular "service of song in the house of the Lord" (see Hengstenberg, 'On the History of the Psalmodic Poetry'), due in part to the influence of Samuel and his prophet-associates (1 Sam. xix. 20), but having him for its real author, and receiving its mightiest impulse from his sublime compositions. He was a *prophet* as truly as Samuel or Moses (Acts ii. 30). "David, as well as Moses, was made like to Christ the Son of David in this respect, that by him God gave a new ecclesiastical establishment and new ordinances of worship" (Jon. Edwards). "*On that day* then David ordered for the first time to thank the Lord by Asaph and his brethren" (1 Chron. xvi. 7).

> "Thank ye the Lord, call on his Name,
> Make known his deeds among the people," etc.
>> (1 Chron. xvi. 8—22; Ps. cv. 1—15.)

> "Sing ye to the Lord, all the earth,
> Proclaim from day to day his salvation," etc.
>> (1 Chron. xvi. 23—36; Ps. xcvi. 2—13; cvi. 1, 47, 48.)

"A day to be remembered for all time! Then 'the sweet singer of Israel' first gave the suggestions of his inspiration, and the product of his pen, to embody and guide the praises of the Church. What effects have followed that first hymn! What streams of praise . . . what clouds of incense have gushed and risen and are ever rising and gushing the world over at this moment, from the immortal impulse of that Divine act!" (Binney). Yet it is Christ himself "in the midst of the Church" (Heb. ii. 12) who inspires its noblest praises, and by whom the sacrifice is rendered acceptable to God (Heb. xiii. 15).

III. A GRACIOUS BENEDICTION. "And he blessed the people in the name of the Lord of hosts;" recognizing him as "the God of omnipotent power in heaven, who victoriously accomplishes his work of salvation" (1 Sam. i. 3), and solemnly invoking a blessing on his people in accordance with his Name and covenant. His act, although not strictly an assumption of the office of the Levitical priesthood, was of a *priestly* character (even more so than the patriarchal blessing); "and thus, though but in a passing and temporary manner, he prefigured in his own person the union of the kingly and priestly offices" (Perowne), alluded to in Ps. cx. (written after this event), 'The victorious king and priest.'

> "Jehovah hath sworn, and will not repent:
> Thou art a priest for ever
> After the order of Melchizedek."
>> (Ps. cx. 4.)

It was while the Lord Jesus "lifted up his hands and blessed them" that "he parted from them, and was carried up into heaven" (Luke xxiv. 51)—a sign of his continual intercession and benediction. "Wherefore also he is able to save," etc. (Heb. vii. 25).

IV. A GENEROUS BENEFACTION. "And he distributed to all the people, even to the whole multitude of Israel, as well to the women as to the men, to every one a cake of bread, and a measure [of wine], and a raisin-cake," that they might feast together before the Lord (according to custom in the case of peace offerings, 1 Sam. i. 4; ix. 13) as a nation, with thankfulness, gladness, and charity. "It is a good thing when *benedicere* and *benefacere* go together, and when in a prince is seen, not only piety toward God, but love and liberality toward his people" (Guild). How much greater are the benefits bestowed by the exalted Redeemer than those conferred by any earthly monarch (Mark xvi. 20; Acts ii. 33)! "Christ has risen bodily into heaven that he may be spiritually present in the earthly heaven of the Church; the bodily ascension and the spiritual indwelling are two aspects of the same act. . . . The mystical David, from his own high home, dispenses his own flesh for the life of the world, and that spiritual bread which he that hungers after righteousness shall eat of and be satisfied, and that 'fruit of the vine' which is even now to be drunk in the earthly 'kingdom of the Father'" (W. Archer Butler).—D.

Ver. 17.— *The ark and the Bible.* The ark of the covenant has been taken as representative of religion, of Christ, of the Church, or of the sacraments and means of grace. It may also be compared with the *Bible* (or Scriptures of the old and new covenants), which is of even greater value to us than the ark was to Israel. The resemblance appears in their: 1. *Supernatural origin.* The ark was made according to the pattern shown (in vision) by God to Moses in the mount (Exod. xxv. 9), by Bezaleel, who was "filled with the Spirit of God" (Exod. xxxi. 3), and other wise-hearted men; and the tables of stone which it contained were "written with the finger of God" (Exod. xxxiv. 1). The Bible is the product of Divine inspiration (2 Tim. iii. 16), though, like the ark, in connection with the (literary) skill of man. "It is a Divine-human book." 2. *External characteristics*, such as choice and precious materials (acacia wood and pure gold), durability, painstaking workmanship ("beaten work"), simplicity, compactness, beauty ("a crown of gold round about"), practical utility (rings and staves), which are all apparent in the Scriptures. 3. *Spiritual significance*—the presence of God, the Law (as a testimony against sin and a rule of life), atoning mercy, Divine fellowship and favour. "In the words of God we have the heart of God." The ark was a sign of these sublime realities, "not the very things themselves." With the Bible, wherein they are so much more clearly and fully set forth, it is the same. 4. *Wondrous achievements;* not, indeed, by their inherent virtue, but by the Divine might of which they were appointed instruments; in blessing or bane according to the diverse moral relationships of men. By the ark the Israelites were led through the wilderness, their enemies scattered, the waves of the Jordan arrested, the walls of Jericho demolished, the land subdued, Dagon destroyed, the rebellious punished, the irreverent smitten, the obedient blessed. Who shall describe the achievements of the Word of God? What enemies it has overcome! what reformations effected! what blessings conferred! 5. *Varied fortunes*: after long wanderings finding rest; misunderstood and superstitiously perverted, lost for a season to its appointed guardians, persistently striven against, treated with irreverent curiosity, buried in obscurity and neglect, eagerly sought after and found, cherished in private dwellings, exalted to the highest honour. 6. *Transcendent claims* on human regard— attention, reverence, faith, love, and obedience. 7. *Preparatory purpose* and temporary duration. At the destruction of Jerusalem by the Babylonians the ark perished or was lost beyond recovery; in the new dispensation there is no place for it (Jer. iii. 16); but the mercy and judgment which it symbolized cannot fail (Rev. xi. 19). The Bible is necessary only in a state where "we see by means of a mirror obscurely" (1 Cor. xiii. 12, 13), not where we see "face to face." But, though in its outward form it vanish away, yet in the spiritual realities of which it testifies, the effects which it produces, the fulfilment of its promises and threatenings, "the Word of the Lord endureth for ever."—D.

Ver. 20 (1 Chron. xvi. 43).—(ZION.) *Family worship.* "And David returned to bless his household." A benediction or blessing is essentially a prayer to God that his blessing may be bestowed upon others; and, being uttered in their presence by one who (like the head of a household) holds a position of authority in relation to them, it is also, to some extent, an assurance of the blessing. Of family worship notice—

I. ITS OBLIGATION; which (although it is not expressly enjoined) is evident from: 1. The *relation* of the family to God: its Founder, Preserver, Ruler, Benefactor, "the God of all the families of the earth" (Ps. lxviii. 6; Jer. xxxi. 1; Eph. iii. 15). Out of this relation arises the duty of honouring him (Mal. i. 6); acknowledging the dependence of the family, confessing its sins, seeking his mercy, and praising him for his benefits; nor, without family worship, can its spiritual end be fulfilled (Mal. ii. 15). 2. The *responsibility* of the head of the household to order it in the fear of God (Gen. xviii. 18; Prov. xxii. 6; Eph. vi. 4; 1 Tim. iii. 4), which involves this obligation. 3. *Precepts*, promises, etc., with reference to prayer, which have a manifest application to social worship in the family (1 Chron. xvi. 11; Jer. x. 25; Matt. vi. 9; Rom. xvi. 5; 1 Tim. ii. 8; iv. 5). 4. The *conduct* of good men, approved of God, and therefore indicative of his will and recorded for imitation. Abraham (Gen. xii. 7, 8), Jacob (Gen. xxxv. 2, 3), Job (i. 5), Joshua (xxiv. 15), David, Daniel (vi. 10), Cornelius (Acts x. 1), and others. "Wherever I have a tent, there God shall have an altar" (John Howard).

II. ITS MANNER. It should be performed: 1. With *regularity* and constancy; other family duties being arranged with reference to it, and public worship made, not a substitute, but a preparation for it or an adjunct to it. 2. In such a way as is *suitable* and profitable to those who take part in it. 3. Always with thoughtfulness, *reverence*, and cheerfulness. 4. Accompanied by the reading of the Scriptures, by instruction, discipline, and consistent practice, and by holy *purposes*, such as are expressed in Ps. ci. (written shortly before this time), 'David's mirror of a monarch' (Luther).

> "Of mercy and judgment will I sing,
> Unto thee, O Jehovah, will I harp.
> I will give heed to a perfect way—
> When wilt thou come unto me?—
> I will walk with a perfect heart within my house," etc.

III. ITS BENEFITS. 1. The sure approbation and rich blessing of God (Prov. x. 22), temporal and spiritual. By its means, perchance, a parent effects "the saving of his house" (Heb. xi. 7; Luke xix. 9). 2. The worthy performance of all the duties of life. 3. Abounding affection, harmony, peace, happiness, and hope that

> "When soon or late they reach that coast
> O'er life's rough ocean driven,
> They may rejoice, no wand'rer lost,
> A family in heaven!"

4. Holy influences, not only on all the household—parents, children, domestics—but also on the neighbourhood and society. What a mighty reformation would be implied in the general adoption of family worship! And to what a moral and spiritual height would it exalt our land!—D.

Vers. 20—23.—(ZION.) *Unholy scorn.* The greatest day of David's life did not end without a cloud. His wife Michal, "Saul's daughter" (ver. 16; ch. iii. 13; 1 Sam. xix. 11—17), had not, from whatever cause, gone forth to meet him with the other women (ver. 19) on his return to Jerusalem with the sacred ark; on beholding from a window of the palace, as the procession swept past, the enthusiasm which he displayed, "she despised him in her heart;" and when, after he had blessed the people, he returned to bless his household, she met him with sarcastic reproaches. "When at a distance she scorned him, when he came home she scolded him" (Matthew Henry). "Whereas David came to bless his house, she, through her foolishness, turneth his blessing into a curse" (Willet). Her scorn (like that of others) was—
I. INDULGED IMPROPERLY. 1. *Without adequate cause;* and even on account of what should have had an opposite effect. Fervent piety is not understood by those who do not possess it, and is therefore wrongly and uncharitably judged of by them (1 Sam. i. 13—18). "In Saul's time public worship was neglected, and the soul for vital religion had died out of the family of the king" (Keil). 2. *From want of spiritual sympathy;* in love to God and joy in his service. Her religion (like her father's) was marked by superstition, formality, and cold conventional propriety. She "knew nothing of the impulse of Divine love" (Theodoret). "The life from and in God remains a mystery to every one until, through the Spirit of God himself, it is unsealed to his experience" (Krummacher). 3. *With a sinful mind*—vain, proud, discontented, unwifely, irreverent (Eph. v. 33), and resentful. "Probably she bitterly resented her violent separation from the household joys that had grown up around him in her second home. Probably the woman who had teraphim among her furniture cared nothing for the ark of God. Probably, as she grew older, her character had hardened in its lines, and become like her father's in its measureless pride, and in its half-dread, half-hatred, of David. And all these motives together pour their venom into her sarcasm" (Maclaren). She had not "a meek and quiet spirit" (1 Pet. iii. 4).
II. EXPRESSED OFFENSIVELY. "How glorious the King of Israel made himself to-day," etc.! 1. At an *unseasonable time;* when, full of devotional feeling, he was returning from public worship "to bless his household," and when such language was calculated to be a cause of pain and of stumbling. But scoffers are inconsiderate, and reckless of the mischief their words may occasion. 2. With exaggerated statements and *misrepresentation* of motives. David had neither committed any impropriety, nor been desirous of vain display in the eyes of others, nor careless of affording occasion for their contempt. Mockers often ridicule in others what is really the creation of their own imagination or suspicion, and the reflection of the evil that is in their own hearts. 3. With *bitter irony* and derision. How keenly it was felt by the sensitive spirit of David may be learnt from what he says of an evil tongue (Ps. lii. 2; lvii. 4; cxx. 3). "Scoffing at religion is irrational; rude and uncivil; a most cruel and unhuman sin;

a most hardening vice; its impiety in the sight of God surpasses all description; it is a contagious and injurious vice" (J. A. James).

III. ANSWERED CONCLUSIVELY. By: 1. A sufficient *explanation* and defence. "It was before Jehovah" that he had "played;" conscious of his presence and desirous of giving him honour. He was not insensible to his own royal dignity; but recognized the surpassing greatness and goodness of Jehovah, from whom it was derived, and acted only in accordance therewith by giving free expression to his humble gratitude and abounding joy. His language was restrained (Ps. xxxix. 1; cxli. 3); though not without rebuke of the proud daughter of the king in preference to whom, and all his house, himself had been chosen. 2. An expression of his *resolve* to proceed still further in his course of self-humiliation (Ps. cxxxi. 1). 3. And of his *expectation* of finding honour instead of reproach among others. In the affectionate regard of those who sympathize with fervent piety, there is abundant compensation for the contempt of those who despise it. "In this incident we have the clue to that spiritual conception of his duties and position which distinguished David from Saul. It was, in fact, his spiritual conception of the true Israel, of the high privileges and duties of worshippers in the holy place, and above all of the privileges and duties of a king, as one who should carry out Jehovah's counsels upon earth, which distinguished David's reign, not only from that of Saul, but from that of any subsequent Jewish monarch" ('The Psalms chronologically arranged,' by Four Friends).

IV. PUNISHED DESERVEDLY. "Michal's childlessness is specially mentioned as a punishment of her pride. This was the deepest humiliation for an Oriental woman" (Erdmann). The scorner: 1. Inflicts a *self-injury*, by hardening the heart and rendering it less capable of faith, love, hope, sympathy, and joy; more solitary, discontented, useless, and unhappy. 2. Becomes unamiable and odious in the sight of *others*. 3. Incurs the displeasure of *God*; for "surely he scorneth the scorners" (Prov. iii. 34). "Now therefore be ye not mockers, lest your bands be made strong" (Isa. xxviii. 22).

EXHORTATION. 1. Expect to meet with opposition and contempt in your zeal for God. Even Christ himself was despised and mocked. 2. Count it no strange thing, if in your household, which you desire to bless, there should be those who deprive themselves of the blessing and dislike your devotion. 3. Suffer not their scorn to quench your zeal for God and your love for their souls. 4. Seek in Divine fellowship consolation amidst human reproach.—D.

Vers. 6, 7.—*The death of Uzzah.* A startling event. Startling to us to read of. How much more to witness, in the midst of all the pomp and joy with which David was bringing the ark to consecrate his newly founded capital, to inaugurate a revival of religion amongst the people, and thus make some fitting return to God for all his goodness to monarch and subjects, and promote in the best and surest way the welfare of all! It is by sudden, startling, and terrible events that God very commonly calls attention to his laws, and avenges the breach of them. By such means the laws of nature come to be known, reverenced, and obeyed; and are thus brought into subjection to man, and made to promote his well-being. And by similar means men are made to reflect upon the laws of God with respect to religion and morals, and so the spiritual good of men is promoted. With reference to the sudden death of Uzzah, we remark—

I. IT WAS THE PUNISHMENT OF HIS SIN. "The anger of the Lord was kindled against Uzzah." Every sudden death is not a judgment, even when the result of disobedience of some law. Instances: a child killed while playing with fire or deadly weapons; a man struck dead by the electric fluid while experimenting with it. But the phrase we have quoted compels us to regard Uzzah's death as a punishment of sin. At first it seems difficult to discover in what the sin consisted. His conduct, in reaching out his hand to the ark and laying hold of it, seems to have been at least well-meaning: he desired to preserve it from falling to the ground. But well-meaning acts may be wrong and severely punished. In this case there were: 1. *Disobedience to a plain law, with the penalty of death attached.* (See Numb. iv. 15.) Indeed, the method of bearing the ark on this occasion was altogether contrary to the Law (Exod. xxv. 14; Numb. vii. 9), as David learned by this event (see 1 Chron. xv. 13—15). There appears to have been at this period a general neglect of the Law of Moses, and ignorance of its requirements. How, otherwise, can we account for the ark itself lying so long neglected (1 Chron. xiii. 3)? But, surely, those who had the care of the ark ought to have known the law of God respecting it, or searched it out diligently when a new departure was contemplated, that they might both act rightly themselves and prevent the king from copying the Philistines (1 Sam. vi. 7) instead of obeying the Divine Law. In the swift punishment that followed Uzzah's act, the memorable maxim was again, and most impressively, proclaimed, "To obey is better than sacrifice" (1 Sam. xv. 22)—better than the most splendid pageant in honour of religion from which obedience is absent. 2. *Irreverence.* The ark was one of the most sacred things in the religion of Israel. It was a symbol of God's presence, his local dwelling-place, "called by the Name, even the Name of the LORD of hosts, that sitteth upon the cherubim" (ver. 2, Revised Version); a witness, therefore, for him: an assurance that he was with them while they were loyal and obedient; the central point of worship and national life. It was, therefore, to be treated with utmost reverence. In the services of religion it was, as a witness for the invisible God, to be itself invisible, concealed by the second veil; it was to be approached only by the high priest, and by him only once a year, and with incense, the smoke of which should prevent his beholding it (Lev. xvi. 13). But it had long been separated from its proper place in the tabernacle, and kept in a private house, the inmates of which had probably become so familiar with it that they ceased to cherish due reverence for it. Hence the rash act of Uzzah. True, the temptation was sudden and strong. But so are many temptations. All the more need to cherish such habitual piety, self-control, and watchfulness, as shall preserve us in the hour of peril. The recollection of the circumstances under which the ark had been brought into the house of Abinadab should have been sufficient to arrest the impulse to lay hold of it (1 Sam. vi. 19—21). 3. *Presumption.* In pushing himself forward without warrant, and against the law, to preserve the ark from injury. Better to have left it to the care of him to whom it belonged, and who had shown in former days his care for it and his power to protect it (1 Sam. v.). It was an instance of zeal without knowledge and faith, and in which self was prominent rather than God.

II. THE DEATH OF UZZAH WAS FOR THE INSTRUCTION AND WARNING OF DAVID AND HIS PEOPLE. David was seeking to revive and re-establish religion, and this act of God appeared to be a hindrance to his good design; but in fact it tended to promote it more effectually than all the measures of the king. 1. *It was an impressive demonstration that Jehovah their God was still among them, the living God, the Almighty, the Holy One, observing and punishing sin.* It showed that his laws were still living laws, not obsolete, though forgotten; that the sacred things which he had appointed were still sacred in his eyes, however neglected, and were to be so esteemed by the people; that, in particular, the ark was still the symbol and pledge of his living presence, as a God to be approached and worshipped with reverence, yet also with confidence in the covenant of which it was the sign. Thus the impression produced by the terrible event would tend to the revival of religious faith and feeling, and secure that David's endeavours should not end in the establishment of a mere ritual, however orderly and stately, but in sincere worship and corresponding life. It was not the first time, nor would it be the last, that the revival of religion began with terrible judgments. We also need a living faith in the living God—faith in his relation to us and presence with us; faith in his love, awakening our confidence and affection; faith also in his majesty, holiness, and justice, awakening our "reverence and godly fear." To this end we should meditate on the awe-inspiring aspects of the Divine character and government, as they appear in nature and providence and in the inspired book. Otherwise our religion is likely to become a weak, superficial, and sentimental thing, without depth and power. 2. *It was a warning that was adapted to guide and restrain the religious zeal of the king.* There was danger that, in his ardent desire for the re-establishment of the national worship with fitting circumstances of splendour and orderliness, he should not pay due attention to the instructions of the Law, but should violate the will of God in the endeavour to pay to him and secure for him due honour. Uzzah's death would teach him that the Divine will must be first regarded. He learnt this lesson so far as the mode of removing the ark was concerned. He could scarcely fail to keep it in mind in all his subsequent proceedings. Great zeal for religion has ever a similar peril. Under its influence there is danger of adopting, with the best intentions, means and methods which are not according to the Divine Word. The most powerful persons are the most likely to feel as if their own will might be their law. Thus carnality and worldliness come to regulate the affairs of the Church, and the Law of God is violated in letter or in spirit. Hence the "will-worship, the volunteered, self-imposed, officious, supererogatory service" (Lightfoot on Col. ii. 23), which has so extensively prevailed in Christendom, and which has originated or fostered errors of doctrine; hence also the terrible crimes against Christian liberty and love which have been committed *ad majorem Dei gloriam*, and thought to be sanctified thereby. 3. *There remain the common lessons taught by every death, especially by sudden deaths*, and yet more especially by sudden deaths in the midst of displays of human power and glory. The uncertainty of life, the certainty of death, the awfulness of death in sin (John viii. 21, 24), the vanity of earthly pomp and splendour, the necessity of habitual preparedness, the value of sincere and spiritual worship and service of God, the appropriateness of the admonition, "Be ye also ready," and of the prayer, "So teach us to number our days, that we may apply our hearts unto wisdom."— G. W.

Ver. 9.—*Dread of God*. The death of Uzzah made David "afraid of the Lord," and deterred him from fulfilling his purpose to bear the ark into the place which he had prepared for it in his newly founded metropolis. He seems for the time to have dreaded lest it should bring evil with it instead of good—a curse instead of a blessing. So the vast assembly was dispersed, and the day which was to have been so glorious and auspicious ended in disappointment and gloom. David's feeling is an illustration of religious terror, or the dread of God.

I. ITS NATURE. 1. *It is to be distinguished from that "fear of the Lord" which is so often inculcated in the Word of God*, and which is especially characteristic of the piety of the Old Testament. This is *reverence* of God, of his nature, authority, and laws. It includes, indeed, a dread of offending him, because of the certainty and terribleness of punishment; but it includes also veneration, esteem, and love. The feeling which is described in the text is simply alarm, terror. 2. *It may be awakened by various causes.* (1) Terrible acts of God: sudden deaths, as that of Uzzah, those of Ananias and Sapphira (Acts v. 5, 10, 11); violent tempests; earthquakes; deadly pestilence. (2) Terrible aspects of his nature. Holiness and hatred of sin; justice, displeasure against sinners; together with his perfect knowledge and unbounded power. (3) His threatenings. (4) The consciousness of sin. This is the secret of the dread which springs from the thought of God. A solemn awe is compatible with innocence, but the holy would not be "afraid of God," or if for a moment, at some startling and threatening event, only for a moment.

II. ITS VALUE. In itself and standing alone, it is of no religious worth at all. It is compatible with enmity to God, which is the opposite of true religion. When it springs into the heart of a good man it may be associated with very wrong feeling. David was "displeased" with God, while "afraid" of him (ver. 8). It tends to drive men from God rather than draw them to him (comp. Luke v. 8; viii. 37). It may drive them from him while seeming to draw them to him; for it is apt to generate a religion without love, without even reverence—an obedience which is slavish and destitute of true virtue. It is favourable to superstition, indeed, and may stimulate to great liberality; but, while acting alone, it cannot produce genuine godliness and true holiness. It is the feeling on which priestcraft in all lands flourishes. Yet it is good as a first step in those that need it, and a preparation for what is better; and some measure of it, blended with other emotions, is always of value to many, if not all. In Ps. cxix., where every feeling of a pious soul finds expression, this is included (ver. 120). And our Lord enjoins it as a safeguard against the fear of man (Luke xii. 4, 5). This fear is of great value: 1. To arouse the conscience and prepare for better things. Many are so hardened that they are incapable of being, in the first instance, drawn by love; their fears must be excited. 2. To make the gospel welcome; which, revealing the love of God and the redemption which is by Jesus Christ, is fitted and intended to allay the dread of God and awaken confidence and affection. 3. To stimulate in obedience to God and deter from sin. It is true that love is the noblest stimulus, and that perfect love casts out fear (1 John iv. 18); but love is not perfect in this world, and fear is needed when temptation is strong and the better feelings are for the time dormant.—G. W.

Ver. 11.—*God's blessing abiding with the ark.* Divine chastisements and Divine benedictions have in this world the same end in view—the promotion of true religion. The judgment on Uzzah and the blessing on the house of Obed-Edom were alike intended to reawaken a living faith and piety in the nation, by showing that Jehovah, the living God, was amongst them, and was still prepared to honour his own institutions and bless those who honoured them, whilst those who dishonoured them would incur his displeasure. Obed-Edom honoured God by receiving the ark into his house and caring for it; and, in return, God's blessing rested on him and all his. They act a similar part who receive into their homes and honour there God's book, God's servants, God's poor; those also who establish in their houses the practice of family worship, and keep alive in their families a warm interest in all that concerns the Church and kingdom of God. They and theirs enjoy the abiding presence and blessing of him who has said, " Them that honour me I will honour, and they that despise me shall be lightly esteemed " (1 Sam. ii. 30). Notice—

I. THE INTRODUCTION OF THE ARK INTO THE HOUSE OF OBED-EDOM. It was owing to the panic occasioned by the death of Uzzah. May illustrate the apparently accidental circumstances which have sometimes introduced religion and the practice of family worship into families.

II. THE WELCOME IT RECEIVED. Obed-Edom, in this instance, excelled David. The alarm excited by Uzzah's death did not deter him from receiving the ark into his house. Faith subdued fear. He may well have felt that the act would be well-pleasing to God; that it would bring him and his nearer to God; that the ark would sanctify his home and turn it as into a temple; and that it could and would occasion no harm to those who honoured it for God's sake. So should the things, persons, and practices that bring God nearer to a household be welcomed; and so will they be welcomed by such as have begun to reverence and love him.

III. THE BLESSING WHICH ACCOMPANIED IT. " The Lord blessed Obed-Edom, and all his household." What form God's blessing took in this case, so that in the course of three months it could become manifest to others, we are not told; perhaps some marked increase of worldly prosperity. And such an indication of God's blessing is not uncommon in households where piety rules. But there are other blessings of God which to his children are more precious, and which are to be confidently expected by families which honour him. 1. *A pervading sense of God's presence and love.* This would surely result from having the ark in the house; and not less is it the result of having a Bible which is really valued and consulted, and a family altar. 2. *The enjoyment of the Divine Spirit.* The actual living operation of the present God on the conscience, heart, and life. He " gives his Holy Spirit to them that ask him." As the result of these: 3. *A new sacredness given to family life and duty.* The presence of the ark in the house would sanctify everything there, making the relationships sacred, and turning common duties into holy rites. Hence: 4. *Higher and more steadfast family affections.* Love to each other sanctified and elevated by common love to the heavenly Father and Divine Brother and Friend; unselfishness; unity; mutual helpfulness. 5. *More cheerful and free, and therefore stricter, obedience to the Divine laws.* The will of God as to the duties of parents, children, and servants, and of all towards those without, shining in a diviner light, better understood, and better practised. Hence the virtues which promote material and social welfare. 6. *Family happiness.* Springing naturally, as we say, but none the less as the result of the Divine appointment and active blessing, from such living. Happiness in and from the daily round of duty and affection. Happiness in the enjoyment together of God's gifts. Peace in trouble. Hope when one departs to the better home; a sense of union still (" We are seven "), and assurance of reunion in due time. 7. *Moral and spiritual fruitfulness.* Such a family dwells in an atmosphere highly favourable for the production and growth of piety and all moral excellence in those connected with it. It is a nursery for the Church. From such the best Christians and Christian workers go forth. Similar family life is multiplied and perpetuated in the subsequent homes of sons and daughters.

IV. THE EFFECT OF THE BLESSING ON DAVID. He was reassured, and took measures, at once more according to the Law and more successful, for fulfilling his purpose to bring the ark to Zion. Similarly, the aspect presented by families which serve God and manifestly enjoy his blessing is adapted to incite, and has often incited, others to go and do likewise. Finally, families which regard not God may have many desirable things, but cannot really enjoy the Divine blessing. "The curse of the Lord is in the house of the wicked," while " he blesseth the habitation of the just " (Prov. iii. 33).—G. W.

Vers. 12—19.—*The ark brought to Zion.* A grand day for Israel, and indeed for the world; the beginning of the religious significance of "Zion " and " Jerusalem," and the mighty spiritual influence which has gone forth far and wide from that centre. With respect to the bringing of the ark "into the city of David," we remark—

I. IT WAS THE ACCOMPLISHMENT OF A DELAYED PURPOSE. Although David was shocked and alarmed by the event which compelled him to desist from his first endeavour, he did not give up his purpose, but evidently set himself to prepare for a more imposing and appropriate introduction of the sacred symbol into his metropolis than he at first contemplated. The narrative in 1 Chron. xv. and xvi. shows this ; for such elaborate arrangements could not have been made in a short time. Delay tests the resolutions and purposes of men, reveals their quality, intensifies those which spring from true and reasonable zeal, and issues in their fuller execution.

II. IT WAS MARKED BY STRICT OBEDIENCE TO THE LAW OF GOD. The death of Uzzah had led to careful study of the Divine directions, which were now rigidly obeyed (1 Chron. xv. 12—15, with which corresponds ver. 13 of our text, " they that *bare* the ark of the Lord"). It is well when painful experience of the penalties of disregard to God's laws leads to inquiry and improvement. Unhappily, multitudes who suffer the penalties fail to profit by them.

III. IT WAS ACCOMPANIED WITH MUCH WORSHIP. Sacrifices were offered when a successful start had been made. Others, in greater number, when the ark had been placed in the tent prepared for it. The praises of God were sung as the procession moved on ; and at the close of the ceremonies David " blessed the people in the name of the Lord of hosts." The suitableness of all this to the occasion is obvious.

IV. IT WAS A SEASON OF GREAT GLADNESS. Indicated by David's dance " before the Lord with all his might." Also by the shouting and the noise of musical instruments ; and the royal gifts to the people at large, that all might feast.

V. IT WAS A NATIONAL TRANSACTION. All the tribes, by their representatives in great numbers, and all classes of the people—the king, the priests and Levites, the nobles, the officers of the army and their forces, the rich and the poor—united in the celebration. It was an act of national homage to the supreme Sovereign of the people— a kind of enthronement of him in his metropolis. It was intended and well adapted to make the people realize afresh that they were one nation, and to bind them in a closer unity hereafter, religious as well as civil.

VI. IT WAS THE INAUGURATION OF A NEW AND BETTER ERA IN RELIGION. The ark was not thus brought to Jerusalem to remain solitary and neglected, as it had so long been, but that before it Divine worship might be conducted daily in a manner becoming the new circumstances of the people. For this David had made careful preparation, organizing part of the priests and Levites for the purpose, while others were appointed to minister at Gibeon, where the tabernacle proper and the altars were (1 Chron. xvi. 4—42). For the national worship was not even now conducted in strict accordance with the Mosaic Law, since that required the ark and the altars, and the priestly and Levitical ministrations, to be all in one place. On account of circumstances which are not explained, though they may be surmised, the king could not do all that he would, but he did what he could ; and this prepared the way for the more exact obedience to the Law which was rendered when the temple was built.

VII. IT MADE MANIFEST THE CHARACTER OF THE KING. His convictions as to the claims of God over him and his people ; his zeal for the worship of God, and desire to infuse a similar spirit into the nation ; his humility in descending from his elevation and fraternizing with, whilst he led, the people.

By the whole narrative we are reminded of : 1. The necessity and worth to a nation of true religion. To elevate its life, unite its various parts and classes, promote mutual justice and a spirit of brotherhood, regulate its conduct towards other peoples, and withal secure the blessing of God. 2. The worth of godly rulers. From their position, rulers necessarily exercise a wide influence, and it is a happy circumstance when their example is in favour of religion and virtue. 3. The difference between national

religious pageants and ceremonies, and true national religion.   Many will unite in the
former who have no part in the latter.   The former are often more brilliant and
imposing as the latter decays.   National Christianity can exist only as the individuals
who compose the nation are sincere Christians.   4. The lessons which the proceedings
here recorded suggest to those engaged in opening a new Christian sanctuary.   Concern
to secure the abiding presence and blessing of God.   Much praise and prayer: praise
for all the mercies which have led up to the day, and all the revelations and promises
that give hope to its proceedings ; prayer for the help of God in all, his acceptance of
the work done in his Name, his use of it for the promotion of his kingdom, the good of
his Church, and the salvation of those without.   Much gladness and mutual congratulation on account of the work accomplished, and the good that may be hoped for from it
to individuals, families, the neighbourhood, etc.   A hearty union of all classes in the
services, introductory to permanent union in mutual love and combined effort.—G. W.

Ver. 16.—*Religious zeal despised.*   "She despised him in her heart."   A graphic
picture here.   A numerous and joyous procession marching into the city with the ark
of God, with sacred music and singing and dancing ; the king at the head of all, more
joyous and enthusiastic than all the crowd besides ; and Michal, behind her window,
cool and collected, without sympathy with the object or spirit of the proceeding, yea,
looking on with contempt, especially for her husband, who was so demonstrative in his
display of zeal and gladness.   She has many imitators.   There are many who regard
fervid zeal in religion with contempt.
I. WHY FERVENT RELIGIOUS ZEAL IS DESPISED.   1. *Alleged reasons* ; as (1) that it
is fanatical; or (2) unintellectual, a sign of weak mind; a style of religion fit only
for women and weak-minded men; or (3) hypocritical; or (4) not respectable.   The
better sort of people, it is alleged, keep their religion within due bounds ; certainly will
eschew forms of religious earnestness which associate closely the upper classes with
the common people.   2. *Secret causes.*   May be : (1) Ignorance.   Want of knowledge of
Christianity.   Acquaintance with its great facts, doctrines, and precepts, and the
exemplification of them in the lives of our Lord and his apostles, would make it clear
that they demand and justify the utmost warmth of love and zeal; so that for
Christians to be zealous in holding, practising, and propagating their religion is simply
to be consistent.   (2) Irreligion, with or without knowledge.   Unbelief or disbelief.
The absence of religious faith and feeling.   Possibly a settled hatred of religion and
goodness.   Men of this class cannot possibly understand or appreciate the operations of
religion in the heart.   The sincerely religious may disapprove of certain forms in which
others display their zeal, but they will not indulge contempt of them.   (3) Formalism
or superficiality in religion.   To which ardent devotion and self-consecration are
unintelligible.   (4) Pride of intellect, taste, or station.   "Hath any of the rulers
believed on him, or of the Pharisees ?   But this multitude which knoweth not the Law
are accursed" (John vii. 48, 49, Revised Version).   (5) Sometimes would be found
secret uneasiness.   Zeal in others awakens conscience, which utters condemnation ; and
conscience is relieved (or attempted to be) by fixing attention on what is regarded as
objectionable in the religious zeal of others, and cherishing contempt for them.
(6) Religious bigotry, which has no tolerance for forms of religion, however sincere and
good those who adopt them may be, that differ from those of the bigot himself.   The
piety of many good men is sadly marred by this spirit, and its earnestness feeds
something very like hatred of fellow-Christians.   In this case also contempt springs
largely from ignorance, as well as from a lack of that principle of religion which is
supereminent, viz. love.
II. WHY SUCH ZEAL OUGHT NOT TO BE DESPISED.   1. *It is in harmony with right
reason.*   In view of the nature and works of God and our obligations to him, especially
the redeeming love of God in Christ, the evils from which we are redeemed, the blessings which are brought within our reach, the cost of our redemption.   It is not zeal, but
indifference and coldness, which are irrational.   Nothing but the willing devotement of
heart and life to Christ is suitable as a return for his love.   Devotion without warmth,
service which is ever measured and stinted, are absurd.   2. *It is required by Holy
Scripture.*   The great duties of Christianity, love to God and man, necessarily include
warmth and earnestness.   And the terms in which we are exhorted to seek our own

salvation and the good of others all imply zeal; the production of which is represented as one great end of the offering of himself by Christ (Titus ii. 14). 3. *It is countenanced by the highest and best society.* By cherubim and seraphim, angels and archangels, apostles, prophets, martyrs, saints in heaven and on earth, and him who is higher than them all, the Lord Jesus Christ, to whose burning zeal we owe everything. The grandest intellects in the universe may be appealed to by the zealous Christian. 4. *It is productive of the greatest good.* Christianity has conferred and is conferring the greatest blessings on mankind, and is ever extending the area of its beneficial influence. But it is its zealous, not its cold-hearted, adherents to whom men owe its extension and powerful operation. 5. *It secures the approbation of God, and final acceptance and reward.* He who zealously uses his talents is to be received into the joy of his Lord, while the slothful servant is rejected and punished. The highly respectable and self-complacent Church at Laodicea is severely reproved and threatened on account of its lukewarmness (Rev. iii. 15, 16). Only religion in earnest fits for heaven. There are no lukewarm Christians there.

Finally : 1. Let despisers of zealous Christians beware lest they be found despising Christ and God (Luke x. 16). 2. Let zealous Christians take heed of needlessly exposing their religion to contempt. As by associating it with things unworthy of it, such as narrowness of mind, cant, eccentricity, worldly policy, excessive ceremonialism, great ardour about small matters, little ardour about great matters, uncharitableness. 3. Some zeal in religion deserves to be despised. That, in particular, which is dissociated from truth, uprightness, holiness, or love. True religious zeal includes zeal for these; and no ardour of professed religion can be a substitute for them.—G. W.

Ver. 20.—*Domestic religion.* "Then David returned to bless his household." An interesting contrast with what precedes. Would have been a pleasing close of the narrative but for what follows. Presents David in an attractive light. His piety did not shine merely in public before a crowd; it illuminated and blessed his home. He did not regard his high station and the weight of the cares of state as raising him above, or releasing him from, his duties as head of a household. Nor did he, after that busy and exciting day, think himself excused from family duty. He had blessed the people in the name of the Lord; he now returns to bless his household, *i.e.* to invoke God's blessing on them.

I. How A MAN MAY BLESS HIS HOUSEHOLD. 1. *By maintaining and conducting family worship.* Praising God with his family. Praying with and for them. Giving the worship a family character by the mention of family blessings, needs, sorrows, joys; the especial mention of special circumstances and events which affect the family, as they arise. Doing this regularly and perseveringly. 2. *By the religious instruction of his family.* Reading the Word of God as part of the daily worship. Teaching the children the truths and duties of Christianity, formally and informally. The latter as important, to say the least, as the former. Let the New Testament be the recognized guide of the house, to which everything is brought for judgment. Let its teaching be instilled insensibly as occasions arise in family life. 3. *By family discipline.* "Ruling well his own house, having his children in subjection with all gravity" (1 Tim. iii. 4); encouraging right, forbidding and suppressing wrong conduct; regulating the companionships and occupations of his children. Family government on Christian principles and in a Christian spirit is itself a mode of instruction, and blesses a household. 4. *By leading and accompanying his family to the house of God.* 5 *By setting a good example.* The head of a household cannot perform his duties aright without personal piety. He cannot teach what he does not value and practise; his instructions and prayers will lack the reality which impresses; his character will deprive his words of their proper force. But a good life is a constant lesson. Children will learn from the spirit and conduct of a good father how to think of their Father in heaven, and how they may serve and please him. The unconscious influence of the parent's life will be a perpetually operating power for good.

II. WHY HE SHOULD DO SO. 1. *It is his manifest duty.* Seen as we contemplate : (1) The relation of the family to God, as its Founder, the Originator of each household, the Lord of family life, the Source of all its peculiar affections, the Bestower of all its blessings, the Guardian of its weaker members (Christ's "little ones"). (2) The relation to God of the head of a household. His servant, his representative, appointed for this very service. (3) The promptings of parental affection and godly principles, which are from God. (4) The express injunctions of Holy Writ. (5) The just claims of society, which has a right to expect that in the household good citizens should be trained and good members of the Church. The character and welfare of a people depend more on family life than on public law and force; and most fathers can best serve their country by training well their children. Let them render more public services if they are capable of them, but ever let them " return to bless their households." 2. *He will thus best promote the welfare and happiness of his household.* (See division III. of homily on ver. 11.) 3. *His own happiness in his family will be greatly increased.* If his desires for their good are granted, he will be a necessary partaker of their happiness, will rejoice that he has so largely contributed to it, and will receive a constant reward for his endeavours in their love and gratitude. If, through untoward circumstances, or counteracting influences against which he had no power to defend them, or through their own perversity, his efforts should fail, he will at least have the satisfaction of a good conscience.

In conclusion, what has been said of the duty of fathers applies equally to mothers, who have more influence than fathers over the younger children, and often over the elder also, and always have most to do with the order and comfort and moral atmosphere of the home.—G. W.

Vers. 20—22.—*A despiser rebuked.* The history of Michal is rather an unhappy one. In early life she became enamoured of David, to whom she was reluctantly given by her father. Afterwards, when Saul became the enemy of David, she was given to another, from whom, after many years, she was torn by her first husband, more, probably, from policy than affection. It is likely she had no warm affection for him now. She may have resented his succeeding to her father's throne. She had no sympathy with his religious zeal. Probably she originally admired the hero rather than loved the saint; and now that his fervour in religion has so strangely displayed itself, she can contain herself no longer. She felt herself—a king's daughter—disgraced by his vulgar conduct; and she resolves to tell him her mind about it; and so, as he returns to his house in joyous religious excitement, eager to bless his family, as he had just blessed the people, she meets him with bitter reproaches, to which he, surprised and mortified, returns a bitter answer, in which are, nevertheless, good reasons for his conduct.

I. HER REPROACH. It was in substance that his conduct had been undignified and indecent. The charge was plausible, but unjust. Her anger and want of sympathy with her husband's zeal led her to misrepresentation of proceedings which were innocent and praiseworthy. Similar lack of sympathy with ardent piety often leads to similar unjust judgment. Many are ready to condemn modes of expressing or promoting religion which are foreign to their own habits. But what would be unsuitable and unprofitable to one class of persons may be the reverse to another; and what would not be suitable as an ordinary practice may be allowable and commendable under special circumstances. In times of general excitement men will do what would be ridiculous at other times. Zacchæus climbed a tree to get a good view of Jesus, regardless of dignity and the possible ridicule of the crowd; and he was rewarded for it. David would not have displayed his zeal by leading the multitude in music and singing and dancing under ordinary circumstances. Reproach and condemnation are to be estimated partly according to the persons who utter them. Many who are ready to do so are incapable of passing just judgment, on account of a total or partial want of religion. "The natural man receiveth not the things of the Spirit of God: for they are foolishness unto him : neither can he know them, because they are spiritually discerned " (1 Cor. ii. 14). And some who are not destitute of religion are so contracted in their views and feelings that they are unable to estimate rightly the religion of others. John the Baptist practised abstinence, and was said to have a demon. Jesus lived as ordinary men, and was condemned as a glutton and winebibber. The apostles on the Day of Pentecost were said to be "full of new wine." Those who are fond of orderliness and dignity in religion are prone to condemn all kinds of excitement and the freedom of form and expression which it favours. But it is possible to sacrifice efficiency to order.   While the lovers of order and good taste are exclusively indulging their preferences, multitudes may be left uncared for and untouched.   When, therefore, by means which are thought objectionable, they are attracted and benefited, the objectors may properly be asked to find and employ better methods *which shall answer the same end*; and meanwhile to bear with, yea, thank God for, those who are doing a good work in a manner which they cannot wholly approve.   On the other hand, those who love and employ excitement and freedom may well be warned lest they frustrate their aim to save men by using means inconsistent with that reverence and thoughtfulness which are essential to true religion, and lest they unjustly condemn their fellow-Christians who pursue their ends by calmer methods.   There are room and need for variety of modes of worship and activity with one spirit and aim.   Let us not condemn those who, in the Name of Jesus, are really casting out evil spirits, and bringing men to a right mind, though they do not follow with us (Luke ix. 49, 50).

II. DAVID'S REPLY.   It was severe, and likely, as it was doubtless meant, to sting. Notice: 1. *His defence.* That what he had done he had done for Jehovah.   (1) Him who in himself was worthy of all possible honour and public praise and confession. (2) Him who had chosen and exalted him, in the place of Saul and his house, to be ruler over his people.   Piety and gratitude combined to impel him to rejoice before the Lord on an occasion so remarkable and auspicious.   All of us have similar reasons for honouring God to the utmost of our power.   In view of them, the most ardent zeal for the worship of God and the promotion of his kingdom is justified, and cold and measured service stands condemned.   2. *His determined resolve.* To do as he had done.   Yea, to surpass his recent displays of zeal for the Lord.   If this was accounted vile, he would be viler still; if this were to lower himself, he would sink lower still. Similar should be the effect upon us of the reproach which fervent piety may subject us to.   If, indeed, objection be made to some of the ways by which we show it, we should reconsider them, especially when the objection comes from Christian brethren; but undeserved reproach should stimulate us to greater devotedness and more resolute determination.   3. *His assurance of honour.* From "the maidservants" of whom Michal had spoken so disparagingly.   He virtually appealed from her judgment to theirs.   What just foundation is there for satisfaction in the approval of the humbler classes?   (1) They may be more capable of right judgment in matters of religion than many who are above them in worldly condition, and even in general education and intelligence.   They may have more spiritual susceptibility and fewer prejudices.   They may feel more their ignorance, and be more humble and teachable.   They at least know what does them good, which is the end of all religious ministrations.   Hence they are often right when their scorners are wrong.   Our Lord was accepted and listened to gladly by many of the common people, while few of the upper and the learned classes received him; and he rejoiced and thanked his Father that, while the truths he taught were hidden from "the wise and understanding," they were revealed unto "babes" (Luke x. 21).   And in the early Churches St. Paul tells us that there were "not many wise after the flesh, or mighty, or noble;" but that these were put to shame by the weak and despised (1 Cor. i. 26—28).   (2) The good of the humbler classes is to be sought.   To secure this end they must be interested, and their approval won; and he who can, without unworthy arts, succeed in winning them so as to lead them to Christ, may well rejoice and be thankful.   David's language may be in substance adopted by preachers who are despised because approved and followed by the common people; while the ministry or Church which fails to lay hold of them ought to mourn and reconsider its spirit and methods.

To conclude: 1. It is an unhappy thing when man and wife differ radically in matters of religion.   It deprives them of the unspeakable benefits of mutual sympathy and helpfulness.   It is the occasion of dispute and unhappiness, if not settled alienation. It hinders very seriously the religious and moral education of the children.   Let these things be thought of before the irrevocable steps are taken which bind two lives together.   2. There are worse faults in relation to religion than vulgarity, undue excitement, or eccentricity.   These may be in some degree injurious, but indifference or hostility is fatal.—G. W.

EXPOSITION.

CHAPTER VII.

Ver. 1.—**When the king sat in his house.**
The order is not chronological; for the words,
Jehovah had given him rest from all his
enemies round about (so the Revised Version, rightly), imply the successful termination, not of all wars necessarily, but certainly
of something more than that with the
Philistine invaders in the Rephaim valley.
A general summary of all David's wars is
given in ch. viii., and it was probably after
he had subdued the Philistines and Moab,
and his throne was now fully established,
that in some time of peace, possibly before
Hanun forced him into wars which won
for him an empire, David sent for Nathan,
and told him his full desire. Its position
here immediately after the account of the
bringing of the ark to Zion has a higher
unity than that of chronology. It shows
that David had always a larger purpose
than the mere placing of the ark in its tent;
and, as soon as a period of tranquillity
arrived, he confided his thoughts to the
prophet. Thus, with only one step taken
towards his whole plan, David exercised
a wise moderation in leaving the service at
Gibeon unmolested. As regards the word
"rest," we have to distinguish between the
first series of wars, which established David
firmly on his throne, and the second series,
which gave him widespread dominion.

Ver. 2.—**A house of cedar**; Hebrew,
cedars. As these trees were sent by Hiram,
and as the house was built, and David now
settled in it, some considerable time must
have elapsed since his accession. Moreover,
the league with Hiram would be the result
of David's successes recorded in ch. viii. 1;
for the bond of union between the two was
their mutual fear of the Philistines. As we
have seen before, the alliance with Tyre
had a very civilizing effect upon the Hebrews, who were far inferior to the Tyrians
in the mechanical arts; and David's house
of hewn cedar logs was marvellous in the
eyes of a people who still dwelt chiefly in
tents. David purposed to build even a more
sumptuous palace for Jehovah, and advised
with Nathan as his chief counsellor, and the
person to whom subsequently the education
of Solomon was confided. **Within curtains**;
Hebrew, *the curtain;* that is, the tent. The
tabernacle prepared by Moses for the ark
was formed of ten curtains (Exod. xxvi. 1),
but the significance lay, not in their number,
but in the dwelling of Jehovah still being
a mere temporary lodging, though his people
had received from him a settled land.

Ver. 3.—**Go, do all that is in thine heart.**
Nathan rashly approves. The king's purpose seems so pious that he does not doubt
its acceptance by God.

Ver. 4.—**The word of Jehovah came unto
Nathan.** Not every word of a prophet was
inspired, and only a very few of the prophets,
and those only upon great and solemn
occasions, spake under the direct influence
of the Spirit of God. In his usual relations
with the king, Nathan was simply a wise,
thoughtful, and God-fearing man. In giving
his approval he probably meant no more
than that a permanent dwelling for Jehovah
was what all pious men were hoping for.
But from the days of Samuel to those of
Ezra, there was never wanting one or even
more holy men who were, on fit occasions,
commissioned to bear a message from God
to man; and as these generally belonged to
the prophetic order, men too often now
confound prophecy with prediction. So
inveterate is this confusion that even in the
Revised Version Amos is made to say, "I
was no prophet, neither was I a prophet's
son," whereas the Hebrew distinctly is, "I
am no prophet, nor a prophet's son [that is,
one trained in the prophetic schools], but
I am a herdsman" (Amos vii. 16). But
though not a prophet by profession, yet
Amos was discharging a prophet's higher
duty in testifying against wickedness and
impiety, and was acting under a special
Divine call. Still, he did not belong to the
prophetic order, nor wear the garment of
black camel's hair, which was their professional dress. On the present occasion,
Nathan, in approving, had spoken as a man,
but now a Divine message comes to him.
How we know not, but in ver. 17 it is called
a "vision;" and it is also said that it came
"that night."

Ver. 5.—**Shalt thou,** etc.? The question
implies an answer in the negative; but there
is no disapproval of David's purpose as such;
but only the deferring of its full execution
unto the days of his son. There is more
than this. The idea which runs through
the Divine message is that the dwelling of
Jehovah in a tent was a fitting symbol of
Israel's unquiet possession of the land. It
was David's mission to give them tranquillity and security in the region which they
had conquered long ago, but wherein they
had never hitherto been able to maintain
their liberty unimpaired. Then, upon the
accomplishment of David's special duty, his
son, Shelomo, *i.e.* the peaceful, was to build
the solid temple, as the proof that Jehovah
had now taken permanent possession of
the land. We find also a further thought,
namely, that the building of the temple

signified " the making for David of a house."
In its full significance this means that the
tribe of Judah and the lineage of David
were now chosen by God as the ancestors of
the Messiah.

Ver. 6.—**I have walked in a tent and in
a tabernacle**; literally, *I have walked continually;* that is, I have ever been a wanderer,
first, in the wilderness, and subsequently
at Gilgal, Shiloh, Nob, and Gibeon. Instead of a " tabernacle," the Hebrew has
a " dwelling." This may refer to the houses
of Abinadab and Obed-Edom, but the words
more probably signify " a tent that was my
dwelling."

Ver. 7.—**In all** the places **wherein I have
walked**; Hebrew, *in all wherein I continued
walking;* that is, in all my walking, in all
the whole time wherein I have been a
wanderer. Instead of *tribes*, the Chronicler
(1 Chron. xvii. 6) reads "judges," the
words in the Hebrew being almost identical.
"Judges" is, of course, the more easy and
natural reading, but " tribes " gives a fuller
sense, and is supported by all the versions.
For in the troubled anarchy which lasted
until Saul's reign, first one tribe and then
another was called to the front, and had
a temporary ascendancy; but neither did
Jehovah give it any command to provide
a settled place for his worship, nor did any
one of the judges conceive the thought of
making his tribe permanently the chief,
by providing a fixed abode for the ark and
for God's worship within its borders. **To
feed my people Israel.** The shepherd, in
biblical language, is the ruler, and *to feed*
is to govern, yet in a kindly way, going in
front as the shepherd before his flock, to
bear the brunt of danger, to clear the road,
and to guide into the safe pastures. So
tribe after tribe had been called to bear the
brunt of war, and, after winning deliverance,
it became its duty to guide and lead the
people. In 1 Kings viii. 16, 18, 25, and
still more remarkably in 1 Chron. xxii. 8,
9, we find large additions made to the
account here given. It follows that we
have in this place only a brief summary of
the message brought by Nathan, but one
containing all the chief points.

Ver. 8.—**I took thee from the sheepcote.**
There is in Nathan's message a marked
advance upon the words of all previous
prophecies. Hitherto God's promises had
been general, and no tribe, and much less
any special person, had been chosen as the
progenitor of the Messiah. The nearest
approach to the selection of a tribe had been
the prediction of Judah's supremacy until
Shiloh came (Gen. xlix. 10); but it was not
even there expressly declared that Shiloh
should be of Judah's race. But now David
is clearly chosen. Jehovah takes him from

the sheepcote ; Hebrew, " the meadow " (see
Ps. lxxviii. 70). It was in the meadows,
the Naioth, round Ramah, that Samuel had
gathered the young men of Israel to study
their ancient records, and raise their country
to a sense of its high calling. In those
meadows David had been formed for his
high vocation ; but he had returned from
them to Bethlehem, to feed his father's
sheep. And now, " from following the
ewes that gave suck," Jehovah takes him
to be " his servant," a word of high dignity,
applied to but few persons in the Old
Testament. It signifies the prime minister,
or vicegerent of Jehovah, as the theocratic
king, and is the special title of Moses
among God's people, and, among the heathen,
of Nebuchadnezzar, as one summoned to do
a great work for God. But it is in the last
twenty-seven chapters of Isaiah that the
title reaches its full grandeur. For there,
first of all, Israel is called Jehovah's servant, because it was Israel's office to be the
witness for the oneness of God amidst the
debasing polytheism of all the nations
round. And then, finally, the servant is
Messiah, as being the personal Representative of God upon earth. The title is now
given to David as the type of Christ's kingly
office, and also as the sweet singer, who
added a new service to the worship of God,
and made it more spiritual, and more like
the service of angels round God's throne.

Ver. 9.—**I have made thee a great name**.
The widespread conquests of David, and
his great empire, were not for the sake of
mere earthly dominion. It was, first of all,
a type of Messiah's reign, to whom God has
promised the heathen for his inheritance,
and that his gospel shall be carried to the
ends of the earth. But, secondly, if Messiah
was to be " David's Son," it was necessary
that that king should hold a special place
in the hearts of all Israelites. In the fables
and tales of the Arabs, it is Solomon who
holds the foremost place. Just as our forefathers showed the native qualities of the
race by making Arthur's court the abode
of prowess and chivalrous bravery ; so the
Arabs made Solomon's court the representative of that dazzling splendour and magnificence which they so admired; and invested
him with superhuman knowledge and
magical power, such as made janns and
ifreets the humble slaves of his will. In
the Old Testament no king is " Jehovah's
servant " but David; no king is ever connected with Messiah but David. The
religious fervour of the people may gather
round a Hezekiah or a Josiah, and prophets
may encourage them in their work; but
no prophet sees in either of them the
ancestor of Christ. It is, however, in the
Psalms that we learn the full meaning of

Nathan's words. Here a veil is partly drawn over them. But it would be a wilful closing of the eyes to read this message and not bear in mind the clear light with which every word is illumined by the inspired outpouring of David's own heart. He thoroughly understood the fulness and blessedness of God's revelation, and has taught us that it all looked onward to Christ.

Vers. 10, 11.—**Moreover I will appoint . . . will plant.** For "moreover," the Hebrew has "and." The tenses also continue the same: "And I have appointed . . . and have planted." It is all part of the same act. As regards the second verb, the past tense alone makes sense. Jehovah was not about to plant Israel in a place of their own, but had just done so completely. For David's kingdom had given them security, and with it the power of doing for God that duty which was Israel's special office in the world. Had the anarchy of the times of the judges continued, and the energies of the nation been spent in a hard struggle for existence, that rapid advance in literature which followed upon the institution of Samuel's schools, and which filled David's court with poets and chroniclers, never could have existed, and prophecy would have been impossible. The age of Hezekiah was apparently the culminating period of Hebrew civilization, after which came the depressing influences of the Assyrian invasions, and then long exile, followed by a second weary struggle for existence. If writing was at first a mystery and an art known only to priests, it became throughout the monarchy the possession especially of the prophets, who were Israel's learned men. At the head of their roll stands the matchless Isaiah, and to render it possible for his genius to display itself, not only Samuel's schools, but the security of David's era of conquest, and the long peace and magnificence of Solomon's reign, were all necessary. When "God had given David rest from his enemies round about," he had thereby finally appointed a place for Israel and had planted them there. There is, perhaps, some difficulty in the verb-forms at the end of ver. 11, but none in the meaning. The reign of David marks an era in the national life. Under him Israel obtained secure possession of the place appointed for it; and now, having no longer to waste its energies in perpetual fighting, the national life grows upwards, and attains to culture, to thought, and civilization. Canaan is now their own, and instead of being mere warriors, they develop national institutions and a national character. What could men do that belongs to a higher and nobler life who were in daily fear of being swept away

by Canaanites and Midianites, by Philistines and Ammonites? This miserable period is described as "beforetime," and as "since the day that I commanded judges to be over my people Israel." And here a colon should be placed; and the Hebrew will then proceed, "But now I have caused thee to rest from thine enemies:" the anarchy and its attendant weakness is over; "and Jehovah telleth thee that Jehovah will make thee a house." Rest has been given; the establishment of David's family as the Messianic lineage is to follow (see on this promise, 1 Sam. ii. 35).

Ver. 12.—**Thy seed . . . which shall proceed.** As the son is to be established in the kingdom and to build the house, he must be Solomon, who plainly, therefore, was not as yet born (see note on ver. 1).

Ver. 13.—**I will establish the throne of his kingdom for ever.** The temple which Solomon was to build was the symbol of the new development of Israel, and naturally these words suggest a meaning not unworthy of so great an advance in the accomplishment of the nation's mission. Had we, indeed, only this passage, we might be content to take it in a popular sense, as signifying that, whereas Saul's throne (and subsequently that of the many usurpers in Samaria) had but a brief existence, Solomon's descendants should hold for many centuries undisputed possession of the kingdom of Jerusalem. But in Ps. lxxxix. 29 we read, "His (David's) seed will I make to endure for ever, and his throne as the days of heaven." And again in vers. 36, 37 a continuance is assured to it as lasting as that of the sun and moon. We can scarcely, therefore, be wrong in the conviction that these promises pointed onwards to the establishment of Christ's kingdom, and that the great importance attached to the building of the temple finds its explanation in its relation to him. This full establishment after so long a delay of the Mosaic typical ritual, the addition to it of psalmody, giving it a spiritual side, and making the worship that of the heart, the bestowal of empire, and the rapid development of the people under David and Solomon, were all steps in that wonderful series of special providences which made the Jews fit to be the progenitors of the Messiah, which surrounded him during his ministry with companions capable of understanding and recording his teaching, and provided for him, after his death, missionaries, not merely with zeal enough, but with intellectual gifts sufficient to enable them to persuade both Greece and Rome to listen to tidings so wonderful and mysterious as that God for our salvation had become man. Keil also well points out that the temple was a symbol of Christ's incarnation; for it meant the dwelling of God on earth. "I have surely," says Solomon, "built thee a house of habitation, a place for thee to dwell in for ever" (1 Kings viii. 13). The same thought was in St. John's mind when he said, "The Word became flesh, and dwelt as in a tabernacle among us" (John i. 14). For the verb used by him, literally "tabernacled," is a comparison between Christ's life on earth, and the dwelling of God in "the tent of meeting." But there is more than this. Christ himself calls his body "the temple" (John ii. 19, 21). At the Resurrection he raised up again the temple of his body which the Jews had destroyed, and at the Ascension it was removed from the earth, to be reserved in heaven until his second advent. His reign now is spiritual, and his temple is not a building made with hands, but is the heart of the renewed believer (1 Cor. vi. 19). And this indwelling of Christ in the heart will continue unto the end of the present dispensation. For Christ's indwelling is that also of the Holy Spirit (1 Cor. iii. 16); and the gift of the Spirit continues unto the end of the world. "The Father shall give you another Comforter, that he may abide with you for ever" (John xiv. 16).

Ver. 14.—**I will be his Father, and he shall be my son.** Between father and son there is not only love, but oneness. Whatsoever the father hath, that belongs also to the son by natural right. But this sonship is magnified in the Psalms beyond the measure of Solomon or any natural limits. The Son there is "the Firstborn," which Solomon was not, "higher than the kings of the earth" (Ps. lxxxix. 27); and he must have "the nations for his inheritance, and the uttermost parts of the earth for his possession" (Ps. ii. 8). Psalms like the second and seventy-second belong, not to Solomon personally, but to him as the type of the Prince of Peace; and they help to show us what is the true meaning and fulfilment of the words here. **The rod of men**; that is, such punishment as men fitly receive for their faults. David's natural posterity was to be exempt neither from human depravity, nor from punishment, nor from the changes and chances of mortal life. With them, as with men generally, there would be a tangled skein, of virtue and sin, of folly and wisdom, of terrible fall and penitent recovery. But there was to be no blotting out of David's lineage. Great earthly houses, in the long course of events, one after another become extinct, and even the tabernacle of David was to fall (Amos ix. 11), but not for ever. God would "raise up its ruins" in Christ, and "build it as in the days of old." So in Isa. ix. 1 there is the same thought of the complete down-hewing of

David's earthly lineage, yet only to rise again to nobler life and vigour, in the Branch, or Sucker, that was to spring from the fallen trunk.

Vers. 15, 16.—**Before thee.** This does not refer to time, but means "in thy presence," or "before thy face," that is, "as thou hast thyself been witness." There is a strong contrast between the fate of Saul's house and this eternal endurance promised to that of David. The lineage of Saul might have made a new start in Jonathan, and even when he died at Gilboa, he left a son behind him. Still, no one ever looked upon Mephibosheth as having any title to the throne; and though Shimei (ch. xvi. 5) may have conceived the hope that, if David were overthrown, the kingdom might return to Saul's family, yet, as a matter of fact, among the many vicissitudes of the ten tribes, the attempt never was made to search for a descendant of Saul to be Israel's king. Saul's was a royalty for one generation; David's throne was to be established for ever. Not because David was sinless. His character is sullied by crimes of the darkest hue. But he never sank into a mere tyrant, such as Saul was towards David and towards the priests at Nob. Nor did David ever become an irreligious man (1 Sam. xxii. 18, 19; xxviii. 15), though there is in him a strange and painful mixture of great good and great evil. The salt that preserves his character is his genuine sincerity and earnestness both towards God and man; and these qualities make him not unworthy of the high place he holds among God's people. Still, the promise was not because of David's deserts, but because from him was to come the Christ, who is blessed for evermore.

Ver. 17.—**Vision.** This word does not imply that Nathan saw anything with the natural eye, but signifies that sort of prophecy which was vouchsafed to a "seer." Thus the prophecies of Isaiah, of Nahum, and of Obadiah are called "visions." Probably the word is taken from the fixed gaze, with which the seer looked into the far-off world with unmoved eyes, yet seeing not with them, but with the spiritual sight within. It would thus be an intellectual process accompanied by a rigidity of the natural organs, caused partly by intensity of feeling, but chiefly by mental preoccupation, which left no faculty at liberty to discharge its ordinary function.

Ver. 18.—**David . . . sat before the Lord.** The word "sat" is usually explained by commentators as meaning "tarried." The rabbins give the word its ordinary meaning, and say that it was the privilege of kings to pray in a sitting posture. But we cannot possibly believe that kings at this early stage had established a special etiquette for observance in prayer, and the difficulty is merely imaginary. Because the Jews prayed standing, and we moderns pray kneeling, we both assume that to pray sitting was an irreverent act. It was not so, nor are we to think of David as sitting at ease in a chair. He sat upon the ground, as was the Oriental custom, with his feet doubled under him, and his head bent forward; and in this posture meditated upon Jehovah's message, and then poured out his thoughts. As it is expressly said that "he sat before Jehovah," the place must have been the outer court of the tabernacle. **Who am I, O Lord Jehovah?** In the Authorized Version *Jehovah* is rendered "God," because it has the vowels of the word *Elohim;* usually it is rendered "Lord," because the Massorites attached to it the vowels of *Adonai,* "lord," equivalent to *Dominus.* As *Adonai* here precedes *Jehovah,* the Massorites were driven from their usual practice, and were so superstitious as to suppose it more reverent to pronounce the name *Elohim* than that of *Jehovah,* to which the Jews attached magical powers. David's words are not so much a prayer as a meditation, full of thanksgiving, and even of wonder at the greatness of God's mercies to him. In it he first acknowledges his own unworthiness and the meanness of his father's house compared with the high dignity which God is bestowing upon him. For not only has he raised him to the kingly office, but promised him the continuance of his house "for a great while to come." Whether David understood as yet that he was now placed in the same position as Abraham of old, in that "in his seed all the families of the earth should be blessed," is uncertain, and depends upon the interpretation put upon the following words. This only we may affirm, that what he says in this place of his house remaining until a distant future falls far short of the meaning of the passages quoted above from the Psalms.

Ver. 19.—**And is this the manner of man, O Lord God?** Hebrew, *and this is the law of man, O Lord Jehovah.* In the parallel passage (1 Chron. xvii. 17) the Hebrew has, "And thou hast regarded me according to the law of a man of high degree." The rendering of the Authorized Version here, which, by making the clause interrogative, implies a negative, gives absolutely no sense; but some commentators render, "And this is the manner of men, O Lord Jehovah," understanding thereby that God was acting towards David in a human manner, that is, as an earthly friend and benefactor would do. But though the Revised Version favours this rendering, the Hebrew word *torah* never has this meaning, and, unless, the attempt be made to amend the text, for which the versions

give no help, we must take *torah* in its usual sense, and understand that this continuance of David's house into the distant future has now become a human law, that is, a divinely constituted ordinance, which must now take its place among the laws which govern human affairs. The words are undoubtedly difficult, and we feel that David was speaking in an ejaculatory manner, in sentences but half expressed, breaking forth from him bit by bit, under the pressure of deep excitement within. We notice too that, while there is no direct reference to the Messiah in David's words, yet that the Psalms indicate that he did connect the duration of his house with the Messiah's advent; and this ejaculation may have sprung forth, if not from a fully formed conviction, yet from the feeling that the permanence of his house was for the purpose of a higher kingdom than that of Jerusalem; and so the promise was a "law of man," and the promulgation of a decree which affected the whole human race. This may be the meaning of the Vulgate, which renders "a law of Adam," that is, one embracing within its scope all Adam's race.

Ver. 20.—**Thou, Lord God, knowest thy servant.** The Hebrew throughout has *Lord Jehovah,* except in vers. 22, 25, where it has "Jehovah God," the title of Deity used in Gen. ii. The repeated use of this covenant and personal name of God is very emphatic; and the appeal to Jehovah's knowledge of his heart reminds us of similar outpourings of David's consciousness of his sincere devotion to his Maker, as for instance in Ps. xvii. 3.

Ver. 21.—**For thy word's sake.** In 1 Chron. xvii. 19 we read, "For thy servant's sake." The phrase seemed, perhaps, to the Chronicler difficult, but it does not mean "because of thy previous promise," for no such promise had been given, but "because thou hast now said it." Nor does it imply pre-existing merit in David, but that God had now chosen to declare his will, and what was **according to his own heart.** It thus makes God's own good will and pleasure the cause of the great honours bestowed upon David. Instead of **these great things,** the Hebrew has *this great thing;* that is, the lasting continuance of David's family.

Ver. 22. — **Wherefore thou art great.** God's goodness is to David a proof of his greatness, and he sees it displayed, not only in his dealings with himself, but also in the past history of the Jewish nation. There is in this a depth of evangelic piety. An unconverted heart would see the greatness of God in the majesty of creation, or in severe dealings with the impenitent. David saw it in acts of mercy and kindness.

We look upon Elijah as the very type of sternness, yet he too recognized the presence of God in " the still small voice " of gentleness and love (1 Kings xix. 13).

Ver. 23.—**And what one nation,** etc. ? The translation should be, *And who is like thy people, like Israel, the one nation upon earth which God went to redeem for himself to be his people, and to make for him a name, etc. ?* Israel both was and remains to this day a nation unique in its history, both in those early dealings of God with it, and also in its later history and its marvellous preservation unto this day. It is remarkable that in this place the word for " God," *Elohim,* is followed by a verb plural, the almost invariable rule in Hebrew being that, though *Elohim* is itself plural, it takes a verb singular whenever it refers to the true God. In the corresponding passage (1 Chron. xvii. 21) the verb is in the singular. No adequate reason has been given for this deviation, but probably the usage in these early times was not so strict as it became subsequently. It is the influence of writing, and of the eye becoming conversant with writing, that makes men correct in their use of language and in the spelling of words. In the Syriac Church, God the Word and God the Holy Ghost were at first spoken of in the feminine gender, because " Word " and " Spirit " are both feminine nouns ; but grammar soon gave way to soundness of thought and feeling. So probably in colloquial language *Elohim* was often used with a verb plural, but correct thinking forbade and overruled grammar. We may regard this, then, as one of the few passages in which the colloquial usage has escaped correction, and attach no further importance to it. **For you.** " You " is plural, and refers to the people. The Vulgate has " for them," which is in accordance with the greater exactness of modern grammar. But sudden changes of person are very common in Hebrew, which follows the rules of thought rather than of written composition ; and so David speaks of Israel as *you,* because they seemed to him to be present. We must note, however, that in the words that follow, **for thy land,** and **thy people,** the pronoun is singular, and refers to God. **From the nations and their gods.** Both the Authorized Version and the Revised Version, by inserting " from," which is not in the Hebrew, take "nations" as in apposition with " Egypt ; " but a moment's consideration shows that this is untenable, as " nations " is plural. But the whole verse is so full of grammatical difficulties as to make it extremely probable that the text is corrupt, and that we ought to supply the verb " to drive out," which is actually read in 1 Chron. xvii. 21, or even to substitute it in the place

of " for thy land," which is omitted in the parallel passage. The nations which God drove out had nothing to do with Egypt, but were the seven dominant tribes of Canaan ; and the bestowal upon Israel of their territories was as essential a part of Jehovah's dealings with his people as the Exodus itself. Thus the reading will be, *To drive out before thy people, whom thou purchasedst for thee from Egypt, nations and their gods.*

Ver. 24.—**For thou hast confirmed.** The word means " thou hast firmly and securely established Israel to be thy people." This plainly refers to the settlement in Canaan, now at last completed by David's victories, and not to the deliverance from Egypt. In the words that follow David recognizes the spiritual importance, not only of the permanent continuance of his house, but also of the empire given unto him. For Israel is now to be **a people for ever: and thou, Jehovah, art become their God.** It is very necessary to retain here the personal name, Jehovah, as it is in the Hebrew, and not dilute it down to the *Lord* of the Septuagint. For now, to David's mind, the covenant seemed complete, and ratified for ever. Israel is to have an everlasting existence—a promise belonging to it in its full sense only spiritually. For as long as the world lasts, it is against the spiritual Israel that the gates of hell shall never prevail. And next, first as the theocratic people, and then as the Church, it is to hold a unique relation to Jehovah, who is to be its God. For Israel, that is, the Jewish and the Christian Church, worships, not the God of nature, *Elohim,* but *Jehovah,* the God of grace ; and they learn his attributes, not from philosophy, nor by metaphysical inquiry, but from his own revealed will, in which he teaches us what he is, what we are, and how we are to become one with him.

Vers. 25, 26.—**And now, O Lord God ;** Hebrew, *Jehovah God.* Similarly, in ver. 26 the Hebrew is " Let thy Name be magnified for ever, saying, Jehovah Sabaoth is God over Israel." The special relation of Jehovah to Israel is throughout kept constantly in view ; for Jehovah is the Name of Deity in covenant with his people, and it is in the confirmation and permanence of the covenant that David sees the true value of the lasting continuance of his own house.

Ver. 27.—**Thou hast revealed to thy servant ;** Hebrew, *thou hast uncovered the ear of thy servant.* (see note on 1 Sam. ix. 15). **Hath thy servant found in his heart ;** Hebrew, *hath found his heart.* The word " heart " has a wide meaning in Hebrew, embracing both our intellectual and our moral powers. Here it simply means " courage," as in,

1 Sam. xvii. 32. The Revised Version puts this in the margin : "Therefore hath thy servant been bold to pray this prayer."

Ver. 28.—**And now, O Lord God, thou art that God.** The pronoun rendered "that" is really a personal pronoun used as the copula, which the Authorized Version inserts in italics. As this grammatical usage, which is common to all the Semitic languages, was not understood at the time when our version was made, we find all the parts of the verb "to be" constantly printed in italics, as though absent, while really they are expressed in the Oriental way. This has the advantage, however, of reminding the reader that wherever the verb "to be" is printed in Roman characters it has a much stronger meaning than the mere union of subject and predicate. Thus in Gen. i. 2 the first "was," in Roman type, means "existed," or possibly "became;" the second "was," in italics, is simply the copula. Here the correct translation is, *And now, O Lord Jehovah, thou art the God;* i.e. the one real, true God.

Ver. 29.—**Let it please thee to bless; or,** *begin and bless.* Literally, the verb signifies to make up the mind and set about the doing of the thing purposed. Thus David prays that the blessing may now at once begin to take effect. It is often rendered "please" in our version, because the verb is one used only of a determination resolved upon of the free-will of the purposer. Its force is well seen in Job vi. 9, where what Job prays for is that God would deliberate no longer, but decide the matter and set about destroying him. The Authorized Version was led, by the use of this verse "please," to adopt the optative form. Really, it is the language of firm faith, and should be rendered, *And now* [there is no "therefore"] *begin of thy own good will, and bless the house of thy servant.*

HOMILETICS.

Vers. 1—11.—The facts are : 1. David, being settled in his kingdom and furnished with a permanent place of abode, is dissatisfied that the ark of the Lord should remain in a frail tent. 2. He sends for Nathan, and intimates his desire to build a fitting house for the Lord, and receives encouragement from the prophet. 3. During a vision of the night Nathan is directed to inform David that his desire cannot be realized; that all along it had been God's will to move from place to place in a tent (ver. 6); that it was never his purpose to have any other abode while Israel was unsettled (ver. 7). 4. He is further to inform David that the dwelling in a tent, and his own call from the sheep-cote (ver. 8) to be a leader of Israel, were both parts of one design, and that the success vouchsafed to him (ver. 9) was evidence of this. 5. Also, David is to know that, in pursuance of the same purpose, God gave his people a land of their own, and planted (these verbs to be taken as perfects, not as converted into futures) them in a permanent abode, free from the embarrassment of such powerful assailants as annoyed them in the time of the judges, and from which they now have rest. 6. The good desire of David, though not to be now realized, is acknowledged by the assurance that God has further purposed to establish his house in Israel.

Commendable but unseasonable zeal. Every reader of the narrative at once feels how natural and beautiful it was in David to desire, for the symbol of God's presence among his people, an abode somewhat commensurate with its glory and suggestive of permanence. It was in keeping with all the antecedents of his life, and there was manifested an exquisite spiritual sensibility in mentioning first of all so important a subject as a change in the abode of the ark to the prophet who represented the Divine source of guidance as distinguished from civil authority. What are the elements which render such zeal commendable and at the same time unseasonable ?

I. THERE IS A PERSONAL ABSORPTION IN THE INTERESTS OF GOD'S KINGDOM AMONG MEN. God's kingdom among men was the great fact to be emphasized and illustrated in the life of the chosen race, suggestive of a more developed kingdom in later times. This fact had absorbed the energies of Moses, but was somewhat obscured when the people, weary of the existing form of the theocracy, asked for and obtained a king in Saul. From the first David had, in his own life, restored the idea of the Divine kingdom to the distinctness of Mosaic times, and counted himself to have no function in the world apart from seeking to realize it in the national experience. For it he lived and ruled; for it he prayed, and of it he sang. This was the fountain-head of all his zeal, and the key to the communication made to Nathan. Herein also is the secret of all acceptable Christian zeal. We are right in feeling and purpose only in so far as our entire life is one with Christ's. Human life rises to its highest level only when it causes all its strength to flow in with the great stream of spiritual force which one day is to cover the earth. It is not patronage of institutions, study or criticism of Christian forms of thought and action, friendly feeling towards workers in mission fields, but personal identification with the interests of Christ's kingdom as the most vital and precious of all interests. This is a practical illustration of the phrase, " We have the mind of Christ."

II. There is a wholesome fear lest private and secular prosperity should generate selfishness. David was blessed with great prosperity in home and in state. In clearer, more reflective moods, he saw that this was connected with the furtherance of the great purpose of God in the world; but amidst the hurry of life and inevitable weaknesses of the moral nature, it was liable to produce a feeling of selfish content with his own condition. The dangers of prosperity are proverbial. His words to Nathan, contrasting his own permanent dwelling with the slender covering of the ark, revealed the thoughts and feelings of a man sensible of a grave spiritual danger, and anxious not to fall into it. It is sometimes, in the course of doing God's work, or what may be called secular work in a Christly spirit, that Providence grants men secular prosperity. Then comes the testing-time of the religious life. Many fall under the spell, and undue absorption in temporal personal comfort robs the kingdom of Christ of much thought and energy it otherwise would have received. The pleasures of the "house of cedar" shut out the condition of the spiritual kingdom. But where zeal is sound, watchfulness is maintained, and spiritual growth keeps pace with worldly prosperity, there will be cherished a wholesome dread lest the blessings which come from God should in any measure wean the heart from him and the supreme interests of his kingdom.

III. There is a perception of the temporary character of existing religious appliances. Spiritual instinct led David to feel that the tent was not suited as the abode in perpetuity of the eternal, unchangeable God. There was an incongruity between the nature of the occupant and the frailty and transitoriness of the dwelling-place. Apart, then, from the contrast with his own "cedar house," he saw that the arrangement which had received Divine sanction through many generations was not to be considered as perfect and unalterable. This was confirmed by the faith he cherished that the presence of God among his people was in pursuance of the great historic promise made to Abraham (Gen. xxii. 17, 18), and preparatory to some further unfolding of the plan which embraced within its scope all the nations of the earth. So far his zeal in seeking a permanent abode for the ark was enlightened. And this is a characteristic of all true zeal. It does not merely proceed from impulse and strong feeling; it has respect to the nature of the kingdom of Christ and the variability of its outward appliances according to the stages of its development. The visible forms and arrangements adapted to one state of society may need revision and change more or less radical to render the deposit of truth more effective in its influence on a different state of society. A mere love of change is not identical with commendable zeal; a bare feeling that simple variation in outward forms will strengthen the power of religion is no sure guide; but a distinction between the permanent truth centring in Christ, and the transitoriness of the setting of that truth, will lead to a desire, when occasion offers, to make such modifications in the circumstantials of religion as may best accord with the nature of the truth on the one side and the development of human society on the other.

IV. The imperfection of the zeal may lie in the error as to seasonableness. In this case all seemed right and sound, in accordance with the purest love and devotion, both to David and to Nathan. Subsequent light from God himself showed that here feeling was right and thought also up to a given point, but that the zeal was inappropriate by reason of a defective knowledge of the specific purposes of God. There were reasons in the Divine mind why David, at this juncture, should not build a house for the Lord. Probably his work of consolidation was not sufficiently advanced, and either then or later on he was reminded that a man of peace was alone suited for such work (1 Chron. xxii. 8; xxviii. 3). The defectiveness of the judgment even of good men is cause of much mistake in altering the institutions and visible agencies of the

Church. There are times when neither David nor Nathan may depend on their present feelings and knowledge, but more light must be sought from the Head of the Church. However sound the principle that forms and circumstantials do not possess the permanence belonging to the central truth they cover, still a busy zeal eager to introduce something new as more suited to a later development, even though shown by the most sincere of men, must be regarded with distrust unless Providence, by some means as good to us as was Nathan's vision to David, makes it quite clear that the time has come when the old should give place to the new. Holy desire, even when conjoined with knowledge of a limited experience, may not be fitly realized because God's time is not quite come.

GENERAL LESSONS. 1. Where there is sincere piety there will be jealousy lest the cause of God should not receive its due consideration. 2. It will be a mark of prosperous piety amidst prosperous circumstances when men deliberately study how they may more worthily serve God and give him the honour due to his Name. 3. We should always anticipate that, as time advances, there will be fresh opportunities for manifesting our devotion, even though our specific methods be not wisest. 4. It is a noble ambition to seek to render the house of God as perfect as human means can make it, and in this often we see contrasts in character (vers. 1—3; cf. Hag. i. 2, 5). A good man's life's work attains completion in so far as he combines, with advancing secular prosperity, regard for the prosperity of religion.

The historic development of God's purpose concerning man. In vers. 4—11 we have an exposition of the grounds on which God declined to accept David's proposal to build a house for him. The motive was good, and there was a certain perception of propriety in the design, but as its unseasonableness resulted from imperfect knowledge of the Divine will, that will is here made known.

I. GOD HAS A PURPOSE CONCERNING MAN. This is the basis of the declaration to David. It may, indeed, be said that there is a Divine purpose in the existence of every atom and form of force, since each is what it is by the will of God, and is related to all the rest of the universe in a definite way, so as to issue in a progressive order. Every change is thus the working out in the material world of a purpose of the eternal mind. But while this is true of man also considered as an organized creature in the world, it is further true of him that there is a purpose in the eternal mind of which he is the object, and to work out which all other things are means and agents. God has something to effect for man as well as by man. The New Testament informs us that it is spiritual in its nature, and abounding with good to man and glory to God.

II. GOD'S PURPOSE CONCERNING MAN IS INCORPORATED WITH HUMAN AFFAIRS. It is pointed out to David that the history of his ancestors in Egypt and under the judges, and also his own personal history, have been the vehicle through which this purpose has been gradually working. God's thoughts for man assume concrete forms. They enter as the golden thread into the rough web of human life. Human wills work in their own free way, but another will works with them, and uses them in their free course for the manifestation of itself. Abraham's domestic life, Israel's sojourn in Egypt and the desert, the struggle for existence during the period of the judges, and the raising up and fall of Saul, and the exploits of David, were occasions and forms by which that redemptive purpose revealed itself which later on in Judæa, in Pilate's hall and in the ages of Christendom, became more distinct and yet more one with human interests.

III. IN THE OUTWORKING OF THE PURPOSE TEMPORARY INSTITUTIONS ARE CREATED. The ark and the tabernacle were the creation of the Divine purpose working along the line of human history. They were the product of two things—the purpose and the incidents of Israel's existence. David was right in viewing the tabernacle as essentially temporary; but he is reminded (ver. 6) that it expressed the Divine will for the time because of the human element through which that will was working onwards. A succession of temporary expedients is traceable from the first to the second Adam. One by one they disappeared before the approach of the true Light. Many of the modern expedients of the Church will prove their temporary character in so far as Christ's holy will works its way into the heart of the world, and men, possessing this life, become in the best sense a law to themselves (1 Cor. xiii. 8—10).

IV. THE DIRECT CONTROL OF GOD SECURES TRANSITION FROM STAGE TO STAGE. The words to David were, " I brought up the children of Israel;" "I have walked in a tent;" "I commanded to feed;" "I took thee from the sheepcote;" "I have appointed a place." Thus men were free, and history was formed by the free action of man; but, still, in pursuance of the Divine purpose, an unseen hand so fashioned the sum of human free action that captivity in Egypt yielded to a settled home, and a good shepherd appeared to care for the flock in that settled home. It was this recognition of the actual control of God so as to shape the items of human history and secure a succession of transitions towards a definite goal that distinguished the teaching of the prophets. It is this which gave such assurance to apostles (Rom. viii. 22, 28, 31). The contending forces of each age are subject to him who by his mighty working can subdue all things unto himself (Phil. iii. 21).

V. THE VALUE OF MEANS IN THE WORKING OUT OF THE PURPOSE IS RELATIVE. David's pious dissatisfaction with the tabernacle as an abode for the ark was met by the assurance (vers. 6, 7) that God was not dissatisfied, but had shown his approval of his servants who were identified with its maintenance. The tabernacle may have been inadequate to the later stage, but it was perfect in its adaptation to the early stage of God's method of working. He never complained of disrespect to his Name; he even honoured his servants who served him with such humble means. This applies to the methods by which, in different ages, revelations came to men—agencies for diffusing and preserving the truth, the condition of the Churches by which his will is still done and the individual efforts of Christians to bring on the final triumph of Christ. Those who will not approve of action and appliances and methods till they meet with what is absolutely perfect, do not know history, or else, knowing it, are unwilling to accept its lessons. In an imperfect world where perfect holiness has to be attained through means inferior, and out of perfect relation to the end in view, we have to estimate each method and agency by its fitness to raise us to a stage above the present, and in which it may be dispensed with for something that will be a stepping-stone to a still higher point.

VI. THE WHOLE OF THE SUCCESSIVE STAGES TEND TO THE PERMANENT DWELLING OF GOD WITH MAN. David was right in his ambition and faith. To have God permanently among Israel was the perfection of holy desire. All hitherto had pointed in that direction; and though in the visible sense in which David desired it his wishes were not to be granted, yet he was pointed on to the reality of a "house" (ver. 11), which we know involved the raising up of Immanuel. This is the goal of all Old Testament revelations and ancient forms of instruction and discipline. And now that God has been visibly manifest in the flesh, the process is going on by which spiritually the dwelling of God with man in permanent union is to be realized (2 Cor. iii. 7—11; cf. Eph. ii. 18—22).

GENERAL LESSONS. 1. Life should be conducted on the principle that God is with man and working with and for him. 2. The comparison of events illustrated by the Bible teaching will enable us to trace out the line of God's working. 3. Although occasions may arise, as during periods of Israel's history, when the signs of God's working are obscured (Isa. xlv. 15), our faith should rest on the general revelation. 4. However unable we may be sometimes to see the unity of God's working, Providence will throw light upon it, and by some explicit "I have walked," "I took thee," our confidence will be confirmed. 5. All our desires and efforts and methods should, in their nature, have reference to the great issue—God's habitation of the Church through the Spirit.

Consolation in disappointment. Although vers. 11, 12 of Ps. cxxxii. make it clear that the psalm was written after the date of Nathan's visit to David, it is highly probable that the sentiments expressed in vers. 3—5 of that psalm were cherished before the king unbosomed himself to the prophet. In the fallibility characteristic of prophets when not authorized to speak by God, Nathan piously encouraged his king in his cherished wishes, and it is certain that that night David went to rest believing that now, with the concurrence of so good a man, the great ambition of his heart would soon be realized. The authorized revelation of the prophet on the following day must have brought with it a disappointment corresponding in bitterness to the previous elevation of feeling. But the gentle, kindly way in which it is allowed to fall is a beautiful instance of God's tenderness toward his people.

I. GOD RECOGNIZES US AS HIS OWN. There was balm in the words, "tell *my servant* David." In the beginning of his career David knew that he was called of God, but many a year had passed, and many a sore spiritual conflict with varied success had been endured. It was then refreshing to his spirit to be thus distinctly acknowledged to be the servant of the Most High—one honoured in heaven and identified with the carrying out of God's will on earth. To be owned of God, to have the witness of his Spirit with ours that we are his, to know on good evidence that our life is moving along the lines of his purpose,—what more satisfying and comforting when some cherished desire is denied? Paul's thorn in the flesh and consequent disappointment of holy ambition was even welcome when the Lord sent a message assuring that he was his "servant"—to do some work in the world, though not in the form desired. It is much in life if, amidst many failures of character and frustration of cherished desires, a man is permitted to know that God is not ashamed of him, and still honours him with a place among the great body of co-workers with himself.

II. PROVIDENCE GRADUALLY MAKES CLEAR, IN PART AT LEAST, THE WISDOM OF THE DISAPPOINTMENT. The first note of Nathan's message brought sorrow and even anguish of spirit. Fond hopes of joyous activity in a blessed cause were crushed. The dream of holy hours vanished. Loving toil was rejected. The heart sank. But by degrees, as the message unfolded and the course of Providence in reference to the tabernacle and settlement of Israel were unfolded, and probably reference made to wars yet impending (vers. 6—10; cf. ch. viii. 1—8; 1 Kings v. 3, 4; viii. 19), the reasons of the Divine conduct became manifest, and the troubled heart could rest in an unerring wisdom alone. A similar course was taken with the apostles when their Lord soothed their disappointment at his expected departure by partially expounding the reason of his conduct (John xiv. 1—4). Sometimes Christian workers who have, through sickness, failing opportunities, temporal disasters, and defective holiness of life, been denied the privilege of accomplishing all that was in their heart for Christ, have had to dwell in dense darkness for a while; but gradually events have occurred and light from God's Word has come which have shown how just and even kind it was that, under all the circumstances of the case, the disappointment came. The day will come when the bitter experiences of life will be so seen in their varied relations to ourselves and others as to give occasion for thankfulness.

III. THERE IS EVIDENCE THAT GOD WILL USE US IN OTHER WAYS. "My servant" meant to David that there was yet noble work to do for God. Human choice of the old form of work is not always best. In the great kingdom that is being established there is scope for many energies in manifold forms; and as the kingdom is one, every worker is honourable and every work essential. To keep the door of the sanctuary, to wash the feet of weary pilgrims, to give a cup of cold water, to feed the hungry, to place a mite in the treasury, and visit the widow and fatherless, are services honoured as truly as erecting a temple and as necessary to the perfection of the kingdom of God on earth. The Apostle Paul could not charm men by unfettered eloquence, but he could bless the universal Church by his example of loving acquiescence in the Lord's will (2 Cor. xii. 8—10). Even the very ambitions that have not been gratified may be used up by God as means to inspire others with generous aims and lofty aspirations.

IV. GOD REVEALS TO THE SPIRIT A CROWNING BLESSING. It was a repayment of David's loving devotion in his own kind when the prophet was instructed to reveal to him that God would "make *him* a house." To an Oriental monarch, especially after the sad failure of Saul, there could not have been a more coveted distinction than being blessed with a posterity that should hold his place in the kingdom. The blessing in this case, we know, carried with it also a spiritual significance embodied in the expression applied to Christ, "the Son of David." This cannot be regarded simply as a reward for the design to build a house for the Lord—it was part of a great purpose from the beginning; but it was clearly brought in here as a matter revealed for the soothing of David's spirit in a season of disappointment. In this way the future blessedness of the faithful is revealed in order that they may have abundant consolation. Good men do not live and labour for future rewards, but from love of Christ and passionate sympathy with the purposes of his heart; nevertheless, the pastor, missionary, and parent whose hopes sometimes seem blighted, rejoice to be able to think of an issue of their life which, in spite of all appearances, redounds to the glory of God. "Here am I, and the souls thou hast given me," is to be true of multitudes. God will give a godly seed, "a house" better and more enduring than any we could build for him (Ps. cxxvi. 5, 6; Matt. xix. 29).

Vers. 12—29.—The facts are: 1. The prophet declares to David (1) that he shall have a seed who shall build a house for the Lord; (2) that this successor shall be regarded as a son, and, while the subject of discipline, if needed, shall not be cast off as was Saul; and (3) that the house and kingdom thus established shall endure for ever. 2. David, in response to the message, acknowledges the condescension and bounty of God in what he had done and promised. 3. He confesses that all is of the free unmerited loving-kindness of God, and regards this wonderful superhuman goodness as being an illustration of the existence of a love transcending all that is known to man. 4. He recognizes the blessedness of Israel in being under the care and guidance of One so supremely good, and in being honoured to be distinctively his people. 5. He prays that the good and glorious things said of his house and of Israel may come to pass, and so bring out into public view and for ever the glory of God. 6. He concludes with a prayer, based on the faithfulness and goodness of God, that grace may be bestowed on the house of David, so that it may fulfil the purpose so graciously formed and now more explicitly revealed.

The testing period, and its rewards. We have here brought out a contrast between Saul and David. Both were accepted of God (1 Sam. ix. 15—17; xvi. 7—12, 13). A period of testing was assigned to each of them, and Saul failed in his (1 Sam. xiii. 13, 14), while David succeeded (ch. vii. 8—12, 15). The whole facts show that for each of them, in his official capacity, there was a probation or testing-time, which was not coextensive with the duration of life, but sufficient to prove fitness for being the instrument for the furtherance of the Divine purpose of redemption through the Messiah. David was found fit for Divine use, and hence, in the prime of his days, he was assured of the completion of his life's work and of issues most glorious.

I. THE EARLY STAGES OF A CAREER DETERMINE ITS ISSUE. From his call and anointing up to his desire to build a house for the Lord, David had been taking the first steps of his public life; on the whole, he had been wise, devout, loyal to God, zealous for the Divine kingdom among men. The great work of his entire life was thereby virtually ensured. All future successes were now germinal. Saul's future was blasted because the early testing years were unimproved; David's future was made sure because his trial had proved his sterling qualities. The years of early manhood carry in them the future of the man. A Christian "found faithful" enters on a wider ministry (1 Tim. i. 12). The Church that has kept true in trial is safe in view of future perils (Rev. iii. 10—12). The proper use of five talents carries with it the promise of use of ten talents. According to the development of Christian character in the early stages of religious life will be its power and victories unto the very end. The beginnings of things are the ends of things in miniature. Character is a prophecy. Ultimate successes lie hidden in first adjustments.

II. THE BLESSED ISSUES OF A PROBATION ARE IN THE ORDER OF NATURE. The bestowment of the honour of being founder of a great line of kings on David was an act of Divine favour, marking approval of his fidelity during the testing-time of life; but it was not a mere artificial, arbitrary arrangement. It was the announcement of the fact that God had so ordered things that he, by faithfulness, thus far had acquired the qualities which a holy God could and would use up in bringing to pass his great purposes. Saul was proved naturally unfit to inaugurate a permanent line; David was proved naturally suited for that end. This runs through all things. A sapling that has, in spite of storms, passed well through the ordeals of early life contains within itself the vital qualities which will develop into a perfect tree. It is by force of the virtues and acquirements of the testing-time of early manhood that subsequent achievements are won. The spiritual characteristics of the man "counted worthy" of a ministry explain the triumph of his life's work; for, though the blessing of God is essential, yet it is the order of nature in the religious sphere that the blessing comes where those characteristics find exercise. The future blessedness of the saints is the outgrowth of the individual character acquired during the earthly period of trial. Continuity, order, and, in proper sense of the term, nature, characterize the succession of events in individual and Church experience from first to last.

III. THE ASSURANCE OF FINAL SUCCESS HELPS A TRUE MAN TO ITS REALIZATION. The promise of a "house" and a permanent "kingdom" would not excite vanity and presumption in David, because he was a true man of God. There is an adaptation in the assurance given to the tested character of the man. It was to David as the warm sun and gentle dew to the good seed hidden in good ground. A true heart responds to God's love and bounteous gifts by increased devotion. Thus the assurance has a natural tendency in a true heart to fulfil itself. Wherever other tendencies appear, it is evidence that the heart is not right, and that the assurance is not intended for the individual. The free grace of God and abounding assurances that he will keep his people from falling are never abused except by those who are not children of God (Rom. vi. 14, 15; 2 Cor. v. 14, 15).

The blending of the temporal and the eternal. The prophecy in vers. 12—16 is not to be regarded as a sudden and isolated revelation of the purpose of God, which burst upon the mind of one who had no previous conceptions of a great purpose being wrought out in the line of human history. All along David was aware of his being used for more than ordinary issues in relation to the great promise made to Abraham. The Aurora Borealis seems, to ignorant men, a disconnected unaccountable phenomenon, but others know it to be a natural occurrence in a beautiful order of things correlated to all else in the material world. In like manner, we now know that this prophecy is part of an order of revelation, coming in at just the right time, and interpretable on principles well ascertained. The temporal and eternal are blended—

I. IN THE MATERIAL ORDER. The results of research into the constitution and order of material things show that the visible, changeable forms of matter coexist with a permanent something which works in and through them. They vary; it abides. They prepare the way for others of kindred nature and form; it uses up the old and the new and marks out its eternal course by means of them. Men call it force. Possibly, probably, there is a persistent something answering to that name—the correlative of our exertion of will-power—but it, at all events, is only the mode in which the Divine purpose works itself out into visible forms and changes. The temporal and eternal are ever blended.

II. IN THE CONSTITUTION OF MAN. The changeful form, the visible appearance, is ever associated with the permanent invisible spirit; the one exists for the other, and is used by the other for expressing its thoughts and purposes. "Mortal and immortal" may be written of man. He comes forth and passes away: he abideth for ever. Paradox is true, because the perishable and imperishable coexist and work one through the other.

III. IN THE PERSON OF JESUS CHRIST. Our Saviour was frail, subject to death; and yet the strong, unchangeable, deathless Son of God. The temporal and eternal were most mysteriously united in him, and the visible and perishable were the vehicle through which the unseen and eternal worked out our redemption. There is language by which men, if they will, can prove his simple humanity, and other language by which they can prove his true Divinity. It is the ignoring of this blending of the temporal and eternal which accounts for certain heresies and perversities of thought.

IV. IN THE PROGRESS OF REVELATION. The revelation which God is pleased to give of his will concerning our redemption is intended for the entire race, and adapted in matter and form to the progressive character of the race. It was not given once for all in concise abstract form; nor was its matter and form given to suit the later ages of the world only; it ran along the line of history from the very first, and was suited as time went on to men of diverse ideas and conditions. But from first to last the Divine imperishable truth was blended with the temporal history of men. The natural development of families and nations was the vehicle through or along which, as occasion required, the one unchangeable purpose gradually marked itself out into the clear light that shone in the face of Christ.

V. IN THE PROPHETIC REFERENCES TO THE MESSIAH. The duality of temporal and eternal thus seen to run through all things, becomes, therefore, *a priori* natural in any predictions concerning him whose throne is from everlasting to everlasting. That in vers. 12—16 we have reference to a mortal Solomon, who should build a perishable temple, sit on a visible throne, and hand down to a terminable though long succession of kings an earthly kingdom, is the interpretation required by subsequent facts. That the "seed" refers also to Christ the "Son of David," the house to a spiritual temple, the "throne" and "kingdom" to the absolutely everlasting dominion of Christ over the redeemed people of God, is the sense put on this and kindred passages by the New Testament (Ps. lxxii. 17; lxxxix. 35—37; cf. Luke i. 31—33, 68—79; Heb. i. 5—13). That the two references should be couched in one form of expression is natural when we consider (1) that the temporal and eternal are blended, as just seen, in one form of nature, in one human being, in the one Christ Jesus, and in the one historic revelation; (2) that this harmonizes with the twofold sense of the prediction made to Abraham (Gen. xxi. 12; xxii. 17—19; cf. Rom. ix. 7—9; Acts iii. 25; Gal. iii. 26), and with the twofold meaning of our Lord's words in reference to "the end" (Matt. xxiv. 9—14, 29—44). The human relationship, the human throne, the possible human frailty, and the human relative permanence, are the lower earthly vehicle by which the Divine and absolutely enduring are set forth and inaugurated.

GENERAL LESSONS. 1. God secures to all his truly faithful ones the realization of their highest and holiest ambitions, as surely as he secured to David the realization of his desire for a *seed*, and the completion of his life's work in the establishment of his throne; for he makes life here to issue in the glory of the kingdom of Christ. 2. It behoves us to remember that there is an eternal element interwoven with common life, and to subordinate everything temporal to its action. 3. The fact that chosen instruments are used in working out eternal purposes does not exempt them from the frailties of their nature and the corrections necessary to their preservation for the service of God (ver. 14). 4. The chastisement due to the literal son of David for sins of his own foreshadows dimly the spiritual fact that *the great* Son of David took upon himself the iniquities of us all, and experienced the "chastisement of our peace." 5. The strong and repeated assurances of the universality and permanence of Christ's reign should inspire us with calm confidence and untiring zeal. 5. Human fidelity in God's service is a condition of the progressive bringing into clearer view and nearer realization the glorious end for which all things consist.

The educational influence of God's great love. In vers. 18—29 we have described, in broken sentences, the effect on the spirit of David of the marvellous loving-kindness of God in having guaranteed unto him such a glorious completion of life's work, and the unspeakable honour of being associated in name and work with the Redeemer of the world. The real nature of a man is tested in seasons of great prosperity as well as in adversity. David bears the strain. Never in the past history of the world had God spoken so distinctly and emphatically to any of his people of the personal honour he would confer. In the effect of this on David we may see an illustration of the general educational influence of God's love on his people.

I. IT INDUCES INEXPRESSIBLE WONDER. When David had heard the strange words he at once went and "sat" before the Lord! The first impulse was to get near to the visible symbol of the Divine presence, and simply sit still in amazement. That silence held his tongue for a while seems indicated in the embarrassment (ver. 20). What *could* a devout man do but muse and wonder at the largeness of the grace? There was a marvel in what God had done in the past (ver. 18), in what was to be in the future, and in the ordination or law, תּוֹרָה, in respect of the man, or otherwise in the superhuman bearing towards one so unworthy (cf. Isa. lv. 8). This is the general effect of a recognition of God's love to us, whether seen in the unspeakable gift of Christ, in the greatness of his long-suffering, in the tenderness of his pity, in the provision for our temporal and eternal good, in the use he makes of us in his service, or in the blessed inheritance promised in the future. There is a devotion of feeling which consists in a permanent silent wonder that God should have dealt so with us. This tones our spirit into quiet gentleness, and we can in some measure understand why seraphim and cherubim should be absorbed in wonder at his ways.

II. IT INDUCES DEEP HUMILITY. It was not because of any good in himself that all these things were done to David, but because God was pleased out of his own heart so to deal with him (ver. 21). Nothing tends more to develop humility than a survey of the wonderful love of God. The contrast of our deserts with his grace bows the spirit down, not to abjectness and loss of heart, but to the tender feeling of self-depreciation and self-abnegation which ever becomes a sinful creature in the presence of the Eternal. Great grace bestowed is an educator in what most befits one who was lost but is now found (Ps. cxv. 1; Rom. iii. 27; 1 Cor. xv. 10; 1 John iii. 1).

III. IT FEEDS THE SPIRIT OF ADORATION. The word "wherefore" (ver. 22) seems to complete the silent reasoning which must have gone on in the mind of David for many a year. The general care of man (Ps. viii.), the heavens (Ps. xix.), and the terrible works of God among the nations (Ps. xlviii. 4—7, 10, 11), had ever furnished occasion for adoration; but all this is surpassed by the great love wherewith he has now loved his servant, and in this lies the moral greatness which most of all wins the adoring love of the soul. It is a well-known psychological truth that the feelings are not under the direct control of the will, and especially not obedient to a bare command. Nor are they developed in noblest form by mere externals. It is when the actual love of God, as seen in deeds done for us and blessings freely showered on us, is manifest to the eye of the soul, that true worship arises. The greatness of love draws forth the homage of the redeemed (Rev. i. 5, 6; v. 9, 10).

IV. IT STRENGTHENS INTEREST IN OTHERS. Some who do not know what personal piety is imagine that it consists in selfish delight in one's own favoured condition— a continuous self-congratulation that we are snatched as brands from the burning. David's deep interest in others, as seen in vers. 23, 24, establishes the reverse. The love we share in is a love embracing others, and it awakens and nourishes a joy in them and their happy lot. It is an unspeakable delight to a true Christian that a multitude that no man can number are the people of God, "redeemed" by the wondrous grace which amazes while it blesses himself.

V. IT LEADS TO EVER-INCREASING CONSECRATION. Such is the meaning of David in vers. 24—27. He surrenders his heart and life afresh to the one great purpose which has been graciously revealed. It is not mere acquiescence that so it should be, but intense desire, self-identification afresh with the work and ways of God. He wants to be used in the accomplishment of the great design. This was the secret of the Apostle Paul's ever-deepening consecration. The love of God to him and others was a constant subject of thought, and hence he was daily "constrained" to live for him who had died to make him what he was (2 Cor. v. 14—16). The love of God contemplated and felt renders every yoke welcome and easy.

VI. IT DRAWS OUT A SPIRIT OF TRUSTFUL DEPENDENCE. To be the instrument of this working in the line of the great purpose required distinguished qualities, and a revelation of it (ver. 27) very naturally made David sensible of the insufficiency of himself and successors, and called forth the prayer for a blessing on his house (vers. 28, 29). The blessing of God is necessary to man's successful working-out of the Divine will; and the heart that appreciates the honour of being so employed will earnestly plead the promises in seeking the grace required.

ADDITIONAL NOTES AND OBSERVATIONS. 1. It is one of the sweetest joys of life granted by God when, in his providence, he gives intimation to parents that their immediate posterity are likely to take up the religious work they love, and carry it on towards the completion of God's will on earth (ver. 12). 2. What parents need is that God would "set up," in positions of righteousness and true honour, their offspring, and "establish" whatever work or interest they may have in hand (ver. 12). 3. To "build a house" for God is an unspeakable privilege (ver. 13). It may be done variously: (1) by rearing up a personal character of our own on the One Foundation (1 Pet. ii. 6), so that it may be a fit habitation of God through the Holy Spirit (1 Cor. iii. 16; vi. 19); (2) by teaching the cardinal truths of the gospel among men, so that on the One Foundation (1 Cor. iii. 9—11) there may be reared a Christian Church, as is still often done by missionaries in heathen lands; (3) by devoting money to the erection of a sanctuary where needed (Luke vii. 5). A more noble use of wealth can scarcely be conceived. 4. God's purposes are unfolded and wrought out in human history with full prevision of the imperfections and sins of his people, and with providential provision for their correction (ver. 14). Not one of the distinguished men who prepared the way for Christ was perfect. The Antitype alone is free from sin. It was in the *occupying of a throne*, not in the details of private conduct, that Solomon the son of David prefigured the true Son of David. 5. There are fundamental errors and failures in the lives of some men which disqualify them utterly from sharing in the highest and noblest work. Saul's obstinacy, self-will, and inability to rise to the conception of the purpose and scope of the theocracy, rendered it unfit that he should found the line by which the Christ should come (ver. 15). Solomon's imperfections were those of another character, springing more from unwatchfulness against certain snares of his position. These imperfect workers suffer loss and shame, but the substantial part of their work abides (1 Cor. iii. 12—15). 6. It is a great consolation to a Christian that God *knows* him (ver. 20). He knows our unexpressed thoughts and feelings, our depth of love and gratitude, our sorrow over sin, our most secret motives, and the path we take. Our ease of mind in remembrance of this is one of the marks of true sonship and service. 7. A review of the gradual revelation of God's purposes will surely induce a profound conviction of his greatness and glory (ver. 22). Men who study only the physical aspects of nature lose much. The moral universe is the grandest arena on which the power and blessedness of the Eternal shines forth. 8. It was ancient Israel's being chosen and used as the people of God (ver. 23) which conferred on them the most enduring distinction. As a fact, Israel has done more than either Egypt, Greece, or Rome for the true elevation of mankind; for Israel was the means of bringing into universal operation the mighty renovating principles of the kingdom of God, which alone can secure the permanence of civilization, and also educate the higher nature of man for time and eternity. "Blessed is that people whose God is the Lord!" 9. The whole question of the final triumph of Christ rests on the word of God, "Thou, O Lord God, hast spoken it" (ver. 29). Modern speculations are beside the mark. The first question covers all. Have we historically the declaration of God? Then, if he has said a thing, it must be so. Difficulties are relative to man's ignorance and weakness, and have no place with the Eternal. Faith in God is a rational exercise of the human mind; it is not blind superstition.

HOMILIES BY VARIOUS AUTHORS.

Vers. 1, 2 (1 Chron. xvii. 1).—(THE KING'S PALACE IN ZION.) *David's purpose to build a house for the Lord.* (*References:* 1 Kings v. 3; vi. 12; viii. 17—19; 1 Chron. xxii. 7—10; xxviii. 2—7; xxix. 1—3; 2 Chron. vi. 7—9.) The king's palace of cedar on Mount Zion had been completed. In the adjacent tabernacle or dwelling-place of Jehovah (ver. 6) the ark had found rest, and a regular order of public worship had been instituted. Surrounding enemies had been subdued, and there was at least a temporary cessation from war. Jerusalem was the civil, military, and ecclesiastical centre of the kingdom. And now another step in advance was taken. Whilst contemplating the lowly abode of the ark of the Lord in comparison with his own palace, the thought arose in David's mind of building a splendid and durable temple "for the Name of the Lord God of Israel" (1 Kings viii. 17), "a house of rest for the ark of the covenant of the Lord, and for the footstool of our God" (1 Chron. xxviii. 2), "exceeding magnifical of fame and of glory throughout all countries" (1 Chron. xxii. 5); and "when the king sat in his house" he intimated his wish (for it scarcely amounted to a distinct and definite resolution) to Nathan the prophet, doubtless in order to obtain his advice concerning its propriety and accomplishment. What followed was of the highest importance in relation to the permanence of his dynasty, the prosperity of his people, the worship of God, and the development of Messianic purposes. "The word of the Prophet Nathan and the thanksgiving of David mark the culmination of David's history" (Baumgarten). This chapter affords a glimpse into his innermost heart, and reveals the devotional feelings, patriotic desires, and lofty aspirations and hopes that dwelt therein. In him we here see an example of—

I. DEVOUT OCCUPATION IN THE RETIREMENT OF HOME. Such retirement, necessary for all, is not always spent wisely and well; but often in sensuous indulgence, frivolous amusement, self-adulation (Dan. iv. 29, 30), envious discontent (1 Kings xxi. 4), or meditating secular and selfish schemes (Luke xi. 17, 18). The godly man not only "returns to bless his household," but also: 1. *Meditates on the best things:* the Name of the Lord, his greatness and goodness, his works, his ways, his Word, his worship, and the welfare of men. He considers "the days of old," and "communes with his own heart" (Ps. lxxvii. 5, 6) of his benefits, obligations, condition, and prospects (Ps. lv. 17; Matt. vi. 5; John i. 48). 2. *Talks of these things in a right manner.* 3. *Cultivates social intercourse with good men,* "the excellent, in whom is all his delight" (Ps. xvi. 3; cxix. 63). He prefers their society to any other, befriends them, and makes them his friends (Luke xvi. 9). Nor is there any greater treasure on earth than a faithful friend, such as David had in Nathan. The manner in which men spend their leisure hours is a sure indication of their real character.

II. ARDENT GRATITUDE TO GOD FOR SUCCESS in his undertakings, labours, conflicts (ver. 1), and whatever rest and prosperity he enjoys. 1. These he *ascribes,* not to his own skill or power (Deut. vii. 17), but *to the Divine hand;* and, in considering what God "hath done for his soul" (Ps. lxvi. 16): 2. He is *deeply affected* by his exceeding kindness, so condescending, undeserved, and inexpressible (vers. 8, 9, 20)! While he muses the fire burns (Ps. xxxix. 3). 3. And he is constrained to *testify* his thankfulness in word and deed. "Those who stretch themselves upon beds of ivory (Amos vi. 4—6), and were not grieved for the affliction of Joseph, though they had David's music had not David's spirit" (Matthew Henry). "Though the Prophet David was guilty of many of the most deadly sins, yet he was said to be a man after God's own heart, because he abounded more with thankfulness than any other that is mentioned in Holy Scripture" (Isaac Walton).

III. TENDER CONCERN FOR THE DIVINE HONOUR. "See now I dwell in a house of cedar," etc. The devout and grateful heart feels: 1. That with the honour of God *the house of God* is intimately connected. No material fabric, however stately, can now possess the same significance or relative importance as the tabernacle or temple (1 Sam. i. 3, 9). But wherever God's children meet for Divine worship and spiritual fellowship (thus constituting the true temple and Church), the place is "hallowed ground." Standing amidst other dwellings, the house of God is a constant witness for him; and, by its sacred associations, religious exercises, and the holy influences therein received and thence diffused, it greatly conduces to his glory, as well as to the good of men. 2. That it ought to *correspond with its declared purpose,* and the circumstances and abilities of those by whom it is erected and attended. All "temples made with hands" fall infinitely beneath the dignity of the Eternal (1 Kings viii. 27; Acts xvii. 24); yet it is becoming that "strength and beauty should be in his sanctuary," that men should offer their best in his service (ch. xxiv. 24), and that, while they dwell in "ceiled houses," his house should not "lie waste" (Hag. i. 4). 3. That it is a *duty and a privilege* to employ the gifts bestowed by God for the improvement of his house and the promotion of his honour. When he has done much for us we should do much for him. "Four great means for administering the religion of Christ have been divinely appointed: the Book of God, the day of God, the worship of God, and the house of God. This last is for the sake of the former three. Without it they cannot be upheld. In *the house of God* the truth of God is proclaimed, the day of God is hallowed, and the worship of God is solemnized. All good gathers into and around God's house. 'I will make,' saith he, 'the places round about my hill a blessing.' There gather pious families. There arise schools for neglected children. There benevolent activities prevail. There spring up fountains of missionary liberality. And from humble sanctuaries in England, gospel light streams forth to distant regions of the earth—the wilds of Southern Africa, or the populous hives of Chinese idolatry" (Algernon Wells).

IV. HIGH ESTIMATION OF FRIENDLY COUNSEL. Unlike some successful and powerful men, who take counsel of their own hearts and despise the advice of others, David valued, sought, and received the advice of Nathan as the counsel of God himself. "The first great office of a friend is (1) *to try our thoughts* by the measure of his judgment, and to taste the wholesomeness of our designs and purposes by the feelings of his heart. As this office of a good friend is to guard us against the imperfections of our own nature, and protect the world from the effects and ourselves from the responsibility of our folly, the next office of a friend is (2) *to protect us* from the selfish and wilful and malicious part of our nature. A third great office of friendship is (3) *to awaken us and lift us up,* and set us on nobler deeds. The fourth good office of a friend is (4) *to rally us when we are defeated* or overtaken with adversity. And so much is the world alive to this office as to have chosen it out as the true test; it being one of our best proverbs that 'a friend in need is a friend indeed'" (E. Irving).—D.

Ver. 3.—*The Prophet Nathan.* (*References:* ch. xii. 1, 25; 1 Kings i. 10, 22; iv. 5; 1 Chron. xvii. 1; xxix. 29; 2 Chron. ix. 29; xxix. 25; Zech. xii. 12.) This is the first mention of his name. He may have been trained by Samuel at Naioth, and become acquainted with David there; was now the confidential friend and spiritual adviser of the king; subsequently reproved him for his sin; gave him counsel concerning the accession of Solomon; aided him in the reorganization of public worship; and wrote annals of his reign. It was his vocation to interpret and announce the Divine mind to others (see 1 Sam. iv. 1). "The calling of a prophet was that of a preacher or pastor with reference to the congregation as a whole and its individual members; but was distinct from our modern ideas with reference to the calling as thus explained in his drawing directly from Divine revelation. The prophets have been rightly called 'the conscience of the Israelitish state.' . . . They held intercourse with God by means of prayer. They questioned God (Hab. ii. 1), and he answered; but they did not receive Divine disclosures until they had first occupied an attitude of waiting and praying" (Delitzsch; Oehler, 'Theology of the Old Testament;' Riehm). 1. *All men, and especially those who are in authority, have need of wise and faithful counsel.* The king himself is only a man; his position is apt to blind his judgment and corrupt his heart; whilst his responsibilities and the consequences of his actions are very great. 2. *Even the wisest of counsellors are liable to err in judgment.* (Job xxxii. 9.) "All that is in thine heart go, do." But herein Nathan spoke "out of his own mind, and not by Divine revelation" (J. H. Michaelis). The prophet, like the king, was only a man (Acts x. 26), imperfect and fallible, and often mistaken, when giving counsel according to his natural judgment and first impressions, without seeking and obtaining the counsel of God, It is not said that he spoke by "the word of the Lord," as he did afterwards (ver. 4). "Ofttimes our thoughts, although springing from motives of real religion, are. not God's thoughts; and the lesson here conveyed is most important—not taking our own impressions, however earnestly and piously derived, as necessarily in accordance with the will of God, but testing them by his revealed Word" (Edersheim). 3. *The errors of human judgment are rectified by Divine communications.* Such communications have been actually made; and they are unspeakably precious. The prophet clearly distinguished them from his own thoughts, and had an inward assurance and overpowering conviction that he was the organ of God. It is the privilege of all Christians to be "taught of God," and "led by the Spirit;" but unless their convictions and impulses accord with the revealed Word, they must be rejected. 4. *The Word of Divine revelation admits of no questioning or contradiction;* but should be received "with meekness," uttered with simplicity and fidelity (Deut. xii. 32), and obeyed humbly, cheerfully, and fully. The prophet hesitated not to acknowledge his mistake, nor the king to lay aside his purpose in obedience to the will of the Lord (vers. 17, 18).—D.

Ver. 3.—"*The Lord is with thee.*" This brief and significant language has often been addressed to good men. And what can be more encouraging! 1. It describes *an invaluable privilege.* "Jehovah," the Eternal, the Unchangeable, the Faithful, the Covenant-God of Israel, "is with thee;" not simply in his special presence, but also in his effectual grace, approving, directing, protecting, qualifying, helping, prospering thee. "I am with thee" (Gen. xxvi. 24; Exod. xx. 24). 2. It expresses *a personal assurance.* "With *thee.*" Such assurance is given by the word of the prophet, the covenant of God, the argument of experience (ver. 9; 1 Sam. xviii. 32—37), and the conviction of the heart in the way of faith and obedience. 3. It furnishes *a powerful incitement* to thanksgiving, prayer, conflict, labour, perseverance, hope (Hag. ii. 4; 1 Cor. xv. 58). "Lo, I am with you always." The spiritual presence and fellowship of Christ are the secret of all spiritual strength and success.—D.

Vers. 4—11 (1 Chron. xvii. 3—10).—(ZION.) *A forbidden purpose.* "Shalt thou build me a house for me to dwell in?" On reflection, the prophet, perhaps, felt some misgiving as to the wisdom of the counsel he had given to the king ; and (in prayer) the same night (before any steps could be taken to carry it into effect) he received a Divine communication which he faithfully announced. The chief significance of this communication lies in the promise it contained with respect to " the house of David." But it was primarily and directly a prohibition of the king's resolve. "Thus saith the Lord, *Thou* shalt not build me a house to dwell in " (1 Chron. xvii. 4). The purpose of a good man is often " broken off " (Job xvii. 11 ; xxix. 18); not always, however, because of the clearer knowledge of the mind of God vouchsafed to him, but more commonly because of the difficulty and opposition he meets with in seeking its accomplishment, and his inability to overcome them. Of the purpose of David (as illustrative of that of others) observe that—

I. ALTHOUGH FORBIDDEN, IT WAS NOT ALTOGETHER DISAPPROVED. " Thou didst well that it was in thine heart " (1 Kings viii. 18); spoken of : 1. The *spirit* in which his purpose was formed—grateful devotion and sincere desire of honouring God and bene-fiting men. This is always the chief thing " in the sight of God, who searches the heart." 2. And the *object* toward which it was directed. It was not *in itself* displeas-ing to God, but received his sanction (Deut. xii. 10, 11 ; ver. 13). Yet : 3. How seldom is a human purpose, though in the main good, entirely unmingled with human imper-fection ! The language in which the purpose of David was forbidden seems to indicate that " his generous impulse was outrunning God's commandment, and that his ardour to serve was in some danger of forgetting his entire dependence on God, and of fancy-ing that God would be the better for him " (A. Maclaren).

II. IT WAS NOT FORBIDDEN WITHOUT SUFFICIENT REASON (vers. 7, 8), viz. : 1. *The dealings of God with his people* in past time ; showing that it was his pleasure that his dwelling-place should be *adapted* to their unsettled condition ; and that " a house of cedar " was not indispensable to his presence and blessing. He was satisfied to share their wanderings. 2. *The absence of a Divine direction* to build a permanent house. " It was not because of any negligence on the part of the former leaders of the people that they had not thought of erecting a temple " (Keil). Until the " word " should be spoken, no one might enter upon such an undertaking. 3. *The unsuitableness of the present time*—the still disturbed and warlike state of the kingdom (ver. 11). "Inas-much as these wars were necessary and inevitable, they were practical proofs that David's kingdom and government were not yet established ; and therefore that the time for the building of the temple had not yet come, and the rest of peace was not yet secured." 4. *The incongruity of his career* with the nature and design of the building. An abode of peace should be erected by a man of peace. " Thou hast shed blood abundantly, and hast made great wars ; thou shalt not build a house to my Name," etc. (1 Chron. xxii. 8 ; xxviii. 3 ; 1 Kings v. 3). "From whence could so sublime a precept descend, amidst a people constituted as the Jews were, unless from the Father of love and mercy ? " (Milman). " War, however necessary it may be in certain circum-stances for the kingdom of God, is only something accidental, the result of human corruption. The true nature of the kingdom of God is peace " (Hengstenberg). Still other reasons appear in what was promised to David (vers. 11, 12), without which the accomplishment of what he purposed in his heart was impossible.

III. IT WAS FORBIDDEN IN THE MOST GRACIOUS MANNER. (Vers. 8—11.) For God : 1. Assured him of the *regard* in which he was held by him. " David is here called God's servant, who is King of kings—the fairest flower in any king's crown, and highest title he can claim " (Guild). 2. Reminded him of the great things which he had *already done* for him ; and which were an earnest of " still greater things than these " (Ps. lxxviii. 70—72). 3. Informed him of the safety and stability, the peace and prosperity, which (in continuance of his former mercies) he was about to grant to *his people* under his rule. 4. Promised to him rest from all his enemies, and an *enduring dynasty* (ch. i. 1, 2). "Jehovah telleth thee that Jehovah will make thee a house " (Ps. cxxxii. 11). What an abundant compensation was thus afforded for any dis-appointment that might be at first experienced ! " Our own plans, though well intended, are often fit for nothing but to be laid aside to make way for the Lord's purposes respecting us, of which perhaps we had no conception " (Scott).

IV. IT WAS FORBIDDEN ONLY THAT IT MIGHT BE MORE EFFECTUALLY FULFILLED. (Vers. 12, 13.) " ' Thou shalt not build a house for me ' (vers. 5—7) ; but I, who have from the beginning till now glorified myself in thee and my people (vers. 8—11), will build a house for thee (ver. 11); and then thy son shall erect a house for me" (Thenius). 1. The purpose of man depends for its fulfilment upon the purpose of God.   2. The purpose which one man is unable to accomplish is often wrought out by another, who comes after him, under more favourable circumstances.   3. Although the former is not permitted to see the execution of his purpose, he may contribute greatly towards it, and does not go unrewarded.   4. Many a seeming failure is a real and glorious success; and "heaven is made for those who fail in this world."—D.

Ver. 9.—(JERUSALEM.) *A great name.* Among the great things which God did for David, he gave him a great name, like that of others, statesmen, warriors, kings, who, on account of their abilities, successes, power, and influence, were renowned "in the earth." "The fame of David went out into all lands" (1 Chron. xiv. 17).   "Glory consists in the honourable and widespread reputation of numerous and important services rendered to one's friends, his country, or the whole human race" (Cicero).   It is: 1. *A desired possession.* The love of human esteem, praise, and honour is natural, universal, beneficial, though often perverted to unworthy ends, and not subordinated to the voice of conscience and of God.   "That characteristic of man which is at once the most unworthy and the most exalted is his desire of glory.   It is the last passion that becomes extinct in the heart of man.   There is such a charm in glory that, whatever we connect with it, even death itself, we love it still" (Pascal).   "Desire of glory is the last garment that even wise men lay aside" (O. Felltham). 2. *A Divine gift.* "And in thine hand it is to make great" (1 Chron. xxix. 12). Although it necessitates, in most instances, strenuous human endeavour, it is never attained apart from or in opposition to the working of Divine providence; which in this, as in other things, is frequently mysterious, but always wise and just and good. How many strive after it in vain!

> "Some sink outright;
> O'er them, and o'er their names, the billows close;
> To-morrow knows not they were ever born.
> Others a short memorial leave behind,
> Like a flag floating when the bark's engulf'd—
> It floats a moment, and is seen no more:
> One Cæsar lives, a thousand are forgot."
>
> (Young, 'Night Thoughts,' viii.)

3. *A weighty responsibility.* As it is given by God, so it should be ascribed to him and used for him, according to his will, not for selfish but beneficent ends (ch. v. 12). Even when righteously gained, it is not always righteously maintained. Some of "the great men that are on the earth" have, by its abuse, fallen from their nest among the stars (Obad. 4), like "Lucifer, son of the morning" (Isa. xiv. 12). 4. *An unsatisfying portion.* In the midst of its enjoyment the soul craves something higher, and can find rest only in the approbation and fellowship of God (Ps. iv. 6; lxxiii. 25; cxix. 57). It cannot impart inward peace; it endures but for a season, and then passes away. "Where are those rulers of the earth gone, with their guards, armies, and carriages, of whose departure the earth stands a witness unto the present day?" ('The Hitopadesa').

> "The noise
> Of worldly fame is but a blast of wind,
> That blows from diverse points, and shifts its name—
> Shifting the point it blows from. Shalt thou more
> Live in the mouths of mankind, if thy flesh
> Part shrivel'd from thee, than if thou hadst died
> Before the coral and the pap were left;
> Or ere some thousand years have past? and that
> Is, to eternity compared, a space
> Briefer than is the twinkling of an eye
> To the heaven's slowest orb."
>
> (Dante, 'Purg.')

Remarks. (1) A great name is not always a good name.   (2) A good name may be possessed, though a great name may be unattainable. (3) To some men (like David) it is given to possess both. (4) True greatness consists in Christ-like goodness (Matt. xx. 25—28), and true glory in "the honour which cometh from God only" (John v. 44).—D.

Ver. 12.—(JERUSALEM.) *The prospect of death.* The view of earthly glory is apt to suggest, by contrast, the thought of its transitory duration, and no one can look forward to the days to come without having "the shadow of death" presented before his mind. Of its unavoidable approach, the message which David received, telling of his present prosperity and future prospects, reminded him. It is: 1. *An event of inevitable occurrence.* "What man is he that liveth, and shall not see death?" (Ps. lxxxix. 48). "The small and great are there" (Job iii. 19). "The path of glory leads but to the grave."

> "Death comes with irrespective feet,
>   And beats upon the door
> That shuts the palace of the great,
>   The cabin of the poor."
>
> (Horace.)

2. *An end of allotted time.* "When thy days be fulfilled." There is "an appointed time to man upon earth" (Job vii. 1; xiv. 5; Ps. xxxi. 15), in which to pass his probation, form his character, and perform his work. Unknown to him, it is determined by God, and, however brief, it is sufficient for that purpose. Happy is he who therein "serves his own generation by the will of God" (Acts xiii. 36). 3. *An exit from earthly cares,* labours, conflicts, and sorrows. "Thou shalt sleep," and be at rest (Job iii. 17; John xi. 11; 1 Thess. iv. 14); not necessarily in absolute unconsciousness and inactivity. Death is a "decease" (2 Pet. i. 15), departure, exodus of the spirit from "this tabernacle" to an eternal home (2 Cor. v. 1, 8). 4. *An entrance into heavenly fellowship.* "With thy fathers;" in the possession of conscious, personal, immortal life, of a common heritage in God, and happy communion with each other (ch. xii. 23; Ps. xvi. 11; xvii. 15). David's hope of this, indeed, was dim, in comparison with the Christian hope, as the morning twilight compared with the perfect day (2 Tim. i. 10; Matt. viii. 11). 5. *An enlargement of beneficent influence.* "I will set up thy seed after thee," etc. He lives in his children; his words; his works; the manifold influences which he exerted on others, and which continue operating after his decease, and contribute to the building up of the temple and kingdom of God. His departure is even expedient and necessary in order to the activities of others; and, instead of becoming extinct, his power for good is thereby extended and exalted. His name "liveth for evermore" (Ecclus. xliv. 14). 6. *An object of profitable contemplation.* By meditating on it, especially in its moral and spiritual aspects, he learns to moderate earthly attachments, sanctify earthly relationships, to be humble in prosperity, patient in trial, and diligent in duty. "Thou must shortly die! O man, set thy house in order. There is a house of thy conscience, a house of thy body, a house of thy family, a house of eternity. All these must be set in order" (Christopher Sutton, 'Disce Mori'). Learn to die. Learn to live. Learn to pray.—D.

Vers. 12—16 (1 Chron. xvii. 11—15).—(JERUSALEM.) *The promise of an everlasting kingdom.*

> "And thy house and thy kingdom shall be permanent;
> Thy throne shall be established for ever."
>
> (Ver. 16.)

1. The position of David was a very exalted one. He was the chosen earthly head of the theocracy, or kingdom of God; and on him rested the hope of its glorious consummation. He was the Lord's messiah—"the mediator through whom Jehovah dispensed help, safety, and blessing" (Riehm). 2. But was the hope of Israel to be completely realized in him? And were his dynasty and kingdom to be permanent, or to pass away, like others? 3. To these questions the promise now given furnished an adequate answer. David would be succeeded in the theocratic throne by his posterity, and his dynasty and kingdom would endure for ever. 4. This promise, *the great charter*

of the house of David, was "the foundation of all Messianic prophecies and hopes in the prophets concerning the completion of the kingdom of God, its revelations of grace and its blessings of salvation" (Erdmann). It was—

I. AN EXPRESSION OF ABOUNDING GRACE. The free, condescending, unspeakable favour of God toward David, this it was which so deeply affected him (vers. 19—21). The good pleasure of the Lord had been shown in "the word of the Lord by Samuel," in David's exaltation to the throne after long suffering and trial (ver. 8), and in his subsequent prosperity (ver. 9); and it was further manifested in this great promise of *continued* grace to his house, "for a great while to come;" whereby his noblest aspirations would be fulfilled (ch. xxiii. 5), and through him and for his sake blessings would abound unto many. In like manner "the exceeding riches of his grace" are apparent in all the promises pertaining to eternal life and salvation, and the whole history of the progress of the kingdom of God from its commencement· to its consummation. "The progress of God's kingdom, or of true religion, should be the progress of David's line. This point constituted the Messianic element in the prophecy. It limited the hopes of the world's redemption to David's line, as Jacob's prophecy had long ago limited it to the tribe of Judah" (P. Thomson).

II. AN ASSURANCE OF EXTRAORDINARY GOOD. To the view of David the future was, by means of the promise, lighted up with glory. He beheld: 1. *The existence of the royal house*, of which he was the founder, made sure by the Divine oath. "Jehovah telleth thee that Jehovah will build thee a house" (ver. 11; Ps. cxxxii. 11; lxxxix. 3, 4). This was the general substance of the promise. "The royal office was elevated to the position of being the controlling and centralizing point of all the theocratic main elements of the national life." 2. *The elevation of his posterity*, and especially of one of his sons, to the royal dignity. "I will set up thy seed after thee" (ver. 12; 1 Chron. xvii. 11). "Behold, a son shall be born to thee . . . Solomon," etc. (1 Chron. xxii. 9; xxxviii. 10; 1 Kings v. 5; viii. 19). 3. *The establishment of the kingdom* in security, peace, and happiness, all enemies being subdued; "and I will establish his kingdom;" which was necessary to the fulfilment of David's purpose. 4. *The erection of the temple* and the dwelling of the Divine King in the midst of his people. "He shall build a house for my Name, and I will stablish the throne of his kingdom for ever" (ver. 13). "The building of the house here goes hand-in-hand with the eternity of the kingdom. . . . The essence of the temple consists in its being a symbol—an outward representation of the kingdom of God under Israel. The real import of our passage, then, is that henceforth the kingdom of David and the kingdom of God should be closely and inseparably linked together" (Hengstenberg, 'Christology'). "The idea of a number of descendants following one another (a line of kings) is evidently contained in the promise" (Keil); and in this sense David must have understood it. "The collective *he* (vers. 13, 14) includes in itself (like Gen. iii. 15) the Son of David in the highest sense and the Founder of the true temple of God, which is his Church." 5. *The relation of Father and son* subsisting between God and the theocratic king. "I will be to him a Father, and he shall be to me a son." Such was the relationship between Jehovah and Israel (Exod. iv. 22; Deut. xiv. 1; xxxii. 6; 1 Chron. xxix. 10; Isa. lxiv. 8; Jer. xxxi. 9; Hos. xi. 1), and it would be made specially manifest in the head and representative of the chosen people. A son (1) derives his being from his father, bears a close resemblance to him, stands near him, represents him, and shares his possessions; (2) is an object of his tender affection, under his protecting care, and subject to his merciful discipline; and (3) is bound to reciprocate his affection, to honour him, and obey his commandments. *The fatherly love of God* is here more particularly presented to view; and "whom the Lord loveth he chasteneth" (Heb. xii. 6). "If he commit iniquity, I will chasten him," etc. (ver. 14). 6. *The unchanging mercy of God*, founded on this relation. "But my mercy shall not depart away from him, as I took it from Saul," etc. (ver. 15). If, indeed, the individual king should forsake the Lord, he would be "cast off for ever" (1 Chron. xxviii. 9). "The contrast is that between the punishment of sin in individuals and the favour that remains permanently with the family, whereby the promise becomes an *unconditional* one" ('Christology'). The kingdom of God is a kingdom of righteousness. 7. *The eternal duration* of his dynasty and kingdom once more assured, with all the advantages of a government faithfully exercised according to the will of God. This was "the everlasting covenant, ordered in all things, and sure;" and these were the "sure mercies of David" (Isa. lv. 3). "This revelation was an epoch-making one for his inner life. It brought an entirely new element into his consciousness, which, as his psalms show, moved him powerfully. He received the promise of the perpetual ascendency of his tribe, of the establishment of his kingdom amid the changing of all earthly things" ('History of the Kingdom of God under the Old Testament'). "This promise, like that made to Abraham, has a twofold aspect. One points to David's natural posterity and temporal kingdom; the other to the Messiah and the kingdom of Jehovah, which respected the former only as types and pledges of the latter."

III. A FOUNDATION OF IMPERISHABLE HOPE. The promise was one of an eternal monarchy rather than directly of an eternal Monarch, "the King Messiah;" but it could only be completely fulfilled in such a Person, "since the eternity of a purely human kingdom is inconceivable;" and it became the basis of a hope of "his power and coming," which, notwithstanding repeated failure and disappointment, was to be renewed with undying strength. David was himself the centre of the Messianic *idea* and hope. "He regarded himself as the messiah of God; although, through his experience and words, he was only a means for representing the future One before his coming" (Delitzsch, 'Messianic Prophecies'). And, amidst the glorious prospect which the promise presented before him, he perceived (all the more clearly because of his own conscious infirmities) the ideal theocratic monarch; "a kingly image, in which all that the present manifests is far surpassed, and the kingship of David and Solomon seen in typical perfection" (Oehler, 'Theology of the Old Testament.' See ch. xxiii. 4; Ps. ii.; cx.; lxxii.; xlv.). The promise "refers neither only to Solomon nor only to Christ; nor has it a twofold application; but it is a covenant promise, which, extending along the whole line (of David's posterity), culminates in the Son of David, and in all its fulness applies only to him" (Edersheim). "Of the increase of his government and peace there shall be no end," etc. (Isa. ix. 6; Luke i. 32, 33; Acts ii. 25—36).

Observe that: 1. *Men's views of the glory of the future age* are naturally and necessarily formed according to the facts and ideas with which they are already familiar. 2. *The Word of God, in promise and prophecy* (being the gradual unfolding of his eternal purpose), had a larger signification than was understood by those to whom it at first came (1 Pet. i. 11). "Divine prophecies are of the nature of their Author, with whom a thousand years are but as one day; and therefore are not fulfilled punctually at once, but have a springing and germinant accomplishment throughout many ages, though the height or fulness of them may refer to one age" (Bacon, 'Advancement of Learning'). 3. *The promises of God* are faithful and true; his covenant is a sure foundation of hope amidst human failures and earthly changes (Ps. lxxxix. 1—37; 2 Cor. i. 20; Heb. vi. 18). 4. *The hope of humanity* is in "the Root and the Offspring of David, and the Bright and Morning Star!" (Rev. xxii. 16).—D.

Ver. 16.—*Glimpses of the King Messiah.* Looked at in the light of the development of the Divine purpose, rather than of the conscious knowledge of the time, (1) the royal office of David and Solomon (in its typical significance), and (2) the promises and prophecies uttered more or less directly in connection therewith, especially as recorded in the last words of David (ch. xxiii.) and in the Psalms, clearly pointed to the coming of an extraordinary, theocratic, Divine *King.* They indicate that he would be: 1. *The Anointed of Jehovah.* His Servant, chosen and beloved (ver. 8; ch. v. 3; Acts iv. 27; x. 28). Ps. lxxxix., 'The faithfulness of the Lord.'

> "Once thou spakest in vision to thy beloved and saidst:
> I have laid help upon a mighty one,
> I have exalted one chosen out of the people.
> I have found David my servant,
> With my holy oil have I anointed him."
>
> (Ps. lxxxix. 19, 20.)

2. *The Son of David* "according to the flesh" (ver. 12; Acts ii. 29—31; xiii. 22—23).

> "Jehovah hath sworn unto David
> In truth that which he will not recall:
> Of the fruit of thy body
> Do I appoint a possessor of thy throne."
>
> (Ps. cxxxii. 11.)

3. *The Son of God.* (Ver. 14; Ps. xvi. 10; Luke i. 35; Acts iv. 25—27; Rom. i. 4.) Ps. ii., 'The triumph of the Lord's Anointed.'

> " Jehovah saith unto me: Thou art my Son:
> I have this day begotten thee."
> (Ps. ii. 7.)

> " He shall cry unto me: My Father art thou,
> My God, and the Rock of my salvation!
> Also I will make him my Firstborn,
> Highest of the kings of the earth."
> (Ps. lxxxix. 26, 27.)

"In the Old Testament the relation between father and son denotes the deepest intimacy of love; and love is perfected in unity of nature, in the communication to the son of all that the father hath. 'The Father loveth the Son, and hath given all things into his hand' (John iii. 35). Sonship, therefore, includes the government of the world" (Keil). 4. *The King of righteousness and peace;* Prophet and Priest; the Conqueror of all opposing powers (through conflict and suffering); the Saviour and Benefactor of those who trust in him; the supreme Lord (ver. 13; Ps. xxii.; xl. 6; Matt. xxii. 45; Heb. i. 8).

> " The oracle of Jehovah unto my Lord:
> Sit thou at my right hand
> Until I make thine enemies thy footstool."
> (Ps. cx. 1.)

> " Thy throne, O God, is for ever and ever;
> A sceptre of uprightness is the sceptre of thy kingdom."
> (Ps. xlv. 6.)

5. *The Builder of the temple.* (Ver. 13; Zech. vi. 12, 13; John i. 14; ii. 19; xiv. 23; 1 Cor. vi. 19; Eph. i. 20—23; ii. 20—22; 1 Pet. ii. 5; Rev. xxi. 1—3.)

> " Thou hast received gifts among men,
> Yea, even the rebellious, that the Lord Jehovah might dwell among them."
> (Ps. lxviii. 18.)

6. *The Possessor of universal dominion.* (1 Sam. ii. 10; ch. xxii. 44; Ps. xxii. 27.)

> " He shall have dominion from sea to sea,
> And from the river to the ends of the earth."
> (Ps. lxxii. 8.)

7. *The King who should reign for ever.* (Ver. 16; Ps. lxi. 6, 7; lxxxix. 36, 37.)

> " His Name shall endure for ever;
> His Name shall be continued as long as the sun."
> (Ps. lxxii. 17.)

" An allegory may serve to illustrate the way in which the Old Testament proclamation of salvation unfolds itself. The Old Testament in relation to the day of the New Testament is night. In this night there rise in opposite directions two stars of promise. The one describes its fall from above downwards; it is the promise of Jehovah who is about to come [Ps. xcvi. 13; xcviii. 9]. The other describes its path from below upwards; it is the hope which rests on the seed of David, the prophecy of the Son of David, which at the outset assumes a thoroughly human and merely earthly character. These two stars meet at last, they blend together in one star; the night vanishes, and it is day. This one star is Jesus Christ, Jehovah and the Son of David in one Person; the King of Israel and at the same time the Redeemer of the world; in one word, the God-Man" (Delitzsch, in Ps. lxxii.).—D.

Vers. 18—24 (1 Chron. xvii. 16—22).—(THE TABERNACLE ON ZION.) *Thanksgiving and praise.* The duty of rendering thanksgiving and praise to God is seldom disputed, though its performance is often neglected. It is beneficial to the offerer himself, as well as to others. The conduct and language of David, on receiving the

Divine communication here recorded, furnish an admirable example of the *spirit* in which " the sacrifice of thanksgiving " should be presented.

I. DEEP HUMILITY before the presence of God. "Then went King David in" from his palace of cedar to the lowly tent (the palace of the Divine King of Israel), "and sat" on the ground in a lowly posture, according to Eastern custom (expressive of his lowly state of mind), "before Jehovah," the symbol of whose presence stood veiled before him. "And (after devout thought on the communication) he said, Who am I, O Lord God ? " etc. (ver. 18). Although in comparison with other men he "might have whereof to glory," yet in the conscious presence of God he had a profound sense of his weakness, insignificance, dependence, and unworthiness (Gen. xxxii. 10; Job xlii. 5, 6; Isa. lvii. 15; Eph. iii. 8; 1 Pet. v. 5, 6). The proud heart is never a thankful heart. The poorer we are in our own estimation the more disposed we are to "praise the Lord for his goodness." Humility is the first step of a ladder whose top reaches heaven (Matt. v. 3).

II. CALM REFLECTION on his benefits. "And this was yet a small thing in thy sight, O Lord God," etc. "And this [which thou hast graciously promised concerning my house] is the law [established order or decree] of [or pertaining to a mortal] man, O Lord God ! " (ver. 19). "Is this the law of one who is a mere man created from the dust as I am, that I should be elevated to such a glorious altitude as this ?" (Words-worth). "Thou hast regarded me according to the estate of a man of high degree" (1 Chron. xvii. 17). An expression of humble astonishment. The more he pondered it in his heart, the more he was humbled, surprised, and filled with thankfulness. We have not less cause for gratitude (Ps. viii. 4, 5; 1 Cor. ii. 9, 10). "Forget not all his benefits," past, present, or to come. We are apt to forget them, and therefore should contemplate them frequently, enumerate them one by one, and endeavour to estimate their exceeding worth. Meditation is like a lens, by which the rays of the sun are collected into a focus and produce so intense a heat that coals of fire are kindled by it (Ps. xxxix. 3; xlviii. 9; lxxvii. 11, 12; Luke ii. 19).

III. INTENSE CONVICTION of his claims. "And what can David say more unto thee ? for thou knowest thy servant, O Lord God !" (ver. 20). The great things which had been promised, the obligations under which they laid him, and his conviction and impression thereof, were all indescribable. Words failed him; and he could only appeal to Omniscience to witness the sincerity and depth of his grateful feeling (John xxi. 17). Every additional benefit conferred upon us increases the claims of our Divine Bene-factor on our love and devotion. His mercies are "new every morning" (Lam. iii. 23); and the debt we owe is ever accumulating.

> "How can I repay to Jehovah
> All his benefits toward me ?"
>
>   (Ps. cxvi. 12.)

IV. FERVENT GRATITUDE for his grace. "For thy Word's sake ;" in fulfilment of thy purpose and promise formerly expressed, "and according to thine own heart," of thy spontaneous, sovereign, unmerited favour, "hast thou done all these great things to make thy servant know them," for his consolation and encouragement (ver. 21). It is the disinterested love and abounding grace of God, displayed in his gifts, that more than anything else touches the heart and constrains it to fervent gratitude. "To my eye the workings of a heart oppressed and overflowing with gratitude are painted stronger in this prayer than I ever observed them in any other instance. It is easy to see that his heart was wholly possessed with a subject which he did not know how to quit, because he did not know how to do justice to the inestimable blessings poured down upon himself and promised to his posterity; much less to the infinite bounty of his Benefactor" (Delany).

V. LOWLY ADORATION of his perfections. "Wherefore thou art great, O Lord God," etc. (ver. 22). The greatness of Jehovah, the incomparable One, the only God, was manifested in his dealings with his servant, as in the whole history of Israel, "according to all that we have heard with our ears." David had the most exalted views of his character as the All-wise and All-powerful, the Condescending, Faithful, Gracious, Merciful, and Just (1 Sam. ii. 2 ; Ps. cxiii. 6); and he delighted in the contemplation and praise of his infinite excellence. God himself is greater than anything he has done or promised to do; but by means of his doings and revelations we are enabled to know him and draw nigh to him in worship and adoration, wherein the soul finds its noblest activity, rest, and joy.

VI. GENEROUS SYMPATHY with his people. "And what one nation in the earth is like thy people," etc. (vers. 23, 24)? An incomparable people! 1. Redeemed by mighty acts. 2. Designed for a special purpose—to be his possession or property, and to "show forth his praise." 3. Established in covenant relationship for ever (ver. 16; Rev. xxi. 3, 7). David "glorified God" in them; and in doing so he showed his love for them, his sympathy and identity with them (ch. v. 12). His thanksgiving and praise were large-hearted and disinterested. The selfish heart (like the proud heart) is never a thankful heart. The more we esteem others the more numerous the occasions we find for gratitude to God, and the more we abound therein.

VII. ENTIRE CONSECRATION to his service and glory. He avowed himself the servan of God (ver. 21), freely and gladly surrendered his will to him, sought what he promised, and desired that his Name might be "magnified for ever" (ver. 26). This is the essence of the sacrifice of praise. "Father, glorify thy Name" (John xii. 28; Phil. i. 20).

> " As of their will, the angels unto thee
> Tender meet sacrifice, circling thy throne
> With loud hosannas ; so of theirs be done
> By saintly men on earth."
>
> (Dante, ' Purg.,' xi.)
>
> D.

Vers. 25—29 (1 Chron. xvii. 23—27).—(ZION.) *Promise and prayer.* "Do as thou hast said" (ver. 25). 1. God has *spoken* to men. "His greatness is unsearchable" (ver. 22; Ps. cxlv. 3); nevertheless, he has surely spoken to them in his Word (ver. 4; Heb. i. 1). 2. He has spoken in the way of *promise* (ver. 28). A large portion of Divine revelation consists of promises, "exceeding great and precious" (2 Pet. i. 4), pertaining to the life that now is, and that which is to come. 3. And as God has spoken to men in the way of promise, so they should speak to him in the way of *prayer* (1 Sam. i. 9; viii. 6; xiv. 16, 36).

> " A breath that fleets beyond this iron world,
> And touches him who made it."
>
> (Tennyson.)

I. PROMISE SUPERSEDES NOT THE NECESSITY OF PRAYER; inasmuch as the latter is commonly the expressed or implied condition of its fulfilment. As a bank-note must be presented that we may obtain the gold which it represents, so the Divine promise must be sought in prayer that we may receive the good of which it gives assurance. A child does not refrain from asking his father for what he wants because it has been promised, but rather asks him all the more. David prayed for what he had been promised. "I will yet for this be inquired of," etc. (Ezek. xxxvi. 37). "Ask, and it shall be given you" (Matt. vii. 7; Ps. l. 15; Zech. x. 1). "The prayer that prevails is a reflected promise."

II. PROMISE CONFIRMS THE DUTY OF PRAYER; by indicating the will of God concerning us. To neglect the condition of receiving the blessing, or to refuse to comply with it, is to despise the blessing itself. Why such a condition? 1. To give to God the honour which is his due. 2. To teach a spirit of dependence. 3. To promote personal and direct intercourse with God. 4. To call into exercise the noblest principles of our nature. 5. To incite co-operation towards the attainment of what is promised. 6. To make its bestowment more beneficial to the recipient. Some things may be beneficial in connection with prayer that would not be so without it.

III. PROMISE AUTHORIZES THE PRIVILEGE OF PRAYER. What greater privilege can there be than that of "making known our requests unto God"? But who, without his promise, could venture to believe that these requests would be heard; especially when made for the "great things" contained in it? Even now, how doubtful and timid are we in claiming the privilege! The promise gives encouragement and confidence; and should, therefore, be pondered in the heart, as it was by David; who was thereby emboldened (Authorized Version, " found in his heart ") " to pray this prayer " (ver. 27). " Thy words are truth " (ver. 28). " When thou saidst, Seek ye my face; my heart said unto thee, Thy face, O Lord, will I seek " (Ps. xxvii. 8; cxix. 49; Gen. xxxii. 12).

IV. PROMISE TEACHES THE MATTER OF PRAYER. " We know not *what* we should pray for as we ought," and are apt, in this respect, to " ask amiss." But the promises constitute an invaluable " directory of prayer," teaching us: 1. The things for which we ought to ask, both temporal and spiritual. 2. Their relative importance. 3. Their application to others as well as to ourselves (vers. 25, 29). 4. Their chief design (ver. 26). " If ye abide in me, and my words abide in you," etc. (John xv. 7; Rev. xxii. 20). " Pause over each promise, and let your faith in it blossom into a prayer for it. This will be the true, responsive reading of the sacred Scriptures, wherein there shall be not simply the answering of voice to voice as among men, but the responding of your heart to God. Happy are they in whose souls there is thus a continual recurring 'Amen' to the benedictions of the Lord " (W. M. Taylor).

V. PROMISE INCITES THE SPIRIT OF PRAYER. 1. A reverent regard for God. 2. A lowly estimate of ourselves. 3. Fervent desire for the blessing of God. 4. Childlike confidence in his Word. 5. Unreserved submission to his will. 6. Patience and perseverance. " Wait on the Lord," etc. (Ps. xxvii. 14; Luke xi. 1—13; xviii. 1). " Prayer is nothing else but the language of faith, love, and hope: of *faith*, a believing of God's being and bounty, that he is willing and able to succour us; of *love*, which directeth us to the prime Fountain of all the good we have and would have, and to the end and glory of God, and regulateth all our choices by it, and to those means which conduce to the enjoying of God; and of *hope*, which is a desirous expectation of the promised blessing " (T. Manton, 'Works,' xviii. 72).

VI. PROMISE ENSURES THE ANSWER OF PRAYER; not always in the immediate and conscious experience of the petitioner, but always at the proper time (Dan. x. 12), the delay being needful and beneficial; not always in the literal terms of the promise, but often in a more spiritual and glorious manner; and never wholly withheld (1 John v. 14, 15). " He is faithful that promised " (Heb. x. 23). " The promises of God are the free expressions of his goodness and beneficence; but then their *meaning* has in it something of that Divine attribute. Nothing that he says can be in the mere narrow proportions of man. The words are necessarily those used by man, but the meaning is that of God; and we may be confident that what will be given in fulfilment of them will be according to the magnitude of the Divine goodness; as far, at least, as the faculties of the recipients will admit, and *these* can be enlarged. The Divine goodness being transcendently above all other goodness, the gifts of it will be according to its own manner, and not limited to the human import of the words, as if merely preserving the bare truth of the words. So that he will surprise his servants, as they find the earthly terms of his promises translated as it were into celestial language, when they arrive in his presence and have those promises acknowledged " (John Foster, 'Literary Remains').—D.

Ver. 27.—(ZION.) *A prayer found in the heart.* When a prayer such as David's is found in the heart, it is: 1. *Found in the right place.* If only on the tongue it is not really found at all. Its proper abode is the heart; yet it is not always found there, even when renewed, as the heart must be for its dwelling. 2. *Possessed of priceless worth;* in contrast with other things that are often found in the heart (Matt. xv. 19). A rare flower among weeds, a fountain in the desert, a treasure in poverty, a friend in need! " I have no earthly friend," said one; " but I have a praying heart." 3. *Derived from a Divine source.* It is not indigenous. Its origin is in " the Father of lights," from whom comes " every good gift and every perfect boon; " its production is due to the teaching of his Word and the operation of his Spirit (Zech. xii. 10). 4. *Designed for a proper use.* Not to be neglected, repressed, or restrained (Job xv. 4); but appreciated, guarded, cherished, freely and fully " poured out " at the feet of the Giver, that he may be glorified.—D.

Vers. 1, 2.—*David's desire to build a temple.* After the conquest of Jebus by David and his appointment of the spot to be the capital of the united kingdom of which he was now the ruler, it soon became his earnest purpose to bring thither the long-neglected ark of the covenant, that the city might be the sacred as well as the civil metropolis. This purpose was at length fulfilled. The ark was settled on Zion in a tent prepared for it, and a daily service established in connection with it. But the king was not long satisfied with what he had done. Larger and more generous thoughts took possession of his mind, and stirred within him eager desire.

1. WHAT WAS THE KING'S DESIRE? To erect a solid, permanent building, of suitable magnificence—a temple—in which the ark should be placed, and where the services of worship should be constantly maintained. Most likely he contemplated what was afterwards effected, the reunion on one spot of the ark and the altars; and the presentation of the daily and other sacrifices and offerings at their proper place before the symbol of the Divine presence—the revival, in fact, of the Mosaic ritual under circumstances and with accompaniments adapted to the existing condition of the nation. The purpose was good and tended to good. It was time that the irregularity and negligence which had prevailed should come to an end, and the requirements of the Law should be obeyed. It was fitting that the unity of the people should be fully symbolized, expressed, and promoted by such a united worship as the Law enjoined. It was also suitable to the more settled state which, under David, the people had reached, that a solid fixed building should supersede the tent which was adapted to the time of wandering and unsettlement; and, as the nation's resources had increased, it was right that the building to be reared should be proportionately costly.

II. HOW IT ORIGINATED. 1. *A time of peace favoured it.* (Ver. 1.) Giving the king leisure for thought as to how he could further promote the nation's welfare; awakening gratitude; affording means and opportunity. Times of war are greatly unfavourable to such enterprises, forcing minds and hearts into other channels, and swallowing up the resources which might otherwise be expended on them. 2. *The solidity, beauty, and comforts of David's own house suggested it.* "I dwell in a house of cedar, but the ark of God dwelleth within curtains." David had known for years what it was to have no settled abode, but to wander about the land, taking refuge in woods and caves; and afterwards he was much away from home, engaged in wars. Lately he had built himself a handsome palace, and now for a time he was able to sit quietly in it and meditate; and as he did so, it one day struck him that his abode was superior to that of the ark of God, and the desire was kindled to put an end to the incongruity. Not every one would have been thus moved. How differently the rich man of whom our Lord speaks in Luke xii. 16, *et seq.*, "thought within himself"! And how many prosperous people there are, professing to have given themselves to God, who, as they increase in wealth and enjoy comfort and luxury, never turn a thought towards God's house or cause, or inquire what they can do for them! They reflect much, it may be, on the question how best to invest their increasing gains; but it never seems to occur to them that the most suitable and profitable investment might be in the cause of religion or charity. A more fervent piety would suggest such thoughts. Gratitude for the abundance bestowed on them; the contrast presented (see Hag. i. 4) between their residences and their churches, between what they spend on their establishments and what they spend in the promotion of the kingdom of God; the witness which their mansions and surroundings bear to the ample means with which God has endowed them—the large trust he has committed to them;—all would be fruitful of thoughts and emotions to which they are now strangers, and of a style of giving which they have never allowed themselves. It was David's piety more than the surrounding circumstances that originated his generous purpose.

III. HOW IT WAS TESTED. As to its propriety and probable acceptance with God. He consulted his friend and adviser, Nathan the prophet. The more important the steps we contemplate, the more needful is it, before we are openly and irrevocably committed to them, that we should ascertain how they appear to others, especially to the wisest and best whom we know. Feeling is not a sufficient guide, not even pious feeling; and our own judgment may not be of the soundest. Another may put the matter in a new light, which shall convince ourselves that, however good our motives, our purpose is not wise or not practicable. We cannot directly consult a prophet, but we may find good and enlightened and trustworthy men who will be glad to aid us to a right conclusion. And what joy it gives to Christian ministers to be consulted by such as come saying, "God has prospered me, I have done well for myself and my family, and I should like to do something proportionate for my God and Saviour: advise me as to how I may best fulfil my desire"! Such applicants are few and far between; such a style of thought and purpose is rare. But it ought not to be. It is a sin and shame that God's work should be hindered for want of money in a thriving community which can spend freely in all other directions.

IV. How IT WAS REGARDED BY NATHAN. He approved and encouraged the desire, assuring David of the Divine approval and co-operation (ver. 3). He spoke on the impulse of the moment, with the feeling natural to a pious Israelite and prophet, thankful that his king should cherish such a design. He did well, but had he paused and proposed to "sleep upon" the matter, he would have done better, as appeared next day. We should ever be ready to encourage others in good thoughts and purposes, yet in important matters it is well to take time to consider before we advise as to definite proposals.

V. How IT WAS REGARDED BY GOD. The proposal was approved, commended, rewarded, and—rejected. The refusal was softened by the terms in which it was conveyed, and the representations and promises by which it was accompanied (vers. 4—17; 2 Chron. vi. 8); declaring that it was well that it was in his heart to build a house for God's Name, although it was a matter of indifference to the Most High what sort of dwelling-places men provided for him; reminding David of what he had done for him; assuring him that he would continue to favour the nation, that he would build a house for him as he had sought to build one for himself, and that his son should fulfil the father's desire, and the throne should continue in his family for ever. This was the greatest promise David had received, greater than he himself could then understand, for it looked forward to the everlasting kingdom of his Son Jesus Christ our Lord. But though his knowledge of its purport was imperfect, his pain at the rejection of his proposal was more than soothed; his heart was filled with adoring gratitude and joy.

VI. How ITS SINCERITY WAS PROVED. If he might not do all he desired, he would do all he might and could. He, therefore, prepared plans for the building, accumulated materials for its erection, and urged the work on his son Solomon and the chief men of the nation. An example for us if, setting our hearts on some particular work for God, our purpose is frustrated. Let the diverted energies be employed all the more in such services as are within our reach. A contrast to the conduct of many who, disappointed in reference to some cherished desire (e.g. to become clergymen or missionaries), allow their zeal to decline to the common level, if it do not pass away altogether.

In conclusion: 1. *Christian piety will kindle earnest desires to do the greatest possible work for God.* Such desires should be cherished in subordination to the Divine will. For though approved of God, they may be denied (Prov. x. 24 notwithstanding). If denied, we should be content, assured of the perfect wisdom and goodness of the purpose of God which has frustrated ours, and that for us and others he has some better thing in store than we had thought of. Though denied, our desire may be fulfilled (as David's by Solomon). Whether denied or gratified, good desires (such as are really good, and not mere idle wishes) are always valuable, for what they indicate in ourselves, for the Divine approval they elicit, for their influence on ourselves, and their influence on others (as David's on his successor and on the chiefs of the nation). 2. *The desire to build or aid in building a house for the worship of God is good.* 3. *We may all assist in the erection and adornment of a nobler temple than that which David sought to build.* "The house of God is the Church of the living God" (1 Tim. iii. 15), and all who labour for the conversion and spiritual improvement of men are helping in the glorious work of building and adorning this spiritual house. Let all Christian workers realize the dignity and glory of their work. Let us all ask ourselves whether we have any heart for it, are doing anything towards it; whether we are capable of doing anything in it that shall be acceptable to God, having first given our own selves to him, and received his Spirit.—G. W.

Vers. 12—16.—*David's everlasting kingdom.* These words relate, first, to Solomon; then to successive generations of David's posterity; and, finally, to the Christ. They promise that David's son should be God's son, and should build the house for God which David had desired to build. They promise also that the rule over Israel should continue in the line of David's posterity, and that his house and kingdom should be established for ever. They were partly fulfilled in the long continuance of the reign of David's descendants. They receive their most ample and splendid fulfilment in the eternal kingdom of the greatest Son of David, our Lord and Saviour—a fulfilment beyond all that David could ask or think.

I. THE GREAT KING. 1. *Is David's son.* He is much more than this; but he *is* this. *A man* is at the head of God's kingdom! 2. *Is God's Son.* (Ver. 14; comp. Heb. i. 5 and Rom. i. 3, 4.) Both as to his human and his Divine natures, Jesus Christ is the Son of God as none other—"the only begotten Son of God." This shows his greatness, and accounts for his triumphs. The Eternal and Almighty Father recognizes and proclaims him as his Son; declares by the miracles accompanying the personal mission of Jesus, by his Word, Spirit, providence, through the ages, "This is my beloved Son, in whom I am well pleased: hear ye him." 3. *And this illustrious person is King.* King over God's people, his true Israel; King of men; "King of kings, Lord of lords;" King of angels, King over all things in heaven and earth. The kingdom of David has expanded till it extends over the universe.

II. THE PERPETUITY OF HIS REIGN. It shall be literally eternal. "He shall reign for ever and ever" (Rev. xi. 15). It is surely more than a coincidence that a system of dominion over men, originating in a Man who had sprung from the reduced family of David, and was accepted by many of his fellow-Jews as the Son of David, the Messiah foretold by the prophets—a system proclaimed at the first as the kingdom of God—should have taken root in the world, have spread so widely and lasted so long; that it should have proved to be the system in and through which especially the best influences of Heaven operate, and the divinest principles rule the hearts and lives of those who receive it; and that it should to-day be more extensively prevalent than ever, and *that* amongst the most enlightened and powerful nations (to whose enlightenment and power it has so largely contributed), and giving promise of becoming the ruling power everywhere. It is a veritable kingdom, uniting all who belong to it as one "holy nation" which acknowledges Jesus of Nazareth as its King, and submits to his rule. It has continued nearly nineteen centuries, and gives no sign of decay. In all this the Christian recognizes the fulfilment of the promise made to David and repeated so frequently afterwards by the prophets; and through his faith in that promise he anticipates the everlasting duration of the reign of Christ, the eternity of the King, and the eternity of his reign. We are sure that he must reign for ever; and our assurance rests on: 1. *The promises of God.* The "God who cannot lie," and who has power to fulfil all his Word, and subdue all that opposes. 2. *The nature of the kingdom.* "A kingdom which cannot be moved" (Heb. xii. 28). It is spiritual, and cannot be put down by the material forces which destroy other reigns. It is the reign of Divine truth, righteousness, and love; and we cannot doubt but that these will triumph and be perpetuated. 3. *The nature of the King.* "The First, and the Last, and the Living One," who, though he "was dead," is "alive for evermore" (Rev. i. 17, 18, Revised Version). This King literally "lives for ever." He is Divine as well as human. His reign is the reign of the Almighty God, which cannot be destroyed. 4. *Past experience.* The kingdom of Jesus Christ has survived in spite of all opposition. All possible hostile powers have done their utmost, and have failed. Christianity has outlived many kingdoms, which to human appearance promised to survive it. It has been assailed by brute force in a variety of forms, and by the forces of intellectual subtlety, of political power, and of spiritual error, and it has conquered. It has seemed to be seriously endangered by the folly and wickedness of its professed friends, but still it survives and flourishes. In a word, the prince of this world has used all arts and energies at his command to crush the power of Christ, but in vain. "He that sitteth in the heavens laughs" at all that opposes his Son, saying, "Yet have I set my King on my holy hill of Zion" (Ps. ii. 4, 6). And in the everlasting future this kingdom will continue. A great change is, indeed, predicted in 1 Cor. xv. 24. But as the kingdom of the Son is the kingdom of the Father, so the kingdom of the Father will still be that of the Son. Let, then, all the loyal subjects of Christ cast away fear for his kingdom, whatever forms opposition to it may take, and however formidable they may appear. And let all be concerned to *be* his loyal subjects.

III. THE GREAT WORK HE WOULD EFFECT. "He shall build a house for my Name" (ver. 13). The words may be taken as applicable not only to the temple which Solomon built, but to the nobler structure which our Lord is rearing, of which he is the chief Corner-stone (1 Pet. ii. 4—6)—"the temple of the living God" (2 Cor. vi. 16), built of "living stones" quickened and consecrated by the Holy Spirit—"the habitation of God through the Spirit" (Eph. ii. 20—22). From age to age the work of erecting this spiritual temple goes on in the conversion of men to Christ, and their addition to his Church; and, when completed, the building will be for the everlasting honour of the Builder. May we all have a place in it!—G. W.

Ver. 18.—*Meditation before the Lord.* David, with a heart filled with wonder and gratitude by the message from heaven communicated to him by Nathan, "went in and sat before the Lord," and poured forth his thoughts and feelings in the words which follow. He probably went into the tent in which he had placed the ark, and there meditated and prayed. But the phrase, "before the Lord," is very frequently employed without any reference to the ark, the tabernacle, or the temple. God is everywhere, and everywhere we may place ourselves as in his special presence, and with acceptance and profit offer him our thoughts and worship; and we do well often to imitate David in this respect.

I. The conditions favourable, and indeed essential, to right thought and worship which are found in the felt presence of God. 1. *The exclusion of the world and its influences.* "Before the Lord," the world, with its gains, pleasures, opinions, applause, or disapproval, vanishes from view, or appears as nothing; and thus we are delivered from its blinding and perverting influence. 2. *Intense consciousness of God.* He is for the time our *All.* His character, works, relation to us, dealings with us, claims upon us, judgment respecting us, stand forth glorious and impressive. 3. *Intense consciousness of ourselves, our real nature, relationships, responsibilities to God and man.* In the light of the Divine presence these things appear quite otherwise than when we regard only the material and the human. 4. *Greater susceptibility to Divine influences, and receptivity of Divine gifts.* Our hearts are prepared to receive more of the Holy Spirit; and we do receive more.

II. The spiritual profit thus secured. 1. *Fuller and truer knowledge.* "In thy light shall we see light" (Ps. xxxvi. 9), which includes knowledge and much besides. "Until I went into the sanctuary of God; then understood I their end" (Ps. lxxiii. 17). In the presence of God we obtain deeper insight into his nature and character, understand better his plans and methods. Our thoughts of him are enlarged and quickened. And in knowing him we come to know ourselves; his greatness reveals our littleness; his holiness, our sinfulness; and his fatherly love and redeeming grace, the true worth and dignity of our souls. Coming to him, as the disciples to Christ, to tell him what we have been doing and teaching, the poverty and imperfections of our lives become manifest to us. In his presence, too, we learn the relative values of holiness and sin, time and eternity, this world and the next. 2. *Richer and deeper emotions and affections.* Penitence and humility, gratitude and love, confidence and hope, peace and joy, are all nourished best in the presence of God. Coming to him to confess our sins and failures, we shall, as we look into his face, be inspired with new and more hopeful resolve. Bringing our cares and fears to him, as Hezekiah the letter of Sennacherib (Isa. xxxvii. 14), we shall be relieved of them, and gain new courage and patience. 3. *Ever-better worship.* Which will naturally spring from an enriched and spiritual life. Worship which is not offered "before the Lord" is not worship at all; and the more his presence is felt the worthier will our worship be. 4. *Ever-growing power to live according to our convictions and resolutions.* "Before the Lord," his children grow brave and strong to do and endure. His eye felt to be upon them, they act nobly; his love realized by them, their hearts are filled with a love mighty to serve him and their brethren, and to conquer the evil powers. Finally: *The measure of our disposition to go before God for converse with him, instruction, stimulus, consolation, etc., is the measure of our actual piety.* We lose much of the highest happiness and profit through negligence in this respect. All that occupies our minds and moves our hearts becomes sanctified and elevated as we go aside and bring it "before the Lord." On the other hand, the greatest attention to religious observances which are not, through faith and love, done in the presence of God, is worthless, dishonouring to God, and useless, yea, worse than useless, to the worshipper.—G. W.

Vers. 18, 19.—*Effects of God's goodness on the heart.* (Suitable for a birthday or the new year.) David, having retired into the presence of God, pours out before him the feelings of his heart, in view of what God had done for him, and what he had just promised to do.

I. THE MERCIES CONTEMPLATED. 1. *Past leading.* "Thou hast brought me hitherto." How much this included in David's case! How much in the case of every one of us! Each should recall in God's presence the particulars of his own life. Life itself, reason, health, preservation, supply of wants, home surroundings and comforts, the love of parents, etc., education, advancement in life, deliverances from perils and sicknesses, honours, the advantages of living in a country civilized, free, Christian; the Word and ordinances of God, connection with his Church and ministers, and all that has flowed therefrom—the life of God in the soul, pardon, peace, hope, the Spirit of adoption, love to God and men, access to God, the communion of saints, growth in grace, victory over temptations, opportunity and will to do good, success in Christian labours, support in troubles and benefit from them. Also the blessings of one's "house"—wife, children, good children especially, and their happiness. It is an endless task to remember and recount all the mercies of God; but the attempt is always salutary. 2. *Promises as to the future.* "This was yet a small thing in thy sight, but thou hast spoken also of thy servant's house for a great while to come." Astonished and grateful as David was in view of his past experience of God's goodness, the promises he had now received respecting the perpetuation of his kingdom into the distant future still more affected him. We also have "given unto us exceeding great and precious promises," stretching onward into the eternal future. The kindness of God in the past is but "a small thing." Even his spiritual gifts, great as they are, and the necessary preparation for the eternal, are but a slight foretaste and pledge of the exaltation, perfection, glory, and bliss which he will bestow upon his children in increasing abundance for ever and ever.

II. THEIR GIVER. The contemplation of our history and prospects will have a beneficial or injurious effect as we do or do not recognize God as the Giver of all. Some men regard themselves as the architects of their own fortunes, and are correspondingly filled with self-satisfaction. David ascribed all to God; and we ought to be like him in this. For if we have done much for ourselves, the power, opportunity, and will to do so came from him; if friends have greatly aided us, these also were God's gifts. In spiritual things it is especially obvious that "by the grace of God" we are what we are.

III. THEIR RECEIVER. "Who am I," etc.? The thought of David's insignificance and that of his family rendered the Divine goodness to him more conspicuous and impressive. So we shall more duly estimate the goodness of God to us, if we think rightly of ourselves; and a due impression of the greatness of his goodness will lead us to a just estimate of ourselves. At every step of our review of the past and anticipation of the future shall we be reminded of the many exhibitions of our own unworthiness. "Who am I?"—a frail and insignificant creature, a sinner, a great and persistent sinner; at best, a very imperfect Christian; proved to be such by innumerable instances—that I should be so favoured now, and should have such hopes of everlasting blessing set before me?

IV. THE EMOTIONS AWAKENED BY THEM. 1. *Astonishment.* At the Divine goodness, sovereign, free, unbounded, condescending. At the return made, which would appear incredible were it not for the sure testimony of memory and consciousness. 2. *Gratitude and love.* Expressed in praise and self-consecration (Rom. xii. 1). 3. *Humility.* The mercies of God revealing the more our unworthiness. The perception of his hand in our lives making our own part in the good they have contained seem insignificant. "Not unto us," etc. (Ps. cxv. 1). "Who maketh thee to differ from another? and what hast thou that thou didst not receive?" (1 Cor. iv. 7). 4. *Benevolence.* His loving-kindness producing loving-kindness in our hearts, as we contemplate it; and prompting to a return of benefits, which, as they cannot be conferred on God himself, we bestow on his representatives. "Be imitators of God, as beloved children; and walk in love" (Eph. v. 1, 2, Revised Version). "Beloved, if God so loved us, we ought also to love one another" (1 John iv. 11).—G. W.

Ver. 20.—*Unutterable thoughts and feelings known to God.* God's knowledge of the heart, which is a terror to evil men who think upon it, is often a joy to his servants.

"Lord, thou knowest all things; thou knowest that I love thee" (John xxi. 17). So David, with his heart too full for adequate utterance, finds satisfaction in the thought that God knew what his thoughts and feelings were.

I. THE FELT INADEQUACY OF LANGUAGE TO EXPRESS THE DEEPEST THOUGHTS AND FEELINGS OF THE GODLY SOUL. In our ordinary condition we feel not this difficulty. Our expressions are more likely to go beyond our thoughts and feelings, especially when we use forms of devotion prepared by others. But when the soul is deeply stirred, as David's at this time, we struggle in vain to express fully what is within. It is thus with 1. *Our sense of the value of God's gifts.* Christ, God's "unspeakable Gift" (2 Cor. ix. 15). Salvation. Everlasting life. Gifts of God associated with these which are from time to time bestowed—special help in temptation, comfort in trouble, guidance in perplexities as to truth or duty, etc. 2. *Our sense of the love which bestows them.* We can only say, "How great is thy goodness!" "How excellent is thy loving-kindness!" "God *so* loved the world;" "The love of Christ, which passeth knowledge" (Ps. xxxi. 19; xxxvi. 7; John iii. 16; Eph. iii. 19). Or, as David (ver. 22), "Thou art great, O Lord God; for there is none like unto thee." 3. *The emotions excited by them.* Our gratitude, affection, penitence, humility, confidence, joy ("unspeakable," 1 Pet. i. 8), longing for fuller experience of them ("groanings which cannot be uttered," Rom. viii. 26), anticipations of their perfect enjoyment (2 Cor. v. 2—4). In our times of intense devotion we feel how utterly impossible it is fully to express what is in our hearts.

II. THE SATISFACTION WHICH ARISES FROM GOD'S PERFECT KNOWLEDGE OF US. "What can David say more unto thee?" I cannot express what I feel; and I need not labour to do so, "For thou, Lord God, knowest thy servant." It is the same thought which St. Paul expresses, when, speaking of the unutterable groanings with which the Holy Spirit intercedes in the Christian soul, he says, "He that searcheth the heart knoweth what is the mind of the Spirit" (Rom. viii. 27). God knows much more about us than our words express; is not dependent for his knowledge of us on our own account of ourselves. As we cannot by any words conceal from him the evil which is in us, so our deficiencies of expression will not hinder his discernment of the good. Even earthly parents see the meaning which their children try to express in stammering words and broken sentences; how much more does the heavenly Father, who is not at all dependent for his knowledge of us on our words, see beyond the poor utterances of his children, into their hearts! This is (1) a comfort under the consciousness of imperfect and unworthy utterance in our addresses to God; and (2) a reason for not labouring too much to express ourselves fully and worthily. But it is not a reason for either (1) declining to speak to God at all,—David did not actually sink into silence because he felt that he could not adequately express himself, and that God knew him (see what follows); or (2) accustoming ourselves to careless expression before him. Since (1) the endeavour to speak aright aids right thought and feeling, these grow in the endeavour to utter them; (2) in family and social worship our language aids or hinders others; and (3) we should ever offer to God our best, poor as we may feel it to be. And we may indefinitely improve both in thought and expression by the careful employment of the helps presented in Holy Scripture and uninspired devotional books. Christian poets, too, may much assist us to find suitable, though it may be still inadequate, utterance for our deepest thoughts and emotions.

Finally: 1. *David's emotions on this occasion are at once an example and a reproach to us.* For the gifts and promises of God to us, if not greater than those to him, are greater than his understanding of them could be. They stand out to us in the light which streams from Jesus Christ, unfolding into all the precious revelations and assurances of the gospel, and all the happy experiences which the Holy Spirit produces. Yet how seldom are we so affected as to feel language too poor for the expression of the wonder, love, and gratitude which we feel! 2. *How sad to be utterly insensible to the goodness of God and the greatness of his gifts to us!*—G. W.

Ver. 21.—*God's works and God's heart and words.* David looks on those great things which God had promised him as if already accomplished, so great confidence had he in the power and faithfulness of the Promiser; and, conscious that they were due to no worthiness or power of his own, he acknowledges that all originated in the heart of God and were simply in fulfilment of his word, by which they had become known to himself. For the will and the work and the word he praises God.

I. GOD DOES GREAT THINGS ON BEHALF OF HIS PEOPLE. The works of creation are great and according to his own heart, originating in himself, and on a scale proportionate to his own greatness. So with the works of his providence. But we will apply the words to redemption. The works included in this are indeed great. They are on a scale of grandeur worthy of God. 1. *The methods employed are great.* The Incarnation—the union of God and man in one Person. The display of the glory of God in the earthly life of Christ, and at his death, resurrection, and ascension. His exaltation to be "Lord of all." The descent and operations of the Holy Spirit. 2. *The work effected on behalf of man is great.* The atonement especially, and all involved in it. The conquest over sin and Satan and death. The opening of the way to God and heaven. 3. *The work wrought in and towards men is great.* (1) In respect to each believer. Illumination, regeneration, pardon, peace, holiness, perfection, glory everlasting, together with the special guidance and government of God's providence tending to and issuing in these great results. (2) In respect to the multitude redeemed and saved. (3) In respect to the final deliverance and exaltation with the Church of the whole creation (Rom. viii. 19—22 ; Eph. i. 10).

II. GOD DOES THESE GREAT THINGS "ACCORDING TO HIS OWN HEART." 1. *They spring from his heart.* They are done spontaneously, of his own free grace and will— "his own good pleasure." Not at the prompting of others, for none other could have conceived them. Not under a sense of obligation, for we had no claim upon him, except that our sin and misery appealed to his compassion. They originated in the Divine mind, sprang from the Divine love. 2. *They befit his heart.* They bear the stamp of the Divine nature; are worthy of his infinite wisdom, righteousness, benevolence, and power; are the grandest display of them. "It *became* him," etc. (Heb. ii. 10).

> "All thy ways
> Are worthy of thyself—Divine;
> But the bright glories of thy grace
> Beyond thine other wonders shine."

III. GOD DOES THESE GREAT THINGS IN FULFILMENT OF HIS OWN WORD. "For thy Word's sake." 1. *He announces them by his Word.* "To make thy servant know them." The things which God has done and will do he makes known. It is thus they become available to each and all to whom the Word is communicated. For the knowledge is the chief part of the means by which salvation is wrought. "The gospel . . . is the power of God unto salvation to every one that believeth" (Rom. i. 16 ; see also Rom. x. 13, 14 ; 1 Cor. i. 17, 18, 23 ; Jas. i. 18 ; 1 Pet. i. 22, 23). Thus also we are assured of the completion of the work of redemption. For by the promises our God lays himself under obligation to perfect the salvation of all believers. It is, therefore, a great privilege to *know* these great things which God works. 2. *He accomplishes them according to his Word.* He cannot do otherwise. He "cannot lie" (Titus i. 2). "He abideth faithful; he cannot deny himself" (2 Tim. ii. 13). Moreover, "what he hath promised, he is *able* also to perform" (Rom. iv. 21). Now that he has given his Word, "for his Word's sake," if there were no other reason, he will do "all these great things."

Then :· 1. *Let us, like David, adore and praise our God for his wondrous works, and for making them known to us.* How glorious he appears in these works! Let us ascribe glory to him. 2. *Let believers rest assured of the complete accomplishment of the work of their own redemption.* They have the Word and the heart of God, and his actual works for them and in them, to give them assurance. 3. *Let us fear, lest we should fail, through negligence and unbelief, to appropriate the redemption so wondrously wrought for us, notwithstanding our knowledge of it.* (See Heb. ii. 1—4.)—G. W.

Ver. 22.—*God surpassingly great and ever the same.* "Wherefore," because thou doest these great things, extending on through the ages, and because thou canst and dost foresee and predict them, "thou art" manifestly "great" thyself, surpassing all others; the very God our fathers worshipped and have told us of. David's knowledge of God becomes to a greater degree personal insight and conviction through the new revelation with which he is favoured. It is well when living conviction as to God is wrought through experience of his kindness rather than his severity.

I. THE SURPASSING GREATNESS OF GOD. 1. *God is great.* (1) In his nature. Infinite in all his perfections. Great, not only in power and knowledge, but in righteousness and love. "His greatness is unsearchable" (Ps. cxlv. 3). (2) In his operations. In these his greatness is exercised and displayed. In his works of creation, preservation, redemption, and government, we see how great he is. David saw it in his dealings towards himself and his posterity. In the nature of his plans and purposes; in his ability to rule a free world through successive ages, so as to effect their accomplishment; and in the power to predict and promise the result with certainty, God appears unspeakably great. Thus prophecy as well as creative energy manifests the greatness of God, both in the Divine plan itself—a grand scheme of justice and love stretching from the beginning to the end of time, and on throughout eternity—and in the revelation of it to man. 2. *God is great beyond all others.* "There is none like unto thee, neither is there any God beside thee." He has no equal, none that approaches him in majesty. (1) No creature. All are at an infinite distance beneath him. He has made some creatures to resemble him in a measure in their intelligence, goodness, and position over other creatures; but their resemblance is like that of the image of the sun in a dewdrop to the sun itself. Whatever his creatures may be, they and their capacities are derived and dependent; he is underived and independent ("from everlasting"); their powers are very limited, his unbounded; none of them can create or give life; he is the "Fountain of life" (Ps. xxxvi. 9); they are mutable, he immutable; they mortal, he "only hath immortality" (1 Tim. vi. 16). (2) No god. David would think of the divinities worshipped by the peoples around; we may think of all the objects of worship in idolatrous nations, ancient and modern. Regarding them as they exist in the minds of men, producing certain effects upon them, how utterly unlike our God! We feel it almost profane to compare them with him. But in reality they are nonentities, "vanities," as they are so frequently called in Holy Scripture. There is no God beside our God.

II. HIS IDENTITY WITH THE GOD MADE KNOWN TO US FROM FORMER TIMES. "According to all that we have heard with our ears" (comp. Ps. lxxviii. 3, 4). David recognizes that the God who was so wondrously and graciously revealing himself to him was the same God whom he had been taught to revere and trust on account of the great things he had done for Israel in former days. The form of manifestation was different; the things done were different; but there were the same Divine perfections apparent, the same care for the people whom he had chosen. It was a joy to the king to discern that Jehovah, the God of the fathers, was communicating with him; and that what he was doing and promising corresponded with what he had heard of him. The revelation which God has given of himself in Christ differs in many respects from the old revelations; the operations of God under the new covenant differ from those under the old. But as we come into living communion with God in Christ, and become ourselves the subjects of his grace; as also we learn the great things which God has done and is doing under the gospel, and the promises he makes to those who receive it; —we too shall rejoice to discern that our God is the same as was worshipped by the faithful of old, and all through the ages—Jehovah, the living God, still righteous and merciful and almighty; still doing wonders of power and grace; and doing them on a vastly wider scale, no longer chiefly in Israel, but amongst all nations. One God unites all generations, is to unite all peoples. The God of our fathers is our God, and our experience of him corresponds with theirs. Thus the records of his revelations and proceedings in all the past become available for instruction, and the encouragement of faith and hope, in the present and the future.

From the whole subject let us learn: 1. *To rejoice in and praise God.* It is matter for just thankfulness that we have a God so great and glorious to worship and confide in, One who lives and works evermore, and is throughout all ages the same God. 2. *To expect great things from One so great, for ourselves and the whole Church.* He "is able to do exceeding abundantly above all that we ask or think, according to the power which worketh in us" (Eph. iii. 20); and which has ever wrought among and on behalf of his people "according to all that we have heard with our ears." 3. *To realize conscious communion with the saints of all ages.* And so with all saints in earth and heaven. 4. *To abjure the folly, sin, and peril of declining the friendship of this great Being, and living in enmity with him.*—G. W.

Vers. 23, 24.—*The blessedness of God's people.* The thought of the greatness of God, in contrast with other objects of worship, naturally leads to that of the happiness of the people to whom he has revealed himself, and on whose behalf he has shown his greatness by his works. Israel was thus blessed above all other nations; Christians inherit the same blessedness with large increase. The people of God are distinguished above all others by—

I. THEIR REDEMPTION. (Ver. 23.) 1. *The nature of it.* Israel was redeemed from bondage in Egypt, and afterwards from the Canaanite "nations and their gods." A wonderful and happy deliverance. Christians are the subjects of a higher redemption. They are delivered from sin, from a bondage more cruel and degrading than that of Egypt. They are redeemed "from all iniquity" (Titus ii. 14), "from this present evil world" (Gal. i. 4); "from their vain manner of life handed down from their fathers" (1 Pet. i. 18, Revised Version). They are redeemed from the consequences of sin. They have "redemption, even the forgiveness of sins" (Col. i. 14); they are redeemed "from the curse of the Law" (Gal. iii. 13); from the power of the devil, and so from the power and the dread of death (Heb. ii. 14, 15); they await "the redemption of their body" (Rom. viii. 23); they are delivered "from the wrath to come" (1 Thess. i. 10). Such are some of the statements of Scripture respecting the "redemption that is in Christ Jesus" (Rom. iii. 24). 2. *The manner of it.* The deliverance from Egypt was effected by marvels of Divine power. God "went" forth to their rescue, doing "great things and terrible," in which the people themselves had and could have no part. In the destruction of the Canaanitish peoples they did take part, but their deliverances were by the power of God as really as their redemption from Egypt. For the spiritual and eternal redemption God has interposed in ways yet more marvellous. By wonders of love and righteousness and power combined, he delivers men from sin and death and hell. "He sent his Son to be the Propitiation for our sins" (1 John iv. 10). "We have redemption through his blood" (Eph. i. 7); and so the saints on earth and those in heaven unite in praise of him who, by his blood, washed them from their sins, and redeemed them to God (Rev. i. 5; v. 9). Mere power could not effect this redemption. (1) God must, in redeeming men, "declare his righteousness . . . that he might be just," as well as "the Justifier" (Rom. iii. 26); and this is effected by the death of Jesus, "the Just for the unjust" (1 Pet. iii. 18). (2) Men are to be delivered from sin by moral suasion; and this also is effected by the manifestation at once of the evil of sin, and the greatness of the Divine love, in the sacrifice of Christ. Thus the great redemptive act is the sacrificial death of the Lord Jesus. But this is rendered effectual in the experience of men by (3) the power of the Holy Spirit, revealing to the heart the gospel of redemption, which then becomes "the power of God unto salvation" (Rom. i. 16). To have thus realized redemption is the greatest blessedness and honour, and those who have this experience are the true "Israel of God" (Gal. vi. 16). 3. *The glory which this Redemption brings to the Redeemer.* "God went to redeem, . . . and to make him a Name." This aspect of the deliverance of Israel is not unfrequently presented in Holy Writ (see Exod. ix. 16; Isa. lxiii. 12, 14). Similarly, the Christian redemption is said to be "to the praise of the glory of his grace" (Eph. i. 6, 12; ii. 7; 2 Cor. iv. 15). It is not that, like some ambitious human hero, he cares for a great name for his own sake; but by his Name he is known, and men are drawn to him and saved (see John xvii. 26). In like manner, our Lord is said to have acquired through his humiliation and obedience unto death "a Name which is above every name," even "the Name of Jesus," and this also "to the glory of God the Father" (Phil. ii. 9—11).

II. THE RELATION ESTABLISHED BETWEEN THEM AND GOD. (Ver. 24.) This also distinguishes them above all others. They are constituted the people of God; he becomes their God. It is for this purpose they are redeemed. This representation of the relation between God and his people appears first in a promise made to Abraham (Gen. xvii. 7, 8), is repeated in promises given through Moses (Exod. vi. 7, etc.), is adopted by David here, reappears in the prophets (*e.g.* Jer. xxxi. 33), is applied in the New Testament to Christians (2 Cor. vi. 16, etc.), and is finally used in a description of the perfect blessedness of the inhabitants of the New Jerusalem (Rev. xxi. 3). It comprehends all that the most enlightened and holy can desire. 1. *They are constituted the people of God.* Thus to Israel it is said by Moses, "Thou art an holy people unto the Lord thy God, and the Lord hath chosen thee to be a peculiar people unto himself, above all the nations that are upon the earth" (Deut. xiv. 2; see also xxvi. 18). St. Peter employs similar language to describe the position of Christians (1 Pet. ii. 9); and St. Paul says (Titus ii. 14) that our Lord "gave himself for us, that he might . . . purify unto himself a peculiar people ['a people for his own possession,' Revised Version]." The representation includes: (1) Ownership. They are his by right of creation and of purchase. "I gave Egypt for thy ransom" (Isa. xliii. 3); "Ye are not your own; for ye are bought with a price" (1 Cor. vi. 19, 20). (2) Appropriation. God takes possession of the people who are his; in the case of Christians, by his Spirit. (3) Self-consecration. (4) Homage, including trust, love, worship (while other peoples worship other gods, the people of God worship him), and obedience. (5) Glorification. They "show forth his praise" (Isa. xliii. 21; 1 Pet. ii. 9). They promote his kingdom. 2. *He is their God.* All that men expect from their God he is to his people, and far more. He is theirs by covenant and promise. He gives himself to them. He exercises authority over them. They enjoy his love, his presence, the employment of his power to teach and guide, to purify, to comfort, to chastise, to protect, to employ, to perfect, to honour, to save. 3. *The relation is eternal.* "For ever." This is true in a sense of the relation between Israel and God. Although no longer a nation, they still are used to witness for him as no other people; and by their inspired men, and especially by him who is of them "according to the flesh," they have become the chief religious teachers and benefactors of mankind. And the day is coming when they will accept their Messiah, and, "with the fulness of the Gentiles," form one people of God. The real, spiritual Israel of all ages and lands are God's, and he is theirs for ever and ever.

Then: 1. *Happy are the people thus favoured by the Most High!* He confers on them greater honour and blessing than on any others. This is true of Israel; of any nation who have the Word and ordinances of God amongst them; of the visible Church of Christ; and emphatically of the true spiritual Church. The distinction and glory become more marked as the reality of what is included in the title, "people of God," increases. To have a Divine revelation is a great privilege; but greater to receive and be renewed by it, and thus be heirs of all its promises. 2. *Be concerned to be one of the true people of God, who have Jehovah for their God for ever.* 3. *Take heed to live in a manner becoming your relation to him whom you acknowledge as your God.* (See Lev. xix., *passim*.) The people of a God of holiness and love should be distinguished by these qualities. Only thus can they prove themselves to be his. Only such people are his in any lastingly happy sense. Would that it were possible to point to every Christian Church, and challenge the world to produce any communities equal to them in all that is pure, righteous, and benevolent!—G. W.

Ver. 25.—*God's promises and our prayers.* "Do as thou hast said." The words are used by David of the promises given to him respecting himself and his house. They are applicable to all the promises.

I. They furnish a guide to our prayers. What God has said shows us what we should ask. His promises indicate: 1. *The kind of blessings which we should most earnestly seek.* The promises of God—those given us in Christ especially—assure us of temporal good so far as is needful; but relate chiefly to spiritual and eternal blessings. The "good things" of Matt. vii. 11 are interpreted for us by Luke xi. 13 to be mainly "the Holy Spirit," which comprehends all good for our spirits, all the best things for time and eternity. While, therefore, we may pray for things temporal with moderated and submissive desire, we should most earnestly and constantly pray for things spiritual. In praying according to what God "has said," we are guided by infinite wisdom and love; we are asking "according to his will" (1 John v. 14). To permit ourselves to be prompted in prayer by our own worldly, carnal inclinations, is to turn our worship into sin, and to ask for evil instead of good. 2. *The degree of these blessings which we should seek.* The promises of God encourage us to open our mouths wide for him to fill (Ps. lxxxi. 10). They are without limit in extent and duration of blessing. Let us not limit ourselves in our desires, nor limit in our thoughts the bounty or power of God (Ps. lxxviii. 41). What he "has said" includes all we can need, but no more than we need for our highest blessedness; let us not be content with less. Let us study the promises, stretch our minds to grasp them, and then turn them into prayer; and, certain that our thoughts have not attained to the full extent of their meaning, let us yield ourselves to the influences of the Holy Spirit, that he may intercede within and "for us with groanings which cannot be uttered," but which "he that searcheth the hearts" can interpret and respond to (Rom. viii. 26, 27).

II. THEY FURNISH AN ALL-POWERFUL PLEA IN OUR PRAYERS. "Do as thou hast said" is an appeal to the faithfulness and kindness of him to whom we pray. "Thou canst not break thy word ('Thy words be true,' ver. 28); thou art too kind to trifle with those who confide in it. For thy Name's sake, therefore, fulfil thy promises."

III. THEY ASSURE US OF A FAVOURABLE ANSWER TO OUR PRAYERS. When our prayers are according to the Divine promises, we should be absolutely certain of their success. For: 1. God is able to do as he has said. 2. He is most willing. His promises spring from his love to us, and express what he is most desirous of conferring upon us, and which only our indifference, unwillingness, unbelief, and consequent unfitness prevent our receiving. 3. His word binds him. "God is not a man, that he should lie; neither the son of man, that he should repent: hath he said, and shall he not do it? or hath he spoken, and shall he not make it good?" (Numb. xxiii. 19). 4. He has given confirmations of his promises and pledges for their fulfilment, especially in the gift of his Son (2 Cor. i. 20; Rom. viii. 32). Therefore "let us ask in faith, nothing doubting" (Jas. i. 6, Revised Version). Were it not for what he has said, we might reasonably hesitate to ask for such great things as we are taught to pray for; but, having his word, there is no room for hesitation (ver. 27). However conscious of sinfulness and unworthiness, we may and should "come boldly unto the throne of grace" (Heb. iv. 16; also x, 19, 22).

Let us, then: 1. *Familiarize ourselves with the promises of God, that we may pray with understanding and largeness of heart, and with confidence, importunity, and perseverance.* 2. *Use the promises when we pray, whether for ourselves, our families, our country, the Church, or the world.* 3. *Abandon whatever would turn the words, "Do as thou hast said," into a fearful imprecation.* For think of what God has said as to what he will do with the impenitent, the unbelieving, the disobedient, the unforgiving, etc., even if they offer prayers to him (see *e.g.* Matt. vi. 12, 14, 15).—G. W.

Ver. 26.—*God's Name magnified in his people.* Any name of God is magnified when it is made to appear great in the eyes of his intelligent creatures, and they esteem and declare it great. This is done when he himself adds to the significance of the name by yet more glorious works or revelations; and when they come to larger conceptions of its significance, and consequently use the name with greater fulness of meaning. Thus as "the sons of God" watched the various stages of creation, the name of "Creator" would acquire greater significance and glory. The name "Jehovah of hosts" would become more glorious as the hosts themselves in the heavens and on earth grew more numerous. But David here assumes that additional glory to this great name of God might and would arise from his relation to Israel; that to say, "Jehovah of hosts is the God over Israel," would be to add lustre to the name. And rightly, for his Name has been magnified by what he did amongst and for that people, by the revelations of himself which he gave them, and by the results in their national history, in the character and deeds of many of them, and in the history of the world. He made through them such manifestations of his greatness and goodness, righteousness and mercy, as befitted himself; and for which vast multitudes have magnified and do magnify him in their thoughts and thanksgivings. Until the Christ came, no name of God was more illustrious than this, "Jehovah of hosts, the God of Israel." In fact, the coming of Christ and all that has grown out of it was included in that name. Hence another name of God greater still, "the God and Father of our Lord Jesus Christ," and "the God and Father of Christ's people." Yea, the whole Name of God, his whole character, all the terms and declarations by which he is made known, is magnified by what he has said and done in Christ. The great threefold name, Father, Son, and Holy Spirit, is as never before declared and glorified in the work of salvation.

I. How God's Name is magnified in and by his people. This is effected by:
1. *The work wrought for them.*

> " 'Twas great to speak a world from nought;
>   'Twas greater to redeem."

2. *The revelations made to them.* In the Person, teaching, miracles, death, resurrection, and ascension of the Lord Jesus; and by the teaching of the Holy Spirit through the evangelists and apostles. In these God is manifested more fully and clearly than by all his works besides. Never before did his Name appear so great and glorious. 3. *The work wrought in them.* The regeneration and sanctification of souls is a more interesting and illustrious display of Divine power than the creation of suns and stars, and reveals more of the Divine nature. The spiritual beauty and glory thus produced surpass all the beauty and glory of the natural world, and in them more of God appears. In "the fruit of the Spirit" (Gal. v. 22) God is magnified more than in all other products of his power. 4. *The works done by them.* The witness they bear for God by their worship and teaching, and sometimes their sufferings as confessors and martyrs; their godly and loving endeavours for the good of others; the courage and self-sacrifice, faith and patience, with which many of them labour for the spread of the gospel; and the good thus effected;—all magnify the Name of God, from whom all proceed, and to the fulfilment of whose gracious purposes all conduce. The changes wrought by the labours of Christians—the whole influence and results of Christianity, notwithstanding all drawbacks (serious as these are), are of such a nature and magnitude as to exalt the Name of God more than anything else in the world. 5. *The condition they at length attain.* Their ultimate moral and spiritual perfection, their perfect happiness, their vast number. "He shall come to be glorified in his saints, and to be admired in all them that believe" (2 Thess. i. 10). 6. *The praises which are given to him on their account.* From themselves, from the angelic hosts; on earth, in heaven; for ever. In these ways God appears great and ever greater because of his relation to Christ and the Church.

II. The prayer of good men respecting it. "Let thy Name be magnified;" let it become greater and greater in the sight of the intelligent universe, and become more and more admired and praised, through what is done in and for and by thy people. 1. *Such a prayer is natural to good men.* Because they love God, because they have received so much from him, and because they desire the welfare of others, which is involved in the magnifying of the Name of God. 2. *There is much to intensify such a prayer.* (1) The condition of the Church. In which there is so much that does not glorify the Name of God, so little comparatively that does. To say that the Lord of hosts is God of such a people does not tend to honour him so greatly as his zealous servants desire. The prayer from their hearts and lips will mean, "Let Christ's people become so Christ-like as to make it manifest that their religion is from God, that they themselves are specially his, and that he is indeed a Being glorious in holiness and lovingkindness." (2) The condition of the world. In which God is so little thought of, his Name so little esteemed; in which idols and all manner of vain and even wicked things are magnified more than God; in which men give to themselves and their fellow-men the honour which should be his; and whose salvation and whole well-being would be ensured by those changes which would magnify the Name of God. (3) The slow progress of the kingdom of God. The apparent weakness of the Church in reference to her great work, and her real insufficiency for it, should lead all Christians to pray that God would so "arise" and "let his work appear" in the spread and establishment of his kingdom that his Name may be magnified in the earth as it has never yet been. 3. *Let the prayer be accompanied by practice.* Let each of us who pray, "Hallowed be thy Name," so live as to aid in fulfilling our prayer; first, in our general character and conduct, and then by faithful endeavours to promote the honour of God amongst professing Christians and throughout the world. Also by hearty praise to God for all he has done in connection with Christ and Christianity to make his Name great and glorious.

Observe, finally, that the Name of God is magnified in the punishment of his enemies. Let us beware lest we be made in this manner to glorify him. Let us rather honour his Name as it appears in Jesus Christ by our faith and obedience; then he will honour it in our salvation.—G. W.

Ver. 27.—*Prayer induced and encouraged by promise.* David gives the promise of God to him as a reason for praying that his house might be established for ever. He intimates that otherwise he would not have found it in his heart to do so. In like manner, the promises of God to Christians incite and encourage them to pray for bestowments that they would not have otherwise ventured to ask for. I. THE GREATNESS OF GOD'S PROMISES. They set before us blessings so precious, vast, and enduring, that, apart from the declarations of God, we should never have dared to think of them as possible for us, or to pray for them. From the goodness and power of God in general we might have ventured to hope and pray for some blessings, but not such as are now the common subjects of Christian prayer. Look in this view at some of the Divine promises, or declarations which are equivalent to promises. 1. *As to the believer himself.* Promises as to: (1) Pardon of great and numerous sins, long practised. Repeated pardons. (2) Renewal of nature and character. Deliverance from slavery to sins the most natural, the most habitual. "A new heart," etc. (3) Adoption into the family of God. The Spirit of adoption. Participation of the Divine nature. Free access to God. Fellowship with him. (4) Victory over the mightiest enemies. (5) "Grace sufficient" for all circumstances, and highest good from them. (6) Fulness of spiritual life, of knowledge, holiness, strength, joy. "Filled unto the fulness of God;" "Filled with the Spirit." The indwelling in the heart of Christ, of God, by the Holy Spirit. Truly there are heights of godliness, goodness, and blessedness attainable in this life, to which most of us are strangers. (7) Heaven. Seeing God face to face; being with Christ, being like him in body, soul, condition; reigning with him as kings; experiencing "fulness of joy, pleasures for evermore." Let any one examine the statements of Holy Scripture on these subjects, and consider what they mean; and he must perceive that they set forth blessings which, apart from the assurances thus given, men could not have conceived of, much less imagined that they could ever be their own. 2. *As to the future of the kingdom of God on earth.* The attraction of all men to Christ; the universal spread of the knowledge, worship, and service of God; and consequently of peace, union, and brotherhood; obedience on earth to God's will as it is obeyed in heaven. In opposition to such a prospect is the whole history and experience of the world, with the exception of a small fraction; the depravity of mankind, the power of error, superstition, idolatry, priestcraft, old habits of wickedness, etc. Such a vision could never have appeared to men; or, if it had occurred to an active imagination, could never have been regarded as a matter for serious prayer and endeavour, if God had not given it by his prophets and by his Son. II. THE EFFECT WHICH THESE PROMISES SHOULD HAVE ON OUR PRAYERS. They should: 1. *Impel us to pray.* Not lead us to neglect prayer, as if the Divine purpose and promise superseded all need for prayer. "Thus saith the Lord God: I will yet for this be inquired of by the house of Israel, to do it for them" (Ezek. xxxvi. 37). The blessings promised are for those who seek them. 2. *Enrich and enlarge our prayers.* The measure in which we receive is according to the measure in which we desire and ask (Luke xi. 5—13; 2 Kings xiii. 18, 19). 3. *Greatly encourage them.* Leading us to pray with confidence and importunity. Petitions that would have been presumptuous without the promises are now sober and reasonable. We need not and ought not to be deterred either by: (1) Our sinfulness and God's holiness and threatenings. (2) Our insignificance and God's majesty. (3) The greatness of the blessings promised, and our incapacity to receive them; or (4) the difficulties in the way of the fulfilment of the promises. Sufficient that they are the promises of God, and he (1) "Jehovah of hosts," having all things under his control, unchanging and eternal and; (2) "God of Israel," our God, our covenant God, who has taken us to be his, and given himself to be ours in Christ Jesus. All that he has promised appears only to befit such a sublime relationship. (See further in homily on ver. 25.)—G. W.

Ver. 28.—*Truth of God's words.* "Thou art God, and thy words are truth" (Revised Version). David may be thinking only of the promises of God, and expressing his own confidence in their fulfilment to himself and his family. But his assertion applies to all the words of God, declarations and threatenings as well as promises; and, as his language is general, his thought may be general also; and his faith in the truth of all the words of God might then be regarded as the ground of his faith in the promise made to himself. The words, "Thou art God," give the reason of his confidence in the Divine words. " Because thou art God, we know that 'thy words are truth,' and only truth." I. THE GROUNDS OF OUR ASSURANCE OF THE TRUTH OF GOD'S WORDS. "Thou art God." 1. *His nature and character.* (1) His universal knowledge. He cannot, like men, be mistaken, and honestly assert that for truth which is untrue. (2) His essential truthfulness. Because he is God we are intuitively sure of this. As he cannot be mistaken, so he "cannot lie." (3) His goodness. Which of itself would prevent him from misleading and deceiving his dependent creatures. (4) His unbounded power. Men who are not untrue to their promises may be unable to fulfil them. Not so God. (5) His unchangeableness. As well in faithfulness as in goodness and power. He can never become either unable or unwilling to fulfil his Word. 2. *His doings.* The actual fulfilment of his words. (1) In the history of the world; especially the promises respecting the Christ, the blessings he would bestow, and the changes he would effect. The faithfulness of God to his Word, as shown in the previous history of Israel, would assure David of the fulfilment of the promises to himself. (2) Within the range of our own observation and experience. The words of God as to the results of faith and unbelief, of holiness and sin, of prayerfulness and prayerlessness, are continually being accomplished. Our personal experience testifies to their truth, and we can witness their fulfilment in others.

II. THE WORDS RESPECTING WHICH WE HAVE THIS ASSURANCE. All declarations that can be traced to God, whether ascertained by unaided reason (as we say, though the living God through the eternal Word is ever working in the human reason) or by the inspired Book. God speaks in nature as well as in the Bible. Scientific truth, and moral truth known by the conscience, are from him as well as religious. But as Christians we have to do with the words of God in Holy Scripture, and especially with the "truth which is in Jesus." As he declared in language almost identical with David's, "Thy Word is truth" (John xvii. 17), so he said of himself, "I am the Truth" (John xiv. 6). And it is of unspeakable importance to be assured that he is and gives the revelation of God; that all that he is and says is the truth. And as he declares of the Old Testament that "the Scripture cannot be broken" (John x. 35), we have his warrant for full confidence also in the more ancient revelation. God's words as thus ascertained relate to: 1. *Existences.* God himself, his Son, his Spirit. Inhabitants of the invisible world— angels, Satan, demons. Mankind—the nature of man, purposes of his creation, the relations he sustains, his fallen condition, etc. For our knowledge of the invisible beings and things we depend on the Word of God, mainly the Scriptures; and the knowledge thus acquired is, we may be sure, truth. 2. *Moral laws.* Known partly by reason, partly by Scripture. However ascertained, we know them to be truth. 3. *Spiritual truths and laws.* The redeeming love and works of God and our Saviour; the way in which they become effectual for ourselves; the duties thence arising. 4. *The results of our conduct in respect to these truths and laws.* That is, the promises and the threatenings of God, as to both the present life and the eternal future.

Observe, that it is the words of God about these things which are the truth; not necessarily the assertions of men—individuals or Churches—respecting them. It is for human teachers, not to require of their brethren unquestioning faith in their statements, but to lead them up to where they may hear the utterances of God himself. And this is to be done, not merely by proving their assertions by the letter of Scripture, but by cherishing themselves, and fostering in others, the spirit which enables communion with "the Father of spirits" (Heb. xii. 9). If God's words be truth: 1. *We should seek full knowledge of them.* 2. *We should exercise undoubting faith in them.* (1) The faith which realizes the invisible and eternal; apprehends and feels them to be as God says. (2) The faith which is full confidence in the Divine promises and threatenings, assurance that our own future and that of others will be according to them. We have such a faith only when our belief sways and rules our hearts and lives. 3. *We should imitate God as to our truthfulness and the actual truth of our words.* Being true and sincere in our character and utterances, and taking care that what we truly say shall be truth.—G. W.

Ver. 29.—*A good man's prayer for his family.* David's prayer has especial reference to the promise given him that his family should continue for ever to rule Israel. We may take the prayer as suitable to be used by any godly father for his children and children's children.

I. THE PRAYER. That God would bless the family. A Christian father offering this prayer would have regard to: 1. *Temporal blessings.* Prolonged life, good health of body and mind, success in worldly pursuits, competence. Asking for these as a blessing from God implies the desire that they should be granted only so far as they will be blessings; that they should come as the result of God's blessing on upright means (not from fraud, injustice, or violence; see Prov. x. 22); and that they should be accompanied with God's blessing, so that they may not ensnare and injure the soul, but promote its prosperity and highest happiness. Thus regarded, such a prayer is not unbecoming the heart and lips of any good man. 2. *Spiritual blessings.* That the family may be worthy the name of a Christian household, all being truly the children of God, worshipping and serving him faithfully and to the end. A Christian parent will be more desirous that his house should be good than great—"rich in faith, and heirs of the kingdom" (Jas. ii. 5) rather than possessed of material wealth. For such blessings he need not restrain his desires, as they are good in and for themselves, good always and for ever. The poorest may seek these for his children, who may enjoy them equally with the wealthiest: they are open to all. 3. *Eternal blessings.* That he and his may "continue for ever before God" (comp. Gen. xvii. 18), and "be blessed for ever"— numbered with the saints in the glory everlasting. The words translated, "let it please thee to bless," may be more literally rendered "begin and bless" (Revised Version, margin). As if David's thoughts reverted from the distant future to the present; and he became acutely alive to the fact that, for the accomplishment of the promise in the future, it was necessary that God should be with him and his at once and all along. In the heart of a Christian the meaning may well be, "Let thy blessing come at once, without any delay, on my house, to correct what is wrong, to increase what is right, to produce those conditions which are most favourable to all good, as they most fully ensure thy constant favour."

II. WHENCE IT ARISES. 1. *Godliness.* Sense of the value of God's blessing; preference of it over all else; confidence in God's fatherly love and sympathy with the love of earthly parents for their children; and faith in his promises. 2. *Parental feeling.* Love for his family; longing for their true and lasting happiness and well-being. 3. *Regard for his own happiness.* Which is necessarily bound up with the goodness and happiness of his children.

Finally: 1. *Such prayer, when real, will be accompanied by Christian instruction and training.* (Eph. vi. 4.) 2. *Let children thank God for praying parents.* Let them keep before them the image of their fathers and mothers daily kneeling before God, and imploring his blessing on them. Let them, however, not trust to their prayers as sufficient to ensure their salvation; but pray for themselves. (See more on ch. vi. 20.)—G. W.

EXPOSITION.

CHAPTER VIII.

Ver. 1.—**David smote the Philistines.** In the previous chapter we have seen that the empire of David not only marked an era in the development of Israel nationally, but was also the reaching of a new stage in the preparation for the advent of the Messiah; and we saw that without this the development of prophecy would have been impossible, and the people have remained unfit for the high mission to which they were called as the witnesses to the unity of God. We have in this chapter a brief summary of the wars which raised Israel from the position of a struggling and oppressed race to the possession of widespread empire. With this narrative the first history of David ends, and in the subsequent narratives many of the events referred to here are more fully detailed, and given with additional incidents. **David took Metheg-ammah out of the hand of the Philistines.** Metheg-ammah means "the bridle of the mother-city." We learn from the parallel place (1 Chron. xviii. 1) that the city of Gath is meant by this phrase. Gath was at this time the metropolis of Philistia, and had reduced the other four chief towns to a state of vassalage. Thus by taking Gath, his old city of refuge (1 Sam. xxvii. 2), David acquired also the supremacy which she had previously exercised over the whole country, and by placing a strong garrison there, as previously the Philistines had done in the towns of Israel, he kept that martial race in awe. It denotes great progress in the arts of war that David could besiege and capture a town so strong as Gath.

Ver. 2.—**He smote Moab.** In the previous history we find David and Moab on such friendly terms that he entrusted his father and mother into their king's keeping (1 Sam. xxii. 3, 4). Now he not only subjugates them, but puts two-thirds or, according to the ancient versions, half of the captured combatants to death. Compared with the custom of the Romans, and with the attempt to destroy all the males in Edom, this was mild treatment: for we find Cæsar in his Gallic wars putting all his prisoners to death, and using for their execution the mere phrase, "he counted them in the number of enemies," as if the killing of enemies was a matter of course. The customs of the Israelites in war were not so cruel, and this treatment of the Moabites seems to be mentioned as showing that they received exceptionally severe treatment. The justification of this is found by Jewish commentators, on the authority of the Midrash, in the supposed fact that the King of Moab had put David's father and mother to death. But as Philippson adds, even so it was an instance of the extreme barbarity of ancient warfare. **Casting them down to the ground**; Hebrew, *making them to lie down on the ground;* and so the Revised Version. It is plain that those who were made to lie on the ground were combatants who had been made prisoners, and the Hebrew seems to mean that, while they were thus prostrate, they were measured off into three divisions, whereof two were put to the sword, and one permitted to live. All the versions, however, understand that only half were put to death, making the sense to be that he measured them with two cords, one to kill, and one full cord—one, that is, of larger size, to save alive. We get no help from 1 Chron. xviii. 2, where this treatment of the Moabites is omitted. It is probable that it was in this war that Benaiah slew "two lion-like men of Moab" (1 Chron. xi. 22), who were its champions and perhaps members of the royal house. **They brought gifts** means that they paid an annual tribute; but the phrase shows that, though now they were **David's servants**, that is, *subjects*, yet that they were left in possession of their independence, and that their internal affairs were managed by native authorities.

Ver. 3.—**Hadadezer.** The name is spelt Hadarezer in ch. x. 16 and in 1 Chron. xviii. 3, and such is the reading of the versions here and of many Hebrew manuscripts. The other reading has been defended on the ground that Hadad is the name of the Syrian sun-god, but the cuneiform inscrip-

tions show that his real name was Hadar. The King of Syria, mentioned in 1 Kings xx. 1, is called in Assyrian Ben-Hidri. **Zobah.** Ewald identifies Zobah with the "Sabo" mentioned by Ptolemy. This is uncertain, but evidently Zobah lay north-east of Damascus and south of Hamath, in the region between the rivers Orontes and Euphrates. In 1 Sam. xiv. 47 it appears as a powerless country governed by a multitude of petty kings; but evidently now Hadarezer had made himself supreme, and become a powerful monarch whose authority extended even across the river into Mesopotamia (ch. x. 16). Having crushed his rivals at home, he had next endeavoured to extend his dominion abroad. **As he went to recover his border at the river Euphrates.** The word "Euphrates" is inserted in the Authorized Version, because the margin says, "Euphrates read but not written." In the Revised Version it is omitted, because the unauthoritative nature of these directions to read something not in the text has been demonstrated. Technically these readings are called *K'ri*, and the written text *K'tib*. In 1 Chron. xviii. 3 the reading is, "as he went to stablish his dominion by the river"—a change which involves the alteration of only one letter, as the word rendered here "his border," and in 1 Chron. xviii. 3 "his dominion," is the same, signifying literally, "his hand." For this reason the Revised Version renders it correctly in both places "his dominion." Now, David never had possessed up to this time any dominion upon the Euphrates, but in the fuller narrative in ch. x. we learn that these Syrians of Zobah had sent powerful reinforcements to the Ammonites in their war with David; and he might reasonably, therefore, determine to follow up his victory over them by extending his power up to the river, so as to guard the fords, and prevent all future invasions. And this Hadarezer would resent. As an able and enterprising man, he had succeeded in making Zobah a powerful realm, and was not likely to submit to having a bridle put upon his adventurous spirit by the posting of an Israelitish garrison on the borders. We learn from ch. x. 19 that David's object was to prevent aid coming to Ammon from Zobah, and that he succeeded in putting a barrier in Hadarezer's way. We can scarcely doubt, therefore, that the reading in the Chronicles is to be preferred. In 1 Sam. xiv. 47 we read that Saul had waged war with Zobah, and as David had probably served in it, he would have thereby acquired both a knowledge of the country, very useful in this present more serious expedition, and also have learned the necessity of guarding his dominions against perpetual invasions from that quarter.

Ver. 4.—**David took from him a thousand chariots, and seven hundred horsemen, and twenty thousand footmen.** The word " chariots " is inserted in the Authorized Version after " thousand," from the parallel place in 1 Chron. xviii. 4, where also it is said that David captured seven thousand horsemen. The numbers of the Chronicler are more in proportion to one another than those mentioned here, provided we assume that the word " chariots " ought to be supplied, which, as it is not the only difference, is uncertain. Until the Arabs invented our present system of notation, the ancient methods of representing numbers were so liable to error that little dependence can be placed upon them. The Hebrews used their letters for numerals, but after 400 their system breaks down. Any number higher than 400 can be represented only by long sums in arithmetic, or by an intricate system of points above and below, which were sure to get into confusion. **David houghed all the chariot** horses. There is good reason for concluding that the word used here, *recheb*, is a collective, and signifies animals used either for riding or driving. What David reserved was not a hundred chariots, but a hundred riding-horses, which would be useful to him for rapid communication, and could scarcely be regarded as a violation of the command in Deut. xvii. 16. Both the Authorized and Revised Versions are wrong, but the Authorized Version at least makes the word *recheb* have the same meaning in both clauses, whereas the Revised Version makes it signify chariot-horses in the first clause, and the chariots themselves in the second. The defeat by David, with infantry only, of an army provided with so powerful a force of cavalry and chariots, proves his great military skill, and their capture bears even more emphatic testimony to his generalship. In the Psalms we find horses often referred to as objects regarded with terror, and which gave a great advantage to their enemies (Ps. xx. 7; xxxiii. 17; lxxvi. 6; cxlvii. 10), but over which they had triumphed by Jehovah's aid. This method, however, of rendering them useless, though practised by Joshua (Josh. xi. 6), was most cruel; as the poor things, unable to move about with the sinews of their hind legs severed, would perish of hunger.

Ver. 5.—**The Syrians of Damascus**; Hebrew, *Aram-Dammesek ;* that is, Aram-Damascus. The inhabitants of these regions and of Mesopotamia were descended from Aram, the son of Shem (Gen. x. 22), and bore his name. Thus Zobah is called Aram-Zobah in the title of Ps. lx. As members of a kindred race, and speaking the same language, all the clans of the Aramean family would naturally combine to check the growing power of Israel.

Ver. 6.—**Garrisons.** This is the word used in 1 Sam. x. 5 and xiii. 3. The Arameans were left free to manage their internal affairs themselves, but they had to pay tribute (see on ver. 2) ; and to prevent the assembling of troops to contest David's authority and shake off his yoke, garrisons were stationed in such places as commanded the country. The Philistines had done the same in Israel when they were masters there.

Ver. 7.—**Shields of gold.** Probably they were plated with gold, and were borne by Hadarezer's body-guard. But it is very uncertain whether shields are really meant. The word in Syriac means " quivers." Jerome evidently could not at first find out what it signified, as he in this place translates in the Vulgate " arms," but subsequently he became better informed. The LXX. renders " bracelets," and adds that they were carried away from Jerusalem by Shishak in the days of Rehoboam. There is no contradiction in this with what is said in 1 Kings xiv. 26, as what Solomon made were undoubtedly shields, such being the certain meaning of the word in the Hebrew, and its rendering in all the versions. No version renders the word used here " shield." In the parallel place (1 Chron. xviii. 7) the Syriac and Vulgate render it " quivers," the LXX. " collars," and the Arabic " plates of gold hung on the trappings of the horses." As they were captured from a Syrian king, they probably retained their Syriac name, and if so they were " quivers."

Ver. 8.—**Betah . . . Berothai.** Of these cities nothing certain is known, and in 1 Chron. xviii. 8 the names are changed to *Tibhath* and *Chun.* An interesting addition is made there, inserted also by the LXX. in this place, that it was from this brass (that is, copper) that Solomon made the great laver, the pillars, and many other vessels for the temple service.

Ver. 9.—**Toi,** called in Chronicles Tou, **King of Hamath.** This was a famous city upon the river Orontes, afterwards called by the Greeks Epiphania, and was situated upon the northernmost boundary of Palestine. Its interest in the present day lies in its having been the capital of the Hittites—a race whose very existence was doubted a few years ago, in spite of the testimony of Holy Scripture; but whose marvellous empire has been lately proved to be historical by Egyptian records on the one side, and cuneiform inscriptions on the other. Unfortunately, inscriptions which they have themselves left behind have not yet found any one capable of deciphering them. In the twelfth century B.C. they were the paramount power from the Euphrates to the Lebanon. For many centuries they contended with the Pharaohs for the possession of Egypt, and while Rameses II. had to make an inglorious peace with the Kheta, as they are called, and marry the king's daughter, Rameses III. won a great victory over them, and saved Egypt from thraldom. In the cuneiform inscriptions we find the record of a struggle between Assyria and the Hittites, lasting for four hundred years, during which Shalmaneser made thirty campaigns against them, but they were not finally conquered until B.C. 717, during the reign of Sargon. Fuller details will be found in Dr. Wright's 'Empire of the Hittites,' published by Messrs. Nisbet.

Ver. 10.—**Joram.** In 1 Chron. xviii. 10 he is called Hadoram, and this was apparently his real name, Joram being merely the substitution of the nearest Hebrew word for something foreign and therefore unintelligible. So among the descendants of the French refugees settled in England similar changes are common. Thus Pillons becomes Pillow; Chevallier, Shoveller; St. Amour, Stammers. As Hamath bordered upon Zobah, and apparently had waged unsuccessful war with the vigorous Hadarezer, Toi was grateful to David for smiting his rival, and sent this embassy of congratulation for the purpose of ensuring the conqueror's friendship. For this end he also sent rich presents; and as a present is called in the Hebrew a *blessing* (1 Sam. xxv. 27; xxx. 26, margin), the phrase used here, **to bless him,** contains the idea, not only of congratulation, but of offerings. There is something admirable in this high Oriental courtesy. The material value of the gifts is left in the background. Their worth lies in their being the acknowledgment of the Divine favour resting upon David, and in the prayer that that favour may continue. In Ps. xviii. 43, 44 we have proof of the great pleasure which this embassy from so great a nation gave to David.

Ver. 11.—**Which also King David did dedicate.** The blessing became more blessed by this use of it, and it shows how strong were David's feelings, that he thus gave to God's house, not only the spoils of war, but also gifts of friendship. It was in this way that he accumulated those large stores of the precious metals enumerated in 1 Chron. xxix., and employed in making the sacred vessels of the temple. Their vast amount is the more remarkable because Palestine previously was almost destitute of them. Wherever the armies of Israel went, they made diligent search after everything that would serve towards the building of their sanctuary.

Ver. 12.—**Of Syria;** Hebrew, *Aram.* The reading in 1 Chron. xviii. 11 is *Edom,* which differs from Aram in only one letter. The two words are constantly confused in manuscripts, and "Edom" is probably right here, first, because it is coupled with Moab and Ammon, which were its neighbours; but chiefly because the spoil of Hadarezer, mentioned at the end of the verse, is the spoil of Aram. It would not be enumerated twice.

Ver. 13.—**From smiting of the Syrians;** Hebrew, *of Aram.* Here "Edom" is certainly right (see 1 Chron. xviii. 12), unless we accept Keil's conjecture, and suppose that "he smote Edom" has dropped out of the text, and must be inserted. In the superscription of Ps. lx. we find the wars with Aram-Naharaim (Mesopotamia) and Aram-Zobah coupled with this smiting of Edom in the valley of salt, which lay to the south of the Dead Sea, and was a fatal place to the Edomites in their war subsequently with Amaziah (2 Kings xiv. 7). Such a double victory over the Arameans first, and immediately afterwards over Edom, would account for the "name," that is, the reputation, which David gained. The course of events seems to have been as follows. The Edomites, believing that David was engaged in a struggle beyond his powers with the Syrians, took the opportunity to invade Israel. But the campaign in Aram was quickly decided, and David was able to send Abishai with a detachment of his forces to repel the Edomites. On hearing of his approach, they retired before him, and, making a stand in their own territories, were defeated in the valley of salt, with the loss of eighteen thousand men (1 Chron. xviii. 12). In this place the victory is ascribed to David, because it was won by his general acting under his orders. For some unexplained reason, the feelings of the Israelites against Edom were very vindictive, and Joab followed with larger forces, and not only slew twelve thousand in a second battle (Ps. lx., title), but remained six months in the country, ruthlessly putting every male to death (1 Kings xi. 15, 16). From this time the Edomites and Israelites were implacable foes, and in later Jewish literature the Jews gave vent to their intense hatred of the Roman empire by giving it the name of Edom.

Ver. 14.—**Throughout all Edom put he garrisons.** In a country naturally so strong as Edom, and with neighbouring states ready to give shelter to their fugitives, Joab's attempt would cause great misery, but only a moderate loss of life. And as soon as he withdrew, the exiles would return to their old homes. To keep them, therefore, in entire subjection, the country was held by strong garrisons, and the Edomites became David's servants, being apparently deprived for the present of any form of independent government. We have, then, in this chapter, a brief summary of David's wars, whereby he established his supremacy over the extensive region from Hamath on the north to the salt plains on the south of the Dead Sea, and from the Mediterranean to the Euphrates.

Ver. 15.—**David executed judgment and justice.** There was very little real truth in Absalom's fault-finding with the administration of justice (ch. xv. 3, 4), unless we suppose—what is only too probable—that David, after his terrible crimes of murder and adultery, became lax in the discharge of his judicial duties. Here, at this period of his life, he was a zealous judge at home, as well as a brave and skilful general. He was one of those many-sided characters who are great in a multitude of ways. Like Julius Cæsar and our own Alfred, he was as distinguished in the arts of peace as in those of war. And thus, while his first care was for the establishment of religion, and while even the singing in the sanctuary was not beneath his notice, he also, even in the midst of dangerous wars, gave careful attention to the orderly government of his kingdom and the maintenance of right and law. We have already seen with what consummate skill he selected a capital immediately that he was made king of all Israel. Saul had done much in war. Though finally defeated at Gilboa, he had taught the Israelites their strength, and laid the foundations of David's empire; but he had done nothing to consolidate the tribes, or provide tribunals for the settlement of disputed legal rights or the punishment of crimes. Israel was as loose an aggregate of discordant atoms at his death as it was at his appointment; and the maintenance of order was left to the caprice of local sheiks. Samuel had done far more for the internal development and consolidation of the people than Saul; but it was David who made them into a nation. The continuance of his work was frustrated by the extravagance of Solomon, the folly of Rehoboam, and the ambition of the restless tribe of Ephraim; but the two parts into which his realm was broken at least held together, and there never again was danger of such anarchy and threatened disintegration as existed in the times of the judges.

Ver. 16.—**Joab . . . was over the host.** Twice in this book we have lists of David's chief officers—here and at the end of ch. xx. The present list belongs to the period of David's greatest prosperity, when all went well with him in peace and war, and when Jehovah had elevated him to the unique rank of Messianic king—a distinction which belonged to him personally, and was inherited by none of his successors. Between it and the second

list there lies a tragic tale of sin and shame, of crime and merited punishment, of the realm rising in rebellion against the adulterous king, and of his own family breaking away from the bonds of godly discipline, and giving way to licentiousness, to bloodshed, and to parricidal ambition. But probably David's character had then gained in spirituality and singleness of heart; whereas now prosperity must already have begun its work of sapping the foundations of his moral nature. Joab, who had been stripped of his command for the murder of Abner, had regained it by his bravery at the capture of Jerusalem. We have seen also that David entrusted to him the building of Jerusalem, and apparently he was prime minister in all matters except probably the king's judicial functions. **Jehoshaphat . . . was recorder;** literally, *remembrancer.* It was his office to reduce the king's decrees to writing, and also to see that they were carried into execution. Probably after they had been committed to writing, they were laid before the king for his approval, and, when confirmed by his hand or seal, were entered in the book of remembrance.

Ver. 17.—**Zadok . . . and Ahimelech . . . were the priests.** We have already seen that this was contrary to the letter of the Mosaic Law, and yet that there was no schism, and that by patience matters came back to the right groove. Zadok, of the elder line of Eleazar (1 Chron. vi. 4—8, 50—53), was high priest at Gibeon, and Ahimelech, of the junior line of Ithamar, was the high priest at Jerusalem. Instead of *Ahimelech the son of Abiathar,* the Syriac transposes the names, and reads, " Abiathar the son of Ahimelech." This agrees with the list in ch. xx. 25, and it is certain that Abiathar outlived David (1 Kings ii. 26), and that he was David's high priest throughout his reign, though Zadok is not only constantly associated with him, but is placed first, as the man of higher rank (ch. xv. 24—35; xvii. 15; xix. 11; xx. 25). It is also remarkable that our Lord makes Abiathar the person who gave David the shewbread (Mark ii. 26), whereas in 1 Sam. xxi. he is repeatedly called Ahimelech. As both the LXX. and the Vulgate support the Hebrew against the Syriac, and as the reading "Ahimelech" is confirmed by 1 Chron. xviii. 16 and xxiv. 3, 6, 31, we must reject the emendation of the Syriac, and conclude that there was a double tradition respecting these names, some manuscripts making Abiathar the father, and others giving the seniority to Ahimelech. Our Lord made Abiathar the father, but the scribes, in their editing of the Hebrew text, gave that place to Ahimelech, yet did not carry out their restoration so thoroughly as not to

leave proof that the names probably ought
to be reversed. **Seraiah was scribe.** His
office was similar to that of a secretary of
state with us. For *Seraiah* we have *Shavsha*
in 1 Chron. xviii. 16, *Shisha* in 1 Kings
iv. 3, and *Sheva* in ch. xx. 25. This illustrates what has just been said as to the
uncertainty about proper names. They are
always most difficult to read, as the sense
gives no aid, and these various forms of a
name that does not occur elsewhere really
bear witness to the high antiquity of the
manuscripts used by the scribes in settling
the text of the Old Testament; and also to
their self-restraint in not making them all
forcibly agree.

Ver. 18.—**The Cherethites and the Pelethites.** As we have already seen (1 Sam.
xxx. 14), the Cherethim were an insignificant tribe inhabiting the southern part
of the country of the Philistines. Nor is
that place the only proof of this fact; for
they are connected with the Philistines also
in Ezek. xxv. 16 and Zeph. ii. 5. David
made their acquaintance when at Ziklag;
and probably the Pelethim dwelt in the
same neighbourhood, and were a still more
unimportant clan or family. Much ingenuity has been expended in finding for
their names a Hebrew derivation, and
Gesenius explains them as meaning "cutters
and runners," though for the latter signification he has to go to the Arabic, where
he finds a verb *falata*, "to run away," "flee."
But this craze of explaining the names of
aboriginal tribes and their towns by Hebrew
words is not only absurd in itself, but bars
the way to sounder knowledge. For it is
possible that, by the study of names not
belonging to the Hebrew language, we
might arrive at some correct ideas about the
races who had previously occupied Palestine.
Instead of this, the whole system of derivation is corrupted, and philology made
ridiculous. What can be more ludicrous
than to explain these Pelethim as "runners
away," unless it be the notion that the
Rephaim took their name from the Hebrew
word for "a ghost"? In his "mighties"
David had a powerful body-guard of native
Israelites, and Saul previously had formed
a similar force of three thousand men, not
merely for the protection of his own person,
but to guard the land from marauding
incursions of Amalekites and other freebooting tribes. Such a body of men was of
primary importance for police purposes and
the safety of the frontiers. How useful
such a force would be we can well understand from the history of the marches between England and Scotland (see also note
on ch. iii. 22); but I imagine that the
Cherethites and Pelethites were used for
humbler purposes. While "the mighties"

guarded the frontiers, and kept the peace
of the kingdom, these men would be used
about the court and in Jerusalem, to execute
the commands of the king and his great
officers. Native Israelites would refuse
such servile work, and the conquered
Canaanites might become dangerous if
trained and armed; while these foreigners,
like the Swiss Guard in France, would be
trustworthy and efficient. As for the true-
born Israelites, they probably did not form
the mass of the population, but, like the
Franks in France, were the privileged and
dominant race. We read that even from
Egypt, besides their own dependents, there
went up with Israel "a great mixture" (Exod.
xii. 38, margin). In Numb. xi. 4 these are
even contemptuously designated by a word
which answers to our "omnium gatherum;"
yet even they, after the conquest of Palestine, would be higher in rank than the
subjugated Canaanites, from whom, together
with another "mixed multitude" spoken of
in Neh. xiii. 3, are descended the felahin of
the present day. David's armies would be
drawn from the Israelites, among whom were
now reckoned the mixed multitude which
went up from Egypt, and which was ennobled
by taking part in the conquest of Canaan.
In the army "the mighties" would hold the
chief place; while the mercenaries, recruited
from Ziklag and its neighbourhood, which
continued to be David's private property
(1 Sam. xxvii. 6), would be most useful in
the discharge of all kinds of administrative
duty, and would also guard the king's
person. In ch. xx. 23 for *Cherethi* we
find *Cheri*, which word also occurs in 2
Kings xi. 4, 19. In the former passage the
spelling is a mistake, the letter *t* having
dropped out, and it is so regarded by the
Jews, who read "Cherethi." The versions
also translate there just as they do here,
namely the Vulgate and LXX., "Cherethi
and Pelethi;" and the Syriac by two nouns
of somewhat similar sound to the Hebrew,
and which signify "freemen and soldiers."
In the latter place in Kings it is probable
that some other tribe supplied the body-
guard in Queen Athaliah's time. **David's
sons were chief rulers;** Hebrew and Revised
Version, *priests*. Similarly, in ch. xx. 26,
"Ira the Jairite was David's priest," Hebrew,
cohen; and in 1 Kings iv. 5, "Zabud was
Solomon's priest." Gesenius and others
suppose that they were domestic chaplains,
not ministering according to the Levitical
law, but invested with a sort of sacerdotal
sacredness in honour of their birth. But if
we look again at 1 Kings iv. 5 we find
"Zabud was priest, the king's friend;" and
the latter words seem to be an explanation
of the title *cohen*, added because the word in
this sense was already becoming obsolete.

In 1 Chron. xviii. 17 the language is completely changed, and we read, "and David's sons were chief at the king's hand." We may feel sure that the Chronicler knew what was the meaning of the phrase in the Books of Samuel, and that he was also aware that it had gone out of use, and therefore gave instead the right sense. Evidently the word *cohen* had at first a wider significance, and meant a "minister and confidant." He was the officer who stood next to his master, and knew his purpose and saw to its execution. And this was the meaning of the term when applied to the confidential minister of Jehovah, whose duty it was to execute his will according to the commands given in the Law; but when so used it gradually became too sacred for ordinary employment. Still, there is a divinity about a king, and so his confidants and the officers nearest to his person were still called cohens; and we find the phrase lingering on for another century and a half. For Jehu puts to death, not only Ahab's great men and kinsfolk, but also "his cohens," the men who had been his intimate friends (2 Kings x. 11).

HOMILETICS.

Vers. 1—18.—*The historic mirror.* The narrative relates a succession of victories and conquests over the Philistines, the Moabites, the Zobahites, the Syrians, the Ammonites, the Amalekites, and the Edomites; the placing of garrisons in Syria and Edom; the voluntary recognition of David's supremacy by the King of Hamath; the military, ecclesiastical, and civil appointments of the kingdom; the dedication of treasure won in conquest and diplomacy to the service of God; the maintenance of a righteous administration throughout Israel; and the safe keeping of David in all his undertakings. History is a record of human acts. Sacred history is a record of human acts in some special relation to the working out of the spiritual issues of the kingdom of God. In all history we see mirrored human thought and feeling. It gives us a glimpse of an invisible world of energy, that is ever seeking to find full expression for itself. In this portion of sacred history we see mirrored not only the strivings of the inner nature of men, but also outlines of truth pertaining to the invisible kingdom which is ever being extended over men. The early and lower developments in Davidic times indicate permanent truths for all Christian times.

I. THERE ARE GRADES OF SERVICE IN THE KINGDOM OF GOD. The conquest of these alien peoples, the rough and thorough crippling of their powers (vers. 2, 4, 8, 14), and the distribution of office among competent men (vers. 16—18), was a form of service far below, in the feelings involved, in the tone running through it, the other service rendered by David in the form of a holy, just life amidst his people, and a contribution by speech and song to the spiritual education of Israel. Yet this lower form of service was necessary, and had its proper place in the great scheme of government whereby God was preparing the world for the Prince of Peace. The actual state of mankind, and not some hypothetical state of perfection, conditioned the means by which gradually the final blessing should come. God is not responsible for the imperfect feelings with which David and others may have done certain work. He allows men in his service to apply themselves to the actual circumstances of their position according to the light they have, and then makes their general course of action subservient to the development of his own gracious purposes. The same is true now. In the Church there are higher and lower forms of service. In consequence of the imperfection of some of the workers and of their surroundings, the service draws out, not the highest feelings of which man is capable. There are rough men for rough work. Superior men may do such work, but they are not so much at ease in it as when engaged in purely spiritual efforts. It was more congenial to David to write psalms than to hough horses. The actual state of the world required both just then.

II. THE SUBJUGATION OF EXTERNAL EVILS SHOULD GO ALONG WITH INTERNAL RENOVATION. The first aim of David was, as we have seen, to restore unity, justice, peace, and religion to Israel. He worked on the central spring of national life. But the heathen and restless foes around were an incessant trouble as long as the political and military strength of Israel under the new *régime* were untested. Their subjugation was therefore the necessary complement of the internal consolidation. Taking the Davidic kingdom as representing in general features the kingdom of Christ, we see the same truth. Its settlement among men means internal change, reformation, and consolidation of all that is good; but it is bound, for its own peace and extension, to make war on all that is alien to the mind of Christ. Hence his Church is militant. He is our Captain. We are soldiers sworn to preserve our heritage and extend his domain by actual destruction of the forces of evil that lie around. The same applies to our own life viewed as a domain over which Christ rules. Internal harmony should be accompanied by an effort to overcome everything in our daily circumstances which, if not overcome, may mar our peace, and possibly gain an unhallowed influence over us.

III. The dedication of material wealth to the service of God is an evidence of godly wisdom. The prohibition to apply the spoils of war to private uses (Josh. vi. 19; cf. 1 Sam. xv. 23) was a wholesome restraint on a low class of human feelings. There was a strong temptation for David to enrich himself by conquest, and, reasoning as an ordinary man, he could have made out a good case for himself. But he was a man of God; he saw things, as it were, with the eyes of God, and therefore, apart from specific injunction for each case, acted in harmony with the mind of God. It was godly wisdom thus to devote to the service of God what had been acquired by his own strong arm; for very great wealth brings very great spiritual dangers (Matt. xix. 23, 24). The blessed temporal condition does not lie in abundance (Prov. xxx. 8, 9; Luke xii. 15). The possession of great wealth, combined with slender gifts to the cause of Christ, reveals a lack of spiritual perception and of sympathy with the heart and purpose of Christ. The devotion of wealth to Christ is the safest investment, for it brings blessings on the donor and on others through all ages. The spiritual results of material wealth, well employed, are beyond calculation. It is said of the true King in Zion, "To him shall be given of the gold of Sheba" (Ps. lxii. 15). He also is "worthy to receive riches" (Rev. v. 12). There are thousands of ways in which wealth may now be dedicated to God. The earnest heart will find out the right channel for its devotion. The demand for sanctuaries, labourers, and the claims of Christ's poor, are ever before the rich (cf. Hag. i. 4—6; Matt. ix. 36, 37; Rom. x. 14, 15; Matt. xxv. 35—40). In so far as Christians enter into the spirit of their Lord will they rejoice in consecrating wealth to him (2 Cor. viii. 9; cf. v. 13—15).

IV. The blessing of God in our endeavours is the spiritual condition of success. It is said twice (vers. 6, 14) that God "preserved David whithersoever he went." It is obvious that these various enterprises were full of danger to a man like David—danger to his life, his spirituality of mind, his moral conduct, his political reputation. His natural qualities of courage, thoroughness, and his laudable ambition as a monarch, might urge him on to positions of extreme peril; and the incidents of warfare are proverbially prejudicial to piety. The secret of his success lay in his being kept of God. The servant of God, doing rough, dangerous work, not for self-aggrandizement, but for God and his people, is surrounded by an unseen shield which no dart can penetrate. Here we see a truth ever being realized in private and public life—a true man of God, a man of undivided heart, setting himself to necessary but undesirable work, pressing on every day amidst dangers to life and religion, keeping the one thought of pleasing God clear before him, and ever everywhere guarded by him whom he serves. Till our work is done no "arrow that flieth by day" can touch us. It is a fact which should be much insisted on, that God does preserve his saints (Ps. xxxvii. 23, 24, 28). No outward sign was visible, yet God was with David. The absence of visible signs with us is no evidence that God is not our Shield and Helper. The chief thing for us is to see that we are his, that we do his will and not our own, and that we have a holy method in our enterprises, be they strictly spiritual or related to ordinary affairs.

V. The glory of an active man lies in his being true to his calling. David was a king, bound by virtue of his position to rule in equity and righteousness. A greater distinction could not have been awarded to him in that office than that conveyed in the declaration that "he executed judgment and justice unto all his people" (ver. 15). He was true to his vocation. No man can rise higher than that. The glory of a man does not lie in being or doing as others have been and done, for talents, opportunities, and occupations differ; but in performing the part to which Providence has called him thoroughly well. Every star is perfect in its own full lustre. Every man is noble when his whole nature is developed in harmony with the purpose of his Maker. "Well done, good and faithful servant," is said of the lowliest of Christ's servants who has been faithful in "a few things" (Matt. xxv. 22, 23). A monarch, a bishop, a pastor, a Sunday school teacher, a pious domestic servant, and a day-labourer, may each be distinguished by faithfulness to the work in hand. True spiritual honour lies more in the spirit of loyalty to our divinely appointed calling than in the specific deeds transacted. Hence the moral prospects of all Christ's servants. It is extremely important to impress this on the young, and on those who are prone to be discouraged by reason of the lowliness of their position in society and in Christian endeavour.

GENERAL LESSONS. 1. The disorganization produced in the world by the action of sin renders it inevitable that much human suffering, much collision of man against man, be endured even in the historical processes of Providence, by which the blessings of redemption are finally brought into full operation. The woes of the Moabites (ver. 2) and of others were humanly necessitated incidents in the ages, giving birth to the promised Christ; and much suffering will yet be endured ere the full triumph of good over evil is achieved (Rom. viii. 18—22). 2. The most certain of the promises of God should be embraced in full confidence, and yet the most strenuous exertion on our part to bring about their fulfilment is reasonable. David's kingdom had been assured (ch. vii. 27). But, nevertheless, he set garrisons in defence of his heritage, and took pains to organize his administration on a judicious basis (vers. 16—18). Fatalism or presumption is irreligious as truly as is unbelief. 3. Resources obtained from men not religious may be used in the service of God (vers. 9—11). The deference paid by Toi to David is similar to that paid by many men destitute of vital godliness to Christians, and their gifts, though not in the most enlightened spirit, may be employed for the holiest of purposes. 4. There is a prophetic truth in the turning of the golden shields and other instruments of the heathen into the peaceful uses of the sanctuary (vers. 7, 9, 10). As a fact, the weapons and splendour of kings will some day be turned into uses subservient to the reign of Christ, the Prince of Peace (Isa. ii. 2—5; lx. 5—11).

HOMILIES BY VARIOUS AUTHORS.

Vers. 1—14 (1 Chron. xviii. 1—13).—(JERUSALEM.) *David's wars and victories.* *Summary*: (1) The Philistines (ver. 1). (2) The Moabites (ver. 2; Numb. xxiv. 17). (3) The Ammonites (ver. 12; ch. x.). (4) The Syrians of Zobah, under Hadadezer (ver. 3; ch. x. 15, 16). The point here touched (ver. 4) in the struggle appears to have been *after* the Ammonites had commenced hostilities, aided by Hadadezer, (5) the Syrians of Beth-Rehob, (6) the King of Maachah, and (7) the men of Tob; and had been defeated (in a *first* campaign) by Joab and Abishai at Medeba (ch. x. 1—14). Hadadezer now recruited his forces in Mesopotamia, and made immense preparations; but he was defeated by David, who took the field in person (in a *second* campaign), at Helam; his general, Shobach, being slain (ch. x. 15—19). (8) The Syrians of Damascus (vers. 5, 6). (9) Toi, King of Hamath (vers. 9, 10). "Thus the Aramean supremacy, which had in previous centuries become so formidable to the Hebrews, and even to the Ammonites, was now broken once more by the heroic arm of David" (Ewald). (10) The Edomites, in league with (11) the Amalekites (ver. 12) and others, threatening to render previous victories fruitless, overcome (in a *third* campaign) by Abishai and by Joab (vers. 13, 14; 1 Chron. xviii. 12; 1 Kings xi. 15; Ps. lx., inscription). "David himself came at the close of the campaign to arrange the conquered territory" (Stanley). (12) The siege of Rabbah, the capital of the Ammonites, which still held out, by Joab (in a *fourth* campaign), while the king remained at Jerusalem (ch. xi. 1); and its capture by David (ch. xii. 26—31; 1 Chron. xx. 1—3). These wars of Israel with surrounding nations were not ordinary wars (ch. ii. 24—29). They were a special embodiment of the great conflict which was ordained from the beginning (Gen. iii. 15), and of which the sacred history is a record. They involved principles and issues of vast importance; and they must be considered in the light of the peculiar position of the people of Israel, the measure of Divine revelation vouchsafed to them, and the "ruling ideas in early ages," in order that they may be judged of correctly, and just inferences drawn from them in relation to the conduct of Christian nations. They were waged—

I. WITH POWERFUL ADVERSARIES. Numerous, varied, confederated, selfish, proud, and "delighting in war" (Ps. lxviii. 30). The Ammonites (1 Sam. xi. 1—15) first attacked

Israel (as the Philistines and others had previously done), assisted by the Syrians, "for reward." "The first recorded example of mercenary warfare" (Kitto). They "succeeded in girdling the whole eastern frontier with steel." They were idolaters, fought against Jehovah, sought to exterminate his people, and would have been satisfied with nothing short of their entire subjugation. Never had their peril been more imminent. It was such as is described by the psalmist—

> "Why do the nations rage,
> And the people imagine a vain thing?
> Kings of the earth set themselves up,
> And rulers take counsel together
> Against Jehovah, and against his anointed:
> Let us burst their bonds asunder,
> And cast away their cords from us!"
>
> (Ps. ii. 1—3.)

II. ON JUSTIFIABLE GROUNDS. For: 1. *The defence of person and property,* and the preservation of the worship of Jehovah (ch. x. 12). The right of self-defence is a law of nature, extending to the relations of states and kingdoms, as well as of individuals. Without its exercise the destruction of Israel by their fierce and powerful enemies could have been averted only by a continuous miracle. 2. *The punishment of evildoers,* and the execution of a Divine judgment upon the heathen and their gods. Of this David deemed himself an appointed agent, fulfilling a Divine commission, like that given to Saul concerning Amalek, and the command under which Joshua acted in the conquest of the land. 3. *The attainment of the destination* of the chosen people to rule over the nations according to former promises and predictions. "The chief aim of the writer is to show the growth of God's kingdom" (see the martial Psalms, ix., x., xviii., xx., xxi., xliv., lx., lxviii., cx.). Ps. ix., 'The righteous Judge of the heathen'—

> "I will praise thee, O Jehovah, with my whole heart;
> I will recount all thy wonderful works.
> Arise, O Jehovah, let not mortal man be defiant;
> Let the heathen be judged in thy sight.
> Put them in fear, O Jehovah;
> Let the heathen know that they are but mortal men!"
>
> (Ps. ix. 1, 19, 20.)

III. IN A DEVOUT SPIRIT. Faith in the immediate presence of God, reverence for his righteous laws, dependence upon his mighty arm, zeal for his universal honour; prayerfulness, confidence, thankfulness. "The whole nation was at once a nation of soldiers and a nation of priests. They were the soldiers of God, pledged to a crusade—a holy war; pledged to the extermination of all idolatry and all wickedness wherever existing" (Perowne, in Ps. cx.). Ps. xx., 'Going forth to battle'—

> "Jehovah answer thee in the day of distress;
> The Name of the God of Jacob set thee up on high.
> We will shout for joy because of thy salvation,
> And in the Name of our God will we raise our banners.
> O Jehovah, save the king!
> May he hear us in the day we call."
>
> (Ps. xx. 1, 5, 9.)

In a reverse, such as may have taken place just before the overthrow of the Edomites, they turned to God in supplication, and girded themselves afresh for the conflict. Ps. lx., 'Confidence in disaster'—"the most martial of all the Psalms"—partially repeated in Ps. cviii. 7—14.

> "O God, thou hast cast us off, thou hast broken us;
> Thou hast been angry, restore us again.
> Thou hast given to them that fear thee a banner,
> That they may muster (around it) from before the bow.
> Who will conduct me into the fortified city?
> Who will bring me into Edom?
> Through God shall we do valiantly;
> And he will tread down our adversaries."
>
> (Ps. lx. 1, 4, 9, 12.)

IV. WITH EXTRAORDINARY SUCCESS; in which the hand of God was manifested, especially in the preservation of David "whithersoever he went" (vers. 6, 14), and was recognized in the dedication to Jehovah of the spoils of war (vers. 7, 10—12) amidst general thanksgiving and praise. One victory rapidly succeeded another until the whole region from the Nile to the Euphrates (Gen. xv. 18) was subdued, peace was established, and Israel occupied a position of unrivalled power and glory. "David erected, on Joab's return (ver. 13), a monument of thanksgiving for his victory; and we may imagine how brilliant was the triumphant procession in Jerusalem when we recollect the hundred war-chariots with their horses which were spared when Hadarezer was conquered" (Ewald). Ps. xxi., 'Returning in triumph'—

> "O Jehovah, in thy strength shall the king be glad,
> And in thy saving help how greatly shall he exult!
> Be thou exalted, O Jehovah, in thy strength;
> So will we celebrate with voice and harp thy might."
>
> (Ps. xxi. 1, 13.)

V. NOT WITHOUT DEPLORABLE CONSEQUENCES. Even when waged on justifiable grounds and from religious motives, war is associated with manifold evils. It was not the loss of life that occurred, nor the cruel severities that were practised (ver. 2; ch. xii. 31), characteristic of the age, in the wars of David, which wrought the mischief, so much as the fierce passions, the pride, ambition, luxury, and vice they engendered, the heavy burdens they imposed, and the neglect of the humbler pursuits and more orderly virtues they involved. "The one blot upon the time is David's lust of war, bringing men like Joab to the front, and debasing David's own character. . . . If ever God wrote his verdict plainly upon ambition and aggressive war, he wrote it upon the wars of David. They brought the stain of two foul crimes on David himself; ruined his own domestic peace and happiness; ruined, by the possession of too-great power, the one of his sons who started so wisely and well; and ruined the kingdom, which broke asunder of its own weight" ('Prophecy a Preparation for Christ,' p. 216). Yet these effects have not always been considered in later times; while the record of his successes has sometimes been regarded as affording a sanction and an incentive to the martial spirit under different circumstances and a better dispensation. "It was among the Teutonic race that the Church first manifested warlike propensities. They were emphatically men of blood. The chief difficulty of the Church was to teach them to love peace. According to a well-known story, the Gothic bishop, Ulphilas, showed his special sense of the special weakness of his Teuton converts by refraining from translating the Books of Samuel and Kings into their language, as he did the rest of the Scripture. His reason, we are told, was that they contained 'the history of wars;' and the nation was already very fond of war, and needed the bit rather than the spur so far as fighting was concerned" (British Quarterly Review, January, 1881). Nevertheless, the wars and victories of David (allowed for "the hardness of men's hearts" until "the times of reformation")—

VI. FORESHADOWED NOBLER CONFLICTS AND TRIUMPHS by One greater than David— the Prince of Peace, and his faithful followers (1 Sam. xiii. 1—7; xvii. 47); in which the elements of good that existed therein are retained and perfected, and those of evil set aside; "the weapons of our warfare are not of the flesh, but" spiritual (truth, righteousness, love) and "mighty before God to the casting down of strongholds" of error and unrighteousness (2 Cor. x. 4; Luke ix. 56; John xviii. 36); and the effects, enduring peace, security, and happiness (Isa. ix. 5, 6). "Since the time that Jesus Christ said, 'Put up thy sword into its scabbard,' Christians ought not to go to war, unless it be in that most honourable warfare with the vilest enemies of the Church—the inordinate love of money, anger, and ambition. These are our Philistines, these our Nebuchadnezzars, these our Moabites and Ammonites, with whom we ought never to make a truce; with these we must engage without intermission till, the enemy being utterly extirpated, peace may be firmly established. Unless we subdue such enemies as these, we can neither have peace with ourselves nor peace with any one else. This is the only war which tends to produce a real and lasting peace" (Erasmus).—D.

Ver. 11.—(JERUSALEM.) Dedication of property to God. According to the custom of the time, the most valuable of the spoils of war became the property of David; and these, along with the presents brought to him, he devoted to a sacred use—in preparation for the building of the temple (1 Chron. xviii. 8). The spirit which he displayed had been shown at the erection of the tabernacle (Exod. xxxv. 29); and it was participated in by many (1 Chron. xxvi. 26—28; xxix. 5—9). Other instances occurred at a much earlier period (Gen. xiv. 30; xxviii. 22). David's act was: 1. *Unselfish.* The evil of selfishness specially appears in undue attachment to earthly possessions; "which is idolatry," and "a root of all evil." It ofttimes increases with the increase of worldly good, "like the Indian fig tree connecting itself vitally at a hundred spots, with the soil over which it spreads." Hence the injunction, "If riches increase," etc. (Ps. lxii. 10). A good man receives that he may give, and feels that "it is more blessed to give than to receive." 2. *Grateful.* David recognized the hand of God in his victories; and herein testified his thankfulness to his Divine Helper and Benefactor. Wealth is his gift; so is the power to acquire it (Deut. viii. 17, 18). But how often are its possessors forgetful of this, proud, and unthankful! "All things come of thee, and of thine own have we given thee" (1 Chron. xxix. 14). 3. *Faithful.* Earthly good is not an absolute gift, but a trust; it is put into our power only for a brief season; its possession involves the responsibility of its employment according to the will of the Owner; and its faithful use is conducive to the possession of "the true riches" (Luke xvi. 9—12). Whilst it should be altogether employed according to his will, a due proportion of it should be set apart as sacred to the claims of the needy, the support of Divine worship, and the spread of the gospel. It would appear that every Jewish family in ancient times devoted as much as a fourth part of its income to religious and charitable purposes. But inasmuch as no definite rule is now enjoined, every man must determine the proportion for himself by earnest thought and prayer, without reference to what others may do, and with a view to giving, not as *little*, but as *much* as possible. It has been stated that more wealth has been made in England during the last fifty years than during the preceding eighteen centuries. But notwithstanding numerous examples of noble beneficence, how small a part of it comparatively has been devoted to the highest ends (Deut. xvi. 17; Prov. iii. 9, 10; Luke xix. 13; 1 Cor. iv. 2; xvi. 1; 2 Cor. viii., ix.; 1 Tim. vi. 17—19)! 4. *Devotional.* David's offering was religious; in it he offered himself to God; and sought to fulfil his purposes concerning the welfare of his people and the promotion of his honour and glory in the earth. This is the highest motive; and those who are actuated by it obtain an unspeakable blessing both here and hereafter (Mal. iii. 10; Matt. xxv. 21).

> "Largely thou givest, gracious Lord,
> Largely thy gifts should be restored;
> Freely thou givest, and thy word
>   Is, 'Freely give.'
> He only, who forgets to hoard,
>   Has learnt to live."
>
> (Keble.)

Ver. 14.—*God's preserving care.* "And the Lord preserved David whithersoever he went" (ver. 6; 1 Chron. xviii. 6, 13). The providence of God (his preservation and government of all things), which embraces the creation in *general* (Ps. xxxvi. 6; Neh. ix. 6) and man in *particular* (Ps. viii. 4, 5; Luke xii. 7), is exercised with *special* regard to the good of those that love him (Matt. vi. 32; x. 29, 30). This is evident from his relation and love to them (Deut. xxxii. 9; Luke xii. 32), the promises and declarations of his Word (Ps. xxxvii. 28; cxxi. 8), and the facts of observation and experience (Gen. xlv. 5; Esth. vi. 1). The life of David is full of illustrations thereof (1 Sam. xix. 10; xxiii. 28). "The Lord preserveth the faithful" (Ps. xxxi. 23)—

I. IN LOYAL OBEDIENCE to his will, such as David exhibited.

> "For he will give his angels charge over thee,
> To keep thee *in all thy ways*."
>
> (Ps. xci. 11.)

i.e. the ways of duty; not of presumption, like those which the tempter (omitting these words in his quotation) sought to induce the Son of man to pursue (Matt. iv. 6). "He that walketh uprightly walketh surely" (Prov. x. 9), and "shall be saved; but he that is perverse in his ways shall fall at once" (Prov. xxviii. 18). We must keep the commandments of God if we would be "kept by the power of God." "Who is he that will harm you, if ye be followers of that which is good?" (1 Pet. iii. 13; iv. 19).

II. AMIDST IMMINENT PERIL, arising from attacks of numerous foes; which must often be met in the path of duty, and cannot be avoided without sin (ch. iv. 9—11). "And, indeed, there is a great deal of reason why we should respect him that, with an untainted valour, has grown old in arms and hearing the drum beat. When every minute death seems to pass by and shun him, he is one that the supreme God cared for, and, by a particular guard, defended in the hail of death" (O. Felltham). There is a holy strife (Phil. i. 27; Jude 3; Eph. vi. 12), and in it we may sometimes be exposed to as great danger as David was (ch. xxi. 16); but the eye of God sees it and his hand wards it off. "No weapon," etc. (Isa. liv. 17).

> "O Jehovah Lord, thou Strength of my salvation,
> Thou hast covered my head in the day of battle."
> (Ps. cxl. 7.)

III. BY MANIFOLD MEANS. Not without prudence and effort on the part of men; not by direct, extraordinary and miraculous interposition; but by: 1. The salutary influence of a devout spirit on conditions favourable to safety. 2. Special impressions on the minds both of the good and of the bad, conducive to the preservation of the former. 3. A peculiar concurrence of circumstances having the same effect; and other ways, still more wonderful, and not less effectual (Prov. xxi. 31). Nothing is more mysterious to our partial comprehension of them than the methods of providence by which God accomplishes his designs. "A mighty maze! but not without a plan."

IV. FOR BENEFICENT ENDS. Not only "the good of his chosen" (Ps. cvi. 5), whom he preserves; but also the good which they may effect on behalf of others, the manifestation of his great Name, the complete establishment of his kingdom. "We know that all things work together for good," etc. (Rom. viii. 28). "This is the sun in the heaven of all the promises."—D.

Vers. 15—18 (1 Chron. xviii. 14—17).—(JERUSALEM.) *David's administration.* From the wars and victories of David we turn to contemplate his administration of the internal affairs of the kingdom. By his skill and energy, united with the services of many eminent men, and aided by the favour of Heaven, he raised the nation, in an incredibly short period, to a position of extraordinary power and glory. "More than Charlemagne did for Europe, or Alfred for England, David accomplished for the tribes of Israel" (W. M. Taylor). What is here recorded (taken along with what is elsewhere stated) affords an illustration of—

I. A JUST REIGN. "And David executed judgment and justice unto all the people" (1 Sam. vii. 15—17; x. 24). It was as important a part of his office to judge them as to lead them forth to battle (ch. xv. 2—4); and, in its fulfilment, he acted: 1. According to *the laws of Jehovah*, the supreme King and Judge, whose servant he was. 2. With proper discernment, *strict equity and impartiality*, and great diligence. 3. So that, either by his own decisions or those of judges appointed and superintended by him, right was done to *all his subjects*, wrongs redressed, and wrong-doers punished. He was a king who

> "In the royal palace gave
> Example to the meanest of the fear
> Of God and all integrity of life
> And manners; who, august yet lowly; who,
> Severe yet gracious; in his very heart
> Detesting all oppression, all intent
> Of private aggrandizement; and, the first
> In every public duty, held the scales
> Of justice, and, as the law which reigned in him
> Commanded, gave rewards; or with the edge
> Vindictive smote now light, now heavily,
> According to the stature of the crime."
> (Pollok, 'The Course of Time.')

II. A SKILFUL ORGANIZATION, indicated by the mention of the chief officers of state, who formed the king's council and acted as his confidential advisers, along with his sons (ver. 18), the prophets, and others (see for later enumeration, ch. xx. 13—26; 1 Chron. xxvii. 32—34). 1. *Military.* (1) The host (1 Chron. xxvii. 1—15), or national militia (under Joab), consisting of all the males capable of bearing arms, and arranged in twelve bodies of twenty-four thousand each, whose turn of service came every month. (2) The body-guard (under Benaiah), Krethi and Plethi (lictors and couriers; Cretans or Carians, and Philistines), "formed at Ziklag, and afterwards recruited from foreigners (ch. xv. 18; xx. 23), having their quarters in Jerusalem, not far from the royal castle" (Ewald). (3) The heroes (Gibborim), mighty men or veterans (under Abishai); the old guard, who had gathered to David in his wanderings, constituting "the first standing army of which we have any special knowledge," the number six hundred being maintained, "divided into three large bands of two hundred each, and small bands of twenty each; the small bands commanded by thirty officers, one for each band, who together formed 'the thirty,' and the three large bands by three officers, who together formed 'the three'" (Stanley). 2. *Civil;* pertaining to the registering and publication of the royal edicts, the regulation of judicial, financial, and other matters, the management of the royal demesnes, etc. (1 Chron. xxvii. 25—31), from which the revenue was largely derived. "Each tribe had still its *prince* or ruler, and continued under a general superintendence from the king to conduct its local affairs (1 Chron. xxvii. 16—22). The supreme council of the nation continued to assemble on occasions of great national importance; and, though its influence could not have been so great as it was before the institution of royalty, it remained an integral part of the constitution. Without superseding the tribal governments, David greatly strengthened them by a systematic distribution through the country of a large number of Levites (six thousand) as officers and judges (1 Chron. xxvi. 20—32). It is extremely probable that this large and able body of Levites were not limited to strictly judicial duties, but that they performed important functions also in the education, the healing, and the general elevation of the people" (Blaikie). 3. *Ecclesiastical;* the Levites (1 Chron. xxiii.); the priests, in twenty-four classes, and their attendants (1 Chron. xxiv.); the choristers, in twenty-four courses (1 Chron. xxv.); the porters and officers (1 Chron. xxvi.). "Order is Heaven's first law." It is an essential condition of peace, safety, and power. "The solemn transfer of the ark of the covenant, at which almost all the people were present, had made a deep impression on their minds, and had awakened them to a sincere adoration of Jehovah. These favourable dispositions David wished to strengthen by suitable regulations in the service of the priests and Levites, especially by the instructive and animating psalms, which were composed partly by himself, and partly by other poets and prophets. By such instructive means, David, without using any coercive measures, brought the whole nation to forget their idols, and to worship Jehovah alone" (Jahn, 'Heb. Com.').

III. AN ABLE EXECUTIVE. The best organization avails little unless there be men of ability to carry it into practical effect. David's reign was singularly rich in such men. 1. *Warriors* like Joab, Abishai, Benaiah, and other "heroes who had vied with him in valour and self-sacrifice for the community of Israel and the religion of Jehovah," and "whose names lived on, linked for ever with his memory" (ch. xxiii. 8—39). 2. *Ministers* like Jehoshaphat, Sheva, Adoram, Ira the Jairite; counsellors like Ahithophel and Hushai. 3. *Priests* like Zadok and Abiathar; "masters of the song" like Asaph, Heman, Jeduthun; prophets like Nathan and Gad. "All is now in full movement and almost in its original life, while around the chief hero a crowd of other figures are woven into the mighty drama, and even these are illumined by the bright rays of his sun; nay, even what would be insignificant elsewhere acquires importance here from the conspicuous eminence of Israel's greatest king" (Ewald). A wise ruler discerns the ablest men, attaches them to him, and profits by their wisdom, appoints them to offices in which they can most effectually promote the common good, and upholds and encourages them in their faithful endeavours to that end. It has been said that "a ruler who appoints any man to an office when there is in his dominions another man better qualified for it, sins against God and against the state" (Koran).

IV. A MIGHTY NATION; united, prosperous, powerful, imbued with lofty principles and aims, "as an eagle muing her mighty youth and kindling her undazzled eyes at the full midday beam" (Milton). To this many influences contributed, one of which was a just, wise, and strong administration (Ps. lxxii.). "David's own moral exaltation, and still more the spirit of fearless justice in which he ruled, had its effect on the nation at large. The theocracy became real to them in a sense in which it had never been before. They saw that an organized system, which was based upon religion and built up of justice, was more truly the embodiment of the Divine government than the fitful inspiration of the judges. Thus they won the might that comes from right: they felt that a war in defence of this new organization was most truly a holy war, and that if David was at the head of it, he was not only the king but the high priest of the people. Animated by this feeling, they forgot all the old 'divisions and searchings of heart,' and flocked around the standard of their king in such numbers and with such a spirit that they crushed the greatest coalition that ever threatened to destroy their religion and their nation" ('The Psalms chronologically arranged'). "The enlargement of territory, the amplification of power and state, leads to a corresponding enlargement of ideas, of imagery, of sympathies; and thus (humanly speaking) the magnificent forebodings of a wider dispensation in the prophetic writings first became possible through the court and empire of David" (Stanley).—D.

Ver. 6.—*Divine preservation*. The Revised Version translates, "The Lord gave victory to David;" but in the margin, "saved David," which is equivalent to the translation in the Authorized Version, and is the more literal meaning of the original, from which there is no necessity to depart. In the Psalms, in which David praises God for his help against his enemies, he speaks as much of the protection he experienced as of the victories he won. His preservation in so many perils of war was worthy of special mention. The record is one that might be made in an account of the lives of most of us; in some respects, of all.

I. THE PRESERVATION EXPERIENCED. 1. *Physical*. That of bodily life and health and of the senses. Protection in perils by land or water. Preservation from serious illnesses, or deliverance from them. The uniformity of good health and wholeness of limbs is a greater blessing than restoration from sickness or repair of fractures, although it does not usually excite so much notice or call forth so much gratitude. 2. *Mental*. That of the soundness of the mind, of perception, memory, reason. It might be salutary for each of us to pay one visit to a lunatic asylum. Such impressions of the value of our reason may be obtained there as can be obtained nowhere else. 3. *Moral and spiritual*. That of faith and a good conscience, of principles and habits of religion and virtue. Protection from specially powerful temptations which, yielded to, would have been our ruin. 4. *Of reputation*. From slander or misunderstanding. A good name is conducive, not only to our comfort, but to our success in life, and to our usefulness. To some, owing to peculiar circumstances, its continuance is marvellous. 5. *Prolonged*. In many cases for very many years, in which dangers numerous, various, repeated, and imminent, have been met with. The greater the perils and the longer the period, so much the more noteworthy the preservation.

II. To WHOM IT IS TO BE ASCRIBED. "The Lord." David owed much to faithful friends and brave soldiers, who regarded his life as their special care, and defended it at the peril of their own (see ch. xxi. 15—17); but the historian ascribes all to God; and David, when he reviews his life, or any part of it, does the same. In like manner, as we look back, we may remember many who have in various ways ministered to our preservation, and towards whom we rightly cherish gratitude; but these, and all else that has contributed to our well-being, we rightly ascribe to God (comp. 2 Tim. iii. 11; iv. 16, 17).

III. THE EMOTIONS IT SHOULD AWAKEN. 1. *Gratitude*. Expressed in praise and renewed self-dedication.

> "My life, which thou hast made thy care,
> Lord, I devote to thee."

Also in zealous endeavours to preserve others from evil, especially the young and inexperienced (see Ps. cxvi., cxvii.) 2. *Confidence and hope*. As to future physical and mental preservation, so far as seems good to the infinite wisdom and goodness; but especially as to the moral and spiritual (see Ps. xci. and cxxi.; 2 Cor. i. 9, 10; 2 Tim. iv. 18).

> "We'll praise him for all that is past,
> And trust him for all that's to come."

G. W.

Ver. 11.—*Dedication of treasure to God.* The dedication in this instance doubtless consisted in placing the spoils of war and other valuables named in the sacred treasury, whether for present use, or, as is probable, with a view to their employment in the erection or services of the future temple. The king presents in this act of piety an example which all should follow. I. WHAT WE SHOULD DEDICATE TO GOD. 1. *Ourselves.* We must begin with this. All true godliness does begin with the surrender of self, with all its powers of soul and body, to God, to be saved and sanctified by him, and devoted to his service. No other gift can be truly presented while this is withheld; none can be a substitute for it; none acceptable without it. True offerings to God are the offerings of his true servants. 2. *Our material treasures.* Gold and silver, houses and lands. All are to be dedicated to God. What we have inherited, what we have gained by industry and enterprise, and what may have been given to us, as the vessels of gold and silver and brass which the King of Hamath sent to David. But if we have gained aught by fraud, injustice or other iniquity, we may not present this to God, but return it to its rightful owners (see Luke xix. 8). 3. *Our mental gifts and acquisitions.* Spoils won from the heathen, it may be, by victorious study. All our abilities and culture; all our knowledge. 4. *Our spiritual acquirements.* All we have of spiritual life and power; all the grace given to us. These are bestowed, not to be merely enjoyed, but used for God and the good of our brethren. 5. *Our influence.* Whether obtained through our abilities, or wealth, or station, or character, all is to be exercised for God. In a word, whatever we are, and whatever we have, are to be devoted to God. Nothing can be rightly withheld. II. IN WHAT MANNER. 1. *In our ordinary life.* By employing our powers and possessions according to God's will, in uprightness and kindness. By enjoying God's gifts with thankfulness and temperance. By "setting the Lord always before us," and doing and enjoying all as his children and servants. Thus the whole of life becomes religion, and common actions are as acceptable to God as prayers. "HOLINESS UNTO THE LORD" is written upon everything (see Zech. xiv. 20, 21). But no greater mistake can be made than to think that, in giving a portion of our substance and time to religion, we are set free to use the rest as we please. 2. *By devoting a due portion of our powers and possessions to religious and charitable uses.* First, to the support of the worship of God in the congregation to which we belong; then to the relief of the poor with whom we are personally acquainted, and the education of the young in our own locality; and then to such religious and charitable institutions as commend themselves to our judgment, and appear to have a just claim upon our liberality. What proportion of our income should be given away must be left to each person's conscience as in the sight of God. Only we must let conscience decide, not mere inclination. Certainly we ought not to give what belongs to creditors, or the reasonable wants of our families. Our aim should be to ascertain the will of God; and this will vary according to the various circumstances of individuals, and of the same individual at different times. "As he may prosper" (1 Cor. xvi. 2, Revised Version) is the general rule; and any special increase of prosperity (as with David at the time spoken of in the text) justly calls for special liberality. In general, our danger does not lie in the direction of excessive generosity. Few give away as much as they ought, on any just interpretation of our Lord's precepts. "The liberal," who "deviseth liberal things" (Isa. xxxii. 8), is an exceptional person, although there are, thank God, many such. III. MOTIVES TO SUCH DEDICATION. 1. *The claims of God.* As our Proprietor and the Proprietor of all we possess; by right of creation and redemption. "Ye are not your own" (1 Cor. vi. 19). "All things come of thee, and of thine own have we given thee" (1 Chron. xxix. 14). As our liberal Benefactor, who gave us his Son, and is ever bestowing good upon us (2 Cor. ix. 15). As our supreme Ruler, who by innumerable commandments enjoins upon us devotement to his service and kindness to our brethren, and to whom we must give account of our use of what he has entrusted to us. As our Father, who desires that we should resemble him, and thus at once prove our sonship and do honour to his Name (Eph. v. 1, 2). 2. *The love of Jesus Christ to us, and the example he has given us.* (2 Cor. v. 14, 15 ; viii. 9.) 3. *Our professions of self-devotement.* 4. *The good of others.* 5. *Our own good.* A life of self-dedication is the true, the noblest, the happiest life. We grow in all that is good by the practice of good. Our being is enriched, our happiness increased. "It is more blessed to give than to receive" (Acts xx. 35). We have now the testimony of a good conscience, which is the witness of God's approval. We shall hereafter be acknowledged and rewarded by him. In devoting ourselves and our substance to him, we are laying up treasures in heaven (Matt. vi. 20), which will reappear transfigured, for our everlasting enrichment. Good done to others as unto the Lord will be reckoned and rewarded as done to himself; good withheld from them, as withheld from him (Matt. xxv. 34—45). Faithful service now will issue in larger and higher service hereafter (Luke xix. 17, 19). Those to whom we have ministered on earth will welcome us into heaven (Luke xvi. 9), and our eternal glory and joy will be increased by knowing how much we have contributed to theirs (1 Thess. ii. 19).—G. W.

Ver. 13.—*Getting a name.* "David gat him a name." There appears to have been something special in the campaign against the Syrians (or rather Edomites, 1 Chron. xviii. 12), and in David's part therein, which rendered his victory peculiarly signal and memorable. Hence he obtained an honourable "name;" his reputation and fame were greatly increased. A large proportion of the names that men have won have been gained in war. But others more honourable have been obtained by the arts and victories of peace. Most to be valued are those acquired by eminence in goodness and usefulness.

I. NAMES WORTH GETTING. 1. *A good name—a reputation for what is good.* Better than a merely great name. Some names, widely known and for centuries, are so much infamy. Better be totally unknown than have a name for ill doing. All may have some reputation, though in a small circle and for a brief period, for sincere piety and Christian excellence ; for unselfishness, benevolence, activity in doing good, liberality, self-denial in helping others, meekness, humility, long-suffering, patience, and the like. And such a name is more to be desired than riches (Prov. xxii. 1), infinitely more than a great name which has been obtained by unscrupulous ambition. 2. *A good name which arises from and represents reality.* A *mere* name conferred through ignorance or flattery, or assumed and pushed into notice to gratify vanity or secure gain, is utterly worthless, and worse than worthless. So it is with a mere name for wisdom, or learning, or liberality (Isa. xxxii. 5), or public spirit, or philanthropy ; worst of all the name which a hypocrite sometimes gets for sanctity. How withering the reproach addressed to the Church at Sardis, "Thou hast a name that thou livest, and art dead " (Rev. iii. 1) !

II. THE VALUE OF A GOOD NAME. 1. *It is a just source of satisfaction to ourselves,* when our own consciousness testifies to its substantial truth. The good opinion of others, especially of the good and discerning, is part of the reward of goodness. It is one of the ways by which God expresses his favourable judgment of us. 2. *It sustains and stimulates in the course of conduct from which it has arisen.* We are influenced by it to strive more and more to be worthy of it. 3. *It is adapted to do good to others.* It attracts attention to the excellence it designates, and may lead to imitation. It awakens confidence in those who have won it, which gives force to their instructions or admonitions, and it gives them in other ways greater influence for good. On all these accounts it is a heinous sin to injure or destroy another's deserved good name by slander.

III. HOW IT SHOULD BE SOUGHT. It should scarcely be sought at all. The way to obtain it is, not to seek it, but to practise the virtues from which it arises. To seek it is to set our hearts on the approval of men, which is perilous. Let us labour to be accepted of God, and he will take care of our reputation among men, so far as it is good for us and adapted to honour him and benefit our fellow-men. "It is a very small thing to be judged of man's judgment. . . . He that judgeth us is the Lord" (1 Cor. iv. 3, 4). At the same time, for the reasons given under division II., we should not needlessly defy or sacrifice the good opinion of others, though we should willingly do so when fidelity to truth and God requires the sacrifice.

In conclusion. The grandest instance of getting a name is that of our Lord and Saviour. By his self-humiliation and self-sacrifice, in love to us and obedience "unto death, even the death of the cross," he obtained "a Name which is above every name," as well in its significance as in its power with God and men (Phil. ii. 5—11).—G. W.

EXPOSITION.

CHAPTER IX.

Ver. 1.—**Is there yet any that is left of the house of Saul?** As Mephibosheth was five years old at his father's death (ch. iv. 4), but now had a son (ver. 12), a sufficient time must have elapsed for him to grow up and marry; so that probably the events of this chapter occurred seventeen or eighteen years after the battle of Gilboa. As David was king at Hebron for seven years and a half, he had been king now of all Israel for about nine years. But during this long period he had been engaged in a weary struggle, which had left him little repose, and during which it might have been dangerous to draw the house of Saul out of obscurity. But he was at last firmly established on the throne, and had peace all around; and the time was come to act upon the promise made to Jonathan (1 Sam. xx. 14, 15), and which we may be sure David had never forgotten.

Ver. 2.—**A servant whose name was Ziba.** It is evident from this that David was not certain that Jonathan had left behind him a son; but not because of the change of name from Meribbaal (1 Chron. viii. 34); for *Baal* retained its innocent meaning of "lord" until the time of Jezebel. It then became the title of the Phœnician sun-god; and Jezebel's shameless worship of this deity, and her cruelty to Jehovah's prophets, made the people henceforth change the name Baal into Bosheth, "the shameful thing" (see note on ch. ii. 8). Mephibosheth had not changed his name, but had lived in obscurity in the wild region beyond Mahanaim. Meanwhile Ziba had probably taken care of Saul's property in the tribe of Benjamin. There is no reason to doubt that he had been steward there for Saul, and after his master's death had continued in possession of the estate. David, we may feel sure, would not interfere with it, and Ziba would hold it for Saul's heirs, who could not themselves take possession. To him David now sends, not because he expected to hear of a son of his dear friend Jonathan, but because he was ready to show kindness to any representative of the fallen monarch.

Ver. 3.—**The kindness of God.** That is, extraordinary kindness. The devout mind of the Orientals saw in everything that was more than common a manifestation of God, and thus the epithet "of God" came to be applied to anything that was very great (comp. Gen. xxx. 8, margin; xxxv. 5; Ps. lxv. 9; Jonah iii. 3, margin). David would show Saul's seed kindness as wonderful as are God's dealings with man.

Ver. 4.—**Machir, the son of Ammiel, in Lo-debar.** Of Lo-debar nothing is known, but it must have been east of the Jordan, near Mahanaim. Of Ammiel we read again in ch. xvii. 27, where we find that he was a man of wealth, who helped to supply the wants of David and his men during the rebellion of Absalom. Possibly this kindness of David towards one for whom he had feelings of loyalty, as representing a royal house to which he had remained faithful, won his heart. There was a magnanimity about it which would commend it to a man who was himself generous and true.

Ver. 6.—**He fell on his face.** Mephibosheth probably expected the fate which in the East usually befalls the members of a dethroned dynasty. Subsequently in Israel each new line of usurpers put to death every male relative of its predecessor, and it was with difficulty that one babe was rescued from the hands of its own grandmother, Athaliah, when she usurped the throne. Looked at, then, in the light of Oriental policy, David's conduct was most generous.

Ver. 7.—**All the land of Saul thy father.** David probably restored to Mephibosheth not only the lands at Gibeah, which Ziba had managed to hold, but Saul's estates generally. There seems, nevertheless, to have been on Ziba's part a grudge against Mephibosheth for thus getting back from the king what he had hoped to keep as his own. The privilege of being the king's friend, and eating at his table, was an honour that would be more highly prized than even the possession of the estates.

Ver. 8.—**A dead dog.** At first sight this extreme self-humiliation makes us look on Mephibosheth as a poor creature, whom early misfortune and personal deformity had combined to depress. But really this is to impose on an Oriental hyperbole a Western exactness of meaning. When in the East your entertainer assures you that everything he has to his last dirhem is yours, he nevertheless expects you to pay twice the value for everything you consume; but he makes his exaction pleasant by his extreme courtliness. So Ephron offered his cave at Machpelah to Abraham as a free gift, but he took care to obtain for it an exorbitant price (Gen. xxiii. 11, 15). Mephibosheth described himself in terms similar to those used by David of himself to Saul (1 Sam. xxiv. 14); but he meant no more than to express great gratitude, and also to acknowledge the disparity of rank between him and the king.

Ver. 9.—**Thy master's son.** Strictly Mephibosheth was Saul's grandson, but words of relationship are used in a very general way in Hebrew.

Ver. 10.—**That thy master's son may have food to eat.** Instead of "son," Hebrew *ben*, some commentators prefer the reading of a few Greek versions, namely, "house," Hebrew, *beth*. But the difficulty which they seek to avoid arises only from extreme literalness of interpretation. Though Mephibosheth ate at the king's table, he would have a household to maintain—for he had a wife and son—and other expenses; and his having "food to eat" includes everything necessary, as does our prayer for "daily bread." He would live at Jerusalem as a nobleman and Ziba would cultivate his estates, paying, as is usual in the East, a fixed proportion of the value of the produce to his master. **Ziba had fifteen sons and twenty servants** (slaves). He had evidently thriven; for, beginning as a slave in Saul's household, he had now several wives and many slaves of his own, and had become a person of considerable importance. He would still remain so, though somewhat shorn both of wealth and dignity in becoming only Mephibosheth's farmer.

Ver. 11.—**As for Mephibosheth, said the king, he,** etc. These words are difficult, because they make David say the same thing thrice. The text is probably corrupt, as it requires the insertion of some such phrase as the "said the king" of the Authorized Version to make it intelligible. Of the many emendations proposed, the most probable is that of the LXX. and Syriac, which make this clause an observation of the historian pointing out the high honour done to Mephibosheth in placing him on an equality with David's own sons. It would then run as follows: *So Mephibosheth ate at the king's table as one of the king's sons.*

Ver. 12.—**Micha.** This son of Mephibosheth became the representative of the house of Saul, and had a numerous offspring, who were leading men in the tribe of Benjamin until the Captivity (see 1 Chron. viii. 35—40; ix. 10—11).

HOMILETICS.

Vers. 1—13.—The facts are: 1. David, remembering his love for Jonathan, inquires whether there were any survivors of the house of Saul; and being informed of the proximity of Ziba, an old servant, he sends for him. 2. He is told that a son of Jonathan, lame of foot, is a sojourner in the house of Machir. 3. Being sent for, Mephibosheth, on appearing before the king, falls on his face and pays reverence, but is spoken to kindly. 4. Being assured by David that there was no need for fear, that kindness for his father's sake was in store, and that all his grandfather's property should be restored, he expresses by deed and word his sense of unworthiness. 5. David informs Ziba of his decision as to the property, and orders him to act as steward for the benefit of Mephibosheth, who was to be henceforth a guest at the royal table. 6. The arrangements are carried out, and so is explained the fact of Mephibosheth's residence in Jerusalem.

The power of hallowed associations. Scripture, in common with all history, usually gives us the outward facts of life, leaving to be inferred the private mental and moral processes which must have lain in their rear. There is an abruptness in the transition of the historian from an account of David's victories and general administration to this record of an act of personal kindness. But if the laws of the human mind were the same then as now, we may be sure there was no such disconnection in the inner course of David's experience. During the few years of public activity in seeking the consolidation of his power, covered by the preceding chapters, there had often risen up in his mind memories of former days of trial, and of names of friends and foes now no longer among the living; and if thought breeds emotion, he would, on these occasions, experience feelings corresponding to the subject-matter of his thoughts. Among these thoughts, with their corresponding feelings, were doubtless those relating to his beloved

Jonathan; and what the historian here places before us in the narrative concerning Mephibosheth is simply the ultimate welling up, from the depths of the memory, of the old associations clustering around the name of Jonathan in such strength as to issue in the deeds here recorded.

I. HALLOWED ASSOCIATIONS ARE A GREAT POWER IN LIFE. Human life is not determined in its condition or conduct at any particular hour by what is purely new in thought, in feeling, or in circumstance. The past furnishes the seed on which the present acts as new environment, and the nature of that past is a more potent element in determining the conduct than is the new environment. The chief clue to David's later character is to be sought in his earlier experiences. The mightiest inner forces that thus influence life are those which centre in strong and sacred associations. The memory of Jonathan's love worked unconsciously as a spell throughout David's career. Every man is subject to this law of life. As a rule, the early mental associations of our life give tone and colour to all that comes after. The power lying in the memory of a mother's love over even the vagaries of later years is proverbial. The mention of a name may suffice to flood the eyes with tears and break down the stoutest heart. David never knew how much of restraint, of tenderness, of noble aspiration, and of fidelity to truth and honour he owed to the associations carried in his memory with the name of his friend Jonathan. So to us the " Name that is above every name " is the centre of associations as powerful as they are blessed; and the more we can enrich our nature with kindred associations, the richer and more Christlike will our lives become.

II. THERE ARE OCCASIONS WHEN HALLOWED ASSOCIATIONS CAN EXERT THEIR PROPER INFLUENCE. During the first few years of his reign David seems to have been utterly absorbed with the work of restoring the civil and religious order of his kingdom, and of securing it against the pressure of surrounding foes. A consideration of the actual state of things consequent on the misgovernment of Saul, and of the enormous labours involved in an absolute monarchy when its obligations are faithfully carried out, will account for the apparent neglect of Jonathan's house till the present date. It is only reasonable to suppose that David had sometimes thought of this matter, and the manner in which it is introduced in ver. 1 suggests that now was the time to give effect to his own previously cherished desires. It might have been politically unwise, and to Saul's descendants personally injurious by placing them in the way of temptation to conspiracies, had he sought to reinstate any of them during the rebellion of Ishbosheth and immediately on his decease. The safe and full establishment of his authority was evidently the occasion for the old and piously cherished associations with the name of Jonathan to put forth their strength. We all have within us a reserve power in the hallowed associations we cherish. They are never without an unconscious influence; but there may come seasons when we may do well to open the doors and let them come forth in full force to sway our conduct. Thus at Easter and Christmas do Christians give free scope to blessed memories. Thus our family birthdays, and days sacred to the memory of those now more blessed than ourselves, are times when our nature becomes enriched with holy feelings, and our vows become more influential. Sometimes, apart from our will and special seasons, by the spontaneous force of mental laws, sacred memories pour forth into our barren experience streams of blessing; and if by pressure of secular business the channels of thought and emotion are clogged, it is well now and then to pause, and, by an effort in quiet solitude, to open some sacred spring within our nature, so that it shall send forth its blessed streams to quicken and beautify our spiritual life.

III. A TRUE HEART WILL SEIZE OCCASION FOR REVIVING THE POWER OF HALLOWED ASSOCIATIONS. The occasion arose in the course of David's public life, and because his heart was still true to God and man, he seized it. The cares of official life and the attractions of exalted position had not yet done him spiritual damage. The David that swore love and fidelity to his friend (1 Sam. xx. 13—17, 42) was still alive. The man was not lost in the king. There are sad instances of the reverse. Old friends, former vows, are forgotten in the satiety of wealth or power, or, if not entirely forgotten, no occasion is sought to let the love of former days assert itself. Much of our power over our future lies in the use we are disposed to make of the fountains of holy thought and feeling which have been formed within by the experiences of former days.

The pressure of business may cause them to lie unnoticed for months and years; but now and then opportunities will occur which an uncorrupted heart will gladly use for bringing them into the current of daily life. There may be an abuse of "days and seasons;" but a well-regulated life will not, on that account, be hindered from taking pains to sweeten and subdue the present, and prepare for a better future, by a distinct and deliberate revival of the most sacred and tender experiences of the past.

IV. This deliberate use of hallowed associations secures a continuity of goodness. There was a native force in David's generous sentiments toward Jonathan in early days which would tend to their continuous assertion. The main elements of a man's moral life will abide in spite of counteracting evils. Yet as limbs maintain their muscular power by exertion, so the special qualities of David's character, as seen in his early friendship for Jonathan, would form a continuous feature of his life only in so far as he availed himself of passing opportunities for reviving the sentiments associated with the name of his departed friend. To this habit of allowing the feelings peculiar to such associations to act again and again, as occasion permitted, upon his life, in combination, of course, with other forms and methods of spiritual culture, we may ascribe the freshness and force of the kindly, generous sentiments which were a distinctive feature of his character to the very end. The characters of some men are disjointed. The main qualities of one part of their life are not conspicuous later on. The good has been overlaid, crushed down, by an enormous pressure of thought and sentiment of an adverse kind, and no care has been taken to give new force to latent memories. Their later good qualities are not of the same order as their earlier. This is not true growth. The true continuity of goodness is that seen in David's case, and is promoted by the same careful use of the power that lies in the best associations of our earlier life.

General lessons. 1. Let us see to the storing of the mind in early years with facts and experiences that will be as fountains of blessing to freshen life amidst the carking cares of a busy life. 2. We should be careful to cast out low thoughts, lest they occupy, in the mental and moral area, ground on which holy and generous feelings may take root and flourish. 3. It is desirable to make seasons when the best memories of the past are allowed to exercise their full power over us. This seems to be one reason, at least, for the institution of the Lord's Supper. 4. It is by cultivating the memories of departed friends, and cherishing the sentiments associated with their name, that the communion of the saints on earth and in heaven is promoted. 5. It is by the deliberate cultivation of sacred memories that we shall be able to conserve the more gentle virtues of life, and so give tone and purity to the otherwise hard and unsympathetic life of the world. 6. It behoves us to consider well what sacred vows of our earlier years are yet waiting to be redeemed. 7. In the remembrance of former friendships we may do well to inquire whether there are any in trouble and need on whom the spirit of the old friendship may exercise itself.

A spiritual parallel. Great mischief may arise from the endeavour to trace spiritual analogies in the ordinary historical narratives of Scripture, in consequence of the licence of an over-active imagination. It is not a safe canon of interpretation to say that sacred history is throughout an allegory. That an apostle saw an allegory in one or two cases is not proof of a general rule (Gal. iv. 24). But, under limitations, we are warranted in tracing parallels between the temporal and spiritual, the earthly and the heavenly: the one may exhibit features which serve to illustrate the other. Much of our Saviour's teaching partook of this character. In this lies the essence of parable. In this light we may regard the story of David's conduct toward Mephibosheth: it serves to illustrate the bearing and action of the true King of Zion toward the weak and lowly. Naaman's cleansing and Mephibosheth's elevation are historic facts shedding light on spiritual realities. Note—

I. A pledge to be kept. The events here recorded have their root in the free pledge given by David many years before that he would care for the seed of Jonathan (1 Sam. xx. 15). He had undertaken to bless when need should arise. In a deeper sense the whole merciful transactions recorded in New Testament history are the outcome of a "covenant ordered in all things." Christ's interposition on behalf of the fallen was not a casual act called forth by a passing incident in human history.

Before the mountains were set fast his "delights were with the sons of men." The purpose and, speaking in human phrase, the plan of redemption were in the original order; and hence Christ's coming was, as it were, to redeem his own pledge, to keep his own vow, to fulfil the covenant. "Lo, I come: in the volume of the book it is written of me." Virtually he was "slain before the foundation of the world;" for all that happened was consequent on "the eternal purpose" (Eph. iii. 11), though not in violation of human freedom (Acts ii. 23).

II. A DEFERRED FULFILMENT. We have seen that some years elapsed, not only after the vow, before any ostensible steps were taken to fulfil it, but also after David came to the kingdom. In this there is no cause for reflection on his sincerity. Providence has many things to bring about in a monarch's wise policy, and he may have to wait till events are ripe for certain lines of action. Here, on a small scale, we have an illustration of the apparently deferred fulfilment of the merciful undertaking of our Saviour. Generations passed ere the set time had come when he could, consistently with the working out of other issues, subordinate or co-ordinate, come to "perform the mercy promised" in the past (Luke ii. 72). Now that we have the complete history of David, we can see the propriety of his not taking measures for the elevation of the seed of Jonathan while his work of consolidation was incomplete; and so now that we have the full record of the Old and New Testaments, we can see the wisdom of the manifestation of the covenanted grace being deferred till the "fulness of time" (Gal. iv. 4). Many threads were being woven by the hand of Providence to meet in the revelation of Christ.

III. A SEARCH FOR THE FALLEN. David inquired after the seed of Jonathan and Saul. The sons of the distinguished were in obscurity and, in a social and political point of view, lost. As compared with the position once held by their father and grandfather, they were indeed degraded and outcast. Their splendid inheritance had vanished. They had to be sought out. How truly their relative social condition represents our spiritual condition is obvious. We have fallen far below the original state of our great ancestor. The effect of sin on man, in so far as it touches his relative social position in the enduring spiritual world, is to lower him, to render him inferior to the holy beings who constitute the members of the eternal kingdom of God. "Thou hast *fallen* by thine iniquity" (Hos. xiv. 1). The mission of Christ, in one aspect of it, is said to be a search for that which is lost—an effort to find and rescue from degradation and shame those who are living below their proper position in the spiritual life (Luke xv. 3—10, 32; xix. 10). This is true of the race; and his work considered as "finished" on Calvary is an effort to find out and save mankind. It is also true of us as individuals that Christ does, like the good shepherd (John x. 16; cf. Luke xv. 4), search for us. He follows us in our wanderings, comes near to our loneliness, and calls us by his Word, his providence, and his Spirit.

IV. A YEARNING COMPASSION. "Is there not yet any of the house of Saul, that I may show the kindness of God unto him?" (ver. 3). How this reveals the deep longings of the heart! David is not satisfied with the desire to show ordinary attentions to the fallen house; he must show such kindness as God would show. The thought of Jonathan evidently brought up again the old love; and it must, if possible, pour itself forth in some unwonted form. There can be no question that, in the regal and better qualities of his life, David illustrates the more perfect King who comes to reign in righteousness and save the poor and needy. This strong yearning compassion was conspicuous in our Lord in the days of his flesh, when he was seeking a lost race. In this he is unapproachable. It appears in his deeply pathetic tone whenever referring to sin and sorrow, in his patient unwearying toil, in his pleadings with the weary and heavy laden, in his looking with compassion on the people as sheep without a shepherd, in his tears over Jerusalem, and in the sweet and gentle submission with which he drank the cup in Gethsemane, and poured out his life on the cross. Overflowing love! And he is the same now (Heb. xiii. 8). His life, sufferings, and death were the revelation of a permanent character, and therefore of an ever-yearning compassion for the fallen.

V. A GRACIOUS BEARING. Mephibosheth trembled in the presence of David, and was overcome by the sense of his own unworthiness (vers. 6—8). No doubt he was surprised at such wondrous conduct on the part of the king as to send for him. But the king in a tone which no written words can indicate, said, "Mephibosheth!" We all know what volumes of meaning may be conveyed by addressing an individual by his name in a certain tone. And, lest this should not suffice, there came the words, "Fear not!" As a brother and friend, on the same level, he speaks to the heart of the weak and troubled one. Foreshadow is this of him who was "meek and lowly in heart;" who would not "break the bruised reed or quench the smoking flax;" who touched the outcast leper and inspired the fallen one with hope. No reproach, no coldness of heart, no imposition of impossible burdens, but the gentleness and grace that banish fear and cause the poor outcast to feel that in him there is a tender, loving Friend!

VI. AN ELEVATION TO HONOUR. David would be content with nothing less than that Mephibosheth should be a free and constant guest at his table. He was to be raised from social degradation and obscurity to a position of greatest distinction. No mere pension, no formal expression of personal interest, no delegation to others of attention to be paid to him, would suit the largeness of the king's heart. His idea of "the kindness of God" (ver. 3) far transcended the best human conceptions of generosity, and this unwonted elevation to honour was but the index of it. What a marvellous change in the condition of this poor, feeble outcast! How contrary to all the usages of monarchs, to the offspring of the fallen, was this overflow of "the kindness of God"! Than this there is not in the Bible a more apt illustration of the exceeding grace of the Lord Jesus Christ, who condescends to our low estate, seeks us out, bows us down in wondering submission by his matchless gentleness, and then raises us to the honour of being members of his household, of free access to his Person and closest fellowship with himself and those most dear to him. "Neither do I condemn thee" (John viii. 11; cf. Rom. viii. 1). He gives "power to become the sons of God" (John i. 12, 16; 1 John iii. 1, 2). The "far-off" are made "nigh" (Eph. ii. 13), and are called "friends" (John xv. 15), blessed with constant fellowship (1 John i. 3), and even made heirs of "the glory" given to himself (John xvii. 22—24). It is in the Antitype alone that we find the full and true expression of "the kindness of God" (ver. 3). "Eye hath not seen, nor ear heard, neither have entered into the heart of man, the things which God hath prepared for them that love him" (1 Cor. ii. 9).

VII. A PERSONAL GUARANTEE. A personal guarantee, involving the king's honour, and backed by all the resources at his command, was given that Mephibosheth should henceforth be regarded "as one of the king's sons" (ver. 11), and that ample provision should be made for all his wants (ver. 10). Whatever demands came on him for the sustenance of his dependents, they were met by the arrangement, under royal warrant, with Ziba. Thus all his interests, present and future, personal and relative, social and material, were provided for. The king guaranteed all. Now, this is beautifully illustrative of what Christ does for those whom he raises from degradation to be his friends. He cares for all their interests. He so orders providence that they shall "want no good thing." It is said of them, "All things are yours" (1 Cor. iii. 22); and, to scatter all fear and afford abundant consolation, the King has said, "Because I live, ye shall live also" (John xiv. 19). Mephibosheth rested under the care of a faithful David. All the power and all the high moral qualities of David were pledged to secure to him all his life long the blessings now enjoyed; so all the power and all the ineffable qualities of Christ are pledged to secure to us the possession and enjoyment of glorious heritage as Christians as long as we live, i.e. for ever.

GENERAL LESSONS. 1. It becomes us to follow the example of David and of Christ, and seek out those who may be in need of blessing, and who may have a special claim on our sympathy. 2. We should make the Divine character and conduct the model of our bearing towards those in trouble. "The kindness of God" is the ideal to be converted into the realities of our life. 3. The lowly and despised may take encouragement from all that is recorded of Christ's gracious bearing and deeds of kindness. 4. We may trace, in every instance of Christ's mercy to the fallen, the permanently elevating tendency of Christianity. It is the one element which alone lastingly raises mankind in material and social good. 5. The resources of Christ for securing the fulfilment of his promises are so vast as to remove all fear. He is more to the universe at large than David was to his kingdom. 6. We see the dignity of bearing that becomes those who are honoured with the royal friendship of Christ.

HOMILIES BY VARIOUS AUTHORS.

Ver. 1.—(JERUSALEM.) *For Jonathan's sake.* David had sworn to his friend Jonathan that he would "not cut off his kindness from his house for ever" (1 Sam. xx. 15). He had been probably unaware of his leaving a son behind him (for Mephibosheth was born while he was in exile, five years before the battle of Gilboa); or, if acquainted with the fact, supposed that he perished in the destruction of the house of Saul. But surmising, perhaps, from something he heard, that a son of his friend survived, he made the inquiry, "Is there yet any that is left," etc.? It was a practice only too common in the East, on a change of dynasty, for the reigning monarch to put to death the surviving members of the family of his predecessor, in order to make his own position more secure. And the conduct of David, in contrast therewith, evinced his gratitude, fidelity, piety, and noble generosity. "Neither the splendour of victories, nor the pleasures of prosperity, nor the lustre of his crown, could make him unmindful of his covenant and oath to his former friend. A suspicious, faithless tyrant would at least have kept the family that imagined they had a right to his kingdom low enough to have prevented the possibility of their ever disputing it with him; or at least have shut up the heir of it in close imprisonment, or got rid of his fears upon his account by totally destroying him; thinking he might reasonably dispense with his oath to his deceased friend through the necessity of self-preservation, and securing to his own family the peaceable succession to his crown" (Chandler). The words "for Jonathan's sake"—

I. EXPRESS A PRINCIPLE OF HUMAN CONDUCT. It is not unusual for one person to show kindness to another for the sake of *some one else,* for whom, whether living or dead, he entertains a high regard, on account of his excellent character or eminent services; with whom the object of his kindness is closely connected, and without whom he would not have shown it. How often has a king exercised his prerogative of mercy toward an offender, or bestowed riches and honour on a subject, for the sake of the faithful service of his father! "The fruit of well-doing lives longer than himself who is the doer, and thereby he leaves a blessing and good treasure behind him to his posterity" (Guild). "There are thousands of young men and women who are daily receiving kindness for their fathers' and mothers' sakes. And this is, in fact, one of the incidental blessings connected with having parents who, though now dead, were, when living, persons of worthy and estimable life. Their children inherit the advantages which the love of others for their memory can bestow, and many an applicant for some office of trust and emolument would be turned away from the door were it not that his face bears the lineaments of a departed and cherished friend, or his tones call back to memory the voice which will speak no more" (E. Mellor).

II. ILLUSTRATE A METHOD OF DIVINE DEALINGS. God deals with men, not merely in their separate individuality, but also in their relationship to one another; spares and blesses them, not only directly and immediately, but also indirectly and mediately, through and on account of each other; and shows kindness to many for the sake of one. This: 1. *Occurs in various ways.* By means of the hereditary influence of a good man on his descendants, and the moral influence on others of his example, utterances, labours, and sufferings; and (with more special reference to the case under consideration) by granting his intercessory requests, fulfilling the promises made to him on their behalf, and doing them good out of regard to him, or because of something he has done which was necessary to that end. 2. *Appears in numerous instances.* With respect to individuals, "The Lord hath blessed me for thy sake" (Gen. xxx. 27; xix. 29; 1 Kings xi. 12); families (Gen. xxxix. 5; Ps. lxix. 26; Prov. xiii. 22); Churches, cities, and nations (Gen. xviii. 26; Exod. xxxii. 14; 1 Kings viii. 19); "beloved for the fathers' sakes" (Rom. xi. 28); "As the new wine is found in the cluster," etc. (Isa. lxv. 8; i. 9). So God testifies his love of righteousness, teaches the worth of a good man in relation to the unworthy, and causes his sovereign mercy to abound toward them. 3. *Has its highest application in Christ,* "the one Mediator between God and man," (1) who is very dear to God (Matt. iii. 17; Eph. i. 6); (2) who is closely allied to men (Heb. ii. 16); (3) who has laboured, interceded, and suffered for us (1 Pet. iii. 18); and (4) to whom many promises have been made on behalf of those who are in him

(Gal. iii. 20 ; 2 Cor. i. 20).   The nature, grounds, and extent of his mediation cannot be fully explained ; but the fact is certain, that it is " for Christ's sake " (Eph. iv. 32), " in Christ " (Revised Version), and " for his Name's sake" (1 John ii. 12), we are forgiven, have access to the Father, and are " blessed with every spiritual blessing " (Eph. i. 3).   " He comprises in his own Person all and everything that is most desirable " (Gregory Nazianzen).

III. SUGGEST A GROUND OF DEVOUT CONFIDENCE.   When Mephibosheth appeared before the king, " he doubtless was in fear for his life (vers. 6. 7).   Such generosity to a fallen rival as David showed in restoring him to his paternal property, seemed to him scarcely credible" ('Speaker's Commentary').   But the assurance that it was "for Jonathan's sake" must have inspired him with confidence.   And similarly, " for Jesus' sake" affords a (1) needful, (2) effectual, and (3) abiding ground of hope, and

> " Provides for those who come to God
> An all-prevailing plea."

" Whatsoever ye shall ask the Father in my Name, he will give it you " (John xvi. 23 ; xiv. 13).

IV. INDICATE A MOTIVE TO PRACTICAL BENEVOLENCE, after the example of David and from love to our Divine Friend (ch. i. 26) ; in : 1. Forgiving each other (Eph. iv. 32).   2. Kind and comforting speech.   " Fear not" (ver. 7).   3. Generous gifts.   4. Self-denial.   5. Suffering (Matt. v. 11 ; Phil. i. 29).   6. Prayers (Rom. xv. 30).   7. Personal, diligent, and constant service on behalf of "the Church which is his body," and of all " for whom Christ died " (2 Cor. iv. 5 ; 3 John 7).   " For his Name's sake ; " " For my sake."   This is the Christian's peculiar, highest, and mightiest motive ; implying not only supreme affection toward him who " alone is worthy," but also sincere sympathy with his spirit and purposes ; and producing most beneficent effects.—D.

Ver. 3.—(JERUSALEM.)   *Showing the kindness of God.*   David remembered the request of Jonathan to show him " the kindness of Jehovah" (1 Sam. xx. 14, 15) ; felt the obligation of his former promises and covenants (1 Sam. xxiv. 21, 22 ; xxiii. 18) ; and now purposed, in accordance therewith, to " show the kindness of God," *i.e.* " love from religious motives, or as God shows it " (Thenius) ; " in God and for his sake " (Keil) ; " in the Lord's sight, and according to the Lord's example, pure, perpetual love, and not such love as arises from mere human respects and is shown in the eye of man " (Wordsworth) ; and not simply "great and eminent kindness " (Poole, Patrick).   There are benevolent affections in our nature ; but they must be imbued with religious motives and principles in order that their exercise may be of the highest kind.   " The kindness of God " is such as is shown : 1. *Out of reverence for his Name.*   Holy, just, and true ; merciful and gracious ; delighting in loving-kindness.   " God is love ; " and the eternal Fountain of love in his creatures.   2. *In obedience to his will,* as expressed in numerous injunctions to the faithful performance of what has been promised ; in " the royal law" (Jas. ii. 8) ; and in manifold exhortations to compassionate love. 3. *From gratitude for his benefits.*   These had been bestowed on David in abundant measure (ch. vii. 18 ; viii. 6).   The acts of kindness which God performs toward men both enable and incite them to perform acts of kindness toward their fellow-men. " What goodness the Lord shall do unto us, the same will we do unto thee " (Numb. x. 32).   " Freely ye have received, freely give."   4. *In imitation of his example ;* of faithfulness, goodness, unsought, abounding, unfailing, and everlasting love.   David was specially called, as king, to exhibit in his character and conduct an image of the moral excellences of the Divine King of Israel ; and to this Christians are likewise called.   " Be ye therefore perfect," etc. (Matt. v. 43—48), "merciful" (Luke vi. 36), "imitators of God as beloved children," etc. (Eph. v. 1).   5. *Under the inspiration of his grace,* his love, his Spirit ; and, indeed, " it is the merciful love of God himself that dwells in the heart of the truly pious, and works therefrom ; for he that lives in fellowship with God receives into his heart, through the Holy Ghost, the love that is in God, and lives and moves in that love" (Erdmann).   " He that dwelleth in love dwelleth in God, and God in him " (1 John iv. 16).   He not only reflects the Divine love on others, but is also the medium of its communication to them.   6. *With the desire of his approval,* of pleasing him rather than men, and of partaking more fully of his loving-kindness, which " is better than life." 7. *For the promotion of his glory;* "that they may see your good works, and glorify your Father which is in heaven."—D.

Ver. 4.—(GILEAD.) *The kindness of Machir Ben-Ammiel.* One of the obscure characters of Scripture. He dwelt at Lo-debar, among the mountains of Gilead, "a favourite asylum for refugees;" was, probably, a descendant of Machir the son of Manasseh; and "the principal man of Gilead" (Josephus). Of his generosity two notable instances are recorded (ch. iv. 4; xvii. 27). From these it may be inferred that he was *rich* in earthly possessions, and (what is of much greater importance) in: 1. *Grateful memories.* Like the men of Jabesh-Gilead, he remembered the heroic enterprise of Saul on behalf of his people (1 Sam. xi. 9; xxxi. 11; ch. ii. 4—7).

> " But, O Saul, do not fail us.
> *Saul.*   Fail ye?
> Let the morn fail to break; I will not break
> My word. Haste, or I'm there before you.
>   Fail?
> Let the morn fail in the east; I'll not fail you;
> But swift and silent as the streaming wind,
> Unseen approach, then gathering up my force
> At dawning, sweep on Amnon, as night's blast
> Sweeps down from Carmel on the dusky sea."
>   (C. Heavysege, ' Saul: a Drama.')

Hence he afforded ready shelter and hospitality to his grandson, and may have assisted the revival of his house at Mahanaim (ch. ii. 8); and when, subsequently, David was in exile at the same place, remembering his kindness to Mephibosheth, rendered him generous aid. 2. *Tender compassion* toward the orphan, unfortunate and friendless. The sight of human distress drew forth his sympathy; and (like the good Samaritan) he suffered no other considerations to hinder its practical expression. 3. *Constant friendship.* During many years (ver. 12), with all their changes, he provided, apparently " without fee or reward," a peaceful home for the crippled prince, and continued his steadfast protector. 4. *Active benevolence.* He was " rich in good works" (2 Tim. vi. 18). "Sensibility, as the word is generally used, is a mere animal instinct, useless when it does not immediately lead to active benevolence; and in such cases not only useless, but pernicious, because it has a tendency to produce a resting satisfied with the emotion and a neglect of the action" (W. Cooke Taylor). 5. *Beneficent influence.* His conduct could not but produce a good effect on the rude, warlike tribe of which he was chief; and possibly incited others (Shobi and Barzillai) to the like.

> " Great deeds cannot die:
> They with the sun and moon renew their light
> For ever, blessing those that look on them."
>   (Tennyson.)

6. *Noble recompense.* "The blessing of him that was ready to perish" (Job xxix. 13), the approval of his own conscience, the enduring memorial of a good name. Although (like that of Abou Ben-Adhem) his name has not been written in the sacred record among "the names of those who love the Lord," but only "as one that loves his fellow-men," it could not fail of being divinely honoured.

> 'The angel wrote, and vanished. The next night
> It came again, with a great wakening light,
> And show'd the names whom love of God had bless'd,
> And lo! Ben-Adhem's name led all the rest."
>   (Leigh Hunt.)
>   D.

Vers. 5—13.—(THE KING'S PALACE.) *Mephibosheth before the king.* We have here a picture of—
I. EXTRAORDINARY VICISSITUDES IN LIFE. A prince by birth, deprived of his father, crippled by a heedless footstep, carried into exile and poverty, recently a helpless

dependent in a remote district, is conducted into the presence of one who was once a shepherd-boy, afterwards a wandering outlaw, and now the greatest monarch on earth! Such changes: 1. May be largely, though not entirely, traced to moral causes, personal character, hereditary relationships. 2. Are wrought by Divine providence (1 Sam. ii. 7, 8; Ps. cxiii. 7, 8). 3. Are designed for human welfare; being not only corrective, but also tentative and disciplinary (Ps. lv. 19; Job xxiii. 10; Heb. xii. 6). 4. And should be regarded in an appropriate spirit (Jas. i. 9, 10).

II. THE DEPRESSING INFLUENCE OF MISFORTUNE. "He fell on his face, and did reverence" (ver. 6); "And he bowed himself, and said, What is thy servant, that thou shouldest look upon such a *dead dog* as I am?" (ver. 8). His physical infirmity, combined with long-continued dependence, made him not merely humble, but timid, anxious, abject, and self-depreciatory. Hence his language (due in part to Oriental exaggeration) is excusable, though scarcely to be commended (Kitto, 'Daily Bible Illus.'). The natural tendency of heavy affliction to enfeeble and crush the spirit is effectually overcome only by the aid of Divine grace.

III. AN ADMIRABLE EXHIBITION OF KINDNESS; spontaneous, faithful, considerate, magnanimous, practical, enduring, Divine. 1. In gracious and encouraging *words*. "Mephibosheth!" (ver. 6). "Fear not!" etc. (ver. 7). To David himself, in a time of dejection, Jonathan had said, "Fear not!" (1 Sam. xxiii. 17); and how often has the Lord spoken the same comforting word to his servants (Gen. xv. 1; Luke xii. 32; Rev. i. 17)! 2. In becoming and beneficent *acts*; fulfilling what had been promised (vers. 9—11), restoring an alienated inheritance, and making a sure, permanent, and abundant provision (ver. 12). 3. In honoured, intimate, and abiding *friendship*. "Mephibosheth, thy master's son, shall eat bread alway at my table" (vers. 10, 11, 13). Such kindness, like sunshine after rain, and as a visit of "the angel of God" (ch. xix. 27, 28), dispersed his fear, alleviated his misfortune, and filled him with grateful devotion; whilst his presence at the royal table would daily remind the king of his deceased friend, and incite him to renewed generosity.

IV. THE IRREMEDIABLE DEFECTS OF THE MOST FAVOURED EARTHLY CONDITION. "And he was lame on both his feet" (ver. 13). His deformity was incurable; his infirmity became an occasion of complaint and slander (ch. xvi. 2—4); and his dejection and distress returned "as the clouds after the rain" (ch. xix. 24—30). The king himself often longed to flee away and be at rest (Ps. lv. 6). And it is vain to expect perfection in character or condition except in the heavenly mansions.

> "There is a spot in every flower,
>   A sigh in every gale,
> A shadow in the brightest hour,
>   Thorns in the smoothest vale.
>
> "To smile and weep, and weep and smile,
>   To man alternate given;
> To cling to earth permitted while
>   We learn to long for heaven."

Ver. 13.—*Lost and found: a sermon to young people.* The story of Mephibosheth may be used as a little *parable* of the spiritual history of every one who is restored to God. He was: 1. *A prince.* To you belongs a more than princely dignity; for you are all "the offspring of God," and bear on you traces of "the image and glory" of "the Father of spirits." 2. *Lost.* You belong to a sinful and fallen race; and your condition is one of deprivation, helplessness, obscurity, and misery. "A true religion ought to instruct man both in his greatness and his misery" (Pascal). 3. *Sought.* Infinite piety has sought and is still seeking every one of you, and employs many means to find and save you (Matt. xviii. 10—14; Luke xv.). 4. *Found;* unexpectedly to himself and to the joy of the seeker. So is it when the gracious message of the gospel comes to you, "not in word only, but in power." 5. *Self-abased;* in the presence of the king. When you see the height of Divine greatness and goodness, you also see the depth of your own unworthiness and shame. 6. *Comforted.* "Fear not; only believe." 7. *Exalted;* endowed with more than had been lost; and adopted as "one of the king's sons" (ver. 11). The gifts of God are worthy of himself. When one, to whom Alexander gave a city, declined to accept it, on the ground that it was unsuitable to his condition, he said, " I do not ask what is becoming in you to receive, but what is becoming in me to give " (Seneca, ' De Beneficiis ').—D.

Ver. 3.—" *The kindness of God.*" David, settled on the throne and in his new metropolis, recalls to mind the fallen house of Saul, not to destroy them, as was usual with Eastern monarchs, but to show them kindness for Jonathan's sake. In his inquiry after them he uses substantially the same phrase which Jonathan had used (1 Sam. xx. 14) when he took an oath of him that he would be kind to himself and his family. " The kindness of the Lord," or " the kindness of God," is an expression descriptive of the highest and best kindness possible to man or angel. It is kindness which—

I. Flows from God. This is true of all the kindness which exists amongst men. " Love is of God." All the love of men towards each other streams forth from the fountain of Divine love, and should be thus regarded by those who are the objects of it, he being praised for all. But this is emphatically true of Christian kindness. It originates in, and is a manifestation of, the love of God in Christ. It is produced by the Holy Spirit as given to the disciples of Christ, and by means of the truth respecting him (1 Pet. i. 22, 23). It is a product of regeneration. It is God's love dwelling in human hearts and revealing itself in human lives. It is an element of "the Divine nature " of which Christians are "partakers" (2 Pet. i. 4).

II. Is exercised from regard to God. 1. It has its root, like all Christian graces, in faith towards God (Gal. v. 6). 2. It springs from gratitude and love to him for all his goodness, especially for his redeeming love (1 John iv. 11). 3. It is practised in obedience to his commandments (1 John iv. 21). 4. It aims at his approval. 5. It imitates him (Luke vi. 36; Eph. iv. 32). Hence it—

III. Is God-like. As it is: 1. *Disinterested.* "Seeketh not her own" (1 Cor. xiii. 5). Kindness which is exercised with a view to personal advantage is not kindness but policy and commercial subtlety. 2. *Expansive.* Ready to help all who need, as far as power permits. Not restricting itself to the good and worthy, but "kind unto the unthankful and the evil" (Luke vi. 35); nor yet to friends, but extending to enemies (Matt. v. 44, 45, 48); nor to one's own sect in religion, but regarding with love all Christian brethren (1 John v. 1; Eph. vi. 24). Yet it is: 3. *Discriminating.* The Divine love is united with righteousness, and seeks righteous ends. Hence it cannot be the same thing, and displayed in the same manner, towards the righteous and the unrighteous, the obedient and the disobedient; and it mainly seeks to promote righteousness and salvation in all, and varies its methods accordingly. Christian love and kindness will be exercised with similar discrimination as far as is possible to men; and will seek supremely the moral and spiritual benefit of its objects. Indiscriminate benevolence does more harm than good. 4. *Unsparing.* "He spared not his own Son " (Rom. viii. 32), and in him the love of God appears as self-sacrificing (1 John iii. 16) and bountiful (Eph. i. 3). Christian love possesses the same qualities of bountifulness (2 Cor. viii. 2, 3, 9—11), self-denial, and self-sacrifice. It "endureth all things" (1 Cor. xiii. 7). 5. *Constant.* The love of God is long-suffering, persistent, and eternal (Ps. ciii. 17; cxxxvi., *passim*). His children are like him in this respect also (1 Cor. xiii. 4, 8, 13).

IV. Is nourished by converse with God. The acts and habits of devotion—reading, meditation, prayer, praise—bring us into closer communion with God, secure us more of his Spirit, open our hearts to receive the impress of his character, promote in us all those sentiments and principles towards him which issue in hearty love and kindness towards our brethren. Let us draw nigh continually to him whose name is Love, and we shall find it ever more easy to be loving.—G. W.

Ver. 13.—*Eating at the king's table.* David, out of regard to the memory of his dear friend Jonathan, and mindful of his oath to him, not only restores to his son Mephibosheth the forfeited property of Saul, and arranges for its cultivation by Ziba and his sons, but exalts Mephibosheth to the position of a constant guest at his own table, " as one of the king's sons." So Mephibosheth " did eat continually at the king's table." The circumstance may serve to remind us of the greater honour which good men enjoy : it is theirs to eat continually at the table of the King of kings.

I. This is true as respects their participation of the gifts of God's providence. All creatures depend upon him, and he supplies their wants (Ps. civ. 27, 28; cxlv. 15, 16). But the lower creatures partake of his bounty unconscious of the hand which feeds them. They are, in relation to God, rather like the horses in the stable, or the cattle and sheep in the fields, than the children at the table. And what these are through incapacity, ungodly people are through unbelief and forgetfulness. They live on the bounty of God, unmindful of him and unthankful. His children, however, even in the enjoyment of their daily food, "sit at his table." As he provides, so they recognize his care and bounty, and give him thanks. As he is present, so they are conscious of his presence. They regard him as presiding at their meals, and are glad to discern him so near. They ask for his blessing, and receive it. They "eat to the Lord, and give God thanks" (Rom. xiv. 6). They satisfy their appetites and gratify their tastes as in his sight. They aim "to eat and drink . . . to the glory of God" (1 Cor. x. 31). They not only enjoy his gifts, but commune with himself. They talk with him, and he with them. Common meals thus enjoyed become as sacraments and means of grace. Let it be our endeavour to enjoy them thus more than we have done.

II. The words are more emphatically applicable to the Christian's enjoyment of spiritual blessings. In this sense, "he eats continually at the king's table." The image reminds us of: 1. *His exaltation.* Once, like Mephibosheth, living far away from the king, now brought near, and associated with, yea, made really one of, his children. Still "lame" and otherwise defective, and unfit perhaps for much service, yet admitted to favour and honour. 2. *The abundance of the best provisions he enjoys.* At the King's table is plenty, and of the best. At the table of the heavenly King, spread under the gospel, are provisions the choicest and rarest, to be found nowhere else; and which nourish, not for this short earthly life, but for life eternal. The best intellectual food is here; but especially that food which quickens and nourishes the soul, in faith, and love, and hope, and holiness. Divine truth and whatever it reveals and presents—the pardoning mercy and fatherly love of God, the love and sacrifice of Christ, his body and his blood, which are the real food and drink of men. Of these the believing and loving soul may partake at will, anywhere and everywhere. The King's table is not confined to place; but especially in the house of God and at the Lord's Supper, the table is spread, and Christians gather together to feed and feast. 3. *At the King's table is the best society.* At the table of the Divine King we associate with the Father and the Son, by the Spirit; and by him also with saints and angels, "the excellent of the earth" and the excellent of heaven. The Lord fulfils his promise, "I will sup with him, and he with me" (Rev. iii. 20). 4. *At the King's table is gladness.* The honour, the provision, the company, all tend to give pleasure. 5. *There also is safety.* The palace of a king is commonly the securest spot in the land. Far more assured is the safety of those who sit at the table of the heavenly King. Angels guard them; God himself is their Dwelling-place and Defence. 6. *The privilege of eating at the table of our King is perpetual.* As in the case of Mephibosheth. If it is not continually enjoyed, it is our own fault. The privilege enjoyed by Mephibosheth would be a constant solace to him in his helplessness; and the spiritual counterpart is to Christians a constant source of comfort and support under their troubles.

III. The words are perfectly fulfilled in the heavenly world. The future blessedness of God's people is often compared to a feast (see Matt. viii. 11; Rev. ii. 7; xix. 9). It is, in fact, the continuance and the perfecting of the blessedness now enjoyed. The King himself is perfectly "manifested." "They shall see his face" (Rev. xxii. 4); "We shall see him as he is" (1 John iii. 2). His love and favour are so displayed as not to admit of a doubt. The provisions at his table are the same as on earth; but the guests are better able to enjoy them, their spiritual appetite and tastes being freed from all that lessens their fitness to do so. The society is the same, but those imperfect on earth are perfected in spirit and in body (Heb. xii. 23; Phil. iii. 21). The security is absolute; the joy unmingled with sorrow; the feast is perpetual and without end. "Blessed is he that shall eat bread in the kingdom of God" (Luke xiv. 15). Who shall partake of that bliss? All are invited by the gospel; and none will be excluded but such as exclude themselves by refusing to accept the invitation, and obtain the necessary preparation for the feast, which consists in reconciliation to the King through Jesus Christ, constant loyalty and obedience to him, and joyful partaking now of his spiritual gifts. To "eat continually at the King's table" here is the necessary condition of our doing so hereafter, as it is also the preparation for that happiness and the evidence that we shall enjoy it.—G. W.

EXPOSITION.

CHAPTER X.

Ver. 1.—**The king of the children of Ammon died.** This war is very briefly referred to in ch. viii. 12; but we have now entered upon a narrative, the interest of which is altogether unlike all that has gone before. There we saw David crowned with earthly glory, and made the monarch of a vast empire; he is also a prophet, and, as such, not only restores, but enriches and enlarges, the worship of the sanctuary; and, as prophet and king, he becomes not only the type, but the ancestor of the Messiah. In this narrative he is a sinner, punished with terrible, though merited, severity, and must henceforth walk humbly and sorrowfully as a penitent before God. From 1 Chron. xix. 1 we learn that the king's name was Nahash; but whether he was the same as the Nahash mentioned in 1 Sam. xi. 1 is uncertain. There was an interval of more than forty years between, but Nahash was probably a young man, just seated on the throne, when he attacked Jabesh-Gilead; and Saul, who repelled him, might have been still alive but for the battle of Gilboa. The name means a "serpent," and is used in Job xxvi. 13 of the constellation Draco. It may thus have been a name assumed by several Ammonite kings, the dragon representing majesty and power, and being the symbol on their seal, just as it is the Chinese imperial emblem now. The phrase, "It came to pass after this," has no chronological significance either here or in ch. viii. 1. It is simply a form of transition from one subject to another.

Ver. 2.—**His father showed kindness unto me.** This makes it probable that it was the same Nahash as Saul's enemy. The smart of the defeat caused by Saul's energy would make him regard with friendship any one who was a thorn in the side of the man who had so unexpectedly stopped him in his career, and hence his kindness to David.

Ver. 3.—**Thinkest thou that David doth honour thy father?** This insinuation arose probably from ill will, stirred up by David's success in war; and, with that distrust with which neighbouring nations too often regard one another, they see in his embassy only a purpose of spying into their defences with a view to future attack. Rabbah, their city, was a place strong both naturally and by reason of its fortifications.

Ver. 4.—**Hanun . . . shaved off the one half of their beards.** To an Oriental the beard was the mark of his being a free man, and to cut it off on one side was not merely an insult to David's ambassadors, but the treating them like slaves. Moreover, as only the priests wore underclothing, and as the ordinary dress of men consisted of a tunic and a loose flowing robe thrown over it, the cutting of this robe short up to the hip was a vile and abominable affront. Of course, Hanun intended this as a challenge to war, whereas David had meant peace and friendship.

Ver. 6.—**That they stank** (see notes on 1 Sam. xiii. 4; xxvii. 12). As the Hebrew literally means, *had made themselves stink*, the Revised Version rightly translates, "had made themselves odious." **The children of Ammon sent and hired the Syrians.** From 1 Chron. xix. 6 we learn that his mercenaries from Aram cost Hanun a thousand talents of silver, or nearly five hundred thousand pounds—a vast sum, especially considering the great relative value of silver in those days. The mercenaries, moreover, were gathered out of numerous districts of Aram—from Rehob, Zoba, Beth-Maacah, and Tob; the margin being right in rendering "the men of Tob," instead of "Ish-tob." So, too, the Revised Version, "The men of Tob twelve thousand men." It was to this land that Jephthah fled (Judg. xi. 3). The whole number of the allies was thirty-three thousand, with which total the parallel place agrees, as they are described there as "thirty-two thousand, and the King of Maacah and his people," who are here said to have been a thousand strong. The text, however, there must be corrupt, as it describes them all as horsemen (Authorized Version, "chariots;" 1 Chron. xix. 7); here footmen only are mentioned, with which the narrative agrees (see note on ver. 18).

Ver. 7.—**And all the host of the mighty men.** The Hebrew is, *and all the host, even mighty men.* By this is meant, not "the mighties," but that the Israelites had now become practised in war, and veterans.

Ver. 8.—**The Syrians . . . were by themselves in the field.** We learn from 1 Chron. xix. 7 that the rendezvous of the Arameans was at Medeba, a small town situated upon a hill in the Mishor, or treeless prairie-land, called "the plain" in Josh. xiii. 16. As it was four miles south-east of Heshbon, and more than twenty miles distant from Rabbah, it is plain that they were marching northward, and that Joab was only just in time to prevent a junction of the two armies. The Ammonites, who were expecting their allies, and knew of their approach, had come outside of Rabbah, but had only posted themselves in fighting order "at the entering in of the gate."

Ver. 9.—**The front of the battle.** The object of Joab was to prevent at all hazards the junction of the Syrians with the Ammonites, and he was only just in time to throw himself between them. This was resolute but dangerous policy, as, in case of defeat, he would have a powerful enemy in his rear. Apparently, however, he was aware that his real work lay with the Syrian mercenaries, who were dangerous enough by themselves, and would become more than a match for him if they were reinforced by the men of Rabbah. He therefore leaves Abishai with such troops as he could spare to watch the Ammonites, feeling sure that they would not hazard an attack unless they saw matters going ill with him; and, taking with him all his bravest men, "the choice men of Israel," he prepares with them to give battle to the Syrians.

Ver. 11.—**And he said,** etc. Thenius remarks, "We have here the briefest of war-like exhortations, but one most full of point and meaning." Joab recognized the full danger of their situation; for should he meet with any check in his attack on this vast host of mercenaries, he was well aware that the Ammonites, watching the battle with eager interest, would, on the first news of victory, rush upon Abishai with exulting fury; and the men with him, being only ordinary troops, would be disheartened by Joab's failure, so that without extraordinary bravery on their leader's part, they would give way, and all would be lost.

Ver. 12.—**Be of good courage, and let us play the men.** The Hebrew employs two conjugations of the same verb, literally, *be strong, and let us show ourselves strong.* And need there was for bravery; for the welfare, as he went on to show, of all Israel, and the honour of Israel's God, were in jeopardy. Finally he adds, **The Lord do that which seemeth him good.** They are the words not so much of confidence as of determined resolution. Come good or ill, he and Abishai would do their utmost.

Ver. 14.—**So Joab returned.** It seems strange to us that Joab should have made no attempt to follow up his victory. But as the Ammonites were posted close to the gate of their city, they would withdraw into it without loss as soon as they learned that their allies were defeated. There was thus the certainty of a long siege before Rabbah

could be taken. We gather from ch. xi. 1 that it was late in the year when Joab won this victory, and it was part of the weakness of ancient warfare that a long campaign was beyond the power of either side.

Ver. 16.—**Hadarezer** (see note on ch. viii. 3). Hadarezer probably had been well content to let his subjects receive the pay of the Ammonites, and extend his empire at their cost. But as paramount king in Aram, the defeat of the mercenaries obliged him to make the war a national affair, and undertake the management of it himself. He therefore summons troops from all the Aramean states on both sides of the Euphrates, and places his own general, Shobach, in command, and makes Helam the place of gathering. **Helam.** No such place is known, and the word might mean "their army," in which case the translation would be, "and they came in full force." The Vulgate takes it in this way, but makes the verb the causative singular, and translates, "and he brought their army." On the other hand, the LXX., the Syriac, and the Chaldee make it a proper name here, as even the Vulgate necessarily does in ver. 17, where there can be no doubt. In the parallel place (1 Chron. xix. 16, 17) it is omitted in the first place, and in the second we find in its stead, "upon them." Either, therefore, the chronicler did not know of such a place, or the text is corrupt. Ewald and others suppose that Helam may be identified with Alamata; but we learn from 1 Chron. xviii. 3 that the battle was fought near Hamath, and Alamata is on the Euphrates, too far away for David to have made his attack there.

Ver. 17.—**David . . . gathered all Israel together.** Some commentators see in this an indication of dissatisfaction with Joab. Really it was a matter of course that in so great a war the king should place himself at the head of his levies. For not only was he possessed of great military genius, but his personal presence would make the men of Israel, a race of sturdy free men, assemble in greater numbers, and would give them confidence. If David himself went there would be no shirking the war and finding excuses to stay at home, and in the camp there would be prompt alacrity and zeal.

Ver. 18.—**David slew,** etc. (see note on ch. viii. 4). We have seen there that the word translated "chariots" means any vehicle or animal for riding. The numbers here are seven hundred chariots with their charioteers, and forty thousand horsemen; in ch. viii. 4 we have seventeen hundred horsemen and twenty thousand footmen; finally, in 1 Chron. xix. 18 we find seven thousand chariots and charioteers, and forty thousand footmen. It is impossible to reconcile these conflicting numbers, but as David had no cavalry, the numbers in ch. viii. 4 are the more probable, namely, seventeen hundred cavalry and chariots, and twenty thousand infantry. The Syriac Version gives us here very reasonable numbers, namely, "seven hundred chariots, four thousand cavalry, and much people."

Ver. 19.—**The kings . . . served them.** It is evident from this that the petty kings of Rehob, Tob, and Maacah had been subject to Hadarezer; they now acknowledged the supremacy of David, and paid to him the tribute which they had previously paid to Zobah, and would be bound to supply him with a contingent of men in case of a war in their neighbourhood. The wars with Damascus and Edom, mentioned in ch. viii. 5, 13, probably followed immediately upon Hadarezer's defeat, but are not referred to here, as the interest now centres in David's personal conduct.

HOMILETICS.

Vers. 1—5.—*Rejected friendliness.* The facts are: 1. On the death of the King of Ammon, David resolves to send a kindly message to Hanun, in remembrance of favours received from his father Nahash. 2. On the arrival of David's servants, the chief men of Ammon suggest to the new king that their message of condolence is a piece of trickery on the part of David for political ends. 3. Listening to these insinuations, Hanun shows his contempt for David by cutting off one side of the beard of his ambassadors, and exposing the lower part of their person. 4. On hearing of this humiliation, David sends a message to them on their way home, directing them to remain at Jericho till their beards were grown again. The question as to the chronological order of the events mentioned in this chapter as compared with ch. viii. does not affect the character of the facts or the lessons conveyed. The supposition that David deserved the insult he met with at the hand of Hanun, in consequence of showing friendliness to one of Israel's traditional foes, is not justified, because of the explicit reference to David's remembrance of acts of kindness. As in the case of Mephibosheth remembrance of Jonathan's kindness is referred to by way of explaining the conduct described, so here it is evidently regarded as a corresponding excellence in David that he was mindful also of the kindness of aliens. The object of the historian is obviously to bring out into view the king's broad generosity. In this light, then, we may regard the narrative as showing—

I. THE EXISTENCE IN HUMAN INTERCOURSE OF UNREQUITED AND UNRECORDED ACTS OF KINDNESS. Had not this ver. 2 been written we might never have known that the pagan Nahash had showed kindness to the Lord's anointed. Possibly few in Israel knew of the actual service rendered by Nahash to David at some period of his exile. No record of it existed save in the king's memory; and Nahash died before his consideration for one in trouble was acknowledged in regal form. Possibly he may have felt it strange that no notice was taken of the past when David came into power. The fact that we have this incidental reference to the kindness suggests what we often observe to be true, that many kindly deeds are done of which history takes no note, and which in the hurry and strife of life are lost to sight and mind. There is more good in the world than is tabulated. Thousands of considerate friendly deeds, revealing the true brotherhood of man and the latent worth of human nature, are being daily performed, but of which the mass of mankind will know nothing, and which, perhaps, will lie for a long time, through unavoidable circumstances, unrequited. We ought to bear this in mind when we strive to form an estimate of the state of the world, and it should set us at ease if our own generous acts do not figure in the annals of our time, and are to all appearance disregarded and unproductive of reciprocal conduct. It is the course of life; and yet nothing is lost, nothing is in vain.

II. THE GENEROSITY OF A TRUE HEART PASSES BEYOND CONVENTIONAL BOUNDS. To some it would seem strange that the King of Israel should cherish kindly sentiments towards an alien monarch, and even go out of the ordinary course to express those sentiments. Bigotry and a narrow interpretation of fidelity to the theocratic principle on which David's government was based would restrict generous feelings to one's own nationality. But David saw that man was before citizen, and the law of love before political expediency; and, as the Saviour later on saw a man and brother in the Samaritan and in every human creature, so now David saw in a kindly Nahash a kinship prior to and more radical than even the bonds which held him to his own nation. It is in these goings out of the best hearts of ancient times in kindliness towards the politically alien that we see a prefigurement of the broad evangelical charity which would embrace in its consideration every child of Adam. It is the delight of the good to recognize good in all men. The restrictive influences of sect and party, of nationality and race, are to be guarded against. The conventional is transitory ; nature is permanent. The sentiments proper to nature must, if possible, rise above the accidental sentiments springing from the casual and fleeting forms of life.

III. IT IS SOMETIMES THE MISFORTUNE OF THE BEST CONDUCT TO BE MISJUDGED. David's conduct was pure in motive, correct in form, and beneficial in tendency ; yet it was regarded by astute men with suspicion, and repaid by the most malicious insult. This was no new thing in his experience. We have seen how again and again, during his early trials, he was misunderstood by Saul, and his very deeds of kindness returned by more bitter persecution. This is the portion of not a few in all ages. The world is dark, and men cannot or will not see the colours of good. It is one of the sad forms of confusion brought about by sin. The merciful Redeemer blessed men, but he was despised and rejected of them. The most lovely character that ever adorned the earth was clothed by the foul imagination of men with the horrible attributes of Satan (Luke xi. 15—18). The same treatment in a milder form was to be expected by his disciples (Matt. v. 11 ; x. 17, 18). We may be comforted, when the like experience happens to us, that it is all foreseen and provided for. The clouds that pass over the sky are not endued with permanence. They are incident to a changeful atmosphere.

IV. THE SOURCE OF THE MISJUDGMENT IS INTELLECTUAL AND MORAL. The men who persuaded Hanun to scorn David's friendliness did not know David. It was ignorance of the actual intentions and the inner character of the king that gave scope for the base moral element to come in and impute to him vile motives (ver. 3). They really supposed him to be a man like unto themselves, and, cherishing ill will, they found no difficulty in tracing his conduct to such considerations as would have influenced themselves had they been in his position. There is in all men affected by what is called the spirit of the world, a primary suspicion and distrust of others. It is a sort of first principle in business, in diplomacy, in casual intercourse. In the absence of perfect knowledge of the heart, the imagination is set to work to find out the possible motives at work. The existence of the slightest dislike will assuredly cause the imagination to see something evil, and hence the deeds most worthy in origin and design may be treated as base and deceitful. Ignorance and dislike combined to slay the Lord of glory (John viii. 37—45 ; 1 Cor. ii. 8). If such things happened to the Master, the servants may be patient and trustful should they also happen to them.

V. WICKEDNESS AND FOLLY, BY THEIR MISJUDGMENT, TURN AN ACT OF FRIENDLI- NESS INTO AN OCCASION OF DESTRUCTION. The conceit and ill will of these Ammonites, acting on Hanun, first misjudged David's conduct, and then, by a natural process of evil, gave rise to a deed which proved the occasion of turning the friendliness of David into retributive anger which issued in their ruin. The men capable of reasoning and feeling as these did were certainly capable of the deed of shameful insult to David in the persons of his ambassadors (ver. 4). When men allow an ill-informed mind to be swayed by a malicious spirit, there is no telling to what lengths they may go in sin. Evil deeds are blind deeds. Their folly is parallel with their depravity. The most conspicuous instance of this is in the case of the people who misjudged Christ and rejected his friendliness. That which was to have been a rock on which they could build a great and blessed future became a stone to grind them to powder (Matt. xxi. 40—44 ; xxiii. 37 ; 1 Pet. ii. 7, 8). It is also the wanton rejection of Christ's kindness which will prove the occasion of the bitterest woe to individuals (Matt. x. 14, 15 ; xi. 20—24 ; cf. Prov. i. 24—27). All rejections of friendliness involve ultimate loss ; rejection of Christ's friendliness involves loss proportionate to his greatness and glory.

Vers. 6—19.—*International quarrels.* The facts are : 1. The Ammonites, discovering the displeasure of David, hire mercenaries of the neighbouring peoples. 2. As a counter-movement, David sends out a strong force under Joab. 3. The opposing forces coming into contact, Joab arranges that he should confront the Syrians, while Abishai deals with the Ammonites. 4. Joab, exhorting Abishai to courage, in dependence on God, arranges also for mutual support, in case of need, in their respective attacks. 5. On the Syrians yielding to the assault of Joab, the Ammonites also flee from before Abishai, whereupon Joab returns to Jerusalem. 6. Another effort of the Syrians under Hadarezer, aided by others from beyond the Euphrates, draws out David at the head of a large army to the eastern side of Jordan. 7. A great battle, issuing in the complete defeat of the Syrians; the tributary kings under Hadarezer make peace with Israel and serve them. We have here a record of quarrels and entanglements, which to the eye of a sacred historian have a bearing on the development of the kingdom of Israel, and consequently on the ultimate advent of the "Prince of the kings of the earth." In that respect the events form a section of the intricate movements of Providence for the furtherance of spiritual interests, and they have their natural place in the Divine moral order, allowing for human freedom, as truly as the formation of the igneous and sedimentary rocks have in the physical order. The narrative may thus be taken as typical of a class. But we may regard the record as suggesting, or illustrating, truths which, while prominent in international quarrels, have also a wider application to human life in general. These chiefly are as follows.

I. THE MAINTENANCE OF HONOUR IS A DUTY. It was right for David to resent the indignity and insult. Meekness and gentleness are qualities consistent with assertion of what is due to self as a man, as a ruler, as a representative of a people and of a Divine institution. A king's honour is his strength, because of the trust of his people, the sentiment of loyalty, the force of his decrees, his silent restraint of the turbulent, and, in David's case, also because of the Divine institution of his government. How kings and individuals may best maintain their honour is a question to be decided by the circumstances of the case; in some way the holiest and kindest may do it and ought to do it.

II. THE REPROACH AND DISPLEASURE OF THE JUST IS ITSELF THE BEGINNING OF PUNISHMENT. That the Ammonites "stank before David"—a monarch so wise, just, and generous—was a brand on them of demerit, and the natural forerunner of chastisement to come. Whoever by his deeds falls righteously under the displeasure of a just man, is *ipso facto* branded as base, is classed by his own conscience and all honourable observers as a criminal. This changing of the face of the just towards the wicked is the primary social punishment of sin ordained by God, and, as the gathering clouds precede the storm, it is the token of further providential chastisements. The course of nature in the long run follows in the course of moral right.

III. SINFUL FOLLY IS SURE TO BRING ON PERPLEXITIES AND PERILS. No doubt there was great mirth in the court of Hanun when the Hebrew ambassadors were half shorn of their beards and apparel. But the mirth was as "the crackling of thorns under a pot" (Eccles. vii. 6). It was soon found that this cheap mirth was, in fact, dearly bought; for the displeasure of so mighty a king as David was soon discovered to mean for them great perplexity and peril. So is it with all sin, which is a sort of moral madness. It may give passing gratification, and all may seem secure, but it leads to perplexities and perils from which there is no escape as long as a Righteous One sits on his throne. The irony of the preacher is painfully true (Eccles. xi. 9).

IV. ONE EVIL DEED REQUIRES OTHER DEVICES TO SUSTAIN IT. The sinful folly of the Ammonites necessitated the device of hiring mercenary troops to ward off the blow that was impending as a consequence of their sin. It is quite true that in any progressive life action must be sustained by action, but in the case of evil-doing the device is to stave off something which ought not to come, and which would not be feared but for the previous wrong. Sin cannot remain sole. If there is not immediate repentance there will be an effort to get out of the self-caused difficulties by other questionable means. The liar has to take ceaseless precautions because of his lie. The man who rejects Christ is conscious of much uneasiness, and has to exercise ingenuity to escape this consequence. Troops of mercenaries are hired.

V. WELL-STORED RESOURCES ADMIT OF PROMPT ACTION IN EMERGENCIES. David had during the five years of his reign paid great attention to the administration of the affairs of his kingdom, and, as a consequence, he was now able at once to avail himself of the resources that had been treasured up. He sent "Joab, and all the host of mighty men" (ver. 7). The fruits of prescience and care were now available without confusion or delay. In kingdoms, as in homes and in business, providence and orderly arrangement give great advantages for action when unexpected and trying events transpire. The same is true of early education and culture, of Church organization, of the personal spiritual life. The world is evil; events at cross-purposes with our plans and adverse to our peace will arise; it is "impossible but that offences come." The moral is, lay up in store continuously, and so be ready for action, and therefore ready for victory.

VI. SOUND PRINCIPLES PERTAINING TO CONDUCT AFFORD MORAL SUPPORT IN TIMES OF GREAT STRESS AND DANGER. Joab showed the better side of his nature when he exhorted Abishai, in face of the foe, to act as a man for the honour and safety of his people and cities, leaving the consequences in the hands of God (ver. 12). Not for military display, not for aggrandizement, not for personal gain, but to vindicate a people whose head had been insulted,—this was the principle on which the battle should be fought. In this was duty; consequences were with God, who cares for the just. History reveals instances in which men have been made strong by the just principle for which they contended. A righteous cause is itself equivalent to an armed force, both in the moral tone it gives to those engaged in it, and in the secret depression of those on the other side. It would be interesting to trace out the physical bearings of moral influences. Let us see to it that our great efforts are under the guidance of clear moral principles.

VII. IN THE CONFLICTS OF LIFE AN ASSURANCE OF MUTUAL HELPFULNESS IS A HELP AGAINST DISASTER. The arrangement for mutual help in case of pressure (ver. 11) was helpful, in that it anticipated a possible evil, and it inspired each with the courage that comes of sympathy and support. In human affairs, secular and religious, the possibility of disaster must be taken into account, because of personal imperfection and of the unascertained forces against us. We do not possess the knowledge by which we can always dispose of our strength in the right quarter, and, even when we do possess it, there may be sudden moral paralysis. None of us contend alone, or for self only. Hence we can be mutually helpful, as were Joab and Abishai. More of this in things sacred and secular would save from many a disaster.

VIII. UNWISE ALLIANCES LEAD ON TO SERIOUS ENTANGLEMENTS. The Syrians lent themselves for gain (ver. 6) to an alliance with the Ammonites. This compact, destitute of sound principle, involved the Syrians in what appeared to them to be the necessity of maintaining their reputation in spite of defeat; and hence further arrangements were made with Syrians "beyond the river." A Syrian war, with the whole of Israel's army under the leadership of the invincible David, was the consequence. Such difficulties arise when men make unholy alliances against a just cause. If men cannot unite without evil it is better to stand aloof. Nature has formed certain elements to combine, and others to keep apart. Whoever tries to put together what is contrary to nature will get into difficulty. Whoever forms an unholy alliance in human affairs, national or personal, is seeking to bring about advantages which it is in the course of moral order to prevent; and sooner or later greater embarrassments will arise. In moral matters simplicity and direct submission to the moral order are true wisdom.

IX. ADVERSE BEGINNINGS MAY, FOR THE JUST, ISSUE IN GOOD ENDINGS. It is a pain and annoyance to David to have his friendliness so wantonly rejected (ver. 4), but the event issued in the extension of his power and the surer peace of his people (vers. 18, 19). Man has the beginnings of things in his hand, but a Mightier One works them up towards issues of his own. The persecution of the early Church resulted in the wider diffusion of the gospel. The rejection of Christ by the Jewish nation is to issue in a greater glory. Many things in our personal experience may pain and injure us, but by stirring up our strength, by awakening more trust in God and leading to greater caution and courage, we may in the end achieve conquests once never thought of.

HOMILIES BY VARIOUS AUTHORS.

Vers. 1—4 (1 Chron. xix. 1—4).—(RABBAH.) *Requiting evil for good.* The Ammonites appear to have remained quiet since their defeat by Saul, nearly half a century before (1 Sam. xi.). Nahash their king (perhaps a son of the former Nahash) had rendered friendly service to David. But on the accession of Hanun, his son, the old hostility of the children of Ammon revived, and showed itself in a way that made conflict inevitable. To this the growing power of David and his recent subjugation of their kindred, the Moabites (ch. viii. 2), doubtless contributed. Their deliberate, wanton, and shameless *treatment of his messengers* was the occasion of "the fiercest struggle, and, so far as the Israelitish kingdom of God was concerned, the most dangerous, that it ever had to sustain during the reign of David." In it we see—

I. A PERSONAL CONTRAST. David requited the kindness of Nahash with kindness to his son; condolence on his bereavement, congratulation on his accession (ver. 2); but Hanun requited the kindness of David with insult and injury to his servants (ver. 4; Isa. xx. 4). The conduct of the one displayed gratitude, sympathy, confidence, and benevolence; that of the other ingratitude, contempt, distrust, and malignity. 1. How different in *character* the men who hold similar positions! David and Hanun were both kings, their heads were pressed by the same "crown of pure gold" (ch. xii. 30; Ps. xxi. 3); but in spirit they were wholly unlike. 2. How different the *construction* put on similar actions! Such actions are regarded by men as good or evil, according to their ruling disposition; just as the same objects appear of different hue according to the colour of the medium through which they are viewed. Hence what is well meant is often ill interpreted. 3. How different the *consequences* that flow from similar influences! *Kindness* is like sunshine, that melts the ice and hardens the clay; causes pleasure to the healthy and torture to the diseased eye. It tests, manifests, and intensifies the good or evil in the heart, and leads to opposite courses of conduct. Its proper tendency is to produce its like; but its actual effect is often the contrary (John xiii. 27). Even the kindness of God is perverted by hardness of heart to more abounding wickedness (Isa. xxvi. 10; Rom. ii. 4, 5). If it be sinful to "recompense evil for evil" (Rom. xii. 17), how much more to recompense evil for good (1 Sam. xxv. 21)!

II. A PUBLIC DISHONOUR. It was not a private and personal indignity put on these ambassadors, but an open and national insult offered to their king and people, by Hanun and his court (ver. 3), who probably expressed therein the prevalent suspicion and hatred of the children of Ammon. 1. How prejudicial the indulgence of jealousy and *suspicion* to the maintenance of peace and good will among nations! 2. How pernicious the influence of *evil counsel* and calumny on the political principles and policy of rulers! "We see in this the bitter fruits which evil counsel to princes, especially to those who are young and inexperienced, produces" (Guild). "The slanderer inflicts a threefold wound at one stroke. He wounds himself by his breach of charity; he wounds his victim by injuring his good name; he wounds his hearers by poisoning their minds against the accused" (St. Bernard). 3. How provocative the exhibition of *ingratitude, injustice, and contempt* to resentment and retaliation (ver. 6)! It turns kindness into wrath, seems to justify the drawing of the sword, and inspires the hope of victory (ver. 12). "Thou knowest not what may show itself when thy contempt awakes the lion of a sleeping mind."

III. A PRESUMPTUOUS AND FATAL DEFIANCE. It was a challenge by the worshippers of Moloch, confident in their strength and success, to the people of Jehovah; the first step of a renewed attack "against Jehovah and against his Anointed" (Ps. ii.). The opposition of the ungodly to the kingdom of God, though it slumber for a season, ever breaks forth afresh. 1. How infatuated their hostility! They are heedless of the warnings afforded by the past. 2. How groundless their confidence! "They trust in vanity." 3. How certain their overthrow!

> "He that sitteth in the heavens laughs,
> The Lord hath them in derision," etc.
>
> (Ps. ii. 4—9.)

The evil which they do returns on their own heads (ver. 14); and "their end is destruction" (ch. xii. 31). "These shall make war with the Lamb," etc. (Rev. xvii. 14).

CONCLUSION. 1. We should not be deterred from doing good by the fear that it may be requited with evil. 2. Although others may render evil for good, we should render good for evil (1 Sam. xi. 12, 13). 3. The noblest victories are those which are gained by patience, forbearance, and all-conquering love (Rom. xii. 21).—D.

Vers. 4, 5 (1 Chron. xix. 4, 5).—(JERICHO.) *Ridicule.* "Tarry at Jericho until your beards be grown, and then return " (ver. 5). It has been the endeavour of men in all ages to make the objects of their aversion appear contemptible and ridiculous. Few things are more painful and humiliating than exposure to popular derision. The fear of it, no doubt, sometimes exerts a salutary influence in restraining from what is unseemly and wrong; but it also frequently exercises an opposite influence in deterring from what is becoming and right. Of *ridicule*, together with the sense of dishonour (ver. 5, former part) which it naturally produces, observe that it is often—

I. INCURRED BY FIDELITY. Like the servants of David, the servants of Christ are made the object of scornful raillery (a common and effective instrument of persecution): 1. In the faithful performance of *duty*, in obedience to the will of their Lord; conveying his message of kindness, acting as his representatives. "For righteousness' sake; " "For my sake " (Matt. v. 10, 11; x. 22). It is not the suffering, but the cause, that makes the martyr (1 Pet. ii. 20; iv. 15). 2. By those who hate and *misrepresent* them and him whom they serve, and whose hostility is due to their diverse character and principles. "If ye were of the world," etc. (John xv. 19). 3. After the *example* of the faithful in past time. "Others had trial of mockings " (Heb. xi. 36). "Herod with his soldiers set him at nought, and mocked him," etc. (Luke xxiii. 11, 35, 36).

II. MODERATED BY SYMPATHY. "And they told it unto David, and he sent to meet them," etc. Those who, in the way of duty, suffer the reproach of the bad, enjoy the sympathy of the good; and especially of the *Master* himself: 1. Whose sympathy is inexpressibly precious. 2. Who has suffered the same, and is therefore able to *feel with them* and for them (ch. vi. 20). 3. Who also *expresses it* in the most appropriate and effectual manner. He regards what is done to them as done to himself, affords them wise and friendly counsel, takes them under his protection, and stands ready to defend and avenge them. "They departed, . . . rejoicing that they were counted worthy to suffer dishonour for the Name " (Acts v. 41; xvi. 25; 1 Thess. ii. 2).

III. REMEDIED BY PATIENCE. "Tarry," etc. They were probably disposed to go up at once to Jerusalem, and proclaim their wrongs, but David, out of consideration for their position in public estimation, bade them remain in obscurity, and "bide their time "—a piece of advice sometimes given (though not always in a like spirit) to persons who are about to attempt something for which they are unfit, on account of their immaturity or want of due preparation; or in which they have already failed. 1. Those who would attain success and honour in any position or enterprise should *consider well their ability* to accomplish what is necessary for their purpose (Luke xiv. 28). 2. Inconsiderate and *rash endeavours* are likely to issue in a result which those who make them neither expect nor desire. 3. The *lapse of time* soothes many a smart; and the wise and patient employment of it qualifies for and ensures honourable achievements. "Ye have need of patience " (Heb. x. 36). "Let us learn not to lay too much to heart unjust reproaches; after a while they will wear off of themselves, and turn only to the shame of their authors; while the injured reputation in a little time grows again, as these beards did " (Matthew Henry).

IV. SUCCEEDED BY HONOUR. "And then return " to the holy city, where they would be honoured (instead of being despised) with: 1. The public commendation of the king. 2. The general admiration of the people. 3. All the more because of the indignity and ridicule which they had previously endured. "If ye are reproached for the Name of Christ, blessed are ye," etc. (1 Pet. iv. 14); "great is your reward in heaven " (Matt. v. 12).—D.

Vers. 6—11 (1 Chron. xix. 6—12).—(MEDEBA.) *An agreement of mutual help.* "If the Syrians be too strong for me, then thou shalt help me: but if the children of Ammon be too strong for thee, then I will come and help thee " (ver. 11). 1. On perceiving the effect of their treatment of David's ambassadors (ver. 6; "That they had made themselves odious," 1 Chron. xix. 6), *the Ammonites* obtained, for "a thousand talents of silver," the aid of *the Syrians* of Beth-rehob and of Zobah (under Hadarezer, the most powerful of David's adversaries), the King of Maacah and the men of Tob; "who came and pitched before Medeba " (1 Chron. xix. 7), twenty miles south-west of Rabbah, with their infantry, cavalry, and war-chariots. "And the children of Ammon gathered themselves together from their cities " to the capital (Rabbah), and put themselves in battle array before the gate. 2. Hearing of their warlike preparations,

David had sent forth " all the host, the mighty men," under *Joab* (ch. iii. 22—30), who now found himself between the two hostile forces; and, selecting a portion of the army, placed himself opposite to the Syrians, whilst he left the rest, under Abishai, to cover his rear and hold the Ammonites in check. He doubtless hoped to defeat the enemy in successive engagements. 3. But fearing a simultaneous attack, he made an agreement with his brother, that if either of them were worsted, the other should hasten to his relief. Such an agreement is prudent, needful, and beneficial among those also who are engaged in spiritual warfare against the enemies of the kingdom of God. It—

I. CONFIRMS AN OBVIOUS DUTY. For it is plainly the duty of *brethren* : 1. To *consider* each other's condition, to sympathize with each other's weakness and distress, and not to be concerned about themselves alone. " Not looking each of you to his own things," etc. (Phil. ii. 4; 1 Cor. x. 24). 2. To make use of their *power*, to " strengthen their brethren," especially when taking part in the same conflict as themselves. The strong should help the weak. 3. To afford them *help*, opportunely, promptly, with all their might, and even at much sacrifice and hazard to themselves. If the ungodly " helped every one his neighbour; and every one said to his brother, Be of good courage " (Isa. xli. 6), much more ought the godly to do the same. " But if ye will not do so, behold ye have sinned against the Lord : and be sure your sin will find you out " (Numb. xxxii. 23). And the agreement to render mutual help in time of need makes the obligation to do so more distinct, impressive, and effective.

II. CONTEMPLATES A POSSIBLE REVERSE. " If the Syrians be too strong for me," etc.; indicating a conviction of : 1. The great power of the *enemy* and the serious nature of the struggle (1 Sam. xiii. 1—7). It would be madness to despise them. 2. The possibility of *failure* in the wisest plans and disappointment in the most sanguine expectations. " We do not hinder our successes by preparing for disappointment." Although those who " contend earnestly for the faith once for all delivered to the saints " cannot be generally and permanently defeated, yet particular organizations, methods, and hopes may be overthrown. None, however strong, can be certain of never needing help; whilst the promise of help furnishes the weak with a special claim to it. 3. The necessity of taking every *precaution* for repairing defect in the weakest part, lest it should issue in disaster to the whole. " Bear ye one another's burdens, and so fulfil the Law of Christ " (Gal. vi. 2).

III. CONDUCES TO SIGNAL SUCCESS. By : 1. Giving them to feel their mutual dependence, and bringing them into closer *union* in the spirit of a common enterprise. 2. Affording assurance of the advantages arising from *co-operation* toward a common end. These advantages are inestimable. " Two are better than one . . . And if one prevail against him, two shall withstand him; and a threefold cord is not quickly broken " (Eccles. iv. 9—12). 3. Inspiring them with increased confidence arising therefrom; and inciting them to greater *individual effort* than they might otherwise have put forth on behalf of each other and their common safety, welfare, and honour. Both the Syrians and Ammonites were routed (vers. 13, 14). " It was, perhaps, the first time in his life that Hadarezer suffered defeat " (Ewald); and this defeat was followed ere long by another (by David at Helam) still more overwhelming; so that " all the kings that were servants to Hadarezer made peace with Israel, and served them," etc. (vers. 15—19; ch. viii. 3, 4).—D.

Ver. 12 (1 Chron. xix. 13).—(MEDEBA.) *Martial courage.* " Be of good courage," etc. Human life is a warfare, unavoidable, arduous, enduring; and spiritual life, more especially, is a warfare of a similar kind. In this conflict nothing is more needful than manly or martial courage ("virtue," 1 Pet. i. 5). It is that quality of mind which meets difficulty, danger, pain, or death, calmly and fearlessly. It has been reckoned by moralists among the four cardinal virtues (prudence, temperance, fortitude, justice), and, in its highest form, it is often enjoined in the Scriptures. " As it is necessarily requisite to the susception of all other virtues, so it is their main support, guardian, and establishment. Without this, every other virtue is precarious, and lies at the mercy of every cross accident " (J. Norris). " All the noble deeds that have beat their marches through succeeding ages have proceeded from men of courage " (O. Felltham). This brief and significant warlike exhortation of Joab was pitched in a higher key than we might have expected; but the devout feeling which it expressed, though genuine, was probably superficial and transient, passing away with the critical occasion which called it forth. We have now to consider, not the character of the speaker, but the import of his words. They indicate the nature, motive, and pervading principle of godly martial *courage*; that it should be displayed—

I. IN STRENUOUS OPPOSITION TO THE ENEMIES OF THE KINGDOM OF GOD. "Be strong" (in spirit), "and show yourselves strong" (in action) in your struggle with numerous and powerful foes; not private, but public enemies; not men as such, but as imbued with principles and devoted to practices which are antagonistic to the righteous and beneficent purposes of God; "principalities and powers," etc. (Eph. vi. 12). "Who will rise up for *me* against the evil-doers?" etc. (Ps. xcvi. 16). There must be: 1. *Firm resistance* to their attack. "Whom resist steadfast in the faith" (1 Pet. v. 9). 2. *Patient endurance* of the sufferings which such resistance involves. "Here is the patience of the saints." 3. *Active endeavour* for their defeat and subjection. "The people that do know their God shall be strong, and do exploits" (Dan. xi 32). "Watch ye, stand fast in the faith, quit you like men, be strong" (1 Cor. xvi. 13). The chief instrument of this opposition is "the sword of the Spirit." "A humble Christian battling against the world, the flesh, and the devil, is a greater hero than Alexander the Great."

II. FROM SINCERE DESIRE FOR THE WELFARE OF THE PEOPLE OF GOD. Not for pay and plunder (like the mercenary Syrians), nor for glory, nor even for personal safety or life; but "for our people" (to whom we are bound by the closest ties), "and for the cities of our God" (his chosen property and possession, the many separate centres where his people dwell and his worship is maintained), imperilled by the attack of his enemies and ours. *Pro aris et focis.* "Thrice is he armed that hath his quarrel just." This, however, is an appeal, not merely to a sense of *justice*, but also and chiefly to *patriotism* and *piety*, which, in the men of Israel, were inseparably blended. There is a place for patriotism in the heart of a Christian (1 Sam. xxiii. 1—6). But his love for his country must be held in harmony with and subordination to his love for the Christian brotherhood, united in spiritual fellowship and confined to no nation; "the people of God" (1 Pet. ii. 9, 10), "his inheritance" (Eph. i. 18), "the Church which is his body" (Eph. i. 22; v. 25; Acts xx. 28), the light of the world, and the salt of the earth. "I endure all things for the elect's sakes" (2 Tim. ii. 10; Col. i. 24). 1. The preservation of their faith and holiness, their unity and peace, from corrupting and destructive influences. 2. The maintenance of their privileges and services, their freedom and independence. 3. The promotion of their prosperity and progress. 4. The fulfilment of their purposes, aims, and hopes. "They shall prosper that love thee" (Ps. cxxii. 4—9; cxxxvii. 7).

III. WITH STRONG CONFIDENCE IN THE RECEPTION OF THE HELP OF GOD. "And the Lord do that which seemeth him good" (Authorized Version); expressive of humble submission to the Divine will. "It may be understood as the language of: (1) Uncertainty and modesty. (2) A firm persuasion that the event of war entirely depends upon the providence of God. (3) A humble submission to the disposal of Providence, let the event turn out as it would. (4) And it may intimate that, let the event be what it will, it will afford us satisfaction to think that we have done the best we could" (Samuel Davies). But the proper reading is, "And Jehovah will do that which is good in his sight," really good for his people. The root of Christian courage, as of every Christian excellence, is faith in God. 1. In his *readiness* to co-operate with us, when we strive against the enemies of his kingdom and for the welfare of his people. "The Lord is on my side, I will not fear." 2. In the *sufficiency* of his might to strengthen the weakest and overthrow the strongest. "Fear not; for they that be with us are more than they that be with them" (2 Kings vi. 16; 1 Sam. xiv. 1—15). 3. In the *certainty* of his affording to his faithful servants all the help they need. Even though he should permit a temporary reverse, he will surely give them the victory over all their adversaries. Such confidence is warranted by his relation to them, his regard for them, his express promises, and his past achievements. "The battle is the Lord's." "If God is for us, who is against us?" (Rom. ix. 31—39).—D.

Vers. 2—4.—*Kindness misinterpreted and ill-requited.* "I am for peace; but when I speak, they are for war" (Ps. cxx. 7). It is not probable that these words were written by David, but they might have been with truth. It does not appear that he desired war with the neighbouring peoples; but for a time he was continually at war with one or other of them. Jealous of the growing greatness and power of Israel under his rule, they sought to humble them, but only to their own discomfiture and subjugation. And as the kingdom extended, more distant nations feared for themselves, and were ready to combine against what seemed the common foe. This is probably the real explanation of the transactions recorded in this chapter, including the most serious struggle which the rising kingdom had had to maintain. Nahash, "the king of the children of Ammon," having died, David, to whom Nahash had in some way shown kindness, sent ambassadors to Hanun, his son and successor, with a message of condolence. But the young king, induced by the princes to regard the ambassadors as spies, who had been sent to obtain such knowledge of the city as might facilitate its overthrow, treated them with the grossest contumely and indecency, and so dismissed them. Hence sprang a deadly war, in which the Ammonites were aided by other and more powerful peoples—a war which taxed to the utmost the strength of Israel, and issued in the complete overthrow of their enemies. The first step in all this commotion and destruction was the false interpretation put upon the kind act of David; and, regarding it as an illustration of a too-common evil, we take occasion to remark upon the evil itself—misinterpretation of good deeds.

I. THE CAUSES OF IT. 1. *Knowledge of the world.* There is so much evil in it, so much evil which conceals itself under the pretence of good; the actions which at first appear good are so often, on closer acquaintance, discovered to be evil; that experience of the world tends to produce a suspicious spirit, which is slow to believe in the reality of goodness in any particular instance, quick to think the worst of the conduct of others, especially of strangers. 2. *Evil in one's self.* Which may be conscious or unconscious. We are indisposed to believe others to be better than we know ourselves to be; and prone to suspect others of motives we are conscious of indulging ourselves. And, without distinct consciousness, we are influenced in our judgments of others by our own character; and may be so far under the influence of evil as to be blind to the good in others. The cold, selfish, illiberal, cannot credit others with the opposite virtues; but suspect the appearance of them to be only a semblance adopted for some unworthy purpose. 3. *Enmity.* If on any account we cherish ill will towards another, we are ever ready to think evil rather than good of him; and specially slow to think he can intend good to us. If another has failed to show as high an esteem for ourselves as we think we deserve, our mortified pride is apt to vent itself in depreciation of him. Prejudice is one kind of enmity, more or less virulent. It commonly exists in those of one party in religion or politics towards those of the opposite party, and predisposes them to misinterpret whatever they do. 4. *Fear.* Which was one of the motives that prompted Hanun and his advisers. 5. *Conceit of sagacity.* A cheap and easy way of appearing very wise, and of obtaining from some a reputation for wisdom, is to affect to discover unworthy motives in good actions. 6. *Bad advisers.* Such as those of Hanun. Those who might be otherwise disposed to a just estimate of good deeds will seldom want advisers to poison their minds, if they will listen to them.

II. THE EVIL OF IT. 1. *In itself.* It is inherently base. It is contrary to: (1) Charity, which "believeth all things, hopeth all things" (1 Cor. xiii. 7), whenever it is not manifestly impossible. (2) Justice. Judgments which seem to be only charitable will often be simply just. (3) Gratitude, in the case of actions kind to ourselves. Better to waste a little gratitude than indulge needless suspicion. (4) The plain commands of our Lord. Such as "Judge not;" "Whatsoever ye would that men should do to you, do ye even so to them" (Matt. vii. 1, 12). It involves, further, an assumption of knowledge such as men do not possess, and a usurpation of the office of him who alone searches the heart (1 Cor. iv. 5). We are not, however, required to cherish a blind credulity, nor to trust men with important interests without positive knowledge of their moral worth, still less against plain evidence of the contrary. Prudence is a virtue as well as charity. The Ammonites might have rightly exercised such caution towards David's messengers as would have prevented their obtaining so much knowledge of the city as would facilitate hostile measures against it, if these were really contemplated. They did wrong in concluding that the seeming kindness was covert hostility. To have returned civility for civility could have done them no harm, and would have prevented the severe retribution for their barbarity which followed. 2. *In its effects.* (1) On those who are guilty of it. It deprives them of the happiness and other good which they would gain from kindness exercised towards them, were it duly appreciated and acknowledged ; and of the benefit which it would impart in the way of example and influence. It strengthens the bad dispositions and habits from which it springs. It prompts to conduct (as in this case) which may work incalculable mischief. (2) On those towards whom it is indulged. Inflicting pain, producing resentment, and perhaps active revenge, and discouraging them in the practice of virtues which are liable to be so maligned. (3) On others. Infecting with unjust suspicions some who would not otherwise cherish them ; encouraging disbelief in genuine goodness, and thus loosening the bonds of mutual confidence by which society is held together ; disinclining also from good deeds, and so lessening the amount of goodness in the world.

III. How it should affect us. 1. *It should not surprise us.* Considering what men are, we should regard it as quite possible that any good we may do will be misrepresented, or at least fail to be duly appreciated and acknowledged even by those whose benefit we seek. 2. *It should not deter us from doing good.* The great motives for good deeds abide the same. They are quite independent of human appreciation. They should be our chief motives, the hope of approval or suitable return from men occupying a very subordinate position. Let us study and labour to be accepted of God (2 Cor. v. 9), and be content with his approval, let men think what they may. 3. *If men misrepresent our conduct, let us exercise charity towards them,* hoping, if we cannot confidently believe, that they have sinned through ignorance or inconsideration rather than ill will. If compelled to vindicate ourselves, let us do it with meekness. We should also reflect whether we have given any occasion in the manner of our conduct for misunderstanding of its real quality ; and avoid the error in future. And, if we are really reproached for that which is good, without just occasion, let us be mindful that we are fellow-sufferers with our Lord and many of the best men of all ages. 4. *Let us be watchful against every temptation to depreciate and misrepresent the good which is practised by others.*—G. W.

Vers. 11, 12.—*Co-operation, courage, and resignation.* Joab here appears at his best. A great occasion, involving great peril for the army and the kingdom, calls forth, not only his eminent military qualities, but sentiments of piety and religious patriotism worthy of David himself. He presents an example worthy of imitation by commanders of armies ; but we take his words as adapted to guide and animate the soldiers of Christ in their warfare against error and sin. They call attention to three duties incumbent upon individual Christians, the several bands of each division of the Christian army, and the several divisions themselves.

I. Mutual help. (Ver. 11.) The servants of Christ are engaged in the endeavour to conquer the world for him, and, in pursuing it, have to fight against enemies of various kinds. In this warfare they ought to cheerfully co-operate, and, as opportunity may arise, help each other. Much mutual assistance they cannot but render, however any might desire to confine the benefits of their activity to their own party. Every hymn-book testifies to this. No individual or section can do good work without helping others. But there should be more of conscious and hearty co-operation. 1. *Why it should be so.* (1) The cause is one—the cause of Christ our King, the defence and extension of his kingdom, the cause of truth and righteousness and human salvation. (2) Christians are comrades in the same army. They should cherish the feeling of brotherhood, realize that they are fighting against common foes, and be glad to encourage and help each other. The success of any is the success of all, and should be so regarded ; the failure of any should be a trouble to all ; and, if any can aid their brethren to turn threatening defeat into victory, their aid should be cheerfully afforded and joyfully accepted. (3) The need is urgent. The spiritual necessities of men, the special needs in particular cases. The field is extensive ; the opposing forces numerous, powerful, and incessantly vigilant and active. The utmost exertions of all are required. To hold back, to refuse co-operation with fellow-soldiers because they belong not to our regiment or division of the army, to observe with pleasure the failure of any of them, or to waste energies and resources in fierce conflicts with one another, is to be disloyal to their Sovereign, unbrotherly to each other, and unfaithful to the souls of men. 2. *Why it often is not so.* (1) Deficiency of spiritual insight. Incapacity, voluntary or involuntary, to discern: (*a*) The real nature of the kingdom of Christ. That it is essentially spiritual, consisting in "righteousness and peace and joy in the Holy Ghost;" that "he that in these things serveth Christ is acceptable to God, and approved of men" (Rom. xiv. 17, 18); and that in Christ Jesus nothing avails but "a new creature," "faith which worketh by love," and "the keeping of the commandments of God" (Gal. vi. 15; v. 6; 1 Cor. vii. 19). (*b*) The essential qualities of Christ's soldiers, which are not the dress they wear, nor the particular drill to which they are accustomed, but love and loyalty to Christ. (2) Deficiency of spiritual affections. Want of supreme and ardent love for Christ and his kingdom, and for his servants as such. These deficiencies of mind and heart act and react on each other, and they open the way for all kinds of blundering and perversity. Fellow-soldiers are mistaken for enemies, and treated as such. The great cause is made practically subordinate to matters infinitely small in comparison. Sectarian rivalry takes the place of Christian co-operation; or a worse thing happens—petty personal ambition and selfishness, or likings and dislikings, dominate, separating those who should be acting together, and introducing low, worldly principles into a region where the spiritual should alone reign. Pride, jealousy, envy, uncharitableness, perhaps the merest avarice, reduce to a fraction, if they do not altogether extinguish, those noble Christian feelings which Christianity inspires, and which would impel brothers to own brothers, cordially to render or receive help in the common work, to rejoice in each other's successes, and sorrow for each other's reverses. 3. *Who should take the lead in effecting co-operation?* Joab addresses Abishai, his fellow-commander; and it is just the leaders and commanders in Christ's army who should be foremost in promoting a good understanding between its various bands, and inducing them to work together. But, alas! they are often foremost in promoting alienation and separation. The people are frequently more disposed to be friendly towards each other than the clergy.

II. COURAGE. (Ver. 12.) In war this is essential to success. In the Christian warfare it is not so obviously or universally required. It is, however, still required in many cases. When unpopular truth has to be proclaimed, when strongholds of sin or superstition have to be assailed, when the evangelization of barbarous tribes is attempted, or perilous climates have to be encountered, the Christian soldier must be prepared to endure hardship, suffering, or death. Even the ridicule which not unfrequently assails the earnest Christian calls for a good deal of courage. Joab sought to inspire his brother, and through him the soldiers under his command, with courage, by reminding him that it was "for our people, and for the cities of our God," that they were about to fight. In like manner Christians may be exhorted to "be of good courage" and "play the men" for the Church of God, and for the sake of the world which they aim to conquer for Christ. Joab might have added, "for our king;" and the strongest and most animating consideration for us is that we are witnessing and working and fighting for our great King, the Lord Jesus Christ. He is worth living for, suffering for, dying for. He has gone before us in the labour and the suffering. He is present with us. His eye is upon each of us. He will overlook no true-hearted soldier of his when he distributes the rewards of victory. "If we suffer, we shall also reign with him" (2 Tim. ii. 12).

III. RESIGNATION. Those who engage in war, though they may hope for victory, must be prepared for defeat. "The battle" is not always "to the strong" (Eccles. ix. 11) or the brave. Nor in the better warfare can we "command success" in this or that particular encounter, however faithful or brave or zealous we may be. We are to recognize, like Joab, that "the Lord" is over all, and be content that he should "do that which seemeth him good." Not that we are required to be resigned to ultimate failure, for we are assured of final and complete victory.

> "The saints in all this glorious war
> Shall conquer, though they're slain."

Nor are the courage and devotedness of any single soldier lost. All the faithful contribute to the final triumph, and all shall unite in the song of victory, "The kingdoms of this world are become the kingdoms of our Lord, and of his Christ." "Alleluia : for the Lord God omnipotent reigneth!" "And he shall reign for ever and ever" (Rev. xi. 15; xix. 6).—G. W.

EXPOSITION.

CHAPTER XI.

Ver. 1.—**After the year was expired;** Hebrew and Revised Version, *at the return of the year;* that is, as Josephus paraphrases it, "the next spring." It seems quite certain that the war with Hadarezer did not take place in the same year as the defeat of the Syrians at Medeba. For the gathering of his mercenaries by Nahash would occupy a long time, and it was done so leisurely, that not only did news of it reach Jerusalem, but David was able to collect his forces, and instead of awaiting the invasion, could deliver his attack on the enemy's ground. The battle at Medeba took place in the autumn, and, as it was impossible to keep the field with winter so near, Joab marched back to Jerusalem, intending in the spring to return to the siege of Rabbah. But David quickly had information that a more serious war was impending, and, instead of sending Joab, he now gathers "all Israel," and, after gaining a victory, it is plain that he marched into the Syrian territories, and compelled by his presence the allies of Hadarezer to transfer their allegiance to him. Simultaneously with this war he had to meet the attack of the Edomites, for which purpose he detached Abishai with a portion of his army; and it was necessary also to post garrisons in their country, and in Aram of Damascus. It was while he was thus occupied in the Aramean states that he gathered the "much brass" spoken of in ch. viii. 8. The Ammonites would necessarily be left to themselves while these great events were going on, but now, after a respite of a year and a half, David **sent Joab, and his servants,** that is, his officers—the word "servant" in Oriental courts being constantly used to designate those high in rank near the king's person—**and all Israel;** that is, an army gathered from all the tribes. In accordance with the cruel customs of ancient warfare, they began by laying the whole country waste, and putting all whom they found to the sword, and thus **destroyed the children of Ammon** before laying siege to the capital, into which all the people by these harsh measures had been forced to go for refuge. In the Hebrew there is a curious spelling, the word "kings" being written *melâkim,* with an *aleph* to represent the long *â.* It is a mistake to suppose that a different word, *malâkim,* "angels" or "ambassadors," is meant, as it is nothing more

than an archaic method of spelling, instances of which have been made rare by the extreme fastidiousness of Hebrew scribes. There is, however, another example not far off, where the Hebrew word for "poor" is also written with an inserted *aleph.*

Ver. 2.—**David arose from off his bed.** It was usual in Palestine, and remains so in all hot countries, to take a siesta in the heat of the day (ch. iv. 5); and, on awaking, David walked backward and forward on the flat roof of his house (1 Sam. ix. 25), to enjoy the cool breezes of the evening. In so doing he was probably following his usual habits; but temptation came upon him, as so often is the case, unexpectedly. We are told that it is regarded in the East as improper for one neighbour to look over the battlement of his house into the inner court of the next dwelling (Philippson). Considering the jealousy with which Orientals guard the female members of their family from intrusion, it was a wrong act on the king's part to spy into what was going on in the recesses of the adjoining house. But he did so, and suffered for it years of disgrace and misery. For he saw a beautiful woman, the wife of one of his high officers, bathing, probably to purify herself from some legal uncleanness, such as those mentioned in Lev. xv. No blame, so far, must be attached to her. The place was regarded as perfectly secluded, and probably neither she nor Uriah had ever suspected that what went on there could be observed from the roof of the king's palace.

Ver. 3.—**Bathsheba, the daughter of Eliam.** In ch. xxiii. 34 Eliam is said to be the son of Ahithophel, and thus Bathsheba would be his granddaughter. Mr. Blunt, in his 'Undesigned Coincidences,' p. 143, *et seq.,* sees in this the explanation of the adherence to the side of Absalom of a man so high in King David's service. It was the result of his indignation at David's profligate treatment of so near a relative. In 1 Chron. iii. 5 she is called "Bathshua, the daughter of Ammiel." The latter is a transposition of Eliam, both names being compounded of *Am,* people, and *El,* God. **Uriah the Hittite.** We read in ch. xxiii. 39 that he was one of David's "mighties," and it is remarkable that we should thus find high in rank in David's army a member of that grand race who had disputed with Egypt and Assyria the empire of the East. Their head now was Toi, King of Hamath.

Ver. 4.—**David sent messengers, and took**

her. David's fall seems as sudden as it was complete; but we may feel sure that there had been gradual preparation for it during the previous period of great prosperity. David had always been a man of strong passions, and the large harem he had set up at Jerusalem, so far from satisfying him, only intensified his lust. And now he who had previously shown himself so chivalrous and noble stoops to robbing one of his own officers of his honour. And stern and terrible was the punishment. When he sent those messengers, who were some of the vile people who hang about great personages, ready to minister to their sins, he was preparing the way for his daughter's disgrace, for the murder of Amnon, for Absalom's rebellion and death, and for the death of Adonijah. From that day his own house was the scene of horrible crimes, feuds, scandals, and miseries of every kind; and the long interval after his repentance, between the birth of Solomon and David's death, is passed over in gloomy silence. No act of the penitent king after his restoration to the throne is deemed worthy of record. He was pardoned, but his place henceforward was not in the light of God's favour, but in shadow and retirement. Men who fall so grievously must be content to be removed into the outer court. Of Bathsheba it must be said that she remained a faithful wife, and bare David four sons besides the one who was the fruit of their adultery, and that she retained her influence over him to the last (1 Chron. iii. 5; 1 Kings i. 15—31). **For she was purified from her uncleanness**; Hebrew, *and she purified herself from her uncleanness;* that is, having committed an act of gross immorality, she nevertheless carefully observed the ceremonial enactment commanded in Lev. xv. 18. She went home unrepentant, and with her conscience defiled, but was all the more scrupulous in performing the rite that purified her outwardly.

Ver. 5.—**The woman . . . told David.** Her crime was one that made her liable to the penalty of death (Lev. xx. 10), and Uriah was a man likely to exact it; consequently she was in great alarm, and the king shared her anxiety. Already was the punishment beginning to be required from both the guilty sharers in the wickedness.

Ver. 8.—**A mess** (of meat); really, *a royal present* (see Esth. ii. 18; Jer. xl. 5; Amos v. 11, where it is translated *burdens of wheat*, but really means *presents of wheat*, forced from the poor); though originally a portion of food sent to a guest from the table of the giver of a feast (Gen. xliii. 34). Uriah, as one of David's thirty-seven heroes, would hold a high rank in the army, though the statement given by Josephus, that he was Joab's armour-bearer, is probably a mere conjecture,

made with the view of explaining what seemed to him strange, that a foreigner should hold so distinguished a place among the captains of Israel. David sends for him, on the pretext that he wanted full information of Joab's plans, and the state of the army, and the progress of the siege of Rabbah. And so prompt is Uriah, that he goes to the king still soiled with travel, and without calling at his house. And David makes his inquiries, listens with apparent interest to the narrative of the war, and, after receiving a full report, bids Uriah go home and rest and refresh himself after the journey. He sends him, moreover, a present, such probably as was usual after special service, but large and liberal, so as to put Uriah in good humour. But the old soldier cared for war more than for pleasure, and, instead of going to his house, spent the night in the guard-room with the soldiers and others who were in attendance upon the king (see 1 Kings xiv. 27, 28). All would be eager for news of friends and relatives, and it was a far greater delight to Uriah to chat with his old comrades than to be resting luxuriously in his own home.

Ver. 11.—**The ark, and Israel, and Judah, abide in tents.** The presence of the ark with the army in the field is puzzling, and shows us how little we know of the religious practices of the Jews, as, but for this chance mention of it, we should have affirmed that it was never taken out of its place in Zion, and that in previous times the conduct of Eli's sons in carrying it out of the sanctuary to war was an irregular act. The Jews themselves feel the difficulty, and some of their rabbins affirm that this was not the ark of the covenant, but a chest containing the ephod whereby inquiries were made of Jehovah. Certainly in 1 Sam. iv. 3, 4 it is expressly called "the ark of the covenant;" and in ch. vi. 2 "the ark of God." The use in our version of the special word "ark" obliges us to think of the ark of the covenant, whereas really it is a general word, rendered "chest" in 2 Kings xii. 9, 10. It is said, too, that the war with Ammon was not a holy war, nor was it of such importance as to call for David's presence at the head of his troops. But, on the other hand, if it was not the ark of God, why did Uriah lay so great stress upon its presence in the field? Moreover, we find the ark with Saul in his war with the Philistines (1 Sam. xiv. 18), where it is expressly called "the ark of God," and is used for the purpose of inquiring the will of Jehovah. On comparing 1 Sam. vii. 2 with ch. vi. 3, we should have imagined that the ark abode uncared for at the house of Abinadab at Kirjath-jearim, did we not plainly find it in attendance upon Saul. We are thus compelled to conclude that David sent it, with its attendant priests, with Joab, that he might consult the Deity by its means. In the Talmud ('Shek. Jerus.,' 9. 2) the idea of there being an inferior or second ark used for this purpose is condemned. David, in his remonstrance with Uriah, shows signs of displeasure, and the conduct of the latter suggests the idea that his suspicions had been aroused. The war was going on prosperously; he had been summoned home on an honourable pretext to give the king a report of it; and it is, to say the least, strange that he should have cared so little for a wife, to whom apparently he had not long been married, and for his domestic affairs, as not even to go to his house, which was close by. The tone, too, of Uriah's answer is excited, and his military ardour too warm. David had assumed that, as a matter of course, he would hasten to visit his wife, and Uriah's unexpected refusal upsets his devices, and leaves him with all his difficulties increased rather than done away with. Very probably, in the conversation in the guard-room, Uriah had received hints that his wife was too high in the royal favour. For "tents" the Hebrew has "booths," and so the Revised Version; and for "fields" the singular, "field." The Israelites still lived mostly in tents, and in war were content with very slight and temporary shelter, and if there were any parks, or enclosures, they were called Naioth, while "the field" was the open unenclosed land, which formed the mass of the country. The separate mention of "Israel and Judah" is no indication of the book having been written after the disruption of the kingdom. Uriah had been in David's service when he was king only at Hebron, and had taken part in the long war between Judah and the house of Saul.

Ver. 13.—**He made him drunk.** David thus adds sin to sin, and, in order to accomplish his vile end, he degrades the brave soldier whom already he had dishonoured. But even when intoxicated Uriah kept to his determination; and though on this second night there would not be the same pleasure in chatting with old comrades seen again after long absence, he still sleeps in the guard-room. And thus there were witnesses that he had not gone to his house.

Ver. 14.—**David wrote a letter.** David now uses the knowledge he had acquired in the schools of the prophets for vicious purposes. For it to be a blessing, knowledge must be sanctified to holy use. The letter would conceal from Joab the truth, and only let him know that Uriah, during his visit to Jerusalem, had incurred the king's serious displeasure; and we may be quite sure that Joab would be very indignant

when he learned, as he certainly soon would, that David had made him his tool, and caused him to murder one of "the mighties" in order to cover the shame of his adultery. The only fair side of the picture is that it shows the high state of morality among the people. The crimes of kings and great men are usually lightly pardoned, and especially that of adultery. Even in our own and other Christian countries this is the case; but David has to resort to extreme measures rather than face the indignation of his subjects. Unfortunately, the shedding of blood was not looked upon with equal horror. Possibly the leaving it to the relatives to requite it made the suppression of murder the business, not of the state, but of "the avenger of blood." At all events, Joab without much compunction carries out David's orders, caring to know no more than that Uriah was out of favour. And what is more extraordinary, David remains utterly callous for a whole twelvemonth (see ch. xii. 15), and his conscience does not even smite him for the additional meanness of sending the order for Uriah's murder by the hand of the injured man himself.

Ver. 16.—**When Joab observed the city;** Revised Version, *kept watch upon the city.* This does not mean, as some suppose, that Joab sent a body of men to examine the fortifications with a view to an assault, and so provoked a sally. The verb simply refers to the ordinary operations of a siege, which usually resolved itself into a long blockade, continued until starvation compelled a surrender; and to hasten this the people of the villages were forced into the town, by the rule that all left outside were put to the sword. To maintain the blockade, men were posted at all fit points round the city, and these were constantly assailed by the besieged. Joab then placed Uriah at a post which was especially the object of attack; and when the usual sally took place and was repulsed, Joab seems to have ordered Uriah to pursue them up to the very gate, where they would be exposed to a shower of arrows from the walls. Others fell besides Uriah, and that the loss was considerable, and the result of bad generalship, though designedly such, seems probable from the deprecation of the king's anger in ver. 20.

Ver. 18.—**Then Joab sent.** Joab now performs another act in this iniquitous drama, and goes through the form of sending the king a report of the disaster which had followed upon his approaching too near the walls. With well-feigned hypocrisy, he makes the messenger believe that David will be displeased at the loss of life, and will blame him for his want of caution. But it is curious that the messenger is instructed to mention the death of Uriah only after the king has given utterance to his anger. Possibly the meaning of this is that the loss of one so high in rank, and the king's near neighbour, is so serious a matter that it must be gradually broken to him, lest his indignation at Joab should be too violent. Probably there was also the suggestion that Uriah had been himself too rash, and had incurred his fate by his own fault. The reference to the fate of Abimelech (Judg. ix. 53) proves that the history of the times of the judges was generally known. Very probably not only records of the several events existed, but the Book of Judges was already written In Samuel's schools the youth of Israel were instructed in the annals of their country, and men like Nathan and Gad, and others who aided Samuel in his work, would be sure quickly to turn their attention to the orderly arrangement and digest of the records in their possession.

Ver. 21.—**Jerubbesheth**; in Judg. vi. 32 called *Jerubbaal*, that is, Gideon. (On the substitution of Besheth, or more correctly Bosheth, for Baal, see notes on ch. ii. 8; ix. 6.) It is remarkable that the LXX., Vulgate, and Syriac all read here Jerubbaal, though, like the Hebrew, they have Ishbosheth and Mephibosheth. Probably the change, which was not made until after the days of Jezebel, was only gradually carried out by the scribes.

Ver. 23.—**The men prevailed against us.** The real meaning is "the men made a sortie against us in force, and came even to the open field; but we were upon them (and drove them back) unto the entry of the gate, and the archers from off the wall shot at thy servants," etc.

Ver. 25.—**Let not this thing displease thee.** David professes to be satisfied with Joab's apology, and bids him, if the war is in the main going on prosperously, not to be too much distressed at a temporary reverse. As for Uriah's death, of course it is to be regretted, but such is the fortune of war, and the sword devours now one and now another. The last words, **encourage thou him,** have provoked comment, as though the messenger was to aid and abet Joab. They simply mean "Give him a message of encouragement from me," the exact form of which is left to the messenger, but of which his report would be that the king wished Joab to take courage.

Ver. 26.—**And when the wife of Uriah heard that Uriah her husband was dead, she mourned for her husband.** There is something pathetic in this repetition of the name of the murdered man, and his close relation-

ship with Bathsheba is dwelt upon by his being twice called " her husband," and she " Uriah's wife." Having been the cause of his murder, she is careful to make for him the customary mourning. How long it lasted is uncertain. The mourning for Aaron (Numb. xx. 29) and that for Moses (Deut. xxxiv. 8) were each for thirty days; while that for Jacob at Atad (Gen. l. 10) and that of the men of Jabesh-Gilead for Saul (1 Sam. xxxi. 13) lasted only for seven days. Both these, however, were under such exceptional circumstances as made them no rule; but in Ecclus. xxii. 12 we read, "Seven days do men mourn for him that is dead," and the national lamentation for Judith lasted the same time (Judith xvi. 24). Probably, however, the mourning of a widow for her husband would last a month.

Ver. 27.—**She . . . bare him a son.** This would be the child whose death is recorded in the next chapter. Afterwards she bare David four sons (1 Chron. iii. 5), of whom one was Solomon, and another Nathan, the ancestor of our Lord. **The thing . . . displeased the Lord.** It was probably during the time of David's victories that success began to work in him its usual results. Too commonly men who have conquered kingdoms have been vanquished by their own strong passions; and David had always evinced a keen appetite for sensuous pleasures. Even at Hebron he had multiplied unto himself wives, and now, raised by repeated victory to be the lord of a vast empire, he ceased to be "base in his own sight" (ch. vi. 22), and lost his self-control. And, as was to be expected in a man of such strong qualities, his fall was terrible. But this declaration of the inspired narrator is not made solely for ethical reasons, but is the key to all that follows up to the end of ch. xx. In this chapter we have had the history of David's sin; a year's respite succeeds, as if God would wait and see whether the sinner's own conscience would waken up, and bring him to repentance; but it slumbers on. Then comes the message of reproof, followed by earnest penitence, and severe punishment. It was, perhaps, during this year of hardened persistence in crime that Amnon and his cousin Jonadab also gave the reins to their passions, and prepared the way for the first of the series of crimes that polluted David's home. An early repentance might have saved the son; but the absence of paternal discipline, the loss of respect for his father, and the evil influence of that father's bad example, all urged on the son to the commission of his abominable crime.

HOMILETICS.

Vers. 1—17.—The facts are : 1. During the prosecution of the war against Ammon in the spring, David remains in Jerusalem. 2. Walking one evening on his house-top, he sees a woman washing herself, and observes her beauty. 3. Curiosity being awakened, he sends to inquire after her, and learns that she is the wife of Uriah. 4. Sending a royal message to her, she, as a loyal subject, waits upon him, whereupon he commits adultery. 5. Discovering in the course of a little time that the fact would come to light, he sends for Uriah from the war, under pretext of gleaning information concerning it, but really that, by Uriah's sojourn with his wife, the fact may be concealed. 6. Uriah, possibly suspicious of wrong, excuses himself from doing as David desires, on the plea that military duty and patriotism required of him absolute abstention from domestic pleasures. 7. Failing in the first attempt, David makes him drunk, in hopes that, when stupid, he would go to his home ; but in this also he fails. 8. Subsequently he sends him back to Joab, with a secret instruction that he would set him in such a position as to ensure his death, which instruction Joab faithfully carries out.

The beginnings of great sins. By universal consent the deed of David here recorded is regarded as a great sin—a *very* great sin, because it was a breach of the commandment which guards the purity of human life, and because committed by one blessed with more than ordinary privileges, and in an abuse of regal authority over a probably unsuspicious subject. The deed is ever base and criminal, but that such a man should commit the crime when God was prospering him in all his affairs, when his people were bravely risking their lives in defence of their country, and after he had spent so long and blessed a life in fellowship with God, is one of the marvels and mysteries of human nature. In the narrative we have set forth the origin and progress of the sin, so far as relates to its ostensible character. Scripture gives us outward facts in their natural order. But we know that in one outward fact of human life there are involved many mental and moral movements, and these are connected in the continuity of life with antecedents which, in part at least, account for their occurrence. It is not difficult, by bringing our knowledge of the laws of mental and moral movement to bear on the facts here recorded, to get a clue to the real beginnings of this great sin, and of great sins in general.

I. INTENSE ABSORPTION IN PROSPEROUS AFFAIRS DIMINISHES THE ENERGY THAT OTHERWISE WOULD GO TO SPIRITUAL CULTURE. Man, considered physiologically and physically, is a store of energy, and he can give out only what he possesses. The totality of his thoughts and acts is the outcome, and generally speaking the measure, of his store. What portion of it is spent in excess in one direction is just so much taken from another direction. The usual law of forces here applies. For some time David had been intensely absorbed in consolidating his power. The amount of work involved in all the changes he initiated and brought to completion must have been far in excess of what falls to an ordinary monarch, and this in proportion to the utter disorganization of affairs under Saul and Ishbosheth. Such an absorption most probably trenched upon the nervous and moral energy he had at one time concentrated directly on the culture of the spiritual life. Some few men seem gifted with the faculty of sudden transitions of energy, so that, while intensely absorbed in business or secular studies at one moment, they can, by an act of will, become equally absorbed at once in religious pursuits. Possibly David was one of these ; but even in their case they cannot escape the weakening effect on the finer sensibilities of a protracted absorption in purely temporal affairs, especially if they are very prosperous. We see many instances of this in the lives of professedly religious men.

II. HABITS OF LIFE MAY UNCONSCIOUSLY BE FORMED WHICH GENERATE A CLASS OF FEELINGS PROVOCATIVE OF TEMPTATION. Habits grow in silence and too slowly to be noted, and every unconsciously formed habit brings with it its corresponding class of feelings, which also, rising gradually, are apt to obtain an unobserved permanence in life. The usages of Eastern courts in reference to polygamy acted in a subtle way on David's life, so that he gradually formed the habits peculiar to that abnormal form of domestic life, and we need no Divine revelation to inform us of the class of inferior feelings that would thereby be surely though slowly engendered. The man in modern times who, by reason of his affluence, combined with a certain habit of body, fares sumptuously every day, does not, while he is getting into the practice of so doing, reflect on the possible effect of all this, in days not far distant, upon his animal tendencies in a certain direction, and his corresponding moral safeguards.   There can be no question that the physical, mental, and moral habits of life of a polygamous household are such as would furnish good soil for a sensual temptation, which, in the case of a man unduly absorbed and preoccupied in mere secularities, would be still more perilous. Many a religious man is weak from sources similar to this.   Our Lord even warned his apostles, after they had had the benefit of his teaching for two years, to take heed lest at any time their hearts be "overcharged with surfeiting and drunkenness, and the cares of this life" (Luke xxi. 34).

III. LEISURE SUPERVENING ON GREAT ACTIVITY BRINGS THE WEAKER SIDE OF NATURE INTO PROMINENCE.   The protracted exertions of years had now issued in a compact kingdom and internal order.   Saul's family was cared for.   Administration was organized and labour divided (ch. viii. 14—18).   The war against the Syrians was in the hands of a powerful force, under a skilful general.   David, in Jerusalem, had leisure unknown in former years.   Now it is a fact in the history of human nature that, when great energies cease to be in demand, and the force of life no longer goes out in its wonted volume in its ordinary course, then the feelings and tendencies which, meanwhile, have been unconsciously generated by slowly formed habits of social life, are apt to take more prominence, and find less resistance, in consequence of the probably impaired power of the spiritual element (see division I).   It is well known among young men that more moral falls occur during seasons of leisure than at any other time.   Leisure following on great prosperity requires for its safe use more than ordinary wisdom and spiritual health.   Adversity, though taxing energy to the utmost, tends to draw the heart nearer to God, so that when there is leisure from it the soul is in a better condition to guard against the evils incident to such a season.

IV. AN UNCONSCIOUS DECLINE OF REALITY IN COMMUNION WITH GOD MAY SET IN ON A MAN'S OBTAINING A RECOGNIZED POSITION IN THE RELIGIOUS WORLD.   The subtlety with which spiritual declension sets in is admitted by all who know anything of religious experience.   The best of men are the objects of assault from the powers of darkness, clothed, it may be, as angels of light (2 Cor. xi. 14).   Once let a man, by some subtle insinuation, begin to think that now, having served God so many years and written such useful and sincere utterances of his experience, he has a distinctly recognized position,—then, in that very thought, there is an element of danger.   From that hour watchfulness may be less keen, routine may set in, and grey hairs may come "here and there upon him" while he "knoweth it not" (Hos. vii. 9).   Undoubtedly David had attained such a recognized position in the religious world.   His people would accord it; and, in the cessation of strain in civil and political exertions, he might, in an unguarded hour, especially if the lower feelings (see division II.) began to put forth their force, indulge in self-complacence.   Communion with God might continue in full form, but its original intense reality would have passed away.   Herein, perhaps, is the secret of the decline of religion in many a *quondam* professor.   There are in the Church not a few who have left to them only "the form of godliness."

V. UNDER THE CONDITIONS THUS FAR CONSIDERED DISTINCT SUGGESTIONS COME THROUGH THE SENSES WITH DOUBLE FORCE.   There are conditions under which suggestions through the eye, ear, or animal passions fall as powerless as snow on the solid rock.   The real power of a temptation through the senses lies in the state of mind which we are in at the time.   David had probably seen beautiful women many a time during his exile, and while king in Jerusalem; but the healthy, well-guarded spirit was unhurt by the sight.   Beauty anywhere is, to a healthy spiritual nature, an object of pure admiration as a work of God.   It was because David was not his old self that this sight was as fuel to a smouldering flame.   It takes but little to create radical changes and commotions, as seen in chemistry, when the primary elements of things are brought into contact; and so is it when certain elemental conditions of the moral man and his surroundings are concerned.   Joseph was pure and spiritually healthy when the suggestion of evil came upon him, and it only produced a recoil (Gen. xxxix. 8, 9).   Great stress is laid on this in the Bible.   "To the pure all things are pure." "Keep thy heart with all diligence; for out of it are the issues of life."

VI. There is a disturbing force in certain passions by which reason, the will, and spiritual instincts are weakened. It is a psychological fact that all emotion affects the exercise of the pure reason for the worse. It is in the experience of men that such passions as were aroused in David by the sight he witnessed from the roof of his house, more than any—except, perhaps, those involved in drunkenness—disturb or cripple the action of reason and of the will. Of course, they weaken the spiritual instincts in proportion as they find scope. Thus the powers which may be considered as the guardians of purity, the foes of evil, are not in their normal condition, and consequently the chances are, unless something happens to prevent such an issue, that the unhallowed feelings will gain further ascendency. In this we see that the perfect man is attainable only in Christ. The triumph of spiritual religion in our nature is coincident with the most perfect development of that nature. Hence, also, spiritual power among men is dependent on inner purity.

VII. When once the rein is given to such passions, the fall has taken place in essence. When David saw and looked on her, with a certain thought in his mind and feeling in his heart, he had virtually done the deed of which we have a record. In the spiritual sphere, thought and desire are tantamount to deed. The one is but the fuller form of the other. Sin lies in intent and purpose, whether it be actualized in outward fact or not. Hence our Lord's strong words (Matt. v. 27, 28). The mystery of David's sin really lies in the creation within himself of the base feeling indicated in the terms of ver. 2. All that followed was a development of this (Jas. i. 14, 15). It is a question whether Christian people have, as a rule, recognized the solemn truth taught by Christ and seen in David's case. The seventh commandment has a bearing on the daily mental life.

VIII. An inward fall brings on spiritual darkness, loss of self-respect, with further enfeebled reason and will-power. Such an inward fall as David's on the roof of his house at once brought a cloud between him and his God, caused him to feel that he was a degraded man, and placed him, in that abandoned mood, under weaker safeguards against the growth of the evil passion. Unless a sudden and sharp repentance—a shocked cry to God for special help—came forth, there was no hope of his being the same man as formerly. Every hour during which the intrusive evil passion retained ascendency only hastened his final overthrow. Men so circumstanced become blind and stupid; they know their degradation, but are under a spell by which it becomes greater; consequences suggested in feeble or strong tones by the reason are not considered; the will, lately crippled for good, now goes over in full strength to the side of evil. *Facilis descensus Averni.* The particular passion may vary in the different deeds of evil which occasionally shock the religious world, but in every case there is a gradual decline, and it is only the last few stages of it which form the subject of surprise among men. Not murder as seen in Shakespeare's 'Macbeth,' nor fraud as seen in occasional modern revelations, nor youthful excesses as when the parent's heart is broken, are sudden in origin. A series of mental and moral changes precede that which attracts the notice of men and forms the occasion of a social condemnation.

General lessons. 1. The fidelity of Scripture writers may be referred to as evidence of Divine inspiration. The cool impartiality with which the best king of Israel is represented as having fallen into the vilest of sins, and this without note or comment, is certainly not of man. 2. Moral causes are deepest and most wide-reaching in the sphere of human life; the change here indicated in David's moral condition was of pernicious influence ever after on his rule, his court, his private life, and the general prosperity of the kingdom. 3. The season of great prosperity in temporal affairs, and of elevation in religious privilege, should, on account of the peril it brings, be a season of keenest and most earnest watchfulness. 4. So powerful are the inferior propensities of human nature, even in the case of most favoured men, that it is possible for them to sweep away in their outburst the reputation built up on the best purposes and actions; and hence the importance of a most jealous guard against everything in appetite, sight, and sound, that may develop their power. 5. Seeing the extraordinary extremes of human experience in the life of David, we may note and weigh well the undeveloped possibilities for good or evil, for joy or pain, for usefulness or harm, that lie within the scope of every human being in the future state, even more than in this. 6. Feminine obtrusiveness, even when no danger is actually perceived in it, may all the time be operating on some one for evil; and hence the duty of the most guarded modesty of manner and personal appearance. We do not fully estimate the harm done to human thought and feeling by the ocular impressions produced by certain forms of dress and bearing. 7. It is good to have leisure from toil, but much grace is needed to use leisure so that in it the tempter may not gain power over us. 8. The dangers of eventide leisure are conspicuous, especially to the young and to the ardent. 9. It adds to the guilt of a man if, being in a position of authority or influence, he exercises his official influence to gain power over others for purposes of evil.

The crooked ways of sin. We have in vers. 6—13 an account of the devices by which David sought to escape the human discovery of his guilt. The perhaps sleepless nights spent in painful thought as to what could be safely done are not alluded to—only the product of his thinking. After what was said in ver. 5, it was certain that exposure in the most palpable form would ensue if the woman's husband remained away at the war. To bring him home, and get him in an apparently natural way to spend a little time with his wife, at once seemed most feasible. The failure of this scheme, either through the patriotism or the awakened suspicions of Uriah, caused another night of thought and scheming, and, as the case was urgent, he was made drunk, in hope thereby his patriotism or suspicions would yield to natural propensities. Once more the force of events is against the scheme; and, as a last resort, seeing that Uriah could not be made out to be the father of the coming child, he must, with as good an appearance as possible, be put out of the way so that the king, in accordance with the rights of Eastern monarchs, might take his wife, and the expected one thus appear to be prematurely born in wedlock. Concerning these crooked ways of sin observe—

I. THE FIRST STEP OF THE IMPENITENT SINNER IS TO CLING TO HIS SIN. When such a sin as David's is committed, God is offended, conscience outraged, self-respect disregarded, and human condemnation rendered imminent. The whole of this disruption and confusion in the moral sphere is recognized at once as being a consequence of the deed done. Now, it is obvious that these consequences are not only to be dreaded, and, if possible, to be avoided, but also that the first act of a sound mind would be to abominate and seek to get dissociated, in every sense of the term, from the sin which entailed them. The sin, and not the consequences, is the evil thing—the most terrible and hurtful thing. And the first step of a truly penitent mind would be to shrink from it, to loathe it, to seek to cut it off if possible from self as the accursed thing. But note here that David shows no sign of this. The evil nature adopts the deed, identifies itself with it, seeks to live on in association of thought, feeling, and interest with it. God, purity, conscience, self-respect,—all may go; the soul will have its sin, and, by cherishing this sentiment towards it, virtually persists in its repetition. So did Adam, Achan, and Ananias; and so do all the poor debased souls that sink into iniquity without the grace of true repentance.

II. THE SECOND STEP IS TO RECOGNIZE THE POSSIBILITY OF EXPOSURE BEFORE MEN. The guilty man knows that God is aware of his crime. His action in this respect is a very singular phenomenon. There may be secret dread of God's coming judgment; the certainty of God's knowledge and power to punish may be so strong as even to render life inwardly wretched, and to produce the passivity and helplessness proper to an unavoidable fate. Possibly this sort of desperation urges to a warding off of such consequences as would come did men but know as much of the sin as God. At any rate, what the narrative sets before us is not an endeavour to escape from God and his anger; it shows us rather that, as soon as the mind can collect itself after the indulgence in sin, it recognizes the possibility of men becoming acquainted with the deed done. That was the thought which lay at the basis of Achan's covering up his spoils; that is the thought which starts in the mind of the thief, the liar, the adulterer, the false professor. The fear of man is a very potent influence. The fear of God is real, but it carries with it a hopelessness of effort. This induces gloomy desperation, but not thought and action to prevent discovery.

III. THE NEXT STEP IS TO CONSIDER THE POSSIBLE MEANS OF ESCAPE FROM HUMAN EXPOSURE. A guilty man pays unconscious homage to holiness in that he begins to think how he can prevent men knowing what he has done. David the hero, who trembled not before Goliath, now spends hours in thinking how he may escape the consequences of his own people knowing what he has done in private. Is it simply fear of civil and social loss? Is it merely dread of physical pain? No; even the guilty testify that sin is abominable; that sin is deepest personal disgrace; that sin is too black and ugly to bear even the gaze of imperfect men. No doubt David saw that he would suffer loss of respect among the best of the land; that the force of law would be weakened; that turbulence might arise in his kingdom by reason of others following his example; and that he would no longer be able to figure before the nation as the illustrious reformer of religion. The thousands who daily live in dread of, and consider how they may escape, human exposure! What restless nights! what deep-laid plans! what feverish concern!—all to cover up sin from feeble man! And yet God knows all, and will bring to judgment. Truly sin renders the operation of the mind very perverse. God knows all and judges all, and yet all effort is to keep man from knowing! Nothing is done Godward, except to harden the heart against him, and go on in sullen desperation. This is sin!—this the accursed evil of the universe!

IV. In seeking to escape human exposure, the first contrivance is to simu-late the order of providence; *i.e.* to create, by innocent natural means, an order of events that shall have in them and their results an appearance of providential succes-sion. David does not commit another positive sin to cover up the first. The sin-stained soul again, notwithstanding its degradation, pays homage to righteousness, in its deliberate effort to hide its past deed by deeds that are within the province of right; for David had a right to send for any officer to give him imformation as to the progress of the war (vers. 6, 7), and it was only generous to allow him to go and rest at home (ver. 8). Lord Bacon has taught us that, by carefully studying the processes of Nature to see how she works, we, on submitting to her ways, become her conquerors, by being able to set her at work in circumstances of our own creation. The scheme of an impenitent sinner, when wishing to hide his sin from the knowledge of man, is very much of that kind. He knows the order of providential events, and he tries to create circumstances by which, in the judgment of men, Providence shall be credited with the deed he himself has done. Uriah, not David, shall be made to appear as the father of the child. How this perverse ingenuity works still is familiar to all who know only a little of mankind. The cleverness with which trains of events are set in motion so as to assuredly direct attention from the doer of evil, is amazing. The devil was always a great schemer, and his dupes catch his spirit.

V. The failure of schemes involving no positive sin in the details is soon followed by deeds distinctly evil. If Providence cannot be simulated, because of the uncontrollable nature of its agents (vers. 9—11), then homage to righteousness must cease, and positive evil must be done (vers. 13—15). The one desired end—escape from human exposure—must, by good or evil means, be secured. The knowledge that God knows and is angry counts for nothing. The despair of escaping God, combined with a mad identification of one's interests with the evil committed and still cherished in the heart, seems to operate on the mind in such a way as practically to banish him from thought or care. All thought is on man, and at any cost man must be kept in ignorance. It is against even the conscience, stained and hardened as it is, to do definite evil, if possible—so mighty is the moral law in the worst of men—but preservation of self from exposure is now the first law, to which right, generosity, every true and holy sentiment and obligation, must bow.

VI. In having recourse to desperate measures of evil, there is some regard to appearances. It is only the very uttermost moral degradation—that, perhaps, of fiends in hell—that can perpetrate fresh evils with utter freedom, and without any reserve of decency or tacit recognition of the majesty of law. Every hour spent by David in elaborating his scheme brought him more within the coil of iniquity, and gradually reduced his moral sensibilities towards zero; but even when in his despair he meditated the death of the man whose life might lead to exposure of his sin, he could not slay him with his own hand, he could not say even to Joab, "Slay him." Appear-ances must be saved, and some homage paid, by the lingering sense of right, to the Law of God, by a contest being created in the interests of the kingdom, so that in fighting for his country the doomed man might die by the hand of the enemy. Of course, David did not kill him! Of course, it was an incident in the natural order of warlike events!

It was not the King of Israel that raised the arm to slay, but the wicked Ammonites!
Such is the crooked logic of sin. Our Saviour has described Satan as a liar as well as
a murderer (John viii. 44). It is evidently very difficult to crush out all light from the
conscience. There is a continuous protest in the performance of guilty deeds; but so
obstinate and desperate in alliance with sin is the heart of an impenitent man, that
this protest, this remnant of light, is only used to grace the performance of positive evil
with a semblance of naturalness and innocence. The crooked ways of sin are traversed
by all men who in any measure hug their iniquities, and try to avoid the consequences
which it is feared would come were the deeds of darkness exposed to view. There
are many acting in this way every day.

GENERAL LESSONS. 1. Men in positions of power have many means at hand for
hiding their sins from public view (ver. 6); but they should be warned of their corresponding peril and increased guilt if they use those means. 2. Real hypocrisy lies in
doing things with the appearance of right and to give an impression of right conduct,
when the real aim is evil, and the present motive is subordinate to that aim (vers.
6—11); consequently, just pains should be taken in exposing to men the horrible
wickedness of their course, and in getting them to recognize more distinctly, as a governing power in life, the perfect knowledge of God. 3. There are always forces working
unconsciously against the designs of hypocritical men, rendering, as the action of Uriah
did (vers. 11—13), the way of transgressors hard. It is vain to fight against God. 4.
The man who, in the day of success and real goodness, scorns the unprincipled and hard-
hearted (ch. iii. 29—39), may so fall as to be glad of such men to carry out his evil designs
(ver. 15)—a warning this to him "who thinketh that he standeth." 5. He who makes
use of another as his instrument of evil henceforth becomes weak in all his relations to
him. Masters who employ their servants to carry on evil transactions lose influence
over them, and virtually place themselves in their power.

Vers. 18—27.—*Complicity in evil.* The facts are: 1. Joab, having executed the
wicked commission, sends word to David as to the progress of the war. 2. He furnishes
the messenger with a means of appeasing the probable wrath of David on his learning
that the conflict was more serious than either he or Joab looked for, namely, an
announcement of Uriah's death. 3. The messenger carefully describes the seriousness
of the engagement with the enemy, and concludes by referring to the death of Uriah.
4. David sends back an encouraging message to Joab, and professes to acknowledge
the inevitable losses and chances of war. 5. On suitable sorrow being shown by the
widow for the loss of her husband, David takes her to himself as a wife. 6. The deed
of David is displeasing to God. The narrative here gives us the maturing of David's
scheme, and the general character of the secret negotiations carried on with Joab in
order to bring his purpose to pass. We have, then, an instance of accomplices in crime,
revealing to us truth, and illustrating facts in connection with human life in all ages.

I. MEN INTENT ON A GREAT EVIL ARE FORCED TO BRING OTHERS INTO THEIR WICKED
SECRETS. Providence kindly frustrated David's attempt to cover his sin by means of
Uriah's free action; and it therefore became necessary, in his desperate wickedness, to
seek the end in view by means of Uriah's death. But unless David committed murder
with his own hand, which his conscience would not allow, he must find some one whose
ingenuity, with his own, would bring it to pass, and save appearances. Such is the
logic of evil. God in his mercy has filled the world with obstacles to the committal
of sin and to persistence in it when once committed; but such is the baseness of the
human heart that this, instead of being regarded as a help in the warfare with evil
propensity, is turned into a reason for seeking the aid of another's wits and agency.
It is a further fall in evil when men are thus impelled to drag others into the meshes of
their sin. So hardened does the heart become by dalliance with sin and indulgence in it,
that even the character and souls of others are to be ruined in order to gratify self and
hide iniquity for a few years from human view.

II. THERE ARE GENERALLY MEN TO BE FOUND READY TO CARRY OUT THE EVIL
PURPOSES OF THEIR SUPERIORS. Even in the chosen nation a Joab was to be found,
cruel, hard of heart, habituated to acts of severity, and glad to have the opportunity of
retorting in spirit, if not in words, the former reproaches of his master (ch. iii. 29, 39). It
is a sign of the marvellous change that had come over David, that he, who had so bitterly

reproached this man for cruelty and hard-heartedness, now turns to him for the purpose of using those very qualities for accomplishing his own cruel design. The presence of such a man in Israel for doing the evil work of his superior is typical of a universal fact. There is a vast amount of reserve evil in the world, waiting only for some influential will to draw it out into activity. The power of superiors over subordinates sometimes extends to the moral sphere. In strict fact, a king has only power, in virtue of his office, over the legal actions of his subjects, and a master over the legal actions of his servants; but when a king or a master, in excess of his right, extends his authority into the moral sphere, it too often happens that the subordinate whose conscience is not sensitive allows the authority due to the legal position to pass over to the moral sphere and break down the defences of conscience. This is an abuse of influence on the one side, and an abandonment of most sacred duties on the other. The wicked heart is apt to find excuses in the fact that a superior leads the way, and that, if guilt lies anywhere, it is on him.

III. MEN BENT ON AN EVIL DESIGN WILL EVEN RISK THE RUIN OF THE INNOCENT IN CARRYING OUT THEIR SCHEMES. David knew very well that Joab could not carry out his instructions without, not only exposing Uriah to the certain risk of death, but also placing other men, not concerned in this domestic trouble, in positions of peril; for the meaning of the instructions was plainly to create a position of extreme peril, which in war can only be done by engaging a troop. What if several innocent men fell in this "hottest battle"! Uriah, at all events, would be amongst them! The more the progressive conduct of the king is scrutinized, the more base and abominable does it appear. This dreadful sin is not confined to David. Monarchs and diplomatists, who from motives of vanity or mere love of power bring on war, really cause the death of innocent men and the wailings of widows in carrying out their designs. What if thousands of men fall! Some regal or other obstacle to ambition or pride will at least be got rid of! That is the moral side of too many wars. The same in a measure applies to men who will be rich, though it cost the health, the poverty, and often lives of workmen. What of all that? Wealth must be secured! Other instances are to be found in modern life.

IV. MEN IN CARRYING OUT NEFARIOUS DESIGNS ARE CAREFUL TO CONFORM TO THE DECENCIES OF OUTWARD LIFE. Bad men understand one another. There is a free-masonry in evil. Joab knew what he was about when he anticipated that David would manifest signs of wrath on hearing of his fruitless attack on the city. Each evil-doer played his part with skill. The messenger was to remind David of historic parallels (ver. 21), and to tell him that the rash man Uriah, who led the bootless assault, had been punished for his rashness by death. No court-martial would be necessary, lamentable as the affair certainly was! Heart answers to heart. The anger ceases; maxims concerning the chances of war come to one's aid (ver. 25); the lessons of failure must be laid to heart; the general at the head of the army must not be discouraged. All this was very proper—in harmony with the proprieties of life. Men doing evil are inwardly ashamed of it, and are compelled to keep up the appearance of doing and being good. It is the outward conformity with the decencies of life that enables wicked men to go on in their evil ways for years. They follow the teaching and example of their chief, who is a liar in deed and word, and who, to perfect his schemes, assumes, if necessary, the form of an "angel of light."

V. EVIL MEN BRING THEIR DEVICES TO A SUCCESSFUL ISSUE WITH ONE NOTABLE EXCEPTION. The success of David was complete. Uriah was safely put away; Bathsheba was the king's wife within a date to prevent convincing exposure; the army and the people were kept in ignorance of actual facts; the future was hopeful; but there was one fact on which the infatuated king did not reflect—*the Lord was displeased.* The brethren of Joseph seemed to succeed in getting rid of a troublesome brother, but God saw their wickedness, and this counted for more than they then imagined. The wicked husbandmen succeeded in freeing themselves from annoyance when they killed the heir (Matt. xxi. 38); but there was One to reckon with of whom they did not think. The conspiring scribes and Pharisees doubtless congratulated themselves that their plans for getting rid of the "babbler" who caused them so much trouble were wonderfully successful; but there was One whose "power" was not secured to their side (Acts ii. 23, 24). Kings and diplomatists and exactors of unjust labour, and secret defrauders, and evil livers may succeed in keeping up appearances, in passing as honourable men, and in securing their heart's desire; but there will always be one factor in the case with which they some day will have to reckon—*the displeasure of the Lord.*

GENERAL LESSONS.   1. It is a disgrace to a master to be in league with a servant, and it puts the master within the servant's power.   Many a subordinate is in possession of secrets which, if used, would blast character and ruin earthly prospects.   The coils of iniquity!   2. Every new device to hide sin, and every effort to keep up appearances, only blinds the mind the more to the actual state of the soul in its relation to God.   3. In all our affairs, and especially when tempted to persist in courses of sin, we should endeavour to remember that we shall have to reckon with One who knows all and is already displeased.   4. That a man professing religion can go on in a secret course of sin without giving due heed to the knowledge which he must possess of God's knowledge of himself and deeds, is a striking sign of the utter deterioration of his spiritual sensibilities and his being nigh unto perdition.

HOMILIES BY VARIOUS AUTHORS.

Vers. 1—5.—(THE KING'S PALACE.)   *David's fall into sin.*   "But David tarried still at Jerusalem" (ver. 1; 1 Chron. xx. 1).   1. He was about fifty years of age; had been reigning in Jerusalem upwards of twelve years; dwelt in a stately palace on Mount Zion; and possessed numerous sons and daughters, a splendid court and a powerful army.   He had been "preserved whithersoever he went," subdued his enemies, and returned in triumph.   His natural gifts and fervent piety (Ps. xxiv. 4; ci. 7) were even more extraordinary than his material prosperity; and he now stood on the pinnacle of human greatness and glory.   2. "We might well wish, in our human fashion, that, as he stood at this elevation, he had closed a life hitherto (as far as was possible before Christianity) almost entirely spotless, and bequeathed to posterity a wholly unclouded memory, and the purest type of true royalty.   But the ascent of the dizzy height is always attended by the possibility of a slip and then of a headlong fall" (Ewald).   3. "Rising from the couch where he had indulged in his noonday siesta to an undue length, David forthwith ascended to the roof of his house.   So ambition commonly follows excess; nor do they whom the contagion of luxury once corrupts readily seek after moderate and lowly ways.   But that ascent of David, alas! was a prelude to his deplorable downfall.   For he ascended only that he might fall, beholding thence, as from a watch-tower, Bathsheba the wife of Uriah, and immediately becoming passionately enamoured of her" (J. Doughty, 'Analecta Sacra:' 1658).   4. It was the turning-point of his career, which was henceforth marked by a long series of calamities.   And "it is sad to think that the cup of life, after being filled for him by God and made pure and sweet by previous suffering and self-restraint, should have been recklessly poisoned by his own hand" (Binney).

> "His steps were turn'd into deceitful ways,
> Following false images of good, that make
> No promise perfect."
>
> (Dante.)

His fall occurred (serving as an instructive warning to others)—

I. AT A SEASON OF SLOTHFUL RELAXATION.   In the spring of the year, "when kings go forth to war," instead of going forth with his army to complete the subjugation of Ammon, "David sent Joab," etc., and abode in Jerusalem.   Formerly, when "the Lord had given him rest" (ch. vii. 1), he spent his leisure in a worthy manner, and displayed an ardent and even excessive zeal; but now, in choosing rest for himself, he showed a lack of zeal, and his unhappy choice was followed by disastrous consequences. "His actual fall into sin seems to have begun by the abdication of his functions as captain of Israel" (Maclaren); which was itself the effect of "previous relaxation of the girded loins and negligence of the untrimmed lamp."   *Inactivity* (voluntarily chosen, without adequate reason, and regardless of opportunities of useful service) is commonly: 1. *Induced by a course of successful enterprise,* and the attainment of great prosperity. If adversity has slain its thousands, prosperity has slain its tens of thousands.   "When his pillow was the rock and his curtain the cave; when his sword, under Providence, procured him his daily bread from the foes of his country, and the means of existence formed the object and pursuit of life,—he was pious and immovable; he must have been active or he must have resigned his life.   But now the case was widely different.   He had not only all the necessaries, but all the luxuries which the most refined voluptuousness could devise, attending in rich profusion around him.   He had certainly the duty of his charge to impress its importance on his mind; but then he had the opportunity of neglecting it, and even David, it appears, was not proof against the solicitations of this opportunity" (Thompson, 'Davidica').   2. *Indicative of a state of spiritual declension.*   (1) Of a gradual decay of faith and neglect of watchfulness and prayer, and so leaving his hold of God; (2) of a defective sense of responsibility to God; (3) of pride and security, "mortal's chief enemy," so that the self-denying labours and hardships of the battle-field seemed no longer necessary; and (4) of undue love of ease and sensuous pleasure, fostered in David's case by polygamy.   "The sense of delicacy and chastity, which has such a purifying and preserving influence on the life, could not flourish side by side with the polygamy in which he permitted himself" (W. M. Taylor).   The majestic forest tree falling suddenly beneath the blast excites our surprise; but, on examination, it will be found to have been undergoing at heart a gradual process of decay, which at length brought the giant to the ground.   3. *Conducive to the indulgence of sinful propensities;* exposing to the peril of falling into "the snare of the devil."   Want of proper occupation tends to develop the hidden evil of the heart.   "Standing waters gather filth" (Matthew Henry).   "Idle hours bring forth idle thoughts, and idle thoughts are nothing but dry kindling wood that waits only for a spark to be suddenly ablaze" (Disselhoff).   "The industrious man hath no leisure to sin; the idle hath no leisure or power to avoid sin" (Hall).   David "may have been quite unconscious of bad habits of mind; but they must have been there growing in secret.   The tyrannous *self-will,* which is too often developed by long successes and command; the unscrupulous *craft,* which is too often developed by long adversity and the necessity of sustaining one's self in a difficult position;—these must have been there.   But even they could not have led David to do the deed he did had there not been in him likewise that fearful moral weakness which comes from long indulgence of the *passions*—a weakness which is reckless of conscience, of public opinion, and of danger either to earthly welfare or everlasting salvation" (C. Kingsley).   "This single act can only be regarded as the expression of his whole disposition of mind" (Hengstenberg).

II. UNDER THE INFLUENCE OF STRONG TEMPTATION; or the desire of self-gratification.   For "each man is tempted, when he is drawn away by his own lust [desire], and enticed," etc. (Jas. i. 13—15).   "Lust is egoistic desire under the incitement of impulse.   But the action is not yet performed; it still lies with the man to combat the lust, or by the free choice of his will to yield himself to it" (Martensen, 'Christian Ethics').   It: 1. *Arises in most cases from impressions made upon the senses by external objects.*   "And it came to pass in an eventide," etc. (ver. 2).   The eye is the most common inlet of temptation.   "And when the woman saw that the tree was good for food," etc. (Gen. iii. 6).   Achan first saw, then coveted and took (Josh. vii. 21).   "David at this time had forgotten the prayer, 'Turn away mine eyes from beholding vanity.'   We see, therefore, how dangerous a thing it is to suffer the eyes to wander.   Job made a covenant with his eyes" (Willet).   "They who abuse the eye deserve to have the inward eye darkened" (Gregory).   2. *Derives its force from various circumstances;* such as (1) the unexpected, sudden, and deceitful manner of its occurrence; (2) the power and opportunity of its gratification; (3) the temperament, predisposition, and besetting sins of its subject; (4) the entertainment of it in the fancy, which forms false images of good, and invests them with a perilous fascination; and (5) the delay of endeavour to overcome it, wherein there always lies peculiar and most imminent danger (Gen. xxxix. 9).   3. *Becomes by such means an absorbing passion* (Matt. vi. 28, 29); blinding the mental vision, perverting the moral judgment, and influencing (though not absolutely compelling) the choice of the personal will, by which sin comes into actual existence.   "There is a black spot, though it be no bigger than a bean's eye, in every soul, which, if once set a-working, will overcloud the whole man in darkness, and something very like madness, and will hurry him into the night of destruction" (Arabic saying).   To escape this fatal issue there is need, not merely of resolute resistance and fervent prayer, but also of instant flight. "The temptation of the flesh is overcome and impure passion mortified by flight, and not by fighting face to face. He then who flies fastest and furthest is most sure of victory. Once more I say to thee, Fly! for thou art as stubble. Therefore fly, fly, if indeed thou wouldest not be overtaken, led captive, and slain!" (Scupoli).

III. AGAINST THE RESTRAINTS OF RECOGNIZED OBLIGATION. "And David sent and inquired after the woman. And one said, Is not this Bathsheba," etc.? (ver. 3). Whilst he knew not who she was, there might be at least some excuse (considering the position of an Oriental monarch, and the common practices of the age) for his passion (ch. iii. 1—5); but now that he was informed that she was "the wife of Uriah," the claims of a higher law than his own inclination must have risen up distinctly before him; and he had to choose between renouncing his evil desire or breaking through the numerous restraints placed in his path. These restraints are: 1. Set up by the *express commandments* of the Divine Law, which says, "Thou shalt not covet thy neighbour's wife;" "Thou shalt not commit adultery;" "Thou shalt not steal" (ch. xii. 4—6). 2. Strengthened by the *special responsibilities* of peculiar position and relationship; such as David held, as King of Israel, under Jehovah, with respect to his subjects, and more particularly his faithful servant Uriah. 3. Enforced by the *terrible consequences* threatened against transgressors (Lev. xx. 10; Deut. xxviii. 15). It is nevertheless possible to burst through all such restraints. And in the exercise of his freedom and the abuse of his power, David set them at nought, and "despised the commandment of the Lord" (ch. xii. 9). "When lust has conceived, every restraint generally increases its vehemence, the thoughts of future consequences and the consideration of the presence, purity, and justice of God are excluded; his Law and authority are disregarded; faith and fear and love are out of exercise; and the enhanced imagination of the satisfaction to be found in indulgence possesses and engrosses the soul" (Scott).

IV. WITH THE PERSISTENCY OF WILFUL PRESUMPTION. "And David sent messengers, and took her," etc. (vers. 4, 5). Regarding himself as a special favourite of Heaven, he perhaps imagined (as others have done) that he might leave the ways of lowly obedience and self-denial, and go whithersoever he pleased, and yet be preserved from harm (Deut. xxix. 19; Ps. xix. 13; Matt. iv. 6); and under this delusion he persisted in his purpose, and fell from his moral elevation into the depths of sin and to the verge of destruction. "How are the mighty fallen!" By such persistency: 1. The sinful purpose of the heart is confirmed and completed in outward action. 2. The guilt incurred is aggravated. 3. The natural consequences of sin become more serious and extensive; and, in some respects, they cannot possibly be averted (ch. xii. 11—14).

OBSERVATIONS. 1. No man, however holy, is exempt from the liability of falling into sin. "Be not highminded, but fear;" "Let him that thinketh he standeth," etc. "If such a strong and tall cedar as David fall, how ought weaker Christians to fear and to pray that God would deliver them from temptation!" (Guild). 2. Material prosperity and outward show are frequently associated with moral failure and secret iniquity. Whilst the conquest of Rabbah went forward, David became the victim of his own unfaithfulness. 3. The fall of men into sin is to be attributed to themselves—their voluntary choice of evil; and not to their circumstances, or constitution, or the withholding from them of the help of God. "Let no man say when he is tempted, I am tempted of God," etc. 4. It is of unspeakable importance to maintain the exercise of the spiritual life in full vigour, and to watch against the first approach of evil. "The narrow way has precipices on both sides; let us walk it awake and watchful, for we are not more exact than David, who by a moment's neglect was precipitated into the very gulf of sin" (Chrysostom). 5. By the record of the sins of good men (1 Sam. xxi. 2), the truth and worth of the Word of God are plainly shown. "If such a story does not give one a view of the unfathomable depths of sin and of its power, he will never learn what sin is" (Schmid). 6. In the whole course of history One alone has appeared "without sin;" he was tempted and overcame, and he is the Succourer of them that are tempted.—D.

Ver. 4.—*Bathsheba.* The Books of Samuel furnish abundant materials for instructive studies of female character, in (1) the praying Hannah, (2) the provoking Peninnah, (3) the broken-hearted wife of Phineas, (4) the proud Michal, (5) the persuasive Abigail,

(6) the beautiful Bathsheba, (7) the unfortunate Tamar, (8) the wily woman of Tekoah, (9) the devoted Rizpah, (10) the peaceable woman of Abel, and (in a minor degree) (11) the terrified nurse of Mephibosheth (ch. iv. 3), (12) the faithful maidservant at En-rogel, (13) the sympathizing woman of Bahurim (ch. xvii. 17, 18). Bathsheba was the daughter of Eliam (Ammiel, 1 Chron. iii. 5), the granddaughter of Ahithophel the king's counsellor (ch. xxiii. 34), and well known (ver. 3) as the wife of Uriah the Hittite. "Eliam and Uriah must have been thrown much together, being both of the same rank, and being each one of the thirty-seven officers of the king's guard" (Blunt, 'Undesigned Coincidences'). She was: 1. *Endowed with perilous gifts*—extraordinary beauty (ver. 2), ardent temperament, quick perceptions, ambitious aims. Something of her natural character may be inferred from 1 Kings i. 15—21 and 1 Kings ii. 13—21, "a woman ignorant of ruling, but skilled in love-matters." 2. *Destitute of adequate safeguards*, such as would have been afforded by the presence of her husband, who was away at the siege of Rabbah; careful moral training; and firm religious principles (Prov. xi. 22). 3. *Overcome by a great temptation.* "And David sent messengers, and took her; and she came," etc. "There is no intimation whatever" (as Delany endeavours to show) "that David brought Bathsheba into the palace through craft or violence; but rather that she came at his request, without any hesitation, and offered no resistance to his desires. Consequently, she is not to be regarded as free from blame" (Keil). "One is even disposed to suspect that she was a designing, ambitious woman, who laid a snare for the king. Nothing is told us concerning her in order that the iniquity of David might not be relieved" (R. Tuck, 'The First Three Kings of Israel'). She, like others, admired the king, felt flattered by his attentions, and had not sufficient moral strength to resist his wishes or control her own inordinate vanity. "Had she been mindful of her matrimonial fidelity, perhaps David had been soon checked in his inordinate desire" (Hall). Yet she was a woman "more sinned against than sinning" (ver. 27; ch. xii. 4). 4. *Observant of customary ceremonies.* "And she was purified," etc. "More scrupulous about the ceremonial law than the moral" (Lev. xv. 18). "She also mourned for her husband when she heard of his death (ver. 26), but not for her sin which caused it" (Guild); being chiefly concerned about appearances; for her sin had been kept, as far as possible, a profound secret. 5. *Visited by deserved chastisement.* Beset by tormenting anxieties and terrible fears, knowing the penalty due to her transgression; and, subsequently, overwhelmed with grief on account of the affliction and death of her child; nor was this the only retribution she experienced. 6. *Treated with merciful consideration.* (Ver. 27.) As David himself, the supreme administrator on earth of the Divine Law, did not suffer death, "and it is easy to perceive that, to leave this single act of criminality unpunished in a great king, was for the advantage of the people" (Michaelis, 'Laws of Moses,' i. 37), as he was expressly exempted from it by the word of the prophet (ch. xii. 13); so, in the exercise of his royal prerogative, he very properly dispensed with the penalty in the case of the partner of his guilt. Like him, also, she probably repented of her sin; and "mercy glorieth against judgment" (Jas. ii. 13). Evil was even overruled for good (ch. xii. 24; 1 Chron. iii. 5; Matt. i. 6; Luke iii. 31). It has been thought (though without sufficient reason) that the counsels contained in Prov. xxxi. were given by her to her son Solomon. "Favour is deceitful, and beauty is vain: but a woman that feareth the Lord, she shall be praised."—D.

Vers. 5—15.—(JERUSALEM, RABBAH.) *Entanglements of sin.* He who once leaves the right path little knows how far he may go astray or how great will be his perplexities and perils. Possibly he may never return; certainly he will not return without overcoming immense difficulties, and finding out by bitter experience his folly and perversity.

> "The gates of hell are open night and day;
> Smooth the descent, and easy is the way;
> But to return and view the cheerful skies,
> In this the task and mighty labour lies."
> (Dryden's 'Virgil.')

Sin is commonly attended (as in the case of David) by—

I. GUILTY FEARS. After his sudden fall he probably felt some measure of compunction; but repressed the reproaches of conscience, and continued, in the view of men, the same as he had ever been. It is evident that, when the message (ver. 5) came to him, he was not truly penitent. 1. It awakened his fears concerning the possible *exposure* of his sin. Would not the wife of Uriah, on the return of her husband, be constrained to declare the author of her shame? 2. His fears were intensified by the probable *consequences* of such exposure. Even if he should be able to save Bathsheba, and himself escape legal punishment, by virtue of his high position as the Lord's anointed, how could he avert the private vengeance of Uriah, or maintain the confidence, affection, and allegiance of his army and people? What other Eastern monarchs did with impunity, could not be done by him in Israel without incurring the moral indignation of the people, and causing the enemies of the Lord to blaspheme. 3. He was impelled by his fears to use his utmost efforts with a view to the *concealment* of his sin. "And David sent to Joab, saying, Send me Uriah the Hittite" (ver. 6). His endeavour to hide his transgression "as Adam" (Job xxxi. 33) was itself a tacit acknowledgment of its disreputable character. And "he that covereth his sins shall not prosper," etc. (Prov. xxviii. 13). Would that men, after their first wrong step, immediately confessed their error, made reparation, and returned to the way of truth and righteousness!

II. FRUSTRATED DEVICES. 1. In their attempts at concealment men are wont to employ extraordinary *ingenuity* (1 Sam. xviii. 17—30), and to hide their base designs under the cover of kindness (vers. 7—9). 2. Their crafty purposes are often *defeated* by simplicity and sincerity, beyond their calculation. "The ark," etc. (vers. 9—12). "This answer expressed the feelings and the consciousness of duty which ought to animate one who was fighting for the cause of God, in such plain and unmistakable terms, that it was well adapted to prick the king to the heart. But David's soul was so beclouded by the wish to keep clear of the consequences of his sin in the eyes of the world, that he did not feel the sting, but simply made a still further attempt to attain his purpose with Uriah" (Keil). 3. Although defeated, their attempts are usually repeated (ver. 13), but only to issue in greater *disappointment*, perplexity, and anxiety. The devices of sin are like a labyrinth, in which the sinner becomes more and more inextricably involved. They are like the meshes of a net, in which he becomes more and more hopelessly entangled.

III. INCREASING CRIMINALITY. (Vers. 14, 15.) "He sent back the unsuspicious warrior to Rabbah, to Joab, with a letter, which, under the name of 'Uriah's letter,' has become notorious throughout the world. It was written with the same pen with which the sweet psalmist had written his psalms" (Krummacher). 1. The course of sin is *downward* into ever deeper moral abasement. "It is the nature of sin to multiply itself, and to draw the wretched sinner on to greater and greater enormities." Adultery was followed by (1) deception, (2) ingratitude, (3) injustice, (4) meanness, (5) temptation (ver. 13; Hab. ii. 15), (6) treachery, (7) murder.

"One sin another doth provoke ;
Murder's as near to lust, as flame to smoke."

2. It is so because of its blinding, hardening, and *enslaving power* (2 Pet. ii. 19 ; Prov. vi. 22), its delusive promises of good, its specious pleas of necessity, its urgent impulses to desperate expedients. "Such are the accursed entanglements of sin ; such the workings and gradations of it in the distracted, bewildered breast that admits it. Millions have been lost in these labyrinths of guilt; but none, sure, in any more intricate and perplexing than this!" (Delany). 3. Although it may be followed by apparent and temporary success, it *cannot ultimately prosper*. "The Lord shall reward," etc. (ch. iii. 39; Prov. xi. 21; Isa. v. 18). "The means which David took to extricate himself from the complications in which his adultery involved him appeared well chosen; but there was one thing he had not taken into consideration—that he could not here, as in former embarassments, confidently expect the assistance of God. It was God's design that David's sin should be fully manifested, for only in this way was perfect cure possible, and therefore he suffered the means to fail" (Hengstenberg). —D.

Ver. 6.—*Uriah the Hittite.* Like Ahimelech (1 Sam. xxvi. 6), he belonged to a notable people (Gen. xxiii. 3; Ezek. xvi. 3; 1 Kings x. 29; 2 Kings vii. 6), had adopted the faith of Israel, and joined David in exile; he was one of the famous "thirty" (1 Chron. xi. 41; ch. xxiii. 39), married Bathsheba (the young and beautiful daughter of a brother officer), to whom he was fondly attached (ch. xii. 3), and had a house overlooked by the king's palace. The story of this man, "immortal by his wrongs," constitutes a little tragedy. He was: 1. *Greatly distinguished for his heroic courage.* For more than twenty years he had taken part in the conflicts of David, and contributed to his victories; and, by the valour which he displayed, gained and kept an honourable position. 2. *Grievously wronged by his royal master.* Having been secretly dishonoured by the king, he was specially sent for, treated with guile, and tempted to become an unconscious agent in concealing the crime. "Were honour driven out of the world, it should find a refuge in the breast of kings." 3. *A noble example of patriotic devotion.* "The ark, and Israel, and Judah, abide in tents," etc. (ver. 11). He "may be regarded from a moral standpoint as a type of the marvellous power and self-control for which those troops, then in their prime, must have been distinguished" (Ewald). In contrast with the indulgent habit (ver. 1) of the king, he exhibited sympathy, self-denial, zeal, and determination: "I will not do this thing."

> "The ark of God is in the field,
> Like clouds around the alien armies sweep;
>   Each by his spear, beneath his shield,
> In cold and dew the anointed warriors sleep.
>
> "And can it be? thou liest awake,
> Sworn watchman, tossing on thy couch of down;
>   And doth thy recreant heart not ache
> To hear the sentries round the leaguered town?
>
> "Oh, dream no more of quiet life;
> Care finds the careless out; more wise to vow
>   Thine heart entire to faith's pure strife;
> So peace will come, thou knowest not when or how."
>
> ('Lyra Apostolica.')

4. *A pitiable instance of a common failing.* (Ver. 13.) He was susceptible to the power of temptation, even as others. Though proof against indulgence in one form, he was overcome by it in another. But he did not entirely lose his self-control. And the guilt of the tempted is far surpassed by that of the tempter. Intoxication weakens the sense of duty, strengthens the force of the passions, is often used as an incitement to vice, and is a fruitful source of incalculable moral, and physical evil in the individual, the family, and society (1 Sam. xxv. 37, 38; ch. xiii. 38). 5. *The unsuspecting bearer of his own death-warrant.* "And David wrote a letter to Joab," etc.—the first letter mentioned in the Bible—telling him "that he had offended him," etc. (Josephus). And without suspecting its contents, he delivered the treacherous missive. 6. *The hapless victim of his unswerving fidelity.* "He assigned Uriah a place where he knew that valiant men were" (ver. 16). "Honour is pretended to poor Uriah; death is meant. He was not the first or last that perished by his friends" (Hall). "He fell unconscious of his wife's dishonour" (Stanley). "Thus fell this brave man, a sacrifice to his own heroic virtue and his prince's guilt. He fell, but not alone; some of his brave companions in arms stood by him to the last, nor deserted him in death" (Delany). The report of his fate was received by the king with the cold and commonplace reflection, "The sword devoureth one as well as another" (ver. 25). "That the sin of David was fulfilling some righteous judgment of God against Uriah and his house, I doubt not—for God often makes his enemies his instruments and, without sanctifying the means, strikes out of them good. Still, a sin it was, great and grievous and offensive to that God to whom the blood of Uriah cried from the ground" (Blunt).—D.

Vers. 16—21.—(RABBAH.) *Complicity in sin.* Here are three men: David, a great but sinful king, bent on the destruction of a faithful servant; Uriah, a brave but injured soldier, sent unconsciously to his doom; and Joab, an able but unscrupulous general (ch. iii. 22—30), become a willing agent and ready accomplice in his execution "with the sword of the children of Ammon" (ch. xii. 9). 1. *There is seldom wanting a suitable accomplice in effecting a sinful purpose,* however iniquitous it may be. The character of Joab was well known to David. "It was his very wickedness that commended him to the king as the most fitting instrument for carrying out his infamous design." He had formerly deprecated his wickedness (ch. iii. 29, 39); but now that he had himself fallen into sin, he associated himself with it, and made use of it for his own ends, although, as he afterwards found, to his own cost. "How Joab must have rejoiced when David sank down to his own level!" 2. *In serving another, such an accomplice is chiefly concerned about serving himself.* He seeks supremely his own advantage. Joab acted not from loyalty, but self-love. "To make himself great, powerful, indispensable, was the object of his life" (Plumptre). "Possibly he had some information that Bathsheba had been with David" ('Speaker's Commentary'). Anyhow, perceiving the design of the king against Uriah, he served him, in order that he might gain complete power over him; and in this he succeeded. "When David made him a partner and secret agent of his guilty purpose touching Uriah, he sold himself into his hands, and in that fatal letter he sealed away his liberty and surrendered himself up to this his unscrupulous accomplice" (Blunt). "All fellowship in sin begets despotism." Henceforth Joab did with the king very much as he pleased. 3. *No authority of man can justify the violation of the Law of God.* How often have men imagined that the command or sanction of one in authority has been a sufficient warrant for doing what their own consciences condemned, and laid the blame of their conduct on the instigator thereof rather than on themselves! Joab probably needed little self-excuse; but if ever he should want a defence, he might plead the king's letter. He was reckless of human life; to effect his purpose made a greater sacrifice of it than the king intended (ver. 17), and became more hardened than ever in wickedness. "We ought to obey God rather than men." 4. *There may be exemption from punishment when there is no exoneration from blame.* "How must this example needs harden Joab against the conscience of Abner's blood! while he cannot but think, ' David cannot avenge that in me which he acteth himself'" (Hall). Nevertheless, his guilt, in the sight of God, remains; and judgment comes at last (Eccles. xii. 14).—D.

Ver. 21.—(JERUSALEM, RABBAH.) *Warnings from history.* "Who smote Abimelech," etc.? "History is philosophy teaching by example." It is full of doctrines, principles, examples, warnings (1 Sam. xii. 8—12). This event, which had taken place two hundred and thirty years before, was familiar to Joab and others; and, viewed as a warning, likely to be recalled by the king to point his reproof (Judg. ix. 53). Of such warnings observe that they—

I. ARE OF IMMENSE SERVICE; in making general lessons concerning danger and duty: 1. More distinct. 2. More impressive. 3. More beneficial. They are beacon-lights, danger-signals, startling voices; and teach that in the way of inconsideration, rashness, and presumption, there is imminent peril; that destruction may come unexpectedly, suddenly, and by a feeble hand—"a woman slew him;" and that (although neither Joab nor David laid it to heart) every violation of God's Law is surely followed by retribution (Judg. ix. 56, 57). They are "written for our admonition" (1 Cor. x. 11).

II. SHOULD BE DULY HEEDED. 1. Intelligently studied. 2. Constantly remembered. 3. Practically observed. They are "written for our learning" (Rom. xv. 4). "The world exists for the education of each man. There is no age or state of society or mode of action in history to which there is not something corresponding in his life. Everything tends in a most wonderful manner to abbreviate itself and yield its whole nature to him" (Emerson).

III. MAY BE DELIBERATELY SLIGHTED. 1. For some immediate personal advantage. 2. From the persuasion of immunity, though others perish (ver. 17). 3. With a plausible excuse, when remonstrated with. "Thy servant Uriah the Hittite is dead also." "Joab quoted God's Word, but was not careful to keep it" (Wordsworth).

IV. WILL BE ASSUREDLY VINDICATED. 1. By the occurrence of similar events (1 Kings ii. 34). "The history of the past is a prophecy of the future." 2. In the bitter experience of the obdurate. 3. With ever-increasing clearness and force to successive generations. "Remember the days of old," etc. (Deut. xxxii. 7).—D.

Vers. 22—27.—(JERUSALEM, RABBAH.) *Concealment of sin. Order of events:*
1. Report of Uriah's death (vers. 22—25). 2. Bathsheba mourns (seven days, 1 Sam.
xxxi. 13) for her husband (ver. 26), being probably unacquainted with the manner in
which it was brought about. 3. David makes her his wife. 4. Joab takes Rabbah,
except the citadel (ch. xii. 26). 5. David, on receiving Joab's message, goes to Rabbah
and conquers the city (ch. xii. 27—31). 6. David and all the people return to
Jerusalem. 7. Bathsheba bears a son (ver. 27).

> "When I kept silence my bones waxed old
>   Whilst I continually groaned;
>   For day and night thy hand was heavy upon me:
>   My moisture was turned into the drought of summer."
>
> (Ps. xxxii. 3, 4.)

The life of David has an *outward* and an *inward* aspect: the one described in the
history, the other by himself in his psalms; each the necessary complement of the
other. They are, in general, closely connected and correspond, the outward being
the expression of the inward, and explained by it. But sometimes they appear at
variance, and in some respects present a melancholy contrast; as in the period that
followed his transgression. He had succeeded in hiding it from public view; but he could
not hide it altogether from himself. Consider concealment of sin in relation to—

I. THE OUTWARD LIFE. Many a man carries in his breast a guilty secret, unsuspected by others. He may be the object of their admiration and envy, and distinguished (as David was) by: 1. *Apparent sincerity* in public and in private life. He
judges offenders in the gate, or receives news (from the battle-field) with words of
resignation or encouragement (ver. 25). "Alas! how often do men hide baseness and
satisfaction at successful plotting under the commonplace of resignation to the
inevitable, of submission to the conditions of existence!" He goes to the house of God
(ch. vii. 8), "returns to bless his household" (ch. vi. 20), and maintains the form of
private devotion. Yet he is inwardly "like the troubled sea when it cannot rest," etc.
(Isa. lvii. 20). 2. *Restless activity* (ch. xii. 29), which, though it appear to be a display of admirable energy, is really pursued as a welcome diversion from disquieting
thoughts. "The enterprise promised an opportunity of escaping from himself; and he
probably went thither in the maddest of all attempts, that, namely, of outrunning
a guilty conscience" (W. M. Taylor). 3. *Earthly prosperity.* "And he took the
king's crown," etc. (ch. xii. 30). In this there was, probably, something of vain-glory
(1 John ii. 16). It was the culmination of his victories over the heathen. But the
honour of wearing the crown of "their king" (or Milcom, Moloch) was a poor compensation for the dishonour he had done to his own, and the loss of uprightness of heart;
his triumph over idolatry a miserable set-off against his overthrow by Satan. 4.
Unusual severity. (Ch. xii. 31.) The effect of sin is to harden the heart.

> "I waive the quantum o' the sin,
>   The hazard of concealing;
>   But och! it hardens a' within,
>   And petrifies the feeling!"
>
> (Burns.)

It also perverts the judgment. He who is wanting in a due sense of his own sinfulness
is apt to be a severe judge of others (ch. xii. 5; Matt. xviii. 28; xxi. 41; Rom. ii. 21).
A conscience ill at ease makes the temper sullen and irritable; and a repressed feeling
of justice in relation to a man himself sometimes finds relief in the infliction of cruel
vengeance on other men. "An evil conscience is the concealed root of bitterness from
which spring a thousand poisonous plants, to shed their baleful influence upon the
possessor and upon society at large" (McCosh).

II. THE INWARD LIFE. The experience of David was marked by: 1. *Obstinate
silence.* (Ps. xxxii. 3.) He not only sought to conceal his transgression from men, but
also sullenly refused to admit "the iniquity of his sin" to himself, or acknowledge it
before God. The impulse to confession in such a man must have been strong; but he
struggled against it with all his might (Ps. xxxii. 9), as others have done. 2. *Self-
deceiving guile.* "The deceit of the impenitent heart consists in its seeking to excuse

and justify itself despite the condemnation of conscience, while it obtains no relief from the feeling of guilt, but rather brings about a sharper *reaction of conscience,* and increases the pains that come from the conflict of mutually accusing and excusing thoughts" (Erdmann). "The roots of this deceit, which makes its appearance immediately after a fall into sin, are pride, lack of trust in God, and love of sin" (Hengstenberg). 3. *Spiritual deprivation.* For during these long, weary months of silence the light of God's countenance was hidden, the joy of his salvation lost (Ps. li. 8, 12). "His harp was out of tune, and his soul like a tree in winter, with the life in the root only" (Matthew Henry). "We are not to conceive of him as one who had quite fallen, nor as one spiritually dead, but as sick unto death. It is certain that he had not quite lost all desire after God, that he had not entirely given up prayer; doubtless there were still many fruits of faith perceptible in him; but his soul was checked in its flight toward God, a curse rested upon him, which made solitary communion with the Divine Being for any length of time intolerable, and moved him to seek distractions in order to escape the torment of conscience and keep it from attaining to full life." 4. *Inexpressible misery;* consisting of "the burden of the heart weighing on itself, the burden of a secret, the sense of hypocrisy, the knowledge of inward depravity, while all without looks pure as snow to men" (F. W. Robertson); the remembrance of sin that cannot be forgotten (Ps. li. 3), the remorse of conscience that cannot be quieted, the sense of Divine displeasure, the dread of approaching woes (Ps. li. 11); continuing without cessation; consuming the vital energies, and exhausting the physical strength (Ps. xxxviii. 6). "Whithersoever the sinner may turn himself, or however he may be mentally affected, his malady is in no degree lightened nor his welfare in any degree promoted until he is restored to God" (Calvin, in Ps. xxxii.). "I will reprove thee" etc. (Ps. l. 21). Although for a season concealed, it will be in due time revealed (Matt. x. 26). "Not only was the fruit of the sin to be first of all brought to light (ver. 27), and the hardened sinner to be deprived of the possibility of either denying or concealing his crimes; God would first of all break his unbroken heart by the torture of his own conscience, and prepare it to feel the reproaches of the prophet. . . . Nathan's reproof could not possibly have borne its saving fruit if David had been still living in utter blindness as to the character of his sin at the time the prophet went to him" (Keil). "No language ever described so vividly the sense of a weight at the heart— a weight that cannot be uplifted; and it was the weight of God's own presence, of that presence which he had once spoken of as the fulness of joy. With this oppression, like that of the air before the thunderstorm, came the drying up of all the moisture and freshness of life, the parching heat of fever. Did the Prophet Nathan bring all this to his consciousness? No, surely. The Prophet Nathan came at the appointed time to tell him in clear words, by a living instance, that which he had been hearing in muttered accents within his heart for months before. He came to tell him that the God of righteousness and mercy, who cared for Uriah, the poor man with the single ewe lamb, was calling him, the king, to account for an act of unrighteousness and unmercifulness. Nathan brought him to face steadily the light at which he had been winking, and to own that the light was good, that it was the darkness which was horrible and hateful, so that he might turn to the light and crave that it should once more penetrate into the depths of his being, and take possession of him" (Maurice). —D.

Ver. 27.—(JERUSALEM.) *God's displeasure at sin.* "And the thing that David had done displeased Jehovah" (1 Chron. xxi. 7). This is the only remark which the sacred historian makes on the conduct of David. It reveals its true nature as with a sun-beam; "contains the moral decision from a theocratic point of view, and is, as it were, a superscription of the following history of the Divine judgments on David and his house on account of this sin" (Erdmann). The Divine displeasure (indignation, anger, wrath) is—

I. REAL. Jehovah is the living, personal, supreme Ruler of men, and to him each man is responsible for his actions. As he is capable of being pleased, so he is of being displeased. His wrath is no less real than his love, wisdom, or power; like, yet unlike, that of man, being above all human imperfection. The Scriptures declare that he is displeased with men when they do evil (Ps. ii. 5; vi. 1; vii. 11; Mark iii. 5).

"The wrath of God is revealed," etc. (Rom. ii. 18). This is confirmed by conscience, in which his displeasure is reflected as a clouded sky in the surface of a lake.

II. DESERVED. Sin is rebellion against his authority, disobedience to his Law, opposition to his holiness, ingratitude toward his goodness; a transgression of the covenant, "a coming short of the mark," iniquity (Ps. xxxii. 1). Every wrong done to man is a dishonouring of God (Ps. li. 4). In the sin of David there were elements of peculiar and aggravated guilt (ch. xii. 7—9). But in every case it is "exceeding sinful," "the abominable thing which he hates" (Jer. xliv. 4). It is the one real evil in man.

> "Sin alone is that
> Which doth disfranchise him, and make unlike
> To the chief good; for that its light in him
> Is darken'd."
>
> (Dante.)

III. IMPARTIAL. The Holy One of Israel is unaffected by any of those influences that make human displeasure at wrong-doing partial and defective. He is neither blind nor indifferent to the sins of his children (ch. vii. 14). They have not, any more than others, a licence to sin. David, "his chosen," is not above the Law, nor exempt from due punishment. "For there is no respect of persons with God" (Rom. ii. 11). "Without respect of persons, the Father judgeth according to every man's work," etc. (1 Pet. i. 17; Amos iii. 2); estimating it according to its exact moral "weight" (1 Sam. ii. 3).

IV. UNAVOIDABLE. However men may conceal it from others, or endeavour to hide it from themselves, they cannot hide it from God (Job xxii. 13). What pleases men may displease him (1 Thess. ii. 4). His knowledge is infinite; his righteousness and justice essential, unchangeable, and eternal. Wherever and whenever sin exists, the holy energy of his wrath must burn against it; "for our God is a consuming fire," an "almighty foe to ill." Although delayed, it is not extinct. "A year had passed since his fall. The child of his sin had been born. And all this time God was silent. Yet like a dark cloud on a summer's day hung this sentence over him, 'But the thing that David did,' etc. Soon it would burst in a storm of judgment."

V. EFFICENT AND DREADFUL. As "in the king's favour there is life," so in his displeasure there is death. It is manifested in the punishment of the sinner, both inwardly and outwardly; as in the case of David (ch. xii. 10, 11). Every future moment must answer for the present. The penalties of transgression in this life are numerous and terrible. And who shall tell what will follow hereafter, when the wind becomes a whirlwind?

VI. MINGLED WITH MERCY. God is displeased with *sin* rather than with the *sinner* (except in so far as he voluntarily identifies himself with it); whom, in his essential nature, he loves; who possesses the capacity of restoration; whose salvation he seeks; and to whom, on his repentance, punishment becomes chastisement, a means of purification and blessing (ch. vii. 15). "There is no more terrible, there is no more instructive, portion of the Word of God than this whole record. The long death-sleep of that once living soul; its awakening under the prophet's voice; its deep repentance; its free forgiveness; its long, heavy, repeated, almost incessant chastisement;—speak to every ear which is not altogether deaf lessons of the holiness and truth, of the severity and love, of the justice and mercy, of the Lord our God, which is borne perhaps with equal force in no other record of his ways with man" ('Heroes of Hebrew History'). "O God, thou hadst never suffered so dear a favourite of thine to fall so fearfully, if thou hadst not meant to make him a universal example to mankind, of not presuming, of not despairing. How can we presume of not sinning, or despair for sinning, when we find so great a saint thus fallen, thus risen?" (Hall).—D.

Ver. 27.—*David's fall.* "But the thing that David had done displeased the Lord." One guarantee, even to the most unlettered, of the truthfulness of sacred history is the impartiality of its accounts of its greatest heroes, whose sins and follies are faithfully recorded as well as their virtues. Noah, Abraham, Moses, Peter, are cases in point. David is another instance, whose fearful sins are recorded in this most distressing chapter, ending with the significant words of our text, "But the thing that David had done displeased the Lord."

I. THE WICKEDNESS WHICH DISPLEASED GOD. Many things done by good men of old times which appear to us very culpable, were in them innocent or excusable, on account of the different standard by which their conduct was regulated, and the different public opinion of their days. But the sins of David recorded in this chapter were not of such a description. The law of nature everywhere and in all times, as well as the laws of the revelation known to David, are clear and emphatic in condemning them. 1. *The sins themselves.* (1) *Adultery* ; and, growing out of this, (2) *deceit.* Pretences to Uriah of concern about the war, and about Uriah's comfort while in Jerusalem (vers. 7—10); and to Joab's messenger, of regarding the deaths of Uriah and other brave soldiers whose lives had been sacrificed through his directions, as being ordinary casualties of war (ver. 25). (3) Murder of Uriah and the soldiers who fell with him. (4) Leading others into crime: Uriah into drunkenness, Joab into murder. 2. *Their aggravations.* (1) His age, position, knowledge, experiences, and reputation. He was between fifty and sixty years old. As king, he was the highest guardian of justice and protector of innocence. He knew well the wickedness of his conduct. He had been marvellously guided, advanced, and blessed by God, with whom he had been accustomed to maintain the closest converse. He was well known as a devout man, professing himself a devoted servant of God. He had thus a reputation to sustain. (2) The difficulties in his way. The necessity of sending messengers (ver. 4) to Bathsheba. Think of his stooping to that ! Difficulties, necessitating some consideration and calling for determined resolution to conquer them, increase the guilt of sin. (3) His abundant harem, as contrasted with Uriah's one wife; hinted at in ch. xii. 2, 3. (4) Uriah's position and conduct. His relation to David, as one of his chief military officers, and distinguished for his valour (ch. xxiii. 39 ; 1 Chron. xi. 41). He was at the time with the army in the field, and might justly look to the king to be the protector (if necessary) of his wife from evil. He cherished noble sentiments (ver. 11) of duty and honour as a soldier. (Did he, however, know or suspect how matters stood ; and frame his language to the king as a subterfuge?) (5) The deliberateness of the later crimes. (6) The time consumed, giving ample opportunity for reflection. When these things are considered, the wickedness of David assumes proportions which are appalling. 3. *How they were possible.* (1) There must have been secret and very serious declension in piety. Had he been in the state of mind and heart which is revealed in ch. vii., it is impossible that he could have so sinned. The height of prosperity and power which he had reached had corrupted him. (2) There is much in what Dean Stanley says of " that abyss which yawns by the side of lofty genius and strong passions," which " opened and closed over him." (3) His position as an Eastern monarch, accustomed to polygamy, accustomed also to act in many things according to his own will. (4) Some think that his being in the way of temptation arose from a self-indulgent neglect of duty in remaining at Jerusalem instead of leading his army in the field. (5) He found in Bathsheba a ready consent to his will. (6) The later sins and crimes seemed necessary, after the first step, to save himself and his companion in guilt from utter disgrace and ruin. Such considerations may help to explain, but cannot be accepted as excusing, his wickedness.

II. HOW THE DISPLEASURE OF GOD WAS MANIFESTED. 1. *The message by Nathan* (ch. xii. 1—12); who boldly reproved David in the name of the Lord, and announced the punishments which would fall upon him. 2. *The death of the child.* 3. *Family scandals, sins, and sorrows.* 4. *Absalom's rebellion, and all the humiliations and troubles it involved.* 5. *Joab's increased ascendency.* " There was a guilty secret between the two " (Trench). The worst part of his punishment sprang from sins like his own, and was probably occasioned by them, at least in part.

LESSONS. 1. *Do nothing, however pleasant, or gainful, or common among men, or seemingly safe, to the account of which may be appended the terrible words,* "The thing . . . displeased the Lord." 2. *Let none presume on their security against even disgraceful sin.* " Let him that thinketh he standeth take heed lest he fall " (1 Cor. x. 12); " Watch and pray, that ye enter not into temptation " (Matt. xxvi. 41). 3. *Guard against the beginnings of evil.* " Keep thy heart with all diligence; for out of it are the issues of life " (Prov. iv. 23). David had already committed adultery when he gazed lustfully on Bathsheba (comp. Matt. v. 28). Pray, as David did afterwards, " Create in me a clean heart " (Ps. li. 10). The beginning of sin is, like that of strife, "as when one letteth out water" (Prov. xvii. 14). The trickling of water through a small crevice in an embankment may seem inconsiderable; but, unless stopped, it may issue in widespread devastation and misery. One sin leads to another and another, and all to pain and sorrow. Gehazi's covetousness led him to falsehood and robbery, and then to lifelong leprosy, transmitted to his children's children (2 Kings v. 20—27). Peter's self-confidence prepared the way for cowardice, falsehood, and profanity, followed by bitter anguish. The pilferings of Judas from "the bag" issued in the betrayal of his Lord; and then remorse and suicide. 4. *How vain are all attempts to conceal sin and prevent punishment!* God is looking on all the time the sinner is cunningly endeavouring to hide his sin (see Job xxxiv. 21, 22). "Be sure your sin will find you out" (Numb. xxxii. 23).—G. W.

EXPOSITION.

CHAPTER XII.

Ver. 1.—Jehovah sent Nathan unto David. Though David had remained unrepentant for nearly a year, for we read in ver. 14 that the child was born, yet we are not to suppose that there had been no compunctions of conscience. A man could scarcely pass from utter callousness to a state of mind so tender as that depicted in Ps. li. without some preparation. Assuredly David had suffered much mental distress, but he had given no outward sign of contrition, and possibly, but for Nathan's message, he might have overpowered his conscience, and his self-reproaches have become less frequent and agitating. More probably he was slowly ripening for repentance, and Nathan's words let loose the agonizing feelings which had more and more struggled within him against his baser lusts. And the prophet's apologue was exactly suited to rouse up that strong sense of justice which was so noble an element in David's character. Doubtless it was framed for this purpose, and Nathan knew what was the right chord to touch. But we must not, because he was wise and skilful, refuse Nathan our fullest admiration for his manly courage. It is a very dangerous thing to tell princes of their sins, and especially when that prince is an absolute monarch, and his sins adultery and murder. But the position which Nathan held in David's court made it his duty so to do, and there is no stronger testimony to the power of religion and of God's grace than that it makes men so brave in doing their duty. We may feel sure that Nathan had long grieved over David's fall, and reflected upon the steps which ought to be taken for his admonition. And now, in answer to prayer, the command came from Jehovah bidding him go and bear his testimony. Nathan's parable is admirably adapted for its purpose. While making no direct reference to adultery or murder, it puts very strongly the injustice and heartlessness of the oppression of the weak by the strong, as exemplified in the deed of the rich man. On many occasions David had shown a warm and generous indignation at injustice, and a righteous pity for those wronged. Would such a feeling be called out now? David's conduct was bad enough, and if there was no outburst of anger at the base deed reported to him, and no welling-up of pity for the poor man robbed of his one joy, then was his case hopeless, and Nathan must withdraw in despair, and leave David to his fate. But his better feelings were not destroyed, and when Nathan saw them deeply stirred, he broke in with the stern application to the king's own sin, "Thou art the man!" The courage and the skill of the prophet are alike admirable.

Ver. 3.—Was unto him as a daughter. The Orientals are excessively fond of pet animals, and, as the dog is with them unclean, its place is taken by fawns, kids, or lambs. The description, therefore, is not overcharged, for in many an English home the dog or cat takes its place as one of the family. The Revised Version preserves the tenderness of the original in translating "it did eat of his own morsel."

Ver. 4.—A traveller, . . . wayfaring man, . . . man that was come to him. Nathan probably used these three terms chiefly to diversify his language, but it has served as a handle for much allegorizing. Thus Rashi explains it of covetousness, which comes at first as a mere "passer-by," the literal meaning of the word rendered "traveller." But, if admitted, it grows into "a wayfaring man," who comes and goes on business, and stays a longer time. Finally it changes into "one who has come to him," and remains permanently. Such allegorical interpretations are common in the Fathers, and thus Augustine compares the three stages of sin to our Lord's three miracles of raising the dead. The sinner is at first like Jairus's daughter, just dead, and repentance can restore him immediately to life; but, if sin be persisted in, he becomes like the son of the widow of Nain, carried away to burial; and finally like Lazarus, given over to corruption.

Ver. 5.—**Shall surely die.** It is strange language to declare that a man shall be put to death and then fined four lambs. But David says nothing of the sort, but that the man is "a son of death," that is, a wretch who deserves to die. The Revised Version correctly renders, "is worthy to die." The sentence actually passed, of fourfold restitution, is exactly in accordance with the Mosaic Law (Exod. xxii. 1), but the moral turpitude of the offence was far greater than could be atoned for by the legal penalty. Rightly, therefore, David expressed his indignation, and regretted that the sentence was so light; but a judge must not strain the law, which necessarily has regard chiefly to the outward offence.

Ver. 7.—**Thou art the man!** Abruptly and with sudden vehemence comes the application to David himself. So skilfully had the parable been contrived, that up to this point David had had no suspicion that he was the rich man who had acted so meanly by his poorer neighbour Uriah. And now he stood self-condemned. Yet even so self-love might have made his indignation break forth against Nathan; but probably the reproof only completed a work that had long been secretly in progress, and brushed away the last obstacles to repentance. **I anointed thee.** The solemn anointing made David the representative of Jehovah, and thus his sin was aggravated by the degradation in the eyes of the people, both of the kingly office and also of Jehovah himself. Rank and authority are given to men that they may lead others to do right; it is a fearful misuse of them when they give prestige to sin.

Ver. 8.—**I gave . . . thy master's wives into thy bosom.** These words probably mean that, as the whole possessions of his predecessor belonged, by Oriental custom, to the next occupant of the throne, David might have claimed the entire household and the wives both of Saul and Ishbosheth as his own, though apparently he had not done so. As far as we know, Saul had but one wife (1 Sam. xiv. 50) and one concubine, Rizpah (ch. iii. 7). Of Ishbosheth's family arrangements we know little, but his harem, if he had one, would become the property of David. But independently of this, the permission of polygamy had made it possible for him to take any of the daughters of Israel and Judah to wife, and he had freely availed himself of this licence. Yet, not content, he had lusted after a married woman, and had got rid of her husband by murder, meanly using the sword of the Ammonites to accomplish his own criminal purpose. The word used in this clause, and rendered "thou hast slain him," is a very

strong one, and literally means "thou hast murdered him," though the sword was that of the enemy.

Ver. 10.—**The sword shall never depart from thine house**; that is, thy crime shall not be expiated by one slaughter, but by many, so that thy punishment shall cease only at thine own death. This sentence was fulfilled in Amnon's murder (ch. xiii. 28), who had been encouraged in his crime by his father's example. Upon this followed Absalom's rebellion and death (ch. xviii. 14); and finally, when in his last hours David made Solomon his successor, he knew that he was virtually passing sentence on Adonijah, the eldest of his surviving sons. But what a fearful choice! for had he not done so, then Bathsheba and her four sons would doubtless have been slain, whereas there was some hope that Solomon might spare his brother. That Adonijah was unworthy we gather from the fact that he had ceased to be cohen, and that this office was conferred, after Absalom's rebellion, on Ira the Jairite (ch. xx. 26), Solomon being then too young to hold such a position. Until he committed this crime, David's family had probably dwelt in concord, and it was his own wickedness which broke up their unity, and introduced among them strife, mutual hatred, and the shedding of blood.

Ver. 11.—**He shall lie with thy wives.** Fulfilled for political purposes by Absalom, under the advice of Bathsheba's grandfather (ch. xvi. 22). The punishment was thus complete. For the murdered Uriah there was fourfold restitution, according to David's own sentence. First there was Bathsheba's child lately born, then Amnon, thirdly Absalom, and lastly Adonijah. For the adultery there was open disgrace wrought upon his royal dignity "before the sun," in open daylight. As he had brought shame and dishonour upon the family relations of his neighbour, so were his own family rights violated by his rebellious son. And, as is often the case, the sins which followed were worse than those which prepared the way. Vice begins as a small stream trickling through the opposing dam, but it quickly breaks down all moral restraints, and rushes along like a destroying flood.

Ver. 13.—**I have sinned against Jehovah.** Saul had used the same words, and had meant very little by them; nor had he added "against Jehovah," because his purpose was to appease Samuel, and prevail upon him not to disgrace him before the people. David's confession came from the heart. There is no excuse-making, no attempt at lessening his fault, no desire to evade punishment. Ps. li. is the lasting testimony, not only to the reality, but to the tenderness of his repentance, and we may even feel here that confession was to him a relief. The deep internal wound was at length disclosed, and healing had become possible. Up to this time he had shut God away from his heart, and so there had been no remedy for a soul diseased. It was because his sorrow was genuine that comfort was not delayed. Jehovah also hath put away thy sin; thou shalt not die. Now, death was the legal penalty for adultery (Lev. xx. 10), and though it might not be easy to exact it of a king, yet, until it was remitted, David would be in the eyes of all "a son of death" (see on ver. 5); and how could he administer justice to others while the death-sentence for a capital crime was hanging over himself? Had not the prophet been authorized to use his dispensing power as the mouthpiece of Jehovah, David could not have remained king. And we can see no reason for supposing, with Ewald and others, that a substantial interval of time elapsed between David's confession and Nathan's absolution. The sole conceivable reason for such a view would be the supposition that David's repentance began and was completed with the one stab of shame which pierced through him when he heard Nathan's sudden reproach. Such a mere thrill, following upon such persistent callousness, would have merited little attention. But if months of brooding sorrow and secret shame had been humbling David, then his open confession was the proof that the Spirit's work had reached the goal, and was now complete. And we gather from Ps. li. 3 that such was the case. "My sin," he says, "is ever before me." It had long haunted him; had long occupied his thoughts by day, and broken his rest at night. Like a flood, his iniquities had gone over his head, and threatened to drown him; like a heavy burden, they had pressed upon him so as to break him down (Ps. xxxviii. 4). Both these psalms tell of long-continued sorrow of heart; but with confession had come relief. He had offered to God the sacrifice of a broken spirit, and knew that it had not been despised. We shall see subsequently that his time and attention had been much occupied with the Ammonite war, and this had probably helped him in evading the secret pleadings of his own conscience.

Ver. 14.—Thou hast given great occasion to the enemies of Jehovah to blaspheme; Hebrew, *thou hast made the enemies of Jehovah to despise;* that is, to despise Jehovah's government, the theocracy, of which David was the visible head and earthly representative. Jehovah's enemies are not the heathen, but Israelitish unbelievers, who would scoff at all religion when one in David's position fell into terrible open sin.

But the death of the adulterous offspring of David and Bathsheba would prove to these irreligious men that Jehovah's righteous rule could reach and punish the king himself, and would thus vindicate his justice from their reproach.

Ver. 16.—David ... went in. He went, not into the sanctuary, which he did not enter until after the child's death, but into some private room in his own house. There he remained, passing his nights stretched on the ground, and fasting until the seventh day. His fasting does not imply that he took no food during this long interval, but that he abstained from the royal table, and ate so much only as was necessary to maintain life. Now, what was the meaning of this privacy and abstinence? Evidently it was David's acknowledgment, before all his subjects, of his iniquity, and of his sorrow for it. The sickness of the child followed immediately upon Nathan's visit, and we may feel sure that news of his rebuke, and of all that passed between him and the king, ran quickly throughout Jerusalem. And David at once takes the position of a condemned criminal, and humbles himself with that thoroughness which forms so noble a part of his character. Grieved as he was at the child's sickness, and at the mother's sorrow, yet his grief was mainly for his sin; and he was willing that all should know how intense was his shame and self-reproach. And even when the most honourable of the rulers of his household (Gen. xxiv. 2), or, as Ewald thinks, his uncles and elder brethren, came to comfort him, he persists in maintaining an attitude of heart-stricken penitence.

Ver. 20.—Then David arose from the earth. If David's grief had been occasioned by love for the child, then its death and the consciousness that, while his guilt had caused its sickness, his prayers had not availed to save it, would have aggravated his anguish. There was much personal regard for the child, which had been made the more precious by these very events. But David's sorrow was, as we have seen, that of penitence, and not that of natural affection. When, therefore, the threatened penalty had been paid by the death of the child, David felt it to be his duty to show his resignation, and therefore he went into the sanctuary and worshipped, in proof that he acknowledged the justice of God's dealings, and was content to bear the punishment as his righteous desert.

Ver. 22.—God; Hebrew, *Jehovah,* usually rendered "Lord." Similarly in Gen. vi. 5 in the Authorized Version we find *God* in capital letters, as here, for the Hebrew *Jehovah.*

Ver. 23.—I shall go to him, but he shall

not return to me. These words indicate, first of all, much personal feeling for the child. Hence some have supposed that, as Solomon is placed last of Bathsheba's four sons in ch. v. 14 and 1 Chron. iii. 5, three other sons had already been borne by her, and that consequently this child, the fruit of their adultery, would now have been seven or eight years of age. It is certainly remarkable that in ver. 16 David calls him "the lad" (so the Hebrew), though in every other place he is styled "the child." On the other hand, we gather from ver. 14 that probably he was as yet the only child, and this is the more reasonable view, even if Solomon was the youngest son (but see note on ver. 24). But secondly, the words indicate a belief in the continued existence of the child, and even that David would recognize and know him in the future world. Less than this would have given no comfort to the father for his loss. Now, it is true that we can find no clear dogmatic teaching in the early Scriptures upon the immortality of the soul. Job could give expression to no such hope in vii. 6—10, and the belief in a world to come would have solved the difficulties of himself and his friends, which really are left unsolved. Even in the Psalms there are words that border on despair (see vi. 5; xxx. 9; lxxxviii. 11; cxv. 17); nor had Hezekiah any such belief in continued existence as could solace him in the expectation of an early death (Isa. xxxviii. 18, 19). This hopelessness was not unnatural at a time when the doctrine had not been as yet clearly taught. On the other hand, in Ps. xvii. 15 and xvi. 9—11 we find proof that David did believe in his own immortality. For though the latter words have a second and higher meaning, yet the primary sense of Ps. xvi. 10 is that David's own soul (or self) would not always remain in Sheol, the abode of the departed, nor would he, Jehovah's anointed one, see such corruption as would end in annihilation.

Ver. 24.—He called his name Solomon. It is rashly assumed that Solomon's birth followed next in order after that of the deceased child. More probably there was a long interval of time, and son after son was born, with little increase of happiness to the family polluted by Amnon's sin and troubled by its miserable consequences. While we must not lay too great stress upon Solomon calling himself "a little child" (1 Kings iii. 7) after his accession, yet it forbids our believing that he was more than just grown up. It was the remarkable ability of Solomon, his goodness and precocious talent, which made him so great a comfort to his parents, and which received Jehovah's seal of approval in the name *Jedidiah*. This name would scarcely

be given him until his good and great qualities were developing; and as it was a sort of indication that he was the chosen and elect son of David, and therefore the next king, we shall probably be right in believing that this second mission of Nathan, and this mark of Divine favour to David's youngest child, did not take place until after Absalom's death, possibly not until Solomon was ten or twelve years of age. The name *Solomon* means "the peaceful," and answers to the German *Friedrich*. It was given to the child in recognition that David's wars were now over, and that the era of quiet had begun, which was to be consecrated to the building of Jehovah's temple. It was the name given to the infant at his birth, and was a name of hope. Alas! this peace was to be rudely broken by the rebellion of the son whom David, in vain expectation and with all a father's pride, had named *Ab-salom*, "his father's peace."

Ver. 25.—He sent. Some commentators make David the subject of the sentence, and translate, "And he, David, sent in the hand of Nathan, and called," etc. They suppose that this means that Nathan was entrusted with Solomon's education; but "in the hand" is the ordinary Hebrew preposition, meaning "by," and the sense plainly is that God sent a message by Nathan. David had already called the child Solomon, and now Jehovah, some years afterwards, gives him an indication of his special favour by naming him Yedidyah. The word is formed from the same root as *David*, that is, "lovely," with the addition of the Divine name. As we have already pointed out, this was no slight matter, but the virtual selection of Solomon to be David's successor, and probably, therefore, was delayed until he had given indication of his great intellectual gifts. His elder brothers would not be passed over without valid reasons.

Ver. 26.—Joab . . . took the royal city. As the siege of Rabbah would be conducted by the slow process of blockade, it might easily be prolonged into the second year, and so give ample space for David's sin and its punishment by the death of the child. But more probably the narrator, having commenced the history of David's sin, completes the story before returning to his account of the war. Thus the capture of Rabbah would occupy some of the interval between David's adultery and Nathan's visit of rebuke, and would lessen the difficulty, which we cannot help feeling, of David remaining for nine or ten months with the guilt of adultery and murder resting upon him, and no open act of repentance. Some short time, then, after Uriah's death, Joab captured "the city of waters." This is not a poetical name for Rabbah, but means the "water-city," that is, the town upon the Jabbok, whence the supply of water was obtained. The citadel, which occupied a high rock on the north-western side, must, therefore, soon be starved into submission, and the whole of "the royal city," that is, of the metropolis of the Ammonites, be in Joab's power. He therefore urges David to come in person, both that the honour of the conquest may be his, and also because probably the blockading force had been reduced to as small a body of men as was safe, and the presence of a large army was necessary for completing the subjugation of the country, which would follow upon the capture of the capital.

Ver. 30.—**Their king**; Hebrew, *Malcam.* This is another mode of spelling Milcom, the god of the Ammonites, and is found also in Zeph. i. 5, and probably in Jer. xlix. 1, 3; Amos i. 15. Strictly, Milcom or Malcom is a proper name for the supreme deity, formed from the word *melec.* a king, or, as it was pronounced in other Semitic dialects, Moloch. Grammatically, *Malcam* also means "their king," and even so belongs to Milcom. For the crown weighed a hundred pounds, a ponderous mass, which no man could possibly bear, and, least of all, when making, as was the case with the Ammonite king, his last stand for his life. But after the capture of the city, it was lifted from the head of the idol, and placed formally upon David's head, and held there for a few moments, as a sign of victory and of rejoicing over the fall of the false god. There is no reason for supposing that there is any exaggeration in the weight, nor will the Hebrew allow us to understand the talent of gold as referring to its value.

Ver. 31.—**The people that were therein.** The cruel treatment described in this verse was inflicted, first of all, upon those who had defended Rabbah, now reduced to a small number by the long siege; but David next proceeded through all the cities, that is, the fortified towns of the Ammonites, inflicting similar barbarities. They were confined probably to the fighting men, and most of these would make their escape as soon as resistance became hopeless. The general population would, of course, scatter themselves in every direction, but the misery caused by such a breaking up of civil life, as well as by the cruel bloodshed, must have been terrible. Instead of " he put them in a saw," we find, in 1 Chron. xx. 3, " he sawed them with a saw." This reading differs from what we have here only in one letter, and is plainly right, as the translation, " under saws," " under harrows of iron," etc., found both in the Authorized and Revised Versions, is simply an expedient, rendered necessary by the corruption of the text. If we restore the passage by the help of the parallel place, it runs on thus : " He sawed with a saw, and with threshing-sledges of iron, and with cutting instruments of iron." What exactly the second were we do not know, as the word does not occur elsewhere. The Vulgate renders it " wains shod with iron," meaning, apparently, those driven over the corn for threshing purposes, and now driven over these unfortunate people. The barbarity is not more horrible than that of sawing prisoners asunder. **He made them pass through the brick-kiln.** Both the Septuagint and Vulgate have " brick-kiln," Hebrew, *malban,* which the Massorites have adopted, but the Hebrew text has *malchan.* No commentator has given any satisfactory explanation of what can be meant by making the Ammonites pass through a brick-kiln; but Kimchi gives a very probable interpretation of the word really found in the Hebrew, and which, not being intelligible, has been corrupted. For the Malchan was, he says, the place where the Ammonites made their children pass through the fire to Moloch. He thinks, therefore, that David put some of the people to death in this way. We cannot defend these cruelties, but they unhappily were the rule in Oriental warfare, and would have been inflicted on their enemies by the Ammonites. We have proof in 1 Sam. xi. 2 and Amos i. 13 that they were a barbarous race; but this did not justify barbarous retaliation.

HOMILETICS.

Vers. 1—14.—The facts are : 1. God sends Nathan the prophet to David, who tells him a story of the greed of a wicked rich man, who, to satisfy his avarice, took away and slew the pet ewe lamb of a poor man. 2. David, accepting the story as a matter of fact, is very angry with this man, and swears that for his deed and lack of compassion he ought to die and restore fourfold. 3. Nathan thereupon reveals the parabolic character of his narrative, by saying unto David, " Thou art the *man!*" 4. He then proceeds to state (1) the goodness of God to him in anointing him king, in delivering him from Saul, in giving him the royal succession, and in guaranteeing all else that might be needed; (2) his despite to the commands of God—his murder of Uriah, and his taking possession of Uriah's wife.   5. He also declares, by way of punishment, that war would arise in his own house; that the purity and safety of his domestic life would be invaded; and that the punishment of his secret sin would be open.   6. On David confessing his guilt, Nathan assures him that the Lord had so far put away his sin that he should not die, but that the child of his guilt should.

Nathan's parable.   This remarkable parable is, perhaps, the most exquisite gem of the kind in the Old Testament.   Its beauty and pathos are enhanced by the plain matter-of-fact way in which the historian narrates, in ch. xi., the fall of David and his subsequent crime.   Apart from its specific purpose, it indicates to us the occasional functions of the prophets in those times as admonishers of kings and rulers, and consequently as representatives of the Divine element in the history of Israel.   The great variety of teaching in this parable may be briefly indicated thus—

I. A DOUBLE LIFE.   At least ten months had elapsed from the date of David's fall to the visit of Nathan.   During that period many public and private acts had been performed by the king in the ordinary course of life, in addition to those referred to in ch. xi. 14—27.   It was his policy to keep up a good appearance—to be in administration, in public worship, in regard for religious ordinances, and in general morality all that he had ever been.   He passed still as the pious, just ruler and exemplary man.   That was one life.   But inwardly there was another.   The conscience was dull, or, if it spoke plainly, was constantly being suppressed.   The uncomfortableness of secret sin induced self-reproach and loss of self-respect.   He was an instance of a man " holding the truth in unrighteousness" (Rom. i. 18).   This double life is the experience of every good man who falls into sin and seeks to cover it up.   He knows too much to be really happy, but he is too enslaved by his sin to be truly godly.   The outside is fair; within is desolation.

II. FELLOWSHIP IN SIN.   David and Bathsheba shared in a fellowship of sin.   They, most probably without words, communed with each other over their guilt, and so far strengthened the chains of iniquity.   Two individuals in possession of a dreadful secret do not, dare not, speak about it.   There is simply a common understanding and a mutual support in keeping up the appearance necessary to social reputation.   It is a pitiable sight before God and holy angels!   It is a case of the fallen, the defiled, the inwardly wretched, and the prospectively condemned, seeking to find comfort and strength in each other's sympathy.   The channels of sympathetic feeling are filled by a polluted stream of affection and interest.

III. A LOST CHARM.   It is well known that a pure disposition and a clear conscience lend a charm to personal life; much more does such deep and strong piety as once characterized the "man after God's own heart."   If we, in reading the historic narrative of David's early years, and the psalms, in which his best thoughts are embodied, feel the spell of his spirit, we may be sure that those in daily converse with him recognized a charm of the most exalted kind.   But all that was now gone, because the honesty and the purity from which it sprang were no more.   In vain did he strive to maintain the form of godliness; in vain his careful discharge of official duties and kindly bearing towards his friends.   The "secret of the Lord" was lost.   The salt had lost its savour.   To truly spiritual men he would not be as in former times.   This loss of a spiritual charm always takes place when good men fall into sin and cover it up.   The light of the spiritual eye is dim.   The pure ring of the voice is gone.   The "form of godliness" is left, but the " power " is no more.

IV. THE DIVINE RESERVE.   At least ten months elapsed before Nathan was commissioned by God to speak to David.   The lustful look, the secret deed, the scheme for concealment and for the death of Uriah, were allowed to pass and issue in seeming success without one act of a decidedly positive character, as far as we know, on the part of God either to smite with punishment or bring to penitence.   The "workers of iniquity" flourished, and the innocent perished unavenged (Ps. xcii. 7; cf. xii. 5; Prov. i. 11—19).   That conscience uttered its protest, and that the laws of mind as constituted by God worked misery from the first in the inner life of David, is no doubt true; but there was no open justice, no obvious interposition on behalf of the oppressed, no distinct and proportionate chastisement, no special call to repentance.   Human nature took its course, and human society remained in relation to the sinner unchanged.

Yet God is not indifferent. He slumbereth not. Government does not relax its hold on each man. The explanation is that God is in no haste in what he does; he reserves his action for a while for reasons more complicate and far-reaching than we can trace. The very reserve only renders the judgment, when it comes, more impressive. Human nature is evidently favoured as a free power, which must have certain scope both for origination of evil, maturing of evil, and filling up its own measure of chastisement. There is a patience, a goodness, in the reserve which need to be studied (Rom. ii. 4—9; 1 Pet. iii. 20; 2 Pet. iii. 9. 15). This reserve attends many a modern sinner's cause.

V. The Divine beginning of salvation. Had David been left to himself the probability is that the coils of iniquity would have been formed around him more and more as time advanced; for the law of habit here holds good. It is instructive to observe that the first step towards a change in his condition was on the Divine side. God sent his prophet Nathan, charged with a merciful purpose, though mercy was to be tempered with judgment. Certainly David might well say in days subsequent, "My salvation cometh from him" (Ps. lxii. 1, 7). Here we have an illustration of the great truth that God is the Author of our salvation. He seeks us. He comes to us in our low estate. This is true of mankind as a whole (John iii. 16, 17; 1 John iv. 9, 10), of each one brought from the ways of sin (1 John iv. 19), and of the backslider (Ps. xxiii. 3). It is all of grace. Our Saviour's earthly life of pleading and seeking was a visible and audible illustration of the outgoing of the heart of the Father towards the fallen.

VI. The defensive attitude of impenitence. The elaborate simplicity of Nathan's parable, in order to reach the conscience and heart of David, suggest to us the fact of a certain defensive attitude of David's mind, which had to be broken down. It is a special weapon in a "holy war," designed to attack a peculiar line of defence. It is well known how men, when they have done a wrong, are on the *qui vive* lest the wrong should be detected and brought home to them; and the resources of reason, ingenuity, and cunning are employed to ward off any approach to the inner life. Any attempt to touch the springs of penitence or remorse, or to arouse the fears which attend conviction, is neutralized by some counter-move of thought or resolve. Hearers of the gospel know, if they would only testify honestly, how they too often fortify themselves against statements, arguments, and appeals. The failure of some ministers and teachers lies in their not knowing enough of human nature to direct their statements so as to meet the actual mental attitude of those who live in sin. A study of this subject is of extreme importance to all who seek to convince and to save men. There are various avenues to the conscience and heart. Some are so utterly closed and guarded that it is a waste of power to seek to penetrate through them. A fortress should be attacked in its weakest point, and only a very special survey can find out where it is. Nathan had reconnoitred the position, and assailed David along the best line.

VII. The use of the good element in man. Nathan approached David in friendliness, recognizing him as a man generally mindful of his people, pitiful towards the poor and weak, and a lover of justice. He knew that there were still elements of good in the fallen saint. The great transgression had not obliterated all trace of the noble qualities of former days. Where these did not come in the way of the one selfish lust which had for the time gained dominion, they were not only cherished, but were at hand for expression when occasion required. In proportion as these could be strengthened and utilized, there would be hope of bringing them to bear, by a reflected light, on the one deed in which they had been suppressed. By a flank movement, and using a piece of history as the instrument, he hoped to turn the whole force of David's better qualities on the cherished secret sin. It was an instance of a wise setting of one part of a man's nature against another part, so that, by a sort of moral dynamic, the worse should be forced out. In dealing with men we ought to avail ourselves of their good qualities and bring them to bear on the removal of the bad. When Christ dealt with publicans and sinners he did not make a direct attack on their sins. There was a something in them which he made the ground of appeal. In the vilest sinner there is some human love, or kindliness, or sense of right. Who is wise to *win* souls? What are the methods, according to varying temperaments, education, habits, and indulgences?

VIII. God's judgment forestalled by conscience. History is a mental reflector. In Nathan's story, which was not a parable to David when he heard it, David saw a sin and a judgment. He was true to his better qualities when he denounced the sin and pronounced sentence of death. The story became to David a parable the moment the prophet said to him, "Thou art the *man!*" The whole figures then become specific, and he was the one most conspicuous against whom the judgment was pronounced. The psychological and moral changes involved in this we cannot now deal with; the point is that, when David's aroused righteous indignation pronounced judgment on the evil man, the human conscience really forestalled the judgment of God on David's sin by declaring its deserts. God does not, in providence or on the day of judgment, declare anything really new to the impenitent sinner. Conscience some time or other has virtually given the sentence of condemnation. Those who worked themselves up to a state of self-delusion (Matt. vii. 22, 23) knew a time when the conscience witnessed against the formalities which issued in its being seared (Eph. iv. 19; 1 Tim. iv. 2). It is this assent of conscience which will render the sense of injustice impossible in the future judgments God may see fit to bring on those who "hold the truth in unrighteousness."

GENERAL LESSONS. 1. We should take warning from the instances in the Bible, and not presume on God's silence, or think that, because we are left to pursue our own courses, it will always be so. 2. There are always in existence agents or agencies by which in due time sin will be rebuked and exposed either in this life or in the life to come (Matt. x. 26; 2 Cor. v. 10). 3. In dealing with the lapsed we should not act on the same rule in all cases, but deal with each according to his peculiar character. 4. It will repay parents, teachers, and evangelists to study human nature and the records of biography and sacred history to find out the best methods of reaching the conscience of the impenitent. 5. We should be ready, as was Nathan, to carry through the most painful duties when God calls us in his providence to them.

The convicted sinner. The fitness of the parable is revealed in its sequel. Nathan, laying aside the character of a friendly visitor relating a story of wrong, now assumes the functions of the prophet of God, and turns the whole light and force of David's just indignation in upon himself, and, with an incisiveness most irresistible, brings an accusation of guilt without naming the actual deed done; states the aggravating circumstances arising out of the exceeding goodness of God in the past; declares the retribution about to come; and, on witnessing the true penitence of the sinner, announces the fact of forgiveness, but qualifies the announcement by foretelling an event of blended justice and mercy. The commission of sin is unhappily common enough, and also, we may thankfully admit, the conviction of sinners is an event of frequent occurrence. Few sins exhibit the peculiar aggravations of this one of David, and few convictions are more sudden and thorough than his; but as there are common qualities in all sins and true convictions of sin, we may regard this case of David's as setting forth features in human experience and Divine procedure universally true.

I. THE FACT OF SIN IS BROUGHT HOME TO THE CONSCIENCE. David all along knew of the existence of the sin, but had conducted himself as though it were not. In general terms he would doubtless speak of sin as an evil of deepest dye, and desire its banishment from mankind. Such sentiments were at the base of his deep interest in Nathan's story, and gave rise to the outburst of indignation. Sin was evil, the sinner ought to be punished, the doer of this deed must come under the ban of law. All this was quite correct. It was orthodoxy. The friendly visitor could not but admit its force. But it was just here, when David was dealing with generalities, and was eager to see general principles applied to a particular case, that Nathan brought him away from the general to the particular, from others to himself. "Thou art the *man!*" This was a straight charge. Nathan held a twofold position—he was a man in Israel, a subject and neighbour, a pious friend of David's; he was also a prophet, a representative of God, and in that capacity a superior to David. When, then, the friendly visitor said, with an unrecordable tone and gesture, "Thou art the *man!*" it was evident to David (1) that his deed, long kept secret, was known to his most influential and incorruptible subject and friend; and (2) that God was speaking straight to his conscience. Even so far as related to Nathan as a good man in Israel, the revelation of his acquaintance with the deed was startling and astounding; but the most potent element in the utterance was the direct charge of God. A sinner cannot look on the Holy One—he dare not.   The conscience knows the awful voice of God, and, when that voice speaks straight to it, all thought of men and opinions vanishes, and the soul in its solemn individuality feels itself in the actual presence of the Eternal.   In true conviction the man "comes to himself."   The deed of evil is brought home.   In a light not of earth, self is seen to be undone, because the sin, hitherto professedly not a reality, is now forced on self as its own offspring.

II. THE AGGRAVATION OF SIN IS SET FORTH.   As soon as the charge is brought home, and before the paralyzed man can speak, the prophet, in the name of God, with swift words reminds him of his privileges and the manifold blessings and honours God had showered on him or was ready to grant if needed.   He was a chosen servant of the Eternal, called to perform a part in the working out of a great future for the world; he had filled a position of honour and influence; he had been charged with high and holy duties; he had been blessed with plenty, and more than ordinary provision for the necessary cravings of nature (vers. 7, 8).   Yet, "Thou art the *man!*"   None can doubt that here was sin of the most aggravated character.   No sin is excusable or free from Divine condemnation; otherwise it were not *sin*, but weakness or fault.   But some sins are worthy of being punished with "many stripes" because of being committed under special circumstances, *e.g.* the possession of religious light and feeling; the occupation of a position of power, and the being recipient of manifold tokens of Divine care and love.   But be the privileges many or few, when God brings home the guilt to the conscience, the sin is revealed in the light of past mercies.   The swift review of David's advantages by Nathan finds its analogue in the swift floating before the mind of the circumstances of one's position which render the sin so utterly inexcusable.   Men see in a few moments the reasons for their utter shame and self-abasement.   This is a feature in all true conviction, and tends to the proper prostration of the soul before God.   Saul of Tarsus knew this.   It is an unspeakable mercy that God does set our sins in the light of his great goodness.

III. THE HEART IS PROBED TO REVEAL THE CAUSE OF SIN.   "*Wherefore* hast thou despised the commandment of the Lord?" (ver. 9).   No sooner did the light flash on the conscience to set forth the aggravated character of the sin, than with unrelenting incisiveness the "wherefore" followed to probe those depths of the heart from whence the evil sprang.   The question really contains an inquiry and a statement.   Why?   "Thou didst *despise.*"   The eye of the sinner is turned in upon himself, to search out and behold those vile feelings and false principles out of which issued the preference of self-will over the holy will of God, which had been so clearly expressed in the Law of the Lord and in the special intimations of Providence.   "The heart is deceitful above all things, and desperately wicked: who can know it?"   The time of conviction is a time of probing and searching.   It is well for men under conviction to face the real facts, and get at the causes that lie out of sight.   There must be some dreadfully subtle evils lurking within to induce a man to "despise" the august majesty of God's will by setting it aside.   Was it not in reference to this probing, and probably in reference to this very deed, that the psalmist said, "Search me, O God" (Ps. cxxxix. 23; cf. li. 5, 6, 10)?

IV. THE PUNISHMENT OF SIN IS BROUGHT TO MIND.   The prophet ceases not; without giving the convicted man time to speak, he passes on to tell of the retribution that is sure to come by the will of God.   The man of whom Nathan once spoke such good things (ch. vii. 12—17) is now informed of coming trouble in life; that this trouble will be the same in kind with that of his sin—murder and adultery; that it will not be secret, as was his, in performance, but open, to his disgrace; that it will arise out of his own house, consequent in a measure on the mischief wrought by his own sin on his domestic life.   Had David not fallen, he would have been a different man, and consequently his private influence at home among his children would have been more holy and powerful; his relation to his kingdom would have been more satisfactory, and therefore moral and political circumstances would probably arise of so important a character as to have prevented the creation of the conditions out of which the troubles now recorded in his later history arose.   He was to reap according to his sowing.   In the conviction of sin, the recognition of personal guilt is the chief element, as we have seen (division I.); but just as here the messenger revealed the aggravation of the guilt, probed the heart for causes, and referred to coming retribution, so in the simple processes of mind attending true conviction there is an anticipation of punishment—an assurance that evil is coming on the soul as a consequence of sin done. Sin is transgression of law; law involves authority to vindicate its righteousness; and, as soon as the conviction of sin is real, the logic of conscience points to coming judgment. Whether it be a temporal judgment, as in Old Testament references, or eternal, as in New Testament references, the experience is virtually the same.

V. The confession of guilt is absolute. The guilty king sat in silence till the prophet had delivered his charge. The time was brief, but the power accompanying the words was Divine. Swifter than lightning the spell of hypocritical concealment was broken. The bonds in which the unholy passion had long held the soul were snapped asunder. The eye of conscience, turning in upon self, gave fresh life to the old suppressed loyalty to righteousness and God, and, as a consequence, the confession came, "I have sinned against the Lord." The question as to whether the historian here simply gives a summary of what passed, and intended to include also the fifty-first psalm, or whether literally this is all that was said and done, does not affect our purpose. There is here a *recognition* prompt, unqualified, *of sin*, not as a fault, a weakness, but of *sin* as known by conscience and stamped with the curse of God and man. It is also a recognition of sin as *against God*, not as a wrong done to Uriah, Bathsheba, or Israel, or his own family. The conscience is not indifferent to the injuries done to men, but when fully aroused, and face to face with *sin* as sin, it seems to see only God. Hence the expression in Ps. li. 4. Again, there is *pain and shame*, not because of what men may say or do, not because personal influence will now be weakened, but because it is *sin*. It is the *sin* which troubles and appals the truly convicted soul. Moreover, there is *abstention* from all *claim to consideration*; no excuse, no palliation. The convicted one can only say, "I have sinned." There is obviously an inward bowing of the spirit before the holy God; an absolute surrender as undone, condemned, helpless, lost. The very brevity of the confession bespeaks the depth of penitential woe. Contrast the wordy confession (1 Sam. xv. 17—25; cf. Luke xv. 18, 19; xviii. 13).

VI. Forgiveness is free, full, but qualified. How long Nathan stood by the prostrate silent king, and whether this confession was the literal whole or not, we do not know; but he saw enough to enable him to say in the name of God, "The Lord hath put away thy sin"—a statement clear and unreserved, intended to go home to the smitten heart. The forgiveness of sin has to do with a personal relation of God to man. It is the restoration of the personal relation of favour and fellowship which had been interrupted by sin. It is conditional on true repentance, the objective ground being the sacrificial death of Christ—under the Old Testament dispensation by anticipation (Rom. iii. 25), and under the New by retrospective reference. God is the sole Judge of the reality of repentance. He looketh at the heart. He knew that David's conviction had issued in the state of mind known as true repentance, and foreseeing this before it occurred, he commissioned the prophet to "declare and pronounce" to David, "being penitent," the remission of his sin. "Thy sins are forgiven thee!" Blessed words! How often brought to penitents since our Lord uttered them! But the pardon left untouched the natural consequences of sin referred to in vers. 19, 20, because a personal relation does not alter the course of the forces which a man sets in motion on earth by his sin. Also, the child born must die, not to its injury, but gain, yet in judgment, so that the father should not find comfort in the fruit of his sin, and in mercy, lest there should be a living memorial of his guilt and shame to which men might point and further blaspheme the Name of the Lord. The same holds good of our forgiveness; it is free, full, but qualified by the continuance of some ill consequences which chastise us all our days. The sinner never entirely gets rid of all the earthly effects of his sin while on earth; they work in his flow of thought and feeling, and often in the checks on his influence, and possibly on the character and health of others. The full redemption comes with the glorified body and the new heavens and earth.

General lessons. 1. The first thing to be sought in men in order to their salvation is a due recognition of themselves as sinners in the sight of God. A general recognition of the evil of sin as distinct from consciousness of personal guilt may really be a cover for unpardoned sin. 2. The tendency and drift of God's messages to men living in sin is to bring them to a right mind in reference to their personal position in his sight, as a preliminary to their seeking forgiveness. 3. Much will be found to depend, in respect to religious views and action, on the apprehension men have of what sin really is and their own guilt. A prepared state of mind is necessary to get good out of gospel state-ments. 4. The Christian religion especially lays stress on intense individuality in our relationships to God and to good and evil, and aims to bring us to a true self-knowledge. 5. It is an astonishing illustration of the tremendous power of our lower tendencies that they may even gain ascendency over men of most exalted privileges and whose very position would suggest superiority to them. 6. It behoves Christian people living in the enjoyment of many advantages to consider well their conduct in comparison with that of others less favoured. 7. The essence of sin abides in all times, though the form may vary; for as Adam preferred the suggestion of the evil one and so despised the word of the Lord, so did David; and on this method did Satan seek to win over Christ in the wilderness. 8. It is of extreme importance to remember that we may carry about with us deep-laid and subtle tendencies which may assert their power in an unguarded hour; and hence we should often probe our heart, and search and see by the help of God whether there be any evil way within us. 9. It should operate as a deterrent to know that our sins will entail unavoidable social and physical troubles as long as life lasts. 10. We are authorized in speaking to the truly penitent of the free and full forgiveness which God has in store for them, and which through his abounding grace they may have at once. 11. In the fuller sense of the words it may be declared to the penitent that they shall not die (John iii. 16). 12. The evil deeds of professors are a stumbling-block to other men, and give occasion to them to blaspheme, and as this must be a most bitter element in the life of the restored backslider, so it is a warn-ing to all Christians to take heed lest they fall, and so bring occasion for reproach on the Name which is above every name.

Vers. 15—31.—The facts are: 1. The child born to David becoming very sick, he entreats God for its life by prayer and fasting. 2. He persists in refusing the consola-tions which the elders of his household offer him. 3. The child dying on the seventh day, and David observing the whisperings of his servants, at once ascertains by direct inquiry the certainty of it. 4. His servants noticing that, on ascertaining the fact of the child's death, he lays aside the tokens of grief and resumes his wonted manner, are amazed at his conduct. 5. Whereupon he justifies his conduct, and intimates his expectation of some day going to the child. 6. Bathsheba is comforted by David, and bears to him another son, Solomon. 7. Joab, carrying on war against Rabbah of the Ammonites, and being about to bring the war to a conclusion, urges on David that he should come and enjoy the honour of taking the city. 8. David, complying with this request, takes possession of Rabbah, and acquires the king's crown with much spoil. 9. He completes his conquest of the Ammonites by causing some of them to endure great sufferings.

Providence and natural affection. The mercy of God to David was immediate, and it continued throughout his life; the judgment with which it was tempered was chiefly to come in days hence, but it began in the severe sickness of Bathsheba's child. It is not an unusual thing for a father to have to face the loss of an infant; in such cases natural affection will manifest itself in unmistakable forms. The extraordinary way in which David's feelings were excited by the apprehended death of this child is to be accounted for by reasons springing out of the peculiar circumstances of his position. These will appear as we proceed to consider the struggle between natural affection and the order of Providence.

I. THERE IS A CERTAIN REASONABLENESS IN THE PLEADING OF NATURAL AFFEC-TION AGAINST WHAT SEEMS TO BE THE ORDINATION OF GOD. The declaration of the prophet (ver. 14), that the child should die, was accepted by David as an ordination of God, and the severe sickness which came on soon after Nathan's departure was interpreted by the king as the first stage in the execution of it. But David was not conscious of a rebellious spirit in the exhibition of such distress, and in such earnest entreaty that the intended cause of providential judgment might be averted. Human affection is as much a part of the order of Nature as is the law of gravity, and its spontaneous action is as natural as is the falling of a weight to the earth. Affection is nothing if it does not feel. There is no law requiring it to be annihilated, if that were possible, in presence of the inevitable. To the pious Hebrew all changes in nature were brought about by God; they were the outcome of his will, as surely as would be the death of this child according to the word of the prophet. Divine ordinations were silent and spoken. Yet the silent ordinations in daily providence were modified by prayer and to meet new conditions; and why, then, might not this spoken one be modified at the entreaty of an agonized parent? As a father, he could not help thinking of this infant as a severe sufferer in being deprived of the blessing of life through no fault of its own. If spared, the child might be a perpetual memorial of befitting sorrow and shame, and so would help to keep him lowly and penitent. Nor could he but feel for the poor woman cruelly sinned against, and whose grief would be consequent on her husband's sin. Moreover, precedents were not wanting in the case of Abraham (Gen. xviii. 20—33) and of Moses (Exod. xxxii. 30—35), in which men pleaded against what seemed to be inevitable. Subsequent to David's time, we know that men were permitted to pray against the apparently inevitable (Joel ii. 12—14). Our Saviour gave utterance to human sensibility when he prayed that, if possible, the cup might pass from him. God has never expressed displeasure at the utterance of the sorrows which spring from natural affection, for feelings often struggle thus with the course of providence. Stoicism has no place in Christianity. The physical order is subordinate to the moral.

II. Intense feeling is reasonable where our sins have to do with the anticipated disaster. The intensity of David's anguish arose, not from the fact that he was a father, but from the knowledge he had that the providence that was bringing death to his child was connected with his own sin. That another should suffer for his sin, and this other a little child, was indeed a bitter reason for pleading with God. Although the course of providence, which connects the suffering of offspring with the sins of parents, is in the widest moral bearings of the fact, both just and merciful, yet it is not always seen to be so. Nevertheless, the great anguish of the evil-doer on that account is not a protest so much as a lament over his own sin, and a prayer that, if possible, this organic issue of sin may, by some intervention, be prevented or modified. The educational value of that feeling on the life of a repentant sinner is of great worth in itself, and really leads to the formation of a character that shall, in the order of providence, do much to lessen the evils that otherwise would arise.

III. The resort of natural affection when struggling against the order of providence is to God. A great change had recently come over David. The alienation of the backsliding heart was gone. As of old, so he now brings his sorrows and troubles to his God. The overwhelmed heart flies to the Rock that is high. He sits not with the scornful, mocking at the ways of Providence, and seeing evil where only there is mysterious judgment. The best and tenderest feelings of human nature, where sanctified by the spirit of piety, turn instinctively to God for help, and they find prayer as the form in which their yearnings are expressed. Some men fancy that they only see and feel the apparent severities of the providential order, and that sullen vexation and displeasure are the only appropriate conditions of mind in relation to it. Christians see and feel quite as much, but their bruised spirit finds refuge in him who ordains all in justice and mercy, and implores him, so far as may be wise and good, to let the penitent, entreating heart count for something among the elements which determine the ultimate issues.

IV. When the course of providence is found to be unalterable, natural affection is subordinated to the higher principle of acquiescence in the will of God. David was right in feeling as he did, in expressing his feeling in earnest prayer, in waiting as long as there was hope of reversal of the sentence. He acted as a father, as a husband, as a penitent. But when once the human desire and human view of wisdom and kindness were proved, by accomplished fact, not to be in accord with Divine wisdom, then, as became a trustful, restored child of God, David ceased to plead and to be in anguish. "Not my will, but thine be done!" was the spirit of his action. It was his duty and privilege now to rest in the Lord, and believe that he will bring to pass the kindest and wisest issue. The death of the child is accepted as the best thing, and the evils once supposed to issue from the event are now believed to be qualified by a love which maketh all things work together for good. It is the sign of an enlightened mind when a man can thus rise from his griefs, and conform his mental and moral and social life to the unalterable will of God. It takes time for a good man to recover from the natural, and, therefore, reasonable, outflow of his feelings; but when he does recover, he retains all the sanctity and softening influence of his anguish in combination with a calm spirit, concerned now in ministering to the consolation of others (ver. 24), and cheered by the hope of a time when the breaches caused by sin will be healed (ver. 23).

GENERAL LESSONS. 1. It becomes us to regard all death in our homes as connected with sin, and we should always give due weight to its moral causes in our consideration of the course of providence. 2. There may exist high moral reasons why intense earnestness in prayer is not always successful; and yet it may be true that God does answer fervent prayer. 3. Men not familiar with the secret life of a Christian are not in a position to understand his conduct on special occasions, just as David's servants could not understand his conduct in relation to the death of the child. 4. We should avail ourselves of such light concerning the future as may be vouchsafed, in order to obtain consolation amidst the bereavements of life (ver. 23). 5. The doctrine of recognition in heaven is certainly in accord with sanctified instincts, and may be held as variously hinted at in Scripture (ver. 23 ; cf. Matt. xvii. 3, 4; 1 Thess. ii. 19).

Tokens of restoration. In vers. 23, 24 we have two statements which incidentally reveal the reality and completeness of the restoration of the fallen king to the favour and care of God. (1) The name (Solomon) given by himself, probably at circumcision, to his son ; (2) the name (Jedidiah) which the prophet was instructed to give to the son, not as a substitute, but as a supplement. The one indicated David's sense of *peace* with God and in himself, the other God's abiding favour. Here, then, we may observe—

1. THAT RESTORATION TO GOD AFTER A FALL IS A REALITY. It is not a state rendered problematical by the observance of conditions extending over a long period. David *was* at peace with God, and God did regard him with unqualified favour. Old things had passed away—the displeasure of God, the fear and apprehension of the man ; the relation of complacent delight and tender care on the one side, and filial love and trust on the other, was now complete. It is important to keep this truth clear. It is bound up with the great doctrine of justification. God once accepting and forgiving a sinner becomes and remains to him a gracious God, forgetting all the past and cherishing only love and tender interest. It is a misreading of the gospel, and implies an ignorance of the most blessed Christian experience to imagine that a really forgiven one is kept in suspense and dread, or that God is holding back the fulness of his favour till we have repented a little more, or more fully perfected our general life. We are accepted in Christ. When he "restoreth" our "soul" (Ps. xxiii. 3), it is actual, not possible, germinal restoration.

II. THAT THE TOKENS OF RESTORATION VARY ACCORDING TO CIRCUMSTANCES. The inward token in David's case was the assured peace of a conscience purged by the grace of God (Ps. li. 7—10, 12), which came in answer to his penitential cry. The outward token was the life of another child, the peaceful order of the kingdom, and especially this welcome message of the prophet (ver. 25). The reality of restoration was known as soon as the almighty word of pardon was spoken, the confirmatory signs of it—to strengthen the heart and ward off subtle temptations of the evil one—came in process of time. No doubt fallen Peter found pardon during the dark night of his penitence ; but the outward token, which was also an instruction to the other disciples not to distrust and shun him, came in the gracious message of the angel of the Lord, "Tell his disciples, *and Peter*" (Mark xvi. 7), and again in the exhortation and encouragement given in the presence of those who might otherwise have distrusted him, "Feed my sheep" (John xxi. 15—17). The ordinary sign of full restoration is in the "witness of the Spirit" (Rom. viii. 14—16), and the outward care and blessing vouchsafed to our work of faith and labour of love (John xv. 7, 8). God will be sure to give his people some "token for good" (Ps. lxxxvi. 17).

III. THAT SIGNS OF GOD'S FAVOUR SHOULD BE GIVEN IS AN ILLUSTRATION OF HIS WONDERFUL CONSIDERATION FOR HIS PEOPLE. There is something truly wonderful in this grace shown to David. Not only is he forgiven and treated in all things spiritual as though he had not sinned ; not only permitted to reign over Israel, and enter into close, though it may be very subdued, fellowship with God ; but God goes, as it were, out of the ordinary course of providence, and sends a messenger to give him, in this other name for his child, a special sign of full restoration. Thus the occasional doubts suggested by the evil one, the possible distrust of the prophet in Israel and those under him, and the sneers of the profane, are all anticipated by the love that slumbers not and that cares most tenderly and minutely for all the need of the reconciled ones. " How excellent is thy loving-kindness, O God!" (Ps. xxxvi. 7); " He is rich in mercy, and plenteous in redemption."

Rabbah's lesson to mankind. The fall of David occurred while the war was going on under Joab (ch. xi. 1, 7, 25). It is probable that, as the historian began to tell the story of the fall, he thought well to finish it, with the account of the restoration, before he took up again the account of the campaign being carried on against the Ammonites. We shall assume, therefore, that the fall of Rabbah referred to in vers. 26—31 took place in the interval between the sin of David and the birth of Solomon (ver. 24). The narrative is inserted here doubtless with the primary design of completing the history of David's wars, and thus keeping up the continuity of his exploits. But as all Scripture is written for our learning, we may notice a few incidental lessons suggested by the capture of the city of Rabbah.

I. A GOOD MAN'S FALL INTO SIN UNFITS HIM FOR MANY OF THE DUTIES OF HIS DAILY LIFE. Joab was not only left to carry on the war alone, but he even felt it to be right (ver. 28) to stir up the king that he might come and take part, and so share in the honour about to be won. The secret of this most probably lay in the fact that, during and after David's entanglement with Bathsheba and crime against Uriah, he was not in a mind to enter upon the perils of war. A woman's spell was on him; his conscience was secretly troubled; he who feared not the lion or the giant now fears lest, if he go to the war, he should be slain. Therefore he tarries in Jerusalem (ch. xi. 1—25). His sins rendered him incompetent to do what otherwise he would have done, and it required even an urgent request from his general, coupled with an assurance that the city was virtually captured already (vers. 27—29), to induce him to move. There are sins which sometimes drive men to desperate deeds and perilous places, and give apparently more zest to life; but in the case of good men, a known habit of sin impairs their energy in life; it creates an abiding fear; it paralyzes certain incumbent moral actions; it keeps from entering on work which otherwise would be cheerfully undertaken; it makes him less a man.

II. THOSE WHO DO DELIBERATE DEEDS OF WRONG TO OTHERS COURT·AN INFLICTION ON THEMSELVES OF SIMILAR EVILS. This account of the infliction of tortures on the Ammonites (ver. 31) is the first instance in Hebrew history of such a deed, and it seems strange that David should have ordered it. But without justifying the retaliation, the point here to be noted is that the Ammonites laid themselves open to such treatment by their own actions. They had proposed barbarous conditions of servitude to men of Israel in the time of trouble (1 Sam. xi. 1, 2), and they had cruelly insulted David's ambassadors (ch. x. 1—6). It is also probable that in this protracted war they may have carried out these barbarous tendencies towards prisoners taken in war. They thus, by deeds of cruelty, sought for deeds of cruelty to themselves in their day of defeat. There is doubtless a principle of retaliation in kind recognizable in the law of nature. As a man soweth so he reapeth. What they do to others they so far justify others to do to them, that they have set an example and are incapable of protest. In some guarded form this principle enters into human law, national and international. In the Mosaic code it received specific illustration (Exod. xxi. 22—25). Whether David was right or wrong, the Ammonites courted torture by evil deeds, as men now court evil from their imperfect fellow-men by evil deeds to them. The harsh employer courts distrust and injury from the *employés.* Tyrannical rulers court plots, conspiracies, and possibly assassinations, from oppressed subjects.

III. THERE ARE PROPHETIC SYMBOLS OF HONOUR FALLING ON THE RIGHT HEAD. It was, perhaps, on the part of Joab and the army, a mere feat of military triumph to place the heavy crown of the Ammonite god (for so we take it to be) on the head of David; but it was suggestive at the time to all spectators of the honours that ought to come, and in course of years were coming, on One who was the Anointed of the Lord. And to us it seems to suggest the ultimate passing of all highest honours, long usurped, to him whose right it is to reign, and who is not only said to be worthy of all honours

(Rev. iv. 11; v. 12, 13), but is so gradually acquiring them that he at last shall be crowned with many crowns (Heb. ii. 9; Rev. iv. 10; xix. 12). In the triumph of every good man over evil, we see a symbolic intimation of the final triumph of the Son of man over all enemies (1 Cor. xv. 25). In the distinction awarded to any of Christ's servants, who are really his representatives in the world, because of the destruction of some monstrous evil, we have a symbolic representation of the glory and honour that will come on the head of the great Deliverer, when to him every knee shall bow, and the last enemy shall have been destroyed. Faith can see coming victories in passing events.

IV. THE EDUCATION OF THE CONSCIENCE IN HUMAN RELATIONS IS VERY SLOW. The principle of retaliation is in all legal punishments (division I.), but the application of the principle is a matter of judgment, and the judgment depends on the culture of the conscience. There are co-ordinate powers in human nature. The feeling of benevolence has a place as truly as a sense of justice. It depends on the degree in which conscience is cultivated as to whether the rigid carrying out of what justice may seem to demand, *i.e.* the spirit of retaliation in the name of love, not of self, should be tempered by kindly consideration, and to what extent. Probably David at this time was in the degenerate mood of mind brought on by his fall, and therefore restive and harsh, as men are when the heart is corroded by guilt. But at all events, in those times there was not that fine sense of delicacy in regard to human suffering as now. The same mental and moral condition prevailed during the ages of persecution for religion. Romanists and Protestants did once what now their descendants would be shocked at. It is a defective education of conscience which enables men to live in careless ease and luxury while thousands are lacking food. Christ only was perfect Man. If all were like him, every consideration would be paid to human feeling in the administration of justice, and in the private relations of life.

HOMILIES BY VARIOUS AUTHORS.

Ver. 1.—(JERUSALEM.) *A faithful reprover of sin.* "And Jehovah sent Nathan to David." The sin of David could not be hid. It was known to his servants (ch. xi. 4) and to Joab; it must have been surmised by many from his hasty marriage; and now it was fully manifest (ch. xi. 27). About a year had elapsed. "What a year for David to have spent! What a joyless, sunless, godless year! Were God's words still sweet to his taste? Were they still the rejoicing of his heart? or had he come to hate the threatening of the Law?" (J. Wright). At length Nathan (ch. vii. 3) came—an example of a faithful reprover (Ps. cxli. 5; Prov. xxvii. 6; 1 Sam. i. 13; ii. 22). Consider—

I. His DIVINE COMMISSION. He came, not because he was sent for by David, nor because he was prompted by natural reason or impulse (ch. vii. 3), but in obedience to the word of the Lord (ver. 7), and in fulfilment of his prophetic calling. "It was the true mission of the prophets, as champions of the oppressed in the courts of kings; it was the true prophetic spirit that spoke through Nathan's mouth" (Stanley). 1. Reproof should be administered *only according to the will of God.* It is not for every one to assume the office of reprover (Ps. l. 16); nor to administer reproof to every one who may deserve it, especially when holding a position of authority. In this matter men are apt to run before they are sent. The duty is a relative one, and demands careful consideration before it is undertaken. 2. The will of God concerning the administration of reproof is *indicated in various ways;* such as the authority given to parents, magistrates, pastors, and teachers—"reprove, rebuke," etc. (2 Tim. iv. 2; v. 1); the teachings of the Divine Word; the guidance of the Divine Spirit. 3. When the will of God is clearly made known, it should be humbly, readily, and diligently *obeyed;* both when it requires his servants to testify his favour (ch. vii. 4, 25) and his displeasure (ch. xi. 27).

II. His CONSUMMATE WISDOM. In nothing are wisdom and prudence more needed than in reproof. If given unwisely it is likely to excite opposition, produce equivocation, repel and harden. "A word fitly spoken," etc. (Prov. xxv. 11, 12). It should be given: 1. At a proper *time*—when the proof of wrong-doing admits of no denial, and the mind of the wrong-doer is duly prepared. It is not probable that Nathan came immediately after he first heard of David's transgression. "His task was not to gain a confession, but only to facilitate it. He was appointed by God to await the time of the internal crisis of David" (Hengstenberg). 2. When the offender is *alone* (Matt. xviii. 15), and is likely to pay greater heed to it and to be less influenced by what others think. Sometimes, however, sinners must be "rebuked before all, that others also may fear" (1 Tim. v. 20). 3. In a *manner* adapted to produce the most salutary effect; with harmless wisdom (Matt. x. 16) and holy and beneficent "guile" (2 Cor. xii. 16) displayed in; (1) A respectful, courteous, and conciliatory bearing. To begin with rude reproaches is to ensure failure. (2) An ingenious invention of a "form of speech" (ch. xiv. 20) and illustration suitable to the case. (3) A generous recognition of the better qualities in men. "David's goodness is not denied because of his sin, nor is David's sin denied because of his goodness." (4) A clear statement of the truth, avoiding exaggeration and everything that may hinder its illuminating force. (5) A strong appeal to the conscience, so as to quicken its action as a witness and judge. (6) A dexterous application of admitted principles and expressed judgments and emotions. (7) An effectual removal of the mists of self-deception, so as to enable the evil-doer to see his actual character and conduct, and constrain him to reprove and condemn himself. The wisdom of the prophet in fulfilling his mission to the king was "inimitably admirable." "Observing that this direct road (the recommendation of self-knowledge) which led to it (the reformation of mankind) was guarded on all sides by self-love, and consequently very difficult to open access, public instructors soon found out that a different and more artful course was requisite. As they had not strength to remove this flattering passion which stood in their way and blocked up the passages to the heart, they endeavoured by stratagem to get beyond it, and, by a skilful address, if possible to deceive it. This gave rise to the only manner of conveying their instructions in parables, fables, and such sort of indirect applications; which, though they could not conquer this principle of self-love, yet often laid it asleep, or at least overreached it for a few moments, till a just judgment could be procured. The Prophet Nathan seems to have been a great master in this art of address" (Laurence Sterne).

III. HIS HOLY COURAGE. His mission was as perilous as it was painful; and might, if it failed, have cost him his life. But he feared not "the wrath of the king" (Prov. xvi. 14; xix. 12; Heb. xi. 27). Such moral courage as he exhibited: 1. Is inspired by *faith in God*, whose face it beholds, and on whose might it relies. 2. Consists in the *fearless fulfilment of duty*, whatever consequences it may involve—the loss of friendship or other earthly good; the endurance of bonds, suffering, and death. "None of these things move me," etc. (Acts xx. 24). 3. Appears in simple, bold, direct, and unreserved *utterance* of God's Word (Ezek. xxxiii. 7). At the proper moment the prophet changed his style of address; gave it a particular application, "the very life of doctrine;" and, in the name of the supreme King and Judge, arraigned the offender, declared his guilt, and pronounced his sentence. "His example is especially to be noted by all whose office is to 'rebuke with all authority'" ('Speaker's Commentary').

IV. HIS BENEVOLENT AIM. He came not only to testify against sin, to maintain the authority of the Law, etc.; but also (in connection therewith) to benefit the sinner, by: 1. Leading him to repentance. 2. Assuring him of forgiveness. 3. Restoring him to righteousness, peace, and joy (ver. 13; Ps. li. 12). "Reproofs of instruction are the way of life" (Prov. vi. 23; xiii. 18; xvii. 10). Sympathy with the holy love of God toward sinners is an essential qualification of a faithful reprover of sin; and as it is God's mercy that employs agents and means for their restoration, so it is his grace alone that makes them effectual (John xvi. 8).

> "And so wide arms
> Hath goodness infinite, that it receives
> All who turn to it."
>
> (Dante.)

D.

Vers. 1—4.—(THE KING'S PALACE.) *The parable of the rich oppressor; or, the poor man's lamb.* 1. This is the first and almost the only *parable* contained in the Old Testament. There is one instance of a *fable* of earlier date (Judg. ix. 8—15). The former belongs to a higher order of teaching than the latter (Smith's 'Dict. of the Bible,' art. "Fable;" Trench, 'Notes on the Parables'); and it was employed most perfectly by the great Teacher. Compare his parables of the unmerciful servant, the rich fool, the rich man and Lazarus. 2. It was in part an *acted* parable (like ch. xiv. 5—7; 1 Kings xx. 35—43); and was at first regarded by the king as the simple, literal statement of a case in which one of his subjects, a poor man, had suffered wrong at the hands of another, a rich man; and with reference to which the prophet appeared as an advocate on behalf of the former against the latter, seeking justice and judgment. "Nathan, it is likely, used to come to him on such errands, which made this the less suspected. It becomes those who have interest in princes and free access to them to intercede for those that are wronged, that they may have right done them" (Matthew Henry). 3. Its moral and spiritual *aim* (which is always the chief thing to be considered in the interpretation of a parable) was to set forth *the guilt of a rich oppressor,* and thereby to awaken the general sense of outraged justice in the king concerning his own conduct. 4. "It is one of those little gems of Divinity that are scattered so plentifully through the sacred Scriptures, that sparkle with a lustre, pure and brilliant as the light of heaven, and attest the sacred origin of the wonderful book that contains them" (Blaikie). Consider the guilt of this rich man in the light of—

I. HIS POSITION compared with that of the poor man, and his relation to him. "There were two men in one city," etc. (vers. 1—3). 1. He had much possessions, "exceeding many flocks and herds." Providence had been very kind to him. He had abundance for personal gratification and princely hospitality and liberality. But the poor man had nothing "save one little ewe lamb," which he valued all the more on that account, and reared amidst his family with the utmost care and tenderness. 2. He had great power, which he might use for good or evil; in fulfilment of the Law or in frustration of it; to protect and benefit "the poor and needy" or to oppress and rob them. 3. He dwelt in the same city with the poor man, and was well acquainted with his circumstances. He knew the story of the little lamb. The picture is exquisitely drawn by one who was familiar with many such scenes in humble life, and adapted to excite sympathy and pity. The obligations of the rich man toward his "neighbour" are manifest; and they shadow forth the greater obligations of others in a still higher position (vers. 7, 8). Although the king had well-nigh absolute power over the property and lives of his subjects, it belonged to the true idea of his office to "reign, command, and punish, as though it were not he that reigned, commanded, and punished, but the One to whom he never ceases to be responsible, and as though he might himself be in the position of any other member of the community and the latter in his own" (Ewald, 'Antiquities').

II. HIS DISPOSITION. "And there came a traveller," etc. (ver. 4). "The Jewish doctors say, it represents that which they call 'the evil disposition,' or desire that is in us, which must be diligently watched and observed when we feel its motions. 'In the beginning it is but a traveller, but in time it becomes a guest, and in conclusion is the master of the house'" (Patrick). This is pressing the imagery of the parable too far. Nevertheless, "the sin is traced to its root, viz. insatiable *covetousness;* this hidden background of all sins" (Keil); sinful, selfish, inordinate *desire* (ch. xi. 1—5). It is a "root of bitterness." And in the case supposed what evils it involved! 1. Discontentment with a man's own possessions, notwithstanding their abundance. "Nature is content with little, grace with less, sin with nothing." 2. Ingratitude toward the Giver of them. 3. Envy of another man on account of some imaginary advantage he possesses, notwithstanding its comparative insignificance —"One little ewe lamb." 4. Avarice. 5. Voluptuousness. 6. Pride in the possession of power; and its irresponsible exercise. There was no sense of personal accountability to God. 7. Vanity or love of display, though at the expense of another; an undue regard for outward appearance. 8. Deceitfulness. Did the guest who enjoyed the rich man's hospitality dream at whose cost it was provided? 9. Pitilessness and obduracy. "Because he had *no pity*" (ver. 6). 10. Idolatry (Col. iii. 5). It is only when sin is viewed in the light of the spirituality of the commandment, that its "exceeding sinfulness" becomes manifest (Rom. vii. 13). "Covetousness is a subtle sin, a dangerous sin, a mother sin, a radical vice, a breach of all the ten commandments" (T. Watson).

III. HIS CONDUCT. "And he spared to take of his own flock," etc. It was: 1. Unjust. 2. Tyrannical. 3. Cruel; "a wanton aggravation of the evils of poverty, humbling the poor man with a sense of injustice and inability to protect himself, deriving a momentary gratification from seeing his neighbour laid low at his feet, as if no lamb was so savoury as that which had been torn from the poor man's bosom amidst the tears of his children." 4. Lawless and reckless; "a despising of the commandment of the Lord" (ver 9). The poor man's complaint is unheard. But is there not in Israel a just God, who notices and punishes such acts as these? "It was a cruel and wicked deed. It was! Who says so? Speak not hastily, lest in so speaking you condemn yourself. This is a parable; and I would have you consider whether under another name it is not spoken concerning you. Reserve your rebuke, lest it come back upon yourself" (R. Halley).—D.

Vers. 5, 6.—(JERUSALEM.) *The blinding influence of sin.* "David's anger was greatly kindled against the man;" he declared with a solemn oath (ch. iv. 9—11) that he deserved to die (literally, "was a son of death," 1 Sam. xxvi. 16; 1 Kings ii. 26), and ordered restitution according to the Law (Exod. xxii. 1). His severity displayed the fiery temper of the man, and the arbitrary power of the monarch, rather than the calm deliberation of the judge; and (like the treatment of the Ammonites, ver. 31) indicated a mind ill at ease (ch. xi. 22—27; Ps. xxxii. 3, 4); for he was not *totally* blind to his sin, nor "past feeling" (Eph. iv. 19); though he had no thought of the application of the case to himself. We have here an illustration of—

I. AN ASTONISHING FACT; viz. the self-ignorance, self-deception, internal hypocrisy, of men. Nothing is more important than self-knowledge. It is often enjoined. "From heaven came the precept, 'Know thyself.'" And it might naturally appear to be easily attained, seeing that it lies so near home. Yet how certain, how common, and how surprising its absence! "There is not anything relating to men's characters more surprising and unaccountable than this partiality to themselves which is observable in many; as there is nothing of more melancholy reflection respecting morality and religion" (Butler, 'Upon Self-Deceit'). They are blind (at least *partially*) and deceived as to their sin; notwithstanding: 1. Their perception of the evil of sin in general or in the *abstract.* Ingratitude, selfishness, oppression, pitilessness; who is not ready to denounce these vices? 2. Their sinfulness in the sight of other people. Although David had sought to conceal his sin from others, perhaps still flattered himself that it was known only to a few, and justified or palliated its guilt to himself, many others besides Nathan saw and abhorred it (Ps. xxxvi. 2).

> "O wad some power the giftie gie us
> To see oursels as others see us!
> It wad frae monie a blunder free us,
> And foolish notion."

3. Their condemnation of sin in others, of the very same kind as that which they tolerate in themselves. The resemblance between the rich oppressor and David was so close that it is astonishing it was not detected. 4. Their abhorrence at another time and under other circumstances of its guilt when thought of in relation to themselves (1 Sam. xxiv. 5). "What! is thy servant a dog, that he should do this great thing?" (2 Kings viii. 13). "Yet the dog did it" (Matthew Henry). "Next to these instances of self-deceit of our true disposition and character, which appear in not seeing *that* in ourselves which shocks us in another man, there is another species still more dangerous and delusive, and which the more guarded perpetually fall into, from the judgments they make of different vices according to their age and complexion, and the various ebbs and flows of their passions and desires" (L. Sterne, 'Self-Knowledge'). 5. Their culpability beyond that of those whom they condemn. It was not a little lamb of which he had robbed the poor man, but his dearly loved wife, his one earthly treasure. It was not a lamb that he had killed, but a man, his neighbour and faithful defender. His superior position and possessions aggravated his guilt. Was he not himself "a son of death'"? "What a sad proof of the blinding influence of self-love, that men are ready to form so different an estimate of their conduct when it is not seen to be their own! How ignorant are we of ourselves, and how true it is that even when our own hearts

condemn us, God is greater than our hearts, and knoweth all things!" (Blaikie). For this fact let us seek—

II. AN ADEQUATE CAUSE. It is seldom due to insufficiency of light or means of knowing sin. Is it, then, due to men's inconsideration of themselves? or to the perversion of their moral judgment? Doubtless to both; but still more to *sin itself*, which is essentially selfishness—a false and inordinate love of self. "For consider: nothing is more manifest than that affection and passion of all kinds influence the judgment" (Butler); prejudicing its decisions in their own favour. Even when there is more than a suspicion that all is not well, it stifles further inquiry and prevents full conviction by: 1. Producing a general persuasion in men that their moral condition is better than it really is. 2. Directing exclusive attention to those dispositions and actions of which conscience can approve. 3. Inducing unwillingness to consider the opposite, and to know the worst of themselves. The glimpse of the truth which they perceive is painful, and (as in the case of diseased vision) it causes them to shut their eyes against perceiving the whole truth (John iii. 20). 4. Inventing specious arguments in justification of the course to which they are disposed. 5. Dwelling upon supposed compensations for injury done or guilt incurred. Self-love is wondrously fertile in devising such excuses and palliatives. David may have thought that the standard by which others were judged was not applicable to him. "Perhaps, as power is intoxicating, he conceived of himself as not subjected to the ordinary rules of society. In sending an order to his general to put Uriah 'in the hottest of the battle,' he probably found a palliative for his conscience; for what was it but to give to a brave soldier a post of honour? No doubt the victim considered himself honoured by the appointment, while it gave occasion to the king to solace himself with the thought that it was an enemy and not he who put an end to the life of his subject" (W. White). His marrying Bathsheba, also, he may have supposed, made amends for the wrong he had done to her. But the means which he adopted to conceal his sin from others, and deemed a palliative of his guilt, were a special aggravation of it (vers. 9, 10).

OBSERVATIONS. 1. Nothing is more ruinous than self-deception (Heb. iii. 13; Jas. i. 12; 1 John i. 8). 2. To avoid it there must be honest self-examination (Ps. iv. 4; 2 Cor. xiii. 5). 3. We should especially guard against the blinding influence of undue self-love (Ps. xix. 12; Jer. xvii. 9). 4. There should also be earnest prayer to him who searcheth the hearts, for true self-knowledge (Ps. cxxxix. 23; Job xiii. 23; xxxiv. 32).—D.

Vers. 7—10.—(THE PALACE.) "*Thou art the man!*" The proper purpose of reproof is *conviction of sin*. This purpose was accomplished by the words of the prophet. They were like a "two-edged sword" (Heb. iv. 12), the point of which was, "Thou art the man!" "If ever a word from human lips fell with crushing weight and with the illuminating power of a gleam of lightning, it was this" (Krummacher). "His indignation against the rich man of the parable showed that the moral sense was not wholly extinguished. The instant recollection of guilt breaks up the illusion of months" (Stanley). Observe that: 1. One of the most effectual means of convincing a man of sin is by setting it before him *as existing in another person*. "Thou art *the man!*" the story of whose crime has stirred thine indignation and called forth the sentence of death from thy lips. Self-interest, passion, and prejudice, that darken a man's view of his own sin, have comparatively little influence upon him when looking at the sin of another. Here the veil is removed; he sees clearly and judges impartially. For this reason (among others) our Lord "spake many things unto them in parables." 2. The force of truth depends upon the *particular application* which is made of it. "*Thou* art the man who hast done this!" (LXX.); against thyself thine indignation should be directed; upon thyself the sentence has been pronounced. It is as if hitherto only the back of the offender was seen, when, suddenly turning round, his face appeared, and David beheld *himself!* "Men often correctly understand a message of God without observing its personal application to them." Hence the preacher, like the prophet of old (1 Kings xiv. 7; xviii. 18; xxi. 19; 2 Kings v. 26; Dan. v. 22; Matt. xiv. 4), must directly, wisely, and faithfully apply the truth to his hearers. "'Thou art the man!' is or ought to be the conclusion, expressed or unexpressed, of every practical sermon." What is a sword without a point? "Here also is a lesson to hearers. David listened to a sermon from Nathan, which exactly suited his own case, and yet he did not *apply it to himself*. He turned the edge of it from himself to another. The benefit of sermons depends more upon the hearer than the preacher. The best sermon is that which is *best applied* by those to whom it is preached " (Wordsworth). " Application is the life of preaching; and self-application is the life of hearing." "They profit most, not who hear most, but who apply most what they hear to their own hearts." 3. Every man is *responsible to God* for the sin which he has committed. " Thou art inexcusable, O man " (Rom. ii. 1), however thou mayest have persuaded thyself to the contrary. Is the man whom thou judgest accountable for his conduct; and art not thou for thine? Is he accountable to thee? How much more art thou to God? No position, however exalted, can release from responsibility to him or exempt from obedience to his commandment; no constitutional tendency, no temptation, expediency, or necessity be an adequate reason for despising it (Ezek. xviii. 4; Rom. iii. 6).

> " And self to take or leave is *free*,
> Feeling its own sufficiency :
> In spite of science, spite of fate,
> The judge within thee, soon or late,
> Will blame but thee, O man !

> " Say not, 'I would, but *could not*. He
> Should bear the blame who fashioned me.
> Call a mere change of motive choice?'
> Scorning such pleas, the inner voice
> Cries, 'Thine the deed, O man !'"

> (J. A. Symonds.)

4. A *messenger of Heaven* is always in readiness to single out the sinner, bring his sin to remembrance, and call him to account. "Thus saith the Lord God of Israel," etc. (ver. 7), "Wherefore hast thou despised the commandment of the Lord, to do evil in his sight?" etc. (ver. 9). Every wrong done to man, yea, every sin, is a factual contempt of his commandment (Ps. li. 4). Whilst the supreme King and Judge observes it, and is long-suffering towards the doer of it, he provides many witnesses, holds them in reserve, and sends them with his word at the proper moment to declare all its enormity—its ingratitude (ver. 8), presumption (ver. 9), disloyalty before him, its "intense and brutal selfishness," sensuality, cruelty, and craft. Conscience also awakes to confirm their testimony, with " a thousand several tongues, and every tongue " crying, " Thou art the man ! " 5. The *less expected the charge* preferred against the sinner, the more overwhelming his conviction of guilt. "The further David was from thinking of a reference to himself, the greater the force with which the word must have struck him " (Erdmann). There could be no defence, no extenuation, no answer (Acts xxiv. 25 ; Matt. xxii. 12). 6. The *condemnation* which one man pronounces on another sometimes recoils upon himself with increased severity. "Out of thine own mouth," etc. (Luke xix. 22). " Now therefore the sword shall never depart from thine house," etc. " For a single moment the features of the king are charged with the expression of astonishment. He gazes eagerly at the prophet like one at a loss to divine his meaning. But, almost instantly, as if an inward light had burst upon his soul, the expression changes to one of agony and horror. The deeds of the last twelve months glare in all their infamous baseness upon him, and outraged justice, with a hundred glittering swords, seems all impatient to devour him " (Blaikie). " O wicked man, thou shalt surely die ! " (Ezek. xxxiii. 8). 7. The conviction of sin is the first step in the way of *restoration* to righteousness. The sense of sin is the beginning of salvation. " He that humbleth himself," etc. (Luke xiv. 11 ; 1 John i. 9). " If we would judge ourselves," etc. (1 Cor. xi. 31, 32). Every man must be revealed to himself in the light of God's righteous judgment here or hereafter (Eccles. xi. 9; xii. 14).—D.

Vers. 10—12.—(THE PALACE.) *The penalties of sin.* "Now therefore the sword shall never depart from thine house," etc. 1. Sin is *connected with* suffering. The connection is real, intimate, inevitable. Nothing is more clearly manifest or more generally admitted; yet nothing is more practically disregarded. Men commit sin under the delusion that they can do so with impunity. But " they that plough iniquity, and sow wickedness, reap the same" (Job iv. 8; Gal. vi. 7). 2. Sin serves to *account for* suffering; explains and justifies its existence under the righteous and beneficent government of God. The subsequent sufferings of David would have been inexplicable if his great transgression had not been recorded. "The remainder of David's life was as disastrous as the beginning had been prosperous" (Hale). Personal suffering, however, often appears disproportionate to personal transgression (1 Sam. iv. 3); and its reason in such cases must be sought in hereditary or other relationships, and in the purposes to which it is subservient. The penalties of sin (such as David suffered) take place—

I. BY DIVINE INFLICTION. "Behold, I will raise up evil against thee," etc. (ver. 11; ch. ix. 27). They are: 1. Necessitated by the *justice* of God. "Justice is that causality in God which connects suffering with actual sin" (Schleiermacher). He who "despises the commandment of the Lord" *ought* to be punished. 2. Declared by the *Word* of God, both in the Law and the prophets. The word of Nathan was a sentence, as well as a prediction of judgment. 3. Effectuated by the *power* of God, which operates, not only by extraordinary agencies, but also, and most commonly, in the ordinary course of things, and by way of natural consequence; directs and controls the actions of men to the accomplishment of special results; and often makes use of the sins of one man to punish those of another. Natural law is the regular method of Divine activity. In accordance therewith the violation of moral law is followed by internal misery and external calamity, which are closely associated (Isa. xlv. 7; Amos iii. 4). "Vengeance is mine," etc.

II. WITH SIGNIFICANT SEVERITY; which appears in: 1. The *peculiarity* of their form. Not only do they follow sin by way of natural consequence, but also the manner of their infliction corresponds with that of its commission; as that which is reaped resembles that which is sown (1 Sam. iv. 1—11). "The seeds of our own punishment are sown at the same time we commit sin" (Hesiod). Having sinned with the sword, his house would be ravaged with the sword; and having sinned by the indulgence of impure passion, he would be troubled in like manner. "Amnon, Absalom, Adonijah! Amnon thought, 'Has my father indulged in it?—Absalom relied on the resentment of the people on account of the double crime. Adonijah fell because he wished to make the best of the precedence of his birth in opposition to him who had been begotten with Bathsheba" (Thenius).

> "The gods are just, and of our pleasant vices
> Make instruments to plague us."

There is a tendency in the sin of one to perpetuate itself in others over whom his influence extends, and so to recoil upon himself. 2. The *publicity* of their exhibition. "For thou didst it secretly," etc. (ver. 12). Falsehood and injustice seek darkness; truth and justice seek light. The evil, which is concealed for the sake of public honour, is followed by public shame. 3. The *extent* and *perpetuity* of their infliction. "The sword shall never depart from thine house." "The fortunes of David turned upon this one sin, which, according to Scripture, itself eclipsed every other" (Blunt). "One sin led to another; the bitter spring of sin grew in time to a river of destruction that flowed over the whole land, and even endangered his throne and life" (Baumgarten). Who can tell the far-reaching effects of one transgression (Eccles. ix. 18)?

III. FOR MANIFOLD PURPOSES. 1. To manifest the justice of God and uphold the authority of his Law. 2. To exhibit the evil of sin, and deter the sinner himself and others from its commission. 3. To humble, prove, chastise, instruct, purify, and confirm the sufferer. "If he commit iniquity, I will chasten him," etc. (ch. vii. 14; Deut. viii. 3, 5; Job v. 17; Ps. xciv. 12; Heb. xii. 6). This last effect is wrought only on those who turn to God in penitence and trust. The forgiveness of sin and restoration to righteousness do not counteract, except in a limited degree, the natural consequences of past transgression; but they transform punishment into chastisement, and alleviate the pressure of suffering and sorrow by Divine fellowship, and the inward peace, strength, and hope which it imparts. "In general the forgiveness of sin has only this result—punishment is changed into fatherly chastisement, the rod into the correction of love. Outwardly the consequences of sin remain the same; their internal character is changed. If it were otherwise, the forgiveness of sins might too readily be attributed to caprice" (Hengstenberg). "The personal forgiveness indulged to the King of Israel, in consideration of his penitence, did not break the connection between causes and their effects. This connection is stamped on the unchanging laws of God in nature; and it becomes every man, instead of arraigning the appointment, to bring support to his domestic happiness by the instrumentality of a good example" (W. White). His family, his kingdom, and even his own character, were permanently affected by his sin. "Broken in spirit by the consciousness of how deeply he had sinned against God and against men; humbled in the eyes of his subjects, and his influence with them weakened by the knowledge of his crimes; and even his authority in his own household, and his claim to the reverence of his sons, relaxed by the loss of character; David appears henceforth a much-altered man. He is as one who goes down to the grave mourning. His active history is past—henceforth he is passive merely. All that was high and firm and noble in his character goes out of view, and all that is weak and low and wayward comes out in strong relief. The balance of his character is broken. Alas for him! The bird which once rose to heights unattained before by mortal wing, filling the air with its joyful songs, now lies with maimed wing upon the ground, pouring forth its doleful cries to God" (Kitto, 'Daily Bible Illust.').—D.

Ver. 13.—(THE PALACE.) *The acknowledgment of sin.* "And David said unto Nathan, I have sinned against the Lord." 1. The words of the prophet were a decisive *test* of the character of David. Had he treated the messenger and his message as others have done (1 Sam. xv. 12—21; 1 Kings xiii. 4; xxi. 20; xxii. 8; Jer. xxxvi. 23; Luke iii. 10; Acts xxiv. 25), his partial blindness to his sin would have become total, and he would have fallen to a still lower depth, perhaps never to rise again. But his genuine piety, as well as the exceeding grace of God (ch. vii. 15), ensured a better issue; and the confidence in his recovery, which Nathan probably felt in coming to him, was fully justified. 2. Hardly was the sentence pronounced, "Thou art the man!" before the long-repressed *confession* broke from his lips (1 Sam. vii. 6; xv. 24—31), "*I* am the man! Who says this of me? Yet—God knows all—yes, I *am* the man. I have sinned against the Lord."

> "Never so fast, in silent April shower,
>   Flushed into green the dry and leafless bower,
>   As Israel's crowned mourner felt
>   The dull hard stone within him melt"
>
>   (Keble.)

The ruling principle of his nature was like a spring of water which, though choked and buried beneath a heap of rubbish, at length finds its way again to the surface. "The fundamental trait in David's character is a deep and tender susceptibility, which, although even for a time it may yield to lust or the pressure of the world, yet always quickly rises again in repentance and faith" ('Old Test. Hist. of Redemption'). "If in this matter Nathan shows himself great, David is no less so. The cutting truth of the prophetic word shakes him out of the hollow passion in which he has lived since first he saw this woman, and rouses him again to the consciousness of his better self. His greatness, however, is shown in the fact that, king as he was, he soon humbled himself, like the lowliest, before the higher truth; and, although his penitence was as deep and sincere as possible, it did not cause him either to lose his dignity or to forget his royal duties" (Ewald). 3. There is no part of his life for the proper under-standing of which it is so necessary to read the history in connection with what he himself has written—"the songs of sore repentance," which he "sang in sorrowful mood" (Dante). Ps. li. (see inscription), 'The prayer of the penitent;' the germ of which lay in this confession, but which was composed after the utterance of the word, "The Lord also hath put away thy sin;" for "the promise of forgiveness did not take immediate possession of his soul, but simply kept him from despair at first, and gave him strength to attain to a thorough knowledge of his guilt through prayer and suppli-cation, and to pray for its entire removal that the heart might be renewed and fortified through the Holy Ghost" (Keil). "It is a generally acknowledged experience that there is often a great gulf between the objective word of forgiveness, presented from without, and its subjective appropriation by man, which hesitating conscience is unable to bridge without great struggles" (Tholuck).   Ps. xxxii., 'The blessedness of forgiveness;' written subsequently.   Other psalms have been sometimes associated with his confession, viz. Ps. vi., xxxviii.; three others, viz. Ps. cii., cxxx., cxliii., make up "the seven penitential psalms."   4. David is here set before us as "the model and ideal of and the encouragement to true penitence."   Consider his acknowledgment of sin as to—

I. ITS MATTER; or the conviction, contrition, change of mind and will, which is expressed.   For words alone are not properly confession in the view of him who "looketh at the heart."   Having, by means of the prophetic word, been led to enter into himself (Luke xv. 17), and had his sin brought to remembrance ("the twin-brother of repentance"), its aggravation described and its punishment declared, he not only recognizes the fact of his sin; but also: 1. Looks at it as committed *against the Lord*; the living God, the Holy One of Israel; and not simply against man.   "Thou hast despised me" (ver. 10).

> "For my transgressions do I know,
> And my sin is ever before me.
> Against thee only have I sinned,
> And done that which is evil in thine eyes," etc.
> (Ps. li. 3, 4.)

2. Takes the blame of it entirely to *himself*, as individually responsible, inexcusable, and guilty; thus accepting the judgment of conscience, without indulging vain and misleading thoughts.   3. Feels sorrow, shame, and self-condemnation on account of its *nature and enormity*; transgression, iniquity, sin (Ps. xxxii. 1, 2); rebellion against the supreme King, disobedience to his Law; debt, pollution, guile, leprosy, bloodguiltiness (Ps. li. 14).   He expresses no *fear* of consequences, and deprecates them only in so far as they include separation from God and loss of the blessings of his fellowship.   4. Puts it away from him with *aversion and hatred*, and purposes to forsake it completely (Prov. xxviii. 13); which confession implies and testifies.

> "For mine iniquity will I confess;
> I will be sorry for my sin."
> (Ps. xxxviii. 18.)

II. ITS MANNER; or the evidence afforded of its sincerity by the language employed and the attendant circumstances.   Observe: 1. Its *promptness*, readiness, and spontaneity.   As soon as he became fully alive to his sin, he said, "I will confess my transgressions unto Jehovah" (Ps. xxxii. 5).   2. Its *brevity*. Two words only: "I-have-sinned against-Jehovah."   "There is in the Bible no confession so unconditional, no expression of repentance so short, but also none so thoroughly true" (Disselhoff).   "Saul confessed his sin more largely, less effectually.   God cares not for phrases, but for affections" (Hall).   3. Its frankness and *fulness*, without prevarication or extenuation.   "The plain and simple confession, 'I have sinned against God,' is a great thing, if we remember how rich the corrupt heart is in the discovery of excuses and apparent justification, and that the king was assailed by one of his subjects with hard, unsparing rebuke" (Hengstenberg).   4. Its *publicity*.   He had sought to hide his sin, but he did not seek to hide his penitence.   He would have it set "in the sight of this sun," even as his chastisement would be; in order that the ways of God might be justified before men, and the evil effects of transgression upon them in some measure repaired.   It is for this purpose, among others, that confession is made a condition of forgiveness (Job xxxiii. 27, 28; 1 John i. 9).   "The necessity of confession (to God) arises from the *load* of unacknowledged guilt.   By confession we sever ourselves from our sin and we disown it.   Confession relieves by giving a sense of honesty.   So long as we retain sin unconfessed, we are conscious of a secret insincerity" (F. W. Robertson, vol. v.).

III. ITS ACCOMPANIMENT; or the further thoughts, feelings, and purposes which should be present in every penitential confession.   1. Faith in the "loving-kindness and tender mercies" of God (Ps. li. 1).

> "But with thee is forgiveness,
> That thou mayest be feared."
> (Ps. cxxx. 4, 7.)

2. Prayer for pardon, purity, the Holy Spirit (1 Sam. xvi. 4—13); steadfastness, freedom, joy, and salvation (Ps. li. 7—12). 3. Submission to the will of God (Ps. xxxii. 9; xxxviii. 13). 4. Consecration to his service (Ps. li. 13—17). " They were not many words which he spoke, but in them he owned two realities—*sin* and *God*. But to own them in their true meaning—sin as against God, and God as the Holy One, and yet God as merciful and gracious—was to return to the way of peace. Lower than this penitence could not descend, higher than this faith could not rise; and God was Jehovah, and David's sin was put away" (Edersheim). " It was not his sin, but his struggle with sin, which makes his history remarkable" (D. Macleod). " David experienced in a greater degree than any other Old Testament character the restlessness and desolation of a soul burdened with the consciousness of guilt, the desire for reconciliation with God, the struggle after purity and renovation of heart, the joy of fellowship, the heroic, the all-conquering power of confidence in God, the ardent love of a gracious heart for God; and has given in his psalms the imperishable testimony as to what is the fruit of the Law and what the fruit of the Spirit in man" (Oehler, ' Theology of the Old Test.,' ii. 159). " The charm of his great name is broken. Our reverence for David is shaken, not destroyed. He is not what he was before; but he is far nobler and greater than many a just man who never fell and never repented. He is far more closely bound up with the sympathies of mankind than if he had never fallen" (Stanley). Even *Bayle* is constrained to say, " His amour with the wife of Uriah and the order he gave to destroy her husband are two most enormous crimes. But he was so grieved for them, and expiated them by so admirable a repentance, that this is not the passage in his life wherein he contributes the least to the instruction and edification of the faithful. We therein learn the frailty of saints, and it is a precept of vigilance; we therein learn in what manner we ought to lament our sins, and it is an excellent model."—D.

Ver. 13.—(THE PALACE.) *The forgiveness of sin.* " And Nathan said unto David, The Lord also hath put away thy sin; thou shalt not die."

> " The absolver saw the mighty grief,
> 　　And hastened with relief;—
> ' The Lord forgives; thou shalt not **die:**
> 'Twas gently spoke, yet heard on high,
> And all the band of angels, us'd to sing
> In heaven, accordant to his raptured string,
> Who many a month had turned away
> With veilèd eyes, nor own'd his lay,
>
> " Now spread their wings and throng **around**
> 　　To the glad mournful sound,
> And welcome with bright, open face
> The broken heart to love's embrace.
> The rock is smitten, and to future years
> Springs ever fresh the tide of holy tears
> And holy music, whispering peace
> Till time and sin together cease."
> 　　　　(Keble, ' Sixth Sunday after Trinity.')

In the interview of Nathan with David much may have passed which is not recorded. But it is improbable that (as some have supposed) there was a long interval between the confession of sin and the assurance of forgiveness, or that the latter was given at a second interview (ver. 15). Perceiving the sincerity of the king's repentance, the prophet forthwith declared that Jehovah also put away (literally, " caused to pass over," ch. xxiv. 10; Zech. iii. 4) his sin, remitting the penalty of death, which the Law appointed and himself had pronounced (ver. 5); and became a messenger of mercy, " one of a thousand" (Job xxxiii. 23), as well as of judgment. " Where sin abounded, grace did much more abound." Consider remission, pardon, forgiveness of sin, as—

I. NEEDED BY A SINFUL MAN. Forgiveness of sin is a change of personal relation between God and man; in which there is: 1. *Release from condemnation* incurred by the latter, through his violation of Divine Law; the removal of the displeasure (ch. x .

27) and wrath (Ps. xxxviii. 1) of God; the blotting out of transgressions (Ps. li. 1; xxxii. 1, 2; Isa. xliii. 25; Rom. viii. 1); deliverance from death (Ezek. xviii. 21). Since "all have sinned," all have need of it; but only those who are convinced of sin value, desire, and seek it. It also involves: 2. *Restoration of communion* with God; which is hindered by sin, as the light of the sun is intercepted by a cloud. "It is the foundation of all our communion with God here, and of all undeceiving expectations of our enjoyment of him hereafter" (Owen, in Ps. cxxx.). 3. *Renewal of the heart* in righteousness; which, though separate from it in thought, is never so in reality, and which was longed for by David with the same intensity and prayed for in the same breath (Ps. li. 9, 10). How lamentable is the condition of that man on whom the wrath of eternal, holy love "abideth" (John iii. 36)!

II. GRANTED BY A MERCIFUL GOD. Forgiveness of sin is an act or gift, which: 1. *God alone can perform* or bestow; the prerogative of the supreme Ruler, against whom it has been committed (Dan. ix. 9; Mark ii. 7). "*The Lord* hath put away thy sin." "To pardon sin is one of the *jura regalia,* the flowers of God's crown " (T. Watson). 2. *Proceeds from his abounding mercy* and grace (Exod. xxxiv. 7). "It is impossible this flower should spring from any other root " (Ps. li. 1). 3. *Rests upon an adequate ground* or moral cause; which, although little known to David, was always present to the mind of God (1 Pet. i. 20), shadowed forth in the "mediatorial sovereignty" of former ages and manifested in Jesus Christ, "in whom we have forgiveness of sins" (Acts xiii. 38; Eph. i. 7).

> "Here is the might,
> And here the wisdom, which did open lay
> The path, that had been yearned for so long,
> Betwixt the heaven and earth."
>
> (Dante, 'Par.,' xxiii.)

III. ANNOUNCED BY A FAITHFUL MINISTER. The prophet said not, "I forgive ; " he simply *declared* what God had done or purposed to do (1 Sam. xv. 28); and in this sense only can there be *absolution* by man. "To forgive sins is the part and inalienable prerogative of God. To absolve is to dispense and convey forgiveness to those who have the right dispositions of heart for receiving it; and this is the part of God's messengers and representatives, whether under the Old or New dispensations" (E. M. Goulburn). The claim of any other power is a groundless assumption. The language employed in the New Testament refers either to cases of discipline in the Church, or to the declaration of the forgiving love of God, the reconciliation of God in Christ, and the assurance of its reality (Matt. xviii. 15—20; John xx. 23; 2 Cor. ii. 10); this assurance depending, for its beneficial influence, on: 1. Its accordance with the *revealed Word of God* (Jer. xxiii. 28; Gal. i. 8). 2. Its utterance by a faithful, holy, merciful *servant of God,* in his ministerial and representative character. "The power of absolution belonged to the Church, and to the apostle through the Church. It was a power belonging to *all* Christians: to the apostle, because he was a Christian, not because he was an apostle. A priestly power, no doubt, because Christ has made all Christians kings and priests " (F. W. Robertson, vol. iii.). 3. Its communication to and reception by such as are *truly penitent.* "The poet said with a great deal of justice, that no sinner is absolved by himself; yet, in another sense, the sinner is absolved by that very self-accusation; and, sorrowing for his sins, is freed from the guilt of them" (Leighton).

IV. APPROPRIATED BY A BELIEVING HEART. The inward assurance of the blessing of forgiveness: 1. Is usually gained through many struggles and fervent *prayers.* David prayed for pardon after the prophet's assurance of it. "Ps. li. shows us how David struggles to gain an inward and conscious certainty of the forgiveness of sin, which was announced to him by Nathan" (Delitzsch). "Under the Old Testament none loved God more than he, none was loved by God more than he. The paths of faith and love wherein he walked are unto the most of us like the way of an eagle in the air—too high and hard for us. Yet to this day do the cries of this man after God's own heart sound in our ears " (Owen). 2. Is personally realized through *faith* in the Word inspired by God and declaring his mercy. "They that really believe forgiveness in God do thereby obtain forgiveness." 3. Is commonly attended with *peace*, refreshment, and gladness, "sweet as the living stream to summer thirst." Happy is he who can say from the heart, "I believe in the forgiveness of sins!"

> "Blessed is he whose transgression is taken away,
>   Whose sin is covered;
>   Blessed is the man to whom Jehovah doth not reckon iniquity,
>   And in whose spirit there is no guile."
>
> (Ps. xxxii. 1, 2; Rom. iv. 7.)
>
> D.

Ver. 14.—(THE PALACE.) *Giving occasion to blaspheme.* "Nevertheless, because by this deed thou hast surely caused [literally, 'causing,' etc., 'hast caused,' etc.] the enemies of Jehovah to speak evil ['despise,' 'contemn,' 'abhor,' 'provoke,' 'blaspheme ']," etc. A scorner, being in company with a devout man, took occasion to speak contemptuously of those whom he called "the Old Testament saints," and especially of David as "a man after God's own heart," asking, "And what did *he* do?" "He wrote the fifty-first psalm and the thirty-second," was the reply; "and if you cherish such feelings as he there expresses, you will be a man after God's own heart." "But," he persisted, "tell me what he did besides." "He did that which the Prophet Nathan said would 'cause the enemies of God to blaspheme.'" The scorner felt the rebuke, and was silent. Even to this day the pernicious influence of his sin appears; but, on the other hand, the fact of its having been recorded is an evidence of, at least, the truthfulness of Scripture; whilst the invaluable lessons taught by it more than compensate for the evil effects it produces. "The sacred writer is perfectly aware of the tendency of this passage of David's history, and yet he is not directed by the Holy Spirit to suppress it. It might have been suppressed. The failings of David are not less useful than his virtues, if we will only faithfully improve the warnings they afford us. It is only to the enemies of the Lord that they afford occasion of blasphemy. They, indeed, will never want occasion; and we are not to be denied the salutary examples which the Scriptures hold forth to us because there are those who wrest them to their own destruction. But it is chiefly in the failings of the good that the enemies of the Lord find cause of triumph" (Thompson, 'Davidica'). Concerning the *sin* of David and other godly men, observe that—

I. IT IS RENDERED ALL THE MORE CULPABLE AND CONSPICUOUS BY THEIR PREVIOUS EXALTATION. *Culpable*, inasmuch as their profession of godliness, especially when united with eminent position, increases their responsibility, and furnishes special motives to a consistent course of conduct; *conspicuous*, inasmuch as their apparent superiority to others: 1. Attracts the *attention* of men to them more than others, and makes it impossible that their failings should pass unnoticed. 2. Naturally leads men to *expect* more from them than others. 3. Produces a deeper impression by the *contrast* exhibited between what is expected from them and what is actually done by them. The transgression of David was in itself great; but it was all the greater, in the view of men, because committed by one of his acknowledged piety, and "in the fierce light that beats upon the throne, and blackens every blot."

II. IT IS CALCULATED TO EXERT A MOST INJURIOUS INFLUENCE ON OTHER MEN. The sin of every man has a baneful effect on his fellow-men; but that of a godly man, in an eminent degree, by: 1. Causing them not only to despise him, but also others, who are *associated* and identified with him in religious faith and service, as (like him) unworthy of respect, insincere, and hypocritical. 2. Inciting them to contemn *religion* itself; doubt the Word of God, distrust the reality of piety everywhere, and even speak evil of God himself; wherein it is commonly implied that sin is sanctioned by religion, or at least is not prevented by it because of its essential weakness. A false impression of the requirements and character of God is given. 3. Lessening the restraints of holy example, hindering the acceptance of the truth, multiplying excuses for neglect, encouraging *indulgence in sin*. 4. Affording means of *opposition to the faith*, whereby others still are made to stumble. "This observation gives us a deep insight into the whole position of David. In him the good principle had attained to supremacy; the *godless party* had seen this with terror, and now they mocked piety in its representative, who, because he held this position, ought to have kept watch over his heart the more carefully, and afterwards made use of the first opportunity of throwing off the burdensome yoke"

(Hengstenberg). "Towards the *heathen* Israel's duty was, by obedience to God's Word and commands, to set forth the theocracy, and bring it to honour and recognition. Transgressions of God's command by the king himself must lead the heathen to heap shame and reproach on Israel and on Israel's God " (Erdmann).

III. ITS INJURIOUS EFFECT ON OTHERS DEPENDS UPON THEIR OWN CHARACTER. It is only " the enemies of the Lord " who despise the Lord, his Word, or his people. 1. Their enmity disposes them to make use of the sin of another as a reason in favour of the course upon which their heart is already set; thus silencing the voice of conscience, increasing their pride and self-deception, and confirming themselves in unbelief and disobedience. 2. It also indisposes them to regard it in a proper manner; to consider the strength of his temptation, the depth of his penitence, the earnestness of his aspirations after righteousness; that the conduct of one man does not prove the character of all with whom he is associated, still less the truth of the religion they profess, or the character of the God they serve ; that it may not be sanctioned by God, but forbidden, reproved, and punished by him; that it is not the standard of practice, which is found in the Law of God alone; and that "every man must give account of himself to God." Those who stand may be led by it to take heed lest they fall, and those who fall to hope to rise again; but the enemies of the Lord see in it nothing but an excuse for persisting in the evil of their way. "Bees will collect honey and spiders poison from the same plant, according to their different natures " (Scott). 3. Their sin is not lessened by the sin of another, but rather increased by the use they make of it. Nevertheless, "all conduct of ours which tends in the slightest degree to strengthen that system of false reasoning, by which sinners confirm themselves in their sins, and undermine the faith and practice of others, is sin of the deepest dye " (Thompson).

IV. ALTHOUGH IT MAY BE PARDONED, IT CANNOT GO UNPUNISHED. "The child also that is born unto thee shall surely die." 1. To manifest the justice and righteousness of God. The penalty of death which he had incurred was transferred from the guilty father to the innocent son. 2. To humble him more deeply on account of his sin, and to produce in him "the peaceable fruit of righteousness " (Heb. xii. 11). "For the most grievous sins a provision of mercy is so made as to secure long and humbling recollections of the aggravated guilt " (Halley). 3. To counteract the evil effects of his sin, and "that the visible occasion of any further blasphemy should be taken away." " God in his wisdom did take away this child, because he should have lived but to be a shame unto David " (Willet). This was only the beginning of a long course of chastisement in his family (ch. xiii.), his person (Ps. xli., lv., xxxix.), and his kingdom (ch. xiv.). Judgment was mingled with mercy; yea, it was itself the chastisement of love. " What was the answer to his prayer? First, the death of Bathsheba's child. Next, the discovery of hateful crimes in his household. Finally, the revolt of the beloved Absalom. These answers to a prayer for forgiveness? Yes, if forgiveness be what David took it to mean—having truth in the inward parts, knowing wisdom secretly " (Maurice).—D.

Vers. 15—23.—(THE PALACE AND THE TABERNACLE.) *David's behaviour in affliction.* In one of the chambers of David's palace his little child lies smitten with a fatal malady. In another the king, divested of his royal robes and clothed in sackcloth, prostrates himself in profound sorrow and abasement. He prays, weeps, fasts, and lies all night upon the ground. His oldest and most confidential servants endeavour to comfort him, and beseech him to take food, in vain. At length the blow falls ; and his servants fear to communicate the intelligence, lest it should plunge him into a dangerous paroxysm of grief. But their reserved demeanour and soft whispering among themselves indicate what has happened; and their answer to his question, " Is the child dead ? " confirms his conclusion. Contrary to their expectation, however, he rises up, washes and anoints himself, puts on becoming garments, goes into the house of the Lord (the tabernacle adjoining the palace), and pours forth his heart in lowly adoration. Then, returning, he asks for bread, and eats. Astonished at his conduct, they inquire the reason of it ; and he replies (in effect) that he has acted, not from thoughtlessness or indifference, but from a due regard to the will of God and the altered circumstances of the case. Whilst the life of the child hung in suspense, he might hope, by prayer and humiliation (since

God deals with men according to their moral attitude toward him), to avert the threatening calamity; but now he is gone it is useless to indulge in lamentation; the will of God must be submitted to without repining (1 Sam. iii. 18). "Those who are ignorant of the Divine life cannot comprehend the reasons of a believer's conduct in his varied experiences" (Scott). "How little can any one of us understand another! The element of conscious sin gave to David thoughts and feelings other than the ordinary ones, and beyond the appreciation of those who looked for the usual signs of grief" (R. Tuck). "In the case of a man whose penitence was so earnest and so deep, the prayer for the preservation of his child must have sprung from some other source than excessive love of any created object. His great desire was to avert the stroke, as a sign of the wrath of God, in the hope that he might be able to discern, in the preservation of the child, a proof of Divine favour consequent upon the restoration of his fellowship with God. But when the child was dead he humbled himself under the mighty hand of God, and rested satisfied with his grace, without giving himself up to fruitless pain" (O. von Gerlach). Consider—

I. His BELIEVING RECOGNITION OF THE HAND OF GOD. "David was a great lover of his children" (Patrick); and to such a father the sufferings of his child must have been *naturally* a severe affliction. But: 1. He also perceived therein a *just chastisement* of his transgression. It is a common fact of experience (no less than a solemn declaration of Scripture) that the sufferings of a child are often the immediate and inevitable fruit of the father's sin. This is, indeed, by no means always the case. In most instances no moral cause thereof can be discerned, save the sinfulness of the race to which he belongs, and which is subject to the universal law of sorrow and mortality. 2. He perceived therein, moreover, a *merciful administration* of such chastisement. "Thou shalt not die. Howbeit," etc. (ver. 14). His life was spared in mercy to himself and his people. He was afflicted in such a manner as would be most conducive to his benefit. His child was smitten to stop the mouths of blasphemers. The innocent suffers for the guilty; suffers—who shall say (believing in the perfect wisdom, righteousness, and love of God) either unjustly or to his own ultimate disadvantage? 3. And he believed in the *Divine susceptibility* to human entreaty; and that it might be possible for the impending blow to be turned aside. "Who can tell whether God will be gracious to me?" (ver. 22). He evidently regarded the prediction of the prophet, though absolute in form, as really conditional (Isa. xxxviii. 1; Jer. xviii. 7, 8). We have to do, not with an iron fate, but with a loving Father, "full of pity and merciful" (Jas. iv. 11; Ps. xxxiv. 15; ciii. 13).

II. His PRAYERFUL HUMILIATION IN THE PRESENCE OF GOD. 1. His grief was not merely natural, but spiritual; *penitential sorrow* for sin, exhibited in solitary, thoughtful, continued self-abasement, fasting, weeping, and genuine purposes of amendment (Ps. li. 3, 4, 13). This is the end of God's afflictive discipline; and, when attained, it may be hoped that the immediate occasion thereof will be removed. Even when affliction is not directly due to personal transgression, it should lead to reflection, humiliation, and "godly sorrow." 2. It was associated with *fervent supplication*. "And David besought God for the child" (ver. 16). "He herein only showed his natural affection, still subordinating his prayer to the will of God; as Christ did to show his human condition when he prayed that the cup might pass from him" (Willet). What evils does prayer avert, what blessings does it obtain, both for ourselves and others! 3. Although the immediate object in view was not gained, his prayer was *not unavailing*. He received light, strength, and comfort; was kept from despair and enabled to endure in a right spirit whatever might occur. God always hears the cries of his children; but he often withholds what they ask. He fulfils their requests in a higher way, transforms the curse into a blessing, and gives them abundant tokens of his favour (ver. 25). "If we ask anything according to his will, he heareth us," etc. (1 John v. 14, 15).

III. His CHEERFUL ACQUIESCENCE IN THE WILL OF GOD. "And David arose from the ground," etc. (ver. 20). Deeming it vain to strive against and mourn over an event which could not be altered, and which he regarded as the expression of the settled determination of God (Deut. iii. 26), he acted accordingly: 1. With *loyal submission* to his sovereign, wise, and beneficent will; strengthened by the conviction that he himself would, ere long, "go the way of all the earth," and be at rest; and by the hope of meeting his child again in God (ver. 23). "Religion," it has been remarked, " is summed up in one word—submission. The chief virtue of Christianity and the root of all the rest is readiness under all circumstances to fulfil the will of God in doing and suffering." 2. With *resolute restraint* upon his natural feelings of sorrow and regret. "The unprofitable and bad consequences, the sinful nature, of profuse sorrowing for the dead, are easily deduced from the former part of this reflection ('Wherefore should I fast?' etc.); in the latter ('I shall go to him') we have the strongest motives to enforce our striving against it—a remedy exactly suited to the disease" (John Wesley). 3. With *cheerful performance* of immediate, practical, appropriate duties; in due attention to personal appearance and needs, public worship in the house of God ("weeping must not hinder worship"), edifying conversation with friends, consoling counsel to the sorrowful (ver. 24). In this manner bereavement is most easily borne and most effectually sanctified, and God is most worthily served and glorified.—D.

Ver. 23.—(THE PALACE.) *The death of a child.* "I shall go to him." David had at least a *glimpse* of the future life. The expectation of going to his child in the grave would have afforded him little comfort. But whatever meaning may be attached to the words as uttered by him, they may be profitably considered by us in the light of the gospel. Reason sheds only *starlight* on the future; the revelations of the Old Testament only *twilight*; but Jesus Christ, the Sun of Righteousness, illumines it with *daylight*. The Christian parent, bereaved of his little child, has—

I. THE PERSUASION OF THE CONTINUED EXISTENCE OF THE DEPARTED, in the unseen, spiritual, eternal world, "the Father's house;" where he: 1. Retains his conscious *personality* (neither ceasing to be, nor "swallowed up in the general sea of being"). 2. Attains the highest *perfection* of which his nature is capable (his capacities of knowledge, holiness, and happiness being gradually developed). 3. Remains in permanent *security* (for ever freed from the temptations and sorrows of this life). On what grounds does such a persuasion rest? (1) The nature of a child—spiritual, immortal, blameless, "having no knowledge between good and evil" (Deut. i. 39). (2) The character of God; his justice and benevolence, and his fatherly relationship (Jer. xix. 4; Ezek. xvi. 21; Joel ii. 16; Jonah iv. 11), which, though consistent with the suffering of the innocent in this world (because of the beneficent purposes to which it is subservient), is not so with their final condemnation. (3) The teachings and actions of Christ, and his redemptive work (Matt. xviii. 1—14; xix. 13—15; xxi. 16; 1 Cor. xv. 22). "They belong to the kingdom of heaven." Whatever disadvantages they suffer from their relation to Adam are more than surpassed by the abounding grace of God in Christ. "He shall gather the lambs with his arm, and carry them in his bosom" (Isa. xl. 11).

II. THE ANTICIPATION OF FUTURE REUNION WITH THE DEPARTED; implying: 1. Hope of personal salvation on the part of him who cherishes it. 2. Belief in the individual recognition of those who are known on earth.

> "I have heard you say
> That we shall see and know our friends in heaven;
> If that be true, I shall see my boy again."
>
> ('King John,' act iii. sc. 4.)

3. Expectancy of common participation in the heavenly fellowship, service, and joy of the Lord.

> "Ah! thy merciless stern mercy hath chastised us,
> Goading us along the narrow road;
> Thy bird, who warmed and dazzled us a moment
> Hath returned to thine abode.
> Lord, when we are purged within the furnace,
> May we have our little child again?
> All thine anguish by the olives in the garden,
> All thy life and death are vain,
> If thou yield us not our own again!"
>
> (Roden Noel, 'A Little Child's Monument.')

III. CONSOLATION IN THE PAINFUL LOSS OF THE DEPARTED; derived from what has been said, the fact that it comes from a Father's hand, and the *benefits* which it brings by (1) teaching patience in the trials of life; (2) moderating attachment to its blessings; (3) spiritualizing affection for those who are left; (4) intensifying desire for the heavenly home. "Let us consider to whom they have gone, from what they have been taken, for what they have been taken, and how this bereavement will appear to us when we come to die ourselves" (W. M. Taylor).

> "'Tis sorrow builds the shining ladder up,
> Whose golden rounds are our calamities."

D.

Vers. 24, 25.—(JERUSALEM.) *The birth of Solomon.* (*References:* 1 Kings i.—xi.; 1 Chron. xxii.—xxix.; 2 Chron. i.—ix.; Ps. lxxii.; Prov. i. 1; Eccles. i. 1; Cant. i. 1.) Where a while ago a dead child lay amidst signs of grief, there now lies a living child amidst signs of gladness. In him David sees a gift of God, an answer to prayer which seemed to be denied, "a pledge of pardon and a sign of hope." In him we see one who was destined to become the wisest of men, the most glorious of monarchs—*Solomon* (whose name occurs only here and ch. v. 14, in this book)—

> "The lofty light, endow'd
> With sapience so profound, if truth be truth,
> That with a ken of such wide amplitude
> No second hath arisen."

(Dante, 'Par.,' x.)

Notice: 1. *His parentage.* David, Bathsheba; from whom he inherited physical strength and beauty, mental and moral qualities, a piercing insight, large-heartedness, skill in ruling, sensuous susceptibilities, etc., royal rank and privileges. "The history of a man's childhood is the description of his parents' environment" (Carlyle). 2. *His birth.* After David's fall, repentance, and forgiveness, and the death of his unnamed infant (see, however, 1 Chron. iii. 5); when Rabbah had fallen, peace was established, and prosperity abounded. The time was propitious. 3. *His name.* (1 Sam. i. 20.) "And he called his name Solomon" (equivalent to "the man of peace," "pacific," *Friedrich*), "because he regarded his birth as a pledge that he should now become a partaker again of the peace of God" (Keil); or perhaps in allusion to the peaceful condition of the kingdom and "from the wish that peace might be allotted him as a gift of God, in contrast with the wars of his father's life" (Erdmann; ch. vii. 12; 1 Chron. xxii. 9). "And Jehovah loved him," and spared his life, in contrast with that of the dead child. "And he [Jehovah] sent by the hand [through] Nathan the prophet; and he [Nathan] called his name *Jedid-jah* [*Jedid* equivalent to 'David,' 'darling;' 'beloved of Jah,' his own name being combined with that of Jehovah], because of the Lord," who loved him; "a practical declaration on the part of Jehovah that the Lord loved Solomon, from which David could and was intended to discern that the Lord had blessed his marriage with Bathsheba. Jedidiah, therefore, was not actually adopted as Solomon's name" (Keil). "The pious father, in his happiness, entreated the oracle, through Nathan, to confer on the new-born child some name of lofty import, and Solomon, as his parents called him, received through the prophet the glorious additional name of Jedidiah. The sadness of the fate of his first child rendered the omens under which the second stepped into its place the more auspicious; and we can easily understand that of all his sons this one became the dearest" (Ewald). 4. *His education;* or the influences that went to form his character; of Nathan, to whom it may have been entrusted; of David, during his declining years; of Bathsheba (ch. xi. 3); of a home and court where polygamy prevailed; of all the learning of the age; of the revolt of Absalom, and other public events. "A shepherd-life, like his father's, furnished, we may believe, a better education for his kingly calling. Born to the purple, there was the inevitable risk of a selfish luxury. Cradled in liturgies, trained to think chiefly of the magnificent 'palace' of Jehovah, of which he was to be the builder, there was the danger first of an æsthetic formalism, and then of ultimate indifference" (Smith, 'Dict. of the Bible'). 5. *His prospects,* after the death of Absalom, if not even before (ch. vii. 12; 1 Chron. xxii. 9; 1 Kings i. 13); his accession and eminence. 6. *His closing years.* 7. *His prefigurement,* not in personal character but royal office, of "the Prince of Peace." "We must not confine our view to David's personal life and reign. After we have seen him fallen and suffering for sin, we must see him rising again and reviving in a more glorious reign, in Solomon his son, who began to reign while David his father was still alive, in order that the continuity might be more clearly marked. And above all, we must contemplate him as culminating upward and attaining the climax of his glory, which God had revealed to him, and for which he yearned with devout aspiration, in Christ, the Divine David and the Son of David, the Solomon, the Jedidiah, the Builder of the Church visible on earth and glorified in heaven " (Wordsworth).—D.

Vers. 26—31 (1 Chron. xx. 1—3).—*The fall of Rabbah.* This event, which occurred after a two years' siege, between the fall of David and his repentance, presents several significant contrasts. 1. *Material success associated with moral failure.* His army victorious, his enterprise terminating in triumph; David himself overcome by temptation, and troubled with a guilty conscience. Worldly success and prosperity are no true measure of moral worth and inward peace and happiness. 2. *Praiseworthy conduct displayed by an unworthy character.* Having captured the lower city, Joab, before attacking the citadel, "sent messengers," etc. (ver. 27). The politic general may have wished to escape the envy and secure the favour of the king; apparently, however, his conduct exhibited consideration for the honour of his master, modesty, and humility. Even the worst men have some good qualities, and often perform excellent actions. "It is possible for a man to be faithful to some one person, and perfidious to others. I do not find Joab other than firm and loyal to David in the midst of all his private falsehoods" (Hall). 3. *A disastrous end following a presumptuous beginning.* (Ver. 29.) In this city the great conflict was commenced, wantonly, proudly, and contemptuously (ch. x. 1—4). On the king (slain in battle) and the people a terrible retribution fell; and their confidence in Moloch (Malcom) was disappointed. 4. *Excessive severity practised by a generous-minded ruler* (ver. 31); not sanctioned by God; but expressive of David's present temper (ch. xi. 22 27), and demanded by the excitement of popular indignation. (1) The cruel conduct of the Ammonites (1 Sam. xi. 2; Amos i. 8); (2) the common practices of the age; (3) an intense zeal against idolatry; (4) the strong conviction of being an appointed instrument of executing Divine vengeance (Ps. cxlix. 7);—may palliate the culpability, though they cannot justify the procedure of David; which, in the light of truth and righteousness, must be condemned and regarded as a blot upon his great renown. This proceeds on the assumption of the correctness of the explanation usually given of the text, which is by no means certain (see critical Commentaries).—D.

Vers. 5—7.—*Unconscious self-condemnation.* Great sinners are generally able to discern and condemn in others wickedness similar to their own. This gives an advantage to those who would convince them of their sins. Nathan made use of it in dealing with David, and with good effect.

I. NATHAN'S PARABLE. It presents a picture of conduct sufficiently like that of David to prepare the way for his self-condemnation, and yet so far different that its drift should not be at once detected. It is a picture of: 1. *Gross covetousness.* For a poor man to covet some part of a rich man's abundance is natural, though wrong; but for a rich man to covet the little of a poor man is monstrous wickedness. Such had been David's conduct towards Uriah. 2. *Robbery.* 3. *Oppression of the weak by the strong.* 4. *Violation of feelings which should have been tenderly respected.* The attachment of the poor man to his pet lamb. The counterpart was the affection of Uriah for his wife, and, till she was seduced, of the wife for her husband.

II. ITS EFFECT ON THE KING. It seems surprising that he did not at once see the prophet's meaning and intention. Perhaps Nathan had been accustomed to come to him to plead the cause of the injured who could obtain no redress otherwise, and David imagined this to be his errand now. Besides, it was a good while since David's sins were committed; yet the prophet had hitherto been silent about them, and would the less be suspected of coming to administer reproof for them now. Hence, all unconsciously, he: 1. *Displayed hot anger against the wrong-doer.* 2. *Passed a severe sentence upon him;* saying that he deserved death, and condemning him to the fourfold restitution which the Law required (Exod. xxii. 1)—a remarkable illustration of Rom. ii. 1. Had he been aware that he was passing sentence upon himself, he would probably have been less severe. Or if he had remembered his own greater crimes, he would hardly so harshly have condemned a man whose crime was so much less heinous. But it is no uncommon thing for great offenders to be harsh in their judgment of others who are far less culpable than themselves.

III. NATHAN'S REJOINDER. 1. *He applied to David himself the judgment he had pronounced.* "*Thou art the man!*" With what terrific force this must have fallen upon the king's ears! He was self-convicted, self-condemned. To such self-condemnation it should be the aim of religious teachers to lead their hearers. It is not permissible, indeed, unless in very extreme cases, to address individuals in public in such words as Nathan's to David; but the preacher's work is not effectually done until each hearer whose sin is described is brought to say to himself, "I am the man!" To use the language of a great preacher of a former generation (Robert Hall), "Without descending to such a minute specification of circumstances as shall make our addresses personal, they ought unquestionably to be characteristic, that the conscience of the audience may feel the hand of the preacher searching it, and every individual know where to class himself. The preacher who aims at doing good will endeavour, above all things, to insulate his hearers, to place each of them apart, and render it impossible for him to escape by losing himself in the crowd. At the day of judgment, the attention excited by the surrounding scene, the strange aspect of nature, the dissolution of the elements, and the last trump, will have no other effect than to cause the reflections of the sinner to return with a more overwhelming tide on his own character, his sentence, his unchanging destiny; and amid the innumerable millions who surround him, he will *mourn apart.* It is thus the Christian minister should endeavour to prepare the tribunal of conscience, and turn the eyes of every one of his hearers on himself." Hearers should welcome such preaching, and thank God for the convictions it produces, as a necessary step in the process of their salvation. 2. *He faithfully delivered God's message to him.* (1) Reminding him of the great kindness of God to him. (2) Charging him distinctly with his crimes. (3) Pronouncing upon him the Divine sentence. In the whole interview, Nathan acted with singular courage, and fidelity to him who sent him.

IV. THE RESULT. David's frank and penitent confession of his sin; and his pardon. Had he been utterly hardened, he might have resented the prophet's faithfulness, dismissed him with anger, or even ordered him to prison or death. But the workings of his own conscience had prepared him to recognize the justice of Nathan's words; and these now melted into contrition the long-burdened yet stubborn heart, which at length found relief in the brief but sincere words, "I have sinned against the Lord;" to which the prophet was able to return the consoling reply, "The Lord also hath put away thy sin; thou shalt not die" (comp. Ps. xxxii. 3—5).

Learn: 1. *The duty of reproving sin in others.* (Lev. xix. 17.) 2. *The value of a minister or other friend faithful enough to administer reproof.* 3. *The responsibility which attaches to the power to discern and condemn sin in others.* (1) It should induce us to avoid the sins which we condemn, and others like them. (2) It increases our guilt if we commit such sins. (3) It ought to induce hearty self-condemnation and penitence when we fall into them. The indignation we feel against the sins of others should be turned on our own, in dealing with which there is more hope than in endeavouring to convince and reform our neighbours; besides which, when we have forsaken our own sins, we shall be better fitted to reprove and amend other offenders (see Matt. vii. 4, 5). 4. *The goodness of God in first sending reprovers to warn and convert, rather than inflicting swift punishment.*—G. W.

Ver. 9.—*Despising the commandments of God.* David, by his grievous sins, had virtually shown contempt for the well-known commandments of God against coveting the wife of another, and against adultery and murder. Hence the force of this remonstrance. It may be properly addressed to all who in any way show contempt for any of the Divine commandments; to all men, therefore, since all are in some respects and in some degree guilty of this sin.

I. WHO MAY BE SAID TO DESPISE THE COMMANDMENTS OF GOD? 1. *Those who take no pains to know and understand them.* Who do not think it worth while to inquire, in reference to their course of life, their duty to others, or any particular action, or even their religious faith and observances, what the will of God is; but are content to follow without question the customs of the world around them, or their own inclinations and habits. 2. *Those who refuse to give heed when their attention is called to them.* Which may be by their own consciences, or by other men. 3. *Those who disobey them.* And the degree of contempt shown by disobedience will be in proportion to (1) their knowledge; (2) their remembrance, at the time, of the commandment, its Author, and its sanctions; (3) the difficulties of disobedience which have to be overcome; and (4) the remonstrances of conscience, and of the Spirit of God, which are resisted and conquered.

II. THEIR SIN AND FOLLY. They may be addressed as the prophet addressed David, "Wherefore," etc. 1. *What rational ground have you for doing it?* Seeing the commandment (1) is "of the Lord," who has the highest right to the obedience of his creatures; (2) proceeds from the perfect reason and the infinite love; and therefore (3) is adapted to promote the good of each and all. "The Law is holy, and the commandment holy, and just, and good (Rom. vii. 12). Consider any particular commandment you have disregarded, and you will see that all this is true of it; and that, therefore, your conduct is foolish and wicked. 2. *How can "you" do it?* Who have been laid under obligations so weighty by the kindness of God; who know so well his character, claims, and laws; who have so often and in such various ways professed love and loyalty to him; who are bound by so many considerations to set a good example; or (as in David's case) are appointed to be an upholder of law, a guardian of innocence, a protector of the public morals. 3. *How "dare" you do it?* In view of the shame and moral injury you bring on yourself; the evil you do to others; the terrible threatenings of the Word of God against sinners; his knowledge of all you do; his awful holiness and justice; and his almighty power to execute his threatenings. In view also of death, and of the day of judgment, when your most secret sins will be brought to light and punished.—G. W.

Ver. 10.—*Despisers of God.* "Thou hast despised me." In the dreadful sins of which David had been guilty he had treated God with contempt. He had treated as of no account all the kindness of God to him; had disregarded his claims; shown contempt practically for his authority, his precepts, his observance of his conduct, his justice and its penalties, his favour, his voice in the conscience. The charge brought against David may be brought against many who are not guilty of gross and flagrant crimes like his.

I. WHO ARE GUILTY OF DESPISING GOD? 1. *All sin involves contempt of him.* It shows: (1) Indifference as to his Being and perfections. If the sinner does not boldly say, "no God," he practically ignores him, leaves him out of account in his conduct, and treats his presence and observation of him, his hatred to sin, his threatened judgments, as of no importance, not worthy of serious consideration (see Ps. x. 13). (2) Contempt for his authority. (3) Despisal of his kindness (Rom. ii. 4). (4) Contempt of his wisdom, as expressed in his laws. As if the sinner thought he could guide and govern himself better than God. (5) Disesteem of his favour and friendship. 2. *Certain kinds of sin may be mentioned as showing such contempt.* (1) Unthankfulness and discontent. As if God's gifts were not worth having. (2) Rejection of Christ and salvation—his best gifts, in which he appears more fully and manifestly than in aught else. "He that despiseth me despiseth him that sent me" (Luke x. 16). "Hath done despite unto the Spirit of grace" (Heb. x. 29). (3) Neglect of the Holy Scriptures. In them God comes to instruct us, to make us partakers of his own wisdom, to make known his will, etc. To neglect them is to show contempt of him. (4) Negligence as to his service. As to the hours and exercises of devotion. God invites us to converse with him, to make known our requests, with the promise of gracious answers. To disregard prayer, or offer unreal worship, is to treat him with contempt. He is most worthy to be praised. To decline to praise him, or to praise in words only, is to despise him. In the sacrament of the Lord's Supper he comes specially near to us, to commune with us in Christ, to feed us with the body and blood of his Son. To turn away from the holy feast, or come with hypocrisy, or with hearts or hands stained with unrepented sin, is to treat him with contempt. And in more active life, to be slovenly, slothful, indifferent; to offer him a half-hearted service; to present him with niggard offerings; is to show grievous disrespect to him (see Mal. i. 6—8). (5) Contempt for his people, or any of them. As if the godly were necessarily fanatical. Or because they may be feeble, or inexperienced (Matt. xviii. 10), or poor (Jas. ii. 6). Or because they differ from us in judgment or observances (Rom. xiv. 3, 10). "He that despiseth you, despiseth me" (Luke x. 16).

II. THEIR FOLLY AND WICKEDNESS. Considering: 1. *Who is despised.* "*Me.*" The infinite Majesty, the Source and Sustainer of all beings, the Giver of all good, the Creator, Preserver, and Benefactor of those who despise him, without whom they have nothing and can do nothing; perfect in all that is good, and worthy of all esteem and love; who is reverenced, adored, loved, and served by the loftiest intelligences, by all the wise and good in all worlds; the Father of our Lord Jesus Christ, in whom all that is glorious in holiness and love appears, revealing the glorious excellences of God. 2. *Who is the despiser.* "*Thou.*" So ignorant, so needy, so dependent, so greatly blessed, so sinful, so perverted in mind and heart, and incapable, while untaught of God, of judging aright as to the best things. It is the creature despising his Creator, folly despising wisdom, weakness despising Omnipotence, the lost despising his Deliverer, the destitute despising him who would enrich him with everlasting riches. 3. *The contrast between him who is despised and the things which are valued.* God is rejected and treated as of little or no account; while things which are worthless or injurious, or which if valuable have only a limited and transient worth, are highly prized and pursued as if of supreme worth and importance. 4. *What is involved in despising God.* It is to despise ourselves, our own souls and their salvation, the true riches and honour, our true and everlasting happiness, eternal life, all that most deserves to be valued.

III. THEIR DOOM. 1. *To be themselves despised.* "They that despise me shall be lightly esteemed" (1 Sam. ii. 30). They shall rise "to shame and everlasting contempt" (Dan. xii. 2), exposed and regarded as fools, and treated as worthless. "Reprobate silver shall men call them, because the Lord hath rejected them" (Jer. vi. 30). 2. *To find by wretched experience how real and how essential to their happiness* is he whom they have slighted. To learn the value of his favour by the irreparable loss of it. The sin of *despising* him they will no longer be able to commit. But the doom may be averted by repentance, as David's case teaches (ver. 13).—G. W.

Ver. 13.—*Confession and pardon.* Two things are very surprising in this narrative —the awful wickedness of David, and the abounding mercy of God.

I. DAVID'S CONFESSION. It was: 1. *Very prompt.* The prophet's address awakened no resentment. There was no attempt at evasion, palliation, or self-justification. How could there be? He at once acknowledged his sin. This was the result, not only of Nathan's faithful reproof, but of the king's own previous mental exercises. The time which had elapsed since the commission of his sins, or some part of it, had been a sorrowful time for him. Burdened with conscious guilt, but not subdued to contrition, he had been wretched (see Ps. xxxii. 3, 4). Nathan's admonitions completed the work; the king's heart was melted to penitence, and he unburdened his soul by a frank confession. 2. *Very brief.* Like the prayer of the publican (Luke xviii. 13). When the heart is fullest, the words are fewest. Not the length of a confession, but its meaning and sincerity, are the important thing. It is so with confessions of men to each other: a word, a look, or an action without a word, is often sufficient, always better than a long speech. 3. *Very appropriate.* Acknowledged *sin*—sin "against the Lord." Nathan had laid stress on this point, and David responds accordingly. He had grievously wronged Uriah, Bathsheba too, and had sinned against the people under his rule; but most had he sinned against God. Hence his language in Ps. li. 4. Only as sin is thus viewed is "*godly* sorrow" possible.

II. HIS FORGIVENESS. Which was: 1. *Immediate.* It startles us that so great a sinner should have been so speedily pardoned, so soon assured of pardon. We might have deemed some delay more suitable. But God is ever ready to forgive; he waits only for the sinner's penitent confession. There is no reason for delay of forgiveness except the sinner's impenitence and unbelief. The moment these are subdued, pardon

is granted. This was assured by the promises of the Old Testament, such as Isa. lv. 7.
In the New we have the same assurances, and the difficulties which arise from the
penitent sinner's conviction of the rightness of the punishment threatened to transgressors (his conscience being on the side of the Divine justice) are removed by the atoning
sacrifice of Christ. 2. *Free.* Burdened with no conditions, no demand for penances,
or compensations, or sin offerings. The sin was too serious for these. So David felt
(Ps. li. 16). Only a perfectly free pardon could meet the case. New love and service
would follow; but these would spring from gratitude for forgiveness, not from the
expectation of securing it. The attempt to merit or earn pardon for past transgressions
by voluntary sufferings, by multiplied prayers or ceremonies, or by future obedience, is
absurd on the face of it, and as contrary to the Old Testament as to the New. It was
to the "multitude of God's tender mercies" (Ps. li. 1) that David appealed; and it is
to the same abounding grace as shown in the gospel that we must trust. 3. *Declared.*
Nathan pronounced the king's absolution: "The Lord also hath put away thy sin;
thou shalt not die." Men would like a similar assurance to themselves individually;
and the system of some Churches is constructed to meet this wish. On confession of
sin to a priest, he pronounces absolution. But this practice is unwarranted and
delusive. Confessedly the absolution is worthless unless the sinner be truly penitent;
and if he be, it is useless; and in multitudes of cases it is most pernicious, fostering
baseless hopes. If men could read the heart, or had, like Nathan, a special message
of pardon from God in each case, they might safely pronounce absolution. But in
ordinary cases none can know the reality of repentance until it is proved by the life;
and therefore none can safely assure the sinner of his actual forgiveness until such
assurance is needless. The repenting sinner, coming to God by faith in Jesus Christ,
is assured of pardon (1) by the promises of God, and (2) by the Spirit of God in his
heart applying the promises to the individual and enabling him to confide in them,
and commencing in him the Christian life. A new heart is given with pardon; and
this, with its fruit in the conduct, becomes a growing evidence of pardon. 4. *Yet with
a reservation.* The penalty of death, to which David had virtually condemned himself,
was remitted; but other penalties were not. One was specifically mentioned—the
death of the child (ver. 14); and the others, denounced (vers. 10—12) before the
confession and forgiveness, we know from the subsequent history were inflicted. And
it is often the case that the painful consequences of sin continue long after pardon is
granted, perhaps till death. Shall we say, then, that the forgiveness is not real and
full? By no means. But because it is real and full the pardoned sinner must suffer.
Suffering, however, changes its character. As from God, it is no longer penal infliction,
but fatherly chastisement and discipline (1) to maintain a salutary remembrance of
the sin, and produce constant gratitude and humility; (2) to preserve in obedience and
promote holiness; (3) to vindicate to others the justice of God, and warn them against
sin. And as to the penitent himself, his suffering produces no bitterness, abjectness, or
sullenness. Love to him that chastises, kept alive by the sense of his forgiving and
fatherly love, enables him to yield himself to the chastisement, thankful, resigned,
acquiescent, and earnestly seeking to realize the intended profit.

In conclusion: 1. *Admire, adore, trust, and proclaim the pardoning love of God.* 2.
Let sinners repent of, confess, and forsake their sins, that they may obtain forgiveness.
For, notwithstanding the love of God and the sacrifice of Christ, no impenitent sinner
shall be forgiven. 3. *Let no penitent despair.* Not even the backslider, and though
his sins have been as bad as David's. 4. *Let none presume.* One of the worst and
most persistent consequences of David's sin and pardon has been the encouragement
to sin, which foolish and wicked persons have derived from them, or—shall we say?—
pretended to derive. For so foolish and impious is it to turn the narrative to such a
purpose that it is difficult to believe in the sincerity of those who do so. Rather they
love their sins, and are glad of anything that may quiet somewhat their consciences in
committing them. Let any such consider that the proper effect of the narrative is to
render sin odious and to awaken a dread of it; and that the sins of those who read it
and persist in sin are rendered doubly guilty. Such are hardening their hearts and
promoting in themselves incapacity to repent, and so incapability of being forgiven.
—G. W.

Ver. 14.—*Religion reproached through the conduct of the religious.* David's wickedness gave occasion for reproach of religion by the ungodly among his subjects, and by the heathen peoples around. Indeed, it occasions blasphemy and contempt of religion down to the present day.

I. CONDUCT WHICH OCCASIONS CONTEMPT AND REPROACH OF RELIGION. The conduct must be that of professedly religious men, and the more strict their profession, and the more prominent their position, so much the greater the mischief they do. 1. *Great inconsistency between profession and conduct.* Gross immorality, fraud, falsehood, avarice, intemperance, hasty temper, revenge, etc. 2. *Unworthy presentation of religion itself.* Ignorant rant, unctuous cant, too much insistence on mere doctrinal refinements which have little or no bearing on practical life, elaborate ceremonialism, fierce strife in a Church, sectarian bitterness and exclusiveness, indifference to the well-being of the general population, clerical pretensions, ambition, or avarice,—all in their various ways and degrees occasion "the enemies of the Lord to blaspheme."

II. THE CLASS OF PERSONS LED THEREBY TO DESPISE AND REPROACH RELIGION. "The enemies of the Lord." Not his friends; they know too well the value of religion; reverence and love it too much. The effect of such conduct on them is sorrow, self-examination, and greater watchfulness and prayer, lest they also should be overcome by temptation. Also prayer and effort (if possible) to restore those who have sinned. To take occasion from the inconsistencies of Christians to despise and revile their religion is a manifest sign of enmity to God. It is also a mark of great ignorance of the religion they revile; for, did they understand it, they would perceive its opposition to the sins and follies of its professed adherents; and that its truth and goodness remained the same, whatever their conduct. Or, if it be said that it is only the profession of religion that is spoken of with contempt, it is plainly unjust to cast a slur on all who make it because of the sins of a few of their number.

III. THE SERIOUS EVILS THUS WROUGHT. 1. *The slanderers are themselves injured.* To occasion them to blaspheme is to occasion the increase of their guilt, and the greater hardening of their hearts; whereas it should be the aim of good men to do all that is possible to bring them to the knowledge of the truth and the experience of salvation. 2. *Discredit is brought upon religion.* Hence some who might have been disposed to inquire into its claims, and others who were preparing to make an open profession of godliness, are deterred from doing so. In this view the inconsistencies of Christians are a serious matter. They help to promote in society a sentiment adverse to earnest godliness and the profession of it. 3. *The hearts of true-hearted and consistent Christians are wounded and distressed.* 4. *Above all, and including all, the Name of God is dishonoured, and the progress of his kingdom checked.*

Finally, let inconsistent professors of religion ponder the words of our Lord (Matt. xviii. 7, Revised Version), "Woe unto the world because of occasions of stumbling! for it must needs be that the occasions come; but woe to that man through whom the occasion cometh!"—G. W.

Vers. 22, 23.—*An infant's illness and death.* This part of the narrative introduces us to a spectacle which, in its main features, is common enough. A child sickening and dying, a parent striving with God in prayer and fasting for its life, but striving in vain. But there are peculiar circumstances here which give the scene a special interest.

I. THE CHILD'S FATAL SICKNESS. 1. *The cause of it.* The sufferings and deaths of little children are painful to witness, and awaken many questionings. Why should these innocent lambs suffer? Why should the sinless die? To which we may reply, Why should they not, seeing that to them death is an escape from a world of sin and misery, with its awful possibilities of evil, into the world of perfect and eternal purity, safety, and bliss? Besides, he who gave life may take it at his pleasure. Holy Scripture throws some further light upon the mystery. It teaches us in general, that, death came into the world through sin. Children die because they belong to a sinful, dying race. Their deaths are part of the penalty of the sins of men. In them the innocent suffer for the guilty, because of their guilt, and to promote their deliverance from sin. Amongst the forces at work to promote repentance and holiness, not the least powerful are the deaths of little children. God thus finds a way to the hearts of parents and their surviving children. In the case of David we have express Divine explanation of the death of the babe (ver. 14). It was inflicted on account of the sin to which it owed its existence, and to vindicate the justice of God as against the blasphemies of his enemies. And not unfrequently now the child's death is the direct consequence and penalty of the sins of its father or mother. But in such cases, as in David's, love is revealed as well as righteousness. "The Lord struck" David's child, not only to show his displeasure at David's sin, but to deepen his penitence, and promote his godliness and holiness. 2. *Its effect on David.* It might have seemed probable that, when the babe was taken ill, the father, while not actually desiring its death, would at least not have been much grieved at the prospect of it. For it was a child of shame, and as long as it lived would be a perpetual reminder of the dreadful past, and would keep alive the memory of it in the court and nation. And it is a striking proof of the tenderness and strength of the monarch's affections that the prospect of the death of his little boy was so distressing to him. Partly, however, his intense longing that the child's life should be spared sprang probably from the feeling that this would be a fresh assurance to him that his sins were forgiven. In his distress he resorted to prayer for the child's restoration. How could he do this, seeing Nathan had expressly told him that it should certainly die? It seems that Divine announcements of punishments were not regarded as irrevocable, however positive their terms. Compare the cases of Hezekiah (2 Kings xx. 1—6) and of Nineveh (Jonah iii. 4—10). So David said, "Who can tell whether God will be gracious to me, that the child may live?" and he persevered in prayer and fasting and self-humiliation until the death of the child extinguished all hope. He "went in" to a retired part of his palace, and cast himself on the ground, beseeching God for the child, and fasting (ver. 16); and in these exercises he continued day and night, until on the seventh day the child died (ver. 18). Doubtless, during that period of solitary communion with God, not only did he pray for the child's life, but reflected much on his sins, indulged anew his penitential grief, prayed for forgiveness and a cleansed heart, surrendered himself and his babe to the Divine will, sought strength to endure whatever might be before him, and grace to derive lasting profit from all that he was passing through, whatever the issue might be. In all which we do well to take him as an example.

II. THE CHILD'S DEATH. The prayers offered for the restoration of the child were sincere, importunate, persevering; but they were offered in vain. "The child died." Yet not in vain. No true prayer is in vain. It brings blessing to him who offers it greater than that which is denied to him. God gives "more than we ask," better than we ask. The effect of his child's death on David astonished his servants. He "arose from the earth, and washed, and anointed himself, and changed his apparel, and came into the house of the Lord, and worshipped," etc. (ver. 20). 1. *He laid aside all signs of mourning.* 2. *He went into the holy tent, and worshipped.* His worship would now be of a different character from that which he had offered in his own privacy. No longer entreaties for the life of the child, but expressions of submission to the will of God at length made plain; acknowledgment of God's righteousness and loving-kindness in what he had done; prayers for support and consolation and sanctifying grace, for himself and the sorrowing mother, and that God would, through this painful stroke, glorify his own Name. 3. *He explained and justified his conduct to his astonished servants.* They expressed their perplexity. He explains by reminding them of the utter uselessness of further fasting and weeping. The dead cannot be recalled to life. The living will go to the dead; the dead will not come back to the living. It is true that this consideration has often a terrible effect in increasing the anguish of bereavement. It adds despair to sorrow. The feeling that it is impossible to recall the departed; that no more will the loved one be seen, or heard, or embraced; that the rest of life must be spent without the society that was so dear and seemed so essential to happiness, is overpowering. Nevertheless, the sense of the unalterableness of the fact, and the utter uselessness of prolonged sorrow, has ultimately a calming effect. Men come at length to reconcile themselves to the unchangeable. But there is greater peace and consolation in the truth that the unchangeable is the expression of the will of the infinitely Wise and Good. Believing this, we reconcile our minds, not to a mere hard, stern fact, but to the will of our Father in heaven, who loves us, and pains us because he loves us. The second expression employed by David in reference to the impossibility of regaining his child is worthy of notice. "He shall not return to me." It reminds us that when our friends are dead all opportunity, not only of enjoying their presence and society, but of benefiting them, and otherwise doing our duty to them, is gone. A cause for regret and penitential sorrow if we have failed in our duty to them; and a reason for greater care in doing our duty to those that remain, and for seeking their forgiveness while we may for any wrong we have done to them. There is consolation, too, in reference to those who have been taken from us, that they cannot return, when we have good assurance that they are in heaven. We cannot wish them to return from heaven to earth. We thank God for their complete deliverance from sin and sorrow, and all liability to those evils. 4. *He expressed his own expectations as to the future.* "I shall go to him" (ver. 23). Whither? To the grave? to Sheol (equivalent to Hades)? or to heaven? The precise thought of David in these words is hardly ascertainable. He may have intended to say only that he must join the child in the region of death. Probably, however, he expressed a hope of conscious reunion in the future world; and the Christian, taking up the words, can express by them a fuller and more confident hope of rejoining his little children and Christian relatives and friends in a state of blessedness than was possible to Old Testament believers, though glimpses of the glorious future were at times enjoyed by them. "Not lost, but gone before" is a thought that is daily comforting thousands. And it is felt how much better it is that the desire for reunion should be fulfilled yonder rather than here—that we should go to our departed friends into that world of perfection and joy, not they come back to us into this world of imperfection and trouble. Only let us take care so to live that such hopes may be reasonable. Think how terrible the thought, "I shall go to him," as cherished by one impenitent sinner in respect to another who has gone to his doom! How dreadful the reunions hereafter of those who have lived together in ungodliness and sin here, and encouraged and helped each other in the practice of them! Better to have died in infancy! Better not to have been born!—G. W.

EXPOSITION.

CHAPTER XIII.

Ver. 1.—After this. This phrase, as we have seen on ch. x. 1, has little chronological force, but the date of the sad event which formed the second stage in David's punishment can be settled with considerable certainty. Tamar was the daughter of Maacah, a princess of Geshur, and David's marriage with her, while still at Hebron, is mentioned as a proof of his growing power, and consequently some time must have elapsed after his appointment as king before this alliance took place. As Absalom was apparently older than Tamar, if she were now fifteen or sixteen years of age, David would have been king of all Israel at least thirteen or fourteen years, and would have reached the summit of his glory. His wars would be over, Rabbah captured, and his empire firmly established. For twenty more years he must sit upon his throne, but as a culprit, and bear the many sorrows resulting from his sin. Amnon was David's firstborn, the son of Ahinoam of Jezreel; and probably he would never have committed his shameless crime had not David's own sin loosed the bonds of parental authority. As it was, he hesitated, but was encouraged to it by his cousin, who was too subtle a man not to weigh David's character well before coming to the conclusion that Amnon might safely gratify his lusts. The name Tamar means "palm tree," and both she and Absalom were remarkable for their personal beauty.

Ver. 2.—Amnon was so vexed, that he fell sick. The Hebrew literally is, *and it was narrow to Amnon, even to becoming sick.* To an Oriental a feeling of narrowness means distress, while in joy there is a sense of largeness and expansion. Our words for distress have lost this picturesque force. That Amnon **thought it hard** does not mean that he had any feeling for his sister's disgrace, but that he knew that his attempt was difficult. He did not see how he could get Tamar into his power, and feared the consequences. The wives had each her own dwelling, and the daughters were kept in strict seclusion.

Ver. 3.—Jonadab, the son of Shimeah. He is called Shammah in 1 Sam. xvi. 9, and is there described as Jesse's third son. A brother of Jonadab, named Jonathan, is mentioned in ch. xxi. 21 as a valiant soldier who slew one of the Philistine giants. **Subtil** is not used in a bad sense, but means clever, ready in devising means.

Ver. 4.—Why art thou, being the king's son, lean? The Hebrew is, *Why, O son of the king, dost thou pine away morning by morning?* There was probably a gathering of friends every morning at the young prince's house, and his cousin, attending this levee, noticed Amnon's melancholy, and, having forced a confession from him, is unscrupulous enough to suggest a plan that would make Tamar her brother's victim.

Ver. 5.—**When thy father cometh to see thee.** While the daughters lived in Oriental seclusion in the dwellings of their mothers, the sons seem to have had separate apartments assigned them in the palace. And David evidently was an affectionate father, who even went to the abodes of his sons in a loving and unceremonious way, to see how they fared. But Jonadab abused the king's affection, and made it the very means of removing the obstacles in the way of his daughter's disgrace. And like the whole tribe of flatterers and time-servers, he employed his cleverness to gratify his patron's momentary passion, indifferent to the miserable consequences which must inevitably follow. For the least punishment which Amnon would have to bear would be exclusion from the succession to the crown, besides disgrace and his father's anger. Absalom, who was three or four years younger than Amnon, he despised, and counted for nothing.

Ver. 9.—**She took a pan.** Many of the words are difficult because, being the names of ordinary domestic articles, they do not occur in literature. A man may be a good French scholar, and yet find it difficult in France to ask for things in common use. Here the Syriac is probably right in understanding, not a pan, but the delicacy Tamar had been cooking. In ver. 8 the word rendered "flour" is certainly "dough," and is so rendered in the Revised Version. The cakes were a kind of pancake, fitted to tempt the appetite of a sickly person. The picture is a very interesting one: the palace parcelled out into separate dwellings; the king kindly visiting all; the girls on friendly terms with their brothers, yet not allowed to go to their rooms without special permission; and finally Tamar's skill in cookery—an accomplishment by no means despised in an Oriental *ménage*, or thought unworthy of a king's daughter.

Ver. 12.—**Do not force me**; literally, *do not humble me.* It is to be regretted that the word should be changed, as it bears testimony to the nobleness of the Hebrew women, who regarded their chastity as their crown of honour. The word **folly** is used in the sense of unchastity in Gen. xxxiv. 7 and elsewhere, and it is noteworthy that the Jews thus connected crime with stupidity. Vain, that is, empty persons were the criminal part of the population (Judg. ix. 4), and to call a man "a fool" was to attribute to him every possible kind of wickedness (Matt. v. 22). The thought which lay at the root of this view

of sin was that Israel was a peculiar people, sanctified to God's service; and all unholiness, therefore, was not merely criminal in itself, but a proof that the guilty person was incapable of rightly estimating his privileges. Tamar urges this upon her "empty" brother, and then pathetically dwells upon their mutual shame, and, finding all in vain, she even suggests that the king might permit their marriage. Such marriages between half-brothers and half-sisters were strictly forbidden, as tending to loosen the bonds of family purity (Lev. xviii. 9; Deut. xxvii. 22); but possibly the Levitical code was occasionally violated, or Tamar may have suggested it in the hope of escaping immediate violence.

Ver. 15.—**Amnon hated her exceedingly.** Amnon had not really ever loved Tamar; his passion had been mere animal desire, which, by a well-known psychological law, when gratified turned to hatred. Had he possessed any dignity of character or self-respect, he would have resisted this double wrong to one so near to him, and whom he had so terribly disgraced; but he can only remember the indignant words she had spoken—her comparison of him to "the fools in Israel," and her obstinate resistance to his wishes. With coarse violence he orders her away; and when, humbled and heartbroken, she begs for milder treatment, he adds insult to the wrong, and bids his manservant push her out, and bolt the door after her. By such an order the manservant and all Amnon's people would be led to believe that she was the guilty person, and Amnon the victim of her enticements.

Ver. 16.—There is **no cause.** This is certainly not a possible translation of the Hebrew, which is probably corrupt; and though Tamar's words may have been broken and hysterical, we cannot suppose that the narrator intended to represent her sobs. The text is rendered by Philippsohn, "And she said to him respecting the evil deed, Greater is this than the other." Similarly Cahen renders it, "au sujet de ce mal." Flat as this is, no better rendering is possible; but the Vatican copy of the Septuagint has a reading which suggests the line of probable emendation: "Nay, my brother, this evil is greater than the other." It was greater because it cast the reproach upon her, refused her the solace of his affection, and made her feel that she had been humbled, not because he loved her, but for mere phantasy. He has had his will, and, careless of her sorrow, he sends her contemptuously away, indifferent to the wrong he has done her, and piqued and mortified at her indignant resistance. However much we may disapprove of Absalom's conduct, Amnon richly deserved his punishment.

Ver. 18.—**A garment of divers colours.** This was probably a long tunic with sleeves, so woven as for the colours to form patterns like those of the Scottish tartans (see on Gen. xxxvii. 3). The next sentence is probably a note, which has crept from the margin into the text, and which literally is, " For so king's daughters, while unmarried, wore over-mantles" (*me'ils*; see note on 1 Sam. ii. 19). Both the Authorized Version and the Revised Version so render as if the coloured chetoneth and the me'il were the same; but the meaning of the note rather is to guard against the supposition that the princess, while wearing the close-fitting long tunic with sleeves, had dispensed with the comely mantle. It is, indeed, possible that, while busy in cooking, she had laid the me'il by, and now rushed away without it. But it was the tunic with its bright colours which made both Amnon's servitor and also the people aware that she was one of the king's daughters.

Ver. 19.—**Tamar put ashes.** There was no concealment of her wrong, but, thrust out of the inner chamber into which Amnon had enticed her (ver. 10), she cast ashes upon her head from the very fire which she had just used in cooking, and, rending her garment, hastened away with her hand on her head, and with cries of lamentation. If David had foreseen this sad sight when giving way to his passion for Bathsheba, he would have felt that sin is indeed "folly," and that its pleasure is followed by shame and bitter anguish.

Ver. 20.—**Hath Amnon?** The Hebrew has *Aminon*, a diminutive, which some authorities regard as expressive of contempt. More probably it is an accidental variety of spelling. **Hold now thy peace.** We must not suppose that Absalom did not comfort his sister, and make her conscious of his love. He was, in fact, so indignant at her treatment as to have purposed the sternest vengeance. But this he concealed from her, and counselled patience, not merely because she would have dissuaded him from a course so full of danger to himself, but because it was the duty of both to wait and see what course David would take. Where polygamy is permitted, it is the duty especially of the brothers to defend their sisters' honour (Gen. xxxiv. 31). But David was both her father and the chief magistrate; and, moreover, he had been made an instrument in his daughter's wrong. They must be patient, and only if David failed in his duty would Absalom's turn come. Meanwhile, Tamar dwelt in his house desolate, as one whose honour and happiness had been laid waste.

Ver. 21.—**David . . . was very wroth.** The legal punishment for Amnon's crime was "the being cut off in the sight of the people " (Lev. xx. 17). But how could David, who had himself committed crimes for which death was the appointed penalty, carry out the law against his firstborn for following his example? Still, he might have done more than merely give Amnon words of reproof. Eli had done as much, and been punished with the death of his sons for his neglect of duty (1 Sam. ii. 34). The sin of David's son had been even more heartless than theirs; and could David hope to escape the like penalty? It would have been wise to have given proof that his repentance included the suppression of the crime to which his previous conduct had given encouragement. But David was a man whose conduct was generally governed by his feelings. He was a creature of warm and often generous impulse, but his character lacked the steadiness of thoughtful and consistent purpose.

Ver. 22.—**Absalom spake . . . neither good nor bad.** (On this phrase, see Gen. xxiv. 50; xxxi. 24.) Absalom's outward demeanour was one of utter indifference, concealing a cruel determination. It is strange how unlike the son was to the father.

Ver. 23.—**Absalom had sheep-shearers in Baal-hazor.** The sheep-shearing was a usual occasion for feasting and holiday-keeping (see 1 Sam. xxv. 2, 8). Baal-hazor was apparently the name of Absalom's estate, situated near the town Ephraim (2 Chron. xiii. 19), which, according to Eusebius, lay about eight miles north of Jerusalem. As Ephraim was near the wilderness of Judah, it was probably the same town as that to which our Lord withdrew (John xi. 54). The phrase **beside**, literally, *near*, Ephraim, shows that it must be the town, and not the tribal territory, which is here meant. **Two full years;** Hebrew, *years of days.*

Ver. 25.—**But blessed him.** These words, in the courtly language of the East, not only mean that David parted from Absalom with 'kindly feelings and good wishes, but that he made him a rich present (see note on 1 Sam. xxv. 27, where the same word occurs; and observe the nature of Abigail's blessing described there). David's court had evidently become lavish, when thus a visit from him to his son's farm would be too costly for the young prince's means; but had he so increased his present as to have made it reasonable for himself and his chief officers to go, Absalom must have deferred his crime. As it was, the invitation put David off his guard, and, forgetting the fatal consequences of his good nature in permitting Tamar's visit to Amnon, he allowed his sons to go to the festival. Nor must we blame him for his compliance. He had probably at first been full of anxiety as to the course Absalom might pursue, but his silence and forbearance made him suppose that Tamar's wrong had not caused her brother any deep sorrow. Himself a man of warm feelings, he had expected an immediate outburst of anger, but such stern rancour persevered in for so long a time with such feline calmness of manner was beyond the range of his suspicions ; and the invitation, first to himself and then to all his sons, made him suppose that Absalom had nothing but affectionate feelings toward. them all.

Ver. 28.—**Smite Amnon.** The order was given before the banquet began, and every arrangement made to render the attack successful. Though Tamar's wrong was the mainspring of Absalom's conduct, yet neither he nor his men would forget that Amnon stood between him and the crown ; and Amnon, entirely off his guard, never very wise at his best, and with his senses made dull by wine, seems to have fallen an easy prey. And as soon as the murder was committed, the rest of the king's sons, though all had attendants with them, fled in dismay, not knowing what might be the extent of Absalom's purpose. It is said that they fled on mules, this being the first place in which this animal is mentioned, as the word so translated in Gen. xxxvi. 24 really means "hot springs," and is so translated in the Revised Version. The breeding of hybrids was forbidden in Lev. xix. 19, and probably they were procured, as were horses, by trade. Up to this time the ass had been used for riding ; but now David had a favourite mule (1 Kings i. 33), and Solomon received mules as tribute (1 Kings x. 25). Horses seem to have been used chiefly for chariots.

Ver. 30.—**Tidings came.** Some of the servants seem to have fled immediately that the attack was made, and in their terror reported, not what had really happened, but what they assumed was Absalom's purpose. It shows, however, how thoroughly Absalom had dissembled when thus they entirely forgot that he had a grudge against Amnon. And David, in utter misery, tears his robes, and throws himself prostrate on the ground, while his courtiers, with rent garments, stand speechless round him. But the guilty Jonadab guesses more correctly the truth. He had probably watched Absalom closely, and distrusted his silence. Nothing, perhaps, had happened to justify his suspicions, but as soon as the tidings came he divined the real meaning. And, wicked as he was, he could never have supposed that Amnon would turn upon the woman he had wronged, and insult and disgrace her. He probably imagined that Amnon really loved her, and that the matter would be patched up. But when the wretched youth acted so shamelessly, Jonadab probably felt sure that

Absalom would sooner or later take his revenge.

Ver. 32.—**By the appointment;** literally, *for upon the mouth of Absalom it was laid from the day he humbled Tamar his sister.* "Mouth" is not the word we should have expected here, and the Syriac instead has "mind," and the Chaldee "heart." But the mouth often expresses determination, and Jonadab may have noticed Absalom looking at his brother with compressed lips. More probably, however, it is a colloquial phrase, with no special application to Absalom ; and the Syriac gives the true sense.

Ver. 34.—**But Absalom fled.** These words break the form of the narrative, but complete the sense. They briefly state that Jonadab was right ; for, so far from molesting any of the rest of the king's sons, Absalom had no other thought than for his own safety. He had avenged his sister, but had at present no other sinister design. It was David's method of treating him which drove this youth, with a nature fit for treachery, into schemes of rebellion. **The way of the hillside behind him.** This may mean " from the west," as, in taking the points of the compass, the Hebrews looked to the east, which would thus be " before them." Compare " the backside of the desert," that is, " the western side," in Exod. iii. 1 ; and " the Syrians before and the Philistines behind," that is, on the east and west (Isa. ix. 12). But the versions differ so strangely in their renderings that they could scarcely have been made from our present text.

Ver. 36.—**The king also and all his servants wept very sore.** The narrative sets very clearly before us the great terror of the king, who at first supposes that all his sons are murdered ; there is then suspense while Jonadab suggests that one only has been sacrificed to private vengeance ; then quickly comes the watchman's report of the appearance of much people rapidly descending the hillside, and this is followed by the hasty rush of the fugitives into his presence, and the terrible certainty that one son has, with long-premeditated malice, murdered his brother. And as he wept, David, we may feel sure, thought of Uriah, murdered because of his own base passions, whereas Amnon had brought death upon himself by following, alas! the example of his own father. He would think, too, of the words of his sentence, that "the sword should never depart from his house." It had claimed one victim, and who could now stop the outburst of angry passions in a family which previously had dwelt in kindly friendship? Probably, too, he reproached himself for not punishing Amnon. Had he done so with sufficient severity to have satisfied Absalom, he would have saved the life of his firstborn, and not have driven his second son into terrible crime. He had not done so because his own sins had tied his hands. Yes; David had good reason for weeping sore.

Vers. 37, 38.—**So Absalom fled.** The triple repetition of these words, and the fragmentary style, make it probable that we have here an abridgment of a longer narrative. So in ver. 34 the words probably are a summary of a more circumstantial account of Absalom's doings after his young men had slain Amnon. (On Talmai and Geshur, see notes on ch. iii. 3.)

Ver. 39.—**And** (*the soul of*) **king David longed to go forth unto Absalom.** This translation has the support of the Jewish Targum, and, as the verb is feminine, the insertion of the added word is possible, though the sense seems to require " anger " instead of " the soul." But the versions (Septuagint, Syriac, and Vulgate) all give the verb its ordinary meaning of " ceasing," and, though there is something harsh in taking it impersonally, yet their authority is too great for us to say that such a mode of rendering it must be wrong. And if the grammar be difficult, the sense put upon the words by the versions is excellent. Literally they are, *As to King David, there was a ceasing to go forth after Absalom; for he was comforted,* etc. At first he had demanded of Talmai the surrender of the offender, and, when Talmai refused, David tried other means; but in time, when his grief for Amnon was assuaged, he desisted from his efforts. But even so it required much subtlety on Joab's part to obtain Absalom's recall, which would scarcely have been the case if David's soul was longing for his son's return; and, even after his coming, David long maintained an unfriendly attitude. Amnon was his firstborn, and evidently dearly loved, but David's culpable leniency had borne bitter fruit. And again he acts without thoughtful sense of justice, and though at first he would have given Absalom merited punishment, yet gradually paternal feeling resumed its sway, unhappily only to be miserably abused.

HOMILETICS.

Vers. 1—22.—*The firstfruits of iniquity.* The facts are: 1. Amnon entertains an improper affection for his half-sister Tamar, and meditates evil. 2. Making known his secret passion to Jonadab, he is prompted to a device for securing a personal interview with her. 3. The king, visiting Amnon in his pretended sickness, kindly arranges that Tamar should wait upon him with special food in his chamber. 4. Seizing an opportunity in the absence of attendants, he accomplishes his purpose in defiance of her protests and pretexts. 5. By a sudden revulsion of feeling, he now hates her, and causes her to be driven away in disgrace. 6. Her trouble becoming known to the king and to Absalom, the one is very wroth and does nothing, and the other conceals his cherished hatred and revenge. The rather long account given of the base sin of Amnon is no doubt intended to show how the chastisements pronounced by Nathan (ch. xii. 10, 11) were brought about. In this way the spiritual character of the narrative shines through all the details, which in themselves seem worthy of being for ever lost in oblivion. It is in connection with the evil, and often through the evil, of life that the righteousness of God is historically revealed. Those who object to such passages as these in the Bible know not the principle on which it, as a book, is constructed. It is not the deeds that are the object of thought and instruction, but the fulfilment of the righteous judgments of God, brought to pass in the fact and consequences of their occurrence. In the deeds here recorded we have a graphic description of the firstfruits of the dreadful sin of David.

I. ALL SIN SOONER OR LATER BEARS FRUIT IN HUMAN SOCIETY. "Sin" is a term descriptive of the moral quality of thought or action. It is a demonstrable fact in the sphere of mind and life, that every distinct thought and mental act, to say nothing of the outward expression of it, is a power or force contributed towards a modification of the existing forces at work in the world. No mental life is the same after a given thought has been formed as it would have been had some other been in its place. The law of dynamics, by which every wave of motion produces an effect for ever, holds good in the mental and moral sphere. Sin is a wave of evil, a force in an oblique direction, or as a seed to germinate and reproduce its kind. David's dreadful deed could not but be an instance of this inevitable law. Other counter-influences of good might arise, but they would not annihilate the fact of the evil influence, and social life would not be the same as it would have been in case his energy had all gone in the line of good, and the energy of the counteraction had been, not counteractive, but supplementary to the force of his unbroken holy life. It is an awful fact that the universe, after sin, is a changed place, and that the trace of the curse in some form, though not necessarily active, will ever be found in the thought and constitution of society.

II. THE IMMEDIATE ACTION OF CONSPICUOUS SIN IS TO WEAKEN THE RESTRAINTS ON EXISTING EVIL TENDENCIES. There are always in the human heart propensities urgent for activity, and they are kept back very much by reason of the force of goodness in the good, as well as by the natural action of conscience. There can be no question that Amnon was, like many, prone to the lusts of the flesh, and that the fact of David's fall had lessened the restraints upon him. The secrecy encouraged by Jonadab might well be stimulated by the previous secrecy of David in his sin, so far as it was known to his family. The influence of David's sin on the mind of Joab could not fail to render court life more corrupt in its springs; for it is a mournful fact that, while we by our sins set a new force for evil at work which gives momentum to those already active, we do not convey to society the blessedness which subsequently may come to us in a free pardon. A notorious sin in high stations is the foster-parent of kindred sins. A parent by his known sin sheds influences around his children that tend to develop the worst elements of their nature. It is fuel to fire.

III. THOSE WHO HAVE COMMITTED OPEN SINS MUST ESPECIALLY FEEL THE PAIN OF WITNESSING THE FRUIT OF THEIR DEEDS. The enlarging family of David offered wider scope for the ill effects of his conduct to work upon. The addition of Bathsheba to the harem under the peculiar circumstances could not but awaken jealousies, and among the various children loosen the bonds of restraint on the lower tendencies of life. He who had so cleverly sought to cover sin in the case of Uriah and his wife, could not detect the secret plot covered by the sickness of his son, whom he with paternal kindness visited and comforted (ver. 6). The iniquity thus coming to maturity at last came to his knowledge in a form little suspected. Its distinctly incestuous character, and the cool cunning with which it was prepared for and perpetrated, must have given intense pain to David, apart from the evil of the act, inasmuch as it would forcibly remind him of days and nights of scheming to accomplish a horrid crime, and compel him to see that the son has learnt too well to imitate the deeds of the father. The more sincere his recent penitence, and the more perfect his restoration to God's favour, the more keen the anguish that now would fill his spirit; for he would see and feel as a holy reconciled man only can. A similar experience is that of parents who witness in their sons, it may be, bolder forms of the sin to which they were once the victims. There are such in Christian society. Their peace with God may be real through the merits of Christ, but their pathway is beclouded by a terrible sorrow. The terrible evils of sin in this life, even to the good! Bitter is the firstfruit!

IV. THOSE WHO HAVE COMMITTED OPEN SIN ARE PARALYZED IN THEIR ACTION TOWARDS SINS OF THE SAME CHARACTER. It is said that when David learnt the full facts of Amnon's conduct towards Tamar, he " was very wroth " (ver. 21). No doubt. Every kind and holy feeling of the restored man would be outraged by this vile conduct. But it is significant that nothing further is said. No action of a legal character was taken. The sentence of the Mosaic Law was not enforced. The remembrance of his own sin unfitted him to deal with Amnon as was due. Direct action on his part for his punishment would, he thought, be met by the reproach of his own deeds. " Physician, heal thyself," had a paralyzing meaning for him. The reference to Absalom nourishing revenge till occasion offered is an historical set-off to David's inactivity. There is nothing unusual in David's conduct. It is repeated every day. The liar's tongue is deprived of its power in reproving lies in others. The deceiver in business affairs cannot with energy and force warn others against fraud. Men who have openly indulged in the lusts of the flesh speak with bated breath and act with indecision when public questions concerning the suppression and punishment of licentiousness are discussed. They may be sincere in their expression of pain, and be intensely angry if any of their offspring fall into vile ways, but they are conscious of a secret force checking the action which otherwise would have been taken. None can speak and act on moral questions as the pure. Our Saviour's words on all moral subjects carry with them the force of his unsullied life. Herein is an example for teachers and taught.

GENERAL LESSONS. 1. There should be an avoidance of all customs in society that in any way tend to strengthen, and give occasion for the development of, the baser feelings of human nature. Oriental harems may have their counterparts in certain usages of Western life. Whatever weakens the feelings of purity and chastity is a positive evil. 2. Care should be taken to avoid the company and services of men clever in evil. There are Jonadabs in society, whose services are ready, but are fraught with woe. 3. The man who can make use of the kindly sympathies of others in order to encompass their ruin is already far gone towards perdition; and inasmuch as there are many such still in society, men who abuse the tenderest affections for lustful ends, their persons should be abhorred and shunned by all Christian people. 4. The selfishness and cruelty of sin is a universal quality (vers. 15—17), and as such it deserves the utmost detestation. All sin is self against God and God's holy order. The adulterer in his lust, the defrauder in his deceit, the extortioner in his greed, the rebellious son in his disobedience, know this too well. Their deeds are damage to the universe for sake of self. 5. There is always being treasured up somewhere retribution for those who seem to escape the punishment due to their sin. Absalom's self-control (ver. 22) is suggestive of restraint on the forces which at last cannot but overwhelm the wicked with destruction (2 Pet. ii. 3; Jude 15).

Vers. 23—39.—The facts are : 1. Absalom, holding a sheep-shearing festival at Baal-hazor, invites the king and his sons. 2. The king, declining to go on account of being unnecessarily burdensome, gets rid of Absalom's entreaty, and bestows on him a parting blessing. 3. After some persuasion, Absalom obtains permission for all the king's sons to accompany him. 4. During the festivities the servants of Absalom, in obedience to their master, smite Amnon, whereupon all the other of the king's sons flee. 5. A false report having reached the king that all his sons were slain, he gives vent to his grief in most distressing form, until Jonadab, who was in the secret of the affair, informs him of the actual facts of the case. 6. Absalom flees, and the rest of the sons return home, and join their father in lamentation over the event. 7. During Absalom's exile for three years, David, while recovering from his grief over Amnon, was in a mind to go out after him, were it possible.

Home troubles. The words of the prophet were being swiftly and terribly fulfilled in the experience of the king. His own crimes of adultery and murder by stealth were now bearing retributive fruit in his own family in the form of adultery and murder, with the increment of incest. That these young men acted as free agents and were responsible for their deeds makes no difference to the fact that, in relation to the previous conduct of their father, it was a terrible retribution in the order of providence. God does chastise his people with the human rod. The blessed covenant made with the chosen one was not broken—his soul was delivered from the mouth of destruction (Ps. lxxxix. 33—36); but a harvest of evil had to be reaped in the place where the dreadful seed had been sown—in the family. Never, perhaps, has this family trouble been paralleled in the experience of good men; but though its precise features are mercifully exceptional, we may see mirrored in this family trouble elements of evil found in some form or other in other domestic circles.

I. JEALOUSIES AND HATREDS CONSEQUENT ON DEEDS OF WRONG. There were signs of ill feeling in this home sprung from an Oriental harem, before the vile deed of Amnon was perpetrated; but this act developed and intensified whatever feeling of that character was in existence. In the most imperfect and unhappy homes a positive deed of wrong to a member of the family is sure to be resented by some other member whose temperament or sympathies flow in a certain direction. The world does not see the acts of harshness and even cruelty sometimes done within the sphere of home; these acts are the parents of a brood of ill feelings, which rankle and burn, waiting for occasion to vent their force on some marked object of hatred. And as the love of home is the tenderest and sweetest of all loves, so, when it is lost, there rises in its place the bitterest and most irreconcilable of hates. The best wine makes the sourest vinegar.

II. PARENTS CRITICIZED. Reading between the lines of this piece of domestic history, we can see that the past conduct of David was not only known, so far at least as Bathsheba was concerned, but that it had not escaped the critical observation of his sons. How could it? A father's domestic conduct is in open light to his children, and, although natural reverence may sway their bearing toward him, they cannot help making critical observations on anything that undermines the respect due. A really pious son would have wept in solitude over the father's sin, and have tenderly covered his shame; but the base tendencies of such young men as Amnon, and the pride of an Absalom, would only have given keenness to the critical spirit. It is a sad prophecy of trouble when children begin to criticize a parent's conduct, and it is moral ruin in a home when a father does deeds which his children, even with their slight knowledge of things, cannot but deplore. Once break down respect for moral conduct, and the home is open to the invasion of numberless ills.

III. PARENTS' APPREHENSION. There is always some room for apprehension in connection with domestic life; for the powers of evil are active, and the best-guarded home may be occasionally invaded from without by a foul spirit. But, as a rule, where prudence in management is combined with correctness of conduct and a spirit of true practical godliness, confidence is in the ascendant. The blessing of God is on the abode of the faithful. In David's house at this time, consequent on the influence of his recent sin and the crime of Amnon, there was evident fear in the father's heart (vers. 26, 27). He had secret reasons for not going or wishing Amnon to go to the feast. Fears of business failures, and of possible changes in domestic material comforts, are common and not to be altogether avoided, yet they may carry with them no secret sting; but anticipations of possible moral disasters and complications in the home life are of all things most fearful burdens to bear, and their gravity is the greater when they are felt to be connected with one's own misconduct. Fathers and mothers should take care that they lay no foundation for painful apprehensions concerning the conduct of their children in deeds of their own performance.

IV. DEVELOPMENTS OF SUPPRESSED ANIMOSITIES. The spirit of David was evidently troubled by observing the strained relations between his sons Amnon and Absalom. The probability is that they were not on terms of familiarity, and seldom visited each other. The ill feeling created by the ruin of his sister had been secretly but steadily cherished for two years, and the treasured revenge at last broke forth in the murder at the festival of sheep-shearing. It is the pain of a father still sometimes to witness the development in violent and distressing forms of passions which he either, through loss of personal influence, could not or would not seek to remove or tone down. The first part of the prophet's prediction had now been fulfilled two years; the other part was on its way, and only awaited the maturity of the forces that were being secretly gathered. When domestic troubles, having a root in moral evil, begin in a home, it is hard to say how long it will be before the powers of evil assume a portentous development. David was fearful, but he scarcely looked for such an issue of a family festival. Literally, in this, as in other cases, sin when it is finished brought forth death (Jas. i. 15). The harvest came after the sowing and germinating of the seed.

V. A FATHER'S DEEDS THE JUSTIFICATION OF EVIL. The bitterest element in David's domestic trouble was not simply the death of an incestuous son, sad as the death of a firstborn always is, but the knowledge that his own conduct was, in the mind of Absalom, the justification of the murder. Absalom seems to have reasoned thus: "Amnon has done a guilty deed worthy of death; no severe punishment has been inflicted on him by my father, perhaps because of his own previous adultery with Bathsheba, or because this is his firstborn; shame has been brought by this crime on the entire family; as the brother of the disgraced and ruined woman, I am her legitimate avenger in the failure of law; and as the injury has been an open one in the centre of the family life, the doom shall be open, in the presence, if possible, of father and brothers." If David was the man of discernment now as formerly, he could scarcely have failed to see that there was something like this current of thought in the mind of his son Absalom, and that it formed a specious justification of his daring deed. Rightly or wrongly, some do reason in defence of their rash and evil deeds, and it is the most serious element of the domestic trouble when the foundation of their reasoning is found in the deeds or neglect of their parents. The devil encourages those who do wrong to get all possible support from the actions of those professing to be good.

VI. A FOMENTER OF MISCHIEF AND EVIL. One of the troubles in David's home life was the presence of an influential double-faced man, who, being in the secrets, entered as adviser into the schemes of some of the family, and was instrumental in promoting incest, and then, on his own showing, knew that it was a settled thing to murder the incestuous man (vers. 3—5; cf. vers. 32, 33). This cunning man, who had not the courage or honesty to tell David of the design of Absalom, was a moral plague in David's family connection. It is an instance of how much evil may come to a home by cultivating the friendship and intimacy of unprincipled or cowardly relatives. Alas! for the home (and there are such in our country) that is invaded by the pestilential influence of men who trample under their feet chastity, love, and, if need be, life itself! There are vipers and dragons in the world still (Matt. iii. 7; cf. Ps. xci. 13).

GENERAL LESSONS. 1. We see the wonderful contrast in domestic life where piety is maintained in unfading beauty. Instead of jealousies and hatreds, parents blamed by sons and full of fear, evil feelings maturing into developed deeds of violence and cruelty, justified by reference to parental conduct, and stimulated or connived at by base friends, we shall see love and consideration, reverence for parents, confidence in children, generous sentiments ripening into holy deeds, encouragement for kind actions found in parental example, and friendships formed conducive to peace and harmony. 2. We learn the danger of deliberately nourishing feelings of revenge even when wrong has been done. It is for God to vindicate his own justice (Rom. xii. 9). Just sentiments of anger may, unless guard be kept over them, burn into more questionable forms. 3. The festive scenes of wicked men should be avoided, because of the evil communications which corrupt good manners, and the possible incidental evils arising therefrom. 4. When men are known to be proud and imperious and revengeful, they are likely to be credited with more evil than they have really done (ver. 30); hence avoid such a spirit. 5. It is a shame to a man to be in the secrets of those intent on evil (vers. 3—5; cf. ver. 32); and, though such may escape punishment in human society, God will visit their sins on their own head. 6. Rulers and parents who show an unwise partiality (vers. 21, 22) in not adequately chastising evil-doers, only defer the day of trouble and increase its sorrows (ver. 36).

Lost and exiled. The closing verses of this chapter are very obscure in their construction and meaning. The sense most probable, and which we here proceed upon, is that Absalom's asylum with the King of Geshur was a reason why David did not follow after him with a view to his apprehension and chastisement, and that while at first he mourned for Amnon every day, he was in process of time able to bear up under his loss. The calamity brought on by his own sins (ch. xii. 9—12) had now culminated in one son lost and another in exile.

I. THERE IS A NATURAL PROGRESSION IN THE TROUBLES CONSEQUENT ON SIN. The first temporal human trouble attendant on David's sin was dislike and aversion of his other wives, and this small beginning was followed by his being put under the power of Joab (ch. xi. 6, 18—21), his exposure to others, the incest of his children, the loss of influence by refraining from duty (vers. 21, 22), and now it came to a climax in the firstborn being in his grave, and the second son being banished as an exile. It is an evil and a bitter thing to sin against God, the more so according to the station and privileges of the sinner. A firstborn lost! A young man cut down with, so far as we can see, the vilest sins unforgiven on his head! The flower of the family, the man of spirit, and avenger in daring way of a sister's wrong, in a foreign land, finding refuge from a father's wrath with the heathen! Fathers and mothers, read the lesson well, and seek for grace to be in the home pure and wise and loving, like unto the holy Saviour.

II. THERE IS SHEER HELPLESSNESS IN FACE OF THE ACCUMULATED CALAMITIES CONSEQUENT ON SIN. David could only mourn over the lost one. And what bitterness in the mourning! The dire chain of moral causes ending in that wretched death could not be broken; for an inscrutable and just Providence had welded them to the first adulterous link of his own manufacture. Whatever anger was cherished against the brother-assassin, and whatever desire to vindicate the law against him, policy and other considerations prevented his going out after him to drag him from the asylum afforded by another king. It was a time of correction in righteousness when the bitter but wholesome lessons of his life were to be taken to heart. It is fortunate if men, having by a succession of faults and sins brought themselves face to face with hard unalterable facts, apply their hearts with all earnestness to God for his sanctifying grace.

III. The discharge of the duties of life becomes increasingly difficult when the joys of home life are destroyed. Though dwelling in distinct abodes in Jerusalem, the royal family had a common home life, and, under hallowed influences, this might have been to David a source of strength in the administration of affairs. Now, however, the joy of his heart was gone. Energy was spent in sorrowful memories and thoughts concerning the possible future efforts of the ambitious and now reckless exile, which otherwise would have gone in the direction of cheerful daily work for the nation. Fears of yet further troubles, and passionate desire to remove the public reproach of letting crime in his house go by default, were not helpful to calm effort for public good. Many a man loses energy for business consequent on the loss of domestic joys. Home is the proper place for weary men to find refreshment after toil, and cheer for new endeavours. We may truly pity the man whose domestic troubles come in such form as to impair his strength for the battle of life. If he has not the grace of God in his heart, it is not surprising if he yields to temptation and seeks relief in sinful pleasures.

HOMILIES BY VARIOUS AUTHORS.

Vers. 1—33.—(Jerusalem.) *The crime of Amnon.* The chastisements which David experienced came upon him chiefly through his family. The misconduct of his sons was largely due to his own "in the matter of Uriah," and his defective discipline (1 Sam. iii. 13; 1 Kings i. 6) in connection with *polygamy* (ch. iii. 1—5). "This institution is the absolutely irrepressible source of numberless evils of this description. It ever furnishes a ready stimulus to unbounded sensual desire in the sovereign, and, should he be exalted above it, is likely to introduce a dissolute life among the very different children of different mothers, by bringing the pleasures of sense so prominently and so early before their eyes. The subsequent troubles with Amnon, Absalom, and Adonijah were all connected with this fundamental wrong; and on the same thread hung many of the evils which were felt under David's successors" (Ewald). "Having grown up without strict paternal discipline, simply under the care of their different mothers, who were jealous of one another, his sons fancied that they might gratify their own fleshly lusts, and carry out their own ambitious plans" (Keil). Amnon his eldest son (by Ahinoam of Jezreel, whom David married during his exile, 1 Sam. xxv. 43; and born in Hebron, ch. iii. 2) was now about twenty years of age. "His character and conduct were doubtless affected by the fact that he was the firstborn son, and of a mother apparently not of the noblest birth." In him (regarded as a warning especially to *young men*) we notice—

I. Impure affection, springing up in the heart, and not repressed, but fondly cherished. His passion was contrary to the Divine Law, not merely because the object of it was his half-sister (ver. 13), but also because of its licentious nature (Matt. v. 28). His subsequent conduct indicates that it was not

> "True love, that ever shows itself as clear
> In kindness as loose appetite in wrong."
>
> (Dante.)

It is not improbable, from his ready entertainment of it, and the question of Absalom (ver. 20), that already he had given himself to unrestrained indulgence of his passions. When once "reason by lust is swayed," the heart becomes a congenial soil for all unholy affections. And the only sure safeguard is to "keep the heart with all diligence," by giving no place to an impure thought, avoiding every incentive to "fleshly lusts, which war against the soul," the exercise of habitual self-denial, and prayer for Divine grace (Matt. v. 29; xv. 19).

II. Inward misery, proceeding from restless passion and fretful discontent at hindrances and restraints in the way of its gratification (ver. 2). It is well that such hindrances and restraints exist (in Divine Law, public opinion, providential circumstances); for they afford opportunity for reflection, conviction of its sinful nature, and the adoption of all proper means whereby it may be overcome. Where it is still cherished, its strength increases and its force is felt more powerfully, as that of a river appears when a rock opposes its progress (Rom. vii. 7). "There is no peace to the wicked." "Amnon here neglected, indeed, the right means; viz. in time to have resisted his affections and not to have given way unto them; to have given himself to abstinence and some honest exercises which might have occupied his mind; then by some lawful matrimonial love to have overcome his unlawful lust; and to have prayed unto God for grace" (Willet).

III. DELIBERATE DISSIMULATION, displayed in crafty devices, adopted in accordance with evil suggestion, in order to selfish indulgence. He who suffers a sinful desire to reign within him is peculiarly susceptible to temptation, and readily yields to it; sometimes pursues a course of guile, and takes advantage of affection, kindness, and unsuspecting confidence. "The seducer is brother to the murderer." Blinded and infatuated, he resorts to the most subtle and contemptible expedients. And, alas! he too often succeeds.

IV. WILFUL PERSISTENCY in wickedness, notwithstanding the strongest inducements to the contrary (vers. 12, 13). "It is enough to suppose that the king had a dispensing power, which was conceived to cover even extreme cases." When persuasive craft is employed in vain to entice into sin, and the slave of passion meets with another merciful check by the opposition of virtue and piety ("in Israel"), he is driven on to more brutal, though less diabolical methods of accomplishing his base designs. The dishonour done to the highest claims (of God, religion, his people), the disgrace incurred, the misery inflicted, should be sufficient to deter from "foolish and hurtful lusts;" but with him they are of no avail. "The unjust knoweth no shame" (Zeph. iii. 5; Isa. xxvi. 10). Then one evil passion is replaced by another.

> "Sweet love, I see, changing his property,
> Turns to the sourest and most deadly hate."
>
> (Shakespeare.)

"He hated her, but did not hate his own sin. Thus he showed that the love he had professed to her was not love, but lust; that it was not of God, but of the evil one" (Wordsworth). "It is characteristic of human nature to hate whom you have injured" (Tacitus). "Such are the baits and allurements of sin, which have a pleasant taste at the first, but in the end bite like a serpent; therefore one saith that pleasures must be considered, not as they come, but as they go" (Willet). "He feedeth on ashes," etc. (Isa. xliv. 20). The victim of evil desire becomes an object of bitter aversion, is pitilessly thrust away, maliciously defamed, and thus more grievously wronged: the true picture of many a desolated life! "What men dignify with the name of love is commonly a base sensual inclination, entire selfishness, which triumphs over the conscience and the fear of God, and without pity consigns its object to irreparable disgrace and misery for the sake of a momentary gratification! How different from that love which the Law of God commands! yea, how contrary to it!" (Scott).

V. DELUSIVE SECURITY, arising from the persuasion that secret iniquity may escape retribution. The transgressor thinks, perhaps, that it cannot be proved, no one will venture to call him to account for it, and that it is not worse than other crimes that go unpunished. Whatever fears (ver. 21) or suspicions he may at first entertain, are laid asleep by the lapse of time (ver. 23). He is not led to repentance by the long-suffering of Heaven, and he heeds not its wrath. But "judgment lingereth not," etc. (2 Pet. ii. 3).

VI. SUDDEN DESTRUCTION, inflicted by an unexpected hand (vers. 20, 28, 32). Where public law fails to do justice, private hostility finds means to take vengeance. One sin produces another, and is punished by it; craft by craft, violence by violence, hatred by hatred. "The way of transgressors is hard" (Prov. xiii. 15; vi. 15; xxix. 1).—D.

Ver. 3.—(JERUSALEM.) A false friend. "And Jonadab was a very subtil man." Every virtue has its counterfeit. As there is a friendship which is true and beneficial, so there is what appears to be such but is false and injurious. Of the former we have an instance in David and Jonathan (1 Sam. xviii. 1—4), of the latter in Amnon and Jonadab (his cousin, a son of Shammah, 1 Sam. xvi. 9; ch. xxi. 21), "one of those characters who in great houses pride themselves on being acquainted and on dealing with all the secrets of the family" (Stanley). In Jonadab, the daily companion of

Amnon (ver. 4), we see the kind of friend that should *not* be chosen. 1. *He is distinguished for subtlety, not for virtue and piety.* "In the choice of a friend, let him be virtuous; for vice is contagious, and there is no trusting of the sound and the sick together" (Seneca). "Friendship is nothing else but benevolence or charity, under some modifications, viz. that it be in a special manner intense, that it be mutual, and that it be manifest or mutually known. It cannot be but between good men, because an ill man cannot have any true charity, much less such an intense degree of it as is requisite to friendship" (J. Norris, 'Miscellanies'). A companion is sometimes chosen solely for his cleverness and insinuating address; but his superior intelligence (however desirable in itself), unless it be combined with moral excellence, enables him to do all the greater mischief (Jer. iv. 22). 2. *In professing concern for another's welfare he seeks only to serve his own interests;* his own pleasure, gain, influence, and advancement (ver. 4). True friendship is disinterested. Jonadab appears to have cared only for himself. Hence (to avoid getting himself into trouble) he gave no warning to others of what he foresaw (ver. 32). "This young man, who probably desired to make himself of some importance as David's nephew, was clever enough to guess the truth from the first; but it is sad to think that his thought and his advice were never founded on anything but a knowledge of the devil in man" (Ewald). 3. *When he is acquainted with the secret thoughts of another, he fails to give him faithful counsel.* (Ver. 5.) Such acquaintance is often obtained by flattery—"thou a king's son"—and frequent questioning; but it is not followed, in the case of improper desires and purposes, by admonition. "No flatterer can be a true friend." "Had he been a true friend, he had bent all the forces of his dissuasion against the wicked motions of that sinful lust" (Hall). "Faithful are the wounds of a friend." 4. *Whilst he devises means for another's gratification, he smoothes his way to destruction.* His aim is only to please. He advises what is agreeable, but what is morally wrong; and thus incites to sin; for which, with all its consequences, he is, in part, responsible. "In wise counsel two things must be considered—that both the *end* be good, and the *means* honest and lawful. Jonadab's counsel failed in both." "The rapacious friend, the insincere friend, the friend who speaks only to please, and he who is a companion in vicious pleasures,—recognizing these four to be false friends, the wise man flies far from them, as he would from a road beset by danger" (*Contemporary Review*, xxvii. 421). "A companion of fools shall be destroyed" (Prov. xiii. 20; i. 10).—D.

Ver. 7.—*Tamar.* A princess; the daughter of David and Maacah (of Geshur), and sister of Absalom; distinguished for her beauty, modesty, domesticity, obedience (ver. 8), tender-heartedness, piety, and misfortunes. In her we see an illustration of (what has often occurred): 1. Purity pursued by licentious desire (ver. 2). 2. Simplicity beset by wily designs (ver. 5). 3. Kindness requited by selfish ingratitude (vers. 9, 10). 4. Confidence exposed to enticing persuasions and perilous temptation (ver. 11). 5. Virtue overpowered by brutal violence (ver. 14). 6. Innocence vilified by guilty aversion (ver. 17). "So fair had she gone forth on what seemed her errand of mercy, so foully had she been driven back" (Edersheim). "Let no one ever expect better treatment from those who are capable of attempting their seduction; but it is better to suffer the greatest wrong than to commit the least sin" (Matthew Henry). 7. Sorrow assuaged by brotherly sympathy (ver. 20). 8. Injury avenged with terrible severity (ver. 28).—D.

Ver. 21.—*Impunity.* "And King David heard of all these things, and was very wroth;" but "he did not grieve the spirit of his son Amnon, because he loved him, for he was his firstborn" (LXX.). And he did not punish him (1 Sam. iii. 13); which must be looked upon as—
I. AN OMISSION OF MANIFEST DUTY. If he had been only a father, he would have been bound to chastise his children for their misbehaviour; but, being also a king, he was under still stronger obligation to punish the guilty. To do this: 1. Properly belonged to the *authority* delegated to him. 2. Was expressly enjoined in the *Divine Law* (Lev. xx. 17). 3. Urgently demanded by *the sense of justice.* 4. Indispensably necessary to the *protection* of his subjects. "Kings, then, have not absolute power to do in their government what pleases them; their power is limited by God's Word; so

that if they strike not where God has commanded to strike, they and their throne are criminal and guilty of the wickedness which abounds upon the face of the earth for lack of punishment" (John Knox).

II. UNWARRANTED BY ADEQUATE REASONS. In Israel (as in Persia and other Eastern countries) the king, as vicegerent of heaven, had a large discretionary power of dispensing with the penalties of the Law; but it behoved him to exercise it without partiality and on sufficient grounds. Although David's omission to punish is not expressly condemned, yet the consequences by which it was followed show that it took place (not, as some have supposed, on "principle," or because it was "impossible" for him to do otherwise, but) without such grounds. 1. *The affection of a father.* This, however, ought not to have prevented punishment by a father or judge; as it did, being inordinate and blamable, in Eli (1 Sam. ii. 22, 30). 2. *The rank of the offender;* the king's son, his firstborn, heir to the crown. But he was not above the law; nor less guilty than another of inferior position would have been. "God is no respecter of persons." 3. *The transgression and forgiveness of the king himself.* Nevertheless, whilst both may have exerted a pernicious influence, Amnon was responsible for his own conduct; and David's exemption (only from legal punishment) rested on grounds which did not exist in the case of his ungodly and impenitent son. The king's wrath proves his full conviction of Amnon's guilt and his moral abhorrence of its enormity; his failure to "grieve," or inflict suffering upon him, indicates his own weakness and dereliction of duty. "Punishment is an effort of man to find a more exact relation between sin and suffering than this world affords us. A duty is laid upon us to make this relationship of sin to suffering as real, and as natural, and as exact in proportion as it is possible to be made. This is the moral root of the whole doctrine of punishment. But if the adjustment of pain to vice be the main ground of punishment, it must be admitted that there are other ends which society has in view in its infliction. These secondary elements in punishment appear to be (1) the reformation of the offender; (2) the prevention of further offences by the offender; (3) the repression of offences in others" (Edward Fry, *Nineteenth Century,* No. lxxix. p. 524).

III. PRODUCTIVE OF DISASTROUS EFFECTS. 1. It does not appear to have produced any other effect *on the offender* than to confirm him in recklessness and fancied security. "Punishment connected with sin operates towards reform in two ways: (1) by the association of ideas—the linking together of that from which our nature shrinks with that from which it ought to shrink, so that the temptation to sin recalls not only the pleasure of sin, but the pain of suffering; (2) by the shock to the habits of thought and of practice which suffering produces, by the solution of continuity in the man's life which it causes, by the opportunity for reflection and thought which it thus affords" (Lord Justice Fry). 2. *On others,* also, it was injurious; weakening respect for royal authority and public justice, causing the law to be despised, furnishing grounds for private revenge, leading to further impunity (ver. 39; ch. xiv. 24, 33), more daring crimes (ch. xv. 7; xvi. 21), widespread disaffection and rebellion. 3. *On the king himself.* Further impairing his personal, moral, kingly energy, and accumulating "sorrow upon sorrow" (vers. 31, 37; ch. xv. 13). It was another link in the chain of painful consequences resulting from his great transgression; naturally, slowly, effectually wrought out under the direction and control of the perfect justice of the supreme King; accomplishing a beneficent end, in purifying his heart, restoring him to God, averting his final condemnation, and teaching, warning, benefiting mankind. "The dark sin of which he had been guilty spoke of a character that had lost its self-control, its truthfulness, its generosity. His penitence was not able to undo all its consequences and to bring back the old energy and life. Over and above its direct results in alienating the hearts of his most trusted counsellors, and placing him at the mercy of a hard taskmaster, that dark hour left behind it the penalty of an enfeebled will, the cowardice of a hidden crime, the remorse which weeps for the past, yet cannot rouse itself to the duties of the present. He leaves the sin of Amnon unpunished in spite of the fearful promise it gave of a reign of brutal passion, 'because he loved him, for he was his firstborn.' Half suspecting, apparently, that Absalom had some scheme for revenging the wrong which he had failed to redress, he has no energy to stop its execution. He shrinks only from being present at a meeting the meaning and issues of which he does not comprehend, and yet dimly fears. When the exaggerated report is brought back that Absalom had slain all his brothers—sure sign, if it had been so, that he was claiming the throne, and marching to it through the blood of his kindred—David's attitude is that of passive, panic-stricken submission" (E. H. Plumptre, 'Biblical Studies,' p. 89). Who can say that he sinned with *impunity*? "Thenceforward the days of his years became full of evil, and if he lived (for the Lord *caused death to pass* from himself to the child by a vicarious dispensation), it was to be a king, with more than kingly sorrows, but with little of kingly power; to be banished by his son; bearded by his servant; betrayed by his friends; deserted by his people; bereaved of his children; and to feel all, all these bitter griefs, bound, as it were, by a chain of complicated cause and effect, to this one great, original transgression" (Blunt, 'Undesigned Coincidences,' p. 146).

> " It often falls, in course of common life,
>   That right long time is overborne of wrong;
> Through avarice, or power, or guile, or strife,
>   That weakens her, and makes her party strong.
> But justice, though her doom she do prolong,
> Yet at the last she will her own cause right."
>
> (Spenser.)
>
> D.

Vers. 22—29.—(BAAL-HAZOR.) *The revenge of Absalom.* "Absalom hated Amnon." *References:* 1. Third son (Chileab, probably, being dead) of David, by Maacah, daughter of Talmai, King of Geshur; born at Hebron, his name ("father of peace") indicating, perhaps, the hope entertained at his birth (ch. iii. 1—5). "The young handsome hero must have been conspicuous among the soldiers of Israel, and taken his place among the sons of David, who were 'chief rulers.'" 2. Hatred (when about eighteen years old) and murder (after two years). 3. Flight to Geshur (ver. 38) and residence there (three years). 4. Return (ch. xiv. 23, 24) and partial reconciliation (during two years); married about this time, and father of three sons (dying in infancy, ch. xiv. 27; xviii. 18) and one daughter (Tamar, named after his sister). 5. Full reconciliation (ch. xiv. 33; xv. 1—11) and preparation for revolt (four years). 6. Conspiracy in Hebron (ch. xv. 12, 13). 7. Occupation of Jerusalem (ch. xv. 37; xvi. 15—19), possession of the palace (ch. xv. 20—23), anointed king (ch. xix. 10), consultations (ch. xvii. 1—14). 8. Pursuit of David, and defeat in battle (ch. xvii. 24—26; xviii. 1—8). 9. Slain by Joab (ch. xviii. 9—18). 10. Lamented by David (ch. xviii. 33; xix. 1—4). Revenge is sinful resentment. It is felt, on account of real or supposed injury, toward the person rather than the conduct of the offender; desires his suffering, not his improvement; and seeks it maliciously, deliberately, and unlawfully. "All pain occasioned to another in consequence of an offence or injury received from him, further than what is calculated to procure reparation or promote the just ends of punishment, is so much revenge" (Paley, 'Mor. Ph.'). It is "a kind of wild justice" (Bacon, 'Essays'). Of the spirit of revenge, which was embodied in Absalom, and too often finds a place in others, observe—

I. ITS SEEMING JUSTIFICATION; for he who indulges it commonly seeks to justify himself therein (ch. xiv. 32), it may be, on account of: 1. The *grievous wrong* suffered, directly or in the person of another with whom he is closely connected. The more this is brooded over, the greater it appears and the more it incites to wrath. 2. The *natural instinct* of anger and retaliation, which is

> " Far, far too dear to every mortal breast,
> Sweet to the soul as honey to the taste."
>
> (Homer.)

But it must be directed, controlled, often completely repressed by justice and love. "The taking vengeance on a foe is honourable," it has been said, "rather than the being reconciled" (Aristotle, 'Rhetoric'). True wisdom teaches otherwise (1 Sam. xi. 12, 13; Prov. xx. 22; xxiv. 29). 3. The *culpable failure* of justice, on the part of the civil magistrate, "the minister of God," etc. (Rom. xiii. 4). It may be a temptation to private vengeance; but it does not warrant any one in taking the law into his own hands; whilst by doing so he becomes a breaker of the law and justly liable to its penalty. "The revenge which he took for the foul wrong that his sister had suffered at the hands of Amnon did not shock the men of Israel as it shocks us. To him, by the feeling of all Oriental nations, belonged the special guardianship of her honour; and subtly as the punishment was inflicted, it was nothing more than the monstrous turpitude of the guilt deserved. Had David been true to his kingly calling, instead of passing the crime over with a weak sorrow and a yet weaker leniency, there would have been no occasion for the vengeance which Absalom felt himself bound to take. The two long years of waiting which followed on his revenge, must have been a time in which disappointment, irritation, bitterness against his father, were gaining, slowly but surely, the mastery over him" (Plumptre).

II. ITS SPECIAL CHARACTERISTICS. 1. Enduring and implacable *hatred* (ver. 23); a malicious purpose formed from the first (as his intimate companion read in his countenance, ver. 32), but concealed that it might be the more effectually accomplished when opportunity served. "A man that studieth revenge keeps his own wounds green, which otherwise would heal and do well" (Bacon). 2. Subtle and deceitful *scheming* (vers. 24, 26); under pretence of kindness; and taking a base advantage of affection, consideration, and confidence. Ver. 25 is "the first instance history offers of the ruinous cost of royal visits to those who are honoured with them" (Kitto). 3. Pitiless and treacherous *cruelty* (ver. 28; ch. xi. 13). Another instance of indulgence in intoxication (1 Sam. xxv. 36, 37; ch. xi. 13). "Absalom calls the execution of this base cruelty in his servants, courage and valour; being indeed but treacherous and cowardly murder; which shows that vices are ofttimes coloured with the name of virtues, as drunkenness is called good fellowship, avarice good husbandry, subtlety to deceive wisdom, and pride magnanimity" (Guild). It is not improbable that he wished to get rid of Amnon as an obstacle in the way to the throne. "The wild acts of Absalom's life may have been to some extent the results of maternal training; they were at least characteristic of the stock from which he sprang" (Smith, 'Dict.'). "From his father he inherited nothing but his regal pride" (Ewald). "He was a man who could scheme deeply, bide his time patiently, and then strike with decision and daring" (D. Macleod).

III. ITS EXCEEDING SINFULNESS. 1. Disbelief in the presence and justice of God, who, though man fails to punish, "will by no means clear the guilty." 2. Insensibility to his forbearance, which should teach the like (1 Sam. xxiv. 13; Matt. v. 48). 3. Disobedience to the Divine Law, which is "fulfilled in one word," etc. (Gal. v. 14), and to many special injunctions (Rom. xii. 9; Matt. vi. 15). 4. Fruitfulness in wickedness and crime (1 John iii. 15), with all their evil consequences to others and to a man himself (vers. 36, 37). "Absalom fled from man, who only could kill the body; but he could not fly from blood-guiltiness and an accusing conscience, nor yet from the hand of God's justice, which did reach him afterwards" (Guild). "It was asked of the sage, 'In what one virtue are all the rest comprised?' 'Patience,' was his answer. 'And in what single vice are all others concentrated?' 'Vindictiveness'" (Rabbi Salomon Ibn Gabirol). "Whereas some may be apt to suspect that the patient bearing of one injury may invite another, I believe it will be found quite otherwise, that the revenging of one injury brings on another; the one is like the withdrawing of fuel or combustible matter, which will soon put out the fire, and the other is continually furnishing fresh fuel, mixed with oil and gunpowder and such inflaming materials as are apt to spread the fire of contention, but not to extinguish it" (J. Blair: 1740).

CONCLUSION. How odious is the spirit of revenge! He who gives way to it might as well cherish a venomous serpent in his bosom. "Be not overcome of evil, but overcome evil with good" (Rom. xii. 21).—D.

Vers. 30—39.—(JERUSALEM.) *Parental sorrows.* "And the king also and all his servants wept very sore" (ver. 36). David's intense feeling appears in his affection (vers. 6, 25, 39), his wrath (ver. 21), and his grief (ver. 31). The delight which a father finds in his children is seldom unalloyed. His sorrows, on their account, are—

I. OFTTIMES PECULIARLY SEVERE. 1. Their misbehaviour. "A 'house-cross' is the heaviest of all earthly crosses. The gall which is mingled in our cup by those who are nearest to us surpasses all others in bitterness" (Krummacher).

> " How sharper than a serpent's tooth it is
> To have a thankless child ! "
>
>   (' King Lear.')

2. Their misfortune (ver. 19).   3. Their disappointment of his hopes ; his consternation, trembling anxieties, exaggerated fears (ver. 30); his bereavement by death (ver. 32) and by enforced exile through crime (ver. 34); his son a fratricide, like Cain, alive yet dead.   What a heavy burden of trouble was thus laid upon David !   It is not surprising that it was followed by serious and protracted *bodily affliction*, favourable to the designs of his enemies and conducive to still deeper distress (ch. xv. 4, 30), as several psalms seem to indicate (Ps. xxxviii., xxxix., xli., lv.).

> O Jehovah, rebuke me not in thine anger,
> Nor chasten me in thy hot displeasure.
> For thine arrows stick fast in me,
> And thy hand presseth me sore," etc.
>
>   (Ps. xxxviii. 1, 2.)

II. SOMETIMES DUE TO HIS OWN FAULT.   1. His sinful example.   Children are more ready to imitate their father's vices than his virtues.   2. His defective discipline. " David's failure in the government of his family was due in part to the excessive, even morbid, tenderness of his feelings towards his children, especially some of them. He may also have thought of his family circle as too exclusively a scene for relaxation and enjoyment; he may have forgotten that even there there is a call for much vigilance and self-denial " (Blaikie).   " By this example we see that children whom their parents spare to correct will in the end be a grief unto them " (Willet). " Chastisement without love is an outrage; no father is at liberty to plague or torture his child; but a love that cannot chastise is no love, and reaps a poor reward.   A child that does not at the proper time feel the father's rod becomes at last a rod for his father " (Schlier).   " Ofttimes the child whom the father loves most (as David did Amnon) becomes his greatest grief by too much indulgence " (Guild).   3. His culpable clemency in the case of a great crime (ver. 21).   Even if David did inflict some punishment on Amnon, as it has been supposed (Chandler), yet it was altogether inadequate to the offence.   The sorrows of a father over the sins and sufferings of his children are intensified by the knowledge that they are, in some degree, the result of his own errors and transgressions.   " A parent can have no sharper pang than the sight of his own sin reappearing in his child.   David saw the ghastly reflection of his unbridled passion in his eldest son's foul crime (and even a gleam of it in his unhappy daughter) and of his murderous craft in his second son's bloody revenge " (Maclaren).

III. NOT WITHOUT MERCIFUL ALLEVIATION.   1. The occasion of trouble is less calamitous than it might have been; less than it was feared to be (ver. 32).   2. Grief is assuaged by the lapse of time (vers. 37, 38).   3. It is vain to mourn over what is irreparable (ver. 39; ch. xii. 23; xiv. 14).   4. These afflictions are chastisements from the heavenly Father's hand, and should be endured with patience and hope (Ps. xxxix. 7, 9; xxxviii. 15).   5. They are mingled with tokens of Divine favour (ch. xii. 13, 25; Ps. xli. 1—3; Isa. xxvii. 8).   6. Their purpose is morally beneficial (Heb. xii. 11).   " It may seem strange to say it, but it is most true, that the tears which flow from the eyelids of a man are as needful to the fruitfulness of his heart as the dews which descend from the eyelids of the morning are to the thirsty ground " (E. Irving).—D.

Ver. 3.—*A diabolical friend : a homily for young men.*   This chapter contains a dreadful story.   The unnatural lust of Amnon, the vile counsels of Jonadab, the unsuspiciousness of the king, the confiding innocence of Tamar, her unavailing remonstrances and resistance, the hardened villainy of her half-brother, his hatred and cruel expulsion of his innocent victim, her bitter anguish and lamentations, the unjust leniency of David towards the offender (although "very wroth"), the vengeance so quietly prepared and so sternly executed by Absalom, the king's lamentations over the death of Amnon, his subsequent longing after the fugitive Absalom,—present a picture of horrible wickedness, of helpless misery, of weak negligence, of fierce and deadly revenge, which moves us with alternate detestation and pity, as well as wonder that so much depravity should have been found in the family of a man so godly and devout, until we remember the unfavourableness of polygamy to the right training of families, the foolish indulgence of David towards his children, and his own evil conduct, which weakened his authority. Passing by, however, all other particulars, let us consider awhile this statement, "Amnon had a friend, whose name was Jonadab . . . a very subtil man."

I. A KIND OF FRIENDSHIP TO BE ABHORRED AND AVOIDED. At first view the friendship of Jonadab and Amnon seems natural and proper. They were first cousins; Jonadab was a man of intelligence ("subtil," equivalent to "wise," not necessarily "subtle" in the bad sense); he "showed himself friendly" by noticing his friend's doleful appearance and inquiring the cause. Not until we observe the advice he gave, and see how it was accepted and followed, do we discover how base he was, how base they both were. Amnon's vileness appears, indeed, earlier, in his indulgence of a passion for his beautiful half-sister, and that so violent, while so seemingly hopeless, that it affected his health. A case, surely, calling for pity and sympathy! No wonder that his dear friend so feelingly inquired after his health, and employed his subtlety to find a remedy! They must have known each other very well for one to acknowledge so disreputable a cause of his ill looks, and the other to suggest so infamous a restorative. What a real friend would have advised is obvious. He would have urged Amnon, by every consideration of morality and religion, of regard for the honour of his family and nation, the happiness of his father, and the duty he owed to his sister, to conquer his guilty passion. But Amnon knew well that he was in no peril of being troubled with such counsel, or he would not have acknowledged his shameful lust. Observe, too, how utterly this pair of friends, like all their tribe, disregarded the ruin and misery which they were plotting for the innocent Tamar. They seem to have been tolerably sure that the offence would not be thought very serious by "society," and that the law would not be put in force by David. His own sins of a similar kind would give them confidence of impunity. Even after committing the foul crime, Amnon does not seem to have thought it necessary, for the sake either of safety or decency, to retire for at least a time from Jerusalem until the affair had "blown over." What a contrast between this friendship and that of David and Jonathan! Many such friends, alas! are to be found in the world; men who are counselling and aiding and hardening each other in licentiousness, whose delight is to ruin the innocent, and bring dishonour and misery on their families; and who are preparing each other for well-merited damnation. Yet their debauchery is overlooked by "society," especially if they be of high rank, while their victims receive no pity. It would be of little use to address such wretches, even if we could gain access to them. But we may warn young men who have not yet come under their deadly influence, but who may be in danger of doing so. For in all classes of society persons are to be found who, corrupt themselves, delight in corrupting others. Young men coming from the country to great cities, where at present they have no friends, are in peril, not only from prostitutes or sometimes from loose married women, but from men of the class referred to. These will test them by using *double entendres*, advancing to outspoken ribaldry and freer conversation about sexual indulgences. If discouraged, they will laugh at the "innocence" and "squeamishness" of the youth they would corrupt. If he at all encourage them, they will introduce him to indecent books, or offer themselves as guides to the places where he may safely indulge his passions. To an inexperienced youth, not yet well grounded in Christian principles, such approaches present very powerful temptations. The assault from without meets with auxiliaries within, in the awakening passions themselves, and in a curiosity "to see a little life." The manner in which such temptations are met at the beginning is likely to determine the character of the youth's whole future life. To yield is to be undone; to resist and conquer is to gain new strength for future conflict and victory. Let, then, those who are thus tempted shrink back from their tempter as from a viper. At the first indication of such depravity let them "cut" those who display it, however related to them by blood, however agreeable as companions (the more agreeable the more dangerous), however able to help them in their worldly career. If their counsel be not followed, yet friendly association with them in any degree must exercise a debasing influence. It may not be possible to avoid them altogether; they may be employed in the same establishment, and indulge themselves in loose language in the hearing of their fellows; but let a loathing of them be cherished, and every practicable effort be made to silence and suppress them.

II. THE SUREST SAFEGUARDS AGAINST SUCH FRIENDSHIP. 1. *Close and decided friendship with Christ.* Begun early, cultivated diligently by daily communion with him in secret, through devout study of his Word, believing meditation, fervent prayer. Thus the heart will become filled with the purest and noblest affections, leaving no room for the vile; and thus will the youth become "strong in the Lord, and in the power of his might," and "be able to withstand in the evil day" (Eph. vi. 10, 13). 2. *Friendship with the best Christians.* Union and communion with them in Church fellowship, in Divine ordinances, in Christian work, in social life and its pure enjoyments. Christian people should interest themselves in the young (especially young men from home), and welcome them to their confidence, their friendship, their homes. For the young must have friends; and if there be difficulty in associating with the good, they are in so much greater danger of contenting themselves with the evil or the doubtful. But if they form Christian friendships, these will be as an impassable barrier against the advances of such as would lead them astray. 3. *Constant watchfulness and prayer.* Against everything that, if indulged, would make the society of the wicked welcome. Guard the heart, for out of it springs the life (Prov. iv. 23). Seek of God a clean heart (Ps. li. 10). Suppress every impure thought and feeling (see Matt. v. 28), and every impulse to utter impure words (Eph. iv. 29; v. 3). Let the psalmist's prayers (Ps. cxli. 3, 4; cxxxix. 23, 24) be yours. Ever cherish the thought, "Thou God seest me" (Gen. xvi. 13). 4. *Consideration of the certain result of following evil counsellors.* "A companion of fools shall be destroyed" (Prov. xiii. 20). Amnon found it so. Let the young man think, when sinners entice him, "They are inviting me to misery, death, *hell!*"

Finally, it is not only those who are unchaste and the abettors of unchastity whose close acquaintance and counsel are to be avoided, but the irreligious and immoral in general; all who are "lovers of pleasure rather than lovers of God" (2 Tim. iii. 4, Revised Version); all who adopt, practice, and tempt to infidelity, sabbath-breaking, intemperance, gambling, untruthfulness, dishonesty, or any other form of evil. "Be not deceived: evil company" of any kind "doth corrupt good manners" (1 Cor. xv. 33, Revised Version).—G. W.

Ver. 12.—*Things that ought not to be done in Israel.* The plea of Tamar, "no such thing ought to be done in Israel," is interesting, as showing that the sentiment was prevalent amongst the Israelites, morally imperfect as they were, that they were not to be as the nations around them; that practices prevalent elsewhere were altogether out of keeping with their position and calling. "It may be so elsewhere; but it must not be so *in Israel.*" A similar sentiment as to what is suitable and becoming is appealed to in the New Testament. Christians are exhorted to act "as becometh saints" (Eph. v. 3; Rom. xvi. 2), to "walk worthy of the Lord," "worthy of their vocation," etc. (Col. i. 10; Eph. iv. 1).

I. THE GROUNDS OF SUCH A SENTIMENT. Why should the people of God regard themselves as under special obligations to live pure and holy lives? 1. *The character of their God.* "Ye shall be holy, for I am holy" was the language of God to Israel (Lev. xi. 44); and it was repeated to Christians (1 Pet. i. 15, 16). The injunction could not have been addressed—cannot now—to the worshippers of other gods. 2. *Their own consecration to God.* Israel was separated by God from other people to be his own people, devoted to the practice of purity and righteousness (Lev. xx. 24, 26). All their history, laws, and institutions had this for their aim, and were adapted to it. In like manner Christians are "called to be saints" (Rom. i. 7), chosen of God, "that they should be holy and without blame before him in love" (Eph. i. 4). The Son of God is called Jesus, because he came to "save his people from their sins" (Matt. i. 21). The purpose of his love and self-sacrifice for them is to "redeem them from all iniquity, and purify unto himself a people for his own possession, zealous of good works" (Titus ii. 14, Revised Version). This aim is expressed by the rite by which they are consecrated to God and introduced into his kingdom—it is a baptism, a washing from uncleanness. For this they are united into a holy fellowship, with sacred ministries and services, and godly discipline; and all the inspired instructions and admonitions addressed to them, and expounded to them by their teachers, have manifestly the same end and tendency. With all and above all, the Spirit which dwells amongst them and gives life and reality to all their communion, worship, and service, is the *Holy Spirit*, and his work is to regenerate and sanctify their nature, and produce in them all goodness. 3. *The wonders by which they have been redeemed and consecrated.* Ancient Israel, by a long succession of supernatural revelations, marvellous miracles, and providential interpositions. The Church of Christ, by the incarnation of the Eternal Word, and all that followed in the life, death, resurrection, and ascension of our Lord, and the miraculous bestowment and works of the Holy Ghost. Yea, every true Christian is himself, as such, a product of the Spirit's supernatural power, being "born again," "born of the Spirit" (John iii. 3, 6). Thus it is that this "holy nation" is perpetuated in the earth. 4. *Their privileges and hopes.* "The children of Israel" were "a people near unto God" (Ps. cxlviii. 14). He was their "Portion;" they enj yed his special presence, guidance, government, and defence. In a yet more emphatic sense Christians have God as their God, enjoy constant union and communion with him, and are assured of his love and sympathy, care and protection. Moreover, to them is given, more clearly and fully than to the Old Testament Church, the hope of eternal life. And what is this hope? It is that of seeing God and being like him (1 John iii. 2), of becoming "a glorious Church, not having spot, or wrinkle, or any such thing, but ... holy and without blemish" (Eph. v. 27), presented "faultless before the presence of his glory" (Jude 24). It is to be admitted into the "New Jerusalem," into which nothing unholy can enter (Rev. xxi. 27). The condition of realizing this blessedness is purity of heart—that "holiness without which no man shall see the Lord" (Matt. v. 8; Heb. xii. 14). It is clear that in such a community nothing unholy "ought to be done," however common elsewhere. Such things are utterly inconsistent with their position, their knowledge, their professions, and their prospects.

II. THE CONDUCT WHICH THIS SENTIMENT CONDEMNS. We need not dwell on gross sensuality, such as that against which the words of the text were first used. They were appropriate then, because the standard of morality "in Israel" was so much higher in respect to such practices than in the surrounding nations. But the respectable part of general society in our time and country recognizes "no such thing" as Amnon proposed as lawful. And as to many other departments of morality, the moral standard of society has been elevated by the influence of Christianity. In using the words, therefore, we do well to think of practices which are permitted or at least thought lightly of by others, but which are nevertheless contrary to the precepts or spirit of our religion. Amongst these may be named: 1. *Selfishness.* Including covetousness, worldly ambition, illiberality, etc., with the disregard or violation of the claims and rights of others that are allied to them. These are common enough in Christian countries, but ought not to exist amongst Christian people, whose religion is a product of Divine love, whose great Leader and Master is the incarnation of love, who have received numberless precepts enjoining the love of others as of themselves, and have been assured that love is greater than faith and hope (1 Cor. xiii. 13), much greater, then, than religious ceremonies, and ecclesiastical forms and observances. Covetousness in particular is closely associated in the New Testament with sensuality, as a vice not even to be named amongst Christians, and is declared to be idolatry (Eph. v. 3, 5; Col. iii. 5; 1 Cor. v. 10, 11). 2. *Pride.* Whether of rank, or wealth, or intellect. Holy Scripture, in both Testaments, abounds in precepts and examples against pride. The Lord Jesus "humbled himself" in becoming man, and in the whole of his life on earth, and frequently enjoined humility on his disciples, and reproved every indication of a proud spirit in them. Common, therefore, as pride is in the world, "no such thing ought to be" in the Church. 3. *Similar remarks may be made as to unkindness, the revengeful spirit, the unforgiving spirit, quarrelsomeness, uncharitableness, evil-speaking, and the like.* 4. To these may be added *frivolity, gaiety*—dissipation, a life of mere amusement, with no serious, worthy purpose or pursuit. These are not becoming in those who are enjoined to work out their salvation with fear and trembling; to be sober and vigilant because of the activity of Satan in seeking their destruction; to deny themselves, etc. (Phil. ii. 12; 1 Pet. v. 8; Luke ix. 23). 5. *Indifference* to the spiritual welfare of others. The gospel brings into prominence the claims which men have upon Christians in this respect. Jesus very solemnly warns against "offending," others, even the least, by doing or saying what would lead them into sin or hinder their salvation (Matt. xviii. 6, 7). He repeatedly teaches his disciples that he gave them light in order that they might "shine before men," and so lead them to glorify God (Matt. v. 14—16; Mark iv. 21, 22). St. Paul commends the Philippians for their "fellowship in furtherance of the gospel," and urges them to "strive" on its behalf (Phil. i. 5, 27, Revised Version). St. Peter enjoins that "as every man hath received the gift" he should use it for the good of others, in teaching and ministering (1 Pet. iv. 10, 11). And in general, the cause of Christ is committed to his disciples, that they may sustain and extend it both by active service and by pecuniary gifts. To the discharge of this duty by others we owe our own Christian privileges and character. If we disregard it, we display ingratitude, unfaithfulness to our Lord, insensibility to his great love to ourselves. Unconcern as to the salvation of men is natural enough in men of the world, but "no such thing ought to be" found amongst Christians.

Finally, in the absence of specific precepts, we may settle many a doubt as to our duty by considering whether the act or habit in question is suitable and becoming in those who profess themselves earnest disciples of Jesus Christ; whether it is in harmony with his spirit and character, and conducive, or at least not hostile, to our spiritual benefit, or that of others.—G. W.

Ver. 13.—*Fools in Israel.* Sad as was the case of the injured Tamar, that of her wicked brother was sadder still. She was outraged, but innocent; he was "as one of the fools in Israel."

I. WICKED MEN ARE "FOOLS." The term is often used in Holy Scripture as synonymous with "godless," "lawless," "sinful;" especially in the Book of Proverbs, where piety and holiness are designated "wisdom." The folly of sinners appears in that : 1, *Their life is opposed to right reason.* To wisdom, as recognizable by the intellect and moral sense, and as revealed in the Sacred Word. They reject the guidance of "the only wise God"—the Infinite and All-perfect Wisdom. This is true, not only of gross and brutal sinners like Amnon, but of the most refined and intellectual. Either they know not how to live, or, worse, will not live according to their knowledge. Of many in our day we may use the words of St. Paul (Rom. i. 22), "Professing themselves to be wise, they became fools." 2. *They act contrary to their own well-being.* They reject the greatest blessings for this life and the next; and choose for themselves degradation, destruction, and misery. They sell their souls for transient gain or pleasure, or surrender them to destruction because they are too proud to learn or to accept salvation as a free gift of God to the undeserving. 3. *They are in many instances the subjects of strange and fatal delusions.* Believing themselves Christians, though destitute of the most essential characteristics of Christ's true disciples; imagining themselves safe for eternity because of their devotion to ritual observances and dutiful submission to their priests, although they continue in their sins.

II. SUCH FOOLS ARE TO BE FOUND EVEN "IN ISRAEL." In the most enlightened communities; in Christian congregations; in the purest Churches.

III. FOOLS "IN ISRAEL" ARE THE WORST FOOLS. The most guilty, the most hopeless of the class. Because of: 1. *The light which shines there.* Revealing God, truth, duty, sin and holiness, life and death. They "rebel against the light" (Job xxiv. 13), either by ignoring it, or hating and consciously rejecting it. 2. *The influences enjoyed there.* From the examples of good men; from the institutions and life of the Church; from the presence and operation of the Holy Spirit. 3. *The privileges accessible there.* The friendship of Christ and Christians; approach with assurance to the throne of grace in prayer for all needful Divine guidance and strength. 4. *The convictions produced there.* Living "in Israel," it is scarcely possible to escape impressions and convictions which especially bring wisdom within reach, and render continuance in folly and sin the more deplorable. They furnish opportunities of repentance and salvation which, being neglected, greatly increase guilt. 5. *The heavier doom incurred there.* By those, that is, to whom the advantages there enjoyed become occasions of greater sin. To them belong the "many stripes" (Luke xii. 47) and the "sorer punishment" (Heb. x. 29). Let each of us, then, be concerned not to be "as one of the fools in Israel."—G. W.

EXPOSITION.

CHAPTER XIV.

Ver. 1.—**The king's heart** was **toward Absalom.** Again there is a diversity of view as to the right rendering. The preposition does not usually mean " toward," but " against," and is so rendered in ver. 13. The whole phrase occurs again only in Dan. xi. 28, and certainly there implies enmity. The whole attitude of David towards Absalom is one of persistent hostility, and, even when Joab had obtained his recall, for two full years he would not admit him into his presence. What has led most commentators to force the meaning here and in ch. xiii. 39 is the passionate burst of grief when news was brought of Absalom's death following upon the anxious orders given to the generals to be careful of the young man's life. But David was a man of very warm affections, and while this would make him feel intense sorrow for the death of a son by his brother's hand, and stern indignation towards the murderer, there would still lie deep in the father's heart true love towards his sinning child, 'and Absalom's fall was sad enough to cause a strong revulsion of feeling. David's grief would be not merely for the death of his son, but that he should have died so miserably, and in an attempt so shameful. Was not, too, the natural grief of a father made the more deep by the feeling that this was the third stage of the penalty denounced on his own sin, and that the son's death was the result of the father's crime?

Ver. 2.—**Tekoah.** This town, famous as the birthplace of the Prophet Amos, lay upon the borders of the great wilderness south-east of Jerusalem. As it was only five miles to the south of Bethlehem, Joab's birthplace, he had probably often heard tales of this woman's intelligence; and, though he contrived the parable himself, yet it would need tact and adroitness on the woman's part to give the tale with tragic effect, and answer the king's questions with all the signs of genuine emotion. If her acting was bad, the king would see through the plot, and only by great skill would his heart be so moved as to force him to some such expression of feeling as would serve Joab's purpose.

Ver. 4.—**When the woman of Tekoah spake.** All the versions and several manuscripts read, as the sense requires, " when the woman of Tekoah came." There is an interesting article in De Rossi, fixing with much probability the twelfth century as the date of this error. Though Absalom subsequently (ch. xv. 4) complained of the lax administration of justice in the realm, yet evidently this woman had the right of bringing her suit before the king; and we may be sure that Joab would take care that nothing unusual was done, lest it should awaken the king's suspicions. But possibly there was a want of method in judicial matters, and very much was left in the hands of the tribal officers, such as we find mentioned in Josh. xxiv. 1.

Ver. 7.—**The whole family.** This does not mean the kinsfolk, in whom such a disregard of the mother's feelings would have been cruel, but one of the great divisions of the tribe (see note on the *mishpachah*, in 1 Sam. xx. 6, and comp. 1 Sam. x. 21). In ver. 15 she rightly calls them " the people." We have thus a glimpse of the ordinary method of administering the criminal law, and find that each portion of a tribe exercised justice within its own district, being summoned to a general convention by its hereditary chief; and in this case the widow represents it as determined to punish the crime of fratricide with inflexible severity, and we may assume that such was the usual practice. The mother sets before David the other side of the matter—her own loneliness, the wiping out of the father's house, the utter ruin of her home if the last live coal on her hearth be extinguished. And in this way she moves his generous sympathies even to the point of overriding the legal rights of the mishpachah. In modern communities there is always some formal power of softening or entirely remitting penalties required by the letter of the law, and of taking into consideration matters of equity and even of feeling, which the judge must put aside; and in monarchies this is always the high prerogative of the crown. **And we will destroy the heir also.** The Syriac has the third person, "And they will destroy even the heir, and quench my coal that is left." This is more natural, but there is greater pungency in the widow putting into the mouth of the heads of the clan, not words which they had actually spoken, but words which showed what would be the real effect of their determination. There is great force and beauty also in the description of her son as the last live coal left to keep the family hearth burning. In another but allied sense David is called " the lamp of Israel " (ch. xxi. 17, marg.).

Ver. 9.—**The iniquity be on me.** The king had given a general promise to help the widow, but she wants to lead him on to a definite assurance that her son shall be pardoned. Less than this would not help Absalom's case. Instead, therefore, of withdrawing, she represents herself as dissatis-fied, and pleads for full forgiveness; and as this would be a violation of the letter of the Levitical Law, in order to remove David's supposed scruples, she takes upon herself the penalty.

Ver. 11.—**I pray thee, let the king re-member**, etc. Thenius says that the woman plays well the part of a talkative gossip, but really she was using the skill for which Joab employed her in bringing the king to give her son a free pardon. Nothing short of this would serve Absalom, who already was so far forgiven as to be in no fear of actual punishment. It is remarkable that David does not hesitate finally to grant this without making further inquiry, though he must have known that a mother's pleas were not likely to be very impartial. Moreover, while in ver. 9 she had acknowledged that there might be a breach of the law in par-doning a murderer, she now appeals to the mercy of Jehovah, who had himself provided limits to the anger of the avenger of blood (see Numb. xxxv.). He had thus shown himself to be a God of equity, in whom mercy triumphed over the rigid enactments of law. The words which follow more exactly mean, " That the avenger of blood do not multiply destruction, and that they destroy not my son." Moved by this en-treaty, the king grants her son full pardon, under the solemn guaranty of an oath.

Ver. 13.—**Against the people of God.** Very skilfully, and so as for the meaning only gradually to unfold itself to the king, she represents the people of Israel as the widowed mother, who has lost one son; and David as the stern clan-folk who will de-prive her of a second though guilty child. But now he is bound by the solemn oath he has taken to her to remit the penalty; for literally the words are, *and by the king's speaking this word he is as one guilty, unless he fetch home again his banished one.* She claims to have spoken in the name of all Israel, and very probably she really did express their feelings, as Absalom was very popular, and the people saw in Tamar's wrong a sufficient reason for, and vindica-tion of, his crime.

Ver. 14.—**Neither doth God**, etc. This translation is altogether wrong. What the woman says is, " God taketh not life [He-brew, 'a soul '] away, but thinketh thoughts not to banish from him his banished one." Her argument is that death is the common lot, and that there is no way of bringing back the dead to life. But though death is thus a universal law, yet God does not kill. Death is not a penalty exacted as a punish-ment, but, on the contrary, he is merciful, and when a man has sinned, instead of put-ting him to death, he is ready to forgive and

welcome back one rejected because of his wickedness. The application is plain. The king cannot restore Amnon to life, and neither must he kill the guilty Absalom, but must recall his banished son. The argument is full of poetry, and touching to the feelings, but is not very sound. For God requires repentance and change of heart; and there was no sign of contrition on Absalom's part. The power of the woman's appeal lay in what she says of God's nature. He is not intent on punishing, nor bent on carrying out the sentences of the Law in their stern literalness; but he is ready to forgive, and " deviseth devices " to bring home those now separate from him. There is also much that is worth pondering over in the distinction between death as a law of nature, and death as a penalty. The one is neces-sary, and often gentle and beneficial; but death as a penalty is stern and terrible.

Vers. 15—17.—**Now therefore that I am come**, etc. The woman now professes to return to her old story as the reason for her importunity, but she repeats it in so eager and indirect a manner as to indicate that it had another meaning. Instead, too, of thank-ing the king for fully granting her petition, she still flatters and coaxes as one whose purpose was as yet ungained. The king's word is, **for rest** (see margin): it puts an end to vexation, and, by deciding matters, sets the disputants at peace. He is **as an angel of God**, as God's messenger, whose words have Divine authority; and his office is, not **to discern**, but " to hear the good and the evil," unmoved, as the Vulgate renders it, by blessing and cursing. His mission is too high for him to be influenced either by good words or by evil, but having patiently heard both sides, and calmly thought over the reasons for and against, he will decide righteously. Finally, she ends with the prayer, **And may Jehovah thy God be with thee**! By such words she hoped to propi-tiate the king, who now could not fail to see that the errand of the woman was personal to himself.

Ver. 19.—**Is the hand of Joab with thee in all this?** The "not," inserted by the Authorized Version, must be omitted, as it alters the meaning. The king really was uncertain, and asked dubiously, whereas the Authorized Version admits only of an affirmative answer. David had seen the general drift of the woman's meaning, but she had involved it in too much obscurity for him to do more than suspect that she was the mouthpiece of Joab, who was stand-ing by, and whose face may have given signs of a more than ordinary interest in the woman's narrative. She now frankly acknowledges the truth, but skilfully inter-weaves much flattery in her answer. And her words are far more expressive than what is given in our versions. Literally they are, *By thy life, O my lord the king, there is nothing on the right or on the left of all that my lord the king has spoken.* His words had gone straight to the mark, without the slightest deviation on either side.

Ver. 20.—**To fetch about this form of speech**; correctly, as in the Revised Version, *to change the face of the matter hath thy servant Joab,* etc. The matter was that referred to in ver. 15, which the king now understands to refer to Absalom. For **in the earth,** translate *in the land.* The Hebrew has no means of distinguishing the wider and narrower significations of the word; but while the king would be flattered by the supposition that he knew all that happened in his dominions, the assertion that he knew all that was done in all the world was too broad and general to be agreeable. The Authorized Version has been misled by the thought of what an angel might know; but while it was a compliment to ascribe to the king an angel's intelligence in his own sphere, it would have been bad taste and unmeaning to ascribe to him omniscience. Nay, it is an assumption without proof that even an angel knows "all things that are in the earth."

Ver. 21.—**I have done this thing**. This is an Oriental form of assent, just as we say in English, "It is done," that is, as good as done, now that the order is given. A few manuscripts, nevertheless, support a Massoretic emendation (K'ri), namely, "Thou hast done this: go therefore," etc. But both the Septuagint and Vulgate agree with the written text (K'tib), and it is less flat and commonplace than the supposed emendation.

Ver. 22.—**In that the king hath fulfilled the request of his servant.** Keil concludes from this that Joab had often interceded for Absalom's pardon, and that this had made the king suspect him of being the prime mover in the affair. But this is to force the meaning. Joab now stood confessed as the person who had brought the woman before the king, and had employed her to gain a hearing. Had he been allowed to plead freely, her intervention would not have been necessary. We have seen, too, that the king's suspicions have been made in the Authorized Version much stronger - than they really were. Many commentators also assume that Joab had a friendship for Absalom, but there are few traces of it in his conduct, and more probably Joab was chiefly influenced by politic motives. It was injurious to the well-being of the nation that there should be discord and enmity between the king and his eldest son, and that the latter should be living in exile. The K'ri, *thy* **servant**, placed in the margin,

is to be decidedly rejected, with all other attempts of the Massorites to remove little roughnesses of grammar.

Ver. 24.—**Let him turn to his own house,** etc. This half-forgiveness was unwise, and led to unhappy results. It seems even as if Absalom was a prisoner in his house, as he could not leave it to visit Joab. Still, we must not assume that even kind treatment would have made Absalom a dutiful son, or weaned him from his ambitious purposes. The long-plotted revenge, carried out so determinately, gives us a low idea of his character, and probably during these two years of waiting, he had brooded over David's criminal leniency, and regarded it as a justification for his own foul deed. And now, when allowed to come home, but still treated unkindly, thoughts condemnatory of his father's conduct were cherished by him. It seems, too, as if a protracted punishment is always dangerous to the moral character of the criminal. And must we not add another reason? Absalom, we may feel sure, saw with indignation the growing influence of Bathsheba over the king. A granddaughter of Ahithophel, she was sure to be an adept in those intrigues in which the women of a harem pass their time; and even if, upon the whole, we form a favourable judgment upon her character, yet undoubtedly she was a very able woman, and could have no affection for Absalom.

Ver. 26.—**Two hundred shekels after the king's weight.** Unless the royal shekel was smaller than the shekel of the sanctuary, the weight of Absalom's hair would be six pounds. But we cannot believe that the king's shekel was not full weight; for to imagine this is to suppose that the king had tampered with the coinage; for the shekel was a coin as well as a weight, being originally a fixed quantity of silver. As a matter of fact, David had amassed too much silver to have need of resorting to what is the expedient of feeble and impoverished princes. Nor can we grant an error in the number; for the versions all agree with the Hebrew, so that any mistake must, at all events, be of great antiquity. Josephus says that Solomon's body-guard wore long hair powdered with gold dust, and undoubtedly Absalom's hair was something extraordinary (ch. xviii. 9). But six pounds is so enormous a weight that it is just possible that some ancient copyist has enlarged the number, to make it accord with a legend current among the people, in which this feature of Absalom's beauty had been exaggerated.

Ver. 27.—**Three sons.** Their names are not given, because they died early (see ch. xviii. 18). Of his daughter **Tamar,** named after her aunt, and, like her, possessed of great beauty, the Septuagint adds that she became the wife of Rehoboam, and mother of Abijah. In 1 Kings xv. 2 we are told that Abijah's mother was "Maachah the daughter of Abishalom;" and in 2 Chron. xiii. 2 that her name was "Michaiah the daughter of Uriel of Gibeah." We thus gather that Tamar married Uriel, and that it was the granddaughter of Absalom who became Rehoboam's queen. It is strictly in accordance with Hebrew custom to call Absalom's granddaughter his daughter, and, as Uriel was a man of no political importance, he is passed over, as the narrator's object was to show that Abijah's mother was sprung from the handsome and notorious son of David (see also 2 Chron. xi. 20, 21).

Ver. 29.—**Absalom sent for Joab.** As Joab had been the means of bringing him back, Absalom naturally regarded him as a friend. But Joab had performed the former service for other reasons, and it does not seem as if he really had any affection for Absalom.

Ver. 30.—**Go, and set it on fire.** The Hebrew has, *Go, and I will set it on fire.* Absalom represents himself as doing in his own person what his servants were to be his instruments in accomplishing. The versions, however, agree with the Massorites in substituting the easy phrase in the text. But few languages are so indifferent to persons and numbers as the Hebrew.

Ver. 31.—**Then Joab arose.** This high-handed proceeding forced Joab to pay the wished-for visit. But, while we cannot acquit Absalom of petulance, we must not regard his act as one of angry revenge; had it been so, Joab would have openly resented it, and he was quite capable of making even the heir-apparent feel his anger. It was probably intended as a rough practical joke, which taught Joab better manners, and which he must laugh at, though with inward displeasure.

Ver. 32.—**If there be (any) iniquity in me, let him kill me.** The word "any," wrongly inserted in the Authorized Version, is omitted in the Revised Version. It would have been monstrous for Absalom to profess innocence, with the murder of Amnon fresh in his memory; but the phrase, "if there be iniquity in me," means, "if my offence is still unpardoned." If year after year he was to be treated as a criminal, then he would rather be put to death at once. And Absalom's plea succeeds. Joab, who had been unwilling to visit the prisoner, now consents to act as mediator, reports to David his son's vexation at such long-continued coldness, and obtains full pardon.

Ver. 33.—**The king kissed Absalom.** The father's kiss was, as in the case of the prodigal son (Luke xv. 20), the sign of perfect reconciliation, and of the restoration of Absalom to his place as a son, with all its privileges. But God's pardon was immediate (ch. xii. 13), while David's was unwilling, and wrung from him. The kiss, we may feel quite sure, was preceded by a conversation between David and his son, the record of which is omitted simply for the sake of brevity. Evidently it satisfied the king, and ended in the kiss which gave the son all he desired. But whatever may have been his professions, Absalom's subsequent conduct is proof that he still regarded Amnon's death as a just retribution for his conduct to Tamar, and secretly cherished a sullen anger against his father for not having punished the wrong-doer himself. It was the contrast between his own five years of punishment and the mere verbal reproof which was all that Amnon had to suffer for his shameless conduct, which rankled in Absalom's mind, and gave him an excuse for finally plotting his father's ruin.

HOMILETICS.

Vers. 1—20.—The facts are : 1. Joab, observing that the king's heart was still adverse to Absalom, devised, in order to bring him round to a different feeling, that a wise woman from Tekoah should appear before him and plead a cause. 2. The woman appears before the king, and narrates as facts certain circumstances, namely, (1) that she was a widow, and that on two of her sons falling into strife, one slew the other; (2) that all the rest of the family connections were urging that the survivor should be put to death, much to her grief. 3. David, touched with her story, undertakes to grant her request, whereupon the woman, recognizing the usage in such cases, desires to exonerate the king from blame in this exercise of his clemency. 4. The king giving her a renewed assurance of safety, should any reproach her for thus trading on his clemency, she again, by a reference to God's presence and knowledge, dwells on the royal promise; whereupon he swears most solemnly that the son shall be spared. 5. The woman then ventures to bring the royal concession to her to bear on the case of Absalom, by suggesting that, in granting her request as a just one, he virtually brings blame on himself for cherishing revengeful feeling against a banished one, and he one of the people of God. 6. She fortifies her argument by alluding to man's inevitable mortality and to God's way of dealing with wrong-doers, namely, that he devises means of restoring the exile. 7. Reverting to her own suit, she next pretends that the people's desire for vengeance has caused the fear which prompts this her request, believing, as she does, in the king's magnanimity and superior discrimination. 8. David, perceiving that she is presenting a parabolic case, now asks whether Joab is not at the origin of it, which, with an Oriental compliment to his discernment, she candidly admits.

Astuteness in human affairs. There are a few facts which, put together, seem to warrant the conclusion that David was hostile in mind to Absalom, and that therefore the expression in ver. 1, rendered " toward," should be " adverse to," על. These facts are, his evident sorrow for Amnon; the related flight of Absalom and absence for three years, but no mention of any messenger of peace being sent to him ; the necessity of the device of the wise woman to awaken kindly interest in the king ; and his unwillingness to see Absalom for two years after having yielded to the force of the argument for his restoration (ver. 28). It was in the endeavour to overcome the king's hostility that Joab manifested the remarkable astuteness of his nature. Taking Joab's conduct in this instance as our exemplar, we may get an insight as to what constitutes the astuteness in human affairs which then gave and always has given some men an advantage over others.

I. There is a shrewd observation of events. Joab was not a mere military man, whose range of observation was limited by his profession. He had his eyes wide open to notice, in their bearing one on the other, the various incidents in the history of Israel, embracing both the private and public life, king and people. The remark that he perceived that the king's heart was adverse to Absalom is but an index of the man's character. Some generals would simply have confined their attention to military duties, paying little or no heed to what passed in the mind of the king, and what was the effect of his attitude on the nation. The widely and minutely observant eye is a great blessing, and, when under the government of a holy purpose, is a means of personal and relative enrichment. All men astute in affairs have cultivated it with zeal, and its activity and range account in part for the superiority they have acquired over their fellow-creatures. Human life is a voluminous book, ever being laid, page by page, before us ; and he who can with simple and steady glance note what is there written, and treasure up the record for future use, has procured an advantage, which, in days to come, will be converted into power. "The wise man's eyes are in his head ; but the fool walketh in darkness" (Eccles. ii. 14).

II. There is a constant looking ahead. This characteristic of Joab is seen in many instances (*e.g.* ch. xi. 16, 18—20 ; xii. 28 ; xiii. 19). He was a man who sought to forecast the issue of events at present transpiring, or conditions that might arise to modify his plans. He seemed to see the complications that might arise should Absalom be kept in perpetual exile, both on account of his fine manly bearing being popular with the people, and of the possible strife should the king die, and the exile then return to contend with a nominee of David's. The prophetic forecast is a vision of coming reality ; the forecast of astuteness is the clever calculation of the bearings of passing events on what may be, the tracking out by anticipation the working on men and things of the various forces now in operation. In so far as a man possesses this quality, he certainly is a power in society, and his opinions with reference to contingencies, and the provision wherewith to meet them, should have weight. The degree to which some men injure themselves and others because they have no prevision, no power of anticipating events, is often very painful. In so far as this kind of prevision can be cultivated in early years, apart from the cunning with which it is sometimes allied, so will be the gain for the entire life.

III. There is a seeking of personal ends combined with public good. Selfish cunning looks on, but looks only for self, and cares not for general interests. Astuteness looks on, but seeks deliberately to combine the personal and the general good. The former may be a prominent consideration, but the latter has a real place sincerely given. In Joab we have a striking example of this. Even in the killing of Abner Joab probably felt that the presence of such a rival might bring on troubles in Israel.

When, by complicity with David's sin (ch. xi. 17), he advanced his own ambition by gaining power over David, he had an idea that the country would be the stronger for king and general to be of one mind. His sending for David to conquer Rabbah (ch. xii. 26—30) promoted his own influence over the king, and at the same time gave the nation the advantage of a regal triumph. No doubt he foresaw that, as Absalom was now the eldest son, he might possibly come to the throne, and hence it was important to secure his favour by being the instrument of procuring his recall; at the same time, he saw it would be better for king and people that this family quarrel should be adjusted. There is no astuteness in pure benevolence, and there is no pure benevolence in astuteness. Its characteristic is that it uses a knowledge of men and things, and an anticipation of coming and possible events, in such a way as to secure personal interests in promoting public good. There is too much conscience for pure selfishness, and too little for pure benevolence. These children of the world are certainly wise in their generation (Luke xvi. 8).

IV. THERE IS A SPECIAL KNOWLEDGE OF HUMAN NATURE, AND OF THE MEANS OF ACTING ON IT. Joab knew men—their foibles and their strength. He had acquired that kind of penetration which comes of having much to do with men of divers temperaments and preferences. He knew how to touch David's natural ambition at Rabbah (ch. xii. 28—30). He understood how he would feign displeasure and sorrow at the assault which brought about the death of Uriah, and how the courtiers could be put off suspicion (ch. xii. 20, 21). He knew that a story appealing to generous, magnanimous feelings would be sure to touch the king's heart (ver. 2). This knowledge of men is an inestimable treasure for practical purposes. Some persons never acquire it, and consequently are at a great disadvantage in the struggle for life. Others avail themselves of it for low, cunning purposes, which are more becoming fiends than men. The astute man, whose character is toned by a moral aim, uses his knowledge to avoid some and secure the favour of others, and also to bring men round to the furtherance of the objects he has in hand. There is not in such a quality the simplicity which sometimes passes for Christian guilelessness; it may even seem, in some cases, to savour of cunning; but there are instances in which it combines the wisdom of the serpent and the harmlessness of the dove. The Apostle Paul was certainly an astute Christian. He knew men, and how to deal with them on Christian principles. His addresses before his judges and his Epistles bear witness.

GENERAL LESSONS. 1. All who wish to be effective in Christian service should endeavour to extend their knowledge of human nature; for it is said of Christ that he knew what was in man (John ii. 25). 2. In seeking a more thorough knowledge of human nature, we should avoid the risking the habitual feeling of distrust and suspicion which many of the sad facts of life may well suggest; for our Saviour, who knew all that is in man, the worst and the best, acted in his relations to them on the principle of generous consideration. 3. We should see to it that the intellectual qualities of astuteness are allied in us with Christian qualities that will save us from low cunning and mere utilitarian motive, and make duty the guide of action. 4. It behoves us to make use of all innocent means—"wise women," if need be—parables, or direct argument, to bring others to act in accordance with the will of God. 5. In dealing with men we should endeavour to touch the better springs of action in their nature, and assume that they are prepared to do justly and generously.

Means to bring back the banished. The woman of Tekoah showed her wisdom in very deftly blending the argument suggested by Joab with thoughts and pleadings designed to meet the successive replies of the king. To gain her point, she proceeded from the assumption of his natural sympathy with a distressed widow up to the overwhelming argument derived from a consideration of God's method in dealing with his children when they are, by reason of their sins, banished from his presence. There may seem to be a weakness in the parallel she implies between the case of her sons and the case of Absalom and Amnon, inasmuch as the death of Amnon was brought about by a deliberate design, while the death of the other was a consequence of a sudden strife; but in reality she was right. The strife of her sons was "in the field," but there may have been antecedents which led to that mortal conflict; and, so far as concerned the sons of David, it was to all intents and purposes a family quarrel, brought on by the wrong done to Absalom in the ruin of his sister, and the wise woman evidently regarded the whole affair as a "strife in the field." Provocation had been given by Amnon, and the anger of Absalom, thus aroused, occasioned his death. Amnon would not have died, but for his attack on the honour of Absalom. Two things in the final argument come home to David. (1) The reference to *the ways of God*. David, as a pious man and as a righteous ruler, rejoiced in the ways of the Lord; to him they were just and true and wise; they were the professed model of his own conduct. This moral argument to a good man is perfectly irresistible. (2) The reference to *God's banished ones*. David had of late been a banished one. He had known the anguish of being far from his heavenly Father, a spiritual exile, no longer permitted or inclined to the close and blessed fellowship of former times. The widow's word "banished" brought back the sad remembrance, followed in a moment by the remembrance of the mercy that had blotted out all his sins and restored him to the joys of salvation. Wise woman, thus to touch the deepest and tenderest springs of the heart! Consider what is implied in the blessed words, "He doth devise means, that his banished be not expelled from him."

I. MAN'S CONDITION BY REASON OF SIN IS ONE OF BANISHMENT. As truly as Absalom was now banished from David as a consequence of his transgressions, so man is separated from God. The information given us of the fallen angels is slight, but it amounts to this—that they are banished because of sin (2 Pet. ii. 4; Jude 6). Our first parents were banished from Paradise because of sin. Those who are not welcomed at last to heaven will have to refer the banishment to sin (Matt. vii. 23; xxv. 45, 46; Rev. xxi. 27). The state of mankind, while sin is loved and followed, is one of alienation. The carnal mind is not subject to the Law of God. We are as sheep going astray. Apart from any positive decree, the fact of sin constitutes moral severance from God. The child wanders, heedless of the Father's love, and all the moral laws of the universe combine with psychological laws to keep him, while in that state, outside the blessed sphere of fellowship and rest. It was instinctive for Absalom to flee from the face of the king. He banished himself by his deed, and the king could not render it otherwise. It is instinctive for one in sin to flee from the face of the holy God, and the Eternal, though omnipotent, cannot render it otherwise. The constitution of nature renders it inevitable. To suppose that it is an arbitrary arrangement is to imagine an impossibility. No power can make sin equivalent to holiness, and consequently no power can confer on sin the blessedness of the Divine favour.

II. GOD NEVERTHELESS REGARDS THE BANISHED AS HIS. Absalom was the son of David, though an exiled wanderer. David felt for him the mingled sorrow and displeasure of a just and good parent. The change of character and position does not destroy natural relationship. Adam was God's wandering child when, with sad heart, he turned his back on Paradise. The prodigal son is represented as being a son, though wasting his substance with riotous living. Our Saviour, in teaching us how to pray, would have us think of God as our Father. The whole tenor of his life on earth was to cause sinful men to feel that God the Father looks on them as his, even while in rebellion against his will. Had he disowned us in this respect, there would indeed have been no hope. It is much to know, in our sins and errors and dreadful guilt, that we are God's offspring, that he has a proprietary right in us, and thinks of us as only a father can think of his children (Ezek. xxxiii. 11).

III. GOD MAKES PROVISION FOR BRINGING THE BANISHED BACK TO HIMSELF. "He doth devise means, that his banished be not expelled from him." Wonderful words for that age, and from a widow! The great and precious truth is the comfort of myriads all over the world, and the occasion of wonder and joy in heaven. Such an incidental statement reveals to us that the pious of Israel in those times possessed much fuller and clearer knowledge concerning God and his salvation than they sometimes get credit for, or would be inferred from the outlines of national history contained in the Bible. The history is designed to trace the great historic line along which Christ came, and the fact that God was, through the Jewish people, working out a great purpose to be gradually revealed in Christ. We are not told of all the detailed teaching of holy priests and prophets. We may fairly regard this wonderful statement of the widow as an index of truth widely possessed, distinct from the provision of such means of blessing as the brazen serpent and the cities of refuge. There is a twofold sense in which the expression may be understood. 1. God *provides means for the redemption of the world.* The Mosaic economy was, in some of its institutions, a shadow of the provision that centres in the cross of Christ. Our salvation is of God. If he does not find means to cover sin and influence our evil hearts, there is no hope. We cannot, and are unwilling. He deviseth means (John iii. 16). There is an intimation of the wisdom requisite. Sin produces such confusion in the moral sphere, and runs so against the order of government, and lays so strong a hold on the human heart, that only infinite wisdom could find out the way by which we might come back to God. Hence the atoning sacrifice of Christ, the gift of the Holy Spirit, the appointment of faith as the condition and of preaching as the instrumentality, are all ascribed to the wisdom and goodness of God. It is by the Church thus saved that the wisdom of God is revealed to all ages (Rom. iii. 23—26; iv. 16; viii. 14; 1 Cor. i. 21—30; Eph. iii. 10). 2. *God provides means for the restoration of those who backslide from him.* By chastisements, by the voice of prophets and conscience, by the pleading of the Spirit, by the varied events of providence causing the erring child to feel how evil and bitter a thing it is to depart from God, he opens a way by which they are brought back again. David knew this. "He restoreth my soul" (Ps. xxiii. 3). How wonderfully wise and gentle these means often are is well known to many who once were as sheep going astray, and had lost the blessedness of fellowship formerly known.

> "Return! . . . O chosen of my love!
> Fear not to meet thy beckoning Saviour's view
> Long ere I called thee by thy name, I knew
> That very treacherously thou wouldst deal;
> Now I have seen thy ways, yet I will heal.
> Return! Wilt thou yet linger far from me?
> My wrath is turned away, I have redeemed thee."
> ('Life Mosaic,' by F. R. Havergal, p. 72.)

IV. GOD'S WAYS IN DEALING WITH HIS BANISHED ONES ARE A MODEL FOR US. The wise woman had spoken of the ways of God with his banished ones in order to induce David to follow in the same course with respect to Absalom—the implication being that, when once a good man is reminded of the ways of God, he will without further urging act in the same manner. The parallel between the relation of Absalom to David and the relation of a sinner to God may not in every detail be perfect; but there being a resemblance in the substantial facts—banishment of a son because of high-handed deeds of wrong—it follows that there should be a resemblance, in the bearing of the earthly father-king to his son, to that of God to his sinful child. The two features of God's bearing toward his own are: (1) He does not take away life; but (2) devises means by which those who deserve to die are brought back to him (ver. 14). The reference evidently is not to the legal code, which in several cases recognizes capital punishment for certain offences, for ends civil and social, but to the general principle and method of God's dealing with sinful man in his highest relations to himself. He desireth not the death of the sinner, and therefore he, speaking after the manner of men, finds out some way of bringing about a restoration to favour consistent with his own honour and the claims of righteousness. In the New Testament this example is set forth in strong and varied terms (Matt. v. 43—48; vi. 14, 15; Eph. iv. 31, 32). The fact that there is a model in God's bearing toward us is only half the truth. It is our duty and privilege to act according to it. It is not enough to be kindly disposed. We are to "devise devices"—take the initiative—in seeking to restore those who may have done wrong and merited our displeasure. This is the hard lesson taught by Christ, which even his own people are so slow to learn. When will Christians be as Christ was and act as Christ did? It is often easier to sing hymns, hear sermons, and bow the knee in prayer.

GENERAL LESSONS. 1. The proper course for the poor and sorrowful and oppressed is, after the example of this widow, to have recourse to him who sitteth as King in Zion; for his ear is ever open to their cry, and there is an open way of access to his throne. 2. In all our approaches to the supreme throne we may, with more confidence than was displayed by this widow in David, act on the assumption of a mercy and wisdom that never fail. 3. It is not only a solace to the weary heart, but a sure means of help in our domestic cares, if we bring them before the notice of our God. 4. We see how often the best and most exalted of men, in their conduct and feelings, come far short of the character they should manifest, and how they may require even the teaching which comes from the spirit and deeds of the poor and troubled to raise them to a higher level of life. 5. It is possible for good men to be kind and generous towards others, and at the same time be unaware, till forced to see it, that there are features in their personal conduct day by day not in accord with the general generosity which they recognize and display. 6. We need to be reminded that the death of those we have cared for, should it come about while we are not acting kindly toward them (ver. 14), is an unalterable event, a change which renders acts of kindness impossible—as water spilt on the ground cannot be gathered up again; and consequently we should seize passing opportunities of blessing them. 7. The sinful state of man is as unnatural as is exile to a king's son, and should ever be so represented (Isa. i. 2, 3). 8. All thanks and praise are due to God, in that he needed not any one to procure our restoration; all is of his own eternal love and free grace. 9. We should distinguish between the human setting of a truth and the truth itself. To "devise a means" is a human way of expressing the truth that God, from the beginning, before the foundation of the world (Eph. i. 4; Rev. xiii. 8), ordained and arranged for our salvation, but that we see the pre-arrangement coming into form subsequent to the advent of sin, and think of it as being devised to meet that event after its occurrence. We say, "the sun rises," but it does not. Our forms of expression consequent on the appearance of things to us is not the exact utterance of absolute truth. 10. The force of a Divine example, when brought to bear on men who recognize the government of God, will often compel conviction when other means fail.

Vers. 21—33.—*Imperfect reconciliation.* The facts are: 1. David, referring to the promise he had made, sends Joab to bring Absalom from Geshur, Joab expressing in lowly form his thanks for the king's gracious attention to his request. 2. On Absalom's return he is ordered to abide in his own house, and not to see the king's face. 3. The personal beauty of Absalom is famous throughout Israel, and of his four children the only daughter is also reputed to be fair. 4. For two years Absalom remains in Jerusalem without seeing the king, whereupon he becomes dissatisfied, and sends to Joab, hoping to send him to the king. 5. Joab, for some unexpressed reason, declines to give heed to the message, and, as a consequence, Absalom orders his field of barley to be burnt. 6. This event bringing Joab to him, Absalom remonstrates with the king through him against this semi-imprisonment, and demands to see the king. 7. The king yielding to the request, Absalom presents himself, and receives his father's kiss. Whatever may have been the secret causes operating on both sides, the course of the narrative clearly shows us that, although Joab seemed to have gained his point through the wise woman of Tekoah, yet the restoration of Absalom to his father's love and confidence was not perfect. There are, in the account here given of the relation of David to his son, illustrations of several important truths or recurring incidents of human life.

I. CONCESSIONS WITH RESERVATIONS. In the interview with Joab (vers. 21, 22) David distinctly intimated to him that he had "done this thing"—consented to Absalom's return in consequence of having been caught within the coils of the parabolic pleadings of the wise woman whom he had employed for that purpose. Apart from the force of the argument, the king was no doubt willing in some degree to comply with the request of so influential a man, especially as he knew more of his own life than was comfortable to reflect upon. Joab regarded it as a work of special grace that his wishes were thus considered; and most probably he went to Geshur to fetch Absalom, with cheerful expectations of a speedy removal of family difficulties. But although the king kept the letter of his concession in Absalom's permitted return, it is evident that he either repented of his original decision or had made, when giving it, a private reservation that, though returned, he should not give him a hearty welcome. Both Joab and Absalom (ver. 24) appear to have reported themselves at the king's house, in expectation of full restoration, for he "returned to his own house." Such concessions as this are valuable in so far as they confer privileges otherwise not attainable, but they lose much value in being extracted by pressure and especially by the reservation which becomes subsequently known. It had been well, perhaps, had conditions been stated from the first. If possible, our agreements and promises should be expressed in terms that cover all we think and intend. The mutual confidence of society depends on the cultivation of frankness and candour. The first inconvenience is the least. The promises of God are "yea and Amen." There is no disappointing reservation for us when we arrive at the palace of the great King.

II. EMBARRASSMENTS OF PATERNAL CONDUCT. Great consideration is due to David when we endeavour to form an estimate of his conduct. His position, brought on, it is true, by his own sad sin, was most perplexing. On the one side there was (1) the very natural and great displeasure against a son who could cherish revenge for two whole years, and then presume to take upon himself the vindication of justice, thus reflecting on royal authority; (2) the absolute need of chastisement for a young man of violent spirit and haughty temper; (3) the importance of maintaining influence over the people by not seeming to palliate the violence of his own family; (4) the temptation to which so handsome and attractive a young man would be exposed were he to be prematurely welcomed into society again; (5) the secret influence of his favourite wife, Bathsheba, who could not but remind him of the claims on the succession of the son specially named by the prophet as "beloved of the Lord" (ch. xii. 24, 25). Then on the other side there was (1) his natural yearning over a hitherto favourite son, the more so as he feared lest he should fall a victim to evil ways; (2) Joab's evident interest in Absalom, and the expediency of conciliating so powerful a man; (3) the near connection of Absalom with the tribe of Judah, and the danger of raising up a party should there be an appearance of harshness; (4) the remembrance of the unqualified promise virtually given to the wise woman of Tekoah, that he would regard God's mercy to his banished ones as his model; (5) the reflection that, after his own dreadful sin in the case of Uriah, God had restored him to personal favour. Under some such conflicting influence David could not grant all that was desired. Happily modern parents have not to decide on the doom of fratricides; but troubles do arise which place them in most embarrassing circumstances. Much charity is needed in our judgments on the action taken in cases of difficulty. There is much unknown to the outward observer. It is important, in all these times of perplexity, to cast our care on the Lord, and seek the special guidance which he has promised. Divine influence alone can keep us from being unduly biassed in either direction. Our decisions may mean perpetual weal or woe to children.

III. THE DISCIPLINE OF PARTIAL PRIVILEGE. It is a severe but wholesome discipline for Absalom to be kept two years without full restoration. Possibly David may have ascertained from others that his temper was not much improved, and that he did not show the signs of penitence or regret becoming one who looked for full restoration to paternal favour. Then, also, David could not but remember that, with his own restoration to God, there was attached a temporal chastisement, which, while it did not touch the reality of the Divine forgiveness, was designed for public good; and possibly he may have thought that the privilege of returning to Jerusalem only might be accepted as a sign of actual personal forgiveness, and at the same time put Absalom under wholesome restraints. This kind of discipline does exist in human affairs and in Church life. Children and men are caused to feel that some inconvenience has resulted from their conduct, even though they are no longer punished. In so far as we fall in with the natural or designed tendency of this discipline, we may turn its annoyances into a means of recovery from the moral failings which have been our bane.

IV. THE PERILS OF PERSONAL ATTRACTIONS. The beauty of Absalom is referred to in such a way as to suggest that he was not only aware of it, but that it exercised a fascinating influence over others, and tended to gather around him persons likely to be influenced by personal appearances, and therefore not the most helpful to one who needs the stimulus and support of high moral principles. Personal beauty is a gift of God, and, were not sin in the world as a disturbing element in the physical and moral development of the human race, the probability is that the average beauty of form and expression would equal or surpass what is now regarded as exceptional. Unfortunately, it is sometimes allied to a vain and frivolous spirit, and in that case it becomes a snare. There are instances in which beauty has been associated with the devout earnest spirit of religion, and has been made tributary to obtaining a hallowed influence over others. Special prayer and strong safeguards are required for our sons and daughters whose personal attractions may lay them open to the flatteries and friendships of the unwise and unholy.

V. THE INTIMATIONS OF DANGEROUS TENDENCIES. It was natural for Absalom to be restless under the restraint of two years, though, had his spirit been very lowly and penitent, he would have kept it within due limits. The treatment of Joab was an intimation that the daring temper which slew Amnon was still there. He who could set a field of barley on fire in order to get his messages attended to was capable, unless the tendencies were checked, of producing a more serious conflagration. The presence within a young man of strong passions, a violent temper, a hatred of restraint or love of pleasure, is a sign of danger. It is in the nature of forces to work their way outward. If we say, "the child is father to the man," we may also say that the moral forces within are the creators of the life without. Unless strong counter-influences are brought to bear to neutralize their action or to extirpate them, they will gain power by being daily cherished, and a free, jovial, handsome Absalom may become the notorious rebel, whose hand turns against his own father. Human life exhibits such developments still. Young men should interrogate their own nature, and fairly face the moral dangers that may lie there, before their power renders introspection and suppression difficult if not impossible. Those who have charge of the young should note signs of struggling forces, and adapt the moral education according to the individual requirement.

HOMILIES BY VARIOUS AUTHORS.

Vers. 1—20.—(JERUSALEM.) *The woman of Tekoah.* 1. In *David* "the king" we here see that fatherly affection may come into conflict with regal justice. He must have perceived the ill effects of sparing Amnon, and felt constrained to punish Absalom. But his grief and resentment were mitigated by the lapse of time (ch. xiii. 39). Nevertheless, though prompted by natural affection to recall his son, he was deterred from doing so by political and judicial considerations. And to overcome his reluctance a stratagem was devised, which, as the sequel shows, was only too successful. For by his weakness towards Absalom "he became guilty of the further dissolution of the theocratic rule in his house and in his kingdom" (Erdmann). 2. In *Joab* "the son of Zeruiah" (ch. iii. 39) we see that a man may promote another's interest out of regard for his own (ch. iii. 22—30; xi. 16—21). "He may have been induced to take these steps by his personal attachment to Absalom, but the principal reason no doubt was that Absalom had the best prospect of succeeding to the throne, and Joab thought this the best way to secure himself from punishment for the murder which he had committed. But the issue of events frustrated all such hopes. Absalom did not succeed to the throne, Joab did not escape punishment, and David was severely chastised for his weakness and injustice" (Keil). "Joab formed a project by which the king, in his very capacity of chief judge, should find the glimmering fire of parental love suddenly fanned into a burning flame" (Ewald). 3. In the "*wise woman*" of *Tekoah* we see that skilful persuasion may so work upon natural feeling as to induce a course which is neither expedient nor just. The cleverness, insight, readiness of speech, tact, boldness mingled with caution, and perseverance, which she displayed (under the direction of Joab, who perhaps "stood by at some distance whilst she addressed herself to the king," ver. 21) are remarkable. Such qualities may be employed for a good or an evil purpose. In contrast with the reproof of Nathan, her persuasion (1) was inspired, not by God, but by man; (2) was addressed, not to conscience, but to pity and affection; (3) aimed, not to manifest the truth, but to obscure it; (4) and "to give effect, not to the convictions of duty, but to the promptings of inclination" (Blaikie); (5) sought to do this, not sincerely and openly, but insincerely and insidiously; (6) and not by proper motives alone, and honest, though unpleasant speech, but by improper motives and "with flattering lips;" and (7) produced, not a beneficial, but an injurious effect. In her persuasive address we notice, more particularly—

I. AN AFFECTING BUT FICTITIOUS APPEAL. (Vers. 4—11.) "And the woman of Tekoah came to the king," etc., making her appeal for help in an acted parable, like that of Nathan (ch. xii. 1—4). "Parables sped well with David; one drew him to repent of his own sin, another to remit Absalom's punishment" (Hall). This parable of *the hapless son*, or the avengers of blood, was intended, adapted, and employed : **1.** *To excite compassion toward the unfortunate* : a son who had slain his brother "unawares" (Numb. xxxv. 11) in the field, and whose life was imperilled by the avengers, "the whole family" (ver. 7); and his widowed mother, whose only stay and comfort he was, whose "live coal which is left" would be quenched, and whose husband's "name and posterity" would be destroyed. "The power of the discourse lies in the fact that they are represented as already doing what their words show to be their purpose." **2.** *To procure protection against the avengers* ; who, according to ancient custom, sought to take his life (ch. iii. 22—30); their conduct being portrayed as persistently pitiless (ver. 11), "and actuated, not so much by a wish to observe the Law, as by covetousness and a desire to share the inheritance among themselves" (Kirkpatrick); obscurely suggestive of the hostility exhibited toward Absalom. "Her circumstances (as a widow and living at some distance from Jerusalem, which rendered the case difficult to be readily inquired into), her mournful tale, her widow's weeds, her aged person, and her impressive manner, all combined to make one united impression on the king's heart" (A. Clarke). "In all this she intended to frame a case as like to David's as she could do; by determining which in her favour, he might judge how much more reasonable it was to preserve Absalom. But there was a wide difference between her case and his, however plausible soever their likeness might appear" (Patrick). **3.** *To obtain assurance of preservation from the king* ; which was given at first as an indefinite promise (ver. 8), afterwards (through her importunity) in a more definite engagement (ver. 10), and finally confirmed by an oath (ver. 11). "Had David first proved and inquired into the matter which with cunning and deceit was brought before him, he would not have given assurance with an oath" (Schlier). "We should learn from David's example to be more guarded over all our feelings and affections, even such as are in their proper degree essential to a religious character" (Lindsay). "Neither shalt thou countenance a poor man in his cause" (Exod. xxiii. 3).

II. AN EFFECTIVE BUT FALLACIOUS ARGUMENT (vers. 13, 14); based upon the assumed resemblance between the case of the hapless son, of whom she had spoken, and that of Absalom, to whom she alluded as fully as she might venture. For her appeal had " a double sense," or twofold purpose—one clear, immediate, feigned, subordinate ; the other dark, ultimate, real, supreme ; and to the latter she now comes. "And why dost thou think [devise] such a thing [as that of which I am now permitted to speak] against people of God? And by the king's speaking this word ['As Jehovah liveth,' etc., ver. 11] he is as one that is guilty [or, 'self-condemned'], in that the king does not bring back *his banished one*." "My banished one!" he must have thought, as the main object of the woman's appeal flashed upon him. But she went on : "For we must die ['shall surely die,' Gen. ii. 17], and are as water poured out on the ground that is not gathered up. And God takes not away a soul [*nephesh*, equivalent to 'individual life'], but thinks thoughts [devises devices] to the end that he may not banish from him [utterly] a banished one." She thus sought to persuade the king to recall his son by : **1.** *The obligation of his oath*, in which "he had acknowledged the possibility of an exception to the general rule of punishment for murder;" sworn to save her son, who had killed his brother under severe provocation; and was consistently bound to spare and restore his own son in similar circumstances. But the difference between them, here kept out of view, was fatal to the argument. Absalom's crime was deliberately planned, executed by his servants under his order, and seen by many witnesses. **2.** *The welfare of the people of God*, involved in the preservation and return of the heir to the throne. Although the king's sons and the whole court were against Absalom (ver. 7), a large party of the people was in his favour. But the general welfare would have been more promoted by his just punishment, or continuance in exile, than by his restoration, as the subsequent history shows. **3.** *The mortality of men*—the inevitable and irreparable decease of Amnon, Absalom, the king himself; the consideration of which should induce compassion and speedy help, lest it should be too late. But "even compassion, amiable as it is, will not justify our violation of the Divine Law, or neglecting the important duties of our station" (Scott). **4.** *The clemency of God* ; in forbearance and long-suffering toward sinful men, and devising means for their restoration to his presence; such as David himself had experienced (ch. xii. 13 ; Ps. li. 11). His example should be imitated. But his forbearance is limited—he pardons only those who repent, and punishes the guilty; and for the king to spare the guilty on insufficient grounds, or pardon the impenitent, would be to harden the wicked in their wickedness, and to act contrary to the purpose for which he is made "an avenger for wrath to him that doeth evil." The reasons assigned, though excellent in themselves, were inapplicable and fallacious. The noblest truths may be perverted to a bad purpose. A weak argument appears strong to one who is already disposed to accept its conclusion; and is a sufficient excuse for a course which he is inclined to pursue. By the manner in which her words were received by the king, the "wise woman" perceived that her point was practically gained; enough had been said, and leaving it to work its effect on his mind, she returned to the ostensible occasion of her petition for help; and "now she would go home happy (she said), as if this reference to the king's behaviour had been only the casual chatter of a talkative woman" (P. Thomson).

III. AN APPROPRIATE BUT FLATTERING APOLOGY for intrusion on the king (vers. 15—20); expressive of: 1. The anxious *fear* and hope with which she had been impelled to make her request (ver. 15). 2. The joyful anticipation and grateful *assurance of rest* which she now felt (vers. 16, 17). 3. Devout admiration and *praise* of the king, on account of his wisdom in judgment; with a prayer for his prosperity: "May Jehovah thy God be with thee!" Fully acknowledging that, as the king surmised, she had acted under the direction of Joab, "in order to bring round the face [aspect] of the matter" (to alter Absalom's relation to his father), she again commends the discernment of the king: "My lord is wise," etc. (vers. 18—20). "When we are most commended for our discernment we generally act most foolishly; for those very praises cloud and pervert the judgment" (Scott). "And the king said unto Joab, Behold now, I have done this thing: go and bring the young man Absalom back" (ver. 21). "The feelings of the father triumphed over the duty of the king, who, as supreme magistrate, was bound to execute impartial justice on every murderer, by the express Law of God (Gen. ix. 9; Numb. xxxv. 30, 31), which he had no power to dispense with (Deut. xviii. 18; Josh. i. 8; 1 Sam. x. 25)" (Jamieson). Although neither the end of the woman's address nor some of the means she employed can be approved, yet much may be learnt from it concerning *the art of persuasion*; e.g. the importance of (1) knowing the character and sentiments of those who are addressed; (2) having a definite aim in view; (3) arresting attention and awakening interest and sympathy; (4) earnestness and fervency of manner; (5) using argument and illustration adapted to present the matter in the most attractive light; (6) saying enough and no more, especially on a difficult and delicate subject; (7) advancing step by step with a persistent determination to succeed.—D.

Ver. 14.—"*As water spilt upon the ground.*" Water is a gift of God, very precious, especially in lands where it is scarce, and often longed for as a means of quenching thirst, renewing strength, and preserving life (ch. xxiii. 15; Ps. lxiii. 1). But it may be thrown away, poured out and lost, by design or accident, through the overturning or fracture of the vessel in which it is contained. Human life, also, is a Divine gift, precious beyond all earthly possessions. But it is contained in "a body of fragile clay" (2 Cor. iv. 7), which is sooner or later destroyed like "the pitcher shattered at the well" (Eccles. xii. 6); and thus "we are as water," etc. We have here—

I. AN IMPRESSIVE ASPECT OF DEATH. 1. It *must* take place in all, without exception. "It is appointed," etc. (Gen. iii. 19; Rom. v. 12; Heb. ix. 27). 2. It *may* occur to each of us at any moment (1 Sam. xx. 3). 3. It puts an *end* to the useful service which might have been rendered. Only while the water remains in the vessel can it be of immediate use. 4. It cannot by any possibility be *repaired*, or "gathered up again." "As the waters fail from the sea," etc. (Job xiv. 11; vii. 10); "as waters melt away," etc. (Ps. lviii. 7; xxxix. 13; xlix. 7—10; ciii. 16). "Death is of all things the most terrible, for it is the end" (Aristotle).

> "What is your life? 'Tis a delicate shell,
>   Cast up by Eternity's flow;
> On Time's bank of quicksand to dwell,
>   A moment its loveliness show.
> Returned to its element grand
>   Is the billow that brought it on shore;
> See, another is washing the strand,
>   And the beautiful shell is no more."

II. AN INSTRUCTIVE ADMONITION FOR LIFE. Is it so? Then: 1. Restrain immoderate indulgence in *sorrow*, "the grief that saps the mind, for those on earth we see no more." No weeping, anger, nor endeavour can bring back Amnon (ch. xii. 23). Accept calmly what cannot be altered. 2. Repress improper feelings of *resentment* toward others. Even though it be just, it should not be perpetual (Eph. iv. 26). They and you alike must die and pass away. "Be reconciled." 3. Regard all around you with sympathy and kindly affection. Before to-morrow they may be gone. 4. Redeem the rest of your time "in the flesh," by prompt, diligent, zealous use of every opportunity of serving God and doing good, according to the pattern of long-suffering and benevolence which he has set before you, in "not taking away a soul," etc. (latter part of the verse).

Consider : 1. The death of the body is not the end of the man. He disappears here only to appear elsewhere as water in the cloud ; gathered "with sinners" (Ps. xxvi. 9; Matt. xiii. 30) or with saints (Gen. xxv. 8; 2 Kings xxii. 20; 2 Thess. ii. 1). 2. The life which a man leads "in the body" determines his condition in the unseen and eternal world. 3. The conviction of these things makes the view of death more impressive, and should make the course of life more just, merciful, and devout.—D.

Ver. 14.—*God's restoration of his banished.* It is hardly possible for a father to be so completely estranged from his child as to lose all affection for him. He may have just cause to feel angry with him; but, with absence and the lapse of time, his anger dies away, and his natural affection springs up afresh. It was thus with David in relation to his son Absalom. Yet he hesitated to give way to his parental feelings, to set aside the claims of public justice, and exercise his royal prerogative of showing mercy toward the guilty. And to induce him to do this it was urged (among the means devised for the purpose) that God, who has ordained that men should die, permits them to live, and even devises means for their restoration. Was not this an indication that Absalom should be spared? Was not this an example which the king should imitate? It has been supposed that there is allusion to the cities of refuge (Numb. xxxv. 9—34; Deut. xix. 6; Josh. xx.), where the manslayer, "though banished from his habitation for a time, was not quite expelled, but might return again after the death of the high priest" (Patrick). The argument used was not properly applicable to the particular instance, but the truth expressed is profound and striking. Notice—

I. THE ALIENATED CONDITION OF MAN. "Banished ;" estranged, separated, "cast out of God's presence," away from his sanctuary, fellowship, and inheritance (ver. 16), in "a far country" (Luke xv. 13). That this is the moral and spiritual state of man (naturally and generally) is not only testified by the Scriptures, but also by his own heart and conscience ; his aversion and dread with respect to God. It is : 1. *Voluntary.* By his own free act Absalom broke the Law, incurred the displeasure, fled from the face of his father, and continued in exile. So has it been with man from the first.

> "The nature with its Maker thus conjoin'd,
> Created first was blameless, pure, and good;
> But, through itself alone, was driven forth
> From Paradise, because it had eschew'd
> The way of truth and life, to evil turn'd."
>
> (Dante, 'Paradise,' vii.)

Of his own accord he departs from God and seeks to hide himself from him. 2. *Unhappy.* Absalom found friendly associates and material comforts in Geshur, but he could not have been at home there, and must have carried in his breast a restless and troubled heart. And it is impossible for him who departs from God, and tries to live without him, to possess inward rest and peace. The soul is made for God: how can it be satisfied with anything short of him? Oh the misery that multitudes at this moment endure because they have forsaken the "Fountain of living waters," and seek their happiness where it can never be found! 3. *Perilous.* The sinner is under condemnation. The "avengers of blood" are on his track. Life is precarious and must soon terminate, with all its alleviations, privileges, and possibilities; "and after that the judgment," when voluntary exile becomes involuntary, partial unhappiness complete wretchedness, temporary estrangement "everlasting destruction from the presence of the Lord" (2 Thess. i. 9). 4. *Not hopeless.* Absalom was still a son, though a disobedient one; still "in the land of the living;" and might entertain the hope that, through his father's affection, his banishment would not be perpetual. However far man may have wandered from the Father's house, he is still an object of the Father's love. "Behold, all souls are mine," etc.; "I have no pleasure in the death of him that dieth," etc. (Ezek. xviii. 4, 32; xxiii. 11); "Turn you to the stronghold, ye prisoners of hope" (Zech. ix. 12).

II. The merciful means devised for his restoration. Man's misery is from himself, but "salvation is of the Lord" (Ps. iii. 8; Jonah ii. 9). It is effected by and through: 1. *The long patience* and forbearance which he shows toward the transgressor; restraining the outgoings of wrath (Luke xiii. 7), sparing forfeited life, affording space for repentance, "making his sun to rise," etc. (Matt. v. 45). "The long-suffering of our Lord is salvation" (2 Pet. iii. 15; Rom. ii. 4). 2. *An extraordinary provision,* whereby the way of his return is opened, consistently with the requirements of eternal righteousness, and his fatherly love is revealed in the highest degree. By restoring Absalom without due regard to the demands of justice, and even without repentance, David weakened his own authority as king, contributed to a popular rebellion, and well-nigh lost his throne and life. But in the method which God in infinite wisdom has "devised" for the restoration of man, *justice and mercy* are alike manifested, an adequate ground or reason for forgiveness is furnished, sinners are "put in the capacity of salvation" (Butler), and the Law is magnified and "established" (Rom. iii. 19—31). "God commendeth his own love toward us, in that, while we were yet sinners, Christ died for us" (Rom. v. 8); "redeemed us from the curse of the Law, having become a curse for us" (Gal. iii. 13); "suffered for sins once, the Just for the unjust, that he might bring us to God" (1 Pet. iii. 18).

> "Man in himself had ever lacked the means
> Of satisfaction. . . . Then behoved
> That God should by his own ways lead him back
> Unto the life from whence he fell, restored;
> By both his ways, I mean, or one alone.
>   But since the deed is ever prized the more,
> The more the doer's good intent appears;
> Goodness celestial, whose broad signature
> Is on the universe, of all its ways
> To raise ye up, was fain to leave out none.
>   Nor aught so vast or so magnificent,
> Either for him who gave or who received,
> Between the last night and the primal day,
> Was or can be. For God more bounty show'd,
> Giving himself to make man capable
> Of his return to life, then had the terms
> Been mere and unconditional release.
>   And for his justice, every method else
> Were all too scant, had not the Son of God
> Humbled himself to put on mortal flesh."
>
>   (Dante, 'Paradise,' vii.)

3. *Numerous messages, efficient motives, and gracious influences,* in connection with that provision, to dispose him to avail himself thereof: the Word, with its invitations, warnings, appeals to reason, affection, conscience, hope and fear; messengers (ver. 31)—ministers and teachers of the Word; above all, the Holy Spirit, striving with sinners, convicting of sin, etc. (John xvi. 8), and renewing the heart in righteousness. 4. The end of all is reconciliation (ver. 33), filial fellowship, perfect holiness, and endless blessedness in God. "Return;" "Be ye reconciled to God."

Conclusion. 1. How wonderful is "the kindness of God our Saviour, and his love toward man" (Titus iii. 4)! 2. How entirely is man his own destroyer (Hos. xiii. 9)! 3. "Beloved, if God so loved us, we also ought to love one another;" and to devise means in order that no "banished one" may be utterly banished from him.

> "Oh let the dead now hear thy voice;
> Now let thy banished ones rejoice."
>
>   D.

Ver. 20.—*Flattery.* "My lord is wise, according to the wisdom of an angel of God," etc. Commendation is often proper and beneficial (ch. ii. 5—7). But flattery (false, partial, or extravagant praise) is always improper and pernicious. This language was not mere Oriental compliment, but a flattering speech, intended to make the king pleased with himself in doing what he was urged to do. 1. It is *agreeable* to most persons when skilfully administered. "Flattery and the flatterer are pleasant; since the flatterer is a seeming admirer and a seeming friend" (Aristotle, 'Rhetoric').

> "When I tell him he hates flatterers,
> He says he does; being then most flattered."
>   (Shakespeare.)

"We believe that we hate flattery, when all which we hate is the awkwardness of the flatterer" (La Rochefoucault). 2. It assumes *various forms*, and is usually obsequious and disingenuous; is direct or indirect; is shown in praising personal qualities, advantages, achievements, etc., giving "flattering titles" (Job xxxii. 31—32), "good Master" (Mark x. 17; xii. 14), "my Lord," etc. Making or suggesting favourable comparisons, it may be, by detracting from the good name of others (ch. iv. 8). It is sometimes sincere; but "people generally despise where they flatter and cringe to those they would gladly surpass." 3. It is commonly designed by those who employ it to serve some *interest* of their own (ver. 22). Hence it is so frequently used to gain the favour of kings, and such as possess authority, influence, or wealth (Jude 16). When Alexander the Great was hit with an arrow in the siege of an Indian city, and the wound would not heal, he said to his flatterers, "You say that I am Jupiter's son, but this wound cries that I am but man." 4. It *blinds* those who listen to it to their defects, ministers to their vanity, and fills them with perilous self-complacency. "It's the death of virtue." 5. It also induces them to pursue erroneous and *sinful courses*, which they might otherwise have avoided. "A man that flattereth his neighbour spreadeth a net for his feet" (Prov. xxix. 5; xxvi. 28). "Ah! how good might many men have been who are now exceedingly bad had they not sold their ears to flatterers! Flatterers are soul-murderers. Flattery is the very spring and mother of all impiety. It put our first parent on tasting the forbidden fruit. It put Absalom upon dethroning his father. It blows the trumpet and draws poor souls into rebellion against God, as Sheba drew Israel to rebel against David. It makes men call evil good and good evil, darkness light and light darkness" (T. Brooks). 6. It is only less *culpable* in those who listen to it than in those who employ it. They are willing captives. "As a wolf resembles a dog, so doth a flatterer a friend. Take heed, therefore, that, instead of guardian dogs, you do not incautiously admit ravening wolves" (Epictetus). 7. Its folly and guilt are sometimes discovered too late; when its *ruinous consequences* cannot be repaired (ch. xv. 13; Ps. xii. 3; Acts xii. 23).—D.

Ver. 25.—*Physical beauty.* "And in all Israel there was none to be so much praised as Absalom for his beauty," etc. (see 1 Sam. xvi. 7, 12; ch. xi. 2; xiii. 1; ver. 27).

> "Of all God's works, which do this world adorn,
>   There is no one more fair and excellent
> Than is man's body, both for power and form,
>   Whilst it is kept in sober government;
>   But none than it more foul and indecent,
> Distempered through misrule and passions base;
>   It grows a monster, and incontinent
> Doth lose its dignity and native grace:
> Behold, who list, both one and other in this place"
>   (Spenser, 'The Faërie Queene,' canto IX.)

It is—

I. An ADMIRED ENDOWMENT; involuntarily conferred, without personal effort and beyond human control (Matt. v. 36; vi. 27); yet one of the most personal and enviable of human possessions. "Beauty is a thing of great recommendation in the correspondence amongst men; it is the principal means of acquiring the favour and good-liking of one another, and no man is so barbarous and morose that does not perceive himself in some sort struck with its attraction" (Montaigne). "Beauty is, indeed, a good gift of God; but that the good may not think it a great good, God dispenses it even to the wicked" (Augustine).

> "A beautiful and fair young man is he;
> In all his body is no blemish seen;
> His hair is like the wire of David's harp,
> That twines about his bright and ivory neck;
> In Israel is not such a goodly man."
>
> (Geo. Peele, 'The Tragedy of Absolom:' 1599.)

II. A SUPERFICIAL DISTINCTION; shadowing forth, indeed, beauty of mind and character; and heightened by the latter, when present; but often, in fact, disassociated from it; and covering, "skin-deep," dreadful moral deformity (Prov. xi. 22). Absalom was beautiful externally, but not "beautiful within." Wisdom, truth, humility, modesty, purity, patience, meekness, piety, mercy, charity,—these constitute inward, substantial, spiritual beauty, "the beauty of holiness," the product of the grace and the reflection of the beauty and glory of the Lord (Ps. xc. 17; cxlix. 4); in which he delights, and which all persons may acquire (Eph. iv. 24; Gal. v. 22; Phil. ii. 5). "Whatsoever things are lovely," etc. (Phil. iv. 8). "The graces of the Spirit are the richest ornaments of the reasonable creature."

III. A DANGEROUS INFLUENCE; on its *possessors*, making them vain and presumptuous, and exposing them to many temptations; on its *beholders*, directing undue attention to "the outward appearance," disposing to excuses for mental and moral defects, alluring to evil (ch. xv. 1—6). The beauty of Absalom was a snare to the people. "His hair was his halter" (ch. xviii. 9).

> "Where is the virtue of thy beauty, Absolon?
> Will any of us here now fear thy locks,
> Or be in love with that thy golden hair,
> Wherein was wrapt rebellion 'gainst thy sire,
> And words prepared to stop thy father's breath?"
>
> (Geo. Peele.)

IV. A TRANSIENT POSSESSION. Precarious, short-lived, inevitably turning to dust (ver. 14); "a fading flower" (Isa. xxviii. 4; xl. 8; Ps. xxxix. 11), whose "root is ever in its grave."

> "A doubtful good, a gloss, a glass, a flower,
> Lost, faded, broken, dead, within an hour."

"So have I seen a rose newly springing from the clefts of its hood, and at first it was fair as the morning, and full with the dew of heaven as a lamb's fleece; but when a ruder breath had forced open its virgin modesty, and dismantled its too youthful and unripe retirements, it began to put on darkness, and to decline to softness and the symptoms of a sickly age; it bowed the head, and broke its stalk, and at night, having lost some of its leaves and all its beauty, it fell into the portion of weeds and outworn faces. The same is the portion of every man and every woman" (Jeremy Taylor, 'Holy Dying'). But goodness is immortal; it "fadeth not away" (1 Pet. i. 4). "Beauty belongs to youth and dies with it, but the odours of piety survive death and perfume the tomb."

> "Only the actions of the just
> Smell sweet and blossom in the dust."

D.

Vers. 28—33.—*Restored, but not reformed.* "Wherefore am I come from Geshur? it were better for me that I were there still; and now I will see the king's face; and if there be any iniquity in me, let him put me to death" (ver. 31). While in Geshur Absalom showed no repentance for his crime; sought no forgiveness of it; rather justified himself in its commission. On this account, perhaps, David would not permit him, when recalled, to see his face, but ordered him to remain at his own house (ver. 24); testifying his abhorrence of the crime, and desiring "to carry further the discipline of approval, to wait till his son was more manifestly penitent." If Absalom had been in a proper frame of mind, it might have been beneficial; as it was, "this half-forgiveness was an imprudent measure, really worse than no forgiveness at all, and bore very bitter fruit" (Keil). "The end showed how fatal the policy of expectation was, how terribly it added bitterness to the sense of alienation that had already been growing only too strong within him" (Plumptre). "A flash of his old kingliness blazes out for a moment in his refusal to see his son. But even that slight satisfaction to justice vanishes as soon as Joab chooses to insist that Absalom shall return to court. He seems to have no will of his own. He has become a mere tool in the hands of his fierce general; and Joab's hold upon him was his complicity in Uriah's murder. Thus at every step he was dogged by the consequences of his crime, even though it was pardoned sin" (Maclaren). Yet immediate and full forgiveness might have failed to subdue the heart of Absalom, and win filial confidence and affection. "Let favour be showed to the wicked, yet will he not learn righteousness," etc. (Isa. xxvi. 10). In his spirit and conduct we observe: 1. *Ingratitude* for the favour shown toward him. He estimated it lightly (knowing little of the fatherly love from which it proceeded), save as a means to his own honour and advancement. Than ingratitude nothing is more odious. 2. *Impatience*, fretfulness, discontent under restraint and chastisement; which a true penitent would have endured humbly and cheerfully; increased as time passed away (two years) and no further sign of royal favour appeared. 3. *Presumption* on account of the privilege already granted to him, but which he repudiated as worthless, unless followed by other privileges, such as became his royal birth and involved his reinstatement in his former dignity. He looked upon himself as rightful heir to the throne. He may, however, have suspected a rival in the youthful Solomon (now six or eight years old), and feared the influence of Bathsheba on behalf of her son. 4. *Resentment* and revenge for the neglect, contempt, and wrong which (as he conceived) he suffered (ver. 29). "See, Joab's field is beside mine, and he has barley there; go and set it on fire" (ver. 30). This appears to have been an act of passion rather than of policy. Joab's slackness, in contrast with his former zeal (ver. 23), was doubtless due to his desire to make the most of his influence with the king, to constrain Absalom humbly to entreat his intercession, and so to increase his feeling of dependence and obligation; it was only when he perceived that he had to deal with "a character wild, impulsive, and passionate," that he deemed it necessary again to alter his tactics. 5. *Wilfulness* in seeking the attainment of his ambitious aims. "I *will* see the king's face." His presence at court was essential to the accomplishment of the daring design upon the crown, which he may have already formed; and he would brook no denial. Possibly his bereavement (ver. 27; ch. xviii. 18) intensified his determination. "The strongest yearning of an Israelite's heart was thrown back upon itself, after a short-lived joy, and his feelings towards his own father were turned to bitterness and hate." 6. *Defiance* of conviction of guilt. "If there be any iniquity in me," etc. "The manner in which he sought to obtain forgiveness by force manifested an evident spirit of defiance, by which, with the well-known mildness of David's temper, he hoped to attain his object, and in fact did attain it" (Keil). He also doubtless relied on the support of a party of the people, dissatisfied with the king's severity toward him, and favourable to his complete restoration. Even Joab yielded for the present to his imperious and resolute demand. 7. *Heartless formality*. "He bowed himself on his face to the ground before the king: and the king kissed Absalom" (ver. 33). His heart was not humbled, but lifted up in pride; yet he openly received the pledge of reconciliation; and herein David's blindness and weakness reached their culmination. "He did not kiss the ill will out of the heart of his son" (Krummacher). "When parents and rulers countenance such imperious characters, they will soon experience the most fatal effects." (Here is another "meeting of three remarkable men," 1 Sam. xix. 22—24, Joab, Absalom, David.) *Remarks.* 1. No hard and impenitent heart is prepared to receive and profit by forgiveness. 2. Such a heart is capable of turning the greatest benefits into means of further and more daring rebellion; and "treasures up for itself wrath against the day of wrath." 3. Whilst "God is good and ready to forgive," he grants forgiveness only to those "who call upon him" in humility and sincerity, confessing and forsaking their sins (Ps. lxxxvi. 5; cxxxviii. 6; xxxii. 5; li. 17).—D.

Ver. 11.—*Remembrance of God.* "Let the king remember the Lord thy God." This passage occurs in a singular bit of history, which illustrates, *inter alia*, the carefulness which even the most favoured and powerful of the subjects of an Eastern monarch must at times exercise in seeking to influence him; and, on the other hand, the accessibility of such a monarch to the meanest subject desirous of his interposition. Perhaps, however, this "wise woman" may have belonged to a class which, like prophets, could (or would) take special liberties with royal and other great persons (comp. ch. xx. 16—22, the only other passage in which the phrase, "wise woman," occurs in the same sense). This woman showed herself "wise" in her management of the case which Joab had entrusted to her. It was after she had succeeded in making a favourable impression upon David, that, desirous of a more solemn and specific assurance, she addressed him in the words of the text. This appeal had the desired effect: the king declared with an oath that no harm should be done to her son, whom she had represented as in danger of death from having killed his brother. The exhortation is ever suitable and seasonable.

I. THE REMEMBRANCE OF GOD WHICH SHOULD BE PRACTISED. It includes mindfulness of: 1. His existence and perfections. 2. His relation to the universe and to ourselves—Creator, Sustainer, Ruler, Redeemer, Father of spirits, etc. 3. His revelations and commands. 4. His goodness to us. What he has done, is doing, and has promised to do.

II. WHEN WE SHOULD REMEMBER HIM. When should we not? The remembrance should be: 1. Habitual. "I have set the Lord always before me" (Ps. xvi. 8); "Be ye mindful always of his covenant" (1 Chron. xvi. 15). 2. At stated times. Without special remembrances the habitual will not be maintained. Hence the value of the hours of devotion, private and public. 3. At times of special need. When duty is hard, temptation urgent, trouble pressing.

III. WHO ARE REQUIRED TO REMEMBER HIM. All—kings as well as subjects. The higher men are raised above their fellow-men, the more they need to keep in mind him who is higher than they, and who will call them to account. The greater the trust God has committed to any, and the more they are independent of others in discharging it, the more they need to look to God for help in discerning and practising what is right. In an unlimited, or only partially limited, monarchy, the king has peculiar reason to keep the King of kings in mind, that he may be preserved from injustice, partiality, and oppression. But people of all classes are bound to remember God, and live as in his sight.

IV. WHY WE SHOULD CHERISH SUCH REMEMBRANCES. 1. *It is our plain duty.* From our relation to God, and from his commandments. And it is no less absurd than impious to forget him "with whom we have to do" (Heb. iv. 13) more than with any and all others. 2. *It is greatly for our profit.* It will be productive of: (1) Piety and holiness. These spring from the knowledge of God, but only as it is kept in mind. To have God in our creed, but not in our memory, is much the same as to have no God at all. It is thought which stirs emotion and nourishes moral principle. (2) Strength and safety under temptation. (3) Happiness. In ordinary life, and in times of trial and suffering. Remembrance of God will sanctify all things, heighten all innocent pleasures, turn duties into delights, afford consolation and support when all else fails. 3. *It will save from the pangs of too-late remembrances on earth or in hell.* (See Prov. v. 11—14; Luke xvi. 25, "Son, remember.") Mindfulness of God is universal in the eternal world, for joy or sorrow.

V. THE NEED THERE IS TO REMIND MEN OF THIS DUTY. "Let the king remember," etc. Men are apt to forget God, even when the memory of him is most desirable and incumbent. Such forgetfulness may spring from: 1. Negligence. 2. The pressure of other thoughts. The worldly. The anxious and troubled. It is often a great kindness to remind troubled Christians of their God. 3. Dislike of God. Unwillingness that he should interfere with life and action. 4. Love of sin. The pleasure of sin, if not sin itself, would be impossible if God were thought of. 5. Pride and self-satisfaction (Deut. viii. 10—19).

Finally: 1. *Remembrance of God, spontaneously and lovingly cherished, is a good evidence of sincere piety.* 2. *The compatibility or incompatibility of it with any act or habit furnishes a safe guide when distinct precepts are wanting.*—G. W.

Ver. 14.—*God fetching home his banished.* The "wise woman," having succeeded in that which she pretended to be her object in coming to David, skilfully approached the real purpose of her visit. She insinuates, in general and guarded language, that he was cherishing thoughts which were "against the people of God," and that the decision he had given in favour of her son was inconsistent with his not fetching home again his own banished one. Then, in our text, she presents, still in a general and indefinite way, reasons why the king should restore his banished one. 1. *The universal mortality of mankind.* "We must needs die," etc. This may contain a hint that it was useless longer to be grieved or angry about Amnon's death—nothing could restore him to life. Or, just as likely, it may be mentioned as a reason for doing rightly (in this case, exercising mercy) while we may, since we and those we can benefit will soon be alike in the grave; and for doing nothing to embitter this brief life to any while it lasts, or to shorten it needlessly by our conduct. Or it may be intended to soften the king's heart and prepare him to exercise compassion, as God is said to pity us because "he knoweth our frame; he remembereth that we are dust" (Ps. ciii. 13, 14). 2. *The long-suffering of God.* "Neither doth God take away life" (Revised Version); *i.e.* He does not usually strike down the sinner at once in his sins, but bears long with him, and gives him space for repentance. This may be a skilful allusion to the mercy shown to David himself (ch. xii. 13, "Thou shalt not die"). 3. *The provision which God makes for the return of sinners to himself.* "He deviseth means, that he that is banished be not an outcast from him" (Revised Version). In this also there may be an allusion to God's treatment of David, in sending to him Nathan to rouse his conscience, bring him to repentance, and then assure him of pardon. Or the woman may have in her mind the provisions of the Mosaic Law for restoring to the congregation and the temple services those who had been separated from them through contracting some uncleanness or committing some sin (see Lev. iv., v., vi. 1—7). Or she may, by a flash of inspiration, have had a glimpse of the great principles underlying these legal and ceremonial appointments, and which are more fully made manifest in Christ. We, at least, can hardly err in interpreting her words in the light of the gospel. Thus regarded, they suggest to us—

I. THE CONDITION OF SINNERS. That is, of mankind apart from Christ. They are "banished," and in danger of being "expelled," from God, and becoming utterly outcast. 1. *"Banished;" self-banished, like Absalom.* (1) Sin separates between man and God; severs from the Divine friendship and favour; from the Father's home, society, and blessing; from the family of God, its occupations, privileges, and joys. Men may be externally associated with the godly in worship and service, yet banished spiritually, cut off from real communion. Two persons may sit side by side in the same church, one holding converse with God and having fellowship with his people in their worship, the other having no real participation in these exercises, far from God even in his house. Of the banished there are two classes—those who have never known God, and those who, having known him, have turned away from him. The case of the latter is the saddest (2 Pet. ii. 20, 21). (2) Sin ever tends to produce increased separation from God. In heart, and also outwardly. When the heart is alienated from God, distaste for the forms of worship, and all that reminds of him, increases; and often ends in the entire abandonment of them. As the prodigal son went "into a far country" (Luke xv. 13). "Banished." It is a wretched condition. To depart from God is to commit great sin; to be destitute of the highest blessings and exposed to the worst miseries. To be without him is to be without true life, solid happiness, and well-grounded hope. 2. *"Banished," but not yet utterly outcast.* (1) Although they have forsaken God, he has not quite forsaken them. He does them good continually in his providence; and, by the blessings he bestows upon them, protests against their unnatural conduct, and urges them to return to him. (2) They are in constant peril of becoming entirely and hopelessly outcast; for the practice of sin hardens the heart increasingly, and threatens to obliterate in the sinner's nature whatever might leave a hope of repentance and reconciliation. And "the wrath of God" ever "abideth on him" (John iii. 36), and may at any moment banish him "into the outer darkness" (Matt. viii. 12, Revised Version).

II. THE PURPOSE OF GOD. To secure "that his banished be not expelled from him;" but be brought back, reconciled, restored to himself, his family, and service. To "fetch home again his banished." Whence this purpose? 1. *The Divine knowledge of the nature and consequent worth of man.* That he is not as the brutes, but was "made after the similitude of God" (Jas. iii. 9). That, though he "must needs die" and become as spilt water, he must needs also live after death. Hence he is worthy of much Divine expenditure in order to his salvation. The spiritual nature and the immortality of man render him an object of intense interest to his Maker, and to all who recognize them. 2. *The desire of God that his purpose in the creation of mankind should not be frustrated.* 3. *The abounding love of God.* Though the sinner is banished from his favour, he is not from his heart. He yearns over him while he expresses his displeasure with his conduct. He expresses his displeasure as one step towards his restoration. He desires the happiness of the sinner, but knows he cannot be happy apart from himself. He is "not willing that any should perish, but that all should come to repentance" (2 Pet. iii. 9).

III. THE MEANS HE DEVISED FOR THE ACCOMPLISHMENT OF HIS PURPOSE. 1. *The incarnation and work of his Son Jesus Christ.* He came "to seek and save the lost" (Luke xix. 10). By his personal manifestation of God, his teaching, example, and especially his death, he became the Way to the Father (John xiv. 6). He "suffered for sins, the Just for the unjust, that he might bring us to God" (1 Pet. iii. 18). 2. *The gospel.* Which is God's message to his banished ones, calling them back to him, and showing the way of return. 3. *The Church, its ordinances and ministries.* One main business of the Church, its ministers, yea, of all its members, is to labour to "fetch home again" God's banished ones. 4. *The events of life.* The providence of God is subservient to his grace. The Lord Jesus is "Head over all things," that all may further the accomplishment of the purposes for which he lived and died on earth, and lives and reigns in heaven. Hence providential events, on the wide scale and in individual life, are often rendered effectual unto salvation. 5. *The gift of the Holy Spirit.* To render all other means effectual in the hearts and lives of men. To convince, incline, persuade, convert, sanctify, save.

IV. THE IMITATION OF GOD IN THIS RESPECT TO WHICH WE ARE CALLED. The woman thus spoke that she might induce David to recall his banished son, Absalom. So we are called to imitate God: 1. *By a readiness to forgive and restore our own banished ones;* those who have forfeited our favour by misconduct. Some are implacable even toward their own children, however penitent they may be; but this is contrary to Christ, and quite unbecoming those who owe their own place in God's family to his forgiving mercy. 2. *By hearty co-operation with God in the work of restoring those who have departed from him.* This is the most glorious purpose for which we can live, the Divinest work in which we can engage. In this work we must bear in mind that to be successful we must conform to the methods which God has devised and furnished; as, in fact, in all departments of life, success springs from learning the Divine laws, and acting in harmony with them. There is no room for our own inventions, no possibility of independent action. In such imitation and co-operation we should be impelled to faithfulness and diligence by the consideration that both ourselves and those we are to benefit "must needs die" (see John ix. 4). And let the same consideration lead those who have departed from God to return with all speed (see John xii. 35; 2 Cor. vi. 1, 2). Let not all the Divine thoughts and methods of mercy be, in your case, in vain. For all had respect to you individually. This we may be aided to realize by the singular number used here, "his banished one." "It was for *me* that all this movement of Divine love took place, and all these wonderful means have been employed. For *me* the Saviour died; to *me* the Divine message is sent," etc. Let not your return, however, be like Absalom's, in outward act only, but in heart. "Let the wicked forsake his *way*, and the unrighteous man his *thoughts*: and let him return unto the Lord, and he will have mercy upon him; and to our God, for he will abundantly pardon" (Isa. lv. 7).—G. W.

Ver. 17.—*An all-comprehensive blessing.* "The Lord thy God be with thee" (Revised Version). The "wise woman," in closing her address to David and taking leave, as. she thought, of him, pronounces this blessing upon him. It was a usual form of salutation amongst the Israelites ; and, like our similar forms ("Adieu," equivalent to "to God [I commend thee] ; " "Good-bye," equivalent, perhaps, to "God be with thee "), was doubtless often employed without thought or feeling as to its significance. But in its full meaning it is the best blessing we can pronounce on our friends, the most comprehensive prayer we can offer for them. "The Lord Jesus be with thy spirit" (2 Tim. iv. 22) is a similar benediction.

I. IT IS A PRAYER OF TRUE FRIENDSHIP. We can desire nothing more or better for our friends than what these words express. For consider : 1. *What is included in God being "with" men.* Not simply his nearness, but : (1) His favour. His presence as a Friend with friends. Not merely as he is near to all men, the Upholder of their being and the Source of whatever they enjoy ; but as he is near to those who are reconciled to him, whom he has forgiven and received into his spiritual family, who love him and delight in his love. (2) His constant help. To defend, uphold, guide, supply with all needed and real good, temporal and spiritual ; to impart to them wisdom, holiness, strength, and happiness. (3) His converse with them. The manifestation of his presence and loving-kindness ; so that they discern his nearness, are conscious of his love and care and co-operation. 2. *Whose friendship is thus invoked.* That of "Jehovah thy God." The living God, the Eternal, the Almighty, the All-wise, the All-good, etc. Better to have him with us than all the world, all the universe. In fact, if God is with us, all things are really with us (see Rom. viii. 28, 31—39 ; 1 Pet. iii. 13).

II. IT IS A PRAYER NATURAL TO A PIOUS MAN. Springing from his personal experience of the blessedness of those who have God with them, and his desire that all, and especially those in whom he feels the deepest interest, should be partakers of the same blessedness.

III. IT IS A PRAYER ESPECIALLY SUITABLE TO BE OFFERED ON CERTAIN OCCASIONS. To express feelings of friendship, gratitude, benevolence, affection : (1) To benefactors, whose kindness we feel we cannot requite. "I cannot repay you, but God can. May he be with you!" (2) To needy persons, whose necessities we feel we cannot meet. Whether the need be temporal or spiritual. The poor, the sick, the perplexed ; friends engaged in difficult enterprises or going into perilous circumstances ; such as are leaving home or country ; friends from whom we are parting, not knowing what may befall them or us. (3) To dying friends, or those near us when we die. "I die, but God shall be with you" (Gen. xlviii. 21). It is a prayer that gives comfort and peace to him who presents it, quieting the tumult excited by the combination of strong desire with conscious helplessness.

IV. IT IS A PRAYER WHICH WILL BE FULFILLED TO THE RIGHTEOUS. The unrighteous can only secure the blessing for themselves by becoming righteous (see 2 Chron. xv. 2), through repentance and faith in Immanuel (equivalent to "God with us ").—G. W.

Ver. 25.—*Absalom's beauty.* This remark, thrown in by the way, has more to do with the main course of the narrative than at first appears. The personal beauty of Absalom accounts in part for the excessive fondness of David for him, for his vanity and ambition, and for his powerful influence over others ; and, so far as it consisted in abundance of fine hair, appears to have been the immediate occasion of his miserable end. It may serve us as the starting-point of some remarks on beauty of person.

I. ITS WORTH. 1. *It is in itself good as a fair work and gift of God.* A sober divine (Manton) calls it "a beam of the majesty of God." 2. *It is pleasant to look upon.* Beautiful people are so many pictures moving about in society for the innocent gratification of beholders, with this superiority to other pictures, that they are alive and present continual variety. 3. *It may be of great advantage to its possessor.* It attracts others ; makes it easier to secure friends. A comely face and form are an introduction to notice and favour. 4. *It may be a power for good to others.* In a ruler, a preacher, any leader in society, it is an element of influence. Is not, therefore, to be despised either by its possessor or by others.

II. ITS PERILS. 1. *It is apt to excite vanity and pride—themselves the parents of many sins.* 2. *When overvalued, it leads to the neglect of higher things—*the culture of mind, heart, and character. 3. *In children it may awaken in their parents a foolish fondness which hinders parental discipline.* (Comp. 1 Kings i. 6.) 4. *It attracts flatterers and seducers, and thus often occasions moral ruin.* It was Tamar's beauty that kindled Amnon's lust (ch. xiii. 1). It is a very perilous endowment to young women, especially among the poor. 5. *It may lead its possessor to become a tempter of others; and renders his (or her) temptations all the more seductive.* Lord Bacon (in his essay 'On Beauty') says, "For the most part it makes a dissolute youth, and an age a little out of countenance; but yet certainly again, if it light well, it maketh virtues shine and vices blush."

III. Its inferiority. In comparison with mental, moral, and spiritual beauty. 1. *In essential nature.* The latter belong to a far higher region, are a far more valuable product of the Divine hand. The beauties of holiness are the features of the Divine Father appearing in his children, and manifesting their parentage. 2. *In appearance.* Moral loveliness is far more beautiful than physical in the sight of God and the good (comp. 1 Sam. xvi. 7), and it has the power of rendering very plain faces interesting and attractive, if not beautiful. 3. *In value to its possessor and to others.* Beauty of character is a priceless treasure (1 Pet. iii. 4), indicating one still more precious—the character itself; it excites the deepest and best kind of admiration and commendation (Prov. xxxi. 30); and it gives those in whom it appears a power over others for their good which incalculably surpasses the influence of mere beauty of person; and which "adorning the doctrine of God our Saviour" (Titus ii. 10)—the chief instrument of good to men—wins for it a readier acceptance. 4. *In facility of attainment.* Beauty of person, if not a gift of nature, cannot be acquired; but that of the soul can. The Lord Jesus came to earth to make it possible for the ugly and deformed to become lovely; he lives to effect this great transformation. Those who are in him become the subjects of a new creation: "Old things are passed away; all things are become new" (2 Cor. v. 17). The Holy Ghost adorns the soul with heavenly grace and attractiveness (Gal. v. 22, 23). And when the process is complete on the whole Church of Christ, he will "present it to himself" as his beauteous bride, "a glorious Church, not having spot, or wrinkle, or any such thing, but . . . holy and without blemish" (Eph. v. 27). Faith in, and habitual converse with, him who is "altogether lovely," is the way to experience for ourselves this wondrous change. "Beholding as in a mirror the glory of the Lord, we are changed into the same image from glory to glory, even as by the Spirit of the Lord" (2 Cor. iii. 18). Even the body will at length be beautified (Phil. iii. 21). 5. *In duration.* The beauty which is of earth fades and passes away, but that which is of heaven abides evermore. The former may vanish even in youth through the ravages of disease; will almost certainly in after-life, unless heightened and ripened by sense and goodness; and certainly will turn to corruption after death. But the latter will survive the decay and destruction of all things, and adorn the "Father's house" for ever.

In conclusion, this subject appeals especially to the young. Let them seek with all their heart the beauty which is spiritual and everlasting; and regard as of small account that which is in itself of little value, and at best of short duration; and which, if separate from moral excellence, is like the beauty of a sepulchre, covering death and corruption.—G. W.

EXPOSITION.

CHAPTER XV.

Ver. 1.—**After this.** The Hebrew is a more precise phrase than that on which we have commented on ch. x. 1 and xiii. 1, and implies that Absalom began his devices soon after obtaining his liberty. **Chariots and horses;** Hebrew, *a chariot and horses;* that is, a chariot for state occasions, in which Absalom rode, while fifty footmen ran at his side. Probably his grandfather Talmai practised similar magnificence at Geshur. In India it is still common for men of rank to be attended by runners on foot, who will keep up with horses or elephants for an incredible distance.

Ver. 2.—**The way of the gate.** The gate would be that of the royal palace, where the king gave audience and administered justice. At the gate of the city the elders were the judges, and, though the higher authority of the king may have weakened the action of this citizen court, yet passages such as Isa. 1, 23 and Jer. v. 28 imply, not only its continued existence, but also that it retained much importance. Probably all causes between citizens were tried by it, just as causes in the country were tried by the mishpachah (see note on ch. xiv. 7); but with an appeal in weighty matters to the king. It is a mistake to suppose that David altogether neglected his judicial functions. On the contrary, the woman of Tekoah obtained an audience, as a matter of course; and Absalom would not have risen up thus early unless David had also taken his seat in the early morning on the royal divan to administer justice. It was the suitors on their way to the king whom Absalom accosted, and made believe that he would be more assiduous in his duties than his father, and that he would have decided every suit in favour of the person to whom he was talking, whereas really one side alone can gain the cause. Still, we may well believe that, guilty himself of adultery and murder, and with his two elder sons stained with such terrible crimes, David's administration of justice had become half-hearted. And thus his sin again found him out, and brought stern punishment. For Absalom used this weakness against his father, and, intercepting the suitors on their way, would ask their city and tribe, and listen to their complaint, and assure them of the goodness of their cause, and lament that, as the king could not hear all causes easily himself, he did not appoint others to aid him in his duties. It was delay and procrastination of which Absalom complained; and as many of the litigants had probably come day after day, and not succeeded in getting a hearing, they were already in ill humour and prepared to find fault. Now, as David possessed great powers of organization, we may well believe that he would have taken measures for the adequate administration of law had it not been for the moral malady which enfeebled his will. In the appointment of Jehoshaphat and Seraiah (ch. viii. 16, 17) he had made a beginning, but soon his hands grew feeble, and he did no more.

Ver. 6.—**Absalom stole the hearts.** By professing anxiety to devote himself to the hearing and deciding of the people's causes, by flattering each one with the assurance that his case was so good that it needed only a hearing to be decided in his favour, and by his affability, made the more charming and irresistible by his personal beauty, he won the love of the people almost without their knowing how devoted they had become to him.

Ver. 7.—**After forty years.** As Absalom was born in Hebron after David was made king (ch. iii. 3), and as David's whole reign lasted only forty years and six months, the reading "forty" is evidently incorrect. Suggestions, such, for instance, as that the forty years are to be reckoned from the desire of the Israelites to have a king, or from the anointing of David by Samuel, are merely methods of evading a difficulty. The Syriac, however, and the Vulgate—except the Codex Amiatinus, which reads "forty," supported by Josephus and some manuscripts—have "four years," which would give ample, yet not too long, time for the growth of Absalom's popularity, and of dissatisfaction at David's tardy administration of justice. **In Hebron.** Absalom chose this town, both as being his birthplace, and also because it was on the road to Geshur (1 Sam. xxvii. 8), whither flight might be necessary should the enterprise fail. He hoped also to win to his cause some of the powerful tribe of Judah, though it generally was the mainstay of David's throne. Local sacrifices were still customary (see note on 1 Sam. xvi. 2), and the visit of the king's son for such a purpose would be celebrated by a general holiday and much feasting at Hebron. As Ewald remarks, David's confidence and want of suspicion were the results of a noble-minded generosity. And besides, there was no state police ever on the watch, and ready to put an unfavourable construction on all that was done; and probably David was even pleased at his son's popularity, and took his professions as proof that he would be a just and wise ruler on succeeding to his father's place. Perhaps, too, he was glad at this indication of religious feeling on Absalom's part; for a father is sure to look on the better side of his son's acts. He had been tardy enough in fulfilling his vow, but it seemed to David that conscience had at last prevailed, and that right was to be done.

Ver. 10.—**Absalom sent spies.** The word means "those who go hither and thither," and, as the object of such journeying would usually be to gather information, the right translation often is "spies." Here there was no such purpose, nor were they to report to Absalom, but to disperse themselves everywhere, and, when the signal was given at Hebron, they were to endeavour to gather the people to Absalom's standard. Some simple-minded commentators wonder how one trumpet could be heard throughout the land. It was heard only at Hebron, but the news of the proclamation would rapidly spread; and, though the rumour might be vague and confused, yet these emissaries, fully acquainted beforehand with its meaning, would turn it to Absalom's advantage, and urge the people to confirm the choice, made, as they would affirm, by the whole tribe of Judah. In such attempts everything depends upon gathering a powerful following at first; and usually a good deal of vigour and even force is necessary to make men take part in a revolt. But as the numbers swell, adherents readily flock in to what seems to be the winning side.

Ver. 11.—**Two hundred men.** These, doubtless, were courtiers and men of rank, who were so accustomed to Absalom's love of display, that, when called, that is, invited, they would go without suspicion. To Absalom their attendance was most important, not only because, being compromised, many would join him, and even all of them for a time be forced to yield obedience, but because they would make the people of Hebron suppose that Absalom had a powerful body of supporters at Jerusalem. It is quite possible that at Hebron, and generally in Judah, there was great discontent because David had left their tribe to choose a capital elsewhere, and because he did not show them any decided preference over the other tribes, whose good will he would rightly seek to conciliate. The existence of much jealousy between Judah and the ten tribes is plain from ch. xix. 41—43.

Ver. 12.—**Ahithophel the Gilonite.** The desertion of David by Ahithophel is in every way remarkable, even if he were Bathsheba's grandfather (see note on ch. xi. 3). For he was far too subtle a man to have joined the conspiracy unless he had felt reasonably sure that it would be successful. Successful it would have been had his advice been followed; but so correctly did he estimate the result if David were allowed time to gather his friends, that, when his counsel was rejected, he withdrew immediately to Giloh, and committed suicide. Still if the revolt had been successful, it would have involved, if not the death of Bathsheba, yet certainly that of her sons, and the exclusion of Ahithophel's great-grandchildren from the throne. In Ps. xli., written at this time, we learn what were David's feelings when he heard the news of this conspiracy, and Ahithophel is the familiar friend, in whom he had trusted, and who had eaten at his table, but now raised up his heel to kick at him. In John xiii. 18 the words are quoted of Judas Iscariot, of whom Ahithophel was a type in his treachery and in his death by his own hand. The translation, "sent for Ahithophel," cannot be maintained. The Hebrew is "sent Ahithophel," but for what purpose or on what embassy is not mentioned. As thus something must have dropped out of the Hebrew text, it possibly may be the preposition "for," as this gives a good sense. For Giloh, Ahithophel's town, was situated a few miles to the south of Hebron (Josh. xv. 51), and Ahithophel had probably been

working there secretly for Absalom for some time. As David's counsellor, his proper place of residence would have been Jerusalem, but the conspiracy had been kept so secret that he had been able to get away without suspicion. He is now summoned to Absalom's side, and his presence there brings in so many adherents that a rapid march on Jerusalem might have put David into their power. The Revised Version is right in translating, while he offered the **sacrifices**; namely, those which he had vowed, and which were the reason given for his visit to Hebron.

Ver. 14.—**Arise, and let us flee.** The rebellion of Absalom, and David's humiliating flight, bring out all the better parts of the king's character, and set him once again before us as a man after God's own heart. For this period is richly illustrated by the psalms which were written under the pressure of this great affliction, and which are marked by firm confidence in God, and an assured sense of the Divine nearness and protection. Ps. xli. shows how poignant was his anguish at Ahithophel's treachery, but it inspired no fear: "As for me, thou upholdest me in mine integrity, and settest me before thy face for ever" (Ps. xli. 12). It was a firm faith which prompted such words. In Ps. lxiii., written "in the wilderness of Judah," before David had reached the Jordan, he gives utterance to his grief at the loss of his religious privileges at Jerusalem; but Jehovah is still his strong Tower, and his dwelling will be in God's tabernacle for ever. Ps. iii. and iv. are his morning and evening hymns written "when he fled from Absalom his son." Ps. lv. is one more sad even than Ps. xli. He describes in it his panic-stricken feelings when the news reached him, his longing to escape from the turmoil of life, and flee into the wilderness and be at rest; and his grief at his desertion by men in whose company he had worshipped in the house of God. Upon this follows an outburst of vehement indignation, made the more bitter by the sense of the treachery whereby he had been duped into connivance with Absalom's plans (ver. 21); but amidst it all his confidence was unshaken that if he cast his burden upon God, "he would sustain him, and never suffer the righteous to be moved." Finally, in Ps. xxvii. we have the contrast between Jehovah's abiding goodness and the inconstancy of men; while Pss. lxi. and lxii. were probably written at Mahanaim, when David's anguish of mind was being assuaged, and a calm confidence was taking its place. Everywhere in all of them David speaks as one who had now given all his heart to God. As regards his terror and flight (Ps. lv. 5—8), it may seem strange that David should have withdrawn so hurriedly from a city so strong as Jerusalem. But we must not suppose that he had a standing army, and his few Cherethites and Pelethites could have made no head against the nation. Probably, too, the fortifications of the city were incomplete (Ps. li. 18); and even if in good order, yet, cooped up in Jerusalem, David would have left the whole country in Absalom's power, and finally, after a long blockade, he must have been driven by famine to surrender. Away from Jerusalem he was the centre whither all who disliked Absalom's attempt would gather, and every day as it passed would make men reflect more and more upon what David had done for them, and the more steady and thoughtful of them would finally decide in his favour. There would be, moreover, the secret conviction that David, with such men round him as Joab and Abishai, if free to take his own course, would be more than a match for Absalom and his larger numbers. This was what Ahithophel foresaw, and was so convinced that, if David were not crushed at once, he would gain the day, that he did not even wait to see, but destroyed himself. Abarbanel thinks that the wish of the people had never been for more than the association of Absalom with David on the throne, according to what he had himself suggested (ver. 4); and that there was a great revulsion of feeling when they saw that they must choose absolutely between father and son, and that whoever lost the crown must lose his life as well. Some commentators consider that Ps xxxi. also belongs to this period, though others ascribe it to Jeremiah. Parts of it are singularly applicable to the circumstances of David's flight, as where the psalmist speaks of Jehovah as being his Fortress in contrast with Jerusalem, and adds, "Thou hast not shut me up into the hands of the enemy, but hast set my feet in a large space," as though "the net which the conspirators had privily laid for him" had been the design to coop him up within the walls of the city. There are touching words, too, of distress at the slander and reproach breaking forth on every side, and at the completeness of his fall, so that whereas but a few days before he had been a king, now "he was clean forgotten, as a dead man out of mind; and cast aside as though he were now of no more account than the sherds of a broken vessel." But, with the calm strength of faith he adds, "My times are in thy hand;" "Thou shalt hide all who trust in thee in the secret of thy presence;" "Oh, then, love Jehovah, and be of good courage! for he shall strengthen the heart of all whose hope is fixed on him."

Ver. 15.—**The king's servants.** These were the officers of David's court and household, numerous enough to hamper his movements, but not enough to protect him. All David's wives, moreover, went, and his children, and some of his concubines (ch. xix. 5), ten, however, being left in charge of the palace.

Ver. 17.—**And tarried in a place that was far off**; Revised Version, *in Beth-merhak.* "The Far House"—so we may translate this proper name—was probably not a dwelling, but a pavilion overlooking the Kidron valley; and here David halted his household until all were assembled, and arrangements made for their journey. Here, too, the body-guard would gather, and they would cross the Kidron only when everything was ready for their orderly progress. Confusion at such a time would breed a panic and invite an attack.

Ver. 18.—**All the Gittites, six hundred men which came after him from Gath.** The Septuagint reads "Gibborim," and without doubt these are the persons meant; but while they were styled Gibborim, the "mighties," for honour's sake, because of their prowess, they probably were popularly called David's Gittites, because they were the six hundred men who had formed his little army when he sought refuge with Achish, King of Gath (1 Sam. xxvii. 2; xxx. 9). They were not Philistines, but Israelites of desperate fortune (1 Sam. xxii. 2); and it is a proof of David's great ability, and of the moral influence of his character, that he was successful, not only in controlling them and maintaining discipline, but also in forming them into as noble a set of heroes as ever existed, and who were faithful to him in all his fortunes. To their number belonged the thirty-seven champions enumerated in ch. xxiii., and possibly the title "Gibborim" strictly belonged to them only. As they are still called "the six hundred," it is probable that the corps was maintained at this number by new appointments, and that they had special privileges which made their position very desirable. Certainly David would never forget men who had shared all his fortunes, and been so true and so useful to him; and it is evident, from Hushai's counsel (ch. xvii. 8), that Absalom feared their resolute valour, and hesitated to attack without overwhelming numbers. Thenius compares these veterans to Napoleon's Old Guard.

Ver. 19.—**Ittai the Gittite.** Ittai was not one of the six hundred, though there was an Ittai among them, a Benjamite. He was a citizen of Gath, who had lately come ("yesterday," see ver. 20), with all his household of slaves and dependents, his clan, Hebrew, his *taf*—translated in ver. 22 his "little ones." He had evidently been a person of importance in his own country, whence he had been driven, perhaps by political troubles, and was now, therefore, an exile and a foreigner (Authorized Version, "stranger") at Jerusalem. As David made him joint commander of his army with Joab and Abishai (ch. xviii. 2), he must also have been a general of recognized military skill. As he was thus not personally interested in the government of Israel, and, in fact, had only lately come thither, David recommends him to return . . . and abide with the king, that is, with the *de facto* king, Absalom. But so great was the fascination which David exercised upon those around him, that this foreigner boldly threw in his lot with him, and accompanied him in his flight. **Return to thy place.** This is a very daring transposition, as the Hebrew is, *Return and abide with the king; for thou art a foreigner, and also an exile art thou to thy place.* The Revised Version gives the same sense as the Authorized, though it shows more respect to the grammar. But the Septuagint, Syriac, and Vulgate, by "his own place" understand Gath, either taking the words as meaning "an exile as to thy own place," or having a different reading. The Hebrew then proceeds, *Yesterday was thy coming, and shall I to-day make thee wander to go with us, seeing I go whither I go?* that is, I go I know not whither. *Return thou, and take back thy brethren—in mercy and truth.* This gives a very good sense, but the Septuagint and Vulgate have a different reading: "Take back thy brethren with thee, and the Lord shew thee mercy and truth." The Syriac gives the general sense of the Hebrew, rendering, "Take back thy brethren well."

Ver. 22.—**All the little ones;** Hebrew, *all the taf;* in ver. 20 called "his brethren," that is, all the relatives and dependents who had accompanied him in his exile. Their presence with him proves that he had entirely broken with the Philistines, and left his country for good. He may have taken this step for religious reasons, though his swearing by Jehovah (ver. 21) does not prove it, as Achish did the same (1 Sam. xxix. 6); or Ittai, after the capture of Gath by David (ch. viii. 1), may have made himself unpopular by becoming the ally of the conqueror, and so finally have determined to leave the city, and find a home in Israel.

Ver. 23.—**All the country wept.** This general lamentation proves that David was not really unpopular in Jerusalem, though it was there that Absalom had dazzled the people by his magnificence, and sought to win favour by his gracious ways. By the *country* the inhabitants are meant, who watched the king's departure; while the *people* are David's followers—his retinue and attendants. **The brook Kidron.** This is a winter torrent, dry during most of the year, but serving at the rainy seasons to carry off the rainfall from the Valley of Jehoshaphat. It lay on the east of Jerusalem, and beyond it was Mount Olivet. The direction of David's flight was toward the wild country on the east of the Jordan, in which Ishbosheth had found a refuge after the defeat of Gilboa. To reach it he must pass by Jericho, and thence through the Arabah (Jer. xxxix. 4) to the ford of the Jordan, after crossing which he would be in comparative safety. Ahithophel would have followed that very night, and have attacked before David had placed the river between himself and his pursuers.

Ver. 24.—**And Abiathar went up.** This rendering, though confirmed by the versions, is very unintelligible. Whither did Abiathar go up? And moreover it is said that he continued going up until all David's followers had passed out of the city. Another possible rendering is, "And Abiathar offered (sacrifices) until all the people had done passing out of the city." Passages quoted in proof that the verb may be so rendered without the addition of the word "sacrifice" are 1 Sam. ii. 28 and ch. xxiv. 22; but in both these places the context makes the sense plain. Such a sacrifice would, of course, sanctify both king and people in their flight; but as none of the versions support this method of translating the text, it seems unsafe to adopt it, and the passage must remain obscure. On the one hand, it is unlikely that there would be time to offer sacrifices at so hasty a flight; but on the other hand, the removal of the ark was a solemn thing, which probably required some such religious ceremonial, and Cahen and other Jewish authorities translate, "Abiathar offered burnt offerings."

Ver. 26.—**Let him do to me as seemeth good unto him.** David's answer is full, not only of devout resignation and trust in God, but is remarkable also for the absence of superstition. He feels that God will not judge him by any mere outward sign or privilege, but in truth and equity. If he deserves condemnation, he will not escape it by carrying the ark about with him. If, on the contrary, God accepts him, he will restore him to the enjoyment of his spiritual privileges, and bring him back to worship at the place which he has chosen for his dwelling. We must notice that he addresses these words to Zadok, who had remained with the ark. This was natural if Abiathar was occupied in offering, but hard to understand if he had gone up, that is, in advance of the ark, to acquaint David with their purpose.

Ver. 27.—**Art thou (not) a seer?** Both the Authorized Version and the Revised Version evade the difficulty of this passage by inserting the word "not." It is one of the merits of the Revised Version that usually it does not take these liberties. But "Art thou a seer?" is meaningless; and the attempts, moreover, to show that Zadok was a seer fail entirely in proof. The receiving revelations by Urim and Thummim was a priestly, and not a prophetic, function. Without altering the text, the words may be correctly translated, "Seest thou?" This was probably a colloquial phrase, cf which the Septuagint gives the sense by rendering it in the imperative, "See;" while the Syriac, regarding it as an expletive, boldly omits it.

Ver. 28.—In the plain of the wilderness. The Revised Version has "at the fords of the wilderness," that is, it rightly keeps to the written Hebrew text (the K'tib), while the Authorized Version adopts a conjecture of the Massorites (the K'ri). This conjecture is the substitution of *arboth* for *abroth*, and they have made the same alteration at ch. xvii. 16. But the substitution is uncalled for and mischievous; for David would not halt indefinitely in the plain, the Arabah (of which Arboth is the plural), but would press on to the fords, where some delay must take place, and where the king's presence would be important in giving instructions for what was by no means an easy operation (comp. ch. xix. 18). At the river, moreover, David could be assailed only in front, where his "mighties" would make a strong defence, while in the Arabah they might be surrounded; and, encumbered as they were with women, their line must be so extended as to be weakened. We find, too, in Judg. iii. 28 that the fords of the Jordan formed a good military position. In ch. xvii. 22 it is expressly said that the fording of the river did not take place until Jonathan and Ahimaaz came with their report; and their words there, in ver. 21, show that David was on the bank when they arrived, with his preparations so complete, that, in the next few hours, all his company were safely carried over to the other side. Ahimaaz was a famous runner (see ch. xviii. 27), and, if David was ready, the time gained by him upon any body of troops leaving Jerusalem at the same hour, would have enabled the king to get his people across; but if he had still some miles to march, with a number of women and children, Ahimaaz's fleetness would have been rendered useless.

Ver. 30.—The ascent of mount Olivet; Hebrew, *the ascent of the olive trees.* The hill never was called Olivet, which is a word formed from the Latin *mons oliveti,* the mount of the olive grove. David had his head covered. This was a sign of grief among the Persians, Egyptians, and Romans,

as well as the Hebrews (for whom see Ezek. xxiv. 17), it being originally a natural movement to conceal an outburst of tears. So we in great sorrow bury our faces in our hands. In this mark of mourning all joined, but David added the going barefoot as a sign of deeper humiliation. According to the Jewish Midrash, it was upon the Mount of Olives that David composed the third psalm. More probably it was at the fords of the Jordan, after David, wearied with the fatigues of the march, had enjoyed a short refreshing slumber, and while he was waiting for his two young friends, that he comforted himself by this outpouring of his heart to God.

Ver. 31.—And one told David. The Hebrew literally is, *and David told.* But we cannot suppose that David had previously known of Ahithophel's defection. The text is evidently corrupt, and the Authorized Version gives the right sense. On hearing of the defection of a man so famous for practical sound judgment, David prays to God to frustrate his counsel, and the opportunity for devising means for this end quickly follows.

Ver. 32.—Where he worshipped God; more correctly, *where God was worshipped,* and so the Revised Version. The summit of the Mount of Olives was one of the many bamoth, or high places, situated on the top of hills, where, in the old Canaanitish time, men had worshipped their heathenish deities. They were still regarded as consecrated places, but the worship had now been transferred to Elohim, the true God. They continued to be hallowed spots, with Levitical priests to minister at them, until the stricter times of Josiah (2 Kings xxiii. 8), when such worship was forbidden; but even then these priests seem to have retained considerable privileges, though their position was inferior to that held by the priests of the temple. It was at this hallowed spot that David's old friend and privy counsellor (ver. 37), Hushai, met him, with his coat rent—not the upper garment, but the *kuttoneth,* the under tunic, the rending of which was a sign of deeper sorrow. We read of "the border of the Archites" (so the Revised Version, rightly) in Josh. xvi. 2, near Bethel, in the tribe of Manasseh; and Hushai's birthplace was probably there.

Ver. 33.—A burden unto me. Most likely because Hushai was old and infirm. Others, with less probability, think that it was because of his rank, which would demand special attendance.

Ver. 34.—Then mayest thou for me defeat the counsel of Ahithophel. David was thus meeting treachery by treachery, and we cannot approve of it, even granting that Ahithophel's conduct was base and selfish, while Hushai was risking his life for his master. Still, he was sent back to tell a falsehood, and his excuse was necessity; for Ahithophel was so sagacious that, if his counsel were not upset, David's cause was lost. It was not Christian morality, but yet it has a sort of nobleness about it in Hushai's devotion to his king. And even now, in war and diplomacy, such acts are not uncommon, and a distinction is unhappily drawn between political and social morality. Even in common life immoral doings are often sanctioned by use. Thus many customs of trade are frauds, considered legitimate because generally practised. Even among ourselves Christian morality is far below the level of our Master's teaching; and the Old Testament must not be taken as approving all that it records. Similar blame does not attach to Zadok and Abiathar. They were known to be David's friends, and had even tried to go with him, bearing with them the ark. They professed no friendship for Absalom, and returned for no covert purpose, looking for protection, not to guile, but to their sacred office. And Absalom would be glad to have them in his power,

and would make them continue the customary sacrifices, and, if his rebellion proved successful, would force them to anoint him, and so give his usurpation a religious sanction. But he would tell them none of his plans, nor would they try to insinuate themselves into his confidence. They would have a perfect right to be useful in any way they could to their true master, but would do so at the risk of severe punishment. Hushai's way of defeating Ahithophel was treacherous; but there was no deceit in the young men carrying a message from him, for they were openly David's friends.

Ver. 37.—**Absalom came into Jerusalem.** Absalom had evidently pushed rapidly forward from Hebron, in hopes, perhaps, of surprising David in the city. Evidently he entered it on the day of David's flight (ch. xvii. 1), and Ahithophel's proposal to select twelve thousand men from Absalom's followers shows how very powerful the conspiracy was. Had this advice been followed, the decisive battle would have been fought that evening at the fords of the Jordan, a few miles only from Jerusalem.

HOMILETICS.

Vers. 1—12.—*The shady side of human nature.* The facts are: 1. Absalom sets up a large domestic establishment with a semblance of royalty. 2. Rising early in the morning of each day, he is first to meet the suitors for judgment at the gate of the city, and seizes the occasion for insinuating that there is defect in the king's provision for the administration of justice. 3. He also professes to manifest sympathy with suitors, by expressing the wish that he were in a position to do them justice, and gives outward evidence of his concern for them by taking each one by the hand and kissing him. 4. These plans being in progress, he next asks permission of David to go to Hebron, on the plea that he desired to redeem a vow which he had sacredly made to God while in exile; and David granting his request, he sets out for Hebron, with a company of men ignorant of his design. 5. Meanwhile he sends spies throughout Israel, so that on a given signal they might simultaneously make the announcement, "Absalom reigneth in Hebron." 6. He moreover gains to his side Ahithophel, David's counsellor, and so advances his cause among the people. The narrative gives us in brief form the scheme, the principles, the methods, and early form of Absalom's conspiracy. He knew his own mind, and was set on the overthrow of his father's authority, from sheer vanity and lust of power. The outline of his method was clearly defined: (1) to win over the people by criticizing the king's administration, and gratifying them by a showy establishment, professed zeal for justice, and marked personal attentions; (2) to secure a good centre for proclaiming his authority, and this by a hypocritical profession of religion which required him to go there; (3) by scattering agents through the land, and gaining to his side the king's most sagacious adviser. There is not one relieving feature to the dark picture of pride, ingratitude, filial alienation, low cunning, and religious hypocrisy. It is, however, our province to extract good out of evil, and in the early stages of Absalom's rebellion we may see illustrations of the shady side of human nature, which, if noted and applied to conduct, may warn against often-recurring evils, and put us on our guard against the same tendencies in other departments of life.

I. THE PRINCIPLES AND METHODS OF UNJUSTIFIABLE REBELLION. Rebellion against existing authority may perhaps be right under special circumstances. People do not exist for governments, but governments for the people; and it is possible that the rights of the people may be so utterly trodden upon that it is the duty of self-preservation to rebel. Even parental authority must be resisted when it comes into direct collision with conscience and with Christ (Matt. x. 33—38). But rebellion is wicked when, as in this case, it springs from a blending of conceit, dislike of constituted authority, and lust for power. This may characterize rebellion originating in an individual or in a restless people. Talk of oppression, justice, kindness and consideration for the oppressed, may be but a cloak for a selfish aversion to restraint and a love of self-will. Even where there is justification for resistance to an evil rule, it is wicked to have recourse to flattery, deceit, hypocrisy, and low cunning to accomplish the end in view. In times of turbulence and agitation it is important that men scrutinize the secret motives of their actions. As a rule, injustice in rulers can be best resisted by the calm, sober protest and passive resistance of conscientious men. Faith in God, and in the force of true principles, with patient persistence, will in the end accomplish more than can be secured by violence ; and where injustice exists only in the imagination of the restless, and the evils of life spring from their own habits and practices, then rebellion is one of the greatest crimes of which man is capable.

II. INCIDENTAL REVELATIONS OF CHARACTER. The character of a man lies primarily in the main principles and passions that are deep down in his nature, and which in course of years shape his outward conduct. Absalom's real character was in existence long before it came out to the eye of the public in the form of rebellion against his father's authority. Probably David discerned its incipient form, and hence his extreme slowness in recalling him to a position of prominence. The setting up by Absalom of a large princely establishment, with chariots and horses and runners, was really an incidental revelation in palpable form of a character internally maturing. It was a sign to such men as David and Nathan of what they had believed to exist—a vain, proud, ostentatious spirit. So in course of time men generally do something in their domestic arrangements or business developments which, if the world will only read aright, brings into public view tendencies and tastes which hitherto have been kept under restraint. Our visible acts and creations are the successive revelations of our condition. A man's dress, his handwriting, his domestic establishment, his bearing before the public, his mode of transacting business, is a manifestation of the hidden man —the indicator of the elements entering into the permanent character. The outward aspects of a man's life may be studied with a view to a knowledge of the habits and tastes of his mind.

III. EVIL TENDENCIES IN CONGENIAL ENVIRONMENT. The evil tendencies of Absalom were somewhat pronounced when he set up his pretentious establishment, but by his own act those tendencies were placed in the midst of circumstances eminently calculated to strengthen and develop them further. The heart of man can devise things out of its own tastes and propensities which become at once food on which those tastes and propensities grow to further power. A man of pleasure out of his own desires creates occupations and pursuits which become the nourishers of the passion for pleasure. The same holds of dreadful vices and blessed virtues. There is a self-promotive power in the forces that dwell within our moral nature. Intellectual and physical forces are not so recuperative of themselves by means of what they create as are the moral. We are to ponder the path of our feet, for every step increases the momentum in the road, be it good or bad.

IV. LUST OF POWER MINUS FITNESS FOR ITS EXERCISE. Absalom set his heart on being King of Israel. The vision of a throne and a submissive people had great attractions for him. The princely establishment, with chariots and horsemen, was only the first instalment of a splendour soon to be won. Like all such men, he had unlimited confidence in himself. He could administer justice ! He could win the people and hold them in subjection ! And yet this vanity, this low cunning, this love of outward show, and mean lying flattery of the people, disqualified him for ruling as a king. Morally speaking, he was a handsome fool, and knew it not. The lust for power is common, and often very strong in men. As manifested in bad men, it is an abnormal development of a love of mastery over what is not self. The possession of power over man is safe and good only when there coexist with it justice, generosity, considerateness, and honesty.

V. ALIENATION FROM A FATHER'S HEART THE CLIMAX OF EVIL. Absalom was no longer a true son. No man could have entered on such a scheme and have devised such means unless he had lost all true natural affection. To find fault with a father's administration, to expose a father to ridicule, to seek to alienate men from attachment to a father, and, in short, crush a father's hopes and life's work, could only proceed from a heart utterly alienated. And such a father! Weak and erring as David in a notable instance had been, he was the most generous, and magnanimous of men, and had brought peace and plenty and honour to Israel. Absalom's crime was one of the basest ever recorded. And all alienation from a true father's heart is utterly base and deserving the strongest detestation. There is hope for sons when they still cherish love and reverence for parents; none when these are gone. Every feeling, and act, and companionship, and habit which tend towards this awful separation of heart, should be shunned as men shun the road to death. And yet this is the real state of the human heart in relation to God. The gulf is awful; and nothing but a new creation will lead to a reconciliation (John iii. 5 ; Rom. viii. 7).

VI. PSEUDO-PATRIOTISM AN ASSUMED VIRTUE. Patriotism is strong in men whose country has been associated in memory with great deeds. To care for one's land and people, to be more concerned for the maintenance of justice and adjustment of the claims of the poor than for the form and *personnel* of government,—this is always commendable; and so much is this virtue esteemed that it is assumed by Absalom for his own purposes. We cannot believe in the patriotism of any man who shuts his heart against a good father. Civil virtues cannot make amends for the absence of the domestic and primary virtues. It is easy to prate about justice and the oppressed, and to speak smoothly to the populace; to keep the heart pure, loving, true toward man and God, is not so easy. There is much pseudo-patriotism in political life. Men claim virtues they do not possess, and use the claim for gaining an influence that else would be unattainable.

VII. RELIGION A CLOAK FOR EVIL DESIGNS. Absalom knew his father to be a pious man, and therefore seeks to accomplish his purpose by a profession of piety. The heartless son finds no difficulty in taking the holy name of God in vain, and concocting a tissue of lies. To the populace he can be a critic of the government; to the pious king he can be a devout man, intent on keeping sacred vows. No clearer proof of a Satanic spirit than when men dare to lay hold of the most sacred things and use them for vile and selfish purposes. Righteous, indeed, was the indignation of Christ against such "hypocrites." "Woe" from the lips of love came upon them. Manifold are the forms and degrees in which this evil appears. To worship in order to be respectable, to profess religion for the sake of trade, to utter pious phrases in order to win popular applause, are but the less repulsive forms of the very crime of Absalom. How abominable such persons must appear in the sight of the all-searching God!

VIII. TAKING UNDUE ADVANTAGE OF ANOTHER'S DIFFICULTY. In consequence of the immense work thrown on an absolute monarch, the growing complications of a flourishing state, and the incompetence of subordinates, there would necessarily arise many difficulties in the administration of the affairs of the kingdom. In all lands people have to wait for justice when others are being served. But the evil heart of Absalom showed itself in using whatever incidental delays arose as an occasion of promoting its own wicked schemes. There is too much of this in the world. The rich have often taken advantage of the ignorance and helplessness of the poor to secure ends otherwise unattainable. In political life it is a maxim to seize the hour of weakness for a party triumph. It is the devil's opportunity with feeble souls to render more sure their destruction. Trouble in state, Church, or family affords opportunity for testing the qualities of men. Love or hate, sympathy or antagonism, will thereby be revealed. How different to others the blessed Saviour in presence of human infirmity!

IX. POPULARITY ON AN UNSTABLE AND HOLLOW BASIS. The people's hearts were won to Absalom. It seems a great triumph to win the hearts of multitudes; it is an indication of great power on the part of the conqueror or of fickleness on the part of the conquered. But in this, as in many instances, the conquest was a revelation of shallow thinking on the one side and basest cunning on the other. There is in most men a soil for receiving the seeds of discontent from the hand of a deft sower. People are easily caught by flatteries and personal attentions. A visible parade of splendour dazzles and pleases the crowd, who think modest, quiet bearing a sign of mediocrity. The dash and careless promises of a young and handsome man excite the imagination, and raise up pictures of great possibilities. The mass of men do not think; they feel, and are led by the clever orator who can stir up their feelings. It is not always a credit to " go with the multitude," and fall in with an order of things because it is popular. The *vox populi* maxim is often false. Of One it was once true, " Of the people there was none with him." He was " despised and rejected of men."

X. An illustration of the most dreadful of conspiracies. It is not necessary to endeavour to trace resemblance in all details between antagonism to the mortal king in Zion and opposition to the immortal King in Zion. But there has been and still is a plot to destroy the authority of him whose right it is to reign. Fashion, wealth, power of speech, wit, and alliances with wise Ahithophels, continue to undermine and eventually overthrow the influence of Christ over the hearts of men. The " gates of hell " take counsel against the Lord and his Anointed. Another seat of supreme influence is being set up as a substitute for that occupied by the Anointed One, and " spies " are abroad seeking to create doubt and distrust in the hearts of the faithful. As we read the account of Absalom's ingratitude, daring, and baseness, and feel for his deeds the utmost detestation, so holy beings who look on the endeavour to destroy the authority of Christ over men cannot but regard the deed as the basest, most daring, and at the same time most fatal to the perpetrators, ever attempted. The wicked may seem to triumph, but their end is destruction.

Vers. 13—30.—The facts are: 1. David, being informed of the rising in favour of Absalom, calls upon his friends to flee from Jerusalem, in order to avoid its being smitten by a sudden attack. 2. His servants being willing to go with him, he leads out his entire household, with the exception of a few to take care of the house. 3. In his departure he is accompanied by his body-guard, and the six hundred men which followed him from Gath. 4. Observing Ittai in the company, he suggests that, being a stranger and exile, he should not risk his fortunes with his own; but, on receiving an assurance that it was his deliberate desire so to do, he permits him to pass on. 5. The people of the district weep with a loud noise as he crosses the brook Kidron, and passes on toward the wilderness. 6. The ark of the covenant being brought out into the procession, when the people have passed the brook, David urges on Zadok that the ark be conveyed back to the city, expressing his humble hope that it might please God to allow him to see it once more, and, in any case, he submits to the appointments of Providence. 7. David requests Zadok and others with the ark to return to the city, and to inform him in the wilderness should anything of great importance arise. 8. The king expresses his grief by passing up the Mount of Olives, with covered head and weeping, accompanied by a covered and weeping multitude.

Submission in the day of adversity. The order of the narrative of David's departure from Jerusalem is rather involved, as may be seen by comparing vers. 17, 19, 23, 30; but the actual facts are clear enough. As soon as he became aware of the extent of the rebellion, he resolved to leave the city, and we have a record of the fact and the incidents accompanying it. The first and most obvious impression produced on the mind of the reader is the prompt and quiet submission of the king to the force of circumstances, not because he was of cowardly spirit, but because he saw in what was happening the providence of God. If we analyze the conduct and words of David in their relation to the great fall and Nathan's prophecy (ch. xii. 9—13), we shall see the leading features characterizing his submission, and in so doing we shall get a view of the main characteristics of all true Christian submission in the day of adversity.

I. A recognition of personal desert. The prompt action, the surrender of regal state, the broken spirit, the barefooted departure from the seat of authority, and the tender references to God doing with him as seemed him good (ver. 26), all point to more than a forced submission to mere military necessity. There may have been a deep inexpressible anguish on account of filial ingratitude, and the father's heart could not but weep in silence over an erring lost child; but the remembrance of his own great sin, and the words of the prophet of God, furnished the chief theme of reflection; for the son's ingratitude base as it was, had become the rod to chastise for the errors of the past. A forgiven man does not the less think of the sin as a disgrace and worthy of being branded as evil. Adversities come to us all—happily, few know the sorrow of such filial ingratitude—and the enlightened mind sees in them more than physical sequence. The doctrine that every sorrow that falls is for a specific sin need not be held. Yet all trouble is connected with the fact that sin is in the world, and a consciousness of personal shortcomings makes us feel, when adversity in home, estate, or health falls, that we deserve every pain that enters the heart. There is no assertion of right to be free from the trouble; rather the true heart says, "It is of the Lord's mercies that we are not consumed" (Lam. iii. 22).

II. ACQUIESCENCE IN GOD'S RIGHTEOUSNESS. To a human observer it might seem that it was a very unrighteous thing for the Supreme Ruler to allow so wise and good a king to be set aside and humiliated by a man so base and vain as Absalom, and many a man in his anguish might question the equity which allowed such sorrow to fall upon him when he had recovered from his special sins. David's spirit was the reverse of this. Not a word of complaint, not a murmur or a fret in trouble. During his long exile, when death encompassed him about, and he had washed his hands in innocency, and all the blame lay with Saul and Doeg the Edomite, he trusted in the justice of God; and this confidence, won in the days of comparative innocence, failed him not now, when, after his recovery from a fall, the storm burst upon him with more terrible violence. He knew and rested in the precious truth that the Lord reigned in righteousness and brought correction to his servants for their good. Yes; this is the faith of the faithful. Never do they, however terrible the disaster in this life, distrust the righteousness of God. "Though he slay me, yet will I trust him," was true for Job and all of kindred spirit. Men who know not the new life cannot understand this. It is the alphabet of religious experience to all who are really born again and accepted in Christ. None of these things move them.

III. ACCOMMODATION TO NEW CIRCUMSTANCES. David does not yield to fretfulness and irresolution. He vacates his home, provides for his house, goes out to a place of safety, and, by his discreet arrangement with Zadok and Abiathar, keeps up means of connection with the city (vers. 27, 28). Utter prostration under calamity does not come where there is the counteractive element of recognition of personal unworthiness and of the righteousness of God. Whether this trouble would pass he knew not, but as a wise man he adapted himself to the storm. As Jacob to his exile (Gen. xxviii. 10—22), as Moses to his deprivation (Deut. iii. 25—27; cf. xxxiv. 1—6), so David makes the best of his position. Providential chastisements are not designed to paralyze action; their benefit is secured when, in a spirit of resignation and trust, we use our powers to bear them and to mitigate their incidence (Heb. xii. 5—12). Adversity becomes truly educational when we are stirred up to adjust our life to its conditions.

IV. CONSIDERATION FOR OTHERS, THAT THEY BE NOT UNNECESSARILY DRAWN INTO OUR SORROWS. David's removal into the open country was partly from policy and partly from feelings of kindness. He probably had suspicions, seeing that his trusty counsellor had been drawn over to Absalom (ver. 12; cf. Ps. xli. 9; lv. 10—14), that Absalom had many friends in the city, and should he in concert with them come suddenly upon him and his friends, multitudes would fall victims to his malice. It was the same generous feeling that prompted him to suggest that Ittai, not being a Hebrew, should not embroil himself in this sad conflict, and so run a risk in case another king should reign. We see the same David as in earlier years, ever mindful of others, and magnanimous to the extreme. The dreadful sin had not destroyed his noble qualities, but had given a sadly tender form to their expression. There are beautiful instances in Christian life of this kindly consideration for others. Fathers and mothers strive to shield their children from the woes which they may connect with their own want of wisdom or goodness. The great Saviour himself, in his dire trouble, sought to shield his faithful followers (John xiv. 1, 27; xvii. 9—12; xviii. 8).

V. GRATEFUL ACCEPTANCE OF SYMPATHY AND AID. The voluntary sympathy and aid of the faithful body-guard, and the six hundred who had shared his fortunes prior and subsequent to his departure from Gath, was as cool water to a thirsty soul; and the free services of Ittai and Zadok were greatly valued. In the adversities which Providence permits to come for purposes of discipline there is the merciful admixture of some provision to meet the pressing need of the hour—some human channel for Divine sympathy and compassion to enter the heart. Submission to the inscrutable will always includes a grateful recognition of this relief. The love and presence of Ruth was as balm to the desolate heart of Naomi as she mourned her forlorn condition, imparted a sweet gentleness to her, and enabled her to submit to the blow that had shattered her early joys. David and she had herein a common experience.

VI. A THOUGHTFUL SELF-SACRIFICING CARE FOR THE INTERESTS OF RELIGION. It was very beautiful conduct on the part of Zadok and Abiathar to bring out the ark of the covenant (ver. 24), to form a prominent object in the sad procession out of the city; it revealed a tender consideration for the man who in his prosperity had associated his purest joys and most glorious triumphs with that precious symbol of the Divine presence. The ark could not but remind David of the mercy that endureth for ever, and its presence with him would be regarded as a pledge of blessing in his wandering. But he desired the priests to take back the treasure, and he, meekly bowing to the chastisement, would go out and suffer the loss of the outward privileges of the sanctuary. The reason of this no doubt was that, as he had been the means of procuring a permanent resting-place for the ark (ch. vi. 17—19), and constituting Jerusalem the centre of religious influence for the nation, he would not now undo that work and serve his own personal advantage at the cost of the people. No; the religious institutions should remain intact, the blessings of public worship and spiritual comfort should abide for Jerusalem, though he a poor exile pine in solitude and peril for the "beauty of the Lord" (Ps. xlii. 1—4; xliii. 1, 2). How beautiful this tender care for the interests of religion appears in true submission to adverse providences is known to all acquainted with Christian biography. Not a deed, not a word, not a thought is allowed that might be prejudicial to the kingdom of God. Storms may come, hopes may be blasted, if only the Name that is above every name be still honoured.

VII. A DELIBERATE COMMITTAL OF PRESENT AND FUTURE INTERESTS INTO THE HANDS OF GOD. "If I shall find favour in the eyes of the Lord, he will bring me again, and show me both it, and his habitation. But if he thus say, I have no delight in thee; behold, here I am, let him do to me as seemeth good unto him" (vers. 25, 26). O blessed trust! O sweet resignation! O modest, yet unshaken hope! Truly the discipline was already bearing precious fruit. The spiritual barrenness of those hot days of prosperity (ch. xi.) was clean gone. The temporal chastisement was in process, but the wandering child was a wanderer no more. Enviable beyond expression is this surrender of all interests to the wise and gracious hands of the covenant-keeping God. Here comes out the essence of the true submission in the season of adversity. "He will," if he "delight" in me! "Let him do as seemeth him good!" No self-will, no boast of claim, no thought of shame; God is over all and can do all; all is in his care, and what he does shall be deemed the best and kindest and most just. Who does not see the purifying power of the grace of God? Holy David once fallen!

APPENDIX. The sorrowing king, passing over the ridge of the Mount of Olives, on bare feet and weeping, bearing on his heart a terrible woe, and full of pity for the people rejecting his authority, and at the same time entirely submissive to the sovereign will that so ordains, reminds us of the other King, greater, wiser, more holy, and bearing on his heart the woes of many sins not his own, pacing the slopes of that same mount, weeping bitter tears, lamenting for the rebellious people, bearing all for others' good, and submitting with unparalleled gentleness and trust to the sovereign will that ordained that so he must suffer.

Fidelity in misfortune. It is believed by many that more remarkable virtues are developed in seasons of adversity than in those of prosperity. Their precise form will depend on the individuals concerned and the stress of the time. The conduct of the Gittites, and Ittai, and Zadok, and Abiathar is in pleasing contrast with that of Ahithophel and his co-conspirators. In these men we may trace the characteristics of fidelity in misfortune.

I. IT IS ROOTED IN INTELLIGENT SYMPATHY. The six hundred had probably been with David and shared in his trials prior to his departure from Gath (1 Sam. xxvii. 2). They knew him better than any others; they had formed a sympathy for him based on true knowledge, and they stood the test of the evil time. Of Ittai we do not know so much, but the words of the man prove that he appreciated the real character of David in spite of the slanders which such men as Ahithophel may have insinuated. The priestly functions of Zadok and Abiathar account for their interest in so devout a man as David. Their fidelity was not based on personal beauty, vague promises, and outward splendour (vers. 1—6), but on intelligence and the feeling which accompanies it in a pure heart. So Ruth was true to Naomi (Ruth i. 16, 17). Any promise of attachment not resting on this foundation is worth nothing.

II. IT IS NOURISHED BY REFLECTION ON THE PAST. There were probably hours when the voice of temptation would come to allure them from a course so perilous in appearance, to a course promising reputation, wealth, and honour; for these men were of like passions with us all, and had no love for poverty and exile in themselves. But they knew David's history, and when temptation to prefer the winning side came they would nourish their vow by thinking of what he had been, how God had befriended him before, and how he had risen from the fall which once was his shame. It is something to be attached to a man with a good history. When we have pledged ourselves to a just though suffering cause, we may ward off many a temptation by allowing the reflective powers to work on the antecedents of the cause to which we are pledged. Thus the early Christians, by reflecting on Christ, his words and work, and all he had been to them, could endorse the dying words of the aged Polycarp.

III. IT IS RESPONSIVE TO FRANKNESS AND MAGNANIMITY. The frank and magnanimous way in which David offered to release them from all risks only drew out into stronger and more pronounced form the attachment already cherished (vers. 19—21). Zadok could not but feel a profounder regard for the king after hearing his words concerning the ark (ver. 25). There is something so noble in this frankness and magnanimity in misfortune that a faithful heart recruits its strength by the very sight and sound of the nobleness. Holy sentiments grow in exchange. There is no sure bond between the wicked. Sin is morally a weakness. Holiness is a strength.

IV. IT IS CAPABLE OF RISKS. Whatever might befall the king in his trouble, these faithful ones were prepared to share in it. True affection is not blind, as some would say; it sees, but it fears not. The faithful mind is intent on being on the side of right and weakness, not on securing anything for self. There are risks in adherence to a righteous cause in the day of adversity. Christ points this out to his followers, and it is the sign of true as distinguished from professional fidelity that it can bear and is determined to bear whatever may come. The real clue to the determination is the conviction that right is supreme in its claims, and that present suffering is only an incident of a well-directed human existence (Matt. x. 16—18, 38; xx. 22; Phil. iii. 7—9).

Vers. 31—37.—*Prayer for Divine intervention.* The facts are: 1. David, hearing that Ahithophel was among the conspirators, prays that God would turn his counsel into foolishness. 2. On reaching the top of the Mount of Olives, the aged Hushai expresses his desire to go with David into exile, but David declines his offer on account of his infirmities. 3. On the other hand, David suggests that he can render him good service by returning to the city and living as a servant of Absalom, and he advises him to act in concert with Zadok and Abiathar. 4. Acting on this suggestion, Hushai returns to the city, and, some time after, Absalom also enters. There passed a pang through the heart of David as he heard of the treachery of his trusty counsellor Ahithophel, bitter because he had relied so much on this wise man's honesty and sagacity, and more bitter still as he remembered the cruel conspiracy which he once entered into with Joab against the life of Uriah. Yet the forgiven and renewed king, in the fulness of his anguish, was true to his revived religious instincts in at once raising his heart to God with the prayer that he would bring his own wisdom to bear so as to defeat the wisdom of this man. We see here—

I. THAT THERE IS IN THIS WORLD A CONFLICT BETWEEN HUMAN AND DIVINE WISDOM. David was well acquainted with two great facts: (1) that the wisdom of God had designed him to be king over Israel to the end of his days (ch. vii. 11—16, 28, 29); (2) that the wisest man in the land was devising means to frustrate this purpose, not perhaps consciously, yet practically. This is an epitome of the history of mankind. God has a purpose to carry out, and employs good men as his instruments,—all is arranged according to his infinite wisdom; but, on the other hand, there are men who bring their powers to bear so as to frustrate this purpose. They may not know that they are setting their wisdom against the wisdom of God, but the facts are to that effect. Adam and Eve went against wisdom in the exercise of their wisdom. Pharaoh contrived to prevent what wisdom had ordained. The wisdom of scribes and Pharisees was arrayed against him who was the "Wisdom of God." In the antagonism of men to the gospel the apostle saw a case of the "wisdom of the world" striving against the wisdom which was so far above theirs that their wisdom was more properly folly (1 Cor. i. 18—25). Men who live in sin, who try to dispense with Christ, really set their wisdom against the great and blessed order which is founded on eternal wisdom. The attitude of the world to the Church may be expressed in the terms just stated. Oh that men *were* wise!

II. THAT A GOOD MAN BELIEVES IN GOD'S POWER TO COUNTERACT THE WISDOM OF MEN. This was the intellectual basis of David's prayer for intervention against the devices of Ahithophel. Faith in God's appointment of prayer is associated with a perception of the fact that God can and does so control human action as to restrain it within definite lines, and to secure in spite of it certain issues that are for the good of the world. A theism that renders God inactive, or bound in the unbreakable chains of a physical necessity, had better be frank and renounce the sacred name, and say once for all, "Force is in eternal motion along lines eternally fixed." God is a Spirit, and as such has free access to the spirits of men. His unseen and unconscious contact may paralyze or divert thought, and render possible ideas which, when carried out, will prove to be subversive of the very ends which the wicked thinker once had set his heart upon. We don't know how much we owe to this silent action of God on evil men. He also, as a free Spirit, is in contact with the ultimate elements of things, and can act on them without dislocation of the order of nature, more perfectly than we can in the effort of our will. Many Christian people do not, it is feared, half believe in this great truth, and do not sufficiently see its ample bearing on the great stress of life. God not only looks into men and sees them through and through; he is an Actor, and brings his wisdom to put to nought the wisdom of the wise.

III. THAT A GOOD MAN IN EXTREMITY NATURALLY PUTS THIS BELIEF INTO PRACTICE. David felt that he could not cope with the combination against him. His heart fainted at the thought of the sagacity of the counsellor uniting with the daring and dash of the ambitious usurper. His prayer was true to nature. We do not in ordinary circumstances allow our faith to have sufficient influence over our lives. Trouble brings us straight to God. Our vast resources are drawn upon when heart and flesh begin to fail. All prayer is a cry for God's help, or it is nothing; but the earnestness and intensity of the cry are proportioned to the perception of peril.

IV. THAT PRAYER FOR HELP, IN THE CASE OF A GOOD MAN, IS ATTENDED WITH A DISCREET USE OF MEANS TO SECURE THE END IN VIEW. The practical character of David's religion is seen in this—that, as soon as he had committed his desperate case to God, he took steps, through Hushai, to counteract the wisdom of Ahithophel. He knew that God worked on the minds of men partly by the agency of other men, to whom he secretly imparts wisdom and discretion. Not only would secret unconscious influences operate within Ahithophel to cause him to blunder in advice, but thoughts would be directed in the minds of Hushai and Zadok so that they would act at the right season and in the right way. This combination of trust in God and action among men is characteristic of all true religious life. "The effectual fervent prayer of the righteous man availeth much," and his labour also "is not in vain in the Lord."

GENERAL LESSONS. 1. In all our dealings with men, and efforts to get them to act, we should remember that we can get at them through God. 2. The Church, in its conflict with the world, should rest in the consolation that the wisdom of God can never fail. 3. Much of our success in Christian work depends on our assigning men to duties suited to their character, age, and position. 4. Good men who are compelled by force of circumstances to live among men of evil purpose may use their knowledge of the world and its ways so as to promote the best interests of the kingdom of God.

HOMILIES BY VARIOUS AUTHORS.

Vers. 1—12.—(JERUSALEM, HEBRON.) *The rebellion of Absalom.* About twelve years had elapsed since David's fall into sin. One of its effects was the rebellion of Absalom. The history of this event—most critical for the theocratic monarchy, and "revealing the thoughts of many hearts "—sheds a clear light upon the condition of Israel. "We seem to know all the people; the natural manners and vivid outbursts of feeling make the scene stand out with a kind of homely poetry." In it we discern the presence and influence of: 1. *Divine chastisement*, announced by the prophet (ch. xii. 10), "The sword shall never depart from thine house," etc. Forgiveness of sin does not annul its natural consequences. Such consequences are sure, however they may appear to be delayed; and, though inflicted by the hand of man, they do not less really proceed from the hand of God. Already David had experienced the effects of his transgression in his family; he must now experience them, on a larger scale, in his kingdom. 2. *Defective administration* of judgment by the king (ver. 3); due, not so much to advancing age (over sixty), as to timidity, irresolution, and want of energy, consequent on what had taken place; and "a tendency to shrink into private life, with a preference for such duties as preparing materials for the future temple rather than those of active government;" perhaps also to serious illness, brought on by trouble of heart, and partially incapacitating him from performing the increasing duties of his office (Ps. xxxviii., xxxix., xli., lv.). 3. *Prevalent dissatisfaction* among the people. His sin "broke the powerful spell which had hitherto bound the whole nation to the name of David" (Ewald). "The imperfections and defects of his internal administration of the kingdom, when the time of his brilliant victories was past, became more and more perceptible to the people, and furnished occasion for dissatisfaction with his government" (Keil). "His pious actions, his attention to the public ordinances of worship, perhaps even his psalms, had for the time lost their credit and their sacredness. Not every one was capable of estimating aright the repentance of the fallen man, and his humiliation before the Almighty. It was almost forgotten that he was king by the grace of God" (Krummacher). "The infirm condition of the king, his eminent godliness and opposition to popular feelings, and the distance of age that now separated him from the sympathies of the younger portion of the people" (Blaikie); some discontent in his own tribe of Judah (ver. 10); "the still lingering hopes of the house of Saul and of the tribe of Benjamin (ch. xvi. 3, 8); and the deep-rooted feeling of Ephraim and the northern tribes (ch. xix. 41) against Judah" (Stanley);—all combined to make the people ripe for insurrection. 4. *Private animosity* on the part of its leaders: Absalom, on account of his long banishment in Geshur and exclusion from court; Ahithophel, the grandfather of Bathsheba (ver. 12; ch. xi. 3), on account of the dishonour done to his house; Amasa, son of Abigal, David's half-sister (ch. xvii. 25), possibly on account of some neglect or discourtesy shown toward him. "These four years (ver. 7) were for David a time of increasing care and anxiety, for that which was planned cannot have remained altogether concealed from him; but he had neither the courage nor the strength to smother the evil undertaking in the germ" (Delitzsch, in Ps. xli.). The course of Absalom (now twenty-seven years of age) was marked by—

I. AMBITION CRIMINALLY INDULGED. Sinful perversion of the natural desire of pre-eminence; unhallowed love of power and glory (as in the case of Adonijah, his brother, 1 Kings i. 5), the bait by which Satan seeks to allure men to a false worship (Matt. iv. 9; 1 Sam. xv. 1—9).

> "He showed him in a jewell'd wreath-
> All crowns the earth bestows;
> But not the rankling thorns beneath,
> That pierce the wearer's brows."

Absalom's ambition was peculiarly culpable; because of his: 1. Self-conceit; his selfish, proud, and false estimate of his own worth. He was "the representative of vain-glory and self-conceit" (Wordsworth). "Those are commonly most ambitious of preferment that are least fit for it" (Matthew Henry). 2. Covetousness; the object of his desire belonging to another, and unattainable save by injustice. It is not likely that he wished simply to share the sovereignty of Israel. 3. Disaffection and unnatural envy toward his father. 4. Disloyalty toward the king. 5. Rebellion against God, the supreme King of Israel, by whose ordinance David had been appointed. He had, apparently, "no spark of religious principle in his breast." 6. Self-will; indisposition to submit to the will of Jehovah, to defer to the nomination of the king, or to wait for his decease. He resolved to anticipate all, and have his own way. "He that destroys self-will, destroys hell." 7. Suspicion and jealousy of his brother. " It is our impression that David already knew that Solomon was, by the Lord's appointment, to be his successor to the throne. In the promise made to David through Nathan, it was clearly indicated that a son not yet born was to sit upon his throne, and when Solomon was born he could not but understand that this applied to him. If he had any doubt of this, it must have been removed by his knowledge that the ' Lord loved him,' and had, through Nathan, bestowed upon him the new name of Jedidiah (ch. xii. 24, 25). It is even probable that he had, long before the present time, if not from the first, received those more distinct intimations of the Lord's will in this matter, which he mentions in 1 Chron. xxviii. 5—7. . . . As the intimations we have traced were long before afforded, it is likely that the pledge (1 Kings i. 17) which was founded on them had not been so long delayed" (Kitto, ' Daily Bible Illust.'). " Absalom was a bold, valiant, revengeful, haughty, enterprising, magnificent, eloquent, and popular prince ; he was also rich, ambitious, and vain of his personal accomplishments ; and, after the death of Amnon and his reconciliation with his father, he saw no hindrance in his way to the throne. He despised Solomon because of the meanness of his birth and his tender years. He was himself of the blood-royal, not only by his father, but also by his mother; and doubtless in his own apprehension of sufficient age, authority, and wisdom to sustain the weight of government. He seemed to stand nearest to the throne ; but his sin was that he sought it during his father's lifetime, and endeavoured to dethrone him in order to sit in his stead" (Calmet).

> " O sacred hunger of ambitious minds,
>   And impotent desire of men to reign !
> Whom neither dread of God, that devils binds,
>   Nor laws of men, that commonweals contain,
>   Nor bands of nature, that wild beasts restrain,
> Can keep from outrage and from doing wrong,
>   Where they may hope a kingdom to obtain ı
> No faith so firm, no trust can be so strong,
> No love so lasting then, that may endure long."
>
>   (' The Faërie Queene,' canto xii.)

II. POPULARITY FRAUDULENTLY ACQUIRED. " Absalom stole the hearts of the men of Israel " (ver. 6); by methods which many a demagogue has since adopted. " David won their hearts by noble deeds of generosity, as well as by deeds of prowess; " but Absalom stole them by : 1. *Subtlety and guile.* 2. *Ostentation ;* affecting royal state. " Absalom prepared him chariots," etc. (ver. 1; ch. xiii. 23, 27; 1 Sam. viii. 4—22). 3. *Assiduity,* in attending to public affairs. " Absalom rose up early," etc. (ver. 2). "Those who least understand the duties and could least endure the burdens of authority are commonly most desirous of it ; but when ambition prompts, the most self-indulgent assume the appearance of diligence, and the most haughty that of affability and condescension ; and while men aspire to the pinnacle of earthly grandeur, they, for the time, pay the most abject court to the meanest of the mob! " (Scott). 4. *Courtesy* and pretended sympathy. " Absalom called unto him, and said, Of what city art thou ? " etc. ; " He put forth his hand, and took him, and kissed-him " (ver. 6).

> " And then I stole all courtesy from heaven,
> And dressed myself in such humility,
> That I did pluck allegiance from men's hearts,
> Loud shouts and salutations from their mouths,
> Even in the presence of the crownèd king."
>
>   (' King Henry IV.,' Part I. act iii. sc. 2.)

5. *Flattery.* " Absalom said unto him, See, thy matters are good and right " (ver. 3). 6. *Disparagement* of the existing administration, and insinuation of the king's incapability and neglect. " But there is no man deputed of the king to hear thee." 7. Fair and lavish *promises,* and holding out the prospect of a golden age under his reign. " And Absalom said, Oh that I were made judge in the land ! " etc. (ver. 4). It is not to be wondered at that, by such arts as these, aided by his ready speech and attractive person and manners, he turned the hearts of the people, already prepared for change, from their rightful monarch. " After thus flattering the people, and ingratiating him-

self into their favour during four years, he decides upon the execution of his cunningly devised project" (Ewald). "The success of this godless rebel shows a lack of true theocratic feeling in the mass of the people, who, in abandoning the king's government, were guilty of opposition to the government of God" (Erdmann).

III. CONSPIRACY CRAFTILY CARRIED OUT (vers. 7—12); apparent in : 1. The selection of the place, Hebron (his birthplace), notable on many accounts, especially as the chief city of Judah, where sympathy could be calculated upon. "There may have been many persons there who had been displeased by the removal of the court to Jerusalem" (Keil). "Accustomed from the earliest times to independence and pre-eminence, Judah stood proudly apart under David even after Saul's death, and now probably offered some opposition to the growing unity of the kingdom" (Ewald). 2. The profession of a religious purpose—the fulfilment of a vow (vers. 7, 8; 1 Sam. i. 11). "With a subtle refinement of hypocrisy, he pretended that his thank-offering was for his return to Jerusalem" (Plumptre). "No villainy can be termed complete which is not disguised under the mask of religion, especially at those times when the profession of godliness is treated with general respect." 3. The obtaining of the king's sanction : "Go in peace" (ver. 9); thereby disarming suspicion and winning confidence. 4. The despatch of emissaries through all the tribes, to prepare for the simultaneous proclamation, "Absalom reigneth in Hebron!" (ver. 10). 5. The securing of the presence of numerous persons from Jerusalem; depriving the king of their aid, and making them unwittingly adherents of Absalom (ver. 11). 6. The gaining of the open support of Ahithophel, whose secret counsel had doubtless been long before afforded (vers. 12, 31). He was "the sinews of Absalom's cause" (Blunt). "While the sacrifices were proceeding, Absalom sent for him from Giloh, and the presence of this influential personage appears to have caused the final outbreak of a conspiracy which had been carefully prepared, and which immediately spread with amazing rapidity, and pouring like a wild mountain torrent from the ancient capital of Judah, soon threatened to flood the whole country" (Ewald).

IV. INSURRECTION SUCCESSFULLY INCITED, only to be disastrously defeated. "And the conspiracy was strong," etc. Its success was: 1. Great, swift, surprising. A few hours later, Jerusalem was in the hands of Absalom. 2. Temporary. The prosperity of the wicked is but for a moment. 3. Followed by signal retribution, whilst itself employed as an instrument thereof, by Divine providence, whose ways, though mysterious, are always just and right. The death of Absalom (ch. xviii. 14) was "the end of a bitter family history, whose every sorrow was linked to the father's blame." The people who shared his crime shared his punishment. The fatal spark of tribal enmity kindled under his influence, though quenched for the moment, soon burst forth again, and ultimately destroyed the unity, independence, and strength of the nation.—D.

Vers. 13—18.—*David's flight from Jerusalem.* "Arise! and let us flee" (ver. 14). *References* : 1. Leaving the palace, on receiving news from Hebron (after the harvest and vintage, ch. xvi. 1 ; xvii. 28 ; Ps. iv. 7). 2. At "the Far House" (Beth-hammerhak), on the outskirts of the city (ver. 17) ; and at "the olive tree in (on the road to) the wilderness of Judah" (LXX.) ; the procession formed ; Ittai the Gittite. 3. Passing over the Kidron ; the signal of flight ; loud and general wailing (ver. 23). 4. Commencement of the ascent of Mount Olivet ; Zadok and Abiathar (vers. 24—29). 5. Ascending the mountain amidst loud wailing (ver. 30) ; tidings concerning Ahithophel (ver. 31). 6. At the top (about noonday), "where God was worshipped" (ver. 32) ; Hushai the Archite (vers. 32—37). 7. Descending, on the other side ; Ziba, with refreshments (ch. xvi. 1—4). 8. At Bahurim ; Shimei (ch. xvi. 5—13). 9. Coming "weary" (or, to "Ayephim") (ch. xvi. 14) ; to the fords (Authorized Version, "plains") of the wilderness, or passages of the wilderness leading to the Jordan ; and resting there for the night. 10. Crossing the river (after midnight), on the arrival of Ahimaaz and Jonathan with news from Jerusalem (ch. xvii. 21, 22) ; and marching onward "by the morning light" toward Mahanaim (ch. xvii. 24, 27—29). "There is no single day in the Jewish history of which so elaborate an account remains as of this memorable flight" (Stanley). It was probably the morning after Absalom's revolt when news came from Hebron. Of all the "evil tidings" that David ever received (ch.

xiii. 21, 30), none were more unexpected or alarming. He must determine at once whether to face the gathering storm or flee before it. With something of his former decision he chose the latter course; his servants (state officers, attendants, soldiers) declared themselves ready to do his bidding; and " he went forth and all his household" (wives, sons, daughters), " all the people" ("servants," LXX.) " after him," etc. At first, no doubt, struck with consternation, he yet speedily regained his composure (Ps. cxii. 12); and came to his decision not from abject fear, or personal cowardice (ch. xviii. 2), but (as others should do in similar critical and perilous positions) from motives of—

I. PIETY; or humble submission to the chastisement of God. Lest he "bring evil upon us;" or "drive over us the evil" or calamity which now threatens, and in which David sees the fulfilment of predicted judgment (ch. xii. 10, 11). 1. He discerns therein the operation of Divine justice on account of his sin (ch. xvi. 11). Trouble and danger bring sin to remembrance; and those who remember their sin are quick to perceive the chastening hand of God where others see only the wrathful hand of man. In the view of faith, wicked men are instruments employed by the supreme and righteous Judge. Resentment toward them is thereby moderated, the sense of sin deepened, and suffering borne in a different manner. "Wherefore doth a living man complain?" etc. (Lam. iii. 39; Micah vii. 9). 2. He is persuaded of the folly of resistance to the Divine power. Such resistance can be of no avail against the Almighty; it ought not to be attempted; and it can only result in defeat and ruin (as in the case of Saul). If he should remain and defend the city, David had no inward assurance, as in former conflicts, that God would be with him. He rather felt that in resisting Absalom at this moment he would be resisting God. He did not even deem it needful to consult the oracle (ver. 24). 3. He acquiesces without murmuring in the Divine will (ver. 26), "accepts the punishment of his iniquity" (Lev. xxvi. 41), and patiently endures the wrath of man, knowing that it is subject to Divine control. When a hurricane sweeps over the land, the things that cannot bend are broken; but those that bow beneath it are preserved, and rise up again when it has passed by. "Humble yourselves," etc. (Jas. iv. 10). 4. He hopes for deliverance in the Divine mercy (ver. 25; ch. xvi. 12). "But as for me, I trust in thee" (Ps. lv. 23). Herein lay the secret of David's passivity, tranquillity, and forbearance during his flight.

II. POLICY; or prudent counsel against the assaults of the wicked. Piety without policy is too simple to be safe. 1. He does not presume upon the protection of God, without, on his part, exercising proper caution and energy. A good man's submission to Divine chastisement does not require that he should always remain in the way of danger or voluntarily invite human hostility and cruelty. "When they persecute you in this city, flee ye into another" (Matt. x. 23). 2. He does not undertake an enterprise rashly, or without adequate means of success. David probably deemed the number of his "servants" present with him in Jerusalem insufficient for the defence of the city. If, indeed, he had the assurance of Divine help, he might have thought otherwise (ch. v. 19). "His departure was an admirable means of testing the real strength of both parties" (Ewald). 3. He does not place an undue confidence in man. "David was perhaps afraid that Jerusalem might fall into Absalom's power through treachery" (Keil). "Beware of men" (Matt. x. 17; John ii. 24; Ps. cxviii. 8, 9). 4. He makes use of the means which are most likely to ensure safety and success. "A prudent man foreseeth the evil, and hideth himself" (Prov. xxii. 3). If there must be conflict, delay appeared to him desirable; it would afford time for his faithful adherents to assemble; and, in the open field, the tried valour and discipline of his veterans would give them an advantage. Pious men are not unfrequently deficient in prudence (Luke xvi. 8); since, however, they are sometimes beset by ravening wolves, it is necessary that they should be "wise as serpents" (Matt. x. 16), taking care nevertheless to avoid guile, and to be "harmless as doves." "When he was reviled," etc. (1 Pet. ii. 23).

III. PITY; or generous concern for the preservation of the imperilled. Foreseeing the misery and bloodshed likely to ensue from awaiting the attack of Absalom, he sought by flight not merely to save his own life, but chiefly: 1. To secure the safety of his helpless household, and aid the escape of his faithful followers (vers. 19, 20). 2. To spare the city the horrors of a siege. "He preferred the safety of the people to his own; and was thus also a figure of him who said, in the garden of Gethsemane, 'If ye seek me, let these go their way'" (Wordsworth). 3. To save the life of his rebellious son (ch. xviii. 12); for which he would have given his own (ch. xviii. 33). 4. To prevent the miseries of civil war (ch. ii. 26; iii. 1), and promote the welfare of the divided and misguided people. If collision could be now avoided, it might perchance be altogether averted (ver. 25), or at least occur with less injurious consequences. He was willing to sacrifice himself for the good of the "sheep" (ch. v. 2; xxiv. 17). "Let thy blessing be upon thy people" (Ps. iii. 8). His piety was honoured, his policy justified, his pity succeeded by renewed attachment (ch. xix. 14), and, in all, the overruling providence of God was displayed. He left Jerusalem in humiliation and grief; he returned (three months afterwards) in triumph (ch. xix. 39, 40). Having practically resigned his sceptre to God, from whom he received it, God gave it back into his hands. "As David falls away from Jehovah to be more firmly bound to him, so Israel turns away from David to be (as the close of the history shows) more devoutly attached to him. The prelude to this first clearing-up of the relations between king and people is given in the conduct of the faithful band who stand firmly by David in the general defection" (Baumgarten).—D.

Vers. 19—22.—(BETH-HAMMERHAK.) *The devotedness of Ittai.* "As Jehovah liveth," etc. (ver. 21). In his flight from Jerusalem: 1. *David experienced much alleviation of his trouble;* as in his flight from the court of Saul (nearly forty years before). He was not left alone (1 Sam. xxii. 1, 2). His "servants" gathered round him, and professed their readiness to follow him (ver. 15). Halting with his household at "the Far House," he found himself accompanied by his body-guard, the Cretans and Philistines (under Benaiah, ch. viii. 18); his six hundred veterans (under Abishai, ch. xxiii. 17—39) who had been with him in his early wanderings and followed him from Gath onward (Gittites, equivalent to "Gibborim," 1 Sam. xxiii. 13; xxvii. 2; xxx. 9; ch. ii. 3; v. 6); and a part at least of the regular soldiery—the host (under Joab, ch. viii. 16; xviii. 1, 2). His attention was arrested by the presence of Ittai the Gittite (who, from some unknown cause, had recently come from Gath) with his brethren (kinsfolk) and children. "The Lord has the hearts of all men in his hands, and if he be our friend, we shall not want friends" (Guild). "Our foremost friends are sometimes raised up among persons from whom we had the least expectations" (Scott). 2. *He exhibited noble generosity in his conduct.* "Wherefore goest thou with us?" etc. (vers. 19—21). "This unexpected meeting with Ittai appeared to the royal fugitive almost like a friendly greeting of his God, and dropped the first soothing balsam-drops into the painful wounds of his deeply lacerated heart" (Krummacher). But David, now himself a wanderer, had no desire to make the condition of this "stranger and exile" more homeless and distressing by dragging him into his own misfortunes; released him from whatever obligations of service he may have incurred; advised him to offer his services to the new king; and expressed the wish, "Mercy and truth [from God] be with thee" (ch. ii. 6).

> "I am a poor fallen man, unworthy now
> To be thy lord and master; seek the king . . .
> Neglect him not; make use now, and provide
> For thine own future safety."
>
> ('King Henry VIII.')

3. *He exerted a powerful attraction on his followers;* as aforetime. His language was really a pathetic appeal; not unlike that of Jesus, "Will ye also go away?" etc. (John vi. 66—69). "Ittai declared his resolution (with a fervour which almost inevitably recalls a like profession made almost on the same spot to the great Descendant of David, Matt. xxvi. 35, centuries afterwards) to follow him in life and death" (Stanley). It was "a beautiful instance of loyal constancy and faithful devotion in a Philistine soldier at a time of apostasy and defection. His truth and fidelity are brought out in a stronger and clearer light by the contrast with the treachery of Absalom, Ahithophel, and eventually of Joab and Abiathar" (Wordsworth). He may be regarded, in his *devotion* to David, as a pattern of devotion to Christ. It was—

I. SEVERELY TESTED. Like him, the follower of Christ is often tried and proved, by :

1. The prospect of *difficulties, privations, and perils* in his service. These are all known to the Lord, for he has himself endured them ; and he forewarns his disciples of them (Luke ix. 57, 58 ; xiv. 25—33). He would not have them follow him from mere impulse. 2. The promise of *ease, safety, and advantage* in other service ; worldly pleasure, treasure, power, honour, in devotion to the prince and " god of this world." 3. The *example and influence* of many persons ; bound by stronger ties to serve their rightful king ; but forsaking their allegiance to him, joining in revolt against his authority, seeking his life, and heaping reproaches on his head (ch. xvi. 11). "From that time many of his disciples went back," etc. (John vi. 66 ; Mark xiv. 50 ; 2 Tim. iv. 10 ; 2 Pet. iii. 17). 4. The *peculiar circumstances* in which he is placed, the special inducements suggested thereby, and the favourable opportunities afforded for the exercise of his freedom. There are times in which the Lord (however much he values and desires his aid) does not urge him to continue, but seems to do the opposite, and give him liberty, if he be disposed, to depart. So he tests his disciples, sifts the false from the true, and, though it cause the former to fall away, it makes the latter cling to him more closely than ever. The decision between Christ and antichrist has to be made, not only at first, but also often afterwards.

II. WORTHILY DISPLAYED, as it should be by every follower of " the Son of David," in : 1. The *deliberate preference* of his service to any other. "Just as in the great French Revolution, the famous Swiss Guard showed a brave, though mercenary fidelity, so Ittai, having eaten of the king's salt, determines that where his lord the king is, in life or death, he will be." 2. The *disinterested motives* by which he is actuated (Ruth i. 16). Ittai was not a mere mercenary, serving David for advantage (Job i. 9). He was influenced possibly by gratitude for the kind reception he met with on coming from Gath as " a stranger and an exile," by a sense of obligation imposed by friendship and previous engagements, by a conviction of the rectitude of the king's cause ; certainly by admiration and affection for his person. Hence he wished to be *with him*, to share his sufferings and to aid in his defence. He was ready "to lay down his life for his sake." An intelligent, sincere, passionate love to the Person of Christ is essential to his service. "Lovest thou me?" 3. The open and *solemn pledge* of loyalty and fidelity. "As Jehovah liveth," etc. (1 Sam. xxix. 6 ; ch. iv. 9). Ittai was doubtless a convert to the faith of Israel. " Whosoever shall confess me before men," etc. (Matt. x. 32 ; Rom. x. 10). 4. The practical, unconditional, *whole-hearted consecration* of himself and all he possessed to the king's service. "And Ittai the Gittite passed over, and all his men, and all the *little ones* that were with him." " Who then is willing to consecrate himself this day unto the Lord?" (1 Chron. xxix. 5).

III. GRACIOUSLY APPROVED. " And David said to Ittai, Go and pass over " (ver. 22), " with me " (LXX.). If he said no more, his look and manner would give peculiar significance to his words. The Lord testifies his reception and approval of every devoted servant by : 1. Giving him the assurance thereof in his heart. 2. Fulfilling his desire to be with him. "If any man serve me," etc. (John xii. 26). 3. Appointing him to his post of duty, and making his way plain (John xi. 9, 10). 4. Exalting him to a position of responsibility and honour (ch. xviii. 2), in which he aids the king in gaining a great victory, and shares the joy of a great triumph. The latter, like the former life of this Philistine, is wrapped in obscurity. But his devotion to " the Lord's anointed " shines like a star among the heathen, and condemns the lukewarmness, selfishness, and unfaithfulness of many " who profess and call themselves Christians."

> " Lo ! of those
> Who call, ' Christ ! Christ !' there shall be many found,
> In judgment, further off from him by far
> Than such to whom his Name was never known.
> Christians like these the Ethiop shall condemn ;
> When that the two assemblages shall part—
> One rich eternally, the other poor."
>
> (Dante, ' Purg.,' xix.)

D.

Vers. 23—29.—(ACROSS THE KIDRON.) *The ark restored to its place.* " Carry back the ark of God to the city " (ver. 25). Having crossed the Kidron ravine amidst the loud wailing of the people, and halted for a moment in the ascent of Olivet, David was met by Zadok (of the elder branch of the Aaronic family), with the Levites, carrying the ark (ch. vi.), and by Abiathar (a descendant of Eli, of the younger branch). The former had come to him at Hebron (about thirty years before), "a young man mighty of valour" (1 Chron. xii. 28); the latter was a still older friend of David (1 Sam. xxii. 23), occupying the highest official position (Zadok being his vicar only, or *sagan*, 1 Kings ii. 27, 35; 1 Chron. xvi. 39), but not taking the most prominent part in active service, and perhaps entertaining "jealousy of his rival" (Blunt). They doubtless intended to render valuable service to the king by bringing the ark. *Why, then, did he send it back?* Not from want of proper regard for it (ver. 25, latter part). He did not, indeed, put a superstitious confidence in it, like Hophni and Phinehas. He esteemed and reverenced it as an appointed symbol of the Divine presence and "favour," and a valuable means of Divine worship and service (1 Sam. iv. 11), just as highly as when he conducted it in triumph to its resting-place (ch. vi. 16). But "he would not use the ark as a charm; he had too much reverence for it to risk it in his personal peril" (Stanley). He looked upon it as belonging to God and to his people, not to himself; considered, not only that it would be of no advantage to him in present circumstances, but also that he was not justified in removing it from the city and depriving the people of its presence; that rather it was the will of God that he should himself be deprived of it, at least for a season; and thus he honoured God in *adversity* as he had formerly done in prosperity. "David is always great in affliction. His conduct throughout, his goodness, resignation, and patience, are clearly evinced in all these trying scenes" (Kitto). Consider him as an *example* of: 1. *Spiritual insight.* He perceived the true nature and worth of the ark; that the symbol was distinct from the reality of the Divine favour, did not necessarily ensure its possession, was not an essential condition of it; that its value depended upon the relation of men to God (1 Sam. vi. 1—9). Affliction often teaches us how to regard the outward privileges and ordinances of religion. "He was contented at this time to forbear the presence of the ark, having his confidence in God, and not relying altogether upon the external sacrament" (Willet). 2. *Deep humility.* Having acted unworthily of the ark of the "testimony," and disobeyed the commandments of God, he deemed himself unworthy of the honour of its presence. His deprivation of it was a just chastisement for his misuse and abuse of it. "I am not worthy," etc. (Gen. xxxii. 10; Luke v. 8; Matt. viii. 8). 3. *Holy affection* toward the "habitation" of God (Ps. xxvi. 8); toward God himself; and toward his people. Hence, although banished from the ark of God, he desired that the God of the ark should still be honoured by others, and do them good. "Observe his disinterested self-sacrifice for the good of the people. He would not punish his subjects for his son's sins" (Wordsworth). "It argues a good principle to be more concerned for the Church's prosperity than for our own, to prefer Jerusalem before our chief joy, the success of the gospel and the flourishing of the Church above our own wealth, credit, ease, safety, even when they are most at hazard" (Matthew Henry). "Let thy Name be magnified for ever" (ch. vii. 26). 4. *Lofty faith* in the presence of God in all places, his superintendence of all events, his acquaintance with all hearts, his righteousness and goodness, favour, guidance, mercy, and truth (ver. 20). It is "an instance of David's clear faith in the omnipresence of God and of his spiritual elevation from the outward symbols of the sanctuary to the Divine essence that was symbolized by them." "Salvation belongeth unto the Lord," etc. (Ps. iii. 8; iv. 3; v. 7). 5. *Unquenchable hope.* "If I find favour," etc. (ver. 26). So far from despairing of God's favour, he cherished the expectation of being delivered "out of all his troubles," brought back to Jerusalem, seeing the ark again, and worshipping in his tabernacle with joy. "My hope is in thee" (Ps. xxxix. 7; xlii. 5; lxxi. 14). 6. *Entire resignation.* "And if he thus say, I have no delight in thee; behold, here am I, let him do to me as seemeth good unto him" (ver. 26; 1 Sam. iii. 18; ch. xii. 15—23). "He besought God, as Alexander Severus told his soldiers a generous and a wise man should; praying for the best things and bearing whatever should befall" (Delany). "This marks strongly his subdued and right spirit, partly induced, we doubt not, by the humility of his own conscious transgressions. He fell; but it was the fall of the upright, and he rose again; submitting himself meekly in the mean time to the will of God" (Chalmers). 7. *Practical wisdom.* "Art thou a seer? return to the city," etc.

(vers. 27—29); "Behold! return," etc. (LXX.). "The peculiar exercises of religion ought to precede, but not to exclude, the use of every prudent means of securing success in lawful undertakings" (Scott). When, in time of adversity, we decline the aid of our friends in one form, because it seems to us injudicious and improper, we should gladly avail ourselves of it in another; knowing that by such instrumentality the help for which we look to God is most commonly vouchsafed. "Among the few faithful amidst the faithless, the first place belongs to the priests, whom loyalty and interest alike bound to the throne. So they were ready if they had been permitted to have carried even the ark to share the exile of the king. They will have their loyalty crowned by seeing the ark, the tent of a once nomad worship, signifying by its flame a spiritual life, set up in Jerusalem; the younger amongst them may see a temple rise, the scene of as noble a worship as the world has yet known" (R. Williams).—D.

Ver. 30.—*David's tears on Olivet.* 1. What a scene of fallen greatness and bitter grief is here depicted! He who yesterday reigned in Jerusalem, as the anointed (Messiah) of Jehovah, is to-day a homeless fugitive (ver. 20), toiling up the ascent of Olivet, in deep humiliation and undisguised sorrow, with head covered (ch. iii. 31, 32; xix. 4) and feet bare; accompanied by stern warriors and tender women and children, all, like himself, with covered heads "going and weeping." It is "as one long funeral procession of men wailing over the fall of all their hopes" (Plumptre). 2. What an instance of moral excellence and overcoming faith is here afforded! "The greatness of David did not depend on his royal state; it was within his lofty soul and inseparable from his commanding character" (Milman). He is considerate, generous (ver. 19), submissive (ver. 26), prayerful (ver. 31), grateful (ch. xvi. 4), forbearing (ch. xvi. 10), and hopeful (ch. xvi. 12). His suffering manifests his sincerity, his outward shame his inward worth; and "out of the depths" of his trouble he rises to the loftiest elevation (Ps. cxxx. 1; lxxxiv. 6; ch. xxiii. 13, 14; Hos. ii. 15). 3. What an outline is here furnished of the *ideal* representation, given by psalmist and prophet, of the suffering Servant of Jehovah (Ps. xxii.; Isa. liii.), and fully realized in him who, on the same spot, a thousand years afterwards, wept over the sinning and perishing city! "And when he was come near," etc. (Luke xix. 41—44; xxiii. 27—31). Consider—

I. THE SORROWS OF DAVID. Why did he weep? Not so much on account of his exile, privation, etc., as on account of: 1. The *grievous transgressions* which he had formerly committed (Ps. xxxix. 12; vi. 6), and which were now brought afresh to remembrance. "My sin is ever before me." 2. The *ungrateful treatment* which he received, from his son whom he tenderly loved (ch. xvi. 11), from his subjects whom he faithfully served, from his adversaries who hated him "wrongfully" and "without a cause" (Ps. lxix. 3—5). Neither his former transgressions nor his recent defects justified rebellion against his authority as king. Indeed, his personal piety and theocratic policy made him to many an object of hatred and reproach; and in him the Divine King of Israel himself was despised (Ps. v. 10; xxii. 8; xlii. 3; lxix. 7, 9, 20). "Though David suffered for his many sins, he had yet through penitence already obtained forgiveness of sins. Thus he was the righteous sufferer, who could appeal to God for the purity of his heart and the holiness of his cause" (Erdmann). 3. The *national calamity* which he beheld—the distress of "all the people that was with him" (ver. 23), the distracted condition of the country, the ruin which thousands would bring upon themselves; filling him with commiseration (1 Sam. xv. 35; Ps. cxix. 136). 4. The *Divine displeasure* which he experienced against his sin and the sins of the people; regarding this calamity as a sign thereof, enduring it in common with them, and bearing it, as far as possible, in his own person (ch. xxiv. 17). "Behold, and see if there be any sorrow like unto my sorrow," etc. (Lam. i. 12; Jer. ix. 1). "When I fall I shall arise," etc. (Micah vii. 8, 9; Ps. xxxi. 5).

II. THE SORROWS OF CHRIST; arising from: 1. *His relation to a sinful race,* whose nature he assumed and among whom he dwelt, "yet without sin;" the suffering "which a pure and holy nature must feel from the mere contiguity of evil; and the reflected and borrowed shame and pain which noble natures feel for the sins of those with whom they are closely connected" (Caird). 2. *His rejection by the world,* which he came to save; being reproached, persecuted, betrayed, deserted, condemned, and crucified; and thus made the victim of human wickedness. His righteousness and love, his Divine dignity, as the Son of God, the King Messiah (ch. vii. 16), rendered his treatment peculiarly sinful, and reveals the sin of men in its true light. 3. *His compassion for human misery*—loss, suffering, bondage, death, in the present and the future; the necessary fruit of human sin (Matt. viii. 17; John xi. 35; Luke xiii. 34, 35). 4. *His endurance of Divine abandonment* to the power of darkness and death (Ps. xxii. 1; Luke xxii. 44; Mark xv. 34; Heb. v. 7); wherein (without the sense of personal guilt and remorse) he gathered into his experience all the griefs endured by the servants of God in all ages from and for transgressors, and all the woes of humanity arising from alienation from God; and whereby, in unfaltering trust and entire self-devotion, he fulfilled the Father's will, overcame sin, death, and hell, and " became unto all them that obey him the Author of eternal salvation." "The chastisement was laid upon him for our peace; and through his stripes we were healed " (Isa. liii. 5, 10; Ps. xxii. 8, 16, 18, 24—31).

III. THE SORROWS OF THE CHRISTIAN. For every one who follows Christ must tread the path of sorrows (not only such as are natural, but such as are spiritual and Divine), on account of: 1. The *manifold sins* of which he has been guilty against the Lord (Matt. v. 4).

> "We have not time to mourn. The worse for us.
> He that lacks time to mourn lacks time to mend;
> Eternity mourns that."
>
> ('Philip van Artevelde.')

2. The *evil effects* wrought thereby in himself and others.

> "Weep not for broad lands lost;
> Weep not for fair hopes crost;
> Weep not when limbs wax old;
> Weep not when friends grow cold;
> Weep not that death must part
> Thine and the best-loved heart;
> Yet weep, weep all thou can—
> Weep, weep, because thou art
> A sin-defiled man."
>
> (Trench.)

3. The *sinful opposition* of men to Christ, his kingdom, and his people; unbelief, enmity, and persecution; the effects of which he shares with his Lord and for his sake (John xvi. 33; 1 Pet. iv. 13; Phil. i. 29; Col. i. 24). "For many walk, of whom I told you often, and now tell you even weeping," etc. (Phil. iii. 18). 4. The *miserable condition* and gloomy prospects of the impenitent. He mourns over them " with many tears " (Acts xx. 19, 31) "in the tender mercies of Jesus Christ" (Phil. i. 8), and is willing to undergo the greatest sacrifice and suffering for their salvation (Rom. ix. 2, 3). "If we suffer we shall also reign with him " (2 Tim. ii. 12).—D.

Ver. 31.—(MOUNT OLIVET.) *The counsel of Ahithophel.* "Turn, I pray thee, the counsel of Ahithophel into foolishness, O Jehovah." (*References:* ch. xv. 12, 34; xvi. 15, 20—23; xvii. 1—7, 15, 23; 1 Chron. xxvii. 33.) While ascending the Mount of Olives, David received intelligence that his counsellor, Ahithophel the Gilonite, had gone over to Absalom. He was the wisest statesman in Israel, and nothing was more adapted than his counsel to ensure the success of the revolt. The effect which his defection produced upon David is evident from the prayer (suggested probably by his name, " brother of a fool ") that forthwith broke from his lips. As he continued his journey, he, perhaps, reflected on the former course of Ahithophel (the Old Testament Judas) in the light of present knowledge, and indulged some such sentiments as are expressed in Ps. xli., 'The comfort of the afflicted and betrayed;' Ps. lv., 'Prayer against a treacherous friend;' Ps. lxix., cix. Observe that—

I. A FAMILIAR FRIEND MAY BECOME A DEADLY FOE.

> "Also my friend [literally, 'man of my peace'], whom I trusted,
> Who did eat of my bread,
> Hath lifted up his heel against me."
>
> (Ps. xli. 10; John xiii. 18.)

> " For it is not an enemy, etc.
> But thou wast a man on an equality with me,
> My companion and familiar friend," etc.
>
> (Ps. lv. 13—15.)

The motives of Ahithophel are not expressly stated; but they were probably: 1. *Dislike* of the religious earnestness and theocratic policy of David. 2. *Ambition* to be the sole adviser and prime minister of Absalom. " There may have been jealousy of Joab, or the natural tendency to worship the rising instead of the setting sun, or the impatience of a hypocrite at the round of religious services in which he was compelled to bear a part, affecting a devotion he did not feel, Ps. lv. 13, 14 " (Plumptre). 3. *Revenge* " for the dishonour done to his family in the person of Bathsheba, which no subsequent marriage could repair or efface " (Delany). " He was urged by the desire of punishing David's greatest crime, if he were not at the bottom of the movement. It is but reasonable to trace in the conspiring Ahithophel one of the intricate methods by which the judicial providence of God works out its own ends; suffering a great offender, notwithstanding his penitence, to eat the fruit of his deeds; yet reserving for treachery in time its reward " (R. Williams). " This text is a glass wherein God's justice is plainly to be seen. David had formerly forsaken Uriah, and now God suffers Ahithophel to forsake David. (1) Let us learn, when our friends forsake us, to enter into a serious scrutiny with our own souls. (2) The most politic heads have not always the faithfullest hearts. (3) False friends will forsake thee in times of adversity " (T. Fuller). " My brethren have dealt deceitfully as a brook," etc. (Job vi. 15; Jacox, 'Stray Side-Lights on Scripture Texts').

II. GREAT GIFTS ARE SOMETIMES PERVERTED TO UNGODLY USES. " That oracular wisdom which made his house a kind of shrine (ch. xvi. 23) seems to move the spirit of the sacred writer with an involuntary admiration " (Stanley). " His great crimes were enhanced by his immense talents, of which God gave him the use and the devil the application." His criminality appears not only in (1) his sanctioning and promoting rebellion against the authority of the king; but also in (2) his lawless and shameless advice against his honour (ch. xvi. 21, 22), whereby he sought to make reconciliation and compromise impossible in the view of all, and to gratify his revenge in the most effective and significant manner (ch. xi. 2, 4, 11); becoming, consciously or unconsciously, an instrument of retribution. " This cursed policy showed him rather an oracle of the devil than of God " (Matthew Henry). (3) His malicious and cruel proposal to take away his life (ch. xvii. 2). None but a man devoid of all moral and religious principle could have given such counsel. A powerful intellect is, alas! too often united with a depraved heart. " It is often found true by experience that persons of superior penetration and wisdom are of bad intentions; they see further than other men, and are under a temptation to turn their minds to the overreaching of others, and effecting mischief; their ability in accomplishing wickedness is a snare and a temptation to them; they find they *can* do it, and therefore are ready and *willing* to do it " (W. Jones, of Nayland). " This man, while he was one of David's deep counsellors, was one of David's fools, that said in their hearts, ' There is no God;' else he could not have hoped to make good an evil with worse, to build the success of treason upon incest." " Oh the policy of this Machiavelli of Israel, no less deep than hell itself! Oh the wisdom of the Almighty, that can use the worst evils well, and most justly make the sins of man his executioners! " (Hall).

III. GOD IS ABLE TO FRUSTRATE THE CRAFTIEST COUNSELS. " Turn," etc., " either infatuate him, that he may give foolish counsel; or, let his counsel be rejected as foolish, or spoiled by the foolish execution of it " (Poole). " He taketh the wise in their own craftiness," etc. (Job v. 13; 1 Cor. iii. 19). Of this David was persuaded from: 1. His supreme and infinite wisdom, in comparison with which the highest human wisdom is foolishness. 2. His abundant and varied resources for the direction and control of men's purposes and actions, so that they are made of none effect, or turn out contrary to what was intended and expected. 3. His frequent and extraordinary interpositions for that end. History is full of such instances (Acts iv. 28). So are individual lives (1 Sam. xxiii. 24—28). " Though Ahithophel spoke as an oracle of God (as we often see statesmen wiser than priests), yet as he turned to treachery his counsel turned to foolishness."

IV. A GOOD MAN HAS AN UNFAILING RESOURCE IN EVERY TROUBLE, viz. sincere, believing, fervent prayer. "Call upon me," etc. (Ps. l. 15). 1. However beset by the craft and power of his adversaries, he cannot be deprived of this privilege, but has access to God in all circumstances, at all times, and in all places (ver. 32). "A Christian cannot always hear, or always read, or always communicate, but he may pray continually. If he be on the top of a house with Peter, he may pray; if he be in the bottom of the ocean with Jonah, he may pray; if he be walking in the field with Isaac, he may pray when no eye seeth him; if he be waiting at table with Nehemiah, he may pray when no ear heareth him; if he be in the mountains with our Saviour, he may pray; if he be in the prison with Paul, he may pray; wherever he is, prayer will help him to find God out. Every saint is God's temple; and he that carrieth his temple about him, saith Austin, may go to prayer when he pleaseth. Indeed, to a Christian every house is a house of prayer; every closet a chamber of presence; and every place he comes to an altar whereon he may offer the sacrifice of prayer" (Swinnock, 'The Christian Man's Calling'). 2. The depth of his helplessness and peril is an incentive to higher earnestness and an argument for the fulfilment of Divine promises. "Ejaculations are short prayers darted up to God on emergent occasions. When we are time-bound, place-bound, or person-bound, so that we cannot compose ourselves to make a large solemn prayer, this is the right instant for ejaculations, whether orally uttered or only poured forth inwardly in the heart" (T. Fuller). 3. And his prayer is not offered in vain. Sometimes while he is "yet speaking" (Isa. lxv. 24) the answer comes (ver. 32). "In answer to a single emphatical ejaculation the counsel of the prudent is carried headlong" (Scott).

> "As for me—unto God will I cry,
> And Jehovah will save me.
> Evening and morning and at noon will I complain and groan,
> And he will hear my voice.
> Cast thy burden upon Jehovah,
> He—he will sustain thee."
>
> (Ps. lv. 16, 17, 22.)
>
> D.

Vers. 32—37.—(THE TOP OF MOUNT OLIVET.) *The friendship of Hushai.* (*References:* Josh. xvi. 2; ch. xvi. 16—19; xvii. 5—15; 1 Chron. xxvii. 33; 1 Kings iv. 16.) Like Uriah and Ittai, he may have been of Gentile origin and a proselyte; was far advanced in life (ver. 33), "the king's friend" or confidential adviser, and doubtless, in disposition, more congenial with David than the cool and calculating Ahithophel. "In him David saw the first gleam of hope. For warlike purposes he was useless; but of political stratagem he was master. The moment before the tidings had come of the treason of Ahithophel. To frustrate his designs, he was sent back just in time to meet Absalom arriving from Hebron" (Stanley). Notice: 1. *His opportune presence;* in answer to prayer (ver. 31); at a time of need, when others were unfaithful, trouble oppressed, and danger threatened. A faithful friend is one of Heaven's best gifts. "When friends come to us just at the moment when we want them, and for a purpose which no one else could accomplish as well as they, and for a time which is precisely conterminous with our necessity, it is hard not to look on them as much sent from God as the angels who met Jacob at Mahanaim, or who stood by the open tomb to tell Mary of Christ" (Thorold, 'On the Use of Friends').

> "When true friends meet in adverse hour,
> 'Tis like a sunbeam through a shower;
> The watery ray an instant seen,
> The darkly closing clouds between."
>
> (Sir W. Scott.)

"A faithful friend is the medicine of life" (Ecclus. vi. 16, 14). "The Lord has the hearts of all men in his hands, and if he be our Friend he will not let us want friends; yea, will make our most cruel enemies to be our friends" (Guild). 2. *His genuine sympathy;* voluntarily and appropriately expressed; and adapted to cheer and strengthen. "There are eight chief uses in the gift of friendship—viz. counsel, defence, appreciation, correction, society, intercession, aid, sympathy" (ch. vii. 1, 2; 1 Sam. xviii. 1—4). 3. *His tested loyalty.* Would he prove his fidelity, not by going into exile (ver. 21), but by returning to Jerusalem, professing allegiance to Absalom, endeavouring to frustrate the counsel of Ahithophel, and communicating secretly with David? "The boldness and originality of this step revealed the remarkable genius which, on former occasions, as in the contest with Goliath, had devised methods so original yet simple for the attainment of its object" (Blaikie). This deceptive policy is recorded, but not commended; it was not contrary to the ideas which prevailed among Eastern nations at the time on the subject of veracity; it has been since practised by Christian monarchs, statesmen, and warriors, toward their enemies, in perilous emergencies, as a justifiable stratagem; and often approved, like a skilful choice of weapons in conflict with an enemy, or like a clever move in a game of chess. It ought not, therefore, to be censured in David with undue severity; and "we must not think that the king's religion was a hypocrisy because it did not bear at once the fruit of the spotless honour and unswerving truth that mark the highest forms of Christian goodness" (Plumptre). But such duplicity cannot be justified on the ground of necessity; or that those against whom it is practised may have (like Absalom) "forfeited all the rights of society" (Delany); or that the end which is aimed at is good. In the light of revelation it must be condemned (Lev. xix. 11). "And in this respect we have (in David) a contrast with the Divine Antitype, the Son of David, who in all his sorrows and sufferings retained his holiness, purity, and truth unsullied and undefiled" (Wordsworth). 4. *His ready service.* (Ver. 37.) He at once complied with the wishes of the king, and evidently without any conception that what he was about to do was morally wrong. "We can hardly excuse his thrusting himself even upon a traitor's confidence in order to play the traitor; though the picture is character-istic of the East; and this is one of many drawbacks which remind us that the Bible embodies an experience and a tone of sentiment which are not always perfect models for the franker races of the West. At least let us remember, though a friend may ask many things of us, he should not ask us to sacrifice the truth and the right; for these are not ours to give him" (R. Williams). 5. *His daring courage.* Should his treachery be discovered, he might have to pay the penalty with his head. 6. *His skilful and prompt activity.* (Ch. xvi. 16; xvii. 7, 15.) 7. *His complete success.* (Ch. xvii. 14.) "In justifying the ways of God to men, and admiring the issues of his will, we are in no case obliged to approve actions which have nothing but their success to commend them" (Kitto, 'Cyc.').—D.

Vers. 7—9.—*Absalom's pious vow.* David and his ministers must have been singularly blind and negligent to have allowed Absalom so far to have prepared the way for the revolution he contemplated as he must have done before asking permission to go to Hebron. Nor does the permission itself show less blindness. David should have known his son better than to have so readily believed that he was likely to have made a pious vow, and to be burdened in conscience by its long non-fulfilment, especially as he had allowed four years (ver. 7, not "forty") to elapse before taking steps for its fulfilment. But David's foolish fondness prepared him to be easily imposed upon by favourite children. The purport of the pretended vow appears from what follows. It was to hold solemn sacrificial services at Hebron in thanksgiving for his return to his home and reconciliation with his father. Hebron was chosen because it was the place of his birth and early life, where he would have many friends; and the first capital of the kingdom, where many may have been still disaffected to David on account of his transfer of the court to Jerusalem. Sacrificial services were chosen as furnishing a plausible pretext for a large gathering of leading men who either were already disaffected, or, if going to the festival (like the two hundred from Jerusalem, ver. 11) "in their simplicity," knowing nothing, might be won over by Absalom's representations. In his representations to his father we have a glaring instance of—

I. HYPOCRITICAL PRETENCES IN RELIGION. 1. *Their nature.* They are imitations of real piety; and the closer the imitation the more likely are they to deceive and be successful in their object. Hypocrites are actors of a part, and the more skilful the actor the stronger the impression of reality. What more natural than the vow Absalom said he had made, and the language in which he describes it? A good

Hebrew prince, banished from home and kingdom, and with his prospects for the future darkened thereby, might well have longed to return, prayed to God to restore him, and vowed that, if his prayer were answered, he would make some singular demonstration of his gratitude. Absalom most likely lied when he said he had so vowed, as well as offered the sacrifices only as a cloak of wickedness. The counterfeit, however, illustrates the genuine; and in this case suggests that in great trouble we should seek relief and deliverance from God; that earnest prayer may be accompanied by promises of special acts of thanksgiving, and that, when deliverance comes, we should scrupulously perform the vows we have uttered (see Ps. lxvi. 13, *et seq.*). 2. *The motives from which they proceed.* These are as various as the objects which men pursue, and the attainment of which they think may be furthered by the appearance of piety. In Absalom the ultimate aim was the throne; the intermediate were the concealment from David of his purposes, the obtaining of leave of absence from Jerusalem, and opportunity for assembling his partisans and others around him, and maturing his plans with them, before striking the decisive blow. Hypocrites sometimes pretend to piety in order to conceal their wickedness and practise it without suspicion; sometimes with a view to gain (Matt. xxiii. 14); sometimes to obtain credit for virtues they do not possess (Acts v. 1—8), and secure praise from men (Matt. vi. 2). In times of persecution the object may be to avoid penalties; and any measure of favour shown to the professors of a particular creed, or of disability imposed on others, is a direct incentive to hypocrisy. How much do they promote hypocrisy amongst the poor who administer their charity in the form of "doles" given away after public worship, or carefully limited to those who attend particular religious services! Again, the hypocrite may pretend to a religion he does not possess, in order to obtain customers in his business from religious people, or to ingratiate himself with his piously disposed fellow-citizens, in order to obtain a seat in the town council, or in parliament, or other position in public life. How many large gifts to churches and chapels might be thus accounted for! Or the motive may be to secure the favour of parents, uncles, or aunts, with a view to a good place in their wills. Or, again, the forms of religion may be kept up because it is the habit of respectable society, without any real attachment to religion. Nor must we omit another motive. Piety may be seen to be necessary to secure deliverance from hell and admission to heaven; and, in total ignorance of the nature of piety, its forms may be adopted with that view. But this is rather formalism than deliberate hypocrisy. The two run into each other. It follows that hypocrisy is a sin most likely to be committed where real religion is prevalent and honoured. Absalom would not have pretended to piety if his father had not been religious; and when and where religion is disregarded, no one would think of professing it from unworthy motives. Though, to be sure, the general prevalence of formal religion may present the same temptation as that of real godliness. When, however, ungodliness and vice prevail in the neighbourhood or the circle in which a man moves, he may pretend to be worse than he is from motives similar to those which induce others to pretend to be better than they are.

II. THEIR ENORMOUS WICKEDNESS AND SURE DOOM. 1. *They evince such knowledge of the nature, grounds, and obligations of piety as enhances the guilt of their impiety.* 2. *They insult God.* By offering him what is worthless as if it were precious; and treating him as if he were unable to distinguish between the real and the unreal, or did not care, so long as his creatures pay homage to him, whether it be with the heart or not. 3. *They deceive and defraud men.* Imposing upon them with a mere appearance of goodness; inducing them to honour what is detestable and reward the unworthy; and diverting from genuine goodness its due notice and reward. 4. *They seriously injure those who are guilty of them.* They eat like a canker into the moral nature. A single act of hypocrisy affects injuriously the whole character, and throws suspicion on all that looks good. Habitual hypocrisy tends to destroy the possibility of sincere goodness, and to render salvation impossible. 5. *They deserve and ensure "the greater damnation"* (Matt. xxiii. 14). It is impossible that the imposition can last or ultimately be successful. It will be exploded, exposed, and punished in the great day of revelation and judgment (1 Cor. iv. 5).—G. W.

Ver. 20.—*A farewell blessing.* "Mercy and truth be with thee." Times of adversity are testing-times. They try and make manifest the character both of the sufferer and of his friends. The base and the noble in men, their selfishness and their disinterestedness, their faithlessness and their fidelity, are revealed and heightened. David never appeared in better light (in all but, perhaps, courage) than at the fearful crisis when his son was usurping his throne and ready to take his life, and he himself became for a time an exile from home and metropolis and sanctuary; and while some of his servants made manifest their inherent baseness, the virtues of others shone forth in new lustre. The conversation between David and Ittai illustrates these remarks. It is a contest of nobleness, in which both appear to great advantage. The words of the text were intended by David as a farewell. Ittai would not, however, accept them as such, but persisted in accompanying him whithersoever he might go. They contain a prayer suitable for all in addressing their friends in parting, or indeed at any time. " Mercy and truth" are, of course, those of God. " May God exercise towards thee his mercy and truth."

I. "MERCY:" HERE EQUIVALENT TO GRACE, KINDNESS, LOVE. Man is entirely dependent on the kindness of God both as a creature and as a sinner. All in some degree are its objects; but in desiring that it may be with any, we wish that they may enjoy it to the fullest extent, both in body and soul, in time and in eternity. It thus includes all manifestations and exercises of Divine grace. 1. Providential. 2. Pardoning. 3. Sanctifying. 4. Defending and preserving. 5. Comforting and gladdening. 6. Eternally saving.

II. "TRUTH:" EQUIVALENT TO TRUTHFULNESS, FAITHFULNESS. That perfection of the Divine nature which assures us that God will ever act in a manner true to himself as he reveals himself in his Word, and to the promises he has given us. In desiring that the truth of God may be with any, we pray that they may to the fullest extent experience how trustworthy are the revelations he has made of himself, how faithfully his promises are fulfilled, how happy they are who confide in him.

III. THE "MERCY AND TRUTH" OF GOD ARE OFTEN PRESENTED TOGETHER IN THE HOLY WRITINGS, ESPECIALLY IN THE BOOK OF PSALMS. They exhibit the two aspects of the nature of God with which we are chiefly concerned; and, taken comprehensively, include his whole moral character. To desire, therefore, that they may be with any one is to pray that God may be with him in the fulness of his Being, as his God; that he may experience for himself all that he can be to one of his creatures—his kindness in the utmost meaning of his faithful representations; his truth, not in the accomplishment of his threatenings, but in the amplest fulfilment of his gracious promises.

IV. THESE DIVINE PERFECTIONS ARE "WITH US" WHEN THEY ARE EXERCISED FOR OUR GOOD. This often takes place when they are not present to our consciousness. But the highest blessedness is to enjoy their exercise in the full consciousness that it is the "mercy and truth" of God that are blessing our lives. The crowning bliss is to enjoy their uninterrupted exercise towards us, and that for ever.

V. FOR TO HAVE GOD'S "MERCY AND TRUTH" WITH US IS TO ENJOY ALL REAL GOOD, AND TO BE SURE OF ITS ENJOYMENT FOR EVER. Hence these words express all that the wisest, kindest, and best can address to their friends in parting with them, or on birthdays, new year's days, etc. We cannot be so certain that we are pronouncing a blessing on them when we wish them health, wealth, long life, abundance of friends, etc.

VI. ONE OF THE BEST EFFECTS OF GOD'S "MERCY AND TRUTH" is to produce their own likeness in those with whom they dwell, making them kind and loving, true and faithful. The possession and cultivation of these qualities are a necessary part of the evidence that we have savingly experienced the Divine grace and faithfulness, and a necessary condition of our continuing to enjoy them (see Prov. iii. 3, 4).—G. W.

Ver. 21.—*Ittai an example to Christians.* It is interesting to find a Gentile, and he a Gittite, so attached to David, so devoted in duty to him, and so honoured as to have (ch. xviii. 2) been entrusted with the command of one-third of the army in the battle with Absalom and his forces. The proposal of David (vers. 19, 20) was generous and reasonable; but to Ittai's loyal spirit was quite inadmissible. He expresses his determination to cleave to David whether for life or for death; and swears to do so by the life of God and the life of the king. His devotedness presents an example to subjects and soldiers, to servants and friends. His language is worthy of adoption by us in addressing our glorious King, the Divine Son of David. It reminds us of the words of Peter, when speaking for all the twelve (John vi. 68) and when speaking only for himself (John xiii. 17), and which expressed his genuine determination, notwithstanding his subsequent fall. It reminds us also of the exhortation of Barnabas to the new converts at Antioch, "that with purpose of heart they would cleave unto the Lord" (Acts xi. 23)—an exhortation which meets with a cordial response in every Christian's heart. His resolve, his vow, is to cleave unto Christ for life and death; to follow him whithersoever he may lead.

I. WHENCE THIS DETERMINATION ARISES. Primarily from the marvellous power of Christ to attract and attach to himself the hearts of men. David had a similar power, of an inferior kind and on a smaller scale. Christ draws and influences, not only by his character and works, but by his Spirit working directly in the heart. But regarded as springing from the Christian's heart, the resolve and vow are the result of: 1. *Faith in Jesus Christ as the Son of God, the Saviour and King of men.* Who has, therefore, a right to supreme homage and service (John vi. 69). 2. *Ardent love to him.* In return for his love (2 Cor. v. 14, 15); and as the result of knowledge and experience, perception of his Divine and human excellences, delight in his society and service. 3. *Desire and hope to make him some suitable return for his love and self-sacrifice,* and the invaluable blessings he has secured and conferred. The ardent Christian will pant for, and delight in, opportunities for serving Christ at the cost of peril, loss, suffering, disgrace with the world, or even sacrifice of life; and for showing his fidelity when others forsake him. 4. *Conviction that safety, happiness, and life everlasting are to be found only with Christ.*

> "Whither, ah! whither should I go,
> A wretched wanderer from my Lord?
> Can this dark world of sin and woe
> One glimpse of happiness afford?
> Depart from thee! 'Tis death; 'tis more—
> 'Tis endless ruin, deep despair!"

5. *Memory of past vows.* "I have sworn, and I will perform it" (Ps. cxix. 106).

II. HOW IT IS TO BE FULFILLED. Not merely by warm feelings at times of special devotion, or by words of endearment, or promise, or lavish praise; but by: 1. *Bold confession of Christ before men.* Wearing his uniform, marching under his banner, acknowledging him openly as King and Captain. 2. *Union and communion with his people.* In profession of his Name, in worship, at the Lord's table, in social life, etc. Christ is in his Church; they are his visible representatives; openly with them all should be who wish to be "in what place their Lord the King may be." 3. *Visiting constantly the places where Christ is specially to be found, and avoiding those which he avoids.* Frequenting the closet, the sanctuary, the houses of poor, sick, and dying brethren. Avoiding the haunts of dissipation and iniquity. Going nowhere where we cannot think with satisfaction that Christ is near and approving. 4. *Active and zealous co-operation with him.* Doing, daring, enduring, in promoting his kingdom and the welfare of mankind. "Always abounding in the work of the Lord" (1 Cor. xv. 58). "Enduring hardship, as a good soldier of Jesus Christ" (2 Tim. ii. 3). Pressing eagerly to the front with Christ where his battles are to be fought, as Ittai with David, regardless of difficulties, danger, or death. 5. *Perseverance in all.* Which is the crowning proof of the deep sincerity of the determination.

III. THE REWARDS OF SUCH DEVOTEDNESS. 1. *Now.* Further opportunities of, calls to, and fitness for, service, suffering, and honour.

> "What his guerdon here?
> Many a sorrow, many a labour,
> Many a tear."

But with these, the manifested presence of Christ, and his smile and words of approval; the pleasures which accompany the exercise of the powers in the noblest possible employment, and those which arise from association with the noblest of God's creatures in earth and heaven. 2. *Hereafter.* To be with Christ and share his glory and bliss evermore. "Enter into the joy of thy Lord" (Matt. xxv. 21). "If we endure, we shall also reign with him" (2 Tim. ii. 12, Revised Version).—G. W.

Vers. 25, 26.—*David's resignation to the will of God.* David's character shone most brightly amid the darkness of adversity—in the early struggles and perils, and in these later ones. In these verses we see his superiority to a superstitious dependence on the presence of the 'ark as ensuring the presence and aid of God. He was thus much in advance of the Israelites, elders and people alike, in the days of Eli (1 Sam. iv. 3—5). We take the verses, however, as evidencing David's profound submission to the will of God, and illustrating the nature and excellence of godly resignation.

I. To WHAT HE WAS RESIGNED. To whatever might be the will of God. To the enjoyment of the Divine favour, or the experience of the Divine displeasure. In particular: 1. *To defeat or victory in the contest with his unnatural son;* and, as results of one or the other: 2. *To the permanent loss or the regaining of his throne.* 3. *To exile from Jerusalem or return to it.* 4. *To banishment from the ark and house of God or restoration to them.* This is specially referred to in ver. 25. 5. *To death or life.*

II. THE NATURE OF HIS RESIGNATION. 1. *It was not insensibility or indifference.* How much he felt the position in which he was placed is evident from his language here, and his tears and other signs of mourning referred to in ver. 30. Those who do not feel their troubles cannot cherish resignation to them. Troubles which do not trouble require no exercise of submission. Resignation may be most eminently displayed by those who are most susceptible of suffering. 2. *It was not a stoical submission to the inevitable.* This is better than vain struggles and useless murmurs, but is not godly resignation. 3. *Nor did it involve abandonment of all prayer and effort to secure what was felt to be desirable.* David, while surrendering himself to the disposal of the Most High, carefully planned and laboured, and was prepared to fight, that he might obtain the victory. Christian resignation is not fatalism. 4. *It was trustful, loving submission to whatever might prove to be the will of God.* David recognized the hand of God in his adversities, saw that the issue of events would be according to the Divine appointment, and on this account was prepared to acquiesce in it. "Let him do to me as seemeth good unto him."

III. MOTIVES TO SUCH RESIGNATION. 1. *The rightful sovereignty of God.* He does rule over all, whether we will or no; and the recognition of his right to rule will much aid in producing willing submission to his will. "You know, my dear," said a poor man to his wife, when they were mourning the loss of a peculiarly interesting and affectionate child, "this family is God's garden, and he has a right to come into it and pluck any flower that pleases him best." 2. *His omnipotence.* "Humble yourselves under the mighty hand of God" (1 Pet. v. 6). Because he is almighty, his will must be accomplished; resistance is futile. At the same time, he is almighty to support, to bring good out of evil, and to "exalt in due time" (1 Pet. v. 6). 3. *His wisdom and goodness.* Which assure us that he does not act according to arbitrary choice, but that what "seemeth good unto him" is really good; so that in submitting to him we are acquiescing in our own ultimate well-being. 4. *Our sinfulness and unworthiness.* David was doubtless aided in resigning himself to the will of God by the memory of his heinous sins (comp. Judg. x. 15; Neh. ix. 33; Lam. i. 18; iii. 39; Dan. ix. 14; Micah vii. 9). We deserve more suffering than is inflicted upon us; we merit no good thing; the more readily, therefore, should we resign ourselves to whatever may be appointed for us. 5. *The blessings enjoyed by us or assured to us.* The memory of past enjoyments, which tends to embitter present griefs, should nevertheless awaken a gratitude which tends to reconcile us to them. "Shall we receive good at the hand of God, and shall we not receive evil?" (Job ii. 10). The mercies still remaining to us, duly appreciated and acknowledged, will have a similar beneficial effect. The way in which God has led us through past difficulties should strengthen confidence in him, and render us willing to trust him with our future. Specially, if we are Christians indeed, let us keep in mind: (1) The relation in which we stand towards God, as his children, redeemed, reconciled, renewed; and the childlike spirit which becomes us. (2) The unspeakable blessings which as Christians we enjoy. Pardon, peace with God, access to him, assurance of his fatherly pity and love, the indwelling of the Holy Spirit, with his special guidance, support, and consolation. (3) The promises made to us of all needful good (Ps. lxxxiv. 11; Matt. vi. 33); the co-operation of all things for our good (Rom. viii. 28); the Divine care, sympathy, and support (Ps. lv. 22; Heb. xiii. 5, 6);

and final deliverance from all affliction, and enjoyment of eternal glory—glory far outweighing all present trouble, and prepared for and increased through its right endurance (Rev. xxi. 4; Rom. viii. 18; 2 Cor. iv. 17, 18). 6. *The cross of Christ illustrates and enhances all other motives.* The love of God in Christ assures us in the darkest hours that he is love, and his ways are love. The sufferings of Jesus as our atoning Saviour make sure to us all spiritual and eternal blessings. His greater sufferings are adapted to reconcile us to our so much lesser ones. In his resignation we have the brightest and most powerful example, and reasons for imitation of it. As our fellow-Sufferer we know that he can, and are assured that he does, sympathize with us; and that he is the better able to succour us. 7. *The benefits* which flow from resignation. (1) "The peace of God" (Phil. iv. 7), and with it strength to endure: power also to do whatever may be possible towards deliverance. (2) Evidence to our own consciousness that we are the children of God. (3) Good influence over others. Proof to them of the worth of religion.

In conclusion, let us lay to heart that in any case we must suffer affliction. The only question is how and with what results? Shall we suffer in faith and hope and submission, and thus secure Divine approval, support, and blessing? or shall we suffer impatiently and rebelliously, thus adding to our sufferings, and gaining no blessing from them? "Woe unto him that striveth with his Maker!" (Isa. xlv. 9).—G. W.

Ver. 32.—*The place of worship.* "The top of the mount where God was worshipped" (Revised Version). This "top of the mount" is one of the most sacred spots in the world —the universe. For here the Son of God wept over Jerusalem, which lay full in view at his feet, as he thought of its coming destruction, and declared the cause of it (Luke xix. 41). In David's time there appears to have been a "high place" there, where men were accustomed to worship God. It seems strange that so near to the tabernacle such a place should have been tolerated, however difficult it was to abolish such separate worship elsewhere. Perhaps, however, this was simply "a place of prayer" (Acts xvi. 13), not of sacrifice or incense-burning, in which case it would not come under the condemnation of the Mosaic Law. One can hardly doubt that such places of worship must have been scattered over the land long before the known existence of synagogues. How otherwise could social religion, or religion at all, have been maintained? Three visits a year to the tabernacle or temple, and those of the men only, could not have been sufficient. How also could the sabbaths have been kept as days holy to the Lord? But without attempting to settle such questions, this Scripture may be used as suggesting some thoughts on places of worship.

I. THEIR SANCTITY. 1. *Because specially set apart and used for the worship of God.* Consecrated in the purpose of men, and by their devotions; by the prayers by which they are dedicated, and the worship constantly offered afterwards. 2. *Because they are scenes of Divine manifestation and gracious operation.* (Exod. xx. 24; Ps. lxiii. 2; Matt. xviii. 20.) They are meeting-places, not only between men and men, but between God and men, heaven and earth, consecrated by the presence and blessing of God.

II. THEIR VALUE. 1. *As witnesses.* (1) For God; reminding men of him, and calling on them to worship and serve him. (2) Of the nature of men; as spiritual, fitted and designed for worship, and immortal. 2. *As inviting to rest from ordinary occupations and employment in spiritual exercises.* 3. *As furnishing valuable opportunities for the exercise of gifts for the good of others.* Gifts of teaching, singing, organization, etc. 4. *In uniting men to each other in sacred bonds, and fostering mutual love and service.* 5. *In promoting piety, holiness, and happiness.* The moral virtues, as well as the godliness, of a people depend to a large extent on their places of worship.

III. THEIR BLESSED ASSOCIATIONS AND MEMORIES. There "our fathers praised" God (Isa. lxiv. 11); thither "we walked in company" with our own parents and best friends (Ps. lv. 14); there many of our most happy and profitable hours have been spent. There, it may be, we were first led to Christ; there we have often met with God, and consciously received his blessing; there we have received instructions and influences which have moulded our character and elevated our lives. There we have been relieved of anxieties, calmed when agitated, comforted when sorrowful, revived when languid, recalled to duty when we have wandered, strengthened in faith and courage when we have become enfeebled. There many a glimpse of heaven has been gained, and many a foretaste of its bliss enjoyed. Many have attended their place of worship from childhood to old age; and esteem it one of the chief blessings of their life. "Planted in the house of the Lord," they "flourish in the courts of our God," and still "bring forth fruit in old age" (Ps. xcii. 13, 14), waiting to be transplanted to "the paradise of God" (Rev. ii. 7).

IV. OUR CONSEQUENT DUTY IN RESPECT TO THEM. 1. *To be thankful for them.* 2. *To take our part in establishing and maintaining them.* 3. *To attend them.* Frequently, regularly, punctually. To be negligent in these respects is to dishonour God, and to rob ourselves of blessing. 4. *To induce others to do so.* Happy the city, happy the land, in which places where men worship God abound, and are attended by crowds of true worshippers!—G. W.

EXPOSITION.

CHAPTER XVI.

Ver. 1.—Ziba the servant of Mephibosheth. It is the misfortune of troubled times like those in which David found himself, that unscrupulous men use them for selfish purposes. For those in danger have no time for careful examination, nor are their minds sufficiently calm for impartial judgment, but they act on first impressions, and catch at every straw. Ziba's present would naturally raise everybody's spirits, and be taken as a good omen; for it showed that David had adherents in unlikely quarters, when thus a servant of the house of Saul of his own accord brought so timely an offering. The asses saddled for riding contradict the idea that Ziba met David by chance as he was bringing the produce of the farm for the use of Mephibosheth's household. More probably the asses had been saddled for Mephibosheth's own use (comp. ch. xix. 26), and the provisions had been prepared as a contribution to the king's needs: but at the last moment the cunning Ziba managed to hurry away with his men, leaving his master in the lurch, and unable to get anything to ride upon in the short interval between David's escape and Absalom's entry. Moreover, possibly from being a cripple, and from the distressing circumstances of his early life, Mephibosheth always seems deficient in energy, and perhaps David's conduct in mulcting him of half his property may not really have been so unjust as it looks, supposing that it was his dilatoriness which gave Ziba the chance of going away with the whole convoy while he was wasting time. It was this apparent desertion of him by one whom he had so befriended which may have made David say, "All men are liars" (Ps. cxvi. 11), though subsequently he learned that the lie was Ziba's. The food consisted of two hundred loaves, or rather flat cakes of bread, a hundred bunches of dried grapes, a hundred cakes of pressed dates, and a skin of wine. Instead of "date-cakes," some of the versions render "fig-cakes;" but for this there is a special Hebrew word (see 1 Sam. xxx. 12).

Ver. 3.—Thy master's son; that is, the son of Jonathan, or even of Saul, as the word "son" is used very indefinitely in Hebrew. Mephibosheth held the property as their representative. **To-day shall the house, etc.** Ziba's slander was absurd. Mephibosheth was likely to meet with no kind treatment from Absalom; but perhaps he was a visionary, and David may have thought that he was holding back for any chance that might turn up. But upon this slander David acts with blamable impetuosity, and, indignant that the son of his old friend should so desert him, he gives Ziba all his lands. The grant would be valid only if David's cause prevailed, and Ziba so far deserves credit in that he attached himself to a ruined man; but his motive was not love to David, but selfish calculation.

Ver. 4.—I humbly beseech thee that, etc. The words are really a form of grateful acceptance. "I do obeisance" (see margin), that is, "I make my humble bow: may I find favour," etc.; may the king continue to look favourably upon me.

Ver. 5.—Bahurim. The exact site of this place is unknown (see note on ch. iii. 16). Lieut. Conder, following a Jewish tradition, identifies it with *Almit,* a village about four miles north-east of Jerusalem. If so it lay, not on the direct road to the fords, but on a side route. **A man of the family of the house of Saul.** The words do not mean that he was a near relative of Saul, but that he was a member of the mishpachah, the larger division of the tribe of Benjamin, to which the house of Saul, a much smaller subdivision of the family, belonged (see note on ch. xiv. 7). But he was a strong partisan, and so fanatical as to care little for his life, if only he could annoy the usurper. For besides "all the people," David had with him "the mighty men," a few of whom could easily have punished him.

Ver. 7.—Come out; rather, *out, out;* that is, "get out; begone, begone, thou murderer and worthless man." Shimei could scarcely have referred to the murders of Ishbosheth and Abner, which were too remote to have so rankled in his memory; but as ch. xxi. is not in its chronological order, what probably called forth his anger was the surrender of Saul's sons and grandsons into the hands of the Gibeonites. Shimei, probably, even resented David's taking the side of the Gibeonites, and treating as a crime to be severely punished what he and all Saul's partisans regarded as righteous zeal for Israel. The three years' famine, followed by the execution of Saul's sons, made more tragic by the noble conduct of Rizpah, contributed largely to the revolt of the nation from David, and helps to explain that abandonment of him by the people, which otherwise seems so hard to understand (on the date of the famine, see note on ch. xxi.).

Ver. 9.—**Then said Abishai.** Abishai's indignation was natural, and it is evident, from ver. 10, that Joab shared it. Shimei's conduct was abominable, and David finally condemned him to death for it (1 Kings ii. 8, 9), having probably found that, even after his pardon, he was an implacable enemy. His revilings now must not only have been painful to David, but depressing to all the people that were with him, and there must have been many a murmur in the ranks at the king allowing such conduct to go unpunished. But he was in a state of great mental distress and self-condemnation. He had borne sorrow after sorrow since the day when, by his own great sin, he had opened the floodgates of wickedness; and now the son whom he dearly loved, and who had first been put wrong by a crime which might never have been committed but for his own example, was seeking both his crown and his life, and had made his cup of sorrow full to the brim and running over. At such a time of agony it was even a relief to have outward affliction to bear; for it brought the consoling thought that the Divine chastisement had its merciful limit. Jehovah had bidden Shimei revile him, and he would bear it because it was Jehovah's doing. " It may be that Jehovah will look upon my wrong, and that he will requite me good for his cursing of me this day." **Go over.** Abishai's word is explained by ver. 13. David's route seems to have lain in a narrow valley, and Shimei, running along the ridge on one side, was near enough for his words to be heard, and for his stones to come near the king's retinue. Abishai, therefore, asked permission to cross over to Shimei's side of the steep ravine with a few men, who would seize him and put him to death.

Ver. 12.—**Mine affliction.** This reading is supported by the Septuagint and Vulgate. The Syriac has " my subjection," possibly a free translation of the same reading. But the written text (K'tib) has " my wrong," either the wrong I have done, and of which I am bearing the punishment, or, as in the Revised Version, " the wrong done unto me." The correction of the Massorites (K'ri), is literally " my eye," that is, " my tears."

Ver. 14.—**Weary.** Evidently the name of a place; for David " refreshed himself there." It was probably a caravanserai, the full name of which was, " Rest for the weary," but gradually the title was shortened down to the last word, " Weary," Hebrew *Ayêphim*, which the Revised Version puts as a proper name in the margin.

Ver. 17.—**Is this thy kindness to thy friend?** After carrying the king to Ayêphim, on the banks of the Jordan, the narrator now turns back to Absalom, because David was to wait at the caravanserai for news from Jerusalem. And immediately on his arrival, Hushai hastens into Absalom's presence, loudly exclaiming, " Long live the king! " for such is the meaning of the Hebrew. The young man is surprised; for Hushai was David's friend and trusted confidant. Yet he does not suspect this sudden breaking of old ties, but, looking at the bright side only, sees in it a proof that his party was looked upon as sure of success, and David's cause as hopeless. He welcomes, therefore, so notable an adherent, and Hushai's pretences confirm his self-deceit; for he professes to regard Absalom as king, not by fraud and violence, but by the formal choice of both Jehovah and the people. On this assumption, obedience to the nation's choice became a religious duty, and Hushai's love to the father was a pledge of love to the son. We must not, however, condemn Absalom for too easy credulity. The nation was in his favour, and, had he acted with promptitude, David's cause would have been lost.

Ver. 18.—**The men of Israel.** Here and in ver. 15 the men of Israel are not contrasted with the men of Judah, but include them (see ch. xv. 10). Absalom's rebellion began at Hebron, in Judæa, and the selection of Amasa, a first cousin both of David and Joab, as commander-in-chief, suggests the conclusion that Absalom's chief strength lay in David's own tribe, though men from all the tribes on the west of the Jordan had also flocked to his standard. Besides them, Hushai speaks of **this people**, that is, the citizens of Jerusalem. For, while there had been general lamentation at David's departure (ch. xv. 23), yet the citizens had admitted Absalom without a struggle, and submitted to him. David's adherents are also constantly called " the people," because they did not belong to any special tribe, but were drawn indifferently from them all.

Ver. 20. — **Give counsel among you;** Hebrew, *for you;* but we have no way in English of expressing the force of this phrase. In Greek it is called the ethic dativo, and is supposed to give character to the address, and indicate that those to whom the words are spoken have also an interest in the matter.

Ver. 21.—**Ahithophel said.** Ahithophel's counsel was utterly abominable, even though the deed would not be regarded by any of the Israelites as incestuous. A king inherited his predecessor's harem, and Absalom's act was a coarse and rude assertion that David's rights were at an end, and that crown and lands and property, even to his wives, now all belonged to the usurper. But, while polygamy had thus degraded the wives and concubines into mere chattels, the harem was the property most jealously guarded by its owner (ch. iii. 7; 1 Kings ii. 22); and Absalom's act was an outrage which David could never have pardoned. And this was what Ahithophel wanted. He was afraid that if Absalom's cause began to decline, he might come to terms with his father, who would readily forgive a son if he submitted, but would certainly punish Ahithophel. For his own selfish purposes, therefore, he led Absalom on to a crime which rendered a reconciliation with David impossible, and pledged all the conspirators to carry out the matter to the bitter end; and that end could only be the death of David if the conspiracy succeeded. But this bitterness to David would vex all moderate men, and weaken Absalom's cause. It was of advantage only to such as were deeply committed to the rebellion, and bent on killing David. To him it was terrible sorrow; for he knew that this open shame was the punishment of his own secret infamy (ch. xii. 11, 12); and in it, again, he saw the meshes of the avenger's net tightening around him.

Ver. 22. **A tent;** Hebrow, *tho tent;* that constantly used by David and his family for the enjoyment of the cool evening breeze, and which the citizens of Jerusalem had frequently seen erected on the flat roof of David's house. It was when walking on this roof that David had given way to guilty passion, and now it is the scene of his dishonour.

Ver. 23.—**The counsel of Ahithophel,** etc. These words form a sort of apology for Absalom. He ought to have had more respect for his father than to offer him so grievous an insult, and aggravate by so terrible a deed the quarrel between them. But his conduct from first to last was utterly mean and selfish, and his only excuse here is that there was such a glamour round Ahithophel, that men yielded up their own judgment to him without an effort, and did what he advised as if it had a religious sanction. **At the oracle of God;** Hebrew, *had asked the Word of God;* that is, had consulted God by Urim and Thummim. When a man went to the priest to inquire in this way, he did whatever he was told; and the word of Ahithophel was accepted with equal deference.

HOMILETICS.

Vers. 1—14.—The facts are: 1. David, passing on his way, is met by Ziba with a present for the king and his servants. 2. On inquiring after Mephibosheth, David is told by Ziba that he was staying in Jerusalem in expectation that, as a result of the present revolt, the kingdom would be restored to him as representative of the house of Saul. 3. Accepting this statement as correct, David assigns Mephibosheth's property (ch. ix. 9—12) to Ziba, who thereupon makes obeisance. 4. Proceeding to Bahurim, David is assailed by Shimei, who curses him, casts stones at him, reproaches him with deeds of evil, and avers that, as a punishment, God had taken the kingdom from him and given it to Absalom. 5. Astonished at the insolence, Abishai seeks permission to slay the man; but David, piously recognizing a providential chastisement in the event, will not have it so, and points out further to his people that this was but a small trouble in comparison with Absalom's conduct, and that probably God would have compassion and vouchsafe a compensating blessing. 6. David and his company proceed on their way, still insulted by Shimei, till they come to a place where they can refresh themselves.

The cruelty of avarice. In this chapter the historian gives us a foil to the loyalty and devotion of the men referred to hitherto. Ittai, Zadok, Abiathar, and Hushai have their opposites in Ziba and Shimei and Ahithophel. It is said that the beasts of prey and creeping things come forth in the night; and so in this dark and sad time for David, the foul creatures come forth and manifest their full strength. Good men are always encompassed by evils, but they are kept in check by the very force of the prosperity of the good. When once that begins to wane, they revive and put forth their destructive powers. The time had now come for their appearance. In the case of Ziba we see avarice in its most hideous form.

I. It CAREFULLY FRAMES ITS SCHEMES. An avaricious man is usually endowed with a good measure of prevision, and his success lies very much in the wicked perversion of this gift. The elaborate present of Ziba to David (vers. 1, 2), and the meeting with him just when a token of kindness would be most acceptable, was the result of hours and days of scheming. The end in view is so precious to the greedy soul that trouble and toil to attain to it go for nothing. There is a spontaneous avarice, as when men suddenly seek to grasp what is apparently within their reach, for the evil principle, like a slumbering hungry dog, is ever quick to discern and to act; but the great achievements of avarice, by which men become rich or gain some swift advantage, are the result of the prostitution of the gifts of foresight and skill in arrangement to low cunning and selfishness. There is many a scheme being concocted at this hour, in commercial and political circles, for the circumvention of others to the enrichment of self.

II. It CONFORMS ITS PLANS TO THE NATURE OF MEN AND CUSTOMS OF THE AGE. Ziba knew what David had done for Mephibosheth (ch. ix. 1—10), how generous was the king's heart, how he would appreciate fidelity in the time of trouble and scorn ungrateful conduct, how his associates in trial would approve any favour conferred on the loyal at the cost of the disloyal, and how it was within the prerogative of a monarch to confiscate the property of a traitor. Avarice is a careful student of human nature and of the usages of the world. Its success often depends on quickness of discernment, and a practical application of the knowledge of men and things to the purposes of a base, greedy heart. A good and generous man may be as quick in discernment, and may in the intercourse of life gather as much knowledge of human nature, but he differs from the avaricious man in that he scorns to turn all this to the sole promotion of purely selfish interests.

III. It TAKES SPECIAL ADVANTAGE OF THE TROUBLES AND WEAKNESS OF OTHERS. There is a fiendish sagacity in avarice. Ziba saw that the sorrows of David furnished a choice opportunity for making an impression on his generous sympathetic nature by a manifestation of loyal interest and kindly consideration for his comfort; and he saw also that the bodily infirmity of Mephibosheth (ch. ix. 13; xix. 25, 26) would prevent his going out to David to express his own loyalty. How splendid the opportunity of so representing matters as to secure the confiscation of Mephibosheth's inheritance to himself as a reward for his personal faithfulness! How this is too often illustrated, in the eager rush after wealth, in the conduct of certain nations towards others, is well known. There are hard-hearted men who rejoice in the commercial calamities of others, because they see their chance of turning them to their own advantage, and not a few are willing to profit by the incapacity, physical, social, and intellectual, of others, by not providing them with the means by which they can rise above it, and act their own part in the world's affairs. The curse of God surely rests on such evil-doers.

IV. It IS HEEDLESS OF THE PAIN IT INFLICTS. David's heart was sad enough. Trouble in most fearful form had come on him. His anguish is seen in the comfort he felt in the fidelity of the high priests and in the presence of the ark. But what though his heart was smitten! Avarice can rive it the more by concocting a lie most suited for such a purpose. Ziba knew that the story about Mephibosheth would rend further the sore wounds of the much-riven heart. What of that? Property would be acquired. What of blasting the reputation and scattering the fortunes of an innocent cripple? His property would become Ziba's. Such things do occur still in the earth. There may be degrees in avarice, but in every case there is a heedless infliction of pain and a positive injury to the innocent. Is there a God to avenge wrong? Is there a future retribution? Seeing that many avaricious men escape positive punishment in this life (Ps. xlix. 16—20; lxxiii. 1—17), a righteous moral order must either be denied or we must look on to the day when God shall give to every man according to the deeds done in the body (2 Cor. v. 10).

V. It ASSUMES THE FORM OF NOBLEST VIRTUES. Ziba comes to David as a kindly, faithful, generous subject, sorrowful for his affliction, ready to minister to his comfort, and even prepared to break the ties which for years had held him to Mephibosheth. Loyalty and religion are publicly professed. The assembled friends of the king are witnesses to his noble conduct. Wolves may come in sheep's clothing, Satan may assume the appearance of an angel of light, and, in the same way, avarice may, if occasion requires it, hide its hateful form under the guise of the two most reputable of all qualities—loyalty and religion. This is done in varying degrees. There is a conformity to prevalent political opinion, to social customs, to decency of bearing, and to the observances of the sanctuary, not because of a thorough conviction of right founded on knowledge and principle, but because it will contribute to swell the amount of one's gains and elevate one's position in the world. God desireth *truth* in the inward parts (Ps. li. 6). The whited sepulchre is no screen from his eye (Matt. xxii. 27; cf. Ps. cxxxix.).

The reproaches of the wicked. A more graphic account of insult and personal wrong than this is not found in the Bible. The language of the sixty-ninth psalm is fitly descriptive of the events of this sad day, as also of Ps. iii. and iv. The harsh voice of Shimei, it is to be feared, was but the index of a feeling in many hearts towards the unfortunate man of God. The political element enters into the attack (ver. 8), but there was a deeper sentiment of hostility in which the ungodly of Jerusalem would be predisposed to share. Everything seems intense in David's life, as a consequence of the natural force of his character, the depth of his feelings, and the corresponding strength of emotion, whether of love or hate, which his conduct aroused. Except in seasons of fierce persecution, and most of all in the instance of our Redeemer, the reproaches of the wicked do not assume the violent form here indicated, but in every instance of their occurrence we may trace features in common with this.

I. THEY PROCEED FROM RELIGIOUS AVERSION. David was a religious man. His kingly position was won by virtue of his being a man after God's own heart (1 Sam. xv. 28; xvi. 7—13). In spite of his great fall, he was a lowly, devout servant of God, intent on the spiritual welfare of the people. When Shimei assailed David as a usurper (ver. 8), and so made a political allusion, he revealed his own intense aversion both to David's piety and the religious reason for his elevation to the throne in the place of Saul. He evidently did not enter into the theocratic views of Samuel (1 Sam. xv., xvi.). He was a man who preferred the unspiritual order of Saul's government to the Divine order of David's. Here lay the real secret of the reproaches heaped upon the unfortunate king. No godly man, no man of elevated views or of spiritual sympathies, could originate such malicious words. This was the secret also of the reproaches heaped on Christ. He was better than his haters liked him to be. Intense aversion to his superior spirituality was the spring of their conduct. They hated him without a cause, *i.e.* a valid reason. In looking at the reproaches against the persecuted Christians, we find the same to be true. The evil words spoken nowadays against good men have their root in a dislike of the holy life which, by contrast, is a reminder of sin and guilt.

II. THEY ARE PROFESSEDLY BASED ON DEFECTS OF CHARACTER. It might be inferred from the words of Shimei (ver. 7) that he was a very righteous, peaceful, God-fearing man, for he comes forth as the accuser of the king, and pleader for what is just to man and God. But we know that this was only a cover for the real feeling. Those who are not holy are obliged, by compulsion of conscience, to find a plea for deeds of shame. The failure of David in one period of his life was most probably known to Shimei, and it is seized with eagerness and made the justification of a reproach bearing on his entire life, and imputing deeds of which David was innocent. Saving the case of Bathsheba and Uriah, David's life was anything but one of blood and worthlessness (Belial). To Saul and his sons he had been unusually kind. The elevation of his character had given dignity and power to the kingdom. These tactics of wicked men are constant; the occasional weaknesses of life are laid hold of, and magnified so as to be representative of the entire life. The free and frank words of Christ, true as they were, not long before his death, were laid hold of and used as though blasphemy and evil works were his general characteristics (Matt. xii. 24; John x. 32—36). Our failings in Christian life doubtless are a reproach to us, and give occasion to the enemy to blaspheme; but the malice of the wicked is seen in that they gladly lay hold of these as a plea for gratifying the feeling of aversion they cherish towards the religion we profess.

III. THEY ARE ESPECIALLY DEVELOPED IN THE DAY OF ADVERSITY. The slumbering aversion of Shimei found expression in form of outrageous insult when David's fortunes began to wane. Malice is associated with cowardice, and it is only when fear of punishment passes away that the malice puts forth its vigour. Malice is cruel, and therefore it adds wound to wound. The history of Christian persecution illustrates this. The very sorrows which ordinarily would draw forth sympathy only induce the feeling expressed in "There is no help for him in God." The natural tendency of the multitude to adhere to the prosperous and stand aloof from the failing cause, becomes intensified into active opposition when a lurking aversion to the individual and his cause has been cherished (Ps. xxxv. 15; xlix. 18). Even the patience and sorrow displayed in the season of providential trial are turned against the sufferer by the keenness of an evil ingenuity. So much freedom does the evil spirit find in the day of calamity that the whole life is charged with the faults that belong only to a portion of it. No consideration is given to repentance and amendment. To crush and ruin are the sole aim of the reproach.

IV. THEY ARE CHARACTERIZED BY THE DARING ENCOURAGED BY A SENSE OF SECURITY. Shimei knew his victim well enough to believe that he would not have the heart to allow the sword to smite him down; for all the antecedents of David's life were in the direction of leniency and gentleness towards those who sought his hurt, though he spared not the man who sought or professed to take away the life of Saul. He was shrewd enough to notice that the grief of the king was so intense, as barefooted and in silence he passed out of the city, as not to allow of his finding room for thoughts of vengeance, and thus, being secure, the reproaches poured forth. The same conclusion was arrived at by the vindictive Pharisees, who loaded the Saviour with reproach. They knew, from all they had seen and heard, that he would not use force against them, and would not avail himself of the Roman authority in self-defence, and hence, secure in these directions, they were very daring, and spared not words and deeds to crush still further the spirit of the illustrious Man of sorrows. In daily life young Christians are often loaded with reproaches by wicked young men, with a boldness that gains strength from the fact that there is no one present to rebuke them, and that the assailed youth is prohibited by the principles he professes from using reproach and violence in return (Matt. v. 39, 43, 44).

GENERAL LESSONS. 1. In the providential discipline of life, we may look for a combination of sorrows from independent sources, but yet all subservient to good for the children of God. 2. We should be so careful of our life every day that we give no apparent occasion for any one to bring charges against us when the failure of our earthly prosperity arouses attention. 3. The freedom exercised by wicked men in pouring forth their hatred against the good is of short duration, and cannot really hurt those who bear their reproaches in a right spirit. 4. We ought to discount largely the accusations brought against good men by those whose life and conduct reveal an absence of sympathy with the kingdom of God.

The waves and billows of God. The events narrated in vers. 5—13 have an aspect towards man and towards God. The scene of a rejected monarch leaving his seat of government, and, while so doing, assailed by an enemy, is a vicissitude in human affairs which, though special in its colouring, is frequent in the annals of the world. It is a case of human ingratitude and violence on the one side, and human suffering on the other. But to the mind of David the sufferer, and to the sacred historian, the vicissitude is seen to stand in direct relation to the government of God, and is invested with its deepest interest in that aspect. The expression of the psalmist here finds exemplification: "All thy waves and thy billows are gone over me" (Ps. xlii. 7). The troubles are earthly; they roll on according to fixed laws, and are raised by agencies that seem to act by virtue of their own nature; and yet they are God's. The Hebrew discernment of the Divine element in the bitterest trials is clear and sure. We learn here the following truths.

I. THERE ARE GRADATIONS OF TROUBLE IN THE EXPERIENCE OF THE GODLY. There are distinct troubles in David's experience as here described, and they are graduated in weight. It was something to leave the city and worship he loved; it was more to break up a home; it was worse to lose regal authority; it was worse still to pass out in sight of the thousands of Israel, poor and powerless; it was a greater wave to have to listen to the reproaches and cursings of the wicked; but the greatest billow of all was the knowledge that his now eldest son, his former pride and delight, was in rebellion against him, and was seeking his life (ver. 11). Fathers, kind and loving, only can estimate the greatness of this swelling billow. Compared with this, all else in form of loss of property and home and friends, must be expressed by the inferior term "waves." And, as we shall see, the magnitude of this is the greater still, because perceived to be in some sort the consequent of the former errors of the sufferer. There are many tribulations for the righteous, in many instances arising out of their own conduct, and it may seem a truism to say that some are greater than others; but the fact deserves noting, inasmuch as material and social troubles, which to an observer seem to press most heavily, are often slight compared with others that enter more into the depths of the soul.

II. The real gradation of trouble is often not discernible by any but the sufferer. To Joab and men of his character it would seem to be the climax of all calamity that a "dead dog" should curse and throw stones at a king. It was a climax in the sense of coming upon other calamities, but only David could perceive its relative weight in the storm then passing over him. His fatherly heart alone could feel the full crushing force of the son's ingratitude and cruelty. He alone could discern with agonizing feeling the relation between his own sin and this dire evil. He only knew the rebound in this dreadful form of the recent alienation of his own heart from purity and God. We often spend our pity on suffering men and women when visible disasters fall, and perhaps fix on some loss of property, or health, or children, or some terrible blasting of a life's hopes, as the item most oppressive to the smitten one. Possibly, in the unrevealed record of their own personal experience in relation to God, there is a fact which does more to bow down the spirit than all else beside. The heart of each man knoweth its own bitterness. There are secrets never to be unravelled here below, or, if made known in words, fully realized in their sorrow-causing power only by those whose past experience is bound up with their existence.

III. They are associated in the mind of the sufferer with a sense of personal demerit. The connection of the events of this period of David's life with his past life was not simply discerned to be organic, but in that discernment there was a distinct recognition of his own unworthiness in the sight of God, yea, of his richly deserving these troubles of varying gravity. Probably not one man in that strange procession, except Nathan, divined the real thoughts and feelings of David. The curses of Shimei were as the echo of his own conscience on that dark and dreadful day when love to God yielded to unchastity and design to slay. The horrible sin came forth, and, though truly forgiven, was now "ever before" him (Ps. li. 3). No curses of the wicked were too bad for him! No rebellion of cherished son was too severe a chastisement for him! The "waves and billows" rolled on. Were they not fitly framed to swallow up one so self-condemned, so unworthy of pity? Yes; here lies the meaning of those bared feet, that bowed head, that silence under the curse, that moral inability to raise a finger to stay the swelling flood of troubles. Nor are we to wonder that this should be so in the case of a forgiven and restored soul (ch. xii. 13); for the more pure the heart of the restored one, the more blessed the sense of actual forgiveness, the keener will be the feeing of demerit when the old sin is brought to the memory by calamitous events which it set in train. It takes a very holy nature to appreciate properly what sin really is. In the instance of all who experience the "waves and billows" of God, there is, with a clearness more or less full, an association of the trouble with their own past demerit. Whether they can, as David did, actually trace the lines, they know that all trouble is in some way connected with the presence of sin in the world, and that their own past relation to God was at one time such that no earthly disaster could be too great as a chastisement. Irreligious men don't know what this is; but it is a real fact in Christian life. "I am not worthy of the least of thy mercies;" "It is of the Lord's mercies that we are not consumed" (Gen. xxxii. 10; Lam. iii. 22).

IV. There is a distinct recognition of the will of God in them. There is an instructive difference in the conduct of Abishai and David. The man of the world saw the passion and heard the voice of Shimei, and his anger was roused accordingly; the sorrowing man of God saw only the will of God. He seemed deaf to the torrent of curses; with head bowed to the earth, he saw not the man, and the thud of the stones made no impression. "The Lord hath said unto him, Curse David." Yes; it was the Lord. The words of the prophet were true (ch. xii. 10—14). Spiritual perception is spontaneous, and, to the godly man, infallible. It passes by the visible to the invisible. Second causes are lost in the efficient Cause. Speculative questions as to human freedom and consecution of events are left behind. The solution of the actual experience in the passing events is found. It is God. This is the significance of all to David. The "waves and billows" are *his*. They roll to do his will. The force of almightiness is in them. This spiritual discernment plays an important part in the lives of all true Christians. It is not ignorance, it is not a disregard of philosophy on their part, it is not a violation of the sequences of scientific law, when, with an intuition clear and irresistible, they see God in the troubles that fall upon themselves. For spiritual intuition is a higher faculty than logical judgment, and relates to a sphere above all physical sequences. There is no more possibility of men setting this aside by reasonings and discussions concerning physical laws, than the perception of an external world by vision can be set aside by the proof of the existence of a physiological structure of the eye. If commercial disaster falls, if health fails, if friends die, if children become rebellious, if the seeds of former sins bear their bitter fruit,—in all God is seen. Nothing comes in form of trouble to his children but that he has a will in it. There may be a human, even physical side, but the child will discern the Father's will (Heb. xii. 5—10).

V. THE SENSE OF PERSONAL DEMERIT AND DISCERNMENT OF THE WILL OF GOD TONE DOWN THE HARDER TENDENCIES OF HUMAN NATURE. Abishai was true to his nature in wishing to cut off the head of the "dead dog;" and David was true to the chastening effect on his nature of these terrible trials when he resisted the suggestion (ver. 10). The heart becomes tender and gentle when under the chastening hand of God, provided, as in David's case, there is a due discernment of personal unworthiness, and of the gracious though just purpose of God in the trouble. We are reminded of One who also endured the contradiction of sinners against himself; who when reviled, reviled not again, and even when bearing more than David could here was pitiful and kind to his foes (Heb. xii. 2, 3; 1 Pet. ii. 23; Luke xxiii. 34). It is the mark of a true endurance of the righteous will of God, and conformity of self to the scope of the Divine purpose, that there is in time of trouble no fretting and chafing against the instruments which he may use, be they men or things. Who can curse when the holy will is doing its work? Who can be in wrath and find time for antagonisms when the soul is absorbed in contrite recognition of sin and humble prostration before a storm designed to purify the heart? What gratitude is due to God for the softening influences of calamity! How much richer in meekness and gentleness and the milder and more Christly virtues are many for the poverty and pain they have experienced! The sons of Zeruiah, still so strong and fierce in the world, little know the blessedness of being like unto him who was "meek and lowly in heart."

VI. WITH SILENT HOMAGE TO THE MAJESTY OF GOD THERE IS BLENDED TRUST IN HIS MERCY. David was not playing a part before the eye of man. There was nothing histrionic in his conduct. The profound homage to the Holy One which underlay his confession before Nathan, "I have sinned" (ch. xii. 13), was now again rendered in the secrecy of his own soul. The head bowed in submission to the fierceness of the storm indicated an acknowledgment of the righteousness of God. Much rather would the humbled king have been free from the necessity of speaking with the "sons of Zeruiah," and have borne the terrible storm without a thought of protest or feeling of complaint. It is in the most critical moments of life that the soul shrinks from the outward strife of tongues, and in the solemn silence of its own thoughts renders to God a sinful creature's homage. But with this utter surrender to the rights and punitive appointments of the Eternal there is blended a quiet, modest trust in his great mercy. "It may be that the Lord will look on mine affliction" (ver. 12). "It may be." Note the content of the words: "He is merciful and gracious. It is inherent in the nature of the Author of the covenant with Israel to be so. The words of the past are evidence of this. I am undone and have no claim; all that comes to crush me comes justly; what he does he does for his Name's sake. Other poor sinners have waited not in vain; the hour may come when he will see his glory to be one with my deliverance, and then the storm will cease. 'He will requite me.' Mercy will find a way of enriching my poor troubled soul out of the very ills which so justly have come upon me." The true heart in its deepest sorrows never loses faith in God's goodness and care. It holds to the possibility of a turn in the tide. It rests not on its merits, not on speculations upon what is unknown, but upon the assured character of God as revealed in Christ. It assumes and presumes nothing, but leaves all with him, and so finds comfort in the hope that through his free unmerited grace all things shall be found to work together for good (Rom. viii. 28).

GENERAL LESSONS. 1. It is an illustration of the dreadful nature of sin that it deposits seeds of trouble which may be inactive during a season of prosperity, but which put forth their strength when adversity falls upon us (vers. 5, 6). 2. The children of God may do well to remember that there are watchful foes, human and Satanic, ready to take advantage of any circumstance that may bring reproach on them as servants of the living God (vers. 5, 6). 3. Our faithful attachment to those bearing sorrow because of their shortcomings is a duty, when they bear it in a submissive spirit, even though it cause us to be sharers in their sufferings (vers. 6, 13, 14). 4. In seeking to alleviate the sufferings of the oppressed, we should abstain from vindictive passions (ver. 10). 5. The most tender consideration and sympathy should be extended towards those whose hearts are crushed by the ingratitude and cruelty of their own children (ver. 11). 6. The most effective way of ministering to those whose spirits are broken down by providential chastisements is to foster in their hearts simple trust in God's great mercy (ver. 12). We obtain evidence of our being true children of God when, in the time of our calamity and amidst persecutions, we are followers to those who, when "reviled, reviled not again" (ver. 11; cf. 1 Pet. ii. 23).

Vers. 15—23.—*Illustrations of facts and principles.* The facts are: 1. Absalom enters Jerusalem with his adherents and Ahithophel. 2. Hushai presents himself before Absalom, with a salutation in ambiguous language. 3. On Absalom expressing surprise that he had not gone with David, he, with studied caution, expresses his readiness to serve whom the Lord and all the men of Israel might choose, and further declares his intention to "serve" in the son's presence as he had in the father's. 4. Absalom, seeking counsel, is advised by Ahithophel to strengthen his position by taking possession of his father's concubines. 5. Whereupon Absalom, in the view of the people, conforms to the advice. 6. Ahithophel is represented as a man whose reputation as a counsellor was of the highest character. The historian passes from the sorrows of David to the aspirations and first measures of Absalom, and reveals another line of providential events apparently working in another direction, and yet, in the light of Nathan's words (ch. xii. 7—12), clearly tending to the realization of one purpose. It is only the religious man that can discern the mind of God in occurrences utterly dissimilar in their bearing. The good are crushed and the vile are exalted, but the crushing and the elevation are but products of free human instrumentality, taken hold of by an unseen Power, to bring about the ends of a righteous administration of justice. In the opening accounts of Absalom's entrance on political power we have instructive illustrations of facts and principles.

I. DEFERENCE WON BY AGE AND CHARACTER. The rash and reckless Absalom treats the aged Hushai with unwonted respect, even while regarding him as a "friend" of David (vers. 16, 17). The violence usually accompanying a bold revolt was evidently restrained by the will of God acting through the natural influence of years combined with reputation for moral worth. Occasionally wicked men have been heedless of infancy and age, and the better the men associated with their opponents, the more readily have they cut them off. But as a rule it is not so. History records cases of the kind here narrated. The reason is plain: sin is ashamed in presence of goodness, and the sinner's arm is weak to smite down what is its own condemnation. Conscience revives and restrains action in the presence of goodness; and the heart must be brutal beyond all relief if hoary hairs do not touch it. They speak of the coming grave, and the voice is not in vain. *Integer vitæ scelerisque purus,* man wields a silent power, not only over the fabled wolf, but over wolf-like men (Horace, I. ode xxii.).

II. THE PART OF SAGACIOUS MEN IN HUMAN AFFAIRS. Hushai and Ahithophel differed much in moral character, but they were similar in their position as advisers in the affairs of state. Their acts show them to have been men of sagacious mind, able to apply the results of extended observation and insight into character to the changing circumstances of the day. As a matter of fact, they played the most important part, by means of their sagacity, in the events of this part of David's life; and their action suggests to us how much of human life in its social and political relations is connected with the thoughts and plans of men of this class. As in a ship a few really control the fate of the many, so in nations a few regulate affairs that involve the weal or woe of millions. No system of government can avoid this fact. Mental power is supreme in the state. Moral influences from the mass may set limits to its action, and open lines along which it must work, but its mighty force is manifest. It is a case of mind rising above mind. Hence the need of prayer that our mentally gifted men may be good men. Hence, also, their solemn responsibilities before God.

III. The responsibility of a post of extreme delicacy and danger. Hushai was just now entering on his perilous duties as friend of David in the court of Absalom, and the utmost care was requisite that he might both save his own head and serve his beloved king. Had he not been sustained by the confidence that God would bring to nought the devices of the wicked, he must have often been overwhelmed by the pressure of his responsibilities. There are analogous positions still in life. Diplomacy knows them; commerce is not a stranger to them; the Church furnishes them; benevolent men have often to work in secrecy, though not by deceit; peacemakers find that they may mar their work for lack of discretion, and run the risk of losing reputation with one or both parties. In all such instances the consciousness of being in the right, that wit and wisdom are devoted to unselfish ends, and that God may be asked to give his help, will sustain the heart, give penetration to moral perceptions, and ensure self-possession. All honour to the men who for a good cause assume such responsibilities!

IV. The coexistence with evil of neutralizing forces. Ahithophel had a great reputation, and devoted the force of his sagacity to the evil cause of a rebel. The forces of evil at work against David were strong, and, to ordinary men in Israel, invincible. Yet we who know more than Absalom and his friends then knew, can see that all this time there were, coexisting with and working secretly and silently against all the forces of evil, other forces which could not but tend to neutralize their action. In this we have on a small scale an illustration of the fact that, though there are in the world many pronounced forms of evil at work against the good of man and the rightful authority of Christ over mankind, there is also a silent, and in its operation a secret, force at work, through the agency of the faithful few, which all the time tends to check the evil, and must in the end overcome it. It has been so from the day when the Seed of the woman was promised to bruise the serpent's head. This fact should inspire the hearts of the faithful in every land in spite of outward appearances.

V. The city of God is sometimes the scene of contending powers. The holy city, the joy of the whole earth, the chosen abode of the Eternal, and the natural abode of peace, was now the scene of a strife between adverse powers of good and evil. The happy days when the people sang for joy and felt secure in the presence of the symbol of the Divine favour (ch. vi. 12—19) were no more. As in some great historic wars the conflict becomes concentrated on the seat of government and influence, so now the great question which involved the welfare of Israel and the Gentiles was being fought out in Jerusalem. Here we certainly find an analogue to times of trouble when the city of God—the Jerusalem of the Christian dispensation—has been the scene of conflict between the powers that would get rid of the Divine authority and set up an order of things not of God. Men have contended within the Church to rob Christ of his Divine rights, and the faithful few have striven to render service for him according to the measure of their wisdom and goodness. The apostles seem to have anticipated such seasons (2 Pet. ii. 1, 2). As this trouble in Jerusalem was connected with the failings of David as well as the vices of Absalom, so the contentions and sorrows that have been experienced in the Church have not been unconnected with the shortcomings of the elect of God.

VI. Ambiguous fidelity is a purely human expedient. The words of Hushai to Absalom were understood by the latter to be the expression of his loyalty to himself; and, on the surface of them, the words doubtless had that meaning. But as a matter of fact, Hushai's heart was with David, and his language was capable of being interpreted in accordance with his true feelings. It is a question of casuistry as to whether, under the circumstances, he was warranted in devising means for deluding Absalom. The Bible does not commit itself to all the acts of its characters; and in our judgment on men we ought to have some regard to the moral atmosphere of their daily lives. But in this ambiguous expression of fidelity we have an instance of what largely prevails in the world. Men still coin phrases to afford satisfaction to others while keeping peace with their own convictions. Forms are adopted which are unimpeachable; but the real feeling is kept secret. In some countries there are current forms for expressing loyalty to the " powers that be," freely employed to the satisfaction of rulers and the safety of those who use them. Attachment to certain political principles is announced while the particular application of them is a matter of private reservation. In commercial houses a form of loyalty to employers' interests often passes with a purpose to sacrifice them to a rival interest. In Church affairs it is possible to accept standards in form and empty them of essential content. The practice is to be condemned in every case. Strong faith in God can dispense with such expedients. He who was chastising David through Absalom knew how to restore the chastened one in due time, without the expedients of human duplicity. The example of Christ and his apostles is better than that of Abraham, Jacob, and Hushai (cf. Gen. xii. 13—20; xxvii. 20—27; John xviii. 33—37; Acts iv. 7—12).

VII. GREAT PRINCIPLES ARE LIABLE TO ABUSE. Hushai evidently laid down a great and sound principle as the rule of his conduct when he declared that, as for himself, he was prepared to serve him whom the " Lord, and this people, and all the men of Israel " might choose. Had Absalom been as keen as he was ambitious, he would have seen that this was a principle which so far could not ensure attachments to himself, because two of the conditions were not fulfilled at present. No doubt he hoped that, in some strange way, his choice by " this people " would be supplemented by the choice of God and all Israel. There was here an abuse of a principle, commonly recognized in those times, by both Hushai and Absalom. Hushai took it as a mere cover for saving his conscience, while getting Absalom to believe in his fidelity. The same twofold object was sought by the following question and the very safe assertion, " As when (כַּאֲשֶׁר) I served in thy father's presence, so will I be (כֵּן אֶהְיֶה) in thy presence." He would be the same man while professing to serve Absalom. On the other hand, Absalom evidently thought the principle laid down very pious and patriotic, and to be respected because it was a principle, and in his superstitious and superficial deference to an orthodox utterance, he detected not the purpose for which it was stated. In the one case a principle was subordinated to cunning in a good cause; and in the other it was simply admired as a platitude by a bad man. The trade in important principles of action is very common. They are made to subserve ends by no means good. Advantage is taken of their natural influence over men, by reason of their clearness and moral force, to hoodwink them for carrying out special designs. Platform and press too frequently have dealt with great truths for no special love of the truths, but for party purposes, and to save credit for intelligence and good sense. Also there is a superstitious regard for a certain class of religious, moral, and political principles which causes many persons to think well of those who proclaim them, simply because of proclaiming them. This unreality in both public and private life should be discountenanced.

VIII. GREAT POWERS CONCENTRATE AGAINST THE LORD'S ANOINTED. The followers of Absalom, under the guidance of Ahithophel, confer with him as to the best course to pursue in order to effectually establish the position of the usurper, and cut off the fugitive king. In a measure, the second psalm is now fulfilled, substituting "counsellors" for " kings " (Ps. ii. 2). The fact that David had been anointed by God must have been familiar to them all. This evidence of his right to reign was clear enough, and no counter-deposition had come from God; and yet such is the blindness and desperate nature of men when alienated from God, that they meditate the destruction of a rule guaranteed from on high. Sin is madness as well as vileness. Our Saviour reminds his disciples that the same combination will take place against his authority (Ps. ii.; Matt. xvi. 18). The conspiracy was formed when keen and crafty men sought his death (Matt. xii. 14; xxvii. 7; John xviii. 14); it was revived when they sought to crush his disciples (Acts v. 33); and it is in force now when men presume to dispense with his teaching and saving power. It is the old antagonism of the serpent and the Seed. Let every Christian brace himself to the conflict.

IX. THERE IS AN UNCONSCIOUS FULFILMENT OF PROPHECY. It is not likely that either Nathan or David proclaimed to the world the terrible prediction that was to be fulfilled within a few years (ch. xii. 7—12). Ahithophel was, therefore, an unconscious instrument in fulfilling the Word of God when he gave the desperate advice to Absalom (vers. 21, 22). It is thus that, in the perfectly free action of men, God's purposes are realized. He chastises his children by using men who at the same time are unconscious of being so used. This wonderful foreknowledge of what free men will do, and the execution of moral ends by the action of responsible agents, is possible alone to the Infinite One. There is involved in it a mystery before which we do well to bow with all humility. Men little think how their very deeds of evil are being worked into the warp and woof of the world's life, so as at last to bring out to view the wisdom and righteousness of God.

X. PUBLIC MEN HAVE IT IN THEIR POWER TO DEBASE PUBLIC MORALS. By the counsel given to Absalom, Ahithophel no doubt widened the breach between father and son beyond the point of reconciliation, and by a bold stroke inspired confidence in the minds of waverers; but he did it at the cost of public morality. The tone of public life was lowered. Vice became familiar. A blow was struck in an ostentatious way at purity of thought and feeling. A voluptuous throne meant a sensual people. There is always a temptation to public men to strike for power by deeds of doubtful and sometimes immoral character. Political ends may be secured at the cost of loss of moral tone to the community. Those who do this may be great and wise in the eye of the world, but they are the real enemies of the people, and deserve, as they will experience, the retribution of God.

XI. REPUTATIONS GREAT IN THE WORLD ARE NOT, THEREFORE, GREAT WITH GOD. Ahithophel was a man in great repute as a counsellor (ver. 23), but he was not in honour with God. The clever head was associated with a base and treacherous heart. The standard of distinction on earth is not the same as that in heaven. Intellectual powers are often grand in their range, but the excellence of the man lies in the subordination of them to high and holy moral principles. The greater the abilities, the greater the sin of not using them for God and his kingdom. There are many "first" in this life who will some day be "last" (Matt. xix. 30). The worship of intellect is one of the banes of modern times. Conformity to the sermon on the mount is more honourable than cleverness in human affairs.

GENERAL LESSONS. 1. It is a safe rule of life to commit ourselves to an undertaking only on the condition that God approves as well as "all the men." 2. It is of immense advantage in times of perplexity to have in the mind a few clear and well-defined principles of conduct to which we may refer for guidance. 3. It is legitimate to bring the force of first principles to bear on those who are bent on evil ways, though it is not right to use them as a cloak for double-facedness. 4. In the midst of contending claims on our allegiance, we should give due force to the inquiry as to whom we are under the most binding obligations to serve, and it will be seen that Christ has the prior claim.

HOMILIES BY VARIOUS AUTHORS.

Vers. 1—4.—(OLIVET.) *The benefaction of Ziba.* (*References* : ch. ix. 3, 9—13; xix. 24—30.) David had taken his last look at Jerusalem, and was "a little past the top" of Mount Olivet in his descent on the other side, when he was met by Ziba, the servant of Mephibosheth, with an apparently thoughtful and generous present. This man was originally a slave of the house of Saul; became a freed-man at its downfall; made his fortune out of its ruins; and had fifteen sons and twenty slaves. About seventeen years before, when inquiry was made for "any of the house of Saul," he gave information concerning the son of Jonathan. By the restoration of Mephibosheth to his patrimony, Ziba was reduced to his former status, and thenceforward cultivated the land for his master. And now, foreseeing the issue of the conflict, he sought to ingratiate himself with the king, regain his position, and obtain his master's estate. Such appears to be the key to his conduct. We have here an illustration of a benefaction: 1. Occurring at a *seasonable moment;* when most needed and least expected; valuable in itself, and still more for the faithfulness and kindness it seemed to manifest. A man of David's generosity could not but be greatly affected by it. But an admirable gift does not always express a commendable purpose (Deut. xvi. 19; Eccles. vii. 7). "Whatever Ziba intended in this present, God's providence sent it to David for his support" (Matthew Henry). 2. Proceeding from *unworthy motives:* selfishness, covetousness, cunning craftiness (ch. i. 2—10), hidden under an ostentatious display of loyalty, sympathy, and benevolence. Ziba was well acquainted with the character of David, and shrewdly calculated upon the means of improving his present necessities to secure his own advantage. Impure motives often lurk, sometimes unconsciously, beneath imposing benefactions. 3. Conferred at *another's expense;* and by the employment of deceit, treachery, and robbery. "The whole, though offered as Ziba's, is the property of Mephibosheth: the asses are his, one of them his own riding animal: the fruits are from his gardens and orchards" (Smith, 'Dictionary'). Poor Mephibosheth! He was at this moment waiting for the return of his faithless and pitiless slave with the ass, to enable him to follow the king. His own account of his absence was consistent with his actions (ch. xix. 24); and the treachery of Ziba could not be denied. "Treacherous servants are a curse to their masters." It is no uncommon thing for one man to seek the credit which is due to another, and obtain it by deceiving, disappointing, and injuring him. 4. Accompanied with a *false accusation.* "And Ziba said," etc. (ver. 3). It was not improbable that the adherents of the fallen dynasty might seize the opportunity to attempt its restoration (ver. 5; ch. xx. 1); and already, perhaps, David entertained some suspicion of the loyalty of Mephibosheth. Hence Ziba might calculate on finding a ready hearing for his calumny. But "every tie, both of interest and gratitude, combined to keep Mephibosheth faithful to David's cause." Innocent men are often suspected and accused groundlessly. "When much treachery and ingratitude have been experienced, men are apt to become too suspicious, and to listen to every plausible tale of calumny" (Scott). "I cannot but pity the condition of this good son of Jonathan; into ill hands did honest Mephibosheth fall, first of a careless nurse, then of a treacherous servant; she maimed his body, he would have overthrown his estate" (Hall). "A false witness will utter lies" (Prov. xiv. 5). 5. Receiving an *undeserved recompense.* "Behold, thine is all that belonged to Mephibosheth" (ver. 4). "David, in the excitement of a momentary misfortune, is here guilty of a double wrong—first in treating the faithful Mephibosheth as a traitor, and then in royally rewarding the false and slanderous Ziba" (Erdmann). "Hearsay is no safe ground of any judgment. Ziba slanders, David believes, and Mephibosheth suffers" (Hall). 6. Followed by *flattering servility.* "I humbly beseech thee," etc. "He pretends to value the king's favour more than the gift he had bestowed" (Patrick). 7. Revealed at length in its *true character* (ch. xix. 27), as a selfish, deceitful, and base procedure; though even then the wrong done to the master is not fully repaired, nor the wickedness of the servant adequately punished.

APPLICATION. 1. Look beneath the outward appearance (John vii. 24). 2. Guard against plausible detractors. 3. Avoid hasty judgments (Ps. cxvi. 11; Prov. xiv. 15); and hear the other side. 4. Wait for the revelation of the righteous judgment of God.—D.

Vers. 5—13.—(BAHURIM.) *The reviling of Shimei.* (*References:* ch. xix. 16; 1 Kings ii. 8, 9, 36—46.) On pursuing his flight until he reached the Benjamite village of Bahurim (ch. iii. 6), David was encountered by another man connected with the house of Saul, who, instead of bringing flatteries and presents, flung "grievous curses" and stones; and (from a safe distance) gave vent to the long-repressed rage which, in common with other partisans of the fallen dynasty, he felt on account of David's exaltation (ver. 8). "Along the ridge he ran, throwing stones, as if for the adulterer's punishment, or when he came to a patch of dust on the dried hillside, taking up and scattering it over the royal party below, with the elaborate curses of which only Eastern partisans are fully masters—curses which David never forgot, and of which, according to Jewish tradition, every letter was significant" (Stanley). Abishai returned reviling for reviling, and wished to take instant vengeance. But David said, "Let him a one," etc.; presenting an instructive contrast to both. "He strikes the same string of nobleness as before." We have here—

I. AN INSTANCE OF RAILING ACCUSATION. "Out, out [of the kingdom], thou man of blood," etc.! The language and conduct of Shimei were: 1. *Cruel.* He rails against David in the day of his calamity, and has "no pity." 2. *Cowardly.* Fear had kept him silent all these years; but "he that smiled on David on his throne curseth him in his flight" (Hall). Seeing that he is not pursued, he is encouraged to continue his imprecations, and becomes more furious (ver. 13). 3. *Malicious;* imbued with personal hatred. "The ungodly are always selfish. They judge of others, not by the laws of impartial justice, but by the standard of self-interest. David was called a usurper, a man of Belial, a murderer; and why? Because he had made himself the slave of lust, and had cruelly slain the noble Uriah? No; because he had been elevated by God to the throne of Israel, and had thus marred the prospects of the ambitious Shimei" (C. Bradley). 4. *Unfounded* and unjust. "Every word of Shimei was a slander." His accusations of wickedness in general, and of "the blood of the house of Saul" in particular (ch. iv. 11; xxi. 6), are the offspring of a wicked heart. "Shimei curses and stones at David, and barks like a live dog, though Abishai calls him a dead one. The only unjust act that ever David had done against the house of Saul he had newly done; that was, giving Mephibosheth's land; and here a man of the house of Saul is soon upon him" (Lightfoot). 5. *Misinterpretive.* (Ver. 8.) Whilst recognizing the judgment of God, he makes a wrong application of it. "We may here learn how falsely and wickedly men sometimes wrest the providence of God, to justify their unjust surmises and gratify their malignant passions" (Lindsay). 6. *Criminal.* He is guilty of high treason and blasphemy, and might justly suffer the penalty of the Law (Exod. xxii. 28; ch. xix. 21; 1 Kings xxi. 13); and if David had put him to death at the time, he would not have been condemned for injustice. 7. *Provocative* of wrath. Surely no man might more reasonably feel resentment than David; no man was ever more strongly incited to inflict punishment; and nothing but "a spirit of meekness" could have restrained him. It is not improbable that Ps. cix. records "the very words of Shimei, and the curses which he threw out against David, and which, as they could not but make a deep impression on his memory, he here repeats and then condemns. They are directly contrary to that temper and disposition shown by David in the other parts of the psalm; and they run all along in the singular number, whereas David speaks of his enemies in the plural" (C. Peters, 'Sermons:' 1776; see 1 Sam. xxii. 18, 19; xxvi. 13—25; *Expositor*, ii. 325).

> "O God of my praise, be not silent!
> For a wicked mouth and a deceitful mouth have they opened against me;
> They have spoken against me with a lying tongue," etc.
>
> (Ps. cix. 1—5.)

> "And they have requited me with evil for good,
> And with hatred for my love (saying):
> Set thou a wicked man over him,
> And let an adversary stand at his right hand;
> When he is judged, let him go forth guilty,
> And let his prayer become sin," etc.
>
> (Ps. cix. 6—19.)

> "This will be the reward of mine adversaries from Jehovah,
> And of those who speak evil against my soul.
> But thou, O Jehovah Lord, deal with me for thy Name's sake;
> Because thy loving-kindness is good, deliver thou me!
> They curse, but thou blessest;
> They arise and are ashamed, and thy servant is glad," etc.
>
> (Ps. cix. 20—31.)

II. AN EXAMPLE OF PATIENCE AND FORBEARANCE. "Let him curse," etc. (vers. 10—12). The manner in which David endured it was: 1. *Uncomplaining.* He does not retaliate; does not even vindicate himself; but is *silent* (1 Sam. x. 26, 27; Isa. liii.

5; Luke xxiii. 9). "When Shimei railed on him, he held his peace, and, though he had many armed men about him, yet did he not retort aught savouring of revenge, yea, repelled with the high courage of a patient spirit the instigation of the son of Gera. He went, therefore, as one dumb and humbled to the dust; he went as one mute and not moved at all. . . . Consider not what is rendered by others, keep thou thy place, preserve thou the simplicity and purity of thine own heart. Answer thou not the angry man according to his anger, nor the unwise man according to his indiscretion; one fault quickly provoketh another. If thou strikest two flints together, doth not fire break forth?" (Ambrose, 'De Officiis'). 2. *Repressive* of resentment, not only in himself, but also in others. "Answer him not" (Isa. xxxvi. 21; xxxvii. 3, 4). 3. *Self-accusing.* Although guiltless of the crimes imputed to him, he feels himself guilty of others not less heinous. "Conscience in that hour had her own tale to tell, of the Almighty Disposer of events, who speaks to us by the reproaches of men as well as by his own blessings. Had he not merited from God, if not from men, whatever disaster could befall the murderer of Uriah? David feels within him that destitution of the Divine presence of which the absence of the ark is but an outward type" (R. Williams).

> "Pure from the blood of Saul in vain,
> He dares not to the charge reply;
> Uriah's doth the charge maintain,
> Uriah's doth against him cry.
> Let Shimei curse: the rod he bears
> For sins which mercy had forgiven;
> And in the wrongs of men reveres
> The awful righteousness of Heaven."
>
> (C. Wesley.)

4. *Reverential;* looking devoutly (as others did not) beyond Shimei to the All-seeing, All-holy, and Almighty One, by whom he was permitted to be an instrument of retribution, and even employed as such, although not thereby exonerated from guilt (ch. xix. 18—20). "Abishai looked only to the stone (as it were), an instrument; but David looked higher, to the hand that was the supreme caster, and chastiser of him, as all the godly do (Gen. l. 20; Job i. 21); which is the ground of their patience under sufferings" (Guild). His vision of the supreme Judge fills him with holy awe and lowly penitence; his conscious offences against God make him reluctant to punish offences against himself; his dependence upon mercy disposes him to show mercy (Matt. v. 44; vi. 14, 15; Rom. xii. 19—21). 5. *Submissive;* humbly accepting the chastisement of God; and deeming this to be his proper business now, rather than seeking to execute justice on another (Micah vii. 9). "Behold, here am I, let him do to me as seemeth good to him" (ch. xv. 26). "The ways of Providence interlace, not only in capacity, but in retribution; one thing is set over against another. Yet the payment comes, not in the manner nor at the time we might expect, it seems not in the connection we think due; but it comes, like doom. Call Absalom thankless, Shimei brutal, etc. All these things read half a riddle, unless we own that God, in whose counsels these are all as instruments in the hand of a man of war, is just. He gave us wine, let us take also the gall from his hands. If it is not due to us now, nor for this, it was for something else at some other time." 6. *Palliative.* "Behold, my son seeketh my life," etc. (ver. 11). He makes light of present wrongs by comparing them with other and greater. "It is the advantage of great crosses that they swallow up the less." 7. *Hopeful.* "It may be that Jehovah will look upon my guilt [tears]," etc. (ver. 12). "This consciousness of guilt also excited the assurance that the Lord would look upon his sin. When God looks upon the guilt of a humble sinner he will also, as a just and merciful God, avert the evil and change the suffering into a blessing. David founded upon this the hope that the Lord would repay him with good for the curses with which Shimei pursued him" (Keil). "Ziba's gifts did more harm than Shimei's curses; for those betrayed him into an act of injustice, but these proved his patience" (T. Fuller). They also had the effect of making him more humble, pure, prayerful, and filling him with new confidence and joy in God (Ps. cix. 30, 31). "A curse is like a cloud, it passes." "All things work together for good," etc.

> " Lord, I adore thy righteous will ;
> Through every instrument of ill
> My Father's goodness see ;
> Accept the complicated wrong
> Of Shimei's hand and Shimei's tongue
> As kind rebukes from thee."

(C. Wesley.)

REMARKS. 1. The best of men have been maligned ; of the Son of God himself it was said, " He hath a devil." Can we expect to escape insult and provocation ? 2. The maledictions of the wicked can do us no harm unless we suffer ourselves to imbibe their spirit. "No man is ever really hurt by any one but himself " (Chrysostom). 3. When reviled of men, instead of considering how little we have deserved their displeasure, we should rather consider how much we have deserved the displeasure of God. 4. We should also consider how little, in comparison with God, do we endure at their hands ! 5. "Bless, and curse not" (Prov. xxv. 21, 22 ; xvi. 32). 6. Imitate "the meekness and gentleness of Christ" (2 Cor. x. 1). 7. So what is meant for evil will turn to good.—D.

Vers. 9, 10.—(BAHURIM.) *The zeal of Abishai.* (*References :* 1 Chron. ii. 6 ; 1 Sam. xvi. 6 ; ch. ii. 18 ; x. 14 ; xxi. 17 ; xxiii. 18 ; 1 Chron. xviii. 12.) Of the three sons of Zeruiah (ch. v. 39), the youngest, Asahel, was slain in early life (ch. ii. 23) ; the oldest, Joab, was now present (ver. 10), " little trusting the revolution which a capricious stripling (like the Stuart Monmouth) was to lead ; " the second, Abishai, was one of the earliest, bravest, and most faithful of David's supporters. As on a former occasion, when he sought to destroy Saul with a stroke, so now his thoughtless, headstrong, and undevout impulses needed to be checked. " The characteristic trait of his nature was a blunt, impetuous ferocity." His passionate emotion was—

I. NATURALLY EXCITED by the conduct of Shimei ; and was, in some respects, commendable ; inasmuch as it showed : 1. An *ardent affection* toward the king, his " lord ; " like that of James and John toward Jesus (Luke ix. 54), and of Peter and the other disciples (Luke xxii. 49 ; Matt. xxvi. 51). The zeal of the Lord's enemies against him calls forth the zeal of his friends on his behalf. 2. A *burning indignation* against wrong-doing. "Ye that love the Lord, hate evil." 3. A *vehement desire* for the triumph of justice. He doubtless felt that the offender deserved to die ; and was eager to " take off his head," in order to the vindication of the royal honour, the maintenance of the Divine Law, and the promotion of the public good. He thus displayed something of the zeal of Phinehas (Numb. xxv. 13 ; Deut. xxxiii. 9) and of Elijah (1 Kings xviii. 40 ; 2 Kings i. 10) ; without, however, being justified therein by the same necessity and authority, or imbued with the same simple, pure, and lofty spirit. It is difficult to indulge in resentment, even when proper to do so, without sin (John ii. 17 ; Eph. iv. 26).

II. WRONGLY INDULGED. " Let me go over," etc. This request was marked by : 1. *Inconsideration* and want of judgment. It is doubtful whether his attempt, if permitted, would have succeeded, for Shimei was hardly likely to be without defenders (ch. xix. 17) ; it could scarcely fail to hinder the king's flight and imperil his safety ; and its success would have effected no useful purpose at such a crisis. Zeal is often blind and misguided (Rom. x. 2 ; Phil. iii. 5 ; Acts xvii. 5) as to the right *end*, the proper *means*, and the suitable *time*. "Zeal without knowledge is as wild-fire in a fool's hand." 2. *Vindictiveness ;* such as frequently mingles with deserved indignation toward evil-doers ; is bitter (Jas. iii. 14) and violent ; and makes him who entertains it partaker of the evil which he condemns. " The wrath of man worketh not the righteousness of God." 3. *Presumption* and vain-glory ; not altogether unlike that of Saul (ch. xxi. 2) and of Jehu (2 Kings x. 16). How often do men feel confident of the rectitude of their course, although acting contrary to the will of God ! and how often, whilst apparently full of zeal for public justice and " the glory of God," are they really full of pride and self-will !

> " True zeal is merciful and mild,
> Can pity and forbear ;
> The false is headstrong, fierce, and wild,
> And breathes revenge and war."

III. Rightly reproved. "What have I to do with you," etc.? The spirit of Abishai and Joab (who, perhaps, joined in the request) was different from that of David; which, in its self-control, patience, and forbearance, displayed the highest heroism, and foreshadowed the meekness of Christ. "True Christian zeal is no other than the flame of love. This is the nature, the inmost essence of it" (Wesley). What is contrary to it should be rebuked by: 1. The indication of the will of God (ver. 10). 2. The exemplification of a spirit of submission (John xviii. 11) and charity. 3. The assurance of the blessing with which it will be followed (ver. 12). "So the travellers went on. The roads diverged. The curses died away. The stones fell short of their aim. The evening closed on that long day of weariness and sorrow—the dreariest day that David had ever known; and he and the partners of his exile rested for the night" (Plumptre).—D.

Vers. 15—19.—(Jerusalem.) *An inconsistent friend.* "Is this thy kindness to thy friend?" (ver. 17; ch. xv. 37). On his unresisted and triumphant entrance into Jerusalem, Absalom was met by Hushai with the exclamation, "Long live the king!" (1 Sam. x. 24). Such a display of loyalty to himself on the part of "David's friend" (companion, favourite) appeared to him so inconsistent that he asked, in ironical astonishment, "Is this," etc.? "One might have said to him, 'Is this thy duty to thy father?'" (Patrick). But Hushai's answer was, in effect, that (being bound to prefer the public good before his own private obligations or affections) he could do no other than abide with him whom Jehovah and the people had chosen king, and would as gladly and faithfully serve the son as he had served the father. Although proceeding from a good motive and serving its special purpose, it was marked by flattery and dissimulation; and these, in common with other sins, are certainly inconsistent with the proper character of a "friend of God" and of Christ (1 Sam. xviii. 4). The question may be regarded (in the latter application) as expressive of—

I. Recognized obligation. (Prov. xviii. 24; Job vi. 14.) "Absalom had not so little sense as not to consider that no man ought to forsake a friend in his distress" If kindness (love, gratitude, faithfulness, useful service) be due to others, how much more to him who said, "I have called you friends" (John xv. 15)! What does his friendship require? To be with him, to follow him, to share his sufferings; to "walk as he walked" (1 John ii. 6), without guile, in truth, purity, self-denial, etc.; to be separate from "the evil that is in the world," to confess his Name before men, to seek his honour, to aid his friends, and to promote the accomplishment of his purposes.

II. Surprising inconsistency; too often observed (1 Sam. xxix. 1—11) in those who are his real or supposed friends: 1. When they exhibit indifference to his transcendent claims. 2. When they refuse to bear "the cross." 3. When they love "the friendship of the world" (Jas. iv. 4). 4. When they solace themselves with his friendship in secret, but shrink from confessing him openly. 5. When they profess that they know him, but "in works deny him." 6. When they employ deception and other "carnal weapons" (2 Cor. x. 4) in his behalf. 7. When they honour success irrespective of the means by which it is attained. 8. When they neglect and despise those whom he loves. 9. When they are zealous for him in some things, but not in others of greater moment. 10. When they are much concerned for their own safety and advantage, and little concerned for his glory and the welfare of mankind. Alas! how often is he "wounded in the house of his friends"!

III. Searching inquiry. Is there not ground for it in the conduct and speech of many? Is the answer which may be given to it satisfactory? Will good intentions and beneficent ends justify unrighteous means (Rom. iii. 8)? Should the answer satisfy others and even ourselves, will it satisfy him "who searcheth the heart"? "Search me, O God," etc. (Ps. cxxxix. 23).

IV. Deserved reproach; which the enemies (and not merely the friends) of Christ are ready to utter, and an enlightened conscience confirms. "As many as I love I rebuke," etc. (Rev. iii. 10). But he rebukes that he may restore. "When thou hast driven him away and lost him, to whom wilt thou then fly? and where wilt thou find a friend? Without a friend, life is unenjoyed; and unless Jesus be thy chosen Friend, infinitely loved and preferred above all others, life will be to thee a scene of desolation and distress. Of all that are dear to thee, then, let Jesus be the peculiar and supreme Object of thy love" (À Kempis, 'Of the Friendship of Jesus').—D.

Vers. 5—13.—*Shimei's curses.* There are peculiar bitterness and moral peril in troubles which spring from, or are mingled with, human malevolence. Such was David's affliction at this time. Absalom's unnatural conduct, Ahithophel's faithlessness, and Shimei's cursing rendered his misfortunes much harder to bear than similar misfortunes coming from the ordinary vicissitudes of human life.

I. SHIMEI'S CURSING. A striking picture here: David, in the midst of his people and servants, including his famous "Ironsides," marching along the ravine; and from a town on the heights, this fierce Benjamite rushing forth, cursing and throwing stones as he comes; and then, moving along the ridge which overlooked the line of march, keeping pace with the king and his company, vomiting forth his rage in bitter taunts and reproaches, and casting down stones and dust; his fury increased by the calmness with which those below marched on, heedless of his impotent rage. It was an outburst of feelings long pent up which dared not express themselves until David seemed to have fallen from his throne beyond recovery. Shimei was a relative of Saul, and chose to regard David as the author of that king's downfall, and of the humiliation of his house, and chargeable with all the bloodshed that had accompanied these changes. And now, in his view, the Divine retribution has at length visited David for his usurpation of the throne, and the "bloody" measures by which he had reached it; and he triumphs over the fallen monarch with bitter resentment and scorn, and unmeasured invective, unsoftened by the spectacle of humiliation and grief which presented itself to his view. In his passion, like most angry people, he is not scrupulous in adherence to the truth. David was not guilty of wantonly shedding blood to reach the throne; he had spared Saul again and again when he might have slain him; and he had punished with death one who professed to have killed him, and others who had treacherously murdered his son. Nor was it nearer the truth to call David a "man of Belial" (a worthless, wicked man). But Shimei cursed the more freely because that was the only way by which he could vent his malice: he was powerless to do anything else. Yet he showed some courage, or at least recklessness, in so freely reviling one who, though fallen, was surrounded by brave warriors, any one of whom could so easily have effectually silenced him (as Abishai desired to do), if permitted by their king. Violent anger is, however, often as regardless of prudence as of truth. Its courage is as that of a maniac.

II. DAVID'S MEEK ENDURANCE OF IT. He doubtless felt it to be annoying and humiliating to be thus bespattered in the presence of his friends, and trampled on so savagely by so contemptible a foe. To be falsely charged with crimes he had carefully avoided was no small addition to his already too heavy affliction. A very natural and justifiable resentment would prompt him to permit the swift punishment that Abishai begged to be allowed to inflict. But he restrained such feelings, and meekly endured the insults heaped upon him. His words reveal the secret of his meekness 1. *He recognized the infliction as from God.* With the freedom which the sacred writers employ when speaking even of human wickedness as it fulfils Divine purposes, he declares that God had bidden Shimei to curse him (ver. 10), and no one must forbid him. Besides his general faith in God as universal and rightful Ruler, just and good, the memory of his own ill desert doubtless aided him, and the conviction that God was chastising him for his sins. Contrition prompted and nourished submission. He no longer saw in Shimei the cruel and vindictive slanderer, but the rod in the hand of his righteous yet merciful God. To his tormentor he would not have submitted, but to his heavenly Guide and Friend he could and would. And evermore the best remedy for impatience and resentment under afflictions and provocations is the recognition of our Father in heaven as ordering and appointing all; and the exercise towards him of confidence and love, humility and self-surrender. Thus Job discerned, behind and above Sabeans and Chaldeans, lightnings and tempest; and would have discerned behind and above Satan, if he could have known him as his accuser and the prompter and mediate cause of his calamities,—the Lord; and therefore could say, "The Lord gave," etc. (Job i. 21). Thus also One who was greater than Job or David could say, "The cup which my Father hath given me, shall I not drink it?" (John xviii. 11). 2. *The thought of the greater trouble of his son's conduct helped to reconcile him to the lesser trouble of Shimei's.* (Ver. 11.) What was chiefly burdening and paining his heart is shown in these words. The ravings of "this Benjamite" was a small matter in

comparison. 3. *The hope that God would regard him with pity soothed him.* (Ver. 12.)
He felt that he was in a condition fitted to awaken the Divine compassion, and hoped
it would be exercised towards him.   In like manner, we may yet more confidently be
assured that he who chastises pities us, as a father the children he is correcting (Ps.
ciii. 13). 4. *He trusted that God would render him good in place of the evil he was
suffering.* (Ver. 12.) Not that he thought he deserved it, or that his sufferings gave
him a claim on God for it; but, confiding in the mercy which had pardoned him, he
could hope for it.   Shimei might curse, but if God would bless (Ps. cix. 28), all would
be well.   So may we be sure that all that God appoints us to endure from men or from
circumstances and events, he will cause to issue in a thousandfold more of blessing, if
we trust and serve him, and resign ourselves to his will (see further in homily on ch.
xv. 25, 26).

In conclusion: 1. *In Shimei we see an example to be carefully avoided.* Let any
who permit themselves outbursts of passionate anger and railing, see here what a repulsive spectacle they present to others, and how sad a spectacle to him whom they call their
Master. Let all give heed to St. Paul's injunctions in Eph. iv. 31, 32. 2. *In David's
meek endurance we see an example to be closely imitated;* yea, by Christians exceeded.
For we have a still better Example, corresponding to a higher Law than David knew
(see 1 Pet. ii. 23; Matt. v. 44, 45; 1 Pet. iii. 9).—G. W.

Ver. 17.—*Unfaithful friends.* Bad men may and often do see and reprove in others
the baseness they are themselves practising, and thus unconsciously condemn themselves.   Absalom reproves his father's friend Hushai for supposed unkindness and
unfaithfulness to him, while he himself, not merely a friend, but a fondly loved son,
was usurping his father's throne, and ready to take away his life (see ch. xvii. 2, 4).
Nevertheless, the sentiment which underlies his remonstrance is just, and Hushai
would have deserved severe rebuke if he had really been guilty of the conduct he was
charged with   It was a time for David's friends to prove themselves to be friends
indeed; and to desert him at such a time (as Ahithophel did) would have been perfidious in the extreme.   Hushai, however, was serving him by obeying his directions
and promoting his interests.   Whether the deception he practised on Absalom was
justifiable is another question, depending for its solution on the answer to be given to
the larger question whether and how far belligerents are bound by the ordinary laws
of truth and righteousness.   The remonstrance of Absalom is suitable to be addressed
to any who are acting in a manner contrary to the duties of friendship.   As one and
another instance of unfaithfulness or unkindness occurs, the question might well be
put to those guilty of them, " Is this thy kindness to thy friend ? " The force of the
remonstrance would be proportionate to the degree of friendship which had existed, the
benefits received, the professions made, etc.; and also the degree of flagrant violation of
the laws of friendship which each act exhibited.   And if to the obligations of friendship are to be added those of some other relationship, as here that of subject and
servant of a sovereign, the guilt of unfaithfulness is increased, and remonstrance may
well be more severe.   The words are very suitable to be addressed to professed friends
of our Lord Jesus Christ who act a faithless and disloyal part towards him.

I. CHRIST IS OUR ROYAL FRIEND. King, and yet Friend; Friend, and yet King.
The claims of each relation to us strengthen those of the other.   Although he is so
glorious a King, he stoops to be and act the part of a Friend to the meanest and most
sinful of his subjects. 1. *He fills this position towards them:* (1) By his self-sacrificing
services on their behalf (John xv. 13). (2) By admitting them to the closest and
most confidential intimacy of which each is capable (John xv. 15). (3) By the greatness and abundance of the benefits he confers on them. 2. *And they on their part
take the position of friends to him:* (1) By their acceptance of his friendship. (2) By
their vows of eternal love, loyalty, and service to him. The relation of sovereign and
subject is, in the best Christians, more and more lost in, though not destroyed by, that
of friend and friend.   A love boundless in its promptings and requirements overflows
and obliterates the limits of mere law.

II. TO ACT AN UNFRIENDLY PART TOWARDS HIM IS DESERVING OF THE SEVEREST
REBUKE. "Is this thy kindness to thy friend?" 1. *Conduct to which the words are
applicable.* (1) Desertion of Christ in times of difficulty. "Why wentest thou not

with thy friend?" (comp. Heb. xiii. 13); "Let us go forth unto him without the camp, bearing his reproach." (2) Moral cowardice in respect to him. The words might well have been addressed to Peter when denying his Lord and Friend—were virtually addressed to him when "the Lord turned and looked" upon him (Luke xxii. 61). It would be well if they could ever be heard by us whenever, from fear of man, we are silent when we ought to speak for Christ, inactive when we should act for him. (3) Parsimony in gifts and services for the promotion of his cause. (4) Failure in duties of love to his friends and representatives—our fellow-Christians, especially the poor and suffering. A timely reproach, reaching the heart, might prevent more terrible words at the day of judgment (Matt. xxv. 41—45). (5) Any act whatever of inconsistency with our position and professions as disciples of Christ. 2. *Their peculiar force.* Arising from the words, "thy Friend." (1) Who has proved himself a Friend indeed. (2) Whom thou hast often addressed and rejoiced in as such. (3) Whom thou hast often been glad to appeal to in that character for help and deliverance. (4) To whom thou hast many times vowed eternal friendship, and fidelity unto death. The reproach, thus viewed, is adapted to break the offender's heart, producing the deepest shame and self-humiliation, and leading to the most earnest penitence and prayers for forgiveness. 3. *From what quarter the remonstrance might come.* (1) From a man's own conscience and heart. It is well when these are sufficiently loyal to Christ to speedily address the offender after this manner. (2) From other friends of Christ. Christians should be sufficiently faithful to their brethren and their Lord to lovingly reprove serious inconsistencies. (3) From the enemies of Christ. As by David's enemy the words were originally spoken. Those who are not themselves Christ's disciples are often quick to detect the faults of those who are, and to taunt them with them. They sometimes thus render good service to Christians. *Fas est et ab hoste doceri.*—G. W.

EXPOSITION.

CHAPTER XVII.

Ver. 1.—**Let me now choose out twelve thousand men.** The advice of Ahithophel was such as would have made success almost certain. The rebellion had taken David by surprise, and he was quite unprepared to resist the large forces which Absalom had gathered round him. But the better part of the nation disapproved of the enterprise, especially when they perceived that David's life was in danger; and consequently his followers, in course of time, would increase. Moreover, the day had been one of extreme moral and mental trial to David. Upon the sudden news of Absalom's approach, he had to arrange for the flight of his wives and children; to provide supplies for their wants, and for those of their attendants on the march; to give orders to his officers, and take means to prevent their flight degenerating into a panic. Then, with covered head and feet unshod, he had descended into the Valley of Jehoshaphat, and slowly traversed the Mount of Olives; thence, in deep distress, he had advanced to the way of the wilderness towards Jericho, and there had been assailed by Shimei with bitter revilings. His progress after this was unimpeded, and at Ayêphim he and the other fugitives had needful rest and refreshment. As Bahurim was about four miles from Jerusalem, this caravanserai a little further on was probably

about six miles from the city, and about half-way towards the fords of the Jordan. The march was probably continued at sunset, and the fords reached before midnight; and there David halted, waiting for the arrival of Jonathan and Ahimaaz, and making preparations for the passage. Now, if Ahithophel's advice had been followed, he would have reached the fords as quickly as the young men did; for they lost time at Bahurim. Upon this David had not calculated, but supposed that anyhow he should have the interval won by Ahimaaz's fleetness. With twelve thousand picked troops unencumbered with baggage, Ahithophel would thus have found David still on the west of the Jordan, and though Joab and Abishai would have done all that brave men could, yet they would scarcely have been in a position to make a long defence. And the command was to "smite the king only." A panic was inevitable, and confusion among David's followers, who had women and children to defend; and in the midst of it Ahithophel would direct his main attack on the part where David was, and single him out for slaughter. When this was done all would be accomplished; for Absalom would become king by right of succession. Even Joab and the Gibborim would acknowledge him, and the whole nation be at peace.

Ver. 3.—**The man whom thou seekest is as if all returned;** Hebrew, *as the return of the* *whole is the man whom thou seekest.* Both the amendments of the text and the various translations offered are innumerable, but nothing is really more satisfactory than the literal rendering of the words, virtually given us in the Authorized Version. Naturally, Ahithophel did not wish to parade David's death too openly. In his heart Absalom must have known that the safe possession of the kingdom could be assured him only by his father's death, but yet he might have shrunk from publicly avowing this, and having it talked of before his courtiers as a settled purpose. One reason why he adopted the counsel of Hushai may have been his reluctance to commit parricide : for plainly the one main purpose of Ahithophel was David's death. This thorough traitor may have seen even a tremor of alarm in Absalom's countenance when he spake out his purpose so frankly of "smiting the king only," and may have felt that, slumbering in the bosom of the son, was something of that generous spirit which had made the father condemn the Amalekite to death for boasting that he had slain Saul. At all events, he was unwilling to dilate upon so ghastly a theme, and this general reference to David, as the man whom Absalom sought, without dwelling upon the subject, is in far better taste than the coarse open villainy so unreservedly expressed in ver. 2. The reading, however, of the Septuagint has many followers : "And I will bring back all the people to thee as a bride returns to her husband, excepting the life of the one man thou seekest ; and for all the people there shall be peace." Ahithophel was bad enough, but scarcely so brutal as to compare to a bridal procession the sad return of David's mourning friends and companions-in-arms weeping round the corpse of their master murdered at the bidding of his own son.

Ver. 4.—**All the elders of Israel.** Their presence seems to show that Absalom professed to act in an orderly and constitutional manner, and with the advice of those in authority. It was possibly this wish to keep up appearances which made him command Hushai to be summoned, as he was one whose advice would certainly have been asked had matters gone on in their ordinary channel. So again in vers. 14, 15, Absalom acts only with the popular consent. Very probably the royal power was gradually superseding that of the tribal authorities, and this may have made David unpopular with many of the great nobles. Absalom would thus gain many adherents by associating " elders " and " men of Israel " with him in his councils.

Ver. 7.—**And Hushai said.** Hushai gives his advice with much Oriental exaggeration, such as ought to have put Absalom on his guard. His main points are that David was

too practised a soldier to let himself be surprised. In his adventures with Saul he and his men had been trained to hold large bodies of pursuers at bay, and evade them. The men, too, who were with him were warriors of desperate valour, whose first thought would be the king's personal safety, and to ensure this they would conceal him in some pit, some cave or ravine, safe and inaccessible by nature ; or in some place (omit the inserted word "other"), that is, in some camping-place, made strong with ramparts, so as to resist the first attack. "To smite the king only " is, therefore, an impossibility ; and if the attack fail, and David's mighties, in their irritation, slaughter a large number of their assailants, and a panic be the result, men will hesitate before they attack such redoubtable champions a second time. A check is fatal to a rebellion, and Absalom was staking his chance on one hasty encounter. Better leave the decision to all Israel. Their hearts were with Absalom, and, when there has been time for them to gather in their thousands, success is certain. Their numbers will be countless as the sands on the shore, or as the dew upon the grass ; while David and his heroes will shrink to so small a body as to be scarcely able to man the walls of one small city. And fighting there will be none ; for the myriads of Israel will drag city and fugitives with ropes down into the nearest torrent-bed, where the next floods will wash all away. There was more in this than an appeal to Absalom's vanity. If all Israel did take his side, then David's cause would soon be hopeless, and there would be no need of parricide. David's death would be the act of Israel, and not of Absalom. Evidently Absalom believed that all Israel was on his side, and his success hitherto had been so rapid as almost to justify the assumption. To us this success is almost unaccountable, but it suggests that there were great faults in David's administration. Yet even so we wonder at the existence of such general dissatisfaction. **At this time.** A wrong translation. The Hebrew is, *Ahithophel's counsel this time is not good,* whereas last time, what he advised about the concubines was good.

Ver. 9.—**When some of them be overthrown** at the first ; Hebrew, *in the falling on them ;* that is, at the first onslaught of David's champions. Even though overpowered finally by force of numbers, they are sure to make a large slaughter at first, which may easily lead to a panic.

Ver. 11.—**And that thou go to battle in thine own person** ; literally, *and that thy presence go to the battle.* The versions have preserved a much better reading, " And that thy presence go in the midst of them."

Ver. 12.—**In some place** ; Hebrew, *in one*

of the places; one of the fortified camps already described in ver. 9.

Ver. 13.—**The river.** The word does not signify a river, but a ravine or gorge worn away by the action of a torrent. Such ravines are common in Palestine, where the streams rush along with resistless fury after the rains, but in summer are dry (Job vi. 17); and their desolate beds, bordered by precipitous cliffs, are described by Isaiah as favourite places for the cruel rites of Moloch (Isa. lvii. 5). Dragged to the edge of one of these gorges, the city, with its few defenders, would topple over, and in the next rainy season be entirely swept away.

Ver. 14.—**The counsel of Hushai is better.** It seemed safer. Nothing in it was left to chance, and Absalom, already at the head of such numbers as to be able to select from them twelve thousand picked men, saw himself, in fancy, marching forward with all Israel at his feet. As a matter of fact, he did advance with so large an army that David was saved only by the skilful strategy of Joab. Like other king-makers, Ahithophel had put himself too forward. He asked for twelve thousand men to be placed under his command, that he might smite David, and so be, not only Absalom's counsellor, but also his commander-in-chief. Amasa and the other commanders would be displeased at this, and Absalom would feel that he was himself placed in a very secondary position. Ahithophel may have asked for the command solely because no one's presence would so ensure success as his own, but he wounded the vanity both of Absalom and Amasa, and made them ready to listen to any other advice that might be offered. **The Lord had appointed;** literally, *and Jehovah had commanded to bring to nought,* etc. So plain did it seem to the writer that Absalom's success depended upon rapid action, that nothing less than the direct interference of the Divine providence could account for the infatuation of Absalom and his counsellors.

Ver. 16.—**Lodge not this night in the plains** (at the fords) **of the wilderness.** The plan of Ahithophel made David's position so dangerous, that he must hesitate no longer, lest, on second thoughts, Absalom should still adopt it. Hushai had frustrated it for the present; but Ahithophel might urge it again, and get the necessary permission; and then David and all the people that were with him would be **swallowed up,** that is, destroyed utterly, and with ease.

Ver. 17.—**Stayed by En-rogel.** The two youths were posted at En-rogel, that is, the "Fuller's spring," near Jerusalem (Josh xv. 7; 1 Kings i. 9), and probably the place now known as "Job's Well," situated at the point where the valleys of Jehoshaphat and Hinnom meet. They were placed there because, though they would have been admitted into the city, they would scarcely have been allowed to leave it. Instead of **wench**—a term less disrespectful when the Authorized Version was made than it is now—the Hebrew has *the maidservant.* Probably the maid is meant whose usual duty it was to fetch water for domestic purposes, and thus her journey to the well would excite no suspicion.

Ver. 18.—**A lad saw them.** Probably Absalom had sent out spies to watch the route which David had taken, to prevent any friends joining him from the city, who would give him information as to the progress of events there. The word "lad" does not mean a boy; more probably he was one of the young men who formed Absalom's body-guard, like the ten "lads," translated "young men," in ch. xviii. 15, who bare Joab's armour. It would be his duty to seize them, but when he tried to approach them, they fled, and made their way at full speed to Bahurim, where they were saved by the shrewdness and fidelity of a woman. Two such fleet runners would have had no difficulty in outstripping a boy, but one of Absalom's young men would have roused the neighbourhood to join in the pursuit. The **well in his court** really signifies a cistern for storing rainwater; but it was at that time dry, and served as a convenient hiding-place for the two messengers.

Ver. 19.—**A covering;** Hebrew, *the cover;* that is, the usual cover of the cistern, which had been taken off to let the young men descend into it. Over it she spread, not **ground corn,** but brayed or peeled corn (see Prov. xxvii. 22), probably barley-groats. She was probably busy in removing the husks of the barley with a pestle in a mortar when Jonathan and Ahimaaz sought refuge with her; and thus her whole proceeding was so natural as to excite no suspicions.

Ver. 20.—**They be gone over the brook of water.** The word *michal,* translated "brook," does not occur elsewhere, and probably it was a local name for some stream near Bahurim. It was, we may suppose, in the right direction, but when the pursuers had followed for some time, and caught no glimpse of the runners, knowing their swiftness of foot, they concluded that they had outstripped them, and, giving up the chase as hopeless, returned to Jerusalem. It was only when she had seen them far on their way back that she removed the cover and allowed the young priests to resume their journey. The delay would have been fatal to David if vigorous counsel had been followed at Jerusalem; as it was, they reached David's camp without further incident, and acquainted him with Ahithophel's plan; and the king at once recognized his danger, and without more delay, commenced at once the passage of the Jordan, and carried it out so skilfully and rapidly, that by the morning every one of his company was safe on the other side.

Ver. 23.—**Ahithophel . . . hanged himself.** There is an old fancy, put down by Thenius as one of the curiosities of interpretation, that Ahithophel died of a quinsy; for the word might mean "was strangled or choked." But the act seems mentioned as a proof of Ahithophel's unerring judgment. Indignation at Absalom's folly, and at the slight cast upon himself, is not a sufficient reason for so violent a deed. He must have foreseen the certain ruin of the conspiracy if David was allowed time; and he knew that upon its failure would follow his own punishment. It is proof also that he was a fierce and ill-tempered man, and animated for some reason or other with a malignant hatred of David. The parallel between Ahithophel and the traitor Judas must strike every one.

Ver. 24.—**Then** (Hebrew, *and*) **David came to Mahanaim.** (On Mahanaim, see note on ch. ii. 8.) It was now a fortified city, with walls and gates (ch. xviii. 24), and its strength of position, which had made it a safe capital for Ishbosheth, who had probably added to its defences, made it also a safe retreat for David while gathering his forces. As it was only about fifty miles distant from the fords of the Jordan, David had not retreated far; and, meanwhile, Absalom was wasting time in gathering "all the men of Israel" for the attack. During this interval Absalom was anointed king (ch. xix. 10) by the priests, with all due solemnity.

Ver. 25.—**Ithra an Israelite.** In 1 Chron. ii. 17 he is called "Jether the Ishmeelite." The first name is the same, Ithra being the emphatic form of Jether; and as it is difficult to find a reason for mentioning so ordinary a fact as that his father was an Israelite, we may conclude that "Ishmeelite" is the correct reading. Bishop Wordsworth, however, suggests that "Israelite" was in contrast to "Judahite;" but this distinction did not come into use until after the disruption of the kingdom. The Vatican text of the Septuagint has "Jezreelite," which is probably a conjecture to get rid of the obvious error of calling him an Israelite. Amasa was an illegitimate son, which confirms the reading "Ishmeelite" in 1 Chron. ii. 17, as a marriage between Abigail and a foreigner would be sure to be opposed by all the members of Jesse's family. **Nahash.** Jewish interpreters regard Nahash (equivalent to "serpent") as another name for Jesse, quoting in proof, "Out of the root of Nahash (the serpent) shall come forth the basilisk" (Isa. xiv. 29), which in the Chaldee Paraphrase is ex-

plained as meaning, "out of the root of Jesse shall come forth the Messiah." This conceit would scarcely have deserved mention, had it not found a place in the margin of the Authorized Version. Some few commentators regard Nahash as a woman's name, and think that she was a wife of Jesse, and mother of Abigail and Zeruiah, but not of David. But Nahash is so constantly a man's name that it is easier to believe that Nahash was the first husband of David's mother, and Abigail and Zeruiah his half-sisters, not on the father's, but on the mother's side. Joab and his brothers are always described as sons of Zeruiah, both to mark their relationship to David, and also because the rank was on her side. Amasa was probably the Amasai mentioned in 1 Chron. xii. 18 as bringing a powerful reinforcement to David while at Ziklag; but the ambition of supplanting Joab made him now forget David's long friendship.

Ver. 27.—**Shobi.** It is evident that the most powerful chieftains in Gilead were on David's side, and supported him with men as well as with provisions. Adherents, too, would constantly cross the Jordan, and gather round the old king; and thus, when Absalom arrived, he found himself in face of an army estimated at about twenty thousand men. Among these chiefs it is interesting to find Shobi, son of Nahash, the Ammonite king, and David's friend (ch. x. 2). When Hanun, the elder son, on succeeding to the throne, brought ruin upon himself by his misconduct to David's ambassadors, Shobi apparently remained faithful to David, and received the grant of a district in Gilead, where he settled with his followers. Some, with less probability, suppose that he had withdrawn to Gilead in the lifetime of his father, to be out of Hanun's way. **Machir** was the generous man who had given the crippled son of Jonathan a refuge (ch. ix. 4); and David's honourable treatment of Mephibosheth may have won his patron's heart. Of **Barzillai**, and his abode, **Rogelim**, nothing more is known than what is said here, and in the very interesting narrative in ch. xix. 31, etc. David's lasting gratitude to him is shown by his care for his sons (see 1 Kings ii. 7). A clan of priests called themselves "the children of Barzillai," and claimed to be the descendants of his daughter. They could not, however, produce their genealogy, and were therefore degraded from the priestly office (Ezra ii. 61—63). Their claim, nevertheless, is a proof that Barzillai was a little king in Gilead, when thus a priestly race thought their alliance with him so honourable as to make them forget that they were of the lineage of Aaron.

Ver. 28.—**Beds.** These would be for the

women and children, and were scarcely more than rugs and small carpets. **Basons**; pots of metal for cooking, while the earthenware would be vessels for holding their food. **Parched** (corn) . . . **and parched** (pulse); Hebrew, *kali . . . and kali.* The word includes all kinds of parched grain. The Septuagint and Syriac rightly omit it in the second place, as it is probably a mere error of some ancient copyist; but for what word it has been substituted we have no means of ascertaining.

Ver. 29.—**Sheep.** This is the only kind of flesh food mentioned. The change in the meaning of the word "meat," which still in America is used simply for "food," as in the Authorized Version, bears witness to

the great change in our diet which has taken place in recent times. **Cheese of kine.** The word occurs only here, but the Syriac and the Targum both support the rendering of the Authorized Version. The Bedaween, after removing the butter, make a kind of cheese from the remaining milk. It is as hard as the cheese made from skimmed milk in Dorsetshire, but wholesome. It must, however, be soaked before eating, or softened with butter. Generally in the East, cow's milk is regarded as coarse, and camel's milk is used for drinking, while that of sheep and goats, and cheese made from it, holds the next place in general estimation. It is curious that "butter" literally means "cheese of kine."

HOMILETICS.

Vers. 1—14.—*Conflicting counsels.* The facts are: **1.** Ahithophel, in advising Absalom, suggests that he himself should fall upon David by night, when weary, with twelve thousand select men, and urges that by so doing a final blow will be so struck as to secure the fealty of all Israel. **2.** The suggestion is pleasing to Absalom, but he, before deciding, wishes to have the counsel of Hushai. **3.** On being called to give counsel, Hushai expresses distrust of the counsel of Ahithophel, and assigns as reasons (1) the known valour and caution of David; (2) the possibility of a panic among the troops of Absalom on a slight reverse at the outset; (3) the natural apprehension of the people on approaching for attack one so famed for courage and strategy. **4.** As a counter-proposal, he counsels (1) a gathering of the entire forces of Israel; (2) the personal leadership of Absalom; and points out the certainty of success whether by attack in the open country or by an assault on a city. **5.** Absalom and his people decide to reject the counsel of Ahithophel and adopt that of Hushai, being overruled in this by the will of God. The bold assumption of regal powers by publicly taking possession of the king's harem was only a formal act, which necessitated other measures if the authority thus usurped was to be maintained. The existence of so valiant and able a man as David, and the attachment to him of a select body-guard, were facts which could not but weigh heavily on the mind of one who knew how his father, in the days of Saul, defended himself amidst rocks and caves against a vindictive and powerful enemy. Hence the natural coherence of the narrative with which this chapter opens, and the account of Absalom's conduct referred to in the previous chapter. In considering the conflicting counsels brought out by the first act of Absalom, we may notice several truths bearing widely on human affairs.

I. POSITIONS IN LIFE ARE ENTERED UPON WHICH RENDER MEN VERY DEPENDENT ON THE SUPERIOR JUDGMENT OF OTHERS. Absalom had aspired to a position of power, and on reaching it found that his difficulties were not materially diminished. The presence in the country of such a man as David, with such a body-guard, was a fact of serious moment, and the well-known hesitancy of the populace as long as there are chances of vicissitude had to be provided against. His early habits of life and his natural gifts by no means qualified him to meet emergencies of this character; and hence he found himself, on usurping the throne, dependent on men of larger experience than himself. It was not preference but necessity which led him to seek the counsel of Ahithophel and Hushai. Occasionally there are men in similar positions of usurped authority who by nature and experience can dispense with the advice of others, but it is more often not so. Young men entering on public life need more wisdom than can be gathered from their own personal experience, and they will do well to consult the wise who have written or may speak. In any position of difficulty, when embarrassed by dangers we cannot escape, whether in professions, commerce, education, morals, or religion, we need not hesitate to act even as did wicked Absalom in this particular—seek out the most accredited guides and advisers. If it is permitted to learn from an enemy, it is certainly allowable for the good to extract wisdom from the actions of the bad. The " children of light " are advised to learn lessons from the conduct of the " children of this world " (Luke xvi. 8). We may, like Absalom, though not with his evil intent, enter on positions by our free choice, for meeting the difficulties of which we are personally ill prepared; or we may, like Joseph, Moses, and Paul, be forced into positions of delicacy and peril. In either case we shall require more than our own sagacity; and no mere pride should deter us from seeking help of others. Possibly ours may be a case in which no human adviser is available. Be it so; Joseph, Moses, and Paul sought counsel of God, and they found, as we shall, that he directeth the way of those who acknowledge him (Prov. iii. 6). There are many advisers, many professing to know what is best. Let us ponder the path of our feet, that all our ways may be established. The good may adopt the policy of Absalom, while shunning his principles.

II. GREAT POWERS BRING CORRESPONDING DISGRACE WHEN EMPLOYED IN DIRECT ANTAGONISM TO GOD'S GRACIOUS DESIGNS FOR MANKIND. Ahithophel was unquestionably a man of great ability. There is in human nature a profound respect for power of intellect. Men feel instinctively that it is a gift of God, and carries with it the key to unlock many of the mysteries that lie hidden in nature. It rests with the moral disposition as to the application of these powers. The true order is for them to run in the line of God's great purpose of mercy to mankind, as a co-operating force to bring about the redemption of the world from the evils incident to the existence of sin. Thus it is that the highest honours are won. But Ahithophel brought on himself everlasting disgrace in that he laid all his native talents, all his acquired experience, all his personal influence, at the service of one who sought to set aside the Lord's anointed. He must have known all David's antecedents. He had taken " sweet counsel " with him (Ps. lv. 14). His deliberate counsel now, to select choice men who should fall on the weary king in the dead of night, and, in the panic, slay him alone so as to secure ultimately the allegiance of those not slain, was crafty, bold, and cruel in the extreme. Humanly speaking, it meant success to the vices of Absalom, and ruin to the holy cause embodied in the Lord's anointed. The treachery to a former friend counts for much; the inhumanity counts for more; but the crowning crime is war upon God's revealed method for bringing on that glorious time when righteousness shall be established in the earth, and all men shall be blessed (Ps. lxxii.). The same plain issue is involved in the antagonism of men now to the appointed order of providence and grace. God has a kingdom, ruled by the Anointed One, and designed to bring peace and joy and holiness to all mankind. Gigantic intellectual powers are now running along a line in direct antagonism to it. The practical issue of their success would be moral and spiritual ruin to man. The more their strength and enrichment by learning, culture, and experience, command respect, the deeper the disgrace and the more dreadful their doom for daring to seek to destroy the authority of Christ's blessed yoke (Matt. xi. 28—30; cf. Ps. ii.). The daring deeds of the Hebrew secular plane are being repeated in the deeds of the modern spiritual plane.

III. THERE ARE EMERGENCIES IN THE HISTORY OF THE KINGDOM OF GOD ON EARTH DEMANDING UNUSUAL EFFORTS ON THE PART OF THE FAITHFUL. To ordinary human view the kingdom of God, as represented by the cause of David, was now in great peril. The most sagacious counsel of the age had been given; an eager young prince, proud of the wisdom of the counsellor, was intent on action, and a hesitant people were waiting for the turn of the balance. Hushai had, with remarkable foresight and courage, though doubtless under unconscious direction from above, placed himself in a position to meet the emergency; and now came the call for him to put forth his strength. Absalom little knew what he was doing when he called on Hushai to speak on the question at issue. The venerable man, strong as he was in his own secret and in the help of God, could not but realize the immense responsibility now devolving upon him. A false step, hesitancy, inappropriate suggestions, and feeble arguments, would be disastrous to the dearest of interests. In that critical hour it was as though the fate of Israel and Israel's banished king, and of the blessed world-wide purpose they were working out, rested entirely on his judgment and skill. Angels could not but hearken with intense interest to his words, and watch their gradual effect on the mind of the rebel son. Corresponding occasions, varying in circumstance and magnitude, though virtually one in principle, have occurred, and will perhaps occur again. The most conspicuous and, in some respects, of course, the unparalleled, instance was that of our Saviour when the " gates of hell " had taken counsel to virtually prevent the salvation of the world by the only method approved of God. Of the people there was none with him. All depended on what he would do. The fate of the world rested with himself. In Caleb and Joshua, in Athanasius *contra mundum*, in the leaders of the Reformation, in the noble men and women who suffered martyrdom in Madagascar, and in many private instances in which family religious interests have been at stake, we may see emergencies demanding of the faithful the exercise of the highest qualities.

IV. UNDISCIPLINED MINDS ARE INFLUENCED BY WHAT WORKS ON THEIR SUSCEPTIBILITIES. Hushai displayed his sagacity and skill by adapting his argument to his man. He wisely did not controvert the particular advice of Ahithophel, but so far complimented him and conciliated Absalom by simply saying that, though good, it was not so just now (ver. 7). And while tacitly recognizing the valour of the twelve thousand, he suggested that there was special danger in attacking men " chafed in their minds." His line of argument was to work upon Absalom's *fears, vanity,* and *suspicions.* David and his men were not ordinary men ; they were bold, desperate, watchful, and gifted in strategy, and the possibility of a reverse would produce a panic among Absalom's followers. Thus fear is awakened. The whole of the forces of Israel should be gathered, and Absalom himself should set out at the head of an imposing army, and so concentrate enthusiasm around his own person, and gain the renown of being conqueror of the mighty one. Thus vanity is aroused. No one else should take the lead, but the prince himself should, by maintaining a personal influence and winning a victory, keep power in his own hand, and so prevent the uprising of a powerful rival. Thus suspicions are awakened. Hushai was a good rhetorician in assailing the will through a graphic description of details, which in their effect could not but call forth fear, vanity, and suspicion—those prompters of the will. All men, but mostly the undisciplined in mind, are liable to be influenced to action by such appeals. This method explains how masses of men are often swayed by a clever presentation of facts blended with possibilities. There is a legitimate use of this method in seeking to win men over to action in harmony with the gospel. The Word of God is not handled deceitfully (2 Cor. iv. 2) when we set forth facts and possibilities to awaken godly fear and prompt to repentance ; for this is only part of the function of the teacher and preacher. Men may be caught by such guile in order to be trained in the knowledge of the truth.

V. THERE IS AN UNTRACEABLE ACTION OF GOD IN THE MINDS OF MEN. The explanation given of the superiority of Hushai's counsel in its influence over Absalom is that it was the determination of God to defeat the good counsel of Ahithophel (ver. 14). Unquestionably his counsel was the best for Absalom's purpose. But the wise man is not to glory in his wisdom ; all hearts are naked and open to him who brings to nought the wisdom of the wise and the understanding of the prudent (Ps. xxxiii. 10; Isa. viii. 10 ; 1 Cor. i. 19; ii. 6). All through Hebrew and Christian history there are evidences of God's action on the minds of men, sometimes causing them blindness, sometimes inspiring with unusual courage and wisdom, and sometimes filling them with dread (John xii. 40 ; Luke xxi. 15; Deut. ii. 25 ; Ps. ix. 20). This direct action of God on the human mind is involved in any just conception of his freedom as an Infinite Spirit, is in harmony with our action on one another, is essential to moral government, is implied in the work of regeneration, is the ground of faith in prayer, and is a basis of our belief that he will in due time defeat the wiles of the devil and bring all things into subjection to himself. We ought to lay hold of this truth with all firmness, and carry on Christian work in the assurance that greater is he that is for us than all who can be against us, and that he has ways of reaching men of which we have no visible trace.

Vers. 15—29.—The facts are: 1. Hushai, having informed Zadok and Abiathar of his counsel, urges them to send quickly to David, advising him to flee at once beyond the river. 2. Their two sons, staying out of the city in order to be of service as occasion required, are informed by a girl of the duty required, and at once go on their errand. 3. In spite of being recognized by an enemy who told Absalom, they go on their way, and take refuge in a well at Bahurim, where they are secreted by the woman of the house. 4. The pursuers, being deceived by the woman, return to Jerusalem, while the two young men escape and tell all to David, who at once, before the morning dawns, passes with all his men over Jordan. 5. Ahithophel seeing that his counsel is not followed, goes home, arranges his affairs, and destroys himself. 6. David passing on to Mahanaim, Absalom also crosses the Jordan with his forces, making Amasa chief captain in place of Joab. 7. On David's arrival with his men at Mahanaim, hungry, thirsty, and weary, he receives gifts of food and clothing from Shobi, Machir, and Barzillai.

Division of labour in doing good. From vers. 15—22 we have a record of the course adopted by the secret friends of David after that Absalom had heard the counsel of Ahithophel and Hushai. Jerusalem was the scene of an evil and a good combination ; and as the drift of Scripture is to record the accomplishment of the Divine purposes in the history of the Hebrew people, we have here a more detailed record of the individuals and work of the good combination than of the evil. The work these four faithful ones had in hand was very clearly defined and most persistently pursued. With a wisdom and skill highly creditable to all concerned, the perilous yet immensely important service was carried out on the principle of the division of labour, which obtains in modern times in the best-conducted spheres of activity. Although we may not see here parallels to all the work we have to do for Christ, we may notice features which are also found in well-directed Christian co-operation, and which it behoves us to reproduce in all we do.

I. There is scope for variety in the nature of the work to be done. The work to be done, stated in general terms, was to advance the interests of the anointed king. The circumstances in which this general aim was to be carried out necessitated varied conduct and action, both of which must be included in the service rendered, since conduct often produces great effects. There was obviously scope for influences around the person of Absalom—subtle assaults on the very seat of mischief and wrong ; for reticent watchfulness in order to take advantage of any movements adverse to David ; for fleet runners to convey to him tidings of importance, and for assistance to them when engaged in their perilous undertaking. The work of Hushai in the counsel chamber, of Zadok and Abiathar in the centre of public influence and information, of their sons outside the city, of the wench passing unsuspected for a country walk, and of the hospitable housewife of Bahurim, was in each case different, but all parts of one service. We are engaged in advancing the interests of the Anointed One against the combinations of spiritual wickedness in high places, and, while the service is one, there is great variety in the nature of the work to be done. There is scope for wise, shrewd men, who know how to confront and confound the enemy in high places ; for quiet, consistent characters, watching with patient concern over the holiest of functions, and eager to use any new light that may hasten on the triumph of the King of Zion ; for vigorous young men, true as steel, accustomed to hardness, prepared to enter on dangerous work in missionary lands, or among the snares and evils of our modern civilization ; little ones, acting as links in the great chain of moral influence ; and sympathetic helpers, who can feed the hungry, shelter the oppressed and fearful, and frustrate the designs of the cruel. The Christian Church is recognizing more than ever this division of labour, and each one who does a part towards bringing on the triumph of Christ is an important worker in the most blessed of all undertakings.

II. There is scope for variety in the qualities employed. In the service rendered in and near Jerusalem we see room for the exercise of discrimination of human character, prudence in adoption of methods, a shrewd consideration of the assailable points in the enemy's position (see previous homily, division IV.), courage, self-possession in counteracting the influence of the most powerful of antagonists, reticence in council, and fidelity in redeeming pledges made (ch. xv. 35), promptitude in action, and ingenuity in rendering aid in times of danger. The interests of David were promoted by a few persons, but the promotion of them called forth very diverse moral and intellectual qualities. On a small scale we see here a picture of what is true of the promotion of the interests of the Eternal King of Zion. The work is so wide and complicated, and the agencies so numerous, that there is not a native talent, not an acquired gift, not a shade of good influence, but it may find scope in his Name. It will be found that, as in building a temple, all the powers of body and mind find scope, and all the influences of sun and air are requisite, so, in raising up the vast superstructure of Christ's kingdom, there is room for the constant exercise of all the qualities possessed by humankind not under the domination of sin. The wisdom of the wise, the sanctity of the holy, the enthusiasm of the young, the gentleness of the maid, and the pity and sympathy of the faithful villager, all can be used up as occasion offers.

III. God raises up instruments for this service as occasion requires. Was it necessary that the powerful influence of Ahithophel should be counteracted? A Hushai is raised up. Must discreet and influential men be retained on David's side? Zadok and Abiathar are forthcoming. Are links of communication necessary between the friends of the king and himself? The two young men have their hearts inclined aright. Are the spies of the enemy to be eluded? A girl is found to carry a message, and a kindly woman to offer shelter. The solution of these facts is assuredly indicated in the assertion that God had "appointed to defeat the counsel of Ahithophel." He raises up his servants to do his will, little as they know the working of his mighty power within them. So it has always been, and will be in the future. Abraham was raised up to lay the foundation of national life for Israel; Moses to lead the people to the promised land; Elijah and seven thousand to protest against the worship of Baal; the little girl to speak in the house of Naaman the Syrian; Nehemiah and his coadjutors to restore the walls of the city; apostles endowed "with power from on high" to inaugurate the new order of things; and Paul, the apostle of the Gentiles, as one "born out of due time." We need never fear but that, in answer to prayer, God will ever do these things for his people. There will be wise men, saintly men, men of vigour and enterprise, maidens to win their way for Christ, and kindly souls to feed the hungry and shelter the distressed.

General lessons. 1. In all our Christian organizations we should strive to be influenced by the remembrance that the enterprise is one with that of other organizations; that the interests at stake are most momentous; and that every power and faculty and influence of the community of the faithful should find some scope for exercise. 2. Personally we should cultivate our best talents with a view to lay them at the service of our Eternal King. 3. We should take heed and never despise services which seem inferior to our own, or the full bearing of which we cannot at the time trace. 4. We should be patient, and allow time for influences to operate.

The end of the wicked. The course run by Ahithophel was very wicked. It combined some of the basest crimes of which human nature is capable, the more base because of the intelligence and former professions of the man. His name is the symbol of craftiness, cunning, faithlessness, cruelty, pride of intellect, and ambition. Every reader of the narrative feels that he was most justly cut off from the land of the living, and is not much surprised that he should be cut off by his own hand. The end seems in some dreadful sense natural and befitting. But while that is, perhaps, the spontaneous judgment of men because of what may be termed his exaggerated vileness, yet, looking at the facts in the light of Scripture, we really see here, in very dark colours, what is virtually the end of all who are guilty of treason against Christ, the Anointed One, and seek to frustrate his righteous purposes in the world. Observe that in antagonism to Christ—

I. There is an anointed King opposed. Ahithophel's crime lay chiefly in being in antagonism to one whom God had anointed to be king over Israel. The qualities of craft and cunning and cruelty were incidents of the antagonism. The essence of his guilt lay in the fact of setting himself against the Lord and his anointed. And those who persist in a sinful life and will not, because of the love of their own way, bow to the yoke of Christ (Matt. xii. 28—30), are as truly guilty of rebellion. In so far as they thus seek to dispense with his authority, they are guilty of high treason. To say that there is no intention to do so counts for nothing in a matter of resistance to his authority. The facts of life are the tests of loyalty. The position of an impenitent sinner is one of enmity against God. This the Apostle Paul declares, and it is the admission of all who awake to a sense of their state and cry for mercy. The tendency to tone down resistance to Christ's personal authority over the entire life is dangerous.

II. THERE IS INGRATITUDE AND CRUELTY IN THE RESISTANCE TO CHRIST. We can easily see the ingratitude and cruelty of Ahithophel. He had been cared for by the king, and blessed with many favours (Ps. lv. 13). And yet what David had been and done for this man was as nothing compared with what Christ, our anointed King, has been and has done for men who rebel against his authority. He has loved them; suffered and died for them; he has crowned their lives with loving-kindness, and even conferred on them the very powers which they refuse to submit to his governance. If Christ was once wounded in the house of his friends by their rejection of him, he surely feels the pain of beholding the ingratitude of those who say in their hearts, "We will not have him to reign over us." There is positive cruelty in deliberately rejecting One who so tenderly loves and has suffered so much for those who scorn him. The appeal of the prophet to heaven and earth as to whether there could be found any parallel to Israel's crime (Isa. i. 2—4) certainly applies in the instance of those who enjoy clearer light and listen to more earnest exhortations, and yet rebel against him who has brought them up.

III. THERE IS NO PALLIATION OF THE CRIME. No ingenuity can find an excuse for Ahithophel. As to the character and qualities of the two, he knew that Absalom was not to be thought of for a moment in comparison with David. As to the administration of government, no good could possibly come from exchanging a wise, generous king for a vain and selfish young man. Reason and good sense and policy alike condemn the deed of Ahithophel. And those who reject the Son of God are without excuse. No other authority can compare with his in wisdom, goodness, or range of beneficence. No single fault can be found with his holy administration. No policy so sound as the policy of the sermon on the mount, and the submission demanded (Matt. xii. 28). The extreme evil as well as folly of the sin of rebellion should be insisted on with all urgency.

IV. THERE IS AN END OF DISAPPOINTMENT AND DOOM. Ahithophel came to his violent end with pride mortified and prestige gone. The cause in which he had so wickedly embarked was seen to be hopelessly lost by the adoption of the counsel of Hushai. Nor was he free from the terrors of an evil conscience. The suicide was an incident only—the result of the interaction of these causes. The actual inner facts of his end find a counterpart in the experience of all who die in rebellion against Christ. They cease to be the great ones, and are classed among those of whom the obscurity of "I never knew thee" is true (Matt. vii. 23). Whatever social prestige they had in the conventional life of this world, they lose it all where only the obedient and faithful are recognized as blessed of the Father, and are as kings and priests unto God for ever (Rev. i. 5, 6). They become aware of the presence of a conscience which is as a worm that dieth not, and as a fire that is not quenched. There is no hiding these great facts concerning the end of the wicked. They are declared in the Word of God.

Sympathy in the day of adversity. The brief record of the kindness of Shobi, Machir, and Barzillai is refreshing after the previous account of the devices of the wicked against the life and authority of David. The conduct of these men, and the reference to it in the sacred record, bring under our notice the subject of sympathy in the day of adversity. Consider, then—

I. THE CHARACTERISTICS OF TRUE SYMPATHY. So far as the conduct of these three men reveals the characteristics of true sympathy, they are seen to be these. 1. It is *spontaneous*. As soon as David's trouble was known, their hearts went forth towards him; they took to themselves his sorrows. There was no effort *ab extra* to produce it, and no inward process of reasoning to call forth deeds which would have the semblance of coming from deep compassion and sincere regard. It was natural to the men and the circumstances. That had been the character of David's sympathy for those in trouble when he was in prosperity (1 Sam. xxix. 21—24; ch. i. 11, 12, 19—27). It was pre-eminently so with Christ in all his relations to sorrow and need. It is a test by which we can estimate our own and others' professions. 2. It is *practical*. It did not spend itself in mere feeling cherished or word spoken, but found expression in abundant provision for David's wants (ver. 28). The measure of the feeling can be seen in an estimate of the pains and toil required to bring so great an amount of food and comforts to David's camp. Our Saviour, during his earthly life, left us an example of this. His sympathy produced food for five thousand. The whole of his life and sufferings were the cost by which he procured for us the blessings of salvation. In this he is infinitely removed from poets who feel and think, and philosophers who discuss the causes and relations of things. 3. It is *timely*. The gifts of these men came just in the hour of extreme need. There is a sympathy which is always too late. Right feeling is not always attended by prompt action. A ready will and quick intelligence are the proper attendants on genuine sympathy. The good Samaritan passed by the scene of sorrow just at the right time, and he acted at once. *Bis dat qui cito dat.* Christian people should cultivate promptitude. It may save many a poor soul from crushing sorrows. 4. It is *discriminating*. These generous men evidently studied the case of David's need, and brought just the things in variety that were most serviceable to a large company of hungry and weary travellers. David's heart must have been deeply affected by observing the care with which their sympathy had expressed itself. Much of the value of acts of kindness lies in this. A blind, blundering sympathy is valuable because it reveals a communion of spirit when the heart is sad; but its value is in the lowest scale. Judgment should guide the expression of feeling if we would make the most of it and secure the highest good of those for whom it is cherished. 5. It is *courageous*. Considering that David was a fugitive, and that to all appearances his friends would be regarded as the foes of the new power rising in Israel, it required some courage in these men to identify themselves in this practical way with the unfortunate king. Herein lies much of the virtue of their conduct. It does require considerable courage to manifest sympathy with the fallen, the shunned, the outcast. Our Saviour's sympathy was of this kind, and it was one of the things that led to his own rejection of men and his cruel death (Matt. ix. 10, 11; xi. 19; Luke xv. 1, 2). There is abundant scope for this virtue.

II. Its PLACE IN THE WORKING OUT OF GOD'S PURPOSES. The sorrows of David were for purposes of discipline—to chastise and train his spirit so that it might be more fully purged from the evil taint of his terrible sin (ch. xii. 7—12), and be more fitted to perform his part as a servant of God in raising the religious tone of the nation, and, indeed, of the whole world. But God is very pitiful even in his anger. "He knoweth our frame." He will not "always chide." The rough wind is "stayed in the day of his east wind." With the wound he sends the balm. He raises up instrumentalities to cause his people to feel that there is a hand to heal as well as to smite. And the appearance of these men, with their considerate provision for his wants, was a means of revealing the goodness of God, and of assuring David that his compassion was not clean gone for ever. All true sympathy in our adversity is a revelation. It brings hope and courage to the crushed spirit, and strengthens faith in the love which never fails, even in the darkest hour. The storm and sunshine are alike God's servants: they "work together" under his direction to sweeten life and endow it with freshness and beauty of eternal spring.

III. Its RECOGNITION BY GOD. The sacred historian was doubtless guided by a principle of selection when he inserted the names of these three men in a book that is to abide through all time. It was the will of God that reference should be made to their conduct. Thus has God expressed approval of their regard for his anointed. In the same way our Saviour gave honour to the sympathy of the woman who poured on him the box of ointment, by declaring that what she had done should be told in all the world for a memorial of her (Matt. xxvi. 13). The sympathy of David for the poor is in like manner divinely recognized. The Bible is a book of instances for mankind. Other deeds of sympathy were performed which have left only the trace which belongs to all good deeds, namely, in the higher and gentler tone given to the world's general life : these are referred to in order to encourage all in the same cause of comforting and helping the needy in their season of sorrow.

GENERAL LESSONS. 1. In the friendships and kindnesses of one part of our life we are sowing the seeds which may return to us in their own kind when later on we may experience trouble (cf. ch. x. 1; xii. 27), and hence we should be encouraged to do good to all men, "especially to the household of faith." 2. In our acts of sympathy we are to remember that they reach beyond the individual—they are helpful in marking out God's gracious purposes toward mankind. 3. Christ has given encouragement to acts of kindness done to the poor and needy, and conferred great honour upon them in that he regards them as done to himself (Matt. xxv. 34—40). 4. While we should not cramp and weaken our generous impulses by over-much introspection and supervision, yet we ought to be careful that the forms they assume are such as will most surely benefit those concerned in them.

HOMILIES BY VARIOUS AUTHORS.

Vers. 1—14.—(JERUSALEM.) *The council-chamber of Absalom.* "And Jehovah had appointed," etc. (ver. 14). The success of the rebellion seemed well-nigh complete. Absalom occupied the capital; was proclaimed by "all Israel;" supported by the wisest statesman, and, apparently, by "the king's friend" and the high priests; held his council (ch. xvi. 20); and took possession of the harem, "the first decided act of sovereignty" (subsequently he was also solemnly anointed, ch. xix. 10, probably by Zadok and Abiathar). "Absalom's next step was to endeavour his father's destruction, in the conviction that his own throne would never be secure so long as he lived. The son had no relentings. He had knowingly subjected himself to the inevitable necessity of taking his father's life, and he only desired to learn how that object might be most effectually secured. A council was held on this question, and it is *the first cabinet council* to which history admits us. It was doubtless conducted in the same form as other royal councils; and, from the instance before us, it appears that the members who had anything to suggest, or rather such as the king called upon for their opinion, described the course they thought best suited to the circumstances" (Kitto, 'Daily Bible Illust.'). It was the turning-point of the revolt (Ps. xcii. 7—9); and in it we see—

I. A RENOWNED COUNSELLOR urging promptitude with oracular wisdom. "And Ahithophel said," etc. (vers. 1—5; ch. xv. 31); "*this night*" (ch. xvi. 14; vers. 2, 16); *instant action* being, in his view, necessary to the accomplishment of the death of David and the success of the revolution. His counsel was the result of an unerring judgment, expressed with the utmost confidence, and thoroughly adapted (ver. 14, "good counsel") to effect its end. It was worthy of his great reputation. Extraordinary human wisdom is sometimes: 1. Employed *against the servants of God* and against his kingdom, of which they are the most conspicuous representatives. "This wisdom descendeth not from above," etc. (Jas. iii. 15). 2. Stimulated, in its exercise, by *personal hatred* toward them. "I will smite the king only" (perhaps exulting in the prospect of inflicting vengeance with his own hand). 3. Fraught with *deadly peril* to them (ver. 4). David himself, as he came "wearied and weak-handed" to the plain of the Jordan and rested there, knew not yet his imminent danger and "marvellous escape" (1 Sam. xxiii. 24—28). "But a higher power than the wisdom of the renowned Gilonite guided events." The Lord is the Defence of his people; and his promise concerning his Church is that "the gates (counsels) of Hades shall not prevail against it."

II. A RIVAL ORATOR advising delay with plausible arguments. "And Hushai said," etc. (vers. 7—13). "He was not a member of the council; but he had been well received by Absalom, whose greater treachery against his father made him give ready credence to the pretended treachery of his father's friend. It was at Absalom's suggestion that he was called in, and, being informed of the course Ahithophel had advised, he saw at once the danger that this course threatened to David; and, in fulfilment of his mission to defeat this man's counsel, he advanced divers reasons against it, all tending to *delay*" (Kitto). "It would not only ward off David's present danger, but would also, as Tacitus observes, give ill men time to repent, and the good to unite" (Delany). His counsel was the result of a profound acquaintance with human nature, and given with a persuasive eloquence equal to his wisdom. Advice favourable to God's servants: 1. Is often given in *unlikely places*, among their adversaries and by persons unsuspected of sympathy with them (Acts v. 38). 2. Derives its power from the *selfish dispositions* of the ungodly themselves: their fears (vers. 8—10) and their vainglory (vers. 11—14). Hushai's speech was "full of a certain kind of boasting which pleased the younger men" (Clericus). 3. *Succeeds* far beyond what might have been naturally expected, in making wisdom appear foolishness (vers. 4, 14).

> "His tongue
> Dropp'd manna, and could make the worse appear
> The better reason, to perplex and dash
> Maturest counsels."
>
> (Milton.)

III. AN INFATUATED USURPER adopting a policy fatal to his own designs. His decision was the result of: 1. His *misjudgment* of the effect of delay upon the nation; for he did not consider that "only the discontented part of the people formed the kernel of the insurrection, that no small portion still remained true to David, and that another part, now for the moment fallen away, would return after the first fit of revolution had passed" (Erdmann). 2. His *over-confidence* in his power and success. 3. His love of *personal display* (his ruling passion). "The new-made king gave the preference to a proposal which promised him, at any rate for a few days, the enjoyment of complete repose and the gratifications of his high position" (Ewald). 4. But herein the sacred historian indicates (what so often appears in the Books of Samuel) the overruling *providence of God* (1 Sam. ii. 1—10; ix. 1—25; xxxi. 7—10; ch. i. 19) which: (1) Pervades all thoughts and actions of men; all places and events. In the council-chamber of Absalom, where there seemed to be nothing but godless ambition, political wisdom, and "the strife of tongues," there was an unseen presence, observing, directing, controlling all. "The king's heart," etc. (Prov. xxi. 1). (2) Employs (without approving) the cunning craftiness of some men to check and punish that of others. (3) "Permits evil to work out its own consequences, and the wicked to entangle themselves in their own snares, that he may reveal his justice and holiness in the self-condemnation and self-destruction of the power of evil" (ver. 23; ch. xviii. 7, 14). "When God is contriving misfortunes for man, he first deprives him of his reason" (Euripides).—D.

Vers. 15—22.—*Slight services: a sermon to young persons.* "And a wench [the maidservant] went and told them, and they went and told King David" (ver. 17). The people of Israel were divided into two parties—the good and the bad; the servants of King David, who had been driven away from Jerusalem, and the servants of Absalom, who had taken possession of the city and were now intent upon his destruction. The world is also divided into two parties, consisting of those who are for Christ and those who are against him. And the slight but useful services rendered to David illustrate similar services to Christ. 1. *It is a good thing to be on the right side*—to be a servant of "the King of kings and Lord of lords." Outside the city, two young men, Jonathan and Ahimaaz, hiding themselves at En-rogel (the Fuller's Fountain), and waiting to carry news to the king; inside the city, their fathers (the high priests Abiathar and Zadok) and Hushai (the king's friend), preparing to send it: these were "faithful among the faithless found." 2. *One who cannot do much can yet do something* for his lord and master. If he cannot lead an army or give counsel in "the assembly of the elders," he can at least carry a message, like the brave Jonathan (1 Kings i. 42) and the swift-footed Ahimaaz (ch. xviii. 23); or, like the trusty maidservant of one of the high priests, who (as though going to the well for water) conveyed intelligence to them without suspicion. She could perform this service even more effectively than others in a higher station (2 Kings v. 2). The servant who has only "one talent" must not "hide it in the earth" (Matt. xxv. 25). Consider what you can do for Christ. 3. *Small services may display great principles* and qualities: love, obedience, diligence, veracity, fearlessness, faithfulness, self-control, self-denial, and self-sacrifice. "He that is faithful in that which is least," etc. (Luke xvi. 10). 4. *Hardly any service can be performed without difficulty* and danger. "And a lad [probably on the watch] saw them," and gave information; so that they were closely pursued by Absalom's servants (soldiers) as far as Bahurim (ch. xvi. 5). It was a race for life. 5. *The servant who does his best will seldom fail to obtain opportune help.* "And the woman took and spread the covering over the well's mouth," etc. (vers. 19, 20). "It was not the first nor yet the last time that an Israelitish woman wrought deliverance for her people" (Edersheim). Her motive was good; not her equivocation and deceit. Many circumstances and casual events, under the ordering of Divine providence, conduce to the safety and success of a faithful servant. 6. *There is as much need of small services as great;* and such services have frequently important issues; it may be escape from death. The message of Hushai, carried by the maidservant and communicated by the young men, contributed to the security and welfare of the king, "and all the people that were with him" (ver. 22). "In this information sent to him so opportunely, David believed that he had reason to recognize a new sign that the Lord still thought of him in love and cared for his deliverance" (Krummacher).

> "Like the coolness of snow on a harvest day
> Is a faithful messenger to them that send him:
> He refresheth the soul of his master."
>
> (Prov. xxv. 13.)

7. *They are surely noticed,* and will be abundantly recompensed. "And the king said, He is a good man," etc. (ch. xviii. 27). "And whosoever shall give to drink," etc. (Matt. x. 42).—D.

Vers. 21, 22.—*David's escape across the Jordan.* "And they passed over Jordan," etc. (ver. 22). Leaving Bahurim behind them, David and his company pursued their rough and dreary way along the wilderness of Judah until they descended into the plain of the Jordan; and there in some place (Ayephim, equivalent to "weary," Authorized Version; "The Traveller's Rest") at an easy distance from the ford of the river (opposite Jericho, and near Gilgal, ch. xix. 15) they rested at nightfall. "Amongst the thickets of the Jordan the asses of Ziba were unladen, and the weary travellers refreshed themselves, and waited for tidings from Jerusalem" (ch. xv. 28, 36; xvi. 14; ver. 16). David had been uncertain whether to cross the river; but during the night the messengers arrived, saying, "Arise," etc.; the encampment was broken up, and "by the morning light there lacked not one of them that was not gone over Jordan." *That night was another memorable one* (1 Sam. xix. 8—18). "It has been conjectured with much probability that as the first sleep of that evening was commemorated in the fourth psalm, so in the third is expressed the feeling of David's thankfulness at the final close of those twenty-four hours, of which every detail has been handed down, as if with the consciousness of their importance at the time" (Stanley). Ps. iv. 'An Even-song'—

> "In peace will I lay me down and straightway sleep;
> For thou, Jehovah, alone wilt make me to dwell securely."
>
> (Ps. iv. 8.)

Ps. iii. (see inscription), 'A Morning Prayer'—

> "I laid me down and slept;
> I awaked, for Jehovah sustaineth me."
>
> (Ps. iii. 5.)

What a brilliant light do these psalms cast upon the inner life of David! Consider him at this time as—

I. BESET BY FEROCIOUS FOES; numerous, powerful, and crafty (ch. xv. 12, 13; xvi. 15; vers. 1—3); seeking to take away his crown, his honour, and his life; by fraud, treachery, and violence. His trouble represents that of the persecuted and afflicted servant of God in every age. 1. The feeling of trouble is usually intensified with the approach of night, the season of peril and emblem of distress. 2. The good man in trouble seeks relief in God (Ps. cxxi. 4); whilst acknowledging his sins, he is conscious of sincerity, trusts in Divine mercy, and derives from his experience of former mercies an argument for his prayer. 3. He regards his adversaries in no vindictive spirit; and, although he desires their overthrow as the enemies of God, still more he desires their conversion. "The address is directed to the aristocratic party, whose tool Absalom had become" (Delitzsch).

> "When I cry, answer me, O God of my righteousness,
> Who hast made room for me in straitness;
> Be merciful unto me, and hear my prayer!
> Ye sons of men! how long shall my glory become shame?
> How long will ye love vanity, will ye seek after lies?" etc.
>
> (Ps. iv. 1—5.)

II. AIDED BY FAITHFUL FRIENDS, who sympathize with him, strive to defeat his enemies, give him useful counsel, and share his dangers (ch. xv. 15, 21, 23; vers. 7, 15, 17). 1. A time of adversity tests the fidelity of friends; and manifests it, as the night brings out the stars that were unseen by day. 2. It also makes their aid peculiarly precious; and is a sign of the favour of the Eternal Friend. 3. When friends begin to despond in a time of trouble, it is the part of a good man, "strong in faith," to encourage them, by directing their thoughts to the Divine Source of consolation, his own "exceeding joy."

> "Many say, Who will show us good?
> Lift up the light of thy countenance upon us, O Jehovah!
> Thou hast put gladness into my heart
> More than when their corn and wine abound," etc.
>
> (Ps. iv. 6—8.)

III. DELIVERED BY DIVINE FAVOUR; shown in his preservation, the salutary warning received during the night, the safe passage of the Jordan, so that "by the morning light," etc. (ver. 22), and the complete defeat of Ahithophel's counsel (vers. 14). 1. In their hostility to the good, wicked men rely on their own wisdom and strength alone, ignoring God; but "the Lord knoweth how to deliver the godly," etc. (2 Pet. ii. 9). 2. Often when a good man is despised as one abandoned of God, he is taken into closer fellowship with him and more signally protected and delivered. 3. In the morning light of every day he perceives fresh tokens of Divine favour. Whilst God "giveth songs in the night" (Job xxxv. 10), "his mercies are new every morning" (Lam. iii. 23; Ps. v.; xxx. 5; cxliii. 8).

> "Jehovah, how many are mine adversaries!
> Many rise up against me,
> Many say of my soul,
> There is no help for him in God.
> But thou, Jehovah, art a Shield about me,
> My Glory and the Lifter-up of my head.
> I cry to Jehovah with my voice,
> And he answereth me from his holy mountain," etc.
>
> (Ps. iii. 1—6.)

IV. INCITED TO VICTORIOUS CONFIDENCE; by the contemplation of what God is to him and has done for him (Gen. xv. 1); as, having now escaped his most immediate peril, he travels on "by the morning light" toward Mahanaim (ver. 24). Troubles do not always "pass away with light." Enemies still threaten (Ps. iii. 1), and with each returning day the servant of God has to begin the conflict afresh (ch. v. 22, 23). But: 1. Even when most formidable, they do not terrify him whose hope is in Jehovah. 2. They are regarded as if already overthrown. 3. And to Jehovah alone is the victory ascribed.

> "I will not be afraid of ten thousands of the people
> Who have set themselves against me round about.
> Arise, O Jehovah! Help me, O my God!
> For thou smitest all mine enemies on the cheek,
> Thou breakest the teeth of the ungodly.
> To Jehovah belongeth the victory!
> Upon thy people be thy blessing!"
>
> (Ps. iii. 7—9.)

To the period of David's exile beyond Jordan have been also referred many other psalms: Ps. lxi., lxii., lxiii. (see inscription), cxliii. (Septuagint, "when his son pursued him"), xxvi., xxvii., xxviii., etc. "A man who can, like David, amidst the first mutterings of an unexpected storm display such lofty composure and submission, and then amidst its fiercest outbursts sing hymns like the third and fourth psalms, penetrated with the purest trust in God, is already raised in an eminent degree above human weakness and frailty, and, whatever be his outward fate, he can only quit this life as one of God's victors" (Ewald).—D.

Ver. 23.—(GILOH.) *The suicide of Ahithophel.* Displeased with the decision of the council (ver. 14), Ahithophel left the city and returned to his own house, whence he had been summoned the day before (ch. xv. 12). While Ahimaaz and Jonathan hurried eastward toward the Jordan with their message (the decision of the council being as yet unknown publicly, or its reversal feared), the renowned counsellor rode southward toward Giloh, brooding over what might have been (ver. 2) and what would be; the shadows of night thickening around him (1 Sam. xxviii. 1—10); and the same night (or soon afterwards) "his lamp was put out in darkness" (Prov. xiii. 9). "With the deliberate cynicism of a man who had lost all faith, he committed that rare crime in Israel, suicide" (Edersheim). "He was probably not the first man who hanged himself, but he bears the unenviable distinction of being the first whose hanging himself is recorded; and society would have little reason to complain if all who have since sentenced themselves to this doom were as worthy of it as this father of self-suspenders." (Kitto). "So perished the great Machiavelli of that age, the very wisest of the very wise men of this world!" (Delany). We have here—

I. A DISAPPOINTED POLITICIAN. Like many other eminent politicians, he was destitute of religious principles; set his heart upon the world, and had "his portion in this life" (Ps. xvii. 14); was proud of his own wisdom, ambitious of wealth, fame, honour, and power, and hostile to godliness and godly men; the leading mind of the ungodly party in Israel. "He had no regard either to the ways of God or the laws of God. Providence made no part of his plan. He considered with great sagacity how *he* was to act; but he never considered how God would act; and therefore all his wise designs must have been very defective. The rich man said, 'I shall want room for my stores,' etc. But the Gospel calls him a fool, for not considering that God might call him out of the world that night, and that then all his schemes of happiness and prosperity would die with him. Such is he who is wise without God; and such was this Ahithophel" (Jones of Nayland). We now see him under the influence of: 1. *Wounded pride*, frustrated ambition, and, probably, ungratified malice (ver. 1). The rejection of his counsel was regarded by him as a personal affront, and a fatal blow to his position and prospects; for "he had been impelled by nothing else than a mad ambition, so that life itself became insupportable when the attainment of the position he had hankered after proved insufficient to satisfy his desires" (Ewald). He would be revenged on Absalom himself, by leaving him to pursue his own course. 2. *Unavoidable fear* of the disgrace, infamy, and punishment that awaited him. For, by the adoption of Hushai's counsel, he foresaw that all was lost, and that David would live and reign. Although he had the "Roman" courage (or rather, cowardice and impatience) to face death, he had not courage enough to face disaster.

> "He's not valiant that dares die;
> But he that boldly bears calamity."

3. *Bitter remorse*, desperation, and despair. "Perhaps he now began to see for the first time that, as he had been against God, God was against him, and, according to the prayer of David, was turning his counsel into foolishness. Under this calamity, what had he to support him? Nothing but that policy of a wicked man which never supported anybody long. In the trouble of a righteous man there is hope; but in the trouble of the wicked there is none. And, for a man like him, there is no refuge but in despair" (Ps. vii. 15, 16).

II. A DELIBERATE CRIME. "And put his household in order," etc.; *i.e.* "he settled his affairs, he made his will, as a person of sound mind and memory; as he would have done if death had been coming upon him in a natural way." He did not commit the deed in an outburst of passion, but with deliberation and forethought. Suicide is often due to insanity, and without blame (except in so far as it is induced by previous misconduct); but in his case there is no indication of it; nor was there the same justification or the same extenuation of guilt as in other cases (Judg. xvi. 30; 1 Sam. xxxi. 4, 5). Whatever may have been the measure of his culpability, suicide is a crime: 1. Against a man *himself*; a violation of the law of self-preservation written upon his nature. 2. Against *society*. "Nor can any case be put which is not concluded under sin by the peculiar injury or general mischief" (Paley, 'Sermons'). 3. Against *God*, who has "fixed his canon 'gainst self-slaughter" (Exod. xx. 13);

who has committed life to men as a trust; and whose will in relation to it is intimated in various ways. "In every society where the Christian and old Pythagorean idea of life, as a talent and a trust, is unknown or forgotten, and where its value is measured by enjoyment, suicide will be likely to become common" (Thirlwall, 'Letters to a Friend'). It is "a complication of ingratitude, contempt of the Lord's gift of life, defiance, impatience, pride, rebellion, and infidelity" (Scott; Wardlaw, 'Sys. Theol.'). "What a mixture do we find here of wisdom and madness!" (Hall). "Thus he displayed the miserable infatuation of worldly policy" (Wordsworth). Under the light which the gospel sheds upon the present and the future, the act of the self-destroyer is rendered peculiarly criminal and awful.

III. A DREADFUL RETRIBUTION. (Ch. xii. 10—12.) The course of sin on which he had entered was attended (as it ever is in others) by most baneful effects on himself, and ended in destruction; the culmination at once of his sin and of his punishment. He became: 1. His own *tormentor*; rushing against impassable barriers, and bringing upon himself irreparable misery. 2. His own *tempter*; being urged onward by inward impulses to further transgression. 3. His own *executioner*; inflicting with his own hand the extreme penalty of the law; a retribution more dreadful than when inflicted by the direct stroke of Heaven (ch. vi. 6—8) or the hands of other men (ch. iv. 12; xviii. 7, 14). "The wages of sin is death" (Prov. xiv. 32). "Thus it falleth out that wicked counsel doth chiefly redound to the hurt of the author thereof" (Willet). Like Judas, Ahithophel went to "his own place" (Acts i. 25).

IV. AN ADMONITORY END; the consideration of which should lead to: 1. The conviction of the enormous evil of suicide; which may exert a preserving influence in an hour of temptation. 2. The abhorrence of the principles which induce its commission, and the avoiding of every sinful way. The sinner is a self-destroyer (Hos. xiii. 9). 3. The cherishing, with renewed earnestness, of the opposite principles of humility, faith, patience, godliness, uprightness, charity, etc. "If the affections are violently set upon anything in this world, whether fame, wealth, or pleasure, and are disappointed, then life becomes insupportable. Therefore, the moral is this: 'Set your affection on things above, not on things on the earth.'"—D.

Vers. 24—29.—(MAHANAIM.) *Hospitality.* Shobi (ch. x. 1—4; xii. 26—31); Machir (ch. ix. 4); Barzillai (ch. xix. 31—40). On hearing of the arrival of David at Mahanaim, these three men came with one accord, bringing presents, and "provided the king of sustenance while he lay" there (ch. xix. 32). "We are inclined to regard them as representative men: Shobi, of the extreme border-inhabitants, or rather foreign tributaries; Machir, of the former adherents of Saul; and Barzillai, of the wealthy landowners generally" (Edersheim). Whilst acting, specially, from feelings of loyalty, gratitude, and affectionate regard, they displayed a *hospitality* such as is often enjoined (Lev. xxv. 35; Isa. lviii. 7; Luke xiv. 13; Rom. xii. 13), but frequently omitted (Heb. xiii. 2). It was: 1. *Much needed* by David and his followers, "who were like a band of beggars or marauders" (Delitzsch), driven from their home, in a comparatively strange land (Ps. lxi. 2), beset by hostile forces (ver. 25), in want of shelter, rest, and provision (ver. 29). "The Son of man had not where to lay his head" (Luke ix. 58); and in his "brethren" he is often persecuted and in want of all things (Matt. xxv. 35; Gal. vi. 10; 1 Tim. v. 10; 3 John 5, 6). 2. *Admirably exemplified.* (1) Spontaneously, without being solicited. (2) Promptly, without delay. (3) Cordially, with sympathy and pity; for they said, "The people have become hungry, and weary, and thirsty in the wilderness." (4) Considerately; those things which were most necessary and agreeable being supplied. (5) Generously; according to ability, and "without grudging" (1 Pet. iv. 9). (6) Disinterestedly, unselfishly, with self-denial and at no little risk. (7) Perseveringly; not (as in another familiar instance) for three days (Acts xxviii. 7), but for nearly as many months. It not unfrequently happens that the poor and the stranger receive the most hospitable treatment from those on whom they have the least claim. 3. *Eminently helpful*, comforting and encouraging; a sign of the Divine care for him (Gen. xxxii. 2)—a proof that he was not forsaken by all the people, and an influence adapted to gather others around him. "The faithfulness of human love, strengthening in need and cheering in misfortune is not only the copy, but also the means and instrument of the faithfulness of the Divine love, granted to those who bow humbly beneath God's hand and wholly trust him" (Erdmann). 4. *Abundantly requited.* Those who exercise it "are blessed in their doing" (Jas. i. 25); and receive unexpected honour and benefit from their guests (ch. xix. 33, 38, 39; Gen. xviii.; Acts xxviii. 8) and from the Lord himself (Heb. vi. 10; Matt. xxv. 34).—D.

Ver. 23.—*Suicide.* Such was the end of the great counsellor of the age, who was regarded as an "oracle of God" (ch. xvi. 23). Astute as he was, he was evidently unprincipled. His desertion of David for Absalom, and the advice he gave the latter, show this. His wisdom did not avail for his own good. He died "as a fool dieth," and by his own hand. Yet there was a thoughtfulness and deliberateness about the deed such as was in a certain keeping with his intellectual ability. It is not difficult to account for the desperate course he took. He was mortified that Absalom, for whom he had incurred so much guilt, and made so great sacrifices, and who knew and revered his wisdom (ch. xvi. 23), should have rejected his counsel for that of Hushai; and, because of his confidence in the wisdom of his own advice, he felt sure that David would be victorious, and he himself, not only disgraced and ruined, but executed as a traitor. Rather than face this prospect, he hanged himself. Self-murder is not an agreeable subject, yet it may be salutary occasionally to reflect upon it. Many do put an end to their own lives; and doubtless many others are more or less tempted to do so. It may be hoped that consideration of the matter may fortify the minds of some against the first approaches of such temptation.

I. THE CAUSES OF SUICIDE. 1. *Mental derangement is doubtless a common cause.* Not so common as we might infer from the verdicts of coroners' juries, anxious to relieve surviving relatives from the pains and penalties inflicted by antiquated civil and ecclesiastical laws; yet still the most common cause. It is virtually the same thing to say that disease of the brain is the common cause. This is often hereditary, or it may be induced by overwork, or by excessive indulgence of the appetites and passions, or by the pressure of worldly anxieties. Insanity relieves of the guilt of self murder; nevertheless, where the insanity is the result of habits which are sinful, the guilt of these remains; and, if the probable issue of them was foreseen, the sinner cannot free himself altogether from the guilt which attaches to the act of self-destruction. 2. *The pressure or dread of troubles often leads to this crime.* Not only as they produce insanity, but as they operate on a sane mind. Intense pain, great misfortunes, disgrace, or the dread of it, fear of destitution, etc. Instances: Saul and his armour-bearer (1 Sam. xxxi. 4, 5); Zimri (1 Kings xvi. 18); Ahithophel; and the Philippian jailor (Acts xvi. 27). 3. *Remorse and despair.* Judas (Matt. xxvii. 5).

II. ITS SIN AND FOLLY. 1. *It is contrary to nature.* The love of life is one of the strongest principles implanted in us by our Creator. "Self-preservation is the first law of nature." The natural conscience, which teaches the criminality of taking the life of another, equally teaches that of taking our own. We may for adequate reasons, in serving God or men, expose our lives to peril; but we must not ourselves extinguish them, and thus cut short our opportunities of service. 2. *It is daring impiety towards God.* It is a cowardly abandonment of our trust; an act of rebellion against him who has assigned us our post and work; a contemptuous casting away as worthless, or worse, of God's precious gift. It springs from distrust of God, discontent with his appointments, a proud refusal to serve him unless under such conditions as are agreeable to ourselves. 3. *It is a serious injustice to our friends and society.* Our life is given us for the sake of others as well as ourselves. To abandon it is to rob and injure them. It is vain to say we can no longer be of service to them. Under the worst circumstances a man can set an example of patience and submission such as is much needed in this world of suffering. And if he have become a burden to others, in bearing the burden they may be enriched and blessed. 4. *It is in direct opposition to the revealed will of God.* No distinct prohibition can, indeed, be quoted, unless it is included in the command, "Thou shalt do no murder;" which is doubtful. But it is entirely opposed to all the precepts of Scripture which enjoin patient endurance of trials, and that to the end; and to the examples of such endurance which are set before us, especially that of our Lord Jesus Christ. The instances in Holy Writ of fleeing from suffering by rushing out of the world, are all those of either wicked or deranged persons. 5. *It is a desperate plunge into worse miseries than can be experienced in this life.* The self-murderer rushes red-handed into the presence of the awful Judge, depriving himself of all possibility of repentance.

III. PRESERVATIVES AGAINST THIS DREADFUL SIN. In this case emphatically " prevention is better than cure "—preservation, that is, from that condition of mind from which suicide springs. And this is to be found in vital godliness in all its branches. In particular : 1. *Constant faith in God.* Confidence that he is, and that he is the Rewarder of those who seek him, however he may try them. Unbounded trust in his goodness and wisdom, as exercised in respect to ourselves. Earnest and cheerful service of him under whatever conditions he may place us. Profound submission to his will. Dread of his displeasure. 2. *Moderation in respect to worldly things.* In our estimates of their worth, and of the evil of being deprived of them ; in the pursuit of them ; in their enjoyment ; in sorrow at their departure. Habitual self-control. Intemperance partakes of the guilt of suicide. 3. *Prayer.* Habitual. Special when cares and temptations press with special weight. " Casting all your care upon him ; for he careth for you " (1 Pet. v. 7 ; comp. Ps. lv. 22). " In nothing be anxious, but in everything by prayer," etc. (Phil. iv. 6, 7, Revised Version). "The peace of God " thus obtained will best " guard " the heart and the thoughts against all that tends to despondency. 4. *The communion of saints.* Christian society ; social worship ; visitation of the Christian poor, whose privations and sufferings will often make our own seem small, whose cheerfulness and resignation will shame our discontent and impatience, and assist us to a better mind. 5. *Prompt and resolute* rejection, with loathing, of every thought of this as a possible way out of trouble. Probably many persons of a nervous and desponding temper are visited with such thoughts. Let them be instantly dismissed, lest they grow in frequency and power, and in a weak moment produce the corresponding deed.

In conclusion, all sin is of the nature of suicide. He who impenitently persists in it destroys the life of his own soul. All they that hate the Divine wisdom and forsake its ways " love death " (Prov. viii. 36).—G. W.

Vers. 27—29.—*Supplies for the king's army.* Mahanaim is memorable in the history of Jacob ; derived, indeed, its name from the circumstance that there " the angels of God met him " (Gen. xxxii. 1) on his way back to the promised land, and just before his interview with Esau, about whose present disposition towards him he was doubtful. In our text also we read of veritable angels (messengers) of God, though human, coming to the same place to succour and encourage another of his servants when in circumstances of great difficulty. David had with him a large company of friends and subjects, who remained faithful while so many were faithless ; but their very number was an embarrassment, and they arrived in the neighbourhood " hungry, and weary, and thirsty." Very welcome, therefore, were the supplies which these chieftains brought for their relief, and which the historian enumerates with so much evident pleasure. They thus cheered the heart of David, contributed very materially to his final victory over his rebellious son and subjects, and obtained for themselves a good name. In the Christian warfare against error and sin there is room and need for this kind of service. The progress of the spiritual cause depends no little on the material aids. As soldiers must eat and drink in order that they may fight, so Christian ministers and missionaries, however spiritual and holy and disinterested, cannot preach and teach unless they are fed and clothed, and their work facilitated by various appliances which are only to be obtained and maintained by money or money's worth. It is only in exceptional cases that competent labourers are able to support themselves by the labour of their hands or from their private fortunes. Hence the absolute necessity that Christians should furnish material supplies, and the certainty that the progress of the Christian cause in the world will be greatly hindered if, through indifference or avarice, such supplies are scantily furnished. In our time the duty of furnishing them more abundantly needs to be pressed on the attention of the disciples of Christ with much urgency. The world is almost everywhere open to the missionary ; devoted men and women offer themselves, ready to go anywhere to make Christ known ; but in many instances they cannot be sent forth for want of the means of sending and sustaining them. That the ability of Christ's servants in this direction is being employed to the utmost is incredible in view of the lavish expenditure of many of them on worldly display and luxury. The disposition is wanting; and this in part because a conviction has not yet been awakened in their hearts of the necessity and worth of pecuniary supplies, and the imperative duty and high honour of furnishing them. Such a conviction may be promoted by due attention to the following considerations.

I. THE OBLIGATIONS OF ALL CHRISTIANS IN RESPECT TO THE PROMOTION OF THE KINGDOM OF GOD IN THE WORLD ARE THE SAME. The character, the toils, the self-denying endurance of hardships and privations, of many missionaries and other ministers of the gospel, awaken admiration and applause. But, amongst those who applaud, the feeling is often wanting that they are themselves as really and truly bound to devoted service of Christ as the men whom they admire. 1. Objects of the same Divine love, redeemed by the same precious blood, called by the same grace, partakers of the same privileges and hopes, they ought to cherish a like ardent love to Christ, and with a like zeal seek to fulfil the purposes for which he lived and died. 2. They are equally "stewards of the manifold grace of God" (1 Pet. iv. 10; 1 Chron. xxix. 14, 16). 3. They are equally bound to love their fellow-men, and seek their good to the utmost of their power

II. THE NECESSITY OF MATERIAL SUPPLIES AFFORDS TO ALL THE OPPORTUNITY OF BEING PARTNERS WITH THE NOBLEST WORKERS IN SUSTAINING AND EXTENDING THE KINGDOM OF GOD. The good women who ministered to our Lord of their substance (Luke viii. 2, 3) became thus partakers in his work. The Philippians who showed hospitality to St. Paul when amongst them (Acts xvi. 15), or sent gifts to him afterwards (Phil. iv. 14—16), are recognized by him as having "fellowship" (partnership) with him, "in furtherance of the gospel" (Phil. i. 5, 7, Revised Version). St. John describes those who were hospitable to evangelists as their "fellow-helpers to the truth" (3 John 8). In like manner, all who subscribe of their money towards the support of Christian ministries and missions, have the honour of being fellow-workers with those who give the ablest personal service. This was recognized by the lad who hastened to a missionary meeting, and being asked the reason of his eagerness, replied, "I have a share in the concern." Bible, missionary, and other societies have, by awakening such thoughts and feelings, done much to enlarge and elevate the minds of the myriads of their supporters in every part of Christendom.

III. GIVING EXERCISES THE SAME CHRISTIAN VIRTUES AS PERSONAL SERVICE. For right and sufficient contribution of substance, as for right preaching and teaching, are required: 1. Faith and love. 2. Conscientiousness. 3. Self-denial. Indeed, all Christian principles and affections are brought into play in the course of earnest service of either kind. Both are processes of education of the Christian soul, by which the lessons of Christ are more thoroughly learnt.

IV. IT IS EQUALLY ACCEPTABLE TO GOD. St. Paul calls the present he had received from the Philippians "an odour of a sweet smell, a sacrifice acceptable, well-pleasing to God" (Phil. iv. 18; see also Heb. xiii. 16). Right motives are, of course, presupposed; but, when these are present, both kinds of service are equally acceptable. "He that receiveth a prophet in the name of a prophet shall receive a prophet's reward" (Matt. x. 41).

V. IT SHALL OBTAIN A SIMILAR RECOMPENSE. In: 1. *The consciousness of Divine approval.* 2. *The pleasure of serving Christ.* 3. *The joy of doing the highest and most enduring good to men.* 4. *The rewards of the last day.* The expressed approval of Christ. Admission to "the joy of the Lord" (Matt. xxv. 21, 23). Participation with Christ and the saints in the joy of final and complete victory over the powers of evil. Every true-hearted sharer in the work and conflict shall share in the gladness of the triumph, when not only the sower and the reaper (John iv. 36), but those who have furnished them with needful support, shall "rejoice together."

Finally, we must not think of workers and givers as two distinct classes of persons, having no part in each other's functions. All Christians can and ought to render personal service as well as contributions. There is need and room for all to labour as well as give. In maintaining Church-life, in teaching the ignorant, in seeking and saving the lost, in comforting the sorrowful, etc., there is scope for the talents of all. No one can by his gifts purchase freedom from such services. We must give account of every talent committed to us.—G. W.

EXPOSITION.

CHAPTER XVIII.

Ver. 1.—And David numbered. The verb really means that he organized his army, and arranged it in companies and divisions. As Absalom gathered all Israel to him, there would be some delay; and David, like a wise general, made use of it for training the brave but undisciplined men who had joined him, chiefly from Gilead. Besides these, he had with him numerous veterans, whose skill and experience would be invaluable in such service. The result was that when the rebels came to close quarters, they had a vast body of men, but David a disciplined force, which, under skilful generalship, scattered Absalom's raw levies with ease. The arrangement into thousands and hundreds was in accordance with the civil divisions (Exod. xviii. 25), both being, in fact, dictated by nature as multiples of our hands.

Ver. 2.—A third part. Armies are usually divided into three divisions: a centre and two wings when drawn up for battle; a van, the main body, and a rearguard when on the march. But the Israelites had no settled rule upon the point, and, when occasion required, Joab divided his army into two parts (ch. x. 9, 10). The reason of the threefold division in this case was that Ittai had brought his clan, or *taf*, with him, and as these would certainly not have fought under an Israelite leader, nor the Israelites under Ittai, David placed all foreigners under his command, while he gave his own nephews the command of the native troops. He thus avoided all jealousies; and Ittai's men, honoured by being made a distinct portion of the army, would feel their reputation at stake, and would rival the Israelites in valour.

Ver. 3.—It is better that thou succour us out of the city. David thought it to be his duty to go out with the men who were risking their lives in his cause, but they felt not only how painful it would be for a father to fight against his son; but also that there would certainly be a picked body of men who would try to bring the battle to a rapid end by slaying David. But while they partly urge personal considerations, their chief argument is that David would be of more use if, posted with a body of troops at the city, he held himself in reserve to succour any division that might be in danger. And David, seeing how earnest their wish was, yielded to this representation, feeling that it would give steadiness to his men if they knew that so experienced a general was watching the fight, and was ready to succour them if they needed aid. As the people say

that it would not matter "if half of us die," and that David "is worth ten thousand of us," Ewald draws the reasonable conclusion that their whole number was about twenty thousand men. The Hebrew literally is, "For now (*'attah*) as us are ten thousand," which might mean, "There are ten thousand such as we are, but no one like thee." But the Septuagint and Vulgate read, "But thou (*attah*) art as ten thousand of us." The Syriac, however, like the Hebrew, reads "now."

Ver. 5.—All the people heard. The king spake so earnestly and strongly to the generals that the words ran from rank to rank as they marched forward. So in ver. 12 the man says to Joab, "In our hearing the king charged thee and Abishai," etc. It does not follow that each one heard the sound of the king's voice, but only that the command was given publicly again and again, and in the presence of the army.

Ver. 6.—The wood of Ephraim. There is a diversity of opinion as to the locality thus described. It might mean the large forest tract in the highlands of Ephraim; but if so, the battle must have been fought on the west of the Jordan, whereas the general tenor of the narrative makes it plain that it took place on the eastern side, near Mahanaim. It is true that no wood of Ephraim is ever mentioned elsewhere in the Bible as situated in Gilead, and those who cannot believe in such a wood except within the borders of the tribe, argue that, after the three divisions had marched out to battle, there was long skirmishing, in which Absalom drew David's men across the Jordan, and there gave battle. But Absalom's army evidently surprised, and as we are told that "he pitched in the land of Gilead" (ch. xvii. 26), for him to have retired would have been a confession of weakness; and Joab, after seeing him cross the Jordan, would not have followed him, but let this retrograde movement have its effect upon his followers. Such a movement is absolutely incredible on the part of an army at least three times as numerous as those whom they attacked, and confident of victory. Moreover, armies in those days were not composed of men receiving pay, and bound to remain with their colours, but of yeomen unwilling to be kept long absent from their farms, and liable, therefore, rapidly to melt away. A quick decision was plainly necessary for Absalom, while David could afford to wait. But besides this, when his forces moved out of Mahanaim, David took his post at the gate with the reserves, and he was still there, sitting "between the two gates," when news was brought him of the victory (ver. 24). The only real argument in support of the view that the battle was fought on the west of the Jordan is that "Ahimaaz ran by the way of the plain" (ver. 23), Hebrew, the *kikkar*— a name specially given to the valley of the Jordan near Jericho. But then Cushi must also have run through the same valley, and it is evident that his route was in this very respect different from that taken by Ahimaaz. Really, *kikkar*, which in Hebrew means "circuit," may be used of the country round any city, and is applied in Neh. xii. 28 to the environs of Jerusalem. Here the meaning probably is that, while the Cushite took the route back over the battle-field through the wood, Ahimaaz went to the left of it, over the more level ground, nearer the Jordan. And though the name is chiefly used of that part near Jericho, it was probably applied popularly to every stretch of level ground near the river. This argument, therefore, is inconclusive; while, on the other side, it is plain that David's army returned that same day to Mahanaim, that they knew at once of his distress, and that they were beginning to steal away home when Joab made David come forth to thank them, and encourage them to remain with him. The most probable explanation of the difficulty is that "the wood of Ephraim" was so called because it was the spot where Jephthah defeated the Ephraimites when they invaded Gilead to punish him for daring to go to war without their consent, they being then the dominant tribe, to whose arbitrament belonged all imperial matters (Judg. xii. 4—6).

Ver. 8.—**The battle was there scattered.** The word in the Hebrew is a noun, which the Massorites have changed into a participle. But the noun is right: "The battle became a scattering," that is, it was a series of disconnected encounters, in which David's three divisions attacked and routed Absalom's men, while still on the march, without giving them an opportunity of collecting and forming in order of battle. **And the wood devoured more people that day than the sword devoured.** The woodland was difficult, full of gorges and bogs and steep defiles leading down to the Jordan, and the fugitives easily lost their way in it, and wandered about till they were hopelessly entangled in thicket and morass.

Ver. 9.—**Absalom met the servants of David.** The verb means that he came upon them by chance. Evidently in the intricacies of the forest, Absalom had lost his way, and, finding himself suddenly in danger of being captured by some of David's men, he urged his mule through a thicket, as the open ground was blocked by his pursuers. But in the attempt his head was jammed

between the boughs of a great terebinth, and the mule, struggling onward, left him hanging in mid-air. Nothing is said about his hair having caused the accident, and apparently it was his neck which became fixed. Probably, too, he was half stunned by the blow, and choked by the pressure; and then his hair would make it very difficult for him to extricate himself. And so, after one or two efforts, in which he would be in danger of dislocating his neck, he would remain suspended to await his fate. Now, this adventure makes the whole affair perfectly plain. Absalom was riding his mule, evidently unprepared for battle. The chariot and horses, with fifty men as his body-guard, used by him at Jerusalem (ch. xv. 1), are nowhere near him. Chariots, of course, would have been useless on such rough ground, but Absalom would have had a picked body of young men round him in the battle; and mules were only for use on the march, and were sent into the rear when the fighting began. But the last thing that Absalom expected was that he should be attacked on the march. He was advancing with an army infinitely more numerous than that of David, and assumed that David would wait at Mahanaim, and, if he fought at all, would fight under its walls. His defeat he regarded as certain, and then the vain-glorious prince and all Israel would drag the city into the nearest ravine. In this over-confidence he was riding in advance of his army, which was struggling on over most difficult ground. For "rising as the country does suddenly from the deep valley of the Jordan, it is naturally along its whole western border deeply furrowed by the many streams which drain the district; and our ride," says Canon Tristram, "was up and down concealed glens, which we only perceived when on their brink, and mounting from which on the other side, a short canter soon brought us to the edge of the next" (Tristram, p. 462). Struggling along over such ground, Absalom's men were not merely tired and weary, but had lost all order, and "become a scattering," and probably Absalom had cantered on in order to find some suitable spot for re-forming them. Suddenly he sees at a little distance before him one of the three detachments of David's army, which had marched out a few miles from Mahanaim, and posted themselves on some fit spot to attack the rebels on their march. Apparently they caught no glimpse of him, but he immediately became aware of the tactics of the king's generals, and discerned the extreme danger of his position. Everything depended upon celerity. If he could warn his men, the foremost would halt until the others came up, and a sufficient force be gathered to resist Joab's onslaught. There was no cowardice on his part, but simply the discharge of his duty as a general. He turns his mule round, and dashes away in order to halt and form his men, keeping to the wood that he may not be seen. In his great haste he is not careful in picking his route, and possibly his mule was stubborn, and swerved; and so, in attempting to force his way through the thicket, he is stunned by a blow from a branch of a terebinth tree, and so entangled in its boughs that he cannot free himself; and as none of David's men had seen him, he might have hung there to be the prey of the vultures, and only his riderless mule have been left to bear witness to his having met with some disaster. Meanwhile his followers struggle on, until they come upon David's men, who put them to the sword. There is no battle, but the three divisions, advancing in order, make merciless slaughter of their opponents. For some time Absalom's forces, extended over many miles of march, do not even learn what is going on in their front, and twenty thousand men had fallen before, becoming aware of their defeat, they fly in wild confusion, to lose more men in their panic than had fallen in fighting. Their loss would even have been greater had not Joab stopped the pursuit upon Absalom's death. But where was Amasa, and what was he doing? He had led his troops miserably, had taken no precautions against surprise, and did nothing to rally them. Had Absalom got back in safety to the van, he might have saved his men from so disastrous a defeat; but Amasa, doubtless a brave soldier, proved himself quite incompetent to the duties of a commander-in-chief, and no match for the sagacious Joab.

Ver. 11.—**A girdle**. This was an important article of dress (Ezek. xxiii. 15), and was often richly embroidered. Absalom's death was well deserved, and there can be little doubt that, if he had gained the victory, he would have massacred David and all his family. The dishonour done to his father at Jerusalem was even intended by Ahithophel to render all reconciliation impossible. But Joab was disobeying the king's express orders, and as Absalom was incapable of making resistance, he ought to have taken him prisoner, and left it to David to decide what his punishment should be.

Ver. 12.—**Though I should receive**. The Hebrew text expresses the horror of the man at Joab's proposal much more vividly than the tame correction of the Massorites admitted into the Authorized Version: "And I, no! weighing in my palm a thousand of silver, I would not put forth my hand against the son of the king."

Ver. 13.—**Against mine own life**. Again the K'tib is better: "Or had I wrought perfidiously against his life—and nothing is hidden from the king—so wouldst thou have set thyself against me." Not only was the man faithful to the king, but he was perfectly aware of Joab's unscrupulous character. If only Absalom were put out of the way, Joab would have readily consented to the execution of the unimportant person who had been the means of gratifying his wish.

Ver. 14.—**Three darts**; Hebrew, *three staves* (see ch. xxiii. 21). The weapons of the ancients were of a very inferior kind, and stakes sharpened at the end and hardened in the fire were used by the infantry, until the increasing cheapness of iron made it possible to supply them with pikes. Joab's act was not one of intentional cruelty, but, picking up the first weapons that came to hand, he hurried away to kill his victim. His thrusts with these pointed sticks were brutal, and inflicted mortal wounds; but as they were not immediately fatal, Joab's armour-bearers, who had followed him, and who had with them Joab's own better weapons, were called upon to put an end to Absalom's sufferings. His **heart** does not mean that organ anatomically, but the middle of his body. So at the end of the verse, **in the midst of the oak**, is, in the Hebrew, *in the heart of the terebinth*.

Ver. 16.—**Joab blew the trumpet**. Stern and unscrupulous as he was, yet Joab is always statesmanlike. He had slain Absalom more for public than for private reasons, though he may have grimly remembered his own blazing barley-field. But the rebellion being now crushed, further slaughter was impolitic, and would only cause sullen displeasure. **The people**, at the end of the verse, are those under Joab's command, and a translation proposed by some, "Joab wished to spare the people," is to be rejected.

Ver. 17.—**A great pit**; Hebrew, *the great pit;* as though there was some great hollow or well-known depression in the wood, into which they cast Absalom's dead body, and raised a cairn over it. Such cairns were used as memorials of any event deemed worthy of lasting remembrance, but the similar cairn piled over the dead body of Achan (Josh. vii. 26) makes it probable that the act was also intended as a sign of condemnation of Absalom's conduct. **All Israel fled every one to his tent**. The Israelites were still a pastoral people, with tents for their abodes, though houses were gradually taking their place. The cry, "To your tents, O Israel!" (1 Kings xii. 16), meant, "Go away to your homes!" and not "Gather for war!" It is remarkable how constantly Absalom's followers are described as "Israel," while the loyal men are "David's

servants." Absalom's was evidently the
popular cause, and, besides Uriah's murder,
there must have been political reasons for
discontent at work to make David's government so distasteful.

Ver. 18.—**Absalom ... had taken and reared
up for himself a pillar.** In contrast with
the heap of stones cast over his dishonoured
body, the narrator calls attention to the
costly memorial erected by Absalom in his
lifetime. The three unnamed sons mentioned in ch. xiv. 27 seem to have died in
their infancy, and probably also their
mother; and Absalom, instead of taking
other wives to bear him sons, which would
have been in unison with the feelings of the
time, manifested his grief by raising this
monument. We have no reason for supposing that it was the result of vanity and
ostentation. Ostentatious he was, and magnificent, but his not marrying again is a
sign of genuine sorrow. **The king's dale** is
"the Valley of Shaveh," mentioned in Gen.
xiv. 17; but whether it was near Jerusalem,
as Josephus asserts, or near Sodom, is uncertain. The pillar was probably an obelisk,
or possibly a pyramid, and certainly was
not the Ionic column of Roman workmanship shown in the Middle Ages and at the
present time as "Absalom's grave." This
is in the Kidron valley, about two furlongs
from Jerusalem. **Absalom's place**; literally,
Absalom's hand; that is, memorial (see note
on 1 Sam. xv. 12).

Ver. 21.—**Cushi.** This is not a proper
name, but signifies that he was an Ethiopian, that is, a negro slave in Joab's service.
Joab was unwilling to expose Ahimaaz to
the king's displeasure, and we gather from
ver. 27 that the sending of a person of low
rank would be understood to signify evil
tidings. The bearer of good news received
a present, and therefore the passing over
all Joab's personal friends to send a slave
was proof that the message was not expected
to bring the bearer honour or reward. And
Joab was quite right in supposing that
David would be more displeased at his son's
death than pleased at the victory.

Ver. 22.—**Seeing ... thou hast no tidings
ready.** This was not true; there were most
important tidings ready. But it is the translation which is in fault. What Joab said
is, "Seeing thou hast no tidings that find,"
that is, no message that will find for thee
the king's favour and a reward.

Ver. 23.—**Ahimaaz ran by the way of the
plain**; Hebrew, *the kikkar*, or *Jordan valley*.
The battle, as we saw in ver. 6, was fought
on the eastern side of the river, and Absalom's army, in their flight, would endeavour
to reach the fords of the Jordan (comp. Judg.
xii. 5); and probably Joab had pursued them
for some distance before the man found in

the thicket the body of the unfortunate Absalom. The large slaughter of twenty thousand
men (ver. 7) proves that the defeated rebels
were vigorously followed. In carrying the
news the negro evidently went back by the
route which the troops had followed; while
Ahimaaz, using his more developed intellect,
took a longer course to the west, but one
that avoided the tangles and the deep defiles of the forest. Strictly, the Kikkar, as
we have seen, was the name of the Jordan
valley near Jericho; but it was probably
applicable also to the same sort of formation
further north. On approaching Mahanaim,
Ahimaaz would strike inland, and the two
routes would join one another; and one
reason which made Ahimaaz go more to the
west was that he did not wish the Cushite to
know that he had a rival. He would thus
go at a steady pace, picking his way through
the forest, while Ahimaaz was using his
utmost speed.

Ver. 24.—**David sat between the two
gates.** The gateway was in a tower in the
city walls, and David was sitting in the
space between the inner and outer gates.
Over this space was a chamber, mentioned
in ver. 33, while the sentinel was posted
upon the front wall over the outer gate.

Ver. 25.—**If he be alone.** In case of
defeat there would have been a crowd of
runaways in eager flight. And when soon
afterwards a second courier is seen, as he also
is alone, and comes by a different route, his
appearance only suggests the idea of com-
pleter tidings. And quickly the foremost is
recognized by his running as the son of the
high priest, and David is then assured that
all has gone well, because Joab would not
have sent a man of such rank to be the
bearer of bad news. The word **good** may
also mean that Ahimaaz was too brave a
man to have fled from the battle, and must,
therefore, have come on an errand from Joab.

Ver. 28.—**And said unto the king, All is
well**; Hebrew, *Peace.* This was the ordinary salutation among the Israelites, but its
hurried exclamation on the part of the
breathless runner was probably intended to
convey the idea given in the Authorized
Version. **Hath delivered up the men**, etc;
Hebrew, *hath hedged*, or *shut in* (see upon
this expression the note on 1 Sam. xvii. 46,
and comp. Ps. xxxi. 8). Both there and in
ch. xxii. 20 prosperity is compared to the
being in a broad place, where there is freedom to act (see also note on ch. xiii. 2).

Ver. 29.—**Is the young man Absalom safe?**
literally, *Is there peace to the lad Absalom?*
Was this mere love for the handsome but
rebellious son, whose image comes back to
the father as he was when just reaching
manhood? Certainly not. David was
thinking of the ominous words, "The sword

shall never depart from thine house" (ch. xii. 10). The sword had devoured one son; was it now to claim another? And then? and then? Where would it stop? And Ahimaaz saw the king's distress, and gave an evasive answer. He understood now Joab's unwillingness to let him carry such painful tidings, and was glad that this part of the news had been entrusted to the Cushite. When Joab sent the king's servant, and (me) thy servant. This distinction is strange, and probably one of these phrases has crept in from the margin. But if the Ethiopian was technically "the king's slave," and Ahimaaz "thy slave" (by courtesy), we might imagine that negro attendants already formed part of the state of kings. It was long afterwards that Ebedmelech was a Cushite in the service of Zedekiah (Jer. xxxviii. 7).

Ver. 31.—Tidings, etc. The literal meaning is more fit for the mouth of a slave. "Let my lord the king learn the tidings that Jehovah hath judged (and delivered) thee this day from the hand," etc., that is, God, sitting as Judge at the assize of battle;

hath given sentence for thee, and pronounced thy acquittal. The same phrase occurs in ver. 19.

Ver. 32.—Is the young man, etc.? Alarm for Absalom is the dominant feeling in David's mind; and as Cushi had been sent for the very purpose, he at once communicates the news to him in words that leave no doubt of his meaning.

Ver. 33.—The king was much moved. The Hebrew word properly refers to agitation of body. A violent trembling seized the king, and, rising, he went up to the guard-chamber over the two gates, that he might give free course to his lamentation. The whole is told so vividly that we can scarcely doubt that we have here the words of one who was present at this pathetic scene, who saw the tremor which shook David's body, and watched him as he crept slowly up the stairs, uttering words of intense sorrow. And it was conscience which smote him; for his own "sin had found him out." In Ps. xxxviii. and xl. he has made the confession that it was his own iniquity which was now surging over his head.

HOMILETICS.

Vers. 1—18.—The facts are: 1. David, refreshed by the aid sent him, sets himself to the work of organizing his followers, and divides them into three corps, under Joab, Abishai, and Ittai respectively. 2. On his proposing to head the force, the people urge him to desist from doing so, pointing out that, in case of a conflict, the enemy would be sure to make an endeavour to kill him rather than to fight a regular battle. 3. The king yields to their persuasions, and, as they suggest, abides by the city to render succour if required. 4. Having seen his men march out, he lays strict injunction on his captains, in the hearing of their forces, to deal gently with Absalom for his sake. 5. A severe battle takes place, in which the followers of Absalom are defeated with great slaughter. 6. Absalom, in riding through a wood, is entangled in the branches by his head, and, while hanging there, is seen by a man who reports the fact to Joab. 7. On being reproached for not slaying Absalom, the man reminds Joab of the solemn injunction of the king, and that he was restrained by that, as also by the fear of being discovered should he attempt the deed in secrecy. 8. Joab in a rage takes three darts, and thrusts them through the heart of Absalom, and his armour-bearers also join in the infliction of wounds on his body. 9. Joab thereupon recalls the people from the pursuit, and causes Absalom to be buried in a pit and covered by a heap of stones, the only monument in his memory being the pillar which he himself had erected during his lifetime. 10. On the death and burial of Absalom becoming known, his forces are dispersed, each man fleeing to his tent.

The discharge of painful obligations. The hasty flight of David from Jerusalem was not the result of cowardice, but of prudence and of spiritual penetration. He thought it possible that a movement which had won over so able a man as Ahithophel, and which had developed so secretly, might issue in a sudden rising which would involve the city in bloodshed. Moreover, with the keen spiritual insight which ever characterized him, he could not but see in this rebellion the chastising hand before which it became him in his lifelong penitence, mingled with sincere trust, to bow. But now that Jerusalem was safe from bloodshed, and the sanctuary of God was undefiled, and his faithful adherents were refreshed and in personal safety, the time had come to consider his position and devise such measures as Providence might render possible; and he thus at once found himself face to face with the unwelcome necessity of waging war against his own son. We may, then, take this as illustrating the obligations under which good men sometimes find themselves to pursue a course most distressing to their feelings.

I. As a matter of fact, obligations involving much pain in their discharge, do arise some time or other in the course of a good man's life. Our entire life' is a continuous duty. Obligations attend us every day. Right action means fulfilment of purposes, obeying laws, harmony with moral necessity. The pressure is incessant, and ordinarily is, for the Christian, a not-unwelcome yoke. But now and then duty is in forms requiring all the resources of a strong will, and in a direction against some of the most cherished feelings of the heart. David was bound to care for the kingdom over which he had been appointed by God. The validity of his anointing was still unrevoked by him who ordained it. It was, therefore, due to himself, his kingdom, and his God that he should take means to put down the usurpation of his own son. Paternal feeling might be pained, but the obligation was imperative. The Church furnishes many such instances. The most tender of ties have been severed in order to be true to Christ's commands. The doing of his work in the world often costs much pain because of its apparent antagonism to those best loved. Peter did not exercise discipline in the early Church without anguish of spirit (Acts v. 1—5). The reproofs of the Apostle Paul were with much sorrow of heart. Letters are daily written with tears. Parents daily have to resist the self-will of sons and daughters, and they mourn the sad necessity. Fidelity to right is, in many instances, a secret martyrdom.

II. In the mental conflict incident to the discharge of duty, the sense of right rises above personal considerations. The whole history of David proves that when, at Mahanaim, he began to collect his thoughts and consider the path of wisdom, a most painful conflict must have arisen in his mind as to the course to be taken. The clearer the conviction that, as God's anointed, he was bound to put down the force that was driving him from the throne, the sharper the pang awakened by the thought of raising the sword against his own child. The battle had to be fought out within his own nature before it was transferred to the open field. The human spirit is the arena of great struggles and victories, before men see visible triumphs. The dreadful disaster had for a time taken away David's strength; the pains of hell got hold of him: he was poor, weak, and forlorn. But now the recollection of duty to God and man brought back his old courage and resolution; and the calm and sober way in which he began to marshal his forces showed that help had come from God to subordinate the anguish of his heart to the sense of duty. Providence seems to work along these lines in the training of the best men. Character is strengthened by the triumph of conscientious regard for the will of God over the strivings of personal considerations. If to fight against a son, to face the possibility of much slaughter, and to see a prosperous reign darkened by civil war, were evils endured by David in order to carry out the kingly purposes of his anointing, how does it become Christians, in carrying out the purposes of their special anointing, to bring every thought, desire, and preference into subjection? Christ has left us the noblest example of this.

III. A resolve to subordinate personal considerations to a sense of duty being taken, a good man will devise means of meeting difficulties and securing the end in view. The season of mental conflict being passed, and stern duty being accepted, David proves his courage and sagacity by his calm determination, his collection of resources, his estimate of his numerical strength, his dispositions for meeting difficulties and accomplishing the end in view, his preparedness to incur personal risks, his acceptance of good and generous counsel, and his precautions against disaster at the outset (vers. 1—5). The king's soul was evidently sustained by the assurance often expressed in the Psalms that the Lord was his Salvation; and this, instead of encouraging neglect and carelessness, stimulated, as it always does, energy to work along the lines of the Divine purpose. The emotions of the father are kept under by prompt and energetic application of all the powers of body and mind to the performance of kingly duty. Our faith in God and in the realization of his purpose will appear in the zeal with which we work to bring that purpose to pass.

IV. In subordinating personal considerations to a sense of duty, a good man will nevertheless cherish sentiments natural to his relationships. David suppressed the pain of making war on his son because it was right so to do; but that did not imply the uprooting from his heart of those feelings of tenderness and compassion and yearning sorrow which are proper to a father, even for a prodigal son. He did not waver in his kingly design to subdue rebellion, nor did he show a wicked leniency towards an evil life in the son, when he, in the presence of the whole army, enjoined on Joab to "deal gently with the young man Absalom." The rebel was his own child, and a pious heart could not but wish to have opportunity once more to pour upon that child the full force of its sorrowful love, in hopes of winning him over to a sense of his guilt. No feeling so natural as the wish that a prodigal may not be cut off by unpitying hands in the midst of his sins. The legal question as to what would have to be done with a captured rebel was not yet for decision. Sanctified human nature simply yearned to save the sinner from men as cruel as the grave. Knowing the character of Joab, and being a stranger to mere personal revenge, David urged upon him, as a strong restraint, consideration for himself as king and father. There are many Christian parents to-day who feel for their erring ones just as David did for his, although, like him, they are obliged, out of regard to their families and themselves, to pursue a line of rigid duty. Hope of salvation never dies from a parent's heart. Beautifully does this adumbrate the compassion of God towards his prodigals! "Deal gently with him" seems to be the message sent forth to the forces which work out the king's purposes in the discipline of life. "Do not crush him" is the spirit of God's government. How much we each owe to that!

V. THERE ARE PROVIDENTIAL ENCOURAGEMENTS TO THE SUBORDINATION OF PERSONAL CONSIDERATIONS TO A SENSE OF DUTY. David was helped in his mental conflict by reflection on the past and present. He was so far spared by God. Sympathetic friends had brought him aid when in great distress. His own followers were intelligently loyal (ver. 3), and were obviously strong in their confidence in the justice of his cause. This kind of external support is of great service when a man is passing through a struggle as to whether he can perform a painful duty. Generally when God assigns duties involving pain in the performance, provision is made for encouragement. When our Saviour required his apostles to renounce all and to look on to persecution like that which he was suffering from, he cheered them by the promise of the Comforter, and a peace which the world could not give. The Resurrection made them strong to endure the loss of all things, and to subordinate love of home, friends, and country to the obligation of fighting against evil in the world.

GENERAL LESSONS. 1. In the time of disaster it behoves us, when occasion arises for reflection on the situation, to avail ourselves with vigour of the resources for recovering our position which God places around us. 2. One of the best preservatives from utter despondency is a remembrance that God has a work for us to accomplish in life, and hence, the more clearly this is kept in view, the more readily shall we be able to face disagreeable duties. 3. It is the duty of citizens to take precautions for the safety of those in high positions, since the welfare of the state is involved in their lives. 4. One of the elements of a perfect moral character to be attained to is the balance between the most rigid justice and the cherishing of feelings free from the taint of personal revenge. 5. As in the state we ought to do things for the "king's sake" which do not involve a breach of morality, so in the Church there are things we should do for Christ's sake, which would not be done did we simply follow out the bare tendencies of our imperfect nature and conform to the usages of society.

A revelation of sin and its issue. The remarkable space given in the sacred history to the life and conduct of Absalom in their relation to David may arouse the question as to the reason. It is not easy to assign all the reasons that may have operated in the mind of the inspired collector of the annals of Israel to give such prominence to these details; but we may be safe in saying that it was the Divine will to set forth, for the instruction of all ages, the discipline of the "man after God's own heart," and also, for the same object, the development and issue of sin in a conspicuous instance. Men learn a lesson written out in large bold characters; and herein lies most of the teaching value of the Old Testament histories. We may, then, trace here, in a concrete instance and striking form, illustrations of what all sin more or less is and involves, though the particular forms it assumes may vary.

I. ALIENATION OF HEART AND LOSS OF THE GENUINE FEELING OF SONSHIP. Absalom had known a time when, in the assertion within his own spirit of self-hood, he virtually ceased to be a true son. This was his fall. The old child-affection became weak; an aversion sprang up; father was no longer regarded as a father should be, and child ceased to be genuine child. This was the secret of all. It was a sort of moral death. The schism was more than political. Virtually he had said, "I will be free and do as I wish." This is also the essence of our sin against God. Adam lost somehow the sonship feeling. Self-will asserted its power. God became one, and he another. Union was gone. This is our Saviour's teaching in the parable of the prodigal son. The young man was weary of his father, and wanted to do as he liked away from him. If we examine our hearts, it will be found to be the same with ourselves. Sin is, negatively, destitution of the sonship feeling; positively, the assertion of self-hood as against God. In this lies its desperate evil, its incurable vice, its secret of doom.

II. A PERVERSION OF GIFTS. As soon as Absalom's heart was gone, he began to use up his beauty, his eloquence, his scheming, every faculty of his nature, to render himself happy in his self-hood, and to be able to dispense with his father's favour. In human nature all gifts flow in the line of one master-feeling. Hence when the dominant feeling is alienation from God, the entire man goes away, and all powers are made subservient to self as against the rightful dominion of God. The prodigal son used his patrimony away from his father. Sinners use up their patrimony for self, and not in harmony with God. Kindness is abused.

III. A RESOLVE TO GET RID OF AUTHORITY. For a time Absalom simply cherished the feeling of alienation and knew the misery of a lost love. But evil is a force, and we cannot remain as we are when it once enters the soul. The wretchedness of a lost love put him on the way to get rid of the authority which existed in spite of his loss of loving delight in it. Thought begets thought, and so in due time positive rebellion arose. The royal father must be formally dethroned. There is a corresponding phase in the life of many a sinner. It is misery to be loveless and to know at the same time that God lives. Hence, thoughts flow in suggesting how, by what scepticism, or disbelief, or defiance, or desperation in vice, he can be dislodged from the conscience. Possibly the war becomes violent. No more welcome thought to some men than that God is not. Lost love means in the end antagonism.

IV. THERE IS FOR A WHILE AN APPEARANCE OF SUCCESS. Unhappy Absalom found abettors and flatterers. His independent spirit accorded with the temper of others. His endeavours to live without his father's love and blessing seemed most successful, for never did men make so much of him as now when he has shaken off the yoke of dependence and has gone in for a free life. His "strength was firm." The aim of his ambition seemed within reach. Wise and astute men encouraged and helped him, and forces were placed at his disposal. So all seems to go well for a while with those who are alienated from God the Father. No visible punishment comes on them. They are free from restraints to which once they submitted. They "become as gods, knowing good and evil." Others, some of them wise and learned and astute, encourage them in their mode of life and join in their aims. The forces of wit, learning, science, worldly sagacity, combine to enable them to put down the authority to which they ought to submit. These are the wicked who prosper in the world.

V. THERE ARE THE BEGINNINGS OF REVERSE. Absalom finds his forces scattered by a force the strength of which he did not expect to meet. The mighty array of power on his side receives a check (vers. 6—8). He has to learn that the authority despised can make itself felt. And in the course of Providence there are times when events remind sinners that God still rules over forces which they cannot resist, that powers are at work before which they have to bow. Sickness, bereavement, adverse conditions of life, ruin of wicked helpers, pangs of conscience, and personal wretchedness, come and beat down the proud array of wit, learning, jovial companionship, and stoutness of will, as the rebel army was beaten down in the wood of Ephraim. Wicked men have intimations of destruction before it falls on them. The conscience sees, as with prophet's eye, the dark shadows of the future in passing events.

VI. VALUABLE GIFTS HASTEN DESTRUCTION. The pride of Absalom's person was the means of hastening his death. The hair which had been so much admired, which he counted as a treasure, and made him conspicuous in Israel, now combined with the silent forces that ran through the forest trees to bring him into the judgment for which his course of rebellion had been preparing him.   When God's time has come, he has many instruments for effecting his purpose.   The best gifts of sinful men sometimes get so entangled with the stable order of nature as to prematurely bring their life to an end.   There are always "branches" stretching out in the natural order of things, forming objects against which the powers and possessions of men run, to their detriment and speedy death.   The young man's natural vigour, of which he is proud, may run against a resisting force which shatters it in proportion to its strength. Brilliant intellects, in their defiance of God, have, in modern times, become so absorbed in literary work bearing on their infidelity, as to be caught early in the arms of death. Of how many may it be said that their beauty has been their destruction!

VII. THEIR MEMORY IS DESTINED TO BE UNHONOURED.   Absalom, proud of his name and ambitious of posthumous fame, erected a memorial pillar for himself—a mournful premonition, as it were, of his miserable end.   Nothing could have been more mortifying to him, had he known it, than to be cut down from a tree like a common felon and be buried as a dog.   The wicked are cut off; their memorial perishes.   It may be that men who die in sin have reared to their memory tablets or monuments of marble or brass; but the truth remains that they shall have no everlasting memorial in the assembly of the upright in the new Jerusalem.   Earthly monuments are perishable.   It is said of those who are so unfortunate and guilty as to die in a state of alienation from God, that their name shall "rot" (Prov. x. 7).   The only enduring order of things is that of the kingdom of God : it "cannot be shaken," and a place in that kingdom alone can ensure a perpetual memorial.   Those who are true sons, who have recovered the lost feeling of love, shall shine in the kingdom of the Father, and shall be heirs with Christ of his glory and joy.   The wicked shall go into "outer darkness."

GENERAL LESSONS.   1. The attention of all, especially of the young, should be called to the fact that the right feeling of sonship is that of loving submission, and that the loss of this towards earthly parents is really the fruit of a loss of the filial feeling towards the heavenly Father.   2. If we would form right notions of the guilt of sin, the need and nature of atonement, and the punishment awarded to sin in Scripture, we must pay due regard to what sin is in its essence—the assertion of self against God.   3. We see here the real nature of the change that is necessary in order to adoption into the redeemed family of God—a radical change of the governing feeling of the heart in relation to God.   Regeneration is the inner antecedent of the conversion of the entire man.   4. Young men may take warning against the terrible power of evil when once they break the bonds of love to parents, and in this first and chief sin they have the germ of unspeakable crimes and woes.   5. Let those who in the height of sinful prosperity imagine that all is going well, remember that, though they thus rejoice, yet for all these things God will bring them into judgment (Eccles. xi. 9).   6. Both the righteous and the wicked may accept it as a certainty that, in some way or other, the very inanimate creation will sooner or later be subservient to the ends of justice.   7. The best monument we can rear to ourselves, or that others can raise to our memory, is that blessed memory of the just which rests on a life of love to earthly parents and righteous fulfilment of all the obligations we owe to God and man.

The place of principles in conduct.   The controversy between the "certain man" and Joab near the oak where Absalom was hanging was natural, and sprang from diversity of views, which took their shape in each case from the character of the individuals.   The man was an ordinary loyal subject of David's, simple in life and thought, governed, as such men generally are, by a few great first principles of conduct.   Joab was an astute man of the world, true to David for reasons of a compound nature, entertaining such views of duty and life as generally sway the minds of men of the world, who regard present facts in the light of an unsentimental expediency.   Each one was true to himself, and the discussion raised was well sustained on each side by reasons cogent to the men themselves who expressed them, but of no force beyond the individual to convert the other to his view.   We see, then—

I. THAT LIFE MAY IN DIFFERENT MEN BE CONDUCTED ON DIFFERENT AND TOTALLY IRRECONCILABLE PRINCIPLES.   Here was a simple countryman unwilling to touch the life of Absalom, solely because of the king's commandment (vers. 5, 12, 13). The question of the prudence or imprudence of the act was not for a moment entertained. Obedience to the royal authority was the prime duty. This belief was the governing rule of conduct. No imaginary advantage to Israel, no example or persuasion of a great general, could turn the man from this fixed principle. On the other hand, Joab swept aside all such forceful pressure of supreme obligation to the royal will, because his conduct was governed, in this case at least, by a worldly wisdom, a consideration of what seemed to himself to be the best thing to do—a policy of expediency. There was a general admission of the existence and value of what the countryman regarded as primary principles of conduct on the part of subjects; but theory was good for theorists, and Joab was a man of deeds when matters were urgent! These men certainly represent two classes—those who accept first principles of obligation, primary conceptions of duty as lying at the very basis of society and of the individual life; and those who, while formally admitting the existence and propriety of such principles, nevertheless set them aside whenever, for prudential reasons, they think it well to do so. There are such primary principles: in government, the law of the ruler is supreme; in the family, e.g., the expressed will of the father is binding; in matters of religion, e.g., God prohibits unholiness of feeling, malice, cruelty, and commands men to repent, believe, and in all things do justly, irrespective of consequences. There are men who do base their action on these principles. But there are men who, like Joab, break the law of their land, and set aside supreme authority for reasons of their own; there are children who violate the fundamental principle of domestic order, because their judgment goes against their parents; there are men of the world who dare to disobey the Eternal King's commandment in relation to repentance, faith, and unswerving righteousness of life, for reasons which seem to them sufficient at the time. Do all Christians follow out the regal commands as to righteousness in all things? Is there not too much expediency in Christian conduct (cf. Matt. vi.)?

II. CONDUCT BASED ON PROMPT RECOGNITION OF FIRST PRINCIPLES IS MORE LIKELY TO CHARACTERIZE UNSOPHISTICATED MEN THAN MEN IMMERSED IN THE PUBLIC AFFAIRS. This plain countryman simply followed the order of the king because the king's will to him was sacred. He was not learned in casuistry, not versed in diplomacy, not skilled in keeping the letter and violating the spirit of the Law. He was amazed that any one should think of deviating from a command so plain. Its justice or injustice, its prudence or imprudence, were no matters for him to settle. Law was binding. The king must be obeyed. This was the instinct of a guileless nature. The force of the principle of obedience to the authority of God's anointed was recognized, because his spirit was politically and morally sound and pure. Joab was a man of the world, a man of many designs and combinations of thought, a man whose purity and guilelessness were gone. In the struggle of high and low principles within his nature, pure principle was deprived of its native force. Our Saviour, in reference to much higher matters, points out this difference of conduct proceeding from difference of character, when he thanks his Father that "these things," which were hidden from the "wise and prudent," were "revealed unto babes" (Matt. xi. 25, 26). We must become as little children—guileless, unsophisticated, quick to act on primary principles apart from the warping influences of worldly prudence, if we would enter his kingdom and be as he was. There may be advantages in being versed in affairs, familiar with the tricks and ways of men, and famed for astuteness and such-like qualities; but on the whole, in matters of pure right and strict adherence to clear duty to God and man, the guileless man is most likely to be the most dependable. Moral intuitions are swift in the pure-hearted, and to debate their applicability is at once to weaken their force.

III. CIRCUMSTANCES MAY ARISE IN WHICH DEVIATION FROM PRIMARY PRINCIPLES MAY AT FIRST APPEAR MOST CONFORMABLE TO REASON. On the face of it most men would have said that Joab was justified in setting aside conscientious scruples about the sacredness of the royal command. The rebel deserved death, the only place of restraint for him was the grave, the king's paternal feelings were a danger to the state, Providence had evidently put Absalom's life in the hands of Joab, and the king would be sure to condone the deed,—all this might be said with force. So may it be argued still. Immediate repentance may be right; but surely a man whose livelihood is at stake may be cautious, and not by a sudden change of life bring himself and family into poverty!

"Love your enemies" is a Divine command; but we are not so good as was he who gave the command, and so he will condone our cherishing some hatred! Be truthful in word and deed is the meaning to us all of Christ's life; but the pressure of business and the difficulties of diplomacy in national affairs are such that we cannot take this grand law of life into all departments of activity! Thus by arguments apparently conclusive the "commandments of God" are "made of none effect."

IV. THE TRUE INTERESTS OF ALL LIE IN ADHERENCE TO PRIMARY PRINCIPLES. Joab, by his deviation from the king's command, while seeming to secure an advantage to the state, was really sowing the seed of rebellion; for it set aside the supreme law, and its natural tendency was to weaken the royal authority throughout Israel. To gain a temporary advantage at the cost of damaging the force of a cardinal truth is no real gain in the end, for the consequences of such an injury are incalculable. Once impair the supremacy of right principles in the national or individual mind, and you have prepared the way for all kinds of degeneracy. God never departs from right, and his ways always come out right. Moral principles are as rigid in their demand for implicit and full recognition as any laws of physics, and they vindicate their neglect with as absolute a certainty. Christ has made it clear that strict and severe adherence to his authority alone will issue well. The sermon on the mount is a statement of unconditioned practical truth. The Church of Christ would have done more for the world had this sermon been more recognized, apart from the limitations of accommodating rules of interpretation.

Vers. 19—33.—The facts are: 1. Ahimaaz being eager to convey tidings of victory to the king, is denied permission by Joab, who, however, sends Cushi. 2. Persisting in his desire to run after Cushi, Joab at last allows him to go. 3. The watchman at the gate of the city reports to the king that a runner is in sight, followed by another, whereupon David takes courage, and hopes for good news. 4. On Ahimaaz being the first to arrive, he briefly announces that all is well, and then prostrates himself before the king, and blesses God for having brought victory to the king's cause. 5. David, in his deep concern for Absalom, inquires after his safety, and receives from Ahimaaz an evasive reply. 6. Just then Cushi comes in and announces tidings of victory, and, in answer to the question as to Absalom's safety, bluntly makes known the fact of his death. 7. The king, overwhelmed with anguish, enters his chamber, and there pours out his soul in a most pathetic lamentation.

The relation of character to work. The work recently accomplished by Joab now gave rise to another, which included elements of good and evil. He was keen enough to see that the communication of the fact of victory would be most welcome to David, but that a statement of the particulars would be most distressing; and, therefore, with his usual practical sagacity, he sought out for the work of conveying tidings to the king a man whose character would fit him for dealing with the evil side of the message very much as he himself would.

I. IN CARRYING ON HUMAN AFFAIRS THERE ARE OCCASIONS REQUIRING THE PERFORMANCE OF DISAGREEABLE WORK. It was a pleasant thing to have to announce to David a great victory over his foes, but far from pleasant to have to tell him what had become of his son, and who had slain him. On a former occasion, when evil tidings, blended with news of the fall of a foe, was brought to him, it went ill with the bearer (ch. i. 13—16). In this case the disagreeable work arose out of the wrong deeds of Joab. One evil created another. Disobedience to absolute authority cannot but bring the transgressor into an awkward position and impose unpleasant obligations. The flow of human life is a flow of work. In consequence of transgression against God, and violation of social order, an immense amount of annoying work has to be done. The sons of Jacob, after the sale of their brother, found difficult work on their hands. The imperfect life in the Church creates the necessity of doing things that pain the tender heart, and which is more adapted to rough and hard men. Evil deeds create duties which always carry with them more or less of pain and sorrow.

II. THERE IS A NATURAL AFFINITY BETWEEN CERTAIN CHARACTERS AND DISAGREEABLE FORMS OF WORK. The reasons for Joab's rejection of Ahimaaz were probably these: fear lest he should so state the facts as to prejudice David against himself, and belief that his nature was too tender and sympathetic for what he regarded as the proper delivery of the dark side of the message. Joab was a hard and blunt man, and he wanted such a man for a work which, because disagreeable, had better be got rid of as quickly as possible. If David should be angry with the Cushite, and slay him, Joab would not care for that, provided, in the blunt and straight announcement of Absalom's death, no tenderness was displayed and no effort made to compromise himself. Such men as he scorn tenderness as weakness. They abhor what they term " sentiment." Joab's character fitted him to send the painful tidings so bluntly and unfeelingly announced by Cushi (vers. 31, 32). As a rule, character finds work in affinity with itself, and Joab was right in the adaptation he sought for his purpose. As character is often a prophecy of work that will be done when occasion arises, so work done is often a revelation of character. Not any one can be a hangman. Not any one can be a consoler of the sick and dying. Even in the Christian Church there are kinds of work for which a peculiar firmness and almost severity of character is most suited. Only an Ambrose could overawe an emperor. On the other hand, most departments of Church work give scope for men of the Ahimaaz stamp rather than that of Cushi.

III. An injured conscience readily adapts itself to painful work issuing out of former violence to itself. Joab had done violence to his conscience in positive disobedience to the king's commands (vers. 12—14). As every wrong to conscience renders its testimony for right the feebler, it was comparatively easy to frame a blunt, unsympathizing message for the Cushite to deliver to the king. There was as real disregard for David's feelings in the framing of the hard, unfeeling message as in setting aside his command to spare the life of Absalom. Thus it is seen that the human conscience has the wonderful and terrible power of adapting itself to the environment produced by its own abuse, and so of being continuously affected for evil. A " seared conscience " is another expression for the gradual deterioration of sensibility produced by the enforced habit of accommodating itself to deeds which are the natural outcome of former misdeeds.

Sympathetic enthusiasm. The son of Zadok espoused the cause of David (ch. xv. 27, 36) in spite of the attractions for young men of Absalom's manners (ch. xv. 1—6). It was a noble thing for this young man to hold to a right cause in the day of adversity, and to place the fleetness of his feet and the vigilance of his ears and eyes at the command of the exile. The zeal with which he offered his services to Joab to convey the news of success to the king, was in keeping with his past reputation, and, as the sequel shows, was blended with a tender regard for the king's feelings. In contrast with the action of Joab and his servant Cushi in relation to David, that of Ahimaaz is an instructive example of the elements that enter into a commendable, sympathetic enthusiasm.

I. A just and good cause. There may be great enthusiasm, but it may be wicked because manifested in an evil cause. It was to the honour of the son of Zadok that all the force of his nature was devoted to the righteous claims of the Lord's anointed. He had identified himself with the servant of Jehovah in the day of trouble. In the great conflict of his age he was on the right side. This is the primary consideration with us all in the exercise of our powers, whether the questions at issue be political, social, or religious. We can take no credit for enthusiasm, and indeed it will be otherwise our sin, unless we take pains to see that we side with what is essentially just and good. Energy spent in advocacy or encouragement of a party, a movement, a system, a belief, or a practice, is not of moral worth apart from conscientious motive. Especially in the supreme question of every age, the claims of Christ as against the demand on our submission and service of lower and often unholy claims, the question comes—On which side are we? Are we with the rightful King or with his adversaries?

II. Entire self-devotion. Ahimaaz had deliberately identified the whole interests of his life with the cause of the exiled king. He was not a mere observer of the conflict. His very life had been at stake when he entered into the compact (ch. xv. 27, 33) and sought out the banished monarch. He had gone out to fight the battle with Joab, and was most eager to render the choicest service on the close of the day of victory. Enthusiasm which consists of approval and delight in the season of prosperity, or in verbal admiration, is of no substantial worth. The men who crossed hill and dale and lake because of the bread they ate (John vi. 24—27) were not the whole-hearted disciples Christ cared to have.   Christ would have the entire life (Luke ix. 59—62).

III. PROMPT ACTION IN EMERGENCIES.   The reality of this young man's enthusiasm appeared in his ready offer of the special powers with which he was endowed to the urgency of the hour.   He laid his best and most cultivated gifts at the service of his king just when they were most required.   It is a characteristic of entire absorption in Christ's work that there is not only the primal and unreserved surrender of life and all its interests to him and his kingdom, but also, as time passes on, a quick perception of entire work is needed, and an instant readiness to use any aptitude possessed for doing the work.   "Here am I ; send me," is the feeling of true enthusiasm when any emergency arises.   There are beautiful instances of the free and prompt devotion of special gifts to the service of Christ when occasions suddenly arise requiring them.   Are men smitten with plague or sword ?   Nurses skilled in care of the sick are at hand.   Does calamity come on a house or village ?   There are eager feet swift to carry gospel consolations.

IV. TRUE SYMPATHY GUIDING ACTION.   It was the deep and genuine sympathy of Ahimaaz with what he knew were the most tender and sacred feelings of the king's heart that made him eager to go, and both gladden him with news of God's deliverance, and at the same time gently break the news of his personal loss.   This gave extra speed to his fleet steps, and this explains his reference to God's goodness (ver. 28), and also his evident desire to prepare the king for sad tidings (ver. 29).   He felt too much for that noble, generous heart to blurt out the intelligence which he knew would crush it.   There is great value in a servant who understands and appreciates the most tender and cherished feelings of his master.   This sympathy is a discriminating guide to words and actions.   It is this intense sympathy with the heart of Christ, this power to enter more than others do into the very passion of the Redeemer for saving men, that accounts for the remarkable zeal and discriminating conduct in doing religious work which have characterized some of the noblest Christians.   The nearer we get to the heart of Christ, the more true will our enthusiasm be.   The natural gifts and aptitudes of body and mind then turn with zest to all wise devices for advancing the interests most dear to him.

Miscellanies.   In connection with the main event referred to in the narrative, there are incidents and statements which suggest a variety of truths bearing more or less on ordinary life or finding their parallels therein.   Briefly stated, these are as follows.

I. EAGER MEN AWAITING GREAT ISSUES.   David and his followers at the gate of Mahanaim, looking out for news of the issue of the conflict then being carried on, sensible that interests more precious than life were involved, are but types of men still intent on learning the issue of undertakings in which they have embarked or in which they have an inexpressible interest.   The disciples once awaited a wonderful issue when Christ was, during his trial and death, in conflict with powers of darkness.   For forty days before Pentecost, men and women waited for signs of a great event.   Often has the Church, in seasons of peril, waited in agony during the crisis.   Men engaged in ordinary business know what it is to look out for the issue of great ventures ; and in private religious experience there are times when the soul waits and watches more than those who watch for the morning.   What great and momentous issues are being wrought out every day in this world for some of our fellow-creatures !

II. QUALIFIED OPTIMISM.   "All is well," said Ahimaaz, to break the painful suspense of the watchers, and bring early consolation to the king's heart.   The words are few, but wonderful.   Taken in their strict sense, they meant to David more than could ever be expressed.   Happy, indeed, is the man of whom and to whom these words can be unconditionally spoken.   "All " is the term of widest range in human language ; and " well " is the greatest and best affirmation that can ever be made.   In David's circumstances the phrase at least meant that his cause was triumphant, that God had come to his help.   Ahimaaz was not insincere in saying what he did, knowing all the time that one event of the day would be most distressing to David.   His optimism was qualified by a reservation, as is common in human life.   There is a sense in which every good is qualified by a shade of ill.   Even so great a boon as redemption bears on it the dark shadow of a Suffering One.   The greatest victory of things is announced amidst the wail of widows and orphans.   The possession of great wealth brings with it carking cares. Perhaps, in the final issue of all events, when Christ shall have put down all authority and power (1 Cor. xv. 27), and the universe has gained its moral equilibrium after the long struggle between good and evil, it may be true in an absolute sense that " all is well; " but till then our optimism must be qualified.

III. A PIOUS PARENT'S ABSORBING THOUGHT. David did not lose his character of parent in his character as king. As the anointed one he was intent on seeing his authority duly established, but as a father he was anxious for the safety of his rebellious son. By no process could he divest himself of his parental relation—dim shadow is this of the fatherly relation which permeates all God's regal relations to mankind! No one as he could pity the erring youth. He still yearned to have opportunity of bringing some influence to bear on his ungrateful heart. The direst thought to him was the possibility of life being cut short before such opportunity arose. " Is the young man safe? " This question has deep significance to multitudes as they think of their children out on the wide world, exposed to its deadly ills. It comes in the morning with the light of day; it intrudes amidst the busy thoughts of daily business; and it is often the last thought when sleep quiets the heart. It is also a question, in its spiritual application, above all questions of health and secular prosperity. To be " safe " in Christ is the prime concern; for usefulness to others and growth in moral good are then ensured, while at the same time the dreadful guilt of the past is covered.

The great lamentation. On hearing of the death of his son, David retired into secrecy and poured out his soul in perhaps the most touching language to be found in the Bible. The strength and depth of feeling expressed were evidently in proportion to the interest which all along he had cherished in this abandoned child. Some writers have reproached David for yielding to what is termed " weakness " for a son whose just punishment ought to have been accepted with a calm acquiescence. But the criticism on his conduct is not really justified when all the facts are considered. He was a man constitutionally of strong, generous feelings—kindly and tender in his bearing toward others. A father cannot forget that he is a father; and the more holy and generous his nature, the more powerfully will the fatherly feeling assert itself. As seen in our Saviour's case, when he wept over Jerusalem already doomed because of sin against him, equal to, yea, worse even than, that of Absalom, the natural feelings of the heart may flow forth in most touching strains, while there is in the soul a most perfect accord with the righteous judgment of God. Nowhere does Scripture require men to suppress natural sentiments, or, in other words, require us to cease to be true human beings when we are brought face to face with the appalling judgments of God. Moreover, it is given to all parents to cherish hope of the most prodigal of sons while life continues, and David's personal experience of the mercy of God was such as certainly warranted his cherishing hope of the renewal and salvation of even this wicked son; and if such a long-cherished hope was suddenly crushed, and that, too, when care had been taken to prevent its being crushed (ver. 5), surely it was no sin for him, but an acceptable deed in the sight of God, when he vented his grief that now all hope of such a change was gone. There is no complaint against the wisdom and justice of God, no trace of a spirit of discontent with the administration of Divine love; it was pure sorrow for a ruined life. David's humanity was not lost in his kingly office. The love of a father's heart is not eradicated by a son's ingratitude. The parable of the prodigal son is evidence of this and also of its Divine counterpart. And in the case of David, the remembrance of his own sad fall having possibly exercised a detrimental influence over Absalom, just in the most critical period of his life, could not but render both just and natural this great lamentation. Taking, then, this view of David's conduct, we briefly notice the following truths.

I. RELIGION INTENSIFIES AND PURIFIES NATURAL AFFECTION. Had not David been a very devout man, he would not have felt such deep sorrow over the death of Absalom. Religion makes a father a true father; it renders love of offspring a more sacred thing. This follows from the more general truth that religion restores man to his normal state. Such affection has no relation to the sin of the child, except, perhaps, that the sin observed tends to render the affection more yearning and pitiful.

II. WE ARE JUSTIFIED IN CHERISHING HOPE WHILE LIFE LASTS. David did, and had good reasons for it. The gospel encourages it; the revelation of the Father's great love to the "greatest of sinners" justifies it. Man is not a judge of what may be done either by the most guilty or for them. That many for whom parents pray and strive do, as far as we can see, perish in their sins, is no reason against hope while life continues. Thousands have been brought to God in the eleventh hour.

III. THE DEATH OF OFFSPRING PRESUMABLY RECKLESS AND IMPENITENT IS THE GREATEST OF PARENTAL TROUBLES. To die is the common lot, and natural affection, though strong and pure, does not face death without consolations. But when death means the passage into eternity of a soul laden with guilt, and that soul once the object of delight and occasion of fondest hopes, then the most terrible of woes comes on a pious parent's heart. The "Redeemer's tears over lost souls," on which Howe has so wonderfully dwelt, are best understood by those who, like David, have wept over sons cut off in their sins.

IV. ONE OF THE BITTEREST INGREDIENTS IN SORROW OVER THE LOST IS THAT OF REFLECTION ON PERSONAL CONTRIBUTION TOWARD BRINGING ON THAT CONDITION. David could not but think of the effect on his son's views of life and tendencies of heart produced by his own great sin, and the months of alienation from God which ensued. How far parents are answerable for the character and destiny of their children is a grave question, but unquestionably a bad example in their early years cannot but tell perniciously on their future, and woe cannot but come on the father in darkest form when he connects his own misconduct with the hopeless death of his offspring. What manner of persons ought parents to be? Who knows what a turn a single lapse into sin may give to a youth's destiny?

V. IN THE PUREST HUMAN LOVE WE SEE A SHADOW OF GOD'S GREAT LOVE. David's lamentation, Jeremiah's wail over a ruined people (Jer. ix. 1, 2), the Apostle Paul's anguish on account of his brethren (Rom. ix. 1—3), and especially the Saviour's sorrow over Jerusalem (Matt. xxiii. 34—38), set forth, so far as we can know of such a mystery, the sorrowful feeling of the eternal Father (John xiv. 7—9) towards those who live and die in sin. God's great love for us has been seen in this, that, while we were yet sinners, Christ died for us (Rom. vi. 6—10). He actually did what David longed to do for Absalom. Redemption in Christ embodies the best and noblest of all feelings, and transcends the human ideal.

HOMILIES BY VARIOUS AUTHORS

Vers. 1—8.—(MAHANAIM.) *David's victory over his rebellious subjects.* Having found refuge in the fortified city of Mahanaim (ch. ii. 8), and recruited their exhausted energies, David and those who were with him prepared for the conflict which now seemed inevitable. Meanwhile (during several weeks) Absalom collected a great army (ch. xvii. 11), appointed Amasa captain, crossed the Jordan, and encamped in the land of Gilead (ch. xvii. 24—27). Here, "in the wood of Ephraim" (ver. 6; Judg. xii. 4), he was met by the forces of David, and the issue was quickly decided. "The traveller who only knows Palestine to the west of the Jordan, can form no idea of the luxuriance of the hillsides of Gilead. Here we crossed sparkling rivulets, where the sunlight glinted through the foliage of handsome oak, terebinth, and carob trees, and traversed glades seldom disturbed by the foot of man, which led into the deep solitudes of the forest. In one of these Absalom met his end; and one could well understand, as one came suddenly upon the brink of some rock or gorge, why possibly, in headlong and disastrous flight, so many of the combatants on that fatal day should have been numbered among the missing, that it was said the wood devoured more than the sword" (Oliphant). Attention is especially directed to David, concerning whom observe—

I. THE RENEWED ENERGY OF HIS CHARACTER. After his deep humiliation, the old king is himself again. His youth is "renewed like the eagle's." Passive submission is succeeded by active exertion, to which he is urged by inward impulses and new circumstances. There is a time to pray, and a time to work. 1. He actively musters his friends around him; and constantly attracts and receives reinforcements from the people who dwell on the east of the Jordan (ch. xvii. 27—29; Ps. xxvii.; xxviii.; cx. 3). 2. He skilfully organizes his forces, appointing captains of thousands and captains of hundreds, and arranging them in three divisions under Joab, Abishai, and Ittai (ch. xv. 19—22), well knowing the worth of able leaders and of strict order and discipline (ch. viii. 15—18). 3. He courageously purposes to go forth himself into the conflict (ch. xxi. 17), and is prevented from doing so only by their considerate determination (ver. 4). "Those who engage others in arduous and perilous attempts must be willing to take their full share of hardship; but true courage and firmness of mind are very different from rashness and obstinacy, and wise men are always most ready to listen to prudent counsel, even from their inferiors" (Scott). 4. He specially charges them to do his son no harm. "Gently for me with the young man Absalom" (ver. 5); "Beware, whoever it be," etc. (ver. 12). A general and intense feeling of resentment is naturally felt against him; and none are concerned about his welfare, save his father, whom he has chiefly wronged. "See what a thing a godly father's affection is to his child. No undutifulness, no practice on a child's part, no, nor death itself, can divide between him and his child. What though Absalom can forget David, yet David cannot forget him; what though he be a very ungracious imp, yet ' he is my child, my child,' saith David, 'I cannot but love him;' and, indeed, he over-loves him; which I do not commend, but only observe, to note the strength of parents' love, if it be natural—a love indeed as strong as death. Is the love of an earthly father so great? What, then, is the affection of our heavenly Father towards us?" (R. Harris: 1610).

II. THE ARDENT ATTACHMENT OF HIS FOLLOWERS; in contrast with the disaffection and hostility of others. 1. They offer themselves willingly to his service, and readily risk their lives for his sake. 2. They set an inestimable value on his life in comparison with their own. "Thou art worth ten thousand of us" (ver. 3). How much often depends on one man! The safety, unity, religion, prosperity, of a whole nation. Both patriotism and piety require the utmost care for his preservation. 3. They see the peculiar peril to which he is exposed, and seek to guard him against it. "They will pay no attention to us," etc. Of Washington, one of his officers wrote, "Our army love their general very much; but they have one complaint against him, which is the very little care he takes of himself." 4. They deem it expedient to provide, in case of need, for receiving his aid. "It is better that thou succour us out of the city." Their proposal is prudent, courteous, and honourable. Whilst he waits in the city with the "reserves," he still commands them, prays for them, and co-operates with them. They go forth under his sanction (ver. 4), are animated on the battle-field by the remembrance of him, and look forward to his approval as their recompense (ch. xix. 3). Such devotion is rare, not merely towards an earthly commander, but even on the part of those who war a spiritual warfare towards the heavenly Leader and "Captain of their salvation."

III. THE SIGNAL OVERTHROW OF HIS ADVERSARIES (vers. 7, 8); which is accomplished by the valour, discipline, and devotion of his "servants," and chiefly : 1. By the interposition of Divine providence (vers. 28, 31). "The race is not to the swift, nor the battle to the strong" (Eccles. ix. 11). "Providence is" by no means "always on the side of big battalions." 2. In retribution upon the disobedient and ungodly, over whom mercy lingers long, but not for ever, and who, though used as instruments of chastising others, are themselves ultimately broken in pieces. 3. For the deliverance of the faithful, the restoration of the "Lord's anointed," and the maintenance of the theocracy. 4. As a preparation for, and a foreshadowing of, the nobler victories of the King Messiah. It was another of the decisive battles of the world. "The contest was of short duration. The victors were soon vanquished. The storm was like a whirlwind, and like a whirlwind it passed away, leaving the enemies of God under the foot of the Messiah. To the depth of David's fall, to the height of his exaltation, there is but one parallel. We see it in the Passion, death, and resurrection of Jesus Christ. The two Davids fell in a manner alike mysterious to their astonished friends. The two Davids rose again in a manner alike terrible to their astonished foes" (M. Hill, 'The Typical Testimony to the Messiah').—D.

Vers. 9—14.—(THE WOOD OF EPHRAIM.) *A faithful soldier.* "Though I should receive [literally, 'weigh'] a thousand pieces of silver in mine hand, yet would I not put forth mine hand against the king's son" (ver. 12). While pursuing the enemy, a brave soldier came upon their leader, suspended from "the entangled branches of the great terebinth," in which his head was fastened so that he could not extricate himself. He forthwith reported what he had seen to Joab, who asked him why he had not despatched him, and said that he would have given him ten pieces of silver and a military girdle for doing so. A less scrupulous man might have sought even yet to secure the reward. But he replied that nothing would induce him to disobey the king. "So genuine was the reverence with which the loyalty of even a common soldier then invested the royal dignity" (Ewald). His fidelity may serve to illustrate that of "a good soldier of Jesus Christ" (2 Tim. ii. 3), as it appears in—

I. His RESPECT FOR THE KING'S COMMANDMENT; which, unlike that of an earthly ruler, is *always* wise, just, and good. 1. He reverences the authority by which it is given, as rightful, all-powerful, supreme. 2. He regards it as obligatory on each and all to whom it is given (ver. 12). 3. He remembers it constantly in the absence as well as the presence of the King, from whom "there is no matter hid" (ver. 13). 4. He is resolved on performing it with all his might. "Thou hast commanded us to keep thy precepts diligently" (Ps. cxix. 4, 11, 106).

II. His REJECTION OF STRONG TEMPTATION. He will not disobey the order received, though urged to do so by: 1. The impulse of resentment against the common enemy. 2. The plea of expediency, or what may seem to be for the common good. 3. The approval of a fellow-soldier, or the sanction of any "captain" inferior to the King. 4. The promise of reward, certain, immediate, and great. "The Law of thy mouth is better unto me than thousands of gold and silver" (Ps. cxix. 72, 31, 36).

III. His REBUKE OF ANOTHER'S PRESUMPTION. Joab must have felt himself reproved by this faithful and honest soldier; though he turned away contemptuously, recklessly, and presumptuously to do the deprecated deed. A dutiful soldier may and ought to rebuke the undutifulness of another by: 1. Reminding him of the word which has been spoken by the King. 2. Avowing his own determination to obey it in spite of all inducements to the contrary. 3. Predicting the certainty of the King's displeasure, which outweighs all present gain (Prov. xvi. 14; xix. 12). "What is a man profited," etc.? "In the King's favour is life." 4. Intimating the unreliability of one who favours disobedience and presumes on impunity. "Thou thyself wouldest have set thyself against me;" leaving me alone to bear the blame and suffer the penalty. "He must be a very bad man who is not attracted to what is good by the good example of his subordinates" (S. Schmid). "Then shall I not be ashamed when I have respect to all thy commandments" (Ps. cxix. 6, 29, 51, 53).—D.

Vers. 14—18.—(THE WOOD OF EPHRAIM.) *The end of Absalom.* After a long course of flagrant and persistent wickedness, Absalom (at the age of twenty-seven) met his deserved doom. There is not in all history a more signal instance of retribution. In it we see punishment following crime, in the way of natural consequence, and corresponding with it in the manner of its infliction. The sinner reaps as he sows.

> "But Justice hastes t' avenge each impious deed:
>   Some in day's clear and open light;
>   Some in the dusky evening's twilight shade;
>   Or, by delay more furious made,
>   Some in the dreary gloom of night."
>
>   (Æschylus.)

Absalom was—

I. ARRESTED BY DIVINE JUSTICE, IN THE PERVERSITY OF HIS WAY. (Vers. 9, 10.) When the battle went against him he sought to escape. Possibly he met with some of David's soldiers, who durst not "touch" him (ver. 12); "but though they let him go, yet God met with him, and put a stop to his flight" (Patrick). His eagerness and impetuosity, his tall form, his long hair, "the king's mule" on which he rode, all contributed to the result. Entangled by the tresses of his hair, and fastened by his neck in a forked bough, he was left hanging "between heaven and earth" (Deut. xxi. 23); "rejected as a traitor by both." None of his companions in crime remained with him, but all left him *alone* to his fate. "A man whom the Divine vengeance is pursuing does not escape" (S. Schmid). Insensate trees, dumb animals, apparently trivial and accidental circumstances, the devices and efforts of the transgressor, are so ordered that he shall not go unpunished (Prov. xi. 19, 31; xiii. 21; xxii. 5; xxviii. 17, 18).

II. EXECUTED BY HUMAN VIOLENCE, SIMILAR TO HIS OWN. (Vers. 14, 15.) As he had slain Amnon (ch. xiii. 28, 29), so was he slain by Joab. "He that was a solicitor for the king's favour (ch. xiv. 1, 2, 33) is his executioner against the king's charge" (Hall); influenced partly by zeal for the king's interest and the public good, partly by revenge for private injury (ch. xiv. 30), and jealousy for his own position (ch. iii. 27; xix. 10). He shared the resentment felt by his men against Absalom; was an instrument by which the wrath of Heaven was inflicted; and perhaps deemed himself justified in becoming such, because of the excessive fondness and blamable weakness of David toward his son; but herein he punished disobedience by disobedience, exhibited a pitiless severity and daring presumption, incurred the king's displeasure (ch. xix. 13), involved himself in deeper crime (1 Kings ii. 5), and ultimately in a violent death (1 Kings ii. 32).

III. BURIED IN A SHAMEFUL GRAVE, in contrast with the splendid monument which "in his lifetime he had taken and reared up for himself," etc. (ver. 18). "He had thought that he would be there, some time or other, buried as *king*; but he is now buried as an outlawed *evil-doer*, as an outcast from among men. Till this hour that grave speaks to us with a loud awakening voice. Violations of the commandment, 'Honour thy father and thy mother,' for the most part, indeed, escape the judgment of human authorities; but the Almighty has reserved it to himself to inflict punishment with his own hand, and for the most part even on this side eternity, as he has promised for this world also a gracious reward to those who keep it holy, according to the promise annexed to the commandment, 'that it may go with thee'" (Krummacher). "The great pit in the wood," with "a very great heap of stones laid upon him"—this was the end of his ambitious career (Deut. xxi. 22, 23; Josh. vii. 26; viii. 29). The site both of his grave and of the "marble pillar in the king's dale, two furlongs distant from Jerusalem" (Josephus), has been for ages unknown; and even the monolith in the valley of the Kidron (probably of the Herodian age, but associated with his name) is "unto this day" regarded with scorn by the passer-by, as he casts another stone, and mutters a curse upon his memory. "Shame shall be the promotion of fools" (Prov. iii. 35; xxx. 17). "Hear this, ye glorious fools, that care not to perpetuate any memory of yourselves to the world, but of ill-deserving greatness. The best of this affectation is vanity; the worst infamy and dishonour; whereas the memory of the just shall be blessed, and, if his humility shall refuse an epitaph and choose to hide himself under the bare earth, God himself shall engrave his name upon the pillar of eternity" (Hall).—D.

Ver. 18.—(THE KING'S DALE.) *Posthumous fame.* "Absalom's place" (literally, "hand," equivalent to "monument," or "memorial," 1 Sam. xv. 12). To live in the memory of men after death is, in a sense, to be immortal on earth (ch. vii. 9). Of this earthly immortality observe that: 1. *It is an object of natural and legitimate desire.* To be wholly forgotten as soon as we are laid in the dust is a prospect from which we instinctively turn away with aversion, as from death itself. The natural love of life, of reputation, of power, of pre-eminence, implies the desire of their continuance, in so far as it is possible, not merely of exerting a continued *influence* (as every one must do), but also of having one's name kept in continued *remembrance*; and this desire exists in those who have little or no knowledge of *personal immortality*. It is well that men's thoughts should extend beyond the narrow span of their own lifetime. But the memory of themselves which they wish to be perpetuated should not be of their shining qualities and extraordinary achievements, but of their genuine faith, their holy character, and their beneficent deeds, as an incentive to the like (Ps. lxxviii. 7; Prov. xiii. 22; Heb. xi. 4); for such a wish alone is of any moral worth. 2. *The desire of it often leads to mistaken and unworthy endeavours in order to its attainment.* Absalom "had taken and reared up for himself the pillar," etc. Imbued with selfish and vainglorious ambition, he imagined that the sight of it would call forth the admiration of posterity. In the same spirit he subsequently made his attempt upon the throne. So others have reared imposing monuments, built huge pyramids and palaces, fought great battles, and rushed into daring enterprises, heedless of the rectitude of their conduct or the welfare of mankind (Gen. xi. 4; Ezek. xxix. 3; Dan. iv. 30). "Their inward thought is," etc. (Ps. xlix. 11—13). The character of their aim determines the nature of their efforts; and only those efforts which proceed from a right spirit ensure an enduring and honourable "name." 3. *The result of such endeavours is shame and ever-lasting contempt, instead of immortal honour and glory.* "Absalom's hand," which was intended to indicate to future generations his magnificence, indicated only his ignominy. Even that at length perished (Ps. ix. 6; Prov. x. 7). And his memory remains as a solemn warning against transgression. "In what different lights, in what different aspects of character, the human beings of past time are presented to our thoughts! How many of them are there that an odious and horrid character rests upon! They seem to bear eternal curses on their heads. A vindictive ray of Heaven's lightning seems con-tinually darting down upon them. They appear as the special points of communication and attraction between a wicked world and the Divine vengeance" (J. Foster). But "the righteous shall be in everlasting remembrance" (Ps. cxii. 6; Matt. xxvi. 13; Acts x. 4; 2 Pet. i. 15).—D.

Ver. 29.—(MAHANAIM.) *"Is the young man . . . safe?"* Youth is a season of intense activity, favourable opportunities, and glowing promise.

> "The passion, which in youth
> Drives fast downhill, means that the impulse gained
> Should speed us up the hill that's opposite."
>
> (Sir H. Taylor.)

This question is specially suggestive of—

I. DANGER. No soldier on the battle-field, no traveller on "dark mountains," no ship on a tempestuous sea, is exposed to greater peril than a young man. Of what? Not so much of physical suffering and death, as of *sin*—the only real evil, and one which involves the loss of his highest life (Matt. x. 28). From what? Chiefly from *himself*—his "own heart" (Jer. xvii. 9); inexperience; susceptibility to impressions; personal endowments (ch. xiv. 25); "youthful lusts" (2 Tim. ii. 22), the love of pleasure, excitement, "name and fame;" impatience of control, self-confidence, rash-ness, and presumption. Also from false friends (ch. xiii. 3), rather than open enemies; sceptical and sensuous literature; "the defilements [miasma] of the age" (2 Pet. ii. 20); and the peculiar temptations of the place, the occupation, and the society with which he is connected. "Rejoice, O young man," etc. (Eccles. xi. 9).

II. SAFETY. "To be forewarned is to be forearmed." "Wherewithal, etc.? By taking heed thereto according to thy Word" (Ps. cxix. 9). The most essential thing is a right state of heart; its supreme affection set on God, its ruling purpose directed to the doing of his will (Prov. iv. 23), its varied powers "united to fear his Name" (Ps. lxxxvi. 11; Prov. i. 7). There is also need of watchfulness (1 Cor. xvi. 31), keeping out of the way of temptation, trusting in God to be kept by him, unceasing prayer, association with good men, the cultivation of proper habits, profitable reading, seasonable recreation, useful employment, and advancement toward the true end of life. "If ye do these things, ye shall never stumble," etc. (2 Pet. i. 10, 11).

III. ANXIETY; on the part of parents, instructors, Christian friends; arising from sincere affection, a clear perception of his danger, and an ardent desire for his welfare; expressed in fervent prayer, appropriate endeavour (ver. 5), and frequent inquiries (ver. 32). Alas! that a young man for whom others are so tenderly concerned should recklessly and wilfully "lose himself and become castaway"!—D.

Ver. 33.—(MAHANAIM.) *David's lament over Absalom.* "Would that I had died in thy stead, O Absalom! my son! my son!" In a little court between the inner and the outer *gate* of the fortified city wall, where (in the early morning) he stood and watched his brave soldiers going forth to battle (ver. 4), sits the aged king at eventide (ch. xix. 3, 7), awaiting tidings from the battle-field. The watchman, "from the roof of the gate at the wall," calls out to him that he descries, first one man "running alone" (not with others, as in flight, ver. 25), then another, and, as the foremost approaches nearer, says that he thinks his running is like that of the swift-footed Ahimaaz (ch. xvii. 17). On the arrival of the news of victory ("Peace!"), the first words of David (like his last, ver. 5) are of Absalom ; " Is there peace (*shalom*) to [is it well with] the young man Absalom ? " and, perceiving his deep concern, Ahimaaz dares not reveal the whole truth (ver. 20).   Again, the king makes the same inquiry of the Cushite, who (with less sympathy, but greater fidelity) utters the wish that *as the young man*, so might all the king's enemies be!   "And the king was much moved (greatly agitated with grief), and went up to the upper chamber of the gate, and wept; and thus he said, as he walked (to and fro): My son Absalom! my son! my son Absalom ! " etc.

> " Is it so far from thee
> Thou canst no longer see
> In the chamber over the gate
> That old man desolate,
> Weeping and wailing sore
> For his son who is no more?
>   ' O Absalom, my son !'
>
> " Somewhere at every hour
> The watchman on the tower
> Looks forth, and sees the fleet
> Approach of hurrying feet
> Of messengers, that bear
> The tidings of despair.
>   ' O Absalom, my son !'
>
> " That 'tis a common grief
> Bringeth but slight relief;
> Ours is the bitterest loss.
> Ours is the heaviest cross;
> And for ever the cry will be,
> ' Would God I had died for thee,
>   O Absalom, my son !' "
>
>   (Longfellow.)

" Absalom afflicted his father more by his death than by his life" (Augustine).   **This** expression of intense and absorbing grief (in which all joy of victory is swallowed up, ch. xix. 2) is indicative of—

I. PARENTAL AFFECTION from which it springs.   Five times the afflicted father cries, " My son ! " (*B'ni*); thrice, " Absalom ! "   A father's love (especially in such a fervid soul as David's) is : 1. The natural, instinctive, spontaneous effect of the relationship which subsists between him and his child.   It is the closest relationship of life, and is mercifully joined by the Creator and Father of all with a great and peculiar *affection* ; which, nevertheless (whilst it is intensified and exalted by a proper appreciation of its object, as " the offspring of God ") requires to be regulated by intelligence and piety. 2. Deeply rooted, enduring, indestructible.   It is not eradicated by a son's estrangement (Luke xv. 12), wilfulness, manifold transgressions, or even open rebellion.   It makes large allowances, has much patience and forbearance; " believeth all things," etc. (1 Cor. xiii. 7), " covereth all sins " (Prov. x. 12).   It feels persuaded that he has " some good thing in him," and cannot endure the thought of his entire abandonment. " Not only the question itself (ver. 29), but the very terms of it, breathe the tenderness of David's feelings.   Absalom is ' the youth,' as if his youth were a full excuse for his conduct" (' Speaker's Commentary ').   3. Pitiful, sympathetic, self-sacrificing (Ps. ciii. 13).   " My son, my beloved, my beautiful Absalom! miserably slain, and now lying dead !   Would that I had died for thee ! " (ch. xxiv. 17; Exod. xxxii. 32; Rom. ix. 3).

> " Thou seest the braided roots that bind
> Yon towering cedar to the rock ;
> Thou seest the clinging ivy twined
> As if to spurn the whirlwind's shock ;—
> Poor emblems of the strings that tie
> His offspring to a parent's heart ;
> For those will, mouldering, yield and die,
> But these can never, never part."

II. DISAPPOINTED EXPECTATION AND HOPE. All through the course pursued by Absalom, David doubtless cherished the hope that: 1. He might see the error of his way, and, constrained by his father's affection, repent of his sins. He may have supposed him penitent at the time of his return (ch. xiv. 23), and that his reconciliation (ch. xiv. 33) would be followed by filial love and obedience. 2. He might fulfil the anticipations formed at his birth, strengthened by the brilliant promise of his early youth, and apparently justified by his more recent diligence and religious zeal (ch. xv. 2, 8). The love of a parent often blinds him to the many defects and malicious designs of his son. Until this moment David hoped (ver. 5) that: 3. His life, at least, might be spared and his destruction averted. All is suddenly extinguished; his "sun is gone down while it was yet day;" and the remembrance of its brightness remains only to deepen the gloom of the succeeding night.

III. PERSONAL COMPUNCTION. Had the righteous judgment of God overtaken Absalom because he had "risen up against him" (ver. 31)? Was David himself, then, blameless? He could not but remember that: 1. He had despised the commandment of the Lord, and rebelled against the Divine King of Israel. 2. He had contributed by his own conduct to the misconduct of his son. "The worst ingredient in this cup of anguish would be, I think, the consciousness in David's heart that, if he had himself been all he ought to have been, his son might not thus have perished" (W. M. Taylor). 3. He was now suffering the chastisement of Heaven, of which his son's death was a part. "Absalom's sin and shame had two sides—there was in it the curse that David's sin brought on David's house (ch. xii. 10), the misdeed of the father's that is visited on the children (Exod. xx. 5); and not less, Absalom's own wickedness and recklessness, which made him the bearer of the family curse. David looks at Absalom's deed not on the latter side, but on the former (for his own guilt seems to him so great, that he looks little at Absalom's); hence his deep, boundless compassion for his misguided son" (Kurtz). "The heart-broken cry, 'Would God I had died for thee!' was not only the utterance of self-sacrificing love, but the confession that he himself deserved the punishment which fell upon another" (Kirkpatrick).

IV. IRREPARABLE LOSS AND SEPARATION. "As that young man is;" his life "as water spilt upon the ground," etc. No cries nor tears can restore him to his father or "the land of the living" (1 Sam. xxv. 29; ch. iv. 11; Ps. xxvi. 9; xlix. 8). Whatever David may have thought of his condition in *Sheôl*, no parent can contemplate the death of a rebellious and impenitent son without heart-rending grief, arising from the fear of his exclusion from the presence of God, sharing the doom of the Lord's enemies, and endless separation from the fellowship of saints. "All hope abandon, ye who enter here!" (Dante, 'Inferno,' iii.).

REMARKS. 1. It is possible, under circumstances most favourable to goodness, to become exceedingly bad. 2. One of the greatest evils in the world is that of disobedience to parents (2 Tim. iii. 3). 3. The love of an earthly parent toward his children is a shadow of the eternal Father's love to men. "He is affected with fatherly love towards the whole human race. Inasmuch as we are men, we must be dear to God, and our salvation must be precious in his sight" (Calvin, on Ezek. xviii. 4). 4. The Divine sorrow over men when they fall into sin and ruin, as revealed in the holy tears of Jesus, indicates their final state in "the world of infinite mourning."—D.

Ver. 3.—*The surpassing worth of Christ.* "Thou art worth ten thousand of us." The doctrine that all men are equal is true in some important respects, but its application and use are very limited. It is equally true that all men are unequal, that no man is of exactly the same weight and worth as any other man. Men differ infinitely in body and mind, in intelligence and goodness, in position and influence, in their value to society; and so in the degrees of their responsibility to God. In domestic and social, civic, national, and Church life, one man is often worth many others. David's "people" felt this now that they were going forth to meet the forces of Absalom in battle; and they give as a reason why he should be content to remain in the city instead of exposing himself to the dangers of the battle-field, that he was worth ten thousand of them; that it was better that ten thousand of them should be slain than he, though he was only one. This sentiment underlies and justifies the natural feeling of loyalty to a sovereign, the willingness to protect him at the cost of many lives. In personal worth he may not be equal to many a single soldier or subject; but he represents the state; in his life may be involved the welfare of a nation, to protect which it is worth while for many to die. Such thoughts might well console the private soldier dying in obscurity on the field or in hospital. His king, his country, is worth a multitude of such as he. His life is worthily sacrificed for them. The same sentiment is applicable to the commanders of an army in contrast with common soldiers; to great statesmen and other leaders of men in contrast with the multitude. It is no disparagement of these to say that it would require many of them to equal in value to society one of those; and that, if necessary, it would be better that the many should die rather than the one. We may use the words emphatically in reference to our great King and Captain, the Lord Jesus Christ. True, he is no longer in personal peril from his enemies. " He lives beyond their utmost rage " (Watts). But his cause, influence, hold of mankind, place in their esteem and affection, in a word, his kingdom, may be endangered; and his true disciples will be ready to die in thousands rather than he should in these respects perish or even suffer loss. And the justification of their feeling is that he, personally and in his cause, " is worth ten thousand of them."

I. THE SURPASSING WORTH OF CHRIST. 1. *In personal excellence.* It is well when the monarch of a country is distinguished for mental and moral endowments. Even when the personality of the ruler is of less account in the actual government, it adds much to the welfare of the state that he is noble in the qualities of his mind and heart. This has been made manifest in the long reign of our beloved and honoured queen. Where the power of government is very largely trusted to the will of the sovereign, it is of incalculable importance that he should be both wise and good. David's kingdom sprang very mainly from, and was maintained by, his personal qualities. And this is more emphatically true of his great Son Jesus. He is " chiefest among ten thousand," chiefest among and above all creation. The perfections of God and the perfections of man are combined in this one glorious Person. In himself he is worthy of the utmost love and self-devotion. 2. *In position and dignity.* As " King of kings and Lord of lords; " " Lord of all; " King of souls; " Head of the Church; " " Head over all things." These are not empty titles; but represent facts, actual glory and power. To serve such a King may well be esteemed the highest possible honour; to die for him, a great glory. 3. *In relation to the good of men.* Who shall say how much Christ is " worth " in this view? of how much value his work for and amongst men? how essentially their welfare in time and in eternity is bound up with his unchanging existence and power, and the manifestation of himself in the world through his Church? Every believer experiences his preciousness (1 Pet. ii. 7), and desires that all should have a like experience, through a " like precious faith " (2 Pet. i. 1); and to keep him living in the memory of men, and secure the wider exercise of his saving power, would cheerfully sacrifice himself. We are insignificant, and if we die it matters little; but for him to perish from the life of men, or become feeble in his influence among them, would be disastrous indeed. 4. *In power to succour and aid his servants.* David was requested to remain in the city with the reserves, that, if it were required, he might send them to the succour of those fighting in the field. Our Lord can, " out of the city " in which he dwells, aid his servants in more effectual manner. Not only has he numberless reserves eager to do his bidding, but he is able to gather around him, from the very ranks of his foes, fresh hosts to fight his battles. And, beyond all this, he can himself be—yea, he is—with his people everywhere and evermore, to inspirit them by his presence, and render them victorious. Who of them, what " ten thousand " of them, could fill his place? 5. *In power to reward those who die in his service.* Earthly rulers are powerless to recompense the soldiers who are slain in fighting their battles. Not so our great King. He is able to promise eternal life and glory to his faithful followers; and what he promises he performs (see Mark viii. 35; John xii. 25).

II. THE EFFECT WHICH CONTEMPLATION OF THE SURPASSING WORTH OF CHRIST SHOULD HAVE UPON US. 1. *Satisfaction that he lives safe above all the hostility of his enemies.* Lives, not in heaven only, but on earth in spirit and power, working in and with his people and confirming his Word (John xiv. 19; Mark xvi. 20). Human leaders and teachers die, but " Jesus Christ is the same yesterday, and to-day, and for ever " (Heb. xiii. 8). That One of so much worth to men, and so needful to them, should be thus immortal and immutable, is matter for joy and thankfulness. He needs not, like David, the plans and efforts of his servants to preserve him; but we can and should rejoice that he lives and reigns, and "must reign till he hath put all enemies under his feet" (1 Cor. xv. 25). 2. *Devoted loyalty to him even unto death.* The readiness with which David's friends hazarded and gave up their lives for him, nay, the similar devotedness of many a common soldier, may well put most Christians to the blush. 3. *Contentment in view of the enormous sacrifice of human lives which has been made for his sake.* It is not waste; the willing deaths of martyrs, missionaries, Christian workers of all grades, have not been unreasonable. He and his cause are worthy of it all. 4. *Confidence in respect to ultimate victory over all his foes.* With such a King and Captain, final defeat is impossible. 5. *Assurance of ample recompense for whatever we lose, were it life itself, in his service.* 6. *Concern to be on the side of Christ rather than of a multitude in opposition to him.* We are tempted to follow the crowd, and (with or without thinking) to esteem that to be the right course which the greater number pursue. But truth goes not necessarily, or even ordinarily, with the majority. With the one Person, the Lord Jesus Christ, are truth, safety, victory, ultimate gain. His judgment is worth more than that of "ten thousand" others; his favour of infinitely more value than theirs. If adherence to him were to lead to the separation from us of all besides, and we were to find ourselves alone, we might say after his manner, "I am not alone, because the Master is with me" (John xvi. 32). —G. W.

Ver. 13.—*Dealing falsely against our lives.* "I should have wrought falsehood against my own life." Another reading, preferred by the Old Testament Revisers, substitutes "his" for "my own;" but they place in the margin that adopted in the Authorized Version. Taking the passage, then, as it stands in the Authorized Version, the meaning of the speaker is that if he had slain Absalom, he would have brought death upon himself, since the king would have been made acquainted with the deed, and would have sentenced him to death. The form of the expression is worthy of notice. Doing what would have cost him his life is called working *falsehood* against it. A man's life is entrusted to him to guard and nourish. When he does this, he acts truly towards it; when he does what injures or destroys his life, he acts falsely towards it; he violates his trust. Every man virtually professes to be concerned for the safety and well-being of his life; when he does what endangers or terminates it, he may be said to deal falsely with it, to act treacherously towards it. This is the case with those who put themselves to death, or shorten their days by intemperance or licentiousness; or who, by crime, bring themselves to the gallows (see homily on ch. xvii. 23). But we may take the words as suggesting that there are persons who work falsehood against their lives in the higher sense, as beings immortal, and capable of that life which is life indeed,—the life everlasting.

I. How DO MEN COMMIT THIS SIN? 1. *By taking the course which surely leads to death.* In violating the laws of God they bring on themselves the sentence of death, and separate themselves from God, in whose favour is life. 2. *By refusing the new life which is proffered them in the gospel.* Life under the Law having become impossible through sin, God has interposed with another method of imparting life. His Son came to be our Life. He died that we might live. He lives evermore to bestow life on all who believe on him. "He that hath the Son hath life," etc. (1 John v. 12); "He that believeth on the Son hath everlasting life," etc. (John iii. 36). To reject him is to reject life. It is to deal falsely with our own lives, our own souls. 3. *By neglecting the means by which the life of the soul is preserved and nourished.* Reading of the Word, meditation, prayer, watchfulness, ordinances of public worship, union and communion with Christians, etc., whatever is intended and adapted to keep the soul in vital union with him who is "the Life" (John xiv. 6).

II. Its UNNATURALNESS AND WICKEDNESS. The man implied that to deal falsely with his own life was a thing utterly inadmissible. So it ought to be in respect to the life of the soul. For: 1. *It is the life which is concerned.* It is not a mere question of more or less health, comfort, or other subordinate good. "It is not a vain thing for you, because it is your life" (Deut. xxxii. 47). 2. *It is the most precious kind of life.* Unspeakably more important than the life of the body, or even of the mind, or of any of the principles and affections which relate us to the family or society. Because of (1) its nature, (2) its blessedness, (3) its duration. 3. *It is our own life.* Which should be specially dear to us, and has been specially entrusted to us : which we are therefore especially bound to care for and conserve. 4. *To imperil or sacrifice it is to deal falsely against it and against God.* We are under a covenant to care for it. Nature binds us, and Scripture, and perhaps religious vows, voluntarily made and often repeated. 5. *Such a course will bring upon us the Divine displeasure.* We shall not only lose our souls, but shall find ourselves involved in awful penalties for doing so; not only shall we fail of " eternal life," but shall " go away into eternal punishment " (Matt. xxv. 46). The words may be a safeguard against temptation. " In doing this thing I should deal falsely against my own life."—G. W.

Ver. 13.—*The omniscience of our King.* " There is no matter hid from the king." This is given, by the man who informed Joab that Absalom was hanging in an oak, as a reason why he might have been sure of death himself if he had killed Absalom. It shows how well informed David was understood to be of all that took place amongst his subjects. Such an impression respecting governors and magistrates in general as this man had respecting David, would go far to extinguish crime. The assertion here made as to King David's knowledge may be made absolutely, and without exception, in reference to our great King.
    I. THE OMNISCIENCE OF CHRIST. This is claimed for and by him in Holy Scripture (see John ii. 24, 25 ; Rev. ii. 23 ; and the repeated declarations in the letters to the seven Churches, Rev. ii. and iii., as to his acquaintance with their works and condition. Also John x. 14, 15). 1. *The sources of his knowledge.* His own essential Divine faculty of knowing. He does not depend, like ordinary rulers, on informants. His " *eyes are in every place,* beholding the evil and the good " (Prov. xv. 3). 2. *The extent of his knowledge.* He knows, not only the actions of men, but their hearts; all thoughts, emotions, motives, plans, purposes; all movements and events that can affect his kingdom. His enemies take counsel against him under his very eyes. 3. *The impossibility of concealing anything from him.* " There is no matter hid from the King." Nothing can hide aught from him. Not physical darkness ; not distance; not efforts at concealment; no hypocrisy ; no simulation or dissimulation ; no excuses, contradictions, or evasions. The assertions in Ps. cxxxix.; Job xxxiv. 21, 22 ; 2 Tim. ii. 19; Heb. iv. 13, are as applicable to the Son as to the Father.
    II. THE EFFECT WHICH THE KNOWLEDGE OF THE OMNISCIENCE OF CHRIST SHOULD HAVE UPON US. 1. *To confirm our confidence in his fitness to be King.* Rule over such a kingdom as his—extending over numbers so vast, and reaching to the inmost souls of his subjects—requires omniscience as one of the attributes of the Ruler. 2. *To deter us from wrong-doing.* As a similar knowledge deterred this Israelite from slaying the king's son. 3. *To assure us that judgment will fall on the guilty, and only on them ; and on each according to the measure of his guiltiness.* For want of better knowledge in human rulers and magistrates, some innocent persons suffer as guilty, and many guilty ones escape punishment. 4. *To encourage us in all that is good.* Christ's perfect knowledge of us is a great comfort for Christians who are unknown or unacknowledged amongst men; for the maligned and misunderstood; for workers in obscurity ; for such as do good quietly and secretly. " Lord, thou knowest all things ; thou knowest that I love thee " (John xxi. 17). " Thy Father "—thy Redeemer and Lord—" which seeth in secret shall recompense thee " (Matt. vi. 4, Revised Version). " Who will both bring to light the hidden things of darkness, and make manifest the counsels of the hearts; and then shall each man have his praise from God " (1 Cor. iv. 5, Revised Version).

> " Men heed thee, love thee, praise thee not.
>   The Master praises: what are men ? "

5. *To comfort us in all troubles.* " Thou hast seen my affliction ; thou hast known my soul in adversities " (Ps. xxxi. 7, Revised Version). A special comfort for those whose troubles are too peculiar or too sacred to communicate to others. Though our King be so exalted, he interests himself in each one of his subjects, even the least, knows all that pains them, and sympathizes with them in all.—G. W.

Ver. 18.—*Absalom's monument.* The contrast between ver. 17 and ver. 18 is touching. Absalom, whose three sons (ch. xiv. 27) were dead, desirous that his name should not therefore die, erected a monument to perpetuate it, probably connecting with it a tomb in which he purposed that his body should lie, and in which possibly he may have placed the remains of his deceased children. But he was buried in another sepulchre, and had another monument reared to his memory. A pit in the forest of Ephraim became his grave, and "a very great heap of stones" his memorial. The contrast appears more marked in the original than in our version. The same Hebrew word is translated "laid" in ver. 17, and "reared" in ver. 18. "They *took* Absalom . . . and *raised* a very great heap of stones upon him . . . Absalom in his lifetime had *taken* and *raised* up for himself a pillar," etc. The desire to have our name perpetuated is natural, and in some becomes a passion. It is one of the pleasures parents have, that, when they are gone, their children (especially their sons) will keep their names in the memory of men. Failing this, the hope of a tombstone to fulfil in some measure the same purpose may give satisfaction; it is only a very few who can hope for a "pillar" as a monument. But, after all, these are poor memorials, and they may preserve a very undesirable memory of a deceased person. There are better methods of ensuring that we shall not be soon forgotten amongst men, and, at the same time, that the image thus perpetuated shall be both desirable and useful. These methods, moreover, are open to the multitude who cannot hope for either pillar or tombstone to commemorate them. "The righteous shall be in everlasting remembrance" (Ps. cxii. 6).

I. How to build monuments to our memory. 1. *By eminent piety and holiness.* "The memory of the just is blessed; but the name of the wicked shall rot" (Prov. x. 7). 2. *By the faithful discharge of private and public duties.* 3. *By zeal for the spiritual good of others.* Instructing them ourselves. Providing for their instruction. Those who have wealth may erect a house of prayer, which will be a better monument than a pillar. The childless man may thus have spiritual children that shall perpetuate his memory and good influence. Loving work amongst the young is likely to be most successful, both in respect to their good and the long perpetuation of our memory. Our name will be written on their hearts, and repeated by them with gratitude in their conversation and in their thanksgivings to God. 4. *By large general benevolence.* Devotedness in the relief of suffering and the promotion in other ways of the good of others. Some secure a lasting name by building, enlarging, or endowing hospitals, almshouses, or schools. But little acts of kindness, especially if they become the habit of a life, may secure even a warmer place in the memory and affection of those whom we benefit.

II. The monuments thus erected. It follows from what has been said that these will be : 1. *Souls saved or greatly profited.* 2. *Happiness produced or increased.* 3. *Grateful remembrance and mention of us.* By those we have benefited. By all acquainted with our lives who rightly estimate goodness and benevolence. 4. *In the case of some, religious and philanthropic institutions and agencies, which they have founded or greatly strengthened, and with which their names will continue to be associated.*

III. The superiority of such monuments. In comparison with pillars, etc., erected to our memory. 1. *In their nature.* Memorials of stone bear no comparison with those written on the hearts, and in the characters and happiness, of men; or indissolubly associated with permanent agencies for their well-being. 2. *In their fruitfulness.* The good done reproduces itself; the memory of the doer, thus perpetuated, more surely excites to imitation of his character and works. 3. *In their duration.* The less durable of such memorials will outlast any material monument; the spiritual ones will survive the last fires, and be everlasting.

To conclude : 1. *It is a solemn thing to reflect that shortly all that will remain of us in this world will be our memorials.* We ourselves must soon be gone, be we princes or peasants, rich or poor, learned or ignorant. The only advantage of the rich over the poor is that of more costly monuments. But the choicest monuments may be secured by the poor as well as the rich. 2. *The securing for ourselves a lasting name amongst men ought not to be the chief motive, nor one of the chief motives, of our conduct.* It should hardly be a *motive* at all. Of *Christian* conduct and works, it cannot be a main motive; for a life so produced is not Christian. To act in order to "have glory of men" (Matt. vi. 2) after our death differs not in principle from seeking to have such glory now. Had Mary (Matt. xxvi. 6—13) lavished her precious ointment on our Lord in order that she might be memorable to all ages, he would not have commended her. Our chief motives should be love to God and Christ and men, the desire to be approved of God, and to have our names recorded indelibly in the book of life (Phil. iv. 3; Rev. iii. 5). 3. *An enduring name may be obtained by ill-doing as well as by well-doing.* The name of Judas will last as long as that of Mary, and be perpetuated by the same means. And the memory of a good man's failings may be as enduring as that of his virtues. 4. *The grand instance of a Name after death synonymous with all that is great and good in the highest sense and degree,* without any admixture of evil, and productive of the highest and most lasting good in others, is that of our blessed Lord.—G. W.

Ver. 27.—*A good messenger of good news.* "He is a good man, and cometh with good tidings." Underlying this phrase is probably the feeling that there is a congruity between good tidings and a good man. David may have thought that such a messenger as Ahimaaz would not have been sent with bad news; and, indeed, Joab was unwilling that he should run with the news, because he knew how grievous part of it would be to David. It may be permissible to take these words as applicable to the proclaimers of the heavenly good news—the gospel of God. It should be true of every Christian minister and teacher, yea, of every Christian, that "he is a good man, and cometh with good tidings." We are the more readily led to such an accommodation of the words, because the terms used throughout this section of the narrative are in the Septuagint identical with those (εὐαγγέλια, εὐαγγελίζω) with which we are so familiar in the New Testament.

I. THERE ARE GOOD TIDINGS TO BE PROCLAIMED. Christianity is pre-eminently "gospel" (equivalent to "good news"), and is often called by this name. It is good tidings from the region and the Person from whence we might reasonably expect bad; and about the Being and the things which are of most importance to us. It declares to us the love of God to sinful men. It announces the coming and the work of a Divine Saviour; the reign of a Divine King; an all-sufficient propitiation for sin; a full and free redemption; an almighty, most loving and ever-abiding Comforter and Helper. It proclaims pardon for the guilty, cleansing for the impure, life for the dead, comfort for the sad and sorrowful, Divine righteousness for the unrighteous, Divine strength for the weak, peace and joy on earth, perfection alike of holiness and happiness in heaven. It offers all these blessings on the simple condition of "repentance toward God, and faith toward our Lord Jesus Christ" (Acts xx. 21).

II. THESE GOOD TIDINGS ARE COMMITTED TO GOOD MEN TO MAKE KNOWN. Only good men, real Christians, have a Divine commission to engage in this work. God does not need the services of his enemies in the work of turning enemies into friends and ministering to their good. No unconverted man, no one that is carnal, worldly, unholy, can be a true Christian preacher or teacher. 1. *Only good men really know the gospel.* (See 1 Cor. ii. 14; Matt. xi. 25.) We need to be "taught of God" (John vi. 45) in order to our real reception and understanding of Christian truth. 2. *Only good men can rightly make it known.* We cannot teach what we do not know; we cannot teach aright that with which we are out of harmony and sympathy. The work of teaching the gospel requires love to God, to the Lord Jesus Christ, to the truth, to the souls of men; sympathy with the mind and heart and purposes of God as revealed in the gospel; a character consistent with it, and adapted to illustrate and recommend it; and the earnest and believing prayerfulness which secures the Divine aid and blessing. "But unto the wicked God saith, What hast thou to do to declare my statutes, or that thou shouldest take my covenant in thy mouth?" (Ps. l. 16).

III. GOOD MEN SHOULD MAKE KNOWN THE GOOD TIDINGS ZEALOUSLY. All Christians should do this according to the measure of their abilities and opportunities. They should be incited to do this by: 1. *The nature of the tidings.* With which only intense earnestness in the messenger is in harmony. 2. *Their personal obligations to the redeeming love which they announce.* 3. *The unspeakable blessings they have received through the knowledge of them.* 4. *The commands of their Lord.* 5. *The natural impulses of the Christian heart.* Which are the promptings of the Holy Ghost.

6. *The good they can thus confer on their fellow-men.* Good of the most important and lasting kind, and of which they are most of all in need.

IV. THOSE WHO MAKE KNOWN THE GOOD TIDINGS OUGHT MORE AND MORE TO BECOME GOOD. The work of learning and teaching the gospel ought to greatly benefit the teachers. It is adapted to do so, on account of: 1. *The nature of the gospel.* Its every truth is sanctifying. 2. *The special character of the work.* It exercises and trains every Christian virtue. It brings into close communion with the infinitely Good, who is also the Inspirer of all good in his creatures. 3. *The regard for consistency which the worker is likely to cherish.* 4. *His desire for success in his work.* This will increase his desire and endeavour after greater personal consecration and holiness. 5. *The concern which he will feel to be accepted of God.* " Lest that by any means, when I have preached to others, I myself should be a castaway " (1 Cor. ix. 27).

In conclusion : 1. *The subject appeals to all who have part in the teaching of Christianity.* Not only preachers, but parents and other teachers of the young, district visitors, etc. 2. *Some need to be reminded that the Christian religion is not all of the nature of good tidings to each one to whom it comes.* If it says, " He that believeth and is baptized shall be saved," it says also, " He that believeth not shall be damned" (Mark xvi. 16). If of the righteous it declares, " It shall be well with him," it also says, " Woe unto the wicked, it shall be ill with him ! " (Isa. iii. 10, 11). But its tidings of evil, as well as of good, need good men to bear them properly. It needs faith and faithfulness toward God, tender love and pity toward men, to utter them aright, and with probability of success.—G. W.

Ver. 29.—*Concern for the welfare of young men.* " Is the young man Absalom safe ? " or, as in the Revised Version, " Is it well with the young man Absalom ? " The inquiry reveals what was on David's heart equally with, if not more than, the welfare of the state and the continuance of his own reign. While Absalom had accepted with approval plans for accomplishing his father's death, David was more solicitous for the preservation of Absalom's life than his own ; and now that the victory of his forces is announced, he cannot rejoice at the tidings until he knows whether his son still lives ; and when he learns that he is dead, his grief quite overwhelms his joy, and bursts all bounds. It is not uncommon for worthless sons, who have lost all affection and dutifulness towards their parents, to have parental love still lavished and wasted upon them. The reprobate is not unfrequently the favourite. The inquiry of David is one that may be, and often is, put respecting young men, with reference to various kinds of well-being. Is it well with him ? Is he in health ? Is he getting on in business, etc. ? It may well be directed towards welfare of a more essential kind— Is it well with him morally, spiritually, and with reference to eternity ?

I. WHEN IS IT WELL WITH YOUNG MEN ? 1. *When they have become decided Christians.* When of their own free choice they have accepted Christ as their Saviour and Lord, and manfully owned him before men. It cannot be really well with those who are without Christ, living in rebellion towards their heavenly Father, and walking in the way that leads to destruction. 2. *When living lives of watchfulness and prayer.* Sensible of the perils to which they are exposed, guarding against temptation, and ever imploring Divine protection and help. In such a world as this, it cannot be well for the young and inexperienced to be unaware of their dangers, or heedless respecting them. 3. *When carrying Christian principles into consistent practice in every depart-ment of their lives.* 4. *When earnestly devoting themselves to works of piety and benevolence.* To do this is well, not only for those whose good they may be seeking, but for themselves. It is a safeguard and an education. Let young men (young women too) thus live, and : (1) It *is* well with them whatever their position in life. Such living *is* well-being. (2) It is likely to be well with them in their relations to others. They will secure esteem, affection, friendships that are worth having, and great influence for good in the Church and the world. (3) It will probably be well with them as to worldly success and comfort. (4) Persevering in such a course, it will be well with them throughout this life and for ever. Such a youth will lead on to an honourable and happy manhood ; such a life on earth to a glorious and blissful life in heaven.

II. THE CONCERN WHICH IS FELT IN RESPECT TO THE CHRISTIAN WELFARE OF

YOUNG MEN. **1.** *By their Christian parents.* Natural affection and religious faith combine to produce an anxiety which young people can very partially understand. The happiness of parents is bound up with that of their children. Christians "live" (1 Thess. iii. 8) when their sons and daughters live to Christ, and "stand fast" in him. Their anxiety on their account is greatly intensified when they have left home for new scenes and associations, involving new perils to character, without the preservative influence of home and known friends. **2.** *Ministers and Churches ought to be more concerned about the spiritual welfare of young men than they always are.* Their mission is to care for souls; and no souls are more interesting, more exposed to danger, more needing and ready to appreciate sympathy and friendly offices, than those of the young. None are of so much value for the advancement of religion at home and abroad. And of the young, none so need guidance and wise influence as young men; young women are drawn to Christ more readily, and are usually exposed to less powerful temptations. Measures for the good of young men should occupy a prominent place in the agencies of every congregation. **3.** *Christian citizens may well cherish a like concern.* For on the direction that the youth of a country take depends to a large extent the welfare of the state. If the young could but be generally brought under the power of godliness, with its accompanying intelligence, purity, uprightness, and benevolence, a new era of national glory and happiness would have commenced. Is it well with the young, especially with young men? should, then, be a common inquiry from all good men and women; and should be accompanied with such practical proofs of interest in the inquiry as are possible. There are few Christians who could not do something to bring Christian influences to bear upon the young men they know, and to shield them from the opposite influences, which are so numerous and powerful.

Finally, young men should be concerned for their own best interests. Because it is right; because the practices of godliness and virtue bring solid happiness; because thus they will make the most of their lives; and because of the concern which those who love them feel on their account. Let them, when tempted to neglect or forsake that which is good, or practice wickedness, remember the counsels and prayers of their fathers and mothers, and the pain they will inflict on them if they go wrong.—G. W.

Ver. 33.—*A father's anguish at his son's death.* The stroke which David feared fell upon him at last. In spite of all his desire to save his rebellious son, and his commands to each of the generals to "deal gently" with him for his sake, he had been slain. When the father learnt the unwelcome truth from "the Cushite" (Revised Version), he was overwhelmed with grief; and retiring to "the chamber over the gate" he burst out in the pathetic lamentation, "O my son Absalom!" etc., and continued crying with a loud voice, "O my son Absalom! O Absalom, my son, my son!" (ch. xix. 4). These loud demonstrations of grief were in a high degree impolitic, as Joab soon convinced him (ch. xix. 5—8), but they were the natural outburst of his tender heart and his unquenchable love for his worthless son. He had grieved sorely in the expectation of the death of his infant child (ch. xii. 16, 21, 22); much more must he grieve over this young man, on whom his heart had been set for so many years, and for whom he had done and borne so much. Moreover, Absalom had died suddenly, and by violence, and in sinful war against his father—unrepentant, unforgiven. David might even, in his passionate grief, reflect on himself as the occasion, however innocently, of his death, since it arose from the measures he had taken in defence of himself and his throne. Still more bitter would be the reflection that, by his foolish fondness, his evil example, his laxity of discipline, his refraining from merited punishment of his son's earlier sins and crimes, and his neglect to crush his treasonable practices at their commencement, he had greatly contributed to the formation of his evil character, and to his untimely and miserable end.

I. THE SORROW OF PARENTS BEREFT OF GROWN-UP CHILDREN. It is composed of various elements. **1.** *Sorrow of natural affection.* Which cannot always give account of itself, but is implanted by the Creator for most important purposes, is increased by years of exercise and mutual endearments and services, and often survives when these have ceased, and parental love is requited with ingratitude, neglect, injury, or deadly hostility. **2.** *Sorrow of disappointed hope.* Parents picture to themselves a career of prosperity and honourable activity for their children, and try to ensure it by the education and start in life which they give them. Or they may have looked to their son to be the prop of their own old age. How can they but sorrow bitterly when all their hopes are scattered by death? 3. *Their sorrow may be increased by painful fears.* It may be a sorrow uncheered by hope, because over the death of one who lived and died in sin. 4. *Self-reproach may, as in the case of David, accompany and embitter the grief.* The highest parental duties—those which have respect to the souls of children—may have been neglected. The home may have been, through parental indifference and worldliness, if no worse, a quite unfit place of preparation for holy service on earth or entrance into heaven. The sorrow arising from the consciousness of this cannot be assuaged by remembrance of the education given to prepare for this world's business, or the accomplishments imparted to render life refined and agreeable. 5. *The sorrows of bereaved parents are increased and from time to time renewed by observing the happiness of other parents whose children are continued to them, and are living in habits of piety, rectitude, and benevolence.*

II. CONSOLATIONS FOR SUCH SORROW. These are to be found in: 1. *Profound submission to the will of God.* The death we mourn, however it comes, was his doing who has the right to dispose of us and ours according to his pleasure; and who is infinite in wisdom and goodness—"our Father." "Thou didst it" (Ps. xxxix. 9); "The Lord gave, and the Lord hath taken away" (Job i. 21). 2. *Assurance of his fatherly compassion.* That he sympathizes while he chastises (Ps. ciii. 13). 3. *A good conscience.* Happy the fathers, the mothers, who have the consoling reflection that they did their best to fit their departed children for this world or the next. 4. *In the case of the death of godly children, the assurance of their blessed existence and happy commencement of nobler careers than those cut short by death.* The assurance also of future reunion where "there shall be no more death" (Rev. xxi. 4).

In conclusion: 1. *Let parents think of their children as mortal;* and be concerned so to train and influence them as to fit them for both living and dying. 2. *Let children live in view of a possibly early death.* Seek safety in Christ. Let life be a constant following of him. Dread to have life shortened and death made terrible by sins and vices. Let your parents have the consolation of knowing, should you die young, that you are "not lost, but gone before."—G. W.

EXPOSITION.

CHAPTER XIX.

Ver. 2.—**The victory** (Hebrew, *the salvation*) **that day was** turned **into mourning.** Naturally, the people did not understand the poignant emotions caused by the activity of David's conscience, and were pained at this seeming ingratitude to them for their brave exertions in his behalf, and at what they must have regarded as indifference to the welfare of the nation. Nor would it be easy for us to understand his conduct during the flight from Jerusalem, and in bearing Shimei's imprecations so tamely, did we not find in the psalms written at this time that David was suffering extreme and even excessive self-reproach and mental anguish at his past sin. It was a relief to bear Shimei's rudeness, for God might remember it for good. Racked thus with self-reproach, he had urged upon his generals to spare the young man (ch. xviii. 5), whose sin was part of a web which he had himself begun to spin, and in terror he waited for the result. Mentally it would have been better for him if he had gone to the battle instead of sitting in gloomy self-reproach between the gates. His eager inquiries, "Is the lad safe?" meant—Has the hand of justice again smitten me? and when he found that a second blow had fallen, his self-control gave way. Joab, more statesmanlike, and with his personal feelings unmoved, notices the fresh wrong that David is committing, and is vexed at seeing his brave warriors slink into Mahanaim ashamed, instead of being welcomed with deserved praise. But their conduct in being so depressed at David's sorrow is a proof of their affection for him, and it was plainly his duty to master his feelings, and to think of making a due return for the great service they had rendered him. The Hebrew word "salvation," that is, deliverance, gives the better side of the idea, while "victory" is a coarser word, taken from the language of a people whose trade was war.

Ver. 5.—**And Joab . . . said.** Joab's speech puts the alternative in a very incisive and even rude way before the king. But what he says is true, namely, that Absalom's success would inevitably have been followed by the massacre, not only of David himself, but of his sons and daughters, and of the women who had accompanied him in his flight. Nor would it have stopped there, but the officers of his court, the captains of his army, his mighties, and all who had long cared for and loved him would have been put to the sword. It was this horrible certainty, according to Oriental usage, which made Absalom's rebellion so abominable, and which steeled the heart of Joab against him when he saw him hanging in the tree. He regarded him as a fratricide and parricide, who had plotted murder on a large scale; and Joab was not made milder by the thought that this would have included himself and the heroes who had made David's throne so great. With stern good sense he, therefore, bids the king suppress his mere personal feelings, and leave the chamber in which he had concealed himself, to go forth and "speak to the heart of his servants," that is, thank and praise them in a friendly manner. For otherwise they would disperse and leave him; and this would be followed by the uprise of some other claimant of the throne—some relative, perhaps, of Saul, backed by the tribes of Benjamin and Ephraim; and David, abandoned by the nation, would fall an easy victim, with all his family, of this second rebellion. Absalom's rapid success proved that David had many enemies, and without great prudence he might be left at Mahanaim as powerless as Ishbosheth had been. The long delay between the death of this puppet-king and David's appointment to be sovereign of all Israel was probably owing to the same want of enthusiasm for David which had made the nation transfer its allegiance so lightly to the handsome Absalom. But with all his good sense Joab was coarse and rude. He was, moreover, utterly incapable of understanding David's real feelings. He saw only a father giving way to an exaggerated loss for a handsome but worthless son. David really was condemning himself for having brought lust and murder into his own house by abominable sin.

Ver. 8.—**All the people came before the king.** Probably they passed in review before him, and received his thanks. By thus acting in accordance with Joab's wise counsel, David probably saved the nation from years of anarchy, and a fresh civil war. **For Israel had fled every man to his tent;** Hebrew, *and Israel*, that is, Absalom's partisans, *fled each man to his tent*—to his home. The Authorized Version confounds Israel with David's soldiers, but consistently throughout the narrative "the hearts of the men of Israel are after Absalom" (ch. xv. 13; and see xvi. 15, 18; xvii. 14, 15, 24, 26; xviii. 6, 7, 16, 17).

Ver. 10.—Absalom, **whom we anointed over us.** It is evident from these words that there had been some solemn anointing and appointment of Absalom, and this accounts for the manner in which his partisans are always described as "Israel," while David's men are simply "his servants." With this anointment there must also have been a formal renunciation of David's rule, and, being thus dethroned, he does not attempt to return until the nation summons him back. As the flight of David narrated in ch. xvi. was extremely hurried, the conspirators must have kept their counsel well, and whatever rumours reached him apparently he disregarded. But meanwhile representatives of the tribes secretly convened at Hebron had claimed to act in the name of Israel, and, chosen a new king. The words certainly imply that, had Absalom lived, the Israelites would have considered themselves bound to obey him.

Ver. 11.—**David sent to Zadok and to Abiathar.** The two high priests had remained behind at Jerusalem, to watch over David's interests, and he now, by a messenger, probably Ahimaaz or Jonathan, urges them to quicken the proceedings of his own tribe. We may feel quite sure that there was discussion in Judah as well as in the other tribes; but the rebellion had begun at Hebron, and probably many of the leading chiefs were deeply implicated in Absalom's proceedings. Probably they now regretted it, but hung back through fear of punishment. It was politic, therefore, to assure them of David's kindly feelings, and that overtures on their side would be readily received, and the past forgiven.

Ver. 12.—**My bones**; Hebrew, *my bone and my flesh*, so nearly related as to be part of my own self (Gen. ii. 23).

Ver. 13.—**Of my bone, and of my flesh;** Hebrew, *art thou not my bone and my flesh?* —a most near and dear relative. It is difficult to understand why in the Authorized Version this common metaphor in the Hebrew has been so meddled with. Ewald thinks that this purposed degradation of Joab and the substitution of Amasa in his stead was a wise and politic act. It was to some extent just, for Joab was a man stained with many murders; but politic it was not. Passing over the fact that Amasa had actually taken the command of the rebel army, he was an ambitious and selfish man, and could lay no claim to that sturdy fidelity which had characterized Joab throughout his long service. For all he had done had been for David's good, and his advice, however roughly given, had averted grave misfortunes. Joab's murder of Absalom was an act of wilful disobedience; but David had used Joab for a far meaner murder, committed, not for reasons of statesmanship, but for purposes of lust. The guilt of slaying Absalom was as nothing compared with that of slaying Uriah, nor was it so base as the assassination of Abner, which David had tolerated, though made angry by it. The dismissal of Joab could have been effected only by putting him to death, and this certainly he did not deserve at David's hands; and the attempt, unless carried out secretly, would have led to tumult and insurrection. Joab, too, was a far more skilful general than Amasa, who, with larger forces, had just suffered a disastrous defeat; and if Joab was removed secretly, his brother Abishai remained to avenge him. David was, in fact, blinded by love for the son whom for so many years he had treated with coldness. There was a strong reaction now in the father's mind, and under its influence he was prepared to sacrifice the nephew who had been faithful to him and saved him, for the nephew who had joined in Absalom's rebellion. But possibly it had an immediate good effect, as Amasa, assured of forgiveness and promotion, now took David's side.

Ver. 14.—**And he bowed**, etc. It was not Amasa, but David, who made all the members of his tribe unanimous in his recall. And not only were the high priests active in his cause, but David, we may feel sure, sent numerous messages to all the more powerful men, assuring them of forgiveness and favour. In his general policy he was right. After the solemn anointing of Absalom, it was necessary for him to wait until some equally public and national act authorized his resumption of the royal power; and delay was dangerous. Every day now spent at Mahanaim might give the opportunity for fresh troubles.

Ver. 15.—**Gilgal.** As Gilgal lay upon the west bank of the Jordan (Josh. v. 9), near Jericho and the fords, it was a convenient place for the elders of Judah to await there the king. During the crossing, two interesting events happened—the meeting of Shimei and David, and the leave-taking of Barzillai the Gileadite. Shortly afterwards came the apology of Mephibosheth but it is uncertain whether he was among those who had come to Gilgal to welcome the king.

Ver. 16.—**Shimei the son of Gera.** The fact that he came attended by a thousand men of the tribe of Benjamin is a proof, not only that he was a person of influence, but that he had exerted himself to bring over his tribesmen to David's side. His adherence was, therefore, of importance. Ziba had always professed allegiance to David, and as he virtually represented the house of Saul, his presence was also valuable, even if prompted by the desire to keep Mephibosheth's land. For though Absalom seemed to be the nation's choice, yet there would

be many legitimists who would consider that the crown belonged to Saul's heirs, and who would watch the course of events for any opportunity favourable to their views. David's victory ruined their hopes, and the public acts of Shimei and Ziba removed all fear of public disturbance on the part of Saul's friends.

Ver. 17.—**They went over Jordan before the king.** This might mean that, in bringing the king across, Shimei and the Benjamites led the way. But, first, the verb, which is a rare one, means that they dashed through the river impetuously; and secondly, *before the king*, means "in the king's presence." While the tribe of Judah remained on the left bank to receive the king on his landing, Shimei and Ziba sought favour by a show of excessive zeal, and forded the Jordan, so as to be the first to welcome him (see ver. 20).

Ver. 18.—**And there went over a ferryboat**; more correctly, *and the ferry-boat kept crossing*, went backwards and forwards to bring the king's household over. **Shimei . . . fell down before the king, as he was come over Jordan.** If this translation were right, instead of fording the river, Shimei would have waited on the western bank. Some commentators do take this view, but it is contradicted by the latter part of ver. 17. Really the Hebrew words signify no more than "at his crossing the Jordan," that is, at some time or other during the passage. Shimei's course was not only the boldest, but also the wisest. For, in the first place, his prompt surrender would commend itself to David's generosity; and, secondly, had Abishai's counsel been taken, it would have offended the thousand Benjamites who formed his escort, and also all the warriors present there from Israel (see ver. 40). Trouble and discontent would certainly have followed upon any attempt on David's part to punish any of his enemies, and there might even have been armed resistance to his crossing.

Ver. 20.—**The first . . . of all the house of Joseph.** Shimei, who was a Benjamite, could not have thus claimed to be the representative of the northern tribes, had he remained on the western bank, where "half the people of Israel" were assembled. Strictly, "the house of Joseph" signified the tribe of Ephraim (Judg. i. 22, 35; and comp. Ps. lxxviii. 67), and in this sense Shimei did not belong to it. But Ephraim claimed a supremacy over all Israel; and one cause of the opposition to David certainly was the transference of the leadership to the tribe of Judah. Even the long reign of Solomon failed to weld the tribes together, and as soon as the reins of power fell into the weak hands of Rehoboam, an Ephraimite.

Jeroboam, whom Solomon had made "ruler over all the charge of the house of Joseph" (1 Kings xi. 28), quickly wrested the ten tribes from him. In Amos v. 6 "the house of Joseph" signifies all the northern tribes, for the reason given in 1 Chron. v. 1, 2 ; and such is its sense here. And Shimei compressed many powerful arguments in the phrase. For as a Benjamite he offered David the allegiance of the tribe which had given Israel its first king; while, as an Israelite, he professed also to represent the leading house of Ephraim, and all the northern tribes which usually followed its bidding.

Ver. 22.—**Ye sons of Zeruiah . . . adversaries unto me**; literally, *that ye be to me for a Satan;* rendered "adversary" in Numb. xxii. 22, but by Ewald in this place "tempter." It probably means "one who would do me harm." Though David speaks of the sons of Zeruiah in the plural (as in ch. xvi. 10), there is no reason to suppose that Joab shared in Abishai's impetuosity. Indifferent as he was to the shedding of blood, he was too prudent and politic to put the people out of temper by an execution on the day of David's return. **In Israel . . . over Israel.** There is much force in this repetition. A short time before Israel had been for Absalom, but now, by Shimei's submission, and that of the large body of Benjamites with him, David felt that once again he was king over the whole people.

Ver. 23.—**The king sware unto him.** David's magnanimity was not the result merely of policy, but also of joyful feeling at seeing all the tribes so readily welcome him back to the throne. But in spite of his oath, he orders Solomon to execute him, regarding what he had done as a sin past forgiveness. In so doing we can hardly acquit David of breaking his oath, even granting that Shimei's repentance was insincere, and that the motive of his actions was the desire simply to save his life. But we must remember that our Lord described his injunction, "that ye love one another," as "a new commandment" (John xiii. 34); and the utmost that can be said in David's favour is that his character was generous and full of chivalry. A half-excuse may be found for his order in the supposition that Shimei was an inveterate conspirator, and dangerous to Solomon's peace. This view seems confirmed by the command given to Shimei to build a house at Jerusalem (1 Kings ii. 36), where he would always be under surveillance. But had not David himself praised the man who "sweareth to his own hurt, and changeth not" (Ps. xv. 4)?

Ver. 24.—**Mephibosheth.** The meeting of David and Mephibosheth possibly took place at Jerusalem (see on ver. 25), and, if

so, the order of events is not chronological. Ziba certainly came to the Jordan fords, and the narrative may have been introduced here to complete the account of his doings. In neglecting his person and his dress, Mephibosheth was showing signs of heartfelt sorrow, and as he thus mourned during Absalom's tenure of power, it exposed him to the usurper's displeasure, and was a public avowal that his sympathies were with David. And his treatment was unjust; but David was in a strait. Ziba had been actively useful to him in his flight, and had also aided greatly in his recall. It was, probably, even owing to his influence that Shimei came with a thousand men of Benjamin. He deserved, therefore, a reward, but not at his master's cost. **His beard;** Hebrew, *the upper lip* (see Lev. xiii. 45; Ezek. xxiv. 17, 22).

Ver. 25.—**When he was come to Jerusalem to meet the king.** This certainly looks as if the meeting took place at Jerusalem, and apparently when David had reached the royal palace (see ver. 30). But what, then, is meant in ver. 24 by his "going down" to meet the king? If, too, he had been at Jerusalem all the while, how could he come there? Some, therefore, translate, "Then Jerusalem came to meet the king"—a possible, but not a natural, rendering, nor one that agrees with ver. 30. Others consider that he had withdrawn to his house in the highlands of Benjamin at Gibeah of Saul; but David had given these lands to Ziba, and the crippled Mephibosheth would have met with rough treatment had he endeavoured to contest the ownership. The Arabic Version reads, "when he came from Jerusalem;" but it is not confirmed by any trustworthy authorities. The view of Kimchi is probably right, that Mephibosheth did go down to the Jordan fords to meet David, and certainly his duty required of him no less. He had been slandered and ill used, but the king believed him to be guilty, and regarded him with displeasure. To have remained, therefore, at home when all Judah and half Israel had gone to welcome David back, would have been culpable remissness. And though he was lame, yet the ride was not so long as to be very fatiguing. But he did not rush through the river, as Shimei and his thousand men had done; and when David had crossed, there was too much going on for him to get an audience. He followed, therefore, in David's suite; but in Jerusalem the meeting actually took place. Thus the verses briefly record different facts: ver. 24 that Mephibosheth went with the vast crowd to welcome the king back; ver. 25 that in due time, in Jerusalem, the explanation was given, and Mephibosheth restored to favour.

Ver. 26.—**Thy servant said, I will saddle me an ass.** This would mean, "Thy servant purposed, said within himself, that he would saddle an ass, not by his own hands, but by those of his servants." All the versions, however, except the Chaldee, read, "Thy servant said to him, Saddle me an ass." With this agrees the narrative in ch. xvi. 1. Mephibosheth ordered Ziba to saddle for him an ass, and one for an attendant, and to put hastily together a supply of food for the journey. And Ziba does so; but when everything is ready, he leaves his master in the lurch, and carries all away to David, to whom he falsely represents Mephibosheth as a traitor. In the words that follow, he unreservedly submits himself to David, on the ground that, though innocent in this affair, yet that, as a member of a dethroned dynasty, his life was forfeit (comp. ch. xxi. 7), and that, in permitting him to live, and placing him among his friends, the king had done him an act of grace.

Ver. 29.—**Thou and Ziba divide the land.** Two views are taken of this decision—the one, that it was a complete reversal of the command in ch. xvi. 4, placing matters upon the old footing, by which Ziba was to have half the produce for cultivating the estate; the other, and apparently the most correct view, is that Ziba was now made actual owner of half the land, and Mephibosheth, instead of a half, would henceforth have only a quarter of the crops. The decision was not equitable, and David speaks in a curt and hurried manner, as though vexed with himself for what he was doing. As a matter of fact, Ziba's treachery had been most useful to David. Besides the pleasure at the time of finding one man faithful, when "all men were liars" (Ps. cxvi. 11), Ziba had been most active in bringing over the tribe of Benjamin to David's side; and though his motives were selfish and venal, yet, as the king reaped the benefit of his conduct, he was bound not to leave him without reward.

Ver. 30.—**Yea, let him take all.** These words betray a feeling of resentment. Though outwardly they profess to regard the loss of the property with indifference, as compared with the joy of the king's return, yet this sort of "I don't care" answer usually covers anger. Blunt's arguments ('Undesigned Coincidences,' p. 157, etc.), to show that Mephibosheth really was a traitor, are ingenious, but not convincing.

Ver. 31.—**Barzillai.** Barzillai was so wealthy a man that, with some help from others, he had provided the king "of sustenance," or, in more modern English, "with sustenance," while his army lay encamped at Mahanaim; and now, though he was eighty years of age, he wished to attend the king

in person until he reached the other side of Jordan.

Ver. 33.—**And I will feed thee.** This is the same verb as that used in ver. 32, and translated "to provide of sustenance."

Ver. 37.—**That I may die in mine own city,** ... **by the grave of my father and of my mother.** The inserted words, "and be buried," are very matter-of-fact and commonplace. What Barzillai wished was that, when death overtook him, it should find him in the old abode of his family, where his father and mother had died, and where their tombs were. This regard for the family sepulchre was hereditary among the Israelites, who followed in it the example of their forefather (see Gen. xlix. 29—31). **Chimham.** David remembered Barzillai's kindness to the last, and on his dying bed specially commended Chimham and his brothers to the care of Solomon. In Jer. xli. 17 we read of "the habitation of Chimham, which is by Bethlehem," whence it has been supposed that David also endowed the son of Barzillai with land near his own city. Stanley ('Jewish Church,' ii. 201) considers that this was a caravanserai founded by Chimham for the hospitable lodging of travellers on their way to Egypt, and that Mary and Joseph found shelter there. It lay to the south of Bethlehem; but there is nothing more than the name to connect it with the son of Barzillai. In ver. 40 he is called in the Hebrew *Chimhan*.

Ver. 40.—**Half the people of Israel.** The northern tribes had been the first to debate the question of the king's recall (ver. 9), while the men of Judah hung back. But at the instigation of the high priests and of Amasa, who was actually in command, they determined upon David's restoration, and acted so promptly and so independently of the rest of Israel that, when they reached Gilgal, only the delegates of a few tribes were in time to join them. As we read in ver. 41 of "all the men of Israel," it is evident that the rest had rapidly followed. It would have been well if the tribe of Judah had informed the rest of their purpose, as the bringing of David back would then have been the act of all Israel; but tribal jealousies were the cause of Israel's weakness throughout the time of the judges, and broke out into open disunion upon the death of Solomon.

Ver. 41.—**Why have our brethren the men of Judah stolen thee away?** Why, that is, have they acted by stealth and without our concurrence? As they were discussing the matter, their decision should have been awaited, and David should not have crossed until formally invited so to do. The half of Israel consisted, probably, of the trans-Jordanic tribes, upon whom those on the west of the river looked contemptuously, and of Shimei and his Benjamites, and a few more in the immediate neighbourhood. The trans-Jordanic tribes are probably those described in ver. 39 as "the people who went with David over Jordan;" for certainly a powerful body of the men who had defeated Absalom would escort David back to Jerusalem, to overawe the malcontents and prevent any opposition to his return.

Ver. 42.—**The king is near of kin to us.** The pronouns are singular throughout: "He is near of kin to me. Why art thou angry? Have I eaten . . . I have ten parts . . . Why didst thou despise me?" and so everywhere. This is much more piquant; but such personification is contrary to the genius of our language. **Have I eaten, etc. ?** Saul had boasted of enriching the Benjamites (1 Sam. xxii. 7), but probably the speaker intended only to protest the purity of his motives.

Ver. 43.—**I have ten parts in the king.** One tribe disappears, which certainly was not Benjamin; nor was this warlike state thus early awed into obedience to Judah. In 1 Kings xi. 31, 35, again, we have ten tribes given to Jeroboam, and here, also, not only must Benjamin be counted, but be included in the tribes rent from the house of David. The tribe that had disappeared was that of Simeon, partly lost among the desert races south of the Negeb, and partly absorbed by Judah. Its position always made it unimportant, and no trace can be found of its taking any part in the political life of Israel. Some strangers from Simeon are mentioned in 2 Chron. xv. 9 as coming to the great gathering of Judah and Benjamin at Jerusalem after Asa had defeated Zerah the Ethiopian; and Josiah carried out his reformation in Simeon as well as in Manasseh, Ephraim, and Naphtali (2 Chron. xxxiv. 6). But it never seems to have emerged from a state of semi-barbarism, and no town can be found within its territories. We must, therefore, omit Simeon, and of course the Levites, who took no part in politics, and thus we have Judah standing alone, and all the rest determined to resist any attempt on its part to establish a hegemony, and restless even at having to endure the more ancient claims of Ephraim to be the leading tribe. By the ten parts which they claim in the king, they meant that, as king, he belonged equally to all, and not to his own tribe only. In this they were expressing a sound view of the royal position. The next words, literally, are, "And also in David I am more than thou;" to which the Septuagint adds, "And I am the firstborn rather than thou." This is in accordance with 1 Chron. v. 1, and states an important claim always made by Ephraim; whereas the Hebrew, "I in David am more than thou," is unintelligible. Except upon the score of numbers already stated, the right of each tribe in David was equal. **Why then, etc.?** rather, *Why hast thou despised me? Was not my word the first for bringing back the king?* (see ver. 9, and note on ver. 40). **Were fiercer.** While the Israelites debated the matter calmly, the men of Judah met their complaint with harsh and bitter rejoinders. This explains the feud which followed.

HOMILETICS.

Vers. 1—15.—The facts are: 1. In consequence of David's sorrowful isolation, the people mourn and betake themselves to the city ashamed and discouraged. 2. Joab, being informed of the fact, enters the king's house, and sharply rebukes him for his conduct, charging him with disregarding the sacrifices his people had made, and caring more for his rebellious son than for his attached friends. 3. Joab then advises him at once to arise and go forth to encourage the people, pointing out that otherwise the greatest trial of his life will be sure to come in the alienation of his subjects. 4. The king thereupon sits in the gate of the city, and all the people come to him. 5. Meanwhile, during David's sojourn at Mahanaim, the people of Israel are at variance as to the course to be pursued with reference to bringing him back to rule over them, and it is urged that, under all the circumstances of the case, something should be done in that direction. 6. David, hearing of the intentions of Israel, sends to Zadok and Abiathar to suggest to the elders of Judah the impropriety of their being forestalled in the movement by their brethren of Israel. 7. He also instructs them to inform Amasa of his purpose to displace Joab in his favour. 8. The heart of the people of Judah being entirely won, they send unto him a message that he should return, and the king acting upon it, they meet him at Gilgal to conduct him over Jordan.

Solitariness in religious experience. The isolation of David from his people during this absorption in what appeared to be a domestic sorrow caused pain to his staunchest friends, was very near imperilling his influence as sovereign, and gave some ostensible ground for the ungracious remonstrance of Joab. But the fact is, David was true to himself as a man of deepest piety, and the people were unable to enter into the actual struggle through which he was passing. Like One greater, he "trod the wine-press alone." It was not mere natural affection for a son, it was not pain that a son had been ungrateful, that crushed him and rendered him for the time forgetful of the claims of his people and the duties of his office. The key to the whole is to be sought in the prediction of Nathan (ch. xii. 9—12), the fulfilment of this in its severest form in the tragedy of the life just ended, and the keen perception of this in relation to his own dreadful sin. His distinct recognition of the chastising hand of God (ch. xv. 24—30) when, with bare feet and broken heart, he passed in silence and tears over Mount Olivet, was now repeated with, of course, the fuller and more overwhelming anguish attendant on the ruin of a life, yea, of a soul, as he felt, through his own great sin. Joab and the people never, perhaps, knew of Nathan's declaration. It was always a latent element in David's restored life of piety; but now it was the crushing force before which he could not hold up. He saw, as he believed, how his spiritual degeneracy, during those dark months of horrible sin and guilt, had acted perniciously on the spirit of his son; and he could not but feel that, in the temporal and spiritual destruction of his son, he was now reaping just what he had sown. Yet all this he had to bear alone! No one could share the dreadful secret; and in proportion as he saw what was involved in a ruined soul, so would be the utterness of his anguish. No wonder if in his solitary experience he forgot all earthly things, and gave himself up to the bitterness of his grief.

I. There are crises in spiritual experience. David was a man of many crises. The history and the Psalms reveal them. His call to kingship by Samuel meant an unrecorded experience of a most extraordinary kind. His anguish in exile when pursued by Saul put his faith to a terrible test. His sad fall was a descent into a pit of horrors. The tremendous conflict involved in his restoration is indicated in the fifty-first psalm, and now, when the judgment of God for his sin falls in heaviest form, he descends into the depths (Ps. cxxx.) further, perhaps, than was ever known by any other man. We see similar crises in the lives of some others. Jacob knew the desolation of Bethel and the pains of the wrestling with the angel. Paul was dumb and blind before God till prayer brought him forth to light and peace; and he later on had experiences of things which it was "not lawful" to utter. Most men whose religion has depths have known times when anguish before God has shut out all thought and care of earthly things. Some have seasons of temptation equal to that of Bunyan's Pilgrim in the Valley of the Shadow of Death. As a rule, religious life is a steady growth, but there are checks and disasters when the question of life itself is at stake. We can understand David's experience in the case before us without having recourse to the hypothesis of a weak mind overborne by natural sorrow for the death of a favourite son.

II. Crises in religious experience are often most absorbing. David was so absorbed in the spiritual anguish springing from a religious view of the ruin of Absalom in connection with his own great sin, as practically to forget that he was a king, and that a nation needed his guidance. The narrative is true to the spiritual facts that may be traced by a comparison of this event with the king's previous conduct. The intensity of his nature, as revealed in the strong and passionate utterances of the psalms, whether in joy or sorrow, would add to the tendency to yield himself utterly to this greatest of all the calamities consequent on his sin. The passion with which he once pleaded for Bathsheba's child (ch. xii. 16—20) was an instance of the same kind, only less than this, because here the trouble was the more serious in so far as the moral and bodily ruin of a son was a greater consequence of his sin. All who have entered into the solitariness of the great crises in the soul's career know how at such times all earthly things seem to vanish into insignificance; and it is with extreme difficulty that ordinary and necessary duties can be attended to. Men have been known to forget to take food, and to isolate themselves from their friends. And no wonder, when the soul sees its sins in the awful light of God's judgments, or is made to feel the consequences to others of its past deeds. Peter did not associate freely with friends that night on which he "went out and wept bitterly."

III. There are qualifying circumstances that determine the degree of

ABSORPTION IN THE SORROWS OF A RELIGIOUS EXPERIENCE. David never felt anything like this. But the reason is plain. Never before did he see a connection between his own past conduct and so awful an event. The special elements contributing to his self-absorbing misery were a vivid remembrance of his dreadful sin in the case of Bath-sheba and Uriah; a spiritual appreciation of the awful issue of his son's life; a deep conviction that that issue was, in the judgment of God, in some way connected with his own sin; a contrast, inevitable in the association of ideas, of the end of Absalom with the hopes once cherished concerning him; a reflection, which could not but occasionally force itself in (ch. xii. 13), that he only was forgiven and saved; a feeling that no one on earth could enter into his sorrows and afford him consolation. All these circumstances gained force by the fact that constitutionally he always felt strongly, and religiously his superior spiritual discernment rendered sin and its effects the more terrible. So in our own experience there will be, perhaps, specialities which may render our absorption much more absolute than is that of others. The natural mental and moral texture of our nature, the conditions under which our sins were committed, the consequences which we can trace from our former sins, the vividness with which an ideal past is con-trasted with present facts, the relative clearness of our spiritual perceptions and tender-ness of our susceptibilities, and degree of homage paid to the majesty of God's holy Law,—all these may qualify the self-surrender to the experience of the time. We can-not expect cold and stolid men to bear the same troubles in the same way as do men of quick and highly developed spiritual sensibilities.

IV. THE SORROWS OF SUCH CRISES CANNOT BE SHARED. A community of experience is necessary to the creation of a sympathy coextensive with the depth of the sorrow. There were parents in Israel and Judah who had lost sons, and they would be able to enter into David's grief to that extent, and he could so far speak to them of his trouble. There were sinful men at Mahanaim who knew what trouble of conscience was, and who might afford comfort to their neighbours when mourning over their guilt; but there was no man in all the world who had sinned as David had, and no one in the world, perhaps, who now saw what an unutterably awful thing sin in general was, and espe-cially his sin. To no one except Nathan, who probably kept aloof from him, had the connection of David's sin with this judgment on it been known. Consequently, David felt shut up to his own anguish. "Of the people there was none with him." The transaction was between himself and God. He knew that the people did not under-stand him, and he could not explain himself to them. So is it with all our deepest experiences before God. We see our sins set in the light of his countenance, and no one can share the experience involved therein. Reversing the picture, it may be said that there are also seasons of blessedness in the course of life when the "joy is unspeakable and full of glory," and which can never be fully told or even understood.

GENERAL LESSONS. 1. Let us remember that there are daily some persons passing through fearful crises in their religious life, and that it is possible to help all such by our prayers. 2. We should be very considerate of others who may appear to be unduly cast down, as there may be circumstances which, if known, would strengthen our pity. 3. It is very possible for us to misjudge others in the conduct they adopt, and make our own contracted experience a standard of judgment. 4. We may expect that those who are utterly broken down in spirit will be called out of their self-absorption by the voice of Providence. 5. It is a comfort to us all to know that God understands our real thoughts and feelings, and that we have a High Priest who is touched with a feeling of our infirmities, he having entered into deeper depths of sorrow than we can ever know.

The remoter consequences of sin. The narrative sets forth the action of Joab to arouse the king from his self-absorption, and the changed attitude of the people towards him, as also the measures taken by David to bring about a reconciliation between himself and the entire nation. The great judgment on David's sin was now passed. Nathan's words had been fearfully fulfilled, but in what followed we see also some of the remoter consequences of the sin. Thus Joab's rough treatment and unbecoming familiarity in the discharge of an honest duty were connected with the fact that David had put himself in Joab's power by making him privy and accessory to the death of Uriah. The people were now almost alienated because of the absorption of the king in sorrow.

which would not have happened but for the sin which created the sorrow. The question of the precedence of Judah in the matter of his restoration was the distinct formulation of a jealousy and sectional interest which subsequently resulted in a schism of the kingdom, and this question would not have arisen but for the chastisement for sin in the form of a son's rebellion. Likewise the ultimate death of Amasa came through David's having, probably because Joab had been insulting and because a complete amnesty was deemed desirable, displaced Joab in his favour. These bitter streams all flowed into the remoter ramifications of life from the fountain of trouble opened by the fall of David. Hereon we may observe—

I. THE FORGIVENESS OF SIN MAY COEXIST WITH THE ONWARD FLOW OF SOME OF ITS CONSEQUENCES. There is a certainty that David's great guilt was covered (ch. xii. 13). The prayer of the fifty-first psalm had been fully answered, and privately he had been able to rejoice again in the God of his salvation. But we have in this history the spectacle of a pardoned, reconciled man, confident in his personal salvation, and the onward flow of a stream of social and material evils which, so far at least as they were related to him, sprang from his sin. The prediction of Nathan did not establish an arbitrary relation between his conduct to Bathsheba and Uriah, and the whole mental and moral condition implied therein, and the rebellion of Absalom and the perplexities of the situation after its suppression. There was an organic connection between the spiritual fall and the civil troubles. The spiritual element in us is the centre of our composite nature. A change for the worse in it radiates through the entire being, and as the outward relations are affected by the condition and direction taken by our various powers, so the inmost change is the spring of manifold and ever-flowing consequences. The deteriorated influence on others, consequent on a period of spiritual declension, cannot but act dynamically as a wave long after we have by repentance and faith been restored to God. The personal condemnation is gone, but the injury done on society is not gone. The intricate mass of material and social evils now afflicting the world is the outcome of deviation from the perfect will of God, and though some who thus deviated are now blessed in heaven, the quota they contributed by their former sins is still somewhere in the tangled mass.

II. SIN IS A DISTURBER OF MANY RELATIONS. David's sin affected his relation to God and to his own family and people. It touched his personal influence among friends, his administration, and indirectly, through the rebellion, the lives and dearest interests of multitudes. The distress and uncertainty at Mahanaim after the defeat of Absalom and the hesitancy of the tribes to welcome him back, were traceable to what he had formerly done. Who can describe the manifold disturbances in the order of things produced in our world by the sin of Adam? The ramifications of the wave of disturbance created by any one sin are more than can be numbered. It is in the more conspicuous acts of transgression that we get visible traces of a widespread disturbance similar to what is caused by every inconspicuous act. A rebellious son in a home, a dishonest deed in business, a vicious habit,—these reveal a manifest series of troubles in private, social, and public connections. No sinner sins to himself. Moral evil gives colour and form to all things. It infuses an element of defect, if not of positive evil, into every bodily, mental, and moral relation sustained by the sinning man.

III. THE DISTURBANCE CAUSED BY SIN FLOWS ON INTO THE REMOTE FUTURE. The great moral shock involved in David's great sin produced effects which for years flowed on, and which, in fact, are flowing on now. The great storm in mid-ocean sends the under swell into far-distant bays, and long after quietude has been restored at the centre the sullen roll falls on the beach. The whole subsequent course of Hebrew history was modified by the deed of evil done in secret. In so far as the power of David over the world is less, and different in kind, from what it would have undoubtedly been had he kept himself pure, so far his sin is still at work shaping the destinies of men. We can never call back the waves of pernicious influence we send forth in a single sinful act or feeling. It is the law of the universe that they go on. The supposed counteraction of them by subsequent repentance and amendment only means that we modify the influence previously sent forth,—we make the world somewhat better than it would have been had the sinful influence gone out alone. We cannot annihilate it any more than we can annihilate force. The future is the sum of all the influences of the past.

IV. THE MANIFOLD AND EVER-FLOWING CONSEQUENCES OF SIN ARE NOT ADEQUATELY RECOGNIZED BY MANKIND. David recognized the rebellion and death of Absalom and the associated civil inconveniences as being in some way connected with his sin; but even he did not see, when at Mahanaim, that the subsequent death of Amasa and the schism of the two kingdoms were also a consequence of his conduct, and therefore of his sin. His own people probably did not even connect the troubles of the times with his sin, but rather with what they regarded as a foolish over-fondness for a favourite son. In our life we do not sufficiently connect our bodily and mental imperfections with the sins of others in the past, or, in some cases, especially with our own sins. Political bodies and publicists fail to recognize the spiritual origin of vast and complicated social troubles. The Bible in this respect is the most statesmanlike and philosophical of all books, in that it gives prominence to sin as the determining factor in all our material and social troubles. A spiritual mind discerns the spiritual causes.

Vers. 16—30.—The facts are: 1. Shimei, with a considerable Benjamite following, including Ziba and his household, joins the men of Judah to meet David at the Jordan. 2. Previous to the king being ferried over, Shimei falls down before him, confesses his past sins, and pleads for mercy, and urges as evidence of sincerity that he is the first to come and bid the king welcome. 3. On Abishai expressing his feeling that Shimei should rather be put to death for his evil deeds, David resents the suggestion, and in honour of the day of his restoration declares to Shimei that his life shall be spared. Mephibosheth also comes, with his person uncared for, to welcome the king at Jerusalem, and on being asked why he had not gone out with him into exile, explains that it was owing to the deception of his servant Ziba. 5. Placing himself and all his interests entirely at the king's disposal, admitting that all his rights and privileges were, according to political custom, of pure clemency, he is told that he need not enter further into the question, but that he and Ziba should divide the land between them.

The influence of superior minds. The section now under notice cannot be separated in import from the preceding words (vers. 14, 15), which relate that David bowed the heart of all the men of Judah so that they came to conduct him over Jordan. The particular instances of Shimei and Mephibosheth are special illustrations of the general truth expressed in David's bowing the hearts of men. The mighty power of the king's words and methods gathered around him the most bitter of foes and the most lonely and helpless of his friends. The facts bring out into view the influence which a superior mind exercises over others; and on the nature and conditions of this influence we may, by the help of the narrative in addition to broad facts in human life, make a few observations, noting—

I. THE NATURAL BASIS. The bowing of the hearts of all the people indicates the swaying of an influence of an unusual kind. Whatever the means and whatever aids to this end came from the sudden transition of public feeling produced by Absalom's death, the fact remains that there was in David's nature as a man something which, when aroused, gave him a mental and moral power over others. Intellectually and morally he was a born king of men. If "king" = *könig* = *können*, "to be able," then he, by virtue of his nature, was king—was above others, and there went forth a spell which all recognized. Apart from special endowments, he was the superior man of the age. There were elements in him which, under evil disposition, would render him most capable of leading people captive in evil ways, and which, under a good disposition, did lay hold of them for their good. The history of mankind and the observation of daily life reveal the domination of one mind over others. The influence of mind is the most subtle and mighty thing we know. Millions sometimes submit to its spell. It is the proud prerogative of the select few to bow down the hearts of their fellows. All attempts to explain the fact by psychological analysis are insufficient. No analysis can get at the mysterious nature of the impact of one spirit on another: yet we know that the reality has its root in the peculiar constitution of the individual. This applies to preacher, statesman, philosopher, poet, king. The Apostle Paul's power was in its basis a constitutional power. Grace is grafted on nature, not a force apart from nature.

II. ACQUIRED INCREMENT. The native qualities of David determined the fact and the kind of his superior influence over other minds, though not its moral direction. But his education and experience in the gradual exercise of his powers in lower spheres of activity contributed to the mature form and range of his influence. The conqueror of lion and giant became, by an educational process, a conqueror of the hearts of men. The development of natural powers, whether of oratory, administration, will-force, moral suasion, or the more nameless thing which goes out from one's personal presence, is another way of saying that we have added to the store of influence which lay in the mental constitution from the first. The difference in the degree to which some men acquire this increment accounts, in large measure, for their ascendancy over the equally gifted. Perhaps this is the meaning of those who regard genius as a name for great powers duly developed by continuous exercise.

III. SPIRITUAL ENDOWMENT. In the case of David we must recognize this element in his superior power over the hearts of good and bad. Grace in him had perfected and beautified a fine nature. The spiritual is always the most subtle and subduing influence over men, when brought fairly into play. In spite of sin, men acknowledge the spell. The anointing by Samuel in the name of God was more than a formal act. David was indeed the Lord's anointed. Hence all the natural and acquired qualities received an elevation and a tone which, when the dire evils of the great fall were not at work on him, gave to his words, his counsels, his movements, and commands a charm and force over men of most diverse temperament and character. In this he was like the apostles when they stood before men. We occasionally see now how greatly the power of certain minds is increased over others when they have the natural and acquired gifts baptized with the anointing of the Holy Spirit. A consecrated heart and intellect gains influence by its consecration. There are men who by oratory have bowed the hearts of thousands; but when such men have became true Christians, the bowing of the hearts under their words is a much more thorough and enduring victory. "Covet earnestly the best gifts" (1 Cor. xii. 31).

IV. CIRCUMSTANTIAL AIDS. The circumstances of the time gave advantage to David in the exercise of his ordinary powers. His friends had mourned his sorrowful isolation; his enemies had felt that, by defeat, they had placed themselves in an awkward position; his being aroused from his self-absorbing grief led him to calmly review the position of advantage in which now the goodness of God had placed him; the reflection that now a supreme effort was needed if he was to prevent the alienation of friends and follow up the fruits of victory so as to save the nation from anarchy, drew forth his entire soul into sympathy with the purpose of God in making him king; and, as a consequence, he so infused into his conversation with the people of Mahanaim, and into his messages to the elders of Judah, the whole power of his nature that he bowed the hearts of all. Events had prepared the minds of the people to receive the influence going forth from his very soul. The narrative evidently implies that there was some unusual persuasiveness in his manner and language, and it reached even to Shimei and Mephibosheth, who certainly were rendered more accessible to his influence by the change in affairs. Seasons of excitement and public interest are favourable to the putting forth of the influence which superior minds can exercise. The Day of Pentecost was a time which brought aid to the efforts of the apostles. A grave responsibility rests on gifted men to use their influence under such favouring circumstances as occasionally occur in human affairs.

GENERAL LESSONS. 1. It behoves us not to allow our gifts to be long unused, by reason of absorption in purely personal interests. 2. It is a scripturally enforced duty that we stir up the gifts that may lie in us. 3. Among the various powers that may be exercised in the world, we should especially desire and seek that of bowing down the hearts of men to the interests of God's kingdom. 4. We may rest assured that, if we use our powers to the utmost in a good cause and in dependence on God, we shall overcome many an obstacle and win over even adverse hearts.

Royal clemency. The sudden collapse of the rebellion placed David in a position of advantage, and yet of difficulty. He was not the man to care for sovereignty over a disunited people, and the attitude of those who had been in rebellion was not quite certain. Those who do wrong are suspicious of those against whom the wrong has been done when power comes into their hands. It was, therefore, the policy of David to convince them that they need not be under any apprehension of his using the recovered power to punish them. This was the evident meaning of the deputation of the high priests to the men of Judah, and the reason of the promotion of Amasa (together with his reasonable desire to express his sense of Joab's dangerous liberty in disobeying a positive public command). The noble-hearted king felt the importance of the restoration of peace and unity so deeply, and was so sensible of the mercy of God in answering his desire when in anguish (ch. xv. 25, 26), that, on this occasion of joy, sobered though it was by thoughts of chastisement just past, he cannot but grant an amnesty to all his foes. In the exercise of this royal clemency we see set forth the following truths.

I. THE INFLUENCE ON MEN OF ALL CONDITIONS OF A TIDE OF SUCCESS. The turn of the tide had come for David, and with it men good and bad, great and small, throughout the land began to consider how they had better comport themselves under the new circumstances. Israel hastened to indicate readiness (ver. 11). Judah was waiting for some encouragement to yield (vers. 12—14), and receiving it, hasted to be first at Jordan (vers. 15, 41). And such representative men as Shimei and Ziba show eagerness to find favour with the victorious monarch. Probably only an active section of the less thoughtful people had really rejected David; the great mass were won over to the winning side because it was the winning side, and, now that David was returning to power, they, and also the real leaders of the rebellion, move on with the tide. Success has a great charm for some minds. The day of prosperity draws out many friends. In national and religious affairs multitudes are influenced, not by a calm and independent consideration of the merits of the question or system, but by the fact that there is a semblance of prosperity. Men are not without reason spoken of as a "flock;" they are disposed to go in with the rest. This is not the highest type of humanity.

II. DOUBTFUL LOYALTY IN THE RELATIONSHIPS OF LIFE. The real friends of Absalom and such men as Shimei fell in with the change in public opinion, and professed, the latter most eagerly and humbly, to welcome the king back. Allegiance is a matter of degrees, and springs from mixed motives. David had to feel for the rest of his days that policy governed the loyalty of some of his people. In national life there are many causes of unsteadiness of loyal attachment to the head of the state—some lying in the seat of authority, and some in ignorance, prejudice, or occasionally the convictions of the people. Every bond of union between moral beings implies a loyalty more or less defined to persons and interests. Master and servant, husband and wife, partners in business and government, teachers and pupils, create, by the relation formed, a demand for loyalty the one to the other and to the common interests professedly sought by the union. The fellowship of the saints in Church life especially creates scope for mutual loyalty and common loyalty to Christ. We may see many things in one, for all truth is related; and therefore, in the doubtful loyalty of men in David's time, with its necessary weakness to the national life, and injury to the highest interests of the kingdom, we see the evil brought on the world by defective loyalty in the various relationships men enter into; and especially do we see the pernicious effect of defective loyalty of professing Christians to the Church and to Christ. The practical bearings of this are very many and very wide.

III. INDICATIONS OF AN UNEASY CONSCIENCE. The moral value of actions is not to be seen by looking at them simply as actions; their form may be perfect, their real value is seen in their connections. It was a beautiful action to hasten over Jordan and be first to bid the king welcome; the most devoted of his friends could not do more; but for Shimei to do it, after his conduct towards David, took away from the deed the flow of its natural beauty. The act was evidence of an uneasy conscience conjoined with a cowardly, time-serving policy. That he was truly penitent is not admissible from the tenor of his words—they sound hollow. It is not the custom of the true penitent to refer to his good deeds in proof of penitence (ver. 20). Nor, perhaps, was Ziba without a restless conscience in thus seeking early to court the favour of the king, who would soon learn the facts concerning his former deception (ch. xvi. 1—4). We here see that conscience is alive, even in very base men; that it is quiescent and seemingly at ease when either possibility of exposure or punishment is far off; that it is nevertheless sensitive to any change in events which tend to hasten exposure or punishment; that its greatest dread is falling into the hands of a supreme power; and that, instead of elevating the man, and prompting to renovation, it rather drags him down to the low and plausible means of avoiding what it knows is deserved. Let the religious teacher see how this action of conscience is verified in the case of many who have rejected Christ, the Lord's Anointed. Once let them know that he is coming into his kingdom, and uneasiness will appear.

IV. The influence in life of dominating ideas. The son of Zeruiah (ver. 21) wished to slay Shimei at once, and, had he done so, many would have said that the wicked man reaped the desert of his crimes. The anointed of the Lord desired that the man should not die, and many doubtless thought that the clemency was ill-judged. But the reason of the totally diverse desires and judgments was that the two men were on that day governed by totally diverse ideas. Abishai was the hard, stern soldier, ruled in this instance by the sentiment of rigid discipline, and acting in all things under the idea of power; whereas David was the wise, generous king, ruled by the sentiment of love for his people, and acting in this instance under the idea of kingly grace. The one saw no reason in the event of the day for sparing an unworthy life; the other saw that kingly grace found befitting exercise when prosperity and joy were returning to all. The ideas that ruled the one life left no room for variation; those that ruled the other required variation. It is an important inquiry to what extent men's lives are ruled by a few leading ideas, and what is the relation of these ideas to the impulses and dispositions that seem to lie next to the will. The Christian man has certain clear and definite conceptions concerning God, Christ, himself, the relation of the present to the future, which mark him off from the *non*-Christian man, and these form the intellectual elements that determine all his conduct toward God and man. Men of diverse ages differ much in the general conceptions they entertain on the details of life, and hence we get differences in the degree of conformity of conduct to an absolute standard of morality. In so far as we can procure unity of perception and unity of disposition, so far do we lay the basis for harmony of conduct and the welfare of civil society. Hence the radical and yet progressive work of true Christianity: it will bring "eye to eye" and heart to heart, and so establish peace for evermore. Hence also the importance of instilling in young and old such views as shall, by their range and controlling influence over the mind, practically determine conduct along the Christian line.

V. The patient waiting of the deceived and oppressed. The personal appearance of Mephibosheth when he came to welcome David to Jerusalem was indicative of trouble and sorrow arising from neglect and poverty, and possibly real grief, experienced during the time of the rebellion. The conduct of Ziba and the loss of David's table (ch. ix. 9—13; xvi. 1—4) account for his poverty, and it is not likely that such a man as Absalom would make ample provision for one of the house of Saul. There is no trace of Mephibosheth having by treasonable means done wrong to David, though it is possible that, in real Oriental manner, he, like the sons of Zadok, may have assumed an outward prudential appearance of fidelity to the cause of Absalom. He was a helpless man, deceived and oppressed, and placed, by reason of his physical infirmity, in such a position as not to be able to extricate himself from trouble. His only chance was to wait and cherish hope that the generous king, who had so bountifully befriended him for his father's sake, would return to power. A fair illustration is this of the patient waiting of men suffering from craft and wrong. The African race in slavery, deceived and robbed of their patrimony by men more strong and crafty, waited and hoped almost against hope for the day of freedom. Their only hope was in the rise of the beneficent kingly power of the Lord's Anointed, and it did come. Others, such as the Waldenses and Malagasy, wronged and oppressed, waited for the coming of the better day, and it did come. Many a soul, deceived by the cunning craft of the father of lies, and robbed of moral and material wealth, has known the pains of poverty of spirit, and waited for the king's gracious restoration. The Apostle Paul tells us, too, of the "whole creation," afflicted with the ills consequent on the great rebellion against God, travailing in pain, and waiting for a better time (Rom. viii. 18—22). It is the joy of the preacher to be able to announce "the acceptable year of the Lord" to all who mourn. They shall not wait in vain (Isa. lxi. 1—4).

VI. A practical view of the anomalies of life. The position in which David found himself when, on hearing the story of Mephibosheth and observing his distressed circumstances, he had to decide with respect to the property at stake, was one of extreme delicacy and difficulty. In all good faith he had handed over the property to Ziba, and

Ziba had befriended his friends in a time of need (ch. xvi. 1, 2), and had been foremost to welcome himself back (ch. xix. 17). The kindness of the man in the hour of need was a set-off to his deceit. On the other hand, the forfeiture of the property of Mephibosheth by royal decree was based on false information; and being a member of a royal house, and not proved to have been openly disloyal, he certainly had a claim to restoration to rights. The brevity of the narrative leaves the actual decision of David in some obscurity (ver. 29). But the sense seems to be that David solved the difficulty by restoring the old relations as a matter of practice (ch. ix. 9—11), without formally revoking the legal right of Ziba. As formerly, so now, the two families were to live on the produce of the soil, and in this there was great consideration, for Mephibosheth was physically incapable of looking after his own affairs. The example of David, as a matter of procedure, is worthy of attention. Life is crowded with difficulties analogous to this. Claims and counter-claims force themselves on our attention. Wrongs have to be righted and merits have to be considered in alleviation of judgment. The principle on which David acted was a sound one, and can be used by us in all things, namely, to deal with anomalies practically, not merely speculatively, and to aim at a restoration of things to their natural basis. To bring men and things back to nature, so far as circumstances admit, is a safe and prudent rule. The old relationship of Ziba to Mephibosheth (ch. ix. 2—4), and the incapacity of the latter, rendered it most unwise to cut the knot of present complications by having recourse to the practical division indicated in ch. ix. 9—12. There is a natural basis, if we will only take pains to find it, in our modern complications.

GENERAL LESSONS. 1. We should see in the returning success of the servant of God after a season of severe chastisement a token of our joyous return to the possession of privilege when we have been duly exercised by the chastisement of Providence (Heb. xii. 5—7). 2. Success is not to be regarded as less real because imperfect and weak men crowd in with it, though we ought to separate their attachment from the elements of endurance in the success. 3. In selecting friends we should not place much reliance on those most eager in their expression of interest. Words are to be tested by deeds. 4. It is incumbent on all Christians to purge from their relationships, whether of master, servant, professor of religion, member of Church, or subject of the realm, every trace of doubtful loyalty. 5. The profession of interest in religion is to be carefully weighed, seeing that an uneasy conscience will often prompt to a formal profession when there is not sincere love and faith. 6. It will be a great gain to the Church if we can instil into the minds of the young the most cardinal principles of Christianity, which, by their dominating power, will expel inferior views and lead to right action. 7. We may encourage the poor and oppressed to take heart from seeing how in the course of history God does vindicate the needy. The great vindications will be when the King of kings comes to judgment.

Vers. 31—43.—The facts are: 1. Barzillai, having provided sustenance for David while he was at Mahanaim, and accompanying him over Jordan, is entreated to go and live with him at Jerusalem. 2. Barzillai, having no relish for the kind of life which he thought prevailed at court, pleads age and infirmity and a fear of being an incumbrance to David, as a reason for not complying with his request, but asks that his own son Chimham may be permitted to go. 3. David consents, promises to do for Barzillai all that he may require, kisses and blesses him, and, while the good old man returns home, David passes on to Gilgal, conducted by all the people of Judah and half the people of Israel. 4. The men of Israel protest against what they conceive to be the stealthy way in which the men of Judah forestalled them in bringing back the king. 5. The men of Judah assign, as the explanation of their conduct, that they were not mercenary, but that their near kinship was the clue to their zeal. 6. The controversy waxes strong on the men of Israel asserting in their rejoinder that, being ten tribes, they had more right in the king than had Judah.

A beautiful old age. The scene described by the historian of the parting of Barzillai and David is one of the most touching to be found in Old Testament story; and the two elements which chiefly contribute to its interest are—the return of the banished king to his beloved city and his throne at the close of a most anxious season; and the beautiful character of the venerable man who had befriended him in his misfortunes, and now, with a consciousness that his own earthly course is nearly run, bids him an affectionate farewell. There are many venerable saints referred to in the Bible—from the time of Enoch to the beloved exile of Patmos—and they all convey to us a certain common instruction concerning life and its destiny, blended with what is peculiar to each; but we shall here confine attention to those features of a beautiful old age which are specially brought out in the description given of Barzillai.

I. OLD AGE ITSELF NATURALLY AWAKENS A TENDER INTEREST. This is the natural basis of all our regard for the aged, and is an element entering into the beauty which in some cases we recognize. In every age and clime, and among all except the most savage, age has won respect and developed tender feelings in the younger. We regard it as a sign of moral debasement when men fail to cherish tender consideration for the aged. The reasons that account for our best feelings are not always definite, and in this case they are certainly very subtle—being hidden away in the thoughts and sentiments that grow with our growth. If we seek the analysis of our sentiment towards age, we shall find these items: a sense of our inferiority in all that makes up the deepest experiences of life; a conviction that the venerable form is the symbol of many a veiled sorrow and buried hope; a perception of traces of unrecorded conflicts; a feeling of sympathy with increasing infirmities; a remembrance of the fleeting character of the best and most vigorous manhood; and a reflection that a responsible being is getting near to the eternal world. In the presence of age we cannot but feel that to live is a grave and solemn business.

II. OLD AGE EXHIBITS A SPECIAL BEAUTY WHERE IT IS PERVADED BY KINDLY FEELINGS AND EARNEST PIETY. Sometimes we meet with old age rendered hard, bitter, venomed, and remorseful, and, while our hearts are touched with tender interest, we feel that we can only pity—there is no admiration, because there is no moral, and probably no physical, beauty. In Barzillai we see all the natural, physical beauties of age crowned by virtues of the most attractive kind. His generous provision for the king when in need, and his making an effort to see him happily on his way home, revealed *kindliness*. His desire to share in such valued society so far as strength permitted, his right estimate of what befits the closing days of life, and his quiet content with the comforts and joys of home, show his *wisdom*. His anxiety not to be a burden to the king amidst the duties and cares of government, and his request for a favour to his son (1 Kings ii. 7), prove his *considerateness*. His wish to live and die and be buried among the kindred whom he had loved so long, was evidence of his *domestic affection*. His having befriended, honoured, and loved the banished king when appearances were against him, and his being privileged to take so tender a leave of the Lord's anointed, was a sign of distinguished *loyalty*. His obvious faith in the right cause when the rebellion was at its height, his bold identification of his interests with those of the Lord's afflicted servant, his doing all for the right cause without any idea of compensation, was proof of deep *piety*. Thus the beauty of old age lies much in years being crowned with kindliness of disposition, wisdom of conduct, consideration of feeling, deep affection for one's own people, faithfulness in the relationships of life, and calm and strong piety. How lovely is old age when so adorned!

III. AN OLD AGE THUS BEAUTIFIED IS VERY HELPFUL TO OTHERS. Barzillai was helpful to David in his trials and triumphs; but it was not the mere food (ch. xvii. 28, 29) which he, with others, brought that gave strength to David's heart and raised his hope in God. The hoary head, crowned with the glory of true goodness, was more to David than all the material supplies. To have the friendship and the kindly attentions of a venerable man of God, was to the king a real spring of new life and vigour. The vain and trifling young man might go off to take sides with rebellion, but age, with its wisdom, its deep experience, its large-heartedness and settled piety, was with him. As cold water to a thirsty soul was the loyalty and affection of so honoured a man. It is a blessing and real help to have the favour and sympathy of men who have had large experience in life, and have won for themselves imperishable honours; and, though the infirmities of age may seem to set a narrow limit to the usefulness of the aged, yet their moral power is very great. Their influence is quiet, but real and pervading. The tone they impart to home affects the world outside, and their known interest in Christ's servants and the work they are doing, is power and cheer to many a heart.

IV. A BEAUTIFUL OLD AGE IS AN ABIDING CHARM IN THE MEMORY. David and Barzillai never met again on earth. Their parting partook of all the sweet tenderness of a final severance. Before David had finished his career, the venerable man had passed away to his blessed reward (1 Kings ii. 7). But it could not but be, as was evident from his charge to Solomon, that throughout his life David cherished the memory of the good old man, and found amid the cares and sorrows of life much comfort therein. The vision of that bent form, laden with precious fruits of a long and godly experience, bending before him and bidding him God-speed in his high vocation, would often rise up and again cheer his spirit. The dead yet speak to us. Our memories retain the cherished form and words and tender embraces of venerable saints, and, as we think of their faith and hope and triumph over the world, we take fresh courage and struggle on. Thank God for aged Christians living or departed!

GENERAL LESSONS. 1. We see how wondrously God does, in his kind providence, sweeten the bitters of life by friendships which would not have been formed but for the trouble. 2. There is great blessedness in being enabled to render encouragement to God's servants when they are engaged in arduous and perplexing service, and this form of usefulness may be sought by all, especially by the aged. 3. We should, in our own lives and in others, look for an advance of moral powers proportionate to the advance of age. 4. We should covet the honour of bringing our ripest and best attainments and placing them at the service of Christ.

The uses and perils of rivalry. It was natural that, at first, there should be some hesitation in at least the leaders of the people, both in Judah and Israel, in making overtures to David and in sending deputations to welcome him back. Israel, however, overcame this feeling first, and David, reasonably anxious that Judah, so near to him, should not be outdone, took means to inform them of what was in contemplation, and urged that they certainly need not hesitate, seeing that his promotion of Amasa was proof of his unchanged feelings of interest in them (ch. xix. 11—13). Influenced by desire not to be outdone in expressions of loyalty, they were first at Jordan, and carried off the honour of accompanying the king to Jerusalem. There is no evidence that David wished Judah to steal a march on Israel, and so embitter the feeling between them. Probably he thought that a conference would take place for joint action. His sole anxiety was that Judah should not be tardy in indicating restored allegiance and taking measures for showing it. For reasons not stated, Judah acted alone, much to the chagrin of Israel, and hence the controversy (vers. 41—43) as to the relative right to manifest special interest in the king. It was a rivalry in good works, not unmixed with questionable feelings. Rivalry has its uses and its dangers.

I. IT TENDS TO STIMULATE ACTION AND DEVELOP LATENT POWERS. The thought that Israel might reach Jordan first, and so get the honour of showing attachment to the king, stirred up zeal in Judah, and drew forth whatever feeling of loyalty was latent in the community; and the fact that Judah outstripped Israel roused the heart of Israel to give verbal evidence of strong attachment to the king. This rivalry in accomplishing a common work enters into all life; it seems to have its roots deep down in our nature. It is associated with the conviction that duties have to be attended to, and that our honour is concerned in attending to them, at least as well as other people. Thus it is a side issue of the action of conscience, though it may easily develop unworthy feelings which will render its connection with conscience very obscure. Leaving out the question of improper feelings for the present, it doubtless does develop our powers, and even draws out latent forces, the existence of which had not been known. By the parallel action of the rivals much mutual instruction is gained as to methods of work, and weakness and strength of character, which instruction being applied, renders effort more successful.

II. IT TENDS TO KEEP THE IDEAL OF DUTY MORE CONSPICUOUSLY BEFORE THE MIND. The suggestion that Israel was about to welcome the king at once set before Judah in striking form the highest ideal of allegiance. Any thoughts concerning it hitherto cherished now were cleared of obscurity, and the duty was manifest. Rivalry among pupils, workmen, statesmen, and literary men necessarily causes all who enter into it to direct their attention from their own achievements as adequate, to the ideal towards which all are striving. This constant presence of a lofty ideal is a great gain to humanity. It is the absence of ideals which marks off the beast from man. When we are expected to provoke one another to love and good works, we at once think of the standard after which we are, as Christians, bound to strive (Phil. iii. 12—14). The fact that others surpass us is a reminder of the vows we have taken, and so, setting the "mark" before us afresh, we press forward with renewed zeal. The healthful effect on us of the presence of a superior Christian is well known. The sight of holy men and women devoting their energies to the service of Christ in the world rebukes sloth, points to "what manner of persons" we ought to be, and so, by rendering the ideal more real to the mind, enable us to be more faithful to our Lord.

III. There is, however, a risk of losing sight of broad principles, and being absorbed in side issues. Judah and Israel were right in provoking to loyalty and reassertion of allegiance, and so far as they purely followed out the first impulse of rivalry all was well; but the ideal before them became obscured as soon as they began to dispute on a matter of detail as to precedence and personal motive. The question as to whether the motive of Judah was pure arose out of the zeal of Judah on the one side and the zeal of Israel on the other. Probably Judah did design to outwit Israel. The secrecy was not purely for the sake of loyalty to David, but to gratify pride in being first. It was not an open competition. Thus, by the minor feelings of the rivalry being allowed to gain ascendancy, there arose an issue which exposed a wholesome rivalry to the danger of being the occasion of sowing the seeds of permanent mischief. Here lies the great danger of rivalry in deeds and enterprises perfectly good in themselves. Especially is there a great risk in the matter of the competition of denominations and religious parties. Work is done, perhaps, to outstrip others, to gain notoriety, to gratify a love of pre-eminence, and also, in the heat of zeal, motives are impugned, and time and strength spent in mutual recriminations which had better be spent in rendering service to Christ.

IV. Rivalry brings forth its worst fruit when it issues in permanently debased feelings and mutual estrangement. We see in this controversy the beginning of an unholy feeling of jealousy and ill will, which, we know, issued at last in positive aversion and enmity. They were one people, the people of God, called to do a good and holy work in the world, and held under the government of God's anointed. This consideration ought to have been uppermost in all times of effort and of difficulty. For one to seek to gratify pride at the cost of another was base; for the other to cherish bitterness of spirit was wrong; for both to weaken, by fierce controversy, the brotherly sentiment, and to create separate interests, instead of being one in devotion to their king and country, was a moral debasement from which they never recovered. To do Christian work well in rivalry requires watchfulness over motives, generous consideration of others, and delight in what they accomplish for the Master's sake, and a conscientious maintenance of the honour and glory of Christ above all the petty considerations of personal or denominational interest. The mutual estrangement of Christians is a great calamity. It has its root in the inferior feelings which have been allowed to mingle with genuine zeal for the kingdom of God; and the removal of it is to be sought in deep searching of heart, and a return to the simplicity of entire consecration to Christ's service.

General lessons. 1. The holy rivalry of the primitive Christians (John xx. 1—4) to be first at the sepulchre should be preferred as a model, both as to aim and spirit, to that of Judah and Israel. 2. The temptation to indulge in a feeling of personal pride should be met by a reflection on the serious evils that may issue from even one departure from purity. 3. In all our Christian enterprises it should be our endeavour to keep Christ and his honour clearly in view, and get inspiration from the zeal of others, not simply to outstrip them, but to bring more glory to him than any one else can. 4. In our efforts we should remember that we are all equally "kin" to Christ, and are equally dear to his heart. 5. In our estimate of Churches we are to give more weight to spiritual qualities than to numbers. 6. If on our guard against lurking evils, we may frequently ask ourselves how we can more perfectly prove our fidelity to our Lord and advance the honour of his Name.

HOMILIES BY VARIOUS AUTHORS.

Vers. 1—8.—(MAHANAIM.) *Immoderate grief.* This interview between David and Joab throws light upon the character of both, and the relations subsisting between them. 1. The *best* of men are by no means perfect. David's grief, although natural, and, in some respects, commendable, was unseasonable, excessive, and injurious; and exposed him to just reproof. 2. The *worst* of men are not altogether bad, but often exhibit admirable qualities. When Joab put Absalom to death against the king's order he was actuated partly by regard for the king's interest and the national welfare, "loyal disobedience;" he was also desirous of preventing unnecessary slaughter (ch. xviii. 16), and showed a thoughtful concern for Ahimaaz (ch. xviii. 19, 20, 22); and now, although his bearing toward the king was harsh and cruel (ch. iii. 24), he was fully justified in expostulating with him (as on another occasion, ch. xxiv. 3). 3. The worst of men are often intimately *associated* with the best of men, and render them invaluable services; but their association is usually uncongenial, and productive of trouble and mischief (ch. iii. 39). By his great abilities Joab made himself necessary to David, and became confirmed in his high position (1 Chron. xi. 6); and by his complicity "in the matter of Uriah," he gained a despotic influence over him; hence his daring disobedience and overbearing attitude, and when the king, resenting his conduct, seeks to replace him as captain of the host, he strikes down his rival, then "calmly takes upon himself to execute the commission with which Amasa had been charged; and this done, 'he returns to Jerusalem, unto the king,' and once more he is 'over all the host of Israel'" (Blunt, 'Coincidences'). David's inordinate grief was—

I. REALLY REPREHENSIBLE. "And the king covered his face," etc. (ver. 4). It was connected (as cause or effect) with: 1. The lack of due *consideration* of the moral causes of the event which he mourned over, and which was their natural and deserved consequence; and of the salutary influence which that event would have upon the nation. In surrendering himself to sorrow for the loss of his son, he was in some measure blind to the justice of his doom. 2. The absence of humble *submission* to the Divine will, such as he had previously displayed in "the day of his calamity" (ch. xii. 20; xv. 26; xvi. 10). 3. The feeling of bitter *resentment* against those who had despised his commandment and disappointed his hopes. He would at first, perhaps, blame all his "servants;" and, when he was informed (ch. xviii. 13) of the circumstances under which Absalom came to his end, would naturally regard the conduct of his executioners in its darkest aspect. "To understand this passionate utterance of anguish, we must bear in mind not only the excessive tenderness, or rather weakness, of David's paternal affection toward his son, but also his anger that Joab and his generals should have paid so little regard to his command to deal gently with Absalom. With the king's excitable temperament, this entirely prevented him from taking a just and correct view of the crime of his rebel son, which merited death, and of the penal justice of God, which had been manifested in his destruction" (Keil). 4. The neglect of urgent *duties:* thanksgiving to God for victory, the commendation of his faithful soldiers, the adoption of proper measures to confirm their attachment and secure peace and unity, the subordination of private grief to the public weal. "The deliverance that day was turned into mourning unto all the people," etc. (ver. 2). "Their hearty participation in the sorrow of their beloved king, for whom they had perilled their lives, soon changed to gloomy dissatisfaction at the fact that the king, absorbed in private grief, did not deign to bestow a look upon them" (Erdmann).

II. RUDELY REPROVED. "And Joab came into the house of the king," etc. (vers. 5—7). His reproof (ch. xii. 1) was: 1. *Unfeeling,* hard-hearted, pitiless. He had no respect whatever for the natural feelings of the father; no sympathy with David's intense and peculiar emotion. 2. *Unscrupulous* and reckless; whilst declaring the truth in part (ver. 5), and as it appeared on the surface, casting unjust reproaches on the king for his heartless selfishness, ingratitude, and hatred (ver. 6). 3. *Unbecoming* the relation of a subject to his sovereign; in language and manner, as well as in substance. 4. United, nevertheless, with wise *counsel* and solemn warning. "And now arise, go forth," etc. (ver. 7). No doubt David felt greatly hurt; and "the immediate effect of his indignation was a solemn vow to supersede Joab by Amasa;

and in this was laid the lasting breach between himself and his nephew, which neither the one nor the other ever forgave" (Stanley). But, convinced that he had given occasion for reproof, he now patiently submitted to it (Ps. cxli. 5). "Hard natures and harsh words have their uses in life after all" (Scott). "The undisciplined word of Joab became a means of discipline to David, and the king turned from the destructive path into which unbridled feeling had led him."

III. READILY RESTRAINED and laid aside. "And the king arose," etc. (ver. 8). "He was stung into action, and immediately roused himself to the discharge of his royal duties." Would we overcome immoderate grief? We must: 1. Listen to the admonitions of truth, however disagreeable; and learn the evil of indulging it. 2. Receive the consoling assurances of Heaven, and pray for needful strength. 3. Repress it with prompt and determined effort. 4. Devote ourselves with diligence to necessary and useful activities.

> "Heaven hath assigned
> Two sovereign remedies for human grief :
> Religion, surest, firmest, first, and best,
> Strength to the weak, and to the wounded, balm ;
> And *strenuous action* next."
>
> (Southey.)

Ordinary grief *must* be restrained within due bounds. But there is a sorrow—tender, hopeful, godly sorrow for sin, to which we may freely and fully surrender ourselves; for it always conducts to greater purity, strength, and joy.—D.

Ver. 15.—*David's return to Jerusalem.* "And David returned, and came to the Jordan" (the eastern bank; while Judah came to Gilgal, joined by Shimei and Ziba; and a ferry-boat was passing to and fro to carry over the king's household, ver. 18); crossed over (to the western bank, conducted by Judah and *half* the people of Israel, vers. 39, 40); came to Gilgal (where *all* the men of Israel met him, and a new contention arose, ver. 41; ch. xxi. 1); and finally (conducted by the men of Judah) to Jerusalem (ch. xxi. 3). The return of David, like his flight, is described minutely and graphically. As he had been called to the throne by the voice of the people (ch. v. 1—3), so he desired to return to it, not by force, but by their free consent; and would take no active measures for his restoration until he should receive some intimation thereof. "Our Lord Jesus will rule only in those that invite him to the throne in their hearts, and not till he is invited. He first bows the heart, and makes it willing in the day of his power, then rules in the midst of his enemies (Ps. cx. 2, 3)" (Matthew Henry). David's restoration was distinguished by: 1. *The returning allegiance of the rebellious.* (Vers. 9, 10.) "All the tribes of *Israel*" (except Judah). Popular revolutions are usually followed by speedy reactions. Convinced of their error, ingratitude, and injustice by their defeat, remembering the great services which David had rendered on their behalf, and considering the present condition of affairs, "all the people" manifest a disposition to "bring the king back;" and this gratifying intelligence is reported to him while waiting at Mahanaim. 2. *The decisive action of the dilatory.* (Vers. 11—15.) "The men of Judah," who, since the rebellion arose in their territory, feared the king's displeasure, or proudly held aloof in continued disaffection under Amasa. But when assured of his regard, reminded of their kinship, and urged to activity, they are at once "drawn" unto him "as one man;" send the message, "Return," etc.; and come to conduct him across the Jordan. Judah is again to the front. David's appeal was conciliatory, and seems wise and just (though some think otherwise), however disastrous its ultimate effect. 3. *The humble submission of the guilty.* (Vers. 16—23.) Shimei, with a thousand men of *Benjamin*, and Ziba," etc. "They went eagerly [prosperously, Hebrew, *tzalach*] over the Jordan in the presence of the king" (ver. 17); and "Shimei fell down before the king in his crossing over (*abar*) the Jordan" (while the transit was going on). "With a self-control rare in Western no less than Eastern history, every step in his progress was marked by forgiveness" (Maclear). 4. *The joyful welcome of the suspected.* (Vers. 24—30.) The innocent Mephibosheth, the grandson of *Saul*, now vindicated and restored to "all that he most cared for—the king's favour, his old place at the king's table, and the formal recognition of his ownership" of the inheritance. 5. *The friendly greeting of the faithful.* (Vers. 31—39). Barzillai, an aged and " very great man," representative of the *trans-Jordanic inhabitants;* testifying his devotion to the king in prosperity, whom he had aided in adversity, and receiving his grateful benediction. How different is it with David now from what it had been at his former crossing (ch. xvii. 22)! " This passage of the Jordan was the most memorable one since the days of Joshua." 6. *The zealous emulation of the tribes.* (Vers. 40—43.) Their strife for pre-eminence ; " *Ephraim* envying *Judah,* and Judah vexing Ephraim " (Isa. xi. 13), leading to a fresh revolt, which, however, is speedily overcome. David's troubles, so incessant, so varied, so great, "from his youth" (ver. 7), are not yet ended; but they are all ordered by the hand of God for his good. "Sanctified affliction is spiritual promotion."   7. *The complete establishment of the kingdom.* (Ch. xx. 3, 22—26.) He sees again the habitation of the Lord (ch. xv. 25), and rules over a peaceful and united nation. His return is like the commencement of a new reign (ver. 22). " The remainder of David's life—a period probably of about ten years —flowed on, so far as we can gather, in a bright calm, and an undisturbed course of improvements " (Ewald).—D.

Vers. 16—23.—(The Jordan.)   *The pardon of Shimei.* The conduct of Shimei towards David in his flight (ch. xvi. 5) was base and iniquitous. "The wheel turns round once more ; Absalom is cast down and David returns in peace. Shimei suits his behaviour to the occasion, and is the first man, also, who hastes to greet him; and had the wheel turned round a hundred times, Shimei, I dare say, in every period of its rotation would have been uppermost" (Sterne). But he may have been actuated by something better than selfish and time-serving policy ; at least, the history affords no intimation that his repentance was insincere and hypocritical. And he was forgiven by David (of whose clemency he had been persuaded)—

I. On the confession of wrong-doing (vers. 19, 20) with : 1. Deep *abasement.* He "fell down before the king." 2. Free, full, unqualified, and open *self-condemnation.* "Thy servant did perversely," and "doth know that I have sinned."   3. Fervent *petition* for mercy. "Let not my lord impute iniquity unto me," etc.   4. Professed *devotion* and zealous endeavour to repair the wrong which had been done. "And behold I am come the first this day," etc. He had brought with him a thousand men of Benjamin, to do honour to the king whom he had formerly despised; perhaps, also, to show the value of his reconciliation and services (which were really important at such a time, in the light of subsequent events, ch. xx. 1). Confession must precede the assurance of forgiveness; and, when made in a becoming manner, should be graciously treated (Luke xvii. 3, 4). God alone knows the heart.

II. Against the demand for punishment (vers. 21, 22); in which Abishai displayed, as before (ch. xvi. 9): 1. An impulse of *natural vengeance* toward the evildoer; unaltered by change of circumstances, unsoothed by Shimei's repentance.   2. A desire for the *rigorous execution* of the Law, according to which the traitor and blasphemer should suffer death "without mercy." Its stern and relentless requirements, unmodified by its deeper and more merciful principles, are represented in " the sons of Zeruiah." 3. A spirit of *reckless imprudence;* not less injurious to the king's interests on "this day" of his triumphant return than it was on the day of his perilous flight. 4. An assumption of *unjustifiable authority,* and interference with the king's rights and privileges, feelings and purposes; incurring a repetition of the rebuke, "What have I to do with you," etc. ?   " Ye will be an adversary [*satan,* Numb. xxii. 22; 1 Chron. xxi. 1] to me;" hindering the exercise of mercy and the joy of my return (1 Sam. xi. 12, 13). "Get thee behind me, Satan " (Matt. xvi. 23). "Our best friends must be considered as adversaries when they would persuade us to act contrary to our conscience and our duty " (Scott).

III. With the assurance of mercy. "Thou shalt not die " (ver. 23 ; ch. xii. 13). "And the king sware unto him." From: 1. An impulse of *personal feeling* of the noblest nature; by which (regarding Shimei's offence as a personal one) he was raised above the level of "the Law," and anticipated the forgiving spirit of a higher dispensation. 2. A sense of the *exceeding mercy* of God toward himself; by which he was disposed to show mercy toward others. 3. A perception of the *wisest policy* to be adopted on such an extraordinary "day" as that of his restoration to the throne.

"Shall there any man be put to death this day in Israel? For do I not know that I am this day king over Israel?" (It is noticeable how frequently he is designated "the king" in this chapter.) 4. An exercise of the *royal prerogative* of pardon. This prerogative, indeed (though prompted by a generous impulse), he no doubt stretched beyond due bounds. Hence, reflecting on the matter at the close of his life (during which he kept faithfully to his oath), he committed (not from a feeling of personal revenge, but of sacred duty) the vindication of the Law to his successor (1 Kings ii. 8, 9). "It can be explained only from the fact that David distinguished between his own personal interest and motive, which led him to pardon Shimei, without taking the theocratic-legal standpoint and the theocratic interests of the kingdom, of which Solomon was the representative, and so held himself bound on theocratic-political grounds to commit to his successor the execution of the legal prescription which he had passed over" (Erdmann).

REMARKS. 1. In showing mercy to private as well as public offenders, due regard must be paid to the claims of public justice. 2. It is better to err on the side of too much mercy than too much severity. 3. How vast is the mercy of God toward men, in him whom he has "exalted to be a Prince and a Saviour," etc. (Acts v. 31)! 4. Those who have received mercy must live in the sphere of mercy and obedience, otherwise mercy ceases to be of any avail (1 Kings ii. 42—46; Matt. xviii. 32—35).—D.

Vers. 24—30.—(THE JORDAN.) *The vindication of Mephibosheth.* "He hath slandered thy servant unto my lord the king" (ver. 27). The lame son of Jonathan comes upon the scene once more before his final disappearance. During the rebellion he seems to have continued at Jerusalem; and a strange spectacle he must have presented there, with his neglected person and mournful countenance. On hearing that the king was returning, he set out *from* Jerusalem (Hebrew, *to;* or "Jerusalem came," Keil) to meet him. But he had been preceded by Ziba, who was present, when, in answer to the inquiry, "Wherefore," etc., he said, "My lord, O king, my servant deceived me," etc. (ch. xvi. 1—4). 1. *The unfortunate and helpless are commonly made the victims of a slanderous tongue.* Others may not escape its venom; but these become its ready prey. Ziba knew that he could not be pursued and punished; and destroyed the reputation of his master with the king for the sake of his own profit. 2. *The voice of slander is put to silence in the presence of honesty and truth.* Already, before Mephibosheth spoke, his appearance must have borne witness to his innocence. His explanation of his conduct, the tone of his defence, and the silence of his accuser, would hardly fail to convince the king that, whatever may have been the designs of others concerning the house of Saul (ch. xvi. 5), the son of his friend Jonathan was not implicated therein. Slander may remain long unchallenged; but it is sure to be ultimately put to shame. 3. *No vindication from slander is able to do away with all its mischievous effects.* The property of which Mephibosheth had been deprived might be restored in whole or in part; but the feelings and actions induced in others could not be obliterated. "Reluctant to think that he had been too hasty; having a royal aversion to admit that he could err and had been duped; and being, in his present humour of overlooking and pardoning everything, indisposed to the task of calling to account a man of such influence as Ziba, who had been forward in his cause when many tried friends forsook him, the king's answer was something less than generous and much less than kind to the son of Jonathan" (Kitto). 4. *Notwithstanding the wrong which he suffers, a man of humble and grateful heart still possesses abundant satisfaction.* Seeking no revenge, acknowledging his dependence even for life, thankful for the kindness formerly shown toward him, and foregoing every claim (vers. 27, 28), he is little concerned about worldly possessions in comparison with the honour and welfare of his lord, and finds his chief delight in "the king's favour." "True to his noble saintly nature, all that he desires is to love and to be loved again" (Plumptre). "Let him also take all," etc. (ver. 30).

"Fret not thyself because of the evil-doers,
    Be not envious against the workers of iniquity, . . .
      The meek shall inherit the land,
    And shall delight themselves in the abundance of peace," etc.
                                        (Ps. xxxvii. 1—11.)
                                                          D.

Vers. 31—40.—(THE JORDAN.) *Old Barzillai.* "How long have I to live?" (ver. 34). Barzillai dwelt at Rogelim (his own city, ver. 37), in Gilead, where, amidst the rich highland pastures, diligently superintending his flocks and herds, he spent his days in peace. He enjoyed "the blessing of the Old Testament"—prosperity; and was "a very great [wealthy] man." Like Machir ben-Ammiel (ch. ix. 4), he was loyal, hospitable, and generous (ch. xvii. 28). One of his sons (1 Kings ii. 7), named Chimham, accompanied him to do honour to the king at his restoration. He was an octogenarian, his memory reaching back to the appointment of the first King of Israel, and Saul's brilliant exploit on behalf of Jabesh-Gilead (1 Sam. xi. 11). Of his genuine piety, his answer to the king's invitation, "Come over with me, and I will provide (ver. 32) for thee in Jerusalem," leaves no room for doubt. "May we not legitimately infer that his conduct was influenced, not merely by loyalty to his earthly sovereign, but by the recognition of the higher spiritual truths, and the hope for Israel and the world, symbolized by the reign of David?" (Edersheim). More especially, he furnishes a picture of *a beautiful old age* (1 Sam. xii. 2). To every one, if he should live long enough, old age will come, with impaired powers of judgment, sensibility, and activity (Eccles. xii. 1); but whether it will be honourable, useful, and happy depends on the course previously pursued and the character possessed. "Clearness and quickness of intellect are gone; all taste for the pleasures and delights of sense is gone; ambition is dead; capacity of change is departed. What is left? The old man lives in the past and in the future. The early child-love for the father and mother who hung over his cradle eighty years ago remains fresh. He cannot 'hear any more the voice of singing men and singing women;' but he can hear, stealing through almost a century, the old tones, thin and ghostlike, of the dear ones whom he first learnt to love. The furthest past is fresh and vivid, and in memory of it is half his life. Also he looks forward familiarly and calmly to the very near end, and thinks much of death. That thought keeps house with him now, and is nearer to him than the world of living men is. Thus one-half of his life is memory, and the other half is hope; and all his hopes are now reduced to one—the hope to die, and then to be laid down and go to sleep again beside his father and mother. And so he returns to his city, and passes out of our sight" (Maclaren). Notice—

I. HIS CLEAR RECOGNITION OF THE NEARNESS OF HIS APPROACHING END. "How many are the days of the years of my life?" etc. (vers. 34, 35; Gen. xlvii. 9). Many an old man considers not that he *is* old, and must shortly leave the world; he rather strives to keep both his age and his departure out of sight. But such a man as Barzillai is accustomed to reflect on his actual condition, deems himself a "stranger and pilgrim on the earth" (Heb. xi. 13; 1 Chron. xxix. 15); and feels certain that a few more steps will bring him to the end of his journey. He also understands what is possible and becoming during his brief continuance, and acts accordingly. "Can anything be more amiable than these simple and sensible words? What a cheerful and peaceful spirit do they breathe! and how does he put to shame very many old men of our day, who, the more the years perform their dismantling work upon them, are so much the more zealously bent on concealing the decay of their strength behind the glittering surroundings of vain dignities, titles, and high alliances!" (Krummacher). "Usually the nearer men approach to the earth, they are more earthly minded; and, which is strange to amazement, at the sunset of life are providing for a long day" (W. Bates).

II. HIS CHEERFUL RESIGNATION UNDER THE INFIRMITIES OF ADVANCED AGE. He utters no complaint (such as is too common with others) at the failure of his mental and bodily powers, the loss of earthly pleasures formerly possessed, his incapacity for new enterprises and excitements, which, at an earlier age, might have been suitable and desirable. His language is singularly free from fretfulness, disappointment, and discontent. He perceives and acquiesces with a "glad contentment" in the will of God, who "hath made everything beautiful in its season" (Eccles. iii. 11), and, although deprived of some enjoyments, he is not destitute of others of a higher order. "It is this, the tasteless meats, the deafness to the singing men and singing women, the apathy to common pleasures, for which old age is pitied and deplored; but this is God's mercy, it is not his vengeance; he deadens the keenness of our bodily senses only to guide us to immortality; we are disgusted with the pleasures of youth, we deride the objects of manly ambition, we are wearied with one worldly trifle or another, that our thoughts may centre at last in God" (Sydney Smith. 'On the Pleasures of Old Age'). "Old age may be not only venerable, but beautiful, and the object of reverence untinctured by compassion. The intellect, the emotions, the affections (the best of them) all alive, —it is the passions and appetites only that are dead; and who that is wise and has felt the plague of them, does not, with the aged Cephalus, in Plato's 'Republic,' account a serene freedom from their clamorous importunities a compensation for the loss of their tumultuous pleasures?" ('Sel. from the Correspondence of R. E. H. Greyson, Esq.').

III. HIS COURTEOUS REFUSAL OF THE PROFFER OF EARTHLY FAVOURS. What can even a monarch give him now? The society, the pleasures, the honours, of a court; enlarged influence, increased responsibility, more abundant wealth. Is it worth while for their sake to be transplanted to a new soil from the place where he has been so long growing; and when he must so soon be removed from the world altogether? If he had been a sensual, ambitious, or avaricious man, the craving for such things would have remained, and led him (like others) to grasp at their possession, though no longer able to enjoy them or employ them aright. "What so distressing as to see the withered face of old age dull and dead to every consideration of eternity, and kindling with life only at the mention of earthly vanities?" (Blaikie). He declines them, not because they are sinful and worthless in themselves, but because they are unsuitable to him. His heart is set on other pleasures; his immediate duties are determined and sufficient for his strength. He will not take new burdens on himself, nor be a burden to others. He will accompany the king "a little way," to show his loyal devotion, and then return (2 Kings iv. 13). "With all the dignity of self-respect, with the courtesy of a true gentleman, undervaluing not the king's offers, but his own service to him, with the prudent love of a father for the son whom he recommends to his kindness, having outlived nothing really belonging to the true character of the life of man, he returned with the royal kiss and blessing, master of his own will, to his own place" (W. Romanis).

IV. HIS CHERISHED REMEMBRANCE OF PARENTS AND THE FAMILIAR SCENES OF HIS EARLY DAYS. "Let thy servant, I pray thee, turn back," etc. (ver. 37). His thoughts turn back to his native place, his childhood, his father and his mother, whom he must have loved and honoured (Exod. xx. 12); and the memory of whom, tender, affectionate, and reverent, is a fountain of pure and undying joy in his breast. How much does the happiness of old age depend upon its memories! Whilst in one case old age is tormented by the recollection of "the pleasures of sin," in another it is gladdened by the recollection of the practice of piety; and such recollections mingle with and, in great measure, determine its anticipations.

> "Son of Jesse, let me go;
> Why should princely honours stay me?
> Where the streams of Gilead flow,
> Where the light first met mine eye,
> Thither would I turn and die;
> Where my parents' ashes lie,
> King of Israel! bid them lay me."
>
> (Sigourney.)

V. HIS CONSTANT DESIRE FOR REST in his "long home" (Eccles. xii. 5), "the house of eternity." It is now a pervading and increasing feeling. He longs for repose in the sacred spot where his parents lie, as a pilgrim longs for home. The grave for him has no terrors. "He looks for a city which hath foundations," etc. (Heb. xi. 10, 16); and desires to be "gathered with his fathers," and to be for ever at rest in God (1 Sam. xxv. 1; ch. vii. 12; Ps. xlix. 15; Prov. xiv. 32; Dan. xii. 13). "Lord, now lettest thou thy servant depart in peace" (Luke ii. 29). "A man should still be bound for home as you see all creatures be. Let a bird be far from the nest, and it grow towards night, she will home even upon the wings of the wind. Every poor beast, and every creature, though the entertainment be but slender at home, yet if you let it slip loose, it will home as fast as it can. Everything tends to its place; there is its safety, there is its rest, there it is preserved, there it is quiet. Now, since it is so with every creature, why should it not be so with us? Why should not we be for our home? This is not our home; here is not our rest. That is our home where our chief friends be, where our Father God is, where our Husband Christ is, where our chief kindred and acquaintance be, all the prophets and apostles and martyrs of God departed are; that is our home, and thither should we go" (R. Harris). "I am now passing through the latest stage of my pilgrimage on earth. My sun is speedily going down; but ere it wholly disappear, its parting beams stream sweetly forth upon the face of all things, and cover all the horizon with a blaze of glory. My Father's house shines bright before my eyes. Its opening door invites me onward, and fills me with an earnest longing to be safe at home. My richest treasures and my dearest hopes are all packed up and gone before, while my whole soul is on the wing to follow after" (W. Gilpin).

VI. HIS CONSIDERATE REGARD for the welfare of those who survive him. "Let thy servant Chimham go over," etc. (vers. 38, 40). He is not wholly absorbed in thoughts of past time or of his final rest; but is interested in the younger man now present with him, and sympathizes with his enjoyments and aspirations. He remembers his own youth. What he declines for himself, he seeks and obtains for his son (Jer. xli. 17). "When the king could not persuade the father, he gladly accepts the charge of his son. He seems to feel as if the care of this young man would bring comfort to his heart, which was still bleeding for the loss of Absalom. It was not in lightness that he made the request, and when on his death-bed he remembered it and charged Solomon to show kindness to the son for the sake of what his father had done for him when he fled from the face of Absalom. In Barzillai we have (1) a man who knows that he is old, but is not distressed by the thought of it; (2) who is rich, but is satisfied with his natural possessions; (3) of long experience, who has kept up his love of simple pleasures; (4) and is attached to the past, but does not distrust the future" (John Ker). "It is a very reasonable conjecture of Grotius, that David, having a patrimony in the field of Bethlehem, the place of his nativity, bestowed it on Barzillai's son; and from thence this place took the name of Chimham, which remained unto the days of Jeremiah" (Patrick). His descendants continue for ages to partake of the fruit of his piety and beneficence, to perpetuate his name and honour his memory (Ezra ii. 61; Neh. vii. 03; Ps. cii. 28).—D.

Ver. 6.—*Loving enemies and hating friends.* "Thou lovest thine enemies, and hatest thy friends." Joab's remonstrance with David was rude, and in the language of exaggeration; yet in substance it was wise, as the issue proved. The king's lamentations did show excessive love for his deceased son, who had been his deadly enemy; and his abandonment of himself to grief when he ought to have been thanking his brave friends as they returned from the battle, and congratulating them on the victory they had won for him, did indicate a present insensibility to their services and claims which might easily be construed as enmity. It is, however, no unusual thing for men to love their enemies and hate their friends; or at least, by their conduct, to give good reason for others to charge them with doing so.

I. THOSE DO SO WHO LOVE ERROR AND HATE THE TRUTH. For truth is one of our best friends, error one of our worst enemies. Moral and religious truth especially is life, health, guidance, happiness, to the soul; it leads to God and goodness and heaven. But error in such matters is death, disease, delusion; producing false peace and leading to destruction. Yet men often love the errors which favour what they are inclined to, and hate the truth which shows them their duties, sins, and dangers. They "love darkness rather than light, because their deeds are evil" (John iii. 19). "Fools hate knowledge" (Prov. i. 22). Hence they love false teachers and hate the true. "I hate him," said Ahab of Micaiah, "for he doth not prophesy good concerning me, but evil" (1 Kings xxii. 8).

II. THOSE WHO LOVE THEIR LOWER RATHER THAN THEIR HIGHER SELF. Our lower nature is good in itself, but is very prone to run to excess, and become evil. Then, from a friend, it is transformed into an enemy. Our higher nature is a friend, especially when informed and directed by the Holy Spirit. Man's worth and blessedness depend on his obeying the latter and subduing the former. Too often, however, he takes the opposite course, yielding himself to the government of the flesh, and resisting the promptings of the spirit.

III. THOSE WHO LOVE THE WICKED AND HATE THE GOOD. Associating with the former and finding pleasure in their practices, but avoiding the society of the latter;

loving flatterers, and hating faithful reprovers and advisers. Ungodly and unholy men are necessarily, though it may be unconsciously and unintentionally, the enemies of the souls of those whom they influence, whether by conversation or example; and the more attractive they are, so much the more dangerous. "Evil company doth corrupt good manners" (1 Cor. xv. 33, Revised Version).

IV. THOSE WHO DELIGHT IN BAD BOOKS, AND DISLIKE AND NEGLECT GOOD ONES. Good books are good friends, promoting in us that which is good. The Bible is the best of books. Bad books, books which suggest and foster evil, are enemies; and the more they interest their readers, the more they injure them. Yet many delight in them, and dislike the books which would profit them.

V. THOSE, IN A WORD, WHO LOVE, IF NOT SATAN, HIS WAYS, AND LIVE IN ENMITY WITH GOD AND CHRIST. Satan is our chief enemy, the head and ruler of all other spiritual foes. He seeks our ruin by manifold devices, and, so that we serve him, is quite content that we should do so in the fashion we most approve. We may join which company of his servants—the coarser or the more refined, the open or the secret —we may prefer. But to follow him in any way is, in effect, to love our worst enemy. Christ, on the other hand, and God in him, is our best Friend, who loves us most truly and most wisely, who has made greater sacrifices for us than any other can make, who has done for us what no other can do, who proffers us blessings beyond the power of any other to confer, who exalts those who love him to a position of honour and happiness to which no other can raise their friends, and lives on to bless them when others die and pass away. To reject him, to refuse him the love, allegiance, and obedience which he claims, is, in effect, to hate the Friend who is most of all needed by us, and most worthy to be loved with all the power of loving which our hearts possess.

Let those to whom these representations apply reflect on the sin and folly of which they are guilty; the incalculable good they are losing; the incalculable evils they are choosing. Their eyes will at length be opened; may it be in time!—G. W.

Ver. 9.—*Late reflection and appreciation.* The rebels against King David having been defeated, and their chosen leader slain, they bethink themselves of their position and of the claims of their injured sovereign; and begin to stir up each other to obtain his return and reinstatement. Their words are obviously true; but the facts they now recognize were as truly facts when they rose in rebellion. It was only their feeling with respect to them that had changed. So it is commonly. Under the excitement of sinful feeling, the most obvious truths are forgotten and neglected. Well is it when there is a reawakening to their significance, and a consequent return to the path of duty. Especially desirable is it that all who are living without any due feeling of the claims of their great King should become sensible of them, and begin to render them a practical recognition.

I. THE ACTUAL AND ABIDING CLAIMS OF CHRIST TO BE ACCEPTED AND OBEYED AS KING. 1. *His nature.* Divine and human; including all qualifications for rule. 2. *His Divine appointment.* Signified in manifold ways. 3. *The deliverance he has wrought.* It is here said of David, "The king saved us," etc. Our Lord has saved us in a more marvellous way, from enemies more to be dreaded than the heathen that harassed Israel. He has conquered, in personal conflict and through suffering unto death, Satan, the world, sin, and death. He has thus "saved us out of the hand of our enemies," including those that, like the Philistines in relation to Israel, are nearest to us and most ready and able to harass us—our own special besetting sins. True, the deliverance is not yet completely accomplished in actual experience; but it is assured, and as really ours, if we are Christ's, as if we were already perfectly freed from all evil.

II. THE INSENSIBILITY TO THESE CLAIMS WHICH COMMONLY PREVAILS. Looking at the lives of most men, even where Christ is made known, it is painfully manifest that they have no due sense of his rights and their duty to him; for they do not submit their minds, hearts, and lives to his government. 1. *Causes of such insensibility.* (1) A depraved nature, whose spiritual sensibilities are further suppressed and benumbed by the practice of sin. (2) Absorption in worldly pursuits. Leaving no opportunity for higher matters to attract attention, no time to think of them. (3) Unconcern as to the enemies from whom Christ delivers. No conviction of sin; no sense of the evil of it; no desire for rescue from its guilt or power. The Deliverer, therefore, excites no real interest. (4) Familiarity with the truth. The habit of hearing, or reading, or even repeating it, without accepting it; or of assenting to it without really believing it; or of accepting (in a sense) the atonement, and relying on Jesus for pardon, without receiving him as King. The process also of indulging feeling and sentiment about Christ, without rendering obedience; and of resisting the feelings which prompt to obedience, thus resisting and grieving the Holy Spirit. In this way the gospel becomes a means of hardening the heart against itself. (5) The attractions of some pretender to the throne. As Absalom "stole the hearts of the men of Israel" (ch. xv. 6) by his youth, beauty, activity, assiduous attentions, insinuating address, and hints as to the defects of his father's government, and the improvements which he would make if he were in power; so the hearts of many are withdrawn from the Lord Jesus by the attractions of some newly revived system of error in philosophy or religion, or anti-religion, of which the novelty (to them) is charming, and the representations of human nature more flattering, and the demands less exacting. The old king comes to be regarded and treated as worn-out, quite unsuited to the needs of an enlightened and scientific age; and the young pretenders are welcomed, one by one class, and another by another, with shouts of joy and pæans of anticipated victory. 2. *Effects of such insensibility.* (1) Negatively, in the prevention of faith and love, loyal obedience and active service. (2) Positively, by leading to disaffection and active rebellion; as in the case of Israel and David.

III. The happy awakening which is often experienced. As in the case of the Israelites in respect to David. This may be produced: 1. *By calamity.* As the Israelites were awakened by defeat and disaster. Troubles stir the conscience, lead the soul to look around for support, throw an unusual light on objects, reveal the vanity of cherished dependencies, prepare for due appreciation of those which are solid and satisfying; and so lead to a right appreciation of Christ. 2. *By impressive presentation of forgotten facts.* As by the tribes of Israel to each other, reminding of their obligations to David, and the ill requital he had received from them. It may be a sermon heard with unaccustomed interest, or some part of the Holy Book read with a new perception of the significance and importance of its teaching, or the appeals of a friend, or the statements of a tract, or words of parents or teachers long ago, recurring with new power to the mind; whatever it be that stirs the heart to consideration and renders it sensible of the rights and worth of Christ, blessed are the means, blessed the moment when such effects are produced. 3. *Always by the enlightening and convincing Spirit.* Whose work it is to reveal and glorify the Son of God (John xvi. 14).

IV. The change produced by this awakening. Similar to that in the text. 1. *In conduct.* (1) Return to allegiance, loyalty, and service to the rightful Sovereign. (2) Incitement of others to return. 2. *In position.* The returning rebels are accepted, and restored to the privileges of faithful subjects. Not because the heavenly King is, like David, dependent on his subjects, needing them as much as they him, but of pure grace. However long they may have been insensible and rebellious, on coming to a sense of their duty, and seeking forgiveness, they are pardoned and restored to favour.

Lastly, the awakening may come too late, producing terror and remorse, but not repentance, and importunate prayers which are unavailing (see Luke xiii. 24—28). —G. W.

Vers. 24—30.—*Inability hindering desired service.* Although some are disposed to accept Ziba's account of his master's conduct (ch. xvi. 3) rather than Mephibosheth's own, as given in these verses, there seems to be no just reason to doubt his truth and sincerity. He did not go with David because, owing to his lameness and the treachery and cunning of Ziba, he was unable to do so. The narrative suggests such thoughts as follow.

I. Inability debars many Christians from some demonstrations of love and loyalty to their King which they would fain make. Indeed, every one, however strong in some respects, is weak in others. The inability may be in body or mind, in understanding, or heart, or speech, or in purse; but to its extent it disables from forms of service which others can adopt. We can only serve Christ with the faculties and powers we have. To attempt what we cannot accomplish is to be hindrances rather than helps.

II. INABILITY IN SOME RESPECTS WILL NOT PREVENT THE TRUE-HEARTED FROM MAKING SUCH MANIFESTATIONS OF LOVE AND LOYALTY AS ARE WITHIN THEIR POWER. If Mephibosheth could not follow David in his exile, or take part in the contest, he could mourn for him, and exhibit signs of mourning; and this he did. He thus showed a courage as great as, or greater than, that of those who took part in the war. In like manner, every one, however feeble, poor, or obscure, may do something for Christ; and, if his heart be right, he will. He who cannot preach can speak to a neighbour. He who cannot say much for Christ can bring others where they can hear of him, or give them an instructive book or tract. He who cannot give much money towards the evangelization of the world can give a little, and at least can pray. He who cannot found a hospital can visit the sick poor. All have some power, and, according to the measure of their power, are responsible. All who love their King will employ such ability as they have in serving him. And the service is accepted by him which comes from a true heart and is according to the ability possessed. Work or gift for Christ is valued by him, not for its quantity, or even quality of the material, or merely mental kind, but for the love to him which it expresses; and many a man who wins the plaudits of men for his talents, his outward success in religious work, or his large gifts for its sustentation, is less pleasing to Christ than some poor and humble friend of his who can give and do but little, but thinks much of him, mourns in secret the dishonour done to him, and prays without ceasing for his triumph. Ziba's handsome and timely presents were really of far less worth than helpless Mephibosheth's mourning and self-neglect.

III. INABILITY IS LIABLE TO BE MISUNDERSTOOD AND MISREPRESENTED. Not only by the malicious or designing, as here, but by the inconsiderate. Men judge of others by their own peculiar standards. If truly zealous in a good cause, they show their zeal in the way most natural and available to themselves, and are ready to condemn as lukewarm those who do not adopt their methods, though these may with equal zeal seek the same ends by the means natural and available to them. Even David judged harshly and unjustly of Mephibosheth. It was, in truth, unreasonable to expect his lame friend to accompany him. He could only have been a burden. It was absurdly unjust to accept Ziba's insinuation that his master was hoping to be placed on the vacant throne. But judgments equally unjust are constantly being pronounced upon zealous servants of Christ, whose only fault is that they are not of the same order of mind, or cannot practise the same bustling activity as their accusers, or have not equal incomes, or equal physical strength or energy, or do not care to exhibit their " zeal for the Lord " (2 Kings x. 16) in the same manner or to secure similar results. Happily, the King knows his servants better than they know each other.

IV. INABILITY IS OFTEN ASSOCIATED WITH QUALITIES THAT RECONCILE TO THE DISADVANTAGES WHICH BELONG TO IT. Mephibosheth was enabled to bear meekly what he had to endure, because he was humble, thankful, sincerely and disinterestedly devoted to the king, and ready to submit without murmuring to his will. Similar qualities are of great value to those servants of our Lord who are deficient in some endowments or possessions by which others are equipped for Christian service. 1. *Thankfulness for, and contentment with, the powers and opportunities granted to them, and the kind and measure of success accorded to them.* 2. *Humility arising from the consciousness of their defects or unworthiness.* 3. *Absence of envy of those who are more abundantly favoured in respect to talents or success.* 4. *Consciousness of sincere devotion to the King, however men may reflect on them.* 5. *Joy that, by whomsoever and in whatever way, the King's cause is triumphing.* Such qualities are frequently found associated with deficient abilities, and go far to compensate those who possess them for the lack of power, or obvious efficiency, or appreciation of them and their work, which may be their lot. Let the less liberally endowed cultivate them.

V. INABILITY WILL AT LENGTH BE EXPLAINED AND JUSTIFIED. When the King comes back, all his servants will receive commendation and reward, not according to their several abilities, but according to their fidelity. Mistakes will be rectified, unjust judgments reversed. Many a plaudit will be hushed; many an inflated reputation will collapse; many a brave-looking building will be reduced to a mass of rubbish by the searching fires, and the builder put to shame, if not utterly rejected (1 Cor. iii. 12—15).

On the other hand, many an obscure and perhaps disregarded servant of Christ will find himself unexpectedly applauded and exalted. "Lord, when saw we thee," etc.? (Matt. xxv. 37).

Wherefore: 1. "*Judge nothing before the time*" (1 Cor. iv. 5).   2. *Let Christians of limited powers and opportunities be encouraged to do their best.* Their Lord appreciates their spirit and services, though men may mistake and misjudge; and he will pass a juster judgment than David did (ver. 29) in the case of Mephibosheth.—G. W.

Ver. 35.—*The privations of old age.* Barzillai graphically depicts these as experienced by himself. All old men have not exactly the same experience; but all who live to a great age must expect a similar diminution of their powers.

I. THE PRIVATIONS OF THE AGED.   1. *Enfeebled or annihilated powers.* Blunted or extinct senses; dulness or loss of sight, hearing, taste, smelling; feebleness of body and mind. Consequent inability for active employments. Loss of the pleasures which the exercise of vigorous faculties confers.   2. *Increasing dependence on others.* Possibly, unlike Barzillai, for the means of subsistence; certainly for much besides. Hence the old man is apt to become, and feel himself to be, "a burden," putting the kindness and patience of others to a severe test. The discomfort arising from such dependence is often very great.   3. *The sense of loneliness.* Sometimes the aged survive all who have loved and cared for them, and, if not, they commonly feel themselves cut off from the interests and pleasures of the new generation.

II. HOW THESE PRIVATIONS SHOULD BE BORNE.   1. *With cheerful submission and patience.* Remembering that the order of nature which brings such ills to the aged, and the circumstances which occasion their own particular troubles, are the appointment of the infinitely wise and good Creator and Father. Recalling also their many years of vigorous faculty and lively enjoyment, and cherishing a gratitude which will suppress discontent.   2. *With thankfulness for what remains.* The love and care which provide for, or minister to, their needs and alleviate their troubles. Above all, the unchanging love of God and the Redeemer, and the spiritual blessings hence enjoyed.   3. *With watchfulness against the temptations incident to old age.* Such as those to fretfulness, irritability, impatience, envy of the young, and needless interference with their enjoyments. The revival with new power of old sinful propensities, ill tempers, and bad habits.   4. *With joyful hope.* Of speedy deliverance from all burdens and troubles, and the recommencement of life with renewed and perfected energies. Nothing can keep the aged Christian long out of heaven.

III. HOW OTHERS SHOULD REGARD THEM.   1. *With respectful tenderness, sympathy, and readiness to alleviate them.*   2. *With diminished desire for the great prolongation of their own lives.*   3. *With steadfast aim and endeavour so to live that, if old age come, it may not be oppressed with the needless burdens and anxieties which a godless life leads to.* Let the young keep in mind the admonition, "Remember now thy Creator in the days of thy youth, while the evil days come not, nor the years draw nigh, when thou shalt say, I have no pleasure in them" (Eccles. xii. 1).—G. W.

EXPOSITION.

CHAPTER XX.

Ver. 1.—**There happened to be there a man of Belial.** The fierce words of the men of Judah led to evil results. It was a time when all wise and thoughtful persons would have laboured for peace, and tried to soothe and appease the angry passions fomented by the late war. Instead of this, the men of Judah irritated the Israelites with insult and contumely, and the day, intended as one of rejoicing and of the restoration of David to his throne by common consent, saw the rebellion break forth afresh. Among those who had taken part in the discussion with Judah was Sheba, a man of Belial, that is, a worthless fellow, but possibly possessed of rank and influence; for, according to many commentators, *ben-Bichri* does not mean **the son of Bichri**, but "a descendant of Becher," the second son of Benjamin (Gen. xlvi. 21), and possibly the representative of the mishpachah descended from him. But it is remarkable that this son of Benjamin disappears from the genealogies, and that no mishpachah of Bichrites is mentioned either in Numb. xxvi. 38 or in 1 Chron. viii. 1. In both places Ashbel, who is enumerated as the third son in Gen. xlvi. 21, takes the second place. We must be content, therefore, to leave this matter in uncertainty; but evidently Sheba had come with Shimei and Ziba to welcome David back, and, with the rest of the thousand Benjamites, had rushed with loud cries of welcome across the Jordan, and, but for this altercation, would have remained faithful. But tribal jealousies were always ready to break forth, and were a permanent source of weakness; and now, stung by some jibe at Benjamin, Sheba gave orders to a trumpeter to give the signal for the breaking up of the meeting, and, as is commonly the case in large and excited gatherings, the crowd obeyed the unauthorized dictation of one man. His words are contemptuous enough. David is no king, but a private person, and the son, not of a great chief, but of Jesse merely, a yeoman of Bethlehem. **Every man to his tents.** "To his tent" meant "to his home" (see ch. xviii. 17). But this withdrawal home signified the rejection of David's government. Almost the same words are used in 1 Kings xii. 16.

Ver. 2.—**So every man of Israel**, etc.; literally, *so all the men of Israel went up from after David after Sheba.* They had come down to Jordan to bring the king back in triumph, but, on finding that the men of Judah had forestalled them, they had a quarrel, and as no one endeavoured to allay it and mediate between them, it ended in open revolt, and they transferred their allegiance to the worthless Sheba. Nothing could more clearly prove the want of cohesion among the tribes, and how little Saul and David had done to knit them together. We need not, therefore, seek for any deep reasons of state, or for proofs of failure in David's government, to account for the rapid success of Absalom's rebellion. Israel was a confused mass of discordant elements, kept in a state of repulsion by the sturdy independence of the tribes and their jealousy one of another. Even David's victories had failed to infuse into them any feeling of national unity, nor did the long glory of Solomon's reign and the magnificence of the temple succeed better. The kings were not as yet much more than the judges had been—leaders in war, but with little authority in times of peace. What is so extraordinary is that David had lost the allegiance of his own tribe; and it now, on returning to its duty, spoiled by its violence the whole matter. The day must have been a great disappointment to David. He was to have gone back conducted gloriously by all the tribes of Israel; but he had fancied that Judah was holding back, and grieving over Absalom. He had secret dealing there-

fore with it, in order that the day might not be marred by its absence. It came, but only to do mischief; and David went home with only its escort, and with all the rest in open rebellion.

Ver. 3.—**They were shut up.** We are not to conclude that all widows had to live in seclusion, but only that those women who belonged to the royal harem, but had been taken by another, were not allowed to return to it, but condemned to a sort of imprisonment. **Living in widowhood.** This is explained by the Chaldee as lasting only during David's life, its rendering being, " in widowhood while their husband was alive."

Ver. 4.—**Then said the king to Amasa.** David thus takes the first step towards depriving Joab of the command (see ch. xix. 13). This was a most unwise step, however guilty Joab may have been in slaying Absalom. With all his faults, Joab had always been faithful to David, and it was chiefly his skill in war and statesmanlike qualities which had raised the kingdom to a position of great power. Just now, too, he had crushed with smaller forces a rebellion in which Amasa had taken the lead. To cast him off and put Amasa in his place might please conspirators, and reconcile them to their defeat, but it would certainly offend all those who had been faithful to David in his troubles. Throughout David acts as one whose affections were stronger than his sense of duty, and his conduct goes far to justify Joab's complaint, "This day I perceive, that if Absalom had lived, and all we had died this day, then it had pleased thee well" (ch. xix. 6). If David, in the administration of his kingdom, acted with as little forethought as in the slight he cast upon the ten tribes in negotiating with Judah to be the first to restore him, as it had been the first tribe to rebel, instead of waiting for the rest, and doing his best to make the day of his return one of general concord and good will; or with as little justice as in the matter of Ziba and Mephibosheth; or with as little tact and good sense as in substituting at the end of a revolt the rebel general for the brave soldier who had "saved his life, and the lives of his sons and of his daughters, and the lives of his wives and of his concubines" (ch. xix. 5);—we cannot wonder that he had failed to secure the allegiance of a race so self-willed and stubborn as the Israelites. One cannot help half suspecting that Joab had used the power he had gained over the king by the part he had taken in the murder of Uriah tyrannically, and for cruel purposes, and that David groaned under the burden. But if so, it was his own sin that was finding him out.

Ver. 5.—**He tarried longer than the set**

time. But not longer than was to be expected. For the appointment was so surprising that everybody must have been agape with astonishment. They would naturally have expected that Amasa would be punished. Instead of this, he is commissioned to gather the militia in David's name. And men would hesitate about joining such a leader. Was he really loyal? or would he embark them in a new rebellion? And what would Joab do? He was not a man likely to bear such a slight tamely, and David ought to have foreseen that he was sowing for himself a crop of discord and enmity.

Ver. 6.—**David said to Abishai.** David thus gives the command to the younger brother, and we find in ver. 7 that even ".Joab's men," his own special troop, were placed under Abishai's command. There seems always to have been a firm friendship between the brothers, and at first Joab acquiesces. The king was, in fact, in so grim a humour that he probably felt that he had better keep with his men, who would protect him, instead of remaining at Jerusalem, where he would be in David's power. When Amasa joined them, Abishai would have to resign to him the command; and David probably expected that, after a successful campaign, and with the aid of the men of Judah, who were rebels like himself, Amasa would be able to crush Joab. But Joab did not intend to wait for this; and immediately on meeting his rival he murders him, and assumes the command. **Thy lord's servants.** These are the men enumerated in ver. 7, and formed David's usual military attendants. When war broke out, they were reinforced by a levy of the people. **And escape us.** The meaning of the Hebrew is uncertain. It may signify, "and withdraw himself from our eyes," which gives the sense of the Authorized Version, and is supported by the Vulgate. The Septuagint renders, "and overshadow our eyes," which might have the same meaning, but, as others think, may signify, "and cause us anxiety." Many modern commentators render, "and pluck out our eye;" that is, do us painful damage. Either this or the Authorized Version gives a good sense, and, anyhow, rapid action was necessary, or Sheba's revolt might become dangerous.

Ver. 7.—**There went out after him**—that is, under Abishai's command (comp. ver. 2)—**Joab's men.** The men who formed his regular attendants, and to whose number belonged the ten armour-bearers who slew Absalom (ch. xviii. 15). Joab retained their command, and probably they would not have served under any other person. It is evident from the enumeration in this verse that the "men of Judah," after escorting David to Jerusalem, had all dispersed to their own homes.

Ver. 8.—**The great stone which is in Gibeon.** Gibeon is situated in the mountains of Ephraim, in the tribe of Benjamin, north-west of Jerusalem. The great stone was probably some isolated rock well known in the neighbourhood. **Amasa went before them;** Hebrew, *Amasa came before them;* that is, came in view with the levy of men he had raised in Judah. **And Joab's garment,** etc.; more correctly, *and Joab was girded with his military coat as his garment, and over it was the strap of his sword in its sheath, and it* (masculine, equivalent to "the sheath") *came out, and it* (feminine, equivalent to "the sword") *fell.* This change of gender is very harsh, and has caused the Authorized Version to apply the masculine verb to Joab, and translate, **and as he went forth it fell**; but a very slight change, supported by the Septuagint, gives us a more satisfactory sense, namely, *and it (the sword) came out and fell.* It is generally assumed that all this was arranged beforehand on Joab's part, who had so placed his sword that he could shake it out of the sheath. More probably it was an accident, of which he took instant advantage. He had felt that his position was insecure, and that if David had the support of Amasa, and a powerful band of the men of Judah at Jerusalem, he would probably order his execution for slaying Absalom ; and Amasa would carry out the command willingly enough, as he thereby would secure the high position offered him. We know David's feelings towards Joab from his dying command to Solomon (1 Kings ii. 5), and probably he had given various indications of his deep-seated resentment. Joab, therefore, determined to stop Amasa's growth in power, and also to give David a rough lesson. And this accident gave him an early opportunity, which he used with ruthless energy.

Ver. 10.—**In the fifth rib**; *in the abdomen* (see note on ch. ii. 23). **He struck him not again.** When his sword fell out of its sheath, Joab picked it up with his left hand, which was not the hand for action, and as he could not put it into its place without taking it into his right hand, his continuing to hold it while he took his cousin's beard in his right hand and kissed him, was too natural to awaken any suspicion. But holding down Amasa's head, he struck him with his left hand so fiercely that no second blow was necessary; and then continued his march forward as if what had occurred was a matter of little importance.

Ver. 11.—**One of Joab's men.** Joab left one of his personal followers to prevent any halt of the people round Amasa's body, and to suggest that he was a traitor. For he was to say to them as they came up, not only that " whosoever had pleasure in Joab," but also that " all who were for David, were to go after Joab." All loyal men were to regard him as captain of the host, and to disobey him would be rebellion. Naturally they would conclude from this that Amasa had not really been true to David, and that his death was the punishment inflicted on him for his past guilt.

Ver. 12.—**He removed Amasa.** The admonition to move on failed; for the sight was terrible and tragic, and all as they came along stopped to see what had happened, and inquire the cause (comp. ch. ii. 23). The man, therefore, had the corpse carried out of the way, and threw over it a cloth, really a coat—the loose upper mantle worn over the tunic (see note on *beged*, 1 Sam. xix. 13). Whereupon the people renewed their march, most of them not knowing what had occurred, and the rest urged to it by the warning voice of Joab's servitor.

Ver. 14.—**And he went through,** etc. It was not Joab, but Sheba, who, by David's prompt action, was compelled to make a rapid retreat, seeking help in vain from tribe after tribe, but rejected of all, and unable to make any defence until he had reached the extreme north of the land of Israel. **Unto Abel, and to Beth-Maachah.** The conjunction probably ought to be omitted, as the proper name of the place is Abel-beth-Maachah, and it is so given in ver. 15 (see below), and in 1 Kings xv. 20; 2 Kings xv. 29. It is the place called Abel-Maim, the "water-meadow," in 2 Chron. xvi. 4—an *abel* being a place where the grass grows rankly from the abundance of springs. It thus forms part of the name of various places, as Abel-Mizraim (Gen. l. 11), Abel-Meholah (1 Kings iv. 12), etc. Abel-beth-Maachah was a fortress in the most northerly part of the tribe of Naphtali, and is identified with the modern village of *Abel*, a few miles above Lake Huleh, the ancient "Waters of Merom." **And all the Berites.** No place or people of this name can be found, but Jerome, when translating the Vulgate, had before him a different reading, which seems clearly right, " And all the chosen men of war were gathered together, and went after him."

Ver. 15.—**It stood in the trench.** This is a literal translation, and yet gives a wrong sense. The Hebrew " stood" means " rose up to," " stood level with;" and the "trench" is what in modern fortifications is called " the glacis," and includes the outer wall of defence. The Revised Version renders, "it stood against the rampart." The usual way of capturing cities in ancient times was to cast up a bank or mound of earth against them (Isa. xxix. 3; xxxvii. 33; Jer. vi. 6); and Joab's work had advanced so far as to be level with the outer line of defence. The name of the city in the Hebrew is not **Abel of Beth-Maachah,** but *Abel-beth-Maachah.* **Battered.** This is a word taken from Roman warfare. The Hebrew says, "And all the people that were with Joab were destroying the wall to make it fall," most probably by undermining it. Ewald even asserts that this is the meaning of the verb, and translates, " were digging pits under the wall." The Revised Version adopts this for the margin, where it gives "undermined." The Septuagint and Chaldee have a different and probable reading, " And all Joab's people were devising (contriving) means to throw down the wall." This would be the next operation after the mound had been carried up to a level with it.

Ver. 18.—**They were wont to speak,** etc. The Hebrew literally is, *they used to say in old time, They shall surely ask at Abel; and so they finished (the matter).* But of these words two completely distinct interpretations are given. The Jewish Targum records the one: " Remember now that which is written in the book of the Law, to ask a city concerning peace at the first. Hast thou done so, to ask of Abel if they will make peace?" The woman, that is, was referring to the command in Deut. xx. 10, not to besiege a city until peace had been offered to the inhabitants on condition of their paying tribute. When a city was captured the lot of the inhabitants, as the woman declares in ver. 19, was utter destruction; and the Law mercifully gave them the chance of escaping such a fate. Joab had not complied with this enactment, but had assumed that the people would support Sheba, and was proceeding to the last extremity without consulting them. This interpretation gives an excellent sense, but cannot be wrung out of the present Hebrew text without violence. The other interpretation is that of the Authorized Version, that the woman was commending her words to Joab, by reminding him that Abel had been famed in early times for its wisdom, and had probably been the seat of an oracle in the old Canaanite times. When, therefore, people had carried their dispute to Abel, both sides were content to abide by the answer given them, and so the controversy was ended. Literally, these words mean, " they shall surely inquire at Abel," the verb being that specially used of inquiring of God.

Ver. 19.—**I am one of them that are,** etc. The Authorized Version translates in this way, because, while " I" is singular, " peaceable" and " faithful" are plural. Really this construction shows that the woman speaks in the name of the city, and consequently the Authorized Version, while preserving the grammar, loses the sense. It should be translated, *we are peaceable, faithful people in Israel.* **A city and a mother;** that is, a mother-city, a metropolis, the chief town of that district.

Ver. 21.—**The matter is not so.** It seems from this verse that the citizens did not quite understand why Joab attacked them. Sheba had thrown himself into the city, and Joab, in hot pursuit, finding the gate closed—a measure of ordinary precaution upon the approach of a body of men—at once blockaded the town, and began to cast up the mount. At all events, they were ready to come to terms now, and would probably have given up Sheba at first, if Joab had demanded his surrender. **A man of Mount Ephraim.** Sheba was a Benjamite, but the hills of Ephraim extended into the territory of Benjamin, and retained their name (see 1 Sam. i. 1). **Over the wall;** Hebrew, *through the wall*, being the word rendered "at" a window in Gen. **xxvi.** 8. It probably means through one of the apertures made for the archers.

Ver. 22.—**In her wisdom;** that is, with her wise counsel. The story in Eccles. ix. 13—15 probably refers to this narrative. **They retired;** Hebrew, *they dispersed themselves each to his tent;* that is, his home. This refers to Amasa's levies, who were glad to depart, and whom Joab did not want at Jerusalem. He took thither with him all those mentioned in ver. 7. Incensed as David must have been at the murder of Amasa following so quickly upon that of Absalom, yet that very act proved Joab's determination, and left the king powerless. He must have felt, too, that Joab was indispensable for the maintenance of peace and order in his dominions, and that he was at the least faithful to himself.

Ver. 23.—**Now Joab,** etc. With this list of his chief officers, the narrator closes the history of David's reign; for the remaining four chapters form a kind of appendix. A similar list closes ch. viii., where, too, there is a break in the history, the previous narrative having been a summary of the rapid rise of David's empire. In this section, ch. ix.—xx., we have a more full and detailed account of David's wars, leading on to his crime and its punishment. The rest of David's life we may trust was calm and uneventful, but it was the life of a sorrow-stricken man; and the sword again woke up against his family when his end was approaching, and filled his dying hours with grief and trouble. This list is much later in date than that previously given, though most of the officers are the same. **Cherethites.**

This is a correction of the Massorites to make the passage agree with ch. viii. 18. The K'tib has *cari*, a word which occurs in 2 Kings xi. 4, 19, where in the Authorized Version it is translated "captains," but in the Revised Version *Carites*, which here appears only in the margin. But there is no reason why the place of the Cherethites should not have been taken by Carian mercenaries later on in David's reign, though really we know too little about such matters to be able to form a judgment. Some commentators translate *cari* "digger," and suppose that it means executioner; but why a digger should have such a meaning is inexplicable. It may be interesting to add that the Carians were famous in old times as mercenaries. During the reign of Manasseh, Psammetichus won the throne of all Egypt by the aid of Carians, and from that period they took a leading part in all Egyptian wars. The age of David is much more antique, but as there was constant communication between Phœnicia and Asia Minor and Greece, there is nothing improbable in David taking Carians into his service in place of the Philistine Cherethites. His connection with them would soon cease after he left Ziklag.

Ver. 24.—**Adoram was over the tribute.** This was a new officer, and a new thing. For the Hebrew word *mas* does not mean "tribute," but "forced labour." This was one of the most oppressive exactions of old time, and it continued to be practised in Europe throughout the Middle Ages until it was abolished at the end of the eighteenth century by the French Revolution, except in Russia, where the serfs were freed from it by the late emperor Alexander II. Nevertheless, it was probably made almost necessary at first by the absence of money. As there was no money for the payment of taxes, the dues of the king or lord could only be rendered by personal service. Yet even so it was exceedingly liable to be abused, and the people might be taken from their own homes and fields just when their presence there was most needed. One most painful result was that the women had to endure, upon the farm and among the cattle, a drudgery to which they were unsuited. We gather from this passage that it was David who began this practice in Israel, exacting probably only from the descendants of the Canaanites (who, nevertheless, formed a considerable portion of the inhabitants of Palestine) forced labour employed in preparing for the building of the temple, and in the fortifications of his fenced cities. Under Solomon it seems to have been extended to other classes (1 Kings v. 13, 14; but see 1 Kings ix. 20—22), and reduced to a system, which pressed so heavily upon the people that it was the principal cause of the revolt of the ten tribes from Rehoboam (1 Kings xii. 4). Unless the Israelites had themselves suffered severely from this exaction, they would not have been driven into rebellion by sympathy with the remains of the native races. Subsequently we find Jeremiah accusing Jehoiakim of employing forced labour (Jer. xxii. 13), but the severity with which he condemned it suggests that it had then ceased to be customary. *Adoram.* His appointment to this office was probably at a late period in David's reign, as he continued to hold the office under Solomon (1 Kings iv. 6; v. 14, where he is called *Adoniram*), and even down to the beginning of Rehoboam's reign (1 Kings xii. 18). We there read that he paid the penalty of his hateful office with his life. In 2 Chron. x. 18 he is called *Hadoram.*

Ver. 25.—**Sheva.** He is called *Seraiah* in ch. viii. 17.

Ver. 26.—**Ira . . . was a chief ruler;** Hebrew, *cohen*, priest, minister (see on this term, ch. viii. 18). We there find David's sons holding this confidential office; but the feuds which resulted from David's sin had destroyed the concord of the family, and the usefulness of David's children. In their degradation from this office we see also a preparation for their being set aside from the succession, and the throne given to Solomon.

ADDITIONAL NOTE.

With this chapter ends the second section of David's history; for, as we have already seen, the last four chapters are not arranged in chronological order, but form an appendix remarkable both for the singularly varied nature of its contents, and also for its omissions. The Second Book of Samuel is so thoroughly a history of David, that we should naturally have expected some account of his latter years, and of his manner of government after his return to power. But such details would have been interesting politically rather than spiritually, and the two narratives which have gone before are complete each in itself; and in each David is regarded from an entirely distinct point of view. In the first eight chapters we have the history of David as the theocratic king. As such he takes the heathen for his inheritance, and founds an empire. Even more remarkable are the alterations he makes in the worship of Jehovah. To the old Levitical sacrifices he added a far more spiritual service of psalms and minstrelsy, without which Judaism would have been unable to develop the evangelical realities which lay embedded in its ritual and legal ordinances. And it is important to notice that his service of sacred song is called

"prophecy" (1 Chron. xxv. 1—3), from which we learn two things. The first that David's service was essentially the same as that established by Samuel at Ramah. There, too, we read of the company of the prophets prophesying (1 Sam. xix. 20), their service undoubtedly being one of minstrelsy (1 Sam. x. 5, 10, 11); and without Samuel's authority David would scarcely have ventured upon so great an innovation. Even so, this consecration of music by Samuel, and David's ordinance whereby there was established a daily service, morning and evening, of thanksgiving and praise (1 Chron. xxiii. 30; Neh. xii. 24), is a most remarkable step forward; and by it the service of God ceased to be mere ritual, and became "a reasonable service" (Rom. xii. 1), such as was repeatedly commended by St. Paul to the members of the Christian Church (Col. iii. 16, etc.). But secondly, it drew the minds of the people to the evangelic meaning of the Levitical ordinances. To this day hymns form a most important part of our solemn services, and seem especially adapted to draw out the inner and deeper meaning of rites and doctrines. They did not, indeed, begin with David. There are psalms older than his reign; but this consecration of them to the public daily service of God led to an outburst of Divine psalmody which raised the minds of the people above the material and grosser elements of their worship, and taught them the true nature of God, and made them ascribe to him high and spiritual attributes in wonderful contrast with the grovelling frivolities of heathenism. The Levitical worship was necessarily typical: in the psalms the people learned that God desireth not sacrifice, but the offering of a broken and contrite heart. Even prophecy, in its sense of speaking for God, would scarcely have reached the high eminence of future days but for the psalms. For only in a nation deeply imbued with poetry and song could an Isaiah have arisen, capable of giving in so perfect an outward form the mysteries of Christ's incarnation, his vicarious sacrifice, and universal kingdom.

In the second section, neither the theocratic nor the prophetic element is in the forefront. It is the history of a fearful sin, and of its stern punishment. The sinner is the theocratic king: the punishment is the pollution of his house by incest and murder; the ruin of the glory of his realm, the rending asunder of his empire, begun in his days and consummated in those of his grandson; his own disgrace and flight; and his sorrowful return to his throne, impotent to avenge either the murder of his son or that of the man whom he had chosen in the hope that he would release him from the stern grip of the ruthless Joab. The moral lessons of this sad story are beyond number. We see the saint changed into a sinner. No privileges save him from hateful crime; no repentance from draining the last dregs of the bitter cup of retribution. But never was the power of repentance in cleansing the heart and giving peace to the conscience more clearly shown; and the psalms written by David as a penitent, and during his flight from Absalom, are the most spiritual and choice and edifying of the whole Psalter. Without them the depths of self-abasement would have been left without inspired expression. The sinner in his greatest need, when crushed with the conviction of sin, when earnestly longing for forgiveness, when thirsting for the restored presence of God within his soul, and when feeling that, vile as he was, yet that he was not shut out from mercy, but that access to God's presence was still permitted him;—at all such times he would have gone to his Bible, and it would have been silent. These psalms are still the sinner's comfort, and give him the words which best express what is present in his heart. Without them the Jewish Church would never have reached that fervid purity of spiritual feeling which so animated the prophets; and even the Christian Church would possibly have stopped short of that full doctrine of repentance which she now holds. It is, indeed, the Christian's privilege to unite the doctrine of repentance with the thought of all that Christ has done and suffered for us, and so to understand why repentance avails to cleanse the heart; but even with this knowledge no Christian writer has ever reached so high a level of spirituality as David, though we may thankfully acknowledge that many of our best hymns do not fall far short of it.

It is easy, then, to see that these two histories are not only of primary importance, but that no narrative after the time of the Exodus equals them in value. They form the very kernel of the Book of the Earlier Prophets, giving us, in the first, the true meaning and spiritual import of the settlement of Israel in Palestine; and setting before us, in the second, the nature of repentance, and so preparing the way for the revelation of the gospel of pardon and peace.

They are followed by an appendix containing several narratives recorded apparently for their intrinsic value. Commentators have endeavoured to trace a connection between them, but their arguments are farfetched, and their conclusions unsatisfactory. It is better to regard them as separate and complete, each one in itself. They are six in number: (1) the visitation of famine because of Saul's cruelty to the Gibeonites; (2) some incidents in the war with the Philistines, illustrating the heroic character of David's worthies; (3) David's psalm of deliverance; (4) David's last words; (5) a list of the Gibborim, with special records of acts of bravery and devotion; (6) the visitation of pestilence because of David's numbering the people. The third and fourth sections especially are of the highest interest; while the second makes it plain that David's bravery in encountering the giant of Gath lit up an equally bright flame of patriotic heroism in the armies of Israel.

HOMILETICS.

Vers. 1—13.—The facts are: 1. Among the men who discuss the question of priority with Judah is a worthless man named Sheba, and he raises the cry of revolt against David, and the men of Israel follow him, while those of Judah cleave to the king. 2. David enters his house and makes arrangement for the sustenance of his concubines, who henceforth live in virtual widowhood. 3. David, observing that Amasa was tardy in executing his orders to gather the men of Judah, directs Abishai to go out with Joab's men in pursuit of Sheba. 4. While they are obeying the king's orders, Amasa joins them at Gibeon; whereupon Joab, under pretext of saluting Amasa and inquiring concerning his health, smites him, while off his guard, unto death. 5. While the pursuit after Sheba continues, one of Joab's partisans calls upon the people to show their preference for Joab and David by following after Joab, which they do when the bleeding corpse is no longer on the road to arrest their progress.

Man's revolt against Christ. The hot controversy between the men of Israel and Judah issued in more than words. The discussion took its rise in a pretended interest in the restoration of David to the throne, but, becoming mixed up with personal matters, it first developed an alienation of one part of the nation from another; and then the more humiliated section turned their alienation from their brethren into the more dangerous form of revolt against the authority of the king whom those brethren claimed as specially theirs (ch. xix. 42, 43). There is always in human society some restless, unscrupulous spirit ready to take advantage of divergent sentiments, and form them into expressions of positive opinion and antagonistic action. The man of Belial used up the elements of discord for securing what, at first, was not contemplated —namely, an open repudiation of the right of David to exercise kingly authority over the people. In this revolt against David, the Lord's anointed, we have an illustration of the nature and some of the causes and pleas of man's revolt against Christ.

I. MAN'S REVOLT AGAINST CHRIST CONSISTS ESSENTIALLY OF A REJECTION OF A DIVINE CLAIM. Sheba not only would not have David as his king, but he distinctly indicates as chief reason his rejection of the Divine claim of David to the throne, and which the nation had previously recognized. In speaking contemptuously of him as the "son of Jesse," he clearly ignores the selection and anointing of him by Samuel in the name of God. David is not the Lord's anointed; only Jesse's son—a mere man, to be treated as any other man. The people also who followed Sheba did so on this basis—that whatever may have been once, there was now in David no more right than in any other man; he was not endowed with Divine authority. This is exactly the case with modern infidelity—men will not submit to Christ. They repudiate all claim to Divine authority. To them he is a mere man—possessing no eternal and unchallengeable right to demand the obedience of all men to his yoke. He is the Nazarene, the carpenter's Son, not the beloved Son of God, anointed of God to be Prince and Saviour. It is a simple matter of choice whether they shall accept his testimony and do what he declares is right. This spirit of revolt against the Divine in Christ is the essence of every form of modern infidelity, be it scientific rejection of the supernatural or pure agnosticism. Once recognize him as the anointed Lord of all, all forms of submission to his teaching and will follow; once reject him in this respect, and high treason is the practical issue.

II. A REJECTION OF CHRIST'S DIVINE CLAIM PROCEEDS FROM UNBELIEF IN GOD'S SELF-REVELATION TO MAN. If ever Sheba was a believer in Samuel's mission, he had certainly ceased to be so now, or else had come to believe that revelation had ceased. No one could hold to the Divine appointment of Moses and of Samuel to gradually unfold the purpose of God to Israel, and at the same time logically refuse to submit to David as king, unless he could show that God had set up another. This revolt, therefore, was the expression of a practical unbelief in the fact of a revelation of God to the Jewish people. In like manner, when we look into the reason for the rejection of the Divine claim of Christ, it is to be found in a prior assumption, namely, that a self-revelation of God to mankind by special means distinct from natural law, though not in contra-vention of it, is a fiction. With a dogmatism evidently based on ignorance, the super-natural is said to be impossible, i.e. we know so well the constitution of all things, and the only possible relation of God to all things, that we can affirm that no such a Divine Lord and King as Christ is said to be, could be a reality. He was simply a much-mis-understood man. It is obvious that, as Sheba's unbelief in Samuel's mission was no credit to his memory or historic knowledge (1 Sam. xvi. 13), so the unbelief in God's self-revelation to man is no credit to man's humility or judgment.

III. REVOLT AGAINST CHRIST'S CLAIMS THUS ORIGINATING IS SUSTAINED BY VARIOUS PLEAS. Sheba's unbelief was in the background, his pleas were in front. He could not have gained so many over to his side by any enunciation of abstract views as to the reality or continuance of a revelation of God's purpose. Men are influenced in action by more superficial and concrete forms of thought. The mistakes of David's govern-ment, his reputed partiality to the son whom he fought against, his errors of conduct in the case of Bathsheba, his apparent preference for Judah, and the apprehension that Judah would gain an ascendency in public affairs,—these pleas would give an appearance of public reason for the conduct pursued. Nor did he or his followers care to consider that incidents in a fallible life do not annihilate a Divine purpose running through that life. We find the same course adopted in relation to the authority of Christ. Though none can convict him of sin, advantage is taken of the mistakes of the Church, the seemingly tardy progress of Christianity, the peculiar structure of Old Testament history, and what seem to be occasional discrepancies in the gospel record, and, in fact, anything that can be construed into a weakness, in order to justify a total rejection of Christ's supreme authority. An ingenious mind, bent on resisting the holy Saviour, will never lack plausible reasons for open revolt.

IV. REVOLT AGAINST CHRIST IS A COURSE OF CONDUCT DEVOID OF POSITIVE REGULA-
TIVE PRINCIPLE. Sheba's principles, so far as he had any, were negative. There was
nothing in his words or deeds that indicated any definite principle on which the state
was to be governed. Hitherto the theocratic principle, enunciated and enforced by
Samuel, regulated the setting up and setting aside of rulers. The spiritual interests of
the nation were the prime concern. Now, Divine authority being ignored, there was no
principle to determine the destiny of the people. The conflicting whims and passions
of men were to contend for supremacy, and the grand purpose for which the nation had
been hitherto supposed to exist in relation to Messiah and the world was lost to view.
In the same way, the course of human affairs, without Christ, is aimless, chaotic.
Infidelity and agnosticism rest on negations. Individual life is as a ship without a
helm.

GENERAL LESSONS. 1. There is always in human nature a latent tendency to restlessness under authority, and we should both be on our guard against this in our own
lives, and also avoid whatever may develop it in others. 2. The quarrels and disputes
of Christian men on matters of government and precedence may generate, by degrees,
feelings of alienation from religion. 3. In this life we should not be surprised if, like
David, we find the pathway of returning prosperity shaded by some transient clouds.
4. The zeal of crowds in a bad cause is more due to the influence of clever and restless
leaders than to any profound convictions or intelligent views in the people themselves.

Unsanctified power. We pass over David's provision for his concubines, simply
noting how wise and considerate he was in thus cutting himself free from old associations full of reminiscences of sorrow, and at the same time doing no injustice to any
one concerned. The chief figure in the narrative before us is Joab, who here stands
out as a strong man bent on a definite purpose, and able to carry out his will in spite
of moral, social, and loyal considerations. All the other men referred to are as pigmies
beside him, and the orders even of the king are so far bent to his will that he becomes
practically master of the situation. Regarding him as an illustration of unsanctified
power, we notice—

I. GREAT ABILITIES. Joab was a man of great natural abilities. This is obvious
throughout his career. There was not one in the army to compare with him. Great
natural abilities are the base of power among men. In some men they are purely
intellectual, in others they are those of will. For influencing action and obtaining an
ascendency over multitudes, will-force must be strong. This partly accounts for success
in commerce, in statesmanship, in Church government, in popular movements.

II. STRONG PASSIONS. Passions are not abilities; they are rather the fire that feeds
the energy of the will. Joab was a man whose passions were very strong, though not
boisterous and impulsive. His jealousy and hatred of Amasa, who had been appointed
to supersede him in command, were intense. These, blended with contempt for his
inferiority, disgust at David's choice, and a lofty pride which would not deign to
remonstrate with the king, formed such a strenuous force on the naturally powerful
will, that to kill his rival was a decision which no ordinary obstacles could hinder
in accomplishment. When unholy passions, deliberately cherished, concentrate on a
powerful will, there results one of the most formidable instances of unsanctified power.
Such men are to be dreaded. They cannot but make a great impression on weaker
natures, and bend them to their own designs. They are illustrations of what woe comes
to mankind when distinguished powers, incorporated in the constitution of man, receive
a bent of evil rather than of good. A being who becomes a Miltonic Satan might be
a real archangel. It is the spirit that makes the one or the other.

III. A DREAD SECRET. To many the bearing of Joab toward the authority of David
in this matter of Amasa may be an enigma, seeing that he raised no revolt, but was
rather zealous for the king. But that which made Joab so terrible an example of
unsanctified power was his possession of the dreadful secret of Uriah's death (ch. xi.
14—25). He knew too much of David's former guilt; and so all his great natural
abilities were concentrated in holding a firm grip on the king's public reputation. It
is true, David had found forgiveness with God, and was a new man; but he knew that
Joab had him in his power in matters that came nearest to a man's life, and Joab
perfectly understood that David dared not do what otherwise he would doubtless have

done. This possession of secret knowledge concerning others always gives increased power. Whoever knows of the financial weakness of a commercial firm, or the private delinquencies of individuals, or of original social inferiority of persons aiming to figure in society, if it be known that he knows, holds a power over these parties which they dread, and which, if he be unholy, he can use in most painful form. Those are to be pitied indeed who have caused their failings and sins to become the secret of unholy men.

IV. FAMILIARITY WITH SUFFERING. Bad as great power is in a man of strong passions and possessed of special knowledge, it is a more terrible thing when the moral sensibilities have been blunted by familiarity with sufferings. Joab had seen many a man dying in agonies. War does not improve the feelings of men. It was with no compunctions of conscience, as far as we can see, that he slew Amasa. What was a bleeding corpse to the man who had smitten many a hero, and who now was governed by jealousy, hatred, contempt, and pride? It is this loss of moral sensibility which has made such men as Napoleon I. so terrible a scourge. There are other men of, perhaps, equally strong will, but their moral susceptibilities restrain them from brutality.

V. CLEARLY DEFINED PURPOSE. Joab knew what he intended to do. The narrative shows that he watched for opportunity. He did not wish to encourage revolt against royal authority, but he did wish and purpose to avenge his displacement from supreme command by the death of his rival, to prove his power to David by actually assuming the leadership and suppressing the revolt, and to vindicate before the people his superiority in the state. Purpose, clearly defined, is a practical addition to power. It avoids waste of energy, and converts subsidiary appliances into instruments of great significance. By such purpose the whole nature of the man and all his strong and unhallowed passions are condensed and concentrated into one channel.

GENERAL LESSONS. 1. We see the supreme importance of prayer for the converting power of the Holy Spirit, so that men of great natural powers may have them governed by a principle according to the will of God. 2. The appearance of unhallowed feelings in the heart should be at once an occasion of prayer and self-control, as they will be sure to combine to influence us to deeds of wrong. 3. There is more real honour in being a man of lowly abilities, but under the sway of holy dispositions, than in possessing the highest powers destitute of such a disposition. 4. If we can only secure progress in life or continued possession of privileges by using abilities wickedly, it is infinitely better to lose all than thus sink deeper in moral and spiritual degradation. 5. According to our abilities will be the account we shall have to give unto God.

Vers. 14—26.—*The causes and remedies of religious strife.* The facts are: 1. Joab and his forces, pursuing Sheba till they came upon him in the city of Abel, lay siege to it. 2. A wise woman of the city remonstrates with Joab for attacking the city, and refers to the fact that when Sheba with his armed followers threw themselves into the city, the people felt sure that when the pursuing foes came up they would open negotiations with the authorities, and so bring the conflict to an end. 3. Urging the impolicy and wrong of seeking to destroy a part of the inheritance of the Lord—a city which was as a mother in Israel—she obtains from Joab a disclaimer, and a declaration that it was only the rebel and traitor Sheba that he was fighting against. 4. The wise woman, conferring with the inhabitants, secures that the head of Sheba be thrown over the wall to Joab, who then retires with his men to Jerusalem. 5. A reorganization of the officers of state is made, and Joab regains his former position as head of the army. The patriotism of Joab and a rough kind of fidelity to David manifested itself in his prompt and eager pursuit of the rebel force till it took refuge in a city and began to act on the defensive. There is no evidence that the inhabitants had formally identified themselves with the cause of Sheba, though probably there as elsewhere some disaffected men of Belial were to be found. It is not always within the competence of a city to prevent an armed force entering within its walls and virtually turning its resources against pursuers. The conflict between the opposing forces was becoming desperate, and threatened, if persisted in, to result in the destruction of the city. The horrors and wasting issues of civil war were impending. At this juncture, the more peaceably inclined portion of the inhabitants, encouraged by a woman who had gained reputation for wisdom, were anxious to avoid the calamities of continued strife, and probably having in mind the old law of Deut. xx. 11, 12, remonstrated with Joab because he had not sought to come to terms before having recourse to arms. And here we see a fact embodying a principle, namely, that a people of one nation, speech, religion, and covenant relation to God, pause while engaged in a ruinous strife, and that it is pre-eminently desirable and right on occasions of strife to seek some basis of reconciliation.

I. THE TRUE CONDITION OF THE PROFESSED SERVANTS OF CHRIST IS THAT OF UNITY AND CONCORD. The strife between Joab's forces and the people of this city was unnatural. They were brethren, the chosen race, called and separated from all nations to work out a blessed purpose in which all men were concerned. Unity and concord became them. How good and beautiful a thing for them to dwell in harmony! The siege of Abel was a sign of an abnormal state of things. This is just what is taught in the New Testament. Christ's disciples are a holy nation, a peculiar people, called to show forth the glory of God and to bless mankind, and in his last most solemn discourses and great prayer he sets forth their unity and concord as the only state befitting them, and congruous with his spirit (John xiv.—xvii.).

II. THE BREAKING OUT OF RELIGIOUS STRIFE IS PRODUCTIVE OF SERIOUS MISCHIEF, AND THREATENS THE CHURCH AND THE WORLD WITH GREAT CALAMITIES. The fact of the strife is itself an evil, and indicates the presence somewhere of a mind alien to the mind of Christ; but also it generates evils of varied form, and intensifies their action in proportion as the spirit of strife is intense. Leaving out of view just now the revolt of Sheba against the lawful authority of David—regarding him in that respect as a type of the men who reject the authority of Christ—we see that there existed a strife between men who had not rejected David's authority. Joab was contending against the whole city of Abel as though it were hostile to him, and many in the city were contending against him as though he were an enemy. The evils of this were obvious: bad feelings were engendered and strengthened the longer the siege continued, desolation and anguish were being brought on many homes, the city as a centre of influence—a mother of children—was having its power for good cut off, and the one kingdom to which all belonged was being checked in its progress. That was the belief of the wise woman and her friends, and it was in accordance with facts. Precisely the same evils attend our more modern strifes. When subjects of the same Lord are engaged in conflict, whatever the passing occasion, there is not only a dire evil in the fact itself, but inevitably bitter unhallowed feelings find scope, many a Christian heart and home are made desolate and sad, Churches and organizations that should embody in themselves all the kindly fostering influences of mothers have their proper spiritual influence weakened, and the progress of the kingdom of love, peace, and righteousness receives a check. "The inheritance of the Lord" is laid waste. "The boar out of the wood doth waste it" (Ps. lxxx. 13).

III. THE CAUSES OF RELIGIOUS STRIFE MAY LIE IN MUTUAL MISUNDERSTANDING AND NEGLECT OF PRIMARY OBLIGATIONS. Joab fought against this city on the supposition that it was in sympathy with Sheba; and the people themselves for a while were constrained by his assaults to assume a defensive attitude. Had he at first, in accordance with Deut. xx. 11, 12, sought an interview with the elders, and had they been willing, in the spirit of that ancient rule, to receive his communications, the strife had earlier come to a close, and brethren would have been one. The beginnings of strife are very subtle, and it is hard to unravel the true causes from among the intricate thoughts and feelings of the human mind; and the incidents which occasion the appearance of strife may be as far beyond the control of communities as was the sudden throwing of an armed force by Sheba into this unguarded city. But most often strife is kept up through mutual misunderstandings. Opinions are supposed to be held which, if fairly looked at in an early stage, would not be ascribed, and motives are imagined which would disappear on closer acquaintance. Perhaps it is inevitable that, differently constituted and educated as men are, judgments must differ as to the form of expressing truth and doing Christian work; but these need not cause actual strife, if formed in a prayerful loving spirit, and all for the glory of Christ, and especially may much contention be avoided if men will but discharge the primary obligation laid down in the ancient law (John xv. 12; Matt. v. 44), of loving and praying for one another, and being frank and generous in intercourse (Matt. xviii. 15, 16).

IV. IT IS THE DUTY OF PERSONS OF REPUTED WISDOM TO BRING ALL THEIR INFLU-
ENCE TO BEAR ON THE PROMOTION OF PEACE AND HARMONY. The "wise woman"
and those of her mind in the city were but discharging a duty they owed to their city,
their king, and the kingdom, when, amidst the discords of the time, they brought
their superior intelligence to bear on a solution of the difficulties of the case. They
evidently saw that, if more light were thrown upon the affair, and proper kindly
influences were brought to bear on Joab, those would become friends who now were in
the unnatural position of enemies. The leaders of opinion in the city showed their
good feeling in being willing to come to terms, and their discretion in availing themselves of the superior gifts and qualities of this "wise woman." The proper place of
intelligence and wisdom is at the head of movements in the direction of concord. A
serious injury is inflicted on the Church in seasons of trial and conflict when men of
character and repute keep in the background, and leave the conduct of affairs to
inferior minds. Acquired reputation is a precious gift that should be cheerfully laid at
the service of the Church, especially in seasons of sorrow. The soothing, healing power
of the noblest minds is a great blessing.

V. THE OCCASION OF STRIFE BEING ASCERTAINED, EVERY EFFORT SHOULD BE MADE
TO PUT IT AWAY. The occasion of the strife in this instance was the presence within
the city of a rebel and a traitor. Had it not been for Sheba entering the city, Joab and
the people would not have so misunderstood each other as to come to actual conflict.
Mutual inquiry and explanations revealed the fact that he was the occasion of trouble;
and therefore the citizens devised means of getting rid of him in accordance with the rude
and swift justice of those times. If in our religious strifes, whether as between communities or within separate organizations, we, in our desire for peace, search out some
removable occasion of them, it then becomes an imperative duty that we not only wish
to see the occasion removed, but that we make vigorous efforts, though full of pain and
sorrow, to put them away. What the disturbing cause may be—evil-minded men,
or narrow ideas of our own, or unhallowed feeling, or an exacting temper, or undue
pressure of the influence of the world—can only be found out by conscientious rigorous
search; and, when found out, it will probably demand a very high and holy resolve to
cast it away. Probably one chief reason why there is not more peace and harmony
among Christians is that they have not the heart to go deep down into the moral
causes of strife, and less heart to cut off those causes when discovered. It takes very
much grace to be a thoroughgoing Christian.

GENERAL LESSONS. 1. Communities and individuals should watch carefully against
the intrusion within themselves of whatever may bring on a disruption of our peaceable
relations to the fellowship of the saints. 2. It is possible to imagine others to be hostile
in feeling to us, when, on full inquiry, it may turn out that they have been misjudged;
and hence we should be careful not to be rash in imputing motives to persons who are
casually placed in circumstances of seeming antagonism. 3. The influence of cities in a
nation and of Christian communities in the world being maternal in character, their
purity, peacefulness, and power should be most jealously guarded. 4. The influence of
woman in promoting peace in the Church of God is worthy of the consideration of all,
seeing that it is often under-estimated, and that its power is of the most subtle and
persuasive kind. 5. We see in the removal of Sheba, the occasion of the trouble in the
earthly kingdom, and the subsequent harmony of the chosen nation during the reign of
David, a foreshadowing of the final removal of the great spirit of discord from the Church
of God, and the consequent peace and unity of the redeemed.

HOMILIES BY VARIOUS AUTHORS.

Vers. 1—3.—(GILGAL.)   *The insurrection of Sheba.*

> "We have no part in David,
>   And we have no inheritance in the son of Jesse;
>   Every man to his tents, O Israel!"
>
> (Ver. 1; 1 Kings xii. 16.)

Before the restoration of David was completed, a new rebellion broke out. The people were still disquieted, like the sea after a storm; the independent action of Judah in conducting the king over the Jordan aroused the jealousy of the other tribes; at Gilgal (1 Sam. xi. 15; xiii. 8—10; xv. 12, 13), where the representatives of the latter assembled and met the king, a fierce altercation ensued (ch. xix. 40—43); and shortly afterwards the trumpet was blown by Sheba the Bichrite (Gen. xlvi. 21). "He who lately (with the rest of Israel) claimed ten parts in David as king, disclaims and disowns him now, as having no part in him at all. David before had raised his hand against a faithful subject, Uriah, and therefore now a faithless subject raises his hand against him; as a man sinneth, so ofttimes he is punished. And as bees, when they are once up in a swarm, are ready to light upon every bough, so the Israelites, being stirred up by the late rebellion of Absalom, are apt here also to follow Sheba; especially finding nothing but clemency, and David's passing by their former revolt" (Guild). Concerning this insurrection, observe that (like others which have since occurred)—

I. IT AROSE OUT OF AN EVIL DISPOSITION INDULGED BY THE PEOPLE. They were: 1. *Discontented* with the government of David; the restlessness, lawlessness, and ungodliness which they displayed in joining Absalom's revolt were only partially corrected by recent chastisement (ch. xix. 9, 10); their complaint to the king concerning the conduct of "the men of Judah" (ver. 41) was due more to regard for their own honour than zeal for his; and was an indirect expression of their dissatisfaction at the disrespect which he had shown toward them, for "very probably it had been learned that he had a hand in the movement." 2. *Contentious* in their treatment of their "brethren;" ready to find occasion of offence "because of envy" and ill will; their anger being increased by the proud and contemptuous bearing of the latter. Whatever may have been the motives of the men of Judah in their recent action, they were now as blamable as the men of Israel; each party sought to exalt itself and depreciate the other; and "the words of the men of Judah were more violent than the words of the men of Israel" (ver. 43). "Grievous words stir up anger" (Prov. xv. 1, 18; xxv. 15; xxix. 22). How differently had Gideon spoken to the men of Ephraim under similar circumstances (Judg. viii. 1—3)! 3. *Self-blinded.* Indifferent to their true interests, without proper self-control, liable to surrender themselves to the guidance of an ambitious leader, and prepared for open rebellion. Having violated the spirit of unity, they were ready to destroy the formal union of the tribes, which it had cost so much to bring about, and on which their strength and prosperity so much depended. "Where jealousy and faction are, there is confusion and every vile deed" (Jas. iii. 16; iv. 1, 11).

II. IT WAS INSTIGATED BY A WORTHLESS LEADER. "A man of Belial, a Benjamite" (like Shimei, ch. xvi. 11); "a man of the mountains of Ephraim" (ver. 21); who probably took an active part in the late rebellion, and had numerous dependents. "He was one of the great rogues of the high nobility, who had a large retinue among the people, and consideration or name, as Cataline at Rome" (Luther). 1. The worst (as well as the best) elements of a people find their chief embodiment in some one man, who is the product of the prevailing spirit of his time, and adapted to be its leader.

> "Avarice, envy, pride,
> Three fatal sparks, have set the hearts of all
> On fire."
>
> (Dante.)

In his selfish ambition, Sheba sought for himself individually what the men of Israel sought for themselves as a whole. 2. Such a man clearly perceives the popular feeling and tendency, with which he sympathizes, and finds therein his opportunity for effecting his own purposes. The design of Sheba was, doubtless, to become head of a new combination of the northern tribes. 3. He seizes a suitable moment for raising his seditious cry; and, instead of quenching the sparks of discord, kindles them into a blaze. "They claim David as their own. Let them have him. We disclaim him altogether. The son of Jesse! Let every man cast off his yoke, return home, and unite with me in securing liberty, equality, and fraternity!" What at another time would have been without effect, is now irresistible with the people. Nothing is more unstable than a multitude; one day crying, "Hosanna!" another, "Not this Man, but Barabbas!"

III. IT ATTAINED A DANGEROUS MAGNITUDE. "And all the men of Israel went up from after David, and followed Sheba the son of Bichri" (ver. 2); "Now will Sheba do us more harm than Absalom" (ver. 6). The insurrection: 1. Was joined in by great numbers of the people. 2. Spread over the greater portion of the country. "He went through all the tribes of Israel," rousing them to action, and gaining possession of the fortified cities. 3. Threatened to produce a permanent disruption of the kingdom. "It was, in fact, all but an anticipation of the revolt of Jeroboam. It was not, as in the case of Absalom, a mere conflict between two factions in the court of Judah, but a struggle arising out of that conflict, on the part of the tribe of Benjamin to recover its lost ascendency" (Stanley). With what anxieties must it have filled the mind of the restored monarch! And how must it have led him to feel his dependence upon God! The influence for evil which one bad man sometimes exerts is enormous (Eccles. ix. 18). It is, nevertheless, limited; and, though it prevail for a season, it is at length "brought to nought" (Ps. xxxvii. 12, 20, 35—40).

IV. IT ENDED IN UTTER DISCOMFITURE. The first act of David, on arriving at Jerusalem, attended by the men of Judah, who "clave unto the king" (after setting his house in order, ver. 3), was to adopt energetic measures to put down the insurrection; and these succeeded (though in a different manner from what he expected). 1. Many who at first followed Sheba deserted him when they had time for reflection and saw the approach of the king's army; so that he found it necessary to seek safety in the far north. 2. He was beheaded by those among whom he sought refuge; and "rewarded according to his wickedness" (ch. iii. 39). "Evil pursueth sinners" (Prov. xiii. 21; xi. 19). 3. All the people returned to their allegiance. "While to men's eyes the co-operation of many evil powers seems to endanger the kingdom of God to the utmost, and its affairs appear to be confused and disturbed in the unhappiest fashion, the wonderful working of the living God reveals itself most gloriously in the unravelment of the worst entanglements, and in the introduction of new and unexpected triumphs for his government" (Erdmann).—D.

Vers. 4—13.—(GIBEON.) *The murder of Amasa.* "And Amasa took no heed to the sword that was in Joab's hand" (ver. 10). Amasa (son of Abigail, David's sister, and Jether an Ishmaelite, and first cousin of Joab, ch. xvii. 25) joined Absalom in his rebellion; and must have been a man of great ability, courage, and influence, from the fact that he was appointed by him "captain of the host instead of Joab," and afterwards promised by David the same post (ch. xix. 13). This promise "involved no injustice to Joab himself, for he had long been notorious for too great severity in war, and had just acted with such direct disobedience to the royal command in Absalom's case, that it was impossible to overlook his offence without endangering the royal prerogative" (Ewald). Whilst it was adapted to conciliate the men of Judah, it was, nevertheless, certain to give offence to Joab and cause future trouble. It does not appear that he was formally replaced by Amasa; but the commission given to the latter (ver. 4) "was intended as the commencement of the fulfilment of the promise" (Keil). And when he exhibited undue delay in its fulfilment (ver. 5), David, "wishing to have nothing to do with Joab," sent Abishai to pursue after Sheba (ver. 6). "And there went out after him Joab's men" (ver. 7) under Joab (who deemed himself still commander-in-chief). At "the great stone which is in Gibeon" (ch. ii. 13; xxi. 1; 1 Chron. xxi. 29) he met Amasa returning with his military levies, and on saluting him with the kiss of peace, dealt him his death-blow (vers. 8—10); passed on, followed (after a brief hesitation at the spectacle of their murdered captain) by "all the people;" finished the war, and returned to Jerusalem. In this tragedy notice: 1. *The danger of holding a responsible position by one who is ill qualified for it* through want of natural ability, proper antecedents, timely appointment, public confidence, adequate zeal and energy. "The cause of Amasa's delay is not stated. It may have been the unwillingness of the men of Judah to place themselves under the orders of Amasa (contrast vers. 13 and 14), or it may have been caused by a wavering or hesitation in the loyalty of Amasa himself. This last is evidently insinuated in ver. 11, and no doubt this was the pretext, whether grounded in fact or not, by which Joab justified the murder of Amasa before David" ('Speaker's Commentary'). 2. *The tendency of repeated crimes to induce more daring criminality.* This was Joab's third murder (ch. iii. 27; xviii. 14), in addition to his complicity in the death of Uriah; less excusable, more guileful, malicious, and reckless than any other; his motive being jealousy of a rival. "No life is safe that stands in his way, but from policy he never sacrifices the most insignificant life without a purpose" (ch. ii. 27—30; xviii. 16; xx. 20). "By degrees men grow more and more bold and unfeeling in the commission of crimes of every kind; until they vindicate and glory in their villainies; and when such daring offenders are actuated by ambition or revenge, they will not be restrained by the ties of relationship or friendship; nay, they will employ the guise and language of love to obtain the opportunity of perpetrating the most atrocious murders. The beginning of evil should therefore in everything be decisively resisted" (Scott). 3. *The infliction of deserved punishment by an unauthorized and wicked hand.* "Amasa is innocent of the crime of seeking Joab's place, for which he is murdered by him, yet he is guilty before God for his siding with Absalom. Whereupon we collect that ofttimes men suffer innocently for some crimes that are laid to their charge, and in respect of the persons who are the pursuers; yet in God's judgment they are justly punished for other sins, wherein either they have been spared or else have not been noted to the world; and as many at the hour of their death and execution, publicly have acknowledged" (Guild). 4. *The commission of a great crime by one who possesses great abilities and renders great public services.* Alas! that a man of such military skill, practical sagacity, and tried fidelity as Joab (now far advanced in life), should have been so "hardened by the deceitfulness of sin"! Once more he saved the monarchy; and once more David was compelled to bear with him (ch. iii. 39; xix. 13). "He probably felt obliged to show some indulgence to a man who was indispensable to him as a soldier, and who, notwithstanding his culpable ferocity, never lost sight of his master's interests." His indulgence was doubtless also due, in part, to the consciousness of his own sin (Ps. li. 3), which made him unwilling to inflict the penalty of the law on one who had been his partner in guilt. But at length judgment overtakes the transgressor; the Law is vindicated; and the ways of God to men are justified (1 Kings ii. 5, 6, 28—35). Near the very spot where his crowning act of perfidy was perpetrated, Joab received his death-blow from the hand of Benaiah (1 Chron. xvi. 39).—D.

Vers. 15—22.—(ABEL-BETH-MAACAH.) *A peacemaker.* "Then cried a wise woman out of the city, Hear! hear!" (ver. 16). 1. Hard pressed by the forces of Joab, Sheba threw himself into the fortified city of Abel-beth-Maachah (in the north-west extremity of Palestine). The feelings of its inhabitants toward him are not stated. But Joab soon appeared; and, without entering into any negotiations with them, made preparations for attack. "Taking advantage of an oblong knoll of natural rock that rises above the surrounding plain, the original inhabitants raised a high mound sufficiently large for the city. With a deep trench and strong wall it must have been almost impregnable. The besiegers cast up a mount against the city, 'and it stood in the trench'" etc. (Thomson, 'The Land and the Book'). A deadly conflict was imminent. 2. At this juncture a wise woman presented herself at the wall; and, having obtained a hearing, sought to make peace; nor was her endeavour fruitless. "There was a little city," etc. (Eccles. ix. 14, 15). "Wisdom is better than strength. Wisdom is better than weapons of war; but one sinner destroyeth much good" (Eccles. ix. 16, 18). As one bad man exposed the city to destruction, so one good woman effected its deliverance. 3. There is often much *need* of a *peacemaker* to heal the strife that arises between individuals, families, cities, Churches, and nations. Regarded as an example to others, this "wise woman" of Abel—

I. POSSESSED AN EXCELLENT SPIRIT; observant, prudent, sagacious, peaceful, faithful, just, and benevolent. Hence she was prompted to go of her own accord, individually and independently, to "seek peace, and pursue it" (1 Pet. iii. 11; Ps. xxxiv. 12—16; Gen. xiii. 8, 9). 1. Being *grieved at the sight of strife between brethren*, and the prospect of the miseries which they were about to inflict on each other. 2. Being *desirous of preventing the evil* which threatened them, and promoting their welfare. Her chief concern was about her own city, which was likely to be the greater sufferer; but she was also (like Joab, ver. 20) concerned about others, and the general good of Israel, in which Abel was "a mother-city," a part of "the inheritance of Jehovah" (ver. 19). 3. Having *faith in the common sense of men*, their regard for their own interest (when they saw it, not blinded by prejudice), their love of justice, their generally good intentions (when not under the influence of wrath and revenge), and their susceptibility to the power of persuasion. 4. Being *determined to make every possible effort* and sacrifice, and undergo any personal risk and suffering for the sake of peace. She was doubtless willing (as others have been) to lay down her own life if thereby the lives of others might be spared. "Peacemakers are fire-quenchers, who, although they may with plying of engines and much ado, rescue a pile of buildings from the flames, yet their eyes will be sure to smart with the smoke" (R. Harris).

II. ADOPTED AN ADMIRABLE METHOD; thereby justifying the "wisdom" with which she was credited. Perceiving that there was some misunderstanding between the contending parties, her aim was to clear it up; if there were any real cause of contention, to remove it; and thus dispose them to peace. This she endeavoured to effect by: 1. Seizing the *opportune moment* for interposition; promptly availing herself of the pause before the attack. Instead of "battered the wall" (Authorized Version), read, "were devising to throw down the wall." There is generally such a time for the work of a peacemaker, which, if it be neglected, may be afterwards too late. 2. Making use of *courteous, gentle, reasonable, and impressive speech*. "Hear the words of thine handmaid." Like the woman of Tekoah (ch. xiv. 4), she was a mistress in the art of persuasion. "The tongue of the wise is health" (Prov. xii. 18); "a tree of life" (Prov. xv. 4; x. 20; xviii. 21). 3. *Ascertaining the nature of the misunderstanding,* and the occasion of complaint; and, for this purpose, going directly and separately to the persons concerned, and learning it from their own lips. She knew the sentiments of her people, especially that they felt aggrieved that no communications should have been made to them by Joab, and suspected his destructive and merciless designs. And now she sought to discover what were his real thoughts and purposes in relation to them. How much mischief would be prevented if contending parties would only be at pains to understand one another! 4. *Removing all misconception,* and producing the conviction in each party of the just aims and good intentions of the other. To Joab she said, "You evidently deem this city deficient in good sense; whereas it has been always noted for its wisdom and conciliatory disposition and counsel. You think the people contentious and rebellious; I assure you in their name that we are among the most peaceable and faithful in Israel. Yet, without any communication with us, so as to ascertain our feelings, and without any reasonable cause, you are about to give an important city of Israel to the devouring sword. Why will you bring to ruin what belongs to the Lord?" On the other hand, from his reply, it was made apparent that he was not desirous of their destruction (as they supposed), but only sought to inflict a just punishment on a notorious traitor in their midst, and was under the necessity (if, as he had supposed, they harboured him, participated with him in rebellion, and resolved to defend him to the utmost) of making an attack upon them for that purpose. "Far be it, far be it from me . . . The matter is not so," etc. (vers. 20, 21). Misunderstanding was now at an end, but a real occasion of difference remained. 5. Obtaining *needful concessions* on both sides. "Deliver him only, and I will depart from the city . . . Behold, his head shall be thrown to thee through the wall." If (as is doubtful) the people had (from whatever reason) at first shown favour to the cause of Sheba, they were now persuaded by her to do otherwise, "and so they ended the matter." 6. Requiring *no sacrifice of principle*; but only urging a course conformable to "goodness, righteousness, and truth," and consistent with professed obedience to the will of the Lord. "The just punishment of one atrocious criminal is frequently mercy to great numbers" (Scott). "Follow peace with all men, and holiness" (Heb. xii. 14; Rom. xiv. 19; Jas. iii. 17, 18).

III. ACHIEVED AN EMINENT TRIUMPH—the triumph of peace. "And he blew the trumpet" (ver. 22) summoning to peace, as Sheba had blown it summoning to war (ver. 1). It was a victory over error, distrust, wilfulness, wrath, injustice, rebellion; and one by which: 1. An immense evil was prevented. 2. The general good was promoted. 3. The Divine kingdom (as represented in the government of David) was confirmed. 4. The peacemaker's joy was fulfilled. The wise woman accomplished what she had set her heart upon; and in blessing others was herself blessed. "Blessed are the peacemakers," etc. (Matt. v. 9). "Of the following things," said a Jewish rabbi, "men reap the fruits both in the present and the future life—honouring father and mother, bestowing benefits, and making peace between men."

REMARKS. 1. It is hardly possible to estimate too highly the worth of peace among men. 2. Those who would make peace between others must themselves be at peace with God, with their own hearts, and with their neighbours. The peacemaker must not be a peacebreaker. 3. The greatest Peacemaker the world has ever seen is Jesus Christ, who is "our Peace" (Eph. ii. 14). 4. In proportion as we partake of his spirit we shall endeavour to heal all unholy strife and promote "peace on earth."—D.

Vers. 1, 2.—*Departure from and adherence to Christ.* A sudden change in the aspect of affairs. The occasion was a fierce dispute between the Israelites and the men of Judah as to the right of the latter to go so far towards the restoration of the king without consulting the former. The causes, however, are to be found partly in old jealousies between the tribes; partly in the unallayed resentment of the Benjamites on account of the setting aside of the house of Saul from the royalty, and its transfer to the tribe of Judah; partly in the excitement of men's minds by the rebellion under Absalom, and its suppression. A spark only was wanted to produce another desolating flame, and that was supplied by the sudden summons of Sheba to the men of Israel. Hence another insurrection, which seems to have been begun without consideration, and which was brought to an end speedily and ignominiously. The men of Israel followed Sheba; but those of Judah "clave unto their king," and conducted him "from Jordan even to Jerusalem." The division thus for the time produced has its counterpart in the spiritual sphere. It may serve to illustrate especially the more open and manifest departures from the Divine King which at times occur, under, perhaps, some leader, and the steadfast adherence to him of his friends, which, at such times, becomes more pronounced and manifest.

I. THE NATURE AND CAUSES OF DEFECTION FROM CHRIST. 1. *Its nature.* It is the casting off of his rule over mind, heart, life. It may be secret or it may be open, and may be with or without emphatic declaration, with or without open adherence to a leader of rebellion against him. But it ought not to be confounded with separation from a particular Church, or renunciation of a particular humanly constructed creed. We do wrong if we condemn any one as having departed from Christ because he has departed from us. There is room for great variety of conception and expression as to Christian truth, and of modes of sincerely and truly serving Christ; and he recognizes, as loyal subjects of his, many in all Churches, and not a few outside all Churches. At the same time, it must be, and ought to be, distinctly maintained that to reject his supreme authority in matters of belief and practice, to think and express our thoughts without regard to his teaching, to feel and act without recognition of his commands, is to reject him; to openly declare that we no longer recognize his authority is open rebellion against him. 2. *Its causes.* (1) Original unreality in professed adherence to Christ. The religion of many is hereditary and traditional, and therefore only formal. They have experienced no radical change of heart. They are without true faith and love. "They have no root," and so "in time of temptation fall away" (Luke viii. 13). (2) Dislike of the government and laws of Christ. Their holiness, the extent of their requirements, their unbending nature, the restraints they impose. Pride revolts against them, and self-will, and carnality in general; and the propounders of religions that are more indulgent to the lower nature are eagerly listened to and accepted. (3) Superficial feeling as to the need of Christ. He is not felt to be indispensable to the soul; to part from him is not felt to involve very serious loss. (4) Neglect of devotion. It is by habits of prayer and other spiritual exercises that the soul is kept in communion with Christ, and his Spirit received, through whose influences faith, love, and obedience are maintained in vigour. The kingdom of Christ is spiritual, and can be realized only through the power of the Holy Ghost. (5) Dissatisfaction with the results of serving Christ. A superficial religion must be unsatisfactory; and when the vanity of its exercises and fruits is felt, no wonder if it should be given up altogether. To experience the substantial blessedness of serving Christ, we must commit ourselves to him heartily and wholly. Then we shall know too well his preciousness to heed those who would entice us to forsake him. (6) The influence of others. The men of Israel would not have deserted David when they did, if Sheba had not blown his trumpet and summoned them to follow him. In like manner, the latent disloyalty of men to Christ may remain concealed, and they may appear to be, and regard themselves as being, his good subjects, until some bolder spirit heads a revolt, and "draws away disciples after him" (Acts xx. 30). Or the pernicious influence may come from inconsistent Christians, unworthy ministers of religion, or corrupt Churches. Men do not sufficiently distinguish between Christ and his professed representatives, and find in the evil discerned in them an excuse for deserting him. (7) Disbelief of Christ's power, or will, to execute justice on those who are unfaithful to him. Did men realize the tremendous issues involved in cleaving to or rejecting Christ, they would not so loosely hold their religion or so readily abandon it. Did they seriously regard his picture of the doom of those who will not have him for their King (Luke xix. 27) as representing an awful reality, they would be more concerned to escape it.

II. REASONS WHICH INDUCE THE FAITHFUL TO CLEAVE TO THEIR KING, WHOEVER MAY DESERT HIM. 1. *Faith in his Divine authority.* That he is King by Divine right, and must and will reign, and make all his foes his footstool (Ps. ii.; cx. 1; 1 Cor. xv. 25). 2. *Love to him.* Originating in gratitude for his redeeming love, becoming attachment to him from discernment and approval of his infinite excellences, and to his government and laws, because the renewed heart is in harmony with them. 3. *Experience of the blessings of his reign.* In the heart, the home, the people who truly serve him. Hence, intense satisfaction with his service. 4. *Hope of a yet happier experience when his reign is fully established and perfected.* Hope, as the "anchor of the soul, both sure and steadfast" (Heb. vi. 19), keeps the soul steadfast when storms of temptation arise. To give up Christ would be, it is felt, to give up hope of glory in his "everlasting kingdom" (2 Pet. i. 11). 5. *Perception of the worthlessness of his rivals.* Observe the contrast presented between Sheba and David—the one "a man of Belial" (worthlessness), the other "their king." Similarly, when "many of Christ's disciples went back, and walked no more with him," and he, turning to the twelve, asked, "Will ye also go away?" Peter exclaimed, "Lord, to whom shall we go? thou hast the words of eternal life. And we believe and are sure that thou art the Christ, the Son of the living God" (John vi. 66—69). And still we may ask, "To whom shall we go?" Where shall we find one to take the place of Christ? Who has equal claims on our confidence and affection? Who can confer equal benefits? Not the irreligious multitude, whether of the coarser or the more refined sort. Not the leaders of sceptical thought, some of whom simply ignore all that renders Christ precious to the Christian; others maintain that nothing can be known of God, and that all that is believed respecting him and his relation to men belongs to the region of imagination, not of truth; and others proffer a religion without a God. The Christian sees that all who would tempt him to forsake his Lord can offer him as substitutes only "vain things, which cannot profit nor deliver" (1 Sam. xii. 21). 6. *Expectation of the coming of Christ.* The account to be then rendered, the judgments to be pronounced, the rewards and punishments to be distributed. The certainty that "he," and only he, "that shall endure unto the end shall be saved" (Matt. xxiv. 13). For these reasons, and such as these, some of which are felt most by one, and some by another; whilst many may follow this or that pretender, Christians who are really such will "cleave unto their King." —G. W.

Ver. 19.—*Peaceableness and faithfulness.* "I am one of them that are peaceable and faithful in Israel." The wise woman probably spoke in these words, not so much for herself, as for the inhabitants of her town, which Joab was besieging. Hence the adjectives are plural. She pleads the peacefulness and fidelity of the people as a reason for sparing them. It was no fault of theirs that a traitor had taken refuge amongst them. Joab acknowledges the force of her plea, and promises to depart if Sheba were delivered up to him—a promise which he fulfilled when the head of the traitor had been flung to him over the wall. The qualities here mentioned are of inestimable value; in an individual in relation to his neighbours, fellow-citizens, and fellow-Christians; in a family as between its members, and in relation to other families; in a town, between its inhabitants, and in respect to other towns; in a country, between the various classes of the people, between the people and their rulers, and in relation to other countries; and in a Church, as between its members, and in its relations with other Churches and with the community at large. They are the subject of many Scripture injunctions and promises. They are fruits of the Spirit; essential parts of the character of a Christian;

the natural product of the gospel in those who really believe it. "The kingdom of God is righteousness and peace" (Rom. xiv. 17); "The fruit of the Spirit is love, joy, peace, long-suffering, kindness, goodness, faithfulness, meekness" (Gal. v. 22, Revised Version); "Love truth and peace" (Zech. viii. 19, Revised Version).

I. PEACEABLENESS. This Christian virtue is very frequently inculcated in the Scriptures, especially the New Testament. 1. *Its nature.* It consists in a disposition to live in harmony and friendliness with all. It shows itself by courtesy and kindness; by avoidance of contention and quarrels; by carefulness not to give just or needless provocation to others; by meek endurance of provocation and even injustice from others; by readiness to give and receive explanation and apology; by quiet, unobtrusive performance of one's own duties, and abstinence from intermeddling with other people's business; by overlooking small offences, and readiness to forgive greater. 2. *Its sources.* In some it is a natural disposition. As a Christian virtue it springs from: (1) Christian love—love to Christian brethren as such, and love to all. This prompts those in whom it reigns to seek the happiness of others, and to put the most charitable construction on their conduct. It also subdues the irascible dispositions, and the selfishness which so readily leads to alienation and contention. (2) Christian humility. "By pride cometh contention" (Prov. xiii. 10). The proud exaggerate their own claims, expect too much from others, resent slight offences, insist on unreasonable reparation. But the humble avoid, without effort, such occasions of strife. Thus love and humility promote peace; and all the influences and motives which produce and foster the former are equally favourable to the latter. 3. *Its benefits.* (1) To the peaceable themselves. It is itself happiness. It secures the good will of others, the enjoyment of which is happiness. It is a frame of mind favourable to the cultivation and growth of all Christian virtues; and to all those devout exercises by which these are nourished and the favour of God realized. (2) To society. The absence of the annoyance and discomfort which the contentious occasion. The enjoyment of quietness and rest. The peaceable are also peacemakers, and promote a pacific disposition in others. If all men were peaceable, wars, small and great alike, would cease.

II. FAITHFULNESS. "Faithful," on the lips of the wise woman, probably meant "loyal" to the king. It might well include also uprightness in general. "We are a people not only peaceful, but (as the word is) reliable, trustworthy. We are honest, just, steadily occupied with a faithful discharge of our duties, at once to God, to each other, and to the state." Fidelity must be associated with peaceableness to form a noble Christian character; fidelity to Christ and God, to conscience and conviction, to truth and duty, to promises and engagements; fidelity to those to whom we are variously related in family, social, ecclesiastical, and national life. This gives strength to the character, as gentleness and peacefulness give beauty. The two qualities are not incompatible, but mutually helpful. A peaceful spirit prevents fidelity from becoming harsh, censorious, meddlesome, fierce. Fidelity prevents peacefulness from becoming an immoral weakness, which disregards justice and truth, is ever making unworthy compromises, and would rather sacrifice the highest principles than run the risk of arousing the passions of men by asserting and defending them. Only "the wisdom that is from above," which "is first pure, then peaceable, gentle, easy to be entreated, full of mercy and good fruits, without variance, without hypocrisy" (Jas. iii. 17, Revised Version); in other words, the teaching of the Holy Spirit,—can enable us to give to each of these virtues, peacefulness and faithfulness, its due place.—G. W.

Ver. 19.—*Seeking to destroy God's inheritance.* "Why wilt thou swallow up the inheritance of the Lord?" The nation of Israel was called the "inheritance" of God, because specially chosen and set apart for himself, and therefore specially valued and cared for (see Deut. iv. 20; ix. 26, 29). The "wise woman," in remonstrating with Joab against his assault on Abel, applies the term to that part of the people which dwelt there. It was an assertion of their right, as belonging to the chosen people, to be protected, not destroyed. The corresponding word in the New Testament is used of the everlasting possession which Christians will inherit, not of Christians themselves (unless Eph. i. 18 be an exception). But the idea is presented in other words (see 1 Pet. ii. 9, "a people for God's own possession," Revised Version); and the remonstrance might be appropriately addressed to any who seek to destroy the Church of God.

I. CHRISTIANS ARE THE LORD'S INHERITANCE. That part of mankind which is specially his. 1. Which he has peculiarly appropriated. All the world is his; but, while he has left the larger portion of it for a time comparatively waste, he has in a special manner claimed and separated this for himself. 2. For which he specially cares, bestowing upon it peculiar culture, watching over it with special interest. 3. From which he expects and receives special returns. Of thought, love, confidence, praise, "fruits of righteousness" (Phil. i. 11), glory (Matt. v. 16). The words, "inheritance of the Lord," may be applied to the whole Church; or (according to the analogy of the text) to any part of it, any Christian society; or to individual Christians. And it is fitted to awaken in them reflections as to the degree in which they are worthy of the name, and to encourage the sincere to expect the special protection and blessing of God.

II. THERE ARE ATTEMPTS TO DESTROY GOD'S INHERITANCE. Some are wrongly charged with such attempts. Joab declared truly that his aim was not to "swallow up or destroy" (ver. 20). He only wished to punish a traitor, by doing which he would serve instead of injuring "the inheritance of the Lord." In like manner, men who endeavour to purify the Church from error and sinful practices may be wrongly charged with seeking to destroy what their desire is to conserve. Reformers are often regarded as destructives. Such, however, do need to be cautioned lest anything in their spirit or measures should injure what is good more than correct what is evil. Some, again, injure God's inheritance without deliberate intention. Unworthy ministers of religion, hypocrites, and inconsistent Christians are of this class. But others are chargeable with *endeavouring* to destroy God's inheritance. 1. *Such as attempt to destroy faith in the great Christian verities.* Could they succeed, there would be no Christianity, no Church, no "inheritance of the Lord," left in the world. 2. *Persecutors of Christians in general, or of particular sections of them.* Various bodies of Christians have in turn sought not to convince (which is right), but to root out, their fellow-Christians, employing the civil power, if that were at their command, or, if not, using their wealth or social influence to oppress or entice in order to suppress.

III. THE EXPOSTULATION OF THE TEXT MAY BE JUSTLY ADDRESSED TO THOSE WHO MAKE SUCH ATTEMPTS. "Why wilt thou swallow up," etc.? The words may be used to urge consideration of: 1. *The reasons and motives which prompt the attempts.* Such as: (1) Hatred of piety and holiness. This often impels infidels in their assaults on the faith of Christians; but many who are called Christians, if they examined themselves, would find that it was also the motive of their endeavours to suppress Christians more in earnest than themselves. (2) Love of domination. (3) Pride of superiority, real or supposed. (4) Indignation at faithful testimony or reproof. (5) Inability to discern the marks of God's true people. The external being regarded to the exclusion of the internal and spiritual; the essential qualities being overlooked because dissociated from certain over-estimated accidentals. A blindness produced by a narrow education, or exclusive intercourse with one kind of Christians. (6) Unholy zeal, such as actuated St. Paul before his conversion (Acts xxvi. 9; Phil. iii. 6; comp. John xvi. 2). The assailants of the Church or any part or member of it may well be urged to pause and consider their real spirit and motives; and whether these will bear reflection, or are capable of justification. 2. *The impiety and unrighteousness of such attempts.* The wise woman suggests to Joab, by the words she uses, that he would be guilty of these sins if he persisted in his assault on the town. So those who assail the Church of God: (1) Sin against God. Whose inheritance they are invading. So far as they succeed, they lessen God's part in society and its affairs; they injure those who are precious in his sight ("He that toucheth you toucheth the apple of his eye," Zech. ii. 8; comp. Acts ix. 4; Rom. iv. 15, 20; 1 Cor. viii. 12). The friends of God should shrink from any conduct which tends to lessen the testimony for him in the world, and cripple those who are desirous of promoting his kingdom according to their lights. (2) They violate the rights of Christians. Every part of the Christian community is entitled to liberty of profession and "prophesying" (see Bishop Jeremy Taylor's treatise on this subject), and to sympathy and all possible help from the rest. All good citizens are entitled to the protection of the state, and cannot be justly persecuted by it on account of their religion. 3. *Their futility.* "The inheritance of the Lord" cannot be really "swallowed up," although certain portions of it may for a time be injured. "Upon this rock I will build my Church; and the gates of Hades shall not prevail against it"

(Matt. xvi. 18). 4. *The retribution which will surely follow them.* Christians who, in their blindness, make them in any degree, receive loss and injury thereby in their own souls and in their influence for good; the enemies of God will find that he is too mighty for them. He will "plead his own cause" (Ps. lxxiv. 22), and "avenge his elect" (Luke xviii. 7).—G. W.

EXPOSITION.

CHAPTER XXI.

Ver. 1.—**There was a famine in the days of David**; Hebrew, *and there was.* There is an entire absence of any mark of time to show in what part of David's reign this famine took place. It does not even follow, from the mention of Mephibosheth's name, that it must have happened at a time subsequent to the sending for that prince from Machir's house; for it may have been the search after the descendants of Saul which made David remember the son of his old friend. The burial, however, of the bones of Saul and Jonathan as an act of respect to the slaughtered king makes it probable that the narrative belongs to the early part of David's reign, as also does the apparent fact that the seven victims were all young and unmarried. Mephibosheth, we read, had a young son when David sent for him. Now, he was five years old when his father was slain (ch. iv. 4), and thus at the end of David's reign of seven years and a half at Hebron, he would be twelve and a half years of age. The famine lasted three years, and if David had been king four or five years when the famine began, Mephibosheth, at the age of twenty, might well have a "young son" in a country where men marry early. We cannot believe that the famine occurred long after David had been king of all Israel, because manifestly it would have been unjust and even monstrous to punish a nation for the sins of a king who had long passed away. The sins of its rulers are visited upon a nation constantly through a long series of years, but it is always in the way of natural development. A statesman may put a nation upon a wrong track, and may involve it in serious difficulties, and even in irretrievable disaster, unless some one be raised up able to make it retrace its steps and regain the rightful direction. But this famine was a direct interference of Providence, and to justify it the sin must be still fresh in the national remembrance. Had it been an old crime long ago forgotten, instead of leading men to repentance, this long and terrible punishment would have hardened men's hearts, and made them regard the Deity as vindictive. It is even probable that the sin was still being committed; for though commenced and approved by Saul, his oppression and purpose of gra-

dually destroying the native races was too much in accord with men's usual way of acting not to be continued, unless stopped by the justice of the ruler. We all know how the Red Indian, the Bushman, the Maori, and the Australian disappear before the advance of the white man. It needs only apathy on the part of the government, and rougher methods for clearing them off are practised than men would care to own. So with Gibeonites and Perizzites and other native races, a similar process would be going on. The lands they held, their little villages, their pastures, and above all their strongholds, would be coveted by the dominant race, and encroachments would lead to quarrels, in which the natives would find any resistance on their part punished as rebellion. Even David seized the hill-fortress of Jebus for his capital, though he still left Araunah the nominal title of king (ch. xxiv. 23). Saul had lent all the weight of the royal authority to the extermination of the natives, and this chapter records the Divine condemnation of wrong done by the dominant race to the aborigines. It remains to this day the charter for their protection, and not only forbids their extinction, but requires that they shall be treated with fair and even justice, and their rights respected and maintained. It has been objected that the execution of Saul's seven sons was a political crime committed to render David's throne secure. If at all to his advantage, it was so only to a very slight extent. The sons of Rizpah could never have become pretenders to the throne; nor were the sons of Merab likely to be much more dangerous. In a few years they would have married, and formed other ties, and been merged in the general population. Mephibosheth was the heir of Saul, and David protected him and Micha his son. It was quite in the spirit of the times to visit upon Saul's house the sins of its chief. The principle was the same as when all Israel stoned Achan, his sons and his daughters, his oxen and his asses, his sheep and his tent, for bringing iniquity upon the people (Josh. vii. 24, 25). We keep chiefly in view the doctrine of personal responsibility; in the Old Testament the other doctrine of the collective responsibility of a family, a city, a nation, was made the more prominent. It was the Prophet Ezekiel who in ch. xviii. stated clearly and with Divine force that "the soul that sinneth it shall die;" but that the sinner's son, if he walk in God's statutes, shall not die for the iniquity of his father; he shall surely live. But the collective responsibility enacted in the second commandment is still God's law. In the philosophic jargon of our times the two factors which form human character and decide our fortunes are "heredity and environment." Heredity was the prevailing sentiment in David's days; and it seemed right to the Gibeonites that the sons of the man who had slaughtered them should die for their father's sins; and it seemed just to David also. But he spared the heir to Saul's throne. There is no adequate reason for supposing that David was influenced by political motives, and the more important lesson of the narrative is the emphatic condemnation given in it of wrong and cruelty to aboriginal tribes. **David inquired of the Lord**; Hebrew, *David sought the face of Jehovah*. The phrase is remarkable, and not found elsewhere in Samuel. Probably it means that he went to Gibeon to pray in the sanctuary, and consult God by Urim and Thummim. **His bloody house.** The Hebrew means "the house on which rested the guilt of murder."

Ver. 2.—**Saul sought to slay them in his zeal.** We gather from various incidental circumstances that Saul, in some part of his reign, manifested great zeal in an attempt to carry out literally the enactments of the Levitical Law; but he seems to have done so with the same ferocity as that which he displayed in slaughtering the priests at Nob with their wives and children. Thus he had put to death wizards and all who dealt with familiar spirits (1 Sam. xxviii. 9), in accordance with Exod. xxii. 18 and Lev. xx. 6. In the same way he seems to have tried to exterminate the aboriginal inhabitants of Palestine, in accordance with Deut. vii. 2, and had especially massacred a large number of Gibeonites, in violation of the covenant made with them by Joshua and all Israel (Josh. ix. 3, 15—27). And as he would thus acquire "fields and vineyards" robbed from them to give to his captains, his conduct was probably popular, and the cause of a general system of wrong and oppression practised upon all the natives. It had thus become a national sin, and as such was punished by a national calamity. **Amorites**; that is highlanders, mountaineers. Strictly they were Hivites (Josh. ix. 7).

Ver. 3.—**Wherewith shall I make the atonement**, etc.? Literally the verb means to "cover up," the idea being that of a veil drawn over the offence to conceal it by means of a gift or offering. Thence gradually it attained to its religious idea of an expiation.

Ver. 4 —**No silver nor gold.** It is a common practice in most semi-civilized nations for a fine to be accepted as compensation for the shedding of blood. As no distinction was drawn between murder and homicide, and as the nearest relative was bound in every case to revenge the blood shed, the custom of receiving a money compensation gradually grew up to prevent the tribe or nation being torn to pieces by interminable revenge. The Arabs still retain this usage, but it was forbidden by the Levitical Law (Numb. xxxv. 31), and rightly so, because a distinction was there made between murder and accidental bloodshed, and precautions taken for the rescue of one who had not acted with malice. **Neither for us shalt thou kill any man in Israel.** The singular is used at the beginning of their answer, in the same way as in ch. xix. 42, 43. Literally their words are, *It is not to me a matter of silver and gold with Saul and his house, nor is it for us to put to death any one in Israel;* that is, "We refuse a money compensation, and it is beyond our power to exact the blood-penalty which would gratify our anger." They make it quite plain that they do want blood, while the Authorized Version makes them say that they do not. The Revised Version more correctly translates, "Neither is it for us to put any man to death in Israel."

Ver. 5.—**The man that consumed us**, etc. The strong language of this verse makes it plain that Saul had been guilty, not merely of some one great act of cruelty, but of a long series of barbarities intended to bring about their utter extirpation.

Ver. 6.—**We will hang them.** The punishment indicated here really was impalement, but in Numb. xxv. 4, where the same verb is used, we find that the criminals were put to death first, and that the impalement was for the purpose of exposing their bodies to view, like the practice a century ago of gibbeting. But the Gibeonites were probably very barbarous, and, when David had delivered the seven lads into their hands, would perhaps wreak upon them a cruel vengeance. *Seven* were chosen, because it is the perfect number, with many religious associations; and **unto the Lord** means "publicly." So among the Romans *sub Jove* meant "in the open air" (comp. Numb. xxv. 4). **In Gibeah.** This was Saul's native place and home, and was selected by the Gibeonites as the spot where the bodies should be exposed, to add to the humiliation and shame of the fallen dynasty. **Saul, whom the Lord did choose.** If this reading is correct, the phrase can only be used as a taunt. But in ver. 9 we find *bahar*, "on the hill," instead of *behir*, "chosen," and the right reading probably is, "in Gibeah, on the hill of Jehovah."

Ver. 8.—**Michal.** It was Merab who became the wife of Adriel the Meholathite (1 Sam. xviii. 19). Michal was childless (see ch. vi. 23). **Whom she brought up for.** This is one of the many cases of untrustworthiness in the renderings of the Authorized Version. We have noticed a very flagrant instance before in ch. v. 21. The object of these mistranslations is always the same, namely, to remove some verbal discrepancy in the Hebrew text. The Hebrew says here "five sons of Michal, whom she bare to Adriel;" but Michal never bore a child, therefore something must be substituted which will save the Hebrew from this verbal inaccuracy, and Michal must be represented as having taken Merab's place (perhaps at her death), and been foster-mother to her children. This explanation is, it is true, taken from the Jewish Targum; but the Targum never professes to be an exact translation, and constantly perverts the meaning of the plainest passages for preconceived reasons.

Ver. 9.—**The beginning of barley harvest.** The barley became ripe in April, about the time of the Passover (Deut. xvi. 9). The wheat was not ripe till Pentecost.

Ver. 10.—**Rizpah ... took sackcloth, and spread it for her upon the rock;** rather, *against the rock*, so as to form a little hut or shelter to protect her from the glaring blaze of the sunshine. The word "upon" has led many commentators to suppose that she used it as a bed; but this is not the meaning of the Hebrew, though given by the Vulgate. The sackcloth was the loose wrapper or cloak which formed the outer dress of mourners. As regards the bodies of those crucified or impaled, the Law required that they should be taken down and buried that same evening (Deut. xxi. 23). Here they remained exposed for six months, as a grim trophy of Gibeonite vengeance. **Until water dropped upon them out of heaven;** Hebrew, *was poured upon them;* until copious and heavy rains came. The outpouring of these rains would put an end to the famine, and be regarded as a proof that the wrath of Heaven was appeased. There is no reason for supposing that these rains came before the usual period, in autumn, which was about the middle of October. Thus, for six months, with no other protection than her mantle of sackcloth hung against the rock, this noble woman watched the decaying bodies of her loved ones, until at last her devoted conduct touched David's heart, and their remains were honourably interred.

Ver. 12.—**The street of Beth-shan;** Hebrew, *the broad place*, or square, just inside the gate, where the citizens met for business. It was upon the wall of this square

that the Philistines had hanged the bodies of Saul and of his sons (1 Sam. xxxi. 12). **The men of Jabesh-Gilead;** Hebrew, *the lords* or owners *of Jabesh-Gilead.* The phrase occurs also in 1 Sam. xxiii. 11, 12 of the citizens of Keilah, and is found also in the Books of Joshua and Judges. (For the brave exploit of these men in rescuing the bodies of their king and his sons, see 1 Sam. xxxi. 11—13; and for David's generous approval, ch. ii. 5.)

Ver. 14.—**The bones of Saul and Jonathan.** The Septuagint adds, "and the bones of them that were hanged." As it is expressly said in ver. 13 that these bones were collected, we cannot doubt but that the remains of the seven grandsons were interred with those of Saul and Jonathan, in the tomb of Kish, their common ancestor. But whether the Septuagint has preserved words that have dropped out of the Hebrew text, or has added them to make the fact plain, is more than we can answer. **Zelah.** Nothing more is known of this place than that it was in the tribe of Benjamin.

Ver. 15.—**Moreover.** A new narrative begins here, and the heroic acts related in it are taken probably from some record of the martial deeds of David and his mighties. We have already seen that the Book of Jasher (ch. i. 18) was a national anthology, full of ballads and songs in praise of glorious exploits of Israel's worthies. The source of the narratives recorded here apparently was a history in prose, and commenced, perhaps, with David's own achievement in slaying Goliath —a deed which called forth the heroism of the nation, and was emulated by other brave men. These extracts were probably given for their own sake, and are repeated in 1 Chron. xx. 4—8, where they are placed immediately after the capture of Rabbah; but they here form an appropriate introduction to the psalm of thanksgiving in ch. xxii. It was usual in Hebrew, in making quotations, to leave them without any attempt at adapting them to their new place; and thus the "moreover" and "yet again," which referred to some previous narrative in the history, are left unchanged.

Ver. 16.—**Ishbi-benob.** The Hebrew has *Ishbo-benob*, which Gesenius interprets as meaning "dweller upon the height." But surely the man's name would not be Hebrew; he was a Raphah, and we shall not be able to explain his name until we know the language of the Rephaim. **Of the sons of the giant;** Hebrew, *of the children of the Raphah;* that is, he belonged to the race of the Rephaim, the word not signifying "sons," but the members of a stock. It is translated "children" in Numb. xiii. 22, 28, etc. (For the Rephaim, see note on ch. v. 18.) "The Raphah" may be the mythic progenitor of the Rephaim, but more probably it is simply the singular of "Rephaim," and "children of the Raphah" a more poetic way of describing the race. **Three hundred shekels.** It weighed, therefore, about eight pounds; the spear-head of Goliath was just twice as heavy (1 Sam. xvii. 7). **Girded with a new.** The Vulgate supplies "sword," which the Authorized Version has adopted. The Septuagint reads a "mace" instead of "new;" others think that he had a new suit of armour. If the narrator had thought it of sufficient importance to let us know that the article was new, he would scarcely have left the thing itself unspecified. It is evident, however, that the Septuagint did not read *hadasha*, "new," but the name of some strange warlike instrument, which being unknown to the scribes, they substituted for it a word which they did know, but which makes no sense. We cannot, however, depend upon the translation of the Septuagint, "mace." The want of special knowledge on the part of the translators of the Septuagint, though partly accounted for by the long absence from Palestine of its authors, and their having to depend entirely upon such knowledge of their language as survived at Alexandria, is more than we should have expected or can quite understand. Here, however, there is nothing remarkable in their not knowing the exact meaning of this curious weapon of the Rephaite; but plainly it could not be a mace, but must have been something that could be girt upon him. The Authorized Version, moreover, gives a look of probability to the insertion of "sword," which is wanting in the Hebrew; for it does not connect his purpose of killing David with the hadasha. The Hebrew is, "And Ishbo-benob, who was a Rephaite, and whose spear weighed three hundred shekels, and who was girt with an hadasha; and he thought to smite David."

Ver. 17.—**The men of David sware unto him.** David's men were specifically the mighties, who had so long been his friends and companions. They now bound him by an oath never again to fight in person, lest he should be singled out for combat by some warrior among the enemy and slain. **The light of Israel.** The lamp in the dwelling was the proof that there was life there, and so it became the symbol of prosperity. In Job xviii. 5, 6 the extinction of the lamp signifies the destruction of the family. David was evidently now king, and under him Israel was advancing to freedom and empire. His death would have plunged the nation back into weakness and probable ruin.

Ver. 18.—**Gob.** In the parallel passage (1 Chron. xx. 4) this place is called *Gezer*, and the Septuagint has *Gath*. It was probably some unimportant spot, except as being the site of this battle, and the scribes, knowing nothing about it, made corrections at their fancy. **Sibbechai the Hushathite.** The name is spelt in the same way in 1 Chron. xi. 29 and xx. 4, but in the list of the mighties he is called Mebunnai (ch. xxiii. 27). In 1 Chron. xxvii. 11 we find that he had the command of the eighth division of the army, consisting of twenty-four thousand men. He is called "the Hushathite," as being a descendant of Hushah, of the family of Judah, in 1 Chron. iv. 4. **Saph, which** was of the sons of the giant; Hebrew, *of the Raphah*. He is called *Sippai* in 1 Chron. xx. 4.

Ver. 19.—**Elhanan the son of Jaare-oregim, a Beth-lehemite, slew Goliath the Gittite.** The words "the brother of" are inserted by the Authorized Version in order to bring this place into verbal agreement with 1 Chron. xx. 5, where we read that "Elhanan the son of Jair slew Lahmi the brother of Goliath the Gittite." The Jewish Targum had the same reading as that still found in the text, but regards Elhanan, "God is gracious," as another name for David, and, instead of Jair or Jaare, reads Jesse. Its translation is as follows: "And David the son of Jesse, the weaver of veils for the sanctuary, who was of Bethlehem, slew Goliath the Gittite." Possibly the Authorized Version is right in concluding that the present text is a corruption of that in 1 Chron. xx. 5. For, first, the repetition of *oregim*, "weavers," is suspicious, the Hebrew being, not "weaver's beam," but the plural "weavers' beam," *menor oregim*. Next, *Jaare* is a transposition of the letters of Jair (in the Hebrew) made probably in order that the compound *Jaare-oregim* may obey the rules of Hebrew grammar. More important is it to notice that *Lahmi* is part of the word "Bethlehemite" (Hebrew, *Beth-hallahmi*), and might thus easily suggest to the eye of a scribe the completion of so well-known a word. We must add that among the thirty Gibborim is "Elhanan the son of Dodo of Bethlehem." Whoever slew Goliath's brother would certainly attain to high rank among the heroes, but if the name *Jair* is right, the Elhanan there spoken of is not the person who slew Lahmi.

Ver. 21.—**Jonathan.** He was brother to the subtle Jonadab who helped Amnon on his way to ruin. The spelling of the father's name shows how little importance we can place on the Hebrew text in the matter of names. He is called here in the Hebrew Shimei, which the Massorites have changed into Shimeah. In ch. xiii. 3 we have *Shimeah*, in 1 Sam. xvi. 9 *Shammah*, and in 1 Chron. ii. 13 *Shimma*.

Ver. 22.—**These four were born to the giant**; Hebrew, *were born to the Raphah;* that is, belonged to the race of the Rephaim, who seem to have settled in Gath in large numbers, and to have been a fine race of men. (For their antiquity, see Gen. xiv. 5.) **By the hand of David.** Not necessarily in personal conflict, though the Hebrew in ver. 17 would admit of the translation that, with the aid of Abishai, David himself slew Ishbi-benob. But the glory of all that the Gibborim did belonged also to David their king.

HOMILETICS.

Vers. 1—14.—*A story of deferred retribution.* The facts are: 1. A famine continuing for three years, and inquiry being made of the Lord by David, he is informed that it was in consequence of Saul's sin in slaying the Gibeonites. 2. David, asking of the Gibeonites what he shall do for them by way of atonement for the wrong done, is informed that they seek not gold or the life of any man of Israel, but require that seven of Saul's family should be put to death, and hung up in Gibeah of Saul. 3. David at once yields to the demand, but spares Mephibosheth in consequence of the special bond between himself and Jonathan. 4. On the seven men being put to death, Rizpah spreads out sackcloth on a rock, and keeps watch by the corpses against beasts and birds of prey till the rain falls. 5. David is told of the deed of Rizpah, and he soon after obtains the bones of Saul and Jonathan from Jabesh-Gilead, and causes the remains of the seven sons to be collected, and has the bones of Saul and Jonathan interred in the family burying-place in Zelah of Benjamin. We assume that the record in this chapter refers to an earlier period in the life of David than does the narrative in the few preceding chapters, which evidently are designed to set forth the connection of David's great sin with its punishment. The story relates the incidents connected with an otherwise unrecorded sin of Saul's, and the retribution which came in due course upon his house. The varied questions and topics of interest and difficulty suggested by the narrative may be best seen and considered by taking them in their natural order.

I. PROVIDENTIAL CALLS TO THE CONSIDERATION OF FORGOTTEN SINS. Whatever physical account may be possible of the famine referred to, looked at in its relation to God's education and discipline of his ancient people, it is here to be viewed as a providential call to the nation to reflect on sins committed during the reign of Saul. The conduct of Saul was a most scandalous sin (Josh. ix. 8—17). When the sin was committed we know not; probably in the latter part of his reign, when all was in confusion. His family were, it would seem from vers. 1, 4—6, implicated in the deed. It is obvious that the nation had condoned the action of Saul, and for some years subsequent to his death there was no conscience in the people with respect to this great sin. It was for the purpose of arousing the public conscience and giving occasion for bringing this sin to mind that the famine was permitted to arise. Even though the famine was by natural causes, yet it was used by God for this special moral end. There is a tendency in nations especially to be unmindful of their sins, and individuals also are liable to the same danger. The eager rush of affairs and absorption of energy in new lines divert attention from the moral character of acts. The forgotten sins of men are countless. But God does not forget, and now and then events arise—calamities, personal troubles, and disagreeable consequences of former deeds—which are practically God's calls to us to remember our transgressions. The prophet no longer proclaims, but God reaches the conscience in manifold ways, and to many an easy-going soul the words will come some day, " Son, remember."

II. THE CONNECTION BETWEEN MORAL AND PHYSICAL EVIL. The mention of famine in the land, and the public sin of the late king as being related the one to the other, establishes in this instance, on the authority of God, the close connection of moral and physical evil. Whether famines do not arise where there is no special moral evil of which they are the chastisements or reminders, is not the question, and makes no difference to the fact in this case. God would have his people know that their past sins were now bearing fruit in physical form. Nor is there anything really wonderful or exceptional in the truth here established. To man, physical evil is, as a whole, the fruit of sin. Man's moral nature is in contact with the physical order by means of a material vehicle, and as his moral nature is supreme and cannot but affect, by its deterioration and wrong direction, the vehicle by which it acts, so the lesser must be disordered by the disorder of the greater. The miseries of human life would not have come had man kept his first estate. All our painful struggles in commerce and war, our diseases and poverty, are the outcome of a heart not as the heart of God. That Sodom should fall under fire, that Pharaoh should be swept into the sea, that Jerusalem should be trodden down, were but physical facts consequent on sin, bold and striking, yet not different in essence from the general connection of sin and suffering. Hence, Christ's mission to make man's physical environment for ever helpful and not hurtful to him, by rendering his moral nature perfect, and therefore his whole nature in perfect adjustment to all that is.

III. THE DUTY OF SEARCHING OUT THE MORAL ELEMENTS CONNECTED WITH OUR PHYSICAL TROUBLES. The famine was a reality in the experience of every one; but it was the will of God that the people should notice its connection with national sin. They must consider its spiritual bearings; they must associate their difficulties with previous conduct. As a rule, there is an indisposition to do this. Physical law, fate, chance, almost anything, is referred to as being occasion or cause of present difficulties and sufferings, rather than personal sin. Of course, individual sin is not the cause of great public calamities, and not immediately of private sufferings. Yet we ought, as a matter of rigid thought, to trace back the physical troubles of the world, so far as man is sufferer, to the moral cause. In nations troubles are referred to the restlessness of other nations, or ignorance of political economy, or of sanitary laws, or decaying commerce; but we should go deeper, and see what pride and arrogance and defiant tone may have done to inflame other nations, and what sinful neglect in spending money on wars rather than on instruction of the people. In personal life we should search and see to what extent failures in business, in health, and enterprise are connected with persistent violation of some of the primary laws which God has given for our guidance.

IV. MISSING CLUES TO THE SOLUTION OF DIFFICULTIES. There are evident difficulties connected with this narrative which press upon the ordinary reader at once. The demand for seven lives, and the yielding to the demand, both perplex us. The pressure of a famine on a whole people, and the use of that famine for purposes of chastisement for a sin of years past, do not lessen the perplexity. Apart from this narrative, we know nothing of any act done by Saul toward the Gibeonites. Now, if instead of this abrupt declaration of the existence of a national sin, and of the retribution for it in the terrible form of seven deaths, we were told of the precise circumstances under which Saul violated the national compact of Josh. ix. 15—17, we should then certainly see the wisdom and appropriateness of the famine to arouse the national conscience, and the justice of the terrible retribution on Saul's family. The clue here missing because of the incompleteness of history is but an instance of what constantly occurs. In the Bible there are many facts which doubtless would lose all their strangeness and seeming discrepancies and moral difficulties did we but know the details left unrecorded. Historians are guided by this remembrance of missing clues in their estimate of men and characters. In our judgment on conduct we often fail or are in suspense because a clue to some strange feature is lacking. Especially are we at present lacking the clue to many events in the government of God. When we know more perfectly, we shall see that to be just which is now perplexing, and, as a rule, we may say that our ignorance of hidden facts ought to count in our judgments on revealed truth as much as our knowledge.

V. GOD HAS IN RESERVE AGENCIES FOR BRINGING THE FACT OF SIN STRAIGHT HOME TO THE CONSCIENCE. The famine aroused conscience. The men of Gibeon were God's agents in bringing all the facts home to the conscience of the nation. The confusion and change of government in the last days of Saul and early years of David, before he left Hebron to be king over the entire people, will explain why the Gibeonites did not press their suit earlier. Although the sin was so grievous, it must have appeared to any who now and then reflected on it as though it were being passed by, and that no means were at hand to bring the new king face to face with the wrong done. But at the proper season God found means for calling forth the Gibeonites to declare the full facts and to bring the sin home to the national conscience. They proved what the famine only indicated.   According to Scripture, all sin is to be brought home to the sinner.   The time may pass, and means for so doing may seem to be lacking; but the universe is God's, and he has in reserve agencies by which the guilty will be found out and the claims of a violated law will be vindicated (Eccles. xi. 9).

VI. THE PRINCIPLE OF RETRIBUTION IN HUMAN AFFAIRS.   The charge of the Gibeonites against the house of Saul was that he, contrary to the solemn compact with Israel, had cruelly slain their countrymen, and the demand was that for this wicked violation of a treaty the lives of his sons should be forfeited.   Here was an appearance of hardship on the sons; but, had we the missing clue, it would probably appear that they were parties to the deed.   The deed, however, was national, being wrought by the representative of the nation; and, acting on the usage of the age in such matters, the Gibeonites demanded that the lives of the representatives of the nation of that date should be sacrificed.   The principle was that of *lex talionis*—"an eye for an eye." We are not called upon to pronounce a harsh judgment on their demand.   It may, however, be said, in extenuation, that if Saul and his family were the real murderers of the Gibeonites, there was no more wrong in their execution than in the execution of any modern murderer.   The principle on which the claim proceeded was that of all criminal law in relation to human life.   The Law of Moses was based on it.   " An eye for an eye " (Exod. xxi. 24) is but a statement of the principle that runs through all the Mosaic laws (cf. Lev. xxiv. 17—22).   Ox for ox, sheep for sheep, life for life,—this was the form of the old jurisprudence.   It is also, so far as circumstances permit, the principle of modern law and modern punishment.   According to a man's crime so is his punishment.   With us the loss of liberty is the form punishment takes, but its degree depends on the degree of the crime.   Proportion is kept in view in every sentence.   The words of our Saviour (Matt. v. 38, 39) are not intended to set aside the administration of justice by the state, but to indicate that the personal feeling of his followers is not to be vindictive.   In the spiritual kingdom all are brethren beloved, and love is to be the dominant feeling.   Moses was speaking of what "judges," administrators of the public laws of the state, should do (Deut. xix. 16—21), and in the discharge of official duty they were to be impartial, and not pity or spare.   Christ speaks of what his individual followers should do and be in their personal relations to brethren in the new spiritual kingdom; they must not imagine, with the Pharisees, that a principle of action designed for " judges " in a state is to be transferred to their private relationships in his kingdom.   Moses distinguishes between the rigid execution of justice on crime and the individual cherishing of tender and pitiful feelings (Deut. xix. 16—21; cf. Exod. xxii. 21—27).   The rules for a state are not to be confounded with rules for individual life.

VII. THE DUE MAINTENANCE OF NATIONAL HONOUR.   The honour of Israel was at stake in the deed of Saul.   Kings compromise the nation.   David was quick to see that the wrong done in cruelly violating a national treaty must be atoned.   Apart from the form of atonement in this case, the principle recognized is most important. When nations lose faith in nations, trouble must come in terrible form.   A nation's word should be sacred, and in relation to the weakest and most barbarous as to the mightiest and most civilized.   The methods adopted for upholding national honour will vary with the conceptions of what that honour is.   To keep faith, to be courteous and considerate to the weak, to allow of no unjust concessions to the great because they are great, and to promote peace and righteousness in all relationships,—this is that in which honour lies.   There is no true glory, no maintenance of honour, in creating wars, in mere military triumphs, or in vaunting of greatness.

VIII. THE SACREDNESS OF PROMISES MADE BY RELIGIOUS MEN.   The promises made to the Gibeonites in the days of Joshua differed from all engagements entered into by other people, in that they were the promises of the chosen race, whose conduct towards others was based on higher principles.   David felt at once that it would be shocking to allow heathen men to imagine that the servants of the covenant-keeping God could break their vows.   The possession of a religious character or the adoption of religious professions lends a special sacredness to our engagements.   It is no wonderful thing if one who believes in no eternal morality easily sets aside what others hold to be binding engagements; and a careless man of the world, whose religion is only a name, may not excite surprise if he sometimes violates his word or does a mean action.   But to be a follower of Christ lends an unusual sanctity to everything in life. The Apostle Peter has suggested "what manner of persons" we ought to be by virtue of our holy profession, and our Lord himself expects more of his followers than can be looked for from others (Matt. v. 43—48). We should not forget that we may compromise the honour of our Lord in our words and deeds.

IX. THE CONFLICTING OF PUBLIC OBLIGATIONS WITH PRIVATE ENGAGEMENTS. David, acting according to the light and usage of the age, felt bound to give up the male members of the house of Saul; but he had made a personal promise to Jonathan (1 Sam. xx. 14—17; xxiii. 16—18) to spare the members of his house, and had especially taken Mephibosheth under his care out of love for his father. Here, then, was a conflict of opposing obligations. The solution was obvious. He had kept his promise, and had not, as kings too often were accustomed to do with the families of rivals, cut off the house of Saul on ascending the throne. If he gave them up now it was not a personal act, but an act in the administration of law. But, further, he seems to have regarded the oath to Jonathan as relating to his own immediate descendants, and hence he spared Mephibosheth in order to keep his kingly promise while making acknowledgment for the sin of Saul. Rulers are bound to be true to national obligations, though at the cost of much feeling, and sometimes it will require more than mere casuistry to be true to private sentiments and obligations while discharging public duties. Self is never to be degraded in public affairs. If in nation or Church the rulers cannot conscientiously discharge obligations involved in the office, the proper alternative is to vacate the office.

X. THE HONOUR DUE TO MORTAL REMAINS. The conduct of Rizpah in keeping off birds and beasts of prey from the corpses, and of David in collecting the bones and placing the remains of Saul and Jonathan in their family burying-place, was worthy of their character; it indicated a refined feeling, a reverence for the dead, a deep sense of the sanctity of all that pertains to human life and human destiny. The mortal remains of friend and foe are touchingly suggestive of the greatness and littleness of man, of his checkered lot on earth, and the strange unknown experience on which his higher nature enters while his perishable remains abide with us.

Vers. 15—22.—*The difficulty of establishing the kingdom of God in the world.* The facts are: 1. In one of his wars with the Philistines David waxes faint in personal conflict with a giant, and is succoured by the intervention of Abishai. 2. Observing the failing strength of the king, his people deprecate his going forth with them to battle, lest by personal failure he should be a means of general discouragement. 3. On each of three subsequent occasions of battle, a Philistine giant is slain respectively by Sibbechai, Elhanan, and Jonathan son of Shimeah. It is of no moment as to what precise period in David's life the battles with the Philistines belonged. The first impression on reading the narrative and, at the same time, remembering the promise that Israel was to subdue and hold the land, is the tediousness of the process by which the complete subjugation of the heathen was effected, and the imperfection of the result even at this late period in the national history. Israel all along had represented the principles of true religion as against idolatry, and the special object of David's wars was to render the cause he represented triumphant over all enemies, and so establish the theocracy on an enduring basis. The difficulties of achieving the end in view are suggested by the necessity of these successive conflicts with a most active and stubborn foe. In general outline we have here an analogy with the work which the Christian Church has in hand, and the difficulties attending its speedy and complete accomplishment. The difficulties attending the subjugation of all opposing forces to the kingdom of Christ, and so permanently establishing a reign of righteousness in the earth, may be indicated as follows.

I. THERE IS A WIDESPREAD AND TENACIOUS PREOCCUPATION BY EVIL. The Philistines were a numerous people, spread over a considerable area of country, bold, resolute, powerful, and therefore very tenacious of their possessions and of their local influence. They did not always wait to be subdued, but became active in their assaults on the kingdom ordained of God. As compared with them, the Israelites were not so hardy, so desperate in fighting, and so strongly influenced by the thought of ancient pre-eminence. It is not surprising that the conflict should extend through long and weary years. And is there not some resemblance here to modern facts? The earth is preoccupied by forces of evil—numerous, strong, tenacious. The power of sin has laid hold of every form of human activity, and has entered into all the public and private ramifications of life. Our preachers at home and missionaries abroad have to face evils hoary with age, and yet strong with the vigour of youth. Nothing is more conspicuous to Christian workers than the terrible grip with which sin holds the human soul to prevent the enthronement there of the King of righteousness.

II. THERE ARE MANY IMPERFECTIONS INHERITED WITH THE WORK WE HAVE TO DO. David's people had not been as true to God as was required of Israel by the great Law laid down for their guidance; and much of this imperfection of character was an inheritance from the generations which had also failed to fulfil the moral conditions of conquest as laid down by the great lawgiver (Deut. xxviii. 1, 7—10, 15, 25). Because Israel of the past had not been fully faithful, Israel of David's age found many conquests unachieved. Failure in moral character ensured to posterity an inheritance of difficulty and sorrow. The work which a thoroughly righteous people could have accomplished remains unfinished, with the additional difficulties created by unfaithfulness. Unfortunately, the Christian Church has too closely followed the example of ancient Israel. There has been, in ages past, sometimes a deviation from the principles laid down by Christ for the casting out of sin and the subjugation of the world to himself, and sometimes a very inefficient application of his instructions. Instead of pure truth, love, faith, holiness of life, prayer, and unity of spirit, there has been a blending of the truth with human errors, and a manifestation of a worldly, time-serving spirit. This age inherits not only the honour of subduing the world to Christ, but the results of the imperfect work done in days gone by. Our own spirit is not so pure and fit as it otherwise would have been; unfinished undertakings are on hand, and the prejudice created by the sins and errors of the Church has to be overcome in addition to the ordinary power of sin.

III. THERE ARE OCCASIONALLY PRESENT GIANT FORMS OF EVIL WHICH, BESIDES BEING ACTIVE CAUSES, TEND ALSO INDIRECTLY TO EMBARRASS THOSE WHO OPPOSE THEM. Philistine giants not only had stout arms wherewith to slay, but their proportions, striking on the senses of men, had the effect of rendering the existing means of resistance and attack less easily available. Giant forms excite fear and awaken self-distrust. The indirect influence on good men of great evils is helpful to the perpetuation of those evils. The monstrous forms of idolatry in vast populations, the magnitude of the influence of Mohammed, the terrible hold of intemperance on multitudes, and the greatness of evil as a whole in the world, when looked at with ordinary eyes, at once bring on a temporary paralysis of energy. Many a brave heart faints in contemplation of the dreadful forms of evil that afflict the world. The Apostle Paul felt this when he reminded his friends to "put on the whole armour of God" (Eph. vi. 11—13), seeing that they had to wrestle with "principalities and powers."

IV. THE VARIABLE CHARACTER OF PROFESSING CHRISTIANS INJURIOUSLY AFFECTS THE PROGRESS OF THEIR ENTERPRISE. There was a day when David, fresh, young, pure, full of faith and courage, without after-thoughts concerning himself, could calmly face and slay a giant (1 Sam. xvii. 39—47). But David, passing the meridian of life, sensible of failing powers, and moreover not free from the remembrance of sad departures from his God, could not perform exploits as of old, and was even in need of succour from another in the field. A true picture is this of many in the Christian warfare. They do not retain all the old vigour. The freshness and power of godliness fail. Were every Christian to grow in spiritual strength from first to last, were the spiritual forces in our religious life to gain momentum the longer we live, and none to become weak, what a mighty army would the Church become! The difficulty of subduing the world to Christ lies very much in the variability of spritual strength in those who form the Church. Many are feeble who ought to be strong.

V. THE NEGATIVE INFLUENCE OF LEADERS IS WIDESPREAD. The friends of David were wise in wishing him not to go out to battle. The negative effect of his weakness would be so much positive advantage to the Philistines. If he could no longer positively inspire by his courage and exploits, that very circumstance would tell against the cause he and they had at heart. Leaders have great power by virtue of their position; and when, by any failure of character, or wisdom, or knowledge, any inaptitude for the special circumstances of the time, they dishearten those who expect example and guidance, they really, by such negation of good, add to the difficulties of the situation, and unwittingly strengthen the position of evil in the world. It would form an instructive study to trace in history the connection of the slow progress of Christianity with the negative influence of its leaders.

HOMILIES BY VARIOUS AUTHORS.

Vers. 1—14.—(GIBEON, GIBEAH.) *Famine.* "And there was a famine in the days of David three years, year after year" (ver. 1). [*Summary* of the remaining portion (or appendix) of this book: 1. The famine. 2. Victorious acts in wars with the Philistines (vers. 15—22). 3. David's song of thanksgiving (looking backward); ch. xxii. 4. His last prophetic words (looking forward); ch. xxiii. 1—7. "These two lyrical and prophetic productions of David, the ripest spiritual fruit of his life, form a worthy conclusion to his reign" (Keil). 5. List of his heroes (forming, with 2, an historical framework for 3 and 4); ch. xxiii. 8—39. 6. The pestilence (with the famine, "two Divine punishments inflicted upon Israel, with the expiation of the sins that occasioned them"); ch. xxiv.] This famine took place after Mephibosheth was brought to Jerusalem (ver. 7; ch. ix.); and, perhaps, about seventeen years after the death of Saul (ch. iv. 4; ix. 12). It is mentioned here "as a practical illustration, on the one hand, of the manner in which Jehovah visited upon the house of Saul, even after the death of Saul himself, a crime which had been committed by him; and, on the other hand, of the way in which, even in such a case as this, when David had been obliged to sacrifice the descendants of Saul to expiate the guilt of their father, he showed his tenderness towards him by the honourable burial of their bones." After long prosperity and plenty there came adversity and destitution. No rain "out of heaven" (ver. 10) for three successive years! What a scene of general, intense, and increasing distress must have been witnessed (Gen. xii. 10; xxvi. 1; xlvii. 13; Ruth i. 1; 1 Kings xviii. 5; 2 Kings vi. 25; xxv. 5; Jer. xiv. 1—10; Acts xi. 28). Nor has it been unknown in modern times. Consider it (with its attendant circumstances) as—

I. CALLING FOR SPECIAL INQUIRY. "And David sought the face of Jehovah" (ver. 1), equivalent to "inquired of Jehovah" (ch. v. 19), by means of the Urim and Thummim through the high priest (the last recorded instance of this method of ascertaining the Divine will, henceforth more fully revealed through the prophets); urged by the cry of distress, especially among "the poorest sort of the people of the land" (2 Kings xxiv. 14), on whom the famine pressed with peculiar severity. 1. The misery of the poor and afflicted produces in every faithful ruler and in every right-hearted man a feeling of compassionate and *anxious concern.* 2. Physical calamities are often due to *moral causes;* they follow human disobedience to moral laws; being in some cases manifestly connected with such disobedience (as when famine follows desolating wars, agricultural neglect, etc.), in others, however, not directly and apparently so connected. This connection is evident (1) from the common convictions of men who instinctively associate calamity with crime; (2) from the plain teachings of Scripture (Deut. xxviii. 15, 23, 24; Ezek. xiv. 21); and (3) from the moral government of the living, personal God, wherein all things are ordered with a view to moral ends. 3. These causes should be diligently *searched out,* by proper means—observation, consideration, prayer—in order to their removal. "It is not superstition, but rather the highest piety and the highest philosophy, which leads a people, under such a visitation as that of famine, to turn to Jehovah, saying, 'Show us wherefore thou contendest with us'" (W. M. Taylor). "Let us search and try our ways," etc. (Lam. iii. 40; 1 Sam. iv. 3).

II. LEADING TO UNEXPECTED DISCOVERY. "And Jehovah said (through the oracle), Concerning Saul and concerning the blood-guilty house, because he slew the Gibeonites." A crime which had been committed, not recently, but twenty or even thirty years before, was brought to remembrance, and set before the national conscience, quickened in its sensibility by the experience of affliction. "David must hitherto have ruled in a very irreproachable manner to render it necessary to go further back to find a cause for the calamity" (Ewald). 1. *Its iniquity was great.* An attempt was made to exterminate (consume and destroy, ver. 5) a poor, dependent, and helpless people; of the original inhabitants of the land (ver. 2; Josh. ix. 3—27), spared by solemn oath, devoted to the service of the sanctuary (now at Gibeon), for more than four hundred years dwelling peaceably among "the children of Israel and Judah" (Josh. ix. 17; ch. iv. 3), professing the same faith, and guilty of no offence; many of them being ruthlessly slain, others escaping by flight.   2. *Its effects were still felt* by the "hewers of wood and drawers of water" (*Nethinim*, bondmen), who survived, in bitter grief, popular odium, heavier servitude.   Their cries "entered into the ears of the Lord of sabaoth" (Jas. v. 4).   3. *Its guilt was unacknowledged* and unexpiated; the wrong unredressed, the sin unrepented of, and even ignored and well-nigh forgotten.   "It would seem that Saul viewed their possessions with a covetous eye, as affording him the means of rewarding his *adherents* (1 Sam. xxii. 7) and of enriching his *family*; and hence, on some pretence or other, or without any pretence, he slew large numbers of them, and doubtless seized their possessions.   It is said that he did this in his zeal for Israel and Judah, and this cannot be explained but on the supposition that the deed was done in order to give the tribes possession of the reserved territories of the Gibeonites.   And there is no doubt this would be, as it was designed, a popular and acceptable act (Josh. ix. 18).   Saul's own family must have been active in this cruel wrong, and must have had a good share of the spoil; for we find them all, when reduced to a private station, much better off in their worldly circumstances than can else be accounted for" (Kitto).   Here lay the secret of the famine, which was interpreted as a sign of Divine wrath.

> "He turneth a fruitful land into a salt-marsh,
>   Because of the wickedness of them that dwell therein."
>   (Ps. cvii. 34.)

III. INVOLVING IMPORTANT PRINCIPLES; not merely that sin and crime are followed by Divine punishment, and the wrongs of the poor and needy avenged (1 Sam. xxx. 15—17), but also that men are dealt with by God (in the way of chastisement) as communities, as well as separate souls (Ezek. xviii. 2—4).   1. The *guilt* incurred by individuals is participated in by the nation to which they belong when their wrong-doing is connived at, profited by, and not repudiated; and especially when the wrong-doer is its recognized representative.   2. The infliction of *suffering* on a whole nation, on account of the sins of one or more persons therein, is often needful for the vindication of public justice, the reparation of wrong-doing, and the general welfare.   3. Although a nation may be exempted for a season, through the forbearance of God, from the chastisement due to sin, it does not escape altogether, but is *surely called to account* in this world.   "Nations as nations will have no existence in another world, and therefore they must look for retribution in this" (Wordsworth).   "I can perceive in the story a recognition of the continuance of a nation's life, of its obligations, of its sins from age to age.   All national morality, nay, the meaning and possibility of history, depends upon this truth, the sense of which is, I fear, very weak in our day" (Maurice).   "Time does not wear out the guilt of sin, nor can we build hopes of impunity on the delay of judgments" (Matthew Henry).

IV. EVOKING RECOGNIZED OBLIGATION.   "And the *king* called the Gibeonites, and said . . . What shall I do for you? and wherewith shall I make the atonement [expiation, satisfaction, means of reconciliation], that ye may bless [and no more curse] the inheritance of Jehovah?" (vers. 2, 3); "What ye say, I will do for you" (ver. 5). Whilst acknowledging the national wrong, he also acknowledged the national obligation, and expressed his purpose: 1. To redress their grievance, satisfy *their claim for justice*, and secure their favour and intercession.   2. To respect *the justice of God* (by whom their cause was manifestly maintained), so that prayer might be heard, and the famine removed.   Unless right is done, prayer is vain (Ps. lxvi. 18).   3. And to do *whatever might be possible and necessary* for these ends.   "The land must expiate the king's wrong. This is rooted in the idea of the solidarity of the people, and the theocratic king as representative of God's people, whence comes solidarity of guilt between king and people" (Erdmann).   David herein acted wisely and in a theocratic spirit.

V. REQUIRING ADEQUATE SATISFACTION.   (Vers. 7—9.)   The expiation was made by the crucifixion of the two sons of Rizpah and the five sons of Merab (Hebrew, Michal), "whom she bare to Adriel," according to the demand and by "the hands of the Gibeonites" (ver. 9), under the authority and sanction of the king (and doubtless with the approval of the nation).   The demand: 1. Could be satisfied with *nothing short of this.* "We will have no silver nor gold," etc. (ver. 4); no private compensation could atone for such a public crime and wilful sin "before the Lord." 2. Accorded with *the requirements of the Law* (Gen. ix. 5, 6; Numb. xxxv. 31); or at least with the custom of blood-vengeance, and the then prevalent ideas of justice. If (as is probable, ver. 1) the hands of the sons of Saul were stained with blood, the Law demanded their death; if (as may have been the case) they were personally guiltless, they *suffered* from their intimate relationship to the murderer, as a "vicarious sacrifice," and for the benefit of the nation. "To understand this procedure, we must bear in mind the ancient Oriental ideas of the solidarity of the family, strict retaliation and blood-revenge—ideas that, with some limitation, remained in force in the legislation of the old covenant" (Kurtz). 3. Was restricted by *merciful consideration* for the assuredly innocent and steadfast fidelity to a solemn engagement. "And the king spared Mephibosheth," etc. (ver. 7). "The obscurities of this narrative probably may never be entirely cleared up. One thing, however, is certain—these seven descendants of Saul were not pretenders to the crown; and David cannot be suspected of having embraced such an opportunity to put them out of the way. Neither is it to be supposed that David delivered up the innocent contrary to the Law (Deut. xxiv. 16). They were, therefore, delivered up to the avengers of blood and punished with death, not on account of the crimes of Saul, but for the murders which they themselves, with the connivance of Saul, had committed on the Gibeonites, and for which they had hitherto remained unpunished" (Jahn, 'Heb. Com.,' xxxii.).

VI. AFFORDING SALUTARY INSTRUCTION (whether the victims be regarded as having actually taken part in the crime or not). "As seen by the people, the execution of Saul's sons (who were not charged with being in any way personally accessory to their father's crime) was a *judicial* act of retribution; but this aspect of the transaction was only an 'accommodation' to the current ideas of the age. Viewed in its essential character as sanctioned by God, it was a *didactic* act, designed to teach the guilt of sin" (Kirkpatrick); to produce repentance, and prevent its recurrence. That melancholy spectacle of a sevenfold crucifixion "on the mountain before Jehovah," in "Gibeah of Saul" (1 Sam. x. 5; xxii. 6), declared: 1. The exceeding *culpability* of unrighteous zeal, of the wanton violation of sacred pledges, of the unjust taking away of human life. "Let us here learn the danger of trifling with oaths and solemn engagements. Four hundred years had elapsed since the treaty made with the Gibeonites; and yet in the sight of God it was as sacred as ever; so that he who presumed to infringe it drew down a severe judgment on the whole nation" (Lindsay). 2. The inevitable, rigorous, and impartial execution of Divine *justice*. Princes are not above its correction, nor bondsmen below its protection. 3. The far-reaching *consequences* of transgression; to the children and children's children of the transgressor. "The evident intention of God in ordering the death of so many of Saul's family" (which, however, is not expressly stated) "was to give public attestation of the abhorrence of Saul's perfidy and cruelty, and to strike into the hearts of his successors on the throne a salutary dread of committing similar offences. The death of these seven persons, therefore, is not to be regarded as a punishment inflicted upon them for personal offences, even though they might have a share in their father's persecution of the Gibeonites, but an act commanded by God in virtue of his sovereign rights over the lives of all men, to teach princes moderation and equity, and to prevent the perpetration of enormous crimes, which are inconsistent with the welfare of the civil government as well as incompatible with the principles of true religion" (Chandler).

VII. FOLLOWED BY MERCIFUL DELIVERANCE. "And after that [the expiation] God was entreated for the land" (ver. 14). "Long-forgotten sin had been brought to mind and acknowledged and expiated; homage had been paid to justice; the evil of unfaithfulness had been exposed; the honour of the nation had been purged from foul stains; it had been shown that neither kings nor princes can do wrong with impunity; maternal fondness had been touchingly displayed; a long-forgotten duty had been attended to; a noble example had borne fruit; *and after that God was entreated for the land.* The generous heavens poured down their showers, the languishing life of field and vineyard revived, and the earth was clothed with beauty and teemed with fruitfulness again. There was one more proof of the everlasting truth, 'Righteousness exalteth a nation'" (C. Vince).—D.

Ver. 2.—(GIBEON.) *Unrighteous zeal.* "And Saul sought to slay them in his zeal to the children of Israel and Judah." When his attempt was made is not certainly known; possibly soon after his sparing Amalek (and to make amends for it); or at the time of his massacre of the priests at Nob (where the Gibeonites then assisted the Levites, before the removal of the altar and tabernacle to Gibeon); more probably at the time of his expulsion of the necromancers and soothsayers (1 Sam. xxviii. 3); being "one of those acts of passionate zeal in which he tried to drown the remorse of his later years." His zeal (like that of others in later times) was: 1. Religious and patriotic in intention and profession; to purge the land of the remnant of the heathen (Deut. vii. 2, 24), to honour God, to benefit his people. Good intentions are not enough to constitute good actions. 2. Blind and wilful, "not according to knowledge" (Rom. x. 2; Acts xxvi. 9). 3. Irreverent and ungodly; in violation of a solemn compact in the name of God, and against those who were consecrated to his service. His humblest ministers should be held in respect. 4. Unjust and ungrateful; for they had done no wrong, but had performed useful service. 5. Proud and tyrannical; regarding them with contempt, and taking advantage of their defenceless condition (1 Sam. xxii. 6—19). 6. Cruel and murderous. 7. Selfish and covetous; to appropriate the spoil to his family and adherents. 8. Popular and acceptable. The people never forgave the crafty manner in which they had originally been induced to spare their lives, looked upon them with suspicion and dislike, and readily sympathized with Saul's attack upon them (as they did not in the case of the priests at Nob), and consented to share the plunder. 9. Restrained and unsuccessful. Some survived. It is seldom that persecutors are able to do all they endeavour to do. 10. Infectious and disastrous, in its influence on his family and the nation.—D.

Vers. 8—14.—(GIBEAH.) *Rizpah.* "And Rizpah the daughter of Aiah took sackcloth," etc. (ver. 10; ch. iii. 7). The days of harvest had come; but not the fruits of harvest. The heaven was brass, and the earth iron (Deut. xxviii. 23). The misery of famine was accompanied by a sense of Divine wrath on account of sin. The guilt of blood was on the land, and especially on "the house of Saul," for the destruction of the Gibeonites. Nothing would satisfy the demand of the sorrowing bondservants of Israel, or (as it was believed) restore Divine favour, save the death of seven men of Saul's family (John xi. 50). These, therefore, two of them being sons of *Rizpah*, were taken and crucified (Numb. xxv. 4) at once on the hill before Jehovah, and their remains left unburied, a prey to ravenous birds and beasts. And in her *maternal grief and affection*, spreading sackcloth on the rocky floor (either for her bed or as a rough tent to shelter her), she watched them there, under the scorching sun by day and the drenching dews by night, and protected them from molestation until they received an honourable burial. "They were accounted as accursed and unworthy of the burial of dogs; but she would not cast them out of her heart. The more they were shunned by others, the more she clung to them; and the deeper the disgrace, the deeper her compassion." Observe—

I. HER SPECIAL DESIRE AND AIM; for it was more than an instinct of natural affection that prompted her watching near the dead. Regarding their unburied condition as one of ignominy (Ps. lxxix. 2), and perhaps as, in some way, affecting their happiness in the future life, she was desirous of their being honourably interred. It was deemed necessary (unlike what was required in other instances, Deut. xxi. 22, 23) that they should remain exposed before Jehovah till assurance was given, by the fall of rain, that the satisfaction was accepted. If she could not do what she would, she would do *what she could* (Mark xiv. 8); and, by preventing further injury, render the fulfilment of her desire possible. Her intense maternal love led her to seek the safety and honour of the *dead*; well may a similar love lead others to seek the safety and honour of the *living!*

II. HER EXTRAORDINARY DEVOTION; as it appears in: 1. Her unquenchable attachment. Others might despise them as criminals, but she could only regard them and cling to them as children (Song of Sol. viii. 7). 2. Her humble submission and resignation to what was unavoidable. "Truly this is a grief, and I must bear it" (Jer. x. 19). 3. Her entire self-surrender and self-sacrifice. If she could not remove their reproach, she could share it with them. 4. Her patient endurance of suffering; through long and lonely nights, and dark and dreary days. 5. Her ceaseless vigilance, zeal, and courage. 6. Her unwearied, faithful, hopeful perseverance. "The emotions in woman act as powerful motives on the will, and, when strongly called forth, produce a degree of vigour and determination which is very surprising to those who have usually seen the individual under a different aspect" (Carpenter). 7. Her importunate prayers for the fulfilment of her desire. "She refrained from all violent and illegal methods of gaining her object. She used no force or stratagem to secure for her beloved ones a safe and decent burial; but waited watchfully, meekly, and humbly, for the time appointed by the Lord. Neither did she give way to despondency, and quit the melancholy scene in wild despair; but did what she could to alleviate the dreadful evil. Though her heart was broken and her grief too bitter for utterance, she still hoped in God; still looked for his merciful interposition, and waited day after day, and night after night until the rain of heaven came down and released the bodies of her beloved ones" (Hughes, 'Female Characters of Holy Writ').

III. HER EFFECTUAL ENDEAVOUR. At length (how long is not stated) "showers of blessing" fell, and her wish was accomplished. Loving, faithful, devoted service: 1. Exerts an undesigned influence on others. "And it was told David," etc. (ver. 11). 2. Fails not, sooner or later, to receive its due reward. 3. Is followed by effects greater than any that were desired or expected. "David was pleased with her tenderness, and was excited by her example to do honour to the bodies of *Saul* and *Jonathan* (1 Sam. xxxi. 12, 13; ch. ii. 5—7), and thus showed that he did not war with the dead, and that his recent act in delivering up Saul's sons was not one of personal revenge, but of public justice" (Wordsworth). She did more than she intended; and what she did is to this day "told for a memorial for her."—D.

Vers. 15—22 (1 Chron. xx. 4—8).—*Giants: a sermon to young people.* "As for these four, they were born to the giant (*Ha-rapha*) in Gath, and fell by the hand of David, and by the hand of his servants" (ver. 22). Of the age before the Flood it is said, "In those days were the giants [*Nephilim*, men of lofty stature and ferocious character] upon the earth" (Gen. vi. 4; Numb. xiii. 32, 33). At a subsequent period there was a like formidable race called Rephaim (Gen. xiv. 5; xv. 20), to which belonged the Emim, the Zuzim (Zamzummim), and the Anakim (Deut. ii. 10, 11, 20, 21; ix. 2). One of this race, of extraordinary stature, was Og, King of Bashan (Deut. iii. 10; Josh. xii. 4). Others, more recently, dwelt among the Philistines (Josh. xi. 12), like Goliath (1 Sam. xvii. 4—11) and the four here mentioned, who were either sons of a celebrated giant (the Rapha) or descendants of the original founder of the tribe. They were all idolaters and formidable opponents of Israel. *And there are giants among us now.* I do not mean such ogres as children read of in story-books; or such harmless persons of exceptional height as are sometimes seen; or even such as appear in any bodily form; but, nevertheless, real, powerful, and terrible giants, aptly represented by "these four" slain by David and his heroes.

I. THEY BELONG TO ONE FAMILY. It is: 1. An *ancient* family; as old as *sin,* and came into the world with it. It survived the Deluge; spread, among the dispersed nations, over all the earth; had one of its principal settlements in Canaan; and, amidst all the conflicts and changes of mankind, has continued to this day. 2. An *ungodly* family. None of its members believe in the living and true God or obey his commandments; yet they have many gods (1 Sam. xvii. 43). 3. A *selfish* family. They all seek their own, and often contend against one another. 4. A numerous, mighty, and *destructive* family. They have their walled cities and strongholds, defy the armies of the living God (ver. 21), and sometimes terrify them (1 Sam. xvii. 1—11) by their imposing appearance and evil doings (Ps. xiv. 1—3; Rom. iii. 10—18). What is this giant family? You have doubtless already discovered that it consists of sins, vices, and wickedness of all kinds.

II. THEY ARE KNOWN BY VARIOUS NAMES. Here are long lists of them (Matt. xv. 19; Gal. v. 19—21; Col. iii. 5—9). But notice especially these four: (1) *Pride,* or undue self-esteem and contempt of other persons (vers. 16, 17). The name *Ishbi-benob* signifies "my dwelling is on the height;" and was possibly given to him because he had his castle on a lofty, inaccessible rock. The brazen head of his lance was eight pounds in weight; and, arrayed in new armour, he resolved to kill David, and nearly succeeded;

but was himself smitten down by the aid of Abishai. Pride is haughty, self-confident, contemptuous, and presumptuous. It has overthrown many mighty men; and is an ungodly, selfish, and most dangerous adversary. "Be not proud" (Jer. xiii. 15; ch. xxii. 28; Obad. i. 3, 4; Jas. iv. 6). (2) *Falsehood*, or deceit (1 Sam. xxi. 1—8). "There was again a battle with the Philistines at Gob [Gezer]: then Sibbechai the Hushathite [1 Chron. xxvii. 11] slew *Saph* [Sippai]." This is a double-faced giant; exceedingly crafty, mean, and mischievous. "Lying lips are abomination to the Lord" (Prov. xii. 22; Rev. xxi. 8). (3) *Hatred*, or ill will; and (in various forms) envy, revenge, anger, and strife. "Elhanan, the son of Jaare-oregim [Jair] the Bethlehemite [ch. xxiii. 24] slew Goliath the Gittite"—possibly a son of the giant whom David slew, and of the same name; or (more probably, as in Chronicles), "*Lahmi* the brother of Goliath, the shaft of whose spear was like a weaver's beam." He is a powerful, fierce, and obstinate foe; and only by the strength which God gives [Elhanan] can he be overthrown. (4) *Dishonesty;* "a man of stature [measure or length] that had on each hand six fingers, and on each foot six toes, four and twenty in number," etc.; slain by Jonathan, David's nephew (1 Sam. xvi. 9; xvii. 3; ch. xiii. 3). He has a powerful grasp; covets, seizes, and steals the possessions of others, in defiance of right and justice. There are many other giants, such as (5) Ignorance, (6) Sloth, (7) Intemperance, (8) Impurity, (9) Profanity, (10) Infidelity, (11) Superstition, and (12) Idolatry.

III. THEY MUST BE FOUGHT AGAINST AND OVERCOME; in their onslaught upon ourselves and others. If we do not conquer them, they will conquer us. And we can conquer them only by: 1. Faithfully following "the Captain of our salvation;" obeying his commands, and depending on his might. 2. Incessant vigilance and firm resistance. 3. Ever-renewed and courageous effort. 4. Confident assurance of victory, inspired by many promises, the presence of our Divine Leader, and the success which has been already achieved. "These conflicts of David's servants are typical of the spiritual combats of Christ's soldiers with the family of the evil one" (Wordsworth). "Fight the good fight of faith" (1 Tim. vi. 12; 1 Sam. xiii. 1—7; xiv. 1—15).—D.

Ver. 17.—*The lamp of Israel.* In the view of his followers, David was the lamp (Hebrew, *naer*) or glory of the nation, and the continuance of his life and reign was essential to its welfare. This is a striking testimony to their estimate of his personal character and faithful and prosperous rule. Similar language is used of others. "He was the lamp that burneth and shineth," etc. (John v. 35; viii. 12; Matt. v. 14). And every faithful servant of God is "a light-giver in the world" (Phil. ii. 15). Such a lamp is—

I. KINDLED BY THE GRACIOUS HAND OF GOD, the true Glory of Israel, the Father of lights, the Fountain of life and light (Ps. xxxvi. 9). None are so ready to recognize dependence upon God for life and all good as the devout man himself.

"Thou art my Lamp, O Jehovah,
And Jehovah enlightens my darkness."
(Ch. xxii. 29; Ps. xviii. 28; xxvii. 1.)

"David's regal life and actions were the light which the grace of God had kindled for the benefit of Israel." · Whatever his gifts, his graces, his position, his success, they are all humbly, gratefully, and constantly ascribed to their Divine Source by the faithful servant; and, whilst we admire him, we should "glorify God in him" (1 Cor. xv. 10; Gal. i. 24).

II. CONDUCIVE TO THE REAL WELFARE OF MEN. "Neither do men light a lamp and put it under the bushel," etc. (Matt. v. 15).

"Heaven does with us as we with torches do,
Not light them for themselves," etc.
('Measure for Measure,' act i. sc. 1.)

By his counsel, his example, his endeavours, his prayers, he renders invaluable service to others in directing them in perplexity and peril; preserving them from error and evil; stimulating them to effort and conflict; and contributing to their safety, prosperity, and lasting happiness.

III. EXPOSED TO IMMINENT DANGER OF EXTINCTION. The light is liable to be quenched. Life is always precarious; the life of some peculiarly so; like that of David when he went down into the conflict (vers. 15, 16; ch. v. 17—25), waxed faint, and was set upon by the giant Ishbi-benob, in a new suit of armour. And it is not only natural life, but also moral and spiritual life, that is beset by danger. The part which a good man takes in the conflict between good and evil attracts the attention of his adversaries, makes him a special object of attack (1 Kings xxii. 31); his efforts are exhausting, and his zeal is apt to consume him (Ps. lxix. 9; cxix. 139). "Ernestus, Duke of Luneburg, caused a burning lamp to be stamped on his coin, with these four letters, A. S. M. C., by which was meant, *Aliis serviens meipsum contero*, 'By giving light to others I *consume myself*'" (Spencer).

IV. WORTHY OF BEING HIGHLY ESTEEMED, carefully sustained, and zealously guarded. "And Abishai succoured him, and he [Abishai, or perhaps David, ver. 22] killed him," etc. The preserving care of God (ch. viii. 14) does not render needless human sympathy, assistance, prudence, resolution (ch. xviii. 3). He who freely spends his strength and risks his life for others ought to be esteemed, considered, defended, and helped by them (1 Thess. v. 12, 23; 2 Thess. iii. 2; Heb. xiii. 17); and, herein, they also benefit themselves and the whole community. "If any man serve me, let him follow me," etc. (John xii. 26—28).—D.

Ver. 1.—*Seeking God's face.* "David sought the face of the Lord" (Revised Version). The Authorized Version has here "inquired of the Lord," as in ch. ii. 1, where it is the translation of a different phrase. Doubtless the substantial meaning is the same. But, as with words, so with phrases, two are seldom wholly synonymous; and the differences are often instructive, suggesting each its own train of thought. So it is with these two phrases. That in the Revised Version leads us to think of—

I. THE NATURE OF TRUE WORSHIP. It is seeking the *face* of God, to realize his presence, behold his glory, be made sensible of his majesty, holiness and loving-kindness. Or, in greater strictness, this may be said to be preliminary to the worship of him. We come into his presence that we may present to him our adoration, praises, confessions, and prayers. We must not be content with coming into his house, seeing his servants, joining in ceremonies—leaving, as it were, our names and messages, engaging and depending on the intercession of those who are supposed to approach nearer to him. Our heavenly Father does not keep such state as to exclude or repel any one from coming near to him. He wishes to see his children, to smile upon them, to embrace them, to speak with them. Any methods of worship which keep men at a distance from him are contrary to his will. The mediation of Christ is not a substitute for intimate converse with God, but a means of attaining it, as we may see by considering—

II. THE POSSIBILITY AND WARRANT OF SUCH WORSHIP. There are, doubtless, difficulties in the way of the approach of men to God. These are removed pre-eminently by the mediation of our Lord. 1. *Ignorance separates from God; Christ makes him known.* By his teaching, by his own character, and by the Spirit he imparts to his disciples. "In the face of Jesus Christ" we see that of the Father (2 Cor. iv. 6; John xiv. 8, 9). 2. *Sin separates from God; Christ delivers from sin.* (1) He has atoned for sin by his death. He "suffered for sins, the Just for the unjust, that he might bring us to God" (1 Pet. iii. 18). He has thus removed the barrier presented by the justice of God and "the curse of the Law" (Gal. iii. 13). And through faith in Christ the conscience is purged from sin by his blood (Heb. ix. 14), and the believer has "boldness to enter into the holiest" (Heb. x. 19—22). Through Christ the face of God shines with a benignant brightness on those who approach him. (2) Christ cleanses the nature and character from sin. He thus produces that purity of heart which is necessary for those who would "see God" (Matt. v. 8). 3. *Not only the putting away of sin, but certain positive dispositions are necessary in seeking the face of God.* Christ has secured and he imparts these. To his disciples is given "the Spirit of adoption" (Rom. viii. 15), and thus they come to God with confidence, affection, and self-surrender. Thus Christ is "the Way" by which we "come to the Father" (John xiv. 6). "Through him we have access by one Spirit unto the Father" (Eph. ii. 18).

III. THE NECESSITY OF SUCH WORSHIP. We must *seek* God's face if we would behold it with joy. He sometimes surprises men by sudden and unexpected manifestations of himself to them; but this will ordinarily be to those who love him and are in the habit of seeking him (see John xiv. 19—23). Hence the exhortations, "Seek the Lord, . . . seek his face evermore" (Ps. cv. 4); "Seek, and ye shall find" (Matt. vii. 7; comp. 2 Chron. vii. 14).

IV. GODLY MEN ARE DISTINGUISHED BY SUCH WORSHIP. "This is the generation of them that seek him, that seek thy face, O God of Jacob" (Ps. xxiv. 6). "When thou saidst, Seek ye my face; my heart said unto thee, Thy face, Lord, will I seek" (Ps. xxvii. 8). 1. *The godly are impelled to this:* (1) By love to God, and consequent longing after him (Ps. xlii. 1, 2; lxiii. 1, 2). (2) By faith in him and in his promises (Heb. xi. 6). (3) By the sense of needs which only God can supply. (4) By memory of former converse with God, and of the enjoyment and profit derived from it. 2. *Hence they seek God's face daily;* and with special earnestness in times of special difficulty or danger. David felt how much he needed Divine guidance in reference to the famine which for three years had harassed the country; hence he "sought the face of the Lord." In trouble the Divine call may be heard, "Seek ye my face;" and many begin to do so when trouble is upon them.

V. SUCH WORSHIP IS FRUITFUL OF BLESSING. It is never in vain (Isa. xlv. 19), although at times it may appear to be so (Job xxiii. 3—9). "Ye shall seek me, and find me, when ye shall search for me with all your heart" (Jer. xxix. 13) is a promise of universal applicability. And to gain the vision of God's face is to be blessed indeed. The sight of him: 1. *Calms and soothes and comforts the heart.* As a mother's face soothes the suffering child.

> " Sorrow and fear are gone,
> Whene'er thy face appears:
> It stills the sighing orphan's moan,
> And dries the widow's tears:
> It hallows every cross;
> It sweetly comforts me,
> Makes me forget my every loss,
> And find my all in thee."

2. *Encourages to pray.* When his face is seen, we are enabled to tell him all that is in our heart, with the assurance of success in our suit. 3. *Sheds light into the soul.* The "light of his countenance" scatters the darkness. Perplexities are half solved as soon as we have caught sight of the face of God. 4. *Produces likeness to him.* "We shall be like him; for we shall see him as he is" (1 John iii. 2) is a promise partially fulfilled in the present life. 5. *The crowning result is to "see his face" in the fulness of its glory, and for ever.* (Rev. xxii. 4.) But to those who refuse to seek him, turning to him their back, and not their face (Jer. ii. 27), he says, "I will show them the back, and not the face, in the day of their calamity" (Jer. xviii. 17); and they will at length say "to the mountains and rocks, Fall on us, and hide us from the face of him that sitteth on the throne, and from the wrath of the Lamb" (Rev. vi. 16).—G. W.

Ver. 10.—*A mother's love and grief.* This verse is part of a narrative full of difficulty and darkness. It stands out a bright light in the midst of the darkness—a grand exhibition of a mother's love.

I. A MOTHER'S LOVE IS MUCH TRIED. Not often as Rizpah's was; but always in some way or other; as: 1. By the conduct of her children. 2. By the conduct of others towards them. 3. By their troubles. 4. By their deaths; especially when untimely or by violence; and most of all when their untimely or violent deaths are the penalty of their misconduct, which was, however, not the case with the sons of Rizpah.

II. IT OCCASIONS HER MUCH SORROW. Love, in this world, always brings grief, through making the sorrows of others our own, as well as rendering us sensitive to their treatment of ourselves. The more deep and tender the love, so much the more poignant the grief. And, as a mother loves most, she is most susceptible of sorrow. She is often pained by her children when they do not think it; and every stroke inflicted on them strikes her to the heart.

III. IT IS UTTERLY UNSELFISH. She loves because it is her nature—freely, spontaneously, making no calculation, asking for no return. Not without hope, indeed, that she may one day be rewarded by her children's welfare and affection; but far from regulating her love by this: rather she lavishes it most on those from whom she cannot expect recompense—the weakest, the most sickly, those most likely to die; yea, as Rizpah, those who are dead. "Death might bereave her of them, not them of her love" (Bishop Hall).

IV. IT IS MOST SELF-DENYING. Prompting to and sustaining in arduous labours, long and wearisome watchings, self-inflicted privations, for the good of her children. For the sake of their health, she willingly hazards, and even sacrifices, her own. For the sake of their education and advancement, she cheerfully gives up, not only luxuries, but comforts, and even necessaries. And when they have gone beyond her reach into the unseen world, their mortal remains are dear to her, and she will spare nothing that may honour them or prevent dishonour to them. Of such affection Rizpah is a signal instance.

V. IT IS MOST PERSISTENT. Through six months Rizpah continued watching day and night (with the aid, doubtless, of her servants) by the crosses on which the bodies of her sons and other relatives hung, that neither vulture, nor jackal, nor any other "bird of the air" or "beast of the field" might devour, or mangle, or even "rest on" them, until she had gained her point in their honourable burial. A striking example of the persistence of a mother's love. But this was only the crowning proof of her affection. A mother's love is lifelong. "A mother's truth keeps constant youth." It endures through years of toil, hardship, and suffering; when feebly responded to, or quite unappreciated, or requited by neglect, hardness, or cruel wrong. When son or daughter is utterly debased and degraded, the mother clings and hopes; when cast off by all the world, she does not abandon them.

> "Years to a mother bring distress,
> But do not make her love the less."
>
> (Wordsworth.)

VI. IT IS SOMETIMES BROUGHT INTO NOTICE AND HONOURED. Thus it was with Rizpah. What she had done was reported to the king; it aroused his attention to his neglect to give honourable burial, in the family sepulchre, to the bones of Saul and Jonathan. He now repaired the neglect, and buried, not only them, but (as is implied) the remains of the seven which had so long been hanging exposed, "in the sepulchre of Kish his (Saul's) father." Thus a mother's love, in this case, exercised a powerful beneficial influence. Moreover, it received honourable mention in the holy records, and wherever the Bible comes, "there shall also this, that this woman hath done, be told for a memorial of her" (Matt. xxvi. 13). And although usually the light of a mother's love shines chiefly in the privacy of home, and she neither asks nor expects applause or record, it is impossible that she can act a noble part without exercising an influence for good which may widen and ramify far more than she could have imagined, and may secure her an honour she never desired. And if no others, "her children arise up, and call her blessed" (Prov. xxxi. 28), and tell of her character and works to their children.

In conclusion: 1. *If human love be so deep and strong, what must be the love of God*, from whom it springs, and of which it is one great sign and proof? All the love of all parents, of all human beings, flows from this original Fountain. The Fountain is greater than the streams. 2. *Mothers should seek to have their love perfected*, by being sanctified and elevated by the love of God, and directed supremely to the ends which he seeks—the moral, spiritual, and eternal welfare of their children. With this view, they should watch carefully their living children (as Rizpah her dead ones), and especially whilst they are young, that they may not be defiled or injured by foul bird or beast. 3. *How strong and constant should be the love of children for their mothers!* Prompting them to all that would gratify and honour them and promote their happiness; to self-denial and self-sacrifice for their good, should they live to need the help of their children; and to patience and forbearance towards them, should they, under the infirmities of old age, make demands on these virtues. "Despise not thy mother when she is old" (Prov. xxiii. 22). 4. *How base the conduct of many children (especially of many sons) to their mothers!* Selfishly wasting their resources, imposing on their credulity, abusing their indulgence, disgracing their name, breaking their hearts. "A foolish [wicked] son is the heaviness of his mother" (Prov. x. 1).—G. W.

Vers. 16—22.—*Giant-killers.* These huge monsters were dangerous enemies. To slay them was to do valuable service to king and country. To assail them required much courage. Those who killed any of them gained great renown; and their names and deeds were recorded in the chronicles of the kingdom, and, as to some of them, have found a place in the Book of books.

I. SOME GIANT FOES OF THE DIVINE KING AND KINGDOM THAT NEED TO BE DESTROYED. We may name *superstition,* whether pagan, papal, or protestant; *infidelity; selfishness; pride; tyranny,* ecclesiastical or political; *slavery; sensuality; intemperance; war; mammon.* Singly, or in partial union, they assail the subjects of Christ, and oppose them in their endeavours to extend his kingdom. And behind lie the devil and his angels, ever active and formidable (Eph. vi. 11, 12).

II. TO BATTLE AGAINST THESE MONSTERS IS THE DUTY OF ALL CHRIST'S SERVANTS. 1. *It is involved in their Christian calling.* The new nature which is given to them is instinctively hostile to Satan and his works. The endeavour to serve God and benefit men necessarily brings them into conflict with these powers of darkness. The attacks made on themselves compel them to fight in self-defence (1 Pet. v. 8, 9). 2. *They are supplied with arms and armour for the purpose.* (Eph. vi. 11—17.) 3. *The enslaved and degraded condition to which these giant evils have reduced their victims appeals to and stimulates them.* 4. *Their own happy condition under the reign of Christ supplies them with a powerful motive.* 5. *Regard for him impels and strengthens them.* Loyalty, desire for his glory, the hope of his approval, and of the honours and rewards he bestows.

III. HEROES IN THE FIGHT ATTAIN TO DISTINCTION AND REWARD. 1. *Who are the heroes?* Not those who engage these giants (nominally) as a profession and for the sake of earthly rewards. But such as (1) renounce for themselves their service, which all who profess to oppose them do not; (2) show great zeal in contending against them; (3) cheerfully expose themselves to hardship and peril in doing so, displaying conspicuous courage and endurance. Those faithful in times of persecution—confessors, martyrs. Those who bear the gospel to savages, or encounter dangerous climates in seeking its extension. 2. *Their honours and rewards.* (1) In many cases, success; not, alas! in *killing* these giants—they are not dead yet—but in preserving themselves, and rescuing others from their power, and in diminishing their dominions. (2) Enrolment in the Divine records. Many illustrious names are written in human records; more have been overlooked; but all are in the "book of remembrance written before" God (Mal. iii. 16). (3) Final promotion to honour, power, and blessedness (see 2 Tim. iv. 7, 8; and the promises made in Rev. ii. and iii. to "him that overcometh ").—G. W.

Ver. 17.—*The unquenchable Light.* "That thou quench not the light of Israel." "The men of David" who thus speak, and doubtless the multitude of his subjects, regarded him as the light (literally, as in Revised Version, "the lamp") of the nation —its guiding mind, its safety, glory, and joy. His death would involve the nation in darkness—in perplexity, confusion, peril, and trouble. Such was likely enough to be the consequence of his death at that period. Nevertheless, David, as a moral and spiritual light, burns on still for all peoples and generations. Death did not quench this light. More emphatically is this true of Jesus Christ our King.

I. HE IS THE LIGHT OF MEN. Intended ultimately to "lighten every man;" actually enlightening those who receive him. He is their: 1. *Teacher and Guide.* Through whose revelations they know God and himself and themselves; sin and righteousness; heaven, and the way to it; perdition, and how to escape it; the real worth of things; the wisdom needful for the guidance of life. Christ sheds light upon all things— the light by which their true character and relations are made apparent. 2. *Safety and Salvation.* In darkness is peril; in light security. 3. *Glory.* Imparting to them of his own lustre. 4. *Joy.* In knowledge and conscious safety are peace and happiness and hope; in ignorance, doubt, and perplexity, is unhappiness.

II. HIS LIGHT CANNOT BE QUENCHED. 1. *Not the light of his personal glory* In the battle with his foes and ours, he fell and died; but he rose again, and to a greater brightness of glory, in consequence of his death. His cross itself is a great light for men. He lives above all the power of his enemies. He goes with his people to battle, but cannot be touched by the foe. 2. *Nor the Light he has become to men through the knowledge he has given to the world.* Great and formidable and persistent have been the efforts to extinguish the light; but it burns on unquenched and unquenchable. It may be obscured here and there, and for a time, but it can never go out. It will yet shine forth over the whole earth, and scatter all the darkness of error and sin. 3. *Nor the Light he is to each of his believing people.* Through life, and in death, and for ever, he remains their Light. His presence in their hearts is their wisdom and joy under all circumstances.

Then: 1. Be grateful for him. 2. Accept the light he sheds. 3. " Walk as children of light." 4. Be lights yourselves. Shine by speech, and especially in your lives.—G. W.

EXPOSITION.

CHAPTER XXII.

DAVID'S PSALM OF THANKSGIVING.

This song, which is identical with Ps. xviii., though with many verbal differences, is so universally acknowledged as a genuine composition of King David, that the objections taken by one or two critics serve only to give us greater security by reminding us that the other side has been carefully argued. The differences between its form here and in the Book of Psalms suggest many important considerations with regard to textual criticism. From the absence of manuscripts, we have very scanty means of judging of the correctness of the ordinary Hebrew text. We have, indeed, abundant proof that the Jews took extreme care of their sacred text in the early centuries of our era; but we nevertheless find, most frequently in names, mistakes which have arisen from the carelessness of scribes, and especially from the confusion by them of similar letters. Thus the *Sibbechai* of ch. xxi. 18 becomes *Mebunnai* in ch. xxiii. 27, owing to some scribe having mistaken two letters in the name. And as the similarity between them exists, not in the old Hebrew writing, but in the square character substituted after the exile, the confusion must be subsequent to that date. In comparing the two texts of this psalm, we find similar instances of confusion of letters in vers. 11, 42, 43; we find words transposed in vers. 5, 6; and clauses repeated or omitted in vers. 13, 14. In short, all the phenomena with which we are familiar in the textual criticism of the New Testament are also found here. And may we not add that they end in the same result? The general sense and meaning remain much the same. The variations of reading do not affect the teaching of Holy Scripture on any

important point. It may be asked, then—Why should we notice them at all? And why urge them upon the attention of scholars? The answer is that there exist flaws and blemishes in the Massoretic, that is, the ordinary Hebrew, text, and that the removal of them is prevented by the strange idea which accords infallibility to the Massorites, and will not concede to the far more difficult problem of the ancient Hebrew text that which is granted as a matter of course to the comparatively modern Greek text of the New Testament. And thus the Old Testament is neglected, and left outside that careful and minute study so lavishly expended on the New, and so rich in useful results.

Of the date when David wrote this psalm there can be little doubt. It was at the close of his first great series of victories, after Toi, the Hittite King of Hamath, had sent to him an embassy of congratulation (ch. viii. 9, 10), referred to very triumphantly in vers. 45, 46. But there is no trace in it of the sorrow and shame that clouded over his latter days; and no man whose conscience was stained with sins so dark as those of adultery and murder could have written words so strongly asserting his integrity and the cleanness of his hands as are found in vers. 21—25. The psalm belongs to David's happiest time, when he had won for Israel security and empire. It is written from first to last in a tone of jubilant exultation, caused, as we may well believe, by Nathan's acceptance of his purpose to build the temple, and by the solemn appointment of David as the theocratic king. If it were arranged according to time and matter, it would be placed immediately after ch. viii., as it is evidently David's thanksgiving for the benefits and blessings just promised to him and his seed.

But the scribes inserted it here, not so much because of its historical value, as because it is a national thanksgiving for the founding of that empire by which Israel became verily the theocratic people, and the type upon earth of the kingdom of the Messiah. The prophet who compiled the Books of Samuel rejoiced in David's victories, not because they gave Israel worldly dominion, but because they were a fulfilment of past prophecy, and a necessary part of the preparation for the religious position which Israel was to hold. Such as it had been under the judges, Israel would have been no fit home for the prophetic light. It could not have grown and developed, nor the race have become a Church fit to be the teacher of all mankind. And in this hymn the Church expresses her joy at the high office and extended usefulness to which God has seen fit to call her.

The spiritual exposition of the psalm will naturally be sought in commentaries on the Book of Psalms. But such matters as its outward form, and the differences between the two texts, will not be out of place here.

Ver. 1.—**David spake.** The introduction was probably written by the prophet who compiled the Books of Samuel. The scribe who collected the Book of Psalms would be a priest, and he has repeated it with one or two additions, the most important of which is that the psalm was written "by David the servant of Jehovah." This title, meaning the minister or vicegerent of Jehovah, is one so high that it would certainly not have been given to David in his lifetime; nor was it even until Moses was dead that he was honoured with this rank (Deut. xxxiv. 5). But what was David's right to this title, which put him on a level with Moses? It was this: In adding to the sacrificial ritual enacted by Moses a daily service in the temple of sacred minstrelsy and songs, David was acting with higher powers than were ever exercised by any other person. For though, as we have seen, Samuel was the originator of these services in his schools, yet there is a wide difference between private and public services; and David made his anthems part of the national liturgy. But it would only be when the halo of long use had gathered round his holy psalmody that David would be placed on an equality with Moses, and his authority to institute a new ritual for the nation be recognized.

Vers. 2—4.—

" Jehovah is my Cliff and my Stronghold
    and my Deliverer;

The God of my rock, in whom I take
    refuge:
My Shield and the Horn of my salvation,
My Fastness and my Place of refuge:
My Saviour: thou savest me from violence.
I call upon Jehovah, the praised One,
And I am saved from my enemies."

The Syriac in ver. 2 inserts, "Fervently do I love thee, Jehovah my Strength;" but it probably only borrows the words from Ps. xviii. 1. For we may well believe that it was at a later period of his life, after deeper and more heart-searching trials, that David thus felt his love to Jehovah only strengthened and made more necessary to him by the loss of his earthly happiness. In ver. 3 **The God of my rock** is changed in Ps. xviii. 2 into "My God my Rock" (Authorized Version, "strength")—probably an intentional alteration, as being far less rugged and startling than this bold metaphor of the Deity being his rock's God. In the original the words present each its distinct idea. Thus in ver. 2 the *rock* is a high cliff or precipice. It is the word *sela*, which gave its name to the crag-city of Idumea. **Fortress** really means a rock, difficult of access, and forming a secure retreat. It is entirely a natural formation, and not a building. In ver. 3 *rock* is a vast mountainous mass (Job xviii. 4), and, as it suggests the ideas of grandeur and immovable might, it is often used for God's glory as being the Strength and Protection of his people (Deut. xxxii. 15, 31; Isa. xxx. 29, margin). Next follow two ordinary metaphors, the *shield* for defence, and the **horn** for attack; after which David, who had so often sought safety among the cliffs and fastnesses of the mountains, returns to the same circle of thoughts, and calls God his **High Tower**, the word signifying, not a building, but a height, a lofty natural stronghold; and finally *his Refuge*, a place of safe retreat among the mountains. This and the rest of the verse are omitted in Ps. xviii. 2. In ver. 4 the words are as literally translated above, and signify, "Whenever I call, I am saved." In all times of difficulty, prayer brings immediate deliverance.

Vers. 5—7.—

" For the breakers of death surrounded me;
    Torrents of wickedness [Hebrew, 'of Belial'] terrified me;
Cords of Sheol surrounded me;
Snares of death came suddenly upon me.
In my distress I cried unto Jehovah,
And to my God I cried.
And he heard my voice out of his palace,
And my cry was in his ears."

Instead of *breakers*—waves dashing violently on rocks—Ps. xviii. 4 has "cords of death" translated "sorrow" in the Authorized Version. But "cords of death" mean the fatal snares of the hunter, and are not in keeping with "torrents of wickedness." "Belial," literally, "worthlessness," is by many supposed from the context to mean here "destruction," that is, physical instead of moral wickedness. So in Nah. i. 11 "a counsellor of Belial" means a ruinous, destructive counsellor. **Sheol** is the world of the departed, and is equivalent to "death." **Cried** is the same verb twice used. In Ps. xviii. 6 it is altered, in the former part of the verse unto "I called"—a change probably suggested by the more fastidious taste of a later age. For **temple** we should translate *palace*, or *heavenly temple*. It is not the temple in Jerusalem, which was not yet built, but God's heavenly dwelling, that is meant. Instead of the terse ellipse, "And my cry in his ears," the full but heavy phrase, "My cry before him came into his ears," is substituted in Ps. xviii. 6.

Vers. 8—10.—

" And the earth quaked and trembled ;
   The foundations of the heavens shook,
   And quaked because he was wroth.
   A smoke went up in his nostril,
   And fire out of his mouth devoured ;
   Red hot cinders burned from him.
   And he bowed the heavens and came down,
   And darkness was under his feet."

In describing the manifestation of God for his deliverance, David bore in mind and repeated the description of God's descent to earth given in Exod. xix. 16, 18. But the poetic vigour of David's imagination intensifies the imagery, and makes it more grand and startling. Not merely is there the earthquake and the volcano and the storm-cloud, but the dim form of the Almighty is present, with the smoke of just anger at unrighteousness ascending from his nostrils, and the lightnings flashing forth to execute his wrath. But David certainly intended that these metaphors should remain ideal; and it was quite unnecessary for the Targum carefully to eliminate all such expressions as seem to give the Almighty human shape. In so doing it merely changes poetry into prose. But even more dull and commonplace is the explanation given by some modern commentators, that all that is meant is that David was once saved by a thunderstorm from some danger or other. Really this glorious imagery, taken from all that is grandest on earth, is intended to magnify to us the spiritual conception of God's justice coming forth to visit the earth and do right and equity. In ver. 8 for "the foundations of the heavens," we find in Ps. xviii. 7 "the foundations of the hills." The former is the grander metaphor, and signifies the mighty mountain ranges, like those of Lebanon, on which the skies seem to rest. **The smoke** signifies hailstorms and, perhaps, also the rain driven in wreaths along the ground by the wind. **Red hot cinders burned from him** describes the flashing lightnings that were shot forth like the coals from the refiner's furnace when heated to the full. It is to be regretted that the Revised Version retains the bathos of the old rendering, that God's fiery breath set coals on fire.

Vers. 11—13.—

" And he rode upon a cherub, and did fly ;
   And he was seen upon the wings of the wind.
   And he made darkness booths round about him ;
   Gathering of waters, thickenings of clouds.
   Out of the brightness before him
   Coals of fire burned."

In ch. vi. 2 Jehovah is described as sitting upon the cherubim; his presence there, called by the rabbins his Shechinah, that is, *dwelling*, being indicated by a cloud of light. In this psalm the cherub is his chariot, on which he rides forth to judgment. **He was seen.** There can be little doubt that the right reading is preserved in Ps. xviii. 10, where we find a verb signifying the swooping down of a bird of prey upon its quarry (Deut. xxviii. 49; Jer. xlviii. 40). The two words differ only in the substitution of *r* for *d*, and these letters are so similar in Hebrew that they are constantly interchanged. **Booths** ; made of branches of trees, and forming a temporary abode. So the dark storm-clouds are gathered round the Almighty to veil his awful form from sight as he goes forth for judgment. **Gathering of waters**; probably the right reading, instead of which in the psalm we find "dark waters." The gathering of waters would describe the massing of the rain-clouds. The difference here also consists only in one letter. **Out of the brightness**, which closely surrounds the Deity in the midst of the black mass of the tempest, the lightning flashes forth. This brightness is the Shechinah (see above), to which St. Paul also refers where he says that God's dwelling is in "the unapproachable light" (1 Tim. vi. 16).

Vers. 14—16.—

" Jehovah thundered from heaven,
   And the Most High uttered his voice.
   And he sent forth arrows, and scattered them [the evil-doers];
   Lightning, and terrified them.
   And the sea-beds became visible,
   The foundations of the world were laid bare,
   At the rebuke of Jehovah,
   By the breath of the wind of his nostril."

Terrified. The verb signifies " to strike with sudden terror and alarm " (see Exod. xiv. 24 ; Josh. x. 10). It describes here the panic caused by the lightning, and by the violent throes of nature, so powerfully described in ver. 16. **Laid bare.** This is the meaning of the word "discovered " in the Authorized Version. When the version was made, it was equivalent to " uncovered," but has now changed its signification.

Vers. 17—20.—

" He stretched forth *his hand* from on high ; he took me,
He drew me out of many waters.
He delivered me from my strong enemy,
From them that hated me ; for they were too mighty for me.
For they attacked me in the day of my misfortune.
But Jehovah became my Staff,
And he brought me forth into a wide place ;
He delivered me, because he had pleasure in me."

In the midst of this fearful convulsion of nature, while all around are stricken with panic, David sees a hand stretched out from above, ready to deliver him from the overwhelming flood of hatred and peril. **Attacked me.** The word does not signify "to prevent," or "anticipate," but "to assail." So in ver. 6, " The snares of death assailed me ;" and in Isa. xxxvii. 33, " The King of Assyria shall not attack this city with shield." It is the same verb in all these places. **Staff**; in the Authorized Version, " stay." But it means something to lean upon, and is rightly translated " staff " in Ps. xxiii. 4. **A wide place** ; in opposition to the straits of affliction. **He had pleasure in me.** In ch. xv. 26 this confidence is gone, and David doubts whether the favour of Jehovah had not been forfeited by him.

Vers. 21—25.—

" Jehovah hath requited me according to my righteousness,
According to the cleanness of my hands hath he recompensed me.
For I have kept the ways of Jehovah,
And sinned not so as to depart from my God.
For all his judgments have been kept in sight,
And from his statutes I have not departed.
I was also perfect towards him,
And was on my guard against my sin.
Therefore hath Jehovah recompensed me according to my righteousness,
According to my cleanness in his eyesight."

It is impossible to suppose that these verses could have been written after David's fall.

For while he acknowledges in them a tendency to sin, he affirms that he had been on his guard against it, and that he had ever kept God's statutes present before his view. However complete may be the penitent's recovery, yet can he never again be " perfect," the word applied to an animal without blemish, and therefore fit for sacrifice. The crime remains a blemish, even though the intense sorrow for the sin may make it the means of even attaining to a higher stage of spirituality and devotion. In ver. 22 the words literally are, " I have not sinned away from God," sin necessarily removing the sinner away from that nearness to God which is the privilege of the saint.

Vers. 26—28.—

" With the pious man thou wilt show thyself pious ;
With the perfect man thou wilt show thyself perfect ;
With the pure thou wilt show thyself pure ;
And with the crooked thou wilt show thyself perverse.
And the afflicted people thou wilt save ;
And thine eyes are upon the haughty, to bring them down."

Having affirmed his integrity, and that God therefore had pleasure in him and rewarded him, David now asserts that this is the unfailing rule of God's dealings with men. The general current of their lives is so ordered as to be in harmony with their characters. It is not by luck or good fortune that prosperity attends the righteous, nor is it by chance that things go awry with the fraudulent, but it is by the law of God's providence. **Pious.** The Hebrew word means " pious " in the original sense of the word, which includes kindness to men as well as love to God. **Perverse.** In the Authorized Version " unsavoury." Really it is the same word as that used in Ps. xviii. 26, and signifies " thou wilt make thyself twisted," only the form is archaic, as is the case with some other words here. Experience confirms the psalmist's verdict. For constantly a strange perversity of fortune and an untowardness of events are the lot of those whose hearts are crooked. **Afflicted.** The word in the original includes the idea of humility, and so leads naturally on to the thought of the abasement of the proud. In the psalm the somewhat harsh expression used here has been softened into the more easy phrase, " The haughty eyes thou wilt bring down."

Vers. 29—31.—

" For thou, Jehovah, art my Lamp ;
And Jehovah will make my darkness light.

For by thee do I run upon a troop;
In my God I leap over a wall.
God—his way is perfect;
The word of Jehovah is purified.
He is a Shield to all that trust in him."

Lamp. The lamp burning in the house is the proof of life and activity present there; and thus the extinguishing of the lamp means ruin and desolation (Job xxi. 17). So David is called "the lamp of Israel" (ch. xxi. 17), because the active life of the nation centred in him. In a still higher sense the life and being of his people centres in God, and without him the soul is waste and void, like the universe before God said, "Let there be light." **I run.** To the warrior in old time speed was as important as strength, and thus Homer constantly calls Achilles "fleet of foot." It was his fleetness which gave Asahel a high place among the mighties (ch. ii. 18), and to this quality David now refers. The **troop** signifies a light-armed band of marauders, whom with God's aid David could overtake, and stop in their course of rapine. The **wall** means fortifications like those of Jerusalem (ch. v. 7). Sieges were tedious affairs in old time, but David had captured that city with a rapidity so great that the metaphor in the text is most appropriate. **Purified;** or, *refined.* This does not mean that it is proved by experience and found true, but that it is absolutely good and perfect like refined gold (see Ps. xii. 6).

Vers. 32—34.—

" For who is God, save Jehovah ?
And who is a rock, save our God ?
God is my strong Fortress,
And he guideth the perfect in his way.
He maketh my feet like the hinds,
And upon my high places he doth set me."

God; Hebrew, *El;* the Mighty One, used several times in this psalm. In the second clause the word is *Elohim,* the ordinary name of God. The psalmist's question is a strong assertion that Jehovah alone is God, and that he alone is a Rock of safety for his people. **He guideth,** etc. In Ps. xviii. 32 "He maketh my way perfect," like his own. The phrase here is probably that which David wrote, as being less usual, and it signifies that God will direct the upright man in his good way. **Hinds.** David's feet are swift as hinds, an animal famous for its speed and sureness of foot. **My high places.** The tops of the mountains are the favourite resort of the antelope (ch. i. 18); and so with David, the possession of such rocky citadels as Bozez and Seneh (1 Sam. xiv. 4) made him master of the whole country.

Vers. 35—37.—

" He teacheth my hands to war;
And mine arms can bend a bow of bronze.
And thou hast given me thy saving shield;
And thy hearing of me hath made me great.
Thou hast enlarged my steps under me;
And my feet have not slipped."

Bow of bronze. In Job xx. 24 we also read of bows made of this metal, or compound of metals, which was a far more ancient material for weapons than steel. The bending of such a bow was proof of great strength, and the last artifice of Penelope, to save herself from the suitors, was to promise her hand to the man who could bend Ulysses' bow. **Thy hearing of me;** in Ps. xviii. 35, and Authorized-Version and Revised Version here, "thy gentleness." The words in the Hebrew are very nearly alike, but the Septuagint notices the difference, and translates "hearing" in this place, but "chastisement" in the psalm. The Vulgate has "gentleness" or "mildness" here, and "discipline" in the psalm. The Syriac alone has "discipline" in both places. **My feet;** literally, *ankle-bones,* the weakness of which causes men to totter.

Vers. 38—40.—

" I have pursued my enemies and destroyed them;
Neither did I turn again until I had consumed them.
And I have consumed them, and smitten them through, and they arose not;
Yea, they fell under my feet.
For thou hast girded me with strength unto the battle;
Thou hast made them that rose against me to bow under me."

In the Psalms, for **destroyed** we find "overtaken," and the second "I have consumed them" is omitted. This exultation of David at the result of his wars is in accordance with the harsh treatment inflicted by him upon the vanquished. His enemies were God's enemies, whom he must consume. The "new commandment" of Christianity forbids and condemns this delight in conquest.

Vers. 41—43.—

" And mine enemies thou hast made to turn upon me their back,
Even those that hate me; and I have utterly destroyed them.
They looked, but there was none to save,
Even to Jehovah, but he answered them not.
And I beat them small as the dust of the earth;
As the mire of the streets I stamped upon them, I trode them down."

Those that hate me. The sentence is to be completed from the previous clause, "my haters" and "my enemies" being equivalent. There are several small variations between the text here and in Ps. xviii., such as "they cried" for **they looked**; and "I emptied them out" for **I stamped upon them**, the difference in both cases consisting in a single letter.

Vers. 44—46.—

"And thou hast delivered me from the strivings of my people;
Thou hast protected me that I might be head of the nations.
A people whom I knew not have become my servants;
Children of strangers have submitted themselves to me;
At the hearing of the ear they obeyed me.
The children of the strangers faded away;
They fled trembling out of their fastnesses."

People, in the singular, means the Jewish people as opposed to the nations, that is, the heathen world. **The strivings** here referred to are the long dissensions which followed Ishbosheth's death, and delayed for many years the appointment of David as king of all Israel. He now feels that the watchful care which had protected him during that dangerous period had a higher purpose than the union of the twelve tribes under one head. He was to be the founder also of that empire over the nations which symbolized the gift of the heathen world to Christ. And this empire had been extended to people previously unknown to David. Such might be the case with Hadarezer, King of Zobah, but it more especially referred to Toi, and the Hittite kingdom of Hamath (ch. viii. 9). It was not from force of arms, but from the hearing of the ear, that is, from the wide-extended fame of David's conquests, that Toi sent ambassadors to offer allegiance and presents. **They fled trembling.** This is certainly the sense in Ps. xviii. 45, where, however, there is a transposition of letters. Probably it is the sense here. But if we might go to the cognate languages for an explanation of a rare word, it would mean "came limping out of their fastnesses," as men worn out with fatigue and exhaustion.

Vers. 47—49.—

"Jehovah liveth; and blessed be my Rock,
And exalted be the God of the rock of my salvation,
Even the God that giveth me avengements,
And bringeth down peoples under me.
And bringeth me forth from my enemies.
Yea, thou liftest me up above those that rise up against me;
From the violent man thou deliverest me."

In Ps. xviii. 46 we find simply "the God of my salvation." Perhaps there seemed to the compiler to be some confusion in calling Jehovah, first David's Rock, and then the God of his rock (but see note on ver. 3). **Avengements, in** the plural. In the Law the sanctions were chiefly temporal, and therefore the saints of old watched anxiously for, and were strengthened by observing, the constantly recurring proofs of God's righteous government of men. **Peoples, in** the plural; heathen nations. **The violent man** may especially be Saul, as is supposed in the title prefixed to this song in the Book of Psalms. There probably it is general, and includes all who were bitter in their hostility to David.

Vers. 50, 51.—

"Therefore will I praise thee among the nations,
And to thy Name will I sing.
Great deliverance giveth he to his king,
And showeth grace to his messiah—
To David, and to his seed for ever."

Great deliverance; literally, *he maketh great the salvation of his king;* that is, he rescueth him marvellously again and again. The K'ri substitutes *tower*, but it has no support either from the versions or from Ps. xviii., though admitted into the Authorized Version. The difference between the two words "making great" and "tower" is, in the Hebrew, trifling. **To his messiah.** This mercy was shown to David as the anointed theocratic king, whose rule was the symbol of that of Christ.

HOMILETICS.

Vers. 1—4.—*Songs of deliverance.* The facts are: **1.** David composes a song at the end of all the deliverances which during his life God had wrought for him. **2.** He describes God as being to him a Rock, a Fortress, a Shield, a High Tower, a Place of Refuge, and represents him as being actively his Deliverer and Saviour. **3.** He, in looking on to the future, resolves to trust in him who had been so much to his life in the past, and expects to be saved from his enemies. **4.** He, reviewing the past, feels that God is worthy of the praise expressed in this song. There is a beautiful congruity in the place of this song being at the close of the most detailed and protracted narrative of personal history to be found in the Old Testament, and even in the entire Bible with the exception of that referring to Christ—seeing that that history was one of most strange vicissitudes, and full of dangers. The story of David's life is so necessarily occupied with events as they appeared to men and as they pertain to visible history, that this song is a true supplement, inasmuch as it brings into view the deep spiritual feelings that influenced him in the midst of those events, and so furnishes a key to the religious life of the great king. This song of deliverances reminds us of the song of Moses when Israel triumphed over Pharaoh and his hosts at the Red Sea (Exod. xv.), of the song of the ransomed as they were to return to Zion with everlasting joy on their heads (Isa. xxxv. 10), and of the still more wonderful new song by the redeemed from all nations and kindreds of the earth (Rev. v. 9—13; xiv. 1—3). In these historic and prophetic instances we have illustrations of songs of deliverance ever rising from grateful hearts, establishing thus with the past and the future a community of religious experience which is at once a fruit and an evidence of the Divine redemption wrought out by our Saviour. Taking the experience of David as our guide, we may observe—

I. The perils of life are sometimes so extreme as to induce immense efforts to escape them. History tells us some of the perils of David's life, both when Saul pursued him with relentless cunning and cruelty, and when, as king, kindred, friend, and foe, and also the unseen powers of darkness, sought his ruin. The subsequent references in vers. 5, 6 give his impression of the greatness of his distress; and the allusions to "rock," "high tower," and "fortress" remind us of the time when his extremity was such that he climbed the craggy cliff or hid himself in the inaccessible clefts of the rocks. No man was so near to death as was David, and no good man came nearer to moral and spiritual destruction than did he in the case of Bathsheba and Uriah. This is the common lot of men on earth, though some find their perils less than those of their fellows. In business affairs, in statesmanship, in special enterprises, in matters of health, in common intercourse with men, and in spiritual experience, there are seasons when it seems to be a question of a few hours whether we make wreck or escape. Then comes a strain, a demand on our fullest resources, corresponding to that on David when Saul sought his life, or when spiritual destruction was in the train of Bathsheba's unholy love.

II. No high character raises us above liability to these extreme perils. The world is infested with evil, and the best characters find that, as mortal, fallible men, they are liable to the exigencies of life, and as good men they are objects of attack by the powers of darkness. David was an honest, sincere, devout man, and specially dear to God when Saul hunted his life; and he was superior to many before the horrible temptation to depart from purity fell upon his soul. Character is a defence against some dangers, else were it of little worth; but danger to our calling, our enterprises, our health, our moral position—subtle and serious—cannot but be our earthly lot. Even our Lord knew the tempter's power in the bitterness of poverty; and he warned the best men around his Person to expect peril to earthly interests, and to watch lest at any time even their devouter hearts should be overcharged with surfeiting and drunkenness and the cares of this life (Luke xxi. 34; cf. 16).

III. Truly religious men will use every effort to escape these perils. In his reference to "rock," "refuge," and "fortress," David at once carries us back to the time when he used his utmost endeavours to escape from Saul by climbing the rocks and taking refuge among the fastnesses of the mountains (1 Sam. xxii. 1, 5; xxiii. 14, 15). David acted as though all depended on himself. The cave, the cliff, the gorge, the lofty peak, were sought to cover him as a "shield," or to raise him as on a "high tower." So far as the two men were concerned, it was a case of skill against skill, endurance against endurance. So, also, in the more spiritual conflicts of his life, he laboured hard to save himself from destruction. Prayer, meditation on the Divine Law, taking heed to his steps, going to the house of the Lord, were so many forms of personal exertion to escape the foes of his highest life. So is it with the followers of Christ. They strive daily to ward off the ills which threaten their temporal interests, and when peril becomes extreme, they stir up all their energies to maintain their head high above all impending evils; and what is true of temporal is true also of spiritual interests—they give all diligence to make their calling sure.

IV. THE VISIBLE MEANS OF SAFETY USED BY RELIGIOUS MEN ARE AN INDEX OF AN INVISIBLE RESOURCE. It is just here that we get at the heart of David's meaning. A spectator, observing how he set his skill against that of Saul, how he baffled the cruel persecutor by feats of daring among the caves and clefts of the rock, might conclude that success was decided by a mere balance of ingenuity and agility—the rock, the cave, were his defence. But no; he used these visible things, but all the time his soul was resting in the protection of God. There was a double exercise of energy—that which expressed itself in agility of movement among the mountain fastnesses, and that which expressed itself in calm trust in the care of God. *God* was his Rock, his Shield, his Fortress. As Elijah saw chariots of fire where others saw nothing but vacant air, so he saw the Eternal Rock, and in him made his refuge. The same double exercise of energy was at work in his strenuous efforts to maintain his piety. It was not prayer, use of the Divine Law, and watchfulness that he trusted in, but the ever-present and faithful God. Herein is the characteristic of a truly godly man. An inner spiritual activity accompanies all the external forms. His soul goes out after the living God. He finds safety in the invisible Rock of Ages. God in Christ is his actual Hiding-place.

V. THE BEST THINGS IN NATURE ARE BUT SYMBOLS AND SHADOWS OF EXCELLENCE IN GOD. The rock and the high tower were the very best things nature afforded to David in his dreadful season of trial. Those wilds then answered indeed a noble purpose. But David saw in their protecting powers only a shadow of the real protecting power of which he was in need. All the saving virtues of the mountain fastnesses were to him the index of the boundless resources that lie in God. He is *the Rock*. Throughout Scripture there seems to be an effort to set forth, if possible, the reality and vastness and sufficiency of the treasures which are in God for us. Thus Christ is represented as being the chief and best of all things in nature—among stars, the Bright and Morning Star; among fruit-bearing trees, the luxurious Vine; of members of the body, the Head. Nature can only indicate what wealth of resources we have in him. His riches are unsearchable (Eph. iii. 8).

VI. A REVIEW OF PAST SIGNAL DELIVERANCES ENCOURAGES CONFIDENCE IN RESPECT TO THE FUTURE. Reviewing the wonderful deliverances wrought for him, David says, "In him will I trust;" "I shall be saved from mine enemies." The conflict of life was not over. New dangers will arise, and other enemies will fill the ranks of the fallen. But experience of God's merciful help keeps the spirit calm, and every triumph in the past by his favour is a guarantee that he will be a very present Help in every time of need. How could David doubt the goodness and power of God after so rich an experience of his aid? If for no other reason than the confidence it inspires, an occasional deliberate review of what great things God has done for us is very desirable. Doubt and fear spring from too much attention to ourselves. Security lies in the covenant of God, and not in our own powers, and a remembrance of actual help received is a reading afresh of the many Divine ratifications of the covenant. The din and hurry of daily life are adverse to reflective habits. It is well to make positive efforts at certain stages of life to resist the hindrances to reflection, and allow to pass before the mind the varied instances in which God has rescued us from impending ruin, both temporal and spiritual.

VII. A RATIONAL BASIS FOR PRAISE IS LAID IN A CONSIDERATION OF GOD'S GREAT DELIVERANCES. It is not without solid reason that David says, "I will call on the Lord, who is worthy to be praised." There are manifold reasons why praise should be rendered to God, but here the basis in view is that found by a consideration of the various acts of mercy he has shown. David's deliverance from Saul, from the treachery of Doeg and Ahithophel, from the sorrows and shame of the banishment from throne and city, and from the more fearful woes of backsliding, were indeed events never to be forgotten. They meant to him life, joy, honour, instead of death and disgrace. All that is valuable in life, in distinction, in personal holiness, and victory over spiritual evil, appealed to his generous nature to acknowledge in thankful form the great things which God had done. It is the wont of some agnostic writers to represent the requirement of praise to God as essentially immoral—as a low representation of God as selfishly egotistic. It might be enough to say that agnostics have no right to speak of essential morality, since on their principles there can be no such thing. But apart from that, it overlooks the real teaching of Scripture and the natural action of human hearts. Men are not condemned for not praising God, but for being lovers of sin in thought, feeling, and deed. Their condition necessarily involves a condemnation, as surely as an anarchical state involves, by its condition, its own destruction. Their not rendering acknowledgments to God for his mercies is only a symptom of the real evil, and not the actual cause of condemnation. A heart true to generous and pure instincts will always admire power blended with goodness, and be thankful for good placed within reach by that beneficent power. " Praise is comely."

VIII. The deliverances wrought for us by God are only preliminary bless-ings. All through these verses David speaks of deliverance, of being saved from certain evils, and God as a Deliverer, a Saviour. This, of course, is a negative good; it is doing something that he may *not* die, and *not* be lost. But it is only a superficial view to say that this was all that David was thinking of. His present position as honoured king, ruling over a united nation, and blessed with a moral elevation superior to any other man then living, is the counterfoil to this negative aspect. There was no need to say in words what he now was. His life tells that side of the record of God's mercy and power. He refers to the deliverances as blessings preliminary to his positive elevation to honour·and distinction. Being delivered from the hand of Saul, he was made king in succession; being saved from the banishment consequent on Absalom's rebellion, of course he was positively restored; being rescued from the sin of back-sliding, of course he was reinstated in the Divine favour and holiness of life. This is the correct and New Testament view of the great deliverance, or salvation, wrought for us by Christ. We are delivered from the curse and guilt of sin; but that is the negative good, preliminary, necessary to the implied positive elevation to sonship and eternal holiness. He saves from condemnation, but does not leave us as merely liberated souls. He gives us therewith " power to become the sons of God." He makes us " kings and priests unto God." The positive aspect of salvation means elevation, progress, con-formity of nature to the Divine will.

Vers. 5—19.—*God's answer to the cry of distress.* The facts are: 1. David repre-sents death, the grave, and ungodly men, under various figures, as causing him deep distress. 2. He states that, on crying unto God out of the greatness of his distress, his voice entered even into his ears. 3. He thus indicates, in strong figurative language, the tokens of God's attention to his cry. (1) Some manifest signs of his displeasure against his foes (vers. 8, 9). (2) A speedy and yet mysterious condescension to the need of his servant (vers. 10, 11). (3) The blending of concealed purpose with distinct manifestations of the reality of his interposition (vers. 12—14). (4) The pressure of his agencies on David's enemies (ver. 15). (5) The thorough rending of all barriers by his mighty power so as to effect deliverance for his servant (vers. 16—19). David represents his condition as one of isolated anguish—he is cut off from God and man, standing in a position of peril and suffering, from which there is no chance of escape. Doubtless there were several occasions in his checkered life when this was true; but he describes them in the terms more strictly appropriate to the time when, being pursued by Saul and his emissaries, he took refuge in mountains. Like one standing on a slight elevation when the floods are gathering around, he sees only, on every side, death as waves eager to sweep him away. The ungodly men with Saul rush on as a torrent from which there is no escape. The sorrows arising from the thought of all his youthful and patriotic aspirations being soon buried in a premature grave, and a once promising life being cut off as a worthless thing, gather irresistibly around his soul. Whichever way he turns, to the cliffs or the plain, to the ravine or the cave, he sees that death is there spreading out snares to catch him. Neither God nor man is nigh to rescue. Life's great and holy purposes are being crushed and blighted for ever. No one cares for his soul. It was then, when destruction was inevitable, that, as a last desperate resort, he poured out his anguish before God and *cried* for help. The help came, and the fact and form of the interposition are the theme of his song. Here we notice—

I. Providence permits men to come into great extremities. David's life was especially providential. He was from his youth the child of Providence, and yet, for no other traceable reason than his patriotism and his goodness, he was persecuted by Saul, a jealous, suspicious king, even to the degree that life was despaired of. All the forces of society and of nature seemed to go against him, and meanwhile the God of his youth and early manhood was silent and apparently far away. Our only interpretation of the facts is that God allows his servants sometimes to be brought very low. He does not give them the immunity from pain and peril which their relative goodness and fidelity would seem to warrant. Yet this is not the result of mere arbitrariness or neglect. It is part of an educational purpose, and inseparable from a government of men free in their deeds of wrong. The latent qualities of the righteous and their powers for future use can often be best developed by means of adverse events which throw them more absolutely on God than under smooth and easy conditions they ever could be. We need not be surprised if we fall into manifold trials (1 Pet. iv. 12).

II. The extremities of life develop the full strength of prayer. David had been accustomed, like all pious men, to pray, but now he *cried* unto God. There was a reserve store of prayer in him which now became developed. He realized as never before his need of God, his helplessness, apart from pure Divine interposition and aid, to accomplish the purpose for which he had been selected by Samuel. There was more faith in him than he had been aware of, and now it was brought into exercise. This was the first gain in the educational process. In the spiritual life, as in the physical and mental, our capacities become atrophied if not well used, and circumstances that draw them forth in unusual degree enrich us with a permanent legacy of increased power. There is a natural tendency to *inertia*, which the stress of our environment urges us to overcome. How great is the power placed in our hands by the privilege of prayer, who can tell? There are indications of its greatness in particular instances recorded in the Bible and known in modern life. It availeth much. It is the human agency by which the exercise of the Almighty Power has conditioned its own exercise. How seldom do we *cry* unto God as though we really wanted him and his aid!

III. The interposition of God on behalf of his people is a reality in life. David contrasts in thought his position and that of his enemies. He was apparently left alone by God and man; they were prosperous, numerous, strong, and eager as rolling waves. Death was before and behind him, so that he could not move; they were free to act, and no one to put them in peril. But a change came; the cry of distress had entered into the very ear of God, and, as though there were a sudden change in the Divine relationship to human forces, rescue came. To David the interposition was as real as the previous peril and agony. It was not mere faint-heartedness in Saul, not accidental diversion of his thoughts, not a simple refusal of his men to go further in pursuit of the victim of his malice; it was God who had somehow so acted on men and things as to bring about deliverance. The strong figures used by David in vers. 8—12 express the conviction that God had come to his help, not simply by the action of normal laws, but by the invisible contact of the eternal energy with those laws, wondrously subordinating them to a special design. The true believer still sees God in his great deliverances. The answer to prayer is a great reality. God can and does get at his suffering children. Men see not the invisible hand, but those who *cry* to God recognize it. The profoundest matters of life are objects of faith, and in faith, as in intention, there is a transcendent knowledge passing all demonstration and all communication.

IV. A review of Divine interpositions brings out to the eye of faith their strong characteristics. David here reflects on the deliverances wrought for him in answer to earnest prayer, and their characteristics appear to him to be best represented by the bold and vigorous language in vers. 8—16. Among these we may notice: 1. *A twofold revelation*—to himself, as the God of power actually stooping to his help, and holding in his hand the most terrible and most subtle forces of nature; and to his enemies, as the great God causing his voice so to be heard in the course of things as to reveal his wrath and impress men with a sense of his greatness and majesty. 2. *An assurance blended with uncertainty.* The coming down and the Divine brightness brought assurance unmistakable; but the darkness and mystery of his movements indicated that his methods of working out a saving purpose were beyond human penetration. 3. *Use of appropriate agencies for frustrating wicked purposes.* The Divine "arrows" were so directed by unerring wisdom as to scatter those who hitherto were bent on pursuit. 4. *Thoroughness in clearing away all natural obstacles to the perfecting of the deliverance.*   So thorough was the reserve to be that the swollen torrents and deep places were to be entirely made bare of water in order to render escape complete.   We may look at our deliverances as from enemies human or fiendish, and we shall find that God does make himself known as our Friend, and causes our foes to feel his displeasure.   We know that he helps, but we know not all his ways. He brings influences to bear on our foes, so that they are weakened, and what he does he does perfectly, clearing away whatever may hinder our safety.   The same general truths will hold good if we look at our many deliverances from spiritual peril. He sets himself against evil, and comes to our sorrowing soul.   He lets us know enough for our cheer, but does not throw full light on all his methods.   He brings the mighty influences of his Word and Spirit to destroy the power of sin, and by the tremendous work of Christ clears away every obstacle to our full salvation.

GENERAL LESSONS.   1. When we come into great troubles let us take comfort that in this matter we are sharing in an experience which, in the case of some of the best of men, has developed a more earnest spirit of prayer.   2. The records of God's dealings with his saints shows that there is no distress too deep for him to reach and remedy.   3. There is no place on earth but that the voice of prayer is free to enter into God's holy temple and even to his ear.   4. Although for a season during the prosperity of those who persecute the pious it may seem as though they were exempt from displeasure, yet God is angry with them, and will in some significant way cause them to know it.   5. However desperate our case, we may rest assured that God is in possession of all the means of gaining access to our need, and of scattering whatever evils threaten us with ruin.   6. There are no powers, however deep-seated and established, but that, if we trust in God, he will clear them out of the way, so that we may find a position of safety, and consequent elevation to honour and blessedness.

Vers. 20—30.—*God's righteousness in saving the righteous.*   The facts are: 1. David states that, in delivering him from his enemies, God recognized his uprightness and purity.   2. He affirms that, as a matter of fact, he had in his conduct endeavoured to live according to the will of God.   3. He declares the general truth that, in thus rescuing him the upright, and showing disfavour to the perverse persecutor, there was exemplified the principle of the usual Divine procedure.   4. He ascribes the successes of the past, not to himself, however upright, but to God, his Light in darkness and his Strength for deeds of daring.   There is, in David's references to his own righteousness and purity, an appearance of what is now called self-righteousness.   He seems to violate the primary canons of Christian propriety and to establish a doctrine of merit. But this interpretation of his words is an utter misconception of his meaning, and proceeds from an ignorance of the historical circumstances he had in mind when penning the words.   It is a wrong done to personal experiences of the Old Testament to approach their interpretation with certain prepossessions based on New Testament teaching with reference to our personal unworthiness before God on account of our essential sinfulness.   David was not speaking of his state absolutely before God; he was not thinking of the question as to whether he or any one else was a sinner.   His sole thought was of the distinct charges brought against him by such men as Doeg the Edomite, and believed by the foolish king Saul; and he was conscious that his being hunted by Saul was a grievous wrong, a treatment he did not deserve.   *He* was the righteous man, for he loved Saul, showed him kindness, and paid him honour; *Saul* and *Doeg* and *others* in the conspiracy were the unrighteous men, uttering falsehoods, using cruelty, and cherishing malice.   God came as Judge between them, and by interposition showed his delight in what his servant had been and done in this particular matter, and his displeasure with Saul for his wicked conduct.   He vindicates the gracious interposition of God on the ground that it is a righteous and glorious thing on the part of God to rescue those who suffer unrighteously, and to declare, by his rescue of them, his delight in them as compared with the men who cause their sufferings (cf. 1 Sam. xxi. 7; xxii. 9—13, 18—23; xxiv. 7—15; xxvi. 10—20). The vindication and illustration of God's righteousness in saving his people may be considered as follows.

I. THERE ARE SPECIAL INSTANCES IN WHICH IT MAY BE SAID THAT GOD SAVES THE RIGHTEOUS.   In ordinary speech we say that God saves sinners.   That is true in the sense that all men saved, whether temporally or spiritually, are, in their relation to him, sinful, or transgressors of the Law. But in relation to others and in relation to specific obligations which he may impose on them, they may be relatively righteous, and his saving them may be because they are so. Thus: 1. *Those who are righteous in life, as compared with others, are saved from calamity and suffering.* Noah was a righteous man, and therefore was spared, while the Flood carried away the wicked. Lot was a righteous man in comparison with the Sodomites, and therefore was delivered by Divine pressure put upon him from the destruction which befell the rest. Some of the better Churches in Asia were not doomed to the woe that was to come on others, because God "knew their works" (Rev. ii., iii.). The more holy and devoted to Christ we are, and the more minutely our lives are regulated by the laws of God as written in his Word and works, and in our own mental and physical nature, the more shall we be saved from woes that come upon others who violate laws physical, moral, and spiritual. 2. *Those who suffer as being unrighteous, when all the time they are not so.* This was the case of David, who was persecuted most bitterly by Saul on the ground that he hated his king and sought his life, when all the time he loved his king and guarded his life. It was as a righteous man in this particular that God saved him from distress. The same was true of Joseph in prison; of the Apostles Peter and Paul; yea, of our Saviour himself. And often still does God save his people from the reproach and sorrow brought on them by being represented as being other than they really are (Matt. v. 11, 12; 1 Pet. iv. 14—17). 3. *Those who conform to the gospel law of salvation.* Before God all are sinners, and condemned by their own consciences as also by the broken Law. But Christ has made full atonement for sin, and now therefore God, in his sovereign grace, has laid down a new law for us to keep, based upon his acceptance of Christ's perfect work, namely, that we exercise faith in Christ as our atoning Saviour. We are not to try and keep the Decalogue as a condition of being accepted; we cannot attain to the righteousness of the moral Law. We are not to plead the value of repentance and a future life better than the past; all that is indefinite, uncertain. But we are simply to have faith in Christ as set forth in the gospel, *that* is all that God requires for our acceptance; that is the newly created law, the sum of all obligations in reference to obtaining justification before God. In other words, we are to attain to the "righteousness of faith," the righteousness which consists in fulfilling the obligation created by gospel grace, and then there is no condemnation: we walk then as freed sons in the glorious liberty of the children of God.

II. IN ALL THESE INSTANCES IT IS CONSONANT WITH GOD'S NATURE TO SAVE THE RIGHTEOUS. God's treatment of Noah and Lot, and of all who keep his truth in the midst of prevailing degeneracy, marks his distinction of character on the basis of goodness. It is the Divine nature to love the good and hate the evil tendencies of men. When the persecuted are delivered, there is a vindication of character and a repressing of wrong which cannot but accord with God's natural love of justice. When he graciously accepts us on the condition that we have fulfilled all that he requires under the gospel order, and in our justification recognizes the "righteousness of faith" (Rom. iii. 25—28; iv. 5, 6, 11, 13), he, accepting that kind of righteousness, that fulfilment of all obligation, maintains the honour of the violated Law under which we had lived, and glorifies the sacrificial work of his beloved Son. There is therefore nothing arbitrary in the "law of faith."

III. THESE SPECIAL INSTANCES OF SALVATION ARE IN ACCORD WITH THE GENERAL PRINCIPLE OF GOD'S GOVERNMENT. David was quite warranted in saying that when God, in the matter of the deliverance from the persecutions of Saul, recompensed him according to his righteousness (ver. 25), he was simply acting in harmony with his general kindness to the merciful and upright, and his stern and repressive ways of providence toward the perverse (vers. 26, 27). The actual laws revealed in the Decalogue, in the civil institutions of Moses, in the precepts of the New Testament, in the constitution of the physical and mental worlds, all go for the good and against the wicked, whatever be the form or degree of the goodness or wickedness. It may be that, for reasons not yet made clear, the wicked triumph for a while and the righteous cry out in agony, "O Lord, how long!" but God's government is vast, intricate, and stretching far into the future, and there are forces at work by which at last the righteous shall be exalted and the wicked abased (Ps. v. 4—6, 11, 12; xxxvii. 6, 7, 23—40).

IV. THOSE WHO ARE SAVED BY GOD ON THE GROUND OF RIGHTEOUSNESS LAY NO CLAIM TO MERIT. The object of David in this passage is not to proclaim his own deeds and claim a right to God's favour, but rather to set forth the righteousness and goodness of God in saving those who conform to his will. He had kept the ways, the statutes, and the judgments of God (vers. 23, 24) in respect to his behaviour toward Saul,—he could honestly say that; and he considers it a matter of praise and glory to God that he manifested his love of what is just in coming to the rescue of such a one. To have allowed Saul to triumph would have been a reflection on Divine justice. In all this, therefore, there is no reference to merit in the sight of God, any more than Noah felt that he merited God's favour. It was in neither case a question of the desert of the entire life, but of the state of the life in relation to other men. So in our personal salvation through faith, there is no claim of merit. It is all of grace. The "law of faith" is the creation of grace, and the heart to conform to it is of grace. The light in which we see spiritual things, and in which we rejoice, is not our own. The Lord is our Lamp, and he lightens our darkness (ver. 29). If we are able to break through troops of spiritual foes, and leap over walls (ver. 30) that hem us in, it is not because of our strength; it is only by our God, who of his free mercy supplies all our need.

Vers. 31—51.—The facts are: 1. David asserts the exclusive perfection of God. 2. He states that his strength and power are from God, and that God teaches him to move and act with advantage in times of war and difficulty. 3. He refers to the help received through the graciousness of God, and the fact that thereby he was able to subdue all his enemies. 4. He alludes to the subjugation of the people to himself as the consequence of Divine help, and looks on to further triumphs over strangers. 5. He recounts the fact of his deliverance, and makes the final reference to them a fresh reason for thanksgiving.

Knowledge of God founded on experience. From vers. 31 to 37 David seems to state some of the results arising out of his experience of God's dealing with him during the earlier portion of his life. He can now say with emphasis what at one time could only be said as a matter of general profession on the part of a pious Hebrew; and there is in ver. 31 an implied contrast with certain apprehensions entertained during those seasons of isolation and distress, when no one cared for his soul, and the course of providence seemed to be all against him. And in this respect others are like him; the more profound their personal experience in life, the more clear and sure are their conceptions of the ineffable perfections of God.

I. A KNOWLEDGE OF GOD IS MORE A QUESTION OF PERSONAL EXPERIENCE THAN OF SPECULATION. Among the Hebrews there were grand traditional beliefs and conceptions which placed their pure monotheism far above the theistic faiths of other nations, and David in early years inherited these, and could give beautiful expression to them. But the traditional and even reasoned views which he had acquired were not his greatest treasure. A long life of communion, service, conflict, and patient trust had caused him to see that experience was the most important element in this matter of knowledge of God. No doubt it is possible to reason up to God. The logical outcome of the principle of causation is God, and the moral nature of man is only intelligible on the hypothesis of a supreme personal Ruler. It is not true that speculative philosophy leads away from God. All its lines, when straightly pursued, converge on him. The question is one of personal relations, and it is not within the competence of a speculative inquirer to settle this great question regardless of the deep, ineradicable, and most sacred experience of which human nature is capable.

II. AS A MATTER OF FACT, EXPERIENCE GIVES A CLEARER, FULLER, AND MORE ASSURED KNOWLEDGE THAN ANY OTHER MEANS. Experience is of first importance in matters pertaining to spiritual things. We know the reality of unseen beings existing beneath the fleshly covering of the body more truly by the mysterious contact of our self with an invisible counterpart, than by any physiological or psychological arguments. There is an inexpressible knowledge in our conscious intuitions of other minds being in communion with our own, which is the more clear, sure, and satisfying, in that it is inexpressible in words. Likewise the personal experience of holy men brings them so near to the living God, so directly in contact with his Spirit, and gives them such clear and irresistible convictions of his Being and his glorious character, that to such men the light thrown on the question of the Divine existence and character by processes of reasoning seems very cold and dim. They can dispense with it for themselves. Like the Apostle John, they have tasted and handled and felt the Divine reality (1 John i. 1—3).

III. THE CLEARER AND MORE SURE KNOWLEDGE RELATES ESPECIALLY TO HIS EXCLUSIVE PERFECTIONS. After his deep and often trying experience, David could speak most confidently of God as "perfect" in all things. He alone was worthy of the name God. The points referred to are : 1. His methods. 2. His Word. 3. His care. His *methods* of discipline, of guidance, of instruction, and of working out purposes seemed strange and obscure while David was in trial, but in the end he saw that all was *perfect*. So is it ever. The more we experience of his "ways," the more do we learn their wisdom, goodness, and justice. His "*Word*," considered as promise, covenant, revelation, or manifestation in Christ, requires personal experience to enable us to see how *perfect* it is. How hearty an "Amen" can multitudes give to this statement ! His *care* is discovered by our experience through scenes of danger and peril to be indeed sufficient, suited to every emergency, and most gentle and considerate. As our "Buckler," "Shield," and "Rock," we know him more truly, as life advances and the heart becomes charged with unutterable experiences, to be *perfect*. How vain are all the negations and disputations of restless speculators to the soul rich in such experience !

IV. THE KNOWLEDGE OF GOD GAINED BY EXPERIENCE ISSUES IN DEVELOPMENT OF CHARACTER AND FITNESS FOR HIGHEST FORM OF WORK. The holy man enriched by such knowledge is not a mere knowing creature ; he becomes a man of higher character and more extended activity. His way is made perfect ; his feet are those of the hind ; he rises to the best positions in the spiritual sphere ; his hands are fit for warfare ; he becomes calm and strong in the guarantee of a perpetual shield ; and distinction in the highest society and fitness for the holiest service are the outcome of God's gracious dealings. As David, after all his strange experience of God's power and gentleness, was more strong in faith, more skilful in administration, more apt at spiritual warfare, and more conformed to the Divine will ; so all who follow on to know the Lord more perfectly, and enter more deeply into the secret of the Lord, rise in spiritual character, and become more fit instruments for doing the purest form of work in the world.

The gentleness of God. This beautiful saying of David's, in ver. 36, is a wonderful illustration of the tenderness of his own heart, and of the deep and thoroughly evangelical thoughts he entertained of the character of God. There is much in this song to remind us of terrible power (vers. 7—18) ; but it was to David the power and terribleness of One who pities the poor and needy, and, out of his deep compassion, throws the shield of his almightiness over them. In one respect this display of power is an expression of gentleness ; it is tender care and loving-kindness for the needy in their defensive aspect. It was gentleness that took David from the sheepcote to make him King of Israel ; that succoured and consoled him when exiled in lonely mountains and heathen lands ; that spared his soul and healed his wounds when he fell into his dreadful sin ; that upheld his broken spirit when the crushing blow of rebellion came as chastisement for sin ; that gradually fashioned his character in spite of adverse influences of the age, and made him a blessing to Israel ; and that so toned his life that now in old age, instead of being a proud monarch boasting of his strength, he is constrained to ascribe all the glory of his life to God. It is the gentleness of God that elevates and ennobles all his people.

I. THIS QUALITY IS MOST CHARACTERISTIC OF GOD IN HIS DEALINGS WITH US. To it —called in the New Testament, *love*—we owe our redemption through Christ. The revelation of "righteousness," of which the Apostle Paul speaks (Rom. i. 17), is made because of the deep love of God, his tender pity for his erring children. Our Saviour, who is the express Image of his Person, was, during his earthly course, the *embodiment of all that is sweet, tender, pitiful, gentle.* The bruised reed, the smoking flax, knew his gentleness. Weeping widows, fallen women, outcast lepers, despised sinners, little children, a sorrowing Mary at the cross, were only a few instances in which the infinite tenderness of his nature went forth in words and deeds of blessing. The *spirit of his gospel* is that of *tender compassion* for all men. In our *personal experience* the same spirit is revealed. He found us bruised, defiled, without hope; and he tenderly bound up our wounds, took away our guilt, and gave us power to become his sons. In our *occasional lapses*, how tender, how patient, and pitiful! When *adversity has come*, home laid desolate, or health taken away, how gently his hand has held us up and assuaged our grief! And when by the open grave, and broken down with sorrow, his all-sufficing gentleness has come and turned our sorrow into joy. O blessed gentleness! How dear and precious is our God to our often weary and sinful hearts!

II. The influence of God's gentleness on us is to elevate our life. It made David "great." That was its object, and he, appreciating its blessedness, found that it did secure its object. A knowledge of this as the distinguishing quality in God's dealings with men, tends in itself to raise our conceptions of God, and of the order of his government. The end for which his gentleness found expression in the work of Christ is that we may be raised from our low estate, and be heirs of his own glory. When we open our hearts to his gentle Spirit, we, like the prodigal, rise from our degradation and become reinstated as beloved and honoured children. In seasons of calamity it gives us strength to endure and to wait, and a deep consciousness of its reality often throws over the character a more than earthly beauty; and when his love has done all its blessed work in us, we shall rise to a far more glorious position than that occupied by David when, as king, he reached the highest honour attainable among men (John xvii. 24).

III. The remembrance of his gentleness in the past is an encouragement to us for the future. David was evidently able to look on to the future with perfect composure. The love of the past was pledge for the future. Our review of God's gracious dealings with us will cause us to sing of his loving-kindness, and to fear no evil. Having given us his beloved Son, we are sure he will give us all things.

Life's warfare. From ver. 38 to ver. 44 David takes a general survey of his life's conflicts, and is able to say at the close that his triumph over enemies is complete. The language is strong, and to modern ears fierce and vindictive; but we have to consider the position which he believed himself to hold under God, and which he believed to be imperilled by his adversaries. He was, and knew it well, the anointed of the Lord, set over the people as the representative of God, and for the distinct purpose of preparing the way for the realization of those vast promises of good to the world made to Abraham, and devoutly cherished by every enlightened Hebrew. Consequently, the personal element in his case largely disappeared. The attacks on him were attacks on God's government, an effort to frustrate God's purposes; and, believing those purposes to be the wisest and best, he regarded the attempt to put them aside as most wicked; indeed, as the crime of high treason against the Eternal King. That men who thus oppose the Lord's anointed, and are instrumental in committing so great a sin or doing so serious a mischief in the world, deserved the judgment which God allowed to come is obvious, or he would not have allowed it; and, admitting this, there is no obvious sin in David expressing in figurative terms his acquiescence and even satisfaction in that judgment. There is no sin in a man's spiritual vision being so high and wide that he sees justice, and is glad that justice is done. It is only when we introduce the more personal element, and judge by it alone, that David's words are felt to be improper. His life's warfare suggests ours, and that being led on by the Captain of our salvation.

I. There are strong and bitter foes around us. Cruel men under Saul's leading, Amalekites, Philistines, and rebels within the kingdom, sought the ruin of David, both personally and in his capacity as anointed king. No words can set forth adequately the number, strength, activity, and combinations of the spiritual foes that practically seek our spiritual life, and also oppose the claims and prerogatives of Christ. Every Christian life is a spiritual reproduction of David's temporal life; and in the antagonism of our own Christian experience we have a miniature view of the great conflict going on between the King in Zion and the principalities and powers of darkness and the countless forces that lie concealed in the depths of human depravity.

II. The conflict is protracted and characterized by vicissitudes. From the day that Saul entertained a wicked jealousy of his powers (1 Sam. xviii. 8) till the revolt of Sheba, David had to be on his guard, and in some form or other defend his person and his right to the kingdom. Now he is in deepest distress, and now rescued by the interposition of God. Sorrow and joy were his portion. The lesson for us is obvious. Our warfare is lifelong. As long as there is lurking evil within the domain of our nature, as long as strong and subtle temptations come upon us, and the great enemy seeketh our life, so long we must stand in the whole armour of God, and watch and strive (Eph. vi. 10—17). And, also, we have our seasons of anguish and desolation, our faintings and fears, our falls and wounds, as well as our songs of triumph and joy. The Apostle Paul wrote at the close of his toils and conflicts as one who had suffered much and accomplished much. What is true of us personally is true in a way of the great Church militant; there are, as history reveals, times of sore defeat and sorrow and apparent abandonment, and times again of magnificent triumphs.

III. There is, through the conflict, abiding trust in God and use of gifts. The language in which David describes the issue of his conflicts reveals that all through he cherished unceasing faith in God, and used well the fingers to fight which Providence had trained. In darkest seasons his hope was in God. Not armies, but God, formed his Refuge, Strength, and Defence (vers. 40, 41). Saving the great lapse, when for a time the soul was estranged from its Source of blessing, there was a calm and unshaken confidence that the great purpose for which he was called to the throne would be realized, and this rendered moral support to all material means employed for subduing foes. It is the characteristic of our warfare that it is the "good fight of faith." From first to last, trust in the presence, help, and succour of God enters into the exercise of all watchfulness, prayerfulness, and resolute endeavours to subdue everything to Christ. Success in Christian warfare springs from a subtle blending of the most absolute faith in the almighty grace of God with the most energetic use of knowledge and resolve. By this combination also, the Church, in its corporate action, seeks to banish spiritual foes from the kingdom, and to extend Christ's supremacy over all people and lands.

IV. Certain and complete victory is the issue. If we compare David when an outcast among the caves of the mountains, or a wanderer among an alien people, dependent on heathen hospitality for his sustenance and protection (1 Sam. xxvii. 1—7), with David at the close of his reign, dwelling in regal splendour, and in peace from all his foes, we can see how complete his triumph, and how true in effect is the bold language of this song. Helpless, unbefriended by the Judge of all the earth, his oppressors are as the beaten dust and trampled mire. Aliens and the rebellious among his own people (vers. 41—44) alike are brought low, and all their pride and strength has vanished. It is only when we come to the end of our Christian career that we can say this of all our foes; but it can even now be said of many in the past. The strongest language of David will be inadequate to express the completeness of the victory we shall at last obtain over all spiritual foes. As Israel saw no living Egyptian as they stood on the shore of the Red Sea, and as the multitude in Rev. xv. 2—4 looked over the calm glassy scene of a former arena of conflict and peril, so we each shall, through Christ, be able to survey the past and see our enemies no more. More than conquerors, we shall sing the song of triumph. Sin and temptation, the horrible dangers, the slippery places, the roaring torrents, the deep waters, will have been overcome, and our sanctified nature will constitute a domain in which the voice of tumult is no more heard. Our personal triumph will be analogous to the triumph of Christ over all the evil forces that once opposed his blessed reign.

The glory of the accomplishment of life's purpose due to God. In the section from ver. 45 to ver. 51 David looks on to what God will yet do for him ; he reflects on what is now his happy position, and on the connection of this with the great deliverances of the past ; and, thus taking a threefold view of his life, he ascribes all the glory of real and possible achievements unto God (ver. 50). His own people and the heathen would regard him as a great king, and ascribe his wonderful successes to his superior prowess in war, and skill in administration. Not so the man of God. To his God he ascribes all the glory. Taking the particulars of David's life as means of illustration, we also may see that the accomplishment of our life's highest purpose is no occasion of praise to ourselves, but solely of glory to God.

I. GOD HAS CHOSEN US. David was called to leave the sheepfold, and raised by the distinct will of God to be what he subsequently came to be. Never does he forget this. It was all of free sovereign grace. No conquests over Philistines, no succession to Saul, no subjugation of people under him, no lofty piety for the enrichment of the world by its poetic utterances, would have had place but for the Divine choice. It is so of all men after God's own heart. He hath begotten them. He hath made them kings and priests unto himself. "We love him, because he first loved us." Whatever conquests we achieve in the spiritual life are an outcome of our having that life which, as clearly taught in the New Testament, is not of man, but of God (John iii. 5—8).

II. IN OURSELVES WE ARE UNWORTHY OF ANY BLESSING. David knew and felt that there was no worthiness in him that he should be called to be king. Whatever moral and mental fitness there may have been in him as compared with others, it was all of God, and constituted no more merit than the sweetness of the rose gives merit to the rose. And during his career he fell again and again, so that his spiritual condition was, so far as it depended on his watchfulness and care, not so perfect as it should have been. It was God's wonderful "gentleness" (ver. 36), and not his superior spiritual qualities or natural force of character, that had made him what he was. The experience of good men is the same in all ages. The ancient patriarch (Gen. xviii. 27), the evangelical prophet (Isa. vi. 5), and the Christian apostle (Rom. xv. 10), are one with the "sweet psalmist of Israel" in confessing entire unworthiness of the least of God's mercies. Self-renunciation before God is essential to true godliness. All the honour and glory are due to him.

III. GOD PROVIDES THE MEANS BY WHICH OUR LIFE'S PURPOSE IS WROUGHT OUT. The natural gifts that distinguished David, and the wisdom to use them, and the disposition to use them for the right ends, were provided for him. The mountain fast-nesses in which he found a shield from the oppressor, belonged to him who claims the "strength of the hills." The repressive influences brought to bear on the rebellious factions, and the concurrent events which issued in their death or depression, were ordered by a higher wisdom. The gift or non-withdrawal of the Holy Spirit on the occasion of the dreadful fall (Ps. li. 10, 11) was all of pure mercy. And thus it was through God alone that the tempted, tried, sorrowing king was enabled to pursue his course. In his case we have in miniature an illustration of the great provision which God makes for us. We are stewards only of gifts of God. The life and death of his beloved Son is the great Gift by which all else is guaranteed. He directs us to the Rock of Ages. His Spirit worketh within us to will and to do. The faith by which we cling to him in the dark and cloudy day is his own gift (Eph. ii. 8). If we conquer our spiritual foes, it is he who teacheth our hands to war and our fingers to fight. By him alone we are more than conquerors. If we arrive at last "perfect" in Zion, it is because he has led us on by ways we knew not.

IV. HE CONTROLS THE INFLUENCES AT WORK AGAINST US. The "strangers" and his own "people" are brought under him because there is an unseen power so working on them that their force is weakened and their will turned. The life of David is full of this Divine control of adverse influences. Saul and Doeg were baffled and restrained. Philistines at Gath (1 Sam. xxvii. 4—7) were favourably disposed to him in the bitter time of his exile. The nation was made willing to accept him in place of the successors in the line of Saul. The wise counsel of Ahithophel was turned to foolishness, and when for a time the chastisement of rebellion seemed to crush his heart, the hour of deliverance came, and the people were made willing to welcome him once more to his beloved Jerusalem. So is it still. Land and sea, men and evil spirits, life and death, are all alike in the hands of God, and he can say, "Thus far, and no further ; " "Touch not mine anointed." Our Lord is Lord also of all. Our highest interests are in his holy hands, and there is nothing, seen or unseen, that can sever us from the love of God that is in Christ our Lord (Rom. viii. 35—39). How natural, then, the words "Therefore, I will give thanks unto thee, O Lord" (ver. 50)! "He" showeth mercy for evermore.

Additional topics—
1. The influence of success in promoting success (ver. 45).

2. The accelerated influences of the spiritual world analogous to the laws of motion (ver. 45).

3. The inherent sense in all men of the majesty of righteousness (ver. 45).

4. The power of reputed character and of deeds in extending personal influence over strangers (ver. 46).

5. Foreshadows of the final collapse of the forces of evil before the victorious Christ (ver. 46).

6. The *ever-living* God the Joy and Hope of the Christian amidst the vicissitudes of life (ver. 47).

7. The adoration of God a natural expression of the sanctified heart, and its Christian element based on an experience of his mercy (ver. 47).

8. The qualities of the rock as illustrating the Divine perfection (ver. 47).

9. The reality of providential retribution for the oppression of the righteous and the needy, as seen in individuals and nations, and revealed in history and Scripture (ver. 48).

10. The various methods by which God acts on human souls to bring them into submission to Christ (ver. 48).

11. The Divine process of bringing souls out from embarrassing circumstances, temporal and spiritual (ver. 49).

12. The concurrence of Divine and human action in spiritual conquests (ver. 49).

13. The setting forth of the wonders of redeeming mercy before men who profess no interest in Christ. How to do it (ver. 50).

14. All the resources of the Divine nature in their pledged relation to the accomplishment of the purpose of Christ, the Anointed One (ver. 51).

15. The inheritance of Christ's people in the resources belonging to him (ver. 51).

16. The permanent character of the work of redemption (ver. 51).

HOMILIES BY VARIOUS AUTHORS.

Vers. 1—51 (Ps. xviii.).—(JERUSALEM.) *David's song of praise.* "And David spake unto Jehovah the words of this song," etc. (ver. 1). It is a song of: 1. *The anointed (messiah) of the Lord,* his king (ver. 51), his servant (Ps. xviii., inscription). Like Moses and Joshua, David held a peculiar and exalted position in the kingdom of God under the Old Testament. He was "a man [unlike Saul] of God's own choosing" (1 Sam. xiii. 14; xvi. 28), to fill the office of theocratic king, and to fulfil his purposes concerning Israel and the world; he was also specially fitted for his vocation, faithfully devoted to it, and greatly blessed in it. And in the consciousness of this he here speaks. 2. *Praise to the Lord,* on the ground of his perfections, his relations, his benefits; prompted by the desire to render to him the honour which is his due (1 Sam. ii. 1—10). "To praise God means nothing else than to ascribe to him the glorious perfections which he possesses; for we can only give to him what is his own" (Hengstenberg). And, more especially, of: 3. *Thanksgiving for past deliverance,* from imminent perils, to which, as the servant of God, he was exposed through the hatred and opposition of his enemies. Of these Saul was the most formidable; and, after becoming King of Israel, David was attacked by numerous heathen nations, both separately and in combination (ch. v. 17; viii.; x.). It was probably when "the Lord had given him rest round about from all his enemies" (ch. vii. 1), and after the promise of an everlasting kingdom (ch. vii. 12—16), that the song was uttered; though by some it is regarded as "a great hallelujah, with which he retired from the theatre of life." "Having obtained many and signal victories, he does not, as irreligious men are accustomed to do, sing a song of triumph in honour of himself, but exalts and magnifies God, the Author of these victories, by a train of striking and appropriate epithets, and in a style of surpassing grandeur and sublimity" (Calvin). 4. *Confidence in future triumph* over all the enemies of the kingdom of God; of which the success already attained is an assurance. God is praised, not only for what he is and has been to him, but also for what he will be to "David and *his seed for ever*" (ver. 51). Of this song, consider—

I. ITS SUBSTANCE; or, the reasons for praise. 1. *The personal and intimate relationship of Jehovah* to his servant (vers. 2—4).

> "Jehovah is my Rock, and my Fortress, and my, yea, my Deliverer,
> My Rock-God, in whom I trust," etc.
>
> (Vers. 2, 3.)

(1) He stands in a *peculiar* relation (beyond that which he bears to all men) to those to whom he reveals his Name, whom he takes into his fellowship, and to whom he promises to be "their God." These things make it possible to say, "my God," and (along with his gracious acts) incite the personal and ardent affection expressed at the commencement of Ps. xviii. (a liturgical variation of the song), "Fervently do I love thee, O Jehovah my Strength," etc. (2) Nature, history, and experience furnish manifold *emblems* of his excellences, and of the blessings which he bestows on those who trust in him (1 Sam. ii. 2; Deut. xxxii. 4; Gen. xv. 1). These images were suggested by the physical aspect of Palestine, and by the perilous condition and special deliverances of David in his early life, as a fugitive and a soldier, beset by many foes. (3) He is all-sufficient for the *needs* of his people, however numerous and great, for their rescue, defence, permanent security, and complete salvation.

> "As worthy to be praised, do I call on Jehovah,
> And (whenever I call) I am saved from mine enemies."

"Faith knows no past and no future. What God has done and will do is present to it." 2. *His marvellous deliverance.* (Vers. 5—20.) In a single comprehensive picture David describes the many dangers that encompassed him during his persecution by Saul, and the many providential interpositions (1. Sam. xxiii. 24—28) that were made on his behalf. (1) Even those whom God loves (ver. 20) are sometimes "greatly afflicted," and reduced to the *utmost extremity* (1 Sam. xxx. 1—10).

> "For breakers of death surrounded me,
> Streams of Belial terrified me;
> Cords of Sheol girt me about,
> Snares of death overtook me."
>
> (Vers. 5, 6.)

(2) Their extreme need impels them to rely upon God all the more entirely, and to *call upon him* all the more fervently; nor do they call in vain. "In my distress I called," etc. (ver. 7), "and he heard my voice (instantly) out of his (heavenly) temple." (3) Very wonderful is *the answer* of God to their cry, in the discomfiture of their adversaries and their complete deliverance. "The means by which this deliverance was achieved were, as far as we know, those which we see in the Books of Samuel—the turns and chances of providence, his own extraordinary activity, the faithfulness of his followers, the unexpected increase of his friends. But the act of deliverance itself is described in the language which belongs to the descent upon Mount Sinai or the passage of the Red Sea" (Stanley). The unseen and eternal King was moved with wrath, at which the whole creation trembled (vers. 8, 9); he approached in the gathering thunder-clouds, and upon the wings of the wind, armed as "a man of war" (Exod. xv. 3), and preceded by his arrows of lightning (vers. 10—13); then, in the full outburst of the tempest, with the thunder of his power, "hailstones and coals of fire," he scattered the enemy, and disclosed the depths from which the cry for help arose (vers. 14—16); finally, with distinguishing, condescending, and tender care (ver. 36)—

> "He reached from above, he laid hold of me,
> He drew me out of great waters," etc.
>
> (Vers. 17—20.)

"It is true that the deliverance of David was not actually attended by any such extraordinary natural phenomena; but the saving hand of God from heaven was so obviously manifested that the deliverance experienced by him could be poetically described as a miraculous interposition on the part of God" (Keil). 3. *His righteous procedure.* (Vers. 21—28.) "He delivered me *because* he delighted in me" (ver. 20). He acted toward David in accordance with his gracious choice of him to be his servant, and delivered him because he was "well pleased" with his faithful service; the ground of this deliverance being now stated more fully—

> "Jehovah rendered me according to my righteousness,
> According to the cleanness of my hands hath he recompensed me," etc.

This language (comp. 1 Sam. xxvi. 13—25) neither implies entire freedom from sin nor indicates a boastful spirit, but is expressive of sincerity, integrity, fidelity; in contrast with the calumnies and wickedness of enemies, in fulfilment of a Divine call, in obedience to the Divine will generally, and in the main course of life, as : (1) An expression and justification of the ways of God in a particular instance.   (2) An illustration of the law of his dealings with men (vers. 26, 27).   "The truth which is here enunciated is not that the conception which man forms of God is the reflected image of his own mind and heart, but that God's conduct to man is the reflection of the relation in which man has placed himself to God (1 Sam. ii. 30 ; xv. 23)" (Delitzsch).   "Jehovah is righteous; he loveth righteousness" (Ps. xi. 7).   This is a most worthy reason for praise.   (3) An admonition and encouragement; "with the design of inspiring others with zeal for the fulfilment of the Law."

> " And oppressed people thou savest;
> And thine eyes are against the haughty : them thou humblest."

4. *His continued and effectual help.* (Vers. 29—46.) The righteousness and faithfulness of God are further confirmed by the experience of David (after his deliverance from the hand of Saul) in his wars with the external enemies of the kingdom.   (1) Having rescued his servant from destruction, he calls him to active conflict with surrounding enemies (vers. 29—32).   In the former part of the song, David is represented as a *passive* object of his aid ; in the latter, as an *active* instrument for effecting his purposes. (2) He prepares him for the conflict, and strengthens him in it (vers. 33—37).   (3) He enables him to overcome his enemies and utterly destroy their power (vers. 38—43). (4) He extends and establishes his royal dominion, making him to be "head of the heathen" (vers. 44—46).   Herein *the Messianic element* of the song specially appears. Not, indeed, that "it is a hymn of victory, spoken not in the person of the prophet himself, David, but in the Person of his illustrious Son and Lord" (J. Brown, 'The Sufferings and Glories of the Messiah'), nor that there is here a direct and conscious prediction of the future Christ; but that the assured triumph of "David and his seed" over the nations, the extension of the theocratic kingdom, prefigured the more glorious victories of "the King Messiah."   "David's history, from first to last, was a kind of acted parable of the sufferings and glory of Christ" (Binnie).   "Prophecy reveals to us the foreknowledge of God ; but typical institutions reveal, not only his foreknowledge, but his providential arrangements.   The facts of history become the language of prophecy, and teach us that he with whom a thousand years are but as yesterday guides the operations of distant ages with reference to each other ; and thus in a typical economy we trace not only the all-beholding eye, but the all-directing hand of the Deity ; not only the Divine omniscience, but the Divine omnipotence.   The foretold and minute resemblance between characters and transactions, separated from each other by an interval of a thousand years, is too striking an argument of the hand of God to be controverted or explained away" (Thompson, 'Davidica').   The kingdom of Christ, nevertheless, is of a higher nature, and established by other means, than the theocratic kingdom of David.   "This was the foundation of that resplendent image of the Messiah which it required the greatest of all religious changes to move from the mind of the Jewish nation, in order to raise up instead of it the still more exalted idea which was to take its place—an anointed Sovereign conquering by other arts than those of war, and in other dominions than those of earthly empire" (Stanley).   "Thus all David's hopes and all his joy terminate, as ours always should, in the great Redeemer" (Matthew Henry).
II. ITS SPIRIT ; as it appears throughout the song, and particularly in its conclusion—

> " Living is Jehovah, and blessed is my Rock ;
> Exalted is the Rock-God of my salvation," etc.

(Vers. 47—51.)

1. Personal, appropriating *faith.*   "Faith it is which gives its peculiar grandeur to David's song of triumph ; his masterpiece, and it may be the masterpiece of human poetry, inspired or uninspired.   What is the element in that ode, which even now makes it stir the heart like a trumpet ?   What protects such words (vers. 7—17) from the imputation of mere Eastern exaggeration ?   The firm conviction that God is the Deliverer, not only of David, but of all who trust in him ; that the whole majesty of

God, and all the powers of nature, are arrayed on the side of the good and the opprest"
(C. Kingsley, 'David: Four Sermons'). 2. Heartfelt *delight* in God. 3. Fervent
gratitude. 4. Unreserved *consecration* to his service, his honour, his glory.

> " Therefore will I give thanks unto thee, O Jehovah, among the heathen;
> And sing praises unto thy Name."
>
> (Vers. 50, 51.)

(See on this song, Chandler, Maclaren, W. M. Taylor, and commentaries on Ps. xviii.)
" David, King of Judah, a soul inspired by Divine music and much other heroism, was
wont to pour himself forth in song; he with a seer's eye and heart discerned the God-
like among the human! struck tones that were an echo of the sphere-harmonies, and
are still felt to be such. Reader, art thou one of a thousand, able still to *read* the
psalms of David, and catch some echo of it through the old dim centuries; feeling far
off in thine own heart what it once was to other hearts made as thine?" (Carlyle,
' Miscellaneous Essays ').—D.

Ver. 24 (Ps. xviii. 23).—*Self-preservation.* " I kept myself from mine iniquity "
(perversion, distortion, departure from the line of truth and rectitude). The life of a
good man is a conflict (ch. x. 12). " A man will never persevere in the practice of
uprightness and godliness, unless he carefully keep himself from his inquity " (Calvin).
His self-preservation—
    I. IMPLIES EXPOSURE TO A DANGEROUS ENEMY. 1. There is none greater than sin.
Every other evil is slight compared with it. 2. Each man has "his besetting sin."
"I kept myself," not merely against iniquity becoming my own, but against the iniquity
which lies near to me, and to which I am specially liable from my constitution or condition (1 Sam. xxiv. 5). A traitor within the fortress is a more dangerous foe than
any other. 3. It besets him at all times, in all places, and by manifold "devices."
4. To be overcome by it is inexpressibly disastrous.
    II. REQUIRES THE ADOPTION OF PROPER METHODS. 1. Due consideration of the
danger. To be forewarned is to be forearmed. 2. Constant and resolute vigilance
against the first approaches of the enemy (Heb. iii. 13). 3. The habitual practice of
self-restraint and self-denial. 4. The daily exercise of the virtues and graces that are
most opposite to the sins to which he is disposed (Gal. v. 16). 5. Familiar acquaintance with the Word of God (Eph. vi. 13—17). 6. Continual looking unto God for his
effectual aid. " Kept [guarded] by the power of God through faith," etc. (1 Pet. i. 5).
7. Unceasing prayer. " Keep yourselves in the love of God " (Jude 21); " Keep yourselves from idols " (1 John v. 21).
    III. DESERVES TO BE SOUGHT WITH THE UTMOST EARNESTNESS, because of the
advantages by which it is attended. 1. An assurance of personal sincerity (1 John v.
18; Heb. iii. 14). "The careful abstaining from our own iniquity is one of the best
evidences of our own integrity; and the testimony of our conscience that we have done
so will be such a rejoicing as will not only lessen the grief of an afflicted state, but
increase the comfort of an advanced state" (Matthew Henry). 2. An experience of
Divine help, of which it is an indispensable condition. 3. An increase of moral
strength. 4. A preparation for future victories. " To mortify and conquer our own
appetites is more praiseworthy than to storm strong cities, to defeat mighty armies,
work miracles, or raise the dead " (Scupoli).—D.

Vers. 26—28 (Ps. xviii. 25—27).—*Divine rectitude.* Consider the righteousness of
God as it appears in: 1. *The supreme importance which he attaches to moral distinctions
amongst men.* Such distinctions are often made light of in comparison with wisdom,
might, and riches (Jer. ix. 23); and those who possess the latter despise and trample
upon the ignorant, the weak, and the poor (ver. 27). But God has chiefly respect to
men in their moral attitude toward himself, their relation to the law of right, their
personal character (1 Sam. ii. 30). With him the great distinction is that between
the righteous and the wicked (Ps. xxxiv. 15, 16). Whilst his infinite greatness dwarfs
earthly power and honour into insignificance, his perfect righteousness exalts moral
worth beyond measure. 2. *The different treatment which he adopts toward men of
different character.* In himself he is always the same (1 Sam. xv. 29); but the aspect

which his character and dealings assume toward them is determined by their own character and conduct, and is the necessary manifestation of his unchangeable rectitude—on the one hand, toward the "loving," etc., full of love (all that is kind, desirable, and excellent); on the other, toward the "perverse," perverse (contrary, antagonistic, "as an enemy," Lam. ii. 5; Lev. xxvi. 23, 24; Hos. ii. 6), inflicting severe chastisement. "There is a higher law of grace, whereby the sinfulness of man but draws forth the tenderness of a father's pardoning pity; and the brightest revelation of his love is made to froward prodigals. But this is not the psalmist's view here, nor does it interfere with the law of retribution in its own sphere" (Maclaren). 3. *The signal change which he makes in their relative positions*; saving and exalting the oppressed and afflicted, and humbling the proud oppressor; his purpose therein being to vindicate, honour, and promote righteousness, and to restrain, correct, and put an end to iniquity (1 Sam. ii. 8, 10). "What is God doing now?" it was asked of Rabbi Jose, and the reply was, "He makes ladders on which he causes the poor to ascend and the rich to descend" (The Midrash).—D.

Ver. 31 (Ps. xviii. 30).—*God's way, Word, and defence.* "I can overcome all opposition in and with my God" (ver. 30); for: 1. *His way is perfect.* His providential dealings, especially in leading his servant forward in the conflict. Although ofttimes mysterious and different from what might have been expected, it is marked by perfect rectitude, perfect wisdom, perfect love; and is exactly adapted to effect his holy and beneficent purposes (Job xxiii. 8—10; Ps. lxxvii. 19; xcvii. 2). 2. *His Word is tried* (purified as silver and gold, without dross, and very precious). It is the chief means of preparation, instruction and help; "the sword of the Spirit." Its declarations are true, its directions good, its promises faithful (Prov. xxx. 5; Ps. xii. 6, 7). The more it is tested, whether by friends or foes, by examination or experience, the more it proves itself to be indeed the Word of God, and of unspeakable worth. "There is none like that; give it me" (1 Sam. xxi. 9). 3. *His defence is sure*; himself effectuating his Word, and being "a Shield to all that trust in him," affording certain, constant, and complete protection. Faith is the bond of union between men and God, the "taking hold of his strength," a necessary means of defence, and hence often called a shield (Eph. vi. 16; Heb. x. 35); but it is God himself who is such in the highest sense (Jer. li. 20; Deut. xxxiii. 29; Ps. v. 12). He is God alone (ver. 32); the absolute, incomparable, perfect One; worthy to be trusted and praised (ver. 4).—D.

Ver. 33.—*God is my Strength.* "The God who girdeth me with strength" (Ps. xviii. 32). Physical strength is derived from God. Much more is spiritual. It is obtained through faith. And every believer may say, "His strength is mine." Thereby: 1. *I live*—live unto God, "soberly, righteously, and godly in this present world" (Titus ii. 12; Hab. ii. 4; Gal. ii. 20). 2. *I stand*—stand fast in temptation, attack, danger (Rom. xiv. 4; 2 Cor. i. 24; Phil. iv. 1). 3. *I walk*—walk forward, in the way of the Lord, surely, swiftly (ver. 34), perseveringly (2 Cor. v. 7; Isa. xl. 31). 4. *I labour* —labour with and for God, zealously, patiently, and not in vain (Isa. xxvi. 12; 1 Cor. xv. 58). 5. *I endure*—endure "hardness," afflictions, reproaches, yea, all things, supported and "strengthened with power through his Spirit in the inward man" (2 Tim. ii. 3; Heb. xi. 27; Ps. cxxxviii. 3). 6. *I fight*—fight "the good fight of faith," against his enemies, courageously and effectually (ver. 35). 7. *I overcome*—overcome in life and death (1 Cor. xv. 57).—D.

Ver. 36.—*True greatness.* "Thy answering hath made me great." Ps. xviii. 35, "Thy gentleness" (humility, meekness, condescending grace). True greatness consists not in external prosperity, nor in splendid achievements, but in moral and spiritual excellence. "The good alone are great." Notice—

I. ITS CONDITIONS, on the part of man. 1. Conscious weakness, the sense of utter helplessness in himself (1 Sam. xxx. 1—10; John xv. 5; 2 Cor. xii. 10; Heb. xi. 34). 2. Believing prayer (ver. 7). "By showing us our own nothingness, humility forces us to depend upon God; and the expression of that dependence is prayerfulness." 3. Ardent aspiration. "When sea-water rises into the clouds it loses its saltness and becomes fresh; so the soul when lifted up to God" (Tamil proverb).

II. Its BESTOWMENT; by "that practical hearkening on the part of God when called upon for help, which was manifested in the fact that God made his steps broad" (Keil). 1. In wonderful condescension (Ps. cxxxviii. 6). 2. By manifold methods; preserving, instructing, strengthening, exalting those who trust in him. 3. With considerate adaptation to their nature and capacities. "The great God and Father, intent on making his children great, follows them and plies them with the gracious indirections of a faithful and patient love" (Bushnell, 'Christ and his Salvation'). "Like as a father," etc. (Ps. ciii. 13).

III. Its MANIFESTATION. As the effect of sunshine and rain, received and appropriated by a plant, appears in its abounding strength, beauty, and fruitfulness, so the effect of Divine grace appears in enlargement and elevation of mind, sincere and fervent love to God, a set purpose to do his will, eminence in "love, joy, peace, gentleness," etc. (Gal. v. 22), maturity of character (Hos. xiv. 5—7), holy and beneficent activity, growing conformity to the perfect Pattern of true greatness (Matt. xx. 25—27). "Have the mind in you which was also in Christ Jesus" (Phil. ii. 5).—D.

Ver. 50 (Ps. xviii. 49).—*The praise of God among the heathen.* "Therefore will I give thanks unto thee, O Jehovah, among the heathen" (Rom. xv. 9). The purpose of God to bestow the blessings of salvation upon *all nations* was made known in the earliest ages (Gen. xii. 3; Numb. xiv. 21; Deut. xxxii. 43). "From the beginning there existed a power to rise above the exclusiveness of Old Testament religion, namely, the vital germ of knowledge, that the kingdom of God would one day find its completion in a universal monarchy embracing all people" (Riehm, 'Messianic Prophecy'). In sympathy and co-operation with the Divine purpose David here speaks. That purpose is, in its highest sense, fulfilled in the extension of the kingdom of Christ (1 Sam. ii. 10; v. 3). This language is such as might be adopted by Christ himself (Ps. ii. 8; Heb. ii. 9—13). It should be that of all his followers; to whom he said, "Go ye, therefore" (Matt. xxviii. 18—20), "proclaim the good news to every creature" (Mark xvi. 15); "Ye are witnesses of these things" (Luke xxiv. 48; Acts i. 8). As such it indicates—

I. A JOYFUL PROCLAMATION of the Word of truth, by which God is glorified in his Son (ch. vii. 14, 26); pertaining to: 1. *His marvellous doings*, in conflict with the powers of evil and in victory over them, through humiliation, suffering, and sacrifice (Ps. xxii.). "Make known his deeds among the people" (Ps. cv. 1, 2; John xii. 31, 32). 2. *His glorious exaltation* and reign (ver. 47). "Say among the heathen, The Lord is King" (Ps. xcvi. 10; Phil. ii. 9—11). His reign is righteous, beneficent, and universal. 3. *His saving benefits*—the remission of sins, deliverance from oppression, "righteousness, peace, and joy in the Holy Ghost." "Praise him, all ye people: for his merciful kindness is great," etc. (Ps. cxvii. 1, 2). "The means of bringing them to the knowledge of God is not the sword, but the proclamation of God's great deeds for his people. As David in his character of missionary to the heathen world praises his God's grace, so at bottom all missionary work among the heathen is, in the announcement of the Word of the God who is revealed in Christ, a continuous praise of the Name of the living God" (Erdmann).

II. A SACRED RESOLVE. "I will praise thee." This determination, or "vow of thanksgiving," ought to be made by every one who has himself received the knowledge of salvation, from: 1. A feeling of *compassion* for the urgent need of the heathen (Acts xvi. 9). He may not keep the "good tidings" to himself (1 Kings vii. 9). 2. A conviction of *duty*, arising from acquaintance with the merciful purpose and express commands of the Lord. 3. An impulse of *grateful love*, on account of the condescending grace shown toward himself, constraining him to obey the Lord's will, promote his purpose, and glorify his Name. It will also lead him to employ every means in his power that "Christ may be magnified" (Phil. i. 20).

III. A CONFIDENT PERSUASION that the heathen will listen to "the joyful sound," freely submit themselves (vers. 44—46), and join in the praise of God; founded on: 1. His *power* to effect his purposes. 2. His *faithfulness* in fulfilling his promises. 3. His past *achievements* (vers. 48, 49). "They shall come and declare his righteousness" (Ps. xxii. 27—31). "Above eighteen centuries have verified the prediction of the permanency of his kingdom, founded as it was by no human means, endowed with inextinguishable life, ever conquering and to conquer in the four quarters of the world; a kingdom one and alone since the world has been, embracing all climes and times, and still expanding, unworn by the destroyer of all things, time; strong amid the decay of empires; the freshness and elasticity of youth written on the brow which has outlived eighteen centuries" (Pusey, 'Daniel,' p. 62).—D.

Vers. 2—4.—*God the Refuge and Deliverer.* The psalm was composed as a thanksgiving for the safety and deliverances David had experienced when Saul so persistently sought to destroy him, and afterwards in the wars with the house of Saul, and with the heathen tribes that set themselves against him. It appears to belong to an earlier period than the place it occupies in the book would indicate. It is scarcely possible that David could have asserted his uprightness and innocence in the strong terms of vers. 21—25 after his great sins. These verses form the introduction to the psalm, and express in emphatic language the safety and salvation which David had found in God. The Christian may use the words of the similar perils to which he is exposed, and of others not immediately in the psalmist's view.

I. The dangers to which we are exposed. Bodily, mental, spiritual. To reputation. From our own constitutional tendencies. From diseases and accidents. From the malice of men, and their favour. From prosperity and adversity. From solitude and society. From labours, rest, and pleasures. From Satan and his angels. From the broken Law and injured justice of God. Always and everywhere, under all circumstances and conditions, we are all exposed to perils.

II. The safety and deliverance to be found in God. The psalmist labours to express his sense of the protection, safety, and deliverance which God had vouchsafed to him, yea, which God himself had *been* to him. The imagery he uses is taken chiefly from natural features of Palestine, with which he had become especially familiar as affording refuge and safety during the time that he was hunted by Saul. He calls him "my Rock," in the heights and recesses of which he had been safe from his foes; "my Fortress," his fortified castle, too high to be reached, too strong to be broken into; "my Deliverer," by whose aid he had escaped from many a peril; "the God of my Rock," equivalent to "my mighty God;" "my Shield and the Horn of my salvation," at once protecting him in battle and pushing his enemies to their destruction; "my high Tower," or lofty Retreat; "my Refuge and my Saviour." What the Almighty was to David he is to all his people. We may use similar language. Our dangers may not be so fearful in appearance, or so numerous, or so obvious; but they are as real and serious. And our safety and deliverance must come from "the Lord." The words of the text show that it is not only what he employs for our good, nor what he himself does, but what he *is*, that assures of safety. Not only does he afford protection and secure deliverance; he is our Protector and Deliverer. In his almightiness, love, knowledge, wisdom, universal presence, observation, and operation, we realize salvation. In Jesus Christ, his very righteousness has become our friend, and assures us of victory. The safety thus assured is not absolute immunity from trouble, but protection from the evil it might produce, and change of its character. The righteous are visited with calamities similar to those which befall the wicked, and in some conditions of society with calamities peculiar to themselves. But in their case they lose their unfriendly character, and become visitations of a Father's love, means of deliverance from worse evils, and of obtaining greater good. The evil which they might do God will defend us from, if we trust and obey him. Nor are the righteous sure of absolute preservation from sin, though they would enjoy perfect immunity if they fulfilled the necessary conditions on their part. But they have a right to feel sure of preservation of body and soul in this world, until their appointed work is done; and of final deliverance from all evils (2 Tim. iv. 18). They should not desire more.

III. The conditions of safety and deliverance. 1. *Faith.* "In him will I trust" (ver. 3). Confidence in God as our Friend, Protector, and Saviour. Especially as he is revealed to us in the gospel. Faith assures us of the Divine love, lays hold of the Divine strength, enables us to flee to God as our Refuge, to rise to the lofty Rock and Tower where we are above all adverse powers, and safe from their assaults, and gives the calmness needful for employing such means as tend to safety and victory. "All things are possible to him that believeth" (Mark ix. 23). 2. *Prayer.* "I will call on the Lord . . . so shall I be saved from mine enemies " (ver. 4). Faith prompts obedience, as in other respects, so in respect to prayer. Divine help and protection are promised to those who pray. "Call upon me in the day of trouble: I will deliver thee, and thou shalt glorify me " (Ps. l. 15). The sense of peril, the knowledge that there is safety in God, and that his delivering power is exercised on behalf of those who seek him, cannot but lead the Christian to that earnest and believing prayer which prevails. The Apostle Paul, after pointing out other methods of ensuring victory over our enemies, adds, "Praying always," etc. (Eph. vi. 18).

IV. The return to be made for safety and deliverance realized, and anticipated. Praise. This psalm is one of the returns of praise which David made to his Deliverer, of whom he speaks in ver. 4 as "the Lord who is worthy to be praised." Many are ready to pray to God in danger, who forget or refuse to praise him when they have experienced deliverance. The Christian will not fail to give thanks, not only for what he has experienced of Divine protection, but for what he feels sure he shall experience, up to and including victory over death itself, "the last enemy," in view of whose approach he sings, "Thanks be to God, who giveth us the victory through our Lord Jesus Christ " (1 Cor. xv. 26, 57).—G. W.

Ver. 4.—*God worthy to be praised.* The conjunction of ideas here is a little singular. "I will *pray* to the Lord, who is worthy to be *praised*." It may originate in the feeling that it is fitting that, when we seek new blessings from God, we should not be unmindful of those which he has already bestowed. Praise should accompany prayer (see Phil. iv. 6, "prayer . . . with thanksgiving "). Add that the subjects of praise are encouragements to prayer. In the act of praising him we are reminding ourselves of the strong reasons we have for hopefully seeking further mercies from him.

I. God is worthy to be praised. Not merely to be feared, entreated, strictly obeyed, and submitted to. He is worthy of thankful and rejoicing obedience and submission. It is not fitting that he should be served sullenly or silently; or that prayer to him should be as a cry of a slave to his master, or of one oppressed to his oppressor, or as a request for help addressed to a stranger. We should speak to him with the confidence and love which his relation to us and past goodness are fitted to inspire. One way of ensuring this is to blend praise with prayer.

II. What it is that renders him worthy to be praised. Some obtain praise who are not worthy of it in any measure; others, much more than they deserve. But God is worthy of and "exalted above all blessing and praise " (Neh. ix. 5). Whether we consider his nature, his regard for his creatures, his works or his gifts, we must feel that it is impossible to render him praise worthy of him. But to the utmost of our power we should praise him for: 1. *His glorious perfections.* Especially his infinite moral excellences—his truth, holiness, righteousness, and love. 2. *His wonderful works.* In creation, providence, and grace. 3. Specially, *his redeeming mercy.* His kindness to us in Christ. The display of his perfections in the gift, the Person, and the work of our Lord and Saviour. The mercy he exercises in the forgiveness of sin, the admission of sinners into his family, and all the operations by which he brings his "many sons [and daughters] unto glory," (Heb. ii. 10). The gift of the Holy Spirit for this purpose. The final bliss and glory. 4. *The goodness of God to ourselves.* Not forgetting that he is "worthy to be praised " for the commonest blessings we enjoy, as well as those distinguishing blessings which we receive as his children through faith in Christ. And not only for the blessings which give us pleasure, but for those which give us pain, but are bestowed that we may become in a greater measure "partakers of his holiness " (Heb. xii. 10).

III. By whom he ought to be praised. 1. *By all his creatures according to their capacity.* All his inanimate and irrational creatures do praise him. Their existence, qualities, order, and (as to the living creatures) their happiness "show forth the excellences " of their Creator. "All thy works shall praise thee, O Lord " (Ps. cxlv. 10; comp. Ps. cxlviii.; xix. 1—4). All intelligent beings ought to praise him; all the right-minded of them do. Those who enjoy least of his bounty have much to thank him for, and often praise him more than those who enjoy most. We do not say that those who are suffering in hell the penalty due to their sins can be expected to praise him whose wrath abides so terribly upon them ; although, if a somewhat fashionable doctrine be true, they have strong reasons for giving him thanks, since he is taking the wisest and best means to make them meet for the glory and joy in heaven which will at length be their portion! 2. *Especially by his redeemed people.* Who are the objects of his special regard and gracious operation, and to whom the work of praise on earth is peculiarly committed (Isa. xliii. 21; 1 Pet. ii. 9). On some accounts the redeemed and regenerate have more reason to give thanks to God than those who have never sinned.

> " They see
> On earth a bounty not indulged on high,
> And downward look for Heaven's superior praise. **. . .**
> They sang Creation, for in that they shared:
> Creation's great superior, man, is thine;
> Thine is redemption; they just gave the key,
> 'Tis thine to raise and eternize the song."
>
> (Young.)

Nevertheless, angels do give thanks for redemption, and with good reason. For it is the work of the God whom they love; it enriches their conceptions of him; it enlarges their service of him; and it supremely and eternally blesses vast multitudes in whom they feel the deepest interest. It thus gratifies their desires, and adds to their wealth of knowledge, goodness, and happiness.

IV. THE KIND AND DURATION OF THE PRAISE OF WHICH HE IS WORTHY. 1. *The kind.* Clearly the best possible; which is not necessarily that which is most poetical or most musical, though in these respects man should do his best. But that is best of all which comes from the heart, and from a heart fullest of admiration, adoration, love, and gratitude. Much which professes to be praise of God is heartless mockery. 2. *The duration.* For ever and ever (Eph. iii. 21). While we have any being, in this world and the next (Ps. cxlv. 1, 2; cxlvi. 2). For, as God is everlasting, the reasons for praising him can never end.—G. W.

Ver. 7.—*Prayer in distress heard.* The distress referred to is graphically described in vers. 5, 6, 17, 18. The interposition of God for the psalmist's deliverance is poetically depicted in vers. 8—20. The connecting link is given in this verse. David, in his danger and trouble, called on God, and therefore he was delivered. We have here—

I. DISTRESS. This may arise from various causes; such as: 1. *Enemies.* As in David's case, with the dangers of the battles fought against them. There are many forms less extreme in which the enmity of men may show itself and occasion pain or peril. 2. *Circumstances.* Worldly losses and anxieties. 3. *Personal affliction.* Of body or mind. Special distress from afflictions which implicate the nerves, and so the mind itself. 4. *Death of dear friends.* 5. *Conviction of sin.* (See Ps. xxxii. 3, 4.) It would be well if this form of distress were more common. 6. *Pressure of powerful temptation.* The mighty and threatening uprising of inward corruptions, or the pressing solicitations of evil from without. 7. *Fear of calamities or of death.*

II. PRAYER. Natural for men to call upon God when they are in great trouble or danger. Yet all do not; and of many the prayers are unacceptable, because they lack the moral and spiritual elements of successful prayer (see Hos. vii. 14). Prayer, to be acceptable, must be: 1. *That of a righteous man.* (Vers. 21—25; Jas. v. 16; Ps. lxvi. 18.) Yet the prayers of one who is stirred by his affliction to sincere repentance are heard; for repentance is the beginning of righteousness. 2. *Offered in faith.* (Matt. xxi. 22.) 3. *Importunate and persevering.* (Luke xi. 8, *seq.*; xviii. 1—8.) 4. *Accompanied, where practicable, with the use of appropriate means.* David fought vigorously as well as prayed earnestly.

III. DELIVERANCE. The Almighty heard the psalmist's voice "out of his temple" (equivalent to "the heavens"), and, interposing in majesty and power, delivered him, discomfiting and scattering his foes. True prayer is always heard and answered; but the deliverance granted is often not according to our conceptions and desires, yet ever according to the perfect wisdom and goodness of our heavenly Father. Sometimes the causes of our distress are removed; sometimes they are allowed to continue, but the distress is allayed, and the causes turned into blessings. So it was with St. Paul's "thorn in the flesh," although he prayed earnestly and repeatedly (2 Cor. xii. 8—10)

Spiritual deliverance, however, is always granted to those who truly seek it; and ultimately complete rescue from all that afflicts the Christian.

IV. Grateful remembrance and thanksgiving. Although David's victories were wrought through the skill and valour of himself and his troops, he gives to God all the glory of them; for he knew that all was due to him. His example will be followed by the Christian, as he reviews life and calls to mind his distresses and deliverances. He will recognize the hand of God in all, and render praise to him who both furnishes the means of deliverance and exercises the power which renders them successful. Finally, let none wait for trouble before they begin to pray. Live in the habit of prayer, and you will be able, when trouble comes, to pray truly and successfully. Otherwise you may find yourself in the miserable condition of those described in ver. 42, who "looked even unto the Lord, but he answered them not."—G. W.

Vers. 17—20.—*Rescue from mighty foes.* In vers. 8—16 the psalmist depicts Jehovah as appearing in his glory for the deliverance of his servant. The picture may have been occasioned by a storm which, in one of his battles, had terrified his enemies and aided in their discomfiture (comp. Josh. x. 11; 1 Sam. vii. 10). In the text he narrates the deliverance itself.

I. The enemies. Who were: 1. *Malignant.* "Hated me." There was not only opposition and contest, but personal hatred. Many of the Christian's foes have this quality in a high degree (John xvii. 14), notably their great leader and chief, Satan (equivalent to "adversary," 1 Pet. v. 8). 2. *Powerful.* "My strong enemy . . . too strong for me." In physical strength, or military, or in numbers. David may have had in view such instances as those recorded in ch. viii. 3—5 and xxi. 15—17. The Christian's foes also are "powers" (Eph. vi. 12). Wherein consists the power of the enemies of the righteous? (1) Their inherent vigour; (2) their adaptation to our lower nature; (3) their number. 3. *Subtle.* "They prevented me in the day of my calamity." They rushed upon him unexpectedly, when he was enfeebled by calamity, and poorly prepared for them. David may be thinking of the attack of the Syrians of Damascus, while he and his army were engaged with Hadadezer or exhausted by the contest with him (ch. viii. 5); or of the assault of the giant Ishbi-benob, while he was faint from fighting against the Philistines (ch. xxi. 15, 16). Thus, also, the Christian's foes often surprise him when he is preoccupied or distressed by troubles. The day of calamity is a day of spiritual danger. 4. *In a measure successful.* So that he became as a man struggling for life in "great waters" (comp. vers. 5, 6). It seemed as if he must be swallowed up. Thus, also, the enemies of the Christian may do him much mischief, temporal and even spiritual; but there is a limit to their power. "For the eyes of the Lord run to and fro throughout the whole earth, to show himself strong in the behalf of them whose heart is perfect toward him" (2 Chron. xvi. 9).

II. The Deliverer. Jehovah, the Almighty, whose glorious interposition on behalf of his servant, in answer to his cry of distress, is described in the previous verses. They set forth: 1. *His awful majesty.* 2. *His power over all the forces of nature.* 3. *The intensity of his interest in his troubled servants.* How he rouses himself, as it were, for the rescue of those in whom he delights (ver. 20). 4. *His anger against their enemies.* (Vers. 8, 9.) With such a Friend, who can neither be surprised, evaded, or resisted, the righteous need not dread the might of any adversary, nor despair of deliverance from the direst troubles.

III. The deliverance. God: 1. *Supported him in his perils.* "The Lord was my Stay." 2. *He saved him from them.* "He stretched forth his hand from on high; he laid hold of me; he drew me out of great waters; he delivered me," etc. God's hand can reach his servants in the lowest depths of trouble, and is strong to rescue them from the strongest of their foes. 3. *He brought him into a condition of freedom and safety.* "Into a large place," a broad, open space, where no "cords of Sheol," or "snares of death" (ver. 6, Revised Version), would embarrass or endanger him; where he could move about with perfect freedom, and yet perfect security. Such help from on high is realized by God's people in this world; perfectly when the hand of their God lays hold of them and raises them from earth to heaven.

IV. The praise. (See homilies on vers. 2—4, 4, and 7.) The perfections and acts of Jehovah are of such a nature that to merely recite them is to praise him. We should acquaint ourselves as fully as possible with his excellences and works, that we may better praise him by declaring them; but our own experience of his power and goodness will give us the liveliest apprehension of them, and stimulate us to the most ardent praise.—G. W.

Vers. 21—25.—*God rewarding the righteous.* "He delivered me because he delighted in me," the psalmist had just said. The reasons of the Divine delight in him, and his consequent deliverance, are given in these verses. They at first startle us, as inconsistent with the humility which is part of the character of a godly man, and as peculiarly unsuitable in the mouth of one who had been guilty of adultery and murder. The latter part of the difficulty is removed if, as is most probable, the psalm belongs to the earlier period of David's reign, before his commission of those grievous sins. As to the former, we should hardly find the Apostle Paul writing in this strain; but rather referring all his successes to the exceeding grace of God (see 1 Cor. xv. 9, 10). His consciousness of sin in general, and of his special guilt on account of his persecution of Christians, prevented everything that savoured of boasting, at least before God. But even he, in appealing to men, did not shrink from reciting his excellences and devoted labours (see 2 Cor. i. 12; vi. 3—10; xi. 5—31), though ready to call himself a "fool" for recounting them. And, after all, the truth that God does reward the righteous according to their righteousness is as much a doctrine of the New Testament as of the Old; and there are occasions when Christians may fittingly recognize and declare that the favour God is showing them is according to their righteousness; although the deeper consciousness of sin, and of entire dependence on the mercy of God, which is awakened by the revelations of the gospel, makes the Christian more reluctant to mention his virtues as a reason for the kindness of God to him. As the meritorious ground of such kindness, David would have been as far as St. Paul from regarding them. Notice—

I. THE PSALMIST'S CHARACTER. This he describes by various words and phrases, which only in part differ from each other. 1. *Righteousness.* Uprightness, rectitude, moral and spiritual goodness in general. 2. *Cleanness of hands.* Hands free from the stain of innocent blood, of "filthy lucre," etc. 3. *Observance of God's ways.* The ways he prescribes of thought, feeling, speech, and action. These are inquired after and followed by the good man. 4. *Adherence to God.* "Have not wickedly departed from my God"—from his presence, worship, the ways he prescribes, and in which he is to be found. Some degree of turning from God at times, every one who knows himself will be conscious of; but "wickedly" to depart from him, to do so consciously, deliberately, persistently, this is apostasy, the very opposite of godliness and righteousness. The Christian will esteem the slightest deviation from God as wicked; but he justly recalls his perseverance in the habits of piety and holiness, in spite of all temptations, with thankfulness. 5. *Mindfulness of his Word, and persevering obedience to it.* God's Word is "his statutes," what he has determined and appointed, and "his judgments," what he declares and prescribes as just and right. These the psalmist "kept before" him, and from them he "did not depart." And his attention and obedience to them were universal—they extended to "all" of them. One necessary quality of a true obedience. "Then shall I not be ashamed when I have respect unto *all* thy commandments" (Ps. cxix. 6). 6. *Uprightness before God.* With regard both to him and to men. 7. *Avoidance of the besetting sin.* "I have kept myself from mine iniquity." There is a particular sin to which each is specially prone. To keep one's self from that, by watchfulness, prayer, and resolute resistance, is special evidence of genuine piety. 8. *Purity of life in general.* "My cleanness," and that "in his eyesight," a very different thing from being pure in the eyes of men. Includes purity of heart as well as conduct, such as is so true and genuine as to bear the Divine inspection.

II. THE PSALMIST'S RECOMPENSE. In his preservation and deliverance from so many perils and enemies, he recognized the Divine reward of his righteousness, the Divine reply to the calumnies of his enemies, the Divine attestation of his innocence. 1. *There is a real righteousness in the character of godly men.* By this they are essentially distinguished from others. It is not a mere difference of taste. 2. *The Divine recompense of such righteousness is certain.* On account of: (1) The character of God. "The righteous Lord loveth righteousness" (Ps. xi. 7). (2) His relation to the righteous.

As their Father, etc. (3) His promises. (4) His almighty power. He is able to do all that is suitable to his nature, and that he has bound himself to do by his Word. 3. *Those who receive such recompense should recognize and acknowledge it.* The righteous do continually receive recompense for their righteousness; rewards, both spiritual, material, and social. But sometimes the happy results of their piety are very manifest, and then they should be specially noticed. (1) To the glory of God. Praising him and inciting others to praise him. (2) For encouragement of themselves and their brethren. Increasing their faith, and strengthening their determination to continue in their chosen course, and their assurance of ultimate, complete recognition and reward. For the whole reward is not yet. "Great is your reward *in heaven*" (Matt. v. 12); but on earth the "guerdon" may be

> "Many a sorrow, many a labour,
> Many a tear."

Finally, in the Lord Jesus Christ we have the perfect Example of righteousness and its recompense; how it may be tried, and how sure is its reward. In him, too, we behold the Source of righteousness for us, and the Pledge of its ultimate triumph.— G. W.

Vers. 26, 27.— *Correspondence between the character of men and the conduct of God towards them.* The psalmist, having spoken of God's treatment of himself according to his righteousness, now shows that his case was no exception to the general rule of the Divine proceedings, but an illustration of it; that, universally, God renders to men according to their character and works.

I. THE MERCIFUL EXPERIENCE HIS MERCY. Our Lord declares the same truth, when he says, "Blessed are the merciful: for they shall obtain mercy" (Matt. v. 7); and when he declares, "If ye forgive men their trespasses, your heavenly Father will also forgive you" (Matt. vi. 14); and teaches us to pray, "Forgive us our debts, as we also have forgiven our debtors" (Matt. vi. 12, Revised Version). But how does this consist with the doctrine of justification by faith? It *must* be in harmony with it, since both are Divine. If it do not accord with some human statements of the doctrine, it must be because these are erroneous or defective. Faith is not a mere assent to the truth, or reliance on the atonement of Christ and the mercy of God in him; but it involves acceptance of Christ as Teacher and Lord as well as Redeemer, and therefore a willing obedience to his instructions, of which part is that we should be forgiving, and that only those who are shall be forgiven—only the merciful shall find mercy. Moreover, faith in the love of God in Christ works love in the heart; a faith which does not is of no avail. From another point of view, "repentance toward God" is as essential to salvation as "faith toward our Lord Jesus Christ" (Acts xx. 21), and will be produced by it. It is vain, therefore, for the unmerciful to trust in the mercy of God, or to cry to him for mercy; his mercy is shown only to the merciful. But to them it is shown; and that not only in the forgiveness of their sins, but in the bestowment of all needful blessings. They also should bear in mind that their enjoyment of the love of God will be in proportion to the love which they cherish and display; and that every degree of selfishness will deprive them of some blessing.

II. THE UPRIGHT EXPERIENCE GOD'S UPRIGHTNESS. He is essentially upright, just, faithful; but the happy experience of his uprightness is for those who "walk uprightly" (Ps. lxxxiv. 11)—those who are sincere and true-hearted towards God and men. To these he will show himself upright by manifesting to them his favour, and fulfilling to them all his promises (comp. Ps. xcii. 12—15); while to others he will show the same quality by the execution of his threatenings.

III. THE PURE EXPERIENCE HIS PURITY. "Blessed are the pure in heart: for they shall see God" (Matt. v. 8). 1. *Genuine Christians are holy.* Truly so, though not perfectly. They have been cleansed by the Word and Spirit of God, and "the blood of Jesus Christ his Son" (1 John i. 7). They have turned from sin, and it is their abhorrence. They watch and pray against it; and, when they fall into it, mourn with sincere grief. They cherish purity of heart, lip, and life. They desire and strive after perfect holiness. 2. *To such God shows himself holy.* (1) He reveals to them his holiness. They are capable of such a revelation, because of their purity of heart. Sin blinds the soul, incapacitating it from discerning and appreciating the holy.   (2) He acts towards them holily.   He requires holiness of them, and works it in them.   All his dealings with them are in accordance with holiness, and have for their end to promote their sanctification.   Hence he does not indulge his children, but, when necessary, afflicts them, that they may become more and more "partakers of his holiness" (Heb. xii. 10).   He will not be satisfied until they perfectly reflect his image, and he can "present them holy and unblameable and unreproveable in his sight" (Col. i. 22).

IV. THE FROWARD FIND HIM FROWARD.   1. *Sinners are froward.*   They are perverse, unreasonable, ungovernable, impracticable.   They show this in their feeling and conduct towards God, his Word and ways.   They will not submit to his instructions or obey his commands.   They "walk contrary unto" him (Lev. xxvi. 21), do the opposite to that which he enjoins.   2. *To them God shows himself froward.*   It is a bold expression, and therefore, perhaps, the translators of this book softened it into "unsavoury," or distasteful.   But the same word is rightly translated in Ps. xviii. 26, "froward."   The meaning is clear.   God acts as if perverse towards the perverse.   As they will not pay regard to his will, he will not to their desires and prayers.   As they oppose him, he opposes them, thwarts their purposes, disappoints their hopes.   As they "walk contrary unto" him, he "will also walk contrary unto" them (Lev. xxvi. 24).   It is a universal truth, discernible: (1) In nature.   If we would have nature work good to us, we must learn and obey its laws.   If we will not, they will work us harm.   (2) In the affairs of life—in business and association with men.   If we will not ascertain and live according to the laws which should regulate our conduct, they will avenge themselves, inflicting pain, loss, perhaps utter ruin.   (3) In respect to religion and salvation.   These originate in the benevolent will of God; and if we would experience their benefits, we must have humble and obedient regard to that will.   We must ask of him, "What must I do to be saved?" and "What wilt thou have me to do?"   If we choose to reject the Divine revelations and requirements, and in pride and perversity take a course opposed to them, the Almighty will not alter his plans to please us, but will bring upon us the just consequences of our frowardness.   He will appear froward to the froward, in that, when they call upon him, he will not answer; when they seek him early, they shall not find him (see Prov. i. 24—29).   It is vain and foolish for man to assert his own proud, capricious will; he will find that there is another and stronger will, that will assert itself to his discomfiture and destruction, unless he repent. —G. W.

Ver. 28.—*God observing and humbling the proud.*   "Thine eyes are upon the haughty, that thou mayest bring them down."   The mention of "afflicted people" in the first clause of this verse renders it probable that the psalmist, in the second, referred to proud oppressors who had afflicted them.   But the words express a general truth.

I. GOD'S OBSERVATION OF THE PROUD.   "His eyes are upon the haughty."   1. *He sees them*; knows who they are, distinguishes them from others, overlooks none of them. 2. *He sees through them, with those piercing eyes of his*, that search the hearts of men. However they may conceal or disguise their pride before men, they cannot before him. 3. *He notices all the exercises and manifestations of their pride.*   Their self-complacency and self-laudation; their contempt of others, their insolence, their injustice, their oppression of the meek and humble, their self-assertion as towards him, their resistance and unsubmissiveness, etc.; all is open to his view; and he notes all for remembrance, exposure, and punishment.   If the proud did but realize that the eyes of the Infinite One were upon them, how ridiculous would their pride soon appear to themselves! how unbecoming and contemptible as well as impious!   How would the things on which they pride themselves—their strength, intellect, knowledge, wealth, honours, mastery of men, virtues, etc., shrivel into insignificance as they looked upon them with the consciousness that God was looking on!   4. *He keeps them ever in sight.*   So that nothing can escape his view, and they cannot elude him or do anything to the real injury of his servants.

II. HIS HUMILIATION OF THEM.   At the right time and in the most effectual way. "Every one that exalteth himself shall be abased" (Luke xviii. 14).   1. *Jehovah sometimes brings down the haughty from the position which fosters or displays their pride.*   He may deprive them of that on which they pride themselves—their property, mental vigour, physical strength, reputation (by permitting them to fall into some disgraceful sin, or otherwise), power over others. He may bring reverses upon them in the full career of their prosperity or enterprises; snatch from them the coveted prize just as they are about to grasp it; rescue the humble victims of their oppressions. While reducing them to a lower level, he may exalt above them some whom they have despised. In the height of their glory he may strike them suddenly down. Pharaoh, Sennacherib, Nebuchadnezzar, Haman, Herod, are illustrations of the humbling which God may administer to the haughty. In every case of impenitent pride terrible humiliation comes at death and judgment. 2. *He sometimes brings the proud down in their own esteem—humbles their spirit.* This may be by such methods as have just been referred to; and the spirit may be humbled without being really changed. But the happiest humiliation is that which is wrought in the heart by the Word and Spirit of God, aided by such methods or apart from them. The man thus affected comes to see his true position as a creature and a sinner. He discerns and recognizes his entire dependence on God; that whatever he has he has received (1 Cor. iv. 7). He perceives and acknowledges the sin and folly of his pride, humbles himself before God on account of it, casts himself on his mercy, gladly accepts pardon and salvation as a free gift of God's grace in Christ Jesus; and thus receives a better exaltation than ever he had known or imagined before. Happy those haughty ones whom God thus brings down!

Then, eschew pride; and "be clothed with humility" (1 Pet. v. 5, 6). This grace may best be learned at the cross of Christ. There we see our condition of evil and peril as sinners, our entire dependence for salvation on the mercy of God and the merits of his Son, our equality in respect to sin and salvation with the meanest of those we are tempted to despise. There also we have presented to our contemplation the noblest model of humility and self-humiliation (Phil. ii. 5—8).—G. W.

Ver. 29.—*God the Lamp of his people.* The image of a lamp seems at first too humble to be employed of God. "The Lord God is a Sun" (Ps. lxxxiv. 11) appears more suitable for One so great, who is the Light of the universe. Still, the humbler and homelier image is expressive. A lamp is of service where the sun is of none—in mines, dark cellars and dungeons, etc. Its light is more readily commanded and appropriated. We can say, "*My* lamp," we cannot so well say, "*My* sun." And so this image may convey to us more readily how God is a Light in the darkest places and obscurest recesses; available to each for his own particular needs and for the humblest uses of daily life. But the distinction need not and should not be pressed. The word is an image of light.

I. A FACT STATED. "Thou art my Lamp, O Lord." 1. *He shines as a bright lamp.* (1) He is Light without darkness (1 John i. 5); essential, independent, unchangeable, and eternal Light. Not needing to be or capable of being replenished, as all other lamps, literal or figurative. (2) He shines pre-eminently in his Son Jesus Christ. (3) In and by his Word—its declarations, precepts, promises, threatenings. "The commandment is a lamp, and the Law is light" (Prov. vi. 23). (4) By his Spirit, in the reason, conscience, and heart of man. Thus "the spirit of man is the lamp of the Lord" (Prov. xx. 27, Revised Version). (5) In and by his people. He so shines on them as to make them lights. 2. *He thus fulfils the various purposes of a lamp.* (1) Revealing. Himself, and in his light all other persons and things in their true nature and relations to him and each other (comp. Eph. v. 13). Bringing into view what had been hidden in the heart, etc., by the darkness. (2) Guiding. In the way that is right and safe, and leads to salvation (Ps. cxix. 105). He thus gives "the light of life" (John viii. 12). (3) Cheering (Ps. iv. 6, 7; xcvii. 11; comp. Esth. viii. 16). 3. *He is a Lamp to each believer.* "*My* Lamp." Similarly, "The Lord is *my* Light" (Ps. xxvii. 1). The godly man accepts the Divine light, uses it in practical life, enjoys the comfort of it. Others reject it, and wander and stumble on in darkness.

II. AN ASSURANCE CHERISHED. "The Lord will lighten my darkness." From his knowledge of God and his promises, and his past experience, the psalmist felt assured that, whatever darkness might come upon him, God would be his light in and through it, yea, would turn the darkness into light. Such an assurance may be cherished by all the people of God. He will lighten the darkness which may arise from: 1. *Perplexity.* As to Divine truth and as to the path of duty. 2. *Sin.* The memory of sins long past or recent; the consciousness of proneness to evil. 3. *Spiritual gloom*. When the lights of heaven seem blotted out, and God seems himself to have deserted the soul (Ps. xxii. 1, 2; xlii.). 4. *Troubles*. Afflictions of body; bereavements, making dark the home; unkindness or unfaithfulness of friends; worldly losses. When all other lights go out, and leave in gloom, God remains, the Light of his friends, and will in due time lighten their darkness.

Let all, then, accept this glorious Lamp for their guidance and comfort. How blessed the world of which it is said, "There shall be no night there . . . for the Lord God giveth them light;" and again, "The glory of God did lighten it, and the Lamb is the Light thereof" (Rev. xxii. 5; xxi. 23)!—G. W.

Ver. 31.—*Perfection of God's way and Word*. These words may be regarded as a brief summary of the lessons which David had learned from his varied experiences and meditations. They are the perfection of God's way, the unmixed truth of his Word, and the safety of all who flee to him for protection.

I. THE PERFECTION OF GOD'S WAY. "His way is perfect." This is true of all his proceedings, in every department of his operations. His ways in nature are to a large extent inscrutable; but we are sure they are infinitely wise and good. His method of redeeming and saving sinners is perfect. But here the reference is rather to the course of his providence—the way in which he leads, governs, protects, and delivers his servants. 1. *The meaning of the assertion*. That God's way is perfectly wise and good and holy, perfectly adapted to fulfil the purposes of his love towards his children, and leads to an end that is perfectly good. That, in comparison with the way we might have preferred, it is infinitely superior. 2. *The grounds of the assertion*. It expresses a conviction which springs from: (1) Reason. Because God is perfect, his way must be. Perfect Wisdom and Goodness cannot err; unbounded power carries into effect the determinations of perfect Wisdom and Goodness. (2) Revelation. Holy Writ is in most cases our first source of knowledge as to God and his ways; and it abounds in declarations adapted to assure us, in the midst of all our perplexities respecting the mysteries of Divine providence, that the ways of God are right and good, and will issue in good to those who love and obey him. (3) Experience. Looking back on his own life, with its many difficulties, struggles, and perils, David could see enough of the way of God in it all to awaken in him a profound conviction that it was a perfect way. And no one who serves God can fail to recognize this truth in his own life, however much may remain at present dark and difficult. (4) Observation. By which the experience of others becomes available for ourselves. In this we may include the *recorded* experience of others in biography and history, in the sacred or other books. The history of the Church and of individuals abounds in instances adapted to increase our confidence in the perfection of the Divine way, while leaving vast spaces of unsolved mystery. 3. *The influence which this truth should have upon us*. (1) Thankfulness and praise. (2) Unwavering confidence, however dark some of the Divine proceedings may be, whether towards ourselves or others. (3) Cheerful submission to the guidance and government of God.

II. THE PURITY OF GOD'S WORD. It is "tried;" literally, "smelted," and so purified and refined, as metals by fire (comp. Ps. xii. 6, "The words of the Lord are pure words: as silver tried in a furnace of earth, purified seven times"). The meaning is that God's Word is thoroughly genuine, true, sincere, free from every particle of opposite qualities. The statement applies to every word of God—his declarations, revelations, precepts, promises, and threatenings. It is most probably made here as to his promises. These are all thoroughly true and reliable, free from error, free from deceit. For God: (1) Cannot lie (Titus i. 2). (2) Cannot mistake. Knows perfectly all the future, all possible hindrances to the accomplishment of his purposes, and his own power to conquer them. (3) Cannot change. Not in purpose; not in power. Thus whatever tends to throw more or less of uncertainty upon human promises is absent from the Divine (see further on ch. vii. 28). The Word of God is "tried" in another sense of the Hebrew word. It has been "tested," put to the proof, in ten thousands of instances, and has ever been found true. The experience of every believer testifies to its perfect truth; and the experience of the Church, and of the world in its connection with the Church, throughout all ages, gives the same assurance. Then: 1. *Let us trust the Word* of God with a confidence suited to its entire trustworthiness. 2. *Let us be glad and thankful that, amidst so much that is unreliable, we have here a firm foundation on which to rest our life and hopes.* 3. *Let our word correspond with that of God in its freedom from all insincerity and untruthfulness,* if it cannot be free from the uncertainty which springs from ignorance, inability, or mutability.

III. THE PROTECTION WHICH GOD AFFORDS TO HIS PEOPLE. 1. *The protection itself.* "He is a Buckler [Shield] to all them that trust in him." Not only he secures protection, he is himself the Shield that protects. As a hen protects her chickens under her own wings (Ps. xci. 4), so the Lord covers and defends his people with his own Being and perfections. Their enemies have to conquer him before they can injure them. They are under the guardianship of his knowledge, power, goodness, faithfulness; and these must fail before they can perish. 2. *The persons who enjoy such protection.* "All them that trust in him"—all, as the word is, who flee to him for refuge. (1) It is one of the characteristics of the godly, that in their perils they flee for refuge to God. It is to God they flee; not to some merely imaginary being whom they call God— a God, for instance, who, however despised in the time of prosperity, is always at the call of men in trouble; too merciful to punish his foes severely; too tender-hearted to disregard the cry of distress, although it come from impenitent hearts. Such confidence is vain. God's Word contains not a promise to the ungodly and unholy, however troubled they may be, unless the trouble subdue their hearts to a true repentance. But those who live by faith in God naturally turn to him in danger and distress. (2) To them he is a Shield. Their faith itself, God-produced and God-sustained, is a shield (Eph. vi. 16); it inspires their prayers and struggles after safety; and in response to their confidence and their prayers the Almighty becomes their Defence, and they are safe. (3) Their safety is according to their faith. Faith which is mixed with doubt is an occasion of peril. Intermittent faith brings intermittent safety. If for a time we flee *from* our Refuge, we are exposed defenceless to the assaults of our enemies, and shall be wounded and distressed. Then, "trust in him at *all* times" (Ps. lxii. 8); and let your prayer be, "Lord, increase our faith" (Luke xvii. 5), and, "Pray for us that our faith fail not" (see Luke xxii. 32).—G. W.

Ver. 32.—*Jehovah the only God, the only Rock.* David's experience of what Jehovah his God had been to him impels him triumphantly to contrast him with all other that men called gods.

I. JEHOVAH ALONE IS GOD. David was thinking of the idols worshipped by the nations around, which had proved themselves unable to protect their worshippers from his victorious arms. The question may be asked as to all other idols, and all persons and things that men serve as if they were gods—self, wealth, the world, etc.: 1. *Which of them has perfections like those of Jehovah?* He is the living God, the everlasting, infinite in power, wisdom, and love; perfect in holiness and righteousness. To whom besides can such attributes be ascribed? "There is none else" (Deut. iv. 39). 2. *Which of them has done or can do works like his?* "All the gods of the peoples are idols: but the Lord made the heavens" (Ps. xcvi. 5, Revised Version; comp. Isa. xlv. 18). 3. *Which of them can help their worshippers as he can?* They are "vain things, which cannot profit nor deliver; for they are vain" (1 Sam. xii. 21). 4. *Which of them, then, is worthy to receive homage such as is due to him?* Fear, trust, love, worship, obedience. Yet the unregenerate do honour one or other of these vanities more than God. They, as truly as the heathen, "worship and serve the creature rather than the Creator, who is blessed for ever" (Rom. i. 25, Revised Version).

II. JEHOVAH ALONE IS A ROCK. 1. *God is a Rock.* A term applied to him by Moses (Deut. xxxii. 4), and afterwards very frequently, especially in the Book of Psalms. God is to those who trust in him what a rock, lofty and difficult of ascent and access to strangers, is to a people invaded by powerful foes. In him they find safety and protection. And as a rock is marked by strength, stability, and permanence, so God is mighty to protect, unchangeable, a Rock of ages, "an everlasting Rock" (Isa. xxvi. 4, Revised Version), a Refuge available through each life and for all generations. 2. *He alone is worthy of the name.* There are other persons and things which minister strength and safety to men. "Wisdom is a defence, and money is a defence" (Eccles. vii. 12), friendship also, and civil government and military force, etc. But none besides

God deserves the name of a Rock. (1) They are limited in their worth; he, unbounded One or another of them may be a refuge against some dangers; he, against all. They may not be at hand in the time of most pressing need; he is always near. (2) They are feeble and unstable; he, strong and firm. (3) They are transient; he, everlasting. (4) They are dependent; he, their independent Source. All their fitness and ability to aid us is from him; so that, when they are of service to us, it is he that is showing himself to be our Rock.

Then: 1. *Accept thankfully the good they can do;* but trust in the Lord alone with absolute and unwavering confidence. 2. *Beware of resorting to God's gifts as a refuge from himself.* From the thought of him; from the reproaches of a guilty conscience; from the penalties of his Law 3. *If you reject or neglect God for others, bethink you what help they can give you when he executes his judgments upon you.* (Judg. x. 14; Jer. ii. 28.)—G. W.

Ver. 33.—*Divine protection and guidance.* The experience of David, and the purpose of the psalm, naturally lead to repetition of declarations and images descriptive of the protection and guidance which had been vouchsafed to him. They are not unsuitable to record the convictions and feelings of every good man as he reviews the past and anticipates the future. This verse in the Revised Version reads, "God is my strong Fortress, and he guideth the perfect in his way."

I. GOD IS OUR STRONG FORTRESS. A fortress is a protection against enemies. 1. *We have powerful foes.* The world and the flesh, the devil and his angels, assault us continually, and would destroy, not only our peace, but our souls. They are too strong and numerous for our power and skill; and no creature-power is sufficient for our defence. 2. *God is our Almighty Protector.* The Fortress into which we can flee, and where we are safe; which no enemy can scale or breach. His presence surrounds us; his power defends us. Yea, he is in our hearts to strengthen and protect us. Everywhere, and under all circumstances, we can resort to this Refuge, and defy our foes. We should therefore be ready to go anywhere and do anything at God's command. He may lead us where temptations are numerous and powerful; but obeying and trusting him, we are secure.

II. GOD IS OUR ALL-WISE GUIDE. The reading and translation preferred by the Revisers gives a good sense, harmonizing with many statements of Holy Writ. "He guideth the perfect in his way," or, perhaps, "his [God's] way." The man who is "perfect" in the sense of "upright," sincere, true, righteous, whole-hearted, may be assured of Divine guidance; while the insincere, hypocritical, double-minded, shall be left to go astray. In the margin of the Revised Version, however, another reading and rendering are given, viz. "guideth my way in perfectness," which appears to be substantially in agreement with the Authorized Version, "maketh my way perfect." 1. *God leads his people in their way.* By his providence, Word, Spirit. In respect to the affairs of this life, and those of the soul and eternity. He guides them into the position he has chosen for them, and to and in the work he appoints for them. "The steps of a good man are ordered by the Lord" (Ps. xxxvii. 23). 2. *His lead is perfect.* Such was the conclusion of the psalmist in reference to his own way. He could see that all had been ordered aright for the accomplishment of the Divine purposes respecting him. Such will be the conclusion of all God's servants at the last; and their faith in God will enable them to cherish this conviction now, notwithstanding all the perplexities in which they may be involved. The way in which they may be led may not be always pleasant; but it is: (1) The best way. The way of holiness; the way in which they can gain most real good, serve and honour God most, be most useful, attain ultimately the greatest glory and felicity. (2) The safe way. Sometimes a way which avoids enemies and perils; in other cases, a way through the midst of them, which God makes safe by his protection. (3) The way that ends in eternal glory and blessedness. It is "the way of life which goeth upward" (Prov. xv. 24, Revised Version). "The end" is "everlasting life" (Rom. vi. 22). It may be asked how it comes to pass that those who have God for their Guide nevertheless make such grievous mistakes, and fall into so much trouble. (1) The troubles which spring from want of worldly wisdom, as well as those which arise from circumstances, are under Divine guidance. It is the will of God that his people should suffer, and his benevolent purpose is often made manifest in the spiritual profit and greater usefulness of the sufferers. (2). Even good men do not fully seek and follow the guidance of God. They too frequently choose their own way, and thus fall into mischief. But God, in his goodness, does not therefore forsake them. He leads those who are true at heart out of the evils into which they have brought themselves, turns their very sins and follies to account in training them for further service, and brings them safe home at last.

The lessons are: 1. *Be thankful for such a Guide.* 2. *See to it that you ever honestly seek and submit to his guidance.* By the study of his Word and providence, and by earnest prayer, inquire what is the way in which he would have you go; and, when you see it, walk in it.—G. W.

Ver. 36.—*Greatness from God's condescension.* "Thy gentleness hath made me great." David had been raised from a humble position to one of greatness. He had become great in arms, in royal dignity, in the extent of his dominion. In these words he ascribes all his greatness to the condescending goodness of God. The word translated "gentleness" is elsewhere used only of men, and signifies "humility" (Prov. xv. 33; xviii. 12; xxii. 4). But in speaking of God, we use the word "condescension" rather than "humility." Yet it is said of him (Ps. cxiii. 6) that "he humbleth himself to behold the things that are in heaven and in the earth;" *i.e.* he stoops to regard them; it is condescension in him to notice them. The words of the text may be used by all Christians; especially by some of them.

I. The greatness to which Christians are exalted. 1. *All of them are made great.* For they are made: (1) Sons and daughters of the great God, brothers and sisters of Jesus the Son of God, having a nature corresponding with the names. They are "partakers of the Divine nature" (2 Pet. i. 4), and therefore God-like, in holiness, righteousness, and love. (2) Wise with heavenly wisdom. A nobler wisdom than that of philosophers. "Taught of God" (John vi. 45), who reveals to them what he hides from the worldly wise (Matt. xi. 25). (3) Powerful with the noblest power, that which is moral and spiritual, by which they "overcome the world" (1 John v. 4), rule their own spirits (Prov. xvi. 32), and subdue others to the obedience of faith. (4) Friends and associates of the best of God's creatures—holy angels and redeemed men; with whom they form one family (Eph. iii. 15). (5) Heirs, and at length possessors, of a grand and enduring estate (1 Pet. i. 4). These things are not mere names or fancies; they are solid and enduring realities, to have the lowest place and the humblest share in which is, in the nature of things, to be greater than the greatest of earthly dignitaries who have no part in them. 2. *Some of them are made specially great.* They realize, in a larger measure than others, the various elements of greatness mentioned above. They have more of God in them; and hence are richer in spiritual wisdom and goodness, exercise a wider and stronger influence, do a greater work, attain to greater honour and renown in this world and the next. Apostles, martyrs; eminent teachers, evangelists, missionaries, and reformers; monarchs, too, and statesmen, poets, etc., who are also devoted Christians. Such special greatness arises sometimes and in part from: (1) Greater natural endowments. More of physical energy, or intellectual power, or emotional force, to begin with. (2) Or greater opportunities, which may be such as rank and fortune give, or the state of things around them, or such as poverty, affliction, and persecution afford. (3) Special earnestness, faithfulness, and diligence in the cultivation and employment of powers and opportunities (Luke xix. 16—26). (4) Special prayerfulness. Hence abundant impartation of the Holy Spirit, the Source and Sustainer of all spiritual excellence. (5) Deeper humility. Without this all seeming greatness is not greatness at all "in the kingdom of heaven," and will shrivel into nothingness (Matt. xviii. 1—4; Luke ix. 48; xiv. 11).

II. To what such greatness is to be ascribed, and is ascribed by those who attain to it. To the condescension of God. David recognized that all his greatness was owing to the goodness and power of God, and in their exercise on his behalf he discerned unspeakable condescension. Similar should and will be the feeling of all who are raised to spiritual greatness. 1. *The work of God in their exaltation is a work of condescension.* This appears as we consider: (1) His greatness and holiness, and their littleness and sinfulness (Ps. viii.; Isa. lvii. 15). God must *stoop* to reach and raise such creatures. (2) His various operations upon and for them. When we consider what is involved in the Divine processes by which they are exalted, they resolve themselves into attention (so to speak) to, and animating or controlling influence over, a countless multitude of small matters. Yet we shall not be astonished at this when we remember that not a sparrow is forgotten by God, and that his children "are of more value than many sparrows" (Luke xii. 6, 7). Also that great results depend on small things; and that, in fact, to the Infinite Mind there is nothing great, nothing small. (3) And pre-eminently, the incarnation and work of the Son of God. The self-humiliation of the eternal Word in becoming man (John i. 1—3, 14), and of the God-Man in lowly service to lowly people, patiently enduring the greatest indignities and most painful and ignominious sufferings, "obedient unto death, even the death of the cross" (Matt. xx. 28; Luke xxii. 27; John xiii. 2—5; Phil. ii. 6—8). (4) The work of the Holy Spirit. Stooping to dwell in the hearts of the mean and sinful, bearing with neglect, waywardness, resistance, and disobedience. 2. *The condescension thus displayed promotes spiritual greatness.* Not only as it is exercised in the ways before mentioned, but: (1) As it is apprehended and realized. The majesty, holiness, and justice of God tend to humiliate and repress the human spirit, and discourage aspiration and effort. At best it produces only a "spirit of bondage" (Rom. viii. 15). But under the influence of condescending love, love is enkindled, confidence is awakened, the heart expands and enlarges, is inspired with the freedom and courage which prepare for noble service of God and man, rises heavenward and yet looks on earth with kindlier eye, and more resolute purpose to labour and suffer for its good. (2) As it incites to imitation. Contemplating the grandeur and beauty of the Divine condescension, we become transformed into its image. We learn to stoop to the lowly and even the degraded. We are content to serve in lowly offices, if thereby we can benefit our fellow-men. It no longer seems strange that we should be required "to wash one another's feet" (John xiii. 14). And this is the way to become great (Mark x. 43, 44). Yet we must not indulge the thought or assume the air of condescension, or we shall fail both to benefit others and to secure honour for ourselves. Rather let us accustom ourselves to think in how many and important respects we are on a level with those whose good we seek. This will produce in us genuine humility, and enable us to feel towards our brethren a brotherly sympathy which will banish the sense of superiority.—G. W.

Vers. 44, 45.—*The head of the nations.* David once more records how God had delivered him in and from the contests in which he had been involved; and declares that he had thus kept him "to be the head of the nations" (Revised Version), not only Israel, but foreign peoples. He, or, if not he, the Spirit which spake by him (ch. xxiii. 2), may have had in view the ultimate purpose of God respecting him and his posterity, viz. the exaltation of his great Son to be, in a wider sense than was applicable to David himself, "the Head of the nations." We may at least take the words as applicable to the Lord Jesus Christ.

I. THE OPPOSITION HE ENCOUNTERS. Like David, he has to withstand many "strivings of the people." 1. *In his life on earth he was much opposed.* He endured the "contradiction of sinners against himself" (Heb. xii. 3). "He came unto his own, and his own received him not" (John i. 11)—his own people, his own family (John vii. 5). All classes, with a few exceptions, rejected him—Pharisees and Sadducees, elders and scribes, ecclesiastics and politicians, rulers and people. The multitude sought once to make him king (John vi. 15), and, when he entered Jerusalem for the last time, welcomed him, in the hope that he was about to ascend the throne; but he would not be such a king as they desired, and they cared not to have such a King as he was to be. Hence they united with their superiors in saying, "We will not have this Man to reign over us" (Luke xix. 14); and, to put an end to his pretensions, put him to death. They did not know that they were thus very effectually promoting his victories and reign. 2. *He has met with various and constant opposition ever since.* His cause has advanced in spite of perpetual "strivings" against it. Jews and Gentiles, kings and subjects, rich and poor, the intellectual and the ignorant, the refined and the coarse, have "set themselves . . . against the Lord, and against his Anointed" (Ps. ii. 2). He, too, can speak still of the "strivings of *my* people." As at first amongst the Jews, so since amongst Christians (so-called), and amongst those in high positions in his Church, have been found his worst foes. Men are willing to bear his Name, to receive some of his doctrines, and even contend for them, to appropriate the comfort he gives; but to *obey* him, to let him *rule* in their minds and hearts and lives, in their homes, in their business, in their pleasures, in their social life, in their national affairs,—that is quite another matter. And those who strive earnestly to obey him themselves, and to induce others to do so, must be prepared for opposite "strivings," and even persecution. Nor do they wonder, seeing they find, more or less, in their own nature, elements of opposition to the rule of the Christ which explain the hostility of others.

II. THE EXALTED POSITION HE NEVERTHELESS OCCUPIES. "Head of the nations." The answer of the Almighty to all the rebellious counsels and works of men is, "Yet have I set my King upon my holy hill of Zion" (Ps. ii. 6). The kingdom of Christ is the kingdom of Jehovah; vain, therefore, must be all strivings against it. Its opponents can only dash themselves to pieces, but "he *must* reign" (1 Cor. xv. 25). 1. *The extent of his dominion.* "The nations," in a wider sense than was true of David. "All nations shall serve him" (Ps. lxxii. 11). And not only all nations in existence at any one time, but all that may come into existence while the world endures. 2. *The nature of his dominion.* (1) He is "Head of the nations" by *right*. By the appointment and gift of the Father (Ps. ii. 7, 8; Matt. xxviii. 18). As the result and reward of his own righteousness and self-sacrificing love (Phil. ii. 8, 9). He redeemed men by his blood, to make them "a kingdom" (Rev. i. 5, 6; v. 9, 10, Revised Version). As truth, righteousness, and love are rightful rulers, however far they may be from actually ruling, so is it with our Lord. (2) He actually rules *over* all nations. "He is Lord of all" (Acts x. 36). All authority *on earth*, as well as in heaven, has been given to him (Matt. xxviii. 18). Whether men know him or not, acknowledge him or not, he is their King; he so orders, controls, and directs the affairs of the nations as to make them subserve the advancement and ultimate universal establishment of his spiritual reign. (3) He has already a vast multitude of willing and obedient subjects in many nations. "A people which he knew not," gathered from the Gentiles, serves him; as well as many from the people whom he knew. (4) Many render him feigned obedience (ver. 45, margin). It is an evidence of his great power among the nations that many find it to their interest, or credit, or convenience, to profess his Name, who are still opposed to him in heart. They call him Lord, though they do not the things which he says (Luke vi. 46). (5) All nations will at length own him as their Head, and heartily and lovingly submit to his sway. The prophecy will yet be fulfilled: "There followed great voices in heaven, and they said, The kingdom of the world is become the kingdom of our Lord, and of his Christ: and he shall reign for ever and ever" (Rev. xi. 15, Revised Version). In the assurance of this, let his people labour and give and pray with joyful hope for the extension of his reign in the earth.—G. W.

Ver. 47.—*Praise to God as the ever-living Saviour.* The whole psalm is a song of praise to God, but some parts bear more distinctively this character. This verse is one of them.

I. THE TITLES HERE GIVEN TO GOD. 1. *Rock.* (See on ver. 32.) "*My* Rock." The Rock to which I have fled, and where I have found safety and repose. The Rock in which I still trust and will trust with full assurance of its stability and security, whatever be the confidences of others. It is a blessed thing, in speaking of God, to be able to use this word "my," as expressive of personal experience, choice, and confidence. 2. *The God of the Rock of my salvation;* equivalent to "the God who is the Rock of my salvation," "my mighty Saviour." David had experienced salvation from enemies and dangers many times and in many ways; and he ascribes all to God. By whatever means and instruments, it was God who had delivered him. He had been manifested in his history as the God of salvation; and in saving him had shown himself a Rock, *the* Rock in which alone safety was to be found. The higher and better salvation which is presented to us in the gospel is from God. With him it originated; by him in Christ it is wrought. Christians joyfully recognize God as the God of salvation, the Rock of salvation. It is for men one of the most glorious and encouraging names of God. God the Creator, God the Preserver, God the Ruler, are glorious names; but unless to them could be added God the Saviour, they would afford no hope or comfort. It is this which renders all other names of God attractive and inspiring. Specially gladdening is it to be able to say, "The God of *my* salvation," the Rock of ages in which

I find refuge, the God who has saved me and is saving me, and in whom I trust that he will fully save me, from the guilt, power, and consequences of my sins, and all the assaults of the deadly enemies of my soul.

II. THE DECLARATION MADE RESPECTING HIM. "The Lord liveth." Which expresses: 1. *His real existence.* In contrast with idols, which are dead, helpless, and unable to help. 2. *His continued existence.* In contrast with men, who die and pass away. 3. *His manifested existence.* He lives and works in the world, in the Church, in each believer. By his operations for the good of his people, he shows himself the living God. 4. *The satisfaction which his servants feel in him as ever-living.* (1) Joy that such a Being is their God. That they know and worship the true and living God. (2) Confidence that his life renders all their interests secure for this world and the next. And not only their interests as individuals, but those of the whole Church of God. Because he lives, his Church cannot perish. (3) Comfort under the death of Christian friends. He lives; and therefore their death was his act. It did not befall them because he had ceased to be or to be able to deliver. He lives, to support and comfort those who survive. He lives, to supply the place of the departed in the family, the Church, the world. He lives, and therefore they live and will live for ever. For through Christ their life was and is rooted in his. He is their abiding Dwelling-place.

III. THE PRAISE RENDERED TO HIM. "Blessed" (equivalent to "praised"), "exalted." 1. Praise is the utterance of exalted thoughts and feelings respecting him. Without these the language of praise is of no value. 2. To publish his praise by speech or writing is to exalt him in view of others. 3. Praise in such words as are here employed expresses the desire that all should exalt him by accepting, loving, obeying, and extolling him. 4. The publication of his praise is adapted to produce this result. 5. The exaltation of God should ever be sought in our services of praise. Some such services tend rather to the exaltation of musical composers, organists, and choirs.—G. W.

Vers. 50, 51.—*Praising God among the nations.* In bringing to a close this grand psalm of praise, the royal writer looks around and forward. He reveals a purpose and expectation that his song will be heard among the nations at large, and he expresses his assurance that the kindness of God which he had experienced would be extended to his family down to the latest ages, yea, for evermore. The two verses are closely connected. Translate "nations" instead of "heathen;" and instead of "He is the Tower of salvation for his king," read, "Effecting great salvations [deliverances] for his king." Thus the verses will run, "Therefore I will give thanks unto thee, O Lord, among the nations, and to thy Name will I sing praises; who effecteth great deliverances for his king, and showeth loving-kindness to his anointed, to David and to his seed for evermore."

I. THE GROUNDS OF THE PSALMIST'S PRAISE. 1. *His position.* God's "king," "his anointed," the messiah (Christ) of God. David was literally anointed by Samuel as the future king of Israel, and had been prepared for and brought to the throne in marvellous ways. He recognized, as Saul had failed to do, that he was God's king and representative, ruling God's people in subjection to him. The position was far more honourable than that of any heathen monarch, however much wider his dominion. 2. *His experience of the goodness and power of God.* Protecting, delivering, giving victory, exalting to the throne, and preserving in it. "Therefore," because of all that I have here recorded of the Divine favour to me, "I will give thanks," etc. Note the value of experience as a help and incentive to praise. It gives reality to our thoughts of God, and personal knowledge of his power and goodness. It stirs the heart to gratitude, and to a desire that all should know and praise him. It furnishes interesting subjects for praise. 3. *The assurance he had of the future kindness of God to himself and his family.* This assurance sprang from the promise of God by Nathan (ch. vii. 12—16), and which finds its ultimate and complete fulfilment in the exaltation of the Christ, the Son of David, to be King of all men, of all beings and things in heaven as well as earth. It was a great honour conferred on David and his family to be made rulers for many generations of the people in and through whom true religion was preserved, to be at length diffused through all the earth; it was a far greater for HIM to spring from them who should be the Saviour of all men, and the eternal King. For consider: (1)

His personal glory. Not only Son of David, but Son of God, filled "with all the fulness of the Godhead" (Col. ii. 9); the incarnate Word. (2) The nature of his rule. Especially his spiritual reign—the reign of Divine truth, holiness, and love in the hearts and lives of men; the reign of peace and joy. (3) Its extent. Far wider than that of David or Solomon. To include at length all nations (Ps. lxxii. 8, 11). (4) Its duration. "For evermore." David discerned, in the Divine promise to him and his, enough to fill his heart with gladness and thankfulness; if he could have seen even as much as we are permitted to behold, his wonder and gratitude would have known no bounds.

II. THE SPHERE OF HIS PRAISE. "Among the nations." 1. *The fulness of his gratitude moved him to make known God's goodness as widely as possible.* 2. *He desired to instruct other nations, and bring them to worship a God so able and willing to bless his worshippers.* He may have felt a special obligation to instruct and benefit the peoples who had been brought into subjection to himself. 3. *The interest which the nations at large had in what God had done and promised to him.* See Rom. xv. 9, where ver. 50 is quoted by St. Paul in proof that it was the purpose of God that the Gentiles should "glorify God for his mercy."—G. W.

EXPOSITION.

CHAPTER XXIII.

Ver. 1.—Now these be the last words of David. A long interval separates this psalm from the preceding. The one was written when David had just reached the zenith of his power, and, when still unstained by foul crime, he could claim God's favour as due to his innocence. These last words were David's latest inspired utterance, written, probably, towards the end of the calm period which followed upon his restoration to his throne, and when time and the sense of God's renewed favour had healed the wounds of his soul. **David the son of Jesse said.** It was probably this account of the author, and its personal character, which caused the exclusion of this hymn from the Book of Psalms. It seemed to belong rather to David's private history than to a collection made for use in the public services of the temple. **Said.** The word is one usually applied to a message coming directly from God. It is used, however, four times in Numb. xxiv. of the words of Balaam, and in Prov. xxx. of those of Agur. The solemnity of the word indicates the fulness of its inspiration. **The sweet psalmist;** literally, *he who is pleasant in the psalms of Israel.* David might well claim this title, as, under God, we owe the Psalter to him.

Vers. 3, 4.—He that ruleth, etc. This rendering of the Hebrew is very beautiful, and fit to be graven on the hearts of rulers. There is often almost an inspiration in the renderings of the Authorized Version. Grammatically, nevertheless, the psalm declares the blessedness of the king who is just, and may be translated as follows:—

"He that ruleth over men righteously,
That ruleth in the fear of God—
And as the morning light shall he be,
when the sun riseth,

A morning without clouds;
Yea, as the tender grass from the earth,
from sunshine, from rain."

A king who rules his people justly is as glorious as the sun rising in its strength to drive away the works of darkness, and give men, by precept and example, the light of clear knowledge of their duty. But the last metaphor is especially beautiful. In the summer, vegetation dries up under the burning heat of the sun; all is bare and brown, and a few withered stalks of the coarser plants alone remain. But when the rains come, followed by bright sunshine, nature at one burst flashes into beauty, and the hillsides and plains are covered with the soft green of the reviving grass, through which myriads of flowers soon push their way, and clothe the landscape with bright colours. So a just and upright government calls into being countless forms of human activity, and fosters all that is morally beautiful, while it checks the blighting influences of unregulated passion and selfish greed.

Ver. 5.—Although my house, etc. The rendering of the Authorized Version is that of the ancient versions, and is to be retained. David could not but feel that his house was too stained with sin upon sin for him to be able to lay claim to have been in fact that which the theocratic king was in theory, and which David ought to have been as the representative of Christ, and himself the christ, or anointed of Israel's God. But most modern commentators take the negatives as interrogative, and, therefore, as strong assertions.

"For is not my house so with God?
For he had made with me an eternal covenant,
Ordered in all things, and secure:

For all my salvation and all my desire,
Shall he not make it to grow?"

But surely David had failed in realizing the better purposes of his heart, and it was of God's good pleasure that the covenant, in spite of personal failure, remained firm and secure.

Vers. 6, 7.—The sons of Belial; Hebrew, *belial;* not a proper name, but a word signifying "worthlessness," and especially vicious worthlessness (see note on 1 Sam. i. 16). It is from this worthlessness that opposition arises to the just king, and he recognizes it as that which thwarts his efforts. The words may be rendered—

"But the ungodly are as thorns, to be all of them thrust away;
For they may not be taken hold of with the hand.
And the man that would touch them
Must arm himself with iron and the staff of a spear;
And they shall be utterly burned with fire unto nothingness."

The vicious worthlessness which opposes righteous government must be treated like thorns, too prickly and sharp-pointed for gentle dealing. They must be torn up by an iron hook fixed to the end of a spear-handle, and then burnt. The word translated in the same place in the Authorized Version is rendered by Jerome "even to nothing;" and it is just the sort of phrase for which his authority is greatest; for he went to Palestine, and remained there several years, to study the language under Hebrew teachers on the spot. The Septuagint must have had a different reading, as it translates "their shame."

Ver. 8.—These be the names. A similar list is given in 1 Chron. xi. 10—47, with several variations, and sixteen more names. It is given there in connection with David's elevation to the throne of all Israel, and the conquest of Jerusalem. Such catalogues might possibly be revised from time to time, and new names inserted as there were vacancies caused by death. And this seems to have been the case with the list in Chronicles, which contains the names of all who were admitted during David's reign into the order of the mighties. The present is the actual list of the order as it existed on the day when David, at Hebron, was anointed king over all the twelve tribes. And we can well conceive that, on so grand an occasion, David founded this, the first order of chivalry, and gave his thirty knights, as they would be now called, their special rank and high privileges. The Tachmonite. This verse is extremely corrupt. A man could not be a Tachmonite and an Eznite at the same time.

In the Revised Version the corruption is confessed in the mildest terms, but there is something painfully ludicrous in giving Josheb-basshebeth as the man's name. The reading "Jashobeam the son of a Hachmonite," in 1 Chron. xi. 11, is confirmed by 1 Chron. xii. 6, where Jashobeam is mentioned among those who joined David at Ziklag, and by 1 Chron. xxvii. 2, where we find him appointed commander of the first brigade of twenty-four thousand men. The error in the present text arose from the scribe's eye being misled by catching sight of *basshebeth* in the line above, it being the word translated "in the same place" in the Authorized Version. He Adino the Eznite. These unmeaning words are a corruption of the right reading preserved in Chronicles, "he lifted up his spear." The number of men whom he slew at one time is there stated as having been three hundred; but, as Abishai accomplished this feat, and yet held only inferior rank, eight hundred is probably right. And possibly it is not meant that he slew them all with his own hand, though that is quite possible. He was chief of the captains. The word for "captain," *shalish,* is derived from the numeral "three;" and probably it was the title of the three who formed the first rank of the mighties. But in course of time it seems to have been applied to the commanders of the body-guard (2 Kings x. 25); and we find Bidcar so styled when in personal attendance upon Jehu (2 Kings ix. 25); and Pekah used the opportunities afforded by this office for the murder of Pekahiah (2 Kings xv. 25). It is not used of military officers generally. Those admitted to the list were evidently the outlaws who had been with David in his wanderings and at Ziklag. They now received their reward, and became, moreover, the stay of David's throne. It is their past history which accounts for the strange composition of the list. A large number came from Judah, and especially from Bethlehem. Several are David's own relatives. Seven towns or families furnish sixteen out of the whole list. We find a father and his son, and pairs of brothers. There are, moreover, numerous foreigners—Hittites, Ammonites, Moabites, a Syrian from Zobah, and Gideonites, descended from the aboriginal inhabitants of the land. Such a list would have been sorely resented had it not been formed out of men who had earned it by their past services and their fidelity to David.

Ver. 9.—Dodo. The Hebrew has *Dodai,* and "Dodo" is a mere correction of the Massorites to bring the name into verbal agreement with 1 Chron. xi. 12; but in 1 Chron. xxvii. 4 he is called *Dodai,* and we there find him in command of the second division of the army. For "Dodai," however, we ought to read there "Eleazar the son of Dodai." **Ahohite**; Hebrew, *the son of an Ahohite*, and probably a member of the family descended from Ahoah, a son of Benjamin (1 Chron. viii. 4). He would thus belong to the most warlike tribe of Israel, though not mentioned among the Benjamites who joined David at Ziklag (1 Chron. xii. 1—7). He joined him, apparently, at an earlier date. That **were there gathered together**. The word "there" implies the previous mention of some place, and though the text in the parallel passage in Chronicles is more corrupt than that before us, it has, nevertheless, preserved the name of the spot where the encounter took place. In Chronicles the name of Shammah is omitted, and his achievement is mixed up in a strange fashion with that of Eleazar. Here the two heroes have each his separate record, and it is only on minor matters that the text there is more correct. Restored from the readings in Chronicles, the narrative is as follows: "He was with David at Pas-dammim, and the Philistines were gathered there to battle, and the men of Israel were gone up: and he stood (that is, made a stand) and smote," etc. *Pas-dammim* is called *Ephes-dammim* in 1 Sam. xvii. 1. It was situated in the valley of Elah, and, as being upon the border, was the scene of numerous conflicts, whence its name, "the boundary of blood." It was there that David slew Goliath. **Were gone away**; Hebrew, *went up*; that is, to battle. The idea that the Israelites had fled is taken from the parallel place in Chronicles, where, however, it refers to Shammah's exploit. In vers. 9 and 11 there, the phrase, "the Philistines were gathered together," occurs twice, and the scribe, having accidentally omitted the intervening words, has confused together the exploits of Eleazar and Shammah. In this battle Eleazar withstood the Philistine onset, and smote them till his hand clave to his sword-hilt. Many such instances of cramp are recorded, and Mr. Kirkpatrick, in his commentary, quotes one in which the muscles of a warrior's hand could be relaxed, after hard fighting, only by fomentations of hot water.

Ver. 10.—**Victory**; Hebrew, *salvation*; and so also in ver. 12 and 1 Sam. xi. 13; xix. 5. **Returned after him**. This does not imply that they had fled, but simply that they turned in whichever way he turned, and followed him. Battles in old time depended very much upon the prowess of the leaders.

Ver. 11.—**Into a troop**. Josephus renders it "to Lehi," the scene of Samson's exploit. The word is rare, but occurs again

in ver. 13, where, however, we find in Chronicles the ordinary name for a *host* substituted for it. The Revisers have retained in the margin, "or, for foraging;" but its occurrence in Ps. lxviii. 10, where it is rendered "thy congregation," and in the margin of the Revised Version, "troop," makes it probable that "troop" is the right rendering here. **Lentiles**. In 1 Chron. xi. 13, "barley." The difference is probably caused by a transposition of letters. The Philistines seem to have made this incursion in order to carry off or destroy the crops of the Israelites.

Ver. 13.—**And three**. The Hebrew text has "thirty," for which both the Authorized Version and the Revised Version silently substitute "three," as is correctly given in Chronicles. The absence of the article shows that these three were not Jashobeam, Eleazar, and Shammah, but probably Abishai, Benaiah, and another whose name and exploits have been purposely omitted both here and in Chronicles. Apparently this narrative, so interesting as showing the fascination which David exercised over his men, is given as having led to the institution of this second order of three in the brotherhood of the mighties. **In the harvest time**. The Hebrew is "to harvest," but in 1 Chron. xi. 15 "to the rock." As the preposition used here cannot mean "in," this is probably the right reading. In this case, also, it is the similarity of the words that has led to the confusion. Is it possible that these lists were taken from very old and worn catalogues, which it was very difficult to decipher?

Ver. 14.—**An hold**; Hebrew, *the hold*. The definite article here and in ch. v. 17, and the mention of the Philistines as being in the valley of Rephaim, seem to indicate that David had abandoned Jerusalem upon the invasion of the Philistines, and sought refuge at Adullam (see note on ch. v. 17). In its neighbourhood is an isolated hill, on which, probably, was a frontier fortress, in which David prepared to defend himself.

Ver. 15.—**The well of Bethlehem, which is by the gate**. Bethlehem is now supplied with water by an aqueduct, and the wells close to the town have ceased to exist. The cistern of "deep, clear, cool water," described by Ritter, in his 'Geography of Palestine,' and now called David's Well, is three quarters of a mile to the north of Bethlehem, and too distant to be that which David meant.

Vers. 16, 17.—**Brake through the host** (or, *camp*) **of the Philistines**. The Philistine camp was pitched in the valley of Rephaim, and to reach Bethlehem, which was more than twenty or twenty-five miles distant, these three heroes must pass close to the ground occupied by the enemy. The valley of Rephaim, in fact, extended from Jerusalem to Bethlehem, and, to guard their position, the Philistines held Bethlehem with a strong garrison. Of course the heroes would use every precaution; for to be discovered would be certain death. The story of their perils and presence of mind in danger, and hairbreadth escape, would be full of interest; but we are told only that they succeeded, and returned in safety, bearing their precious burden; but David would not drink, and **poured it out unto Jehovah.** The word is that used of a sacrificial libation; for David regarded it as holy, and consecrated to God, because it had been bought with blood—at the risk, that is, of the lives of these gallant men. Nothing is recorded in the romances of the Middle Ages, when knightly chivalry was at its height, more gallant and noble than the exploit of these men. And the very essence of its devotion lay in the fact that it was done to gratify a mere sick longing, and therefore out of pure love. Sick, no doubt, David was, and burning with fever; and even more depressed by the apparent hopelessness of his position. The exploit changed the course of his thoughts. What could he not do with such heroes! Though racked during their absence with anxiety and self-reproach, yet on their return he would be dispirited no longer, but filled with confidence. The words, "Shall I drink?" inserted in the Revised Version, have apparently dropped out of the text by accident. They are found in the parallel place in Chronicles, and in the Septuagint and Vulgate here. The Syriac has, "At the peril of their life's blood these men went."

Ver. 18.—**Abishai . . . was chief among three.** The sense is obscured in the Authorized Version by the translators having failed to notice the presence of the definite article. Abishai, by reason of this exploit, became "chief of the three;" that is, of the second order of three established in the fraternity of the mighties. At the end of the verse, and in ver. 19, the Authorized Version strangely puts the article where it is absent in the Hebrew, and omits it where it is present. The right rendering and meaning is, "He had a name, that is, rank, reputation, among the three. Was he not the most honourable of the three? For this he was made their captain: yet he attained not to equal dignity with the first three."

Ver. 20.—**Benaiah the son of Jehoiada.** He was a very important person throughout David's reign, being the commander of the body-guard (ch. viii. 18), and general of the third brigade of twenty-four thousand men (1 Chron. xxvii. 5). The meaning of the description given of him there is disputed; but probably it should be translated, "Benaiah the son of Jehoiada the priest, as head," that

is, of the brigade. He was thus the son of the Jehoiada who was leader of the house of Aaron, and whose coming to Hebron with three thousand seven hundred martial priests did so much to make David king of all Israel (1 Chron. xii. 27). Subsequently he took the side of Solomon against Adonijah, and was rewarded by being made commander-in-chief, in place of Joab (1 Kings ii. 35). **Kabzeel.** An unidentified place in the south of Judah, on the Edomite border (Josh. xv. 21), called *Jekabzeel* in Neh. xi. 25. **Two lionlike men of Moab.** The Septuagint reads, "the two sons of Ariel of Moab," which the Revised Version adopts. "Ariel" means "lion of God," and is a name given to Jerusalem in Isa. xxix. 1, 2. The Syriac supports the Authorized Version in understanding by the term "heroes," or "champions;" but the use of poetical language in a prosaic catalogue is so strange that the Septuagint is probably right. If so, Ariel is the proper name of the King of Moab, and the achievement took place in the war recorded in ch. viii. 2. **A lion.** This achievement would be as gratefully remembered as the killing of a man-eating tiger by the natives in India. A lion, driven by the cold from the forests, had made its lair in a dry tank near some town, and thence preyed upon the inhabitants as they went in and out of the city. And Benaiah had pity upon them, and came to the rescue, and went down into the pit, and, at the risk of his life, slew the lion.

Ver. 21.—**A goodly man.** The Hebrew text has "who a sight," for which the Massorites read, "a man of sight," that is, handsome, and worth looking at. In 1 Chron. xi. 23 we find what, no doubt, is the right reading, "a man of measure [equivalent to 'a tall man'], five cubits high." The height of Goliath was six cubits and a span (1 Sam. xvii. 4).

Ver. 23.—**David set him over his guard.** We have already seen (upon 1 Sam. xxii. 14) that the words mean that David made him a member of his privy council. Literally the words are, *and David appointed him to his audience.* In 1 Chron. xxvii. 34 mention is made of "Jehoiada the son of Benaiah" as being next in the council to Ahithophel, and many commentators think that the names have been transposed, and that we ought to read, "Benaiah the son of Jehoiada."

Ver. 24.—**The thirty.** This order of knighthood consisted originally of thirty-three men, of whom three were of higher rank, and presided, probably, each over ten, while Joab was chief over them all. This arrangement of men in tens, with an officer over them, was, in fact, the normal rule among the Hebrews. The second triad is unusual, but is explained by the history. In honour of the exploit of bringing the water from the well of Bethlehem, this second order of three was instituted, lower than the three chiefs, but higher than the rest. The third of these is not mentioned, and the disappearance of the name is not the result of accident, but of purpose. Had it been a scribe's error, there would have been some trace of it in the versions. But if the name was erased, it must have been blotted out for treason, and we thus have two candidates for the vacant niche: one is Amasa, and the other Ahithophel. The name of Joab we cannot for one moment admit. He never was a traitor to David, nor would the latter, though king, have ventured to degrade one so powerful, and who continued to be commander-in-chief until David's death. Now, if Amasa is the same as the Amasai in 1 Chron. xii. 18, who was chief of the captains who came from Judah and Benjamin to David when he was in the hold, it is difficult to account for the absence of his name from the list of the thirty. Plainly, however, David did not regard his treason with strong displeasure, but was prepared, after Absalom's death, to make him commander-in-chief. But we must remember that a place in this second triad was gained by one exploit. The three were those who broke through the Philistine host, and fetched the water from Bethlehem. Such a deed would account for the close attachment between David and Ahithophel. He was the king's companion, and his familiar friend. It would account also for his suicide. His love to David had, for some unknown reason, turned to bitter hatred. He sought, not only David's life, but his dishonour. His feelings must have been highly excited before he could have worked himself up to such a pitch; and the reaction and disappointment would be equally extreme. He never could have faced David again, remembering the warmth of former love, and the shamelessness with which he had sought, not only his life, but to bring upon him public shame and ignominy. And his name would have been totally erased, and gone down into silence. Of Ahithophel's personal accomplishments as a brave warrior, we cannot doubt (see ch. xvii. 1), and his son Eliam was one of the mighties. (On a son and father both belonging to the order, see note on ver. 33.) **Elhanan** (see note on ch. xxi. 19).

Ver. 25.—**Shammah the Harodite.** The town Harod was in the plains of Jezreel, near Mount Gilboa. In 1 Chron. xi. 27 he is called "Shammoth the Harorite," the latter word being an easy corruption of *Harodite;* and in 1 Chron. xxvii. 8 he appears as "Shamhuth the Izrahite," and has the command of the fifth brigade. "Izrahite" is by some regarded as an error for "the Zarhite," that is, a member of the clan descended from Zerah the son of Judah. But if so, how did he get to Harod? **Elika.** Omitted in Chronicles, probably through the repetition of the word "Harodite."

Ver. 26.—**Helez.** He is twice called a *Pelonite* in Chronicles, and was general of the seventh brigade (1 Chron. xxvii. 10), where he is said to have belonged to the tribe of Ephraim. Whether *Paltite* or *Pelonite* is right, no one knows; but Beth-Palet was a town in the tribe of Judah, and not in Ephraim. **Ira.** Ira had the command of the sixth brigade (1 Chron. xxvii. 9). **Tekoah** (see note on ch. xiv. 2). This Ira is a distinct person from his namesake, David's confidential minister (ch. xx. 26).

Ver. 27.—**Abiezer.** He had the command of the ninth brigade (1 Chron. xxvii. 12). Anathoth, now *Mata*, was a priestly city in Benjamin (Josh. xxi. 18), the home of Abiathar (1 Kings ii. 26), and the birthplace of Jeremiah (Jer. i. 1). *Anethothite* and *Antothite*, in the parallel places in Chronicles, are merely different ways of pronouncing the same Hebrew consonants. **Mebunnai.** Written *Sibbechai* in ch. xxi. 18, and, as the name is so written in both the parallel places in Chronicles, *Mebunnai* is probably a mistake. In 1 Chron. xxvii. 11 he is said to have been commander of the eighth brigade, and to have been a Zarhite of the town of Hushah, in the tribe of Judah (see 1 Chron. iv. 4).

Ver. 28.—**Zalmon.** He is called *Ilai* in 1 Chron. xi. 29. **Ahohite** (see note on ver. 9). **Maharai the Netophathite.** Netophah, in the neighbourhood of Jerusalem (Ezra ii. 22), was chiefly inhabited, after the exile, by the singers (Neh. xii. 28). Robinson identifies it with *Beit-Netif*, to the south of Jerusalem; but probably erroneously, as Beit-Netif is too far from Bethlehem. Maharai was commander of the tenth brigade, and was a Zarhite, and therefore belonged to the tribe of Judah.

Ver. 29.—**Heleb.** He is called *Heled* and *Heldai* in the parallel places in Chronicles, where we are told that he was a descendant of Othniel, and commander of the twelfth brigade. **Ittai.** He is called *Ithai*, by a very slight change, in Chronicles. **Gibeah** is the *Geba* so closely connected with the history of Saul (see 1 Sam. xiii. 3, 15, etc.). (For Ittai the Philistine, a distinct person, see ch. xv. 19.)

Ver. 30.—**Benaiah.** He was an Ephraimite, and had the command of the eleventh brigade. Pirathon was a town in Ephraim (Judg. xii. 15). **Hiddai.** Called *Hurai* in 1 Chron. xi. 32, by the common confusion of *d* and *r*. **The brooks of Gaash.** "Nahale-

Gaash," the ravines of Gaash, was probably the name of some village, of which nothing is now known.

Ver. 31.—**Abi-albon.** He is called *Abiel* in 1 Chron. xi. 32. He belonged to the town of Beth-Arabah (Josh. xv. 61; xviii. 22), called also Arabah (Josh. xviii. 18), in the wilderness of Judah. **Azmaveth the Barhumite.** He was of Bahurim, for which see note on ch. iii. 16.

Ver. 32.—**Eliahba.** He was of Shaalabbin, in the tribe of Dan (Josh. xix. 42). St. Jerome calls the place Selebi, the modern *Sebbit*. **Of the sons of Jashen, Jonathan, Shammah the Hararite.** In 1 Chron. xi. 34, "The sons of Hashem the Gizonite, Jonathan the son of Shage the Hararite." The word "of" is not in the Hebrew, and is inserted in the Authorized Version to make sense. Really, *b'ne*, sons, is a careless repetition of the three last letters of the name "Shaalbonite," and should be omitted. The text in Chronicles then goes on regularly, "Hashem the Gizonite, Jonathan the son of Shage the Hararite;" but see note on next verse.

Ver. 33.—**Shammah the Hararite.** He was really one of the first three (see ver. 11). (For the reading in Chronicles, see above.) A very probable correction would be "Jonathan the son of Shammah, the son of Agee the Hararite." Thus both father and son would be in the number of the thirty. **Ahiam.** He is called "the son of Sacar" in 1 Chron. xi. 35.

Ver. 34.—**Eliphelet the son of Ahasbai, the son of the Maachathite.** In Chronicles this becomes "Elipha the son of Ur, Hepher the Mecherathite." If the text here is correct, Eliphelet must be a native of Beth-Maachah, a town in Naphtali (ch. xx. 14). **Eliam the son of Ahithophel the Gilonite.** Instead of this, we find "Ahijah the Pelonite" in 1 Chron. xi. 36. Eliam is supposed by many to have been Bathsheba's father (see note on ch. xi. 3; and for Ahithophel the Gilonite, note on ch. xv. 12).

Ver. 35.—**Hezrai.** The Hebrew text has *Hezro*, as in 1 Chron. xi. 37. His native place was Carmel, for which see note on 1 Sam. xv. 12. **Paarai the Arbite.** A native of Arab, in Judah. In Chronicles he is called "Naarai the son of Ezbai."

Ver. 36.—**Igal the son of Nathan of Zobah.** In Chronicles, "Joel the brother of Nathan," *Igal* and *Joel* in Hebrew being almost the same. If the text here is correct, he was by birth a Syrian of Zobah, for which see note on ch. x. 6. **Bani the Gadite.** In Chronicles, "Mibhar the son of Haggeri," "Mibhar" taking the place of "from Zobah;" " "the son," *ben*, that of "Bani;" and Haggadi, "the Gadite," becoming "Haggeri."

Ver. 37.—**Zelek the Ammonite.** The presence of an Ammonite among the thirty reminds us of the fidelity of Shobi, the son of Nahash the Ammonite king, to David (see ch. xvii. 27). **Armourbearer.** The written text has the plural, "armourbearers," for which the K'ri has substituted the singular. The plural is probably right, and if so, both Joab's chief armourbearers, or squires, were foreigners, Zelek being an Ammonite, and Nahari a Gibeonite (see note on ch. iv. 2). In actual warfare we find Joab attended by ten esquires (ch. xviii. 15).

Ver. 38.—**Ithrite.** Of the family of Jether, of Kirjath-jearim (1 Chron. ii. 53), unless Ira and Gareb were two brothers of Amasa, and sons of Jether the husband of Abigail, David's sister (ch. xvii. 25).

Ver. 39.—**Uriah the Hittite** (see note on ch. xi. 3). **Thirty and seven in all.** "The thirty" became a technical name, and might receive additional members. But if we suppose Asahel's place to have been filled up, the number is exact, there being thirty ordinary members, three chiefs of the first class, and three of the second, of whom, however, one name is omitted. In Chronicles sixteen additional names are given, who were probably men admitted to the order to fill up vacancies.

HOMILETICS.

Vers. 1—7.—*The fruitful lessons of David's last words.* The facts are: 1. There is a statement that these are the last words of David, who is spoken of in a fourfold respect. 2. It is affirmed that the utterance which follows is expressly by the Spirit of God. 3. The true ruler is described as one who is just and one fearing God; and the effects of his government are compared to the light of a bright morning, and the tender grass after rain. 4. David affirms that his house is specially characterized as one with which God has made a sure and everlasting covenant, and that, consequently, the whole salvation he cares for and desires will be advanced and realized. 5. He refers to worthless men having no sympathy with the desires of his heart and the purposes of his house—as being like thorns fit only to be ultimately burned. A larger space is given in the Bible to the life of David than to any other except that of his great Antitype; and herein do we see the beautiful harmony of the sacred book as an organic whole, for just as in the New Testament there is great prominence given to the death of Christ and its relation to sin, corresponding to the prominence in the Old Testament of the sacrifices which foreshadowed it, so the position of the eternal King in Zion in the one book is in the same relative proportion to that of the temporal king who so conspicuously shadowed forth his reign in the other. The great interest thus attaching to the life of David renders his last words of unusual importance. We shall best bring out their teaching by noting in succession the very fruitful topics suggested by this section.

I. THE INFLUENCE OF DYING WORDS OF GOOD MEN. We feel that there is a value in these last words of David, not simply by what an examination of their strict sense may yield, but because they are his last words. All last words are weighty in comparison with others; for they close the record, or end the intercourse, or give, as in dying words, the matured expression of one's long experience. The last words of Jacob, of Moses, of Paul, and above all of Christ, are very rich in instruction by virtue of being last. The last words of children, parents, friends who sleep in Jesus, are most precious; they are treasured for ever. There are special reasons for attaching weight to them. 1. They are *reflective, and touched by the influence of the eternal world*. Men are earnest, sincere, uttering only what a review of the past and a prospect of the future will warrant. 2. The *mind is usually calm*. The passions of life are gone, the strife of tongues is no more heard, the spirit is open to the still, small voice. 3. *Worldly influences are in abeyance*. The pomps and fashions of this world are reduced to their proper position. There is scope for things eternal to get their legitimate hold on the thoughts, and so to form aright the conceptions of duty. 4. The *action of the Holy Spirit* is more direct and strong. The great hindrances to his blessed fellowship are reduced to a minimum, and hence a truer estimate is formed of life, its purpose and perils; of Christ, his love and power. 5. The *affections are most pure and tender*. The heart goes out freely toward the Saviour and toward men. Silver and gold and the perishable things of active life are now as dross, and words flow forth steeped in love and tender concern for others, and delight in God's great salvation. Dying saints preach powerful sermons. Their memory is blessed. Their words are rich in all that is good and helpful.

II. THE HONOUR AND RESPONSIBILITY OF RICH MENTAL ENDOWMENTS. David was the man raised up on high, the anointed of God, the sweet psalmist of Israel. These words necessarily imply the coexistence in time of varied mental endowments—wisdom and discretion for ruling, lofty conceptions of the theocracy and the far-reaching character of God's dealings with Israel, and all the qualities requisite for the sweetest poetry. He was certainly most honoured of men in that age, and hence his responsibility was very great. The references to the ideal ruler (ver. 3) indicate how conscious he was of solemn obligations. The fact is, every gift of God bestowed on man is honour put on him, and in its nature it is a talent for use, that the world may be the better for its existence. The possession of great and varied gifts—of thought, emotion, will-power, and of aptitude to do the right thing at the right time—is a wonderful boon. The men of ten talents may well ponder their responsibilities to God and man. What blessing or woe comes to the world according to the direction in which great gifts are used!

III. THE INFLUENCE OF SACRED SONG ON THE RELIGIOUS LIFE. The incidental reference to the "sweet psalmist" throws a sudden and unexpected light on the immense influence exerted by David on the spiritual thought and feeling of his own and subsequent ages. He had touched the deepest feelings of the people, and by his psalms done, perhaps, more to conserve their faith and hope than by all his acts of formal legislation and words of distinct exhortation. His influence will never cease. The saints of all ages are cheered and comforted by his sweet words of song; and they find relief in using language which so aptly expresses the holiest and purest feelings and thoughts of their life. He blessed Israel with a wise and just rule, and the entire world by the most enduring influence of sacred song. The place of sacred song in the Church is most important. It elevates thought, nourishes the more fine and tender sentiments, strengthens the most secret and radical elements of the religious life by giving form and occasion for their exercise, enriches the memory with strains that spring up in hours of weakness and sorrow, and stores the minds of young and old with a treasury of precious Christian truth. He who writes a good hymn blesses the generations to come.

IV. The unknown work of the Holy Spirit. When David said, "The Spirit of the Lord spake by me," he seemed to speak of what was a familiar truth. He was no stranger to such Divine help, as our Lord's testimony to the Psalms indicates (cf. Ps. li. 11). Yet if we confine our attention to the bare historic record of his life, we find scarcely any distinct reference to his consciousness of the direct aid of the Holy Spirit. For aught we can see in distinct words, there was none. His holy influence has no full record. Thus the most important spiritual element in David's spiritual life was to onlookers unknown. There are two aspects of this fact in our Christian life. 1. We do not know the *great extent* to which we are *indebted to the Holy Spirit* for our perseverance, our highest thoughts, our purest feelings, and general growth in excellence. 2. *The non-Christian world does not know the great work which the Holy Spirit achieves in Christian lives.* "The world knoweth him not" (John xiv. 17). It becomes us to remember what we owe to him, and how incessant his action, though men live as though he were not. Religion is at a low ebb whenever the work of the Holy Spirit is forgotten.

V. The model ruler. In his closing days David remembered that he had been raised on high to be a ruler over Israel; and doubtless, in reviewing the past, he was humbled in observing the instances in which he had failed to be as a man after God's own heart. But in the assurance of forgiveness he could now reflect on the ideal which had ever stood before him, and for the instruction of others he indicates his hope of the ideal being approximately realized in his immediate successor, and his faith that in the coming Christ it would be perfectly realized. The two *elements* of the ideal ruler are *justice* and *the fear of God*. These qualities being in full exercise, all things will be done for the good of man and the glory of God. Human obligations—morality on the human side—must be combined with religious feeling—supreme regard in everything to the Divine will. The *effect* of such ruling on saints is (1) what the bright light of morning is on the earth, *i.e.* it is conducive to safety, cheerfulness, full development of activities, and extended knowledge and usefulness; (2) what the abundance of rich verdure is in a tropical climate, *i.e.* it is wealth, beauty, restfulness, contrast. The history of civil and ecclesiastical communities illustrates the truth of this. There are conditions of prosperity which can only be fulfilled by the ruled, but here we have to do with the natural tendency of the just and godly ruling. The ruler may be king, president, parent, or pastor, and wherever the standard of ruling is high, so in proportion will these effects follow. Bad as the subjects ruled may be, the model ruler will to some extent secure for them these blessings. The most perfect illustration of the truth is to be found in Christ. He rules justly, and in harmony with the mind of the Eternal. An examination of the principles of his kingdom, its discipline and spirit, will show that it is perfectly equitable and is an expression of the Divine mind. The effects that flow from it in proportion as it is submitted to, are exactly those here set forth. Heaven and earth testify (Ps. lxxii.).

VI. The ordered covenant. Through Samuel and Nathan (1 Sam. xv. 28; ch. vii. 12—17), God had declared his promise to David, and David on his part had solemnly recognized the goodness of God, and virtually pledged himself to fulfil his side of the sacred engagement (ch. vii. 24—29). Throughout his singular life, amidst all his frailties, he had found God gracious and merciful. Though manifold dangers had arisen which seemed at one time to frustrate the promise and hand over his kingdom to anarchy and his family to disgrace, Divine wisdom had so ordered all things that now, at the close of life, the throne is firm and succession is sure and promising. His mind evidently ponders a threefold covenant: 1. *Personal.* This God was his God, and he could say, "I am thine" (Ps. cxix. 94; cf. lxi. 5). 2. *Official.* He had been chosen to be king, and God had guaranteed to him all needful help and blessing. 3. *Messianic.* The private and official covenant was to him a type of that wider and more blessed covenant of grace which is exemplified in the working out of the redemptive purpose in Christ (Ps. ii.; cf. Isa. liii. 10—12). In respect to each of these the characteristics "everlasting," "ordered in all things," and "sure," were most precious to David's heart. The covenant made with us in Christ is thus most blessed. It is a covenant of pure mercy, originated by God, designed to elevate us to highest dignity, sustained in its development by all the resources of the Eternal; and as to *duration*, from everlasting to everlasting (Matt. xxv. 34; John xvii. 24; Eph. i. 4; 1 Pet. i. 20; Rev. xvii. 8; cf. John iii. 16); as to *execution*, "ordered in all things," everything pertaining to its development and issue being so foreseen and provided for that nothing is left to chance or the exigencies of the hour (Luke xxiv. 26, 27; Acts ii. 23—28; Gal. iv. 4; Eph. i. 10; 2 Pet. iii. 9; cf. Gen. xxii. 14; Rom. xi. 33; Phil. iv. 19); as to *stability*, "sure," resting on the unchangeable faithfulness of the all-wise and all-powerful God (Ps. lxxxix. 1; Isa. xxv. 1; 1 Thess. v. 24; 2 Thess. iii. 3; cf. Acts ii. 30; Heb. vi. 17).

VII. GOD'S FAITHFULNESS MAN'S CONSOLATION. Who can tell the consolation brought to David by the fact that the covenant of God was so "sure"? Reflection on his own frailty and on the dangers of life could not but awaken shame and dread; but this sure, well-ordered, enduring covenant, no words suffice to set forth its preciousness! In this we have a common experience with David. Our hearts are sad and pained by our own shortcomings; we see perils to our salvation on every side; the resolutions we frame for the future partake of our infirmity; the struggle to attain to the likeness of Christ seems to be interminable; and the possibility of so changing our discordant and shattered nature as to present it blameless before his face, seems to us very slight. But the bruised and crushed spirit finds healing and rest in this—that God is true, and has resolved to save us. Blessed knowledge! Instead of inducing indifference or carelessness, it supplements the comfort it brings by a calm and steady flow of energy toward the holy goal, and develops gratitude in form of more entire consecration. In health, in sickness, amidst earthly strifes and fears, and when the chilly hand of death lays hold of us, we rest in him who cannot die, and who has said, "Because I live, ye shall live also." Truly we have "abundant consolation."

VIII. JOY IN THE REVEALED PURPOSE OF GOD. To see God's blessed covenant unfold towards realization of the Divine purpose was all David's salvation and desire. His heart was bound up with it. His joys and his sorrows were more deeply interwoven with the spiritual kingdom than with personal ease or regal splendour. Our Saviour sets forth the same more illustriously in his life. It was his meat and drink to do his Father's will. To see the blessings of the covenant spread to all mankind was the absorbing passion of his heart. For this he endured the cross and despised the shame. The prospect of the issue of his death gave him satisfaction in the hour of death (Ps. liii. 10). The secret of his life was oneness with the Father's will. The Apostle Paul exhibits, in his measure, the same delight in God's purpose. It is a mark of high Christian feeling that we pass from our own personal interest in redemption to delight in the merciful purpose being realized in others. This is the spring of enterprise, the purifier of the heart from spiritual selfishness, the sure mark of having the mind that was in Christ.

IX. THE CHARACTERISTICS OF A WICKED LIFE. David, in vers. 5, 6, contrasts the men of Belial with those who rejoice in and work along the lines of God's covenant. Their power often terrifies the good, causes much mischief, and seems for a while to tend to their permanent prosperity. But their power is barren of good result, noxious in its influence, and destined to be cut short. Here we have the truth exemplified in the case of all who are alien to the gracious purpose of God as revealed in his covenant of mercy. The life of the wicked is: 1. *Barren* as thorns. Whatever promise of good there may be at one time, it never passes from the bare thorn condition to that of fruitfulness. In highest moral and simplest religious fruitfulness their lives are worth nothing. 2. It is *noxious* as thorns. A wicked life pierces and wounds those who come under its influence; it tends not to healing and comfort, but to pain and distress. 3. It is *fleeting* in power, as thorns destined to be crushed by a mightier force and consumed. The wicked may be in great power, but the day will come when it will be said of him, "He is not" (Ps. xxxvii. 35, 36). These contrasts of the righteous and the wicked should strengthen the hearts of those who endure persecution and trial.

Vers. 8—39.—The facts are: 1. A general statement of the names of David's mighty men, with a comparative reference to some of their deeds. 2. A more special account of the daring of three who procured water for David at the risk of their lives. 3. The refusal of the king to drink that which had been obtained at so great a risk.

Mighty men. The account here of the heroes who figured in the course of David's life is supplementary to the general history, and, while intended to set forth incidents in his career, is also most probably designed to give a place of honour in the national records to those whose strength and valour contributed to establish the kingdom. There are deeds of mighty men recorded in the annals of the Church, and we may note—

I. THAT A PLACE OF HONOUR IS IN RESERVE FOR THOSE WHO RENDER HIGH SERVICE. Because of great service these men were honoured with a place in the record which is to be read by all mankind. In subduing the world to Christ there is scope for great energies and efforts. Those who by prayer, self-denial, holy living, written or spoken words, or other means and weapons, go forth daily in the name of Christ and achieve great things, will be honoured in the esteem of the coming ages and in the esteem of Christ. While all good men shall shine as with the brightness of the firmament, these shall shine forth more distinctly as the "stars" for ever and ever (Dan. xii. 3; 1 Cor. xv. 41).

II. THAT THE GROUND OF THE HONOUR LIES IN THEIR OVERCOMING MUCH EVIL. These men smote gigantic foes. They contributed to the stability and splendour of David's reign by sweeping away the evils which would have checked the progress of his wise and just methods of government. The honour of Christian soldiers lies in ridding the world of gigantic evils, the preliminary step to the perfection of good. Those who smite the greatest evils or a multitude of the most pervasive sins, confer unspeakable benefits on mankind, and clear the way for the positive development of those holy principles which are the glory of the kingdom of Christ. The riddance of sin and the introduction of holiness are concurrent acts in Christian warfare. Some men are marvellous warriors as compared with others.

III. THAT THE SPIRIT WHICH RENDERS SUCH TRIUMPHS POSSIBLE IS THAT OF DEVOTION TO THE KING. These men followed David, were under his guidance, caught his spirit, sought to establish his supremacy, and hence were nerved by a definite inspiring purpose. Consecration to Christ is the key to our victories. Wherever there is true devotion to him, and in proportion to its depth, there will be great deeds done in his name. Hence the apostolic allusions to fighting the good fight under the leadership of the great Captain of our salvation.

Christ's tribute to Christian devotion. The exclamation of David, "Oh that one would give me drink of the water of the well of Bethlehem!" was probably the natural unpremeditated outcome of an intense feeling of thirst when hemmed in by the Philistines. There is no evidence that it was a pretext to draw forth some special proof of devotion to himself. The incidental knowledge acquired of his actual need, nevertheless, developed in the hearts of these brave men a determination to obtain drink for him, even at the risk of their own lives. Where true loyalty exists there is no waiting for formal commands. The refusal of the king to drink what they so nobly obtained, doubtless, at first, filled them with surprise, and possibly caused annoyance. But the generous sentiment expressed—that he valued their generous devotion so highly that he could not at such a risk indulge in any personal satisfaction, deeming the offering too costly for mortal acceptance—this must have removed all disappointment, and strengthened the bond of allegiance. Here we may see a parable setting forth Christ's tribute to the devotion of his followers.

I. THE HIGHEST DEVOTION RISKS ALL FOR CHRIST. As these men went forth, risking life for their king, so the truest devotion leads men to risk all for Christ. There are forms of devotion in which little is given up, and much reserve is made. The stories of the rich young man in the gospel and of the going first to prove the purchased oxen exhibit a profession of attachment too frequent in Christendom. The Apostle Peter came nearer the truth of the case when he declared that he and others had "left all" to follow Christ. The mind to forsake, if need be, father and mother, houses and land, and to give up life, is stated to be the condition of the acceptable service. Wherever there is a real appreciation of who Christ is, what we are, what his vast mercy to us is, and the infinite claims of his love upon heart and life, devotion to him becomes so complete and absorbing that pain, loss, and possibly death among the heathen are faced with composure when they stand between the soul and the advancing of his interests.

II. THIS RISK OF LIFE IS AN OFFERING WORTHY OF CHRIST. The position of David as the anointed of the Lord and distinct ruler of the kingdom of God on earth, rendered it right and reasonable for the personal risk on his account. For the covenant with David and all the great issues involved were at stake. And so, apart from the subjective feeling which prompts to full devotion to Christ, there is in him and the vast enterprise of working out the redemption of man everything to justify this devotion. The surrender of life and all is an offering most worthy. Our mortal interests are as nothing compared to the requirements of his kingdom. He is worthy of all might, all riches, all life, all that men or angels can lay at his feet.

III. CHRIST HAS NO JOY IN THE LOSS OF HIS SERVANTS WHEN SEEKING TO SERVE HIM. David felt no satisfaction that such valued lives were risked for him. It was no pleasure to think that widows might have had cause to weep in consequence of noble devotion in his service. He was always tenderly regardful of the lives and comfort of his people. And although, from the necessities of the case in a world where evil has to be fought at all costs, many a noble life has to be sacrificed and many a pain endured, yet Christ finds no pleasure in the sufferings of his people any more than he had in his own. His and their sufferings were to him a painful condition of conquest over sin. He feels for them in their woes.

IV. BUT CHRIST PAYS HONOUR TO THE SPIRIT WHICH FREELY FACES GREAT RISKS. David's refusal to drink the water, and his pouring it out before the Lord as though it were too sacred for mortal lips to touch, was his way of paying honour to these devoted men. His feeling in regard to their personal devotion is, so far as the human may be a symbol and measure of the Divine, a representation of the feeling cherished by Christ with respect to noble deeds in his service and the spirit from which they spring. He looks with admiration on the self-consuming zeal of his followers; he sees in it the reflection of that spirit of self-sacrifice which enters into his own sufferings and death for men. They are partakers with him of the cup of which some have not the courage to drink (Matt. xx. 20—23). Those who have won great honours in his service are to be welcomed as "good and faithful servants," and to be made "rulers over many things." The loss of parents and houses and lands is to be compensated by others more enduring, with life eternal (Mark x. 30). His care and love assured to them in trial, his grace given according to their need, his distinct promise of distinction among the redeemed, all point to the tribute which he bears to the noble self-sacrificing spirit which animates them (John xiv. 18, 19, 27; xv. 18—21; 2 Cor. xii. 7—10; Rev. ii. 10; iii. 10—12).

HOMILIES BY VARIOUS AUTHORS.

Vers. 1—7 (Matt. i. 1).—*The son of Jesse, and the Son of David.* The relation of David to Jesus, regarded in the light of prophecy and history, was one of: 1. *Hereditary connection*; inasmuch as he not only belonged to the tribe of Judah (Gen. xlix. 10; Heb. vii. 14; Rev. v. 5) and the house of Jesse the Bethlehemite (Isa. xi. 1), but was ancestor of Jesus (Matt. i. 16; Luke iii. 23); who was thus legal heir to "the throne of his father David," and was born in "the city of David" (Micah v. 2; Matt. ii. 6). 2. *Typical representation*, in his *office* as theocratic king, divinely chosen, "the Lord's anointed" (messiah, christ), the representative of God and of the people; his *devotion* to the purpose of his calling, fulfilling the will of God, contending against his enemies, and ruling his people righteously; his *exaltation*, through suffering (1 Pet. i. 11), by the mighty hand of God, to power, honour, and dominion; his *influence* in securing national deliverance, religious benefits, temporal order, prosperity, and happiness; whereby he foreshadowed an incomparably greater Ruler of a kingdom "not of this world," who saves his people from their sins, reconciles them to God, and gives them eternal life. 3. *Historical resemblance* (closely associated with the former, but without, so far as is revealed, being expressly designed by God), in his lowly birth, youthful consecration (1 Sam. xvi. 12; Luke ii. 49), and humble occupation; his decisive conflict (1 Sam. xvii. 50; Matt. iv. 11), public services, and bitter persecutions; his attracting around him a band of faithful followers (1 Sam. xxii. 1; Matt. x. 1), increasing fame, and popular recognition (ch. ii. 4; John vi. 15; Matt. xxi. 9); his great achievements, spiritual utterances, and beneficent influence (ch. vi., viii.); his rejection (ch. xv. 13), betrayal, and overwhelming sorrows (ch. xv. 30); his final victory (ch. xviii.; John xii. 31, 32), glorious restoration, and diligent preparation for an enduring reign of peace. 4. *Extraordinary contrast.* Even wherein the first prefigured the second David (Ezek. xxxiv. 23), the imperfection of the former stands opposed to the perfection of the latter. And Jesus is "the Son of God" (Luke i. 35) in the highest sense, David's Lord (Mark xii. 37); was without sin and always well-pleasing to the Father; came to establish, not an earthly kingdom (as the Jews expected), but a spiritual one, and only by moral means (truth, righteousness, and love); died as a sacrifice for sin, rose again, and ascended into the heavens" (Acts ii. 34); "who is God over all, blessed for ever. Amen" (Rom. ix. 5).—D.

Vers. 1—3.—(JERUSALEM.) *David's last words.* [The closing years of David's life (after the insurrection of Sheba was subdued, ch. xx.) were spent in peace. Having secured a site for the altar (ch. xxiv. 25; 1 Chron. xxi. 28), he made preparations for the building of the temple (1 Chron. xxii.). At length his strength began to fail; but, when made acquainted with the conspiracy of Adonijah, he displayed something of his former energy in hastening the accession of Solomon (1 Kings i.). He also "gathered together the princes of Israel," etc. (1 Chron. xxiii. 1, 2), made numerous arrangements, sacred and civil (1 Chron. xxiii. 3—32; xxiv.—xxvii.), addressed a convocation of princes, gave a charge to his successor, and offered thanksgiving to God (1 Chron. xxviii.; xxix. 1—25). He subsequently gave further counsel to Solomon (1 Kings ii. 1—9). About the same time, probably, he uttered these last prophetic words; and then, at the age of seventy, he "fell on sleep" (1 Kings ii. 10; 1 Chron. xxix. 26—28). "The omission of David's death in the conclusion of this work is satisfactorily explained from the theocratic character and aim of the composition, since in this conclusion the fulfilment of the theocratic mission of David is completed" (Erdmann).]

> "And these are the last words of David:
> An oracle of David, son of Jesse,
> And an oracle of the hero highly exalted,
> Anointed of the God of Jacob,
> And pleasant (in) Israel's songs of praise.
> The Spirit of Jehovah speaks within me,
> And his word is on my tongue;
> Says the God of Israel,
> To me speaks the Rock of Israel," etc.

How varied are the last words of men! How significant of their ruling passion! And how instructive to others (Gen. xlviii. 21, 22; xlix. 1; Deut. xxxiii. 1; Josh. xxiii. 14; xxiv. 27; 2 Kings xiii. 19; Luke ii. 29; Acts vii. 59; 2 Tim. iv. 6—8)! Here is David, "the man of God's own choice," about to go "the way of all the earth" (ch. vii. 12; 1 Kings ii. 2). Highly exalted as he was, he must die like other men. "We walk different ways in life, but in death we are all united." Ere he departs his spirit kindles with unwonted lustre, as not unfrequently happens in the case of others; he is under the immediate inspiration of God (Numb. xxiv. 3, 4), and sings his last song of praise, sweet as the fabled notes of the dying swan. "No prince, and certainly no one who had not acquired his kingdom by inheritance, could possibly close his life with a more blessed repose in God and a brighter glance of confidence into the future. This is the real stamp of true greatness" (Ewald). "These are the words of the prophecy of David, which he prophesied concerning the end of the age, concerning the days of consolation which are to come" (Targum). They show that he has in death (what it is also the privilege of other servants of God in some measure to possess)—

I. GRATEFUL MEMORIES of the favour of God; which has been manifested: 1. Toward one of *lowly origin* and condition. "A son of Jesse." "Who am I?" etc. (1 Sam. xviii. 18). "I am the least in my father's house" (Judg. vi. 15). He recognizes his natural relationships, recalls his early life, renounces all special claim to Divine favour, and is filled with humility. "What hast thou that thou didst not receive?" (1 Cor. iv. 7). 2. In raising him up to *exalted honour.* "The man [hero] who was highly exalted." Earthly distinction is the portion of a few, but spiritual distinction is the possession of every good man ; he is a partaker of the Divine nature (2 Pet. i. 4), raised up with Christ, and made to sit with him in heavenly places (Eph. ii. 6), and an heir of all things (1 Cor. iii. 23). " The Christian believes himself to be a king, how mean soever he be, and how great soever he be ; yet he thinks himself not too good to be servant to the poorest saint " (Bacon, ' Christian Paradoxes '). 3. In appointing him to *royal dominion* over men. " Anointed," etc. He has " an anointing from the Holy One," and shares in the dominion of Christ. " To him will I give power over the nations," etc. (Rev. ii. 26). 4. In conferring upon him *excellent endowments*, in the exercise of which he quickens the spiritual susceptibilities of men, furnishes them with " acceptable words " in their approach to God, and becomes a helper of their noblest life and joy. " Pleasant [lovely] in [by means of] the praise-songs of [sung by] Israel." " He was not only the founder of the monarchy, but the founder of the Psalter. He is the first great poet of Israel. Although before his time there had been occasional bursts of Hebrew poetry, David is he who first gave it its fixed place in Israelite worship " (Stanley).

> " The harp the monarch-minstrel swept,
>   The king of men, the loved of Heaven,
> Which Music hallow'd, while she wept
>   O'er tones her heart of hearts had given;
>   Redoubled be her tears, its chords are riven !
> It soften'd men of iron mould,
>   It gave them virtues not their own;
> No ear so dull, no soul so cold,
>   That felt not, fired not to the tone,
> Till David's lyre grew mightier than his throne ! "
>   (Byron, ' Hebrew Melodies.')

Although his greatness was peculiar, yet a measure of true greatness belongs to every one of the " royal priesthood " (1 Pet. ii. 6, 9; Rev. i. 6) of the spiritual Israel. He has power with God and with men, represents God to men and men to God, employs his power with God on behalf of men, and his power with men on behalf of God ; and if, by the culture and use of the gifts bestowed upon him, he has contributed to the highest good of men—this (together with all the Divine benefits he has received) is a matter of grateful remembrance and fervent thanksgiving (Ps. xxxvii. 25, 37, 39; ciii.). " It is not what we have done, but what God has done for us and through us, that gives true peace when we come to the end."

II. GRACIOUS COMMUNICATIONS by the Spirit of God ; inasmuch as he is : 1. Filled with *Divine inspiration*. " The Spirit of Jehovah speaks within me." Such inspiration is of various kinds and degrees, and given for different special purposes. " Men spake from God, being moved by the Holy Ghost " (2 Pet. i. 21; 2 Tim. iii. 16). But every one who has fellowship with God is inhabited, pervaded, inspired by his Spirit, enlightening, purifying, elevating, gladdening, and strengthening him. Some are " full of the Holy Ghost." In a dying hour, what a marvellous elevation of thought and feeling have they sometimes attained ! " Holy men at their death have good inspirations " (see ' Last Words of Remarkable Persons;' ' Life's Last Hours;' Jacox, ' At Nightfall,' etc.; S. Ward, ' The Life of Faith in Death;' J. Hawes, ' Confessions of Dying Men,' etc.). 2. Enabled to utter the *Divine Word*. " And his Word is on my tongue." Even though there be no new, definite, and infallible revelation of the Word of God, there is often a new indication of its meaning and application, and a fresh, fervid, and forcible expression thereof. " As the Spirit gave them utterance." 3. Made a recipient of *Divine promises*. " The God of Israel says." He who entered into a covenant-relation with Israel, and promised to be their God, gave to David the promise of an ever-lasting kingdom (ch. vii. 12—16), and still gives it, with an inner voice that cannot be mistaken. He also " speaks all the promises," not only in the written Word, but also in the soul of every one to whom that Word comes in " much assurance."

> " Oh, might I hear thy heavenly voice
>   But whisper, ' Thou art mine ! '
> Those gentle words should raise my song
>   To notes almost Divine."

4. Constituted a witness of the *Divine faithfulness* in the fulfilment of the promises.

"To me speaks the Rock of Israel" (1 Sam. ii. 2; ch. xxii. 2, 3, 32, 47). "He is faithful that promised" (Heb. x. 23). His faithfulness is the foundation of his promises. "And the heavens shall praise thy wonders, O Jehovah: and thy *faithfulness* in the assembly of the holy ones" (Ps. lxxxix. 1, 2, 5, 8, 24, 33). On this the believer rests when all things fail, and of this he testifies in death, committing his soul into the hands of God, as "unto a faithful Creator" (1 Pet. iv. 19; Ps. xxxi. 5).

III. Glorious anticipations of the kingdom of God; wherein the glory of the present merges into the greater glory of the future, and earth and heaven are one (vers. 3—5; Ps. lxxxv. 11). He sees: 1. The majesty of *the King of righteousness;* like the splendour of the rising sun. His view of the ideal theocratic ruler of the future has its perfect realization in him who is "King of kings, and Lord of lords." The chief object of the Christian's contemplation in death is the glory of Christ. "Herein would I live; herein would I die; herein would I dwell in my thoughts and affections, to the withdrawing and consumption of all the painted beauties of this world, unto the crucifixion of all things here below, until they become unto me a dead and deformed thing, no way meet for affectionate embraces" (Owen). 2. The brightness of *a heavenly day;* "the drawing near of the kingdom of the heavens," and abounding life and happiness for ever (ch. xxii. 51; ver. 5). "Nevertheless we according to his promise," etc. (2 Pet. iii. 13). 3. The realization of a blessed hope; the hope of *personal salvation* (ver. 5), associated with and assured in the immortal life of the King and his people (Ps. xvi. 9—11; xvii. 15; xlix. 15; lxxiii. 24; John xiv. 19). 4. The *destruction of all iniquity.* (Ver. 6.) The people shall be all righteous. "The dying eyes see on the horizon of the far-off future the form of him who is to be a just and perfect Ruler; before the brightness of whose presence, and the refreshing of whose influence, verdure and beauty shall clothe the world. As the shades gather, that radiant glory to come brightens. He departs in peace, having seen the salvation from afar. It was fitting that this fullest of his prophecies should be the last of his strains, as if the rapture which thrilled the trembling strings had snapped them in twain" (Maclaren).

> "They who watch by him see not; but he sees—
> Sees and exults. Were ever dreams like these?
> Those who watch by him hear not; but he hears,
> And earth recedes, and heaven itself appears."
>
> (Rogers.)

"His funeral obsequies were celebrated with the greatest pomp ever yet known in Israel, and his arms were preserved as sacred relics in the temple; but the lapse of time only increased the reverence in which his memory was held in the national heart, until it finally culminated in a glowing desire to behold him once again upon the earth, and to see the advent of a second David" (Ewald).—D.

Vers. 3—7.—*An oracle concerning the King Messiah.* 1. The hope of salvation, and more especially of the establishment of the kingdom of heaven upon earth, was, in some measure, fulfilled in the reign of *David, the Lord's messiah.* In his character as theocratic ruler he was a type (prefigurement or anticipatory outline) of Christ (1 Sam. ii. 10). "The type is prophecy in deed." 2. Under Divine inspiration, *he formed an ideal of a theocratic ruler,* in connection with his own personality and history. Hence the representations contained in the Messianic psalms (xvi., xxii.), in some things transcend his experience, and in others are mingled with his infirmities. 3. In this oracle or Divine saying (as in Ps. cx., and perhaps others) *he looked forward to the realization of his ideal at a future time.* "No part whatever of the Old Testament is introduced with a greater majesty of language, or more excites the expectation of some splendid and glorious sense, than the last words of David" (Kennicott). The promise of eternal dominion to his house was joined with an intimation of his death (ch. vii. 12); and "these last words show how, in consequence of the consciousness of his own guilt, the image of the Messiah was separated from his subjectivity, and came before him as a majestic form of the future. He, the highly favoured one, who had considered himself immortal (Ps. xvi.), must now die! He therefore grasps the pillars of the promise, ceases to connect the Messianic hopes with himself, and as a prophet beholds the future of his seed" (Delitzsch). "These words are not merely a lyric effusion of the promise, but a prophetic declaration concerning the true king of the kingdom of God" (Keil). "They form the key-stone of his life; his prophetic legacy; to which the cycle of psalms cxxxviii.—cxlv. must be regarded as supplementary" (Hengstenberg). "If there is any part of Scripture which betrays the movements of the human individual soul, it is this precious fragment of David's life. If there be any part which claims for itself, and which gives evidence of the breathings of the Spirit of God, it is this also. Such a rugged two-edged monument is a fitting memorial of the man who was at once the king and the prophet, the penitent and the saint of the ancient Church" (Stanley). 4. The ideal of a theocratic ruler was *only partially realized in Solomon* and other kings of the house of David (Ps. xlv.; lxxii.; Isa. xxxii.). 5. Although the hope of a more adequate realization thereof was again and again disappointed, it was not extinguished, but *became more and more spiritual and exalted* (Riehm, 'Messianic Prophecy;' C. A. Row, 'The Jesus of the Evangelists;' W. F. Adeney, 'The Hebrew Utopia'). 6. At length the hope of Israel *was perfectly fulfilled in the Person, work, and glory of our Lord Jesus Christ.* (Luke i. 32; Matt. xxii. 43; Acts ii. 36; Eph. i. 20—22; Rev. i. 18.) "In using the Old Testament now, especially for purposes of edification, we should feel that we fail to do justice to the Old Testament, if, when expounding any truth taught in it, we do not bring into connection with the passage explained the highest form of the truth as revealed in the New Testament" (A. B. Davidson, 'Messianic Prophecy,' *Expositor,* viii.). What is here said must, on this principle, be referred to Christ; and it may be referred to him, with more or less propriety, in his earthly life, in his heavenly dominion, or at his second appearing. It indicates—

I. His EXALTED CHARACTER and principles of government. As if present at the commencement of "the golden age," David beholds

> "A ruler over men [literally, 'in man'], just!
> A ruler fearing God!"

Many a ruler, like "the unjust judge," neither fears God nor regards man. He acquires his position by craft and bloodshed, and exercises his power in oppression and ungodliness. Not so the ruler here depicted; who is distinguished by: 1. *Rectitude* of heart, of speech, and of conduct; in the laws according to which he rules, and his administration of them, rendering to every man according to his deeds; herein resembling, reflecting, and representing the rectitude of God; and protecting and promoting the best interests of men (Ps. lxxii. 4; Isa. ix. 7; xi. 1—10; Jer. xxiii. 5; xxx. 9; Ezek. xxxiv. 23, 24; Hos. iii. 5; Micah v. 1—5; Zech. ix. 9, 10). "The history of the actual David supplies the subject-matter for these idealizations. David is the original prototype on which they are formed, and round whose person they cluster. They may be described as David idealized" (C. A. Row). 2. *Piety;* the fear of offending God, reverence for his Name, delight in his fellowship, obedience to his will, opposition to his adversaries, dependence on his strength, and devotion to his honour and glory. "When he that rules is just, it is as if he did not rule, but the fear of the Lord ruled in the earth" (Barrett, 'A Synopsis of Criticisms'). 3. *Rectitude united with piety;* founded upon it, pervaded by it, and expressive of it; his supreme aim and constant endeavour being the establishment of the kingdom of God. All this is realized, even beyond expectation, in the wonderful Person of Christ, and his just and merciful reign over mankind. "Put together your ideal of true greatness of soul—power combined with gentleness; dignity with no pride; benevolence with no weakness; sympathy and love for humanity as it is, and especially for the poor, the sad, the suffering. Let your ideal be stainless, and even unsuspected of stain; and let him cheerfully and patiently live and die for men who misunderstood and even hated him. This is what you will see in the history of Christ . . . the Messiah of humanity as well as the Jews" (J. M. Wilson). "The *type* set up in the Gospels as the Christian type is the essence of man's moral nature clothed with a personality so vivid and intense as to excite through all ages the most intense affection; yet divested of all those peculiar characteristics and accidents of place and time by which human personalities are marked. What other notion than this can philosophy form of Divinity manifest on earth?" (Goldwin Smith, quoted by Liddon, 'Some Elements,' etc., p. 218).

II. His BENEFICENT INFLUENCE.

> " And (his appearance is) as the light of morning, (at) the rising of the sun,
> A morning without clouds ; (and the effect thereof as when)
> From brightness (and) from rain verdure (springs) from (out of) the earth."

As the influence of an unjust and ungodly ruler is powerful for evil, so the influence of the King Messiah is powerful for good, and much more abundantly (Ps. lxxii. 6, 7, 16). It is like that of

> " . . . the great minister
> Of nature, that upon the world imprints
> The virtue of the heaven, and doles out
> Time for us with his beam.".
>
> (Dante.)

The sun is the source of light, heat, and force; of life, health, fertility, beauty, and gladness. What a change takes place in the whole aspect of nature at the approach of " the powerful king of day " ! A similar change takes place in the moral and spiritual world at the rising of the Sun of Righteousness (Mal. iv. 2 ; Isa. lx. 2). In him, who is " the Light of the world," Jehovah himself becomes manifest to men, " visits and redeems his people," and " gives light to them that sit in darkness and in the shadow of death," etc. (Luke i. 68—79). "Even as the light of the morning shall he arise, Jehovah the Sun" (Pye Smith, 'Scripture Testimony to the Messiah'). At his appearance, and under his influence: 1. *Darkness is dispersed ;* the long dreary night of ignorance, error, injustice, impiety, oppression, discord, and misery, "and the veil that is spread over all nations" (Isa. xxv. 7). 2. *Light is diffused ;* the light of truth, pure and bright; revelations of heavenly love and mercy; a spirit of gentleness and tenderness, "of wisdom and might;" guiding, quickening, healing, and saving. 3. *Life abounds* with the peaceful fruits of righteousness; spontaneously, readily, universally; as, when (after a season of drought, or in spring) heavy showers have fallen and bright sunshine breaks forth, the earth clothes itself in fresh and "tender green" (Isa. xxxv. 1, 2). "The kingdom of God is righteousness, peace, and joy in the Holy Ghost." The one true King of men has come, his influence is powerfully and widely felt, and it is constantly increasing; nevertheless we see not yet all things subdued unto him. Like prophets and kings of old, we still wait for his appearing. "For he must reign till he hath put all enemies under his feet" (1 Cor. xv. 25).

III. His ASSURED MANIFESTATION.

> " For (there is sure ground for my expectation, for) is not my house (not myself merely) thus with (related to) God (that out of it such an exalted ruler and his beneficial influence shall proceed) ?
> For (because) he has established to me an everlasting covenant (to this effect),
> Arranged in all (respects) and kept ;
> For (therefore) all my salvation (involved therein) and all (his) good pleasure (expressed therein)—
> For (therefore, I say) will he not cause (them) to sprout (to be fully accomplished)?"

" The pledge of this just ruler was the eternal covenant which God had concluded with him" (Tholuck). The whole oracle is founded upon this *covenant* (solemn promise, sacred engagement, arrangement, constitution, dispensation), securing eternal dominion to his house and the blessings of salvation to the subjects of his kingdom (ch. vii. 13, 10, 24). "The Davidic covenant is the embodiment of the hope of David, and the theme of his last meditations. In this swanlike song David clings to the Messianic promise as his greatest delight" (C. A. Briggs, 'Messianic Prophecy'). 1. *It cannot fail of fulfilment,* in the appearing and reign of the Messiah; because of: (1) The faithfulness of God, "the Rock of Israel" (ver. 3), its Author; (2) its having been actually made, (3) with the express assurance of these things, (4) "to David, and his seed *for ever*" (ch. xxii. 51); (5) carefully arranged, provided with everything adapted to effect the proper end thereof, and to avert failure, even through apostasy (ch. vii. 14, 15); (6) and its being constantly preserved, guarded, watched over, until completely fulfilled. 2. In its fulfilment, *the promised salvation of the people of God, and his gracious purposes concerning them, will be accomplished.* "All my salvation," etc. "The dying Israelite looked forward to the grand destiny of his people, and lost his personality in the larger life of the nation, and thus triumphed over death through the thought of the immortality and future blessedness of the collective Israel " (W. F. Adeney) ; or rather he expected to share with them, in some way, their glorious inheritance (Ps. lxi. 5, 6 ; lxxiii. 23, 26 ; Isa. liv. 10—14 ; lv. 3, 4 ; Dan. xii. 3, 4, 13). 3. On this the servant of God *rests with strong confidence* and blessed hope, in life and death (Gen. xlix. 18). " We are saved by hope." And " when Christ, who is our Life, shall be manifested, then shall ye also with him be manifested in glory " (Col. iii. 4 ; 1 John iii. 2 ; 2 Pet. iii. 13).

> " My God, the covenant of thy love
> Abides for ever sure ;
> And in its matchless grace I feel
> My happiness secure."

IV. His FINAL JUDGMENT on the wicked.

" And worthlessness [literally, ' Belial, ungodly men '] as thorns thrust away (are) all of
    them ;
For (because) not with the (unarmed) hand are they seized ;
And (but) the man who touches them
Is filled (fills his hand, provides himself) with iron,
And shaft of spear (*i.e.* a long spear),
And with fire are they utterly burned on the spot."

It is the part of a just and godly ruler to punish evil-doers. The undue leniency of David was followed by disastrous consequences (ch. iii. 39 ; xiii. 21 ; xiv. 33 ; xix. 23 ; xx. 10) ; and, at the close of his life, he charged his successor to vindicate the Law wherein he had himself failed to do so (1 Kings ii. 1—9). The coming King is not only a Saviour, but also a Judge ; and to him all judgment is committed (John v. 22, 27). " There rises up before him (David) a field overrun with thorns, which the Divine ministers pluck up with gauntleted hands, and beat down with their burnished spears, and commit to the consuming flames " (S. Cox, ' Expositor's Note-Book '). His judgment is : 1. Just. 2. Certain. 3. Irresistible. 4. Complete. The day of grace, during which forbearance has been shown in vain, is followed by the day of wrath (Mal. iv. 1 ; Matt. iii. 12 ; xiii. 40—43 ; Heb. vi. 7).—D.

Vers. 8—12 (1 Chron. xi. 10—14).— *The first three heroes. Jashobeam* the son of Hach-moni (*Zabdiel,* 1 Chron. xxvii. 2), who came to David at Ziklag (1 Chron. xii. 6), and became general of the first division of the army ; *Eleazar* the son of Dodo the Ahohite, general of the second division (1 Chron. xxvii. 4) ; and *Shammah* the son of Agee the Hararite. " They served in the most direct manner by their work one who was the representative of the Divine government on earth " (Krummacher). " Such traits of warlike courage (as they displayed) are more significant than anything else ; they recall to us completely those few periods of history, otherwise unknown to us, in which a marvellous aspiration for the possession of some higher blessing, such as freedom or immortality, has taken hold of an entire nation, and so has produced, through special instruments of exceptional power, even military exploits which appear incredible to ordinary men " (Ewald). " Christ the Son of David has his worthies too, who, like David's, are influenced by his example, fight his battles against the spiritual enemies of his kingdom, and in his strength are more than conquerors " (Matthew Henry). In these battles, neither physical prowess nor intellectual strength is of so much importance as moral and spiritual qualifications, and especially *eminent faith* ; such as that by which many " from weakness were made strong, waxed mighty in war, turned to flight armies of aliens " (Heb. xi. 34). It ensures success by means of—
I. FEARLESSNESS and daring courage (ver. 8). " He lifted his spear against eight hundred [three hundred], slain at one time ; " went undismayed " against a multitude " (2 Chron. xiv. 11), and alone (or possibly aided by others) overcame them (Judg. iii. 31 ; xv. 15). Instances of a similar kind are recorded in history (see ' Pictorial Bible ' in 1 Chron. xi.) : " Ajax beating down the Trojan leader with a rock which two ordinary men could scarcely lift ; Horatius defending the bridge against an army ; Richard, the lion-hearted, spurring along the whole Saracen line without finding an enemy to stand his assault ; Robert Bruce crushing with one blow the helmet and the head of Sir Henry Bohun, in sight of the whole army of England and Scotland ;—such are the heroes of a dark age. In such an age, bodily vigour is the most indispensable

qualification for a warrior" (Macaulay, 'History of England'). Even in modern times (when the superiority of strength of mind has been so manifest) it has accomplished extraordinary feats. But how much greater and nobler have been the achievements wrought by moral courage and spiritual weapons (2 Cor. x. 4)!

II. INDEPENDENCE and single-handed effort (vers. 9, 10). When "he alone remained" (Josephus), "he arose and smote the Philistines, until his hand was weary, and his hand clave unto the sword," etc. In like manner, when "the people fled from the Philistines" (vers. 11, 12), Shammah stood alone against their attack. The valour of some men depends upon the presence, sympathy, and help of others, and fails when they are left to themselves. 1. Under such circumstances, the courage of a true hero is fully brought out (Isa. lxiii. 3). 2. He is independent of men because he depends upon God. 3. By his single-handed effort, one such man is sometimes able to "chase a thousand" (Josh. xxiii. 10). 4. His courage and success infuse fresh vigour into fearful hearts; and "the people return after him," though it be "only to spoil." He alone is fit to be a leader of men.

III. STEADFASTNESS in passive endurance and active endeavour. "He stood in the midst of the ground" which was "full of lentiles," or barley, "defended it, and slew the Philistines" (who had probably come up to carry away the ripe crops); like Eleazar, he "endured to the end," and conquered. It is not enough to exhibit fearlessness and independence at first; we must continue to do so (Luke ix. 51), otherwise nothing will be gained, but everything be lost. "Whatever is each man's post, chosen by himself as the better part, or appointed by his leader, there, as it appears to me, he ought to stay in spite of danger; taking no account of death or anything else in comparison with dishonour" ('The Apology of Socrates'). This is the crowning quality: "Having done all, to stand [hold the field]. Stand therefore," etc. (Eph. vi. 14); "Be ye steadfast," etc. (1 Chron. xv. 58; Gal. vi. 9); "Stand fast in the Lord."

IV. DIVINE HELP. "And Jehovah wrought a great deliverance" (ver. 10, repeated in ver. 12). Here is the chief source of success. Human effort is needful, but in itself ineffectual. It avails only through the help of God (Ps. cxxvi. 1; cxxi. 2). Nor is this withheld from such as seek and rely upon it. He will fight for those who fight for him. How often has he enabled them to prevail against an overwhelming host! "Salvation is of the Lord." To him it should be ascribed. And every great deliverance calls for great thanksgiving.—D.

Vers. 13—17 (1 Chron. xi. 15—19).—*The well of Bethlehem.* When a shepherd-youth, David doubtless often sat beside "the well by the gate," and refreshed himself with its cold, clear, sparkling water. But those days have long since departed; and he is now a king, with many cares. Bethlehem is occupied by a part of the Philistine host, and he is once more in "the hold" (ch. v. 17; 1 Sam. xxi. 1), accompanied by his heroic band of men, to whom his every wish is equivalent to a command. "What a circle of names are associated with his name, some of them names and scarce anything beside—men who would have been unheard of but for the occasions which brought them into temporary connection with so famous a man, and of whose lives, apart from that connection, we know nothing; yet all of whom had a life, had a character, were as precious as individuals in the eye of God as the great soul to whom they owe what little interest they have in the eyes of men!" The names of these three "knights" are not recorded; but their chivalrous achievement is immortalized. "God knows them, as he knows the noble acts of all his saints and martyrs, and will reward them at the great day" (Wordsworth). In the threefold scene here described we have—

I. THE NATURAL WISH expressed by the king. "Oh that one would give me drink!" etc. (ver. 15). It is: 1. *Involuntarily excited.* "In the harvest-time," oppressed with heat, and exhausted by conflict and toil, David is parched with thirst, and overcome with a great longing for a refreshing draught from the well of Bethlehem, whose familiar walls he, perchance, sees from a distance. So men sometimes desire, not merely the satisfaction of bodily appetites, but also the gratification of deeper yearnings, for youth and home, and happier conditions and experiences. "Oh that I had wings like the dove!" etc. (Ps. lv. 6). 2. *In itself innocent.* Many a wish, even for objects at present out of reach and beset by difficulty and peril, is as blameless as the thirst of a traveller "in a dry and weary land where no water is." Although it may be

" according to nature " (in the best sense), it nevertheless requires to be controlled, regulated, and subordinated to a higher law than that of pleasing ourselves; and it is, too frequently : 3. *Inordinately indulged;* so that it becomes a dominant selfish impulse. " The habit of wishing and hankering for those things which Providence denies, though natural to us and often given way to, even by godly men, in an unguarded hour, is a degree of rebellion against the Lord; and it shows the remaining sensuality and selfishness of the heart, and leads to many snares and evils " (Scott). 4. *Inconsiderately uttered.* David may not intend his men to hear what he says (still less to challenge their devotion); he may hardly be aware of their presence. But, knowing their character and his relation to them, he is none the less responsible for the effect of his words upon them; and should have put a bridle on his tongue (Ps. xxxix. 1; cvi. 33; cxli. 3). Unregulated impulses and imprudent speech—what mischief have they wrought in the world! " Watch and pray, lest ye enter into temptation."

II. The heroic deed performed by his followers. " And the three mighty men broke through the host," etc. (ver. 16). " It was a foolhardy thing to do," some one says; " they might easily have seen that a draught of water was not worth the conflict and hazard necessary to obtain it." Happily they did not see it; else we had never heard of their heroic enterprise. Without calculating consequences, they act from a sense of duty, an impulse of unselfish devotion, a spirit of chivalry, " which shrinks from no sacrifice in order to do the smallest service for the object of its devotion ; " therein exhibiting : 1. *An intense attachment* to their leader, love to his person, sympathy with his need, loyalty to his office, desire to please him and to do his will (as they interpreted it). It could have been inspired in them only by a man of great ability, generosity, and enthusiasm. They learnt it of him (1 Sam. xvii. 50). His self-indulgent and momentary wish was no true index of his prevailing disposition. 2. *A spontaneous, prompt, and cheerful purpose* and endeavour. They say nothing and do not hesitate, but go together " into the jaws of death." 3. *Invincible courage;* a principle which is as needful in moral and spiritual conflict as in physical warfare (ch. x. 12). " Most probably it made such an impression as rendered the host of the Philistines an easy prey to the Israelites " (Blaikie). 4. *Entire self-denial and self-sacrifice;* disregarding alike their own pleasure and peril, and laying down their lives for his sake. " Greater love hath no man," etc. (John xv. 13). " Pure love has its measure in itself, and disregards in its outward expression every critic (Matt. xxvi. 7—13). This exploit of the three heroes was a sacrifice offered, not so much to the *man* David, as rather in him to the ' Anointed of the Lord,' and therefore to the Lord himself " (Krummacher). How does it rebuke our lack of devotion to our Divine King! Were we as ardent, loyal, courageous, and self-sacrificing as they, what victories should we gain over his adversaries and ours !

III. The sacred offering presented before the Lord. " And he would not drink thereof," etc. For the first time, probably, he becomes acquainted with their desperate exploit, when they come into his presence, stained with blood, and place the vessel, containing the water for which he longed, in his hands. To him it is as if it were their blood, and he cannot drink it (Lev. xvii. 11, 12). To do so would be to justify his former wish, and gratify himself at the hazard of their lives. Their devotion evokes within him a nobler feeling and impulse than he before displayed; so that he practically confesses his fault, personally shares their suffering and self-denial, and publicly testifies his thankfulness for their preservation and his devotion to their welfare. And this he does in the highest and most effectual manner—by making of their gift a libation (1 Sam. vii. 6), or drink offering, and thereby *giving honour to God.* " It was too sacred for him to drink, but it was on that very account deemed by him as worthy to be consecrated in sacrifice to God as any of the prescribed offerings of the Levitical ritual. Pure chivalry and pure religion there found an absolute union " (Stanley). Alexander denied himself of a draught of water because he could not bear to drink it alone, and the cup was too small to be divided among all his soldiers; Sir Philip Sidney, that he might give it to a wounded soldier, whose necessity appeared to him greater than his own (' Percy Anecdotes '); David, that he might present it unto God. " He never was more magnanimous than at this moment. This deed was a psalm, sublime in its significance, and for ever sweet to all loving hearts in its pure simplicity." In his offering there is : 1. An exalted estimate of the value of human life. 2. A humble renunciation of the power even of a king to make use of it according to his own pleasure or for a selfish end. 3. A solemn recognition of the sovereignty of God over "life and breath and all things." 4. An unreserved submission, surrender, and sacrifice of every gift to him who alone is worthy. David's offering must have deepened the attachment of his three heroes, and exerted no small moral and spiritual influence on all his followers. How much greater is the "offering" of the Son of David (Eph. v. 2; Heb. ix. 14), and his claim on our affection, gratitude, and self-consecration! Constrained by his love, we should live in the spirit of his life (Rom. xii. 1; 2 Cor. v. 15; Phil. ii. 17, "poured out as a libation;" 2 Tim. iv. 6).

REFLECTIONS. 1. An impulse of a lower kind is most effectually overcome by one of a higher order. 2. A wish in itself blameless may, in certain circumstances, be sinful and injurious. 3. An action which is mistaken and imprudent sometimes affords occasion for the display of the noblest principles. 4. The self-denial of some silently reproves the self-indulgence of others, and incites in them a similar spirit. 5. The highest return that can be made of gifts received from men is to consecrate them to God. 6. A gift made to God is not "wasted," but is a means of conferring manifold benefits on men. 7. The sacrifice of self enriches the soul by enabling it to partake more fully of the life and love of him for whose sake it is made.—D.

Vers. 18—23 (1 Chron. xi. 22—25).—*The heroism of Benaiah.* He was son of Jehoiada, chief priest and leader of the Aaronites who came to David at Hebron (1 Chron. xii. 27); one of (a second) three "mighties" (with Abishai and, perhaps, Asahel), and above the thirty (1 Chron. xxvii. 5, 6); captain of the host for the third month; and commander of the body-guard (ch. viii. 18; xx. 23). He remained faithful to Solomon in the conspiracy of Adonijah, was commissioned to execute Joab, and appointed commander-in-chief in his stead (1 Kings i. 26, 36; ii. 29, 35). He was "a valiant man, of many illustrious deeds." His name (equivalent to "built by Jah") is suggestive of the Divine source of his strength, valour, and successful conflicts with the enemies of the people of God. He slew (1) *two Moabitish champions,* or princes, "lions of God" (ch. viii. 2); (2) *a ferocious lion,* which had been driven by a heavy fall of snow into the neighbourhood of human habitations, to the terror of the inhabitants, and had taken refuge in a pit or (empty) cistern; and (3) *an Egyptian giant* (fighting on the side of the Philistines). "His valour and virtues are recorded, not only for commemoration and remembrance, but likewise for example and imitation of his virtues, and to show how great works the Lord wrought by weak means" (Guild). 1. We ought never to contend, except in *a good cause;* for truth, justice, and liberty, the honour of God, the kingdom of Christ, and the welfare of men. "If it be possible," etc. (Rom. xii. 18). 2. We *cannot avoid conflict* altogether without sin, captivity, dishonour, and destruction. In a world like this there is often no choice but to fight or be slain. "Curse ye Meroz," etc. (Judg. v. 23). "Contend earnestly for the faith," etc. (Jude 3). "Now we must fight if we would reign." 3. We *must not be dismayed* by the power of the enemy; "in nothing affrighted by the adversaries" (Phil. i. 28); their strength, their number (two to one, ver. 20), their formidable appearance, their varied character, natural or spiritual; lionlike men, real lions, or "your adversary the devil," who, "as a roaring lion, walketh about," etc. (1 Pet. v. 8). Be strong and fear not. 4. We should not be unduly concerned about *our own safety;* but seek, above all things, to do our duty faithfully, and use our best endeavours to secure the ends for which we strive. Having traced the footprints of the lion in the snow, "he went down" (voluntarily placing his own life in imminent peril to secure the safety of others) "and slew the lion in the pit" (knowing that he must succeed or perish) "in a time of snow" (which is apt to benumb man's strength and to cool their courage, and when beasts of prey are most fierce and ravenous from hunger). "None of these things move me," etc. (Acts xx. 24; xxi. 13; 2 Tim. iv. 16, 17). 5. We must *make the best of our resources,* however inadequate they may appear; and not shrink from the conflict until we are as fully armed as our opponents. "He went down to him with [only] a staff" (ver. 22); skilfully and adroitly deprived him of his spear ("like a weaver's beam"), rendered him defenceless, and turned his weapon against himself. We must fight with such means as we have. 6. We should never forget the example of *our great*

Leader (1 Sam. xvii. 50); that he sees us, is ready to help us, and will greatly honour "him that overcometh" (vers. 22, 23; Rev. ii. 26).

> "Though the sons of night blaspheme,
> More there are with us than them;
> Hell is nigh, but Christ is nigher,
> Circling us with hosts of fire."

7. We should be encouraged by the remembrance of *past successes*, achieved by ourselves and others. These are a sure earnest of the final victory of the kingdom of light over the kingdom of darkness. "Greater is he that is in you," etc. (1 John iv. 4).—D.

Vers. 1—7.—*The righteous Ruler.* David, in his last days, like Jacob and Moses, received the spirit of prophecy, and was thus enabled to predict the coming of the perfect King, sprung from himself; the blessings of his reign, and his triumph over his enemies. These "last words" of his are, indeed, regarded by some as primarily a description of what a ruler of men should be, and as only secondarily, if at all, relating to the Christ. Our Authorized Version favours this interpretation by introducing in ver. 3 the words, "must be." But the obvious truth that rulers ought to be just would hardly have been prefaced by so solemn an introduction, asserting in such varied words and phrases that the declaration was owing to the special inspiration of God. Nor would the reference to the "everlasting covenant" be so appropriate.

I. THE HUMAN SPEAKER. The terms used indicate: 1. *His origin.* "David the son of Jesse." The royal son was not ashamed of his father. 2. *His exaltation.* "Raised up on high" (comp. ch. vii. 8, 9). 3. *His Divine appointment as king.* "The anointed of the God of Jacob." 4. *His gifts and works as a sacred poet.* "The sweet psalmist of Israel" (Hebrew, "pleasant in the psalms of Israel"). "As David, on the one hand, had firmly established the kingdom of God in an earthly and political respect as the anointed of Jehovah, *i.e.* as king; so had he, on the other, as the composer of Israel's songs of praise, promoted the spiritual edification of that kingdom" (Keil and Delitzsch).

II. THE DIVINE SPEAKER. This is intimated by the word used twice in ver. 1 and translated "said." It is the word commonly used of the utterances of God by his prophets, and, without any addition, indicates that the saying is a Divine oracle. Further, that what is said here is from God is distinctly declared by the assertion, "The Spirit of the Lord spake by me, and his Word was in my tongue; the God of Israel said, the Rock of Israel spake to me" (vers. 2, 3). Such a preamble prepares us for an utterance of great weight and importance, and is adapted to excite the utmost confidence in it as one of "the true sayings of God" (Rev. xix. 9).

III. THE WORDS SPOKEN. David was himself a divinely appointed king over God's nation. He had ruled on the whole justly, and had, with his people, enjoyed much of the benefit which righteous rule secures. He was, however, conscious of not having realized his ideal, partly through his own weakness and sinfulness, partly through the opposition he had encountered and the impracticableness of the materials which he had had to mould. But before he leaves the world he has a Divine assurance that One should arise out of his own house, who should be, as a Ruler, all, and more than all, that he had himself aimed to be—should diffuse amongst his subjects the greatest blessings, and thoroughly master and destroy all that should oppose his designs. Note: 1. *His descent.* The reference to the "everlasting covenant" in ver. 5, compared with the covenant itself in the promise of God through Nathan (ch. vii. 16), sufficiently indicates that David discerned that the King of whom he was prophesying would spring from himself. He was to be "of the seed of David according to the flesh" (Rom. i. 3). 2. *His character.* "Just, ruling in the fear of God." (1) The fear of God (equivalent to "godliness, piety") would be at the foundation of his character. He would rule with constant regard to the will and the glory of God (comp. Isa. xi. 2, "the spirit of . . . the fear of the Lord"). How much this feature was found in the character of our Lord Jesus the Gospels everywhere testify. (2) He would be eminently "just." This characteristic of the coming King of men appears frequently in the prophecies respecting him (see Ps. xlv. 6, 7; lxxii. 2; Isa. ix. 7; xi. 3—5; Jer. xxiii. 5; Zech. ix. 9). It was a welcome thought in a world filled with injustice, which was unredressed by its rulers, yea, often perpetrated by them—a world in which the poor and feeble, the widows and the fatherless, instead of being protected by the mighty, were often trampled down by them, that at length a Ruler would arise who would be just, and would cause justice everywhere to triumph. These prophecies receive their fulfilment in the character and reign of the Lord Jesus. (a) He is personally just. Hence he is called "that Just One" (Acts xxii. 14); "the Holy One and the Just" (Acts iii. 14). He was like other men in all but this, that he was "without sin" (Heb. iv. 15). He "knew no sin" (2 Cor. v. 21). He "did no sin" (1 Pet. ii. 22). In his addresses to God there is no confession of sin or prayer for pardon. Before men he could boldly say, "Which of you convicteth me of sin?" (John viii. 46, Revised Version). His exaltation is attributed to his love of righteousness and hatred of iniquity (Heb. i. 9). (b) Justice distinguishes the salvation he effects. For this King is also Saviour (Zech. ix. 9). David felt that in some way his own salvation depended on him (ver. 5). In the light of the New Testament the truth becomes clear. Jesus the Son of David, the Divine King, works salvation. Now, in doing this, he displays the highest regard for righteousness. He does not deliver in violation of justice; does not take the part of the sinner against God as righteous Ruler. By his death he makes propitiation for sin, that God "might be just" while "the Justifier of him which believeth in Jesus" (Rom. iii. 25, 26). Moreover, he saves from sin to righteousness (Rom. viii. 4), so that all who are his become just. (c) His laws are just. The very laws of some kingdoms are tainted with injustice. They are oppressive or partial, favouring one class of the people at the cost of others, etc. Not so with the laws of the Christ. They prescribe all that is right, and only what is right, both towards God and towards men. Were they obeyed, all injustice and wrong-doing would cease, and all the evil dispositions from which they proceed. (d) His rule is just. Good laws are sometimes ineffective through bad administration of them. Commonly the enforcement of them requires money; and those who have little of it must submit to injustice for want of the means to set the machinery of the law in motion. Sometimes the magistrates are corrupt, and decide in favour of those who bribe them, or too indolent and indifferent to examine sufficiently into the merits of the cases brought before them. Practical injustice also springs from the ignorance or weakness of rulers. But this Ruler will see that full justice is done to all under his sway. He knows exactly the character of each and all; he is powerful to execute judgment. Mighty oppressors find him stronger than they. Secret plotters against the just discover that nothing is hidden from him. With him sophistry has no weight, rank and wealth no influence. "He shall reward every man according to his works" (Matt. xvi. 27). (e) His whole power and influence are promotive of righteousness, and ensure its ultimate prevalence. 3. The blessings of his reign. "[He (or, 'it') shall be] as the light of the morning when the sun riseth, a morning without clouds; [when] the tender grass [springeth] out of the earth, through clear shining after rain" (ver. 4, Revised Version). Under the reign of this Ruler shall be: (1) Unclouded light in place of darkness. Truth, holiness, and happiness shall abound. (2) Fruitfulness. Growth and increase of goodness and the good (Ps. lxxii. 6, 7, 16). (3) Beauty. Like the flush of the tender grass just sprung up and shining in the light of the morning sun. These are the effects which the Lord Christ does produce in heart and home and country, wherever and so far as he is received and obeyed. History confirms prophecy, and gives additional assurance of its fulfilment. 4. The fate of the wicked under his rule. (Vers. 6, 7.) The reign of One so just and powerful ensures the destruction of the wicked as well as the salvation of the righteous. He comes, indeed, to subdue the wicked by truth and love, and render them righteous. But many remain obdurate, refuse submission to him, perhaps oppose him actively; these he destroys. Note: (1) Their worthlessness. They are "Belial" (equivalent to "worthlessness"); good for nothing; "thorns, to be thrust away" and "burned." (2) The difficulty of getting rid of them. Like thorns, difficult to handle and "thrust away," requiring whoever would deal with them to be "armed with iron and the staff of a spear." Laws cannot restrain them, example is lost upon them, benevolent efforts are wasted upon them, legal punishments only harden them, the gospel itself renders them more perverse. (3) Their certain destruction. "They shall be utterly burned with fire in their place" (Revised Version); "on the hearth" (Dean Stanley). See Matt. iii. 10, 12; John xv. 6; Heb. vi. 8. Let sinners tremble and repent before it is too late.

IV. THE COMFORT WHICH THE PROPHECY GAVE TO DAVID HIMSELF. (Ver. 5.) The words are obscure, and variously interpreted. Most modern scholars translate substantially as in the margin of the Revised Version, "For is not my house so with God? for he . . . for all my salvation and all my desire, will he not make it to grow?" So taken, the words are altogether words of assured confidence and hope. But taken as in the Authorized Version, and substantially in the text of the Revised Version, shadows mingle with the brightness. The glorious vision of the future reminds David of the contrast presented by the past and present. His own reign has not corresponded, or only in a small measure, with the picture he has drawn. Yet he finds consolation in the "everlasting covenant, ordered in all things, and sure." He doubts not that the promise given him through Nathan (ch. vii.) will be fulfilled; and in its fulfilment he recognizes the fulfilment of his own ardent "desire," and the accomplishment of his "salvation."

So let us, amid all the blighted hopes, the fears and troubles of the present, stay ourselves on God, and admit to our hearts the comfort which springs from his covenant in Christ, and the conviction that it cannot but be faithfully and fully performed.—G. W.

Ver. 5.—*Comfort from the everlasting covenant.* David, as he approached the close of life, had this vision (vers. 2—7) of the just king, and the happiness which would attend his reign. It reminded him of what ought to have been the character of his own rule, and what might have been its blessedness. The perfect realization of the picture by himself and his subjects was not, indeed, possible; but the actual condition of things was not inevitable. He knew that he himself had largely contributed to the sins and troubles of his "house" and of the nation. And now life was nearly over; and as the past could not be undone, neither could he hope to repair the mischief it had produced. Under the sadness of his reflections, he finds relief and consolation in the memory of the "everlasting covenant" which God had "made with" him, which ensured that from his house should arise One in and by whom would be realized the perfect ideal of a Divine King and kingdom. His utmost "desire" would then be fulfilled, and his "salvation" effected. For it seems that as David, in the hundred and tenth psalm, calls his great Son his "Lord," so here he recognizes him as his Saviour. These words of David have often been used by godly people for their own comfort; and the hymn of Dr. Doddridge, founded upon them, commencing, "My God, the covenant of thy love," has ministered consolation to thousands. We shall see that there is good reason for such an application of them.

I. THE COVENANT. The word properly signifies a mutual agreement between two or more persons. When used, however, of a transaction or arrangement between God and men, the idea of agreement as between two contracting parties retires into the background, or vanishes altogether; and the word designates, on the one hand, the promises of God, and, on the other, his requirements. In this passage it refers to the Divine promise to David and his house of an everlasting kingdom (ch. vii. 12—16), which was in fact the promise of the Christ, and of all the blessings (poetically set forth in ver. 4) which his coming and reign involved. In the time of Isaiah it was seen that this covenant was in effect made with all repentant and believing souls, and that the "sure mercies of David" (the blessings promised to him) included the spiritual mercies for which they hunger and thirst (see Isa. lv. 1—3). Indeed, in the fourth verse of that chapter, David and his illustrious Descendant are identified, as in other Scriptures the latter is called "David" (Jer. xxx. 9; Ezek. xxxiv. 23, 24; xxxvii. 24, 25; Hos. iii. 5). It will thus be seen that our text may be used by Christians in its original purport. But if there were any doubt of this, the direct application of the term "everlasting covenant" to the promises of God in and through the "Lord Jesus," and sealed with his "blood" (Heb. xiii. 20)—promises made to all who have faith in Christ— establishes the propriety of the use of the words by Christians, though it were in a sense only analogous to that which they originally bore. Notice: 1. *The contents of the covenant.* (1) The promises of "all spiritual blessings," yea, of all needful temporal blessings—pardon, renewal, adoption, sanctification, guidance, support, comfort, preservation, etc., terminating in eternal life; in a word, salvation. (2) The requirements of faith in Christ and obedience to his laws. 2. *Its qualities.* (1) "Ordered in all things." Well arranged; the product of perfect wisdom, and worthy of it; so constituted as to be adapted to its purpose, fitted for the wants of men, suited to reveal and glorify God. (2) "Sure." More literally, "guarded," "preserved," and therefore secure and sure. God takes care of his own Word. Enemies may assail it, but he watches over and preserves it. Foolish friends or professed friends may misinterpret it, may narrow it so as to make it speak the language of their own particular sect, and promise good only to its members, may overlay it by traditional interpretations, or otherwise veil it from the sight of men as if it were too sacred for common eyes, or substitute for it "another gospel, which is not another" (Gal. i. 6, 7), which they regard as more in harmony with the advanced intelligence of the times; but, amid and through all, God's covenant abides sure, the only basis of his gracious dealings with men, the secure basis of men's hopes and life. (3) Everlasting. An assertion that *might* be made in respect to its origin in the eternal thought and purpose of God, but which *is* made of its enduring character. It is a covenant which abides the same evermore, which God will never alter, and will be eternally fulfilling in the experience of his children. "The Word of the Lord endureth for ever. And this is the Word which by the gospel is preached unto you" (1 Pet. i. 25). 3. *With whom it is made.* "With me." The covenant was made to David directly and personally, through Nathan. The covenant of God in the gospel is with all those who conform to its requirements—all who repent, believe, and obey. Whoever sincerely accepts Christ as Saviour and Lord, is warranted to regard the promises of God as made to himself, and will be able to do so with increasing confidence as his faith, love, and holiness increase. These are at once the work of the Holy Spirit, and his witness to each Christian that he is a Christian indeed, one of "the children of God," who are "heirs of God and joint-heirs with Christ" (Rom. viii. 16, 17).

II. The estimation in which it is held. The believer values it as beyond all price, because : 1. *It assures him of salvation.* "This is all my salvation"—salvation in the fullest sense, salvation from all evil to the enjoyment of all blessing, a salvation everlasting as the covenant. 2. *It meets and satisfies his best, his utmost longings.* "All my desire"—delight, pleasure. The aspirations after perfect communion with God, and likeness to him and eternal happiness in him, all are met and satisfied by the promises of God.

III. The comfort it affords. "Although my house, . . . yet," etc. Similarly, the Christian may realize unfailing support and consolation from the consciousness of being interested in the everlasting covenant. 1. *In view of his past and present life.* Its unfulfilled ideals, disappointed hopes, broken vows, wasted energies, poor results (material or spiritual); in view of sins committed, work undone or ill done; after sad experience of the unreliableness of the promises of men (whether through changed mind, or changed circumstances, or death); or again, when he thinks with sad heart of the moral condition of his "house" (often a distressing sight to godly parents), or the painful circumstances in which it may be placed through bereavements or worldly misfortunes; or finally, when he looks upon himself, contrasting what he might have become with what he is—it is a thought to bring rest and hope that God has made with him an everlasting covenant, which remains secure and unchanged amid all changes, and assures of forgiveness of all that has been wrong and defective, and eternal profit from all that has been painful, and final and complete deliverance from all sin and sorrow. 2. *In anticipation of the future.* (1) The future of this life. Its uncertainties, its possible or probable troubles, personal, domestic, national, etc. "I know not what is before me, but this I know, that God has made with me a covenant which cannot fail." (2) Its approaching end and the eternal future. The possible suddenness or painfulness of the end; its possible loneliness, through the deaths or removals of those who it had been hoped would be near to impart consolation; in the case of the aged, the certainty that departure from this world cannot be long delayed; the dimness and strangeness of the invisible world, and the awfulness of eternity; the constitutional dread of death which haunts some; the dread, at least the awe, which sometimes visits all as they think of the account to be given of life to the holy Judge. How blessed under all anxieties and forebodings to say, "'I know whom I have believed' (2 Tim. i. 12); I am sure he will not forsake me, but will 'deliver me from every evil work, and will preserve me unto his heavenly kingdom' (2 Tim. iv. 18); for 'he hath made with me an everlasting covenant,' etc."!

Let Christians aim so to live that they may ever enjoy such consolation. Let all seek to make it their own; for it is available for all. Hear the Word of the Lord before referred to: "Incline your ear, and come unto me: hear, and your soul shall live; and I will make an everlasting covenant with you, even the sure mercies of David" (Isa. lv. 3).—G. W.

Ver. 8.—*The king's mighty men.* From this verse to the end of the chapter is given an account of men who had distinguished themselves in the service of David by their might and prowess, and who were rewarded with promotion and a place in this honourable list. Our King, Jesus Christ, has also his mighty ones—men, women, and children —whose exploits are not forgotten.

I. THEIR QUALITIES. 1. *What they are.* They are the ordinary characteristics of a Christian existing in a high degree of strength and fervour. (1) Strong faith. The eye that sees the invisible; the hand that grasps the promises; strong confidence in God and Christ (see Heb. xi.). (2) Ardent love. Warm attachment and devoted loyalty to their King; love to his kingdom and all who belong to it; love to men in general; love disinterested, unselfish. A selfish man cannot be a hero. (3) A strong sense of duty, overpowering the desire for ease, safety, pleasure, or gain. (4) Intense prayerfulness. Earnest prayer is "power with God and with men" (Gen. xxxii. 28). (5) Clear and impressive knowledge. "Knowledge is power." "A wise man is strong; yea, a man of knowledge increaseth strength" (Prov. xxiv. 5). Knowledge adds strength to the character of its possessor, and is a powerful weapon in the service of our King. It is by "the truth" that Christ's battles are fought and victories won. "The gospel is the power of God unto salvation" (Rom. i. 16). Christ's "mighty men" are "mighty in the Scriptures" (Acts xviii. 24). (6) Dauntless courage. (7) Unwavering constancy and perseverance. 2. *Whence they spring.* David was brave himself, and inspired his men with bravery. They became "mighty men" through the influence of a mighty leader. Consciously or unconsciously, they imbibed his spirit and imitated him. In like manner, our "Leader and Commander of the people" (Isa. lv. 4) infuses his own Spirit into his faithful followers. They become mighty through close union and association with him. They are "strong in the Lord, and in the power of his might" (Eph. vi. 10); "strengthened with might by God's Spirit in the inner man" (Eph. iii. 16).

II. THEIR WORKS. Their might is exercised: 1. *In resisting and overcoming temptation.* In conquering the enemies of Christ as they assail and would destroy themselves. A man may be a hero in the service of his country and a miserable coward and slave morally and spiritually, yielding without resistance to the impulses of lust and passion, covetousness and ambition, led "captive by the devil at his will" (2 Tim. ii. 26). 2. *In patient endurance of suffering.* Martyrs, confessors, ordinary sufferers. Some of the noblest of Christ's "mighty ones" are found in sick-chambers, enduring pain and perhaps privation for long months or years without a murmur. 3. *In assailing and conquering religious errors or practical evils.* Especially when the many favour them, and not only opposition, but obloquy, has to be encountered. 4. *In promoting the salvation and welfare of men.* David's "mighty men" displayed their strength and courage chiefly in destroying men's lives; Christ's in saving and blessing; though occasionally they too are called to take up material weapons in the service of their King. In this service the noblest heroic qualities are often called into exercise, as in the case of missionaries bearing their message among savages or into perilous climates; ministers of religion at home patiently and lovingly labouring on in obscurity and poverty; visitors of those suffering from infectious diseases; teachers in ragged schools, etc.

III. THEIR VARIETIES. David's "mighty men" were from various tribes of Israel, some even Gentiles, and had each his own peculiarities of character and achievement. But all were alike loyal to their king and brave in serving him. Thus it is also with Christ's mighty ones. They are from every country and nation where he is known, from every section of his Church, from every class of society; and they all bear some marks of their origin. But they all are one in their devoted love to their King, and their readiness to labour and suffer for him even unto death. They differ also in respect of the special elements and manifestations of their power. Some owe their pre-eminence in part to physical peculiarities; others are great in spite of theirs. Some have the might of intellect; others, of heart. Some, the power of inflexible determination; others, of gentleness and tenderness. Some conquer by intense activity; others, by passive endurance or quiet influence. Some are powerful through their ability to attract and lead numbers; others, acting alone. The special sphere of some is the home; of others, the Church; of others, the exchange, the factory, the workshop, or the public meeting. Some are mighty in argument; others, in appeal; some, in instructing; others, in consoling, etc.

IV. THEIR REWARD. 1. *Promotion.* David promoted those of his men who distinguished themselves by their bravery to posts of honour (ver. 23). Similarly, our Lord teaches us that those who are faithful to him shall be advanced to higher positions of trust and power (Luke xix. 17, 19; Rev. ii. 26—28; iii. 12, 21). The display and exercise of noble qualities increases their vigour, and thus prepares for and ensures higher and wider service. 2. *Honourable record.* As here, " These be the names," etc., Christ's heroes also have their names, characters, and deeds recorded. (1) Some on earth. In the Divine book; in ordinary biographies; in the memories of men. (2) All in heaven (comp. Phil. iv. 3). Not all who are mentioned in the earthly lists are in the heavenly; for some obtain a reputation here to which they are not justly entitled. Not all in the heavenly list are in the earthly; for good men are not omniscient, nor can they always discern superior worth, though it be before their eyes. The chief desire of us all should be to have a place in the heavenly records—to be " accepted of *him* " (2 Cor. v. 9), whoever may reject or overlook us.

In conclusion: 1. *We should not be content just to exist as Christians, but should aim to be " mighty."* This is possible to all, through union with the " strong Son of God," maintained and increased by vigorous exercises of faith, meditation, and prayer; and through faithful use of such power as they possess. 2. *Whatever our might or achievements, we should ascribe all, and be sincerely concerned that others should ascribe all, to God.* (Vers. 10, 12.)—G. W.

Vers. 15—17.—*Love, courage, and self-sacrifice.* This narrative is highly creditable to both David and these three brave men. It shows the power he had of awakening in his soldiers passionate attachment and devotedness to himself, his high appreciation of such qualities, and at the same time his unwillingness that they should be displayed in enterprises which hazarded precious lives for no corresponding advantage. In the pouring of the water out as an offering unto the Lord, because it was too costly and sacred for ordinary use, " pure chivalry and pure religion found an absolute union " (Dean Stanley). On the other hand, the heroism of these men, stirred by their love and loyalty to their chief, although displayed in a rash enterprise, is worthy of great admiration. We are reminded of similar qualities found amongst the servants of the Son of David, our Lord Jesus Christ. Notice—

I. THE DEVOTED LOVE OF CHRIST'S FAITHFUL SERVANTS TO HIMSELF. 1. *They show sincere and practical regard to his every wish.* They do not need explicit commands in detail, still less accompanying threatenings. Enough if they can ascertain what he desires; and their love for him and converse with him enable them to know his wishes without definite verbal revelations or laws. A large portion of the life of many modern Christians, especially in the departments of Christian zeal and benevolence, is founded on no express command, but springs from love and sympathy—from that participation of the Spirit of Christ which produces intuitive discernment of his will, and that devoted attachment which prompts to the gratification of his every wish. 2. *They are ready to encounter danger in his service.* The work of Christ makes at times great demands on love, zeal, and courage. It cannot be done without hazard; but his true-hearted friends are prepared to endure the toil and brave the peril. Not a few in our own day may be described as " men that have hazarded their lives for the Name of our Lord Jesus Christ " (Acts xv. 26). This spirit of Christian heroism is not confined to the more hardy races, but among the softer tribes of Polynesia and India, the knowledge of Christ has produced a similar courage. Converted natives offer themselves for service in the most dangerous fields of missionary enterprise; and when some fall at the hand of savages, or through attacks of deadly diseases, others eagerly press forward to take the vacant places. The language of St. Paul is still the language of faithful Christians, " None of these things move me, neither count I my life dear unto myself," etc.; " I am ready not to be bound only, but also to die . . . for the Name of the Lord Jesus " (Acts xx. 24; xxi. 13). 3. *They are sometimes moved to extraordinary manifestations of their regard.* Like the three heroes whose exploit is here recorded. Like Mary in her lavish anointing of her Lord (John xii. 3). Warm love prompts to generous deeds and gifts. There is need of these in the service of Christ; and if ardent love to him were more common, they would be more frequent. Love should, however, submit to the guidance of wisdom, lest it become wasteful or injurious. Our Lord will accept mistaken offerings, but it is well that the offerings should themselves be such as he can approve. One safeguard against mistake is the remembrance that he desires no display of love which is fantastic or useless, no self-denial or daring which answers no proportionate end in the advancement of his kingdom and the promotion of the good either of our own souls or of our fellow-men. There is abundant room for all possible generosity, self-denial, and bravery in the practical service of Christ and man; to expend these in fruitless ways is to expose our works to condemnation, however good and acceptable may be our motives. We are to serve God with our reason as well as our feelings.

II. THE REASONABLENESS AND RIGHTNESS OF SUCH LOVE. Because of: 1. *His self-sacrificing love for them.* "The love of Christ constraineth us" (2 Cor. v. 14) is their sufficient answer to any who allege that they are "beside themselves" (2 Cor. v. 13). His love requires and justifies the utmost consecration to him of heart and life. 2. *His injunctions.* He claims from all who follow him that they should love him more than their nearest relations, more than their own life (Matt. x. 37; Luke xiv. 26), and that, in serving him, they should be fearless of death (Luke xii. 4). 3. *His example.* Of love to the Father, and complete devotedness to his will and glory (John xiv. 31; iv. 34; Matt. xxvi. 39, 42; John xii. 27, 28). 4. *The effects of such love.* In purifying and ennobling the character of those who cherish it, and promoting through them the well-being of mankind. It is love for all excellence, stimulates to its pursuit and greatly aids its attainment. It is the inspiration and support of the highest and most persistent benevolence; for he who is loved is the Incarnation of Divine holiness and love, and the great Friend and Benefactor of the human race, and the return he asks for his love to us is not a barren, sentimental devotion, but practical obedience (John xiv. 15, 21, 23), and especially a fruitful love to our brethren (John xv. 12—14; 1 John iii. 16—18), whom he teaches us to regard as being himself (Matt. xxv. 35—45). Love to Jesus Christ has been, and still is, the strongest motive-power in the world in favour of all godliness and goodness. 5. *Its rewards.* Love to Christ is not mercenary, and makes no stipulation for recompense. It is its own reward. Yet in the midst of a cold and unbelieving world it needs all supports. These are to be found in the assurance of the approval and affection of Christ himself, and of the Father (John xiv. 21, 23; xvi. 27), and the prospect of sharing the glory and joy of Christ for ever (John xvii. 24; 2 Tim. iv. 8; Matt. xix. 29; Jas. i. 12; ii. 5). On the other hand, to be destitute of love to Christ is to be lost (1 Cor. xvi. 22).—G. W.

EXPOSITION.

CHAPTER XXIV.

Ver. 1.—And again the anger of Jehovah was kindled against Israel. It is probable that this chapter once stood in intimate connection with ch. xxi., and that the famine therein described was followed by a pestilence, of which the blame largely rested upon David, though the sin punished by it was fully shared by the people. In saying that David was moved of Jehovah to number Israel and Judah, the writer acknowledges the great truth that all action, both good and evil, is of God. "Shall there be evil in a city, and Jehovah hath not done it?" (Amos iii. 6). While we are taught to pray that we may not be led into tempta-

tion, yet trial and temptation are by God's ordinance for man's good. Man falls only when the temptation gives the opportunity for the outbreak of that which already was at work within (Jas. i. 14). If the previous watch over the heart has been careful and earnest, then the temptation is a stepping-stone to a nobler and more pure godliness; and if a man fall, yet even so he learns by outward proof what was secretly ruining his soul, and may by its manifestation be led to repentance. There were festering in David's heart a thirst for war, and pride in his victories; a growing ambition, and, as its necessary result, a disregard of the rights of other nations. The same passions were gaining a daily increasing influence over the people generally. It is too often the case that a nation uses the bravery which has obtained for it freedom from foreign oppression, to impose the yoke of slavery upon others. But this chastisement brought back David and his subjects to more upright counsels. In 1 Chron. xxi. 1 the temptation is ascribed to Satan, because David fell. God tempts, that is, tries men that they may stand more firmly and advance in all that is true and good. Satan tempts men that he may find out their weaknesses and effect their ruin. Yet David fell only to rise again. Satan's triumph was but temporary, and the result was good for king and people, who would have suffered far more terribly from the effects of their lust of war than from the pestilence. Temptation, then, has two sides, and is good or evil according to the use we make of it; but in itself it is a necessity for our probation. The trials and sorrows of life serve but to break up the fallow ground (Jer. iv. 3); and without them our hearts would remain hard as the roadway; and the good seed, which may spring up to eternal life, would lie unheeded upon the surface, and find no entrance into their depths. (On the word "Satan," nevertheless, see note on ch. xix. 22. The Revised Version in 1 Chron. xxi. 1 puts in the margin, "or, an adversary." But in such matters our constant adversary is the devil.) As regards the exact time to which this pestilence may be referred, we cannot draw any certain conclusion from its place in 1 Chron. xxi., because it seems to have been inserted there in connection with the arrangements for the building of the temple, which was erected upon the site purchased from Araunah. As Joab, however, could be spared for nine months and twenty days for the making of this census, it is plain that it took place in a time of profound peace. Probably, therefore, its position in 1 Chronicles is right, namely, at some time after the termination of David's great wars. About twelve years elapsed between the capture of Rabbah and the rebellion of Absalom, and if during this period the respect of the people for David was first damaged by the revelation of his adultery with Bathsheba, and the murder of her husband, and then rudely shaken by the repeated manifestation of the displeasure of the Most High, it is not so surprising, perhaps, that his hold upon his subjects was so small as to make them ready to favour the designs of his ambitious son. But wherein lay the sin? Not only was a census lawful, but it was actually commanded (Exod. xxx. 12, *sqq.*); and the idea of the Jewish commentators, that the sin consisted in neglecting to pay the half-shekel there enjoined upon each man numbered, is not merely gratuitous, but is disproved by Joab's remonstrance; for he objects to the census absolutely. From what, too, we know of Joab's character, we cannot suppose that he would be particularly shocked at this being a census of the fighting men. Yet these Israelites were very noble men in their love of freedom and their respect for their national constitution; and if Joab observed in David a growing disposition towards despotism, and foresaw danger to the nation's liberty from the king's lust of foreign conquest, he was too upright a statesman not to oppose a measure which would strengthen the king in his dangerous tendencies. His words in 1 Chron. xxi. 3, "Are they not all my lord's servants?" seem to have this meaning. David was the master of all these fighting men. If their vast number was paraded before his imagination, it might lead him, flushed with past successes, into aggressive war; and victory abroad would lead to the destruction of freedom at home. The sin plainly lay in the violation of the principles of the theocratic government, which fostered personal independence in every member of the nation, and were opposed to every war except one of self-defence; and it was the fact that a nation so governed was weak and almost powerless even to protect itself, that had made the people clamour for a king. And now the opposite dangers were developing themselves, and the Israelites, dazzled by the glamour of victory, were joining with their king in a longing after extended empire. The pestilence stopped them for the present in their ambitious course; the disruption of the kingdom under Rehoboam dispelled their dream for ever. In 1 Chron. xxvii. 23 we also find the thought that the taking of a census, though several times practised by Moses (Exod. xxxviii. 26; Numb. i. 2; xxvi. 2), was in itself presumptuous, because it seemed to contradict the promise in Gen. xv. 5, that the seed of Abraham should be past numbering. **He moved.** It is impossible to translate, "and one moved," understanding thereby Satan, as stated in Chronicles. It was Israel which had incurred the Divine anger by its lust of war, and Jehovah used David, who was himself the victim of the same evil passions, to take a step which led on to the just chastisement. **Number**; Hebrew, *count*. It is a different word from that translated "number" in the rest of the chapter.

Ver. 2.—**For the king said**; Hebrew, *and the king said*. David's command was not the cause of Jehovah's anger, but the result of his having himself given way to ambition; and, as he yielded to the temptation, it so far became an act of Satan, in that it led to sin; but in its final result it led to good, in that the chastisement cured the people of their thirst for war. And as Satan can act only so far as the Divine will permits, the temptation was most truly the doing of Jehovah (but see note on 1 Sam. xxvi. 19). **Captain of the host, which was with him.** There is a good deal of difficulty about this passage, as the word for "host" is not that elsewhere used, and the last phrase is somewhat meaningless. In 1 Chron. xxi. 2 we find "David said to Joab and to the rulers of the people." Without the concurrence of these rulers, who were the princes of the tribes, the census could not have been taken. But as the ancient versions confirm the reading of the Hebrew here, no change of the text is admissible. **Number ye.** This is distinctly the war-word, for which see note on ch. xviii. 1. It proves that the census was taken for military reasons. Even this in itself was not wrong (Numb. xxvi. 2), but it is indicative of David's purpose. When, moreover, Moses numbered the people, the census was taken by the priests (Numb. i. 3; xxvi. 1, 2), and from the payment of the half-shekel to the sanctuary, it appears that it was to some extent a religious ceremony. All this David neglects, and the employment of Joab goes far to prove that what David wanted was an examination of the military resources of his kingdom.

Ver. 3.—**Why doth my lord the king delight in this thing?** Joab was an unscrupulous and irreligious man; but he was clear-headed, and far more statesmanlike than David (ch. xix. 5—7). He saw whither the king was drifting, and that the increase of the royal power, resulting from successful war, would be fatal to the liberties of Israel. Probably, too, though he had consented to carry out Uriah's murder, yet he despised David for it. When he had murdered Abner to avenge Asahel, David had deprived him of his command, and he had to endure a long period of disgrace; and now David uses him to murder one altogether innocent. Joab, we may feel sure, noted the degradation of David's character, and drew the conclusion that he was not the man to be trusted at the head of a military despotism. Warned thus by what he saw, his mind reverted to the principles of the theocracy, and their truth and value became more clear to his understanding; and honourably he remonstrates with David for violating them.

Ver. 4.—**The captains of the host.** The matter was not undertaken without a council being held, and at it David's chief officers agreed with Joab; but David had made up his mind, and would take no advice.

Ver. 5.—**Aroer.** There is some uncer-

tainty as to the Aroer here meant. There is first a city of that name in the tribe of Gad facing Rabbah (Josh. xiii. 25), and this is apparently the city meant; for it is said that "Joab and his men pitched in Aroer, on the south side of the city situated in the middle of the valley of Gad, and unto Jazer." Now, Jazer is also in Gad, about seven miles west of Rabbah, and as Rabbah is on the extreme east of the Israelite territory towards Ammon, it would be a very convenient spot from which to commence the numbering. But there is another Aroer on the Arnon, to the south of Reuben, and many commentators think that this Aroer must be meant, as otherwise the tribe of Reuben would seem to have been omitted. But this Aroer is regularly called "Aroer on the brink of the valley of Arnon" (Deut. ii. 36; iv. 48; Josh. xii. 2; xiii. 9, 16); or simply Aroer "in the valley of Arnon" (Deut. iii. 12; 2 Kings x. 33); and cannot possibly be "the city in the midst of the valley of Gad," nor can this Aroer be "toward Jazer." Really the difficulty is made by commentators whose idea of the method of the census is superficial. Joab, in commencing it, formed an encampment in the open country on the right-hand side, that is, on the south of Aroer in the tribe of Gad, as being central, with Reuben on the south, and Manasseh on the north. It was "toward Jazer," that is, it was on the Jazer side of Aroer, and not on the side opposite Rabbah. We, with our simpler way of describing the points of the compass, would merely say that Joab's camp was in the open pasture-land southwest of Aroer. Joab probably selected this spot because, though on the eastern border, it was yet not too far from Jerusalem, was central, and because a brook from Jazer flowing eastward for some distance, and thence to the north past Rabbah, would supply his people with water; and from this camp he would direct the proceedings of those who were to take the census. And as probably there would be considerable opposition—for the people would see in an act which for four centuries had been in desuetude threats of heavier taxation, of heavier forced labour, and of longer service with the army—Joab would require the presence of a body of troops sufficiently powerful to overawe malcontents. And these would be of no use at Aroer on the Arnon, in the distant south, but must lie encamped in some central position, whence detachments could rapidly be moved to any place where there was danger of resistance.

Ver. 6.—**Then they came to Gilead.** When the enumerators had finished their labours in Reuben and the region south of Aroer,

Joab moved his camp northwards, and pitched in Gilead, on the river Jabbok; and, having completed the counting in this part of the tribe of Gad, would next enter the wild regions of Manasseh. It is probable that the tribal princes and local officers actually numbered the people, and that Joab, with a powerful force, constrained them to obedience often against their will. It was possibly this danger of resistance which made David entrust the business to Joab, instead of employing the Levites. **The land of Tahtim-hodshi.** Gesenius dismisses this name with the remark that it can scarcely be regarded as genuine. The versions give little help; but Thenius cleverly extracts from the LXX., "unto Bashan, which is Edrei." Others, by a slight change in the Hebrew, read, "the land of the Hittites," and suppose that Hodshi is a corruption of the Hebrew word for "month," so that the whole might have been, "They came to the land of the Hittites in the (third) month." Others, again, suppose that Hodshi is a corruption of the name of the town Kadesh. But the versions would certainly have preserved anything so commonplace as this. When they make mistakes, it is almost invariably in proper names or unusual phrases. The emendation of Thenius is too ingenious to be accepted, but it gives the right sense, namely, that from Gilead and the tribe of Gad the numerators went northward through Bashan and the rest of the half-tribe of Manasseh till they came to Dan, the town on the extreme northeast border, and the limit in that direction of the Israelite realm, as Beersheba was its limit on the south. **Dan-jaan.** Nowhere else is Dan found with this addition, and the Syriac omits it even here. The Vulgate, and Septuagint (Codex Alex.) read *Dan-jaar* the woodland Dan. Possibly the names of two towns have been run into one, and the original reading was "unto Dan and Ijon" (see 1 Kings xv. 20). Ijon was on the direct road from Dan to Sidon. **Zidon.** This was on the extreme north-western boundary. It did not actually belong to David, but both it and Tyre had apparently placed themselves under his protection, and were bound to render some kind of military service.

Ver. 7.—**Tyre** (comp. Josh. xix. 29). Tyre and the whole coast-land between it and Sidon had been too strong for the tribe of Asher, and remained unsubdued. But, like the independent states in India, it acknowledged the supremacy of the paramount power. **The cities of the Hivites, and of the Canaanites.** It is evident from this that even in David's time there were towns and districts were Hivites and Canaanites dwelt as distinct communities, governed probably by their own laws. But as they were bound to serve in the Israelite armies, they were included in the census, and possibly one of its main objects was to learn the number of fighting men of alien races dwelling in Israel. They seem to have been reckoned as belonging to the tribe in whose borders they dwelt. So Baanah and Rechab, the murderers of Ishbosheth, though Beerothites (and therefore Gibeonites, who again were Hivites), were counted to Benjamin (ch. iv. 2). These Gentile communities were chiefly to be found in the north, for which reason it was called "the circuit (*Gelil*) of the nations" (Isa. ix. 1), and in later times from *Gelil* came the name Galilee. The Syriac adds "Jebusites," and we find Jerusalem occupied by a community of Jebusites living in independence in the very neighbourhood of the warlike tribe of Benjamin (ch. v. 6). This numbering of the aborigines by David is referred to in 2 Chron. ii. 17, where it is added that Solomon made a separate census of them, and found that there were in Israel no fewer than a hundred and fifty-three thousand six hundred of these aliens.

Ver. 8.—**Nine months and twenty days.** This long period seems excessive, if nothing more was intended than merely counting the heads of the people, especially as the census was left unfinished. But there might very probably be difficulties with the aliens dwelling in Israel; and it is still more probable that there was a complete examination of all the military resources of the land. The result showed a very different state of things from that described in 1 Sam. xiii. 19—22, and we can well understand the existence of much elation and war-lust among the Israelites on the first flush of pride in their new empire.

Ver. 9.—**There were in Israel eight hundred thousand valiant men that drew the sword; and the men of Judah were five hundred thousand men.** In Chronicles the numbers are, "of Israel eleven hundred thousand men, and of Judah four hundred and sixty-five thousand men." These discrepancies are a remarkable confirmation of the truth of what is said in 1 Chron. xxvii. 24 that because of the outbreak of the Divine wrath, "the number was not put in the account of the Chronicles of King David." Neither the writer of the Books of Samuel nor of Chronicles had any official document to refer to; and as the numbers are lump sums, and derived probably from what was said by the enumerators, the more exact four hundred and sixty-five thousand men of the Chronicles might easily in round numbers be called a half-million. The other is a much larger discrepancy, and no satisfactory explanation of it has been given. It is, however, quite possible that the additional three hundred thousand men were made up of the thirty-eight thousand Levites, as numbered on a later occasion by David, of the Benjamites, and of the aborigines, who belonged to the northern part of the kingdom, and might be included among "all they of Israel" (1 Chron. xxi. 5). The numbers are further attacked on the ground of exaggeration. A million and a half of fighting men means a general population of six or seven millions. Now, Palestine at most does not contain more than eleven thousand square miles, and a population of six millions means five hundred and forty-five persons to every square mile, or one to every acre. The country was undoubtedly very fertile in ancient times, and the ruins of populous cities are found where now there is a waste. But there were vast forests and pasture-lands and downs, where there were the means of subsistence for only a few. But we must remember that the enumerators went as far north as Tyre, and counted the inhabitants, therefore, of the seaboard between it and Sidon. Probably they also acted in the same way in the south, where the limits of Simeon were very uncertain. Besides this, there is a very remarkable undesigned coincidence. We read in 1 Chron. xxvii. that David had a force of two hundred and eighty-eight thousand men, who formed his regular army, and of whom twenty-four thousand were called up for training every month. But there are reasons for believing that David took for this purpose each fifth man of those of the military age (see Sime, 'Kingdom of All Israel,' p. 389); and thus the whole number of such men would be one million four hundred and forty thousand. This, as Mr. Sime has shown (ibid., p. 378), holds a middle place between the one million three hundred thousand of the Book of Samuel, and the one million five hundred and seventy thousand of Chronicles, and shows that these numbers are not to be rejected on the score of exaggeration.

Ver. 10.—**David's heart smote him.** It appears from 1 Chron. xxvii. 24 that the census was not completed, and, though Joab had visited Judah, he had not even begun to enrol the names of the men of the tribe of Benjamin (1 Chron. xxi. 6). It appears also that the displeasure of God was manifesting itself before David repented (1 Chron. xxi. 7; xxvii. 24). Some sign of this, either in public trouble, or in the brooding of the pestilential miasma over the land, brought home to David's mind the conviction of sin; and he at once humbled himself before God, for the vanity of mind which had engendered in him a wicked lust after martial glory and thirst for bloodshed. **I have done very foolishly** (comp. 1 Sam. xiii. 13; 2 Chron. xvi. 9).

Ver. 11.—**For when,** etc.; Hebrew, *and David arose in the morning, and a word of Jehovah came unto Gad, a seer of David, saying.* The visit of the seer was the result of David's repentance, and not its cause. And he was sent in mercy, that, after such punishment as would cure both king and people of their folly, there might be for both forgiveness. The name for *seer* is not *roëh*, the old word used in 1 Sam. ix. 9, and which simply means "one who sees;" but *chozeh*, a gazer, one who looks with fixed eyes, that penetrate into the hidden world.

Ver. 13.—**Seven years of famine.** In 1 Chron. xxi. 12 and here in the Septuagint we find "three years." This is probably right as being in harmony with the rest. Three years of famine, three months of defeat, or three days of pestilence. In Ezek. xiv. 21 famine, pestilence, and the sword are mentioned as three of God's four sore judgments. But a fourth judgment is there enumerated, namely, that of the increase of wild beasts, and Joshua the Stylite says that in Mesopotamia, as a result of the desolating war between the Romans and Persians, about A.D. 505, beasts of prey had become so numerous that they entered the villages and carried off the children from the streets, and were so bold and ferocious that even the men scarcely dared go about their labours in the fields (Jos. Styl., edit. Ur., chap. 85). **Now advise, and see;** Hebrew, *now know, and see.* The phrase is common in the historical books (see 1 Sam. xii. 17; xiv. 38; xxiii. 22; xxiv. 11; xxv. 17, etc.). Our translators render the phrase in a multitude of ways without greatly improving it.

Ver. 14.—**Let us fall now into the hand of Jehovah.** David had sinned against God, and to God he humbly submitted himself. There would thus be nothing to come between the soul and God, and prevent the chastisement from having its due effect upon the heart. A famine would indeed equally come from God, but would necessitate effort and exertion on man's part. In the pestilence he would wait patiently, nor look to anything but prayer for averting God's judgment. In Ps. li. 1 David refers to God's mercies, in much the same way as here, as being a motive to repentance.

Ver. 15.—**Even to the time appointed.** This rendering, though very uncertain, is retained in the Revised Version. It would mean, of course, the end of the third day, as the pestilence was to last for that time. The objections to it are that there is no article in the Hebrew, so that literally it would be "unto a time appointed." Secondly, the pestilence did not continue unto the time appointed, but was mercifully stayed. And thirdly, these words are a literal translation, indeed, of the Vulgate, but a violation of its meaning. For Jerome, who made the translation, says, "'tempus constitutum' means the hour when the evening sacrifice was offered" ('Tradd. Heb. in Duos Libros Regum'). The versions all agree that the pestilence lasted only a few hours. Thus the Syriac translates, "From morning until the sixth hour," *i.e.* noon. So too the Septuagint, "From morning until the midday meal." The Vulgate adds on three hours, as the evening sacrifice was at the ninth hour; and this is the meaning of the Chaldee Paraphrase: "From the time the daily sacrifice was slain until it was burnt." As the word *moëd* used here means both a time or place appointed for a meeting, and also the meeting itself, the right translation probably is, "From the morning even to the time of assembly," or, as we should say, "the hour of service." *Moëd* was the regular word for the time of the temple service, derived from the old name of the tabernacle, which was called "the tent of *moëd*" (see Numb. xvi. 19, etc.), rendered in the Authorized Version, "the tabernacle of the congregation," and in the Revised Version, "the tent of meeting." The hour would thus be the ninth, or three o'clock in the afternoon. **Seventy thousand men.** This is a vast number to fall victims of the pestilence in so short a time, as even the most dangerous forms of sickness take some days for their development. But similarly the army of Sennacherib was cut off in a night (Isa. xxxvii. 36); as were the firstborn in Egypt, whose visitation more nearly resembles the course of this pestilence; and the rapidity of the death-blow, striking down so vast a multitude suddenly throughout all parts of the land, would be proof to every mind that the mortality was the Divine chastisement for national sin. It is possible, nevertheless, that the black death-cloud, bringing with it the plague, may have been settling down upon the land previously, and have alarmed David, and brought him to repentance; and though no new cases occurred after the offering of his burnt offerings (ver. 25), yet it by no means follows that all cases of infection were miraculously cured. The malady may have run in them its normal course. It was Jerusalem that was saved from the blow, and, after the offering of the burnt offering, the pestilence smote down no more.

Ver. 16.—**The angel.** In the next verse we are told that David saw the angel, and more fully in 1 Chron. xxi. 16 that he beheld him "standing between the earth and the heaven, having a drawn sword in his hand." The pestilence plainly was not a natural visitation; though possibly the means used was a simoom, or poisonous wind, advancing with terrible rapidity throughout

Israel. **The Lord repented.** In all the dealings of God's providence, his actions are made to depend upon human conduct. Looked at from above, from God's side, all things are foreknown and immutably fixed; looked at from man's side, all is perpetually changing as man changes. The rescue of Jerusalem as the result of David's penitence and prayers, is thus to human view a change in the counsels and even in the feelings of him who changeth not. **The threshing-place.** "The threshing-floor," as rightly translated in vers. 18, 21, 24. Threshing-floors were constructed, whenever possible, on eminences, that the wind might drive the chaff and dust away. Araunah's was on the east of Jerusalem, outside the walls, upon Mount Moriah, and was the site on which the temple was built (see 2 Chron. iii. 1). **Araunah.** The name is so spelt seven times in vers. 20—24, for which reason the Massorites have substituted it for *Avarnah*, found in this verse in the Hebrew text, and for *Aranyah* in ver. 18. In 1 Chron. xxi. the name is spelt *Ornan;* in the Septuagint in all places, Ὀρνά, *Orna,* and in the Syriac, *Oron.* The name is, of course, a Jebusite word, and the variation arises from the narrators having written down the sound as it caught their ears. In this, as in many other particulars, it is clear that the chronicler derived his account from independent sources.

Ver. 17.—**I have done wickedly;** Hebrew, *I have done perversely,* or crookedly. David acknowledges that his conduct had not been upright and straightforward, but that he had turned aside into the paths of self-will and personal aggrandizement. **These sheep, what have they done?** The sin had been quite as much that of the people as of the king; for the war-lust had entered into the very heart of the nation. But David, with that warmth of feeling which makes his character so noble, can see only his own fault. It is not a true repentance when the sinner looks for excuses, and apportions the blame between himself and others. To David the people seemed innocent, or, if at all to blame, he felt that it was he who had set them the example and led them on. The narrative in this place is much briefer than in Chronicles.

Ver. 18.—**Go up.** David probably, on receiving God's message, had gone to the tent which he had pitched for the ark in Zion (ch. vi. 17), in order that he might pray there; and while on his way he saw the dark plague-cloud coming as the messenger of God's wrath to smite Jerusalem. In an agony of grief, he poured out his prayer that Jerusalem might be spared, and God heard him, and sent Gad a second time to bid him offer sacrifice, that, by making an atonement, he might stand between the dead and the living, as Aaron had done in the wilderness (Numb. xvi. 46—48). He is therefore to leave the tabernacle, and mount up to the summit on which Araunah's threshing-floor was situated. We read in 1 Chron. xxi. 28—30 that David wished to go to Gibeon, where the Mosaic tabernacle and altar of burnt offering were, to inquire of God, but that he was afraid, as the angel of the pestilence was smiting outside the walls. This is mentioned as an excuse for his offering at an unconsecrated spot. But it also suggests that David's choice was a submission to a chastisement already at work.

Ver. 20.—**Araunah . . . saw the king.** In 1 Chron. xxi. 20, "saw the angel;" but the text there is apparently corrupt, the difference, moreover, in Hebrew between "king" and "angel" being very slight. The addition there of the story of Araunah's four sons hiding themselves is very lifelike and natural. For these remnants of the aborigines, though tolerated, yet held a very insecure position, as we have seen in the dealings of Saul with the Gibeonites; and the coming of the king with his retinue to the out-of-the-way spot where Araunah was at work, no doubt filled them all with terror.

Ver. 22.—**Behold,** here be **oxen.** Araunah was threshing out his wheat by dragging sledges or frames of wood without wheels over it. All these he at once gives to David, that the sacrifice may be offered without delay, as it would have cost much time and labour to bring wood up from the city. Instead of **and** other **instruments of the oxen,** the Hebrew has "the harness or furniture of the oxen," all of which was of wood.

Ver. 23.—**All these did Araunah, as a king, give unto the king.** The Hebrew is, "The whole gave Araunah the king to the king;" and so the Vulgate, *dedit Areuna rex regi.* The rendering of the Revised Version (and Keil), "All this, O king, doth Araunah give unto the king," requires a change both of the order and of the tense. It is, of course, possible (though highly improbable) that Araunah was the representative of the kings of Jebus, and a titular monarch, like the Maori king in New Zealand. But the word is omitted in the Septuagint and Syriac, and is probably a mere repetition of the following word. The remark is made in order to point out Araunah's generosity; and to mark even

more clearly how hearty and sincere he was in his offering, the narrator adds, in Araunah's own words, his prayer for God's acceptance of David and his offering.

Vers. 24, 25.—**David bought the threshing-floor and the oxen for fifty shekels of silver.** In 1 Chron. xxi. 25, "So David gave to Ornan for the place six hundred shekels of gold by weight." There is a superficial, but no real discrepancy between these two narratives. David gave the fifty shekels for the immediate use of the place, and for the oxen and implements. He had no idea at the time of permanently occupying it, and probably the note in the LXX., interpolated by scribes from the margin into the text, is true, "And Solomon added to the altar afterwards, for it was small at the first." It was a small altar hurriedly put together for the purpose of offering one sacrifice; and fifty shekels would be full compensation. But the sacrifice had hallowed the spot, and, when finally it was selected as the site for the temple, David bought the whole area and all that Araunah possessed there. Fifty shekels of silver would be about £9; six hundred shekels of gold would be about £1500; so that there is no comparison between the two sums. But the precious metals were worth very much more in David's time than in ours, so that the smaller sum was adequate compensation for David's first acquisition, while the larger implies the purchase of an extensive and valuable estate. Substantially the fuller narrative in Chronicles agrees with this. David refuses to sacrifice of that which cost him nothing, and must therefore have at once paid for what he took. But when God accepted his offering, and answered him by fire from heaven, then David said, "This is the house of the Lord God, and this is the altar of the burnt offering for Israel." And as the Chronicler has in view throughout the selection of the site for the temple, he naturally mentions its full cost. In the Book of Samuel this purpose is not expressly mentioned, and the narrative closes with the forgiveness of the sin both of David and his people. Jehovah was entreated for the land, and the plague was stayed. But this sudden smiting down of so large a host humbled both king and people, and their eagerness for war and their lust of empire ceased.

DEO GLORIA.

HOMILETICS.

Vers. 1—9.—The facts are: 1. On account of some transgressions, God, being angry with Israel, permits some one to incite David to number the people. 2. David, on issuing his commands to Joab, is met with a remonstrance from him and the captains of the host. 3. But the king persisting in his desire, Joab and his officers and men apply themselves to the work, and at the end of nine months and twenty days return the number of men capable of serving in war at 1,300,000. The difficulties involved in the statements of this section may be, at least, lightened by a few considerations. The parallel passage in 1 Chron. xxi. mentions, in an indefinite way, *an adversary* as the instrument of inciting the mind of David. It is in accordance with the order of the Divine government sometimes to allow agencies to act on the minds of men for purposes of trial and especially for discipline. Adam was assailed. Satan had permission to tempt Job. David recognizes the possibility of Saul being incited against himself by God (the Hiph. as here, הֱסִיתְךָ); 1 Sam. xxvi. 19. A spirit or agency inclining to evil is said to go forth or be sent from God, when the idea of permitting the free action of evil influences as a means of punishment for previous sins is to be inculcated (Judg. ix. 23; 1 Sam. xvi. 14; ch. xvi. 10; 1 Kings xxii. 21—23). The ascription of actions to God in almost absolute terms, where in reality the Divine action is a withdrawal of restraint, is a strong Hebraism, as seen in the hardening of Pharaoh's heart (cf. Isa. vi. 9, 10; lxiii. 17; Matt. xiii. 13—15). It is no uncommon thing for sin to be punished by sin (Ps. xvii. 13, 14; cf. Isa. x. 5, 6). Now, accepting this general teaching as to some of God's methods when trial or chastisement are in view, we find in ch. xxi. that the nation was chastised for a previous national or semi-national sin. It seems, therefore, natural that the expression (ver. 1), " And *again* the anger of the Lord was kindled against Israel," really sets forth the event of this chapter as being a second instance of national suffering on account of public sin; the difference being that in ch. xxi. the famine became a fact before the occasion is revealed, while here the fact of sin is first stated, and the human instrumentality of bringing on the punishment is then set forth. David had sinned in the matter of Uriah, and been punished. Absalom had sinned in rebelling, and had also been punished. But he was not the only sinner. Israel had revolted under him against the Lord's anointed, and was there to be no punishment for Israel as a people? The whole history of the dealings of God with them gives the reply. Apart from any recent unrecorded sin, there is, then, historical continuity in the words, " The anger of the Lord " was *again* " kindled against Israel." The peculiarity of the case is this—that the free falling of David into a snare of pride and undue reliance on material strength became the occasion and means by which the transgression of Israel was chastised, while he, being quite free in his sin, was also caused to suffer for it.

Deferred chastisements. Some time evidently had elapsed between the sin of Israel and the expression of Divine anger against it (ver. 1). This and the other Book of Samuel sets forth the chief cases of public visitation on account of sin, *e.g.* Eli, Saul, David, Absalom; and, in keeping with this, the conduct of the people in revolting against the Lord's anointed is now made the occasion of Divine displeasure. With reference to deferred chastisements observe—

I. That God sometimes waits till events serve the purpose of chastisement. The chastisement of Eli did not come till national affairs so far developed as to issue in a disastrous defeat of Israel. David's sin bore its bitter fruit some months and years after committal. The sin of the house of Saul was brought home to the conscience of the nation after his death (ch. xxi. 1). So here the wicked conduct of the nation in rejecting David, God's chosen servant, was allowed to remain relatively unnoticed, as though God were waiting for such a development of events in the natural course of things as would serve the purposes of chastisement. Nations, Churches, and individuals are still allowed to go on for a while till events mature for bringing upon them the reward of their deeds.

II. That the events which serve for chastisement are brought about by the free action of others. The free action of the Philistines brought on Eli's trouble. The free action of Absalom and Israel was the means of chastising David for his sin in the case of Uriah. The natural development of famine, united with a revelation of God's overruling purposes, smote Israel for the national crime against the Gibeonites (ch. xxi. 1—4). So here the free action of some evil person or agent on the free mind of David was the natural event which issued in his official sin, and in his punishment in such a form as to bring on Israel the chastisement which all along they were deserving for their revolt. The same is seen in the free action of Babylon bringing on the chastisement of captivity, and of Rome in bringing on the chastisement of the dispersion due for rejection of Christ. God may wait long before he brings on what is due to sin; but all free events are in his hands, and he will use up some of them when fit conditions arise.

III. THE FREE ACTION OF MEN BY WHICH THEY ARE MEANS OF CHASTISING OTHERS; FOR SIN MAY BE ITSELF SINFUL AND SUBJECT TO PUNISHMENT. David's free act in yielding to the inducement to number the people was a sin. It was displeasing to God. It was a case of sin opening the way for a chastisement for sin. There were circumstances in David's personal and official position which rendered it natural that his deed should be at once disowned, and in that disownment there came the rod which smote also for the past sin of Israel. The acts of Babylon and Rome were wicked, though they were the rod by which God smote his people. It is by a most wonderful adjustment that God thus makes sin the avenger of sin; and so, in course of ages, sin tends to establish that very righteousness of God which in its initiation it sought to set aside. All the resources of God are at his command at any time for expressing his anger against sin; but he does not create new agencies—he uses up what is in existence, and utilizes the successive acts even of the wicked. It is a solemn fact that though judgment be deferred it is not the less sure (2 Pet. ii. 3). Here is a warning to the impenitent, and a restraint on all. The injured may rest assured that God will bring a recompense (Rom. xii. 19).

The subtle power of a sinful motive. The narrative simply states outward facts; but the form of them compels the belief that David's actions were now governed by a subtle motive, sinful in its nature, complete in its mastery over intellect and will, and so able to dominate his entire nature that its own real character should all the time be disguised. It is a difficult matter to disintegrate the complex movements of the mind or to present an accurate psychological analysis of an act of sin; but we may trace in David's case a few features of sin in its subjective workings. An underlying sinful motive may so operate as—

I. To SECURE BEFORE THE INTELLECT A GOOD ARRAY OF REASONS FOR AN ACT. David must have formulated reasons for his proposal to number the people. Most probably he thought it was a natural thing after all the vicissitudes the nation had passed through. It would afford an occasion of showing how God had blessed and prospered the people. He would be in a better position to make up any defects that might be discovered in the defences of the country. The knowledge of their unity and strength would give encouragement and confidence to men apprehensive of danger from without. The result, becoming known among neighbouring nations, would act as a check on their aggressiveness. His successor to the throne would be in possession of facts that would help his administration of affairs, and there would be some comfort in seeing how far Israel was realizing the hopes held out to their ancestors. Such reasons may seem to be the outcome of mere intellectual activity; but in reality they are set in order by the subtle influence of the ruling motive over the intellectual powers. Men do not know to what extent the form and order of their thinkings are determined by the governing desire. Herein lies much of the deceitfulness of sin. The useful nature of facts can easily be seen when the disposition would have it so. The devil was a clever reasoner in Eden. The inner adversary of our soul, be it evil motive or propensity, practically, by influence over the intellect, performs the part of a cogent reasoner, and makes out a case for the consent of the reason.

II. To DIVERT CONSCIENCE FROM ITSELF. Conscience was alive in David when first the question of numbering occurred to him, but when once the idea is entertained and the subtle unspoken motive has strengthened its hold on the mind by being temporarily cherished, it so operates as to weaken the gaze of conscience on itself and virtually divert it to more incidental circumstances. An evil motive cannot live face to face with a live conscience; but if by persistence it can get lodgment among the many feelings of the heart, and as it were be hidden from direct single gaze, it can, by its contagious nature, create a condition of things that the conscience shall be occupied with other evils inferior in rank, while it does its deadly work almost without coming into consciousness. So many a man finds his conscience busy with straining out a gnat while the evil disposition most cherished is free to devour a camel. Hence, even great sinners are sometimes precise and punctilious in minor matters.

III. To GIVE OBSTINACY TO THE WILL. It seems strange that David should have ventured to go against the deliberate protest of Joab and the chief military men. His disregard of Joab's wishes can, perhaps, be explained by his previous quarrels with him; but that he should have gone against the judgment of the chief men in the army is explicable only on the moral and psychological principle that the subtle power of an evil motive, when cherished, imparts a peculiar obstinacy to the will. We see this in human life. The persistence of men in carrying out a sinful feeling, active though not perhaps distinct in consciousness, is amazing. The will is so imbued with the feeling as to be proof against all reason and all but physical force. This is the real bondage. This led Augustine to say that man, as a sinner, is not free. There is something akin to the blindness and insensibility and mechanical necessity of physical forces in a will subject to the rule of a sinful motive.

IV. To ENSURE SELF-COMPOSURE. David seems to have set about this business with coolness, and to have been calmly determined to see it through. There was no excitement, and whatever occasional gleams of conscience may have fallen on the dark recesses where the hidden sinful motive lay doing its subtle work, they did not permanently affect the self-possession of his life. The sudden breaking of the spell came after the nine months and twenty days. Restlessness and anxiety during a sinful course can only arise when conscience and desire are face to face, and conscience is not diverted from its gaze. When the governing feeling has, by subtle action, brought intellect, conscience, and will into subjection, or rather when its nature has somehow tainted and weakened them all, there is a peace and composure which, if not of God, is nevertheless serviceable for the execution of a purpose. It is the bane of some wicked men that their strength is firm. It is an evil omen for a religious man when he is undisturbed in doing what others know to be wrong. "Grey hairs are upon him, and he knoweth it not."

GENERAL LESSONS. 1. It becomes men in the most favourable circumstances to remember that they are open to incitements to evil as truly as the most unfavoured. 2. The more elevated our position in the religious life the more subtle are the temptations of the great adversary. 3. It is possible for a really good man to becloud his last days by falling into sin through lack of watchfulness and prayer against the more secret forms of evil.

Vers. 10—17.—*A king's sin and a people's chastisement.* The facts are: 1. David, reflecting on the accomplishment of his purpose, comes to a consciousness of his sin, and makes confession before God. 2. In the morning the Prophet Gad is sent to him from the Lord, offering him, as a choice of a chastisement, either seven years' famine, or three months' defeat before his enemies, or three days' pestilence. 3. David, in his anguish, elects to fall into the hands of God. 4. Thereupon God sends a pestilence which carries off seventy thousand men. 5. There being some relenting in the anger of God when the pestilence reached Jerusalem, David entreats with the angel of the Lord by the threshing-floor of Araunah, that he would have pity on the people and rather smite him and his house. The various truths taught in this section may be briefly set forth thus.

I. THE REACTION OF MAN'S SPIRITUAL NATURE. For more than nine months the unhallowed feeling which prompted the numbering of the people had held sway, and now during the silence of night the spiritual man that had been suppressed again asserts his power. David comes to himself, and sees his conduct in a Divine light. The supremacy of sin means a depression of the better nature. The awakening to a sense of sin is the reaction of that better nature. The same was seen in the matter of Bathsheba and Uriah. The prodigal son's coming to himself is an instance; as also the repentance of every sinner. The causes and occasions of the reaction may come from without, but there can be no doubt that the change does lie in a reaction. The spell is broken, and the higher nature of man once more asserts itself.

II. THE CAUSES AND OCCASIONS OF THE SOUL'S BREAKING THE SPELL OF SIN ARE DEFINITE. David came to himself most probably for three reasons. 1. *Difficulties of carrying out his project* may have pressed on him the need of reflection; for not only were Joab and the captains reluctant workers, but long time elapsed, and so strong was the opposition that two tribes were not counted (1 Chron. xxi. 4). 2. The *strain of persistence* would, by psychological law, enfeeble purpose.   He could not go on for ever in a line of sin; exhaustion of moral motive is a reality.   3. The *gracious action of God* would revive the latent and suppressed sense of right; for though the Holy Spirit is grieved, he does not depart for ever from the erring.   The same is true still.   External difficulties of a sinful course make the way hard, and so give chance for reflection and reaction of the better self.   The exhaustion and satiety of persistence in evil tends to open a way for the action of Divine influence.   The misery of the prodigal, the weariness of sin, the loss of early novelty, do not turn men, but they render other more spiritual action more timely.   The real cause which turns these occasions to account is the gracious action of the Holy Spirit.

III. The changed estimate of conduct under the light of God's Spirit. As we have seen (vers. 1—9), plausible reasons could be assigned for numbering the people, but now that in the silence of night the light had come, that which once was reasonable and proper, and persisted in as essential, is folly and sin.   It is only in the light which God causes to shine into our hearts that we can see what is the real character of some of the motives lurking there.   Saul of Tarsus came to see himself in the light of God, and the old life in which he had prided himself became his shame.   No man knows himself apart from Divine illumination.   Repentance marks the change undergone in a man's estimate of himself in the sight of God.

IV. The antithesis of sin and right reason.   When David confessed before God that in what he had done he had acted foolishly, he not only expressed a changed estimate of his conduct, but also illustrated a universal truth.   Sin and wisdom are incompatible; they are mutually exclusive.   The lie from the beginning has been that it is good for man to do his own will.   The wisdom of being "as gods" was the first of snares.   The votaries of pleasure and the scornful rejecters of the supernatural Christ deem themselves wise in following the bent of their unholy and proud disposition.   The wise "disputer of this world" looks with contempt on "the foolishness of preaching" and of the obedience to Christ which is its object.   Yes, like David, in his sin, they have their day; but just as he found at last that his wisdom was all the time folly, so others will find that wisdom is utterly removed from their preference of their own to the will of Christ.   Sin is the most desperate folly.   It debases man's nature, entails numberless ills for body and spirit, interferes with the true development of the mind and the acquisition and enjoyment of the treasures of good hid in nature, inflicts a stigma and leaves a stain that unfit for the highest society in the universe, and, moreover, mars the future possibly beyond recovery.   Holiness and wisdom alone coincide.   To go against the will of God is a species of madness.   The history of individuals and of nations is proof of it.

V. God's watchfulness over repenting sinners.   It was a long solitary night when David came to see the folly and sin of his conduct.   The outpouring of his penitent heart was known to no human being.   The most sacred experiences of life are secrets between the soul and God.   But yet in the morning, just at the right time, the messenger of God came to him.   His mission was to offer alternative chastisements, but there was implied in it forgiveness.   The eye of God had seen the inner workings of the broken spirit, and the occasion was seized to bring David again into more direct communication with his God.   In the case of Bathsheba Nathan had awakened penitence; here Gad came to help forward the good work begun in penitence.   The cry of Saul of Tarsus was heard in heaven, and to help him a servant of God was prepared to speak the words suitable to his case.   The ear of the Lord is ever open to the cry of the humble, and his eye is on their sorrows.   Some message or messenger will be sent to them to confirm the fact of their awakening to a sense of sin, and do what is best for their restoration.   Let every penitent remember that God hears the cry in the night, and sees all the desires of the broken heart.

VI. The adaptation of chastisement to sin.   In the alternative choice of David as to the form of chastisement there is secured the same adaptation of the infliction to the nature of the sin.   Many explanations have been offered of this sin, but we prefer to consider its essence to lie in a sense of elation in the strength of the nation, and a consequent desire to be assured of its sufficiency for all contingencies.   David was thinking of strength and glory in numerical form.   In this he was going counter to the letter and spirit of the Law laid down for him and his people (Lev. xxvi.).   Success and prosperity were to be dependent on perfect obedience to God's commands (Lev. xxvi. 3, 4). It is expressly added that then a few men will suffice against a host, and, on the other hand, disobedience and "pride of power" (vers. 14, 15—19) will entail defeat and desolation. That this "pride of power" was the real sin in David's case is seen in this—that the three alternatives offered to him are the very three forms of chastisement alluded to in Lev. xxvi. 3—10 (cf. 16—20). But the point is this, that, whichever form of chastisement is taken, the effect is the same—a *diminution of the power* which was an object of pride. The sin of rejoicing in the "arm of flesh" (Jer. xvii. 5; cf. Isa. xxx. 2) was visited by a weakening of that "arm." Famine, war, pestilence, either, would take away from that very *number* which it was David's ambition to know and have as large as possible. This adaptation of chastisement to sin is seen elsewhere. The infliction for wicked craving for flesh in the wilderness (Numb. xi. 33), the confusion and helplessness of those who sought help in Egypt rather than in God (Isa. xxx. 2, 3, 16, 17), the turning of Laodicean outward respectability into a loss of all respectability (Rev. iii. 14—18), the change from boasted glory to corruption in the case of Herod (Acts xii. 21—23),—are instances of a certain adaptation of chastisement to the particular sin committed. All who make self, or personal merits, or created power, a substitute for God, will find that on which they rest vanishing just when they most need comfort.

VII. THE PENITENT'S TRUST IN THE JUSTICE AND MERCY OF GOD. Of the three dreadful alternatives, David took the pestilence, on the ground that his broken heart could rest more calmly in God's judgments, where the human element was not employed as agent. Here was the true instinct of the soul. God is just and good, and in his hands all is sure to be right and kind. Man is weak and evil, and as an agent may blend his own base passions with the execution of a Divine decree. Even in the hour of suffering, when sin is to be punished, the heart has faith in God. Here is homage to God's justice and mercy. Many a man, who by his sins brings terrible wars on himself and family, bows in entire submission, and rests in blended justice and mercy. This is the essence of our faith in Christ as Sacrifice for sin.

VIII. THE RELATIVE CHARACTER OF OPEN MANIFESTATIONS OF GOD'S PRESENCE. There is nothing really surprising in the appearing of the angel of the Lord to David; for it is in keeping with the theophanies of the early dispensation, when men had special need to be reminded of the reality of God's presence. Abraham, Jacob, Moses, Joshua, Manoah, were predecessors of David in this respect. The step from the message of God by the Seer Gad to a visible manifestation is not very great to any one who believes at all in the supernatural; indeed, the final manifestation of God in Christ covers all prior manifestations. Those who profess to see difficulties in these Old Testament accounts do not understand the logic or the historical congruity of their position as believers in the visible incarnation of the Son of God. Manifestations of God's presence are relative. Creation is an expression of the being and presence of God. The voice which comes to prophet or apostle, the glory on which Moses gazed, the pillar of cloud and of fire, the appearance of manna after the promise of it, the vision of the seer, the still small voice to Elijah, the coming of the Holy Spirit at Pentecost, the frustration of the scheme of the wicked and the furtherance of those of the good, and the spiritual revelation to the soul in fulfilment of the precious words (John xiv. 21, 22),—these are all manifestations of God. Christ differs from all in that he is the Fulness of the Godhead bodily. It is a mercy that our poor dull nature has been blessed by these demonstrations of the reality of things unseen and eternal.

IX. MENTAL SUFFERING THE CHIEF PENALTY OF SIN. David sinned in numbering the people; the pestilence smote many of them, but touched him not. Nevertheless, he was the greatest sufferer; for no physical death could equal, in the pain it brings, the anguish of his soul in seeing that his sin had brought such trouble and pain on "these sheep" (ver. 17). To a man of his generous nature, with all the ambition to be a good and wise ruler (ch. xxiii. 3—5), it must have been torment unspeakable to see that he was an occasion of bringing woe to thousands of homes. His punishment was heavy indeed. A similar terrible mental punishment comes to the parent who sees, in his reformed years, his children diseased or ruined by former sins of his own. In this mental anguish lies, perhaps, the hell which men so much dread.

X. THE PARCIMONY OF PROVIDENCE. David was not correct in his supposition that "these sheep" had not gone astray. We are not certain whether they had indulged in feelings of pride in the strength of Israel, and so were virtually one with their king in the sin of numbering; but we know that they had sinned in the revolt of Absalom and Sheba, and the anger of the Lord against Israel may, as we have seen (vers. 1—9), be referred to those acts. The fact that they had not been chastised for so great a sin is manifest, so far as the history is any guide, though, if Absalom's sin deserved special visitation on him, theirs equally deserved a visitation on themselves. The sense of the whole history, therefore, is that God waited, and made the occasion of the new sin of their king the opportunity of visiting them with stripes while visiting him with stripes for his own. Indeed, the severity of his chastisement lay much in this, that he was the instrumental occasion of their woe. By one pestilence the double chastisement was secured. Philosophy has dwelt much on the "law of parcimony" in nature. It seems also to run through many providential dispensations in relation to man. By the Flood God punished wicked men and set forth his faithfulness to the righteous. The institution of the Hebrew ritual both educated men in spiritual conceptions, and kept them distinct from the nations for the ulterior purpose of Christ's coming. The sacrifice of Christ is at the same time an objective ground of forgiveness, and the most impressive source of moral influence in winning men over to God. There are manifold forms of the same law in daily life.

Vers. 18—25.—The facts are: 1. The Seer Gad having directed David to rear an altar to the Lord in the threshing-floor of Araunah, he proceeds to carry out the instruction. 2. Araunah, observing the approach of David and his servants, makes obeisance, and desires to know the purport of his visit. 3. Ascertaining that David desired to buy the threshing-floor that he might there entreat for the staying of the plague, he generously offers all that was requisite for the sacrifices, and expresses the hope that God might be propitious. 4. But David, not caring to offer to God what cost him nothing, insists on purchasing the place and the oxen required. 5. The offering being presented on the altar, the plague ceases to trouble Israel.

The way to reconciliation with God a matter of Divine revelation. God had graciously condescended to reveal himself in visible form both to assure David that the plague was more than a mere natural course of disease (ver. 17), and to render an approach to himself more accessible. The chief effect, however, on David was to deepen his conviction of sin and his pity for his suffering people. His prayer, like that of Moses, was that he might suffer if so be they be set free. It was not till the seer came the next day that David learnt what course to take in order to secure reconciliation, not only for the people, but for himself also. God reveals to man the way of reconciliation.

I. THIS IS TRUE OF THE GROUND OF OUR SALVATION IN CHRIST. As surely as the prophet from God informed David as to what was to be done in order to find favour with God and escape the plague, so surely has God revealed in his Word the fact that through Christ alone do we find favour and eternal life. The work of redemption by the sacrifice of Christ was not discovered by the exercise of human reason. In the desert, when Israel was perishing, God ordained the lifting up of the serpent, and caused information of the fact to be given. In our desert life God sent his beloved Son, independently of our asking or knowledge, and commissioned his servants to announce the way of salvation. Reason may enable us to ascertain the reality of the historic fact, but reason could not discover the way of reconciliation. The Apostle Paul declares that he received it not of man, but of God. They do not understand the gospel who imagine that man, by his learning or reason, could ever find out, apart from special revelation, the only way to God.

II. IT IS TRUE OF THE MEANS BY WHICH SALVATION BECOMES PERSONAL. Salvation may be spoken of in general terms, and in this sense is too often the subject of discussion. But it is, also, a matter of personal experience. The end for which Christ lived and died becomes realized in individual souls, in the form of actual forgiveness, restoration to favour, newness of life and progressive holiness. By what means this is to be brought about, so far as our action is concerned, is purely a matter of revelation. It is revealed from heaven to be of faith (Rom. i. 17). As Christ was the Gift of God, so the revelation that we are saved by Christ on condition of our faith is also the gift of God. It was made known to David that sacrifice would be the ground of pardon, and that his personal use or application of that to the need of the hour was the means of his obtaining the benefit of it. The place of our faith in our salvation from the plague of sin is not a question of human speculation: it is fixed by him who gave the sacrifice.

III. IT IS TRUE OF OUR INDIVIDUAL APPRECIATION OF WHAT GOD HAS ALREADY MADE KNOWN. The spiritual bearing of the acts enjoined on David could only be spiritually discerned. That Christ is our great Sacrifice, and that faith is the means by which we are to appropriate it,—these are things plainly revealed in Scripture, and could only be known as Divine ordinations by special revelation; but they are a dead letter to multitudes. We need the revelation of their spiritual bearing to our own souls by the Holy Spirit; and it is only as the Holy Spirit takes of these things pertaining to Christ and reveals them to our individual spirit that we see their force and value their application. Hence a revelation of the matter of revelation is needful to conversion. Hence many read and speak about salvation who never see its real significance or know it as a matter of personal experience. The invisible messenger of God must come to us as truly as the seer came to David, if we are to *see* his salvation (John iii. 5).

Devotion of property to God's service. Araunah was eager to provide a place and oxen for the celebration of the services about to be rendered to God. His interest in David, in Israel, and his homage for God seem to have prompted the generous proposal. On the other hand, David's sense of what was due to God from himself, and his personal interest in the solemn transaction, would not suffer him to be spared cost through the generosity of Araunah. He must honour God with his own and not with another man's possessions.

I. ALL OUR POSSESSIONS ARE GOD'S. This is the basis of our devotion of what we hold to his service. We are really but stewards. Our mental powers, our wealth, our personal influence, our very life, are lent to us for a season, and lent with a view to use in God's Name. This is laid down in the words, "Ye are not your own;" in the parable of the talents; in the very constitution and dependence of our lives; in the specific commands concerning "firstfruits;" and this was practically recognized by both David and Araunah in their emulation in self-sacrifice. It would be a great gain to the Church and world if Christian people would only let this truth sink deeply into their hearts. What elevation, tone, and nobility it would import to life!

II. THERE IS NO NOBLER USE OF POSSESSIONS THAN IN GOD'S SERVICE. David and Araunah were one in this belief. They strove for the honour of devoting substance to God. In a well-ordered Christian life *all* is devoted to God. The entire life, embracing mental powers, occupations, property, time, is a sacrifice (Rom. xii. 1). But by reason of custom we recognize that as specially devoted to God which is directly employed in maintaining his holy worship or diffusing a knowledge of his great mercy to mankind. The wonderful way in which the priesthood was set apart, the distinction put in Scripture on men whose lives were chiefly spent in witnessing for God, the significant words of our Saviour in reference to the widow's mite and the box of ointment, and the glorying of the Apostle Paul in that he was called and counted worthy of a special ministry,—these things point out the honour of using our gifts and possessions in furtherance of God's gracious purposes to mankind.

III. THE USE OF OUR POSSESSIONS IN GOD'S SERVICE IS A MEANS OF VAST BLESSING TO MANKIND. By devoting their substance to God on this occasion, David and Araunah knew that they would be doing that which, being graciously accepted, would issue in the removal of the plague from Israel. No wonder that they were ambitious to lay their gifts at the mercy-seat! It was a question of staying the plague. Equally in our case it is daily a question of staying the plague, lifting the curse of sin and scattering the wholesome blessings of salvation over the land. He who builds a sanctuary, or endows a college, or send forth missionaries, turns his money into streams of spiritual good.

IV. A TRUE HEART WILL FIND PURE SATISFACTION IN DEVISING MEANS OF DEVOTING GIFTS TO GOD. David honoured the noble impulse of Araunah, but he could not be deprived of the satisfaction claimed by every true man of giving of his own. There is a real blessedness in laying our gifts of mind and body and our material possessions at the altar of God. The meanness which would worship at others' expense, or look on spiritual good done at others' cost, can never dwell in a Christly soul. As the Saviour himself counted it a deep and holy joy to lay down his life for others, so all who enter into his spirit feel it to be a matter of thankfulness when occasion arises for some surrender in his service. The bountiful soul is always rich. The large heart is never in poverty. The joy of their Lord is their portion.

V. IT IS BY THE USE OF SUCH ACTS OF DEVOTION TO HIS SERVICE THAT GOD HAS HITHERTO BLESSED THE WORLD. The self-surrender of Abraham when he left Ur of the Chaldees, the devotion by Moses of his great powers to the leadership of Israel, were simply conspicuous instances in the entire history of redemption of God's acceptance and use of human powers and possessions for carrying out his great purpose of mercy. David was following the usual order in the case before us. Even our blessed Lord came to earth by means of the devotion of a virgin life. The "good news" has been sent abroad by consecration of human speech. Who would not fall in with this glorious succession till the world is saved?

Plague and prayer. The narrative plainly teaches that this plague was ordained of God for moral ends, and that it was stayed by means of the intercession offered in the manner suited to the age of shadowy sacrifice before the offering of the eternal sacrifice by Christ.

I. AFFLICTIVE EVENTS ARE SOMETIMES TO BE REGARDED AS DIVINE CHASTISEMENTS. This was true of the event here referred to. No sensible man can doubt it. The only way to get rid of the fact is to regard this portion of Scripture as a mere superstitious legend—human superstitions being infused into a natural occurrence. The bad logic of this, in the case of one who accepts the supernatural in the incarnation of Christ, is obvious. If God thought fit to deal supernaturally with men at one time, why not at another? In Scripture many afflictive events are set forth in the same light, and we may fairly say that God's government of men has not yet ceased, and that men, especially communities, need discipline as much now as ever. If men are moral beings under government, and if the order of nature is not beyond the reach and control of God, we have a right to regard the events of Scripture as examples of what God does to the sons of men (1 Cor. x. 11).

II. THERE IS MORE IN THESE EVENTS THAN THE NECESSARY ACTION OF PHYSICAL LAWS. The presence of the angel here shows that there was a special Divine element in the event. The same is true of other similar events recorded in Scripture. In modern Divine chastisements of men there may be physical order, but that will not be the interpretation of the moral bearing of the events. There seems to be more than a foreseen coincidence of a chain of physical necessities issuing in an event just at the time when some national or individual sin transpires. Bare prevision of a coincidence that could not be helped is a poor explanation of Divine government. The scriptural idea is the best—that God is *free* and *above* and *behind* all the forces at work, and in some way not revealed and not certainly discoverable by physical science, he does so regulate the succession of physical events as to make them subserve a moral purpose when, in the development of human history, there arises a need of such subservance. We must either admit this, or place God practically outside his own possessions as a helpless spectator, less able to strike in than are we ourselves. The mystery may be great, but it is more mysterious, and certainly more absurd, that there should be such a God deprived of freedom of action.

III. THE REMOVAL OF AFFLICTIVE EVENTS IS CONNECTED WITH THE WORK OF CHRIST. The offering of sacrifice by David was a divinely appointed means of accepting the repentance and homage of the nation. "Without the shedding of blood there is no remission." This deep spiritual truth was doubtless recognized by all the truly pious of those times. Thus it sets forth the greater truth that the sacrifice of Christ is the ground on which God exercises his mercy in forgiving our sins and healing our wounds. The far-reaching benefits of his death deserve more consideration than they commonly get. Thousands enjoy the fruit of his sacrifice who know him not. For all men-he has lifted up the curse, so that its pressure is not so great as once it was or might have been. When the rod is laid by, and the sinful nation or individual is no longer smitten, it is for "Christ's sake."

IV. Prayer is the human means by which chastisements are removed. On the basis of the sacrifice typical of Christ's death, David's prayer was accepted and the plague was stayed. In like manner Moses intreated for Israel, and David for his people. The nature of prayer and its place in the Divine government have not changed with years. It is a spiritual power as truly as that gravity is a physical force. Its exercise, according to Scripture, is not exclusive of the use of personal effort to remove physical evils, and certainly not exclusive of moral conduct. As a spiritual power, it is part of our endowment, and to be employed along with our other endowments of good sense, prudence, and correctness of life. It does not follow that answer to prayer is a violation of the order of things. We do not know how far God's personal contact with every force in action is or is not part of the order, and hence we do not know but that his free energy may so modify the course of events as to maintain what seems to us to be natural order, and yet to be the product of his own will. The pointsman on a railway may suddenly save a train from destruction without violating the order of nature. Who shall say that the watchful energy of the Eternal may not, in answer to our urgent cry, so act as to obviate what otherwise would be a great disaster? "The effectual fervent prayer of a righteous man availeth much." It is mighty only as it is the concentrated voice of a "newness of life" lifted up to heaven in the all-prevailing Name of the Lord Jesus Christ.

HOMILIES BY VARIOUS AUTHORS.

Vers. 1, 2 (1 Chron. xxi. 1, 2).—(Jerusalem.) *A sinful census.* 1. This census appears to have been ordered by David in one of the *later years* of his life. The word "again" (ver. 1) indicates that it was subsequent to the famine (ch. xxi. 1, 14; ver. 25); and a measure that occupied Joab and the captains of the host nine months and twenty days could only have been accomplished during a time of settled peace, such as succeeded the rebellions of Absalom and Sheba. "Three great external calamities are recorded in David's reign, which may be regarded as marking its beginning, its middle, and its close—a three years' famine, a three months' exile, a three days' pestilence" (Stanley). No man, however advanced in life, or whatever the wisdom he may have "learnt by experience," is wholly exempt from the power of temptation. 2. It was a census of those who were capable of bearing arms (ver. 9), and of the nature of a *military organization* (ch. viii. 15—18). "But David took not the number of them from twenty years old and under," etc. (1 Chron. xxvii. 23, 24). The result showed a great increase of the people—800,000 (1,100,000) warriors of Israel, 500,000 (470,000) of Judah, omitting Levi and Benjamin (1 Chron. xxi. 6); representing a population of about five millions. 3. Its direct and *declared object* was that David might "know the number of the people," or become fully acquainted with its military strength, "its defensive power" (Keil). Of any additional object, except what is implied in the words of Joab, "Why does my lord the king *delight* in this thing?" nothing is stated. 4. It, nevertheless, was wrong and *exceedingly sinful.* This is evident, not only from the expostulation of Joab, but also from the confession of David himself (ver. 10), and the Divine chastisement that followed. Wherein consisted his sin? A census was not in itself and always sinful; for it had been expressly directed by God (Exod. xxx. 11—16; xxxviii. 26; Numb. i. 2; xxvi. 1—4, 63—65), and it was (as it still is) attended with important advantages. But this census was determined upon by David, (1) apparently without due inquiry, by means of oracle (1 Chron. xxi. 30) or prophet (ver. 11), concerning the will of the Divine King of Israel; without adequate grounds in relation to the welfare of the people; and without proper consideration of the danger of promoting a spirit of pride, and producing other evil consequences (Exod. xxx. 11, 12). "David forgot the commands of Moses, who told them beforehand that if the multitude were numbered, they should pay half a shekel (the price of a sin offering) to God for every head" (Josephus). In its omission "he invaded the rights of the supreme King of Israel, and set aside a positive command of God. The demanding the tax by his own authority might have created a national disturbance, and therefore should have prevented him from numbering his people" (Chandler). (2) Probably with warlike thoughts and intentions, for the strengthening of the army and the further extension of

Israel's dominion by foreign conquests (ch. xxii. 44, 45). " Warlike thoughts certainly stand in the background; if we fail to see this, we lose the key to the whole transaction, and the Divine judgment is incomprehensible " (Hengstenberg); but it can hardly be supposed that he formed the definite purpose of "transforming the theocratic state into a conquering world-state " (Kurtz). (3) Possibly with a view to " the development of the royal power in Israel" and "general taxation" (Ewald); which made it obnoxious to Joab and the council (for something of the kind seems necessary to account for the opposition of such a man). (4) Certainly with vain-glorious pride, self-elation, distrust of God, who "said he would increase Israel like to the stars of the heavens" (1 Chron. xxvii. 23), and presumptuous confidence in himself (1 Sam. xv. 1—9; Luke iv. 5—12). "David's heart was lifted up to rejoice in the number and strength of the people" (Willet). "The very same action, apparently performed with different intentions, becomes essentially different in a moral point of view. It is the *motive* in which it originates, or the spirit with which it is carried on, that gives it its distinctive character in the sight of God. David was actuated by a vain-glorious spirit, which is always an abomination in the sight of God. He was thus indulging a vain conceit of his own strength, a proud confidence in his own greatness, as if his chief dependence were on an arm of flesh; forgetting his own devout profession that the Lord was his Rock and his Fortress and his Deliverer, in whom he would trust" (Lindsay). "From its first origin Israel was called to *the supremacy of the world* (Deut. xxxiii. 29). David now thought that he could rise step by step to such elevation without the help of God, who had provided for the beginning. The records should bear witness for all time that he had laid a solid foundation for this great work of the future" (Hengstenberg). "It was a momentary apostasy from Jehovah; an oblivion of the spirit of dependence inculcated on the rulers of Israel." This was the root of the offence; and in it the whole nation participated. "This history shows that the acts and fortunes of rulers and people are closely connected together; and that the sins and virtues of the one exercise great influence on the happiness of the other" (Wordsworth). Consider that—

I. GOD IS NEVER ANGRY WITH ANY PERSON OR PEOPLE EXCEPT ON ACCOUNT OF SIN. "David's causing the people to be numbered was the *immediate* cause of the pestilence; for the procedure originated in motives which the Lord condemned. But the *primary* and *real* cause is to be found in the verse which introduces the narrative, and which is almost invariably lost sight of in the common accounts of this transaction. It is that 'the anger of the Lord was kindled against Israel.' Now, the anger of the Lord could only be awakened by unfaithfulness and evil-doing; and that, whatever its precise nature, was the real cause of the calamity that followed, and relieves the case of the apparent harshness, of which so much has been said, of making the people suffer for the offence of their king" (Kitto, 'Daily Bible Illus.'). 1. *Sin alone excites the anger of God*; which is his holy opposition to sin and sinners, and not inconsistent with his love, but rather the effect of resistance to it (ch. xi. 27). 2. *Whenever sin dwells in the heart*, no less than when it is expressed in outward actions, God observes it, and is displeased with those who are guilty of it. "For he knoweth the secrets of the heart" (Ps. xliv. 21). 3. His displeasure with a whole people implies *prevalent and persistent sin* among them, such as the spirit of unbelief, disobedience, vain-glorious pride, and presumption, which was manifested in the recent rebellions of Israel, and appears to have been subsequently indulged. 4. So far from being palliated or passed over because of *their exalted position and privileges*, their sin is aggravated, and more fully ensures their chastisement on that account. "You only have I known," etc. (Amos iii. 2). "It may be not unreasonably surmised that they were smitten with the same unhallowed elation of heart (as the king); that they were tempted to exult in their own strength; that they rejoiced in the prospect of beholding the proud array of their multitudes of fighting men; and that dreams of grandeur and glory may have been before their eyes, and may have caused them to depart from the Lord" (Le Bas). "The important lesson for all here is this—that even the smallest feeling of *national pride* is a sin against God, and, unless there be a powerful reaction, calls down the judgments of God. With this feeling even the Romans presented offerings of atonement at their census."

II. SIN IN A PEOPLE IS USUALLY ASSOCIATED WITH SIN IN THEIR RULER. 1. The former may be incited by the latter (1 Kings xv. 30). Or: 2. It may be an incitement to it (John xix. 12). "The people had infected the king with their own arrogance, which had been called forth by their success." Or: 3. Both people and ruler may alike participate in the same prevalent, sinful disposition or tendency of the age. As formerly (ch. xv. 1—5), "soft indulgence" and sensual desire; so now, "the lust of the eyes and the pride of life" (1 John ii. 16) seem to have taken possession of his mind. 4. The sin of a people may culminate in, and be manifested and represented by, the sin of their ruler. For this he is eminently responsible, and when his piety, which should have checked the evil tendency of the people, and may hitherto have restrained the righteous judgment of God, begins to fail, it becomes the occasion of the breaking forth of his fiery indignation. "It was the final offence which filled up the cup of wrath, and the punishment smote the nation, and, through the nation, its ruler" (Kirkpatrick, *Hom. Quart.*, vi.). "The Lord was wearied with the sins of Israel and Judah; and he likewise beheld the *secret pride* of David's heart; and for these things he was resolved to visit both the people and the king." "Pride, or vain-glory, or self-sufficiency, which was the sin of David, and which, for the very reason that it effects us less, because it is not so much against man as against God, offends him the more. It is a substitution of ourselves in his place; an impious thought of independence, and transference to ourselves of that confidence and admiration which are due to him alone. It is an invasion of his throne, an assumption of his sceptre, an attempt to rob him of that glory which he will not give to another, a removing of the crown from his head to put it on our own. 'Wherefore it is said, God resisteth the proud'" (J. Leifchild). "He was, for the time, the image and emblem of all who in any age, or in any country, love to have arrayed before them the elements of their worldly strength; who delight to see spread out the full enrolment of their powers and resources, and who forget that there is One before whose breath all these things shall be even as the cloud-capped towers and palaces before the breath of the whirlwind."

III. The sinful measures of a ruler are sometimes the effect of the Divine displeasure with his people, whose sin he shares, and of whose punishment he is made the instrument. "And he [Jehovah] moved [incited, provoked] David to say," etc. "The thought is—there should come a pestilence over Israel, and David become the occasion thereof" (Thenius). "The ruler's sin is a punishment to a wicked people." Sin implies personal responsibility; and "God tempts no man" (Jas. i. 13). But in his universal sovereignty: 1. He appoints the *circumstances*, which are adapted to test and manifest character, and often conduce to sin. 2. He suggests *thoughts* which, although right and good in themselves, are sometimes perverted to wrong and evil by human folly and infatuation (ver. 10). "All good thoughts, counsels, just works, come from the Spirit of God; and, at the same time, we are in the most imminent peril at every moment of turning the Divine suggestions into sin by allowing our selfish and impure conceits and rash generalizations to mix with them" (Maurice). 3. He withdraws his *restraining grace* in consequence of sin, and permits men to be tempted of Satan (1 Chron. xxi. 1), who readily seizes the opportunity to lead them into transgression. *Deus probat, Satan tentat.* 4. He even constrains the *manifestation of the iniquity of the heart* for holy and beneficent ends. "God's influence, making use of Satan as its instrument, leads the corrupt germ to its development, rousing into action that which slumbers in the soul, in order to bring about the retributive judgment in which man, if otherwise well-intentioned, learns fully to recognize his sinful condition, and is moved to repentance. The question is not of simple permission on the part of God, but of a real action, and that of the nature which each one may perceive in his own tendencies. Whoever once yields to his sinful disposition is infallibly involved in the sinful deed which leads to retributive judgment, however much he may strive against it" (Hengstenberg). "Though it was David's sin that opened the sluice, the sins of the people all contributed to the deluge" (Matthew Henry).

IV. An adequate reason is afforded by such measures for the chastisement of ruler and people. "It was needful for an external, visible manifestation of the sin to precede the judgment, in order to justify the ways of God to men. The temptation was presented to David; he fell, and in his fall represented truly and faithfully the fall of the nation. The nation was not punished vicariously for its ruler's sin, but for a sin which was its own, and was only embodied and made visible by its ruler's act. And the punishment struck the very point of their pride, by diminishing the numbers which had been the ground of their self-confident elation" (Kirkpatrick, 2 Samuel).

"Because David was about to boast proudly and to glory in the number of his people, God determined to punish him by reducing their number, either by famine, war, or pestilence" (S. Schmid). 1. Sinful *actions* serve to manifest the hidden sin of the heart. 2. They show the connection between such sin and its just retribution. 3. They make chastisement more signal and salutary. 4. They are often overruled to the glory of God and the welfare of men. [*Note:* Some of the difficulties indicated above would be removed by regarding the first sentence as "the heading of the whole chapter, which goes on to describe the sin which kindled this anger, viz. the numbering of the people" ('Speaker's Commentary'); and by reading, "And one moved David," etc.; *i.e.* "one of his courtiers or attendants, who is therefore called satan, or an adversary, either designedly or consequentially both to David and his people. The people were themselves very culpable; as they knew, or might have known, that, upon being numbered, they were to pay the prescribed ransom, which yet they neglected or refused to do; as partners in the offence, they justly shared in the penalty inflicted" (Chandler). But this explanation is not satisfactory.]—D.

Ver. 2 (1 Chron. xxi. 2).—(THE KING'S PALACE.) *Self-elation.* This chapter contains the spiritual history of a great soul in its "fall and rising again," its sin and recovery—its (1) self-elation, (2) self-will (vers. 3, 4), (3) self-deception (during many months), (4) self-conviction (by self-examination, ver. 10), (5) self-abasement, (6) self-surrender (ver. 14), (7) self-devotion for the people (ver. 17), and self-dedication to God (vers. 24, 25). Of self-elation, pride, presumption, vain-glory (the sin of David), it may be said that it is—

I. A COMMON EFFECT OF EXTRAORDINARY PROSPERITY, temporal or spiritual. Pride; war, famine, or pestilence; suffering and humiliation; peace and industry; prosperity —pride again; such is the melancholy circle of human affairs (Exod. viii. 14). "If we knew how to enjoy our blessings in the fear of God, they would be continued unto us; but it is the sin of man that he extracts, even from the mercies of God, the poison which destroys his comforts; he grows fat upon the bounties of Heaven, spurns its laws, and awakens its vengeance" (R. Watson).

II. AN UNGRATEFUL PERVERSION OF DIVINE BENEFITS. "The grave sin of proud exaltation, which David and the people of Israel here had in common, presupposed the elevation to victory and power that God had bestowed by his gracious mind; and its consequence was the judgment that revealed God's anger against the perversion of his favours into plans of self-aggrandizement" (Erdmann). What should produce thankfulness and humility too often results in unthankfulness and vain-glory (2 Kings xx. 13).

III. A SPECIAL TEMPTATION OF THE EVIL ONE. (1 Tim. iii. 6.) "And Satan [an adversary] stood up," etc. (1 Chron. xxi. 1). "We see that God and Satan both had their hand in the work; God by permission, Satan by suggestion; God as a Judge, Satan as an enemy; God as in a just punishment for sin, Satan as in an act of sin; God in a wise ordination of it to good, Satan in a malicious intent to confusion" (Hall).

IV. A GRIEVOUS EXHIBITION OF SPIRITUAL BLINDNESS; inconsideration of dependence, self-ignorance, self-deception, and foolish infatuation (Jer. xlix. 16). "David, when strongly tempted to this gratification of his vanity, was not at all sensible of the evil of such an act; while Joab was. Joab, though a man of blood, and apparently hardened in iniquity, could see through David's vain and arrogant feelings, while David himself, whose mind was under ordinary circumstances eminently sensitive and pious, could not discover the impiety of his proceeding, but persevered in evil for several months. Such is the infatuation of sin!" (Lindsay).

V. A PECULIAR PROVOCATIVE OF DIVINE WRATH (1 Sam. ii. 3; Prov. xvi. 5); most odious of all things in the sight of God, because most directly opposed to him. "Pride is the beginning of sin" (Ecclus. x. 13). "And what is pride but the craving for undue exaltation? And this is undue exaltation when the soul abandons him to whom it ought to cleave as its end, and becomes a kind of end to itself. This happens when it becomes its own satisfaction. And it does so when it falls away from that unchangeable good which ought to satisfy it more than itself" (Augustine, 'The City of God,' xiv. 13).

VI. A PERNICIOUS INFLUENCE IN RELATION TO OTHER PEOPLE; inciting in them a similar spirit, and bringing untold miseries upon them. What oppression, strife, and other deadly fruits grow out of this "root of bitterness" (Exod. xiv. 5)!

VII. A RUINOUS TENDENCY IN RELATION TO MAN HIMSELF. (Dan. iv. 28; Prov. xvi. 18.) "Pride wishes to dethrone God. Pride takes occasion from virtue itself. Pride was particularly odious in David, who was exalted from so lowly a state. His pride was accompanied by falsehood; for he had protested his humility in the psalms which he made for all the people to sing. David was a just man; but this was a reason why God should punish him more severely. For it is certain that the sins of the children of God are more deserving of condemnation than the sins of reprobates and slaves of the devil. These only offend their master, but those do outrage to their Father; these are only rebel subjects, but those are unnatural children and barbarians; these only abuse the gifts of nature, but those profane miserably the gifts of grace. And how much more abominable is Judas than Pilate! Be not surprised, then, that when David, who was complete in a thousand graces, committed the crime of felony against him, the Eternal could not suffer such an indignity without punishing him severely " (Du Bosc, in Vinet's 'Histoire de la Prédication ').—D.

Vers. 3, 4 (1 Chron. xxi. 3, 4).—(THE ROYAL COUNCIL-CHAMBER.) *Unheeded remonstrance.* This was not the first time that Joab remonstrated with David (ch. iii. 24; xix. 5); but his manner was now very different from what it had been before; arising, perhaps, from his recollection of the consequences of his former rudeness (ch. xix. 13), and his fear of the displeasure of the king, whose authority was fully restored. His remonstrance appears to have been made in a council of the captains of the army (ch. xxiii. 8), to whom the king declared his purpose, and by whom Joab's objection to it was supported (ver. 4). As often happens in other instances, it was : 1. *Greatly needed,* on account of a sinful and dangerous course about to be pursued. (1) Men of the most exalted position and excellent character sometimes go astray from the right path. (2) The error of their way is often perceived by others, when they are blind to it themselves. (3) One of the principal means of preventing their continuance therein is to reason, expostulate, and remonstrate with them concerning its real nature and probable consequences (Ps. cxli. 5). 2. *Properly offered.* (1) By those to whom the matter is one of just concern. Joab was captain of the host; and, although a man of depraved character, he possessed a sound practical judgment, and had rendered great services to the nation and the king. (2) From sincere conviction. "No man is so wicked but that sometimes he will dislike some evil, and it will be abominable (1 Chron. xxi. 6) to him" (Guild). (3) On reasonable grounds. It can neither increase the number of the people (which is with God) nor the power and honour of the king (already supreme, 1 Chron. xxi. 3), and it will be "a cause of trespass." "Why doth my lord," etc.? "There are many who can give good counsel to others, for the avoiding of some sins, who in grosser trespasses have not grace to take good counsel themselves" (Matt. vii. 3). (4) In a right spirit; devout, loyal, humble, and courteous. There is nothing to indicate that Joab was actuated by sinister motives; and the event justified the wisdom of his counsel. 3. *Impatiently received,* and imperfectly considered; it may be because of : (1) Distrust of the person from whom it comes. "Let none look who gives the counsel, but what it is; and, if good, not to reject it for him who gives the same." (2) A determination to have one's own way; and the wish to show independence of and superiority to other persons. (3) Dislike to the nature of the advice itself, and indisposition to abandon a course on which the heart is set. 4. *Resolutely rejected* and wholly overborne. "The word of the king prevailed," etc. His persistency in his purpose, after the remonstrance, (1) increases his responsibility, (2) aggravates his guilt, (3) consummates his transgression. "And Joab and the captains went out from the presence of the king," reluctantly to fulfil their commission ; and it was only when it was well-nigh accomplished (1 Chron. xxvii. 24) that he became aware of his sin and folly. "Men seldom accomplish to good purpose those services in which they reluctantly engage; and God does not generally allow those whom he loves the satisfaction which they sinfully covet " (Scott).—D.

Vers. 5—10 (1 Chron. xxi. 5—8).—(THE ROYAL BED-CHAMBER.) *An awakened conscience.* The taking of the census occupied over nine months; and during this time

David remained insensible to his sin, and waited for the result. At length the work was finished (about wheat-harvest), and the number given to the king; but, whilst he looked at the definite proof of the nation's increase, and at first, perhaps, felt elated at the thought of commanding an army of more than a million soldiers (with something of the spirit of another monarch, Dan. iv. 30), the same night "David's heart smote him; and he said unto Jehovah, I have sinned," etc.; "and David arose in the morning," etc. (ver. 11). What the remonstrance of Joab failed to effect was wrought by the operation of his own conscience. "It was well for him that his own ways reproved him, and that conscience sounded the first trumpet of alarm. This is characteristic of the regenerate. Men who have no light of grace, no tenderness of conscience, must have their sin recalled to them by the circumstances which at once reveal its enormity and visit it with punishment; but the regenerate have an inward monitor that waits not for these consequences to rouse its energy, but lights up the candle of the Lord within them, and will not let them rest after they have done amiss till they have felt compunction and made confession" (J. Leifchild). *Conscience* is of a threefold nature—a law, a judgment, a sentiment (1 Sam. xxii. 20—22). Observe, with respect to it—

I. THE CAUSES OF ITS CONTINUING LONG ASLEEP. These are summed up in "the deceitfulness of sin" (ch. xii. 5, 6). More especially: 1. The persistency of the influence under which sin is at first indulged; viz. the pleasing *illusion* (arising from partial views, strong passions, and self-will) that it is different from what it really is, and the agent better than he really is; which (even when the true standard of right is recognized) perverts the moral judgment and deadens the moral emotion. "A concrete fact is presented in a partial aspect; conscience pronounces its judgment according to the representation made to it; this representation, or rather misrepresentation, is made, directly or indirectly by the influence of the rebellious will, the true seat of all moral evil" (McCosh). Hence evil is often deemed good, and self-glory the glory of God. 2. The *assumption* (arising from self-confidence) that what has been resolved upon is justifiable and right; and indisposition to review the grounds of the determination or to examine one's self so that a too favourable estimate of his character may be corrected. 3. The *absorption* of the mind in the pursuit of the object sought and in other occupations, preventing due consideration of the state of the heart. Alas! how many on this account "regard iniquity in their heart" with an easy conscience!

> "Great crimes alarm the conscience; but she sleeps
> While thoughtful man is plausibly amused."
>
> (Cowper.)

"And Satan is so far from awaking him, that he draws the curtains close about him that no light nor noise in his conscience may break his rest" (Gurnall). "If a man accustoms himself to slight or pass over the first motions to good, or shrinkings of conscience from evil, which originally are as natural to the heart as the appetites of hunger and thirst are to the stomach, conscience will by degrees grow dull and unconcerned, and, from not spying out motes, come at length to overlook beams; from carelessness it shall fall into a slumber; and from a slumber it shall settle into a deep and long sleep; till at last, perhaps, it sleeps itself into a lethargy, and that such a one that nothing but hell and judgment shall be able to awaken it" (South, Serm. xxiii.).

II. THE MEANS BY WHICH IT IS SUDDENLY AROUSED. In some cases the publication of the offence, the reprobation of society, the threatening of punishment; in others, serious consideration, deliberate *reflection*, deeper self-inspection (1 Sam. xxiv. 5; Ps. iv. 4), induced by: 1. The feeling of disappointment and *dissatisfaction* which commonly attends the attainment of an earthly end, or the accomplishment of a selfish purpose. David has the number of the people before him; yet, after all, he cannot "delight in this thing" (ver. 3). "All is vanity." Where shall the heart find rest (Ps. cxvi. 17; lxxiii. 25)? 2. The occurrence of *circumstances* naturally adapted to fix attention on a particular subject and excite inquiry concerning the motives by which one is actuated: a pause in "life's fitful fever;" the necessity of contemplating—what next? and next? a sleepless night (Esth. vi. 1); "sleep that bringeth oft tidings of future hap" (Dante)—"a dream, a vision of the night" (Job xxxiii. 15). "David had made spiritual progress since the time when it required the parable of Nathan, and the prophetic announcement, 'Thou art the man,' to awaken him from his spiritual slumber. At this period of his life he examined himself and weighed his own actions in private, especially at night-time; and no sooner was the census of the men of war reported to him than, instead of being elated with self-confidence and puffed up with vain-glory, 'his heart smote him,'" etc. (Wordsworth). "*Night and sleep* bring us times of revision or moral reflection, such as greatly promote the best uses of existence. Whatever wrong has been committed stalks into the mind with an appalling tread. All those highest thoughts and most piercing truths that most deeply concern the great problem of life will often come nigh to thoughtful men in the dusk of their evenings, and their hours of retirement to rest. The night is the judgment-bar of the day. About all the reflection there is in the world is due, if not directly to the night, to the habit prepared and fashioned by it. Great thoughts and wonderfully distinct crowd in, stirring great convictions—all the more welcome to a good man; to the bad, how terrible! ' Thou hast visited me in the night,' says David ; ' thou hast tried me;' and again, 'My reins instruct me in the night season.' What lessons of wisdom have every man's reins given him in the depths of the night!—things how high, how close to other worlds! reproofs how piercing in authority, how nearly Divine !" (Bushnell, 'Moral Uses of Dark Things '). 3. The operation of Divine *grace* (in connection with a man's own thoughts), which visits the upright in heart, dispels every illusion, and strengthens every holy and God-ward aspiration. Did the Lord in judgment move David to number Israel? His judgment was founded on love, and his goodness led him to repentance.

III. THE EFFECT OF ITS RENEWED ACTIVITY. "And David said unto Jehovah, I have sinned greatly in that I have done," etc. 1. A right knowledge of himself and a correct judgment of his conduct. 2. A painful sense of his guilt and folly. In the truly penitent: 3. A humble confession before the Lord (1 Sam. vii. 6); and: 4. Fervent prayer for forgiveness (ch. xii. 13). Of the way of forgiveness and its own pacification, indeed, conscience is unable to declare anything; the knowledge thereof is afforded by the Word of God alone (ver. 18). Nevertheless, its awakening tests and manifests the character, and results in peace and righteousness, or in increased "hardness of heart," confirmed rebellion, remorse, and despair. The hour of its awakening comes to all; but it may come too late, when there is found "no place for repentance" (ver. 16).—D.

Vers. 9—13, 18, 19 (1 Chron. xxi. 9—13, 18, 19).—*The Prophet Gad.* "And when David was up in the morning," etc. Gad had formerly given valuable direction to David (1 Sam. xxii. 5); and he must have been now far advanced in life. He was "David's seer," or spiritual counsellor ; a true prophet of God (1 Sam. ii. 27 ; iii. 19 ; ch. vii. 3); assisted in the arrangements for the temple service (1 Chron. ix. 22), and (like Samuel and Nathan) wrote a (theocratic) history of his time (1 Chron. xxix. 29). "The most celebrated representatives of special prophecy in David's period were Nathan the prophet and Gad the seer. As Nathan connected Messianic prophecy for ever with the house of David, so Gad was instrumental in moulding the history of salvation even till the period of the New Testament, since, by directing David to build an altar on the threshing-floor of Araunah the Jebusite, he laid the foundation of the temple upon Mount Moriah, in which Israel, by prayer and sacrifice, honoured his God for more than a thousand years" (Delitzsch). He was fully acquainted with the king's purpose, the remonstrance of Joab, the completion of the census ; and may possibly already, from his intimacy with David, have observed misgivings in him concerning the measure, and surmised his present state of mind. "He said nothing to him about his sin, but spoke only of correction for it; which confirms it that David was made sensible of his sin before he came to him" (Gill). Notice: 1. *His Divine mission.* "The word of Jehovah came unto the prophet," etc. (1) It came to him *directly*, by inward intuition, when "in a state most nearly related to communion with God in prayer" (Oehler). (2) With the irresistible *assurance* of its Divine origin. "The prophets themselves had the clearest and most profound consciousness that they did not utter their own thoughts, but those revealed to them by God" (Riehm). (3) With a powerful *impulse* to give it utterance, in "fulfilment of a definite duty laid upon him by God." (4) And it *proved* whence it came, by its manifest adaptation and actual accomplishment; the Divine wisdom and might with which it was imbued (vers. 15, 25). "The three elements which enter into the true conception of a prophet are *revelation, inspiration, and utterance*; for the prophet is the inspired medium of truth to other minds. Revelation, the inner disclosure of the Divine thought and will to the human soul, is an essential element of genuine prophecy. But this revelation cannot become realized, cannot become a real disclosure of thought and purpose to the individual as a preparation for prophecy, without inspiration. The soul of the prophet must be ethically quickened and elevated in order that the word of Jehovah may reach the people through him. Nor can the message remain concealed in the prophet's own soul; for it is a *message*, a Divine commission, to communicate a revealed truth to those for whom it is divinely intended" (Ladd, 'The Doctrine of Sacred Scripture,' i. 124). 2. *His prophetic message.* More than what is recorded may have been spoken in his two interviews with the king; but his words contain: (1) An assertion of the sole *sovereignty* of Jehovah, which had been for a season practically ignored. "Thus saith Jehovah," etc. (ver. 12). The office of a prophet was that of "watchman to the theocracy" (Jer. vi. 27); he had to observe and denounce every departure from its principles on the part of the king or people, and give warning of coming danger. (2) An announcement of the approach of *judgment.* "I lay before thee three things," etc. Already, perchance, the king had a presentiment thereof; but now it was rendered plain and certain. Yet "mercy is mixed with judgment; the Lord is angry, yet shows great condescension and goodness." "His mercies are great" (ver. 14). (3) An appointment of the means of *deliverance.* "Go up, rear an altar unto Jehovah," etc. (ver. 18). (4) An injunction of those duties or *conditions*, in the fulfilment of which the favour of God would be enjoyed—submission, trust, and unreserved self-devotion. 3. *His faithful obedience.* "And Gad came to David," etc., with: (1) Simplicity; uttering the word of God, just as it was revealed to him, adding nothing, and withholding nothing. (2) Fearlessness. (3) Earnestness. "Now advise," etc. (4) Diligence and perseverance. 4. *His salutary influence* (in accordance with the purpose of his mission), not only in the removal of the pestilence, but also in (1) checking the spirit of presumption and of rebellion against Jehovah, (2) pacifying a troubled conscience, (3) restoring both king and people to their allegiance, (4) promoting the interests of the kingdom of God.—D.

Ver. 13 (1 Chron. xxi. 12).—(JERUSALEM.) *Preachers and hearers.* "Now advise [know], and see what answer I shall return to him that sent me." The intercourse of the prophet with the king, especially his language at the close of the first interview, is suggestive of—

I. THE VOCATION OF THE PREACHER of the gospel. 1. Every true preacher is sent forth by God. 2. He is put in trust with the Word of God, and is sent to proclaim it to others, as his messenger and ambassador (2 Cor. v. 20); not to teach his own speculations. 3. The purpose of the proclamation is their spiritual welfare—their instruction, edification, salvation. "They watch on behalf of your souls" (Heb. xiii. 17). But, too often,

> "The aim of all
> Is how to shine: e'en they whose office is
> To preach the gospel, let the gospel sleep,
> And pass their own inventions off instead.
> The sheep, meanwhile, poor witless ones, return
> From pasture, fed with wind: and what avails
> For their excuse, they do not see their harm?
> Christ said not to his first conventicle,
> 'Go forth and preach impostures to the world,'
> But gave them truth to build on."
>
> (Dante, 'Par.,' xxix.)

4. The fulfilment of his calling demands the highest qualities—wisdom, sincerity, sympathy, disinterestedness, self-denial, fidelity, courage, zeal, assiduity. 5. The manner of his reception varies (Acts xvii. 34), and tests the character of those to whom he is sent (Matt. x. 11—13; 2 Cor. ii. 16). 6. He must return to him who sent him, and give account, not only of his own conduct, but also of the manner in which they have

treated him and his message (Ezek. xxxiii. 30—33), and the effect produced in their lives. His return takes place in private communion with God on earth, and at " the end of his life" (Heb. xiii. 7). "What answer," etc.?

II. THE RESPONSIBILITY OF THE HEARER of the Word. 1. He receives through the preacher a message from God of unspeakable importance; not, indeed, an announcement of judgment, but a revelation of mercy and of his will concerning him; repentance, faith, and obedience; "all the words of this life" (Acts v. 20). 2. He has the power of considering and understanding it, and of accepting or rejecting it. 3. He is under the strongest obligation to accept and not reject it. 4. He cannot avoid doing the one or the other; indifference, inattention, or procrastination being itself an "answer" little short of positive rejection. 5. Whatever may be his treatment thereof, it is fully known to God. 6. According to the manner in which he treats the message of God, is he justly treated by God, both here and hereafter. "The word that I have spoken, the same shall judge him in the last day" (John xii. 48). "Now therefore advise thyself." "Consider" (1 Sam. xii. 24). "Take heed therefore how ye hear" (Luke viii. 1—18).

III. THE MUTUAL DEPENDENCE OF PREACHER AND HEARER. 1. On the preacher, his character, adaptation, diligence (as well as on himself), depend the hearer's acceptance of the message and his spiritual benefit. 2. On the hearer, his attention, acceptance, obedience (as well as himself), depend the preacher's efficiency, success, and present joy. "That they may do this [watch, etc.] with joy, and not with grief; for this were unprofitable for you" (Heb. xiii. 17). 3. The relation in which they stand to each other will fully appear in the light of the great day; when the salvation of the hearer will be clearly seen to have been connected with the faithful labours of the preacher (Dan. xii. 3), and the reward of the preacher will be *proportioned* to his success (and not merely to his fidelity). "For what is our hope, or joy, or crown of rejoicing?" etc. (1 Thess. ii. 19, 20; 1 John ii. 28). 4. For his own benefit, therefore (as well as that of the hearer), the preacher should seek that the hearer may be believing, obedient, and fruitful in good works (1 Thess. iii. 2; v. 12, 13). 5. For his own benefit, also, the hearer should seek that the preacher may be faithful and successful. 6. Each should pray for the blessing of God upon the other, so that the proper end of preaching and hearing may be accomplished.—D.

Ver. 14 (1 Chron. xxi. 13).—(THE KING'S PALACE.) *Submission to Divine chastisement.* "Let us now fall into the hand of Jehovah." Already David had been convinced of his sin. He had also confessed it and sought forgiveness. Nor had he done so in vain. But, as formerly (ch. xii. 10—12), so now, the (temporal) penalties of sin must follow. Throughout he exhibited a spirit the exact reverse of that in which he had numbered the people. Consider—

I. THE CHASTISEMENT OF SIN which was laid before him. 1. It was consequent upon his sin, and *adapted* to its correction. A vain-glorious pride and warlike policy result (in the providence of God, sometimes by means which can be clearly seen) in the destruction of human life; not only directly by war (Matt. xxvi. 52), but also by famine (through lack of proper cultivation of the soil, wasting consumption of its produce, etc.) and by pestilence (to which both contribute); and are rebuked and chastised thereby (Rev. vi. 4—8). 2. It was a necessity, from which there was no escape. He and his people *must* suffer, according to the fixed and just method of the Divine procedure, for the vindication of the honour of God and the promotion of their own welfare. Herein no choice is left. 3. But it was also *optional*, within certain limits (Jer. xxxiv. 17). "Every example, public or private, of a sin brought face to face with its suffering, presents an aspect of choice as well as of compulsion. The mere question of confession or denial, with the consequences of either, is such an alternative in the case of individual wrong-doing. The adoption of this expedient rather than that, in the way of avoidance or mitigation of consequences, is an alternative" (C. J. Vaughan). Why was such a choice submitted to him? To test his character; to deepen his sense of sin, by the consideration of its terrible effects; to induce the open acknowledgment of his guilt; to perfect his submission; "to give him some encouragement under the correction, letting him know that God did not cast him out of communion with himself, but that still his secret was with him; and in afflicting him he considered his frame, and what he could best bear" (Matthew Henry). 4. And it caused him great *distress;* all the greater because he was required, not merely to submit passively to chastisement, but to choose the form thereof, and thus make it, in some sense, his own. "All chastening seemeth for the present to be not joyous, but grievous," etc. (Heb. xii. 11).

II. The spirit of submission which he displayed. "Is it a choice made? or, is it a choice referred back to the offerer? Is it, 'I choose pestilence'? or is it, 'Let God choose'? Whatever the application, the principle stands steadfast—In everything let me be in God's hand; whether for the choice of my punishment, or for the infliction of it, he shall be my Judge; for his mercies are great—greater than man's; the more free his choice, the more direct his dealing, the better is it for the man, the better is it for the nation that must suffer." "And David chose for himself the mortality [death]" (LXX.); "that affliction which is common to kings and to their subjects, and in which the fear was equal on all sides" (Josephus). Of famine and war, with their untold miseries, he had had experience, not of pestilence. By the former he would become dependent on men (for the sustaining or the sparing of life); by the latter, more directly on God; and whilst "the tender mercies of the wicked are cruel," his "anger endureth but a moment" (Ps. xxx. 5), and "his mercies are great." The spirit evinced is one of: 1. Self-abasement, before the majesty of the supreme King and Judge. 2. Self-abnegation; with noble disinterestedness, setting aside all care for his personal safety, and enduring, in common with the meanest of his subjects, the just chastisement of Heaven. His position might secure him against suffering and death by famine and "the sword of his enemies;" not by "the sword of the Lord" (1 Chron. xxi. 12)—

> "The pestilence that walketh in darkness,
> And the sickness that wasteth at noonday."
>   (Ps. xci. 6.)

3. Self-surrender; the sacrifice of his own will to the will of God (1 Sam. iii. 18; ch. xv. 23—29; Ps. cxxxi.).

> "And in his will is our tranquillity:
> It is the mighty ocean, whither tends
> Whatever it creates and nature makes."
>   (Dante, 'Par.,' iii.)

"Though he slay me," etc. (Job xiii. 15). "If Christ stood with a drawn sword in his hand pointed at my breast, yet would I rush into his arms" (Luther). 4. Confidence in the abounding mercy of God. For he is not like man, ignorant, inconsiderate, unjust, wilful, selfish, cruel, and malicious; but knows all things (the secrets of the heart, the force of temptation, the sincerity of penitence, the reality of love), is considerate (of human infirmities, Isa. lvii. 16), righteous, "merciful, and gracious," etc. (Exod. xxxiv. 6), very pitiful (Ps. ciii. 13, 14), mitigates affliction (Isa. xxvii. 8), mingles with it many consolations, and "repents him of the evil" (Jonah iv. 4; 1 Sam. xv. 29; ver. 16). Such trust is the spring of true submission, and it is fully justified by the event. 5. Co-operation with the merciful and holy purposes of God in relation to the moral welfare of those whom he afflicts. The selfishness of men in famine and their cruelty in war tend to evoke rebellion, wrath, and retaliation; the recognition of "the mighty hand of God" (Jas. iv. 10; 1 Pet. v. 6) tends to produce lowly obedience, tenderness, and kindness. 6. Concern for the welfare of the nation, which would suffer less by the last than by the first two of the calamities; and: 7. Zeal for the interests of religion and the glory of God. "Let thy Name be magnified for ever" (ch. vii. 26). "When the apostle said to the Hebrews that it is a fearful thing to fall into the hands of the living God, does it not contradict the decision of David? By no means. The apostle meant to speak of those who fall *without repentance* into the hands of God for punishment; but, in a penitent disposition, nothing is so sweet as to fall into the loving and most gracious hands of the living God" (Du Bosc).—D.

Vers. 15, 16 (1 Chron. xxi. 14, 15).—(Jerusalem.) *Pestilence.* Pestilence, even more than famine and war, was regarded by David as directly inflicted by the hand of God. How far, in this instance, it occurred in connection with secondary causes is unknown.

But doubtless, ordinarily, it depends on such causes; the crowding together of great numbers of people, the accumulation of filth, the state of the atmosphere, the susceptibilities of the persons affected by it. "The peculiar source of the thought that a numbering of the people brought mischief lies probably in the experience that epidemic sicknesses often broke out in such numberings, because therein a great mass of people was crowded together, to facilitate the business, in a proportionally small space" (Thenius). Most of the great plagues that have afflicted mankind appear to have originated in the East, where the climate, the soil, and the social habits of the population afford conditions favourable to their production. In all cases, however, the hand of God must be recognized in the consequences of violating his laws, physical and moral; and in the employment of them "for correction." Consider—

I. Its MOURNFUL PREVALENCE; as at this time in Israel, so in other ages and nations (Exod. xii. 29; Numb. xxv. 9; 2 Kings xix. 35; Jer. xxvii. 13). 1. Its sudden appearance. 2. Its rapid diffusion; "from the morning to the [a] time appointed [the time of assembly]." "It burst upon the people with supernatural strength and violence, that it might be seen at once to be a direct judgment from God" (Keil). 3. Its extensive presence; "from Dan to Beersheba." 4. Its dreadful destructiveness; "seventy thousand men" (fourteen in the thousand of the whole population). "Such a pestilence and loss of life as this [at Athens, 430 B.C.] was nowhere remembered to have happened" (Thucydides, ii. 47). At Rome (A.D. 80) ten thousand perished daily; in England (1348) more than half the population; in London (1603) over thirty thousand; and again (August, 1665) eight thousand persons weekly. These are only a few of the many recorded instances of the awful "visitation of God."

II. Its MERCIFUL ARREST. "And the angel" (1 Sam. xxix. 9; ch. xiv. 17; xix. 27; Ps. civ. 4; xxxiv. 7; xxxv. 5; xci. 11), who had been "destroying through all the territories of Israel" (1 Chron. xxi. 12), "stretched out his hand" (having a drawn sword therein, 1 Chron. xxi. 6) "upon Jerusalem to destroy it," etc. The pestilence approached the city, threatening its destruction, and filling all hearts with terror (1 Chron. xxi. 16, 20). We can conceive that it might have spread until the whole human race perished. But its destructive force was limited (as it always is): 1. When its purpose was accomplished and the law of retribution satisfied. "It is enough." 2. By the same Divine power as sent it. "Stay now thine hand." God has placed in the human constitution a self-healing power. "Our natures are the physicians of our diseases" (Hippocrates). He provides special remedies for special diseases; alleviates and often cures them in unexpected, extraordinary, and mysterious ways. The Christian religion is a remedial system by which mortality itself is "swallowed up of life." "I am Jehovah thy Physician" (Exod. xv. 26; Matt. viii. 16; John iii. 14, 15; Rev. xxii. 2). 3. With tender pity toward the afflicted, involving a change of his procedure. "And Jehovah repented him of the evil" (1 Sam. xv. 24—31). 4. In connection with the moral condition of men and their altered relation to himself—humiliation (ver. 10), trust (ver. 14), and prayer (ver. 17). "Then David and the elders, clothed in sackcloth, fell upon their faces" (1 Chron. xxi. 16), their spirit being doubtless shared in by the people, whose representatives they were. God deals with men according to the state of their hearts (ver. 1), and commences doing so even before it is fully expressed in outward actions. Ps. xci. ("by David," LXX.), 'Under the shadow of the Almighty.'

"Because he hath set his love upon me,
Therefore will I deliver him," etc.
(Ps. xci. 14.)

"Some years ago an eminent physician in St. Petersburg recommended this psalm as the best preservative against cholera" (Perowne).

III. Its MORAL USES, with respect to those who suffer from it or to mankind generally, in: 1. Producing efficient impressions of the majesty of God; his sovereignty, justice, and might. 2. Proving the real condition of the hearts of men; whether they will "keep his commandments or no" (Deut. viii. 3). 3. Inducing, in those who are rightly disposed, proper feelings of penitence, humility, dependence, submission; and correcting vanity, pride, and self-will. 4. Inciting a purer and loftier trust in God, and more complete devotion and self-sacrifice. "Plagues to us are not funerals of terror, but exercises of holiness. We understand their meaning. They are messages sent to us by God, to explore our hearts, to sound the depth of our love to him, and to fathom our faith in God" (Cyprian, 'De Mortalitate'). 5. Presenting a terrible picture of the evil of sin, by exhibiting, not only the natural consequences thereof, but also its degrading effect on the ignorant and unbelieving, who pass rapidly from the extreme of fear to the opposite extreme of recklessness, licentiousness, and despair (1 Cor. xv. 32). "So they resolved to take their enjoyment quickly, and with a sole view to gratification; regarding their lives and their riches alike as things of a day. And fear of gods or law of men there was none to stop them" (Thucydides). 6. Teaching the solidarity of the race; and, more especially, constraining "the higher and more privileged ranks of mankind to own their oneness of life with the humbler and more degraded or even savage classes" (Bushnell). 7. Promoting, in still other ways, the advancement of mankind in knowledge, virtue, and piety; for it is through the discipline of suffering that the race, like the individual, "learns obedience." "The Lord's dealing herein is not penal, but paternal and medicinal" (Guild).—D.

Vers. 17—19 (1 Chron. xxi. 16—19).—(ZION.)   *Self-devotion.* "These sheep, what have they done?" etc. (ver. 17). As through one man many suffer, so through one man many are delivered from suffering and greatly benefited. This is especially the case when, like David, he is their head and representative, the shepherd of the flock of God (ver. 17; ch. v. 2). His numbering the people in a spirit of self-exaltation was the occasion (not the cause, ver. 1) of the pestilence; his *intercession* for them in a spirit of self-devotion is now the means in connection with which the calamity is limited in its duration (from three days to nine hours) and wholly removed (ver. 25). Already, with an "awful rose of dawn," the agent of destruction goes forth on his mission, and a "great cry" of distress reaches the city (Exod. xii. 30). Then the king gathers the elders together (at the tabernacle and before the curtained ark, ch. vii. 2; xii. 20; xv. 25; adjoining the palace in Zion, ch. v. 7); they are clothed with sackcloth, and overwhelmed with fear and grief (1 Chron. xxi. 16; ch. xii. 16; xv. 30); and at length, "about the time of assembly," or evening oblation (Acts iii. 1), there appears (beyond the Tyropœan Valley) on Mount Moriah (2 Chron. iii. 1), "by the threshing-floor of Araunah the Jebusite" (just outside the city), "the angel of the Lord standing between the earth and the heaven, having a drawn sword in his hand stretched out over Jerusalem;" and they "fell upon their faces" in humiliation before the Lord. "Significantly, it was as the Divine command of mercy sped to arrest the arm of the angel-messenger of the judgment, that he became visible to David and his companions in prayer" (Edersheim). "As in 2 Kings vi. 17 the source of seeing the heavenly powers was in Elisha, and by his mediation the eyes of his servant were opened, so here the flight of David's mind communicated itself to the elders of his retinue, whom he collected about him; and, after he had repaired to the place where he saw the vision, was revealed even to the sons of Araunah" (Hengstenberg). "And David said unto God," etc. "And Gad came *that day* to David," etc. (ver. 18; 1 Chron. xxi. 18). Here is—

I. A FEARFUL VISION OF JUDGMENT impending over the people. This judgment may be regarded as representing that to which nations are exposed in this world, and individuals both here and hereafter; real, terrible and imminent; the result and reflection of human sin and guilt, which

> " Blackens in the cloud,
> Flashes across its mass the jagged fire,
> Whirls in the whirlwind and pollutes the air,
> Turns all the joyous melodies of earth
> To murmurings of doom."
>
> (Talfourd.)

1. Similar judgment has been already executed (ver. 15; Jude 7; Rom. v. 12; Rev. ii. 11; xxi. 8). "The wages of sin is death." 2. Solemn warnings of its certain and speedy approach have been repeatedly given (vers. 13, 17; 2 Pet. ii. 3; 1 Thess. v. 2, 3). 3. Only a few persons have any adequate impression thereof; whilst they behold "the wrath to come," the rest are blind and unconcerned, immersed in the pleasures and

cares of this life (Luke xxi. 34; Matt. vii. 14).   4. They whose eyes are opened are naturally impelled to seek the salvation of themselves and others, and are under the obligation of doing so (Jude 22, 23).   "Take a censer," etc.; "and he stood between the dead and the living; and the plague was stayed" (Numb. xvi. 46—68; Joel ii. 17).

II. A FERVENT ENTREATY FOR THE PEOPLE, that they may be spared.   In his intercession for them (1 Sam. xii. 23; xv. 10, 11, 35) David: 1. Takes the burden of their guilt upon himself; whilst he recognizes his responsibility, openly confesses his transgression in "commanding the people to be numbered" (1 Chron. xxi. 17), and honours the justice of God in inflicting punishment; he "forgets their sin is his own," regarding them, "not indeed as free from every kind of blame, but only from the sin which God was punishing by pestilence" (Keil).   "Many of those sheep were wolves to David.   What had they done?   They had done that which was the occasion of David's sin and the cause of their own punishment; but that gracious penitent knew his own sin; he knew not theirs" (Hall).   2. Feels a tender compassion for them in their misery and danger.   His language " shows the high opinion he had of them, the great affection he had for them, and his sympathy with them in this time of distress " (Gill).   3. Offers himself freely, and his " father's house " (his life and all his most cherished hopes) to the stroke, that it may be averted from his people.   " Hitherto David offered not himself to the plague, because, as Chrysostom conjectureth, he still expected and made account of himself to be taken away in the plague, but now seeing that it was God's will to spare him, he doth voluntarily offer himself" (Willet).   4. Urges an effectual plea on their behalf; not merely that they are blameless (in comparison with himself), and may be righteously spared, but that they are the chosen flock of the Divine Shepherd, whose mercies are great, whose promises to them are numerous and faithful, and whose glory they are designed to promote in the earth (1 Sam. xii. 22; Ps. lxxiv. 1; xcv. 7).   " Wilt thou also destroy the righteous with the wicked?" (Gen. xviii. 23); " Yet now if thou wilt forgive their sin," etc. (Exod. xxxii. 32; 1 Kings xviii. 36; Dan. ix 3); " I could wish that I myself were accursed from Christ on behalf of my brethren," etc. (Rom. ix. 3); " Father, forgive them; for they know not what they do" (Luke xxiii. 34); " The good Shepherd giveth his life for the sheep " (John x. 11); " He ever liveth to make intercession" (Heb. vii. 27).   " In his hands intercessory prayer is the refuge of the guilty, the hope of the penitent, a mysterious chain fastened to the throne of God, the stay and support of a sinking world."

III. A FAVOURABLE ANSWER FROM THE LORD.   Although David sees not the interposition of God, by which the hand of the angel is stayed, yet his prayer " availeth much in its working " (Jas. v. 16).   "And the angel of the Lord [now transformed from a minister of wrath into a minister of mercy] commanded Gad [who previously announced the message of judgment] to say," etc. (1 Chron. xxi. 18); "And Gad came that day to David, and said unto him, Go up, rear an altar," etc.; "And David went up as the Lord commanded " (vers. 18, 19).   The answer is propitious; a sign of Divine reconciliation.   But why the command to rear an altar, instead of the direct assurance of forgiveness (ch. xii. 13)?   1. To show forth to all the people (who confess by their elders and representatives that they have part in the king's transgression) that forgiveness is possible only in connection with sacrifice, wherein justice and mercy are alike exhibited.   2. To call forth their renewed and open obedience and self-devotion.   3. To give there a public sign of the Divine acceptance and removal of the judgment (1 Chron. xxi. 26, 27).   4. To establish a new and permanent centre of Divine worship, in fulfilment of previous promises (ch. vii. 13); so overruling the evil for good, and turning the curse into a blessing (1 Chron. xxii. 1).   This was a turning-point in the history of the nation; and henceforth the service of the tabernacle began to be superseded by that of the temple.

CONCLUSION.   Let it be remembered that the intercession of Christ (unlike that of David) is the intercession of the Innocent for the guilty; that he is also himself the Altar, " which sanctifieth the gift," and " the Propitiation for our sins; " and that in dependence upon him, as well as after his example and in his spirit, all our prayers and " spiritual sacrifices " must be presented unto God.—D.

Vers. 20—23 (1 Chron. xxi. 18—23).—(MORIAH.) *Araunah the Jebusite.* Araunah (Aravnah, Avarnah, Aranyah, Ornan) was: 1. A *Gentile* by birth; almost the last relic of the Canaanitish tribe whose fortress was taken nearly thirty years before (ch. v. 6). "He was not slain by David in the siege of Jerusalem, because of the good will he bore to the Hebrews, and a particular benignity and affection which he had to the king himself" (Josephus); with whom, during his exile, he may have become acquainted. 2. A *proselyte* to the faith of Israel (ver. 23). "There was no other people who were specially called the people of God; but they (the Jews) cannot deny that there have been certain men of other nations, who belonged, not by earthly but heavenly fellowship, to the true Israelites, the citizens of the country that is above" (Augustine). 3. A *prosperous owner* of property on the hill Moriah (at that time outside the city), where he had his threshing-floor, and dwelt with his four sons. His prosperity was due, not merely to his own industry, but chiefly to his friendship with David and his people. 4. A *partaker of the sufferings*, as well as the privileges, of the inhabitants of Jerusalem. Whilst occupied in threshing wheat (by means of sledges drawn by oxen), it was given him to see the supernatural messenger of wrath (1 Chron. xxi. 20); and "his four sons with him, hid themselves" from fear. 5. A *loyal subject*; respectful, courteous (ver. 20), and grateful for the king's visit to him in his threshing-floor (ver. 21). "It was a piece of condescension to be marvelled at; and the language expresses a desire to know his pleasure concerning him, supposing it must be something very urgent and important" (Gill). 6. A *generous donor* and public-spirited man (ver. 22). "All does Araunah, O king, give to the king" (ver. 23). "His liberality and princely munificence is registered to all after-ages in the Holy Scripture; what is done by a pious heart to the honour and worship of God shall never want its own reward and blessed remembrance; as was the breaking of the box of precious ointment" (Guild). 7. A *devout worshipper* of God. "Jehovah thy God accept thee." 8. A *ready helper* toward the building of the altar and temple of God. 9. A *pattern* to Christians. 10. A *pre-intimation* of the willing homage of the Gentile world to Christ (ch. xxii. 50); an earnest or firstfruits of the harvest (Ps. lxxii. 10, 11). "In every place incense shall be offered," etc. (Mal. i. 11).—D.

Ver. 24 (1 Chron. xxi. 24, 25).—(MORIAH.) *Personal sacrifice.* "And I will not offer unto Jehovah my God of that which doth cost me nothing." The gift of Araunah would have enabled David to perform a religious service in a cheap and inexpensive manner. But, (1) humbly recognizing the obligations that rested upon him, and animated by a spirit of self-devotion, (2) he nobly repudiates an offering which would have been, not really his own, but another's; or rendering to God a selfish and mercenary service; "which rebukes and condemns the avaricious disposition of many in this age, who can part with nothing for the maintenance of God's worship or promoting religion or any good work" (Guild). "It is a heartless piety of those base-minded Christians that care only to serve God good-cheap" (Hall). (3) He also generously resolves (acting toward the Divine King of Israel in the same spirit as Araunah acted toward himself) to purchase all that was required at "the full price," and thus serve God at his own cost, with self-denial and self-sacrifice. "And David bought the threshing-floor and the oxen for fifty shekels of silver" (1 Chron. xxi., "the place," the whole hill perhaps, for "six hundred shekels of gold by weight"). The principle applies not only to gifts of money (ch. viii. 11); but also to the employment of thought, effort, time, talents, relationships, influence; the renunciation of ease, pleasure, convenience, name, and fame; the endurance of privation, pain, opposition, dishonour, and shame; its highest application is to the "whole burnt offering" of a man himself (heart, soul, will), which virtually includes all other offerings, and without which they are vain. "What a change it would make in the Christian world if Christians of all sorts would put this question seriously to their souls, 'Shall I serve God with that which costs me nothing?'" (Manton, xxii. 94). Personal sacrifice is: 1. *Enjoined by the express commands of God.* "None shall appear before me empty" (Exod. xxxiv. 20); "Every man as he is able," etc. (Deut. xvi. 16); "It shall be perfect to be accepted; there shall be no blemish therein. Neither from a stranger's hand," etc. (Lev. xxii. 21, 25). Men were required to offer what was valuable, not worthless; what was their own, not another's. Even the poorest were not exempt. Self-denial is also "the law of Christ" (Mark viii. 34; x. 21—27). 2. *Incited by the supreme claims of God;* arising from his greatness and goodness, his ownership of all things (1 Chron. xxix. 14), his manifold mercies (ver. 14), above all, the unspeakable Gift of his only Son (Rom. viii. 32 ; xii. 1). 3. *Expressive of a right feeling toward God.* Reverence, gratitude, love, self-consecration, holy zeal (John xii. 3). "Everything depends on the predominant principle and purpose. If a man's prime feeling be that of self, he will go the easiest and most economic way to work and worship ; if a man's prime feeling be that of God, he will rebuke all thoughts of cheapness and facility. In the first case, he will seek the largest possible results from the least possible expenditure ; in the second, the expenditure will be itself the result. Now, it is the end and essence of all religion to turn the mind from self to God ; to give it absorbing views of the Divine beauty and glory ; to fill it with Divine love and zeal ; to make it feel honoured in honouring God, blessed in blessing him ; to make it feel that nothing is good enough or great enough for him ; and when the mind is thus affected and thus possessed, it will understand and share the spirit of David's resolve " (A. J. Morris, 'The Unselfish Offering'). 4. *Essential to the true service of God ;* for this depends not so much upon the form or amount of the offering as upon its relation to the offerer ; its being the genuine expression of the heart (as it professes to be) ; without which the service is formal, unreal, and insincere. That which costs nothing is worth nothing (Mal. i. 8 ; Isa. i. 11 ; Ps. li. 16, 17). 5. *Necessary to the assured acceptance of God.* It alone is attended with the sign and sense of his approval (1 Chron. xxi. 26). 6. *Conducive to the proper honour of God* amongst men ; in whom it begets a spirit like its own. 7. *Embodied in highest perfection in Christ ;* "who gave himself up for us, an Offering and a Sacrifice to God," etc. (Eph. v. 2). "A Spanish proverb says, 'Let that which is lost be for God.' The father of a family, making his will and disposing of his goods upon his death-bed, ordained concerning a certain cow which had strayed, and had been now for a long time missing, if it were found it should be for his children, if otherwise for God. Whenever men would give to God only the lame and blind, that which costs them nothing, that from which they hope no good, no profit, no pleasure to themselves, what are they saying in their hearts but that which this man said openly, 'Let that which is lost be for God'?" (Trench, 'Proverbs').—D.

Ver. 25 (1 Chron. xxi. 26—30; xxii. 1).—(MORIAH.) *The new altar.* "And David built there an altar unto Jehovah," etc. 1. An altar was *a place of sacrifice* (Gen. iv. 3, 4 ; viii. 20 ; xxii. 14) ; consisting (according to Divine direction, Exod. xx. 24, 25) of earth or unhewn stone, and constituting (according to Divine assurance) a point of meeting or reconciliation between God and men ; the offerings which it sustained and sanctified (and with which it was identical in purpose) being of divers kinds, symbolic of certain truths, and expressive of various feelings on the part of those who brought them. It was a prime necessity of religious worship in ancient time ; the appointed way of access to God ; the table at which Divinity and humanity held fellowship with one another. 2. The altar erected by David on the threshing-floor of Araunah marks the commencement of a new chapter in the history of the kingdom of God *under the old covenant.* Heretofore sacrifice was offered in different places (1 Sam. i. 3 ; ii. 33 ; vi. 15 ; vii. 9, 17 ; ix. 12 ; xi. 15 ; xiv. 35 ; xvi. 3 ; xx. 6 ; ch. vi. 13, 17 ; xv. 12) ; and the requirement of the Law (Deut. xii. 13, 14) was imperfectly fulfilled, in consequence of the unsettled condition of the nation and the disorganized state of religious worship (1 Kings iii. 2). Whilst the ark was at Jerusalem, "the altar of the burnt offering" remained at Gibeon (1 Chron. xxi. 29, 30) ; and although not finally abandoned till some time after (1 Kings iii. 4), it henceforth began to be superseded by *the new altar,* which was divinely appointed and consecrated by fire from heaven (1 Chron. xxi. 26), and chosen by Jehovah (Deut. xvi. 15) as the place of his worship, the central sanctuary for succeeding ages. "Now when King David saw that God had heard his prayer, and had graciously accepted of his sacrifice, he resolved to call that entire place *the altar of all the people*" (Josephus). "And David said, This is the house of the Lord God," etc. (1 Chron. xxii. 1, 2 ; Gen. xxviii. 17) ; "And Solomon began to build the house of the Lord at Jerusalem in Mount Moriah, where the Lord appeared unto David," etc. (2 Chron. iii. 1). Ps. xxx., inscription : 'A song at the dedication of the house' (see Hengstenberg). "I will extol thee, O Lord," etc.

"And as for me—I had said, in my prosperity,
I shall not be moved for ever," etc.

(Ps. xxxi. 6—10.)

3. The chief interest for us of this altar (as of every other) arises from the fact that it was not merely symbolic of spiritual truth, but also typical of its embodiment *in Christ*—the Altar (as well as the Offering and the Offerer), the new and only true (Heb. vii. 2), perfect, effectual, central, universal, and enduring Altar and Temple (John ii. 21), where God records his name, and where we draw nigh to God, offer spiritual sacrifices, and find acceptance with him.   It was "a shadow of things to come; but the body is of Christ" (Col. ii. 17).   "We have an altar [his cross and sacrifice], whereof they have no right to eat who serve the tabernacle" (Heb. xiii. 10).   Consider, with this reference—

I. THE ERECTION OF THE ALTAR, as (in connection with the offerings, apart from which it cannot be fully contemplated) : 1. *Rendered necessary* by human sin, through the temptation of Satan : estrangement from God through pride and disobedience to his Law ; exposure to condemnation and death (Heb. ix. 22).   2. *Ordained* by Divine wisdom and love, "before the foundation of the world" (1 Pet. i. 20), in order to the remission of sins and the restoration of sinners to the fellowship of God (Heb. ix. 26). 3. *Adapted* to the fulfilment of that purpose ; by the atonement there made (ch. xxi. 3 ; Lev. i. 4 ; Isa. liii. 6 ; John i. 29 ; 1 John ii. 2 ; 2 Cor. v. 19 ; Gal. iii. 13) ; by the exhibition of the duty, sinfulness, and desert of men, and the sovereignty, righteousness, and mercy of God (Rom. iii. 21—26).   "When sinful souls approached the altar of God, where dwelt his holiness, their sinful nature came between them and God, and atonement served the purpose of covering their sins, of cancelling the charges on which they were arraigned" (Küper).   4. *Designed* to do away with every other altar and to afford free access to God for all people in all places and ages (Isa. lvi. 7 ; John iv. 23 ; Eph. ii. 18).   The language in which the death of Christ is described in the New Testament is derived from the sacrifices of the former dispensation, and can only be properly understood by some acquaintance with them.   It is no longer needful or possible to *set up an altar* (according to a common mode of expression), except in the sense of recognizing, approaching, and making known "the altar of God" which is set up in Christ Jesus (Ps. xliii. 4 ; John xiv. 6).   "Let us draw near," etc. (Heb. x. 22).

II. THE OFFERINGS PRESENTED THERE.   "And offered burnt offerings and peace offerings" (1 Sam. i. 3 ; ch. vi. 17—19).   In becoming himself an Offering (Isa. liii. 12) and Propitiation for our sins (complete and incapable of being repeated or rendered more efficacious), Christ displayed a spirit (Heb. x. 5—7) in which (coming to him with penitence, ver. 10, and faith) we must participate, and thus "offer up spiritual sacrifices," etc. (1 Pet. ii. 5).   1. The free, entire, and continual surrender (ver. 14) and dedication of ourselves, spirit, soul, and body, to God (Rom. xii. 1).   2. Prayers, supplications and intercessions (ver. 17 ; Judg. xx. 26 ; Ps. li. 17 ; cxli. 2).   "And the Lord Jehovah was *entreated* for the land."   "Sacrifice is in the main embodied prayer."   3. "The sacrifice of praise" (Heb. xiii. 15).   4. Holy obedience (ver. 19), generous gifts (ver. 24), and benevolent activities.   "To do good and to communicate forget not : for with such sacrifices God is well pleased" (Heb. xiii. 16 ; Phil. iv. 18).   "The altar is not to stand in its beauty and stateliness a solemn, unapproachable thing, on which we may reverently gaze, but which we may not touch without sacrilege.   It is for use ; its broad summit is to be laden with oblations and crowded with victims ; it stands in the midst of us ; it accompanies us wherever we wander, that it may invite our offerings, and be always ready to receive what we should always be ready to give" (Ps. iv. 5 ; xxvi. 6 ; cxviii. 27).

III. THE ACCEPTANCE OF THE OFFERER.   "Jehovah thy God accept thee" (ver. 23) ; "And the plague was stayed from Israel."   Christ's offering was well-pleasing to God ; and we are accepted in him (Eph. v. 2 ; i. 6, 7).   1. There is now no condemnation (Rom. viii. 1 ; Heb. x. 16—18).   The sword is put up again into the sheath thereof. 2. The presence, favour, and sanctifying power of God are manifested to us (Acts ii. 3, 4).   3. Peace with God, and "the communion of the Holy Ghost," are vouchsafed to us.   4. And we "rejoice in hope of the glory of God" (Rom. v. 1, 2 ; Eph. ii. 19—22 ; Rev. xxi. 3, 4).

"Thou didst turn for me my mourning into dancing ;
Thou didst put off my sackcloth, and didst gird me with joy ;
To the end that my glory should sing praise to thee, and not be silent.
O Jehovah my God, for ever will I give thanks unto thee."

(Ps. xxx. 11, 12.)

CONCLUSION. 1. " Jesus Christ is the Object of the two Testaments : of the Old, its expectancy ; of the New, its model; of both, the centre " (Pascal). As in every part of the country there is a way which leads to the metropolis, so in every part of Scripture there is a way which leads to Christ. 2. The method of human salvation has always been the same in the mind of God; but it has been gradually revealed to the mind of man ; and wherever faith has been exercised in God, in so far as he has revealed his saving purposes, it has been accounted for righteousness. 3. " To the cross of Christ all eternity looked forward; to the cross of Christ all eternity will look back. With reference to it all other objects were created and are still preserved ; and every event that takes place in heaven, earth, and hell is directed and overruled " (Payson). 4. " Wherefore, receiving a kingdom," etc. (Heb. xii. 28). " Now the God of peace," etc. (Heb. xiii. 20, 21).—D.

Ver. 10.—*Sinful numbering.* This is part of a narrative which presents various serious difficulties. The chief is that which arises from the statement that God moved David to commit the sin for which he afterwards punished him. In 1 Chron. xxi. 1 the instigator is said to be Satan, or "an adversary;" and it is possible to translate here ('Speaker's Commentary') "one moved David." Still, the translation in our English versions (both Authorized and Revised) is more natural. The statement reminds us of Numb. xxii. 20, 22, and is probably susceptible of a similar explanation. God gives permission to men who indulge sinful desires to gratify their desires. He says "Go" when they strongly desire to do so, and thus punishes them by allowing them to sin, and then inflicting the penalty due to such sin. Moreover, the sacred writers speak more freely than we are accustomed to do of the agency of God in connection with the sins of men (see ch. xii. 11; xvi. 10; Exod. vii. 3; 1 Sam. xxvi. 19; 1 Kings xxii. 20—23; Ezek. xiv. 9, 10; Mark iv. 12; 2 Thess. ii. 11, 12). Our Lord teaches us to pray, "Lead us not into temptation," which implies that God may thus lead men. However, if David knew that in some sense God had bidden him number the people, he none the less felt that the sin of the proceeding was great, and that it was *his own.*

I. DAVID'S SIN. In what did it consist? As the narrative does not explain, and no law or statement of the Scriptures can be adduced in explanation, it is impossible to answer the question satisfactorily. That there was sin in the numbering of the people at this time, the strong remonstrance of the by-no-means-over-scrupulous or pious Joab (ver. 3) makes manifest. It may have been done in a spirit of pride and vain-glory, that the king might delight himself in the contemplation of the greatness of his armed forces. For it should be noted that only those that "drew the sword" (ver. 9) were counted. The kings of Israel were not, like other monarchs, to trust in the multitude of their armed men, but in their God, who could save or give victory by many or by few (1 Sam. xiv. 6; 2 Chron. xiv. 11). Possibly David may have had ulterior designs that were opposed to the will of God. He may have proposed to himself to reduce the people, as into more complete unity, so into more slavish subjection to the throne (comp. 1 Sam. viii. 11—18); or he may have had designs of unjust aggression on other peoples. Similar sins are committed: 1. When men reckon up their achievements or possessions, or the number of their servants and retainers, in a spirit of pride, self-satisfaction, or false confidence (Dan. iv. 30). 2. When they sum up their wealth, not to consider how they may best employ it for the good of men and the glory of God, but to frame schemes of sinful indulgence (Luke xii. 19). 3. When the calculation of numbers or resources is made in order to determine the safety or otherwise of perpetrating or continuing some injustice to others. Rulers increasing and reckoning their hosts, etc., with a view to unjust wars, or the suppression of the liberties, or other violation of the rights, of their subjects. 4. When numbers are counted, instead of arguments weighed, previous to adopting a religious or political creed, or to obtain encouragement in the practice of any wickedness (John vii. 48; Exod. xxiii. 2).

II. DAVID'S REPENTANCE. It was long in coming—so long as to excite our amazement. It included: 1. Conviction. "His heart smote him." His conscience accused him. He saw the greatness of his sin and folly. Sin is always folly, though folly is not always sin (see on ch. xiii. 13). 2. Humble confession made to God. 3. Earnest prayer for pardon.

III. HIS PUNISHMENT. The reply to his prayer was not such as he may have hoped.

The Prophet Gad was sent to him, not to assure him of pardon, but to offer him a choice of punishments (vers. 12, 13). He chose pestilence, as being more immediately from "the hand of the Lord," whose "mercies are great." Accordingly, a terrible plague fell on the people, destroying seventy thousand men in less, apparently, than one day. For although three days had been named as the duration of the pestilence, the time was evidently shortened, and the plague ceased as it threatened to destroy Jerusalem (ver. 16). To that extent the prayers of David (vers. 10, 17), and the sacrifices which he hastened to offer by direction of the prophet, prevailed. The king had sinned; the punishment fell on the people. David felt and pleaded the incongruity (ver. 17). What can we say respecting it? 1. *It is according to a universal law of Divine procedure.* The difficulty meets us everywhere. Subjects suffer on account of the sins, and even the mistakes, of their rulers; children, of their parents; and, more widely, the innocent, because of the sins and follies of others. It is useless to argue against facts. 2. *Events which are judgments to the guilty are simple trials to the innocent, and may be unspeakable blessings.* When the godly are struck down with others in a time of general calamity they exchange earth for heaven.

> "The sword, the pestilence, or fire,
> Shall but fulfil their best desire;
> From sins and sorrows set them free,
> And bring thy children, Lord, to thee."
>   (Watts.)

3. *In this case the people suffered for sins of their own.* It was because "the anger of the Lord was kindled against Israel" for their sins (ver. 1), that David's sin was permitted and its punishment inflicted. Many other cases would admit of a similar explanation. 4. *Although the calamity which fell on the nation was great, a greater would have been the death of its sovereign by the plague.* 5. *David suffered severely in the destruction of so many of his subjects.* If his sin was that of pride in the number whom he ruled and could lead to war, the punishment corresponded to the sin. He was made to feel how soon God could deprive him of that in which he boasted. 6. When all has been thought and said that is possible, it is for us (1) to recognize that God's ways are necessarily beyond our comprehension—we are soon out of our depth as we contemplate them; (2) to cherish undoubting confidence in his wisdom, righteousness, and love in all his proceedings, whether they are discernible by us or not. Such confidence is required and justified by what we do distinctly know of him; and it is the only way to settled peace in a world so full of misery and mystery. 7. Let us *carefully avoid sin*, not only because it is evil in itself and will bring pain and sorrow to ourselves, but because others will inevitably be involved in the consequences of our conduct. Many children are sufferers for life through the wickedness of their parents.—G. W.

Ver. 13.—*Pressing for an answer to God's message.* "Advise, and see what answer I shall return to him that sent me." These words of Gad to David might well be addressed by religious teachers, and especially ministers of the gospel, to those whom they instruct. Notice—

I. GOD'S MESSENGERS. "Him that sent me." 1. *True ministers of Christ are God's messengers.* Their office is not a human invention. They are not mere lecturers, who may choose their own themes and aims; not mere philosophers, free to speculate at will and give the people the result of their speculations; still less mere performers, whose business is to amuse. They are sent of God, by the operations of his Spirit, the guidance of his providence, and the appointment of his Church; and have a definite message from him to their hearers, viz. the gospel (in the wider sense) of Jesus Christ—its revelations, precepts, promises, and threatenings. In delivering this message, they have a definite end to seek—the salvation of their hearers. He who is not convinced that he is God-sent—"inwardly moved by the Holy Ghost to take upon him this office and ministration" (Prayer-book)—ought not to assume it. 2. *They should cherish a due sense of their position.* Which will keep alive: (1) The feeling of responsibility to God. "As they that must give account" (Heb. xiii. 17). (2) Humility. The consciousness of a Divine mission might tempt them to pride and arrogance, but the consciousness of unworthiness and unfitness for so sacred a work will keep them humble. "Who is sufficient for these things?" (2 Cor. ii. 16). (3) Care as to what they teach. That it may be the very message of God. "Preach the preaching that I bid thee" (Jonah iii. 2). (4) Care as to the spirit and aim of their teaching. Not to exalt or enrich themselves, or merely please men, but to glorify God and promote the salvation of their hearers (John vii. 18; Gal. i. 10; Col. i. 28). (5) Faith and hope. That he whose messengers they are will guide and support them, give success to their endeavours, and amply reward them. 3. *Hearers should recognize the position of their ministers.* Such recognition will: (1) Regulate their expectations from them. They will not expect them to flatter, or merely entertain, or to suppress unwelcome truths. They will desire them to be faithful to their convictions as to the message God would have them deliver. (2) Induce them to give earnest heed to their instructions and admonitions. Their attitude will be that of Cornelius and his friends (Acts x. 33): "Now therefore are we all here present before God, to hear all things that are commanded thee of God;" and, when the words addressed to them are perceived to be Divine truth, they will receive them "not as the word of men, but as the Word of God" (1 Thess. ii. 13), with faith and obedience. (For the opposite spirit and practice, see Ezek. xxxiii. 31, 32.)

II. THE ALTERNATIVES THEY PRESENT. Happily they have not, like Gad, to offer a choice of fearful calamities, but of: 1. On the one hand, eternal life; commencing now in the enjoyment of pardon and peace, holiness and hope; and perfected in heaven. This to be secured by faith in the Son of God as Saviour and Lord, with corresponding love and obedience. 2. And, on the other, eternal punishment; "indignation and wrath, tribulation and anguish" (Rom. ii. 8, 9); to be assuredly secured by rejection of Christ, and of God in him. These solemn alternatives must not, cannot, be kept out of view by a faithful messenger of God; and the thought of them will give earnestness to his ministrations, and to the treatment of them by his hearers (comp. Deut. xxx. 15—19).

III. THE ANSWER FOR WHICH THEY PRESS. Christian ministers should endeavour as far as possible privately to urge *individuals* to consider what answer they will give to the Divine message, what choice they will make between the alternatives presented to them. This cannot be always done; but in their public addresses they ought to be urgent in pressing their hearers to definite consideration and decision. They should show them: 1. *That an answer has to be given, and that to God,* who searches the heart. That, in fact, they are ever giving a reply; ever choosing the evil, if not the good. 2. *That their answer should be the result of careful consideration.* "Advise, and see;" consider and determine. A great point is gained when men are induced to *consider* the claims of God and their souls. 3. *That such consideration should be prompt.* It is both sinful and perilous to delay. To put off attention to God's message is insulting to him, and may end in his deciding suddenly and unexpectedly for us which of the two alternatives shall be ours. 4. *That they are themselves intensely concerned that the answer given should be that which is alone wise and good* —the hearty acceptance of Christ and salvation. "As though God did beseech you by us: we pray you in Christ's stead, be ye reconciled to God" (2 Cor. v. 20).—G. W.

Ver. 14.—*God's treatment preferred to man's.* David had good reasons for the choice he made. He knew well, from his own treatment of defeated enemies (ch. xii. 31; 1 Chron. xx. 3), how fearfully cruel were conquerors in war in those days, what an awful scourge to his subjects would be the ravages of a victorious invading army. He also doubtless dreaded the disgrace and permanent damage to the kingdom which would be thus wrought, and the dishonour, in the view of the heathen, which would be cast on the Name of Jehovah its God (see Josh. vii. 8, 9). Taking the words in a wider application, they express what will be the natural preference of good men.

I. GROUNDS OF THE PREFERENCE HERE EXPRESSED. 1. *The great mercy of God and the unmercifulness, or limited mercy, of men.* 2. *The righteousness of God and the unrighteousness of men.* We can never be sure that in a particular case righteousness will guide human proceedings; we know that the Divine are always thus guided. Many men are utterly regardless of what is right where their own interests, inclinations, or passions are concerned; and even the best men are liable to fail in respect to pure and constant regard for rectitude. 3. *The knowledge and wisdom of God, and the ignorance and folly of men.* Much of the misconduct and untrustworthiness of men springs from ignorance and folly. When they mean well, they often do ill through not knowing the actual state of the affairs with which they are called to deal, not taking the trouble, perhaps, to ascertain it; or, when they know it, not understanding how to treat it. But the Divine knowledge and wisdom are perfect. 4. *The power of God and the weakness of men.* Men are often incapable of doing the good they know, and even strongly desire to do; and their weakness often causes them to do mischief while endeavouring to do good. God is Almighty to effect what his wisdom, mercy, and rectitude prompt. 5. *The relation of God to good men.* Their Father, their covenant God. The certainty that he will honour those that honour him, and turn all things, including his own chastisement of them, to their good, and ultimately bring them to eternal glory. The preference will be strong in proportion to the actual contrast between the men with whom we have to do and God. There are some men who are so God-like that we should not be averse to falling into their hands in a considerable variety of circumstances. It would be to a limited extent like falling into the hands of God.

II. CASES IN WHICH THE PREFERENCE WOULD BE EXERCISED. 1. *The endurance of suffering.* As in the text. It is better to suffer from disease than from human violence. The suffering will be easier to bear, more likely to profit, less likely to excite resentment and other evil passions. The infliction will be more tempered with mercy, and promote in a greater degree the ends of mercy. 2. *Judgment of character and actions.* To be judged by God is preferable to being judged by men. Men are often fond of passing judgment, but for the most part very incapable. They commonly judge ignorantly, or from prejudice, and therefore unjustly. They are apt to be wrong alike in their favourable and unfavourable opinions of others. When condemned by them, it is well if we can appeal with confidence to the judgment of God, which is always just. 3. *Forgiveness.* Men forgive reluctantly, in a limited measure, with reserves; and soon grow weary of pardoning the same offender. To pardon "seven times," much more "seventy times seven" (Matt. xviii. 21, 22), seems to them an impossibility. Indeed, repeated offences, as they appear incompatible with real repentance, may justify hesitation to pardon repeatedly, since the state of the offender's heart cannot be known. But God, who knows the heart, discerns where it is true, notwithstanding frequent falls; and, pitying human weakness, forgives many times a day. And his pardons are full and complete. Add that forgiveness from men does not ensure forgiveness from God, and that having the latter we can, if need be, dispense with the former. There is then abundant reason why, in the matter of pardon, we should prefer to have to do with God rather than men. 4. *Spiritual guidance and help.* God has appointed that men should instruct and aid their fellow-men in matters of religion and morals. But those who offer themselves as spiritual guides are fallible, and they differ widely on important points. It is then encouraging and assuring that Divine guidance and help are available. By the devout study of God's holy Word, and earnest prayer for the Holy Spirit, whose aid is promised to those who seek it (Luke xi. 13), all may obtain such heavenly wisdom and strength as shall ensure them against serious error and failure. And after listening to the conflicting statements of human teachers, and their denunciation of those who decline their counsel, a religious inquirer may in many instances wisely turn from them to God, saying, "Let me fall into the hand of the Lord rather than of man."

In conclusion: 1. *It is a great comfort to sincere Christians to know that they are ever in the hand of the Lord.* When they seem to be most left to the will of arbitrary, unjust, and cruel men, God is over all, controlling, overruling, sanctifying, compelling their most malignant foes to promote their real and lasting good. He will rectify and compensate for all the injustice and injury which he permits men to inflict upon them. 2. *Impenitent sinners might well prefer to fall into the hands of men rather than of God.* The limited knowledge and power of men, as well as their feeble hatred of sin, would be in their favour; at the worst, they can only "kill the body." But God abhors sin with a perfect hatred, knows fully the guilt of each sinner, and "hath power to cast into hell" (Luke xii. 4, 5). "Who knoweth the power of *thine* anger?" (Ps. xc. 11).—G. W.

Ver. 23.—*Acceptance with God.* "The Lord thy God accept thee." A good wish, flowing from good will, and all the heartier because of the occasion. For Divine acceptance of the king and his offerings meant deliverance for the nation, Araunah included, from the ravages of the pestilence. The sincerity of his wish was proved by the substantial offers with which it was accompanied.

I. THE BLESSING DESIRED. Araunah referred to the favourable reception by God of David's offerings. In the widest sense, acceptance with God includes: 1. *Acceptance of ourselves.* Our reception by God into his friendship and favour. Unless the *man* is accepted, his offerings cannot be. God receives nothing from his enemies—a truth which should be very seriously pondered by multitudes of his professed worshippers, who give him outward homage, but withhold from him *themselves.* Who, then, are accepted by God? Those who come to him according to his appointment, with repentance, faith, self-devotement, confessing sin, trusting to the mercy and entering on the service of God. Under the Christian dispensation, men are accepted through faith in Jesus Christ. When we receive him as Saviour and Lord, God receives us (comp. Rom. v. 1, 2). 2. *Acceptance of our worship.* Which includes devout exercises of mind and heart, study of the Word of God, pious meditation, praises and thanksgivings, prayers. What worship is accepted? Such as is offered in the name of Jesus (John xvi. 23, 24; Eph. iii. 12; Phil. ii. 10, Revised Version). Sincere (Isa. xxix. 13; John iv. 24), humble (Luke xviii. 10—14), reverential (Heb. xii. 28), yet trustful and affectionate as children (Rom. viii. 15). Not that of slaves or mercenaries. 3. *Acceptance of our gifts.* We give to God when we give for the support of his worship and the spread of his kingdom, and when we give to the poor for his sake (Matt. xxv. 40). Our gifts are acceptable (1) when presented with pure hearts, not ostentatiously to gain human applause (Matt. vi. 2—4), not with a view to atone for sin and obtain pardon, not to bribe men to unholy compliances; (2) when they are our own property, not the fruit of dishonesty, oppression, or injustice; (3) when they are in due proportion to our ability (2 Cor. viii. 12). 4. *Acceptance of active service.* Labours for the good of others, temporal and spiritual. All honest work springing from and guided by Christian principles.

II. THE DESIRE ITSELF. In this case it was a *patriotic* desire. It is always *pious* and *benevolent.* Pious, as it recognizes the necessity of God's favour and approbation to the well-being of men, and implies his willingness to be favourable to them. Benevolent, as it is a desire that others should enjoy the most essential and all-comprehensive of blessings, without which other blessings are of small and temporary value. Not health or wealth, not acceptance with men, not long life, not intellectual superiority, not refinement of taste, etc., are of primary importance; and these should not be first in our minds when seeking the welfare whether of ourselves or of others; but the favour of Almighty God, and, as the sure means of securing this, the possession of Christian faith and holiness. "Wherefore" let us "labour that, whether present or absent" (living or dying), "we," and all in whom we are interested, yea, all mankind, "may be accepted of him" (2 Cor. v. 9).—G. W.

Ver. 24.—*Cheap religion repudiated.* "Neither will I offer burnt offerings unto the Lord my God of that which doth cost me nothing." We have in the context "a laudable contention between a good king and a good subject" (Manton). Araunah wished to give the site for an altar, the animals and fuel for sacrifice, taking, on account of the necessity for haste, the threshing oxen and implements for the purpose. David insisted on paying for all. The text expresses his reason. He felt it was unworthy of his position and means as monarch, of the greatness of God, and of his own relation and obligations to him, to offer sacrifices which had cost him nothing. His determination is worthy of adoption by all, and will be adopted by all true-hearted Christians. They will not worship and serve God without cost to themselves. In considering the words, we need not confine attention to gifts of money or other property. In the worship and service of God, expenditure of thought, feeling, time, strength, etc., is required as well as of property; and, in relation to each and all, the true Christian, when the need for such expenditure arises, and he is tempted to avoid it, will be ready to exclaim, "I will not serve the Lord my God without cost." His motives are such as follow.

I. REVERENCE FOR GOD. Sense of his majesty and excellence. The feeling that he who is so great and glorious should be served with the best we can present to him, internal and external; and that to come before him without any worthy gift is to insult him (see Mal. i. 7, 8, 14).

II. GRATITUDE TO GOD. For his great and manifold gifts to us, especially that of his Son, with all the unspeakable blessings which come to us with and through him. If duly sensible of what we have received from God, we shall be eager to make him such return, poor though it is, as is possible to us, and shall feel that we can never do enough for him who has done so much for us.

III. LOVE TO GOD AND MAN. The substance of true religion. Love to God, awakened and kept alive by his love to us and by increasing knowledge of his all-perfect and lovely character, will produce love for his worship, his people, his cause in the world, our fellow-men. In helping these by deed and gift, we offer sacrifices to him (Phil. ii. 17; iv. 18; Heb. xiii. 16), and all who love him will offer such sacrifices. In proportion to the ardour of their love will be the measure of their services; and they will never grow weary of them, since love makes them a delight.

IV. JUSTICE TO OTHERS. The worship of God cannot be maintained, nor his kingdom extended, nor his will as to the poor done, without cost of various kinds, in which it is right that all should do their part according to their capabilities. If some shirk their duty, others may be compelled to do more than fairly belongs to them. The thought of this will move each to take his proper share of gift or labour.

V. THE EXAMPLE OF OTHERS. 1. *The liberal expenditure of some on their idols.* Heathen. Worldly men. Ourselves, perhaps, before we were converted. 2. *The liberality of many Christians.* In every circle a few are known who are generous in deed or gift, or both, in the service of God and the poor. Their zeal incites others by the power of sympathy and the feeling that they are themselves under equal obligation to their Saviour and their God. 3. *The cost at which multitudes of Christians have had to serve God.* In times of persecution their religion has cost many their property, liberty, or lives; and they have borne the cost bravely and gladly (Heb. x. 34; Acts vi. 41; Phil. ii. 17; Col. ii. 24). Shame on us if we grudge the much smaller cost of religion to us. 4. *Above all, the example of our Lord and Saviour.* (2 Cor. viii. 9; Titus ii.. 14.) Remembrance of the cost to him of our opportunity of serving God acceptably will strengthen us when tempted to make our religion as cheap as possible.

VI. PERCEPTION OF THE WORTHLESSNESS OF A RELIGION THAT COSTS US NOTHING. 1. *It is unreal.* A mere name and pretence. Real religion begins and is maintained at the cost of much thought, feeling, and prayer. Where it exists it must move the heart to zeal and generosity in the service of God, cannot but manifest itself in works and gifts. 2. *It is unacceptable to God.* Instead of accepting, he abhors it. It is contrary to his will. The spirit of the old injunction, "They shall not appear before the Lord empty," is plainly of universal application; and the New Testament abounds in precepts enjoining zeal and generosity in the service of God. 3. *It is therefore fruitless of good*, now and hereafter. It may be correct in creed, fair in profession, interesting in sentiment, beautiful in phrase; but it is useless. It answers no substantial end of a religion. It does not elevate and improve the worshipper. It can hardly secure even the approval of men. It does not avert, but ensure and increase, the judgments of God. Those who practise it will justly have their "portion with the *hypocrites*" (Matt. xxiv. 51).

VII. ASSURANCE OF RECOMPENSE. God will not let any man be a loser in his service. 1. *He gives valuable rewards now to those who expend their energies or substance for him.* The practical manifestation of Christian principles strengthens them. Talents employed are multiplied. "Unto every one that hath shall be given, and he shall have abundance" (Matt. xxv. 29). Service opens opportunities and develops capacities for service. Influence for good widens, honourable positions in Christ's Church are reached without ambitious striving for them, the esteem and affection of the good are enjoyed. The pleasure of doing good is experienced, and, withal, the pleasures of a good conscience —the consciousness of Christian principles, affections, and aims, and of the approval of God. 2. *Great is their reward in heaven.* Perfected character; enlarged and exalted service; the unclouded light of the Divine countenance; the blessings of those whom they have helped to save; the eternal joy and glory of the Lord.

In conclusion: 1. This resolution deserves the serious consideration and adoption of: (1) Ministers and other teachers of religion, who are often tempted to do their work with as little trouble to themselves as possible. The help afforded by such books as this may be abused by the indolent. (2) All who have opportunity to expend money, time, or talents in the service of Christ. Cordially adopted, it will make the numerous calls on Christian zeal and liberality in our day matter of thankfulness rather than of annoyance. It will induce even the poor to render aid according to their means. 2. The subject shows the disadvantages attending endowments of religion. They tend to deprive worshippers of the pleasure and profit of worshipping God with cost to themselves. Where they exist, Christians should compensate themselves for the loss thus inflicted on them by exercising all the greater generosity towards other branches of Divine service, such as missions at home and abroad, charity to the poor, etc.—G. W.

Ver. 25.—*Efficacious sacrifices.* These sacrifices of David illustrate the nature and purpose of such offerings under the Law. David acted in obedience to a message from God (ver. 18). He did not offer sacrifices in order to render God merciful; it was the mercy of God which originated them. It was because he would stay the destroying pestilence that he directed David to offer them. Still, the sacrifices were a condition of the exercise of his mercy. It was when they had been offered that "the Lord was entreated for the land, and the plague was stayed from Israel." Hence the question arises—Why should the Merciful One have required the death of innocent victims in order that his mercy might be displayed in the cessation of the pestilence? If it be said that this method of entreating him was a solemn and expressive acknowledgment that the sins which occasioned the pestilence were deserving of death, the answer may be accepted as a partial explanation. But the question recurs—Why should not the confession of sin, with sincere penitence, be accepted without the infliction of death on the innocent? The only satisfying answer is that which takes into account the justice as well as the mercy of God, and recognizes in the death of the innocent an atonement for the guilt of those to whom mercy is shown. In exercising his mercy, God would also "declare his righteousness . . . that he might be just" while justifying the sinner (Rom. iii. 25, 26), and that men, while seeking and obtaining forgiveness, might discern more clearly, feel more deeply, and acknowledge more heartily, the righteousness of the sentence which condemned them to death. These remarks apply more especially to the "burnt offerings." The "peace offerings" (thank offerings) were added apparently as an expression of joyful gratitude for the deliverance which was confidently expected through the sacrifice of the burnt offerings. The text reminds us of another sacrifice which was offered ten centuries later near the site of David's altar, and which has rendered all other offerings for sin superfluous and unlawful. It may tend to the better understanding of both to view them together, noting their resemblances and contrasts.

I. THEIR RESEMBLANCES. 1. *In their origin.* Both were of Divine origin and appointment. They originated in the love and righteousness and wisdom of God—his perception of what "became him" (Heb. ii. 10). 2. *In their nature.* As making atonement for sin, by which God was "entreated," and the exercise of his forgiving mercy rendered consistent with a due regard for justice. 3. *In their significance for men.* Displaying the evil of sin and the Divine displeasure against it, and at the same time the loving-kindness of God—his readiness to pardon; and thus tending to produce at once abhorrence of sin and penitential grief, and the assured hope of pardon. 4. *In their results.* Reconciliation between God and sinners; forgiveness of sin and deliverance from its penalties; renewed enjoyment of the favour of God; renewed confidence in and obedience to him; added strength to resist temptation.

II. THE INCALCULABLE SUPERIORITY OF THE SACRIFICE OF OUR LORD. 1. *David offered the lives of animals; our blessed Lord offered himself.* They were of little value; but who shall calculate the worth of him who was not only the perfect Man, but the Word Incarnate, the only begotten Son of God? They could not understand the transaction in which they were made to participate, and could take no voluntary part in the sacrifice. But Jesus entered fully into the mind of God, shared to the utmost his love to sinners and hatred of their sins, made the Divine purpose his own, and in devoted obedience to the will of the Father surrendered himself willingly to suffering and death for our salvation. The virtue of his sacrifice arose from his Divine dignity, his perfect oneness with the Father in mind and heart, and his perfect obedience unto death (John x. 17, 18; Phil. ii. 6—8; Heb. ix. 14; x. 5—10). 2. *David provided his own sacrifices; Jesus was the Gift of God.* (1 John iv. 9, 10.) No man, no creature, could provide a sacrifice of sufficient worth to really and effectually atone for the sins of men.   3. *The moral significance of the sacrifice of Christ is immeasurably greater than of the offering of any number of animal sacrifices.*   As a revelation of God and man, of holiness and sin, of the Divine hatred to sin and love to sinners, of the beauty and glory of self-sacrifice, etc., it is altogether unique.   4. *The efficacy of the sacrifice of Christ transcends incalculably that of the sacrifices offered by David.*   (1) The value of the latter for atonement depended wholly on the will and appointment of God; the worth of the former was essential and intrinsic.   (2) The one atonement was of limited, the other of boundless, efficacy.   The former removed limited guilt—of a single nation, and for the time; the other was for the sins of all men, everywhere, and in all ages of the world (John i. 29; 1 John i. 7; ii. 2; Heb. x. 14).   (3) The sacrifices of David arrested a pestilence, and thus lengthened the lives of many; that of Christ saves from eternal punishment, and secures eternal life (1 Thess. i. 10; John vi. 51—54). (4) The former had doubtless some influence on some of the Israelites, favourable to repentance, faith, and obedience; the latter has produced and will yet produce a complete revolution in the position and character of vast multitudes belonging ˙to many nations.   Those who believe are by the death of Christ brought to God (1 Pet. iii. 18; Heb. x. 19, 20), made partakers of the Holy Spirit (Gal. iii. 13, 14), pardoned and justified (Eph. i. 7; Rom. v. 9), sanctified (Rom. viii. 3, 4; Eph. v. 25—27), led to thorough consecration of life to him who died for them (2 Cor. v. 14, 15), and to assured hope and unspeakable happiness (Rom. v. 5—11; viii. 32—39), issuing in the perfection, glory, and bliss of heaven (Rev. vii. 9, 10, 13—17).   5. *The animals offered by David ceased to exist; the great Redeemer obtained for himself by his self-sacrifice exaltation to universal dominion and immortal glory,* including the honour of leading and saving those for whom he died, and of receiving their loving and devoted homage (Rom. xiv. 8, 9; Eph. i. 19—23; Phil. ii. 8—11; Heb. xiii. 20; Rev. i. 17, 18). 6. *The benefits of David's offerings came to the people through his faith, penitence, and obedience; those of the sacrifice of Christ come to each Christian as the result of his own.* Its moral and spiritual power is thus enhanced.   7. *The burnt offerings of David laid the foundation for his thank offerings; much more does the death of Christ call for, induce, and render acceptable, thank offerings of a nobler kind, and these innumerable, unceasing, and throughout eternity.*   Such are the presenting of ourselves to God, and the offerings of praise, prayer, and beneficence (Rom. xii. 1; Phil. iv. 18; Heb. xiii. 15, 16; Rev. viii. 3, 4).   Let us not fail to present such thank offerings.   Let us take up the song of the banished apostle (Rev. i. 5, 6), "Unto him that loved us, and washed us from our sins in his own blood . . . to him be glory and dominion for ever and ever." Let us now join angels and the Church and all creation, and purpose and hope to join them for ever, in the sublime anthem (Rev. v. 12, 13), "*Worthy is the Lamb* that was slain to receive power, and riches, and wisdom, and strength, and honour, and glory, and blessing . . . Blessing, and honour, and glory, and power, be unto him that sitteth upon the throne, and unto the Lamb for ever and ever.   Amen."—G. W.

HOMILETICAL INDEX

TO

THE SECOND BOOK OF SAMUEL